THE ROUGH GUIDE TO

France

There are more than two hundred Rough Guide titles
covering destinations from Alaska to Zimbabwe
and subjects from Acoustic Guitar to Travel Health

Forthcoming travel guides include
The Algarve • The Bahamas • Cambodia • Caribbean Islands
Costa Brava • New York Restaurants • Bolivia • Zanzibar

Forthcoming Reference guides include
Elvis • Online Travel • Internet Radio • Cult TV

Rough Guides on the Internet
www.roughguides.com

ROUGH GUIDE CREDITS

Text editor: Sam Thorne
Series editor: Mark Ellingham
Editorial: Martin Dunford, Jonathan Buckley, Jo Mead, Kate Berens, Amanda Tomlin, Ann-Marie Shaw, Paul Gray, Helena Smith, Judith Bamber, Orla Duane, Olivia Eccleshall, Ruth Blackmore, Geoff Howard, Claire Saunders, Gavin Thomas, Alexander Mark Rogers, Polly Thomas, Joe Staines, Richard Lim, Duncan Clark, Peter Buckley, Lucy Ratcliffe, Clifton Wilkinson, David Glen (UK); Andrew Rosenberg, Mary Beth Maioli, Stephen Timblin, Yuki Takagaki (US)
Production: Susanne Hillen, Andy Hilliard, Link Hall, Helen Ostick, Julia Bovis, Michelle Draycott, Katie Pringle,

Robert Evers, Mike Hancock, Zoë Nobes, Rachel Holmes
Cartography: Melissa Baker, Maxine Repath, Ed Wright, Katie Lloyd-Jones
Picture research: Louise Boulton, Sharon Martins
Online: Kelly Cross, Anja Mutić-Blessing, Jennifer Gold, Audra Epstein, Suzanne Welles (US)
Finance: John Fisher, Gary Singh, Edward Downey, Mark Hall, Tim Bill
Marketing & Publicity: Richard Trillo, Niki Smith, David Wearn, Chloë Roberts, Birgit Hartmann, Claire Southern (UK); Simon Carloss, David Wechsler, Kathleen Rushforth (US)
Administration: Tania Hummel, Demelza Dallow, Julie Sanderson

ACKNOWLEDGEMENTS

Thanks to Nuria Silleras Fernández, Elena Aznar, Peter Catlos, Robin Vose, Gîtes de France, Jean-François Pouget (CDT l'Hérault), Sylvie Bonnafond (OT Lyon), Christian Rivière (OT Albi), Natalie Steinberg (CDT Bouches-de-Rhône), Sylvie Joly (OT Avignon), Valérie Crouineau (CDT Ariège-Pyrénées), Myriam Journet-Fillaquier (CDT Aude), Fabrice Marion (CRT Provence-

Alpes-Côte d'Azur). Thanks also to Mike Hancock for typesetting, Sharon Martins for picture research, Melissa Baker, Ed Wright and Sam Kirby for mapping, Jennifer Speake for proofreading, Kate Davies, Narrell Leffman and Judith Bamber for additional research, and Mandy Tomlin for her editorial advice.

PUBLISHING INFORMATION

This seventh edition published May 2001 by Rough Guides Ltd, 62–70 Shorts Gardens, London WC2H 9AH. Reprinted March 2002
Distributed by the Penguin Group:
Penguin Books Ltd, 80 Strand, London WC2R ORL
Penguin Putnam, Inc. 375 Hudson Street, NY 10014, USA
Penguin Books Australia Ltd, 487 Maroondah Highway, PO Box 257, Ringwood, Victoria 3134, Australia
Penguin Books Canada Ltd, 10 Alcorn Avenue, Toronto, Ontario, Canada M4V 1E4
Penguin Books (NZ) Ltd, 182–190 Wairau Road, Auckland 10, New Zealand
Typeset in Linotron Univers and Century Old Style to an original design by Andrew Oliver.
Printed in England by Clays Ltd, St Ives PLC.
Illustrations in Part One and Part Three by Edward Briant.

Illustrations on p.1 & p.1095 by Mike Hancock
© Rough Guides Ltd 2001
No part of this book may be reproduced in any form without permission from the publisher except for the quotation of brief passages in reviews.
1184pp – Includes index
A catalogue record for this book is available from the British Library
ISBN 1-85828-697-2

The publishers and authors have done their best to ensure the accuracy and currency of all the information in *The Rough Guide to France*, however, they can accept no responsibility for any loss, injury, or inconvenience sustained by any traveller as a result of information or advice contained in the guide.

THE ROUGH GUIDE TO

France

written and researched by

Kate Baillie, Tim Salmon, Brian Catlos, Amy K. Brown, Rachel Kaberry, Greg Ward, Jan Dodd, Marc Dubin, Ruth Blackmore and David Abram

ROUGH GUIDES

TRAVEL GUIDES • PHRASEBOOKS • MUSIC AND REFERENCE GUIDES

 We set out to do something different when the first Rough Guide was published in 1982. Mark Ellingham, just out of university, was travelling in Greece. He brought along the popular guides of the day, but found they were all lacking in some way. They were either strong on ruins and museums but went on for pages without mentioning a beach or taverna. Or they were so conscious of the need to save money that they lost sight of Greece's cultural and historical significance. Also, none of the books told him anything about Greece's contemporary life – its politics, its culture, its people, and how they lived.

So with no job in prospect, Mark decided to write his own guidebook, one which aimed to provide practical information that was second to none, detailing the best beaches and the hottest clubs and restaurants, while also giving hard-hitting accounts of every sight, both famous and obscure, and providing up-to-the-minute information on contemporary culture. It was a guide that encouraged independent travellers to find the best of Greece, and was a great success, getting shortlisted for the Thomas Cook travel guide award, and encouraging Mark, along with three friends, to expand the series.

The Rough Guide list grew rapidly and the letters flooded in, indicating a much broader readership than had been anticipated, but one which uniformly appreciated the Rough Guide mix of practical detail and humour, irreverence and enthusiasm. Things haven't changed. The same four friends who began the series are still the caretakers of the Rough Guide mission today: to provide the most reliable, up-to-date and entertaining information to independent-minded travellers of all ages, on all budgets.

We now publish more than 150 titles and have offices in London and New York. The travel guides are written and researched by a dedicated team of more than 100 authors, based in Britain, Europe, the US and Australia. We have also created a unique series of phrasebooks to accompany the travel series, along with an acclaimed series of music guides, and a best-selling pocket guide to the Internet and World Wide Web. We also publish comprehensive travel information on our Web site:

www.roughguides.com

HELP US UPDATE

We've gone to a lot of effort to ensure that the seventh edition of *The Rough Guide to France* is accurate and up to date. However, things change – places get "discovered", opening hours are notoriously fickle, restaurants and rooms raise prices or lower standards. If you feel we've got it wrong or left something out, we'd like to know, and if you can remember the address, the price, the time, the phone number, so much the better.

We'll credit all contributions, and send a copy of the next edition (or any other Rough Guide if you prefer) for the best letters. Please mark letters: "Rough Guide France Update" and send to:

Rough Guides, 62–70 Shorts Gardens, London WC2H 9AH, or Rough Guides, 4th Floor, 345 Hudson St, New York, NY 10014.

Or send email to: mail@roughguides.co.uk
Online updates about this book can be found on Rough Guides' Web site at www.roughguides.com

Thanks to all the readers who took the trouble to write in with their comments on the sixth edition (apologies for any omissions or mis-spellings): Angela Achi, Alex Allan, J. Anstey, J. H. Aston, C. P. Aylott, Alexandra Baker, Charles Baker, James M. Barisic, Mrs D. Barnes, M. C. Barrés-Baker, Mrs S. Barret-Hill, Alex Bartram, Jerry van Beers, Stanley Blenkinsop, R. H. Bradbery, Claire Bradfield, Janet Bradley, Pamela Brankin, Paul Brookes, Ann M. Brooks, Chris Burin, Nick and Annie Cannan, Wendy Carlyle, Jackie Cartledge, Brian Catlos, June Caustick, Chuck, Rosemary Clemence, Jeremy Close, Ruth N. Cohen, Wim De Connick, Maureen Constable, Alasdair Cook, Stella Coombe, Elisabeth Mendes da Costa, Desmond Coughlan, Marjorie L. Cox, Paola Cremonini, Kevin Cronin, Christopher Cunliffe, A. A. Cutts, Gwenno Dafydd, Donald Dean, A. Dinno, Michael Donley, Kristie Drummond, Wendy and Christopher Dunn, Olivia Eccleshall, David Ellis, John Elmes, Ann Fergus, Pauline Ferguson, Deborah Fink, Alex Fisher, Jon Fletcher, Rev. Paul Flowers, A. F. Ford, Penny Foulkes, Samantha Franklin, Chris Frean, Martin Garvey, K. B. Gilkes, Stuart Gill, S. Goodman, Patrick Graham, Glen Grundle, Nicky Halton, W. K. Hamilton, U. Hamnett, Jenny Harris, Mrs Hazel Harrison, Stephen Hartley and Michaela Jautz, Penelope Hasler, Louis Hemmings, G. W. Henton, Martin Hillman, Simon Hope, Knut Hordnes, E. Hudson, Sara Humphreys and Adrian Cashman, Stefania Igor, Steve Inwood, Mr R. Irani, John and Jackie Jackson, John W. Jackson, Marc and Nancy Jackson, Adam Jeff, Rod and Margaret Jenkins, Geraint Jennings, Christine Johns, Gordon Johnson, Scott Johnson, Hazel Johnstone, Ed Kaye, Andrew and Sarah Kenningham, Stanley Klar, N. Kutty, Stephen Lamley, Stephen Larkin, John Law, Chris Leavy, Eddy Le Couvreur, Philip LeRoux, Elizabeth L'Estrange, Lucy Liddell, Jenny Lunnon, Deirdre Madden, Malcolm, John Malloch, I. W. and D. Martin, Emily Mathieson, Brian Mcgarrigle, Christine McKee, Mrs McReilly and Mrs Boudinet, Audrey B. Moore, Jenny Morris, Mr and Mrs N. A. Muir, David Murray, Susan Murray, Ken Napia, Andrew Neather, Lisa Nellis, Charlotte Newell, Johanna and Charlotta Nilsson, Peter Noel-Storr, Steve P., J. Pagni, Ed Papworth, Colin Parker, Steve Parkes, G. A. Parkinson, Michael Parl, Carol and Den Pardy, Clare Partridge, Jo Patrick, Ian Payne, Helen Pearce, Alan Penfold, Stefanie Ponting, Mrs Jane Powell, Jill Prime, Quadling, Andrew Reid, Denise Riley, John Roberts, Lindsay Roberts, Ian Robinson, John Rogers, Mr and Mrs M. H. Rogers, David Rowe, Steve Rowe and Jennifer Smiley, Su Roxburgh, Hillary and Barry Samuels, Hannah Saxton, J. H. Schultz, Mike Scott, Mrs C. J. Scovell, Julian Seeley, Anamaria Crowe Serrano, Matt Shaw, Jim and Ann Skipper, Mrs C. A. Smith, J. A. Smith, Fay Stevens, Eira Stone, Leanne Stone, Charles Stuart, Julie Summers, Douglas Swanson, Daniel Sweeney, Mrs P. Sweetlove, Taku Tada, Peter Talbot, Martin Thomas, M. Thorncroft, Peter and Jane Thurman, Simon Tombs, Alan Tomlinson, Martin Tordoff, John Trevitt, Ewan and Joanne Turner, Winfried Van Gool, Terry Walton, Steve Waring, Julie Warner, Maria Warren, Bill White, Rose White, Mrs Brigitte Whitehead, Mike Williams, Alison Yates, Igor Zamberlan and Stefania Consigliere.

CONTENTS

Introduction xii

PART THREE CONTEXTS 1095

LIST OF MAPS

MAP SYMBOLS

– – – –	Chapter division boundary	✈	Airport
▪–▪–▪	International boundary	◉	Youth Hostel
▪ ▪	Regional boundary	⚠	Campground
▬▬	Motorway	⌂	Refuge
══	Road	——	Fortified wall
	Pedestrianised street	⚔	Fort
▥▥▥▥▥	Steps	◗	Cave
━━━	Railway	∴	Ruin
	Waterway	⚲	Monastery
— —	Ferry route	⌂	Abbey
- - - - -	Footpath	🏛	Château
☀	Lighthouse	⚔	Battlefield
⬠	Rock outcrop	ⓘ	Information office
▲	Mountain peak	✉	Post office
⤫⤫	Mountain range	★	Bus/tram stop
)(	Bridge/mountain pass	⊠–⊠	Gate
▼▼▼▼▼▼	Cutting	■	Building
☞	View point	✚	Church
⬥	Point of interest	▨	Park
P	Parking	▨	National Park
Ⓡ	RER station	✝	Cemetery
Ⓜ	Metro station	▨	Beach

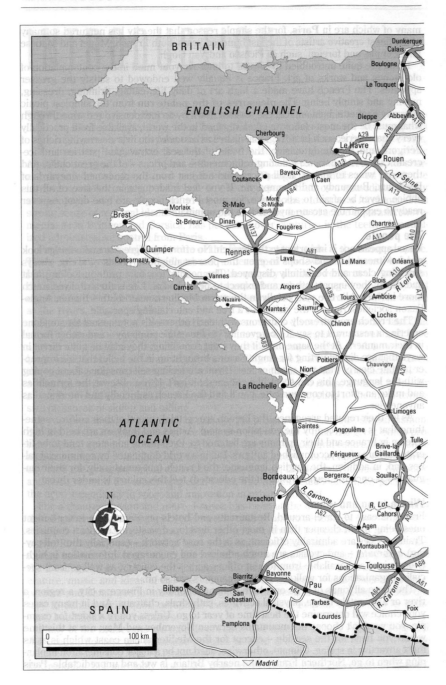

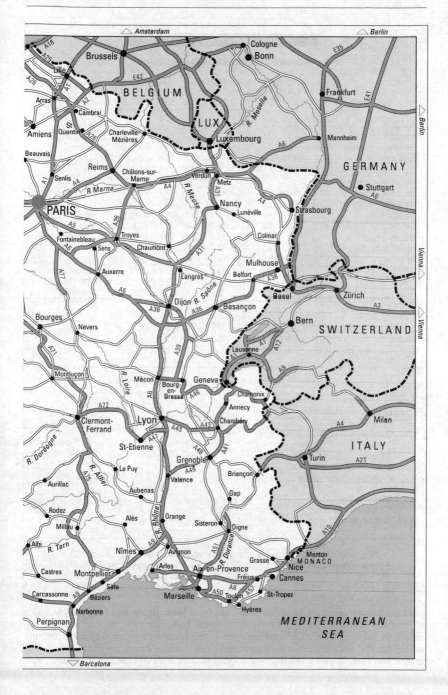

THE CLIMATE OF FRANCE

Average Daily Maximum Temperatures

	Jan	Feb	March	April	May	June	July	Aug	Sept	Oct	Nov	Dec
Paris/Île de France	7.5	7.1	10.2	15.7	16.6	23.4	25.1	25.6	20.9	16.5	11.7	7.8
Alsace	5.5	5.3	9.3	13.7	15.8	23.0	24.1	26.3	21.2	14.9	7.6	4.7
Aquitaine	10.0	9.4	12.2	19.5	18.0	23.7	27.2	25.7	24.2	19.7	15.4	11.0
Auvergne	8.0	6.4	10.1	15.9	17.1	24.2	27.0	24.5	23.3	17.0	11.0	8.3
Brittany	9.3	8.6	11.1	17.1	16.0	22.7	25.1	24.2	21.2	16.5	12.1	9.3
Burgundy	6.1	5.9	10.3	15.3	15.8	23.8	25.8	26.1	21.2	15.5	9.1	6.2
Champagne-Ardennes	6.2	5.6	8.9	13.8	15.1	22.5	23.8	24.9	19.3	15.0	9.6	6.2
Corsica	13	14	16	18	21	25	27	28	26	22	17	14
Franche-Comté	5.4	4.8	9.8	14.6	15.5	23.0	25.0	26.5	21.8	15.2	9.6	5.8
Languedoc-Roussillon	12.4	11.5	12.5	17.6	20.1	26.5	28.4	28.1	26.1	21.1	15.8	13.5
Limousin	6.1	6.1	9.6	16.1	14.9	22.1	24.8	23.6	21.0	16.2	12.8	8.5
Lorraine	5.5	5.3	9.3	13.7	15.8	23.0	24.1	26.3	21.2	14.9	7.6	4.7
Midi-Pyrénées	10.0	9.0	12.3	18.3	19.1	26.4	27.6	27.2	25.0	19.3	15.5	9.8
Nord/Pas de Calais	6.6	5.6	8.3	13.7	14.9	21.5	22.7	24.0	19.3	15.3	8.3	6.9
Normandy	7.6	6.4	8.4	13.0	14.0	20.0	21.6	22.0	18.2	14.5	10.8	7.9
Picardy	6.6	5.6	8.3	13.7	14.9	21.5	22.7	24.0	19.3	15.3	8.3	6.9
Poitou-Charentes	10.0	8.7	11.7	18.2	16.4	22.4	25.3	24.6	22.0	18.4	14.0	9.8
Provence	12.2	11.9	14.2	18.5	20.8	26.6	28.1	28.4	25.2	22.1	16.8	14.1
Rhône Valley	7.4	6.7	10.8	15.8	17.3	25.6	27.6	27.6	23.5	16.5	10.4	7.8
Riviera/Côte d'Azur	12.2	11.9	14.2	18.5	20.8	26.6	28.1	28.4	25.2	22.2	16.8	14.1
Savoy/ Dauphiné Alps	3.1	3.7	7.9	13.8	15.7	22.4	26.8	25.7	22.7	15.9	10.7	6.3
Val de Loire	7.8	6.8	10.3	16.1	16.4	23.6	25.8	24.5	21.1	16.2	11.2	7.0
Western Loire	9.9	8.6	11.3	17.7	16.7	23.3	25.7	24.6	21.8	16.9	12.4	9.5

Average Sea Temperatures

	May	June	July	Aug	Sept	Oct
Channel						
Calais to Le Havre	10	13	16	17	16	14
Cherbourg to Brest	11	13	15	17	16	14
Atlantic						
Brest to Bordeaux	13	15	17	18	17	15
Bordeaux to St-Jean-de-Luz	14	15	18	19	19	17
Mediterranean						
Montpellier to Toulon	15	19	19	20	20	17
Île de Levant to Menton	17	19	20	22	22	19

All temperatures are in **Centigrade**: to convert to **Fahrenheit** multiply by 9/5 and add 32.
For a recorded **weather forecast** you can phone the Paris forecasting office at ☎01.45.55.91.09
(☎01.45.55.95.02 for specific enquiries).

perhaps has a marginally better climate than New York, rarely reaching the extremes of heat and cold of that city, but only south of the Loire does the weather become significantly warmer. West coast weather, even in the south, is tempered by the proximity of the Atlantic, subject to violent storms and close thundery days even in summer. The centre and east, as you leave the coasts behind, have a more continental climate, with colder winters and hotter summers. The most reliable weather is along and behind the Mediterranean coastline and on Corsica, where winter is short and summer long and hot.

The single most important factor in deciding when to visit France is tourism itself. As most French people take their holidays in their own country, it's as well to avoid the main French holiday periods – mid-July to the end of August, with August being particularly bad. Almost the entire country closes down, except for the tourist industry itself. You can easily walk a kilometre and more in Paris, for example, in search of an open boulangerie, and the city seems deserted by all except fellow tourists. Prices in the resorts rise to take full advantage and often you can't find a room for love nor money, and not even a space in the campsites on the Côte d'Azur. The seaside is the worst, but the mountains and popular regions like the Dordogne are not far behind. Easter, too, is a bad time for Paris; half Europe's schoolchildren seem to descend on the city. For the same reasons, ski buffs should keep in mind the February school ski break. And no one who values life, limb, and sanity should ever be caught on the roads the last weekend of July or August, and least of all on the weekend of August 15.

PART ONE

THE

BASICS

GETTING THERE FROM BRITAIN

The quickest way of reaching France from most parts of Britain is by air, though in the southeast this is now rivalled closely by the Channel Tunnel London–Paris rail link, which makes the 340-kilometre journey in just three hours. The standard rail- or road-and-sea routes are significantly more affordable, but can be uncomfortable and tiring – and if you're just going for a short break, the journey time can significantly eat into your holiday.

BY AIR

If your destination is other than Paris, where the entire journey takes about the same time as by Eurostar, **flying** from London can represent a considerable saving in time compared to other methods of getting there: Nice, Toulouse and Lyon, for example, are less than two hours away. As often as not, if you live outside London, you'll find it pays to go to the capital and fly on to France from there. The cheapest fares are generally on the London–Paris route. Prices are highly competitive with those of Eurostar and can cost as little as £80 even with the big airlines; you should add on at least £40 to fly to a regional airport such as Nice, and around £120 to fly into Corsica. Direct flights from British regional airports do exist, and are detailed below: prices are not unfavourable compared with London fares. To find the best deals you should shop around, ideally a month or so before you plan to leave.

Air France, British Airways and British Midland are the main carriers to France from Britain, offering **scheduled flights** and Apex fares; the latter must be reserved one or two weeks in advance (depending on the route taken), and must include one Saturday night. Your return date must be fixed when purchasing, and no subsequent changes are allowed. Several **low-cost airlines** also offer scheduled flights to France, namely Buzz, EasyJet, Go and Ryanair. There are no advance-purchase conditions with these airlines, but obviously the earlier you book your seat the greater chance you have of taking advantage of special offers and availability – EasyJet offers deals from Luton airport to Paris for as little as £17.50 one way, for example. Alternatively, you can take the London–Paris leg of a long-haul flight to more distant destinations with airlines such as MAS (Malaysian) or PIA (Pakistan International) – STA Travel (see box on p.4) are specialists in this.

Air France flies to Paris Charles de Gaulle (abbreviated as Paris CDG) around ten times daily from Heathrow, four times daily (Mon–Fri) from London City airport, and daily from Manchester, Birmingham, Edinburgh and Glasgow. From Heathrow there is at least one flight a day direct to Lyon, Nice and Toulouse. Flights to Corsica – into Ajaccio, Bastia or Calvi – involve a change in Paris, including a swop from Paris CDG to Paris Orly. **British Airways** flies to Paris CDG three times daily from Gatwick, eight times daily from Heathrow and at least once daily from Birmingham, Manchester, Newcastle, Aberdeen, Edinburgh and Glasgow. BA also flies three times daily from Gatwick to Lyon and Marseille, and once daily to Montpellier. **British Midland** flies to Paris CDG at least five times daily from Heathrow, and at least once daily from East Midlands, Leeds-Bradford, Manchester, Edinburgh and Glasgow; also twice daily to Nice from Heathrow, and on weekdays from Leeds-Bradford, Manchester, Edinburgh and Glasgow.

With more competition between low-cost airlines, there are even cheaper flights available, though often to destinations other than Paris and not generally from Gatwick or Heathrow. **Buzz** flies from Stansted to Paris CDG three times daily, and once daily to Lyon, while **Ryanair** flies once daily out of Stansted to Carcassonne, Nîmes and St-Etienne, and **EasyJet** flies four times daily from Luton airport to Nice. At the time of writing, BA's low-cost sister company **Go** still offered daily

AIRLINES AND TRAVEL AGENTS IN BRITAIN

AIRLINES

Air France ☎0845/084 5111, *www.airfrance.fr.*
British Airways ☎0345/222 111, *www.britishairways.com.*
British Midland ☎0870/6070 555, *www.britishmidland.co.uk.*
Buzz ☎0870/240 7070, *www.buzzaway.com.*

Go ☎0845/605 4321, *www.go-fly.com.*
EasyJet direct sales ☎01582/702 900, *www.easyjet.com.*
Ryanair direct sales ☎0541/569 569, *www.ryanair.com.*

TRAVEL AGENTS

Campus Travel (*www.campustravel.co.uk*), 52 Grosvenor Gardens, London SW1W 0AG (☎0870/240 1010). There are also branches in Birmingham (☎0121/414 1848); Brighton (☎01273/570 226); Bristol (☎0117/929 2494); Cambridge (☎01223/324 283); Edinburgh (☎0131/668 3303); Glasgow (☎0141/553 1818); Manchester (☎0161/273 1721); and Oxford (☎01865/242 067). Student/youth travel specialists, with branches also in YHA shops and on university campuses all over Britain.

Flightbookers, 177–178 Tottenham Court Rd, London W1P 0LX (☎020/7757 2000, *ebookers.com*); Gatwick Airport, South Terminal inside the British Rail Station (☎01293/568 300). Low fares on a wide selection of scheduled flights.

North South Travel, Moulsham Mill Centre, Parkway, Chelmsford, Essex CM2 7PX (☎01245/608 291). Friendly, competitive travel agency, offering discounted fares to most destinations – profits are used to support projects in the developing world, especially the promotion of sustainable tourism.

STA Travel (*www.statravel.co.uk*), London: 86 Old Brompton Rd, SW7 3LH; 117 Euston Rd, NW1 2SX; 38 Store St, WC1E 7BZ; and 11 Goodge St, W1P 2SX (☎020/7361 6161). There

are also branches in Brighton (☎01273/728 282); Bristol (☎0117/929 4399); Cambridge (☎01223/366 966); Manchester (☎0161/834 0668); Leeds (☎0113/244 9212); Liverpool (☎0151/707 1223); Newcastle-upon-Tyne (☎0191/233 2111); Oxford (☎01865/792 800); Aberdeen (☎0122/465 8222); Edinburgh (☎0131/226 7747); and Glasgow (☎0141/338 6000); and on university campuses throughout Britain. Worldwide specialists in low-cost flights and tours for students and under-26s.

Thomas Cook, 45 Berkeley St, London W1X 5AE; and high streets across London and the UK (nationwide ☎0990/666 222; Flights Direct ☎0990/101 520; *www.tch.thomascook.com*). Long-established travel agency for package holidays and scheduled flights, with bureau de change (issuing Thomas Cook travellers' cheques), own travel insurance and car rental.

Trailfinders (*www.trailfinders.com*), London: 1 Threadneedle St, EC2R 8JX (☎020/7628 7628); 215 Kensington High St, W6 6BD (☎020/7937 5400). There are also branches in Birmingham (☎0121/236 1234); Bristol (☎0117/929 9000); Manchester (☎0161/839 6969); Glasgow (☎0141/353 2224). One of the best-informed and most efficient agents for independent travellers.

flights from Stansted to Lyon, though its forthcoming sell-off has left the future of this service uncertain.

A good place to look for **discount fares** from London to France is the classified travel sections of papers such as the *Independent* and the *Daily Telegraph* (Saturday editions), the *Observer*, *Sunday Times* and *Independent on Sunday*, where agents advertise special deals; if you're in London, check the back pages of the listings mag-

azine *Time Out*, the *Evening Standard* or the free travel mag *TNT*, found outside main-line train stations. Independent travel specialists such as STA Travel and Campus Travel do deals for students and anyone under 26, or can simply sell a scheduled ticket at a discount price. All these are worth contacting to see what deals they currently have on offer, whether these involve seats on their own or a tour operator's **charter flight** – in theory this is supposed to be sold in conjunction with accommodation, but it is sometimes possible just to buy the air ticket at a discount through your travel agent. Bear in mind that any travel agent can sell you a **package deal** with a tour operator (see p.9) and these can often offer exceptional bargain travel.

BY TRAIN

The **Channel Tunnel** has slashed travelling time by train from London to Lille and Paris and has also led to a multitude of cut-rate deals on regular train and ferry or hovercraft fares via Calais, Boulogne and Dieppe. Crossing the Channel **by sea** can work out to be slightly cheaper than using the Channel Tunnel, but you should note that it does take considerably longer, unless you are heading for the area close to one of the French ports or live in the southeast of England, and is generally less convenient.

Eurostar (☎0990/186 186, *www.eurostar.com*) operates high-speed passenger trains daily from London Waterloo to the continent via Ashford in Kent (itself 1hr from London) and the Channel Tunnel. There are at least thirteen daily to Paris-Gare du Nord (3hr), though only around half of these also stop at Ashford; a few of the services also stop at Calais-Fréthun (1hr 30min) and at Lille (2hr), and there's a separate, direct service to Lille (2hr), which runs around nine times daily. The service to Brussels (at least six daily) also stops in Lille. There's also a daily and direct train to Disneyland Paris (3hr); and a ski-season-only direct service from Waterloo/Ashford to Moutiers-Salins and Bourg-St-Maurice in the French Alps which runs twice weekly (mid-Dec to April; around 8hr); skis are carried free.

The Eurostar can also be used to make fast and affordable train **connections** to other parts of France, particularly from Lille where you can connect at the same station with the high-speed TGV network to Lyon, Bordeaux, Nice and Cannes. For example, you can travel from London to Lille (2hr) and change for the TGV to Bordeaux (5hr).

Standard-class return **fares** from London to Paris range from £70 (weekend day-trip) to £290, but frequently advertised special offers can go as low as £59. Besides such offers, and day-trips, the cheapest ticket to Paris is the "Leisure Apex 14", which must be bought up to fourteen days before departure and must include a Saturday night, with fixed outward and return dates and no refunds; it costs £70 through to Paris, £60 to Lille.

There are other cheap deals – such as the "Leisure Flexi", which can be purchased up to thirty minutes before departure for £140/110 – but for a high-season ticket with changeable departure and return times, bought close to your departure date, you're looking at £290/220. Standard return fares to Disneyland Paris are £220 for adults, £58 for children aged 4–11 and £75 for youths aged 11–25. A standard return on the Eurostar Ski train is £220 (with less flexible Ski Saver tickets from £169 return). Youth-fare **concessions** are available on all the routes (student discounted tickets are only available from STA, USIT Campus Travel and Wasteels, not directly from Eurostar) – there are concessions also for over-60s, and for holders of an international rail pass.

You can also get **through-ticketing** – including the tube journey to Waterloo International – from other mainline stations in Britain; typical add-on prices for a return ticket to Paris from Edinburgh or Glasgow are £30, from Manchester £20 and Birmingham £10. However, there is still no sign of the promised direct high-speed Eurostar services from the north of England, Scotland and the Midlands, which means that add-on time to your journey is around four or six hours if you're travelling from the north of England or southern Scotland respectively.

Tickets can be bought directly over the phone from Eurostar (see box on p.7), from most travel agents, from all main rail stations in Britain and from the Waterloo International and Ashford ticket offices.

TRAIN PASSES

If you plan to use the rail network to get around France, there are several **train passes** you might consider buying before you leave.

The **Euro Domino Pass**, available from Rail Europe (SNCF), Wasteels and USIT Campus offers unlimited rail travel through France for any three (£99), four (£119), five (£139), six (£159), seven (£178) or eight (£198) days within a calendar month; passengers under 25 pay £79, £95, £111, £127, £143 and £159 respectively. Children under 4 travel free, and those aged between 4 and 11 are charged half the adult price. The pass also entitles you to reductions on rail-ferry links to France.

InterRail passes cover eight European "zones" and are available for either 22-day or one-month

SEA CROSSINGS AND PRICES FROM BRITAIN

The following services are ferry crossings, unless otherwise stated.

Route	Operator	Crossing Time	Frequency	One-Way Fares Small car + 2 adults	Foot passengers
BRITTANY					
Portsmouth–St-Malo	Brittany Ferries	8hr 45min–11hr	7 weekly	£97–203	£24–47
Poole–St-Malo (via Jersey and Guernsey)	Condor Ferries	5hr 25min	1 daily	£95–187	£26
Plymouth–Roscoff	Brittany Ferries	6hr–7hr 30min	2–12 weekly	£110–189	£27–48
Weymouth–St-Malo (via Jersey and Guernsey)	Condor Ferries	5hr	May–Oct 1 daily	£95–187	£27
NORMANDY					
Newhaven–Dieppe (catamaran)	Hoverspeed	2hr	1–3 daily	£139–195	£28
Portsmouth–Cherbourg	P&O Portsmouth	2hr 45min–7hr 30min	1–7 daily	£95–178	£20–41
Poole–Cherbourg	Brittany Ferries	4hr 15min–5hr 45min	1–2 daily	£100–171	£21–42
Portsmouth–Le Havre	P&O Portsmouth	5hr 30min–7hr 30min	2–3 daily	£95–178	£20–41
Portsmouth–Caen (Ouistreham)	Brittany Ferries	6hr	2–3 daily	£80–185	£19–43
PAS-DE-CALAIS					
Folkestone–Boulogne (catamaran)	Hoverspeed	55min	4 daily	£115–155	£24
Dover–Calais	P&O Stena	1hr 15min	30–35 daily	£105–123	£24
Dover–Calais	Sea France	1hr 30min	15 daily	£118–163	£15
Dover–Calais (hovercraft)	Hoverspeed	35min	9–16 daily	£125–169	£24
BELGIUM					
Hull–Zeebrugge	P&O North Sea Ferries	3hr 15min	1 daily	£152–188	£37–46

FERRY COMPANIES IN BRITAIN

Brittany Ferries ☎0870/901 2400, *www.brittany-ferries.co.uk.*
Condor Ferries ☎01305/761 551, *www.condorferries.co.uk.*
Hoverspeed ☎0870/524 0241, *www.hoverspeed.co.uk.*
P&O North Sea Ferries ☎01482/377 177, *www.ponsf.com.*
P&O Portsmouth ☎0870/242 4999, *www.poportsmouth.com.*
P&O Stena ☎087/0600 0600, *www.posl.com.*
Sea France ☎0870/571 1711, *www.seafrance.com.*

periods; you must have been resident in Europe for at least six months before you can buy the pass.

The passes for those over 26 have now been extended to cover the same territory as for those

USEFUL TRAIN AND BUS ADDRESSES

USIT Campus (see box on p.4).

Eurolines, 52 Grosvenor Gardens, London SW1W 0AU (bookings and enquiries ☎020/7730 8235 or 01582/404 511, *www.eurolines.co.uk*). Tickets can also be purchased from any National Express agent (☎0990/808 080).

Eurostar, Eurostar House, Waterloo Station, London SE1 8SE (☎0990/186 186, *www.eurostar.com*).

Eurotunnel, Customer Services Centre, PO Box 300, Dept 302, Folkestone, Kent CT19 4QD (information and bookings ☎0990/353 535, *www.eurotunnel.com*).

Rail Europe, 179 Piccadilly, London W1V 0BA (☎0990/848 848).

Wasteels, Platform 2, Victoria Station, London SW1V 1JY (☎020/7834 7066).

under 26 and the only difference now is the price. France is in the zone including Belgium, the Netherlands and Luxembourg. A 22-day pass to travel this area is £159/229; a two-zone pass valid for a month is £209/279, a three-zone £229/309, and an all-zones pass £259/349. The pass is available from the same outlets as the Euro Domino (see above) and from STA Travel. InterRail passes do not include travel between Britain and the continent, although InterRail pass-holders are eligible for discounts on rail travel in Britain and Northern Ireland and cross-Channel ferries.

Both the Euro Domino and InterRail passes entitle you to a discount on the London–Paris Eurostar service.

BY BUS

Eurolines run regular bus-ferry services from London Victoria to over sixty French cities. Prices are very much lower than for the same journey by train, with adult return fares at the time of writing £45 for Paris, £35 for Lille, £92 for Lyon, and £89 each for Bordeaux and Toulouse. Regional return fares from the rest of England and from Wales are available as are student and youth discounts. Again, prices are very much lower than for the same journey by train. As well as ordinary tickets on its scheduled coach services to an extensive list of European cities, Eurolines offers a pass for Europe-wide travel, for either thirty days (over-26s £245, youth pass and over-60s £195) or sixty days (£283/227). **Tickets** are available directly from the company, from National Express agents and from most high-street travel agents.

EUROTUNNEL AND MOTORAIL

The most convenient way of taking your car across to France is to drive down to the **Channel Tunnel**, load your car on the train shuttle, and be whisked under the Channel in 35 minutes, arriving at Coquelles on the French side, near Calais. The Channel Tunnel entrance is off the M20 at junction 11A, just outside Folkestone, and the sole operator, **Eurotunnel**, offers a frequent, daily service (☎0800/969 992, *www.eurotunnel.com*). Because of the frequency of the service, you don't have to buy a ticket in advance (though this might be advisable in mid-summer and during other school holidays), but you must arrive at least 30 minutes before departure; the target loading time is just ten minutes. Inside the carriages, you can get out of your car to stretch your legs during the crossing. Tickets are available through Eurotunnel's Customer Service Centre, on the Internet or from your local travel agent. Fares are calculated per car, regardless of the number of passengers. Rates depend on the time of year, time of day and length of stay (the cheapest ticket is for a day-trip, followed by a five-day return); it's cheaper to travel between 10pm and 6am, while the highest fares are reserved for weekend departures and returns in July and August. As an example, a five-day trip at an off-peak time starts at £95 (passengers included) in the low season and goes up to £135 in the peak period.

If you don't want to drive far when you've reached France, you can take advantage of SNCF's **motorail**, which you can book through Rail Europe (☎0870/584 8848, *www.raileurope .co.uk*), putting your car on the train in Calais for Avignon, Biarritz, Bordeaux, Brive, Narbonne, Nice or Toulouse, or in Paris for Avignon, Biarritz, Bordeaux, Briancon, Brive, Evian, Frejus, Lyon, Marseille, Moutiers, Narbonne, Nice, St-Gervais, Tarbes, Toulon or Toulouse. This is a relatively expensive option: Calais–Nice, for example, costs from £560 return for car and driver, plus £115 for each additional adult and £60 for children aged between 4 and 11.

BY FERRY AND HOVERCRAFT

If you are heading to France from the southeast of Britain, you will find that Eurotunnel and Eurostar are quicker and more convenient than the **ferries** plying the same route, even though the ferry and hovercraft/catamaran services between Dover and Calais, and Folkestone and Boulogne are the most frequent services crossing the Channel. However, if your starting point is further west than London, it may well still be worth heading direct to one of the south-coast ports and catching one of the ferries to Brittany or Normandy – the crossings from Portsmouth to St-Malo, Cherbourg, Caen and Le Havre are amongst the most competitively priced sea crossings from Britain. If you're coming from the north of England or Scotland, you should consider the Hull–Zeebrugge (Belgium) overnight crossing with P&O North Sea Ferries.

Ferry **prices** are seasonal and, for motorists, depend on the size of your vehicle. The popular Dover–Calais routing costs from £105 one way for a car and two adults. Note that return prices are substantially cheaper than one-way fares, but generally need to be booked in advance – details of routes, companies and current fares are given in the box on p.6. You can either contact the companies direct to reserve space in advance –

essential in peak season if you're intending to drive – or any travel agent in the UK or France will do it for you. All ferry companies also offer foot passenger fares only, from £20 one way; accompanying bicycles can usually be carried free, at least in the low season, and for a charge of around £5 one way in mid- and high seasons.

The ferry companies will often offer **special deals** on three-, five- and ten-day returns, or discounts for regular users who own a property abroad. The tour operator **Eurodrive** (☎020/8324 4007, *www.eurodrive.co.uk*) can also arrange discounts on ferry crossings for people taking their cars across the Channel, and can book accommodation in northern France at competitive rates.

HITCHING

Hitching from Calais or Boulogne to Paris is notoriously difficult, so you'd be well advised to accept through-lifts only. The worst black holes – where hitchers become invisible to drivers – are Abbeville and Beauvais, and if you can possibly afford one of the cheaper bus or train tickets from the UK, you'll save yourself a lot of trouble. If not, get friendly with drivers on the boat over and try to get a promise of a lift before docking. It is not much easier hitching from any of the other ports either, and it may well be worth contacting the

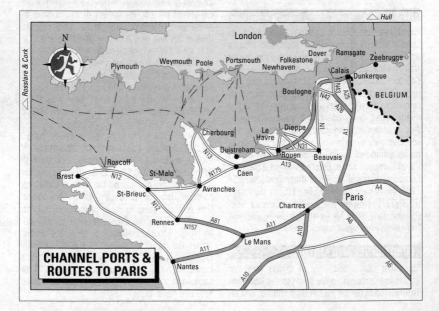

CHANNEL PORTS & ROUTES TO PARIS

ride-share organization Allostop Provoya; see p.40 for information.

PACKAGE TOURS

Any travel agent will be able to provide details of the many operators running **package tours** to France (see box below), which can be a competitively priced way of travelling. Some deals are straightforward travel-plus-hotel affairs, while others offer tandem touring, air-and-rail packages and stays in country cottages. If your trip is geared around specific interests – like cycling or self-catering in the countryside – packages can work out much cheaper than the same arrangements made on arrival. Packages can also be a good idea if you are on a tight

schedule – particularly if you are planning a city break, as these deals often include free transfers to your hotel and guided tours or theatre tickets as well as flights and accommodation, leaving you more time to enjoy your holiday.

In addition to the addresses in the box below, bear in mind that most of the ferry companies (see box on p.6) also offer their own travel and accommodation deals. The **French Holiday Service** at 178 Piccadilly, London W1V 0AL (☎020/7355 4747) can book the largest range of package holidays in France. A complete list of package operators is available from the **French Government Tourist Office**, also at 178 Piccadilly, London W1V 0AL (☎0906/824 4123).

TOUR OPERATORS AND VILLA AGENCIES IN BRITAIN

Allez France (☎01903/742 345, www.greatescapes.co.uk). Self-drive and fly-drive accommodation packages (cottages, villas, hotels and caravans) throughout France.

Bike Tours (☎01225/310 859, www.biketours.co.uk). Biking trips to France.

Corsican Affair (☎020/7385 8438, www.frenchaffair.com). Fly-drive, hotel packages and self-catering to the island, plus some villa rental on the mainland.

Dominique's Villas (☎020/7738 8772, www.dominiquesvillas.com). Small, upmarket agency with a diverse and tempting range of mostly older properties (some quite historic) in the Loire, Dordogne, Provence and on the Côte d'Azur. Most are for large groups, sleeping six to eight or more.

Gîtes de France Ltd. The UK operation of this French Government letting service was taken over in 1997 by Brittany Ferries (☎0870/901 2400, www.brittany-ferries.co.uk), although you can still deal directly with Gîtes de France (see p.44). Comprehensive list of houses, cottages and chalets all over France; ferry crossing extra.

Keycamp Holidays (☎020/8395 4000, www.keycamp.com). Mobile homes and tents for rent; deals may include ferry or Channel Tunnel tickets.

Martin Randall Travel (☎020/8742 3355, www.martinrandall.com). Small-group cultural tours led by experts on art, architecture, archeology and music. Tours are very specialized, and this is reflected in the price, but for opera buffs or art enthusiasts they may well prove a rewarding investment.

Paris Travel Service (☎01992/456 000, www.paristravel.co.uk). Good for regional flights from across the UK and rail deals via London to the French capital. Also offers accommodation packages.

Plas y Brenin National Mountain Centre (☎01690/720 214, www.pyb.co.uk). Springtime ski-mountaineering courses in the Alps, including parts of the High Level Route.

Susie Madron's Cycling for Softies (☎0161/248 8282, www.cycling-for-softies.co.uk). An easy-going cycle holiday operator to most regions, including Provence. Although luggage transfer is not included in the deals, this can be arranged for an additional fee.

Time Off (☎0870/584 6363 or 0845/733 6622). Short breaks to Paris and Nice, with accommodation in comfortable and central surroundings; flight, Eurostar and Orient Express packages available.

Travelscene Ltd (☎020/8427 4445, www.travelscene.co.uk). Short breaks to Disneyland Paris or Northern France, travelling by air or Eurostar or self-drive via the Channel Tunnel or ferry.

VFB Holidays (☎01242/240 310, www.vfbholidays.co.uk). Good-value self-catering, ferry and road holidays, plus alpine resorts in the Midi, Alsace and Burgundy and fly-drive holidays to Corsica and city-breaks in Nice, Paris and Lille. Their brochure has a huge range of well-detailed cottages, farmhouses and villas to choose from.

Voyages Ilena (☎020/7924 4440). Specializing in self-catering villas, this helpful and friendly agency can also arrange accommodation in luxury hotels; flights, fly-drives and tailor-made holidays can be arranged too.

GETTING THERE FROM IRELAND

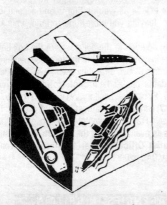

The fastest and most cost-effective way of getting to France from Ireland is by plane. There are good deals out of the regional airports as well as out of Dublin to Paris. It is also possible to fly direct from Belfast, but there are fewer options and the costs are generally much higher. Your best bet is to get a flight into Paris, from where you can make connections to France's regional airports, or book a flight to London or Amsterdam and travel on to France from there. It is also possible to sail to northern France from Cork and Rosslare, though the journey time is long (around 15hr) and the costs are not significantly lower than the deals offered by the airlines that fly out of western Ireland; however, if you do need to take your car, and northern France is your main destination, then sailing – especially for groups of two or more – could prove to be a cheaper and more convenient option.

BY AIR

In the **Irish Republic**, Aer Lingus flies direct from Dublin and most other regional airports to Paris CDG with a few seats at IR£102/€129 return and a standard fare of IR£199/€253. Ryanair offers two flights daily from Dublin to Beauvais Tillé airport outside Paris for IR£97.50/€124. Go Holidays arranges charter flights in high season (April–Sept)

AIRLINES, TRAVEL AGENTS AND TOUR OPERATORS IN IRELAND

AIRLINES

Aer Lingus Republic: ☎01/705 3333; Northern Ireland: ☎0845/973 7747; *www.aerlingus.ie*.

British Airways Republic: ☎1800/626747; Northern Ireland: ☎0845/722 2111; *www.british-airways.com*.

Ryanair Republic: ☎01/609 7800; Northern Ireland: ☎0870/156 9569; *www.ryanair.com*.

TRAVEL AGENTS

Joe Walsh Tours, 69 Upper O'Connell St, Dublin 2 (☎01/872 2555); 8–11 Baggot St, Dublin 2 (☎01/676 3053); 117 St Patrick St, Cork (☎021/277 959). Discounted flight agent.

Thomas Cook, 118 Grafton St, Dublin 2 (☎01/677 0469); 11 Donegall Place, Belfast (☎01232/550 232 or 554 455). Package holiday and flight agent who can also arrange travellers' cheques, insurance and car rental.

Trailfinders, 4–5 Dawson St, Dublin 2 (☎01/677 7888, *www.trailfinders.ie*). Competitive fares out of all Irish airports, as well as deals on hotels, insurance, tours and car rental.

USIT (*www.usitnow.ie*), 19 Aston Quay, Dublin 2 (☎01/602 1777 or 677 8117; Fountain Centre, College St, Belfast (☎01232/324 073); plus branches in Cork, Galway, Limerick, Waterford and Derry. Student and youth specialists for flights and trains.

TOUR OPERATORS

Go Holidays, 28 North Great George St, Dublin 1 (☎01/874 4126). French holiday specialists offering city breaks to Paris. Also Disneyland Paris packages, fly-drive packages, and charter flights to regional destinations.

Irish Ferries, 2–4 Merrion Row, Dublin 2 (☎1890/313 131, *www.irishferries.ie*). Self-drive, self-catering package holidays – camping, mobile homes, apartments – to all coastal regions of France.

Neenan Travel, 12 South Leinster St, Dublin 2 (☎01/676 5181, con@neenantrav.ie). Packages to Paris and Disneyland Paris.

FERRY ROUTES AND PRICES FROM IRELAND

Route	Operator	Crossing Time	Frequency	One-Way Fares	
				Small car + 2 adults	Foot passenger
Cork–Roscoff	Brittany Ferries	14hr	April–Sept 1 weekly	IR£140–330/ €178–419	IR£45–85/ €57–108
Rosslare–Cherbourg	Irish Ferries	16hr	March–Oct 2–3 weekly	IR£140–330/ €178–419	IR£45–85/ €57–108
Rosslare–Cherbourg	P&O Irish Sea	18hr	3 weekly	IR£110–260/ €140–330	not allowed
Rosslare–Roscoff	Irish Ferries	15hr	April–Sept 1–3 weekly	IR£140–330/ €178–419	IR£45–85/ €57–108

FERRY COMPANIES IN IRELAND

Brittany Ferries Republic: ☎021/277 801; Northern Ireland: 0870/536 0360; *www.brittany-ferries.com*.
Irish Ferries 24hr information ☎1890/313 131, *www.irishferries.ie*.

P&O Irish Sea Republic: ☎1800/409 049; Northern Ireland: 0870/598 0777; *www.poirish-sea.com*.

from Shannon, Cork and Dublin to Nantes, Toulouse, Montpellier, Marseille, Lyon, Paris and Nice, from £179 return.

In **Northern Ireland**, British Airways flies directly from Belfast City Airport to Paris CDG, but prices are generally much higher than taking a routing through London or Amsterdam. Go, BA's low-cost arm, currently offers one-way deals from Belfast to London Stansted for around IR£60/€76.18. The Paris Travel Service (see box on p.9) has package deals including flights from Belfast.

BY CAR AND FERRY

The cheapest way of getting to France – though far from the quickest – is by **ferry** from Cork or Rosslare outside Wexford to Cherbourg or to Roscoff in Brittany.

Ferry **prices** vary according to season and, for motorists, the size of their car; note that return prices are substantially cheaper but generally need to be booked in advance. Services are run by Brittany Ferries and Irish Ferries, and prices are around IR£140/€178 to IR£330/€419 for a small car and two adults one way; foot passengers will pay between IR£45/€57 and IR£85/€108; P&O Irish Sea offers a slightly cheaper service for cars with no foot passengers. Often ferry companies will offer special deals on return fares for a specified period, so check first. You can either contact the companies direct to reserve space in advance (essential at peak season if you're driving), or any competent travel agent at home can do it for you. Details of routes, companies and fares are given in the box above.

GETTING THERE FROM NORTH AMERICA

Getting to France from North America is straightforward; there are direct flights from over thirty major cities to Paris, with connections from all over the continent. Nearly a dozen different scheduled airlines operate flights, making Paris one of the cheapest destinations in Europe. If France is part of a longer European trip, a Eurail train pass may be a useful option (see box on p.14).

SHOPPING FOR TICKETS

Barring special offers, the cheapest fare is usually an **Apex** ticket, although this will carry certain restrictions: you have to book – and pay – at least 21 days before departure, spend at least

---

AIRLINES AND DISCOUNT TRAVEL COMPANIES IN NORTH AMERICA

AIRLINES

Air Canada in US ☎1-800/776 3000; in Canada ☎1-800/555 1212; *www.aircanada.ca.*

Air France in US ☎1-800/237 2747; in Canada ☎1-800/667 2747; *www.airfrance.fr.*

American Airlines ☎1-800/433 7300; *www.aa.com.*

AOM French Airlines ☎1-800/892 9136; *www.aom.com.*

British Airways ☎1-800/247 9297; *www.british-airways.com.*

Canadian Airlines in US ☎1-800/426 7000; in Canada ☎1-800/665 1177; *www.cdnair.com.*

Continental Airlines ☎1-800/231 0856; *www.flycontinental.com.*

Delta Airlines ☎1-800/241 4141; *www.delta-air.com.*

Iceland Air ☎1-800/223 5500; *www.icelandair.com.*

Northwest Airlines ☎1-800/225 2525; *www.nwa.com.*

TWA ☎1-800/892 4141; *www.twa.com.*

United Airlines ☎1-800/538 2929; *www.ual.com.*

US Air ☎1-800/622 1015; *www.usairways.com.*

Virgin Atlantic Airways ☎1-800/862 8621; *www.virgin-atlantic.com.*

DISCOUNT TRAVEL COMPANIES

Air Brokers International, 150 Post St, Suite 620, San Francisco, CA 94108 (☎1-800/883 3273; *www.airbrokers.com*). Consolidator.

Air Courier Association, 15000 W 6th Ave, Suite 203, Golden, CO 80401 (☎1-800/282 1202; *www.aircourier.com*). Courier-flight broker.

Airhitch, 2641 Broadway, New York, NY 10025 (☎1-800/326 2009 or 212/864 2000; *www.airhitch.org*). Standby-seat broker: for a set

price, they guarantee to get you on a flight as close to your preferred destination as possible, within a week.

Airtreks.com, 442 Post St, Suite 400, San Francisco, CA 94102 (☎1-800/428 8735; *www.airtreks.com*). Travel company with a highly recommended interactive Web site.

Council Travel, 205 E 42nd St, New York, NY 10017 (☎1-800/226 8624;

seven days abroad (maximum stay three months), and you tend to get penalized if you change your schedule. On transatlantic routes there are also winter **Super Apex** tickets, sometimes known as "Eurosavers" – slightly cheaper than an ordinary Apex, but limiting your stay to between 7 and 21 days. Some airlines also issue **Special Apex** tickets to people younger than 24, often extending the maximum stay to a year. Many airlines offer youth or student fares to **under-25s**; a passport or driving licence are sufficient proof of age, though these tickets are subject to availability and can have eccentric booking conditions. It's worth remembering that most cheap return fares involve spending at least one Saturday night away and that many will only give a percentage refund if you need to cancel or alter your journey, so make

sure you check the restrictions carefully before buying a ticket.

You can normally cut costs further by going through a specialist flight agent – either a **consolidator**, who buys up blocks of tickets from the airlines and sells them at a discount, or a **discount agent**, who deals in blocks of tickets offloaded by the airlines, and often offers special student and youth fares and a range of other travel-related services such as travel insurance, rail passes, car rental, tours and the like. Bear in mind, though, that penalties for changing your plans can be stiff, and that these companies make their money by dealing in bulk – don't expect them to answer lots of questions. Some agents specialize in **charter flights**, which may be cheaper than anything available on a scheduled flight, but again

www.counciltravel.com). Nationwide US student travel organization with branches in (among others) San Francisco, Washington DC, Boston, Austin, Seattle, Chicago, Minneapolis.

Educational Travel Center, 438 N Frances St, Madison, WI 53703 (☎1-800/747 5551; *www.edtrav.com*). Student/youth discount agent.

Flight Centre, 3030 Granville St, Vancouver, BC V6H 3J9 (☎1-604/739 9539; *www.flightcentre.com*). Discount air fares from Canadian cities.

Interworld Travel, 800 Douglas Rd, Suite 140, Coral Gables, FL 33134 (☎1-800/468 3796; *www.interworldtravel.com*). Consolidator.

Last Minute Travel Club, 100 Sylvan Rd, Suite 600, Woburn, MA 01801 (☎1-800/ LAST MIN). Travel club specializing in standby deals.

New Frontiers/Nouvelles Frontières, 12 E 33rd St, New York, NY 10016 (☎1-800/366 6387 or 514/526 8444; *www.newfrontiers.com*). French discount-travel firm; also markets charters to Paris and Lyon. Branches in New York, Montréal, Los Angeles, San Francisco and Québec City.

Now Voyager, 74 Varick St, Suite 307, New York, NY 10013 (☎212/431 1616; *www.nowvoyagertravel.com*). Agent specializing in courier flights.

STA Travel, 10 Downing St, New York, NY 10014 (☎1-800/777 0112; *www.sta-travel.com*).

Worldwide specialist in independent travel with branches in the Los Angeles, San Francisco and Boston areas. STA also has French branches in Paris and Grenoble.

TFI Tours International, 34 W 32nd St, 12th Floor, New York, NY 10001 (☎1-800/745 8000). Consolidator; offices in New York, Las Vegas, San Francisco, Los Angeles.

Travac, 989 6th Ave, 16th Floor, New York, NY 10018 (☎1-800/872 8800; *www.thetravelsite.com*). Consolidator and charter broker; branches in New York and Orlando.

Travel Avenue, 10 S Riverside Plaza, Suite 1404, Chicago, IL 60606 (☎1-800/ 333 3335; *www.travelavenue.com*). Discount travel agent.

Travel Cuts, 187 College St, Toronto, ON M5T 1P7 (☎1-800/667-2887 or 416/979 2406; *www.travelcuts.com*). Canadian specialist student and discount travel organization with branches all over the country.

Travelers Advantage, 3033 S Parker Rd, Suite 1000, Aurora, CO 80014 (☎1-800/548 1116; *www.travelersadvantage.com*). Discount travel club.

Unitravel, 11737 Administration Dr, Suite 120, St Louis, MO 63146 (☎1-800/325 2222; *www.flightsforless.com*). Consolidator.

Worldtek Travel, 111 Water St, New Haven, CT 06511 (☎1-800/243 1723; *www.worldtek.com*). Discount travel agency.

EUROPEAN TRAIN PASSES

There are a number of European **train passes** that can only be purchased before leaving home, though consider carefully how much travelling you are going to be doing: these all-encompassing passes only really begin to pay for themselves if you intend to see a fair bit of France and the rest of the Europe.

The best-known and most flexible is the **Eurail Youthpass** (for under-26s), which costs US$388/A$733 for fifteen days, and there are also one-month and two-month versions; if you're 26 or over you'll have to buy a first-class **Eurail** pass, which costs US$554/A$1046 for the fifteen-day option. You stand a better chance of getting your money's worth out of a **Eurail Flexipass**, which is good for a certain number of travel days in a two-month period. This, too, comes in under-26/first-class versions: ten days for under-26s costs US$458/A$865, for over-26s US$654/A$1234; and for fifteen days US$599/A$1131 and US$862/A$1627.

A scaled-down version of the Flexipass, the **Europass** allows travel in France, Germany, Italy, Switzerland and Spain for US$233/A$440 and US$348/A$657 for five days in two months, on up to US$513/A$968 and US$728/A$1374 for fifteen days in two months; there are also cheaper three- and four-country combinations, as well as the option of adding adjacent "associate" countries. A further alternative is to attempt to buy an **InterRail Pass** in Europe (see "Getting there from Britain", p.5) – most agents don't check residential qualifications – but once you're in Europe it'll be too late to buy a Eurail pass if you have problems. You can purchase Eurail passes from one of the agents listed below.

In addition to the passes outlined above, you can buy **more specific passes** valid for travel in France only. North Americans can take advantage of the **France Railpass** which provides 3 days, unlimited travel in a one-month period: they are available for first- and second-class travel, costing $210 and $180, respectively, or, if travelling in groups of two or more, $171 and $146 per person. Up to six additional days of travel may be purchased for $30 per day. For under-26s, the **France Youthpass** provides four days of unlimited travel in a two-month period for $164; up to six additional days may be purchased for $20 per day. All passes must be purchased before departure and are available through travel agents or with rail specialists (see below). There is also a **France Rail n' Drive** pass starting at $175 which provides three days' of unlimited train travel and two days' car rental; price increases with size of car and class of ticket.

In addition, the SNCF has a range of other reductions and passes, which can be purchased once in France: details of these can be found in "Getting around", p.36.

RAIL CONTACTS IN NORTH AMERICA

CIT Rail, 15 W 44th St, 10th Floor, New York, NY 10036 (☎1-800/223 7987; *www. fs-on-line.com*). Eurail passes only.

Rail Europe, 226 Westchester Ave, White Plains, NY 10604 (☎1-800/438 7245; *www.raileurope.com*). Official Eurail pass agent in North America; also sells the widest range of European regional and individual country passes.

ScanTours, 3439 Wade St, Los Angeles, CA 90066 (☎1-800/223 7226 or 310/636 4656; *www.scantours.com*). Eurail, and many other European country passes.

RAIL CONTACTS IN AUSTRALIA AND NEW ZEALAND

CIT World Travel, 2/263 Clarence St, Sydney, Australia (☎02/9267 1255; *www.cittravel.com.au*). For Eurail and Europasses.

Rail Plus, Level 3, 459 Little Collins St, Melbourne, Australia (☎03/9642 8644 or 1300/555 003; *info@railplus.com.au*); Level 2, 60 Parnell Rd, Auckland, New Zealand (☎09/303 2484). For Eurail and Europasses.

Thomas Cook, 175 Pitt St, Sydney, Australia (for the nearest branch call ☎13 1771; for telesales call ☎1800/801 002; *www.thomascook.com.au*); 191 Queen St, Auckland, New Zealand (☎09/379 3920, *www.thomascook.co.nz*).

departure dates are fixed and withdrawal penalties are high (check the refund policy). If you travel a lot, **discount travel clubs** are another option – the annual membership fee may be worth it for benefits such as cut-price air tickets and car rental.

A further possibility is to see if you can arrange a **courier flight**, although the hit-or-miss nature of these makes them most suitable for a single traveller who travels light and has a very flexible schedule. In return for shepherding a parcel through customs and possibly giving up your baggage allowance, you can expect to get a deeply discounted ticket. For more options, consult *Courier Bargains: How to Travel Worldwide for Next to Nothing* by Kelly Monaghan ($17.50, postpaid, from The Intrepid Traveler, PO Box 438, New York, NY 10034). Flights are issued on a first-come, first-served basis, and there's no guarantee that the Paris route will be available at the time you want. Round-trip fares cost from around $350, with last-minute specials as low as $150 for flights booked within three days of departure.

Don't automatically assume that tickets purchased through a travel specialist will be the cheapest – once you get a quote, check with the airlines and you may turn up an even better deal. Be advised also that the pool of travel companies is swimming with sharks – exercise caution and never deal with a company that demands cash up front or refuses to accept payment by credit card.

Note that fares are heavily dependent on **season**, and are highest from around early June to the end of August; they drop during the "shoulder" seasons (Sept–Oct & April–May) and you'll get the best deals during the low season (Nov–March, excluding Christmas). Note that Friday, Saturday and Sunday travel tends to carry a premium, and that one-way fares are generally slightly more than half the round-trip.

If you have a specific French destination in mind outside Paris and you're in a hurry – and if you're prepared to pay extra – it's possible to be ticketed straight through to any of more than a dozen **regional airports**. Most of these entail connecting flights on Air Inter, Air France's domestic arm, and require a change of planes in Paris (check to make sure there's no inconvenient transfer between Charles de Gaulle and Orly). Low-season round-trip add-on fares from Paris will cost around $60–100.

Air passes, coupons and discounts on further flights within Europe vary with airlines, but the basic rules are that they must be pre-booked with the main ticket, are valid for three months, and are available only with a return fare with the one airline – for example, you have to fly to France with KLM alone to be eligible for their air pass deals. Air France offers a Euroflyer for use in France and Europe at US$99 each flight (min 3, max 9). KLM's Passport to Europe uses coupons for single flights within Europe and are $100 (min 4, max 12). Lufthansa's start at US$89 (max 12) during the low season up to US$159 in the high season per coupon. British Airways has a "One World: Visit Europe" programme that offers flights within Europe from US$92 to US$145 depending on the destination (min 2, max 12).

If France is only one stop on a longer journey, you might want to consider buying a **Round-the-World (RTW) ticket**. Some travel agents can sell you an "off-the-shelf" RTW ticket that will have you touching down in several cities. Others will have to assemble one for you, which can be tailored to your needs but is apt to be more expensive. Sample itineraries: Los Angeles–Hong Kong–Bangkok–Delhi–Paris–Los Angeles (about $1195), or Vancouver–San Francisco–Paris –Casablanca–Cairo–Bombay–Kathmandu –Bangkok–Vancouver (about CAN$3449).

FLIGHTS FROM THE US

Transatlantic fares to France from the US are very reasonable, thanks to intense competition. Any local travel agent should be able to access airlines' up-to-the-minute fares, although they may not have time to research all the possibilities, and you could call the airlines direct. The lowest discounted scheduled fares you're likely to get in low and high season flying midweek to Paris are $448/966 from Chicago, $468/876 from Houston, $498/1116 from Los Angeles, $368/866 from New York and $408/635 from Washington DC.

Most airlines use Paris as the transatlantic gateway to France. Some charter carriers offer direct flights to Nice, Marseille and Lyon in late spring to early autumn. In addition, Air France has regular scheduled non-stop services into Nice from New York. Nearly a dozen different **scheduled** airlines operate flights to Paris. Air France has the most frequent and convenient service, but their fares tend to be on the expensive side. Other

TOUR OPERATORS IN NORTH AMERICA

Abercrombie & Kent, 1520 Kensington Rd, Oak Brook, IL 60523 (☎1-800/323 7308; *www.aber-crombieandkent.com*). Walking tours, barge and canal trips all over France. A walking tour in Burgundy with barge accommodation is $1990.

Adventure Center, 1311 63rd Street, Suite 200, Emeryville, CA 94608 (☎1-800/227 8747; *www.adventurecenter.com*). Small-group hiking or cycling tours in France and Corsica. Ten-day "Cycling in the Loire Valley" costs $750; fifteen-day "Hiking in Provence", $820.

Adventures on Skis, 815 North Rd, Westfield, MA 01085 (☎1-800/628 9655; *www.advonskis.com*). Skiing and sport packages throughout France from $745.

AESU Travel, 3922 Hicory Ave, Baltimore, MD 21211 (☎1-800/638 7640; *www.aesu.com*). Riviera packages, tours, independent city-stays and discount airfares for under-35s.

Back Door Travel, 130 4th Ave North, Edmonds, WA 98020 (☎425/771 8303; *www.ricksteves.com*). Off-the-beaten path, small-group travel with budget travel guru Rick Steves and his enthusiastic guides. Twenty-day "Best of Village France", $3200; fourteen-day tours of East or West France, $2300.

Backroads, 801 Cedar St, Berkeley, CA 94710-1800 (☎1-800/462 2848; *www.backroads.com*).

Trendy hiking tours. A six-day trip in Bourgogne, Dordogne or the Basque country is $2698.

Butterfield & Robinson, 70 Bond St, Suite 300, Toronto, ON M5B 1X3 (☎1-800/678 1147; *www.butterfield.com*). Biking and walking trips all over France. An eight-day bike tour of Alsace wine villages costs $3395.

CBT Bicycle Tours, 2506 North Clark St, Suite 150, Chicago, IL 60614 (☎1-800/736 BIKE; *www.biketrip.net*). Bike tours throughout France from $110 to $125 per day, some starting or ending in Paris.

Contiki Tours, 300 Plaza Alicante, Suite 900, Garden Grove, CA 92640 (☎1-800/CONTIKI). Budget tours to Europe for under-35s. A fourteen-day "Best of France" tour costs $1395 including airfare from NY.

Cosmos Tourama/Globus, 5301 S Federal Circle, Littleton, CO 80123-2980 (☎1-800/221 0090; *www.globusandcosmos.com*). Group tours and city-breaks. The fourteen-day "Grand Tour of France" is $1311 with airfare included.

EC Tours, 12500 Riverside Drive, Suite 210, Valley Village, CA 91607 (☎1-800/388 0877; *www.ectours.com*). City tours and individually planned tours of regions like Normandy, the Loire and the French Riviera.

airlines offering non-stop services to Paris from a variety of US cities are: United, daily from Chicago, San Francisco and Washington DC; Delta, daily from Cincinnati, Atlanta and New York; TWA, daily from New York and St Louis; and AOM French Airlines from Los Angeles three to five times a week, depending on the season. For the best fares, check the ads in Sunday newspaper travel sections and book with a discount agent or consolidator. It's also worth considering **charter flights**, which operate from late spring to early autumn. New Frontiers, a Canadian discount travel agency, has summer non-stop charters from Los Angeles to Paris on Corsair from $800 round-trip.

FLIGHTS FROM CANADA

The strong links between France and Québec's Francophone community ensure regular air ser-

vices from **Canada to Paris**. The main route is Vancouver–Toronto–Montréal–Paris Charles de Gaulle, although most departures originate in Toronto.

Air France and Air Canada offer non-stop services to Paris from the major Canadian cities. There are also some excellent charter deals. Travel Cuts is a good source of general information on flights. The lowest discounted scheduled **fares** for midweek travel to Paris will be around CDN$976/1316 from Montréal, CDN$976/1316 from Toronto, CDN$1360/1728 from Vancouver, and CDN$1008/1258 from Halifax on Iceland Air.

PACKAGE TOURS

A tour is inevitably more confining than independent travel, but it can help you make the most of time if you're on a tight schedule; a tour can also ensure a worry-free first few days of a

ETT Tours, 7578 North Broadway, Suite 4, Red Hook, NY 12571 (☎1-800/551 2085; *www.ett-tours.com*). Independent travel with some possibilities for group tours.

Euro-Bike Tours, PO Box 990, DeKalb, IL 60115 (☎1-800/321 6060; *www.eurobike.com*). Luxury bike tours in Provence, Brittany, Normandy and the Loire: $2095 for a seven-day tour of Burgundy; $3095 for a fourteen-day tour of Brittany, Normandy and the Loire valley.

France Vacations, 9841 Airport Blvd, Suite 1120, Los Angeles, CA 90045 (☎1-800/332 5332; *www.francevacations.net*). Air/hotel and car rental packages.

The French Experience, 370 Lexington Ave, #812, New York, NY 10017 (☎1-800/28 FRANCE). Self-drive tours, apartment and cottage rentals, air-fare arrangements. A three-day Château Country tour in Brittany or the Loire Valley, including car costs $405, land only.

Himalayan Travel, 110 Prospect St, Stanford, CT 06901 (☎1-800/225 2380; *www.gorp.com/himtravel.htm*). Trekking and cycling in the French and Corsican interior. $1095 for an seven-day self-guided bike trip around Alsace.

Holidaze Ski Tours, 810 Belmar Plaza, Belmar, NJ 07719 (☎1-800/526 2827; *www.holidaze.com*). Ski specialist.

International Study Tours, 225 W 34th St, New York, NY 10122 (☎1-800/833 2111; *www.ist.com*). Theme tours such as "Provencal Voyage of Discovery" cost between $3000 and $4000. Nine- to ten-night river cruises on the Rhone and barge trips for $2000–3000, land only.

Mountain Travel-Sobek, 6420 Fairmount Ave, El Cerrito, CA 94530 (☎1-800/227 2384; *www.mtsobek.com*). Hiking in Haute Savoie and Provence. A nine-day hiking trip in Provence is $2390; the "Mont Blanc" circuit, a thirteen-day hike through France, Italy and Switzerland around Mont Blanc is $2390.

REI Adventures, PO Box 1938, Sumner, WA 98390 (☎1-800/622 2236; *www.rei.com/travel*). Hiking trips in France. Nine-day hiking trip in Provence is $1495; ten-day cycling trip in the Loire Valley, $1595.

Saga International Holidays, 222 Berkeley St, Boston, MA 02116 (☎1-800/343 0273; *www.sagaholidays.com*). Specialist in group travel for 50s-plus.

Vacances en Campagne, PO Box 299, Elkton, VA 22827 (☎1-800/327 6097; *www.britishtravel.com*). Short-term rentals of châteaux and country houses in France and Corsica.

Worldwide Adventures, 1170 Sheppard Ave W, Suite 45, Toronto, ON M3K 2A3 (☎1-800/387 1483; *www.worldwidequest.com*). Adventure holidays.

---

trip, and time to find your feet. Hundreds of tour operators specialize in travel to France, and many can put together very **flexible deals**, sometimes amounting to no more than a flight plus car or train pass and accommodation. If you're planning to travel in moderate or luxury style, and especially if your trip is geared around special interests, such packages can work out cheaper than the same arrangements made on arrival.

Of greater interest are the **package-tour operators** that help you explore the country's unique points: many organize walking or cycling trips through the countryside, boat trips along canals and any number of theme tours based around history, art, wine and so on. The box above mentions a few of the possibilities, and a travel agent will be able to point out others. Remember: bookings made through a travel agent cost no more than going through the tour operator.

Many **airlines** have reasonably priced packages including round-trip airfare, hotel, some sightseeing tours and, in the case of fly-drive packages, a rental car. Delta offers a seven-day fly-drive package to Paris starting at $599 for New York departures. British Airways has a seven-day "Treasures of Paris" tour starting at $699, including transatlantic airfare via London, hotels, sightseeing and a métro pass. American Airlines offers a seven-day England–France fly-drive package, including Channel Tunnel crossing, from around $900 per person for hotel, breakfast, rental car and Channel tickets. American also has a variety of flight/hotel/sightseeing packages, such as its seven-day Paris package for around $860, and the "Paris Stopover" from around $472 per person for one night's hotel and breakfast.

GETTING THERE FROM AUSTRALIA AND NEW ZEALAND

Many people travelling to France from Australia and New Zealand will choose to travel via London although there are scheduled flights to Paris from Sydney, Melbourne, Brisbane, Cairns, Perth and Auckland. Most airlines can add on a Paris (or any other major French destination) leg to any Australia/New Zealand–Europe ticket. Travelling time is around 22 hours via Asia and 30 hours via the US – not counting time spent on stopovers.

Fares to France vary according to the season and the carrier. In general, low season lasts from mid-January to the end of February, and from the beginning of October to mid-November; high sea-

---

AIRLINES, DISCOUNT TRAVEL AGENTS AND TOUR OPERATORS IN AUSTRALIA AND NEW ZEALAND

AIRLINES

Air France in Australia ☎02/9244 2100; in New Zealand ☎09/308 3352; *www.airfrance.fr.*

British Airways in Australia ☎02/8904 8800; in New Zealand ☎09/356 8690; *www.british-airways.com.*

Canadian Airlines in Australia ☎1300/655 767; in New Zealand ☎09/309 9159; *www.cdnair.ca.*

Cathay Pacific in Australia ☎13/1747 or 02/9931 5500; in New Zealand ☎09/379 0861; *www.cathaypacific.com.*

Garuda in Australia ☎1300/365 330; in New Zealand ☎09/366 1855 or 1800/128 510.

Japan Airlines (JAL) in Australia ☎02/9272 1111; in New Zealand ☎09/379 9906; *www.japanair.com.*

KLM in Australia ☎1300/303 747; in New Zealand ☎09/302 1452; *www.klm.com.*

Lauda Air in Australia ☎02/9251 6155 or 1800/642 438; *www.lauda-air.com.*

Lufthansa in Australia ☎1300/655 727 or 02/9367 3887; in New Zealand ☎09/303 1529 or 008/945 220; *www.lufthansa.com.*

Malaysian Airlines in Australia ☎13/2627; in New Zealand ☎09/373 2741 or 008/657 472; *www.malaysiaair.com.*

Olympic Airways in Australia ☎02/9251 2044 or 1800 221 663; *www.olympic-airways.com.*

Qantas in Australia ☎13/1313; in New Zealand ☎09/357 8900 or 0800/808 767; *www.qantas.com.*

Singapore Airlines in Australia ☎02/9350 0262 or 13/1011; in New Zealand ☎09/303 2129 or 0800/808 909; *www.singaporeair.com.*

Sri Lankan Airlines in Australia ☎02/9244 2234; in New Zealand ☎09/308 3353.

Thai Airways in Australia ☎1300/651 960; in New Zealand ☎09/377 3886; *www.thaiair.com.*

United Airlines in Australia ☎13/1777; in New Zealand ☎09/379 3800; *www.ual.com.*

DISCOUNT TRAVEL AGENTS

All the agents listed below offer competitive discounts on airfares as well as a good selection of packaged holidays and tours, and can also arrange car rental and bus and rail passes.

Anywhere Travel, 345 Anzac Parade, Kingsford, Sydney (☎02/9663 0411; *anywhere@ozemail.com.au*).

Budget Travel, 16 Fort St, Auckland (☎09/366 0061 or 0800/808 040, *www.budgettravel.co.nz*); plus branches around the city.

son is from mid-May to the end of August, and from the beginning of December to mid-January. Seasonal fare increases are A\$/NZ\$200–400.

SHOPPING FOR TICKETS

Tickets purchased direct from the airlines tend to be expensive; the **discount agents** listed in the box below offer much better deals, and have the latest information on limited special offers. Some of the best discounts are offered by companies such as Flight Centre, STA and Trailfinders (see box below); they can also help with visas, travel insurance and tours. You might also want to have a look on the **Internet**: *www.travel.com.au* and *www.sydneytravel.com* offer discounted fares online.

If you're planning to visit France as part of a wider world trip, then **Round-the-World (RTW)** **tickets** offer greater flexibility and better value than a standard return flight. There are numerous airline combinations to choose from: for example, a straightforward ticket (no backtracking) from Sydney or Auckland to Honolulu, then Vancouver, London, Paris, Bangkok, Singapore and back home, starts at A\$2099. However, the most comprehensive and flexible routes are offered by One World and Star Alliance, allowing you to take in destinations in the US and Canada, Europe, and Asia, as well as South America and Africa; prices are mileage-based from A\$2700, for a maximum of 29,000 miles up to A\$3700 for 39,000 miles.

If you intend to do a fair amount of travelling within a limited time, it's worth considering an **air pass**. Air passes, coupons and discounts on further flights within Europe vary with airlines, but the basic rules are that they must be pre-booked

---

Destinations Unlimited, 220 Queen St, Auckland (☎09/373 4033).

Flight Centre (*www.flightcentre.com*) Australia: 82 Elizabeth St, Sydney (☎02/9235 3522); plus branches nationwide (for the nearest branch call ☎13/1600). New Zealand: 350 Queen St, Auckland (☎09/358 4310 or 0800/354 448); plus branches nationwide.

Northern Gateway, 22 Cavenagh St, Darwin (☎08/8941 1394; *oztravel@norgate.com.au*). Discount flights to France from Darwin.

STA Travel (*www.statravel.com*) Australia: 855 George St, Sydney; 256 Flinders St, Melbourne; other offices in state capitals and major universities (for nearest branch call ☎13/1776; telesales ☎1300/360 960). New Zealand: 10 High St, Auckland (☎09/309 0458); other offices in major cities and university campuses (for nearest branch call ☎0800/874 773; telesales ☎09/366 6673). Fare discounts for students and those under 26, as well as visas, student cards and travel insurance.

Student Uni Travel, 92 Pitt St, Sydney (☎02/9232 8444; *sydney@backpackers.net*); plus branches in Brisbane, Cairns, Darwin, Melbourne and Perth. Student/youth discounts and travel advice.

Thomas Cook Australia (*www.thomascook.com.au*): 175 Pitt St, Sydney (☎02/9231 2877); 257 Collins St, Melbourne (☎03/9282 0222); plus branches in other state capitals (for nearest branch call ☎13/1771; telesales ☎1800/801 002). New Zealand (*www.thomascook.co.nz*): 191 Queen St, Auckland (☎09/379 3920). Bus and rail passes and reasonable rates on currency exchange.

Trailfinders (*www.travel.com.au*), 8 Spring St, Sydney (☎02/9247 7666); 91 Elizabeth St, Brisbane (☎07/3229 0887); Hides Corner, Shield St, Cairns (☎07/4041 1199).

Usit Beyond (*www.usitbeyond.co.nz*), cnr Shortland St & Jean Batten Place, Auckland (☎09/379 4224 or 0800/788 336); plus branches in major cities. Student/youth travel specialists.

TOUR OPERATORS

Adventure Specialists, 69 Liverpool St, Sydney, (☎02/9261 2927 or toll-free 1800/634 465). Overland specialist and agent for numerous adventure-travel operators that offer walking and camping trips through France.

Adventure World Australia: 73 Walker St, North Sydney (☎02/9956 7766 or local call rate 1300/363; *www.adventureworld.com.au*); plus branches in Adelaide, Brisbane, Melbourne and Perth. New Zealand: 101 Great South Rd, Remuera, Auckland (☎09/524 5118; *www.adventureworld.co.nz*). A wide selection of city ministays and active holidays throughout France.

Alpine World, Inski, 343 Pacific Hwy, Crows Nest (☎02/9955 7100 or toll-free ☎1800 063 063). Tailored skiing holidays in France.

continued overleaf

continued from previous page

Australians Studying Abroad (ASA), 1st Floor, High Street, Armadale, Victoria (☎03/9509 1955 or toll-free 1800/645 755; *www.asatravinfo.com.au*). All-inclusive 22-day lecture tours exploring the cultural landscapes of France.

CIT, 2/263 Clarence St, Sydney (☎02/9267 1255); plus offices in Melbourne, Brisbane, Adelaide and Perth. Specializes in city tours and accommodation packages, plus bus and rail passes and car rental.

Contiki, 35 Spring St, Bondi Junction, Sydney (☎02/9511 2200 or local call rate 1300/301 835; *www.contiki.com*). Specializes in extended coach tours for 18- to 35-year-olds. Bookings can also be made through travel agents.

Destinations Adventure, 2nd Floor, Premier Building, cnr Queen & Durham streets, East Auckland (☎09/309 0464). Agent for "The Imaginative Traveller" trekking holidays in France.

European Travel Office (ETO), 122 Rosslyn St, West Melbourne (☎03/9329 8844); Suite 410/368 Sussex St, Sydney (☎02/9267 7714); 407 Great South Rd, Auckland (☎09/525 3074). Offers a wide selection of tours and accommodation, from hotels to country inns, palaces and monasteries.

Explore Holidays, 2nd Floor, 55 Blaxland Road, Ryde (☎02/9857 6200; *www.exploreholidays.com.au*). Offers a wide range of accommodation from B&B home-stays and hotels to châteaux and historic monuments; mini city stays in Paris and regional capitals; plus car rental and coach and rail passes.

France Unlimited, 16 Goldsmith St, Elwood, Melbourne (☎03/9531 8787). All French travel arrangements, individually tailored holidays and guided walking and cycling holidays.

French Cottages and Travel, 674 High St, E Kew, Melbourne (☎03/9859 4944). International and domestic travel, independent tours and cottage rental.

French Travel Connection, Level 6, 33 Chandos St, Sydney (☎02/9966 8600). French travel arrangements, city accommodation and regional country cottages from A$400 to A$1500 per week, depending on the size and time of year.

IT Adventures, Level 4, 46048 York St, Sydney (toll-free ☎1800/804 277). Agent for Kumuka and Exodus' extended overland camping/hostelling expeditions through France.

Peregrine Adventures (wholesaler), 258 Lonsdale St, Melbourne (☎03/9663 8611); offices in Brisbane, Sydney, Adelaide, Perth and Hobart. Agents for Headwater's graded seven- to eleven-day walking and cycling holidays through the regions of Provence, Lot and Dordogne, Languedoc, Burgundy, the Pyrenees and the Loire.

Silke's Travel, 263 Oxford St, Darlinghurst, Sydney (☎02/9380 6244 or toll-free 1800/807 860; *www.silkes.com.au*). Specially tailored packages for gay and lesbian travellers.

Snow Bookings Only, 1141 Toorak Rd, Camberwell, Melbourne (☎03/9809 2699 or toll-free 1800/623 266). Can arrange skiing and snow-boarding holidays.

The Adventure Travel Company, 164 Parnell Rd, Parnell, Auckland (☎09/379 9755; *advakl@hot.co.nz*). The NZ agent for Peregrine (see above).

Travel Notions, 136 Bridge Rd, Glebe, Sydney (☎02/9552 2852). "Cycling for Softies" seven- to fifteen-day centre-based and go-where-you-please cycling holidays throughout rural France.

Walkabout Gourmet Adventures, PO Box 52, Dinner Plain, Victoria (☎03/5159 6556; *www.reho.com/walkabout*). All-inclusive classy fourteen-day food-and-wine walking trip through regional France, plus cooking seminars in Provence.

Yalla Tours, 661 Glenhuntley Rd, Caulfield, Melbourne (local call rate ☎1300/362 844; www.*yallatours.com.au*). Wide range of accommodation, rail and coach passes, car hire, Paris city stays, plus self-skippered canal and river cruises.

YHA Travel Australia (*www.yha.com.au*): 422 Kent St, Sydney (☎02/9261 1111); 205 King St, Melbourne (☎03/9670 9611); 38 Sturt St, Adelaide (☎08/8231 5583); 154 Roma St, Brisbane (☎07/3236 1680); 236 William St, Perth (☎08/9227 5122); 69 Mitchell St, Darwin (☎08/8981 2560); 28 Criterion St, Hobart (☎03/6234 9617). New Zealand: 173 Gloucester St, Christchurch (☎03/379 9970, *www.yha.co.nz*). Accommodation and adventure tours throughout France (adult membership rate A$47/NZ$40).

with the main ticket, are valid for three months and are available only with a return fare with the one airline – for example, you have to fly to France with British Airways alone to be eligible for their air-pass deals. Air France offers a Euroflyer for use in France and Europe at A$200 each flight (minimum 3, maximum 9). KLM's Passport to Europe uses coupons for single flights within Europe: three coupons for A$480, up to six for A$840 in the low season, A$550 and A$980 in the shoulder period, A$650 and A$1170 in the peak period; Lufthansa's start at A$90 (max 9) during the low season up to A$140 in the high season per coupon. British Airways has a zone system: around A$140 for each flight within France, A$210 each for single flights to and around Germany, Italy and Belgium, although you may originally have to travel via London, from where it will cost an extra A$170 to get to France (min 3, max 12).

If you're planning to visit France as part of an extensive European trip, it's worth looking into a variety of **rail passes**, valid in most other European countries. Details of passes on offer and rail contacts in Australia and New Zealand are given in the box on p.14.

Finally, if you're planning to travel in style, and especially if your visit is going to be geared around special interests, such as walking, cycling, art or wine, you may want to consider one of the **package tours** offered by the operators in the box opposite. Though these tours are inevitably more restrictive than independent travel, they may work out cheaper than making the same arrangements on arrival in France and can help you make the most of time if you're on a tight schedule.

FLIGHTS FROM AUSTRALIA

Airfares **from east-coast gateways** are common rated, with Ansett and Qantas providing a shuttle service to the point of international departure. **From Perth and Darwin** they're around A$100–300 less via Asia, and A$400 more via the US. There's a host of airlines operating a service between major cities in Australia – with either a transfer or overnight stop in their home ports – to Paris.

Flights **via Southeast Asia**, with either a transfer or overnight stop in the airlines' home ports, are generally the cheaper option. The lowest fares are with Sri Lankan Airways and Garuda for A$1400 in the low season rising to A$2400 in the high season, while Alitalia/Qantas, Olympic Airways and JAL are both A$1500 low season to A$2600 high season. Mid-range fares are with KLM, Malaysian Airlines, Lauda Air, Thai International, Air France (on to 87 destinations within France), Cathay Pacific and Lufthansa, all costing A$1600–2600. Qantas/Air France, British Airways and Singapore Airlines are higher still at A$1900–2800.

Generally flights to Paris are pricier **via the US**, with the best deals offered by United Airlines (via LA, Miami and Washington), from A$2100 to 3000; Canadian Airlines (via Toronto or Vancouver) are more expensive at A$2200 low season and A$3000 high season.

FLIGHTS FROM NEW ZEALAND

From New Zealand, there is also a good range of airlines flying to Paris with either a transfer or overnight stop in their home ports. The best discounted deals to Paris from Auckland are **via Southeast Asia** with Garuda at NZ$1800 low season to NZ$2400 high season. Mid-range fares are with Japanese Airlines, Thai International, Malaysia Airlines, Cathay Pacific and Singapore Airlines, all costing NZ$2000–2400. For **stopovers** in Europe, British Airways fly via LA and London (NZ$2399); Qantas/Alitalia (via Rome and London) costs slightly less at NZ$2295. Most of these airlines also include a **side-trip** within Europe in their fare.

As with Australia, flights **via the US** are more expensive, the best deals being with United Airlines (via LA, Miami and Washington) for NZ$2200 and NZ$3000. Fares with British Airways (via LA and London) and Canadian Airlines (via Vancouver or Toronto) cost NZ$2399 to NZ$3000.

RED TAPE AND VISAS

Citizens of EU (European Union) countries can travel freely in France; and citizens of

Australia, Canada, the United States and New Zealand, among other countries, do not need any sort of visa to enter France, and can stay for up to ninety days. However, the situation can change and it is advisable to check with your embassy or consulate before departure. Note that the British Visitor's Passport is no longer available.

EU citizens (or other non-visa citizens) who **stay longer than three months** are officially supposed to apply for a **carte de séjour**, for which you'll have to show proof of income at least equal to the minimum wage (at least 6700F/€1025 per month). However, EU passports are rarely stamped, so there is no evidence of how long you've been in the country. If your passport does get stamped, you can cross the border

FRENCH EMBASSIES AND CONSULATES OVERSEAS

BRITAIN

Embassy: 58 Knightsbridge, London SW1X 7JT (☎020/7201 1004).

IRELAND

Embassy: 36 Ailesbury Rd, Ballsbridge, Dublin 4 (☎01/260 1666).

US

Embassy: 4101 Reservoir Rd NW, Washington DC 20007 (☎202/944 6195, *www.info-france -usa.org*).

Consulates: Prominence in Buckhead, Suite 1840, 3475 Piedmont Rd NE, Atlanta, GA 30305 (☎404/495 1660, *www.consulatfranceatlanta.org*); 31 St James Ave, Park Square Building, Suite 750, Boston, MA 02116 (☎617/542 7374, *www.france-boston.com*); 737 North Michigan Ave, Suite 2020, Chicago, IL 60611 (☎312/787 5360, *www.france -consulat.org/chicago*); 777 Post Oak Blvd, Suite 600, Houston, TX 77056 (☎713/572 2799, *www.consulatfrancehouston.org*); 10990 Wilshire Blvd, Suite 300, Los Angeles, CA 90024 (☎310/235 3200, *www.etats-unis.com/consulat -la*); One Biscayne Tower, 17th Floor, South Biscayne Blvd, Miami, FL 33131 (☎305/372 9799, *www.info-france-usa.org/miami*); 1340 Poydras St, Amoco Building, Suite 1710, New Orleans, LA 70112 (☎504/523 5772, *www.info-france -usa.org/nouvelle-orleans/index.html*); 934 Fifth

Ave, New York, NY 10021 (☎212/606 3689, *www.franceconsulatny.org*); 540 Bush St, San Francisco, CA 94108 (☎415/397 4330, *www.accueil-sfo.org*).

CANADA

Embassy: 42 Sussex Drive, Ottawa, ON K1M 2C9 (☎613/789 1795, *www.amba-ottawa.fr*).

Consulates: 777 Main St, Suite 800, Moncton, NB E1C 1E9 (☎506/857 4191, *www .moncton.consulfrance.org*); 1 place Ville Marie Bureau 2601, Montreal, QC H3B 4S3 (☎514/878 4385, *www.montreal.consulat france.org*); 25 rue St-Louis, Québec, QC G1R 3Y8 (☎418/694 2294, *www.quebec.consulatfrance.org*); 130 Bloor St West, Suite 400, Toronto, ON M5S 1N5 (☎416/925 8044, *www.toronto .consulatfrance.org*); 1100–1130 West Pender St, Vancouver, BC V6E 4A4 (☎604/681 4345, *www.vancouver.consulatfrance.org*).

AUSTRALIA

Consulates (*www.france.net.au*): 492 St Kilda Rd, Melbourne, VIC 3001 (☎03/9820 0921); 31 Market St, Sydney, NSW 2000 (☎02/9261 5779).

NEW ZEALAND

Embassy: 34–42 Manners St, PO Box 11-343, Wellington (☎04/384 2555, *www.ambafrance.net.nz*).

– to Belgium or Germany, for example – and re-enter for another ninety days legitimately.

CUSTOMS

With the Single European Market you can carry most things between EU countries, as long as you have paid tax on them in an EU country and you intend them for personal consumption. Customs will only start asking questions if your car is groaning under the weight of goods and they think you are going to resell them. Duty-free restrictions for non-EU residents are standard in EU countries at 200 cigarettes, 250g tobacco or 50 cigars; one litre of spirits or two litres of fortified wine, or two litres of sparkling wine; two litres of table wine; 50mg of perfume and 250ml of toilet water.

Americans can bring home up to $400-worth of goods purchased overseas duty-free, including a litre of alcohol or wine, 200 cigarettes and 100 cigars. If you carry back between $400 and $1000 worth of stuff you'll have to go through the red lane and pay ten percent of the value in duty; above $1000 and the duty depends on the items. For the full rundown on customs niceties, request a copy of the pamphlet *Know Before You Go* from the US Customs Service, 1300 Pennsylvania Ave, Room 6.3-D, Washington DC 20229. Their information line (☎202/354 1000) lists other publications for travellers, though they must be requested by mail. All their pamphlets can be viewed online at *www.customs.gov.*

Canadians are exempt from paying duty on up to CAN$750-worth of goods after spending seven days out of the country (or CAN$100-worth after a trip lasting two to six days). Those goods may include up to 1.5 litres of spirits or wine, 24 355ml bottles of beer and 200 cigarettes. For more details contact the Canada Customs and Revenue Agency, Sir Richard Scott Building, 191 Laurier Ave West, Ottowa, ON K1A 0L5 (☎1-506/636 5064, *www.ccra-adrc.gc.ca*), and request a copy of the government's *I Declare* brochure.

Travellers returning to **Australia** from abroad can bring in $400-worth of "gifts" duty-free (for under-18s this is reduced to $200) – not including personal purchases such as clothing which don't incur duty – plus 250 cigarettes or 250g of tobacco and one bottle of alcohol (beer, wine or spirits). **New Zealand** permits $700-worth of "gifts", plus six 750ml bottles of wine or beer (4.5 litres in all), 1125ml of spirits, and 200 cigarettes, or 250g tobacco, or 50 cigars, or a mixture of these not exceeding 250g. In both countries, certain goods must be declared for inspection and may be prohibited: these include cordless phones purchased overseas, artefacts containing wood or other plant material, and foodstuffs.

COSTS, MONEY AND BANKS

Until the euro currency is introduced in 2002 (see box on p.24), the French unit of money is the franc (abbreviated as F or sometimes FF), divided into 100 centimes. Francs come in notes of 500, 100, 50 and 20F, and there are coins of 20, 10, 5, 2 and 1F, and 50, 20, 10 and 5 centimes. During most of 2000, the exchange rate hovered around 11.10F to the pound, 7.60F to the US dollar, 5.10F to the Canadian dollar, 4.10F to the Australian dollar, and 3.40F to the New Zealand dollar. The euro was initially pegged at just under one US dollar, but it suffered a series of declines and by late 2000 had plummeted to near the US$0.80 mark; at that stage the exchange rate was €1.67 to the pound, €1.17 to the US dollar, €0.75 to the Canadian dollar, €0.60 to the Australian dollar, and €0.47 to the New Zealand dollar. For the most up-to-date

THE EURO

France is one of twelve European Union countries who have changed over to a single currency, the **euro** (€). The transition period, which began on January 1, 1999, is, however, lengthy: euro notes and coins are not scheduled to be issued until January 1, 2002, with francs remaining in place for **cash transactions**, at a **fixed rate** of 6.55957 francs to 1 euro, until they are scrapped entirely at the end of February July 1, 2002. The euro will come in coins of 1 to 50 cents, €1 and €2, and notes of €5 to €500.

Even before euro cash appears in 2002, you can opt to pay in euros by **credit card** and you can get **travellers' cheques** in euros – you should not be charged commission for changing them in any of the eleven countries in the euro zone (also known as "Euroland"), nor for changing from any of the old Euroland currencies to any other (Italian lira to francs, for example).

All **prices** in this book are given in francs and the exact equivalent in euros. When the new currency takes over completely, prices are likely to be rounded off – and if decimalization in the UK is anything to go by, rounded up.

exchange rates, consult the useful Currency Converter Web site *www.oanda.com*.

COSTS

Because of the relatively low **cost** of accommodation and eating out, at least by northern European standards, France may not seem an outrageously expensive place to visit, though this will depend on the relative strength of your own country's currency. When and where you go also makes a difference: in main resorts hotel prices can go up by a third during July and August, while places like Paris and the Côte d'Azur are always more expensive than the other regions. For a reasonably comfortable existence, including a hotel room for two, a light restaurant lunch and a proper restaurant dinner, plus moving around, café stops and museum visits, you need to allow at least 600F/€90 a day per person. But by counting the pennies, staying at cheap **hostels** (around 100F/€15.25 for bed and breakfast) or **camping** (from 30F/€4.58), and being strong-willed about extra cups of coffee and doses of culture, you could manage on 250F/€38 a day, to include a cheap restaurant meal – less if your eating is limited to street snacks or market food.

For two or more people, **hotel accommodation** is nearly always cheaper and better value than hostels, which are only worth staying at if you're by yourself and want to meet other travellers. A sensible average estimate for a double room would be around 280F/€43, though perfectly adequate but simple doubles can be had from 190F/€29. Single-rated and -sized rooms are often available, beginning from 140F/€21 in a cheap hotel. **Breakfast** at hotels is normally an extra 30F/€4.50, for coffee, croissant and orange juice –

about the same as you'd pay in a bar (where you'll normally find the coffee and ambience more agreeable). As for other **food**, you can spend as much or as little as you like. There are large numbers of reasonable **restaurants** with three- or four-course menus for between 65F/€10 and 120F/€18; the lunchtime or *midi* menu is nearly always cheaper. **Picnic fare**, obviously, is much less costly, especially when you buy in the markets and cheap supermarket chains, and takeaway baguette sandwiches from cafés are not extortionate. **Wine** and **beer** are both very cheap in supermarkets; buying wine from the barrel at village co-op cellars will give you the best value for money. The mark-up on wine in restaurants is high, though the house wine in cheaper establishments is still very good value. **Drinks** in cafés and bars are what really make a hole in your pocket: black coffee, wine and draught lager are the cheapest drinks to order; glasses of tap water are free; and remember that it's cheaper to be at the bar than at a table.

Transport will inevitably be a large item of expenditure if you move around a lot, which makes some kind of train pass a good idea, although French trains are in any case good value, with many discounts available – two sample one-way fares are Paris to Toulouse, 445F/€67.86, and Paris to Montpellier, 379F/€57.80. Buses are cheaper, though prices vary enormously from one operator to another. Bicycles cost about 80F/€12 per day to rent. Petrol prices shot up in late 2000, and at the time of writing were around 7.70F/€1.17 a litre for unleaded (*sans plomb*), around 7.80F/€11.90 a litre for Super and around 5.50F/€8.40 a litre for diesel; there are 3.8 litres to the US gallon. Most *autoroutes* have tolls:

rates vary, but to give you an idea, travelling only by motorway from Calais to Montpellier would cost you around 379F/€57.80.

Museums and monuments can also prove a big wallet-eroder. Reduced admission is often available for those over 60 and under 18 (for which you'll need your passport as proof of age) and for students under 26 (for which you'll need an International Student Identity Card, or ISIC). Many museums and monuments are free for children under 12, and nearly always for kids under 4. Under-26s can also get a free **youth card**, or *Carte Jeune*, available in France from youth travel agencies like USIT and from main tourist offices (120F/€18.30; valid for a year), which entitles you to reductions in France and throughout Europe. Several towns operate a global ticket for their museums and monuments (detailed in the *Guide*).

CHANGING MONEY

Standard **banking hours** are Monday to Friday 9am to 4pm or 5pm. Some close at midday (noon/12.30pm–2/2.30pm); some are open on Saturday 9am to noon. All are closed on Sunday and public holidays. They will have a notice on the door if they do currency exchange. **Rates and commission** vary from bank to bank, so it's worth shopping around; the usual procedure is a 1–2 percent commission on travellers' cheques and a flat-rate charge on cash (a 30F/€4.58 charge for changing 200F/€30.50 is not uncommon). Be wary of banks claiming to charge no commission at all; often they are merely adjusting the exchange rate to their own advantage.

There are **money-exchange counters** (*bureaux de change*) at all the French airports and at train stations of big cities, with usually one or two in town centres as well, often keeping much longer hours than the high-street banks. You'll also find **automatic exchange machines** at airports and train stations and outside many money exchange bureaux. They accept £10 and £20 notes as well as dollars and other European currency notes, but offer a very poor rate of exchange.

TRAVELLERS' CHEQUES AND THE VISA TRAVELMONEY CARD

Travellers' cheques are one of the safest ways of carrying your money. Worldwide, they're available from almost any major bank (in most cases whether you have an account there or not), and from special American Express or Thomas Cook offices, usually for a service charge of 1 percent on the amount purchased. Banks may charge more to purchase, but check first with your own establishment as some offer cheques free of charge to customers meeting certain criteria. The most widely recognized brands of travellers' cheques are Visa, Thomas Cook and American Express, which most banks will change, and there are American Express and Thomas Cook offices in France; American Express travellers' cheques can also be cashed at post offices.

French franc travellers' cheques can be worthwhile: they may often be used as cash, and you should get the face value of the cheques when you change them, so commission is only paid on purchase. Banks being banks, however, this is not always the case.

The latest way of carrying your money abroad is with a **Visa TravelMoney Card**, a sort of electronic travellers' cheque. The temporary disposable debit card is "loaded up" with an amount between £100 and £5000 and can then be used (in conjunction with a PIN number) in any ATM carrying the Visa sign in France (and 112 other countries). When your funds are depleted, you simply throw the card away. It's recommended you buy at least a second card as back-up in case your first is lost or stolen, though like travellers' cheques the cards can be replaced if such mishaps occur. Up to nine cards can be bought to access the same funds – useful for couples/families travelling together. Charges are 2 percent commission with a minimum charge of £3. The card is available from, among other places, Colombus Bank in the US and Thomas Cook in the UK. For further information, call Visa's 24-hour toll-free customer services line on ☎1-410/581-9091 or check out their Web site at *www.visa.com*.

CREDIT AND DEBIT CARDS

Credit cards are widely accepted; just watch for the window stickers. Visa – known as the *Carte Bleue* in France – is almost universally recognized; Access, Mastercard – sometimes called Eurocard – and American Express rank a bit lower. It's always worth checking, however, that restaurants and hotels will accept your card; some smaller ones don't. Be aware, also, that French cards have a smart chip, and machines may reject cards with a magnetic strip even if they are valid. If your card is refused because of this, you may be able to get them to confirm it by explaining the problem to the cashier or waiter in question: "Les cartes britanniques/américaines/canadiennes/

LOSS OR THEFT OF CREDIT CARDS

If your credit card is lost or stolen you should ring your credit card company to cancel it. Some companies, like Diners' Club in the UK, allow you to reverse the charges; others will pay for the call if you're absolutely desperate. It is very important to cancel cards straight away as purchases can be made without the signature even being glanced at. If you don't have the relevant number to call, contact the French 24-hour lines below; they will speak English.

Access, Mastercard, Eurocard
☎01.45.67.53.53.

Visa ☎01.42.77.11.90.

American Express lost or stolen cards☎01.47.77.72.00; lost or stolen travellers' cheques ☎08.00.90.86.00.

Diners' Club ☎01.49.06.17.50.

You can also use credit cards for **cash advances** at banks and in ATMs. The charge tends to be higher – for example 4.1 percent instead of the 1.5 percent at home for Visa cards. The PIN number should be the same as you use at home but check with your credit card company before you leave. Also, because French credit cards are smart cards, some ATMs baulk at foreign plastic and tell you that your request for money has been denied. If that happens, just try another machine. All ATMs give you the choice of instructions in French or English. Post offices will give cash advances on Visa credit cards if you are having a problem using them in ATMs. **Debit cards** can also be used in ATMs or to pay for goods and services if they carry the appropriate Visa symbol or there's an "edc" (European acceptance) sign. British cards are charged around 1 percent or a minimum of £1.50 when used in an ATM, so it makes sense not to take small sums out constantly, whereas North American cards tend to charge a flat rate of $1–2, making it the most economical and convenient method. You would not want the use of ATMs to be your sole source of money on a long trip far from home as a lost, stolen or malfunctioning card would leave you with nothing, so always have some spare currency or travellers' cheques as a back-up.

australiennes/de Nouvelle Zealand ne sont pas cartes à puce, mais à piste magnétique. Ma carte est valable et je vous serais très reconnaissant(e) de demander la confirmation auprès de votre banque ou de votre centre de traitement."

HEALTH AND INSURANCE

Citizens of all EU and Scandinavian countries are entitled to take advantage of French health services under the same terms as res- **idents, if they have the correct documentation. British citizens need form E111, available from post offices. North American and other non-EU citizens have to pay for most medical attention and are strongly advised to take out some form of travel insurance.**

Under the French Social Security system, every hospital visit, doctor's consultation and prescribed medicine incurs a charge. Although all employed French people are entitled to a refund of 70–75 percent of their medical and dental expenses, this can still leave a hefty shortfall, especially after a stay in hospital (accident victims even have to pay for the ambulance that takes them there).

The phone numbers and addresses of hospitals and the phone numbers for SOS Médecins (for emergency doctor call-out) are given in the *Guide* for all the main cities; the national number for medical emergencies is ☎15. You will also find the number for the local police station, which can provide addresses of doctors on call, and for pharmacies open after hours. In smaller towns, to find a **doctor**, stop at any pharmacy and ask for an address, or look under "Médecins qualifiés" in the Yellow Pages of the phone directory. To qualify for Social Security refunds, make sure the doctor is a *médecin conventionné*. An average consultation fee would be between 150F/€22.88 and 180F/€27.45. You will be given a *Feuille de Soins* (Statement of Treatment) for later documentation of insurance claims. Prescriptions should be taken to a **pharmacie**, signalled by an illuminated green cross, where they must be paid for; the medicines will have little stickers (*vignettes*) attached to them, which you must remove and stick to your *Feuille de Soins*, together with the prescription itself. In addition to dispensing medicine, all pharmacies are equipped, and obliged, to give first aid on request – though they will make a charge. When closed, they all display the address of the nearest open pharmacy, day or night. In serious emergencies you will always be admitted to the nearest **hospital** (*hôpital*), either under your own power or by ambulance, which even French citizens must pay for; many people instead call the *pompiers* (fire brigade), who are trained for such circumstances and whose number is ☎18.

TRAVEL INSURANCE

A typical **travel insurance** policy usually provides cover for the loss of baggage, tickets and – up to a certain limit – cash or cheques, as well as cancellation or curtailment of your journey. Most of them exclude so-called **dangerous sports** unless an extra premium is paid. Read the small print and benefits tables of prospective policies carefully; coverage can vary wildly for roughly similar premiums. Many policies can be chopped and changed to exclude coverage you don't need – for example, sickness and accident benefits can often be excluded or included at will. If you do take **medical coverage**, ascertain whether benefits will be paid as treatment proceeds or only after return home, and whether there is a 24-hour medical emergency number. When securing baggage cover, make sure that the per-article limit – typically under £500 equivalent – will cover your most valuable possession. If you need to make a claim, you should keep receipts for medicines and medical treatment, and in the event you have anything stolen, you must obtain an official statement from the police.

British bank and credit cards often have certain levels of medical or other insurance included and you may automatically get travel insurance if you use a major credit card to pay for your trip. If you have a good all-risks home insurance policy it may cover your possessions against loss or theft even when overseas. Many private medical schemes such as BUPA or PPP also offer coverage plans for abroad, including baggage loss, cancellation or curtailment and cash replacement as well as sickness or accident.

Americans and **Canadians** should also check that they're not already covered. Canadian provincial health plans usually provide partial cover for medical mishaps overseas. Holders of official student/teacher/youth cards are entitled to meagre

---

ROUGH GUIDES TRAVEL INSURANCE

Rough Guides now offer their own **travel insurance**, customized for our readers by a leading UK broker and backed by a Lloyds underwriter. It's available for anyone of any nationality travelling anywhere in the world. There are two main plans: **Essential**, for effective, no-frills cover, starting at £10 for two weeks; and **Premier** – more expensive but with more generous and extensive benefits. Each offer European or Worldwide cover, and can be supplemented with a "Hazardous Activities Premium" if you plan to indulge in sports considered dangerous, such as skiing, scuba-diving or trekking. Unlike many policies, the Rough Guides schemes are calculated by the day, so if you're travelling for 27 days rather than a month, that's all you pay for. You can alternatively take out annual **multi-trip insurance**, which covers you for all your travel throughout the year (with a maximum of sixty days for any one trip).

For a **policy quote**, call the Rough Guides Insurance Line on UK freefone ☎0800/015 0906, or, if you're calling from outside Britain on ☎(+44) 1243/621 046. Alternatively, you can **buy** online at *www.roughguides.com/insurance*.

accident coverage and hospital in-patient benefits. Students will often find that their student
health coverage extends during the vacations and
for one term beyond the date of last enrolment.

Homeowners' or renters' insurance often covers
theft or loss of documents, money and valuables
while overseas, though conditions and maximum
amounts vary from company to company.

DISABLED VISITORS

France has no special reputation for providing facilities for disabled travellers. For people in wheelchairs, the haphazard parking
habits and stepped village streets are serious obstacles, and public toilets with disabled access are rare. In the major cities
and coastal resorts, however, ramps or other
forms of access are gradually being added
to hotels, museums and some theatres and

concert halls. APF, the French paraplegic
organization (see box below), which has an
office in each *département*, will be the most
reliable source of information on accommodation with disabled access and other facilities.

Public **transport** is certainly not wheelchair-
friendly, and although many train stations now
have ramps to enable wheelchair users to board

CONTACTS FOR TRAVELLERS WITH DISABILITIES

FRANCE

APF (Association des Paralysés de France), 17
bd Auguste-Blanqui, 75013 Paris
(☎01.40.78.69.00, *orphanet.infobiogen.fr/asso-
ciations/APF*). National organization providing
useful information and lists of new and accessible accommodation. Their guide *Où Ferons-Nous
Étape* is available at the office or by post to a
French address.

CNRH (Comité National Français de Liaison pour
la Réadaptation des Handicapés), 236bis rue de
Tolbiac, 75013 Paris (☎01.53.80.66.66).
Information service whose various useful guides
include the *Guide Touristique pour les Personnes
à Mobilitée Réduite*, available in English for
60F/€9.15.

UK

Access Travel, 6 The Hillock, Astley, Lancashire
M29 7GW (☎01942/888 844, fax 891 811, *www
.access.co.uk*). Tour operator that can arrange
flights, transfer and accommodation. This is a
small business, personally checking out places
before recommendation. They can guarantee
accommodation standards in several regions of
France: Pas de Calais, Loire Valley, Normandy and
Puy de Dôme. Established 1991; ATOL bonded.

Disability Action Group, 2 Annadale Ave,
Belfast BT7 3JH (☎01232/491 011). Offers infor-

mation about travel and access for disabled travellers abroad.

Holiday Care, 2nd Floor, Imperial Building,
Victoria Rd, Horley, Surrey RH6 7PZ (☎01293/774
535, fax 784 647. Minicom 01293/776 943,
www.holidaycare.org.uk). Provides free lists of
accessible accommodation throughout France.
Information on financial help for holidays available.

RADAR (Royal Association for Disability and
Rehabilitation), 12 City Forum, 250 City Rd,
London EC1V 8AF (☎020/7250 3222, Minicom
☎020/7250 4119). A good source of advice on
holidays and travel abroad. They produce a guide
for European holidays (£5 inc. p&p) alternate
years, and the useful publication *Access in Paris*
is available through them.

Tripscope, Alexandra House, Albany Rd,
Brentford, Middlesex TW8 0NE (☎08457/585
641, fax 020/8580 7022,
www.justmobility.co.uk/tripscope). Registered
charity providing a phone-in travel information
service that offers free advice on transport for
those with a mobility problem.

IRELAND

Irish Wheelchair Association, Blackheath
Drive, Clontarf, Dublin 3 (☎01/833 8241, fax 833
3873, *iwa@iol.ie*). Offers information about
travel and access for disabled travellers abroad.

and descend from carriages, at others it is still up to the guards to carry the chair. The high-speed **TGVs** (including Eurostar) all have places for wheelchairs in the First Class saloon coach, which you must book in advance, though no higher fee is charged; on other trains, a wheelchair symbol within the timetable denotes whether that service offers special features, and you and your companion will again be upgraded to first class with no extra charge. The *Guide du Voyageur à Mobilité Réduite*, available free at main train stations, details all facilities. **Taxis** are obliged by law to carry you and to help you into the vehicle, also to carry your guide dog if you are blind. Specialist taxi services are available in some towns: these are detailed in the Ministry of Transport and Tourism's pamphlet *Guide des Transports à l'Usage des Personnes à Mobilité Réduite*, available at airports, main train stations and some tourist offices. The guide also gives some indication of the accessibility of urban public transport systems, and the availability of cars for hire with hand controls. Hertz has a fleet at the airports of Paris, Lyon, Marseille and Nice which can be booked 48 hours in advance (in France ☎08.00.05.33.11).

Up-to-date information about handicap accessibility, special programmes and discounts is best obtained from organizations at home before you leave or from the French disability organizations. The publication *Touristes Quand Même!*, produced by the CNRH (see box below), lists facilities throughout France but is not updated regularly. Some tourist offices have information but, again, it is not always very reliable. For Paris, *Access in Paris* by Gordon Couch and Ben Roberts, published in Britain by Quiller Press and available from RADAR (£6.95), is a thorough guide to accommodation, monuments, museums, restaurants and travel to the city. The Holiday

---

US

Access First Travel, 239 Commercial St, Malden, MA 02148 (☎1-800/557 2047). Offers up-to-date information for disabled travellers.

Directions Unlimited, 123 Green Lane, Bedford Hills, NY 10507 (☎1-800/533 5343). Tour operator specializing in customized tours for people with disabilities.

Mobility International USA, PO Box 10767, Eugene, OR 97440 (☎541/343 1284 voice & TDD, *www.miusa.com*). Offers information and referral services, access guides, tours and exchange programmes. Annual membership $25 (includes quarterly newsletter).

Society for the Advancement of Travel for the Handicapped (SATH), 347 Fifth Ave, Suite 610, New York, NY 10016 (☎212/447 7284, *www.sath.org*). Non-profit-making travel industry referral service that passes queries on to its members as appropriate.

Travel Information Service (☎215/456-9600). Telephone-only information and referral service for disabled travellers.

Wheels Up!, PO Box 5197, Plant City, FL 33564-5197 (☎1-888/389 4335, *www.wheelsup.com*). Provides discounted airfare, tour and cruise prices for disabled travellers, as well as publishing a free monthly newsletter. Their Web site is comprehensive.

CANADA

Twin Peaks Press, Box 129, Vancouver, WA 98666 (☎360/694 2462 or 1-800/637 2256, *www.pacifier.com/twinpeak*). Publisher of the *Directory of Travel Agencies for the Disabled* ($19.95), listing more than 370 agencies worldwide; *Travel for the Disabled* ($19.95); the *Directory of Accessible Van Rentals* ($9.95); and *Wheelchair Vagabond* ($14.95), which is loaded with personal tips.

Jewish Rehabilitation Hospital, 3205 Place Alton Goldbloom, Chomedy Laval, PQ H7V 1R2 (☎450/688 9550, ext 226). Provides guidebooks and travel information.

AUSTRALIA

ACROD (Australian Council for Rehabilitation of the Disabled), PO Box 60, Curtin, ACT 2605 (☎02/6282 4333); 24 Cabarita Rd, Cabarita, NSW 2137 (☎02/9743 2699). Provides lists of travel agencies and tour operators for people with disabilities.

Barrier Free Travel, 36 Wheatley St, North Bellingen, NSW 2454 (☎02/6655 1733). Independent consultant – draws up individual itineraries for people with disabilities for a fee.

NEW ZEALAND

Disabled Persons Assembly, PO Box 10, 138 The Terrace, Wellington (☎04/472 2626, *www.dpa.org.nz*). Provides details of tour operators and travel agencies for people with disabilities.

continued from previous page

CANADA

Montréal Ulysses Travel Bookshop, 4176 St-Denis, QUE H2W 2M5 (☎514/843 9447, *www.ulyssesguides.com*).
Toronto Open Air Books and Maps, 25 Toronto St, ON M5R 2C1 (☎416/363 0719).

Vancouver International Travel Maps and Books, 552 Seymour St, BC V6B 3J5 (☎604/687 3320, *www.itmb.com*).

AUSTRALIA

Adelaide The Map Shop, 16a Peel St (☎08/8231 2033).
Brisbane Worldwide Maps and Guides, 187 George St (☎07/3221 4330).
Melbourne Map Land, 372 Little Burke St (☎03/9670 4383).

Perth Perth Map Centre, 884 Hay St (☎08/9322 5733).
Sydney Travel Bookshop, Shop 3, 175 Liverpool St, 2000 (☎02/9261 8200).

NEW ZEALAND

Auckland Specialty Maps, 58 Albert St (☎09/307 2217).

Christchurch Mapworld, 173 Gloucester St (☎03/374 5399, *www.mapworld.co.nz*).

Guide). For the practical purposes of visitors, there is little difference between them: SIs have wider responsibilities for encouraging business, while Offices du Tourisme deal exclusively with tourism; sometimes they share premises and call themselves an OTSI. In small villages where there is no OT or SI, the Mairie, or town hall, will offer a similar service. Before you go, it's worth checking out the official French Tourist Board Web site, *www.tourisme.fr*.

From all these offices you can get specific local information, including listings of hotels and restaurants, leisure activities, car and bike rental, bus timetables, laundries and countless other things; many can also book accommodation for you. Most offices will provide a free town plan (though some places charge a nominal 5–10F/€0.76–1.53), if asked, and will have maps and local walking guides on sale. In mountain regions they display daily meteorological information and often share premises with the local hiking and climbing organizations. In the big cities you can usually also pick up free *What's On* guides. The regional or departmental tourist offices also offer useful practical information (their Web sites can be accessed on the Net via *www.tourist-office.org*).

MAPS

In addition to the various free leaflets – and the maps in this guide – the one extra map you'll probably want is a reasonable **road map** of France. The Michelin map no. 989 (1:1,000,000) is the best for the whole country. A useful free map for car drivers, obtainable from filling stations and traffic information kiosks in France, is the Bison Futé map, showing alternative back routes to the congested main roads, clearly signposted on the ground by special green Bison Futé road signs. For more regional detail, the Michelin yellow series (1:200,000) is best for the motorist. You can get the whole series in one large spiral-bound *Atlas Routier*.

If you're planning to **walk or cycle**, check the IGN (Institut Géographique National) maps – either green (1:100,000 and 1:50,000), or the more detailed blue (1:25,000) series. The IGN 1:100,000 series is the smallest scale available that has the contours marked – essential for cyclists, who tend to cycle off 1:25,000 maps in a couple of hours. Didier Richard maps (1:50,000) show walking paths in Corsica, the Alps, Provence and the Southern Rhône, while routes in the French Pyrenees are well covered by the twelve maps in the *Randonnées Pyrénées* series (1:50,000).

For those wanting to plan a visit to the **battlefields of northern France**, the two maps of Major and Mrs Holt's *Battle Map Series* are available direct from its English authors (T. & V. Holt, Oak Housem, Woodnesborough, Sandwich CT13 0NJ, England; ☎ & fax 01304/614123).

GETTING AROUND

With the most extensive train network in western Europe, France is a country in which to travel by rail. The nationally owned French train company, the SNCF (Société Nationale des Chemins de Fer), runs fast, modern trains. In rural areas where branch lines have been closed, routes are covered by buses operated by the SNCF. It's an integrated service, with buses timetabled to meet trains and the same ticket covering both.

The private **bus** services that supplement the SNCF services are confusing and unco-ordinated. Approximate journey times and frequencies can be found in the "Travel details" at the end of each chapter, and local peculiarities are also pointed out in the text of the *Guide*.

Flying within France has the obvious advantage of speed, but is only recommended for those short on time and long on cash. Aside from Corsica, which can also be reached by air, France's islands are serviced only by **ferries**, some of which are seasonal and not all of which are equipped to carry vehicles.

For a more private kind of independent transport, by **car** or **bicycle**, you'll need to be aware of a number of French road rules and peculiarities. **Hitching** is also an option, but is not easy and is becoming less and less popular. **Walking** (see p.73), on the extensive network of "GR" footpaths, is recommended, as are the more specialist realms of inland **boating** and **cross-country skiing** (see p.73), both of which have a high profile in France.

TRAINS

The SNCF has pioneered one of the most efficient, comfortable and user-friendly railway systems in the world. Its staff are, with a few exceptions, courteous and helpful, and its trains – for the most part, fast, clean and frequent – continue, in spite of the closure of some rural lines, to serve a vast part of the country. For national train **information**, you can either phone (☎08.36.35.35.35; 2.23F/€0.34 per minute) or check on the Internet at *www.sncf.fr*.

Pride and joy of the system are the high-speed **TGVs** (*trains à grande vitesse*), capable of 300kph, and their offspring **Eurostar**. The continually expanding system has its main hub at Paris, from where a main line heads northeast to Lille, and two other trunk routes head south: one reaching down the east side of the country to Marseille and the Mediterranean, the other down the west to Bordeaux and the Spanish frontier. Spur lines service Brittany and Normandy, the Alps, Pyrenees and Jura. Although the whole service is much faster than ordinary trains, the special high-speed TGV track, which alone permits top speeds, at the moment stretches from Lille (with a branch to the Channel Tunnel at Calais) to Paris, then southeast to Valence and southwest to Tours and Le Mans. The only difference between TGV and other train fares is that you pay a compulsory reservation charge (from 20F/€3), plus a supplement on certain peak-hour trains. It is easiest to

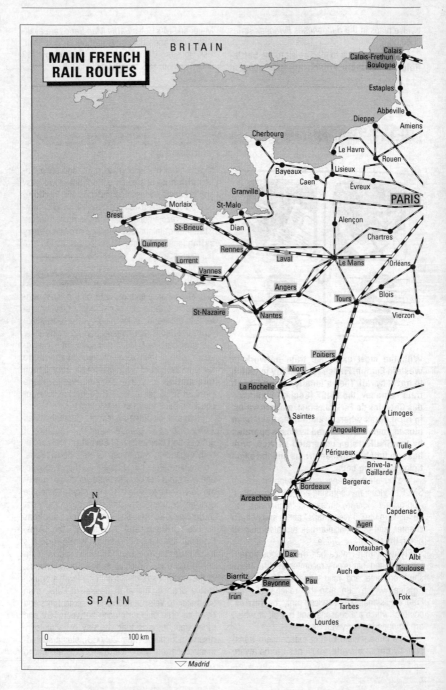

MAIN FRENCH
RAIL ROUTES

Motoring Assistance (☎0800/550055, www.*rac.co.uk*), the AA's Five-Star Europe cover (☎0800/444500, www.*theaa.co.uk*), or Europ Assistance (☎0645/947000). In the US, contact the American Automobile Association (☎1-800/222-4357, www.*aaa.com*); in Canada, the Canadian Automobile Association (☎1-800/267-8713, www.*caa.ca*); in Australia, the Australian Automobile Association (☎02/6247 7311, www.*aaa.asn.au*); and in New Zealand, the New Zealand Automobile Association (☎09/377 4660, www.*nzaa.co.nz*).

RULES OF THE ROAD

British, EU, Australian, Canadian, New Zealand and US **driving licences** are valid in France, though an International Driver's Licence makes life easier if you get a police officer unwilling to peruse a document in English. If the vehicle is rented, its registration document (*carte grise*) and the insurance papers must be carried. GB stickers are, by law, meant to be displayed, and a Green Card, though not a legal requirement, might save some hassle. If your car is right-hand drive, you must have your headlight dip adjusted to the right before you go – it's a legal requirement – and as a courtesy change or paint them to yellow or stick on black glare deflectors. Remember also that you have to be 18 years of age to drive in France, regardless of whether you hold a licence in your own country.

The law of *priorité à droite* – **giving way** to traffic coming from your right, even when it is coming from a minor road – is being phased out as it is a major cause of accidents. It still applies in built-up areas, so you still have to be vigilant in towns, keeping a lookout along the roadside for the yellow diamond on a white background that gives you right of way – until you see the same sign with an oblique black slash, which indicates vehicles emerging from the right have right of way. At roundabouts the *priorité à droite* law no longer applies. *Stop* signs mean stop completely; *Cédez le passage* means "Give way". Other signs warning of potential dangers are *déviation* (diversion), *gravillons* (loose chippings), *nids de poules* (potholes) and *chaussée déformée* (uneven surface).

Fines of up to 2500F/€381.25 for driving violations are exacted on the spot, and only cash is accepted. The fines for exceeding the speed limit by 1–30kph (1–18mph) range from 900F/€137 to 5000F/€763. Speed limits are: 130kph (80mph)

ROAD INFORMATION

For information on traffic and road conditions on *autoroutes* throughout France, ring the multilingual service, Autoroutel (☎08.36.68.10.77) or consult their Web site www.*autoroutes.fr*. Traffic information for non-motorway routes can be obtained 24 hours per day at ☎01.56.96.33.33.

---

on the tolled *autoroutes*; 110kph (68mph) on dual carriageways; 90kph (56mph) on other roads; and 50kph (37mph) in towns. In wet weather, and for drivers with less than two years' experience, these limits are 110kph (68mph), 100kph (62mph), and 80kph (50mph) respectively. Random breath tests are common, and the legal blood alcohol limit (0.05 percent alcohol) is lower than in the UK and North America; fines range from 900F/€137 to 30,000F/€4575.

CAR RENTAL

Car rental in France costs upwards of 2000F/€305 a week (from around 290–520F/€44.23–79.30 a day), but can be cheaper if arranged before you leave home – in the UK, Holidays Autos offer competitive deals on car rental in France. You'll find the big firms – Hertz, Avis, Europcar and Budget – at airports and in most big cities, with addresses detailed throughout the *Guide*. Rental from airports normally includes a surcharge. Local firms can be cheaper but you need to check the small print and be sure of where the car can be returned to. It's normal to pay an indemnity of around 1000F/€152 against any damage to the car – they will take your credit card number rather than cash. You should return the car with a full tank of fuel. Extras are often pressed on you, like medical cover, which you may already have from travel insurance. The cost of car rental includes the basic legally necessary car insurance. North Americans and Australians in particular should be forewarned that it is very difficult to arrange the hire of a car with **automatic** transmission – not popular in France; if you can't drive a manual you should try to book an automatic well in advance, possibly before you leave home, and be prepared to pay a much higher price for it.

Most rental companies will only deal with people over 25 unless an extra insurance premium, typically around 130–150F/€20–23 per day, is paid (but you still must be over 21 and have driven for at least one year). OTU Voyage (Paris office ☎01.40.29.12.12), the student travel agency, can arrange car rental for young drivers, with prices beginning at 459F/€70 for three days, insurance extra.

MOPED AND MOTORBIKE RENTAL

Mopeds and scooters are relatively easy to find: everyone in France, from young kids to grandmas, rides one of them, and although they're not built for any kind of long-distance travel, they're ideal for shooting around town and nearby. Places that rent out bicycles will often also rent out mopeds; you can expect to pay 175F/€26.69 a day for a 50cc Suzuki. No licence is needed for 50cc and under bikes, but for anything larger you'll need a valid **motorbike** licence. Rental prices are around

220F/€33.55 a day for an 80cc motorbike, 300F/€45.75 for a 125cc; also expect to leave a hefty deposit by cash or credit card – 6000F/€900 is not unusual – which you may lose in the event of damage or theft. Crash helmets are now compulsory on all mopeds and motorbikes.

HITCHING

If you're intent on **hitching**, you'll have to rely almost exclusively on car drivers, as lorries very rarely give lifts. Even so, it won't be easy. Looking as clean, ordinary and respectable as possible makes a very big difference, as conversations with French drivers soon make clear. Experience also suggests that hitching the less-frequented D roads is much quicker. In mountain areas a rucksack and hiking gear will help procure a lift from fellow aficionados.

CAR RENTAL AGENCIES

BRITAIN AND IRELAND

Autos Abroad (in the UK ☎08700/667788; www.autosabroad.co.uk).

Avis (in Britain ☎0870/606 0100; Northern Ireland ☎0990/900 500; Irish Republic ☎01/874 5844; www.avis.com).

Budget (in Britain ☎0800/181181; Irish Republic ☎0800/973159; www.budgetrentacar.com).

Europcar (in Britain ☎0345/222 525; Northern Ireland ☎0345/222 525; Irish Republic ☎01/874 5844; www.europcar.com).

Hertz (in Britain ☎0870/844 8844; Northern Ireland ☎0990/996 699; Irish Republic ☎01/676 7476; www.hertz.com).

Holiday Autos (in Britain ☎0870/400 0011; Northern Ireland ☎0990/300400; Irish Republic ☎01/872 9366; www.kemwel.com).

National Car Rental (in Britain ☎01895/233 300, www.nationalcar.com).

Thrifty (in Britain ☎01494/442 110, www.thrifty.com).

US AND CANADA

Alamo (☎1-800/522 9696, www.alamo.com).

Auto Europe (☎1-800/223 5555).

Avis (☎1-800/331 1084).

Budget (☎1-800/527 0700).

Dollar (☎1-800/421 6868, www.dollar.com).

Europe by Car (☎1-800/223 1516, www.europe bycar.com).

Hertz (in US ☎1-800/654 3001; in Canada ☎1-800/263 0600).

Holiday Autos (☎1-800/422 7737).

National (☎1-800/CAR-RENT).

Thrifty (☎1-800/367 2277).

AUSTRALIA AND NEW ZEALAND

Avis (in Australia ☎13/6333; in New Zealand ☎09/526 5231 or 0800/655 111).

Budget (in Australia local-call rate ☎1300/362 848; in New Zealand ☎0800/ 652 227 or 09/375 2270).

Fly and Drive Holidays (in New Zealand ☎09/529 3709).

Hertz (in Australia toll-free ☎1800/550 067; in New Zealand ☎09/309 0989 or 0800/655 955).

Renault Eurodrive (☎02/9299 3344).

Autoroutes are a special case. Hitching on the *autoroute* itself is strictly illegal, but you can make excellent time going from one service station to another, and if you get stuck, at least there's food, drink, shelter and washing facilities at most service stations. It helps to have the *Guide des Autoroutes*, published by Michelin, which shows all the rest stops, service stations, tollbooths (*péages*), exits, etc. Remember to get out at the service station before your driver leaves the *autoroute*. The tollbooths are a second best (and legal) option; ordinary approach roads can be disastrous.

For major long-distance rides, and for a greater sense of safety, you might consider using the national **hitching organization**, Allostop Provoya, 8 rue Rochambeau (on square Montholon), 17009 Paris (Mon–Fri 9am–7.30pm, Sat 9am–1pm & 2–6pm; ☎01.53.20.42.42, fax 01.53.20.42.44, *pcb.ecritel.fr/allostop/welcome*; M° Cadet/Poissonnière). The cost comprises a registration fee (30F/€4.58 for a journey less than 200km, 50F/€7.63 if less than 400km, 60F/€9.15 if less than 500km and a maximum of 70F/€10.68 if more than 500km, or you can buy a 180F/€27.45 membership card which is good for eight trips over two years), plus a charge of 22 centimes for every kilometre of the journey.

BICYCLES

Bicycles (*vélos*) have high status in France. All the car ferries carry them for nothing; the SNCF makes minimal charges; and the French (Parisians excepted) respect cyclists – both as traffic and, when you stop off at a restaurant or hotel, as customers. In addition many municipalities and *départements* are actively promoting cycling, not only with city paths, but comprehensive networks linking rural areas (frequently utilizing disused roadways and rail right-of-ways). These days more and more cyclists are using **mountain bikes**, which the French call VTTs (*vélos tout terrain*), even for touring holidays, although it's much less effort, and much quicker, to cycle long distances and carry luggage on a traditionally styled touring or racing bike.

Restaurants and hotels along the way are nearly always obliging about looking after your bike, even to the point of allowing it into your room. Most large towns have well-stocked retail and **repair shops**, where parts are normally cheaper than in Britain or the US. However, if you're using a foreign-made bike with non-stan-

dard metric wheels, it's a good idea to carry spare tyres. Inner tubes are not a problem, as they adapt to either size, though make sure you get the right valves.

The **train** network runs various schemes for cyclists, all of them covered by the free leaflet *Guide du Train et du Vélo*, available from most stations. Trains marked with a bicycle in the timetable allow you to take a bike as free accompanied luggage. Otherwise, you have to send your bike parcelled up as registered luggage for a fee of 150F/€22.88. Although it may well arrive in less time, the SNCF won't guarantee delivery in under five days; and you do hear stories of bicycles disappearing altogether.

You can normally load your bike straight onto the train at the **ferry** port – as on the boat train at Dieppe – but remember that you must first go to the ticket office of the station to register it. Don't just try to climb on the train with it, as both you and your bike will end up left behind. Ferries either take bikes free or charge a maximum of £5 one way. British Airways and Air France both take bikes free – you may have to box them though, and you should contact the airlines first. **Eurostar** allow you to take your bicycle as part of your baggage allowance provided it is dismantled and stored in a special bike bag, and the dimensions don't exceed 120cm by 90cm. Otherwise it needs to be sent on unaccompanied, with a guaranteed arrival of 24 hours (you can register it up to ten days in advance; book through Esprit Europe ☎0800/186186); the fee is £20 one way.

Bikes – usually mountain bikes – are often available to **rent** from campsites, hostels and *gîtes d'étapes*, as well as from specialist cycle shops and some tourist offices for around 80F/€12.20 per day; these machines are likely to be more reliable, though more expensive, than those of the SNCF. The bikes are often not insured, however, and you will be presented with the bill for its replacement if it's stolen or damaged. Check whether your travel insurance policy covers you for this if you intend to rent a bike.

As for **maps**, a minimum requirement is the IGN 1:100,000 series – the smallest scale that carries contours. In the UK, the Cyclists' Touring Club, Cotterell House, 68 Meadrow, Godalming, Surrey GU7 3HS (☎01483/417 217, fax 01483/426 994, *cycling@ctc.org.uk*), will suggest routes and supply advice for members (£25 p.a. or £12.50 for unemployed). They run a particularly good insur-

A CYCLING VOCABULARY

to adjust	*régler*	loose	*déserré*
axle	*l'axe*	to lower	*baisser*
ball-bearing	*le roulement à billes*	mudguard	*le garde-boue*
battery	*la pile*	pannier	*le pannier*
bent	*tordu*	pedal	*le pédale*
bicycle	*le vélo*	pump	*la pompe*
bottom bracket	*le logement du pédalier*	puncture	*la crevaison*
brake cable	*le cable*	rack	*le porte-bagages*
brakes	*les freins*	to raise	*remonter*
broken	*cassé*	to repair	*réparer*
bulb	*l'ampoule*	saddle	*la selle*
chain	*la chaîne*	to screw	*visser/serrer*
cotter pin	*la clavette*	spanner	*la clef*
to deflate	*dégonfler*	spoke	*le rayon*
derailleur	*le dérailleur*	to straighten	*redresser*
frame	*le cadre*	stuck	*coincé*
gears	*les vitesses*	tight	*serré*
grease	*la graisse*	toe clips	*les cale-pieds*
handlebars	*le guidon*	tyre	*le pneu*
to inflate	*gonfler*	wheel	*la roue*
inner tube	*la chambre à air*		

ance scheme. Companies running specialist bike touring holidays are listed in the boxes on pp.9 and 16–17.

BOATING

With some 7500km of navigable rivers and canals, **boating** can be one of the best and most relaxed ways of exploring France. Except on parts of the Moselle, there is no charge for use of the waterways, and you can travel without a permit for up to six months in a year. For information on maximum dimensions, documentation, regulations and so forth, ask at a French Government Tourist Office for their booklet *Boating on the Waterways*, or contact Voies Navigables de France, 175 rue Ludovic Boutleux, 62408 Bethune (☎03.21.63.24.24, fax 03.21.63.24.42, *www.vnf.fr*), which has information on boating throughout France, and lists of firms that rent out boats. British companies organizing **boating holidays** include Hoseasons (☎01502/500 555), Crown Blue Line (☎01603/630513, *boathols @crown-blueline.com*) and Abercrombie & Kent (☎0171/730 9600). The most attractive boats, based on a scaled-down version of real commercial barges, are run by French Country Cruises (☎01572/821 330, fax 821 072), although Locaboat (☎03.86.91.72.72, *www.locaboat.com*) also has good modern vessels (expect to pay between 5250F/€800 and 10,000F/€1500 per week,

depending on season, for a 3–5 person boat). Details of North American and Australian firms offering boating holidays can be found in the boxes on pp.16–17 and 20. For a full list of rental firms operating in France write to the Syndicat National des Loueurs de Bateaux de Plaisance, Port de la Bourdonnais, 75007 Paris (☎01.44.37.04.00, fax 01.45.77.21.88).

The principal **areas** for boating are Brittany, Burgundy, Picardy-Flanders, Alsace and Champagne. Brittany's canals join up with the Loire, but this is only navigable as far as Angers, with no links eastwards. Other waterways permit numerous permutations, including joining up via the Rhône and Saône with the Canal du Midi in Languedoc and then northwestwards to Bordeaux and the Atlantic. The eighteenth-century Canal de Bourgogne and 300-year-old Canal du Midi are fascinating examples of early canal engineering. The latter completely transformed the fortunes of coastal Languedoc, and in particular Sète, whose attractive harbour dates from that period. Together with its continuation, the Canal du Sète à Rhône, it passes within easy reach of several interesting areas.

The through-journey from the **Channel to the Mediterranean** requires some planning. The Canal de Bourgogne has an inordinate number of locks, while other waterways demand consider-

fortable but still affordable chain hotels are **Campanile** (*www.campanile.fr*), **Ibis** (*www.ibis.fr*) and **Clarine** (*www.clarine.fr*), which all have en-suite rooms with cable TV and direct-dial phones from 270–320F/€41–49. All three of these hotel chains can be reached by Internet and will accept reservations by email. They will also send a complete list of their locations in France by email request within a few days. Ibis provides a very affordable, dependable level of comfort, which makes its hotels highly suitable for families; prices start from about 300F/€45 per en-suite double, including cable TV. In the UK, call ☎0181/746 3233 and request a detailed location booklet.

Aside from the chains, there a number of **hotel federations** in France. The biggest of these is **Logis de France**, an association of over 3000 hotels nationwide. They have a central reservation number (☎01.45.84.83.84, fax 01.45.83.59.66) and Web site (*www.logis-de-france.fr*), which you can contact to obtain their free yearly guide (or write 88 av d'Italie, 75013 Paris).

Over sixty cities in France now participate in the "Bonne Weekend en Ville" programme, whereby you book through the local tourist office and get two nights for the price of one (Oct–May only) at participating hotels, as well as an array of discount coupons and special deals.

BED AND BREAKFAST AND RENTED ACCOMMODATION

In country areas, in addition to standard hotels, you will come across *chambres d'hôtes* and *fermes auberges*, **bed-and-breakfast accommodation** in someone's house or farm. These vary in standard and are rarely a cheap option, usually costing the equivalent of a two-star hotel. However, if you're lucky, they may be good sources of traditional home-cooking and French company. The brown leaflets available in tourist offices list most of them.

If you are planning to stay a week or more in any one place it might be worth considering **renting a house**. You can do this by checking adverts from the innumerable private and foreign owners in British Sunday newspapers (*Observer* and *Sunday Times*, mainly), or trying one of the numerous holiday firms that market accommodation /travel packages (see the boxes on pp.9, 16–17 and 18–20 for a brief selection of these).

Alternatively you could contact **Gîtes de France**, 59 rue St-Lazare, Paris 75009 (Mon–Sat 10am–6.30pm; ☎01.49.70.75.75, *www.gites-de-france.fr*), a government-funded agency which promotes and manages a range of bed-and-breakfast and self-catering accommodation in France, the latter usually consisting of a self-contained country cottage, known as a **gîte rural** or **gîte de séjour**. Further details can be found in their two very useful national guides – *Chambres et Tables d'Hôtes* (120F/€18.30) and *Chambres d'Hôtes de Prestige et Gîtes de Charme* (120F/€18.30) – which are also sometimes on sale in bookstores and tourist offices. The national guides, however, are not exhaustive; complete listings (with photos) are available in the guides (60F/€9.12) distributed by departmental Gîtes de France offices – you can either contact the main office for a complete list, or pick up copies from local and departmental tourist offices.

HOSTELS, FOYERS AND STUDENT ACCOMMODATION

At between 60F/€9.15 and 120F/€18.30 per night for a dormitory bed, and generally breakfast thrown in, **hostels** – *auberges de jeunesse* – are invaluable for single travellers on a budget. Many of the modern ones now offer rooms for couples, with en-suite showers, but they don't necessarily work out cheaper than hotels – particularly if you've had to pay a bus fare out to the edge of town to reach them. However, many hostels are beautifully sited, and they allow you to cut costs by preparing your own food in their kitchens (not often possible), or eating in their cheap canteens. Normally, to stay at FUAJ or LFAJ hostels (see opposite) you must be a member of Hostelling International (HI) or the International Youth Hostel Federation (IYHF). Head offices and membership fees, which differ from country to country, are listed in the box opposite. If you don't join up before you leave home, you can purchase a **membership card** in relevant French hostels for 100F/€15.25.

Slightly confusingly, there are three rival French **hostelling associations** (see box opposite): the main two being the Fédération Unie des Auberges de Jeunesse (FUAJ; 180 hostels), which has its hostels detailed in the *International Handbook*, and the Ligue Française pour les Auberges de Jeunesse (LFAJ; 100 hostels). HI membership covers both organizations, and you'll find all their hostels detailed in the text. The third organization is the Union des Centres de Recontres Internationales de France (UCRIF), with 60 hostels in France; membership is not required.

HOSTELLING ASSOCIATIONS

France Fédération Unie des Auberges de Jeunesse (FUAJ), 27 rue Pajol, 75018 Paris (☎01.44.89.87.27, fax 01.44.89.87.10, *www.fuaj.org*); Ligue Française pour les Auberges de Jeunesse (LFAJ), 38 bd Raspail, 75007 Paris (☎01.45.48.69.84, fax 01.45.44.57.47); Union des Centres de Recontres Internationales de France (UCRIF), 27 rue Turbigo, 75002 Paris (☎01.40.26.57.64, fax 01.40.26.58.20, *ucrif@aol.com*).

England and Wales Youth Hostel Association, Trevelyan House, 8 St Stephen's Hill, St Albans, Herts AL1 2DY (☎0870/870 8808, *www.yha.org.uk*); London membership desk and booking office: 14 Southampton St, London WC2 7HY (☎020/7836 8541). Annual membership £12.

Scotland Scottish Youth Hostel Association, 7 Glebe Crescent, Stirling FK8 2JA (☎01786/451 181, *www.syha.org.uk*). Annual membership £6.

Ireland Republic: 61 Mountjoy St, Dublin 7 (☎01/830 4555, *www.irelandyha.org*); annual membership IR£10. Northern Ireland: 22 Donegal Rd, Belfast BT12 5JN (☎028/9031 5435, *www.hini.org.uk*); annual membership £8.

US Hostelling International, 733 15th St NW, Suite 840, PO Box 37613, Washington DC 20005 (☎202/783 6161, fax 202/783 6171, *www.hiayh.org*).

Canada Hostelling International/Canadian Hostelling Association, Room 400, 205 Catherine St, Ottawa, ON K2P 1C3 (☎1-800/663 5777 or 613/237 7884, fax 613/237 7868).

Australia Youth Hostel Association of Australia, 422 Kent St, Sydney (☎02/9261 1111, www.*yha.com.au*).

New Zealand Youth Hostels Association of New Zealand, 173 Gloucester St, Christchurch (☎03/379 9970, *www.yha.co.nz*).

There are now also several independent hostels, particularly in Paris, where dorm beds cost from 95F/€14.49 to 120F/€18.30 with breakfast thrown in, though these tend to be party places with an emphasis on good times rather than sleep.

A few large towns provide a more luxurious standard of hostel accommodation in Foyers des Jeunes Travailleurs/euses, **residential hostels** for young workers and students, where you can usually get a private room for around 60F/€9.15. They normally have a good cafeteria or canteen.

At the height of summer (usually July & Aug only), there's also the possibility of staying in **student accommodation** in university towns and cities. The main organization to contact for this is CROUS, Académie de Paris, 39 av Georges-Bernanos, Paris 75005 (☎01.40.51.36.00, www.*crous.fr*). Prices are similar to the official hostels, from around 70F/€10.68 per person, and you don't need membership.

GÎTES D'ÉTAPE AND REFUGES

In the countryside, another hostel-style alternative exists: **gîtes d'étape**. *Gîtes d'étape* are often run by the local village or municipality (whose mayor will probably be in charge of the key) and are less formal than hostels. They provide bunk beds and primitive kitchen and washing facilities

from around 40F/€6.10, and they are marked on the large-scale IGN walkers' maps and listed in the individual GR *Topoguides*. In addition, mountain areas are well supplied with **refuge huts**, mostly run by the Club Alpin Français (CAF) and mostly only open in summer. These huts are staffed in hiking season and offer dorm accommodation and meals; they are the only available shelter once you are above the villages. Costs are from around 60F/€9.15 for the night, less if you're a member of a climbing organization affiliated to the CAF. Meals – invariably four courses – cost around 80F/€12.20, which is not unreasonable when you consider that all supplies have to be brought up by mule or helicopter.

More information can be found in the guides *Gîtes d'Étapes et Sejours* (60F/€9.12) and *Chambres d'Hôtes de Prestige et Gîtes de Charme* (120F/€18.30), published by Gîtes de France (see opposite), and *Gîtes d'Étape et Refuges*, published by Guides La Cadole, available in French book shops for 110F/€16.78. Gîtes de France also publishes more detailed departmental guides (60F/€9.12); you can order them from their main office or pick up copies from local and departmental tourist offices.

CAMPING

Practically every village and town in France has at least one **campsite** to cater for the thousands of people who spend their holiday under canvas – camping is a very big deal in France. The cheapest – at around 25–35F/€3.80–5.30 per person per night – is usually the *Camping municipal*, run by the local municipality. In season or whenever they're officially open, they are always clean and have plenty of hot water; often they are situated in prime local positions. Out of season, those that stay open often don't bother to collect the overnight charge.

If you're planning to do a lot of camping, an **international camping carnet** is a good investment. The carnet serves as useful identification, covers you for third party insurance when camping, and helps you get 10 percent reductions at campsites listed in the CCI information booklet that comes with your carnet. It is available in the UK from the AA, the RAC and the Carefree Travel Service (☎01203/422024), who also book inspected camping sites in Europe and arrange ferry crossings; in the US from Family Campers and RVers (FCRV), 4804 Transit Rd, Building 2, Depew, NY 14043 (☎1-800/245 9755); and in Canada from FCRV, 51 W 22nd St, Hamilton, ON LC9 4N5 (☎1-800/245 9755). FCRV annual membership costs $20, and the carnet an additional $10.

On the coast especially, there are **superior categories** of campsite where you'll pay prices similar to those of a hotel for the facilities – bars, restaurants and sometimes swimming pools. These have rather more permanent status than the *Campings municipaux*, with people often spending a whole holiday in the one base. If you plan to do the same, and particularly if you have a caravan, camper or a big tent, it's wise to book ahead – reckon on paying at least 35F/€5.34 a head with a tent, 40F/€6.10 with a camper van. Inland, *camping à la ferme* – on somebody's farm – is another possibility (generally without facilities). Lists of sites are detailed in the Tourist Board's *Accueil à la Campagne* booklet.

A number of companies also specialize in selling **camping holidays**, including Allez France (see box on p.9), Canvas Holidays (☎08709/022 022, *www.canvasholidays.com*), Keycamp (see box on p.9) and Sunsites (☎01606/787 555, *www.sunsites.co.uk*). Twelve nights' camping at Argelès, near Perpignan, with Sunsites, for example, costs from £862 for two adults, with up to four children under 18 free, which includes the price of the Channel ferry.

Lastly, a word of **caution**: never camp rough (*camping sauvage*, as the French call it) on anyone's land without first asking permission. If the dogs don't get you, the guns might – farmers have been known to shoot before asking questions. On the other hand, a politely phrased request for permission will as often as not get positive results. Camping on public land is not officially permitted, but is widely practised by the French, and if you are discreet you will likely not meet with problems. On beaches, it's best to camp out only where other people are doing so.

EATING AND DRINKING

French cuisine has taken a bit of a knocking in recent years. The wonderful ingredients are still there, as every town and village market testifies. But those little family restaurants serving classic peasant dishes that celebrate the region's produce in each exquisite mouthful – and where the bill is less than 100F/€15 – are few and far between nowadays. The processed, boil-in-the-bag and ready-to-microwave productions of the global food industry, all so inimical to the basic culinary arts of France, are making serious inroads. That's not to say you can't eat well in France – far from it – but be prepared for disappointments at run-of-the-mill establishments.

In the rarefied world of **haute cuisine**, where the top chefs are national celebrities, a battle is currently raging between traditionalists, determined to preserve the purity of French cuisine, and those who experiment with different flavours from around the world to create novel combinations, for example seafood and cinnamon. At this level, French food is still brilliant – in both camps – and the good news is that prices are continuing to come down. Many gourmet palaces offer weekday lunchtime menus where you can sample culinary genius for around 290F/€44.

France is also a great place for **foreign cuisine**, in particular North African, Caribbean (known as *Antillais*) and Asiatic. Moroccan, Thai or Vietnamese restaurants are not necessarily cheap options but they are usually good value for money.

On the whole, **vegetarians** can expect a somewhat lean time in France. A few cities have specifically vegetarian restaurants (detailed in the text), but elsewhere you'll have to hope you find a sympathetic restaurant (crêperies and pizzerias can be good standbys). Sometimes they're willing to replace a meat dish on the *menu fixe* with an omelette; other times you'll have to pick your way through the *carte*. Remember the phrase "Je suis végétarien(ne); il y a quelques plats sans viande?" (I'm a vegetarian; are there any non-meat dishes?). **Vegans**, however, should probably forget all about eating in French restaurants and stick to self-catering.

BREAKFAST AND SNACKS

A croissant, *pain au chocolat* (a square-shaped chocolate-filled light pastry) or a sandwich in a bar or café, with hot chocolate or coffee, is generally the best way to eat **breakfast** – at a fraction of the cost charged by most hotels. (The days when hotels gave you mounds of croissants and brioches for breakfast seem to be long gone; now it's virtually always bread, jam and a jug of coffee or tea for about 30F/€4.50.) Croissants and sometimes hard-boiled eggs are displayed on bar counters until around 9.30am or 10am. If you stand – cheaper than sitting down – you just help yourself to these with your coffee; the waiter keeps an eye on how many you've eaten and bills you accordingly.

At **lunchtime**, and sometimes in the evening, you may find cafés offering a *plat du jour* (chef's daily special) at between 40F/€6.10 and 75F/€11.44, or *formules*, a limited or no-choice menu. *Croques-monsieur* or *croques-madame* (variations on the toasted-cheese sandwich) are on sale at cafés, brasseries and many street stands, along with *frites* (potato fries), crêpes, *galettes* (wholewheat pancakes), *gauffres* (waffles), *glaces* (ice creams) and all kinds of fresh-filled baguettes (these very filling sandwiches usually cost between 18F/€2.75 and 28F/€4.27 to take away). For variety, there are Tunisian snacks like *brik à l'œuf* (a fried pastry with an egg inside), *merguez* (spicy North African sausage), Greek souvlaki (kebabs) and Middle Eastern falafel (deep-fried chickpea balls in flat bread with salad). Wine bars are good for regional

continued from previous page

Meat (*viande*) and Poultry (*volaille*)

agneau (de pré-salé)	lamb (grazed on salt marshes)	*lapin, lapereau*	rabbit, young rabbit
andouille, andouillette	tripe sausage	*lard, lardons*	bacon, diced bacon
bifteck	steak	*lièvre*	hare
bœuf	beef	*merguez*	spicy, red sausage
boudin blanc	sausage of white meats	*mouton*	mutton
boudin noir	black pudding	*museau de veau*	calf's muzzle
caille	quail	*oie*	goose
canard	duck	*onglet*	cut of beef
caneton	duckling	*os*	bone
contrefilet	sirloin roast	*poitrine*	breast
coquelet	cockerel	*porc*	pork
dinde, dindon	turkey	*poulet*	chicken
entrecôte	rib steak	*poussin*	baby chicken
faux filet	sirloin steak	*ris*	sweetbreads
foie	liver	*rognons*	kidneys
foie gras	(duck/goose) liver	*rognons blancs*	testicles
gigot (d'agneau)	leg (of lamb)	*sanglier*	wild boar
grenouilles (cuisses de)	frogs (legs)	*steak*	steak
		tête de veau	calf's head (in jelly)
grillade	grilled meat	*tournedos*	thick slices of fillet
hâchis	chopped meat or mince hamburger	*tripes*	tripe
		tripoux	mutton tripe
langue	tongue	*veau*	veal
		venaison	venison

meat and poultry dishes and terms

aïado	roast shoulder of lamb stuffed with garlic and other ingredients	*choucroute*	pickled cabbage with peppercorns, sausages, bacon and salami
aile	wing	*civit*	game stew
au feu de bois	cooked over wood fire	*confit*	meat preserve
au four	baked	*côte*	chop, cutlet or rib
baeckoffe	Alsatian hotpot of pork, mutton and beef baked with potato layers	*cou*	neck
		coq au vin	chicken cooked until it falls off the bone with wine, onions and mushrooms
blanquette, daube, estouffade, hochepôt, navarin, ragoût	types of stew		
		cuisse	thigh or leg
		épaule	shoulder
blanquette de veau	veal in cream and mushroom sauce	*en croûte*	in pastry
		farci	stuffed
bœuf bourguignon	beef stew with Burgundy, onions and mushrooms	*grillade*	grilled meat
		garni	with vegetables
		gésier	gizzard
canard à l'orange	roast duck with an orange and wine sauce	*grillé*	grilled
		hâchis	chopped meat or mince hamburger
canard pâté de périgourdin	roast duck with prunes, foie gras and truffles		
		magret de canard	duck breast
carré	best end of neck, chop or cutlet	*marmite*	casserole
		médaillon	round piece
cassoulet	casserole of beans and meat		

mijoté	stewed	*steak au poivre*	steak in a black (green/red)
pavé	thick slice	*(vert/rouge)*	peppercorn sauce
pieds et paques	mutton or pork tripe and trotters	*steak tartare*	raw chopped beef, topped
poêlé	pan-fried		with a raw egg yolk
poulet de Bresse	chicken from Bresse – the best	*tagine*	North African casserole
râble	saddle	*tournedos*	beef fillet with foie gras
rôti	roast	*rossini*	and truffles
sauté	lightly cooked in butter	*viennoise*	fried in egg and breadcrumbs

terms for steaks

bleu	almost raw	*à point*	medium	*très bien cuit*	very well done
saignant	rare	*bien cuit*	well done	*brochette*	kebab

garnishes and sauces

américaine	white wine, cognac and tomato	*chasseur*	white wine, mushrooms and
arlésienne	with tomatoes, onions,		shallots
au porto	aubergines, potatoes and	*châtelaine*	with artichoke hearts and
	rice in port		chestnut purée
auvergnat	with cabbage, sausage and	*diable*	strong mustard seasoning
	bacon	*forestière*	with bacon and mushroom
béarnaise	sauce of egg yolks, white	*fricassée*	rich, creamy sauce
	wine, shallots and vinegar	*mornay*	cheese sauce
beurre blanc	sauce of white wine and	*pays d'auge*	cream and cider
	shallots, with butter	*périgourdine*	with foie gras and possibly
bonne femme	with mushroom, bacon, potato		truffles
	and onions	*piquante*	gherkins or capers, vinegar
bordelaise	in a red wine, shallot and		and shallots
	bone-marrow sauce	*provençale*	tomatoes, garlic, olive oil and
boulangère	baked with potatoes and onions		herbs
bourgeoise	with carrots, onions, bacon,	*savoyarde*	with gruyère cheese
	celery and braised lettuce	*véronique*	grapes, wine and cream

Vegetables (*légumes*), Herbs (*herbes*) and Spices (*épices*)

ail	garlic	*choufleur*	cauliflower	*menthe*	mint
anis	aniseed	*concombre*	cucumber	*moutarde*	mustard
artichaut	artichoke	*cornichon*	gherkin	*oignon*	onion
asperge	asparagus	*echalotes*	shallots	*panais*	parsnip
avocat	avocado	*endive*	chicory	*pélandron*	type of string
basilic	basil	*épinard*	spinach		bean
betterave	beetroot	*estragon*	tarragon	*pâte*	pasta or pastry
blette/bette	Swiss chard	*fenouil*	fennel	*persil*	parsley
cannelle	cinnamon	*férigoule*	thyme (in	*petits pois*	peas
capre	caper		Provençal)	*piment*	pimento
cardon	cardoon, a	*fèves*	broad beans	*pois chiche*	chick peas
	beet related	*flageolets*	white beans	*pois mange-*	snow peas
	to artichoke	*gingembre*	ginger	*tout*	
carotte	carrot	*haricots (verts,*	beans (French/	*pignons*	pine nuts
céleri	celery	*rouges,*	string, kidney,	*poireau*	leek
champignon,	types of	*beurres)*	butter)	*poivron (vert,*	sweet pepper
cèpe,	mushrooms	*laurier*	bay leaf	*rouge)*	(green, red)
chanterelle		*lentilles*	lentils	*pommes de*	potatoes
chou (rouge)	(red) cabbage	*maïs*	corn	*terre*	

continued overleaf

continued from previous page

primeurs	spring vegetables	*salade verte*	green salad
radis	radish	*sarrasin*	buckwheat
riz	rice	*tomate*	tomato
safran	saffron	*truffes*	truffles

vegetable dishes and terms

alicot	puréed potato with cheese	*à la parisienne*	sautéed in butter (potatoes); with white
allumettes	very thin chips		wine sauce and
à l'anglaise	boiled		shallots
beignet	fritter	*parmentier*	with potatoes
biologique	organic	*petits farcis*	stuffed tomatoes,
duxelles	fried mushrooms and shallots with cream		aubergines, courgettes and
farci	stuffed		peppers
feuille	leaf	*pimenté*	peppery hot
fines herbes	mixture of tarragon, parsley and chives	*piquant*	spicy
		pistou	ground basil, olive
gratiné	browned with cheese or butter		oil, garlic and parmesan
à la grecque	cooked in oil and lemon	*râpée*	grated or shredded
jardinière	with mixed diced vegetables	*sauté*	lightly fried in butter
		à la vapeur	steamed
mousseline	mashed potato with cream and eggs	*en verdure*	garnished with green vegetables

Fruit (*fruit*) and Nuts (*noix*)

abricot	apricot	*groseille*	redcurrant	**fruit dishes and terms**	
acajou	cashew nut	*mangue*	mango	*agrumes*	citrus fruits
amande	almond	*marron*	chestnut	*beignet*	fritter
ananas	pineapple	*melon*	melon	*compôte*	stewed fruit
banane	banana	*mirabelle*	small yellow	*coulis*	sauce of
brugnon, nectarine	nectarine		plum		puréed fruit
		myrtille	bilberry	*crème de marrons*	chestnut purée
cacahouète	peanut	*noisette*	hazelnut		
cassis	blackcurrant	*noix*	nuts	*flambé*	set aflame in
cérise	cherry	*orange*	orange		alcohol
citron	lemon	*pamplemousse*	grapefruit	*fougasse*	bread
citron vert	lime	*pastèque*	watermelon		flavoured
datte	date	*pêche*	peach		with
figue	fig	*pistache*	pistachio		orange-
fraise (de bois)	strawberry (wild)	*poire*	pear		flower water
		pomme	apple		or almonds
framboise	raspberry	*prune*	plum		(can be
fruit de la passion	passion fruit	*pruneau*	prune		savoury)
		raisin	grape	*frappé*	iced
grenade	pomegranate	*reine-claude*	greengage		

Desserts (*desserts* or *entremets*) and Pastries (*pâtisserie*)

bombe	moulded ice-cream dessert	*charlotte*	custard and fruit in lining of almond fingers
brioche	sweet, high yeast breakfast roll		
calisson	almond sweet	*chichi*	doughnut shaped in a stick

clafoutis	heavy custard and fruit tart	petits fours	bite-sized cakes/pastries
crème Chantilly	vanilla-flavoured and sweetened whipped cream	poires belle hélène	pears and ice cream in chocolate sauce
crème fraîche	sour cream	tarte tatin	upside-down apple tart
crème pâtissière	thick, eggy pastry-filling	tarte tropezienne	sponge cake filled with custard cream topped with nuts
crêpe suzette	thin pancake with orange juice and liqueur		
fromage blanc	cream cheese	tiramisu	mascarpone cheese, chocolate and cream
gaufre	waffle	yaourt, yogourt	yoghurt
glace	ice cream		
île flottante/ œufs à la neige	soft meringues floating on custard	**dessert dishes and terms**	
macaron	macaroon	barquette	small boat-shaped flan
madeleine	small sponge cake	bavarois	refers to the mould, could be a mousse or custard
marrons Mont Banc	chestnut purée and cream on a rum-soaked sponge cake	coupe	a serving of ice cream
		crêpe	pancake
mousse au chocolat	chocolate mousse	gênoise	rich sponge cake
omelette norvégienne	baked alaska	pâte	pastry or dough
palmier	caramelized puff pastry	sablé	shortbread biscuit
parfait	frozen mousse, sometimes ice cream	savarin	a filled, ring-shaped cake
		tarte	tart
petit-suisse	a smooth mixture of cream and curds	tartelette	small tart

Service compris or *s.c.* means the **service charge** is included. *Service non compris, s.n.c.* or *servis en sus* means that it isn't and you need to calculate an additional 15 percent. **Wine** (*vin*) or a **drink** (*boisson*) is occasionally included in the cost of a *menu fixe*. When ordering house wine, the cheapest option, ask for *un quart* (0.25 litre), *un demi-litre* (0.5 litre) or *une carafe* (1 litre). If you're worried about the cost ask for *vin ordinaire* or the *vin de table*. In the *Guide* the lowest price menu or the range of menus is given; where average à la carte prices are given it assumes you'll have three courses and half a bottle of wine.

The French are much better disposed towards **children** in restaurants than other nationalities, not simply by offering reduced-price children's menus but in creating an atmosphere – even in otherwise fairly snooty establishments – that positively welcomes kids; some even have in-house games and toys for them to occupy themselves with. It is regarded as self-evident that large family groups should be able to eat out together.

A rather murkier area is that of **dogs** in the dining room; it can be quite a shock in a provincial hotel to realize that the majority of your fellow diners are attempting to keep dogs concealed beneath their tables.

One final note is that you should always call the waiter or waitress *Monsieur* or *Madame* (*Mademoiselle* if a young woman), never *Garçon*, no matter what you've been taught in school.

DRINKING

Wherever you can eat you can invariably drink, and vice versa. **Drinking** is done at a leisurely pace whether it's a prelude to food (*apéritif*), a sequel (*digestif*), or the accompaniment, and *cafés* are the standard places to do it. Every bar or café has to display its full price list, usually without the fifteen percent service charge added, with the cheapest drinks at the bar (*au comptoir*), and progressively increasing prices for sitting at a table inside (*la salle*), or outside (*la terrasse*). You pay when you leave, and it's perfectly acceptable to sit for hours over just one cup of coffee.

Wine (*vin*) is drunk at just about every meal or social occasion. Red is *rouge*, white *blanc* and rosé *rosé*. *Vin de table* or *vin ordinaire* – table wine – is generally drinkable and always cheap, although it may be disguised and priced-up as the house wine, or *cuvée*. The price of AOC (*appellation d'origine contrôlée*) wines can vary from 10F/€1.53 to 100F/€15.25 and over, and that's the vineyard price. You can buy a very decent bottle of wine for 20F/€3.05 or 30F/€4.58, and 60F/€9.15 and over will buy you something really nice. By the time restaurants have added their considerable mark-up, wine can constitute an alarming proportion of the bill.

The basic **wine terms** are: *brut*, very dry; *sec*, dry; *demi-sec*, sweet; *doux*, very sweet; *mousseux*, sparkling; *méthode champenoise*, mature and sparkling. There are grape varieties as well, but the complexities of the subject take up volumes. A glass of wine is simply *un rouge*, *un rosé* or *un blanc*. You may have the choice of *un ballon* (round glass) or a smaller glass (*un verre*). *Un pichet* (a pitcher) is normally a quarter-litre. A glass of wine in a bar will cost around 30F/€5.58.

The best way to **buy bottles** of wine is directly from the producers (*vignerons*), either at vineyards, at Maisons or Syndicats du Vin (representing a group of wine-producers), or at Coopératifs Vinicoles (wine-producer co-ops). At all these places you can sample the wines first. It's best to make clear at the start how much you want to buy (if it's only one or two bottles) and you will not be popular if you drink several glasses and then leave without making a purchase.

The most economical option is to buy *en vrac*, which you can also do at some wine shops (*caves*), taking an easily obtainable plastic five- or ten-litre container (usually sold on the premises) and getting it filled straight from the barrel. In cities supermarkets are the best places to buy your wine, and their prices often beat those of the *vignerons*.

Familiar light Belgian and German brands, plus French brands from Alsace, account for most of the **beer** you'll find. Draught beer (*à la pression*) – usually Kronenbourg – is the cheapest drink you can have next to coffee and wine; ask for *un pression* or *un demi* (0.33 litre). A *demi* costs around 17F/€2.59. For a wider choice of draught and bottled beer you need to go to the special beer-drinking establishments or English-style pubs found in most city centres and resorts. A small bottle at one of these places will cost at least twice as much as a *demi* in a café. In supermarkets, however, bottled or canned beer is exceptionally cheap.

Strong alcohol is consumed from as early as 5am as a pre-work fortifier, and then at any time through the day according to circumstance,

---

WINES

French **wines** are unrivalled in the world for their range, sophistication, diversity and status. Individual wines from other countries may be able to compete with the best of French wines, but however hard foreign producers try, the French market is uncrackable. The French simply see no reason to try any wines but their own. Sipping a Nuits St-Georges, Sancerre, Chablis, Châteauneuf-du-Pape or one of the top champagnes, it's hard to disagree.

With the exception of the northwest of the country and the mountains, wine is produced just about everywhere. The great **wine-producing regions** are Champagne, Bordeaux and Burgundy, closely followed by the Loire and Rhône valleys. Alsace also has some great wines, and there are some beautiful wines to be had in the lesser wine regions of Bergerac, Languedoc, Roussillon and Provence.

The quality of the *vins de pays*, though very variable, is still exceptional for the price. Quality wines are denoted by the *appellation d'origine contrôlée* (AOC), which strictly controls the amount of wine that a particular area, whether

several hundred square kilometres or just two, may produce. Within each *appellation* there is enormous diversity generated by the different types of soil, the lie of the land, the type of grape grown – there are over sixty varieties – the ability of the wine to age, and the individual skills of the wine-grower.

It's an extremely complex business and it's not difficult to feel intimidated by the seemingly innate expertise of all French people. Many individual wines and *appellations* are mentioned in the text, but trusting your own taste response is the most important thing. Knowing the grape types that you particularly like (or dislike), whether you like wines very fruity, dry, light or heavy, is all useful when you are discussing your choice with a waiter, wine-grower or wine merchant. The more interest you show, the more helpful advice you are likely to receive. The only thing the French cannot tolerate is people ordering Coke to accompany a gourmet meal. We've detailed the main wine-growing regions – and their produce – throughout the *Guide*.

though the national reputation for drunkenness has lost much of its truth. Brandies and the dozens of *eaux de vie* (spirits) and liqueurs are always available. *Pastis* – the generic name of aniseed drinks such as Pernod or Ricard and a favourite throughout Languedoc – is served diluted with water and ice (*glaçons*). It's very refreshing and not expensive. Among less familiar names, try Poire William (pear brandy), or Marc (a spirit distilled from grape pulp). Measures are generous, but they don't come cheap: the same applies for imported spirits like whisky (*Scotch*). Two drinks designed to stimulate the appetite – *un apéritif* – are Pineau (cognac and grape juice) and Kir (white wine with a dash of Cassis – blackcurrant liquor, or with champagne instead of wine for a Kir Royal). **Cocktails** are served at most late-night bars, discos and music places, as well as at upmarket hotel bars and at every seaside promenade café; they usually cost at least 45F/€6.86.

On the **soft drink** front, you can buy cartons of unsweetened fruit juice in supermarkets, although in the cafés the bottled (sweetened) nectars such as apricot (*jus d'abricot*) and blackcurrant (*cassis*) still hold sway. You can also get fresh orange or lemon juice (*orange/citron pressé*), at a price. A *citron pressé* is a refreshing choice for the extremely thirsty on a hot day – the lemon juice is served in the bottom of a long ice-filled glass, with a jug of water and a sugar bowl

to sweeten it to your taste. Other drinks to try are syrups (*sirops*) of mint, grenadine or other flavours mixed with water. The standard fizzy drinks of lemonade (*limonade*), Coke (*coca*) and so forth are all available. Bottles of **mineral water** (*eau minérale*) and spring water (*eau de source*) – either sparkling (*gazeuse*) or still (*eau plate*) – abound, from the big brand names to the most obscure spa product. But there's not much wrong with the tap water (*l'eau de robinet*) which will always be brought free to your table if you ask for it.

Coffee is invariably espresso – small, black and very strong. *Un café* or *un express* is the regular; *un crème* is with milk; *un grand café* or *un grand crème* are large cups. In the morning you could also ask for *un café au lait* – espresso in a large cup or bowl filled up with hot milk. *Un déca* is decaffeinated, now widely available. Ordinary **tea** (*thé*) is Lipton's nine times out of ten and is normally served black, and you can usually have a slice of lemon (*limon*) with it if you want; to have milk with it, ask for *un peu de lait frais* (some fresh milk). *Chocolat chaud* – **hot chocolate** – unlike tea, lives up to the high standards of French food and drink and can be had in any café. After eating, **herb teas** (*infusions* or *tisanes*), served in every *salon de thé*, can be soothing. The more common ones are *verveine* (verbena), *tilleul* (lime blossom), *menthe* (mint) and *camomille* (camomile).

COMMUNICATIONS AND THE MEDIA

You should have no problem keeping in contact with people at home while you are in France. The country has an efficient postal system and you can have letters and packages sent general delivery to any of the official branches. The Internet is widely accessible, and is gradually displacing the now-primitive Minitel telnet system which France pioneered. Should you need to use the phone, you can use cheap pre-paid phone cards or access home-country operators via free numbers.

French **newspapers** (not to mention **radio** and **television**) will be of less interest if you are not a reader (or speaker) of French. There are some local English-language magazines, but you will probably find yourself reaching for an international edition of a British or American newspaper or an international news magazine to keep up on current events. These are available in major cities and tourist centres, though they can get to be an expensive habit.

MAIL

French **post offices** (*bureaux de poste* or *PTTs*) – look for bright yellow La Poste signs – are generally open 9am to 7pm Monday to Friday, and 9am to noon on Saturday. However, don't depend on these hours: in smaller towns and villages offices may close earlier and for lunch, while in Paris the main post office is open 24 hours.

You can receive mail at the central post offices of most towns. It should be addressed (preferably with the surname first and in capi-

tals) "**Poste Restante**, Poste Centrale", followed by the name of the town and its postcode, detailed in the *Guide* for all the main cities. To collect your mail you need a passport or other convincing ID and there may be a charge of around a couple of francs. You should ask for all your names to be checked, as filing systems are not brilliant.

For sending letters, remember that you can buy **stamps** (*timbres*) with less queuing from *tabacs*. Standard letters (20g or less) and postcards within France and to European Union countries cost 3F/€0.46, to North America 4.40F/€0.67 and to Australia and New Zealand 5.20F/€0.79. Inside many post offices you will find a row of yellow-coloured *guichet automatiques* – automatic ticket machines with instructions available in English with which you can weigh packages and buy the appropriate stamps; sticky labels and tape are also dispensed. A machine can change notes into change, so there is no need to queue for counter service. If you're sending parcels abroad, you can try to check prices on the *guichet* if available or in various leaflets available: small post offices don't often send foreign mail and may need reminding, for example, of the reductions for printed papers and books.

You can also use Minitel (see below) at post offices, change money, make photocopies, send faxes and make phone calls. To post your letter on the street, look for the bright yellow **postboxes**.

PHONES AND FAXES

You can make domestic and international **phone calls** from any telephone box (*cabine*) and can receive calls where there's a blue logo of a ringing bell. A 50-unit (40.60F/€6.19) and 120-unit (97.50F/€14.87) phone card (called a *télécarte*) is essential, since coin boxes are being phased out. **Phone cards** are available from *tabacs* and newsagents as well as post offices, tourist offices and some train station ticket offices. You can also use **credit cards** in many call boxes. Coin-only boxes still exist in cafés, bars, hotel foyers and rural areas; they take 50 centimes, 1F, 5F or 10F pieces; put the money in after lifting up the receiver and before dialling. You can keep adding more coins once you are connected. Local calls are costed in France at

TELEPHONES

IDD CODES

From France dial ☎00 + IDD code + area code minus first 0 + subscriber number.

Britain ☎44	Ireland ☎353
US and Canada ☎1	Australia ☎61
New Zealand ☎64	

From Britain to France: dial ☎00 33 + nine digit number (leaving out the first 0).

From the US and Canada to France: dial ☎011 33 + nine digit number (leaving out the first 0).

From Australia to France: dial ☎011 33 + nine digit number (leaving out the first 0).

From New Zealand to France: dial ☎0044 33 + nine digit number (leaving out the first 0).

Within France: telephone numbers have **ten digits**; the first eight digits are preceded by by 01 for the Parisian and Île de France area, 02 for the northwest, 03 for the northeast, 04 for the southeast and 05 for the southwest. Even when you are within the same area, you must dial all ten digits.

USEFUL NUMBERS WITHIN FRANCE

Weather ☎08.36.68.02 + the number of the *département*.

Telegrams by phone Internal ☎36.55; external ☎08.00.33.44.11 – all languages.

Time ☎36.99.

International operator For Canada and the US ☎00 33 11; for all other countries ☎00 33 followed by the country code.

International directory assistance For Canada and the US ☎00 33 12 11; for all other countries ☎00 33 12 followed by the country code.

French operator ☎13 to signal a fault.

French directory assistance ☎12.

Traffic and road conditions Paris and Île de France ☎01.48.99.33.33; rest of France ☎08.36.68.20.00.

0.813F/€0.123 for three minutes (1F/€0.15 minimum); long-distance calls within France cost up to 2.44F/€0.37 for three minutes depending on the distance. Off-peak charges apply on weekdays between 7pm and 8am and after noon on Saturday until 8am Monday.

For calls within France – local or long-distance – simply dial all ten digits of the number. Numbers beginning with ☎08.00 are free numbers; those beginning with ☎08.36 are premium-rate (from 2.23F/€0.34 per minute), and those beginning with 06 are mobile and therefore also expensive to call. The major international calling codes are given in the box above; remember to omit the initial zero of the local area code from the subscriber's number.

Cheap rates operate between 7pm and 8am Monday to Friday, from midnight to 8am and noon to midnight on Saturday, and all day Sunday. From a private phone, a call to the UK (*Royaume-Uni*) will cost between 1.64F/€0.25 and 2.47F/€0.38 per minute, from a public phone 2.17–2.57F/€0.33–0.39; to Ireland 1.95–2.97F/€0.30–0.45 per minute or 2.85–3.52F/€0.45–0.54; to the US

(*États-Unis*) and Canada 1.95–2.97F/€0.30–0.45 per minute or 2.85–3.52F/€0.45–0.54; to Australia and New Zealand 4.31–6.55F/€0.66–1 per minute or 7.99–10.16F/€1.23–1.55. By far the most convenient way of making international calls is to use a **calling card**, opening an account before you leave home; calls will be billed monthly to your credit card, to your phone bill if you are already a customer or to your home address. However, the rates per minute of these cards are many times higher than the cost of calling from a public phone in France, with flat rates only. The best value is offered by Interglobe (☎020/7972 0800; 50p/min to the UK), followed by AT&T (☎0500/626262; $US1.50/min to the UK), then Cable and Wireless Calling Card (☎0500/100505; 68p/min to the UK), and Swiftcall Global Card (☎0800/7691444; 70p/min to the UK). British Telecom's BT Charge Card (☎0800/345600 or 0800/345144) offers the worst value with calls from France to the UK charged at 90p per minute. But since all of these cards are free to obtain, it's certainly worth getting one at least for emergencies. You dial a free number (make sure you have with you the relevant number for France), your account number and then the number you wish to call. The drawback is that the free number is often engaged and you have to dial a great many digits. If you need to make many foreign calls from France, several companies offer cheap-rated phone cards, such as the bargain-basement store Tati who sell a 50F/€7.62 or 100F/€15.24 **Intercall Carte Téléphone** (☎08.00.51.79.43) for calling overseas which you can use in a public or private telephone; a 50F/€7.62 card gives you, for example, 15 minutes to Australia, 32 minutes to Canada or the US and 49 minutes to the UK. These rates work out much cheaper than using France Telecom from a public phone.

To avoid payment altogether, you can, of course, make a reverse charge or **collect call** – known in French as *téléphoner en PCV* – by contacting the international operator (see box on p.59). You can also do this through the operator in the UK, by dialling the Home Direct number ☎08.00.89.00.33; to get an English-speaking operator for North America, dial ☎00.00.11.

Some British **mobile phones**, as long as they're digital, will work in France. Getting a mobile phone in France is – in principle – simply a matter of visiting a phone boutique (for instance, a France Telecom store) with identification, proof of address and proof of ability to pay. This involves setting up a French bank account, which will entitle you to the *bona fide* certificate known as an RIB (*Relève d'Identité Bancaire*); to obtain this you will need to provide a copy of a utility bill with your name on it, not necessarily a problem since banks are prepared to accept foreign utility bills.

Faxes can be sent from all main post offices and many photocopy stores: the official French word is *télécopie*, but people use the word fax. A typical rate for sending a fax within France is 25F/€3.81 for the first and 6F/€0.92 for subsequent pages.

MINITEL

Many French phone subscribers have **Minitel**, a dinosaurial online computer that's been around since the early 1980s, which allows access through the phone lines to directories, databases, chat lines, etc. You will also find it in post offices. Most organizations, from sports federations to government institutions to gay groups, have a code consisting of numbers and letters, which you can call up for information, to leave messages,

make reservations, etc. You dial the number on the phone, wait for a fax-type tone, then type the letters on the keyboard, and finally press *Connexion Fin* (the same key ends the connection). If you're at all computer-literate and can understand basic keyboard terms in French (*retour* – return, *envoi* – enter, etc), you shouldn't find them hard to use. Be warned that most services cost more than phone rates. Directory enquiries (☎12) are free.

EMAIL AND THE INTERNET

Email is the cheapest and most hassle-free way of staying in touch with home while in France. Practically every reasonable-sized town has a **cyber café** or connection point of some sort, and in less populated areas, the need is being filled by post offices, many of which now have rather expensive public Internet terminals, which are operated with a prepaid card (50F/€7.63 for the first hour). In addition France Telecom has streetside Internet kiosks in major cities. We have given details of cyber cafés and other Internet access points in the *Guide* so you can stay on line while travelling. Prices range from 15F/€2.29 to 60F/€9.15 per hour, so it can be worth shopping around. It's easy to open a free email account to use while you're away with Hotmail or Yahoo: head for *www.hotmail.com* or *www.yahoo.com* to find out how.

The existence of Minitel and the relatively low level of personal computer ownership in France contributed to the rather slow adoption of the **Internet** here, but in recent years the situation has changed and France as a nation has come fully on-line. Information about practically every aspect of French culture and travel can now be picked up on the Internet: government agencies are now on-line, including even some of the smallest local tourist offices; in the cultural sphere even the most obscure and esoteric associations have discovered the importance of getting their message out over the Web; and the hotel and restaurant businesses have come to realize that the Net is a key to foreign markets. On the down side, many or most of these pages do not have **English-language** versions, although they are gradually coming to be seen as indispensible in all but the most focused sites. As anywhere on the Net, persistent combing of links pages and use of search engines (among the best are *www.google.com* and *www.dogpile.com*, and the French *www.enfin*

FRANCE ON THE NET

TOURISM AND RECREATION SITES

www.tourist-office.org
Handy database of France's municipal and local tourist offices arranged by *région* and *départe-ment*. Town listings have practical and cultural information and links to local Web sites.

www.franceguide.com
The official site of the French Government Tourist Office, with news, information on local festivals and useful links. Has a good English-language version.

www.monuments-france.fr
Good starting point for information on over 200 national monuments and museums across France, including news on special events.

www.fr-holidaystore.co.uk
France Holiday Store is a useful site for planning with tour operators – everything from cycling to canal cruising, fly-drive and short breaks and ski-ing. Property search with over 1000 places listed with photos-plus-brochure searches and regional and tourist info.

www.francesport.com
Links page for French national sports associa-tions, both professional sports and participatory outdoor activities. Everything from hiking to handball.

NEWS AND INFORMATION SITES

www.gksoft.com/govt
Gateway to English-language listings of all French government Web sites, including embassies, departmental and regional tourist boards, political parties, municipalities and media.

www.radio-france.fr
Radio France's official page has national and international news coverage, current affairs, as well as music, culture and the latest in French sports. French language only.

www.lemonde.fr
The French-language Web version of one of France's most reputable daily newspapers. Includes national and international news, culture and sports.

www.france2.fr/cyber
France TV 2's daily Web page has the latest on news, weather, and road conditions as well as listings and reviews of cultural events. Also has a youth section.

ARTS AND CULTURE SITES

web.culture.fr
French Ministry of Culture's page, with informa-tion on everything from monuments to exhibi-tions and also comprehensive lists of links to organizations related to the whole gamut of artistic mediums.

www.bpi.fr
Home page of the Bibliothèque Pompidou, with good links to media and a very comprehensive list of arts and humanities pages for France.

www.irma.assoc.fr
Master page for Centre d'Information et des Ressources pour les Musiques Actuelles – the French music industry's promotional organization. Search for information and organizations repre-senting every genre and style.

www.jazzfrance.com
Brilliant bilingual site for jazz fans with every-thing from venues and festivals covered, and an up-to-date diary. Links to music stores.

www.revue-spectacle.com
Arts page, set up by a group of newspapers and radio stations in co-operation with the Ministry of Culture. Covers theatre, dance and mime events and is updated monthly. No English ver-sion at present, but a link to the Babelfish trans-lation page.

www.ladanse.com
Multilingual site with comprehensive information on French and international dance including news, links and a database of artists and companies.

.com) will almost certainly get you the informa-tion you are looking for.

Email addresses and **Web sites** are given where available throughout the *Guide*, and as a supplement to this you'll find a list of some of the most useful and important French Web sites in the box above.

NEWSPAPERS AND MAGAZINES

English-language newspapers, such as the *European*, the *Washington Post*, *New York Times* and the *International Herald Tribune*, are on sale the same day in Paris, and in most large cities and resorts the day after publication. Of the **French daily papers**, *Le Monde* is the most intellectual; it is widely respected, but somewhat austere, making no concessions to such frivolities as photographs. *Libération*, founded by Jean-Paul Sartre in the 1960s, is moderately left-wing, independent and more colloquial, with good, if choosy, coverage, while rigorous left-wing criticism of the French government comes from *L'Humanité*, the Communist Party paper. The other nationals are all firmly right-wing in their politics: *Le Figaro* is the most respected. The top-selling national is *L'Équipe*, which is dedicated to sports coverage, while *Paris-Turf* focuses on horse-racing. The widest circulations are enjoyed by the **regional dailies**. The most important of these is the Rennes-based *Ouest-France* – though for travellers, this, like the rest of the regionals, is mainly of interest for its listings.

Weeklies of the *Newsweek/Time* model include the wide-ranging and socialist-inclined *Le Nouvel Observateur*, its right-wing counterpart *L'Express* and the boringly centrist *L'Évenement de Jeudi* and the newcomer with a bite, *Marianne*. The best investigative journalism is to be found in the weekly satirical paper *Le Canard Enchaîné*. *Charlie Hebdo* is a sort of *Private Eye* or *Spy Magazine* equivalent. There is also *Paris-Match* for gossip about stars and the royal families. **Monthlies** include the young and trendy – and cheap – *Nova*, which has excellent listings of cultural events, and *Actuel*, which is good for current events. There are, of course, the French versions of *Vogue*, *Elle* (weekly) and *Marie-Claire*, and the relentlessly urban *Biba*, for women's fashion and lifestyle.

Moral **censorship** of the press is rare. On the newsstands you'll find pornography of every shade, as well as covers featuring drugs, sex, blasphemy and bizarre forms of grossness alongside knitting patterns and DIY. You'll also find French **comics** (*bandes dessinées*), which often

indulge such adult interests: wildly and wonderfully illustrated, they are considered to be quite an artform and whole museums are devoted to them.

Some of the huge numbers of homeless people in France (*les sans-logement*) make a bit of money by selling magazines on the streets which combine culture, humour and self-help with social and political issues. Costing 10F/€1.53, the most well-known of these is *L'Itinérant*.

TV AND RADIO

French TV has six channels: three public (France 2, Arte/La Cinquième and FR3); one subscription (Canal Plus – with some unencrypted programmes); and two commercial open broadcasts (TF1 and M6). In addition there are the **cable** networks, which include France Infos, CNN, the BBC World Service, BBC Prime, MTV, Planète, which specializes in documentaries, Paris Première (lots of French-dubbed films), and Canal Jimmy (*Friends* and the like in French). There are two music channels: the American MTV and the French-run MCM, where you can get a real education on French rap.

Arte/La Cinquième is a joint Franco-German cultural venture that transmits simultaneously in French and German: offerings include highbrow programmes, daily documentaries, art criticism, serious French and German movies and complete operas. During the day (6am–7pm), La Cinquième uses the frequency to broadcast educational programmes. **Canal Plus** is the main **movie channel** (and funder of the French film industry), with repeats of foreign films usually shown at least once in the original language. **FR3** screens a fair selection of serious movies, with its *Cinéma de Minuit* slot late on Sunday nights good for foreign, undubbed films. The main French **news broadcasts** are at 8.30pm on Arte and at 8pm on F2 and TF1.

If you've got a **radio**, you can tune into English-language news on the BBC World Service on 648kHz AM or 198kHz long wave from midnight to 5am (and Radio 4 during the day). The Voice of America transmits on 90.5, 98.8 and 102.4 FM. If you're in the Paris area, you can listen to the **news in English** on Radio France International (RFI) for an hour (3–4pm) on 738 kHz AM. For radio **news in French**, there's the state-run France Inter (87.8 FM), Europe 1 (104.7 FM) or round-the-clock news on France Infos (105.5 FM).

OPENING HOURS AND PUBLIC HOLIDAYS

Basic hours of business are 8 or 9am to noon or 1pm, and 2pm or 3pm to 6.30pm or 7.30pm. In big city centres shops and other businesses stay open throughout the day, and in July and August most tourist offices and museums are open without interruption. Otherwise almost everything closes for a couple of hours at midday, or even longer in the south. Small food shops often don't reopen till halfway through the afternoon, closing around 7.30pm or 8pm just before the evening meal.

The standard **closing days** are Sunday and/or Monday, with shops taking turns to close with their neighbours; many food shops such as boulangeries (bakeries) that open on Sunday will do so in the morning only. In small towns you'll find everything except the odd boulangerie shut on both days. This includes **banks**, which in cities are usually open Monday to Friday from 9am to 4pm or 5pm, making it all too easy to find yourself dependent on hotels for money-changing at poor rates and high commission. Restaurants and cafés also often close on a Sunday or Monday.

Museums tend to open between 9am and 10am, close for lunch at noon until 2pm or 3pm, and then run through to 5pm or 6pm, although in the big cities they will stay open all day. **Closing days** are usually Tuesday or Monday, sometimes both. **Admission charges** can be very off-putting, though many state-owned museums have one day of the week (often Sun) when they're free or half-price, and you can often get reductions if you're a full-time student (with ISIC card), under 26 or over 60. **Cathedrals** are almost always open all day every day, with charges only for the crypt, treasuries or cloister and little fuss about how you're dressed. **Church** opening hours are often more restricted; on Sunday mornings (or at other times which you'll see posted up on the door) you may have to attend Mass to take a look. In small towns and villages, however, getting the key is not difficult – ask anyone nearby or seek out the priest, whose house is known as the *presbytère*.

PUBLIC HOLIDAYS

There are thirteen national holidays (*jours fériés*), when most shops and businesses (though not necessarily restaurants), and some museums, are closed. May in particular is a big month for holidays: as well as May Day and VE Day, Ascension Day normally falls then, as sometimes does Pentecost.

January 1 New Year's Day
Easter Sunday
Easter Monday
Ascension Day (forty days after Easter)
Pentecost or Whitsun (seventh Sunday after Easter, plus the Monday)
May 1 May Day/Labour Day

May 8 Victory in Europe Day
July 14 Bastille Day
August 15 Assumption of the Virgin Mary
November 1 All Saints' Day
November 11 1918 Armistice Day
December 25 Christmas Day

FESTIVALS

It's hard to beat the experience of arriving in a small French village, expecting no more than a bed for the night, to discover the streets decked out with flags and streamers, a band playing in the square and the entire population out celebrating the feast of their patron saint. Apart from Bastille Day (July 14) and the Assumption of the Virgin Mary (August 15), there are traditional folk festivals still thriving in Brittany and the remote rural regions of the south, as well as a full calendar of festivals devoted to films and to music from jazz and folk to rock and classical.

Catholicism is deeply ingrained in the culture of French rural areas, and as a result **religious feast days** still bring people out in all their finery, ready to indulge once Mass has been said. Most of these occasions, along with the celebrations

FESTIVALS CALENDAR

AIX Aix en Musique (mid-June to early July); International Dance Festival (mid-July).

ALÈS Festival du Jeune Théâtre (second to third week July).

ANNECY Festival de la Vieille Ville (second week July).

ARLES Gypsy and World Music Festival (mid-July).

AURILLAC International Street Theatre Festival (last week Aug).

AVIGNON Dance and Drama Festival (last two weeks July).

BASTIA (Corsica) Mediterranean Film Festival (Oct).

BELFORT Eurockénnes Rock Festival (first week July).

BORDEAUX Doc Martens Rock Festival (last week July).

CALVI (Corsica) Jazz Festival (third week June).

CANNES International Film Festival (May).

CHALON-SUR-SAÔNE National Festival of Street Artists (third week July).

CHARLEVILLE-MÉZIÈRES Triennial World Festival of Puppet Theatre (last ten days Sept).

CLERMONT-FERRAND Festival of Short Films (end Jan to early Feb).

COLMAR Colmar International Festival/Classical music (end Aug to early Sept).

CRÉTEIL (outskirts of Paris) International Festival of Women's Films (end March/early April).

DIJON International Folk and Wine Festival (first week Sept).

DINARD Chamber Music (late July to early Aug).

DOUAI International Festival of the French Language (May) – drama, dance, music and cinema from Francophone countries.

FORT-LOUIS (nr Strasbourg) Rock Festival (end Aug).

GANNAT (nr Vichy) World Folk Festival (last ten days July).

GRENOBLE Festival of European Theatre (first week July).

JUAN-LES-PINS International Jazz Festival (last two weeks July).

LA ROCHELLE Contemporary Arts Festival (June & July); International Film Festival (end June/first week July).

LES ARCS Chamber Music (late July to early Aug).

LES-STES-MARIES-DE-LA-MER Gypsy Festival (May 24).

LIMOGES International Festival of French-Speaking Communities (end Sept to mid-Oct).

LOCRONAN Breton Troménie Pardon (second Sun July).

around wine and food production, are very genuine affairs. Other festivals, based for example on historical events, folklore or literature, are often obviously money-spinners and shows for municipal prestige – not something to go out of your way for.

One **folk festival** that is definitely worth attending is the **Inter-Celtic** event held at **Lorient** in Brittany every August. Another annual event with deep historical roots is the great gypsy gathering at **Les-Stes-Maries-de-la-Mer** in the Camargue. Though exploited for every last cen-time and, in recent years, given a heavy police presence, it is a unique and exhilarating spectacle to be part of.

Bonfires are lit and fireworks set off for **Bastille Day**, for the **Fête de St-Jean** on June 24, three days from the summer solstice, and for the **Assumption of the Virgin Mary** on August 15. **Mardi Gras** – the last blowout before Lent – is far less of an occasion than in other Catholic countries, although the towns on the Côte d'Azur put on a show at great expense and in questionable taste.

LORIENT Inter-Celtic Festival (first full week Aug).

MARCIAC Jazz in Marciac (second to third week Aug).

MENTON Chamber Music Festival (Aug).

METZ International Contemporary Music Festival (mid-Nov).

MONT-DE-MARSAN Flamenco Festival (mid-July).

MONTPELLIER International Dance Festival (end June to mid-July).

MONTPELLIER Festival de Radion France et Montpellier (mid-July to early Aug) – classical music, early music and jazz.

MURAT International Folklore Festival (first full week Aug).

NICE Mardi Gras (Feb, week before Lent); Festival of Contemporary Music (Nov) – electro-acoustic music.

NÎMES La Féria du Carnaval (Feb, week before Lent).

ORCIVAL Pilgrimage to Notre-Dame d'Orcival (May 24).

PARIS Gay Pride (June 21); New Morning All Stars Jazz Festival (July); La Villette Jazz Festival (first week July); Fête de l'Humanité (early Sept) – cultural festival sponsored by the Communist Party; Festival d'Automne (mid-Sept to Dec) – international theatre, dance and music; JVC Jazz Festival (Oct); Montmartre Vintage Festival (early Oct).

PARTHENAY Jazz Festival (first to second week July); Festival of Traditional Music (Aug).

PÉRIGUEUX International Mime Festival (first full week Aug).

PRADES Festival Pablo Casals (late July to early Aug) – classical music.

PUY-EN-VELAY Festival of the Roi de l'Oiseau (mid-Sept).

QUIMPER Semaines Musicales (Aug) – classical music.

RENNES Tombées de la Nuit (first ten days July) – theatre and music festival; Les Transmusicales (second week Dec) – international rock festival.

ROQUE D'ANTHÉRO International Piano Festival (first three weeks Aug).

ST-LIZIER Chamber Music (late July to early Aug).

ST-MALO La Route du Rock (third week Aug) – rock festival.

STRASBOURG Film Festival (March); International Mime and Clown Festival (Nov).

UZÈS Festival de la Nouvelle Danse (mid-June).

VAISON-LA-ROMAINE L'Été de Vaison Dance Festival (mid-July to early Aug).

VIENNE Jazz à Vienne (first fortnight July).

MUSIC, CINEMA, THEATRE AND DANCE

The best contemporary popular music in France is distinctly un-French, combining sounds from West, Central and North Africa, the Caribbean and Latin America, though the old chanson tradition is undergoing something of a revival, and rap has taken strides. Meanwhile jazz and classical music continues to thrive. The French have treated film as an art form, deserving of state subsidy, ever since its origination with the Lumière brothers in 1895, although today the greatest economic drive for French film comes from the pay television network Canal Plus. In theatre, the French have developed their own heavyweight brand of intellectual drama in which directors (not playwrights) dominate. Innovative dance can't compete with the US, but there are several excellent regional companies and festivals that bring in the best international talent.

MUSIC

Standard **French rock** largely deserves its miserable reputation. Sixties rocker Johnny Halliday is still France's biggest music star; Patrick Bruel, idol of love-lorn adolescents, appeals equally across the generations; and Seventies disco music, epitomized by Claude François, remains depressingly popular. This said, half of all albums bought in France are recorded by British and American bands, and the dominance of Anglo-Saxon music on the radio prompted a recent law insisting that radio stations' output must be at least forty percent French.

However, France is in the forefront of the **World Music** (*sono mondial*) scene. **Algerian raï** flourishes, with singers like Cheb Khaled and Zahouania enjoying megastar status. Daddy Yod from Guadeloupe sings **ragga**; Angélique Kidjo, from Benin, is a brilliant vocalist as is the Senegalese singer Youssou N'Dour; and the best "**alternative**" **rock** band, until their recent demise, was the Franco-Spanish **Mano Negra**, whose music, heavily influenced by Latin American tours, combined rap, reggae, rock and salsa sounds. The "**ethnically French**" have produced their own rewarding hybrids, best exemplified in the Pogue-like chaos of Les Négresses Vertes. Other names to look out for

producing eclectic sounds are Louise Attaque, Mano Solo, Gabriel Yacoub and Thomas Ferson, and groups like Paris Combo, Pigalle and Castafiore Bazooka. French "country music", known as **Astérix rock**, with accordions as the main instruments, has a raucous energy going for it. The culture of the dispossessed suburbs has found musical expression in **rap and hip-hop**. France is the second biggest producer of rap music after the US, and names to look out for include the internationally known MC Solaar, NTM, IAM, Doc Gynéco and Alliance Ethnik.

Electronic music has long been a French obsession, with the world-famous **Jean Michel Jarre** at the fore. With such a tradition, it's not surprising that **house and techno** are popular in France. DJs to look out for are the well-known Laurent Garnier, plus Manu le Malin, Sex Toy, DJ Cam, Chris the French Kiss and the techno twosome Daft Punk. The best **trance/jungle** DJ is Gilb-R, while **Etienne Daho**, who found fame as a pop star in the 1980s, has gained another following with the trance/jungle feel of his 1998 album.

But the French are probably right not to abandon **chansons**, epitomized by Edith Piaf and developed by Georges Brassens and the Belgian Jacques Brel in the Fifties and Sixties, and reaching their sly, sexy best with the legendary Serge Gainsbourg, who died in 1991. Today, the elderly Charles Aznavour and younger singer-composers like Arlette Denis and Dominique A continue the tradition, while Juliette has added a postmodern flavour.

Jazz has long enjoyed an appreciative audience in France: Charlie Parker, Dizzy Gillespie, Bud Powell and Miles Davis were being listened to in the Fifties, when elsewhere in Europe their names were known only to a tiny coterie of fans. Gypsy guitarist Django Reinhardt and his partner, violinist Stéphane Grappelli, whose work represents the distinctive and undisputed French contribution to the jazz canon, had much to do with the music's popularity. But it was also greatly enhanced by the presence of many front-rank black American musicians, for whom Paris was a haven of freedom and culture after the racial prejudice and philistinism of the States. Among them were the soprano sax player Sidney Bechet, who set up in legendary partnership with French clarinettist Claude Luter, and Bud Powell, whose turbulent exile partly inspired the tenor man played by Dexter Gordon (himself a veteran of the Montana club) in the film *Round Midnight*. In Paris you can listen to a different band every night for weeks, from trad, through bebop and free jazz, to highly contemporary experimental. And there are many excellent festivals, particularly in the south (see box on p.64).

If your taste is for **classical music** and its development, you're also in for a treat. Paris has two **opera** houses and in the provinces there are no fewer than twelve companies, of which Strasbourg and Toulouse are said to be the best, and a further dozen orchestras. Monaco's opera house is renowned for drawing the top international stars. The places to check out for **concerts** are the Maisons de la Culture (in all the larger cities), churches (where chamber music is as much performed as sacred music, often without charge), and festivals – of which there are hundreds, the most famous being at Aix in July.

Contemporary and experimental computer-based work flourishes: leading exponents are Paul Mefano and Pierre Boulez, founder of the IRCAM centre in Paris and himself one of the first pupils of Olivier Messiaen, the grand old man of modern French music who died in 1992.

CINEMA

While it's true that over sixty percent of films shown in French **cinemas** are from the US, investment in film production in France is nearly twice the level of that in the UK, and the number of films made annually is three times as great – though, of course, nowhere near the output of the US. There are ciné-clubs in almost every city, censorship is very slight, students get discounts and foreign films are usually shown in their **original language** with subtitles (look for *version originale* or *v.o.* in the listings). In addition there are a number of film festivals, though the most famous of these, the **Cannes Film Festival**, where the prized Palme d'Or is handed out, is not, in any public sense, a festival; it's more a screening of what's new for those in the industry. Filmfests where anyone can go along include those at **La Rochelle** (Rencontres Internationales d'Art Contemporain; June–July); **Créteil**, in the Paris suburbs (festival of women's films; March/April); **La Ciotat** (silent films; July); **Reims** (thrillers; Oct–Nov); **Strasbourg** (general films; March); and **Toulouse** (Cinespaña; Oct).

While the French celebrate contemporary cinema they also treasure the old. The **Paris Archives du Film** possess the largest collection of silent and early talkie movies in the world, and in 1992 they embarked on a fifteen-year, 17-million-franc/2.5-million-euro programme to transfer all the pre-1960 stock onto acetate to avoid disintegration.

Cinema is, of course, a French invention, dating back to 1895 when the **Lumière Brothers**, marrying photography with the magic lantern show, first projected in Lyon their crackly images in the short *Sortie de l'Usine*, whose image of a train leaving a factory sent the audience ducking for cover. The medium was eagerly seized by the artists of the post-World War I avant-garde who realized immediately its potential visual impact. Early twentieth-century films such as **Jean Cocteau**'s *Blood of a Poet* (1930) and *La Belle et la Bête* (*Beauty and the Beast*) (1945), **Jean Renoir**'s *Grand Illusion* (1937) and Spanish expats **Luis Buñuel**'s and **Salvador Dali**'s *Un Chien Andalou* (1929) and *L'Âge d'Or* (1930) were works more of art than entertainment. And after World War II the art-school continued to dominate through directors such as **Robert Bresson**.

In the "mainstream", as early as 1902 the prolific **Georges Mélies** had pioneered special effects with his adaptation of Jules Verne's *Voyage to the Moon*. However, French entertainment cinema didn't truly come into its own until the **New Wave movement** (Nouvelle Vague) of the 1960s. This raw and gritty style – pioneered by the young assistants of the postwar directors – owed its birth to 1959's *Les Quatre Cents Coups* (*The Four Hundred Blows*), by **Jean-Claude Truffaut**, and **Alain Resnais**' *Hiroshima Mon Amour* of the same year. In the years that followed, French cinema exploded with the morally provocative work of **Erich Rohmer**, who debuted with 1962's *Signe du Lion*, and the then-scandalous eroticism of **Roger Vadim**. **Jean-Luc Godard** gained a deserved reputation for well-crafted narratives, and his 1960 film *Au Bout de Souffle* (*Breathless*) made **Jean-Paul Belmondo** and **Jean Seberg** pin-ups around the world. This was the age in which sexy French stars like **Brigitte Bardot**, who first appeared on screen bare-breasted in Vadim's *Et Dieu Créa la Femme* (*And God Created Woman*) in 1956, came to epitomize glamorous sexuality across the Western world. Among male actors, the suave and self-assured **Alain Delon** became something of a Sixties French Bogart.

The post-New Wave era of the Seventies, Eighties and early Nineties was dominated by the towering actor **Gérard Dépardieu**, whose cinema career began in 1965 and whose most memorable roles were in *The Return of Martin Guerre* (1981), *Danton* (1983), *Jean de Florette* (1985) and *Camille Claudel* (1987). However, it was not until the mid-Eighties that French cinema began to find itself again as a new generation of directors emerged, among them **Luc Besson**. His *Subway* (1984) made Christopher Lambert an international star, and was followed by a string of snappy if superficial works like *The Big Blue* (1995), *Nikita* (1990) and *Léon* (1994). He and his contemporaries – Jean-Jacques Beineix (*Diva*, 1981; *Betty Blue*, 1986), Bertrand Tavernier (*Mississippi Blues*, 1994), Patrice Leconte (*Ridicule*, 1996) – garnered considerable attention in the English-speaking world.

As the Nineties progressed French film benefited from an international current which saw foreign directors – notably Roman Polanski, Akira Kurosawa, Andrzej Wajda and the late **Krzysztof Kieslowski**, director of the *Three Colours* trilogy – base themselves temporarily or permanently in France, drawn in part by a programme of generous production subsidies. Meanwhile, French production teams began to seek out foreign collaborators in former colonies, such as Algeria, and also as far afield as Russia and Israel. The Algerian cultural connection has led to a spate of co-productions and French-language Algerian works, like **Merzak Allouache**'s *Le Journal de Yasmine* (2000), while long-time Russophile **Pavel Lounguine** (*Taxi Blues*, 1990; *Luna Park*, 1992) recently released *La Noce* (2000).

Contemporary politics and cinematographic innovation made a dramatic comeback in French cinema with the 1996 winner of the French Césars award for best film, *La Haine*, by **Mathieu Kassovitz**. A brilliant and strikingly original portrayal of exclusion and racism in the Paris suburbs, *La Haine* is worlds away from the early Eighties movies that used Paris as a backdrop, such as *Diva* and *Subway*. This trend has broadened as young film-makers like **Laurent Cantet** confront the socio-economic challenges of their own generation, as in his acclaimed *Ressources Humaines* (2000), and its follow-up *L'Emploi du Temps* (2001). Another southern French director, **Robert Guédiguian**, uses hometown Marseille as the backdrop for his gritty proletarian-flavoured works, like *Marius et Jeanette* (1997) and *À la place du coeur* (1998).

The 2000 Cannes festival was marked by a return to period dramas, including two seventeenth-century dramas: veteran **Roland Joffré**'s *Vatel*, and **Patricia Mazuy**'s *Saint Cyr*, both an improvement on the glossy star-vehicle "heritage" movies of the late Nineties, like *Beaumarchais L'Insolent* (a French equivalent of *The Madness of King George*) and *Le Hussard sur le Toit*, which broke budget records and flopped, lapping up funds. Reasonable thrillers have also surfaced in recent years, such as **Chantal Akerman**'s *La Captive* (2000), and controversial and censored *Baisse-Moi* (2000) by **Virgine Despentes** and **Coralie Trinh Thi**.

Although French cinema has not returned to the world domination of the New Wave period, it is now a healthy and diverse industry. In addition to the film-makers named above, directors to watch out for include **Cédric Klapisch** whose *Chacun Cherche Son Chat* (*When the Cat's Away*) (1996) about day-to-day life in the Bastille area of Paris was followed by *Un Air de Famille* (1998), a black comedy about a dysfunctional family set in a local bar; and **Jacques Dillon**, whose poignant *Ponette* (1996) recounts the tale of a four-year-old girl who refuses to accept the death of her mother.

THEATRE

The earlier **theatre** generation of **Genet**, **Anouilh** and **Camus**, joined by **Beckett** and **Ionesco**, hasn't really had successors. In the 1950s, **Roger Planchon** set up a company in a suburb of Lyon, determined to play to working-class audiences. It became the Théâtre Nationale Populaire, the number-two state theatre after the Comédie Française, and now does the classics with all due decorum. Bourgeois farces, postwar classics, Shakespeare, Racine and Cyrano de Bergerac make up the staple fare in most theatres. But certain directors in France do extraordinary things with the medium. Classic texts are shuffled to produce theatrical moments where spectacular and dazzling sensation takes precedence over speech. Their shows are overwhelming: huge casts, vast sets – sometimes in real buildings never before used for theatre – exotic lighting effects, original music scores. They are a unique experience, even if you haven't understood a word. Directors' names to look out for are **Peter Brook** (the English director who has been in Paris for decades; he is based at the Centre Internationale de Création),

The FNAC shops in all big towns and Virgin Megastores in the main cities have copious listings of what's on and are the best booking agencies for gigs, ballet or theatre. Booking details for festivals are given in the *Guide*.

Ariane Mnouchkine, Patrice Chereau and **Jérôme Savary**.

Café-théâtre, literally a revue, monologue or mini-play performed in a place where you can drink and sometimes eat, is probably less accessible than a Racine tragedy at the Comédie Française. The humour or puerile dirty jokes, wordplay, and allusions to current fads, phobias and politicians can leave even a fluent French speaker in the dark.

For details of **Paris theatres**, see Chapter One. In other cities, the theatres are often part of the Maisons de la Culture or Centres d'Animation Culturelle; local tourist offices usually have schedules and tickets are not expensive. The two major theatre festivals are the **Festival Mondial du Théâtre** in Nancy (June) and the **Festival d'Avignon** (July).

DANCE AND MIME

The French regional **contemporary dance companies** – including Régine Chopinot's troupe from La Rochelle, Jean-Claude Gallotta's from Grenoble, Mathilde Monnier's from Montpellier, Karine Saporta's from Caen, and Joëlle Bouvier and Régis Obadia's from Angers – easily rival the Paris-based troupes, though the exciting choreographers Jean-François Duroure and the Californian Carolyn Carlson are both based in or around the capital. Other names to watch for are Maguy Marin in Créteil and François Verret in Aubervilliers.

Humour, everyday actions and obsessions, social problems and the darker shades of life find expression in the myriad current dance forms. A multidimensional performing art is created by combinations of movement, mime, ballet, music from the medieval to contemporary jazz-rock, speech, noise and theatrical effects. Philippe Genty's company in Paris combines dance, drama and marionettes to astonishing effect while the Gallotta-choreographed film *Rei-Dom* opened up a whole new range of possibilities. Many of the traits of the modern epic theatre are shared with dance, including crossing international frontiers.

Though the famous Lecoq School of Mime and Improvisation in Paris still turns out excellent artists, pure **mime** – as practised by the incomparable Marcel Marceau – hardly exists, except on the streets and at Périgueux's international festival of mime.

For **classical ballet** (again well represented in festivals), the two most renowned companies are the Ballet de l'Opéra National de Paris at the Opéra-Garnier and the Opéra-Bastille, whose dance director is Brigitte Lefèvre, and the Ballet National de Marseille, whose artistic director is Roland Petit. Other classical ballet companies are based in Avignon, Bordeaux, Lyon, Toulouse and St-Etienne.

SPORT AND OUTDOOR ACTIVITIES

France has a wide range of sports on offer, both for the spectator and the participant. It is not difficult to get tickets to domestic and international football and rugby matches, while the biggest event of all, the Tour de France, is free. And if you are interested in expending some energy yourself, you will find a whole host of activities and adventure holidays available.

SPORTING CALENDAR

LE MANS 24-hour car rally (mid-June).
MONTE CARLO Formula 1 Grand Prix (May, Ascension Day to following Sun).
PARIS Rugby Six Nations (Feb–April); Marathon (mid-April); Roland Garros tennis tournament (last week May to first week June).

SPORTS

More than any of the cultural jamborees, it is **sporting** events that really excite the French – cycling, football, tennis and skiing. At the local level, the gentle sobriety of boules is the most obvious manifestation of sporting life.

CYCLING

The sport the French are truly mad about is **cycling**: first and foremost in their sporting calendar is the Tour de France race in July. It was, after all, in Paris's Palais Royale gardens in 1791 that the precursor of the modern bicycle, the *célerifière*, was presented, and seventy years later the Parisian father-and-son team of **Pierre and Ernest Michaux** constructed the *vélocipede* (hence the modern French term *vélo* for bicycle), the first really efficient bicycle. The French can also legitimately claim the sport of cycle racing as their own, with the first event, a 1200-metre sprint, held in Paris's Parc St-Cloud in 1868 – sadly for national pride, however, the first champion was an Englishman.

That most French of sporting events, and the the world's premier cycling race, the **Tour de France**, was inaugurated in 1903. Covering 4000-odd-kilometres, the 25-stage three-week course changes every year but some truly arduous mountain stages and some time trials are always part of the action, and sometimes foreign countries are included in the itinerary (Britain and Ireland, among others, have hosted stages). An aggregate of each rider's times is made daily, the overall leader wearing the coveted **yellow jersey** (*maillot jaune*). Huge crowds turn out to cheer on the cyclists at the finishing line of the ultimate stage on the Champs-Élysées in late July when the French president himself presents the jersey to the overall winner – however, the crowds have

been waiting for a French cyclist to win it since **Bernard Hinault**'s victory in 1985.

Over the last couple of years the event has been rocked by **drug scandals**, beginning in 1998 when evidence of systematic doping within the cycling teams came to light. Nicholas Chaine, of the Crédit Lyonnais bank, which sponsored the race supplied this unusually honest quotable quote: "Let's not be hypocrites. You just don't do that on fizzy mineral water and salads." These scandals have cast a shadow over the American rider **Lance Armstrong**'s monumental achievement of fighting to overcome cancer and later going on to win the race in 1999 and 2000.

Other classic long-distance bike races include the 600-kilometre **Bordeaux–Paris**, the world's longest single stage race, first held in 1891; the **Paris–Roubaix**, instigated in 1896, which is reputed to be the most exacting one-day race in the world; the **Paris–Brussels** held since 1893; and the rugged six-day **Paris–Nice** event, covering over 1100km. The **Grand Prix des Nations**, always held somewhere in France, with locations changing every year, is the world's foremost **time trial**; the Palais Omnisport de Bercy in Paris (see p.184) holds other time trials and cycling events.

FOOTBALL

In France, as in most countries, **football** is the number-one team sport, and French football at present is riding the crest of a wave. Having won the World Cup for the first time in 1998 in front of their home crowd, in 2000 the French national team became the first ever side to add a European Championships title to the world crown.

Up until 1998, most of France's footballing successes had come off the pitch through innovators such as **Jules Rimet**, who created the World Cup in 1930, and **Henri Delauney**, who conceived the European Championships thirty years later. It was not until 1984, when **Michel Platini**'s cavalier side lifted the European Championships cup, that the French were able to translate their influence in the corridors of power onto the pitch.

It was only fitting, therefore, that Platini was chosen as president of his country's bid to host the **World Cup** for the second time in 1998. Having won the right to stage it, the French began the tournament slowly and struggled to convince a traditionally ambivalent French public of their championship potential. But this all changed after close shaves against Paraguay in the second round, Italy in the quarter finals and Croatia in the semis set up a dream final against Brazil, the pre-tournament favourites and defending champions. In the event the final itself was an anti-climax, with two goals by **Zinedine Zidane**, France's best player, and a late effort by **Emmanuel Petit**, being enough to overturn a lacklustre Brazil, whose morale was shattered by the breakdown of their talisman Ronaldo before the game. However, the result was all that mattered to the French, and a million people piled onto the streets of Paris for the biggest street party since the end of World War II.

France's success in the World Cup did not end on the pitch. Of the 32 sides that made it to the finals, France's was the most diverse ethnically, with half of the squad's 22 players of foreign extraction. For the first time, the national team really reflected the **racial diversity** of modern French society. Before the tournament **Jean-Marie Le Pen**'s right-wing **Front National** party had called for a ban on players of foreign extraction playing for France, but the heroics of Zidane, Marcel Desailly and Lillian Thuram, among others, and the sight of black, white and *beurs* embracing in the streets in celebration of victory, caused him to backtrack sharply. Furthermore, the French president, **Jacques Chirac**, chose his Bastille Day conference, two days after the French triumph, as a political platform to denounce the Front National's policies of racial discrimination and to praise France's "tricolour and multi-colour" World Cup win.

Back on the pitch, the only small cloud hanging over the French team was the accusation by some that they had won the World Cup only because they were playing at home: in the **2000 European Championships** they set out to prove those critics wrong. This they did in style, adding pace and flair in the form of young strikers such as **Thierry Henry** and **Nicolas Anelka** to the rock-solid defence and combative midfield – plus the genius of Zidane – that had won France the World Cup. Though they rode their luck in the final, needing an injury time equalizer by **Sylvain Wiltord** and a golden goal winner by **Davide Trézéguet** to beat Italy, the French richly deserved their victory.

The success of the international side has meant that French players are hugely in demand at Europe's richest clubs, and consequently most of the international squad play their **club football** outside France, mainly in England, Italy and Spain. French coaching acumen is also a valuable commodity abroad, especially in England, where **Arsène Wenger** in particular has enjoyed outstanding success.

The drain of talent out of France does not seem to have harmed the **domestic game**, however. Average attendances are on the rise, almost all clubs now have sound financial backing, and the biggest clubs, such as **AS Monaco**, **Marseille** and **Paris St-Germain** (PSG), have all done well in European competition in recent years. More importantly, the infrastructure of French football has never been in better shape. France's main club grounds underwent major reconstruction for the World Cup – some for the first time in sixty years – and the magnificent **Stade de France** was built on the outskirts of Paris to host the final. In addition, the French football federation has invested heavily in a **national football institute** for outstanding young players, based in Clairefontaine, near Paris, which is the envy of the footballing world and which looks set to maintain France's position at the top table of the world game for many years to come.

RUGBY

Although confined mainly to the southwest of the country, the sport that arouses most passion in France is **rugby**. The French have a rich rugby heritage and are renowned throughout the world for the style and spirit of adventure with which they play the game. Their high-risk strategies make the French a fascinating side to watch, capable of the sublime – when everything clicks – and the abject, but rarely anything in between. French rugby's greatest moment to date came in the semi-finals of the **1999 World Cup**, when they stunned the world by trouncing favourites New Zealand with an exhilarating display of attacking rugby. Rather predictably, however, they blew cold in the final, putting up feeble resistance against an Australian side that never had to rouse itself out of second gear.

More staple international fare is provided by the **Six Nations tournament** – the other five nations being England, Wales, Scotland, Ireland and Italy – which takes place every year between February and April. Matches are played alternately at home and away. Over the past few years, France has consistently challenged for the title, and in 1997 and 1998 it achieved the considerable feat of winning back-to-back **Grand Slams** – "Grand Slam" being the term used to describe a clean sweep of victories over the other nations.

Domestically, the **French clubs** have ridden out rugby's occasionally fraught transition from amateur to professional status and look to be in good shape. Though France has lost some of its stars to predatory English clubs, unlike in football the majority of the national side still plays in France. Sides to watch for are **Toulouse** and **Brive** (past winners of the European Heineken Cup), **Dax** and **Agen**, and the Basque teams of **Bayonne** and **Biarritz**, which still have their reputation as keepers of the game's soul.

BOULES

In every town or village square, particularly in the south, you'll see the older generation playing **boules** or **pétanque**. The principle is the same as British bowls but the terrain is always rough (never grass) and the area much smaller. The metal ball is usually thrown upwards from a distance of about 10m, to land and skid towards the wooden marker (*cochonnet*). It's very male-dominated, and socially the equivalent of darts or perhaps pool: there are café or village teams and endless championships.

PELOTA

In the Basque country, the main draw for crowds is the national ball game of **pelota**, which is like a lethally (sometimes literally) fast variety of team squash played in a walled court with a ball of solid wood and wicker slings strapped to the players' arms.

BULLFIGHTING

In and around the Camargue, meanwhile, the number-one sport is **bullfighting**. Though not to everyone's taste, it is at least a considerably less gruesome variety than that practised by the Spanish – usually bloodless and involving variations on the theme of removing cockades from the base of the bull's horns. It's generally the "fighters", rather than the bulls, who get hurt. The big event of the year is the Whitsun Féria de Pentecôte in Nîmes.

OUTDOOR ACTIVITIES

In addition to the old standbys – walking, cycling (see p.40) and skiing, and the traditional French *boules* – France provides a fantastically wide range of **outdoor activities**.

Rafting and **canoeing** are growth industries in France, and practically every stretch of river, particularly in the gorges and ravines of the Pyrenees, the Alps and the Massif Central, has outfits renting boats or organizing excursions. These mountainous areas also provide prime **rock climbing** (*escalade*) territory. **Paragliding** (a combination between parachuting and hanggliding) is another popular and stimulating option; the best areas for this are the Hautes-Alpes of Provence and Corsica.

More placid inland activities include **fishing** (local tourist offices will assist you in obtaining a licence) and **horse-riding**. Practically every town has riding stables (*centre équestre*), although the most famous and romantic region for riding is the flat and wind-swept Camargue – the Rhône Delta. On the scrappy trails of the Pyrenees and Alps, **mule-trekking** is also coming increasingly into vogue. You can also **swim** at many river beaches (usually signposted from highways) and in the real and artificial lakes which pepper France. Many of these have leisure centres (*bases de plein airs*) at which you can rent pedaloes, windsurfers and dinghys, as well as larger boats and jet-skis (on the bigger reservoirs).

France's extensive coasts have also been well developed for recreational activities, and this is especially true in the south. Although in summer, you can swim just about anywhere from Normandy to the Mediterranean, the Côte d'Azur is justly reputed as the best for **beaches**. In the coastal towns and resorts of the Mediterranean coast, you'll find every conceivable sort of beach-side activity, including **boating**, **sea-fishing** and **diving**. If you don't mind high prices and crowds, its too-blue waters and sandy coves are unbeatable. The western Mediterranean coast is much windier, and **windsurfers** delight in the calm of the broad salt-water inlets (*étangs*) which typify the area. The best **surfing** is to be found on the rougher Atlantic coast, where Biarritz is something of a Mecca for the sport, hosting a lively annual championship.

Details of outdoor activities are outlined throughout the *Guide*, and local and regional tourist offices will also provide in-depth information about activities in their area.

WALKING

Long-distance walkers are well served in France by a network of over 30,000km of long-distance marked **footpaths**, known as *sentiers de grande randonnée* or, more commonly, simply as **GRs**. They're fully signposted and equipped with campsites and rest huts along the way. Some are real marathons, like the GR5 from the coast of Holland to Nice, the trans-Pyrenean GR10 or the Grande Traversée des Alpes (the GRX). The Chemin de St-Jacques – GR65 – follows the ancient pilgrim route from Le Puy in the Auvergne to the Spanish border above St-Jean-Pied-de-Port and on to the shrine of Santiago de Compostela, while GR3 traces the Loire from source to sea. There are many more.

Each path is described in a **Topoguide** (available in Britain from Stanfords, see p.31), which gives a detailed account of the route (in French), including maps, campsites, refuge huts, sources of provisions, etc. In addition, many tourist offices can provide guides to their local footpaths, especially in popular hiking areas, where they often share premises with professional mountain guides and hike leaders. The latter organize climbing and walking expeditions for all levels of experience. Topoguides are produced by the principal French walkers' organization, the Fédération Française de la Randonnée Pédestre, 14 rue Riquet, 75019 Paris (☎01.44.89.93.93, fax 01.40.35.85.67). The main climbing organization is the Club Alpin Français, 24 ave de Laumière, 75019 Paris (☎01.53.72.87.00, fax 01.42.03.55.60, *www .clubalpin.com*). In the Pyrenees, CIMES offers similar services and has its own network of refuges. Contact CIMES-Pyrenees 1, rue Maye-Lane, BP 2, 65420 Ibos (☎05.62.90.09.92, fax 05.62.90.67.61, *www.cimes-pyrenees.com*). In Corsica, you can find out details about rambling and climbing from the Parc Naturel Régional de la Corse, 2 rue Major Lambroschini, off Cours Napoléon in Ajaccio (☎04.95.51.79.10, fax 95.21.88.17).

Maps are listed under the "Information and maps" section on p.32; you might also like to look at the specialized walking sheets produced by Didier et Richard of Grenoble for the Alps. **Guidebooks** worth looking out for are listed on pp.1140–1141.

SKIING

One sport that millions of visitors come to France to practise rather than watch is **skiing**. And whether downhill, cross-country or mountaineering, it's also enthusiastically pursued by the French. It can be an expensive sport to practise independently, however, and the best deals are often to be had from package operators (see pp.9,6,19 & 20). These can be arranged in France or before you leave (most travel agents sell all-in packages). In France, the umbrella organization to contact is the Fédération Française de Ski, 50 rue des Marquisats, 74000 Annecy (☎04.50.51.40.34, fax 04.50.51.75.90, *www.ffs.fr*).

The best skiing is generally to be had in the **Alps**. The higher the resort the longer the season, and the fewer the anxieties you'll have about there being enough snow. These resorts are almost all modern, with the very latest in lift technology. They're terrific for full-time skiing, but they lack the cachet, charm or the nightlife of the older resorts such as Megève and Courchevel. The foothills of the Alps in Provence have the same mix of old and new on a smaller scale. The clientele are Riviera residents and prices are not cheap, though at least you can nip down to the coast for a quick swim when you're bored with snow. The **Pyrenees** are a friendlier range of mountains, less developed (though that can be a drawback if you want to get in as many different runs as possible per day) and warmer, which means more problems with the snow.

Cross-country skiing (*ski de fond*) is being promoted hard, especially in the smaller ranges of the Jura and Massif Central. It's easier on the joints, but don't be fooled into thinking it's any less athletic a sport. For the really experienced and fit, though, it can be a good means of transport, using snowbound GR routes to discover villages still relatively uncommercialized. Several independent operators organize ski-mountaineering courses in the French mountains (see pp.9,16 & 19).

TROUBLE AND THE POLICE

Petty theft is endemic in all the major cities and along the Côte d'Azur. Drivers, particularly with foreign number-plates or in rental cars with Parisian registration, face a high risk of break-ins. Vehicles are rarely stolen, but car radios and luggage make tempting targets.

It obviously makes sense to take the normal **precautions**: not flashing wads of notes or travellers' cheques around; carrying your bag or wallet securely; never letting cameras and other valuables out of your sight; and parking your car overnight in an attended garage or within sight of a police station. But the best security is having a good insurance policy, keeping a separate record of cheque numbers, credit card numbers and the phone numbers for cancelling them (see box on p.26), and the relevant details of all your valuables.

If you need to **report a theft**, go along to the *commissariat de police* (addresses are given in the *Guide* for the major cities), where they will fill

EMERGENCY NUMBERS

Fire brigade (*pompiers*) ☎18.
Medical emergencies ☎15.
Police ☎17.
Rape crisis (*SOS Viol*) ☎08.00.05.95.95.
AIDS information (SIDA Info Service) ☎08.00.84.08.00.
All these numbers are free.

out a *constat de vol*. The first thing they'll ask for is your passport, and vehicle documents if relevant. Although the police are not always as co-operative as they might be, it is their duty to assist you if you've lost your passport or all your money.

If you have an **accident** while driving, you have officially to fill in and sign a *constat à l'aimable* (jointly agreed statement); car insurers are supposed to give you this with the policy, though in practice few seem to have heard of it. For **non-criminal driving offences** such as speeding, the police can impose an on-the-spot fine.

People caught smuggling or possessing **drugs**, even a few grams of marijuana, are liable to find themselves in jail, and consulates will not be sympathetic. This is not to say that hard-drug consumption isn't a visible activity: there are scores of kids dealing in *poudre* (heroin) in the big French cities and the authorities seem unable to do much about it. As a rule, people are no more nor less paranoid about cannabis busts than they are in the UK or North America.

Should you be **arrested** on any charge, you have the right to contact your consulate (addresses are given on p.194).

THE POLICE

The two main types of **police** – the Police Nationale and the Gendarmerie Nationale – are for all practical purposes indistinguishable. The CRS (Compagnies Républicaines de Sécurité), on the other hand, are an entirely different proposition. They are a mobile force of paramilitary heavies, used to guard sensitive embassies, "control" demonstrations and generally intimidate the populace on those occasions when the public authorities judge that it is stepping out of line. Armed with guns, CS gas and truncheons, they have earned themselves a reputation for brutality over the years, particularly at those moments when the tensions inherent in the long civil war of French politics have reached boiling point. Not quite in the same league, but with an ugly recent history, is the separate **Paris police force**. This bunch are prone to pulling up "non-conformists" – often just ordinary teenagers and black people – for identity checks. You can be

RACISM IN FRANCE

Racist attitudes in the populace and the police are rife. A survey on French attitudes to race, commissioned by the French government and published in June 1998, resulted in 38 percent of the population declaring themselves racist, double the figures for similar surveys in Britain and Germany, and the **Front National**, a neo-fascist, racist party, headed by **Jean-Marie Le Pen**, won fifteen percent of the vote in the last parliamentary elections. Support for the party was highest in Provence and the Cote d'Azur, where by 1997 four cities had Front National mayors. The Front National's alliance with conservatives has led to changes in educational, cultural and sporting and programmes to suit its policies; the party's fundamental priority is the withdrawal of benefits to immigrants who have not yet been granted French citizenship.

However, the mood in France altered after the 1998 World Cup victory of its multicultural team (see p.71) and Le Pen was forced to modify some of his racist statements. Since then the party has fractured and lost popularity (with it and the splinter group rated at about nine percent), so the next round of elections may change the current unpleasant state of affairs.

It will take a long time for the warm glow created by the World Cup to transform France into a racially tolerant country, and for the moment being black, particularly if you are Arab or look as if you might be, makes your chances of avoiding unpleasantness very low. Hotels claiming to be booked up, police demanding your papers and abuse from ordinary people is horribly frequent. In addition, even entering the country can be difficult. Changes in passport regulations have put an end to outright refusal to let some British holiday-makers in, but customs and immigration officers can still be obstructive and malicious. In North African-dominated areas of cities, identity checks by the police are very common and not pleasant. The clampdown on illegal immigration (and much tougher laws) has resulted in a significant increase in police stop-and-search operations. Carrying your passport at all times is a good idea.

If you suffer a **racial assault**, you're likely to get a much more sympathetic hearing from your consulate than from the police. There are many anti-racism organizations which will offer support (though they may not have English-speakers): Mouvement contre le Racisme et pour l'Amitié entre les Peuples (MRAP) and SOS Racism have offices in most big cities.

stopped anywhere in France and asked to produce ID. If it happens to you, it's not worth being difficult or facetious. The police can also be rather sensitive on political issues: a few years ago a group of Danish students wearing "Chirac Non!" T-shirts against the French nuclear tests in the Pacific were surrounded on their arrival in France, accompanied in force to their hotel and made to change.

Lastly, in the Alps or Pyrenees, you may come across specialized **mountaineering sections** of the police force. They are unfailingly helpful, friendly and approachable, providing rescue services and guidance.

GAY AND LESBIAN FRANCE

France is more liberal on homosexuality than most other European countries. The legal age of consent is 16. Gay communities thrive especially in Paris, Toulouse and Nice and many of the southern towns, though lesbian life is rather less upfront.

Addresses are listed in the Guide, and you'll find details of groups and publications for the whole country in the box below.

In general, the French consider sexuality to be a private matter and homophobic assaults are very rare. On the whole, gays tend to be discreet

GAY AND LESBIAN CONTACTS AND INFORMATION

ARCL (Les Archives, Recherches et Cultures Lesbiennes), based at the Maison des Femmes, below (☎01.46.28.54.94, *www.mrap.asso.fr*). ARCL publishes a biannual directory of lesbian, gay and feminist addresses in France, *L'Annuaire* (70F/€10.68), and organizes frequent meetings around campaigning, artistic and intellectual issues.

ARIS (Accueil Rencontres Informations Services), 16 rue Polycarpe, Lyon (☎04.78.27.10.10). Gay and lesbian centre organizing various activities and producing a bimonthly bulletin.

Centre Gai et Lesbienne, 3 rue Keller, 17011 Paris (Mon–Sat 2–8pm, Sun 2–7pm; ☎01.43.57.21.47, fax 01.43.57.27.93, *www.cglparis.org*; Mº Ledru-Rollin). The main information centre for the gay, lesbian, bisexual and transexual community in the capital. The centre publishes a free map/guide to gay and lesbian Paris and a monthly magazine, *3 Keller*, and is the meeting place for numerous campaigning, identity, health, arts and intellectual groups.

Centre Gai et Lesbienne Toulouse, 4 rue de Belfort (☎05.61.62.30.62). Open for phone calls and visits Mon–Fri 5–8pm, Sat 3–8pm, and on Sunday the *Café Positif*, a great place for meeting people, is open from 3 to 7pm.

Collectif Gai et Lesbien Marseille et Provence, Maison des Associations, 93 La Canebière, Marseille (Mon, Wed & Fri 4–7pm; ☎04.91.42.07.48), and at Le Local, 9 rue Barbaroux, Marseille (☎04.91.92.38.48). Publishes a bimonthly information bulletin.

Collectif Homosexuel d'Aide et d'Information de Loire-Atlantique, Maison des Associations, 42 rue Hauts Pavés, Nantes (☎02.40.93.38.24). Brings together different gay and lesbian groups, ranging from Christian organizations to rambling enthusiasts.

Les Flamands Roses, Centre Culturel Libertaire, 1–2 rue Denis-du-Péage, Lille (☎03.20.47.62.65, *www.france.qrd.org/regions/lille/flamands*). Gay and lesbian social and campaigning group; publishes a monthly bulletin, *Les Flamands Roses*.

Gai Amitié Initiative Lorraine, PO Box 258, Nancy Cedex 54005 (☎03.83.32.63.14). Gay and lesbian social and information network; publishes trimonthly bulletin, *Le Chardon Rose*.

Maison des Femmes, 163 rue de Charenton, 17012 Paris (Mon 5–8pm, Wed 3–8pm, Fri 5–10pm; café Fri 8pm–midnight; ☎01.43.43.41.13, fax 01.43.43.42.13; Mº Faidherbe-Chaligny). The main women's centre in the capital and home to ARCL and other lesbian groups.

Minitel. 36.15 GAY is the Minitel number to dial for information on groups, contacts, messages, etc.

Gay and Lesbian Media

Fréquence Gaie (FG), 98.2 FM. 24-hour gay and lesbian radio station with music, news, chats, information on groups and events, etc.

Guide Gai Pied. The most comprehensive gay guide to France, published annually and carrying a good selection of lesbian and gay addresses, with an English section (79F/€12.05); available in newsagents and bookshops in France. You can look at their Web site at *www.gaipied.fr*.

Lesbia. The most widely available lesbian publication, available from most newsagents. Each monthly issue features a wide range of articles, listings, reviews, lonely hearts and contacts.

Spartacus International Gay Guide. Guidebook in English focusing mainly on gay travel in Europe with an extensive section on France. Geared mostly towards males but with some info for lesbians. Available around the world at travel and gay bookshops.

outside specific gay venues, parades and the prime gay areas of Paris and the coastal resorts. Lesbians tend to be extremely discreet.

Hedonistic lifestyles have changed, here as elsewhere, since the advent of **AIDS** (SIDA in French). The resulting homophobia, though not as extreme as in most parts of the world, has nevertheless increased the suffering among gay men. The Pasteur Institute in Paris is at the forefront of research into the virus, though its gay patients have complained of being treated like cattle. A group of gay doctors and the association AIDES (Association pour l'Entraide et l'Information SIDA), however, have consistently provided sympathetic counselling and treatment, and the gay press has done a great deal to disseminate the facts about AIDS and to provide hope and encouragement. Lesbian organizations fight alongside gays on the general issue of anti-homosexuality, while also lobbying for women's rights.

WORK AND STUDY

Specialists aside, most Britons, North Americans, Australians and Kiwis who manage to survive for long periods of time in France do it on luck, brazenness and willingness to live in pretty basic conditions. In the cities, bar work, club work, freelance translating or teaching English, software fixing, data processing and typing or working as an au pair are some of the ways people scrape by; in the countryside, the options come down to seasonal fruit- or grape-picking, teaching English, busking or DIY oddjobbing. Remember that unemployment is very high; the current rate in France is hovering at around eleven percent.

Anyone staying in France for over three months must have a *carte de séjour*, or residency permit – citizens of the EU are entitled to one automatically. France has a **minimum wage** (the SMIC – Salaire Minimum Interprofessional de Croissance), indexed to the cost of living; it's currently around 40F/€6.10 an hour (for a maximum 169-hour month). Employers, however, are likely to pay lower wages to temporary foreign workers who don't have easy legal resources and to make them work longer hours. By law, however, all EU nationals are entitled to exactly the same pay, conditions and trade union rights as French nationals.

If you're looking for something secure, it's important to plan well in advance. A few books which might be worth consulting are *Work Your Way Around the World* by Susan Griffiths (Vacation Work), *A Year Between* and *Working Holidays* (both Central Bureau) and *Living and Working in France* by Victoria Pybus, published by Vacation Work, 1998. **In France**, check out the "Offres d'Emploi" (Job Offers) in *Le Monde*, *Le Figaro* and the *International Herald Tribune*; keep an eye on the noticeboards at English and North American bookshops and churches; and try the youth information agency CIDJ (Centre d'Information et de Documentation Jeunesse), 101 quai Branly, 17015 Paris, or CIJ (Centre d'Information Jeunesse) offices in other main cities, which sometimes have temporary jobs for foreigners. The national employment agency, ANPE (Agence Nationale pour l'Emploi), with offices all over France, advertises temporary jobs in all fields and, in theory, offers a whole range of services to job-seekers open to all EU citizens, but is not renowned for its helpfulness to foreigners. Non-EU citizens will have to show a work permit to apply for any of their jobs. Vac-Job, 46 av René-Coty, 17014 Paris (☎01. 43.20.70.51), publishes the annual *Emplois d'Été*

DIRECTORY

BEACHES Beaches are public property within 5m of the high-tide mark, so you can kick sand past private villas. Under a different law, however, you can't camp.

CAMERAS AND FILM Film is considerably cheaper in North America than France or Britain, so stock up before travelling. If you're bringing a video camcorder, make sure any tapes you purchase in France will be compatible. Again, American videotape prices are way below French prices.

CHILDREN AND BABIES Kids are generally welcome everywhere, and in most bars and restaurants, though French children seem to be much more well trained at a younger age in restaurant etiquette. Hotels charge by the room, with a small supplement for an additional bed or cot, and family-run places will usually babysit or offer a listening service while you eat or go out. Especially in the seaside towns, most restaurants have children's menus or will cook simpler food on request. You'll have no difficulty finding disposable nappies (*couches à jeter*), but nearly all baby foods have added sugar and salt, and French milk powders are very rich indeed. SNCF charge nothing on trains and buses for under-4s, and half-fare for 4–11s (see p.36 for other reductions). In most museums children under 4 are free and it's usually half price for under-18s, while entry to many monuments is free for under-12s. Most local tourist offices have details of specific activities for children – in particular, many resorts supervise "clubs" for children on the beach. And

almost every town down to small ones has a children's playground with a good selection of activities. Most parks, even in Paris, have a children's play area; unfortunately the majority of parks are gravelled rather than grassed and when there are lawns they are often out of bounds (*pelouse interdite*), so sprawling horizontally with toddlers and napping babies is usually not an option. Something to beware of – not that you can do much about it – is the difficulty of negotiating a child's buggy over the large cobbles that cover many of the older streets in town centres.

CONTRACEPTIVES Condoms (*préservatifs* or *capotes*) are available at all pharmacies, as well as from many clubs and street dispensers (10F/€1.50 for 3–4 condoms) in larger cities. You can also get spermicidal cream and jelly (*dose contraceptive*), plus the suppositories (*ovules, suppositoires*) and (with a prescription) the Pill (*la pillule*), a diaphragm (*le diaphragme*) or IUD (*le sterilet*). Test sticks (*tests réactifs*) for the Persona monitor (only available in Europe) are readily available in pharmacies for 95F/€14.49 per packet.

ELECTRICITY This is almost always 220V, using plugs with two round pins. If you haven't bought the appropriate transformer before leaving home, the best place in France to find the right one is the electrical section of a department store, where someone is also more likely to speak English; cost is around 60F/€9.15.

FISHING You get fishing rights by becoming a member of an authorized fishing club – tourist offices have details.

LAUNDRY Laundries are common in French towns, and some are listed in the *Guide* – elsewhere look in the phone book under "Laveries Automatiques". They are often unattended, so come pre-armed with small change. Machines are normally graded into 5kg, 8kg or 10kg wash sizes, and the smallest costs around 12F/€1.80 for a load, though some laundries only have bigger machines and charge around 20F/€3. If you're doing your own washing in hotels, keep quantities small as most forbid doing any laundry in your room.

PEDESTRIANS French drivers pay no heed to pedestrian/zebra crossings marked with horizontal white stripes on roads. It is very dangerous to step out onto one and assume drivers will stop as in Australia and Britain. Take just as great care as you would crossing at any other point. Also be careful at traffic lights: check cars are not still speeding towards you even when the green man is showing.

PETROL The cheapest gas (*essence*) or diesel fuel (*gasoil*) can be bought at out-of-town super-stores. Four-star is *super*, unleaded is *sans plomb*. See p.24 for average prices.

SAFE SEX Paris has the highest number of people suffering from AIDS of any city in Europe, and studies show that there are almost equal numbers of heterosexual and homosexual people who are HIV-positive. Among heterosexuals (excluding drug users) the number of women who are HIV-positive has overtaken men. See "Contraceptives" above.

SWIMMING POOLS Swimming pools (*piscines*) are well signposted in most French towns and reasonably priced, usually around 16F/€2.44 for a swim. Tourist offices have their addresses. You may be requested to wear a bathing cap, whether you are male or female, so come prepared.

TIME France is one hour ahead of GMT (Greenwich Mean Time) throughout the year. It is six hours ahead of Eastern Standard Time, and nine hours ahead of Pacific Standard Time. This also applies during daylight savings seasons, which are observed in France (as in most of Europe) from the end of March through to the end of September.

TOILETS Ask for *les toilettes* or look for signs for the WC (pronounced "vay say"); when reading the details of facilities outside hotels, don't confuse *lavabo*, which means washbasin, with lavatory. Usually found downstairs along with the phone, French toilets in bars are still often of the hole-in-the-ground squatting variety, and tend to lack toilet paper. Standards of cleanliness are often not high, and men shouldn't expect much privacy in the urinal, which often won't have a door. Both bar and restaurant toilets are usually free, as are toilets in museums, though toilets in railway stations and department stores are commonly staffed by attendants who will expect a bit of spare change. Some have coin-operated locks, so always keep 50 centimes and one and two franc pieces handy for these and for the frequent Tardis-like public toilets found on the streets. These beige-coloured boxes have automatic doors which open when you insert coins to the value of two francs, and are cleaned automatically once you exit. Children under 10 aren't allowed in on their own.

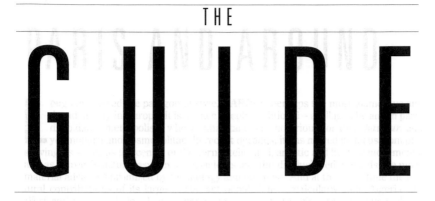

BRITAIN

BELGIUM

GERMANY

LUX.

ENGLISH CHANNEL

SWITZERLAND

ATLANTIC
OCEAN

ITALY

SPAIN

MEDITERRANEAN
SEA

N

0   250 km

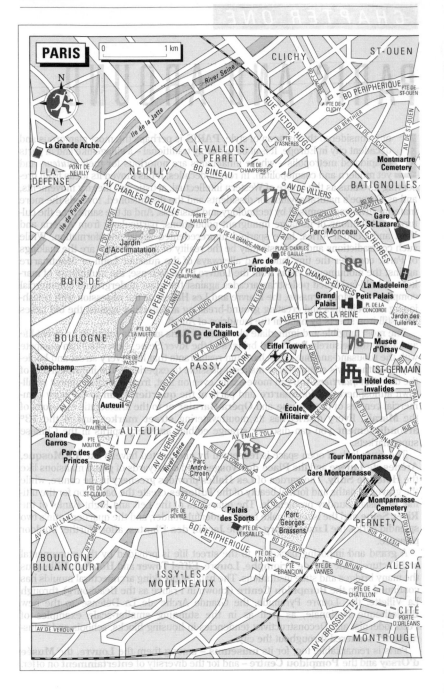

PARIS

0   1 km

N

River Seine

CLICHY   ST-OUEN

RUE VICTOR HUGO

BD PERIPHERIQUE   PTE DE ST-OUEN

Ile de la Jatte

PTE DE CLICHY

PTE D'ASNERES

BD BERTHIER   AV DE CLICHY

AV DE ST-OUEN

La Grande Arche

Montmartre Cemetery

LEVALLOIS-PERRET

BD BINEAU

PTE DE CHAMPERRET

AV DE VILLIERS

BATIGNOLLES

LA DEFENSE

PONT DE NEUILLY

NEUILLY

17e

BD DES BATIGNOLLES

AV CHARLES DE GAULLE

Ile de Puteaux

PORTE MAILLOT

AV DE LA GRANDE-ARMEE

AV DE WAGRAM

AV DE COURCELLES

Gare St-Lazare

BD MALESHERBES

Jardin d'Acclimatation

Parc Monceau

BOIS DE

BD DU COL CHARCOT

PLACE CHARLES DE GAULLE

Arc de Triomphe

AV DES CHAMPS-ELYSEES

8e

La Madeleine

BOULOGNE

PTE DAUPHINE

AV FOCH

AV DE LA GRANDE-ARMEE

Grand Palais

Petit Palais

PL DE LA CONCORDE

Jardin des Tuileries

AV KLEBER

AV VICTOR HUGO

BD LANNES

16e

Palais de Chaillot

ALBERT 1er CRS. LA REINE

PTE DE LA MUETTE

PTE DE PASSY

AV P. DOUMER

Eiffel Tower

7e

Musée d'Orsay

Longchamp

PASSY

AV DE NEW YORK

AV DE ST-CLOUD

AV MOZART

AV BOSQUET

ST-GERMAIN

Auteuil

BD SUCHET

Hôtel des Invalides

AUTEUIL

PTE D'AUTEUIL

École Militaire

AV DE LOWENDAL

BD DU MONTPARNASSE

Roland Garros

PTE MOLITOR

AV DE VERSAILLES

AV EMILE ZOLA

Parc des Princes

BD MURAT

River Seine

15e

RUE DE LA CONVENTION

RUE DE VAUGIRARD

Tour Montparnasse

Gare Montparnasse

PTE DE ST-CLOUD

Parc André-Citroën

Montparnasse Cemetery

PTE DE SEVRES

Palais des Sports

Parc Georges Brassens

PERNETY

RUE D'ALESIA

AV DU MAINE

AV E. VAILLANT

BD VICTOR

PTE DE VERSAILLES

BD LEFEBVRE

BOULOGNE BILLANCOURT

AV P. BRIMER

BD PERIPHERIQUE

PTE DE LA PLAINE

PTE DE BRANCION

BD BRUNE

ALESIA

PTE DE VANVES

ISSY-LES-MOULINEAUX

PTE DE CHATILLON

CITÉ PORTE D'ORLEANS

AV DE VERDUN

AV P. BROSSOLETTE

MONTROUGE

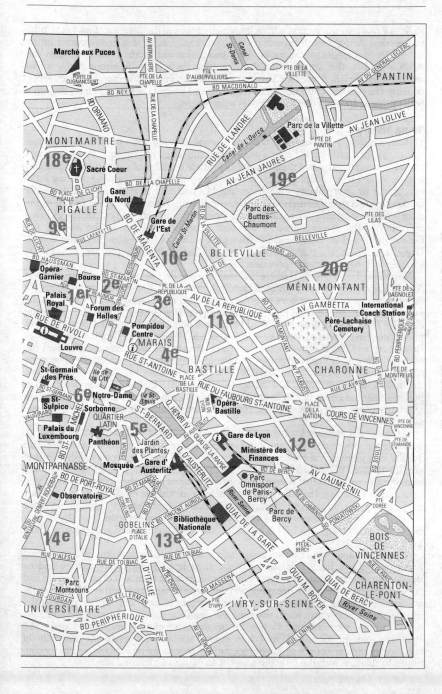

Paris is a real **cinema** capital, with a large percentage of the films on show in the original version. And although French rock is notoriously awful, it is compensated for by the quality of current Parisian music, from **jazz** and **avant-garde** to **West African** and **Arab sounds** – the vibrant cultural mix putting Paris at the forefront of the **world music** (*sono mondial*) scene. **Classical concerts** in fine architectural settings – particularly chapels and churches – are frequent, and entry is sometimes free, though a ticket price of upwards of 80F/€12.20 is more likely.

Some history

The city's history has conspired to create a sense of being apart from, and even superior to, the rest of France. From a shaky start the kings of France – whose seat was Paris – gradually extended their control over their feudal rivals, centralizing administrative, legal, financial and political power as they did so, until anyone seeking influence, publicity or credibility – in whatever field – had to be in Paris. Louis XIV consolidated this process. Supremely autocratic, considering himself the embodiment of the state – "L'état, c'est moi" – he inaugurated the tradition of Paris as symbol: the glorious reflection of the pre-eminence of the state. The Cour Carrée of the Louvre, the Observatoire and Invalides, and the triumphal arches of the Portes St-Martin and St-Denis, are his. It is a tradition his successors have been only too happy to follow, whether as king, emperor or president.

Napoléon I added to the Louvre and built the Arc de Triomphe, the Madeleine and Arc du Carrousel; he also instituted the Grandes Écoles, those super-universities for super-competent administrators, engineers and teachers. **Napoléon III** extended the Louvre even further and had his city planner Baron Haussmann redraw the rest of the city. The **Third Republic** had its World Fairs and bequeathed the Eiffel Tower. Recent presidents have initiated the skyscrapers at La Défense, the Tour Montparnasse, Beaubourg and Les Halles shopping precinct. **President Mitterrand** completed the high-tech Parc de la Villette complex and the Musée d'Orsay and added the glass pyramid entrance to the Louvre, the Grande Arche at La Défense, the Bastille opera house, the Institut du Monde Arabe and the new national library building. The scale of all this publicly financed construction is extraordinary – so, too, is the architecture. The new buildings should, and do, feature as prominently on any visitor's itinerary as the classic city sights.

Yet despite these developments Paris remains compact and remarkably uniform, basically the city remodelled in the mid-nineteenth century by Haussmann, who laid out the long geometrical boulevards lined with rows of grey bourgeois residences that are the hallmark of Paris today. In doing so, he cut great swathes through the stinking wen of medieval slums that housed the city's rebellious poor, already veterans of three revolutionary uprisings in half a century. If urban renewal and modernization were part of the design, so too was the intention of controlling the masses by opening up more effective fields of fire for artillery and facilitating troop movements. Not that it succeeded in preventing the 1871 Commune, the most determined insurrection since 1789.

Although riotous street protests are still a feature of Parisian life, the traditional barricade-builders have long since been booted into the suburban factory-land or depressing satellite towns, leaving behind ever-increasing numbers of people living and begging on the streets. The decaying parts of the city, especially in the east and north, are gradually being rebuilt, introducing a new mix of arty and media types to the underserved and downtrodden communities – made up mostly of immigrants and their descendants – who continue to live in the dank, unsanitary housing of areas like Belleville and the Goutte d'Or. While most Parisians appreciate the diversity of restaurants and music each group brings, racist tensions are undeniable as the city continues to struggle with the growing pains of an expanding cultural identity.

Arrival

Nowadays most British travellers to Paris will find themselves arriving by Eurostar at the very central Gare du Nord **train station**, while flights to the two main **airports**, Charles de Gaulle and Orly (information on both airports at *www.adp.fr*), continue to be the main mode of entry for more far-flung visitors. Those arriving from other parts of France or continental Europe by train arrive at one of the six central mainline train stations. Almost all the **buses** coming into Paris – whether international or domestic – arrive and depart from the main **gare routière** at 28 av du Général-de-Gaulle, Bagnolet, at the eastern edge of the city; métro Gallieni (line 3) links it to the centre. If you're **driving** in yourself, don't try to go straight across the city to your destination. Use the ring road – the **boulevard périphérique** – to get around to the nearest *porte*: it's much quicker, except at rush hour, and far easier to navigate.

Disneyland Paris is linked by bus to both Charles de Gaulle and Orly airports: for details of these services, plus train links from the centre to the purpose-built Marne La Vallée TGV, see p.202.

By air

Roissy-Charles de Gaulle Airport (24hr information in English ☎01.48.62.22.80), often also referred to as Charles de Gaulle and abbreviated to CDG or Paris CDG, is 23km northeast of the city. The airport has two main terminals, referred to as CDG 1 and CDG 2. Make sure you know which terminal your flight is departing from when it's time to leave Paris, so you take the correct bus or get off at the right train station. A TGV station links the airport with Bordeaux, Brussels, Lille, Lyon, Nantes, Marseille and Rennes. CDG is connected with the centre by various forms and combinations of transport. **Roissyrail** runs on RER line B every fifteen minutes from 5am until midnight, from both CDG 1 and 2 (TGV) stations to Gare du Nord, Châtelet-Les Halles, St-Michel and Denfert-Rochereau, at all of which you can transfer to the ordinary métro (for those arriving at CDG 1 airport terminal, take the free airport shuttle to the first station; from terminal CDG 2 there is direct access to the second station). Taking about thirty minutes to Gare du Nord, this is the quickest route and costs 49F/€7.47 one way (second class). Leaving Paris for CDG, all but the first train of the day depart from platform 43 of Gare du Nord where there is an English-speaking **information desk** indicated by a large question mark (daily 8am–8pm); confirm here which station you should get off at by checking the airline code on your ticket against the information board, or ask the staff to help you. **Air France bus** (information in English ☎01.41.56.89.00) offers three services with differing routes, times and prices. The green-coded line 2 (60F/€9.15 one way, 105F/€16 return) leaves from CDG 2 every twelve minutes from 5.40am to 11pm terminating at Porte Maillot (métro) on the northwest edge of the city, stopping at av Carnot, outside Charles-de-Gaulle-Étoile RER/métro between the Arc de Triomphe and rue Tilsitt. The yellow-coded line 4 (70F/€10.67 one way, 120F/€18.29 return) departs from both CDG 1 and CDG 2 every thirty minutes from 7am to 9pm, terminating near Gare Montparnasse and stopping at Gare de Lyon; journey times vary from 25 minutes to over an hour in rush hour. Leaving Paris, the green-coded line 2 (for CDG 2) departs from av Carnot, right outside the RER exit of Charles-de-Gaulle-Étoile, and from Porte Maillot. The yellow-coded line 4 (70F/€10.67; for both CDG 1 and CDG 2) leaves from 2bis bd Diderot outside Gare de Lyon and near Gare Montparnasse at rue du Commandant-René-Mouchotte in front of the Méridien Hotel. **Roissybus** connects CDG 2 with the Opéra-Garnier (corner of rues Auber and Scribe; RER Auber/métro Opéra) every fifteen minutes from 5.45am to 11pm – at 48F/€7.32 this is the cheapest route and takes around 45 minutes. The **Airport Shuttle** is a minibus door-to-door airport service, with no extra charge for luggage, so can work out to be more reasonable

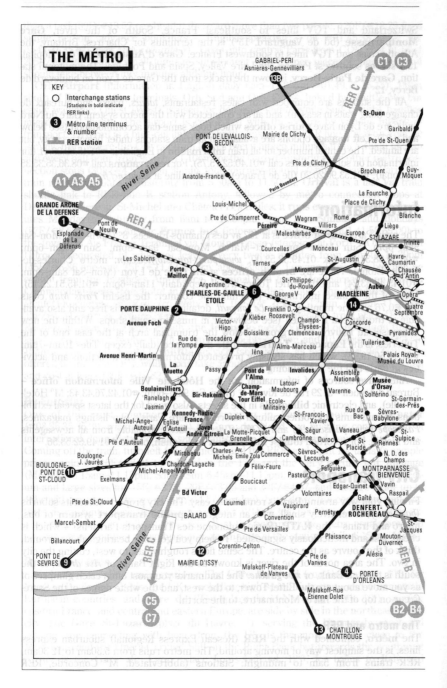

THE MÉTRO

KEY

○ Interchange stations
(Stations in bold indicate RER links)

❸ Métro line terminus & number

▬▬ RER station

A1 **A3** **A5**

GRANDE ARCHE DE LA DEFENSE ❶

Esplanade de La Défense

Pont de Neuilly

Les Sablons

Porte Maillot

Argentine

CHARLES-DE-GAULLE ETOILE ❻

PORTE DAUPHINE ❷

Avenue Foch

Victor-Higo

Kléber

Rue de la Pompe

Boissière

Trocadéro

Iéna

Avenue Henri-Martin

Passy

La Muette

Boulainvilliers

Bir-Hakeim

Ranelagh

Jasmin

Kennedy-Radio-France

Michel-Ange-Auteuil

Eglise d'Auteuil

Javel André Citroën

Pte d'Auteuil

Mirabeau

Charles-Michels

Dupleix

La Motte-Picquet Grenelle

Av. Emile Zola Commerce

BOULOGNE-PONT DE ST-CLOUD ❿

Boulogne-J. Jaurès

Exelmans

Chardon-Lagache
Michel-Ange-Molitor

Félix-Faure

Bd Victor

Pte de St-Cloud

Marcel-Sembat

Billancourt

PONT DE SEVRES ❾

❽ Lourmel

BALARD

Boucicaut

Vaugirard

Convention

Pte de Versailles

❿ **MAIRIE D'ISSY**

Corentin-Celton

Malakoff-Plateau de Vanves

Malakoff-Rue Etienne Dolet

❹ **PORTE D'ORLEANS**

CHATILLON-MONTROUGE ⓭

GABRIEL-PERI
Asnières-Gennevilliers ⓭B

St-Ouen

Garibaldi

Pte de St-Ouen

Mairie de Clichy

Pte de Clichy

Brochant

Guy-Môquet

PONT DE LEVALLOIS-BECON ❸

Anatole-France

Louis-Michel

Pte de Champerret

Wagram

Péreire

Malesherbes

Courcelles

Ternes

Monceau

St-Augustin

Miromesnil

St-Philippe-du-Roule

George V

Franklin D. Roosevelt

Champs-Elysées-Clemenceau

Alma-Marceau

Pont de l'Alma

Champ-de-Mars Tour Eiffel

Ecole-Militaire

Latour-Maubourg

Invalides

Varenne

La Fourche

Place de Clichy

Rome

Villiers

Europe

ST-LAZARE

Havre-Caumartin

Chaussée d'Antin

MADELEINE ⓮

Concorde

Tuileries

Palais Royal-Musée du Louvre

Assemblée Nationale

Musée d'Orsay

Solférino

St-Germain-des-Prés

Rue du Bac

Sèvres-Babylone

St-Sulpice

Blanche

Liège

Trinité

Auber

Opéra

Quatre Septembre

Pyramides

St-François-Xavier

Ségur

Cambronne

Sèvres-Lecourbe

Pasteur

Volontaires

Vaneau

Duroc

St-Placide

Falguière

Rennes

N. D. des Champs

MONTPARNASSE BIENVENUE

Edgar-Quinet

Gaîté

Vavin

Raspail

DENFERT-ROCHEREAU

Pernéty

Plaisance

Pte de Vanves

Mouton-Duvernet

Alésia

St-Jacques

B2 **B4**

C1 **C3**

C5
C7

RER C

RER A

RER B

River Seine

Paris Boundary

Pte de Champerret

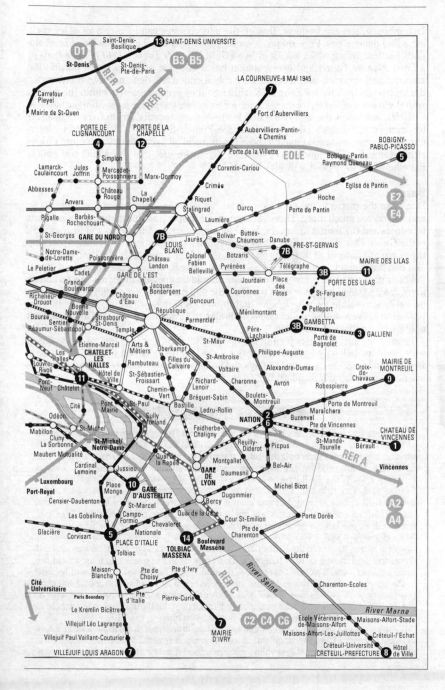

Luxembourg, etc) are frequent, though the interchanges can involve a lot of legwork, including many stairs. Free **maps** of varying sizes and detail are available at most stations (in descending scale, ask for either a *Grand Plan de Paris*, a *Petit Plan de Paris* or a *Paris Plan de Poche*) and every station has a big plan of the network outside the entrance and several inside. The lines are colour-coded and designated by numbers for the métro and by letters for the RER, although they are signposted within the system with the names of the terminus stations: for example, travelling from Montparnasse to Châtelet, you follow the sign "Direction Porte-de-Clignancourt"; from Gare d'Austerlitz to Grenelle you follow "Direction Boulogne–Pont-de-St-Cloud". The numerous interchanges (*correspondances*) make it possible to travel all over the city in a more or less straight line. For RER journeys beyond the city, make sure that the station you want is illuminated on the platform display board.

Buses

Don't use the métro to the exclusion of the city's **buses**. They are not difficult to use and you do see much more. There are free **route maps** available at métro stations, bus terminals and the tourist office; the best bus map, showing the métro and RER as well, is the *Grand Plan de Paris*. Every bus stop displays the numbers of the buses that stop there, a map showing all the stops on the route, and the times of the first and last buses. You can buy a single ticket (8F/€1.23 from the driver), or use a pre-purchased carnet ticket or pass (see box below). A red button should be pressed to request a stop and an *arrêt demandé* sign will then light up. Only the #20 bus route (see p.96) is designed to be easily accessible for wheelchairs and prams. Generally speaking, buses run from 6.30am to 8.30pm with some services continuing to 12.30am. Around half the lines don't operate on Sundays and holidays.

From mid-April to mid-September, a special **Balabus** service (not to be confused with Batobus, below) passes all the major tourist sights between Grande Arche de la Défense and Gare de Lyon, on Sundays and holidays between noon and 9pm. Bus stops are marked "Balabus". Standard bus fares apply.

TICKETS AND PASSES

For a short stay in the city, **carnets** of ten tickets can be bought from any station or *tabac* (55F/€8.34, as opposed to 8F/€1.23 for an individual ticket). The integrated system is divided into five **zones**, though the entire métro system itself fits into zones 1 and 2. The same **tickets** are valid for bus, métro and, within the city limits and immediate suburbs (zones 1 and 2), the RER express rail lines, which also extend far out into the Île de France. Only one ticket is ever needed on the métro system, and within zones 1 and 2 for any RER or bus journey, but you cannot switch between buses or between bus and métro/RER on the same ticket. Night buses require separate tickets costing 30F/€4.57 each, unless you have a weekly or monthly travel pass (see below). For RER journeys beyond zones 1 and 2 you must buy a RER ticket; visitors often get caught out, for instance, when they take the RER to La Défense instead of the métro. Children under 4 travel free and from 4 to 10 at half price. Don't buy from the touts who hang round the main stations – you'll pay well over the odds, quite often for a used ticket – and be sure to keep your ticket until the end of the journey as you'll be fined on the spot if you can't produce one. A *mobilis* **day pass** is also available (from 32F/€4.88 for the city to 70F/€10.67 to include the outer suburbs and airports), which offers unlimited access to the métro, buses and, depending on which zones you choose, the RER.

If you've arrived early in the week and are staying more than three days, it's more economical to have a **Carte Orange** with a weekly coupon (*coupon hebdomadaire*). It costs 82F/€12.50 for zones 1 and 2, is valid for an unlimited number of journeys from Monday

Night buses (*Noctambus*) run on eighteen routes every hour from 1am to 5.30am between place du Châtelet near the Hôtel de Ville and the suburbs, stopping en route. There is a reduced service on Sunday.

Taxis

If it's late at night or you feel like treating yourself, don't hesitate to use the taxis. Their **charges** are fairly reasonable: between 40F/€6.10 and 70F/€10.67 for a central daytime journey but considerably more if you call one out. Before you get into the taxi you can tell which rate is operating from the three small indicator lights on its roof: "A" (passenger side) indicates the daytime rate (7am–7pm) for Paris and the *boulevard périphérique* (around 3.45F/€0.53 per km); "B" (in the centre) is the rate for Paris at night, on Sunday and on public holidays, and for the suburbs during the day (around 5.45F/€0.83 per km); "C" (driver's side) is the night rate for the suburbs (around 7F/€1.07 per km). In addition there's a pick-up charge of around 13F/€1.98, a time charge of around 120F/€18.29 an hour for when the car is stationary, an extra charge of 5F/€0.76 if you're picked up from a mainline train station, and a 6F/€0.95 charge for each piece of luggage carried. Tipping is not mandatory, but ten percent will be expected. Taxi drivers do not have to take more than **three passengers** (they don't like people sitting in the front); if a fourth passenger is accepted, an extra charge of 9F/€1.37 will be added. Waiting at a **taxi rank** (*arrêt taxi* – there are around 470 of them) is usually more effective than hailing one from the street. The large white light signals the taxi is free; the orange light means it's in use. Phone numbers are shown at the taxi ranks, or try Taxis Bleus (☎01.49.36.10.10), Alpha Taxis (☎01.45.85.85.85) or Artaxi (☎01.42.03.50.50).

Disabled travellers

If you are handicapped, **taxis** are obliged by law to carry you and to help you into the vehicle – also to carry your guide dog if you are blind. Specially adapted taxis are available on ☎01.41.83.15.15, and for transportation to and from the airports on

---

morning to Sunday evening, and is on sale at all métro stations and *tabacs* (you'll need a passport photo). You can only buy a coupon for the current week until Wednesday; from Thursday you can buy a coupon to begin the following Monday. There is also a monthly coupon (*mensuel*) for 279F/€42.53 for zones 1 and 2. You need to write your *Carte Orange* number on the coupon.

Other possibilities are the **Paris Visites**, one-, two-, three- and five-day visitors' passes at 55F/€8.38, 90F/€13.72, 120F/€18.29 and 175F/€26.67 for Paris and close suburbs, or 110F/€16.77, 175F/€26.67, 245F/€37.35 and 300F/€45.73 to include the airports, Versailles and Disneyland Paris (make sure you buy this one when you arrive at Roissy-Charles de Gaulle or Orly to get maximum value). A half-price child's version is available for one, two and three days. You can buy them from métro and RER stations as well as tourist offices. *Paris Visites* passes can begin on any day; they also allow you discounts at certain monuments and museums. Both the *Carte Orange* and the *Paris Visites* entitle you to **unlimited travel** (in the zones you have chosen) on bus, métro, RER, SNCF and the Montmartre funicular. On the métro you put the *Carte Orange* coupon through the turnstile slot (make sure to retrieve it afterwards); on a bus you show the whole *carte* to the driver as you board – don't put it into the punching machine.

The RATP also runs numerous **excursions**, some to quite far-flung places, which are far less expensive than those offered by commercial operators. Details are available from the RATP's Bureau de Tourisme, place de la Madeleine, 1ᵉ (☎01.40.06.71.45; Mᵒ Madeleine). For 24-hour recorded **information in English** on all RATP services call ☎08.36.68.41.14 (premium rate) or visit online at *www.ratp.fr*.

Eldorado, 18 rue des Dames; ☎01.45.22.35.21, fax 01.43.87.25.97 (M° Rome/Place-de-Clichy). You can't miss the bright yellow front of this hotel, which sets the tone for the colour scheme within – sunny Mexican colours. A funky, trendy and reasonably priced place to stay. ③.

du Roi René, 72 place Félix-Lobligeois; ☎01.42.26.72.73, fax 01.42.63.74.99 (M° Rome/Villiers). Fairly average hotel in a very nice location by a mini Greek temple and public garden. ⑤.

Savoy, 21 rue des Dames; ☎01.42.93.13.47 (M° Place-de-Clichy/Rome). Typical unmodernized Paris cheapie; basic, but decent. ①.

18ᵉ hotels

André Gill, 4 rue André-Gill; ☎01.42.62.48.48, fax 01.42.62.77.92 (M° Pigalle/Abbesses). Very adequate, quiet rooms in a great location on the slopes of Montmartre, in a dead-end alley off rue des Martyrs. ③.

Burq-Bonséjour, 11 rue Burq; ☎01.42.54.22.53, fax 01.42.54.25.92 (M° Abbesses). Set in a marvellous location on a quiet untouristy street on the slopes of Montmartre, this hotel is run by friendly and conscientious owners, and the rooms, which are basic, but clean and spacious, are Montmartre's best deal. Ask for rooms 23, 33, 43 or 53, which have a balcony. ②.

du Commerce, 34 rue des Trois-Frères; ☎01.42.64.81.69 (M° Abbesses/Anvers). Very basic and cheap hotel; for the hardened traveller only. ①.

Ermitage, 24 rue Lamarck; ☎01.42.64.79.22 (M° Lamarck-Caulaincourt/Château-Rouge). Discreet hotel only a stone's throw from Sacré Coeur yet completely undisturbed by the throngs of tourists. Approach via M° Anvers and the *funiculaire* to avoid the steep climb. ⑤.

Terrass, 12 rue Joseph de Maistre; ☎01.46.06.72.85, fax 01.42.52.29.11 (M° Blanche). Located on the southwest side of the Butte, *Terrass* has magnificent views from the terrace-garden. Spacious rooms are done out with antiques and in warm colours. ⑨.

Versigny, 31 rue Letort; ☎01.42.59.20.90, fax 01.42.59.32.66 (M° Jules-Joffrin). Unmodernized and basic hotel – fine if all you want is a cheap sleep. ②.

19ᵉ hotels

Ibis Paris La Villette, 31 quai de L'Oise; ☎01.40.38.04.04, fax 01.40.38.48.90 (M° Corentin Cariou/Ourcq). Situated right on the canal facing the Parc de la Villette, this good-value modern chain hotel is a great spot to stay if you want to spend a few days exploring the park or attending concerts at the Cité de la Musique. It is also a wise choice for people with their own cars, easily reached from the *boulevard périphérique* exiting at the Porte de la Villette, with free parking included. ③.

Rhin et Danube, 3 place Rhin-et-Danube; ☎01.42.45.10.13, fax 01.42.06.88.82 (M° Danube). Good-value hotel, away from the centre on the airy heights of Belleville; geared to self-catering. ④.

20ᵉ hotels

Ermitage, 42bis rue de l'Ermitage; ☎01.46.36.23.44, fax 01.46.36.23.44 (M° Jourdain). A clean and decent budget hotel, close to the leafy rue des Pyrénées with its provincial feel. ②.

Pyrénées-Gambetta, 12 av du Père-Lachaise; ☎01.47.97.76.57, fax 01.47.97.17.61 (M° Gambetta). Very pleasant hotel, perfect for visiting the Père-Lachaise cemetery. All rooms have cable TV. ④.

Tamaris, 14 rue des Maraîchers; ☎01.43.72.85.48, fax 01.43.56.81.75 (M° Porte-de-Vincennes). Simple, clean and attractive hotel, run by pleasant people. Extremely good value. Close to métro and the terminus of #26 bus route from Gare du Nord. ②.

Hostels, student accommodation and campsites

There are numerous places in Paris offering **hostel** accommodation. The cheapest hostels are those run by the **Fédération Unie des Auberges de Jeunesse** (FUAJ; *www.fuaj.fr*), for which you need Hostelling International (HI) membership (no age limit), and those connected with the **MIJE** (Maison Internationale de la Jeunesse et des Étudiants) and **UCRIF** (Union des Centres de Rencontres Internationaux de France). There is also a handful of privately run hostels.

Current costs for dorm bed and breakfast are: HI hostels from 120F/€18.29, MIJE hostels from 140F/€21.34 and UCRIF hostels 120–130F/€18.29–19.82. Single and double rooms are more expensive. There is no age limit and reservations are not always possible. MIJE hostels, mostly centrally situated in historic buildings, have a seven-day stay limit; for the other hostels it varies but is normally less. Bear in mind, too, that some places have a curfew – usually around 11pm – though you may be able to borrow a key. We've detailed only the most central of the UCRIF hostels: for a full list contact their main office at 27 rue de Turbigo, 2ᵉ (Mon–Fri 10am–6pm; ☎01.40.26.57.64, fax 01.40.26.58.20, *www.ucrif.asso.fr*; Mᵒ Étienne-Marcel). Independent hostels are even cheaper: around 90F/€13.72 for a dorm room off-season, rising to about 120F/€18.29 in summer.

Student accommodation is let out during vacation time. Rooms are spartan, part of large modern university complexes, often complete with self-service kitchen facilities and shared bathrooms. Space tends to fill up quickly with international students, school groups and young travellers, so it's best to make plans well in advance. Expect to pay 100–200F/€15.24–30.49 per night for a single and 80–150F/€12.20–22.87 per person for a double. The organization to contact for information and reservations is CROUS, Académie de Paris, 39 av Georges-Bernanos, 5ᵉ; ☎01.40.51.36.00, *www .crous-paris.fr* (Mᵒ Port-Royal).

The cheapest option is camping, with three **campsites** on the outskirts of Paris. Although pleasant enough, the campsites are a bit of a pain to get to on public transport.

Hostels

D'Artagnan, 80 rue Vitruve, 20ᵉ; ☎01.40.32.34.56, fax 01.42.32.34.55 (Mᵒ Porte-de-Bagnolet). Colourful funky modern HI hostel, with a fun atmosphere and lots of facilities including a small cinema, restaurant and bar, and a local swimming pool nearby. Located on the eastern edge of the city near the village-like Charonne, which has some good bars, close to the Père-Lachaise cemetery. Very popular so try to get here early – reservations by fax or from other HI hostels only.

Auberge International des Jeunes Ste-Marguerite, 10 rue Trousseau, 11ᵉ; ☎01.47.00.62.00, fax 01.47.00.33.16, *www.aij.com* (Mᵒ Bastille/Ledru-Rollin). Despite the official-sounding name, a laid-back (but very noisy) independent hostel in a great location five minutes' walk from the Bastille. Clean and professionally run with 24hr reception, generous breakfast and free luggage storage.

Centre International de Paris/Louvre, 20 rue Jean-Jacques-Rousseau, 1ᵉʳ; ☎01.53.00.90.90, fax 01.53.00.90.91, *www.ucrif.asso.fr* (Mᵒ Louvre/Châtelet-Les Halles; see map, pp.112–113). Clean, modern and efficiently run UCRIF hostel. Bookings can be made up to ten days prior to your stay.

Le Fauconnier, 11 rue du Fauconnier, 4ᵉ; ☎01.42.74.23.45, fax 01.40.27.81.64 (Mᵒ St-Paul/Pont-Marie). MIJE hostel in a superbly renovated seventeenth-century building with a courtyard. Dorms sleep four to eight. Breakfast included.

Le Fourcy, 6 rue de Fourcy, 4ᵉ; ☎01.42.74.23.45 (Mᵒ St-Paul). Another MIJE hostel housed in a beautiful mansion, this one has a small garden and a restaurant with menus from 52F/€7.93. Dorms only, sleeping 4–8.

Foyer International d'Accueil de Paris Jean Monnet, 30 rue Cabanis, 14ᵉ; ☎01.45.89.89.15, fax 01.45.81.63.91 (Mᵒ Glacière). A huge, efficiently run UCRIF hostel in a fairly sedate area. Facilities include meeting rooms and a disco; ideal for groups.

Jules Ferry, 8 bd Jules-Ferry, 11ᵉ; ☎01.43.57.55.60, fax 01.40.21.79.92 (Mᵒ République). Smaller and more central HI hostel than *D'Artagnan*, in a lively area at the foot of the Belleville hill. Very difficult to get a place, but when full they will help you find a bed elsewhere.

Maison Internationale des Jeunes, 4 rue Titon, 11ᵉ; ☎01.43.71.99.21, fax 01.43.71.78.58 (Mᵒ Faidherbe-Chaligny). For 18- to 30-year-olds. Clean, well-run establishment located between Bastille and Nation. Doors close at 2am with lockout from 10am to 5pm. Dorms only, sleeping four.

Maubuisson, 12 rue des Barres, 4ᵉ; ☎01.42.74.23.45 (Mᵒ Pont-Marie/Hôtel-de-Ville). MIJE hostel in a magnificent medieval building on a quiet street. Restaurant has menus from 32F/€4.88. Dorms only, sleeping four. Breakfast included.

Three Ducks Hostel, 6 place Étienne-Pernet, 15ᵉ; ☎01.48.42.04.05, fax 01.48.42.99.99, *www .3ducks.fr* (Mº Commerce/Félix-Faure). A private youth hostel with no age limit; kitchen facilities as well as a bar with the cheapest beer in town. Essential to book ahead between May and Oct: send the price of the first night or leave a credit card number. Lockout 11am–5pm, curfew at 2am.

Woodstock Hostel, 48 rue Rodier, 9ᵉ; ☎01.48.78.87.76, *www.woodstock.fr* (Mº Anvers/St-Georges). Another hostel in the *Three Ducks* stable, with its own bar, and set in a great location on a pretty, untouristy street near Montmartre. Price includes breakfast.

Young and Happy Hostel, 80 rue Mouffetard, 5ᵉ; ☎01.45.35.09.53, fax 01.47.07.22.24 (Mº Monge/Censier-Daubenton). Noisy, basic and studenty independent hostel in a lively, if a tad touristy, position. Dorms, with shower, sleep four to eight and there are a few doubles (137F/€20.88 per person). You can book in advance but you have to turn up early, between 8am and 11am to keep the room.

Campsites

Camping du Bois de Boulogne, Allée du Bord-de-l'Eau, 16ᵉ; ☎01.45.24.30.00, fax 01.42.24.42.95 (Mº Porte-Maillot then bus #244 to Route des Moulins – bus runs 6am–8.30pm). Much the most central campsite, next to the River Seine in the Bois de Boulogne, and usually booked out in summer. The ground is pebbly, but the site is well equipped and has a useful information office. Costs 90F/€13.72 for a tent with two people; and there are also bungalows from 399F/€60.83 per night. A shuttle bus runs between the campsite and Mº Porte-Maillot April–Oct from 8.30am to 1am.

Camping du Parc de la Colline, Route de Lagny, 77200 Torcy; ☎01.60.05.42.32 (RER line A4 to Torcy, then phone from the station and they will come and collect you or take bus #421 to stop Le Clos). Pleasant wooded site to the east of the city near Disneyland, offering the whole gamut of camping possibilities: fully equipped mobile homes (300F/€45.73 per night for two), pre-erected tents complete with beds and fridge, and of course, space to erect your own tent (122F/€18.60 per night for two people and a tent).

Camping du Parc-Étang, Base de Loisirs, 78180 Montigny-le-Bretonneux; ☎01.30.58.56.20 (RER line C St-Quentin-en-Yvelines; métro connections for RER line C at Invalides/St-Michel/Gare-d'Austerlitz). Adequately equipped large campsite in a leisure complex southwest of Paris. Costs 81F/€12.35 for two people and a tent.

The City

Paris is an extremely compact city of twenty **arrondissements** that are strictly confined within the 78-square-kilometre limits of its ring road, the **boulevard périphérique**, built over the nineteenth-century city defences. The **Seine** flows in an arc through the middle from east to west, around its two islands, the **Île de la Cité** – where Notre-Dame sits at the historic heart of the capital – and the **Île St-Louis**. In the centre, north of the river on the **Right Bank**, or *rive droite,* is the Louvre; the banking, media and commercial quarter contained within the *grands boulevards*; **Les Halles**, the nightlife and daytime shopping quarter around the site of the city's former main food market (now the Forum des Halles); the aristocratic **Marais**; and, further to the east, the trendy **Bastille** quarter. South of the islands on the **Left Bank**, or *rive gauche*, is the **quartier Latin**, so called because it was the language of the university founded here in the thirteenth century; and **quartier St-Germain-des-Prés**, which evolved around an abbey, established on the site of a church of the same name in the sixth century.

West of St-Germain is the **7ᵉ**, with the **Eiffel Tower**, Invalides, the parliament and embassies. Across the river the **8ᵉ** has the **Champs-Élysées**, **Arc de Triomphe** and the most expensive shops. The outer *arrondissements*, continuing the clockwise spiral centred on the Île de la Cité, were mostly incorporated into the city in the nineteenth century. Generally speaking, those to the east accommodated the poor and working class, while those to the west were, and still are, the addresses for the aristocracy and new rich.

There are any number of **ways of exploring Paris** – you certainly don't have to start with the Louvre or Notre-Dame. Our account is structured in chunks of territory that share a common identity even though they do not always correspond exactly with the boundaries of the twenty *arrondissements*. We start with the Île de la Cité, then move to the Right Bank and the Voie Triomphale, the city's greatest vista. This leads from the Louvre right out to the northwest perimeter, from where we move east to the Marais and the Bastille. We continue with the inner *arrondissements* on the Left Bank, followed by the southern *arrondissements*, the rich Beaux Quartiers to the west, and beyond them, outside the city, the modern business district of La Défense, then Montmartre and the northern *arrondissements* and, finally, the east of the city, from the old villages of Belleville and Ménilmontant, including the Père-Lachaise cemetery, out to Vincennes.

Île de la Cité

The **Île de la Cité** is where Paris began. The earliest settlements were built here, as was the small Gallic town of Lutetia, overrun by Julius Cæsar's troops in 52 BC. A natural defensive site commanding a major east–west river trade route, it was an obvious candidate for a bright future. The Romans garrisoned it and laid out one of their standard military town plans, overlapping onto the Left Bank. While the Romans never attached any great political importance to it, they endowed it with an administrative centre that became the palace of the Merovingian kings in 508, then of the counts of Paris, who in 987 became kings of France.

Today the lure of the island lies in its tail-end **square du Vert-Galant** and, at the opposite end, the **Cathédrale de Notre-Dame**. The central section has been dulled by heavy-handed nineteenth-century demolition that displaced 25,000 people and replaced them by four vast edifices largely given over to housing the law. The space in front of the cathedral was a by-product, allowing a full-frontal view.

Pont-Neuf and the quais, Ste-Chapelle and the Conciergerie

Arriving on the island by the **Pont-Neuf**, the city's oldest bridge, you will find steps behind the **statue of Henri IV** (who commissioned the bridge) leading down to the **quais** and the **square du Vert-Galant**, a small tree-lined green enclosed within the triangular stern of the island. The prime spot to occupy is the sunny knoll dotted with trees at the extreme point of the island – haunt of lovers, sparrows and sunbathers.

In the opposite direction to the square du Vert-Galant, seventeenth-century houses flank the entrance to the sanded, chestnut-shaded **place Dauphine**, one of the city's most secluded and exclusive squares. The further end is blocked by the dull mass of the **Palais de Justice**, which swallowed up the palace that was home to the French kings until Étienne Marcel's bloody revolt in 1358 frightened them off to the greater security of the Louvre.

The only part of the older complex that remains in its entirety is Louis IX's **Ste-Chapelle** (daily: April–Sept 9.30am–6.30pm; Oct–March 10am–5pm; 32F/€4.88, combined admission to the Conciergerie 50F/€7.62; M° Cité), built to house a collection of holy relics he had bought at extortionate rates from the bankrupt empire of Byzantium. Though much restored, the chapel remains one of the finest achievements of French High Gothic (consecrated in 1248). Very tall in relation to its length, it looks like a cathedral choir lopped off and transformed into an independent building. Its most radical feature is its fragility – created by reducing the structural masonry to a minimum to make way for a huge expanse of exquisite glass in the upper chapel, which is reached via a spiral staircase. The impression inside is of being enclosed within the wings of myriad brilliant butterflies – one of the more beautiful sights in the city.

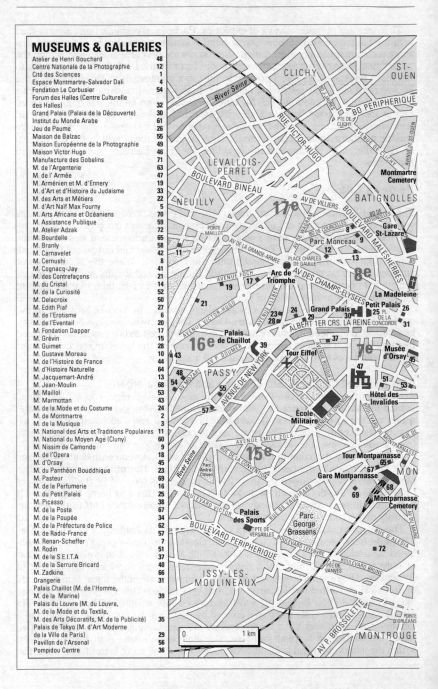

MUSEUMS & GALLERIES

Atelier de Henri Bouchard	48
Centre Nationale de la Photographie	12
Cité des Sciences	1
Espace Montmartre-Salvador Dali	4
Fondation Le Corbusier	54
Forum des Halles (Centre Culturelle des Halles)	32
Grand Palais (Palais de la Découverte)	30
Institut du Monde Arabe	61
Jeu de Paume	26
Maison de Balzac	55
Maison Européenne de la Photographie	49
Maison Victor Hugo	46
Manufacture des Gobelins	71
M. de l'Argenterie	63
M. de l' Armée	47
M. Arménien et M. d'Ennery	19
M. d'Art et d'Histoire du Judaisme	33
M. des Arts et Métiers	22
M. d'Art Naïf Max Fourny	5
M. Arts Africans et Océaniens	70
M. Assistance Publique	59
M. Atelier Adzak	72
M. Bourdelle	65
M. Branly	58
M. Carnavalet	42
M. Cernushi	8
M. Cognacq-Jay	41
M. des Contrefaçons	21
M. du Cristal	14
M. de la Curiosité	52
M. Delacroix	50
M. Edith Piaf	27
M. de l'Erotisme	6
M. de l'Eventail	20
M. Fondation Dapper	17
M. Grévin	15
M. Guimet	28
M. Gustave Moreau	10
M. de l'Histoire de France	44
M. d'Histoire Naturelle	64
M. Jacquemart-André	13
M. Jean-Moulin	68
M. Maillol	53
M. Marmottan	43
M. de la Mode et du Costume	24
M. de Montmartre	2
M. de la Musique	3
M. National des Arts et Traditions Populaires	11
M. National du Moyen Age (Cluny)	60
M. Nissim de Camondo	9
M. de l'Opera	18
M. d'Orsay	45
M. du Panthéon Bouddhique	23
M. Pasteur	69
M. de la Perfumerie	16
M. du Petit Palais	25
M. Picasso	38
M. de la Poste	67
M. de la Poupée	34
M. de la Préfecture de Police	62
M. de Radio-France	57
M. Renan-Scheffer	7
M. Rodin	51
M. de la S.E.I.T.A	37
M. de la Serrure Bricard	40
M. Zadkine	66
Orangerie	31
Palais Chaillot (M. de l'Homme, M. de la Marine)	39
Palais du Louvre (M. du Louvre, M. de la Mode et du Textile, M. des Arts Décoratifs, M. de la Publicité)	35
Palais de Tokyo (M. d'Art Moderne de la Ville de Paris)	29
Pavillon de l'Arsenal	56
Pompidou Centre	36

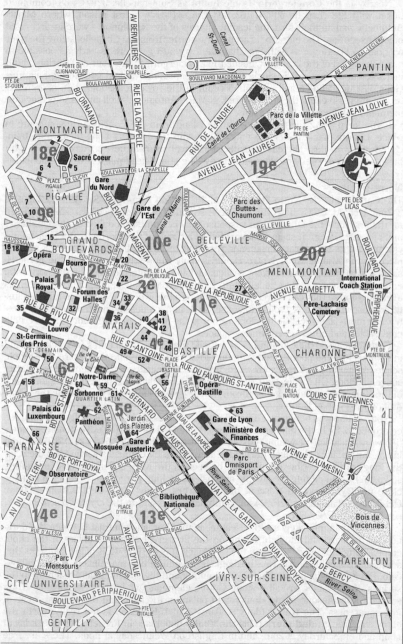

Nearby is the **Conciergerie** (same hours as Ste-Chapelle; 32F/€4.88, combined ticket with Ste-Chapelle 50F/€7.62; M° Cité), Paris's oldest prison, where Marie-Antoinette and, in their turn, the leading figures of the Revolution – were incarcerated before execution. The entrance is around the corner from Ste-Chapelle, facing the river on quai de l'Horloge; as with Ste-Chapelle it pays to get here as early as possible to avoid the worst of the crowds. Outside the Conciergerie is the Tour de l'Horloge, built in 1370, Paris's first public clock. Inside, the enormous vaulted late Gothic Salle des Gens d'Arme, canteen and recreation room of the royal household staff, is architecturally impressive, but the chief interest is Marie-Antoinette's cell and various macabre mementos of the guillotine's victims.

If you keep along the north side of the island from the Conciergerie you come to **place Lépine**, named after the police boss who gave Paris's cops their white truncheons and whistles. There is an exuberant **flower market** here six days a week, with birds and pets – cruelly caged – on Sunday. The police headquarters is right behind.

Notre-Dame

The **Cathédrale de Notre-Dame** (Mon–Fri & Sun 8am–7pm, Sat 8am–12.30pm & 2–7pm; free; M° St-Michel/Cité) has been so much photographed that, seeing it even for the first time, the edge of your response may be somewhat dulled by the familiarity of its form, although it seems rejuvenated as a result of the thorough and painstaking cleaning of the exterior undertaken in recent years. Described as the greatest masterpiece of the Middle Ages, Notre Dame is truly impressive, especially the great H-shaped west front, with its strong vertical divisions counterbalanced by the horizontal emphasis of gallery and frieze, all centred on a rose window. It demands to be seen as a whole, though that can scarcely have been possible when the medieval houses clustered close about it. It is a solid, no-nonsense design, confessing its Romanesque ancestry. For more fantastical Gothic, look rather at the north transept facade with its crocketed gables and huge fretted window space.

Getting in to see the cathedral is easier said than done for at times (at weekends and in summer) it is so popular that there are long queues out onto the square. The whole scene can get uncomfortably crowded, and the immediate area is crammed with tacky souvenir shops. On the fun side, there is always a bunch of spectators jostling for a view of the young rollerbladers going through their gymnastic stunts just outside the cathedral on the Pont au Double.

Notre-Dame was begun in 1160 under the auspices of Bishop de Sully and completed around 1345. In the nineteenth century, Viollet-le-Duc carried out extensive renovation work, including remaking most of the statuary – the entire frieze of Old Testament kings, for instance, damaged during the Revolution by enthusiasts who took them for the kings of France (the originals can be seen in the Musée National du Moyen-Age, see p.132) – and adding the steeple and baleful-looking gargoyles, which you can see close up if you brave the ascent of the **towers** (daily: April–Sept 9.30am–7.30pm; Oct–March 10am–5pm; 32F/€4.88, combined admission to the *crypte archéologique* – see below – 50F/€7.62).

Inside, the immediately striking feature is the dramatic contrast between the darkness of the nave and the light falling on the first great clustered pillars of the choir, emphasizing the special nature of the sanctuary. It is the end walls of the transepts that admit all this light, nearly two-thirds glass, including two magnificent rose windows coloured in imperial purple. These, the vaulting and the soaring shafts reaching to the springs of the vaults, are all definite Gothic elements, while there remains a strong sense of Romanesque in the stout round pillars of the nave and the general sense of four-squareness. The **trésor** (daily 9.30am–6pm; 15F/€2.29) is not really worth the entry fee. Free **guided tours** (1hr–1hr 30min) take place in French every weekday at noon and on Saturday at 2pm, and in English on Wednesday at noon. There are free organ **concerts** every Sunday at 5pm or 5.30pm, plus four **Masses** on Sunday morning and one at 6.30pm.

On the pavement by the west door of the cathedral is a spot known as **kilomètre zéro**, the symbolic heart of the country, from which all main road distances in France are calculated.

Before you leave, it's worth walking round to the public garden at the east end of the cathedral for a view of the flying buttresses supporting the choir, and then along the riverside under the south transept, where you can sit in springtime with the cherry blossoms drifting down. Out in front of the cathedral, in the plaza separating it from Haussmann's police HQ, is the entrance to the **crypte archéologique** (daily: April–Sept 10am–6pm; Oct–March 10am–4.30pm; 32F/€4.88, combined entry with the towers 50F/€7.62), an interesting museum containing the remains of the original cathedral, as well as streets and houses of the Cité as far back as the Roman era.

Le Mémorial de la Déportation

At the eastern tip of the island is the symbolic tomb of the 200,000 French who died in Nazi concentration camps during World War II – Resistance fighters, Jews and forced labourers among them. The **Mémorial de la Déportation** is scarcely visible above ground; stairs hardly shoulder-wide descend into a space like a prison yard and then into the stifling crypt (gates to crypt open daily 10am–noon & 2–5pm; free), where thousands of points of light represent the dead. Floor and ceiling are black, and it ends in a black, raw hole, with a single naked bulb hanging in the middle. On either side are empty barred cells. Above the exit are the words "Forgive. Do not forget." In contrast, the little green park surrounding the memorial is more of a celebration of life and a popular hang-out on a fine evening.

The Voie Triomphale

The **Voie Triomphale**, or Triumphal Way, stretches in a dead straight line from the **Louvre** palace to the modern complex of corporate skyscrapers at La Défense, 9km away. Incorporating some of the city's most famous landmarks – the **Tuileries** gardens, **Champs-Élysées** avenue and the **Arc de Triomphe** – its monumental constructions have been erected over the centuries by kings and emperors, presidents and corporations, to promulgate French power and prestige.

The tradition dies hard. Further self-aggrandizement has been given expression in an enormous, marble-clad cubic arch at the head of La Défense, and in the glass pyramid entrance to the much-expanded Louvre.

The Arc de Triomphe and Champs-Élysées

The best view of the Voie Triomphale's grandiose but simple geometry is from the top of the **Arc de Triomphe**, Napoléon's homage to the armies of France and himself (daily: April–Sept 9.30am–11pm; Oct–March 10am–10.30pm; 40F/€6.10; M° Charles-de-Gaulle-Étoile; access from stairs on north corner of av des Champs-Élysées). Your attention, however, is most likely to be caught not by the view but by the mesmerizing traffic directly below you, around the massive **place Charles-de-Gaulle** (still better known as place de l'Étoile) – the world's first organized roundabout. Twelve wide avenues make up the star (*étoile*), of which the busiest is the **Champs-Élysées**. At Christmas the Champs-Élysées is draped in fairy lights, and on December 31 cars converge here to hoot in the New Year. Bastille Day's procession of president, tanks and guns is less appealing. The avenue's pavements have recently been widened and new trees planted, but there are still too many airline offices, car showrooms, fast-food outlets and over-bright shopping arcades to recuperate the old glamour represented by the

ACCOMMODATION

d'Artois	3
Brighton	6
Le Bristol	2
Centre International de Paris/Louvre	7
des Champs-Élysées	4
Costes	5
de l'Élysée	1

RESTAURANTS

aux Amis du Beaujolais	A
Le Dauphin	D
Dragons Élysées	E
Foujita	C
L'Incroyable	B
Yvan	F

Lido cabaret, *Fouquet's* bar and restaurant, the perfumier Guerlain's shop and the former *Claridges* hotel.

On the north side of the Champs-Élysées is the **Musée Jacquemart-André**, 158 bd Haussmann, 8ᵉ (daily 10am–6pm; 49F/€7.47; Mᵒ Miromesnil/St-Philippe-du-Roule), which features a collection of Rembrandts and works by Botticelli, Titian, Tintoretto, Tiepolo and Donatello. A short way west in the magnificent Hôtel Salomon de Rothschild, 11 rue Berryer, 8ᵉ (Mᵒ George-V), the **Centre National de la Photographie** hosts important temporary exhibitions of photography (daily except Tues noon–7pm; 30F/€4.57).

The stretch of the Champs-Élysées between the Rond-Point des Champs-Élysées, whose Lalique glass fountains disappeared during the German occupation, and place de la Concorde is bordered by chestnut trees and municipal flower beds, pleasant

LA VOIE TRIOMPHALE

enough to stroll among but not sufficiently dense to muffle the squeal of accelerating tyres. The gigantic building with overloaded Neoclassical exteriors, glass roofs and exuberant flying statuary rising above the greenery to the south is the **Grand Palais**, created with its neighbour, the **Petit Palais**, for the 1900 Exposition Universelle. Major temporary art exhibitions are held in the Grand Palais, and one wing is given over to the **Palais de la Découverte**, av Franklin-D.-Roosevelt, 8ᵉ (Tues–Sat 9.30am–6pm, Sun & hols 10am–7pm; 30F/€4.57, combined ticket with planetarium 45F/€6.86; Mᵒ Champs-Élysées-Clemenceau/Franklin-D.-Roosevelt), a science museum with plenty of interactive exhibits, some very good temporary exhibitions and an excellent planetarium. The Petit Palais houses the **Musée des Beaux-Arts** (currently closed for renovation; due to reopen in 2003), which offers the odd Impressionist gem, lots of Art Nouveau furniture and jewellery, and vast canvases recording Paris street battles during the 1830 and 1848 revolutions. At the Seine end of avenue Winston-Churchill, the road running between the Grand Palais and the Petit Palais, the English World War II leader himself is honoured by a statue. Georges Clemenceau, French Prime Minister at the end of World War I, is commemorated by a statue at the other end of the avenue, in place Clemenceau.

On the north side of place Clemenceau, combat police guard the high walls round the presidential **Palais de l'Élysée** and the line of ministries and embassies ending with the US in prime position on the corner of place de la Concorde. On Thursdays and at weekends you can see a different manifestation of the self-images of states in the **postage-stamp market** at the corner of avenues Gabriel and Marigny.

Place de la Concorde and the Tuileries

At the bottom of the Champs-Élysées is the **place de la Concorde**, where more crazed traffic makes crossing over to the middle a death-defying task. As it happens, some 1300 people did die here between 1793 and 1795, beneath the Revolutionary guillotine – Louis XVI, Marie-Antoinette, Danton and Robespierre among them. The centrepiece of the square is an **obelisk** from the temple of Luxor, offered as a favour-currying gesture by the viceroy of Egypt in 1829. It serves merely to pivot more geometry: the alignment of the French parliament, the Assemblée Nationale, on the far side of the Seine, with the church of the Madeleine to the north (see p.119).

The symmetry continues beyond place de la Concorde in the formal layout of the **Tuileries gardens**, disrupted only by the bodies lounging on the grass, kids chasing their boats round the ponds, and gay men cruising the terrace overlooking the river. A major project of replanting and tree surgery, recasting statues and re-landscaping took place between 1991 and 1997 as part of the Grand Louvre Project, and the revamped Tuileries (with 3000 new trees) adds new perspectives to the Louvre whilst retaining features from Le Nôtre's original garden. Unfortunately, the December 1999 storms that ravaged northern France stripped the Tuileries of some of its older specimens.

The two buildings flanking the garden at the Concorde end are the Orangerie, by the river, and the **Jeu de Paume**, by rue de Rivoli (Tues noon–9.30pm, Wed–Fri noon–7pm, Sat & Sun 10am–7pm; 38F/€5.79; M° Concorde), an ex-royal tennis court and ex-Impressionists museum, which has had huge windows cut into its classical temple walls to light what is the city's best exhibition space for contemporary art.

The **Orangerie**, a private art collection inherited by the state with the stipulation that it should always stay together, has also been affected by the Grand Louvre project. The plan was to enlarge, restructure and convert many of the existing exterior walls to glass, in line with Monet's request that as much natural light as possible reach his masterpieces, and the museum is due to reopen at the end of 2001. After all the upheaval the Orangerie's centrepiece, comprising two oval rooms arranged by Monet as panoramas for his largest waterlily paintings, will be rearranged according to Monet's original stipulations. The rest of the collection, containing works by artists such as Renoir, Sisley, Matisse, Cézanne, Utrillo, Modigliani and Soutine, will be rearranged and possibly added to from the collection's reserves.

The new pedestrian **Solférino bridge**, which links the quai des Tuileries to the Musée d'Orsay, was unveiled at the end of 1999. Despite its award-winning design, suspicious vibrations and a wooden floor that slipped underfoot when wet forced it to close a week after opening; it was reopened only towards the end of 2000.

The Louvre

Paris's largest monument, at the start of the Voie Triomphale, is the palace of the **Louvre** – for centuries the site of the French court, and renowned today as one of the world's greatest art galleries. It was begun by Philippe-Auguste in 1200 as a fortress to

THE MUSEUM PASS AND REDUCTIONS

If you're planning to visit a great many museums in a short time, it is worth buying the **Carte Musées et Monuments pass** (80F/€12.20 one-day, 160F/€24.40 three-day, 240F/€36.59 five-day), available from the tourist office, RER/métro stations and museums, and valid for seventy museums and monuments in and around Paris, and allowing you to bypass ticket queues (though not the time-sucking security checkpoints or entry to special exhibitions). Many museums offer **reductions** on admission fees to certain age groups and students: the latter should show an ISIC or Youth Card (though students obviously over 25 may be refused), while under-25s and under-18s will need to show their passports; cheaper admission for over-60s has been cut back at many places, but come armed with your passport just in case. Under-12s are usually free. Some museums have free or half-price admission on Sunday; many are closed on Monday and Tuesday.

store his scrolls, jewels and swords while he himself lived on the Île de la Cité. Charles V was the first French king to make the castle his residence, but not until François I in the mid-sixteenth century were the beginnings of the palace laid and the fortress demolished. From then on, almost every sovereign added to it, with Catherine de Médicis, Henri II's widow, contributing the Palais des Tuileries extension, burnt to the ground during the Paris Commune (1871), across which is now the underpass avenue du Gal-Lemonnier. The whole lot was nearly demolished by both Louis XIV and Louis XV but the Louvre survived to be given further additions by Napoléons I and III, and finally by Mitterrand in the 1980s. It was during the French Revolution that the palace was first opened to the public to display the former kings' art treasures, a collection greatly expanded by Napoléon I's requisitions in his foreign campaigns.

Every alteration and addition up to 1988 created a surprisingly homogeneous building, with a grandeur, symmetry, and Frenchness entirely suited to this most historic of Parisian edifices. Then came the **Pyramide**, bang in the centre of the Cour Napoléon. It was an extraordinary leap of daring and imagination. Conceived by the Chinese-born architect Ieoh Ming Pei, it has no connection to its surroundings, save as a symbol of symmetry. Mitterrand also managed to persuade the Finance Ministry to move out of the northern Richelieu wing, which now, with its two courtyards roofed over in glass, houses the French sculpture and the Objets d'Art collections of the museum. A public passageway, the **passage Richelieu**, linking the Cour Napoléon with rue de Rivoli, allows you to look down into these courtyards – a better view of the Chevaux de Marly (which once graced place de la Concorde) and Puget's monumental sculptures than you get from within the museum.

Mitterrand's project also dramatically extended the Louvre underground, with the **Hall Napoléon** beneath the Pyramide leading into a series of galleries known as the **Carrousel du Louvre**. Very smart shops, cheap and expensive restaurants, exhibition and conference areas fill the vast spaces, and an inverted glass pyramid lets in light from place du Carrousel.

Napoléon's pink marble **Arc du Carrousel**, just east of place du Carrousel, which originally formed a gateway for the former Tuileries Palace, has always looked a bit out of place (though it sits precisely on the Voie Triomphale axis); now it is definitively and forlornly upstaged by the Pyramide.

Access and opening hours

The Pyramide is the **main entrance** to the Musée du Louvre, although alternative access directly from the métro, the Porte des Lions, the Arc du Carrousel or from rue de Rivoli via passage Richelieu allows you to avoid the queue here. **Tickets** can be bought in the Hall Napoléon, below the Pyramide, and at the Porte des Lions entrance.

The *Café Marly*, overlooking the Pyramide from the north wing, is the classiest place to eat and drink here.

Lifts and escalators lead from the Hall Napoléon beneath the Pyramide into the three wings of the **Musée du Louvre**. The permanent collection is open on Monday and Wednesday to Sunday from 9am to 6pm, staying open until 9.45pm on Monday (selected rooms only) and Wednesdays. Everything is closed on Tuesday. The usual entry charge is 46F/€7.01 but after 3pm and on Sunday this is reduced to 30F/€4.57. Under-18s get in free at all times, and on the first Sunday of each month admission is free for everyone else, unless it's a public holiday. Tickets can be bought in advance (advisable because of the queues in the Hall Napoléon for the ticket office) by telephoning ☎08.03.80.88.03; from branches of FNAC (see p.189); or over the Internet at *www .louvre.fr*. Each of the three wings – Sully, around the Cour Carrée; Denon, the southern wing; and Richelieu, to the north – has four floors: the *entresol* (the level reached from the escalators in the Hall Napoléon), the *rez-de-chaussée* (ground floor), then the first and second floors. These are then divided into numbered rooms and colour-coded for the main categories of the collection (see below). At first overwhelming and seemingly nonsensical, the layout of the museum is a delight to discover and following the collections through their arrangements is absorbing and rewarding. The indispensable floor-plan, available from the information desk in the Hall Napoléon, highlights some of the more famous masterpieces, such as the *Mona Lisa*, for those wishing to do a whistle-stop tour, although don't expect to be able to contemplate them peacefully without being jostled by other visitors wishing to take a look. Your ticket allows you to leave and re-enter as many times as you like throughout the day, handy if the crowds get too much and you can't take anything else in.

As well as the Musée du Louvre, the Louvre palace houses three other museums in its northern wing dedicated to fashion and textiles, decorative arts and the art of advertising. The entrance to the **Musée de la Mode et du Textile**, the **Musée des Arts Décoratifs** and the **Musée de la Publicité** can be found at 107 rue de Rivoli, where a combined ticket for all three museums can be purchased (see below for details).

The Musée du Louvre

The **collections** housed in the Musée du Louvre are divided into **seven basic categories**: Oriental antiquities; Egyptian antiquities; Greek, Etruscan and Roman antiquities; Sculpture; Objets d'Art; Painting; and Prints and Drawings. Each category spreads over more than one wing and several floors. An added bonus from all the building works was the opportunity to excavate the remains of the **medieval Louvre** – Philippe-Auguste's twelfth-century fortress and Charles V's fourteenth-century palace conversion – under the Cour Carrée. The foundations and archeological findings are now on show along with a permanent exhibition on the **history of the Louvre**, from the Middle Ages up to the current transformations. The medieval Louvre is all in the *entresol* floor in the Sully wing, and easy to find. A new, probably temporary, eighth category, which contains 120 works of art from **Africa, Asia, Oceania and the Americas** (pavillon des Sessions, nearest entrance Porte des Lions), was opened in 2000 in an attempt to give due respect to an area of art long excluded from the ranks of high art. Whether they will join their compatriots in a new museum at quai Branly (see p.138) is yet to be decided – as is the name of the new museum – but they are being showcased in the Louvre at least until the new museum opens (scheduled for 2004).

Oriental Antiquities – including the newly presented Islamic Art collection – covers the Mesopotamian, Sumerian, Babylonian, Assyrian and Phoenician civilizations, plus the art of ancient Persia. **Egyptian Antiquities** contains jewellery, domestic objects, sandals, sarcophagi and dozens of examples of the delicate naturalism of Egyptian decorative technique, such as the wall tiles depicting a piebald calf galloping through fields of papyrus, and a duck taking off from a marsh. Among the major exhibits are the pink granite *Mastaba Sphinx* (Sully, ground floor, room 1), the *Kneeling Scribe* statue (Sully, first floor, room 22), a wooden statue of Chancellor Nakhti, a bust of Amenophis IV and a low-relief sculpture of Sethi I and the goddess Hathor. The **Greek and Roman Antiquities** include the *Winged Victory of Samothrace* (Denon, first floor, at the top of the great staircase) and the *Venus de Milo* (Sully, ground floor, room 12), the biggest crowd-pullers in the museum after the *Mona Lisa*. *Venus*, striking a classic model's pose, dates from the late second century BC. Her antecedents are all on display, too, from the graceful marble head of the *Cycladic Idol* and the delightful *Dame d'Auxerre* (seventh century BC) to the classical perfection of the *Athlete of Benevento*. In the Roman section are some very attractive mosaics from Asia Minor and luminous frescoes from Pompeii and Herculaneum, which already seem to foreshadow the decorative lightness of touch of a Botticelli, still a thousand years and more away.

The **Sculpture section** covers the entire development of the art in France from Romanesque to Rodin, all in the new Richelieu wing, and Italian and northern European sculpture in Denon, including Michelangelo's *Slaves* (ground floor, room 4), designed for the tomb of Pope Julius II. The huge glass-covered courtyards of the Richelieu wing – the Cour Marly with the Marly Horses which once graced place de la Concorde, and the Cour Puget with Puget's *Milon de Crotone* as the centrepiece – are very impressive, if a bit overwhelming.

The **Objets d'Art** collection is heavily weighted on the side of imperial opulence, with finely crafted tapestries, ceramics, jewellery and furniture executed to impress and suit royal tastes of the day. The exception is the Middle Ages section, of a more pious nature, which includes carved Parisian ivories of the thirteenth century, Limoges enamels and Byzantine ivories. The circuit passes through the former Minister of State's apartments, open to the public since the Finance Ministry was ousted, full of plush upholstery, immense chandeliers, gilded putti and caryatids, and dramatic ceiling frescoes in true Second Empire style.

The largest section by far is the **Paintings**: French from the year dot to mid-nineteenth century, along with Italians, Dutch, Germans, Flemish, Spanish and English. Some are so familiar from reproduction in advertisements and on chocolate boxes that it is a surprise to see them on a wall in a frame. The early Italians (Denon, first floor, rooms 1–5) are perhaps the most interesting part of the collection. All the big names are represented – Giotto, Fra Angelico, Botticelli, Filippo Lippi, Raphael. Works to look out for include Uccello's *Battle of San Romano*, a *Crucifixion* by Mantegna, and Paolo Veronese's *Marriage at Cana*, a huge work painted in 1563. If you want to get near the *Mona Lisa* (Denon, first floor, room 6), go first or last thing in the day. For a less hurried inspection of Leonardo's art, have a look at his *Virgin of the Rocks* and *Virgin and Child with St Anne*, on display in the Grande Galerie. Non-Italian works worth lingering over include Quentin Matsy's moralistic *Moneychanger and his Wife*, Rembrandt's superb *Supper at Emmaus*, and the Goya portraits; the French collection is so vast that a selective approach is necessary unless you intend spending at least a couple of days devoted to the subject. Amongst the multitude are a number of paintings by the master of French classicism, Poussin. There's also a good representation of canvases by French nineteenth-century artists whose most famous images can be seen in the two large-format French painting rooms (Denon, first floor, rooms 75 & 77): David's *Coronation of Napoléon*, Ingres' *La Grande Odalisque*, Géricault's intensely dramatic *Raft of the Medusa*, and, the icon of nineteenth-century revolution, Delacroix's *Liberty Leading the People*. The final part takes in Corot and the Barbizon school of painting, the precursors of Impressionism.

Interspersed throughout the painting section are rooms dedicated to the Louvre's impressive collection of **Prints and Drawings**, including prized sketches and preliminary drawings by Ingres and Rubens and some attributed to Leonardo. Because of their susceptibility to the light, however, they are exhibited in rotation.

Other Palais du Louvre museums

The other museums housed in the Louvre palace (entrance at 107 rue de Rivoli), have been subject to recent reorganization. All are now open, although work is ongoing in the Musée des Arts Décoratifs. The **Musée de la Mode et du Textile** (Tues, Thurs & Fri 11am–6pm, Wed 11am–9pm, Sat & Sun 10am–6pm; 35F/€5.34, combined ticket with Musée des Arts Décoratifs and the Musée de la Publicité) is a museum of fashion, whose exquisite collection is too large to be shown all at once and too fragile to be exposed for long periods, resulting in a yearly rotation of the garments and textiles based on changing themes. The **Musée des Arts Décoratifs** (same hours and ticket as above) starts on the third floor, with a section that covers decorative art from the Middle Ages to the Renaissance. The collection of religious art and everyday bourgeois objects seems rather humble in comparison with the high art next door but the craftsmanship and devotion are nonetheless apparent, and the thematic arrangement with two period mock-ups (a late-fourteenth-century castle bedroom and a fifteenth-century reception room) brings it to life. At the time of writing the rest of the permanent collection was closed but it comprises furnishings, fittings and objects of French interiors such as beds, blankets, cupboards, tools, stained glass and lampshades – almost anything illustrating decorative skills from the Renaissance to the present day. The contemporary section features works by French, Italian and Japanese designers, including some great examples of Philippe Starck. The rest of the twentieth-century collection is fascinating – a bedroom by Guimard, Jeanne Lanvin's Art Deco apartments, and a salon created by Georges Hoentschel for the 1900 Exposition Universelle.

The fourth floor houses the **Musée de la Publicité** (same hours and ticket as above), which creates a neutral space in which to contemplate the inspiration and influence of the persuasive art via multimedia and temporary exhibitions.

Opéra district

In the narrow streets of the 1er and 2e *arrondissements*, between the Louvre and **boulevards Haussmann, Montmartre, Poissonnière** and **Bonne-Nouvelle**, the grandiose financial, cultural and political state institutions are surrounded by well-established **commerce** – the rag trade, media, sex and well-heeled shopping. In contrast to the hulks of the Bourse, Banque de France and the Bibliothèque Nationale, and the monumental style of the **Madeleine, Opéra** and the **Palais Royal**, are the once crumbling and secretive **passages** – shopping arcades long predating the concept of pedestrian precincts, with glass roofs, tiled floors and unobtrusive entrances. Most have now been rendered as chic and immaculate as they originally were in the nineteenth century, with mega-premiums on their leases. Many are closed at night and on Sundays.

The passages

Foremost among the *passages* is the **Galerie Vivienne**, between rue Vivienne and rue des Petits-Champs, with its flamboyant decor of Grecian and marine motifs enticing you to buy Jean-Paul Gaultier or Yuki Torri gear. The neighbouring **Galerie Colbert**, gorgeously lit by bunches of bulbous lamps, contains the 1830s-style brasserie, *Le Grand Colbert*, to which senior librarians and rich academics from the Bibliothèque Nationale retire for lunch. But the best stylistically are the stylish three-storey **passage du Grand-Cerf**, between rue St-Denis and rue Dussouds, and **Galerie Véro-Dodat**, between rue Croix-des-Petits-Champs and rue Jean-Jacques Rousseau, named after the two pork butchers who set it up in 1824. This last is the most homogeneous and aristocratic *passage*, though a little dilapidated, with painted ceilings and panelled shop-fronts divided by black marble columns. At no. 26, Monsieur Capia keeps a collection of antique dolls in a shop piled high with miscellaneous curios. North of rue St-Marc the grid of arcades round the **passage des Panoramas** is still a touch rough, with no fancy mosaics for your feet. An old brasserie with carved wood panelling has been restored, and there are still bric-a-brac shops, bars, stamp dealers, and an upper-crust printshop with its original 1867 fittings. In **passage Jouffroy**, across boulevard Montmartre, a Monsieur Segas sells walking canes and theatrical antiques opposite a shop for dolls' house fittings and furnishings, while Paul Vulin spreads his secondhand books further down along the passageway, and *Ciné-Doc* serves cinephiles. Crossing rue de la Grange-Batelière, you enter **passage Verdeau**, where a few of the old postcard and camera dealers still trade alongside smart new art galleries.

Place du Claire and the rag trade

Mass-produced clothes is the business of **place du Caire**, the centre of the **rag trade** district. The frenetic trading and deliveries of cloth, the food market on rue des Petits-Carreaux, and general toing and froing make a lively change from the office-bound quarters further west. Beneath an extraordinary pseudo-Egyptian facade of grotesque Pharaonic heads (a celebration of Napoléon's conquest of Egypt), an archway opens on to a series of arcades, the **passage du Caire**. These, contrary to any visible evidence, are the oldest of all the *passages* and entirely monopolized by wholesale clothes shops.

The garment business gets progressively more upmarket west of the trade area. The upper end of **rue Étienne-Marcel**, and Louis XIV's **place des Victoires**, adjoined to the north by the appealingly asymmetrical **place des Petits-Pères**, are the centre for new-name designer clothes, displayed to deter all those without the necessary funds. The boutiques on **rue St-Honoré** and its Faubourg extension have the established names, paralleled across the Champs-Élysées by **rue François-1er**, where Dior has at least four blocks on the corner with avenue Montaigne. Hermès, at 24 rue du Faubourg-St-Honoré, displays a small collection of its original saddlery items. The aristocratic **place Vendôme**, with Napoléon high on a column clad with recycled Austro-Russian cannons, has all the fashionable accessories for haute couture, plus the original *Ritz*, various banks and the Ministry of Law and Order.

Madeleine and the Opéra-Garnier

Another obese Napoleonic structure is the church of **La Madeleine**, to the northwest of place Vendôme, which holds society weddings and offers a perspective across place de la Concorde. There's a **flower market** every day except Monday along the east side of the church, and a luxurious **Art Nouveau loo** by the métro at the junction of place and boulevard Madeleine. But the square holds greatest appeal for window-gazing gourmets. In the northeast corner – at Fauchon – are two blocks of the best **food display** in Paris, with a *salon de thé* for epicurean treats.

Set back from the boulevard des Capucines (the continuation of boulevard de la Madeleine), and crowning the avenue de l'Opéra, is the dazzling **Opéra-Garnier**, which was constructed in the scheme of Napoléon III's new vision of Paris. The building's architect, Charles Garnier, whose golden bust, as realized by Carpeaux, can be seen on the rue Auber side of his edifice, pulled out all the stops to provide ample space for aristocratic preening, ceremonial pomp and the social intercourse of Second Empire opera-goers. You can see round the **interior** (daily 10am–5pm; 30F/€4.57), including the auditorium – rehearsals permitting – whose ceiling is the work of Chagall. The visit includes the **Bibliothèque-Musée de l'Opéra**, dedicated to the artists connected with the Opéra throughout history, and containing model sets, dreadful nineteenth-century paintings and rather better temporary exhibitions on operatic themes.

Palais Royal

The **avenue de l'Opéra** was built at the same time as the Opéra-Garnier – and left deliberately bereft of trees lest they mask the vista of the building. The avenue leads down to the **Palais Royal**, originally Richelieu's residence, which now houses various government and constitutional bodies, and the **Comédie Française**, where the classics of French theatre are performed. The palace **gardens** to the north were once a gastronomic, gambling and amusement hotspot overlooked by apartments that were occupied by Cocteau and Colette, amongst others. New shops and cafés have opened in the arcades, and the flower beds are sumptuous. Folly has returned in the form of Daniel Buren's black-and-white pillars in different sizes, which stand above flowing water in the main courtyard of the palace. Kids use these monochrome Brighton-rock lookalikes as an adventure playground, but for most people the palace grounds are just a useful short cut from the Louvre to rue des Petits-Champs. Beyond this street, just to the left, is the forbidding wall of the old **Bibliothèque Nationale** (Mon–Fri 9am–6pm, Sat 9am–5pm); you can enter free of charge and peer into the atmospheric reading rooms or pay to enter the various exhibitions.

Les Halles to Beaubourg

In 1969 the main **Les Halles** market was moved to the suburbs after more than eight hundred years in the heart of the city. There was widespread opposition to the destruction of Victor Baltard's nineteenth-century pavilions, and considerable disquiet at what renovation of the area would mean. The authorities' excuse was that they had to install the RER and métro interchange below. Digging began in 1971, and the hole was only finally filled at the end of the 1980s. Hardly any trace remains of the working-class quarter, with its night bars and bistros serving market traders; rents now rival the 16e, and the all-night places serve and profit from salaried and big-spending types.

The Forum des Halles

From the RER station at Châtelet-Les Halles you surface only after ascending levels 4 to 0 of the **Forum des Halles** centre, which stretches underground from the Bourse du Commerce rotunda to rue Pierre-Lescot. The overground section comprises aquarium-like arcades of shops enclosed by glass buttocks with white steel creases sliding down to an imprisoned patio. To cover up for all this, commerce, poetry, arts and crafts pavilions top two sides in a simple construction – save for the mirrors – that just manages to be out of sync with the curves and hollows below.

The **gardens** above the extensive underground complex do, however, provide much-needed greenery and open space, as well as fountains and a tropical greenhouse within a glass pyramid. Beneath the garden, amidst the uninspiring shops, there's scope for various diversions, such as swimming, billiards, discovering Paris through videos, and movie-going.

After a spate of air-conditioning and artificial light, you can seek relief outside in the water cascading down the perfect Renaissance proportions of the **Fontaine des Innocents**, or in the high Gothic and Renaissance **church of St-Eustache**, where a woman preached the abolition of marriage from the pulpit during the Commune.

There are always hundreds of people around the Forum filling in time, hustling or just loafing about. Pickpocketing is pretty routine; the law plus canine arm is often in evidence, and at night the atmosphere can be quite tense, although the labyrinth of tiny streets southeastwards to **place du Châtelet** teems with jazz bars, nightclubs and restaurants, and is far more crowded at 2am than 2pm.

To the north, rues Montmartre, Montorgueil and Turbigo concentrate on food – strictly not for vegetarians – with shops featuring the cadavers of wild boar, deer and fowl, alongside *pâté de foie gras* and caviar. On the riverfront due south, the three blocks of the **Samaritaine department store** (Mon–Sat 9.30am–7pm, Thurs till 10pm) recall the days when art rather than marketing psychology determined the decoration of a store. Built in 1903 in the Art Nouveau style, its gold, green and glass exteriors, interior ceramic tiles and wrought-iron staircases and balconies have all been restored, though best of all is the view from the roof – the most central high location in the city.

Centre Georges Pompidou

Originally opened in 1977, the **Centre Georges Pompidou** (M° Rambuteau/Hôtel-de-Ville) was known as Paris's most outrageous building, though it has since won over critics and citizens alike and become one of the city's more recognizable landmarks. Architects Renzo Piano and Richard Rogers designed the building placing all infrastructure, including utility pipes and escalator tubes, outside – thus freeing up maximum gallery space inside. Its closure in 1997 for extensive renovation led sceptics to grumble that the young architects had been overly ambitious, but the structure has weathered two years of internal renovations with aplomb. Having been updated, its slick lighting, gleaming polished concrete floors, stylish café and expensive rooftop restaurant combine to create a feeling that is less Seventies and much more Nineties. Sadly, however, the free escalator rides – complete with fabulous views of the city – have become a thing of the past, since access to them now requires paying the admission price.

Once inside, you'll find Levels One, Two and Three devoted to the **Bibliothèque Publique d'Information** (Mon–Fri noon–10pm, Sat & Sun 11am–10pm; free), known as the BPI, which has an impressive collection of 2500 periodicals including international press, 10,000 CDs and 2200 documentary films. The superb **Musée National d'Art Moderne** (see below) presides over the fourth and fifth floors, with the sixth floor reserved for special exhibitions.

On the northern edge of the centre, down some steps off the sloping piazza, in a small separate one-level building, is the **Atelier Brancusi** (Mon & Wed–Fri noon–8pm, Sat, Sun & hols 10am–8pm; closed Tues & May 1; 20F/€3.05). When he died in 1956, the sculptor Constantin Brancusi bequeathed the contents of his 15ᵉ *arrondissement* studio to the state: the condition was that it had to be reconstructed exactly as it was found. The artist had become obsessed with the spatial relationship of the sculptures in his studio, going so far as to supplant a sold work with a plaster copy, and the four interlinked rooms of the studio faithfully adhere to his arrangements. Studios one and two are crowded with fluid sculptures of highly polished brass and marble, his trademark abstract bird and column shapes, stylized busts and poised objects that look as though they want to take off into space. Unfortunately the rooms are behind glass, creating a feeling of sterility and distance. Perhaps the most satisfying rooms are studios three and four, his private quarters, where you really get an idea of how the artist lived and worked.

The surrounding cafés, like the *Café Beaubourg* (see p.159), are still popular – there's the view of the brilliant building after all, and the **Fontaine de Stravinsky** (see below) still provides a colourfully kinetic focus.

MUSEÉ NATIONAL D'ART MODERNE

The **Musée National d'Art Moderne** (daily except Tues 11am–9pm; 30–50F /€4.57–7.62) offers a near-complete visual essay on the history of twentieth-century art, with the fifth floor hosting works from the first sixty years of the century, and the fourth works from the last forty. The museum is easily seen in a half-day, since its collection, though one of the largest of its kind, is densely and efficiently organized, with pieces displayed along the spacious central hallways bisecting each floor and within the many small cubicles off to each side.

Beginning on the fifth floor, Henri Matisse, adhering to the **Fauvists'** creed not to imitate nature but to create form, journeys from a fascination with the nude in *Luxe I* (1907; room 9), to the unexplored frontiers of space and jarring colour of *Grand Intérieur Rouge* (1948; room 30). In the far reaches of rooms 31 and 32, the works of Picasso and Braque share the signs of an emerging **Cubism** in pieces such as Picasso's *Le Joueur de Guitare* (1910) and Braque's *Le Guéridon (nature morte au violon)* (1911). Near room 7 Marcel Duchamp challenges the boundaries of art with his ready-made *Porte-bouteilles* (1914), a bottle rack placed on a pedestal and termed as "art". Further along in rooms 10 and 11, Wassily Kandinsky explores emotions in his two series the *Impressions* and the *Improvisations*, and in doing so makes the shift into **Abstract** art. In room 19, the foreboding *Ubu Imperator* (1927) by the German-born Max Ernst, caught up in the distorted **Surrealism** movement of the inter-war period, is said to challenge the perversion of male authority. In room 39 are Joan Miró's series, *Three Blues*, painted with bright lapis and azure made more intense by watery red dabs and dots of opaque jet black, and Jackson Pollack's splattery *No 26A, Black and white* (1948). Standing guard at the end of the long hallway right outside room 39 is Giacometti's impossibly thin and wonderfully graceful *Femme debout* (1964), while in room 34 a quick peek at Jean Dubuffet's *D'Hôtel Nuancé d'Abricot* (1947) will give you the confidence to face yourself in the mirror each morning.

The fourth floor picks up where the fifth left off, namely **Pop Art** (room 3). Easily recognizable is Andy Warhol's piece *Ten Lizes* (1963), which features the actress Elizabeth Taylor sporting a Mona Lisa-like smile. The **New Realists** (room 4) are odd enough, but there's something strangely serene about Yves Klein's *L'Arbre, Grande éponge bleue* (1962), with its large sponge soaked in plaster, synthetic resin and blue pigment. In the airy open main hall Claes Oldenburg's *Giant Ice Bag* sits "melting", while buried away in room 15 Joseph Beuys' hot, stale and utterly claustrophobic *Plight* (1985) features a forlorn piano surrounded by burlap. Alain Séchas' piece, *Le Mannequin*, gives new meaning to the phrase "bury your head in the sand", while the practically living and breathing blankets that make up Wendy Jacob's piece *The Somnambulist (Blue) A* (1993) are truly shocking. Once you have been fooled, stick around to watch the reactions of others. Continuing on, things become increasingly contemporary: Marie-Ange Guilleminot's sculpture *La Rotateuse* (1995) is an object resembling a dismembered dressmaker's dummy attempting a gymnastic routine on the uneven bars – it is as disturbing as it sounds. Scattered throughout the museum are rooms filled with furniture and architectural plans from the Sixties and Seventies, many unrealized, which feel too familiar to really seem like art, but are ingenious nonetheless.

Quartier Beaubourg and the Hôtel de Ville

Visual entertainments around Beaubourg include the clanking gold *Défenseur du Temps* clock in the quartier de l'Horloge; a *trompe-l'œil* as you look west along rue Aubry-le-Boucher from Beaubourg; and colourful moving sculptures and fountains by Jean Tinguely and Niki de St-Phalle in the pool in front of Eglise St-Merri on **place Igor Stravinsky**. This squirting waterworks pays homage to Stravinsky and shows scant respect for passers-by; beneath it lies IRCAM, founded by the composer Pierre Boulez, a research centre for contemporary music, with an overground extension by Renzo Piano.

Small commercial art galleries where you can browse to your heart's content for free are concentrated north of rue Aubrey-le-Boucher on **rue Quincampoix**.

Rue Renard runs down to **place de l'Hôtel de Ville**, where the oppressively vertical, gleaming and gargantuan mansion is the seat of the city's government. Those opposed to the establishments of kings and emperors created their alternative municipal governments in this building in 1789, 1848 and 1870. But with the defeat of the

Commune in 1871, the conservatives concluded that the Parisian municipal authority had to go if order, property, morality and the suppression of the working class were to be maintained. For a hundred years Paris was ruled directly by the ministry of the interior. The next head of an independent municipality was Jacques Chirac, elected in 1977. Amazingly he even held the position whilst prime minister, eventually relinquishing it in 1995 when he became president. Chirac's successor, the current mayor of Paris, is **Jean Tiberi**.

The Marais, the Île St-Louis and the Bastille

Jack Kerouac translated **rue des Francs-Bourgeois**, the Marais' main east–west axis along with rue Rivoli/rue St-Antoine, as "street of the outspoken middle classes". The original owners of the mansions lining its length would not have taken kindly to such a slight on their blue-bloodedness. The name's origin is medieval, and it was not until the sixteenth and seventeenth centuries that the **Marais**, as the area between Beaubourg and the Bastille is known, became a fashionable aristocratic district. After the Revolution it was abandoned to the masses, who, up until some thirty-five years ago, were living ten to a room on unserviced, squalid streets. Since then, gentrification has proceeded apace and the middle classes are finally ensconced – mostly media, arty or gay, and definitely outspoken.

The renovated mansions, their grandeur concealed by the narrow streets, have become museums, libraries, offices and chic apartments, flanked by shops selling designer clothes, house and garden accoutrements, works of art and one-off trinkets. Though cornered by Haussmann's boulevards, the Marais itself was spared the baron's heavy touch, and very little has been pulled down in the recent gentrification. This is Paris at its most seductive – old, secluded, as unthreatening by night as it is by day, and with as many alluring shops, bars and places to eat as you could wish for.

Rue des Francs-Bourgeois and the Musée Picasso
Rue des Francs-Bourgeois begins with the eighteenth-century magnificence of the **Palais Soubise**, which houses the Archives Nationales de France and the Musée de l'Histoire de France. Opposite, at the back of a driveway for the Crédit Municipal bank, stands a pepperpot tower which formed part of Philippe-Auguste's twelfth-century **city walls**. Further down the street are two of the grandest Marais *hôtels*, **Carnavalet** and **Lamoignon**, housing respectively the Musée Carnavalet and the Bibliothèque Historique de la Ville de Paris.

The **Musée de l'Histoire de France**, within the Palais Soubise, at 60 rue des Francs-Bourgeois (Mon & Wed–Fri noon–5.45pm, Sat & Sun 1.45–5.45pm; closed Tues & hols; 20F/€3.05), shows permanent and temporary exhibitions of historical documents from the national archives; more interestingly the museum provides an opportunity to enter perhaps Marais' most splendid mansion, with some fine Rococo interiors, and paintings by the likes of Boucher.

The **Musée Carnavalet**, whose entrance is off rue des Francs-Bourgeois at 23 rue de Sévigné (Tues–Sun 10am–5.40pm; 27F/€4.12, 35F/€5.34 with special exhibitions; Mº St-Paul), presents the history of Paris from its origins until the Belle Époque in an extensive and beautifully presented collection filling two adjoining converted Renaissance mansions which in themselves repay a visit. Paris's history is presented as viewed and lived by its people: working class, bourgeoisie, aristocrats and royalty. The collection begins with nineteenth- and early twentieth-century shop and inn signs (beautiful objects in themselves) and fascinating models of Paris through the ages, along with maps and plans. The stairwell to the first floor boasts a glorious *trompe-l'oeil*; and decorative arts feature strongly, with numerous recreated salons and boudoirs from the time of Louis XII to Louis XVI from buildings which had to be destroyed for

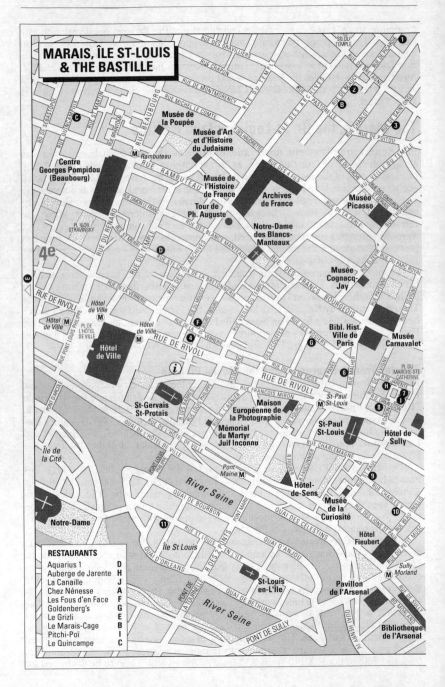

MARAIS, ÎLE ST-LOUIS & THE BASTILLE

Musée de la Poupée

Musée d'Art et d'Histoire du Judaisme

Centre Georges Pompidou (Beaubourg)

Musée de l'Histoire de France

Tour de Ph. Auguste

Archives de France

Musée Picasso

Notre-Dame des Blancs-Manteaux

PL IGOR STRAVINSKY

4e

Musée Cognacq-Jay

Hôtel de Ville

Hôtel de Ville

Hôtel de l'Hôtel de Ville

PL DE L'HÔTEL DE VILLE

Hôtel de Ville

Bibl. Hist. Ville de Paris

Musée Carnavalet

Hôtel de Ville

St-Paul St-Louis

PL DU MARCHÉ-STE-CATHERINE

St-Gervais St-Protais

Maison Européenne de la Photographie

Mémorial du Martyr Juif Inconnu

St-Paul St-Louis

Hôtel de Sully

Île de la Cité

Hôtel-de-Sens

River Seine

Notre-Dame

Musée de la Curiosité

Hôtel Fieubert

QUAI DE BOURBON

Île St Louis

St-Louis en-L'Île

Pavillon de l'Arsenal

Sully Morland

River Seine

PONT DE SULLY

Bibliothèque de l'Arsenal

RESTAURANTS

Aquarius 1	D
Auberge de Jarente	H
La Canaille	J
Chez Nénesse	A
Les Fous d'en Face	F
Goldenberg's	G
Le Grizli	E
Le Marais-Cage	B
Pitchi-Poï	I
Le Quincampe	C

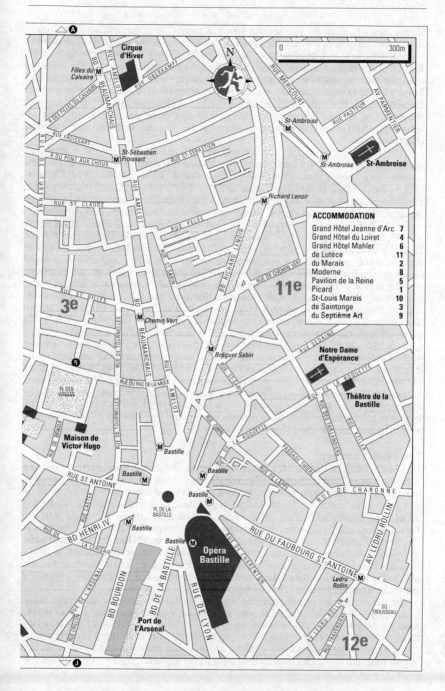

ACCOMMODATION

Grand Hôtel Jeanne d'Arc	7
Grand Hôtel du Loiret	4
Grand Hôtel Mahler	6
de Lutèce	11
du Marais	2
Moderne	8
Pavilion de la Reine	5
Picard	1
St-Louis Marais	10
de Saintonge	3
du Septième Art	9

Haussmann's boulevards. The second floor has rooms full of mementos of the French Revolution: models of the Bastille, original *Declarations of the Rights of Man and the Citizen*, tricolors and liberty caps, sculpted allegories of Reason, crockery with Revolutionary slogans, models of the guillotine and execution orders to make you shed a tear for the royalists as well. Not all the rooms are open at the same time: the Second Empire to the twentieth century section is only open 10–11.50am, and the section on the sixteenth to the eighteenth century from 1.10–5.40pm, so to see everything you should arrive at 10am. However, the ticket lasts all day, so you can return. After an exhausting trawl of the collection, you can rest in the peaceful, formally laid-out garden courtyards.

To the north of the rue des Francs-Bourgeois, at 5 rue de Thorigny, the magnificent seventeenth-century Hôtel Salé houses the **Musée Picasso** (Mon, Wed & Fri–Sun 9.30am–6pm, Thurs 9.30am–8pm; 38F/€5.79, reduced Sun to 28F/€4.27; M° Chemin-Vert/St-Paul), which is the largest compilation of the Paris-based Spanish artist's work anywhere. A large proportion of the pieces in the collection – paintings he bought or was given by his contemporaries, his African masks and sculptures, photographs, letters and other personal memorabilia – were owned by Picasso at the time of his death in 1973, but seized by the state in lieu of taxes owed. The works themselves are not Picasso's most impressive – the museums of the Côte d'Azur and the Picasso gallery in Barcelona are more exciting – but the collection provides what many art-lovers yearn for: an unedited body of work that provides a sense of the artist's growth and an insight into the person behind the myth. The paintings of his wives, lovers and families – the portraits of Marie-Thérèse, Claude Dessinant Françoise and Paloma, for example – are some of his gentlest and most endearing. The portrait of Dora Maar, like that of Marie-Thérèse, was painted in 1937, during the Spanish Civil War – a time when Picasso was going through his worst personal and political crises, and a period when he produced some of his most inspired and passionate work. A decade later, Picasso was a member of the Communist Party – his cards are on show along with a drawing entitled *Staline à la Santé* (Here's to Stalin) and his delegate credentials for the 1948 World Congress of Peace. The *Massacre in Korea* (1951) demonstrates the lasting pacifist commitment in his work. Temporary exhibitions bring works from the periods least represented: the Pink Period, Cubism (though there are some fine examples here, including a large collection of collages), the immediate postwar period, and the 1950s and 1960s. There is also a cinema and reference library.

The Jewish quarter

One block south of the rue des Francs-Bourgeois, the area around narrow **rue des Rosiers** has traditionally been the **Jewish quarter** of the city, and remains so, despite incursions by trendy clothes shops. It has a distinctly Mediterranean flavour, testimony to the influence of the North African Sephardim, who replenished Paris's Jewish population, depleted when its Ashkenazim were rounded up by the Nazis and the French police and transported to the concentration camps. The Hôtel de St-Aignan, at 71 rue de Temple, is now home to the **Musée d'Art et d'Histoire du Judaisme** (Mon–Fri 11am–6pm, Sun 10am–6pm; 35F/€5.34; M°Hôtel-de-Ville), opened in 1998 – a combination of the collections of the now closed Musée d'Art Juif, in Montmartre, and of Isaac Strauss, conductor of the Paris Opera orchestra, and the Dreyfus archives, a gift to the museum from his grandchildren.

The museum is not one of religious artefacts — though there are, understandably, quite a few – but of the culture, history and artistic endeavours of the Jewish people from the Middle Ages to the present day. The focus is on the works of French artists, though pieces from other countries are represented, many of startling historic significance. Some of the most notable exhibits are an Italian gilded circumcision chair, one of only three surviving chairs of its kind from the seventeenth century; an unbelievably well-preserved and completely intact late-eighteenth-century Austrian *Sukkah*, or outdoor dwelling, constructed for the celebration of the Harvest; and the Torah scrolls, covered with the elaborate designs meant to represent the Tree of Life and used to transport sacred scripture. Throughout the museum are vast compilations of prayer books, Hannukkah lamps, wedding garments, rings and other clothing, and gorgeous, almost whimsical, spice containers. Paintings by Marc Chagall, Samuel Hirszenberg, Chaim Soutine and Jacques Lipchitz, among others, round out the collection and are as valuable for their subject matter – daily Jewish life – as for their mastery of technique. The collection comes to a rather abrupt end with Christian Boltanski's outdoor tribute to the Jewish artisans who once lived in the *hôtel* and who lost their lives to the Nazis in the 1930s and 1940s.

Place des Vosges

At the western end of rue des Francs-Bourgeois is the masterpiece of aristocratic urban planning, the **place des Vosges**, a vast square of stone and brick symmetry built for the majesty of Henri IV and Louis XIII, whose statue is hidden by trees in the middle of the grass and gravel gardens. Expensive high-heels tap through the arcades, pausing at art, antique and fashion shops, and people lunch al fresco at the restaurants while buskers play classical music. In the garden, toddlers, octogenarians, workers and schoolchildren on lunch breaks sit or play in the only green space of any size in the locality – unusually for Paris, you're allowed to sprawl on the grass.

Through all the vicissitudes of history, the square has never lost its cachet as a smart address. Among the many celebrities who made their homes here was Victor Hugo: his house, at no. 6, where he wrote much of *Les Misérables*, is now a museum, the **Maison de Victor Hugo** (Tues–Sun 10am–5.40pm; closed hols; 27F/€4.12; M° Chemin-Vert/Bastille); a whole room is devoted to posters of the various stage adaptations of his most famous novel. Hugo was extraordinarily multi-talented: as well as writing, he decorated and drew – many of his ink drawings are exhibited – and even put together the extraordinary Japanese dining room on display here. That apart, the usual portraits, manuscripts and memorabilia shed sparse light on the man and his work, particularly if you don't read French.

From the southwest corner of the square, a door leads through to the formal château garden, *orangerie* and exquisite Renaissance facade of the **Hôtel de Sully**. The garden, with its park benches, makes for a peaceful rest-stop, or you can pass through the building, nodding at the sphinxes on the stairs, as a pleasing short cut to rue St-Antoine. Temporary photographic exhibitions, usually with social, historical or anthropological themes, are mounted in the *hôtel* by the **Mission du Patrimoine Photographique** (Tues–Sun 10am–6.30pm; 25F/€3.81), or you can browse in the history-focused bookshop (Tues–Sun 10am–7pm).

South of rue St-Antoine

In the southern section of the Marais, **south of rue St-Antoine**, the crooked steps and lanterns of rue Cloche-Perce, the tottering timbered houses of rue François-Miron, the medieval buildings behind St-Gervais-et-Protais and the smell of flowers and incense on rue des Barres are Paris at its most atmospheric. Between rues Fourcy and François-Miron, the Hôtel Hénault de Cantoube, with its two-storey crypt, has become the **Maison Européenne de la Photographie** (Wed–Sun 11am–8pm; 30F/€4.57, free Wed after 5pm; M° St-Paul/Pont-Marie), hosting excellent exhibitions of contemporary photography, with a stylish café designed by architect Nestor Perkal; the entrance is at 4 rue du Fourcy. Shift eastwards to the next tangle of streets and you'll find the modern, chi-chi flats of the "Village St-Paul" and its expensive clusters of antique shops. **Rue St-Paul** itself has some good addresses, including the **Musée de la Curiosité et** de la Magie at no. 11 (Wed, Sat & Sun 2–7pm; 45F/€6.86; M° St-Paul/Sully-Morland), dedicated to the art of illusion, with a magician regularly performing seemingly impossible sleights of hand.

Further east again, at 21 bd Morland, the **Pavillon de l'Arsenal** (Tues–Sat 10.30am–6.30pm, Sun 11am–7pm; free; M° Sully-Morland), signalled by a sculpture of Rimbaud entitled *The Man with his Souls in Front*, is an excellent addition to the city's art of self-promotion. It presents current architectural projects to the public and shows how past and present developments have evolved as part and parcel of Parisian history. To this end they have a permanent exhibition of photographs, plans and models, including a model of the whole city linked to a touch-screen choice of 30,000 images.

The Île St-Louis

Often considered to be the most romantic part of Paris, the peaceful **Île St-Louis** is prime strolling territory. Unlike its larger neighbour, the Île de la Cité, the Île St-Louis has no monuments or museums, just high houses on single-lane streets, tree-lined *quais*, a school, church, restaurants, cafés, interesting little shops, and the best sorbets in the world at *Berthillon*, 31 rue St-Louis-en-l'Île (see p.159). It's also where the likes of the Aga Khan and the pretender to the throne of France have their Parisian residences, and the island is indeed the most coveted of the city's addresses. A popular approach to bring you right to *Berthillon* is to cross Pont Louis-Philippe, just east of the Hôtel de Ville; you're then positioned to join the throngs strolling with their ice creams down rue St-Louis-en-l'Île for a spot of window-shopping. Alternatively, you can find seclusion on the **southern quais**, tightly clutching your triple-sorbet cornet as you descend the various steps, or climb over the low gate on the right of the garden across boulevard Henri-IV to reach the best sunbathing spot in Paris. The island is particularly atmospheric in the evening, and dinner in the area (see p.160 for restaurant recommendations), followed by an arm-in-arm wander along the *quais* is a must in any lovers' itinerary.

The Bastille

The landmark column topped with the gilded "Spirit of Liberty" on **place de la Bastille** was erected not to commemorate the surrender in 1789 of the prison – whose only visible remains have been transported to square Henri-Galli at the end of boulevard Henri-IV – but the July Revolution of 1830 that replaced the autocratic Charles X with the "Citizen King" Louis-Philippe. When Louis-Philippe fled in the more significant 1848 Revolution, his throne was burnt beside the column and a new inscription added. Four months later, the workers again took to the streets. All of eastern Paris was barricaded, with the fiercest fighting on rue du Faubourg-St-Antoine, until the rebellion was quelled with the usual massacres and deportation of survivors. However, it is the events of July 14, 1789, symbol of the end of feudalism in Europe, that France celebrates every year on Bastille Day.

The Bicentennial in 1989 was marked by the inauguration of the **Opéra-Bastille** (see p.178), Mitterrand's pet project and subject of the most virulent sequence of rows and resignations. Filling almost the entire block between rues de Lyon, Charenton and Moreau, it has shifted the focus of place de la Bastille, so that the column is no longer the pivotal point; in fact, it's easy to miss it altogether when dazzled by the night-time glare of lights emanating from this "hippopotamus in a bathtub", as one critic dubbed it.

The Opéra's construction destroyed no small amount of low-rent housing, but, as with most speculative developments, the pace of change is uneven, and cobblers and ironmongers still survive alongside cocktail haunts and sushi bars, making the **quartier de la Bastille** a simultaneously gritty and trendy quarter. **Place and rue d'Aligre** still have their raucous daily market and, on **rue de Lappe**, *Balajo* is one remnant of a very Parisian tradition: the *bals musettes*, or music halls of 1930s *gai Paris*, frequented between the wars by Piaf, Jean Gabin and Rita Hayworth. It was founded by one Jo de France, who introduced glitter and spectacle into what were then seedy gangster dives, and brought Parisians from the other side of the city to the rue de Lappe lowlife. Now the street is full of fun, trendy bars, full to bursting on the weekends. You'll find art galleries clustered around **rue Keller** and the adjoining stretch of **rue de Charonne**, and indie music shops and gay, lesbian and hippy outfits on rues Keller and **des Taillandiers**.

Quartier Latin

On the Left Bank of the river, the pivotal point of the **quartier Latin** is **place St-Michel**, where the tree-lined **boulevard St-Michel** begins. It has lost its radical penniless chic now, preferring harder commercial values. The cafés and shops are jammed with people, mainly young and – in summer – largely foreign.

Rue de la Huchette, the Mecca of beats and bums in the post-World War II years, with its Théâtre de la Huchette still showing Ionesco's *La Cantatrice Chauve* (The Bald Prima Donna) over fifty years on, is now mostly given over to indifferent Greek restaurants, as is the adjoining rue Xavier-Privas, with the odd couscous joint thrown in. Connecting it to the riverside is the city's narrowest street, the **Chat-qui-Pêche**, evocative of what Paris must have looked like at its medieval worst.

Around rue St-Jacques

Things improve as you move away from the boulevard St-Michel. At the end of rue de la Huchette, **rue St-Jacques** is aligned on the main street of Roman Paris, and was in medieval times the road up which millions of pilgrims trudged at the start of their long march to Santiago de Compostela in Spain. One block south of rue de la Huchette, and west of rue St-Jacques, is the mainly fifteenth-century church of **St-Séverin**, whose entrance is on rue des Prêtres St-Séverin (Mon–Fri 11am–7.30pm, Sat 11am–8pm, Sun 9am–9pm; Mᵒ St-Michel/Cluny-La Sorbonne). It is one of the city's most elegant churches, with splendidly virtuoso chiselwork in the pillars of the Flamboyant choir, as well as stained glass by the modern French painter Jean Bazaine.

East of rue St-Jacques, and back towards the river, **square Viviani** – with a welcome patch of grass and trees – provides the most flattering of all views of Notre-Dame. The mutilated and disfigured church is **St-Julien-le-Pauvre** (daily 10am–7.30pm; Mᵒ St-Michel/Maubert Mutualité). The same age as Notre-Dame, it used to be the venue for university assemblies until rumbustious students tore it apart in the 1500s. Across rue Lagrange from the square, rue de la Bûcherie is the home of the American-run English-language bookshop **Shakespeare and Co.** (see p.189), haunted by the shades of James Joyce and other great expatriate literati – though Sylvia Beach, publisher of *Ulysses*, had her original shop on rue de l'Odéon.

The river bank and Institut du Monde Arabe

A short walk from square Viviani on the river bank, you'll find books, postcards, prints and assorted goods on sale from the **bouquinistes**, who display their wares in green padlocked boxes hooked onto the parapet of the **riverside quais**. Continuing upstream, you come to the **Pont de Sully** – with a dramatic view of the apse and steeple of Notre-Dame – and the beginning of a sunny riverside garden dotted with interesting though worn pieces of modern sculpture, known as the **Musée de Sculpture en Plein Air** (Tues–Sun 10am–5pm; free; Mᵒ Jussieu/Gare-de-l'Austerlitz).

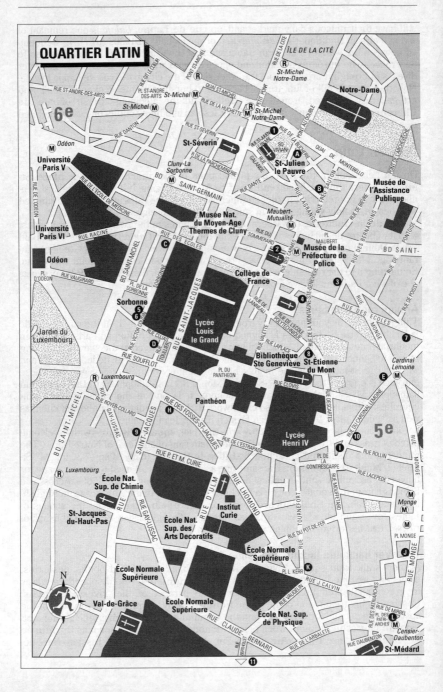

QUARTIER LATIN

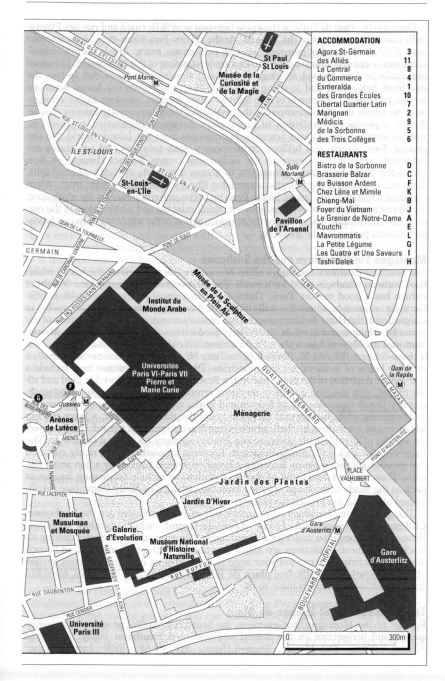

ACCOMMODATION

Agora St-Germain	3
des Alliés	11
Le Central	8
du Commerce	4
Esmeralda	1
des Grandes Écoles	10
Libertal Quartier Latin	7
Marignan	2
Médicis	9
de la Sorbonne	5
des Trois Collèges	6

RESTAURANTS

Bistro de la Sorbonne	D
Brasserie Balzar	C
au Buisson Ardent	F
Chez Léna et Mimile	K
Chieng-Maï	B
Foyer du Vietnam	J
Le Grenier de Notre-Dame	A
Koutchi	E
Mavrommatis	L
La Petite Légume	G
Les Quatre et Une Saveurs	I
Tashi Delek	H

Opposite the mosque is the **Jardin des Plantes** (daily: summer 7.30am–7.45pm; winter 8am–dusk; free; Mº Austerlitz/Jussieu/Monge), founded as a medicinal herb garden in 1626 and gradually evolved as Paris's botanical gardens, with hothouses, shady avenues of trees, lawns to sprawl on, museums and a zoo. Magnificent, varied floral beds make a fine approach to the collection of buildings which form the **Muséum National d'Histoire Naturelle**. Musty museums of paleontology, mineralogy, entomology and paleobotany should be sidestepped in favour of the **Grand Galerie de l'Évolution**, (daily except Tues 10am–6pm, Thurs till 10pm; 40F/€6.10), housed in a dramatically restored nineteenth-century glass-domed building; the entrance is off rue Buffon. You'll be wowed by the sheer scale of the interior, where the story of evolution and the relations between human beings and nature is told using stuffed animals that look real, a combination of clever lighting effects, ambient music and birdsong, videos and touch-screen databases. In a contrastingly small space, real animals can be seen in the small **menagerie** across the park to the northeast near rue Cuvier (daily: summer 9am–6pm, Sun till 6.30pm; winter 9am–5pm, Sun till 6.30pm; 30F/€4.57); it is France's oldest zoo and has operated in the same location since the Revolution. Despite its scale, it's home to a surprising assortment of creatures, from big cats to snakes, possible because of their unacceptably cramped conditions.

The gardens are a pleasant space to while away the middle of a day. By the rue Cuvier exit is a fine cedar of Lebanon planted in 1734, raised from seed sent over from the Oxford Botanical Gardens, and a slice of an American sequoia more than 2000 years old. In the nearby physics labs, Henri Becquerel discovered radioactivity in 1896, and two years later the Curies discovered radium.

A short distance away to the northwest, with an entrance in rue de Navarre, rue des Arènes and another through a passage on rue Monge, is the **Arènes de Lutèce**, an unexpected backwater hidden from the street, and, along with the Roman baths (see p.132), Paris's only Roman remains. It is a partly restored amphitheatre, with a boules pitch in the centre, benches, gardens and a kids' playground behind.

St-Germain

The northern half of the 6ᵉ *arrondissement*, asymmetrically centred on **place St-Germain-des-Prés**, is one of the most physically attractive, lively and stimulating square kilometres in the city. The most dramatic approach is to cross the river from the Louvre by the footbridge, the **Pont des Arts**, from where there's a classic upstream view of the Île de la Cité, with barges moored at the quai de Conti, and the Tour St-Jacques and Hôtel de Ville breaking the skyline of the Right Bank. The dome and pediment at the end of the bridge belong to the **Institut de France**, seat of the Académie Française, an august body of writers and scholars whose mission is to safeguard the purity of the French language. This is the most grandiose bit of the Left Bank riverfront: to the left is the **Hôtel des Monnaies**, redesigned as the Mint in the late eighteenth century; to the right is the **Beaux-Arts**, the School of Fine Art, whose students throng the *quais* on sunny days, sketchpads on knees.

The riverside

The riverside part of the 6ᵉ *arrondissement* is cut lengthwise by **rue St-André-des-Arts** and **rue Jacob**. It is full of bookshops, commercial art galleries, antique shops, cafés and restaurants, and if you poke your nose into the courtyards and side streets, you'll find foliage, fountains and peaceful enclaves removed from the bustle of the city. The houses are four to six storeys high, seventeenth- and eighteenth-century, some noble, some stiff, some bulging and skew, all painted in infinite gradations of grey, pearl and off-white. Broadly speaking, the further west you go the posher the houses.

Historical associations are legion: Picasso painted *Guernica* in rue des Grands-Augustins; Molière started his career in rue Mazarine; Robespierre et al. split ideological hairs at the *Café Procope* in rue de l'Ancienne-Comédie. In rue Visconti, Racine died, Delacroix painted, and Balzac's printing business went bust. In the parallel rue des Beaux-Arts, Oscar Wilde died, Corot and Ampère (father of amps) lived, and the crazy poet Gérard de Nerval went walking with a lobster on a lead.

If you're looking for lunch, you'll find numerous places to snack on **place and rue St-André-des-Arts**, but more tempting is the brilliant food market in **rue Buci** up towards boulevard St-Germain. Before you get to Buci, there is an intriguing little passage on the left, **Cour du Commerce St André**, where Marat had a printing press and Dr Guillotin perfected his notorious machine by lopping off sheep's heads in the loft next door. A couple of smaller courtyards open off it, revealing another stretch of Philippe-Auguste's twelfth-century city wall.

An alternative corner for midday food or quiet is around rue de l'Abbaye and rue du Furstemberg. Halfway down rue du Furstemburg at no. 6, opposite a tiny square, is Delacroix's old studio. The studio backs onto a secret garden and is now the **Musée Delacroix** (daily except Tues 9.30am–5.30pm; 30F/€4.57; 23F/€3.55 on Sun), with a small collection of the artist's personal belongings as well as temporary exhibitions of his work. This is also the beginning of some very upmarket shopping territory, in rue Jacob, rue de Seine and rue Bonaparte in particular.

Place St-Germain-des-Prés

Place St-Germain-des-Prés, the hub of the *quartier*, is only a stone's throw away from the Musée Delacroix, with the *Deux Magots* café (see p.162) on the corner of the square and *Flore* (see p.162) just down the boulevard St-Germain – both renowned for the number of philosophico-politico-literary backsides that have shined their seats, although nowadays you're more likely to be dragged into some street-clown's act than engaged in high-flown debate.

The tower opposite the *Deux Magots* belongs to the **church of St-Germain**, all that remains of an enormous Benedictine monastery. The interior is its best aspect, with the pure Romanesque lines still clear under the deforming paint of nineteenth-century frescoes.

St-Sulpice and the Palais du Luxembourg

South of boulevard St-Germain, the streets round St-Sulpice are calm and classy. **Rue Mabillon** is pretty, with a row of old houses set back below the level of the modern street. On the left are the **halles St-Germain**, on the site of a fifteenth-century market. **Rue St-Sulpice** – with excellent shops for edibles – leads through to the front of the enormous **church of St-Sulpice** (daily 7.30am–7.30pm), an austerely classical church, erected either side of 1700, with a Doric colonnade surmounted by an Ionic, and Corinthian pilasters in the towers, only one of which is finished. For many, however, the main attraction of **place St-Sulpice** is Yves Saint Laurent Rive Gauche, the most elegant fashion boutique on the Left Bank. The least posh bit of the *quartier* is the eastern edge, along boulevard St-Michel, where the university is firmly implanted. Scientific and medical bookshops display skeletons and instruments of torture, and there are a couple of weird and wonderful shops in rue Racine, but really all is elegance round here.

To the south, rue Férou, where a gentleman called Pottier composed the Revolutionary anthem – the *Internationale* – in 1776, connects with **rue de Vaugirard**, Paris's longest street, and the **Palais du Luxembourg**, constructed for Marie de Médicis, Henri IV's widow, to remind her of the Palazzo Pitti and Giardino di Boboli of her native Florence. Today it is the seat of the French Senate and its **gardens** are the

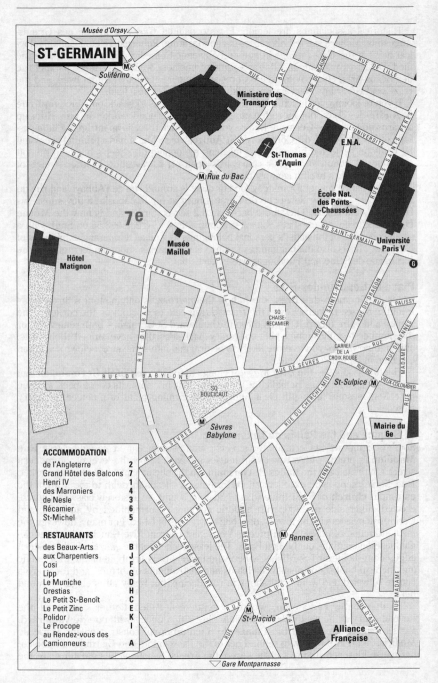

ST-GERMAIN

Musée d'Orsay

Soliférino

Ministère des
Transports

E.N.A.

St-Thomas
d'Aquin

Rue du Bac

École Nat.
des Ponts-
et-Chaussées

7e

Musée
Maillol

Université
Paris V

Hôtel
Matignon

SQ
CHAISE-
RÉCAMIER

CARREF.
DE LA
CROIX ROUGE

RUE DE BABYLONE

St-Sulpice

SQ
BOUCICAUT

Sèvres
Babylone

Mairie du
6e

Rennes

St-Placide

Alliance
Française

Gare Montparnasse

ACCOMMODATION

de l'Angleterre	2
Grand Hôtel des Balcons	7
Henri IV	1
des Marroniers	4
de Nesle	3
Récamier	6
St-Michel	5

RESTAURANTS

des Beaux-Arts	B
aux Charpentiers	J
Cosi	F
Lipp	G
Le Muniche	D
Orestias	H
Le Petit St-Benoît	C
Le Petit Zinc	E
Polidor	K
Le Procope	I
au Rendez-vous des Camionneurs	A

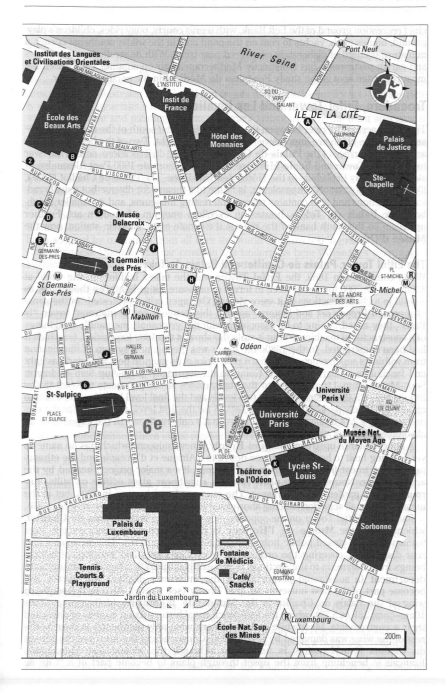

remains of Napoléon. Les Invalides today houses the vast **Musée de l'Armée** (daily: April–Sept 10am–5.45pm; Oct–March 10am–5pm; 37F/€5.64 ticket also valid for Napoléon's tomb, see below), an enormous national war museum whose largest part is devoted to the uniforms and weaponry of Napoléon's armies, with numerous personal items of the emperor, including his campaign tent and bed, and even his dog – stuffed. Later French wars are illustrated, too, through paintings, maps and engravings. The interesting new section on World War II is staged over three floors and is dedicated to General de Gaulle. The battles, the resistance and the slow liberation are documented through the usual displays of maps, uniforms etc, but it's the reels of contemporary footage (with English option) that are the most stirring – the noise of bombs dropping and the overwhelming joy in the faces of the liberated recount the people's story.

Both of the Invalides churches are cold and dreary inside. The **Église du Dôme** (same hours and ticket as Musée de l'Armée above), in particular, is a supreme example of architectural pomposity, with Corinthian columns and pilasters, and grandiose frescoes in abundance. Napoléon lies in a hole in the floor in a cold, smooth sarcophagus of red porphyry, enclosed within a gallery decorated with friezes of execrable taste and grovelling piety, captioned with quotations of awesome conceit from the great man: "Co-operate with the plans I have laid for the welfare of peoples"; "By its simplicity my code of law has done more good in France than all the laws which have preceded me"; "Wherever the shadow of my rule has fallen, it has left lasting traces of its value".

Musée Rodin and around

Immediately east of Les Invalides is the **Musée Rodin**, on the corner of rue de Varenne (Tues–Sun: April–Sept 9.30am–5.45pm, garden closes at 7pm; Oct–March 9.30am–4.45pm, garden closes at 5pm; 28F/€4.27, Sun 18F/€2.74, garden only 5F/€0.76; M° Varenne), housed in a beautiful eighteenth-century mansion which the sculptor leased from the state in return for the gift of all his work at his death. Major projects like *The Burghers of Calais, The Thinker, The Gate of Hell* and *Ugolini and Son* are exhibited in the garden – the latter forming the centrepiece of the ornamental pond. Indoors, which is usually very crowded, are works in marble like *The Kiss, The Hand of God, The Cathedral* – those two perfectly poised, almost sentient, hands. There is something particularly fascinating about the works, like *Romeo and Juliet* and *La Centauresse* (The Centaur), which are only half-created, not totally liberated from the raw block of stone.

The rest of rue de Varenne and the parallel rue de Grenelle is full of aristocratic mansions, including the **Hôtel Matignon**, the prime minister's residence. At 61 rue de Grenelle, an elegant eighteenth-century house has been turned into the **Musée Maillol** (daily except Tues 11am–6pm; 40F/€6.10; M° Rue-du-Bac), showing overbearing numbers of Aristide Maillol's painted and sculpted female nudes, minor works by Matisse, Dufy, Bonnard, Picasso, Degas, Gauguin and Kandinsky, a few Duchamps, and Soviet installation art of the 1970s.

From here, **rue du Bac** leads south into rue de Sèvres, cutting across **rue de Babylone**, another of the *quartier*'s livelier streets, with the crazy, rich man's folly, **La Pagode**, at no. 57bis, brought over from Japan at the turn of the century. Used as a cinema until recently, its future is uncertain.

Musée d'Orsay

Close to the Musée Maillol on the riverfront, in a former railway station whose stone facade disguises a huge vault of steel and glass, is the **Musée-d'Orsay**, at 1 rue de Bellechasse (Tues, Wed, Fri & Sat 9/10am–6pm, Thurs 9/10am–9.45pm, Sun 9am–6pm; 40F/€6.10; M° Solférino/RER Musée-d'Orsay). Housing the painting and sculpture of the period 1848–1914, and thus bridging the gap between the Louvre and

Beaubourg, its highlights are the electrifying works of the **Impressionists** and, scarcely less impressive, of the **Post-Impressionists**.

The design of the Musée d'Orsay is very clever, a combination of well-laid-out galleries, ample lighting, fine presentation and an invigorating pulse reminiscent of its days as a train station. Critics complain that the space is overdesigned and the collection overwhelmingly large, but don't be put off: the collection is unsurpassed in quality as well as quantity. It's well worth taking half a day, if not a whole one, to meander throughout, following the rooms as they are numbered, or just to see the galleries on the top floor.

On the **ground floor**, the mid-nineteenth-century sculptors, including Barye, caster of super-naturalistic bronze animals, occupy the centre gallery. To their right, rooms dedicated to **Ingres** and **Delacroix** (the bulk of whose work is in the Louvre) serve to illustrate the academies of the early nineteenth century. Puvis de Chavannes, Gustave Moreau, the Symbolists and early Degas follow, while in the galleries to the left Daumier, Corot, Millet and the Realist school depart from the academic parameters of subject matter and idealization of the past, and lead on to **Manet's** *Olympia* (1863), as controversial for the colour contrasts and sensual surfaces, as for its portrayal of Olympia as nothing more than a high-class whore.

To get the chronological continuation you have to go straight up to the **top level** where you will pass firstly through the private collection donated by Moreau-Nélaton, room 29. An assiduous collector and art historian, his collection contains some of the most famous Impressionist images: Monet's *Poppies*, as well as Manet's more controversial *Déjeuner sur l'Herbe*, which sent the critics into apoplexies of rage and disgust when it appeared in 1863, and was refused for that year's Salon. The next few rooms are full of the well-known masterpieces which typify Impressionism: **Degas'** ballet-dancers, demonstrating his principal interest in movement and line as opposed to the more common Impressionist concern with light; and numerous landscapes and outdoor scenes by **Renoir, Sisley, Pissarro** and **Monet**, owing much of their brilliance to the novel practice of setting up easels in the open to capture the light. *Le Berceau* (1872), by Berthe Morisot, the first woman to join the early Impressionists, is one of the few to have a complex human emotion as its subject – perfectly synthesized within the classic techniques of the movement. A very different touch, all shimmering light and wide brush strokes, is to be seen in Renoir's depiction of a good time being had by all in *Le bal du Moulin de la Galette* – a favourite Sunday afternoon out on the Butte Montmartre.

The development of Monet's obsession with light continues with five of his Rouen cathedral series, each painted in different light conditions, along with one from his water lilies series painted around fifteen years later; whilst room 35 is full of the blinding colours and disturbing rhythms of **Van Gogh**. **Cézanne**, a step removed from the preoccupations of the mainstream Impressionists, is wonderfully represented in room 36: one of the canvases most revealing of his art is *Still Life with Apples and Oranges* (1895–1900), in which the background abandons perspective while the fruit has an extraordinary solidity.

The rest of this level is given over to the various offspring of Impressionism. Among a number of pointillist works by Seurat (the famous *Cirque*), Signac and various other artists is the dreamlike precursor of the moderns, **Rousseau's** *La Charmeuse de Serpent*, of 1907. There's **Gauguin**, post- and pre-Tahiti, as well as lots of **Toulouse-Lautrec** at his caricaturial nightclubbing best. Take the opportunity for a break on the top level in the *Café des Hauteurs* – the outside terrace offers Seine views, whilst inside you can sit in the light filtering through the huge clock-face.

The **middle level** takes in Rodin and other late nineteenth-century sculptors, several rooms of superb Art Nouveau furniture and *objets*, and the sumptuous reception room (room 51) of the station hotel. Vuillard and Bonnard are tucked away here (rooms 71 & 72), while Klimt and Munch feature in the rooms overlooking the Seine.

Montparnasse and southern Paris

Montparnasse divides the lands of the well-heeled opinion-formers and power-brokers of St-Germain and the 7^e from the amorphous populations of the three southern *arrondissements* which have been subjected to large-scale developments, most notably along the riverfronts both east and west. There are lively areas – **rue du Commerce** in the 15e, **Pernety** in the 14e and the **Buttes-aux-Cailles** in the 13e – plus three good parks: **André Citroën**, **Georges-Brassens** and **Montsouris**.

Like other Left Bank *quartiers*, Montparnasse still trades on its association with the wild characters of the inter-war artistic and literary boom. Many were habitués of the cafés *Select, Coupole, Dôme, Rotonde* and *Closerie des Lilas*, all still going strong on **boulevard du Montparnasse**. Another major subcommunity in the *quartier* in the early years of the century consisted of outlawed Russian revolutionaries. They were so many that the Tsarist police ran a special Paris section to keep tabs on them. Trotsky lived in rue de la Gaîté near the cemetery – a fascinating street of old theatres and cafés – and Lenin lodged further south in the 14e *arrondissement*.

Most of the life of the quarter is concentrated between the junction with boulevard Raspail, where Rodin's *Balzac* broods over the traffic, and at the station end of boulevard du Montparnasse, where the colossal **Tour du Montparnasse** has become one of the city's principal, if unloved, landmarks. You can go up to the top for less than the Eiffel Tower (daily: summer 9.30am–11.30pm; winter 9.30am–10.30pm; 48F/€7.32 to 59th floor, 40F/€6.10 to 56th floor; entrance on the north side), or you could sit down for an expensive drink in the 56th-storey bar, from where you get a tremendous view westwards.

One block northwest of the tower, on rue Antoine-Bourdelle, a garden of sculptures invites you into the **Bourdelle museum**, the artist's old *atelier* (Tues–Sun 10am–5.40pm; 22F/€3.35, or 30F/€4.57 if there's a temporary exhibition).

Montparnasse cemetery, the catacombs and the Observatoire

Just south of boulevard Edgar-Quinet (which has a good street market and cafés full of traders) is the main entrance to the **Montparnasse cemetery** (April–Oct Mon–Fri 8am–6pm, Sat 8.30am–6pm, Sun 9am–6pm; Nov–March closes at 5.30pm), a gloomy city of the dead, with ranks of miniature temples, dreary and bizarre, and plenty of illustrious names, from Baudelaire to Sartre and André Citroën to Saint-Saëns. In the southwest corner is an old windmill, one of the seventeenth-century taverns frequented by the carousing, versifying students who gave the district its name of Mount Parnassus.

If you are determined to spend your time among the dear departed, you can also get down into the **catacombs** (Tues–Fri 2–4pm, Sat & Sun 9–11am & 2–4pm; 33F/€5.03) in nearby **place Denfert-Rochereau**, formerly place d'Enfer (Hell Square). The catacombs are abandoned quarries stacked with millions of bones cleared from the old charnel houses in 1785, claustrophobic in the extreme, and cold.

Rue Schoelcher and boulevard Raspail on the east side of the cemetery have some interesting examples of twentieth-century architecture, from Art Nouveau to contemporary facades of glass in the **Cartier Foundation** at 259 bd Raspail (Tues–Sun noon–8pm; 30F/€4.57). Designed by Jean Nouvel in 1994, this presents all kinds of contemporary art – installations, videos, multimedia – in temporary exhibitions. For a more classical style, there's the **Observatoire de Paris**, on avenue de l'Observatoire, just east of Montparnasse cemetery. From the 1660s, when it was constructed, until 1884, all French maps had the zero meridian through the middle of this building. After that date, they reluctantly agreed that 0° longitude should pass through a small village in Normandy that happens to be due south of Greenwich. The Paris meridian line is visible in the garden behind on boulevard Arago.

The 15ᵉ arrondissement

The western edge of the 15ᵉ *arrondissement* fronts the Seine from the **Porte de Javel** to the Eiffel Tower. From Pont Mirabeau northwards, the river bank is marred by a sort of mini-Défense development of half-cocked futuristic towers with pretentious galactic names, rising out of a litter-blown pedestrian platform some 10m above street level. Far pleasanter riverside strolling is to be had on the narrow midstream island, the **Allée des Cygnes**, which you can reach from the Pont de Grenelle. A scaled-down version of the **Statue of Liberty** stands at the downstream end. South of Pont Mirabeau, between rue Balard and the river, is the city's newest park, the **Parc André-Citroën** (Mᵒ Balard), so named because the site used to be the Citroën motor works. Its best features are the glasshouses full of exotic-smelling shrubs and the fountain display, which on a hot day tempts park-goers to run through. The gardens are less successful, with more concrete than greenery.

It was in the **rue du Commerce**, running down the middle of the *arrondissement* from Mᵒ La Motte Piquet-Grenelle, that George Orwell worked as a dishwasher, an experience described in his *Down and Out in Paris and London*. These days it is a lively, old-fashioned high street full of small shops and peeling, shuttered houses. Towards the end of the street is place du Commerce, with a bandstand in the middle, a model of old-fashioned petit-bourgeois respectability – it might be a frozen frame from a 1930s movie. Cafés and pâtisseries proliferate as rue du Commerce ends at place Étienne-Pernet, where cottagey houses still survive.

The other park in the 15ᵉ *arrondissement*, the **Parc Georges-Brassens**, lies in the southeast corner (Mᵒ Convention/Porte-de-Vanves). It's a delight, with a garden of scented herbs and shrubs designed principally for the blind (best in late spring), puppets and rocks and merry-go-rounds for kids, a mountain stream with pine and birch trees, beehives and a tiny terraced vineyard. The corrugated pyramid with a helter-skelter-like spiral is the Silvia-Montfort theatre.

On the west side of the park, in a secluded garden in passage Dantzig, off rue Dantzig, stands an unusual polygonal building known as **La Ruche**. Home to Fernand Léger, Modigliani, Chagall, Soutine and many other artists at the start of the century, it is still used by creative types. In the sheds of the old horse market between the park and rue Brançion, a **book market** is held every Saturday and Sunday morning.

The 14ᵉ below Montparnasse

The gargantuan development around place de Catalogne gives way to a walkway along the old rue Vercingétorix and to the changing but still cosy atmosphere, long lived in by artists, of **Pernety**. Wandering around Cité Bauer, rue des Thermopyles and rue Didot reveals adorable houses, secluded courtyards and quiet mews, and on the corner of rue du Moulin Vert and rue Hippolyte-Maindron you'll find Giacometti's old ramshackle studio and home. At the end of Impasse Floriment, behind a petrol station on rue d'Alésia, a bronze relief of Georges Brassens smoking his pipe adorns the tiny house where he lived and wrote his songs from 1944 to 1966.

Rue d'Alésia, the main east–west route through the 14ᵉ, is best known for its good-value clothes shops, many selling discounted couturier creations. There are more artistic associations south of rue d'Alésia near the junction with avenue Réné-Coty: Dalí, Lurçat, Miller and Durrell lived in the tiny cobbled street of **Villa Seurat** off rue de la Tombe-Issoire; Lenin and his wife, Krupskaya, lodged across the street at 4 rue Marie-Rose; Le Corbusier built the studio at 53 av Reille, close to the secretive and verdant square du Montsouris which links with rue Nansouty; and Georges Braque's home was in the cul-de-sac now named after him off this street. All these characters would have taken strolls in **Parc Montsouris** (RER Cité-Universitaire). Along with a lake and waterfall, its more surprising features include a meteorological office, a marker of the

you reach **place de Passy** and the crowded but leisurely terrace of *Le Paris Passy* café. From the square, stroll southeast along cobbled, pedestrianized **rue de l'Annonciation**, a pleasant mixture of down-to-earth and well-heeled which gives more of the flavour of old Passy. You may not want your Bechstein repaired or your furniture lacquered, but as you approach the end of the street, past several food shops with delectable displays, there'll be no holding back the salivary glands. When you hit rue Raynouard, cross the road and veer to your right, where at no. 47 you'll discover a delightful, summery little house with pale green-shutters and a decorative iron entrance porch, tucked away down some steps amongst a tree-filled garden. Here Balzac moved in the 1840s to outrun his creditors. In fact the deceptively tiny house extends down the hillside for three storeys, which made it easy for Balzac to slip out of the back door and into town unnoticed. The **Maison de Balzac** (Tues–Sun 10am–5.40pm; 22F/€3.35) repays a visit even if you've never read the writer. Memorabilia include a room devoted to the development of ideas for the creation of a monument to Balzac, resulting in the the famously blobby Rodin sculpture of the writer that was caricatured by contemporary cartoonists (see p.142).

Behind the house, and reached via some steps descending from rue Raynouard, **rue Berton** is a cobbled path with gas lights still in place, blocked off by the heavy security of the Turkish embassy. On the other side, arrived at by heading down avenue de Lamballe and then right into avenue du Général Mangin to cobbled **rue d'Ankara**, you can see the embassy building, an eighteenth-century château half hidden by greenery and screened by a high wall and guards. This was once a clinic where the pioneering Dr Blanche tried to treat the mad Maupassant and Gérard de Nerval, amongst others. It's a short walk from here down to the river which is crossed at this point by the **Pont Bir Hakeim**, a bridge famously featured in *Last Tango in Paris*. You're well placed now to cross the bridge and head north along the water to the Eiffel Tower about 500m along.

Bois de Boulogne

The **Bois de Boulogne**, running all down the west side of the 16ᵉ, is supposedly modelled on London's Hyde Park, though it is a very French interpretation. It offers all sorts of facilities: the **Jardin d'Acclimatation**, with lots of attractions for kids (see p.187); the **Parc de Bagatelle** (M° Port-de-Neuilly, then bus #43, or M° Porte-Maillot, then bus #244), which features beautiful displays of tulips, hyacinths and daffodils in the first half of April, irises in May, water lilies and roses at the end of June; a riding school; **bike rental** at the entrance to the Jardin d'Acclimatation; **boating** on the Lac Inférieur; and **race courses** at Longchamp and Auteuil. The best, and wildest, part for walking is towards the southwest corner.

When it was opened to the public in the eighteenth century, people said of it, "Les mariages du bois de Boulogne ne se font pas devant Monsieur le Curé" ("Unions cemented in the Bois de Boulogne do not take place in the presence of a priest"). Despite a more obvious police presence, the park is not a safe place for a evening stroll as the sex trade practised within is accompanied by a fair amount of crime, rendering it somewhat seedy and potentially dangerous.

If you have any interest in the beautiful and highly specialized skills, techniques and artefacts developed in the long ages that preceded industrialization, standardization and mass production, you should visit the fascinating **Musée National des Arts et Traditions Populaires**, 6 av du Mahatma Gandhi, Bois de Boulogne (daily except Tues 9.45am–5.15pm; 25F/€3.81, 32F/€4.88 with exhibitions; M° Les Sablons/Porte-Maillot), beside the main entrance to the Jardin d'Acclimatation. Boat-building, shepherding, farming, weaving, blacksmithing, pottery, stone-cutting, games and clairvoyance are all beautifully illustrated and displayed.

La Défense

La Défense (M°/RER Grande-Arche-de-la-Défense) has been elevated to one of the top places of pilgrimage for visitors to Paris by the **Grande Arche**, a beautiful and astounding 112-metre hollow cube clad in white marble, standing 6km out from the Arc de Triomphe at the far end of the Voie Triomphale, from which it stands at a slight angle. Suspended within its hollow – which could enclose Notre-Dame with ease – are open lift shafts and a "cloud" canopy. The roof section belongs to the Fondation Internationale des Droits de l'Homme, who stage exhibitions and conferences on issues related to human rights. You can ride up to the roof (daily 10am–7pm; 43F/€6.55) to see these, admire the "Map of the Heavens" marble patios and, on a clear day, scan to the Louvre and beyond.

Between the Grande Arche and the river is the **business complex** of La Défense, a perfect monument to late-twentieth-century capitalism. There is no formal pattern to the arrangements of towers. Token apartment blocks, offices of ELF, Esso, IBM, banks and other businesses compete for size, dazzle of surface and ability to make you dizzy. Mercifully, bizarre **artworks** transform the nightmare into comic entertainment, like **Joan Miró**'s giant wobbly creatures despairing at their misfit status beneath the biting edges and curveless heights of the buildings and Alexander **Calder**'s red-iron offering, a *stabile* rather than a mobile. A statue commemorating the defence of Paris in 1870 (after which the district is named) perches on a concrete plinth in front of a coloured plastic waterfall and fountain pool, while nearer the river disembodied people clutch each other round endlessly repeated concrete flower beds. You'll find details of all the sculptures in the **Art Défense** exhibition space beside the waterfall. A good way to approach the Grande Arche, see the sculptures and watch the main attraction loom is to get out of the métro a stop before at Esplanade-de-la-Défense.

If you're desperate to hand over money to the firms surrounding you, there's the enormous Quatre-Temps shopping centre to the left of the Grande Arche as you face it, and a FNAC bookshop in the CNIT building oppposite. Fun but expensive is **Le Dôme-Imax**, a 180° projection cinema between Quatre Temps and the Grande Arche (daily 12.15–8pm; 60F/€9.15; programme details in *Pariscope*).

The 17ᵉ arrondissement

The 17ᵉ *arrondissement* is most interesting in its eastern half. The classier western end is cold and soulless, cut by too many wide and uniform boulevards. A route that takes in the best of it would be from **place des Ternes**, with its cafés and flower market, through the stately wrought-iron gates of place de la République Dominicaine into the small and formal **Parc Monceau**, surrounded by pompous residences. **Rue de Lévis** (a few blocks up rue Berger from M° Monceau) has one of the city's most strident, colourful and appetizing markets every day of the week except Monday, and is also a good restaurant area, particularly up around rue des Dames and rue Cheroy.

Further north still, across the St-Lazare train tracks, **rue des Batignolles** is the heart of Batignolles "village", now sufficiently self-conscious to have formed an association for the preservation of its "*caractère villageois*". At the north end of the street, the attractive semicircular place du Dr-Lobligeois frames a small colonnaded church whose entrance was modelled on the Madeleine. Behind it is the tired and trampled greenery of square Batignolles, with the marshalling yards beyond. The long **rue des Moines** leads northeast towards Guy-Môquet. This is the working-class Paris of the movies, all small, animated, friendly shops, four- or five-storey houses in shades of peeling grey, and brown-stained bars where men drink standing at the *zinc* (a traditional bar made from zinc).

Montmartre and northern Paris

Montmartre lies in the middle of the largely petit-bourgeois and working-class 18ᵉ *arrondissement*, respectable round the slopes of the Butte, distinctly less so towards the **Gare du Nord** and **Gare de l'Est**, where depressing slums crowd along the train tracks. The Butte itself has a relaxed, sunny, countrified air; **Pigalle**, at the foot of the hill, is full of sex shops and peep-shows, interspersed with tired-looking women in shop doorways. On its northern edge lies the extensive **St-Ouen flea market**.

Place des Abbesses and up to the Butte

In spite of being one of the city's chief tourist attractions, the **Butte Montmartre** manages to retain the quiet, almost secretive, air of its rural origins. The most popular access route is via the rue de Steinkerque and the steps below the Sacré-Cœur (the funicular railway from place Suzanne-Valadon is covered by the *Carte Orange*). For a quieter approach, go up via place des Abbesses or rue Lepic.

Place des Abbesses is postcard-pretty, with one of the few complete surviving Guimard métro entrances. To the east, at the Chapelle des Auxiliatrices in rue Yvonne-Le-Tac, Ignatius Loyola founded the Jesuit movement in 1534. It is also supposed to be the place where St Denis, the first bishop of Paris, had his head chopped off by the Romans around 250 AD. He is said to have carried it until he dropped, where the cathedral of St-Denis now stands north of the city.

Continuing from place des Abbesses to the top of the Butte, two quiet and attractive routes are up rue de la Vieuville and the stairs in rue Drevet to the minuscule **place du Calvaire**, with a lovely view back over the city, or up rue Tholozé, then right below the **Moulin de la Galette** – the last survivor of Montmartre's forty-odd windmills, immortalized by Renoir – into rue des Norvins.

Artistic associations abound hereabouts. Zola, Berlioz, Turgenev, Seurat, Degas and Van Gogh lived in the area. Picasso, Braque and Juan Gris invented Cubism in an old piano factory in place Émile-Goudeau, known as the **Bateau-Lavoir**, still serving as artists' studios, though the original building burnt down some years ago. And Toulouse-Lautrec's inspiration, the **Moulin Rouge**, survives also, albeit a mere shadow of its former self, on the corner of boulevard de Clichy and place Blanche.

The **Musée de Montmartre**, at 12 rue Cortot (Tues–Sun 11am–6pm; 25F/€3.81), just over the brow of the hill, tries to recapture something of the feel of those pioneering days, but it's a bit of a disappointment, except for the occasionally excellent temporary exhibition. The house itself, rented at various times by Renoir, Dufy, Suzanne Valadon and her alcoholic son Utrillo, is worth visiting for the view over the neat terraces of the tiny **Montmartre vineyard** and the north side of the Butte. The entrance to the vineyard is on the steep rue de Saules.

Place du Tertre and Sacré-Cœur

The **place du Tertre** is the heart of tourist Montmartre, photogenic but totally bogus, jammed with tourists, overpriced restaurants and "artists" doing quick portraits while you wait. Between place du Tertre and the Sacré-Cœur, the old church of **St-Pierre** is all that remains of the Benedictine abbey that occupied the Butte Montmartre from the twelfth century on. Though much altered, it still retains its Romanesque and early Gothic feel. In it are four ancient columns, two by the door, two in the choir, leftovers from a Roman shrine that stood on the hill – *mons mercurii* (Mercury's Hill), the Romans called it. Crowning the Butte is the **Sacré-Cœur** (daily 6am–11pm), a romantic and graceful pastiche, whose white pimply domes are an essential part of the Paris skyline. The best thing about it is the view from the **tower** (daily 9am–6pm;

15F/€2.28), almost as high as the Eiffel Tower and showing the layout of the whole city. Construction was started in the 1870s on the initiative of the Catholic Church to atone for the "crimes" of the Commune. **Square Willette**, the space at the foot of the monumental staircase, is named after the local artist who turned out on inauguration day to shout "Long live the devil!"

Montmartre cemetery

West of the Butte, near the beginning of rue Caulaincourt in place Clichy, lies the **Montmartre cemetery**. Ramshackle and peeling, on a tiny courtyard full of plants, it epitomizes the kind-hearted, instinctively arty, sepia-tinged Paris that every romantic visitor secretly cherishes. Most of the guests have been there years. The cemetery is tucked down below street level in the hollow of an old quarry with its entrance on avenue Rachel under rue Caulaincourt. A tangle of trees and funereal pomposity, it holds the graves of Zola, Stendhal, Berlioz, Degas, Feydeau, Offenbach and Truffaut, among others.

St-Ouen flea market

Officially open Saturday to Monday 9am to 7pm – unofficially, from 5am – the **puces de St-Ouen** (M° Porte-de-Clignancourt) claims to be the largest flea market in the world, the name "flea" deriving from the state of the secondhand mattresses, clothes and other junk sold here when the market first operated outside the city walls. Nowadays it is predominantly a proper – and expensive – antiques market (mainly furniture, but including old café-bar counters, telephones, traffic lights, posters, jukeboxes and petrol pumps), with what is left of the rag-and-bone element confined to the further reaches of rues Fabre and Lécuyer.

Pigalle

From place Clichy in the west to Barbès-Rochechouart in the east, the hill of Montmartre is underlined by the sleazy **boulevards of Clichy and Rochechouart**, the centre of the roadway often occupied by bumper-car pistes and other funfair sideshows. At the Barbès end of boulevard Rochechouart, where the métro clatters by on iron trestles, the crowds teem round the Tati department stores, the city's cheapest, while the pavements are lined with West and North African street vendors offering cloth, watches and trinkets. At the place Clichy end, tour buses from all over Europe feed their contents into massive hotels. In the middle, between place Blanche and place Pigalle, sex shows, sex shops, tiny bars where hostesses lurk in complicated tackle, and street prostitutes (both male and female) coexist with one of Paris's most elegant private *villas* on avenue Frochot. In the adjacent streets are the city's best specialist music shops.

Perfectly placed amongst all the sex shops and shows is the **Musée de l'Erotisme** (daily 10am–2am; 40F/€6.10), exploring different cultures' approaches to sex. The ground floor and first floor are dedicated to sacred and ethnographic art, where proud phalluses and well-practised positions in the art from Asia, Africa and pre-Colombian Latin America reveal a strong link between the spiritual and the erotic. European art (apart from the copies of Ancient Greek vases, where there's no beating about the bush), on the other hand, uses sex to satirize and ridicule religion with lots of naughty nuns and priests caught in compromising situations. Humour is the main theme in the basement. Have a go on the metal outline of a naked women with a metal ring and baton attached. The aim is to get the ring from one end to the other without it touching the filament – the longer you succeed the more she moans. Beware, it's quite loud! The rest of the floors upstairs are devoted to temporary exhibitions which change every three months.

over to the east is the **Zenith** inflatable rock music venue. To the south, the largest of the old **market halls** – an iron-frame structure designed by Baltard, the engineer of the vanished Les Halles pavilions – is now a vast and brilliant exhibition space, the **Grande Salle**.

South of the Grande Salle is the brand-new **Cité de la Musique**, in two complexes to either side of the Porte-de-Pantin entrance. To the west is the national music academy; while to the east lies a concert hall, the very chic *Café de la Musique*, a music and dance information centre and the **Musée de la Musique** (Tues–Thurs noon–6pm, Fri & Sat noon–7.30pm, Sun 10am–6pm; 35F/€5.34), presenting the history of music from the end of the Renaissance to the present day, both visually – a collection of 4500 instruments – and aurally, with headsets and interactive displays. Designed by Christian de Portzamparc, the buildings make abstract artistic statements with their wedge, wavy and funnelling shapes, musical patterns, and varied colours and textures. Around the concert hall, a glass-roofed arcade with pale blue sloping walls even gives out deep relaxation sounds.

Belleville, Ménilmontant, Père-Lachaise and the Bois de Vincennes

The **eastern districts** of Paris are no longer the revolutionary hotbeds they were in the nineteenth century, and the predominantly working-class identity of the area is changing as a slow process of architectural and cultural transformation takes place. **Belleville** and **Ménilmontant** have long had large immigrant populations of Slavs, Greeks, Portuguese, Chinese, Vietnamese, Jews, Arabs, Armenians, Senegalese, Malians – still very much in evidence against a backdrop of some much more pleasing architectural additions than the old high-rise shelving-unit housing. Exploring the old villagey streets and admiring the best of the new constructions are the main pleasures of this part of Paris, which also offers wonderful views down onto the city; for a focus to your wandering, there's **Père-Lachaise cemetery**.

Parc des Buttes-Chaumont

At the northern end of the Belleville heights, a short walk from La Villette, is the **parc des Buttes-Chaumont** (M° Buttes-Chaumont/Botzaris), constructed by Haussmann in the 1860s to camouflage what until then had been a desolate warren of disused quarries and miserable shacks. The sculpted beak-shaped park stays open all night and, equally rarely for Paris, you're not cautioned off the grass. At its centre is a huge rock upholding a delicate Corinthian temple and surrounded by a lake which you cross via a suspension bridge or the shorter Pont des Suicides. Louis Aragon, the literary grand old man of the French Communist Party, wrote of this bridge that it claimed victims among passers-by who had no intention of dying but found themselves suddenly tempted by the abyss. Feeble metal grills erected along its sides have put an end to such impulses.

Belleville and Ménilmontant

The route from Buttes-Chaumont to Père-Lachaise will take you through the one-time villages of **Belleville** and **Ménilmontant**. Many of the old village lanes disappeared in the tower-block mania of the 1960s and 1970s, but others have now been opened up, and many of the newest buildings are imaginative infill, following the height and curves of their older neighbours. Dozens of cobbled and gardened *villas* remain intact: east of Buttes-Chaumont towards place Rhin-et-Danube, between rue Boyer (with a 1920s Soviet-style building at no. 25) and rue des Pyrénées just north of Père-Lachaise, and out to the east by Porte de Bagnolet, up the very picturesque steps from place Octave-Chanute.

The first main street you cross coming down from Buttes-Chaumont, **rue de Belleville**, has become the new Chinatown of Paris. Vietnamese and Chinese shops and restaurants have proliferated over the last few years, adding considerable visual and gastronomic cheer to the area. African and oriental fruits, spices, music and fabrics can be bought at the **boulevard de Belleville market** on Tuesdays and Fridays. On the steps of no. 72 rue de Belleville Edith Piaf was abandoned when just a few hours old, and there's a small **museum** dedicated to her at 5 rue Créspin-du-Gast (Mon–Thurs 1–6pm; closed Sept; by appointment on ☎01.43.55.52.72; donation; Mº Ménilmontant/St-Maur). Rue Ramponneau, just southeast of the crossroads with boulevard de Belleville and now entirely rebuilt, was where the last Communard on the last barricade held out alone for a final fifteen minutes.

You get fantastic views down onto the city centre from the higher reaches of Belleville and Ménilmontant: the best place to watch the sun set is the **Parc de Belleville** (Mº Couronnes/Pyrénées), which descends in a series of terraces and waterfalls from rue Piat. And from **rue de Ménilmontant**, by rues de l'Ermitage and Boyer, you can look straight down to Beaubourg.

Père-Lachaise cemetery

Père-Lachaise cemetery (daily 7.30am–6pm; Mº Gambetta/Père-Lachaise/Alexandre-Dumas) is like a miniature city of dead, seemingly empty houses and temples of every size and style. The cemetery was opened in 1804, after an urgent stop had been put to further burials in the overflowing city cemeteries and churchyards, and to be interred in Père-Lachaise quickly became the ultimate symbol of riches and success. A free **map** of the cemetery is available at the entrance on rue des Rondeaux by avenue du Père Lachaise, or you can buy a more detailed souvenir one for 10F/€1.52 at newsagents near here and the boulevard de Ménilmontant entrance.

Swarms of admirers flock to the now-sanitized tomb of ex-Doors lead singer Jim Morrison (division 6), cleansed of all its graffiti and watched vigilantly by security guards. Colette's tomb (division 4), close to the main Ménilmontant entrance, is very plain though always covered in flowers. The same is true of the tombs of Sarah Bernhardt (division 44) and the great chanteuse Edith Piaf (division 97). Marcel Proust lies in his family's conventional tomb (division 85), which honours the medical fame of his father. In division 92, nineteenth-century journalist Victor Noir – shot for daring to criticize a relative of Napoléon III – lies flat on his back, fully clothed, his top hat fallen by his feet.

Corot (division 24) and Balzac (division 48) both have superb busts, Balzac looking particularly satisfied with his life. Géricault reclines on cushions of stone (division 12), paint palette in hand; Chopin (division 11) has a willowy muse weeping for his loss. The most impressive of the individual tombs is that of Oscar Wilde (division 89), adorned with a strange pharaonic winged messenger (sadly robbed almost immediately of its prominent penis by a scandalized cemetery employee, who, so the story goes, used it as a paperweight), sculpted by Jacob Epstein, and with a grim verse from *The Ballad of Reading Gaol* behind. Nearby, in division 96, is the grave of Modigliani and his lover Jeanne Herbuterne, who killed herself in crazed grief a few days after the artist died in agony from meningitis.

But it is the monuments to the collective, violent deaths that have the power to change a sunny outing to Père-Lachaise into a much more sombre experience. In division 97 you'll find the memorials to those who died in the Nazi concentration camps, to executed Resistance fighters and to those who were never accounted for in the genocide of the last world war. The sculptures are relentless in their images of inhumanity,

PÈRE-LACHAISE CEMETERY

of people forced to collaborate in their own degradation and death. There is also the *Mur des Fedérés* (division 76), the wall where the last troops of the Paris Commune were lined up and shot in the final days of the battle in 1871. The man who ordered their execution, Adolphe Thiers, lies in the centre of the cemetery in division 55.

The 11ᵉ and 12ᵉ arrondissements

To the south and west of Père-Lachaise, around **rue de la Roquette** and **rue de Charonne**, there's nothing very special about the passages and ragged streets that make up the **11ᵉ arrondissement**, except that they are utterly Parisian, with the odd detail of a building, the display of veg in a simple greengrocer's, sunlight on a café table or graffiti on a Second Empire street fountain to charm the aimless wanderer. The closer you get to the Bastille, the more chunks are missing – demolition areas of several blocks at a time. It's depressing, but so too is the northeast corner of the 11e, where the buildings are crumbling and the poverty very much in evidence.

There are quiet havens from the mania of the Bastille traffic in the courtyards of **rue du Faubourg-St-Antoine**. Since the fifteenth century, this has been the principal artisan and working-class *quartier* of Paris, the cradle of revolutions and mother of streetfighters. From its beginnings the principal trade associated with it has been **furniture-making**, and the maze of interconnecting yards and passages are still full of the workshops of the related trades: marquetry, stainers, polishers and inlayers.

Alongside **avenue Daumesnil**, the main artery of the **12e arrondissement**, an old railway line has been converted into the **Promenade Plantée**, a "green corridor" for walkers and cyclists running all the way from the junction with rue Ledru-Rollin to the Jardin de Reuilly and on out to Vincennes (see below). Below, the railway arches have been transformed into a string of art workshops and galleries, the **Viaduc des Arts**, running from nos. 15 to 121. South of the avenue is the gorgeous nineteenth-century extravaganza of the Gare de Lyon, a high-rise business area, the Stalinesque 400-metre-long **Ministère des Finances** building, and, facing the national library across the river, the very welcome new green space of the **Parc de Bercy** (M° Bercy) replacing the warehouses where for centuries the capital's wine supplies were unloaded from river barges.

Out to Vincennes

Across the *boulevard périphérique* at the end of avenue Daumesnil, on the edge of the Bois de Vincennes, is the **Musée des Arts Africains et Océaniens**, 293 av Daumesnil (Mon, Wed–Fri & hols 10am–5.30pm, Sat & Sun 10am–6pm; 30F/€4.57; M° Porte-Dorée), with a 1930s colonial facade of jungles, hard-working natives and the place names of the French empire. This strange museum – one of the least crowded in the city – has an African gold brooch of curled-up sleeping crocodiles on one floor and, in the basement, five live crocodiles in a tiny pit surrounded by tanks of tropical fish. Imperialism is much in evidence in a gathering of culture and creatures from the old French colonies: hardly any of the black African artefacts are dated – the collection predates European acknowledgement of history on that continent, and the captions are a bit suspicious too. These masks and statues, furniture, adornments and tools should be exhibited with paintings by Expressionists, Cubists and Surrealists to show the influence they had. Picasso and friends certainly came here often.

In the **Bois de Vincennes** itself, the city's only extensive green space besides the Bois de Boulogne, you can spend an afternoon boating on Lac Daumesnil (by the zoo) or rent a bike from the same place and feed the ducks on Lac des Minimes on the other side of the wood (bus #112 from Vincennes métro). The fenced enclave on the southern side of Lac Daumesnil is a **Buddhist centre**, with a Tibetan temple, Vietnamese chapel and international pagoda – all occasionally visitable (information on ☎01.40.04.98.06). As far as real woods go, the forest itself opens out once you're east of avenue de St-Maurice, but the area is so overrun with roads that countryside sensations don't stand much chance. To the north is the **Parc Floral** (daily: summer 9.30am–8pm; winter 9.30am–dusk; 10F/€1.52; bus #112 or short walk from M° Château-de-Vincennes), one of the best gardens in Paris. Flowers are always in bloom in the Jardin des Quatres Saisons; you can picnic beneath pines while the kids play, then wander through concentrations of camellias, cacti, ferns, irises and bonsai trees. Abutting the Parc Floral is the **Cartoucherie de Vincennes**, an old ammunitions factory, now home to four theatre companies, including the radical Théâtre du Soleil.

On the northern edge of the *bois*, the **Château de Vincennes** (daily 10am–5/6pm; choice of guided visits, 32F/€4.88 or 25F/€3.81; M° Château-de-Vincennes), royal medieval residence, then state prison, porcelain factory, weapons dump and military training school, is still undergoing restoration work started by Napoléon III. The best of the tours available is that to the Flamboyant Gothic **Chapelle Royale**, completed in the mid-sixteenth century and decorated with superb Renaissance stained-glass windows around the choir.

Eating and drinking

Eating and drinking are among the chief delights of Paris, as they are in the country as a whole. There is a tremendous variety of foods, from Senegalese to Caribbean, from Thai to eastern European and North African, as well as regional French cuisines, notably from the southwest. There's also a huge diversity of eating and drinking establishments: luxurious **restaurants** in the traditional style or elbow-to-elbow bench-and-trestle-table jobs; spacious **brasseries** and **cafés** where you can watch the world go by while nibbling on a baguette sandwich; or dark, cavernous **beer cellars** and tiny **wine bars** with sawdust on the floor offering wines by the glass from every region of France. You could take coffee and cakes in a chintzy **salon de thé**, in a bookshop or gallery, or even in the confines of a mosque. **Bars** can be medieval vaults, minimalist or post-modern design units, London-style pubs or period pieces in styles ranging from the Swinging Sixties to the Naughty Nineties. The variety is endless and the distinctions between bars, cafés, pubs, ice-cream parlours, sandwich bars, brasseries and wine bars can't always be clearly drawn. **Gay** establishments proliferate in the Marais and around the Bastille *quartier* (see "Gay and lesbian Paris", p.179).

It's true that the old-time cheap neighbourhood cafés and bistros are a dying breed, while fast-food chains have burgeoned at an alarming speed. Quality is also in decline at the lower end of the restaurant market, particularly in tourist hotspots. Yet, however much Parisians bemoan the changing times, you'll find you're still spoiled for choice even on a modest budget. There are numerous **fixed-price menus** (*prix fixe*) for under 80F/€12.20, particularly at lunchtime, providing staple dishes; for 150F/€22.87 you'll have the choice of more interesting dishes; and for 200F/€30.49, you should be getting some gourmet satisfaction.

STUDENT RESTAURANTS

Students of any age are eligible to apply for tickets for the **university restaurants** under the direction of CROUS de Paris. A list of addresses, which includes numerous cafés and brasseries, is available from their offices at 39 av Georges-Bernanos, 5ᵉ (Mon–Fri 9am–5pm; ☎01.40.51.36.00; RER Port-Royal). The **tickets**, however, have to be obtained from the particular restaurant of your choice (opening hours generally 11.30am–2pm & 6–8pm). Not all serve both midday and evening meals, and times change with each term. Though the food is not wonderful, it is certainly filling, and you can't complain about the price. They will cost you 13.70F/€2.09 if you're studying at a French university; 23F/€3.51 if you can produce an International Student Card; and 28.20F/€4.30 otherwise. The **addresses** of the most conveniently located student restaurants are listed below:

8bis rue Cuvier, 5ᵉ (Mᵒ Jussieu); 31 av Georges-Bernanos, 5ᵉ (Mᵒ Port-Royal); rue de Santeuil, 5ᵉ (Mᵒ Censier-Daubenton); 12 place du Panthéon, 5ᵉ (Mᵒ Cardinal-Lemoine); 8bis rue de l'Eperon, 6ᵉ (Mᵒ Odéon); 46 rue de Vaugirard, 6ᵉ (RER Luxembourg/Mᵒ Mabillon); 21 rue d'Assas, 6ᵉ (Mᵒ Port-Royal/Notre-Dame-des-Champs); 105 bd de l'Hôpital, 13ᵉ (Mᵒ St-Marcel); 13/17 rue Dareau, 14ᵉ (Mᵒ St-Jacques); in the Cité Universitaire, 14ᵉ (RER Cité Universitaire); and 156 rue Vaugirard, 15ᵉ (Mᵒ Pasteur).

PARIS FOR VEGETARIANS

The chances of finding vegetarian main dishes on the menus of regular French restaurants are not good. Though you can choose a selection of non-meat starters or order an omelette or a salad, you'll be much better off going to an ethnic restaurant – Middle Eastern or Indian make a good choice – or a proper **vegetarian restaurant**. There are not many of the latter, and the ones that do exist tend to be based on a healthy diet principle rather than *haute cuisine*, but at least you get a choice. All the establishments listed below are reviewed in the pages that follow.

Aquarius 1, 54 rue Ste-Croix-de-la-Bretonnerie, 4e. See p.160.
Aquarius 2, 40 rue Gergovie, 14e. See p.168.
Au Grain de Folie, 24 rue de la Vieuville, 18e. See p.172.
Grand Appetit, 9 rue de la Cerisaie, 4e. See p.160.
Le Grenier de Notre-Dame, 18 rue de la Bûcherie, 5e. See p.161.
Joy in Food, 2 rue Truffaut, 17e. See p.171.
La Petite Légume, 36 rue Boulangers, 5e. See p.62.
Les Quatre et Une Saveurs, 72 rue du Cardinal-Lemoine, 5e. See p.162.
La Ville de Jagannath, 10 rue St Maur, 11e. See p.167.
La Victoire Suprême du Coeur, 41 rue des Bourdonnais, 1er. See p.158.

The big boulevard cafés and brasseries are always more expensive than those a little further removed, and addresses in the smarter or more touristy *arrondissements* set prices soaring. A snack or drink on the Champs-Élysées, place St-Germain-des-Prés or rue de Rivoli, for instance, will be double or triple the price of Belleville, Batignolles or the southern 14e. Many bars have **happy hours**, but prices can double after 10pm, and any clearly trendy, glitzy or stylish place is bound to be expensive.

The different eating and drinking establishments are listed here by *arrondissement*. They are divided into **restaurants**, including some brasseries, and **bars and cafés**, incorporating snack bars, ice-cream parlours and *salons de thé*. You'll also find boxes listing **vegetarian** (not Paris's strongest suit; see above), **ethnic** (see p.168) and **late-night** (see p.170) possibilities.

1er arrondissement
Bars and cafés

Angélina, 226 rue de Rivoli (M^o Tuileries). Mon–Fri 9am–7pm, Sat & Sun 9am–7.30pm; closed Tues in July & Aug. A long-established gilded cage, where the well-coiffed sip the best hot chocolate in town. Pâtisseries and other desserts of the same high quality. Not cheap.

Aux Bons Crus, 7 rue des Petits-Champs (M^o Palais-Royal). Mon 9am–4pm, Tues–Sat 9am–11pm; closed Sun. A relaxed workaday place that has been serving good wines and cheese, sausage and ham for over eighty years. Wine from 15F/€2.29 a glass; plate of cold meats from 55F/€8.38.

Café Marly, Cour Napoléon du Louvre, 93 rue de Rivoli (M^o Palais-Royale/Musée-du-Louvre). Daily till 2am. Very chic, very classy and very expensive café inside the Louvre, with tables beneath the colonnade overlooking the Pyramide in summer.

Restorama, Le Carrousel du Louvre (M^o Louvre). Daily 9am–9pm. A vast underground fast-food eating hall served by over a dozen different outlets: rôtisseries, hamburgers, pizzas, Tex-Mex, Chinese, Lebanese, Japanese, crêperies, salad bars – easy to eat for under 50F/€7.62. Access from place du Carrousel or the Louvre Pyramide.

Le Rubis, 10 rue du Marché-St-Honoré (M^o Pyramides). Mon–Fri 7am–10pm, Sat 8am–4pm; closed mid-Aug. One of the oldest wine bars in Paris, with a reputation for excellent wines, snacks and *plats du jour*. Very small and very crowded. Glasses of wine from 5.50F/€0.84.

Le Sous-Bock, 49 rue St-Honoré (M° Châtelet-Les Halles). Mon–Sat 11am–5am, Sun 3pm–5am. Hundreds of beers – bottled and on tap (around 40F/€6.10 a pint) – and whiskies to sample, plus simple, inexpensive food. Mussels a speciality (60–75F/€9.15–11.43). Frequented by night owls. Prices go up after 7pm.

Taverne Henri IV, 13 place du Pont-Neuf (M° Pont-Neuf). Mon–Fri noon–10pm, Sat noon–4pm; closed Aug. Yves Montand used to come here when Simone Signoret lived in the adjacent place Dauphine. Good food but a bit pricey for a full meal. Plates of meats and cheeses around 70F/€10.67, sandwiches 30F/€4.57, wine from 20F/€3.05 a glass.

Restaurants

Le Dauphin, 167 rue St-Honoré; ☎01.42.60.40.11 (M° Palais-Royal/Musée-du-Louvre; see map, pp.112–113). Daily noon–2.30pm & 7–10.30pm; June–Oct till 12.30am. A genuine bistro with a menu at 140F/€21.34. Seafood platter during oyster season for 167F/€25.46. Country cooking including pig's cheeks, *lapereau* (young rabbit) *à la grand-mère* and *magret de canard*.

Foujita, 41 rue St-Roch; ☎01.42.61.42.93 (M° Tuileries/Pyramides; see map, pp.112–113). Mon–Sat noon–2.15pm & 7.30–10pm; closed mid-Aug. One of the cheaper but best Japanese restaurants, as proven by the numbers of Japanese eating here. Quick and crowded; soup, sushis, rice and tea for 72F/€10.98 at lunchtime; plate of sushis or sushamis for under 110F/€16.77.

Le Gros Minet, 1 rue des Prouvaires; ☎01.42.33.02.62 (M° Châtelet-Les Halles). Mon & Sat 7.30–11.30pm, Tues–Fri noon–2pm & 7.30–11.30pm. Relaxed, small and charming restaurant, specializing in duck recipes.

L'Incroyable, 26 rue de Richelieu; ☎01.42.96.24.64 (M° Palais-Royal; see map, pp.112–113). Tues–Fri lunch & 6.30–9pm, Mon & Sat lunch only. A very pleasant restaurant, hidden in a tiny passage, serving decent meals for 85F/€12.96 lunch; 115F/€17.53 evenings.

Au Pied de Cochon, 6 rue Coquillière; ☎01.42.36.11.75 (M° Châtelet-Les Halles). Daily 24hr. The place to go for extravagant middle-of-the-night pork chops and oysters. Seafood platter 155F/€23.63. *Carte* up to 300F/€45.73.

Au Rendez-vous des Camionneurs, 72 quai des Orfèvres; ☎01.43.54.88.74 (M° St-Michel; see map, pp.136–137). Daily noon–2pm & 7–11.30pm. Crowded, traditional establishment serving snails, steaks and scallops. Midday menus under 100F/€15.24; evening menu 130F/€19.82; à la carte around 175F/€26.68.

La Robe et le Palais, 13 rue des Lavandières St-Opportune; ☎01.45.08.07.41 (M° Châtelet). Mon–Sat noon–2.30pm & 7.15–10.30pm. Refined, unpretentious cuisine and an excellent wine list served up in a small, busy space. Good lunch menu for 79F/€12.04.

La Tour de Montlhéry (Chez Denise), 5 rue des Prouvaires; ☎01.42.36.21.82 (M° Louvre-Rivoli/Châtelet). Mon–Fri till midnight, Sat lunch only. An old-style Les Halles bistro serving substantial food; always crowded and smoky. *Carte* from 200F/€30.49.

La Victoire Suprême du Coeur, 41 rue des Bourdonnais; ☎01.40.41.93.95 (M° Louvre-Rivoli/Châtelet). Mon–Sat noon–10pm. Vegetarian restaurant of the Sri Chimnoy variety – the Indian guru's photos and drawings cover the walls. The menu offers a wide range of tasty salads, quiches and *plats du jour* (49F/€7.47) – all very wholesome.

2ᵉ arrondissement
Bars and cafés

L'Arbre à Cannelle, 57 passage des Panoramas (M° Rue-Montmartre). Mon–Sat till 6.30pm. Exquisite wooden panelling, frescoes and painted ceilings; puddings, flans and *assiettes gourmandes* for 60–75F/€9.15–11.43.

Le Café, 62 rue Tiquetonne (M° Les Halles/Étienne-Marcel). Daily 10am–2am. Quiet and secluded café on the junction with rue Étienne-Marcel, with old maps adorning the walls and people playing chess. *Plats du jour* 45–55F/€6.86–8.38.

Juveniles, 47 rue de Richelieu (M° Palais-Royal). Mon–Sat noon–midnight. Very popular tiny wine bar run by a Brit. Wine from 85F/€12.96 a bottle; *plats du jour* around 68F/€10.37.

Kitty O'Shea's, 10 rue des Capucines (M° Opéra). Daily noon–1.30am. An Irish pub with excellent Guinness and Smithwicks. A favourite haunt of Irish expats. The *John Jameson* restaurant upstairs serves high-quality, pricey, Gaelic food, including seafood flown in from Galway.

Restaurants

Dilan, 13 rue Mandar; ☎01.42.21.14.88 (M° Les Halles/Sentier). Mon–Sat noon–2pm & 7.30–11.30pm; closed Sun. An excellent-value Kurdish restaurant, offering beautiful starters, stuffed aubergines (*babaqunuc*), fish with yoghurt and courgettes (*kanarya*). Midday menu 64F/€9.76.

Higuma, 32bis rue Sainte Anne; ☎01.47.03.38.59 (M° Pyramides). Daily 11.30am–10pm. Authentic Japanese canteen with cheap, filling ramen dishes and a variety of set menus starting at 63F/€9.60.

Vaudeville, 29 rue Vivienne; ☎01.40.20.04.62 (M° Bourse). Daily 7am–2am. A lively, late-night brasserie, often with a queue to get a table. Good food, attractive marble and mosaic interior. À la carte from 150F/€22.87; *menu* at 138F/€21.04.

3e arrondissement

Bars and cafés

L'Apparemment Café, 18 rue des Coutures-St-Servais (M° St-Sébastien-Froissart). Mon–Fri noon–2am, Sat 4pm–2am, Sun 12.30pm–midnight. Chic but cosy café resembling a series of comfortable sitting rooms, with quiet corners and deep sofas. Popular Sunday brunch until 4pm costs 90F/€13.72.

Web Bar, 32 rue de Picardie (M° Filles-du-Calvaire). Mon–Fri 8.30am–2am, Sat & Sun 11am–2am. Paris's best cyber café, on three levels in a converted industrial space, with fifteen terminals on a gallery level. A real culture zone: pick up a printed programme of the art exhibitions, short film screenings and other arty events or consult their Web site *www.webbar.fr*. Comfy couches to loll on and a resident DJ make it a good place to chill, and simple healthy food comes in generous portions (37F/€5.34 for a delicious quiche with loads of salad; lunch menu 51F/€7.77 or 61F/€9.30).

Restaurants

See map, pp.124–125.

Chez Nénesse, 17 rue Saintonge; ☎01.42.78.46.49 (M° Arts-et-Métiers). Mon–Fri noon–2pm & 7.45–10pm; closed Aug. Steak in bilberry sauce, figs stuffed with cream of almonds, and home-made chips on Thursday lunchtimes are some of the unique delights at this restaurant. À la carte around 160F/€24.40.

Le Marais-Cage, 8 rue de Beauce; ☎01.48.87.44.51 (M° Arts-et-Métiers/Filles-du-Calvaire). Mon–Fri noon–2.15pm & 7–10.30pm, Sat evenings only; closed Aug. Friendly, popular West Indian restaurant, serving good food, especially seafood. 130F/€19.82 menu midday, 160F/€24.40 and 199F/€30.34 evening, wine included with all.

Le Quincampe, 78 rue Quincampoix; ☎01.40.27.01.45 (M° Étienne-Marcel/Rambuteau/RER Châtelet). Noon–11pm; closed Mon, Sat lunch & Sun. Moroccan restaurant and *salon de thé*, with a pleasant atmosphere, serving high-quality food and delicious mint tea. You can eat around a real fire in the room at the back. Tagines, *pastilla* and *plat du jour* 80F/€12.20.

4e arrondissement

Bars and cafés

Bar de Jarente, 5 rue de Jarente (M° St-Paul). Closed Sun & Mon. A lovely old-fashioned café-bar off the pretty place du Marché Ste-Catherine, which remains nonchalantly indifferent to the shifting trends arround it.

Berthillon, 31 rue St-Louis-en-l'Île (M° Pont-Marie). Wed–Sun 10am–8pm. Long queues for these excellent ice creams and sorbets (22F/€3.35 a triple) with a big choice of fruity flavours – like rhubarb – you've probably never tasted before. Also available at *Lady Jane* and *Le Flore-en-l'Île*, both on quai d'Orléans, as well as at four other island sites listed on the door.

Bofinger, 7 rue de la Bastille; ☎01.42.72.87.82 (M° Bastille). Daily until 1am. A popular *fin-de-siècle* brasserie with its original decor, serving sauerkraut and seafood. Weekday lunchtime menu at 119F/€18.14, evening 178F/€27.13, both including wine; otherwise over 200F/€30.49.

Ma Bourgogne, 19 place des Vosges (M° St-Paul). Daily until 12.30am, till 1am in summer. A quiet and pleasant arty café with tables under the arcades on the northwest corner of the square. Best in the morning when the sun hits this side of the square. Serves somewhat pricey meals too – lunch and dinner menu 195F/€29.73.

Café Beaubourg, 43 rue St-Merri (M° Rambuteau/Hôte-de-Ville). Mon–Thurs & Sun 8am–1am, Sat 8am–2am. A seat under the expansive awnings (café designed by Christian de Partzamparc) is one of the best places for people-watching on the Pompidou Centre's piazza; expensive, rather sour service, but very stylish loos.

Café des Phares, 7 place de la Bastille, west side (M° Bastille). Daily 7am–4am. Every Sunday at 11am a public philosophy debate is held in the back room here, run by the somewhat controversial Nietzsche specialist Marc Sautet, who also offers private philosophical consultations.

Dame Tartine, 2 rue Brisemiche (M° Rambuteau/Hôtel-de-Ville). Daily noon–11.30pm. Overlooking the Stravinsky pool, this place serves particularly delicious open toasted sandwiches (from 30F/€4.57). Inside, the relaxed atmosphere matches the mellow yellow walls.

L'Ébouillanté, 6 rue des Barres (M° Hôtel-de-Ville). Tues–Sun noon–9pm, till 10pm in summer. Tiny *salon de thé* in a picturesque, cobbled, pedestrian-only street behind the church of St-Gervais, serving chocolate cakes and pâtisseries as well as savoury dishes. *Plats du jour* for 67F/€10.21, Tunisian crêpes for 45F/€6.86, and generous salads.

Épices et Délices, 53 rue Vieille-du-Temple (M° St-Paul). Daily till midnight. Restaurant and *salon de thé* with very pleasant service and food. Salads from 60F/€9.15; 70F/€13.72 evening menu.

Grand Appetit, 9 rue de la Cerisaie (M° Bastille). Mon–Thurs noon–7pm, Fri & Sun noon–2pm. Vegetarian meals served by dedicated eco-veggies at the back of an unassuming shop.

Le Petit Fer à Cheval, 30 rue Vieille-du-Temple (M° St-Paul). Mon–Fri 9am–2am, Sat & Sun 11am–2am; food noon–midnight. Very attractive small bistro/bar with trad decor, including a huge *zinc* bar, and tables outside; a popular drinking spot. Agreeable wine and good-value *plats*, and sandwiches from 35F/€5.34.

Le Petit Marcel, 63 rue Rambuteau (M° Rambuteau). Mon–Sat till 2am. Speckled tabletops, mirrors and Art Nouveau tiles, cracked and faded ceiling and about eight square metres of drinking space. Friendly bar staff and "local" atmosphere.

Le Rouge Gorge, 8 rue St-Paul (M° St-Paul). Mon–Sat 11am–2am, Sun 11am–8pm. The young, enthusiastic clientele sip familiar wines and snack on *chèvre chaud* and smoked salmon salad, or tuck into more substantial fare (*plats du jour* around 60F/€9.15) while listening to jazz or classical music.

Sacha Finkelsztajn, 27 rue des Rosiers (M° St-Paul; Wed–Sun 10am–2pm & 3–7pm; closed Aug) and 24 rue des Écouffes (M° St-Paul; daily except Wed 10am–1pm & 3–7pm). Marvellous for take-away goodies: gorgeous east European breads, cakes, *gefilte* fish, aubergine purée, tarama, *blinis* and *borscht*.

La Tartine, 24 rue de Rivoli (M° St-Paul). Daily except Tues until 10pm; closed Aug. The genuine 1900s article, which still cuts across class boundaries in its clientele. A good selection of affordable wines, plus excellent cheese and *saucisson* with *pain de campagne*.

Le Temps des Cerises, 31 rue de la Cerisaie (M° Bastille). Mon–Fri until 8pm; food at midday only; closed Aug. It is hard to say what is so appealing about this café, with its dirty yellow decor, old posters and prints of *vieux Paris*, save that the *patronne* knows most of the clientele, who are young, relaxed and not the dreaded *branchés*. 68F/€10.37 menu.

Au Volcan de Sicile, 62 rue du Roi-de-Sicile (M° Hôtel-de-Ville). Flooded with sunshine at midday, this is a good café in which to sit and sip on the corner of the exquisite and minuscule place Tibourg.

Restaurants

See map, pp.124–125.

Aquarius 1, 54 rue Ste-Croix-de-la-Bretonnerie; ☎01.48.87.48.71 (M° St-Paul/Rambuteau). Mon–Sat noon–10pm; closed last fortnight in Aug. Vegetarian restaurant established in 1974: not the austere and penitential place it once was though. Alcohol is now served (Òhard drinks) but there's still no smoking. Also functions as a health-food store, New Age bookshop and *salon du thé* between lunch and dinner, so you can order an omelette, soup or salad throughout the afternoon. Lunch menu at 62F/€9.45, evening 62F/€9.45 and 92F/€14.02. Hot dishes 22–64F/€3.35–9.76.

Auberge de Jarente, 7 rue Jarente; ☎01.42.77.49.35 (M° St-Paul). Tues–Sat noon–2.30pm & 7.30–10.30pm; closed Aug. A hospitable and friendly Basque restaurant, serving first-class food: *cassoulet*, hare stew, *magret de canard* and *piperade* – the Basque omelette. Menus at 117F/€17.84 and 132F/€20.12, and 185F/€28.20 with wine.

La Canaille, 4 rue Crillon; ☎01.42.78.09.71 (M° Sully-Morland/Bastille). Daily till midnight; closed Sat & Sun lunch. Bar in front, restaurant behind. Simple, traditional and well-cooked food in a friendly atmosphere. There are 79F/€12.04 and 89F/€13.56 lunch menus – 130F/€19.82 in the evening – and à la carte at 140F/€21.34.

Les Fous d'en Face, 3 rue du Bourg-Tibourg; ☎01.48.87.03.75 (M° Hôtel-de-Ville). Daily 11.30am–3pm & 7pm–midnight. Delightful little restaurant and wine bar serving wonderful marinated salmon and scallops. Midday menu under 90F/€13.72, otherwise *carte* 140F/€21.34 upwards.

Goldenberg's, 7 rue des Rosiers; ☎01.48.87.20.16 (M° St-Paul). Daily until 2am. The best-known Jewish restaurant in the capital, though success has made service pretty surly. Its *borscht, blinis,* potato strudels, *zakouski* and other central European dishes are a treat. Daily changing *plat du jour* 80F/€12.20, *carte* around 200F/€30.49.

Le Grizli, 7 rue St-Martin; ☎01.48.87.77.56 (M° Châtelet). Mon–Sat till 11pm. *Fin-de-siècle* bistro serving superb food with specialities from the Pyrenees. 115F/€17.53 midday menu; 155F/€23.63 evening.

Pitchi-Poï, 7 rue Caron, cnr place du Marché-Ste-Catherine; ☎01.42.77.46.15 (M° St-Paul). Daily noon–3pm & 7.30–11pm. Excellent Polish/Jewish cuisine in a lovely location with sympathetic ambience and 150F/€22.87 lunch and dinner menu, kids' menu 73F/€11.13, choice of delicious hors d'œuvres from 43F/€6.55.

5ᵉ arrondissement

Bars and cafés

Café de la Mosquée, 39 rue Geoffroy-St-Hilaire (M° Monge). Daily 8am–midnight. You can drink mint tea and eat sweet cakes beside a fountain and assorted fig trees in the courtyard of this Paris mosque – a delightful haven of calm. The salon has a beautiful Arabic interior. Meals are served in the adjoining restaurant. Couscous from 55F/€6.38, tagines from 70F/€10.67.

Cyber Café Latino, 13 rue de l'École-Polytechnique (M° Maubert-Mutualité). Mon–Sat 11am–2am, Sun 4–9pm. Small friendly bar with a Venezuelan owner, Latino sounds on the stereo and fruit smoothies and tapas on the menu; six computers out the back to surf the Net.

La Fourmi Ailée, 8 rue du Fouarre (M° Maubert-Mutualité). Daily noon–midnight. Simple, light fare – including weekend brunch (2–6pm; 100F/€15.24) – in this former feminist bookshop which has been transformed into a *salon de thé*. A high ceiling painted with a lovely mural and a book-filled wall contribute to the rarified atmosphere. Around 69F/€10.52 for a *plat*.

Le Piano Vache, 8 rue Laplace (M° Cardinal-Lemoine). Daily noon–2am. Venerable student bar with canned music and a relaxed atmosphere.

Les Pipos, 2 rue de l'École-Polytechnique (M° Maubert-Mutualité/Cardinal-Lemoine). Mon–Sat 8am–2am; closed three weeks in Aug. Old, carved, wooden bar, serving its own wines at 14–25F/€2.13–3.81 a glass. *Plats*, which change every day, from 50F/€7.62 to 75F/€11.43.

Le Violon Dingue, 46 rue de la Montagne-Ste-Geneviève (M° Maubert-Mutualité). Daily 6pm–1.30am; happy hour 6–10pm. A long, dark, student pub that's also popular with young travellers; noisy and friendly. English-speaking bar staff and cheap drinks.

Restaurants

See map, pp.130–131.

Bistro de la Sorbonne, 4 rue Toullier; ☎01.43.54.41.49 (RER Luxembourg). Mon–Sat noon–2.30pm & 7–11pm. Traditional French and delicious North African food is served here in large portions at reasonable prices. Crowded and attractive student/local ambience. 69F/€10.52 lunch menu; 95F/€14.48 and 140F/€12.34 evening.

Brasserie Balzar, 49 rue des Écoles; ☎01.43.54.13.67 (M° Maubert-Mutualité). Daily until 1am; closed Aug. A traditional literary-bourgeois brasserie frequented by the intelligentsia of the quartier Latin. À la carte about 180F/€27.44.

Au Buisson Ardent, 25 rue Jussieu; ☎01.43.54.93.02 (M° Jussieu). Mon–Fri noon–2pm & 7.30–10pm, Sat evening only; closed two weeks Aug. Copious helpings of first-class traditional cooking: mussels, duck, warm goat's cheese salad, lamb, etc. 70F/€10.67 menu lunch, 160F/€24.39 evenings. Reservations recommended.

Chez Léna et Mimile, 32 rue Tournefort; ☎01.47.07.72.47 (M° Censier-Daubenton). Mon–Fri until 11pm, Sat evening only. The high south-facing *terrasse*, overlooking a shady little square, is the main attraction, and the 185F/€28.20 menu with wine and coffee included is excellent. Serves a 98F/€14.94 menu at lunchtime on weekdays.

Chieng-Maï, 12 rue Frédéric-Sauton; ☎01.43.25.45.45 (M° Maubert-Mutualité). Daily noon–2.30pm & 7–11.20pm. Excellent Thai dishes. Menus 69F/€10.52 at lunchtime; otherwise 122F/€18.60 and 173F/€26.37.

Foyer du Vietnam, 80 rue Monge; ☎01.45.35.32.54 (M° Monge). Mon–Sat until 10pm. Casual, authentic Vietnamese with dishes from 30F/€4.57 and menus for 56F/€8.54 and 67F/€10.21.

Le Grenier de Notre-Dame, 18 rue de la Bûcherie (M° Maubert-Mutualité). Daily noon–11.30pm. Some veggies love this tiny place, which has been operating since 1978. Others hate it and its posh candle-lit atmosphere, cramped tables and cheesy music. Substantial fare, including couscous, fried tofu and cauliflower cheese. Menus at 75F/€11.43 and 105F/€16.

Koutchi, 40 rue du Cardinal-Lemoine; ☎01.44.07.20.56 (M° Cardinal-Lemoine). Mon–Sat noon–2.30pm & 7–11pm. A well-regarded Afghan restaurant, with pretty good prices. Menu 55F/€8.38 at lunchtime, 98F/€14.93 in the evening.

Mavrommatis, 42 rue Daubenton; ☎01.43.31.17.17 (M° Censier-Daubenton). Tues–Sun noon–2.30pm & 7–11pm. A sophisticated Greek restaurant, quite expensive (lunchtime menu 120F/€18.29), but you are definitely tasting Greek food at its best.

La Petite Légume, 36 rue Boulangers; ☎01.40.46.06.85 (M° Jussieu). Mon–Sat noon–2.30pm & 7.30–10pm. This is a health-food grocery that doubles as a vegetarian restaurant, serving quality ingredients in a variety of *plats* for around 58F/€8.84.

Les Quatre et Une Saveurs, 72 rue du Cardinal-Lemoine; ☎01.43.26.88.80 (M° Cardinal-Lemoine). Tues–Sat till 10pm. Inventive high-class macrobiotic vegetarian food. The 120F/€18.29 and 130F/€19.82 menus include coffee.

Tashi Delek, 4 rue des Fossés-St-Jacques; ☎01.43.26.55.55 (RER Luxembourg). Mon–Sat noon & eve until 10.30pm; closed Aug. An enjoyable Tibetan restaurant run by refugees, where you can eat for as little as 52F/€7.93 at lunchtime and 64F/€9.76 in the evening.

6ᵉ arrondissement

Bars and cafés

Le 10, 10 rue de l'Odéon (M° Odéon). Daily 6.30pm–2am. The beer here is very cheap, which is why it attracts youth, particularly foreigners. Small dark bar with old posters, a jukebox and a lot of chatting-up.

L'Alsace à Paris, 9 place St-André-des-Arts; ☎01.43.26.21.48 (M° St-Michel). A very busy and well-worn brasserie. Menus are at 119F/€18.14 and 169F/€25.76 – but they also serve delicious and cheap *tartes flambées* like thin pizzas that you can take away.

L'Assignat, 7 rue Guénégaud (M° Pont-Neuf). Mon–Sat 7.30am–8.30pm, food noon–3.30pm; closed July. *Zinc* counter, bar stools, bar football and young regulars from the nearby art school in an untouristy café close to quai des Augustins. 27F/€4.12 for a sandwich and a glass of wine.

Chez Georges, 11 rue des Canettes (M° Mabillon). Tues–Sat noon–2am; closed July 14–Aug 15. An attractive wine bar in the spit-on-the-floor mode, with its old shop-front still intact, situated in a narrow street off place St-Sulpice.

La Closerie des Lilas, 171 bd du Montparnasse (M° Port-Royal). Daily noon–1.30am. The smartest, artiest, classiest Montparnasse café, with excellent cocktails for around 60F/€9.15 and a resident pianist. The tables are name-plated after celebrated former habitués (Verlaine, Mallarmé, Lenin, Modigliani, Léger, Strindberg). Very expensive restaurant; brasserie main courses for under 100F/€15.24.

Les Deux Magots, 170 bd St-Germain (M° St-Germain-des-Prés). Daily 6.30am–1.30am; closed one week in Jan. Right on the cnr of place St-Germain-des-Prés, this café too owes its reputation to the intellos of the Left Bank, past and present. In summertime it picks up a lot of foreigners seeking the exact location of the spirit of French culture, and buskers galore play to the packed terrace. Come early for an expensive but satisfying 75F/€11.43 breakfast.

Le Flore, 172 bd St-Germain (M° St-Germain-des-Prés). Daily 7am–1.30am. The great rival and immediate neighbour of *Les Deux Magots*, with a very similar clientele. Sartre, De Beauvoir,

Camus and Marcel Carné used to hang out here. Best enjoyed during a late-afternoon coffee or after-dinner drink.

Le Mazet, 60 rue St-André-des-Arts (M° Odéon). Mon–Thurs 10am–2am, Fri & Sat till 3.30am; happy hour 5–8pm; closed Sun. Historically, a well-known hang-out for buskers and heavy drinkers. For an evil concoction, try a *bière brûlée* – it's flambéed with gin. Small glass beer 20F/€3.05, cocktails 49F/€7.47.

La Paillote, 45 rue Monsieur-le-Prince (RER Luxembourg/M° Odéon). Mon–Sat 9pm–dawn; closed Aug. *The* late-night bar for jazz fans, with one of the best collections of recorded jazz in the city. Soft drinks start from 30F/€4.57.

La Palette, 43 rue de Seine (M° Odéon). Mon–Sat 8am–2am. Once-famous Beaux-Arts student hangout, now more frequented by art dealers and their customers. The service can be uncivil, but the murals and every detail of the decor are superb, including, of course, a large selection of colourful, used palettes.

Pub St-Germain, 17 rue de l'Ancienne-Comédie (M° Odéon). Open 24hr. Stocks 26 draught beers and hundreds of bottles. Huge, crowded and expensive. Hot food at mealtimes, otherwise cold snacks. For a taste of "real" French beer, try *ch'ti* (patois for "northerner"), a *bière de garde* from the Pas-de-Calais. Live music nightly from 10pm.

La Taverne de Nesle, 32 rue Dauphine (M° Odéon). Daily 9pm–4am, Fri & Sat till 5am. Vast selection of beers. Full of local night-birds. Cocktails from 45F/€6.86.

Restaurants

See map, pp.136–137.

Des Beaux-Arts, 11 rue Bonaparte; ☎01.43.26.92.64 (M° St-Germain-des-Prés). Daily lunch & evening until 10.45pm. The traditional hang-out of Beaux-Arts students. The choice is wide, portions are generous and queues are long in high season. The atmosphere is generally good, though the waitresses can get pretty tetchy. Menu at 79F/€12.04, including wine.

Aux Charpentiers, 10 rue Mabillon; ☎01.43.26.30.05 (M° Mabillon). Daily until 11pm; closed hols. A friendly, old-fashioned place belonging to the *Compagnons des Charpentiers* (Carpenters' Guild), with appropriate decor of roof-trees and tie beams. Traditional *plats du jour* are their forte – tripe sausage, calf's head and the like – for about 75F/€11.43. Around 200F/€30.49 à la carte; lunch menu at 120F/€18.29.

Cosi, 54 rue de Seine; ☎01.46.33.35.36 (M° St-Germain-des-Prés). Daily noon–midnight. Fantastic sandwiches (30–48F/€4.57–7.32) made on home-made focaccia bread. Mix and match your own ingredients, including roast beef, tomatoes stewed with coriander, cucumbers with chevre, ricotta with nuts, roasted vegetables, smoked salmon, and on it goes. Wine by the glass (18F/€2.74), rich desserts (22F/€3.35). The opera-loving owner has a different opera on the CD player each day.

Lipp, 151 bd St-Germain (M° St-Germain-des-Prés). Daily until 12.30am; closed mid-July to mid-Aug. A 1900s brasserie, and one of the best-known establishments on the Left Bank; haunt of the very successful and very famous. *Plat du jour* 100–115F/€15.24–17.53; no reservations, so be prepared to wait.

Le Muniche, 7 rue St-Benoît; ☎01.42.61.12.70 (M° St-Germain-des-Prés). Daily noon–2am. A crowded old-style brasserie with an oyster bar, mirrors and theatre posters on the walls, serving classic French brasserie fare: seafood, *choucroute*, leg of lamb. Menus at 98F/€14.94 and 149F/€27.44; *carte* 180F/€27.44.

Orestias, 4 rue Grégoire-de-Tours; ☎01.43.54.62.01 (M° Odéon). Mon–Sat lunch & evening until 11.30pm. A mixture of Greek and French cuisine. Good helpings and very cheap – with a menu at 46F/€7.01 (weekdays only until 8pm).

Le Petit St-Benoît, 4 rue St-Benoît; ☎01.42.60.27.92 (M° St-Germain-des-Prés). Mon–Fri noon–2.30pm & 7–10.30pm. A simple, genuine and very appealing local for the neighbourhood's chattering classes. Serves solid, traditional fare in a brown-stained, aproned atmosphere. Menu at 130F/€19.82.

Le Petit Zinc, 11 rue St-Benoit; ☎01.42.61.20.60 (M° St-Germain-des-Prés). Daily noon–2am. Excellent traditional dishes, especially seafood, in stunning Art-Nouveau-style premises (built thirty years ago). Not cheap – menu 188F/€28, seafood platter 450F/€68.60 for two.

Polidor, 41 rue Monsieur-le-Prince; ☎01.43.26.95.34 (M° Odéon). Mon–Sat until 12.30am, Sun until 11pm. A traditional bistro, open since 1845, whose visitors' book, they say, boasts more of history's big names than all the glittering palaces put together. Not as cheap as it was in James Joyce's day, but good food and great atmosphere. Lunches at 55F/€8.38 during the week, and an excellent 165F/€25.15 evening menu.

Le Procope, 13 rue de l'Ancienne-Comédie; ☎01.40.46.79.00 (M° Odéon). Daily noon–1am. Opened in 1686 as the first establishment to serve coffee in Paris, it is still a great place to enjoy a cup and bask in the knowledge that over the years, Voltaire, Benjamin Franklin, Rousseau, Marat and Robespierre, among others, have done the very same thing. Fairly good 130F/€19.82 menu (up to 8pm) and 178F/€27.13 menu with wine included after 11pm, though some say it caters too much to tourist's weary tastebuds.

7e arrondissement

Bars and cafés

Café du Museé d'Orsay, 1 rue Bellechasse (RER Musée-d'Orsay/M° Solférino). Tues–Sun 11am–5pm. Superb views over the Seine in the museum's magnificent rooftop café, which serves snacks and drinks. Quick and friendly service.

Le Poch'tron, 25 rue de Bellechasse (M° Solférino). Mon–Fri 9am–10.30pm. With a fine selection of wines by the glass, this is an excellent place to revive yourself after visiting the museums in the *arrondissement*. Also serves lunch and dinner; main dishes at around 70F/€10.67.

Restaurants

Au Babylone, 13 rue de Babylone; ☎01.45.48.72.13 (M° Sèvres-Babylone). Mon–Sat lunch only; closed Aug. Lots of old-fashioned charm and culinary basics like *rôti de veau* and steak, plus wine on the 100F/€15.24 menu.

Le Bourdonnais, 113 av Le Bourdonnais; ☎01.47.05.47.06 (M° École-Militaire). Daily noon–2.30pm & 8–11pm. A high-class gem of a restaurant. À la carte costs upwards of 400F/€60.98, but there's a superb midday menu including wine for 240F/€36.59, and an evening menu at 340F/€51.83.

Chez Germaine, 30 rue Pierre-Leroux; ☎01.42.73.28.34 (M° Duroc/Vaneau). Daily noon–2.30pm & 7–9.30pm; closed Sat, Sun & Aug. A simple, tiny and unbelievably cheap restaurant, with a mid-day 50F/€7.62 menu and evening 65F/€9.91 menu, including wine; the *carte* costs up to about 90F/€13.72.

8e arrondissement

Bars and cafés

Barry's, 9 rue Duras (M° Champs-Élysées-Clemenceau). Mon–Sat 11am–3pm. Serves salads, snacks and sandwiches for under 30F/€4.57 in a tiny street behind the Élysée palace.

Le Fouquet's, 99 av des Champs-Élysées (M° George-V). Daily till 1.30am. Such a well-established watering hole for stars of the stage and screen, politicians, newspaper editors and advertising barons, that it's now been classified as a Monument Historique. You pay dearly to sit in the deep leather armchairs, and as for the restaurant, don't expect any change from 300F/€45.73.

Musée Jacquemart-André, 158 bd Haussmann; ☎01.45.62.11.59 (M° St-Philippe-du-Roule/Miromesnil). Daily 11am–6pm. A sumptuously appointed *salon de thé* in a nineteenth-century palazzo, with salads at 58–85F/€8.84–12.96, a lunch *formule* at 86F/€13.11 and a popular weekend brunch for 130F/€19.82; museum ticket not needed.

Restaurants

See map, pp.112–113.

Aux Amis du Beaujolais, 28 rue d'Artois; ☎01.45.63.92.21 (M° George-V/St-Philippe-du-Roule). Mon–Sat noon–3pm & 6.30–9pm; closed middle two weeks of July. If you can fathom the handwritten menu, you'll find good traditional French stews and sautéed steaks, and Beaujolais. Evening menu at 120F/€18.29.

Dragons Élysées, 11 rue de Berri; ☎01.42.89.85.10 (M° George-V). Daily 11am–3pm & 7–11pm. The Chinese-Thai cuisine encompasses dim sum, curried seafood and baked mussels, but the overriding attraction is the extraordinary decor. Beneath a floor of glass tiles water runs from pool to pool inhabited by exotic fish. Menu at 80F/€12.20; 220F/€33.34 for *menu royal*; *carte* 250F/€38.11.

Yvan, 1bis rue J-Mermoz; ☎01.43.59.18.40 (Mº Franklin-D.-Roosevelt). Mon–Sat noon–2.30pm & 7pm–midnight; closed Sat lunch & Sun. Fish specialities and pigeon with polenta attract a stylish clientele. Extremely good food and menus from 168F/€25.61.

9e arrondissement

Bars and cafés

Le Dépanneur, 27 rue Fontaine; ☎01.40.16.40.20 (Mº Pigalle). Relaxed and fashionable all-night bar.

Au Général Lafayette, 52 rue Lafayette (Mº Le-Peletier/Cadet). Daily noon–4am. Old-time brasserie where all sorts rub shoulders, while sampling the large variety of beers and wines on offer.

Le Grand Café Capucines, 4 bd des Capucines (Mº Opéra). A favourite all-nighter with over-the-top *belle époque* decor and excellent seafood. Boulevard prices mean 20F/€3.05 for an espresso.

Restaurants

Chartier, 7 rue du Faubourg-Montmartre; ☎01.47.70.86.29 (Mº Montmartre). Daily 11.30am–3pm & 6–10pm. Dark-stained woodwork, brass hat-racks, mirrors, waiters in long aprons – the original decor of an early twentieth century soup kitchen. Though crowded and rushed, it's worth a visit, and the food's not bad at all. Under 100F/€15.24.

aux Deux-Théâtres, 18 rue Blanche, cnr rue Pigalle; ☎01.45.26.41.43 (Mº Trinité). Daily 11.30am–2.30pm & 7pm–midnight. A distinctly bourgeois but welcoming and friendly place, whose 179F/€27.29 menu includes aperitif. The entrées and desserts are particularly good.

Le Relais Savoyard, 13 rue Rodier, cnr rue Agent-Bailly; ☎01.45.26.17.18 (Mº Notre-Dame-de-Lorette/Anver/Cadet). Mon–Sat until 9.30pm; closed Aug. Located at the back of a very ordinary local bar, and serving a very good three-course meal for 115F/€17.53.

La Table d'Anvers, 2 place d'Anvers; ☎01.48.78.35.21 (Mº Anvers). Noon–2.30pm & 7.30–11.30pm; closed Sat lunchtime and Sun. This is one of the city's best restaurants, whose chef is renowned for his original combinations. The menu at 250F/€38.11 gives a good taste of his skills; the full experience of four *plats*, cheese and two desserts will cost you 650F/€99.09.

10e arrondissement

Bars and cafés

L'Atmosphère, 49 rue Lucien-Sampaix (Mº Gare-de-l'Est). Tues–Fri 11am–2am, Sat & Sun 5.30pm–2am. Lively bar with food and occasional live music next to the canal St-Martin. The *Hôtel du Nord* on the opposite bank was the setting for the eponymous film of 1938, and the name of this bar comes from a quote in the film.

China Express Nord, 3 bd Denain (Mº Gare-du-Nord). Daily 11am–10pm; closed Sun in winter. A good place to fill up on chicken and noodles, near the Gare du Nord. Dish of the day and Cantonese rice 30F/€4.57.

Le Réveil du Dixième, 35 rue du Château-d'Eau; ☎01.42.41.77.59 (Mº Château-d'Eau). Mon–Sat 7.15am–9pm. A welcoming, unpretentious wine bar serving glasses of wine and regional *plats*, or a menu at 150F/€22.87, including wine.

Restaurants

de Bourgogne, 26 rue des Vinaigriers; ☎01.46.07.07.91 (Mº Jacques-Bonsergent). Mon–Fri lunch & evening until 10pm, Sat lunch only; closed Aug. Homely, old-fashioned restaurant. Dinner around 80F/€12.20.

Chez Prune, 36 rue Beaurepaire; ☎01.42.41.30.47 (Mº Jacques-Bonsergent). Mon–Sat 7.30am–1.45am, Sun 10am–1.45am. Lovely location for casual canal-side dining. Creative *assiettes* (starting at 40F/€6.10) guaranteed to tempt both meat-eaters and vegetarians, and a romantic place to sip a glass of wine or indulge in a dessert. *Plats* in the 55F/€8.38 to 80F/€12.20 range.

Flo, 7 cours des Petites-Écuries; ☎01.47.70.13.59 (Mº Château-d'Eau). Daily until 1.30am. Handsome old-time brasserie where you eat elbow to elbow at long tables, served by waiters in ankle-length aprons. Excellent food and atmosphere. Good-value menus, including wine, at 189F/€28.81, or 138F/€21.04 after 10pm.

Julien, 16 rue du Faubourg-St-Denis; ☎01.47.70.12.06 (M° Strasbourg-St-Denis). Daily until 1.30am. Part of the same enterprise as *Flo* (above), with an even more splendid decor. Same good traditional French cuisine at the same prices, and it's just as crowded.

Pooja, 91 passage Brady; ☎01.48.24.00.83 (M° Strasbourg-St-Denis/Château-d'Eau). Daily noon–2.30pm & 5–11pm; closed Mon lunchtime. Located in a passage that is Paris's own slice of the Indian subcontinent, *Pooja* serves authentic, good-value Indian cuisine. *Formules* at 45F/€6.86 lunch and 89F/€13.57 evening.

Terminus Nord, 23 rue de Dunkerque; ☎01.42.85.05.15 (M° Gare-du-Nord). Daily until 1am. A magnificent 1920s brasserie where a full meal costs around 250F/€38.11, but where you could easily satisfy your hunger with just a main course and enjoy the decor for considerably less.

11e arrondissement

Bars and cafés

Bar des Ferrailleurs, 18 rue de Lappe, 11e (M° Bastille). Daily 5pm–2am. Dark and stylishly sinister bar, with rusting metal decor, an eccentric owner and fun wig-wearing staff. Relaxed, friendly crowd.

Boca Chica, 58 rue de Charonne (M° Ledru-Rollin). Daily 8am–2am. Popular tapas bar/bodega (tapas 28–78F/€4.27–11.89), heaving by night and restful in the morning, when you can get coffee and croissant for 10F/€1.52, and a newspaper for an extra 5F/€0.76. Colourful arty decor.

Café Charbon, 109 rue Oberkampf (M° St-Maur/Parmentier). Daily 9am–2am. A very successful and attractive resuscitation of a *fin-de-siècle* café, drawing a young and trendy clientele. Nice *plats du jour* for 50–60F/€7.62–9.15 at lunchtime; lots of salads and vegetarian dishes. DJ Thurs, Fri & Sat 10pm–2am, and live music on Sun from 8.30pm.

Café de l'Industrie, 16 rue St-Sabin (M° Bastille). Noon–2am; closed Sat. Rugs on the floor around solid old wooden tables, miscellaneous objects on the walls, and a young, unpretentious crowd enjoying the comfortable lack of minimalism. One of the best Bastille addresses. *Plats du jour* from 48F/€7.32.

Cithea, 112 rue Oberkampf (M° Parmentier). Daily 5pm–2am. Bar and venue next door to the *Café Charbon* for Afro funk, funk reggae, world beat, jazz fusion, etc on Thurs, Fri & Sat nights. Cocktails 45F/€6.86. No admission charge for the music, but busy.

Fouquet's, 130 rue de Lyon (M° Bastille). Mon–Fri till midnight; closed Sat & Sun midday. A smart, expensive café-restaurant underneath the new Opéra, sister establishment to the Champs-Élysées *Fouquet's*. But with perfect French courtesy they will leave you undisturbed for hours with a 15F/€2.29 coffee. Menu, including wine, at 170F/€25.91.

Havanita Café, 11 rue de Lappe (M° Bastille). Daily 5pm–2am; happy hour 5–8pm. Large, comfortable, Cuban-style bar with battered old leather sofa. Cocktails from 48F/€7.32.

Iguana, 15 rue de la Roquette, cnr rue Daval (M° Bastille). Daily 10am–2am. A place to be seen in. Decor of trellises, colonial fans and a brushed bronze bar. The clientele studies *récherché* art reviews, and the coffee is excellent.

Jacques-Mélac, 42 rue Léon-Frot (M° Charonne). Mon–Fri 9am–10.30pm; closed weekends & Aug. Some way off the beaten track (between Père-Lachaise and place Léon-Blum) but a highly respected and very popular *bistrot à vins*, whose patron even makes his own wine – the solitary vine winds round the front of the shop. The food (*plats* around 70F/€10.67, menu 130F/€19.82), wines and atmosphere are great; no bookings.

SanZSanS, 49 rue du Faubourg-St-Antoine (M° Bastille). Daily 9am–2am. Features a Gothic decor of red velvet, oil paintings and chandeliers, with a young clientele in the evening. Drinks reasonably priced; main courses for around 48–65F/€7.32–9.91, and there's always a vegetarian dish on offer.

Restaurants

Les Amognes, 243 rue du Faubourg-St-Antoine; ☎01.43.72.73.05 (M° Faidherbe-Chaligny). Mon–Sat noon–2.30pm & 7.30–10.30pm; closed Mon lunch, Sun & two weeks in Aug. Excellent, interesting food in a very popular place. Booking essential. Menu at 190F/€28.96, otherwise well over 250F/€38.11.

Astier, 44 rue Jean-Pierre-Timbaud; ☎01.43.57.16.35 (M° Parmentier). Mon–Fri until 10pm; closed Aug, fortnight in May & fortnight at Christmas. Very successful and popular restaurant, with simple decor, unstuffy atmosphere and fresh, refined food. Booking essential. Menu at 140F/€21.34.

Bistrot du Peintre, 116 av Ledru-Rollin; ☎01.47.00.34.39 (M° Faidherbe-Chaligny). Mon–Sat 7am–2am, Sun 10am–8pm. Small tables jammed together beneath Art Nouveau frescoes and wood panelling. Traditional Parisian bistro food, with *plats du jour* from 62F/€9.45.

Blue Elephant, 43–45 rue de la Roquette; ☎01.47.00.42.00 (M° Bastille/Richard-Lenoir). Daily except Sat lunchtime till midnight. Superb Thai restaurant, with a tropical forest decor. 150F/€22.87 midday menu, otherwise over 270F/€41.16.

Chez Omar, 47 rue de Bretagne (M° Arts-et-Metiers). Daily noon–2.30pm & 7pm–midnight; closed Sun lunch. Very popular North African resto in a nice old brasserie set with mirrors, attracting a young crowd. Couscous 60–98F/€9.15–14.94. Does not accept credit cards.

Les Cinq Points Cardinaux, 14 rue Jean-Macé; ☎01.43.71.47.22 (M° Faidherbe-Chaligny/ Charonne). Mon–Fri noon–2pm & 7–10pm; closed Aug. An excellent, simple, old-time bistro, still mainly frequented by locals. Prices under 60F/€9.15 for lunch, and under 100F/€15.24 in the evening.

L'Homme Bleu, 57 rue Jean-Pierre-Timbaud (M° Parmentier). Mon–Sat evenings only till 10pm. Very affordable and pleasant Berber restaurant, popular with students.

La Mansouria, 11 rue Faidherbe; ☎01.43.71.00.16 (M° Faidherbe-Chaligny). Tues–Sat lunchtime & evening until 11.30pm; closed two weeks in Aug. An excellent, elegant Moroccan restaurant, serving superb couscous and tagines. Menu at 170F/€25.61.

Au Trou Normand, 9 rue Jean-Pierre-Timbaud; ☎01.48.05.80.23 (M° Filles-du-Calvaire/ Oberkampf/République). Mon–Fri lunch & evening until 9.30pm, Sat evening only; closed Aug. A small, totally unpretentious and very attractive local bistro, serving good traditional food at knockdown prices. *Plat du jour* from 30F/€4.57.

La Ville de Jagannath, 10 rue St Maur, 11 (M° St-Maur). Closed Mon lunch and Sun. Authentic vegetarian Indian food served in thalis. Lunch menu 50F/€7.62. For a small corkage fee you can bring your own wine.

12ᵉ arrondissement
Bars and cafés

Le Baron Aligre, 1 rue Théophile-Roussel, cnr place d'Aligre market (M° Ledru-Rollin). Tues–Sat 10am–2pm & 5–9.30pm, Sun 10am–2pm. Popular local bar. As well as the wines – around 16F/€2.44 per litre from the barrel to take away – it serves a few snacks of cheese, *foie gras* and *charcuterie*.

Le Penty Bar, cnr place d'Aligre & rue Emilio-Castellar (M° Ledru-Rollin). Small, old-fashioned café making no concessions to 1990s sanitation, and still charging only 7F/€1.07 for a sit-down cup of coffee.

Restaurants

L'Ébauchoir, 43–45 rue de Cîteaux; ☎01.43.42.49.31 (M° Faidherbe-Chaligny). Mon–Sat until 11pm. Good bistro fare in a sympathetic atmosphere. Best to book for the evening. Midday menu for 66F/€10.06; *carte* 150F/€22.87 upwards.

Le Gourmandise, 271 av Daumesnil; ☎01.43.43.94.41 (M° Porte-Dorée). Mon–Sat till 10.30pm; closed Mon lunch and first two weeks Aug. Superb and original food with a good menu at 170F/€25.91.

13ᵉ arrondissement
Bars and cafés

La Folie en Tête, 33 rue Butte-aux-Cailles (M° Place-d'Italie/Corvisart). Mon–Sat 5pm–2am. Cheap beer, sandwiches and midday *plat du jour*. Occasional concerts and solidarity events. A very warm and laid-back address.

Le Merle Moqueur, 11 rue Butte-aux-Cailles (M° Place-d'Italie/Corvisart). Daily 9pm–1am. Old-time co-op still going strong and still popular, with live rock some nights.

ETHNIC RESTAURANTS OF PARIS

AFGHAN
Koutchi, 40 rue du Cardinal-Lemoine, 5ᵉ. See p.162.

AFRICAN AND NORTH AFRICAN
Le Berbère, 50 rue de Gergovie, 14ᵉ. See p.169.
Chez Omar, 47 Rue de Bretagne, 11ᵉ. See p.167.
Fouta Toro, 3 rue du Nord, 18ᵉ. See p.172.
L'Homme Bleu, 57 rue Jean-Pierre-Timbaud, 11ᵉ. See p.167.
La Mansouria, 11 rue Faidherbe-Chaligny, 11ᵉ. See p.167.
N'Zadette M'Foua, 152 rue du Château, 14ᵉ. See p.169.
au Port de Pidjiguiti, 28 rue Étex, 18ᵉ. See p.172.
le Quincampe, 78 rue Quincampoix, 3ᵉ. See p.159.

GREEK
Mavrommatis, 42 rue Daubenton, 5ᵉ. See p.162.
Orestias, 4 rue Grégoire-de-Tours, 6ᵉ. See p.163.

INDIAN
La Ville de Jagannath, 10 rue St Maur, 11ᵉ. See p.167.
Pooja, 91 passage Brady, 10ᵉ. See p.166.

INDO-CHINESE
Blue Elephant, 43–45 rue de la Roquette, 11ᵉ. See p.167.
Chieng-Maï, 12 rue Frédéric-Sauton, 5ᵉ. See p.162.
Dragons Élysées, 11 rue de Berri, 8ᵉ. See p.164.
Foyer du Vietnam, 80 rue Monge, 5ᵉ. See p.162.
Lao Siam, 49 rue de Belleville, 20ᵉ. See p.173.

Lao-Thai, 128 rue de Tolbiac; 13ᵉ. See p.167.
Le Pacifique, 35 rue de Belleville, 20ᵉ. See p.173.
Pho-Dong-Huong, 14 rue Louis-Bonnet, 20ᵉ. See p.173.
Phuong Hoang, Terrasse des Olympiades, 52 rue du Javelot, 13ᵉ. See p.169.
Taï Yen, 5 rue de Belleville, 20ᵉ. See p.173.

ITALIAN
Da Attilio, 21 rue Cronstadt, 15ᵉ. See p.171.
Rittal et Courts, 1 rue des Envierges, 20ᵉ. See p.173.

JAPANESE
Foujita, 41 rue St-Roch, 1ᵉʳ. See p.158.

JEWISH
Goldenberg's, 7 rue des Rosiers, 4ᵉ. See p.161.

KURDISH
Dilan, 13 rue Mandar, 2ᵉ. See p.159.

LEBANESE
Aux Saveurs du Liban, 11 rue Eugène-Jumin, 19 ᵉ. See p.172.

POLISH
Pitchi-Poï, 7 rue Caron, 4ᵉ. See p.161.

TIBETAN
Tashi Delek, 4 rue des Fossés-St-Jacques, 5ᵉ. See p.162.

WEST INDIAN
Le Marais-Cage, 8 rue de Beauce, 3ᵉ. See p.159.

Restaurants

Auberge Etchegorry, 41 rue Croulebarbe; ☎01.44.08.83.51 (Mᵒ Gobelins). Mon–Sat till 10.30pm. A former *guinguette* on the banks of the Bièvre, this Basque restaurant has preserved an old-fashioned atmosphere of relaxed conviviality, and the food's good too. Menus from 130F/€19.82.

Chez Gladines, 30 rue des Cinq-Diamants; ☎01.45.80.70.10 (Mº Corvisart). Daily 9am–2am. This small corner bistro is always welcoming. Excellent wines and dishes from the southwest; the mashed/fried potato is a must and goes best with *magret de canard*. Around 120F/€18.29 for a full meal.

Lao-Thai, 128 rue de Tolbiac; ☎01.44.24.28.10 (Mº Tolbiac). Daily except Wed 11.30am–2.30pm & 7–11pm. Big glass-fronted resto on a busy interchange. Finely spiced Thai and Laotian food, with coconut, ginger and lemongrass flavours. Midday menu at 46.50F/€7.09, otherwise around 120F/€18.29.

Phuong Hoang, Terrasse des Olympiades, 52 rue du Javelot; ☎01.45.84.75.07 (Mº Tolbiac; take the escalator up from rue Tolbiac). Mon–Fri noon–3pm & 7–11.30pm. Vietnamese, Thai and Singapore specialities on menus at 50F/€7.62, 70F/€10.67 and 80F/€12.20. If it's full or doesn't take your fancy, try *Le Le Lai* or *New Chinatown* nearby.

Le Temps des Cerises, 18–20 rue Butte-aux-Cailles; ☎01.45.89.69.48 (Mº Place-d'Italie/ Corvisart). Mon–Fri noon–2pm & 7.30–11pm, Sat 7.30–11pm. A well-established workers' co-op with elbow-to-elbow seating and a different daily choice of imaginative dishes. Lunch menu at 58F/€8.84 and evening menus starting at 118F/€17.99.

14e arrondissement

Bars and cafés

L'Entrepôt, 7–9 rue Francis-de-Pressensé (Mº Pernety). Mon–Sat noon–midnight. Cinema with a spacious café. Midday menu at 77F/€11.74; 150F/€22.87 à la carte in the evening.

Mustangs, 84 bd du Montparnasse (Mº Montparnasse-Bienvenue). Daily 9am–5am. Young crowd and happy atmosphere. A good place to finish up the evening after nightclubbing in St-Germain. Tex-Mex food, cocktails and beers.

La Pause Gourmande, 27 rue Campagne-Première (Mº Raspail). Mon–Fri 8.30am–7pm, Sat 8.30am–3pm. Delicious salads and savoury and sweet *tartes* from 28F/€4.27.

Le Rallye, 6 rue Daguerre (Mº Denfert-Rochereau). Tues–Sat until 8pm; closed Aug. A good place to recover from the catacombs or Montparnasse cemetery. The patron offers a bottle for tasting; gulping the lot would be considered bad form. Good cheese and *saucisson*.

Restaurants

Aquarius 2, 40 rue Gergovie; ☎01.45.41.36.88 (Mº Pernety). Mon–Sat noon–2.15pm & 7–10.30pm. Imaginative vegetarian meals served with proper Parisian bustle. Midday menu at 65F/€9.91.

Le Berbère, 50 rue de Gergovie; ☎01.45.42.10.29 (Mº Pernety). Daily lunchtime & evening until 10pm. Very unprepossessing decor-wise, but serves wholesome, unfussy and cheap North African food. Couscous from 50F/€7.62.

La Coupole, 102 bd du Montparnasse; ☎01.43.20.14.20 (Mº Vavin). Daily 8.30am–1am. The largest and perhaps most famous and enduring arty-chic Parisian hang-out for dining, dancing and debate. After 11pm, menu at 138F/€21.04 including wine, or *carte* from 170F/€25.92. Dancing Tues 9.30pm–4am, Fri & Sat 9.30pm–5am (100F/€15.24) and Sun 3–9pm (80F/€12.20).

N'Zadette M'Foua, 152 rue du Château; ☎01.43.22.00.16 (Mº Pernety). Daily 7pm–2am. A small Congolese restaurant, with tasty dishes such as *maboké* (meat or fish baked in banana leaves). Reservations required at weekends. Menu at 85F/€12.96, à la carte around 120F/€18.29.

Au Rendez-Vous des Camionneurs, 34 rue des Plantes; ☎01.45.40.43.36 (Mº Alésia). Mon–Fri lunchtime & 6–9.30pm; closed Aug. No lorry drivers any more, but good food for under 100F/€15.24; menu at 72F/€10.98 and a quarter of wine for under 20F/€3.05. Wise to book.

Restaurant Bleu, 46 rue Didot; ☎01.45.43.70.56 (Mº Plaisance). Tues–Sat lunchtime & evening until 11pm. Excellent high-class cooking in a small and well-tended restaurant. The three-course *menu du marché* is 130F/€19.82, or else you can choose the speciality *truffade* (mashed potato and sausage) amongst others from the à la carte menu for 175F/€26.86.

15e arrondissement

Bars and cafés

Au Roi du Café, 59 rue Lecourbe (Mº Volontaires/Sèvres-Lecourbe). Daily till 2am. Traditional café with a decor that didn't change much during the twentieth century and a pleasant terrace, albeit on a busy road.

LATE-NIGHT PARIS

It's not at all unusual for bars and brasseries in Paris to stay open after midnight; the list below is of cafés and bars that remain open after 2am, and restaurants that are open beyond midnight. Note that the three **Drugstores**, at 133 av des Champs-Élysées and 1 av Matignon in the 8ᵉ, and 149 bd St-Germain in the 6ᵉ, stay open till 2am, with bars, restaurants, shops and *tabacs*.

BARS AND CAFÉS

Bofinger, 3–7 rue de la Bastille, 4ᵉ. Daily till 1am. See p.159.

Café des Phares, 7 place de la Bastille, west side, 4ᵉ. Daily 7am–4am. See p.160.

La Champmeslé, 4 rue Chabanais, 2ᵉ. Thurs–Sun till 4am. See p.180.

Le Dépanneur, 27 rue Fontaine, 9ᵉ. All-nighter. See p.165.

Au Général Lafayette, 52 rue Lafayette, 9ᵉ. Daily till 4am. See p.165.

Le Grand Café Capucines, 4 bd des Capucines, 9ᵉ. All-nighter. See p.164.

Le Mazet, 60 rue St-André-des-Arts, 6ᵉ. Mon–Thurs till 2am, Fri & Sat till 3.30am. See p.163.

Mustangs, 84 Boulevard de Montparnasse 14ᵉ. Daily till 5am. See p.169.

La Paillote, 45 rue Monsieur-le-Prince, 6ᵉ. Mon–Sat till dawn. See p.163.

Pub St-Germain, 17 rue de l'Ancienne-Comédie, 6ᵉ. All-nighter. See p.163.

Le Quetzal, 10 rue de la Verrerie, 4ᵉ. Mon–Thurs till 4am, Fri–Sun till 5am. See p.180.

Le Sous-Bock, 49 rue St-Honoré, 1ᵉʳ. Daily till 5am. See p.158.

La Taverne de Nesle, 32 rue Dauphine, 6ᵉ. Mon–Thurs & Sun till 4am, Fri & Sat till 5am. See p.163.

RESTAURANTS

Brasserie Balzar, 49 rue des Écoles, 5ᵉ. Daily till 1am. See p.161.

Chez Gladines, 30 rue des Cinq-Diamants, 13ᵉ. Daily till 2am. See p.169.

La Coupole, 102 bd du Montparnasse, 14ᵉ. Daily till 1am. See p.169.

Le Dauphin, 167 rue St-Honoré, 1ᵉʳ. June–Oct daily till 12.30am. See p.158.

Flo, 7 cours des Petites-Écuries, 10ᵉ. Daily till 1.30am. See p.165.

Fouta Toro, 3 rue du Nord, 18ᵉ. Daily except Tues till 1am. See p.172.

Goldenberg's, 7 rue des Rosiers, 4ᵉ. Daily till 2am. See p.161.

Julien, 16 rue du Faubourg-St-Denis, 10ᵉ. Daily till 1.30am. See p.166.

Lipp, 151 bd St-Germain, 6ᵉ. Daily till 12.30am. See p.163.

Le Muniche, 7 rue St-Benôit, 6ᵉ. Daily till 2am. See p.163.

N'Zadette, M'Foua, 152 rue due Château, 14ᵉ. Daily till 2am. See p.169.

Le Pacifique, 35 rue de Belleville, 20ᵉ. Daily till 1am. See p.173.

Le Petit Zinc, 11 rue St-Benoît, 6ᵉ. Daily till 2am. See p.163.

Au Pied de Cochon, 6 rue Coquillière, 1ᵉʳ. All-nighter. See p.158.

Polidor, 41 rue Monsieur-le-Prince, 6ᵉ. Mon–Sat till 12.30am. See p.163.

Le Procope, 13 rue de l'Ancienne-Comédie, 6ᵉ. Daily till 1am. See p.164.

Taï Yen, 5 rue de Belleville, 20ᵉ. Daily till 2am. See p.173.

Terminus Nord, 23 rue de Dunkerque, 10ᵉ. Daily till 1am. See p.166.

Vaudeville, 29 rue Vivienne, 2ᵉ. Daily till 2am. See p.159.

Au Virage Lepic, 61 rue Lepic, 18ᵉ. Daily except Tues till 2am. See p.172.

Restaurants

Le Café du Commerce, 51 rue du Commerce; ☎01.45.75.03.27 (Mᵒ Émile-Zola). Daily noon–midnight. A two-storey restaurant that's been catering for *le petit peuple* for over a hundred years. Serves varied, nourishing and cheap fare. *Formules* 87F/€13.26 and 115F/€17.53; *carte* around 145F/€22.11.

Da Attilio, 21 rue Cronstadt; ☎01.40.43.91.90 (M° Convention/Porte-de-Vanves). Mon–Sat till 9.30pm. Close to the Parc Georges Brassens. Unprepossessing decor and run-of-the-mill food, but very friendly service and a great atmosphere. Different Italian specialities each day. *Plats du jour* 50F/€7.62.

Le Bistrot d'André, 232 rue St-Charles; ☎01.45.57.89.14 (M° Balard). Mon–Sat noon–2.45pm & 7.45–10.30pm. A reminder of the old Citroën works before the Parc André-Citroën was created, with pictures and models of the classic French car. Great puds. Midday menu 65F/€9.91, otherwise around 140F/€21.34.

Sampieru Corsu, 12 rue de l'Amiral-Roussin (M° Cambronne). Mon–Fri lunchtimes & 7–9.30pm. Decorated with the posters and passionate declarations of international socialism, this restaurant has as its purpose the provision of meals for the homeless, unemployed and low-paid. The principle is that you pay what you can and it is left to your conscience how you settle the bill. The minimum requested is 45F/€6.86 for a three-course meal with wine. However poor you might feel, as a tourist in Paris you should be able to pay more. The restaurant only survives on the generosity of its supporters, and it's a wonderful place.

16e arrondissement
Bars and cafés

Totem, southern wing of the Palais de Chaillot, place du Trocadéro (M° Trocadéro). Daily noon–2am. Native American-themed restaurant but with French traditional dishes thrown in; the 134F/€20.43 lunch menu isn't bad, but the views from the terrace are magnificent.

17e arrondissement
Bars and cafés

Chamignon, 64 rue des Batignolles (M° Rome/Place-de-Clichy). Daily except Wed till 8pm. A local boulangerie on one side and an old habitués' café on the other where you can sit and snack on quiche, sandwiches and pastries. Tables on the street in the summer.

Restaurants

Joy in Food, 2 rue Truffaut; ☎01.43.87.96.79 (M° Place-de-Clichy). Mon–Sat noon–2.30pm. Minuscule veggie place, with its mind on higher things: meditation sessions at 8pm Mon–Sat. Good, inexpensive food in an attractive atmosphere. Menus at 63F/€9.60 and 75F/€11.43.

La Nonna, 43 rue des Dames; ☎01.45.22.14.14 (M° Place-de-Clichy). Mon–Sat noon–2.30pm & 7–9.30pm. Great little Italian restaurant with pizzas from 30F/€4.57 and salads from 50F/€7.62.

La P'tite Lili, 8 rue des Batignolles; ☎01.45.22.54.22 (M° Place-de-Clichy). Mon–Fri noon–2.30pm & 7–9.30pm. Simple and small menu but carefully prepared and with delicious home-made traditional desserts.

18e arrondissement
Bars and cafés

La Petite Charlotte, 24 rue des Abbesses (M° Abbesses). Tues–Sun till 8pm. Crêpes, pâtisseries and 58F/€8.84 *formule* on sunny tables.

Le Refuge, cnr rue Lamarck & the steps of rue de la Fontaine-du-But (M° Lamarck-Caulaincourt). Mon–Sat till 8.30pm. A gentle café stop with a long view west down rue Lamarck to the country beyond.

Le Sancerre, 35 rue des Abbesses (M° Abbesses). Daily 7am–2am. A fashionable hang-out for the young and trendy of all nationalities on the southern slopes of Montmartre.

Restaurants

L'Assiette, 78 rue Labat; ☎01.42.59.06.63 (M° Château-Rouge). Mon–Sat noon–2.30pm & 7.30–10.30pm; closed Wed evening. A bit out of the way, but a very friendly place, with delicious *champignons forestières, chocolate charlotte* and a surprising beetroot sorbet starter. An extraordinarily good-value 98F/€14.94 menu.

Fouta Toro, 3 rue du Nord; ☎01.42.55.42.73 (M° Marcadet-Poissonniers). Daily except Tues 7.30pm–1am. A tiny, crowded, welcoming Senegalese diner in a very scruffy alley northeast of Montmartre. Be prepared for a wait unless you come at 8pm or after 10.30pm. No more than 70F/€10.67 all-in.

Au Grain de Folie, 24 rue La Vieuville; ☎01.42.58.15.57 (M° Abbesses). Daily 12.30–2.30pm & 7–11.30pm. Tiny, simple, cheap and friendly vegetarian, with just the sort of traditional atmosphere that you would hope for from Montmartre. *Gratin* and fruit compote for 55F/€8.38, menu 100F/€15.24.

Marie-Louise, 52 rue Championnet; ☎01.46.06.86.55 (M° Simplon). Tues–Sat lunchtime & evening until 10pm; closed Aug. A bit of a trek north, but the excellent traditional French cuisine at this renowned restaurant is definitely worth the journey. Menu at 130F/€19.82, otherwise around 180F/€27.44.

Au Port de Pidjiguiti, 28 rue Étex; ☎01.42.26.71.77 (M° Guy-Môquet). Tues–Sun lunchtime & evening until 11pm; closed Jan. Very pleasant atmosphere and excellent food. It is run by a village in Guinea-Bissau, whose inhabitants take turns in staffing the restaurant; the proceeds go to the village. Good-value wine list. Menu 100F/€15.24; à la carte around 120F/€18.29.

Au Virage Lepic, 61 rue Lepic; ☎01.42.52.46.79 (M° Blanche/Abbesses). Daily except Tues 7pm–2am. Simple, traditional fare in a noisy, friendly atmosphere created by the singers – in the French/Parisian idiom. Small, smoky and very enjoyable. Around 100F/€15.24.

19ᵉ arrondissement

Restaurants

Café de la Musique, 213 av Jean-Jaures (M° Porte-de-Pantin). Daily till 2am. Part of the Cité de la Musique, this café, with a popular terrace, was designed by the Cité architect Portzamparc and exudes sophistication, discretion and comfort, but be prepared to pay over the odds for a coffee.

Le Rendez-vous des Quais, 10 quai de la Seine (M° Jaurès/Stalingrad). Daily 11.30am–12.30am. Attached to the MK2 art-house cinema, the outside tables of this café/brasserie sit right on the banks of the Bassin de la Villette providing a relaxing spot for a refreshment before or after the canal cruises which depart opposite.

Aux Saveurs du Liban, 11 rue Eugène-Jumin (M° Porte-de-Pantin). Mon–Sat 11am–11pm. Excellent authentic Lebanese food at this tiny restaurant in a lively local street not far from the Parc

---

GOURMET RESTAURANTS OF PARIS

Unsurprisingly, there are some really spectacular Parisian restaurants. *Alain Ducasse* at 59 av Raymond Poincaré, 16ᵉ (☎01.47.27.12.27), is one of two three-star restaurants – the other being *Le Louis XV* in Monte Carlo – run by Alain Ducasse, who since the early 1990s has been the tidal wave sweeping through French cuisine and is the first-ever chef to have been awarded six stars by Michelin. The other greats include: *Lucas Carton*, 9 place de la Madeleine, 8ᵉ (☎01.42.65.22.90), with splendid Art Nouveau decor and chef Alain Senderens; *Taillevent*, 15 rue Lamennais, 8ᵉ (☎01.45.61.12.90); *Les Ambassadeurs*, in the *Hôtel Crillon*, 10 place de la Concorde, 8ᵉ (☎01.44.71.16.16); *Ledoyen*, 1 av Dutuit, 8ᵉ (☎01.47.42.35.98), headed by a Flemish woman chef, Ghislaine Arabian; *L'Ambroisie*, 9 place des Vosges, 4ᵉ (☎01.43.78.51.45); and *Guy Savoy*, 18 rue Troyon, 17ᵉ (☎01.43 .80.40.61).

Recent trends have guided many great chefs to open smaller, less expensive, more casual, though certainly still very high-quality establishments in order both widen their market and bring the tradition of fine cooking to a public less and less willing to pay the historically high prices – Alain Ducasse, for example, has opened *Spoon, Food & Wine* at 14 rue de Marignan, 8ᵉ (☎01.40.76.34.44). At midday during the week you may find menus of around 300–395F/€45.73–60.21; *prixe fixe* menus range from 480F/€73.17 to 1500F/€228.66; and there's no limit on the amount you can pay for beautiful wines.

de la Villette. Very good value with *plats* for 30F/€4.57 and wine for 9F/€1.37 a glass; sandwiches from 18F/€2.74 to take away; 40F/€6.10 lunch-time *formule*.

20e arrondissement
Bars and cafés

Le Baratin, 3 rue Jouye-Rouve (M° Pyrénées). Tues–Fri 11am–1am, Sat 6pm–1am. Friendly, unpretentious *bistrot à vins* in a run-down area with a good mix of people. Fine selection of lesser-known wines and whiskies. Midday menu 65F/€9.91.

Bistrot Cave des Envierges, 11 rue des Envierges (M° Pyrénées). Wed–Fri noon–midnight, Sat & Sun noon–8pm. Another *bistrot à vins* purveying good-quality, lesser-known wines to connoisseurs. An attractive bar – though more a place to taste and buy wine than eat – in a great location above the Parc de Belleville.

La Flèche d'Or, 102bis rue de Bagnolet, cnr rue des Pyrénées (M° Alexandre-Dumas). Daily 10am–2am. A large, lively café attracting the biker, arty, punkish Parisian young. The decor is *très destroy* – ie railway sleepers and a sawn-off bus front hanging from the ceiling – and the building itself is the old Bagnolet station on the *petite ceinture* railway that encircled the city until around thirty years ago. It's a nightly venue for live world music, pop, punk, ska, fusion and chanson, and the reasonably priced food also has a multicultural slant.

Rital et Courts, 1 rue des Envierges; ☎01.47.97.08.40 (M° Pyrénées). Tues–Sat noon–2am, Sun noon–7pm. Mellow bar/café/trattoria which specializes in showing "Courts Metrages" – short films (Tues–Sun 3.30–7pm, Sat midnight–2am). It's in an unbeatable situation overlooking the Parc de Belleville: get a pavement table on a summer evening and you'll have the best restaurant view in Paris. The Italian food is tasty and affordable, with a large pasta selection, including loads of vegetarian options; 50–90F/€7.62–13.72.

Restaurants

La Fontaine aux Roses, 27 av Gambetta; ☎01.46.36.74.75 (M° Père-Lachaise). Tues–Sat till 10pm; closed Sun evening, Mon & Aug. Small, beautiful restaurant with first-rate menus: midday 120F/€18.29 and evenings 170F/€25.91, both including *kir royale*, wine and coffee.

Lao Siam, 49 rue de Belleville; ☎01.40.40.09.68 (M° Belleville). Daily till 11pm. Extremely good Thai and Laotian food, popular with locals. Dishes 42–60F/€6.40–9.15.

Le Pacifique, 35 rue de Belleville; ☎01.42.49.66.80 (M° Belleville). Daily 11am–1am. A huge Chinese eating house with variable culinary standards but low prices. Main courses from 50F/€7.62; 85F/€12.96 or 100F/€15.24 menu.

Pho-Dong-Huong, 14 rue Louis-Bonnet; ☎01.43.57.18.88 (M° Belleville). Daily except Tues noon–10.30pm. Spotlessly clean Vietnamese resto, where all dishes are under 50F/€7.62 and come with piles of fresh green leaves. Spicy soups, crispy pancakes, but slow service.

Aux Rendez-Vous des Amis, 10 av Père-Lachaise; ☎01.47.97.72.16 (M° Gambetta). Mon–Sat noon–2.30pm; closed last week July to mid-Aug. Unprepossessing surroundings for very good, simple and satisfying family cooking. Main courses 45–78F/€6.86–11.89; menu at 65F/€9.91.

Taï Yen, 5 rue de Belleville; ☎01.42.41.44.16 (M° Belleville). Daily 10am–2am. Admire the koi carp idling round their aquarium like embroidered satin cushions while you wait for the generous soups and steamed specialities of this Chinese restaurant. 65F/€9.91 menu, dishes from 49F/€7.47.

Le Zéphyr, 1 rue Jourdain; ☎01.46.36.65.81 (M° Jourdain). Mon–Sat till 11.30pm. A rather trendy but relaxed 1930s-style bistro with menus at 69F/€10.52 and 130F/€19.82.

Music and nightlife

The strength of the Paris **music scene** is its diversity – a reputation gained mainly from its absorption of immigrant and exile populations. The city has no rivals in Europe for the variety of **world music** to be discovered: Algerian, West and Central African, Caribbean and Latin American sounds are represented in force. **Rap** and **hip-hop** are fashionable, both imported and home-grown, whilst French **techno** – along with its DJs – has proved a hit both abroad and, more recently, in France.

Commercial French **popular music** is, on the whole, to be avoided: bands worth their salt are Les Négresses Vertes, Zebda and the soloist Manu Chau, all of whom employ a fascinating mix of styles, and the rock groups Rita Mitsouko and Louise Attaque.

Jazz fans are in for a treat, with all styles from New Orleans to current experimental to be heard, although in most clubs expense is a real drawback to enjoyment. Admission charges are generally high, and when they're not levied there's usually a whacking charge for your first drink, and subsequent drinks don't come cheap.

Then there is the tradition of **chansons**, epitomized by the sublime Edith Piaf and developed to its greatest heights by Georges Brassens and the Belgian Jacques Brel. This type of music has been undergoing something of a revival, and chanson evenings in restaurants and bars can be great fun and a typically Parisian experience.

Nightlife recommendations – for **dance clubs and discos** – are to some extent incorporated with those for live rock, world music and jazz venues, with which they merge. Places that cater for a primarily **gay or lesbian** clientele are listed in the "Gay and lesbian Paris" section (see p.180). Bear in mind that some clubs operate very snooty door policies.

Classical music, as you might expect in this Neoclassical city, is alive and well and takes up twice the space of "jazz-pop-folk-rock" in the listings magazines. The **Paris Opéra**, with its two homes – the Opéra-Garnier and Opéra-Bastille – puts on a fine selection of opera and ballet. The need for advance reservations (except sometimes for the concerts held in churches) rather than the price is the major inhibiting factor here. If you're interested in the **contemporary** scene of Systems composition and the like, check out the Cité de la Musique auditorium at La Villette. At the end of the section are details of all the **big performance halls** for major events from heavy metal to opera.

On June 21 the **Fête de la Musique** sees live bands and free concerts of every kind of music throughout the city.

Information and tickets

For exhaustive listings of **what's on** in the city, there are two weekly guides, published on a Wednesday: *Pariscope* (*www.pariscope.fr*, 3F/€0.46) and *L'Officiel des Spectacles* (2F/€0.30). *Pariscope* is probably the easiest to find your way around and has a small section in English at the back, but since both guides are just listings, mainly in French with a minimum of comment, there is not much difference between them. The best places to get **tickets** for concerts, whether rock, jazz, chansons or classical, are: FNAC Forum des Halles, 1–5 rue Pierre-Lescot, 1ᵉ (☎01.40.41.40.00, *www.fnac.fr*; Mº Chatelet-Les Halles); the FNAC Musique branches (see p.192); or Virgin Megastore (see p.192).

Music venues

Most of the **music venues** listed below are also clubs. A few of them will have live music all week, but the majority host bands on just a couple of nights, usually Friday and Saturday, when admission prices are also hiked up. See also under "Big performance halls" for concerts that attract big international names in all fields of music, and "Mainly jazz" for venues which programme not only jazz concerts but branch into other genres, such as world music and folk.

Mainly rock

Café de la Danse, 5 passage Louis-Philippe, 11ᵉ; ☎01.47.00.57.59 (Mᵒ Bastille). Good friendly venue playing rock, pop, world and folk music in an intimate and attractive space. Be warned, there's no bar. Open nights of concerts only; check local press or ring for details and prices.

La Cigale, 120 bd de Rochechouart, 18ᵉ; ☎01.49.25.89.99 (Mᵒ Pigalle). Music from 8.30pm. Rita Mitsouko, punk, indie, etc. An eclectic programming policy in an old-fashioned converted theatre, long a fixture on the Pigalle scene. Admission for concerts 120–250F/€18.29–38.11.

Le Divan du Monde, 75 rue des Martyrs, 18ᵉ; ☎01.44.92.77.66 (Mᵒ Pigalle). Daily 7pm–5am. A youthful venue in a café whose regulars once included Toulouse-Lautrec. An eclectic, exciting programming policy that includes a round-the-world theme – the country chosen is represented by food, music and events. Admission for concerts 60–120F/€9.15–18.29.

Élysée Montmartre, 72 bd de Rochechouart, 18ᵉ; ☎01.44.92.45.45, *www.elyseemontmartre.com* (Mᵒ Anvers). Check press for times. A historic Montmartre nightspot, now dedicated to rock. Inexpensive and fun, it pulls in a young, excitable crowd. Around 80F/€12.20.

Le Grand Rex, 1 bd Poissonnière, 2ᵉ; ☎01.45.08.93.89 (Mᵒ Grands-Boulevards). Check press for times. Mythical Rococo-style cinema that doubles up as a concert venue with 2750 places. Varied programming with well-known names. Admission fee depends on who's playing.

La Guinguette Pirate, Bateau quai de la Gare, 13ᵉ; ☎01.44..24.89.89 (Mᵒ Quai-de-la-Gare). Tues–Sat 7pm–2am. Beautiful Chinese barge, moored alongside the quay in front of the Bibliothèque Nationale, hosting funk, reggae, rock and folk concerts; your best bet for a not-too-expensive good night out. Admission 30–40F/€4.57–6.10.

Trabendo, Parc de la Villette, 19ᵉ; ☎01.49.25.81.75 (Mᵒ Porte-de-Pantin). Check press for times. The ex-*Hot Brass* revamped and with a wider range of programming – world, jazz and rock, with big French names such as Les Negresses Vertes. Open nights of concerts only; check local press or ring for details.

Latin & Caribbean

L'Escale, 15 rue Monsieur-le-Prince, 6ᵉ; ☎01.40.51.80.49 (Mᵒ Odéon). Tues–Sat 10.30pm–5am. More Latin-American musicians must have passed through here than any other club. The dancing sounds, salsa mostly, are in the basement, while on the ground floor every variety of South American music is given an outlet. Drinks 80F.

Mambo Club, 20 rue Cujas, 5ᵉ; ☎01.43.54.89.21 (Mᵒ St-Michel/Odéon). Wed–Sat 11pm–dawn, Sun 5pm–dawn for themed *soirées*. Afro-Cuban and Antillais music in a seedy dive with people of all ages and nationalities. 110F/€16.77 admission in the evening, 80F/€12.20 during the day.

Bals musettes

Balajo, 9 rue de Lappe, 11ᵉ; ☎01.47.00.07.87 (Mᵒ Bastille). Daily 10.30pm–5am. The old-style music hall of *gai Paris* – extravagant 1930s decor and vast dance floor. The music encompasses everything from mazurka to tango, cha-cha, twist and the slurpy chansons of between the wars. Admission price is around 100F/€15.24.

Chapelle des Lombards, 19 rue de Lappe, 11ᵉ; ☎01.43.57.24.24 (Mᵒ Bastille). Thurs–Sat 10.30pm–dawn. This erstwhile *bal musette* still plays the occasional waltz and tango, but for the most part the music is salsa, reggae, steel drums, gwo-kâ, zouk, raï and the blues. The doormen are not too friendly and its renown as a pick-up joint means unabashed advances. Thurs 100F/€15.24 entry and first drink, Fri & Sat 120F/€18.29.

Mainly jazz

Le Baiser Salé, 58 rue des Lombards, 1ᵉʳ; ☎01.42.33.37.71 (Mᵒ Châtelet). Mon–Sat 8am–5am. A bar downstairs and a small, crowded upstairs room with live music every night from 11pm – usually jazz, rhythm & blues, Latino-rock, reggae or Brazilian. Admission 30–90F/€4.57–13.72.

Le Bilboquet, 13 rue St-Benoît, 6ᵉ; ☎01.45.48.81.84 (Mᵒ St-Germain). Mon–Sat 9pm–dawn. A rather smart, comfortable bar/restaurant with live jazz every night – local and international stars. The music starts at 10.45pm, and food is served until 1am. No admission charge, but pricey drinks: 120F/€18.29.

Caveau de la Huchette, 5 rue de la Huchette, 5e; ☎01.43.26.65.05 (M° St-Michel). Daily 9.30pm–2am. A wonderful slice of old Parisian life in an otherwise horribly touristy area. Live jazz, usually trad, to dance to on a floor surrounded by tiers of benches, and a bar decorated with caricatures of the barman drawn on any material to hand. Admission Mon–Thurs & Sun 60F/€9.15; Fri & Sat 75F/€11.43; drinks from 26F/€3.96.

L'Eustache, 37 rue Berger, 1er; ☎01.40.26.23.20 (M° Les Halles). Daily 11am–4am. Live jazz 10.30pm–2am on Thurs and cheap beer in this young and friendly Les Halles café – in fact, the cheapest good jazz in the capital.

Instants Chavirés, 7 rue Richard-Lenoir, Montreuil; ☎01.42.87.25.91 (M° Robespierre). Tues–Sat 8pm–1am; concerts at 8.30pm. Avant-garde jazz joint – no comforts – on the eastern edge of the city where musicians go to hear each other play. Admission 40–80F/€6.10–12.20, depending on the celebrity of the band; drinks from 15F/€2.29.

New Morning, 7–9 rue des Petites-Écuries, 10e; ☎01.45.23.51.41 (M° Château-d'Eau). Usually Tues–Sat 9pm–1.30am (concerts start around 9.30pm). This is the place where the big international names in jazz come to play. Blues and Latin, too. Admission around 110F/€16.77.

Le Petit Journal, 71 bd St-Michel, 5e; ☎01.43.26.28.59 (RER Luxembourg). Mon–Sat 10pm–2am; closed Aug. A small, smoky bar with good, mainly French, traditional and mainstream sounds. Admission free; first drink 100–150F/€15.24–22.87, 50F/€7.62 thereafter.

Le Petit Journal Montparnasse, 13 rue du Commandant-Mouchotte, 14e; ☎01.43.21.56.70 (M° Montparnasse). Mon–Sat 9pm–2am. Under the *Hôtel Montparnasse*, and sister establishment to the above, with bigger visiting names, both French and international. Admission free; first drink 100F/€15.24, 50F/€7.62 thereafter.

Le Petit Opportun, 15 rue des Lavandières-Ste-Opportune, 1er; ☎01.42.36.01.36 (M° Châtelet-Les Halles). Tues–Sat 9pm–2.30am. Music from 11pm. Arrive early to get a seat for the live music in the dungeon-like cellar where the acoustics play strange tricks and you can't always see the musicians. Fairly eclectic policy and a crowd of genuine connoisseurs. Admission 50–80F/€7.62–12.20.

Le Sunset, 60 rue des Lombards, 1er; ☎01.40.26.46.20 (M° Châtelet-Les Halles). Mon–Sat 9pm–2am. Restaurant upstairs, jazz club in the basement, featuring the best musicians – the likes of Alain Jeanmarie and Turk Mauró – and frequented by musicians in the wee small hours. Admission and first drink 50F–120F/€7.62–18.29.

Utopia, 79 rue de l'Ouest, 14e; ☎01.43.22.79.66 (M° Pernety). Mon–Sat 10pm–dawn; closed Aug. No genius here, but good French blues singers interspersed with jazz and blues tapes, with a mainly young and studenty audience. Generally very pleasant atmosphere. Admission free; drinks from 50F/€7.62.

Mainly chansons

Casino de Paris, 19 rue de Clichy, 9e; ☎01.49.95.99.99 (M° Trinité). Check press for times. This decaying, once-plush casino in one of the seediest streets in Paris is a venue for all sorts of performances – chansons, poetry combined with flamenco guitar, cabaret, musicals. Check the listings magazines under "Variétés" and "Chansons". Tickets 120–180F/€ 18.29–27.44.

Le Lapin Agile, 22 rue des Saules, 18e; ☎01.46.06.85.87 (M° Lamarck-Caulaincourt). Tues–Sun 9pm–2am. Old haunt of Apollinaire, Utrillo and other Montmartre artists, some of whose pictures adorn the walls. Cabaret, poetry and chansons; you may be lucky enough to catch the singer-composer Arlette Denis, who carries Jacques Brel's flame. Admission 130F/€19.82 including drink, students 90F/€13.72.

Nightclubs and discos

The **clubs** listed below are primarily dance venues, although a couple occasionally also put on live music. It's worth remembering that most of the places listed under "Music venues" (see above) also function as clubs.

Les Bains, 7 rue du Bourg-l'Abbé, 3e; ☎01.48.87.01.80 (M° Étienne-Marcel). Daily midnight–dawn (Sun rock; Mon "disturbance of the peace"; Wed "disco inferno"). This is as posey as they come – an old Turkish bathhouse with plunge pool. The music is house, rap and funk, with occasional live (usually dross) bands. Fussy bouncers and expensive drinks. Admission 100F/€15.24 weekdays, 120F/€18.29 at the weekend.

Batofar, quai de la Gare, 13ᵉ; ☎01.56.29.10.00 (Mᵒ Quai-de-la-Gare/Bibliothèque-Tolbiac). Daily 7pm–1am. An old lighthouse boat moored at the foot of the Bibliothèque Nationale Tolbiac. Brilliant line-up of DJs from all over the world spinning techno for the most part. Your best bet for a not-too-expensive club night out. Admission 30–50F/€4.57–7.62.

El Globo, 8 bd Strasbourg, 10ᵉ; ☎01.42.41.55.70 (Mᵒ Strasbourg-St-Denis). Sat, Sun & public hols 10pm–dawn. Currently very popular with Beaux Quartiers rebels, 10ᵉ *arrondissement* punks and others. Lots of room to dance to international hits past and present. Admission 100F/€15.24; drinks 50F/€7.62, or 25F/€3.81 11pm–midnight.

La Locomotive, 90 bd de Clichy, 18ᵉ; ☎08.36.69.69.28 (Mᵒ Blanche). Daily 11pm–dawn. Enormous high-tech nightclub with three dance floors: one for techno; one for rock, heavy metal and concerts; and one for rap and funk. One of the most crowded and popular clubs in the city. Admission 60F/€9.15 weekdays, 100F/€15.24 weekends, including one drink.

Le Queen, 102 Champs-Élysées, 8ᵉ; ☎01.53.89.08.90, *www.queen.fr* (Mᵒ George-V). Daily 11pm–dawn. Legendary gay club whose success has interested a heterosexual clientele as well. These days everyone is welcome, except on Thurs when the club is strictly gay. "Disco inferno" on Mon, otherwise mainly house music and top name DJs. The crowd includes drag queens and model types. Admission 30F/€4.57 Mon, Tues & Sun, 50F/€7.62 Wed & Thurs, 100F/€15.24 Fri & Sat; prices include one drink

Rex Club, 5 bd Poissonnière, 2ᵉ; ☎01.42.36.10.96 (Mᵒ Grands-Boulevards). Thurs–Sat & occasionally Wed 11.30pm–6am; closed Aug. A happening club in the same building (but different entrance) as the mythical cinema-cum-concert venue *Le Grand Rex* (see p.175), with strictly electronic music – house, drum 'n' bass, etc. Admission 50–80F/€7.62–12.20.

Le Shéhérazade, 3 rue de Liège, 9ᵉ; ☎01.40.16.17.18 (Mᵒ Liège). Mon–Thurs 11pm–dawn, Fri–Sun midnight–dawn. Popular with the youthful, mixed, dancing crowd. House music, with occasional variant evenings. Exotic decor in a former Russian cabaret. 100F/€15.24 admission plus drink; vodka 80–90F/€12.20–13.72 a shot.

Zed Club, 2 rue des Anglais, 5ᵉ; ☎01.43.54.93.78 (Mᵒ Maubert-Mutualité). Wed–Sat 10.30pm–3.30am. The best rock 'n' roll club in town. Entry 50F/€7.62 plus drink Wed & Thurs; 100F/€15.24 plus drink Fri & Sat.

Classical music

Paris is a stimulating environment for **classical music**, both established and contemporary. The former is well represented in performances within churches – sometimes free or very cheap – and in an enormous choice of commercially promoted concerts held every day of the week. Contemporary and experimental computer-based work also flourishes.

Concert venues

The **Cité de la Musique** at La Villette (*www.cite-musique.fr*; Mᵒ Porte-de-Pantin) has given Paris two new, major concert venues: the **Conservatoire** (the national music academy) at 209 av Jean-Jaurès, 19ᵉ (☎01.40.40.46.46); and the **Salle des Concerts** at 221 av Jean-Jaurès, 19ᵉ (☎01.44.84.44.84). Ancient music, contemporary works, jazz, chansons and music from all over the world are featured.

These apart, the top **auditoriums** are: Salle Pleyel, 252 rue du Faubourg-St-Honoré, 8ᵉ (☎01.45.61.53.00; Mᵒ Ternes); Salle Gaveau, 45 rue de la Boétie, 8ᵉ (☎01.49.53.05.07; Mᵒ Miromesnil); Théâtre des Champs-Élysées, 15 av Montaigne, 8ᵉ (☎01.49.52.50.50; Mᵒ Alma-Marceau); and the Théâtre Musical de Paris (see "Opera" below). **Tickets** are best bought at the box offices, though for big names you may find overnight queues, and a large number of seats are always booked by subscribers. The price range is very reasonable.

Churches and **museums** are also good places to hear classical music. The Église St-Séverin, 1 rue des Prêtres st-Séverin, 5ᵉ (☎01.48.24.16.97; Mᵒ St-Michel); the Église St-Julien le Pauvre, 23 quai de Montebello, 5ᵉ (☎01.42.08.49.00; Mᵒ St-Michel); and the Sainte

Chapelle, 4 bd du Palais, 1er (☎01.42.77.65.65; M° Cité), all host regular concerts. The Musée du Louvre, palais du Louvre, 1er (☎01.40.20.84.00; M° Louvre-Rivoli/Palais-Royal-Musée-du-Louvre) and the Musée d'Orsay, 1 rue de Bellechasse, 7e (☎01.40.49.47.17; M° Solférino/RER Musée-d'Orsay), both host chamber music recitals in their auditoriums.

Classical concerts also take place for free at **Radio France**, 166 av du Président-Kennedy, 16e (☎01.56.40.15.16; M° Passy).

Opera

The first performance at the **Opéra-Bastille** – the six-hour-long *Les Troyens* by Berlioz – cast something of a shadow on the project's proclaimed commitment to popularizing its art. Since then it has been plagued by rows and resignations, and opinions differ on the quality of the acoustics and productions. However, the bickering hasn't stopped it being packed at every performance. To judge the place for yourself, tickets (60–670F/€9.15–102.14) can be booked Monday to Saturday 9am to 7pm on ☎08.36.69.78.68 at least four weeks in advance, or at the ticket office (Mon–Sat 11am–6.30pm) within two weeks of the performance. The cheapest seats are only available to personal callers; unfilled seats are sold at discount to students five minutes before the curtain goes up. For programme details, phone ☎08.36.69.78.68, or have a look at their Web site *www.opera-de-paris.fr*.

Big-scale opera productions are usually staged at the **Théâtre Musical de Paris**, 1 place du Châtelet, 1er (☎01.40.28.28.40; M° Châtelet). Smaller, daring classical and modern operatic productions are performed at the **Opéra-Comique**, Salle Favart, 5 rue Favart, 2e (☎01.42.44.45.46; M° Richelieu-Drouot), and productions still take place at the old **Opéra-Garnier**, place de l'Opéra, 9e (☎08.36.69.78.68, *www.opera-de-paris*; M° Opéra). Both opera and recitals are also put on at the multipurpose performance halls (see below).

Contemporary music

Pierre Boulez' post-serialist experiments received massive public funding for many years in the form of a vast laboratory of acoustics and "digital signal processing" – a complex known as **IRCAM** – housed underneath the Beaubourg arts centre. Boulez' Ensemble Intercontemporain is now based in the Cité de la Musique, but IRCAM occasionally has concerts.

Other Paris-based practitioners of contemporary and experimental music include Laurent Bayle, Jean-Claude Eloy, Pascal Dusapin and Luc Ferrarie, who can occasionally be heard at the Cité de la Musique.

Festivals

Festivals are plentiful in all the diverse fields that come under the far too general term of "classical". The **Festival d'Art Sacré** involves concerts and recitals of church music (end of Nov to mid-Dec); concerts feature in the general arts **Festival d'Automne** (end of Sept to end Dec); and a summer **festival of classical chamber music** is held at the Château de Sceaux to the south of the city (mid-July to third week in Sept).

For details of these and more, pick up the current year's **festival schedule** from one of the tourist offices or from the Hôtel de Ville, 29 rue du Rivoli, 4^e (M° Hôtel-de-Ville). During January the Hôtel de Ville sponsors a week of two concert tickets for the price of one.

The big performance halls

Events at any of the **performance halls** listed below will be well advertised on billboards and posters throughout the city. **Tickets** can be obtained at the halls themselves, though it's easier to get them through agents like FNAC or Virgin Megastore (see p.192).

Le Bataclan, 50 bd Voltaire, 11ᵉ; ☎01.47.00.30.12 (Mᵒ Oberkampf). One of the best places for visiting and native rock bands.

Maison des Cultures du Monde, 101 bd Raspail, 6ᵉ; ☎01.45.44.72.30 (Mᵒ Rennes). All the arts from all over the world, for once not dominated by Europeans.

Olympia, 28 bd des Capucines, 9ᵉ; ☎01.47.42.25.49 (Mᵒ Madeleine/Opéra). A recently renovated old-style music hall hosting occasional well-known rock groups and large, popular concert performers.

Palais des Congrès, place de la Porte-Maillot, 17ᵉ; ☎01.40.68.22.22 (Mᵒ Porte-Maillot). Opera, ballet, orchestral music, trade fairs, and the superstars of US and British rock.

Palais Omnisports de Bercy, 8 bd de Bercy, 12ᵉ; ☎01.43.46.12.21 (Mᵒ Bercy). Opera, cycle racing, Bruce Springsteen, ice hockey, and Citroën launches – a multipurpose stadium, with seats to give vertigo to the most level-headed, but an excellent space when used in the round.

Palais des Sports, Porte de Versailles, 15ᵉ; ☎01.48.28.40.48 or 01.44.68.44.68 (Mᵒ Porte-de-Versailles). Another vast-scale auditorium, ideal if you want to see your favourite rock star in miniature 1km away.

Stade de France, St-Denis; ☎01.55.93.00.00, *www.stadefrance.fr* (RER B La-Plaine-Stade-de-France/RER D Stade-de-France-St-Denis). One hundred thousand capacity stadium, purpose-built for France's hosting of the 1998 Football World Cup. As well as hosting major football and rugby events, the stadium is the venue for big names such as Johnny Halliday and Tina Turner.

Zenith, Parc de la Villette, 211 av Jean-Jaurès, 20ᵉ; ☎01.42.08.60.00 or 01.42.40.60.00 (Mᵒ Porte-de-Pantin). Seating for 6500 people in an inflatable stadium designed exclusively for rock and pop concerts. Head for the concrete column with a descending red aeroplane.

Gay and lesbian Paris

Paris is one of Europe's major centres for **gay men**, with numerous bars, clubs, restaurants, saunas and shops catering for a gay clientele. Its focal point is the **Marais**, whose central street, rue Ste-Croix-de-la-Bretonnerie, has visibly gay commerces at almost every other address. **Lesbians** have much fewer facilities, but there are a handful of women-only addresses. The high spot of the calendar is the annual **Gay Pride parade**, which is normally held on the Saturday closest to the summer solstice.

Information and contacts

The gay and lesbian community is well catered for by the mainstream media and support groups. The main information centre for the gay community in Paris is the **Centre Gai et Lesbienne**, 3 rue Keller, 11ᵉ (☎01.43.57.21.47, *www.cglparis.org*; Mᵒ Ledru-Rollin), which is open Monday to Saturday from 4pm to 8pm. It's full of flyers, leaflets and contacts, as well as being the meeting place for numerous campaigning, identity, health, arts and intellectual groups. Also full of information are the *Guide Gai/Gay Guide*, published annually in French and English by Gai Pied (*www.gaipied.fr*), and costing 79F/€12.04 from newsagents and bookshops, which is the most comprehensive **gay guide** to France, and *Têtu* (*tetu.com*), a monthly gay and lesbian **magazine** with interesting news features, and music and books reviews. In addition there is a 24-hour gay and lesbian **radio** station, RadioFG (Fréquence Gaie) 98.2FM, with music, news, chats, information on groups and events, etc. Listed below are a couple of other useful contacts.

Association des Médecins Gais (AMG), 45 rue Sedaine, 11ᵉ; ☎01.48.05.81.71, *www.gaipied.fr/associations/amg* (Mᵒ Bréguet-Sabin). Wed 6–8pm, Sat 2–4pm. Gay doctors' association, offering help with all health concerns relative to the gay community.

Écoute Gaie ☎01.44.93.01.02. Mon, Wed & Thurs 8–10pm, Tues & Fri 6–10pm. Helpline in French with information on the gay community and advice on problems.

Les Mots à la Bouche, 6 rue Ste-Croix-de-la-Bretonnerie, 4ᵉ; ☎01.42.78.88.30, *www.motalabouche.com* (Mᵒ Hôtel-de-Ville). Mon–Sat 11am–11pm, Sun 2–8pm. The main gay and lesbian bookshop, with exhibition space and meeting rooms; a selection of literature in English, too. Lots of free listings maps and club flyers to pick up, and one of the helpful assistants usually speaks English.

Bars, clubs and discos

Paris has a wide range of **gay venues** – the selection given below only scratches the surface – and although lesbians do not enjoy a wide selection of women-only places, they are welcome in some of the predominantly male clubs. The reputation of wild hedonism in gay clubs has transmitted beyond the boundaries of the gay community and attracted heterosexuals in search of a good time. Consequently, heterosexuals are welcome in some gay establishments if in gay company – some gay clubs have all but abandoned a gay policy (the legendary gay club *Le Queen* – see p.177 – is gay only on a Thursday now) – whilst many of the more mainstream clubs have started doing gay nights. For a complete rundown, consult the free magazine *Em@le* (distributed in gay bars) which has a comprehensive weekly listing of gay nights. Alternatively, tune into RadioFG (98.2FM) and keep an eye out for flyers.

L'Alcantara, 30 rue du Roi-de-Sicile, 4ᵉ (Mᵒ St-Paul). Daily 5–11pm. This ex-boulangerie with its relaxed café-style area on the ground floor and bar area downstairs is a welcome addition to the lesbian scene in Paris. The crowd is young, trendy and outgoing.

Le Central, 33 rue Vieille-du-Temple, 4ᵉ (Mᵒ Hôtel-de-Ville). Daily 2pm–2am. The oldest gay local in the Marais. Small, friendly and always crowded.

La Champmeslé, 4 rue Chabanais, 2ᵉ; ☎01.42.96.85.20 (Mᵒ Opéra/Pyramides). Mon–Wed 7pm–2am, Thurs–Sat 7pm–4am; closed Sun. Long-standing lesbian bar with back room reserved for women, front room for mixed company. Cabaret on Thurs. Admission free.

Le Dépôt, 10 rue aux Ours, 3ᵉ; ☎01.44.54.96.96 (Mᵒ Étienne-Marcel). Mon–Sat from 11pm, Sun tea-dance from 5pm; ladies welcome on Wed. Two floors of music in this hardcore gay club which is popular for cruising. Admission 45–60F/€6.86–9.15.

Le Keller, 14 rue Keller, 11ᵉ (Mᵒ Bastille). Daily 10pm–2am. Cruising gay bar where leather, latex and uniform is the requisite dress-code.

Mixer Bar, 23 rue Ste-Croix de la Bretonnerie, 4ᵉ (Mᵒ Hôtel-de-Ville). Daily 4pm–2am. Another popular and crowded Marais gay bar, which the law has been particularly heavy with in the past. Women also welcome.

Open Café, 17 rue des Archives, 4ᵉ (Mᵒ Hôtel-de-Ville). Daily 10am–2am. The first gay bar/café to have tables out on the pavement.

Le Pulp, 25 bd Poissonnière, 2ᵉ; ☎01.40.26.01.93 (Mᵒ Montmartre). Thurs–Sun from 11.30pm; happy hour 11.30pm–1.30am. Lesbian club, playing diverse music – from techno to Madonna. Fri & Sat 50F/€7.62 entrance from midnight.

Le Quetzal, 10 rue de la Verrerie, 4ᵉ; ☎01.48.87.99.07 (Mᵒ Hôtel-de-Ville). Daily noon–5am; happy hours 5–9pm & 11pm–midnight. Lots of beautiful bodies cram into this popular gay nightspot.

Les Scandaleuses, 8 rue des Ecouffes, 4ᵉ (Mᵒ Hôtel-de-Ville). Daily 5pm–2am. Trendy and high-profile women-only bar in the Marais. Lively atmosphere guaranteed.

Le Tango, 13 rue au-Maire, 3ᵉ; ☎01.42.72.17.78 (Mᵒ Arts-et-Métiers). Fri, Sat & public hols 10.30pm–dawn, Sun 6–10pm. Gay and lesbian dance-hall with a traditional *bal* until midnight, then all other types of music except techno. Admission 40F/€6.10 Fri & Sat, 30F/€4.57 on Sun.

L'Utopia, 15 rue Michel le Comte, 3ᵉ (Mᵒ Rambuteau). Mon–Sat 7pm–2am. Bar on two levels, with billiards and chess downstairs. Themed nights, varied music and friendly atmosphere. Predominantly women.

Film, theatre and dance

Cinema addicts have a choice of around three hundred films showing in Paris in any one week. **Theatre**, on the other hand, is less accessible to non-French-speakers, especially the cabaret and comics of the *café-théâtres*. However, there is stimulation in the cult of the director – Paris is home to Peter Brook, Ariane Mnouchkine and other exiles, as well as French talent, whose dazzling productions are highly visual. Suburban theatres rival the city proper for bold experimental theatre. Also, transcending language barriers, there are exciting developments in **dance**, much of it incorporating **mime**. Traditional **circus** has a seasonal home at the Cirque d'Hiver Bouglione (see p.188); more cutting-edge troupes are programmed at the Parc de la Villette, and there's an international festival every January.

The main **festivals** include the Festival de Films des Femmes (end March/beginning of April; see below); the Festival Exit (March), featuring international contemporary dance, performance and theatre at Créteil's Maison des Arts; Paris Quartier d'Eté (July), with music, theatre and cinema events around the city; the Festival d'Automne (Sept–Dec), with traditional and experimental theatrical, musical, dance and multimedia productions from all over the world; and the Festival du Cinéma en Plein Air (mid-July to end Aug) at Parc de la Villette, showing free films in the park.

Information and tickets

The most comprehensive **film listings** are given in *Pariscope*. You rarely need to book in advance; programmes (*séances*) often start around midday and continue through to the early hours. The average price is 40–45F/€6.10–6.86, but some cinemas have lower rates on Monday or Wednesday and for earlier *séances*, and student reductions are available from Monday to Thursday. UGC and Gaumont sell multi-tickets in carnets of five, which work out at around 30F/€4.57 a seat depending on whether you choose to go at the weekend or not, and some independents offer a *carte de fidélité*, giving you a free sixth entry. Almost all of the huge selection of foreign films will be shown at some cinemas in the original language – *version originale* or *v.o.* in the listings. Dubbed films will be listed as *v.f.* and English versions of co-productions as *version anglaise* or *v.a.*

Stage productions are detailed in *Pariscope* and *L'Officiel des Spectacles* with brief résumés or reviews. Prices vary between 30F/€4.57 and 170F/€25.92 for state theatres (around 130F/€19.82 for the suburbs), and 60F/€9.15 and 260F/€39.64 for commercial theatres (most closed Sun & Mon). Half-price previews are advertised in *Pariscope* and *L'Officiel des Spectacles*, and there are weekday student discounts. Prices are high for epic productions by top directors which may be seven hours long or even carry over several days; these always need booking in advance. Tickets can be bought directly from the theatres, from FNAC shops and Virgin Megastores (see p.192), or at the **ticket kiosks** on place de la Madeleine, 8ᵉ, opposite no. 15, and on the parvis of the Gare du Montparnasse, 14ᵉ (Tues–Sat 12.30–8pm, Sun 12.30–4pm). They sell half-price same-day tickets and charge a 16F/€2.44 commission, but be prepared to queue. Tickets for **café-théatres** average around 80F/€12.20, and it's best to book in advance for Friday and Saturday performances, directly from the venues.

In May the Mairie sponsors a week of two theatre tickets for the price of one; in June, three days of 10F/€1.52 cinema tickets if you buy one normal entry; and in February, a week of "18hr–18F" – 18F/€2.74 cinema tickets for 6pm screenings. Many cinemas and theatres have unwaged ushers who will expect a 5F/€0.76 **tip**.

Film and video

Even though many of the smaller movie houses in obscure corners of the city have closed in recent years, and the big chains, UGC and Gaumont, keep opening new multi-screen cinemas, you still have a fantastic choice of non-mainstream **films** in Paris, covering every place and period. You can go and see Senegalese, Taiwanese, Brazilian or Finnish films, for example, that would never be shown in Britain or the US, or choose your own **video** clips at the Forum des Images (see p.182). The **International Festival of**

Women's Films is organized by the Maison des Arts, place Salvador-Allende, 94000 Créteil (☎01.43.99.22.11, *www.gdebussacs.fr/filmfem*; M° Créteil-Préfecture); programme details are available from mid-March. For the biggest screens of all, check-out the 180° Omnimax projection system at La Villette and La Défense (see pp.151 and 147).

In addition to conventional cinemas, **cinémathèques** offer a choice of over fifty films a week, many of which would never be shown commercially (tickets cost 29F/€4.42). The main *cinémathèque* is housed at the Palais de Chaillot, cnr avs Président-Wilson & Albert-de-Mun, 16ᵉ (M° Trocadéro), and the Salle Grands Boulevards, 42 bd Bonne Nouvelle, 10ᵉ (☎01.56.26.01.01; M° Bonne-Nouvelle), but at the time of writing there were plans to move it to a new location – possibly in Bercy (check with the tourist office for details). The Centre Pompidou, 4ᵉ (M° Rambuteau) also has its own *cinémathèque*.

Venues

L'Arlequin, 76 rue des Rennes, 6ᵉ (M° St-Suplice). The quartier Latin's best cinephile's palace, offering special screenings of classics every Sunday at 11pm followed by debates in the café opposite.

L'Entrepôt, 7–9 rue Francis-de-Pressensé, 14ᵉ (M° Pernety). One of the best alternative Paris cinemas, which has been keeping ciné-addicts happy for years with its three screens dedicated to the obscure, the subversive and the brilliant. It also shows videos, satellite and cable TV, and has a bookshop (Mon–Sat 2–8pm) and a restaurant (daily noon–midnight).

Forum des Images, 2 Grande Galerie, Porte St-Eustache, Forum des Halles, 1ᵉʳ (RER Châtelet-Les Halles). Tues–Sun 1–9pm, Thurs till 10pm. This venue screens several films or videos daily, but also has a library of 4000 videos of newsreel footage, film clips, adverts, documentaries, etc – all connected with Paris – that you can access yourself from a computer terminal. You can make your choice via a Paris place name, an actor, a director, a date, and so on; there are instructions in English at the desk, and a friendly librarian to help you out. Internet connection is also available. Entry 30F/€4.57.

Grand Action and Action Écoles, 5 & 23 rue des Écoles, 5ᵉ (M° Cardinal-Lemoine/Maubert-Mutualité); Action Christine Odéon, 4 rue Christine, 6ᵉ (M° Odéon/St-Michel). The Action chain specializes in new prints of ancient classics and screens contemporary films from different countries.

Le Grand Rex, 1 bd Poissonnière, 2ᵉ (M° Bonne-Nouvelle). Just as outrageous as La Pagode (see below), but in the kitsch line, with a *Metropolis*-style tower blazing its neon name, 2750 seats and a ceiling of stars and Moorish city skyline. Foreign films are always dubbed.

Max Linder Panorama, 24 bd Poissonnière, 9ᵉ (M° Bonne-Nouvelle). Opposite Le Grand Rex, and with almost as big a screen, this cinema always shows films in the original and has state-of-the-art sound and Art Deco decor.

MK2 Quai de la Seine, 14 quai de la Seine, 19ᵉ (M° Jaurès/Stalingrad). Part of the MK2 chain but distinctive in style – covered in famous cinematic quotes and on the banks of the Bassin de la Villette – and with a varied art-house repertoire.

La Pagode, 57bis rue de Babylone, 7ᵉ (M° François-Xavier). The most beautiful of the city's cinemas, transplanted from Japan at the turn of the century to be a rich Parisienne's party place. The wall panels of the Grande Salle auditorium are embroidered in silk; golden dragons and elephants hold up the candelabra; and a battle between Japanese and Chinese warriors rages on the ceiling. Financial problems have made its future uncertain but at the time of writing it was due to keep going; check *Pariscope* for details.

Le Studio 28, 10 rue de Tholozé, 18ᵉ (M° Blanche/Abbesses). In its early days, after one of the first showings of Buñuel's *L'Age d'Or*, this was done over by extreme right-wing Catholics who destroyed the screen and the paintings by Dalí and Ernst in the foyer. The cinema still hosts avant-garde premières, followed occasionally by discussions with the director, as well as regular festivals.

Theatre

Bourgeois farces, postwar classics, Shakespeare, Racine and *Cyrano de Bergerac* – all are staged with the same range of talent or lack of it that you'd find in London or New York. What is rare are home-grown, socially concerned and realist dramas, though touring foreign companies make up for that. Exciting contemporary work is provided by the superstar breed of directors such as Peter Brook, Ariane Mnouchkine and Patrice Chereau; spectacular and dazzling sensation tends to take precedence over speech in their productions, which feature huge casts, extraordinary sets and over-whelming sound and light effects – an experience, even if you haven't understood a word.

Venues

Bouffes du Nord, 37bis bd de la Chapelle, 10ᵉ; ☎01.46.07.34.50 (Mᵒ La Chapelle). Peter Brook's permanent base in Paris; the occasional concert is also performed.

Cartoucherie, route du Champ-de-Manoeuvre, 12ᵉ (Mᵒ Château-de-Vincennes). Home to several interesting theatre companies including Ariane Mnouchkine's workers' co-op, Théâtre du Soleil (☎01.43.74.24.08), whose 1996 interpretation of Molière's *Tartuffe*, with the protagonist as a mullah in a North African city, dazzled French and foreign critics.

Comédie Française, 2 rue Richelieu, 1ᵉʳ; ☎01.44.58.15.15 (Mᵒ Palais-Royal). The national theatre, mainly staging the classics but also some contemporary work.

Maison de la Culture de Bobigny, 1 bd Lénine, Bobigny; ☎01.41.60.72.72 (Mᵒ Pablo-Picasso). The resident company, MC93, stages highly challenging productions; there's also dance by François Verret.

Odéon Théâtre de l'Europe, 1 place Paul-Claudel, 6ᵉ; ☎01.44.41.36.36 (Mᵒ Odéon). Contemporary plays and foreign-language productions in the theatre that became an open parlia-ment during May 1968.

Opéra Comique, rue Favart, 2ᵉ; ☎01.42.44.45.46 (Mᵒ Richelieu-Drouot). Jérôme Savary's (ex-Théâtre National de Chaillot) new home as artistic director. The diverse and exciting pro-gramme blends all forms of stage arts: modern and classical opera, musicals, comedy, dance and pop music.

Théâtre des Amandiers, 7 av Pablo-Picasso, Nanterre, 92; ☎01.46.14.70.00 (RER Nanterre-Université & theatre bus). The suburban base for Jean-Paul Vincent's exciting productions; also stages excellent dance.

Théâtre de la Bastille, 79 rue de la Roquette, 11ᵉ; ☎01.43.57.42.14 (Mᵒ Bastille). One of the best places for new work and fringe productions.

Théâtre de la Colline, 15 rue Malte-Brun, 20ᵉ; ☎01.44.62.52.52 (Mᵒ Gambetta). A national theatre putting on works by both epic directors and less well-established innovators.

Théâtre de la Main-d'Or, 15 passage de la Main-d'Or, 11ᵉ; ☎01.48.05.67.89 (Mᵒ Bastille). An inter-esting experimental space, with occasional classics and English productions including a festival of English theatre in the spring.

Théâtre National de Chaillot, Palais de Chaillot, place du Trocadéro, 16ᵉ; ☎01.53.65.30.00 (Mᵒ Trocadéro). With the departure of Jérôme Savary to the Opéra Comique, the role of artistic direc-tor here is to be taken by Dominique Pitoiset and the choreographer José Montalvo, in order to con-secrate more national theatre space to dance. Roger Planchon from Lyon has some of his Parisian showings here, which are accessible to foreign audiences through an innovative individual transla-tion system.

Café-théâtre

Café-théâtre, with its word-play and allusions to current fads, phobias and politicians, can be incomprehensible even to a fluent French-speaker. Puerile, dirty jokes are also its stock in trade. But the atmosphere can be fun, and every so often an original talent will appear.

The Marais has a high concentration of **venues**: you could try the tiny Blancs-Manteaux, 15 rue des Blancs-Manteaux, 4ᵉ (☎01.48.87.15.84; Mᵒ Hôtel-de-Ville/Rambuteau); or the *Café de la Gare*, 41 rue du Temple, 4ᵉ (☎01.42.78.52.51; Mᵒ Hôtel-de-Ville/Rambuteau), which has a reputation for novelty.

Dance and mime

The French **regional dance companies** from La Rochelle, Marseille, Grenoble, Angers and Montpellier easily rival the Paris-based troupes, but Paris-based choreographers Maguy Marin, Karine Saporta and François Verret are worth looking out for. The current trend is in multidimensional performing art, combining movement, mime, ballet, speech, noise, theatrical effects and music from medieval to jazz-rock. Though the famous **mime** schools of Marcel Marceau and Lecoq still turn out excellent artists, pure mime hardly exists except on the streets; Beaubourg's piazza is one of the best place to catch performances.

Many of the theatres listed above under "Drama" include these new forms in their programmes. Plenty of space and critical attention is also given to **tap**, **tango**, **folk** and **jazz dancing**, and to visiting traditional dance troupes from all over the world. As for **ballet**, the principal stage is at the old opera house, the Opéra-Garnier; other major productions are at the Théâtre de la Ville and the Théâtre Musical de Paris.

Venues

Centre Mandapa, 6 rue Wurtz, 13ᵉ; ☎01.45.89.01.60 (Mᵒ Glacière). The one theatre dedicated to traditional dances from around the world.

Centre Pompidou, rue Beaubourg, 4ᵉ; ☎01.44.78.13.15 (Mᵒ Rambuteau/RER Châtelet-Les Halles). The Grande Salle in the basement is used for dance performances by visiting companies.

L'Espace Kiron, 10 rue la Vacquerie, 11ᵉ; ☎01.44.64.11.50 (Mᵒ Voltaire). Venue for experimental dance and performance art.

Maison des Arts de Créteil, place Salvador-Allende, Créteil; ☎01.45.13.19.19 (Mᵒ Créteil-Préfecture). Maguy Marin's company's home base and venue for the Festival Exit (see p.181).

Opéra-Garnier, place de l'Opéra, 9ᵉ; ☎08.36.69.78.68, *www.opera-de-paris.fr* (Mᵒ Opéra). Main home of the Ballet de l'Opéra National de Paris.

Théâtre des Abbesses, 31 rue des Abbesses, 18ᵉ; ☎01.42.74.22.77 (Mᵒ Abbesses). Sister company to the Théâtre de la Ville, with slightly more off-beat and daring performances.

Théâtre Musical de Paris, place du Châtelet, 4ᵉ; ☎01.40.28.28.40 (Mᵒ Châtelet). A major ballet venue where, in 1910, Diaghilev put on the first season of Russian ballet. Today it still hosts ballet companies from abroad.

Théâtre de la Ville, 2 place du Châtelet, 4ᵉ; ☎01.42.74.22.77 (Mᵒ Châtelet). The height of success for dance productions is to end up here. Works by Karine Saporta, Maguy Marin and Pina Bausch are regularly featured, along with modern theatre classics, comedy and concerts.

Sports and activities

When it's cold and wet and you've had your fill of café vistas and peering at museums, monuments and the dripping panes of shop-fronts, don't despair or retreat back to your hotel. As well as movies, Paris offers a whole host of pleasant ways to pass the time indoors – **skating**, **bowling**, **billiards**, **swimming**, **hamams** – or outdoors, with all the **popular sports** to watch or participate in.

Information

L'Officiel des Spectacles has the best listings of **sports facilities** (under "Activités sportives"). Information on municipal facilities is also available from Allo Sports (Mon–Fri 10.30am–5pm; ☎01.42.76.54.54) or Direction Jeunesse et Sports, 25 bd Bourdon, 4ᵉ (Mon–Fri noon–7pm; ☎01.42.76.22.60; Mᵒ Bastille), while the Mairie de Paris gives away a weighty free book, *Le Guide du Sport à Paris* (ask for it at the tourist office, town halls or the Direction Jeunesse et Sports), which provides a list of sporting facilities by *arrondissement*. For details of current **sporting events**, try the daily sports paper *L'Équipe*. A major venue for all sports, including athletics, cycling, show jumping, ice hockey, ballroom dancing, judo and motorcross, is the Palais Omnisport Paris-Bercy (POPB), 8 bd Bercy, 12ᵉ (☎01.44.68.44.68, *www.bercy.com*; Mᵒ Bercy).

Spectator sports

Cycling The biggest event of the French sporting year is the grand finale of the Tour de France on the Champs-Élysées in late July. Huge crowds turn out to cheer on the cyclists at the finishing line of the ultimate stage in the gruelling three-week 4000-kilometre-odd event, and the French president presents the yellow jersey (*maillot jaune*) to the overall winner. Another classic bike event ending in Paris is the 600-kilometre Bordeaux–Paris, the world's longest single stage race, first held in 1891. Races commencing in Paris include the Paris–Roubaix, instigated in 1896, which is reputed to be the most exacting one-day race in the world, and the rugged six-day Paris–Nice event, covering over 1100km. The Palais Omnisport de Bercy (see opposite) holds other bike races and cycling events. For more information on the Tour de France and other cycling events, see "Basics", p.70.

Football and rugby The Parc des Princes, 24 rue du Commandant-Guilbaud, 16ᵉ (☎01.42.30.03.60; Mᵒ Porte-de-St-Cloud), is the capital's main stadium for domestic rugby union and football events: it is home ground for the first-division football team Paris-St-Germain (PSG) plus the rugby team Le Racing. In 1998 France hosted the World Cup and the action in Paris centred around the specially built Stade de France, on rue Francis de Pressensé in St-Denis (☎01.55.93.00.00; RER Stade-de-France-St-Denis), which is now the venue for international football matches and rugby's Five Nations' Cup and other international matches.

Horse-racing The biggest races are the Prix de la République and the Grand Prix de l'Arc de Triomphe on the first and last Sun in Oct at Auteuil and Longchamp, both in the Bois de Boulogne. Trotting races, with the jockeys in chariots, run from Aug to Sept on the Route de la Ferme in the Bois de Vincennes. *L'Humanité* and *Paris-Turf* carry details of all races; admission charges are under 30F/€4.57. If you want to place a bet, any bar or café with the letters "PMU" will take your money on a three-horse bet, known as *le tiercé*.

Running The Paris Marathon is held in May over a route from place de la Concorde to Vincennes. Up-to-date information is available from the runners' shop, Marathon, 26 rue de Lyon, 12ᵉ (☎01.42.27.48.18; Mᵒ Gare-de-Lyon), or online at *www.parismarathon.com*.

Tennis The French Tennis Open takes place in the last week of May and first week of June at Roland-Garros, 2 av Gordon-Bennett, 16ᵉ (☎01.47.43.48.00, *www.frenchopen.org*; Mᵒ Porte-d'Auteuil). A few tickets are sold each day, but only for unseeded matches.

Participatory activities

Billiards and bowling You can do both at Le Stadium, 66 av d'Ivry, 13ᵉ (daily 10am–2am; ☎01.45.86.55.52; Mᵒ Porte-d'Ivry) and at Bowling Mouffetard, Centre-Commercial Mouffetard-Monge, 73 rue Mouffetard, 5ᵉ (daily 11am–2am; ☎01.43.31.09.35; Mᵒ Monge). Bowling costs 15F–33F/€2.29–5.03 a session – more in the evenings and at weekends; shoe rental is 8–10F/€1.22–1.52. Billiards will set you back around 60F/€9.15 an hour, plus an average 100F/€15.24 deposit.

Boules The classic French game involving balls, boules (or pétanque) is best performed (if you have your own set or are prepared to make some new French friends) or watched at the Arènes de Lutèce (p.134) and the Bois de Vincennes (p.155). On balmy summer evenings it's a common sight in the city's parks and gardens.

Cycling Since 1996 the Mairie de Paris has made great efforts to introduce dedicated cycle lanes in Paris, which now add up to 130km. You can pick up a free leaflet, *Paris à Vélo*, outlining the routes, from town halls, the tourist office, or bike hire outlets (p.193). If you prefer cycling in a more natural environment, the Bois de Boulogne and the Bois de Vincennes have extensive bike tracks. On Sundays cycling by the Seine is popular, when its central *quais* (and along the Canal St-Martin) are closed to cars between 10am and 4pm. Excellent half-day bicycle tours (170F/€25.91) are offered by Paris à Vélo C'est Sympa/Vélo Bastille, 37 bd Bourdon, 4ᵉ (☎01.48.87.60.01; Mᵒ Bastille), including a "Paris by night" excursion (190F/€28.96).

Hamams Luxurious, laid-back and very Parisian, the best hamam or Turkish baths is the Hamam de la Mosquée, 39 rue Geoffroy-St-Hilaire, 5ᵉ (☎01.43.31.38.20; Turkish bath 85F/€12.96, massage extra; Mᵒ Censier-Daubenton); times may change, so check first, but generally women on Mon & Wed–Sat 10am–9pm, men Tues 2–9pm & Sun 10am–9pm.

Ice skating From Dec to March a small rink is set up in the place Hôtel de Ville (daily 9am–10pm; Mᵒ Hôtel de Ville); skating is free and skates are available for rental.

In-line skating Roller-blading has become so popular in Paris that it takes over the streets every Friday night from 9.45pm, when between 5000 and 10,000 rollerskaters meet on Place d'Italie in the 13ᵉ (Mᵒ Place d'Italie) for a 40km circuit of the city, accompanied by roller-blading police officers and tag-along cyclists. If you want to join in the fun, the best place to find more information and to hire roller-skates and -blades is Nomades, 37 bd Bourdon, 4ᵉ (Mon–Fri 11am–7pm, Sat & Sun 10am–7pm; ☎01.44.54.07.44; Mᵒ Bastille), with its own bar out back where you can meet other bladers. Hire is a reasonable 50F/€7.62 per day on a weekday and 60F/€9.15 at the weekend (half-day 30F/€4.57 and 40F/€6.10), but the deposit is 1000F/€152.43, and hiring the recommended protective pads will cost another 30F/€4.57. Bike N'Roller, 6 rue St-Julien-Le-Paure, 5ᵉ (Wed–Sat 10am–7.30pm, Sun 9am–8pm; ☎01.44.07.35.89, *www.bikenroller.com*) also hires rollers and blades from 60F/€9.15 per half-day or 80F/€12.20 per day; 5–10F/€0.79–1.52 additional for protective gear. The main outdoor in-line skating and skateboarding arena is the concourse of the Palais de Chaillot (Mᵒ Trocadéro). Les Halles (around the Fontaine des Innocents), the Beaubourg piazza and place du Palais-Royal are also very popular. On Sundays, the central *quais* of the Seine and the stretch of road along the Canal St-Martin are car-free between 10am and 4pm, making way for a stream of rollerbladers and cyclists.

Swimming *L'Officiel des Spectacles* lists all the municipal pools (usually 16F/€2.44), of which the unchlorinated student hang-out Jean Taris, 16 rue de Thouin, 5ᵉ (Mᵒ Cardinal-Lemoine), the Art Deco Butte aux Cailles, 5 place Verlaine, 13ᵉ (Mᵒ Place-d'Italie) and the 50-metre-long Piscine Susanne Berlioux/Les Halles, 10 place de la Rotonde, niveau 3, Porte du Jour, Forum des Halles, 1ᵉʳ (RER Châtelet-Les Halles), are among the best.

Tennis and squash One of the nicest places to play tennis is on one of the six asphalt courts at the Jardins du Luxembourg (daily 8am–9pm; hourly rates are 37F/€5.64 by day, 53F/€8.08 by night; reservations only on Minitel 3615; Mᵒ Notre-Dame-des-Champs). However, to play on municipal courts such as these, you need first to apply for a *Carte Paris-Tennis* from the Mairie, while private clubs demand steep membership fees. It's much easier to play squash, with several dedicated centres, including Squash Montmartre, 14 rue Achille-Martinet, 18ᵉ (01.42.55.38.30; Mᵒ Lamarck-Caulaincourt), which charges 30F/€4.57 for your novice first half-hour, and the Club Quartier Latin, 19 rue de Pontoise, 5e (☎01.43.25.31.99; Mᵒ Maubert-Mutualité), which has courts costing 60–75F /€9.15–11.43 for 40min to an hour.

Kids' stuff

For most **kids** the biggest attraction for miles around is **Disneyland Paris** (see p.201), though within the city there are plenty of other, far less expensive and more educational possibilities for keeping them entertained. Wednesday afternoons, when primary school children have free time, and Saturdays are the big times for children's activities and entertainments; Wednesdays continue to be child-centred even during the school holidays. The tours around the **sewers** and the **catacombs** will delight some children; while smaller ones can enjoy performances of **Guignol** (the equivalent of Punch and Judy) in the city's parks. Many of the **museums** and **amusements** already detailed will appeal, particularly the Musée de la Curiosité (see p.127); and the best treat for children of every age from three upwards is the **Cité des Sciences** (see opposite) in the Parc de la Villette. A number of museums have special children's activities on Wednesdays and Saturdays, details of which are carried in the free booklet *Objectif Musée*, available from the museums or from the Direction des Musées de France, 34 quai du Louvre, 1ᵉʳ (Mon, Wed & Fri 2–6pm; ☎01.40.15.73.00): the Musée du Moyen-

Age, Musée d'Art Moderne de la Ville de Paris, Carnavalet, the Louvre, the Institut du Monde Arabe and the Musée d'Orsay have regular or special programmes but they will of course be conducted in French. Otherwise, the most useful **sources of information** for current shows, exhibitions and events are the special sections in the listings magazines ("Enfants" in *Pariscope*, and "Jeunes" in *L'Officiel des Spectacles*) and the Kiosque Paris-Jeunes at the Direction Jeunesse et Sports, 25 bd Bourdon, 4ᵉ (Mon–Fri noon–7pm; ☎01.42.76.22.60; Mᵒ Bastille), and at the CIDJ, 101 quai Branley, 15ᵉ (Mon–Fri 9.30am–6pm, Sat 9.30am–1pm; ☎01.43.06.15.38; Mᵒ Bir-Hakeim). The tourist office also publish a free booklet in French, *Paris-Ile-de-France Avec Des Yeux Enfants*, with lots of ideas and contacts.

Cité des Sciences

The **Cité des Enfants** (for kids aged 3–12) is a totally engaging special section of the Cité des Sciences et de l'Industrie – detailed on p.151 – in the Parc de la Villette, in the 19ᵉ (Tues–Sat 10am–6pm, Sun 10am–7pm; adults and children over 3 25F/€3.81, children under 3 free; children must be accompanied by at least one adult; Mᵒ Porte-de-la-Villette). As well as single tickets to the Cité des Enfants, you can buy combined tickets with Cité des Sciences (same hours; adults 55F/€8.38, children over 7 45F/€6.86, under 7s free), the Géode (Tues–Sun 10am–8pm; adults and children 50F/€7.62), and with the Cité des Sciences and Géode (adult 92F/€14.02, child 79F/€12.04). The kids can touch, smell and feel things, play about with water, construct buildings on a miniature construction site, experiment with sound and light, manipulate robots, put together their own television news and race their own shadows. It's beautifully organized and managed, and if you haven't got a child it's worth borrowing one to get in here. Sessions run for an hour and a half (Tues, Thurs & Fri 11.30am, 1.30pm & 3.30pm; Wed, Sat, Sun & public hols 10.30am, 12.30pm, 2.30pm & 4.30pm).

A new space on the ground floor, **Techno Cité** (1hr 30min sessions; Tues & Sat 2pm & 4pm; during summer hols Tues–Sat 10.30am, 12.30pm, 2.30pm & 4.30pm; over-11s only; extra 25F/€3.81), offers hands-on application of technology to industry. You can write a program for a robotic videotape selector, for example, or design a prototype racing bike.

The rest of the museum is also pretty good for kids, particularly the planetarium, the various film shows, the *Argonaute* submarine, children's *médiathèque* (noon–8pm) and the frequent temporary exhibitions designed for the young. In the park, there's lots of wide open green space, the dragon slide and seven themed gardens featuring mirrors, trampolines, water jets and spooky music.

Jardin d'Acclimatation

The **Jardin d'Acclimatation**, in the Bois de Boulogne by Porte des Sablons (daily: June–Sept 10am–7pm; Oct–May 10am–6pm; adult 13F/€1.98, child 6.50F/€1, under-3s free; rides from 10F/€1.52; special attractions Wed, Sat, Sun & all week during school hols, including a mini-train from Mᵒ Porte-Maillot, behind *L'Orée du Bois* restaurant, every 10min 1.30–6pm: 25F/€3.81 ticket combines ride and entry to the park; Mᵒ Les Sablons/Porte-Maillot), is a cross between a funfair, zoo and amusement park. Temptations range from bumper cars, go-karts, pony and camel rides, to sea lions, birds, bears and monkeys; plus there's a magical mini-canal ride (*la rivière enchantée*; 11F/€1.68), distorting mirrors, scaled-down farm buildings and a puppet theatre. Astérix and friends may be explaining life in their **Gaulish village**, or Babar the world of the elephants in the **Musée en Herbe**. The **Théâtre du Jardin pour l'Enfance et la Jeunesse** puts on musicals and ballets.

Outside the garden, in the Bois de Boulogne, older children can amuse themselves with **minigolf** and **bowling**, or **boating** on the Lac Inférieur. By the entrance to the garden there's **bike rental** for roaming the wood's cycle trails.

Parc Floral

Fun and games are always to be had at the **Parc Floral**, in the Bois de Vincennes, route de la Pyramide (daily: March–Sept 9.30am–8pm; Oct–Feb 9.30am–5pm; admission 10F/€1.52, 6–10s 5F/€0.76 plus supplements for some activities, under-6s free; M° Château-de-Vincennes, then a seven-minute walk past the Château de Vincennes, or bus #112). The excellent playground has slides, swings, ping-pong (bat and ball 30F/€4.57), pedal carts (42–60F/€6.40–9.15 per half-hour), minigolf modelled on Paris monuments (from 1.45pm; 30F/€4.57, children under 12 18F/€2.74), an electric car circuit and a little train touring all the gardens (April–Oct daily 10.30am–5pm; 6F/€0.91). Tickets for the activities are sold at the playground between 1.45pm and 5.30pm weekdays and until 7pm on weekends; activities stop fifteen minutes afterwards. On Wednesdays at 2.30pm (May–Sept) there are free performances by clowns, puppets and magicians. Also in the park is a children's theatre, the **Théâtre Astral**, which has mime, clowns or other not-too-verbal shows for small children aged 3 to 8 (Wed 3pm, Sun & public hols 4.30pm & during school hols Mon–Fri 3pm; ☎01.43.71.31.10; 34F/€5.18). There are also a series of pavilions with child-friendly educational exhibitions (free entry) which look at nature in Paris; the best is the **butterfly garden** (mid-May to mid-Oct Mon–Fri 1.30–5.15pm, Sat & Sun 1.30–6pm).

Parc Zoologique

The top Paris **zoo** is in the Bois de Vincennes at 53 av de St-Maurice, 12ᵉ (April–Sept Mon–Sat 9am–6pm, Sun & hols 9am–6.30pm; Oct–March Mon–Sat 9am–5pm, Sun & hols 9am–5.30pm; adults 40F/€6.10, children over 4 30F/€4.57, under-4s free; M° Porte-Dorée). It was one of the first zoos in the world to get rid of cages and use landscaping to simulate a more natural environment and give the animals more room to exercise.

Jardin des Enfants aux Halles

Right in the centre of town, just west of the Forum, the **Jardin des Enfants aux Halles** is great if you want to lose your charges for the odd hour (Tues–Thurs & Sat 10am–7pm, Fri 2–5pm, Sun 1–7pm; winter till 4pm; closed Mon & during bad weather; 2.50F/€0.38 for a one-hour slot; M°/RER Châtelet-Les Halles; 7–11s only except Sat am). You may have to reserve a place an hour or so in advance for this small but cleverly designed space filled with a whole series of fantasy landscapes. On Wednesday, animators organize adventure games; and at all times the children are supervised by professional child-carers, who speak several languages, including English. On Saturdays (10am–2pm), adults too can go in and play while they take charge of their under-7-year-olds.

Funfairs and the circus

The Tuileries gardens normally have a **funfair** in July, and there's usually a **merry-go-round** at the Forum des Halles and beneath Tour St-Jacques at Châtelet, with carousels for smaller children on place de la République and at the Rond-Point des Champs-Élysées, by av Matignon; the going rate for a ride is 10F/€1.52. The Cirque d'Hiver Bouglione, 110 rue Amelot, 11ᵉ (M° Filles-du-Calvaire; details in *Pariscope* and *L'Officiel des Spectacles*) is open from October to January, or you can spend an entire day at the **circus** courtesy of the Cirque de Paris in the Parc des Chanteraines, 115 bd Charles-de-Gaulle, Villeneuve-La Garenne (Oct–June Wed, Sun & school hols 10am–5pm; 295F/€44.97, under-12s 230F/€33.06, including a meal; ☎01.47.99.40.40; RER Gennevilliers/St-Denis); lessons in juggling, tightrope-walking, clowning and make-up are followed by lunch in the ring then by the show. You can, if you prefer, just attend the show at 3pm (70–155F/€10.67–23.63, under-12s 45–95F/€6.86–14.48).

Shopping

Even if you don't plan – or can't afford – to buy, browsing Paris's **shops and markets** is one of the chief delights of the city. Flair for style and design is as evident here as it is in other aspects of the city's life. Parisians' epicurean tendencies and fierce attachment to their small local traders has kept alive a wonderful variety of speciality shops, despite the pressures to concentrate consumption in gargantuan underground and multistorey complexes. Among specific areas, the square kilometre around **place St-Germain-des-Prés** is hard to beat, packed with books, antiques, gorgeous garments, art works and playthings. But in every *quartier* you'll find enticing displays of all manner of consumables.

Bookshops

Books are not cheap in France – foreign books least of all – but don't let that stop you browsing. The best areas are the narrow streets of the quartier Latin and along the Seine where rows of **stalls** are perched against the river parapet. Here we've listed a few specialists and favourites. For books in English, head for Abbey Bookshop, Shakespeare & Co or W. H. Smith.

Abbey Bookshop/La Librairie Canadienne, 29 rue de la Parcheminerie, 5ᵉ (Mᵒ St-Michel). Mon–Sat 10am–7pm. A Canadian bookshop round the corner from Shakespeare & Co (see below), with lots of secondhand British and North American fiction; good social science sections; knowledgeable and helpful staff – and free coffee.

Artcurial, 9 av Matignon, 8ᵉ (Mᵒ Franklin-D.-Roosevelt). Tues–Sun 10am–7.15pm; closed two weeks in Aug. The best art bookshop in Paris.

FNAC, at the Forum des Halles, niveau 2, Porte Pierre-Lescot, 1ᵉʳ (Mᵒ/RER Châtelet-Les Halles); 136 rue de Rennes, 6ᵉ (Mᵒ Montparnasse); 74 av des Champs-Élysées, 8ᵉ (Mᵒ George-V); 24 bd des Italiens, 9ᵉ (Mᵒ Richelieu Drouot); and 26–30 av des Termes, 17ᵉ (Mᵒ Termes). Mon–Sat 10am–7.30pm; the bd des Italiens store is open until midnight. Not the most congenial of bookshops, but it's the biggest and covers everything.

Galerie Maeght, 42 rue du Bac, 7ᵉ (Mᵒ Rue-du-Bac). Tues–Sat 9.30am–7pm. Famous art gallery which makes its own beautifully printed art books.

Présence Africaine, 25bis rue des Écoles, 5ᵉ (Mᵒ Maubert-Mutualité). Mon–Sat 10am–7pm. Specialist black African bookshop, with titles ranging from literature to economics and philosophy by Caribbean and North American as well as African writers.

Parallèles, 47 rue St-Honoré, 1ᵉʳ(Mᵒ Châtelet-Les Halles). Mon–Sat 10am–7pm. An alternative bookshop, with everything from anarchism to New Age. Good for info on current events and gigs.

Shakespeare & Co, 37 rue de la Bûcherie, 5ᵉ (Mᵒ Maubert-Mutualité). Daily noon–midnight. A cosy, famous literary haunt, American-run, with the biggest selection of secondhand English books in town. Also poetry readings and the like.

W.H.Smith, 248 rue de Rivoli, 1ᵉʳ(Mᵒ Concorde). Mon–Sat 9.30am–7pm. Paris outlet of the British chain. Wide range of new books and newspapers.

Clothes

The haute couture shows may be well out of bounds, but there's nothing to prevent you trying on fabulously expensive creations by famous **couturiers** in rue du Faubourg-St-Honoré, av François-1ᵉʳ and av Victor-Hugo – apart from the intimidating air of the assistants and the awesome chill of the marble portals. Likewise, you can treat the **younger designers** round place des Victoires and in the Marais and St-Germain areas as stops on your sightseeing itinerary. The long-time darlings of the glitterati are Jean-Paul Gaultier and Azzedine Alaïa who, in 1991, were prevailed upon to design some gear for the city's **cheapest department store** – Tati (whose main branch is at 13 place de la République, 11ᵉ; Mᵒ République). Of the more recent star designers three are British – John Galliano at Dior, Stella McCartney at Chloé and the controversial

---

DESIGNER FASHION

The addresses below are those of the main or most conveniently located shops for designer clothes.

Agnès B, 6 rue du Jour, 1er (M° Châtelet-Les Halles).

Azzedine Alaïa, 7 rue de Moussy, 4e (M° Hôtel-de-Ville).

Chanel, 31 rue Cambon, 1er (M° Madeleine).

Christian Lacroix, 73 rue du Faubourg-St-Honoré, 8e (M° Concorde).

Gianni Versace, 62 rue du Faubourg-St-Honoré, 8e (M° Concorde).

Giorgio Armani, 25 place Vendôme, 1er (M° Opéra).

Inès de la Fressange, 14 av Montaigne, 8e (M° Alma-Marceau).

Issey Miyake, 3 place des Vosges, 4e (M° St-Paul).

Jean-Paul Gaultier, 30 rue du Faubourg St-Antoine, 12e (M° Bastille).

Jil Sander, 52 av Montaigne, 8e (M° Franklin-D.-Roosevelt).

Junko Shimada, 54 rue Étienne-Marcel, 2e (M° Châtelet-Les Halles).

Kenzo, 3 place des Victoires, 1er (M° Bourse).

Sonia Rykiel, 175 bd St-Germain, 6e (M° St-Germain-des-Prés).

Thierry Mugler, 49 av Montaigne, 8e (M° Alma-Marceau).

Yves Saint-Laurent, 6 place St-Sulpice, 6e (M° St-Sulpice/Mabillon).

Alexander McQueen at Givenchy. For **smart clothes** without the fancy labels the best areas are rue St-Placide and rue St-Dominique in the 6e and 7e. The **department stores** Galeries Lafayette and Au Printemps have good selections of designer prêt-à-porter; and the **Forum des Halles** is chock-a-block with clothes shops at less competitive prices. The **sales** take place in January and July, with reductions of up to forty percent on designer clothes. Ends of lines and old stock of the couturiers are sold year round in **discount shops** concentrated in rue d'Alésia in the 14e and rue St-Placide in the 6e. For **shoes**, take a wander down rue Meslay in the 3e.

Department stores

Au Bon Marché, 38 rue de Sèvres, 7e (M° Sèvres-Babylone). Mon–Sat 9.30am–7pm, Sat till 8pm. Paris's oldest department store, founded in 1852. Prices are lower on average than at the chic-er Galeries Lafayette and Printemps. Excellent kids' department and a legendary food hall.

Au Printemps, 64 bd Haussmann, 9e (M° Havre-Caumartin). Books, records, a *parfumerie* even bigger than that of rival Galeries Lafayette, excellent fashion for women – less so for men.

Galeries Lafayette, 40 bd Haussmann, 9^{e} (M° Havre-Caumartin). Mon–Sat 9.30am–6.45pm, Thurs till 9pm. The store's forte is, above all, high fashion. Two complete floors are given over to the latest creations by leading designers for men, women and children. Then there's household stuff, tableware, furniture, a huge *parfumerie*, etc – all under a superb 1900 dome.

La Samaritaine, 75 rue de Rivoli, 1er (M° Louvre-Rivoli/Châtelet). Mon–Sat 9.30am–7pm, Thurs till 10pm. The largest of the department stores, spread over three buildings, whose boast is to provide anything anyone could possibly want. It aims downmarket of the previous two. You get a superb view of Paris from the eleventh-floor rooftop, and from the inexpensive tenth-floor terrace café (closed Oct–March).

Food and drink

You can, of course, find sumptuous food stores all over Paris: the listings below are for the **specialist places**, palaces of gluttony many of them, with prices to match. Economical food shopping is invariably best done at the **street markets** or **supermarkets**, though save your bread buying at least for the local boulangerie. The cheapest supermarket chain is Ed Discount. Food markets are detailed at the end of this section.

Le Baron Aligre, 1 rue Théophile-Roussel, 12ᵉ (Mᵒ Ledru-Rollin). Tues–Fri 10am–2pm & 5–9.30pm, Sat 10am–9.30pm, Sun 10.30am–1pm. Stocks a good selection of dependable lower-range French wines; 7F/€1.07 for a small tasting glass. Very drinkable Merlot at 16F/€2.44 a litre, if you bring your own containers.

Barthélémy, 51 rue de Grenelle, 7ᵉ (Mᵒ Bac). Tues–Sat 8.30am–1pm & 4–7.30pm; closed Aug. Purveyors of cheeses to the rich and powerful.

Carmès et Fils, 24 rue de Lévis, 17ᵉ (Mᵒ Villiers). Tues–Sat 8.30am–1pm & 4–7.30pm, Sun am; closed Aug. Run by a family of experts who mature many of the cheeses sold here in their own cellars.

Caves Michel Renaud, 12 place de la Nation, 12ᵉ (Mᵒ Nation). 9.30am–1pm & 2–8.30pm; closed Sun pm and Mon am. Established in 1870, this wine shop purveys superb-value French and Spanish wines, champagnes and Armagnac.

Comptoir du Saumon, 60 rue François-Miron, 4ᵉ (Mᵒ St-Paul). Mon–Sat 10am–10pm. Specializes in salmon, but also sells eels, trout and all things fishy as well – there's also a delightful little restaurant in which to taste the fare. Three other branches.

Debauve and Gallais, 30 rue des Sts-Pères, 6ᵉ (Mᵒ St-Germain-des-Prés). Mon–Sat 9am–7pm; closed Aug. A beautiful, ancient shop specializing in chocolate and elaborate sweets.

Diététique DJ Fayer, 45 rue St-Paul, 4ᵉ (Mᵒ St-Paul). Mon–Sat 9.30am–1.30pm & 2.30–8.45pm. Tiny shop, one of the city's oldest specialists in dietary, macrobiotic and vegetarian fare.

Divay, 4 rue Bayen, 17ᵉ (Mᵒ Ternes). Tues–Sun 8am–1.30pm & 3.30–7.30pm; closed Wed & Sun afternoon & Aug. Purveyor of *foie gras, choucroute, saucisson* and suchlike.

Fauchon, 26 place de la Madeleine, 8ᵉ (Mᵒ Madeleine). Mon–Sat 9.40am–7pm. Carries an amazing range of super-plus groceries and wine, all at exorbitant prices; there's a self-service counter for pâtisseries and *plats du jour*, and a *traiteur* which stays open a little later, until 8.30pm.

Goldenberg's, 7 rue des Rosiers, 4ᵉ (Mᵒ St-Paul). Daily 9am–2am. Superlative Jewish deli and restaurant, specializing in charcuterie.

Hédiard, 21 place de la Madeleine, 8ᵉ (Mᵒ Madeleine). Mon–Sat 8am–10pm. Since 1850 the aristocrat's grocer. Several other branches throughout the city.

La Maison de l'Escargot, 79 rue Fondary, 15ᵉ (Mᵒ Dupleix). Tues–Sat 9am–7.30pm, Sun 9am–1pm; closed mid-July to Sept. As the name suggests, this place specializes in snails: they even sauce them and re-shell them while you wait.

Mariage Frères, 30 rue du Bourg-Tibourg, 4ᵉ (Mᵒ Hôtel-de-Ville). Daily 10.30am–7.30pm. Hundreds of teas, neatly packed in tins, line the floor-to-ceiling shelves of this 100-year-old tea emporium. There is a *salon de thé* in the back with exquisite pastries (daily noon–7pm).

À la Mère de Famille, 35 rue du Faubourg-Montmartre, 9ᵉ (Mᵒ Le Peletier). Tues–Sat 8.30am–1.30pm & 3–7pm. An eighteenth-century confiserie serving *marrons glacés*, prunes from Agen, dried fruit, sweets, chocolates and even some wines.

Poilâne, 8 rue du Cherche-Midi, 6ᵉ (Mᵒ Sèvres-Babylone). Mon–Sat 7.15am–8.15pm. Bakes bread to ancient and secret family recipes; there is always a queue.

Rendez-Vous de la Nature, 96 rue Mouffetard, 5ᵉ (Mᵒ Cardinal-Lemoine). Tues–Sat 9.30am–7.30pm, Sun 9.30am–noon. One of the city's most comprehensive health-food stores, with everything from organic produce to herbal teas.

Music

New **cassettes and CDs** are not particularly cheap in Paris, but there are plenty of secondhand bargains, and you may come across selections that are novel enough to tempt you. Like the live music scene, there are albums of Brazilian, Caribbean, Antillais, African and Arab sounds that would be specialist rarities in London or the States, and there's every kind of jazz.

Afric' Music, 3 rue des Plantes, 14ᵉ (Mᵒ Mouton-Duvernet). Mon–Sat 10am–7pm. A small shop with an original selection of African, Caribbean and reggae discs.

BPM Records, 1 rue Keller, 11ᵉ (Mᵒ Bastille). Mon–Sat noon–8pm. Specialists in house, including acid, hip-hop, rap, techno and dub. A good place to pick up club flyers.

Camara, 45 rue Marcadet, 18ᵉ (Mᵒ Marcadet-Poissonnière). Mon–Sat noon–8pm. The best selection of West African music on cassette and video in town.

Crocodisc, 40–42 rue des Écoles, 5ᵉ (Mᵒ Maubert-Mutualité). Tues–Sat 11am–7pm. Folk, Oriental, Afro-Antillais, funk, reggae, salsa, rap, soul, country, new and secondhand. Some of the best prices in town.

Crocojazz, 64 rue de la Montagne-Ste-Geneviève, 5ᵉ; 40 & 42 rue des Ecoles, 5ᵉ (all Mᵒ Maubert-Mutualité). Tues–Sat 11am–1pm & 2–7pm. Mainly new imports: jazz, blues, gospel and country.

Dream Store, 4 place St-Michel, 6ᵉ (Mᵒ St-Michel). Mon 1.30pm–7.15pm, Tues–Sat 9.30am–7.15pm. Good discounts on jazz and classical in particular but also rock and folk.

FNAC Musique, 4 place de la Bastille, 12ᵉ, next to opera house (Mᵒ Bastille). Mon–Sat 10am–8pm, Wed till 10pm. Extremely stylish shop in black, grey and chrome, with computerized catalogues, books, every variety of music and a concert booking agency. The other FNAC shops (see above under "Bookshops") also sell music and hi-fi; the branch at 24 bd des Italiens, 9ᵉ, has a greater emphasis on rock and popular music, and stays open till midnight.

Paul Beuscher, 15–29 bd Beaumarchais, 4ᵉ (Mᵒ Bastille). Mon–Fri 9.45am–12.30pm & 2–7pm, Sat 9.45am–7pm. A music department store that's been going strong for over 100 years. Instruments, scores, books, recording equipment, etc.

Virgin Megastore, 56–60 av des Champs-Élysées, 8ᵉ (Mᵒ Franklin-D.-Roosevelt); and Carrousel du Louvre, 1ᵉʳ (Mᵒ Louvre-Rivoli). Mon–Sat 10am–midnight, Sun noon–midnight. The biggest and trendiest of all Paris's music shops. Concert booking agency and expensive Internet connection.

Sport and outdoor activities

Le Ciel Est à Tout le Monde, 10 rue Gay-Lussac, 5ᵉ (RER Luxembourg). Mon–Sat 10am–7pm; closed Mon in Aug. The best kite shop in Europe. It also sells frisbees, boomerangs, etc, plus books and traditional toys.

Nomades, 37 bd Bourdon, 4ᵉ (Mᵒ Bastille). Mon–Fri 11am–7pm, Sat & Sun 10am–7pm. The place to buy and hire roller-blades and equipment, with its own bar out back where you can find out about the scene. See also "In-line skating", p.186.

Au Vieux Campeur, 48 rue des Écoles, 5ᵉ (Mᵒ Maubert-Mutualité). Mon–Fri 10.30am–7.30pm, Wed till 9pm, Sat 9.30am–8pm. Maps, guides, climbing, hiking, camping, ski gear, plus a kids' climbing wall.

Markets

Paris's **markets**, like its shops, are grand spectacles. Mouthwatering arrays of **food** from half the countries of the globe, captivating in colour, shape and smell, assail the senses in even the drabbest parts of town. Though the food is perhaps the best offering of the Paris markets, there are also street markets dedicated to **secondhand goods** (the flea markets, or *marchés aux puces*), **clothes** and **textiles**, **flowers**, **birds**, **books** and **stamps**. Though all have semi-official opening and closing hours, many begin business in advance and drag on till dusk. Note that several of the markets listed below are described in more detail in the *Guide*.

SECONDHAND AND FLEA MARKETS

Marché aux Livres, Pavillon Baltard, Parc Georges-Brassens, rue Brancion, 15ᵉ (Mᵒ Porte-de-Vanves). Sat & Sun 9am–6pm. Secondhand and antiquarian books.

Marché aux Timbres, junction of avs Marigny and Gabriel, 8ᵉ (Mᵒ Champs-Élysées-Clemenceau). Thurs, Sat, Sun & hols 10am–dusk. Paris's best stamp market.

Porte de Montreuil, 20ᵉ (Mᵒ Porte-de-Montreuil). Sat, Sun & Mon 7am–5pm. Best of the flea markets for secondhand clothes – cheapest on Mon when leftovers from the weekend are sold off. Also good for old furniture, household goods and assorted junk.

Porte de Vanves, av Georges-Lafenestre/av Marc-Sangnier, 14ᵉ (Mᵒ Porte-de-Vanves). Sat & Sun 7am–1.30pm. The best choice for bric-a-brac.

St-Ouen/Porte de Clignancourt, 18ᵉ (Mᵒ Porte-de-Clignancourt). Sat, Sun & Mon 7.30am–7pm. The biggest and most touristy flea market, with stalls selling new and secondhand clothes, shoes, records, books and junk of all sorts, as well as expensive antiques.

FOOD MARKETS

Markets usually start between 7am and 8am and tail off around 1pm. Details of locations and days of operation are given below. The covered markets have specific opening hours, which are also detailed below.

Belleville, bd de Belleville, 20ᵉ (Mᵒ Belleville/Ménilmontant). Tues & Fri.

Buci, rue de Buci & rue de Seine, 6ᵉ (Mᵒ Mabillon). Tues–Sun.

Carmes, place Maubert, 5ᵉ (Mᵒ Maubert-Mutualité). Tues, Thurs & Sat.

Convention, rue de la Convention, 15ᵉ (Mᵒ Convention). Tues, Thurs & Sun.

Dejean, place du Château-Rouge, 18ᵉ (Mᵒ Château-Rouge). Tues–Sun.

Edgar-Quinet, bd Edgar-Quinet, 14ᵉ (Mᵒ Edgar-Quinet). Wed & Sat.

Enfants-Rouges, 39 rue de Bretagne, 3ᵉ (Mᵒ Filles-du-Calvaire). Tues–Sat 8am–1pm & 4–7pm, Sun 9am–1pm.

Monge, place Monge, 5ᵉ (Mᵒ Monge). Wed, Fri & Sun.

Montorgueil, rue Montorgueil & rue Montmartre, 1ᵉʳ (Mᵒ Châtelet-Les Halles/Sentier). Tues–Sat 8am–1pm & 4pm–7pm, Sun 9am–1pm.

Mouffetard, rue Mouffetard, 5ᵉ (Mᵒ Censier-Daubenton). Tues–Sun.

Place d'Aligre, 12ᵉ (Mᵒ Ledru-Rollin). Tues–Sun until 1pm.

Port-Royal, bd Port-Royal, nr Val-de-Grâce, 5ᵉ (RER Port-Royal). Tues, Thurs & Sat.

Porte-St-Martin, rue du Château-d'Eau, 10ᵉ (Mᵒ Château-d'Eau). Tues–Sat 8am–1pm & 4–7.30pm, Sun 8am–1pm.

Raspail, bd Raspail, between rue du Cherche-Midi & rue de Rennes, 6ᵉ (Mᵒ Rennes). Tues & Fri. Organic on Sun.

Rue Cler, 7ᵉ (Mᵒ École-Militaire). Tues–Sat.

Rue de Lévis, 17ᵉ (Mᵒ Villiers). Tues–Sun.

Rue du Poteau, 18ᵉ (Mᵒ Jules-Joffrin). Tues–Sat.

Secrétan, av Secrétan/rue Riquet, 19ᵉ (Mᵒ Bolivar). Tues–Sat 8am–1pm & 4–7.30pm, Sun 8am–1pm.

Saint-Germain, rue Mabillon, 6ᵉ (Mᵒ Mabillon). Tues–Sat 8am–1pm & 4–7.30pm, Sun 8am–1pm.

Tang Frères, 48 av d'Ivry, 13ᵉ (Mᵒ Porte-d'Ivry). Tues–Sun 9am–7.30pm. Not really a market, but a vast emporium of all things oriental, where speaking French will not help you discover the nature and uses of what you see before you. In the same yard there is also a Far Eastern flower shop.

Ternes, rue Lemercier, 17ᵉ (Mᵒ Ternes). Tues–Sat 8am–1pm & 4–7.30pm, Sun 8am–1pm.

Listings

Airlines Aer Lingus, 47 av de l'Opéra, 2ᵉ (☎01.47.42.12.50, *www.aerlingus.ie*); Air Canada, 106 bd Haussmann, 8ᵉ (☎08.20.87.08.71, *www.aircanada.ca*); Air France, 119 av des Champs-Élysées, 8ᵉ (☎01.42.99.21.01 or 08.02.80.28.02, *www.airfrance.fr*); British Airways, 12 rue Castiglione, 1ᵉʳ (☎08.25.82.54.00, *www.british-airways.com*); British Midland, 4 pl de Londres, Roissy-en-France 95700 (☎01.48.62.55.65, *www.iflybritishmidland.com*); Delta, 4 rue Scribe, 9ᵉ (☎01.47.68.92.92, *www.delta-air.com*); Qantas, 7 rue Scribe, 9ᵉ (☎01.44.55.52.05, *www.qantas.com.au*).

American Express, 11 rue Scribe, 9ᵉ; ☎01.47.77.79.50 (Mon–Fri 9am–6pm, Sat 9am–5pm, Sun 10am–4pm; Mᵒ Opéra).

Babysitting Two main agencies: Ababa, with English-speakers (☎01.45.49.46.46), and Kid Services (☎01.42.61.90.00, *www.kidservices.fr*). Apart from these, you could scan the notices at the American Church, 65 quai d'Orsay, 6ᵉ (Mᵒ Invalides), or at the Alliance Française, 101 bd Raspail, 6ᵉ (Mᵒ St-Placide).

Banks and change Money-exchange bureaux are at the airports (Charles de Gaulle 6.30am–11.30pm; Orly 6.30am–11pm); train stations (latest at Gare de Lyon: 6.30am–11pm); and CCF, 115 av Champs-Élysées, 8ᵉ (8.30am–8pm; Mᵒ Georges-V). There are also automatic exchange machines at the airports, train stations and outside many money-exchange bureaux. Credit and debit cards can be used in many cash machines. Also see American Express, above.

Bike rental Charges start from about 80F/€12.20 a day with a *caution* (deposit) of 1000–2500F/€152.44–381.10. If you want a bike for Sunday, when all of Paris takes to the *quais*, you'll need to book in advance. Try Paris-Vélo, 2 rue du Fer-à-Moulin, 5ᵉ (☎01.43.37.59.22; Mᵒ

Censier-Daubenton), for 21-speed and mountain bikes; Paris à Vélo C'est Sympa/Vélo Bastille, 37 bd Bourdon, 4ᵉ (01.48.87.60.01; Mᵒ Bastille), who also offer commendable bicycle tours; Bike N'Roller, 6 rue St-Julien-Le-Pauvre, 5ᵉ (☎01.44.07.35.89, *www.bikenroller.com*; Mᵒ/RER St-Michel); or the Maison du Vélo, 11 rue Fénélon, 10ᵉ (☎01.42.81.24.72; Mᵒ Gare-du-Nord/Poissonnière), with summer outlets at the Gare-de-l'Est and Gare-du-Montparnasse.

Buses For national and international buses, including Eurolines (☎01.49.72.51.51), you can get information and tickets at the main terminus, 28 av du Général-de-Gaulle, Bagnolet (Mᵒ Gallieni).

Car rental Local firms include Buchard, 99 bd Auguste-Blanqui, 13ᵉ (☎01.45.88.28.38; Mᵒ Place-d'Italie); Locabest, 3 rue Abel, 12ᵉ (☎01.43.46.05.05; Mᵒ Gare-de-Lyon), and at 104 bd Magenta, 10ᵉ (☎01.44.72.08.05; Mᵒ Gare-du-Nord). Look up "Location" in the yellow pages for others.

Dental treatment Emergency service: SOS Dentaire, 87 bd Port-Royal, 5ᵉ; ☎01.43.37.51.00 (Mᵒ Port-Royal).

Embassies/Consulates Australia, 4 rue Jean-Rey, 15ᵉ (☎01.40.59.33.00; Mᵒ Bir-Hakeim); Britain, 35 rue du Faubourg-St-Honoré, 8ᵉ (☎01.44.51.31.02; Mᵒ Concorde); Canada, 35 av Montaigne, 8ᵉ (☎01.44.43.29.00; Mᵒ Franklin-D.-Roosevelt); Ireland, 4 rue Rude, 16ᵉ (☎01.44.17.67.00; Mᵒ Charles-de-Gaulle-Étoile); New Zealand, 7ter rue Léonardo-de-Vinci, 16ᵉ (☎01.45.00.24.11; Mᵒ Victor-Hugo); US, rue St-Florentin, 1ᵉʳ (☎01.43.12.22.22; Mᵒ Concorde).

Emergencies Call ☎18 or SOS-Médecins (☎01.47.07.77.77) for 24hr medical help; ☎15 for 24hr ambulance (SAMU) service.

Festivals There's not much in the carnival line, though kids armed with bags of flour aiming to make a total fool of you appear on the streets during Mardi Gras (in Feb). There are free concerts and street performers all over Paris for the Fête de la Musique which coincides with the summer solstice (June 21), with Gay Pride around this date. July 14 (Bastille Day) is celebrated with official pomp in parades of tanks down the Champs-Élysées, firework displays and concerts. The French Communist Party, with the left-wing newspaper *L'Humanité*, hosts an annual Fête de l'Humanité in September at La Courneuve, just north of Paris, with representatives of just about every CP or ex-CP in the world, bands and eats that bring in Parisians of most political persuasions. See "Basics" for other music and religious festivals.

Gay and lesbian See "Gay and lesbian Paris", pp.179–80.

Helpline SOS Helpline in English: any problems, call ☎01.47.23.80.80 (daily 3–11pm). The American Church offers help and counselling on ☎01.45.50.26.49 (Mon–Sat 9.30am–1pm).

Hitching Allostop-Provoya, 8 rue Rochambeau, square Montholon, 9ᵉ (Mon–Fri 9am–7.30pm, Sat 9am–1pm & 2–6pm; ☎01.53.20.42.42; Mᵒ Cadet/Poissonnière) is the national hitching organization. See pp.39–40, for more details.

Hospitals English-speaking hospitals include the American Hospital, 63 bd Victor-Hugo, Neuilly-sur-Seine (☎01.46.41.25.25; Mᵒ Porte-Maillot then bus #82 to terminus); and the Hertford British Hospital, 3 rue Barbès, Levallois-Perret (☎01.46.39.22.22; Mᵒ Anatole-France).

Internet access At Forum des Images (see p.182); Virgin Megastore (p.192); British Council Library (see below); *Web Bar* (p.159); and *Cyber Café Latino* (p.161).

Language schools French lessons are available from the Alliance Française, 101 bd Raspail, 6ᵉ (☎01.45.44.38.28), and numerous other establishments. A full list is obtainable from embassy cultural sections.

Laundries Self-service places have multiplied in Paris over the last few years, and you'll probably find one near where you're staying. The smallest machines cost around 22F/€3.35 for a load, though some laundries only have bigger machines and charge around 45F/€6.86. Dryers run about 2F/€0.46 for five minutes. Generally, self-service laundry facilities open at 7am and close between 7pm and 9pm.

Left luggage Lockers are available at all train stations, though security is quite heavy.

Libraries The British Council, 9 rue de Constantine, 7ᵉ, has a paying library, with daily newspapers (Mon–Fri 11am–6pm; ☎01.49.55.73.23; day pass 30F/€4.57, annual pass 250F/€38.11; Mᵒ Invalides); the American Library in Paris, 10 rue du Général-Camou, 7ᵉ (Tues–Sat 10am–7pm; ☎01.53.59.12.60; day pass 70F/€10.67, annual 570F/€86.89; Mᵒ École-Militaire), with American papers and a vast range of books, also charges readers. The library of the Canadian Council, next door to the British, is free. Interesting French collections include the BPI (Bibliothèque Publique d'Information), Pompidou Centre, 3ᵉ (Mon & Wed–Fri noon–10pm,

Sat, Sun & public hols 10am–10pm; closed Tues & May 1; free; M° Rambuteau), with a vast collection, including all the foreign press, videos and a language lab; Bibliothèque Forney at the Hôtel de Sens, with books being a good excuse if you want to visit this medieval bishop's palace at 1 rue du Figuier in the 4ᵉ (Tues–Sat 1.30–8pm; 20F/€3.05; M° Pont-Marie); and the Historique de la Ville de Paris, in the Hôtel Lamoignon, a sixteenth-century mansion housing centuries of texts and picture books on the city at 24 rue Pavée, 4ᵉ (Mon–Sat 9.30am–6pm; 20F/€3.05; M° St-Paul).

Lost property Bureau des Objets Trouvés, 36 rue des Morillons, 15ᵉ (Mon, Thurs & Fri 8.30am–5pm, Tues & Thurs till 8pm; ☎01.55.76.20.00; M° Convention).

Petrol There are 24hr filling stations at all the *portes* of the city and in every *arrondissement*.

Pharmacies 24hr service at Dhery, 84 av des Champs-Élysées, 8ᵉ (☎01.45.62.02.41; M° George-V). When closed, each pharmacy should post the address of the nearest open one.

Police ☎17 for emergencies. To report a theft, go to the *commissariat de police* of the *arrondissement* in which the theft took place.

Post office Main office at 52 rue du Louvre, Paris 75001 (M° Châtelet-Les Halles). Open daily 24hr for letters, poste restante, faxes, telegrams and phone calls; currency exchange Mon–Fri 8am–7pm, Sat 8am–noon.

Train information For the bulk of information, see "City transport", pp.91–4. Eurostar (☎08.36.35.35.39); Hoverspeed SeaTrain Express (☎08.00.90.17.77).

Travel firms Council Travel, 16 rue de Vaugirard, 6ᵉ (☎08.00.14.81.48; M° Odéon), is a dependable student/youth agency as is OTU Voyages, 119 rue St-Martin, 4ᵉ, opposite the Pompidou Centre (☎01.40.29.12.12). Access Voyages, 6 rue Pierre-Lescot, 1ᵉʳ (☎01.44.76.84.50; M° Châtelet-Les Halles), has cheap transatlantic and train fares.

Women's Paris The best place to make contact is the Maison des Femmes, 163 rue de Charenton, 12ᵉ (Wed & Fri 4–7pm, Fri café 7–10pm; ☎01.43.43.41.13; M° Reuilly-Diderot/Gare-de-Lyon), a women's meeting place used by a variety of lesbian and feminist groups.

Around Paris

The region around the capital – the **Île de France** – and the borders of the neighbouring provinces are studded with large-scale **châteaux**. Many were royal or noble retreats for hunting and other leisured pursuits, some – like **Versailles** – were for more serious state show. However, they are all undoubtedly impressive, especially **Vaux-le-Vicomte** for its homogeneity and **Chantilly** for its masterpiece-studded art collection. If you have even the slightest curiosity about church buildings, make sure you visit the **cathedral of Chartres**, which is all it is cracked up to be – and more. Closer in, on the edge of the city itself, **St-Denis** boasts a cathedral second only to Notre-Dame among Paris churches – a visit which can be combined with a wander back into the centre of Paris along the banks of the St-Denis canal. Other **waterside walks** include **Chatou** and the Marne-side towns, with their memories of carousing, carefree painters and musicians in the early 1900s, when these places were open countryside or small villages. **Auvers-Sur-Oise** has a museum that transports you back to Impressionist days and landscapes, as well as laying claim to Van Gogh's final inspiration and resting-place. Whether the various suburban museums deserve your attention will depend on your degree of interest in the subjects they represent – china at **Sèvres**, French prehistory at **St-Germain-en-Laye**, Napoléon at **Malmaison** or horses at **Chantilly**. The biggest pull for kids is without question **Disneyland Paris**, out beyond the bizarre satellite town of **Marne-la-Vallée**, but they might also like the air and space museum at **Le Bourget**.

All of the attractions listed in this section are easily accessible by the region's public transport links of train, RER, métro and bus. We have arranged the accounts geographically, moving in a clockwise direction around Paris from St-Denis in the north to Malmaison in the west.

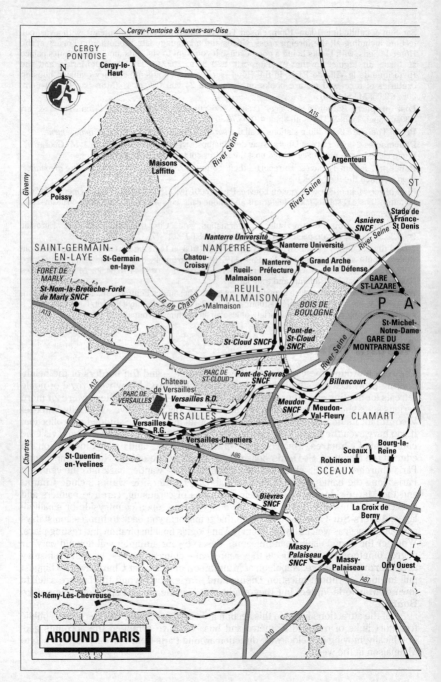

AROUND PARIS

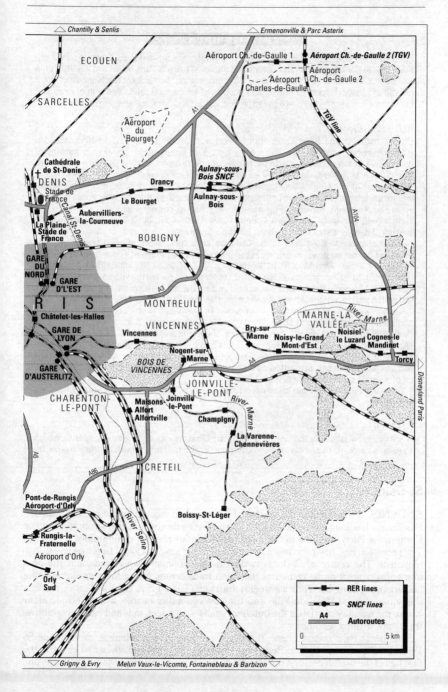

△ *Chantilly & Senlis* △ *Ermenonville & Parc Asterix*

ECOUEN

Aéroport Ch.-de-Gaulle 1 *Aéroport Ch.-de-Gaulle 2 (TGV)*

Aéroport
Ch.-de-Gaulle 2

SARCELLES

Aéroport
Charles-de-Gaulle

Aéroport
du
Bourget

TGV line

A104

Cathédrale
de St-Denis

Aulnay-sous-
Bois SNCF

DENIS

Drancy

Stade de
France

Le Bourget

Aulnay-sous-
Bois

La Plaine-
Stade de
France

Aubervilliers-
la-Courneuve

Canal St-Denis

BOBIGNY

GARE
DU
NORD

GARE
D'L'EST

MARNE-LA-
VALLÉE

River Marne

RIS

A3

MONTREUIL

Châtelet-les-Halles

VINCENNES

Bry-sur-
Marne

Noisiel-
le Luzard

GARE DE
LYON

Vincennes

Noisy-le-Grand
Mont-d'Est

Cognes-le
Mandinet

Torcy

GARE
D'AUSTERLITZ

Nogent-sur-
Marne

BOIS DE
VINCENNES

A4

△ *Disneyland Paris*

JOINVILLE-
LE-PONT

CHARENTON-
LE-PONT

Maisons-
Alfort
Alfortville

Joinville-
le-Pont

River Marne

Champigny

La Varenne-
Chennevières

CRETEIL

A6

A86

River Seine

Pont-de-Rungis
Aéroport-d'Orly

Boissy-St-Léger

Rungis-la-
Fraternelle

Aéroport d'Orly

Orly
Sud

■━■	RER lines
●━●	*SNCF lines*
▬▬	**Autoroutes**

0   5 km

▽ *Grigny & Evry* *Melun Vaux-le-Vicomte, Fontainebleau & Barbizon* ▽

ARTISTIC HAUNTS

For painters in search of visual inspiration, the countryside around Paris began to take a primary role in the late nineteenth century and attracted many a Paris-based artist, either on a day jaunt or on a more permanent basis. The towns along the banks of the Seine read like a roll-call of Musée d'Orsay paintings, and pockets of unchanged towns and scenery remain. Local museums, set up to record these pioneering artistic days, are well worth a visit.

AUVERS-SUR-OISE

On the banks of the River Oise, about 35km northwest of Paris, **AUVERS** makes an attractive rural excursion. It is the place where **Van Gogh** spent the last two months of his life, in a frenzy of painting activity, producing more canvases than the days of his stay. The church at Auvers, the portrait of Dr Gachet, black crows flapping across a wheat field – many of Van Gogh's best-known works belong to this period. He died in his brother's arms, after an incompetent attempt to shoot himself, in the tiny attic room he rented in the **Auberge Ravoux**. The *auberge* still stands, repaired and renovated, on the main street. A visit to Van Gogh's room (daily 10am–6pm; 30F/€4.57) is surprisingly moving. There is a short video about his time in Auvers.

At the entrance to the village is the **Château d'Auvers**, which offers a fascinating tour (infra-red helmet on head) of the world the Impressionists inhabited (Tues–Sun: April–Sept 10.30am–7.30pm; Oct–March 10.30am–6pm; ☎05.34.48.48.48, *www.chateau-auvers.fr*; 60F/€9.15). Most evocative of all is a walk through the old part of the village, past the church and the red lane into the famous wheat field and up the hill to the cemetery where, against the far left wall in a humble ivy-covered grave, the Van Gogh brothers lie side by side.

Auvers boasts a further artistic connection in Van Gogh's predecessor, **Daubigny** – contemporary of Corot and Daumier. A small **museum** (Wed–Sun 2–6pm; 20F/€3.05), dedicated to him and his art, can be visited above the tourist office. His **studio-house** (April–Oct Tues–Sun 2–6pm; 28F/€4.27), built to his own requirements, can also be visited at 61 rue Daubigny. From here, Daubigny would go off for weeks at a time, in his boat, to paint. This is represented by a boat sitting in the garden which is, in fact, a replica of a smaller boat once owned by Monet.

To reach Auvers you can take trains from Gare du Nord or Gare St-Lazare, changing at Pontoise.

CHATOU

A long narrow island in the Seine, the Île de Chatou was once a rustic spot to which Parisians came on the newly opened train line in the mid-nineteenth century to row on

St-Denis

ST-DENIS, 10km north of the centre of Paris and accessible by métro (Mᵒ St-Denis-Basilique), has long been the bastion of the Red suburbs and the stronghold of the Communist Party, and one of the most heavily industrialized communities in France. The recession has, however, taken a heavy toll in the form of closed factories and unemployment. The centre of St-Denis retains traces of small-town origins, but the area immediately abutting its cathedral has been transformed into a fortress-like housing and shopping complex. A thrice-weekly **market** (Tues, Fri & Sun) still takes place in the square by the Hôtel de Ville and the covered *halles* nearby, a multi-ethnic affair where the quantity of offal on the butchers' stalls – ears, feet, tails and bladders – shows this is not wealthy territory.

The town's chief claim to fame, though, is its magnificent cathedral, close by the St-Denis-Basilique métro station. Begun by Abbot Suger, friend and adviser to kings, in the first half of the twelfth century, the **Basilique St-Denis** (April–Sept Mon–Sat 10am–7pm, the river, and to dine and flirt at the *guinguettes*. A favourite haunt of many artists was the **Maison Fournaise**, just below the Pont de Chatou road bridge, which is now once again a restaurant (daily lunch & evening until 10pm; closed Sun in winter; ☎01.30.71.41.91; menu 159F/€24.24, *carte* 200–250F/€30.49–38.11), with a small museum of memorabilia (Thurs & Fri 11am–5pm, Sat & Sun 11am–6pm; 25F/€3.81). One of **Renoir**'s best-known canvases, *Le Déjeuner des Canotiers*, shows his friends lunching on the balcony, which is still shaded by a magnificent riverside plane tree. As well as many Impressionists, Vlaminck, Derain, other Fauves, and Matisse, were also habitués.

Access to the island is from the Rueil-Malmaison RER stop. Take the exit av Albert-1er, go left out of the station and right along the dual carriageway onto the bridge – a ten-minute walk. Bizarrely, the island hosts a twice-yearly **ham and antiques fair** (March & Sept), which is fun to check out.

BARBIZON

The landscape and country-living around **BARBIZON**, southeast of Paris, inspired painters such as **Rousseau** and **Millet** to set up camp here, initiating an artistic movement known as the Barbizon group. More painters followed, as well as writers and musicians, all attracted by the lifestyle and community. The **Auberge du Père Ganne**, on the main road, became the place to stay, not unrelated to the fact that the generous owner accepted the artists' decorations of his inn and furniture as payment. Now home to a museum (Mon & Wed–Fri 10am–12.30pm & 2–5/6pm, Sat & Sun 10am–5/6pm; 25F/€3.81), the inn still contains the original painted furniture as well as many Barbizon paintings.

MEUDON

The tranquil suburb of **MEUDON**, to the southwest of Paris, was where **Rodin** spent the last years of his life. In 1895, he acquired the **Villa des Brillants** at 19 av Rodin (May–Oct Fri–Sun 1.30–6pm; ☎01.45.34.13.09; 10F/€1.52; RER line C to Meudon-Val Fleury, then a fifteen-minute walk along avs Barbusse & Rodin), and installed his studio in the first room you encounter as you enter through the veranda. It was in this room that he used to dine with his companion, Rose Beuret, on summer evenings, and here that he married her, after fifty years together, just a fortnight before her death in February 1917. His own death followed in November, and they are buried together on the terrace below the house, beneath a version of *The Thinker*. The classical facade behind them masks an enormous pavilion containing plaster casts of many of his most famous works.

Sun noon–7pm; Oct–March Mon–Sat 10am–5pm, Sun noon–5pm; closed public hols) is generally regarded as the birthplace of the Gothic style in European architecture. The west front was the first ever to have a rose window, but it is in the choir that you best see the clear emergence of the new style: the slimness and lightness that comes with the use of the pointed arch, the ribbed vault and the long shafts of half-column rising from pillar to roof. It is a remarkably well-lit church thanks to the clerestory being almost one hundred percent glass – another first for St-Denis – and the transept windows being so big that they occupy their entire end walls. Once the place where the kings of France were crowned, the cathedral has been the burial place of all but three since 1000 AD, and their very fine tombs and effigies are distributed about the transepts and **ambulatory** (32F/€4.88; closed during services). Among the most interesting are the enormous Renaissance memorial to François 1er on the right just beyond the entrance, and the tombs of Louis XII, Henri II and Catherine de Médicis on the left side of the church. To the right of the ambulatory steps you can see the stocky little general Bertrand du Guesclin, who gave the English the runaround after the death of the Black Prince, and on the level above him – invariably graced by bouquets of flowers – the undistinguished statues of Louis XVI and Marie-Antoinette. Around the corner on the far side of the ambulatory is Clovis himself, king of the Franks way back in 500, a canny little German who wiped out Roman Gaul and turned it into France, with Paris for a capital.

Not many minutes' walk away on rue Gabriel-Péri, third right off rue de la Légiond'Honneur, the **Musée d'Art et d'Histoire de la Ville de St-Denis** (Mon & Wed–Sat 10am–5.30pm, Sun 2–6.30pm; 20F/€3.05) is housed in a former Carmelite convent. The exhibits are not of spectacular interest, save for the unique collection of documents relating to the Commune: posters, cartoons, broadsheets, paintings, plus an audiovisual presentation. There is also an exhibition of manuscripts and rare editions of works by the Communist poet Paul Éluard, native son of St-Denis.

Most of the visitors to St-Denis, however, will be coming for a match or concert: the **Stade de France** has attracted twice as many visitors since it was opened in 1998 than the cathedral. At least 2.8 billion francs/430 million euros were spent on the construction of this high-tech stadium, whose cosmic elliptic structure is best appreciated at night when lit up. If there isn't an event on, you can visit its grounds and facilities (daily 10am–6pm; 35F/€5.34 to visit the public areas, 90F/€13.72 for the backstage visit).

If you want to **walk back to Paris**, follow rue de la République from the Hôtel de Ville to the church of St-Denis-de-l'Estrée, then go down the left side of the church until you reach the canal bridge. If you turn left, you can walk practically all the way along the towpath (parts of the canalside are being rehabilitated and may necessitate a slight detour) – between an hour-and-a-half and two hours – to Porte de la Villette. There are stretches where it looks as if you're probably not supposed to be there. Just pay no attention and keep going. You pass peeling *villas* with unkempt gardens, patches of greenery, sand and gravel docks, and waste ground where larks rise above rusting bedsteads and doorless fridges. Decaying tenements and improvised shacks give way to lock-keepers' cottages with roses and vegetable gardens, then derelict factories and huge sheds where trundling gantries load bundles of steel rods onto Belgian barges.

Chantilly

CHANTILLY, a small town 40km north of Paris, is associated mainly with horses. Some 3000 thoroughbreds prance the forest rides of a morning, and two of the season's classiest flat races, the Jockey Club and the Prix de Diane, are held here. The stables in the château are given over to a museum of the horse.

Trains take about thirty minutes from Paris's Gare du Nord to Chantilly. Occasional free buses pass from the station to the château, though it's an easy walk away. **Footpaths** GR11 and 12 pass through the château park and its surrounding forest: following them makes a peaceful and leisurely way of exploring this bit of country.

The château and the Musée Vivant du Cheval

The Chantilly estate used to belong to two of the most powerful clans in France: first to the Montmorencys, then, through marriage, to the Condés. The present **Château** (March–Oct daily except Tues 10am–6pm; Nov–Feb Mon & Wed–Fri 10.30am–12.45pm & 2–5pm, Sat & Sun 10.30am–5pm; 42F/€6.40; park open daily same hours, 17F/€2.59) was put up in the late nineteenth century. It's a beautiful structure, graceful and romantic, surrounded by water and looking out over a formal arrangement of pools and pathways designed by the busy Le Nôtre.

The entrance is across a moat, past two realistic bronzes of hunting hounds. The visitable parts are mainly made up of an enormous collection of **paintings and drawings**, of which only the *galeries de peinture* on the first floor are accessible without a guided tour. Stipulated to remain as organized by Henri d'Orléans (the donor of the château), the paintings are not well displayed, and you quickly get visual indigestion from the massed ranks of good, bad and indifferent, deployed as if of equal value. Some highlights, however, are in the Rotunda of the picture gallery; Piero di Cosimo's *Simonetta Vespucci* and Raphael's *Madone de Lorette*. Raphael is also well represented in the so-called Sanctuary, with his *Three Graces* displayed alongside Filippo Lippi's *Esther et Assuerius* and forty miniatures from a fifteenth-century Book of Hours attributed to the French artist Jean Fouquet. Pass through the Galerie de Psyche with its series of sepia stained glass illustrating Apuleius' *Golden Ass*, to the room known as the Tribune, where Italian art, including Botticelli's *Autumn*, takes up two walls, and Ingres and Delacroix have a wall each.

A free guided tour will take you round the main apartments. The first port of call is the well-stocked **library**, where the museum's single greatest treasure is kept, *Les Très Riches Heures du Duc de Berry*, the most celebrated of all the Books of Hours. The illuminated pages illustrating the months of the year with representative scenes from contemporary (early 1400s) rural life – like harvesting and ploughing, sheep-shearing and pruning – are richly coloured and drawn with a delicate naturalism. Only facsimiles are on view, but these give an excellent idea of the original. Thousands of other fine books are also displayed here.

A rather unique view of the château can be experienced by going up in a hot-air **balloon**, the *aérophile*, which is moored in the park (March–Oct daily 10am–7pm; departure every 10 mins, duration of flight 10 mins; 66F/€10.06, 72F/€10.98 combined ticket for the balloon and the château). If the weather's not suitable or if you just don't fancy the hot-air balloon, you can take a 25-minute commentated **boat trip** (March to mid-Oct daily 10am–7pm; 52F/€7.93, or 107F/€16.31 combined ticket for the boat, the balloon and the château) all the way round the château and be dropped off at the entrance to the museum.

Five minutes' walk along the château drive, the colossal stable block has been transformed into a museum of the horse, the **Musée Vivant du Cheval** (April–Oct Mon & Wed–Fri 10.30am–5.30pm, Sat & Sun 10.30am–6pm; May & June also open Tues 10.30am–5.30pm; July & Aug also open Tues 2–5.30pm; Nov–March Mon–Fri 2–5pm, Sat & Sun 10.30am–5pm; 50F/€7.62). The building was erected at the beginning of the eighteenth century by the incumbent Condé prince, who believed he would be reincarnated as a horse and wished to provide fitting accommodation for 240 of his future relatives. In the main hall, horses of different breeds from around the world are stalled, with a ring for **demonstrations** (April–Oct 11.30am, 3.30pm & 5.15pm; Nov–March weekends & public hols 11.30am, 3.30pm & 5.15pm, weekdays 3.30pm only), followed by a series of life-size models illustrating the various activities horses are used for.

Disneyland Paris

Children will love **Disneyland Paris**, 32km east of the capital – there are no two ways about it. What their minders will think of it is another matter. First, there is the question of whether it's worth the money; the admissions price quickly renders other parks and museums in the city more appealing. Second, there's the weather. Parents might well decide that it would be easier, and cheaper, to buy a family package to Florida, where sunshine is assured and where the conflict between enchanted kingdom and enchanting city does not arise. Bad weather does have one advantage, however: on a wet and windy weekday (Mon & Thurs are the best) off-season you can probably get round every ride you want. Otherwise, one-hour waits for the big rides are common.

The resort

Since the opening of Space Mountain, Disneyland Paris has provided a variety of good fear-and-thrill rides, though the majority of attractions remain very safe and staid. It takes its inspiration from film sets, not funfairs or big tops, and the results seem "real" – you can go into them and round them and the characters talk to you. All the structures are incredibly detailed, and their shades and textures worked out with the precision of a brain surgeon. But if you're not a child, solid buildings masquerading as flimsy film sets and constantly being filmed by swarming hordes of camcorder operators can well fail to fulfil any kind of escapist fantasy.

The **Magic Kingdom** is divided into four "lands" radiating out from **Main Street USA**. **Fantasyland** appeals to the youngest kids, with Sleeping Beauty's Castle, Peter Pan's Flight, Dumbo the Flying Elephant, the Mad Hatter's Teacups and Alice in Wonderland's Maze among its attractions. **Adventureland** has the most outlandish sets and two of the best rides – Pirates of the Caribbean and Indiana Jones and the Temple of Doom. **Frontierland** has the *Psycho*-inspired but insipid Phantom Manor and the hair-raising roller coaster Big Thunder Mountain, modelled on a runaway mine train. In **Discoveryland** there's a high-tech 3-D experience called "Honey, I Shrunk The Audience" from which you exit the same size you were when you entered, a 360-degree Parisian exposé in Le Visionarium, the Nautilus submarine of *20,000 Leagues Under the Sea* and the startling Space Mountain (see above). The grand **parade** of floats representing all the top box-office Disney movies sallies down Main Street USA at 3pm sharp every day (a good time to try for the more popular rides). Night-time Electrical Parades and **firework displays** take place several times a week.

Besides the theme park, the complex includes **Festival Disney**, the evening entertainments complex where you can splash out 325F/€49.54 for Buffalo Bill's Wild West Show, with real guns, horses, bulls and bison (nightly 6.30pm & 9.30pm; children 3–11 195F/€29.73); and **grounds** beyond which you can play golf, do workouts, jog, ride bikes or ponies, skate, sail and take part in team sports. Festival Disney and the six themed **hotels** are a mixed bag of hideous eyesores and over-ambitious kitsch designed by some of the world's leading architectural names – Michael Graves, Antoine Predock, Robert Stern and Frank Gehry.

Practicalities

To reach Disneyland from Paris, take RER line A to Marne-la-Vallée Chessy/ Disneyland (about 35–40 min; 76F/€11.59 return, child 38F/€5.79; for prices of one-, two- and three-day Paris Visite transport cards including EuroDisney see box on p.95). If you're coming straight from the airport, you can take a shuttle bus from both Charles de Gaulle and Orly (times and frequencies change seasonally, but roughly every 45min 8.30am–8pm; for recorded information call ☎01.64.30.66.56; adults 85F/€12.96 one way, children 65F/€9.91, under-3s free). Marne-la-Vallée Chessy also has its own TGV train station, linked to Lille, Lyon and London (see p.5 for details of the direct Eurostar from London Waterloo and Ashford in Kent). If you're **driving**, follow the A4 east from Paris for 32km (Exit 13 for Ranch Davy Crockett and Exit 14 for the park and the hotels); from Calais follow the A26 changing to the A1, the A104 and finally the A4.

Admission charges for the "passports" are: October to March excluding Christmas hols – one-day pass 160F/€24.50 (child aged 3–11 130F/€19.90), two-day pass 310F/€47.50 (250F/€38.30), three-day pass 435F/€66.60 (355F/€54.30); April to September & Christmas hols – one-day pass 220F/€33.70 (170F/€26), two-day pass 425F/€65.50 (330F/€50.50), three-day pass 595F/€91.10 (460F/€70.40). Children under 3 are free. Opening hours vary greatly depending on the season and whether it is a weekend, and should be checked when you buy your ticket (or via the Internet on *www.disneylandparis.com*) but they are roughly low season daily 10am to 6pm, Saturday and Sunday till 8pm; high season daily 9am to 11pm.

Special packages are available in advance (for details call ☎01.60.30.60.53 in France, ☎1/407 W. DISNEY in the US and ☎0990/030303 in the UK), or you can buy admission passes and train tickets in Paris at all RER line A and B stations and in major métro stations.

The **accommodation** will be out of many people's price range, the least expensive hotel room – the two-star *Hotel Santa Fé* – off season being 515F/€78.51 a night (two adults, two children), rising to around 2500F/€381.10 peak season for a room in the *Disneyland Hotel* inside the Magic Kingdom on Main Street. The cheapest alternative if you have a car is the park's *Davey Crockett Ranch*, a fifteen-minute drive away, with self-catering log cabins (sleeping four to six) from 350F/€53.35 to 850F/€129.57. To really economize, you could camp at the nearby *Camping du Parc de la Colline*, Route de Lagny, 77200 Torcy (☎01.60.05.42.32), which is open all year.

Vaux-le-Vicomte

Of all the great mansions within reach of a day's outing from Paris, the classical **Château of Vaux-le-Vicomte** (April–Oct daily 10am–6pm; Nov–March group bookings only – phone ☎01.64.14.41.90; 56F/€8.54), 46km southeast of Paris, is the most architecturally harmonious, the most aesthetically pleasing and the most human in scale.

To get there, take a train from Gare de Lyon to Melun (40min), then a bus (weekends only; 6.40F/€0.98), or else taxi (approximately 100–120F/€15.24–18.29) for the seven-kilometre ride to the château.

The château

Louis XIV's finance superintendent, Nicholas Fouquet, had the **château** built at colossal expense, using the top designers of the day – architect Le Vau, painter Le Brun and landscape gardener Le Nôtre. The result was magnificence and precision in perfect proportion, and a bill that could only be paid by someone who occasionally confused the state's account with his own. The house-warming party, to which the king was invited, was more extravagant than any royal event – a comparison which other finance ministers ensured that Louis took to heart. Within three weeks Fouquet was jailed for life on trumped-up charges, and the design team carted off to build the king's own gaudy piece of one-upmanship at Versailles.

Seen from the entrance, the château is a rather austere grey pile surrounded by an artificial moat, and it's only when you go through to the south side – where clipped box and yew, fountains and statuary stand in formal gardens – that you can look back and appreciate the very harmonious and very French qualities of the building: the combination of steep, tall roof and central dome with classical pediment and pilasters.

As to the interior, the main artistic interest lies in the work of Le Brun, who was responsible for the two fine **tapestries** in the entrance, made in the local workshops set up by Fouquet specifically to adorn his house (and subsequently removed by Louis XIV to become the famous Gobelins works in Paris), as well as numerous **painted ceilings**, notably in Fouquet's Bedroom, the Salon des Muses, *Sleep* in the Cabinet des Jeux, and the so-called King's Bedroom, whose decor is the first example of the style that became known as "Louis Quatorze".

Other points of interest are the **kitchens**, which have not been altered since construction, and a room displaying letters in the hand of Fouquet, Louis XIV and other notables. One, dated November 1794 (mid-Revolution), addresses the incumbent Duc de Choiseul-Praslin as *tu*. "Citizen," it says, "you've got a week to hand over one hundred thousand pounds . . .", and signs off with "Cheers and brotherhood". You can imagine the shock to the aristocratic system.

Every Saturday evening from May to mid-October, between 8pm and midnight (80F/€12.20 entrance), the **state rooms** are illuminated with a thousand candles, as they probably were on the occasion of Fouquet's fateful party. The **fountains** and other waterworks can be seen in action on the second and last Saturdays of each month between April and October, from 3pm until 6pm. In the stables, the **Musée des Équipages** comprises a collection of horse-drawn vehicles, including those used by Charles X fleeing Paris and the Duc de Rohan retreating from Moscow.

MUSEUMS AROUND PARIS

The assortment of **museums** in the general vicinity of Paris are of specialist interest: **ceramics** at Sèvres, **prehistory** at St-Germain-en-Laye and **aviation** at Le Bourget. All are excellent and shouldn't be missed if any of the subjects arouse interest.

MUSÉE DE L'AIR ET D'ESPACE

Five kilometres east, and a short hop up the A1 motorway from St-Denis, is **LE BOUR-GET** airport. The French were always adventurous, pioneering aviators, and the name of Le Bourget is intimately connected with their earliest exploits. Lindbergh landed here after his epic first flight across the Atlantic. From World War I to the development of Orly in the 1950s, this was Paris's principal airport, though nowadays it sees only internal flights. Some of the older buildings have been turned into a fascinating museum of flying machines.

The **museum** (Tues–Sun 10am–5/6pm; 40F/€6.10) occupies the old airport buildings, and consists of five adjacent hangars and the Grande Galerie, taking you from the earliest attempts to fly through to the latest spacecraft. The Montgolfier brothers are the first on the scene with their invention of the hot-air balloon. The room dedicated to them shows society going balloon-crazy before real aeroplane madness begins in the **Grande Galerie**; the first contraption to fly 1km, the first cross-Channel flight, the first aerobatics. . . successes and failures are all on display here. The Grande Galerie also showcases World War I planes, whilst highlights of World War II planes are on display with the first Concorde prototype in the Hall Concorde. **Hangars C and D** cover the years from 1945 to the present day. Having lost eighty percent of its capacity in 1945, the French aviation industry has recovered to the extent that it now occupies a pre-eminent position in the world. Its high-tech achievement is represented here by the super-sophisticated best-selling Mirage fighters and two Ariane space-launchers, Ariane I and the latest, Ariane V (both parked on the tarmac outside). **Hangar E** contains light and sporty aircraft and **Hangar F**, nearest to the entrance, is devoted to **space**, with rockets, satellites, space capsules, etc. Some are mock-ups, some the real thing. Among the latter are a Lunar Roving Vehicle, the Soyuz craft in which a French astronaut flew and France's own first successful space rocket. Everything is accompanied by extremely good explanatory panels – though in French only.

Fontainebleau

From the Gare de Lyon it's just a fifty-minute train ride to **FONTAINEBLEAU**, famous for its vast, rambling **Château** (daily except Tues: May–Oct 9.30am–5pm; Nov–April 9.30am–12.30pm & 2–5pm; 35F/€5.34; Musée Chinois open when there's enough staff, entry included with ticket for the château; Musée Napoléon guided tours morning only, Petits Appartements guided tours afternoon only, although both prone to change, both 16F/€2.44; ring for further details ☎01.60.71.50.70). Bus #AB from Fontainebleau-Avon station will take you to the château gates in a few minutes.

The château owes its existence to its situation in the middle of a magnificent forest, which made it the perfect base for royal hunting expeditions. A hunting lodge was built here as early as the twelfth century, but it only began its transformation into a luxurious palace during the sixteenth on the initiative of François 1er, who imported a colony of Italian artists – most notably Rosso il Fiorentino and Niccolò dell'Abate – to carry out the decoration. They were responsible for the celebrated **Galerie François-1er** – which had a seminal influence on the subsequent development of French aristocratic art and design – the Salle de Bal, the Salon Louis XIII and the Salle du Conseil with its eighteenth-century decoration. The palace continued to enjoy royal favour well into the

To get there, take RER line B from Gare du Nord to Gare du Bourget, then bus #152 to Le Bourget/Musée de l'Air. Alternatively, take bus #350 from Gare du Nord, Gare de l'Est and Porte de la Chapelle, or #152 from Porte de la Villette.

MUSÉE NATIONAL DE LA CÉRAMIQUE

The **Musée National de la Céramique** (daily except Tues 10am–5pm; 22F/€3.35) in Sèvres is within easy reach of Paris: take the métro to the Pont-de-Sèvres terminus; cross the bridge and spaghetti junction; the museum is the massive building facing the river bank on your right. If you're interested in ceramics you will find much to savour here – not just French pottery and china, but Islamic, Chinese, Italian, German, Dutch and English. There is also, inevitably, a comprehensive collection of Sèvres ware, as the stuff is made right here. Close by, overlooking the river, the **Parc de St-Cloud** is good for fresh air and visual order, with a geometrical sequence of pools and fountains delineating a route down to the river and across to the city.

MUSÉE DES ANTIQUITÉS NATIONALES

ST-GERMAIN is a pleasant town, but the **Musée des Antiquités Nationales** (daily except Tues 9am–5.15pm; 25F/€3.81) is the main attraction. It is housed opposite St-Germain-en-Laye RER station in the unattractively renovated château, which was one of the main residences of the French court before Versailles was built.

The presentation and lighting make the visit a real pleasure. The extensive Stone Age section includes mock-ups of several cave drawings and carvings, and a beautiful collection of decorative objects, tools and so forth. All ages of prehistory are covered, right down into historical times, with Celts, Romans and Franks: there's a great section on the battle of Alésia when Vercingétorix found himself and his armies besieged by the Romans. A model of Caesar's double fortifications that ringed the hill-top of Alésia shows how, despite being attacked from the inside by Vercingétorix's lot, as well as from the outside by the called-for reinforcements, the Romans managed to win. The end-piece is a room of comparative archeology, with objects from cultures across the globe.

From right outside the château, a **terrace** – Le Nôtre arranging the landscape again – stretches for more than 2km above the Seine, with a view over the whole of Paris. Behind it is the **forest** of St-Germain, a sizeable expanse of woodland that's nowadays criss-crossed by too many roads to make this a convincing wilderness.

nineteenth century; Napoléon spent huge amounts of money on it, as did Louis-Philippe.

The **gardens** are equally luscious, but if you want to escape to the relative wilds, the surrounding **forest** of Fontainebleau is full of walking and cycling trails, all marked on Michelin map #196 (*Environs de Paris*).

Versailles

The **Palace of Versailles** (Tues–Sun: May–Sept 9am–6.30pm; Oct–April 9am–5.30pm; closed public hols; 45F/€6.86, 35F/€5.34 after 3.30pm, or 70F/€10.67 for longer tours) is one of the most visited monuments in France. Apart from a few areas you can visit on your own, most of the palace can only be viewed in guided groups, whose various itineraries can be booked in the morning at entrance D. Long queues are common, though by hiring an audioguide (25F/€3.81 from entrance C) you avoid the queues and have access to many more rooms. Don't set out to see all the palace in one day – it is not possible.

To **get there**, take the RER line C5 to Versailles-Rive Gauche (40min), turn right out of the station and immediately left to approach the palace. The **tourist office** is on the left at 2bis av de Paris (daily: May–Sept 9am–7pm; Oct–April 9am–noon & 2–6pm; ☎01.39.24.88.88, *www.mairie-versailles.fr*), and has free maps of the park.

The palace

The **palace** was inspired by the young Louis XIV's envy of his finance minister's château at Vaux-le-Vicomte (see p.203), which he was determined to outdo. He recruited the design team of Vaux-le-Vicomte architect Le Vau, painter Le Brun and gardener Le Nôtre and ordered something a hundred times the size. Versailles is the apotheosis of French regal indulgence and, even if its extravagant decor and the blatant self-propaganda of the Sun King are not to your liking, it will certainly leave an impression.

Construction began in 1664 and lasted virtually until Louis XIV's death in 1715. It was never meant to be a home; kings were not homely people. Second only to God, and the head of an immensely powerful state, Louis XIV was an institution rather than a private individual. His risings and sittings, comings and goings, were minutely regulated and rigidly encased in ceremony, attendance at which was an honour much sought after by courtiers. Versailles was the headquarters of every arm of the state. More than 20,000 people – nobles, administrative staff, merchants, soldiers and servants – lived in the palace in a state of unhygienic squalor, according to contemporary accounts.

Following Louis XIV's death, the château was abandoned for a few years before being reoccupied by Louis XV in 1722. It remained the residence of the royal family until the Revolution of 1789, when the furniture was sold and the pictures dispatched to the Louvre. Thereafter it fell into ruin and was nearly demolished by Louis-Philippe. In 1871, during the Paris Commune, it became the seat of the nationalist government, and the French parliament continued to meet in Louis XV's opera building until 1879. Restoration only began in earnest between the two world wars.

Of the rooms you can visit without a guide, the most stunning is the dazzling **Galerie des Glaces** – or Hall of Mirrors – where the Treaty of Versailles was signed to end World War I. Overdoses of gilding await you in the **grands appartements**, the state apartments of the king and queen, and the royal **chapel**, a grand structure that ranks among France's finest Baroque creations.

The park and Grand and Petit Trianons

The **park** at Versailles (daily 7am–dusk; fountains play May–Sept Sun 11am–noon & 3.30–5pm) was one of the biggest casualties of the storms that ravaged northern France on December 26, 1999. Ten thousand trees were killed and the Hameau de la Reine, with its thatched roofs, was devastated; as a result parts of the park may be off-limits whilst the massive replanting programme is underway. The park is free except on days when the fountains play (30F/€4.57), and the scenery is better the further you go from the palace. There are even informal groups of trees near the lesser outcrops of royal mania: the Italianate **Grand Trianon**, designed by Hardouin-Mansart in 1687 as a "country retreat" for Louis XIV; and the more modest Greek **Petit Trianon**, built by Gabriel in the 1760s for Louis XV's mistress, Mme de Pompadour (daily: April–Oct noon–6.30pm; Nov–March noon–5.30pm; Grand Trianon 25F/€3.81, Petit Trianon 15F/€2.29, combined ticket 30F/€4.57). More charming than either of these is **Le hameau de Marie-Antoinette**, a play village and farm built in 1783 for Louis XVI's queen to indulge the fashionable Rousseau-inspired fantasy of returning to the natural life (under restoration at the time of writing).

Distances in the park are considerable. If you can't manage them on foot, a *petit train* shuttles between the terrace in front of the château and the Trianons (33F/€5.03). There are **bikes** for hire at the Grille de la Reine, Porte St-Antoine and by the Grande Canal. **Boats** are for hire on the Grande Canal, within the Park.

Near the park entrance at the end of boulevard de la Reine is the **Hôtel Palais Trianon**, where the final negotiations for the Treaty of Versailles took place in 1919; the hotel has a wonderfully posh **tearoom**. The style of the *Trianon* is very much that of the town in general. The dominant population is aristocratic, with the pre-revolutionary titles disdainful of those dating merely from Napoléon. On Bastille Day both lots show their colours with black ribbons and ties.

Chartres

About 80km southwest of Paris, **CHARTRES** is a small and relatively undistinguished town. However, its **Cathédrale Notre-Dame** (Mon–Sat 7.30am–7.15pm, Sun 8.30am–7.15pm) is one of the finest examples of Gothic architecture in Europe and, built between 1194 and 1260, perhaps the quickest ever to be constructed. It is best experienced on a cloud-free winter's day when the low sun transmits the stained-glass colours to the interior stone, the quiet scattering of people leaves the acoustics unconfused and the exterior is unmasked for miles around.

For a medieval pilgrim, the cathedral would have been a glistening, fabulous jewel with all the exterior sculptures brightly painted and the walls inside whitewashed and covered with a myriad of refractions from the stained-glass windows. These, too, in their original pristine state would have been so bright they would have glittered from the outside along with the gold of the crowns and haloes of the statuary. For the contemporary visitor, however, there are more than enough wonders to enthral: the geometry of the building, unique in being almost unaltered since its consecration; the details of the stonework, the Renaissance choir screen and hosts of sculpted figures above each transept door; and the shining circular symmetries of the transept windows, virtually all of which are original, dating from the twelfth and thirteenth centuries. On the floor of the nave is an original thirteenth-century labyrinth comprising a path over 200m long enclosed within a 13-metre diameter, the same size as the rose window above the main doors. It's a great rarity, since the authorities at other cathedrals had them pulled up as distracting frivolities.

Among paying extras, the crypt and treasures can wait for another time but, crowds permitting, it's worth climbing the **north tower** for its bird's-eye view of the sculptures and structure of the cathedral (times vary, check in the cathedral; 25F/€3.81). There are **gardens** at the back from where you can contemplate at ease the complexity of stress factors balanced by the flying buttresses. And if you hear a passionate and erudite Englishman giving **guided tours** as you're wandering around, it is probably Malcolm Miller, almost an institution in himself and a world expert on Chartres cathedral. He does two tours daily from April to November (in the winter he may be away on a lecture tour; telephone for details ☎02.37.21.75.02) at noon and 2.45pm (40F/€6.10), starting just inside the west door.

Though the cathedral is the focus of a visit to Chartres, there are a few other attractions. The **Musée des Beaux Arts** (daily except Tues: May–Oct 10am–noon & 2–6pm; Nov–April 10am–noon & 2–5pm; closed Sun am; 15F/€2.29), in the former episcopal palace just north of the cathedral, has some beautiful tapestries, a room full of Vlaminck, and Zurbaran's *Sainte Lucie*, as well as good temporary exhibitions. Behind it, rue Chantault leads past old town houses to the river Eure and Pont du Massacre. You can follow this reedy river lined with ancient wash-houses upstream via rue du Massacre on the right bank. The cathedral appears from time to time through the trees and, closer at hand, on the left bank, is the Romanesque church of **St-André**, now used for art exhibitions, jazz concerts and so on. Crossing back over at the end of rue de la Tannerie into rue du Bourg takes you back to the cathedral through the medieval town, decorated with details such as the carved salmon on a house on place de la Poissonnerie.

The **memorial** on the corner of rue Collin d'Arleville and boulevard de la Résistance is to Jean Moulin, prefect of Chartres until he was sacked by the Vichy government in

1942. When the Germans occupied Chartres in 1940, he refused under torture to sign a document to the effect that black soldiers in the French army were responsible for Nazi atrocities. He later became de Gaulle's number one man on the ground, co-ordinating the Resistance, and died at the hands of Klaus Barbie in 1943.

Practicalities

From the **gare SNCF** (trains roughly every two hours from Gare du Montparnasse; 1hr), avenue J-de-Beauce leads straight up to place Châtelet. Diagonally opposite is rue Ste-Même, which leads to place Jean-Moulin; turn left at place Jean-Moulin and you'll find the cathedral and the **tourist office** (April–Sept Mon–Sat 9am–7pm, Sun 9.30am–5.30pm; Oct–March Mon–Sat 10am–6pm, Sun 10am–1pm & 2.30–4.30pm; ☎02.37.21.50.00). They can supply **free maps** and help with **accommodation**. Cheap accommodation can be found at Chartres' **hostel** over on the right bank of the river at 23 av Neigre (☎02.37.34.27.64). Cloître-Notre-Dame, along the south side of the cathedral, has plenty of **eating** places, the nicest one being *Café Serpente*, at no. 2. The best meals to be had in Chartres are at *La Truie qui File*, place de la Poissonnerie (☎02.37.21.53.90; closed Sun evening, Mon & Aug).

Malmaison

The **Château of Malmaison** (summer Mon & Wed–Fri 9.30am–12.30pm & 1.30–5.45pm, Sat & Sun 10am–6.30pm; winter Mon & Wed–Fri 9.30am–12.30pm & 1.30–5.15pm, Sat & Sun 10am–6pm; combined ticket with Bois-Préau museum 30F/€4.57), set in the beautiful grounds of the **Bois-Préau**, about 15km west of central Paris, is a relatively small and surprisingly enjoyable place to visit.

It was the home of the Empress Josephine, and – during the 1800–1804 Consulate – of Napoléon, too. According to his secretary, "it was the only place next to the battlefield where he was truly himself." After their divorce, Josephine stayed on here, occasionally receiving visits from the emperor until her death in 1814.

Tours of the château include the private and official apartments, in part with original furnishings, as well as Josephine's clothes, china, glass and personal possessions. There are other Napoleonic bits in the **Bois-Préau museum** (closed for renovation at the time of writing).

To get to Malmaison take the métro to Grande-Arche-de-la-Défense, then bus #258 to Malmaison-Château. Alternatively, if you'd like a walk, take the RER to Rueil-Malmaison and follow the GR11 footpath from the Pont de Chatou along the left bank of the Seine and into the château park.

travel details

TRAINS

Gare d'Austerlitz to: Tours (hourly; 1hr).

Gare de l'Est to: Metz (9 daily; 2hr 30min); Nancy (11 daily; 2–3hr); Reims (8 daily; 1hr 30min); Strasbourg (every 2 hours; 4hr).

Gare de Lyon to: Avignon (6 daily; 4 hr); Besançon (6 daily; 2hr 30min); Dijon (8 daily; 1hr 40min); Grenoble (6 daily; 3hr 20min); Lyon (hourly; 2hr–2hr 30min); Marseille (every 2 hrs; 4hr 40min); Nice (6 daily; 7hr).

Gare Montparnasse to: Bayonne (6 daily; 4hr 30min); Bordeaux (hourly; 3hr); Brest (hourly until 7pm; 5hr 30min–6hr); Carcassonne (4 daily; 8hr); Nantes (frequent; 3hr 30min); Pau (8 daily; 5hr 30min); Poitiers (every 2hr; 1hr 40min); Rennes (hourly; 2hr 30min); Toulouse (6 daily; 6hr–6hr 30min).

Gare du Nord to: Amiens (at least hourly; 1hr 45min); Arras (roughly every 2hr; 50min); Boulogne (at least hourly; 2hr 30min); Lille (hourly; 1hr).

Gare St-Lazare to: Caen (hourly; 2hr–2hr 30min); Cherbourg (roughly every 2hr; 3hr–3hr 30min); Dieppe (2 daily; 2hr 15min); Le Havre (every 2–3hr; 2hr–2hr 30min); Rouen (hourly; 1hr 15min).

CHAPTER TWO

THE NORTH

W hen conjuring up exotic holiday locations, you're unlikely to light upon the **north** of France. Even among the French, the most enthusiastic tourists of their own country, it has few adherents. Artois and Flanders include the most heavily industrialized parts of the country, while across the wheat fields of the more sparsely populated regions of Picardy and Champagne a few drops of rain are all that is required for total gloom to descend. It is likely, however, that you'll arrive and leave France via this region, and there are reasons to stop within easy reach of the Channel ports – of which **Boulogne** is by far the most appealing.

The north of France has been on the path of various invaders into the country, from northern Europe as well as from Britain, and the events that have taken place in Flanders, Artois and Picardy have shaped French history. The bloodiest battles were those of World War I, above all the **Battle of the Somme**, which took place north of Amiens, and **Vimy Ridge**, near Arras, where the trenches have been preserved in perpetuity. Throughout the north, but particularly around the villages of the Somme, monuments and cemeteries are powerful reminders of the devastating human wastage of those years.

Picardy boasts two of France's finest cathedrals, at **Amiens** and **Laon**. Further south, the *maisons*, vineyards and produce of the **Champagne** region are the main draw, for which the best bases are **Épernay** and **Reims,** the latter with another fine cathedral. Other attractions include the bird sanctuary of **Marquenterre**; the wooded wilderness of the **Ardennes**; industrial archeology in the coalfields around **Douai**, where Zola's *Germinal* was set; the great medieval castle of **Coucy-le-Château**; and the battle sites of the Middle Ages – **Agincourt** and **Crécy** – whose names are so familiar in the history of Anglo-French rivalry.

Though the past is not forgotten, the present life of the region does not feed on it. In city centres from **Lille** to **Troyes**, you'll find your fill of food, culture and entertainment in the company of locals similarly intent on having a good time; and in addition to the more obvious pleasures of the Champagne region, there's the possibility of finding relatively lucrative employment during the harvest season towards the end of September.

THE CHANNEL PORTS AND THE ROAD TO PARIS

Apart from their attraction for British day-trippers after a sniff of something foreign, a shopping bag full of continental produce, or more commonly a few crates of cheap beer, the chief function of the Channel ports in this part of France – **Calais** and **Boulogne** – is to provide a cheap, efficient route between Britain and France, though in recent years serious competition has been provided by the **Channel Tunnel**, which emerges at Fréthun, 5km southwest of Calais. The Channel Tunnel has reduced the crossing time to just thirty minutes, either with your car on Eurotunnel trains, or on the passenger train Eurostar. Details of the various train and ferry crossings are listed in "Basics" (see pp.5–8). There are frequent train connections east to **Lille** and beyond, and south

ACCOMMODATION PRICE CODES

Each hotel and guesthouse in this book has been graded according to the following price codes, which indicate the price for the **cheapest double room available during the high season**.

① Under 160F/€24   ④ 300–400F/€46–61   ⑦ 600–700F/€91–107
② 160–220F/€24–34   ⑤ 400–500F/€61–76   ⑧ 700–800F/€107–122
③ 220–300F/€34–46   ⑥ 500–600F/€76–91   ⑨ Over 800F/€122

towards **Paris**, while the *autoroute* system will whisk you quickly off to your ultimate destination.

For a much more immediate immersion into *La France* – little towns, idiosyncratic farms, a comfortable verge to sleep off the first baguette and *vin rouge* – the old **route nationale N1**, which shadows the coast all the way from Dunkerque to Abbeville before heading inland to Paris, is infinitely preferable to the *autoroute*. There are also interesting things to see en route: the cathedrals at **Amiens** and **Beauvais**, the hilltop town of **Montreuil** with its Vauban fortress, the remains of Hitler's Atlantic Wall along the bracing **Côte d'Opale** and the **Marquenterre bird sanctuary** at the mouth of the River Somme.

Dunkerque and around

A one-time competitor in the cross-Channel passenger business, **DUNKERQUE** finally lost out in October 1997 to the heavyweights of Calais and Boulogne and the Channel Tunnel. Although this doesn't bode well for the future of its hotels, restaurants and shops, Dunkerque is still France's third largest port and a massive industrial centre in its own right, albeit now badly hit by unemployment; its oil refineries and steelworks produce a quarter of the total French output. If you fancy a closer look at all this industrial muscle, you could take one of the various themed **boat trips** from place du Minck, Bassin du Commerce, at the northern end of rue Clemenceau (March to mid-June & Sept–Dec first two weekends of the month; mid-June to Aug daily; the tourist office can provide a list of departure times or call ☎03.28.59.11.14; 35–49F/€5.34–7.47).

Frequently under a cloud of chemical smog and unstylishly resurrected from wartime devastation, the only reasons you might want to visit Dunkerque are to pay homage to the events of 1940 – in which case you should head straight for Malo-les-Bains (see p.215) – or to stop off if heading north from Calais. The only buildings of any significance to have survived the last war (or at least to have been rebuilt afterwards) are the tall medieval red-brick **belfry** that is the town's chief landmark (hourly guided tours: June–Aug Mon–Sat 9.30–11.30am & 2.30–5.30pm; July & Aug also Sun 10.30–11.30am & 2.30–3.30pm; 15F/€2.29); the much-restored fifteenth-century church of **St-Éloi**; and, a few blocks south of the church on place Jean-Bart, the turn-of-the-century **Hôtel de Ville**, a Flemish fancy to rival that of Calais.

If, however, you are stuck with time on your hands, you could visit a couple of the town's museums to help while away the hours. The **Musée des Beaux-Arts** (daily except Tues 10am–12.15pm & 1.45–6pm; 20F/€3.05, first Sun of the month free), on place du Général-de-Gaulle near the post office, three blocks along rue Poincaré from the tourist office, has a good collection of seventeenth- and eighteenth-century French, Dutch and Flemish paintings, with bits of natural history and a display on the May 1940 evacuation of Allied troops. The Musée d'Art Contemporain is closed indefinitely, but its **sculpture park** (daily: July & Aug 9am–8pm; rest of year 9.30am–5.30pm; free), beside the canal on avenue des Bains, is still open to the public. More interesting, espe-

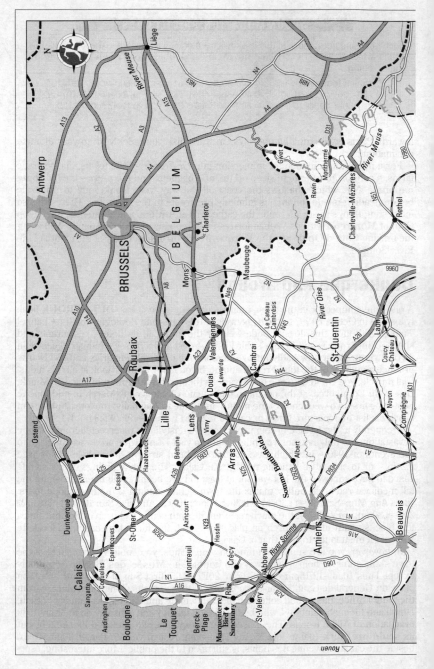

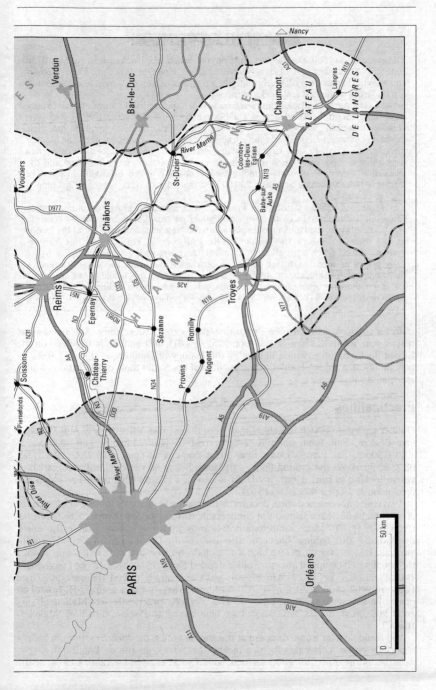

DUNKERQUE 1940

The evacuation of 350,000 Allied troops from the beaches of Dunkerque from May 27 to June 4, 1940, has become a heroic wartime legend. However, this legend conveniently conceals the fact that the Allies, through their own incompetence, almost lost their entire armed forces in the first few weeks of the war.

The German army had taken just ten days to reach the English Channel and could very easily have cut off the Allied armies. Unable to believe the ease with which he had overcome a numerically superior enemy, however, Hitler ordered his generals to halt their lightning advance, giving Allied forces trapped in the Pas-de-Calais enough time to organize Operation Dynamo, the largest wartime evacuation ever undertaken. Initially it was hoped that around 10,000 men would be saved, but thanks to low-lying cloud and the assistance of over 1750 vessels – among them pleasure cruisers, fishing boats and river ferries – 140,000 French and over 200,000 British soldiers were successfully shipped back to England.

In France, the ratio of British to French evacuees caused bitter resentment, since Churchill had promised that the two sides would go *bras dessus, bras dessous* ("arm in arm"). Meanwhile, the British media played up the "remarkable discipline" of the troops as they waited to embark, the "victory" of the RAF over the Luftwaffe and the "disintegration" of the French army all around. In fact, there was widespread indiscipline in the early stages as men fought for places on board; the battle for the skies was evenly matched; and the French fought long and hard to cover the whole operation, some 150,000 of them remaining behind to become prisoners of war. In addition, the Allies lost seven destroyers and 177 fighter planes and were forced to abandon over 60,000 vehicles.

cially for children, is the **Musée Portuaire** (daily except Tues: July & Aug 10am–6pm; rest of year 10am–12.45pm & 1.30–6pm; 25F/€3.81), at 9 quai de la Citadelle on the Bassin du Commerce, which illustrates the history of Dunkerque the port from its beginnings as a fishing hamlet, using models of boats and tools of the various trades associated with the port.

Practicalities

Dunkerque's **gare SNCF** is a short walk from the **tourist office** (July & Aug Mon–Sat 9am–6.30pm, Sun 10am–noon & 2–6pm; rest of year Mon–Fri 9am–12.30pm & 1.30–6.30pm, Sat 9am–6.30pm, Sun 10am–noon & 2–6pm; ☎03.28.66.79.21, fax 03.28.63.38.34) on the ground floor of the town belfry on rue de l'Amiral Ronarc'h. If you're looking to **rent a car**, try DLM Location, 1 rue du Chemin-de-Fer (Mon–Sat 8am–noon & 2–5pm; ☎03.28.66.45.61).

Two cheap **accommodation** options by the station on place de la Gare are *Terminus Nord* (☎03.28.66.54.26; ①) and the comfortable two-star *Le Select* (☎03.28.66.64.47, fax 03.28.66.03.47; ②). More salubrious hotels away from the station include the *Borel*, overlooking the fishing boats of the Bassin du Commerce on rue Hermitte (☎03.28.66.51.80, fax 03.28.59.33.82; ④), a modern three-star with well-set-up rooms; the equally well-equipped but more old-fashioned *Europ*, close by at 13 rue Leughenaer (☎03.28.66.29.07, fax 03.28.63.67.87; ④); and the centrally placed *Welcome*, at 37 rue Poincaré (☎03.28.59.20.70, fax 03.28.21.03.49; ④). There's also a seafront HI **hostel** on place Paul-Asseman, 2km east of the centre, practically at Malo-les-Bains (☎03.28.63.36.34, fax 03.28.63.24.54; take blue bus #3 to Piscine, direction "Malo-les-Bains").

You could do a lot worse than **eat** at the station buffet, the *Richelieu*, though it's not especially cheap. Other possibilities include *La Sirene*, on rue de l'Amiral-Ronarc'h, near the tourist office, for good seafood, with a *menu complet* for 125F/€19.06; or the

Taverne le Tormore, 11 place Charles-Valentin, near the town hall, a brasserie/grill with Flemish dishes. At 6 quai de la Citadelle, *Le Corsaire* has menus from 95F/€14.48, as well as a view over the port and the *Duchess Anne*, a 1901 German ship given to France as part of the war reparations in 1946. For more enjoyable eating options, however, head for Malo-les-Bains (see below).

Malo-les-Bains

MALO-LES-BAINS is a more attractive place to stop off than Dunkerque: it's a surprisingly pleasant nineteenth-century seaside suburb on the east side of town (bus #3 & #9), from whose vast sandy beach the Allied troops embarked in 1940 (see box opposite). Digue des Alliés is the dirtier end of an extensive **beachfront** promenade lined with cafés and restaurants; at the cleaner end, Digue des Mers, the beach can almost seem pleasant when the sun comes out – that is, if you avert your eyes from the industrial inferno to the west. However, the suburb actually reveals its *fin-de-siècle* charm away from the seafront, a few parallel blocks inland along avenue Faidherbe and its continuation avenue Kléber, with the pretty green place Turenne sandwiched in between; around here you'll find some excellent pâtisseries, boulangeries and charcuteries.

   Places to stay include the *Hirondelle*, 48 av Faidherbe (☎03.28.63.17.65, fax 03.28.66.15.43, *www.hotelhirondelle.com*; ③), a modern two-star in a great position; and the unassuming, less expensive *Au Bon Coin*, 49 av Kléber (☎03.28.69.12.63, fax 03.28.69.64.03; ②), whose cosy bar is good for a drink. Both have well-regarded **restaurants** specializing in seafood: menus cost from 65F/€9.91 at the *Hirondelle* and from 90F/€13.72 at the more intimate and relaxed *Au Bon Coin*. Also on avenue Kléber are a few ethnic eateries, including a Vietnamese and a North African restaurant. Two popular beachfront **brasseries**, again specializing in seafood, are *L'Iguane*, 15 Digue des Alliés, a down-to-earth establishment offering generous servings, and the stylish but more expensive *Le Pavois*, at 175 Digue de Mer.

Calais and around

CALAIS is less than 40km from England – the Channel's shortest crossing – and is by far the busiest French passenger port. The port (and its accompanying petrochemical works) dominates the town; in fact, there's not much else here. In the last war the British destroyed it to prevent it being used as a base for a German invasion, but the French still refer to it as "the most English town in France", an influence that began after the battle of Crécy in 1346, when Edward III seized it for use as a beachhead in the Hundred Years War. It remained in English hands until 1558, when its loss caused Mary Tudor famously to say: "When I am dead and opened, you shall find Calais lying in my heart." The association has been maintained by various Brits across the centuries: Lady Emma Hamilton, Lord Nelson's mistress; Oscar Wilde on his uppers; Nottingham lacemakers who set up business in the early nineteenth century; and, nowadays, nine million British travellers per year, plus another million-odd day-trippers.

Arrival, information and accommodation

Don't bother walking into town from the ferry terminal (Calais-Maritime train station): there's a free daytime **bus** service to place d'Armes and the central Calais-Ville train station in Calais-Sud. Buses for the outlying hypermarkets and the **gare TGV** (Calais-Fréthun) leave from in front of Calais-Ville train station. If you're intent on **hitching** to Paris, take a left out of the ferry terminal – the new *autoroute* bypass begins almost

tor at Crécy, Edward III – only to be spared at the last minute by the intervention of Queen Philippa, Edward's wife. For a record of Calais' wartime travails you can consult the fascinating **Musée de la Guerre** (April–Sept daily 10am–6pm; Oct–Nov & Feb–March daily except Tues 11am–5pm; 15F/€2.29), installed in a former German *Blockhaus* in the Parc St-Pierre across the street, with exhibits of uniforms, weapons and models from World War II and a small section devoted to World War I.

Eating and drinking

Calais is full of **eateries**, mostly mediocre, catering for its day-tripper trade – place d'Armes is full of such examples. Rue Royale offers your best bet for eating out, and there are plenty of self-service and fast-food outlets at the beach. **Drinking** establishments are mainly of the Gaelic theme-pub variety and are in abundance on rue Royale and its continuation, rue de la Mer.

Café de Paris, 72 rue Royale. Popular with locals and tourists alike for its cheap fare; *plats du jour* from 49F/€7.47, menu at 65F/€9.91.

Channel, 3 bd de la Résistance, overlooking the yacht basin. Generous menus and stylish decor; the popular 98F/€14.94 menu – the cheapest – is not available on Sun, though a wide range of delicious desserts always is. Closed Sun evening & Tues.

Le Grand Bleu, 8 rue J.-P.-Avron (☎03.21.97.97.98; wise to book). A smart, modern seafood restaurant on the waterfront, with menus from 130F/€19.82.

Histoire Ancienne, 20 rue Royale. Greek-run brasserie with a charming interior, particularly its old bar; the good, mainly French menu includes the occasional Greek dish plus inexpensive, interesting salads that will delight vegetarians. Menus from 63F/€9.60 at lunchtime; otherwise from 99F/€15.09.

Le St-Charles, 47 place d'Armes. By far the best option on the place d'Armes, and consequently often crowded. Menus consist of traditional French and Italian dishes and start from 65F/€9.91. Closed Mon.

Le Troubador, quai du Rhin. Hidden away in a quiet street near the station and tourist office, this bar is a popular hang-out for local music-heads: lots of long hair around the games tables by day and bands by night.

Around Calais

Understandably, most tourists travel non-stop through the **Pas-de-Calais** – France's northernmost *département* – en route to warmer climes and more varied scenery. However, if you're on a short break to one of the Channel ports, it's worth making the effort to venture inland; **Cassel** in particular is a minor gem.

St-Omer

The first stop inland for many visitors to France is **ST-OMER**, a quiet, unassuming and attractive little town. Away from the ports, the landscape becomes more rural and the roads straighter and quieter, while the town itself has flights of Flemish magnificence, especially in the **Hôtel de Ville** and some of the recently restored mansions on rue Gambetta. The Gothic **Basilique Notre-Dame** contains some noteworthy statuary, and there are some handsome exhibits in the eighteenth-century **Hôtel Sandelin** museum on rue Carnot (closed for renovation at the time of writing; due to reopen in 2001 – check with tourist office for details) – in particular, a glorious piece of medieval goldsmithing known as the *Pied de Croix de St-Bertin*.

Aside from visiting the pleasant **public gardens** to the west of town, there's the possibility of exploring the nearby **marais**, a network of Flemish waterways cut between plots of land on reclaimed marshes east of town along the river. You can join a *bâteau-promenade* leaving from the quai du Haut-Pont, north from the *gare SNCF* along the

Canal de l'Aa (June Sat & Sun 3pm & 4pm; July & Aug daily 3pm & 4pm; 42F/€6.40; tickets from the *Café du Haut-Pont* on the *quai*), where you can also rent rowing boats, or from the church in the nearby town of Clairmarais (July & Aug daily 11am & hourly 2–5pm; 38F/€5.79). Round trips on the *bâteaux-promenades* take roughly two hours, and include a commentary on the flora and fauna of the marshes; the longer trip also features a ride down the unique vertical boat-lift at Arques. For further information, including times, visit the tourist office (see below).

To get to the centre of town from the exuberant 1903 **gare SNCF**, cross over the canal and walk ten minutes down rue F.-Ringot, past the post office and into rue Carnot. The **tourist office** is by the **gare routière** on place P.-Painlevé (Easter–Sept Mon–Sat 9am–6pm, Sun 10am–1pm; Sept–Easter Mon–Sat 9am–12.30pm & 2–6pm; ☎03.21.98.08.51, fax 03.21.98.22.82). For **accommodation**, try the pretty old *Hôtel St-Louis* at 25 rue d'Arras (☎03.21.38.35.21, fax 03.21.38.57.26; ②; restaurant from 75F/€11.43); the *Bretagne*, 2 place du Vainquai, near the train station (☎03.21.38.25.78, fax 03.21.93.51.22; ④; restaurant from 90F/€13.72), or the *Vivier*, 22 rue Louis-Martel, on a small pedestrian street near the town hall (☎03.21.95.76.00, fax 03.21.95.42.20; ③; closed beginning of Jan), whose restaurant specializes in fish (menus from 89F/€13.57). The closest **campsite** is near the Forêt de Clairmarais, 4.5km east of St-Omer (☎03.21.38.34.80; April–Oct), although there's no transport out there. For **places to eat** other than the hotels, try the *Auberge du Bachelin*, 12 bd de Strasbourg, on the north side of the town centre (menus from 79F/€12.04), or establishments around place Maréchal-Foch.

The Blockhaus at Eperlecques

In the **Forêt d'Eperlecques**, 12km north of St-Omer (several trains daily from Calais to Watten station, on the eastern edge of the forest, about 4km from the site), you can visit the largest ever **Blockhaus**, or concrete bunker, built in 1943–44 by the Germans – or rather 6000 half-starved slave labourers (March Sun 2.15–6pm; April, Oct & Nov daily 2.15–6pm; May Mon–Sat 10am–noon & 2.15–6pm, Sun 10am–7pm; June & Sept Mon–Sat 10am–noon & 2.15–7pm, Sun 10am–7pm; July & Aug daily 10am–7pm; ☎03.21.88.44.22; 39F/€5.95). It was designed to launch V2 rockets against London, but fortunately the RAF and French Resistance prevented its ever being ready for use by bombing it during construction.

La Coupole

Of all the World War II converted bunker museums **La Coupole** (daily: April–Sept 9am–7pm; Oct–March 10am–6pm; closed first two weeks in Jan; ☎03.21.93.07.07; 55F/€8.38), 5km southwest of St-Omer, is the most modern and stimulating. As you walk around the site of an intended V2 rocket launchpad, you can listen on multilingual infra-red headphones to a discussion of the occupation of northern France by the Nazis, the use of prisoners as slave labour and the technology and ethics of the first liquid-fuelled rocket – advanced through Hitler and taken at the end of the war by the Soviets, the French and the Americans and developed in the space race. Films, models and photographs, all with accompanying text in four different languages help to develop each theme. Getting there by car is easy: it's just off the D928 (A26 junctions 3 & 4), but there are only a few **buses** running from St-Omer train station (ring La Coupole or St-Omer tourist office for times).

Cassel

Twenty-three kilometres east of St-Omer is the tiny hilltop town of **CASSEL**. Hills are rare in Flanders, and consequently Cassel was much fought over from Roman times onwards. Marshal Foch spent "some of the most distressing hours" of his life here during World War I, and it was up to the top of Cassel's hill that the "Grand Old Duke of York" marched his 10,000 men in 1793, though, as hinted in the nursery rhyme, he failed to take the town.

Cassel's train station, 3km west of town, is linked only to Dunkerque, so you really need your own transport to make the trip worthwhile. Once there, however, your efforts will be rewarded with the very Flemish **Grande-Place**, lined with some magnificent mansions, from which narrow cobbled streets fan out. From the **public gardens** you have an unrivalled view over Flanders, with Belgium just 10km away. Here among the trees is Cassel's only remaining wooden **windmill** – there used to be 29 pounding their oil mills day and night – which revolves on its axis every Sunday.

There are two good **places to eat** on the central Grande-Place: *La Taverne Flamande* (closed Tues evening & Wed; from 89F/€13.57), specializing in Flemish cuisine; and the simpler *À l'Hôtel de Ville*, with a filling, tasty menu at 70F/€10.67.

The Côte d'Opale

The **Côte d'Opale** is the stretch of Channel coast between Calais and the mouth of the River Somme, characterized by huge, wild and windswept sandy beaches. In the northern part, as far as Boulogne, the beaches are fringed, as on the English side of the Channel, by white chalk cliffs. Here, between the prominent headlands of **Cap Blanc-Nez** and **Cap Gris-Nez**, the D940 coast road winds high above the sea, allowing you best to appreciate the "opal" in the name – the sea and sky merging in an opalescent, oyster-grey continuum in the prevailing weather conditions. The southern part of the coast is flatter, and the beach, uninterrupted for 40km, is backed by a landscape of pine-anchored dunes and brackish tarns, punctuated every few hundred metres by solid German pillboxes now toppled on their noses by the shifting sand foundations. An organization called Eden 62 publishes ten free leaflets detailing **walks** around the area, which you can get hold of by either writing to them or telephoning (Eden 62, B.P.65–62930 Wimereux; ☎03.21.32.13.74, fax 03.21.87.33.07).

South from Calais: the Channel Tunnel and Wissant

Right on the southern outskirts of Calais, **BLÉRIOT-PLAGE** was thus named to commemorate Louis Blériot's epic first cross-Channel flight in 1909. Six kilometres further along the foreshore of well-conserved dunes, by the dreary village of **SANGATTE**, the Channel Tunnel comes ashore; the actual terminal is 5km to the east outside the village of **COQUELLES**. Thereafter, the D940 winds up onto the grassy windswept heights of **Cap Blanc-Nez**, topped by an obelisk commemorating the Dover Patrol who kept the Channel free from U-boats during World War I. Just off the D940, opposite the turn-off to the Cap Blanc-Nez obelisk, is the **Musée du Transmanche** (April–June & Sept Tues–Sun 10am–6pm; July & Aug daily 10am–6pm; 20F/€3.05), which offers an overall history of Channel Tunnel exploits; the museum is housed in the basement of *Le Thomé du Gamond*, a rather pricey restaurant with panoramic views (open all year round from noon only; menus from 80F/€12.20, plus snacks). From here, 130m above sea level, you can spot the Channel craft plying the water to the north, while to the south you look down on **WISSANT** and its enormous beach between the capes from which Julius Cæsar set sail in 55 BC for a first look at Britain.

Modern Wissant remains a small and quietly attractive place, popular out of season with windsurfers and weekending Britons, and it has some good **places to stay and eat**. First and foremost is the old, red-timbered *Hôtel de la Plage*, 1 place Edouard Houssen (☎03.21.35.91.87, fax 03.21.85.48.10; ③ with buffet breakfast for the modern more expensive rooms; good restaurant from 90F/€13.72), whose rooms are arranged around a wide courtyard. Decent alternatives are the much smaller *Le Vivier*, in the village centre (☎03.21.35.93.61, fax 03.21.82.10.99, *www.levivier.com*; ②; closed mid-Jan to mid-Feb), with a good restaurant offering similar prices; and the clean and modern *Escale*, on the crossroads in neighbouring **ESCALLES** (☎03.21.85.25.00, fax 03.21.35.44.22; ③; restaurant from 75F/€11.43). Wissant also has a municipal **campsite**.

To Cap Gris-Nez and the Blockhaus at Audinghen

The GR du Littoral footpath passes through Wissant and continues up to **Cap Gris-Nez**, just 28km from the English coast. To get to the cape by road, take the turn-off 1km outside **AUDINGHEN**, from where it's a three-kilometre walk, drive or cycle.

Just after the Cap Gris-Nez turn-off beside the D940 is one of the many massive concrete bunkers, or *Blockhäuser* (see also p.219), which stud the length of the Côte d'Opale, and which were part of the German World War II defences known as the Atlantic Wall. Equipped with a gun that could hit the English coast, it has been converted into a rather rough-and-ready **museum** (daily: June–Sept 9am–7pm; rest of year 9am–noon & 2–6pm; closed Dec & Jan; 25F/€3.81), displaying the paraphernalia of war. Burrowing two or three floors below ground level, it has curiosity value rather than any great attractions. The best exhibits are British propaganda material and a poster cautioning troops against the dangers of VD, in which a portly officer, buttons popping with excitement, is propositioned by a German Fräulein ("Komm' mit mi'!").

Audinghen itself is a drab little place. If you're stuck for somewhere to stay, you'd do better to continue south to the charming though faded seaside villages of Audreselles and Ambleteuse.

Wimereux

Just 4km north of Boulogne, **WIMEREUX** is a traditional, *fin-de-siècle* seaside resort. Once favoured by the vacationing miners of the north of France, it still preserves a certain faded charm, only really enlivened in the summer months, when it buzzes to the sound of Dutch, Belgian, English and German voices.

Wimereux is easily reached by local **bus** from Boulogne (line #1 goes via the coast, line #2 via Wimille, the village just inland from Wimereux) or by **train** (to Wimille) about every two hours. The **tourist office** is on quai Alfred-Giard, near the river (April–Sept Mon–Sat 9am–noon & 2–7pm, Sat & Sun 9am–7pm; Oct–March Mon–Sat 9am–noon & 2–6pm, Sun 9am–noon & 2–5pm; ☎03.21.83.27.17, fax 03.21.32.76.91). Opposite is a small **market** on Tuesday and Friday mornings, good for picnic material.

The main street, rue Carnot, has three reasonable **hotels**: the attractive, modernized *Hôtel du Centre* at no. 78 (☎03.21.32.41.08, fax 03.21.33.82.48; ③; restaurant from 99F/€15.09); the simple, old-fashioned *des Arts*, with a popular bar and restaurant, at no. 143 (☎03.21.32.43.13; ①; closed Sun evening); and the *Auberge de Maître Hans* at no. 12 (☎03.21.32.41.04; ②). You can **camp** at *L'Olympic*, on av de la Libération. For a sit-down meal, try *Le Charolais*, 25 rue Napoléon, the narrow road heading for Boulogne (closed Wed evening & Sun); smart but relaxed, it has set menus from 75F/€11. For a real gourmet treat, try the *Atlantic*, on the front at Wimereux (☎03.21.32.41.01; cheapest menu 130F/€19.82, *carte* around 400F/€61), or *La Brocante*, by the church in neighbouring **WIMILLE** (☎03.21.83.19.31; closed Sun evening & Mon; menu from 210F/€32.01, *carte* 400F/€61).

Boulogne

BOULOGNE is quite different from Dunkerque and Calais – recommendation in itself. It has long been an important harbour and claims to be the largest fishing base in Europe. Rising above the port is an attractive medieval quarter, the **ville haute**, contained within the old town walls and dominated by a grand, domed cathedral. Below, amid the newer shopping streets of the *ville basse*, are some of the best charcuteries and pâtisseries in the north, along with an impressive array of fish restaurants. Alone among the northeast Channel ports, this is a place that might actually tempt you to stay.

Arrival, information and accommodation

Ferries dock within a few minutes' walk of the town centre. The **gare SNCF** is a ten-minute walk from the ferry terminal, down boulevard Diderot then left down boulevard Voltaire. If you arrive by **hovercraft**, which docks a little further out, you'll be met by a free shuttle **bus** (☎03.21.30.27.26).

The **tourist office** (July & Aug Mon–Sat 9am–7pm, Sun 10am–12.30pm & 2.30–5pm; Sept–June Mon–Sat 9am–12.30pm & 1.30–6pm, Sun 10am–12.30pm & 2.30–5pm; ☎03.21.31.68.38, fax 03.21.33.81.09) is at Building B, quai Gambetta, across the bridge from the ferry terminal, and can supply a mass of information and advise on availability of rooms – which, in summer, get taken early.

There's plenty of inexpensive **accommodation** in Boulogne to fall back on if you've missed your boat and need somewhere basic to stay; most of the cheap hotels are close to the port area. There are also some upmarket places around the centre, but rates are competitive.

Hotels

des Arts, 102–112 quai Gambetta (☎03.21.31.53.31, fax 03.21.33.69.05). Very reasonable hotel right opposite the port; rooms are clean, light and well set up, and many have a balcony. No lift: be prepared for a long climb. ①.

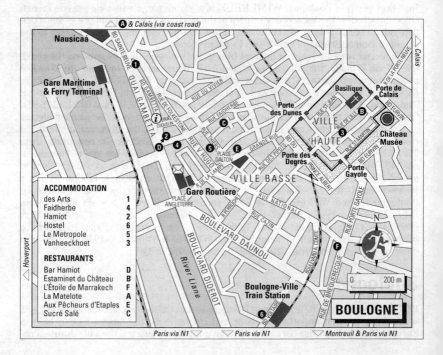

Grande Arche, La Défense, Paris

Pompidou Centre fountains

PETER WILSON

Flower shop, Ile St-Louis, Paris

S. THOMPSON, TRAVEL INK

A. COWIN, TRAVEL INK

Reims cathedral

House nr Mulhouse, Alsace

PETER WILSON

MICHAEL JENNER

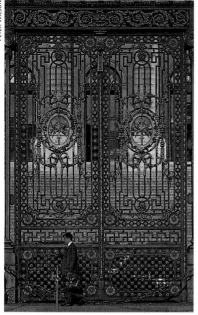

Palais de Justice, Paris

Louvre pyramid, Paris

J. GOODMAN, TRAVEL INK

Monet's garden, Giverny, Normandy

NEIL SETCHFIELD

Strasbourg

CHRIS COE, AXIOM

Scenery near Epernay, Champagne

J. DEGRANGE, GREG EVANS INT'L

Carnac, Brittany

Faidherbe, 12 rue Faidherbe (☎03.21.31.60.93, fax 03.21.87.01.14). Respectable, well-tended and slightly worn central two-star; all rooms have bathroom and TV. ②.

Hamiot, cnr rue Faidherbe & bd Gambetta (☎03.21.31.44.20, fax 03.21.83.71.56). Cheap hotel on the main road above a popular bistro. ①.

Le Metropole, 51 rue Thiers (☎03.21.31.54.30, fax 03.21.30.45.72). A plush three-star with spacious rooms in the midst of a fashionable street; central but not noisy. ④.

Vanheeckhoet Chambres d'Hôte, 24–26 rue de Lille (☎03.21.80.41.50). A pleasant B&B in the centre of the old town. ②.

Hostel and campsite

HI Hostel, place Rouget-de-l'Îsle (☎03.21.80.14.50, fax 03.21.80.45.62), opposite the *gare SNCF* in the middle of a housing estate. Friendly hostel with en-suite double rooms.

Camping municipal at la Capelle-lès-Boulogne, near the Auchan centre on the N42 (☎03.21.83.16.61). Closed mid-Sept to mid-April.

The Town

The quiet cobbled streets of the **ville haute** make a pleasant respite from the noise and congestion of the *ville basse*. Within the walls, the **Basilique Notre-Dame** (closed for 2hr around noon, except during July & Aug) is an odd building – raised in the nine-teenth century by the town's vicar, without any architectural knowledge or advice – yet

---

SHOPPING

You'll find everything in the consumer line – clothes, furniture, sheets, hats, plates – around Grande-Rue, Thiers, Faidherbe and Nationale. For general shopping, head for the Centre Commercial Liane, on the corner of boulevards Diderot and Danou, a down-market shopping mall on two levels – lots of neon, milling teenagers, food stalls, a super-market and a cheap cafeteria. If you want to hit the serious **hypermarkets**, catch bus #20 for the Leclerc or bus #8 for the monstrous Auchan complex, 8km along the N42 towards St-Omer – certainly the most convenient place for large-scale food and wine shopping.

More fastidious foodies should cross the Pont de l'Entente-Cordiale into Grande-Rue. For **charcuterie**, try Bourgeois, on the corner of Grande-Rue and Victor-Hugo; for **chocolates** and other goodies, head for De Marchez, on the corner of Thiers and Faidherbe. Check out the **fish** selection at Aux Pêcheurs d'Étaples, a large poissonnerie on the Grande-Rue, opposite place Dalton. Next door, the Comtesse du Barry specializes in *foie gras* and other gastronomic luxuries, and there's a good selection of **wine** at Les Vins de France on rue Nationale. One other shop that should not be missed is Philippe Olivier's famous **fromagerie**, just around the corner in rue Thiers, which has a selection of over two hundred cheeses – in various states of maturation.

As far as **department stores** go, there's a Nouvelles Galeries on rue Thiers, where you'll also find plenty of fashion boutiques. For Parisian women's clothes, try Cloë, on rue Nationale. A wide selection of **hats** is on sale at Monteil, on the corner of rues Faidherbe and Hugo; and you can choose from over 600 **handbags** at Maroquinerie Florence, on rue Faidherbe between rues Thiers and Victor-Hugo. Roger, at 67 rue Thiers, has a beautiful selection of **shoes**; while Seduction, on rue Nationale, sells exquisite French **lingerie**. At Leclercq, 15 Grande-Rue, you'll find beautiful **homeware**, including glass, cutlery and plates.

The best **bookshop** is Le Furet du Nord, 14 Grande-Rue, with a wide selection of maps and an excellent *papeterie* downstairs. If you're looking to **cycle** or **bike** from Boulogne, Cycles Dufour is a motorbike/cycle shop at 207 rue Nationale; it also sells mountain-bike supplies. From place Lorraine and place Charpentier, rue Faidherbe heads uphill (but downmarket) with lots of **bargain shops**, **hi-fi** and **electronics**. And don't miss the Wednesday and Saturday **markets** on place Dalton.

it seems to work. In the vast and labyrinthine **crypt** (Tues–Sun 2–5pm; 8F/€1.22) you can see frescoed remains of the Romanesque building and relics of a Roman temple to Diana. In the main part of the church sits a bizarre white statue of the Virgin and Child on a boat-chariot, drawn here on its own wheels from Lourdes over the course of six years during a pilgrimage in the 1940s.

Nearby, the **Château Musée** (Mon & Wed–Sat 10am–12.30pm & 2–5pm, Sun 10am–12.30pm & 2.30–5.30pm; 20F/€3.05) has Egyptian funerary objects donated by a local-born Egyptologist and a good collection of Greek pots. Alternatively, you can climb up the most ancient monument in the old town, the twelfth-century **belfry** (Mon–Fri 8am–6pm, Sat 8am–noon; free; access via the Hôtel de Ville), attached to the Hôtel de Ville, at the other end of rue de Lille from the Basilique, or stroll round along the **medieval walls**, decked out with rosebeds, gravel paths and benches for picnicking, with impressive views over the town and port.

Outside the *ville haute* the place to head for is the town's smart new aquarium at the Centre National de la Mer, or **Nausicaá**, on boulevard Sainte-Beuve (daily: July & Aug 9.30am–8pm; rest of year 9.30am–6.30pm; closed 3 weeks in Jan; 68F/€10.37). Ultraviolet lighting and New Age music create a suitably weird ambience, while hammerhead sharks circle overhead and giant conger eels conceal themselves in rusty pipes – definitely not for piscophobes. There's plenty of educational stuff, too (in French and English throughout), and a half-hour film show, though only a passing nod towards environmental issues.

Three kilometres north of Boulogne on the N1 stands the **Colonne de la Grande Armée**, where, in 1803, Napoléon is said to have changed his mind about invading Britain and turned his troops east towards Austria. The column was originally topped by a bronze figure of Napoléon symbolically clad in Roman garb – though his head, equally symbolically, was shot off by the British navy during World War II. It is now displayed in the Château Musée (see above).

Eating and drinking

As you might expect from a large fishing port, Boulogne is a good spot to **eat** fresh fish and seafood. There are dozens of possibilities for eating around place Dalton and the *ville haute*, but bear in mind the day-tripper trade and be selective. If you're after a **drink**, there is a concentration of bars in place Godefroy de Bouillon, opposite the Hôtel de Ville, and several lively bars in place Dalton, with *Au Bureau* and the *Welsh Pub* being most popular.

Bar Hamiot, 1 rue Faidherbe. This brasserie remains as popular as ever with locals and tourists alike, offering a large range of dishes from 38F/€5.79 omelettes and 55–90F/€8.38–13.72 fish dishes to 82F/€12.50 and 110F/€16.77 menus.

Christope et Laurence, 10 rue Coquelin (☎03.21.31.45.64). Friendly service in a small, popular restaurant. Good home-cooking on menus from 75F/€11.43 to 140F/€21.34.

Estaminet du Château, 2 rue du Château, off rue de Lille by the *basilique* (☎03.21.91.49.66). Serving simple food in a prettily decorated old stone building opposite Notre-Dame in the *ville haute*, this restaurant has an excellent menu from 60F/€9.15 and inexpensive à la carte dishes (quarter roast chicken 30F/€4.57). Closed Thurs.

L'Étoile de Marrakech, 228 rue Nationale. A friendly Moroccan restaurant where the chef comes out to shake your hand; olives, bread and spicy sausage come as complimentary starters, and the servings of couscous (from 69F/€10.52) are incredibly generous. Closed Wed.

La Matelote, 80 bd Ste-Beuve (☎03.21.30.17.97). Very smart restaurant, located opposite Nausicaá, featuring a *dégustation* menu at 390F/€59.46. If you'd rather not spend that much, you could go for the 190F/€28.97 menu or à la carte fish from 120F/€18.29. Loving care is taken over the food and service, but it's rather snooty. Closed Sun evening.

Aux Pêcheurs d'Etaples, 31 Grande Rue. The freshest fish and seafood in a smart restaurant hidden behind the poissonnerie front. Menus at 80F/€12.20 upwards.

Sucré Salé, 13 rue Monsigny. Smart, modern eatery combining the roles of restaurant, café, bar, *salon de thé* and pâtisserie; its speciality is gourmet salads, making it a good choice for vegetarians. Light, airy and sparse, with a wonderful range of teas and coffees. Mon–Sat 8am–8pm, Sun take-away only.

South to Amiens

South of Boulogne the coast is even wilder and more magnificent, but without your own transport it's hard to get down to the beach: a band of unstable dunes forces the D940 coast road and the Calais–Paris railway to keep 3 or 4km inland. With the exception of **Étaples**, the seaside towns are artificial resorts of twentieth-century creation – only of interest in that they provide access to the beach. The beach, however, really is worth getting to, and its eerie beauty is best experienced by walking the coastal GR path or any one of the several marked paths which the local tourist offices promote, or by visiting the **Marquenterre** bird sanctuary. For car-drivers, a lane at Dannes leads directly into the dunes.

The quickest route south is the **A16**, recently extended from Boulogne to **Abbeville** and providing non-stop motorway all the way to Paris. More interesting, if you have time and want to take in the battlefield of **Agincourt**, would be a winding cross-country route exploring some of the English-looking side valleys on the north side of the River Canche – such as the Crequoise, Planquette and Ternoise – whose farms and hamlets have been largely bypassed by the onward march of French modernity.

Le Touquet and Étaples

Situated among dunes and wind-flattened tamarisks and pines, **LE TOUQUET** is a kind of French Hollywood on the sea, with ambitious villas freed from the discipline of architectural fashion hidden away behind its trees. Now dully suburban, the town was the height of fashion in the 1920s and 1930s and for a spell after World War II, ranking alongside places on the Côte d'Azur. At one time flights arrived from Britain every ten minutes, but the opening up of long-distance air travel put an end to this era. Nowadays, air traffic consists of private aircraft, most of which are piloted by Brits benefiting from the short hop over the Channel.

To get to Le Touquet, take the **train** from Boulogne to Étaples, from where a local bus covers the last 4km; alternatively, you can take one of the four daily **buses** (Mon–Sat only) directly from Boulogne (☎03.21.31.77.48 for times) from outside the ANPE office on boulevard Daunou; the bus heads on down the coast to Berck. Le Touquet's **tourist office** is in the Palais de l'Europe on place de l'Hermitage (Mon–Sat 9am–7pm, Sun 10am–7pm; ☎03.21.06.72.00, fax 03.21.06.72.01, *www.letouquet.com*) and can furnish you with a free map of the town.

If you're looking for somewhere reasonable to **stay** the night, try the hostel *Riva Bella*, 12 rue Léon Garet (☎03.21.05.08.22), or the *Armide*, 56 rue Léon-Garet (☎03.21.05.21.76, fax 03.21.05.99.77; half-board ③). There's also a **campsite**, on the waterfront of the Canche estuary, but this requires three-nights' minimum stay. If you fancy splashing out, you have the choice of several luxurious hotels: *Le Manoir* on avenue du Golf (☎03.21.06.28.28, fax 03.21.06.28.29, *www.open-golf-club.com*; ⑨) is the most palatial; others include *Le Westminster*, 5 av du Verger (☎03.21.05.48.48, fax 03.21.05.45.45, *www.westminster.fr*; ⑧), and *Le Bristol*, 17 rue Jean-Monnet (☎03.21.05.49.95, fax 03.21.05.90.93, *hotelsletouquet.com*; ⑥). Places to **eat** are also generally expensive in Le Touquet. For a treat, visit *Le Café des Arts*, 80 rue de Paris (☎03.21.05.21.55; closed Mon; menus from 200F/€30.49), or *Auberge de la Dune aux Loups*, on the avenue of the same name (☎03.21.05.42.54; closed Tues & Wed; menus

100F/€15.24 & 165F/€25.15), where you can eat their speciality fish on the terrace. More affordable than these is *Les Sports*, 22 rue St-Jean, a classic brasserie with a menu at 75F/€11.43.

A more affordable treat worth indulging in – especially if you've got kids – is Le Touquet's Aqualud **swimming complex** right on the front (65F/€9.91 upwards), which boasts three giant water slides; there's also the vast Bagatelle **amusement park**, 10km south of Le Touquet, on the D940 (April to mid-Sept daily 10am–7pm; 102F/€15.55).

On the other side of the River Canche is the much more workaday **ÉTAPLES**, a picturesque fishing port whose charm lies in its unassuming air. Between April and September daily **boat trips** departing from the port can be booked via the **tourist office** (Mon–Fri 9am–noon & 2–6pm, Sat 10am–noon & 3–6pm; ☎03.21.09.56.94, fax 03.21.09.76.96), at le Clos St-Victor, bd Bigot Descelers; you can choose between a fifty-minute sea jaunt (42F/€6.40) or a more rigorous twelve-hour fishing stint with experienced fishermen (300F/€45.73). Étaples also boasts a good seafood **restaurant**, the *Pêcheurs d'Étaples*, on quai de la Canche (☎03.21.94.06.90; from 80F/€12.20).

Montreuil-sur-Mer

Once a port, **MONTREUIL-SUR-MER** is now stranded 13km inland from the sea, due to the silting up of the River Canche. Perched on a sharp little hilltop above the River Canche and surrounded by its ancient walls, it's an immediately appealing place. Laurence Sterne spent a night here on his *Sentimental Journey*, and it was the scene of much of the action in Victor Hugo's *Les Misérables*, perhaps best evoked by the steep cobbled street of pavée St-Firmin, first left after the Porte de Boulogne, a short climb from the *gare SNCF*.

Two heavily damaged Gothic churches grace the main square: the **church of St-Saulve** and a tiny wood-panelled **chapelle** tucked into the side of the red-brick Hôtel-Dieu. To the south there are numerous cobbled lanes to wander down, all lined with half-timbered artisan houses. In the northwestern corner of the walls lies Vauban's **Citadelle** (Feb–Nov daily 10am–noon & 2–6pm; 15F/€2.29) – ruined, overgrown and, after dark, pretty atmospheric, with subterranean gun emplacements and a fourteenth-century tower that records the coats of arms of the French noblemen killed at Agincourt. A path following the top of the walls provides views out across the Canche estuary.

The **tourist office** is by the citadel at 21 rue Carnot (April–Sept Mon–Sat 9.30am–12.30pm & 2–6pm, Sun 10am–12.30pm & 2.30–5pm; Oct–March Mon–Sat 9.30am–12.30pm & 2–5.30pm, Sun 10am–12.30pm; ☎03.21.06.04.27, fax 03.21.06.57.85). For **accommodation**, there's the classy and expensive *Château de Montreuil* (☎03.21.81.53.04, fax 03.21.81.36.43, *www.relaischateaux.fr/montreuil*; ⑨; closed mid-Dec to Jan), which overlooks the citadel and is much loved by the English. It also contains a top-class restaurant (closed Thurs lunch & Mon out of season), whose lunchtime menu is good value at 270F/€41.16 with wine. For delightful **food** and accommodation at more manageable prices, there's no beating *Le Darnétal*, in place Darnétal (☎03.21.06.04.87, fax 03.21.86.64.67; ③; closed Mon evening, Tues & first two weeks in July; restaurant from 100F/€15.24). Another good bet is the *Clos des Capucins* on the wide place de Gaulle, the shopping centre of the town (☎03.21.06.08.65, fax 03.21.81.20.45; ③; menu from 98F/€14.94). There's also an **HI hostel** (☎03.21.06.10.83; closed Nov–Feb), housed in one of the citadel's outbuildings and giving access to the place long after the gates have been closed to the public. The municipal **campsite** (☎03.21.06.07.28) is by the River Canche, below the walls.

In the second half of August, Montreuil puts on a surprisingly lively mini-arts **festival** of opera, theatre and dance, *Les Malins Plaisirs*.

The Agincourt and Crécy battlefields

Agincourt and Crécy, two of the bloodiest Anglo-French battles of the Middle Ages, took place near the attractive little town of **HESDIN** on the River Canche (a town that will be familiar to Simenon fans from the TV series *Inspector Maigret*). Getting to either site is really only feasible with your own transport.

Twenty kilometres southwest of Hesdin, at the **Battle of Crécy**, Edward III inflicted the first of his many defeats of the French in 1346, thus beginning the Hundred Years War. This was the first appearance on the continent of the new English weapon – the six-foot longbow – and the first use in European history of gunpowder. There's not a lot to see today: just the **Moulin Édouard III** (now a watchtower), 1km northeast of the little town of Crécy-en-Ponthieu on the D111 to Wadicourt, site of the windmill from which Edward watched the hurly-burly of battle. Further south, on the D56 to Fontaine, the battered **croix de Bohème** marks the place where King John of Bohemia died, having insisted on leading his men into the fight, in spite of his blindness.

Ten thousand more died in the heaviest defeat ever of France's feudal knighthood at the **Battle of Agincourt** on October 25, 1415. Forced by muddy conditions to fight on foot in their heavy armour, the French, though three times as strong in number, were sitting ducks to the lighter, mobile English archers. The rout took place near present-day **AZINCOURT**, about 12km northeast of Hesdin off the D928, and a **museum** in the village (daily: April–Oct 9am–6pm; Nov–March 10am–5pm; 10F/€1.52) includes a short film about the battle; on the battle site itself noticeboards are placed at strategic points to indicate the sequence of fighting. Just east of the village, by the crossroads of the D104 and the road to Maisoncelle, a **cross** marks the position of the original grave pits.

The Marquenterre bird sanctuary

Even if you know nothing of birds, the **Parc ornithologique du Marquenterre** (April–Sept daily 9.30am–7pm; Oct daily 10am–6pm; Nov–March Sat & Sun guided visits only; ☎03.22.25.03.06, *www.marcanterra.fr*; 60F/€9.15), situated off the D940 between the estuaries of the River Canche and the River Somme, 30km south of Éta-ples, will be a revelation. In terms of landscape, it is beautiful and strange: all dunes, tamarisks and pine forest, full of salty meres and ponds thick with water plants. This is "new" land, formed by the erosion of the Normandy coast and the silting of the Somme estuary, where thousands of cattle are grazed today to give their meat the much-prized flavour of the "salt meadows".

One of only two bird sanctuaries in the whole of France, Marquenterre is a tiny reserve in an area that gives new meaning to the word "sanctuary". From the opening of the waterfowl season – July 14, Bastille Day, ironically – gunshots can be heard, day and night, all around. No species, however rare, is spared.

You'll need to rent binoculars unless you carry your own, and there's no point in trying to manage without. Once inside, there's a choice of two itineraries – a longer, more interesting one (2hr 30min–3hr) and a shorter one (roughly 1hr 30min) aimed at children – as well as several themed **guided tours** (40F/€6.10), which last three hours. The routes take you from resting area to resting area whence you can train your glasses on dozens of species – ducks, geese, oyster-catchers, terns, egrets, redshanks, greenshanks, spoonbills, herons, storks, godwits – some of them fat-cat residents, most taking a breather from their epic migratory flights to and from the ends of the earth. In April and May they head north, and they return from the end of August to October, so these are the best times to visit.

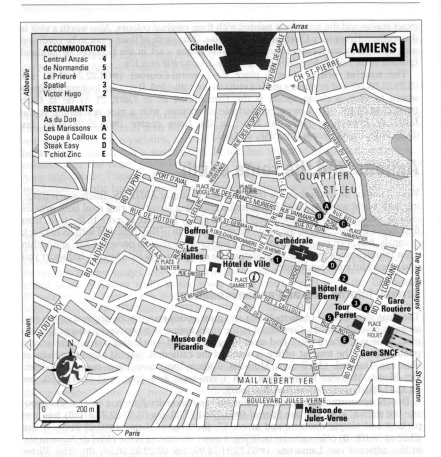

should adorn the sculptures again. An evening multicolour **light show** (daily June–Sept & Dec 15–Jan 6; free) gives a vivid idea of how the west front would have looked when coloured. By way of contrast, the interior is all vertical lines and no fuss: a light, calm and unaffected space. Ruskin thought the apse "not only the best, but the very first thing done perfectly in its manner by northern Christendom". The later embellishments, like the sixteenth-century choir stalls, are works of breathtaking virtuosity. The same goes for the sculpted panels depicting the life of St Firmin, Amiens' first bishop, on the right side of the choir screen. The figures in the crowd scenes are shown in fifteenth-century costume, the men talking serious business, while their wives listen more credulously to the preacher's words. One of the most atmospheric ways of seeing the cathedral is to attend a Sunday morning mass (10.15am), when you will be uplifted by sublime Gregorian chanting.

Just north of the cathedral is the **quartier St-Leu**, a very Flemish-looking network of canals and cottages that was once the centre of Amiens' thriving textile industry. The town still produces much of the country's velvet, but the factories moved out to the suburbs long ago, leaving St-Leu to rot away in peace – until, that is, the local property developers moved in. The slums have been tastefully transformed into neat brick cottages on cobbled streets, and the waterfront has been colonized by restaurants and clubs.

On the edge of town, the canals still provide a useful function as waterways for the **hortillonnages** – a series of incredibly fertile market gardens, reclaimed from the marshes created by the very slow-flowing Somme. Farmers travel about them in black, high-prowed punts and a few still take their produce into the city by boat for the Saturday morning **market**, the *marché sur l'eau*, on the river bank of place Parmentier. If you want to look around the *hortillonnages*, turn right as you come out of the station and continue straight ahead for about five minutes until you reach the river and the *chemin de halage*, or towpath, which you can wander down. A map here shows pedestrian routes and viewpoints. If you walk further up boulevard de Beauvillé to no. 54, you will find the Association des Hortillonnages and the embarkation point for their inexpensive, thirty-minute **boat trips** (April–Oct daily 2–6pm; regular departures, normally depending on a minimum of 12 people; 30F/€4.57), which make for a relaxing glimpse of the market gardens and their way of life.

If you're interested in Picardy culture, you might take a look at Amiens' two regional museums. Five minutes' walk south of central place Gambetta, a nineteenth-century mansion houses the **Musée de Picardie** (Tues–Sun 10am–12.30pm & 2–6pm; 20F/€3.05), whose star exhibits are the Puvis de Chavannes paintings on the main stairwell and a collection of rare sixteenth-century paintings on wood donated to the cathedral by a local literary society, some of the pictures still in their original frames carved by the same craftsmen who worked the choir stalls. Close by the cathedral, in the seventeenth-century **Hôtel de Berny** (May–Sept Thurs–Sun 2–6pm; Oct–April Sun 10am–12.30pm & 2–6pm; 10F/€1.52), is an annexe to the main museum, with *objets d'art* and local-history collections, including a portrait of Choderlos de Laclos, author of *Les Liaisons Dangereuses*, who was born in Amiens. A third museum or documentation centre, at 2 rue Dubois, was the **house of Jules Verne**, who spent most of his life in Amiens and died here (Mon–Fri 9am–noon & 2–6pm, Sat 2–6pm; 15F/€2.29).

Just to the west of the city, at Tirancourt off the N1 to Abbeville, a large museum/park, **Samara**, recreates the life of prehistoric man in northern Europe with reconstructions of dwellings and displays illustrating the way of life, trades and so on (mid-March to mid-Nov daily 9.30am–6pm; *www.samara.fr*; 59F/€8.99).

Eating, drinking and entertainment

There are plenty of cheap brasseries and **restaurants** around the station, but by far the most attractive area to look is **St-Leu**, both for appearance and general ambience. Two favourite places are in the pretty, cobbled place du Don directly below the cathedral, with room to sit outside in good weather. The *Soupe à Cailloux* serves delicious family cuisine, including regional dishes, for a reasonable price (weekday lunch menu at 72F/€10.98, other times from 90F/€13.72; closed Mon in winter), and is consequently very popular. The equally attractive *As du Don*, across the square, does a *formule* for 109F/€16.62, while just over the canal is Amiens' best gourmet restaurant, *Les Marissons* (☎03.22.92.96.66; closed Sat lunch & Sun; menus from 200F/€30.49, *carte* from 300F/€45.73). There are also several **bars** and pubs in the area.

For eating **in town**, one of the nicest places to go is the handsome *T'chiot Zinc* (closed Mon lunch & Sun; menu at 69F/€10.52, *plats* for 49F/€7.47), at 18 rue Noyon opposite the station, which serves traditional country fare. A total contrast is the hip Tex-Mex *Steak-Easy*, with an aeroplane hanging from the ceiling, at 18 rue Metz-l'Évêque (guacamole, spare ribs and other un-Gallic fare; around 90F/€14 for a meal).

For one week in May Amiens bursts into life for its annual international **jazz festival**; on the third weekend in June, the local costumes come out for the **Fête d'Amiens**; and in November there's a **cinema festival**. Traditional Picardy **marionettes** give performances (July & Aug Tues–Sun; rest of year Wed & Sun) at the Théâtre de Chés Cabotans d'Amiens, 31 rue Edouard David: call Théâtre d'Animation Picard (☎03.22.22.30.90) for reservations – tickets are around 55F/€8.38. To purchase or take a look at hand-made marionettes, you should visit the workshop of Jean-Pierre Facquier at 67 rue du Don.

Beauvais

As you head south from Amiens towards Paris, the countryside becomes broad and flat – agricultural, though not rustic. **BEAUVAIS**, 60km south of Amiens, seems to fit into this landscape. Rebuilt, like Amiens, after the last world war, it's a drab, neutral place redeemed only by its radiating Gothic cathedral, the **Cathédrale St-Pierre**, which rises above the town, its roof, unadorned by tower or spire, seeming squat for all its height. It is a building that perhaps more than any other in northern France demonstrates the religious materialism of the Middle Ages – its main intention to be taller and larger than its rivals. The choir, completed in 1272, was once 5m higher than that of Amiens, though only briefly, as it collapsed in 1284. Its replacement, only completed three centuries later, was raised by the sale of indulgences – a right granted to the local bishops by Pope Leo X. This, too, fell within a few years, and, the authorities having overreached themselves financially, the church remained unfinished, forlorn and mutilated. The appeal of the building, and its real beauty, lies in its glass, its sculpted doorways and the remnants of the so-called Basse-Oeuvre, a ninth-century Carolingian church incorporated into the structure. It also contains a couple of remarkable clocks, including one 12m high that features the Archangel Michael helping to weigh souls at the Last Judgement.

Stopping at Beauvais to break your journey, you'll probably want to give the rest of the town no more than a passing look. However, the **church of St-Étienne**, a few blocks to the south of the cathedral on rue de Malherbe, houses yet more spectacular Renaissance stained-glass windows. There's also the **Galerie Nationale de Tapisserie** behind the cathedral (Tues–Sun 9.30–11.30am & 2–6pm; 25F/€3.81), a museum of the tapestry for which Beauvais was once renowned, and the **Musée Départemental** (daily except Tues 10am–noon & 2–6pm; 10F/€1.52), devoted to painting, local history and archeology, in the sharp, black-towered building opposite. The rousing **statue** in the central square is of local heroine Jeanne Hachette, a fighter and inspiration in the defence of the town in 1472 against Charles the Bold, Duke of Burgundy.

Beauvais is an hour by train from Paris, and the **gare SNCF** is a short walk from the centre of town – take avenue de la République, then turn right up rue de Malherbe. Opposite the Galerie Nationale de la Tapisserie, at 1 rue Beauregard, the **tourist office** (Mon 10am–1pm & 2–6pm, Tues–Sat 9.30am–7pm, Sun 10am–5pm; ☎03.44.15.30.30, fax 03.44.15.30.31) can provide exhaustive information. If you want to **stay**, three inexpensive choices are the *Hôtel du Commerce*, 11 rue Chambiges (☎03.44.15.34.34, fax 03.44.15.34.33; ①), *Le Brazza*, 22 rue de la Madeleine (☎03.44.45.03.86; ③), between the station and the centre of town, and *Hôtel du Palais*, within sight of the cathedral, 9 rue St-Nicolas (☎03.44.45.12.58, fax 03.44.45.66.23; ①). There's a *camping municipal* (☎03.44.02.00.22; closed mid-Sept to mid-May) just out of town on the Paris road.

For fine **food** on the square, call in at *Le Marignan*, 1 rue de Malherbe (☎03.44.48.15.15), which has menus from 65F/€9.91 in the brasserie downstairs, and from 99F/€15.09 in the very good restaurant upstairs.

THE INDUSTRIAL NORTH AND THE BATTLEFIELDS

Picardy, Artois and Flanders are littered with the monuments, battlefields and cemeteries of the two world wars, but nowhere as intensely as the region northeast of Amiens, between **Albert** and **Arras**. It was here, among the fields and villages of the Somme, that the main battle lines of World War I were drawn. They can be visited most spectacularly at **Vimy Ridge**, just off the A26 north of Arras, where the trenches have been left *in situ*. Lesser sites, often more poignant, are dotted over the countryside around Albert and along the **Circuit de Souvenir**.

A more enduring and more domestic presence in the life of northern France has been that of the **coalfields** and all their related heavy industrial works. At their peak of production they formed a continuous stretch from Béthune in the west to Valenciennes in the east, though the industry is now in terminal decline. At **Lewarde** you can visit one of the pits, while at the big industrial city of **Lille**, or the pleasant town of **Douai**, you can see what the masters did with takings from the muck.

Lille

LILLE, by far the largest city in the north, is the very symbol of French industry and working-class politics. Its mayor, Pierre Mauroy, was the first Socialist prime minister appointed by Mitterrand in 1981. In every direction the city spreads far into the countryside, a mass of suburbs and heavy industrial plants. Lille exhibits most of the problems of contemporary France: some of the worst poverty and racial conflict in the country, a crime rate rivalled only by Paris and Marseille, and a certain regionalism – *Lillois* sprinkle their speech with a French-Flemish patois and to some extent assert a Flemish identity. But there is also classic French affluence. The city has a lovely centre, Vieux Lille, some vibrant and obviously prosperous commercial areas, modern residential squares, a large university, a brand-new métro system, and a very serious attitude to its culture and restaurants. Although you may not consider Lille a prime destination, if you're travelling through this region it's worth at least a day and a night.

Arrival, information and accommodation

The central Grande-Place is just a few minutes' walk from the **gare SNCF** (originally Paris's Gare du Nord, but brought here brick by brick in 1865). Despite being the fifth-largest city in France, the centre of Lille is small enough to walk round and, unless you choose to visit Villeneuve-d'Ascq on the outskirts, you won't even need to use the city's efficient métro system.

The **tourist office** is in place Rihour (Mon–Sat 9.30am–6.30pm, Sun & public hols 10am–noon & 2–5pm; ☎03.20.21.94.21, fax 03.20.21.94.20), ten minutes' walk from the station along rue Faidherbe and through place du Théâtre and place du Général-de-Gaulle. You should have few problems finding a cheap place to **stay** if you don't mind the slightly seedy station area.

Hotels

Brueghel, 3–5 parvis St-Maurice (☎03.20.06.06.69, fax 03.20.63.25.27). Very attractive two-star hotel with individually styled rooms furnished with antiques, and with charming, understated service. ③.
Carlton, 3 rue de Paris (☎03.20.13.33.13, fax 03.20.51.48.17, *www.carltonlille.fr*). Posh four-star with all the frills, right down to a red carpet outside. ⑨.

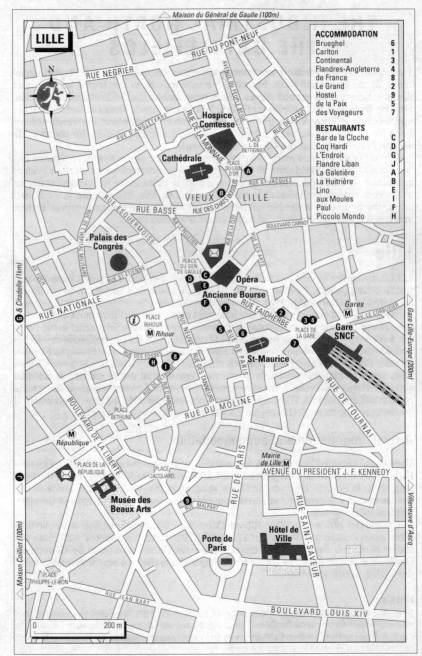

△ Maison du Général de Gaulle (100m)

LILLE

N

RUE DU PONT-NEUF

RUE NEGRIER

RUE D'ANGLETERRE

AVENUE DU PEUPLE BELGE

RUE DE GAND

Hospice Comtesse

PLACE L. DE BETTIGNIES

Cathédrale

PLACE DU LION D'OR

RUE DE LA MONNAIE

Ⓐ

RUE ST-JACQUES

VIEUX Ⓑ **LILLE**

RUE ESQUERMOISE

RUE BASSE

RUE DES CHATS BOSSUS

RUE DE LA CLEF

BOULEVARD CARNOT

RUE DE L'HOPITAL MILITAIRE

Palais des Congrès

RUE LE PELLETIER

RUE DES ARTS

AV. FOCH

RUE ST-ETIENNE

PLACE DU GEN DE GAULLE

Ⓓ Ⓒ **Opéra**

Ⓔ

Ancienne Bourse

Ⓕ

RUE NATIONALE

ⓘ PLACE RIHOUR

Ⓜ *Rihour*

❶ RUE FAIDHERBE

❷

Gares
Ⓜ
AV. LE CORBUSIER

❸❹

RUE NEUVE

❺ ❻

Gare SNCF

RUE DES FOSSES

❼

Ⓗ Ⓘ ❽

RUE DE BÉTHUNE

RUE DES TANNEURS

RUE DE PARIS

St-Maurice

RUE D'AMIENS

RUE DU MOLINET

PLACE BÉTHUNE

Ⓜ *République*

BOULEVARD DE LA LIBERTÉ

PLACE DE LA RÉPUBLIQUE

PLACE JACQUARD

RUE DE TOURNAI

Mairie de Lille Ⓜ

AVENUE DU PRESIDENT J. F. KENNEDY

Musée des Beaux Arts

Ⓙ

RUE DE PARIS

❾ RUE MALPART

RUE SAINT-SAUVEUR

Hôtel de Ville

Porte de Paris

PLACE PHILIPPE-LE-BON

RUE JEAN BART

BOULEVARD LOUIS XIV

0   200 m

◁ G & Citadelle (1km)

◁ Maison Coilliot (100m)

▷ Gare Lille-Europe (200m)

▷ Villeneuve d'Ascq

ACCOMMODATION

Brueghel	6
Carlton	1
Continental	3
Flandres-Angleterre	4
de France	8
Le Grand	2
Hostel	9
de la Paix	5
des Voyageurs	7

RESTAURANTS

Bar de la Cloche	C
Coq Hardi	D
L'Endroit	G
Flandre Liban	J
La Galetière	A
La Huitrière	B
Lino	E
aux Moules	I
Paul	F
Piccolo Mondo	H

Continental, 11 place de la Gare (☎03.20.06.22.24, fax 03.20.51.85.57). More upmarket version of *des Voyageurs*, complete with satellite TV. ②.

Flandres-Angleterre, 13 place de la Gare (☎03.20.06.04.12, fax 03.20.06.37.76). Much the classiest of the hotels near the train station: all rooms with bath or shower and toilet. ③.

de France, 10 rue de Béthune (☎03.20.57.14.78, fax 03.20.57.06.01). In a fantastic location right in the centre of the pedestrianized area, the *France* has big, clean, comfortable rooms, some with balcony. ①.

le Grand, 51 rue Faidherbe (☎03.20.06.31.57, fax 03.20.06.24.44). Comfortable two-star, all rooms with shower, toilet and TV. ③.

de la Paix, 46bis rue de Paris (☎03.20.54.63.93, fax 03.20.63.98.97). Classy two-star in a great position, with leather lounges and a gleaming wooden staircase. All rooms come with shower, toilet and TV. ④.

des Voyageurs, 10 place de la Gare (☎03.20.06.43.14, fax 03.20.74.19.01). A slip of a building directly opposite the station, with basic, cheap rooms – worth it just for the wrought-iron lift. ①.

Hostel and campsite

Hostel, 12 rue Malpart, off rue de Paris (☎03.20.57.08.94, fax 03.20.63.98.93). Recently renovated hostel in a fairly central situation. Dinner and breakfast are served if requested, but kitchen facilities are also available.

Camping Les Ramiers, Bondues (☎ & fax 03.20.23.13.42). Lille's nearest site is located in the village of Bondues, about 10km north of the city and is linked by bus. Closed Nov–April.

The City

The focal point of the city is the **Grande-Place** (otherwise known as place du Général-de-Gaulle), which marks the southern boundary of the old quarter, **Vieux Lille**. To the south is the central pedestrianized shopping area which extends along rue de Béthune as far as the adjacent squares of place Béthune and place de la République. On Saturdays, especially, the area is so jammed with shoppers that you can hardly move, and crowded outdoor cafés add to the street life. The major **festival** of the year, the Grande Braderie, takes place over the first weekend of September, when a big street parade and vast flea market fill the streets of the old town by day, and the evenings see a *moules frites* frenzy in all the restaurants, with empty mussel shells piled up in the streets.

Vieux Lille

The east side of the Grande-Place is dominated by the old exchange building, the lavishly ornate **Ancienne Bourse**, as perfect a representative of its age as could be imagined. To the merchants of seventeenth-century Lille, all things Flemish were the epitome of wealth and taste; they were not men to stint on detail, neither here nor on the imposing surrounding mansions. Recently cleaned up, the courtyard of the Bourse is now an organized flea market, with stalls selling books and flowers. Lounging around the fountain at the centre of the square is a favourite *Lillois* pastime. In the middle of the fountain is a **column** commemorating the city's resistance to the Austrian siege of 1792, topped by *La Déesse* (the goddess), modelled on the wife of the mayor at the time.

In the adjacent square of **place du Théâtre**, you can see how Flemish Renaissance architecture became assimilated and Frenchified in grand flights of Baroque extravagance. The superlative example of this style is the **Opéra**, whose facade sports sculptures symbolizing music and tragedy, with Apollo among the muses. It was built at the turn of the twentieth century by Louis Cordonnier, who also designed the extravagant **belfry** of the neighbouring Nouvelle Bourse and Chamber of Commerce, now the city's main post office.

From the north side of these two squares, the smart shopping streets, rues Esquermoise and Lepelletier, lead towards the heart of old Lille, a warren of red-brick terraces on cobbled lanes and passages. It is an area of great character and charm, successfully reclaimed and reintegrated into the mainstream of the city's life, having been for years a dilapidated North African ghetto. To experience the atmosphere of Vieux Lille, head up towards rue d'Angleterre, rue du Pont-Neuf and the Porte de Gand, rue de la Monnaie and place Lion-d'Or. Places to eat and drink are everywhere.

There are no particular sights apart from the **Hospice Comtesse** on rue de la Monnaie: twelfth-century in origin – though much reconstructed in the eighteenth century – it served as a hospital until as recently as 1945. Its old ward, the **Salle des Malades**, and the chapel can be visited (Mon 2–6pm, Wed–Sun 10am–6pm, Fri till 7pm; 15F/€2.29).

Charles de Gaulle was born in this part of the town, at 9 rue Princesse, in 1890. His house is now a **museum** (Wed–Sun 10am–noon & 2–5pm; 15F/€2.29); among the exhibits is the bullet-riddled Citroën in which he was driving when the OAS attempted to assassinate him in 1962. Another must for military buffs is the nearby **Citadelle** that overlooks the old town to the northwest, constructed in familiar star-shaped fashion by Vauban in the seventeenth century. Still in military hands, it too can be visited, though only on Sundays from May to October and by guided tour (45F/€6.86; tours depart from the citadel's Porte Royale at 3pm).

Amid all the city's secular pomp, Lille's ecclesiastical architecture used to seem rather subdued. However, the façade of the cathedral, **Notre-Dame-de-la-Treille**, just off rue de la Monnaie, breaks this mould. The body of the cathedral is a fairly homogeneous neo-Gothic construction that was begun in 1854, but the new façade, finished just in time for the millennium celebrations in December 1999, is completely different: a translucent marble front supported by steel wires, which is best appreciated at night when lit up from within. More traditional, but also impressive, is the **church of St-Maurice**, close to the station off place de la Gare, a classic red-brick Flemish Hallekerke, with the characteristic five aisles of the style.

South of the Grande-Place

Just south of the Grande-Place is **place Rihour**, a largely modern square with an old palace that now houses the tourist office, hidden behind an ugly war monument of gigantic proportions. Close by, the busiest shopping street, **rue de Béthune**, leads into place de Béthune, which has some excellent cafés, and beyond to the **Musée des Beaux-Arts** on place de la République (Mon 2–6pm, Wed–Sun 10am–6pm, Fri till 7pm; 30F/€4.57). The recent redesign is rather disappointing – too sleek and spacious to create any coherence to the collection – but the museum does contain some important works. Flemish painters form the core of the collection, from "primitives" like Dirck Bouts, through the northern Renaissance to Ruisdael, de Hooch and the seventeenth-century schools. Other works include Goya's interpretation of youth and old age, *Les Jeunes et Les Vieilles*, and a scattering of Impressionists, including Monet and Renoir. Ceramics are well represented in one of the two rooms on the ground floor; the other room displays a small collection of nineteenth-century sculpture.

A couple of blocks to the south of the museum, on rue de Fleurus, is **Maison Coilliot**, a ceramics shop and one of the few houses built by Hector Guimard, who made his name designing the Art Nouveau entrances to the Paris métro. Built at the height of the Art Nouveau movement, it's as striking today as it obviously was to the conservative burghers of Lille (there are no other such buildings in Lille), but it also displays the somewhat muddled eclecticism of the style, coming over as half brick-faced mansion, half timber-framed cottage. East of the museum, near the triumphal arch of **Porte de Paris**, the city's **Hôtel de Ville** is also worth a quick look, executed in a bizarre, Flemish Art Deco style, with a tall belfry and viewing platform (closed at the time of writing but due to reopen sometime in 2001; check for details with the tourist office).

Around the stations: Euralille

Thanks to Eurostar and the international extension of the TGV network, Lille has become the transport hub of northern Europe, a position it is trying to exploit to turn itself into an international business centre, with the appropriate space-age facilities. Hence, **Euralille**, the burgeoning complex of buildings behind the old *gare SNCF*.

One definite success is the new **Lille-Europe TGV and Eurostar station**: composed of lots of props and struts and glass and sunscreens, it's lean, elegant and functional, a fitting setting for the magnificent trains that use it. The other developments smack of a new totalitarianism: manipulation of the consuming masses by the distant powers of international finance. Literally treading on the roof of the new station is an anonymous boot-shaped tower reminiscent of nothing so much as the home of the old woman in the nursery rhyme who lived in a shoe. And opposite is an enormous shopping centre with galvanized walkways, marbled malls and relentless Muzak. This controlled environment is traceable to the utopian dreams of Le Corbusier, whose paternity is acknowledged in the **avenue Le Corbusier**, which sweeps over the plaza to the Lille-Europe station. There are other ironies, too, such as the fashion for "factory" architecture now that there are no more factories – there's more than thirteen percent unemployment in Lille, more than sixteen percent in neighbouring Roubaix, and more than twenty percent among the immigrant community.

Villeneuve d'Ascq: the Musée d'Art Moderne

The suburb of **Villeneuve-d'Ascq** is a mark of Lille's cultural ambition: acres of parkland, an old windmill or two, and a whole series of mini-lakes form the backdrop for the **Musée d'Art Moderne** (daily except Tues 10am–6pm; 25F/€3.81), which houses an unusually good collection in its uninviting red-brick buildings. To get there, take the métro to Pont-de-Bois, then bus #41.

The ground floor of the museum is generally given over to temporary exhibitions of varying quality by contemporary French artists. The permanent collection starts on the first floor with canvases by Picasso, Braque, Modigliani, Miró and a whole room devoted to Fernand Léger and Georges Rouault. On the top floor, a small room – easy to miss but worth the search – contains graphics by many of the above. Meanwhile, outside on the grass, Giacometti and Calder provide some playful picnic backdrops.

Eating

A Flemish flavour and a taste for mussels (*moules*) characterize Lille's cuisine. The main area for **cafés**, **brasseries** and **restaurants** is around place Rihour and along rue de Béthune. Rue Royale has a selection of fairly pricey but generally very good ethnic eateries, from Cambodian to Japanese. The best general area for cheap restaurants is the student quarter along the Solférino and rue Masséna.

Bar de la Cloche, 13 place du Théâtre. Excellent small brasserie, serving twenty different wines by the glass, in a relaxed, casual atmosphere; popular with the older set. *Plats* 60–80F/€9.15–12.20, cheeses and cold meats 30–55F/€4.57–8.38.

Coq Hardi, 44 place Général-de-Gaulle. In a prime position on the main square, you can people-watch whilst eating one of the salads at 40–50F/€6.10–7.62 or specialities of the region from the 88F/€13.42 menu. Also open for drinks outside of meal times.

Flandre Liban, 125 rue des Postes. Excellent Lebanese restaurant in a mainly North African and Middle Eastern quarter. Go for the mezze menu at 95F/€14.48.

La Galetière, 4 place Louise-de-Bettignies (☎03.20.54.89.92). Good-value crêperie in the old town. If full or closed, try the equally good *Beaurepaire II* round the corner on place Lion-d'Or. Closed Sun & Mon.

La Huîtrière, 3 rue des Chats-Bossus (☎03.20.55.43.41). A wonderful, colourful shop tiled with mosaics of seaside and rural working scenes, which sells everything from fish and seafood – with huge lobsters alive in their tanks – to chicken, meats and wine. An expensive, chandelier-hung restaurant at the back specializes in fish and seafood at 150–220F/€22.87–33.54 a dish; there's a staggering 600F/€91.47 menu, and a 260F/€39.64 one for lunch. Closed Sun evening, hols & July 22–Aug 23.

Aux Moules, 34 rue de Béthune (☎03.20.12.90.92). The best place to eat mussels; it's been serving them since 1930 in its Art Deco-style interior. Nothing much costs over 60F/€9, including the other brasserie fare, and it's all excellent value. Daily noon–midnight.

Paul, place du Théâtre, cnr rue Faidherbe (☎03.20.78.20.78). *Paul* is an institution in Lille and here the boulangerie, pâtisserie and *salon de thé* are all under one roof. There are various good breakfast menus served throughout the day, but the main reason to come here is to taste the delights of the pâtisserie in the *salon de thé*. Daily 7am–7.30pm.

Piccolo Mondo, 2 rue des Molfonds, off rue de Béthune. Erratic service but Lille's best pizza place. Also serves pasta and offers several vegetarian alternatives.

Drinking and nightlife

The **cafés** around the Grande-Place and place Rihour are always buzzing with life. Rue de Paris has lots of tacky, loud, crushed **bars** raging at all hours, while rue Basse and nearby place Louise-de-Bettignies have some trendier spots. Bars are thick on the ground in rues Solférino and Masséna, and attract a young crowd. Art and music events are always worth checking up on – there's a particularly lively jazz scene. Pick up a copy of the free weekly **listings magazine**, *Sortir*, from the tourist office, or look in the local paper, *La Voix du Nord*.

L'Angle Saxo, 36 rue d'Angleterre (☎03.20.15.06). Relaxed bar with good jazz – and you can hear yourself speak. Drinks are pricier than the pubs. Daily 9pm–2am, with concerts generally Thurs–Sun.

Bâteau Ivre, 41 rue Lepelletier. Loud music ranging from house to soul in a pleasant street in the old quarter. Mainly young crowd. Mon–Fri 3pm–2am, Sat 11am–2am.

Café au Bureau, rue de Béthune. Done out with plenty of brass and dark woodwork, and offering a hundred kinds of beer. Tables outside are crowded with young things watching the parade.

Les Deux Zèbres, 57 rue Basse. Groovy stripy bar, with an intimate atmosphere, playing Eighties music. Daily 6pm–2am.

Father Moustache, 19 rue Masséna. In a street lined with bars, this is as good a place as any to join a mainly student crowd. Daily 9pm–2am.

L'Imaginaire, place Louise-de-Bettignies, next door to the *Hôtel Treille*. Arty young bar with paintings adorning the walls. Mon–Sat 10pm–2am.

Les Trois Brasseurs, 22 place de la Gare. Dark, smoke-stained dining stalls surround copper cauldrons in this genuine brasserie that brews its own beer. Food is also served but it's the beer that's the main attraction.

Listings

Banks All the banks have big branches on rue Nationale, and you can guarantee to find one open until 4pm on Saturday. There's a branch of Barclays here too.

Books Le Furet du Nord, 11 place Général-de-Gaulle, is a huge bookstore with a wide selection of books in English.

Cinema There are several cinemas in Lille with a concentration on rue de Béthune. Le Métropole on rue des Ponts-de-Comines shows original-language versions with normally a couple in English. Gaumont at no. 25 rue des Alpes and UGC on rue de Béthune will usually have one of their screens in English.

Doctors SOS Médecins (☎03.20.29.91.91).

Hitch-hiking Auto Pass, 21 rue Patou (☎03.20.14.31.91), is an organization that puts hitch-hikers and drivers in touch with each other.

Laundry There are several outlets of Lavotec, the most central being at 72 rue Pierre-LeGrand, 57 rue des Postes and 137 rue Solférino.

Markets The loud and colourful Wazemmes market is centred around place de la Nouvelle Aventure. Main day Sun but also open Tues and Thurs (7am–2pm). A smaller food market takes place in *vieux Lille* on place du Concert (Wed, Fri & Sun 7am–2pm).

Post office place du Théâtre, cnr bd Carnot, and 7 place de la République (both Mon–Fri 8am–6.30pm, Sat 8.30am–12.30pm).

Taxi Gare (☎03.20.06.64.00); Taxi Union (☎03.20.06.06.06).

Douai and around

Right at the heart of mining country, 35km south of Lille, and badly damaged in both world wars, **DOUAI** is a surprisingly attractive and lively town, its streets of eighteenth-century houses cut through by both river and canal. Once a haven for English Catholics fleeing Protestant oppression in Tudor England, Douai later became the seat of Flemish local government under Louis XIV, an aristocratic past evoked in the novels of Balzac.

Centre of activity is the **place d'Armes**, overlooked by the massive Gothic belfry of the **Hôtel de Ville** on rue de la Mairie, popularized by Victor Hugo and renowned for its carillon of 62 bells – the largest single collection of bells in Europe. It rings every 15 minutes, and there are hour-long concerts every Saturday at 10.45am, on public holidays at 11am, and in summer on Monday at 9pm (hourly guided tours: July & Aug daily 10–11am & 2–5pm; rest of year Mon–Sat 2–5pm, Sun 10am, 11am, 3pm & 5pm; 11F/€1.68).

One block north of the town hall, on **rue Bellegambe**, is an outrageous Art Nouveau shop-front serving a very ordinary haberdashery store. At the end of the street, rising above the old town, are the Baroque dome and tower of the **church of St-Pierre**, an immense, mainly eighteenth-century church with – among other treasures – a spectacular carved Baroque organ case. East of the place d'Armes, Douai's oldest church, the twelfth-century **church of Notre-Dame**, suffered badly in the last war but has been refreshingly modernized inside. Beyond the church is the better of the town's two surviving medieval gateways, the **Porte Valenciennes**, now the centre of a triumphal roundabout. With the exception of the 1970s extension to the old Flemish Parliament building, the riverfront west of the town hall is pleasant to wander along. Between the river and the canal to the west, on rue de Chartreux, the **Ancienne Chartreuse** has been converted into a museum (Mon & Wed–Sat 10am–noon & 2–5pm, Sun 3–6pm; 12F/€1.83), with a good collection of paintings by Flemish, Dutch and French masters, including Van Dyck, Rubens, Rodin and Douai's own Jean Bellegambe.

The **gare SNCF** is a five-minute walk from place d'Armes – from the station head left down avenue Maréchal Leclerc, then right onto the place d'Armes. The **tourist office** (July & Aug daily 9am–noon & 2–6pm; rest of year closed Sun; ☎03.27.88.26.79, fax 03.27.99.38.78) is within the fifteenth-century Hôtel du Dauphin, on the square. For **accommodation** there's the *Hôtel au Grand Balcon*, on place Carnot (☎03.27.88.91.07; ②), or the better *Grand Cerf*, 46 rue St-Jacques (☎03.27.88.79.60, fax 03.27.98.05.74; ④). A far classier option is *La Terrasse*, a swanky four-star in the narrow terrasse St-Pierre (☎03.27.88.70.04, fax 03.27.88.36.05; ⑤), to one side of the church of St-Pierre; its restaurant is well regarded, with menus from 145F/€22.11.

Just northeast of the place d'Armes is the **post office**, whence buses leave for Lewarde (Line #1 orange).

Lewarde

A visit to the colliery at **LEWARDE**, 7km east of Douai, is a must for admirers of Zola's *Germinal*, perhaps the most electrifying "naturalistic" novel ever written. The bus from

Douai heads east across the flat and featureless beet fields, down a road lined with poor brick dwellings that recall the company-owned housing of *Germinal*, intersected by streets named after Pablo Neruda, Jean-Jacques Rousseau, Georges Brassens and other luminaries of the French and international Left. This is the traditional heart of France's coal-mining country, always dispiriting and now depressed by closures and recession. Even the distinctive landmarks of slag heap and winding gear are fast disappearing in the face of demolition and landscaping.

The bus puts you down at the main square, leaving a fifteen-minute walk down the D132 towards Erchin to get to the colliery. The **Centre Historique Minier** (guided tours: March–Oct daily 9am–5.30pm; Nov–Feb Mon–Sat 1–5pm, Sun 10am–5pm; visits last 2hr; March–Oct 66F/€10.06, Nov–Feb 58F/€8.84) is on the left in the old Fosse Delloye, sited, like so many pits, amid woods and fields. Visits are guided by retired miners, many of whom are not French, but Polish, Italian or North African – Polish labour was introduced in the 1920s, other nationalities successively after World War II. One Polish guide went down the pit at 14 and was brought up at 38 with silicosis, which had also killed his father at 52. "Ce n'est pas un métier," he said – "It's not what you'd call a career."

The main part of the tour – in addition to film shows and visits to the surface installations of winding gear, machine shops, cages, sorting areas and the rest – is the exploration of the pit-bottom roadways and faces, equipped to show the evolution of mining from the earliest times to today. These French pits were extremely deep and hot, with steeply inclined narrow seams that forced the miners to work on slopes of 55° and more, just as Étienne and the Maheu family do in Zola's story.

Accidents were a regular occurrence in the old days: the northern French pits had a particularly bad record in the last years of the nineteenth century. The worst mining disaster occurred at Courrières in 1906, when 1100 men were killed. Incredibly, despite the fact that the owners made little effort to search for survivors, thirteen men suddenly emerged after twenty days of wandering in the gas-filled tunnels without food, water or light. The first person they met thought that they were ghosts and fainted in fright. More incredible still, a fourteenth man surfaced alone after another four days.

Cambrai and around

CAMBRAI, like Douai 26km to the north, has kept enough of its character to repay a passing visit, despite the tank battle of November 1917 (see box opposite) and the fact that the heavily defended Hindenburg Line ran through the town centre for most of World War I.

The huge, cobbled main square, **place Aristide-Briand**, is dominated by the Neoclassical Hôtel de Ville, and still suggests the town's former wealth, which was based on the textile and agricultural industries. Unlike most places, Cambrai's chief treasure is not its cathedral but the **church of St-Géry**, off rue St-Aubert west of the main square, which contains a celebrated *Mise au Tombeau* by Rubens. The **Musée Municipal** (Wed–Sun 10am–noon & 2–6pm; 20F/€3.05) on rue de l'Épée, south of the town square, is also worth a visit: paintings of Velázquez feature prominently alongside works by various Flemish masters, Utrillo and Matisse, a native of Le Cateau (see below).

Cambrai's **tourist office** is housed in the Maison Espagnole on the corner of avenue de la Victoire, at 48 rue de Noyon (Mon–Fri 9am–noon & 2–6pm, Sat 10am–noon & 2–6pm, Sun 2–6pm; ☎03.27.78.36.15, fax 03.27.74.82.82, *www.villedecambrai.com*). Central **accommodation** includes *Le Mouton Blanc*, 33 rue d'Alsace-Lorraine (☎03.27.81.30.16, fax 03.27.81.83.54; ③), which is a convenient and moderately priced hotel close to the station, with a posh **restaurant** inside (from 98F/€14.94; closed Sun

---

CAMBRAI 1917

At dawn on November 20, 1917, the first full-scale tank battle in history began at **Cambrai**, when over 400 British tanks poured over the Hindenburg Line. In just 24 hours, the Royal Tank Corps and British Third Army made an advance that was further than any undertaken by either side since the trenches had first been dug in 1914. A fortnight later, however, casualties on both sides had reached 50,000, and the armies were back where they'd started.

Although in some respects the tanks were ahead of their time, they still relied on cavalry and plodding infantry as their back-up and runners for their lines of communication. And, before they even reached the "green fields beyond", most of them had broken down. World War I tanks were primitive machines, operated by a crew of eight who endured almost intolerable conditions: with no ventilation system, the temperature inside could rise to 48°C. The steering alone required three men, each on separate gearboxes, communicating by hand signals through the din of the tank's internal noise. Maximum speed (6kph) dropped to almost 1kph over rough terrain, and refuelling was necessary every 55km. Consequently, of the 179 tanks lost in the battle at Cambrai, very few were destroyed by the enemy; the majority broke down and were abandoned by their crews.

---

evening & Mon, plus the evenings of public hols & Aug 1–15). The cheaper hotels are way out on the other side of town on the highway, while the nearest **campsite** is 10km away and is signposted off the D939 to Arras.

Le Cateau

Twenty-two kilometres east of Cambrai along an old Roman road, the small town of **LE CATEAU** is the birthplace of Henri Matisse (1869–1954), and as a gift to his home town, Matisse bequeathed it a collection of his works. Some of them are now displayed in the **Musée Matisse**, housed in the local château in the centre of town (the museum has been redesigned to double its floor-space and is due to reopen in February 2002). Although no major works are displayed at the museum, it's the third-largest collection of his work in France, and includes several studies for the chapel in Vence plus a whole series of his characteristically simple pen-and-ink sketches. Also worth looking at is the work of local Cubist Auguste Herbin, particularly his psychedelic upright piano.

Arras, Albert and the Somme battlefields

Around **Arras**, 35km northwest of Cambrai, and **Albert**, 40km to the southwest of Cambrai, some of the fiercest and most futile battles of World War I took place, and at one time the trenches even cut through the grandiose main square in Arras, now restored to its former glory. At nearby **Vimy Ridge**, the Canadians fell in their thousands; at **Notre-Dame de Lorette**, the French suffered the same fate. Albert is not a place to linger, but makes a convenient base for exploring the many war cemeteries in the area.

Arras

ARRAS, with its fine old centre, is one of the prettiest towns in northern France. It was renowned for its tapestries in the Middle Ages, giving its name to the hangings behind which Shakespeare's Hamlet killed Polonius. Subsequently the town fell under Spanish control, and many of its citizens today claim that Spanish blood runs in their veins. Only in 1654 was Arras returned to the kingdom of France.

Although almost destroyed in World War I, the town bears few obvious battle scars. Reconstruction here, particularly after the last war, has been careful and stylish, and two grand arcaded squares in the centre – **Grand' Place** and the smaller **place des Héros** – preserve their historic, harmonious character. On every side are restored seventeenth- and eighteenth-century mansions, built in relatively restrained Flemish style, and, on place des Héros, there's a grandly ornate **Hôtel de Ville**, its entrance hall housing a permanent photographic display documenting the wartime destruction of the town and sheltering a pair of *géants* (festival giants) awaiting the city's next fête.

Also inside the town hall is the entrance to the **belfry viewing platform** (approximately three visits per day, depending on demand, starting from the tourist office; 15F/€2.29) and **les souterrains** (or *les boves*) – cold, dark passageways and spacious vaults tunnelled beneath the centre of the city (May–Sept Mon–Sat 9am–6.30pm, Sun 10am–1pm & 2.30–6.30pm; Oct–April Mon–Sat 9am–noon & 2–6pm, Sun 10am–12.30pm & 3–6.30pm; 22F/€3.35). Once down, you're escorted around an impressive area and given an interesting survey of local history. During World War I, the rooms – many of which have fine, tiled floors and lovely pillars and stairways – were used as a British barracks and hospital.

Arras's other main sight is its enormous **cathedral** and the Benedictine **Abbaye St-Vaast**, next door, a grey-stone classical building, still pockmarked by shrapnel, that was erected in the eighteenth century by Cardinal Rohen. The Abbaye now houses the **Musée des Beaux-Arts**, whose entrance is at 22 rue Paul-Donnier (April–Sept Mon & Wed–Sat 10am–noon & 2–6pm, Sun 10am–noon & 3–6pm; rest of year Mon & Wed–Fri 10am–noon & 2–5pm, Sat 10am–noon & 2–6pm, Sun 10am–noon & 3–6pm; 20F/€3.05), which contains a mediocre collection of paintings, including a couple of Jordaens and Brueghels, fragments of sculpture, local ceramics and some of the tapestries or *arras* (the final "s" is pronounced) that made the town famous in medieval times.

On the western edge of town, next to the Vauban barracks, is a **war cemetery** and **memorial** by the British architect Sir Edwin Lutyens, a movingly elegiac, classical colonnade of ivy-covered brick and stone, commemorating 35,928 missing soldiers, the endless columns of their names inscribed on the walls. It is a mournful corner of town: around the back of the old brick Vauban fortress, in an overgrown moat, is the **Mur des Fusillés**, where some two hundred Resistance fighters were shot by firing squad in the last war – most of them of Polish descent, most of them miners, and most of them Communists.

Practicalities

From the **gare SNCF** it's a ten-minute walk up rue Gambetta then rue Désiré Delansorne, to the **tourist office**, located in the Hôtel de Ville on place des Héros (May–Sept Mon–Sat 9am–6.30pm, Sun 10am–1pm & 2.30–6.30pm; Oct–April Mon–Sat 9am–noon & 2–6pm, Sun 10am–12.30pm & 3–6.30pm; ☎03.21.51.26.95, fax 03.21.71.07.34, *www.ot.arras.fr*); the tourist office is worth consulting for details of transport and tours of local battlefields (see "Vimy Ridge and around", below). To reach the Vimy memorial, you can also **rent a car** from Hertz, bd Carnot (☎03.21.23.11.14), or Euroto, 15 av Paul-Michonneau (☎03.21.55.05.05).

There are two good, inexpensive **hotels** in the town centre: the *Diamant*, 5 place des Héros (☎03.21.71.23.23, fax 03.21.71.84.13; ③), a comfortable, reliable two-star; and *Hôtel des Trois Luppars*, 47 Grand' Place (☎03.21.07.41.41, fax 03.21.24.24.80; ③), a friendly family-run place with modern facilities in a characterful old building. For a more luxurious night, go to the *Univers*, a lovely classical building round a courtyard in place de la Croix-Rouge, near the Abbaye St-Vaast (☎03.21.71.34.01, fax 03.21.71.41.42;

⑤; restaurant 120–260F/€18.29–39.64). The newly modernized, well-positioned **hostel** is at 59 Grand' Place (☎03.21.22.70.02, fax 03.21.07.46.15; closed Nov–Jan). A **campsite** (closed Nov–March) lies 1km out of town on the Bapaume road.

Restaurants worth trying include *La Rapière*, 44 Grand' Place, with excellent regional food and menus at 88F/€13.42 or 120F/€18.29; and, for a splurge, the gourmet *La Faisanderie*, a few doors away (from 135F/€20.58). Pizzerias abound: two particularly good ones are on rue Petit-Viéziers – *Le Petit Théâtre* and *Aux Petits-Viéziers* – while *Le Palerme* at 50 Grand' Place also serves pasta. For something different, an excellent *shwarma* place (eat in or take away) is tucked away in rue des Trois-Visages, just around the corner from the Hôtel de Ville, with a luscious range of Middle Eastern sweets.

Les Grandes Arcades, the hotel on Grand' Place (☎03.21.23.30.89; menus from 130F/€19.82), also serves good and not wildly expensive **regional food** (including the local speciality *andouillette*, or tripe sausage – an acquired taste), and you'll find a good **fromagerie**, Jean-Claude Leclercq, at 39 place des Héros. Saturdays are a good day for food and wine, when the squares are taken up with a morning **market**, and Esto Cave, an extensive sixteenth-century wine cellar run by the delightfully large and quirky proprietor of *Les Trois Luppars*, is open for the sale of fine wines (10am–1pm & 3–8pm).

Vimy Ridge and around

Eight kilometres north of Arras on the D49, **Vimy Ridge**, or Hill 145, was the scene of some of the direst trench warfare of World War I: almost two full years of battle, culminating in its capture by the crack Canadian Corps in April 1917. It is a vast site, given in perpetuity to the Canadian people out of respect for their sacrifices, and has been preserved, in part, as it was during the conflict. There's an **information centre** (daily 10am–5pm) supervised by bilingual Canadian students, who run free guided tours (April–Nov daily 10am–5.30pm) and can fill you in on all the horrific details. You really need your own transport to get there, as the nearest bus stop is forty-five minutes' walk away (for details contact the tourist office in Arras, see p.242).

Near the information centre, long worms of neat, sanitized **trenches** meander over the now grassy ground, still heavily pitted and churned by shell bursts beneath the planted pines. There are examples of dugouts – hideous places where men used to shelter during heavy bombardments and where makeshift hospitals were set up. Beneath the ground lie some 11,000 bodies still unaccounted for and countless rounds of unexploded ammunition. Signs are still required to warn people against straying from the directed paths.

On the brow of the ridge, 1500m north of the information centre, overlooking the slag-heap-dotted plain of Artois, a great white **monument** towers, like a giant funerary stele, rent down the middle by elemental force, with allegorical figures half-emerging from the stone towards the top, and inscribed with the names of 60,000 Canadians and Newfoundlanders who lost their lives during the war. It must have been an unenviable task to design a fitting memorial to such slaughter, but this one, aided by its setting, succeeds with great drama.

Back from the ridge, there's a subdued **memorial** to the Moroccan Division who also fought at Vimy, and in the woods behind, on the headstones of another exquisitely maintained **cemetery**, you can read the names of half the counties of rural England.

La Targette, Neuville-St-Vaast and Notre-Dame de Lorette

At the crossroads (D937/D49) of **LA TARGETTE**, 8km north from the centre of Arras and accessible from there by bus, the **Musée de la Targette** (daily 9am–8pm;

20F/€3.05) contains an interesting collection of World War I and II *objets de guerre*. It is the private collection of one David Bardiaux, assembled with passion and meticulous attention to detail, under the inspiration of tales told by his grandfather, a veteran of Verdun. Its interest lies in the absolute precision with which the thirty-odd mannequins of British, French, Canadian and German soldiers are dressed and equipped, down to their sweet and tobacco tins and such rarities as a 1915 British-issue cap with earflaps, very comfortable for the troops but withdrawn because the top brass thought it made their men look like yokels. All the exhibits have been under fire; some belonged to known individuals and are complete with stitched-up tears of old wounds.

More **cemeteries** lie a little to the south of La Targette, nominally at **NEUVILLE-ST-VAAST**, though the village is actually 1km away to the east. There is a small British cemetery, a huge French one, and an equally large German cemetery, containing the remains of 44,833 Germans. If you haven't been to a German war cemetery before, the macabre, skeletal black crosses – each one represents four soldiers – come as quite a shock. So, too, do the handful of individual Jewish headstones that stand out from the rest. In the village itself a Polish **memorial** – among the Poles that died in action here was the sculptor Henri Gaudier-Brzeska, in 1915 – and a Czech **cemetery** face each other across the main street.

On a bleak hill a few kilometres to the northwest of Vimy Ridge (and 5km north of Neuville-St-Vaast) is the church of **Notre-Dame de Lorette**, scene of a costly French offensive in May 1915. The original church was blasted to bits during the war and rebuilt in grim neo-Byzantine style in the 1920s, grey and dour on the outside but rich and bejewelled inside. It now stands at the centre of a vast graveyard with over 20,000 crosses laid out in pairs, back to back, each one separated by a cluster of blood-red roses. There are 20,000 more buried in the ossuary, and there's the small **Musée Vivant 1914–1918** (daily 9am–8pm; 20F/€3.05) behind the church, displaying photographs, uniforms and other military paraphernalia. You can reach Notre-Dame de Lorette by bus from Arras, direction "Lens".

Albert and around

The church at **ALBERT**, 30km south of Arras – now, with the rest of the town, completely rebuilt – was one of the minor landmarks of World War I. Its tall tower was hit by German bombing early on in the campaign, leaving the statue of the Madonna on top leaning at a precarious angle. The British, entrenched over three years in the region, came to know it as the "Leaning Virgin". Army superstition had it that when she fell the war would end, a myth inspiring frequent hopeful pot shots by disgruntled troops. Before embarking on a visit of the region's battle sites and war cemeteries, otherwise known as the *circuit de souvenir* (see below), you might want to stop in at the **Musée des Abris** (daily: March–June & Sept–Nov 9.30am–noon & 2–6pm; July & Aug 9.30am–6pm; 20F/€3.05), a museum which has re-enactments of fifteen different scenes from life in the trenches of the Somme in 1916. The mannequins look slightly too jolly and eager but it does go some way to bringing the props to life.

As you arrive (trains from Amiens or Arras), the town's new tower, capped now by an equally improbably posed statue, is the first thing that catches the eye. The **tourist office** is close by on rue Gambetta (April–Sept Mon–Sat 10am–noon & 2–6.30pm, Sun 9.30am–noon; Oct–March Mon–Sat 10am–noon & 3–5pm; ☎03.22.75.16.42, fax 03.22.75.11.72), together with a couple of **hotels**: the moderately priced *Basilique*, 3–5 rue Gambetta (☎03.22.75.04.71, fax 03.22.75.10.47, *hotel-de-la-basilique@wanadoo.fr*, ③; restaurant 68–150F/€10.37–22.87); and the cheaper and friendlier *La Paix*, 43 rue Victor-Hugo (☎03.22.75.01.64, fax 03.22.75.44.17; ②), whose restaurant has simpler menus from 79F/€12.04.

The Circuit de Souvenir

Was it for this the clay grew tall?
O what made fatuous sunbeams toil
To break earth's sleep at all?

Wilfred Owen, *Futility*

The **Circuit de Souvenir** conducts you from graveyard to mine crater, trench to memorial. There's not a lot to see; nothing, at least, that is going to satisfy any appetite for shocking atrocities or scenes of destruction. Neither do you get much sense of movement or even of battle tactics. But you will find that, even if you start out with the feeling that your interest in war is somehow puerile or mawkish, you have in fact embarked on a sort of pilgrimage, in which each successive step becomes more harrowing and oppressive.

The **cemeteries** are the most moving aspect of the region – beautiful, the grass perfectly mown, an individual bed of flowers at the foot of every gravestone. And there are tens of thousands of gravestones, all identical, with a man's name, if it is known (nearly half the British dead have never been found), and his rank and regiment. Just reading the names of the regiments evokes a world of experience quite different from today's: locally recruited regiments, young men from Welsh border farms, mill towns, and villages, who had never been abroad, wiped out in a morning, men from all corners of the Empire. In the lanes between Albert and Bapaume you'll see the cemeteries everywhere: at the angle of copses, halfway across a wheat field, in the middle of a bluebell wood, moving and terrible in their simple beauty. What follows is necessarily just a selected handful of some of the better-known sites.

A good place to start is the station at **HAMEL** (7km north of Albert), where the 51st Highland Division walked abreast to their deaths with their pipes playing. Just across the river, towards the village of **THIÉPVAL**, the 5000 Ulstermen who died in the Battle of the Somme are commemorated by the incongruously Celtic **Ulster Memorial**, a replica of Helen's Tower at Clandeboye near Belfast (information bureau open Mon–Sat 11am–5pm; closed Dec & Jan). Probably the most famous of Edwin Lutyens' many memorials is south of Thiépval: the colossal **Memorial to the Missing**, in memory of the 73,357 British troops whose bodies were never recovered at the Somme. A half-hour hike north of Hamel station is the memorial to the Newfoundlanders at **BEAUMONT-HAMEL**. Here, on the hilltop where most of them died, a series of trenches has been preserved, now grassed over and eroding, where German faced Canadian a few paces apart. It all seems so small-scale now and almost more appropriate to the antics of parties of schoolchildren, who run around here shooting each other with their fingers, than to anything as obscene as what took place.

Five kilometres east at **POZIÈRES**, on the Albert–Bapaume road, *Le Tommy* café has a World War I permanent **exhibition** (daily 9.30am–6pm; free) in its back garden, consisting mainly of a reconstructed section of trench and "equipped" with genuine battlefield relics. It's a bit amateurish, but worth a look if you're passing through. The guide had first collected objects from the battlefield as a boy to sell for pocket money. Farmers apparently still turn up about 75 tonnes of shells every year – not really surprising when you think the British alone fired one-and-a-half million in the last week of June 1916.

Another fine Lutyens memorial stands near **VILLERS-BRETONNEUX**, some 18km southwest of Albert near the River Somme itself. As at Vimy, the landscaping of the **Australian Memorial** is dramatic – for the full effect, climb up to the viewing platform of the stark white central tower. The monument was one of the last to be inaugurated, in July 1938, when the prospects for peace were already looking bleak.

Laon's pride and joy. You board next to the train station and get out by the town hall on place Général-Leclerc; from there a left turn down rue Serrurier brings you nose to nose with the cathedral.

The **tourist office** is right by the cathedral (March–June, Sept & Oct Mon–Sat 9am–12.30pm & 2–6.30pm, Sun 11am–1pm & 2–6pm; July & Aug Mon–Sat 9am–1pm & 2–7pm, Sun 11am–1pm & 2–5pm; Nov–Feb Mon–Sat 9am–12.30pm & 2–6pm, Sun 11am–1pm & 2–5pm; ☎03.23.20.28.62, fax 03.23.20.68.11, *www.ville-laon.fr*), housed within the impressive Gothic Hôtel-Dieu, built in 1209. For **accommodation** in the *ville basse*, try *Le Welcome* (☎03.23.23.06.11; ①), at 2 av Carnot, straight in front of the *gare SNCF*. The cheapest solution in the *ville haute* is the hostel *Maison des Jeunes*, 20 rue du Cloître, by the cathedral (☎03.23.23.27.79). As for hotels, *La Paix*, 52 rue St-Jean (☎03.23.79.06.34; ①; restaurant from 64/€9.76F; hotel closed Sun evening, restaurant closed Sat & Sun), is a good bet, as is the charming and characterful old *Hôtel des Chevaliers*, at 3 rue Serrurier, near the Poma stop (☎03.23.27.17.50, fax 03.23.23.40.71; ①). On the eastern edge of the town, along avenue de Gaulle, there's a concentration of motel-type places: try the *Campanile* (☎03.23.23.15.05, fax 03.23.23.04.25; ③; restaurant from 84F/€12.81) or the adjacent *Première Classe* (☎03.23.23.44.55, fax 03.23.23.21.01; ②). The **camping municipal** is on the south side of the *ville basse*, near the *stade municipal*, just off the N44. Alternatively, there's *Camping La Chenaie* (☎03.23.20.25.56; closed Nov–March), on allée de la Chenaie, on the northwest side of the town.

The Town

Laon's number-one attraction is its magnificent **Cathédrale Notre-Dame** (daily 9am–6.30pm; guided tours from tourist office: July & Aug daily 2pm & 5pm; rest of year Sat, Sun & public hols 3pm). Built in the second half of the twelfth century, the cathedral was a trendsetter in its day, elements of its design – the gabled porches, the imposing towers and the gallery of arcades above the west front – being repeated at Chartres, Reims and Notre-Dame in Paris. When wrapped in thick mist, the towers seem otherworldly. The creatures craning from the uppermost ledges appear to be reckless mountain goats borrowed from some medieval bestiary and are reputed to have been carved in memory of the valiant horned steers who lugged the cathedral's masonry up from the plains below. Inside, the effects are no less dramatic – the high white nave is lit by the dense ruby, sapphire and emerald tones of the stained glass, which at close range reveals the appealing scratchy, smoky quality of medieval glass.

Crowding in the cathedral's lee are a web of quiet, grey, eighteenth-century streets. One – rue Pourier – leads past the post office and onto the thirteenth-century **Porte d'Ardon**, which looks out over the southern part of the *ville basse*. A left turn at the post office along rue Ermant leads to the little twelfth-century octagonal **Chapelle des Templiers** – the Knights Templar – set in a secluded garden by the **Musée de Laon**, 32 rue Georges-Ermant (daily except Tues 10am–noon & 2–6pm; winter 2–5pm; 20F/€3.05), which has a collection of classical antiquities.

The rest of the *ville haute*, which rambles along the ridge to the west of the cathedral into the Le Bourg quarter around the early Gothic **church of St-Martin**, is good to wander in, with grand views from the **ramparts**.

Eating, drinking and entertainment

Rue Châtelaine, in the *ville haute*, has a good range of **boulangeries** and **fromageries** for assembling picnics. Simple **snacks** can be had at the *Le Parvis*, which overlooks the west front of the cathedral; at *Crêperie Agora*, an inexpensive Breton place near the cathedral at 16 rue des Cordeliers (open until 1am; closed Sat lunch & Mon); or at the *Brasserie Chenizelles*, at no. 1 on rue du Bourg, the continuation of rue Chatelaine.

Restaurants in Laon tend to be expensive: *La Petite Auberge*, the gourmets' favourite, at 45 bd Pierre-Brossolette in the *ville basse* near the station, falls into this category, serving traditional French cuisine using the freshest ingredients (menus from 129F/€19.67). Next door, the *Saint-Amour* is more economical and still very good (menus from 75F/€11.43).

There's usually something going on at the Maison des Arts on place Aubrey – including the annual ten-day international **film festival** in early April – and a concentration of events during the *Heures Médiévales* festival in the first week of May. *Le Welcome*, next door to the arts complex, is an Irish-style **bar** and is a good place for just a drink.

Coucy-le-Château and the Forêt St-Gobain

About 30km west of Laon, in hilly countryside on the far side of the forest of St-Gobain (a worthwhile cycling trip in itself), lie the straggling ruins of one of the greatest castles of the Middle Ages, **Coucy-le-Château** (May–Aug Mon–Fri 10am–12.30pm & 2–6.30pm, Sat 10am–12.30pm & 2–7pm, Sun 10am–7pm; March, April, Sept & Oct Mon–Fri 10am–12.30pm & 2–6pm, Sat 10am–12.30pm & 2–6.30pm, Sun 10am–6.30pm; Nov–Feb Mon–Fri 10am–12.30pm & 2–4.30pm, Sat 10am–12.30pm & 2–5pm, Sun 10am–5pm; 25F/€3.81). The power of its lords, the Sires de Coucy, rivalled and often even exceeded that of the king – "King I am not, neither Prince, Duke nor Count. I am the Sire of Coucy" was Enguerrand III's proud boast. The retreating Germans capped the destruction of World War I battles by blowing up the castle's keep as they left in 1917, but enough remains, crowning a wooded spur, to be extremely evocative. A small **museum** (daily: May–Sept 2.30–6.30pm; rest of year 2.30–6pm; free) in the tower at the Porte de Soissons, on the south side of the walled part of town, has a display of photographs showing how it looked pre-1917, which can be compared with today's remains from the vantage point of the roof.

The entire modern village of **COUCY-LE-CHÂTEAU-AUFFRIQUE** is contained within the vast ring of walls, entered through the original gates, squeezed between powerful, round flanking towers; there is a footpath all around the outside. **Bicycles** can be rented from the **tourist office**, in the central square (May–Aug Mon–Fri 9.30am–12.30pm & 2–6pm, Sat closes at 6.30pm, Sun 10am–1pm & 2.30–7pm; Sept–April daily 10am–12.30pm & 2–6pm; ☎03.23.52.44.55), near the Porte de Soissons. Should you need a **place to stay**, try the *Hôtel Bellevue* within the walls (☎03.23.52.69.70, fax 03.34.52.69.79; ②; closed Jan).

It's hard to get to Coucy-le-Château without a car, though several Laon–Soissons trains stop at **ANIZY-PINON**, which, if you're otherwise hitching, cuts the distance by about half – and there is an infrequent bus on to Soissons. If you continue into the nearby **Forêt St-Gobain**, it's worth including **ST-GOBAIN**, 13km north of Coucy, in your itinerary. The original eighteenth-century **glassworks** – the firm is now a vast conglomerate – hides behind a classical facade, pretending it's nothing so vulgar as a factory (visits by appointment only, ☎03.23.52.84.75).

Soissons

Half an hour by train, or 30km down the N2, southwest of Laon, **SOISSONS** can lay claim to a long and highly strategic history. Before the Romans arrived it was already a town, and in 486 AD it was here that the Romans suffered one of their most decisive defeats at the hands of Clovis the Frank, making Soissons one of the first real centres of the Frankish kingdom. Napoléon, too, considered it a crucial military base, a judgement borne out this century in extensive war damage.

The town boasts the fine, if little-sung, **Cathédrale Notre-Dame** – thirteenth century for the most part with majestic glass and vaulting – at the west end of the main square, place F.-Marquigny. More impressive still is the ruined **Abbaye de St-Jean-des-Vignes**, to the south of the cathedral down rue Panleu and then right down rue St Jean. The facade of the tremendous Gothic abbey church rises sheer and grand, impervious to the now empty space behind it. The rest of the abbey complex, save for remnants of a **cloister** and **refectory** (Mon–Sat 9am–12.30pm & 1.30–6pm, Sun 10am–12.30pm & 1.30pm–7pm; free), was dismantled in 1804. Near the *abbaye* is the impressive eighteenth-century **Hôtel de Ville** with its grand stone gate.

Practicalities

Soissons is relatively compact. From the **gare SNCF** (with good services to Laon and Paris) the main square is a fifteen-minute walk away along avenue du Général-de-Gaulle and then rue St-Martin. The **gare routière** is closer to the centre by the river on Le Mail: infrequent buses leave for Compiègne and Laon. The **tourist office** is on place F.-Marquigny by the cathedral (mid-June to mid-Sept Mon–Sat 9.30am–6.30pm, Sun 9.30am–12.30pm & 2–6pm; mid-Sept to mid-June Mon–Sat 9.30am–12.30pm & 2–6.30pm, Sun 9.30am–12.30pm & 2–6pm; ☎03.23.53.17.37, fax 03.23.59.67.72).

The town is a useful and attractive place to stay if you're exploring this part of the country, and there are a couple of moderately priced **hotels**: the *Terminus* by the station (☎03.23.53.33.59; ①; closed Sun & Aug) and the *Pot d' Étain*, 7 rue St-Quentin (☎03.23.53.27.39; ①), which is more central and also has a decent restaurant (from 70F/€10.67). Alternatively there's a **campsite**, 1km from the station on avenue du Mail.

An excellent place for **crêpes** and *galettes* is *La Galetière* (closed Mon) at 1 rue du Beffroi by the cathedral, and there's a good Tunisian **restaurant**, the *Sidi Bou*, on rue de la Bannière, down towards the river.

Compiègne and around

Thirty-eight kilometres west of Soissons lies **COMPIÈGNE**, whose reputation as a tourist centre rests on the presence of a vast royal palace, built at the edge of the Forêt de Compiègne in order that generations of French kings could play at "being peasants", in Louis XIV's words. Although the town itself is a bit of a one-horse place with a bland, Sunday-afternoon feel, it's worth a visit for the opulent palace interiors, and the car and Second Empire museums.

Arrival, information and accommodation

The **gares routière** and **SNCF** are adjacent to each other, just a few minutes' walk away from the centre of town: cross the wide River Oise and go up rue Solférino to place de l'Hôtel-de-Ville. The **tourist office** (Mon–Sat 9.15am–12.15pm & 1.45–6.15pm; Easter–Oct also open Sun 10am–1pm & 2.30–5pm; ☎03.44.40.01.00, fax 03.44.40.23.28) takes up part of the ornate Hôtel de Ville and, for a small fee, will provide you with a plan of the town, on which is conveniently marked an exhaustive visitors' route, including the forest paths (see below).

As for **accommodation**, there are cheapish rooms at the *Hôtel St-Antoine*, 17 rue de Paris (☎03.44.23.22.27; ①), concealed above a Thai restaurant; and the *Lion d'Or*, 4 rue du Général-Leclerc (☎03.44.23.32.17; ①). More comfortable is the *Hôtel de Flandre*, an enormous, recently redecorated place on the riverside at 16 quai de la République (☎03.44.83.24.40, fax 03.44.90.02.75; ②). Much the best place to stay, however, is the *Hôtel de France*, 17 rue E.-Floquet, centrally located right next to the Hôtel de Ville (☎03.44.40.02.74, fax 03.44.40.48.37; ②; good restaurant from 148F/€22.56), a charming old place with very reasonable rates. The town **campsite** is along avenue Royale, into the forest beyond the palace.

The Town

Compiègne itself is plain disappointing, though that shouldn't come as a surprise, as a platoon of German soldiers burnt it down in 1942 to provide their commander with evidence of a subjugated community. Several half-timbered buildings remain on the pedestrianized rue Napoléon and rue des Lombards, south of the main place de l'Hôtel-de-Ville. The most striking building, as so often in these parts, is the **Hôtel de Ville** – Louis XII Gothic – its ebullient nineteenth-century statuary including the image of Joan of Arc, who was captured in this town by the Burgundians before being handed to the English.

By the side of the town hall is the **Musée des Figurines** (Tues–Sat 9am–noon & 2–6pm, Sun 2–6pm; closes at 5pm in winter; 12F/€1.83), which features reputedly the world's largest collection of wafer-thin military figurines in mock-up battles from ancient Greece to World War II. Also of specialist interest is the **Musée Vivenel**, on rue d'Austerlitz (same hours and price), which has one of the best collections of Greek vases around, especially a series illustrating the Panathenaic Games from Italy – a welcome dose of classical restraint and good taste compared with the palace. There is also a section on the flora and fauna of the Forêt de Compiègne, which includes a wild boar the size of an armoured car.

But Compiègne's star attraction is two blocks east of the town hall down rue des Minimes. For all its pompous excess, there is a certain fascination about the seventeenth- and eighteenth-century **Palais National**, particularly its interior (guided tours: April–Sept daily except Tues 10am–6pm; last tour leaves 45min before closing; 35F/€5.34, 25F/€3.51 for just the Musée de la Voiture). The lavishness of Marie-Antoinette's rooms, the sheer, vulgar sumptuousness of the First and Second Empire and the evidence of the unseemly haste with which Napoléon I moved in, scarcely a dozen years after the Revolution, are impressive. The palace also houses the **Musée du Second Empire** and the **Musée de la Voiture**, the latter containing a wonderful array of antique bicycles, tricycles and fancy aristocratic carriages, as well as the world's first steam coach. The **Théâtre Impérial**, planned (but never finished) by Napoléon III, was finally completed in 1991 at a cost of some thirty million francs. Originally designed with just two seats for Napoléon and his wife, it now seats 900 and is regularly used for concerts.

If you don't want to take the guided tour, a visit to the palace gardens or **petit parc** (daily: summer 7.30am–8pm; winter 8am–6.30pm) is a pleasant alternative. Serene and formal, they include a long, straight avenue extending far into the Forêt de Compiègne (see below), which touches the edge of town.

Eating and drinking

Compiègne has no shortage of cheap **eateries**, such as *À la Dernière Minute* on place de la Gare and the crêperie *La Bolée* on rue St Martin. More rewarding **restaurants** are the *Bistrot de Flandre*, 2 rue d'Amiens, and *Le Bouchon* at 5 rue St-Martin, a wine bar offering a lunch menu at 69F/€10.52 and *plats du jour* for 48F/€7.32 (a glass of wine costs about 25F/€3.81). *Le Lombard*, a contemporary bar/brasserie on rue des Lombards, has a good range of gourmet salads which should please vegetarians.

For just a pastry and coffee, try *Les Muscadines*, 1 rue Solférino, just by the bridge, which has a relaxing atmosphere and magazines to browse through. On Saturdays, there's a big all-day **market** in the square by place de l'Hôtel-de-Ville.

Into the forest: the Clairière de l'Armistice

Very ancient, and cut by a succession of hills, streams and valleys, the **Forêt de Compiègne** is grand rambling country for walkers or cyclists – the GR12 goes through

bag – and few are much more than hamlets, with grocery vans doing the rounds once a week, and not a boulangerie in sight.

At least the official capital of Champagne, the cathedral city of **Reims**, is worth a visit in its own right, and it has a reasonably full cultural calendar. For champagne-worshippers, however, **Epernay** is the place to head for, where you can sample vintages to your heart's content and go on several visits to the underground *caves* of the different *maisons*. Across the plains, neither **Châlons-en-Champagne** nor the smaller, further-flung towns like **Chaumont** or **Langres** dotted along the Marne towards its source are much of an incentive to break your journey. The only real attraction in the rest of the region is the town of **Troyes**, some way off to the southwest, which is easily Champagne's most beautiful city.

Reims

Laid flat by the bombs of World War I, **REIMS** (pronounced like a nasal "Rance") may give the first impression of being a large industrial centre with little to redeem it. However, the town is not as large as it looks, and there are other reasons for visiting here: apart from its status as champagne capital of the world, Reims possesses one of the most impressive Gothic cathedrals in France – formerly the coronation church of dynasties of French monarchs going back to Clovis, first king of the Franks – whose 1500th anniversary celebrations in 1996 provoked fierce controversy between Catholics and secularists.

Arrival, information and accommodation

The cathedral is less than ten minutes' walk from the **gare SNCF** and **gare routière**. The **tourist office** (Easter to mid-Oct Mon–Sat 9am–7pm, Sun 10am–6pm; mid-Oct to Easter Mon–Sat 9am–6pm, Sun 10am–5pm; ☎03.26.77.45.25, fax 03.26.77.45.27, *www.tourisme.fr/reims*) is conveniently located next door to the cathedral in a picturesque ruin. **Internet access** is available at *Clique et Croque*, 27 rue de Vesle (daily 9am–midnight), a cyber café serving snacks throughout the day.

Rooms are generally affordable and easy to come by in Reims, with plenty of central hotels, many on place Drouet-d'Erlon. If you're planning on visiting several of Reims' museums, you can pay 15F/€2.27 for a **museum pass**, giving entry to the Musée des Beaux-Arts, Musée de St-Remi, Ancien Collège des Jésuites and the Musée de la Reddition.

Hotels

au Bon Accueil, 31 rue de Thillois (☎03.26.88.55.74, fax 03.26.05.12.38). A small, old hotel in an excellent central location with the cheapest single rates in town – just a little more than the hostel. Basic rooms have toilet and shower. ①.

Continental, 93 place Drouet-d'Erlon (☎03.26.40.39.35, fax 03.26.47.51.12). Well-situated hotel, with quiet rooms, all with bathroom and TV. ④.

Crystal, 86 place Drouet-d'Erlon (☎03.26.88.44.44, fax 03.26.47.49.28). The small courtyard blocks out much of the traffic noise; rooms are small but respectable and the service pleasant. ③.

New Hôtel Europe, 29 rue Buirette (☎03.26.47.39.39, fax 03.26.40.14.37). Quiet *fin-de-siècle* four-storey three-star. ⑤.

Thillois, 17 rue de Thillois (☎03.26.40.65.65). Basic hotel, with shared washing facilities for the cheaper rooms, but well located. ①.

Hostel

Centre International de Séjour, 1 chaussée Bocquaine, Parc Léo Lagrange (☎03.26.40.52.60, fax 03.26.47.35.70). A large, well-run HI hostel with single or double rooms, and self-catering, though

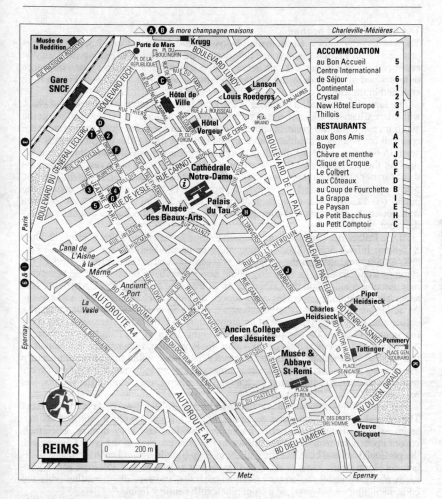

breakfast is available. It's a fifteen-minute walk from the station on the other side of the canal: cross over the big roundabout in front of the station, turn right down bd du Général-Leclerc to Pont de Vesle; chaussée Bocquaine is the first left after the bridge. There's no daytime lockout, but a curfew of 11pm – a late key is available for a deposit; no HI card required.

The City

The old centre of Reims stretches from the **cathedral** and its adjacent episcopal palace north to place de la République's triumphal Roman arch, the Porte de Mars, punctuated by the grand squares of place Royale, place du Forum and place de l'Hôtel-de-Ville. Over to the south, about fifteen minutes' walk from the cathedral, is the other historical focus of the town, the **Abbaye de St-Remi**, and nearby the **Jesuits' College**. To the east of here are most of the **champagne maisons** and, further east still, a museum of cars.

The cathedral and around

The thirteenth-century **Cathédrale Notre-Dame** (daily 7.30am–7.30pm) features prominently in French history: in 1429 Joan of Arc succeeded in getting the Dauphin crowned here as Charles VII – an act of immense significance when France was more or less wiped off the map by the English and their allies. In all, 26 kings of France were crowned in the Gothic glory of this edifice.

The lure of the cathedral's interior is the kaleidoscopic patterns in the stained glass, with Marc Chagall designs in the east chapel and champagne processes glorified in the south transept. But the greatest appeal is outside: an inexplicable joke runs around the restored but still badly mutilated statuary on the west front – the giggling angels who seem to be responsible for disseminating the prank are a rare delight. Not all the figures on the cathedral's west front are originals – some have been removed to spare them further erosion and are now at the former bishop's palace, the Palais du Tau (see below). Between June and September the upper parts of the cathedral are open to the public (10–11.30am & 2–5.30pm; guided tour every 30min; 25F/€3.81); as well as a walk round the transepts and chevet, you get to see inside the framework of the cathedral roof.

At the **Palais du Tau** (daily: mid-March to June & Sept to mid-Nov 9.30am–12.30pm & 2–6pm; July & Aug 9.30am–6.30pm; mid-Nov to mid-March 10am–noon & 2–5pm; 32F/€4.88), next door to the cathedral, you can appreciate the expressiveness of the statuary from close up – a view that would never have been possible in their intended monumental positions on the cathedral. Apart from the grinning angels, there are also some friendly-looking gargoyles and a superb Eve, shiftily clutching the monster of sin. As added narrative, embroidered tapestries of the *Song of Songs* line the walls. The palace also preserves, in a state of unlikely veneration, the paraphernalia of the arch-reactionary Charles X's coronation in 1824, right down to the dauphin's hat box. In being anointed here in purple pomp – after the Revolution, Robespierre and Napoléon had tried to achieve a new France – Louis XVI's brother stated his intention to return the country to the *ancien régime*. His attempt turned out to be short-lived, but the tradition he was calling upon dated back to 496 AD when Clovis, king of the Franks, was baptized in Reims.

Just west of the cathedral on rue Chanzy, the **Musée des Beaux-Arts** (daily except Tues & public hols 10am–noon & 2–6pm; 10F/€1.52) is the city's principal art museum, which, though ill suited to its ancient building and very diverse, effectively covers French art from the Renaissance to the present. Few of the works are among the particular artists' best, but the collection does contain one of David's replicas of his famous Marat death scene, a set of 27 Corots, two great Gauguin still lifes, some beautifully observed sixteenth-century German portraits, and various interesting odds and ends, including an old *tabac* sign from nineteenth-century Reims.

Five minutes away, there's another museum in the **Hôtel de Vergeur**, 36 place du Forum (Tues–Sun 2–6pm; 20F/€3.05): it is a stuffed treasure house of all kinds of beautiful objects, including two sets of Dürer engravings – an *Apocalypse* and *Passion of Christ* – but you have to go through a long guided tour of the whole works. By the museum there's access to sections of the partly submerged arcades of the **crypto portique Gallo-Romain** (mid-June to mid-Sept Tues–Sun 2–5pm; free), which date back to 200 AD. Reims' other Roman monument, the quadruple-arched **Porte de Mars**, on place de la République, belongs to the same era.

The Abbaye St-Remi, Jesuits' College and surrounding museums

Most of the early French kings were buried in Reims' oldest building, the eleventh-century **Basilique St-Remi**, fifteen minutes' walk from the cathedral on rue Simon (Mon–Wed, Fri & Sun 8am–dusk, Thurs & Sat 9am–dusk; closed during services; music & light show July–Sept Sat 9.30pm; free), part of a former Benedictine abbey named after the 22-year-old bishop who baptized Clovis and 3000 of his warriors. An immensely spacious building, with aisles wide enough to drive a bus along, it preserves its Romanesque transept walls and ambulatory chapels, some of them with modern stained glass that works beautifully. The spectacular abbey buildings alongside the church house the **Musée St-Remi** (Mon–Fri 2–6.30pm, Sat & Sun 2–7pm; 10F/€1.52), the city's archeological and historical museum, whose eclectic collection includes some fine tapestries on St Remi's life, plus sixteenth-century weapons and armour.

The **Ancien Collège des Jésuites** (guided tours: daily 10am, 11am, 2.15pm, 3.30pm & 4.45pm, Tues afternoon hours only, Sat & Sun morning hours only; 10F/€1.52), a short walk north on rue du Grand-Cerf, was founded in Reims in 1606, and the building completed in 1678. Guided tours in French take you round the refectory, kitchens and, highlight of the visit, the beautifully ornate carved wooden fittings of the library. The books on the shelves are false (aesthetics aside, the conditions are not ideal for storing books) and remain from the filming of *La Reine Margot* for which they were made.

If you have even a passing interest in old cars you should make for the **Centre de l'Automobile**, 84 av Georges-Clemenceau (daily except Tues 10am–noon & 2–6pm; 35F/€5.34), fifteen minutes' walk southeast of the cathedral. All the vehicles are part of the private collection of Philippe Charbonneaux, designer of a number of the postwar classics on display. In addition to the full-scale cars, there's an impressive selection of models, antique toys and period posters.

On the opposite side of town, behind the station in rue Franklin-Roosevelt, is the rather less interesting **Musée de la Reddition** ("Museum of Surrender"; daily except Tues & public hols 10am–noon & 2–6pm; 10F/€1.52), based around an old schoolroom that served as Eisenhower's HQ from February 1945. In the early hours of May 7, 1945, General Jodl agreed to the unconditional surrender of the German army, thus ending World War II in Europe. The room has been left exactly as it was (minus the ashtrays and carpet), with the Allies' battle maps on the walls. The visit includes a good documentary film and numerous photographs and press cuttings.

Champagne tasting

For the serious business of Reims, head to place des Droits-de-l'Homme and place St-Niçaise, near the Abbaye St-Remi. These are both within striking distance of the majority of the Reims **maisons**, most of which charge an entrance fee for their tours but include a *dégustation* and have English guides. Only three can be visited without an appointment: the houses of Mumm, Taittinger and Piper-Heidsieck.

The best of the regular guided tours is **Mumm** at 34 rue du Champ-de-Mars (March–Oct daily 9–11am & 2–5pm; Nov–Feb Mon–Fri same hours, Sat & Sun afternoons only; tour takes 45min; 25F/€3.81). Established in 1827, Mumm is familiar for its red-slashed Cordon Rouge label – its un-French-sounding name is the legacy of its founders, affluent German wine-makers from the Rhine Valley. The tour is fairly informal – you can wander freely about its cellar museum and throw questions at the approachable guides – though you pick up the basics from a pre-tour video. There's not a lot of walking despite 25km of cellars and a reported 35 million bottles of wine; some of the vintage bottles date from 1911. It all ends with a generous glass of either Cordon Rouge, the populist choice; the sweeter Cordon Vert; or their Extra Dry. At **Taittinger**, 9 place St-Niçaise (Mon–Fri 9.30am–noon & 2–4.30pm, Sat & Sun 9–11am & 2–5pm; Dec–Feb Mon–Fri only; tour takes 1hr; 35F/€5.34), there are still more ancient *caves*, with doodles and carvings added by more recent workers, and statues of St Vincent and St Jean, patron saints respectively of *vignerons* and cellar hands.

Although founded in 1785, **Piper-Heidsieck**, at 51 bd Henry-Vasnier (March–Nov daily 9–11.45am & 2–5.15pm; Dec–Feb closed Tues & Wed; 40F/€6.10), is better known in the New World than the Old, having been the champagne of the American movie industry since first appearing – with Laurel and Hardy – in the 1934 classic *Sons of the Desert*. The champagne of the Oscars gives a fair whack of sponsorship for film prizes and festivals too, and really the only folk who'll get anything out of the tour – which ends up at a gallery of celebrity snaps – are confirmed film buffs and lovers of tackiness: the antique *caves* are toured by automatic five-seater car shuttle resembling a ghost train. Out of the darkness and timed to a cliché-ridden narration loom giant fibreglass grapes and vast hands armed with secateurs, or life-size badly proportioned lumpy figures positioned as cellar masters. You emerge to a glittering photo-studded foyer and a snooty atmosphere and a much-needed drink.

Top of the list of appointment-only houses is the **Maison Veuve Clicquot-Ponsardin**, 1 place des Droits-de-l'Homme (☎03.26.89.54.41; free). In the early days of capitalism, the widowed Mme Clicquot not only took over her husband's business, but later bequeathed it to her business manager rather than to her children – both radical breaks with tradition. In keeping with this past, the *maison* is one of the least pompous and its video the best. The *caves*, with their horror-movie fungi, are old Gallo-Roman quarries. The **House of Pommery**, 5 place du Général-Gouraud (☎03.26.61.62.55; 40F/€6.10), also has excavated Roman quarries for its cellars; it claims – in a case of good champagne oneupmanship – to have been the first to do so. Other appointment-only *maisons* are **Ruinart**, 4 rue des Crayères (☎03.26.77.51.51; 50–120F/€7.62–18.29, depending on number of tastings), **Charles Heidsieck**, 4 bd Henry-Vasnier (☎03.26.84.43.50; 40–60F/€6.10–9.15), and **Lanson**, 12 bd Lundy (☎03.26.78.50.50; 30F/€4.57).

Finally, to get an overview of the various champagnes available (plus wines from all over France), it's worth visiting **La Vino Cave**, 43 place Drouet-d'Erlon (Mon 2.30–7.30pm, Tues–Sat 9.30am–1pm & 2.30–7.30pm), where you can also buy all the paraphernalia of the bubbly business, from champagne flutes to snazzy servers.

Eating and drinking

Place Drouet-d'Erlon, a wide pedestrianized boulevard lined with **bars** and **restaurants**, is where you'll find most of the city's nightlife, such as it is. For self-catering, there's a big Wednesday and Saturday **market** in place du Boulingrin (6am–1pm).

Aux Bons Amis, 13 rue Gosset (☎03.26.07.39.76). Excellent-value traditional French cooking. Lunchtime set menu at 67F/€10.21. Closed Fri evening, Sat & Sun.

Boyer, 64 bd Henry-Vasnier (☎03.26.82.80.80). Reputed to be one of France's finest gastronomic restaurants – with prices and style to match – *Boyer* is set in a restored eighteenth-century château and equipped with a helipad. Closed Mon & Tues lunch. Menus from 990F/€150.92.

Chèvre et Menthe, 63 rue de Barbatre. A very good-value, plain establishment with an interesting range of gourmet salads from 35F/€5.34; recommended for vegetarians. Daily *carte* dishes might include moussaka (45F/€6.86) as well as more traditional choices. Closed Sun evening and Mon.

Le Colbert, 64 place Drouet-d'Erlon (☎03.26.47.55.79). Traditional cuisine – including an excellent regional Champagne-Ardenne menu (158F/€24.09) – in a daintily set-up and popular restaurant. Menus from 100F/15.24, and affordable champagne by the glass.

La Grappa, 49 rue du Colonel-Fabien. Handy for the youth hostel, this Italian is popular – particularly with families – and serves inexpensive pasta and pizza dishes.

Le Paysan, 16 rue de Fismes (☎03.26.40.25.51). Serves genuine peasant dishes, copious and delicious, in suitably rustic surroundings with genuinely warm service. It's some way northwest of the station: follow rue de Courcelles, and rue de Fismes will be on your left. Menus under 100F/€15.24 during the week. Closed Sat lunch & Sun evening.

Au Petit Bacchus, 11 rue de l'Université (☎03.26.47.10.05). Reasonably priced traditional cooking in an interior of sparse brick floor with bare tables. Around 120F/€19. Closed Sun and Mon.

Au Petit Comptoir, 17 rue de Mars (☎03.26.40.58.58). Close to the Marché du Boulingrin, with traditional dishes from 95F/€14.48 (no menus) served in a solid provincial middle-class milieu. Champagne by the glass too. Closed Sat lunch & Sun.

Nightlife and entertainment

For drinking into the early hours there are plenty of large terrace **cafés** on place Drouet-d'Erlon, including *Café Leffe*, at no. 85, which has a wide selection of beers; and *Le Gaulois*, at nos. 2–4, with excellent cocktails and ice creams. If you want to **dance**, try *Le Curtayn Club* at 7 bd Général-Leclere (daily 10pm–4am). *L'Usine*, 115 rue Lesage (☎03.26.04.56.38), hosts a **rock festival** in October, with concerts throughout the year. The Opéra Cinema, 3 rue T.-Dubois (☎03.26.47.29.36), shows undubbed **films**. In the summer, over 120 **classical concerts** – many of them free – take place as part of Les Flâneries Musicales d'Été; pick up a leaflet at the tourist office.

Epernay

EPERNAY, 26km south of Reims, is *the* Champagne town to head for, beautifully situated below rolling, vine-covered hills, with wealth-impregnated tree-lined streets. In addition to some of the most famous *maisons*, there are also several smaller houses to tour, and the town makes a good base for exploring the surrounding villages and vineyards.

Arrival, information and accommodation

Epernay's **gare SNCF** is a five-minute walk north of place de la République, down rue Jean Moet. The **gare routière** is on the corner of rues Dr-Verron and Dr-Rousseau one block northeast from place de la République. The information-packed **tourist office** is at 7 av de Champagne (Easter to mid-Oct Mon–Sat 9.30am–12.30pm & 1.30–7pm, Sun 11am–4pm; mid-Oct to Easter Mon–Sat 9.30am–12.30pm & 1.30–5.30pm; ☎03.26.53.33.00, fax 03.26.51.95.22). If you feel like roaming around the *vignerons*, you could rent a **bike** from Rover Cycles, 10 place Hugues-Plomb (Tues–Sat 9am–noon & 2–7pm; ☎03.26.55.29.61), not far from place de la République at the other end of rue Général-Leclerc.

The cheapest **hotels** in Epernay are *St-Pierre*, 1 rue Jeanne-d'Arc (☎03.26.54.40.80, fax 03.26.57.88.68; ①), in a quiet street away from the centre, and *Le Chapon Fin*, 2 place Mendès-France (☎03.26.55.40.03; ②), by the train station. Classier rooms are to be had at the *Hôtel de Champagne*, 30 rue E.-Mercier (☎03.26.53.10.60, fax 03.26.51.94.63; ④). The *Foyer des Jeunes Travailleurs* **hostel**, within easy walking distance of the station at 2 rue Pupin (☎03.26.51.62.51; Mon–Fri 9am–8pm, Sat 10am–2pm; 16–25s only), has dorm-style accommodation and a cheap cafeteria. The local **campsite** is 1.5km to the north on route de Cumières in the Parc des Sports, on the south bank of the Marne (☎03.26.55.32.14; closed Oct–Feb).

The Town

The loveliest of Epernay's streets is **avenue de Champagne**, running east from the central place de la République. It's worth a stroll for its eighteenth- and nineteenth-century mansions and champagne *maisons*.

The largest, and probably the most famous *maison* of all, is **Moët et Chandon**, 18 av de Champagne (daily 9.30–11.30am & 2–4.30pm; mid-Nov to March Mon–Fri only; visits cost 40F/€6.10 including *dégustation* of the brut Impérial, 65F/€9.91 for two *dégustations*, and 100F/€15.24 for three *dégustations*), which owns Mercier, Ruinart and a variety of other concerns, including Dior perfumes. By its own reckoning, a Moët champagne cork pops somewhere in the world every two seconds. The cellars are adorned with mementos of Napoléon, a good friend of the original M. Moët. True to tradition, the bottles are still turned by hand, a process of *remuage* (riddling) explained in detail by the guide; by the time you reach the generous *dégustation* you appreciate why the stuff costs so much.

Of the other *maison* visits, one of the most rewarding is **Mercier**, 70 av de Champagne (Mon–Fri 9.30–11.30am & 2–4.30pm, Sat & Sun 9.30–11.30am & 2–5pm; Dec–Feb closed Tues & Wed; 30F/€4.57, including *dégustation*), whose glamour relic is a giant barrel that held 200,000 bottles' worth when M. Mercier took it to the 1889 Paris Exposition, with the help of 24 oxen – only to be upstaged by the Eiffel Tower. Visits round the cellars are by electric train and are great fun, climaxing in *dégustation*.

Castellane, by the station at 57 rue de Verdun (April–Oct daily 10am–noon & 2–6pm; 35F/€5.34, including *dégustation*), provides Epernay with its chief landmark: a tower looking like a kind of Neoclassical signal box. As well as the inevitable cellars, the visit takes in a rather good museum displaying bottles and their labels, publicity posters, old tools and tableaux of champagne-making and related processes. Best of all, you get to climb to the top of the tower, which allows unsurpassed views of the town and surrounding vineyards.

Epernay has many other *grandes maisons* that can be visited by appointment, but perhaps more worthwhile are the many smaller houses. Two which offer tours with *dégustation* are located on rue Chaude-Ruelle, west of av de Champagne, with views over the town: **Janisson-Baradon**, at no. 65 (☎03.26.54.45.85; 25F/€3.81), and **Leclerc-Briant**, at no. 67 (☎03.26.54.45.33; 20F/€3.05).

Esterlin, at 25 av de Champagne (Mon–Fri 9am–12.30pm & 1.30–5pm, Sat & Sun 10am–12.30pm & 1.30–5.30pm), don't offer guided tours of their cellars, but if you want to see their ten-minute video on the painstaking process of making champagne then you'll get a free *dégustation* to sip throughout.

Die-hard champagne lovers might wander into the **Musée du Champagne** at 13 av de Champagne (closed in 2000 for restoration). The exhibits themselves are humdrum, but the building is worth a peek, housed as it is in Château Perrier, an impressive example of a nineteenth-century champagne mansion, with a Louis XIII exterior and a flamboyant marble interior featuring a rather grand staircase.

Eating and drinking

Restaurants in Epernay are not cheap, but good food is assured at *La Table Kobus*, 3 rue du Dr-Rousseau (☎03.26.58.42.68; from 135F/€20.58; closed Sun evening & Mon), and at *Les Berceaux*, 13 rue des Berceaux (☎03.26.55.28.84; closed Sun evening & Mon; menus from 180F/€27.44), which also has a wine bar. Several cheaper, culturally varied places are on rue Gambetta, between the gare and place de la République: *Le Bel Azur*, at no. 33, has Tunisian specialities; while *Le Messina*, at no. 17, has pizza and inexpensive pasta. For a major blowout, head 5km north on the N2051 to Champillon and the *Royal Champagne* (☎03.26.52.87.11; surprise *dégustation* menu at 600F/€91.47, weekday lunchtime menus from 155F/€23.63, and evening menus from 300F/€45.73).

Around Epernay

The villages in the vineyards of the Montagne de Reims, Côte des Blancs and Vallée de la Marne which surround Epernay, promote a range of "attractions": the world's largest champagne bottle and cork in **MARDEUIL**; the world's largest champagne glass and an artisan chocolate producer in **PIERRY**; a snail farm in **OLIZY-VIOLAINE**; a museum of marriage in **OGER**; and a traditional *vigneron*'s house and early twentieth-century school room at **OEUILLY**. Full details of these are available from Epernay's tourist office, along with lists of all the champagne producers. But the best reason for taking yourself out into the countryside is to view the vines. Many of the villages have conserved their sleepy old stone charm: **VERTUS**, 16km south of Epernay, is particularly pretty, and so too is **HAUTVILLERS**, 6km north of town, where you can see the abbey of Dom Pérignon fame. Various "champagne excursions" by minibus, horse-drawn carriage or hot-air balloon are touted, but there are regular local **buses** from Epernay's *gare routière*.

Troyes

TROYES, ancient capital of Champagne, is a gem. Its high, narrow streets of restored, half-timbered houses protect an elegant Gothic cathedral, half-a-dozen superb lesser churches, a fistful of Renaissance mansions and several exceptionally good museums.

Arrival, information and accommodation

The **gare SNCF** and **gare routière** are side by side off bd Carnot (part of the ring road). Not all buses use the main station, though, and if you're heading for the countryside it's best to check first with the regional **tourist office** at 16 bd Carnot (Mon–Sat 9am–12.30pm & 2–6.30pm; ☎03.25.82.62.70, fax 03.25.73.06.81, *www.ot-troyes.fr*). Information on the town of Troyes can also be obtained from the tourist office on rue Mignard, opposite the church of St-Jean (July & Aug Mon–Sat 9am–8.30pm, Sun 10am–noon & 2–6.30pm; first two weeks of Sept Mon–Sat 9am–7.30pm, Sun 10am–noon & 2–5pm; rest of year Mon–Sat 9am–12.30pm & 2–6.30pm, Sun 10am–noon & 2–5pm; ☎03.25.73.36.88). Smaller tourist offices can be found in all the churches mentioned below, with the same opening hours as the churches.

Places to stay around the station are plentiful, though for not much more you can find accommodation right in the centre of the old town. Outside term-time there may be room in the city's foyers – the tourist office has details.

Hotels

De la Gare, 8 bd Carnot (☎03.25.78.22.84, fax 03.25.74.16.26, *hotel.de.la.gare@pem.net*). A simple but comfortable two-star near the station. ③.

Grand Hôtel, 4 av Mal-Joffre (☎03.25.79.90.90, fax 03.25.78.48.93). Right opposite the station, a big three-star hotel with swimming pool and garden. ④.

Patiotel, next door to the *Grand Hôtel* (same telephone and fax numbers) and managed by the same people, but with cheaper rates. ③.

Le Relais St-Jean, 51 rue Paillot-de-Montabert (☎03.25.73.89.90, fax 03.25.73.88.60, *relais.st.jean@wanadoo.fr*). Posh hotel in a half-timbered building in a narrow street right in the centre. ⑥.

Splendid, 44 bd Carnot (☎03.25.73.08.52, fax 03.25.93.41.04, *lesplendid@pem.net*). Near the station on a very busy road. Rooms have shower and TV. ②.

Du Théâtre, 35 rue Jules-Lebocey (☎03.25.73.18.47, fax 03.25.73.85.73). In a quiet location virtually opposite the Théâtre Madeleine, *du Théâtre* has a friendly management and a good-value, old-fashioned brasserie downstairs. ②.

Hostel and campsite

HI hostel, chemin Ste-Scholastique, Rosières (☎03.25.82.00.65, fax 03.25.72.93.78). Decent hostel located 5km out of town on the Dijon road in a former fourteenth-century priory; take bus #8 direction "Rosières", stop "Liberté". Opposite the sign saying "Vielaines", a path leads down to the priory. Open year round; HI card required.

Camping municipal, 7 rue Roger-Salengro, Pont Ste-Marie (☎03.25.81.02.64). Attractive grassy campsite, situated 5km out on the N60 to Châlons, on the left, with good facilities including washing machines and children's play area. Closed mid-Oct to March.

The Town

As tourist pamphlets are at pains to point out, the ring of boulevards round the town is shaped like a champagne cork. In fact it's just as much like a sock – a shape that's just as suitable, since hosiery and woollens have been Troyes' most important industry since the end of the Middle Ages, when Louis XIII decreed that charitable houses had to be self-supporting and the orphanage of the Hôpital de la Trinité set their charges to knitting stockings.

Some of the old machines and products used for creating garments can be seen in the **Musée de la Bonneterie** (June–Sept daily except Tues 10am–1pm & 2–6pm; Oct–May Wed–Sun 10am–noon & 2–6pm; 30F/€4.57), in the sixteenth-century Hôtel de Vauluisant, opposite the church of St-Pantaléon at 4 rue de Vauluisant. Beautifully restored and visually appealing, it sets an example for all crafts museums with its respect for traditions and lack of sentimentality. The building also houses the **Musée Historique de Troyes** (same hours and ticket), a small collection of unsophisticated religious art from the Troyes school. Just one block east is **La Maison de l'Outil**, 7 rue de la Trinité (Mon–Fri 9am–1pm & 2–6.30pm, Sat & Sun 10am–1pm & 2–6pm; 30F/€4.57), in the beautiful sixteenth-century Hôtel de Mauroy, a surprisingly fascinating museum of tools, with seventeenth- and eighteenth-century exhibits providing a window into the world of the workers who used them and the people who crafted them.

Despite being raked by numerous fires in the Middle Ages, Troyes has retained many of its timber-framed buildings south of the central main shopping street, in **rue Émile-Zola**, around the cathedral and particularly in the streets and alleyways of the **old town** off the pedestrianized rue Champeaux. The church of **St-Jean-au-Marché**, between rues Émile-Zola and Champeaux (daily: July & Aug 10am–12.30pm & 1.30–7pm; rest of year 10am–noon & 2–4pm), is where Henry V married Catherine of France after being recognized as heir to the French throne in the 1420 Treaty of Troyes. Other churches worth seeking out are the church of **Ste-Madeleine**, on the road of the same name (same hours as St-Jean), whose delicate stonework rood screen – used to keep the priest separate from the congregation – is one of the few left in France; the sumptuous church of **St-Pantaléon** (daily 10am–12.30pm & 2–5.30pm; July & Aug till 6pm), southwest of the church of St-Jean, on rue Vauluisant; and the Gothic **Basilique St-Urbain**, place Vernier (same hours as church of St-Jean), its exterior dramatizing the Day of Judgement with the damned and the devils providing a wicked variety of gargoyles.

Heading east from St-Urbain across the covered canal, you come to **La Cité quartier**, full of more museums and ancient buildings, and centred on the **Cathédrale St-Pierre-et-St-Paul** (daily: July to mid-Sept 9am–1pm & 2–7pm; rest of year 9am–1pm & 2–6pm), whose pale Gothic nave is stroked with reflections from the wonderful stained-glass windows. Next door to the cathedral, housed in the old bishops' palace on place St-Pierre, is the **Musée d'Art Moderne** (daily except Tues 11am–6pm; 30F/€4.57), an outstanding museum displaying part of an extraordinary private collection of art, particularly rich in Fauvist paintings by the likes of Vlaminck and Derain – along with other, first-class works by Degas, Courbet, Gauguin, Matisse (a tapestry and three canvases), Bonnard, Braque, Modigliani, Rodin, Robert Delaunay and Ernst. On the other side of the cathedral, the **Abbaye St-Loup** (daily except Tues 10am–noon & 2–6pm; 30F/€4.57) houses collections of paintings, natural history and archeology, and has a showcase window that gives onto an ornate Baroque library. In similar vein, the **Hôtel-Dieu**, back down rue de la Cité, has a richly decorated sixteenth-century pharmacy (Wed, Sat & Sun 2–6pm; 20F/€3.05; entrance on quai des Comtes de Champagne).

Quite different from the rash of Christian churches in Troyes is the **synagogue** on rue Brunneval, inaugurated in memory of the Jewish scholar Rachi (1040–1105) in 1987. He was a member of the small Jewish community which flourished for a time dur-

CLOTHES SHOPPING

Today the clothes industry still accounts for more than half Troyes' employment, and buying **clothes from the factory** is one of the town's chief attractions: designer-label clothes can be bought at half the normal shop price. Espace Belgrand in rue Belgrand, off bd du 14-Juillet, has quite a number (Mon 2–7pm, Tues–Fri 10am–7pm, Sat 9am–7pm); rues Émile-Zola and des Bas Trévois are also worth a wander. Or you can go out to the manufacturers on the outskirts, where dozens of factory shops sell clothes, shoes and leather goods designed for everyone, from Nike to Laura Ashley and Yves St-Laurent to Jean-Paul Gaultier. The best array is in the four giant sheds of Marques Avenue, 114 bd de Dijon, St-Julien-les-Villas (Mon 2–7pm, Tues–Fri 10am–7pm, Sat 9.30am–7pm), south of the city on the N71 to Dijon. At Pont-Ste-Marie, to the northeast of Troyes along the D960 to Nancy, there's Le Centre des Marques, on rue Marc-Verdier, and McArthur Glen, on rue Danton, both with the same hours as Espace Belgrand. Buses for the outlets on the outskirts of town depart from the bus station by Marché les Halles.

ing the eleventh and twelfth centuries under the protection of the counts of Champagne. His commentaries on both the Old Testament and the Talmud are still important to academics today: the Rachi University Institute opposite is devoted to studying his work.

Eating and drinking

Rue Champeaux is packed with places to **eat**: crêpes are on offer at *Crêperie la Tourelle*, the half-timbered building at no. 9, with its own tiny tower and views of the church of St-Jean. Troyes' top restaurant is *Le Valentino*, 11 cour de la Rencontre (☎03.25.73.14.14; closed Sat lunch, Mon & three weeks in Aug & Sept; menus from 110F/€16.77), whose inventive chef combines different flavours from all over the world, while a good place to try the regional speciality of *andouillette* is the *Cheval de 3* at 31 rue de la Cité (☎03.25.80.58.23; closed in the evening on Tues, Wed & Sun). For brasserie food, try the *Hôtel du Théâtre*'s brasserie (closed Sun evening; menus from 68F/€10.37). *Le Café du Musée*, 59 rue de la Cité, near the cathedral, has a decent upstairs restaurant (closed Sun & Mon evening) and a cool contemporary **bar** downstairs (Mon–Sat until 3am), with a wide range of beers. *Le Tricasse*, 2 rue Charbonnet, is a perennially popular bar, with tables and the occasional live band; a few more bars are on nearby narrow rue Paillot-de-Montabert, including the tiny and consistently packed-out *Bar des Bougnets des Pouilles*.

Self-caterers should head for the Marché les Halles, a daily covered **market** on the corner of rue Général-de-Gaulle and rue de la République, close to the Hôtel de Ville. Vegetarians and the health-conscious will think they're in heaven at Coopérative Hermes, 39 rue Général-Saussier, a surprisingly good – for France – wholesale/health-food store.

The Plateau de Langres

The Seine, Marne, Aube and several other lesser rivers rise in the **Plateau de Langres** between Troyes and Dijon. Hunting for sources is a thankless task – there are no bubbling springs – and you're more likely to be conscious of undifferentiated water everywhere. Main routes from Troyes to the Burgundian capital of Dijon skirt this area; to the east, the N19 (which the train follows) takes in **Chaumont** and **Langres**, two towns that could briefly slow your progress if you're in no hurry, and the home village of General de Gaulle, **Colombey-Les-Deux-Églises**.

the 1980s. The only major investment in the region has been a nuclear power station in the loop of the Meuse at Chooz, to which locals responded by etching "Nuke the Élysée!" high on a half-cut cliff of slate just downstream.

Tourism, the main growth industry, is developing apace – there are walking and boating possibilities, plus good train and bus connections – though the eerie isolated atmosphere of this region remains.

Charleville-Mézières

The twin towns of **CHARLEVILLE** and **MÉZIÈRES** provide a good starting point for exploring the northern part of the region, which spreads across the meandering Meuse before the valley closes in and the forests take over. Of the two, Charleville, with its beautifully arcaded place Ducale, is the one to head for.

The **place Ducale**, in the centre of Charleville, was the result of the seventeenth-century local duke's envy of the contemporary place des Vosges in Paris. Despite the posh setting, the shops in the arcades remain very down-to-earth – *poissonnières* amongst them – and the cafés charge reasonable prices to sit outside: a very good position on Tuesdays, Thursdays and Saturdays, when the **market** is held here.

From 31 place Ducale you can reach the complex of old and new buildings that house the **Musée de l'Ardenne** (Tues–Sun 10am–noon & 2–6pm; 25F/€3.81, or 35F/€5.34 combined ticket with Musée Arthur Rimbaud, see below), which covers the different economic activities of the region over the ages through local paintings, prehistoric artefacts, legends, puppetry, weapons and coins. You need to keep up a good pace to get round all the rooms, but it's fun and informative.

The most famous person to emerge from the town was Arthur Rimbaud (1854–91), who ran away from Charleville four times before he was 17, so desperate was he to escape from its quiet provincialism. He is honoured in the **Musée Arthur Rimbaud**, housed in a very grand stone windmill – a contemporary of the place Ducale – on quai Arthur-Rimbaud, two blocks north of the main square (Tues–Sun 10am–noon & 2–6pm; 20F/€3.05, or 35F/€5.34 combined ticket with Musée de l'Ardenne). It contains a host of pictures of him and those he hung out with, as well as facsimiles of his writings and related documents. A few steps down the quayside is the spot where he composed *Le Bateau Ivre*. After penning poetry in Paris, journeying to the Far East and trading in Ethiopia and Yemen, Rimbaud died in a Marseille hospital. His body was brought back to his home town – probably the last place he would have wanted to be buried – and true Rimbaud fanatics can visit his **tomb** in the cemetery west of the place Ducale at the end of avenue Charles Boutet.

Charleville is also a major international **puppetry centre** (its school is justly famous), and every three years it hosts one of the largest puppet festivals in the world, the **Festival Mondial des Théâtres de Marionnettes** (the next one is in Sept 2003; details can be found at *www.marionnette.com*). As many as 150 professional troupes – some from as far away as Mali and Burma – put on something like fifty shows a day on the streets and in every available space in town. Tickets are cheap, and there are shows for adults as well as the usual stuff aimed at kids. If you miss the festival you can still catch one of the puppet performances in the summer months every year (☎03.24.33.72.50 for booking and information), or if you're passing by the Institut de la Marionnette between 10am and 9pm, you can see one of the automated episodes of the *Four Sons of Aymon* enacted on the facade's clock every hour, or all twelve scenes on Saturday at 9.15am.

Practicalities

From the **gare SNCF**, place Ducale is a five-minute ride away on bus #1, #3 or #5; the **gare routière** is a couple of blocks northeast of the square, between rues du Daga and

Noël. The **regional tourist office** for the Ardennes is at 22 place Ducale (July & Aug Mon–Sat 9am–7pm, Sun 10am–7pm; rest of year Mon–Sat 9am–12.30pm & 1.30–7pm, Sun 2–7pm; ☎03.24.56.06.08, fax 03.24.59.20.10), with Charleville-Mézières' tourist office at no. 4 (Tues–Sat 9.30am–noon & 1.30–6pm; ☎03.24.32.44.80).

Three fairly central **hotels** that are worth trying are the *de Paris*, 24 av G.-Corneau (☎03.24.33.34.38, fax 03.24.59.11.21, *www.hoteldeparis08.fr,* ③); the *Central*, 23 av du Maréchal Leclerc (☎03.24.33.33.69, fax 03.24.59.38.25; ②); and *Le Relais du Square*, 3 place de la Gare (☎03.24.33.38.76, fax 03.24.33.56.66; ③; closed Sat & Sun), a smart three-star hotel in a tree-filled square near the station. The town **campsite** (☎03.24.33.23.60; open May–Sept) is north of place Ducale, over the river and left along rue des Paquis. There are plenty of places to **eat and drink** in Charleville. For something a bit special, *La Côte à l'Os*, at 11 cours Aristide-Briand (☎03.24.59.20.16; closed Sun evening), specializes in *fruits de mer* and local *Ardennais* cuisine; daily chalkboard menus cost from 79F/€12.04. *La Cigogne*, at 40 rue Dubois-Crancé (☎03.24.33.25.39; closed Sun evening, Mon & first week Aug), also serves good regional dishes, with menus from 88F/€13.42. Worth checking out for a drink or a coffee is the *Ideal Bar* on rue de la République – a characterful, down-to-earth local despite its chandelier-style lights and dark wood interior; or you could sit under the arcades on place Ducale at *Au Caveau*.

North of Charleville

George Sand wrote of the stretch of the Meuse that winds through the Ardennes that "its high wooded cliffs, strangely solid and compact, are like some inexorable destiny that encloses, pushes and twists the river without permitting it a single whim or any escape". What all the tourist literature writes about, however, are the legends of medieval struggles between Good and Evil whose characters have given names to some of the curious rocks and crests. The grandest of these, where the schist formations have taken the most peculiar turns, is the **Roc de la Tour**, also known as the Devil's Castle, up a path off the D31, 3.5km out of **MONTHERMÉ**, a slate-roofed little town with nothing of great interest except a twelfth-century **church** with late medieval frescoes.

The journey through this frontier country should ideally be done on foot or skis, or **by boat**. The alternatives for the latter are good old *bateau-mouche*-type cruises (RDTA; July & Aug Tues–Sun; April–June & Sept–Oct weekends only; ☎03.24.33.77.92), which depart from the Vieux Moulin (Musée Rimbaud) in Charleville-Mézières and the quai des Paquis in Monthermé, or live-in pleasure boats – not wildly expensive if you can split the cost four or six ways. These are rented out, with bikes on board, by Ardennes Plaisance in Charleville-Mézières, 76 rue des Forges-St-Charles (☎03.24.56.47.61), and Ardennes Nautisme in Sedan, 16 rue du Château (☎03.24.27.05.15, *www.ardennes-nautisme.fr*), the next town downstream from Charleville. The latter moor their boats just east of Dom-Le-Mesnil on the D764 at the junction of the Meuse and the Canal des Ardennes. The local walking **organization**, Comité Départemental de Randonnée Pédestre des Ardennes (☎03.24.26.55.95), can provide footpath maps; for details of canoeing, biking or riding, contact the regional tourist office at Charleville (see above). For **public transport** from Charleville, trains follow the Meuse into Belgium, and a few buses run up to Monthermé and **LES HAUTES-RIVIÈRES**, the latter on the River Semoy.

The **GR12** is a good walking route, circling the **Lac des Vieilles Forges**, 17km northwest of Charleville – where you can hire canoes – then meeting the Meuse at Bogny and crossing over to Hautes-Rivières in the even more sinuous **Semoy Valley**. There are plenty of other tracks, too, though beware of *chasse* (hunting) signs – French hunters tend to hack through the undergrowth with their safety catches off and are notoriously trigger-happy. Wild boar are the main quarry being hunted, and nowhere near as dangerous as their pursuers: the bristly beasts would seem to be more intelligent, too, rooting about near the crosses of the Resistance memorial near **REVIN**, while hunters stalk the forest at a respectful distance. The abundance of wild boar is partly explained when you rootle around on the forest floor yourself and discover, between the trees to either side of the river, an astonishing variety of mushrooms, and, in late summer, wild strawberries and bilberries. For a quaint insight into life in the forest stop in at the **Musée de la Forêt**, situated right on the edge of the Ardennes forest, 2km north of **RENWEZ** on the D40 (March–May & mid-Sept to mid-Nov daily 9am–noon & 2–5pm; June to mid-Sept daily 9am–7pm; mid-Nov to Feb Mon–Fri 9am–noon & 2–5pm; 25F/€3.81). All manner of wood-cutting, gathering and transporting is enacted by log dummies along with displays of utensils and flora and fauna of the forest; it's also a tranquil spot for a picnic.

A good **place to stay**, overlooking the river at Revin, is the *Hôtel Francois-1er*, 46 quai Camille-Desmoulins (☎03.24.40.15.88, fax 03.24.40.32.93; ③), which rents out bikes and canoes, and gives good advice on walks. There's also a hostel in **GIVET**, route des Chaumières (☎03.24.42.09.60, fax 03.24.42.02.44).

travel details

Trains

Amiens to: Compiègne (5 daily; 1hr 15min); Laon (4 daily; 2hr); Paris (10 daily; 1hr 45min–2hr); St Quentin (5 daily; 1hr).

Beauvais to: Paris (6 daily; 1hr 10min).

Boulogne-Ville to: Amiens (8 daily; 1hr 15min); Arras (4 daily; 2hr); Calais-Ville (9 daily; 30min); Étaples-Le Touquet (9 daily; 20min), Montreuil (7 daily; 30min); Paris (8 daily; 3hr).

Calais-Ville to: Amiens (6 daily; 1hr 45min); Boulogne-Ville (frequent; 30min); Étaples-Le Touquet (9 daily; 1hr); Lille (frequent; 1hr–1hr 30min); Paris (6 daily; 3hr 30min).

Charleville-Mézières to: Givet (10 daily; 1hr).

Dunkerque to: Arras (7 daily; 1hr 20min); Calais-Ville (1–4 daily; 1hr); Paris (6 daily; 3hr 10min).

Laon to: Paris (4 daily; 2hr); Soissons (4 daily; 1hr 40min).

Lille to: Arras (very frequent; 30–40min); Brussels (frequent; 2hr); Lyon (TGV 7 daily; 3hr); Marseille (4 daily; 5hr 30min–6hr 30min); Paris (very frequent; 2–2hr 30min).

Reims to: Charleville-Mézières (8 daily; 1hr); Epernay (frequent; 30min); Paris (frequent; 2hr).

St-Quentin to: Compiègne (12 daily; 30–40min); Paris (frequent; 1hr 45min).

Troyes to: Chaumont (6 daily; 45min); Langres (4 daily; 1hr 10min); Paris (frequent; 1hr 30min).

Buses

Amiens to: Abbeville (2 daily; 1hr 30min); Albert (4 daily; 40min); Arras (2 daily; 2hr); Beauvais (4 daily; 1hr 15min).

Boulogne to: Calais (4 daily; 1hr); Le Touquet (4 daily; 1hr).

Calais to: Boulogne (4 daily; 1hr); Le Touquet (4 daily; 2hr).

Dunkerque to: Calais (2–9 daily; 30min).

Reims to: Troyes (1–3 daily; 2hr 30min).

Ferries See "Basics", pp.6,8.

CHAPTER THREE

ALSACE-LORRAINE AND THE JURA MOUNTAINS

France's eastern frontier provinces, **Alsace**, **Lorraine** and **Franche-Comté**, where the Jura mountains lie, have had a complex and tumultuous history. For a thousand years they have been a battleground, disputed through the Middle Ages by independent dukes and bishops whose allegiance was endlessly contested by the kings of France and the princes of the Holy Roman Empire, and the scene, this century, of some of the worst fighting of both world wars.

The democratically minded burghers of **Alsace** had already created a plethora of well-heeled, semi-autonomous towns for themselves centuries before their seventeenth-century incorporation into the French state. Sharing the Germans' taste for Hansel-and-Gretel-type decoration, they adorned their buildings with all manner of frills and fancies – oriel windows, carved timberwork and Toytown gables – and with Teutonic orderliness they still maintain them, festooned with flowers and in pristine condition. Not that you should ever call an Alsatian German. Their mother tongue, *Elsässisch*, is a Germanic dialect, but their neighbours across the Rhine have behaved in a decidedly unneighbourly fashion twice in the last 130 years, annexing them, along with much of Lorraine, from 1870 to 1918 and again from 1940 to 1944 under Hitler's Third Reich. They remain fiercely and proudly Alsatian and French – in that order.

The combination of influences makes for a culture and atmosphere as distinctive as any in France. It is seen at its most vivid in the numerous little wine towns that punctuate the **Route du Vin** along the eastern margin of the wet and woody Vosges mountains; at **Colmar**; and in the great cathedral city of **Strasbourg**, now one of the capitals of the European Union. But the province is not just a quaint setting for coach tours: it's

---

ACCOMMODATION PRICE CODES

Each hotel and guesthouse in this book has been graded according to the following price codes, which indicate the price for the **cheapest double room available during the high season**.

① Under 160F/€24	④ 300–400F/€46–61	⑦ 600–700F/€91–107
② 160–220F/€24–34	⑤ 400–500F/€61–76	⑧ 700–800F/€107–122
③ 220–300F/€34–46	⑥ 500–600F/€76–91	⑨ Over 800F/€122

also an industrial powerhouse, making cars, locomotives, textiles, machine tools and telephones, as well as half the beer in France.

By comparison, **Lorraine**, a large region taking in the northern border shared with Luxembourg, Germany and Belgium, is rather colourless, although it has suffered much the same vicissitudes as Alsace. However, the elegant eighteenth-century town of **Nancy**, the cathedral city and provincial capital **Metz**, and the depressing and unforgettable World War I battlefield of **Verdun** are well worth visiting.

More impressive are the wooded plateaux, pastures and valleys of the **Jura mountains** abutting the German and Swiss frontiers further south, rural and poor, but partly rejuvenated by the attentions of the leisure industry. *Ski de fond* – cross-country skiing – is the speciality here, and it's ideal terrain. It's good walking country, too, without the grinding ascents of the neighbouring Alps. The Jura has its own **Route du Vin**, without the hordes of tourists, and the mountains and lakes here are also much less congested than the Vosges in summer; if it's peace and quiet you are looking for, it's here you will find it.

LORRAINE

During World War II, when de Gaulle and the Free French chose **Lorraine**'s double-barred cross as their emblem, they were making a powerful point. For it is this region, above all others, that the French associate with war. Its name derives from the Latin, *Lotharii regnum*, "the kingdom of Lothar", who was one of the three grandsons of Charlemagne, among whom his empire was divided by the Treaty of Verdun in 843 AD.

Lorraine has been the principal route of invasion from the German lands across the Rhine ever since, even though the trench-like valleys of the rivers **Meuse** and **Moselle** form a main line of defence. Joan of Arc was born here in 1412, at **Domrémy-la-Pucelle** on the Meuse, when the land was disputed by the dukes of Burgundy and the kings of France – it only finally became part of the kingdom of France in 1766. In 1792 a mixed army of Prussians and other alarmed royalist enemies of the French Revolution was stopped by Revolutionary forces at the battle of Valmy to the west of Verdun. In 1870 Napoléon III's armies suffered a humiliating defeat at the hands of the Prussians on the heights above Metz. Then, this century, the two world wars saw terrible fighting in the area, both ultimately involving American as well as French armies.

Of all the killing fields the bloodiest was **Verdun**, where the French army fought one of the most costly and protracted battles of all time from 1916 to 1918. The battlefield is a site of national pilgrimage. The SNCF still lays on extra trains here for the celebration of Armistice Day, though there are now few left alive who knew and mourn the 750,000 dead. For a fascinating and detailed history of all the various battlefields there is no better account than Richard Holmes' *Fatal Avenue*.

The rest of Lorraine – a rolling, windswept plateau of farmland to the south, moribund coalfields and heavy industry along the Belgian and German frontiers north of **Metz** – seems to stand in the shadows. General Patton, who commanded the US troops which liberated the area in 1944, said he could imagine "no greater burden than to be the owner of this nasty country where it rains every day and the whole wealth of the people consists in assorted manure piles". That is an unnecessarily harsh judgement: the landscape may not be the prettiest in France, but if this is your first stop out of Paris, you will notice that the people seem far friendlier.

Metz and around

METZ (pronounced "Mess"), the capital of Lorraine, lies on the east bank of the River Moselle, close to the Autoroute de l'Est, linking Paris and Strasbourg, and the main train line. Its origins go back at least to Roman times, when, as now, it stood astride major trade routes. On the death of Charlemagne it became the capital of Lothar's portion of his empire, managing to maintain its prosperity in spite of the dynastic wars that followed. By the Middle Ages it had sufficient wealth and strength to proclaim itself an independent republic, which it remained until its absorption into France in 1552.

A frontier town caught between warring influences, Metz has endured more than its share of history's vicissitudes, none more gruesome than those it has suffered in the last 130 years. In 1870, when Napoléon III's defeated armies were forced to surrender to Kaiser Bill, it was ceded to Germany. It recovered its liberty at the end of World War I in 1918, only to be re-annexed by Hitler in 1940 before being liberated again by American troops in 1944.

Although its only really important sight is the magnificent cathedral, Metz is not at all the dour place you might expect from its northern geography and industrial background. The university founded here in the 1970s is at least partly responsible for its liveliness.

Arrival, information and accommodation

The huge granite **gare SNCF** stands opposite the **post office** at the end of rue Gambetta. The **gare routière** is east of the train station and on the other side of the railway tracks on avenue de l'Amphithéâtre. The **tourist office** (July & Aug Mon–Sat 9am–9pm, Sun 10am–1pm & 3–5pm; rest of year Mon–Sat 9am–7pm, Sun 10am–1pm & 3–5pm; ☎03.87.55.53.76, fax 03.87.36.59.43, *www.ot-metz.fr*) is located by the side of the Hôtel de Ville on place d'Armes in the old town (see below). Almost any bus from the station will take you there.

There is a good range of hotels and budget **accommodation** in Metz, including an HI hostel, foyer (the tourist office has information about other foyers available in summer) and campsite, as well as the odd ritzy establishment. The several reasonable hotels in front of the train station tend to fill up fast in season.

Hotels

de la Cathedrale, 25 place de Chambre (☎03.87.75.00.02, fax 03.87.75.40.75). Charming hotel with original beams and stained-glass windows in a wonderful location opposite the cathedral. ④.

du Centre, 14 rue Dupont-des-Loges (☎03.87.36.06.93, fax 03.87.75.60.66). A well-established, comfortably modernized hotel between rue des Clercs and place St-Louis. ③.

Grand-Hôtel de Metz, 3 rue des Clercs (☎03.87.36.16.33, fax 03.87.60.40.38). An ancient, characterful and recently refurbished establishment in the heart of the old town near the cathedral, with friendly staff. ④.

Lafayette, 24 rue des Clercs (☎03.87.75.21.09). Cheap and cheerful place on the busy shopping street leading from place de la République to the cathedral. ②.

Métropole, 5 place du Général-de-Gaulle (☎03.87.66.26.22, fax 03.87.66.29.91). Not a particularly welcoming place but fine for a stopover, located directly in front of the station. ②.

Moderne, 1 rue Lafayette (☎03.87.66.57.33, fax 03.87.55.98.59). Functional and friendly hotel, just a short distance to the left as you come out of the station. ②.

du Théâtre, 3 rue du Pont-St-Marcel, Île Chambière (☎03.87.31.10.10, fax 03.87.30.04.66). Smart hotel in an exquisite location on the island in the Moselle below the cathedral. Facilities include a swimming pool. ⑤.

Hostels and campsite

Camping municipal, allée de Metz-Plage, Île Chambière (☎03.87.32.05.58, fax 03.87.38.03.39). Quiet, grassy campsite right next door to *Metz Plage* (see below). Open May–Sept.

Carrefour, 6 rue Marchant (☎03.87.75.07.26, fax 03.87.36.71.44). Friendly and conveniently located HI hostel, close to place d'Armes and the cathedral. You may want to take your own sheets, as the ones provided here are of disposable paper, but comfortable enough. Internet access available.

Metz Plage, 1 allée de Metz-Plage, Île Chambière (☎03.87.30.44.02, fax 03.87.33.19.80). Clean, friendly hostel on the island by the bridge at the further end of rue Belle-Isle which crosses the end of rue du Pont-St-Marcel. Bus #3 or #11 (stop "Pontiffroy") from the *gare SNCF*.

The City

Metz in effect is two towns: the original **French quarters**, gathered round the cathedral, and the **Ville allemande**, undertaken as part of a once-and-for-all process of Germanification after the Prussian occupation in 1870. The latter, although unmistakably Teutonic in style, has considerable elegance and grandeur. The **gare SNCF** sets the tone, a vast and splendid granite structure of 1870 in Rhenish Romanesque, which looks like a bizarre cross between a Scottish laird's hunting lodge and a dungeon. Its gigantic dimensions reflect the Germans' long-term strategic intention to use it as the fulcrum of their military transport system in subsequent wars of conquest against the French. It is matched by the **post office** opposite as well as by some imposing bourgeois apartment buildings in the surrounding streets. The whole quarter was meant to serve as a model of superior town planning, in contrast to the squalid Latin hugger-mugger of the old French neighbourhoods, which begin five minutes' walk to the north in place de la République.

The place de la République is a main parking area, bounded on the east side by shops and cafés, with army barracks to the south and the formal gardens of the **Esplanade**, overlooking the Moselle, to the west. To the right, as you look down the esplanade from the square, is the handsome classical **Palais de Justice** in yellow stone. To the left, a gravel drive leads past the old arsenal, now converted into a prestigious concert hall by the postmodernist architect Riccardo Bofill. It continues to the **church of St-Pièrre-aux-Nonnains**, not much to look at but claiming to be one of the oldest churches in France, with elements from the fourth century. Nearby is another historic church: the octagonal thirteenth-century **Chapelle des Templiers**.

From the north side of place de la République, **rue des Clercs** cuts through the attractive, bustling and largely pedestrianized heart of the old city, where most of the shops are located. Past the **place St-Jacques**, with its numerous outdoor cafés, you come to the eighteenth-century **place d'Armes**, where the lofty Gothic **Cathedral of St-Étienne** towers above the pedimented and colonnaded classical facade of the Hôtel de Ville. It boasts the tallest nave in France after Beauvais and Amiens cathedrals, but its best feature is without doubt the stained glass, both medieval and modern, including windows by Chagall in the north transept and ambulatory.

From the cathedral a short walk up rue des Jardins brings you to the city's best museum, the **Musée d'Art et d'Histoire**, 2 rue du Haut-Poirier (daily 10am–noon & 2–6pm; 30F/€4.57), a treasure house of Gallo-Roman sculpture, but equally strong on mock-ups of vernacular architecture from the medieval and Renaissance periods. The art section is less impressive, although it includes works by Corot and Delacroix. When the museum was extended in the 1930s, the remains of Roman baths were discovered, and they are now one of the most interesting things about the museum.

For the city's most compelling townscape, as well as the most dramatic view of the cathedral, you have only to go down to the river bank and cross to the tiny **Île de la Comédie**, dominated by its classical eighteenth-century square and theatre (the oldest in France) and a rather striking Protestant church erected under the German occupation. An older and equally beautiful square is the **place St-Louis** with its Gothic arcades some ten minutes' walk to the east of the cathedral along the curiously named rue En-Fournirue. On the way, wander up into the Italianate streets climbing the **hill of Ste-Croix** to your left, the legacy of the Lombard bankers who came to run the city's finances in the thirteenth century. It's worth continuing east from the place des Paraiges, at the end of rue En-Fournirue, down the rue des Allemands to have a look at the **Porte des Allemands** – a massive, fortified double gate that once barred the eastern entrances to the medieval city.

After a long day, you'll have no trouble finding a nice café or bar to relax in. **Rue des Jardins** has some interesting shops – clothes, records and antiques/junk – and at night, the cathedral and other significant buildings are lit up, making for a pleasant late stroll.

Eating and drinking

Eating is easy in Metz, with plenty of cafés on place St-Jacques that are popular with locals and tourists. For night-time **drinking**, you'll find plenty of bars, clubs and music venues.

Restaurants

Café de l'Abreuvoir, 8 rue de l'Abreuvoir, near place St-Louis. Cosy, noisy and fashionable place, with a very French atmosphere and simple, good wine-bar fare (*andouillette* and *quiche Lorraine* at around 50F/€7.62 per *plat*).

La Fleur de Ly, 5 rue des Piques (☎03.87.36.64.51). Charming restaurant between the cathedral and the river offering traditional French food, with excellent service. Menus change regularly and cost from 120F/€18.29. Closed Sat lunch & Sun.

du Pont-St-Marcel, 1 rue du Pont-St-Marcel, Île Chambière (☎03.87.30.12.29). A seventeenth-century establishment on the island, distinctive for its excellent regional cuisine and staff dressed in regional costume. Menus at 98F/€14.94 and 165F/€25.15, including eel and sucking-pig, and wines from the French Moselle. Closed Sun evening & Mon.

Le Relais des Tanneurs, 2bis rue des Tanneurs, off the end of rue En-Fournirue (☎03.87.75.49.09). Unpretentious restaurant, serving traditional French dishes. Lots of specialities, including mussels, scallops and *ris de veau*; menus 65–160F/€9.91–24.39, *carte* around 120F/€18.29, *plats du jour* 40–60F/€6.10–9.15. Closed Sun & Aug 1–15.

À la Ville de Lyon, 7 rue Piques (☎03.87.36.07.01). Located just below the cathedral, this restaurant specializes in the best traditional cooking. The atmosphere is quite formal (you'll wish you weren't wearing jeans). From 200F/€30.49. Closed Mon, Sun evening & Aug.

Cafés and bars

Comédie Café, quai Vautris, just across the Pont-Des-Roches from the theatre. Stylish and cosy bar/café. Open noon–2pm & 5pm–2am.

Irish Pub, 3 place de Chambre. Crowded and smoky bar. Till 1am.

Café Jehanne d'Arc, place Jeanne-d'Arc. Situated a fifteen-minute walk northeast of place d'Armes, this place features medieval beams and frescoes, and occasional music. There are free jazz concerts in the square every Thursday evening in summer. Till 2 or 3am.

Café Mathis, 72 rue En-Fournirue. A minute old-time place spilling over into the garden of the former chapel of St-Genest in summertime, opposite a house where Rabelais once lived. Closed Sun.

Les Trinitaires, 10–12 rue des Trinitaires, north of place Ste-Croix, opposite *Café Jehanne d'Arc*. The place to go for serious jazz, rock, folk and chanson, enhanced by the Gothic cellars. It's hosted such eminent musicians as Dexter Gordon, Max Roach and Archie Shepp. Live music at 9pm. Closed Sun & Mon.

Le Tunnel, 27 place du Quarteau at the south end of place St-Louis. Loud rock music with your drink. Till 12.30am during the week and 2.30/3.30am weekends.

The battlefields of 1870

Just north of Metz, beyond the Moselle, the land rises to a bleak windswept plateau across which the conquering might of German armies has rolled three times in the last hundred years or so. Stone memorials stand among the fields marking the site of individual, particularly German, regiments' actions.

much of it is now reforested, there are parts even today that steadfastly refuse anchorage to any but the coarsest vegetation.

The most visited part of the battlefield extends along the hills north of Verdun, but the fighting also spread well to the west of the Meuse, to the hills of Mort-Homme and Hill 304, to Vauquois and the Argonne, and south along the Meuse to St-Mihiel, where the Germans held an important salient until dislodged by US forces in 1918.

The only really effective way to explore the area is by car. The main sights are reached via the D913 or by a minor road, the D112, that leaves the main N3 to Metz opposite the Cimetière du Faubourg-Pavé on the outskirts of Verdun and is soon enclosed by appropriately gloomy conifer plantations. On the right you pass a **monument** to André Maginot, who was himself wounded in the battle and under whose later stewardship at the Ministry of War the famous Maginot Line (see box below) was built. Shortly afterwards a sign points out a forest ride to the **Fort de Souville**, the furthest point of the German advance in 1916.

The site is not on the main tourist beat, and it is a very moving, if rather frightening, twenty-minute walk over ground absolutely shattered by artillery fire, with pools of black water standing in the now grassy shell-holes, as if the players in some malevolent game had been abruptly and mysteriously removed. The fort itself lies half-hidden among the scrub, the armoured gun turrets still lowering in their pits, the tunnels to their control rooms dank and dangerous with collapse. A little way beyond the fort, where the D112 meets the D913, a stone lion marks the precise spot at which the German advance was checked. To the left the road continues to Fleury and Douaumont.

THE MAGINOT LINE

Like the Séré de Rivières forts constructed along the line of the rivers Meuse and Moselle after the 1870–71 war (such as Génicourt, Paroches and Troyon on the Meuse – not open to the public), the **Maginot Line** was designed to keep the Germans out. Constructed between 1930 and 1940, it was the brainchild of the French Minister of War (1929–31), André Maginot. Spanning the entire length of the French–German border, it comprised a complete system of defence in depth. There were advance posts equipped with anti-tank weapons and machine guns. There were fortified police stations close to the frontier. But the main line consisted of a continuous chain of underground strongpoints linked by anti-tank obstacles and equipped with state-of-the-art machinery. It was of course hugely expensive and, when put to the test in 1940, proved to be worse than useless: the Germans simply violated Belgian neutrality and drove round the other end of the Line.

One of the largest forts, the **Fort de Fermont**, situated about 50km north of Verdun near the small town of Longuyon, is open to the public (guided visits June–Aug Mon–Fri 3pm, Sat & Sun 2pm & 3.30pm; Sept–May weekends only 2pm & 3.30pm; ☎03.82.39.21.21; 30F/€4.57; times are susceptible to change so check in advance). Armed with nine fire points, it was served by 6km of underground tunnels and a garrison of 600. The entrance is hidden in woodland. Nothing shows above ground but the scarcely noticeable cupolas of the gun turrets. Below, the tunnels are equipped with power plants, electric trains, monorails, elevators and all the other technological paraphernalia necessary to support such a lunatic enterprise. The place has the feel of a nuclear bunker.

Getting there without your own transport is not easy. There are trains to Longuyon from Metz and Verdun (change at Conflans), but you'll have to hitch or walk the last 5km to the fort. Over in the Alsace region, 15km north of Haguenau, the **Four à Chaux** fortress, dating from 1930, at Lembach has been restored, and now houses a museum of World War II (guided tours daily: mid-March to June & Sept to mid-Nov 10am, 2pm & 3pm; July & Aug 10am, 11am, and hourly 2–5pm; ☎03.88.94.48.62; 25F/€3.81).

Fleury and the Fort de Vaux

The horrifying story of the battle is graphically documented at **FLEURY**, in the **Musée-Memorial de Fleury** (daily: April to mid-Sept 9am–6pm; mid-Sept to March 9am–noon & 2–6pm; closed mid-Dec to mid-Jan; 30F/€4.57), which is included in the Verdun tourist office's guided tour. Contemporary newsreels and photos present the stark truth; and in the well of the museum, a section of the shell-torn terrain that was once the village of Fleury has been reconstructed as the battle left it.

Also included in the tour is the **Fort de Vaux**, 4km east of Fleury (daily: Feb, March & Oct to mid-Dec 9.30am–noon & 1–5pm; April–June & Sept 9am–6pm; July & Aug 9am–6.30pm; 16F/€2.44), where, after six days' hand-to-hand combat in the confined, gas-filled tunnels, the French garrison, reduced to drinking their own urine, were left with no alternative but surrender. On the exterior wall of the fort a plaque commemorates the last messenger pigeon sent to the command post in Verdun vainly asking for reinforcements. Having safely delivered its message, the pigeon expired as a result of flying through the gas-filled air above the battlefield. It was posthumously awarded the *Légion d'Honneur*.

Douaumont

The principal memorial to the carnage stands in the middle of the battlefield a short distance along the D913 beyond Fleury. It is the **Ossuaire de Douaumont** (daily: March & Oct 9am–noon & 2–5.30pm; April 9am–6pm; May–Aug 9am–6.30pm; Sept 9am–noon & 2–6pm; Nov 9am–noon & 2–5pm; closed Jan; 16F/€2.44), a vast and surreal structure with the stark simplicity of a Romanesque crypt or a Carolingian sarcophagus, from which rises a central tower shaped like a projectile aimed at the heavens. Its vaults contain the bones of thousands upon thousands of unidentified soldiers, French and German, some of them visible through windows set in the base of the building. When the battle ended in 1918, the ground was covered in fragments of corpses; 120,000 French bodies were identified, just a third of the total killed.

Across the road, a **cemetery** contains the graves of 15,000 men who died more or less whole – Christians commemorated by rows of identical crosses, Muslims of the French colonial regiments by gravestones aligned in the direction of Mecca. Nearby, a wall commemorates the Jewish dead, beneath a treeless ridge-top on whose tortured, pitted ground around the remains of the Fort de Thiaumont some of them must have died.

The **Fort de Douaumont** (daily: Feb, March & Oct–Dec 10am–1pm & 2–5pm; April–June & Sept 10am–6pm; July & Aug 10am–7pm; closed Jan; 16F/€2.44) is 900m down the road from the cemetery. Completed in 1912 and commanding the highest point of land, it was the strongest of the 38 forts built to defend Verdun. But, in one of those inexplicable aberrations of military top brass, the armament of these forts was greatly reduced in 1915 – when the Germans attacked in 1916, twenty men were enough to overrun the garrison of 57 French territorials. The fort is on three levels, two of them underground, and its claustrophobic, dungeon-like galleries are hung with stalactites. The Germans, who held it for eight months, had 3000 men housed in its cramped quarters with no toilets, continuously under siege, its ventilation ducts blocked for protection against gas, infested with fleas and lice and plagued by rats that attacked the sleeping and the dead indiscriminately. In one night, when their ammunition exploded, 1300 men died in the blast. When the French retook the fort, it was with Moroccan troops in the vanguard. General Mangin, revered by officialdom as the heroic victor of the battle, was known to his troops as "the butcher" for his practice of shoving colonial troops into the front line as cannon fodder.

Last stop on the guided tour is the so-called **Tranchée des Baïonnettes** (Trench of the Bayonets), where, according to legend, two entire infantry platoons are thought to have been buried alive in an upright position with fixed bayonets during a German

ST-MIHIEL AND THE VOIE SACRÉE

In an attempt to cut Verdun off as early as 1914, the Germans captured the town of **ST-MIHIEL** on the River Meuse to the south of it, which gave them control of the main supply route into Verdun. The only route left open to the French – and that far from safe – was the N35, winding north from Bar-le-Duc over the open hills and wheat fields. In memory of all those who kept the supplies going, the road is called **La Voie Sacrée** (The Sacred Way) and marked with milestones capped with the helmet of the *poilu* (the slang term for the French infantryman).

Just behind the town of St-Mihiel to the east, on the Butte de Montsec, is a memorial to the Americans who died here in 1918 and a US cemetery at **THIANCOURT** on the main road.

bombardment on June 11, 1916. A concrete memorial has been built around the area. Though not particularly interesting to look at, it still makes for a very moving experience. Sadly, the bayonets have been stolen.

Mort-Homme, Vauquois and the Argonne

West of the Meuse there are a number of equally evocative, though much less visited, battle sites. The **hill of Mort-Homme**, above the farming village of **CHATTANCOURT**, was furiously contested in 1916 as the Germans sought to outflank the main French positions above Verdun. The access road comes to an end at the memorial on top of the hill, where the ground is still a chaos of shell-holes. On the way up you get a chillingly clear picture of how exposed these low hills were before the conifer plantations.

A dozen kilometres further west, this exposed country gives way to the friendlier contours of the **Argonne**. Just off the D38, above the prettily rustic hamlet of **VAUQUOIS**, is the steep wooded hill known as the **Butte de Vauquois**. Steps lead to the top, where an astonishing sight awaits you. The whole of the hilltop has been blown away by mine explosions, both French and German. The largest, a German sixty-tonner, killed over a hundred French soldiers on May 14, 1916. Of the village of Vauquois, which once stood here, not a trace survives. Extensive networks of trenches and rusting wire entanglements are visible in the woods round about.

Below the hill lies the village of **VARENNES-EN-ARGONNE**, where Louis XVI and the royal family were recognized and arrested on the night of June 21, 1791, as they tried to escape from Revolutionary France. A plaque marks the spot opposite the Hôtel de Ville and the post office. Just uphill is a memorial to American soldiers from Pennsylvania, and the entire area is riddled with tunnels and bunkers from World War I. One that was known as the **Abri du Kronprinz**, off the D38 4km from Varennes, was used by the German Crown Prince during the battle for Verdun.

Nancy and around

NANCY lies on the banks of the River Meurthe. It was spared the Prussian occupation that afflicted the rest of the region from 1870 to 1918, and its centre, largely unaffected by the undistinguished modern sprawl that blights the valley sides, remains a model of eighteenth-century Classicism. For this, it has the last of the independent dukes of Lorraine to thank, the dethroned King of Poland and father-in-law of Louis XV, Stanislas Leszczynski. During the twenty-odd years of his office in the mid-eighteenth century, he ordered some of the most successful urban renewal of the period in all France.

Arrival, information and accommodation

The part of Nancy that you are likely to want to see extends to no more than a ten- or fifteen-minute walk either side of **rue Stanislas**, the main axis and shopping street connecting the **gare SNCF** and the principal **place Stanislas**. The **tourist office**, on the south side of place Stanislas in the Hôtel de Ville (April–Oct Mon–Sat 9am–7pm, Sun & hols 10am–5pm; Nov–March Mon–Sat 10am–6pm, Sun 10am–1pm; ☎03.83.35.22.41, fax 03.83.35.90.10, *www.ot-nancy.fr*), is well stocked with information about both city and region, and organizes the *petit train touristique*, a frequent 45-minute **guided tour** of the town (May–Sept; 35F/€5.34; departure from place de la Carrière), as well as

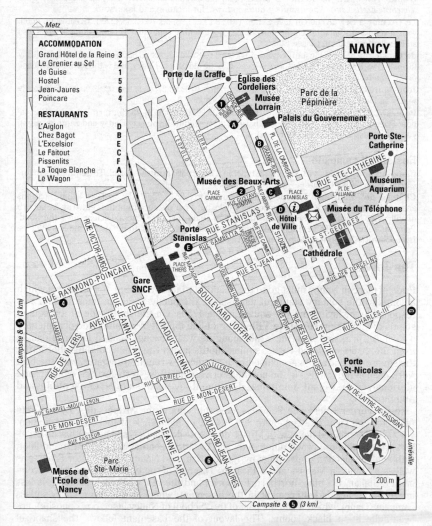

NANCY

ACCOMMODATION

Grand Hôtel de la Reine	3
Le Grenier au Sel	2
de Guise	1
Hostel	5
Jean-Jaures	6
Poincare	4

RESTAURANTS

L'Aiglon	D
Chez Bagot	B
L'Excelsior	E
Le Faitout	C
Pissenlits	F
La Toque Blanche	A
Le Wagon	G

several other themed visits of the town. Regional **buses** depart from rue de l'Île de Corse and boulevard d'Austrasie, both on the eastern side of town. **Internet** access is available at *Voyager*, 57 rue St-Jean, a cyber café located in the new part of town (1F/€0.15 per min).

Reasonable **accommodation** is not hard to find in Nancy. There are plenty of hotels visible from the station, and signs directing you to most of the others – all are within ten to fifteen minutes' walk of the station.

Hotels

Grand Hôtel de la Reine, 2 place Stanislas (☎03.83.35.03.01, fax 03.83.32.86.04, *www .concorde-hotels.com*). The grandest hotel in town, for location and luxury. ⑦.

Le Grenier à Sel, 28 rue Gustave Simon (☎03.83.32.31.98, fax 03.83.35.32.88). Great-value hotel, with seven rooms, all different in appearance, in a beautiful renovated 1714 building. There's also an excellent restaurant. Closed Sun. ②.

de Guise, rue de Guise just off Grande-Rue (☎03.83.32.24.68, fax 03.83.35.75.63). Atmospherically furnished with antiques, the *de Guise* is located in the old part of Nancy, and is the former residence of the countess of Bressy. All rooms have a bathroom. ③.

Jean-Jaurès, 14 bd Jean-Jaurès, south of the station (☎03.83.27.74.14, fax 03.83.90.20.94). Slightly weary and worn, but a friendly place in a pretty location. ②.

Poincaré, 81 rue Raymond-Poincaré (☎03.83.40.25.99, fax 03.83.27.22.43); turn left out of the station. Friendly and clean, with a special bargain at weekends: if you stay Friday and Saturday night, you get Sunday night thrown in free. ①.

Hostel and campsite

Camping de Brabois (☎03.83.27.18.28). Set in a large park near the hostel. To get there take bus #26 direction "Villers Clairlieu", stop "Camping".

Château de Rémicourt, 149 rue de Vandoeuvre (☎03.83.27.73.67, fax 03.83.41.41.35). Spacious and pretty hostel, set in a sixteenth-century castle, but a fair distance from the centre in the suburb of Villers-lès-Nancy to the southwest off the N74 Dijon road/av Général-Leclerc, near the Rond-Point du Vélodrome. To get there, take bus #16 on rue des Carmes, to the end of the line "Villers-Lycée Stanislas", or the #26 direction "Villers Clairlieu", stop "Fiacre".

The Town

Pride of place in Nancy must go to the beautiful **place Stanislas**, the middle of which belongs to the solitary statue of its inspirer, the portly Stanislas himself, who was responsible for laying out the square in the 1750s. On the south side of the square stands the imposing **Hôtel de Ville**, its roof-line topped by a balustrade ornamented with florid urns and amorini, while along its walls lozenge-shaped lanterns dangle from the beaks of gilded cocks; similar motifs adorn the other buildings bordering the square. Its entrances are closed by magnificent wrought-iron gates, with the best work of all in the railings of the northeastern and northwestern corners, which frame gloriously extravagant fountains dominated by lead statues of Neptune and Amphitrite.

In the corner where rue Stanislas joins the square, the **Musée des Beaux-Arts** (daily except Tues 10.30am–6pm; 30F/€4.57, or 35F/€5.34 if there's an exhibition; 40F/€6.10 combined ticket with Musée de l'École de Nancy – see below) has an excellent presentation of French nineteenth- and twentieth-century art on the ground floor, with a good selection of paintings by Émile Friant and Nancy's own Victor Prouvé, as well as a Manet, a Matisse and a Picasso. The rest of the collection upstairs, encompassing Italian, German, northern European and the rest of French painting, is less interesting. Time is better spent in the basement, where works from Nancy's glass company, Daum, which formed a part of the "School of Nancy" (see box opposite), are beautifully lit in black rooms. The layout of the basement follows the shape of

NOUVEAU NANCY

A traditional handicraft and metal-working town, at the turn of the twentieth century Nancy became a centre of **Art Nouveau** to rival Paris. The practitioners of Art Nouveau in Nancy attempted to marry the artistic styles of orientalism and Baroque with the industrial advances of the day, and their style became known as the "School of Nancy" (*l'École de Nancy*). The most illustrious exponents of the "School of Nancy" were the manufacturer of glass and ceramics, Émile Gallé, and the glass manufacturer Daum. But the town's moment of glory was short-lived, and all that now remains are a handful of buildings and the Musée de l'École de Nancy, housed in a *fin-de-siècle* villa. For a post-museum coffee in the same kind of atmosphere, try the Art Nouveau café-restaurant of the former hotel *L'Excelsior* (see p.284), opposite the train station, built in 1910 and pre-served virtually intact to this day. It's worth keeping your eyes open as you walk around Nancy as there are many other expressions of small Art Nouveau. The Nancy tourist office distributes a free leaflet, *École de Nancy – Itinéraire Art Nouveau*, which details several itineraries around Nancy's Art Nouveau heritage.

fortifications dating from the fifteenth century through to Vauban's seventeenth-century alterations, which were found during the recent renovation. For a glimpse of Daum's contemporary creations you can visit their shop, also on place Stanislas. A short walk east of the square is the excellent **Muséum-Aquarium de Nancy**, at 34 rue Ste-Cathérine (daily 10am–noon & 2–6pm; 30F/€4.57). Upstairs is a colossal jumble of stuffed animals and birds, woefully displayed and labelled, while downstairs is a star-tling aquarium of exotic fish whose colours surpass even the daring of Matisse.

On its north side, place Stanislas opens into the long, tree-lined **place de la Carrière**, a fine eighteenth-century transformation of what was originally a jousting ground. Its further end is closed by the classical colonnades of the **Palais du Gouvernement**, former residence of the governor of Lorraine. Behind it, housed in the fifteenth-century Palais Ducal and entered through a handsome doorway sur-mounted by an equestrian statue of one of the dukes, is the **Musée Lorrain**, 64 Grande-Rue (daily except Tues: May–Sept 10am–6pm; Oct–April 10am–noon & 2–5pm; closed public hols; 20F/€3.05, 30F/€4.57 combined ticket with the Musée des Cordeliers). Dedicated to the history and traditions of Lorraine, it contains, among other treasures, a room full of superb etchings by the Nancy-born seventeenth-century artist, Jacques Callot, whose concern with social issues, evident in series such as *The Miseries of War* and *Les Gueux*, presaged much nineteenth- and twentieth-century art. Next door, in the Église des Cordeliers et Chapelle Ducale, is the **Musée des Cordeliers** (same hours as Musée Lorrain; 20F/€3.05, 30F/€4.57 combined ticket with the Musée Lorrain), where rural life in the region in days gone by is illustrated. On the other side of the Palais du Gouvernement, you can play crazy golf, admire the deer or just collapse with exhaustion on the green grass of the **Parc de la Pépinière**, a sort of cross between a formal French garden and an English park – there is also a free zoo. At the end of Grande-Rue is the medieval city gate, **Porte de la Craffe**.

A half-hour walk southwest of the train station, the **Musée de l'École de Nancy**, 36 rue Sergent-Blandan (Mon 2–6pm, Wed–Sun 10.30am–6pm; 30F/€4.57), is housed in a 1909 villa built for the Corbin family, founders of the Magasins Réunis chain of depart-ment stores. Even if you are not into Art Nouveau, this collection is exciting. Although not all of it belonged to the Corbins, the museum is arranged as if it were a private house. The furniture is outstanding – all swirling curvilinear forms, whether the object is mantelpiece or sofa, buffet or piano – and the standards of workmanship are superla-tive, with a fair sprinkling of Gallé's work on display, too. Another quirky sight is the **Musée du Téléphone**, 11 rue Maurice Barres, just off place Stanislas (check with the tourist office for opening hours; 15F/€2.29), which dedicates two floors to the display of telephones and models of telephone exchanges.

Eating and drinking

There are plenty of places to **eat** and **drink** in Nancy. Good streets for restaurants include Grande-Rue, rue Maréchaux and rue des Ponts. Place Stanislas is perfect for a coffee, day or night, with several cafés that make good vantage points to watch Nancy go by. It's a good place to start an evening – later on you can continue along the Grande-Rue and its offshoots, where you will certainly find a late-night bar.

Restaurants

L'Aiglon, 5 rue Stanislas, near the square (☎03.83.32.21.43). An interesting and well-prepared meal here would cost you 110–120F/€16.77–18.29, including wine and coffee. For more sophisticated traditional and local cuisine, with dishes like *choucroute, tourte lorraine, baeckeoffe, poule-au-pot*, there's the *menu terroir* at 88F/€13.42.

Chez Bagot, 45 Grande-Rue (☎03.83.37.42.43). Fresh fish dishes cooked to Breton recipes served up in an appropriately decorated restaurant. Menus from 82F/€12.50. Closed Mon & Tues lunch.

L'Excelsior, 50 rue Henri-Poincaré, cnr rue Mazagran in front of the train station (☎03.83.35.24.57). A *fin-de-siècle* Art Nouveau brasserie, frequented by everyone who aspires to be anyone in Nancy. Now part of the Flo brasserie chain but managing to retain its superb interior and good food (menus at 128F/€19.51 and 172F/€26.22). It's also the best daytime stop for coffee.

Le Faitout, 7 rue Gustave-Simon (☎03.83.35.36.52) Serves delicious, beautifully presented organic food in a chic setting. There is a vegetarian set meal for 85F/€12.96; local specialities are also available.

Pissenlits, 25 rue des Ponts (☎03.83.37.43.97). Real old-fashioned bistro fare on a menu at 99F/€15.09, in an attractive atmosphere. Recently awarded the *Bib Gourmand* by Michelin for well-prepared meals at moderate prices. Closed Sun & Mon.

La Toque Blanche, 1 rue Mgr-Trouillet, just off place St-Epvre (☎03.83.30.17.20). One of the best gourmet restaurants in Nancy. The 125F/€19.06 menu is a bargain; à la carte costs 400F/€60.98 and more. Closed Sun evening & Mon.

Le Wagon, 75 rue des Chaligny (☎03.83.32.32.16). Housed in the original Orient Express dining car from 1927, this restaurant is now stationary and serves traditional French fare. Menus 85–250F/€12.96–38.11.

Cafés and bars

Bar des Carmes, cnr rue du Lycée & rue des Carmes. Straight stand-up shots are the order of the day at this tiny and delightful old-fashioned bar.

Grand Café du Commerce, place Stanislas, cnr of rue Stanislas. Posh café that's perfectly in keeping with aristocratic feel to place Stanislas – an elegant place to be seen. Till 2am.

Grand Café Foy, place Stanislas. Situated next door to the *Commerce* and equally grand.

Kilo What's, rue St Michel, just off Grande-Rue. Hip little café-bar with club-like interior and outdoor tables. Open 5pm–2am.

Pinocchio, place St-Epvre. Features stylish wooden interior furnishings and a terrace facing the church St-Epvre; good for drinks at all hours. Open Mon–Sat 8am–2am.

Queens Pub, place Stanislas, next to the Musée des Beaux-Arts. English theme pub/café, serving the usual French café fare.

Théâtre le Vertigo, 29 rue de la Visitation (☎03.83.36.51.40). Postmodern gargoyles contribute to its interesting theatrical atmosphere. Bands and other performances regularly. Mon–Sat until 2am; open till 5am if there's a show.

Lunéville

LUNÉVILLE is a twenty-minute train ride east of Nancy or a half-hour drive along the banks of the River Meurthe. If you are travelling by train from Nancy, plan ahead because there are not many trains outside peak hours. Everything in this town is closed from noon to 2pm, except the cafés.

Lunéville was renowned for the **faïence** (ceramic tile) works set up by Stanislas. There is now a small collection of it – not worth a detour unless you're a specialist – in a museum in the immense eighteenth-century **Château** (daily except Tues 10am–noon & 2–6pm; 15F/€2.29), dubbed *Le Petit Versailles*, which dominates the town. The rest of the museum is occupied by cavalry uniforms and weaponry, Lunéville being a garrison town; the formal château gardens, host to an extensive rookery, are good for picnicking.

While you're in town, the only thing worth a visit is M. Chapleur's private motorcycle museum, the **Musée de la Moto et du Vélo** (Tues–Sun 9am–noon & 2–6pm; 20F/€3.05), directly opposite the gates of the château. Monsieur Chapleur started collecting in the 1930s when he was a mechanic at Citroën, and the museum has over 200 models of different origins on display, all overhauled and in working order. And they are beauties – works of art in copper, brass, chrome and steel. Some of the bicycles go back to 1865, and the motorbikes date mostly from 1900 to 1940. Several of the older bikes are probably unique; one certainly is – a 1906 René Gillet 4.5hp belt-driven tandem. Many look like flying bombs and must have been incredibly dangerous to ride: bits of Meccano with a couple of hefty cylinders welded on, and capable of 100kph in 1900.

Between the *gare SNCF* and the château run the small-scale cottagey streets of the old town, where the newly restored, splendidly Baroque **church of St-Jacques**, Stanislas' gift to the town, raises its enormous twin towers.

From the **gare SNCF**, the rue Carnot north will bring you to the back of the old theatre which adjoins the château, where the **tourist office** is housed (daily 9am–noon & 2–6pm; ☎03.83.74.06.55, fax 03.83.73.57.95); following the signs, you'll find it right at the front of the château on the place de la 2eme Division du Cavalerie. Should you wish to **stay**, try *Hôtel des Pages*, 5 quai des Petits-Bosquets (☎03.83.74.11.42, fax 03.83.73.46.63; ③), which is close to the château and very peaceful. For something very special, however, the place to go is the *Château d'Adoménil*, a couple of kilometres out of town across the River Meurthe (☎03.83.74.04.81, fax 03.83.74.21.78, *www. relaischateaux.fr /adomenil*; ⑨; closed Sun out of season): its seven beautifully furnished and luxuriously equipped rooms overlook water, orchards and a home farm, and its **restaurant** belongs in the top category (closed Sun evening out of season, Mon & Tues lunch & Jan; cheapest menu 215F/€32.78; *carte* upwards of 400F/€60.98). There's a **campsite** at 69 quai des Beitis Bosquets (☎03.83.73.37.58; April–Oct), near the château. As for eating in town, the *New Vien Tong*, 29 rue de Lorrain (☎03.83.73.33.96), has freshly prepared Chinese, Vietnamese and Thai food (menus from 55F/€8.38); the decor is very French Indo-China and the atmosphere is friendly and calm.

ALSACE

There's no denying **Alsace**'s attractiveness, with its old stone and half-timbered towns set amid the thickly wooded hills of the Vosges, but it's a quaintness that has become a commodity. **Strasbourg**, the Alsatian capital and, along with Brussels, one of the main centres of the European Union, escapes the tweeness of some of the smaller towns of the foothills. **Saverne** and **Wissembourg**, to the north, also avoid the worst of the tourist-brochure image, giving access to some spectacular ruined castles in the **northern Vosges**.

South of Strasbourg, along the **Route du Vin**, there are countless picturesque medieval villages and yet more ruined castles which suffer to varying degrees from the attention of the tour buses. A very different, sobering experience is the concentration

THE FOOD AND WINE OF ALSACE

The cuisine of Alsace is quite distinct from that of other regions of France because of its German origins, albeit tempered by French refinement. The classic dish is the chopped pickled cabbage of **sauerkraut**, or *choucroute*, which includes the use of juniper berries in the pickling stage and is cooked with goose grease or lard and smoked pork, with ham and a variety of sausages added. The qualification *à l'alsacienne* after the name of a dish usually means "with *choucroute*".

Strasbourg **sausages** and boiled **potatoes** are another common ingredient in Alsatian cooking. One of the best culinary incarnations of the spud is the three-meat hotpot, **baeckoffe**, which consists of pork, mutton and beef marinated in wine and cooked between layers of potato for a couple of hours in a baker's oven.

Onions, too, are a favourite dish, either in the form of an onion tart, which is made with a béchamel sauce, or *flammeküche* (*tarte flambée* in French), made with a mixture of onion, cream and pieces of chopped smoked pork breast baked on a base of thin pizza-like pastry. **Noodles** are also a common feature, and don't miss the chance to sample a *matelote* (a stew of river fish cooked in Riesling) or Vosges trout cooked *au bleu* (briefly boiled in Riesling with a dash of vinegar).

Like the Germans, Alsatians are fond of their **pastries**. The dessert fruit tarts made with cherries or yellow *mirabelle* plums – *tartes alsaciennes* – are delicious. Cake-lovers should try *kugelhopf*, a moulded dome-shaped cake with a hollow in the middle, made with raisins and almonds, and *birewecks*, made with dried fruit marinated in Kirsch.

All of these delights can be washed down with the region's **white wines**, renowned for their dry, clean-tasting fruitiness and compatibility with any kind of food. The best-known of them are Riesling, Gewürztraminer, Sylvaner and Tokay, named after the type of grape from which they are made – unlike other wine-growing regions in the country, the taste of Alsatian wines does not vary from locality to locality. There are, incidentally, a few reds – from Ottrott, Marlenheim and Cleebourg – but it is the whites which make the region's reputation. The term *Edelzwicker* on a label means the wine is a high-quality blend.

Alsace also shares the German predilection for **beer** and has long been the heartland of French hop-growing and brewing. Its fruit **brandies** are honoured too, especially Kirsch, which is made from cherries, and *quetsche* and *mirabelle* from different varieties of plum.

camp of **Le Struthof**, hidden away in the Vosges forest. **Colmar** is almost excessively twee, yet still worth a visit for Grünewald's amazing Issenheim altarpiece. By contrast, **Mulhouse** is thoroughly industrial but boasts some unusually good museums devoted to cars, trains, electricity and printed fabrics.

Every town has a **tourist office**, which in smaller places is usually in the Mairie or Hôtel de Ville. Special tourist maps cost around 3F/€0.46, but free maps containing a reasonable amount of information are always available.

Strasbourg

STRASBOURG owes both its name – "the city of the roads" – and its wealth to its position on the west bank of the Rhine, long one of the great natural transport arteries of Europe. The city's medieval commercial pre-eminence was damaged by too close an involvement in the religious struggles of the sixteenth and seventeenth centuries, but recovered with the city's absorption into France in 1681. Along with the rest of Alsace, Strasbourg suffered annexation by Germany from 1871 to the end of World War I and again from 1940 to 1944.

Today old animosities have been submerged in the togetherness of the European Union, of which, as the seat of the Council of Europe, the European Court of Human

Rights and the European Parliament, Strasbourg is one of the capitals. Prosperous, beautiful and modern, with an orderliness that is Germanic rather than Latin, the city is big enough – with a population of over a quarter of a million people – to have a metropolitan air without being overwhelming. It has one of the loveliest cathedrals in France and one of the oldest and most active universities: this is the one city in eastern France that is definitely worth a special detour.

Arrival and information

The **gare SNCF** lies on the west side of the city centre, barely fifteen minutes' walk from the cathedral along rue du Maire-Kuss and rue du 22-Novembre. The **airport shuttle** (*navette*), departing every fifteen minutes (5.30am–11pm), drops off at Baggersee, from where you can catch the very convenient and futuristic **tram** into central Strasbourg.

The main **tourist office** is at 17 place de la Cathédrale (June–Sept Mon–Sat 9am–7pm, Sun 9am–6pm; Oct–May Mon–Sat 9am–6pm, Sun 9am–5pm; ☎03.88.52 .28.28, *www.strasbourg.com*), with the regional office for the Bas-Rhin nearby at 9 rue du Dôme (Mon–Fri 9.30am–6pm, Sat 10am–1pm & 2–6pm; ☎03.88.15.45.80, *alsace-tourism@sdv.fr*). There is also a tourist office just in front of the train station (Mon–Sat 9am–7pm, Sun 9am–6pm), in the new underground shopping complex, and one at the airport (daily 8.30am–12.30pm & 1.15–5pm).

Most of the city centre is now pedestrian-only, but several car parks around Strasbourg cater for those who are **driving** into town. At Parking Rotonde, to the north, and at Parking Étoile to the south, a 15F/€2.29 fee gives you unlimited parking and tram tickets for the journey into the town centre; further south, Parking Baggersee is free and has easy access to the tram, which takes you to the town centre in fifteen minutes. Strasbourg is also France's most bicycle-friendly city, and 300km of **bicycle** lanes and particularly cheap bicycle hire (see "Listings" below) making cycling a tempting option.

Accommodation

When you are looking for a place to **stay**, bear in mind that once a month the European Parliament is in session for three or four days, bringing its hundreds of MPs and their entourages into town, which puts all the city's facilities under pressure, especially hotel accommodation. The hostels, at least, are less affected, though it is said that even they play host to one or two Euro-deputies. The station area has the usual clutch of hotels.

Hotels

Beaucour, 5 rue des Bouchers (☎03.88.76.72.00, fax 03.88.76.72.60, *www.hotel-beaucour.com*). Very central and quite luxurious hotel, just off place du Corbeau, in a handsome old house with its own courtyard. ⑧.

Cerf d'Or, 6 place de l'Hôpital (☎03.88.36.20.05, fax 03.88.36.68.67). Sixteenth-century hotel with its own bar and restaurant (menu from 95F/€14.48) on the south side of the River Ill. Closed Dec 24–Jan 2. ④.

Dragon, 2 rue de l'Écarlate (☎03.88.35.79.80, fax 03.88.25.78.95, *www.dragon.fr*). Fully modernized luxury hotel south of the River Ill. Closed Dec 23–27. ⑥.

Europe, 38 rue du Fossé des Tanneurs (☎03.88.32.17.88, fax 03.88.75.65.45, *www.hotel-europe.com*). Part of a chain but a good option, well situated in the centre of town. ④.

Gutenberg, 31 rue des Serruriers (☎03.88.32.17.15, fax 03.88.75.76.67). Pleasant, quirky hotel in an old house in a central location, with period furniture in some rooms. Closed Jan 1–11. ④.

de l'Ill, 8 rue des Bateliers (☎03.88.36.20.01, fax 03.88.35.30.03). The best bargain in Strasbourg; a quiet, comfortable, family-run place just 50m from the river, in sight of the cathedral. Closed end of Dec to mid-Jan. ③.

THE ALSATIAN LANGUAGE

Travelling through the province, it's easy to mistake the language being spoken in the shops and streets for German. In fact, it is *Elsässisch*, or Alsatian, a High German dialect, known to philologists as Alemannic. To confuse matters further, there are two versions, High and Low Alemannic, as well as an obscure Frankish dialect spoken in the Wissembourg region and a Romance one called *Welche* from the valleys around Orbey. You will hear a different version spoken in almost every town.

Most daily transactions are conducted in French, and *Elsässisch* has still not made it onto the school curriculum. Yet it remains a living language, with a rich medieval literary legacy, and is still spoken by young and old throughout Alsace and even parts of Lorraine. A recent upsurge in nationalist feeling has meant that *Elsässisch* is beginning to reappear on menus and shop signs.

In many ways, it's a miracle that it has survived at all, since both French and German rule have tended to discourage the Alsatian language. During the French Revolution, the language was suppressed in favour of French for nationalistic reasons, only to be ousted by German when the Prussians annexed the region in 1870. On its return to French rule, all things Germanic were disdained, and many Alsatians began to speak French once more . . . until the Nazi occupation brought in laws that made the speaking of French and even the wearing of berets imprisonable offences. To top off the linguistic confusion, a proposal by Strasbourg's socialist mayor in 1991 that street signs should be bilingual has now been passed, so that signs bearing both *Gass* and *rue* are now in evidence around the town.

including, in the apse, the modern glass designed in 1956 by Max Ingrand to commemorate the first European institutions in the city. On the left of the nave, the cathedral's organ perches precariously above one of the arches, like a giant gilded eagle, while further down on the same side is the late fifteenth-century pulpit, a masterpiece of intricacy in stone by the appropriately named Hans Hammer.

In the south transept are the cathedral's two most popular sights. One is the slender triple-tiered central column known as the **Pilier des Anges**, decorated with some of the most graceful and expressive statuary of the thirteenth century. The other is the huge and enormously complicated **astrological clock** built by Schwilgué of Strasbourg in 1842: a favourite with the tour-group operators, whose customers roll up in droves to witness the clock's crowning performance of the day, striking the hour of noon, which it does with unerring accuracy, at 12.30pm – that being 12 o'clock Strasbourg time (tickets can be bought from the postcard stand 9am–11.30am, then at the cash desk at the south door until 12.20pm; 5F/€0.76). Death strikes the chimes; the apostles parade in front of Christ, who occupies the highest storey of the clock; and as each one passes he receives Christ's blessing.

Strasbourg's museums

Most of Strasbourg's **museums** are to be found to the south of the cathedral (the main exception being the Musée d'Art Moderne et Contemporain), between the tree-lined place du Château and the river. Check with the tourist office for museum passes/discounts if you are planning to visit them all.

Right next to the cathedral, place du Château is enclosed to the east and south by the Lycée Fustel and the **Palais Rohan**, both eighteenth-century buildings, the latter designed for the immensely powerful Rohan family, who, for several generations in a row, cornered the market in cardinals' hats. There are three museums in the Palais Rohan itself (Mon & Wed–Sat 10am–6pm; closed public hols; 20F/€3.05 for each of the museums, or 40F/€6.10 for all three): the **Musée des Arts Décoratifs**, **Musée des Beaux-Arts** and **Musée Archéologique**. Of the three collections, only the Arts

Décoratifs stands out – and that's of slightly specialist interest – with its eighteenth-century *faïence* tiles crafted in the city by Paul Hannong. The rooms of the palace are vast, opulent and ostentatious but not especially interesting.

Next door, in the mansion lived in by the cathedral architects, the **Musée de l'Oeuvre Notre-Dame** (Tues–Sun 10am–6pm; 20F/€3.05) houses the original sculptures from the cathedral exterior, damaged in the Revolution and replaced today by copies; both sets are worth seeing. And there are other treasures here: glass from the city's original Romanesque cathedral; the eleventh-century Wissembourg Christ, said to be the oldest representation of a human figure in stained glass; and the architect's original parchment drawings for the statuary, done in fascinating detail down to the different expressions on each figure's face.

The **Musée Historique** (closed for renovation at time of writing; due to reopen 2001), 3 place de la Grande Boucherie by place du Marché-aux-Cochons-de-Lait (Sucking-Pig Market), is mainly concerned with the city, though it also has an oddball collection of mechanical toys upstairs. On the other side of the river, in a typically Alsatian house on qual St-Nicolas across the Pont du Corbeau, is the **Musée Alsacien**, 23 quai St-Nicholas (daily except Tues 10am–6pm; 20F/€3.05), which contains painted furniture and other local artefacts.

The latest addition to Strasbourg's museums is the **Musée d'Art Moderne et Contemporain** (Tues, Wed & Fri–Sun 11am–7pm, Thurs noon–10pm; 30F/€4.57), housed in a purpose-built glass-fronted building overlooking the river and Vauban's dam. It's a light and airy space and its collection is well presented, acknowledging the importance of some lesser-known artists in the scheme of modern art. The ground floor confronts the themes, challenges and roots of modern European art from the late nineteenth century through to the 1950s, by way of the Impressionists, Symbolists, a good section on Surrealism, with plenty of folkloric, mystical paintings by Brauner, and of course a room devoted to the soft curves sculpted by Strasbourg's own Arp. The chronology continues upstairs with conceptual art and Arte Povera, and finishes up with stripy creations by Daniel Buren and video art by Bill Viola.

Another interesting museum, visitable by appointment only, is the **Centre Tomi Ungerer**, 4 rue de la Haute-Montée (Thurs 9am–noon, 2–6pm by appointment; ☎03.88.32.31.54; free), which houses the private collections and works of the Strasbourg-born artist.

The rest of the old town

On the south side of the Pont du Corbeau, the medieval **Cour du Corbeau** still looks much as it must have done in the fourteenth century. Downstream, the **quai des Bateliers** was part of the old business quarter, and the streets leading off it – rue Ste-Madeleine, rue de la Krutenau and rue de Zurich – are still worth a wander. Two bridges upstream, the Pont St-Thomas leads to the **church of St-Thomas** (Jan & Feb Sat & Sun 2–5pm; March & Dec daily 10am–5pm; April–Nov daily 10am–6pm; closed Sun morning for services), with a Romanesque facade and Gothic towers. Since 1549 it has been the city's principal Protestant church. Strasbourg was a bastion of the Reformation, and one of its leaders, Martin Bucer, preached in this church. The amazing piece of sculpture behind the altar is Jean-Baptiste Pigalle's **tomb of the Maréchal de Saxe**, a very capable French military commander active against the Duke of Cumberland in the campaigns of the War of the Austrian Succession in the middle of the eighteenth century.

From here, it's a short walk upstream to the **Pont St-Martin**, which marks the beginning of the district known as **La Petite France**, where the city's millers, tanners and fishermen used to live. At the far end of a series of canals are the so-called **Ponts Couverts** (they are in fact no longer covered), built as part of the fourteenth-century city fortifications and still punctuated by watchtowers. Just beyond is a **dam** built by

Vauban (daily 9am–7pm; mid-March to mid-Oct till 8pm; free) to protect the city from waterborne assault. The whole area is extremely picturesque, with winding streets – most notably rue du Bain-aux-Plantes – bordered by sixteenth- and seventeenth-century houses adorned with flowers and elaborately carved woodwork. Predictably, it's a top-of-the-bill tourist hotspot.

The area east of the cathedral is good for a stroll, too, where rue des Frères leads to place St-Étienne. **Place du Marché-Gayot**, off rue des Frères behind the cathedral, is very lively, with a couple of studenty cafés on the north side. From the north side of the cathedral, rue du Dôme leads to the eighteenth-century **place Broglie**, with the Hôtel de Ville, the *préfet*'s residence and some imposing eighteenth-century mansions. It was at 4 place Broglie in 1792 that Rouget de l'Isle first sang what later became known as the *Marseillaise* for the mayor of Strasbourg, who had challenged him to compose a rousing song for the troops of the army of the Rhine.

The German quarter and the Palais de l'Europe

Across the river from place Broglie, **place de la République** is surrounded by vast German neo-Gothic edifices erected during the post-1870 Imperial Prussian occupation, a good example being the main **post office** on avenue de la Liberté. At the centre of the square is a war memorial showing a mother holding two dead sons in her arms, one German and one French, testifying to the split personality of this frontier city whose inhabitants found themselves fighting, not always willingly, in both Allied and German armies during the war. At the other end of avenue de la Liberté, across the confluence of the Ill and Aar, is the city's **university**, where Goethe studied. Adjacent, at the beginning of boulevard de la Victoire, are the splendidly Teutonic municipal baths, the **Grand Établissement Municipal de Bains**, where you can take a sauna or Turkish bath or just swim.

From in front of the university, the wide, straight allée de la Robertsau, flanked by confident *fin-de-siècle* bourgeois residences, leads to the buildings of the various European institutions: the **Palais de l'Europe**, home of the Council of Europe; the glass and steel curvilinear **European Parliament building**, opened in 1999; and Richard Rogers' contribution for the **European Court of Human Rights**, with its curving glass entrance and silver towers rising to a boat-like superstructure overlooking a sweep of canal. To visit the European Parliament and the Council of Europe you have to book (☎03.88.17.52.85 and ☎03.90.21.49.40 respectively; free).

Opposite the Palais, the **Orangerie** is Strasbourg's best bit of greenery, and hosts a variety of exhibitions and free concerts. Here the *cigognes* (storks), which perch on top of most buildings in the town, have their nests. There is also a zoo with small animals, such as monkeys, and exotic birds.

Eating and drinking

For the classic Strasbourg **eating** experience, you have to go to a **winstub**, usually translated as a "wine bar", a cosy establishment with bare beams, panels and benches, and a noisy, convivial atmosphere. In the classic version there is a special table set aside for the *patron*'s buddies and regulars. The food tends towards *choucroute, tarte à l'oignon*, knuckle of pork and horseradish and ham *en croûte*: the Alsatian classics, washed down with local wines. Place du Marché-Gayot behind the cathedral is full of **cafés**, most open until late, and there is a good selection of **restaurants** in rue du Faubourg Saverne.

Restaurants

La Bourse, place de Lattre-de-Tassigny (☎03.88.36.40.53). Quite a sedate brasserie, in agreeable, spacious surroundings across the river in the direction of place de l'Étoile. Menus 50–200F/€7.62–30.49 (50F/€7.62 lunchtime menu). Closed Mon & Wed lunch.

Les 3 Brasseurs, 22 rue des Veaux. Wonderful *winstub*, which brews its own beer: the enormous copper brewing equipment is part of the decor. *Tarte flambée* from 30F/€4.57. Other Alsatian specialities available. Happy hour 5–7pm.

La Choucrouterie, 20 rue St-Louis, by the church of St-Louis, just across Pont St-Thomas (☎03.88.36.52.87). *Choucroute* specialist with menus at 150–220F/€22.87–33.54, *plats* from about 75F/€11.43. Cabaret acts. Closed Sun & first two weeks Aug.

Flam's, 1 rue de l'Epine, and another at cnr of rues des Frères & du Faisan (☎03.88.75.77.44). *Tarte flambée* restaurant, very popular with locals. A good place to sample the local speciality with the 73.50F/€11.21 all-you-can-eat *tarte flambée* menu (plus dessert). Meals from 34F/€5.18.

Gurtlerhoft, 13 place de la Cathédrale (☎03.88.75.00.75). Downstairs, away from the crowds and very seductive. Not as expensive as it looks. Menus from 89F/€13.57.

Poêles de Carottes, 2 place des Meuniers (☎03.88.32.33.23). Good vegetarian restaurant in the picturesque quarter of Petite France. Lunch 59F/€8.99, dinner 108F/€16.46. Closed Sun.

La Robe des Champs, 4 rue de l'Écurie (☎03.88.22.36.82). Potato-fanciers will enjoy the variety of things they can do – inexpensively – with the spud here. Menu 39–150F/€5.95–22.87. Closed lunchtimes Sat & Sun, last week in July & first week in Aug.

Le Saint-Sépulcre, 15 rue des Orfèvres, off rue des Hallesbardes (☎03.88.32.39.97). Traditional *winstub*. Menu 90–160F/€13.72–24.39. Closed Sun & Mon & first fortnight in July.

La Victoire, 24 quai des Pêcheurs (☎03.88.35.39.35). A *winstub*, worth experiencing for its lively student ambience rather than the food. Menu from 100F/€15.24, *plats* 44F/€6.71. Closed Sat evening, Sun & first three weeks in Aug.

Winstub Strissel, 5 place de la Grande-Boucherie (☎03.88.32.14.73). *Winstub* with Alsatian fare and a menu at 64–125F/€9.76–19.06 (70F/€10.67 or more per *plat*), Closed Sun, Mon & one week in Feb & July,

Zür Zehnerglock, 4 rue du Vieil-Hôpital, near the cathedral (☎03.88.32.87.09). Quality food and a little live music to sweeten the digestion on Fri. Menu 90–120F/€13.72–1.29, *plats* around 75F/€11.43. Closed Sun & Mon.

Cafés and bars

Académie de la Bière, 17 rue Adolphe-Seyboth, near the church of St-Pierre. Strasbourg's most famous *bierstub*. Open daily till 4am.

Café Brant, place Sebastian-Brant. Atmospheric café close to the University. Outdoor tables make it perfect for summer meals.

Montmartre, 6 rue du Vieux-Marché-aux-Poissons (☎03.88.32.40.58). Shiny Parisian-style café near the cathedral.

Monte-Carlo, quai Turkheim. Hip gay bar, with performances and club nights.

Opéra Café, place Broglie. Stylish and friendly café next door to the theatre. Outdoor tables (no plastic chairs in sight). Open even when the theatre season is over.

Rive Gauche, cnr rue Marie Kuss & quai St-Jean. Brasserie-style café, with a Parisian ambience.

La Salamandre, 3 rue Paul-Janet (☎03.88.25.79.42). A popular bar (free entrance) famous for its rock concerts (tickets 50–120F/€7.62–18.29) and theme nights (20–30F/€3.05–4.57).

Tapas Café, south of Petit France, cross the Pont des Moulins and you'll see it next to the fire station. Cool Spanish bar, with wonderful, affordable tapas.

Troc' Café, 8 rue du Faubourg de Saverne (☎03.88.23.23.29). Easy-going café often hosting concerts or theme nights. Also does a good brunch. Closed Sun.

Entertainment

Strasbourg usually has lots going on. In summer, pick up the free *Saison d'Été* **listings** leaflet or the free **magazine** *Spectacles à Strasbourg* (*www.spectacles-strasbourg.presse.fr*), with entertainment info and practical listings, both available from the tourist office. If you're here during university term-time, you might want to check the noticeboards at the university as well. **Free concerts** are held regularly in the Parc des Contades and Parc de l'Orangerie, which also boasts a 24-lane bowling alley. The best of the annual **festivals** starts with music from around the world in mid-June, followed by jazz in July, and contemporary world music in mid-September and early October. In addition, there's **Les Nuits de Strasbourg**, a firework, light and music display at the Ponts Couverts during July and August; and, on July 14, a fireworks display and street entertainment. At the **Marché de Noël** (end Nov to Dec 24), an annual event for over 400 years, you can buy tree decorations, gifts, crafts, sweets and Alsatian Christmas cookies, *bredele*.

Listings

Ambulance (SAMU) ☎15.

Bikes Bicycles can be rented from 4 rue du Maire Kuss, Parking Ste-Aurélie, place du Château and Impasse de la Grande Écluse (near the Ponts Couverts) for 30F/€4.57 a day.

Boat trips Strasbourg Fluvial (☎03.88.84.13.13, *www.strasbourg.port.fr*) runs cruises on the River Ill year round. Cruises depart from the landing stage in front of the Palais Rohan (daily: April–Oct every 30min 9.30am–9pm; Nov–March four departures 10.30am–4pm), and the itinerary includes Petite-France, the Vauban dam and the Palais de l'Europe. Evening cruises depart at 9.30pm and 10pm May to September only. The trip costs 41F/€6.25 (43F/€6.56 for evening cruises) and lasts 1hr 15min.

Books Librarie International Kléber, 1 rue des Francs-Bourgeois, sells new books, French and English; La Librocase, 2 quai des Pêcheurs, sells second-hand books; Quai des Brumes, 35 quai des Bateliers, although small, also has a very good range; Bookworm, 4 rue de Pâques, is a small English bookshop with new and used books, audio books, children's books and greetings cards.

Buses Eurolines has an office at 5 rue des Frères (☎03.88.22.73.74). Some out-of-town buses leave from place des Halles.

Car rental Europcar, at the airport (☎03.88.68.95.55) and 15 place de la Gare (☎03.88.15.55.66); Avis, Galérie Marchande, place de la Gare (☎03.88.32.30.44); Hertz, at the airport (☎03.88.68.93.11) and 6 bd de Metz by the *gare SNCF* (☎03.88.32.57.62).

Cinemas Le Club, 32 rue du Vieux-Marché-aux-Vins (☎03.36.68.20.22) and Le Star, 27 rue du Jeu-des-Enfants, the parallel street (☎03.88.32.44.97). L'Odyssée, 3 rue des Francs-Bourgeois (☎03.88.75.10.47), shows a combination of classic and contemporary films.

Internet Access available at *Midi minuit*, 5 place du Corbeau (Mon–Wed 7am–7pm, Thurs–Sat 7am–10pm, Sun 8am–7pm; access for a minimum of 30min; 1F/€0.15 per minute).

Markets The city's biggest fruit and vegetable market takes place every Tues and Sat morning on bd de la Marne; the Marché aux Puces (Wed & Sat) is on rue du Vieil-Hôpital (near the cathedral).

Post office, 4 av de la Liberté (☎03.88.52.35.18).

Rape crisis SOS Viol (☎08.00.05.95.95); SOS Femmes Solidarité (☎03.88.24.06.06).

Taxis Station Centrale (☎03.88.36.13.13); Novotaxi (☎03.88.75.19.19).

The northern Vosges

The **northern Vosges** begin at the Saverne gap northwest of Strasbourg and run up to the German border, where they continue as the Pfälzerwald. They don't reach the same heights as the southern Vosges, nor do they boast any famous vineyards, but as a result, they are spared the mass tourism of the southern range. Much of the region comes under the auspices of the Parc Régional des Vosges du Nord, and there are numerous hiking possibilities, as well as a couple of attractive towns – **Saverne** and **Wissembourg** – built in the characteristic red sandstone of the Vosges.

Transport here is patchy, as elsewhere in Alsace, though not hopeless. SNCF buses wind their way through the villages and apple orchards around Hagenau, and the Strasbourg–Sarreguemines and Hagenau-Bitche train lines cut across the range. Saverne and Wissembourg are also linked to Strasbourg by rail. Even so, the easiest way to explore the region is with your own transport – hilly work, if it's a bike.

HIKING, CYCLING AND DRIVING IN THE NORTHERN VOSGES

Numerous **cycling** and **motoring** routes designed to bring you into contact with the most interesting sights, villages and landscapes are detailed in various pamphlets published by the Agence de Développement Touristique du Bas-Rhin, 9 rue du Dôme, 67000 Strasbourg (☎03.88.15.45.80, fax 03.88.75.67.64, *alsace-tourism@sdv.fr*). Independent hikers and cyclists will find further routes marked on the Club Vosgien 1:50,000 and 1:25,000 maps (on sale in bookshops and tourist offices), in addition to the three **GRs** (Sentiers de Grande Randonnée), which cross the *parc régional*: GR53–55, GR531 and GR532. Don't get too excited when you see a road sign for a picnic area: in the Vosges this usually means a cleared parking area with some concrete tables. It's a good idea to do some research before you set off, even if you are just planning a short drive and lunch, so that you end up far from camper-van traffic.

One easy cycle route in the region is along the Rhôn–Rhine canal. It's flat all the way from Strasbourg down past Mulhouse, with bars and cafés along the way for regular pit-stops, and places to pitch tents. Again, be wary of the official picnic areas. The *Carte des Parcours Cyclables* is a free map available from Strasbourg's tourist offices, with descriptions of cycle routes in the region from Wissembourg to Colmar. Cycling routes in this region are continually being developed and improved. Possible routes include:

Canal de la Marne au Rhin: 50km Strasbourg to Saverne, and further into the Moselle if you wish.

Haguenau–Woerth–Lembach: 24km circuit through forests and 1870 battlefields.

Geispolsheim–Barr/Geispolsheim–Obernai: 25km each section, through vineyards with beautiful views of the Rhine valley.

If you want your **accommodation** and **baggage transport** taken care of, there are organizations in each town that can arrange this for you (usually around 2500F/€381.12 for six days, including meals); details from tourist offices. For large hiking groups you will need to book in advance; for one or two people, only one day's notice is usually needed.

For further information, the regional tourist office (see above) has the most up-to-date books and maps, or contact the Club Vosgien, 16 rue Ste-Hélène, 67000 Strasbourg (☎03.88.32.57.96). Alternatively, you will find that every tourist office in the Bas-Rhin region has plenty of information and maps, and will be able to give you all the necessary advice about the routes. Some of them even organize cycling and hiking trips with a guide, but with the amount of information available, you should be able to manage on your own quite easily. If you want to stay in a *gîte d'étape*, contact the Gîtes de France Bas-Rhin, 7 place des Meuniers, 67000 Strasbourg (☎03.88.75.56.60, fax 03.88.23.00.97). The Club Alpin Français, Section Strasbourg Bas-Rhin, 2 rue des Écrivains (☎03.88.35.27.62), also arranges various mountain activities.

Saverne and around

SAVERNE, seat of the exiled Catholic prince-bishops of Strasbourg during the Reformation, commands the only easy route across the Vosges into Alsace, at a point where the hills are pinched to a narrow waist. It's a small and friendly town, not as picturesque as some of its neighbours, but possessing the region's characteristic steep-pitched roofs, dormer windows and window boxes full of geraniums. It's also the best launch pad from which to explore the northern Vosges.

The town has a couple of sights worth visiting, not least the vast red sandstone **Château des Rohan**, on place de Gaulle, built in rather austere classical style by one of the Rohans who was prince-bishop at the time, and now housing the **Musée Rohan** (March–June & Sept–Nov daily except Tues 2–5pm; July & Aug daily except Tues 10am–noon & 2–6pm; Dec–March Sun only 2–5pm; 16F/€2.44) and hostel. A feature of the museum is the collection of local Resistance journalist Louise Weiss. The River Zorn and the Marne–Rhine canal both weave their way through the town, the latter framing the château's formal gardens in a graceful right-angle bend. Alongside the château, the **church of Notre-Dame-de-la-Nativité** contains another finely carved pulpit by Hans Hammer. Horticultural distraction can be found in the town's famed rose garden, **La Roseraie** (June–Sept daily 9am–7pm; ☎03.88.71.83.33; 15F/€2.29), to the west of the centre by the river, which boasts over four hundred varieties; and the **botanical gardens** 3km out of town off the N4 Metz–Nancy road (May, June & first two weeks Sept Mon–Fri 9am–5pm, Sun 2–6pm; July & Aug Mon–Fri 9am–5pm, Sat & Sun 2–7pm; 25F/€3.81).

There are several relatively easy **walks** around Saverne (the tourist office can give details), the most popular being the one to the ruined **Château du Haut-Barr** (2hr return). Follow rue du Haut-Barr southeast along the canal past the leafy suburban villas until you reach the woods, where a signboard indicates the various walks possible. Take the path marked "Haut-Barr" through woods of chestnut, beech and larch, and you'll see the castle standing dramatically on a narrow sandstone ridge, with fearsome drops on both sides and views across the wooded hills and eastward over the plain towards Strasbourg. Approaching by road you'll pass an early **telegraph station**, part of the Paris–Strasbourg line dating from around 1800 (July & Aug Tues–Sun noon–6pm; 10F/€1.52).

If you're driving, you can easily get to the several beautiful small towns and villages around Saverne, in particular Bouxwiller, Neuwiller, Pfaffenhoffen and Ingwiller, from where an alternative road to Bitche (see p.299) leads through the densely wooded heart of the northern Vosges. A focus to your explorations could be the **Château of Lichtenburg** (March & Nov Mon–Sat 1–4pm, Sun 10am–7pm; April, May, Sept & Oct Mon 1.30–6pm, Tues–Sat 10am–noon & 1.30–4pm, Sun & hols 10am–7pm; June–Aug Mon 1.30–6pm, Tues–Sat 10am–6pm, Sun & hols 10am–7pm; 15F/€2.29), dating back to the thirteenth century and much restored, situated just a short way outside Ingwiller.

Practicalities

The **tourist office** is at 37 Grand' Rue (Mon–Sat 9am–12.30pm & 2–7pm; May–Oct also open Sun 10am–12.30pm & 2–5pm; ☎03.88.91.80.47, fax 03.88.71.02.90); they will be able to provide you with a map of walks in the area published by the Saverne Centre de Randonnées Pedestres (part of the Club Vosgien).

For **accommodation** in town, try the *Europe*, at 7 rue de la Gare (☎03.88.71.12.07, fax 03.88.71.11.43; ④), with bright, modern rooms. The *Hotel/Restaurant Chez Jean*, 3 rue de la Gare (☎03.88.91.10.19, fax 03.88.91.27.45, *www.chez-jean.com*; ⑤), has a restaurant with good Alsatian food such as *choucroute* and *preskopf de bœuf au Raifort* (menus 98–300F/€14.94–45.73). A less expensive option is the *National*, 2 Grand' Rue (☎03.88.91.14.54; ②), and cheaper still is the friendly HI hostel in the Château Rohan, on place de Gaulle (☎03.88.91.14.84, fax 03.88.71.15.97; reception open 8–10am & 5–10pm). There's also a **campsite** about 1km from town below the Château du Haut-Barr, on rue du Père Liebermann (☎03.88.91.35.65; closed Oct–March). As for **food**, gourmets will appreciate the *Taverne Katz* on the main street, 80 Grand' Rue (☎03.88.71.16.56; closed Tues evening & Wed; menu 89–155F/€13.57–23.63): not only is it a beautiful old house with an ornately carved facade and plush decor within, but the food is excellent, traditional Alsatian cuisine, with very good *baeckoffe* and divine sorbets. More modest, and with a local ambience, is the *Restaurant de la Marne*, 5 rue du Griffon (☎03.88.91.19.18; closed Mon), overlooking the Marne–Rhine canal in the centre of town, serving good copious salads amongst their varied menu. There is also a restaurant at the Château du Haut-Barr (see above).

Wissembourg and around

WISSEMBOURG, 60km north of Strasbourg and right on the German border, is a small town of cobbled and higgledy-piggledy prettiness, largely given over to moneyed German weekenders. The townspeople have a curious linguistic anomaly; they speak an ancient dialect derived from Frankish, unlike their fellow Alsatians whose language is closer to modern German.

At the end of rue Nationale, the town's main commercial street, stands the imposing Gothic **church of St-Paul-et-St-Pierre**, with a Romanesque belfry and some fine twelfth- and thirteenth-century stained glass, once attached to the town's abbey. Beneath the apse, the meandering River Lauter flows under the Pont du Sel beside the town's most striking secular building and first hospital, the **Maison du Sel** (1450). A few minutes' walk away, on the northern edge of the town, another fine old building, with beautifully carved woodwork round its windows, contains the town's folk museum, the **Musée Westercamp**, 3 rue du Musée (Mon, Wed & Thurs 2–6pm, Fri & Sat 9am–noon & 2–6pm, Sun & hols 10am–noon & 2–6pm; closed Jan & Feb; 15F/€2.29). Along the southern edge of town, following the riverbank from the Tour des Husgenossen in the western corner, a long section of the **medieval walls** survives intact, built – like the houses – in the local red sandstone.

Nearby **WOERTH**, 25km southwest along the D27, has a **museum** dedicated to an important engagement in the 1870 Franco-Prussian War, reconstructed here with the aid of 4000 lead soldiers (April–Oct daily except Tues 2–5pm; July & Aug daily except Tues 10am–noon & 2–6pm; Nov–March Sat & Sun 2–5pm; closed Jan; ☎03.88.09.30.21; 15F/€2.29). Those with a sweet tooth can indulge at the *Restaurant Sans Alcool* (☎03.88.09.30.79; closed Mon), noted for its desserts and ice creams – it's moderately priced, with a lunchtime menu at 40F/€6.10, and the quality of cooking compensates for the ban on tobacco and alcohol.

Practicalities

The **tourist office** is at 9 place de la République (June–Sept Mon–Sat 9am–noon & 2–6pm, Sun 10am–noon & 2–5pm; Oct–May Mon–Sat 9am–noon & 2–5pm; ☎03.88.94.10.11, fax 03.88.94.18.82). From the **gare SNCF** the "Office du Tourisme" signs are for cars – if you are on foot the quickest route is to turn left out of the station and walk to the roundabout, where you'll see signs of café life. Turn right and you're in town.

For **accommodation**, much the most attractive hotel is the *Hôtel du Cygne*, 3 rue du Sel, next to the town hall on the central place de la République (☎03.88.94.00.16, fax 03.88.54.38.28; ④; closed two weeks in Feb & two weeks in July; restaurant 120–350F/€18.29–53.36). Otherwise, try the *Hôtel-Restaurant au Moulin de la Walk*, 2 rue de la Walk, by the hospital just outside the old town (☎03.88.94.06.44, fax 03.88.54.38.03; ③; closed Sun evening, Mon, Jan 8–30 & June 15–30), which has a very good but rather pricey restaurant, with the cheapest menu at 180F/€27.44 – easy-listening music included. Friendly and less expensive is the *Hôtel de la Gare*, opposite the train station (☎03.88.94.13.67, fax 03.88.94.06.88; ③), whose restaurant is also cheaper (closed Sun; menu at 78–150F/€11.89–22.87). In the main street, the hotel-restaurant *L'Escargot*, 40 rue Nationale (☎03.88.94.90.29, fax 03.88.94.90.29; ③; menu at 55–130F/€8.38–19.82; closed Sun), is about the same price and its restaurant serves Alsatian cuisine. The nearest **HI hostel** to Wissembourg, and the closest hostel to the Maginot Line is at 10 rue du Moulin in Woerth (☎03.88.54.03.30, fax 03.88.09.58.32; closed Dec to mid-March; bus from Haguenau); there is a kitchen for members and camping facilities.

In addition to the hotel restaurants above there are a couple of reasonable **places to eat** on the main rue Nationale, including *Au Petit Dominicain*, 36 rue Nationale

(☎03.88.94.90.87; closed Mon and Tues; menu at 45–130F/€6.86–19.82), which serves traditional Alsatian food. A much fancier establishment, with a chef who rings his own inventive changes on the traditional regional cuisine, is *À l'Ange*, 2 rue de la République (☎03.88.94.12.11; closed Tues evening, Wed & last two weeks in Feb), in a beautiful old house by the stream next to place du Marché-aux-Choux: the prices reflect the excellent cooking, influenced by the proximity of Germany (the cheapest menu is the lunchtime 165F/€25.15, otherwise you'll be looking at twice that). For simple *tartes flambées*, *Au Saumon*, by little Venice, behind the Maison du Sel (☎03.88.94.17.60), has a nice garden and outdoor oven (from 30F/€4.57). *La Mirabelle*, 3 rue Générale Leclerc (☎03.88.54.82.14) is a nice outdoor café for summer meals, also from 30F/€4.57.

The Route des Châteaux

Scattered among the wooded hills to the west of Wissembourg are a host of ruined castles that once stood guard over the frontier with Germany, and the winding D3 and its smaller tributaries, which cross the now untenanted frontier, take you close to most of them. The ruins of the **Château du Fleckenstein** (daily March 15–March 31 & Nov 1–Nov 15 10am–5pm; April–June & Sept–Oct 10am–6pm; July & Aug 9.30am–6.30pm; 17F/€2.59 in the summer and at weekends, otherwise 12F/€1.83), 7km north of Lembach (see below), are perhaps the most spectacular, rising above the forest on a narrow sandstone outcrop, just a stone's throw from the German border. Six kilometres further on at Obersteinbach, the **Maison des Châteaux-Forts**, at 42 rue Principal (March–Oct Wed 2–5pm, Sat & Sun 3–6pm; call in advance because opening hours are susceptible to change; ☎03.88.09.56.34; 10F/€1.52), is an information centre, with displays and maps on the other castles in the area. A rather more modern fortress, just outside Lembach, is the **Four à Chaux**, part of the Maginot Line (guided tours: mid-March to June & Sept to mid-Nov 10am, 2pm & 3pm; July & Aug 10am, 11am & hourly 2–5pm; ☎03.88.94.48.62; 25F/€3.81).

An agreeable base for exploring this area is the village of **LEMBACH**, where the homely and unpretentious *Hôtel au Heimbach*, 15 rue de Wissembourg (☎03.88.94.43.46, fax 03.88.94.20.85; ③), is a pleasant **place to stay**. Directly opposite, the *Auberge du Cheval Blanc* (☎03.88.94.41.86, fax 03.88.94.20.74; closed Mon & Tues Feb & July; menu at 190–475F/€28.97–72.41) serves exquisite but expensive cuisine.

THE POLES OF WISSEMBOURG

Stanislas Leszczynski, born in the Polish-Ukrainian city of Lemberg (now Lwóv) in 1677, lasted just five years as the elected king of Poland before being forced into exile by the Russian tsar Peter the Great. For the next twenty-odd years he lived on a French pension in Wissembourg, along with a motley entourage of Polish expats. After fifteen years of relatively humdrum existence in the town's Ancien Hôpital south of the main church, Stanislas' luck changed when he managed, against all odds, to get his daughter, Marie, betrothed to the 15-year-old king of France, Louis XV. Marie was not quite so fortunate: married by proxy in Strasbourg Cathedral, and having never even set eyes on the groom, she subsequently had a total of ten children, only to be ultimately rejected by Louis, who preferred hunting and the company of his two more powerful mistresses, Madame de Pompadour and Madame du Barry. Bolstered by his daughter's marriage, Stanislas had another brief spell on the Polish throne from 1733 to 1736, but eventually gave it up in favour of the comfortable dukedom of Barr and Lorraine. He lived out his final years in true aristocratic style in the capital, Nancy, which he transformed into one of France's most beautiful towns.

The road continues westwards through wet, sparsely populated country to the big French army camp at **BITCHE** (in Lorraine), around 32km from Lembach. This garrison town, dominated by a squat dark Vauban **fort** atop its commanding bluff, has nothing to detain you, but if you need a **bed**, you could do worse than the *Hôtel de la Gare*, 2 av Trumelet-Faber (☎ & fax 03.87.96.00.14; ①; closed Sat, Sun & hols), which is friendly and clean; its restaurant is acceptable, too, with a menu at 49F/€7.47.

The southern Vosges

The **southern Vosges** cover a much greater area than the northern range, stretching as far south as Belfort in Franche-Comté. The major tourist attractions are along the **Route du Vin**, which follows the foot of the mountains along the western edge of the wide flat valley of the Rhine; every turn in the road reveals yet another exquisitely preserved medieval village. Many of these, such as **Colmar**, the main centre for the route, suffer from an overdose of visitors. To escape from the crowds, you'll need to head for the hills proper, along the **Route des Crêtes**, which traces the central ridge of the Vosges to the west.

The Route du Vin

Alsace is a region both blessed and cursed by tourism, and no more so than along the so-called **Route du Vin**, which stretches from Marlenheim, west of Strasbourg, to Thann, near Mulhouse. The problem with Alsace is that, left to its own devices, it stays on the right side of Disneyland but, under the impact of tourism and the desire to make money, it comes close to caricaturing itself.

Set against the "blue line of the Vosges", the route winds north–south through endless terraced vineyards which produce the region's famous fruity white wines. Opportunities for tasting the local produce are plentiful, with free *dégustations* along the roadside, in the *caveaux* of most villages and at the region's countless wine festivals. For a closer look at the vines themselves you can follow various *sentiers vinicoles* (vineyard paths); local tourist offices have details. In the midst of this sea of vines are dozens of flowery and typically picturesque Alsatian villages, dominated from the heights above by an extraordinary number of ancient ruined castles, testimony to the province's turbulent past.

The Route du Vin is deceptively hilly work on a bike, but **getting around** is definitely easier with your own transport. Otherwise you're dependent either on the train, which narrowly misses some of the best villages, or the region's poor bus service. In summer there's a **wine festival** each weekend in a different town, with *dégustations*, bargains, *tarte flambée* and traditional Alsatian music.

Obernai and around

Picturesque little **OBERNAI**, on the D422, is the first place most people head for when travelling south along the route from Strasbourg. Miraculously unscathed during the last two world wars, Obernai has retained almost its entire **rampart system**, including no fewer than fifteen towers, as well as street after street of carefully maintained medieval houses. Not surprisingly, it also gets more than its fair share of visitors, though this shouldn't put you off as the town is just about big enough to absorb the crowds. The **tourist office**, on place du Beffroi (May–Oct Mon–Sat 9.30am–12.30pm & 2–7pm, Sun 9am–12.30pm & 2–5.30pm; Nov–April Mon–Sat 9am–noon & 2–5pm; ☎03.88.95.64.13), has lots of useful information about wine and easy-to-follow routes for exploring the region. The only reasonably priced **hotels** are the *Maison du Vin*, 1 rue de la Paille (☎03.88.95.46.82, fax 03.88.95.54.00; ①), whose pretty rooms are above a wine shop; and *La Diligence*, 23 place de la Mairie (☎03.88.95.55.69, fax 03.88.95.42.46; ③), with a charming and reasonably priced *salon de thé* serving *petits plats* all day. *La Halle au Blé* **café** is a good place for a hot chocolate after a hard day's hiking in the Vosges.

ROSHEIM, 7km north of Obernai and up in the hills a little to the west of the D422, is relatively off the beaten track. Its two main sights are the Romanesque **church of St-Pierre-et-St-Paul**, whose roof is peppered with comical sculptured figures contemporary with the building, and the twelfth-century **Heidenhüs**, at 24 rue de la Principale, thought to be the oldest building in Alsace. The simple, clean, friendly family-run *Hôtel Alpina*, 39 rue du Lion (☎03.88.50.49.30, fax 03.88.49.25.75; ①), with an attractive terrace and breakfast room, makes a very nice place to stay. **ROSENWILLER**, a couple of kilometres up the hill among the vineyards, has a prettily sited and atmospherically overgrown **Jewish cemetery** at the edge of the woods, testimony to Alsace's once numerous Jewish community.

From Rosheim's *gare SNCF*, 1.5km northeast of the village, a **steam train** runs up the valley on Sundays and holidays to **OTTROTT**, which produces one of the few red wines of Alsace. An elegantly restored and modernized village house at 11 rue des Châteaux has been transformed into a rather luxurious **hotel**, the *Hostellerie des Châteaux* (☎03.88.48.14.14, fax 03.88.95.95.20; ⑨), with a sauna, swimming pool and overpriced restaurant. Just out of town is the Aquarium d'Ottrot, **Les Naïades** (daily 9.30am–6.30pm; 43F/€6.56), with sharks, crocodiles and thousands of fish from all over the world: follow the signs.

Ottrott brings you within hiking distance – 6km – of **Mont Ste-Odile** (763m), whose summit is surrounded by a mysterious Celtic wall, originally built in the seventh century BC. The wall is almost 10km in length and in parts reaches a height of 3.5m. Ste Odilia herself is buried in the small **chapel** on top of the hill, a pilgrimage site even today. According to tradition, she was cast out by her father at birth on account of her blindness, but miraculously regained her sight during childhood and returned to found the convent on Mont Ste-Odile, where she cured thousands of cases of blindness and leprosy. Accommodation is available here at *Le Mont Ste-Odile* (☎03.88.95.80.53, fax 03.88.95.82.96; ②; bookings advisable).

Barr

For some reason, **BARR**, west of the main road, is bypassed by many coach groups. Every bit as charming as Obernai, it's easy to while away a couple of hours wandering its twisting cobbled streets, at their busiest during the mid-July **wine festival** and on Sundays when the vintners come to ply their wines. The town has just one specific sight, **La Folie Marco**, at 30 rue du Docteur-Sultzer (July–Sept daily except Tues 10am–noon & 2–6pm; June & Oct Sat & Sun 10am–noon & 2–6pm; ☎03.88.08.94.72; 20F/€3.05), an unusually large eighteenth-century house on the outskirts of town along the road to Obernai, which has displays of period French and Alsatian furniture. There are regular *dégustations* in the garden cellar, and a festival of dance and waltz at the end of May. There is also a **restaurant** serving Alsatian specialities (menus 95–130F/€14.48–19.82, *tarte flambée* 35F/€5.34). Some interesting walks begin behind the Hôtel de Ville, including one to Mont Ste-Odile (13.9km; 3–4 hours).

The nearest **gare SNCF** is in the neighbouring village of Gertwiller, 1km to the east. The nicest **place to stay** in Barr is the superb *Hôtel Le Manoir*, 11 rue St-Marc (☎03.88.08.03.40, fax 03.88.08.53.71; ③), on the edge of town, with light, spacious rooms and a superb buffet breakfast. Alternatively, there are two **campsites**: the *Camping St-Martin*, at rue de l'Ill, near the Catholic church (☎03.88.08.00.45; June to mid-Oct), and *Camping Municipal Ste-Odile "Wepfermatt"*, 3km out of town at 137 rue de la Vallée (☎03.88.08.02.38; May–Oct). St-Pierre, 3km south of Barr, also has a camp-

ALSACE AND HITLER'S REICH

When Hitler conquered France in 1940, he not only occupied Alsace, but also incorporated it into the German state, making it subject to German laws and outlawing all manifestations of French and Alsatian culture. Worst of all, he conscripted 140,000 young Alsatian men, citizens of France, into the German armies, on pain of terrible reprisals against their families if they attempted to escape. They are known as the "**malgré-nous**": soldiers against their will.

Most of the *malgré-nous* were sent to the Russian front, where, as one survivor related, they were used as human minesweepers, sent into attack first across the Russian mine-fields. Forty thousand died and forty thousand have never been accounted for. Some deserted, and were hidden by their families, and others mutilated themselves. Many were taken prisoner and ended up in the Soviet Gulag, in the notorious camp at Tambov, in particular, northeast of Odessa, where they either died or were eventually repatriated in broken health. Having experienced the fascist Legion of French Volunteers against Bolshevism, the Russians were understandably not very sympathetic to Frenchmen fighting in German uniform, and dragged their feet over sending them back. The last *malgré-nous* to be released came home in 1955, after ten years in a Siberian camp.

Yet the most bitter experience for these soldiers was finding themselves, after so much suffering, treated as traitors by their fellow Frenchmen. A friend, recounting her father's experience as a *malgré-nous*, said: "The Germans took our children as if they were their own and after all that we were treated by France as the bloody Germans of the east."

For fifty years the veterans' association has fought for recognition of these unwilling soldiers of the Reich and for compensation in the form of pensions and invalidity bene-fits. And still the painful ambiguity endures. Thirteen Alsatian *malgré-nous* fought with the infamous Waffen SS Das Reich division, which was responsible, on its march to join battle with the Allies in Normandy in 1944, for the terrible massacres in Tulle and Oradour-sur-Glane (see p.648). Put on trial in the 1950s, they were granted amnesty for domestic political reasons. But the request in 1996 for a war veteran's pension by one of these old soldiers caused outrage amongst the survivors of Oradour.

site – the *Beau Séjour* (☎03.88.08.52.24 or 03.88.08.90.79; mid-May to Sept). For a real-ly good *tarte flambée* in a **restaurant** with great atmosphere, try *Les Caveau des Tanneurs*, 32 rue Neuve (☎03.88.08.91.50; *tarte flambée* from 40F/€6.10; Wed–Sun din-ner only): the *munster* (a kind of cheese) and cumin version is particularly good. *Winstub S'Barrer Stubbel*, 5 place de l'Hôtel de Ville (☎03.88.08.57.44), also serves good local specialities at reasonable prices.

Le Struthof concentration camp

Deep in the forests and hills of the Vosges, over 20km west of Barr, **Le Struthof-Natzwiller** (daily: March–June 9am–noon & 2–4.30pm; July & Aug 10am–5pm; Sept–Dec 10am–noon & 2–4.30pm; closed Jan & Feb; ☎03.88.97.04.49; 10F/€1.52) was the only Nazi concentration camp to be built on French soil (though at the time, of course, it was part of the Greater German Reich). The site is almost perversely beauti-ful, its stepped terraces cut into steep hillside, giving fantastic views across the Bruche valley. Set up shortly after Hitler's occupation of Alsace-Lorraine in 1940, it is thought that over 10,000 people died here. When the Allies liberated the camp on November 23, 1944, they found it empty – the remaining prisoners having already been transported to Dachau.

The barbed wire and watchtowers are as they were, though only two of the prisoners' barracks remain, one of which is now a **museum** of the deportations. Captions are in French only, but the pictures suffice to tell the story. An arson attack by neo-Nazis in 1976 only served to underline the need for such displays. At the foot of the camp is the crematorium with its ovens still intact. A couple of kilometres down the road to the west, towards Schirmeck, the Germans built a gas chamber – proof that Le Struthof was a fully integrated part of the Nazi killing machine. To the east, the two main granite quarries worked by the internees still survive, clearly signposted from the main road.

Sélestat

Back on the Route du Vin, **SÉLESTAT**, midway between Strasbourg and Colmar, is a delightful, relatively cosmopolitan old town, which makes a good base for exploring the central and most popular section of the route. The choice of reasonable accommodation is better than average, and the town itself contains a couple of interesting churches and a great museum for bibliophiles.

The oldest and finest of the two churches is the **church of Ste-Foy**. Built by the monks of Conques, it has been much restored since but its clean, austerely Romanesque lines have not been entirely wiped out. Close by, to the north, the much larger Gothic **church of St-Georges** sports spectacularly multicoloured roof tiles and some very fine stained glass. For a brief period in the late fifteenth and early sixteenth centuries, Sélestat was the intellectual centre of Alsace, due mainly to its Latin School, which attracted a group of Humanists led by Beatus Rhenanus, whose personal library was one of the most impressive collections of its time. At the **Bibliothèque Humaniste**, housed in the town's former corn exchange just by St-Georges (July & Aug Mon & Wed–Sat 9am–noon & 2–6pm, Sun 2–6pm; rest of year Mon & Wed–Fri 9am–noon & 2–6pm, Sat 9am–noon; 20F/€3.05), Rhenanus' collection is now on display along with some unusual and very rare books and manuscripts from as far back as the seventh century.

Sélestat is comparatively well served transport-wise, with frequent train connections to Strasbourg and Colmar, as well as a branch line that heads north to Strasbourg via Molsheim; the **gare SNCF** is west of the town centre down avenue de la Liberté. For a **place to stay**, there's none better than the comfortable, friendly *Auberge des Alliés*, 39 rue des Chevaliers, in the middle of town (☎03.88.92.09.34, fax 03.88.92.12.88; ③; closed Sun evening & Mon); its restaurant is good value and worth a look for its splendid tiled stove (menus 98–240F/€14.94–36.59). A funky modern alternative is the *Vaillant* on place de la République (☎03.88.92.09.46; ③; restaurant 95–225F/€14.48–34.30) – the groovy lifesize statue in the foyer is called Tom. There's a **campsite**, *Les Cigognes* (☎03.88.92.03.98; May to mid-Oct), south of the centre behind Vauban's remaining ramparts. Further information is available from the **tourist office** by the ring road on boulevard du Général-Leclerc (May–Sept Mon–Fri 9am–12.30pm & 1.30–7pm, Sat 9am–noon & 2–5pm, Sun 9am–3pm; Oct–April Mon–Fri 8.30am–noon & 1.30–6pm, Sat 9am–noon & 2–5pm; ☎03.88.58.87.20, fax 03.88.92.88.63).

Castles around Sélestat

Within easy range of Sélestat is a whole host of **ruined castles**. Seven kilometres north, and accessible by train, the village of **DAMBACH-LA-VILLE**, with its walls and three fortified gates all intact, is one of the highlights of the route. A thirty-minute climb west of the village is the formidable **Castle of Bernstein**. In the Middle Ages, Alsace was culturally more German than French, and this is a typically German mountain keep: tall and narrow with few openings and little use for everyday living. Around it are residential buildings enclosed within an outer wall, the masonry cut into protruding knobs, which gives it a curious pimpled texture. You can also go on a mini-train **tour** of the town and vineyards (July & Aug Mon, Thurs & Sat 5pm; 30F/€4.57), leaving from the main town square. Dambach has a cheap *Camping Municipal* (☎03.88.92.48.60; mid-May to Sept), 1km east on the D210, and a small but most attractive and inexpensive restaurant, *À la Couronne*, 13 place du Marché (☎03.88.92.40.85; closed Thurs, Feb 12–March 1 & Nov 15–30; menus 50–120F/€7.62–18.29).

Just 3km northwest of Sélestat is **SCHIRWILLER**, another attractive village, from where you can climb a steep, marked path to the **Castle of Ortenbourg**. Like Bernstein, it has a lofty refuge-tower with courtyards outside, very well preserved and protected by a rock-cut ditch. A few hundred metres southwest of here is **Ramstein Castle**, built in 1293 to protect the besiegers of Ortenbourg.

The best cluster of castles, however, is southwest of Sélestat. Four kilometres away, **KINTZHEIM** boasts a small but wonderful ruined castle built around a cylindrical refuge-tower. Today it's an aviary, the **Volerie des Aigles**, for birds of prey, with magnificent displays of aerial prowess by eagles and vultures (April–Nov; ☎03.88.92.84.33 for details of afternoon demonstrations; 45F/€6.86). If you have a yen to watch Barbary apes at play in the Vosgian jungle, you can do just that a couple of kilometres further west at the **Montagne des Singes** (daily: April–Oct 10am–noon & 1–5pm; July & Aug no lunchtime closure; ☎03.88.92.11.09; 40F/€6.10). Also on the way to Kintzheim from Sélestat is the rather tacky bird-based amusement park, the **Parc des Cigognes et Loisirs** (April–Sept daily 10am–7pm; March, Oct & Nov Wed, Sat & Sun 10am–7pm; ☎03.88.92.05.94; 45F/€6.86).

Another 5km on from Kintzheim, the ruins of **Oudenbourg Castle**, its sizeable hall preserved among the trees, is dwarfed by the massive **Haut-Koenigsbourg** (daily: March, April & Oct 9am–noon & 1–5.30pm; May, June & Sept 9am–6pm; July & Aug 9am–6.30pm; Nov–Feb 9.30am–noon & 1–4.30pm; ☎03.88.82.50.60; 40F/€6.10), one of the biggest, most popular castles in Alsace, and – astride its 757-metre bluff – by far the highest. Ruined after an assault in 1633, it was heavily restored in the early years of this century for Kaiser Wilhelm II. It's easy to criticize some of the detail of the restoration, but it's an enjoyable experience and a remarkably convincing re-creation of a castle-palace of the age of Dürer. There are guided tours, but it's best explored on your own. The views all around are fantastic. There's a winding road down to Bergheim from here (see below), if you'd rather not retrace your tracks to Sélestat.

Ribeauvillé and around

RIBEAUVILLÉ is the largest town between Sélestat and Colmar – not as pretty as some of its immediate neighbours, but right at the foot of the mountains and well placed for exploring the many castles and villages that surround it.

If you wish to **stay**, you could try the rather fancy and friendly little *Hôtel de la Tour*, in a converted winery at 1 rue de la Mairie (☎03.89.73.72.73, fax 03.89.73.38.74; ④; closed Jan to mid-March), with a Turkish bath and a *winstub*. Two local **campsites** are *Camping des Trois Châteaux* (☎03.89.73.20.00; July & Aug), to the north of Ribeauvillé, and the much plusher *Pierre-de-Courbertin* site (☎03.89.73.66.71; March–Nov) to the south.

In the vicinity of the town is a trio of fortresses built by the counts of Ribeaupierre: **St-Ulrich Castle**, an hour's haul up a marked path; just north of it the smaller **Girsberg Castle**, balanced on a pinnacle which somehow provides room for a bailey, two towers and other buildings; and, further on, the ruins of **Haut-Ribeaupierre**.

BERGHEIM, 3.5km northeast of Ribeauvillé, retains a good part of its old fortifications, with three towers still surviving – despite being one of the most beautiful Alsatian villages, it rarely attracts the attentions of the tour groups. Also within easy walking range of Ribeauvillé, this time to the south, the village of **HUNAWIHR** is another beguiling hamlet, with a fourteenth-century walled **church** standing out amid the green vines. Hunawihr is at the forefront of the Alsatian ecological movement aimed at reintroducing the stork – the *cigogne* – to the region, and there's a **reserve** to the east of the village, **Centre Cigognes et Loutres** (daily: April–June & Sept to mid-Nov 10am–noon & 2–6pm; July & Aug 10am–6pm; call to check show times, ☎03.89.73.72.62; 45F/€6.86). There is also a breeding reserve for otters and other fishing animals.

Lastly, nearer to the hub of Colmar, there are a couple of tourist targets you may want to avoid, or at least for which you should time your visits carefully. A couple of kilometres south of Hunawihr, the walled village of **RIQUEWIHR** is exceptionally well preserved, with plenty of medieval houses and a château containing a **postal museum**, the Musée d'Histoire des PTT d'Alsace (April to mid-Nov daily except Tues 10am–noon & 2–6pm; 20F/€3.05); consequently it suffers more visitors per annum than any other village along the route.

KAYSERSBERG, still further southwest, also plays host to more than its fair share of tour buses. It boasts a fortified **bridge** and a handsome sixteenth-century wooden altarpiece in the main **church**. But the town's principal renown is as the birthplace of Nobel Peace Prize winner Albert Schweitzer, who spent most of his extremely active, and not always peaceful, life at the leprosy hospital he founded at Lambaréné in French Equatorial Africa, now Gabon. During World War I he was interned by the French authorities as an "enemy alien", but nowadays he is suitably honoured with the **Centre Culturel Albert Schweitzer**, 126 rue du Général-de-Gaulle (Easter & May–Oct daily 9am–noon & 2–6pm; 5F/€0.76).

Two kilometres from Kaysersberg in the village of **KIENTZHEIM** (see also box on p.307), the very comfortable *Hostellerie de l'Abbaye d'Alspach*, 2–4 rue Foch (☎03.89.47.16.00, fax 03.89.78.29.73; ④; closed Jan 9–March 10), in a former abbey, makes a good base for visiting Colmar, 10km away. Try some of the home-made wine.

Colmar

COLMAR, a fifty-minute train ride south of Strasbourg, has sprawled unattractively on both sides of the train tracks, but the old centre remains typically and whimsically Alsatian, with crooked houses, half-timbered and painted, on crooked lanes – all extremely pretty and very touristy. Colmar's attractions don't stop at its buildings; it is also the proud possessor of one of the last and most extraordinary of all Gothic paintings – the altarpiece for St Anthony's monastery at Issenheim, painted by Mathias Grünewald.

Arrival, information and accommodation

From the **gare** SNCF it's a ten-minute walk down avenue de la République to the **tourist office** on place d'Unterlinden (April–June, Sept & Oct Mon–Sat 9am–6pm, Sun & hols 10am–2pm; July & Aug Mon–Sat 9am–7pm, Sun 9.30am–2pm; Nov–March Mon–Sat 9am–noon & 2–6pm, Sun 10am–2pm; ☎03.89.20.68.92, fax 03.89.41.34.13, *www.ot-colmar.fr*). Besides selling Club Vosgien hiking maps and a booklet of day walks in the hills behind the town, they'll also give you details of the **buses** to the towns and villages of the Route du Vin, which leave from outside the *gare SNCF*. **Bikes** can be rented from La Cyclothéque, 31 route d'Ingersheim (Mon 2–6.30pm, Tues–Sat 8am–noon & 2–6.30pm; ☎03.89.79.14.18), Cycles Geiswiller, 6 bd du Champ de Mars (Tues–Fri 8.30am–noon & 2–6.30pm, Sat 8.30–noon & 2–6pm; ☎03.89.41.30.59), and Cycles Mayer, 6 rue du Pont-Rouge (Tues–Sat 8.30am–noon & 2–6.30pm; ☎03.89.79.12.47).

Accommodation is not as overpriced as you might expect, with a number of reasonable hotels very close to the *gare SNCF*. Try the quiet and comfortable *Hôtel Colbert*, 2 rue des Trois-Épis, parallel to av de la République (☎03.89.41.31.05, fax 03.89.23.66.75; ③), or *La Chaumière*, 74 av de la République (☎03.89.41.08.99; ②). For more luxury, there's the *Grand Hôtel Bristol*, 7 place de la Gare, directly opposite the station exit (☎03.89.23.59.59, fax 03.89.23.92.26, *www.grand-hotel-bristol.fr*, ⑤), a relic of the grand old prewar days of tourism, now comfortably refurbished and part of a chain. There are also two **hostels**: the central *Maison des Jeunes et de la Culture*, 17 rue Camille-Schlumberger (☎03.89.41.26.87, fax 03.89.23.20.16), two streets over from av de la République; and the HI hostel, *Auberge de Jeunesse Mittelhardt*, at 2 rue Pasteur (☎03.89.80.57.39, fax 03.89.80.76.16); take bus #4 from the station or rue d'Unterlinden, stop "Lycée Technique". This place gets very busy in summer with lots of teenagers – unfortunately the rooms are not insulated as in some of the other hostels in France. The nearest **campsite**, *Camping Colmar-Horbourg-Wihr*, is 2km from the centre of town on Route de Neuf-Brisach (☎03.89.41.15.94; closed Dec & Jan); take bus #1 from the station, direction "Wihr", stop "Plage de l'Ill".

The Town

The *pièce de résistance* of the **Musée d'Unterlinden**, housed in a former Dominican convent at 1 rue d'Unterlinden (April–Oct daily 9am–6pm; Nov–March daily except Tues 9am–noon & 2–5pm; closed public hols; 35F/€5.34) is the **Issenheim altarpiece**, originally designed as a single piece. On the front was the Crucifixion, almost luridly expressive: a tortured Christ with stretched ribcage and outsize hands turned upwards, fingers splayed in pain, flanked by his pale, fainting mother and SS John and Mary Magdalene. Then it unfolded, relative to its function on feast days, Sundays and weekdays, to reveal an Annunciation, Resurrection, Virgin and Child, and finally a sculpted panel depicting saints Anthony, Augustine and Jerome. Completed in 1515, the painting is affected by Renaissance innovations in light and perspective while still rooted in the medieval spirit, with an intense mysticism and shifts of mood in its subject matter. Also worth a look is the collection of modern paintings in the basement, which includes works by Picasso, Léger and Vasarely.

A short walk into the old town, the **Dominican church** on rue des Serruriers (April–Dec daily 10am–1pm & 3–6pm; 8F/€1.22) has some fine glass and, above all, a radiantly beautiful altarpiece known as *The Virgin in a Bower of Roses*, painted in 1473 by Martin Schongauer, who is also represented in the Musée d'Unterlinden. At the other end of rue des Serruriers you come to the **Collégiale St-Martin** on a café-lined square. Known locally as "the cathedral", it's worth a quick peek for its stonework and stained glass, as is the sixteenth-century **Maison Pfister**, on the south side of the church, for its painted panels. Frédéric Auguste Bartholdi, the nineteenth-century sculptor responsible for New York's Statue of Liberty, was born at 30 rue des Marchands. This has been turned into the **Musée Bartholdi** (March–Dec daily except Tues 10am–noon & 2–6pm; closed public hols; 23F/€3.51), containing Bartholdi's personal effects, plus the original designs for the statue, along with sundry Colmarabilia.

Rue des Marchands continues south to the Ancienne Douane or **Koïfhus**, its gaily painted roof tiles loudly proclaiming the city's medieval prosperity. This is the heart of Colmar's old town, a short step away from the archly picturesque quarter down the Grand' Rue, cut through by the River Lauch and known as **La Petite Venise**. The dolly-mixture colours of the old fishing cottages on quai de la Poissonnerie are more touristy even than Strasbourg's Petite France. Twice as tall, but similarly over-restored, are the black-and-white half-timbered tanners' houses on **quai des Tanneurs**, which leads off from the Koïfhus, with open verandas on the top floor originally designed for drying hides.

There are two other museums that you will see if you take a stroll through the old town: the **Musée Animé du Jouet et des Petits Trains**, 40 rue Vauban (July & Aug daily 10am–6pm; Sept–June daily except Tues 10am–noon & 2–6pm; 25F/€3.81), whose collection of toys and toy trains is fun for children; and the unexciting **Museum d'Histoire Naturelle**, 11 rue Turenne (March–Dec Mon & Wed–Sat 10am–noon & 2–6pm, Sun 2–6pm; 25F/€3.81).

Eating and drinking

Restaurants in Colmar are generally overpriced, particularly Alsatian ones. However, *Winstub Brenner*, 1 rue de Turenne (☎03.89.41.42.43; main course from 50F/€7.62;

closed Tues evenings and Wed, second fortnight Jan, third week June & third week Nov), serves delicious, generous meals and has a lovely terrace by Little Venice – ask for a side order of *pommes sautées* if you're really hungry. A fun establishment for both food and atmosphere is *S'Parisser Stewwele*, 4 place Jeanne-d'Arc (☎03.89.24.53.15; main course 60–70F/€9.15–10.67, or from 160F/€24.39 à la carte; closed Tues, second half of Feb, third week June & third week Nov), while a good place for regional food is *Le Petit Gourmand* on quai de la Poissonnerie, in Little Venice (☎03.89.41.09.32; closed Mon & Tues evening; menus from 120F/€18.29). Otherwise, you could amass a sumptuous picnic from the town's numerous pâtisseries and charcuteries. There's a fruit and veg **market** every Thursday around the Koïfhus at place de l'Ancienne-Douane, and every Saturday on place St-Joseph.

Munster and the Route des Crêtes

MUNSTER owes its existence and its name to a band of Irish monks who founded a monastery here in the seventh century, some 19km west of Colmar up the narrowing valley of the River Fecht, overlooked by Le Petit Ballon (1267m) and Le Hohneck (1362m), among the highest peaks of the Vosges. Its name today is particularly associated with a rich, creamy and exceedingly smelly cheese, the crowning glory of many an Alsatian meal. Although of no special interest in itself, the town makes a peaceful and verdant base either for exploring further into the mountain range, much of which lies within the Parc Régional des Ballons des Vosges, or for visiting Colmar and other places along the Route du Vin.

Munster is accessible by **train** from Colmar. The **tourist office**, 1 rue du Couvnet (July & Aug Mon–Sat 9.30am–12.30pm & 1.30–6.30pm; Sept–June Mon–Fri 9.30am–12.30pm & 2–6pm, Sat 10am–noon & 2–6pm; ☎03.89.77.31.80, fax 03.89.77.07.17), has lots of information about hiking in the Munster valley and the *parc régional*. The Maison du Parc, 1 cour de l'Abbaye (May–Sept Tues–Sun 9am–noon & 2–6pm; Oct–April Mon–Fri 10am–noon & 2–6pm, ☎03.89.77.90.20), is the place to get all the information you need about the park.

If you want to **stay**, you could try the large, modern *Hôtel Verte-Vallée*, 10 rue Alfred-Hartmann (☎03.89.77.15.15, fax 03.89.77.17.40, *www.alsanet.com/verte-vallee*; ④), in the depths of the wooded valley, which, with its squeaky-clean and pastel atmosphere, makes a perfect haven for a day or two. It has a good restaurant specializing in traditional French dishes, with a terrace overlooking the stream (closed Jan 3–27; menu at 100–280F/€15.24–42.69, *carte* 180F/€27.44 or more). Less well appointed but blessed with stupendous views are two hotels perched high on the north side of the valley in the hamlet of **HOHRODBERG**: *Hôtel Panorama*, 3 route du Linge (☎03.89.77.36.53, fax 03.89.77.03.93; ③), and, with rather awful decor, *Hôtel Roess* (☎03.89.77.36.00, fax 03.89.77.01.95; ③), 100m higher up. Both have restaurants. Back in Munster, there is a **hostel**, *Luttenbach/Munster*, at 13 rue de la Gare (☎03.89.77.34.20), and a **campsite**, *Camping municipal du Parc de la Fecht*, on the route de Gunsbach (☎03.88.77.31.08).

The Route des Crêtes

Above Munster the main road to Gérardmer crosses the mountains by the principal pass, the Col de la Schlucht, where it intersects the so-called Route des Crêtes, built for strategic purposes during World War I. It's a spectacular trail, traversing thick forest and open pasture, where the herds of cows that produce the Munster cheese graze in summer; in winter it becomes one long cross-country ski route. Starting in **CERNAY**, 15km west of Mulhouse, it follows the main ridge of the Vosges, including the highest peak of the range, the Grand Ballon (1424m), north as far as **STE-MARIE-AUX-MINES**, 20km west of Sélestat, once at the heart of a silver-mining district. From Munster it is also accessible by a twisting minor road through Hohrodberg (see above),

HIKING IN THE SOUTHERN VOSGES

There is no shortage of waymarked paths in the **southern Vosges**. Six **GRs** cross the Vosges: they are a good way to see the less tourist-congested castles.

GR7: Ballon d'Alsace to Remiremont.

GR53: Wissembourg to Belfort (part of the route coincides with GR5).

GR59: Ballon d'Alsace to Besançon.

GR531: Wissembourg to the Ballon d'Alsace.

GR532: Soultz-sous-Forêts to Belfort.

GR533: Sarrebourg to Belfort, along the west flank of the Vosges.

There are five treks of between five and eleven days' duration described in *Les Grandes Traversées des Vosges*, published by the Office Départemental du Tourisme du Bas-Rhin, 9 rue du Dôme, 67000 Strasbourg (☎03.88.15.45.80), with details of accommodation, access and so on. They are structured to show different aspects of the Vosges in landscapes, history and traditional culture. Another useful contact for information is the Association Départmentale du Tourisme du Haut-Rhin, 1 rue Schlumberger, 68006 Colmar (☎03.89.20.10.68, fax 03.89.23.33.91).

Organized walks, involving guides or luggage transport or both, are arranged by various companies and tourist offices. For example, Horizons d'Alsace, 7 Grand' Rue, Kientzheim (☎03.89.78.20.30, fax 03.89.78.12.22), organizes the walk, accommodation and meals, and baggage transport. It is essential to book in advance. A six-day trip will cost around 3000F/€457.

Belfort in Franche-Comté is another good place to base a hiking trip in the southern Vosges. The Ballon d'Alsace, in the centre of the Parc Régional des Ballons des Vosges is the meeting point of the GR5, GR7 and GR59, and a discovery trail has been marked out around the summit. A number of PR trails (rambles) begin from here. The Malsaucy lake along the GR5 trail is another popular hiking area. Contact the Belfort tourist office (see p.311) for maps and information.

which takes you past beautiful glacial lakes, the Lac Blanc and the Lac Noir, as well as the eerie World War I battlefield of Linge, where the French and German trenches, once separated literally by a few metres, are still clearly visible.

Mulhouse and around

Thirty-five kilometres south of Colmar, **MULHOUSE** is a large sprawling industrial city. It was Swiss until 1798 when, at the peak of its prosperity (based on printed cotton fabrics and allied trades), it voted to become part of France. Even now many people who live here work in Basle in Switzerland. It is also the home city of Alfred Dreyfus, the unfortunate Jewish army officer who was wrongly convicted of espionage in 1894 (see "Contexts", p.1105). Not having much of an old town, it is no city for strollers, but there are four or five unusually good – and rather unusual – museums in the town and its vicinity that delve into the region's manufacturing past: wallpaper (see Rixheim, p.309), firemen, railway, automobiles and fabrics are all given their platform. There is also a jazz festival in August, which is a good time to be out partying in this town, with concerts in the museums, the schools and the streets, as well as in the cafés and bars.

Close to the *gare SNCF*, just along the canal to the right, is the excellent **Musée de l'Impression sur Étoffes**, 14 rue Jean-Jacques Henner (daily 10am–6pm; printing demonstration on Mon, Wed, Fri & Sun at 3pm; 36F/€5.49). It contains a vast collection of the most beautiful fabrics imaginable: eighteenth-century Indian and Persian imports that revolutionized the European ready-to-wear market in their time; silks from Turkestan; batiks from Java; Senegalese materials; some superb kimonos from Japan; and a unique display of scarves from France, Britain and the US. Also in the centre, the Hôtel de Ville on place de la Réunion contains a beautifully presented history of Mulhouse and its region in the **Musée Historique** (daily except Tues: May–Oct 10am–noon & 2–6pm; Nov–April 10am–noon & 2–5pm; undergoing renovation at the time of writing, the museum is free until the work is finished), which exhibits local archeological findings and seventeenth- and eighteenth-century furnishings.

Out of the centre of Mulhouse, near the northwestern suburb of **DORNACH**, in the direction of the A36 *autoroute*, is the **Musée Français du Chemin de Fer**, 2 rue Alfred-de-Glehn (daily: April–Sept 9am–6pm; Oct–March 9am–5pm; 46F/€7.01 combined ticket with Musée des Sapeurs-Pompiers, or 60F/9.15 joint ticket with the Electropolis); take bus #17 from Porte-Jeune Place to stop "Musée du Chemin de Fer". Railway rolling stock on display includes Napoléon III's ADCs' drawing room, decorated by Viollet-le-Duc in 1856, and a luxuriously appointed 1926 diner from the *Golden Arrow*. There are cranes, stations, signals and related artefacts, but the stars of the show are the big locomotive engines with brightly painted boilers, gleaming wheels and pistons, and tangles of brass and copper piping – real works of art. In the same complex is the **Musée des Sapeurs-Pompiers** (times and price as above), its antique fire engines and other memorabilia the personal collection of a retired local firefighter. A third museum, **Electropolis – Musée de l'Énergie Électrique**, 55 rue du Pâturage (Tues–Sun 10am–6pm; 48F/€7.32, or 60F/9.15 joint ticket with the Musée du Chemin de Fer and the Musée des Sapeurs-Pompiers), is devoted to the production and uses of electricity.

A couple of kilometres north of the city centre, the **Musée National de l'Automobile**, 192 av de Colmar (daily except Tues 10am–6pm; 60F/€9.15; bus #1, #4 or #17 from Porte-Jeune Schuman or Porte-Jeune Place to stop "Musée Auto"), has a collection of over six hundred cars, originally the private collection of local business sharks, the Schlumpf brothers. The vehicles range from the industry's earliest attempts, like the extraordinary wooden-wheeled Jacquot steam "car" of 1878, to 1968 Porsche racing vehicles and contemporary factory prototypes. The largest group is that of locally made Bugatti models: dozens of glorious racing cars, coupés and limousines, the pride of them the two Bugatti Royales, out of only seven that were constructed – one of them Ettore Bugatti's own, with bodywork designed by his son.

Practicalities

Place de la Réunion, nominally the centre of town, is five minutes' walk north of the **gare SNCF**. The **tourist office** is on the way at 9 av Foch (July & Aug Mon–Sat 9am–7pm, Sun 10am–noon; Sept–June Mon–Fri 9am–7pm, Sat 9am–5pm; ☎03.89.35.48.48, fax 03.89.45.66.16, *www.ot.ville-mulhouse.fr*). As for **accommodation**, rooms are generally overpriced in Mulhouse, but the following hotels are comfortable and affordable: *St-Bernard*, 3 rue des Fleurs (☎03.89.45.82.32, fax 03.39.45.26.32; ②), with Internet access in the "library" in the foyer; *de Paris*, 5 passage de l'Hôtel-de-Ville (☎03.89.45.21.41, fax 03.89.36.08.31; ①); *Schoenberg*, 14 rue Schoenberg, behind the station (☎03.89.44.19.41, fax 03.89.44.49.80; ②); and *Central*, 15–17 passage Central (☎03.89.46.18.84, fax 03.89.56.31.66, ①–③). The **HI hostel** is at 37 rue de l'Illberg (☎03.89.42.63.28, fax 03.89.59.74.95; bus #1 or #2, stop "Salle des Sports"), and also has facilities for camping. There is a pleasant **campsite**, *Camping de l'Ill*, on rue Pierre-de-Coubertin, near the suburb of Dornach, 4km from the city centre on the banks of the River Ill (☎03.89.06.20.66; closed Oct–March); take bus #7 from place Porte-Jeune.

As at Colmar and Strasbourg, Mulhouse's Alsatian **restaurants** are none too cheap, but there are plenty of them – look for the outdoor terraces full of tourists. The *Crêperie*

Crampous Mad, 14 impasse des Tondeurs (☎03.89.45.79.43; closed Sun; menu 50–100F/€7.62–15.24), is a good standby. For a really good seafood meal, try *Le Bistrot à Huitres*, 2 rue Moenschberg (☎03.89.64.01.60; closed Sun & Mon; menus from 130F/€19.82). You can drown your sorrows at *Gambrinus*, 5 rue des Franciscains, north of place de la Réunion (☎03.89.66.18.65; menu 45–150F/€6.86–22.87), which boasts over thirty **beers** on tap and offers simple dishes to wash them down with.

At the beginning of August you can see some of the vintage cars from the Musée de l'Automobile in gear as part of a **Grande Parade**, and in late August, Mulhouse hosts the region's hottest **jazz festival** (festival dates and information: ☎03.89.45.63.95, *www.alsacom.com/jazz-a-mulhouse*). To find out what's going on at other times of the year, get hold of a copy of *Mulhouse Poche*, the free **listings** quarterly, or *Mulhouse Echo*, also free. The tourist office should be well stocked with both of these.

Rixheim and Ungersheim

In the village of **RIXHEIM**, 6km east of Mulhouse, the **Musée du Papier-Peint**, 28 rue Zuber (June–Sept daily 9am–noon & 2–6pm; Oct–May daily except Tues 10am–noon & 2–6pm; 35F/€5.34; train to Rixheim or bus #10 from Mulhouse, direction "Commanderie", stop "Centre Europe"), a subsidiary of the printed fabrics museum, is housed in the former headquarters of the Teutonic Knights. A museum of wallpaper may not be everyone's idea of a fun afternoon out, but this contains a stunning cornucopia of antique painted wallpaper, and there are demonstrations of printing the stuff (Tues, Thurs & Sat at 3pm).

Just past Pulvershalm, 10km northwest of Mulhouse off the D430 at **UNGERSHEIM**, the **Écomusée d'Alsace** (daily: July & Aug 9am–7pm; April–June & Sept 9.30am–6pm; March & Oct 10am–5pm; Nov–Feb 10.30am–4.30pm; ☎03.89.74.44.74; 78F/€11.89) is an open-air museum that presents regional traditions and customs. It's plenty of fun for adults and kids, with over fifty traditional Alsatian buildings spanning the centuries, as well as on-site craft workers doing their various things. It's a vast complex already, and there are plans to enlarge it further to incorporate the nearby potassium mine which recently ceased production. A regional bus runs frequent services Monday to Saturday from the *gare SNCF*, direction "Guebwiller" (40F/€6.16 one way).

FRANCHE-COMTÉ AND THE JURA MOUNTAINS

The **Jura mountains** – gentle in the west, precipitous in the east, with wide, high forested plateaux in between – cover most of the old county of **Franche-Comté**, once part of the realms of the Grand Dukes of Burgundy, but properly French only since the late seventeenth century. The towns, especially the capital **Besançon**, are beautiful and tranquil, with the River Doubs flowing through, and the villages, such as **Baume-Les-Messieurs** and **Château Chalon**, are some of the prettiest in France. Otherwise, what there is to see is countryside – hundreds of square kilometres of woodland, lake and pasture that is hard to get around without a car, and is best explored on foot or by bicycle. There are several **GR footpaths** in the area, including the marathon GR5 from the Netherlands to the Med, and the GR9, which snakes its way through the Parc Régional du Haut-Jura. One of the best things about this part of France in summer is that you will barely notice other tourists. **Franche-Comté** is divided into four *départements*: the Territoire de Belfort, the Haute-Saône, the Doubs (around Besançon) and, largest of all, the Jura.

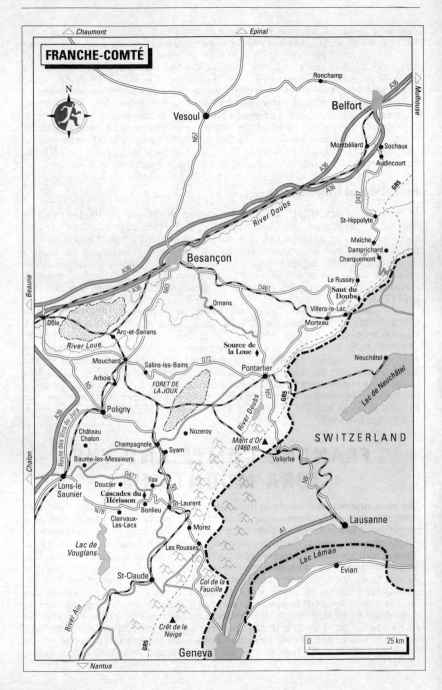

FRANCHE-COMTÉ

N

Chaumont

Epinal

Mulhouse

Ronchamp

A36

Belfort

Vesoul

N57

Montbéliard

Sochaux

Audincourt

A36

A36

GR5

D437

River Doubs

St-Hippolyte

Maîche

Damprichard

Charquemont

Besançon

D461

Le Russey

Saut du Doubs

A36

N83

Ornans

Villers-le-Lac

Beaune

Morteau

Dôle

River Loue

Arc-et-Senans

Source de
la Loue

Neuchâtel

Mouchard

Salins-les-Bains

D72

Pontarlier

Lac de Neuchâtel

Arbois

N5

FORÊT DE
LA JOUX

N57

GR5

Poligny

A39

Château
Chalon

Nozeroy

River Doubs

Champagnole

Syam

Mont d'Or
(1460 m)

SWITZERLAND

Route des Vins du Jura

Baume-les-Messieurs

Vallorbe

Chalon

D471

Doucier

Ilax

N5

Lons-le
Saunier

Cascades du
Hérisson

Bonlieu

St-Laurent

N9

N78

Clairvaux-
Les-Lacs

Lausanne

Morez

A1

Lac de
Vouglans

Les Rousses

Lac Léman

Evian

St-Claude

Col de la
Faucille

GR5

River Ain

Crêt de la
Neige

0   25 km

Geneva

Nantua

Belfort and around

Nestled in the gap between the southern reaches of the Vosges and the northern outliers of the Jura mountains – the one natural chink in France's eastern geological armour and the obvious route for invaders – **BELFORT** is assured of a place in French hearts for its deeds of military daring. Its name is particularly linked with the 1870 Prussian War, when its long resistance to siege spared it the humiliating annexation to Germany suffered by much of neighbouring Alsace-Lorraine. The commanding officer at the time, Colonel Denfert-Rochereau, earned himself the honour of numerous street names as well as that of a Parisian métro station. These days it is an interesting town with a mixed population.

Finding your way around Belfort is easy enough. The town is sliced in two by the River Savoureuse: the **new town** to the west is the commercial hub; to the east lies the quieter **old town**, laid out below the massive red **château.** Built by the ubiquitous fortress-architect Vauban on the site of a medieval fort, it now houses the **Musée d'Art et d'Histoire** (May–Sept daily 10am–7pm; Oct–April daily except Tues 10am–noon & 2–5pm; ☎03.84.54.25.51/52; 18F/€2.74, or 20F/€3.05 including entry to the viewing platform at the lion – see below), containing works by Dürer, Doré and Rodin. The other collections include military objects from Belfort's centuries of conflicts, and artefacts from Bronze and Iron Ages found in the funeral cave at Cravanche in 1876. Vauban is also responsible for the fortifications surrounding Belfort, which created a five-sided old town whose street plan is still largely unchanged. Belfort's other museum, the **Donation Maurice Jardot** (daily except Tues 10am–6pm; 25F/€3.81), is a ten-minute walk away from the tourist office down rue de Mulhouse, at no. 8, and will be of interest to fans of Cubism. Jardot was an associate of Daniel-Henry Kahnweiler, one of the great twentieth-century art dealers: his collection, left to the town of Belfort upon his death in 1997, contains 110 works of art, including some by Braque, Léger and Picasso.

The most famous and photographed phenomenon in town is the eleven-metre-high red sandstone **lion** applied to the rock-face that you pass on the way up to the castle, fashioned by Bartholdi to commemorate the 1870 siege. From the **viewing platform** at the front paw of the lion (April & Oct daily 8am–noon & 2–6pm; May & June 8am–noon & 2–7pm; July–Sept daily 8am–7pm; Nov–March Mon–Fri 10am–noon & 2–5pm, weekends & hols 8am–noon & 2–5pm; 6F/€0.91, or 20F/€3.05, combined ticket to the Musée d'Art et d'Histoire), you get some stunning views over the town and surrounding countryside.

Belfort is a good base for exploring the northeastern corner of the **River Doubs**. After that, it's either follow the *autoroute* directly to Besançon, which is a lively town with lots of good restaurants, or take your time and lose yourself in the hills and forests and pretty towns along the scenic route.

Practicalities

The **gare SNCF** and departure point for local **buses** are at the end of Faubourg-de-France, the main pedestrianized shopping drag in the new town. The **tourist office** (mid-June to mid-Sept Mon–Sat 9am–7pm; mid-Sept to mid-June Mon–Sat 9am–12.30pm & 1.45–6pm; ☎03.84.55.90.90, fax 03.84.55.90.99, *otbtb@essor-info.fr*) is at 2bis rue Clemenceau, a ten-minute walk from the station down Faubourg de France as far as the river, then left along quai Charles-Vallet until you reach rue Clemenceau; the castle houses a tourist information annexe during the summer (July & Aug daily 10am–12.30pm & 2–6.30pm).

There is an excellent choice of **hotels**: the *Au Relais d'Alsace*, 5 av de la Laurencie (☎03.84.22.15.55, fax 03.84.28.70.48; ②), is where out-of-town musicians stay when they perform in Belfort, and they will be happy to advise you about what's happening in the region. Other options include the *Hôtel Vauban*, 4 rue du Magasin (☎03.84.21.59.37, fax 03.84.21.41.67; ③), where the owners are also artists, and, for a bit more grandeur, the *Grand Hôtel du Tonneau d'Or*, 1 rue Reiset (☎03.84.58.57.56, fax 03.84.58.57.50; ⑤). Belfort's **hostel**, *Résidence Madrid*, is 1km west of the railway line at 6 rue de Madrid (☎03.84.21.39.16, fax 03.84.28.58.95), and its **campsite**, *Camping International de l'Etang des Forges*, is on rue du Général Béthouart, north of the old town (☎03.84.22.54.92; May to mid-Oct).

Inexpensive places to **eat** and **cafés** can be found in the place d'Armes and place de la République, in between antique shops and old-fashioned grocery stores such as Épicerie de Lion, on rue de la Porte de France. *Aux Crêpes d'Antan*, 13 rue du Quai, has delicious crêpes, starting from 25F/€3.81. *Bistrot Boeuf-Carottes*, 14 rue Lecourbe (☎03.84.21.15.40; closed Sun evening & Mon), is another good place to eat, with menus from 90F/€13.72. *Café Théâtre*, behind the theatre on place Corbis, has outdoor tables by the river and is a pleasant place for a coffee, while *La Poudrière*, place de l'Arsenal (closed late July & Aug), is the best place for **live music**.

Ronchamp

Before you take to the hills, there is one day-trip from Belfort worth undertaking – to the mining town of **RONCHAMP**, 20km west (connected by train and bus), where the architect Le Corbusier built one of his most enduring and atypical masterpieces in the 1950s, the **Chapelle de Notre-Dame-du-Haut** (daily except Tues: April–Sept 9.30am–6.30pm; Oct–March 10am–4pm; 10F/€1.52). It stands, all in concrete, above the town on the top of a wooded hill, white and reflective, visible from miles away, with its aerodynamic tower and wave-curved roof cutting into the sky beyond. Inside, the rough-textured walls are pierced with unequal embrasures, several closed by patterns of primary glass, whose reds, blues and yellows stain the dipping floor. Simplicity itself, with pared-down crucifix and steel altar rail, it's highly atmospheric.

The **tourist office** is on place 14-Juillet (July & Aug Mon–Fri 9am–noon & 2–6pm, Sat 9am–noon & 2–4pm; Sept–June Mon 2–5pm, Tues–Fri 9am–noon & 2–5pm, Sat 9am–noon; ☎03.84.63.50.82). If it's getting late and you're worried about a place to **stay**, try *La Pomme d'Or*, 34 rue le Corbusier, alongside the train line (☎03.84.20.62.12, fax 03.84.63.59.45; ②; restaurant from 55F/€8.38). Hostellers can take another twenty-minute train ride west to **VESOUL**, where the **HI hostel** is by the Lac de Vaivre–Vesoul (☎03.84.76.48.55; bus #1 to stop "Peugeot"), but check the train timetables: there are not many trains to or from either Belfort or Vesoul.

Montbéliard

MONTBÉLIARD is not far from Belfort and, because of the Peugeot factory (the second car production plant to be created in Europe), is another thriving industrial town. There are some unexpected pleasures in Montbéliard, however: the town has been part of France only since 1793, so the architecture of the old town has a strong Germanic look. The imposing **Château des Ducs de Wurtemburg** (daily except Tues 10am–noon & 2–6pm; 30F/€4.57), constructed during the fifteenth and sixteenth centuries, has been restored to house various exhibitions: there is always a specialist international exhibition as well as the permanent display of the collection of famous French zoologist Georges Cuvier, who was born in Montbéliard and whose work paved the way for Darwin. There is also a display of the Gallo-Roman objects found nearby at the remains of the huge **Roman theatre** at Mandeure, 8km south of Montbéliard, just off the D437 (rue du Theatre, Mandeure; daily 24hr; free). The old houses around the château have been repainted in their original colours. Note the circular stairwells,

CROSS-COUNTRY SKIING AND MOUNTAIN BIKING IN THE JURA

The nature of the Jura's terrain – its high plateaux guaranteeing winter snow but without excessively steep gradients – has made it France's most popular destination for **cross-country skiing**, or *ski du fond*. The goal of any superfit *fondeur* is the 210-kilometre Grande Traversée du Jura (GTJ), which roughly follows the long-distance GR5 footpath across the high plateau from Villiers-le-Lac to Hauteville-Lompnes.

The same gentle topography and established infrastructure which enable cross-country skiing have made this region an ideal high-summer venue for **mountain biking**, currently enjoying an upsurge in popularity in the eastern Jura, with hundreds of way-marked cross-country skiing pistes used out of season as trails for adventuresome mountain bikers. The 300-kilometre **GTJ–VTT**, starting near Montbéliard, has become the greatest long-distance challenge in the area. Many people cycle on the roads in the area; there aren't that many cars, so if you can handle the hills, go for it.

Cycling in the Doubs region is flatter and very scenic, with proper cycling paths. The 65-kilometre **Tour des Lacs** takes in some caves and waterfalls. There are 21 routes listed in the *Guide de Cyclotourisme du Doubs* (35F/€5.34), published by ADED, 7 av de la Gare d'Eau, 25031 Besançon, and also available from the tourist offices in the Doubs.

The headquarters of the departmental tourist board, the **Comité Departemental du Tourisme de Jura**, 8 rue Louis-Rousseau, Lons-le-Saunier (☎03.84.87.08.88), can supply plenty of information, maps and literature – in English – on outdoor leisure opportunities of all kinds in the Jura.

always at the back of the house – an architectural curiosity developed in the days when space was taxed, as part of an elaborate tax-avoidance scheme. The **Bourg des Halles** covered market was built in the sixteenth century, and is another fine Germanic building. Every two years in December there is a fabulous **exhibition** (the next one is 2001) of crazy mechanical vehicles/moveable sculptures, "Quand les Machines Rient: au Pays de Montbéliard", followed by a New Year's Eve **procession**, "Le Réveillon des Boulons", when the machines and their creators fill the streets like surrealist Peugeots. There is an outdoor Christmas **market**, "Lumières de Noël", every year around the St-Martin church, and also a three-kilometre labyrinth at the **Parc du Près-la-Rose**.

The **tourist office** is at 1 rue Henri Mouhot (mid-June to mid-Sept Mon–Fri 9am–noon & 1.30–7pm, Sat 9am–noon & 1.30–6pm, Sun 10am–noon & 2–4pm; mid-Sept to mid-June Mon–Fri 9am–noon & 1.30–6pm, Sat 9am–noon & 1.30–6pm; ☎03.81.94.45.60, fax 03.81.94.14.04, *www.montbeliard.com*). For local events, which may influence whether you stay in Montbéliard or Belfort, which both have some good music and art festivals, get the free cultural magazine *Atmosphere*, or *Montbéliard Magazine*, available in tourist offices. For **accommodation**, the choice is slightly better in Belfort, but Montbéliard does have its fair share: try the *Hôtel-Restaurant l'Auberge Mon Repos*, 8 rue des Grands-Jardins (☎03.81.94.52.67; ②), which is very peaceful with a large garden, or the *Hôtel de la Balance*, 40 rue de Belfort (☎03.81.96.77.41, fax 03.81.91.47.16; ③), in the old town, which also has a restaurant with menus from 69F/€10.52. There are plenty of outdoor **cafés** in the old town area: *Café de la Paix*, 12 rue des Febvres, near Les Halles, is a nice place to relax. There is also an **Internet café** (few and far between in this part of France) in the Centre des Images: *Cybercentre*, 2 cour des Halles (☎03.81.91.10.85; Mon–Fri 4–7pm, Sat 2–6pm; 10F/€1.52 per hour).

The Doubs Valley

The River Doubs runs a course like a hairpin, doubling back on itself repeatedly, with its most dramatic change of course at **AUDINCOURT**, a short way south of Belfort and the place where Peugeots are made. The town's chief sight is the modern **church of Sacré-Cœur**, which has windows and a tapestry by Fernand Léger. Just north of Audincourt, **SOCHAUX** is home to the **Musée Peugeot** (daily: May–Aug 9am–7pm; Sept–April 10am–6pm; 40F/€6.10), which displays the products of over a century of automotive manufacturing, from the Bey of Tunis's one-off quadricycle to contemporary rally winners and concept cars.

From Audincourt, southwards and upstream, the D437 follows the valley of the Doubs, winding and climbing steadily between steep, wooded banks to the bridging point at **ST-HIPPOLYTE**, where you'll find the riverside *Hôtel Bellevue* (☎03.81.96.51.53, fax 03.81.96.52.40; ①) and a **campsite** (May–Sept). Seven kilometres west along the D39, the *Auberge de Moricemaison*, in Valoreille (☎03.81.64.01.72; ①), offers rustic simplicity and wholesome evening meals from 80F/€12.20.

A less congested scenic route from Besançon follows the D464 south of the river, but without a car you'd have to hitch all this – manageable but slow. Beyond St-Hippolyte the road climbs onto a wide plateau at an altitude of around 850m, with grassy cattle pastures encompassed by fir-clad ridges and dotted with broad-roofed farms and barns. Once up here, cycling is easy enough. Alternatively, it's a lovely but long hike of well over 50km along the **GR5 footpath** from St-Hippolyte across the plateau and up the Doubs valley to the plunging waterfall of the **Saut du Doubs** outside Villers-le-Lac – the beginning of the **GTJ** marathon cross-country ski piste. To reach the fall, it's a four-kilometre walk from the last houses above the north end of the lake in **VILLERS** along a track through the woods.

By road, Villers is 47km south of St-Hippolyte along the D437, which turns east at **MORTEAU**, a village with nothing more than a much-altered, thirteenth-century priory church to recommend it. The D437 is part of the Route du Comté, so if you like cheese, it's worth the detour. There is **accommodation** here in the form of a *gîte* on chemin du Breuille (☎03.81.67.48.72) and, up on the plateau, the welcoming *Hôtel des Montagnards* (☎03.81.67.08.86, fax 03.81.67.14.57; ②; closed Sun out of season).

Besançon and around

The capital of Franche-Comté, **BESANÇON** is an ancient and attractive grey-stone town at the northern edge of the Jura mountains, enclosed in a loop of the River Doubs, whose lugubrious meanders define the layout of the old town. The tongue of land it sits on has been protected since Roman times, when it lay on a major trading route; the indefatigable Vauban added the still-extant fortifications and a citadel to guard the natural breach in the river. Once a major centre of French clock-making (until the Far East became important in the manufacturing industry), Besançon was also the birthplace of artificial silk – or rayon – in 1890. It counts among its native sons both the pioneering Lumière brothers and epic novelist Victor Hugo.

The **River Doubs** rises on the high plateau 100km to the south of here, making a diversion far to the northwest of the town, gathering tributaries and broadening as it briefly crosses the Swiss border before entering Besançon. A lazy journey upstream to **Pontarlier** can make a rewarding excursion over a couple of days. From Pontarlier a direct return north to Besançon can be made by following the **River Loue**'s steep descent through its heavily wooded valley past the pretty mill town of **Ornans**.

Arrival, information and accommodation

The **gare SNCF** is at the end of avenue Maréchal-Foch, while the **gare routière** is at 9 rue Proudhon off rue de la République; buses for Pontarlier and Ornans leave from here. The best way to reach the town centre from the train station is to take the underground passage (next to the monument in front of the station) and cut across the park down to the the *quais* – the old town is on the other side of the river. The **tourist office** is upstream on the right bank by the Pont de la République on place de la Première Armée-Française (April–Sept Mon 10am–7pm, Tues–Sat 9am–7pm, Sun 10am–noon, mid-June to mid-Sept Sun also 3–5pm; Oct–March Mon 10am–6pm, Tues–Sat 9am–6pm; ☎03.81.80.92.55, fax 03.81.80.58.30, *www.besançon.com*). On the other side of the Pont de la République from the tourist office is the departure point for the **bâteaux-mouches** (daily April–Oct; 49F/€7.47), which tour round the outer limits of the town centre.

Hotels include the comfortable and friendly family-run *Granvelle*, 13 rue Lecourbe, close to the citadel (☎03.81.81.33.92, fax 03.81.81.31.77; ②); *Florel*, 6 rue de la Viotte opposite the station (☎03.81.80.41.08, fax 03.81.50.44.40; ①); the dead central *Regina*, 91 Grande-Rue (☎03.81.81.50.22, fax 03.81.81.60.20; ②); the *Hôtel de Paris*, 33 rue des Granges (☎03.81.81.36.56, fax 03.81.61.94.90; ②), with free parking for guests; and the *Hôtel du Nord*, at 8–10 rue de Moncey in the centre (☎03.81.81.34.56, fax 03.81.81.85.96; ②). The **hostel** is a couple of kilometres northeast of the train station at 48 rue des Cras (☎03.81.40.32.00, fax 03.81.40.32.01; bus #7, stop "Les Oiseaux"). The *Centre International de Séjour* at 19 rue Martin-du-Gard, 4km northwest of the centre (☎03.81.50.07.54, fax 03.81.53.11.79; bus #8, stop "L'Épitaphe"), fulfils the same function, though at slightly greater expense. Alternatively, there's the *Foyer des Jeunes Filles*, 18 rue de la Cassotte (☎03.81.80.90.01; women only). **Camping** is at Plage de Chalezeule, 5km out on the Belfort road (☎03.81.88.04.26; April–Oct; bus #1 towards Palente).

The Town

Once you're in the old town, getting around is simple, and some of the most interesting things to see are outdoors and free – such as the beautiful bluish stone walls of most buildings, and the signs of Roman life that still remain. Rue de la République leads from the river to the central **place du 8-Septembre** and the sixteenth-century **Hôtel de Ville**. The principal street, **Grande-Rue**, cuts across the square along the line of an old Roman road. At its northwestern end – the livelier part of town with shops and cafés – is the place de la Révolution and the excellent **Musée des Beaux-Arts** (June–Oct daily 9.30am–6pm; Nov–May daily except Tues 9.30am–noon & 2–6pm; 21F/€3.20), with some good nineteenth- and twentieth-century works, two magnificent Bonnards and a wonderful clock collection. Midway down Grande-Rue, the fine sixteenth-century **Palais Granvelle** is due to open some time in 2001 with a new museum paying homage to the town's history of clock-making, the Musée du Temps. Continuing up the street, you pass place Victor-Hugo (he was born at no. 140) and arrive at the **Porte Noire**, a second-century Roman triumphal arch spanning the street and partially embedded in the adjoining houses. Beside it, in the shady little **square Archéologique A.-Castan**, are the remains of a *nymphaeum*, a small reservoir of water fed by an aqueduct. Beyond the arch is the pompous eighteenth-century **Cathédrale St-Jean** (closed Tues) which houses the nineteenth-century **Horloge Astronomique** (hourly guided visits: April–Sept daily except Tues 9.50–11.50am & 2.50–5.50pm; rest of year Mon & Thurs–Sun same hours; closed Jan; 15F/€2.29), detailing over a hundred terrestrial and celestial positions and containing some 30,000 parts.

The spectacular **Citadelle** (daily: July & Aug 9am–7pm; rest of year 10am–5pm; 40F/€6.10) is a steep fifteen-minute climb from the cathedral, and has a crow's-nest view of the town and the noose-like bend in the river that contains it. It houses many worthwhile museums (times as above): for animal lovers there's the **Musée d'Histoire Naturelle** (a noctarium, aquarium, insectarium and zoo); the **Musée Comtois**, with pottery, furniture and a good collection of nineteenth-century marionettes, as well as some marvellous old farming implements; the **Espace Vauban**, devoted to the military architect; and – best of all – the **Musée de la Résistance et de la Déportation**, a superb aid to understanding postwar France's political consciousness (English audio commentary available). The first rooms document the rise of Nazism and French Fascism through photographs and exhibits, including a bar of soap stamped *RIF* – "Pure Jew Fat". In the section on the Vichy government, there's a telegram of encouragement sent by Marshal Pétain to the French troops of the "legion of volunteers against Bolshevism", who were fighting alongside the Germans on the eastern front. Finally, as counterbalance, much is made of General Leclerc's vow at Koufra in the Libyan desert, whose capture in January 1941 was the first, entirely French, victory of the war – "We will not stop until the French flag flies once more over Metz and Strasbourg" – a vow which he kept when he entered the latter city at the head of a division in November 1944.

Eating, drinking and entertainment

There are plenty of lively and inexpensive restaurants, cafés and bars by the river near place Battant, particularly along the little streets running parallel to the river. *Brasserie du Commerce*, 31 rue des Granges, has rather grand decor and ambience, and *Brasserie du Palais Granvelle*, in a lovely shady park next door to the Palais Granvelle, is the best place for breakfast and coffee hits. Two good places for a substantial **meal** are the century-old *Restaurant au Petit Polonais*, 81 rue des Granges (☎03.81.81.23.67; closed Sat evening & Sun; menus from 64F/€9.76), which serves regional food, and, for lunch, the superb *Le Café-Café*, 5bis rue Luc Breton (☎03.81.81.15.24; Mon–Sat lunch only; *plats* from 59F/€8.99).

The two biggest **cultural events** of the year in Besançon are **Jazz en Franche-Comté**, which takes place in June and July, and an international young conductors' competition in the first two weeks of September.

Pontarlier and around

Sixty kilometres southeast of Besançon lies **PONTARLIER**, one of the bigger Jura towns, and not very interesting in itself except as a transit point and recreational base. If you need **accommodation** here, try the *Hôtel de Morteau*, 26 rue Jeanne-d'Arc, near the river (☎03.81.39.14.83, fax 03.81.39.75.07; ②), which has an excellent restaurant (menus from 70F/€10.67). There's also an HI hostel at 2 rue Jouffroy, near the station (☎ & fax 03.81.39.06.57); a *gîte* – the *Chalet-Refuge du Larmont* (☎03.81.46.61.07); plus a municipal campsite in rue de Toulombief. For places to **eat**, try the rue de Besançon, which is full of cafés and brasseries, or, for a fuller meal, the *Brasserie de la Poste*, 55 rue de la République. Good-quality **mountain bikes** can be rented from Vélos Pernet, 23 rue de la République (☎03.81.46.48.00), for 80F/€12.20 per day; and cross-country **ski gear** can be found at Sports et Neige, along the street at no. 4 (☎03.81.39.04.69). The **tourist office**, 14 bis rue de la Gare (Mon–Sat 9am–noon & 2–6pm; June–Sept also Sun 10.30am–noon & 5.30–7pm; ☎03.81.46.48.33, fax 03.81.46.83.32), has some good hiking maps for 12F/€1.83 and 58F/€8.84.

Just south of town, past a divinely aromatic chocolate factory that will have chocoholics drooling, a steep road to the left ascends for 11km to **Le Grand Taureau**, whose 1328-metre summit is just a short walk from the road's end and offers a view over the whole Jura Massif and across Switzerland to the Alps. A couple of kilometres further south of Pontarlier, the **Château de Joux** (guided tours daily: Jan–June & Sept–Oct 10am, 11.30am, 2pm & 3.30pm; July & Aug every 30min 9am–4.30pm; closed Nov & Dec; 32F/€4.88) stands over the defile known as La Cluse et Mijoux, the ancient Franco-Swiss frontier. It was originally constructed in the eleventh century, and Vauban had a hand in remodelling and modernizing it, but most of what you see today is less than a century old. The fort's history and impressive appearance are of more interest than its collection of military uniforms.

Moving on, there are **trains** and **buses** to Besançon, the TGV to Dijon and Paris, and local buses to the six-kilometre-long **Lac de St-Point**, where you can pick up the GR5 again to make the ascent of **Mont d'Or** (1463m) overlooking Lake Geneva and the Alps, and to **Mouthe**, where the River Doubs emerges from an underground cavern.

Ornans and the Valley of the Loue

Some 17km north of Pontarlier, the D67 splits west off the N57 and plunges precipitously into the **Valley of the Loue**. A couple of kilometres above the village of Ouhans lies the source of the river, issuing from an enormous rock beneath a tiered cliff, in winter entirely fringed with icicles. From this point you can continue on foot along the **GR595 footpath** down the valley bounded by densely wooded limestone cliffs, a descent no less dramatic by road, which passes through a string of pretty villages.

Roughly halfway between Pontarlier and Besançon, **ORNANS** is the prettiest of all, an archetypal Franche-Comté town that has become the touristic focal point of the valley. The Loue here is an abrupt trench with the river washing the foundations of ancient balconied houses. The town is easily appreciated from the numerous footbridges spanning the river. Pierre Vernier, inventor of the eponymous gauge, and the painter Gustave Courbet were both born here: the latter's house is now the **Musée de la Maison Natale de Gustave Courbet** (daily 10am–noon & 2–6pm; Nov–March closed Tues; 20F/€3.05), displaying some of his drawings, sculpture and locally painted scenes. The **tourist office** is at 7 rue Pierre Vernier (April–June, Sept, Oct & school hols Mon–Sat 9.30am–noon & 2–6pm; July & Aug Mon–Sat 9am–7pm, Sun 10am–noon & 3–6pm; Nov–March Mon–Fri 10am–noon & 3–5pm; ☎ & fax 03.81.62.21.50). There's **accommodation** in the form of the riverside *Hôtel Le Progrès*, 11 rue Jacques Gervais (☎03.81.62.16.79, fax 03.81.62.19.10; ②), and the pricier but better-placed *de la Cascade* (☎03.81.60.95.30, fax 03.81.60.94.55; ③), in the centre of **MOUTHIER**, further down the D67. There are **campsites** and **gîtes d'étapes** in Ornans, Vuillifans and Mouthier.

Arc-et-Senans and Salins-les-Bains

At the southeastern edge of the Forêt de Chaux, some 35km south of Besançon, is the unfinished eighteenth-century "salt city" of the **Saline Royale d'Arc-et-Senans** (April–June, Sept & Oct 9am–noon & 2–6pm; July & Aug 9am–7pm; Nov–March 10am–noon & 2–5pm; 39F/€5.95), commissioned by royal decree in 1773 to replace the ageing works at Salins-les-Bains (see below). The complex, dreamed up by the Revolutionary architect Claude-Nicolas Ledoux, was to have become a model utopian city. His grandiose project reflected the egalitarian social concerns of the pre-Revolutionary era: the settlement was to have radiated along the primary axes of a clock-face from a nucleus housing the administrative offices, distillation plants, public baths and other municipal utilities.

Sadly, the socio-aesthetic ideals could not overcome the works' functional deficiencies: the pipeworks linking the new plant with Salins deteriorated rapidly and only half of the central arc was ever completed. Salt production continued until the end of the nineteenth century, but all that remains today is the impressively restored semicircle of eleven buildings, a monumental epitaph to Ledoux's unconsummated vision. The beautiful complex now houses two museums, usually with exhibitions about architecture.

SALINS-LES-BAINS, 15km southeast of Arc-et-Senans, is worth a further detour (back along the tree-lined country road that leads to the entrance to the Saline Royale).

some absorbing prehistoric displays, including a touching Neolithic family scene circa 4000 BC, a dug-out canoe found locally and a life-size replica of a 210-million-year-old plateosaurus, France's oldest-known dinosaur. The museum, which also mounts various temporary exhibitions, is housed in the old Bel cheese factory, whose enduringly popular *La Vache Qui Rit* cheese spread is now produced in larger premises near the station (you might see a big lorry with the familiar cow on it). Returning south along rue Richebourg to avenue Jean-Moulin, you come to the inevitable **statue** of Rouget de Lisle, designed by Frédéric Bartholdi, the sculptor who went on to refine de Lisle's stirring pose on a much grander scale in the Statue of Liberty. A left turn here leads to the pleasant **Parc Edouard Guenon**, where you'll find the **Salines** (☎03.84.24.20.34 for admission details), with their ornate *fin-de-siècle* exterior, which are lavishly equipped with a sauna, Turkish bath and jacuzzi: the saline immersions not only soothe the usual aches and pains, but are also renowned for their ability to cure juvenile bed-wetting.

Practicalities

Lons' **tourist office** is in the same building as its theatre (Mon–Fri 8am–noon & 2–6pm, Sat 8am–noon & 2–5pm; ☎03.84.24.65.01, fax 03.84.43.22.59). For information about the Jura region, the **Comité Départemental du Tourisme** is at 8 rue Louis Rousseau (Mon–Fri: April–Nov 8.30am–12.30pm & 2–6pm; rest of year 8.30am–6pm; ☎03.84.87.08.88). Two good **hotels** are the recently renovated *Terminus*, 37 av Aristide-Briand, by the train station (☎03.84.24.41.83, fax 03.84.24.68.07; ②), and the cosy *Nouvel Hôtel*, 50 rue Lecourbe (☎03.84.47.20.67, fax 03.84.43.27.49; ②), just west of place de la Liberté. There's a rather pricey **campsite**, *Camping de la Marjorie* (☎03.84.24.26.94), on the northeast edge of town. For a truly inspired **meal** in a charming setting, pay a visit to the *Bistrot des Marronniers*, 22 rue de Vallière, west off rue St-Désiré (closed Sun; menu from 60F/€9.15). For a coffee or drink, head for the *Grand Café de Strasbourg*, next to the theatre, which has a beautiful interior.

Baume-Les-Messieurs and Château Chalon

Twenty kilometres east of Lons is the tiny village of **BAUME-LES-MESSIEURS**, tucked in a cliff-bound valley festooned with foliage on all but the steepest faces. From Lons, the quickest – as well as most interesting – way to get there is to take the N471 Champagnole road and turn down the narrow and steep lanes descending into the valley from the north; the **Belvédère des Roches de Baume**, signposted off the N471, gives stunning views of the village and the verdant Seille valley out as far as the Château Chalon and beyond if the weather is up to it.

In the village, the main attraction is the **abbey** (guided tours daily: first two weeks June 10am–noon & 2–6pm; mid-June to mid-Sept 10am–6pm; 15F/€2.29). Monks were active in the area in the fourth century, and it is thought that the Irish St Columba was here in the sixth century, along with other monks, before leaving for Cluny (see p.555). In spite of visitors clacking over the ancient stone floors, an atmosphere of monastic tranquillity still pervades the place. Consecrated in 909 by Benedictines, it was disbanded by the newly formed Republic in 1792, and today the interior and its twelfth-century **church**, in whose crypt rest three members of the once-dominant Chalon family, remain open to the public. **Accommodation** is available at the abbey at the *Gothique Café* (☎03.84.44.64.47; ④), which has three beautiful rooms that will make you feel as though you're back in the Middle Ages; the café itself serves lovely meals using local produce (menus from 85F/€12.96).

Two kilometres south of the village, at the very end of the valley, are the **Grottes de Baume** (several 40min guided tours daily: April–June & Sept 10am–noon & 2–5.30pm; July & Aug 9am–6pm; 29F/€4.42), one of the many limestone stalactite cave systems throughout the region. Those who are particularly energetic may wish to ascend the stairway cut into the rock on the valley's eastern face; at times exposed and best avoided if conditions are wet, it leads to the clifftop and the Belvédère des Roches de Baume viewpoint described above. Others may opt for a meal at the *Restaurant des Grottes* (☎03.84.44.61.59; 85–145F/€12.96–22.11; mid-April to Sept lunchtimes only), near the beautiful, fern-draped **waterfall**, with a stunning view back down the valley.

As you head north out of Baume, you'll see the limestone cliffs recede as the valley opens out, revealing miles of vineyards that yield the distinctive yellow wine of Château Chalon, produced from the Sauvignon grape. The fortified hilltop village of **CHÂTEAU CHALON** overlooks the vines and was built around a castle (not open to the public) of the once-influential Comtoise family who give the village its name. A short wander will lead you past promising baskets of Chalon (expect to pay around 160F/€24.39 a bottle) to the fortified **church**, dating from the eleventh century and possessing some impressive stained glass and early examples of vaulting. An archway outside by the porch leads to the **Belvédère de la Rochette**, looking out across the valley back towards Baume. The views from the village are indescribably beautiful.

Poligny and Arbois

Back on the Route des Vins du Jura, the attractive medieval town of **POLIGNY**, at the southern end of the Culée de Vaux valley, is noteworthy for its well-preserved, early Romanesque buildings, including the **church of St-Hippolyte**, which features the characteristic, bell-like tower seen all over Franche-Comté. But the town's principal attraction is the hallowed **Maison du Comté** (July & Aug daily 1hr guided tours at 10am, 11am, 2pm, 3.30pm & 4.30pm; ☎03.84.37.23.51; 12F/€1.83) on avenue de la Résistance, which leads south from the central place des Deportés, an old fromagerie that now forms the headquarters of the Comité Interprofessional du Gruyère du Comté. Displays show the process of cheese-making, from extracting milk to producing the finished article, alongside audiovisual presentations exalting the industry. Gruyère officers, an institution of tax collectors founded by Charlemagne, once collected the 60-centimetre-wide *meules* of cheese as payment – each the product of 500 litres of milk; now, with over 800 years' experience of production, Comté cheese has earned the distinguished *Appellation d'Origine Contrôlée* (AOC) label more commonly reserved for vintage wines.

The attractive medieval houses and other sites of interest in Poligny are indicated on the blue *Walking Through the Old Town* leaflet available from the friendly **tourist office** in rue Victor-Hugo (July & Aug Mon–Fri 9am–12.30pm & 1.30–6.30pm, Sat 9am–12.30pm & 2–6pm, Sun 9am–12.30pm; Sept–June Mon–Fri 9am–12.30pm & 2–6pm, Sat 9am–noon & 2–5pm; ☎ 03.84.37.24.21).

There's no mistaking that **ARBOIS**, 10km to the north, is the capital of this region's viticulture. Glittering wine emporia line the central place de la Liberté, entreating you to sample the unusual local wines, of which the sweet *vin de paille* is rarest – so called because its grapes are dried on beds of straw, giving the wine a strong aftertaste equal to that of the better-known Château Chalon. Chocolatier M. Hirsinger has developed chocolates to eat with wines, especially the Jura's own *vin jaune*, a wine flavoured with walnuts. A visit to the Hirsinger chocolate shop on place de la Liberté is a must: try the delicious ice cream.

Louis Pasteur lived in Arbois after his family moved from Dôle, and his boyhood home, the **Maison de Louis Pasteur** on avenue Pasteur, is open to the public (hourly guided visits daily: April, May & Oct 2.15am–5.15pm; June–Sept 9.45am–11.45pm & every 30min 2.15–6.15pm; 32F/€4.88). The **tourist office** is at 10 rue de l'Hôtel de Ville (July & Aug Mon–Sat 9am–12.30pm & 2–6.30pm, Sun 10am–noon & 2–5pm; Sept–June Mon 3–6pm, Tues–Sat 9am–noon & 2–6pm; ☎03.84.37.47.37); in the basement of the same building is the **Musée de la Vigne et du Vin** (July & Aug daily

10am–12.30pm & 2–6pm; March–June, Sept & Oct daily except Tues 10am–noon & 2–6pm; Nov–Feb daily except Tues 2–6pm; 21F/€3.20), which details the development and production of wine in the Jura.

If you're **staying** overnight in town, try the cheap and friendly *Hôtel Mephisto*, 33 place Faramand, just over the river from the main part of town (☎03.84.66.06.49; ①), or the more luxurious *Les Messageries* (☎03.84.66.15.45, fax 03.84.37.41.09; ②–④), up from the Maison Pasteur. There's a **campsite**, *Camping Les Vignes*, on avenue Général-Leclerc (☎03.84.66.14.12, fax 03.84.66.25.50; April–Sept), 1km east of the centre. For a **meal**, try the *Restaurant La Cuisance*, with lunchtime menus at 40F/€6.10 and evening menus from 75F/€11.43 to 110F/€16.77; or *Au Jardin Venitien*, a good pizzeria at 1 rue Mercière (☎03.84.37.49.22; pizzas from 35F/€5.34).

The Central Plateau and the Jura mountains

On the broad upland plateau, the Jura landscape unrolls, stretches and rises in increasingly abrupt steps to the mountains bordering the Swiss frontier. With its lakes and pine forests, small farming communities and – at the higher altitudes – huge ski resorts enveloping tiny villages, semi-deserted in summer, this is the most beautiful area of the Jura and, as you might expect – despite trains linking **Champagnole**, **Morez** and **St-Claude** with Arbois and Pontarlier – best appreciated with your own transport.

Champagnole and the Forêt de la Joux

Situated at a major crossroads on the plateau, **CHAMPAGNOLE**, an industrial town largely rebuilt after a major fire in 1798, holds little intrinsic interest for the passing visitor, with the exception of an **archeological museum**, 26 rue Baronne-Delfort (July & Aug daily except Tues 2–6pm; 15F/€2.29), above the tourist office, which displays an interesting array of Gallic and Roman artefacts found in the vicinity. However, the town does serve as a useful base for exploring the surrounding countryside, in particular the Forêt de la Joux, to the northeast.

For central **accommodation**, try the *Hôtel de la Londaine*, 31 rue du Général–Leclerc (☎03.84.52.06.69; ①), or, for old-style grandeur, the *Grand Hôtel Ripotot*, 54 rue Maréchal Foch (☎03.84.52.15.45, fax 03.84.52.09.11; ③), which is definitely the nicest hotel in town. The **campsite**, *Camping de Boyse*, is on rue Georges-Vallery (☎03.84.52.00.32; June to mid-Sept). The **tourist office** is in an annexe of the Mairie at 26 rue Baronne-Delfort (Mon–Fri 9am–noon & 2–6pm, Sat 9am–noon & 2–5pm; ☎03.84.52.43.67), and provides lots of information about exploring the surrounding forests and lakes, including a hiking kit for 30F/€4.57.

Out of Champagnole, things start to get remote and beautiful. To the southeast, the D279 passes the **château** at **SYAM**, built in 1818, and continues to the **Gorges de la Langouette**, 17km away. Here, a half-hour walk leads down to the narrow 47-metre-deep gorge sliced through the cretaceous escarpment by the River Saine. Other riverine curiosities in the area include the **Perte de l'Ain**, near the village of Bourg-de-Sirod, where a half-hour walk from an electricity station leads through the woods, past a waterfall and lesser cascades, to a boulder-strewn chasm where the Ain takes a brief subterranean detour. Another pleasant ten-minute walk a few kilometres northeast – just past the village of Conte – leads to a natural amphitheatre from whose base rises the **source of the Ain**.

A couple of kilometres north of the source, spread over a small hill surrounded by pastures, is the old walled village of **NOZEROY**, ancestral home of the Chalon family, who dominated regional politics in feudal times. The town preserves much of its medieval charm today, with the **Porte de l'Horloge** – once part of the town's fortifications – fram-

ing the beginning of the Grande-Rue. This thoroughfare, lined with many ancient houses, ends at the place des Annonciades and the ruins of the thirteenth-century **castle**.

North of Nozeroy, on the other side of the D471 Champagnole–Pontarlier road, the
Forêt de la Joux is considered one of the most beautiful of France's native pine
forests. It is crisscrossed by a net of narrow fire roads, but if you don't have a car, you
can use the Gare de la Joux, in the heart of the forest on the Champagnole–Pontarlier
train line, from where you can explore further on foot or by bicycle. There are many
well-marked walking trails through the forest: the most popular area is the **Sapins de
la Glacière**. The **Route des Sapins** is the approved tourist drive, signposted for 50km
from the D471 to the village of Levier, passing lookouts and the 45-metre-high **Sapin
Président** (a 200-year-old fir tree) along the way. But the less regimented can just as
easily enjoy getting mildly disorientated by following any number of lesser, unmarked
roads and discovering the wonder of the forest for themselves.

The Lake District

South of Champagnole, the flattened plateau, unable to shed the Haute Jura's winter
run-off, collects the meltwaters in a series of natural and not-so-natural lakes, known as
the **Région des Lacs**, loosely strung along the valley of the River Ain. Where the
ground begins to crumple upward to the eastern summits, gorges and waterfalls highlight each successive step, and lookouts survey the tiny villages, each with its characteristic domed belfry beaten from metal or composed from a mosaic of tiles and slates.
Some of the lakes charge parking fees during the day, but after 6pm, when the crowds
and swimming supervisors go home, the lakes are deserted and peaceful – perfect for
an evening picnic watching the sun set.

Clairvaux-les-Lacs and the Cascades du Hérisson

The region's main resort town is **CLAIRVAUX-LES-LACS**. It is here that the northern
tip of the serpentine **Lac de Vouglans**, dammed 25km downstream, reverts to the River
Ain which feeds it. The **Grand Lac**, just south of town, is the focus of summer resort
activity, with a beach area and watersports facilities. It's calm and scenic, in spite of all
the camping activity going on around it. The **Office du Tourisme du Pays des Lacs**,
36 Grande-Rue (Mon–Sat 9am–noon & 2–6pm; July & Aug also Sun 10am–noon;
☎03.84.25.27.47, fax 03.84.25.23.00), is the place to find information about the region and
outdoor activities such as boat hire and bike hire. For hiking, the *63 Circuits de Petite
Randonnée* (45F/€6.86 from the tourist office) has maps and descriptions of the circuits.

Simple, inexpensive **accommodation** can be found at the *Hôtel Raillette*, 50 rue
Neuve (☎03.84.25.82.21; ②). On the Grand Lac, providing more comfortable lodgings,
are the *Chaumière du Lac* (☎03.84.25.81.52, fax 03.83.25.24.54; ②; closed Oct–March)
and the *Bellevue* (☎03.84.25.82.37; ②; closed Oct–May) – the latter offering a view worthy of its name.

Surrounded by hills, **Lac Chalain**, 16km north of Clairvaux and near the village of
Doucier, has a much more impressive setting. It's also a very popular spot for **camping**.
There are five campsites in town: *Fayolan*, on the lake (☎03.84.25.26.19; May–Sept); *La
Ferme du Villaret*, on a farm, route des Moirans (☎03.84.25.26.03; July & Aug); *Le Grand
Lac*, on the lake (☎03.84.25.26.19; May–Sept); *La Grisière et Europe Vacances*, near the
lake with mobile homes for hire (☎03.84.25.80.48; May–Sept); and *Les Tilleuls*, 6 chemin
des Tilleuls (☎03.84.25.81.45; May–Sept), also with mobile homes for hire.

By far the most interesting sight around here – and one of the Jura's best-known natural spectacles – is the **Cascades du Hérisson**, a septet of waterfalls descending nearly
300m in just 3km. Well-marked from either end of the gorge, the easiest walk, accessible
by road via Val-Dessous southeast of Doucier, leads to the best-known and prettiest of the
falls, the **Éventail**. A ten-minute stroll from the car park leads to the cascade, which

spreads out in ever-widening tiers, giving it the fan-like appearance after which it is named. Continuing upstream, you'll shake off most casual spectators and pass through the woods of wild oak and springtime daffodils to the dramatic **Grand Saut**, with its clear drop of 60m; the pathway passes behind the waterfall – an alarmingly windy spot to shower in. A steep climb leads to smaller *sauts* feeding the odd swimming-hole, past a drinks kiosk – at the intersection of another path which leads south to the village of Bonlieu – to the uppermost **Saut Girard**, 3km up from the Éventail and close to the village of **ILAY**. There's a choice of restaurants in Ilay, but only one **hotel**, the *Auberge du Hérisson*, 5 rue des Lacs (☎03.84.25.58.18, fax 03.84.25.51.11; ③; closed Nov–Jan; restaurant from 73F/€11.13); they'll also be able to provide some tourist information.

A short drive up the N78 east of Ilay leads to a lookout atop **Pic de l'Aigle**: at nearly 1000m high, this is one of the best spots from which to view the Jura's topography. On fine days, the views are said to extend as far as Mont Blanc to the east, and west to the plain of the Saône.

The Haute Jura

As you climb from the plateau through the pine forests to the scrawny higher pastures, the temperatures dip and the landscape takes a bleaker turn towards the summits of the **Haute Jura**. The main roads struggle up the valleys towards the Swiss border, but less demanding routes run along the mountains' narrow folds linking Pontarlier to **Morez** and **St-Claude**; when they're not passing through woodland or low cloud, these can provide memorable motoring. While the main towns in the area are valley-bound and claustrophobic, the resort towns tend to be expensive or rather soulless out of season, but most people come up here for the views across Lac Léman (Lake Geneva) in Switzerland towards the perennial snowscapes of the Alps.

Up to Morez and Les Rousses

The main **trans-Jura route** into Switzerland is the N5, which begins its ascent to the frontier around **ST-LAURENT-EN-GRANDVAUX**, which is great for skiing but unmemorable apart from the picturesque **Lac de l'Abbaye**, 4km south of town on the D437. Also on the Arbois–St-Claude train line is **MOREZ**, 12km northwest, a town squeezed along the narrow valley floor and noted for the manufacture of watches and spectacles. Its **tourist office** is in the central place Jaurès (mid-July to mid-Aug Mon–Sat 9am–noon & 2–6pm, Sun 10am–noon; rest of year Mon 2–6pm, Tues–Fri 9am–noon & 2–6pm, Sat 10am–noon; ☎03.84.33.08.73), along with the **gare routière**, from where buses depart for La Cure on the Franco-Swiss border. Once on the Swiss side, you can catch trains down to Nyon on Lac Léman and to Geneva itself.

A couple of kilometres before the frontier, **LES ROUSSES** exists purely for skiing – downhill and especially cross-country – but just before it a lane leads down to a very attractive **HI hostel** in an old, red-shuttered farmhouse by a stream, 2km away at Bief-de-la-Chaille (☎03.84.60.02.80, fax 03.84.60.09.67; closed mid–April to mid-May & Oct to mid-Dec). There's also a **gîte d'étape** at Prémanon on the D25 (☎03.84.60.54.82; closed mid-Nov to mid-Dec & for 1 week at the end of winter). From the hostel you can see the eerie spheres of the satellite-tracking station on the summit of **La Dôle** (1677m), the Jura's highest peak, just over the Swiss border. The **GR9 footpath** passes through here, beginning a magnificent hiking section all along the crest of the ridge to the Col de la Faucille and beyond (see below).

There are plenty of **hotels** in Les Rousses itself: the *Hôtel de France*, 323 rue Pasteur (☎03.84.60.01.45, fax 03.84.60.04.63; ④), is the town's best, but less extravagant lodgings can be found at the *du Gai Pinson*, 1465 route Blanche (☎03.84.60.02.15; ③), or *Le Village*, 344 rue Pasteur (☎03.84.34.12.75; ②). For a **meal**, try the restaurant at the *Hôtel-Restaurant Les Gentianes* (menus from 75F/€11.43), or the *Restaurant Les*

P'Losses (from 85F/€12.96), in the winter-sports centre on the Geneva road southwest of town. There are also plenty of cafés and pizzerias.

St-Claude

From Morez, the train line leaves the N5 and heads along the Gorges de la Bienne to the industrial town of **ST-CLAUDE** to the southwest, hemmed in claustrophobically by even higher mountains than those around Morez. It's famous for pipes (the smokers' kind) and diamonds, and there's a **museum**, the Exposition des Pipes et Diamants (May, June & Sept daily 9.30am–noon & 2–6.30pm; July & Aug daily 9.30am–6.30pm; rest of year Mon–Sat 2–6pm; closed Nov & Dec; 25F/€3.91), dedicated to both of these opposite the fortified cathedral of St-Pierre on rue du Marché. The **tourist office**, 19 rue du Marché (July & Aug Mon–Fri 8.30am–7pm, Sat 9am–noon & 2–6pm, Sun 10am–1pm; Sept–June Mon–Fri 8.30am–noon & 2–6.30pm, Sat 9am–noon & 2–6pm; ☎03.84.45.34.24), distributes a free leaflet in English, *The City's Discovery Tour*, which gives a florid description of a two-hour walk around the town.

Should you wish to **stay** here, try the *Hôtel de la Poste*, on rue Reybert (☎03.84.45.52.34; ①), opposite the tourist office. Plusher accommodation can be found at the *Jura Hôtel*, 40 av de la Gare (☎03.84.45.24.04, fax 03.84.45.58.10; ②), or *Le Joly* (☎03.84.45.12.36; ③) in Le Martinet, 3km southwest of town on the Col de la Faucille road, right next to a campsite. Wholesome, inexpensive food is served at the restaurant of *Hôtel St-Hubert* on the place St-Hubert and at *Brasserie le Lacuzon*, at 5 rue Victor-Hugo.

What gives purpose to the rest of the onward route from either St-Claude or Les Rousses are the superb views from the crest of the great fir-clad ridge that overlooks Lac Léman to the east. The N5 crosses the ridge at the **Col de la Faucille** (1323m). If it's clear, the view is unbelievably dramatic from the Col or the GR footpath; the whole range of the western Alps stretches out before you, dominated by Mont Blanc, with the steely cusp of Lac Léman at your feet. There's an even better view from the top of nearby **Mont Rond** (1534m), accessible by chair lift. Of course, if it's not clear, the journey will have been in vain, but if you're carrying on south of Geneva, 30km away, it's downhill all the way – with the thought of some revitalizing bars of Swiss chocolate at the day's end.

travel details

Trains

Belfort to: Besançon (10 daily; 1hr–1hr 15min); Dôle (5 daily; 1hr 30min); Paris-Est (2 daily; 5hr); Ronchamp (12 daily; 5 min); Montbéliard (hourly; 20min).

Besançon to: Bourg-en-Bresse (4–5 daily; 2hr 30min); Dijon (10 daily; 1hr); Dôle (10 daily; 30min); Lons (several daily; 1hr–1hr 30min); Morez (4 daily; 2hr 10min–2hr 30min); Morteau (4 daily; 1hr–1hr 45min); Paris-Lyon (up to 6 daily; 2hr 30min); St-Claude (4 daily; 2hr 30min–3hr); St-Laurent (4 daily; 1hr 40min–2hr).

Dôle to: Dijon (10 daily; 30min); Paris-Lyon (10 daily; 4hr); Pontarlier (3 daily; 1hr 20min).

Metz to: Longuyon (2 daily; 1hr 30min); Mulhouse (7 daily; 2hr 30min); Nancy (hourly; 1hr); Paris-Est (4 daily; 3hr); Strasbourg (every 2hr; 1hr 30min).

Mulhouse to: Belfort (up to 5 daily; 30–45 min); Colmar (every 30min; 20min).

Nancy to: Lunéville (hourly during peak hours, then every 3 hours; 30min); Paris-Est (hourly; 3hr); Saverne (3 daily; 1hr); Strasbourg (2 daily; 1hr 20 min).

St-Claude to: Bourg (4–5 daily; 1hr 40min–2hr), connecting with TGV to Paris; Champagnole (5 daily; 1hr).

Strasbourg to: Barr (9 daily; 55min); Basle (hourly; 1hr 30min–2hr); Besançon (8 daily; 2hr 15min); Colmar (hourly; 50min); Dambach (9 daily; 1hr); Dôle (10 daily; 3hr 30min); Ingwillen (6 daily; 30min); Molsheim (9 daily; 20min); Mulhouse (hourly; 1hr 20min); Obernai (9 daily; 40min);

Paris-Est (every 2hr; 4hr 30min); Rosheim (9 daily; 25min); Sarreguemines (6 daily; 1hr 20min); St-Dié (3 daily; 1hr 50min); Sélestat (hourly; 20min); Wingen-Moden (6 daily; 40min); Wissembourg (up to 5 daily; 1hr).

Verdun to: Metz (4 daily; 1hr–1hr 15min); Nancy (2 daily; 1hr 40min); Paris-Est (up to 5 daily; 3hr).

Buses

Belfort to: Ronchamp (1 daily; 45min).

Besançon to: Ornans (4 daily; 30min); Pontarlier (4 daily; 1hr).

Colmar to: Mulhouse (at least 1 hourly; 1hr); Sélestat (hourly; 1hr).

Haguenau to: Neuwiller (4 daily; 1hr 10min); Pfaffenhoffen (4 daily; 30min); Saverne (4 daily; 1hr 40min).

Lons-le-Saunier to: Dôle (5 daily; 1hr).

Morez to: St-Claude (3 weekly; 1hr).

St-Claude to: Lyon (daily; 3hr 40min).

Saverne to: Molsheim (2 daily; 1hr).

Sélestat to: St-Dié (5–6 daily; 1hr 10min).

Verdun to: Metz (5 daily Mon–Sat; 2hr).

CHAPTER FOUR

NORMANDY

Though now firmly incorporated into the French mainstream, the seaboard province of Normandy has a history of prosperous independence as one of the crucial powers of medieval Europe. Colonized by Scandinavian Vikings (or Norsemen) from the ninth century onwards, it began to colonize in turn during the eleventh and twelfth centuries, with military expeditions conquering not only England but as far afield as Sicily and parts of the Near East. Later, as part of France, it was instrumental in the settlement of Canada.

Normandy has always had large ports: **Rouen**, on the Seine, is the nearest navigable point to Paris, while **Dieppe**, **Le Havre** and **Cherbourg** have important transatlantic trade. Inland, it is overwhelmingly agricultural – a fertile belt of tranquil pastureland, where the chief interest for most visitors will be the groaning restaurant tables of regions such as the **Pays d'Auge**. Much of the seaside is a little overdeveloped; the last French emperor created, towards the end of the nineteenth century, a "Norman Riviera" around **Trouville** and **Deauville**, and an air of pretension still hangs about their elegant promenades. But more ancient harbours such as **Honfleur** and **Barfleur** remain visually irresistible, and there are numerous seaside villages with few crowds or affectations. The banks of the Seine, too, hold several delightful little communities.

Normandy also boasts extraordinary Romanesque and Gothic architectural treasures, although only the much-restored capital, Rouen, retains a complete medieval centre. Elsewhere, the attractions are more often single buildings than entire towns. Most famous of all is the spectacular *merveille* on the island of **Mont St-Michel**, but there are also the monasteries at **Jumièges** and **Caen**; the cathedrals of **Bayeux** and **Coutances**; and Richard the Lionheart's castle above the Seine at **Les Andelys**. In addition, **Bayeux** has its vivid and astonishing tapestry, while among more recent creations are Monet's garden at **Giverny** and, at Le Havre, a fabulous collection of paintings by Dufy, Boudin, as well as other Impressionists. Furthermore, Normandy's vernacular architecture makes it well worth exploring inland – the back roads through the countryside are lined with splendid centuries-old half-timbered manor houses. It is remarkable how much has survived or been restored since the Allied landings in 1944 and the subsequent **Battle of Normandy**, which has its own legacy in a series of war museums, memorials and cemeteries.

To the French, at least, the essence of Normandy is its produce. This is the land of Camembert and Calvados, cider and seafood, and a butter- and cream-based cuisine

---

ACCOMMODATION PRICE CODES

Each hotel and guesthouse in this book has been graded according to the following price codes, which indicate the price for the **cheapest double room available during the high season**.

① Under 160F/€24   ④ 300–400F/€46–61   ⑦ 600–700F/€91–107
② 160–220F/€24–34   ⑤ 400–500F/€61–76   ⑧ 700–800F/€107–122
③ 220–300F/€34–46   ⑥ 500–600F/€76–91   ⑨ Over 800F/€122

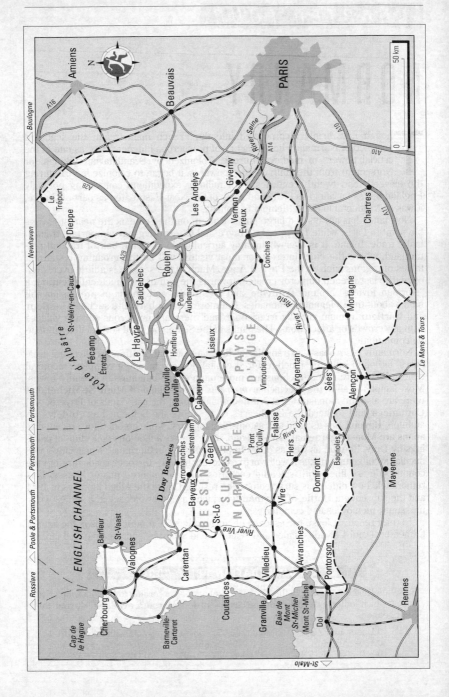

THE FOOD OF NORMANDY

The **food of Normandy** owes its most distinctive characteristic – its gut-bursting, heart-pounding richness – to the lush orchards and dairy herds of its agricultural heartland, and most especially the area southeast of Caen known as the Pays d'Auge. Menus abound in meat such as veal (*veau*) cooked in *vallée d'Auge* style, which consists largely of the profligate addition of cream and butter. Many dishes also feature orchard fruit, either in its natural state or in successively more alcoholic forms – either as apple or pear cider, or perhaps further distilled to produce brandies.

Normans have a great propensity for blood and guts. In addition to gamier meat and fowl such as rabbit and duck (a speciality in Rouen, where the birds are strangled to ensure that all their blood gets into the sauce), they enjoy such intestinal preparations as *andouilles*, the sausages known in English as chitterlings, and *tripes*, stewed for hours *à la mode de Caen*. A full blowout at a country restaurant in one of the small towns of inland Normandy – places like Conches, Vire and the Suisse Normande – will also traditionally entail one or two pauses between courses for the *trou normand*: a glass of Calvados while you catch your breath before struggling on with the feast.

Normandy's long coastline ensures that it is also a wonderful region for **seafood**. Many of the larger ports and resorts have long waterfront lines of restaurants competing for attention, each with its "*copieuse*" *assiette de fruits de mer*. **Honfleur** is probably the most enjoyable of these, but **Dieppe**, **Cherbourg** and **Granville** also spring to mind as offering endless eating opportunities. The menus tend to be much the same as those on offer in Brittany (see p.387), if perhaps slightly more expensive.

The most famous products of Normandy's meadow-munching cows are, of course, their **cheeses**. The tradition of cheese-making in the Pays d'Auge is thought to have started in the monasteries during the Dark Ages. By the eleventh century the local products were already well defined; in 1236, the *Roman de la Rose* referred to *Angelot* cheese, identified with a small coin depicting a young angel killing a dragon. The principal modern varieties began to emerge in the seventeenth century – **Pont l'Evêque**, which is square with a washed crust, soft but not runny, and **Livarot**, which is round, thick and firm, and has a stronger flavour. Although Marie Herel is generally credited with having invented **Camembert** in the 1790s, a smaller and stodgier version of that cheese had already existed for some time. A priest fleeing the Revolution seems to have stayed in Mme Herel's farmhouse at Camembert, and suggested modifications in her cheese-making in line with the techniques he'd seen employed to manufacture Brie de Meaux – a slower process, gentler on the curd and with more thorough drainage. The rich full cheese thus created was an instant success in the market at Vimoutiers, and the development of the railways (and the invention of the chipboard cheesebox in 1880) helped to give it a worldwide popularity.

with a proud disdain for most things *nouvelle*. Economically, however, the richness of the dairy pastures has been Normandy's downfall in recent years. EU milk quotas have liquidated many small farms, and stringent sanitary regulations have forced many small-scale traditional cheese factories to close. Parts of inland Normandy are now among the most depressed of the whole country, and in the forested areas to the south, where life has never been easy, things have not improved.

SEINE MARITIME

The *département* of Seine Maritime comprises three very distinct sections: Normandy's dramatic **northern coastline**, home not only to major ports like Dieppe and Le Havre but also to such delightful resorts as **Étretat**; the meandering course of the **River Seine**, where unchanged villages stand both up- and downstream of the provincial capital of Rouen; and the flat chalky **Caux plateau**, where to be frank there's nothing to detain visitors.

Dieppe in particular makes a much more appealing introduction to France than its counterparts further north in Picardy, and with the impressive white cliffs of the aptly named **Côte d'Albâtre** (Alabaster Coast) stretching away to either side it could easily serve as the base for a long stay. The most direct route to Rouen from here is simply to head due south, but it's well worth tracing the shore all the way west to **Le Havre**, and then following the Seine inland.

Driving along the D982 along the northern bank of the Seine, you'll often find your course paralleled by mighty tankers and container ships out on the water. Potential stops en route include the medieval abbeys of **Jumièges** and **St-Wandrille**, but **Rouen** itself is the prime destination, its association with the execution of Joan of Arc merely the most compelling episode in its fascinating and still conspicuous history. Further upstream, Monet's wonderful house and garden at **Giverny** and the redoubtable English frontier stronghold of Château Gaillard at **Les Andelys** also justify taking a slow route into Paris.

Dieppe

Crowded between high cliff headlands, **DIEPPE** is an enjoyably small-scale port that used to be more of a resort. During the nineteenth century, Parisians came here by train to take the sea air, promenading along the front while the English colony indulged in the peculiar pastime of swimming. These days, it's not a place many travellers go out of their way to visit, but it's one of the nicer ferry ports in northern France, and you're unlikely to regret spending an afternoon or evening here before or after a Channel crossing. With kids in tow, the aquariums of the **Cité de la Mer** are the obvious attraction; otherwise, you could settle for admiring the cliffs and the castle as you stroll the extravagant seafront lawns. Meanwhile, the business of the port goes on as ever, with Dieppe's commercial docks unloading half the bananas of the Antilles and forty percent of all shellfish destined to slither down French throats. The markets sell fish right off the boats, displayed with the usual Gallic flair, and the sole, scallops and turbot available in profusion at the restaurants may well tempt you to stay.

Arrival, information and accommodation

Dieppe's **tourist office** is on the pont Ango, which separates the ferry harbour from the pleasure port; you can't miss it if you're arriving by ferry (May, June & Sept Mon–Sat 9am–1pm & 2–7pm, Sun 10am–1pm & 3–6pm; July & Aug Mon–Sat 9am–1pm & 2–8pm, Sun 10am–1pm & 3–6pm; rest of year Mon–Sat 9am–noon & 2–6pm; ☎02.32.14.40.60, *www.mairie_dieppe.fr*). A beach annexe where quai Duquesne reaches the oceanfront is open in summer only (mid-June to mid-Sept Mon–Thurs & Sun 10am–7.30pm, Fri & Sat 10am–8pm). The main **post office** is at 2 bd Maréchal-Joffre (Mon–Fri 8.30am–6pm, Sat 8.30am–noon; ☎02.35.04.70.14).

Between one and three Hoverspeed SuperSeaCat **ferries** sail daily, all year round, between Newhaven and Dieppe's **gare maritime**, taking little over two hours for the crossing; for information call ☎08.20.00.35.55. Motorists coming off the boats are directed away from the town, and have to double back west to reach it; foot passengers can either walk the 500m to the tourist office, or take the 15F/€2.29 shuttle buses that connect with each sailing.

Dieppe's **gare SNCF** is another 500m south of the tourist office, on boulevard Clemenceau, and trains are much the quickest way to get to Rouen or Paris. Buses along the coast leave from the **gare routière** alongside.

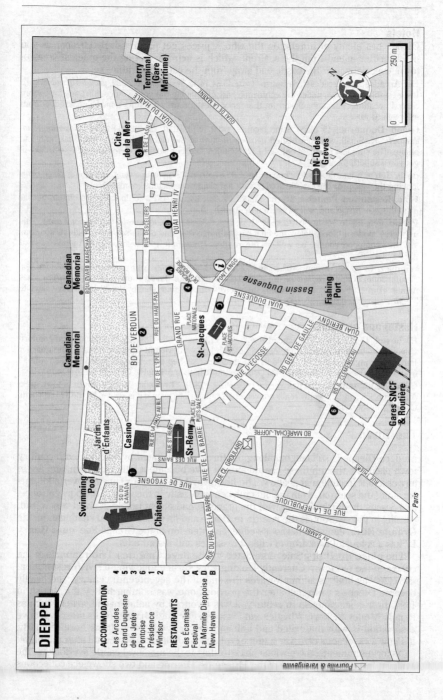

DIEPPE

ACCOMMODATION

Les Arcades	4
Grand Duquesne	5
de la Jetée	3
Pontoise	6
Présidence	1
Windsor	2

RESTAURANTS

Les Écamias	C
Festival	D
La Marmite Dieppoise	A
New Haven	B

Canadian Memorial

Canadian Memorial

Jardin d'Enfants

Swimming Pool

Casino

Château

St-Rémy

St-Jacques

BD DE VERDUN

BOULEVARD MARÉCHAL FOCH

QUAI DU HABLE

RUE DE L'ASILE

Cité de la Mer

Ferry Terminal (Gare Maritime)

QUAI DE LA MARNE

RUE DESCELLIERS

QUAI HENRI IV

N-D des Grèves

Bassin Duquesne

Fishing Port

QUAI DUQUESNE

PONT ANGO

GRANDE RUE DE LA BOURSE

RUE DU HAUT-PAS

GRAND RUE

RUE DE L'ÉPÉE

PLACE NATIONALE

PLACE ST-JACQUES

RUE D'ÉCOSSE

BD GÉN DE GAULLE

QUAI BÉRIGNY

BD A. CLÉMENCEAU

Gares SNCF & Routière

RUE DE LA HALLE AU BLÉ

RUE ST-RÉMY

PLACE DU PUITS-SALÉ

RUE DE LA BARRE

RUE DES BAINS

SQ DU CANADA

RUE DE SYGOGNE

RUE CL. GROULARD

BD MARÉCHAL-JOFFRE

RUE DE LA RÉPUBLIQUE

AV GAMBETTA

RUE THIERS

RUE DU FBG DE LA BARRE

Paris

250 m

Pourville & Varangeville

Hotels

Dieppe has plenty of **hotels**; on the whole, prices get progressively cheaper as you head further inland from the seafront, which is actually among the quietest areas of town, especially near the castle end away from the car ferry traffic.

Les Arcades, 1–3 Arcades de la Bourse (☎02.35.84.14.12, fax 02.35.40.22.29, *www.les-arcades.com*). Long-established hotel, under the eponymous arcades facing the port; you couldn't ask for a more central location, nor one closer to the ferry. Restaurant with full, good-value menus from 98F/€14.94. ④.

Grand Duquesne, 15 place Saint Jacques (☎02.32.14.61.10, fax 02.35.84.29.83, *www.augrand-duquesne.fr*). Small, well-refurbished pension in view of the cathedral; every room has bath and phone. The simplest menu, at 68F/€10.37, includes squid or salmon *choucroute*; 179F/€27.29 will get you a superb meal. ②.

de la Jetée, 5 rue de l'Asile Thomas (☎02.35.84.89.98). Simple but very welcoming place overlooking the sea, near the Cité de la Mer, with ten plain but spacious rooms. ①.

Hôtel-Restaurant Pontoise, 10 rue Thiers (☎02.35.84.14.57). Basic, inexpensive option, not far from the *gare SNCF* and well away from the beach. ②.

Présidence, bd de Verdun (☎02.35.84.31.31, fax 02.35.84.86.70, *www.hotel-la-presidence.com*). This ugly grey modern block, below the château at the far west end of the seafront, holds 89 spacious and well-equipped rooms, as well as the rooftop *Panoramic* restaurant, where menus start at 95F/€14.48. ④.

Windsor, 18 bd de Verdun (☎02.35.84.15.23, fax 02.35.84.74.52). You pay premium rates for sea-facing rooms in this *logis*, where the glass-fronted first-floor dining room – *Le Haut Gallion* – has menus from 110F/€16.77. The rooms themselves can be quite shabby, but they do have satellite TV. ④.

Hostel and campsite

HI hostel, 48 rue Louis Fromager (☎02.35.84.85.73, fax 02.35.84.89.62). Welcoming and comfortable, if somewhat inconveniently located hostel, 2km southwest of the *gare SNCF* in the quartier Janval, offering beds for 55F/€8.38 in two-, four- and six-bed dorms only. Served by bus route #2 from the tourist office (direction "Val Druel", stop "Château Michel"). Closed mid-Nov to mid-Feb.

Camping Vitamin, chemin des Vertus (☎02.35.82.11.11). Three-star site, well south of town in St-Aubin-sur-Scie, and thus only really convenient for motorists, even if it is served by the #2 bus route. Closed Nov–March.

The Town

Modern Dieppe is still laid out along the three axes dictated by its eighteenth-century town planners, though these central streets have become a little run-down, and are in any case left in continual shadow. The **boulevard de Verdun** runs for over a kilometre along the seafront, from the fifteenth-century castle in the west to the port entrance, and passes the Casino, along with the grandest and oldest hotels. A short way inland, parallel to the seafront, is the **rue de la Barre** and its pedestrianized continuation, the **Grande Rue**. Along the harbour's edge, an extension of the Grande Rue, **quai Henry IV** has a colourful backdrop of cafés, brasseries and restaurants.

The **place du Puits Salé**, dominated by the huge **Café des Tribunaux**, is at the centre of the old town. Currently looking very spruce following a lavish restoration, the café was built as an inn towards the end of the seventeenth century, and briefly became Dieppe's town hall after the previous one was bombarded by the British in 1694. In the late nineteenth century, it was favoured by painters and writers such as Renoir, Monet, Sickert, Whistler and Pissarro. For English visitors, its most evocative association is with the exiled and unhappy Oscar Wilde, who drank here regularly. It's now a cavernous café, the haunt of college students and open until after midnight.

As for monuments, the obvious place to start is the medieval **castle** overlooking the seafront from the west, home of the **Musée de Dieppe** and two showpiece collections

(June–Sept daily 10am–noon & 2–6pm; rest of year closed Tues; 15F/€2.29). The first collection is a group of carved ivories – virtuoso pieces of sawing, filing and chipping of the plundered riches of Africa, shipped back to the town by early Dieppe "explorers". The other permanent exhibition is made up of a hundred or so prints by the co-founder of Cubism, Georges Braque, who went to school in Le Havre, spent summers in Dieppe and is buried just west of the town at Varengeville-sur-Mer (see p.334).

An exit from the western side of the castle takes you out onto a path up to the **cliffs**. On the other side, a flight of steps leads down to the **square du Canada**, originally named in commemoration of the role played by Dieppe sailors in the colonization of Canada. Now a small plaque is dedicated to the Canadian soldiers who died in the suicidal 1942 raid on Dieppe, justified later as a trial run for the 1944 Normandy landings.

The **Cité de la Mer**, at 37 rue de l'Asile-Thomas, just back from the harbour, sets out simultaneously to entertain children and to serve as a centre for scientific research, and succeeds in both without being all that interesting for the casual adult visitor (daily 10am–noon & 2–6pm; 28F/€4.27). Kids are certain to enjoy learning the principles of navigation by operating radio-controlled boats (5F/€0.76 for 3min). Thereafter, the museum traces the history of sea-going vessels, featuring a Viking drakkar under construction, following methods depicted in the Bayeux Tapestry. Next comes a very detailed geological exhibition covering the formation of the local cliffs, in which you learn how to convert shingle into sandpaper. Visits culminate with large **aquariums** filled with the marine life of the Channel: flat fish with bulbous eyes and twisted faces, retiring octopuses, battling lobsters and hermaphrodite scallops (the white part is male, the orange, female). Thanks to a typical lack of sentimentality, jars of fish soup, whose exact provenance is not made explicit, are on sale at the exit.

Eating and drinking

The most promising area to look for **restaurants** in Dieppe is along the quai Henri IV, which makes a lovely place to stroll and compare menus of a summer's evening. The beach itself holds no formal restaurants, but it does have a couple of open-air cafés selling mussels, salads and so on, and plenty of crêpe stands. Four of the town's best restaurants are listed below.

As well as the daily spectacle of the fish on sale in the **fishing port**, there's an all-day open-air **market** in the place Nationale and Grande Rue on Saturday. The largest of several hypermarkets in the area is Auchan (Mon–Sat 8.30am–10pm), out of town at the Centre Commercial du Belvédère on the route de Rouen (RN 27), and reached by free courtesy buses from the tourist office.

Les Écamias, 129 quai Henri IV (☎02.35.84.67.67). Small, friendly traditional French restaurant, at the quieter, seaward end of the main quay. Each of its two dining rooms serves the same menu, with a 75F/€11.43 option that includes *moules marinières* and stuffed shellfish; they also offer skate with capers. Closed Mon (except in Aug), and Sun evening in winter.

Le Festival, 11 quai Henri IV (☎02.35.40.24.29). Quick-fire brasserie at the busiest end of the quayside that delivers fishy goods at top speed without skimping on quality. *Moules frites* is a mere 40F/€6.10; on the 110F/€16.77 menu you can get half a lobster, and there's *fruits de mer* literally by the boatload – it comes in blue china ships.

La Marmite Dieppoise, 8 rue St-Jean (☎02.35.84.24.26). Busy little rustic restaurant near St-Jacques church, where the speciality is *marmite Dieppoise* (seafood pot, with shellfish and white fish). Dinner menus start at 150F/€22.87. Closed Sun evening, Mon, and Thurs evening out of season.

Le Newhaven, 53 quai Henri IV (☎02.35.84.89.72). Reliable seafood specialist, at the slightly quieter end of the quayside, serving good menus from 70F/€10.67. The 115F/€17.53 menu of Dieppe specialities includes fish livers and squid; if you go à la carte, 115F/€17.53 will also buy you a *choucroute de la mer*. Closed Sun evening in winter.

The Côte d'Albâtre

The shoreline of the Côte d'Albâtre is eroding at a ferocious rate, and it's conceivable that the small resorts here, tucked in among the cliffs at the ends of a succession of valleys, may not last more than another century or so. For the moment, however, they are quietly prospering, with casinos, sports centres and yacht marinas ensuring a modest but steady summer trade. To the east of Dieppe **Le Tréport** is pleasant enough, but the obvious direction to head is west, where you can take your pick of **St-Valéry**, **Fécamp** and the best of the bunch, **Étretat**.

Le Tréport

Thirty kilometres east of Dieppe, on the border with Picardy, **LE TRÉPORT** is a seaside resort that has clearly seen better days. It was already something of a bathing station when the railways arrived in 1873 and promoted this as "the prettiest beach in Europe, just three hours from Paris". It remained the capital's favoured resort until the 1950s – and is still served by around five trains daily – but it can't ever have been that pretty, and these days its charms are definitely fading.

Le Tréport divides into three sections: the flat wedge-shaped **seafront** area, bounded on one side by the Channel, on another by the harbour at the mouth of the river Bresle, and on the third by imposing 100-metre-high white chalk cliffs; the **old town**, higher up the slopes on safer ground; and the **modern town** further inland. Only the parts closest to the shore are of any interest to visitors. The seafront itself is entirely taken up by a hideous pink-and-orange concrete apartment block, with one or two snack bars but no other sign of life, facing the Casino and a drab grey shingle beach. The more sheltered harbourside quai Francois-1er around the corner holds most of the action, lined with restaurants, souvenir shops and cafés. The assorted stone jetties and wooden piers around the harbour make an enjoyable stroll, watching the comings and goings of the fishing boats.

Climbing up from the *quai*, you come to the heavily nautical **Église St-Jacques**, built in the fifteenth century to replace an eleventh-century original that crumbled into the sea, along with the cliff on which it stood. Nearby, next to the fortified former town hall that is now the local library, successive flights of steps, 365 of them in all, climb to the top of the cliffs.

Practicalities

Trains and **buses** arrive in Le Tréport on the far side of the harbour, a short walk from the main *quai*. Turning left as you hit the main drag will bring you to the **tourist office**, on quai Sadi-Carnot (Easter–Sept daily 10am–noon & 2–6pm; rest of year Mon–Sat 10am–noon & 2–5pm; ☎02.35.86.05.69).

Of the **hotels**, the best in terms of a sea view and good-quality food is the *Riche-Lieu* at 50 quai Francois-1er (☎02.35.86.26.55; ③), which has modernized rooms with showers on four floors and a wide range of menus starting at 90F/€13.72 for a "bistro" meal. The *Matelote*, 34 quai Francois-1er (☎02.35.86.01.13), is a quayside seafood **restaurant** with a high gourmet reputation.

Varengeville

If the museum in Dieppe (see p.333) awakened your interest in Georges Braque, you may be interested in visiting his grave in the clifftop church some way north of **VARENGEVILLE**, 8km west of Dieppe (25min ride on bus #311 or #312, afternoon only). Braque's marble **tomb** is topped by a sadly decaying mosaic of a white dove in flight. More impressive is his vivid blue Tree of Jesse stained-glass window inside the church, through which the sun rises in summer.

Also in Varengeville, 300m south of the D75, is the **Manoir d'Ango**, the "summer palace" of sixteenth-century Dieppe's leading shipbuilder (mid-March to mid-Nov daily 10am–12.30pm & 2–6.30pm; rest of year Sat 10am–12.30pm, Sun 10am–12.30pm & 2–6.30pm; 30F/€4.57). Jean Ango outfitted such major expeditions as Verrazzano's, which "discovered" the site of New York in 1524, and made himself rich from pillaging treasure ships out on the Spanish Main. His former home consists of a rectangular ensemble of fine brick buildings arranged around a central courtyard. The intricate patterning of red bricks, shaped flint slabs, stone blocks and supporting timbers is at its finest in the remarkable central dovecote, topped by a dome that rises to an elegant point, which is aflutter with pigeons.

Back along the road towards Dieppe from the church, the house at the **Bois des Moutiers**, built for Guillaume Mallet from 1898 onwards and un-French in almost every respect, was one of architect Edwin Lutyens' first commissions. Lutyens, then aged just 29, was at the start of a career that was to culminate during the 1920s when he laid out most of the city of New Delhi. The real reason to visit, however, is to enjoy the magnificent **gardens**, designed by Mallet in conjunction with Gertrude Jekyll, which are at their most spectacular in the second half of May (mid-March to mid-Nov Mon–Fri & Sun 10am–noon & 2pm–sunset, Sat 2pm–sunset; admission 40F/€6.10 during May & June, otherwise 35F/€5.34). Enthusiastic guides lead you through the highly innovative engineering of the house and grounds, full of quirks and games. The colours of the Burne-Jones tapestry hanging in the stairwell were copied from Renaissance cloth in William Morris's studio; the rhododendrons were chosen from similar samples. Outside, paths lead through vistas based on paintings by Poussin, Lorrain and other seventeenth-century artists.

St-Valéry-en-Caux

The first sizeable community west of Dieppe is **ST-VALÉRY-EN-CAUX**, a rebuilt town which is the clearest reminder of the fighting – and massive destruction – of the Allied retreat of 1940. A monument on the western cliffs pays tribute to the French cavalry division who faced Rommel's tanks on horseback, brandishing their sabres with hopeless heroism, while beside the ruins of a German artillery emplacement on the opposite cliffs another commemorates a Scottish division, rounded up while fighting their way back to Le Havre and the boats home.

Much the most attractive house to survive in St-Valéry, the Renaissance Maison Henri-IV on the quai d'Aval, serves as the **tourist office** (May to mid-Sept daily 10am–12.30pm & 3–7pm; rest of year Wed–Sat 10am–12.30pm & 3–7pm, Sun 10am–12.30pm; ☎02.35.97.00.63). The *Terrasses*, 22 rue le Perrey (☎02.35.97.11.22; ④; closed Christmas & Jan), is the only **hotel-restaurant** actually facing the sea, but several others surround the main market square. In high season the 149 comfortable if characterless rooms of the *Relais Mercure*, 500m back from the seafront at 14 av Clémenceau (☎02.35.57.88.00; ④), can be a godsend. There are also two year-round **campsites**: the two-star *Falaise d'Amont* (☎02.35.97.05.07) on the eastern cliffs and the larger four-star *d'Etennemare* (☎02.35.97.15.79), set back from the sea southwest of the harbour. If you fancy a **meal**, head for the *Restaurant du Port*, overlooking the harbour at 18 quai d'Amont (☎02.35.97.08.93; closed Sun evening & Mon in low season), which has a delicious 118F/€17.99 seafood menu.

Fécamp

FÉCAMP, roughly halfway between Dieppe and Le Havre, is a serious fishing port with an attractive seafront promenade. One compelling reason to pay a brief visit is to see the

Arrival and information

Three daily P&O **ferries** sail from Portsmouth to the **Terminal de Grande Bretagne**, not far from the train and bus stations in the Bassin de la Citadelle (☎08.03.01.30.13). The **gare SNCF** is 1.5km west of the Hôtel de Ville, on cours de la République, right alongside the **gare routière** across boulevard de Strasbourg. Shuttle buses from the *gare SNCF* run to the ferry terminal.

Le Havre's rather inconspicuous and not very central **tourist office** is on the main oceanfront drag, at 186 bd Clémenceau, near its intersection with avenue Foch (May–Sept Mon–Sat 9am–7pm, Sun 10am–12.30pm & 2.30–6pm; rest of year Mon–Sat 9am–6.30pm, Sun 10am–1pm; ☎02.35.74.04.04, *www.lehavretourism.com*). There's also a tourist information kiosk at the ferry terminal, open in summer to coincide with sailings.

Accommodation

Le Havre holds two main concentrations of **hotels**: one group faces the *gare SNCF*, and most of the rest lie within walking distance of the ferry terminal. The nearest **camp-site** is the surprisingly attractive four-star *Forêt de Montgeon* (☎02.35.46.52.39; closed Oct to mid-April), north of the town centre in a 700-acre forest; take bus #1 from the Hôtel de Ville or *gare SNCF*, direction "Jacques-Monod".

Hotels

Celtic, 106 rue Voltaire (☎02.35.42.39.77, fax 02.35.21.67.75). Friendly and comfortable option, in the long buildings that flank the Espace Oscar Niemeyer, overlooking the Volcano. ②.

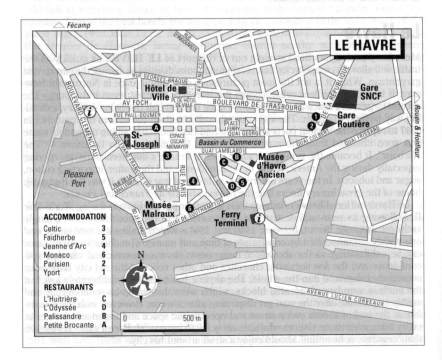

LE HAVRE

ACCOMMODATION
Celtic	3
Faidherbe	5
Jeanne d'Arc	4
Monaco	6
Parisien	2
Yport	1

RESTAURANTS
L'Huitrière	C
L'Odyssée	D
Palissandre	B
Petite Brocante	A

Faidherbe, 21 rue Général-Faidherbe (☎02.35.42.20.27, fax 02.35.42.57.03). Welcoming family hotel offering simple rooms, some with sea views, very near the ferry port in the old town. ①.

Grand Hôtel Parisien, 1 cours de la République (☎02.35.25.23.83, fax 02.35.25.05.06). A well-appointed place, with congenial management, facing the *gare SNCF* on a busy corner. All rooms have shower and TV. Twenty-five percent reductions on Fri & Sat Dec–March. ②.

Jeanne d'Arc, 91 rue Émile-Zola (☎02.35.21.67.27, fax 02.35.41.26.83). Tiny little hotel, with old-fashioned but clean rooms, which are given a personal touch by the owner's needlework. ①.

Le Monaco, 16 rue de Paris (☎02.35.42.21.01, fax 02.35.42.01.01). Bright hotel on a busy corner overlooking the quay; handy for the ferries and with a good-value brasserie downstairs. Closed second fortnight in Feb & Mon July–Oct. ②.

d'Yport, 27 cours de la République (☎02.35.25.21.08, fax 02.35.24.06.34). Another option opposite the train station, this time slightly quieter, being set just back from the street, and unusually hospitable. Guests in the cheaper rooms are charged 25F/€3.81 to have a shower, so you might as well pay for en-suite facilities. ①–③.

The Town

One reason visitors tend to dismiss Le Havre out of hand is that it's easy – whether by train, bus or your own vehicle – to get to and from the city without ever seeing its downtown area, giving the impression that it's merely an endless industrial sprawl.

The Perret-designed central **Hôtel de Ville** is a logical first port of call, a low flat-roofed building that stretches for over a hundred metres, topped by a seventeen-storey concrete tower. Surrounded by pergola walkways, flower beds and flowing water from an array of fountains, it's an attractive, lively place with a high-tech feel, and is often the venue for imaginative civic-minded exhibitions.

Perret's other major creation, clearly visible northwest of the town hall, is the **church of St-Joseph**. Instead of the traditional elongated cross shape, the church is built on a cross of which all four arms are equally short. From the outside it's a plain mass of speckled concrete, the main doors thrown open to hint at dark interior spaces within resembling an underground car park. In fact, when you get inside it all makes sense: the altar is right in the centre, with the hundred-metre bell tower rising directly above it. Very simple patterns of stained glass, all around the church and right the way up the tower, create a bright interplay of coloured light, focusing on the altar.

Le Havre's boldest specimen of modern architecture is even newer – the cultural centre known as the **Volcano** (or less reverentially as the "yoghurt pot"), standing at the end of the Bassin du Commerce, and dominating the Espace Oscar Niemeyer. The Volcano, designed by the Brazilian architect after which the *espace* is named, is a slightly asymmetrical, smooth, gleaming white cone, cut off abruptly just above the level of the surrounding buildings, so that its curving planes are undisturbed by doors or windows; the entrance is concealed beneath a white walkway in the open plaza below.

The **Bassin du Commerce**, which stretches away from the complex, is of minimal commercial significance. Kayaks and rowing boats can be rented to explore its regular contours, and a couple of larger boats are moored permanently to serve as clubs or restaurants – it's all disconcertingly quiet, serving mainly as an appropriate stretch of water for the graceful white footbridge of the Passarelle du Commerce to cross.

Overlooking the harbour entrance is the modern, recently renovated **Musée Malraux** (Mon & Wed–Fri 11am–6pm, Sat & Sun 11am–7pm; 25F/€3.81), which ranks among the best-designed art galleries in France, using natural light to its full advantage to display an enjoyable assortment of nineteenth- and twentieth-century French paintings. Its principal highlights are over two hundred canvases by Eugène Boudin, including greyish landscapes produced all along the Norman coastline, with views of Trouville, Honfleur and Étretat, as well as an entire wall of miniature cows and a lovely set of works by Raoul Dufy (1877–1953), which make Le Havre seem positively radiant, whatever the weather outside.

If you have the time to spare, you might like to see what old Le Havre looked like in the prewar days when Jean-Paul Sartre wrote *La Nausée* here. He taught philosophy for five years during the 1930s in a local school, and his almost transcendent disgust with the place cannot obscure the fascination he felt in exploring the seedy dockside quarter of St-François, in those spare moments when he wasn't visiting Simone de Beauvoir in Rouen. Little survives of the city Sartre knew, but pictures and bits gathered from the rubble are on display in one of the very few buildings that escaped World War II intact, the **Musée de l'Ancien Havre** at 1 rue Jérôme-Bellarmato, just south of the Bassin du Commerce (Wed–Sun 10am–noon & 2–6pm; 10F/€1.52).

The once-great port of **Harfleur** is now no more than a suburb of Le Havre, 6km upstream from the centre. While no longer sufficiently distinctive to be worth visiting, it earned an undying place in history as the landing place of Henry V's English army in 1415, en route to victory at Agincourt. Laid under siege, Harfleur surrendered in late September, following a final English onslaught spurred on – according to Shakespeare – by Henry's cry of "Once more unto the breach, dear friends . . ."

Eating

Few of the **restaurants** in Le Havre are worth making a fuss about, except perhaps for some in the suburb of **Ste-Adresse**. There are, however, lots of bars, cafés and brasseries around the *gare SNCF*, and all sorts of crêperies and ethnic alternatives – North African, South American, Caribbean – in the back streets of the St-François district.

If you're **shopping** for food to take home, you could try the central **market**, just west of place Gambetta and ideal for fresh produce, or two Auchan **hypermarkets** (both open Mon–Sat 8.30am–10pm): the larger, at the Mont Gaillard Centre Commercial, is reached by following cours de la République beyond the *gare SNCF*, through the tunnel; the other, at Montivilliers, is signposted off the Tancarville road.

L'Huitrière, 12 quai Michel Féré (☎02.35.21.24.16). Seafood specialists in the St-François quarter, facing the rotating bridge of the port. Even the simplest 92F/€14.03 *assiette* includes clams, shrimps and langoustines; the two-person 750F/€114.34 *Abondance* menu has to be seen to be believed.

L'Odyssée, 41 rue Général-Faidherbe (☎02.35.21.31.42). First-rate seafood restaurant close to the ferry terminal in the old town, serving a reliable 125F/€19.06 weekday lunch menu and a changing, more adventurous 155F/€23.63 dinner option. Closed Sat lunch, Sun evening, Mon & mid-July to mid-Aug.

Palissandre, 33 rue de Bretagne (☎02.35.21.69.00). Old-fashioned wood-panelled bistro in the St-François quarter, where the conventional menus from 85F/€12.96 feature dishes such as fish stewed in cider, and an express menu guarantees service within 20min. Closed Wed evening, Sat lunch & Sun.

La Petite Brocante, 75 rue Louis Brindeau (☎02.35.21.42.20). Lively central bistro; the set menus are a little pricey at 128F/€19.51 and up, but there's always a good-value *plat du jour*, as often as not fresh fish. Closed Sun & first three weeks in Aug.

Along the Seine to Rouen

Until relatively recently, no bridges crossed the Seine any lower than Rouen, which made the river an all but impassable barrier for motorists heading between Upper and Lower Normandy. Now though an enormous bridge spans its mouth – the **Pont de Normandie**, which opened in 1995 – enabling motorists to zip across from Le Havre to Honfleur for a hefty toll of 33F/€5.03, and further inland, the immense **Tancarville** suspension bridge and the magnificent **Pont de Brotonne**, just upstream from Caudebec, whose yellow stays refract into strange optical effects as you cross, offer alternative routes across the river. If Rouen is your destination from Le Havre, however, it makes much more sense to stick to the north bank of the river. A succession of quiet roads follow the Seine's every loop, leading through sleepy towns such as **Caudebec-en-Caux** and past intriguing ruins like the abbey of **Jumièges**.

Caudebec-en-Caux

The first town of any size on the right bank of the Seine is **CAUDEBEC-EN-CAUX**. Most traces of its long past were destroyed by fire in the last war, after which it was rebuilt. The damage – and previous local history – is recorded in the thirteenth-century **Maison des Templiers**, one of the few buildings to be spared (Easter–June Sat & Sun 3–6pm; July–Sept Tues–Sun 3–6pm; 12F/€1.83). You can **rent bicycles** from M. Jaubert on rue de la Vicomte. A **market** has been held every Saturday since 1390 in the main square.

Caudebec's **tourist office** is slightly south of the centre, in place Charles de Gaulle (April–Nov Mon–Sat 9.30am–1pm & 3–7pm, Sun 3–7pm; rest of year daily 3–7pm; ☎02.32.70.46.32, *caudebec-en-caux.tourisme@wanadoo.fr*). Two absolutely indistinguishable *logis de France* face the river side by side from quai Guilbaud, with all but identical prices: the *Normotel La Marine* at no. 18 (☎02.35.96.20.11; ③; closed Jan), and the *Normandie* at no. 19 (☎02.35.96.25.11; ③; closed Feb). There's also a riverside **campsite** to the north, the *Barre Y Va* (☎02.35.96.26.38; closed Oct–March).

Abbaye de St-Wandrille

Just beyond the Pont de Brotonne as you continue towards Rouen, the medieval **abbey** in **ST-WANDRILLE** was founded – so legend has it – by a seventh-century count who, with his wife, renounced all earthly pleasures on the day of their wedding. The abbey's buildings make an attractive if curious architectural ensemble: part ruin, part restoration and, in the case of the main buildings, part transplant – a fifteenth-century barn brought in a few years ago from another Norman village miles away.

St-Wandrille remains an active monastery, home to fifty Benedictine monks who in addition to their spiritual duties turn their hands to money-making tasks that range from candle-making to running a reprographic studio; they also show visitors around the abbey on **guided tours** (Tues–Sat 3.30pm, Sun 11.30am; 20F/€3.05). You can wander through the grounds for no charge in summer (July & Aug Tues–Sun 10.45am–12.30pm & 3–5pm), and you can also listen to the monks' **Gregorian chanting** in their new church (Mon–Sat 9.45am & 5.30pm, Sun 10am & 5pm).

There's a **crêperie** opposite the abbey, and, a few doors along in the place de l'Église, the more upmarket *Deux Coronnes* **restaurant** (☎02.35.96.11.44; closed Sun evening & Mon), a seventeenth-century inn – half-timbered, naturally – serving delicious menus starting at 135F/€20.58.

Abbaye de Jumièges

In the next loop of the Seine, 12km on from St-Wandrille, comes the highlight of the Seine valley: the majestic **abbey** in **JUMIÈGES** (daily: mid-April to mid-Sept 9.30am–7pm; rest of year 9.30am–1pm & 2.30–5.30pm; 32F/€4.88), said to have been founded by St Philibert in 654 AD, just five years after St-Wandrille. A haunting ruin, the abbey was burned by marauding Vikings in 841, rebuilt a century later, then destroyed again – as a deliberate act of policy – during the Revolution. Its main surviving outline, as far as it can still be discerned, dates from the eleventh century – William the Conqueror himself attended its re-consecration in 1067. The twin towers, over 52m high, are still standing. So too is one arch of the roofless nave, while a one-sided yew tree stands in the centre of what were once the cloisters.

Overlooking the abbey at 17 place de la Mairie is a grand **restaurant**, the *Auberge des Ruines* (☎02.35.37.24.05; ②; closed Sun evening & Mon, plus all evenings except Fri & Sat Nov–Feb), which also offers a handful of simple **rooms**.

Rouen

ROUEN, the capital of Upper Normandy, is one of France's most ancient and historic cities. Standing on the site of Roman Rotomagus, the lowest point on the river then capable of being bridged, it was laid out by the Viking Rollo shortly after he became Duke of Normandy in 911. Captured by the English in 1419, it was the stage in 1431 for the trial and execution of Joan of Arc, and returned to French control in 1449.

Over the centuries, Rouen has suffered repeated devastation; there were 45 major fires in the first half of the thirteenth century alone. It has had to be almost entirely rebuilt during the last fifty years, and now you could spend a whole day wandering around the city without realizing that the Seine ran through its centre. War-time bombs destroyed all its bridges, the area between the cathedral and the *quais*, and much of the industrial quarter. The riverside area has never been adequately restored, and what you might expect to be the most beautiful part of the city is in fact something of an abomination.

Enormous sums have, however, been lavished on an upmarket restoration job on the streets a few hundred metres north of the river, which turned the centre into the closest approximation to a medieval city that modern imaginations could come up with. The suggestion that for historical authenticity the houses should be painted in bright, clashing colours was not deemed appropriate, but so far as it goes, the whole of this inner core can be very seductive, and its churches are impressive by any standards.

Outside the renovated quarters, things are rather different. The city spreads deep into the loop of the Seine, with its docks and industrial infrastructure stretching endlessly away to the south, and it's increasingly expanding up into the hills to the north as well, while the river bank itself is lined with a fume-filled, multi-laned motorway. As the nearest point that large container ships can get to Paris, even in decline this remains the fourth largest port in the country.

Arrival and information

The main **gare SNCF**, Gare Rive Droite, stands at the north end of rue Jeanne-d'Arc; it is connected to the centre by a multibillion-franc **métro** system, completed in 1998, the city's pride and joy. From the train station (M° Gare Rue Verte), the métro follows the line of the rue Jeanne-d'Arc, making two stops before it resurfaces to cross the river by bridge; thereafter the tracks dip below and above ground like a roller coaster. Individual journeys cost 8F/€1.22 and a book of tickets is 59F/€8.99, though in truth the métro is of more use to commuters than tourists. All **buses** except #2A from the *gare SNCF* run down rue Jeanne-d'Arc to the centre, which takes five minutes. From the fifth stop, the "Théâtre des Arts" by the river, the **gare routière** is one block west in rue des Charettes, tucked away behind the riverfront buildings.

Rouen's **tourist office**, opposite the cathedral at 25 place de la Cathédrale, stands in the sixteenth-century Hôtel des Généraux (May–Sept Mon–Sat 9am–7pm, Sun 9.30am–12.30pm & 2.30–6pm; rest of year Mon–Sat 9am–6pm, Sun 10am–1pm; ☎02.32.08.32.40, *www.mairie-rouen.fr*). It serves each day as the starting point for two-hour **walking tours** of different areas of the city, each costing 35F/€5.34. For more sedate visitors, a motorized **petit train** makes a forty-minute loop tour from the tourist office at regular intervals (daily 10am, 11am, 2pm, 4pm & 5pm; 30F/€4.57).

You can rent **bicycles** from Rouen Cycles, 45 rue St-Éloi (☎02.35.71.34.30), as well as at the *gare SNCF*. The **post office** is at 45 rue Jeanne-d'Arc, in the centre of town (Mon–Fri 8am–7pm, Sat 8.30am–12.30pm; ☎02.35.08.73.73). For **Internet** access, head for the café-style *Cybernetics*, 59 place du Vieux-Marché (Mon & Fri 12.30pm–midnight, Tues–Thurs & Sat 12.30–7.30pm; ☎02.35.07.02.77, *www.cybernetics.fr*), or the more

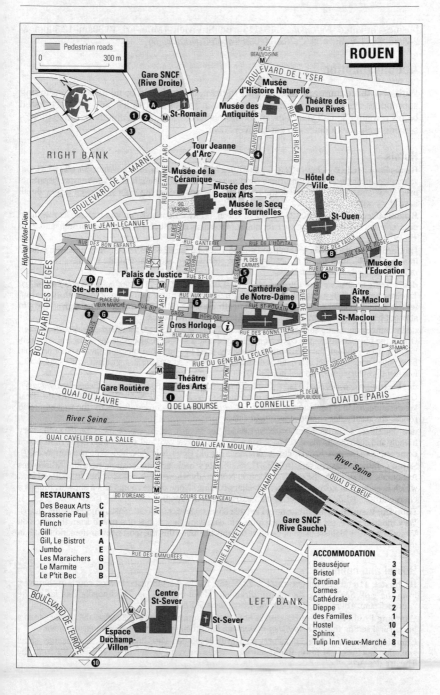

RIGHT BANK

Pedestrian roads
0   300 m

ROUEN

Gare SNCF
(Rive Droite)

Musée
d'Histoire Naturelle

Musée des
Antiquités

Théâtre des
Deux Rives

St-Romain

Tour Jeanne
d'Arc

Musée de la
Céramique

Musée des
Beaux Arts

Hôtel de
Ville

Musée le Secq
des Tournelles

St-Ouen

Musée de
l'Education

Palais de Justice

Ste-Jeanne

Cathédrale
de Notre-Dame

Aître
St-Maclou

St-Maclou

Gros Horloge

Théâtre
des Arts

Gare Routière

River Seine

Gare SNCF
(Rive Gauche)

River Seine

RESTAURANTS

Des Beaux Arts	C
Brasserie Paul	H
Flunch	F
Gill	I
Gill, Le Bistrot	A
Jumbo	E
Les Maraichers	G
Le Marmite	D
Le P'tit Bec	B

ACCOMMODATION

Beauséjour	3
Bristol	6
Cardinal	9
Carmes	5
Cathédrale	7
Dieppe	2
des Familles	1
Hostel	10
Sphinx	4
Tulip Inn Vieux-Marché	8

Centre
St-Sever

St-Sever

LEFT BANK

Espace
Duchamp-
Villon

business-oriented *Netropole*, 113–115 rue St-Vivien (Mon–Fri 10.30am–12.30pm & 2–8pm, Sat 1–7pm; ☎02.32.76.40.90, *netropole@wanadoo.fr*).

Accommodation

With over three thousand **hotel** rooms in town, there should be no difficulty in finding appropriate accommodation in Rouen, even at the busiest times, and all those listed below remain open all year. Few of the hotels have restaurants, chiefly because there's so wide a choice of places to eat all over town.

Hotels

Beauséjour, 9 rue Pouchet (☎02.35.71.93.47, fax 02.35.98.01.24, *beausejour@lerapporteur.fr*). Good-value place near the train station (turn right as you come out), though once you're past the attractive facade and garden courtyard, the rooms themselves are on the plain side, even if they do all have shower and TV. ②.

Bristol, 45 rue aux Juifs (☎02.35.71.54.21). Clean, pretty little nine-room hotel, above its own little brasserie in a half-timbered house overlooking the Palais de Justice. All rooms are en suite and have TV. ③.

Le Cardinal, 1 place de la Cathédrale (☎02.35.70.24.42, fax 02.35.89.75.14). Very good-value hotel in a stunning location facing the cathedral; the rooms have excellent en-suite facilities. No restaurant, but ample buffet breakfasts. ④.

des Carmes, 33 place des Carmes (☎02.35.71.92.31, fax 02.35.71.76.96, *h.des.carmes@mcom.fr*). Twelve-room hotel in a beautifully decorated nineteenth-century house, complete with blue shutters, in a quiet central square a short walk north from the cathedral. Guests are not given keys to stay out late. No restaurant, but buffet breakfasts for 34F/€5.18. ③.

de la Cathédrale, 12 rue St-Romain (☎02.35.71.57.95, fax 02.35.70.15.54, *www.hotel-de-la-cathedrale.com*). One of the most attractive and conveniently located hotels in Rouen, alongside the cathedral and arch-bishop's palace, though the plain rooms themselves don't live up to the appealing facade and quaint old flower-filled courtyard. Set in a quiet pedestrianized street – so parking is a problem – that's lined with fourteenth-century timber-framed houses. ④.

de Dieppe, place Bernard Tissot (☎02.35.71.96.00, fax 02.35.89.65.21, *hotel.dieppe@wanadoo.fr*). Grand traditional hotel, immediately opposite the train station, which is affiliated to the Best Western chain and is home to the top-notch *Quatre Saisons* restaurant. Prices for the well-equipped rooms are greatly discounted at weekends. ⑤.

des Familles, 4 rue Pouchet (☎02.35.71.88.51, fax 02.35.07.54.65, *www.hoteldesfamilles.com*). Very friendly and characterful place, set back beyond a small gravel yard and a short walk to the right as you come out from the gare Rive Droite. Incorporates the old Hôtel de la Paix; hence the two entrances. ②.

Sphinx, 130 rue Beauvoisine (☎02.35.71.35.86). Very basic accommodation, near the Musée des Antiquités, but possibly the only hotel left in Normandy where rates still start below 100F/€15.24, which is enough to keep the budget travellers coming. None of the rooms has a shower; there's a charge of 10F/€1.52 per shower, and an extra bed in the room costs 60F/€9.15. ①.

Tulip Inn Vieux Marché, 15 rue de la Pie (☎02.35.71.00.88, fax 02.35.70.75.94, *tulip.inn@wanadoo.fr*). Very modern place, set around a venerable old courtyard, just a toss of a match from the place du Vieux-Marché. A high standard of comfort has quickly made this the most popular upmarket hotel in town. ⑥.

Hostel and campsites

HI hostel, 118 bd de l'Europe (☎02.35.72.06.45). Fairly spartan place located south of the river; from the *gare SNCF*, take the métro, direction "Hôtel de Ville" or "Technopôle", as far as the "Europe" stop. There's an 11pm curfew. Dorm beds 59F/€8.99.

Camping l'Aubette, 23 Vert Buisson in St-Léger du Bourg-Denis (☎02.35.08.47.69). Basic site in a more rural setting than the *Camping municipal*, but much less accessible, 5km east of town.

Camping municipal, rue Jules-Ferry in Déville-lès-Rouen (☎02.35.74.07.59). Surprisingly small site, 4km northwest of town, that's geared towards caravans rather than tents; bus #2 from the Théâtre des Arts.

The Town

Rouen has traditionally spent a bigger slice of its budget on monuments than any other provincial town, which maddens many a Rouennais. As a tourist, your one complaint may be the lack of time to visit them all.

The place du Vieux-Marché to the cathedral

The obvious place to start sightseeing is the **place du Vieux-Marché**, where a small plaque and a huge cross (nearly 20m high) mark the spot on which Joan of Arc was burnt to death on May 30, 1431. A new memorial **church** to the saint has been built in the square (Mon–Sat 10am–12.30pm & 2–6pm, Sun 2–6pm): it's a wacky, spiky-looking thing, said to represent either an upturned boat or the flames that consumed Joan, but indisputably an architectural triumph, part of an ensemble of buildings that manages to incorporate in similar style a covered food market. The theme of the church's fish-shaped windows is continued in the scaly tiles that adorn its roof, which is elongated to form a walkway across the square. The outline of that vanished church's foundations is visible on the adjacent lawns, which also mark the precise spot of Joan's martyrdom. The square itself is surrounded by fine old brown-and-white half-timbered houses, many of those on the south side now serving as restaurants. The private **Musée Jeanne d'Arc**, tucked in among them in an ancient cellar in the back of a gift shop, draws large crowds to its collection of tawdry waxworks and facsimile manuscripts (Tues–Sun: May to mid-Sept 9.30am–7pm; rest of year 10am–noon & 2–6.30pm; 25F/€3.81).

From place du Vieux-Marché, **rue du Gros-Horloge** leads east towards the cathedral. Just across the intersection with rue Jeanne-d'Arc you come to the **Gros Horloge** itself. A colourful one-handed clock, it used to be on the adjacent Gothic **belfry** until it was moved down by popular demand in 1529, so that people could see it better. At the time of writing restoration work was in progress, but when it is complete you should be able to pay a small fee to climb up rather too many steps to see its workings and, if the sponginess of the lead roofing agrees with your nerves, totter around the top for a marvellous view of the old city.

Despite the addition of all sorts of different towers, spires and vertical extensions, the **Cathédrale de Notre Dame** (March–Oct Mon–Sat 9am–7pm, Sun 8am–6pm; rest of year Mon–Sat 9am–6pm, Sun 8am–6pm) remains at heart the Gothic masterpiece that was built in the twelfth and thirteenth centuries. The west façade of the cathedral, intricately sculpted like the rest of the exterior, was Monet's subject for over thirty studies of changing light, which now hang in the Musée d'Orsay in Paris (see p.140). Monet might not recognize it now, however – in the last few years, it's been scrubbed a gleaming white, free from the centuries of accreted dirt he so carefully recorded. Inside, the carvings of the misericords in the choir provide a study of fifteenth-century life – in secular scenes of work and habits along with the usual mythical beasts. The **ambulatory** and **crypt** – closed on Sundays and during services – hold the assorted tombs of various recumbent royalty, stretching back as far as Duke Rollo, who died "enfeebled by toil" in 933 AD, and the eponymous heart of Richard the Lionheart.

Unfortunately, a violent storm in late December 1999 detached one of the four greenish supports of the nineteenth-century iron spire of the central lantern tower, which fell, piercing the roof of the cathedral itself and destroying a section of the medieval choir stalls below. Repairing that damage forms yet another part of the immense ongoing task of restoring the cathedral as a whole.

St-Ouen and around

The **church of St-Ouen**, next to the Hôtel de Ville (which itself occupies buildings that were once part of the abbey), is larger than the cathedral and has far less decoration, so from the outside there's nothing to diminish the instant impact of its vast Gothic proportions and the purity of its lines. Inside, it holds some stunning fourteenth-century stained glass, though much was destroyed during the Revolution (mid-March to Oct daily except Tues 10am–12.30pm & 2–6pm; rest of year Wed, Sat & Sun 10am–12.30pm & 2–4.30pm; closed mid-Dec to mid-Jan). The world that produced it – and, nearer the end of the era, the light and grace of the **church of St-Maclou** not far to the south – was one of mass death from the Plague: thus the **Aître St-Maclou** immediately to the east, a cemetery for the victims, was an integral part of the St-Maclou complex (daily 8am–8pm; entrance between 184 & 186 rue Martainville; free). It's now the tranquil garden courtyard of the Fine Arts school, but if you examine the one open lower storey of the surrounding buildings you'll discover the original deathly decorations and a mummified cat. In the square outside are several good antique bookshops, and a few art shops.

Just past the Hôtel de Ville, the **Musée des Antiquités**, which occupies a seventeenth-century convent on rue Beauvoisine (Mon & Wed–Sat 10am–12.15pm & 1.30–5.30pm, Sun 2–6pm; 20F/€3.05), is also worth a look: its tapestries and Middle Ages collection are particularly good.

The **rue Eau de Robec**, which runs east from rue Damiette just south of St-Ouen, was described by one of Flaubert's characters in an earlier age as a "degraded little Venice". It's now a textbook example of how Rouen has been restored. Where once a shallow stream flowed beneath the raised doorsteps of venerable half-timbered houses, a thin trickle now makes its way along a stylized cement bed crossed by concrete walkways. It remains an attractive ensemble, if a rather ersatz one, and the houses themselves are now predominantly inhabited by antique dealers, interspersed with the odd café.

The Musée des Beaux-Arts and around

Rouen's imposing **Musée des Beaux-Arts** commands the square Verdrel from just east of the central rue Jeanne d'Arc (daily except Tues 10am–6pm; 20F/€3.05). Even this grand edifice is not quite large enough to display some of its medieval tapestries, which trail inelegantly along the floor, but the collection as a whole is consistently absorbing. Unexpected highlights include dazzling Russian icons from the sixteenth century onwards, and an entertaining three-dimensional eighteenth-century Nativity from Naples. Many of the biggest names among the painters – Caravaggio, Velázquez, Rubens – tend to be represented by a single minor work, but there are several Monets, including a *Rouen Cathedral* from 1894, and a *Vue Générale de Rouen*. The central sculpture court, roofed over but very light, is dominated by a wonderful three-part mural of the course of the Seine from Paris to Le Havre, prepared by Raoul Dufy in 1937 for the Palais de Chaillot in Paris.

Rouen's history as a centre for *faïencerie*, or earthenware pottery, is recorded in the **Musée de la Céramique**, facing the Beaux-Arts from the north (daily except Tues 10am–1pm & 2–6pm; 15F/€2.29). A series of beautiful rooms, some of which incorporate sixteenth-century wood panelling rescued from a demolished nunnery of St-Amand, display specimens from the seventeenth century onwards. Assorted tiles and plates reflect the eighteenth-century craze for *chinoiserie*, although the genuine Chinese and Japanese pieces nearby possess a sophistication contemporary French craftsmen could only dream of emulating. The mood changes abruptly in the Revolutionary era, as witnessed by plates bearing slogans from both sides of the political fence.

Behind the Beaux-Arts, housed in the old and barely altered church of St-Laurent on rue Jacques-Villon, the **Musée Le Secq des Tournelles** (daily except Tues 10am–1pm & 2–6pm; 15F/€2.29) consists of a brilliant collection of wrought-iron objects of all dates and descriptions, among them nutcrackers and door knockers, spiral staircases that lead nowhere and hideous implements of torture.

The Tour Jeanne d'Arc

The pencil-thin **Tour Jeanne d'Arc** (April–Sept Mon & Wed–Sat 10am–12.30pm & 2–6pm, Sun 2–6.30pm; rest of year Mon & Wed–Sat 10am–12.30pm & 2–5pm, Sun 2–5.30pm; 10F/€1.52), a short way southeast of the *gare SNCF* at the junction of rue du Donjon and rue du Cordier, is all that remains of the castle of Philippe-Auguste, built in 1205 and scene of the imprisonment and trial of Joan of Arc. It served as the castle's keep and entrance-way, and was itself fully surrounded by a moat. It was not however Joan's actual prison – that was the Tour de la Pucelle, demolished in 1809 – while the trial took place first of all in the castle's St-Romain chapel, and then later in its great central hall, both of which were destroyed in 1590.

The tall, sharp-pointed tower was bought by public subscription in 1860, and restored to its present state. After seeing a small collection of Joan-related memorabilia, you can climb a steep spiral staircase to the very top, but you can't see out over the city, let alone step outside into the open air.

Eating and drinking

Unlike the hotels, which sometimes have cheaper weekend rates, Rouen's upmarket **restaurants** tend to charge more over weekends, when families eat out. The greatest concentration of restaurants is in place du Vieux-Marché, where there's a daily **food market**, while the area just north is full of Tunisian **takeaways**, **crêperies** and so forth. Some of Rouen's most agreeable **bars** are in the maze of streets between rue Thiers and place du Vieux-Marché. Incoming sailors used to head straight for this area of the city, and the small bars are still there even if the sailors aren't.

Restaurants

Brasserie Paul, 1 place de la Cathédrale (☎02.35.71.86.07). The definitive address for Rouen's definitive bistro, an attractive Belle-Époque place with seating both indoors and on a terrace in full view of the cathedral. Daily lunch specials, such as the goat's cheese and smoked duck salad that was Simone de Beauvoir's regular favourite in the 1930s, cost around 60F/€9.15.

des Beaux Arts, 34 rue Damiette (☎02.35.70.17.15). Very good-value Algerian restaurant, set on a pretty pedestrianized street north of St-Maclou church. Couscous from 50F/€7.62 or tagine from 68F/€10.37, with all kinds of sausages and assorted meats. Closed Mon.

Flunch, 60 rue des Carmes (☎02.35.71.81.81). Large and good self-service on a street running north from the cathedral, with many fresh dishes and a 43F/€6.56 daily *formule*. Daily 11am–10pm.

Gill, 9 quai de la Bourse (☎02.35.71.16.14). Absolutely classic French restaurant, chosen eleven years in a row as the best in the province by a local magazine on account of such specialities as lobster grilled with asparagus and pigeon baked in puff pastry. Weekday lunches start at 185F/€28.20, while the cheapest dinner menu will set you back 220F/€33.54. Closed Sun & Mon June–Sept, otherwise Sun evening & Mon.

Gill, Le Bistrot du Chef . . . en Gare, 1st floor, gare Rive Droite (☎02.35.71.41.15). This bistro in the main train station, run under the auspices of the city's top chef, is a true marvel. There's an excellent self-service cafeteria downstairs, while the more formal dining room upstairs is open for lunch only, with set menus from 89F/€13.57. Closed Mon evening, Sat lunch, Sun & Aug.

Jumbo, 11 rue Guillaume-le-Conquerant (☎02.35.70.35.88). Another good self-service, off the northeast corner of place du Vieux-Marché. Put together your own large salad for under 25F/€3.81, or choose from a variety of cooked dishes. Daily 11.15am–2.30pm & 6.30–9.30pm.

Les Maraichers – Le Bistrot d'Adrien, 37 place du Vieux-Marché (☎02.35.71.57.73). Deservedly the most popular of the Vieux-Marché's many restaurants, with a streetside terrace right in front of the St-Jeanne church. Styled to resemble a *fin-de-siècle* Parisian bistro, serving varied set menus until 11pm nightly and à la carte until midnight. Menus start at 89F/€13.57, with lots of *andouillettes*, snails and tongues, but plenty of wholesome possibilities too, and great desserts.

Le Marmite, 3 rue de Florence (☎02.35.71.55.55). Romantic little place just west of the place du Vieux-Marché, which offers beautiful, elegantly presented gourmet dishes on well-priced menus at 115F/€17.53, 165F/€25.15 (featuring delicious hot oysters) and 250F/€38.11. Closed Sun evening & Mon.

Le P'tit Bec, 182 rue Eau de Robec (☎02.35.07.63.33). Friendly brasserie-cum-tearoom that has become Rouen's most popular lunch spot, with a simple 75F/€11.43 menu. They also serve afternoon tea. There's seating both indoors and outside, on the pedestrianized street, beside the running water and in view of a fine blue half-timbered mansion next door. The only evenings it's open are Fri & Sat; closed all day Sun.

Bars

Le Bateau Ivre, 17 rue des Sapins (☎02.35.70.09.05). Low-key but atmospheric hangout, with wooden tables, which puts on a mostly rock-oriented programme of music and performance, with an open-mike night on Thursdays that attracts lovers of traditional French chansons. Tues & Wed until 2am, Thurs–Sat until 4am. Closed Sun, Mon & Aug.

Big Ben Pub, 95 rue du Gros-Horloge (☎02.35.88.44.50). Right under the big clock – hence the name – this always-packed bar is strictly speaking entered from a side street, at 30 rue des Vergetiers. Usually as crowded inside as is the street outside. Mon–Sat noon–2am.

Le Café Curieux, rue des Fossés Louis VIII (☎02.35.71.20.83). Incredibly loud and hectic bar, where Rouen's beautiful mingle to a techno and drum 'n' bass soundtrack, while cult and avant-garde videos flicker on all sides.

Exo 7, 13 place des Chartreux (☎02.35.03.32.30). Traditionally the centre of Rouen's heavy-rock scene, a long way south of the centre, the *Exo 7* (pronounced "Exocet") is these days becoming a bit more eclectic, with the odd techno dance night as well. Wed–Sat 10.30pm–4am.

La Luna, 26 rue St-Étienne-des-Tonneliers (☎02.35.88.77.18). Glamorous late-night club that specializes in all things South American, with steamy salsa dancing most nights. Thurs–Sat 7pm–4am.

La Taverne St-Amant, 11 rue St-Amant (☎02.35.88.51.34). Popular bar serving draught Guinness and bistro meals, off rue de la République above the cathedral.

Le Traxx, 4 bd Ferdinand-de-Lesseps (☎02.32.10.12.02). Rouen's top gay club offers a regular diet of house and techno to a flamboyant clientele that loves to go wild on a special occasion. Fri & Sat 11pm–4am.

XXL, 25–27 rue de la Savonnerie (☎02.35.88.84.00). Gay bar that's a premier clubbing rendezvous. Stays open all night Sat to serve breakfast on Sun. Closed Mon.

Entertainment

As you would expect in a conurbation of 400,000, there's always plenty going on in Rouen, from classical concerts in churches to alternative events in community and commercial centres. An annual handbook, *Le P'tit Normand*, available in all newsagents, is helpful with addresses and telephone numbers. For current events, pick up the free *Cette Semaine à Rouen* from the tourist office.

Rouen has several **theatres**, which mainly work to winter seasons. The most highbrow and big-spectacle is the **Théâtre des Arts**, 7 rue de Dr Rambert (☎02.35.71.41.36), which puts on opera, ballet and concerts. The more adventurous repertory company of the **Théâtre des Deux Rives** (☎02.35.70.22.82), based opposite the Musee des Antiquités at the top end of rue Louis Ricard (no. 48; happily at the junction with rue de Joyeuse), presents work by playwrights such as Beaumarchais, Shakespeare, Beckett and Gorky.

Major concerts often take place in the **Théâtre Duchamp-Villon** in the St-Sever complex (☎02.35.62.31.31). Also south of the river, but a long way further out, are **Théâtre Charles Dullin**, allée des Arcades, Grand Quévilly (☎02.35.68.48.91), and **Théâtre Maxime Gorki**, rue François Mitterand, Petit Quévilly (☎02.35.72.67.55), which specializes in contemporary and traditional music from around Europe.

Upstream from Rouen

Upstream from Rouen towards Paris, high cliffs on the north bank of the Seine imitate the coast, looking down on waves of green and scattered river islands. By the time you reach **Les Andelys**, 25km southeast of Rouen, you're within 100km of the capital, meaning that accommodation and eating prices tend to be geared towards affluent weekend and day-trippers. Large country estates abound in this agreeable countryside, and public transport is minimal – it's assumed any visitor has, if not a residence, then at least a car. However, infrequent buses run from Rouen to Les Andelys, and trains from Rouen call at **Vernon**, just across the river from one of Normandy's most-visited tourist attractions, the village of **Giverny**.

Les Andelys

The most dramatic sight anywhere along the Seine has to be Richard the Lionheart's **Château Gaillard**, perched high above **LES ANDELYS**. Constructed in a position of impregnable power, it looked down over any movement on the river at the frontier of the English king's domains. It was built in less than a year (1196–97) and might have survived intact had Henri IV not ordered its destruction in 1603. As it is, the dominant outline remains. Visits to the château are permitted between mid-March and mid-November only (Mon & Thurs–Sun 10am–noon & 2–6pm, Wed 2–6pm; 18F/€2.74). On foot, you can make the steep climb up via a path that leads off rue Richard Coeur-de-Lion in Petit Andely. The only route for motorists is extraordinarily convoluted, following a long-winded one-way system that starts opposite the church in Grand Andely.

The **tourist office** for Les Andelys is at 24 rue Philippe-Auguste in Petit Andely (May–Sept Mon–Fri 9.30am–12.30pm & 2.30–6pm, Sat 9.30am–12.30pm & 2.30–5pm, Sun 10am–noon & 2–5pm; rest of year daily 2–5.30pm; ☎02.32.54.41.93). The nicest places to **stay** are the eighteenth-century *Chaîne d'Or* hotel, opposite the thirteenth-century church of St-Sauveur at 27 rue Grande (☎02.32.54.00.31; ⑤; closed Jan, Sun evening, Mon & Tues lunch), and the *Normandie* at 1 rue Grande (☎02.32.54.10.52; ②; closed Dec; restaurant closed Wed evening & Thurs), both on the banks of the Seine. There's also a lovely riverside **campsite**, far below the château, the *Île des Trois Rois* (☎02.32.54.23.79; closed Nov–March).

Giverny

Roughly 15km south of the ancient fortifications of Les Andelys, on the north bank of the river, you come to **Monet's house and gardens** – complete with water-lily pond – at **GIVERNY** (April–Oct Tues–Sun 10am–6pm; last ticket sold 5.30pm, no advance sales; house and gardens 35F/€5.34, gardens only 25F/€3.81). Monet lived here from 1883 till his death in 1926, and the gardens that he laid out were considered by many of his friends to be his masterpiece. In fact art lovers who make the pilgrimage here tend to be outnumbered by garden enthusiasts. None of Monet's original paintings are on display – most are in the Orangerie and Musée d'Orsay in Paris – whereas the gardens are still lovingly tended in all their glory.

You enter the house through the huge studio, built in 1915, where Monet painted his last and largest canvases depicting water lilies (in French, *nymphéas*). It now serves as a well-stocked book and gift shop, albeit disappointingly short of good-quality reproductions of the famous works. A gravel footpath leads from there to the actual house, a long two-storey structure facing down to the river. Monet's bedroom is bedecked with family photos and paintings by friends and family, while his salon holds further washed-out reproductions. All other main rooms are crammed floor-to-ceiling with his collection of Japanese prints, especially works by Hokusai and Hiroshige. Most of the original furnishings are gone, but you do get a real sense of how the dining room used to be, with all its walls and fittings painted a glorious bright yellow; Monet designed his own yellow crockery to harmonize with the surroundings. By contrast, the stairs and upstairs rooms are a pale blue.

Colourful flower gardens, with trellised walkways and shady bowers, stretch down from the house. At the bottom, a dank underpass beneath the road leads to the *jardin d'eau*, focused around the narrow **water-lily pond**. Footpaths around the perimeter, as well of course as arching Japanese footbridges, offer differing views of the water lilies themselves, cherished by gardeners in rowing boats. May and June, when the rhododendrons flower around the pond, and the wisteria that winds over the Japanese bridge is in bloom, are the best times to visit. Whenever you come, however, you'll have to contend with camera-happy crowds jostling to capture their own impressions of the water lilies.

A few minutes' walk up Giverny's village street, the **Musée d'Art Américain** is an unattractive edifice that hides a spacious and well-lit gallery devoted to American artists resident in France between 1865 and 1915 (April–Oct Tues–Sun 10am–6pm; 35F/€5.34). Some took their admiration of Monet to a point that now seems embarrassing, painting many of the same scenes, but there are some interesting works by John Singer Sargent, Winslow Homer and, especially, Mary Cassatt.

Giverny's one **hotel**, the *Musardière*, stands not far beyond Monet's house at 123 rue Claude-Monet (☎02.32.21.03.18; ④); dinner menus in its restaurant start at 145F/€22.11. There's also a pleasant little tearoom and **restaurant**, *Les Nymphéas* (☎02.32.21.20.31), opposite the house itself. The nearest inexpensive accommodation is the *Hôtel d'Évreux*, 11 place d'Évreux (☎02.32.21.16.12; ③), in the heart of **VERNON**, across the river, a fine seventeenth-century town house offering good food and comfortable accommodation.

To reach the gardens from the **gare SNCF** in Vernon, either rent a bike or catch the connecting bus.

BASSE NORMANDIE

As you head west along the coast of Basse Normandie from Le Havre, a succession of somewhat smug and exclusive resorts – of which only **Honfleur** is especially memorable – is followed first by the beaches where the Allied armies landed in 1944, and then by the wilder, and in some places deserted, shore around the **Cotentin Peninsula**. There are two absolutely unmissable sights – the glorious island abbey of **Mont St-Michel** and the **Bayeux Tapestry**.

The Norman Riviera

The only section of the Norman coast to have any serious delusions of grandeur is the stretch that lies immediately West of the mouth of the Seine. The new **Pont de Normandie** across the river estuary from Le Havre is starting to make such places as **Trouville** and **Deauville** too hectic for comfort, though only **Honfleur** could be said to have all that much to lose.

Honfleur

HONFLEUR, the best-preserved of the old ports of Normandy and the first you come to on the eastern Calvados coast, is a near-perfect seaside town that lacks only a beach. It used to have one, but with the accumulation of silt from the Seine the sea has steadily withdrawn, leaving the eighteenth-century waterfront houses of **boulevard Charles-V** stranded and a little surreal. The ancient port, however, still functions – the channel to the beautiful Vieux Bassin is kept open by regular dredging – and though only pleasure craft now use the moorings in the harbour basin, fishing boats tie up alongside the pier nearby, and you can usually buy fish either directly from the boats or from stands on the pier, still by right run by fishermen's wives.

Honfleur is highly picturesque, and has been moving upmarket at an ever greater rate since the opening of the Pont de Normandie. Despite now being just a few minutes' drive from the giant metropolis of Le Havre, however, the old port still feels not so very different to the fishing village that appealed so greatly to artists in the second half of the nineteenth century.

Arrival and information

Honfleur's **gare routière**, just to the east of the Vieux Bassin, is served by over a dozen direct daily **buses** from Caen (#20), and up to eight express services from Le Havre (Bus Verts; ☎02.31.89.28.41). The nearest **train station** is at Pont l'Évêque, connected to Honfleur by the Lisieux bus (#50) – a twenty-minute ride.

The **tourist office** adjoins the glass-fronted *mediathèque* on quai Le Paulmier, just east of the town centre (Easter to mid-July & Sept Mon–Sat 9.30am–12.30pm & 2–6.30pm, Sun 10am–5pm; mid-July to Aug Mon–Sat 9.30am–7pm, Sun 10am–5pm; rest of year Mon–Sat 9am–noon & 2–5.30pm; ☎02.31.89.23.30). Ask about their summer programme of **guided tours** of the town, which range from two-hour walkabouts to full-day excursions including meals.

Accommodation

If finding budget **accommodation** is one of your main priorities, it probably makes sense for you not to stay in Honfleur at all, and simply to visit for the day. Especially on summer weekends, so many visitors turn up that even the most ordinary hotel can get away with charging rates well above the average for Normandy. No hotels overlook the harbour itself.

HOTELS

des Cascades, 17 place Thiers (☎02.31.89.05.83, fax 02.31.89.32.13). Large hotel-restaurant offering slightly noisy rooms upstairs, and a good-value, if not all that exciting, restaurant with outdoor seating on two sides; menus climb upwards from 75F/€11.43. Closed Mon evening, Tues out of season & Dec–Feb. ②.

du Dauphin, 10 place Berthelot (☎02.31.89.15.53, fax 02.31.89.92.06). Grey-slate town house just around the corner from Ste-Catherine church, with a wide assortment of rooms. Closed Jan. ④–⑦.

Le Hamelin, 16 place Hamelin (☎02.31.89.16.25). Five basic rooms, some with showers, in a plain building very near the Lieutenance in the liveliest part of town. The restaurant downstairs has standard seafood menus from 80F/€12.20, and manages to squeeze a few tables onto the street. ②–④.

Motel Monet, Charrière du Puits (☎02.31.89.00.90, fax 02.31.89.97.16, *www.motelmonet.fr*). Not quite a motel, but the modern rooms are arranged around a courtyard, so parking is easy, in a very quiet location ten minutes' walk from the centre. ④.

La Salle des Fêtes, 8 place Albert-Sorel (☎02.31.89.19.69). Clean, well-priced rooms above a friendly family-run bar a short walk inland along the main road from the Vieux Bassin. ②.

CAMPSITE

Camping du Phare, place Jean-de-Vienne (☎02.31.89.10.26). Two-star campsite at the western end of bd Charles-V. Closed Oct to mid-March.

The Town

Visitors to Honfleur inevitably gravitate towards the old centre, around the **Vieux Bassin**. At the *bassin*, slate-fronted houses, each of them one or two storeys higher than seems possible, harmonize – despite their tottering and ill-matched forms – into a backdrop that is only excelled by the **Lieutenance** at the harbour entrance. This latter was the dwelling of the king's lieutenant, and has been the gateway to the inner town at least since 1608, when Samuel Champlain sailed from Honfleur to found Québec. The **church of St-Étienne** nearby is now the **Musée de la Marine**, which combines a collection of model ships with several rooms of antique Norman furnishings (April–June & Sept Tues–Sun 10am–noon & 2–6pm; July & Aug daily 10am–1pm & 2–6.30pm; Oct to mid-Nov & mid-Feb to March Tues–Fri 2–5.30pm, Sat & Sun 10am–noon & 2–5.30pm; 15F/€2.29). Just behind it, two seventeenth-century **salt stores**, used to contain the precious commodity during the days of the much-hated *gabelle*, or salt tax, now serve as the **Musée d'Ethnographie et d'Art Populaire Normand** (same hours; 15F/€2.29, or combined with Musée de la Marine 25F/€3.81), filled with everyday artefacts from old Honfleur.

Honfleur's artistic past – and its present concentration of galleries and painters – owes most to Eugène Boudin, forerunner of Impressionism. He was born and worked in the town, trained the 15-year-old Monet and was joined for various periods by Pissarro, Renoir and Cézanne. At the same time, Baudelaire paid visits to the town, which was also home to the composer Erik Satie. There's a fair selection of Boudin's works in the **Musée Eugène Boudin**, west of the port on place Erik-Satie (mid-Feb to mid-March & Oct–Dec Mon & Wed–Fri 2.30–5pm, Sat & Sun 10am–noon & 2.30–5pm; mid-March to Sept daily except Tues 10am–noon & 2–6pm; 26F/€3.96), and his crayon seascapes in particular are quite appealing here in context, though the Dufys, Marquets, Frieszes and, above all, the Monets are the most impressive paintings on show.

Admission also gives you access to one of Monet's subjects featured in the museum, the detached belfry of the **church of Ste-Catherine** (daily 9am–6pm). The church and belfry are built almost entirely of wood – supposedly due to economic restraints after the Hundred Years War. The church itself makes a change from the great stone Norman churches, and has the added peculiarity of being divided into twin naves, with one balcony running around both. From **rue de l'Homme-de-Bois** behind you can see yacht masts through the houses overlooking the *bassin* and, in the distance, the huge industrial panorama of Le Havre's docks.

Just down the hill from the Musée Boudin, at 67 bd Charles-V, is **Les Maisons Satie** (daily except Tues: mid-June to mid-Sept 10am–7pm; rest of year 10.30am–6pm; closed Jan; 30F/€4.57), the red-timbered house of Érik Satie. From the outside it looks unchanged since the composer was born there in 1866. Step inside, however, and you'll find yourself in Normandy's most unusual and enjoyable museum. As befits a close associate of the Surrealists, Satie is commemorated by all sorts of weird interactive surprises. It would be a shame to give too many of them away here; suffice it to say that you're immediately confronted by a giant pear, bouncing into the air on huge wings to the strains of his best-known piano piece, *Gymnopédies*. You also get to see a filmed reconstruction of *Parade*, a ballet on which Satie collaborated with Picasso, Stravinsky and Cocteau, which created a furore in Paris in 1917.

Eating

With its abundance of day-trippers and hotel guests, Honfleur supports an astonishing number of **restaurants**, most specializing in seafood. Surprisingly few face onto the harbour itself; the narrow buildings around the edge seem to be better suited to being snack bars, crêperies, cafés and ice-cream parlours.

L'Absinthe, 10 quai de la Quarantaine (☎02.31.89.39.00). Imaginative restaurant housed in an eighteenth-century mansion just around the corner from the *bassin*. Such dishes as scallop carpaccio or foie gras in ginger nestle on menus that range from 175F/€26.68 to a seven-course 380F/€57.93 extravaganza. Closed mid-Nov to Dec.

Auberge de la Lieutenance, 12 place Ste-Catherine (☎02.31.89.07.52). Not in fact by the Lieutenance, despite the name. Plenty of outdoor seating on the cobbled pedestrian square, facing both church and belfry. Gourmet dining with a heavy emphasis on oysters; menus start at 120F/€18.29. Closed Sun evening & mid-Nov to Dec.

Au P'tit Mareyeur, 4 rue Haute (☎02.31.98.84.23). No distance from the centre, but all the seating is indoors and there are no views. Very good fish dishes – red crab soup with garlic – plus plenty of creamy pays d'Auge sauces and superb desserts. The main menu, at 125F/€19.06, includes skate marinated in coriander; for a 40F/€6.10 supplement you can also enjoy warm oysters. Closed Mon & Tues.

Taverne de la Mer, 35 rue Haute (☎02.31.89.57.77). Small converted bar, with no outdoor seating, but a magnificent selection of fresh seafood. The main set menu, at 125F/€19.06, consists almost entirely of fish, though there is a token "*pièce de viande*"; you can also get a large *assiette de fruits de mer* for a similar price, or lesser menus at 75F/€11.43 and 95F/€14.48. Closed Mon & Tues lunch.

La Tortue, 36 rue de l'Homme de Bois (☎02.31.98.87.91). A welcoming place near the Musée Boudin, where 100F/€15.24 buys a great-value five-course meal; there's also a 77F/€11.74 vegetarian menu, consisting of apple soup or vegetables followed by cheese or salad. Closed Tues & mid-Jan to mid-Feb.

Le Vieux Honfleur, 13 quai St-Étienne (☎02.31.89.15.31). The best of the restaurants around the harbour itself, with spacious alfresco dining – in shade at lunchtime – on its pedestrianized eastern side. Very simple menus, but the seafood is very good, as befits prices starting at 175F/€26.68. Closed Jan.

Trouville and Deauville

Heading west along the corniche from Honfleur, green fields and fruit trees lull the land's edge, and cliffs rise from sandy beaches all the way to Trouville, 15km away. The resorts aren't exactly cheap but they're relatively undeveloped, and if you want to stop along the coast this is the place to do it. The next stretch, from Trouville to Cabourg, is what you might call the Riviera of Normandy with Trouville as "Nice" and Deauville as "Cannes", within a stone's throw of each other.

TROUVILLE retains some semblance of a real town, with a constant population and industries other than tourism. But it is still a resort, with a tangle of busy pedestrian streets just back from the beach that are alive with restaurants and hotels. It has been a chic destination ever since the imperial jackass Napoléon III started bringing his court here every summer in the 1860s. One of his dukes, looking across the river, saw, instead of marshlands, money – and lots of it, in the form of a racetrack. His vision materialized, and villas appeared between the racetrack and the sea to become **DEAUVILLE**. Now you can lose money on the horses, cross five streets and lose more in the casino, then lose yourself across 200m of sports and "cure" facilities and private swimming huts before reaching the *planches*, 500m of boardwalk, beyond which rows of primary-coloured parasols obscure the view of the sea.

Practicalities

Trouville and Deauville share their **gare SNCF** and **gare routière**, in between the two just south of the marina. Each day, seven of the hourly buses from Caen continue along the coast to Honfleur. Visits to the **tourist office** on place de la Mairie in Deauville (Mon–Sat 9am–12.30pm & 2–6.30pm, Sun 11am–4pm; ☎02.31.14.40.00, *www.deauville.org*), or the one at 32 quai F. Moureaux in Trouville (April–June, Sept & Oct Mon–Sat 9.30am–noon & 2–6.30pm, Sun 10.30am–12.30pm; July & Aug Mon–Sat 9.30am–7pm, Sun 10am–4pm; rest of year Mon–Sat 9.30am–noon & 2–6pm, Sun 10.30am–12.30pm; ☎02.31.14.60.70, *ot.trouville@wanadoo.fr*), are repaid with the usual lavish brochures.

As you might imagine, **hotels** tend to be either luxurious or overpriced. The *Café-Hôtel des Sports*, 27 rue Gambetta (☎02.31.88.22.67; ③; closed Sun in winter), behind

Deauville's fish market, is the least expensive, while *Le Trouville*, 1 rue Thiers (☎02.31.98.45.48; ③; closed Jan), is Trouville's closest equivalent. If you fancy staying right on the seafront, it's hard to beat the *Flaubert*, rue Gustave-Flaubert (☎02.31.88.37.23; ④), a grand faux-timbered mansion at the start of Trouville's boardwalk, which is home to the recommended *Le Vivier* restaurant. Trouville also has a **campsite**, *Le Chant des Oiseaux* (☎02.31.88.06.42; closed Oct–March).

A good place to **eat** in Deauville is *Chez Miocque* at 81 rue Eugène-Colas (☎02.31.88.09.52), a top-quality Parisian-style bistro with prices that are high but not outrageous. Trouville has some good fish restaurants including *Les Vapeurs*, opposite the attractive old half-timbered fish market at 160 bd F. Moureaux (☎02.31.88.15.24), and *La Petite Auberge*, 7 rue Carnot (☎02.31.88.11.07; closed Tues & Wed in winter), though both get very crowded at weekends.

Deauville's **American Film Festival**, held in the first week of September, is the antithesis of Cannes, with public admission to a wide selection of previews.

Houlgate

A hundred years ago, **HOULGATE**, 15km west of Deauville, was every bit as glamorous and sophisticated a destination as its neighbours. What makes it different today is that it has barely changed since then. Its long straight beach remains lined by a stately procession of Victorian villas, with the town's handful of commercial enterprises confined to the narrow parallel street, the **rue des Bains**, fifty metres inland. As a result, Houlgate is the most relaxed of the local resorts, ideal if you're looking for a peaceful family break where the only stress is deciding whether to paddle or play mini-golf.

Houlgate's **tourist office** is well back from the sea on boulevard des Belges (mid-June to mid-Sept Mon–Sat 9am–7pm, Sun 9am–12.30pm & 2–7pm; rest of year Mon–Sat 9am–12.30pm & 2–6.30pm; ☎02.31.24.34.79, *houlgate@wanadoo.fr*). The *Hostellerie Normandie*, just off the rue des Bains at 11 rue E.-Deschanel (☎02.31.28.77.77; ③; closed mid-Oct to mid-March, plus Mon evening & Tues in low season), is a pretty little **hotel** covered with ivy and creeping flowers, with a 65F/€9.91 lunch menu on which you can follow half a dozen oysters with a plate of *moules frites*. Above the Vaches Noires (Black Cows) cliffs on the corniche road east of town, *La Ferme Auberge des Aulnettes* (☎02.31.28.00.28; ③; closed Jan, plus Tues evening & Wed in low season), is a lovely country house set in pleasant gardens, with a good restaurant and room to sit outside in the evening. The best **campsite** in the area, the four-star *Les Falaises* (☎02.31.24.81.09; closed Nov–March), is close at hand.

Dives and Cabourg

DIVES, the port from which William the Conqueror sailed for Hastings, is another 3km west from Houlgate, though like Honfleur it's now pushed well back from the sea. A lively Saturday **market** focuses around the ancient oak *halles*, whose steep tiled roof must be five times the height of its walls; on market days, it's crammed with mouthwatering delicacies and Norman specialities. Dives is also home to an inexpensive **hotel**, the *Hôtel de la Gare* at 10 pace Trefouet (☎02.31.91.24.52; ②; closed Dec & Jan).

At the much newer town of **CABOURG**, across the mouth of the Dives river, the *fin-de-siècle* streets of the town centre fan out in perfect symmetry from what must be the straightest promenade in France, with semi-circular avenues linking them together. The resort, contemporary with Deauville, seems to be stuck in the nineteenth century – immobilized by Proust, perhaps, who wrote for a while in the **Grand Hôtel**, one of an outrageous ensemble of buildings around the **Jardins du Casino**. The **tourist office** in the Jardins du Casino has full details on hotels (July & Aug daily 9.30am–7pm; rest of year Mon–Sat 9.30am–12.30pm & 2–6.30pm, Sun 10am–12.30pm & 2.30–6pm; ☎02.31.91.20.00, *www.cabourg.net*). A pleasant **place to stay and eat** is *L'Oie qui Fume*, 18 av de la Brèche-Buhot (☎02.31.91.27.79; ③; closed Jan to mid-Feb, plus Mon evening, Tues & Wed in low season), 100m back from the sea on a quiet road half a dozen streets west of the centre; its 138F/€21.04 menu features goose (*oie*) as either starter or main course.

Caen

CAEN, capital and largest city of Basse Normandie, is not a place where you'll want to spend much time: in the months of fighting in 1944, it was devastated. Nonetheless, the city that nine hundred years ago was the favoured residence of William the Conqueror remains – in parts – impressive.

Its central feature is a ring of ramparts that no longer have a castle to protect, and, though there are the scattered spires and buttresses of two abbeys and eight old churches, roads and roundabouts fill the wide spaces where prewar houses stood. Approaches are along thunderous dual carriageways through industrial suburbs now prospering once more following an influx of high-tech newcomers.

Arrival and information

The **gare SNCF** is 1km south of the town centre, with the **gare routière** so close that you can walk directly to it from platform 1. The Brittany Ferries service from Portsmouth, promoted as sailing to Caen, in fact docks at Ouistreham, 15km north (see p.360); buses from the *gare routière* connect with each sailing. CTAC, the extensive local **bus** service (☎02.31.15.55.50), makes a one-way circuit between the "Tour le Roi" stop, north of the pleasure port, and the *gare SNCF*, heading north up avenue du 6-Juin and south down rue St-Jean.

Caen's **tourist office** is across the street from the church of St-Pierre in the beautiful sixteenth-century Hôtel d'Escoville at 14 place St-Pierre (July & Aug Mon–Sat 10am–7pm, Sun 10am–1pm & 2–5pm; rest of year Mon–Sat 10am–1pm & 2–6pm, Sun 10am–1pm; ☎02.31.27.14.14, *www.ville-caen.fr*); for details of forthcoming events, pick up a copy of their free weekly *Caen Scope*. The main **post office** is on place Gambetta (Mon–Fri 8am–7pm, Sat 8am–noon).

Accommodation

Caen has a great number of **hotels**, though, as ever in the bomb-damaged cities of Normandy, few could be called attractive. The main concentrations are near the *gare SNCF*, around the pleasure port and just west of the castle and tourist office. With plenty of dedicated restaurants in town, few hotels other than those specifically mentioned below bother to provide food.

Hotels

Bernières, 50 rue de Bernières (☎02.31.86.01.26, fax 02.31.86.51.76, *www.hotelbernieres.com*). Bright, central and very good-value hotel, halfway between the churches of St-Pierre and St-Jean. ②.
des Cordeliers, 4 rue des Cordeliers (☎02.31.86.37.15, fax 02.31.39.56.51). Friendly hotel with a wide range of rooms, in small side street near the castle. Has a bar but no restaurant. Closed Sun. ②.
Courtonne, place Courtonne (☎02.31.93.47.83, fax 02.31.93.50.50). Very welcoming modernized hotel overlooking the pleasure port, that's so narrow it's easy to miss. All rooms have bath or shower, phone and TV. ③.

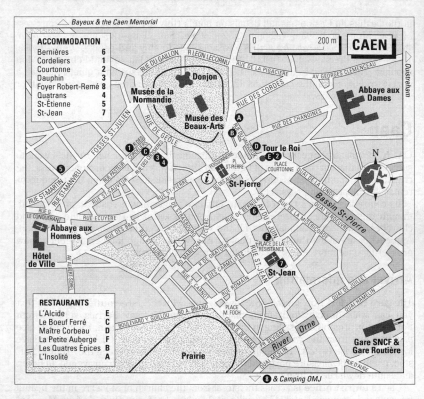

Hôtel-Restaurant le Dauphin, 29 rue Gémare (☎02.31.86.22.26, fax 02.31.86.35.14, *dauphin.caen@wanadoo.fr*). Upmarket central Best Western hotel, tucked away behind the tourist office. Part of it was a priory during the eighteenth century, not that you'd ever guess; the rooms are comfortable without being exciting. Has a grand restaurant, with a 110F/€16.77 weekday menu; weekend menus 175F/€26.68 and 260F/€39.64. Closed Sat & mid-July to early Aug. ⑤–⑨.

des Quatrans, 17 rue Gémare (☎02.31.86.25.57, fax 02.31.85.27.80, *www.hoteldesquatrans.com*). A little way behind the tourist office, but unmissable thanks to its garish neon sign. The pastel theme of the facade continues inside; some might find it all a bit cloying, but the service is friendly, and at least everything works. Cheaper rooms are without showers. ②.

St-Étienne, 2 rue de l'Académie (☎02.31.86.35.82, fax 02.31.85.57.69). Friendly budget hotel in an old stone house in the characterful St-Martin district, not far from the Abbaye des Hommes. The cheapest rooms do not have showers. ②.

St-Jean, 20 rue des Martyrs (☎02.31.86.23.35, fax 02.31.86.74.15). Simple but well-equipped rooms – all have shower or bath – facing St-Jean church near the *Petite Auberge* (see p.358). ②.

Hostel and campsite

Camping OMJ, route de Louvigny (☎02.31.72.60.92). Two-star municipal campsite near the hostel, beside the River Orne (bus #13, direction "Louvigny", stop "Camping"). Closed Oct to mid-May.

Foyer Robert-Remé, 68 bis rue E.-Restout, Grâce-de-Dieu (☎02.31.52.19.96). Lively and welcoming HI hostel, even if it is situated in an otherwise sleepy area about 500m southwest of the *gare SNCF*. Beds in both four-bed dorms or two-bed private rooms cost 62F/€9.45 per person. Take bus #17 from the town centre (stop "Tour le Roi") or *gare SNCF*, direction "Grace de Dieu", stop "Lycée Fresnil". Closed Oct–May.

The Town

A virtue has been made of the necessity of clearing away the rubble of Caen's medieval houses, which formerly pressed up against its ancient **château ramparts**. The resulting open green space means that those walls are now fully visible for the first time in centuries. In turn, walking the circuit of the ramparts gives a good overview of the city, with a particularly fine prospect of the reconstructed fourteenth-century facade of the nearby **church of St-Pierre**. Some magnificent Renaissance stonework has survived intact at the church's east end.

Within the castle walls, it's possible to visit the former **Exchequer** – which dates from shortly after the Norman conquest of England, and was the scene of a banquet thrown by Richard the Lionheart en route to the Crusades – and inspect a garden that has been replanted with the herbs and medicinal plants that were cultivated here during the Middle Ages. Also inside the precinct, though not in original structures, are two museums. Most visitors will probably prefer the **Musée des Beaux-Arts** (daily except Tues 9.30am–6pm; 25F/€3.81, free on Wed), which traces a potted history of European art from Renaissance Italy through such Dutch masters as Brueghel the Younger up to grand portraits from eighteenth-century France in the upstairs galleries. Downstairs brings things up to date with some powerful twentieth-century art, though there are few big-name works. The other museum, the **Musée de Normandie** (daily except Tues 9.30am–12.30pm & 2–6pm; 10F/€1.52, free on Wed), provides a cursory overview of Norman history, ranging from archeological finds like stone tools from the region's megalithic period and glass jewellery from Gallo-Roman Rouen up to the impact of the Industrial Revolution.

The **Abbaye aux Hommes**, at the west end of rue St-Pierre, was founded by William the Conqueror and designed to hold his tomb within the huge, austere Romanesque **church of St-Étienne** (daily 8.15am–noon & 2–7.30pm, free; 1hr 15min guided tours leave adjacent Hôtel de Ville daily 9.30am, 11am, 2.30pm & 4pm; 10F/€1.52). However, his burial here, in 1087, was hopelessly undignified. The funeral procession first caught fire and was then held to ransom, as various factions squabbled over his rotting corpse for any spoils they could grab. A further interruption came when a man halted the service to object that the grave had been constructed without compensation on the site of his family house, and the assembled nobles had to pay him off before William could be laid to rest. During the Revolution the tomb was again ransacked, and it now holds a solitary thigh-bone rescued from the river. Still, the building itself is a wonderful Romanesque monument. Adjoining the church are the abbey buildings, designed during the eighteenth century and now housing the Hôtel de Ville.

At the other end of the town centre, at the end of rue des Chanoines, is the **Abbaye aux Dames**, commissioned by William's wife Matilda in the hope of saving her soul after committing the godless sin of marrying her cousin. Her monument – the **church of La Trinité** – is even more starkly impressive than her husband's, with a gloomy pillared crypt, wonderful stained glass behind the altar and odd sculptural details like the fish curled up in the holy-water stoup. The convent buildings today house the regional council but are open to the public for free guided tours (daily 2.30pm & 4pm).

Most of the centre of Caen is taken up with busy new shopping developments and pedestrian precincts, where the cafés are distinguished by names such as Fast Food Glamour Vault. Outlets of the big Parisian stores – and of the aristocrats' grocers, Hédiard, in the cours des Halles – are here, along with good local rivals. The main city **market** takes place on Friday, spreading along both sides of Fosse St-Julien, and there's also a Sunday market in place Courtonne. The **pleasure port**, at the end of the canal which links Caen to the sea, is where most life goes on, at least in summer.

Just north of Caen, at the end of avenue Marshal-Montgomery in the Folie Couvrechef area, the **Caen Memorial** – "a museum for peace" – stands on a plateau named after General Eisenhower (daily: mid-Jan to mid-Feb & Nov–Dec daily 9am–6pm, last entry 4.45pm; mid-Feb to June, Sept & Oct 9am–7pm, last entry 5.45pm; July & Aug 9am–8pm, last entry 6.45pm; ☎02.31.06.06.44, *www.unicaen.fr/memorial*; 74F/€11.28), on a clifftop beneath which the Germans had their HQ in June and July 1944. Funds and material for it came from the US, Britain, Canada, Germany, Poland, the former Czechoslovakia, the USSR and France. The museum is a typically French high-tech, novel-architecture conception, with excellent displays divided into three sections; it's worth allowing at least two hours for a visit. The first section deals with the rise of fascism in Germany, another with resistance and collaboration in France. A third charts all the major battles of World War II, and visits culminate with three separate film documentaries. In addition, the former German bunkers below have been refurbished as the Nobel Peace Prize Winners' Gallery. Portraits and short essays commemorate each recipient in turn, placing their achievements in context. There's also a good-value self-service restaurant upstairs.

The memorial is on bus routes #17 (Mon–Sat) and #S (Sun) from the "Tour le Roi" stop in the centre of town.

Eating

Caen's town centre offers two major areas for **eating**: with cosmopolitan restaurants in the pedestrianized **quartier Vaugueux** and more traditional French restaurants on the streets off **rue de Geôle**, near the western ramparts, particularly rue des Croisiers and rue Gémare.

L'Alcide, 1 place Courtonne (☎02.31.44.18.06). Anonymous-looking bistro-style place that serves classic French dishes cooked with great attention to detail. Menus from 82F/€12.50 up to 135F/€20.58. Closed Sat.

Le Boeuf Ferré, 10 rue des Croisiers (☎02.31.85.36.40). Gourmet restaurant, with stone walls and timbered ceiling, serving rich and substantial meals; foie gras is the house speciality, as featured in the no-choice 135F/€20.58 menu, and there's always plenty of duck and red meat. Midday menu 75F/€11.43, dinners from 95F/€14.48. Closed Mon & Sun evening, plus the first fortnight in March and the second fortnight in July.

L'Insolité, 16 rue du Vaugueux (☎02.31.43.87.87). Attractive half-timbered restaurant with terrace and indoor seating. A 65F/€9.91 vegetarian menu offers a "*symphonie des crudités*", but the main emphasis is on seafood, with a 95F/€14.48 menu that features a trio of steamed fish, and a knockout 250F/€38.11 *Prestige* menu. Closed Sun evening, plus Mon in low season.

Maître Corbeau, 8 rue Bouquet (☎02.31.93.93.00). Fondue is the speciality in this eccentric little place, and they won't let you forget it, festooning the whole place with cheesy iconography. A typical fondue costs around 80F/€12.20, while set menus start from 92F/€14.03. Closed Sat lunch, Sun & first 3 weeks of Aug.

La Petite Auberge, 17 rue des Équipes-d'Urgence (☎02.31.86.43.30). Plain and simple restaurant, with a nice view of the St-Jean church, serving very good-value Norman specialities – including a daily 68F/€10.37 menu that doesn't force you to eat tripe. Closed Sun evening, Mon & first 3 weeks of Aug.

Les Quatres Épices, 25 rue Porte-au-Berger (☎02.31.93.40.41). Lively West African restaurant, just off rue du Vaugueux. Everything is à la carte – prawns with sweet potato for 95F/€14.48, grilled fish with ginger for 76F/€11.59, plus plantains and meat galore – and African music plays non-stop.

The D-Day beaches

Despite the best efforts of Stephen Spielberg, it is all but impossible now to picture the scene at dawn on **D-Day**, June 6, 1944, when Allied troops landed along the Norman coast between the mouth of the Orne and Les Dunes de Varneville on the Cotentin

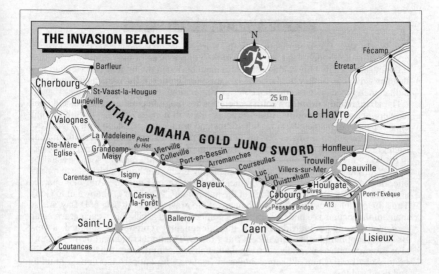

Peninsula. For the most part, these are innocuous beaches backed by gentle dunes, and yet this foothold in Europe was won at the cost of 100,000 soldiers' lives. That the invasion happened here, and not nearer to Germany, was partly due to the failure of the Canadian raid on Dieppe in 1942. The ensuing **Battle of Normandy** killed thousands of civilians and reduced nearly six hundred towns and villages to rubble but, within a week of its eventual conclusion, Paris was liberated.

The **beaches** are still often referred to by their wartime code names: Sword, Juno, Gold, Omaha and Utah. Substantial traces of the fighting are rare, the most remarkable being the remains of the astounding **Mulberry Harbour** at **Arromanches**, 10km northeast of Bayeux. Further west, at **Pointe du Hoc** on Omaha Beach, the cliff heights are still deeply pitted with German bunkers and shell holes, while the church at **Ste-Mère-Église**, from which the US paratrooper who became entangled in the steeple dangled during heavy fighting throughout *The Longest Day*, still stands, and now has a model parachute permanently fastened to the roof.

Just about every coastal town has its **war museum**. These tend as a rule to shy away from the unbearable reality of war in favour of *Boy's Own*-style heroics, but the wealth of incidental human detail can nonetheless be overpowering. Veterans and their descendants apart, visitors these days come to this stretch of coast for its **seaside**: sand and seafood (the best oysters are at Courseulles), plenty of campsites and no Deauville chic.

Bus Verts run all along this coast. From Bayeux, bus #74 goes to Arromanches and Courseulles, and bus #70 to Port-en-Bessin and Vierville. From Caen, bus #30 runs inland to Isigny via Bayeux, express bus #1 to Ouistreham, and express bus #3 to Courseulles. In July and August, Bus Verts' special **D-Day Line** departs daily from Caen's *gare routière* and place Courtonne at 9.30am, calls at Courseulles, and stops at Arromanches, the US cemetery and the Pointe du Hoc, before returning to Caen around 6pm (100F/€15.24 flat fare).

In addition, the Caen Memorial (see p.357) organizes expensive bilingual **guided tours** of the beaches all year round, with four hours on the road and a visit to the Memorial at your own pace (April, May & Sept daily 1pm; June–Aug daily 9am & 2pm; Oct–March Sat & Sun 1pm; 380F/€57.93).

THE WAR CEMETERIES

The **World War II** cemeteries that dot the Norman countryside are filled with foreigners; most of the French dead are buried in the churchyards of their home towns. After the war, some felt that the soldiers should remain buried in the original makeshift graves that were dug where they fell. Instead, commissions gathered the remains into purpose-built cemeteries devoted to the separate warring nations.

The **British** and **Commonwealth** cemeteries are magnificently maintained, and open in every sense. They tend not to be screened off with hedges or walls, or to be forbidding expanses of manicured lawn, but are instead intimate, punctuated with bright flowers. The family of each soldier was invited to suggest an inscription for his tomb, making each grave very personal, and yet part of a common attempt to bring meaning to the carnage. Some epitaphs are questioning – "One day we will understand"; some are accepting – "Our lad at rest"; some matter-of-fact, simply giving the home address; some patriotic, quoting the "corner of a foreign field that is forever England". And interspersed among them all is the chilling refrain of the anonymous "A soldier . . . known unto God". Thus the cemetery at **Ryes**, where so many of the graves bear the date of D-Day, and so many of the victims are under 20, remains immediate and accessible – each grave clearly contains a unique individual. Even the monumental sculpture is subdued, a very British sort of fumbling for the decent thing to say. The understatement of the memorial at **Bayeux**, with its painfully contrived Latin epigram commemorating the return as liberators of "those whom William conquered", conveys an entirely appropriate humility and deep sadness.

An even more eloquent testimony to the futility of war is afforded by the **German** cemeteries, filled with soldiers who served a cause so despicable as to render any talk of "nobility" or "sacrifice" simply obscene. What such cemeteries might have been like had the Nazis won doesn't bear contemplation. As it is, they are sombre places, inconspicuous to minimize the bitterness they still arouse. At **Orglandes** ten thousand are buried, three to each of the plain headstones set in the long flat lawn, almost hidden behind an anonymous wall. There are no noble slogans and the plain entrance is without a dedicatory monument. At the superb site of **Mont d'Huisnes** near Mont St-Michel, the circular mausoleum holds another ten thousand, filed away in cold concrete tiers. There is no attempt to defend the indefensible, and yet one feels an overpowering sense of sorrow – that there is nothing to be said in such a place bitterly underlines the sheer waste and stupidity.

The largest **American** cemetery, at **Colleville-sur-mer** near the Pointe du Hoc, may already be familiar to you from the opening sequences of *Saving Private Ryan*. Here, by contrast, neat rows of crosses cover the tranquil clifftop lawns, with no individual epitaphs, just gold lettering for a few exceptional warriors. At one end, a muscular giant dominates a huge array of battlefield plans and diagrams, covered with surging arrows and pincer movements.

Ouistreham and around

The small community of **OUISTREHAM**, on the coast 15km north of Caen and connected to it by a fast dual carriageway, gives the impression that it can barely believe its luck at having become a major ferry port. Since Brittany Ferries started their service here in 1986, the easternmost of the D-Day resorts has developed an extensive array of reasonable hotels and restaurants.

Several cafés and brasseries in the place Courbonne, immediately outside the *gare maritime*, are eager to liberate passengers from their spare change, while *Le Channel*, just around the corner at 79 av Michel-Cabieu (☎02.31.96.51.69; ②), is the best value for both **eating and sleeping**: menus start with the 55F/€8.38 *menu pêcheur*, while the 88F/€13.42 and 144F/€21.95 options increase in splendour; guest rooms are in a separate building across the street. The smart *Le Normandie et le Chalut*, a few doors down at 71 av Michel-Cabieu (☎02.31.97.19.57, *www.lenormandie.com*; ④; closed mid-Dec to mid-Jan, plus Sun evening & Mon Nov–March), has pleasant, quiet rooms; its *Normand* menu at 95F/€14.48 features a lethal triple plate of tripe, *andouille* and *boudin noir*, while the 199F/€30.34 option makes an excellent last-night blowout.

Pegasus Bridge

Roughly 5km south of Ouistreham, the main road towards Caen passes close by the site now known as **Pegasus Bridge**. On the night before D-Day, the twin bridges here that cross the Caen canal and the River Orne were a crucial Allied objective, and were the target of a daring but successful glider assault just after midnight. The original bridge was replaced in 1994, but is now the focus of the **Mémorial Pegasus** immediately to the east (daily: May–Sept 9.30am–6.30pm; rest of year 10am–1pm & 2–5pm; closed Dec & Jan; 30F/€4.57). This vaguely glider-shaped museum holds the expected array of helmets, goggles, medals and other memorabilia, most captioned in English, as well as various model bridges used in planning the attack.

Arromanches

At **ARROMANCHES**, 10km northeast of Bayeux, an artificial **Mulberry harbour**, "Port Winston", protected the landings of 2,500,000 men and 500,000 vehicles during the invasion. Two of these prefab concrete constructions were built in Britain, while "doodlebugs" blitzed overhead; they were then submerged in rivers away from the prying eyes of German aircraft, and finally towed across the Channel at 6kph as the invasion began. The seafront **Musée du Débarquement**, in Arromanches' main square (daily: May–Aug 9am–6.30pm; rest of year 9am–11.30am & 2–5.30pm; closed first three weeks of Jan; 35F/€5.34), recounts the whole story by means of models, machinery and movies. A huge picture window runs the length of the museum, enabling you to look straight out to where the bulky remains of the harbour, whose sheer scale is impossible to appreciate at this distance, make a strange intrusion on the beach and shallow sea bed (the other one, slightly further west on Omaha Beach, was destroyed by a ferocious storm within a few weeks). There are war memorials throughout Arromanches, with Jesus and Mary high up on the cliffs above the invasion site and helicopter trips available to overlook the area.

Nonetheless, Arromanches somehow manages to be quite a cheerful place to stay, with a lively pedestrian street of **bars** and **brasseries**, and a long expanse of sand where you can rent windsurf boards. *La Marine* at 2 quai Canada (☎02.31.22.34.19; ④; closed Nov to mid-Feb), is a slightly expensive **hotel**, with an excellent sea-view restaurant that serves fishy menus from 99F/€15.09. Across the main square stands the *Arromanches*, 1 rue Maréchal-Joffre (☎02.31.22.36.26; ④; closed Tues evening & Wed in winter), whose restaurant has menus from 70F/€10.67 up to 180F/€27.44, and nearby at 5 place du 6-Juin is the cheaper *Normandie* (☎02.31.22.34.32; ②; closed Jan). The spacious three-star municipal **campsite** is 200m back from the seafront (☎02.31.22.36.78; closed Nov–March).

Bayeux and around

BAYEUX, with its perfectly preserved medieval ensemble, magnificent cathedral and world-famous tapestry, is 23km west of Caen – a mere twenty-minute train ride. It's a smaller and much more intimate city, and, despite the large crowds of summer tourists, a far more enjoyable place to visit.

Arrival, information and accommodation

Bayeux's **tourist office** stands in the centre of town, on the arched pont St-Jean (June to mid-Sept Mon–Sat 9am–6pm, Sun 9.30am–noon & 2.30–6pm; rest of year Mon–Sat 9am–noon & 2–6pm; ☎02.31.51.28.28, *www.bayeux-tourisme.com*). The **gare SNCF** is fifteen minutes' walk away to the south, just outside the ring road, while the **gare routière** is on the other side of town on rue du Manche, alongside place St-Patrice. For information on local **buses**, call Bus Verts du Calvados (☎02.31.92.02.92), whose services stop at both the *gare SNCF* and the *gare routière*.

As one of Normandy's most important tourist destinations, Bayeux is well equipped with **accommodation**. On the whole, however, the hotels are more expensive than usual. There's a large three-star **campsite** on boulevard d'Eindhoven (☎02.31.92.08.43; closed mid-Nov to mid-March), on the northern ring road (RN13) near the river.

Hotels

d'Argouges, 21 rue St-Patrice (☎02.31.92.88.86, fax 02.31.92.69.16, *argouges@mail.cpod.fr*). Quiet, central and very stylish hotel in an eighteenth-century building, with an imposing courtyard, and a well-kept garden around the back. ③–⑥.

BAYEUX

Jardin Botanique

BOULEVARD D'EINDHOVEN

Swimming Pool

St-Patrice

RUE DU DR MICHEL

RUE D'ETERVILLE

RUE MONTFIQUET

Gare Routière

PLACE SAINT-PATRICE

AVENUE DE LA VALLÉE DES PRÉS

AVENUE GEORGES CLEMENCEAU

RUE ST-LAURENT

ACCOMMODATION

d'Argouges	1
Family Home	2
de la Gare	7
Lion d'Or	3
Notre Dame	4
Relais des Cèdres	6
Reine Mathilde	5

RESTAURANTS

La Fringale	B
Le Petit Bistrot	D
Le Petit Normand	E
Le Pommier	A
La Table du Terroir	C

RUE DES BOUCHERS

RUE ST-MALO

RUE GÉNAS DUHOMME

RUE FRANCHE

RUE ST-MARTIN

RUE ST-JEAN

RUE DE LA JURIDICTION

PLACE CHARLES DE GAULLE

Musée Baron Gérard

Musée de Gaulle

RUE BOURBESNEUR

Nôtre-Dame

RUE DE NESMOND

Bayeux Tapestry

RUE ST-EXUPÉRÉ

British War Cemetery

RUE DE VERDUN

RUE TARDIF

Musée de la Bataille de Normandie

BOULEVARD FABIEN WARE

BD MARECHAL LECLERC

BOULEVARD SADI CARNOT

Gare SNCF

0   100 m

Cherbourg

Caen

Saint Lô

Family Home, 39 rue Général-Dais (☎02.31.92.15.22, fax 02.31.92.55.72). Central seventeenth-century house which describes itself as both *maison d'hôtes* (guesthouse) and an *auberge de jeunesse* (youth hostel). Its prices are a little over the usual odds (hostel accommodation is 95F/€14.48 per person) and it's a bit self-consciously jolly – but people return again and again. Rates include breakfast. Meals are taken communally, Madame Lefèvre presiding at the head of a long table in an old oak-beamed dining room, with dinner for 65F/€9.91 at 7.30pm. They also rent bikes and run D-Day tours. ①–③.

de la Gare, 26 place de la Gare (☎02.31.92.10.70, fax 02.31.51.95.99). Old but perfectly adequate basic hotel, with a simple brasserie, beside the station, on the ring road a 15min walk from the cathedral. Tours of D-Day beaches arranged. ①.

Hôtel-Restaurant Lion d'Or, 71 rue St-Jean (☎02.31.92.06.90, fax 02.31.22.15.64). Grand old coaching inn set back behind a courtyard, just beyond the pedestrianized section of the rue St-Jean, outside Les Halles des Grains (now the assembly rooms). The rooms themselves are brighter and newer than the exterior might lead you to expect. Menus from 150F/€22.87. Closed mid-Dec to mid-Jan. ⑤.

Hôtel-Restaurant Notre Dame, 44 rue des Cuisiniers (☎02.31.92.87.24, fax 02.31.92.67.11). Friendly and very pleasant *logis*, with a magnificent view of the cathedral. Menus from 95F/€14.48 (with rabbit in cider), with a special Norman one at 145F/€22.11. Closed mid-Nov to mid-Dec, plus Sun evening & Mon in winter. ②–③.

Reine Mathilde, 23 rue Larcher (☎02.31.92.08.13, fax 02.31.92.09.93). Simple but well-equipped hotel – all rooms have showers and TV – backing onto the canal, between the tapestry and the cathedral. No restaurant as such, but there's a nice open-air summer-only brasserie downstairs, with the cheapest menu at 49F/€7.47 and a good four-course meal for 100F/€15.24. Closed Jan. ③.

Le Relais des Cèdres, 1 bd Sadi-Carnot (☎02.31.21.98.07). Pretty guesthouse, not far from the station but within sight of the cathedral. The rooms are fine, and good value, although the atmosphere is not all that welcoming. ②–③.

The Town

Housed in an impressive eighteenth-century seminary on rue de Nesmond, the **Bayeux Tapestry** – also known to the French as the Tapisserie de la Reine Mathilde – is a seventy-metre strip of linen that recounts the story of the Norman conquest of England (daily: mid-March to April & Sept to mid-Oct 9am–6.30pm; May–Aug 9am–7pm; mid-Oct to mid-March 9.30am–12.30pm & 2–6pm; last admission 45min before closing; 40F/€6.10). Although created over nine centuries ago, the brilliance of its coloured wools has barely faded, and the tale is enlivened throughout with scenes of medieval life, popular fables and mythical beasts. Technically it's not really a tapestry at all, but an embroidery; the skill of its draughtsmanship, and the sheer vigour and detail, are stunning. The work is thought to have been carried out by nuns in England, commissioned by Bishop Odo, William's half-brother, in time for the inauguration of Bayeux cathedral in 1077.

Visits are well planned and highly atmospheric, if somewhat exhausting. First comes a slide show, projected onto billowing sheets of canvas; you then pass along a photographic replica of the tapestry, with enlargements and detailed commentaries. After an optional film show, you finally approach the real thing, to find that it has a strong three-dimensional presence you might not expect from all the flat reproductions. The tapestry looks – and reads – like a modern comic strip. Harold is every inch the villain, with his dastardly little moustache and shifty eyes. He looks extremely self-satisfied as he breaks his oath to accept William as king of England and seizes the throne for himself, but his come-uppance swiftly follows, as William, the noble hero, crosses the Channel and defeats the English armies at Hastings.

The **Cathédrale Notre-Dame** (daily: July & Aug 9am–7pm; rest of year 9am–6pm) was the first home of the tapestry and is just a short walk away from its latest resting-place. Despite such eighteenth-century vandalism as the monstrous fungoid baldachin that flanks the pulpit, the original Romanesque plan of the building is still intact, although only the crypt and towers date from the original work of 1077. The crypt is a beauty, its columns graced with frescoes of angels playing trumpets and bagpipes, looking exhausted by their performance for eternity. Next to the cathedral, in the shadow of the 200-year-old Liberty Tree, the former palace of the archbishops of Bayeux has over the centuries received a considerable quantity of porcelain and lace donated by local families. Named the **Musée Baron Gerard** in honour of its most generous patron, it has recently been renovated to display its collection to far better advantage (daily: June to mid-Sept 9am–7pm; rest of year 10am–12.30pm & 2–6pm; 40F/€6.10, combined admission with tapestry).

Set behind massive guns, next to the ring road on the southwest side of town, Bayeux's **Musée de la Bataille de Normandie** (daily: May to mid-Sept 9.30am–6.30pm; rest of year 10am–12.30pm & 2–6pm; 33F/€5.03) is one of the old school of war museums, with its emphasis firmly on hardware rather than humans. By way of contrast, the understated and touching **British War Cemetery** stands immediately across the road (see box on p.360).

Although Bayeux's newest museum, the **Mémorial Général de Gaulle** at 10 rue de Bourbesneur, near place de Gaulle (mid-March to mid-Nov daily 9.30am–12.30pm & 2–6.30pm; 17F/€2.59), is aimed squarely at French devotees of the great man, it does make an interesting detour for foreign visitors. The sheer obsessiveness of the displays, which focus on the three separate day-trips De Gaulle made to Bayeux during the course of his long life, somehow illuminates the extent to which he came to epitomize the very essence of a certain kind of Frenchness, which seems scarcely removed from self-parody.

Eating

Several of the hotels have good **restaurants**, while the *Family Home* (see p.363) serves a filling and good-value dinner at 8pm each evening for 65F/€9.91. Otherwise, most of Bayeux's restaurants are in the rue St-Jean, leading east from the river, or near the main door of the cathedral. Watch out for Sundays: virtually everywhere is shut.

La Fringale, 43 rue St-Jean (☎02.31.21.34,40). The nicest of the many pavement restaurants along the pedestrian rue St-Jean, offering good-value lunch menus and also generous salads and snacks, as well as more formal fishy dinners. Closed mid-Dec to Jan, plus Wed in low season.

Le Petit Bistrot, 2 rue Bienvenue (☎02.31.51.85.40). Bright-yellow-painted restaurant opposite the cathedral; menus from 98F/€14.94 upwards boast a fine assortment of scallops. Closed Sun, plus Mon in low season.

Le Petit Normand, 35 rue Larcher (☎02.31.22.88.66). Sixteenth-century house by the cathedral, offering good traditional cooking, with seafood specialities and local cider. Lunch menus from 60F/€9.15, dinner from 95F/€14.48. Closed Jan, plus Thurs Oct–April.

Le Pommier, 40 rue des Cuisiniers (☎02.31.21.52.10). Small traditional restaurant near the cathedral, with a tiny terrace. Meat- and dairy-rich Norman cuisine on menus from 76F/€11.59 to 146F/€22.26. Closed Feb, plus Sun evening & Wed in low season.

La Table du Terroir, 42 rue St-Jean (☎02.31.92.05.53). A rendezvous for closet meat freaks, tucked away behind a butcher's shop and serving the freshest, bloodiest flesh on a well-judged quartet of menus, at 60F/€9.15, 98F/€14.94, 115F/€17.53 and 155F/€23.63 – the last features a tureen of sweetbreads. Closed Sun evening, Mon & mid-Oct to mid-Nov.

Cerisy and Balleroy

Heading southwest from Bayeux towards St-Lô, you pass close to the remarkable Romanesque **Abbaye de Cerisy-la-Forêt** (Easter to mid-Nov Tues–Sun 9am–6.30pm, free; guided tours Easter–Sept Tues–Sun 10.30am–12.30pm & 2.30–6.30pm, Oct to mid-Nov Sat & Sun 10.30am–noon & 2–6pm, 10F/€1.52), halfway along the D572 and 5km to the north of it. Its triple tiers of windows and arches and the delicate workmanship of its nave and choir are testimony to the breathtaking skills of medieval Norman masons.

No less notable is the **Château de Balleroy** (mid-March to June & Sept to mid-Oct daily except Tues 9am–noon & 2–6pm; July & Aug daily 10am–6pm; 37F/€5.64), 3km southeast of the same junction, where you switch to an era when architects ruled over craftsmen. The main street of the village leads straight to the brick-and-stone château, a masterpiece of the celebrated seventeenth-century architect, François Mansart, and standing like a faultlessly reasoned and dogmatic argument for the power of its owners and their class. It belongs to the family of the late American press magnate Malcolm Forbes, pal of Nixon, Ford and Nancy Reagan. His is the enlarged colour photograph sharing the stairwell with Dutch still lifes, and he left his mark on most other aspects of the house, too – only the salon remains in its original state of glory, with brilliant portraits of the (then) royal family by Mignard. Admission also includes a **hot-air balloon museum**, which was one of Mr Forbes' hobbies.

The Cotentin Peninsula

Until Brittany Ferries inaugurated its direct services to Brittany, the **Cotentin Peninsula**, in the far west of Normandy hard against the frontier with Brittany, provided many visitors with their first taste of western France. Now that Caen, too, has direct sailings, the port of **Cherbourg** sees only a fraction of the traffic it had twenty years ago, but the peninsula itself remains worth exploring.

Cherbourg

If the murky metropolis of **CHERBOURG** is your port of arrival, it's best to head straight out and on: despite some busy pedestrian streets and lively bars, the town itself lacks anything of substantial interest, and there are some much more appealing places within a very few kilometres to either side. Napoléon inaugurated the transformation of what had been a rather poor, but perfectly situated, natural harbour into a major transatlantic port, by means of massive artificial breakwaters. An equestrian statue commemorates his boast that in Cherbourg he would "recreate the wonders of Egypt", though there are as yet no pyramids nearer than the Louvre.

Arrival and information

Several cross-Channel ferry companies still sail into Cherbourg's **gare maritime**, just east of the town centre (☎02.33.44.20.13). Services from **Portsmouth**, including the new Superstar Express, which takes a mere 2hr 45min for the crossing, are operated by P&O (5–6 daily; ☎08.03.01.30.13, *www.poef.com*), and those from **Poole** by Brittany Ferries (1–2 daily; 4hr 15min; ☎08.03.82.88.28, *www.brittany-ferries.com*) – Cherbourg is twinned with Poole, hence the British red telephone kiosk on quai de Caligny. Irish Ferries also sail to Cherbourg, from **Rosslare** (2–4 weekly; ☎02.33.23.44.44).

Cherbourg's **tourist office** is at 2 quai Alexandre III (June–Aug Mon–Sat 9am–6.30pm; rest of year Mon 1.30–6pm, Tues–Fri 9am–noon & 1.30–6pm, Sat 9am–noon; ☎02.33.93.52.02, *www.cherbourg-channel.tm.fr*). The **gare SNCF**, on avenue François-Miller/place Jean-Jaurès, is served by regular trains to Paris, Bayeux and Caen. Buses to Coutances (☎02.33.98.13.38) and St-Lô, Valognes and Barfleur (☎02.33.44.32.22) run from the **gare routière** opposite.

Accommodation

By usual Norman standards, room rates are very reasonable. The town's newly refurbished and well-equipped red-brick **hostel**, fifteen minutes' walk west of the centre at 55 rue de l'Abbaye (☎02.33.78.15.15), offers dorm beds for 51F/€7.77 per night, serves lunch or dinner for 50F/€7.62, and also rents out bicycles. Two of its bedrooms are designed for

CHERBOURG

Ferry Terminal

QUAI DE FRANCE
QUAI DE NORMANDIE

RUE DE L'ABBAYE
AVENUE CESSART
RUE DE L'UNION

Basilique de la Trinité

BOULEVARD FELIX

RUE EMMANUEL LIAIS
RUE CHRISTINE
RUE TOUR CARRÉE
RUE F. LAVIEILLE
RUE MAHIEU
RUE AU BLÉ
PLACE CENTRALE
RUE DE LA MARINE
RUE DE LA MARNE
QUAI DE CAIGNY

Avant Port

AVENUE A. BRIAND
RUE DE TOURVILLE

QUAI LAWTON COLLINS

PONT TOURNANT

RUE GAMBETTA
RUE DE L'ALMA
RUE MAL FOCH
RUE EMILE ZOLA

Théâtre

RUE DU VAL DE SAIRE

Bassin du Commerce
QUAI ALEXANDRE III
QUAI DE L'ENTREPÔT

AVENUE CARNOT

BD PIERRE MENDES-FRANCE
RUE PRÉSIDENT LOUBERT

Gare Routière

PLACE JEAN-JAURÈS
AVENUE FRANCIS-MILLET

Gare SNCF

RUE SAINT-SAUVEUR
BD DE L'ATLANTIQUE
AV DE PARIS

AVENUE ETIENNE LECARPENTIER

● Roule Fort

0   200 m

▽ *Valognes & Paris*

ACCOMMODATION

La Croix de Malte	5
de la Gare	6
Hostel	1
Moderna	3
La Régence	4
Rénaissance	2

RESTAURANTS

Café de Paris	C
Café du Théâtre	D
Le Faitout	B
Le Grandgousier	A

visitors with limited mobility. The closest **campsite** is the three-star *Camping de Collignon*, 3km east towards Barfleur at Tourlaville (☎02.33.20.16.88; closed Oct–May).

HOTELS

Croix de Malte, 7 rue des Halles (☎02.33.43.19.16, fax 02.33.43.65.66). Simple hotel on three upstairs floors, one block back from the harbour. Clean and recently renovated rooms – all 24 have TV and at least a shower – with the cheapest rates being for the perfectly acceptable ones in the attic. ②.

de la Gare, 10 place Jean-Jaurès (☎02.33.43.06.81, fax 02.33.43.12.20). Very convenient for the *gares SNCF* and *routière*, if not exactly stunning in itself. The cheapest rooms have a shower but no toilet. ②.

Moderna, 28 rue de la Marine (☎02.33.43.05.30, fax 02.33.43.97.37, *www.moderna-hotel.com*). Rooms ranging from basic to lavish, slightly back from the harbour and tourist office; most have phones, showers and British TV. ①–③.

La Régence, 42 quai de Caligny (☎02.33.43.05.16, fax 02.33.43.98.37). Small, neat rooms with balconies overlooking the harbour, near the tourist office. The restaurant downstairs kicks off with a reasonable 70F/€10.67 menu, and ranges up to 185F/€28.20. ③.

de la Renaissance, 4 rue de l'Église (☎02.33.43.23.90, fax 02.33.43.96.10, *renaissance @cherbourg-channel.tm.fr*). Friendly hotel with rooms of all kinds, some with sea views, facing the port in the most appealing quarter of town – the Église of the address is the attractive Trinité. ①–③.

The Town

If you are waiting for a boat, the best way of filling time is to settle into a café or restaurant or do some last-minute shopping. Don't, however, leave your food shopping for the town. Unless you hit the Thursday **market**, held around rue des Halles, your best bets for shopping are the Auchan hypermarket at the junction of RN13 and N13, south of town, or the Carrefour, on the southeast corner of the Bassin du Commerce.

As for walking off lunch, the only area that really encourages a ramble is over by the **Basilique de la Trinité** and the former town **beach**, now grassed over to form the "Plage Vert". Over to the south, you could alternatively climb up to **Roule Fort** for a view of the whole port. The fort itself contains a **Musée de la Libération** (May–Sept daily 10am–6pm; rest of year Tues–Sun 9.30am–noon & 2–5.30pm; 15F/€2.29), with the usual dry maps and diagrams but plenty of contemporary newsreel – much of it, for once, in English – commemorating the period in 1944 when Cherbourg was briefly the busiest port in the world.

Eating

Restaurants in Cherbourg divide readily into the glass-fronted seafood places along the quai de Caligny, each with its "copious" *assiette de fruits de mer*, and the more varied, more adventurous and less expensive little places tucked away in the pedestrianized streets and alleyways of the old town.

Café de Paris, 40 quai de Caligny (☎02.33.43.12.36). Work your way up through the ranks of *assiettes de fruits de mer*, from the 85F/€12.96 *Matelot* to the *Amiral* at 520F/€79.27 for two; there's also a quick 105F/€16.01 menu if you're in a hurry. Here it's the live lobsters in the fish tanks set into the windows that get the sea views, not you – but the food is excellent. Closed Sun evening, plus Mon in low season.

Café du Théâtre, 8 place de Gaulle (☎02.33.43.01.49). Attractive setup adjoining the theatre, with a café behind plate-glass windows on the ground floor and a full-scale brasserie upstairs, arranged on three sides of the central opening. The whole ensemble offers a great sense of participating in the life of the town. The varied menus, from 79F/€12.04, hold more than just seafood; the 115F/€17.53 one, for example, features frogs' legs.

Le Faitout, 25 rue Tour-Carrée (☎02.33.04.25.04). Basement restaurant in the shopping district that offers traditional French cuisine at very reasonable prices; a bowl of mussels can be had for under 40F/€6.10, and there's a daily special for 55F/€8.38. Closed Sun & Mon lunch.

Le Grandgousier, 21 rue de l'Abbaye (☎02.33.53.19.43). The definitive French fish restaurant, well worth the walk to its unprepossessing location at the west end of town. Menus start at 75F/€11.43, but this is a place to expect to spend a lot and dine well. Imagine any combination of fish, throw in a bit of caviar, a few crab claws and a leavening of foie gras, and you'll find it somewhere on the menu. Closed Mon & Fri lunchtime, plus Sun evening.

Around the Cotentin

Once you get away from Cherbourg, the largely rural Cotentin Peninsula is geographically an area of transition. Little ports such as **Barfleur** on the indented northern headland presage the rocky Breton coast, while inland the meadows resemble the farmlands of the Bocage and the Bessin. The long western flank with its flat beaches serves as a prelude to Mont St-Michel (see p.371), and hill towns such as **Coutances** and **Avranches** contain architectural and historical relics associated with the abbey.

Barfleur

The pleasant little harbour village of **BARFLEUR**, 25km east of Cherbourg, was the biggest port in Normandy seven centuries ago. The population has since dwindled from nine thousand to six hundred, and fortunes have diminished alongside – most recently through the invasion of a strain of plankton that poisoned all the mussels. It's now a surprisingly low-key place, where the sweeping crescent of the grey granite quayside sees little tourist activity.

Near the town, about a thirty-minute walk, is the **Gatteville lighthouse**, the second tallest in France. It guards the rocks on which William, son and heir of Henry I of England (and recently "outed" by historians as being gay), was drowned in 1120, together with three hundred of his nobles.

Barfleur has a fine selection of **hotels**. *Le Conquérant* stands a short distance back from the sea at 16–18 rue St-Thomas-à-Becket (☎02.33.54.00.82; ②; closed mid-Nov to mid-March); its nicest rooms face onto a lovely garden, and there's a summer-only crêperie. *Le Moderne* is tucked away south of the main road at 1 place de Gaulle (☎02.33.23.12.44; ②; closed mid-Sept to mid-March); some of the rooms are very inexpensive, while the restaurant is superb, with the 144F/€21.95 menu featuring a fish-shaped *feuilleton* (pastry) of seafood – the house speciality is oysters, stuffed or raw.

St-Vaast

Pretty **ST-VAAST-LA-HOUGUE**, 11km south of Barfleur, is more of a resort, with lots of tiny Channel-crossing yachts moored in the bay where Edward III landed on his way to Crécy and a string of fortifications from Vauban's time. The *Hôtel de France et des Fuchsias*, just back from the sea at 18 rue du Maréchal-Foch (☎02.33.54.42.26; ②–⑤; closed Mon in winter & Jan to mid-Feb), with its splendid gardens and excellent restaurant, is an ideal stopover for ferry passengers – in fact both it and the annexe at the end of the garden are packed throughout the season with British visitors.

Utah Beach

The westernmost of the main Invasion Beaches, **Utah Beach** stretches for approximately thirty kilometres south from St-Vaast. From 6.30am onwards on D-Day 23,000 men and 1700 vehicles landed here. A minor coast road, the D241, traces the edge of the dunes and enables visitors to follow the course of the fighting, though in truth there's precious little to see these days. Ships that were deliberately sunk to create artificial breakwaters are still visible at low tide, while markers along the seafront commemorate individual fallen heroes.

Two museums now tell the story: the **Musée de la Liberté** in **QUINÉVILLE** (daily: mid-March to May & Oct to mid-Nov 10am–6pm; June–Sept 9.30am–7.30pm; 20F/€3.05), which focuses on everyday life for the people of Normandy under Nazi occupation, and the much more comprehensive **Musée du Débarquement d'Utah-Beach** in **STE-MARIE-DU-MONT** (April, May & Oct daily 10am–12.30pm & 2–5.30pm; June–Sept daily 9.30am–6.30pm; Nov–March Sat, Sun & hols 10am–12.30pm & 2–5pm; 27F/€4.12), which explains the operations in exhaustive detail, with huge sea-view windows to lend immediacy to the copious models, maps, films and diagrams.

La Hague and the Nez de Jobourg

If you go west from Cherbourg to **LA HAGUE**, the northern tip of the peninsula, you'll find wild and isolated countryside where you can lean against the wind, watch waves smashing against rocks or sunbathe in a spring profusion of wild flowers. But the discharges of "low-level" radioactive wastes from the **Cap Hague nuclear reprocessing plant** may discourage you from swimming. In 1980, the Greenpeace vessel *Rainbow Warrior* chased a ship bringing spent Japanese fuel into Cherbourg harbour. The

Rainbow Warrior's crew were arrested, but all charges were dropped when 3000 Cherbourg dockers threatened to strike in their support.

The main road, the D901, continues a couple of kilometres beyond the nuclear plant to **GOURY**, where the fields finally roll down to a craggy pebble coastline. Almost the only building here, the *Auberge de Goury* (☎02.33.52.77.01; closed for dinner on Sun & Mon), is a really excellent **restaurant**, facing the octagonal lifeboat station and looking out towards a slate-grey lighthouse. It specializes in charcoal-grilled fish and meat, with a wide-ranging cheeseboard that includes the extraordinary *voluptueuse*, and is very popular at lunchtimes.

South of La Hague a great curve of sand – some of it military training ground – takes the land's edge to **FLAMANVILLE** and another nuclear installation. But the next two sweeps of beach down to **CARTERET**, with sand dunes like mini-mountain ranges, are probably the best beaches in Normandy: there are no resorts, no hotels and just two **campsites** – at **LE ROZEL** and **SURTAINVILLE**.

Château de Pirou

Roughly 30km south of Cartaret, a turn off the main coastal road, the D650, leads to the **Château de Pirou** (Easter–June & Sept–Oct daily except Tues 10am–noon & 2–6.30pm; July & Aug daily 10am–noon & 2–6.30pm; Nov–Easter daily except Tues 10am–noon & 2–5.30pm; 25F/€3.81), a few hundred metres away. Although you see nothing from the road, once you've passed through its three successive fortified gateways you'll find yourself confronted by a ravishing little castle. Some historians have suggested that this is the oldest castle in Normandy, dating back to the earliest Viking raids; it's thought to have taken its current form around the twelfth century.

Coutances

The old hill town of **COUTANCES**, 65km south of Cherbourg, confined by its site to just one main street, has on its summit a landmark for all the surrounding countryside, the **Cathédrale de Notre-Dame**. Essentially Gothic, it is still very Norman in its unconventional blending of architectural traditions, and the octagonal lantern crowning the crossing in the nave is nothing short of divinely inspired. The *son et lumière* on Sunday evenings and throughout the summer is for once a true complement to the light stone building. Also illuminated on summer nights (and left open) are the formal fountained **public gardens**.

Coutances' **gare SNCF**, about 1.5km southeast of the town centre (at the bottom of the hill), also serves as the stop for **buses** heading north and south. The local **tourist office** is housed behind the Hôtel de Ville in place Georges-Léclerc (July & Aug Mon–Sat 10am–1pm & 2–7pm, Sun 3–7pm; rest of year Mon–Fri 10am–12.30pm & 2–6pm, Sat 10am–12.30pm & 2–5pm; ☎02.33.19.08.10). The cream-coloured *Hôtel du Normandie*, behind and below the cathedral at 2 place du Gaulle (☎02.33.45.01.40; ②; closed Fri Sept to mid-May & Sun evening), has the usual assortment of rooms, and a restaurant with menus that range from the good-value 55F/€8.38 option (not Sun) to an excellent 98F/€14.94 spread. A better alternative for motorists is the *Relais du Viaduc* (☎02.33.45.02.68; ②; closed second fortnight of Feb, plus Fri evening & Sat in low season), at the junction of the D7 and D971, south of town, which serves fine food. The excellent year-round municipal **campsite**, *Les Vignettes* (☎02.33.45.43.13), halfway up the hill west of town, stands next to a large, comfortable chain hotel, the *Cositel* (☎02.33.07.51.64; ④).

Granville

From Coutances, the D971 runs down to the coast at **GRANVILLE**, the Norman equivalent of Brittany's St-Malo (see p.395), with a history of piracy and the severe citadel of

VISITING MONT ST-MICHEL

Access to the island of Mont-St-Michel is free and unrestricted, although there's a 15F/€2.29 fee to park on either the causeway or the sands below it (which are submerged by the tides). If you're visiting by car in summer, you might prefer to park on the mainland well short of the Mont, both to enjoy the walk across the causeway and to avoid the dense traffic jams.

Between May and September, the **abbey** is open daily from 9am to 5.30pm; from October to April, it's open daily from 9.30am until 4.30pm, except during school holidays, when the hours are 9.30am until 5pm. It's closed on Jan 1, May 1, Nov 1, Nov 11 and Dec 25. Paying the standard 40F/€6.10 **admission fee** – ages 12–25 25F/€3.81, under-12s free – entitles you to wander the generally accessible areas, and to join an expert-led **guided tour** in the language of your choice. Tours last 45 minutes between mid-June and mid-Sept, and a full hour the rest of the year; the daily schedule for each language is displayed at the entrance. There are also a number of more detailed two-hour tours, in French only, which take you both higher and deeper and cost 65F/€9.91 (ages 12–25 45F/€6.86).

Merveille (The Marvel) – incorporating the entire north face, with the cloister, Knights' Hall, Refectory, Guest Hall and cellars – is visible from all around the bay, but it becomes if anything more awe-inspiring the closer you approach. In Maupassant's words:

> *I reached the huge pile of rocks which bears the little city dominated by the great church. Climbing the steep narrow street, I entered the most wonderful Gothic dwelling ever made for God on this earth, a building as vast as a town, full of low rooms under oppressive ceilings and lofty galleries supported by frail pillars. I entered that gigantic granite jewel, which is as delicate as a piece of lacework, thronged with towers and slender belfries which thrust into the blue sky of day and the black sky of night their strange heads bristling with chimeras, devils, fantastic beasts and monstrous flowers, and which are linked together by carved arches of intricate design.*

The Mont's rock comes to a sharp point just below what is now the transept of the **church**, a building where the transition from Romanesque to Gothic is only too evident in the vaulting of the nave. In order to lay out the church's ground plan in the traditional shape of the cross, supporting crypts had to be built up from the surrounding hillside, and in all construction work the Chausey granite has had to be sculpted to match the exact contours of the hill. Space was always limited, and yet the building has grown through the centuries, with an architectural ingenuity that constantly surprises in its geometry – witness the shock of emerging into the light of the cloisters from the sombre Great Hall.

Not surprisingly, the building of the monastery was no smooth progression: the original church, choir, nave and tower all had to be replaced after collapsing. The style of decoration has varied, too, along with the architecture. That you now walk through halls of plain grey stone is a reflection of modern taste. In the Middle Ages, the walls of public areas such as the refectory would have been festooned with tapestries and frescoes, while the original coloured tiles of the cloisters have long since been stripped away to reveal bare walls.

To get a clearer sense of the abbey's historical development, be sure to take a look at the intriguing scale models in the reception area, which depict it during four different epochs.

The rest of the island

The base of Mont St-Michel rests on a primeval slime of sand and mud. Just above that, you pass through the heavily fortified **Porte du Roi** onto the narrow **Grande Rue**, climbing steadily around the base of the rock and lined with medieval gabled houses and a jumble of overpriced postcard and souvenir shops, maintaining the ancient tradition of prising pilgrims from their money. A plaque near the main staircase records that Jacques Cartier was presented to King François I here on May 8, 1532, and charged with exploring the shores of Canada.

The rather dry **Musée Maritime** offers an insight into the island's ties with the sea, while the Archangel Michael manages in just fifteen minutes to lead visitors on a voyage through space and time in the **Archéoscope**, with the full majestic panoply of multimedia mumbo jumbo. Further along the Grande Rue and up the steps towards the abbey church, next door to the eleventh-century **church of St-Pierre**, the absurd **Musée Grévin** contains such edifying specimens as a wax model of a woman drowning in a sea of mud. (All open Feb to mid-Nov daily 9am–6pm; 75F/€11.43 for all, or 45F/€6.86 each one.)

Large crowds gather each day at the **North Tower**, to watch the tide sweep in across the bay. During the high tides of the equinoxes (March & Sept), the waters are alleged to rush in like a foaming galloping horse. Seagulls wheel away in alarm, and those foolish enough to be wandering too late on the sands toward Tombelaine have to sprint to safety.

Practicalities

Mont St-Michel has its own **tourist office**, in the lowest gateway (mid-June to mid-Sept Mon–Sat 9am–7pm, Sun 9am–noon & 2–6pm; rest of year Mon, Tues & Thurs–Sat 9am–noon & 2–6pm; ☎02.33.60.14.30). Regular **buses** connect it with the SNCF stations at Pontorson (see below), Rennes (see p.388) and St-Malo (see p.395).

The island holds a surprising number of **hotels** and **restaurants**, albeit nothing like enough to cope with the sheer number of visitors. Most are predictably expensive, though virtually all the hotels seem to keep a few cheaper rooms. The most famous hotel, *La Mère Poulard* (☎02.33.60.14.01; ④–⑨), uses the time-honoured legend of its fluffy omelettes, as enjoyed by Leon Trotsky and Margaret Thatcher (not simultaneously), to justify extortionate charges. Higher up the Mont, however, prices fall to more realistic levels. The cheapest option is the *Du Guesclin* (☎02.33.60.14.10; ④; closed mid-Nov to mid-March), where all the rooms have TV, but both the *Hôtel La Croix Blanche* (☎02.33.60.14.04; ⑤; closed mid-Nov to mid-Dec) and the *Mouton Blanc* (☎02.33.60.14.08; ④; closed Jan) serve much better food.

In addition, the main approach road to the island, the D976, is lined shortly before the causeway by around a dozen large and virtually indistinguishable hotels and motels, each with its own brasserie or restaurant. Typical among these are the *Motel Vert* (☎02.33.60.09.33; ③; closed mid-Nov to mid-Feb), the *Hôtel Formule Verte* (☎02.33.60.14.13; ③; closed mid-Nov to mid-Feb) and the *Hôtel de la Digue* (☎02.33.60.14.02; ④; closed mid-Nov to mid-March). The three-star, 350-pitch *Camping du Mont-St-Michel* (☎02.33.60.09.33; closed mid-Nov to mid-Feb) is also on the mainland just short of the causeway.

Many visitors to Mont St-Michel find themselves lodging at **PONTORSON**, 6km inland, which has the nearest **gare SNCF**, connected to the Mont by an overpriced bus service (30F/€4.57 return). The **hotels** here are not especially interesting, but both the *Montgomery*, in a fine old ivy-covered mansion at 13 rue du Couesnon

(☎02.33.60.00.09; ③; closed Nov–March), and the *Bretagne*, 59 rue du Couesnon (☎02.33.60.10.55; ③; closed Mon & Jan), have distinguished restaurants. A recently renovated **hostel** stands near the cathedral, 1km west of the station, in the Centre Duguesclin at 21 rue du Général-Patton (☎02.33.60.18.65, *aj@ville-pontorson.fr*; closed Oct–April).

INLAND NORMANDY

It's hard to pin down specific highlights in **inland Normandy**. The pleasures lie in the feel of particular landscapes – the lush meadows and orchards, the classic half-timbered houses and farm buildings, and the rivers and forests of the Norman countryside. **Gastronomy** is, of course, another major motivation for going there – the cheeses, creams, apple and pear brandies and ciders for which the region is famous. The **Pays d'Auge** country south of Lisieux and the **Vire Valley** to the west are the best for this. The **Suisse Normande** is canoeing and rock-climbing country, and there are endless good walks in the stretch along the southern border of the province designated as the **Parc Naturel Régional de Normandie-Maine**. Of the towns, **Conches** is the most charming, **Falaise** has William the Conqueror as a constant fall-back attraction, and **Lisieux** has religious myths – and a spectacularly unpleasant basilica to back them up.

South of the Seine

Heading south from the Seine you can follow the River Risle from the estuary just east of Honfleur, or the Eure and its tributaries from upstream of Rouen. Between the two stretches the long featureless **Neubourg Plain**. The lowest major crossing point over the Risle is at **PONT-AUDEMER**, where medieval houses lean out at alarming angles over the crisscrossing roads, rivers and canals. From here, perfect cycling roads lined with timbered farmhouses follow the river south.

Le Bec-Hellouin

The size and tranquillity of the **Abbaye de Bec-Hellouin**, upstream from Pont-Audemer just before Brionne, give a monastic feel to the whole Risle valley. Bells echo across the water and white-robed monks go soberly about their business. From the eleventh century onwards, the abbey was one of the most important centres of intellectual learning in the Christian world; the philosopher Anselm was abbot here before becoming Archbishop of Canterbury in 1093. Due to the Revolution, most of the monastery buildings are recent – the monks only returned in 1948 – but there are some survivals and appealing clusters of stone ruins, including the fifteenth-century **bell tower of St-Nicholas** and the cloister. Recent archbishops of Canterbury have maintained tradition by coming here on retreat. Visitors are welcome to wander through the grounds for no charge, though you can also join regular **guided tours** (June–Sept Mon & Wed–Fri 10.30am, 3pm, 4pm & 5pm, Sat 10.30am, 3pm & 4pm, Sun & hols noon, 3pm & 4pm; Oct–May Mon & Wed–Sat 11am, 3pm & 4pm, Sun & hols noon, 3pm & 4pm; 25F/€3.81).

In the rather twee adjacent town of **BEC-HELLOUIN** is a **vintage car museum** (mid-June to mid-Sept daily 9am–noon & 2–7pm; rest of year Mon, Tues & Fri–Sun 9am–noon & 2–7pm; 25F/€3.81), and a distinctly unascetic **restaurant**, the wonderful *Auberge de l'Abbaye* (☎02.32.44.86.02; ⑤; closed Mon evening, all day Tues in winter & all Jan), which also has half a dozen expensive rooms. The *Restaurant de la Tour* on place Guillaume-le-Conquérant nearby (☎02.32.44.86.15; closed Dec, plus Tues evening & Wed in low season) is a more affordable place to eat, with some outdoor tables.

Brionne and Beaumont-le-Roger

BRIONNE, on the Rouen–Lisieux rail line, is a small town with large regional markets on Thursday and Sunday. The fish hall is on the left bank, the rest by the church on the right bank. Above them both, with panoramic views, is an excellent example of a Norman **donjon**. If you decide to **stay**, try the lovely old half-timbered *Auberge du Vieux Donjon*, 19 rue Soie (☎02.32.44.80.62; ③; closed Mon & Sun evening in low season & last fortnight in Oct), which has a good restaurant.

The River Charentonne joins the Risle near Serquigny. The town is also the meeting point of rail lines and main roads and the banks are clogged with fuming industrial conglomerations. But 7km upstream, at **BEAUMONT-LE-ROGER**, you are back in pastoral tranquillity. The ruins of a thirteenth-century **priory church** slowly crumble to the ground, the slow restoration of one or two arches unable to keep pace. In the village, little happens beyond the hammering of the church bell next door to the abbey by a nodding musketeer.

The next riverside village, **LA FERRIÈRE-SUR-RISLE**, has an especially beautiful **church**, with some interesting sculpture, and a fourteenth-century covered **market hall**. Paddocks and meadows lead down to the river and a small and inviting **hotel**, the *Vieux-Marché* (☎02.32.30.25.93; ②; closed mid-Sept to mid-Oct).

Conches-en-Ouche

Fourteen kilometres east of La Ferrière across the wild and open woodland of the **Forêt de Conches**, standing above the River Rouloir on an abrupt and narrow spur, is **CONCHES-EN-OUCHE**, many a Norman's favourite heartland town. At the highest point, in the middle of a row of medieval houses, is the **church of Ste-Foy**, its windows a stunning sequence of Renaissance stained glass. Behind are the gardens of the **Hôtel de Ville**, where a robust, if anatomically odd, stone boar gazes proudly out over a spectacular view. Next to that, you can scramble up the slippery steps of the ruined twelfth-century **castle**. Conches is given a certain edge over other towns with equal lists of historic relics by the pieces of modern sculpture that seem to lie around every other corner.

Across the main street from the castle is a long **park**, with parallel avenues of trees, a large ornamental lake and fountain. The inexpensive **hotel** *Grand'Mare*, in a green and quiet location beside the park at 13 av Croix de Fer (☎02.32.30.23.30; ①), serves up enjoyable dinners in its restaurant, including a good 98F/€14.94 menu with oxtail braised in sherry and some fruit desserts. There's also a two-star municipal **campsite**, *La Forêt* (☎02.32.30.22.49; closed Oct–March). On Thursday the whole town is taken up by a **market**.

Évreux

If you're heading south to Conches from Rouen, you follow first the River Eure, and then its tributary the Iton, passing through **ÉVREUX**, capital of the Eure *département*. It's hardly an exciting place, but an afternoon's wander in the vicinity of the **cathedral** – a minor classic with its Flamboyant exterior decoration and original fourteenth-century windows – and the **ramparts** alongside the Iton river bank is pleasant.

The old *Biche*, at 9 rue St-Joséphine on place St-Taurin at the edge of town (☎02.32.38.66.00; ①; closed Sun in July & Aug, Sun evening Sept–June), is a strange but splendid Belle Époque **hotel**, with a lurid pink interior, a triangular dining room and even some triangular bedrooms. In its **restaurant**, 135F/€20.58 will buy you a magnificent meal of oysters braised in cider and a garlicky seafood *pot au feu*, to the musical accompaniment of an unlikely assortment of funk and disco classics.

Lisieux and the Pays d'Auge

The rolling hills and green twisting valleys of the **Pays d'Auge**, which stretches south of the cathedral town of **Lisieux**, are scattered with magnificent half-timbered manor houses. The pastures here are the lushest in the province, their produce the world-famous cheeses of Camembert, Livarot and Pont L'Évêque. And beside them are hectares of orchards, yielding the best of Norman ciders, both apple and pear (*poiré*), as well as Calvados apple brandy.

Lisieux

LISIEUX, 35 minutes by train from Caen, is the main town of the Pays d'Auge, and a good place to get to know its cheeses and ciders is at the large street **market** on Wednesday and Saturday. Most people, however, come to Lisieux as a place of pilgrimage based around the cult of St Thérèse, the most popular French spiritual figure of the last hundred years. Passivity, self-effacement and masochism were her trademarks, and she is honoured by the gaudy and gigantic **Basilique de Ste-Thérèse**, completed in 1954 on a slope to the southwest of the town centre. The huge modern mosaics that decorate the nave are undeniably impressive, but the overall impression is of a quasi-medieval hagiography. The faithful can ride on a white, flag-bedecked fairground train around the holiest sites, which include the infinitely restrained and sober **Cathédrale St-Pierre**.

Lisieux's **tourist office**, 11 rue d'Alençon, is the best place to gather information on the rural areas further inland (June–Sept Mon–Sat 8.30am–6.30pm, Sun 9am–12.30pm & 2–5pm; rest of year Mon–Sat 8.30am–noon & 1.30–6pm; ☎02.31.48.18.10, *www.ville-lisieux.fr*). The quantity of pilgrims means the town is full of good-value **hotels**, such as *de la Terrasse*, near the basilica at 25 av Ste-Thérèse (☎02.31.62.17.65; ②; closed Jan & Mon in winter), and the exceptionally cheap *des Arts*, backing onto the bishop's gardens at 26 rue Condorcet (☎02.31.62.00.02; ①). There is also a large two-star **campsite**, *de la Vallée* (☎02.31.62.00.40; closed Oct–March), but campers would probably be better off somewhere more rural, such as Livarot or Orbec. If Thérèse isn't your prime motivation, Saturday is the best day to visit, for the large street market – stacked with Pays d'Auge cheeses.

Into the Pays d'Auge

Though the tourist authorities responsible for the Pays d'Auge have laid out a **Route du Fromage** and a **Route du Cidre**, you won't be missing out if you don't follow these itineraries. For really good solid Norman cooking this is the perfect area to look out for *fermes auberges*, working farms which welcome paying visitors to share their meals. Local tourist offices can provide copious lists of these and of local producers from whom you can buy your cheese and booze.

Beuvron-en-Auge

By far the prettiest of the Pays d'Auge villages is **BEUVRON-EN-AUGE**, 7km north of the N13 halfway between Lisieux and Caen. It consists of an oval central square, ringed by a glorious ensemble of multicoloured half-timbered houses, including the yellow and brown sixteenth-century **Vieux Manoir**. Immediately alongside it, the eighteenth-century *Auberge de la Boule d'Or* (☎02.31.79.78.78; ③; closed Jan, plus Tues evening & Wed Oct–June), offers three attractive bedrooms. The very centre of the square is taken up by the *Pavé d'Auge* **restaurant** (☎02.31.79.26.71; closed Mon May–Aug), where menus featuring chicken and *andouille* in cider or salmon start at 145F/€22.11.

Orbec

The larger town of **ORBEC**, 19km southeast of Lisieux, also epitomizes the simple pleasures of the region. Along the rue Grande, you'll see several houses in which the gaps between the timbers are filled with intricate patterns of coloured tiles and bricks. Debussy composed *Jardin sous la Pluie* in one of these, and the oldest and prettiest of the lot – a tanner's house dating back to 1568, and once again called the **Vieux Manoir** – holds a museum of local history. On the whole, though, it's more fun just to walk down behind the church to the river, and its watermill and paddocks. The *Hôtel de France*, 152 rue Grande (☎02.31.32.74.02; ②; restaurant closed Mon), serves good meals for 90F/€13.72 and upwards.

Livarot

The centre of the cheese country is the old town of **LIVAROT**, with the rather faded **hotel** and restaurant *du Vivier* (☎02.31.32.04.10; ③) in its heart. Set in a grand house near the Vie river on its western outskirts, the **Musée du Fromage** illustrates the history and manufacture of Livarot's eponymous cheese, and doles out free samples (March Tues–Sat 2–5pm; April & Sept–Oct Mon–Sat 10am–noon & 2–6pm, Sun 2–6pm; May & June daily 10am–noon & 2–6pm; July & Aug daily 10am–6.30pm; 17F/€2.59).

Vimoutiers and Camembert

VIMOUTIERS, due south of Livarot, contains yet another **cheese museum**, at 10 av Général-de-Gaulle (May–Oct Mon 2–6pm, Tues–Sat 9am–noon & 2–6pm, Sun 10am–noon & 2.30–6pm; March, April, Nov & Dec Mon 2–6pm, Tues–Fri 9am–noon & 2–6pm, Sat 9am–noon; 25F/€3.81). This one specializes in labels – the cheeses underneath are mostly polystyrene.

A statue in the town's main square honours Marie Harel, who, at the nearby village of **CAMEMBERT**, developed the original cheese early in the nineteenth century, promoting it with a skilful campaign that included sending free samples to Napoléon. Marie is confronted across the main street by what might be called the statue of the Unknown Cow.

Vimoutiers is the venue of a **market** on Monday afternoons and Fridays. Its **tourist office**, in the cheese museum (same hours; ☎02.33.39.30.29), has piles of information on local cheese-related attractions. Of its **hotels**, the central *Soleil d'Or*, 15 place Mackau (☎02.33.39.07.15; ②; closed mid-Feb to mid-March), has a good 75F/€11.43 menu and an even better 110F/€16.77 one.

A short way south of Vimoutiers, en route to Camembert, the beautifully sited lake known as the **Escale du Vitou** offers everything you need for windsurfing, swimming and horse-riding, as well as its own new, comfortable, rural **hotel**, *L' Escale du Vitou* (☎02.33.39.12.04; ②). There's also a clean and very cheap year-round **campsite** nearby, the two-star *La Campière*, 9 rue du 8-Mai (☎02.33.39.18.86).

Falaise

William the Conqueror, or William the Bastard as he is more commonly known over here, was born in **FALAISE**, 40km southwest of Lisieux. His mother, Arlette, a laundrywoman, was spotted by his father, Duke Robert of Normandy, at the washing place below the château. She was a shrewd woman, scorning secrecy in her eventual assignation by riding publicly through the main entrance to meet him. During her pregnancy, she is said to have dreamed of bearing a mighty tree that cast its shade over Normandy and England.

Falaise's **castle** keep, firmly planted on the massive rocks of the cliff (*falaise*) that gave the town its name, and towering over the **Fontaine d'Arlette** down by the river, is one of the most evocative historic sights imaginable. Nonetheless, it was so heavily damaged during the war that it took over fifty years to reopen for regular visits (daily 9.30am–6pm, English-language tours daily 11am & 3pm; 30F/€4.57). Huge resources have been lavished on restoring the central **donjon**, reminiscent of the Tower of London with its cream-coloured Caen stone. A guiding principle was to avoid any possible confusion as to what is original and authentic, and what is new. Rest assured you'll be in no doubt whatever. Steel slabs, concrete blocks, glass floors and tent-like canvas awnings have been slapped down atop the bare ruins, and metal staircases even squeezed into the wall cavities. The raw structure of the keep, down to its very foundations, lies exposed to view, while the newly created rooms are used for changing exhibitions that focus on the castle's fascinating past.

The town itself was devastated in the war. The struggle to close the "Falaise Gap" in August 1944 was the climax of the Battle of Normandy, as the Allied armies sought to encircle the Germans and cut off their retreat. By the time the Canadians entered the town on August 17, they could no longer tell where the roads had been and had to bulldoze a new four-metre strip straight through the middle.

The **tourist office** can be found on the boulevard de la Libération (May, June & first half of Sept Mon 10am–12.30pm & 1.30–6.30pm, Tues–Sat 9.30am–12.30pm & 1.30–6.30pm, Sun 10.30am–12.30pm; July & Aug Mon–Sat 9.30am–6.30pm, Sun 10.30am–12.30pm & 3–5.30pm; mid-Sept to April Mon 1.30–6.30pm, Tues–Sat 9.30am–12.30pm & 1.30–6.30pm; ☎02.31.90.17.26, *falaise-tourisme@mail.cpod.fr*). Most of the **hotels** stand along the main, noisy Caen–Argentan road. The *Poste*, near the tourist office at 38 rue Georges-Clémenceau (☎02.31.90.13.14; ③; restaurant closed Sun evening & Mon), serves good food on menus from 87F/€13.26, while rooms and meals at the *de la Place*, 1 place St-Gervais (☎02.31.40.19.00; ②; closed Sun evening & Wed), are significantly cheaper. The three-star **campsite**, *Camping du Château* (☎02.31.90.16.55; closed Oct–Easter), next to Arlette's fountain and the municipal swimming pool, is in a much better location.

The Suisse Normande

The area known as the **Suisse Normande** lies roughly 25km south of Caen, along the gorge of the River Orne, between Thury-Harcourt and Putanges. The name is a little far-fetched – there are certainly no mountains – but it is quite distinctive, with cliffs and crags and wooded hills at every turn. There are plenty of opportunities for outdoor pursuits: you can race along the Orne in canoes and kayaks, cruise more sedately on pedaloes or a bizarre species of inflatable rubber tractor, or dangle on ropes from the sheer rock-faces high above. For mere walkers the Orne can be frustrating: footpaths along the river are few and far between, and often entirely overgrown.

The Suisse Normande is usually approached from Caen or Falaise and contrasts dramatically with the prairie-like expanse of wheat fields en route. On wheels, the best access is via the D235 from Caen (signed to Falaise then right through Ifs). Bus Verts #34 will take you to **Thury-Harcourt** or **Clécy** on its way to Flers, and there are occasional special summer train excursions from Caen.

Thury-Harcourt and Clécy

At **THURY-HARCOURT**, the **tourist office** on place St-Sauveur (mid-June to mid-Sept Tues–Sat 9.30am–noon & 2.30–6.30pm, Sun 10.30am–noon; rest of year Tues &

Thurs 9.30am–noon & 2.30–5pm, Fri 9.30am–noon; ☎02.31.79.70.45) can suggest walks, rides and *gîtes d'étape* throughout the Suisse Normande; SIVOM at 15 rue de Condé rents out **canoes**. **Hotels** are for the most part quite expensive, though the flowery *Hôtel du Val d'Orne*, down by the river at 9 rte d'Aunay (☎02.31.79.70.81; ②; closed Sat lunch in summer, Fri evening & all Sat in low season), keeps its room rates low, and has a decent **restaurant**. There's also an attractive four-star **campsite**, the *Vallée du Traspy* (☎02.31.79.61.80; closed mid-Sept to mid-April).

CLÉCY, 10km to the south, is a slightly better bet for finding a room, although its visitors outnumber its residents in peak season. The **hotel** facing the church in the village centre, *Au Site Normand*, 1 rue des Châtelets (☎02.31.69.71.05; ③; closed mid-Nov to Easter, plus Tues evening & Wed out of season), consists of an old-fashioned and good-value dining room in the main timber-framed building, and a cluster of newer units around the back. The river is a kilometre away, down the hill. En route, in the Parc des Loisirs, is a **Musée du Chemin de Fer Miniature** (March–Easter Sun 2–5.30pm; Easter–June & Sept daily 10am–noon & 2–6pm; July & Aug daily 10am–noon & 2–6.30pm; Oct–Nov Sun 2–5pm; 25F/€3.81), featuring a gigantic model railway certain to appeal to children. Set in spacious grounds on the far bank of the river, the *Moulin du Vey* (☎02.31.69.71.08, *www.oda.fr/aa/moulin.duvey*; ⑤; closed Dec & Jan) is a luxury hotel that takes its name from the restored watermill right by the bridge, which is itself, confusingly, now a restaurant. The western river bank continues in a brief splurge of restaurants, takeaways and snack bars as far as the two-star municipal **campsite** (☎02.31.69.70.36; closed Oct–March).

Pont d'Ouilly

If you're planning on walking, or cycling, a good central spot in which to base yourself is **PONT D'OUILLY**, at the point where the main road from Vire to Falaise crosses the river. It's a small town, with a few basic shops, an old covered market hall and a promenade (with bar) slightly upstream alongside the weir. Continuing upstream from the weir a pleasant walk leads for 3.5km alongside the river to the pretty little village of Le Mesnil Villement.

As well as a **campsite** overlooking the river (☎02.31.69.46.12; closed Oct–Easter), Pont d'Ouilly can offer an attractive **hotel**, the *du Commerce* (☎02.31.69.80.16; ②; closed Sun evening & Mon Oct–May), the quintessential French village hotel, with a friendly welcome and attentive service. Its **restaurant** is very popular with local families, serving superb, definitive Norman cooking, with plenty of creamy Pays d'Auge sauces, on menus that start at 65F/€9.91. About a kilometre north, the more upmarket *Auberge St-Christophe* (☎02.31.69.81.23; ③; closed Sun evening, Mon & mid-Feb to mid-March) stands, covered with ivy and geraniums, in a beautiful setting on the right bank of the Orne.

A short distance south of Pont-d'Ouilly is the **Roche d'Oëtre**, a high rock with a tremendous view into the deep and totally wooded gorge of the Rouvre. The river widens soon afterwards into the **Lac du Rabodanges**, formed by the many-arched Rabodanges Dam. It's a popular spot where people practise every watersport, and with a **campsite**, *Les Retours*, perfectly situated between the dam and the bridge on D121.

Southern Normandy

As an alternative to following the more northerly routes across Normandy, motorists heading west from Paris towards Brittany may prefer to cut directly across the province by following the line of the N12 through **Alençon** and then heading north on the N176. Much of the terrain along Normandy's southern border is taken up by the dense woodlands of the **Forêt d'Écouves** and the Forêt des Andaines, so there's plenty of good walking to be had, while the hill towns of **Carrouges** and **Domfront** make great stopovers.

Alençon and around

ALENÇON, a fair-sized and busy town, is known for its traditional – and now pretty much defunct – lacemaking industry. The **Musée des Beaux-Arts et de la Dentelle** (mid-June to mid-Sept daily 10am–noon & 2–6pm; rest of year Tues–Sun 10am–noon & 2–6pm; 20F/€3.05) is housed in a former Jesuit school and has all the best trappings of a modern museum. The highly informative history of lacemaking upstairs, with examples of numerous different techniques, can, however, be tedious for anyone not already riveted by the subject. It also contains an unexpected collection of gruesome Cambodian artefacts like spears and lances, tiger skulls and elephants' feet, gathered by a "militant socialist" French governor at the turn of the century. The paintings in the adjoining Beaux-Arts section are nondescript, except for a few works by Courbet and Géricault. The **Château des Ducs**, the old town castle close by the museum, looks impressive but doesn't encourage visitors: it is now a prison, and people in Alençon have nightmarish memories of its use by the Gestapo during the war. Wandering around the town might also take you to St Thérèse's birthplace on rue St-Blaise, just in front of the *gare routière*.

The **tourist office** is housed in the fifteenth-century Maison d'Ozé on place La Magdelaine (July & Aug Mon & Sat 9.30am–noon & 2–6.30pm, Tues–Fri 9.30am–6.30pm, Sun 10.30am–12.30pm & 2.30–5.30pm; rest of year Mon–Sat 9.30am–noon & 2–6.30pm; ☎02.33.80.66.33, *www.ville-alencon.fr*). The **gare routière** and the **gare SNCF** are both northeast of the centre, in an area that holds Alençon's prime concentration of **hotels**. The two *logis*, *l'Industrie*, 20 place Général-de-Gaulle (☎02.33.27.19.30; ③; closed Sun evening & Mon), and the *Grand Hôtel de la Gare*, 50 av Wilson (☎02.33.29.03.93; ②), are decent and have fixed-price menus for around 70F/€10.67. Back in the town centre, the *Jardin Gourmand*, 14 rue de Sarthe (☎02.33.32.22.56; closed Sun & Mon), is a romantic little **restaurant** with menus from 98F/€14.94. Alençon has good shops and **cafés** in a few well-pedestrianized streets at the heart of its abysmal one-way traffic system. Good places to sample the thriving local **bar scene** include *La Caves Aux Boeufs*, spreading across the pedestrian rue de la Caves aux Boeufs, and the half-timbered *Café des Sept Colonnes* at 2 rue du Château.

The **Forêt d'Écouves**, north of Alençon and inaccessible by public transport, is a dense mixture of spruce, pine, oak and beech, unfortunately a favoured spot of the military – and, in autumn, deer hunters, too. You can usually ramble along the cool paths, happening on wild mushrooms and even the odd wild boar. The *Camping d'Ecouves* on the edge of the forest in **RADON**, 6km north of Alençon, is an ideal spot from which to explore the woodlands and has its own inexpensive restaurant (☎02.33.28.10.64; ②; closed Oct–April).

Carrouges

An alternative base to Alençon, at the western end of the Forêt d'Écouves, is the hill town of **CARROUGES**, with its fine old-style **château** set in spacious grounds at the foot of the hill (daily: April to mid-June & Sept 10am–noon & 2–6pm; mid-June to Aug 9.30am–noon & 2–6.30pm; Oct–March 10am–noon & 2–5pm; 32F/€4.88). Its two highlights are a superb restored brick staircase and a room in which hang portraits of fourteen successive generations of the Le Veneur family, an extraordinary illustration of the processes of heredity. The town also offers two appealing, very similar and almost adjacent small **hotels**: the *Hôtel du Nord* (☎02.33.27.20.14; ①; closed mid-Dec to mid-Jan, plus Fri Sept–June), with a restaurant serving well-prepared local cuisine on menus that start at 60F/€9.15, and the tiny *St-Pierre* (☎02.33.27.20.02; ②), whose rooms all have showers, and whose restaurant has menus starting at 47F/€7.17.

Bagnoles-de-l'Orne

West of Carrouges, the spa town of **BAGNOLES-DE-L'ORNE** is quite unlike anywhere else in this part of the world. The moneyed sick and convalescent come from all over France to its thermal baths, and business is so good they maintain a reservations office next to the Pompidou Centre in Paris. The layout is formal and spacious, centring on a lake with gardens, from where horse-drawn calèches take the clients to an enormous casino. With so many visitors to keep entertained, and spending money, there are also innumerable cultural events of a restrained and stressless nature.

Whether you'd actually want to spend time in Bagnoles depends on your disposable income as well as your health. Furthermore, the town as a whole operates to a season that lasts roughly from early April to the end of October; arrive in winter, and you may find everything shut. The numerous hotels are expensive and sedate places, in which it's possible to be too late for dinner at seven o'clock and locked out altogether at nine, and the three-star **campsite**, *de la Vée* (☎02.33.37.87.45; closed Nov–March), south of town, is rather forlorn.

The **tourist office** on place du Marché (April–Oct Mon–Sat 9am–1pm & 2–6.30pm, Sun 10am–noon & 3–6.30pm; rest of year Mon–Fri 10am–noon & 2–6pm; ☎02.33.37.85.66, *www.bagnoles-de-lorne.com*) will give details on accommodation in Bagnoles and its less exclusive sister town of **TESSE-MADELEINE**. Despite its ugly would-be-Deco exterior, the *Cetlos*, on rue des Casinos (☎02.33.38.44.44; ④), is the best of the **hotels**, bedecked with balconies and terraces overlooking the lake. Cheaper alternatives near the central roundabout in Bagnoles include the *Albert 1er* at 7 av Dr-Poulain (☎02.33.37.80.97; ②; closed Nov–Jan), which has excellent menus from 85F/€12.96, and the *Grand Veneur* at 6 place République (☎02.33.37.86.79; ③; closed Nov–March).

Domfront

The road through the forest from Bagnoles, the D335 and then the D908, climbs above the lush woodlands and progressively narrows to a hog's back before entering **DOMFRONT**. Less happens here than at Bagnoles, but it has the edge on countryside.

A public park, near the long-abandoned former train station, leads up to some redoubtable **castle** ruins perched on an isolated rock. Eleanor of Aquitaine was born in this castle in October 1162, and Thomas à Becket came to stay for Christmas 1166, saying Mass in the **Notre-Dame-sur-l'Eau** church down by the river, which has sadly been ruined by vandals. The views from the flower-filled gardens that surround the mangled keep are spectacular, including a very graphic panorama of the ascent you've made to get up. A slender footbridge connects the castle with the narrow little village itself, which boasts an abundance of half-timbered houses. Near its sweet little central square, the modern **St Julien church**, constructed out of concrete segments during the 1920s, is bursting with exciting mosaics.

On summer afternoons (July & Aug Mon–Sat 3pm), free **guided tours** of old Domfront leave from the **tourist office**, 21 rue St-Julien (Mon–Sat 10am–noon & 2.30–6.30pm; ☎02.33.38.53.97). Domfront's **hotels**, clustered together at the foot of the hill below the old town, make useful and very pleasant stopovers. Two *logis de France* stand side by side: the *Relais St-Michel* (☎02.33.38.64.99; ②) has widely varied menus at under 100F/€15.24, while the *Hôtel de France* (☎02.33.38.51.44; ②) is a little cheaper, and has a nice little bar and garden. Campers should note that the two-star local **campsite**, *du Champs Passais* (☎02.33.37.37.66; closed mid-Oct to mid-April), is exceptionally small.

The Bocage

The region centring on **St-Lô**, just south of the Cotentin, is known as the **Bocage**, from a word that refers to a type of cultivated countryside common in the west of France, where fields are cut by tight hedgerows rooted into walls of earth well over a metre high. An effective form of smallhold farming – at least in pre-industrial days – it also proved to be a perfect system of anti-tank barricades. When the Allied troops tried to advance through the region in 1944, it was almost impenetrable – certainly bearing no resemblance to the East Anglian plains where they had trained. The war here was hand-to-hand slaughter, and the destruction of villages was often wholesale.

St-Lô

The city of **ST-LÔ**, 60km south of Cherbourg and 36km southwest of Bayeux, is still known as the "Capital of the Ruins". Memorial sites are everywhere and what is new speaks as tellingly of the destruction as the ruins that have been preserved. In the main square, the gate of the old prison commemorates Resistance members executed by the Nazis, people deported east to the concentration camps and soldiers killed in action. When the bombardment of St-Lô was at its fiercest, the Germans refused to take any measures to protect the prisoners and the gate was all that survived. Samuel Beckett was here during and after the battle, working for the Irish Red Cross as interpreter, driver and provision-seeker – for such things as rat poison for the maternity hospitals. He said he took away with him a "time-honoured conception of humanity in ruins".

All the trees in the city are the same height, all planted to replace the battle's mutilated stumps. But the most visible – and brilliant – reconstruction is the **Cathédrale de Notre-Dame**. Its main body, with a strange southward-veering nave, has been conventionally repaired and rebuilt. But the shattered west front and the base of the collapsed north tower have been joined by a startling sheer wall of icy green stone that makes no attempt to mask the destruction.

By way of contrast to such memories, a lighthouse-like 1950s folly spirals to nowhere on the main square. Should you feel the urge to climb its staircase, make your way into the brand-new and even more pointless labyrinth of glass at its feet, and pay the 10F/€1.52 admission fee. More compelling, around behind the Mairie, is the **Musée des Beaux-Arts** (daily except Tues 10am–noon & 2–6pm; 10F/€1.52), which is full of treasures: a Boudin sunset; a Lurçat tapestry of his dog, *Nadir and the Pirates*; works by Corot, van Loo, Moreau; a Léger watercolour; a fine series of unfaded sixteenth-century Flemish tapestries on the lives of two peasants; and sad bombardment relics of the town.

St-Lô's **tourist office** adjoins the "lighthouse" on the main square (mid-June to mid-Sept Mon–Sat 9am–6pm; rest of year Mon 2–6pm, Tues–Fri 9am–noon & 2–6pm, Sat 9am–6pm; ☎02.33.77.60.35, *www.mairie-saint-lo.fr*). Most of the **hotels**, restaurants and bars are across the river, near the **gare SNCF**. Overlooking the river from the brow of a ridge beside the station, the upmarket *logis Hôtel des Voyageurs*, 5–7 av Briovère (☎02.33.05.08.63; ③), is home to the *Tocqueville* **restaurant**, which serves a delicious trout soufflé on its 100F/€15.24 menu. If you'd rather be up in town, try *La Cremaillère*, 27 rue Belle (☎02.33.57.14.68; ②; closed Sat lunch & Sun).

The Vire Valley

Once St-Lô was taken in the Battle of Normandy, the armies speedily moved on south-westwards for their next confrontation. The **Vire Valley**, trailing south from St-Lô, saw little action – and its towns and villages seem to have been rarely touched by any historic or cultural mainstream. The motivation in coming to this landscape of rolling hills and occasional gorges is essentially to consume the region's cider, its Calvados (much of it bootleg), its fruit pastries, and its sausages made from pigs' intestines.

From St-Lô to Tessy

The best section of the valley is south of St-Lô through the Roches de Ham to Tessy-sur-Vire. The **Roches de Ham** are a pair of sheer rocky promontories high above the river. Though promoted as "viewing tables", the pleasure lies as much in the walk up, through lanes lined with blackberries, hazelnuts and rich orchards. Downstream from the Roches, and a good place to stop for the night, is **LA CHAPELLE-SUR-VIRE**. Its church, towering majestically above the river, has been an object of pilgrimage since the twelfth century. Next to the bridge on the lower road is the *Auberge de la Chapelle* (☎02.33.56.32.83; ①), a good but rather expensive **restaurant** with a few cheap rooms. At **TESSY-SUR-VIRE**, 5km on, there's little to see other than the river itself, though the town has a luxurious campsite, along with a couple of hotels and a Wednesday **market**.

Vire

VIRE itself is worth visiting specifically for the **food**; in fact the one problem is what to do when you're not eating. The town is best known for its dreaded *andouille* sausages, but you can gorge yourself instead on salmon trout fresh from the river, accompanied by local *poiré*. Choosing a **hotel**, it makes sense to go for one with a good dining room. At the central *Hôtel de France*, 4 rue d'Aignaux (☎02.31.68.00.35; ③), the 98F/€14.94 menu is packed with local specialities, including *andouille* for both starter and main course, but no one's going to make you eat it if you don't want to – there's always *tripes a là mode de Caen* instead. *Au Vrai Normand*, 14 rue Armand-Gasté (☎02.31.67.90.99), is the best **restaurant**.

Villedieu-les-Poêles

VILLEDIEU-LES-POÊLES – literally "City of God the Frying Pans" – is a lively though touristy place, 28km west of Vire. Copper souvenirs and kitchen utensils gleam from its rows of shops, and the tourist office has lists of dozens of local *ateliers* for more direct purchases, plus details of the copperwork museum.

All of this can seem a bit obsessive, though there is more authentic interest at the **Fonderie de Cloches** at 13 rue du Pont-Chignon, one of the twelve remaining bell foundries in Europe. Work here is only part-time due to limited demand, but it's open to visits all year round, and you may find the forge lit (June & Sept Mon–Sat 8am–noon & 2–5.30pm, Sun 9.30am–noon & 2–5.30pm; July & Aug daily 8am–6pm; rest of year Tues–Sat 8am–noon & 2–5.30pm; 22F/€3.35). Expert craftsmen will show you the moulds, composed of an unpleasant-looking combination of clay, goat's hair and horse shit.

The local **tourist office** is on place des Costils (June–Sept Tues–Sat 10am–noon & 2–6pm; ☎02.33.61.05.69). If you're charmed into staying, head for the comfortable *Fruitier* on place Gostils (☎02.33.90.51.00; ③; closed Sat in winter), which serves a reasonable 68F/€10.37 menu and a 128F/€19.51 menu packed with regional delights. In the heart of the main street, the welcoming *logis Hôtel St-Pierre et St-Michel*, 12 place de la République (☎02.33.61.00.11; ③; closed Jan, plus Fri in low season), houses the stylish *Le Sourdin* restaurant, where the 115F/€17.53 menu features fine local ham, and the 195F/€29.73 menu is seriously gastronomic. There's also a three-star **campsite** by the river, *La Sienne* (☎02.33.61.02.44; closed Oct–Easter).

travel details

Trains

Through services to Paris connect with all ferries at Dieppe, Le Havre and Cherbourg: if you're doing this journey, it's easiest to buy a combined rail–ferry–rail ticket at your point of departure.

Caen to: Bayeux (14 daily; 20min); Cherbourg (10 daily; 1hr 15min); Coutances (4 daily; 1hr 15min); Lisieux (hourly; 30min); Paris-St-Lazare (at least hourly; 2hr); Pontorson (4 daily; 2hr); Rennes (4 daily; 3hr); St-Lô (4 daily; 50min); Rouen (6 daily; 2hr).

Cherbourg to: Caen (10 daily; 1hr 15min); Paris (10 daily; 3hr).

Dieppe to: Paris-St-Lazare (8 daily; 2hr 15min); Rouen (10 daily; 1hr).

Granville to: Cherbourg (frequent; 1hr); Coutances (8 daily; 30min); Paris (frequent; 3hr).

Le Havre to: Paris (12 daily; 2hr 15min); Rouen (12 daily; 1hr).

Le Tréport to: Paris (5 daily; 2hr 45min).

Rouen to: Caen (8 daily; 2hr 15min); Fécamp (at least hourly; 1hr 15min); Paris-St-Lazare (12 daily; 1hr 15min).

St-Lô to: Bayeux (4 daily; 30min); Caen (4 daily; 1hr); Coutances (4 daily; 20min); Pontorson (4 daily; 1hr 15min); Rennes (4 daily; 2hr).

Trouville-Deauville to: Lisieux (6–14 daily; 20min); Paris (6–14 daily; 2hr).

Buses

Alençon to: Bagnoles (3 daily; 1hr); Évreux (1 daily; 2hr); Vimoutiers (1–3 daily; 1hr 30min).

Bayeux to: Arromanches (4 daily; 25min); Ouistreham (4 daily; 1hr 15min).

Caen to: Bayeux (4 daily; 50min); Cabourg (14 daily; 40min); Clécy (3–5 daily; 50min);

Deauville (14 daily; 1hr 05min); Falaise (5–6 daily; 50min); Honfleur (14 daily, 1hr 30min; 2 express services daily, 1hr); Houlgate (14 daily; 55min); Le Havre (4 daily, 2hr 30min; 2 express services daily, 1hr 25min); Thury-Harcourt (3–5 daily; 40min).

Cherbourg to: Barfleur (2 daily; 45min); St-Lô (2–3 daily; 1hr 30min); St-Vaast (2 daily; 1hr).

Dieppe to: Fécamp (2 daily; 2hr 20min); Le Havre (2 daily; 3hr 50min); Le Tréport (3 daily; 30min); Paris (5 daily; 2hr 15min); St-Valéry (2 daily; 1hr).

Mont-St-Michel to: Rennes (4 daily; 1hr 20min); St-Malo (4 daily; 1hr 30min).

Rouen to: Caudebec (2 daily; 1hr 10min); Dieppe (2 daily; 1hr 45min); Fécamp (4 daily; 2hr 30min); Jumièges (2 daily; 45min); Le Tréport (4 daily; 2hr 30min); Le Havre (hourly; 2hr 45min); Lisieux (4 daily; 2hr 30min).

St-Lô to: Bayeux (4 daily; 30min); Cherbourg (4 daily; 1hr 30min); Coutances (6 daily; 30min).

Ferries

Caen (Ouistreham) to: Portsmouth (2–3 daily; 6hr) with Brittany Ferries (☎08.03.82.88.28, *www.brittany-ferries.com*).

Cherbourg to: Poole (1–2 daily; 4hr 15min) with Brittany Ferries (see above); Portsmouth (5–6 daily; 2hr 45min–4hr 45min) with P&O (☎08.03.01.30.13, *www.poef.com*); Rosslare (2–4 weekly; 17hr) with Irish Continental (☎02.33.23.44.44).

Dieppe to: Newhaven (4–5 daily; 2hr 15min–4hr) with Hoverspeed (☎08.20.00.35.55).

Le Havre to: Portsmouth (3 daily; 5hr 30min) with P&O (see above).

For more details, see p.5 onwards.

CHAPTER FIVE

BRITTANY

N o one area – and certainly no one city or town – in **Brittany** encapsulates the character of the province; that lies in its people and in its geographical unity. For generations Bretons risked their lives fishing and trading on the violent seas and struggled with the arid soil of the interior. This toughness and resilience is tinged with Celtic culture: mystical, musical, sometimes morbid and defeatist, sometimes vital and inspired.

Though archeologically Brittany is one of the richest sites in the world – the alignments at **Carnac** rival Stonehenge – its first appearance in recorded history is as the quasi-mythical "Little Britain" of Arthurian legend. In the days when to travel by sea was safer and easier than by land, it was intimately connected with "Great Britain" across the water, and settlements such as St-Malo, St-Pol and Quimper were founded by Welsh and Irish missionary "saints" whose names are not to be found in any official breviary. Brittany remained independent until the sixteenth century, its last ruler, Duchess Anne, only managing to protect the province's autonomy through marriage to two consecutive French monarchs. After her death, in 1532, François I took her daughter and lands, and sealed the union with an act supposedly enshrining certain privileges. These included a veto over taxes by the local *parlement* and the people's right to be tried, or conscripted to fight, only in their province. The successive violations of this treaty by Paris, and subsequent revolts, form the core of Breton history since the Middle Ages.

Even though their language has been steadily eradicated, and the interior of the province severely depopulated, Bretons still tend to treat France as a separate country. Few, however, actively support Breton nationalism (which it's a criminal offence to advocate) much beyond putting *Breizh* (Breton for "Brittany") stickers on their cars. But there have been many successes in reviving the language, and the economic resurgence of the last two decades, helped partly by summer tourism, has largely been due to local initiatives, like Brittany Ferries re-establishing an old trading link, carrying produce and passengers across to Britain and Ireland. At the same time a Celtic artistic identity has consciously been revived, and local festivals – above all August's **Inter-Celtic Festival** at Lorient – celebrate traditional Breton music, poetry and dance, with fellow Celts treated as comrades.

If you're looking for traditional Breton fun, and you can't make the Lorient festival (or the smaller *Quinzaine Celtique* at Nantes in June/July), look out for gatherings

---

ACCOMMODATION PRICE CODES

Each hotel and guesthouse in this book has been graded according to the following price codes, which indicate the price for the **cheapest double room available during the high season**.

① Under 160F/€24	④ 300–400F/€46–61	⑦ 600–700F/€91–107
② 160–220F/€24–34	⑤ 400–500F/€61–76	⑧ 700–800F/€107–122
③ 220–300F/€34–46	⑥ 500–600F/€76–91	⑨ Over 800F/€122

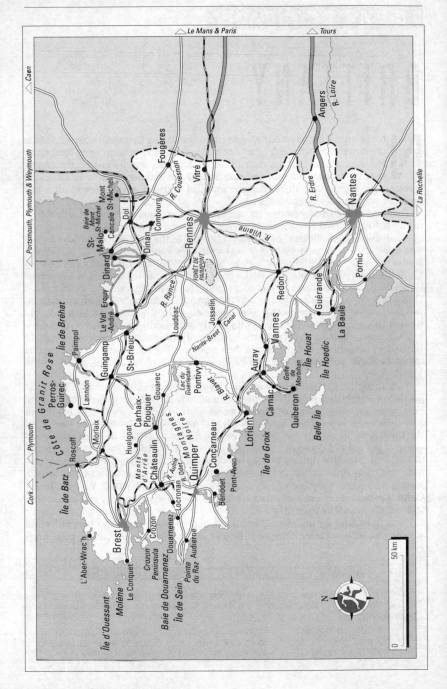

organized by **Celtic folklore groups** – *Circles* or *Bagadou*. You may also be interested by the **pardons**, pilgrimage festivals commemorating local saints, which guidebooks (and tourist offices) tend to promote as spectacles. These are not, unlike most French festivals, phoney affairs kept alive for tourists, but deeply serious and rather gloomy religious occasions.

For most visitors, however, it is the Breton **coast** that is the dominant feature. Apart from the Côte d'Azur, this is the most popular summer resort area in France, for both French and foreign tourists, and although the sinking of the supertanker *Erika* on Christmas Eve 1999 – the most recent of several similar disasters – dented visitor numbers in 2000, visible signs of the oil spill are minimal, and there's no reason for it to deter future tourism. The attractions of the Breton coast are obvious: warm white-sand beaches, towering cliffs, rock formations and offshore islands and islets, and everywhere the stone dolmen and menhir monuments of a prehistoric past. The most frequented areas are the **Côte d'Émeraude**, around **St-Malo** and the **Morbihan coast** below **Auray** and **Vannes**. Accommodation and campsites here are plentiful, if pushed to their limits from mid-June to the end of August, and for all the crowds there are

---

FOOD IN BRITTANY

Brittany's proudest addition to the great cuisines of the world has to be the **crêpe** and its savoury equivalent the **galette**; crêperies throughout the region attempt to pass them off as satisfying meals, serving them with every imaginable filling. However, few people can plan their holidays specifically around eating pancakes, and gourmets are far more likely to be enticed to Brittany by its magnificent array of **seafood**. Restaurants in resorts such as St-Malo and Quiberon jostle for the attention of fish connoisseurs, while some smaller towns – like Cancale, which specializes in oysters (*huîtres*), and Erquy, with its scallops (*coquilles St-Jacques*) – depend wholly on one specific mollusc for their livelihood.

Although they can't quite claim to be uniquely Breton, two appetizers feature on every self-respecting menu. These are **moules marinières**, giant bowls of succulent orange mussels steamed open in a combination of white wine, shallots and parsley (and perhaps enriched by the addition of cream or crème fraiche to become *moules à la crème*), and **soupe de poissons**, traditionally served with a little pot of the garlicky mayonnaise known as *rouille* (coloured by the addition of pulverized sweet red pepper), a mound of grated *gruyère*, and a bowl of croutons. Jars of freshly made *soupe de poissons* – or even crab or lobster – are always on sale in seaside *poissonneries*, and make an ideal way to take a taste of France home with you. Paying a bit more in a restaurant – typically on menus costing 150F/€22.87 or more – brings you into the realm of the **assiette de fruits de mer**, a mountainous heap of langoustines, crabs, oysters, mussels, clams, whelks and cockles, most of them raw and all delicious. **Main courses** tend to be plainer than in Normandy, for example, with fresh local fish being prepared with relatively simple sauces. Skate served with capers, or salmon baked with a mustard or cheese sauce, are typical dishes, while even the **cotriade**, a stew containing such fish as sole, turbot or bass, as well as shellfish, is distinctly less rich than its Mediterranean equivalent, the *bouillabaisse*. Brittany is also better than much of France in maintaining its respect for fresh green **vegetables**, thanks to the extensive local production of peas, cauliflowers, artichokes and the like. Only with the **desserts** can things get a little heavy; **far Breton**, considered a great delicacy, is a baked concoction of sponge and custard dotted with chopped plums, while *îles flottantes* are meringue icebergs adrift in a sea of crème brulée or custard.

Strictly speaking, no **wine** is produced in Brittany itself. However, along the lower Loire valley, the *département* of Loire-Atlantique, centred on Nantes, is still generally regarded as "belonging" to Brittany – and is treated as such in this chapter. Vineyards here are responsible for the dry white Muscadet – which is what normally goes into *moules marinières* – and the even drier Gros-Plant.

resorts as enticing as any in the country. Over in **southern Finistère** (Land's End) and along the **Côte de Granit Rose** in the north you may have to do more planning. This is true, too, if you come to Brittany out of season, when many of the coastal resorts close down completely.

Whenever you come, don't leave Brittany without visiting one of its scores of **islands** – such as the **Île de Bréhat**, the **Île de Sein**, or **Belle Île** – or taking in cities like **Quimper** or **Morlaix**, testimony to the riches of the medieval duchy. Allow time, too, to leave the coast and explore the interior, particularly the western country around the **Monts d'Arrée**. Here you pay for the solitude with very sketchy transport, few hotels and few campsites. This last need not be a problem: Brittany is one of the few areas of France where *camping sauvage* (not in campsites) is tolerated.

EASTERN BRITTANY AND THE NORTH COAST

All roads in Brittany curl eventually inland to **Rennes**, the capital, which lies a short way north of the legendary **Forêt de Paimpont**, the location of the Arthurian tales. To the east of Rennes are the heavily fortified citadels of **Fougères** and **Vitré**, which guarded the eastern approaches to medieval Brittany, which was obliged vigorously to defend its independence against potential incursors. Along the north coast west of Mont St-Michel, only just across the border in Normandy, are some of Brittany's finest old towns. One of the most spectacular introductions to the province is that which greets ferry passengers from Portsmouth; the **River Rance**, guarded by magnificently preserved **St-Malo** on its estuary, and beautiful medieval **Dinan** 20km upstream. To the west stretches a varied coastline culminating in one of the most seductive of the islands, the **Île de Bréhat**, and the colourful chaos of the **Côte de Granit Rose**.

Rennes and around

For a city that has been the capital and power centre of Brittany since the 1532 union with France, Rennes is – outwardly at least – uncharacteristic of the province, with its Neoclassical layout and pompous major buildings. What potential it had to be a picturesque tourist spot was destroyed in 1720, when a drunken carpenter managed to set light to virtually the whole city. Only the area known as **Les Lices**, at the junction of the canalized Ille and the River Vilaine, was undamaged. The remodelling of the rest of the city was handed over to Parisian architects, not in deference to the capital but in an attempt to rival it. The result, on the north side of the river at any rate, is something of a patchwork quilt, consisting of grand eighteenth-century public squares interspersed with intimate little alleys of half-timbered houses. It's quite a pleasant city to stroll around for half a day, but it lacks a cohesive personality.

Arrival, information and accommodation

Rennes' modern **gare SNCF** is located south of the Vilaine, around twenty minutes' walk from the tourist office and a little more from the medieval quarter. The **gare routière** is immediately east of the *gare SNCF* on boulevard Solferino, but most local buses start and finish on or near place de la République. Rennes is a busy junction, with direct services to St-Malo (TIV; ☎02.99.79.23.44), Dinan and Dinard (Armor Express; ☎02.99.50.64.17),

A BRETON GLOSSARY

Estimates of the number of Breton-speakers range from 400,000 to 800,000. You may well encounter it spoken as a first, day-to-day language by the very old and the young in parts of Finistère and the Morbihan. Learning Breton is not really a viable prospect for visitors without a grounding in Welsh, Gaelic or some other Celtic language. However, as you travel through the province, it's interesting to note the roots of Breton place names, many of which have a simple meaning in the language. Below are some of the most common:

aber	estuary	*hen*	old	*nevez*	sea
bihan	little	*hir*	long	*parc*	new
bran	hill	*inis*	island	*mor*	field
braz	big	*ker*	town or house	*penn*	end, head
creach	height	*koz*	old	*plou*	parish
cromlech	stone circle	*lan*	church	*pors*	port, farmyard
dol	table	*lann*	heath	*roch*	stone
dolmen	stone table	*lech*	flat stone	*ster*	river
du	black	*mario*	dead	*stivel*	fountain, spring
gavre	goat	*men*	stone	*trez*	sand, beach
goat	forest	*menez*	mountain	*trou*	valley
goaz	stream	*menhir*	long stone	*ty*	house
guen	white	*meur*	big	*wrach*	witch

and Nantes (Société Transports Tourisme de l'Ouest; ☎02.40.20.45.20). In addition Les Courriers Bretons (☎02.99.19.70.70, *www. lescourriersbreton.fr*) runs **day-trips to Mont-St-Michel** departing from the *gare routière* daily at 11am, timed to connect with the morning TGV from Paris (128F/€19.51 return).

Rennes' **tourist office** stands in a disused medieval church, just north of the river at 11 rue St-Yves (April–Sept Mon–Sat 9am–7pm, Sun 11am–6pm; Oct–March Mon–Sat 9am–6pm, Sun 11am–6pm; ☎02.99.67.11.11, *www.tourisme-rennes.com*). For **Internet access**, head to *Cybernet On Line*, near the Palais du Parlement at 22 rue St-Georges (☎02.99.36.37.41).

Unfortunately, there are very few **hotels** in the old part of Rennes – and those that are there can be very hard to find. If you've arrived by train or bus, it's easier to settle for staying near the *gares SNCF* and *routière*.

Hotels

Garden Hôtel, 3 rue Duhamel (☎02.99.65.45.06, fax 02.99.65.02.62). Comfortable, nicely decorated and very personal hotel, north of the *gare SNCF* not far from the river, with a pleasant little garden café but no restaurant. ②.

de Léon, 15 rue de Léon (☎& fax 02.99.30.55.28). Quiet little eleven-room hotel, off the beaten track northeast of the *gare SNCF*, offering old-fashioned but adequate rooms at knockdown rates. ①.

des Lices, 7 place des Lices (☎02.99.79.14.81, fax 02.99.79.35.44, *hotel.lices@wanadoo.fr*). Very comfortable and friendly modern hotel, with forty rooms, all with TV, on the edge of the prettiest part of old Rennes, very convenient for the place des Lices car park. ③.

Riaval, 9 rue de Riaval (☎02.99.50.65.58, fax 02.99.41.85.30). Friendly hotel with neat budget rooms, on a quiet street well away from the centre, but only a few minutes' walk east of the *gare SNCF*. ①.

Hôtel-Restaurant Au Rocher de Cancale, 10 rue St-Michel (☎02.99.79.20.83). Beautifully restored four-room hotel with modern facilities on a lively pedestrian street, between place Ste-Anne and place St-Michel, in the heart of medieval Rennes. The restaurant, closed at weekends, has lunch menus from 58F/€8.84, dinners from 85F/€12.96; the 130F/€19.82 exclusively fish menu is excellent. ③.

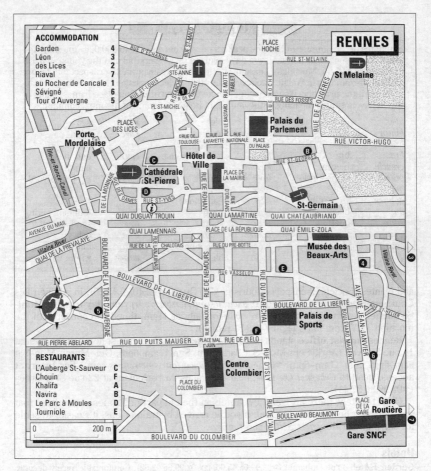

Le Sévigné, 47bis av Janvier (☎02.99.67.27.55, fax 02.99.30.66.10). Smart, upmarket option 100m north of the *gare SNCF* en route to the centre, with a large brasserie next door. All rooms are en suite, with satellite TV. ④.

Tour d'Auvergne, 20 bd de la Tour-d'Auvergne (☎02.99.30.84.16; fax 02.23.42.10.01). Very simple but welcoming option, above the little *Serment de Vin* brasserie, between the *gare SNCF* and the river. Some low-priced rooms have en-suite shower facilities. ①.

Hostel and campsite

Camping municipal des Gayeulles, rue de Professeur-Maurice-Audin (☎02.99.36.91.22). An appealingly verdant site 1km east of central Rennes; take bus #3. Closed Oct–March.

Centre International de Séjour, 10–12 Canal St-Martin (☎02.99.33.22.33, fax 02.99.59.06.21). Welcoming and attractively positioned HI hostel with a cafeteria and a laundry, situated 3km out from the centre, next to the Canal d'Ille et Rance. Costs 72–135F/€10.98–20.58 per person per night for a dorm bed in a small room, or 200F/€30.49 for a private double. Buses #20 and #22 run weekdays only from the *gare SNCF*, direction "St-Gregoire", stop "Coëtlogon"; at weekends catch bus #18.

The City

Rennes' surviving **medieval quarter**, bordered by the canal to the west and the river to the south, radiates from **Porte Mordelaise**, the old ceremonial entrance to the city. Just to the northeast of the porte, the **place des Lices**, nowadays dominated by two empty market halls, was originally the venue for tournaments – that is, jousting "lists". It was here, in 1337, that the hitherto unknown Bertrand du Guesclin, then aged 17, fought and defeated several older opponents. This set him on his career as a soldier, during which he was to save Rennes when it was under siege by the English. However, after the Bretons were defeated at Auray in 1364, he fought for the French, and twice invaded Brittany.

The one central building to escape the 1720 fire was the **Palais de Justice** on rue Hoche downtown. Ironically, however, the Palais was all but ruined by a major confla-gration in 1994; the exact circumstances remain somewhat mysterious, but it's thought the blaze was sparked by a stray flare set off during a demonstration by Breton fisher-men. Since then, the entire structure has been rebuilt and restored, and is once more topped by an impressive array of gleaming gilded statues.

If you head south from the Palais de Justice, you'll soon reach the **River Vilaine**, which flows through the centre of Rennes, narrowly confined into a steep-sided channel. The south bank of the river is every bit as busy, if not busier, than the north, and at 20 quai Émile-Zola on the south bank a former university building houses the city's **Musée des Beaux Arts** (daily except Tues 10am–noon & 2–6pm; 20F/€3.05). Unfortunately many of its finest artworks – which include drawings by Leonardo da Vinci, Botticelli, Fra Lippo Lippi and Dürer – are not usually on public display. Instead you'll find a number of indif-ferent Impressionist views of Normandy by the likes of Boudin and Sisley, interspersed with the occasional treasure such as Pieter Boel's startlingly contemporary-looking seventeenth-century animal studies, Veronese's depiction of a flying *Perseus Rescuing Andromeda*, and Pierre-Paul Rubens' *Tiger Hunt*, enlivened by the occasional lion. The same building was long home also to the Musée de Bretagne, covering the history and culture of Brittany, which has been closed for several years while its exhibits are moved to a new, high-tech museum, due to open on a separate site in 2003.

Heading south away from the river, **rue Vasselot** has its own array of half-timbered old houses, while the giant **Colombier Centre**, just west of the *gare SNCF*, is Rennes at its most modern. It is a vast mall packed with shops of all kinds, plus cafés and snack bars, and featuring an amazing crystal model of itself in its main entrance hall.

Eating and drinking

Most of Rennes' more interesting **bars** and **restaurants** are to be found in the streets just south of place Ste-Anne and St-Aubin church. Rues St-Michel and Penhoët, each with a fine assemblage of ancient wooden buildings, are the epicentre at the moment, while eth-nic alternatives can be found along rue St-Malo just to the north. While you're exploring, look around the back of the excellent crêperie at 5 place Ste-Anne, through an archway off rue Motte-Fablet, to get an extraordinary glimpse of medieval high-rise housing.

Rue Vasselot is the nearest equivalent south of the river, though if you're just look-ing for a quick snack, don't forget the various outlets in the Centre Colombier.

L'Auberge St-Sauveur, 6 rue St-Sauveur (☎02.99.79.32.56). Classy, romantic restaurant, in an attractive medieval house near the cathedral, with rich, meaty dinner menus at 109F/€16.62 and 165F/€25.15, and lighter lunches for 78F/€11.89. Closed for lunch on Sat & Mon and all day Sun.

Le Chouin, 12 rue d'Isly (☎02.99.30.87.86). A fine fish restaurant, a little north of the Centre Colombier towards the river. Lunch costs just 59F/€8.99 or 79F/€12.04, while both the 99F/€15.09 and 129F/€19.67 dinner menus include nine oysters to start. Closed Sun evening & Mon.

drop down through successive tiers of formal public gardens, offering magnificent views of the ramparts and towers along the way, to reach the water meadows of the River Nançon, which you cross beside a little cluster of medieval houses still standing on the river bank.

The **Forêt de Fougères**, a short way out on the D177 towards Vire (see p.383), is one of the most enjoyable in the province. The beech woods are spacious and light, with various megaliths and trails of old stones scattered in among the chestnut and spruce. It's quite a contrast to their normal bleak and windswept haunts to see dolmens sporting themselves in such verdant surroundings.

Fougères' **tourist office**, at 1 place Aristide-Briand, provides copious information on all aspects of the town and local countryside (July & Aug Mon–Sat 9am–7pm, Sun 10am–noon & 2–4pm; rest of year Mon–Sat 9.30am–12.30pm & 2–6pm, Sun 10am–noon & 2–4pm; ☎02.99.94.12.20, *www.ot-fougeres.fr*). The *Hôtel des Voyageurs*, nearby at 10 place Gambetta (☎02.99.99.08.20; ②; closed second fortnight of Aug) is a particularly nice **place to stay**, with a separate but excellent **restaurant** downstairs (closed Sat). There are no hotels in the immediate vicinity of the château, but the squares on all sides are crammed with an abundance of appealing **bars** and **crêperies**. At *Le Medieval* (☎02.99.94.92.59), which has lots of outdoor seating beside the moat, you can snack on *moules frites* or crêpes, or get a full dinner from 79F/€12.04.

Vitré

VITRÉ, just north of the Le Mans–Rennes motorway, rivals Dinan as the best-preserved medieval town in Brittany. Its walls are not quite complete, but the thickets of medieval stone cottages that lie outside them have hardly changed. The towers of the **castle** itself, which dominates the western end of the ramparts, have pointed slate-grey roofs in best fairy-tale fashion, looking like freshly sharpened pencils, though, unfortunately, the municipal offices and **museum** of shells, birds, bugs and local history inside are not exactly thrilling (April–June daily 10am–noon & 2–5.30pm; July–Sept daily 10am–6pm; rest of year Mon, Sat & Sun 2–5.30pm, Wed–Fri 10am–noon & 2–5.30pm; 26F/€3.96).

Vitré is a market town rather than an industrial centre, with its principal **market** held on Mondays in the square in front of **Notre-Dame church**. The old city is full of twisting streets of half-timbered houses, a good proportion of which are bars – **rue Beaudrairie** in particular has a fine selection.

Vitré's **gare SNCF** is a little way south of the centre, where the ramparts have disappeared and the town blends into its newer sectors. Just across the square from the station you'll find the **tourist office** (July & Aug daily 10am–7pm; rest of year Mon–Fri 10am–noon & 1.30–6pm, Sat 10am–noon; ☎02.99.75.04.46, *www.ot-vitre.fr*), and most of the **hotels** too. The *Petit-Billot*, 5bis place du Général-Leclerc (☎02.99.75.02.10; ③), is good value, while rooms on the higher floors of the *Hôtel du Château*, 5 rue Rallon (☎02.99.74.58.59; ③; closed Sun out of season), on a quiet road just below the castle, have views of the ramparts. Of the town's **restaurants**, *Le St-Yves*, immediately below the castle at 1 place St-Yves (☎02.99.74.68.76; closed Mon), serves menus from 50F/€7.62 to 175F/€26.68 (the 72F/€10.98 one should suit most requirements), and *La Soupe aux Choux*, at the top of rue de la Baudrairie at 32 rue Notre-Dame (☎02.99.75.10.86; closed Sun in low season), prepares simple but classic French food.

Dol-de-Bretagne and around

During the Middle Ages, **DOL-DE-BRETAGNE**, 30km west of Mont St-Michel, was an important bishopric. It no longer has a bishop, though its huge granite **cathedral** endures, with its strange, squat, tiled towers. The ambitious new **Cathédraloscope** (daily: mid-Feb to April & Oct to mid-Jan 10am–6pm; May–Sept 9am–7pm; 40F/€6.10), in the cathedral square, sets out to explain the construction and significance of medieval cathedrals in general, but for all its high-tech presentation and flair, non-French-speakers may well find it rather heavy going. Also in the square, the more traditional **Musée Historique de Dol** (Easter–Sept daily 2.30–6pm) holds two rooms of astonishing wooden bits and pieces rescued in assorted states of decay from churches, often equally rotten, all over Brittany.

Dol still has a few streets packed with venerable buildings, most notably the pretty **Grande-Rue**, where one Romanesque edifice dates back as far as the eleventh century, alongside an assortment of 500-year-old half-timbered houses that look down on the bustle of shoppers below.

All approaches to Dol from the bay are guarded by the former island of **Mont Dol**, now eight rather marshy kilometres in from the sea. This abrupt granite outcrop, looking mountainous beyond its size on such a flat plain, was the legendary site of a battle between the Archangel Michael and the Devil. Various fancifully named indentations in the rock, such as the "Devil's Claw", testify to the savagery of their encounter, which as usual the Devil lost. The site has been occupied since prehistoric times – flint implements have been unearthed alongside the bones of mammoths, sabre-toothed tigers and even rhinoceroses. Later on, it appears to have been used for worship by the druids, before becoming, like Mont St-Michel, an island monastery, all traces of which have long vanished. A plaque proclaims that visiting the small chapel on top earns a papal indulgence. The climb is pleasant, too, a steep footpath winding up among the chestnuts and beeches to a solitary bar.

There is not a great deal to keep casual visitors in Dol for very long. However, the **tourist office**, at 3 Grande-Rue (Easter–June & Sept daily 10.30am–noon & 3.30–7pm; July & Aug daily 9.30am–12.30pm & 2.30–7.30pm; rest of year Thurs only 2–4pm; ☎02.99.48.15.37), can direct you eastwards to a reasonable **hotel**, the *Bretagne*, next to the market at 17 place Chateaubriand (☎02.99.48.02.03; ③; closed Oct). Rooms at the back look out across a small vestige of ramparts towards Mont Dol. The best **campsite** in the area is the luxurious *Castel-Camping des Ormes* (☎02.99.73.53.00, *www.lesormes.com*; closed mid-Sept to mid-May), set around a lake 6km south towards Combourg on the N795, which offers horse-riding, golf and even cricket.

A couple of nice **fish restaurants** can be found in the ancient houses on rue Ceinte, as it winds its way from Grande-Rue to the Cathedral: *Le Porche au Pain* at no. 1, and *La Grabotais* at no. 4 (☎02.99.48.19.89; closed Mon).

St-Malo and around

Walled and built with the same grey granite stone as Mont St-Michel, **ST-MALO** was originally in the Middle Ages a fortified island at the mouth of the Rance, controlling not only the estuary but the open sea beyond. The promontory fort of Alet, south of the modern centre in what's now the St-Servan district, commanded approaches to the Rance even before the Romans, but modern St-Malo traces its origins to a monastic settlement founded by saints Aaron and Brendan early in the sixth century. In later centuries it became notorious as the home of a fierce breed of pirate-mariners, who were never quite under anybody's control but their own; for four years from 1590, St-Malo even declared itself to be an independent republic. The *corsaires* of St-Malo not only forced English ships passing up the Channel to pay tribute, but also brought wealth from further afield. Jacques Cartier, who colonized Canada, lived in and sailed from St-Malo, as did the first colonists to settle the Falklands – hence the islands' Argentinian name, Las Malvinas.

Now inseparably attached to the mainland, St-Malo is the most visited place in Brittany – thanks more to its superb old **citadelle** than to the ferry terminal that's tucked into the harbour behind. From outside the walls, the dignified ensemble of the old city might seem stern and forbidding, but passing through into the streets within the walls brings you into a busy, lively and very characterful town, packed with hotels, restaurants, bars and shops. Though the summer crowds can be oppressive, a stroll atop the ramparts should restore your equilibrium, and the presence of vast, clean beaches right on the city's doorstep is a big bonus if you're travelling with kids in tow. Having to spend a night here before or after a ferry crossing is a positive pleasure – so long as you take the trouble to reserve accommodation in advance.

Arrival and information

Though almost all St-Malo buses, whether local or long-distance, coincide also with trains at the **gare SNCF** – 2km out from the citadelle on place Hermine, and convenient neither for the old town nor the ferry – the **gare routière** is officially an expanse of concrete right next to the tourist office. The two main local bus companies both have ticket offices here: the Compagnie de Transport d'Ille et Vilaine (TIV; ☎02.99.40.82.67), which runs services to Dinard, Dinan, Cancale, Combourg and Rennes, and Les Courriers Bretons (☎02.99.19.70.70, *www.lescourriersbreton.fr*), which goes to Cancale, Mont St-Michel, Dol, Rennes and Fougères, and also runs **day-trips to Mont St-Michel** (Tues–Fri 1.35pm; 115F/€17.53).

St-Malo is always busy with **boats**. From the Terminal Ferry du Naye (☎02.99.40.64.41), Brittany Ferries (*www.brittany-ferries.com*) sails to Portsmouth (mid-March to mid-Nov daily at 10.45am, otherwise less frequently; 8hr 45min) and Plymouth (mid-Nov to mid-March Fri noon; 8hr), while Condor Ferries (☎02.99.20.03.00, *www.condorferries.co.uk*) connects with both Poole and Weymouth (May–Oct one sailing daily on each route; 5hr),

Between mid-April and early Oct, regular **passenger ferries**, run by Émeraude Lines (☎02.23.18.15.15; *www.emeraudelines.com*), cross to **Dinard** from the quai Dinan, in front of the port (20F/€3.05 single, 30F/€4.57 return, bikes 15F/€2.29 each way; 10min). Émeraude Lines also conducts **excursions** up the river to Dinan (see p.401), day-trips to Granville in Normandy (see p.369), and cruises along the Brittany coast.

St-Malo's helpful **tourist office** (April–June & Sept Mon–Sat 9am–7pm, Sun 10am–noon & 2–6pm; July & Aug Mon–Sat 8.30am–8pm, Sun 10am–7pm; rest of year Mon–Sat 9am–12.30pm & 1.30–6pm; ☎02.99.56.64.48, *www.ville-saint-malo.fr*) is right in front of the city walls, beside the Bassin Duguay-Trouin in the Port des Yachts. For **Internet access**, head to *Cop' Imprim*, just west of the *gare SNCF* at 39 bd des Talards (Mon–Fri 9am–7pm, Sat 9am–noon; ☎02.23.18.08.18, *copimprim@wanadoo.fr*; 50F/€7.62 per hour).

Bicycles can be rented from Cycles Diazo, 47 quai Duguay-Trouin (☎02.99.40.31.63), Espace Nicole Deux Roues, 11 rue Robert-Schumann in Paramé (☎02.99.56.11.06), and from the *gare SNCF*.

Accommodation

St-Malo boasts over a hundred **hotels**, including the seaside boarding houses just off the beach, along with several **campsites** and a **hostel** – in high season it needs every one of them. If you plan to stay the night before catching a summer ferry, it's best to make a reservation well in advance.

You pay a premium for the privilege of staying within the city walls, since that's where any nightlife takes place, and it's a fair walk in through the docks from any of the surrounding suburbs. Unfortunately, the *intra-muros* hotels tend to take advantage of

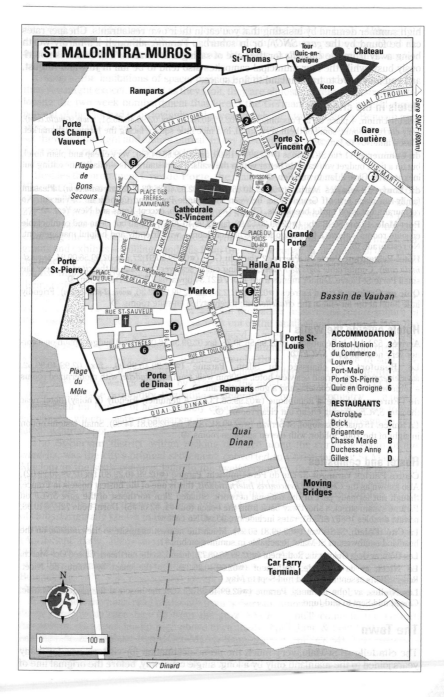

ST MALO: INTRA-MUROS

Porte St-Thomas

Tour Quic-en-Groigne

Château

Keep

Gare SNCF (800m)

Ramparts

QUAI D'TROUIN

Porte des Champ Vauvert

RUE DE LA VICTOIRE

RUE STE-BARBE

RUE DU PUITS AUX BRAIS

Porte St-Vincent

Gare Routière

AV LOUIS-MARTIN

Plage de Bons Secours

RUE ST-ANNE

PLACE DES FRÈRES-LAMMENAIS

RUE DU BOYER

POISSON-ERIE

GRANDE RUE

RUE JACQUES-CARTIER

Cathédrale St-Vincent

PL. AUX HERBES

RUE BROUSSAIS

RUE DE LA BOUCHERIE

PLACE DU POIDS-DU-ROI

Grande Porte

Porte St-Pierre

LE PLACÎTRE

RUE THEVENARD

PLACE DU GUET

RUE DE LA PIE QUI BOIT

RUE DE LA HERSE

Halle Au Blé

RUE DES CORDIERS

Bassin de Vauban

Market

RUE ST-SAUVEUR

RUE DE DINAN

RUE ST-VINCENT

RUE DE TOULOUSE

RUE D'ESTRÉES

Plage du Môle

Porte de Dinan

Ramparts

QUAI DE DINAN

Porte St-Louis

Quai Dinan

ACCOMMODATION

Bristol-Union	3
du Commerce	2
Louvre	4
Port-Malo	1
Porte St-Pierre	5
Quic en Groigne	6

RESTAURANTS

Astrolabe	E
Brick	C
Brigantine	F
Chasse Marée	B
Duchesse Anne	A
Gilles	D

Moving Bridges

Car Ferry Terminal

N

0   100 m

▽ Dinard

of the deep or simply pull faces back at them. Its eight distinct fish tanks include one shaped like a Polo mint, where dizzy visitors stand in the hole in the middle as myriad fish whirl around them. There's actually another aquarium, logically enough named the **Petit Aquarium**, set into the walls of the old city, but this is far superior.

For last-minute **shopping**, St-Malo's *citadelle* contains a few specialists, but buying in any quantity is best done in Le Continent **hypermarket** on the southwest outskirts of the town. There are **markets** in both St-Malo (*intra-muros*) and St-Servan on Tuesdays and Fridays, and in Paramé on Wednesdays and Saturdays.

Eating

Intra-muros St-Malo boasts even more **restaurants** than hotels, with a long crescent lining the inside of the ramparts between the Porte St-Vincent and the Grande Porte. Prices are probably higher than anywhere else in Brittany, however, especially on the open café terraces – the demand is inflated by day-trippers and ferry passengers having last-night blowouts. Bear in mind that most of the crêperies also serve *moules* and similar quasi-snacks. All the restaurants listed below are in the *citadelle*.

Astrolabe, 8 rue des Cordiers (☎02.99.40.36.82). Quality restaurant not far south of the Grande Porte. A full lunch costs 85F/€12.96, while in the evening you can compose your own menu from the extensive *carte*. 160F/€24.39 buys a superb spread, with sensational grilled langoustines and a *gratin du Granny-Smith* from the wide range of desserts. Serves until late. Closed all day Mon & Tues lunchtime.

Le Brick, 5 rue Jacques-Cartier (☎02.99.40.18.88). Perhaps the best of the many seafood restaurants set into the walls near the Grande Porte, with a 75F/€11.43 menu that offers fish soup or "big size winkles" followed by skate, and more lavish options up to 185F/€28.20. Closed Mon in low season.

Crêperie la Brigantine, 13 rue de Dinan (☎02.99.56.82.82). Sweet and savoury pancakes at very reasonable prices – the seafood fillings are exceptional. An individual crêpe can cost under 10F/€1.52, and there's a 58F/€8.84 full menu. Closed Tues evening & Wed in low season.

Le Chasse Marée, 4 rue Grout de St-Georges (☎02.99.40.85.10). Nautical decor and *haute cuisine*, just round the corner from the post office, with a few tables out on the quiet street and more upstairs. The 87F/€13.26 menu, served until 9pm, has oysters followed by red mullet or coley; the 145F/€22.11 features scallop or duck salad to start, and a mixed fish grill or fish couscous. Closed Sun in low season, plus all Feb.

Duchesse Anne, 5–7 place Guy-la-Chambre (☎02.99.40.85.33). The best-known of St-Malo's up-market restaurants, situated right next to the Porte St-Vincent, which continues to work hard to keep up its reputation – and its prices. No set menus; you might manage to get a lunch for under 100F/€15, but dinner will be well over 200F/€30. Whole baked fish is the main speciality. Closed Wed, plus Sun evening in low season, and all Jan & Dec.

Restaurant Gilles, 2 rue de la Pie-qui-Boit (☎02.99.40.97.25). Bright, modern, good-value restaurant, just off the central pedestrian axis. The basic 92F/€14.03 menu is fine, though as it consists of the "*suggestion du jour*" followed by the "*idée du moment*" you'll have to trust the chef; 132F/€20.12 brings you a duck-and pistachio sausage and a rabbit *crêpe* with cider. Closed Wed lunchtime July & Aug, all day Wed rest of year.

The Pointe du Grouin and Cancale

Along the coast east of St-Malo is the **Pointe du Grouin**, a perilous and windy height, which offers spectacular views of the pinnacle of Mont St-Michel and the bird sanctuary of the **Îles des Landes** to the east. Just south of the *pointe*, and less than 15km from St-Malo across the peninsula, **CANCALE** is renowned for its **oysters**. In the old church of **St-Méen** at the top of the hill, the town's obsession is documented with meticulous precision by the small **Musée des Arts et Traditions Populaires** (July & Aug Mon 2.30–6.30pm, Tues–Sun 10am–noon & 2.30–6.30pm; June & Sept Thurs–Sun

2.30–6.30pm, and groups by appointment on ☎02.99.89.71.26; 15F/€2.29). Cancale oysters were found in the camps of Julius Cæsar, taken daily to Versailles for Louis XIV and even accompanied Napoléon on the march to Moscow.

From the rue des Parcs next to the jetty of the port, you can see at low tide the *parcs* where the oysters are grown. The rocks of the cliff behind are streaked and shiny like mother-of-pearl; underfoot the beach is littered with countless generations of empty shells. The port area is very pretty and very smart, with a long line of upmarket glass-fronted hotels and restaurants. Cancale's **hotels** mostly insist that you eat if you want to stay; among the best value are *Le Phare* (☎02.99.89.60.24; ③) and the *Émeraude* (☎02.99.89.61.76; ④) – both set above their own restaurants, at nos. 6 and 7 respectively on quai Thomas – and *La Houle*, 18 quai Gambetta (☎02.99.89.62.38; ②). Budget travellers can head instead for the **hostel** 2km north of town at Port Picain (☎02.99.89.62.62, *cancale@fuaj.org*; closed Jan), where a dorm bed costs 55F/€8.38 for the night. *Au Pied de Cheval*, 10 quai Gambetta (☎02.99.89.76.95), is an informal place to sample a few oysters, with great baskets of them spread across its wooden quayside tables. A dozen raw oysters on a bed of seaweed cost just 26F/€3.96.

Dinan

The wonderful citadel of **DINAN** has preserved almost intact its three-kilometre encirclement of protective masonry, with street upon colourful street of late medieval houses within. Like St-Malo, just 25km to the north, it's best seen when arriving by boat up the River Rance, which allows you to see its castle and fortifications to their best advantage. Behind the houses on the left bank quay where the boats tie up, a steep and cobbled street with fields and bramble thickets on either side climbs up to the thirteenth-century ramparts, partly hidden by trees.

Arrival, information and accommodation

Both the Art Deco **gare SNCF** and the **gare routière** (☎02.96.39.21.05) are in the rather gloomy modern quarter, on place du 11-Novembre, ten minutes' walk west of the walled town. Dinan's **tourist office** is very central, in the sixteenth-century Hôtel Kératry at 6 rue de l'Horloge (mid-June to Sept Mon–Sat 9am–7.30pm, Sun 10am–12.30pm & 2.30–6pm; rest of year Mon–Sat 8.30am–12.30pm & 2–6pm; ☎02.96.87.69.76, *www.dinan-tourisme.com*); they sell a ticket called *Les Clefs pour Dinan* (35F/€5.34 per person; 85F/€12.96 per family), which grants access to a handful of local museums.

Between mid-April and late September, **boats** along the Rance sail between the port downstream and Dinard and St-Malo. The trip takes two and a half hours, exact schedules varying with the tides (95F/€14.48). It's only possible to do a day return by boat (135F/€20.58) if you start from St-Malo or Dinard. For details, contact Émeraude Lines in Dinan, on the quai de la Rance (☎02.96.39.18.04), Dinard (☎02.99.46.10.45) or St-Malo (☎02.23.18.15.15).

Dinan has a surprising shortage of the kind of welcoming mid-range hotel-restaurant **accommodation** that characterizes so many a Breton town, so if that's what you're looking for you might do best to visit only as a day-trip. There are, however, plenty of budget options around.

Hotels and B&Bs

Arvor, 5 rue Pavie (☎02.96.39.21.22, fax 02.96.39.83.09, *www.destination-bretagne.com*). Smart hotel with well-equipped rooms in a renovated eighteenth-century town house, facing the tourist office, with some surviving flourishes of the convent that previously occupied the site. Free parking included. ④,

Café-Hôtel du Théâtre, 2 rue Ste-Claire (☎02.96.39.06.91). Very simple rooms above a bar, right by the tourist office and Théâtre des Jacobins, and under the same efficient management as the nearby *Restaurant Cantorbery* (see opposite). ②.

Hôtel-Restaurant Duchesse Anne, 10 place du Guesclin (☎02.96.39.09.43, fax 02.96.87.57.26). Comfortable if not luxurious rooms on the quieter side of the square, above a basic restaurant where set menus start at 62F/€9.45. Closed mid-Nov to mid-Dec. ③.

Logis de Jerzual, 25 rue du Petit Fort (☎02.96.85.46.54, fax 02.96.39.46.94). *Chambres d'hôte* on the exquisite little lane that leads from the port, halfway up to the porte du Jerzual. Garden terrace looking down onto the street. Inaccessible by car, so deathly quiet in the mornings. ④.

de l'Océan, 9 place du 11-Novembre (☎02.96.39.21.51, fax 02.96.87.05.27). Extremely convenient and well-run (if rather basic) hotel, outside the walls opposite the *gare SNCF*. ①.

de la Porte Saint-Malo, 35 rue St-Malo (☎02.96.39.19.76, fax 02.96.39.50.67). Tasteful small hotel, with very comfortable rooms, situated just outside the walls, beyond the Porte St-Malo. ②.

Hostel and campsite

HI hostel, Moulin de Méen, Vallée de la Fontaine-des-Eaux (☎02.96.39.10.83, *dinan@fuaj.org*). Attractive, rural hostel, set in green fields below the town centre. Unfortunately it's not on any bus route; to walk there, follow the quay downstream from the port on the town side. Dorm bed 50F/€7.62. Closed Jan.

Camping Municipal, 103 rue Châteaubriand (☎02.96.39.11.96). Just outside the western ramparts. Closed Oct–May.

The Town

For all its slightly unreal perfection, Dinan is not excessively overrun with tourists. There are no very vital museums; the monument is the town itself, and time is best spent wandering from crêperie to café, admiring overhanging houses along the way. Unfortunately, you can only walk along one small stretch of the **ramparts**, from the Jardin Anglais behind St Sauveur church to a point just short of Tour Sillon overlooking the river. You can get a good general overview from the **Tour de l'Horloge**, dating from the end of the fifteenth century (daily: April & May 2–6pm; June–Sept 10am–7pm; 16F/€2.44, or *Les Clefs pour Dinan* ticket).

As you might guess from its blending of two separate towers, the fourteenth-century **keep** that once protected the town's southern approach was built by Estienne Le Tour, architect of St-Malo's Tour Solidor (see p.399). It's now known as the **Château de Duchesse Anne**, and houses a small **local history museum** in the ancient Tour Coëtquen (June to mid-Oct daily 10am–6.30pm; rest of year daily except Tues 1.30–5.30pm; 22F/€3.35, or *Les Clefs pour Dinan* ticket). On the lower floor, a group of stone fifteenth-century notables looks for all the world like a medieval time capsule, about to de-petrify at any moment.

St Sauveur church, very much the town's focus, is a real mixture of ages, with a Romanesque porch and an eighteenth-century steeple. Even its nine Gothic chapels feature five different patterns of vaulting in no symmetrical order, and the most complex pair, in the centre, would make any spider proud. A cenotaph contains the heart of Bertrand du Guesclin, the fourteenth-century Breton warrior (and later Constable of France), who fought and won a single combat with the English knight Thomas of Canterbury, in what is now place du Guesclin, to settle the outcome of the siege of Dinan in 1364. Relics of his life and battles are scattered all over Brittany and Normandy; in death, he spread himself between four separate burial places for four different parts of his body (the French kings restricted themselves to three burial sites). North of the church, rue du Jerzual leads down to the gate of the same name and on down (as rue du Petit-Fort) to the lovely **port du Dinan**. Here the river is sufficiently narrow to be spanned by a small but majestic old stone bridge, and artisans' shops and restaurants line the quay.

At some point during each summer (the date tends to vary; check with the tourist office) the **Fête des Remparts** is celebrated with medieval-style jousting, banquets, fairs and processions, culminating in an immense fireworks display. There's a **market** every Thursday in the places du Champ and du Guesclin (the original medieval fairground).

Eating and drinking

All sorts of specialist **restaurants**, including several ethnic alternatives, are tucked away in the old streets of Dinan. Stroll of an evening through the town and down to the port, and you'll pass at least twenty places. For **bars**, explore the series of tiny parallel alleyways between the place des Merciers and the rue de la Ferronnerie. Along rue de la Cordonnerie, the busiest of the lot, the various hang outs define themselves by their taste in music: *À la Truye qui File* at no. 14 is a sort of contemporary folky Breton dive, while *Morgan's Tavern*, next door at no. 12, is considerably more raucous.

Le Cantorbery, 6 rue Ste-Claire (☎02.96.39.02.52). Reasonable food served in an old stone house with rafters, a spiral staircase and a real wood fire. Lunch from 65F/€9.91, while traditional dinner menus start with a good 125F/€19.06 option. Closed Sun evening & Mon, plus all Feb.

Chez La Mère Pourcel, 3 place des Merciers (☎02.96.39.03.80). Beautiful half-timbered fifteenth-century house in the central square. The lunch menu, at 97F/€14.79, is pretty minimal, but the dinners, starting at 168F/€25.61, are gourmet class, featuring *agneau pré-salé* from Mont St-Michel. Closed Sun evening, plus Mon in low season, and all Feb.

Crêperie Connetable, 1 rue de l'Apport (☎02.96.39.02.52). Crêpes and snacks in a magnificent old house opposite the *Mère Pourcel* beside the place des Merciers. Sit if you dare at the pavement tables, where all that prevents the upper storeys from crashing down around your ears are a couple of misshapen pillars.

Le Relais des Corsaires, 7 rue du Quai, port du Dinan (☎02.96.39.40.17). Attractive waterfront restaurant split between a formal dining room and the less expensive all-hours "grill", the *Petit Corsaire*. Both serve much the same wide range of traditional French cuisine, on menus that start with an 89F/€13.57 option that offers shrimp followed by mussels or cod. Closed Sun evening & Wed in low season.

Le Saint Louis, 9–11 rue de Léhon (☎02.96.39.89.50). Very good-value restaurant just inside the Porte St-Louis, specializing in buffets; a 79F/€12.04 menu entitles you to choose at will from extensive buffets of *hors d'oeuvres* and desserts, while the 95F/€14.48 option offers the same deal plus a conventional main course. Closed Sun evening & Wed.

The north coast from Dinard to Lannion

The coast that stretches from the resort town of **Dinard** to Finistère at the far western end of Brittany is divided into two distinct regions either side of the bay of **St-Brieuc**. Between Dinard and St-Brieuc are the exposed green headlands of the **Côte d'Émeraude**, while beyond St-Brieuc, along the **Côte de Goëlo**, the shore becomes more extravagantly indented, with a succession of secluded little bays and an increasing proliferation of huge pink granite boulders seen at their best on the **Côte de Granit Rose** near Perros-Guirec.

Dinard

The former fishing village of **DINARD** sprawls around the western approaches to the Rance estuary, just across from St-Malo but a good twenty minutes away by road. While it might not feel out of place on the Côte d'Azur, with its casino, spacious villas and social calendar of regattas and ballet, here in Brittany it's a little incongruous. Its nineteenth-century metamorphosis was largely thanks to the tastes of the affluent

St Stephen, the fine views of the valley from **Tertre Aubé** and a handful of half-timbered houses in the streets around place au Lin, there's nothing to keep you here.

If you decide to use the city as a base, the best place to **stay** is the central *Champ du Mars*, 13 rue du Général-Leclerc (☎02.96.33.60.99; ③), which offers mussels or fish soup for around 50F/€7.62 in the old-fashioned, green-painted brasserie downstairs. St-Brieuc also has a **hostel**, 2km out, in the magnificent fifteenth-century Manoir de la Ville-Guyomard (☎02.96.78.70.70), on bus route #1 from the station. Some of the nicest **eating** options in town are in the old quarter, behind the cathedral. The traditional French cooking at *Le Madure*, 14 rue Quinquaine (☎02.96.51.20.17; closed Sun & Mon), is served à la carte, with steaks around 87F/€13.26 and salads half that; the fondues at *Le Chaudron*, 19 rue Fardel (☎02.96.33.01.72; closed Sun), start at 80F/€12.20 per person.

The Côte de Goëlo

Moving northwest towards Paimpol along the **Côte de Goëlo**, the shoreline becomes wilder and harsher and the seaside towns tend to be crammed into narrow rocky inlets or set well back in river estuaries. **BINIC** is a narrow port surrounded by meadows, with a thin strip of beach and the decent (if relatively pricey) *Hôtel Benhuyc*, 1 quai Jean-Bart (☎02.96.73.39.00; ④; closed Jan). A little further on at the sedate family resort of **ST-QUAY-PORTRIEUX**, the *Gerbot d'Avoine* (☎02.96.70.40.09; ③; closed Jan), beside the beach, is the best place to stay, despite the hideous decor of its rooms.

After St-Quay, the coastal road shifts inland, through **PLOUHA**, the traditional boundary between French-speaking and Breton-speaking Brittany. It's a viable proposition to hitch from here to **KERMARIA-AN-ISQUIT**, signposted off the D21 from Plouha, to see the extraordinary medieval frescoes of a *Danse Macabre* in the thirteenth-century **chapel** of the village. They show Ankou, who is death or death's assistant, leading representatives of every social class in a Dance of Death. An encounter between three living nobles out hunting and three philosophical corpses is also depicted, and there's a statue of the infant Jesus refusing milk from Mary's proffered breast. In summer, the caretaker, Mme Hervé Droniou, usually keeps the church open (daily 9am–noon & 2–6pm; donation); at other times, you'll have to find her in the house just up the road on the left to let you in.

Paimpol and around

Back on the north coast, **PAIMPOL** is an attractive town with a tangle of cobbled alleyways and fine grey-granite houses, but has lost something in its transition from working fishing port to pleasure harbour. It was once the centre of a cod and whaling fleet, which sailed to Iceland each February after being sent off with a ceremony marked by a famous *pardon*. From then until September the town would be empty of its young men. The whole area was commemorated in Pierre Loti's book, *Pêcheur d'Islande*; the author, and his heroine, lived in the **place du Martray** in the centre of town.

Thanks to naval shipyards and the like, the open sea is not visible from Paimpol; a maze of waterways leads to its two separate harbours. Both are usually filled with the high masts of yachts, but are still also used by the fishing vessels that keep a fish market and a plethora of *poissonneries* busy. This is doubtless a very pleasant place to arrive by boat, threading through the rocks, but from close quarters the tiny port area is a little disappointing, very much rebuilt and quite plain. Even so, it is always lively in summer.

A couple of kilometres short of town, the D786 passes the substantial ruins of the **Abbaye de Beauport** (mid-June to mid-Sept daily 10am–7pm, with regular 90-minute guided tours; rest of year daily except Tues 10am–noon & 2–5pm; 25F/€3.81), established in 1202 by Count Alain de Goëlo. The abbey is currently being restored, but the main appeal for visitors is the sheer romance of its setting. Its stone walls are covered with wild flowers and ivy, the central cloisters are engulfed by a huge tree, and birds fly everywhere. The Norman Gothic chapterhouse is the most noteworthy building to survive, but wandering through and over the roofless halls you may spot architectural relics from all periods of its history. Footpaths lead down through the salt meadows where the monks raised their sheep to the sea, offering the same superb views of the hilltop abbey that must have been appreciated by generations of arriving pilgrims.

Possible places to **stay** in Paimpol include the luxurious *Repaire de Kerroc'h*, overlooking the small-boat harbour from quai Morand (☎02.96.20.50.13; ④), which serves gourmet meals from 125F/€19.06 up to 350F/€53.36; the very hospitable *Hôtel Berthelot* at 1 rue du Port (☎02.96.20.88.66; ②); and the plainer *Hôtel Origano*, just back from the front at 7bis rue du Quai (☎02.96.22.05.49; ③). There's a year-round **HI hostel** in the grand old *Château de Kerraoul* (☎02.96.20.83.60), which also has facilities for **camping**. As for **restaurants**, *La Cotriade*, on the far side of the harbour on the quai Armand-Dayot (☎02.96.20.81.08; closed Wed evening & Thurs), is the best bet for authentic fish dishes, with a simple 95F/€14.48 menu, including a *véritable Cassoulet Paimpolais* and a 165F/€25.15 menu that features a delicious crab mousse.

The Île de Bréhat

Two kilometres off the coast at Pointe de l'Arcouest, 6km northwest of Paimpol, the **ÎLE DE BRÉHAT** – in reality two islands joined by a tiny bridge – gives the appearance of spanning great latitudes. On the north side are windswept meadows of hemlock and yarrow, sloping down to chaotic erosions of rock; on the south, you're in the midst of palm trees, mimosa and eucalyptus. All around is a multitude of little islets – some accessible at low tide, others *propriété privée*, most just pink-orange rocks. All in all, it is one of the most beautiful places in Brittany, renowned as a sanctuary not only for rare species of wild flowers, but also for birds of all kinds. Individual private gardens are also meticulously tended, so you can always anticipate a magnificent display of colour, for example in summer from the erupting blue acanthus.

As you might expect, a high proportion of the homes on this island paradise now belong to summer-only visitors from Paris and beyond, and young Bréhatins leave in ever-increasing numbers for lack of a place of their own, let alone a job. In winter the remaining three hundred or so natives have the place to themselves, without even a *gendarme*; the summer sees two imported from the mainland, along with upwards of three thousand temporary residents and a hundred times as many day-trippers.

All boats to Bréhat arrive at the small harbour of **PORT-CLOS**, though depending on the tide passengers may have to walk several hundred metres before setting foot on terra firma. No **cars** are permitted on the island, so many visitors rent **bikes** at the port, at 70F/€10.67 per day. However, it's easy enough to explore the whole place on foot; walking from one end to the other takes less than an hour.

Each batch of new arrivals heads first to Bréhat's village, **LE BOURG**, five hundred metres up from the port. As well as a handful of hotels, restaurants and bars, it also holds a limited array of shops, a post office, a bank, and an ATM machine, and hosts a small **market** most days. In high season, the attractive central square tends to be packed fit to burst, with exasperated holiday-home owners pushing their little hand-wagons through the throngs of day-trippers.

Continue a short distance north of Le Bourg, however, and you'll soon cross over the slender **Pont ar Prat bridge** to the northern island, where the crowds thin out, and countless little coves offer opportunities to sprawl on the tough grass or clamber across the rugged boulders. Though the coastal footpath around this northern half offers the most attractive walking on the island, the best **beaches** line the southern shores, with the **Grève de Guerzido** at its southeastern corner, being the pick of the crop.

ÎLE DE BRÉHAT

Paon Lighthouse

Pointe du Rosédo

ROUTE DU PAON

Île Ar-Morbic

N

Baie de la Corderie

Pont Ar Prat

D 104

Le Bourg

Île Lavrec

Île Beniguet

Île Logodec

Fort

Port-Clos

Greve du Guerzido

0   500 m

▽ *Point de l'Arcouest (Paimpol)*

Practicalities

Bréhat is connected regularly by **ferry** from the Pointe de l'Arcouest, 6km north-west of Paimpol, and served by summer buses from the *gare SNCF* there. Sailings, with Les Vedettes de Bréhat (☎02.96.55.79.50, *www.vedettesdebrehat.com*), are roughly half-hourly in July & Aug, hourly between April and June and in September, and every two hours otherwise, with the first boat out to Bréhat at 8.30am in summer, and the last boat back at 7.45pm. The return trip costs 40F/€6.10 (bikes 50F/€7.62 extra). The same company also operates boats in summer from Erquy, Dahouët, Binic and St-Quay-Portrieux.

Bréhat's **tourist office** is in the main square in Le Bourg (April–Sept Mon–Sat 10am–1pm & 2.30–6pm; ☎02.96.20.04.15, *syndicateinitiative.brehat@wanadoo.fr*). All three of its **hotels** tend to be booked through the summer, and close for at least part of the winter. Both the *Bellevue* in Port-Clos (☎02.96.20.00.05; ⑤; closed mid-Nov to mid-Feb), and the *Vieille Auberge*, on your left as you enter Le Bourg (☎02.96.20.00.24; ⑤; closed Dec–Easter), insist on *demi-pension* in high season. The smaller *Aux Pêcheurs* (☎02.96.20.00.14; ③; closed Nov–March), on the main square in Le Bourg, has a nice little garden terrace. There's also a wonderful **campsite** in the woods high above the sea west of the port (☎02.96.20.00.36; closed Oct–April).

The Côte de Granit Rose

The whole of the northernmost stretch of the Breton coast, from Bréhat to **Trégastel**, has loosely come to be known as the **Côte de Granit Rose**. There are indeed great granite boulders scattered in the sea around the island of Bréhat, and at the various headlands to the west, but the most memorable stretch of coast lies around **Perros-Guirec**, where the pink granite rocks are eroded into fantastic shapes.

Tréguier

The D786 turns west from Paimpol, passing over a green ria on the bridge outside Lézardrieux before arriving at **TRÉGUIER**, one of the very few hill-towns in Brittany. Its central feature is the **Cathédrale de St-Tugdual**, which contains the tomb of St Yves, a native of the town who died in 1303 and – for his incorruptibility – became the patron saint of lawyers. Attempts to bribe him continue to this day; his tomb is surrounded by marble plaques and an inferno of candles invoking his aid.

The *Hôtel-Restaurant d'Estuaire* on the waterfront (☎02.96.92.30.25; ③) is a nice place to **stay** – the sea views are great – with reasonable menus from 75F/€11.43. Up in town at 2 rue Renan, *La Poissonnerie du Trégor* (☎02.96.92.30.27) is an excellent fish **restaurant** that's no more expensive. During the **market** each Wednesday, clothes and so on are spread out in the square by the cathedral, and food and fresh fish down by the port.

Château de la Roche-Jagu

About 10km inland from Tréguier, on a heavily wooded slope above the Trieux river, stands the fifteenth-century **Château de la Roche-Jagu** (daily: Easter–June & Sept–Oct 10.30am–noon & 2–6pm; July & Aug 10am–7pm; park access free, château 10F/€1.52, or 35F/€5.34 during special exhibitions). It's a gorgeous building – a harmonious combination of fortress and home – and plays host to lavish annual exhibitions, usually on some sort of Celtic theme. The rooms within are bare, but if you climb right up to the top, you can admire the beautiful woodwork of the restored eaves, and walk the two long indoor galleries, which offer tremendous views over the river.

Perros-Guirec and Ploumanac'h

PERROS-GUIREC is the most popular resort along this coast, though not perhaps the most exciting, consisting largely of a network of tree-lined avenues of suburban villas. It does stand, however, at one end of the long **Sentier des Douaniers** pathway, which winds round the clifftops to the tiny resort of **PLOUMANAC'H** past an astonishing succession of deformed and water-sculpted rocks. Birds wheel overhead towards the offshore bird sanctuary of Sept-Îles, and battered boats shelter in the narrow inlets or bob uncontrollably out on the waves. There are patches and brief causeways of grass, clumps of purple heather and yellow gorse. Occasionally the rocks have crumbled into a sort of granite grit to make up a tiny beach; one boulder is strapped down by bands of ivy that prevent it rolling into the sea.

Hotels in Perros-Guirec itself include the old-fashioned *Les Violettes*, 19 rue du Calvaire (☎02.96.23.21.33; ②), which has a seriously cheap restaurant, and two with sea views: the *Gulf Stream*, high on the hillside at 26 rue des Sept-Îles (☎02.96.23.21.86; ②; closed mid-Nov to March), and the *Bon Accueil*, 11 rue de Landerval (☎02.96.23.25.77; ④), which has a gourmet restaurant. Ploumanac'h offers the *St-Guirec et de la Plage* (☎02.96.91.40.89, *www.hotelsaint-guirec.com*; ②; closed mid-Nov to mid-Feb, and most of March), which has some lovely sea-view rooms at bargain rates, and serves a simple good-value menu to all guests in a separate dining room. The *Hôtel du Parc*, on the main square nearby (☎02.96.91.40.80; ③; closed mid-Nov to mid-Dec & all Jan), has more reasonably-priced rooms, and serves good seafood menus from 75F/€11.43. The

(once Lyonesse), the northern peninsula, and its southern neighbour Cornouaille (Cornwall), which both feature prominently in Arthurian legend. In the north of Léon, the ragged **coastline** is the prime attraction, indented with a succession of estuaries or **abers**, each of which shelters its own tiny harbour: heading west from either the thriving historic town of **Morlaix**, or the appealing little Channel port of **Roscoff**, there are possible stopping places all the way to **Le Conquet**. From Le Conquet, you can reach the islands of **Ouessant** and **Molène** across a treacherous stretch of ocean. Inland, by contrast, the ornate medieval village churches known as **parish closes** hold some of Brittany's finest religious architecture.

Morlaix

MORLAIX, one of the great old Breton ports, thrived off trade with England in between wars during the "Golden Period" of the late Middle Ages. Built up the slopes of a steep valley with sober stone houses, the town was originally protected by an eleventh-century castle and a circuit of walls. Little is left of either, but the old centre remains in part medieval – cobbled streets and half-timbered houses. Its present grandeur comes from the pink-granite viaduct carrying trains from Paris to Brest way above the town centre. Coming by road from the north, the opening view is of shiny yacht masts paralleling the pillars of the viaduct.

On her way from Roscoff to Paris, Mary Queen of Scots passed through Morlaix in 1548 and stayed at the **Jacobin convent** that fronts place des Jacobins. She was at the time just five years old, and a contemporary account records that the crush to catch a glimpse of the infant was so great that the inner town's "gates were thrown off their hinges and the chains from all the bridges were broken down". The **Musée des Jacobins** in the convent church contains a reasonably entertaining assortment of Roman wine jars, bits that have fallen off medieval churches, cannon and kitchen utensils, and a few modern paintings (Easter–June, Sept & Oct Mon, Wed–Fri & Sun 10am–noon & 2–6pm, Sat 2–6pm; July & Aug Mon, Wed–Fri & Sun 10am–12.30pm & 2–6.30pm, Sat 2–6.30pm; rest of year Mon, Wed–Fri & Sun 10am–noon & 2–5pm, Sat 2–5pm; 25F/€3.81).

The nearby **church of St Mathieu**, off rue de Paris, contains a sombre and curious statue of the Madonna and Child; Mary's breast was apparently lopped off by a prudish former priest, to leave the babe suckling at nothing. The whole statue opens down the middle to reveal a separate figure of God the Father, clutching a crucifix.

Duchess Anne of Brittany, who had by then become Queen of France, visited Morlaix in 1506. She is reputed to have stayed at the **Maison de la Reine Anne**, 33 rue du Mur, which, although much restored, does indeed date from the sixteenth century. Its intricate external carvings, and the lantern roof and splendid Renaissance staircase inside, make it the most beautiful of the town's ancient houses, each of its storeys overhanging the square below by a few more centimetres. The house is open to the public in summer (May & June Mon–Sat 10am–noon & 2–6pm; July & Aug Mon–Sat 10am–6.30pm, Sun 2–6pm; Sept Mon–Sat 10am–noon & 2–5pm; 10F/€1.52).

Practicalities

The **tourist office** in Morlaix is almost under the viaduct in place des Otages (mid-June to mid-Sept Mon & Sat 10am–noon & 2–6pm, Tues–Fri 10am–noon & 2–7pm, Sun 10.30am–12.30pm; rest of year Tues–Sat 9am–noon & 2–6pm; ☎02.98.62.14.94). All **buses** conveniently depart from place Cornic, right under the viaduct, but the **gare SNCF** is on rue Armand-Rousseau, high above the town at the western end of the viaduct. To reach it on foot, you have to climb the steep steps of Venelle de la Roche.

On the whole Morlaix's **hotels** are fairly uninspiring, but worth a try is the *de l'Europe*, 1 rue d'Aiguillon (☎02.98.62.11.99, fax 02.98.88.83.38; *www.hotel-europe-com.fr*, ④), an eccentric old place, but very central, with modern and well-equipped rooms –

and a separate restaurant downstairs (see below), which is superb. Less expensive options include *Greenwood Café Hôtel*, 25 place St-Martin (☎02.98.88.03.29; ②), with reasonable-value en-suite rooms above an American-themed bar, close to the *gare SNCF*; *Le Roy d'Ys*, 8 place des Jacobins (☎02.98.63.30.55; ②; closed Nov), a small hotel across the square from the town museum (the cheapest rooms do not have their own showers; guests have to pay 15F/€2.29 extra to use shared showers); and the *Hôtel-Restaurant le St-Mélaine*, 75–77 rue Ange-de-Guernisac (☎02.98.88.08.79; ①), a good-value but dull family hotel, with a restaurant (closed Sun & two weeks in May). There's also a **hostel** at 3 route de Paris (☎02.98.88.13.63), 1km from the town centre; take the Kernégues bus to rue de Paris or place Traoulan, and it's just off to the left

The best hunting ground for **restaurants** in Morlaix is to be found between St-Melaine church and place des Jacobins. Try *Brasserie Le Lof*, 1 rue d'Aiguillon (☎02.98.88.81.15), a characterful split-level brasserie below the central *Hôtel de l'Europe*, serving imaginative gourmet menus from 85F/€12.96 – the bizarre *kig ha farz*, a combination of seafood stew and pancake, is a regular feature. Alternatives include the *Brocéliande*, 5 rue des Bouchers (☎02.98.88.73.78; closed Tues; menu 125F/€19.06), in the southeast of town, beyond the place des Halles and St-Mathieu church, which offers elegant evening-only dining in a *fin-de-siècle* atmosphere; and *La Marée Bleue*, 3 rampe Ste-Mélaine (☎02.98.63.24.21; closed Sun evening & Mon Sept–June), a well-respected seafood restaurant, a minute's walk up from the tourist office – the 80F/€12.20 menu is a bit limited, but 165F/€25.15 ensures you a superb *assiette de fruits de mer*, and 235F/€35.83 buys a five-course feast.

The parish closes

Morlaix makes an excellent base for visiting the countryside towards Brest, where **parish closes**, or *enclos paroissiaux* (walled churchyards incorporating cemetery, calvary and ossuary), celebrate the distinctive character of Breton Catholicism – closer to the Celtic past than to Rome – in elaborately sculpted scenes. Stone calvaries are covered in detailed scenes of the Crucifixion above a crowd of saints, gospel stories and legends; in richer parishes, a high stone arch leads into the churchyard, adjoining an equally majestic ossuary, where bones would be taken when the tiny cemeteries filled up. Most of the parish closes date from the two centuries either side of the union with France in 1532, Brittany's wealthiest period.

The most famous *enclos* are in three neighbouring parishes off the N12 between Morlaix and Landivisiau on a clearly signposted route that's served by an SNCF bus. At **ST-THÉGONNEC**, the entire east wall of the church is a carved and painted retable, with saints in niches and a hundred scenes depicted, while the pulpit and the painted oak entombment in the crypt beneath the ossuary are acknowledged masterpieces. At **LAMPAUL-GUIMILIAU**, the painted wooden baptistry, the dragons on the beams and the suitably wicked faces of the robbers on the calvary are the key components. Poor Katel Gollet (Katherine the Damned) is depicted as being tormented in hell at **GUIMILIAU** – for the crime of hedonism rather than manslaughter. In the legend she danced all her suitors to death until the reaper-figure Ankou stepped in to whirl her to eternal damnation. Further on at **LA ROCHE** (15km or so on towards Brest), where the ruined castle above the Elhorn estuary is said to have been her home, it is Ankou who appears on the ossuary with the inscription "I kill you all". A five-kilometre detour southeast of La Roche brings further variations at **LA MARTYRE** (where Ankou clutches his disembodied head) and its adjoining parish **PLOUDIRY**, the sculpting of its ossuary affirming the equality of social classes – in the eyes of Ankou.

St-Thégonnec makes the best base for a tour of the parish closes. The *Auberge de St-Thégonnec*, 6 place de la Mairie (☎02.98.79.61.18, *www.auberge.thegonnec.com*; ④; closed Sun evening & Mon), has a superb restaurant, while the *Moulin de Kerlaviou*,

2km west of St-Thégonnec (☎02.98.79.60.57; ③), is a ravishing farmhouse **B&B** in an almost absurdly pastoral riverside setting.

Roscoff and around

The opening of the deep-water port at **ROSCOFF** in 1973 was part of a general attempt to revitalize the Breton economy. The ferry services to Plymouth and to Cork are intended not just to bring tourists, but also to revive the traditional trading links between the Celtic nations of Brittany, Ireland and southwest England. In fact, Roscoff has long been a significant port. It was here that Mary Queen of Scots landed in 1548 on her way to Paris to be engaged to François, the son and heir of Henri II of France. And it was here that Bonnie Prince Charlie, the Young Pretender, landed in 1746 after his defeat at Culloden.

Roscoff itself has, however, remains a small resort, where almost all activity is confined to **rue Gambetta** and to the **old port** – the rest of the roads are residential back streets full of retirement homes and institutions. One factor in preserving its old character is that both the ferry port and the *gare SNCF* are some way from the centre.

The town's sixteenth-century church, **Notre-Dame-de-Croas-Batz**, at the far end of rue Gambetta, is embellished with an ornate Renaissance belfry, complete with sculpted ships and protruding stone cannon. From the side, rows of bells can be seen hanging in galleries, one above the other like a wedding cake created by Walt Disney. Some way beyond is the grand **Thalassotherapy Institute** of Rock Roum, and a kilometre further on is Roscoff's best **beach**, at Laber, surrounded by expensive hotels and apartments.

The old **harbour** is livelier, mixing an economy based on fishing with relatively low-key pleasure trips to the **Île de Batz** (see opposite). The island looks almost walkable; a narrow pier stretches over 300m or 400m towards it before abruptly plunging into deep rocky waters. The Pointe de Bloscon and the fishermen's white chapel, the **Chapelle Ste-Barbe**, make a good vantage point, particularly when the tide is in; the tide goes out a long way (and dictates the embarkation point for the boat trips).

In 1828, Henri Ollivier took **onions** to England from Roscoff, thereby founding a trade which flourished until the 1930s. The story of the "Johnnies" – that classic French image of men in black berets with strings of onions hanging over the handlebars of their bicycles – is told in **La Maison des Johnnies**, across from the tourist office (daily except Tues 10am–noon & 3–6pm; 10F/€1.52).

Practicalities

Boats run by Brittany Ferries (☎08.03.82.88.28; *www.brittany-ferries.com*) from Plymouth (6hr) and Cork (19hr), and those run by Irish Ferries (☎02.98.61.17.17) from Rosslare (21hr) dock at the Port de Bloscon, to the east (and just out of sight) of Roscoff. From the **gare SNCF**, a few hundred metres south of the town proper, a restricted rail service runs to Morlaix. Most **buses** also go from here, including a direct service to Brest run by Les Cars du Kreisker (☎02.98.69.00.93). The **tourist office** is at 46 rue Gambetta in town (April–June & Sept Mon–Sat 9am–noon & 2–6pm; July & Aug Mon–Sat 9am–12.30pm & 1.30–7pm, Sun 10am–12.30pm; rest of year Mon–Fri 10am–noon & 2–5pm, Sat 10am–noon; ☎02.98.61.12.13).

For a small town, Roscoff is well equipped with **hotels**, which are accustomed to late-night arrivals from the ferries. Good options in the old town include the *Hôtel-Restaurant des Arcades*, 15 rue Amiral-Réveillère (☎02.98.69.70.45, fax 02.98.61.12.34, *www.acdev.com*; ③; closed Oct–Easter; menus from 59F/€8.99), housed in a sixteenth-century building with superb views; family-run *Du Centre*, 5 rue Gambetta (☎02.98.61.24.25; ③; closed Jan to mid-Feb), looking out on the port, above the café-bar *Chez Janie*; and *Les Chardons Bleus*, 4 rue Amiral-Réveillère (☎02.98.69.72.03, fax 02.98.61.27.86; ④; closed Feb), a very friendly and helpful hotel, with a good restaurant (closed Thurs Sept–June, plus Sun in winter). Nearer the ferry terminal is the *Hôtel-Restaurant le Bellevue*, rue Jeanne d'Arc (☎02.98.61.23.38, fax 02.98.61.11.80; ④; closed mid-Nov to mid-March, except Xmas and New Year), which has a lively bar, pleasant rooms and fine views from the dining room. Lower down the price range, there's an **HI hostel** on the Île de Batz (see below) and two **campsites**: *Camping municipal de Perharidy*, 2km west of town (☎02.98.69.70.86; closed Oct–March), just off the route de Santec, and *Camping du Manoir de Kerestat*, 2km south towards St-Pol (☎02.98.69.71.92; closed Nov to mid-April). Very much the obvious places to **eat** are the dining rooms of the hotels themselves, though it's not easy to get a meal much after 9pm.

St-Pol-de-Léon

The main road south from Roscoff passes by fields of the famous Breton artichokes before arriving after 6km at **ST-POL-DE-LÉON**. It's not an exciting place but – assuming you've got your own transport – it has two churches that at least merit a pause. The **Cathédrale**, in the main town square, was rebuilt towards the end of the thirteenth century along the lines of Coutances (see p.369) – a quiet classic of unified Norman architecture. The remains of St Pol are inside, alongside a large bell, rung over the heads of pilgrims during his *pardon* on March 12 in the unlikely hope of curing headaches and ear diseases. Just downhill is the original **Kreisker Chapel**, with access to the top of its sharp-pointed soaring granite belfry (now coated in yellow moss).

The Île de Batz

The long, narrow **ÎLE DE BATZ** (pronounced "Ba") mirrors Roscoff across the water, separated from it by a sea channel that's barely 200m wide at low tide but perhaps five times that when the tide is high. Appearances from the mainland are somewhat deceptive: the island's old town, home to a thousand or so farmers and fishermen, fills much of its southern shoreline, but those parts of Batz not visible from Roscoff are much wilder and more windswept. With no cars permitted, and some great expanses of sandy beach it makes a wonderfully quiet retreat for families in particular, whether you're camping or staying in one of its two old-fashioned little hotels.

Ferries from Roscoff arrive at the quayside of the old town. There's a nice small beach along the edge of the harbour, though the sea withdraws so far at low tide that the port turns into a morass of slimy seaweed. You may well spot the island's best beach from the boat – it's the white-sand **Grève Blanche** towards its eastern end. Walking in that direction also brings you to the hostel (see below), and the 44-metre lighthouse that stands on the island's peak, all of 23m above sea level (June & last fortnight of Sept daily except Wed 2–5pm; July to mid-Sept daily 1.30–5.30pm).

Two separate companies operate ten-minute **ferry** services to the Île de Batz from Roscoff's long pier. Between late June and mid-September, the service is pretty much non-stop between 8am and 8pm daily; for the rest of the year, both Compagnie Maritime Armein (☎02.98.61.77.75) and Compagnie Finistérienne (☎02.98.61.78.87) run eight to ten trips daily between 8.30am and 7pm; the return fare is 34F/€5.18.

The island's nicest **hotel**, at the centre of the harbour, is the *Grand Hôtel Morvan* (☎02.98.61.78.06; ③; closed Dec & Jan), which serves good meals on its large seafront terraces. Its **hostel** is in a beautiful setting, by the beach at the evocatively named Creach ar Bolloc'h (☎02.98.61.77.69; closed Oct–March).

The abers

The coast west of Roscoff is some of the most dramatic in Brittany, a jagged series of **abers** – deep, narrow estuaries – in the midst of which are clustered small, isolated resorts. It's a little on the bracing side, especially if you're making use of the numerous **campsites**, but that just has to be counted as part of the appeal. In summer, at least, the temperatures are mild enough, and things get progressively more sheltered as you move around towards Le Conquet and Brest.

Around the abers

If you're dependent on public transport, bear in mind that the only stop on the Roscoff–Brest bus before it turns inland is **PLOUESCAT**. It is not quite on the sea itself, but there are campsites nearby on each of three adjacent beaches; of the **hotels**, best value is the *Roc'h-Ar-Mor*, right on the beach at Porsmeur (☎02.98.69.63.01; ①; closed Oct–March).

BRIGNOGAN-PLAGE, on the next *aber*, has a small natural harbour, once the lair of wreckers, with beaches and weather-beaten rocks to either side, as well as its own menhir. The two high-season **campsites** are the central municipal site at Kéravezan (☎02.98.83.41.65; closed Nov–April) and the *du Phare*, east of town (☎02.98.83.45.06; closed Oct–March), while the only **hotel**, *Castel Regis* (☎02.98.83.40.22; ④; closed Oct–March), is expensive but beautifully sited among the rocks, right at the headland. There are also schools of sailing and riding.

The *aber* between Plouguerneau and **L'ABER-WRAC'H** has a stepping-stone crossing just upstream from the bridge at Llanellis, built in Gallo-Roman times, and its long cut stones still cross the three channels of water (access off the D28 signposted "Rascoll"), and continue past farm buildings to the right to "Pont du Diable". L'Aber-Wrac'h itself is a promising place to spend a little time. It's an attractive, modest-sized resort, within easy reach of a whole range of sandy beaches and a couple of worthwhile excursions. Beyond the town's little strip of bars and restaurants, the Baie des Anges stretches away towards the Atlantic, with the only sound the cry of seagulls feasting on the oyster beds. At the start of the bay, the irresistible *Hôtel la Baie des Anges*, 350 route des Anges (☎02.98.04.90.04, *www.baie-des-anges.com*; ④; closed Jan to mid-Feb), makes a peaceful and exceptionally comfortable place to **stay**. The best local **restaurant**, *Le Brennig* (☎02.98.04.81.12; closed Tues, plus Oct to mid-March), is back at the other end of town. A municipal **campsite**, *de Penn Enez* (☎02.98.04.99.82; closed Oct–May), nestles among the dunes at the very tip of the headland.

At the small harbour of **PORTSALL**, 5km along the coast from the far side of the next *aber*, l'Aber-Benoît, the **Espace Amoco Cadiz** commemorates a defining moment in local history (daily 9.30am–1pm & 2.30–7pm; free): on March 17, 1978, the sinking of the *Amoco Cadiz* supertanker resulted in an oil spill that devastated 350km of the Breton coastline, and threatened to ruin the local economy. Displays and films document not only the immense task of cleaning up the mess, but also the long legal battle to obtain compensation from the "multinational monster" responsible.

Five kilometres west of Portsall is **TRÉMAZAN**, whose ruined castle was the point of arrival in Brittany for Tristan and Iseult. From here a beautiful corniche road leads further along the coast. Odd little chapels dot the route, and the views of sea and rocks are unhindered before turning inland just before Le Conquet.

Le Conquet

LE CONQUET, at the far western tip of Brittany, 24km beyond Brest, is a wonderful place, scarcely developed, with a long beach of clean white sand, protected from the winds by the narrow spit of the Kermorvan peninsula. It is very much a working fishing village, with grey-stone houses leading down to the stone jetties of a cramped harbour. It occasionally floods, by the way, causing great amusement to locals who watch the waves wash over cars left there by tourists taking the ferry out to Ouessant and Molène. A good walk 5km south brings you to the lighthouse at **Pointe St-Mathieu**, looking out to the islands from its site among the ruins of a Benedictine abbey. A small exhibition explains the abbey's history, including the legend that it holds the skull of St Matthew, brought here from Ethiopia by local seafarers (April & May Wed, Sat & Sun 2.30–6.30pm; June & Sept daily 2.30–6.30pm; July & Aug daily 11am–7pm; Oct & Nov Wed, Sat & Sun 2–6pm; 10F/€1.52).

The *Relais du Vieux Port*, quai Drellac (☎02.98.89.15.91; ②; closed Jan), offers three attractive but inexpensive **rooms** right by the jetty in Le Conquet, and has a simple crêperie downstairs. Nearby, the larger *Pointe Ste Barbe* (☎02.98.89.00.26; ②–⑦; closed Mon out of season & mid-Nov to mid-Dec), offers amazing sea views to guests in its more expensive rooms, and has a great restaurant, where menus start at 100F/€15.24. There are also two well-equipped **campsites**, *Le Théven* (☎02.98.89.06.90; closed Oct–March) and *Quère* (☎02.98.89.11.71; closed mid-Sept to mid-June).

The Îles d'Ouessant and de Molène

The **Île d'Ouessant** ("Ushant" in English) lies 30km northwest of Le Conquet, and its lighthouse at **Creac'h** (said to be the strongest in the world) is regarded as the entrance to the English Channel. It's at the end of a chain of smaller islands and half-submerged granite rocks. Most are uninhabited, or like Beniguet the preserve only of rabbits, but the **Île de Molène**, midway, has a village and can be visited. Both Molène and Ouessant are served by at least one ferry each day from Le Conquet and Brest; however, it is not practicable to visit more than one in a single day.

Île d'Ouessant

You arrive on the **Île d'Ouessant** at the new **harbour** in the ominous-sounding Baie du Stiff. There is a scattering of houses here and dotted around the island, but the single town – with the only hotels and restaurants – is 4km away at **LAMPAUL**. Everybody from the boat heads there, either by the bus that meets each ferry or on bicycles rented from one of the many waiting entrepreneurs – a good idea, as the island is a bit too big to explore on foot.

GETTING TO OUESSANT AND MOLÈNE

Penn Ar Bed (☎02.98.80.80.80, *www.penn-ar-bed.fr*) runs **ferries** to Ouessant and Molène all year, with up to five daily departures from Le Conquet (first sailing at 8am daily in summer; return fare 157F/€23.94), and one daily at 8.30am from Brest (return fare 186F/€28.35). They also depart from Camaret at 8.45am on Wednesday from May until mid-July, and daily except Sunday at 8.45am from mid-July until the end of August (return fare 170F/€25.92).

Finist'Mer operates **high-speed ferries** to Ouessant in summer only, from Camaret (☎02.98.27.88.44; return fare 160F/€24.39), Le Conquet (☎02.98.89.16.61; return fare 148F/€22.56) and Lanildut, 25km northwest of Brest (☎02.98.04.40.72; 155F/€23.63). Bikes cost 65–70F/€9.91–10.67 extra. In June and September, they offer a daily departure from Camaret at 8.30am, calling at Le Conquet at 9.30am; another departure from Le Conquet at 5pm; and an extra departure from Le Conquet at 11am on Saturday. In July and August, they offer a morning departure from Camaret at 9.30am, plus up to seven ferries daily from Le Conquet and an additional service from Lanildut, departing at 9.20am daily and taking just half an hour to reach Ouessant. Certain summer sailings call in at Molène as well.

In addition, you can **fly** to Ouessant with **Finist'Air** (☎02.98.84.64.87). The fifteen-minute flights leave Brest daily at 8.30am and 5pm in summer, 8.30am and 4.45pm in winter. The adult return fare is 340F/€51.84; groups of three or more adults go for 270F/€41.16 each.

Lampaul has not a lot to it and quickly becomes very familiar. The best beaches are sprawled around its bay, and, in case you should forget the perils of the sea, the town cemetery's **war memorial** lists all the ships in which townsfolk were lost, alongside graves of unknown sailors washed ashore and a chapel of wax "*proëlla* crosses" symbolizing the many islanders who never returned.

At nearby **NIOU**, the **Maison du Niou** (April Tues–Sun 2–6.30pm; May to mid-July & Sept daily 10.30am–6.30pm; mid-July to Aug daily 10.30am–6.30pm & 9–11pm; Oct–March Tues–Sun 2–4pm; 25F/€3.81) is actually two houses, one of which is a museum of island history, and the other a reconstruction of a traditional island house, complete with two massive "box beds", one for the parents and the other for the children. Officially, it forms half of the Eco-Musée d'Ouessant, in combination with the **Creac'h lighthouse** (same hours), which stands 1km northwest of Niou. This contains a small museum about lighthouses, and makes a good point from which to set out along the barren and exposed rocks of the north coast. Particularly in September and other times of migration, this stretch of coast is a remarkable spot for birdwatching. The star-shaped formations of crumbling walls that you'll see are not extraterrestrial relics, but built so that the sheep – peculiarly tame here – can shelter from the strong winds.

Lampaul boasts several accommodation options. The adjacent **hotels** *Océan* (☎02.98.48.80.03; ②) and *Fromveur* (☎02.98.48.81.30; ②) both offer a basic standard of accommodation. The *Roch Ar Mor*, just down the street (☎02.98.48.80.19; ②; closed Jan–March), makes a marginally more attractive alternative. There is also a small official **campsite**, the *Penn ar Bed* (☎02.98.48.84.65; closed Oct–March), and a brand new little **hostel**, *La Croix Rouge* (☎02.98.48.84.53). All the hotel **restaurants** serve menus for under 100F/€15.24, but if you just come for a day, it's a good idea to buy a picnic before you set out – the Lampaul shops have limited and rather pricey supplies.

Île de Molène

The **Île de Molène** is quite well populated for a sparse strip of sand. Its inhabitants make their money from seaweed collecting and drying – and to an extent from crabbing and from crayfish, which they gather on foot, canoe and even tractor at low tide. The tides here are more than usually dramatic, halving or doubling the island's territory at a stroke – it's not called "the bald isle" for nothing. Few people do more than look at Molène as an afternoon's excursion from Le Conquet, but it's possible to stay, too. There are **rooms** – very chilly in winter – at *Kastell An Doal* (☎02.98.07.39.11; ④; closed Jan), one of the old buildings by the port.

Brest

Set in a magnificent natural harbour, known as the Rade de Brest, the city of **BREST** is doubly sheltered from the ocean storms by the bulk of Léon to the north and by the Crozon peninsula to the south. It has always played an important role in war, and in trade whenever peace allowed. Today it is the base of the French Atlantic Fleet with a dry dock that can accommodate ships of up to 500,000 tonnes; the town, as a ship repair centre, ranks sixth in the world.

During World War II, Brest was continually bombed to prevent the Germans from using it as a submarine base. When the Americans liberated it on September 18, 1944, after a six-week siege, they found the town devastated beyond recognition. The architecture of the postwar town is raw and bleak. There have been attempts, as in Caen, to green the city, but despite the heaviest rainfall in France the site has proved too windswept to respond.

Arrival, information and accommodation

The **gare SNCF** and **gare routière** (☎02.98.44.46.73) are together in place du 19ème-RI at the bottom of avenue Clémenceau. Bus services include those to Plouescat and Roscoff (Les Cars du Kreisker; ☎02.98.69.00.93); to the Crozon peninsula via Landévennec (☎02.98.27.02.02); and to Le Conquet (Sarl St Mathieu Transports; ☎02.98.98.12.02). Brest's **tourist office** on avenue Clémenceau faces place de la Liberté (mid-June to mid-Sept Mon–Sat 9.30am–12.30pm & 2–6.30pm, Sun 10am–noon & 2–4pm; rest of year Mon–Sat 10am–12.30pm & 2–6pm; ☎02.98.44.24.96, *office.de.tourisme.brest@wanadoo.fr*).

As well as the sailings to Ouessant (detailed in the box on p.417), in summer three or four **boats** per day, run by Société Azenor (☎02.98.41.46.23), make the 25-minute crossing from Brest's Port de Commerce to Le Fret on the Crozon peninsula (June–Sept; 90F/€13.72 return). Sailings are met at the port in Le Fret by buses for Crozon (15min), Morgat (30min) and Camaret (40min). Société Azenor and other operators also run excursions around the harbour and the Rade de Brest (1hr 30min).

The vast majority of Brest's **hotels** remain open throughout the year; only a few, however, bother to maintain their own restaurants. Several lie within easy walking distance of the stations, in the vicinity of the central place de la Liberté. The year-round **hostel** is on rue de Kerbriant, Port de Plaisance du Moulin-Blanc (☎02.98.41.90.41), 3km east of the *gares SNCF* and *routière* in a wooded setting near Océanopolis, on bus route #7 or the Bus Albatros.

Hotels

Astoria, 9 rue Traverse (☎02.98.80.19.10, fax 02.98.80.52.41). Peaceful central hotel with a cheerful ambience and decor, not far up from the port. ②.

Comoedia, 21 rue d'Aguillon (☎02.98.46.54.82). Simple but very cheap rooms in a quiet street just up from the port, with an equally no-frills restaurant downstairs. ①.

de la Gare, 4 bd Gambetta (☎02.98.44.47.01, fax 02.98.43.34.07). En-suite rooms opposite the stations; you can pay a little extra for an uninterrupted view of the Rade de Brest, from the upper storeys. ③.

Pasteur, 29 rue Louis-Pasteur (☎02.98.46.08.73). Clean, good-value budget hotel near the St-Louis church. ②.

The Town

As a tourist centre, Brest has little to offer, and few relics of the past remain. The fifteenth-century **castle** looks impressive on its headland and offers a superb panorama of the city, but once inside it is not especially interesting. Three of its towers house part of the collection of the **Musée National de la Marine** (April–Sept Mon & Wed–Sun 10am–6.30pm, Tues 2–6.30pm; rest of year Mon & Wed–Sun 10am–noon & 2–6pm, Tues 2–6pm; 30F/€4.57). The fourteenth-century **Tour Tanguy** on the opposite bank of the River Penfeld, with its conical slate roof, serves as the **Musée de Vieux Brest** (June–Sept daily 10am–noon & 2–7pm; rest of year Wed & Thurs 2–5pm, Sat & Sun 2–6pm; free). Dioramas convey a vivid impression of just how attractive the city used to be.

Brest's most up-to-the-minute attraction is **Océanopolis**, a couple of kilometres east of the city centre beside the Port de Plaisance du Moulin-Blanc (daily: June–Sept 9am–7pm; rest of year 9am–6pm; 90F/€13.72). This futuristic complex currently consists of three distinct aquariums and a 3-D cinema. The aquarium in the main white dome, known as the Temperate Pavilion, focuses on the Breton littoral and Finistère's fishing industry, holding all kinds of fish, seals, molluscs, seaweed and sea anemones. The emphasis is very much on the edible, with the displays on the life-cycle of a scallop, for example, culminating in a detailed recipe. To that has recently been added a Tropical Pavilion, with a tankful of ferocious-looking sharks plus a myriad of rainbow-hued smaller fish that populate a highly convincing coral reef, and a Polar Pavilion, complete with polar bears and penguins. Everything's very high-tech, and perhaps a little too earnest for some visitors' tastes, but it's quite possible to spend an entertaining day on site – especially if you take the assorted restaurants, snack bars and gift stores into consideration.

Eating

As well as a concentration of low-priced places near the stations, Brest offers a wide assortment of **restaurants**. Rue Jean-Jaurès, climbing east from the place de la Liberté, holds plenty of bistros and bars, while just to the north, place Guérin is the centre of the student-dominated quartier St-Martin.

L'Espérance, 6 place de la Liberté (☎02.98.44.25.29). Busy, inexpensive conventional restaurant in the lively square that faces the Hôtel de Ville, with a wide range of imaginative menus that start at 70F/€10.67 midweek. Closed Sun evening & Mon, plus last 2 weeks in Aug and first week of Sept.

La Maison de l'Océan, 2 quai de la Douane (☎02.98.80.44.84). Blue-hued fish restaurant down by the port, open every day and serving wonderful assortments of seafood from 85F/€12.96.

Ma Petite Folie, plage du Moulin-Blanc (☎02.98.42.44.42). Converted fishing boat, moored in the pleasure port, which serves a wonderfully fishy 110F/€16.77 set menu and also offers a wide range of à la carte dishes and daily specials. Closed Sun & two weeks in mid-Aug.

Le Ruffé, 1 rue Yves-Collet (☎02.98.46.07.70). An attractive place between the *gare SNCF* and the tourist office that prides itself on good, traditional French seafood dishes, served on menus costing 80F/€12.20 and upwards. Daily except Sun until 11.30pm.

The Crozon peninsula

The **Crozon peninsula**, a craggy outcrop of land shaped like a long-robed giant, arms outstretched to defend bay and roadstead, is the central feature of Finistère's torn chaos of estuaries and promontories. Much the easiest way for cyclists, and travellers relying on public transport, to reach the peninsula from Brest is via the ferries to Le Fret (see p.419).

Motorists heading for Crozon have to follow a circuitous route skirting this complex coast through **PLOUGASTEL-DAOULAS**. At the church here, the calvary shows more torment for Katel Gollet (Katherine the Damned), in this case being raped by devils, but with a more sympathetic sculpting of Katel herself than at Guimiliau (see p.413).

As you approach the Crozon peninsula, it's well worth making a slight detour to climb the hill of **Menez-Hom**, "at the giant's feet", for a fabulous view of the land and water alternating out to the ocean. Getting down to the coastal headlands themselves can be a bit of a disappointment after this vision: those extremities that don't house military installations tend to be too crowded. But it is the cliffs that tourists head for here, and some of the **beaches**, like **La Palue** on the southern arm, are almost deserted.

Daoulas and Le Faou

Ten kilometres beyond Plougastel-Daoulas, the **abbey** at **DAOULAS** holds Brittany's only Romanesque cloister. It now stands beautiful and isolated at the edge of cool monastery gardens, since its surrounding buildings were destroyed during the Revolution. Since 1984 it has been used as a cultural centre for Finistère, which stages ambitious historical exhibitions lasting for around six months at a time (usual summer opening hours daily 10am–7pm; current information on ☎02.98.25.84.39 or *centre.culturel.abbaye.daoulas@infini.fr*; 35F/€5.34).

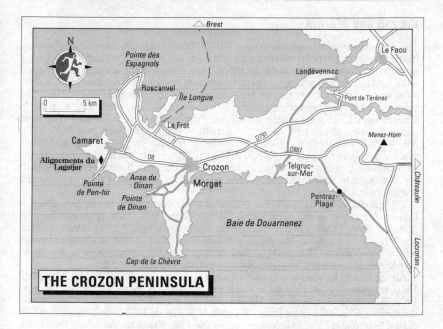

THE CROZON PENINSULA

From Daoulas the motorway and railway cut down to Châteaulin (see p.433) and Quimper. For Crozon, you'll need to veer west at **LE FAOU**, a tiny medieval port, still with some of its sixteenth-century gabled houses and set on its own individual estuary. From beside the pretty little village church – whose porch holds some intriguing carved apostles – a sheltered corniche follows the river to the sea, where there are sailing and windsurfing facilities.

Le Faou holds two good and very similar **hotels**, each with a top-class restaurant – the *Relais de la Place* (☎02.98.81.91.19; ③; closed mid-Sept to mid-Oct), and the Best Western *Hôtel de Beauvoir* (☎02.98.81.90.31, *www.hotel-beauvoir.com*; ④; closed mid-Nov to Dec & Mon Sept–June). The one snag is that they're not in the most attractive part of town, near the river, but a few hundred metres south in the newer and much noisier main square.

Landévennec

Nine kilometres west of Le Faou, by way of a beautiful shoreline road, the **Pont de Térénez** spans the Aulne – outlet for the Nantes–Brest canal – to the Crozon peninsula. Doubling back to the right as soon as you cross the bridge brings you after a further 5km to **LANDÉVENNEC**, where archeologists are uncovering the outline of what may be Brittany's oldest abbey (June & last 2 weeks of Sept daily 2–6pm; July to mid-Sept Mon–Sat 10am–7pm, Sun 2–7pm; rest of year Sat, Sun & hols 2–6pm; 25F/€3.81). Nothing survives above ground of the original thatched hut, constructed in a forest clearing by St Gwennolé around 485 AD. After the abbey had been pillaged by raiding Normans in 913 AD, however, it was rebuilt in stone. Those foundations can now be seen, together with displays on monastic history and facsimile manuscripts. There's a small but attractive **hotel** in the heart of Landévennec, *Le St-Patrick* (☎02.98.27.70.83; ②).

Crozon and Morgat

The first town on the peninsula proper, **CROZON**, is not much more than a one-way traffic system to distribute tourists among the various resorts – though it does keep a market running most of the week. **MORGAT**, just down the hill, is a more realistic and enticing base. It has a long crescent beach that ends in a pine slope, and a well-sheltered harbour full of pleasure boats raced down from England and Ireland. The main attractions are **boat trips** around the various headlands, such as the **Cap de la Chèvre** (which is a good clifftop walk if you'd rather make your own way). The most popular is the 45-minute tour of the **Grottes** (daily May–Sept; ☎02.98.27.10.71; 50F/€7.62), multicoloured caves in the cliffs, accessible only by sea but with steep "chimneys" up to the clifftops, where in bygone days saints would lurk to rescue the shipwrecked. Organized by two rival companies on the quay, the trips run every quarter of an hour in high season; they often leave full, however, so it's worth booking a few hours in advance.

The **tourist office** for the whole peninsula is in what used to be the *gare SNCF* at Crozon (mid-June to mid-Sept Mon—Sat 9am–7pm, Sun 10am–1pm; rest of year Mon–Fri 10am–12.30pm & 2.30–5.30pm, Sat 10am–noon; ☎02.98.26.17.18); an information office for the Crozon–Morgat area stands at the start of Morgat's beach crescent on the boulevard du France (May, June & Sept Mon–Sat 9.15am–noon & 2–6.30pm; July & Aug Mon–Sat 9.30am–7pm, Sun 10am–1pm; ☎02.98.27.07.92).

All the **hotels** in Morgat are quite expensive. Appealing options include the grand *Hôtel-Restaurant de la Ville d'Ys*, which enjoys fabulous views just above the port (☎02.98.27.06.49; ③; closed Oct–March), and has a good dinner-only restaurant, and the quieter *Julia*, 400 metres from the beach at 43 rue de Tréflez (☎02.98.27.05.89; ③; closed Nov to mid-Feb). Immediately below the *Ville d'Ys* at the far end of the beach, *Les Échoppes*, 24 quai du Kador (☎02.98.26.12.63; closed Oct–Easter), a flowery stone cottage with tiny little windows, is Morgat's best **restaurant**, serving good menus from 100F/€15.24. With a total of 865 pitches available, **campers** are spoilt for choice: the best sites are the three-stars at *Plage de Goulien* (☎02.98.27.17.10; closed mid-Sept to mid-June) and *Les Pins*, towards the pointe de Dinan (☎02.98.27.21.95; closed mid-Sept to mid-June).

Camaret

CAMARET is another sheltered port, at the very tip of the peninsula. Its most distinguishing feature is the pink-orange **Château de Vauban**, standing four-square at the end of the long jetty that runs back parallel to the main town waterfront. Walled, moated, and accessible via a little gatehouse reached by means of a drawbridge, it was built in 1689 to guard the approaches to Brest; these days it guards no more than a motley assortment of decaying half-submerged fishing boats, abandoned to rot beside the jetty. There are two beaches nearby – a small one to the north and another, larger and more attractive, in the low-lying (and rather marshy) Anse de Dinan. In summer Penn Ar Bed (☎02.98.27.88.22, *www.penn-ar-bed.fr*) operates an irregular **ferry** service from Camaret to the islands of Ouessant (see box on p.417 170F/€25.92 return) and Sein (see p.425; 170F/€25.92 return), while Finist'Mer sails to Ouessant only (☎02.98.27.88.44; 160F/€24.39 return).

A little walk away from the centre, around the port towards the protective jetty, the quai du Styvel contains a row of excellent **hotels**. Both the *Vauban* (☎02.98.27.91.36; ②; closed Dec & Jan) and *du Styvel* (☎02.98.27.92.74; ②; closed Jan) are exceptionally hospitable, with rooms that look right out across the bay, but only the *Styvel* has a restaurant. There are also various **campsites** to fall back on, such as the four-star *Le Grand Large* (☎02.98.27.91.41, *lglca@club-internet.fr*, closed Oct–March) and the two-star municipal *Lannic* (☎02.98.27.91.31; closed mid-Sept to mid-June). Back along the quay-side in the centre of town, *La Voilerie*, 7 quai Toudouze (☎02.98.27.99.55), is an excellent **fish restaurant**.

South towards Quimper

Moving south of the Crozon peninsula, you soon enter the ancient kingdom of **Cornouaille**. The most direct route to the region's principal city, **Quimper**, leaves the sea behind and heads due south, passing close to the unchanged medieval village of **Locronan**. However, if you can spare the time, it's worth following the supremely isolated coastline instead around the Baie de Douarnenez to the **Pointe du Raz**, the western tip of Finistère. With a few exceptions – most notably its "land's end" capes – this stretch of coast has kept out of the tourist mainstream, and nowhere does that hold more true than on the remarkable, remote **Île de Sein**.

Locronan

LOCRONAN, a short way from the sea on the minor road that leads down from the Crozon peninsula, is a prime example of a Breton town that has remained frozen in its ancient form by more recent economic decline. From 1469 through to the seventeenth century, it was a successful centre for woven linen, supplying sails to the French, English and Spanish navies. It was first rivalled by Vitré and Rennes, before suffering the "agony and ruin" so graphically described in its small **museum** (daily 10am–7pm; 20F/€3.05). As a result, the rich medieval houses of the town centre have never been superseded or surrounded by modern development. Film directors love its authenticity, even if Roman Polanski, filming *Tess*, deemed it necessary to change all the porches, put new windows on the Renaissance houses, and bury the main square in mud to make it all look a bit more English.

Today Locronan is once more prosperous, with its main source of income the tourists who buy wooden statues carved by local artisans, pottery brought up from the Midi and leather jackets of less specified provenance. This commercialization should not, however, put you off making at least a passing visit, for the town itself is genuinely remarkable, centred around the focal **Église St-Ronan**. Be sure to take the time to walk down the hill of the **rue Moal**, where there's a lovely little stone chapel, with surprising modern stained glass, and a wooden statue of a depressed-looking Jesus, sitting alone cross-legged.

Simply to park on the outskirts of Locronan costs 15F/€2.29, though at least your ticket remains valid for a full year. The **tourist office** adjoins the museum (July & Aug Mon–Sat 10am–1pm & 2–7pm; rest of year Mon–Sat 10am–noon & 2–6pm; ☎02.98.91.70.14). The one **hotel**, *du Prieuré*, 11 rue du Prieuré (☎02.98.91.70.89; ③; closed mid-Nov to mid-March), has a good restaurant.

Douarnenez

Sufficient quantities of tuna, sardines and assorted crustaceans are still landed at the port of **DOUARNENEZ**, in the superbly sheltered Baie de Douarnenez, south of the Crozon peninsula, to keep the largest fish canneries in Europe busy. However, the catch has been declining ever since 1923, when eight hundred fishing boats brought in 100 million sardines during the six-month season. Over the last fifteen years or so, Douarnenez has therefore set out – at phenomenal expense, the subject of considerable local controversy – to redefine itself as a living museum of all matters maritime.

Quimper

QUIMPER, capital of the ancient diocese, kingdom and later duchy of Cornouaille, is the oldest Breton city. According to legend, the first bishop of Quimper, St Corentin, came with the first Bretons across the Channel some time between the fourth and seventh centuries to the place they named Little Britain. He lived by eating a regenerating and immortal fish all his life, and was made bishop by one King Gradlon, whose life he later saved when the sea-bed city of **Ys** was destroyed. According to one version, Gradlon built Ys in the Baie de Douarnenez, protected from the water by gates and locks to which only he and his daughter had keys. But St Corentin suspected her of evil doings, and was proven right: the princess's keys unlocked the gates, the city flooded and Gradlon escaped only by obeying Corentin and throwing his daughter into the sea. Back on dry land and in need of a new capital, Gradlon founded Quimper.

Modern Quimper is very relaxed, active enough to have the bars – and the atmosphere – to make it worth going out café-crawling. Still "the charming little place" known to Flaubert, it takes at most half an hour to cross it on foot. The word "kemper" denotes the junction of the two rivers, the Steir and the Odet, around which are the cobbled streets (now mainly pedestrianized) of the medieval quarter, dominated by the cathedral towering nearby. As the Odet curves from east to southwest, it is crossed by numerous low, flat bridges, bedecked with geraniums, and chrysanthemums in the autumn. You can stroll along the boulevards on both banks of the river, where several ultramodern edifices blend in a surprisingly harmonious way with their ancient – and attractive – surroundings. Overlooking all are the wooded slopes of **Mont Frugy**. There is no great pressure in Quimper to rush around monuments or museums, and the most enjoyable option may be to take a boat and drift down "the prettiest river in France" to the open sea at Bénodet.

Arrival, information and accommodation

The **gare SNCF** and **gare routière** (☎02.98.90.88.89) are next to each other on avenue de la Gare, 1km east of the centre. **Bus services** include those to Bénodet, which leave from place de la Résistance (Compagnie Armoricaine de Transport; ☎02.98.95.02.36); to Audierne and Pointe du Raz, from the *gare routière* or boulevard Kérguelen (also CAT); to Pont l'Abbé and St-Guenolé, from place St-Corentin (Cariou Castric Lecoeur; ☎02.98.47.04.08); and to Concarneau and Pont-Aven, also from place St-Corentin (Sarl Transports Caoudal Réné; ☎02.98.56.96.72).

Between July and September you can **sail** from Quimper down the Odet to Bénodet, which takes about 1hr 15min, on Vedettes de l'Odet (Bénodet ☎02.98.57.00.58, Quimper ☎02.98.52.98.41, *www.vedettes-odet.com*; 115F/€17.53 return). Between two and four boats each day leave from the end of quai de l'Odet; times vary with the tides so check with the tourist office (which also sells tickets).

Quimper's **tourist office** is on the south bank of the Odet at 7 rue de la Déesse (May to mid-June & first 2 weeks of Sept Mon–Sat 9am–12.30pm & 1.30–6.30pm, Sun 10am–1pm & 3–6pm; July & Aug Mon–Sat 9am–7pm, Sun 10am–1pm & 3–6pm; mid-Sept to April Mon–Sat 9am–noon & 1.30–6pm; ☎02.98.53.04.05, *www.bretagne-4villes.com*). For **Internet access**, call in at *Cybercopy*, 3 bd de Kerguélen (Mon–Fri 9am–7pm, Sat 9am–6pm; ☎02.98.64.33.99).

There are remarkably few **hotels** in the old streets in the centre of Quimper, though there are some near the station. There's a four-star **campsite**, *Orangerie de Lannion*, 4km out of the centre on the route de Bénodet (☎02.98.90.62.02; *www.lanniron.com*; closed mid-Sept to mid-May).

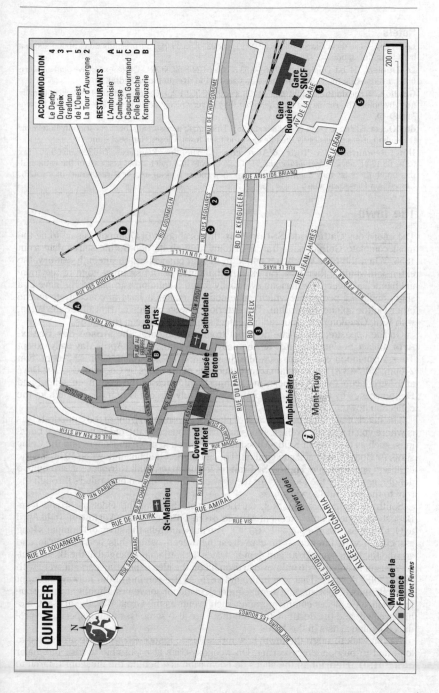

Hotels

Le Derby, 13 av de la Gare (☎02.98.52.06.91, fax 02.98.53.39.04). Surprisingly quiet option above a bar facing the station. ②.

Le Dupleix, 34 bd Dupleix (☎02.98.90.53.35, fax 02.98.52.05.31). Quite expensive and modern hotel, overlooking the Odet, with fine views across the river to the cathedral. ④.

Gradlon, 30 rue du Brest (☎02.98.95.04.39, fax 02.98.95.61.25). Central but quiet and exceptionally friendly hotel. The rooms are not cheap but they're very nicely decorated. Closed mid-Dec to mid-Jan. ④–⑤.

de l'Ouest, 63 rue le Déan (☎02.98.90.28.35). This small, unassuming, but very friendly hotel near the station offers consistently the cheapest rooms in town. Closed Sun Sept–June. ①.

Hôtel-Restaurant La Tour d'Auvergne, 13 rue des Réguaires (☎02.98.95.08.70, fax 02.98.95.17.31, *www.la-tour-dauvergne.fr*). Tucked away in a quiet street just east of the cathedral, this hotel offers 38 very comfortable refurbished rooms and an excellent restaurant (see p.429). Closed Sun Oct–April. ⑥.

The Town

The enormous **Cathédrale St-Corentin**, the focal point of Quimper, is said to be the most complete Gothic cathedral in Brittany, though its neo-Gothic spires date from 1856. When the nave was being added to the old chancel in the fifteenth century, the extension would either have hit existing buildings or the swampy edge of the then-unchannelled river. The masons eventually found a solution and placed the nave at a slight angle – a peculiarity which, once noticed, makes it hard to concentrate on the other Gothic splendours within. The exterior, however, gives no hint of the deviation, with King Gradlon now mounted in perfect symmetry between the spires.

On the opposite side of rue de Frout from the cathedral, the **Musée des Beaux-Arts**, 4 place St-Corentin (July & Aug daily 10am–7pm; Sept & April–May daily except Tues 10am–noon & 2–6pm; Oct–March Mon & Wed–Sat 10am–noon & 2–6pm, Sun 2–6pm; 25F/€3.81), houses amazing collections of drawings by Cocteau, Gustave Doré and Max Jacob (who was born in Quimper), paintings of the Pont-Aven school and Breton scenes by the likes of Eugène Boudin. Only the old Dutch oils upstairs let the collection down.

The heart of old Quimper lies west of place St-Corentin, in front of the cathedral. This is where you'll find the liveliest shops and cafés, housed in the old half-timbered buildings, such as the Breton Keltia-Musique record shop in place au Beurre and the Celtic shop, Ar Bed Keltiek, at 2 rue Grallon. The old market hall burnt down in 1976, but the light and spacious new **Halles St-Francis** in rue Astor, built to replace it, are quite a delight, not just for the food but for the view past the upturned boat rafters through the roof to the cathedral's twin spires.

South of the covered market, on the opposite bank of the Odet at 14 rue Jean-Baptiste-Bosquet, is the excellent **Musée de la Faïence Jules Verlinque** (mid-April to Oct Mon–Sat 10am–6pm; 26F/€3.96). The museum tells the story of Quimper's long association with **faïence** – tin-glazed earthenware – which has been made in and around the town since 1690, and demonstrates that little has changed in the Breton pottery business since some unknown artisan hit on the idea of painting ceramic ware with naive "folk" designs. That was in around 1875, as the coming of the railways brought the first influx of tourists, and a consequent demand for souvenirs. Highlights of the collection include pieces commemorating such events as the Great War, the first automobile accident and the death of Zola, but there are also some fascinating specimens produced by fine artists in the 1920s.

As you walk through the town, it is impossible to ignore *faïence* – you are invited to look and to buy on every corner. On weekdays, it's also possible to visit the major *atelier* **H.-B. Henriot**, in the allées de Locmarion just behind the museum (March to mid-July & Sept Mon–Fri 9am–11.15am & 1.30–4.15pm; mid-July to Aug Mon–Fri 9am–11.15am & 1.30–4.45pm; Oct–Feb tours only Mon–Thurs 11am & 3.45pm; ☎02.98.90.09.36, *www.hb-henriot.com*; 20F/€3.05). H.-B. Henriot maintain a bright, modern **gift shop** alongside; the prices, even for the seconds, are similar to those on offer everywhere else, but the selection is superb.

Eating and drinking

Though the pedestrian streets west of the cathedral are unexpectedly short on places to eat, there are quite a few **restaurants** further east on the north side of the river, en route to the *gare SNCF*. Rue Aristide-Briand here is a particularly promising area, with some lively bars, and place au Beurre, north of the cathedral, is a good bet for crêperies.

L'Ambroisie, 49 rue Élie-Fréron (☎02.98.95.00.02). Upmarket French restaurant a short climb north from the cathedral, with menus from 120F/€18.29. Choice is very restricted, but you can feel safe placing yourself in the hands of the Guyon family. Closed Mon evening, except in summer.

La Cambuse, 11 rue Déan (☎02.98.53.06.06). Lively place, south of the river, serving inexpensive crêpes, salads and quiche-like savoury *tartes*. Behind the bright-orange facade there's more orange panelling, with wooden tables and a little garden as well. Closed Sun lunch and all day Mon.

Le Capucin Gourmand, 29 rue des Réguaires (☎02.98.95.43.12). Gourmet French cooking, not far east of the cathedral. Menus start at 100F/€15.24 and zoom on up to 360F/€54.58; most offer very little choice, though all feature at least some meat dishes. Closed Mon lunch & allday Sun.

La Folle Blanche, 39 bd de Kerguélen (☎02.98.95.76.76). Lovely Art-Deco restaurant, facing the river close to the cathedral, which serves top-value menus at 95F/€14.48 and 145F/€22.11 and often features live jazz at weekends. Closed Sun, plus Tues evening in winter.

La Krampouzerie, 9 rue du Sallé, on the place au Beurre (☎02.98.95.13.08). One of the best of Quimper's many crêperies, with some outdoor seating on the square. Most crêpes cost around 20F/€3.05, though you can get a wholewheat galette with scallops for 42F/€6.40, or with seaweed for 30F/€4.57. Closed Mon in winter & Sun.

La Tour d'Auvergne, 13 rue des Réguaires (☎02.98.95.08.70). Formal hotel dining room that offers high-quality menus from 125F/€19.06 at lunchtime up to 198F/€30.19 in the evening, with an emphasis on fresh local seafood. The mussels and monkfish are excellent and the baked strawberries divine. Closed Sat evening, plus Sun Oct–April.

Entertainment

Quimper's **Festival de Cornouaille** started in 1923 and has gone from strength to strength since. This great jamboree of Breton music, costumes, theatre and dance is held in the week before the fourth Sunday in July, attracting guest performers from the other Celtic countries and a scattering of other, sometimes highly unusual, ethnic-cultural ensembles. The whole thing culminates in an incredible Sunday parade through the town. The official programme does not appear until July, but you can get provisional details in advance from the tourist office. Accommodation is at a premium in Quimper while the festival is on.

Not so widely known are the **Semaines Musicales** which breathe life into the rather stuffy nineteenth-century theatre on boulevard Dupleix during the first three weeks of August. The music is predominantly classical and tends to favour French composers such as Berlioz, Debussy, Bizet and Poulenc.

South from Quimper

More tourists flock to Finistère's southern coast than to any other part of the region, with the busiest segment of all in summer centring on the family-friendly resort of

Bénodet. The beaches between here and **Forêt-Fouesnant** to the east rank among the finest in Brittany. Slightly further east, the walled, sea-circled town of **Concarneau** makes a perfect day-trip destination, though a prettier place to spend a night or two would be the flowery village of **Pont-Aven**, as immortalized by Paul Gauguin, further to the east again.

Bénodet and around

Once out of its city channel, the Odet takes on the shape of most Breton inlets, spreading out to lake proportions then turning narrow corners between gorges. The family resort of **BÉNODET** at the mouth of the river (reachable by boat from Quimper – see p.426) has a long sheltered beach on the ocean side, with amusements for children and beachside nurseries. Among the nicest **hotels** in Bénodet are the *Hôtel-Restaurant Le Minaret*, an odd-looking building in a superb seafront position on the corniche de l'Estuaire (☎02.98.57.03.13; ③; closed mid-Oct to March), and the *Bains de Mer*, 11 rue du Kérguelen (☎02.98.57.03.41; ③; closed mid-Nov to mid-March). Bénodet also has several large **campsites** – if anything, rather too many of them – such as the enormous four-star *du Letty*, southeast of the village by plage du Letty on rue du Canvez (☎02.98.57.04.69; closed early Sept to mid-June).

The coast that continues east of Bénodet is rocky and repeatedly cut by deep valleys. It suffered heavily in the hurricane of 1987, but the small resort of **BEGMEIL** survives, albeit with fewer trees to protect its vast expanse of dunes. These are ideal for **campers**, with several official sites, and just back from the seafront there's also the hotel *Thalamot* (☎02.98.94.97.38; ③; closed Oct–April).

Around the **Forêt-Fouesnant** in particular, 12km east of Bénodet, the hills are much too steep for cyclists to climb, and forbidden to heavy vehicles such as caravans. The Forêt-Fouesnant minor road may look good, but there are few beaches or places to stop. Motorists would do best to take the more direct D44, a few kilometres inland, followed by the D783, which leads close to the major towns along the route.

Concarneau

The first sizeable town you come to east of Bénodet is **CONCARNEAU**, where the third most important fishing port in France does a reasonable job of passing itself off as a holiday resort. Its greatest asset is its **Ville Close**, the small and very well-fortified old city located a few metres offshore on an irregular rocky island in the bay. This can get too crowded for comfort in high summer, but otherwise it's a real delight. Like those of the *citadelle* at Le Palais on Belle-Île, its ramparts were completed by Vauban in the seventeenth century. The island itself, however, had been inhabited for at least a thousand years before that, and is first recorded as the site of a priory founded by King Gradlon of Quimper.

Concarneau boasts that it is a *ville fleurie*, and the flowers are most in evidence inside the walls, where climbing roses and clematis swarm all over the various gift shops, restaurants and crêperies. Walk the central pedestrianized street to the far end, and you can pass through a gateway to the shoreline to watch the fishing boats go by. In summer, however, the best views of all come from the promenade on top of the **ramparts** (daily: May, June & Sept 10am–6pm; July & Aug 10am–9pm; 5F/€0.76).

The **Musée de la Pêche**, immediately inside the Ville Close (daily: mid-June to mid-Sept 9.30am–8pm; rest of year 9.30am–12.30pm & 2–6pm; 36F/€5.49), provides an insight into the traditional life Concarneau shared with so many other Breton ports, illuminating the history and practice of catching whales, tuna – with dragnets the size of central Paris – herring and sardines.

Practicalities

There's no rail service to Concarneau, but SNCF **buses** connect the town with Quimper and Rosporden. The **tourist office** (May & June Mon–Sat 9am–noon & 2–6.30pm, Sun 9.30am–12.30pm; July & Aug daily 9am–8pm; rest of year Mon–Sat 9am–noon & 2–6.30pm; ☎02.98.97.01.44) is on the quai d'Aiguillon, not far from the long-distance bus stop.

The Ville Close is almost completely devoid of **hotels**, so most of those that Concarneau has to offer skulk in the back streets of the mainland, and tend to be full most of the time. Decent options include the bright, modernized *Hôtel de France et d'Europe*, 9 av de la Gare (☎02.98.97.00.64, fax 02.98.50.76.66; ④; closed Sat mid-Nov to mid-Feb), near the main bus stop, and the *Hôtel-Restaurant les Océanides*, 3 rue du Lin (☎02.98.97.08.61, fax 02.98.97.09.13; ②–③; closed Sun evening in May & June, all Sun Oct–April), a *logis de France*, a couple of streets up from the sea above the fishing port, with a highly recommended and far from expensive restaurant – some of the fancier rooms are in the nominally distinct *Petites Océanides* across the street. Opposite the entrance to the Ville Close are the spruce pastel-orange *des Halles*, place de l'Hôtel de Ville (☎02.98.97.11.41, fax 02.98.50.58.54; ④; closed Sun evening in low season), offering well-equipped rooms at reasonable rates, and the more basic *des Voyageurs*, 9 place Jean-Jaurès (☎02.98.97.08.06; ②), above a bar. Probably the best bet of all is the **hostel** (☎02.98.97.03.47; 50F/€7.62; open all year), for once very near the city centre but also enjoying magnificent ocean views. It's just around the tip of the headland on the quai de la Croix, with a good crêperie opposite and a windsurfing shop a little further along.

For an atmospheric meal in Concarneau, choose from any of the **restaurants** along the main street that runs through the Ville Close, or explore the lanes that lead off it. There are, however, plenty of cheaper places back in town. Worth a try on the mainland are *Chez Armande*, 15 av du Dr-Nicholas (☎02.98.97.00.76; closed Wed & Tues in winter; menus from 105F/€16.01), an excellent seafood restaurant not far south of the market; *Le Bélem*, place Jean-Jaurès (☎02.98.97.02.78; closed Wed), a pretty little indoor restaurant, next to the market, serving mussels for 50F/€7.62 and good seafood menus from 79F/€12.04; and *L'Escale*, 19 quai Carnot (☎02.98.97.03.31; closed Sun), a waterfront restaurant on the main road in town that's a favourite with local fishermen, with lunch menus for around 54F/€8.23. In the heart of the Ville Close is *L'Écume*, 3 place St-Guénolé (☎02.98.97.15.98; closed Wed, plus Nov to mid-March; menus from 60F/€9.15), one of several good-value **crêperies** in that part of town, and a great spot to watch the world go by.

Pont-Aven and around

PONT-AVEN, 14km east of Concarneau and just inland from the tip of the Aven estuary, is a small port packed with tourists and art galleries. This was where Gauguin came to paint in the 1880s, before he left for Tahiti in search of a South Seas idyll. He produced some of his finest work in Pont-Aven, and his influence was such that the **Pont-Aven School** of fellow artists – the best known of whom was Émile Bernard – developed here, but for all the local hype, the town has no permanent collection of Gauguin's work. The **Musée Municipal** (daily: mid-Feb to mid-June & mid-Sept to Dec 10am–12.30pm & 2–6pm; mid-June to mid-Sept 10am–7pm; 27F/€4.12) in the Mairie holds changing exhibitions of the school and other artists active during the same period, but you can't count on paintings by the man himself.

Gauguin aside, Pont-Aven is pleasant in its own right. Just upstream of the little granite bridge at the heart of town, the **promenade Xavier-Grall** crisscrosses the tiny river itself on landscaped walkways, offering glimpses of the backs of venerable mansions, dripping with red ivy, and a little "chaos" of rocks in the stream itself. A longer walk – allow an hour – leads into the **Bois d'Amour**, wooded gardens which have long provided inspiration to painters, poets and musicians.

Pont-Aven's **tourist office**, 5 place de l'Hôtel de Ville (April–June & Sept–Oct daily 9.15am–12.30pm & 2–7pm; July & Aug daily 9.30am–7.30pm; Nov–March Mon–Sat 10am–12.30pm & 2–6pm; ☎02.98.06.04.70, *ot.pont.aven@wanadoo.fr*), sells an excellent English-language guide booklet to the town, plus route maps of local walks, for a mere 2F/€0.30. Much the best of the town's three relatively expensive **hotels** is the central *Hôtel des Ajoncs d'Or*, 1 place de l'Hôtel de Ville (☎02.98.06.02.06; ③; closed Jan), where gourmet menus start at 85F/€12.96. The nicest of the local **campsites** is *Le Spinnaker* (☎02.98.06.01.77; closed Oct–April), set in a large wooded park.

From the unremarkable village of **RIEC-SUR-BÉLON**, 5km southeast of Pont-Aven, back roads snake down for another 4km to reach a dead end at the **port du Bélon**, on the sinuous estuary of the Bélon river. The coastal footpath that leads from here along the thickly wooded shoreline is clearly signposted to offer optional loop trails of 3km, 6km and 8km.

Many of the oyster beds visible at low tide in the sands off the port belong to *Chez Jacky* (☎02.98.06.90.32; closed Mon, plus Oct–Easter), a popular seafood **restaurant**. Once past the well-stocked vivarium at its entrance, you'll find bare wooden benches and tables inside, and beyond that a lovely seafront terrace. The ambience is informal, but both the food, and the prices, are to be taken seriously. Local oysters are 80F/€12.20 a dozen, while a huge platter of mostly raw shellfish costs 200F/€30.49 per person.

Quimperlé

The final town of any size in Finistère, **QUIMPERLÉ** straddles a hill and two rivers, the Isole and the Elle, cut by a sequence of bridges. It's an atmospheric place, particularly in the medieval muddle of streets around **Ste-Croix church**. This was copied in plan from schema brought back by crusaders of the Church of the Holy Sepulchre in Jerusalem and is notable for its original Romanesque apse. There are some good **bars** nearby and, on Fridays, a **market** on the square higher up on the hill.

Reasonable **rooms** can be had at *Le Brizeux*, 7 quai Brizeux (☎02.98.96.19.25; ②), and *de Kervidanou*, in the village of Mellac 5km northwest (☎02.98.39.18.00; ③). The nicest **campsite** in the vicinity is the two-star, British-owned *Bois des Ecureuils* (☎02.98.71.70.98), 15km northeast in the verdant countryside at Guilligomarch, north of Arzano.

INLAND BRITTANY: THE NANTES–BREST CANAL

The **Nantes–Brest canal** is a meandering chain of waterways from Finistère to the Loire, interweaving rivers with stretches of canal built at Napoléon's instigation to bypass the belligerent English fleets off the coast. Finally completed in 1836, it came into its own at the end of the century as a coal, slate and fertilizer route. The building of the dam at Lac Guerlédan in the 1920s chopped the canal in two, leaving a whole section unnavigable by barge. Road transport had already superseded water haulage; now tourism is breathing life back into the canal.

En route the canal passes through riverside towns, such as **Josselin** and **Malestroit**, that long predate its construction; commercial ports and junctions – **Pontivy**, most notably – that developed in the nineteenth century because of it; the old port of **Redon**, a patchwork of water, where the canal crosses the River Vilaine; and a sequence of scenic splendours, including the string of lakes around the **Barrage de Guerlédan**, near Mur-de-Bretagne. As a focus for exploring **inland Brittany**, whether by barge, bike, foot or all three, the canal is ideal. Not every stretch is accessible, but there are detours to be made away from it, such as into the wild and desolate **Monts d'Arrée** to the north of the canal in Finistère.

For general information on **renting barges** for use on the inland waterways, contact the Comité de Promotion Touristique des Canaux Bretons, Office du Tourisme, place du Parlement, 35600 Redon (☎02.99.71.06.04).

The Finistère stretch

As late as the 1920s, steamers would make their way across the Rade de Brest and down the Aulne River to **Châteaulin**, the first real town on the canal route. If you're walking the canal seriously, **Pont-Coblant** and **Pleyben** are just 10km further away on the map, but be warned that the meanders make it a several-hour hike. Pick your side of the water, too; there are no bridges between Châteaulin and Pont-Coblant.

Châteaulin
CHÂTEAULIN is a quiet place, where the main reason to stay is the canal itself – or river as it is here. Most bars sell permits for its salmon and trout **fishing** (as do fishing shops, some of which rent out tackle). You should have little difficulty finding a room at the **hotel** *Le Christmas*, 33 Grande-Rue (☎02.98.86.01.24; ②), which serves excellent food. Within a couple of minutes' walk upstream from the statue to Jean Moulin (the Resistance leader who was *sous-préfet* here from 1930 to 1933) and the town centre, you'll find yourself on towpaths full of rabbits and squirrels and overhung by trees full of birds.

Carhaix
CARHAIX, a further 25km east of Châteaulin, is a road junction that dates back to the Romans, with cafés and shops to replenish supplies, but not much to recommend it. The most interesting building in town is the granite Renaissance **Maison de Sénéchal** on rue Brisieux, which houses the **tourist office** (July & Aug Mon–Sat 9am–12.30pm & 1.30–7pm, Sun 10am–1pm; rest of year Mon–Sat 10am–noon & 2–6pm; ☎02.98.93.04.42). The modern *Hôtel Gradlon* at 12 bd de la République (☎02.98.93.15.22; ③), near the church, makes a comfortable if slightly pricey place to spend the night, and serves good food, with dinner menus starting at 85F/€12.96.

Huelgoat and its forest
HUELGOAT is the halfway point between Morlaix and Carhaix on the minor road D769, and it makes a pleasant overnight stop, next to its own small **lake**. Spreading north and east from the village is the **Forêt de Huelgoat**, a landscape of trees, giant boulders and waterfalls tangled together in primeval chaos – or at least it was up until 1987, when the hurricane of that October demonstrated just how fragile the forest really was, just how miraculous had been its long survival, by smashing it to smithereens in the space of fifteen minutes. After several years of cleaning up, the forest has now returned to a fairly close approximation of its former glories, and it is once again possible to walk for several kilometres along the various paths that lead into the depths of the woods.

One or two of the village's **hotels** were too hard hit by the post-hurricane decline in tourism to survive, but the *Hôtel du Lac*, beside the lake at 12 rue du Général-de-Gaulle (☎02.98.99.71.14; ③; closed mid-Nov to mid-Dec), is still there, offering well-refurbished rooms and good food. Also beside the lake, on the road towards Brest, the two-star *Camping du Lac* (☎02.98.99.78.80; closed mid-Sept to mid-June) comes complete with swimming pool.

Le Faouët, St-Fiacre and Kernascléden

Thirty kilometres south of Carhaix on the D769, the secluded town of **LE FAOUËT** is served by neither buses nor trains and is distinguished mainly by its large old **market hall**. Above a floor of mud and straw, still used by local traders, rises an intricate latticework of ancient wood, propped on granite pillars and topped by a little clock tower.

The church at **ST-FIACRE**, just over 2km south, is notable for its rood screen, brightly polychromed and carved as intricately as lace. The original purpose of a rood screen was to separate the chancel from the congregation – the decorations of this 1480 masterpiece go rather further than that. They depict scenes from the Old and New Testaments as well as a dramatic series on the wages of sin. Drunkenness is demonstrated by a man somehow vomiting a fox; theft by a peasant stealing apples; and so on. The **hotel** *Croix d'Or*, opposite the old market in the heart of Le Faouët at 9 place Bellanger (☎02.97.23.07.33; ③; closed mid-Dec to mid-Jan, plus Sun evening & Mon in low season), has a 135F/€20.58 menu that features snail ravioli and skate's wing with thyme.

At the ornate and gargoyle-coated church at **KERNASCLÉDEN**, 15km southeast of Le Faouët along the D782, the focus turns from carving to frescoes. The themes, however, contemporary with St-Fiacre, are equally gruesome. On the damp-infested wall of a side chapel, horned devils stoke the fires beneath a vast cauldron filled with the souls of the damned, and you may be able to discern the outlines of a Dance of Death, a faded cousin to that at Kermaria (see p.406).

The central stretch: Gouarec to Redon

Although the canal is limited to canoeists between Carhaix and Pontivy, it's worth some effort to follow on land, particularly for the scenery from **Gouarec** to **Mur-de-Bretagne**. At the centre is the trailing **Lac de Guerlédan**, created by the construction of a barrage near Mur, and backed, to the south, by the enticing **Forêt de Quénécan**. Approaching by road, the canal path is most easily joined at Gouarec, covered by the five daily buses between Carhaix and Loudéac.

Gouarec

At **GOUAREC**, the River Blavet and the canal meet in a confusing swirl of water that shoots off, edged by footpaths, in the most unlikely directions. The old schist houses of the town are barely disturbed by traffic or development, nor are there great numbers of tourists. For a comfortable overnight stop, the *Hôtel du Blavet* (☎02.96.24.90.03, *louis.le-loir@wanadoo.fr*, ②), is in an ideal waterside position. Don't be put off by its extravagant menus – they have affordable meals as well. There's also a well-positioned two-star municipal **campsite**, the *Tost Aven* (☎02.96.24.85.42; closed Oct–March), next to the canal and away from the main road.

Quénécan Forest

For the 15km between Gouarec and Mur-de-Bretagne, the N164 skirts the edge of **Quénécan Forest**, within which is a series of artificial lakes created when the **Barrage of Guerlédan** was completed in 1928. Though sadly once again damaged by the hurricane, it's a beautiful stretch of river, a little overrun by campers and caravans, but peaceful enough nonetheless.

The best places to stay are just off the road, past the villages of **ST-GELVEN** and Caurel. At the former, the ravishing *Hôtellerie de l'Abbaye Bon-Repos* (☎02.96.24.98.38; ③; closed Tues evening & Wed in low season) is an absolutely irresistible, inexpensive **hotel-restaurant**, nestling beside the water at the end of a venerable avenue of ancient trees, and housed in the intact outbuildings of a twelfth-century Cistercian abbey. Porthole-like windows pierce the thick slate walls of its six cosy guest rooms, to look out across extensive riverfront grounds to the dramatic wooded slopes beyond.

From just before **CAUREL**, the brief loop of the D111 leads to tiny sandy beaches – a bit too tiny in season – with the two-star **campsite** *Les Pins* (☎02.96.28.52.22; closed Oct–March). At the spot known, justifiably, as **BEAU RIVAGE**, a lavish holiday complex features the *Nautic International* campsite (☎02.96.28.57.94; closed Oct–April), and the *Hôtel Beau Rivage* (☎02.96.28.52.15; ③; closed Mon evening & Tues in low season), plus a restaurant, a snack bar and a 140-seat glass-topped cruise boat.

Pontivy

You can again take **barges** all the way to the Loire from **PONTIVY**, the central junction of the Nantes–Brest canal, where the course of the canal breaks off once more from the Blavet. When the waterway opened, the small medieval centre of the town was expanded, redesigned and given broad avenues to fit its new role. It was even briefly renamed Napoléonville, in honour of the man responsible for its new prosperity.

These days, Pontivy is a bright market town, its twisting old streets contrasting with the stately riverside promenades. At its northern end, occupying a commanding hillside site, is the **Château de Rohan**, built by the lord of Josselin in the fifteenth century (June–Sept daily 10.30am–7pm; rest of year Wed–Sun 10am–noon & 2–6pm; 20F/€3.05). Used in summer for low-key cultural events and temporary exhibitions, the castle still belongs to the Josselin family, who are slowly restoring it. At the moment, one impressive facade, complete with deep moat and two forbidding towers, looks out over the river – behind that, the structure rather peters out.

Pontivy's helpful **tourist office** is just below the castle, on place de Gaulle (June–Sept daily 10am–6pm; rest of year Mon–Sat 10am–noon & 2–6pm; ☎02.97.25.04.10). Among local **hotels** are the low-priced *Robic*, 2 rue Jean-Jaurès (☎02.97.25.11.80; ②; closed Sun evening in winter), which has a good restaurant with menus from 60F/€9.15, and the smarter *Porhoët*, near the tourist office at 41 rue du Général-de-Gaulle (☎02.97.25.34.88; ③). In addition, the local **hostel**, 2km from the *gare SNCF* on the Île des Récollets (☎02.97.25.58.27), is in good condition and serves cheap meals.

Josselin

About 30km further along the canal from Pontivy, you come to the three Rapunzel towers embedded in a vast sheet of stone of the **château** in **JOSSELIN**. The Rohan family used to own a third of Brittany, but the present duke contents himself with the position of local mayor. The pompous apartments of his residence are not very interesting, even if they do contain the table on which the Edict of Nantes was signed in 1598. But the duchess's collection of dolls, housed in the **Musée des Poupées**, behind the castle, is something special (château and doll museum open April, May & Oct Wed, Sat, Sun & hols 2–6pm; June & Sept daily 2–6pm; July & Aug daily 10am–6pm; both 33F/€5.03, combined ticket 62F/€9.45).

The town is full of medieval splendours, from the gargoyles of the **basilica** to the castle **ramparts**, and the half-timbered houses in between. **Notre-Dame-du-Roncier** is built on the spot where, in the ninth century, a peasant supposedly found a statue of the Virgin under a bramble bush. The statue was burnt during the Revolution, but an important *pardon* is held each year on September 8.

Josselin's **tourist office** is in a superb old house on the place de la Congrégation, up in town next to the castle entrance (April–June, Sept & Oct daily 10am–noon & 2–6pm; July & Aug daily 10am–6pm; Nov–March Mon–Fri 10am–noon & 2–6pm; ☎02.97.22.36.43, *ot.josselin@wanadoo.fr*). Just across from the basilica, the *Hôtel de France*, 6 place Notre Dame (☎02.97.22.23.06; ②; closed Sun evening & Mon between

Oct and March), is an ivy-covered *logis* which is amazingly quiet considering its central location, where you can choose on the 81F/€12.35 menu between duck *à l'orange* or trout with almonds. The lovely *Hôtel du Chateau*, facing the castle from across the river at 1 rue du Général-de-Gaulle (☎02.97.22.20.11; ③; closed Feb), is also a treat. The nearest good **campsite** is the three-star *Bas de la Lande* (☎02.97.22.22.20; closed Oct–April), half an hour's walk from the castle, south of the river and west of town.

Guéhenno and Lizio

One of the largest and best Breton calvaries is at **GUÉHENNO**, south of Josselin on the D123. Sculpted in 1550, the figures include the cock that crowed after Peter's denials, Mary Magdalene with the shroud and a recumbent Christ in the crypt. Its appeal is enhanced by the naivety of its amateur restoration. After damage caused by Revolutionary soldiers in 1794 – who amused themselves by playing boules with the heads of the statues – all the sculptors approached for the work demanded exorbitant fees, so the parish priest and his assistant decided to undertake the task themselves.

Over to the east, off the D151, **LIZIO** has also set itself up as a centre for arts and crafts, with ceramic and weaving workshops its speciality. One venerable old cottage also houses an **Insectarium** (April–Sept daily 10am–noon & 2–6pm; 35F/€5.34), holding creepy-crawlies that include hairy spiders, giant millipedes, praying mantises and stick insects in amazing colours.

Malestroit and around

Not a lot happens in **MALESTROIT**, which celebrated its thousand-year anniversary in 1987. But the town is full of unexpected and enjoyable corners. As you come into the main square, the **place du Bouffay** in front of the church, the houses are covered with unlikely carvings – an anxious bagpipe-playing hare looking over its shoulder at a dragon's head on one beam, while an oblivious sow in a blue buckled belt threads her distaff on another. The **church** itself is decorated with drunkards and acrobats outside, torturing demons and erupting towers within. Beside the grey canal, the matching grey slate tiles on the turreted rooftops bulge and dip, while on its central island overgrown houses stand next to the stern walls of an old mill.

Two kilometres west of Malestroit (and with no bus connection), the village of **ST-MARCEL** hosts a **Musée de la Résistance Bretonne** (April to mid-June daily 10am–noon & 2–6pm; mid-June to mid-Sept daily 10am–7pm; rest of year daily except Tues 10am–noon & 2–6pm; 25F/€3.81). The museum stands on the site of a June 1944 battle in which the Breton *maquis* (guerrilla Resistance fighters), joined by Free French forces parachuted in from England, successfully diverted the local German troops from the main Normandy invasion movements.

If you arrive in Malestroit by barge (this is a good stretch to travel), you'll moor very near the town centre. The local **tourist office** stands at the edge of the main square at 17 place du Bouffay (Mon–Fri 9am–12.30pm & 2–6.30pm, Sat 9am–noon & 2–6pm; ☎02.97.75.14.57, *www.malestroit.com* or *www.morbihan-valdoust.com*). Sadly, Malestroit no longer has a hotel, but there's a two-star **campsite**, *La Daufresne* (☎02.97.75.13.33; closed Oct–May), down below the bridge in the Impasse d'Abattoir next to the swimming pool.

Rochefort-en-Terre

ROCHEFORT-EN-TERRE, commanding a high eminence 17km south of Malestroit, may be a prettified and polished version of its neighbour, but it ranks nonetheless among the most delightful villages in Brittany. Every available stone surface, from the window ledges to the picturesque wishing well, is festooned with colourful geraniums, a tradition that originated with the painter Alfred Klots, who was born in France to a wealthy American family in 1875, and bought Rochefort's ruined **château** in 1907. Perched on the town's highest point, the castle is now open for guided tours (April, May & Oct Sat, Sun & hols 10.30am–noon & 2–6.30pm; June & Sept daily 10.30am–noon & 2–6.30pm; July & Aug daily 10am–7pm; 25F/€3.81), though not until you go through its dramatic gateway do you find out that in fact that gateway is all that survives of the original fifteenth-century structure.

Rochefort's modern **tourist office**, in the central place des Halles (June & Sept Mon–Fri 10am–12.30pm & 2.30–6pm, Sat & Sun 2–6pm; July & Aug Mon–Fri 10am–12.30pm & 2–6.30pm, Sat & Sun 2–6.30pm; rest of year Mon–Fri 10am–noon & 2.30–5pm, Sat 2–5pm; ☎02.97.43.33.57), displays a list of expensive *chambres d'hôte* in the neighbourhood, and operates the three-star municipal **campsite**, *Le Moulin Neuf*, in the chemin de Bogeais (☎02.97.43.37.52; closed Oct–March). The one **hotel** stands alongside the tourist office: *Le Pélican* (☎02.97.43.38.48; ③) offers reasonable rooms and good food, with dinner menus starting at under 100F/€15.

Redon

Thirty-four kilometres east of Malestroit, at the junction not only of the rivers Oust and Vilaine and the canal, but also of the train lines to Rennes, Vannes and Nantes and of six major roads, **REDON** is not easy to avoid. And you shouldn't try to, either. A wonderful grouping of water and locks, it's a town with history, charm and life.

Until World War I, Redon was the seaport for Rennes. Its industrial docks – or what remains of them – are therefore on the Vilaine, while the canal, even in the very centre of town, is almost totally rural, its towpaths shaded avenues. Shipowners' houses from the seventeenth and eighteenth centuries can be seen along quai Jean-Bart by the *bassin* and quai Duguay-Truin next to the river. A rusted wrought-iron workbridge, equipped with a gantry, still crosses the river, but the main users of the port now are cruise ships heading down the Vilaine to La Roche-Bernard.

Redon was once also a religious centre, its first abbey founded in 832 by St Conwoion. The most prominent church today is **St-Sauveur**. Its unique four-storeyed Romanesque belfry is squat, almost obscured by later roofs and the high choir, and is best seen from the adjacent cloisters; the Gothic tower is entirely separated from the main building by a fire. In the crypt, you'll find the tomb of the judge who tried the legendary Bluebeard – Joan of Arc's friend, Gilles de Rais.

Redon's **gare SNCF** is five minutes' walk west from the **tourist office** in the place de la République (July & Aug Mon–Sat 9am–7pm, Sun 10am–noon & 4–7pm; rest of year Mon–Sat 9am–noon & 2–6pm; ☎02.99.71.06.04, *www.ville-redon.fr*), north across the railway tracks from the town centre. Most of the **hotels** are concentrated in town and near the *gare SNCF* rather than in the port area. The off-white *Hôtel de France* looks down on the canal from 30 rue Duguesclin (☎02.99.71.06.11; ②); its en-suite rooms offer a considerable degree of comfort for the price. Nearer the station, the *Hôtel Chandouineau*, 1 rue Thiers (☎02.99.71.02.04; ⑤), is a luxurious establishment with just seven bedrooms, where the restaurant serves gourmet menus from 120F/€18.29.

THE SOUTHERN COAST

Brittany's **southern coast** takes in the province's – and indeed Europe's – most famous prehistoric site, the alignments of **Carnac**, with the associated megaliths of the beautiful, island-studded **Golfe de Morbihan**. The beaches are not as spectacular as in Finistère, but there are more safe places to swim and the water is warmer. Of the cities, **Lorient** has Brittany's most compelling **festival** and **Vannes** has one of the liveliest medieval town centres. Further east, **La Baule** does a good impression of a Breton St-Tropez, and you can escape to the islands of **Belle-Île**, **Hoëdic** and **Houat**. Inevitably it's popular, and in summer you can be hard pressed to find a room, but if you're prepared to make reservations, or you're camping, there shouldn't be much problem.

Lorient and around

LORIENT, Brittany's fourth-largest city, lies on an immense natural harbour protected from the ocean by the Île de Groix and strategically located at the junction of the rivers Scorff, Ter and Blavet. A functional, rather depressing port today, it was once a key base for French and English colonialism, and was founded in the midseventeenth century for trading operations by the Compagnie des Indes, an equivalent of the Dutch and English East India Companies. Apart from the name, little else remains to suggest the plundered wealth that once arrived here. During the last war, Lorient was a major target for the Allies; the Germans held out until May 1945, by which time the city was almost completely destroyed. The only substantial remains were the U-boat pens – subsequently greatly expanded by the French for their nuclear submarines.

Across the estuary in Port-Louis is the **Musée de la Compagnie des Indes**, a pretty dismal temple to imperialism (Jan–March, Oct & Nov daily except Tues 2–6pm; April & May daily except Tues 10am–6.30pm; June–Sept daily 10am–6.30pm; closed Dec; 30F/€4.57). Time would be more enjoyably spent on a boat trip, either up the estuary towards Hennebont or out to the **Île de Groix**. This 8km-long steep-sided rock is a somewhat smaller version of Belle-Île (see p.440), and holds some gorgeous beaches to encourage day-trippers.

Lorient's **tourist office**, beside the pleasure port on the quai de Rohan (July & Aug Mon–Sat 9am–7pm, Sun 10am–6pm; rest of year Mon–Sat 9am–12.30pm & 2–6pm; ☎02.97.21.07.84, *www.lorient.com*), can provide full details on local boat trips and organizes some excursions itself. Unless you arrive during the festival (see box below), there's a huge choice of **hotels**. Among reasonable, fairly central options are two on rue Lazare-Carnot as it curves away south of the tourist office: the *Victor Hugo Hôtel* at no. 36 (☎02.97.21.16.24, *www.contacthotel.com*; ②), with an action-packed 99F/€15.09 menu offering langoustines, wild pheasant pâté and duck *à l'orange*, and the *Hôtel d'Arvor*, at no. 104 (☎02.97.21.07.55; ②), also with a good-value restaurant. There's also an **HI hostel**, next to the River Ter at 41 rue Victor-Schoelcher, 3km out on bus line C from the *gare SNCF* (☎02.97.37.11.65; closed Jan). Good central **restaurants** include

---

THE INTER-CELTIC FESTIVAL

The overriding reason people come to Lorient is for the **Inter-Celtic Festival**, held for ten days from the first Friday to the second Sunday in August. The biggest Celtic event in Brittany, or anywhere else for that matter, attracts representatives from all seven Celtic countries. In a popular celebration of cultural solidarity, well over a quarter of a million people attend over 150 different shows, five languages mingle and Scotch and Guinness flow with French and Spanish wines and ciders. There is a certain competitive element, with championships in various categories, but the feeling of mutual enthusiasm and conviviality is paramount. Most of the activities – embracing music, dance and literature – take place around the central place Jules-Ferry, and this is where most people end up sleeping, too, as accommodation is pushed to the limit.

For schedules of the festival, and further details of temporary accommodation, contact the Office du Tourisme de Pays de Lorient, 2 rue Paul-Bert, 56100 Lorient (☎02.97.21.24.29, *www.festival-interceltique.com*), bearing in mind that the festival programme is not finalized before May. For certain specific events, you'll need to reserve tickets well in advance.

Yesterday's, 1 cours de la Bôve (☎02.97.84.85.07), a brasserie near the town hall that serves an excellent 98F/€14.94 menu, and *Le Café Leffe* (☎02.97.21.21.30; closed Jan), in the same building as the tourist office, facing the port.

St-Cado

Twelve kilometres east of Port-Louis, a large bridge spans the broad estuary of the Etel river. A short detour north of the village of Belz on the eastern shore brings you to the delightful islet of **ST-CADO**, a speck on the water dotted with perhaps twenty white-painted houses.

From the mainland, you walk across a spindly little bridge to reach the island itself. Its main feature is a twelfth-century chapel that stands on the site of a Romanesque predecessor built by St Cado around the sixth century. Cado, who was a prince of "Glamorgant", returned in due course to his native Wales and was martyred, but Welsh pilgrims still make their way to this pretty little spot. As Cado is a patron saint of the deaf, it's said that hearing problems can be cured by lying on his stone "bed" inside the chapel. A little fountain behind the chapel only emerges from the sea at low tide.

The Presqu'île de Quiberon

The **Presqu'île de Quiberon**, south of Carnac (see p.442), is well worth visiting on its own merits; **Quiberon** is quite a lively port, and you can get boats out to the islands or walk the shores of this narrow peninsula. The ocean-facing shore, known as the **Côte Sauvage**, is a wild and highly unswimmable stretch, where the stormy seas look like flashing scenes of snowy mountain tops. The sheltered eastern side has safe and calm sandy beaches, and plenty of campsites.

Quiberon

The town of **QUIBERON** itself centres on a miniature golf course surrounded by bars, pizzerias and some surprisingly good clothes and antique shops. The cafés by the long bathing beach are the most enjoyable, along with the old-fashioned *Café du Marché* next to the PTT.

Port-Maria, the fishing harbour and **gare maritime** for the islands of Belle-Île, Houat and Hoëdic (see pp.440–1), is the most active part of town and has the best concentration of hotels and restaurants. Port-Maria was once famous for its sardines, canned locally, but those days are long gone.

In July and August, the special Tire Bouchon train links Quiberon's **gare SNCF**, which is a short way above the town proper, with Auray. There are also buses right to the *gare maritime* from Vannes (#23 and #24) and Auray (#24) via Carnac. The **tourist office** at 14 rue de Verdun (July & Aug Mon–Sat 9am–8pm, Sun 9.30am–noon & 3–7pm; rest of year Mon–Sat 9am–12.30pm & 2–6.30pm; ☎02.97.50.07.84, *www.quiberon.com*), downhill and left from the gare SNCF, has an illuminated map outside that purports to monitor exactly which hotels are full, hour by hour.

For most of the year, it's hard to get **accommodation** in Quiberon. In July and August, the whole peninsula is packed, while in winter it gets very quiet indeed. The nicest area in which to stay is along the seafront in Port-Maria. Inexpensive options include the *Hôtel-Restaurant au Bon Accueil*, 6 quai de Houat (☎ & fax 02.97.50.07.92; ②; closed Jan), with a friendly dining room downstairs serving good fish soup and seafood specialities on menus that start at 85F/€12.96, and *L'Océan*, 7 quai de l'Océan (☎02.97.50.07.58, fax 02.97.50.27.81; ②; closed Oct–March), an attractive little hotel, with multicoloured pastel shutters and reasonably priced rooms. More upmarket are the

Hôtel-Restaurant Bellevue, rue de Tiviec (☎02.97.50.16.28, fax 02.97.30.44.34; ④; closed Oct–March), a relatively quiet *logis de France*, set slightly back from the sea near the casino 500m east of the port, with its own pool and a good restaurant; the comfortable *de la Mer*, 8 quai de Houat (☎02.97.50.09.05, fax 02.97.50.44.41; ④; closed mid-Nov to Jan; menus from 89F/€13.57), a blue-trimmed hotel at the western end of Port-Maria's seafront strip; and *Le Neptune*, 4 quai de Houat (☎02.97.50.09.62, fax 02.97.50.41.44; ④; closed Jan & Mon in low season), where some rooms enjoy seafront balconies, and the usual seafood menus range from 89F/€13.57 to 198F/€30.33. There's an HI hostel, *Les Filets Bleus*, 45 rue du Roc'h-Priol (☎02.97.50.15.54; closed Oct–April), 1.5km southeast of the *gare SNCF*, and a couple of decent **campsites**: *Do-Mi-Si-La-Mi*, St-Julien (☎02.97.50.22.52, *www.acdev.com/domisilami*; closed Nov–March), on the sheltered east coast north of Quiberon town and the *Camping municipal*, Kerne (☎02.97.50.05.07; closed Sept–June), one of the few sites on the Côte Sauvage, above the cliffs, 1km north-west of Port-Maria.

Once again, the most appealing area in which to browse the menus is along the waterfront in Port-Maria, with its seafood **restaurants** competing to attract ferry passengers. Hotel-owners are very insistent on persuading guests to pay for half-board – at the *Bon Accueil*, for example, that's no great hardship – but there are plenty of alternatives to choose from if you do manage to escape their clutches. Try *Ancienne Forge*, 20 rue Verdun (☎02.97.50.18.64; closed Jan, & Wed in low season), set back from the road that leads down to the port from the *gare SNCF*, which offers slightly unadventurous but good-value seafood-heavy menus from 85F/€12.96; *Le Corsaire*, 24 quai de Belle-Île (☎02.97.50.15.05), facing the ferry terminal and serving fine seafood spreads on a sprawling terrace for 79F/€12.04 and upwards; and *de la Criée*, 11 quai de l'Océan (☎02.97.30.53.09; closed Jan, Sun pm, & Mon in low season), which serves fish specialities that change every day, fresh from the morning's catch at the quayside as displayed in baskets arrayed along the front; the 89F/€13.57 menu includes stuffed mussels and fish smoked on the premises.

Belle-Île

The island of **BELLE-ÎLE**, 45 minutes by ferry from Quiberon, has its own Côte Sauvage on its Atlantic coast, while the landward side is fertile, cultivated ground, interrupted by deep estuaries with tiny ports. To appreciate the island's contrasts, some form of transport is advisable – you can **rent bikes** at the port and main town of **LE PALAIS**, and if you're in a small car the ferry fare is relatively low.

The island once belonged to the monks of Redon; then to the ambitious Nicolas Fouquet, Louis XIV's minister; later to the English, who in 1761 swapped it for Menorca in an unrepeatable bargain deal. Docking at Le Palais, the abrupt star-shaped fortifications of the **citadelle** are the first thing you see (daily: April–June, Sept & Oct 9.30am–6pm; July & Aug 9am–7pm; Nov–March 9.30am–noon & 2–5pm; 20F/€3.05). Built along stylish and ordered lines by the great fortress-builder, Vauban, it is startling in size – filled with doorways leading to mysterious cellars and underground passages, endless sequences of rooms, dungeons and deserted cells. It only ceased being a prison in 1961, having numbered a succession of state enemies and revolutionaries among its inmates, including Ben Bella of Algeria. Less involuntarily, painters such as Monet and Matisse, the writers Flaubert and Proust and the actress Sarah Bernhardt all spent time on the island. And presumably Alexandre Dumas, too, as Porthos's death, in *The Three Musketeers*, takes place here. A **museum** documents the island's history, in fiction as much as in fact.

For exploring the island, a coastal footpath runs on bare soil the length of the **Côte Sauvage**. At the Sauzon end you'll find the **Grotte de l'Apothicairerie**, so called because it was once full of cormorants' nests, arranged like the jars on a pharmacist's shelves. It's reached by descending a slippery flight of steps cut into the rock. Be careful: most years someone falls and drowns. Inland, on the D25 back towards Le Palais, you pass the two **menhirs**, Jean and Jeanne, said to be lovers petrified as punishment for wanting to meet before their marriage. Another larger menhir used to lie near these two; it was broken up to help construct the road that separates them.

Belle-Île's second town, **SAUZON**, is set at the mouth of a long estuary, 6km to the west of Le Palais. If you're staying any length of time, and you've got transport, it's probably a better place to base yourself.

Practicalities

Throughout the year, at least five **ferries** each day sail from Port-Maria, at the southern tip of the Quiberon peninsula, to Le Palais. They are operated by the Société Morbihannaise et Nantaise de Navigation (Le Palais ☎02.97.31.80.01, Port-Maria ☎02.97.50.06.90, *www.mn-les-iles.com*; 112F/€17.07 return, small car 418F/€63.72 return, bicycles 52F/€7.93 return); the first departure each day from Quiberon is usually at 8am and crossings take 45 minutes. In July and August the same company also sends two or three boats daily direct to Sauzon, which takes 25 minutes, and costs 112F/€17.07 return. In addition it runs a limited service between Le Palais and Lorient (July & Aug departs Lorient daily 8am & 1.30pm; 50min; Lorient ☎02.97.21.03.97; 158F/€24.08 return). **Day-trips** to the island, organized by Navix (May & June Wed–Sun; July & Aug daily; occasionally out of season; ☎02.97.46.60.00, *navix@wanadoo.fr*, 175F/€26.68), set out regularly from Vannes, Port Navalo and La Trinité.

The island's **tourist office** is next to the **gare maritime** in Le Palais (July to mid-Sept Mon–Sat 9am–7.30pm, Sun 9am–1pm; rest of year Mon–Sat 9.30am–6.30pm, Sun 10am–noon; ☎02.97.31.81.93, *www.belle-ile-en-mer.com*).

Accommodation in Le Palais includes the simple *Frégate* at the quayside (☎02.97.31.54.16; ①–③; closed mid-Nov to March) and a couple of more expensive options: the *Hôtel Vauban*, 1 rue des Remparts (☎02.97.31.45.42; ⑤; closed Nov to March), and the recently refitted *Hôtel-Restaurant de Bretagne* on quai Macé (☎02.97.31.80.14; ⑤), both of which have excellent sea-view **restaurants**. There are also three **campsites**, including the three-star *Camping de l'Océan* (☎02.97.31.83.86; mid-Nov to March), and a **hostel** (☎02.97.31.81.33; closed Oct), which despite holding over a hundred beds is always wildly oversubscribed; it's located a short way out of town along the clifftops from the Citadelle, at Haute-Boulogne.

Sauzon has one good hotel in a magnificent setting, the *du Phare* (☎02.97.31.60.36; ③; closed Oct–March) – where guests must eat its delicious 85F/€12.96 fish dinners – and two two-star **campsites**, *Pen Prad* (☎02.97.31.64.82; closed Oct–March) and *La Source* (☎02.97.31.60.95; closed Oct–March).

Houat and Hoëdic

The islands of **Houat** and **Hoëdic** can also be reached by ferry from Quiberon-Port-Maria with the Société Morbihannaise et Nantaise de Navigation (1–7 sailings daily depending on the season; ☎02.97.50.06.90, *www.mn-les-iles.com*; 112F/€17.07 return, bicycles 52F/€7.93). The crossing to Houat takes forty minutes, to Hoëdic another 25. Navix run **day-trips** to Houat only from Vannes, Port Navalo and La Trinité daily in July and August (☎02.97.46.60.00; 120F/€18.29).

You can't take your car to these two very much smaller versions of Belle-Île. Both have a feeling of being left behind by the passing centuries, although the younger fishermen of Houat have revived the island's fortunes by establishing a successful fishing co-operative. Houat in particular has excellent **beaches** – as ever on its sheltered (eastern) side – that fill up with campers in the summer even though camping is not strictly legal. Hoëdic on the other hand has a large municipal **campsite** (☎02.97.30.63.32). There are a couple of small **hotels** on Houat – *L'Ezenn* (☎02.97.30.69.73; ③) and the pricier *Hôtel-Restaurant des Îles* (☎02.97.30.68.02; ⑤; closed Dec & Jan) – and one on Hoëdic, *Les Cardinaux* (☎02.97.52.37.27; ③; closed Sun in winter).

Carnac and around

The **alignments** at **CARNAC** – rows of 2000 or so menhirs, or standing stones, stretching for over 4km to the north of the village – constitute the most important prehistoric site in Europe, long predating Knossos, the Pyramids, Stonehenge or the great Egyptian temples of the same name at Karnak. Mercifully, they now stand a few kilometres in from the sea, meaning you can combine a reasonably tranquil visit to the stones with a stay in the popular, modern seaside resort, pretty hectic by Brittany's mild standards.

The alignments

According to local legend, the standing stones at Carnac are Roman soldiers turned to stone by Pope Cornelius (St Cornély). Another theory, with a certain amount of mathematical backing, says the giant menhir of Locmariaquer and the Carnac stones were an observatory for the motions of the moon – a sort of three-dimensional Neolithic graph paper for plotting the movements of heavenly bodies. But history has seen them used as ready-quarried stone, and dug up and removed by peasants to protect their precious crops from academic visitors when prehistoric archeology became fashionable. It's impossible to say how many have disappeared, nor really to prove anything from what's left; and in any case their actual arrangement may never have been particularly important, with their significance lying in some great annual ceremony as each one was erected.

Thanks to increasing numbers of visitors, the principal alignments have recently been fenced off, and you are no longer free to wander at will among them. The area will be allowed to re-vegetate at a natural pace, but there's no predicting how long that process will take, and even when it's complete the chances are that access will still be restricted. For the moment, a temporary **visitor centre** at the Alignements de Kermario (daily: March–June, Sept & Oct 9am–6pm; July & Aug 9am–10pm; rest of year 10am–5.30pm) sells books and maps of the site, and holds an interesting scale model; a much larger facility is due to be constructed in the near future. The stones themselves are clearly visible on the far side of the fence, though from this or indeed almost any distance they tend to look like no more than stumps in the heather.

The grandly named **Archéoscope**, across the road from the Alignements de Menec, is presumably intended as some sort of substitute for a close-up inspection of the actual megaliths, but in fact is a terribly designed and uncomfortable building, containing a small theatre that puts on over-priced half-hour audio-visual presentations (mid-Feb to mid-Nov daily 10am–noon & 2–6.30pm; for the times of English-language performances call ☎02.97.52.07.49; 50F/€7.62). Some of the effects are quite spectacular, but basically it takes a lot of portentous booming to manage to inform you that no one knows very much.

Carnac's **Musée de Préhistoire**, at 10 place de la Chapelle in town (May–Sept Mon–Fri 10am–6.30pm, Sat & Sun 10am–noon & 2–6.30pm; rest of year daily except Tues 10am–noon & 2–5pm; April–Sept 30F/€4.57, rest of year 25F/€3.81), is a disappointingly dry museum of archeology that's likely to leave anyone whose command of

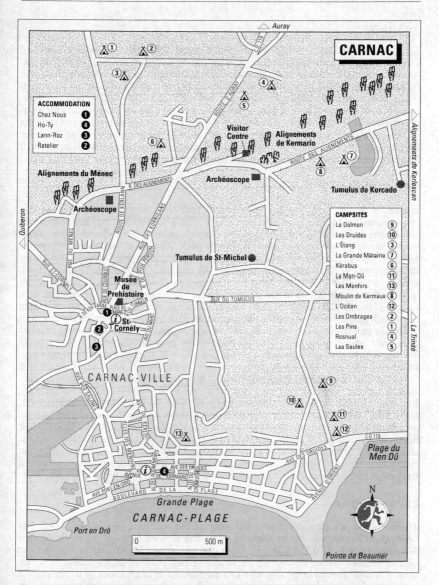

French is less than perfect almost completely in the dark as to what all the fuss is about. It traces the history of the area from earliest times, starting with 450,000-year-old chipping tools and leading by way of the Neanderthals to the megalith builders and beyond. As well as authentic physical relics, it holds reproductions and casts of the carvings at Locmariaquer, a scale model of the Alignements de Menec and diagrams of how the stones may have been moved into place.

The Town

Carnac itself, divided between the original **Carnac-Ville** and the seaside resort of **Carnac-Plage**, is extremely popular and swarming with holiday-makers in July and August. For most of these, the alignments are, if anything, only a sideshow. But, as a holiday centre, it has its special charm, especially in late spring and early autumn when it is less crowded – and cheaper. The town and seafront remain well wooded, and the tree-lined avenues and gardens are a delight, the climate being mild enough for evergreen oak and Mediterranean mimosa to grow alongside native stone pine and cypress.

The town's five **beaches** extend for nearly 3km in total. The two most attractive beaches, usually counted as one of the five, are **plages Men Dû** and **Beaumer**, which lie to the east towards La Trinité beyond Pointe Churchill.

Practicalities

Buses to Auray, Quiberon and Vannes stop near the tourist office on avenue des Druides, and on rue St-Cornély in Carnac-Ville. The Tire Bouchon **rail** link with Auray and Quiberon runs in July and August; the nearest station is at Plouharnel, 4km northwest. Carnac's main **tourist office** is slightly back from the main beach at 74 av des Druides (July & Aug Mon–Sat 9am–7pm, Sun 3–7pm; rest of year Mon–Sat 9am–noon & 2–6pm; ☎02.97.52.13.52, *www.ot-carnac.fr*). An annexe in the place de l'Église in town is open in summer (April–Sept Mon–Sat 9.30am–7pm, Sun 10am–1pm). **Bicycles** can be rented from several local campsites, or from Le Randonneur, 20 av des Druides, Carnac-Plage (☎02.97.52.02.55). The *Grande Metairie* site (see below) also arranges horseback tours. There's a **market** in Carnac on Wednesday and Sunday mornings.

Hotels in Carnac are at a premium in July and August, when you can expect higher prices and intense pressure to take half-board (*demi-pension*). Carnac-Ville is marginally cheaper than Carnac-Plage, although the distinction is blurred where the two merge. In **Carnac-Ville**, *Hôtel Chez Nous*, 5 place de la Chapelle (☎02.97.52.07.28; ③; closed Nov to mid-April), is central and convenient, with a nice garden, while the old stone, ivy-clad *Hôtel le Ratelier*, 4 Chemin de Douët (☎02.97.52.05.04; ③), has menus from 95F/€14.48. In **Carnac-Plage**, the *Hôtel-Restaurant Ho-Ty*, 15 av de Kermario (☎02.97.52.11.12; ②), is the best value. As befits such a family-oriented place, Carnac holds as many as nineteen **campsites**. Among the best are the two-star *Men Dû* (☎02.97.52.04.23; closed late Sept to mid-April) near the sea, inland from the plage du Men Dû, and the more expensive four-star *Grande Metairie* (☎02.97.52.24.01; closed mid-Sept to March), near the Kercado tumulus. Most of the **restaurants** worth recommending are in hotels – one of the best is at the cheerful *Hôtel Lann-Roz*, 36 av de la Poste (☎02.97.52.10.48; ⑤).

Locmariaquer

Thanks to the complex patterning, the stone of the roof on Gavrinis (see p.449) has been identified as part of the same piece as the dolmen known as the **Table des Marchands** at **LOCMARIAQUER**, 12km east of Carnac. Locmariaquer also has the **Grand Menhir Brisé**, supposedly the crucial central point of the megalithic observatory of Carnac. Before being floored by an earthquake in 1722, it was by far the largest known menhir – 22m high and weighing more than a full jumbo jet at 347 tonnes. It now lies on the ground in four pieces, with a possible fifth missing, close to the Table des Marchands (daily: mid-Jan to March & Oct to mid-Dec 2–5pm; April & May 10am–1pm & 2–6pm; June–Sept 10am–7pm; July & Aug 32F/€4.88, rest of year 25F/€3.81).

There are a couple of reasonable small **hotels** in Locmariaquer, both with good restaurants: *L'Escale* (☎02.97.57.32.51; ③; closed Oct–March), is right on the waterfront, with a great view from its terrace, while the *Lautram* is set slightly back from the sea, facing the church (☎02.97.57.31.32; ②; closed Oct–March). **Campsites** include the excellent two-star *La Ferme Fleurie* (☎02.97.57.34.06; closed Dec & Jan), 1km towards Kerinis, and the two-star, summer-only *Lann Brick* (☎02.97.57.32.79; closed mid-Sept to May), 1.5km further on, nearer the beach.

Auray

Some people find **AURAY**, with its over-restored ancient quarter, slightly dull – but it is a lot less crowded than Vannes, a lot cheaper than Quiberon town and usefully placed for exploring Carnac, the Quiberon peninsula and the Gulf of Morbihan.

The centre of the town today is the **place de la République**, with its eighteenth-century Hôtel de Ville. In a neighbouring square, linked to the place de la République by rue du Lait, is the seventeenth-century **church of St Gildas**, with its fine Renaissance porch. A covered market adjoins the Hôtel de Ville, but on Mondays an open-air **market** fills the surrounding streets with colour – and stops all traffic for a considerable radius.

However, Auray's showpiece is undoubtedly the ancient quarter of **St-Goustan**, with its delightful fifteenth- and sixteenth-century houses. The bend in the River Loch, an early defended site, was a natural setting for a town – and, with its easy access to the gulf, it soon became one of the busiest ports of Brittany. Today, as you look at it from the Promenade du Loch on the opposite bank, with the small seventeenth-century stone bridge still spanning the river, it is not difficult to imagine it in its heyday. In 1776, Benjamin Franklin landed here on his way to seek the help of Louis XVI in the American War of Independence.

The **gare SNCF** is twenty minutes' walk from the centre; **buses** run from the station through the centre of Auray and on to La Trinité, Carnac and Quiberon. Auray's **tourist office** is up in town at 20 rue du Lait, very near the Hôtel de Ville on place de la République (Mon–Sat 9.30am–noon & 2–6pm; ☎02.97.24.09.75). A small annexe is maintained in July and August at the train station. The most appealing place to **stay** would be by the port in the St-Goustan quarter, but in the absence of waterfront hotels the best option is the *Hôtel Le Branhoc*, about 300m from the waterfront at 5 route du Bono (☎02.97.56.41.55; ④; closed mid-Dec to Jan), which offers clean, well-equipped rooms and a reasonable restaurant. Up in town, *Hôtel Le Cadoudal*, 9 place Notre-Dame (☎02.97.50.78.51; ②), is a cheaper, more basic alternative, while the *Olympic Bar*, 19 rue Clémenceau (☎02.97.24.06.69), is a friendly restaurant-cum-bar with menus at 49F/€7.47 and 78F/€11.89.

Vannes

Thanks to its position at the head of the Golfe de Morbihan, **VANNES**, 20 km east of Auray, is southern Brittany's major tourist town. Modern Vannes is such a large and thriving community that the small size of the old walled town at its core, **Vieux Vannes**, may well come as a surprise. Its focal point, the old gateway of the **Porte St-Vincent**, commands a busy little square at the northern end of the long canalized port that provides access to the gulf itself. Once inside the ramparts, the old centre of chaotic streets – crammed around the cathedral, and enclosed by gardens and a tiny stream – is largely pedestrianized, in refreshing contrast to the somewhat insane road system beyond.

Arrival, information and accommodation

Vannes' **gare SNCF** is 25 minutes' walk north of the town centre. Buses to Auray, Carnac, Quiberon and other destinations leave from the **gare routière** alongside.

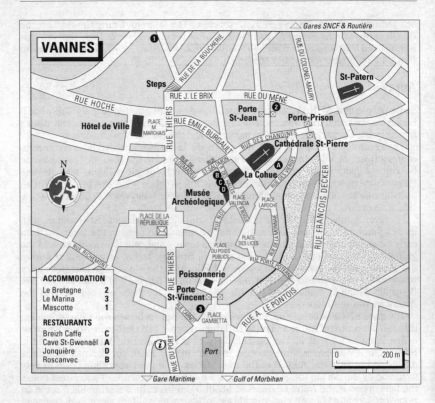

The **tourist office** is at 1 rue Thiers (July & Aug Mon–Sat 9am–7pm, Sun 10am–1pm & 3–7pm; rest of year Mon–Sat 9am–noon & 2–6pm; ☎02.97.47.24.34, *www.vannes -bretagne-sud.com*), on the corner of rue du Drézen, near place Gambetta.

In peak season, Vannes can get claustrophobic, but it offers a better choice of **hotels** than anywhere else around the gulf. The town also has a **hostel**, 4km southeast of the town centre in Séné (☎02.97.66.94.25), on bus route #4 from place de la République. The nearest **campsite** is the three-star *Camping Conleau* at the far end of avenue du Maréchal-Juin, beyond the aquarium, and alongside the gulf (☎02.97.63.13.88; closed Oct–March).

Hotels

Le Bretagne, 36 rue du Méné (☎02.97.47.20.21, fax 02.97.47.90.78, *www.bretagne-hotel.com*). Reasonable hotel situated just outside the walls, around the corner from the Porte-Prison. The rooms aren't fancy, but all have showers or bath plus TV. ②.

Ibis Vannes, rue Emile-Jourdan (☎02.97.63.61.11, fax 02.97.63.21.33; *h0650@accor-hotels.com*). Large, comfortable and dependable chain option, with its own restaurant, in a very unexciting setting 2km north of town, just north of the N165. ④.

Le Marina, 4 place Gambetta (☎02.97.47.22.81, fax 02.97.47.00.34). Fourteen pleasantly refurbished rooms, right in the thick of the things by the port, with sea views and bright sun in the morning. There's a bar downstairs. ②.

Mascotte, av Jean-Monnet (☎02.97.47.59.60, fax 02.97.47.07.54). Functional, reasonable-value hotel a short walk northwest of the walled town, with 65 en-suite rooms and an adequate restaurant. ④.

The Town

The new town centre of Vannes is **place de la République** – the focus was shifted outside the medieval city in the nineteenth-century craze for urbanization. The grandest of the public buildings here, guarded by a pair of sleek and dignified bronze lions, is the **Hôtel de Ville** at the top of rue Thiers. By day, however, the streets of the old city, with their overhanging, witch-hatted houses and busy commercial life, are the chief source of pleasure. **Place Henri-IV** in particular is stunning, as are the views from it down the narrow side streets.

La Cohue, which fills a block between rue des Halles and place du Cathédrale, recently became the **Musée de Vannes** (June–Sept daily 10am–6pm; rest of year Mon & Wed–Sat 10am–noon & 2–6pm, Sun 2–6pm; 26F/€3.96), having served at various times over the past 750 years as high court and assembly room, prison, revolutionary tribunal, theatre and marketplace. Upstairs it still houses the dull collection of what was the local Beaux-Arts museum, while the main gallery downstairs is the venue for different temporary exhibitions.

Opposite La Cohue the **Cathédrale St-Pierre** is a rather forbidding place, with a stern main altar almost imprisoned by four solemn grey pillars. The light – purple through new stained glass – illuminates the desiccated finger of the Blessed Pierre Rogue, who was guillotined on the main square in 1796. For a small fee, in summer you can examine the assorted treasures in the chapterhouse, which include a twelfth-century wedding chest, brightly decorated with enigmatic scenes of romantic chivalry.

West of the cathedral and housed in the sombre fifteenth-century Château Gaillard on rue Noé, the **Musée Archéologique** is said to have one of the world's finest collections of prehistoric artefacts (April–June & Sept–Oct Mon–Sat 9.30am–noon & 2–6pm; July & Aug Mon–Sat 9.30am–6pm; rest of year Mon–Sat 2–6pm; 20F/€3.05). But much like the displays at Carnac, it's all pretty lifeless – some elegant stone axes, more recent Oceanic exhibits by way of context, but nothing very illuminating.

Vannes' modern **aquarium** (daily: June–Aug 9am–8pm; rest of year 9am–noon & 1.30–7pm; 52F/€7.93), in the **Parc du Golfe** 500 metres south of place Gambetta, claims to have the best collection of tropical fish in Europe. Certainly it holds some pretty extraordinary specimens, including four-eyed fish from Venezuela that can see simultaneously above and below the water, and are also divided into four sexes for good measure; cave fish from Mexico that by contrast have no eyes at all; and *arowana* from Guyana, which jump two metres out of the water to catch birds. A Nile crocodile found in the Paris sewers in 1984 shares its tank with a group of piranhas.

Eating, drinking and entertainment

Dining out in old Vannes can be an expensive experience, whether you eat in the intimate little restaurants along the rue des Halles, or down by the port. The leading venues for **live music** are *La Route du Rhum*, 7 place Stalingrad (☎02.97.42.26.94), which puts on local rock, blues and Breton bands, and *John R. O'Flaherty*, at 22 rue Hoche (☎02.97.42.40.11; closed Sun), which is more a jazz hangout. During the first week of August, the open-air **Vannes Jazz Festival** takes place in the Théâtre de Verdure.

Breizh Caffe, 13 rue des Halles (☎02.97.54.37.41). One of the less pricey options on this attractive cobbled street, but every bit as good as its rivals, with a strong emphasis on Breton dishes and ingredients. Weekday lunches for 68F/€10.37, traditional evening menus from 93F/€14.18. Closed Sun & Mon lunchtime in low season.

Crêperie La Cave St-Gwenaël, 23 rue St-Gwenaël (☎02.97.47.47.94). Atmospheric, good-value crêperie in the cellar of a lovely old house, facing the cathedral. Closed Sun, Mon lunchtime & all Jan.

La Jonquière, 9 rue des Halles (☎02.97.54.08.34). Very central option, which manages to squeeze a few tables onto the cobbles. For 76F/€11.59 you can choose a main course plus a buffet of either hors d'oeuvres or desserts; for 99F/€15.09 you can take your pick of both; 117F/€17.84 buys a full *assiette de fruits de mer*.

Restaurant de Roscanvec, 17 rue des Halles (☎02.97.47.15.96). Formal gourmet restaurant in a lovely half-timbered house in the heart of the old town. Lunch at 88F/€13.42 is a bargain, dinner menus go all the way up to 300F/€45.73. Closed Sun evening, plus Mon Sept–June.

The Golfe de Morbihan

It comes as rather a surprise to discover that Vannes is on the sea. Its harbour is a channelled inlet of the ragged-edged **Golfe de Morbihan** – *mor bihan* means "little sea" in Breton – which lets in the tides through a narrow gap between the peninsulas of **Rhuys** and **Locmariaquer.** By popular tradition the **islands** scattered around this enclosure used to number the days of the year, though for centuries the waters have been rising and there are now fewer than one for each week. Of these, thirty are owned by film stars and the like, while two – the **Île-aux-Moines** and **Île d'Arz** – have regular populations and ferry services and end up in summer being like Safeway on a Saturday

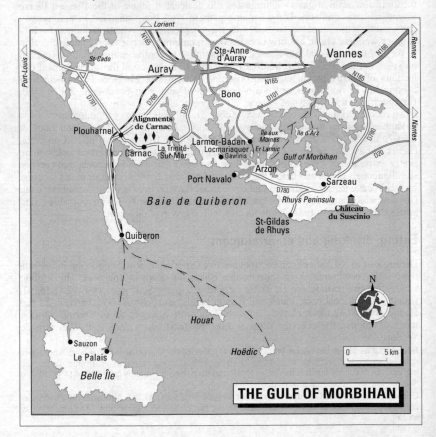

THE GULF OF MORBIHAN

GULF TOURS

In season, dozens of boats leave for **gulf tours** each day from Vannes, Port Navalo, La Trinité, Locmariaquer, Auray and Larmor-Baden. These are among the options:

Navix (☎02.97.46.60.00; *navix@wanadoo.fr*), which is based in Vannes, runs deluxe *vedettes* around the gulf, including half-day (105F/€16.01) and full-day (125F/€19.06) tours, excursions to the Île-aux-Moines and the Île d'Arz, and gastronomic cruises for lunch (July & Aug Tues–Sun, departs 12.30pm; 140F/€21.34 plus food) and dinner (July & Aug Wed & Sat, departs 8pm; 140F/€21.34 plus food). Other Navix sailings depart from Port Navalo and Locmariaquer (60–160F/ €9.15–24.39, plus expensive dinner cruises) and, to no fixed schedule, from Auray, Le Bono and La Trinité. Between May and September, they also go to Belle-Île (up to 175F/€26.68 return) and Houat (150F/€22.87) from Vannes, Port Navalo and La Trinité.

Compagnie des Îles (☎02.97.46.18.19) runs gulf tours (105–160F/€16.01–24.39) and excursions to the Île-aux-Moines (80–105F/ €12.20–16.01) from Vannes. It also operates a more limited programme of similar cruises from Port Navalo (105–145F/€16.01–22.11)

and Port Haliguen in Quiberon (125–145F/ €19.06–22.11).

Izenah Croisières (☎02.97.57.23.24 or 02.97.26.31.45, *www.izenah-croisieres.com*) runs gulf tours in summer (April–June & Sept daily 3pm, 90F/€13.72; July & Aug 11am, 3pm & 5pm, 65F/€9.91) and a year-round ferry service, with departures every half-hour, to the Île-aux-Moines (21F/€3.20 return) from Port Blanc at Baden.

Vedettes l'Aiglon (☎02.97.57.39.15) runs an extensive itinerary of gulf tours from Locmariaquer (mid-June to mid-Sept daily at 9.45am, 11am, 2.15pm & 4.15pm; 60–130F/€9.15–19.82), plus summer day-trips to Belle-Île (July & Aug Tues–Fri & Sun 8.45am; 140F/€21.34).

Vedettes l'Angelus (☎02.97.57.30.29) also runs gulf tours from Locmariaquer (60–130F/€9.15–19.82), as well as excursions on summer Sundays to Belle-Île (July & Aug Sun 8.30am; 150F/€22.87).

morning. The rest are the best, and a **boat tour** around them, or at least a trip out to Gavrinis near the mouth of the gulf, is a fairly compelling attraction. As the boats thread their way through the baffling muddle of channels, you lose track of what is island and what is mainland; and everywhere there are megalithic ruins, stone circles disappearing beneath the water and solitary menhirs on small hillocks.

Er Lannic and Gavrinis islands

A dramatic group of menhirs, arranged in a figure of eight, is to be seen on the tiny barren island of **Er Lannic** – though only at low tide when the water gives these smaller islets the appearance of stranded hovercraft skirted with mud. The best island for megalithic monuments is, however, **Gavrinis**. It contains (almost consists of) a tumulus that has been partially uncovered to reveal a chamber in which all the slabs of stone are carved with curving lines like fingerprints, axeheads and spirals – purely decorative according to archeologists. The island is a fifteen-minute **ferry** ride from Larmor-Baden; in summer, the boat trips include guided tours of the cairn (departures every 30min: April & May Mon–Fri 2–6pm, Sat & Sun 10am–noon & 2–6pm; June–Sept daily 10am–noon & 2–6pm; Oct daily except Tues 10am–noon & 2–6pm; ☎02.97.57.19.38; June–Sept 56F/€8.54, April, May & Oct 51F/€7.77).

The Presqu'île de Rhuys

The tip of the Presqu'île de Locmariaquer is only a few hundred metres away from Port Navalo and the **Presqu'île de Rhuys**. This peninsula has a micro-climate of its own – warm enough for pomegranates, figs, bougainvillea and the only Breton vineyards

Oysters are cultivated on the muddy gulf shores, but the currents of the gulf make this no place for swimming. The ocean beaches are the ones to head for: east from St-Gildas-de-Rhuys is the most enticing and least crowded stretch, with glittering gold- and silver-coloured rocks. For details on the whole peninsula, call in at the new **information centre** just off the main road as you come into Sarzeau (daily: mid-June to mid-Sept 9am–8pm; rest of year 9am–noon & 2–6pm; ☎02.97.26.45.26).

Near **SARZEAU**, the impressive fourteenth-century **Château de Suscinio** is a completely moated castle that was once a hunting lodge of the dukes of Brittany, set in marshland at the edge of a tiny village and holding a sagging but still vivid mosaic floor. You can take a precarious stroll around its high ramparts (April & May daily 10am–noon & 2–7pm; June–Sept daily 10am–7pm; rest of year Mon–Wed & Fri 2–5pm, Thurs, Sat & Sun 10am–noon & 2–5pm; June–Sept 30F/€4.57, rest of year 25F/€3.81).

Near the tip of the peninsula, clearly visible to the north of the main road, is the **Tumulus de Thumiac**, from the top of which Julius Cæsar is said to have watched the sea battle in which the Romans defeated the Veneti. Further on, **PORT NAVALO** has little more character than larger **ARZON** which precedes it, but there's a cute little beach tucked into the headland, and the *Hôtel de la Plage*, 21 av de Gaulle (☎02.97.53.75.92; ②; closed Dec–March), offers some cosy little **rooms** above its busy bar. The *Grand Largue* (☎02.97.53.71.58; ④; closed mid-Nov to mid-Dec) is a considerably more luxurious option, with dinner menus from 140F/€21.34. Vedettes Thalassa (☎02.97.53.70.25) runs **ferries** to the islands and across the gulf from the jetty nearby.

Immediately north of Arzon on the pointe de Kerners is the two-star **campsite** *de Bilouris* (☎02.97.53.70.55; closed mid-Nov to Feb), which is well placed for the less crowded beaches east of St-Gildas.

South to the Loire

When you cross the **Vilaine** on the way south, you are not only leaving the Morbihan *département* but technically also leaving Brittany itself. The roads veer firmly east and west – to Nantes or **La Baule**, avoiding the marshes of the **Grande-Brière**. For centuries these 20,000 acres of peat bog have been deemed to be the common property of all who lived in them. The scattered population, the *Brièrois*, made and make their living by fishing for eels in the streams, gathering reeds and – on the nine days permitted each year – cutting the peat. Tourism has arrived only recently, and is resented. The touted attraction is renting a punt to get yourself lost for a few hours with your pole tangled in the rushes.

Guérande

On the edge of the marshes of the Grande-Brière, just before you come to the sea, is the tiny, gorgeous walled town of **GUÉRANDE**. Guérande gave its name to this peninsula, and derived its fortune from controlling the salt pans that form a chequerboard across the surrounding inlets. This "white country" is composed of bizarre-looking *oeillets*, each 70 to 80 square metres in extent, in which sea water, since Roman times, has been collected and evaporated.

Guérande today is still entirely enclosed by its stout fifteenth-century ramparts. Although you can't walk along them, a spacious promenade leads right the way around the outside, passing four fortified gateways; for half its length the broad old moat remains filled with water. The main entrance, the **Porte St-Michel** on the east side of town, now holds a small **museum** of local history (daily: April–Sept 10am–12.30pm & 2.30–7pm; Oct 10am–noon & 2–6pm; 20F/€3.05).

Guérande's **tourist office** is just outside the Porte St-Michel at 1 place du Marché au Bois (July & Aug Mon–Sat 9.30am–7pm, Sun 10am–1pm; rest of year Mon–Sat 9.30am–12.30pm & 1.30–6pm; ☎02.40.24.96.71, *office.tourisme.guerande@wanadoo.fr*). Tucked out of sight behind the market, the pretty *Roc-Maria*, 1 rue des Halles (☎02.40.24.90.51; ③; closed mid-Nov to mid-Dec, plus Wed & Thurs in low season), offers **rooms** above a crêperie in a fifteenth-century town house. Opposite the Porte Vannetoise and the most impressive stretch of ramparts, to the north, the *Hôtel des Voyageurs*, 1 place du 8 Mai 1945 (☎02.40.24.90.13; ③; hotel closed Sun evening & Mon in low season, restaurant closed Oct–March), is a *logis* serving good menus from 102F/€15.55.

La Baule

There is something very surreal about emerging from the Brière to the coast at **LA BAULE** – an imposing, moneyed landscape where the dunes are no longer bonded together with scrub and pines, but with massive apartment buildings and luxury hotels. Sited on the long stretch of dunes that links the former island of Le Croisic to the mainland, it owes its existence to a storm in 1779 that engulfed the old town of Escoublac in silt from the Loire, and thereby created a wonderful crescent of sandy beach.

Neither La Baule's permanence nor its affluence seems in any doubt these days. It is a resort that very firmly imagines itself in the south of France: around the crab-shaped bay, bronzed nymphettes and would-be Clint Eastwoods ride across the sands into the sunset against a backdrop of cruising lifeguards, horse-dung removers and fantastically priced cocktails. It can be fun if you feel like a break from the more subdued Breton attractions – and the beach is undeniably impressive. It's not a place to imagine you're going to enjoy strolling around in search of hidden charms; the back streets have an oddly rural feel, but hold nothing of any interest.

La Baule has two **gare SNCFs**, the barely used La-Baule-les-Pins, and the main La-Baule-Escoublac near the tourist office on place Rhin-et-Danube, where the TGVs from Paris arrive. The **gare routière** is at 4 place de la Victoire (☎02.40.60.25.58). Full details on staying in La Baule can be had from the **tourist office**, away from the seafront at 8 place de la Victoire (mid-May to mid-Sept daily 9am–7.30pm; rest of year Mon–Sat 9.30am–noon & 2–6pm; ☎02.40.24.34.44), or from the local **Web site** *www.pays-blanc.com*.

Few of the **hotels** are cheap, particularly in high season, and in low season more than half are closed. The cheapest options are near the main *gare SNCF*, less than 1km from the beach. These include *Le Clémenceau*, 42 av Clémenceau (☎02.40.60.21.33; ③; closed Dec), and the *Marini*, 22 av Clémenceau (☎02.40.60.23.29; ③). The finest of the many local **campsites**, 2km back from the beach, is the four-star *La Roseraie*, 20 av Sohier (☎02.40.60.46.66, *la-roserie@post.club-internet.fr*, closed Oct–March).

Le Croisic

The small port of **LE CROISIC**, sheltering from the ocean around the corner of the headland, is a more realistic and more attractive place to stay than La Baule. These days it's basically a pleasure port, but fishing boats do still sail from its harbour, near the very slender mouth of the bay, and there's a modern **fish market** near the long Tréhic jetty, where you can go to see the day's catch auctioned. The hills on either side of the harbour, Mont Lenigo and Mont Esprit, are not natural; they are formed from the ballast left by the ships of the salt trade. If you are staying, choose between the **hotels** *Les Nids*, 15 rue Pasteur (☎02.40.23.00.63; ④; closed mid-Nov to March), or the purple and

Le Petit Bacchus, 5 rue Beauregard (☎02.40.47.50.46). Red-painted half-timbered house, with the atmosphere and decor of a World War I *estaminet*, just off rue des 50-Ôtages in a little alley leading down to the cours F.-Roosevelt. Lovely 89F/€13.57 menu featuring duck *à l'orange* or fish of the day. Closed Sun, plus first three weeks in Aug.

travel details

Trains

Brest to: Morlaix (10 daily; 35min); Paris-Montparnasse (10 daily; 4hr 20min); Quimper (6 daily; 1hr 20min); Rennes (10 daily; 2hr 15min).

Guingamp to: Paimpol (June–Sept only, 4–5 daily; 45min).

Quimper to: Lorient (7 daily; 40min); Vannes (7 daily; 1hr 05min); Redon (7 daily; 1hr 40min).

Rennes to: Brest (10 daily; 2hr 15min); Caen (4 daily; 3hr); Dol (4 daily; 35min); Morlaix (10 daily; 1hr 40min); Nantes (4 daily; 1hr 30min); Paris-Montparnasse (8 daily; 2hr 10min); Pontorson (4 daily; 50min); Quimper (4 daily; 2hr 30min); St-Brieuc (10 daily; 45min); Vannes (4 daily; 1hr).

Roscoff to: Morlaix (2–3 daily; 30min).

St-Brieuc to: Guingamp (June–Sept only, 1–4 daily; 15min); Lannion (June–Sept only, 1–4 daily; 1hr).

St-Malo to: Caen (8 daily; 3hr 30min); Dinan (8 daily; 1hr); Dol (12 daily; 25min); Rennes (12 daily; 1hr; connections for Paris on TGV).

Buses

Brest to: Le Conquet (4 daily; 30min); Quimper (6 daily; 1hr 30min); Roscoff (5 daily; 1hr 30min).

Quimper to: Audierne (3 daily; 1hr); Camaret (5 daily; 1hr 30min); Crozon (5 daily; 1hr 20min); Concarneau (6 daily; 30min); Locronan (5 daily; 30min); Pointe du Raz (3 daily; 1hr 15min); Quimperlé (6 daily; 1hr 30min).

Rennes to: Dinan (6 daily; 1hr 20min); Dinard (8 daily; 1hr 40min); Fougères (7 daily; 1hr); Mont St-Michel (4 daily; 1hr 20min); Vannes (8 daily; 2hr).

Roscoff to: Morlaix (3–6 daily; 50min); Quimper (1 only Mon, Thurs & Sat; 2hr); Vannes (1 only Mon, Thurs & Sat; 4hr).

St-Brieuc to: Dinan (4 daily; 1hr); Guingamp (4 daily; 20min); Lannion (4 daily; 1hr 40min); St-Cast, via Lamballe, Le Val-André, Erquy & Cap Fréhel (4 daily; 1hr 50min); Paimpol (8 daily; 1hr 30min).

St-Malo to: Cancale (4 daily; 35min); Combourg (2 daily; 1hr); Dinan (4 daily; 45min); Dinard (8 daily; 30min); Fougères (3 daily; 2hr); Mont St-Michel (4 daily; 1hr 30min); Pontorson (3 daily; 1hr 15min); Rennes (5 daily; 1hr 30min).

Vannes to: Auray (4 daily; 45min); Carnac (4 daily; 1hr 15min); Josselin (8 daily; 1hr); Malestroit (4 daily; 45min); Quiberon (4 daily; 1hr 45min); Rennes (8 daily; 2hr).

Ferries

St-Malo: Brittany Ferries (☎02.99.40.64.01, *www.brittanyferries.co.uk*) to Portsmouth (1 daily mid-March to mid-Nov, otherwise less frequently; 9hr) and Plymouth (1 weekly mid-Nov to mid-March; 8hr). Regular ferries to Dinard (10min) in season, operated by Émeraude Lines (☎02.23.18.15.15, *www.emeraudelines.com*), which also sail to Dinan up the River Rance, and along the Brittany coast to Cap Fréhel and Île Cézembre (May–Sept). They also go to Jersey, to Guernsey (April–Oct), and Sark (April–Sept), and to the Îles Chausey in Normandy. Condor Ferries (☎02.99.20.03.00, *www.condorferries.co.uk*) runs services to Poole (May–Oct; 1 daily; 5hr), Weymouth (May–Oct; 1 daily; 5hr), Jersey (4 daily April–Sept, 2 daily Oct, 1 daily second half of March and first half of Nov), Guernsey (2 daily April–Oct, 1 daily second half of March and first half of Nov) and Sark (daily April–Oct).

Roscoff: Brittany Ferries to Plymouth (6hr) & Cork (13–17hr).

For details of ferries to Ouessant & Molène, see p.417; to Bréhat, see p.407; to Batz, see p.415; to Groix, see p.438; to Sein, see p.425; to Belle-Île, see p.441; and for tours of the Gulf of Morbihan see p.449.

CHAPTER SIX

THE LOIRE

The density of châteaux and all their great Renaissance intrigues and associations can prove quite intimidating, but if you pick your castles selectively, rid yourself of a sense of duty to guided tours and spend days on river banks with supplies of cheese, fruit and white Loire wines, the Loire can be one of the most enjoyable of all French regions.

The Loire's central region of **Touraine**, known as "the heart of France", has the best wines, the most scented flowers and delicious fruit, two of the best châteaux in **Chenonceau** and **Azay-le-Rideau**, and, it's argued, the purest French accent in the land. It also takes in three of the Loire's most pleasurable tributaries: the **Cher**, **Indre** and **Vienne**, each with its own individual attractions. If you have just a week to spare for the region, then these are the parts to spend it in. The most imposing palaces and hunting lodges are upstream around **Blois** – including the Renaissance turreted fantasy of **Chambord** – with the wild and watery region of the **Sologne** to the east, good for long walks and rides, while downstream around **Saumur** are fascinating troglodyte dwellings carved out of the rock-faces.

As well as the select handful of châteaux, the region has a few unexpected sights, most interesting of which are the gardens at **Villandry**, outside Tours; the Romanesque abbey at **St-Benoît-sur-Loire**; and the stunning tapestries in **Angers**, capital of the ancient wine-producing county of **Anjou**. Of the cities, **Tours** and Angers provide the best urban bases, **Orléans** has charm, and **Le Mans**, though some way north of the Loire valley in the topographically uninspiring *département* of **Sarthe**, is the least touristy and most authentically lively, even outside race times. Further upstream, and quite some distance south of the Loire itself, the marshy farming land of **Berry** contains few sights, though the magnificent cathedral and medieval town of **Bourges**, lying between the Loire and the Cher, is worth visiting.

The lowest – and best – stretch of the Loire flows through Touraine, languidly floating by long islands of reed and willows before it reaches its estuary. But the Loire is still the wild river of whirlpools, quicksands, shifting banks and channels, with vicious currents and a propensity to flood. Thanks to hard campaigning by conservationists, plans to control the water levels of the central stretch with dams have been dropped, despite strong interest from various businesses, including the four nuclear power stations that use the river water for their cooling systems. The longest river in France, the Loire is for the most part too unpredictable for swimming or boating, and no goods are carried along it.

ACCOMMODATION PRICE CODES

Each hotel and guesthouse in this book has been graded according to the following price codes, which indicate the price for the **cheapest double room available during the high season.**

① Under 160F/€24   ④ 300–400F/€46–61   ⑦ 600–700F/€91–107
② 160–220F/€24–34   ⑤ 400–500F/€61–76   ⑧ 700–800F/€107–122
③ 220–300F/€34–46   ⑥ 500–600F/€76–91   ⑨ Over 800F/€122

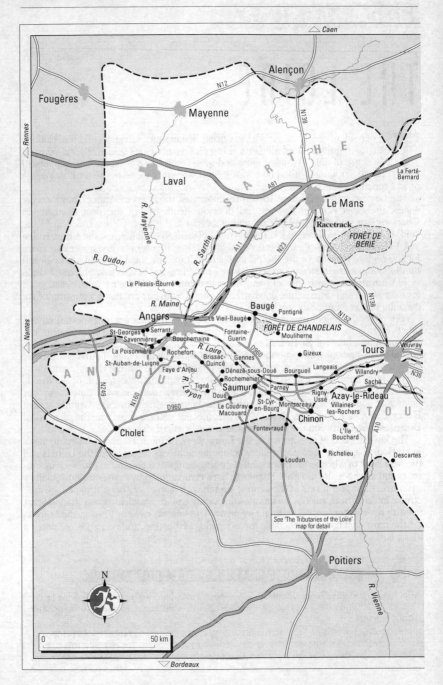

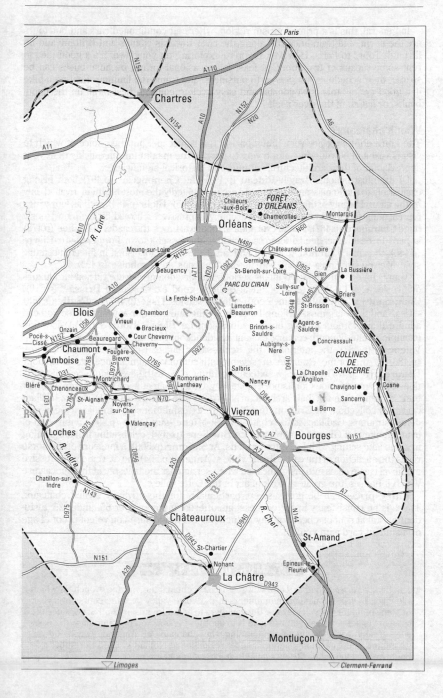

In general, this is a prime tourism region, where air-conditioned cars and bus tours are the norm, and train lines run along the river towards Nantes and Brittany and up through Tours to Paris. However, if you're exploring on your own, it's a good idea to rent some means of **transport**, at least for occasional forays, because buses can be sparse, their schedules not geared to outsiders, and trains too limiting. Renting a bike is a good option: this is wonderful and easy cycling country, best of all on the flood-banks, or *levées*, of the river itself.

Which châteaux?

The Loire **châteaux** are very much part of the landscape, but the choice of which to visit is vast and bewildering, and trying to pack in the maximum can quickly dent your appreciation of their architecture, settings and historical significance.

Of the most famous, **Azay-le-Rideau** (p.497) and **Chenonceau** (p.497) both belong exclusively to the Renaissance period and are undoubtedly the most beautiful, rivalled only by the natural beauty of the gardens of **Villandry** (p.495). **Blois** (p.484), with its four wings representing four distinct periods, is extremely impressive, followed by the monstrously huge **Chambord** (p.487). For an evocation of medieval times, the citadel of **Loches** (p.478) is hard to beat; other feudal fortresses include the lesser-known **Fougères-sur-Bièvre** (p.486), the ruined **Chinon** (p.498), **Langeais** (p.496), still furnished in fifteenth-century style, **Meung-sur-Loire** (p.466), with its vile dungeons, and **Amboise** (p.493).

Many châteaux that started life as serious military defences were turned into luxurious residences by their regal or ducal owners: good examples are **Brissac** (p.510), **Chaumont** (p.486), with its nineteenth-century stables, **Ussé** (p.497) and **Sully** (p.468) – Ussé and Sully are most striking for their setting and exterior appearance, so you can admire them without forking out for admission. **Le Plessis-Bourré** (p.511) is a fine example of late fifteenth-century elegant residence and strong defences combined. At **Valençay** (p.483), the interior of the Renaissance château is Napoleonic; **Cheverny** (p.486) is the prime example of seventeenth-century magnificence; its neighbour **Beauregard** (p.487) encloses a sixteenth-century core with seventeenth-century additions but is most famous for its portrait gallery. Other châteaux are more compelling for their contents than for their architecture: **Argent-sur-Sauldre** (p.471), with a brilliant ceramics collection; **St-Brisson** (p.470), with art exhibitions and medieval weaponry demonstrations; Cadillacs at the château in **St-Michel-sur-Loire** (p.496); a museum of living donkeys at **Gizeux** (p.496); and **La Bussière** (p.469), celebrating fish and fishing in a fine lake setting with Le Nôtre gardens. At **Saumur** (p.500), a museum of the horse rivals the attraction of the castle itself, while at **Angers** (p.504) the extremely impressive medieval castle pales into insignificance when set against the tapestry of the Apocalypse which it houses, the greatest work of art in the Loire valley.

Entry prices can be pretty steep, particularly for the privately owned châteaux. There is no consistency in the concessions offered: if you're over 65, under 25, a student or still at school, check for any reductions and make sure you've got proof of age or a student card with you.

MUSEUM PASS

The handy *Passeport Val de Loire* (130F/€19.82) contains ten entrance vouchers which allow you to visit ten national monuments in the Loire Valley over the course of a year. At some monuments, you may use the vouchers to admit friends or family, and, since the passport is not personal, you can lend it to another person. You may purchase the passport at any participating site, including the châteaux at Angers, Azay-le-Rideau, Chambord and Chaumont, George Sand's residence at Nohant-Vic and the Abbaye de Fontevraud: a full list of sites is available at *www.monuments-france.fr*.

Orléans and around

ORLÉANS is the northernmost city on the Loire, sitting at the apex of a huge arc in the river as it switches direction and starts to flow southwest. Its proximity to Paris, just over 100km away, is a problem for this ancient city. Not only do many Orléanais go to Paris for their evenings out, they commute to work there as well. To counter its subordinate position as a country suburb to the capital, Orléans feels compelled to recoup its faded glory by harking back to the turning point in the Hundred Years War (1339–1453), when Paris had been captured by the English and was infested by disease, and Orléans itself, as the key city to central France, was under siege.

Despite a rich early history of being a centre of revolt against Julius Cæsar in 52 BC (for which it was burnt to the ground), besieged by Attila the Hun in the mid-fifth century, and elevated to the position of temporary capital of the Frankish kingdom in 498, it is **Joan of Arc**'s (Jeanne d'Arc) deliverance of the city in 1429 that the town feels bound to commemorate. Crazed or divinely inspired, the 17-year-old peasant girl presented herself to the Dauphin, the uncrowned Charles VII, at Chinon (see p.499), rallied French troops at Blois and then led them up the Loire to confront the English at

---

THE FOOD AND DRINK OF THE LOIRE

Fish from the river features on most restaurant menus. Favourites are *filet de sandre* (pickerel), salmon (often flavoured with sorrel), stuffed bream and eels softened in mature red wine, and little smelt-like fishes served deep-fried (*la friture de la Loire*). The favoured meat of the eastern Loire is **game**. Pheasant, guinea fowl, pigeon, duck, quails, young rabbit, venison and even wild boar are all hunted in the Sologne. They are served in rich sauces made from the wild mushrooms of the region's forests or the common *champignon de Paris*, cultivated on a huge scale in caves cut out of the limestone rock along the Loire and its tributaries. Both Tours and Le Mans specialize in *rillettes*, or potted pork; in Touraine charcuteries you'll also find *pâté au biquion*, made from pork, veal and young goat's meat.

The Loire valley is also great **fruit-** and **vegetable**-growing country. There are greengages from orchards in Anjou, called *Reine Claudes* after François I's queen. Market stalls overflow with summer fruits, and old varieties of apples and pears can still be found. *Tarte tatin*, an upside-down apple tart, is said to have originated from Lamotte-Beuvron in the Sologne. Tours is famous for its French beans, and Saumur for its potatoes. Asparagus (the best from Vineuil) appears in soufflés, omelettes and other egg dishes as well as on its own, accompanied by vinaigrette made (if you're lucky) with local walnut oil. Finally, from Berry, comes the humble lentil, whose green variety often accompanies salmon or trout.

Though not as famous as the produce of Bordeaux and Burgundy, the Loire valley has some of the finest **wines** in France, and there are well over twenty different *appellations* to discover. Sancerre, halfway along the river, produces some well-known flinty, very dry white wines made from the Sauvignon grape, as well as some good reds and a rosé (see p.470). There are the mellow whites and rosés of the Anjou vineyards in the west (see box on p.511), the fruity sparkling *méthode champenoise* wines around Saumur (see box on p.502), and the sweet, still wines of Vouvray (see p.493). The Cabernet grape is used to produce the rich, ruby reds of Chinon (see p.500) and Bourgueil (see p.496); these are some of the best Touraine wines, and many are capable of maturing over decades.

To go with the wine, Touraine has some of the best soft goat's **cheese**: Ste-Maure, shaped into a long cylinder with a piece of straw running through the middle; the small, round *crottin de Chavignol* goat's cheese from Sancerre, eaten fresh or matured, when it becomes hard with a very sharp flavour; the pyramid-shaped Pouligny-St-Pierre and Valençay; and the flat, round Selles-sur-Cher.

Orléans. She informed the encircling army that God had sent her to throw them out of France, and proceeded to break all military rules and raise the siege. The Maid of Orléans is honoured everywhere in town despite people questioning the story's authenticity.

There's been a lot of new building and tarting up of the city over the last few years. It may not have provided much aesthetic improvement, which is difficult given the beauty of Orléans' ancient buildings, but it's been a valiant and not entirely vain attempt to bring back some pride to the place. One of the best times to visit is May 8 (**Joan of Arc Day**), when the city is filled with parades, fireworks and a medieval fair.

Arrival, information and accommodation

The **Centre d'Arc**, a large modern shopping centre on place d'Arc, is the first thing you'll see as you step out of the **gare SNCF**. The **tourist office** is in the Centre d'Arc on the south side overlooking place Albert-1er (April–Sept Mon 10am–7pm, Tues–Sat 9am–7pm, Sun 10am–noon; Oct–March Tues–Sat 9am–6.30pm; ☎02.38.24.05.05, fax 02.38.54.49.84), and hands out *Orléans Poche*, a free **listings magazine** telling what's going on around the town. Online, *www.orleanscity.com* has plenty of information on special events and cultural happenings in the city, while *www.tourismloiret.com* covers the rest of the region. The **gare routière**, on rue Marcel-Proust, is a short way northeast of the tourist office off rue Prince-Albert-1er.

Accommodation in Orléans is good, with a few cheap hotels near the unusually appealing station area, and a hostel and campsites not too far out – most places are in the habit of closing for a few hours, usually on Sunday afternoon.

Hotels

de Blois, 1 av de Paris (☎02.38.62.61.61). Conveniently placed hotel opposite the station above an interesting, typically French bar. The rooms are a little dingy, but good value. ①.

Charles Sanglier, 8 rue Charles-Sanglier (☎02.38.53.38.50, fax 02.38.68.01.85). Comfortable enough and very central hotel. ③.

Jackotel, 18 Cloître-St-Aignan (☎02.38.54.48.48, fax 02.38.77.17.59). Charming hotel, with a small garden and views onto the cloisters of St-Aignan. ④.

Marguerite, 14 place du Vieux-Marché (☎02.38.53.74.32, fax 02.38.53.31.56). Very average hotel, though it's in a good location on the market square. ②.

de Paris, 29 Faubourg-Bannier (☎02.38.53.39.98, fax 02.38.81.03.97). Small, very cheap but pleasant rooms above a brasserie, just across place Gambetta from the *gare SNCF*. ①.

St-Aignan, 3 place Gambetta (☎02.38.53.15.35, fax 02.38.77.02.36). Good-value hotel, with friendly service. ③–④.

Hostel and campsites

Hostel, 14 rue du Faubourg-Madeleine (☎02.38.62.45.75). Clean and bicycle-friendly hostel, situated on the continuation of rue Porte-Madeleine to the west of town; bus #B, direction "Paul-Bert", from the bus and train stations. Reception 7.15–9.30am & 5.30–10/10.30pm, curfew 10/10.30pm. Closed Dec to mid-Feb & Sat mid-Feb to March.

Olivet, rue du Pont-Bouchet in Olivet (☎02.38.63.53.94). Campsite situated 6km south of Orléans between the River Loiret and the Loire; bus #S to Aumône. Closed Nov–March.

St-Jean-de-la-Ruelle, rue de la Roche, St-Jean-de-la-Ruelle (☎02.38.88.39.39). The closest campsite to Orléans, 3km away out on the Blois road; bus #D, stop "Roche aux Fées". Closed mid-Oct to March.

The City

St Joan turns up all over town. In pride of place in the large, central **place du Martroi**, at the end of rue de la République, rises a bulky mid-nineteenth-century likeness of her

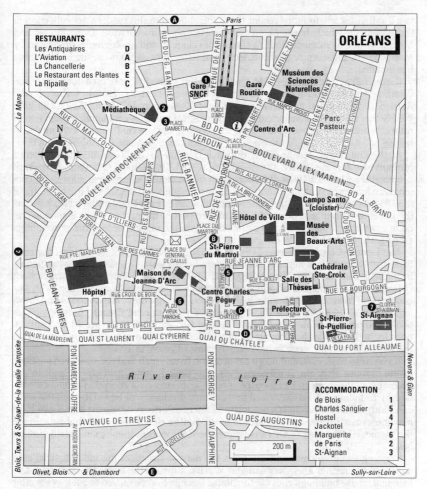

on horseback, with a series of copper-green friezes around the base, depicting scenes from her action-filled life. To the east, the **Cathédrale Ste-Croix** (daily 9am–noon & 2–6pm), battered for the best part of 600 years by various wars, is full of Joan of Arc, who celebrated her victory over the English here. In the north transept, her pedestal is supported by two jagged and golden leopards, representing the English, on an altar carved with the battle scene. In the nave, the late-nineteenth-century stained-glass windows tell the story of her life, starting from the north transept, with caricatures of the loutish English and snooty French nobles. Across place d'Etape from the cathedral, outside the red-brick Renaissance **Hôtel de Ville**, Joan appears again, in pensive mood, her skirt now shredded by twentieth-century bullets.

You are spared the Maid in the **Musée des Beaux-Arts**, opposite the Hôtel de Ville (Tues & Sun 11am–6pm, Wed 10am–10pm, Thurs–Sat 10am–6pm; 20F/€3.05), where the main collections are of fourteenth- to sixteenth-century Italian, Dutch and Flemish works on the second floor, and eighteenth-century French portraits on the first floor. If you'd rather escape to more recent times, head down to the modern art collection in the basement, which houses canvases by Picasso, Miró, Braque, Dufy, Renoir and Monet, as well as Auguste Rodin's studies of Gauguin, and photographs of Picasso by Man Ray. The museum regularly stages good temporary exhibitions; the tourist office has details.

If you follow rue Jeanne-d'Arc east from the cathedral and turn left down rue Charles-Sanglier, you'll find the ornate sixteenth-century **Hôtel Cabu** (daily: April–Sept 10am–noon & 2–6pm; rest of year 10am–noon & 2–5pm; 15F/€2.29, free Wed & Sun morning), a historical and archeological museum containing a collection of rather beautiful bronze animals from the Gallo-Roman period, along with medieval ivories and more Joan of Arc mementos. The entrance is on square Abbé-Desnoyers.

At the end of rue Jeanne-d'Arc, on place Général-de-Gaulle, is the semi-timbered **Maison de Jeanne d'Arc** (Tues–Sun: May–Oct 10am–noon & 2–6pm; Nov–April 2–6pm; 13F/€1.98), a 1960s reconstruction of the house where Joan stayed. Its contents are fun, most of all for children, with good models and displays of the breaking of the Orléans siege. Despite the consistency in artists' renderings of the saint, it seems the pageboy haircut and demure little face are part of the myth – there is no contemporary portrait of her, save for a clerk's doodle in the margin of her trial proceedings (see pp.342 & 1100), kept in the Paris archives.

The **Centre Charles Péguy**, 11 rue Tabour (Mon–Fri 2–6pm; free), down the road from Joan's house in a Renaissance mansion, is also worth a visit. It takes its themes from the life and work of Charles Péguy (1873–1914), a Christian Socialist writer from Orléans, a great humanitarian and supporter of Dreyfus, a Jewish army officer who was convicted of treason in 1894 on forged evidence. Though there are cartoons and drawings, the main exhibits are texts, so it helps if you can read French. Among various books and pamphlets, there's Zola's front-page *J'accuse* letter to the president, explanations by both sides in the Dreyfus affair and documentation of the 1907 general strike call for the forty-hour week (which only became effective in 1936).

If you head back east, and down towards the river, you'll find the scattered vestiges of the old city. **Rue de Bourgogne** was the Gallo-Roman main street, and, in the basement of the modern **Préfecture** at no. 9, a spartan civic reception room provides odd surroundings for an excavated first-century dwelling – or bits of it – and the walls of a ninth-century church. It's not a site as such: ask the receptionist if you can have a look. Across the street is the facade of the **Salles des Thèses**, all that remains of the medieval university of Orléans where the Reformation theologian Calvin studied law.

Between the Préfecture and the river, the narrow streets of the old industrial area surround the former **Dessaux vinegar works**, a turn-of-the-twentieth-century establishment whose buildings encircle the house Isabelle Romée moved to a few years after her daughter Joan was burnt at the stake in Rouen. Down the rue de Bourgogne, a plaque marks the house of Joan's brother and companion-in-arms on the corner of rue des Africains and rue de la Folie. At least two of the quarter's churches are on the list of precious monuments: the remains of **St-Aignan** and its well-preserved eleventh-century crypt; and the Romanesque **St-Pierre-le-Puellier**, an old university church now used for concerts and exhibitions. St-Aignan was destroyed during the English siege, rebuilt by the Dauphin and extended into one of the greatest churches in France by Louis XII, but during the Wars of Religion, more sieges of the city took their toll on the church, leaving just the choir and transepts standing. Visits to the crypt need to be arranged through the tourist office.

North of the city centre, next to the *gare routière*, is the **Muséum de Sciences Naturelles**, at 2 rue Marcel-Proust (daily 2–6pm; 21F/€3.20), a small, but well-organized and educational museum, with a large rooftop tropical greenhouse. A short distance to the east is the **Parc Pasteur**, a pleasant and relaxing spot for a picnic.

Eating and drinking

Rue de Bourgogne is the main street for **restaurants** and **nightlife**. You can choose from among French, Spanish, North African, Middle Eastern, Indian and Asian cuisines, all of which can be sampled at very reasonable prices. For buying your own provisions there are the covered **market halls** on place du Châtelet, near the river.

Restaurants

Les Antiquaires, 2 & 4 rue au Lin (☎02.38.53.52.35). Run by one of the master chefs of France, this is Orléans' best restaurant and must be booked in advance. Seafood and ginger, Loire salmon and a soup of summer fruits and honey are some of its delights, with menus starting at 200F/€30.49. Closed Sun evening, Mon & first three weeks of Aug.

L'Aviation, 473 bd du Faubourg-Bannier (☎02.38.73.91.88). Located 2km north of place Gambetta, *L'Aviation* serves seasonal menus, with plenty of game dishes in autumn and a wonderful crayfish omelette. From 100F/€15.24; gastronomic menu around 200F/€30.49. Closed Mon, Wed evening, Sun evening & Aug.

La Chancellerie, 95 rue Royale, cnr place Matroi (☎02.38.53.57.54). The most prominent brasserie in town for drinking wine, beer or cocktails till midnight, indulging in ice-cream concoctions or eating good solid *plats du jour* from 54F/€8.23; gastronomic menus around 175F/€26.68. Closed Sun & two weeks in Feb.

Le Restaurant des Plantes, 44 rue Tudelle (☎02.38.56.65.55). Situated on the south side of the river, *des Plantes* serves traditional dishes such as *magret de canard* and snails. Menus from 108F/€16.46. Closed Sat lunch, Sun & Mon evenings & first three weeks in Aug.

La Ripaille, 14 place du Châtelet (☎02.38.54.56.85). Simple grilled meat and fish with salads, served up in a convivial atmosphere; menus from 64F/€9.76. Closed Sun.

Bars and nightlife

Majestic Café, 2 rue des Trois Maries. Dance club and bar, playing house music and hosting occasional drag acts. Entry 50F/€7.62 including a drink. Wed–Sun 7pm–3am.

Monté Cristo, 42 rue Étienne Dolet. A bar with billiards, games and Internet access. Tues–Sat 3pm–3am.

Paxton's Head, 264–266 rue de Bourgogne. Funky jazz cellar with live music on Wednesday and Saturday evenings. Tues–Sat 3pm–3am.

Shannon Irish Pub, place du Châtelet. Popular Irish bar, serving a selection of beers and whiskies. May–Sept daily 5pm–3am.

Listings

Banks Several around place Martroi and on the rue de la République.

Bike rental Available from Kit Loisirs in Olivet, just outside Orléans (☎02.38.63.44.34), and from Véloland, 356 rue Cornaillère, St-Jean-Le-Blanc (02.38.56.69.79, *www.veloland.com*).

Car rental Avis, 13 rue Sansonnières (☎02.38.62.27.04); Budget, 5 rue Sansonnières (☎02.38.54.54.30); Europcar, 81 rue A.-Dessaux (☎02.38.73.00.40); Hertz, 47 av de Paris (☎02.38.62.60.60).

Cinemas Select Studios, 45 rue Jeanne-d'Arc, often shows good art-house movies in the original language (☎02.36.68.69.25); cheap tickets for midday and early evening performances.

Festivals Fête de Jeanne d'Arc – a period-piece parade on April 29, May 1 and May 7–8; Festival de Jazz d'Orléans in late June to early July held in the Campo Santo (tickets 130F/€19.82, 300F/€45.73 for three nights; ☎02.38.79.23.77, *www.jazzfrance.com*); Semaines Musicales Internationales d'Orléans, Nov & Dec (programme details and bookings from the tourist office).

Internet Access available at *Monté Cristo* (see above).

Library Médiathèque, 1 place Gambetta (☎02.38.65.45.45); a new state-of-the-art media centre, featuring a library, video library, café and exhibition space.

Medical assistance SAMU ☎15; Centre Hospitalier, 1 rue Porte-Madeleine (☎02.38.69.45.45).

Police 63 rue du Faubourg-St-Jean (☎02.38.24.30.00).

Poste restante place de Gaulle, 45031 Orléans Cedex 1.

Public transport Bus information available from SEMTAO office (☎02.38.71.98.38) in the Centre d'Arc shopping mall, place Albert-1er.

Taxis Taxi Radio d'Orléans (☎02.38.53.11.11).

Meung-sur-Loire

Little streams known as *les mauves* flow between the houses in the village of **MEUNG-SUR-LOIRE**, 14km southwest of Orléans on the Blois rail line. During the summer months they leave slimy green high-water marks, but the sound of water is always pleasant, and Meung is an agreeable place to spend an afternoon.

Meung has accumulated a number of literary associations over the years. Over seven hundred years ago one Jean de Meung added 18,000 lines to the already 4000-line-long *Roman de la Rose*, written half a century earlier in 1225 by Guillaume de Lorris. This extended tale of courtly love, all very formal and allegorical, inspired Chaucer, who wrote his own version before moving onto more material topics. Most recently, the town featured in the works of Georges Simenon – his fictional hero, Maigret, takes his holidays here.

The town's most notable and imposing building is its grisly **Château**, built for the bishops of Orléans in the early Middle Ages (daily: April to mid-Sept 9.30am–12.30pm & 1.30–6.30pm; rest of year 10am–noon & 2–5.30pm; 35F/€5.34). The exterior of the château on the side facing the old drawbridge looks suitably spooky, retaining its thirteenth-century pepperpot towers, though much of the interior was remodelled in the nineteenth century. The highlight of the guided tour is the dreaded **dungeon**, where you're better off with minimal imagination: it was here that the poet François Villon (1431–85) – originator of the much-quoted line *Où sont les neiges d'antan?* ("Where are the snows of yesteryear?") – was imprisoned and supposedly wrote his famous *Grand Testament*. He is the only known survivor of this monstrous dungeon, where people were abandoned to die.

If you feel inspired to pen a few poetic lines yourself while loitering over **lunch**, head for the *Café du Commerce*, on place de l'Église, which provides the ideal atmosphere (Tues–Sun; menus from 75F/€11.43).

Beaugency

Six kilometres southwest of Meung along the Loire, **BEAUGENCY** is a pretty little town, which, in contrast to its innocuous appearance today, played its part in the conniving games of early medieval politics. In 1152, the marriage of Louis VII of France and Eleanor of Aquitaine was annulled by the Council of Beaugency in the church of Notre-Dame, allowing Eleanor to marry Henry Plantagenet, the future Henry II of England. Her huge land holdings in southwest France thus passed to the English crown, which already controlled Normandy, Maine, Anjou and Touraine: the struggles between the French and English kings over their claims to these territories – and to the French throne itself – lasted for centuries afterwards.

Liberated by the indefatigable Joan of Arc on her way to Orléans in 1429, Beaugency was a constant battleground in the Hundred Years War due to its strategic significance as the only Loire bridge-crossing at that time between Orléans and Blois. Remarkably, the 26-arch **bridge** still stands and gives an excellent view of the once heavily fortified medieval heart of the town. The two central squares – **place St-Firmin**, with its statue of Joan and a tower of a church destroyed during the Revolution, and **place Dunois** – are atmospherically lit by flickering gaslights. Place Dunois is bordered by the massive eleventh-century **Tour de César**, which was formerly part of the rather plain fifteenth-century **Château Dunois** (daily except Tues 10am–noon & 2–5pm; Oct–April closes 4pm; 22F/€3.35). It now houses a small museum of traditional Orléanais life, whose guided tours can definitely be given a miss. The square is completed by the rather severe Romanesque **abbey church of Notre-Dame**, the venue for the council's fatal matrimonial decision in 1152.

Today the town casts a much more romantic image of the medieval period, and wandering around the streets of the attractive old town and along the shaded river bank is probably the best way to pass the time peacefully here. But if the urge to sightsee is strong, go and look at the **embroidered wall hangings** in the council chamber of the **Hôtel de Ville** on place du Docteur-Hyvernaud, two blocks north of place Dunois (May–Sept Mon–Fri 11am–4.30pm, Sat 11am–3pm; rest of year Tues–Fri 3–4.30pm, Sat 11am–3pm; 8F/€1.23). One set illustrates the four continents as perceived in the seventeenth century, with the rest dramatizing pagan rites such as gathering mistletoe and sacrificing animals.

Practicalities

For somewhere special to **stay** in Beaugency, try the *Hôtel de l'Abbaye*, 2 quai de l'Abbaye (☎02.38.44.67.35, fax 02.38.44.87.92; ⑥), a beautiful eighteenth-century abbey with painted ceilings and beds on raised platforms. Much cheaper and less grand, though equally pleasant, is the *Hôtel de la Sologne*, 6 place St-Firmin (☎02.38.44.50.27, fax 02.38.44.90.19; ③–④; closed Dec 20–Jan 4), and the cheapest hotel of all is the *Hôtel des Vieux Fossés*, 4 rue des Vieux-Fossés (☎02.38.44.51.65, fax 02.38.46.45.05; ①). There's also an **HI hostel** in the suburb of Vernon at 152 rte de Châteaudun, 2km north off the main Orléans–Blois road from the east side of town (☎02.38.44.61.31; closed Jan & Feb), and a riverside **campsite** (☎02.38.44.50.39; closed Nov–March) in Beaugency.

There are no particularly special **restaurants** in Beaugency, but *Le Relais du Château*, 3 rue du Pont (☎02.38.44.55.10), is plain and unpretentious with menus at 80F/€12.20, 115F/€17.53 and 170F/€25.91. A good place to **drink** is *Le Moulin Rouge*, 2 rue de la Bonde (closed Mon), east of rue du Pont, which has good beers plus live blues, jazz and rock some weekends.

Château de Chamerolles

Situated approximately 30km northeast of Orléans towards Pithiviers, **Chamerolles** is a sixteenth-century chateau (April–Sept daily 10am–6pm; rest of year daily except Fri 10am–5pm; closed Jan; 30F/€4.57), whose pristine condition is devoid of the well-worn patina you may have come to expect. Its history is not particularly exciting, but the south wing now houses the **Château-Promenade des Parfums** (same hours and price), tracing the use of scents from the sixteenth century to the present day. With its "press-and-smell" buttons and reconstructed "toilets" it's great fun, not least for its revelations about European lavatorial habits over the last four hundred years. Behind the château is a reconstruction of a Renaissance garden – interesting more for its construction than its beauty.

To **get there** using public transport, take a bus from Orléans to Chieulleurs-aux-Boix, from where you'll have to walk the last 3km.

East to the Burgundy border

Upstream from Orléans, single-lane roads run along the top of the flood banks of the Loire – these are ideal for cycling. To the north is the rambling **Forêt d'Orléans**, densely planted and crisscrossed with roads. Beyond it, a bland, treeless wheat plain stretches to Paris, and the immediate countryside to the south is likewise drab: sticking to the Loire itself is the best advice.

way and one pepperpot tower are recognizably medieval. Inside, tanks of freshwater fish and a coelacanth, one of the oldest fishes known, with paddle-like fins and a world-weary expression, are the key exhibits, but the seventeenth-century kitchens and old laundry are also quite fun.

On the south side of the Loire, halfway between Sully and Gien, medieval weaponry is the theme at the **Château de St-Brisson** (April–Nov daily except Wed 10am–noon & 2–6pm; 22F/€3.35). Demonstrations are given at 3.30pm and 4.30pm every other Sunday during summer in the moat, using bows and arrows, battering rams and devices for lobbing stones. The château also has an **art gallery**, with changing exhibitions of painting, sculpture and photography, and hosts a **concert** series of jazz, opera and classical music (60F/€9.15) at weekends during the summer, both of which help to make up for the rather unattractive mix of styles (twelfth- to seventeenth-century) of the building itself.

Briare

The small village of **BRIARE**, 10km from Gien on the Orléans–Nevers road and the Paris–Nevers rail line, centres on its Belle Époque iron aqueduct, the **Pont Canal**, linking the Canal de Briare to the north with the Canal Latéral à la Loire, which runs south to the Saône. The design of the Pont Canal came from the workshops of Gustav Eiffel of Eiffel Tower fame, but parts of the canal scheme date back to the early seventeenth century, when internal waterways linking the Mediterranean, Atlantic and Channel coasts were devised. You can walk along the aqueduct's extraordinary 625-metre span, with its wrought-iron crested lamps and railings, hopefully without a *bâteau-mouche* spoiling the effect.

The **tourist office**, 1 place Charles-de-Gaulle (daily 10am–noon & 2–5pm; ☎02.38.31.24.51, fax 02.38.37.15.16), can provide details of canal boats and canoe rental as well as maps of footpaths, towpaths and the locks (the one at Chatillon-sur-Loire, 4km upstream, is particularly appealing). For **accommodation**, try the modern *Hôtel le Canal* at 19 rue du Pont-Canal (☎02.38.31.24.24, fax 02.38.31.92.12; ③), right next to the bridge.

Sancerre and around

Although you can buy its wines anywhere, and there's not much justification for making a detour to visit **SANCERRE**, a village huddled at the top of a steep, round hill with the vineyards below, there is something appealing about seeing the actual vineyards from which the famous grape has sprung. Sancerre is an extremely dry wine made from the Sauvignon grape; the white is the most renowned, but there are good reds as well, and the rarer rosé is exquisite.

Around Sancerre are several **vignerons**, most of them small-scale traditional winemakers. Three you can visit are: M. Raimbault at the Caves de la Mignonne (☎02.48.54.07.06), on the D955 towards St-Satur on the left; M. Archambault at Caves du Clos de la Perrière, on the D134 in Verdigny-en-Sancerre (☎02.48.54.16.93), to the west of St-Satur; and M. Laporte at the Cave de la Cresle, on the D57 (☎02.48.54.04.07), to the northwest of St-Satur. Well suited to the wines is the local *crottin de Chavignol*, a goat's cheese named after **CHAVIGNOL**, the neighbouring village in which it's made; signs in Chavignol direct you to **fromageries** open to visitors, where you can sample the cheese.

If you're planning to **stay** in Sancerre, first choice is the *Panoramic*, Rempart des Augustins (☎02.48.54.22.44, fax 02.48.54.39.55; ③), a lovely hotel with a pool and superb views of the vineyards to the north. There are also two excellent **restaurants**: *La Pomme d'Or*, 1 rue de la Panneterie (☎02.48.54.13.30; closed Mon & Wed evening), with menus from 80F/€12.20; and *La Tour*, 31 place de la Halle (☎02.48.54.00.81), with menus from 80F/€12.20.

La Sologne

Between the Loire and the Cher, from Gien in the east almost as far as Blois in the west, lies the area known as the **Sologne**, marked to the southeast by the low, abrupt **Collines du Sancerrois**, northwest of Sancerre. The *autoroute* and main road from Orléans to Bourges run almost together through the middle of the area.

Depending on the weather and the season it can be one of the most dismal areas in central France: damp, flat, featureless and foggy. But at other times its forests, lakes, ponds and marshes have a quiet magic – in summer when the heather is in bloom and the ponds are full of water lilies, or in early autumn when you can go hunting for wild mushrooms, egg-yolk orange *chanterelles* smelling of apricots, or *cèpes*, with caps like suede and bulging pure white stalks. Wild boar and deer roam here, not to mention the ducks, geese, quails and pheasants, who far outweigh the small human population.

Two *grandes randonnées* run through the Sologne, the **GR41** and **GR3C**, and there are numerous other paths, well signposted and detailing the accessibility for bicycles. From Easter to the end of October, tourist offices in most of Sologne's towns and villages can provide maps and details of bike rental or horse riding, as well as accommodation details. Information about walks is also available from the tourist office at Orléans all year, though you may have to pay for some of the maps. If you're exploring the Sologne during the hunting season (Oct 1–March 1), don't stray from the marked paths: there are endless stories of people being accidentally shot.

Domaine du Ciran

Halfway between Ménestreau-en-Villette and Marcilly-en-Villette and 6km east of La Ferté-St-Aubin, just off the D108, is the little hamlet of **CIRAN**. Its tiny château has a **Musée de la Vie Traditionelle**, with photos showing such delights as dogs being used to pull carts, among other local revelations (daily 10am–noon & 2–5.30/6pm; winter closed Tues; 20F/€3.05). But the main reason to come here is to explore the 300 hectares of the **Domaine de Ciran** and see its working farm, a typical Sologne set up where the principal activities are deer breeding, keeping goats and making *chèvre*, as well as growing acres of asparagus. You may well catch a glimpse of wild deer in the forested parts of the *domaine*, herons and geese around the ponds and sometimes even coypus. It's also possible to come across wild boar, so be careful, though they are not very threatening unless they're with their babies. The 6km signed walk – for which waterproof footwear is advisable – gives you an excellent taste of the different landscapes of the Sologne.

Argent-sur-Sauldre and around

In the grounds of the thirteenth-century château just outside the village of **ARGENT-SUR-SAULDRE**, on the D940 between Gien and Bourges, is the excellent **Musée Vassil Ivanoff** (May–Sept Mon & Wed–Fri 2–7pm, Sat & Sun 10am–noon & 2–6pm; 16F/€2.44), which contains a small, fascinating collection of modern ceramics. The Bulgarian Ivanoff came to France in the 1920s and settled in La Borne, a small village in the Sancerre hills which has mutated into a highly commercialized pottery centre; there he produced a collection that has been described as a revolution in clay. The works on display in the museum – sensual forms expressing all the complexities of the human condition – demonstrate a range of his experimentation with different surface textures and glazes, the most successful of which is a unique, ox-blood red.

The other museum in the château is the **Musée des Métiers et Traditions de France** (mid-April to mid-Oct Mon–Thurs 2–5.45pm, Fri–Sun 10–11.30am & 2–6pm; 25F/€2.44), a nostalgic meander through eighteenth- and nineteenth-century country crafts and trades, including bizarre machines for making brooms and clogs, looms, a

LA FÊTE ÉTRANGE

There is much dispute as to where the magical party in **Alain Fournier's novel** *Le Grand Meaulnes* was set, despite the fact that it was clearly an imaginary mixture of many places. Fournier was born in La Chapelle d'Angillon, 24km south of Argent-sur-Sauldre on the D940. He spent much of his childhood in the château there, but went to school in Épineuil-le-Fleurial (the Ste-Agathe of the novel) well beyond the Sologne and Bourges, some 25km south of St-Armand-Montrond (turn right off the Montluçon road from Bourges to cross the Cher at Meaulne). Albicoco's film of the book was shot around Épineuil, and the elementary school described in the book can be visited outside class hours. But the "domain with no name" where the *fête étrange* takes place is certainly in the Sologne: "In the whole of the Sologne," he wrote, "it would have been hard to find a more desolate spot." Nançay, between Salbris and La Chapelle d'Angillon on the D944, has a **Musée Imaginaire du Grand Meaulnes** dedicated to the novelist within the **Galaria Capazza**, an excellent gallery of contemporary art housed in one of the outbuildings of its château (Sat & Sun only 9.30am–12.30pm & 2.30–7.30pm; 20F/€3.05).

windmill gear and a display about the production of weathercocks. The exhibits continue into the roofspace, giving a good opportunity to view the rafters of the château.

Close to Argent, 11km southeast on the D8 near Concressault, is a new witchcraft museum at La Jonchère, the **Musée de la Sorcellerie** (Easter–Oct daily 10am–6pm; 34F/€5.18). It's a bit over the top with its animated reconstructions of witchcraft trials, but kids will probably enjoy it, and some of the prints and paintings of legendary witches are fun.

For **accommodation** and good **food** in Argent, head for the comfortable *Relais de la Poste* (☎02.48.81.53.90, fax 02.48.73.30.62; ②), directly opposite the château. Otherwise, there's a very pleasant hotel in the village of **BRINON-SUR-SAULDRE**, 16km west of Argent: *La Solognote*, Grande Rue (☎02.48.58.50.29, fax 02.48.58.56.00; ④–⑤; closed Wed out of season, mid-Feb to mid-March, last week in May & three weeks in Sept; restaurant closed Wed & out of season Tues evening).

Romorantin-Lanthenay

ROMORANTIN-LANTHENAY, 67km due south of Orléans, is the biggest town in the Sologne and best visited in the last weekend in October for the **Journées Gastronomiques**, a major food festival when every restaurant and hundreds of street stalls tempt you with traditional and novel dishes centred on game, wild mushrooms, apples and pumpkins. The rest of the year the only sight of interest is the **Musée de Sologne**, in the old mills in the centre of Romorantin (April–Nov Mon & Wed–Sat 10am–6pm, Sun 2–5pm; rest of year Mon & Wed–Sat 10–11am & 2–5pm, Sun 2–5pm; 25F/€3.81), which presents the history, ecology and traditions of the area.

For more information about the Sologne, contact the **tourist office** on place de la Paix (July & Aug Mon–Sat 8.45am–12.15pm & 1.30–6.30pm, Sun 10am–noon; rest of year closed Sun; ☎02.54.76.43.89). If you fancy a splurge, head for *Grand Hôtel du Lion d'Or*, 69 rue G.-Clemenceau (☎02.54.94.15.15, *www.hotel-liondor.fr*; ⑥), an old manor house, with a fabulous courtyard garden, sixteen well-appointed **rooms** and a stellar **restaurant** (meals well over 500F/€76.23).

Bourges

BOURGES, the surprisingly agreeable chief town of the rather bland region of Berry, south of the Sologne, is some way from the Loire valley proper but historically linked to it. The miserable Dauphin Charles VII, mockingly dubbed "King of Bourges" by the English, retreated to the city after Henry V's victory at Agincourt had put all of northern France under English control. Today's unpretentious and handsome city hums along with the business of everyday life and offers a substantial calendar of festivals, some good restaurants, a glorious Gothic cathedral and an impressive mansion belonging to the Dauphin's financial advisor, Jacques Cœur.

Arrival, information and accommodation

The **gare routière** is west of the city beyond boulevard Juranville on rue du Prado, while the **gare SNCF** lies 1km to the north of the centre, on avenue P.-Sémard. The **tourist office**, which faces the south facade of the cathedral, is at 21 rue Victor-Hugo (July–Sept Mon–Sat 9am–7.30pm, Sun 10am–7.30pm; rest of year Mon–Sat 9am–6pm, Sun 10am–12.30pm; ☎02.48.23.02.60, fax 02.48.23.02.69, *www.ville-bourges.fr*), and there is also a regional tourist office at 5 rue de Séraucourt (☎02.48.48.00.10, fax 02.48.48.00.20, *www.berrylecher.com*). **Rue Moyenne** is the main street leading north from rue Victor-Hugo, with rue Porte-Jaune parallel to it from the cathedral parvis. If you feel like pedalling through the surrounding flat countryside, you can **rent bikes** from Loca Bourges, 118 rue Barbès (☎02.48.21.08.33), or from the *Auberge de Jeunesse*.

Hotels

de l'Agriculture, 15 rue du Prinal (☎02.48.70.40.84, fax 02.48.65.50.58). A nondescript but reasonable hotel on the corner of bd Juranville, with only eight rooms, so it's a good idea to call first. ③.

d'Angleterre, place des Quatre-Piliers (☎02.48.24.68.51, fax 02.48.65.21.41). Central three-star located right by the Palais de Jacques-Cœur, and part of the Best Western conglomerate. Pleasant service and a high level of comfort, as you'd expect for the price. ④–⑤.

Le Christina, 5 rue de la Halle (☎02.48.70.56.50, fax 02.48.70.58.13). A large, good hotel on the west of town. ③–④.

L'Étape, 4 rue Raphael-Casanova (☎02.48.70.59.47, fax 02.48.24.57.93). Very good-value hotel on the edge of the old city centre. ①.

Olympia, 66 av d'Orléans (☎02.48.70.49.84, fax 02.48.65.29.06). A small hotel but with pleasant rooms. ②.

Hostels and campsite

HI hostel, 22 rue Henri-Sellier (☎02.48.24.58.09, fax 02.48.65.51.46). Hostel located a short way southwest of the centre, overlooking the River Auron. Bus #1 to "Maison de la Culture", stop "Auberge de Jeunesse"; or a 10min walk from the *gare routière*. Open mid-Jan to mid-Dec Mon–Fri 7am–noon & 2–9pm; weekends and holidays 7am–noon & 5–9pm. HI membership needed.

Centre International de Séjour la Charmille, 17 rue Félix-Chédin (☎02.48.70.63.90, fax 02.48.69.01.21, *www.lacharmille.asso.fr*). This place has sunny, modern dorm-style rooms, equipped with showers, sleeping one to seven people. A skateboarders' haven with every kind of ramp, plus plenty of cultural activities and meals for around 50F/€7.62. For students under 25 only. A short walk north of the *gare SNCF*.

Camping municipal, 26 bd de l'Industrie (☎02.48.20.16.85). Decently sized site located south of the HI hostel, within 100m of a boulangerie and tabac and 800m from a supermarket. Bus #6 from place Cujas, stop "Joffre", or a 10min walk from the *gare routière*. Closed mid-Nov to mid-March.

The City

The centre of Bourges sits on a hill rising from the River Yèvre, in the shadow of its main attraction, the magnificent early Gothic cathedral. Having seen the cathedral, many people move straight on, but the rest of the city is worth at least a couple of hours of wandering. Bourges has its fair quota of ancient *hôtels* and burghers' houses, displaying the wealth of a city that was built to rival the ruling provincial city of Dijon.

The cathedral

The exterior of the twelfth-century **Cathédrale St-Étienne** (daily: April–Sept 8am–7.30pm; Oct–March 8am–6.30pm; 32F/€4.88) is characterized by the delicate, almost skeletal appearance of flying buttresses supporting an entire nave that has no transepts to break up its bulk. A much-vaunted example of Gothic architecture, it is modelled on Notre-Dame in Paris but incorporates improvements on the latter's design, such as the increased height of the inner aisles, which appear to ascend almost to vanishing point.

The **tympanum** above the main door of the west portal could engross you for hours with its tableau of the Last Judgement, featuring carved, naked figures whose faces are alive with expression and bodies full of movement. Thirteenth-century imagination has been given full rein in the depiction of the devils, complete with snakes' tails and winged bottoms and faces appearing from below the waist, symbolic of the soul in the service of sinful appetites. A cauldron filling with merry souls – one of whom appears to be wearing a bishop's mitre – contrasts sorely with the depiction of the gloomy-looking saved, while God, sitting in judgement, appears exceptionally sanctimonious.

The interior's best feature is its mostly twelfth- to thirteenth-century **stained glass**. There are geometric designs in lovely muted colours in the main body of the cathedral, but the most glorious and astonishingly bright windows are around the choir, all created between 1215 and 1225. You can follow the stories of the Prodigal Son, the Rich Man and Lazarus, the life of Mary, Joseph in Egypt, the Good Samaritan, Christ's Crucifixion, the Last Judgement and the Apocalyse – binoculars come in handy for picking up the exquisite detail. But the most memorable way of seeing the cathedral is to come on a Sunday morning, when the powerful eighteenth-century organ is played, or to attend one of the concerts on Tuesday evenings.

In the **crypt**, you can see the design of the fourteenth-century rose window of the west front cut into the floor, suggesting that this was where it was assembled. Tickets for guided visits to the crypt (closed Sun morning; 32F/€4.88) also allow you to climb to the top of the north **tower**, rebuilt in Flamboyant style after the original collapsed in 1506.

The rest of the city

Although Bourges's museums are not particularly interesting, they are housed in some beautiful medieval buildings, the finest of which are contained within the loop of roads northwest of the cathedral to either side of rue Moyenne and rue Porte-Jaune. Next to the cathedral in place E.-Dolet, the recently opened **Musée des Meilleurs Ouvriers de France** (daily 2–6pm; closed Jan; free) has examples of what are considered to be the best works by French artisans; these are gathered under various categories such as pastry-making, musical instruments and glassware. Rue Bourbonnoux, parallel to rue Moyenne to the east of the cathedral, is worth a wander for the richly decorated **Hôtel Lallemant** (daily 10am–noon & 2–6pm; free), now a diverting enough museum of medieval artefacts, with displays of sculpture, tapestries and furniture. Halfway along the street, you can take a narrow passage up to the remains of the Gallo-Roman town **ramparts**, lined with old houses and trees. Rue Gambon is noteworthy for the **Maison de la Reine Blanche** and the **Hôtel-Dieu**, and close by is the pleasant square of **place Notre-Dame**, with its eponymous church, clearly showing the shift from Gothic to Renaissance. On rue E.-Branly, you'll find the fifteenth-century **Hôtel des Échevins** (daily 10am–noon & 2–6pm; free), which was restored in 1985 and became the **Musée de Maurice Estève**, filled with works by the twentieth-century painter.

The continuation of rue E.-Branly, **rue Jacques-Cœur**, was the site of the head office, stock exchange, dealing rooms, bank safes and home of Charles VII's finance minister, Jacques Cœur (1400–56), a medieval shipping magnate, moneylender and arms dealer who dominates Bourges as Joan of Arc does Orléans – Charles VII just doesn't get a look-in. The **Palais de Jacques-Cœur** (daily: April–June, Sept & Oct 9am–noon & 2–6pm; July & Aug 9am–7pm; Nov–March 9am–noon & 2–5pm; guided tours every 1hr 15min beginning at 9.15am; 32F/€4.88) is one of the most remarkable examples of fifteenth-century domestic architecture in France. The visit is memorable, and especially fun for children: it starts with the fake windows on the entrance front from which two realistically sculpted half-figures look down – possibly the man himself and his wife. There are hardly any furnishings inside, but the decorations on the stonework, including numerous hearts and scallop shells, clearly show the mark of the man who had it built. In the Salle du Trésor, there are carved scenes from the romance of Tristan and Iseult. The tour includes the kitchen, with its original water-heating system, and dining hall, with minstrels' gallery; you are also shown the original loos.

Eating and drinking

Bourges's main centre for **eating** is place Gordaine, at the end of rue Coursarlon, off rue Moyenne. The square is attractively medieval, a lovely place to sit and eat in the daytime, despite the continuous piped music: try *Lucky Luke*, a lively place serving hearty American hamburgers and salads from 45F/€6.88; or *Le Comptoir de Paris*, a very popular and friendly restaurant with a terrace overlooking the square (☎02.48.24.17.16), which serves *plats du jour* from 59F/€8.99 with wine and menus from 98F/€14.94. A short walk from here towards the cathedral, *D'Antan Sancerrois*, 50 rue Bourbonnoux (☎02.48.65.96.26; closed Sun & Mon lunch), features local goodies cooked in wine and served in a medieval dining hall (à la carte from 90F/€13.72); and just next to the food **market** (Wed–Sat am), at 28–30 rue des Cordeliers, the *Palais de la Bière* (☎02.48.70.32.22) has menus for 76F/€11.59 and 94F/€14.33, and specializes in seafood. *Les Beaux Arts*, on place Cujas (☎02.48.24.00.30; closed Sun) – above the popular and pleasant *Le Cujas* brasserie (☎02.48.24.52.67; daily 7am–2am) – also offers seafood and plenty of dishes created to include the local asparagus (menus 79–175F/€12.04–26.67).

Those with a sweet tooth should head for the excellent **pâtisserie** Aux Trois Flûtes, on the corner of rues Joyeuse and Bourbonnoux; for chocolates and the local sweet speciality of *fourrées au praliné* try the imposing Maison Forestines, on place Cujas.

Nightlife and festivals

For a small city, Bourges doesn't do too badly for **nightlife**. Late-night venues include *L'Iguana Café*, 3 rue du Prinal, a hot hangout with salsa every Tuesday (Mon–Sat 7pm–3am); the nearby *La Clé*, 5 rue Emile Deschamps, which has live music and cheesy theme nights (Mon–Sat 7pm–3.30am); the *Pub Murrayfield*, 11 rue Jean Girard (Mon & Sun 3pm–2am; Tues–Sat 11am–2am), offering quite a selection of beer and whisky, and dart boards; and the very 1980s *L'Interdit*, 5 rue Calvin (Wed–Sun 5pm–2am), a gay bar that touts itself as a "*bar humain*".

Bourges's **festival** programme is also impressive, with several major events in town. The Printemps de Bourges features every sort of music – including some big names – for one week between mid-April and the beginning of May (☎02.48.24.30.50; tickets from 100F/€15.24). More esoteric are the Festival Synthèse, an electronic and acoustic music bash during the first week of June (☎02.48.20.41.87, fax 02.48.20.45.51), and Un

Été à Bourges (mid-July to mid-Sept), a celebration of theatre, music and open-air street performances.

The upper Indre valley

Although the **Berry** countryside is on the whole rather dismal, the upper valley of the **Indre** has some attractions. **Nohant** and **La Châtre** were home to George Sand and Chopin for some time, while the small village of **St-Chartier**, 9km north of La Châtre, is worth a visit for its huge folk festival around July 14. The main draw along this stretch, however, is **Loches**, with its magnificent medieval citadel.

La Châtre and around

LA CHÂTRE, about 60km southwest of Bourges, is dominated by the nineteenth-century novelist **George Sand**: every other place name is connected with her. The **Musée George Sand et de la Vallée Noire**, 71 rue Venose (daily: May, June & Sept 9am–noon & 2–7pm; July & Aug 9am–7pm; rest of year 9am–noon & 2–5pm; closed Jan; 20F/€3.05), dedicates a floor to the writer, with plenty of pictures, including George Sand's caricatures of her friends, a photo of Chopin, her son Maurice's illustrations for his mother's work and the doodles on her manuscripts. Apart from this, the town's most distinctive feature is the background noise of gentle tapping as competitors in the annual **stone sculpture competition** set to work each June. You can watch them at it and admire the results, which are displayed around the town.

La Châtre's **tourist office** is on square George-Sand (daily 10am–12.30pm & 2–6pm; ☎02.54.48.22.64, fax 02.54.06.09.15). If you want to **stay**, try *Le Paradis Breton*, 4 rue Alphonse-Fleury (☎02.54.48.02.87; ③), a pleasant option with just five very cheap rooms. *Le Lion d'Argent*, 2 av Lion d'Argent (☎02.54.48.11.69, *www.hotel-lion -argent.com*; ③), is well equipped with a swimming pool and has bikes for rental; its restaurant (closed Sun out of season; menus from 75F/€11.43) serves generous helpings of traditional dishes and has a good wine selection. There's also a **hostel** by the River Indre on the east side of the town on rue du Moulin Borgnon (☎02.54.06.00.55, fax 02.54.48.48.10; HI membership required), and a riverside **campsite** (☎02.54.48.32.42; closed mid-Nov to mid-March) at Montgivray, 2.5km from La Châtre. The **restaurant** *Jardin de la Poste*, 10 rue Basse-Mouhet (☎02.54.48.05.62; closed Sun evening, Mon & mid-Sept to Oct 5), should leave you feeling well satisfied for little more than 100F/€15.24.

GEORGE SAND (1804–76)

After the publication of her novel *Valentine*, which was set locally and received considerable publicity, **George Sand** wrote: "This unknown Vallée Noire, this quiet and unpretentious landscape . . . all this had charms for me alone and did not deserve to be revealed to idle curiosity." What the critics jumped on in this novel, and in the rest of her writings, were "anti-matrimonial doctrines"; her view – reasonable enough – that ill-matched couples should be able to separate. Simone de Beauvoir described Sand as a "sentimental feminist", and, except for the brief period of the 1848 Revolution, she was certainly no activist. But her male contemporaries called her a man-eater, and she is still too often referred to simply as Chopin's mistress. Though her literary output was enormous and the French recognize her as one of their great writers, her lasting reputation is based on her – at the time – shocking lifestyle.

Nohant

NOHANT, about 10km north of La Châtre on the main Châteauroux road, is where Sand, or Amandine Aurore Lucie Dupin as she was born, spent half her life. The **Château de Nohant** – not really a château but her very pleasant eighteenth-century country house – is open for quick guided tours (daily: July & Aug 9am–6.30pm; mid-Oct to Jan 2.30–3.30pm; rest of year 9–11.15am & 2–5.30pm; 35F/€3.34). You're shown the dining-room table where Flaubert, Turgenev, Dumas, Delacroix, Balzac and Liszt all dined on many occasions. The piano that George Sand gave Chopin, her guest for ten years, sits in the living room surrounded by the family portraits. There's also the puppet theatre made by Chopin and Sand's son Maurice, the pair no doubt trying to outdo each other in their well-documented rivalry for Sand's attentions.

Chopin's music is honoured in a week-long **piano festival**, Chopin chez George Sand, at Nohant and La Châtre towards the end of July. Tickets range from 30F/€4.57 to 200F/€30.49; bookings and programme details are available from La Châtre's tourist office (see opposite).

St-Chartier

ST-CHARTIER, 10km north of La Châtre, is the venue of one of the best **folk festivals** in Europe, the Rencontres Internationales de St-Chartier, an annual festival of folk and traditional music and dance that started as a hurdy-gurdy and pipe festival but has spread its horizons over the years. It takes place around the old château, the village church and in the surrounding parkland. Traditional-instrument makers set up their stalls, and there are dance workshops, competitions, concerts and a festive ball in the main square every night. To give some idea of the festival's range, past line-ups have included traditional music from Lombardy, folk bands from Moldavia, Spanish bagpipes, English and Irish folk, and a fifty-piece orchestra from Berry.

The festival takes place over four or five days around July 14, and inclusive tickets cost around 380F/€57.93, or you can just go for the day for about 160F/€24.39. There are free **campsites** all around the village for the duration. Details are available from the Comité George Sand, 141 rue Nationale, 36400 La Châtre (☎02.54.06.09.96), or online at *www.saintchartier.com*.

On the route de Verneuil, in St-Chartier, is the *Château de la Vallée Bleue*, a peaceful country park **hotel** (☎02.54.31.01.91; ④), with an excellent restaurant (menus from 130F/€19.82).

On to Loches

If you follow the Indre downstream from La Châtre, the river itself tends to be the only source of interest until you reach Loches – one exception being the Romanesque church in the pretty town of **CHATILLON-SUR-INDRE**, on the Touraine–Berry border. **CHÂTEAUROUX**, the largest town on the banks of the Indre and a local route hub, is a grey and officious sort of place, surrounded by supermarkets and petrol stations. However, it's a good spot to stock up on necessities if you are driving or biking through.

Loches and around

LOCHES is the obvious place to head for in the Indre valley. Its walled **citadel** is by far the most impressive of the Loire valley fortresses, with its unbreached ramparts and the Renaissance houses below still partly enclosed by the outer wall of the medieval town.

The **old town** is announced by the Tour St-Antoine belfry, close to place du Marché (Wednesday market), linking rue St-Antoine with Grande Rue. Two fifteenth-century gates to the old town still stand: the **Porte des Cordeliers**, by the river at the end of Grande Rue, and the **Porte Picois** to the west, at the end of rue St-Antoine. Rue du Château, lined with Renaissance buildings, leads to the twelfth-century towers of **Porte Royale**, the main entrance to the citadel.

The citadel

The Porte Royale contains the **Musée de Terroir**, a traditional museum of rural life and crafts (daily except Wed 9–11.45am & 2–4/5/6pm; 20F/€3.05). Behind the gateway and down to the left is the **Musée Lansyer**, with works by the local nineteenth-century painter Lansyer, overshadowed by a Japanese collection that includes a complete suit of samurai armour (daily except Tues: April–Sept 10am–7pm; rest of year 1.30–5pm; closed Dec & Jan; 25F/€3.81). Straight ahead is the Romanesque church, the **Collégiale de St-Ours**, with its odd roof-line of four turrets, two of which are supported by octagonal pyramids. The porch has some entertaining twelfth-century monster carvings, and the stoup, or basin for holy water, is a Gallo-Roman altar.

The northern end of the citadel is taken up by the **Logis Royal**, or Royal Lodgings, of Charles VII and his three successors (daily: mid-March to June & last two weeks in Sept 9am–noon & 2–6pm; July to mid-Sept 9am–7pm; rest of year 9am–noon & 2–5pm; 23F/€3.51, 31F/€4.73 including *donjon*). The medieval half of the palace was home to two women of some importance to Charles: Joan of Arc, victorious from Orléans, who came here to give the defeatist Dauphin another pep talk about coronations, and later the less significant (but much sexier) Agnès Sorel, Charles's lover. Even the pope took a fancy to Agnès, which allowed Charles to be the first French king to have an officially recognized mistress. She was buried at Loches and her tomb now lies in the fifteenth-century wing, her alabaster recumbent figure restored after anticlerical Revolutionary soldiers mistook her for a saint. Also in the same room there's a portrait of her in full regalia and a painting of the Virgin in her likeness; the semi-nudity in both was no artist's fantasy, but a courtly fashion trend set by Agnès.

While little remains today in the Logis Royal to give much impression of the highlife of kings' favourites, the nastiness of being out of favour is clear at the other end of the citadel. Here are the dungeons and two keeps, the larger one, the **donjon**, initiated by Foulques Nerra, the eleventh-century count of Anjou, with cells and a torture chamber added in the fifteenth century (daily June to mid-Sept 9am–7pm; last two weeks in Sept 9.30am–1pm & 2.30–7pm; rest of year 9.30am–1pm & 2.30–6pm; 23F/€3.51, 31F/€4.73 including château). There is not much left of the fifteenth-century extension, thanks to the people of Loches, who destroyed most of the torture equipment during the Revolution, and although the very professional guides make up for the lack of exhibits with their spiel, they can't quite express the goriness – Louis XI's adviser, Cardinal La Balve, was supposed to have been locked up here in a wooden cage for eleven years. You can climb unescorted to the top of the keep, though the views of the surrounding countryside are unexciting.

Practicalities

From the **gare SNCF** on the east side of the Indre, avenue de la Gare leads to place de la Marne, with the **tourist office** on your left (daily: July to mid-Sept 9am–7pm; rest of year Mon–Fri 9.30am–12.30pm & 2–6pm; ☎02.47.59.07.98, fax 02.47.91.61.50); the **gare routière** is a short way down rue de Tours from the square. Loches is only an hour's train or coach journey away from Tours, but you may well want to stay, particularly if you're **camping** – the *Camping Municipal de la Citadelle* (☎02.47.59.05.91; mid-March to mid-Nov) is between two branches of the Indre by the swimming pool and stadium, looking up at the east side of the citadel. The *George Sand* **hotel**, 37 rue Quintefol (☎02.47.59.39.74, fax 02.47.91.55.75; ⑦), just below the eastern ramparts, has its best rooms at the back, looking onto the river; its restaurant is not at all bad, with menus from 100F/€15.24. The *Hôtel Tour Ste-Antoine*, 2 rue des Moulins (☎02.47.59.01.06, fax 02.47.59.13.80;③–④), is the only hotel in the old town itself, but the *France*, 6 rue Picois, near the Porte Picois (☎02.47.59.00.32, fax 02.47.59.28.66; ④), is more pleasant, with an excellent restaurant (menus start at 85F/€12.95). The best place for a **drink** is the *Café des Arts*, on place du Blé.

Beaulieu-les-Loches

Just across the Indre from Loches is the village of **BEAULIEU-LES-LOCHES** – an extraordinary, little-known place, thoroughly medieval in appearance, with its parish church built into the spectacular ruins of an abbey contemporary with the Loches keep. Its other church, St-Pierre, holds the bones of Foulques Nerra, the eleventh-century count of Anjou responsible for Loches's grisly *donjon*. Next to the ruined abbey, there's a charming low-budget **hotel**, the *Hôtel de Beaulieu*, 3 rue Foulques-Nerra (☎02.47.91.60.80; ②). The **bistro** *L'Estaminet* (☎02.47.59.35.47; closed Mon) next door is run by the hotel owner's son and serves simple country cooking from around 80F/€12.20.

The Cher

Twenty kilometres north of Loches and southeast of Tours, spanning the slow-moving **River Cher**, the **Château de Chenonceau** is perhaps the best of all the Loire châteaux for architecture, site, contents, organization and atmosphere. Further upstream **Montrichard** and **St-Aignan** make nice diversions from the endless stream of castle tours, while for still-unsatiated château buffs, there's **Valençay** further south between the Cher and the Indre.

Château de Chenonceau

Unlike the Loire, the gentle River Cher flows so slowly and passively between the exquisite arches of the **Château de Chenonceau** that you are almost always assured of a perfect reflection (daily: Jan & Dec 9am–4.30pm; early Feb & Nov 9am–5pm; late Feb & Oct 9am–6pm; rest of year 9am–7pm; *www.chenonceaux.com*; 45F/€6.86).

The building of the château was always controlled by women. Catherine Briconnet, whose husband bought the site, hired the first architects in 1515 and had them begin building on the foundations of an old mill that stood on the granite bed of the Cher. The château's most characteristic feature, the set of arches spanning the River Cher, was begun later in the century by Diane de Poitiers (mistress of Henri II) and completed by the indomitable Catherine de Médicis (wife of Henri II), after she had evicted Diane and forced her to hand over the château in return for much less elaborate Chaumont (see p.486). Mary, Queen of Scots, child bride of François II, also spent time here until her husband's early death. Then, after a long period of disuse, one Mme Dupin brought eighteenth-century life to this gorgeous residence, along with her guests Voltaire, Montesquieu and Rousseau, whom she hired as tutor to her son. Restoration back to the sixteenth-century designs was completed by another woman, Mme Pelouze, in the late nineteenth century. It is now a profitable business, owned and run by the Menier chocolate family firm.

Unlike some of its neighbours, Chenonceau is not visible from the road and you will have to pay for access to the grounds before even getting a peek at the residence. While the tree-lined path to the front door is dramatic, for a more intimate approach, head through the gardens laid out under Diane de Poitiers. After the pay-booths, cross the

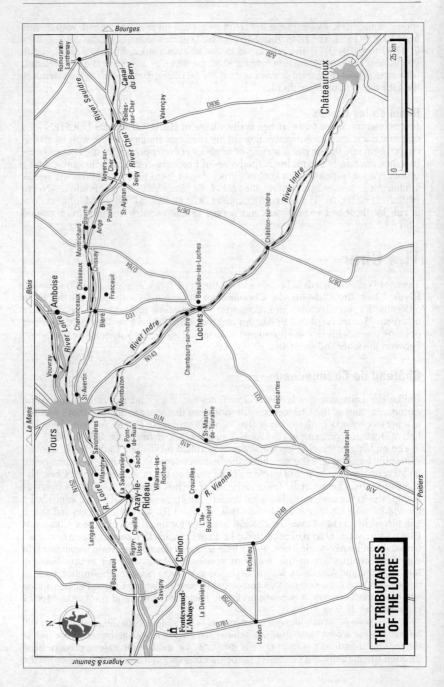

THE TRIBUTARIES
OF THE LOIRE

stream and follow signs to the maze. Walk along the stream through the woods, turn right to the Cher and, upriver, there's a magnificent view of the château.

During summer the place is teeming with people, but visits are unguided – a luxurious relief, for there's an endless number of arresting tapestries, paintings, ceilings, floors and furniture on show. On the ground floor the Chambre de François I features a portrait of Diane de Poitiers by Primaticcio and a case containing copies of her signatures. Another exceptional picture is Zurbaran's half-dressed *Archimedes*, his clothes inside out and his face full of fear and (justified) suspicion that his theories would be misunderstood. The Salle des Gardes on the same floor, its painted rafters emblazoned with the device of Catherine de Médicis, is used to exhibit Flemish tapestries. The elegant gallery across the Cher, despite the plastic potted plants, is worth spending time in if only to evoke the parties – all naked nymphs and Italian fireworks – held there by Catherine.

There's a **son et lumière** show, "Les Dames de Chenonceau", tracing the history of the château from fortified mill to elegant residence, on June 3 and 4, then every evening from June 24 to Sept 3 (10.15pm; 40F/€6.10). In July and August you can take **boats** out onto the Cher, and there's a crèche for small children.

Practicalities

The **tourist office** for Chenonceaux, Chisseaux and Franceuil, three villages in close proximity, is at 13bis rue du Château in **CHENONCEAUX** (☎02.47.23.94.45) – the village is spelt with an 'x' on the end.

All the **hotels** in the village of Chenonceaux are on rue du Docteur-Bretonneau, within easy reach of the station and the château. The *Hôtel du Roy* at no. 9 (☎02.47.23.90.17, fax 02.47.23.89.81; ②) is comfortable and excellent value; at no. 6, the *Hôtel du Bon Laboureur et du Château* (☎02.47.23.90.02, fax 02.47.23.82.01; ④) is the most luxurious option; and *Le Renaudière*, at no. 24 (☎02.47.23.90.04, fax 02.47.23.90.51; ③), is very welcoming, with decent food on menus from 89F/€13.57. If these are all booked up, you could try *Le Cheval Blanc* at 5 place Charles-Bidault in **BLÉRÉ**, 5km downstream (☎02.47.30.30.14, fax 02.47.23.52.80; ④), a very pleasant place serving finely cooked meals (menus from 100F/€15.24), or the *Clair Cottage*, 27 av de l'Europe, at **CHISSEAUX** (☎02.47.23.90.69; ③), 2km east of Chenonceaux. For **camping**, there's *Le Moulin Fort* (☎02.47.23.86.22; closed Oct–March) in **FRANCEUIL**, south of the river.

Montrichard and around

If you're beginning to feel peeved that only dead royals had all the fun, take yourself to the Fraise-Or, 3km east of Chenonceaux, just beyond Chisseaux on the road to **MONTRICHARD**: it's an old-fashioned **distillery** (Easter–Sept daily 9–11.30am & 2–6pm; 17F/€2.59), complete with shiny copper stills, that specializes in fruit liqueurs. The visit includes a *dégustation* of three of their eighteen liqueurs and *eaux-de-vie*, based on various fruits, herbs, spices, nuts and, best of all, rose petals.

Montrichard itself is one of those laid-back market towns with its full complement of medieval and Renaissance buildings, plus a ruined **fortress**, of which just the keep remains. Its Romanesque **church** was where the disabled 12-year-old princess, Jeanne de Valois, who would never be able to have children, married her cousin the Duc d'Orléans, who subsequently became King Louis XII after the unlikely death of Charles VIII at Amboise. Politics dictated that he marry Charles VIII's widow, Anne of Brittany, so poor Jeanne was divorced and sent off to a nunnery in Bourges.

Three kilometres to the east of Montrichard, in **BOURRÉ**, are the quarries for the famous château-building stone that gets whiter as it weathers. Some of the caves are now used to cultivate mushrooms, a peculiar process that you can witness at the **Caves**

Champignonnières, 40 rte des Roches (guided visits daily April–Oct at 10am, 11am & hourly 2–5pm; 28F/€4.27).

Practicalities

Montrichard's **tourist office** is in the Maison Ave Maria (☎02.54.32.05.10, fax 02.54.23.75.29), an ancient house with saints and beasties sculpted down its beams, on rue du Pont. If the gentle pace of Montrichard takes your fancy, some **hotels** to try are *La Tête Noir*, 24 rue de Tours (☎02.54.32.05.55, fax 02.54.32.78.37; ③), by the river, or the cheaper *Hôtel de la Gare*, 20 av de la Gare (☎02.54.32.04.36, fax 02.54.32.78.17; ②). There's also a **campsite**, *L'Étourneau* (☎02.54.32.10.16; closed mid-Sept to May), on the banks of the Cher. You can rent **canoes** from the Club Nautique (☎02.54.71.49.49).

On the D17, the smaller of the two roads from Montrichard to St-Aignan (see below), between Angé and Pouillé, a good-value **restaurant**, *Le Bousquet*, serves simple meat dishes cooked over a charcoal grill and cheap jugs of local AOC wine in an old wine cellar (☎02.54.71.44.44; July & Aug Tues evening to Sun; rest of year Fri, weekends & hols only; menus from 85F/€12.96). There's also a pleasant *gîte d'étape*, offering home-cooked food, in the lock-keeper's house at Bourré, called the *Vallagon* (☎02.54.32.50.59). In **POUILLÉ**, on the N76, the *Auberge Le Bien-Allé* (☎02.54.71.47.45; closed Sun evening), in an attractive eighteenth-century country house overlooking the Cher, has similar fare, with menus starting at 88F/€13.41.

St-Aignan

ST-AIGNAN, 15km south of Montrichard, and a good stopover for cyclists, is a small town comprising a cluster of houses below a huge Romanesque collegiate church and sixteenth-century château. Its main sight is the **Collégiale de St-Aignan** (Mon–Sat 9am–8pm, Sun 1–8pm), which features some of the best ecclesiastical decoration in the region. Its capitals are adorned with mermaids, a multi-bodied snake biting its own necks, a man's head tunnelled by an eagle, doleful dragons and other wonders of the twelfth-century imagination, while in the crypt there are some very well-preserved, brightly coloured late twelfth-century frescoes.

St-Aignan lends itself to aimless wandering, with the **château grounds** accessible to the public and some pleasant walks down by the river – or a swim if you feel inclined. On the road bridge above the long island facing the town is the Maison du Vin, open for tastings and sales of Côteaux du Cher wines (July & Aug). On the mainland east of the bridge, at 21 quai J.-J.-Delorme, Promenades sur le Cher runs **boat trips** (departures 3pm & 5pm: April, June, Sept & Oct Sat, Sun & bank hols; July & Aug daily; ☎02.54.71.40.38; 55F/€8.38); or you can rent a **houseboat** (2100–2500F/€320–380 for four people for a weekend) and explore the Berry Canal, which joins the river at St-Aignan. At the Base Nautique Les Couflons, a couple of kilometres upstream in **SEIGY**, you can windsurf, canoe and sail. **Bikes** can be rented in town from Le Tandem, 54 rue Constant-Ragot.

For a good break from ancient aristocratic artefacts, St-Aignan has the **Zoo Parc de Beauval** (daily 9am–dusk; 62F/€9.45), 2km to the south of town on the D675. The space given to the animals is ample, and it's part of the European programme for breeding threatened species in captivity to reintroduce them to the wild. From a human viewpoint the park is very attractive, with sumptuous flower beds giving way to suitably wild areas of woods, little streams and lakes where the islands provide natural enclosures for some of the monkeys. Two hothouses with tropical flowers and greenery are home to an extraordinary collection of tropical birds and to a large group of chimpanzees and two families of orang-utans. But the creature most children will want to take home with them is the rare white tiger, in particular the ultimate fantasy cuddly pet, Katharina, the first cub to be bred in France.

Practicalities

The **tourist office** (☎02.54.75.22.85, fax 02.54.75.22.85) is on place President Wilson, which is essentially a car park. **Hotels** worth choosing from include *Le Moulin*, 7 rue Novilliers (☎02.54.75.15.54; ③; closed Sun), to the west of the bridge, with meals for only 55F/€8.38, or *Le Grand Hôtel St-Aignan*, 7–9 quai J.-J.-Delorme (☎02.54.75.18.04; ④; Nov–March closed Sun evening; menus from 85F/€12.96). Otherwise, you'll have to look for rooms in **NOYER-SUR-CHER** on the other side of the river. St-Aignan has an excellent **campsite**, near Seigy, the *Camping des Cochards* (☎02.54.75.15.59; April to mid-Sept).

St-Aignan has few **restaurants** and none of them is special. Besides the two hotels, you could try *Le Crêpiot*, 36 rue Constant-Ragot (☎02.54.75.21.39; closed Mon & Tues), with a terrace where you can eat grills, crêpes and so forth.

Valençay

There is nothing medieval about the fittings and furnishings of the **Château de Valençay**, 20km southeast of St-Aignan on the main Blois–Châteauroux road (mid-March to June & Sept to mid-Nov daily 10am–6pm; July & Aug daily 9am–7pm; rest of year weekends only 10am–12.30pm & 1.30–5pm; 40F/€6.10): this proud and overbearing castle was built to show off the wealth of a sixteenth-century financier. Two hundred and fifty years later it was used to illustrate the power of Napoléon's France, as residence of the empire's foreign minister, the Prince de Talleyrand. The contrast of eras is one of the chief interests of Valençay.

Inside the château there hangs a portrait of the minister, a great political operator and survivor, by François Bonneau. A bishop before the Revolution, with a reputation for having the most desirable mistresses, he proposed the nationalization of church property, renounced his bishopric, escaped to America during the Terror, backed Napoléon and continued to serve the state under the restored Bourbons. One of his tasks for the emperor was keeping Ferdinand VII of Spain entertained for six years here after the king had been forced to abdicate in favour of Napoléon's brother Joseph. The Treaty of Valençay, signed in the château in 1813, put an end to Ferdinand's forced guest status, giving him back his throne.

The interior consequently is largely First Empire, with elaborately embroidered chairs on spindly legs, Chinese vases, ornate inlays and studdings to all the tables, finicky clocks and chandeliers: in short, the sort of furnishings dominated by strict rules of etiquette. Some of the Renaissance period rooms, however, in which it's easier to imagine more passionate and rougher lifestyles, are now open to the public.

The château **park** (same hours as above; 8F/€1.22) keeps a collection of unhappy-looking camels, zebras, llamas and kangaroos, and there's also a **car museum** (same hours and ticket as the château), with pre-World War I Michelin maps and guides.

Blois and around

BLOIS, the former seat of the dukes of Orléans, is a handsome town with much character. Its biggest drawback is the modern town around the centre, and particularly the broad, fast-moving boulevard that rings its **château** as if it were a mere traffic island rather than a sensational piece of architecture. There are, however, plenty of places around place Victor-Hugo that offer excellent views of the exterior of the building, Italian loggias and all, and it's worth braving the traffic for the pleasure of a non-guided visit around rooms steeped in power and intrigue.

If you want to get out into the countryside, head for one of the several stretches of woodland around Blois, which include the **Forêt de Blois** to the west of the town on the north bank of the Loire, the **Parc de Chambord** and the **Forêt de Boulogne**, around the Château de Chambord, further upstream. And if you haven't yet tired of châteaux, you have a choice of several fine examples within easy reach of the town.

Arrival, information and accommodation

Blois is easy to get around: avenue Jean-Laigret is the main street leading south from the **gare SNCF** to place Victor-Hugo and the château, and past it to the town centre. The **gare routière** is directly in front of the gare SNCF, with **buses** leaving several times a day for Cheverny and Chambord (mid-June to mid-Sept; 65F/€9.91). The **tourist office**, set back from the road at 3 av Jean-Laigret (April–Sept Mon–Sat 9am–12.30pm & 2–7pm, Sun 10.30am–12.30pm & 4.30–7pm; Oct–March Mon–Sat 9.15am–noon & 2–6pm; ☎02.54.90.41.41, fax 02.54.90.41.49), organizes hotel rooms for a small fee and changes money; during summer it has information desks open in the pedestrian precinct and place du Château (July & Aug daily 10am–7pm). Regional information is available online at *www.chambordcountry.com*. **Bikes** can be rented from Cycles Leblond, 44 Levée des Tuileries (☎02.54.74.30.13) or Ets Bucquet, 33 av Wilson (☎02.54.78.12.94).

Hotels worth trying are the inexpensive and well-maintained *St-Jacques*, 7 rue Ducoux (☎02.54.78.04.15, fax 02.54.78.33.05; ①), near the train station; *À la Ville de Tours*, 2 place de la Grève (☎02.54.78.07.86, fax 02.54.56.87.33; ②), overlooking the river, with a well-priced restaurant below serving traditional cuisine (menus at 75F/€11.43 and 99F/€15.09); and the *Hôtel du Bellay*, 12 rue des Minimes (☎02.54.78.23.62, fax 02.54.78.52.04; ②). *Le Savoie*, across the street from the *St-Jacques* at 6 rue Ducoux (☎02.54.74.32.21, fax 02.54.74.29.58; ③), is more appealing, but if you want somewhere classy, consider the *Mercure*, 28 quai St-Jean (☎02.54.56.66.66, fax 02.54.56.67.00, *mercure-blois@wanadoo.fr*, ⑤), overlooking the river to the east of the town centre. Blois' **HI hostel**, 18 rue de l'Hôtel-Pasquier (☎02.54.78.27.21, *blois@fuaj.org*; March to mid-Nov), is further out at Les Grouets, 5km downstream, between the Forêt de Blois and the river; take bus #4, direction "Les Grouets", stop "Auberge". The town's **campsite** is across the river 2km from the town centre on the Lac de Loire at Vineuil (☎02.54.74.22.78; bus #3C, stop "Mairie Vineuil"), and it offers bike rental.

The château

All six kings of the sixteenth century spent time at the **Château de Blois** (daily: mid-March to Nov 9am–6pm; rest of year 9am–noon & 2–5pm; 35F/€3.34), and in the early nineteenth century it was given to Louis XVIII's brother to keep him away from Paris. Hence the courtiers' mansions that fill the town and, given its earlier non-royal owner-ships, the château's architectural montage of distinct, unmatching wings – medieval, Gothic, Renaissance and Classical. Much of the château can be visited, from its oldest part – the thirteenth-century manorial assembly hall of the Salle des États – to the Flamboyant Gothic east wing of Louis XII and the Italianate north wing of François I, with its double loggias and gallery, and the great staircase with the spiralling balconies and its windows not quite in alignment.

The Blois horror story is the murder by Henri III of the Duc de Guise and his broth-er, the cardinal of Lorraine, the perpetrators of the summary execution of Huguenots at Amboise (see p.494). The king had summoned the States-General to a meeting in the Grande Salle, only to find that an overwhelming majority supported the Duke, along with the stringing up of Protestants, and aristocratic rather than royal power. He panicked and had de Guise ambushed and hacked to death in a corridor of the palace. The cardinal was murdered in prison the next day. Their deaths were avenged a year later when a monk assassinated the king himself. The château was also home to Henri III's mother and manipulator, Catherine de Médicis, who died here a few days after the murders in 1589. The most famous of her suite of rooms is the study, where, according to Alexander Dumas, she kept poison hidden in secret caches in the skirting boards and behind some of the 237 narrow carved wooden panels. In the nineteenth century, revolutionaries were tried in the Grande Salle for conspiring to assassinate Napoléon III, a year before the Paris Commune of 1870.

Otherwise, the interior of the château is wonderfully colourful, or dreadfully garish if you're a purist, thanks to the mid-nineteenth-century restoration. The floors have intricate designs in tiling or parquet, walls are painted with repeating patterns, and the arches, pillars and fireplaces of the superb Salle des États are a riot of colour. Two ornamental regal emblems recur ostentatiously: the porcupine in Louis XII's wing and the salamander in that of François I.

In addition, the château houses three small **museums**: the **Beaux-Arts**, with plenty of regal portraits and a rather good collection of forged ironwork, including locks and keys; a set of seventeenth-century **sculptures** in white Loire tufa, rescued from many of the neighbouring châteaux before their detail weathered away; and an **archeological collection**, with several fine examples of Merovingian and Carolingian glass and ceramics.

Finally, it's worth visiting the extraordinary **church of St Nicholas**, just below the château on rue St-Laumen. Though altered greatly over the centuries, for the most part it is a stunning example of twelfth-century church architecture.

Eating and drinking

There are plenty of cheap **eating** places around Blois' town centre: rue St-Lubin, rue des Violettes and rue Foulérie are good streets to try. *La Garbure*, 36 rue St-Lubin (☎02.54.74.32.89; closed Wed & Sat lunch), serves specialities from the Périgord and Gascogne regions for under 100F/€15.24 – the *garbure*, a filling duck soup, is excellent; *La Tocade*, 9–11 rue Chant-des-Oiseaux, is a popular brasserie with good-value set menus for as little as 65F/€9.91; and, for straightforward meat grills, the friendly *La Forge*, 18 rue du Bourg-Neuf (☎02.54.74.43.45; from 100F/€15.24), is a good option. A more upmarket restaurant is *Au Rendez-Vous des Pêcheurs*, 27 rue Foix (☎02.54.74.67.48; closed Sun & Mon lunch), with delicious fish dishes, especially the salmon, and a menu for around 150F/€22.87.

Around Blois

On the south bank of the river, within a twenty-kilometre radius south and east of Blois, are a handful of impressive and easily visited **châteaux** (information online at *www.loiredeschateaux.com*). By car you could call at all of them in a couple of days, but they also make ideal cycling or walking targets if you arm yourself with a map and strike out along minor roads and woodland rides. Of the two most imposing examples, Chaumont has frequent daily trains from Blois (Onzain *gare SNCF* on the other side of the river), but Chambord is reachable by public transport only on the expensive châteaux tour buses that leave from Blois, Tours or Amboise – it does, however, make a flat, beautiful cycle ride from Blois. The cheapest tour **bus trips** leave Blois from the *gare SNCF* (mid-June to mid-Sept), with two itineraries: Chaumont–Chenonceau–Amboise (110F/€16.77) and Chambord–Cheverny (65F/€9.91); tickets are available from the tourist office in Blois, and prices are exclusive of entry fee.

Château de Chaumont

Catherine de Médicis forced Diane de Poitiers to hand over Chenonceau on the Cher (see p.479) in return for the **Château de Chaumont** (daily: mid-March to late Oct 9.30am–6pm; rest of year 10am–4.30pm; 32F/€4.88; grounds open daily 9am–dusk; free), 20km downstream from Blois. Diane got a bad deal, but this is still one of the more fascinating châteaux.

Chaumont started life as a Gothic fortress – complete with towers, moat and draw-bridge – defending the river and valley below, but during the Renaissance, the carcass of the building was dressed up with Renaissance frippery. The wings you see today form three sides of a square, the fourth side having been demolished in 1739 to improve views over the river, which are spectacular. Chaumont's interior, unlike those of many Loire châteaux, is furnished in an early nineteenth-century style which, combined with its unkempt air, gives it a surprisingly homely feel. Look out for the tiled floor with its depictions of hunting scenes, and a copy of a sixteenth-century portrait of the young Catherine de Médicis in the Salles des Fêtes, on the first floor.

More interesting than anything inside the château, however, are the remarkable Belle Époque **stables**, with their porcelain troughs and elegant electric lamps for the benefit of the horses at a time before the château itself was wired – let alone the rest of the country. The best way to get a further feel of the château's equestrian character is to rent a horse or a pony and trap, available in the château grounds (☎02.54.20.90.60; daily May–Oct; rest of year daily except Tues).

Château de Cheverny

Fifteen kilometres southeast of Blois, the **Château de Cheverny** (daily: April & May 9.15am–noon & 2.15–6.30pm; June to mid-Sept 9.15am–6.45pm; mid-Sept to March 9.30am–noon & 2.15–5/5.30/6.30pm; *www.chateau-cheverny.fr*; 35F/€4.88) is the perfect example of a seventeenth-century château. Built between 1604 and 1634 and never altered, it presents an immaculate picture of symmetry and harmony. The stone, from Bourré on the River Cher (see p.481), from which it is built, lightens with age, so the château looks as if it were whitewashed yesterday. Its interior decoration has only been added to, never destroyed: the display of paintings, furniture, tapestries and armour against the gilded, sculpted and carved walls and ceilings is extremely impressive. Some highlights are the painted wall panels in the dining room telling stories from *Don Quixote*; the lily, daffodil and iris motifs in the Salles des Gardes; the bindings of the books in the library; and the embroidered Persian silk canopy on the king's bed.

The château is still lived in by a descendant of the original owner, whose **deer-hunting expeditions** every Tuesday and Saturday from October to March are something of a spectacle. Tourists are bused in to watch the local aristos tie their silk cravats while huntsmen sound their horns and the hounds mill around. There's a room full of deer-head trophies, and even the feeding of the animals is turned into an event. The **son et lumière** every Saturday evening at 10pm from mid-July to August is also dedicated to the hunting theme.

Near Cheverny you can **stay** at the elegant, rustic *Hôtel des Trois Marchands* (☎02.54.79.96.44, fax 02.54.79.25.60, *www.hoteldes3marchands.com*; ②), in **COUR CHEVERNY**, Cheverny's larger neighbour; the hotel's **restaurant** is not bad at all, with menus from 100F/€15.24. Another good place to eat is *Le Pousse Rapière* in Cheverny (☎02.54.79.94.23). There's a **campsite** on the D102 in Cheverny (☎02.54.79.90.01, *campsaules@aol.com*), and another on rue de Poussard in Cour Cheverny (☎02.54.79.95.63).

Château de Fougères

The grim, medieval **Château de Fougères** (April–Sept daily 9am–noon & 2–6pm; Oct–March daily except Tues 10am–noon & 2–4.30pm; 25F/€3.81) provides a good contrast to Cheverny. It lies in the village of **FOUGÈRES-SUR-BIÈVRE**, 10km south-west of Cheverny, and was built in 1470 by Louis XI's chancellor, who was clearly sceptical about long-term peace. It is a veritable fortress, with spiky towers and the theme of war running through the building, with sculptured soldiers and battle scenes above arches and on door lintels and chimneys. Come the sixteenth century – here as elsewhere – Italianate windows were fashioned onto former blank walls and steep roofs, but it still looks as if it expects an attack and is concealing its defences as a tactic. It could hardly be a more peaceful place now, and is rarely overrun with visitors.

Château de Beauregard

A cyclable ride from Blois, the relatively little-visited **Château de Beauregard**, 7km south of Blois on the D956 to Contres (April–June & Sept daily 9.30am–noon & 2–6.30pm; July & Aug daily 9.30am–6.30pm; rest of year daily except Wed 9.30–noon & 2–5pm; closed first three weeks Dec & first week Feb; 40F/€6.10), lies amid the Forêt de Russy. It was – like Chambord – one of François I's hunting lodges, but its transformation in the sixteenth century involved beautification rather than aggrandizement. It was added to in the seventeenth century; the result is a restrained – by Loire standards – and serene white building, very much at ease in its manicured geometric park.

The highlight of the château is a richly decorated **portrait gallery**, whose floor of Delft tiling depicts an army on the march. The 363 paintings of kings, queens and their cohorts are arranged by reign, beginning with Philippe VI at the start of the Hundred Years War and ending with Louis XIII, who inherited the throne in 1610; also included are some characters, like Rabelais, who were not directly involved with the shifty-eyed monarchs and their power-brokers. The paintings are gradually being restored, often revealing other portraits beneath in the process.

Château de Chambord

The **Château de Chambord**, François I's little "hunting lodge", is the largest of the Loire châteaux (daily: April–June, Sept & Oct 9am–6.15pm; July & Aug 9am–6.45pm; Nov–March 9am–5.15pm; 40F/€6.10) and one of the most extravagant commissions of its age. Its patron's principal object – to outshine the Holy Roman Emperor Charles V – would, he claimed, leave him renowned as "one of the greatest builders in the universe", and the result is undoubtedly impressive. The palace has over 440 rooms and is surrounded by 34km of wall; its construction even involved diverting the Loire to accommodate the grand plan.

The Italian architect Domenico de Cortona was chosen to design the château in 1519 in an effort to introduce prestigious Italian Renaissance art forms to France, but the labour was supplied by French masons; hence the result is essentially French medieval – the massive round towers, with their conical tops, and the explosion of chimneys, pinnacles and turrets on the roof bring to mind Flamboyant Gothic. The details, however, are pure Italian: the Great Staircase (attributed by some to da Vinci), panels of coloured marble, niches decorated with shell-like domes, and free-standing columns. Wandering through, you can get a good feel for the contrasting architectural styles, which have combined to create a very decadent, if at times discordant, whole.

The building has its fans, though for many its mix of styles makes it the single ugliest building in the Loire – except perhaps for the nuclear power station at St-Laurent-des-Eaux, just to the north. Visits are unguided, and there's plenty of entertainment to be had from roaming around inside – up and down the double spiral staircase (devised so courtiers could ascend and descend without meeting up on the steps) around the spectacular chimneys and through endless rooms and corridors.

The **Parc de Chambord** around the château is an enormous walled game reserve – the largest in Europe – red deer being the main beast you're likely to spot. You can explore on foot, bike or on horseback, with mounts rented from the Centre Equestre near the château (☎02.54.20.31.01).

Accommodation in the village of **CHAMBORD** itself can be found at the *Hôtel Le St-Michel* (☎02.54.20.31.31, fax 02.54.20.36.40; ④), which has direct views of the château. In **BRACIEUX**, a small village just beyond the southern wall of the Parc de Chambord, 8km from the château, there are the pleasant little *Hôtel de la Bonnheure*, 9bis rue R.-Masson (☎02.54.46.41.57, fax 02.54.46.05.90; ③), and the *Hôtel du Cygne*, 20 rue R-Brun (☎02.54.46.41.07, fax 02.54.46.04.87; ④). There's also a **campsite** in the village (☎02.54.46.41.84).

Tours and around

Chief town of the Loire valley and capital of the Touraine region, **TOURS** has long had a reputation as a staid, bourgeois city. An English travel writer wrote in 1913:

> *Tours has an immense air of good breeding . . . you have visions of portentously dull entertainments in lofty gilded saloons where everything is rather icily magnificent.*

It is a reputation that Tours doesn't really deserve: it's a bustling urban centre, only an hour's journey from Paris on the TGV line, with a great many restaurants, bars and cafés, and, thanks to the student population, a lively nightlife. These factors, together with the building of a new conference centre, have brought an influx of business people and young commuters into an already large and fairly diverse population. It has a prettified and fairly animated **old quarter**, some good **museums** – of wine, crafts, stained glass and an above-average Beaux-Arts museum – and a great many fine buildings, not least of which is **St Gatien's cathedral**. And if you don't have your own transport, it's the obvious Touraine base, with both bus and train connections to a snatch of notable châteaux – **Villandry**, **Langeais**, **Azay-le-Rideau** and **Amboise** – as well as the celebrated wine-producing towns of **Vouvray** and **Bourgeuil**.

Arrival, information and accommodation

The **gare routière** and **gare SNCF** are situated a short way southeast of the cathedral district, and face the mammoth "hypercentre" that shelters the Centre International de Congrès. Some trains, including most TGVs, stop at **St-Pierre-des-Corps**, an industrial estate outside the city. Frequent shuttles link the two stations (about 8min) or you can take bus #2 or #3 from St-Pierre-des-Corps to place Jean-Jaurès (15min). The huge and excellent **tourist office** is close by, on the corner of rue Bernard-Palissy and boulevard Heuteloup (May–Sept Mon–Sat 8.30am–6.30pm, Sun 10am–1pm & 3–6pm; Oct–April Mon–Sat 9am–12.30pm & 1.30–6pm, Sun 10am–1pm; ☎02.47.70.37.37, fax 02.47.61.14.22, *www.ligeris.com*), and sells a **museum pass** (*carte multi-visites*; 50F/€7.62) that lets you into eight major sites, including the Musée des Beaux-Arts and the Musée du Gemmail. Information on Tours and the surrounding region can be found online at *www.tourism-touraine.com*.

Hotels

au Chien Jaune, 74 rue B. Palissy, (☎02.47.05.10.17). A charming, friendly hotel-brasserie near the train station, with basic clean rooms upstairs. ①.

du Manoir, 2 rue Traversière, cnr rue J.-Simon (☎02.47.05.37.37, fax 02.47.05.16.00). A converted nineteenth-century town house offering exceptional service. ③.

Mon Hôtel, 40 rue de la Préfecture (☎02.47.05.25.36, fax 02.47.66.08.72). Clean and comfortable cheapie near the cathedral, with small rooms. ②.

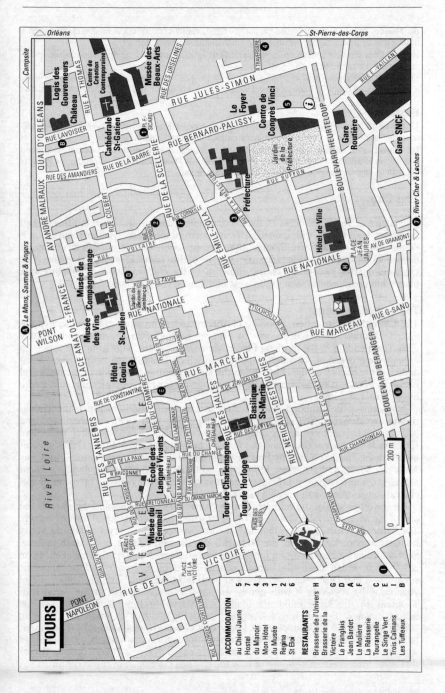

du Musée, 2 place François-Sicard (☎02.47.66.63.81, fax 02.47.20.10.42). A quiet and unassuming hotel, right by the cathedral, overlooking a small public flower garden. ③.

Regina, 2 rue Pimbert (☎02.47.05.25.36, fax 02.47.61.12.72). Large, old hotel with good-sized rooms at a reasonable price. ②.

St-Éloi, 79 bd Béranger (☎02.47.37.67.34, fax 02.47.39.34.67). Excellent-value, intimate hotel run by a friendly young couple. All rooms have TV. Booking is advisable. 50F/€7.62 dinner available. ①.

Hostels

Le Foyer, 16 rue Bernard-Palissy (☎02.47.60.51.51). A recently renovated workers' hostel and cafeteria that sometimes has rooms available for under-25s. Closed Sat afternoon & Sun.

HI hostel, av d'Arsonval (☎02.47.25.14.45). Hostel located in Parc de Grandmont. Reception 5–9/10pm; late-night key available with deposit. Take bus #6 or #2 from place Jean-Jaurès towards Chambray, stop "Auberge de Jeunesse". Closed Dec & Jan.

The City

The centre of Tours lies between the Loire and its tributary, the Cher, but has spread far across both banks, with industrial Tours north of the Loire. Neither river is a particular feature of the town, though there are parks on islands in both rivers and a newish footbridge across the Loire from the site of the old castle on quai d'Orléans. The city's old quarter focuses not on the cathedral or the château, but on the picturesque place Plumereau, some 600m to the west of the main rue Nationale.

The cathedral quarter

The **Cathédrale St-Gatien**, standing on the square of the same name, illustrates the entire evolution of Gothic designs in France, starting with the thirteenth-century chevet and ending in the glorious Flamboyant Gothic of the west front and towers, a mesmerizing overdose of sculpted pattern to which Renaissance belfries have been added as the cherry on the cake. When the sun is shining, the inside of the cathedral becomes a magical kaleidoscope, with the stained-glass windows projecting neat, multihued shards of colour.

Just south of the cathedral, housed in the former archbishop's palace, is the **Musée des Beaux-Arts** (daily except Tues 9am–12.45pm & 2–6pm; free), overshadowed by a 200-year-old Lebanon cedar. The museum has some beauties in its rambling collection: *Christ in the Garden of Olives* and the *Resurrection* by Mantegna; Frans Hals's portrait of Descartes; Balzac painted by Boulanger; prints of *The Five Senses* by the Tourainais Abraham Bosse; and a sombre Monet. Its top treasure, however, Rembrandt's *Flight into Egypt*, is unfortunately difficult to see through the security glass. The roster of special exhibits is also worth keeping an eye out for.

On the other side of the cathedral, between rue Albert-Thomas and the river, is the site of the ancient royal **château** of Tours, of which just two medieval towers remain. The **Tour de Guise**, now embedded in the seventeenth-century Pavillon de Mars, houses a waxworks museum, the **Historial de Touraine** (daily: mid-March to June, Sept & Oct 9am–noon & 2–6pm; July & Aug 9am–6.30pm; Nov to mid-March 2–5.30pm; 35F/€5.33), which makes the various courtly murders, marriages and machinations seem like a bad Disney cartoon. You can push mock-medieval French history out of your mind by replacing it with gently waving multicoloured fish in the **Aquarium Tropical** in the same buildings (daily: mid-March to June & Sept to mid-Nov 9.30am–noon & 2–6pm; July & Aug 9.30am–7pm; mid-Nov to mid-March 2–6pm; 30F/€5.34). In the fifteenth-century **Logis des Gouverneurs** alongside (mid-March to mid-Dec Wed & Sat 3–6.30pm; free), across the remnants of the city's Gallo-Roman wall, there's an exhibition of historical artefacts called "Vivre à Tours" (Life in Tours) that gives quite a plausible sense of how the city has developed over the centuries.

The old quarter

The old part of Tours crowds around **place Plumereau**, over to the west of rue Nationale. Between the two, the **Hôtel Gouin**, 25 rue du Commerce, has a Renaissance facade to stop you in your tracks. Inside, it exhibits a surprising collection for an archeological museum, including a medicine chest belonging to Jean-Jacques Rousseau, and examples of early technical advances in physics, such as the Archimedes screw and a vacuum pump (mid-May to Sept daily 10am–7pm; Oct to mid-March daily except Fri 10am–12.30pm & 2–5.30pm; rest of year daily 10am–12.30pm & 2–6.30pm; 20F/€3.05).

But it's the old town's half-timbered houses and bulging stairway towers dating from the twelfth to fifteenth centuries that are the city's showpiece. Some of the earlier buildings look like cut-out models, but the Renaissance stone-and-brick constructions are sturdier – particularly the **Écoles des Langues Vivantes** on rue Briconnet, with its wonderful sculpted dogs, drunks, frogs and monsters. West of rue Bretonneau, around place Robert-Picou, modern artisans' workshops cluster between medieval dwellings.

Off rue Briconnet, at 7 rue du Mûrier, you'll find the **Musée du Gemmail** (mid-March to mid-Oct Tues–Sun 10am–noon & 2–6.30pm; 30F/€4.57), a museum of non-leaded stained glass. Some of the works are displayed in an underground twelfth-century chapel, and artists include such leading artists as Picasso and Jean Cocteau. Their works shine with an extraordinary intensity and, through the use of layering, have a far greater colour range than traditional stained glass.

To the south, an enormous church once stood, with its nave stretching along rue des Halles from rue des Trois-Pavées-Ronds almost to place de Châteauneuf. Only the north tower, the Tour de Charlemagne, and the western clock tower remain of the ancient **Basilique de St-Martin**. The new church, a late nineteenth-century neo-Byzantine affair, guards the shrine of St Martin, bishop of Tours in the fourth century and famous for giving half his cloak to a freezing beggar.

Around rue Nationale

At the head of **rue Nationale**, Tours' main street, statues of Descartes and Rabelais overlook the Loire. A short walk back from the river and you come to the **church of St Julien**, whose old monastic buildings are home to two of the town's most compelling museums.

The **Musée de Compagnonnage** is housed in the eleventh-century guesthouse and sixteenth-century monks' dormitory at 8 rue Nationale (mid-June to mid-Sept daily 9am–6.30pm; rest of year daily except Tues 9am–noon & 2–5/6pm; 25F/€3.81). Here, for once, the people who built – rather than ordered – the châteaux and cathedrals are celebrated. In addition to documents of the origins and militant activity of the *compagnonnage* (the guilds), you can see masterpieces (in the original sense of the term) of various crafts, from cake-making and carpentry to locksmithery and bricklaying, with their relevant tools exhibited alongside.

The **Musée des Vins** in the twelfth-century cellars of the abbey at 16 rue Nationale (daily except Tues 9am–noon & 2–6pm; 15F/€2.29) takes you through a comprehensive treatment of the history, mythology and production of wine, though there's nothing on recent technical innovations and no quaffing to look forward to. Behind the museum, a Gallo-Roman winepress from Cheillé sits in the former cloisters of the church.

If you take a left into rue Colbert and right into rue Jules-Favre, you can wander into the **Jardin de Beaune-Semblançay**, whose sixteenth-century fountain stands in front of the sad facade of the mansion that belonged to François I's finance minister. Back on rue Colbert, at no. 39, is the house where Joan of Arc is said to have had her suit of armour made.

Eating and drinking

Place Plumereau is set out with the tables of expensive **cafés** and **restaurants**; the bars in this area can be overpriced but many have a lot of character. The most promising restaurant streets are rue du Grand-Marché and rue de la Rôtisserie, on the periphery of old Tours, and rue du Commerce and rue Colbert. Sugar and chocolate freaks should make a detour to **pâtisseries** like La Marotte, 3 rue du Change, and La Chocolatière, 6 rue de la Scellerie. The main **market** halls are to the west of St-Martin at the end of rue des Halles.

Académie de la Bière, 43 rue Lavoisier. A serious establishment near the cathedral for those dedicated to good ale; you can choose from among 200 types of beer while playing darts.

Brasserie de l'Univers, 8 place Jean-Jaurès (☎02.47.05.50.92). Big and beautiful Belle Époque brasserie with its original painted glass. Grilled meat and fish, pizzas and menus from 85F/€12.96. Service till midnight.

Brasserie de la Victoire, place de la Victoire. Simple brasserie in one of the less touristy squares. *Moules frites* for 55F/€8.38.

Au Chien Jaune, 74 rue B. Palissy (☎02.47.05.10.17). Serves simple good food. Menus at 75F/€11.43 and 98F/€14.94.

Le Franglais, 27 rue Colbert. This bar-cum-restaurant serves up enormous plates of meat with chips and salad for 60F/€9.15, including wine. The owner and cook is English, which explains the name, but the cuisine is decidedly French.

Jean Bardet, 57 rue Groison (☎02.47.41.41.11). Tours' top restaurant and one of the best in France. Extremely sophisticated, health-conscious food with a minimum of butter and cream and a maximum of rare herbs and old varieties of vegetables. 500F/€76.22 à la carte, and fixed menus from 250F/€38.11.

Le Molière, cnr rue de la Scellerie & rue Cornielle. Directly in front of the Grand Théâtre, this vast Belle Époque café has faded frescoes and a relaxed atmosphere.

La Rôtisserie Tourangelle, 23 rue du Commerce (☎02.47.05.71.21). Salmon pancakes, beef from Chinon, guinea fowl and other goodies, and excellent-value menus from 95F/€14.48. Closed Sun evening & Mon.

Le Singe Vert, 5 rue Marceau (☎02.47.20.02.76). Another Belle Époque brasserie with lunchtime menus from 68F/€10.37. Open till midnight.

Trois Caïmans, 91 rue Jules-Charpentier (☎02.47.37.71.26). Senegalese-African restaurant serving specialities such as *brochette d'antilope* and *chèvre yassa* (goat in onion and lime sauce). 65F/€9.91 and 95F/€14.48 menus. Closed Sun & Mon.

Les Tuffeaux, 19 rue Lavoisier (☎02.47.47.19.89). An attractive setting for delicious classic cuisine; menus from 110F/€16.77. Closed Sun & Mon lunch.

Nightlife

Nightlife in Tours is a lot more promising than in other Loire towns, with a fairly impressive selection of nightclubs, bars and cabaret-cafés. You can pick up a free copy of the **listings magazine** *Tours Cultures*, which gives day-by-day details of musical and cultural events for the entire summer, from the tourist office or the Maison des Associations Culturelles, 5 place Plumereau (☎02.47.20.71.95).

Clubs worth visiting include *Labo*, 18 rue de la Longue-Échelle, off place du Grand-Marché (free admission, drink obligatory), a café-club open from 6pm to 4am with disco music on Friday and a gay night on Sunday, and *L'Excalibur*, in a vaulted cellar at 35 rue Briçonnet (daily 11pm–4am; admission Mon–Fri 60F/€9.15, Sat & Sun 70F/€10.67), which caters for smart young clubbers. **Cafés with shows** include the popular *Petit Faucheaux*, 23 rue des Cerisiers, best known for jazz but also featuring comedians, darts, cards and chess at any time, and *Le Vieux Mûrier* on place Plumereau, with live music and an amazing decor of diverse objects. For **gigs**, try *Le Bateau Ivre*, 146 rue Édouard-Vaillant (☎02.47.44.77.22), to the south of the *gare SNCF*, where top British and American rap/reggae/hip-hop bands play (entry 50–100F/€7.62–15.24), or *Les 3 Orfèvres*, 6 rue des Orfèvres (☎02.47.64.02.73).

Listings

Bike rental Amster Cycles, 5 rue de Rempart; Grammont Motocycles, 93 av de Grammont. Both closed Mon.

Books English books from 2 rue du Commerce and 20 rue Marceau.

Car rental Avis, gare de Tours (☎02.47.49.21.49); Budget, 2 place de la Gare (☎02.47.46.21.21); Europcar, 76 rue Bernard-Palissy (☎02.47.64.47.76); Hertz, 57 rue Marcel Tribune (☎02.47.75.50.00).

Châteaux tours Service Touristiques de Touraine, *gare SNCF* (☎02.47.05.46.09); Tour Évasion, 19 rue Édouard-Vaillant (☎02.47.63.25.64). Tours from 100F/€15.24 (exclusive of entrance fees).

Cinema Les Studios, 2 rue des Urselines (☎02.47.20.27.00), shows the arty, obscure and old favourites in their original language.

City transport Bus tickets: flat fare of 6.50F/€0.99 for an hour's journey. Route map from SEMI-TRAT on rue de la Dolve near place Jean-Jaurès.

Exchange In the *gare SNCF*, or 24hr automatic change machine on the wall of the Vinci centre on rue Bernard-Palissy. Most banks are on (or close to) place Jean-Jaurès.

Internet *Le Café*, 39 rue Bretonneau (Mon–Fri 11am–2am, Sat & Sun 4.30pm–2am; ☎02.47.61.37.83).

Laundries 21–23 place Michelet; 56 rue du Grand-Marché; 45 rue Georges-Courteline.

Medical assistance SOS Médecins (☎02.47.38.33.33); SAMU (☎15); Hôpital Bretonneau, 2 bd Tonnelé (☎02.47.47.47.47); late-night pharmacy, phone police for address.

Police 70–72 rue Marceau (☎02.47.60.70.69).

Poste restante 1 bd Béranger, Tours, France 37000.

Taxis Groupement Taxis Radio Tours (☎02.47.20.30.40).

Vouvray

The main reason to visit **VOUVRAY**, 10km east of Tours (bus #61) on the north bank, is for its wines, though it has its own charm in the villagey centre clustered around its thirteenth-century **church**. Vouvray's wonderful **Foire aux Vins** takes place from August 11 to 15. The **tourist office** at the Hôtel de Ville (April–Oct Mon–Sat 9am–1pm & 2–6.30pm, Sun 9am–1pm; rest of year Tues, Wed & Sat 9am–1pm, Fri 9am–1pm & 2–5pm; ☎02.47.52.68.73) can provide addresses of **vignerons**, and information on guided tours, but all the roads leading up the steep valleys are lined with *caves*. The view of the vines from the top of the hill is almost intoxicating in itself.

If you decide to **stay** in Vouvray, try the pleasant *Grand Veatel*, at 8 av Brulé (☎02.47.52.70.32, fax 02.47.52.74.52; ②; closed March 1–15). There's also a **campsite** between the Loire and the Cisse (☎02.47.52.68.81).

Amboise

Twenty kilometres upstream of Tours, **AMBOISE** is a prim little town trading on long-gone splendours, its one saving grace being Leonardo da Vinci's residence of Clos-Lucé and its mind-expanding exhibition on the great man's works. It is also one of Mick Jagger's favourite foreign residences – perhaps because few people recognize him here.

The one concession to twentieth-century art in Amboise is a **fountain** by Max Ernst of a turtle topped by a teddy bear (or ET figure), standing in front of the spot where the **market** takes place every Saturday and Sunday morning by the riverside. Behind, rising above the river, are the interesting remains of the **Château** where Charles VIII was born and died (daily 40min guided tours in French: April–June, Sept & Oct 9am–6pm; July & Aug 9am–7.30pm; Nov–March 9am–noon & 2–5pm; 40F/€6.10). It was in the late fifteenth century that Charles VIII decided to turn the old castle of his childhood days into a vast, extravagant and luxurious palace. Not long after the work was completed, he managed to hit his head, fatally, on a door lintel. The château continued to be enlarged under Louis XII and François I, but later wars and lack of finance have left less than half the total standing.

The **Tour des Minimes**, the original fifteenth-century entrance, is architecturally the most exciting part of the castle, designed for the maximum number of fully armoured men on horseback to get in and out as quickly as possible. From the top you step out onto the roof, with the Loire presenting one of its best panoramas. Before you've had time to orientate yourself, the guide launches into the story of how the hooks along the battlements were once smeared with the blood and guts of rebellious Huguenots. Caught plotting to get rid of the Catholic de Guise family, the power behind young François II, they were summarily tried in the Salle des Conseils and their corpses hung around the town.

The last French king, Louis-Philippe, also stayed in the château, hence the abrupt switch from solid Gothic furnishings to 1830s post-First Empire style. People imprisoned in the castle include Louis XIV's finance minister, Fouquet, of Vaux-le-Vicomte fame (see p.203), and, in the mid-nineteenth century, Abd el-Kader, an Algerian Resistance leader who spent fifteen years fighting against the French. A striking portrait of him hangs in the château.

A man of far greater renown today than any of the French kings was invited here by François I to bolster and encourage the French Renaissance: **Leonardo da Vinci** made his home at the **Clos-Lucé**, at the end of rue Victor-Hugo (daily 9am–6pm, July & Aug till 8pm; closed Jan; 38F/€5.79), now a museum to Leonardo and his work, with some forty models of his inventions, constructed according to his detailed plans. It's wonderful to see the mechanical manifestations of his technological achievements, but even the best model – the wooden tank – does not have the same effect as Leonardo's sketch. Leonardo died here in 1519.

A contrast to Leonardo's output is the **Musée de la Poste** in the Hôtel Joyeuse, 6 rue Joyeuse (Tues–Sun: April–Sept 9.30am–noon & 2–6.30pm; Oct–March 10am–noon & 2–5.30pm; 20F/€3.05), whose exhibits trace the history of the postal delivery service, from the pony express to air and sea mail.

If you take the main road south out of Amboise and turn right just before the junction with the D31, you'll come to a very unlikely building in this land of châteaux. It's an eighteenth-century **pagoda** that once formed part of a château. You can climb to the top for fabulous views and also explore the grounds of the surrounding park (daily: March–May & Oct 10am–noon & 2–5pm; June & Sept 10am–7pm; July & Aug 9.30am–8pm; 28F/€4.27).

Close to the château on rue Victor-Hugo, you'll find the **Caveau de Dégustation-Vente des Vins de Touraine Amboise** (June–Aug daily 10am–7.30pm), a good place to try some wines if you haven't got time to visit individual vineyards. Amboise celebrates its wines in a **Foire aux Vins** on August 15. And if you're heading towards Chenonceaux, you'll pass a farmhouse by a crossroads and a petrol station some 4.5km out from Amboise on the D81. Here, M. Delecheneau sells his *sec* and *demi-sec* white wine and sublime *demi-sec* rosé across the kitchen table. He'll show you his barrels, named after cows (Dauphine, Jolie, Violette, etc), and the winepress his grandfather used.

A group of **museums for children** has just opened to the east of Amboise on the D751: the Mini-Châteaux, Aquarium de Touraine and Le Fou de l'Âne (daily: May–Oct 9am–7pm, July & Aug till midnight; 42F/€6.10). Of the three, the first is the best, featuring two hectares of tiny replicas of the Loire châteaux.

WINE AND CHEESE OF TOURAINE

The food markets and vineyards of this fertile, affluent area of the Loire are famous. Chinon, Vouvray and Bourgueil have exceptional **wines**; the early ripening of fruits and vegetables, including asparagus, makes it clear that this is a different climate to northern France.

Vouvray is the *appellation* for one of the most delicious white wines of the Loire. A good vintage lives to be a hundred years old, can be *sec, demi-sec* or *pétillant* (lightly sparkling) and is best from the grape of a single vineyard. The other two famous Touraine *appellations* are **Chinon**, with mostly red wines and also a few very dry whites, and **Bourgueil**, renowned for its long-maturing red wine, but also producing a few dry rosés. Other *appellations* are **St-Nicholas de Bourgueil**, which – like its neighbour Bourgueil – is based exclusively on the Cabernet franc grape; **Montlouis**, with wines similar to Vouvray, which faces it across the Loire; and, with fewer pretensions but still some excellent wines, **Touraine Amboise**, **Touraine** and **Touraine Azay-le-Rideau**.

To go with the wine, Touraine produces *chèvre* (**goat's cheese**): the best of those cylindrical and speckled miniature building blocks that you see on market cheese stalls bear the name of Ste-Maure-de-Touraine, a small town 30km south of Tours. The *appellation d'origine contrôlée* for Ste-Maure-de-Touraine *chèvre* covers a very wide area, stretching to the north bank of the Loire. The tourist offices of Tours, Amboise, Chinon, Bourgueil and Vouvray can provide addresses of farms. If you want to visit Ste-Maure itself and you haven't got wheels, the Richelieu bus from Tours passes through. Ste-Maure's **tourist office** (daily: March–Sept 10am–noon & 2.30–5.30pm; rest of year Mon–Fri 10am–noon & 2.30–4pm) on rue du Château can provide addresses for *dégustations*, and the Friday market is well stocked. Cheese is celebrated on the first weekend in June with a **Foire aux Fromages**.

Practicalities

Information on Amboise and its environs is available at the **tourist office** on quai du Général-de-Gaulle, on the riverfront (mid-June to mid-Sept daily 9am–8pm; rest of year Mon–Sat 9am–12.15pm & 2–6.30pm, Sun 10am–noon & 2–4pm; ☎02.47.57.09.28, fax 02.47.57.14.35). Some of the town's **hotels** are overpriced, but worth trying are the central *Lion d'Or* (☎02.47.57.00.23, fax 02.47.23.22.49; ③; half-board compulsory in season) and *Belle Vue* (☎02.47.57.02.26, fax 02.47.30.51.23; ③), both on quai Charles-Guinot, just below the château. You could also try the pleasantly decorated, good-value *Chaptal*, 13 rue Chaptal (☎02.47.57.14.46; ②), or the more expensive, but thoroughly romantic *Vieux Manoir*, 13 rue Rabelais (☎02.47.30.41.27, fax 02.47.30.41.27, *www.le-vieux-manoir.com*; ⑦–⑧), run by an American couple. At the budget end of the scale, there's a good **campsite** on the island across from the castle, the *Île d'Or* (☎02.47.57.23.37), with a **hostel**, the *Centre Charles Péguy* (☎02.47.57.06.36; reception 3–8pm; closed Mon all year & Sun in winter), next door. **Bikes** can be rented from Cycles Richard, 2 rue Nazelles (☎02.47.57.01.79).

The **restaurants** in town don't stay open beyond 10pm. Try the dependable *Lion d'Or* (see above; menus from 66F/€10.06), or the crêperies on the approach to the château: *Crêperie Anne de Bretagne*, 1 rampe Château (closed Thurs) and *Crêperie L'Ecu*, at 7 rue Corneille (closed Sun & Mon during term-time). A cheap, hearty lunch can be had at 50 rue Rabelais, where a small working-man's café offers a 50F/€7.62 menu.

Villandry and around

Even if gardens aren't really your thing, those at the château in the tiny, peaceful village of **VILLANDRY** (mid-Feb to mid-Nov daily; château 9am–6pm; gardens 9am–7.30pm;

45F/€6.86 château and gardens, 32F/€4.88 gardens only) are well worth a visit. Thirteen kilometres west of Tours along the Cher – a superb cycle trip – this recreated Renaissance garden is no ordinary formal pattern of opposing primary colours, but more like a tapestry that changes with the months and only fades in winter. Carrots, cabbages and aubergines are arranged into patterns beneath ripe rose bowers; herbs and ornamental box hedges are part of the artwork, divided by vine-shaded paths. From a terrace above, you can see the confluence of the Cher and the Loire and châteaux on the northern bank. If you are visiting in late summer, you may be lucky enough to sample some garden-fresh produce.

Just past the château, 1km down the D121 towards Druye, there's an upmarket farmhouse **restaurant**, the *Domaine de la Giraudière* (☎02.47.50.08.60; closed mid-Nov to mid-March), which serves elaborate meals for 150–200F/€22.87–30.49, with cheaper menus for 63F/€9.60, featuring some excellent specialities based on goat's cheese. Alternatively, head back to **SAVONNIÈRES**, between Villandry and Tours, where the *Ferme Auberge de la Tuilerie* (☎02.47.50.04.96; closed Tues & Nov–Easter) serves straightforward and very pleasant family meals, with a set menu from 110F/€16.77; cross the Cher, follow the D288, take the first left along the bank of the Cher and the farm is on your left. For **accommodation** in Savonnières, try *Le Faisan* on route de Villandry (☎02.47.50.00.17, fax 02.47.50.14.90; ②).

Langeais and around

On a high terrace on the river's north bank in the middle of **LANGEAIS** sits the **Château de Langeais**, looking sturdily severe (daily: April–Sept 9am–6.30pm, mid-July to Aug till 9pm; rest of year 9am–noon & 2–5/6.30pm; 35F/€5.34). It is purely fifteenth century, with furnishings to match, and significant to the French because it was built to stop any incursions up the Loire by the Bretons. This threat ended with Charles VIII and Duchess Anne of Brittany's marriage in 1491, which was celebrated in this castle. A diptych of the couple portrays them looking less than joyous at their union – Anne had little choice in giving up her independence. There are fine tapestries on show, but this is a visit only for real château aficionados. Langeais has a pleasant **hotel**, the *Hosten*, 2 rue Gambetta (☎02.47.96.82.12, fax 02.47.96.56.72; ⑤–⑥), with a good but expensive **restaurant**.

Five kilometres further west along the river bank, the little town of **ST-MICHEL-SUR-LOIRE** boasts the **Musée Cadillac**, located in the Château de Planchoury (April–Sept daily 10am–6pm; 40F/€6.10). The museum features the largest collection of Cadillacs outside the US, comprising fifty different models of the American dream machine collected from all over the world, all in remarkable condition.

If you want to do some wine-buying, head for **BOURGUEIL**, just 13km west of St-Michel-sur-Loire. The **Abbaye de Bourgueil** has been making wine for nearly a thousand years and this is the best place to taste it. The Close de l'Abbaye (July & Aug Mon & Thurs–Sun 2–6pm; rest of year Sun only 2–6pm; ☎02.47.97.74.20; 25F/€3.81), just east of the town centre, is open for visits. Bourgueil's **Foire aux Vins** is held the first weekend in March; on the third Tuesday in July the town celebrates garlic; and on the third Tuesday in October, chestnuts are honoured.

If you're heading north towards the Sarthe, an interesting stop is **GIZEUX**, 12km north of Bourgueil, or 15km on a back-road route from St-Michel, whose fourteenth- to sixteenth-century **Château** extends like a game of dominoes around its gardens (May–Sept Mon–Sat 10am–6.30pm, Sun 2–6pm; 35F/€5.34). It contains some fine Renaissance paintings and beautiful seventeenth-century frescoes, but its speciality is the humble donkey: the **Musée Vivant de l'Ane** (daily: April–Sept 9am–7pm; rest of year 10am–5pm; closed mid-Nov to Feb 4; 42F/€6.40) has gathered together pack saddles and all the means of controlling and cajoling these stubborn beasts of burden, and has sixty different breeds for you to sympathize with in the park.

Azay-le-Rideau and around

Even without its **Château** (daily: April–Oct 9.30am–6pm, July & Aug till 7pm; Nov–March 9.30am–12.30pm & 2–5.30pm; 32F/€4.88), the quiet village of **AZAY-LE-RIDEAU** would bask in its serene setting, complete with an old mill by the bridge and Carolingian statues embedded in the facade of the church of St Symphorien. The château exterior, however, on its little island in the Indre, is one of the loveliest in the Loire: pure turreted Renaissance, and required viewing. While the guided tours of the interior, furnished in period style, don't add much to the experience, the portrait gallery is worth seeing, since it has the whole sixteenth-century royal Loire crew – François I, Catherine de Médicis, the de Guises, and the rest – the highlight being a semi-nude painting of Gabrielle d'Estrée, Henri IV's lover.

The downside to Azay is that **hotels** don't come cheap, though *Le Balzac*, 4 & 6 rue A.-Richer (☎02.47.45.42.08, fax 02.47.45.29.87; ③), and *Le Grand Monarque*, 3 place de la République (☎02.47.45.40.08, fax 02.47.45.46.25; ④–⑤; half-board compulsory in season), are both comfortable possibilities. Upstream from the château is a large **campsite**, the *Camping du Sabot* (☎02.47.45.42.72), near to the swimming pool and sports centre, signposted off the D84 to Saché. The **restaurant** of *Le Grand Monarque*, place République (☎02.47.45.40.08), is very acceptable, with a midday menu for around 100F/€15.24, or try *L'Automate Gourmand*, 1 rue Parc (☎02.47.45.39.07; closed Mon evening & Tues out of season), with weekday menus from 120F/€18.29. A rotating gourmet **night-time market** operates between Azay-le-Rideau, Bourgeuil and Langeais (June–Sept 5pm–midnight) and involves lots of drinking and delicious snacks – details are available from Azay's **tourist office**, on place de l'Europe (daily: April–Sept 9am–1pm & 3–7pm; rest of year 2–6pm; ☎02.47.45.44.40). You can rent **bikes** at the station or from Le Provost, 13 rue Carnot.

Rigny-Ussé

Fourteen kilometres west of Azay-le-Rideau, as the Indre approaches its confluence with the Loire, is the **Château d'Ussé** in **RIGNY-USSÉ** (daily: mid-March to June & first three weeks Sept 9am–noon & 2–6/6.45pm; July & Aug 9am–6.30pm; Sept 21–Nov 11 9am–noon & 2–5.30pm; 59F/€8.99). With its shimmering white towers and spires and idyllic wooded setting (best seen after dark when floodlit), this is the ultimate fairy-tale château, so much so that it's supposed to have inspired Charles Perrault's transcription of the Sleeping Beauty fairy story. Going inside for the visit – despite a display of models illustrating the Sleeping Beauty myth which might be of interest to children – isn't half as compelling, and perhaps not worth the rather excessive entrance fee.

Villaines-les-Rochers

Six kilometres south of Azay-le-Rideau is the troglodyte village of **VILLAINES-LES-ROCHERS**, famous for its wickerwork co-operative, set up in 1849 by the local curate to keep the village economically sustainable; you can still visit the **Musée de l'Osier et de la Vannerie** (mid-May to Sept daily 2.30–6.30pm; free). Villaines still produces a third of all wickerwork articles in France: you can visit the **workshops** that are dug into the rock, providing perfect humid conditions for keeping the willow supple, and buy baskets, chairs and so forth from the Maison d'Exposition of the Société Coopérative Agricole de Vannerie, 1 rue de la Cheneillère (☎02.47.45.43.03).

Upstream along the Indre

Following the D84 from Azay-le-Rideau eastwards along the north bank of the Indre you get glimpses of various privately owned châteaux. North of the hamlet of La Sablonnière, on the top of a hill surrounded by vines with beautiful views of the Indre

followers. The sixth-century German princess renounced the world and her husband – probably not a great sacrifice, since he eventually murdered her brother – in order to devote her life to God.

The other good excuse for getting out of Chinon is to discover the delights of the Chinon *appellation* ruby-red **wines**. The vineyards extend from **CROUZILLES**, just beyond L'Île Bouchard, 18km upstream, to **SAVIGNY-EN-VÉRON**, near the confluence of the Vienne and the Loire. *Vin de Pâques* (Easter wine) is the name given to the wine that should be drunk young, but most Chinon will age for thirty years, sometimes even longer. Though reds dominate, there's also a dry white and dry rosé. The Chinon tourist office can provide a list of wine-growers to visit.

The man who vies with Joan of Arc for shops and streets named in his honour in Chinon is François Rabelais (1494–1553), who wrote approvingly of wine, food and laughter in serious and rather difficult humanist texts, and whose most famous creations are the giant father and son Gargantua and Pantagruel. He was born at **LA DEVINIÈRE**, 6km southwest of Chinon, in a steep-roofed farmhouse that is now a **museum** to the prolific man (daily: May–Sept 10am–7pm; rest of year 9am–noon & 2–5/6pm; closed Dec; 21F/€3.20), completely furnished in the style of the time, right down to the stone kitchen sink.

Saumur and around

Unlike many small Loire towns, **SAUMUR** is not completely dominated by its château, nor by the military, though it's been the home of the French Cavalry Academy, and its successor, the Armoured Corps Academy, since 1763. Even the local sparkling wines are based elsewhere. Saumur itself is simply a peaceful and pretty place, spread along both banks of the Loire and over a small island in the middle of the river. The Hôtel de Ville strives busily to attract festivals and conferences, and, when they're successful, finding a room can be a problem – even at the best of times, reservations are essential.

The stretch of the Loire from Chinon to Angers, which passes through Saumur, is the loveliest part of the river, with the bizarre added draw of **troglodyte dwellings** carved out of cliffs as early as the twelfth century. The land on the south bank, under grapes and sunflowers, gradually rises away from the river, with long-inactive windmills still standing. Across the water cows graze in wooded pastures. For **transport** you can either take the train or one of three buses to get to Angers: #5 along the south bank, #11 crossing halfway, or #10 staying north of the river.

Arrival, information and accommodation

Arriving at the **gare SNCF**, you'll find yourself on the north bank of the Loire: turn right onto avenue David-d'Angers and either take bus #A to the centre or cross the bridge to the island on foot. From the island the old **Pont Cessart** takes you to the main part of the town on the south bank; the **gare routière** is in this part of town, a couple of blocks from the Pont Cessart on place St-Nicolas. Saumur's main street, rue d'Orléans, cuts through the south-bank sector from the bridge: the **tourist office** is next to the bridge on place de la Bilange near the theatre (mid-May to mid-Oct Mon–Sat 9.15am–7pm, Sun 10.30am–12.30pm & 3.30–6.30pm; rest of the year Mon–Sat 9.15am–12.30pm & 2–6pm, Sun 10am–noon; ☎02.41.40.20.60, fax 02.41.40.20.69, *www.ot-saumur.fr*). The **old quarter**, around St-Pierre and the castle, is reached by walking two blocks south of the tourist office down rue d'Orléans then following the signs pointing you down rue Dacier to the left.

Hotels

Anne d'Anjou, 32 quai Mayaud (☎02.41.67.30.30, fax 02.41.67.51.00). Comfortable hotel, with excellent service, in an eighteenth-century listed building. Closed Christmas. ④.

La Bouère-Salée, rue Grange-Couronne (☎02.41.67.38.85, fax 02.41.51.12.52). Delightful bed and breakfast situated 500m behind the train station. ③–④.

de Bretagne, 55 rue St-Nicolas (☎02.41.51.26.38). Consisting of a few rooms above a bar, the *Bretagne* is not the quietest place, but is central and clean. Closed Sun. ②.

Central, 23 rue Daillé (☎02.41.67.82.35, fax 02.41.51.05.78). Small, quiet and comfortable hotel. ③.

Le Cristal, 10–12 place de la République (☎02.41.51.09.54, fax 02.41.51.12.14, *www.cristal-hotel.fr*). One of the nicest hotels in town, with river views from most rooms and very friendly proprietors. ④.

du Roi René, 94 av du Général-de-Gaulle (☎02.41.67.45.30, fax 02.41.67.74.59). Pleasant two-star hotel on the Île d'Offard, with lovely river and château views. ③.

St-Pierre, 3 rue Haute-St-Pierre (☎02.41.50.33.00, fax 02.41.50.38.68). Large, well-equipped and very comfortable rooms in the old quarter. ⑥.

Hostel and campsites

Hostel, rue de Verden, Île d'Offard (☎02.41.40.30.00, fax 02.41.67.37.81). Large hostel with laundry facilities, swimming pool access and views of the château. From the station, take the second left off avenue du Général-de-Gaulle; it's at the east end of the island. Reception 8–10am & 5–10pm. Boat and bike rental available.

Camping municipal, rue de Verden, Île d'Offard (☎02.41.40.30.00, fax 02.41.67.37.81). Situated next door to the hostel. You can even swim in the Loire from the north side of the island.

La Chantepie, on the D751, St-Hilaire-St-Florent (☎02.41.67.95.34). An alternative to the municipal campsite, a couple of kilometres west of Saumur. Closed Oct–April.

The Town

Saumur's **Château** (daily: June–Sept 9.30am–6pm; Oct–May 9.30am–noon & 2–5.30pm; closed Tues Oct–March; 37F/€5.64), a great, square building high above the town, is recognizable as the gleaming white, turreted subject of one of the scenes of *Les Très Riches Heures du Duc de Berry*, the most celebrated of all the medieval Books of Hours. Its symmetry and witch-hat towers give it an air of fantasy, particularly on a misty morning or under night-time illumination (July & Aug Wed & Sat 8.30–10.30pm). It was built in the fourteenth century and turned into a much more decorative and comfortable residence by Duke René of Anjou in the fifteenth. The star-shaped fortifications around it were added in 1590 during the Wars of Religion, when Saumur was a Protestant stronghold.

The dungeons and the watchtower can be visited on your own; for the two larger museums within the château, relaxed guides take over. The **Musée des Arts Décoratifs** in the former royal apartments has a huge and impressive collection of European china, plus several fifteenth-century tapestries, one of which portrays wonderfully snooty-looking medieval ladies out hunting. But it's the **Musée du Cheval**, in the attic of the château, that's the real treat. Progressing from a horse skeleton, through the evolution of bridles and stirrups over the centuries, you finally reach an amazing and diverse international saddlery collection. One of the best pieces is a Russian sleigh on which a fishy female figure looks up at a cherub wearing what seems to be a Roman helmet. The **Musée de la Figurine-Jouet**, located in an ancient powder magazine on the ramparts (mid-June to mid-Sept daily except Tues 2–6pm; rest of year reservations only, ☎02.41.83.13.32; 12F/€1.83, separate ticket from château entrance), offers a display of ancient toys: farm and zoo animals, circus and theatre figures, cowboys and Indians, and model soldiers.

Back down in the town, a real soldier will escort you around the **Musée de la Cavalerie** (Tues, Thurs & Sun 9am–noon & 2–5pm, Sat 2–5pm; 20F/€3.05), if you knock at the guarded gate on avenue Maréchal-Foch, west of rue d'Orléans. Among the uniforms, weapons and battle scenes (including some very recent engagements), there's a particularly moving room, dedicated to the cavalry cadets who held the Loire bridges between Gennes and Montsoreau against the Germans for three days in 1940, after the French government had surrendered. The history of tank warfare is covered in the separate **Musée des Blindés**, at 1043 rue Fricotelle, to the southeast of the centre (daily: mid-April to Oct 9.30am–6.30pm; Nov to mid-April 10am–5pm; 25F/€3.81).

The early medieval pointy-spired **church of St Pierre** is most notable for its interesting selection of dragons; there are at least seven monsters carved in stone and wood or woven into the sixteenth-century tapestries that tell the legend of St Florent, an early scourge of the beautiful beasts that symbolize sin. Saumur's oldest church, **Notre-Dame de Nantilly**, by the public gardens south of the château, is notable for its sixteenth-century tapestries, with immensely crowded and detailed scenes; it was closed for restoration at the time of writing, but is due to reopen sometime in 2002.

Beyond the town centre

For a slightly less bellicose diversion you can visit the **École Nationale d'Équitation**, in St-Hilaire-St-Florent, a suburb to the east of the centre; take bus #B from the town centre. The Riding School (Tues–Fri 9.30–10am & 2.30–4pm, Sat 9.30–10am; closed Aug; ☎02.41.53.50.60; 32F/€4.88 for morning visits, 20F/€3.05 afternoons) provides guided tours in which you can watch training sessions (mornings only) and view the stables. Displays of dressage and anachronistic battle manœuvres by the crackshot Cadre Noir, the former cavalry trainers, are regular events (programme details from the tourist office or the school itself).

Performances of a far greater diversity are celebrated in the **Musée du Masque**, a short walk back down towards Saumur from the Riding School, on rue de l'Abbaye (daily: mid-April to mid-Oct 10am–12.30pm & 2.30–6.30pm; rest of year Sat & Sun 2–6pm; closed mid-Dec to mid-March; 25F/€3.81). This is very much geared towards children, with waxwork models of clowns and storybook characters wearing masks dating from the 1870s to the present day.

Another museum in St-Hilaire-St-Florent, of a very different nature, is the **Musée de Champignon** (mid-Feb to mid-Nov daily 10am–7pm; 40F/€6.10), which runs informative (if a bit dank and cold) tours through some of the region's 500km of underground *caves de champignons*, used to grow seventy percent of France's commonest cooking mushrooms, the *champignon de Paris*. The entrance is 1km downriver, along the D751 from the last bus stop in St-Hilaire-St-Florent.

SAUMUR WINES

The **Maison du Vin** at 25 rue Beaurepaire in Saumur (☎02.41.51.16.40) has information on locally produced wines and addresses of wine-growers. The speciality here is sparkling – *méthode champenoise* – wine, which can rival lesser-quality champagnes. Names to look out for are Veuve Amiot and Gratien-Meyer (*www.gratienmeyer.com*). A good red is the Saumur Champigny from around the village of the same name. The **Caves Coopératives** at St-Cyr-en-Bourg (☎02.41.53.06.08), a short train hop south of Saumur and near the station, have kilometres of cellars, and you can taste different wines with no obligation to buy.

Eating and drinking

There are several cheap **eating places** around place St-Pierre: *Auberge St-Pierre*, 6 place St-Pierre (☎02.41.51.26.25; closed Mon out of season), has good 55F/€8.38 and 75F/€11.43 menus ; opposite, at no. 1, *Les Forges de St-Pierre* (☎02.41.38.21.79; closed Sun & Tues evening & Oct) specializes in grilled meat, with an acceptable 75F/€11.43 menu; and *La Quichenotte*, 2 rue Haute-St-Pierre (☎02.41.51.31.98; closed Mon & Jan), serves good crêpes at 55F/€8.38. You can also eat in the château grounds at *L'Orangerie* (☎02.41.67.12.88; closed Sun evening & Mon out of season), a restaurant and *salon de thé*, with a 90F/€13.72 menu.

There are a couple of good **bars** on place St-Pierre: *Le Swing*, with its ancient Wurlitzer jukebox and fruit cocktails, and *Le Richelieu*, with good music, Guinness and pool. The *Café de la Poste*, opposite the post office on place du Petit-Thouars, is a student meeting place that serves cheap snacks and stays open till 2am. The hotel bar of *Le Cristal* (see p.501) is also popular, along with the other bars along the riverfront on place de la République.

Troglodyte dwellings

The "falun" or soft shellstone found in the Loire valley lends itself to **troglodyte dwellings** – homes carved out of rocky outcrops, of which there are more in this area (between Saumur and Angers) than anywhere else in France. It's reckoned that in the twelfth century half the local population lived in homes carved out of the rock. Today, some of the rock dwellings have surprising uses, along with the more predictable "Troglo" bars and restaurants.

Away from the Loire cliffs on the plains to the south, troglodyte villages were built by digging holes like large craters and then carving out the walls. The best example is at **ROCHEMENIER**, north of Doué-la-Fontaine, about 20km southwest of Saumur, where an underground village housed a small farming community with its own underground chapel (daily: April–Nov 9.30am–7pm; rest of the year 2–6pm; closed Dec & Jan; 25F/€3.81), and was only abandoned in the 1930s. The visit includes a typical troglodyte dwelling, along with a museum of domestic items, including wine and oil presses.

Just 3km north, at **DÉNEZÉ-SOUS-DOUÉ**, there are underground carvings thought to have been sculpted by a secret sixteenth-century sect of libertarians. The cartoon-style figures mock religion, morality, the state and the ruling class, with scenes of sex, strange deformities and perverted Christian imagery (Tues–Sun: April & May 2–6.30pm; June & Sept 10am–7pm; July & Aug 9am–7pm; 20F/€3.05). There are also concerts in the cave on Wednesday evenings (April–Oct).

Equally bizarre is the **Zoo de Doué** on the D960 to Cholet, 2km southwest of Doué-la-Fontaine (daily: April–Sept 9am–7pm; Oct–March 10am–noon & 2–6pm; 60F/€9.15), established in one of the region's complexes of quarried falun caverns. The natural setting has been used to full advantage for a cave of fruit bats, a vivarium (formerly a cave dwelling but now home to pythons, anacondas and the like) and a lynx enclosure so spacious and overgrown it's hard to spot a cat.

At **PARNAY**, about 7km upstream from Saumur on the south bank of the Loire, you can taste and buy wines from a troglodyte mansion, the **Château du Marconnay**, 75 rte de Saumur (April–Sept Tues–Sun 10am–12.30pm & 2–6pm; 16F/€2.44). Further on, just before Turquant, in **LE VAL-HULIN**, are the last producers of the once common Saumurois dried whole apples, known as *pommes tapées* – each apple, after drying, is given a little expert tap to make it a more amenable shape for bottle storage. You can tour one of the workshops at **Le Troglo des Pommes Tapées** (Easter–May & Nov

Hotels

Centre, 12 rue St-Laud (☎02.41.87.45.07). Quiet, comfortable and central cheapie. ①.

Continental, 12–14 rue Louis-de-Romain (☎02.41.86.94.94, fax 02.41.86.96.60, *le.continental @wanadoo.fr*). Bright, well-equipped hotel, with good service, located on a quiet street just off place Ralliement. ③.

des Lices, 25 rue des Lices (☎02.41.87.44.10). A real bargain in the centre of town, with fresh baked goods at breakfast; bistro downstairs. Closed August 1–15. ②.

du Mail, 8 rue des Ursules (☎02.41.25.05.25, fax 02.41.86.91.20). Old-fashioned and attractive two-star, offering "silence in the heart of the city". Parking available. ③–④.

St-Julien, 9 place du Ralliement (☎02.41.88.41.62, fax 02.41.20.95.19, *www.destination-anjou .com/saintjulien*). Generous, pleasant and quiet rooms in the centre of the city. ③.

Hostels and campsite

Centre d'Accueil du Lac de Maine, 49 av du Lac de Maine (☎02.41.22.32.10, fax 02.41.22.32.11). Rather expensive hostel-style accommodation accommodation, complete with extensive sports facilities, a 20min ride southwest of the town; bus #6 (#26 on Sun) either from the train station or bd Générale-de-Gaulle to stop "Bouchemaine". You can rent canoes at the Base Nautique in the complex. There's also a campsite here (see below).

Darwin, 3 rue Darwin (☎02.41.22.61.20, fax 02.41.48.51.91). Somewhat austere hostel but cheaper than the *Centre d'Accueil*; take bus #8 to CFA.

Camping du Lac de Maine, av du Lac de Maine (☎02.41.73.02.20, fax 02.41.73.05.03). Sandy campsite next to a lake off the D111 south of the city centre. 40F/€6.10 per person, 100F/€15.24 for a car, tent and three people. Closed Dec–Feb.

The City

Your lasting impression of Angers will be of the **château**, an impressive, sturdy fortress by the river, its moat now filled with striking formal flower arrangements and softened by trees. From here, it's just a fifteen-minute stroll east to the **cathedral** and its entourage of several smaller churches and museums.

Across the pont Verdun from the château is the suburb of **La Doutre**, where the **Hôpital St-Jean** houses the modern response to the castle's Apocalypse tapestry, *Le Chant du Monde*. Further out in the suburbs are a rash of interesting museums, easily reached by bus, exalting everything from early aeroplanes to Cointreau and communication methods.

The château and Apocalypse tapestry

The **Château d'Angers** (daily: mid-March to May & mid-Sept to Oct 10am–6pm; June to mid-Sept 9.30am–7pm; rest of year 10am–5pm; closed Dec–Feb; 32F/€4.88) is a formidable early medieval fortress whose sense of impregnability is created by seventeen circular towers resembling elephants' legs gripping the rock below the kilometre-long curtain wall. Inside there are a few miscellaneous remains of the counts' royal lodgings and chapels, but the immediate and obvious focus is the **Tapestry of the Apocalypse**, whose 100-metre length (of an original 140m) is well displayed in a modern gallery. Woven between 1375 and 1378 for Duke Réné of Anjou, it takes as its text St John's vision of the Apocalypse, as described in the Book of Revelation. A Bible would come in handy, since, though the French biblical quotations are given, the English "translation" is just explanation. The vision is of the lead-up to the Day of Judgement signalled by seven angels blowing their trumpets. After this...

> *hail and fire mingled with blood . . . were cast upon the earth and the third part of trees was burned up and all green grass . . . and as it were a great mountain burning with fire was cast into the sea and the third part of the sea became blood . . .* (Rev. 8:7–8)

The battle of Armageddon rages, as Satan, "the great red dragon" (depicted with seven heads), and his minions of composite animals mark their earthly followers. The holy forces retaliate by breaking the seven vials of plagues. It all ends with heavenly Jerusalem, and Satan buried for a thousand years. The slightly flattened medieval perspective has a hallucinatory quality, extraordinarily beautiful and terrifying, evoking the end of the world either in accordance with the first-century text or as a secular holocaust.

If you can take in anything else after that, there are more tapestries, of a gentler nature, in the sporadically open Royal Lodgings and Governor's Lodge within the castle. Those feeling in need of a drink can head straight out of the castle and into the **Maison du Vin de l'Anjou**, 5bis place Kennedy (daily 9am–1pm & 3–6.30pm; closed Mon year round & Sun in winter), where the very professional and helpful staff will offer you wine to taste before you buy, and provide lists of wine-growers to visit.

The cathedral and around

Ten minutes' walk upstream along the quayside from the château will bring you to a long flight of steps leading up to the **Cathédrale St-Maurice**. It's a dramatic approach, giving you the full benefit of the building's early medieval facade. Inside, the unusually wide, aisle-less nave with its dome-like Plantagenet vaulting is illuminated by twelfth-century stained glass. In the choir one window is dedicated to Thomas à Becket – it was made shortly after his death. The fifteenth-century rose windows in the transepts are particularly impressive, and there are modern examples of stained glass in the chapel of Notre-Dame de la Pitié, right of the entrance. The stone carving on the capitals and the supports for the gallery are beautiful, but the cathedral is overzealously furnished with a grandiose high altar and pulpit and a set of tapestries that can't compete with Angers' other woven treasures.

In front of the cathedral, on place Ste-Croix, is the town's favourite carpentry detail, the unlikely genitals of one of the carved characters on the medieval **Maison d'Adam**. The building is now used by craftspeople for presenting their wares (daily 9.30am–7pm). There's a small daily **market** on the square.

Heading north from place Ste-Croix, you pass **place du Ralliement**, hub of modern Angers, which has just undergone a face-lift, the most impressive result being the facade of the nineteenth-century **Théâtre Municipal**. From here, proceed into rue Lenepveu, where a Renaissance mansion (at no. 32) houses the **Musée Pincé** (mid-June to mid-Sept daily 9am–6.30pm; rest of year daily except Mon 10am–noon & 2–6pm; 10F/€1.52). It's a mixed bag of antiquities, with collections from China and Japan, the latter by far the more interesting, with a reconstruction of a tearoom and a gallery full of delicate prints, including the famous wave engulfing a boat with Mount Fuji in the background by Hokusaï.

Apart from its cathedral, the other great Gothic edifice in Angers is the chancel of the **Abbey of St Serge**, now home to a high school, on avenue Mairie-Talet across boulevard Carnot, north of the centre near the congress centre. Though nothing much to look at from outside, the interior – notably the chapter room, cloister and refectory – has some of the most perfect vaulting rising from the slenderest of columns. Close by is the verdant and relaxing **Jardin des Plantes** (summer 7.30am–8pm; winter 8am–5.30pm; free).

Arguably the greatest stoneworks in Angers, however, are the creations of the famous local sculptor David d'Angers (1788–1856), whose statue of St Cecilia adorns the cathedral chancel; his best works, some original, some copies and casts, are exhibited in the stunning **Galerie David d'Angers**, built by glassing over the ruins of a thirteenth-century church, the **Église Toussaint**, 37bis rue Toussaint (mid-June to mid-Sept daily 9am–6.30pm; rest of year Tues–Sun 10am–noon & 2–6pm; 10F/€1.52). David d'Angers was a prime activist in mid-nineteenth-century republican struggles in

Paris and was close friends with many of the great Romantic artists and thinkers of the time, some of them featured here in busts or bronze medallions.

The **Musée des Beaux-Arts** next door, entered from 10 rue du Musée (closed for restoration until the end of 2002), is home to Boucher's *Génie des Arts*, Lorenzo Lippi's beautiful *La Femme au Masque*, the highly operatic *Paolo et Francesca* by Ingres and other representative works from the thirteenth to the twentieth centuries.

La Doutre and Le Chant du Monde tapestry

The district facing the château from across the Maine is known as **La Doutre** (literally, "the other side"), and still has a few mansions and houses dating from the medieval period, despite redevelopment over the years.

In the north of the area, a short way from the Pont de la Haute-Chaine (about 15 minutes' walk from the château), the **Hôpital St-Jean**, at 4 bd Arago, was built by Henry Plantagenet in 1174 as a hospital for the poor, a function it continued to fulfil until 1854. Today it houses the **Musée Jean Lurçat et de la Tapisserie Contemporaine** (June to mid-Sept daily 9am–6.30pm; rest of year Tues–Sun 10am–noon & 2–6pm; 20F/€3.05), which contains the city's great twentieth-century tapestry, **Le Chant du Monde**. The tapestry sequence was designed by Jean Lurçat in 1957 in response to the Apocalypse tapestry, though he died nine years later before its completion (the artist's own commentary is available in English). It hangs in a vast vaulted space, the original ward for the sick, or Salle des Malades. The first four tapestries deal with *La Grande Menace*, the threat of nuclear war: first the bomb itself; then *Hiroshima Man*, flayed and burnt with the broken symbols of belief dropping from him; then the collective massacre of the *Great Charnel House*; and the last dying rose falling with the post-Holocaust ash through black space – the *End of Everything*. From then on, the tapestries celebrate the joy of life and the interdependence of its myriad manifestations: fire, water, champagne, the conquest of space, poetry and symbolic language.

Modern tapestry is an unfamiliar art, and the colours and Lurçat's style are so unlike anything else that initially you may be overwhelmed. More predictable is the impressive old hospital building with its seventeenth-century pharmacy, the chapel's fine thirteenth-century stained-glass windows and soaring Gothic vaulting. The Romanesque cloisters, with their original woodwork intact, are also worth a peek. There are more modern tapestries, too, in the building adjoining the Salle des Malades: built up around the donation by Lurçat's widow of several of his paintings, ceramics, other tapestries and illustrations for *Le Chant du Monde*, it has become one of the best showcases for contemporary tapestry in a changing programme of exhibitions. If you want to see the different stages involved in carrying out a modern tapestry commission or restoring old tapestries, call in at the neighbouring **Centre Régional d'Art Textile**, 3 bd Daviers (*ateliers* Mon, Tues, Thurs & Fri 10am–noon & 2–4pm; *exposition* Tues–Sat 2–6pm; free), where you can watch artists at work.

South of the Hôpital St-Jean, on La Doutre's central square, place de la Laiterie, the ancient buildings of the **Abbaye de Ronceray** are used as an art and technology college, and when the school mounts exhibitions (or if you take one of the tourist office's guided tours of the town) you can visit the Romanesque galleries of the old abbey and admire their beautiful murals. Inside the adjacent twelfth-century **church of the Trinity** on the square, an exquisite Renaissance wooden spiral staircase fails to mask a great piece of medieval bodging used to fit the wall of the church around a part of the abbey that juts into it.

Suburban museums

The Château de Pignerolle, in the satellite village of **ST-BARTHELÉMY D'ANJOU**, to the east of Angers (signposted off the N147), is home to the **Musée Européen de**

la **Communication** (daily 10am–12.30pm & 2.30–6pm; 50F/€7.62), a typically histri-
onic French science and technology museum, which promises a complete history of
communication "from the tom-tom to the satellite". It's quite good fun, with everything
from Leonardo's helicopter drawings to German submarines brought into play, and fantastic scenes of the future, but don't expect to come out much the wiser. For something
completely different, you could go on a guided tour around the **Distillerie Cointreau**,
just off the ring road between Angers and St-Barthelemy d'Anjou (mid-June to mid-Sept
Mon–Fri 9.30am, 11am, 2pm & 3.30pm, Sat 10.30am, 2pm & 4pm, Sun 4pm; mid-Sept
to mid-June Mon–Fri by appointment, Sun & bank hols 3pm & 4.30pm; ☎02.41.43.25.21;
20F/€3.05), reached on bus #7, where the famous orange liqueur has been distilled
since the mid-nineteenth century. You'll learn a lot about the Cointreau brothers and
how marvellous the drink is, a little bit about distilling techniques, and nothing, of
course, about the recipe. You get a little sip at the end, but the highlight is definitely the
rows of gleaming copper stills.

Northwest of the city at the Aéroport d'Angers Marcé (signposted off the RD766,
direction "Tours"), one of the most romanticized twentieth-century means of transportation – early aeroplanes – are on show in the **Musée Régional de l'Air** (daily
2–6pm; free; take bus #6 from the centre). There are around forty well-restored examples on display, starting with a classic 1935 Potez 60.

Eating and drinking

The streets around place du Ralliement and place Romain have a wide variety of **bars**
and **restaurants**, many of them very inexpensive.

Le Connétable, 13 rue des Deux-Haies (☎02.41.88.57.04). A good Breton crêperie; from
50F/€7.62.

Le Grandgousier, 7 rue St-Laud (☎02.41.87.81.47). Serves traditional regional dishes compliment-
ed by specially chosen local Anjou wines, which are included in the price of the 89F/€13.57 menu.
Closed Wed, Sat lunch & Sun.

La Martinique, 75 rue du Mail (☎02.41.87.22.25). Ignore the tacky decor and enjoy the Martinique
cuisine that includes smoked chicken, lamb curry and coconut-milk crème caramel. Set menus start
at 90F/€13.72.

Papagayo, 44 bd Ayrault (☎02.41.87.03.35). Low-priced bistro, serving straightforward salad and
meat dishes. Closed Sun & Mon evening.

Le Petit Mâchon, 43 rue Bressigny (☎02.41.86.01.13). Low-priced local wines to go with *andouillettes*, pigs' trotters and the like. Closed Sun evening & Mon.

La Rose d'Or, 21 rue Delâge (☎02.41.88.38.38). Serves delicious salmon and trout; menus from
105F/€16. Closed Sun evening & Mon.

Le Soufflerie, 8 place Pilori (☎02.41.87.45.32). Café specializing in soufflés (from 50F/€7.62).
Closed Sun, Mon & first half Aug.

Les Templiers, rue des Deux-Haies, off place Ralliement (☎02.41.88.33.11). Good food in a pleasant, if slightly formal, atmosphere and, perhaps most importantly, open on Sundays. Menus range
from 98F/€14.93 to 165F/€25.15; the 74F/€11.28 lunch Tues–Fri is a real bargain.

Nightlife

Late-opening **bars** congregate around rue St-Laud – *Bar du Centre*, below *Hôtel Centre*,
and *Le Louisiane*, at no. 43, are the liveliest – and the other pedestrian streets around,
and tend to have a young clientele. Over to the east of the city, the *Spirit Factory*, 14–16
rue Bressigny (open till 1am), is a cavernous bar, with beer brewed on the premises,
serving late-night *moules frites*. Over the river in La Doutre, *Le Rockmania*, 18 bd Arago,
has live French rock/fusion/ska (Thurs–Sat 11.30pm–2am), and, in the northern suburbs, *Chabada*, 56 bd du Doyenné (take bus #5) puts on live music; to find out about

gigs, go to the FNAC record store on rue Lenepveu. For something more cerebral, check out the philosophy debates on Wednesday nights at *Le Carpe Diem*, a "café philosophe" at 15 rue St-Maurille (☎02.41.87.50.47).

Listings

Bike rental Anjou Bike Center, in the nearby riverside hamlet of Blaison-Gohier (☎02.41.57.10.52, *www.anjou-bike-center.com*); the industrious owners rent bikes, organize trips and run a bed and breakfast.

Boat rental Anjou Plaisance, rue de l'Écluse, Grez-Neuville (☎02.41.95.68.95), and Maine-Anjou-Rivières, Le Moulin, Chenillé-Changé (☎02.41.95.10.83), rent out boats of all kinds for exploring the Oudon, Mayenne and Sarthe rivers.

Car rental Anjou Location Auto, 32 rue Denis-Papin (☎02.41.88.07.53); Europcar, 26 bd du Général-de-Gaulle (☎02.41.87.87.10); Hertz, 14 rue Denis-Papin (☎02.41.88.15.16).

Emergencies ☎15; Centre Hospitalier, 1 av de l'Hôtel-Dieu (☎02.41.35.36.37); for late-night pharmacies, phone the police on ☎02.41.47.75.22.

Festivals During July and Aug, jazz and Latin-American music concerts are held in the Cloître Toussaint (programme details from tourist office). The Festival d'Anjou is a prestigious theatre festival using châteaux throughout the Maine-et-Loire *département* as venues in July (details on ☎02.41.88.14.14). There is also the World Folklore Festival (1–6 Sept) with acts from all over the globe; ☎02.41.87.28.28.

Laundries 17 rue Marceau; 25 place Grégoire-Bordillon; 15 rue Plantagênet; 5 place de la Visitation.

Market There are a number of markets Tues–Sat throughout the city including a large one held on place Grégoire-Bordillon on Sat.

Police 15 rue Dupetit-Thouars (☎02.41.47.75.22).

Poste restante 1 rue Franklin-Roosevelt, 49052 Angers (☎02.41.87.28.28).

Taxis Allo Anjou Taxi (☎02.41.87.65.00).

Around Angers

Lazing around the Loire and its tributaries between visits to vineyards can fill a good summer week around Angers, as long as you have your own transport. Otherwise it's a two-buses-a-day problem, or no buses at all. Worthy exceptions are the **Savennières vineyards**, which you can reach by train (see box on p.511), and **St-Aubin-de-Luigne**, 20km southwest of Angers and just south of Rochefort, where you can rent rowing boats during the summer at the tourist office, next to the campsite.

If you have your own car, you can easily reach of a couple more châteaux in these parts: **Brissac-Quincé**, 20km south of the town (also bus #9), and **Le Plessis-Bourré** near Ecuillé (impossible to get to by public transport), 17km to the north. For a more accessible glimpse of a real monster of a mansion, head for the **Château de Serrant**, just outside St-Georges-sur-Loire, on bus route #18 from Angers. **Baugé**, north of the Loire and over to the east, is famous for a religious relic and is a pleasant little town for a short stopover, with four or five buses daily from Angers.

Château de Brissac

The **Château de Brissac** at **BRISSAC-QUINCÉ** (April–June & mid-Sept to Oct daily except Tues 10am–noon & 2.15–5.15pm; July to mid-Sept daily 10am–5.45pm; 40F/€6.86) has been owned since 1502 by the same line of dukes. Of the original fortress, only the fifteenth-century fortified towers remain, and they were long due to be pulled down in deference to the symmetry of the seventeenth-century additions.

The interior is a riot of bad taste, but it has some beautiful ceilings, as well as an interesting portrait in the Gallery of Ancestors of Mme Clicquot, the first woman to run a

CHRIS COE, AXIOM

Chenonceau, Loire Valley

M. HUGHES, TRAVEL INK

The château at Vitré, Brittany

M. HUGHES, TRAVEL INK

Côte de Granit Rose, Brittany

M. HUGHES, TRAVEL INK

St-Cirq-Lapopie, in the Lot Valley

B. WEST, TRAVEL INK

Troglodyte dwelling, Saumur, Loire Valley

MARC S. DUBIN

Lescun and its cirque

J. PHILLIPS, TRAVEL INK

CHARLES BOWMAN

Wine shop, Cahors, Lot region

Lourdes

CHRIS PARKER, AXIOM

M. IKEDA, GREG EVANS INTL

Cluny, Burgundy

Beynac, Dordogne

CHRIS PARKER, AXIOM

MICHAEL JENNER

H. SMITH, GREG EVANS INT'L

The Hôtel-Dieu, Beaune, Burgundy

Flea market, Bordeaux

Château de Hautefort, Dordogne

THE WINES OF ANJOU

A few kilometres west out of Angers, along the north bank of the Loire, Bouchemaine, Savennières and La Possonnière are the communes for the dry white **appellation Savennières** – one of the few white wines that can mature for a century. The most famous is Coulée de Serrant, which you can taste and buy at the **Château de la Roche-aux-Moines**, just upstream from Savennières. **Rochefort-sur-Loire**, on the south bank, is the first of the **appellations Côteaux du Layon-Villages**, a sweet golden wine. Following the trail of this wine along the River Layon, as the road winds below vineyard hills as far as **Faye-d'Anjou**, is a hedonist's dream. The road is free of *dégustation* signs, but the *vignerons* are not hard to find. In the fourth village upstream from Faye d'Anjou, the **Château of Tigné** produces a variety of good Anjou reds and whites, a Côteaux de Layon and a Cuvée Cyrano. Its owner is none other than the film actor Gérard Dépardieu who, it's said, thinks nothing of flying from any corner of the globe, mid-shoot, to inspect his grapes.

champagne business, and her granddaughter, the present duke's grandmother, apparently one of the first women to get a driving licence. The château has had a **vineyard** since 1515, with its own label: the current *vignerons* are the brothers Daviau at the Domaine de Bablut (visits by appointment only; ☎02.41.91.22.21).

Château du Plessis-Bourré

Five years' work at the end of the fifteenth century produced the fortress of **Le Plessis-Bourré** (Feb & Nov daily except Wed 2–6pm; March–June, Sept & Oct Mon, Tues & Fri–Sun 10am–noon & 2–6pm, Thurs 2–6pm; July & Aug daily 10am–6pm; closed Jan & Dec; 40F/€6.10), 2km southeast of **ECUILLÉ** between the Sarthe and Mayenne rivers. It still looks as if it expects an attack any day from across its vast, full moat, spanned by an arched bridge with a still-functioning drawbridge. But inside, all is Renaissance elegance and comfort at its best. The treasurer of France at the time, Jean Bourré, built the château to receive important visitors, among them Louis XI and Charles VIII, and it is appropriately flamboyant. Everywhere is painted with secular and allegorical scenes interwoven with mottoes, some enigmatic, some moralistic: a unicorn poses as Lust, a grisly operation is performed by a barber, and people carouse and cook. In one of the turreted staircases, the ceiling supports are carved with symbols from alchemy. Less exotic but still impressive are the furnishings of the state rooms and the collection of fans displayed in the library. A visit to the château is capped by a tour of the attics with their ship's keel rafting, and a stroll out onto the roof to follow the sentry's walk.

Château de Serrant

At the **Château de Serrant**, 15km west of Angers beside the N23 near **ST-GEORGES-SUR-LOIRE**, the combination of dark-brown schist and creamy tufa give a rather pleasant biscuit-cake effect to the outside (guided tours: April–June & Sept to mid-Nov daily except Tues 10–11.20am & 2–5pm; July & Aug daily 10–11.20am & 2–5.20pm; mid-Nov to Dec Sat & Sun only 10.20–11.20am & 2.20–4.40pm; 45F/€6.86). But it has those heavy slate bell-shaped cupolas pressing down on massive towers, which ruin any impression of lightness and grace. The building was begun in the sixteenth century and was added to, discreetly for the most part, up until the eighteenth century. In 1755 it belonged to an Irishman, Francis Walsh, to whom Louis XV had given the title Count of Serrant as a reward for Walsh's help against the old enemy, the English. Walsh had provided the ship for Bonnie Prince Charlie to return to Scotland for the 1745 uprising.

Inside are endless tapestries, paintings and furniture; a Renaissance staircase and some richly carved ceilings; a bedroom prepared for Napoléon (who never came); and a library of well over ten thousand books. If you've already had your fill of château tours, then give this one a miss.

Baugé

In **BAUGÉ** – as easily reached by car from Saumur as Angers, 25km north of the river – the nuns at the **Chapelle des Incurables** claim to have a cross made from the True Cross. The wood is certainly Palestinian, though its history prior to its donation to an Angevin crusader is dubious. It is, anyhow, the double-armed cross that became the emblem of the dukes of Anjou and Lorraine and, in this century, of the Free French Forces. To see it, ring on the doorbell at 8 rue de la Girouardière (daily except Tues 2.30–4.15pm; free).

The **tourist office** in Baugé (mid-June to mid-Sept Mon–Sat 10am–12.30pm & 1.30–6pm; rest of year Mon–Fri 11.30am–12.30pm & 1.30–6.30pm; ☎02.41.89.18.07) is worth visiting merely for its location in a fifteenth-century **château**, one of Duke Réné of Anjou's favourite residences and once home to his magnificent Apocalypse tapestry, now in Angers (see p.506). Take a look, too, at the **Hôpital de Baugé**, east of the château up rue Anne-de-Melun, for its seventeenth-century **pharmacy**, to which the hospital receptionist will direct you (July & Aug Mon–Sat 10am–noon & 3–5pm, Sun 3–5pm; rest of year Mon & Wed–Sat 10am–noon & 3–5pm, Sun 3–5pm; free): it contains beautiful woodwork shelves, parquetry floor and a sculpted ceiling, and its vials, flacons and contents remain just as they were in 1874.

Staying in Baugé, there's a reasonably priced hotel-restaurant, the *Boule d'Or*, 4 rue Cygne (☎02.41.89.82.12; ③; closed Mon & Sun out of season), as well as a pleasant **campsite** by a river just southeast of the town, *Le Pont des Fées*, on chemin du Pont des Fées (☎02.41.89.14.79; closed mid-Sept to mid-May). Decent brasserie fare is available at *Le Commerce* café on place du Marché (☎02.41.89.14.15; closed Wed evening & Sun; menus around 65F/€9.91).

Le Mans and around

LE MANS is 80km northwest of Tours in the *département* of Sarthe, some way from the Loire valley but included here as a good, relatively untouristy base between Normandy and the Loire valley, with swift transport connections down to Angers and Tours. The city is taken over by car fanatics in the middle of June for the famous 24-hour race, but for the rest of the year it's still lively enough, with some interesting museums and one of the most beautiful old quarters of any city in France. It was here, in 1129, that Geoffrey Plantagenet, Count of Maine and Anjou, married Matilda, daughter of Henry I of England, and where their son, the future Henry II, was born.

Arrival, information and accommodation

The hub of Le Mans today is the **place de la République**, with its assortment of Belle Époque facades, fountains and more modern office blocks. Beneath the square in the underground shopping centre is the city **bus terminal**; buses #3, #5 and #16 run between here and the **gare SNCF** via avenue Général-Leclerc, where the **gare routière** is located. From place de la République, rue Bolton leads east into rue de l'Étoile, where you'll find the **tourist office** (Mon–Sat 9am–6pm, Sun 10am–noon, July & Aug also Sun 2–6pm; ☎02.43.28.17.22, fax 02.43.23.37.19) in a turreted seventeenth-century building on the corner with avenue de la Préfecture. **Bikes** can be rented from Top Team, on place St-Pierre in the old town, or from Métayer Loisirs, 73 av Jean-Jaurès (the continuation of rue Nationale).

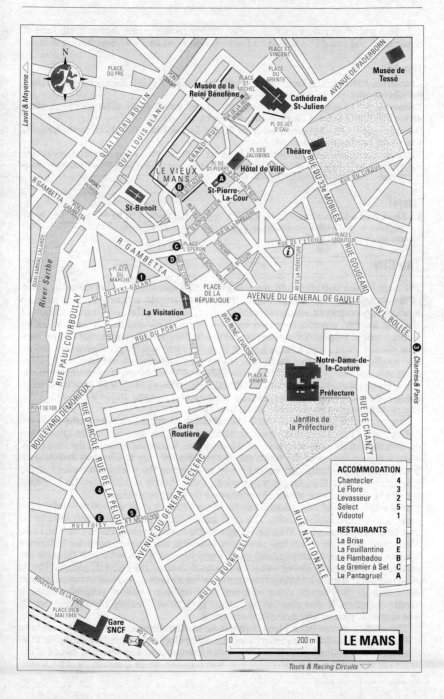

LE MANS

ACCOMMODATION

Chantecler	4
Le Flore	3
Levasseur	2
Select	5
Videotel	1

RESTAURANTS

La Brise	D
La Feuillantine	E
Le Flambadou	B
Le Grenier à Sel	C
Le Pantagruel	A

Tours & Racing Circuits ▽

Unless your visit coincides with one of the big racing events during April, June or September, you should be able to find **accommodation** easily without having to book.

Hotels

Chantecler, 50 rue de la Pelouse (☎02.43.14.40.00, fax 02.43.77.16.28). Slightly impersonal place, but offering quiet, well-equipped rooms and parking. ④.

Levasseur, 5–7 bd René Levasseur (☎02.43.39.61.61, fax 02.43.39.61.65). Good-value hotel, with a decent 67F/€10.21 menu in the restaurant downstairs. ②.

Select, 13 rue du Père-Mersenne, off av du Général-Leclerc (☎02.43.24.17.74). Small and pretty basic hotel, but the price is right. ①.

Videotel, 40 rue du Vert-Galant (☎02.43.24.47.24, fax 02.43.24.58.41). Fairly new hotel overlooking the Sarthe a short way south of the old town, catering mostly to the business crowd; top-floor rooms are the best. Reduced rates on weekends. ③.

Hostel

Le Flore, 23 rue Maupertuis (☎02.43.81.27.55). A clean and modern HI hostel, quite close to the centre. Take av du Général-de-Gaulle from place de la République, continue along av Bollée; rue Maupertuis is the third on the left.

The City

The complicated web of the **old town** lies on a hill above the River Sarthe to the north of the central place de la République. Its medieval streets, a hotch-potch of intricate Renaissance stonework, medieval half-timbering, sculpted pillars and beams and grand classical facades, are still encircled by the original third- and fourth-century **Gallo-Roman walls**, supposedly the best-preserved in Europe and running for several hundred metres. Steep, walled steps lead up from the river, and longer flights descend on the southern side of the enclosure, using old Gallo-Roman entrances. If you're intrigued, you can see pictures, maps and plans of Vieux Mans, plus examples of the city's ancient arts and crafts, most notably the collection of Malicorne ceramics, in the **Musée de la Reine Bérengère** (daily 9am–noon & 2–6pm; 16F/€2.44), one of the Renaissance houses on rue de la Reine-Bérengère.

Rearing up the hill from the east is the immense Gothic apse of the **Cathédrale St-Julien**, with a Romanesque nave and radiating chapels, on place du Grente (also called du Château), at the crowning point of the old town. According to Rodin, the now badly worn sculpted figures of the south porch were rivalled only in Chartres and Athens. Some of the stained-glass windows here were added in the thirteenth century, some time after the first Plantagenet was buried in the church in 1151, but the brightest colours in the otherwise austere interior come from the tapestries.

In the 1850s a road was tunnelled under the quarter – a slum at the time – helping to preserve its self-contained unity. The road tunnel comes out on the south side, by an impressive **monument to Wilbur Wright** – who tested an early flying machine in Le Mans (see opposite) – and into place des Jacobins, the vantage point for St-Julien's double-tiered flying buttresses and apse. From here, you can walk east through the park to the **Musée de Tessé** (daily 9am–noon & 2–6pm; 16F/€2.44), a mixed bunch of pictures and statues including Georges de la Tour's light at its most extraordinary in the *Extase de St-François*, along with copies of brilliant medieval populist murals in Sarthe churches. It also contains an enamel portrait of Geoffrey Plantagenet, which was originally part of his tomb in the cathedral.

The modern centre of Le Mans is **place de la République**, bordered by a mixture of Belle Époque buildings and more modern office blocks, and the Baroque bulk of the **church of the Visitation**, built in 1730, with a balustrade inside designed by one of the sisters of the order. Just south of here is **Notre-Dame de la Couture**, a church with

Plantagenet vaulting and a fine Last Judgement scene over the doorway on an otherwise rather ugly facade. The name has nothing to do with dressmaking but is a corruption of the word *culture* from the days when the church was surrounded by cultivated fields. Inside there are various treasures, including a shroud of the early seventh-century bishop of Le Mans who founded the monastery to which this church belonged.

The racetrack and car museum

Stretching south from the outskirts of the city is the **car racing circuit** (daily 9am–5pm; free), where the world-renowned 24 Heures du Mans car race takes place each year in mid-June, continuing the city's associations with automobiles, begun when local bell-founder Amadée Bollée built his first car back in 1873. Le Mans still has a huge Renault factory operating in its southwest suburbs.

The first big race at Le Mans was the Grand Prix de l'Automobile Club de l'Ouest in 1906, initiated by the newly formed automobile club. Two years later Wilbur Wright took off in his prototype aeroplane, alongside what is now the fastest stretch of the racetrack, remaining in the air for a record-breaking 1 hour and 31.5 minutes. The year 1923 saw the first 24-hour car race, run on the present 13.5-kilometre circuit. Thirty-three contestants took part, and the prize was taken by Lagache and Léonard in a Chenard and Walcker, covering over 2000km at an average speed of 92kph. The distance covered is now over 5000km, with average speeds in excess of 220kph.

Entrance to events at the racetrack is pricey today – around 320F/€48.80 for a seat at the 24 Heures du Mans – but practice sessions are much cheaper, at around 100F/€15.24. Throughout the year motorcycles, go-karts and even trucks race on the 4.25-kilometre Bugatti training circuit, so some practising vehicle is bound to provide you with the appropriate soundtrack for the scene.

The **Musée de l'Automobile** (daily 10am–6pm, June–Sept till 7pm; 40F/€6.10) is on the edge of the Bugatti and 24-hour circuits. It documents the early history of car racing, automobile anatomy and automated assembly. The display includes a superb collection of 150 cars from as far back as 1885 to recent winners, with all the big names represented and in working order. The visit ends with audiovisual displays examining the world of car racing, including a simulated high-speed track.

Eating, drinking and nightlife

In the centre of town, the **cafés** and **brasseries** on place de la République stay open till late, while on nearby place l'Éperon there's a very good, if pricey, restaurant, *Le Grenier à Sel* (☎02.43.23.26.30; closed Sat lunch & Sun; menus from 135F/€20.58), and a very cheap one, *La Brise* (☎02.43.28.20.52). Sophisticated fish dishes are served at *La Feuillantine*, 19bis rue Foisy (☎02.43.28.00.38; closed Sat lunch & Sun), with menus under 100F/€15.24 during the week. The best restaurants, however, are located in the labyrinthine streets of the old town, particularly on and around Grande-Rue. Good value for a special occasion is *Le Flambadou*, 14bis rue St-Flaceau (☎02.43.24.88.38; closed Sun), which offers a very meaty menu, including a fantastic *cassoulet landaise*, from around 200F/€30.49. *Le Pantagruel* on place St-Pierre (☎02.43.24.87.63; closed Mon) is a good bet for fish and *fruits de mer*, with menus from 95F/€14.48.

The **charcuterie** À la Truie qui File, 36 rue du Docteur-Leroy, near place de la République, provides excellent picnic fodder, including the Le Mans version of *rillettes*, or potted pork. There's a daily **market** in the covered halls on place du Marché, plus a bric-a-brac market (with food on Fri) on Wednesday, Friday and Sunday mornings on place du Jet-d'Eau, below the cathedral on the new town side.

Le Mans has a lively **night-time scene**. There are a couple of good late-night **bars** on boulevard Émile-Zola, and a jazz bar, *Le Stan*, on place de l'Éperon (until 4am).

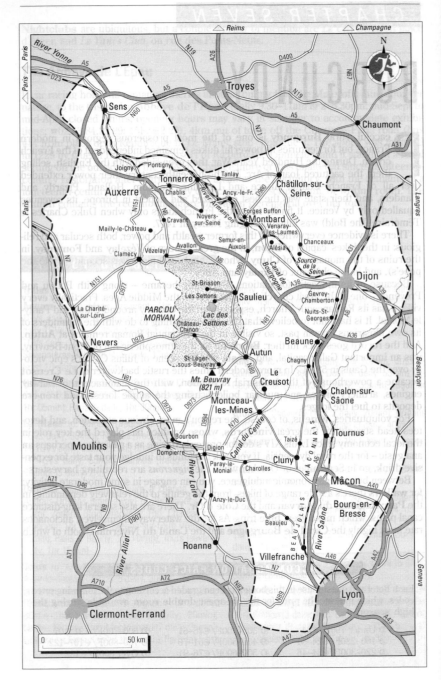

THE FOOD OF BURGUNDY

The **cuisine** of Burgundy is known for its richness, due in large part to two factors: the region's heavy red wines and its possession of one of the world's finest breeds of beef cattle, the Charollais. The **wines** are used in the preparation of the sauces which earn a dish the designation of *à la bourguignonne*. Essentially, this means cooked in a red wine sauce to which baby onions, mushrooms and *lardons* (pieces of bacon) are added. The classic Burgundy dishes cooked in this manner are *bœuf bourguignon* and *coq au vin*. Another term which frequently appears on menus is *meurette*, also a red wine sauce but made without mushrooms and flambéed with a touch of *marc* brandy. It is used with eggs, fish and poultry as well as red meat.

Snails (*escargots*) are hard to avoid in Burgundy, and the local style of cooking them involves stewing them for several hours in the white wine of Chablis with shallots, carrots and onions, then stuffing them with a butter of garlic and parsley and finishing them off in the oven. **Other specialities** include the parsley-flavoured ham (*jambon persillé*); hams from the Morvan hills cooked in a cream *saupiquet* sauce; calf's head (*tête de veau*, or *sansiot*); a *pauchouse* of river fish (that is, poached in white wine with onions, butter and *lardons*); a *poussin* from Bresse; a saddle of hare (*rable de lièvre à la Piron*); and a *potée bourguignonne*, or soup of vegetables cooked in the juices of long-simmered bacon and pork bits.

Like other regions of France, Burgundy produces a variety of **cheeses**. The best-known are the creamy white Chaource, the soft St-Florentin from the Yonne valley, the orange-skinned Époisses and the delicious goat's cheeses from the Morvan. And then there is *gougère*, a kind of cheesecake, best eaten warm with a glass of Chablis.

can be cruised by rented barge; contact the Comité Régional du Tourisme de Bourgogne, BP 1602, 21035 Dijon (☎03.80.50.90.00, fax 03.80.30.59.45, *www.burgundy-tourism.com*).

THE ROAD TO DIJON

The old **road to Dijon**, the Nationale 6, runs from Paris down to the Côte d'Azur, the route taken by the National Guardsmen of Marseille when they marched on Paris singing the *Marseillaise* in 1792. It enters the province of Burgundy just south of Fontainebleau, near where the River Yonne joins the Seine, and follows the Yonne valley through the historic towns of **Sens**, **Joigny** and **Auxerre**. Scattered in a broad corridor to the west and east of the road, in the valleys of the Yonne's tributaries, the Armançon, Serein, Cure and Cousin rivers, is a fascinating collection of abbeys, châteaux, towns, villages and other sites as ancient as the history of France, while further to the southwest lie the wooded hills of the **Morvan**. It makes for a route far more interesting, albeit slower, than speeding around the bland curves of its modern replacement, the **Autoroute du Soleil (A6)**.

Sens

The name of **SENS**, the northernmost town in Burgundy, commemorates the *Senones*, the Gallic tribe whose shaggy troops all but captured Rome in 390 BC; they were only thwarted by the Capitoline geese cackling the garrison awake. Its heyday as a major ecclesiastical centre was in the twelfth and thirteenth centuries, but it lost its pre-eminence in the ensuing centuries largely through damage caused by the Hundred Years War and the Wars of Religion. Nowadays, it is a quiet and unexciting place on the banks of the River Yonne, although the cathedral, its treasury and the adjacent museum make a stop worthwhile.

Contained within a ring of tree-lined boulevards where the city walls once stood, the town's ancient centre is still dominated by the **Cathédrale St-Étienne**, close to the intersection of Grande-Rue and rue de la République, which, together with their prolongations, neatly quarter the town centre. Begun around 1130, it was the first of the great French Gothic cathedrals. Though an early example, the Gothic elements of airiness, space and weightlessness are fully realized in the height of the nave, the arcading of the aisles and the great rose window. The architect who completed it, William of Sens, was later to rebuild the choir of Canterbury Cathedral in England – the link being Thomas à Becket, who had previously spent several years in exile around Sens. The story of his murder is told in the twelfth-century windows in the north aisle of the choir, just part of the cathedral's outstanding collection of stained glass. The **treasury**, which can be entered either from the cathedral or the museum (see below for times), is also uncommonly rich, containing Islamic, Byzantine and French vestments, jewels and embroideries.

Next door is the thirteenth-century **Palais Synodal**, with its roof of Burgundian glazed tiles restored by the nineteenth-century "purist" Viollet-le-Duc, as were those of so many other buildings in this region. Its vaulted halls, originally designed to accommodate the ecclesiastical courts, now house the excellent **Musée de Sens** (July & Aug daily 10am–6pm; Sept–June Mon, Thurs & Fri 2–6pm, Wed, Sat & Sun 10am–6pm; 20F/€3.05, free Wed), which makes all possible use of available space to display a prize collection of exhibits found in the region, including statuary from the cathedral and Gallo-Roman mosaics. Prize exhibits include the Villethierry treasure, which consists of 867 items of bronze jewellery in a jar, and is thought to be a jeweller's hoard; a collection of bone combs; and the facade of Sens' second-century public baths. The vaults of the building – partly constituting the remains of a Gallo-Roman building, including baths heated through the pavement – have also been incorporated into the museum, along with displays of Gallo-Roman metalwork, jewellery and textile crafts, many of which were discovered when the basement was excavated.

Facing the cathedral across place de la République are fine wood and iron *halles*, where a **market** is held on Monday, Friday and Saturday mornings. The square stands right in the centre of town and is intersected by the two main streets, **rue de la République** and **Grande-Rue**. These streets are lined with old houses now converted into shops, and are mainly reserved for pedestrians. There are two particularly finely carved and timbered houses on the corner of rue Jean-Cousin one block south of the square: the **Maison d'Abraham** and the **Maison du Pilier**, with **Maison Jean Cousin** on rue du Général-Alix.

Practicalities

From the **gare SNCF**, Grande-Rue crosses over the two broad arms of the River Yonne and leads straight to the place de la République and the cathedral, about fifteen minutes' walk. The **tourist office** is on place Jean-Jaurès (July & Aug Mon–Sat 9am–12.30pm & 2–7.30pm, Sun 10am–12.30pm & 2–5.30pm; Sept–June Mon–Sat 9am–noon & 1.30–6.15pm; ☎03.86.65.19.49, fax 03.86.64.47.96, *www.mairie-sens.fr*), just north of the Hôtel de Ville, where rue de la République becomes rue Leclerc.

For **places to stay**, try the simple *Hôtel du Centre*, 4 place de la République, above a café opposite the cathedral (☎03.86.65.15.92; ①; closed Wed evening & Thurs, March & Oct), or the pleasant *Esplanade*, 2 bd du Mail (☎03.86.83.14.70, fax 03.86.83.14.71; ②; closed Aug), with a bar downstairs. Also by the cathedral and a cut above the others is the old-time provincial *Hôtel de Paris et de la Poste*, 97 rue de la République (☎03.86.65.17.23, fax 03.86.64.48.45, *www.hotel-paris-poste.com*; ⑤–⑥), with an excellent restaurant specializing in traditional country cuisine (menu at 170F/€25.91, *carte* considerably more). The local **campsite**, *Entre-deux-Vannes*, is on avenue de Sénigallia (☎03.86.65.64.71; closed Nov–March), just out of town.

For **eating**, you'll find pizza, Mexican or French food on place de la République, which is also the place for a coffee or drink. There's a good crêperie, *Aux P'tit Croux*, 3 rue de Brennus, almost on the doorstep of the cathedral (from 45F/€6.86). There's also inexpensive, very good quality Vietnamese food at the *Saigon* on Grande-Rue near the bridge, where a delicious plate of beef and vermicelli is about 30F/€4.57. For excellent seafood, try *Le Soleil Levant*, 51 rue Emile-Zola (☎03.86.65.71.82; closed Sun & Wed evenings & Aug; menus 95–155F/€14.48–23.63).

Joigny

As you travel from Sens towards Auxerre, the next place of any size on the Yonne is the modest town of **JOIGNY**, its elegant old houses ranged up the slope above the river. Its first fort was constructed here at the end of the tenth century, with houses built beneath it, though much of the original settlement was destroyed in a fire in 1530. The town is not worth a prolonged visit, but makes a pleasant rest stop, particularly on market days (Wed & Sat). Buildings worthy of attention are the **Château des Gondi**, built by Cardinal Gondi in the sixteenth century and borrowing Italian influences from the château at Ancy-le-Franc (see p.526), and the remains of the twelfth-century **ramparts** on Chemin de la Guimbard. In addition you can see a few half-timbered houses that somehow escaped the 1530 fire on **rue Montant-au-Palais**, the street leading up to the church of St-Jean, including the best-known **Maison du Pilori**, combining Gothic and Renaissance styles, with some carvings strangely reminiscent of crocodile heads.

The **tourist office** is at 4 quai Ragobert (Mon–Sat 9am–12.15pm & 2–6pm, Sun 10am–noon & 2–4pm; winter closed Mon; ☎03.86.62.11.05, fax 03.86.91.76.38, *www.ville-joigny.fr*), by the **gare routière**. Cheap **hotels** include the simple but adequate *Relais de L'Escargot*, 1 av Roger-Varrey (☎03.86.62.10.38; ①), and the *Relais Paris-Nice*, Rond Point de la Résistance (☎03.86.62.06.72, fax 03.86.62.44.33; ②; restaurant from 75F/€11.43, closed Sun evening & Mon). A much classier and more modern establishment is *Rive Gauche* on chemin du Port-au-Bois (☎03.86.91.46.66, fax 03.86.91.46.93; ④), with a very reasonable restaurant overlooking the river (menus 98–138F/€14.94–21.03). There's a decent **bar**, the *Montmartre*, on place de Jean-de-Joigny. But the nicest place (both to stay and eat) is a little way out of town to the west, 6km along the D182 towards St-Julien-du-Sault – *Le P'tit Claridge*, in Thèmes (☎03.86.63.10.92, fax 03.86.63.01.34; ②; closed Jan & Feb), with a restaurant offering a very good-value menu at 90F/€13.72 (closed Sun evening, Mon, Jan & Feb).

An interesting side trip from Joigny is the village of **ST-SAUVEUR-EN-PUISAYE**, the birthplace, in 1873, of Colette. The **Musée Colette** is in the château (April–Oct daily except Tues 10am–6pm; rest of year Sat & Sun 2–6pm; 25F/€3.81) and includes a reconstruction of her apartment in Paris, as well as personal items and original manuscripts.

Auxerre and around

A pretty old town of narrow lanes and unexpected open squares, **AUXERRE** stands on a hill a further 15km up the Yonne from Joigny. It looks its best seen from Pont Paul-Bert and the riverside **quais**, where houseboats and barges moor, its churches soaring dramatically and harmoniously above the surrounding rooftops. The most interesting of the churches is the disused abbey church of **St Germain**, now a museum (daily except Tues: May–Sept 9.45am–6.30pm; Oct–April 9.45am–noon & 2–6pm; 22F/€3.35), at the opposite end of rue Cauchois from the cathedral. Partial demolition has left its belfry detached from the body of the building, but what gives it special interest is the **crypt**, one of the few surviving examples of Carolingian architecture, with its plain barrel vaults still resting on their thousand-year-old oak beams. Deep inside, the faded ochre frescoes of St Stephen (St Étienne) are among the most ancient in France, dating back to around 850 AD.

The **Cathedral** itself (daily except Sun morning: July–Sept 9am–6pm; rest of year 9am–noon & 2–5/6pm) still remains unfinished, despite the fact that its construction was drawn out over more than three centuries from 1215 to 1560: the southernmost of the two west front towers has never been completed. Compensation for this lies in the richly detailed sculpture of the porches and in the glorious colours of the original thirteenth-century glass that still fills the windows of the choir, despite the savagery of the Wars of Religion and the Revolution. There has been a church on the site since about 400 AD, though nothing visible survives earlier than the eleventh-century **crypt** (10F/€1.52). Among its frescoes is a unique depiction of a warrior Christ mounted on a white charger, accompanied by four mounted angels.

From in front of the cathedral, rue Fourier leads to place du Marché and off left to the Hôtel de Ville and the old city gateway known as the **Tour de l'Horloge**, with its fifteenth-century coloured clock face. The whole quarter, from place Surugue through rue Joubert and down to the river, is full of attractive old houses. Of somewhat recondite interest, the **Musée Leblanc-Duvernoy**, in an eighteenth-century *hôtel* at 9 rue Egleny, contains a collection of faïence and china of local provenance, furniture and tapestries (daily except Tues 2–6pm; 12F/€1.83, free Wed).

If you're finding the narrow streets a bit confining, then take a stroll to the **Clos de Chaînette**, off to the northeast, the only vineyard in Auxerre to be spared in the phylloxera disaster of the nineteenth century.

Practicalities

If you arrive by train at the **gare SNCF** in rue Paul-Doumer, you'll find yourself across the river from the town: to get to the centre, follow signs for the *centre ville*, crossing Pont Paul-Bert. The **tourist office** is by the bridge at 2 quai de la République (summer Mon–Sat 9am–1pm & 2–7pm, Sun 10am–1pm & 2–6.30pm; winter Mon–Sat 10am–12.30pm & 2–6.30pm, Sun 10am–1pm; ☎03.86.52.06.19, fax 03.86.51.23.27, *www.auxerre.com*), with an annexe in place des Cordeliers in summer. The **gare routière** lies in place des Migraines off the *boulevard périphérique*. There's a **market** in place de l'Arquebuse (Wed morning), and another on the *périphérique* at the end of rue du Temple (Tues & Fri morning).

First choice for somewhere to **stay** should be *Hôtel Normandie*, 41 bd Vauban (☎03.86.52.57.80, fax 03.86.51.54.33, *www.acom.fr/normandie*; ④), which is wonderfully luxurious and reasonably priced, considering all its amenities: gym, sauna, room service, a 24-hour porter and a current copy of *The Times* to read over breakfast. *Les Clairions*, on avenue Worms in the Clairions district off the N6 to Paris (☎03.86.94.94.94, fax 03.86.48.16.38, *www.clairions.com*; ④; restaurant from 100F/€15.24), is less characterful but just as pleasant, and, down by the river, *Le Maxime* at 2 quai de la Marine (☎03.86.52.14.19, fax 03.86.52.21.70; ⑤; closed mid-Dec to Jan) is both expensive and elegant, with an excellent attached restaurant (menus 170–400F/€25.91–60.98). For a simple and inexpensive stay, try the central *Hôtel de la Renommée*, 27 rue d'Egleny (☎03.86.52.03.53, fax 03.86.51.47.83; ②; closed Sun, one week in Feb & three weeks in Aug), whose restaurant has menus from 50F/€7.62 to 145F/€22.10. Cheapest of all are the *foyers* (which offer hostel-style accommodation): there is one at 16 av de la Résistance, across the tracks by the footbridge at the train station (☎03.86.46.95.11; canteen 40F/€6.10), and a second at 16 bd Vaulabelle (☎03.86.52.45.58), at the back of the courtyard of the Peugeot and Citroën garage.

There's also a pleasant municipal **campsite**, south at 8 rte de Vaux (☎03.86.52.11.15; closed Oct–March), next to the riverside football ground.

Finding somewhere to **eat** is easy, as there are numerous reasonably priced restaurants. *Le Bistrot de Palais*, 69 rue de Paris (☎03.86.51.47.02; closed Sun & Aug), is a lively place with a changing menu (from 100F/€15.24); *La Primavera*, 37 rue du Pont (closed Sun, Mon & three weeks in Aug; menus 80–130F/€12.20–19.82), does good Greek, Italian and Mediterranean food; and *Le Quai*, in the very pretty place St-Nicholas beside the river not far from the tourist office, does *plats du jour* at lunchtime for 59F/€8.99 – though it is really a place for a drink. For good traditional cuisine, there's *Le Saint Pélerin*, 56 rue St-Pélerin, near the Pont Paul-Bert (☎03.86.52.77.05; closed Sun, Mon & three weeks in Aug), with menus at 110F/€16.77 and 120F/€18.29. Finally, top of the range in culinary terms, the imaginative *Le Jardin Gourmand*, 56 bd Vauban, offers its cheapest menu at 150F/€22.87 (☎03.86.51.53.52; closed Tues & Wed, mid-Aug to Sept).

Around Auxerre

On or close to the D965 and the Paris–Dijon train route in the open, rolling country east of Auxerre lie several minor attractions, ranging from Greek treasures to Cistercian abbeys and Renaissance châteaux. The valley of the aptly named Serein River is the location of the villages of **Pontigny**, of monastic origin, **Chablis**, famed for its excellent vineyards, and the time-locked **Noyers-sur-Serein**; while to the south, a string of villages along the **upper valley of the Yonne** provides a glimpse of a gentler, more intimate countryside, with the possibility of a quiet night's rest for the long-distance traveller keen to get away from the main roads and towns.

Pontigny

The ravages of time – in particular, the 1789 Revolution – have destroyed most of the great monastic buildings of the Cistercian order of monks, whose rigorous insistence on simplicity and manual labour under their most influential twelfth-century leader, St Bernard, was a revolutionary response to the worldliness and luxury of the Benedictine abbots of Cluny (see p.555). Citeaux and Clairvaux, the first Cistercian foundations, are unrecognizable today: the only places in Burgundy where you can get an idea of how Cistercian ideas translated into bricks and mortar are at Pontigny and Fontenay (p.528).

PONTIGNY lies 18km northeast of Auxerre, and its beautifully preserved twelfth-century **abbey church** stands on the edge of the village, where its functional mass rises from the meadows. There is no tower, no stained glass and no statuary to distract from its austere, harmonious lines, though the effect is marred by the seventeenth-century choir that occupies much of the nave. Begun in the early 1100s and finished in the late, it spans the transition between the old Romanesque and the new Gothic, and was much copied in the country round about – in Chablis, for example.

Three Englishmen played a major role in the abbey's early history, all of them archbishops of Canterbury: Thomas à Becket took refuge from Henry II in the abbey in 1164, Stephen Langton similarly lay low here during an argument over his eligibility for the primacy, and Edmund Rich died here – his tomb in the church is a goal of pilgrimages to this day. The abbey was also the origin of a tourist attraction with which a nearby village is more often associated: the famous **Chablis wine**. It was the monks of Pontigny who originally developed and refined the variety, and the village and its unassuming neighbouring hamlets are better places to sample the wine than in the expensive wine bars of Chablis itself.

There is a simple **hotel** in Pontigny: the *Relais de Pontigny* on the N77 (☎03.86.47.96.74; ①; restaurant from 75F/€11.43), whose rooms have neither bath nor shower. With more cash, it's better to go for the *Relais St-Vincent*, 14 Grande-Rue in nearby **LIGNY-LE-CHATEL**, 4km along the D91 (☎03.86.47.53.38, fax 03.86.47.54.16; ③; restaurant from 70F/€10.67, closed Feb). Another hotel possibility is the comfy *Soleil d'Or* at **MONTIGNY-LA-RESLE** on the N77 (☎03.86.41.81.21, fax 03.86.41.86.88; ②; closed Jan; restaurant from 98F/€14.94). Ligny also has a **campsite** by the Serein off the D8 Auxerre road (mid-May to Sept).

Chablis

Sixteen kilometres to the south of Pontigny on winding, rural D965, the pretty red-roofed village of **CHABLIS** is the home of the region's famous light dry white wines. It lies in the valley of the River Serein – brimful of fish waiting to be poached – between the wide and mainly treeless upland wheat fields typical of this corner of Burgundy. While wandering around the village you could take a look at the side door of the **church of St-Martin**, decorated with ancient horseshoes and other bits of rustic ironwork left as *ex votos* by visiting pilgrims. Legend has it that Joan of Arc was one of them.

The **tourist office** (Maison de la Vigne et du Vin) is at 1 rue de Chichée (May–Nov daily 9.30am–12.30pm & 1.30–6pm; ☎03.86.42.80.80). If you need to **stay** the night, try the nearby *Hôtel de l'Étoile*, 4 rue des Moulins (☎03.86.42.10.50, fax 03.86.42.81.21; ②; closed Sun evening, Mon in winter & Jan; restaurant from 90F/€13.72). There's also an attractive **campsite**, the *Camping de Chablis* (☎03.86.42.44.39, fax 03.86.42.49.71; mid-June to mid-Sept), beside the river just outside the village. If you're seeking **sustenance**, *Le Vieux Moulin*, 18 rue des Moulins (☎03.86.42.47.30; closed Mon evening & Tues) is good enough, with menus ranging from 99F/€15.10 to 240F/€36.59.

Noyers-sur-Serein

Twenty-three kilometres to the southeast of Chablis – there's no choice but to hitch if you don't have your own transport – you come to the beautiful little town of **NOYERS-SUR-SEREIN**, sealed from the modern world in a medieval time warp. Its half-timbered and arcaded houses, ornamented with rustic carvings – particularly those on place de la Petite-Étape-aux-Vins and round place de l'Hôtel-de-Ville – are corralled inside a loop of the river and the town walls, and pleasant hours can be passed wandering the path between the river and the irregular walls, with their robust towers. The Serein here is as pretty as in Chablis, but Noyers, being remarkably free of commercialism, has more authentic charm.

The town's main sight is the **Musée de l'Art Naïf** (June–Sept daily 11am–6.30pm; Oct–May Sat & Sun only same hours; 15F/€2.29), comprising the remarkable collec-

---

CHABLIS: THE WINE

The neatly staked Chablis **vineyards**, originally planted by the monks of Pontigny (see p.523), cover the sunny, well-drained, stony slopes on both sides of the valley. The grape is the *chardonnay*, which is to white wine what the *pinot noir* is to red: raw material of all the greatest Burgundies. To taste the wines, avoid Chablis itself: the town milks its product for all it's worth. Overpriced wine bars and stuffy restaurants abound, you don't get the opportunity to taste the cheaper varieties, and there's haughty disapproval if you hope to spend less than 100F/€15.24 a bottle. You'd be better off heading for the co-operative, La Chablisienne, 8 bd Pasteur (Mon–Sat 8am–noon & 2–6pm, Sun 9.30am–noon & 2–6pm; ☎03.86.42.89.98, *www.chablisienne.com*), which offers maximum variety in a casual environment – better still, drink in one of the other villages like Pontigny or Maligny. If you want to buy a good wine, go for one with an *appellation*; the seven distinguished *grands crus*, from the northern slopes of the valley, are the best, with the *premiers crus*, made from more widely planted grapes, next in line. For information on the Chablis *appellation*, ask at the tourist office.

tion of art historian Jacques Yankel. The Naive painters had no formal training and were often workers lacking academic education (one, Augustine Lesage, worked as a miner for sixty years before he started painting). Some star exhibits include Gérard Lattier's morbid comic-strip-style work and the excellent collages of Louis Quilici.

The best place to **stay** is the creeper-covered seventeenth-century *Hôtel de la Vieille Tour* in place du Grenier-à-Sel in the town centre (☎03.86.82.87.69, fax 03.86.82.66.04; ②), with ten beautifully furnished rooms and views across the gardens to the river; it's also the best place to **eat** (excellent *table d'hôte* meal for 75F/€11.43). At the entrance to the village the *Porte Peinte* restaurant (☎03.86.82.81.07; Easter–Oct closed Wed evening & Thurs) has menus at 120F/€18.29 and 180F/€27.44.

South – the valley of the Yonne

If you're travelling south from Auxerre and want a break from the main roads, head along the D163, a twisting minor road which follows the course of the **River Yonne** through a score of peaceful rural villages. Several have places both to stay and eat, making for a much more restful overnight stop than the towns.

VAUX and **ESCOLIVES-STE-CAMILLE**, the first villages you come to, both have attractive Romanesque churches. **VINCELOTTES** and **IRANCY**, on the opposite bank of the river, are flower-decked and picturesque: Irancy produces the only red wine in this area, much loved by Louis XIV, while Vincelottes was the port for shipping it.

A nice place to stay is *Le Castel* on place de l'Église in **MAILLY-LE-CHÂTEAU**, a further 10km along the river (☎03.86.81.43.06, fax 03.86.81.49.26; ③; closed Wed & mid-Nov to mid-March), which has a most attractive and attentive restaurant, serving tasty snails, *coq au vin* and *magret de canard* at around 150F/€22.87 à la carte (menus 75–175F/€11.43–26.67). The main part of the village is on high ground above the river, but there's also a lovely riverside quarter, with ancient houses huddling under cliffs.

Half a dozen kilometres further upstream, more cliffs (the **Rochers du Saussois**) flank the east bank of the river: about 50m high, they are a series of broken rock walls, ideal for rock climbing – which is indeed what they are used for, with routes of all sorts of different grades. From here south to Clamecy, the river is at its most attractive, becoming more and more of a mountain stream.

The Canal de Bourgogne

From Migennes near Joigny on the N6, the River Armançon, in tandem with the **Canal de Bourgogne**, branches off to the north of the River Yonne. Along or close to its valley are several places of real interest: the Renaissance châteaux of **Ancy-le-Franc** and **Tanlay**, the eighteenth-century ironworks and **Fontenay monastery** near **Montbard** and the site of Julius Cæsar's victory over the Gauls at **Alésia**. It is a route which is particularly worthwhile if you don't have your own transport, for all these places are served by trains on the Dijon–Migennes line (with connections to Sens and Auxerre).

Tonnerre and around

On the Paris–Sens–Dijon train route, **TONNERRE** is a useful, though not that inspiring, starting point for exploring this corner of the region. A run-down little town that has clearly not enjoyed the same prosperity as its neighbour Chablis, it has as its principal sight the vast and well-conserved medieval hospital, the **Hôtel-Dieu** (hourly guided tours: June–Sept daily except Tues 10am–noon & 1–7pm; April, May & Oct Sat, Sun & hols only 1–6pm; 23F/€3.51), right on the main road in the middle of town. In the chapel is a super-expressive and realistic piece of Burgundian tableau statuary, an *Entombment of Christ*, in the style pioneered by Claus Sluter.

A couple of blocks from the hospital, the **Hôtel d'Uzès** saw the birth of Tonnerre's quirkiest claim to fame, an eighteenth-century gentleman with the fittingly excessive moniker Charles-Geneviève-Louis-Auguste-André-Timothé Déon de Beaumont (b.1728). He tickled his contemporaries' prurience by going about his important diplomatic missions for King Louis XV dressed in women's clothes. His act was so convincing that while he was in London bookmakers took bets on his real sex. Oddly enough, he was also a fearsome swordsman, though history does not relate what he wore to fight in. When he died, the results of the autopsy were eagerly awaited by the gossip columnists of the day. You can see the house where he lived from 1779 to 1785 at 22 rue du Pont.

The **tourist office** is at 42 rue de l'Hôpital (July & Aug Mon–Sat 9am–12.30pm & 2–6pm, Sun 10am–12.30pm; Sept–June Mon–Sat 9am–noon & 2–5pm; ☎03.86.55.14.48). The cheapest **accommodation** is at the *Hôtel du Centre*, 65 rue de l'Hôpital (☎03.86.55.10.56, fax 03.86.51.10.63; ①), an old-fashioned provincial hotel with a reasonable little **restaurant** (menus from 60F/€9.15). Slightly posher is the *de la Fosse Dionne*, 37 rue de l'Hôtel-de-Ville (☎03.86.55.11.92, fax 03.86.55.21.23; ③), near the beautiful old *lavoir*, or public washing-place, also with a restaurant (menu from 90F/€13.72); or for a touch more luxury, try *L'Abbaye Saint Michel*, montée St-Michel (☎03.86.55.05.99, fax 03.86.55.00.10; ⑦). The local **campsite**, *La Cascade* (☎03.86.55.15.44; May–Sept), is between the River Armançon and the Canal de Bourgogne. If you fancy a **drink**, you can sample the wines of Tonnerre at Les Vinées du Tonnerois, in the cellars of the Hôtel-Dieu.

The châteaux of Ancy-le-Franc and Tanlay

Close to Tonnerre are two of the finest, though least-known and least-visited, châteaux in France: Tanlay and Ancy-le-Franc. The former has the edge for romantic appeal, the latter for architectural purity.

The **Château of Ancy-le-Franc**, 8km from Tonnerre, was built in the mid-sixteenth century for the brother-in-law of the notorious Diane de Poitiers, mistress of Henri II (guided tours March 23–Nov 11 hourly at 10am, 11am & 2–6pm; Sept 15–Nov 11 last visit 5pm; ☎03.86.75.14.63; 42F/€6.40). More Italian than French, with its rather gloomy, austere classical countenance, it is the only accepted work of the Italian Sebastiano Serlio, one of the most important architectural theorists, who was brought to France in 1540 by François I to work on his palace at Fontainebleau. The inner courtyard is more elaborate, and some of the apartments are sumptuous, decorated by the Italian artists Primaticcio and Niccolò dell'Abbate, who also worked at Fontainebleau. The most impressive rooms are La Chambre des Arts, with medallions by Primaticcio, and La Galerie des Sacrifices, with monumental battle scenes in monochrome by Abbate.

Ancy has two small **hotels**, the *Hostellerie du Centre*, 34 Grande-Rue (☎03.86.75.15.11, fax 03.86.75.14.13; ③; closed Fri in winter & Dec 20–Jan 5; good restaurant from 76F/€11.59), and *Hôtel de la Poste*, 79 Grande-Rue (☎03.86.75.11.08; ①; closed Wed & Oct 22–31; restaurant from 75F/€11.43, closed in winter).

The **Château of Tanlay** (guided tours daily except Tues: April to mid-Nov hourly 9.30–11.30am, every 45min 2.15–5.15pm; ☎03.86.75.70.61; 40F/€6.10), 15km along the canal from Tonnerre, is by contrast much more French and full of *fantaisie*. It is only slightly later in date, about 1559, but those extra few years were enough for the purer Italian influences visible in Ancy to have become Frenchified. It also feels much more feudal, the village crouching humbly at its gate and its approach road – a long straight tree-lined avenue – like a private drive, tying down the land on either side, proclaiming ownership.

Encircling the château are water-filled moats, and a wooded hill provides an effective backdrop. Standing guard over the entrance to the first grassy courtyard is the grand lodge, and it's here that you enter the château proper across a stone drawbridge. Domed and lanterned turrets terminate the wings of the *cour d'honneur*, urns line the ridge of the roof, from whose slates project carved and pedimented dormers. The white stone and round medieval towers, leftovers from the original fortress, add to the irregularity and charm. Inside, the most remarkable, if overpowering, room is the Grande Galerie, entirely covered by monochrome *trompe-l'œil* frescoes.

Montbard and around

The area around **MONTBARD** offers some insights into Burgundy's early industrial heritage. Blessed with iron-ore deposits, extensive forest for charcoal burning and water for hydraulic power, this part of the country became the cradle of the French industrial revolution during the eighteenth century (see also "Le Creusot", p.539). The earliest foundries were small-scale rural affairs, dependent on one man's knowledge, with minimal and costly production, despite the invention of the blast furnace (*haut fourneau*) and the use of water power to drive hammers and bellows.

The town itself is of no great interest, and its current predicament is typical of present-day industrial Europe: it's a one-industry town – making steel tubes – so things are economically vulnerable. It was the family home of the celebrated botanist, the Comte de Buffon (see below), and the most interesting things are the pretty terraced gardens of the **Parc Buffon**, laid out by the great man, and the **museum** opposite, Cabinet de Travail de Buffon, devoted to his works (Mon & Wed–Fri 2–5pm, Sat & Sun 10am–noon & 2–5pm; 15F/€2.29, 25F/€3.81 combined ticket with the Musée des Beaux-Arts), and with a rather specialist display of books, manuscripts and drawings. There is also a **Musée des Beaux-Arts**, rue Piron (daily except Tues: April, Sept & Oct 3–6pm; June–Aug 10am–noon & 3–6pm; 15F/€2.29), with works by famous local artists, included the sculptor Pompon.

The **tourist office** is in rue Carnot (April–Oct daily 9am–noon & 2.30–6.30pm; Nov–March Mon–Sat 9am–noon & 2–6/7pm, Sun 10am–noon; ☎03.80.92.03.75), and can provide a list of local *chambres* and *tables d'hôtes*, *gîtes* and *fermes auberges*. Alternatively, there's **accommodation** opposite the train station at *Hôtel de la Gare*, 10 rue Maréchal-Foch (☎03.80.92.02.12, fax 03.80.92.41.72; ③; closed Dec 22–Jan 31), and a **campsite** near the swimming pool on rue Michel-Servet (☎03.80.92.21.60; Feb–Oct).

Forges de Buffon

Just outside Montbard, 6km north on D905, beside the River Armançon and the Canal de Bourgogne, are the remains of one of the most influential eighteenth-century foundries, the **Forges de Buffon** (April–June & Sept Wed–Fri 2.30–6.30pm; July & Aug Wed–Fri 10am–noon & 2.30–6pm, Sat & Sun 2.30–6pm; 25F/€3.81), built in 1768 by Georges-Louis Buffon, distinguished scientist, landowner and lord of Montbard. Production was never more than 400 tonnes of iron a year, but Buffon's main interest was experimental. The site, now owned by an Englishman and being restored as part of the growing French interest in industrial archeology, comprises model dwellings for workers (woodmen, ox-drivers and miners along with foundry workers) as well as the **foundry workshops**. These are situated on the banks of the river, designed in a most unindustrial classical style, with special viewing galleries for royal visitors and a grand staircase. There's not a great deal to see (some reproductions of machinery made by kids from the local school), but you get a unique insight into a pre-capitalist approach to industry. The foundry's most notable product was the railings, still in place, of the Jardin des Plantes in Paris.

The best approach to the Forges de Buffon is a pleasant hour's walk along the canal path. If that doesn't appeal, there are buses to St-Rémy, from where it's a mere two-kilometre hike to **BUFFON**, where you can refresh yourself at the *Marronier* (☎03.80.92.33.65; meals from 60F/€9.14).

Fontenay Abbey

Six kilometres east of Montbard and accessible from the GR213 footpath, the privately owned **Abbey of Fontenay** (daily 45min guided tours: July & Aug hourly 9am–noon & every half-hour 2–6pm; Sept–June hourly 9am–noon & 2–6pm; 45/€6.86F), founded in 1118, is the only Burgundian monastery to survive intact, despite conversion to a paper mill in the early nineteenth century. It was restored earlier this century to its original form and is one of the most complete monastic complexes anywhere, comprising care-taker's lodge, guesthouse and chapel, dormitory, hospital, prison, bakery, kennels, dovecote, abbot's house, as well as church, cloister, chapterhouse and even a forge. There's not much to be seen in the forge, but it is interesting that there should have been such a large one here, where France's industrial ironmasters set up shop 500 years later.

On top of all this, the abbey's physical setting, at the head of a quiet stream-filled val-ley enclosed by woods of pine, fir, sycamore and beech trees, is superb. There is a bucolic calm about the place, but you still feel a *frisson* of unease at the spartan sim-plicity of Cistercian life. Not a scrap of decoration softens the church: there's not one carved capital – the motherly statue of the Virgin arrived after St Bernard's death – and there's no direct lighting in the nave, just an other-worldly glow from the square-ended apse, beautiful but daunting, the perfect structural embodiment of St Bernard's ascetic principles.

Venarey-les-Laumes and around

One train stop south of Montbard (or 3hr on the GR213) brings you to **VENAREY-LES-LAUMES**, home to another ailing metal tube factory. It was here, or rather behind and above the town, on the flat-topped hill of Mont Auxois, that the Gauls, united for once under the leadership of Vercingétorix, made their last stand against the military might of Rome at the **Battle of Alésia** in 52 BC. Julius Cæsar himself commanded the Roman army, surrounding the hill with a huge double ditch and earthworks and starv-ing the Gauls out, bloodily defeating all attempts at escape. Vercingétorix surrendered to save his people, was imprisoned in Rome for six years until Cæsar's formal triumph and then strangled. The battle was a great turning point in the fortunes of the region. Thereafter, Gaul remained under Roman rule for four hundred years. The **site** of Alésia, treeless and exposed, is back along the ridge 3km from the modern village of Alise-Ste-Reine (see below). While you can see little more than the layout today, it is extensive, and the interest of the whole area lies in imagined atmosphere rather than in anything concrete.

There's a **tourist office** in Venarey at place de Bingerbrúck (April–Sept Mon–Sat 9.30am–12.30pm & 2–7pm, Sun 9.30am–noon; rest of year Mon–Sat 10am–noon & 3–6pm, Sun 10am–noon; ☎03.80.96.89.13), offering information about the town and its surroundings. **Accommodation** can be found at *Hôtel-Restaurant de la Gare*, 6 av de la Gare (☎03.80.96.00.46, fax 03.80.96.13.04; ③; restaurant from 85F/€12.96, closed Fri & Sun evening). The local **campsite** is off the D954.

Alise-Ste-Reine

Towards the top of Mont Auxois, the village of **ALISE-STE-REINE** has a small **mu-seum** (daily: April–June & mid-Sept to Nov 10am–6pm; July to mid-Sept 9am–7pm; 17F/€2.59), which displays finds from the Gallic town of Alésia and Cæsar's earthworks (the line of them still clearly visible in aerial photographs). On the first weekend of September the martyrdom of St Reine is celebrated in a **costume procession** through the village, a custom that goes back to the year 866. St Reine was a young Christian girl who was put to death in 262 for refusing to marry the proconsul of the Gauls, Olibrius. This martyrdom was the occasion for the conversion of Alésia.

Directly above the village, steps climb up to a great bronze **statue of Vercingétorix**. Erected by Napoléon III, whose influence popularized the rediscovery of France's pre-Roman roots, the statue represents Vercingétorix as a romantic Celt, half virginal Christ, half long-haired 1970s matinee idol. On the plinth is inscribed a quotation from Vercingétorix's address to the Gauls as imagined by Julius Cæsar: "United and forming a single nation inspired by a single ideal, Gaul can defy the world." Napoléon signs his dedication, "Emperor of the French", inspired by a vain desire to gain legitimacy by linking his own name to that of a "legendary" Celt.

The Château de Bussy-Rabutin

Eight kilometres east of Venarey, on the D954, stands the handsome **Château de Bussy-Rabutin** (guided tours: April–June & Sept daily 9.30–11.30am & 2–5pm; July & Aug daily 9am–6pm; Oct–March Mon & Thurs–Sun 10–11am & 2–3pm; 35F/€5.34), built for Roger de Rabutin, member of the Academy in the reign of Louis XIV and a notorious womanizer. The scurrilous tales of life at the royal court told in his book *Histoires Amoureuses des Gaules* earned him a spell in the Bastille, followed by years of exile in this château, which contains some interesting portraits of great characters of the time, including the famous female beauties of the age, each underlined by an acerbic little comment of this kind: "The most beautiful woman of her day, less renowned for her beauty than the uses she put it to".

Châtillon and the source of the Seine

If you're interested in pre-Roman France, there is one compelling reason for going to **CHÂTILLON-SUR-SEINE**: the so-called **Treasure of Vix**. Housed in the town's **museum** in the Maison Philandrier, 7 rue du Bourg, close to the centre (mid-April to mid-June & mid-Sept to mid-Nov daily except Tues 9am–noon & 2–6pm; mid-June to mid-Sept daily 9am–noon & 1.30–6pm; mid-Nov to mid-April daily except Tues 10am–noon & 2–5pm; 28F/€4.26), it consists of the finds from the sixth-century BC tomb of a Celtic princess buried in a four-wheeled chariot. In addition to pieces of the chariot, the finds include staggeringly beautiful jewellery, Greek vases and Etruscan bowls. But the best on show is a gloriously simple gold tiara, actually found on the princess's head, and the largest bronze vase (*krater*) of Greek origin known from antiquity. It stands an incredible 1.64m high on triple tripod legs, and around its rim is a superbly modelled high-relief frieze depicting naked hoplites and horse-drawn chariots, with Gorgons' heads for handles. How these magnificent objects found their way to such a remote place is a mystery. One explanation lies in the fact that the village of **VIX**, 6km northwest of Châtillon, is the highest navigable point on the Seine, and it is thought that the Celtic chieftains who controlled it received such gifts, possibly from traders in Cornish tin shipped south from Britain via here on its way to the Adriatic, or perhaps to the bronze workers of Bibracte, the capital of the Aedui (see p.538).

The town of Châtillon has a few other points of interest. On the rocky bluff overlooking the steep-pitched roofs of Châtillon's old quarter are the ruins of a **castle** and the early Romanesque **church of St Vorles**. At its foot in a luxuriantly verdant spot, a **spring** swells out of the rock to join the infant Seine.

The **tourist office** is off place Marmont (daily 9am–noon & 2–6pm; Nov–March closed Wed & Sun; ☎03.80.91.13.19). There is a very welcoming **hotel**, the *Jura*, at 19 rue Docteur-Robert (☎03.80.91.26.96, fax 03.80.91.10.52; ②; closed Sun evening). Alternatives are the *Sylvia*, standing in attractive grounds at 9 av de la Gare (☎03.80.91.02.44, fax 03.80.91.47.77; ②–③), and the three-star *Hôtel de la Côte d'Or*, 2 rue Charles-Ronot (☎03.80.91.13.29, fax 03.80.91.29.15; ④; closed Dec 20–Jan 31), with an excellent **restaurant** (from 95F/€14.48).

The source of the Seine

To get to the **source of the Seine** you'll have to hitch 43km down the N71, or take the GR2 footpath, to the hamlet of **COURCEAU**. From there, by road, take D103 through the upland hamlet of St-Germain, all crumbling stone farms and barns; or, better still, because rides are unlikely, pick up the GR2 at the bridge in Courceau for a two-hour walk.

The Seine, no more than a trickle here, rises in a tight little vale of beech woods. The spring is now covered by an artificial grotto complete with a languid nymph, Sequana, spirit of the Seine. In Celtic times it was a place of worship, as is clear from the numerous votive offerings discovered there, including a neat bronze of Sequana standing in a bird-shaped boat, now in the Dijon archeological museum (see p.545). If you're here alone, it's a good place for rustic reverie, but if your arrival coincides with a coachload of Parisian day-trippers (the site belongs to the city of Paris), you'd be wise to retreat downstream. There's a **campsite** at **CHANCEAUX**, 5km away on the N71 (mid-April to Sept).

Semur-en-Auxois

Thirteen kilometres west of Venarey, the small fortress town of **SEMUR-EN-AUXOIS** sits on a rocky bluff, an extraordinarily beautiful little place of cobbled lanes, medieval gateways and ancient gardens cascading down to the River Armançon; only the patina of centuries could achieve such harmony of shape and colour. All roads here lead to place Notre-Dame, a handsome square dominated by the large thirteenth-century **church of Notre-Dame**, another Viollet-le-Duc restoration, characterized by its huge entrance porch and the narrowness of its nave. The twin-towered west front has had many of its statues removed and the niches left bare. The best view is from the east in place de l'Ancienne-Comédie, past the finely sculpted north transept door (depicting the Life of Doubting Thomas), with a couple of Burgundy snails, symbol of Burgundy's culinary traditions, carved on the flanking columns. Inside, the windows of the first chapel on the left commemorate American soldiers of World War I – a reminder that the battlefields were not far away. Also on the left are more fine fifteenth-century windows, dedicated by the butchers' and drapers' guilds and illustrating their trades, and a masterly Sluteresque painted *Entombment*.

Down the street in front of the church and off to the left you come to the four sturdy towers of Semur's once powerful **castle**, dismantled in 1602 because of its utility to enemies of the French crown. There is a dramatic view of it from the **Pont Joly** on the river below. The whole town is full of interesting buildings: there is scarcely a street without something of note, and there's a pleasant shady walk around the **fortifications**. On rue J.-J.-Collenot, the **library** (Wed 2–6pm), which is part of the otherwise not very interesting town **museum** (mid-June to mid-Sept daily except Tues 2–6pm; rest of year Wed & Fri only 2–5.30pm; free), has a fantastic collection of illuminated manuscripts and early printed books.

Cheese connoisseurs might like to take a twelve-kilometre hop further west on the Avallon road to **ÉPOISSES**, not just for its village and **château** (July & Aug daily except Tues 10am–noon & 2–6pm; 30F/€4.57), but for its distinctive soft orange-skinned cheeses washed in *marc de Bourgogne*.

Practicalities

Semur's **tourist office** is on the small place Gaveau (July & Aug daily 8.30am–noon & 2–6.30pm; rest of year closed Sun; ☎03.80.97.05.96), at the junction of rues de l'Ancienne-Comédie, de la Liberté and Buffon, where the medieval Porte Sauvigny and Porte Guillier combine to form a single long, covered gateway.

The cheapest **hotel rooms** in town are at *Hôtel des Gourmets*, 4 rue de Varenne (☎03.80.97.09.41; ②), which has an excellent, reasonably priced **restaurant** (closed Mon evening, Tues & Dec), with good home cooking from 98F/€14.94, and the *Hôtel de la Côte d'Or*, 3 place Gaveau (☎03.80.97.03.13, fax 03.80.97.29.83; ②), whose restaurant serves traditional Burgundy cuisine like *coq au vin, truite farcie* and *ris de veau aux morilles* (closed Wed & Dec 18–Feb 2; from 90F/€13.72). Alternatively, there's the modern and comfortable *Hôtel du Lac* down by the lake at Pont-et-Massène (☎03.80.97.11.11, fax 03.80.97.29.25, *www.hoteldulacdepont.com*; ③), also with a good restaurant, featuring *coq au vin, jambon persillé* and *tête de veau* (closed Sun evening, Mon & mid-Dec to Jan; menus 90–235F/€13.72–35.82). There is a **hostel**, 1 rue du Champs-de-Foire, off rue de la Liberté (☎03.80.97.10.22, fax 03.80.97.36.97), and a similar but more expensive establishment founded by a group of unemployed, the *Centre CRAC*, at 10 rue du Couvent (☎03.80.97.03.81; ①); both provide canteen meals for around 40F/€6.10. The local **campsite** is at Lac-de-Pont, 3km south of town.

The Morvan

The **Morvan** region lies smack in the middle of Burgundy between the valleys of the Loire and the Saône, stretching roughly from **Clamecy**, **Vézelay** and **Avallon** in the north to **Autun** and **Le Creusot** in the south. It is a land of wooded hills, close and rounded rather than mountainous, although they rise to 900m above Autun. The villages and farms are few and far between, for the soil is poor and the pastures only good for a few cattle. In the old days timber was the main business – supplying firewood and charcoal to Paris – but in modern times, far from main roads and rail lines, the region's chief export has been its escaping young. It earned a reputation as one of the poorest and most backward regions in the country, with few resources to trade on and little inspiration for outside investment.

In fine weather it is a lush and verdant home to all manner of foliage, flora and wild animals; in foul it is damp, muddy, lonely and rather depressing. The creation of a **parc naturel régional** in 1970 did something to promote the area as a place for outdoor activities and refuge from commuterdom. But more than anything it was the election of François Mitterrand, local politician and mayor of **Château-Chinon** for years, as president of the Republic that rescued the Morvan from oblivion. In addition to lending it some of the glamour of his office, he took concrete steps to beef up the local economy.

Avallon

Approaching **AVALLON** along the N6 from the north, you wouldn't give the place a second look. But the southern aspect is altogether more promising, as the town stands high on a ridge above the wooded valley of the River Cousin, looking out over the hilly, sparsely populated country of the Morvan regional park. Once a staging post on the Romans' *Via Agrippa* from Lyon to Boulogne on the Channel coast, it is a small and ancient town of stone facades and comatose cobbled streets, bisected north to south by the narrow **Grande-Rue-Aristide-Briand**. Under the straddling arch of the fifteenth-century **Tour de l'Horloge**, whose spire dominates the town, this street brings you to the pilgrim **church of St Lazare**, on whose battered Romanesque facade you can still decipher the graceful carvings of signs of the zodiac, labours of the months and the old musicians of the Apocalypse. Almost opposite, in a fifteenth-century house, is the tourist office, with the municipal **museum** (daily Easter–Nov 10am–12.30pm & 2–6.30pm; 20F/€3.04) behind it; exhibits include a room of modern silverware, designed by local boy Jean Despres, and a second-century mosaic from a Gallo-Roman villa. There is also the **Musée du Costume** at 6 rue de Belgrand (April–Nov 10am–6pm; 25F/€3.81), just off Grande-Rue, with a collection of regional dress. Continuing from St-Lazare down the street, now called rue Bocquillot, brings you to the lime-shaded **Promenade de la Petite Porte**, with precipitous views across the plunging valley of the Cousin. You can walk from here around the outside of the **walls**. From the **Parc des Chaumes**, on the east side of town, there is a great view back to the old quarter, snug within its walls, with garden terraces descending on the slope beneath. You can't miss the **statue of Vauban**, almost like a statue of Vercingétorix, standing guard over the place Vauban – the great military architect was born in the Morvan in 1633.

Practicalities

The **tourist office** is at 4 rue Bocquillot (May, June & Sept daily 9.30am–noon & 2–6pm; July & Aug daily 9.30am–7pm; Oct–April Mon–Sat 9.30am–noon & 2–6pm ☎03.86.34.14.19). You can organize **bike rental** through Touvélo, 26 rue de Paris (☎03.86.34.28.11). The main **shopping** centre is in the new town north of the city walls, and there's a Saturday **market** in place Vauban.

For cheap **accommodation**, head for the bargain-priced *Hôtel du Parc*, opposite the train station at 3 place de la Gare (☎03.86.34.17.00; ①), which is clean and friendly, with an inexpensive restaurant and locals' café. More modern, and comfortable, is the *Dak' Hôtel*, 119 rue de Lyon, 4km from the town centre (☎03.86.31.63.20, fax 03.86.34.25.28; ③), while the most expensive option is the charming *Hostellerie de la Poste*, 13 place Vauban (☎03.86.34.16.16, fax 03.86.34.19.19, *www.hostelleriedelaposte.com*; ⑥), a former coaching inn, with twelve sumptuous rooms, a restaurant serving an overwhelming choice of desserts (menus 155–410F/€23.63–62.50) and a relaxing flower-strewn courtyard. If you have a car, take the scenic, wooded road towards nearby Vézelay, along which, after 5km, you'll find the pleasant riverside *Moulin de Ruats* (☎03.86.34.97.00, fax 03.86.31.65.47, *www.moulin-des-ruats.com*; ④; closed mid-Jan to mid-Feb), with an exceptional restaurant and alfresco rural dining (closed all day Mon, Tues lunch & all day Tues in low season; from 155F/€23.63). The attractive *Camping Municipal de Sous-Roche* (☎03.86.34.10.39; March–Oct), and the *Ferme-Auberge des Chatelaines* (☎03.86.34.16.37; closed Thurs–Sun mid-Oct to April), are a couple of kilometres out of town on the route de Corbigny/Us.

Reasonable **food** can be found at *Grill des Madériens*, 22 rue de Paris (☎03.86.34.31.38), with meals from 60F/€9.15. Most of the hotels in town have their own restaurants, and for picnics there are numerous boulangeries on the streets radiating from place Vauban.

Vézelay

The coach buses winding their way like ants up the steep incline to **VÉZELAY** should not deter you from visiting this picturesque hilltop hamlet, surrounded by ramparts and home to one of the seminal buildings of the Romanesque period, the abbey church, **La Madeleine** (daily sunrise–sunset; closed 12.15–1.15pm & during Sun Mass). Saved from collapse by Viollet-le-Duc in 1840, the church's restored west front looks disappointingly unauthentic, but veer to the right into the garden on the south side and you get an angle on the long buttressed nave and Romanesque tower that corrects the balance and sheds light on the nautical imagery of "nave" – *navis*, ship or hull.

The colossal narthex was added to the nave around 1150 to accommodate the swelling numbers of pilgrims attracted by the presence of bones alleged to be Mary Magdalene's. Inside, your eye is first drawn to the superlative sculptures of the central doorway, on whose tympanum an ethereal Christ swathed in swirling drapery presides over a group of apostles and peoples going about their business with cows, fish, crossbows and so forth – among those featured are giants, pygmies (one mounting his horse with a ladder), a man with breasts and huge ears, and dog-headed heathens. Better preserved are the charmingly small-scale medallions of the zodiac signs and labours of the months in the outer arch. In the flanking portals are depicted Nativity scenes on the right, and Christ on the road to Emmaus after the Resurrection on the left.

From this great doorway you look down the long body of the church, vaulted by arches of alternating black and white stone, to a choir of pure early Gothic (completed in 1215), luminous with the delicacy of the inside of a shell by contrast with the heavier, more sombre Romanesque nave. Its arches and arcades are edged with fretted mouldings, and the supporting pillars are crowned with 99 finely cut capitals, depicting scenes from the Bible, classical mythology, allegories and morality stories. The finest of all is "The Mystic Mill" at the end of the fourth bay on the right, showing Moses pouring grain (Old Testament Law) through a mill (Christ), the flour (New Testament) being gathered by St Paul.

St Bernard preached to the Second Crusade at Vézelay in 1146. Because the church was too small, he preached in the open, down the hill; a **commemorative cross** marks the spot. Richard the Lionheart and Philippe-Auguste, king of France, also made their rendezvous here before setting off on the Third Crusade in 1190. But the abbey's heyday came to an end in 1280 when it was discovered that the supposed Mary Magdalene bones belonged to someone else. Its decline was hastened by Protestant vandalism in the sixteenth century, and the whole establishment was disbanded during the Revolution.

Before moving on, be sure to take a look at the beautiful Gothic **church** in the village of **ST-PÈRE**, a half-hour walk from the abbey at the foot of the hill. The village is also home to one of the greatest restaurants in the land, *Marc Meneau* (☎03.86.33.33.33; upwards of 350F/€53.35).

Practicalities

Despite the final ascent, **cycling** is a pleasant way of covering the 20km from Avallon to Vézelay. Alternatively, you could take a direct **bus** from Avallon (Cars de la Madeleine; 1 daily Mon–Fri), or a **train** to Sermizelles on the Auxerre–Avallon line, which has an SNCF bus link on to Vézelay. Buses arrive in Vézelay at Garage de la Madeleine on the main square.

Vézelay's small **tourist office** (daily 10am–1pm & 2–6pm; Nov–mid-June closed Thurs; ☎03.86.33.23.69) is on the right on rue St-Pierre as you go up towards the abbey. Reasonable-value **hotels** include *de la Terrasse*, right outside the church (☎03.86.33.25.50; ②), with only seven rooms, and *Le Cheval Blanc* on place Champ-du-Foire (☎03.86.33.22.12, fax 03.86.33.34.29; ②; restaurant from 75F/€11.43), although you'll need to book both far in advance at weekends and in high season. There are also two **hostels**: the *Centre de Rencontres Internationales*, on rue des Écoles, run by the Amis de Pax Christi (☎03.86.33.26.73; July & Aug), and a second about 1km along the route de l'Étang (☎03.86.33.24.18; Easter–Sept), which also has **camping** space.

For a rather special and romantic stay, you could try the lovely creeper-covered *Moulin des Templiers* beside the river near **PONTAUBERT**, back towards Avallon (☎03.86.34.10.80; ④; closed Nov to mid-March). Another possibility is Clamecy, or, for **campers**, a beautiful site in the little farming village of **BRÈVES**, right beside the Yonne, midway between Vézelay and Clamecy (closed mid-Sept to mid-June).

Clamecy

In sharp contrast to its rustic neighbours **CLAMECY**, 23km to the west of Vézelay on the banks of the River Yonne, has a distinctly industrial feel as the centre of the Morvan's logging trade from the sixteenth century to the completion of the Canal du Nivernais in 1834. Individual woodcutting gangs working in the hills floated their logs down the Yonne and its tributaries as far as Clamecy, where they were made up into great rafts for shipment on to Paris. This contact with the capital – and cradle of new egalitarian political ideas – led to the early spread of revolutionary thoughts among the workers and peasantry of the Morvan, who staged a number of violent insurrections even before 1789. The history of the logging trade is documented in the **museum** on rue de la Mirandole (daily 10am–noon & 2–6pm; Nov–Easter closed Sun; 20F/€3.05).

There's nothing special to see in town, apart from the many fifteenth- to eighteenth-century buildings in the centre, but it does have an interesting history and a bizarre connection with Bethlehem. In 1168 William IV, crusading Count of Nevers, died in Palestine, bequeathing one of his properties in Clamecy to the bishopric of Bethlehem, to serve as a sanctuary in the case of Palestine falling into the hands of the infidel. When the Latin Kingdom of Jerusalem fell, the first bishop arrived to claim his legacy, and from 1225 until the Revolution fifty bishops of Bethlehem suceeded each other in Clamecy, honouring the little town with the title of bishopric. A curious little **chapel** by the bridge, built in 1927 in reinforced concrete, commemorates the connection.

The **tourist office** is on rue du Grand-Marché, opposite the church of St-Martin (July & Aug Mon–Sat 9am–6.30pm, Sun 9am–noon; Sept–June Mon–Sat 9am–noon & 2–5.30pm; ☎03.86.27.02.51). For places to **stay**, try the lovely old-fashioned *Hostellerie de la Poste*, on place Émile-Zola not far from the bridge (☎03.86.27.01.55, fax 03.86.27.05.99; ③; restaurant from 105F/€16), or the good-value *La Boule d'Or*, 5 place Bethléem (☎03.86.27.11.55, fax 03.86.24.47.02; ②), with an attractive restaurant, located in a renovated thirteenth-century chapel just across the river, near the modern Chapel of Bethlehem on the road to Auxerre. There's also a good riverside **campsite** on the edge of town on the route de Chevroches (☎03.86.27.05.97; May–Sept). For places to **eat** outside the hotels, try *La Vieille Rome*, also by the chapel on place du 19-Août (closed Mon evening & Tues; 70–120F/€10.67–18.29). And if you're travelling south towards Nevers, the *Ferme-Auberge du Vieux Château*, near the village of Oulon just off the D977, makes an ideal place to treat yourself to a little luxury in beautiful surroundings (☎03.86.68.06.77; ③, half-board).

Saulieu

SAULIEU, having suffered something of a decline with the depopulation of the Morvan, then the construction of the A6 *autoroute* that took away the traffic from the old N6, is once more a relatively thriving market town, best known for its gastronomy: every year the town waits hungrily for its Charollais **festival**, on the third weekend of August – a super-gourmet festival featuring lots of meat and other local produce. Halfway between Paris and Lyon, it's a good place to stop for a meal – the D6 is lined with former coaching inns, and most of them have been turned into restaurants with very quiet rooms that face peaceful gardens at the back.

The old town – on the west side of the N6 – is pretty enough, perfect for an after-dinner stroll. Its main sight is the twelfth-century **Basilique St-Andoche**, noted for its lovely capitals, probably carved by a disciple of Gislebertus, the master sculptor of Autun. Next door, the **Musée François-Pompon** (Mon & Wed–Sat 10am–12.30pm & 2–6pm, Sun 10.30am–noon & 2–5pm; 22F/€3.35) is also surprisingly interesting, with good local folklore displays and a large collection of the works of the local nineteenth-century animal sculptor, François Pompon.

The **tourist office** (July & Aug Mon–Sat 9.30am–6pm; rest of year Mon–Sat 9.30am–noon & 2–6pm, Sun 10am–noon; ☎03.80.64.00.21) is on the N6 near the hospital, in the direction of Paris – there is a Pompon statue of a bull in the little garden almost opposite. The **gare SNCF** is straight up avenue de la Gare opposite the market place/car park.

You may want to **stay** the night if you've been tempted by the wine lists at some of the restaurants. *La Borne Imperiale*, 14–16 rue d'Argentine (☎03.80.64.19.76; ②; menus from 125F/€19.05), is a roadside inn with a fantastic atmosphere, a lovely terrace and rooms which all have a view of the garden; it also has a restaurant specializing in *escargots* and, of course, *charollais*. Two other reasonable hotels to try are the old stone coaching inn *La Vieille Auberge*, 15 rue Grillot (☎03.80.64.13.74; ③; restaurant from 75F/€11.43; closed Tues evening, Wed & Jan), and *Le Lion d'Or*, by the hospital at 7 rue Courtépée (☎03.80.64.16.33, fax 03.80.64.14.64; ②), whose restaurant food starts at 96F/€14.63 (closed Mon, Sun evening & Jan 1–15). Higher up the price scale, *La Côte d'Or* at 2 rue d'Argentine in the middle of town (☎03.80.90.53.53, fax 03.80.64.08.92, *www.bernard-loiseau.com*; ⑤), has an outrageously expensive, though exquisite, restaurant run by the famous creative chef Bernard L'Oiseau (menus 490–920F/€74.70–140.24). There are also a couple of *gîtes d'étape* (Easter–Nov) and a **campsite** (☎03.80.64.00.21; April–Oct 20), 1km out along the Paris road.

The Parc du Morvan

The **Parc Régional du Morvan** was only officially designated in 1970, when 170,000 hectares of hilly countryside were set aside in an attempt to protect the local cultural and natural heritage with a series of nature trails, animal reserves, museums and local craft shops. The Maison du Parc, its official **information centre** (Mon–Fri 8.45am–12.15pm & 1.30–5.30pm; ☎03.86.78.70.00), is located 13km from Saulieu in beautiful grounds – which include a deer park – about a kilometre outside **ST-BRISSON** on the D6. There's no public transport to get you there, but if you're walking or cycling it's a good place to head for, as they have all available information on routes and facilities in the park, as well as a small **museum** (July to mid-Sept daily 2–6pm; 15F/€2.29), devoted to the region's World War II Resistance movement, and a **herbarium** of regional plants. At weekends the same service is provided by the exhibition centre next to the museum.

A map, *Saulieu Vélo Tout-Terrain en Morvan*, marks cycling and walking routes. For **walkers** the most challenging trip is the **GR13** footpath, which crosses the park from Vézelay to Mont-Beuvray, taking in the major lakes, which are among the park's most developed attractions. There are also less strenuous possibilities: for example, the four-kilometre walk to Lac Chamboux, leaving Saulieu by the D26 and taking a track to the left (blue and yellow markers) after about ten minutes. For a starting point deeper into the park, there is a bus to Moux.

Accommodation in the park includes a number of hotels and campsites. There are several campsites round the Lac des Settons, and municipal sites in St-Brisson (☎03.86.78.71.48; May–Oct) and in **MOUX** (☎03.86.76.18.81; June–Sept). There's a reasonable hotel in **SETTONS**, *Le Beau Site* (☎03.86.76.11.75, fax 03.86.76.15.84; ②; closed Dec 22–Feb 10, plus Sun & Mon evening out of season), whose good restaurant has meals from 70F/€10.67. **MONTSAUCHE**, northwest of Settons, is a good bet for provisions, including camping gas, and also has a *camping municipal* (☎03.86.84.51.05). **Bikes** are available from a number of outlets, including *Camping du Peron* (☎03.80.64.16.19), *Camping du Midi* on Lac des Settons (☎03.86.84.51.97) and *La Margelle* pizzeria in Montsauche (☎03.06.84.54.55).

Château-Chinon

The most substantial community – approximately 2500 residents – in the park itself is the rather ugly village of **CHÂTEAU-CHINON**, nestled in contrastingly beautiful countryside dotted with evergreens, lakes and limestone deposits (bus connection to Autun). President Mitterrand was a local council member here until 1983, and the town was the home base of his political life for half a century. Thanks largely to him, it now boasts a major hosiery factory and military printing works, both of which have provided much needed employment to an isolated and often forgotten region.

In the **Musée du Septennat** (June–Sept daily 10am–6pm; Oct–May Sat & Sun only 10am–6pm; 26F/€3.96, 40F/€6.10 to include Musée du Costume), you can see the extraordinary variety of gifts Mitterrand received as head of state. The museum is light and airy, purpose-built to hold a collection of some of the finest handicrafts from their many countries of origin: carpets from the Middle East, ivory from Togo, Japanese puppets, beaded spears from Burundi and bizarre gifts, like a table decorated with butterfly wings. Another of the town's attractions is the **Musée du Costume**, 4 rue du Château (daily except Tues: May–June & Sept 10am–1pm & 2–6pm; July & Aug daily 10am–1pm & 2–7pm; rest of year 10am–noon & 2–6pm; closed Jan; 26F/€3.96, 40F/€6.10 to include Musée du Septennat), featuring a collection of over five thousand articles, the biggest collection in France, and interesting temporary exhibitions.

Mitterrand's preferred **hotel** was the *Vieux Morvan*, 8 place Gudin (☎03.86.85.05.01, fax 03.86.85.02.78; ③; closed Jan), with a nice bright restaurant with view (from 100F/€15.24). If you're not budgeting at this level, you might be better off in the *Hostellerie l'Oustalet* on the route de Lormes (☎03.86.85.15.57; ①; closed Dec 20–Jan 1; restaurant from 60F/€9.14), or in the comfortable *Lion d'Or*, rue des Fossés (☎03.86.85.13.56, fax 03.86.79.42.22; ②; restaurant from 70F/€10.67, closed Sun evening & Mon). There's also a **campsite** here, *Le Petit Oiseau* (☎03.86.85.08.17; May–Sept).

Autun and around

With its Gothic spire rising against a backdrop of Morvan hills, **AUTUN**, even today, is scarcely bigger than the circumference of its medieval **walls**, and they in turn follow the line of earlier Roman fortifications. The emperor Augustus founded the town in about 10 BC as part of a massive and, in the long term, highly successful campaign to pacify and Romanize the brooding Celts of defeated Vercingétorix. Augustodunum, as it was called, was designed to eclipse by its splendour the memory of Bibracte (see p.538), the neighbouring capital of the powerful tribe of the Aedui. And it did indeed become one of the leading cities of Roman Gaul.

The Town

Traces of the Roman period are still much in evidence. Two of the city's four Roman gates survive: **Porte St-André**, spanning rue de la Croix-Blanche in the northeast, and **Porte d'Arroux** in Faubourg d'Arroux in the northwest. In a field just across the River Arroux stands a lofty section of brick wall known as the **Temple of Janus**, which was probably part of the sanctuary of some Gallic deity, while on the east side of the town, on avenue du 2ème-Dragon just off the Dijon road, you can see the rather meagre remains of what was the largest **Roman theatre** in Gaul, with a capacity of fifteen thousand – in itself a measure of Autun's importance at that time. It's not an evocative site – the remaining seats now overlook a football pitch – but in July and August its authenticity is enhanced by the performances of a play in which six hundred locals, dressed in period costume, reconstruct the Gallo-Roman past of the town.

The influence of the monuments of this Roman past is very much in evidence in Autun's great twelfth-century **Cathédrale St-Lazare**, built nearly a thousand years after the Romans had gone. It stands in the most southerly and best fortified corner of the town, and although its external appearance has been much altered by the addition of Gothic tower, spire and side chapels in the fifteenth century, and the twin towers flanking the front in the nineteenth, the Romanesque – and Roman – elements are very clear inside. The church's greatest claim to artistic fame lies in its sculptures, the work of Gislebertus, generally accepted as one of the greatest Romanesque sculptors. The tympanum of the Last Judgement above the west door bears his signature – *Gislebertus hoc fecit* ("Gislebertus made this") – beneath the feet of Christ. To the left and right of Christ are depicted the elect entering heaven; the apostles; the Archangel Michael disputing souls with Satan, who tries to cheat by leaning on the scales; and the flames of hell licking at the damned. Luckily, during the eighteenth century the local clergy decided it was an inferior work and plastered it over, saving it from almost certain destruction during the Revolution. The interior, whose pilasters and arcading were modelled on the Roman architecture of the city's gates, was also decorated by Gislebertus, who himself carved most of the capitals. Conveniently for anyone wanting a close look, some of the finest are now exhibited in the old chapter library, up the stairs on the right of the choir, among them a beautiful *Flight into Egypt* and *Adoration of the Magi*.

Just outside the cathedral on rue des Bancs, the **Musée Rolin** (daily except Tues: April–Sept 9.30am–noon & 1.30–6pm; Oct–March 10am–noon & 2–4pm; 20F/€3.04) occupies a Renaissance *hôtel* built by Nicolas Rolin, chancellor of Philippe le Bon, and is definitely worth a look. In addition to interesting Gallo-Roman pieces, the star attractions are Gislebertus's representation of Eve as an unashamedly sensual nude and the Maître de Moulins' brilliantly coloured *Nativity*.

The most enigmatic of the Gallo-Roman remains in the region, however, is the **Pierre de Couhard**, off Faubourg St-Pancrace to the southeast of the town. It's a 27-metre-tall stone pyramid situated on the site of one of the city's necropolises, thought to date from the first century, and most probably either a tomb or a cenotaph.

Practicalities

Whether you arrive at the **gare SNCF** or **gare routière** next door, you'll find yourself on avenue de la République, which is bisected at right angles by avenue Charles-de-Gaulle, which in turn leads to the wide square of the Champs-de-Mars and into the old town. The **tourist office** is at 2 av de Charles-de-Gaulle (Easter–Sept Mon–Sat 9am–noon & 2–6pm, Sun 10am–noon & 3–6pm; Oct–Easter Mon–Fri 9am–noon & 2–7pm, Sat 9am–noon; ☎03.85.86.30.00, fax 03.85.86.80.49).

There is a good choice of **accommodation** in Autun. Opposite the station, the *Hôtel de France*, 18 av de la République (☎03.85.52.14.00, fax 03.85.86.14.52; ①), and *Commerce et Touring*, 20 av de la République (☎03.85.52.17.90, fax 03.85.52.37.63; ②; closed Jan; reasonable restaurant from 65F/€9.91), are both decent and inexpensive. For something a bit more upmarket, there are a couple of old coaching inns just off the Champs-de-Mars: the magnificent *St-Louis*, 6 rue de l'Arbalète (☎03.85.52.21.03, fax 03.85.86.32.54, *www.amadeusprop.com*; ⑤–⑥), where Napoléon slept; and the comfortable *Hôtel Moderne et de La Tête Noire*, opposite at 3 rue de l'Arquebuse (☎03.85.86.59.99, fax 03.85.86.33.90; ②; restaurant from 85F/€12.96). There's also a **campsite** just across the river on the road to Saulieu, *Camping Pont d'Arroux* (☎03.85.52.10.82; Easter–Oct).

In addition to the hotel **restaurants**, there are a couple of brasseries on the Champs-de-Mars, but the best option, in the bottom corner by the Hôtel de Ville, is the innovative *Chalet Bleu*, 3 rue Jeannin (☎03.85.86.27.30; closed Mon evening, Tues & Feb 6–22), which, though expensive à la carte, has a weekday menu at 85F/€12.96 and a very good-value one at 120F/€18.29.

Mont-Beuvray and Bibracte

The base for the climb up Mont-Beuvray to the 2000-year-old site of the Gallic capital of Bibracte is **ST-LÉGER-SOUS-BEUVRAY**, about 26km southwest of Autun and reached along the N81 and D61 through typical Morvan countryside of wooded hills and scattered farms, coarse marshy pastures and brown streams. There's a morning and an afternoon bus from Autun to St-Léger, or you can tackle the seven-hour walk on **GR131** from the Croix de la Libération outside Autun. Should you need to spend the night, St-Léger has a **hostel** (☎03.85.82.55.46) and **campsite** (May–Oct).

From St-Léger, it's the best part of two hours further by the path, or 8km by the road, to **BIBRACTE** at the top of the hill, at an altitude of 800m. If you want to recapture a Celtic mood, it's worth doing this last stretch on foot along a path winding up through woods of conifer and beech. The settlement of Bibracte, the lines of which you can still follow through the trees, was inhabited from 5000 BC. In 52 BC it was the scene of an assembly of all the Gallic tribes, which resulted in the election of Vercingétorix as their commander-in-chief, in one last desperate attempt to fight off Roman imperialism. Although it is two millennia since Bibracte was abandoned – probably on Roman orders – vague memories of its significance were preserved in the folk tales of the Morvan and a fair was held on the summit every May until the beginning of World War I. Close to the fortified earthwork that surrounds the site, great ceremonial stones like the **Pierre de la Wivre** are still standing. The Bibracte **Musée de la Civilisation Celtique** (mid-March to mid-June & mid-Sept to mid-Nov daily except Tues 10am–6pm; mid-June to mid-Sept Mon–Fri 10am–6pm, Sat & Sun 10am–7pm; 25F/€3.81 museum entry, 60F/€9.15 with guided tour of archeological site; ☎03.85.86.52.35 for bookings) is a fascinating state-of-the-art museum displaying the many Celtic coins, jugs, platters and pieces of statues unearthed from the neighbouring archeological site.

Le Creusot

LE CREUSOT means one thing to French ears: the **Schneider iron and steelworks**, maker of the first French locomotive in 1838, the first steamship in 1839, the 75mm field gun – mainstay of World War I artillery – the ironwork of the Pont Alexandre-III and the Gare d'Austerlitz in Paris. Its successor, Creusot-Loire, now manufactures specialized steels and boilers for the nuclear industry, though, like many steelworks in Britain, it employs far fewer people than in the past, thus contributing to the region's unemployment rate which typically hovers well over 12 percent.

As you travel south through the wooded hills from Autun, nothing prepares you for this former industrial powerhouse. You arrive to see, suddenly, over the brow of a hill, spilling down the bottom of a valley, abandoned factories and workers' housing. A small street of rustic-looking workers' dwellings survives in the **Combe des Mineurs**, while in place du 8-Mai on the Montchanin road out of town a colossal 100-tonne Schneider **drop-hammer** has been set up as a monument to past glories. If you climb to the rue des Pyrénées above the Combe des Mineurs, you can see Le Creusot spread before you, including the modern Creusot-Loire steelworks, the gleaming white Château de la Verrerie and the terraces of pastel-coloured houses, against a backdrop of hills which are the northeast border of the Massif Central.

The town's main attraction is the **Écomusée de la Communauté Urbaine du Creusot-Montceau-les-Mines** in the Château de la Verrerie on place Schneider (Mon–Fri 9am–noon & 2–6pm, Sat & Sun 2–6pm; 20F/€3.05). Built as a glassworks in 1786–87 – Louis XVI was a shareholder before losing his head – the château was sold to the Schneider family in 1838 and transformed into their private home and the administrative centre of their business empire. The Schneiders were paternalistic but despotic employers, providing housing, schools and health care for their workers and even a theatre where Sarah Bernhardt once performed, but expecting "gratitude and obedience" in return. When a certain Dumay, one of their workers whose political interests and involvement in strikes they had been watching with disapproval, became mayor in 1870 and proclaimed adherence to the Paris Commune, he was sentenced to hard labour for life, while the army moved in to quell the unrest. They organized a private police force to keep an eye on workers' reading matter and church attendance, handed out building plots for "good behaviour" and rigged municipal elections in favour of "their" candidates. In the end they became so unpopular they had to turn the château into a kind of Fort Knox. But, by one of history's delightful ironies, the last Schneider married the granddaughter of Jules Guesde, father of the French Communist Party. The château remained in the family's possession until the widow of the last incumbent bequeathed it to the town in 1969.

Today, the exhibits in the *écomusée* tell the story of heavy industry and agriculture in the area, with superb period photos, coin-slot push-button models of the works, steam cranes, reconstructed workshops, models of locomotives and a photo record of the great *Mistral* train's run from Paris to Marseille. Many examples of the glass produce are on display, with a video explaining methods of production. The peculiar cone-shaped constructions in the courtyard were the glass furnaces, recently transformed into a theatre and a chapel.

Practicalities

The **tourist office** in the Château de la Verrerie (July & Aug daily 9am–noon & 2–7pm; Sept–June Tues–Fri 10am–noon & 2–6pm, Sat & Sun 10am–noon; ☎03.85.55.02.46, fax 03.85.80.11.03) can provide information on tours of the town, the TGV industry workshops and some of the coal mines in the vicinity. Frequent buses connect Le Creusot with the **TGV station** 6km away in Montchanin, connecting with Paris. There are also good train connections for visiting other towns in the region, such as Cluny or Mâcon.

If you need to **stay** overnight, head for the acceptable *Hôtel des Voyageurs*, 5 place Schneider (☎03.85.55.22.36, fax 03.85.77.48.21; ②), which has a good restaurant (closed Fri, Sat & Sun evenings; from 65F/€9.91). Vegetarians may enjoy lunch at *Les 4 Saisons*, at 37 rue du Président Wilson (☎03.85.56.01.26; closed Sun, Mon, and all evenings except Sat & Aug; 50–60F/€7.62–9.15).

DIJON AND SOUTHERN BURGUNDY

If the much-touted image of "rural Burgundy" has conjured up an image of slightly backward and ramshackle rustic charm in your mind, you'll have to do some adjusting when you encounter the slick prosperity of **Dijon** and the wine-producing country to the south, known as the **Côte d'Or**. It may look peacefully pastoral, but there is nothing medieval about the methods or the profits made in today's wine business. For any trace of the older traditions you have to head into the southwestern corner of the region, into the wine-producing regions of the **Mâconnais** and **Beaujolais**, and the cattle country of the **Charollais**.

Dijon

DIJON owes its origins to its strategic position in Celtic times on the tin merchants' route from Britain up the Seine and across the Alps to the Adriatic. It became the capital of the dukes of Burgundy in around 1000 AD, but its golden age occurred in the fourteenth and fifteenth centuries under the auspices of dukes Philippe le Hardi (the Bold), who as a boy had fought the English at Poitiers and been taken prisoner, Jean sans Peur (the Fearless), Philippe le Bon (the Good), who sold Joan of Arc to the English, and Charles le Téméraire (the Bold). They used their tremendous wealth and power – especially their control of Flanders, the dominant manufacturing region of the age – to make Dijon one of the greatest centres of art, learning and science in Europe. It lost its capital status on incorporation into the kingdom of France in 1477, but has remained one of the country's pre-eminent provincial cities, especially since the rail and industrial booms of the mid-nineteenth century. Today, it is smart, modern and young, especially when the students are around.

Arrival, information and accommodation

Dijon is not an enormous city and the part you'll want to see is neatly confined in the centre and eminently walkable. Whether you arrive by road or rail from either Paris and the north or Lyon and the south, you will find yourself almost inevitably at the **gare SNCF** – the **gare routière** is next door. If you plan to use buses a lot – not especially necessary unless you are staying at one of the hostels – it's worth getting a pass and bus map from STRD, in the middle of place Grangier.

From immediately outside the station, avenue Maréchal-Foch leads to central place Darcy – a five-minute walk away. You'll pass the **tourist office** (daily: May to mid-Oct 9am–9pm; mid-Oct to April 9am–1pm & 2–7pm; ☎03.80.44.11.44, fax 03.80.30.90.02, *www.ot-dijon.fr*) on your left as you reach the square. There's another office at 34 rue des Forges (Mon–Fri 9am–noon & 1–6pm; May to mid-Oct also open Sat same hours; ☎03.80.44.11.44, fax 03.80.30.90.02), which also houses the Club Alpin, who produce a booklet, *Promenez-vous en Côte d'Or*, showing all the region's marked paths. Both offer services such as hotel booking, money changing, guided tours of the city and – most worthwhile – a 45F/€6.86 museum card which allows access to all the museums listed below. *Dijon Nuit et Jour* is a good guide to **what's on**, and has some practical listings too.

Dijon has no shortage of reasonably priced **hotels** in the centre of town, which are a better option than the two **hostels**, inconveniently located on the east side of the city.

Hotels

Le Chambellan, 92 rue Vannerie (☎03.80.67.12.67, fax 03.80.38.00.39). A clean and friendly, if somewhat old-fashioned, hotel. ②.

Continental, 7 rue Albert Remy (☎03.80.53.10.10, fax 03.80.53.10.38). Bright and cheerful hotel, newly modernized, and across the street from the train station. Amenities include car park (30F/€4.57 per night), an all-you-can-eat breakfast buffet (40F/€6.10) and a small indoor pool. ③.

Hostellerie Le Sauvage, 64 rue Monge (☎03.80.41.31.21, fax 03.80.42.06.07). Pleasant option situated in a former coaching inn with a lovely little courtyard for its restaurant tables. ③.

Le Jacquemart, 32 rue Verrerie (☎03.80.60.09.60, fax 03.80.60.09.69). Offers old-world charm close to the dukes' palace. High ceilings, tall windows and a liberal use of floral wallpaper. ②.

du Palais, 23 rue du Palais (☎03.80.67.16.26, fax 03.80.65.12.16). Smart, modern hotel, close to the ducal palace. ②–③.

République, 3 rue du Nord, near place de la République (☎03.80.73.36.76, fax 03.80.72.46.04). A pleasant hotel with a skylit foyer, friendly staff and clean rooms on a quiet side street. They offer a fifty percent discount on Sundays between Oct and March if you stay two nights. ②–③.

Thurot, 4–6 passage Thurot (☎03.80.43.57.46, fax 03.80.42.86.57). A modern, simply and tastefully decorated hotel near the train station, run by the same congenial owner as the *Hostellerie Le Sauvage*. Convenient car park. ③.

Hostels and campsite

Centre de Rencontres Internationales, 1 bd Champollion (☎03.80.72.95.20, fax 03.80.70.00.61). HI hostel in a modern complex, with well-kept dorm rooms, a self-service canteen and sports facilities next door; popular with school groups. Take bus #5, direction "Épirey", from place Grangier. The last bus back is at 9pm, however, so you can't really go out at night.

Foyer International d'Étudiants on rue Maréchal-Leclerc (☎03.80.71.51.01). University accommodation, offering single or double rooms, laundry and kitchen facilities and a cafeteria. Takes visitors when there is room, but don't rely on this option. Take bus #4, direction "St-Apollinaire", stop "Billardon".

Camping du Lac (☎03.80.43.54.72). Pleasant and popular establishment about 1km out of town off boulevard Chanoine-Kir near Lake Kir: follow the signs for Paris. Take bus #12, direction "Fontaine d'Ouche", or #18, direction "Plombières".

The City

The **rue de la Liberté** forms the major east–west axis of the town, running from the wide, attractive **place Darcy** and the eighteenth-century triumphal arch of **Porte**

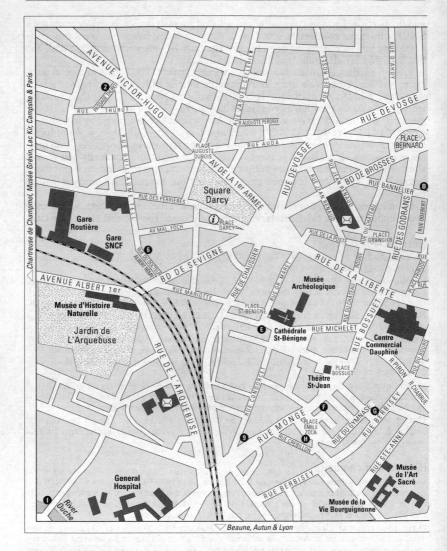

▽ *Beaune, Autun & Lyon*

Guillaume, once a city gate, past the **palace of the dukes of Burgundy** on the semi-circular **place de la Libération**, east to the **church of St Michel**. The street is pedestrianized and lined with smart shops and elegant old houses, and most places of interest are within fifteen minutes' walk to the north or south of it.

The Palais des Ducs

The geographical focus of a visit to Dijon is inevitably the seat of its former rulers, the **Palais des Ducs**, which stands precisely at the hub of the city overlooking Mansart's perfectly proportioned and serene **place de la Libération**, built towards the end of the

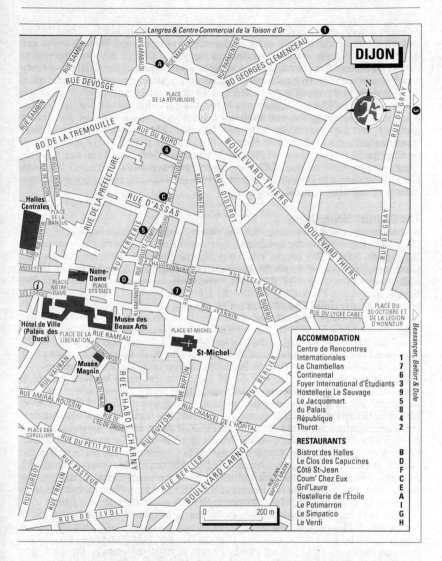

△ Langres & Centre Commercial de la Toison d'Or △ ❶

DIJON

PLACE DE LA RÉPUBLIQUE

RUE SAMBIN
AV GARABALDI
RUE MARCEAU
RUE FARMENTIER
BD GEORGES CLEMENCEAU
RUE DEVOSGE
❹
RUE SAMBIN
BD DE LA TREMOUILLE
RUE DU NORD
BOULEVARD THIERS
RUE DE GRAY
RUE DE SUZON
RUELLE DESNOYER
RUE DE LA PRÉFECTURE
RUE J-J. ROUSSEAU
RUE VANNERIE
RUE DIDEROT
Halles Centrales
PLACE DE LA BANQUE
RUE D'ASSAS ❻
RUE VERRERIE
RUE AUGUSTE COMTE
RUE JEAN-ROUSSEAU
RUE CHAUDRONNERIE
RUE LYCEE CABET
BOULEVARD THIERS
RUE DE GRAY
MUSETTE
CL RAMEY
RUE QUENTIN
❺
Notre-Dame ❹
PLACE DES DUCS
RUE FLAMMONOYE
RUE VANNERIE
RUE LYCEE CABET
RUE DIDEROT
PLACE DU 30 OCTOBRE ET DE LA LEGION D'HONNEUR
ⓘ PLACE NOTRE-DAME
DES FORGES
❼
RUE JEANNIN
RUE DU LYCEE CABET
Hôtel de Ville (Palais des Ducs)
PLACE DE LA LIBERATION
RUE RAMEAU
Musée des Beaux Arts
PLACE ST-MICHEL
St-Michel
RUE DES BONS ENFANTS
Musée Magnin
RUE VAUBAN
RUE DU PALAIS
RUE CHABOT CHARNY
RUE BUFFON
RUE BERLIER
RUE AMIRAL ROUSSIN
❽
RUE DE L'EC DE DROIT
RUE CHANCEL DE L'HÔPITAL
PLACE DES CORDELIERS
RUE DU PETIT POTET
RUE BUFFON
RUE BERLIER
RUE PASTEUR
RUE JEAN BAPTISTE BAUDIN
RUE TURGOT
RUE FRANKLIN
RUE DE TIVOLI
BOULEVARD CARNOT
0   200 m
▷ Besançon, Belfort & Dole

ACCOMMODATION

Centre de Rencontres Internationales	1
Le Chambellan	7
Continental	6
Foyer International d'Étudiants	3
Hostellerie Le Sauvage	9
Le Jacquemart	5
du Palais	8
République	4
Thurot	2

RESTAURANTS

Bistrot des Halles	B
Le Clos des Capucines	D
Côté St-Jean	F
Coum' Chez Eux	C
Gril'Laure	E
Hostellerie de l'Étoile	A
Le Potimarron	I
Le Simpatico	G
Le Verdi	H

seventeenth century as place Royale to show off a statue of the Sun King. Though still functioning as the town hall, the palace's exterior has undergone so many alterations – especially in the sixteenth and seventeenth centuries when it became Burgundy's parliament – that the dukes themselves would scarcely recognize it. The only outward reminders of the older building that stood here are the fourteenth-century **Tour de Bar** above the east wing, which now houses the Musée des Beaux-Arts, and the fifteenth-century **Tour Philippe-le-Bon**, which is unfortunately closed for an indefinite period.

The excellent **Musée des Beaux-Arts** (daily except Tues & public hols 10am–6pm; 32F/€4.88, Sun free) houses an impressive collection of paintings, representing many different schools and periods, from Titian, Rubens and Schongauer to Manet, Monet and other Impressionists, with substantial numbers of Italian and Flemish works and quantities of religious artefacts, ivories and tapestries. One of the most interesting exhibits is a small room devoted to the intricate woodcarving of the sixteenth-century designer and architect Hugues Sambin, whose work appears throughout the old quarter of the city in the massive doors and facades of the aristocratic *hôtels*. Visiting the museum also provides the opportunity to see the surviving portions of the original ducal palace, including the vast **kitchens** needed to service the dukes' gargantuan appetites, and the magnificent **Salle des Gardes**, richly appointed with panelling, tapestries and a minstrels' gallery. Here are displayed the **tombs** from the Chartreuse de Champmol (see opposite) of Philippe le Hardi and Jean sans Peur and his wife, Marguerite de Bavière. Both follow the same pattern: painted effigies of the dead, attended by angels holding their helmets and heraldic shields, and accompanied by a cortege of brilliantly sculpted mourners.

The Quartier Notre-Dame

Architecturally more interesting than the palace, and much more suggestive of the city's former glories, are the lavish town houses of its rich burghers. These abound in the streets behind the palace: rue Verrerie, rue Vannerie, rue des Forges, rue Chaudronnière (look out for no. 28, **Maison des Cariatides**). Some are half-timbered, with storeys projecting over the street, others are in more formal and imposing Renaissance stone. Particularly fine are the **Hôtel de Vogüé**, 12 rue de la Chouette, and at no. 34, the **Hôtel Chambellan** (1490), housing one of Dijon's tourist offices and the Club Alpin. There's a good view of the latter from the courtyard, with its open galleries reached by a spiral staircase and a marvellous piece of stonemason's virtuosity at the top, where the vaulting of the roof springs from a basket held by the statue of a gardener. For a glimpse of what must be nearly genuine medieval character, take a look in the cobbled alleys by the **Tour St-Nicholas**, off rue Jean-Jacques-Rousseau.

Also in this quarter behind the dukes' palace, in the angle between rue de la Chouette and rue de la Préfecture, is the **church of Notre-Dame**, built in the early thirteenth century in the Burgundian Gothic style, with an unusual west front adorned with tiers of spectacularly leaning gargoyles. Inside, the north transept windows contain some beautiful fragments of the original stained glass, while in the south transept there is a twelfth-century black wooden Virgin that has long been an object of veneration to the citizens of Dijon. Outside on rue de la Chouette, in the north wall of the church, is a small sculpted owl – *chouette* – polished by the hands of passers-by who for centuries have touched it for luck and which gives the street its name. High on the south tower of the west front is a Jacquemard clock, taken from Courtrai in Belgium as a present for Dijon in 1382, when Philippe le Hardi defeated the people of Ghent.

From here rue de la Musette leads to the **market square**, the whole area full of sumptuous displays of food and attractive cafés and restaurants, and always thronged with people. The market operates from 6am on Tuesday, Friday and Saturday, spilling over into the surrounding streets, with bric-a-brac in rue de Soissons on the north side and clothes in the beautiful little **place François-Rude**, named after the sculptor, and a favourite hangout, with its cafés and fountain graced by the bronze figure of a grape harvester.

South of the place de la Libération

On the south side of the place Darcy–church of St-Michel axis, and especially in the *quartier* behind place de la Libération, there is a concentration of magnificent *hôtels* from the seventeenth and eighteenth centuries. These were built for the most part by men who had bought themselves offices and privileges with the Parliament of

Burgundy, established by Louis XI in 1477 after the death of Duke Charles le Téméraire (the Bold) as a concession designed to win the compliance of this newly acquired frontier province. One of them, 4 rue des Bons-Enfants, houses the **Musée Magnin** (Tues–Sun: summer 10am–6pm; winter 10am–noon & 2–6pm; free): the building, a seventeenth-century *hôtel particulier*, complete with its original furnishings, is more interesting than the exhibition of paintings by good but lesser-known artists, which constituted the personal collection of Maurice Magnin, and which were donated to the state in 1938. Other noteworthy houses are to be found nearby in rue Vauban, some showing the marks of Hugues Sambin's influence in their decorative details (lions' heads, garlands of fruit, tendrils of ivy and his famous *chou bourguignon*, or "Burgundy cabbage"): notably, nos. 3, 12, 21 and 23. Also worth a look for its elaborate west front is the **church of St-Michel**, a ten-minute walk to the east behind place du Théâtre.

In the same area, in rue Ste-Anne near place des Cordeliers, are two museums. The **Musée de la Vie Bourguignonne**, 17 rue Ste-Anne (daily except Tues 9am–noon & 2–6pm; 18F/€2.74, ticket includes the Musée d'Art Sacré, Sun free), housed in a stark, well-designed modern setting within a former convent, is all about nineteenth-century Burgundian life, featuring costumes, furniture, domestic industries like butter, cheese- and bread-making, along with a reconstructed kitchen. Practically next door at no. 15, the **Musée d'Art Sacré** (same hours and ticket as Vie Bourguignonne) contains an important collection of church treasures, including a seventeenth-century statue of St Paul, the first in the world to be treated with gamma rays – carried out in Grenoble as part of the Nucle-art project. Formerly crumbling to dust, it is now solid. There's a free guided visit that really perks up these special-interest exhibits.

A little further to the west, at the end of rue du Dr-Maret in the direction of place Darcy, the **Cathedral** – the once great abbey church of St-Bénigne – is no longer of very great interest, although its garish tiled roof and nineteenth-century spire dominate the skyline impressively enough. Its circular crypt is the original tenth-century Romanesque church. A little historical curiosity, however, is the fact that Raoul Glaber was a monk here: Glaber is famed as the historian who described the great burgeoning of Romanesque churches across France once the apocalyptic dangers of the first millennium were safely past and the earth began "clothing herself in a white garment of churches".

In a chestnut-shaded garden next to the cathedral, the **Musée Archéologique**, 5 rue du Dr-Maret (daily except Tues: June–Sept 9.30am–6.30pm; Oct–May 9am–noon & 2–6pm; 14F/€2.13, Sun free), has some extremely interesting finds from the Gallo-Roman period, especially funerary bas-reliefs depicting the perennial Gallic preoccupation with food and wine, and a collection of *ex votos* from the source of the Seine, among them the little bronze of the goddess Sequana (Seine) upright in her bird-prowed boat. Also on show is Sluter's bust of Christ from the Chartreuse.

The neighbouring streets – especially **rue Monge** and **rue Berbisey** – are very active at night with lots of bars and restaurants. The latter ends in a curious postmodern perspective joke: a sort of parody of a medieval housing estate. In place Bossuet at the start of rue Monge is the **Théâtre du Parvis St-Jean** (Mon–Fri 9am–noon & 2–6pm; ☎03.80.30.63.53), whose daring and innovative programmes of dance, theatre and performance art are worth keeping an eye on.

The Musée d'Histoire Naturelle and around

One of the greatest of Dijon's artistic monuments, however, lies some 1.5km west of the city centre along avenue Albert-1er, beyond the *gare SNCF*. It is the **Chartreuse de Champmol** (daily 8am–6pm; free), founded by Duke Philippe le Hardi in 1383 to be the burial place of his dynasty – Dijon's equivalent of the cathedral of St-Denis in Paris. To adorn it, Philippe recruited a talented team of artists, foremost among them the

Dutchman Claus Sluter, pioneer of Realism in sculpture and founder of the Burgundian school. Although it was practically destroyed in the Revolution and most of the surviving works of art are in the city's museums, two of Sluter's finest – the so-called *Well of Moses*, featuring six highly realistic portrayals of Old Testament prophets, and the portal of the chapel – remain *in situ*. The site is now part of a psychiatric hospital, and you enter at 1 bd Chanoine-Kir (bus #12 from the station, direction "Fontaine d'Ouche" to stop "Hôpital des Chartreux"). On the way from the station to the Chartreuse de Champmol, you pass Dijon's waxworks, the **Musée Grevin** at 13b av Albert-1er (daily 9.30am–noon & 2–6pm; 30F/€4.57), a not wildly interesting experience, consisting principally of scenes from Burgundy's history. You're better off strolling in the botanical garden, the **Jardin de l'Arquebuse** (daily 7.30am–6/7pm), site of the **Natural History Museum** (Mon & Wed–Sat 9am–noon & 2–6pm; 14F/€2.13), with just about every stuffed bird and mammal you can think of, plus an exquisite collection of butterflies.

Eating, drinking and entertainment

Dijon has an inordinate number of **pâtisseries** in the town, full of high-quality, tempting confectionery in which marzipan and fruit feature prominently. The more exotic places also promote the Dijon specialities: *pain d'épices*, a gingerbread made with honey and spices and eaten with butter or jam (from Mulot et Petitjean, 13 place Bossuet and other branches all over town), and *cassissines* – blackcurrant candies. **Chocolate**, best made on the premises, is another speciality – try Au Parrain Généreux, 21 rue du Bourg. And you can hardly forget that Dijon is also the high temple of **mustard**; there is the shop of leading producer Maille at 30 rue de la Liberté, selling a range from the mild to the cauterizing. Finally, a couple of ideas for buying good but affordable **wine**: first and foremost, there's Nicot, 48 rue Jean-Jacques-Rousseau, where you can taste, seek advice or take courses; alternatively, try La Cave du Clos, 3 rue Jeannin, or Nicolas, 6 rue François-Rude.

There are a large number of excellent **restaurants** in town, some of which are listed below. Lively rue Berbisey and place Emile Zola hold the most promise for both eating and drinking options. There are also three **university restaurants** – 3 rue du Dr-Maret in the town centre; 6 bd Mansart; 6 rue du Recteur-Bouchard, near the university to the southeast of the city – where students can eat for 15F/€2.29 (daily 11.30am–1.15pm & 6.40–7.45pm).

Restaurants

Bistrot des Halles, 10 rue Bannelier (☎03.80.49.94.15). Offers serious gourmet eating, with menus at around 160F/€24.39, lunch menu at 92F/€14.02. Closed Sun evening.

Le Clos des Capucines, 3 rue Jeannin, at the end of rue Jean-Jacques-Rousseau (☎03.80.65.83.03). Situated in a beautiful medieval setting, this restaurant serves very good traditional, rich Burgundy cuisine (*jambon persillé, escargots, bœuf bourguignon*) at very reasonable prices. Menus at 85F/€12.96 and up to 230F/€35.06, *carte* around 200F/€30.49. Closed Sun.

Côté St-Jean, 13 rue Monge (☎03.80.50.11.77). Rather chic restaurant offering such delights as fricassee of lobster, duck tournedos and gratin of pears and almonds. Menus 108–175F/€16.46–26.68, *carte* over 200F/€30.49. Closed Sat lunch, Tues & mid-July to mid-Aug.

Coum' Chez Eux, 68 rue Jean-Jacques-Rousseau (☎03.80.73.56.87). A restaurant that continues to provide genuine homely regional cooking: *jambonneau* with lentils, leek pie, home-made terrines, rabbit sautéed Morvan-style. It also has an informal and agreeable atmosphere. *Carte* around 130F/€19.82. Closed Sat lunch & Sun.

Gril'Laure, 8 place St-Bénigne (☎03.80.41.86.76). Popular with the business lunch crowd for its convenient cathedral-side location, sophisticated atmosphere, and pizzas, pasta and grilled dishes hot out of the wood-fired oven. Menus at 100F/€15.24. Closed Sun lunch.

Hostellerie de l'Étoile, 1 rue Marceau (☎03.80.73.30.72). Serves an excellent traditional meal in an attractive dining room just off place de la République; menus from 120F/€18.29, *carte* around 200/€30.49. Closed Sun evening & Mon.

Hostellerie Le Sauvage, 64 rue Monge (see "Accommodation", p.541). First-class grills in a great little courtyard. Lunch menu at 75F/€11.43, *carte* around 130–150F/€19.82–22.86. Closed Sat lunch & Sun.

Le Potimarron, 4 av de l'Ouche (☎03.80.43.38,07). A bit out of the way, but serves home-made vegetarian and macroblotic dishes as well as organic meat and fish. Menus at 75F/€11.43 and 85F/€12.96, *carte* 70–90F/€10.67–13.72. Closed Sun & Mon.

Le Simpatico, 30 rue Berbisey (☎03.80.30.53.53). Trendy Italian restaurant with funky decor and excellent menus (65–185F/€9.91–28.20). Closed Sun, Mon lunch & Aug.

Le Verdi, 10 place Émile Zola (☎03.80.30.68.41). Wildly popular lunch menu (62F/€9.45) including grills, pizza and fish, all wonderfully prepared and served in an intimate two-room dining area. Dinners in the 95–150F/€14.48–22.87 range. One of the few places open on Sun, though closed Mon & Tues.

Cafés, bars and nightclubs

Dijon is an important university city as well as one of France's main conference centres, so **nightspots** and cultural centres at both ends of the range are worth exploring. Place Émile Zola and rue Berbisey are good places to start a night out. The English theme pubs seem to be the liveliest.

L'Acropole, 4 bd du Dr-Petitjean. Gay bar located near the university on #9 bus route. Mon–Sat till 1am; closed Sun.

L'An-Fer, 8 rue Marceau. One of Dijon's livelier discos. Tues–Sat 10,30pm–3am, Fri & Sat till 4am. Admission weekdays 50F/€7.62; weekends 60F/€9.15.

Le Brighton, 33 rue Auguste-Comte. English pub with 200 different kinds of beer, and dancing. Summer 3pm–3am; winter 5pm–3am.

Café de la Cathédrale, 4 place St-Bénigne, next to the *Café au Carillon*. Two bars popular with students, in front of the cathedral. Both daily 6.30pm–1am.

Le Café des Grands Ducs, 96 rue de la Liberté. Popular rendezvous for young people, with original decor and table jukeboxes. Pricey. Daily till 2am winter, 3am summer.

Le Crocodil, rue Berbisey. Nice atmosphere, a good place for an afternoon coffee leading into an early evening drink. Mon–Sat till 2am.

Le Grand Café, rue du Château. A very pleasant bar/brasserie with an Art Deco interior.

Messire Bar, 3 rue Jules Mercier. Very Seventies bar, tucked away in a side street in the old town. Open till late night every night.

Pub Kilkenny, 1 rue Auguste-Perdrix. Noisy, popular Irish bar: draught Guinness and week-night Irish bands. Daily till 3am.

Rhumerie la Jamaïque, 14 place de la République. Cocktails (38–70F/€5.79–10.67) and ice creams laced with alcohol in an exotic venue. Jazz bar in the basement. Daily except Sun 3pm–3am.

L'Univers, 47 rue Berbisey (☎03.80.30.98.29). Check for rock concerts in the cellar. Open till midnight and later.

Listings

Cinemas L'Eldorado, 21 rue Alfred de Musset (☎03.80.66.12.34; closed July & Aug), is a three-screen arts cinema showing all films in original language with a concentration of foreign films. Devosge, 6 rue Devosge (☎03.80.30.74.79), shows some films in the original, and tries to deviate from the obvious classics. Other general release cinemas are: ABC, 7 rue du Chapeau Rouge, and Darcy Palace, 8 place Darcy (☎03.80.30.50.50 for both).

Festivals The city has a good summer music season, with classical concerts through June in its Été Musical programme. L'Estivade, June 20–Aug 15, puts on endless music, dance and street theatre performances; Fête de la Vigne at the beginning of Sept is a traditional costume/folklore jamboree; while the Foire gastronomique at the beginning of Nov celebrates all things edible.

Markets From 6am Tues, Fri & Sat mornings along the four streets surrounding the covered market – rue Bannelier, rue Quentin, rue C.-Ramey and rue Odebert.

Swimming pool Oxygène-Parc Aquatique, Centre Commercial de la Toison d'Or (daily 10am–8pm, Sun till 7pm; ☎03.80.74.16.16; adults 60F/€9.15, kids 45F/€6.86; bus #16). Toboggans, jacuzzi and water slides.

The Côte d'Or

The attractive countryside of the **Côte d'Or** is characterized by the steep scarp of the *côte*, wooded along the top and cut by steep little valleys called *combes*, where local rock climbers hone their skills (footpaths **GR7** and **GR76** run the whole length of the wine country as far south as Lyon). Spring is a good time to visit this region, when you avoid the crowds and the landscape is a dramatic symphony of browns – trees, earth and vines, along with millions of bone-coloured vine stakes wheeling past as you travel through, like crosses in a vast war cemetery.

The villages, strung along the N74 through Beaune and beyond, have names – Gevrey-Chambertin, Vougeot, Vosne-Romanée, Nuits-St-Georges, Pommard, Volnay, Meursault – that all sound like music to the ears of wine buffs and are familiar to even the most casually interested; but they turn out to be sleepy, dull and exceedingly prosperous places, full of houses inhabited by well-heeled *vignerons* in expensive suits and fat-cat cars. You can make a very good living on a patch of four or five hectares, the average-sized plot, the proof being that none is ever up for sale.

There are numerous **caves** where you can taste (usually for a charge of 30–40F/€4.57–6.10) and buy the local elixir, but remember that the former is meant to be a prelude to the latter. And there's no such thing as a cheap wine here, red or white, 100–120F/€15.24–18.29 being the minimum price you'll pay for a bottle. The Hautes Côtes (Nuits and Beaune) – wines from the top of the slope – are cheaper, but they lack the connoisseur cachet of the big names.

Beaune

BEAUNE, the principal town of the Côte d'Or, has managed to maintain its ancient air, despite rampant commercialism and a near constant stream of tourists. Narrow cobbled streets and sunny squares dotted with cafés make it a lovely spot to sample the region's wine, though you may find it cheaper and easier to use Dijon or the nondescript town of Chalon as a base for getting around in the area, as both are easily accessible by train and Transco buses, which service all the villages down the N74. Beaune is situated at a major *autoroute* junction (A6 from Paris/Lyon–A31 from Metz), and its hotels are pricey and likely to be full.

Beaune's town centre is a tightly clustered, rampart-enclosed *vieille ville*, and its chief attraction is the fifteenth-century hospital, the **Hôtel-Dieu** (daily: mid-April to mid-Nov 9am–6.30pm; rest of year 9–11.30am & 2–5.30pm; 32F/€4.88), on the corner of place de la Halle. Once past the turnstile of the Hôtel-Dieu you find yourself in a cobbled courtyard surrounded by a wooden gallery overhung by a massive roof patterned with diamonds of gaudy tiles – green, burnt sienna, black and yellow – and similarly multi coloured steep-pitched dormers and turrets. Inside is a vast paved hall with a painted timber roof, the Grande Salle des Malades, which until quite recently continued to serve its original purpose of accommodating the sick. The last item on the tour is a splendid fifteenth-century altarpiece of the *Last Judgement* by Rogier van der Weyden, commissioned by Nicolas Rolin, who also founded the hospital in 1443 (King Louis XI commented: "It was only fair that a man who had made so many people poor during his life should create an asylum for them before his death"). A major wine auction takes place here during the annual Trois Glorieuses festival (see p.550), the prices paid setting the pattern for the season.

The private residence of the dukes of Burgundy on rue d'Enfer now contains the **Musée du Vin** (daily 9.30am–6pm; winter closed Tues; 25F/€3.81, same ticket allows entry to the two fine arts museums listed below), with giant winepresses and an interesting collection of tools of the trade. At the other end of rue d'Enfer is the collegiate **church of Notre-Dame**, which is about the only free thing in town (closed mid-Nov to March; guided visit 15F/€2.28, otherwise free). Inside are five very special Tournai tapestries from the fifteenth century, depicting the life of the Virgin and commissioned, once again, by the Rolin family.

There are two other museums, both in the former Ursuline convent that is now the Hôtel de Ville: the not-very-interesting **Musée des Beaux-Arts**, and the **Musée Marey Etienne-Jules**, devoted to early movie photography (both April to mid-Nov daily 2–6pm; 25F/€3.81, same entry ticket as for the wine museum). On the outskirts of the town, by the A6 Beaune–Tailly–Merceuil rest area, there's an open-air park called the **Archéodrome**, illustrating the history of Burgundy, with film and reconstructions of a Neolithic house, Cæsar's siege of Alésia (see p.528), a farm with ancient breeds of farm animals and so on. It costs 20–50F/€3.05–7.62 for adults, 15–40F/€2.29–6.10 for kids, depending on how many of the displays you wish to see.

Practicalities

Beaune's **gare SNCF** is outside the old walls to the east of town in avenue du 8-Septembre. If you arrive by bus, you're likely to be dropped at the main **gare routière** on the southwest side of town, just outside the walls at the end of rue Maufoux, a five-minute walk from the town's highlights. The slick **tourist office**, 1 rue de l'Hôtel-Dieu (April to mid-Nov Mon 9am–6pm, Tues–Thurs 9am–8pm, Fri & Sat 9am–9pm, Sun 9am–7pm; mid-Nov to March daily 9am–6pm; ☎03.80.26.21.30, fax 03.80.26.21.39, *www.ot-beaune.fr*), is the best place to find out about all things to do with the region's wines. You can also rent **bikes** from the tourist office and collect them from avenue du 8-Septembre.

If you're going to **stay** in Beaune, you'll have to be prepared to pay at least 200F/€30.49 a night. Be warned: the cheapest hotels may look good but you may encounter inconveniences (eg no showers after 9pm). The following are worth trying: the well-located *Central*, 2 rue Victor-Millot (☎03.80.24.77.24, fax 03.80.22.30.40; ④–⑤), which also has a good restaurant with a 98F/€14.94 menu; the *Grillon*, 21 route de Seurre (☎03.80.22.44.25, fax 03.80.24.94.89; ③), in an old family home; and, for a more comfortable stay, the vine-covered *Le Home*, 138 rte de Dijon, on the way into Beaune (☎03.80.22.16.43, fax 03.80.24.90.74; ④). The pretty *Les Cent Vignes* **campsite**, 10 rue Dubois (☎03.80.22.03.91; mid-March to Oct), is about 1km out of town, off rue du Faubourg-St-Nicolas (the N74 to Dijon), before the bridge over the *autoroute*; booking is advisable, as it fills up through the day.

Eating can also be an expensive business here. The best places to look for something cheap are rue Monge, place Carnot and rue Madeleine. *Le Carnot*, 18 rue Carnot, is a good cafeteria; and the *Brelinette*, 6 rue Madeleine, where menus start at 60F/€9.15, is also reasonably priced. If you are looking for something more sophisticated, try *Le Bénaton*, 25 rue du Faubourg-Bretonnière (☎03.80.22.00.26; closed Wed evening & Thurs), which has a good-value 105F/€16.01 menu, with a choice of calf's head, *jambon persillé* and *coq au vin* (à la carte will set you back quite a bit more). There's also the upscale *Bernard Morillon*, 31 rue Maufoux (☎03.80.24.12.06; closed Mon & Tues lunch), where menus start at 180F/€27.44, and *Le Gourmandin*, 8 place Carnot (☎03.80.24.07.88; closed summer Tues & Wed lunch, winter Mon & Tues lunch), with a good menu at 120F/€18.29. *Les Tontons*, 22 Faubourg Madeleine (☎03.80.24.19.64; closed Sun & Mon lunch) is stylish and unpretentious, with a more inspired way of interpreting the local specialities (menus 98–250F/€14.94–38.11).

THE WINES OF BURGUNDY

Burgundy farmers have been growing grapes since Roman times, and their rulers, the dukes, frequently put their **wines** to effective use as a tool of diplomacy. Today they have never had it so good, which is why they're reticent about the quirks of soil and climate and the tricks of pruning and spraying that make their wines so special. Vines are temperamental: frost on the wrong day, sun at the wrong time, too much water or poor drainage, and they won't come up with the goods. And they like a slope, which is why so many wines are called "Côte de" something. Burgundy's best wines come from a narrow strip of hillside called the **Côte d'Or** that runs southwest from Dijon to Santenay. It is divided into two regions, **Côte de Nuits** and **Côte de Beaune**. With few exceptions the reds of the Côte de Nuits are considered the best: they are richer, age better and cost more. Côte de Beaune is known particularly for its whites: Meursault, Montrachet and Puligny.

The single most important factor determining the "character" of wines is the **soil**. In the Côte d'Or, the relative mixture of chalk, flint and clay varies over very short distances, making for an enormous variety of taste. Chalky soil makes a wine *virile* or *corsé*, in other words "heady" – *il y a de la mâche*, they say, "something to bite on" – while clay makes it *féminin*, more *agréable*.

These and other more extravagant judgements are made after the hallowed procedure of **tasting**: in order to do it properly, by one account, you have to "introduce a draft of wine into your mouth, swill it across the tongue, roll it around the palate, churn it around, emitting the gargling sound so beloved of tasters, which is produced by slowly inhaling air through the centre of your mouth, and finally eject it". The ejection is what has to be learnt.

For an **apéritif** in Burgundy, you should try *kir*, named after the man who was both mayor and MP for Dijon for many years after World War II – two parts dry white wine, traditionally *aligoté*, and one part *cassis* or blackcurrant liqueur. To round the evening off there are many liqueurs to choose from, but Burgundy is particularly famous for its **marcs**, of which the best are matured for years in oak casks.

Château du Clos-de-Vougeot

If you find the French wine culture fascinating, it's worth visiting the **Château du Clos-de-Vougeot** to see the wine-making process (April–Aug & Oct–Nov 9–11.30am & 2–5.30pm; Sept 9am–6.30pm; 20F/€3.05), 15km north of Beaune between Gévry-Chambertin and Nuits-St-Georges, where you get to see the mammoth thirteenth-century winepresses installed by the Cistercian monks to whom these vineyards belonged for nearly 700 years until the Revolution. The château today is the home of a phoney chivalrous order founded in 1934, the Confrèrie des Chevaliers du Tastevin. Chivalrous or not, the "new" monks continue the good wine work. After you've seen how it's made, you can taste it nearby at La Grand Cave à Vougeot (9am–7pm). There is a three-day wine **festival**, Les Trois Glorieuses on the third Saturday in November, starting in Vougeot and continuing in Beaune and Meursault.

From the Saône to the Loire

The **Saône valley** is prosperous and modern, nourished by the *autoroute*, tourism, industry and the wine trade. But turn your back on the river and head west and at once you enter a different Burgundy: close, hilly pasture and woodland, utterly rural and more populated by cattle than people. This is the hinterland – the Deep South – of Burgundy, where every village clusters under the tower of a Romanesque church, spawned by the influence of Cluny in the 1000s and 1100s. It is only when you reach the Loire and encounter the main traffic routes again that you re-enter the modern world. It is beautiful country for **cycling**, though there are few places actually to rent a bike. There are, however, plenty of bus and train connections, and all these are very conveniently listed in the *Guide des Transports Régionaux* available from any *gare SNCF* in Burgundy.

Chalon-sur-Saône

CHALON, a sizeable port and bustling industrial centre on a broad meander of the Saône, is generally uninteresting, though its old riverside quarter does have an easy charm, and it makes a good base for exploring the more expensive areas of the Côte d'Or. Today it's a thriving business centre, and trade fairs frequently take over the town, but more festive occasions are also an important part of its appeal and good reasons to stop if you're around at the right time. Three major **events** are: a carnival in March, which features a parade of giant masks, confetti battle and "laughter evening"; a national festival of street artists in July; and a film festival in October.

The **old town** is just back from the river around Grande-Rue and rue du Châtelet. At the junction of these two streets you'll see a fifteenth-century timber-framed house, and around the quarter you'll find a number of half-timbered jettied facades. Nearby, 200m to the west on place de l'Hôtel-de-Ville, is the **Musée Denon** (daily except Tues & hols 9.30am–noon & 2–5.30pm; 14F/€2.13, Wed free), whose most vaunted exhibit is the 18,000-year-old Volgu flint, rated one of the finest stone tools yet discovered. Apart from the usual collection of bits and pieces excavated nearby, look out for the local furniture.

More interesting and unusual is the **Musée Niepce**, 28 quai des Messageries (daily except Tues: July & Aug 10am–6pm; Sept–June 9.30–11.30am & 2.30–5.30pm; 14F/€2.13), just downstream from Pont St-Laurent. Niepce, who was born in Chalon, is credited with inventing photography in 1816, and the museum possesses a fascinating range of cameras, from the first machine ever to the Apollo moon mission's equipment, plus a number of 007-type spy-camera devices, all attractively displayed under a set of glass domes. Upstairs is a library of works on the subject of photography, to be thumbed through at leisure, and a space for temporary exhibitions, with some big names in the history of the art.

The other interesting target in town is the **Maison des Vins** on Promenade Ste-Marie (daily 9am–7pm), where you can taste and buy Côte Chalonnaise wines, chosen from the wines of 44 local villages by a choice committee of professional wine tasters; even the cheaper ones are really good.

Practicalities

The **tourist office** is on boulevard de la République (July & Aug Mon–Sat 9am–12.30pm & 1.30–6.30pm, Sun 10.30am–12.30pm & 3–6pm; rest of year Mon–Sat same hours, Sun 10am–noon; ☎03.85.48.37.97, fax 03.85.48.63.55, *www.chalon-sur-saone.net*), and gives out excellent listings and a 5F/€0.76 map. The **gare SNCF** is just five minutes' walk away at the end of avenue Jean-Jaurès.

The most attractive **hotel** in town is undoubtedly the *St-Jean*, right on the river bank at 24 quai Gambetta (☎03.85.48.45.65, fax 03.85.93.62.69; ③). For something a little cheaper, there's *Hôtel au Vendanges de Bourgogne*, 21 rue du Général-Leclerc (☎03.85.48.01.90; ②), with charming rooms and a crêperie downstairs; *Nouvel Hôtel*, 7 av Boucicaut (☎03.85.48.07.31, fax 03.85.48.86.42; ②) – from the station turn left at the end of avenue Jean-Jaurès and left again; and the *Central*, 19 place de Beaune (☎03.85.48.35.00, fax 03.85.93.10.20; ②). The hostel has closed down – ignore the building that is still there. *Camping de la Butte* (☎03.85.48.26.86), 3km east of town in St-Marcel, is accessible on bus #9; if you're walking, cross either Pont St-Laurent or Pont J.-Richard and head east.

ALPHONSE LAMARTINE (1790–1869)

Often referred to as the French Byron, **Alphonse Lamartine** is one of the best-known of the French Romantic poets. He was born and grew up in Milly, about 15km west of Mâcon, and published his first poetic work, *Méditations poétiques*, in 1820. In 1825 he published *Le Dernier Chant du Pélérinage d'Harold* as a tribute to Byron.

After the 1830 Revolution in Paris, he became involved in politics, being elected to the Chambre des Députés in 1833 and quickly acquiring a reputation as a powerful orator on the weighty questions of the day, like the abolition of slavery and capital punishment. His finest hour was as the leading figure in the provisional government of the Second Republic, which was proclaimed from the Hôtel de Ville in Paris on February 23, 1848. He withdrew from politics when reactionary forces, under the leadership of General Cavaignac, let the army loose on the protesting workers of Paris and Marseille in June 1848, after which he retired to St-Point (see p.555).

(☎03.85.39.17.11, fax 03.85.38.02.75; ④; restaurant from 90F/€13.72) and the modern *de Genève*, 1 rue Bigonnet (☎03.85.38.18.10, fax 03.85.38.22.32; ④; restaurant from 70F/€10.67). There's a **campsite** 3km north out of town on the N6 (☎03.86.38.16.22; closed Nov to mid-March).

Mâcon has no shortage of good **restaurants** to choose from. For cheap eats, head for the river: the pleasant *Lamartine*, 266 quai Lamartine (closed Mon evening & Tues), is popular with diners at mealtimes and drinkers later on, while the *St Laurent*, on the other side of the river, has great views and *plats* from 80F/€12.20. For local meat, the place to go is *La Vigne et les Vins (Scoubidou)*, 42 rue Joseph-Dufour (☎03.85.38.65.92), which offers good prices and friendly service, while *Chez Gilou*, 19/21 rue Joseph-Dufour (☎03.85.40.95.47; closed Sun lunch and Mon), does a nice summer paella. However, the best moderately priced option is *Le Rocher de Cancale*, 393 quai Jean-Jaurès (☎03.85.38.07.50; closed Sun evenings & Mon), a superb restaurant, serving wonderful fish (menus from 135F/€20.58, *plats* from 65F/€9.91). And if you're really pushing the boat out, the elegant *Pierre*, 7/9 rue Joseph-Dufour (☎03.85.38.14.23; closed Sun evenings & Mon, last week in June & first two weeks in July) is well worth a splurge for a special occasion, not least for its Grand Marnier soufflé (menus 100–315F/€15.24–48.02).

Brou

BROU is an uninteresting suburban village outside Bourg-en-Bresse, 32km east of Mâcon, which happens to have an early sixteenth-century **church** (daily; 26F/€2.44). If you're heading east to Geneva or the Alps, take a look, but don't lose a lift or miss a train for it. Aldous Huxley found it "a horrible little architectural nightmare", its monuments "positively and piercingly vulgar". Certainly, it was a very rich woman's expensive folly, crammed with virtuoso craftsmanship from the dying moments of the Gothic style; it was undertaken by Margaret of Austria after the death of her husband, Philibert, Duke of Savoy, as a mausoleum for the two of them and Philibert's mother. It's interesting to see, but soulless, without a trace of vision or inspiration – it's no longer a place of worship.

Bourg-en-Bresse

BOURG-EN-BRESSE is the place to base yourself if you want to visit Brou's church, just a short bus (#1) ride away. The **tourist office** (Mon–Fri 9am–noon & 2–6.30pm; ☎04.74.22.49.40, *www.bourg-en-bresse.org*) is in Centre Albert-Camus, 6 av Alsace-Lorraine, with an annexe by Brou church in summer. Wednesday is **market** day in place Carriat, and on the first and third Wednesdays of each month there's a livestock market as well. An attractive place to **stay** is the *Hôtel du Mail* near the station at 46 av du Mail (☎04.74.21.00.26, fax 04.74.21.29.55; ②; closed Dec 5–Jan 12 & July 12–Aug 7). The municipal **campsite** (☎04.74.45.37.21; April to mid-Oct) is on avenue des Sports, the N83 northeast of town heading for Lons-le-Saunier.

The Mâconnais

The **Mâconnais** wine-producing country lies to the west of the valley of the Saône, a strip hardly 20km wide, stretching from Mâcon to Tournus. The land rises sharply into steep little hills and valleys, at its prettiest in the south, where the region's best white wines come from, around the villages of **POUILLY**, **VINZELLES**, **PRISSÉ** and **FUISSÉ**, at the last of which, should you yearn for rustic rest, the *Hôtel La Vigne Blanche* will provide just the setting you're looking for (☎03.85.35.60.50, fax 03.85.35.67.13; ②; closed Dec 20–Jan 6), along with good regional cooking in its restaurant (from 85F/€12.96).

Directly above these villages rises the distinctive and precipitous 500-metre rock of **Solutré**, which in prehistoric times – around 20,000 BC – seems to have served as some kind of ambush site for hunters after migrating animals: the bones of 100,000 horses have been found in the soil beneath the rock, along with mammoth, bison and reindeer carcasses. The history and results of the excavations are displayed in a museum at the foot of the rock, the **Musée Départemental de Préhistoire** (daily except Tues: Feb–May & Oct–Nov 10am–noon & 2–5pm; June–Sept 10am–1pm & 2–7pm; 20F/€3.05). A steep path climbs to the top of the rock, where you get a superb view as far as Mont Blanc and the Matterhorn on a clear day, as well as your immediate surroundings. You look down on the huddled roofs of **SOLUTRÉ-POUILLY** and the slopes beneath you covered with the vines of the Chardonnay grape that makes the exquisite greenish Pouilly-Fuissé wine. It is at its most enchanting in early spring when the earth still shows its *terre-cuite* colours, punctuated by bursts of white cherry blossom and the blue drift of bonfire smoke from prunings amid the neatly staked rows of vines.

Aside from the sheer pleasure of wandering about in such reposeful landscapes – not so, however, if you are trying to tackle this very hilly country on a bike – there are some specific places to make for. One such is the sleepy hamlet of **ST-POINT**, where the poet Lamartine (see box on p.554) spent much of his life in the little medieval **Château de St-Point**, now a museum dedicated to his memory (March to mid-Nov Mon & Thurs–Sat 10am–noon & 2–6pm, Sun 2–6pm; 23F/€3.51), next to the Romanesque church where he is buried. If you continue up the road behind the château you come to an utterly rural farm where you can buy goat's cheese. There is a **campsite** by the Lac St-Point (☎03.85.50.52.31; April–Oct).

Cluny

The abbey of **CLUNY** is the major tourist destination of the region. The voice of its abbot once made monarchs tremble, as his power in the Christian world was second only to that of the pope. The monastery was founded in 910 in response to the corruption of the existing church, and it took only a couple of vigorous early abbots to build the power of Cluny into a veritable empire. Gradually its spiritual influence declined, and Cluny became a royal gift. Both Richelieu and Mazarin did stints in the monastery as abbot.

Now, although the reputation of the place still pulls in the tourist coaches, little remains apart from the very attractive village. The Revolution suppressed the monastery, and Hugues de Semur's vast and influential eleventh-century **church**, the largest building in Christendom until the construction of St Peter's in Rome, was dismantled in 1810. Now all you can see of the former **abbey** (daily: April–June 9.30am–noon & 2–6pm; July – Sept 9am–7pm; Oct 9.30am–noon & 2–5pm; rest of year 10am–noon & 2–4/5pm; 26F/€3.96, 32F/€4.88 combined ticket with museum) is an octagonal belfry, the south transept and, in the impressive granary, the surviving capitals from its immense columns. From the top of the **Tour des Fromages** you can reconstruct it in your imagination; you enter the tower through the tourist office (see below). The **Musée d'Art et d'Archaeologie** (same hours as abbey; 14F/€2.13, 32F/€4.88 combined ticket with abbey), in the fifteenth-century palace of the last freely elected abbot, helps to flesh out the picture with reconstructions and fragments of sculpture, while the octagonal Romanesque belfry of the parish **church of St-Marcel** also recalls the belfries that once adorned the abbey.

There are some interesting old houses in rue Mercière/rue Lamartine and, in particular, rue de la République/rue d'Avril, where nos. 25 and 6 are nearly as old as the abbey itself. At the back of the abbey is one of France's national stud farms, **Haras National** (daily 9am–7pm; free), which can also be visited.

The **tourist office** is at 6 rue Mercière (daily: May–Sept 10am–7pm; rest of year 10am–noon & 2.30–6.30pm; ☎03.85.59.05.34, fax 03.85.59.06.95, *www.perso.wanadoo.fr /otcluny*). For **accommodation**, try the *Hôtel de l'Abbaye* on avenue de la Gare (☎03.85.59.11.14, fax 03.85.59.09.76; ②–③; closed end of Jan to mid-Feb), which has reasonable rooms; the *Hôtel du Commerce*, 8 place du Commerce (☎03.85.59.03.09, fax 03.85.59.00.87; ②); or the *Hôtel St-Odilon*, across the river on the left before the campsite (☎03.85.59.25.00, fax 03.85.59.06.18, *www.acmtel.com/saint-odilon*; ④; closed mid-Dec to mid-Jan). There's a municipal **hostel**, *Cluny Séjour*, on rue Porte-de-Paris (☎03.85.59.08.83; closed Dec & Jan), and a municipal **campsite**, *St-Vital* (☎03.85.59.08.34; May to mid-Sept), across Pont de la Levée in the direction of Tournus, where you can also hire **bicycles.**

For a **meal**, other than a crêpe or snack, try *Les Marronniers*, 20 av de Gaulle (☎03.85.59.07.95), or, for some good country cooking, *Le Potin Gourmand*, 4 place Champ-de-Foire (☎03.85.59.02.06; closed Mon & Jan 4–Feb 5; best-value menus at 78F/€11.89 & 120F/€18.29).

Taizé

Another powerful attraction for the faithful might be the modern ecumenical community at **TAIZÉ**, 10km north of Cluny. It was founded in 1940 by the Swiss pastor Roger Schutz and centres around a restored Romanesque church and the new Church of Reconciliation. Hordes of youngsters come to take part in discussion groups and camp out. If you are seriously interested – and it is not likely to be to the taste of the merely curious – write to Communauté de Taizé, 71250 Cluny.

The Beaujolais

Imperceptibly, as you continue south, the Mâconnais becomes the **Beaujolais**, a larger area of terraced hills producing lighter, fruity red wines, which it is now fashionable to drink very early. The Beaujolais grape is the Gamay, which, in contrast to other parts of Burgundy, thrives here on this granite soil. Of the four *appellations* of Beaujolais, the best are the *crus*, including Morgon and Fleurie, which come from the northern part of the region between St-Amour (the northernmost *cru*), and Brouilly in the south. If you have transport, you can follow the *cru* trail south from Mâcon by turning right at Crêches-sur-Saône up the D31 to St-Amour, and then south along the D68. Beaujolais Villages, which produces the best *nouveau*, comes from the middle of the Beaujolais region, south of the *cru* belt, while plain Beaujolais and Beaujolais Supérieur are produced in the vineyards southwest of Villefranche.

The well-marked **route de Beaujolais** winds down through the wine villages to **VILLEFRANCHE**, not far from Lyon and a good base for the route. Here, the **tourist office** at 290 rue de Thizy (Mon–Sat 9am–noon & 1.30–6pm, Sun 9am–noon; ☎04.74.68.05.18) has all the information about *caves*, visits and wine tours. There are numerous cheap **hotels**, almost all near the **gare SNCF**. A good one to try is the friendly and clean *La Colonne*, 6 place Carnot (☎04.74.65.06.42; ①), with a popular cheap **bar**, open every night – including Sunday, when everything else in the village is dead. Most of the cafés on rue Nationale are good for snacks or cheap menus, too.

Paray-le-Monial

Fifty kilometres west of Cluny, across countryside that becomes ever gentler and flatter as you approach the broad valley of the Loire, is **PARAY-LE-MONIAL**, whose major attraction is its **Basilique du Sacré-Cœur**. Not only is it a superb building in its own right, with a marvellously satisfying arrangement of apses and chapels stacking up in sturdy symmetry to its fine octagonal belfry, it's also the only place, albeit on a smaller scale, where you can get an idea of what the abbey of Cluny looked like (see oppsite). The two churches are contemporary and the result of the same Hugues de Semur's influence.

The town itself is the archetypal country town, quiet and unpretentious, straddling the slow waters of the River Bourbince and the Canal du Centre. The only thing that disturbs its calm is the arrival of pilgrims of the Sacré-Coeur, or "Sacred Heart", a cult which originated here with Marguerite-Marie Alacoque, a local nun who received revelations advocating the worship of the sacred heart. The cult was later adopted by the entire Roman Catholic Church. The first pilgrimage took place in 1873, encouraged as a means of combating the socialist ideas espoused by the Paris Commune, and it raised the money to construct the church of the Sacré-Cœur on the hill of Montmartre in Paris. Paray is now second only to Lourdes as a pilgrim centre.

The one secular building definitely worth a look, aside from just browsing down the main street – rue de la République/rue des Deux-Ponts/rue Victor-Hugo – is the highly ornamented **Maison Jayet**, now the Hôtel de Ville on place Guignaud, built in the 1520s.

Practicalities

The **tourist office** is on avenue Jean-Paul-II (Mon–Sat 9am–noon & 1–6.30pm; ☎03.85.81.10.92, fax 03.85.81.36.61). You can rent **bikes** from André Vaz, 24 rue de la République (☎03.85.81.08.51).

For **accommodation**, try the *Hostellerie des Trois Pigeons*, 2 rue Daugard, just beyond the Hôtel de Ville (☎03.85.81.03.77, fax 03.85.81.58.59; ③; closed Dec–Feb; restaurant from 80F/€12.19), or, near the station, *Hôtel du Nord*, 1 av de la Gare (☎03.85.81.05.12, fax 03.85.81.58.93; ②; closed Dec 25–Jan 25; restaurant from 68F/€10.36). Further possibilities are the *Hôtel aux Vendanges de Bourgogne*, 5 rue Denis-Papin (☎03.85.81.13.43, fax 03.85.88.87.59; ②; closed Nov 25–Dec 15; good-value restaurant from 70F/€10.67), south of the Canal du Centre off the N79, or the *Grand Hôtel de la Basilique*, 18 rue de la Visitation (☎03.85.81.11.13, fax 03.85.88.83.70, *www.hoteldelabasilique*; ②; closed Nov to mid-March; restaurant from 75F/€11.43), bang opposite the chapel that stands on the spot where St Marguerite had her revelations, and consequently rather sought after by the pilgrims. The *Mambré* **campsite** is on route du Gué-Léger (☎03.85.88.89.20; April–Oct). If you want to explore the little villages throughout the Mâconnais (see p.555), there's no better base than the Merle family's organic farm at Vitry-en-Charollais (☎03.85.81.10.79; around 230F/€35.06 with breakfast for two, and 80F/€12.20 a head for dinner), with delicious home-cooking, about 6km southwest of Paray.

The Charollais

The **Charollais** is cattle country, taking its name from the pretty little water-enclosed market town of **CHAROLLES**, with its 32 bridges, on the main N79 road, and in turn giving its name to one of the world's most illustrious breeds of cattle: the white, curly-haired and stocky Charollais, bred for its lean meat. The fields south of Paray are full of the beasts. Throughout this landscape, scattered across the rich farmland along the Arconce River, are dozens of small villages, all with more or less remarkable Romanesque churches, offspring of Cluny in its vigorous youth.

ANZY-LE-DUC, about 15km south of Paray off the main D982 to Roanne, boasts an exquisite complex of buildings: a perfect Romanesque church with jackdaw chatter echoing off the octagonal belfry, side by side with the remains of the old priory incorporated into a sort of fortified farm looking out over the Arconce valley, the whole built in a rich, warm stone. **MONTCEAUX-L'ÉTOILE**, a little nearer to Paray, has its special charm too: a quiet, worn church with beautiful sculptures adorning the porch, standing likewise above the Arconce valley, and, a little way down the village street, a curious tower-like house where a Marquis of Vichy is said to have practised alchemy with the notorious Italian wizard, Cagliostro. There is a farm **campsite** (☎03.85.25.38.66; May–Sept) on the Paray side of the village.

Ten kilometres to the west of Paray, the Arconce flows into the Loire just upstream from **DIGOIN**, France's chief centre of pottery manufacture. Although it's not a place you are likely to do more than pass through, the nineteenth-century **bridge** carrying the Canal du Centre over the Loire is worth a look and the riverside quays make a quiet, sunny picnic spot. The town also has two very good **hotel-restaurants**: *de la Gare*, 79 av de Gaulle (☎03.85.53.03.04, fax 03.85.53.14.70; ③; closed mid-Jan to mid-Feb; restaurant from 135F/€20.58, closed Wed except in July & Aug), and *Les Diligences*, 14 rue Nationale (☎03.85.53.06.31, fax 03.85.88.92.43; ③; closed Nov 20–Dec 10; restaurant from 95F/€14.48, closed Mon evening & Tues except in July & Aug). There's a **campsite**, *de la Chevrette*, by the Loire on the Moulins road (☎03.85.53.11.49; April–Oct).

Nevers

At the western confines of Burgundy, **NEVERS** is a small provincial city on the confluence of the rivers Loire and Nièvre. In France it is known for its *nougatine* candies and fine porcelain, a hallmark since the seventeenth century, still produced in just three workshops and sold in a few elegant, expensive shops (*faïenceries*) around town. Parts of the **old town**, best viewed from the bridge over the Loire, date back to the twelfth century and make for a relaxed stroll away from the busier town centre. Not necessarily a destination in itself, Nevers makes, with its open-air concert programme in summer and a few lively bars and restaurants, a useful and reasonably pleasant stopover if you are travelling in the region.

The Town

Nevers centres around **place Carnot**, close to the fifteenth-century **Palais Ducal**, former home of the dukes of Nevers, with octagonal turrets and an elegant central tower decorated with sculptures illustrating the family history of the first duke, François de Clèves, in the mid-seventeenth century. The building now houses an annexe of the law courts. Nearby, opposite the Hôtel de Ville, the **Cathédrale de St-Cyr** reveals a sort of wall display of French architectural styles from the tenth to the sixteenth centuries; it even manages to have two opposite apses, one Gothic, the other Romanesque. But more interesting and aesthetically satisfying is the late eleventh-century **church of St-Étienne**, on the east side of the town centre. Behind its plain exterior lies one of the prototype pilgrim churches, with galleries above the aisles, ambulatory and three radiating chapels around the apse.

From the station, avenue de-Gaulle leads to place Carnot, where you take a left turn for the **Parc Roger-Salengro**, which has some unexpected sculptures – look out for *Les Sangliers* (wild boar). The north side of the park edges onto the **convent of St-Gildard**, where Bernadette of Lourdes ended her days. Her embalmed body is displayed in a glass-fronted **shrine** (daily: summer 7am–7.30pm; winter 7am–noon & 2–7pm) in the convent chapel. A short walk away is the modern **church of Ste-Bernadette du Banlay**, built in 1966 in the style of *fonction oblique* by the architects Claude Parent and Paul Virilio.

Crossing to the other side of avenue de-Gaulle, five minutes' walk from the station by place Mossé and the bridge over the Loire, you pass a section of the old town walls and the **Tour Goguin**, partly dating back to the eleventh century. If you turn in here to the right you come to the **Porte de Croux**, a cream stone tower with intact machicolations and a steep tiled roof like those of its surrounding buildings; inside, there's a small local **archeology museum** (March–Nov Wed–Sun 2–6pm; 10F/€1.52), displaying mainly Greek and Roman statuary. Nearby in rue du 14-Juillet, a seventeenth-century **faïencerie** sells antique pieces such as huge Nivernais plates. To your right again you get back to the oldest quarter of town around the cathedral – rue Morlon and rue de la Cathédrale – with its dilapidated half-timbered houses, alleys and stairs descending to the river.

To the north of the ducal palace on the way out of town towards Orléans, **Porte de Paris**, a triumphal arch, straddles rue des Ardilliers. It commemorates one of Europe's major conflicts, the battle of Fontenoy, fought out between Charlemagne's sons in 841 AD. The stakes were Charlemagne's empire, and the outcome the division of his lands east and west of the Rhine, which formed the basis of modern France and Germany.

Practicalities

The **gare SNCF** and **gare routière** are on rue du Chemin-de-Fer. The **tourist office**, in the foyer of the Palais Ducal (daily 9.30am–12.30pm & 2.30–6pm; ☎03.86.68.46.00, *www.ville-nevers.fr*), provides maps and information on events in the summer music festival. **Bike rental** is available from Belair, 31bis rue de la Préfecture.

There are plenty of **hotels**, of which the best is the *Beauséjour* at 5 rue St-Gildard (☎03.86.61.20.84, fax 03.86.59.15.37; ②), only ten minutes' walk from the station. *Hôtel Thermidor*, 14 rue Claude-Tillier (☎03.86.57.15.47; ②), reached by turning left out of the station and right after *Bar des Messages*, is also good value and quiet. The municipal **campsite** (☎03.86.37.56.52) is just over the bridge on the other side of the Loire, with the best view of the town. **IMPHY**, 10km from Nevers, has a **hostel**, *Foyer du Vignot*, 8 rue Jean-Sounié (☎03.86.90.95.20).

Avenue de-Gaulle has a few inexpensive **restaurants** and **cafés**, such as the superb *Gambrinus*, 37 av de-Gaulle (☎03.86.57.19.48; closed Sat lunch & Sun; *plats* from 50F/€7.62). *Le Goemon*, 9 rue du 14-Juillet (☎03.86.59.54.99; closed Sun & Mon evening), is a crêperie with good salads, and live jazz on Saturday nights, and *La Crêperie*, 24 av de-Gaulle (☎03.86.57.28.61; closed Sun lunch & Mon), has good cheap meals. For fresh, tasty food in a friendly place, try *La Grignote* at 7bis rue Ferdinand-Gambon near the market (☎03.86.36.24.99; closed Mon, Tues & Wed evening). *Donald's Pub*, on rue François Mitterand near the river, is a good place for a drink.

travel details

Trains

Autun to: Avallon (4–5 SNCF buses or trains daily; 2hr); Le Creusot (2 daily; 1hr).

Auxerre to: Avallon (4–5 daily; 1hr 05min); Paris (7–8 daily; 2hr 15min–2hr 30min); Sens (2 daily; 55min).

Avallon to: Auxerre (4–5 daily; 1hr 05min); Dijon (4 daily; 2hr); Paris (several daily via Laroche-Migennes; 3hr); Sens (2 daily; 55min).

Beaune to: Dijon (about 7 daily; 20min); Lyon (about 7 daily; 2hr); Paris (2 TGVs daily; 2hr).

Bourg-en-Bresse to: Dijon (2 daily; 1hr 45min–2hr 30min); Geneva (4 TGVs daily; 1hr 30min); Lyon (14 daily; about 1hr); Mâcon (12 daily; 20–30min); Paris (4 TGVs daily; 2hr).

Dijon to: Beaune (frequent; 25min); Chalon (frequent; 40min); Laroche-Migennes (6 daily; 1hr 30min); Les Laumes (6 daily; 30min); Lyon (20 daily; 1hr 45min–2hr 30min); Mâcon (frequent; 1hr–1hr 20min); Montbard (6 daily; 35min); Nevers (4–5 daily; 2hr 30min–3hr); Nuits-St-Georges (frequent; 20min); Paris (15 daily; 1hr 40min–3hr); Tournus (frequent; 1hr); Sens (6 daily; 2hr 10min); Tonnerre via Ancy-le-Franc and Tanly (6 daily; 1hr 15min); Villefranche (frequent; around 1hr 40min).

Mâcon to: Bourg-en-Bresse (4 TGVs daily; 20min); Dijon (around 14 daily; 1hr 10min); Geneva (4 TGVs daily; 1hr 50min); Lyon (around 14 daily; 40min); Paris (5 TGVs daily; 1hr 40min).

Nevers to: Autun (3 daily; 1hr 30min); Clermont-Ferrand (5 daily; 1hr 50min); Le Creusot (5 daily; 1hr 30min); Dijon (5 daily; 2hr 30min); Étang (3 daily; 1hr–1hr 50min); Montchanin (6 daily; 1hr 30min); Paris (several daily; 2–3hr).

Paray-le-Monial to: Chagny (5 daily; 1hr–1hr 30min); Chalon (5 daily; 1hr 10min–1hr 40min); Dijon (2 daily; 1hr 45min); Montchanin (2 daily; 50min).

Sens to: Auxerre (3–5 daily changing at Laroche-Migennes; 45min); Autun (1 daily; 4hr); Avallon (3–5 daily; 2hr); Dijon (11 daily; 2hr 10min); Joigny (11 daily; 30min); Laroche-Migennes junction (11 daily; 30min); Montbard (11 daily; 1hr 30min); Paris (frequent; 1hr–1hr 30min); Tonnerre (11 daily; 55min).

Tonnerre to: Dijon (6 daily; 1hr 15min); Paris (6 daily; 1hr 45min).

Buses

Autun to: Beaune (1 daily; 1hr 10min); Chalon (2–3 daily; 1hr 20min); Château-Chinon (1 daily; 1hr); Le Creusot (several daily; 30min); Dijon (1 daily; 2hr 30min); Montchanin TGV station (several daily; 1hr); St-Léger-sous-Beuvray (2–3 daily; 1hr 15min).

Avallon to: Dijon (1 daily; 2hr 30min–3hr); Vézelay (1 daily; 30min).

Bourg-en-Bresse to: Lyon (1 daily; 1hr 40min).

Chablis to: Auxerre (2 daily, 35min); Tonnerre (2 daily; 1hr). No bus service in Aug.

Cluny to: Chalon (7 daily; 1hr 20min); Charolles (2–5 daily; 45min); Mâcon (7 daily; 45min); Paray-le-Monial (2–5 daily; 1hr).

Dijon to: Autun (1 daily; 2hr 30min); Avallon (3 daily; 2hr 30min); Beaune (every half-hour; 1hr); Châtillon-sur-Seine (4 daily; 1hr 30min); Chaumont (1 daily; 2hr 20min); Langres (1 daily; 1hr 40min); Nuits (4 daily; 35min); Saulieu (1 daily; 1hr 30min).

Mâcon to: Chalon (7 daily; 2hr 15min); Charolles (2–5 daily; 2hr); Cluny (7 daily; 45min); Paray-le-Monial (2–5 daily; 2hr 20min).

Semur to: Auxerre (1 daily; 2hr 50min); Les Laumes (1 daily; 40min); Montbard (1 daily; 1hr 10min); Saulieu (1 daily; 45min).

Sens to: Auxerre (4 daily; 2hr 05min); Joigny (4 daily; 1hr 10min); Troyes (4–5 daily; 1hr 45min).

CHAPTER EIGHT

POITOU-CHARENTES AND THE ATLANTIC COAST

News-stands selling *Sud-Ouest* remind you where you are: this is not the Mediterranean, certainly, but in summer the quality of the light, the warm air, the fields of sunflowers and the shuttered siesta-silence of the farmhouses give you the first exciting promises of the south.

The coast, on the other hand, remains unmistakably Atlantic – dunes, pine forest, reclaimed marshland and misty mudflats. While it has great charm in places, particularly out of season on the islands of **Noirmoutier**, **Ré** and **Oléron**, it's a family, camper-caravanner seaside, lacking the glamour and excitement of the Côte d'Azur. The principal port in the north, **La Rochelle**, is one of the prettiest and most distinctive towns in France. The sandy beaches are beautiful everywhere, though can occasionally be disappointing where the water is murky and shallow for a long way out: this applies more to the northern stretches. On the dune-backed **Côte d'Argent**, south of Bordeaux, however, the sea can be lively, not to say dangerous.

Inland, the valley of the slow and green **River Charente** epitomizes blue-overalled, Gauloise-smoking, peasant France. The towpath is accessible for long stretches, on foot or mountain bike, and there are boat trips from **Saintes** and **Cognac**. The **Marais Poitevin**, too, with its groves of poplars and island fields reticulated by countless canals and ditches, is both unusual landscape and easy-going walking or cycling country.

But perhaps the most memorable aspect of the countryside – and indeed of towns like **Poitiers** – is the presence of exquisite Romanesque churches. This region formed a significant stretch of the medieval pilgrim routes across France and from Britain and northern Europe to the shrine of St Jacques (St James, or Santiago as the Spanish know

---

ACCOMMODATION PRICE CODES

Each hotel and guesthouse in this book has been graded according to the following price codes, which indicate the price for the **cheapest double room available during the high season**.

① Under 160F/€24	④ 300–400F/€46–61	⑦ 600–700F/€91–107
② 160–220F/€24–34	⑤ 400–500F/€61–76	⑧ 700–800F/€107–122
③ 220–300F/€34–46	⑥ 500–600F/€76–91	⑨ Over 800F/€122

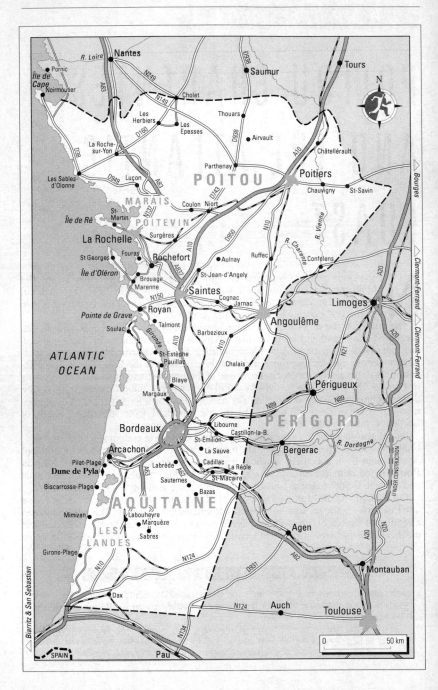

him) at Compostela in northwest Spain, and was well endowed by its followers. The finest of the churches, among the best in all of France, are to be found in the country-side around Saintes and Poitiers: informal, highly individual and so integrated with their landscape they often seem as rooted as the trees.

Lastly, of course, remember that this is a region of seafood – fresh and cheap in every market for miles inland – and, around **Bordeaux**, some of the world's top vineyards.

POITOU

Most of the old province of **Poitou** is a huge expanse of rolling wheat land and sun-flower and maize plantations where the combines crawl and giant sprinklers shoot great arcs of white water over the fields in summertime. Villages are strung out along the valley floors. Heartland of the domains of Eleanor, Duchess of Aquitaine, whose marriage to King Henry II in 1152 brought the whole of southwest France under English control for 300 years, it is also the northern limit of the *langue d'oc*-speaking part of the country, whose Occitan dialect survives among old people even today.

West of **Poitiers** the open landscape of the Poitou plain gradually gives way to *bocages* – small fields enclosed by hedges and trees. The local farmers' co-operatives say that grubbing up woodland and creating vast windswept acreages in the name of efficiency and productivity is going out of fashion. And not just for aesthetic reasons: wind erosion has left scarcely 15cm of top soil.

Poitiers

Heading south from Tours on the Autoroute de l'Aquitaine, you'd hardly be tempted by the cluster of towers and office blocks rising from the plain, which is all you see of **POITIERS**. But approach more closely and things look very different. Sitting on a hill-top overlooking two rivers, Poitiers is a country town with a unique charm that comes from a long and sometimes influential history – as the seat of the dukes of Aquitaine, for instance – discernible in the winding lines of the streets and the breadth of civic, domestic and ecclesiastical architectural fashions represented in its buildings. Its pedestrian precincts, restaurants and pavement cafés – and some wonderful central gardens – make for comfortable sightseeing.

Arrival, information and accommodation

The **gare SNCF** is on boulevard du Grand-Cerf, part of the ring-road system that encir-cles the base of the hill on which Poitiers is built. There is no *gare routière*: out-of-town **buses**, run by Rapides de Poitou (☎05.49.46.27.45, *www.les-rapides-du-poitou.fr*), leave from the train station. The **tourist office** is fifteen minutes' walk away at 8 rue des Grandes-Écoles off place du Maréchal-Leclerc (July & Aug Mon–Fri 9am–7pm, Sat & Sun 9.45am–6.45pm; rest of year Mon–Fri 9am–noon & 1.30–6pm, Sat 9am–noon & 2–6pm; ☎05.49.41.21.24, fax 05.49.88.65.84, *www.mairie-poitiers.fr*), and will supply walkers with a guide to the regional opportunities: the **GR364** sets out from here, reaching the Vendée coast via Parthenay. **Bikes** can be rented from Cyclamen, 49 rue Arsène-Orillard (☎05.49.88.13.25), **cars** from outlets near the train station on boulevard du Grand-Cerf, such as Citer at no. 48 (☎05.49.58.51.58).

There are plenty of **hotels** along boulevard du Grand-Cerf by the train station, but the area is not particularly salubrious; for more entertaining surroundings it's only a short uphill walk – boulevard Solférino, then to the right up the steep steps – to the town centre on place du Maréchal-Leclerc.

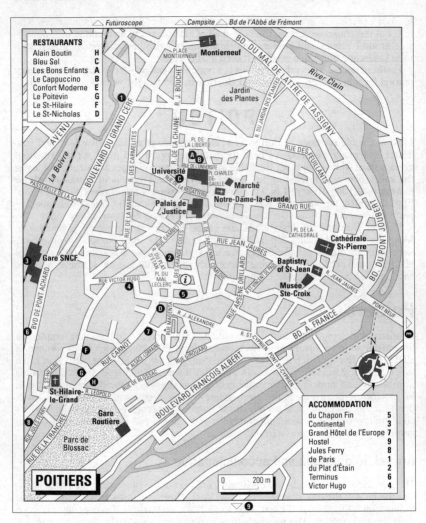

POITIERS

Hotels

du Chapon Fin, 11 rue Lebasdes (☎05.49.88.02.97, fax 05.49.88.91.63). Substantial old two-star hotel in a great position near the grand Hôtel de Ville; the spacious rooms all have showers. Closed mid-Dec to mid-Jan. ②.

Continental, 2 bd Solférino (☎05.49.37.93.93, fax 05.49.53.01.16). Comfortable two-star opposite the train station, whose soundproofed rooms all have bath or shower and TV. ③.

Grand Hôtel de l'Europe, 39 rue Carnot (☎05.49.88.12.00, fax 05.49.88.97.30). Smart and very central hotel; its front courtyard is set back from the street, meaning that it's very quiet. Covered parking 20F/€3.05. ④.

Jules Ferry, 27 rue Jules-Ferry (☎05.49.37.80.14, fax 05.49.53.15.02). Friendly, family-run establishment situated in a peaceful residential street near the church of St-Hilaire; clean and nicely decorated. ①.

de Paris, 123 bd du Grand-Cerf (☎05.49.58.39.37). A once superior hotel by the train station, now run-down and inexpensive; suffers from traffic noise. If a little unfriendly, the simple, good-value restaurant compensates. ②.

du Plat d'Étain, 7 rue du Plat-d'Étain (☎05.49.41.04.80, fax 05.49.52.25.84). An attractive, well-run hotel in a central quiet street just off the main shopping precinct. Closed mid-Dec to early Jan. ③.

Terminus, 3 bd Pont-Achard (☎05.49.62.92.30, fax 05.49.62.92.40). One of the better hotels around the train station, with an excellent brasserie. Rooms are very clean, modern and soundproofed. ③.

Victor Hugo, 5 rue Victor-Hugo (☎05.49.41.12.16). A central bargain above an agreeable bar – only five rooms, most of them simple. ②.

Hostel and campsite

HI hostel, 17 rue de la Jeunesse (☎05.49.30.09.70, fax 05.49.30.09.79). Large, modern hostel next to a swimming pool, often overrun with school groups. Take bus #3 from the *gare SNCF* to Bellejouanne, 3km away. Well signposted, it's to the right off the N10 Angoulême road.

Camping municipal, rue du Porteau (☎05.49.41.44.88). Grassy site with clean facilities situated 2km north of town; bus #7. Closed Oct–March.

The Town

The two poles of communal life in Poitiers are the tree-lined **place du Maréchal-Leclerc**, with its popular cafés and lively outdoor culture, and **place Charles-de-Gaulle** to the north, where a big and bustling food and clothes **market** takes place (Mon–Sat 7am–6pm, Sun 7.30am–1pm). Between the two is a warren of prosperous streets – as far along as the half-timbered medieval houses of **rue de la Chaine** – with the rue Gambetta cutting north past the old **Palais de Justice**, with a nineteenth-century facade that hides a much older core (closed to the public at the time of writing; check with tourist office for reopening date).

The church of Notre-Dame-la-Grande

From the Palais de Justice, you can look down upon one of the greatest and most idiosyncratic churches in France, **Notre-Dame-la-Grande** (daily 8am–7pm), begun in the twelfth-century reign of Eleanor and recently renovated; strangely enough, pigeon droppings and pollution weren't the major concern, but the salt from the market stalls of fishmongers and salt merchants seeping into the ground and up into the church's facade.

The weirdest and most spectacular thing about the church is the west front. You can't call it beautiful, at least not in a conventional sense. It is squat and loaded with detail to a degree that the modern eye could regard as fussy. And yet it is this detail which is enthralling, ranging from the domestic to the disturbingly anarchic: in the blind arch to the right of the door, a woman sits in the keystone with her hair blowing out from her head; in the frieze above, Mary places her hand familiarly on Elizabeth's pregnant belly. You see the newborn Jesus admired by a couple of daft-looking sheep and gurgling in his bathtub. Higher still are images of the apostles, and at the apex, where the eye is carried deliberately and inevitably, Christ in Majesty in an almond-shaped inset. Such elaborate sculpted facades – and domes like pine cones on turret and belfry – are the hallmarks of the Poitou brand of Romanesque. The interior, which is crudely overlaid with nineteenth-century frescoes, is not nearly as interesting.

The cathedral and around

At the eastern edge of the old town stands the **Cathédrale St-Pierre**, an enormous building on whose broad, pale facade pigeons roost and plants take root. Some of the stained glass dates from the twelfth century, notably the Crucifixion in the central window of the apse, in which the features of Henry II and Eleanor are supposedly discernible. The choir stalls, too, are full of characteristic medieval detail: a coquettish Mary and Child, a peasant killing a boar, the architect at work with his dividers, a baker with a basket of loaves. But it's the grand eighteenth-century organ, the Orgue Clicquot, which is the cathedral's most striking feature, often playing deafening tunes, with organized concerts in the summer.

Opposite – literally in the middle of rue Jean-Jaurès – you come upon a chunky, square edifice with the air of a second-rate Roman temple. It is the mid-fourth-century **Baptistère St-Jean** (April–Oct daily 10.30am–12.30pm & 3–6pm; rest of year daily except Tues 2.30–5pm; 4F/€0.61), reputedly the oldest Christian building in France and, until the seventeenth century, the only place in town you could have a proper baptism. The "font" was the octagonal pool sunk into the floor. The guide argues that the water pipes uncovered in the bottom show that the water could not have been more than 30–40cm deep, which casts doubt upon the popular belief that early Christian baptism was by total immersion. There are also some very ancient and faded frescoes on the walls, including one of the emperor Constantine on horseback, and a collection of Merovingian sarcophagi. Striking a postmodern note between the cathedral and baptistry is the small domed shape of **Espace Mendès-France** (Tues–Fri 9.30am–6.30pm, Sat & Sun 2–6.30pm), containing a state-of-the-art planetarium (32F/€4.88) and laserium (10F/€1.52).

Next to the baptistry is the town museum, the **Musée Ste-Croix** (Mon 1.15–6pm, Tues 10am–noon & 1.15–8pm, Wed–Fri 10am–noon & 1.15–6pm, Sat & Sun 10am–noon & 2–6pm; 20F/€3.05, Tues free), featuring an interesting collection of farming implements like its *alambic ambulant*, or itinerant still, of a kind in use until surprisingly recently. There is also a good Gallo-Roman section with some handsome glass, pottery and sculpture, notably a white marble Minerva of the first century. The same ticket is valid for the **Musée de Chièvres** at 9 rue V.-Hugo (Mon 1–6pm, Tues, Wed & Fri 10am–noon & 1–6pm, Thurs 10am–noon & 1–9pm, Sat & Sun 10am–noon & 2–6pm; 20F/€3.05), a rather dusty old collection of not very exciting paintings, pottery, furniture and arms, and the Hypogée (see below).

If you still have an appetite for sightseeing, there's a seventh-century subterranean chapel, the **Hypogée des Dunes** at 44 rue du Père de la Croix (closed for renovation at the time of writing; call ☎05.49.41.07.53 for latest details), and the **Pierre Levée dolmen**, a prehistoric stone chamber located on the eastern side of the river across the Pont Neuf, where Rabelais came with fellow students to talk, carouse and scratch his name.

Alternatively, you could take a more relaxed walk along the **riverside path** – on the right across Pont Neuf – upstream to Pont St-Cyprien. On the far bank, you'll see a characteristic feature of every French provincial town: neat, well-manured *potagers* – vegetable gardens – coming down to the water's edge with a little mud quay at the end and a moored punt.

The Parc de Blossac and St-Hilaire

Towards the southern tip of the old town, where the hump of the hill narrows to a point, the **Parc de Blossac** is a great spot to sit among the clipped limes and gravelled walks, to watch the boules and munch a baguette. Nearby is the eleventh-century **church of St-Hilaire-le-Grand**, on rue du Doyenné, which unbelievably was pruned of part of its nave in the nineteenth century, though the chevet from the outside is still a fine sight; the apse has a particularly beautiful group of chapels surrounding it. Inside, there is the usual ambulatory to accommodate the many pilgrims who flocked here, one of whom perhaps caused the fire around 1100 that destroyed the original wooden roof and necessitated the improvised arrangement that makes St-Hilaire architecturally unique: eight heavy domes introduced for the reroofing had to be supported somehow, hence the forest of auxiliary columns that make three aisles either side of the nave.

Eating and drinking

Poitiers offers good opportunities for fine **food** whatever your culinary persuasions. If you know where to head, you'll find everything from cheap fast food to high-priced restaurants with so many recommendations you can't see in the windows for stickers – and there's a good range of ethnic options to try if you're bored with French cuisine. If you're really keen to make your money last, you can ask for any student/youth offers that may be available at the Centre Information Jeunesse (CIJ), 64 rue Gambetta (☎05.49.60.68.78). The students at the university in Poitiers generate lively **nightlife** particularly in the bars along rue Carnot and on place de la Liberté, and posters announcing live music and dancing are easy to spot throughout town.

Alain Boutin, 65 rue Carnot (☎05.49.88.25.53). A good bet for regional dishes like *cailles au pineau* (quails cooked in a brandy liqueur), with a small, carefully chosen selection; menus from 90F/€13.72. Closed Sat lunch, all Sun & first half of Aug.

Bleu Sel, 40 rue Moulin à Sel. Serves a good range of salads and sandwiches at affordable prices and is popular with students. Closed Sun lunch.

Les Bons Enfants, 11bis rue Cloche-Perse (☎05.49.41.49.82). Good value for money: serves lunchtime menu at 67F/€10.21 on weekdays, evenings 111F/€16.92 and 145F/€22.10. Closed Sun & Mon.

Le Cappuccino, 5 rue de l'Université (☎05.49.88.27.39). One of a number of Italian restaurants in this area with menus starting at 57F/€8.69. Closed Sun & Mon.

Confort Moderne, 185 Faubourg du Pont-Neuf (☎05.49.46.69.61, *www.confort-moderne.fr*), just over the Pont Neuf. French and Moroccan food in café connected to an exhibition centre and record store. Check their Web site for concert listings.

Le Poitevin, 76 rue Carnot (☎05.49.88.35.04). Regional food at decent prices, in an exaggeratedly "rustic" interior. Menus from 95F/€14.48. Closed Sun.

Le St-Hilaire, 65 rue Théophraste-Renaudot (☎05.49.41.15.45). An extraordinary place to dine, in a magnificent medieval cellar with stained glass and ancient columns – and less expensive than it looks. Lunchtime menu at 95F/€14.48, evening menus from 100F/€15.24. Closed Sun.

Le St Nicholas, 7 rue Carnot (☎05.49.41.44.48). Actually located on a small traffic-free lane off rue Carnot, meaning you can eat outside peacefully. Traditional food served with a contemporary feel. Menus 89F/€13.56 and 119F/€18.14. Closed Wed.

Around Poitiers

The area immediately surrounding Poitiers is dominated by the postmodern cinema theme park **Futuroscope**, to the north, though more traditional attractions can be found at nearby **Chauvigny** and **St-Savin**, which boast two fine Romanesque churches, with some great sculpture and frescoes. Less inspired are the small town of **Parthenay** and the larger city of **Niort**, neither of which is worth a special trip, though both make useful stopovers for provisions before heading further westward into the verdant marshes of the **Marais Poitevin**.

Futuroscope

Poitiers' best-known attraction is the giant high-tech film theme park called **Futuroscope: Le Parc Européen de l'Image**, 8km north of the city, a collection of virtual-reality rides which draw onlookers into the action on screen, with the result that you feel you're flying, being flung around, rocketing down a ski slope or catapulting through the solar system in a vertigo-inducing 3-D nightmare. Not for young children or faint-hearted adults.

The futuristic **cinema pavilions** are set in several acres of greenery around a series of undulating lakes. The fifteen screens take some getting around, with plenty of walking between them, so it's wise to arrive early to beat the huge queues. To see everything in the park in one day, with time off for lunch, takes about ten exhausting hours, and as well as seeing the screen entertainment, you should give yourself time to ride the oversized floating bicycles on the park's lakes. To orientate yourself, head first for **La Gyrotour** where a lift takes you to the top of the high rotating tower and you can get the full effect of the futuristic scenario.

All the films are in French, with English commentaries on headphones often available, but as these are not very effective, and as it's the visual impact that's most important anyway, it's better to do without; recommended screenings are listed below. Apart from the films, there's a **laser show**, La Symphonie des Eaux, a display of music, colour and effects focused on the park's dancing fountains (shows are at 10.30pm: April–June & early Sept to Oct Sat only; July to early Sept daily).

The park's opening hours vary with the seasons (daily: July & Aug 9am till end of laser show; rest of year 9am–6pm; ☎05.49.49.30.80, *www.futuroscope.fr*), and the only public **transport** to the park is the #17 bus from Poitiers' Hôtel de Ville, which runs twice a day during school term-time. A system of taxi shuttles from Poitiers' *gare SNCF*, with specific leaving and return times, is the best option (40F/€6.10 per person; you must book your return in advance). **Tickets** are valid for one or two days (one-day pass adult 210F/€32.01, child aged 5–16 145F/€22.11; two-day pass adult 360F/€54.88, child 250F/€38.11); to avoid queues at the park, you can purchase tickets in advance from a booth at Poitiers' *gare SNCF*. **Food** is predictably expensive inside the park, and a picnic lunch can cut costs substantially. There are various deals available that include admission plus a wide selection of accommodation on site, the cheapest of which costs 400F/€60.98 per adult in a four-bed room.

The presentations – a selection

Le Cinéma 360°. Spain's contribution to Seville Expo '92 is now housed here permanently.

Le Cinéma Dynamique. You literally have to hang onto your seat for this one: a fast and thrilling ride as the seats move in sync with the images on the screen, among them a journey through the traps and pits found in the short film *The Mysteries of the Lost Temple*.

Cyber Avenue. To keep the computer kids busy – 72 multimedia kiosks with virtual games and video games.

Imax Solido. An enormous screen, measuring 540 square metres, in conjunction with 3-D vision glasses brings you face to face with T-Rex and his prehistoric cohorts.

Le Pavillon de Communication. A dizzying high-tech system of projection fires multiple images in rapid succession and attempts to tell the story of human communication.

Le Pavillon du Futuroscope. Using holographic images, a robot tells the story of the universe and its atoms.

Le Pavillon de Vienne. Moving seats parade before a huge wall of multiple images patchworking into a film on the region, which also tells the story of Futuroscope.

Paysages d'Europe. Very slow – for a change – and good for the faint-hearted and those in need of a rest, as a boat floats serenely past images of the continent.

Le Tapis Magique. Probably the most stunning presentation, with a vast screen in front of you, and another under your feet, creating the incredible feeling of flying.

Chauvigny

Twenty-three kilometres east of Poitiers, **CHAUVIGNY** is a busy market town on the banks of the Vienne with half a dozen porcelain factories and lumber mills providing work for the area. Overlooking the bustling *ville basse*, the old town boasts five medieval castles whose imposing ruins stand atop a precipitous rock spur, but its pride and joy are the sculpted capitals in the Romanesque **church of St-Pierre**. If you take rue du Château, which winds up the spur from the central **place de la Poste**, you'll pass the ruins of the **Château Baronnial**, which belonged to the bishops of Poitiers, and the better-preserved **Château d'Harcourt**, before coming to the attractive and unusual east end of St-Pierre.

Inside, the church is damp and in poor repair, but the choir capitals are a visual treat. Each one is different, evoking a terrifying, nightmarish world. Graphically illustrated monsters – bearded, moustached, winged, scaly, human-headed with manes of flame – grab hapless mortals – naked, upside down and puny – and rip their bowels and crunch their heads. The only escape offered is in the naively serene events of the Nativity. On the second capital on the south side of the choir, for instance, the angel Gabriel announces Christ's birth to the shepherds, their flock represented by four sheep that look like Pooh's companion Eeyore, while just around the corner the archangel Michael weighs souls in hand-held scales and a devil tries to grab one for his dinner. The oddest scene is on the north side: a Siamese-twin dancer grips the hind legs of two horse-like monsters that are gnawing his upper arms. You get a strong feeling that here was an artist who came from the same peasant background as his audience, prey to the same fears of things that went bump in the night or lurked in the wet woods.

Coinciding your visit with the Saturday, Tuesday (particularly the second Tuesday of each month) or Thursday **market** gives an extra dimension to a day-trip here. Held between the church of Notre-Dame and the river, it offers a mouthwatering selection of food – oysters, prawns, crayfish, cheeses galore and pâtés in aspic. The cafés are fun, too, bursting with noisy wine-flushed farmers mixing business with pleasure.

There are five **buses** a day from Poitiers to Chauvigny, which will drop you in the *ville basse*. The **tourist office** is located in the old town at 5 rue St-Pierre (daily 10am–1.30pm & 2–6pm; ☎05.49.46.39.01, *www.chauvigny.cg86.fr*). If you want to **stay** overnight, your best bet is *Le Lion d'Or*, 8 rue du Marché (☎05.49.46.30.28, fax 05.49.47.74.28; ③; closed mid-Dec to Feb; restaurant with menus from 85F/€12.96). Chauvigny also has a municipal **campsite**, just east of the centre on rue de la Fontaine (☎05.49.46.31.94; fax 05.49.46.40.60).

St-Savin

You need to get an early start from Poitiers if you want to make a single day-trip by public transport to see both Chauvigny and **ST-SAVIN**, which is scarcely more than a hamlet in comparison with bustling Chauvigny.

The bus sets you down beside the abbey near the modern bridge over the poplar-lined River Gartempe; walk downstream a little way to the medieval bridge for a perfect view of the **abbey church**, now listed as a UNESCO monument of universal importance (Jan & Dec Sat & Sun 9am–5pm; Feb–Sept daily 9am–5pm; Oct & Nov daily 2–5pm). Built in the eleventh century, possibly on the site of a church founded by Charlemagne, it rises strong and severe above the gazebos, vegetable gardens and lichened tile roofs of the houses at its feet. Inside, steps descend to the narthex and from there to the floor of the nave, stretching out to the raised choir: high, narrow, barrel-vaulted and flanked by bare round columns, their capitals deeply carved with interlacing foliage. The whole of the vault is covered with paintings. The colours are few – red and yellow ochres, green mixed with white and black – yet the paintings are full of light and grace, depicting scenes from the stories of Genesis and Exodus. Some are instantly recognizable: Noah's three-decked ark, Pharaoh's horses rearing at the engulfing waves of the Red Sea, graceful workers constructing the Tower of Babel.

If you do get stuck in St-Savin, you'll find **rooms** at the squeaky clean *Hôtel de France*, 38 place République (☎05.49.48.19.03, fax 05.49.48.97.07; ③), which has been recently refurbished and has a good restaurant serving menus from 85F/€12.96 (closed Sun evening & Mon except in July & Aug). There's a municipal **campsite**, too (☎05.49.48.18.02; closed mid-Sept to mid-May).

Parthenay and around

Directly west of Poitiers, and served by regular SNCF buses, the attractive small town of **PARTHENAY** was once an important staging point on the pilgrim routes to Compostela and is now the site of a major **cattle market** every Wednesday. It's not a place to make a special detour for, but it's worth a stopover if you're heading north to Brittany or west to the sea.

Parthenay has nothing very remarkable to see, though its medieval heart is quite interesting. The main part of town – essentially the medieval core, and fairly restricted in area at that – lies to the west, towards the River Thouet. Rue Jean-Jaurès and rue de la Saunerie cut in through the largely pedestrian shopping precinct to the Gothic **Porte de l'Horloge**, the fortified gateway to the old citadel on a steep-sided neck of land above a loop of the Thouet.

Through the gateway, on rue de la Citadelle, the attractively simple Romanesque **church of Ste-Croix** faces the Mairie across a small garden, which offers views over the ramparts and the **gully of St-Jacques**, with its medieval houses and vegetable plots climbing the opposite slope. Further along rue de la Citadelle is a house where Cardinal Richelieu used to visit his grandfather, and then a handsome but badly damaged Romanesque door, all that remains of the castle chapel of **Notre-Dame-de-la-Couldre**. Of the **castle** itself, practically nothing is left, but from the tip of the spur where it once stood you can look down on the twin-towered **gateway** and the **Pont St-Jacques**, a thirteenth-century bridge through which the nightly flocks of pilgrims poured into the town for shelter and security. To reach it, turn left under the Tour de l'Horloge and down the medieval lane known as **Vaux St-Jacques**. The lane is highly evocative of that period, with its crooked half-timbered dwellings crowding up to the bridge. Some look as if they have received little attention since the last pilgrim shuffled up the street, and they are only now beginning to be restored.

Practicalities

Finding your way around Parthenay is easy. From the **gare SNCF**, avenue de Gaulle leads directly west to the central square, with the **tourist office** on the right-hand corner (Mon–Fri 8.30am–12.30pm & 2–6pm, Sat & Sun 2.30–6.30pm; ☎05.49.64.24.24, fax 05.49.64.52.29, *www.district-parthenay.fr*). If you're after shelter, you'll find a very reasonable **hotel** by the main square, the *Grand Hôtel*, 85 bd Meilleraye (☎05.49.64.00.16; ①; restaurant from 50F/€7.62, closed Sat evening & Sun out of season). Another possibility is the fancier two-star *Hôtel du Nord*, 86 av de Gaulle, opposite the station (☎05.49.94.29.11; ②–③; restaurant from 76F/€11.59, closed Sat). There is a **hostel** some way from the centre at 16 rue Blaise-Pascal (☎05.49.95.46.89), with a central annexe at 115 bd Meilleraye: phone first and they will let you into the annexe. **Campers** have to head to the three-star site at **LE TALLUD** (☎05.49.94.39.52; open all year), part of the huge Base de Loisirs riverbank recreation area, about 3km west of Parthenay on the D949.

As for **eating**, Parthenay has the usual range of restaurants for a provincial town: Italian, Tunisian and Chinese, as well as traditional French. Best of the latter is *Le Fin Gourmet*, 28 rue Ganne (☎05.49.64.04.53; closed Sun evening & Mon), where high-quality cuisine combines well with a jovial atmosphere; it's affordable for all, with menus from 90F/€13.72, and on up to 185F/€28.20.

Around Parthenay

There are three more beautiful Romanesque churches within easy reach of Parthenay. One – with a sculpted facade depicting a mounted knight hawking – is only a twenty-minute walk away on the Niort road, at **PARTHENAY-LE-VIEUX**. The others are at **AIRVAULT**, 20km northeast of Parthenay and easily accessible on the

Parthenay–Thouars SNCF bus route, and **ST-JOUIN-DE-MARNES**, 9km northeast of Airvault (no public transport). A trip to St-Jouin can easily be combined with a visit to the sixteenth-century **Château d'Oiron**, 8.5km to the northwest. Alternatively, you could go on north to **THOUARS**, 21km from Airvault or 16km from St-Jouin, to see the abbey church of St-Laon; here there are accommodation options in the form of cheap hotels and a *Camping municipal*.

Niort

NIORT, 50km southwest of Poitiers, and connected to it by regular trains, makes a useful stopover if your goal is the Marais Poitevin (see p.572). The town itself has enough of interest to fill a pleasant morning's stroll, and it's the last place before the marshes to get a really wide choice of provisions. The most interesting part of the town is the mainly pedestrian area around **rue Victor-Hugo** and **rue St-Jean**, full of stone-fronted or half-timbered medieval houses. Coming from the *gare SNCF*, take rue de la Gare as far as avenue de Verdun with the tourist office and main post office on the corner, then turn right into place de la Brèche. Rue Ricard leaves the square on the left; rue Victor-Hugo is its continuation, following the line of the medieval market in a gully separating the two small hills on which Niort is built. Up to the right, opposite the end of rue St-Jean, is the old **town hall**, a triangular building of the early sixteenth century with lantern, belfry and ornamental machicolations, perhaps capable of repelling drunken revellers but no match for catapult or sledgehammer.

At the end of the street is the river, the **Sèvre Niortaise**, not to be confused with the Sèvre Nantaise which flows northwards to join the Loire at Nantes. There are gardens and trees along the bank and, over the bridge, the ruins of a glove factory, the last vestige of Niort's once thriving leather industry. At the time of the Revolution, it kept more than thirty cavalry regiments in breeches. Today Niort's biggest industry is insurance: the most bourgeois town in France, so it is said, because of the prosperity brought by the large number of major insurance firms making their headquarters here. Accordingly, restaurants are usually packed at lunchtime, and well-heeled shoppers throng the pedestrianized streets, giving a fairly lively – if affluent – feel.

Just downstream, opposite a riverside car park, is the **market hall** (with a café doing a good cheap lunch) and, beyond, vast and unmistakable on a slight rise, the keep of a **castle** begun by Henry II of England. Now housing a **museum** (daily except Tues 9am–noon & 2–5/6pm; 17F/€2.59, free Wed), it displays mainly local furniture and an extraordinary variety of costumes that were still commonly worn in the villages until the beginning of the twentieth century.

If you want to see the surrounding Marais area, the most pleasurable way is by bike – it's completely flat and small enough to pretty well cover in three days.

Practicalities

The **gare SNCF** is on rue Mazagran and has **bicycles** for rental – note that the station has no *consigne automatique*, charging a hefty 30F/€4.57 for each piece of left luggage. **Buses** leave from the **gare routière**, just off place de la Brèche on rue Viala. The excellent **tourist office** on place de la Poste (July–Sept Mon–Fri 9.30am–7pm, Sat 10am–5pm, Sun 10am–1pm; rest of year Mon–Fri 9.30–6pm, Sat 9.30am–noon; ☎05.49.24.18.79, *www.ville-niort.fr*) has plenty of information about walking itineraries around the Marais, and offers a free room reservation service (☎05.49.24.98.92); for more rustic accommodation in the Marais itself, contact Relais des Gîtes Ruraux, at 15 rue Thiers (☎05.49.24.00.42).

There's the usual crop of **hotels** close to the station, including the *Terminus*, 82 rue de la Gare (☎05.49.24.00.38, fax 05.49.24.94.38; ③), which is a decent budget option,

More centrally, the *St-Jean*, 21 av St-Jean-d'Angély (☎05.49.79.20.76, fax 05.49.35.03.27; ②), is another good bet for cheap, comfortable rooms, while several more upmarket hotels cluster on avenue de Paris, including *Le Paris*, at no. 12 (☎05.49.24.93.78, fax 05.49.28.27.57, *www.groupcitotel.com*; ③–④), and the three-star *Grand Hôtel*, at no. 32 (☎05.49.24.22.21, fax 05.49.24.42.41; ④). The three-star **campsite**, *de Noron* (☎05.49.79.05.06; closed Oct–Jan), is on boulevard S.-Allende next door to the stadium; bus #6 from place de la Brèche. Two **restaurants** to head for are *Les Quatre Saisons* on 247 av de la Rochelle (☎05.49.79.41.06; closed Sun), for traditional Marais Poitevin specialities (menus from 59F/€8.99), and, for lunches, *Sucrée Salée*, at 2 rue du Temple (☎05.49.24.77.16), which specializes in tarts and crumbles *à l'anglaise* (from 69F/€10.52).

The Marais Poitevin

The **Marais Poitevin** is a strange, lazy landscape of fens and meadows, shielded by poplar trees and crisscrossed by an elaborate system of canals, dykes and slow-flowing rivers. Recently declared a regional park, it is known as "La Venise Verte" – the Green Venice – and indeed, farmers in this area frequently travel through the marshes in flat-bottomed punts as their fields lack dry-land access. A tourist industry of sorts has been developing around the villages, so it's best to avoid weekends, when evidence of the transformation is all too clear.

Access to the eastern edge of the marsh is easiest at the whitewashed village of **COULON**, on the River Sèvre, just 11km from Niort by bike or occasional bus. The **tourist office** is at 18 place de l'Eglise (daily: April–June & Sept 10am–noon & 4–7pm; July & Aug 10am–7pm; rest of year Tues–Sat 10am–12.30pm & 2–5.30pm; ☎05.49.35.99.29, *www.ville-coulon.fr*) while **punts** can be rented, with or without a guide, just down the road at no. 6 (☎05.49.35.02.29).

There are two **hotels** in the village, both likely to be full in season: the family-run *Central*, 4 rue d'Autremont (☎05.49.35.90.20, fax 05.49.35.81.07; ③; closed mid-Jan to early Feb, plus Sun & Mon late Sept to mid-Oct), and the pricey *au Marais*, 46–48 quai Louis Tardiy (☎05.49.35.90.43, fax 05.49.35.81.98; ④; closed late Dec to late Jan). If you're **camping**, head for the attractively sited *Camping Venise Verte* (☎05.49.35.90.36), in a meadow about 2km downstream (a 25min walk), or the *Camping Municipal La Niquière* (☎05.49.35.81.19; closed mid-Sept to March), north of Coulon on the road to Benet. The best **eating** option in Coulon is the regional cuisine of *Le Central*'s charac-terful restaurant; with generous servings, a well-deserved reputation and a menu from 96F/€14.63, you would be wise to book.

An excellent place from which to rent **bikes** is La Bicyclette Verte (☎05.49.35.42.56, *www.bicyclette-verte.com*), on rue du Coursault in the village of **ARÇAIS**, 10km west of Coulon; they also have children's bikes and tandems. If you're walking the marshes, it's best to stick to the lanes, since cross-country routes tend to end in fields surrounded by water, and you have to backtrack continually. Once you're away from the riverside road from Coulon to Arçais, there's practically no traffic, just meadows and cows. At the seaward end of the marsh – the area south of **LUÇON** – the landscape changes, becom-ing all straight lines and open fields of wheat and sunflowers. The villages cap low mounds that were once islands.

The Vendée

The northwest of the Poitou region falls within the rural *département* of the **Vendée**, whose main attraction is the eighty-kilometre stretch of coast between chic **Les Sables-d'Olonne** and the northernmost tip of the scenic **Île de Noirmoutier**.

Inland, there is little of interest, aside from a marvellous summertime *spectacle* at **Les Épesses**.

Les Sables-d'Olonne

The area around **LES SABLES-D'OLONNE** and northwards has been heavily developed with Costa-style apartment blocks. If you're passing through, though, it's worth having a look at the surprisingly good modern art section in the **Musée de l'Abbaye Ste-Croix** on rue Verdun (mid-June to mid-Sept Tues–Sun 10am–noon & 2–6.30pm; rest of year guided visits by arrangement only; ☎02.51.32.01.16; 30F/€4.57, free Sun) and a collection of classic autos at the **Musée d'Automobile**, 8km southeast of town on the road to Talmont (mid-March to June & Sept daily 9.30am–noon & 2–6pm; July & Aug daily 9.30am–7pm; rest of year Sat & Sun only 9.30am–noon & 2–6pm; 36F/€5.49). The main reason to stay, though, is the town's vast curve of clean, beautiful **beach**, which lures hordes in the summer.

Hotels get booked up well in advance for July and August, but a couple worth trying are *Le Merle Blanc*, near the beach at 59 av Aristide-Briand (☎02.51.32.00.35; ②), and *Hôtel les Olonnes*, 25 rue de la Patrie (☎02.51.32.04.12, fax 02.51.23.72.63; ②), with a restaurant (closed Sun evening & Mon). Budget options include a beachside **HI hostel**, 3km from the centre at 92 rue du Sémaphore (☎02.51.95.76.21, fax 02.40.20.08.94; closed Oct–March), a bus line #2 ride away in the direction of "Côte Sauvage" (stop "Armandèche"); a municipal **campsite** (☎02.51.95.10.42, fax 02.51.33.94.04; closed Dec–March) on rue des Roses, 400m from the beach; and several more campsites in the Pironnière district, 3km south of town on the D949. For more accommodation options, ask at the **tourist office** on 1 promenade Joffre (June & Sept Mon–Sat 9am–12.15pm & 2–6.30pm, Sun 10am–12.30pm; July & Aug daily 9am–7pm; ☎02.51.96.85.85, fax 02.51.96.85.71, *www.ot.lessablesdolonne.fr*).

The Île de Noirmoutier

The twenty-kilometre-long **Île de Noirmoutier**, approximately 60km north of Les Sables-d'Olonne on the D38, was an early monastic settlement of the seventh century; now it has bowed to pilgrims of a different type, serving as a relatively plush tourist resort, though it has been spared the high-rise development of the adjoining coast. Although tourism is the island's main economy, it doesn't dominate everything. Salt marshes here are still worked, spring potatoes sown and fishes fished. The island can be reached in three hours by bus from Les Sables, and is connected to the shore by a toll bridge.

The island town, **NOIRMOUTIER-EN-L'ÎLE**, is a low-key type of place but still has a twelfth-century **castle**, a **church** with a Romanesque crypt, an excellent **market** (Tues & Fri) in place de la République and most of the island's **nightlife** in the form of piano bars with longer-than-usual café hours. There are campsites dotted around the island – maps are available from the **tourist office** (July & Aug Mon–Sat 9am–7pm, Sun 10am–1pm; rest of year Mon–Fri 9am–12.30pm & 2–6pm, Sat 9.30am–12.30pm & 2–6pm; ☎02.51.39.80.71, fax 02.51.39.53.16) on the main road from the bridge at **MARMATRE**. **Bikes** can be rented from Vel-hop, 55 av Joseph-Pineau in Noirmoutier (☎02.51.39.01.34), or Charier, 23 av Joseph Pineau (☎02.51.39.01.25). Among the **hotels** to try in the town are *Le Bois de la Chaize*, 23 av de la Victoire (☎02.51.39.04.62, fax 02.51.39.11.89; ②), *Hôtel Les Capucines*, 38 av de la Victoire (☎02.51.39.06.82, fax 02.51.39.33.10; ②; closed mid-Nov to mid-Feb), which has a nice restaurant with menus from 75F/€11.43, and the luxuriously appointed *Fleur de Sel*, in rue des Saulniers (☎02.51.39.21.59; *contact@fleurdesel.fr*; ⑤–⑦), with an excellent seafood restaurant (menus 138–225F/€21.03–34.30). A further option in the south of the island is the *Hôtel Goéland*, 15 route du Gois, in **BARBÂTRE** (☎02.51.39.68.66; ②; closed mid-Nov to Jan; restaurant from 75F/€11.43).

As for exploring the island, the western coast, with its great curves of sand, resembles the mainland, while the northern side dips in and out of little bays with rocky promontories between. Inland, were it not for the saltwater dykes, the horizon would suggest that you were far away from the sea. The more southerly resorts, though built up, have not been the main targets for the developers. In the village centres there are still the one-storey houses that you see throughout La Vendée and southern Brittany – whitewashed and ochre-tiled with decorative brickwork around the windows and S- or Z-shaped coloured bars on the shutters. During the spring, the weather is fickle – sunny one moment, stormy the next – and the heat of the summer cultivates a vicious mosquito population.

Les Épesses

Some 80km inland from Les Sables (on the N160 if you're driving), at the ruined **Château du Puy du Fou** in the village of **LES ÉPESSES**, a remarkable lakeside extravaganza takes place during the summer months (end May to early Sept Fri & Sat 10pm or 10.30pm; 1hr 45min; booking essential, ☎02.54.64.11.11, *www.puydufou.tm.fr*; 130F/€19.82, including Vendée museum). It is a weird affair: the enactment of the life of a local peasant from the Middle Ages to World War II, complete with fireworks, lasers, dances on the lake and Comédie Française voice-overs. The story, summarized in a brief English text, is interesting but incidental – the spectacle is the attraction, and all proceeds from the event go to charity The château also houses a **museum** on life in the Vendée (Tues–Sun 10am–noon & 2–6/7pm).

To get to Les Épesses by public **transport**, you'll need to get to **CHOLET** (reasonably connected by train) and take a bus south from there; Puy du Fou itself is 2.5km from Les Épesses on the D27 to Chambretaud. There is one reasonably priced **hotel** in Les Épesses, *Le Lion d'Or*, 2 rue de la Libération (☎ & fax 02.51.57.30.01; ③), and there are three more options, all with restaurants, 10km west in **LES HERBIERS**: the comfortable *Relais* (☎02.51.91.01.64, fax 02.51.67.36.50, *www.cotriade.com*; ③), the well-located *Le Centre* (☎02.51.67.01.75, fax 02.51.66.82.24; ②) and the modern *Chez Camille* (☎02.51.91.07.57, fax 02.51.67.19.28, *www.chezcamille.fr*; ③).

THE COAST AROUND LA ROCHELLE

The coast around **La Rochelle** – especially the **islands** – is great for young families, with miles of safe sandy beaches and shallow water. Be aware, however, that in August, unless you're camping or book in advance, accommodation is a near-insuperable problem. Out of season you can't rely on sunny weather, but that shouldn't deter you since the quiet misty seascapes and working fishing ports have a melancholy romance all their own. La Rochelle and **Royan** in the south are the best bases, and are both served by train. Away from these centres – if you're not driving – you'll have to take potluck with the rather quirky bus routes.

La Rochelle and around

LA ROCHELLE is the most attractive and unspoilt seaside town in France. Thanks to the foresight of 1970s mayor Michel Crépeau, its historic seventeenth- to eighteenth-century centre and waterfront were plucked from the clutches of the developers and its streets freed of traffic for the delectation of pedestrians. A real shock-horror outrage at the time, the policy has become standard practice for preserving old town centres across the country – more successful than Crépeau's picturesque yellow bicycle plan, designed to relieve the traffic problem (see below).

La Rochelle has a long history, as you would expect of such a sheltered Atlantic port. Eleanor of Aquitaine gave it a charter in 1199, which released it from its feudal obligations, and it rapidly became a port of major importance, trading in salt and wine and skilfully exploiting the Anglo-French quarrels. The Wars of Religion, however, were particularly destructive for La Rochelle. It turned Protestant and, because of its strategic importance, drew the remorseless enmity of Cardinal Richelieu, who laid siege to it in 1627. To the dismay of the townspeople, who reasoned that no one could effectively blockade seasoned mariners like themselves, he succeeded in sealing the harbour approaches with a dyke. The English dispatched the Duke of Buckingham to their aid, but he was caught napping on the Île de Ré and badly defeated. By the end of 1628 Richelieu had starved the city into submission. Out of the pre-siege population of 28,000, only 5000 survived. The walls were demolished and the city's privileges revoked. La Rochelle later became the principal port for trade with the French colonies in the Caribbean Antilles and Canada. Indeed, many of the settlers, especially in Canada, came from this part of France.

Arrival, information and transport

Finding your way around La Rochelle is straightforward. Arriving at the elaborate **gare SNCF** on boulevard Joffre, take avenue de Gaulle opposite to reach the town centre; on the left as you reach the waterfront you'll see the efficient **tourist office**, on quai de Gabut (May Mon–Sat 9am–6pm, Sun 10am–noon; June & Sept Mon–Sat 9am–7pm, Sun 11am–5pm; July & Aug Mon–Sat 9am–8pm, Sun 11am–5pm; Oct–April 9am–noon & 2–6pm, Sun 10am–noon; ☎05.46.41.14.68, fax 05.46.41.99.85, *www.ville-larochelle.fr*), which dispenses excellent **maps**, some of which you may have to pay for, and sells a 39F/€5.95 **museum pass** covering the Nouveau Monde, the Orbigny-Bernon and the Beaux-Arts. In addition, the **CDIJ Youth Centre**, 14 rue des Gentilshommes (☎05.46.41.16.36), has an information service for young people. Most things you'll want to see are in the area behind the waterfront; in effect, between the harbour and the place de Verdun, where the **gare routière** is situated.

Getting around

The bus terminal for Autoplus, the town's efficient **public transport** system, is also located on place de Verdun, and there is another local bus terminal at 44 cours des Dames. Once you've stowed your luggage, you can use **bikes** to get around: on quai du Carénage, facing restaurant-lined cours des Dames across the Vieux Port, is the free municipal **bike park**, part of the Autoplus system and heir to Michel Crépeau's original no-identity-check, no-restrictions, pick-up-and-leave scheme. You get two hours of free bike time after handing over a piece of ID; after this it's a generous 6F/€0.95 per hour (office open May–Sept daily 9am–12.30pm & 1.30–7pm). You can also rent bikes from the *gare SNCF* and from Motive Location, opposite the Maritime Museum (☎05.46.31.03.66). **Car rental** is available from Ada/Budget, 1 av de Gaulle (☎05.46.41.35.53), and Rent-a-car, 29 av de Gaulle (☎05.46.27.27.27). Autoplus also has a nifty **taxi system** with flat rates between any two of 46 *"bornes"* – terminal posts with a card-activated calling system, operating 24 hours. You can buy the cards and find out the inexpensive going rate at Boutique Autoplus, 5 rue de l'Aimable-Nanette, near the tourist office (Mon–Fri 9am–noon & 2–6pm, Sat 9am–noon).

Boat trips around La Rochelle and to neighbouring islands are organized by Océcars, on Place de Verdun (☎05.46.00.92.12), and Interîles runs guided day-trips

LA ROCHELLE

Gare Routière
PLACE DE VERDUN
Cathédrale
Marché
Hôtel de Ville
Grosse Horloge
Parc Charruyer
Municipal Campsite
Tour de la Chaîne
Tour de la Lanterne
Piscine
Plage
Tour St-Nicolas

0   200 m

N

J, Musée des Automates & Modèles Reduits ▽   ❾ & ❿ ▽   Gare SNCF ▽ & Bd Joffre

ACCOMMODATION				RESTAURANTS			
Le Bordeaux	7	Henri IV	4	Le Bistrot de l'Entr'acte	H	Richard Coutanceau	G
Comfort St-Nicholas	6	Hostel	9	Café Resto à la Villette	B	Le Soleil Brille pour	
Fasthotel	10	de l'Océan	8	à Côté de Chez Fred	F	Tout Le Monde	A
de France-Angleterre		Le Printania	2	La Marie-Galante	J	La Solette	E
et Champlain	1	La Tour de Nesle	5	Pub Lutèce	C	Le St-Sauveur	D
François I	3			Les Pyramides	I		

from La Rochelle to the Île d'Oléron (July–Sept 9.30am–8.15pm; ☎05.46.50.51.88; 175F/€26.68 – doesn't include lunch); weather and tides may affect crossings. The town's other attractions include a good **beach**, about 2km south of the centre at Les Minimes, reached by bus #10 from place Verdun or by the more entertaining **bus de mer**, a small boat which runs from the old port to Port des Minimes, stopping off at avenue Marillac en route (April–June & Sept Sat & Sun hourly 10am–noon & 2–7pm; July & Aug half-hourly 10am–12.30pm & 1.30–11pm; Oct–March hourly 10am–noon & 2–6pm; 10F/€1.52 one way).

Accommodation

Accommodation in La Rochelle can be a bit of a problem, so you should be sure to book in advance from May until well into autumn, even if you're camping. While there's a handful of inexpensive hotels in the town centre, in general, you can expect to pay resort prices at most establishments, especially in season. A possible alternative to hotels are **self-catering apartments** which abound, particularly around Les Minimes

and its Village Informatique. The tourist office has a handy board of rented accommodation and is able to reserve hotel rooms for a 10F/€1.52 fee.

Hotels

Le Bordeaux, 43 rue St-Nicolas (☎05.46.41.31.22, fax 05.46.41.24.43). Comfortable, friendly hotel
in a characterful pedestrianized street between the train station and the port. ②.

Comfort St-Nicolas, 13 rue Sardinerie (☎05.46.41.71.55, fax 05.46.41.70.46). A very attractive modernized hotel in a pretty street two minutes from the harbour. ④.

Fasthotel, Village Informatique, Les Minimes (☎05.46.45.46.00, fax 05.46.44.72.71). Small, quiet
hotel made up of modern bungalows, near the port des Minimes and the beach. ②.

de France-Angleterre et Champlain, 20 rue Rambaud (☎05.46.41.23.99, fax 05.46.41.15.19).
Comfortable hotel located close to the extensive parklands. The old, venerable half is *Le Champlain*
and the new Great Western addition is the *France-Angleterre*; both are what you'd expect from a
modern and an old-fashioned three-star. ④.

François I, 15 rue Bazoges (☎05.46.41.28.46, fax 05.46.41.35.01). Well-maintained hotel in a historic
building with a walled courtyard. ②.

Henri IV, 31 rue des Gentilshommes (☎05.46.41.25.79, fax 05.46.41.78.64). Excellent and very popular hotel right in the town centre on place de la Caille, a short stroll from the harbourfront. ②.

de l'Océan, 36 cours des Dames (☎05.46.41.31.97, fax 05.46.41.51.12). Comfortable two-star hotel
in an enviable position, with air-conditioned rooms – many with views of the port. ②.

Le Printania, 9 rue Brave-Rondeau (☎05.46.41.22.86, fax 05.46.35.19.58). Pleasant, unpretentious
and central place in a peaceful street. ②.

La Tour de Nesle, 2 quai Louis-Durand (☎05.46.41.05.86, fax 05.46.41.95.17). A large comfortable
old hotel, right in the middle of things. ③.

Hostel and campsites

HI hostel, av des Minimes (☎05.46.44.43.11, fax 05.46.45.41.48). A big modern hostel overlooking the marina at Port des Minimes, a 10min walk from the beach, shops and restaurants, and
with a self-service restaurant and bar. It's wise to book in summer, especially at weekends. Catch
bus #10 from place de Verdun, or walk from the train station, following the signs to the left. When
you get to the roundabout by the Musée Maritime, don't follow the sign to the left: go straight
ahead across the grass past a huge modern building with a distinctive sloping roof, then turn left
on the Avenue Marillac and carry on until you meet the next crossroads where av des Minimes
cuts through.

Camping municipal de Port-Neuf, on the northwest side of town (☎05.46.43.81.20). Well-kept
and shaded campsite about forty minutes' walk from the town centre. Take bus #6 from Grosse
Horloge, direction "Port-Neuf".

Camping Le Soleil, Port des Minimes (☎05.46.44.42.53). In a great location near the hostel and
close to the beaches, this site is often crowded with raucous young holiday-makers. Take bus #10
from place Verdun to Les Minimes. Closed Sept–May.

The Town

The **Vieux Port** is very much the focus of the town, with pleasure boats moored in ser-
ried ranks in front of the two impressive towers guarding the entrance to the port.
Leading north from the **Porte de la Grosse Horloge**, the **rue du Palais** runs
towards the cathedral and several of the museums on rue Thiers. Between the harbour
and the **Port des Minimes**, a new marina development 2km south of the town centre,
there are several excellent museums for children and a large frigate (permanently
moored) providing some insight into the town's seagoing past.

The Vieux Port

Dominating the inner harbour, the heavy Gothic gateway of the **Porte de la Grosse
Horloge** straddles the entrance to the old town. The quays in front of it are too full of

traffic to encourage loitering; for that, it's best to head out along the tree-lined cours des Dames towards the fourteenth-century **Tour de la Chaine** (April–June & Sept daily 10am–1pm & 2–7pm; July & Aug daily 10am–7pm; rest of year daily except Tues 10am–12.30pm & 2–5.30pm; June–Sept 25F/€3.81, otherwise free), so called because of the heavy chain that was slung from here across to the opposite tower, **Tour St-Nicolas**, to close the harbour at night. Today the only night-time intruders are likely to be yachties from across the Channel, whose craft far outnumber the working boats – mainly garishly painted trawlers. Beyond the tower, steps climb up to rue Sur-les-Murs, which follows the top of the old sea wall to a third tower, the **Tour de la Lanterne** or Tour des Quatre Sergents, named after four sergeants imprisoned and executed for defying the Restoration monarchy in 1822 (same times and prices as at Tour de la Chaine). There's a way up onto what's left of the **city walls**, planted with unkempt greenery. Beyond is the beach, backed by casino, hot-dog stands and amusement booths, along with an extensive, truly beautiful belt of park that continues up the western edge of the town centre and along the avenue du Mail behind the beach, where the first seaside village was built by the *Rochelais* rich.

The rue du Palais and around

The real charm of La Rochelle lies on the city's main shopping street, **rue du Palais**, leading up from the Vieux Port to place de Verdun. Lining the street are eighteenth-century houses, some grey stone, some half-timbered, with distinctive *Rochelais*-style slates overlapped like fish scales, while the shop fronts are set back beneath the ground-floor arcades. Among the finest are the **Hôtel de la Bourse** – actually the Chamber of Commerce – and the **Palais de Justice** with its colonnaded facade, both on the left-hand side. A few metres further on, in **rue des Augustins**, there is another grandiose affair built for a wealthy Rochelais in 1555, the so-called **Maison Henri II**, complete with loggia, gallery and slated turrets, where the regional tourist board has its offices. Place de Verdun itself is dull and characterless, with an uninspiring, humpbacked, eighteenth-century classical **cathedral** on the corner. Its only redeeming feature is the marvellously opulent Belle Époque **Café de la Paix**, all mirrors, gilt and plush, where La Rochelle's ladies of means come to sip lemon tea and nibble daintily at sticky cakes – and there is a tempting *charcuterie* and seafood shop next door.

To the west of rue du Palais, especially in **rue de l'Escale**, paved with granite setts brought back from Canada as ballast in the *Rochelais* cargo vessels, you get the discreet residences of the eighteenth-century shipowners and chandlers, veiling their wealth with high walls and classical restraint. A rather less modest gentleman once installed himself on the corner of **rue Fromentin**: a seventeenth-century doctor who adorned his house front with the statues of famous medical men – Hippocrates, Galen and others. In rue St-Côme closer to the town walls is the **Musée d'Orbigny-Bernon** (Mon & Wed–Sat 10am–noon & 2–6pm, Sun 2–6pm; 21F/€3.20), with an extensive section on local history, important collections of local *faïence*, porcelain from China and Japan and some handsome furniture.

East of rue du Palais, and starting out from place des Petits-Bancs, rue du Temple takes you up alongside the **Hôtel de Ville**, protected by a decorative but seriously fortified wall. It was begun around 1600 in the reign of Henri IV, whose initials, intertwined with those of Marie de Médicis, are carved on the ground-floor gallery. It's a beautiful specimen of Frenchified Italian taste, adorned with niches and statues and coffered ceilings, all done in a stone the colour of ripe barley. And if you feel like quiet contemplation of these seemingly more gracious times, there's no better place for it than the terrace of the *Café de la Poste*, right next to the post office, in the small, traffic-free square outside. For more relaxed vernacular architecture nearly as ancient, carry on up rue des Merciers, the other main shopping area, to the cramped and noisy **market**

square, close to which you'll find the **Musée du Nouveau Monde** (Mon & Wed–Sat 10.30am–12.30pm & 1.30–6pm, Sun 3–6pm; 21F/€3.20), whose entrance is in rue Fleuriau. Out of the ordinary, this museum occupies the former residence of the Fleuriau family, rich shipowners and traders who, like many of their fellow *Rochelais*, made fortunes out of the slave trade and Caribbean sugar, spices and coffee. There is a fine collection of prints, paintings and photos of the old West Indian plantations; seventeenth- and eighteenth-century maps of America; photogravures of Native Americans from around 1900, with incredible names like Piopio Maksmaks Wallawalla and Lawyer Nez Percé; and an interesting display of aquatint illustrations for Marmontel's novel *Les Incas* – an amazing mixture of sentimentality and coy salaciousness. Nearby in rue Gargoulleau is the **Musée des Beaux-Arts** (daily except Tues 2–5pm; 21F/€3.20), whose works are centred around a few *Rochelais* artists and illustrate the history of art from the primitives to the present day.

To get back towards the port, from the maze of pedestrianized streets around the Hôtel de Ville, head down rue St-Sauveur, with its large gloomy church, across quai Maubec and quai Louis-Durand to **rue St-Nicolas** and adjoining **place de la Fourche** with its huge shady tree and outdoor café – both pedestrianized and boasting several antiques dealers, second-hand bookshops and a vintage clothes shop. The two streets share a Saturday flea/antiques **market**.

Towards Port des Minimes

On the east side of the old harbour behind the Tour St-Nicolas is the **quartier du Gabut**, the one-time fishermen's quarter of wooden cabins and sheds, now converted into bars, shops and eating places. Beyond it lies an extensive dock and the market and service buildings of the old fishing port. This is now the **Musée Maritime** (daily: April–June & Sept 10am–6.30pm; July & Aug 10am–7.30pm; rest of year 2–6.30pm; 45F/€6.86), which includes an interesting collection of superannuated vessels as well as land-based exhibits. A further ten-minute walk brings you to the **Musée des Automates** (daily: Feb–May, Sept & Oct 10am–noon & 2–6pm; June–Aug 9.30am–7pm; Nov–Jan 2–6pm; 40F/€6.10) on rue de la Désirée, a fascinating collection of three hundred automated puppets, drawing you into an irresistible fantasy world. Some of the puppets are interesting from a historical angle; others, like one that writes the name "Pierrot", are interesting from a mechanical viewpoint. Further down the same street is the **Musée des Modèles Réduits** (same hours & prices as the Automates, joint ticket for both museums 65F/€9.91). The prices may be a bit prohibitive for families – especially considering the whole tour takes barely half an hour – but this does combine well with a visit to the neighbouring Musée des Automates. Scale models of every variety and era are on show, starting with cars and including models of a submerged shipwreck and La Rochelle train station.

The **Port des Minimes** is a large modern marina development with mooring for thousands of yachts, about 2km south of the old harbour or thirty minutes' walk along the waterside. There are shops, restaurants, bars and apartments. The young and beautiful flock out here at weekends and on summer evenings to sun and parade on the beautiful **plage des Minimes**. Right next to the beach is the spectacular brand-new **aquarium** (daily: April–June & Sept 9am–7pm; July & Aug 9am–11pm; Oct–March 10am–noon & 2–7pm; *www.aquarium-larochelle.com*; 42F/€6.40).

Eating and drinking

For **eating**, try the rue du Port/rue St-Sauveur area just off the waterfront, or the attractive rue St-Jean-du-Pérot, which has everything from crêperies and pizzerias to expensive gourmet restaurants and several ethnic eateries including Indian and

Chinese places. Particularly worth seeking out are the town's many excellent **fish restaurants**. *Ernest Le Glacier*, 15 rue du Port, and *Olivier Glacier*, 21 rue St Jean du Pérot, both serve excellent **ice cream** well into the evening.

Popular daytime **bars** to hang out at in the town include the dark and down-to-earth wine bar *Cave de la Guignette* at 8 rue St-Nicolas, the numerous brasseries round the old harbour and the *Lou-Foc*, next to the tourist office in quartier du Gabut. *Corrigans*, 20 rue des Cloutiers, near the market, serves pub grub and has an affable English-speaking owner, Barry – it also has also live music on Thursday nights.

Cafés and restaurants

Le Bistrot de l'Entr'acte, 22 rue St-Jean-du Pérot (☎05.46.50.62.60). A highly regarded place with *fin-de-siècle* decor, little table lamps and a mainly fish and seafood *carte* of some originality; people rave about the 155F/€23.63 menu. Closed Sun.

Café-Resto à la Villette, 4 rue de la Forme, behind the market. Tiny, authentic place popular with locals; good *plats du jour* from 50F/€7.62. Closed Sun.

à Côté de Chez Fred, 30–32 rue St-Nicolas (☎05.46.41.65.76). A small, characterful corner restaurant with all sorts of charming fishing and seafaring paraphernalia; it's very popular, so you're best off booking. A blackboard *carte* changes depending on what's in at Fred the fishmonger's next door – it's guaranteed to be super-fresh and mouthwatering. Fish dishes from 40F/€6.10; around 100F/€15.24 for a full meal. Closed Sun.

La Marie-Galante, 35 av des Minimes (☎05.46.44.05.54). Pretty yellow- and white-striped awnings over the outdoor seating overlooking the yacht basin at Les Minimes. Fish of the day 55F/€8.38; generous menus from 80F/€12.20. Its three neighbours are also good value.

Pub Lutèce, 1bis rue St-Sauveur. Reasonably priced brasserie with outdoor tables.

Les Pyramides, 59 rue St-Jean-du-Pérot. Serves a mixture of expensive Egyptian and Greek food in bright, pleasant surroundings.

Richard Coutanceau, plage de la Concurrence (☎05.46.41.48.19). Located on the seafront just to the west of the old harbour, this place is expensive but it's a veritable palace of gastronomic excellence, renowned for its fish and seafood and specialities. Menus at 220F/€33.54 and 410F/€62.50.

Le St-Sauveur, 24 rue St-Sauveur (☎05.46.41.18.16). Unpretentious restaurant opposite the old Protestant church, with good fish dishes (68–98F/€10.37–14.94 à la carte), particularly the fish soup entrée. It's good for families, with a fish tank filled with tropical types providing some entertainment for bored children. Menus 68F/€10.37, 98F/€14.94 and 128F/€19.51. Closed Sun, and Mon evening out of season.

Le Soleil Brille pour Tout Le Monde, 13 rue des Cloutiers (☎05.46.41.11.42). Cheerful and colourful food in agreeable surroundings. The *tartes* (45F/€6.86) are outstanding and, like almost everything else here, are made from fresh organic ingredients. Mostly vegetarian, though seafood is served. Very popular, so get there early. Closed Sun & Mon.

La Solette, place de la Fourche, off rue St-Nicolas (☎05.40.41.74.45; closed Jan, Feb, and Sun off season). A pleasant little restaurant on a pretty square with menus from 59F/€8.99 and *plats* from 55F/€8.38.

Nightlife and entertainment

To find out **what's on**, pick up the thrice-weekly *Sortir* from the tourist office, with theatre, cinema and mainstream and classical music listings. For **nightlife**, head for the rue St-Nicolas: many bars line the streets, some offering **live music** and most with a lively atmosphere. An older crowd heads for rue des Templiers, where you'll find the *Piano Pub*, the *Mayflower*, the *St-James* and the *Académie de la Bière*. **Nightclubs** worth checking out include *L'Oxford*, plage de la Concurrence, and *Le Triolet*, 8 rue des Carmes.

La Rochelle is also host to the major **festival** of French-language music, Les Francofolies, in mid-July, which features musicians from overseas as well as France and attracts the best part of 100,000 fans to the city.

The Île de Ré

A half-hour drive west from La Rochelle, the **Île de Ré** is a low, narrow island some 30km long, fringed by sandy beaches to the southwest and salt marshes and oyster beds to the northeast, with the interior a motley mix of small-scale vine, asparagus and wheat cultivation. All the buildings on Ré are restricted to two storeys and are required to incorporate the typical local features of whitewashed walls, curly orange tiles and green-painted shutters, which give the island villages a southerly holiday atmosphere.

Out of season the island has a slow, misty charm, and life in its little ports revolves exclusively around the cultivation of oysters and mussels. In season, though, it's extraordinarily crowded, with upwards of 400,000 visitors passing through. The crowds mainly head for the southern beaches; those to the northeast are covered in rocks and seaweed, and the sea is too shallow for bathing.

The island is connected to the mainland at **LA PALLICE**, a suburb of La Rochelle, by a three-kilometre-long toll bridge constructed in 1988 (110F/€16.77 round trip per car). La Pallice was once a big commercial port with important shipyards, and although it still serves as a naval base, times have changed. As you drive past, you'll notice some colossal weather-stained concrete sheds, submarine pens built by the Germans to service their Atlantic U-boat fleet during World War II. Too difficult to demolish, they are still in use. As an alternative to the toll-bridge connection, Interîles, 14 cours des Dames, La Rochelle, also runs a bus and boat service to Sablonceaux on Ré (110F/€16.77 return with a car), and combined trips to the Îles de Ré and Oléron (see p.575).

ST-MARTIN, the island's capital, is an atmospheric north coast fishing port with whitewashed houses clustered around the stone quays of a well-protected harbour, from where trawlers and flat-bottomed oyster boats, piled high with cage-like devices used for "growing" oysters, slip out every morning on the muddy tide.

The quayside *Café Boucquingam* recalls the military adventures of the Duke of Buckingham, who attacked the island unsuccessfully in the mid-seventeenth century. To the east of the harbour, you can walk along the almost perfectly preserved **fortifications** – redesigned by Vauban in the late seventeenth century after Buckingham's attentions – to the citadel, long used as a prison. It was from here that the *bagnards* – prisoners sentenced to hard labour on Devil's Island in Guyana or New Caledonia in the Pacific – set out. Most did not return. One who eventually did was the notorious French general Papillon.

Practicalities

Rébus runs **bus services** all over the island from La Rochelle, leaving from place Verdun via the train station every hour; crossing to Sablonceaux just across the bridge costs 10F/€1.52. For frequent travelling, ten-trip cards are better value: La Rochelle–Sablonceaux costs 72F/€10.98, La Rochelle–St-Martin 195F/€29.73, La Rochelle to anywhere on the island 230F/€35.06, but the timetable can be awkward if you want to tour the island.

The alternative is to **rent a bike** from the Sablonceaux bus depot; from Cyclo-Surf Location, 14 rue Henri-Lainé (☎05.46.09.51.60), in seaside La Flotte between Sablonceaux and St-Martin; Clos Vauban, avenue V.-Bouthillier in St-Martin; or Cycland, 2 route Joachim in La Couarde on the southern side of the island.

Hotels are plentiful in all the island's villages, though obviously packed very full through July and August. Most reasonably priced are the one-star *Le Sénéchal*, 6 rue Gambetta in Ars-en-Ré, in a protected bay on the western side of the island (☎05.46.29.40.42, fax 05.46.29.21.25; ②; closed Oct–March), *L'Océan*, 172 rue St-Martin in Le-Bois-Plage (☎05.46.09.23.07, fax 05.46.09.05.40; ④; closed mid-Nov to Jan), and, in La Flotte, the *L'Hippocampe*, 16 rue du Château-des-Mauléons (☎05.46.09.60.68; ②), and *Le Français*, 1 quai de Sénac (☎05.46.09.60.06, fax 05.46.09.58.77; ③; closed mid-Nov to March).

There are even more **campsites** on the island than there are hotels, and it should not be difficult finding a place, except perhaps in desirable locations near the southern beaches at the height of the summer. A few names, if you want to book ahead, are the *Camping du Soleil* in Ars-en-Ré (☎05.46.29.40.62), *L'Île Blanche* in La Flotte (☎05.46.09.52.43, *www.ile-blanche.com*; closed Nov–March) and *L'Océan*, La Passe in La Couarde (☎05.46.29.87.70; closed Oct–March). Online, *www.campings-ile-de-re.com* lists other options.

Good-value **food** is available on the quayside in St-Martin at *Les Remparts*, 4 quai Daniel-Rivaille, which has a piano bar upstairs. The airy *La Salicorne*, 16 rue de l'Olivette in La Couarde (☎05.46.29.82.37), has a high standard of cuisine starting at 130F/€19.82 for lunchtime menus, as does *Le Bistrot de Bernard*, 1 quai de la Criée, in Ars-en-Ré.

Rochefort and around

ROCHEFORT dates from the seventeenth century, when it was created by Colbert, Louis XIII's navy minister, to protect the coast from English raids. It remained an important naval base until modern times with its shipyards, sail-makers, munitions factories and hospital. Built on a grid plan with regular ranks of identical houses, the town is a monument to the tidiness of the military mind, but is not without charm for all that. The central **place Colbert** is very pretty and the nearby **rue Courbet** is exactly as the seventeenth century left it, complete with lime trees and cobblestones brought from Canada as ships' ballast. The seventeenth-century warehouse buildings and old arsenal as yet are unrestored and cannot be visited, but there are still some sights worth making a special effort for.

Many of the towns along the pretty surrounding coastline are served by the Aunis and Saintonge buses, although you will find the simplest solution to travelling along this whole section of coast is renting a car or even cycling. Unless you have your own transport, Rochefort is a useless base for nearby Royan or the Île d'Oléron. Bus times are inconvenient and buses to Oléron generally involve a wait at Boucrefranc.

Arrival, information and accommodation

The **gare SNCF** is located at the northern end of avenue du Président Wilson, about a fifteen-minute walk from the centre of town. The efficient **tourist office** (daily: mid-June to mid-Sept 9am–7pm, till 8pm in July & Aug; rest of year 9am–12.30pm & 2–6.30pm; ☎05.46.99.08.60, fax 05.46.99.52.64, *www.ville-rochefort.fr*) is on avenue Sadi-Carnot off rue du Dr-Pelletier, two blocks north of the **gare routière**; the staff will reserve rooms for a charge of 15F/€2.29.

Should you want to stay, you'll need to book hotels in advance to ensure reasonably priced accommodation. The cheapest **hotel** rooms in town are at *Les Messageries* on place de la Gare opposite the handsome station buildings (☎05.46.99.00.90; ③). The *Hôtel de France*, 55 rue du Dr-Pelletier (☎05.46.99.34.00, fax 05.46.37.36.08; ①–③), also has some cheap but dingy rooms – much better is the extremely comfortable and friendly two-star *Caravelle*, at 34 rue Jaurès, off avenue Charles-de-Gaulle (☎05.46.99.02.53, fax 05.46.87.29.25; ③). *Hôtel des Vermandois*, 33 rue Émile-Combes (☎05.46.99.62.75, fax 05.46.99.62.83; ④), next door to the Loti museum, is an old hotel but with modern fittings: one room is accessible for the handicapped, and several are family studios. *La Corderie Royale*, within the seventeenth-century ropeworks on rue Audebert (☎05.46.99.35.35, fax 05.46.99.78.72; ⑨; closed Feb 1–19), is the town's poshest place to stay. There's also a new, modern **hostel**, centrally located for once at 97 rue de la République (☎05.46.82.10.40). The municipal **campsite** (☎05.46.99.14.33; closed Dec–Feb) is a long haul if you've arrived at the *gare SNCF*: take avenue du Président-Wilson and keep going straight, until you reach the bottom of rue Toufaire, where you turn right, then left – about half an hour all the way.

The Town

If you have a taste for the bizarre, then there's one good reason for visiting Rochefort – the house of the novelist Julien Viaud, alias Pierre Loti. Forty years a naval officer, he wrote numerous best-selling romances with exotic oriental settings and characters. The **Maison Pierre Loti**, at 141 rue Pierre-Loti (guided tours every 20min: July–Sept Mon–Sat 10–11am & 2–5pm, Sun 2–5pm; rest of year Mon & Wed–Sat 10–11am & 2–4pm; closed Dec 20–Jan 20 & public hols; 45F/€6.86), is part of a row of modestly proportioned grey-stone houses, outwardly a model of petit-bourgeois conformity and respectability, inside an outrageous and fantastical series of rooms decorated to exotic themes. There's a medieval banqueting hall complete with Gothic fireplace and Gobelin tapestries; a monastery refectory with windows pinched from a ruined abbey; a Damascus mosque; and a Turkish room, with kilim wall-hangings and a ceiling made from an Alhambra mould. To suit the mood of the place, Loti used to throw extravagant parties: a medieval banquet with swan's meat and hedgehog and a *fête chinoise* with the guests in costumes he had brought back from China, where he took part in the suppression of the Boxer rebellion.

Also worth a quick look is the **Centre International de la Mer** (daily 9am–6/8pm; 30F/€4.57) situated in the Corderie Royale, or the royal ropeworks, off rue Toufaire. At 372m, the Corderie is the longest building in France and a rare and splendid example of seventeenth-century industrial architecture, substantially restored after damage in World War II. From 1660 until the Revolution, it furnished the entire French navy with rope, and the building now houses an appropriate exhibition on ropes and rope-making, including machinery from the nineteenth century. If you don't fancy visiting the museum, it's definitely worth a wander around the extensive building and its lawns along the River Charente, whose reed-fringed banks support a garden made up of plants brought back from long-forgotten expeditions overseas. One such, financed by Michel Bégon, quartermaster of Rochefort in 1688, brought back the flower we know as the begonia. The small harbour, the **Bassin Laperouse**, next to the Corderie, is also worth a stroll.

If you're interested in finding out more about the town's history and naval importance, head for the **Musée d'Art et d'Histoire**, 63 av Charles-de-Gaulle (July & Aug daily 1.30–7pm; rest of year Tues–Sat 1.30–5.30pm; 10F/€1.52), and the **Musée de la Marine** (daily except Tues 10am–noon & 2–6pm; closed mid-Oct to mid-Nov; 29F/€4.42), in the seventeenth-century Hôtel de Cheusses on place de la Gallosinnière, which houses an excellent collection of model ships, figureheads, navigational instruments and other naval paraphernalia. One other attractive small museum is the **Musée des Métiers de Mercure** at 12 rue Lessan, which displays lovingly and authentically reconstructed shop interiors from the beginning of the twentieth century (July & Aug daily 10am–8pm; rest of year daily except Tues 10am–noon & 2–7pm; 30F/€4.57).

Eating and drinking

Strolling through Rochefort, you should not have trouble finding somewhere to **eat**, though few establishments are culinary standouts. For inexpensive meals, try *Le Galion*, a self-service restaurant by the arsenal on rue Toufaire, and there's a more than adequate Vietnamese/Chinese, *L'Asie*, at 45 rue Toufaire. Probably the best restaurant in Rochefort is *Le Tourne-Broche*, 56 av Charles-de-Gaulle (☎05.46.99.20.19; closed Sun night & Mon, & three weeks in Jan), specializing in *grillades* but offering fish and seafood as well; menus from 110F/€16.77. For an excellent morning *café crème*, try the local bar *La Givelte*. *Le Comptoir des Îles*, also on place Colbert, serves good **beer**, and you can finish the evening playing billiards, snooker or pool around the corner at *Le Roller*, 48 rue de la République.

Fouras and the Île d'Aix

FOURAS, some 30km south of La Rochelle, is the embarkation point for the tiny Île d'Aix (see below), where Napoléon spent his last days in Europe. It's an uninspiring town, redeemed only by a clutch of popular beaches and the *presqu'île*, the peninsula that extends 3km out to sea from the town centre, terminating at the ferry dock, **Pointe de la Fumée**. The peninsula is bordered by oyster beds, and off its westernmost tip at low tide can be seen the *bouchots à moules*, lines of mussel-encrusted stumps of wood. At high tide this is a popular place to fish for *crevettes* – shrimp. The finger of land is hemmed by sea-dashed fortresses – originally intended to protect the Charente, and particularly La Rochelle, against Norman attack – which were later employed against Dutch invasions in the seventeenth century and English ones in the eighteenth. The seventeenth-century **Fort Vauban** (daily 3–5pm) now houses a small, uninspiring, local maritime museum, but its esplanade offers a magnificent panorama of neighbouring forts and islands.

Fouras's **tourist office**, which also serves the Île d'Aix, is situated in the Fort Vauban (mid-June to mid-Sept Mon–Sat 9am–7pm, Sun 10am–12.30pm & 1–6pm; rest of year Mon–Sat 9am–7pm, Sun 9am–12.30pm & 2–6pm; ☎05.46.84.60.69, fax 05.46.84.28.04). As for places to **stay**, Fouras has a posse of overpriced **hotels**, many of which can be contacted online at *www.fouras.net*, but first options should be the good-value *Roseraie*, at 2 av du Port-Nord (☎05.46.84.64.89; ③–④), and the comfortable *Grand Hotel des Bains*, 15 rue Géneral Bruncher (☎05.46.84.03.44, fax 05.46.84.58.26; ③–④), housed in an old post office with a lovely courtyard. There are also three **campsites** around the town: the *Fumée*, near the ferry port (☎05.46.84.26.77; closed Oct–April); the *L'Espérance* off avenue Philippe-Jannet (☎05.46.84.24.18; closed Oct to mid-April); and the *Cadoret*, near to plage Nord on avenue du Cadoret (☎05.46.82.19.19). The best-value **food** in town is probably from *Restaurant La Jetée* at Pointe de la Fumée (☎05.46.84.60.43; closed Jan & Tues out of season), which serves excellent seafood at affordable prices (menus 80–140F/€12.20–21.34).

Île d'Aix

Less frequented than the bigger islands, the crescent-shaped **Île d'Aix** is small enough – just 2km long – to be walked around in about three hours, giving a greater sense of its island status than is felt on the Île de Ré.

The island is well defended, with a pair of forts and ramparts around its southern tip. The island, and particularly **Fort Liédot**, served as a prison for members of the Paris Commune and later held Russian prisoners in the Crimean and First World wars. There's a **museum** (daily 10am–noon & 2–6pm; 25F/€3.81) in the house constructed to Napoléon's orders and inhabited by him for a week in 1815 while he was planning his escape to America, only to find himself en route to St Helena and exile. Extensive displays fill ten rooms with the emperor's works of art, clothing, portraits and arms. The white dromedary from which he conducted his Egyptian campaign is lodged nearby in the **Musée Africain**, with its entire collection devoted to African wildlife (daily except Wed same hours as above; 16F/€2.44).

OYSTERS

Marennes' speciality is fattening the **oysters** known as *creuses*. It's a lucrative but precarious business, extremely vulnerable to storm damage, changes of temperature or salinity in the water, the ravages of starfish and umpteen other improbable natural disasters.

Oysters begin life as minuscule larvae, which are "born" about three times a year. When a "birth" happens, the oystermen are alerted by a special radio service, and they all rush out to place their "collectors" – usually arrangements of roofing tiles – for the larvae to cling to. There the immature oysters remain for eight or nine months, after which they are scraped off and moved to *parcs* in the tidal waters of the sea: sometimes covered, sometimes uncovered. Their last move is to the *claires* – shallow rectangular pools where they are kept permanently covered by water less salty than normal sea water. Here they fatten up and acquire the greenish colour the market expects. With "improved" modern oysters, the whole cycle takes about two years, as opposed to four or five with the old varieties.

Access is by frequent ferry (half-hourly in season) from Pointe de la Fumée (☎05.46.84.26.77), or with Interîles from La Rochelle (May–Sept 2–4 daily). The only **hotel** on the island is the overpriced *Napoléon* on rue Gourgard (☎05.46.84.66.02, fax 05.46.84.69.70; ②), and there's also a **campsite**, the *Fort de la Rade* (☎05.46.84.28.28; closed Oct–April).

Brouage and Marennes

Eighteen kilometres southwest of Rochefort, **BROUAGE** is another seventeenth-century military base, this time created by Richelieu after the siege of La Rochelle. It is surrounded by salt marshes, now reclaimed and transformed into meadows grazed by white Charollais cattle and intersected by dozens of reed-filled drainage ditches, where herons watch and yellow flag blooms. It's a strangely beautiful landscape with huge skies specked with wheeling buzzards and kestrels and, being flat as a pancake, it's good cycling and walking country. To reach the town from Rochefort, you cross the Charente on the D733 near the disused **Pont Transbordeur**, a great iron gantry with a raft-like platform suspended on hawsers, on which a dozen cars were loaded and floated across the river – a technological wonder in its time. From there, you can either turn right for Soubise and Moëze or go on to St-Agnant.

The way into Brouage is through the **Porte Royale** in the north wall of the totally intact fortifications dating from the mid-seventeenth century. Locked within its 400-metre square, the town now seems abandoned and somnolent; even the sea has retreated, and all that's left of the harbour are the partly freshwater pools, or *claires*, where oysters are fattened in the last stage of their rearing.

Within the walls, the streets are laid out on a grid pattern, lined with low two-storey houses. On the second cross-street to the right is a **memorial** to Samuel de Champlain, the local boy who founded the French colony of Québec in 1608. In the same century, Brouage witnessed the last painful pangs of a royal romance: here, Cardinal Mazarin, successor to Richelieu, locked up his daughter, Marie Mancini, to keep her from her youthful sweetheart, Louis XIV. The politics of the time made the Infanta of Spain a more suitable consort for the King of France than his daughter – in his own judgement. Louis gave in, while Marie pined and sighed on the walls of Brouage. Returning from his marriage in St-Jean-de-Luz, Louis dodged his escort and stole away to see her. Finding her gone, he slept in her room and paced the walls in her footsteps.

Half a dozen kilometres south, on a narrow, drier spit of land, past the graceful eighteenth-century **Château de la Gataudière** with its unique interior and original furnishings (March–Nov Mon–Sat 10am–noon & 2–6.30pm, Sun 2–6.30pm; 35F/€5.34) – built by the man who introduced rubber to France – you come to the village of **MARENNES**. This is the centre of oyster production for an area that supplies over sixty percent of France's requirements. If you want to visit the oyster beds and see how the business works, you can do so here; just ask at the **tourist office** on place Chasseloup-Laubat (☎05.46.85.04.36, fax 05.46.85.14.20) or out of season at the Mairie, 6 rue Foch (☎05.46.85.25.55) – visits cost on average 50F/€7.62 for an adult, 20F/€3.05 for a child.

For **accommodation** in Marennes, try the inexpensive *Hôtel du Commerce* at 9 rue de la République (☎05.46.85.00.09; ②), with a restaurant where you can eat generously and well from 65F/€9.91. A good alternative for **eating** is *La Verte Ostréa* at the end of the pier at La Cayenne, where oysters and shellfish form the basis of every menu (from 65F/€9.91).

The Île d'Oléron

The **Île d'Oléron** is France's largest island after Corsica and a favourite of day-trippers and families in the summer months for its beautiful sandy beaches. It's up the road from Marennes, joined to the mainland by a bridge. Buses from Rochefort are awkward, with irritating changes at Saintes or Boucrefranc, and it's easier to go direct from Saintes on one of the several daily Citram buses that stop at all the main towns on the island; alternatively, take one of Interîles' guided day-trips from La Rochelle (see p.575).

Flat and more wooded than the Île de Ré, Oléron has plenty of greenery, with the extensive pine-studded **Forêt des Saumonards** in the northeast of the island; here you can eyeball a dazzling panorama of the surrounding *parcs à huitres* and the mighty **Fort Boyard** stranded in the midst of sea between Oléron and the Île d'Aix to the northeast. At the island's southern tip, the larger **Forêt de St-Trojan** creeps up the western coast along **La Grande Plage**, a popular spot but far enough from the main towns not to be too crowded. The island interior is pretty and distinctive. Waterways wind right into the land, their gleaming muddy banks overhung by round fishing nets suspended from ranks of piers. There are so many oyster *claires* that, from above, the island must look like an Afghan mirrored cushion; the stretch from Boyardville to St-Pierre – with its pines, tamarisks and woods of evergreen oak – is the most attractive.

The island's most interesting attraction is off the D126 between St-Pierre and Dolus, right in the middle of the island. The bird park of **Le Marais aux Oiseaux** (daily: April, May & Sept 10am–noon & 2–7pm; June–Aug 10am–8pm; 25F/€3.81) was originally established as a hospital for injured birds found in the wild, but is now a breeding centre with many examples of rare or endangered species. Some 300 to 400 species of birds are given the freedom of twenty hectares of beautiful countryside, while sixty species are caged for observation alongside public walkways.

Most of the little towns on the island inevitably have been ruined by the development of hundreds of holiday homes – and it can be a real battle in the summer season to find a place to stay. There are a few places that still retain some amount of charm, however, not least of which is the main town in the south of the island, **LE CHÂTEAU**, named after the **citadel** that still stands, along with some seventeenth-century **fortifications**: the town thrives on its traditional oyster farming and boat-building, and there's a lively **market** in place de la République every morning. The chief town in the north – and most picturesque of the island's settlements – is **ST-PIERRE**, whose market square has an unusual thirteenth-century **monument**, or *lanterne aux morts*. A few kilometres to the northeast, **BOYARDVILLE** has no interest except for the ranks of *bouchots* – stakes for growing mussels – along the shore. It's tempting to help yourself, but these are private property and you'll be in trouble if someone sees you. Instead, head to the major attraction around here: the superb stretch of sandy beach at **LA BRÉE-LES-BAINS**. Halfway down the west coast is the pretty fishing port of **LA COTINIÈRE**, with a daily morning fish market (except Sun), Criée aux Poissons, where the fishermen traditionally cry out their wares.

Practicalities

The main **tourist office** is on place de la République in Le Château (July–Sept daily 9.30am–12.30pm & 2.30–7pm; rest of year closed Sun; ☎05.46.47.60.51, fax 05.46.47.73.65), also the location of a couple of affordable restaurants. St-Pierre's tourist office is on place Gambetta (June–Aug Mon–Sat 9am–7pm, Sun 10am–1pm; rest of year Tues–Sat 9.15am–12.30pm & 2–6pm; ☎05.46.47.11.39, fax 05.46.47.10.41). **Bikes** are available in St-Pierre from Lespagnol, rue de la République, and from Lacellerie Michel, rue Maréchal-Foch.

Well-priced **accommodation** on the Île d'Oléron can be had at *Les Tamaris* in the port of St-Denis (☎05.46.47.86.04, fax 05.46.75.73.08; ②), at the *Hôtel de la Petite Plage à Domino*, rue de l'Océan, St-Georges (☎05.46.76.52.28; ③) and at *L'Albatross*, 11 bd du Dr-Pineau, St-Trojan-les-Bains (☎05.46.76.00.08, fax 05.46.76.03.58; ③; closed Oct–Feb). There are **campsites** all over the island: at La Brée, where the best beaches are, there's *Pertuis d'Antioche* (☎05.46.47.92.00), 150m from the beach off the D273. Further down the east coast, *Signol* at Boyardville (☎05.46.47.01.22) is pleasantly sited near pine forests. If you want to stay a week or so, you could rent a **holiday apartment**, easy enough outside of July and August; ask for a list at any of the tourist offices, or contact the Agence Centrale Oléronaise (☎05.46.75.32.53).

Places to **eat** abound on the island, and St-Pierre has the greatest choice of restaurants and brasseries. One place worth mentioning is in La Cotinière: at *L'Écailler*, 65 rue du Port (☎05.46.47.10.31; mid-Nov to Jan closed Sun & Mon), you can have a slap-up, super-fresh seafood meal facing the port from 150F/€22.86.

Royan and around

Before World War II, **ROYAN**, at the mouth of the Gironde, was a fashionable resort for the bourgeoisie. It is still popular – though no longer exclusive – and the modern town has lost its elegance to the dreary rationalism of 1950s town planning: broad boulevards, car parks, shopping centres, planned greenery. Ironically, the occasion for this planners' romp was provided by Allied bombing, an attempt to dislodge a large contingent of German troops who had withdrawn into the area after the D-Day landings. But the **beaches** – the most elegant and fashionable of which is in the suburb of **Pontaillac** to the northwest – are beautiful: fine pale sand, meticulously harrowed and raked near town, and wild, pine-backed and pounded by the Atlantic to the north.

Arrival, information and accommodation

The **gare routière** and **gare SNCF** are located in cours de l'Europe. The nearby **tourist office** (June–Sept Mon–Sat 9am–7.30pm, Sun 10am–1pm & 3–6pm; rest of year Mon–Sat 9am–12.30pm & 2–6pm; ☎05.46.05.04.71, fax 05.46.06.67.76, *www.ot-royan.fr*) and **PTT** are close to the Rond-Point-de-la-Poste at the east end of the seafront. You can rent **bikes** from Cyclojet in the *gare SNCF* or from Cycl'Océan at 23 & 37 cours de l'Europe; **car rental** is available from either Europcar, 13 place du Dr-Gantier (☎05.46.05.20.88), or Avis, 75 av de Pontaillac (☎05.46.38.48.48).

Accommodation in Royan is expensive and in short supply in season, when your best bet is to camp up the coast to the north or visit for the day from Saintes or

Rochefort. If you're booking ahead, try the *Nouvel Hôtel de la Plage*, 18 av de Cognac (☎05.46.39.00.18, fax 05.46.38.41.14; ①), a cheapie at Pontaillac beach to the west of town; frequent Aunis and Saintonge buses run from the train station via place Charles-de-Gaulle. The *Hôtel de l'Hôtel de Ville*, 1 bd Aristide-Briand (☎05.46.05.00.64; ①), is close to the beach, as is *Hôtel de la Plage*, right amidst the action at 26–28 Front de Mer (☎05.46.05.10.27, fax 05.46.38.37.79; ②). There's also the more comfortable and central two-star *Les Bleuets*, 21 facade de Foncillon (☎05.46.38.51.79, fax 05.46.23.82.00, *www.hotel-les-bleuets.com*; ④), with sea or garden views. Finally, the three-star *Family Golf Hotel*, 28 bd Frédéric-Garnier (☎05.46.05.14.66, fax 05.46.06.52.56; ④), has air-conditioning and beachfront balconies, though its 1950s exterior is rather ugly. Alternatively, 3km southeast of Royan, in **ST-GEORGES-DE-DIDONNE**, there's an excellent little hotel, the *Colinette*, 16 av de la Grande-Plage (☎05.46.05.15.75, fax 05.46.06.54.17; ③; half-board only mid-June to mid-Sept), in pleasant surroundings 100m from the sea.

There are a number of **campsites** in the region and around Royan itself, including the *Clairefontaine* (☎05.46.39.08.11, fax 05.46.38.13.79; closed Oct–May), a fairly pricey site at avenue Louise, allée des Peupliers in **PONTAILLAC**, and the municipal *La Triloterie* (☎05.46.05.26.91, fax 05.46.06.20.74) off avenue d'Aquitaine – the road to Bordeaux.

The Town

One sight worth seeing in Royan is the 1950s **church of Notre-Dame**, designed by Gillet and Hébrard, in a tatty square behind the main waterfront. Though the concrete has weathered badly, the overall effect is dramatic and surprising. Tall V-sectioned columns give the outside the appearance of massive fluting, and a stepped roof-line rises dramatically to culminate in a 65-metre bell tower, like the prow of a giant vessel. The interior is even more striking: using uncompromisingly modern materials and designs, the architects have succeeded in out-Gothicking Gothic. The stained-glass panels, in each of which a different tone predominates, borrow their colours from the local seascapes – oyster, sea, mist and murk – before a sudden explosion of colour in the Christ figure above the altar.

The most attractive area in Royan is around **boulevard Garnier**, which leads southeast from Rond-Point-de-la-Poste along the beach and once housed Parisian high society in purpose-built, Belle Époque holiday villas. Some of these have survived, including **Le Rêve**, 58 bd Garnier, where Émile Zola lived and wrote; **Kosiki**, 100 av du Parc (running parallel to bd Garnier), a nineteenth-century folly of Japanese inspiration; and **Tanagra**, 34 av du Parc, whose facade is covered in sculptures and balconies.

Various **cruises** are organized from Royan in season, including one to the **Cordouan lighthouse**, erected by the Black Prince and commanding the mouth of the Gironde River. There's a twenty-minute **ferry** crossing (one way: pedestrians & cycles 17F/€2.59, motorbikes 55F/€8.38, cars 123F/€18.75) to the headland on the other side of the Gironde, the **Pointe de Grave**, from where a **bicycle trail** and the **GR8** head down the coast through the pines and dunes to the bay of Arcachon (see p.613).

Eating, drinking and nightlife

As for **food**, good-value menus can be found at the huge, old-fashioned *Relais de la Mairie*, 1 rue du Chay, quite far from the centre off avenue de Pontaillac (☎05.46.39.03.15), and at *Les Filets Bleus*, near the cathedral at 14 rue Notre-Dame (☎05.46.05.74.00), which specializes in seafood dishes and gourmet salads, with *plats du jour* from 55F/€8.38 and menus from 85F/€12.96. The smart *Le Chalet*, 6 bd de la Grandière (☎05.46.05.04.90; closed Wed), serves imaginative seafood dishes reasonably cheaply and is crammed with French families on Sundays, when you'd be wise to book. Several **crêperies**, **pizzerias** and **snack bars** are situated on Front de Mer, the brassy strip leading from the tourist office to the beach and pleasure boats, with the *Crêperie de la Plage* at no. 40 recommended. The town's best-value bistro, though, is packed-out *Le Tiki*, on the beachfront right by the tourist office: it dishes out an above-average variety of *plats du jour* from 40F/€6.10 as well as fish, pizza and grills. Self-caterers can head for the large covered **market**, the Marché Central, at the end of boulevard A.-Briand, open every day (except Mon out of season) but particularly crowded and lively on Wednesday and Sunday mornings.

Nightlife is fairly restricted, considering the size of Royan: there's a disco, *Tropicana*, and a jazz bar at Plage de Pontaillac; and a piano bar, *Le Mylord*, and jazz bar, *Le Yachtman*, at Voûtes-de-Port.

Palmyre and Talmont

It's worth knowing about the **zoo park** in **PALMYRE** (daily: April–Sept 9am–7pm; rest of year 9am–noon & 2–6pm; *www.zoo-palmyre.fr*; 70F/€10.67), 10km northwest of Royan up the D25 coast road, especially if you're travelling with children, although its tacky advertising, with chimps dressed in human clothes, may put you off. Once you're inside, there are plenty of exotic species – from elephants and wild cats to gorillas and monkeys – housed in spacious enclosures covering fourteen hectares. To reach it, there are **buses** all day from Royan's *gare routière* and the place Charles-de-Gaulle.

An ideal bicycle or picnic excursion just over an hour's ride from Royan is to **TAL-MONT**, 16km up the Gironde on the GR360 – apart from a few ups and downs through the woods outside Royan, it's all level terrain. The low-crouching village clusters about the twelfth-century **church of Ste-Radegonde**, standing at the edge of a cliff above the Gironde. With gabled transepts, a squat tower, an apse simply but elegantly decorated with blind arcading – all in weathered tawny stone and pocked like a sponge – it stands magnificently, in sun or cloud, against the forlorn browny-grey seascapes typical of the Gironde. The entrance is through the north transept, where the rings of carving in the arched doorway depict acrobats standing on each other's shoulders and, in the outer braid, two tug-of-war teams hauling roped lions up the arch. The inside is as unpretentiously beautiful as the exterior.

THE CHARENTE

It is hard to believe that the peaceful fertile valley of the **River Charente** was once a busy industrial waterway, bringing armaments from **Angoulême** to the naval shipyards at Rochefort. Today peaceful, low, ochre-coloured farms crown the valley slopes, with green swathes of vineyard sweeping up to the walls, and the graceful turrets of minor châteaux – properties of wealthy cognac-producers – poke up from out of the woods. The towns and villages may look old-fashioned, but the prosperous shops and classy new villas are proof that where the grape grows, money and modernity are not far behind.

PINEAU DES CHARENTES

Roadside signs throughout the Charente advertise **Pineau des Charentes**, a sweet liqueur that's a blending of grape juice stopped in its fermentation by adding cognac from the same vineyard. It's best drunk chilled as an apéritif; the locals also like it with oysters and love cooking with it. Favourite dishes include *moules au Pineau* (mussels cooked with tomatoes, Pineau, garlic and parsley) and *lapin à la saintongeaise* (rabbit casseroled with Pineau rosé, shallots, garlic, tomatoes, thyme and bay leaves).

The **valley** itself is easy to travel as the main road and train lines to Limoges run this way. North and south, Poitiers, Périgueux (for the Dordogne) and Bordeaux are also easily reached by train. Otherwise, for cross-country journeys, you are heavily reliant on your own transport.

Saintes and around

SAINTES was formerly much more important than its present size suggests. Today a busy market for the surrounding region, it was capital of the old province of Saintonge and a major administrative and cultural centre in Roman times. It still retains some impressive remains from that period, as well as two beautiful Romanesque pilgrim churches and an attractive centre of narrow lanes and medieval houses. It also has the doubtful distinction of being the birthplace of Dr Guillotin, whose instrument of decapitation came into its own during the Revolution.

The Town

The abbey church, the **Abbaye-aux-Dames** (daily: June–Sept 10am–12.30pm & 2–7pm; rest of year 2–7pm only; 15F/€2.29), is as quirky as Notre-Dame in Poitiers. It stands back from the street on rue St-Pallais, in a sandy courtyard behind the smaller Romanesque church of St-Pallais. An elaborately sculpted doorway conceals the plain, domed interior. Its rarest feature is the eleventh-century tower, by turns square, octagonal and lantern-shaped, flanked with pinnacles and capped with the Poitou pine cone.

From here rue Arc-de-Triomphe brings you out on the river bank beside an imposing Roman arch – the **Arc de Germanicus** – which originally stood on the bridge until it was demolished in the mid-nineteenth century to make way for the modern crossing. The arch was dedicated to the emperor Tiberius, his son Drusus and nephew Germanicus in 19 AD. In a stone building next door is an **archeological museum** (summer Tues–Sun 10am–noon & 2–6pm, no midday break in July & Aug; winter Tues–Sat 10am–noon & 2–5.30pm, Sun 3–6pm; 10F/€1.52), with a great many more Roman bits and pieces strewn about, mostly rescued from the fifth-century city walls into which they had been incorporated. This whole area comes alive on the first Monday of every month when a sprawling **market** extends from the abbey right through here and up most of avenue Gambetta.

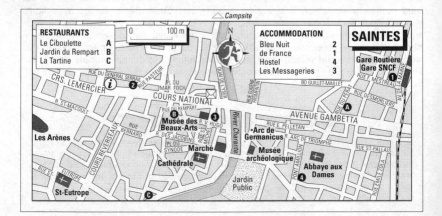

A footbridge crosses from the archeological museum to the covered market on the west bank of the river and place du Marché at the foot of the rather uninspiring **Cathédrale de St-Pierre**, which began life as a Romanesque church but was significantly altered in the aftermath of damage inflicted during the Wars of Religion, when Saintes was a Huguenot stronghold. Its enormous, heavily buttressed tower, capped by a hat-like dome instead of the intended spire, is the town's chief landmark. In front, the lime trees of place du Synode stretch away to the municipal buildings, while up to the right are the old quarter and the Hôtel Martineau library in the rue des Jacobins, with an exquisite central courtyard full of trees and shrubs. North of the cathedral, a seventeenth-century mansion on rue Victor-Hugo houses the **Musée des Beaux-Arts** (Tues–Sat 10am–noon & 2–5.30/6pm, Sun 2–6pm; 10F/€1.52), containing a collection of local pottery and some unexciting paintings.

Saintes' Roman heritage is best seen at **Les Arènes**, an amphitheatre whose ruins lie at the head of a leafy little valley reached by a footpath which begins by 54 cours Reversaux. The amphitheatre was dug into the end of the valley in the early first century, making it one of the oldest surviving examples in France. Although most of the seats are now grassed over, it is still an evocative spot.

On the way back from the amphitheatre, it's no extra trouble to take in the eleventh-century **church of St-Eutrope**. The upper church, which lost its nave in 1803, has some brilliant capital-carving in the old choir, best seen from the gallery. But it's the crypt – entered from the street – which is more atmospheric and primitive: here massive pillars carved with stylized vegetation support the vaulting in semi-darkness, and there is a huge old font and the third-century tomb of Saintes' first bishop, Eutropius himself.

Practicalities

Saintes' **gare SNCF** is on avenue de la Marne at the east end of the main road, avenue Gambetta. The **tourist office** is housed in grand old Villa Musso, 62 cours National (Mon–Sat: July & Aug 9am–6pm; rest of year 9am–1pm & 2–6pm; ☎05.46.74.23.82, fax 05.46.92.17.01, *www.ville-saintes.fr*), and organizes **boat trips** to Cognac during the summer.

There are several **hotels** in the vicinity of the *gare SNCF*, the best of the bunch being the now rather tatty old *Hôtel de France* (☎05.46.93.01.16, fax 05.46.74.37.90; ②). More congenial and more central is *Les Messageries* in tiny rue des Messageries, off rue Victor-Hugo (☎05.46.93.64.99, fax 05.46.92.14.34, *www.hotel-des-messageries.com*; ③), with a laundry available. Another agreeable place is the *Bleu Nuit* at 1 rue Pasteur, the crossroads of cours National and cours Reversaux (☎05.46.93.01.72, fax 05.46.74.43.80; ③; locked garage 30F/€4.57); it has some character and is well insulated against the noise of the street. The **hostel**, 2 place Geoffroy-Martel (☎05.46.92.14.92, fax 05.46.92.97.82), is right behind the Abbaye aux Dames; it has been totally renovated and modernized. The municipal **campsite** (☎05.46.93.08.00) is to the right (if you are coming from the Arc de Germanicus) immediately after the bridge, along quai de l'Yser.

For **eating**, there's a good restaurant, the *Tartine* (☎05.46.74.16.38), by the river on place Blair, and a popular crêperie at 20 rue Victor-Hugo, off rue Alsace-Lorraine, the pedestrianized shopping street. *Le Jardin du Rempart*, 36 rue du Rempart (☎05.46.93.37.66), serves top-value menus from 89F/€13.57, including salads, seafood and grills, while *Le Ciboulette*, 36 rue Pérat (☎05.46.74.07.36; closed Sat lunch & Sun), serves lots of Charentais specialities at moderate prices. Out of town, the *Restaurant de la Charente* (☎05.46.91.03.17; closed Sun), 10km upstream at **CHANIERS**, is the Sunday haunt of prosperous locals and makes a more expensive but fulfilling gastronomic experience.

Around Saintes

If you have a car, you could explore several of the marvellous Romanesque churches within easy reach of Saintes. In **FENIOUX**, 29km to the north towards St-Jean-d'Angély, there is the superb church of St-Eutrope with its mighty spire, while the church at **RIOUX**, 12km to the south, is well worth visiting for its detailed facade. There is also the fine **Château of Roche-Courbon**, 18km northwest off the Rochefort road – once described as the Sleeping Beauty's castle – with some stylish interiors and gardens.

One place worth any amount of trouble to get to is the twelfth-century pilgrim **church of St-Pierre** at **AULNAY**, 37km northeast of Saintes, and sadly not served by public transport. Aulnay church's finest sculpture is on the west front, the south transept and apse, with some more fine work inside. On the building's main facade, two blind arches flank the central portal. The tympanum of the right depicts Christ in Majesty; the left, St Peter, crucified upside down with two extraordinarily lithe and graceful soldiers balancing on the arms of his cross to get a better swing at the nails in his feet. On the south side, the doorway is decorated with four bands of even more intricate carving. The apse, too, is a beauty, framed by five slender columns and lit by three perfectly arched windows, the centre one enclosed by figures wrapped in the finest twining foliage. Inside, there is more extraordinary carving: capitals depicting Delilah cutting Samson's hair, devils pulling a man's beard, human-eared elephants, bearing the Latin inscription *Hi sunt elephantes*, "These are elephants" – presumably for the edification of ignorant locals.

You might also like to visit **NUAILLÉ-SUR-BOUTONNE**, 9km west of Aulnay, which boasts another remarkable church; and, even nearer just down the D129 east of Aulnay, you can walk to **SALLES-LES-AULNAY** (20min), or **ST-MANDÉ** (1hr), with humbler churches of the same period, each in its way as charming as that of Aulnay.

Cognac and around

Anyone who does not already know what **COGNAC** is about will quickly nose its quintessential air as they stroll about the medieval lanes of the town's riverside quarter. For here is the greatest concentration of *chais* (warehouses), where a high-quality brandy is matured, its fumes blackening the walls with tiny fungi. Cognac *is* cognac, from the tractor driver and pruning-knife wielder to the manufacturer of corks, bottles and cartons. Untouched by recession (80 percent of production is exported), it is likely to thrive as long as the world has sorrows to drown – a sunny, prosperous, respectable, self-satisfied little place.

The Town

Cognac has a number of medieval stone and half-timbered buildings in the narrow streets of the old town, of which rue Saulnier and rue de l'Ísle-d'Or make atmospheric backdrops for a stroll, and picturesque **Grande-Rue** winds through the heart of the old quarter to the *chais*. On the right is all that remains of the **castle** where King François I was born in 1494.

To the left are the *chais* and offices of the **Hennessy Cognac Company** (Mon–Fri 10am–5/6pm; 30F/€4.57), a seventh-generation family firm, and widely thought the best of the houses to visit. The first Hennessy, an officer in the Irish brigade serving with the French army, hailed from Ballymacnoy in County Cork and gave up soldiering in 1765 to set up a little business here. The Hennessy visit begins with a film explaining what's what in the world of cognac. Only an *eau de vie* distilled from grapes grown in a strictly defined area can be called cognac, and this stretches from the coast at La Rochelle and Royan to Angoulême. It is all carefully graded according to soil properties: chalk essentially. The inner circle, from which the finest cognac comes – Grand Champagne and Petit Champagne (not to be confused with bubbly) – lies mainly south of the River Charente. Hennessy alone keeps 180,000 barrels in stock. All are regularly checked and various *coupages* (blendings) made from barrel to barrel, of which only the best are kept – depending on the well-honed taste buds of the *maître du chais*.

Another important cog in the cognac mechanism is Europe's second biggest bottle-maker, the modern **St-Gobain glassworks**, which lies 2km south of town; guided tours of the works can be arranged through the tourist office (see below).

Practicalities

From the **gare SNCF**, to get to the central place François-I, go down rue Mousnier, right on rue Bayard, past the **PTT** and up rue du 14-Juillet. The square is dominated by an equestrian statue of the king rising from a bed of begonias. The **tourist office** is on rue du 14-Juillet at no. 16 (daily: July & Aug 9am–6.15pm; rest of year 9am–12.30pm & 2–6.15pm; ☎05.45.82.10.71, fax 05.45.82.34.47, *www.ville-cognac.fr*), where you can ask about visiting the various *chais*, the St-Gobain glassworks (30F/€4.57) and river trips – upstream through the locks to Jarnac, where the late President Mitterrand's modest grave has become a place of pilgrimage for elderly left-wingers, is a particularly beautiful excursion.

As for **rooms**, the cheapest are at *Le Cheval Blanc*, 6–8 place Bayard (☎05.45.82.09.55, fax 05.45.82.14.82; ①), with a simple inexpensive restaurant downstairs, and the *Hotel St-Martin*, 112 av Paul Firino-Martell (☎05.45.35.01.29; ②), whose restaurant serves a respectable 63F/€9.60 dinner menu. For something a bit more comfort, try one of these: the characterful *Hôtel d'Orleans*, 25 rue d'Angoulême (☎05.45.82.01.26, fax 05.45.82.20.33; ②), in a calm pedestrianized street in the old part of town; *La Résidence*, 25 av Victor-Hugo (☎05.45.36.62.40, fax 05.45.36.62.49; ③), an attractive two-star with a clean modern interior; or *L'Étape*, a little further out on the N141 at 2 av d'Angoulême (☎05.45.32.16.15, fax 05.45.36.20.03; ③). Upstream from the bridge, the oak woods of the Parc François-I – where there's swimming in the river or a pool – stretch along the river bank to the Pont Chatenay and the town **campsite** (☎05.45.32.13.32).

Eating out shouldn't pose a problem. The relaxed and friendly *La Bonne Goule*, 42 allée de la Corderie (☎05.45.82.06.37; closed Sun evening; from 60F/€9.15), serves up excellent Charentais specialities at inexpensive prices, and there's a good list of local wines. Those after a dining experience will find it at *La Boîte-à-Sel*, 68 av Victor-Hugo (☎05.45.32.07.68; closed Mon), a seasoned restaurant with an emphasis on fresh natural produce; the good-value 75F/€11.43 menu gets you a *plat* from the 102F/€15.55 *menu de marché* and a dessert or entrée; the excellent *menu des gourmets* will set you back 195F/€29.73. There is also good brasserie fare to be had at the *Coq d'Or* on the central place François-Ier (☎05.45.82.02.56).

Around Cognac

The area around Cognac is gentle enough for some restful walks, taking in some pretty little Charentais villages. The best is the towpath or *chemin de halage* that follows the south bank of the Charente upstream to Pont de la Trâche, then on along a track to the village of **BOURG-CHARENTE**, with an excellent **restaurant** called *La Ribaudière* (☎05.45.81.30.54, *www.laribaudiere.com*; closed Sun evening & Mon; menus 140–330F/€21.34–50.30) at the bridge, an interesting castle and a Romanesque church; the walk takes about three hours in all. A byroad leads back to **ST-BRICE** on the other bank, past sleepy farms and acres of shoulder-high vines. From there, another lane winds 3km up the hill and over to the ruined **abbey of La Châtre**, abandoned amid brambles and fields. Alternatively, at the hamlet of **RICHEMONT**, 5km northwest of Cognac, you can swim in the pools of the tiny River Antenne below an ancient church on a steep bluff lost in the woods.

Further afield, 18km northwest of Cognac between the villages of Migron and Authon, there's the fascinating **Écomusée du Cognac** (daily 9.30am–12.30pm & 2.30–6.30pm; free), which illustrates the history of the distillation process and the various tools involved, finishing off with a tasting of cognacs, liqueurs and cocktails; follow the D731 to St-Jean-d'Angely for 13km as far as Burie, then turn right onto the D131, 4km from Migron.

Angoulême and around

Today, the cathedral city of **ANGOULÊME** has a failing economy. The paper mills that dominated the town used to employ thousands of workers and bolstered the city's prosperity; now they are almost completely defunct. But in the past, the former capital of the Angoumois province was a much-coveted city, being heavily fought over during the fourteenth-century Anglo-French squabbles and again in the sixteenth century during the Wars of Religion, when it was a Protestant stronghold. After the revocation of the Edict of Nantes, a good proportion of its citizens – among them many of its skilled papermakers – emigrated to Holland, never to return.

The Town

The **old town** occupies a high steep-sided plateau overlooking a bend in the Charente, a natural fortress. It has many charms, if few notable sights. The labyrinthine streets to the north of the delightful **place Louvel** and the massive Hôtel de Ville have been largely restored and pedestrianized. It is here that the restaurants and bars are concentrated, while the eastern section, down rue Marango and rue St-Martial, has become the main commercial centre. On the southern edge of the plateau stands the **Cathedral**, whose west front – like Notre-Dame at Poitiers – is a fascinating display board for some expressive and lively twelfth-century sculpture, culminating in a Risen Christ with angels and clouds about his head, framed in the usual blaze of a halo. The lively frieze beneath the tympanum to the right of the west door commemorates the recapture of Spanish Zaragoza from the Moors, showing a bishop transfixing a Moorish giant with his lance and Roland killing the Moorish king.

Next to the cathedral in the old bishop's palace, there's more art on show at the **Musée des Beaux-Arts** (Mon–Fri noon–6pm, Sat & Sun 2–6pm; 15F/€2.29), with an emphasis on seventeenth- to nineteenth-century paintings, many by Charentais artists. From the front of the cathedral, you can walk all around the **ramparts** encircling the plateau, with long views over the surrounding country, now largely filled with urban sprawl. There are **public gardens** below the parapet at the far end of the fortifications, and a gravelly esplanade by the *lycée* where locals gather to play boules.

Angoulême's most fascinating museum lies just below the city walls on the north side close to the River Charente: the **Centre National de la Bande Dessinée**, 121 rue de Bordeaux (Tues–Fri 10am–6/7pm, Sat & Sun 2–6/7pm; open Mon during school hols; 30F/€4.57; bus #3 or #5), devoted entirely to comic strips. Housed in a turn-of-the-twentieth-century brewery, with contemporary high-rise and glass additions, the museum gets across the message that comics ("BD") – from politics to pornography – are regarded as a serious art form in France. The museum owns a collection of some four thousand original drawings, which it displays in rotating exhibitions of about three hundred at a time. They range from the earliest stories with pictures and captions, the nineteenth-century *images d'Épinal*, through the introduction of the speech bubble in the 1920s to some of the darker contemporary productions. Astérix, Peanuts, Tintin and many other characters and artists are represented. There's also a vast library, much of it in English, where you're welcome to relax on cushions and devour comics.

Another riverfront museum close by is the **Atelier-Musée du Papier**, 134 rue de Bordeaux (July & Aug Tues–Sat 12.30–6.30pm; rest of the year Tues–Sun 2–6pm; free), located in a disused cigarette-paper factory – a fitting tribute to the declining Charentais paper industry. While exhibits get into the history and technicalities of paper-making, art isn't forgotten, with contemporary creations on show, utilizing paper, cardboard and pulp.

Practicalities

Angoulême is easily accessible by **train** from Cognac, Limoges and Poitiers. From the **gare SNCF** avenue Gambetta, with the **gare routière** and several cheap hotels, leads uphill to the town centre through place Pérot, a fifteen-minute walk. The main **tourist office**, 2 place St-Pierre (July & Aug Mon–Sat 9.30am–7pm, Sun 10am–noon & 2–5pm; rest of year Mon–Fri 9am–12.30pm & 1.30–6pm, Sat 10am–noon & 2–5pm, Sun 10am–noon; ☎05.45.95.16,84, fax 05.45.95.91.76), is by the cathedral and can provide route details for walks in the area – *circuits pédèstres*; there's another branch office outside the *gare SNCF*.

Both tourist offices can help with **accommodation**, although if you want to go it alone the cheapest rooms in town are at the peaceful family-run *Le Crab*, 27 rue Kléber (☎05.45.93.02.93, fax 05.45.95.38.52; ①), with a decent restaurant serving menus from 60F/€9.15, and at *Hôtel Gasté*, 381 rte de Bordeaux (☎05.45.91.89.98, fax 05.45.25.24.67; ①; closed first three weeks in Aug; restaurant from 60F/€9.15), a long haul from the station on the opposite side of town. But far and away the nicest place to stay is the elegant old *Hôtel du Palais*, overlooking the delightful shady place Louvel in the heart of the old town (☎05.45.92.54.11, fax 05.45.92.01.83; ③; garage 35F/€5.34). Another place worth trying, especially for its excellent regional cuisine, is the *Hôtel La Palma*, 4 rampe d'Aguesseau, on the road leading up into the old town from the station (☎05.45.95.22.89, fax 05.45.94.26.66; ①; restaurant from 65F/€9.91). Alternatively, there's a wonderfully positioned **HI hostel** (☎05.45.92.45.80, fax 05.45.95.90.71), with canteen, on an island in the Charente; take bus #7 from place du Champ-de-Mars. The municipal **campsite** (☎05.45.92.83.22) is nearby, beyond the Pont de Bourgines.

Likely **restaurant** areas are rue de Genève, with a number of options including traditional French and international, and the narrow, pedestrianized rue Massilon. One of the best restaurants in the region, with a number of interesting and inventive menus, starting at 170F/€25.91, is *La Ruelle*, 6 rue Trois-Notre-Dames (☎05.45.95.15.19; closed Sat lunch, Sun, April 8–14 & Aug 5–18). *Le Mektoub*, 28 rue des Trois-Notre-Dames (☎05.45.92.60.96), is good for inexpensive North African cuisine, and just near the excellent daily covered market of Les Halles, *Le Chat Noir*, on rue du Chat, is crowded with lunchers after its cheap salads and snacks. *La Marine* on rue Ludovic-Trarieux a modern and airy oyster/wine bar, while *Chez Paul*, 1 place France Louval (☎05.45.90.04.61), is a friendly and very reasonable restaurant (and bar with live music) with a beautiful garden; the food is fantastic, with menus starting at 59F/€8.99, and it is well worth a visit.

Around Angoulême

LA ROCHEFOUCAULD, 22km east of Angoulême, is the site of a huge Renaissance **château** on the banks of the River Tardoire, which still belongs to the family that gave

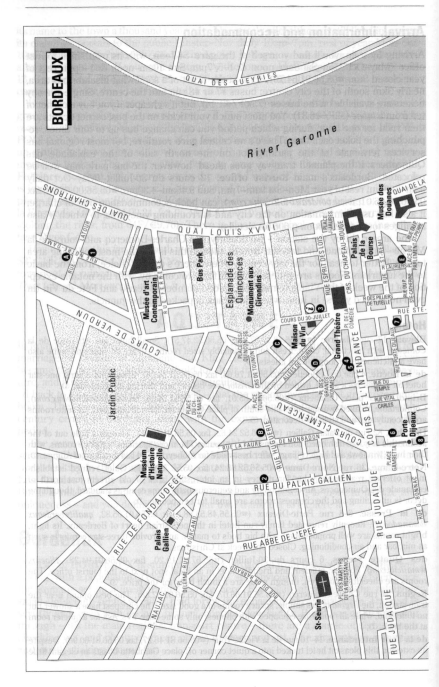

BORDEAUX

River Garonne

QUAI DES QUEYRIES

QUAI LOUIS XVIII

QUAI DES CHARTRONS

Musée des Douanes

Palais de la Bourse

Bus Park

Esplanade des Quinconces

Monument aux Girondins

Musée d'art Contemporain

Maison du Vin

Grand Théâtre

Porte Dijeaux

Jardin Public

COURS DE VERDUN

Muséum d'Histoire Naturelle

Palais Gallien

RUE DU PALAIS GALLIEN

RUE ABBE DE L'EPEE

St-Seurin

COURS DE L'INTENDANCE

COURS CLEMENCEAU

RUE JUDAIQUE

RUE DE FONDAUDEGE

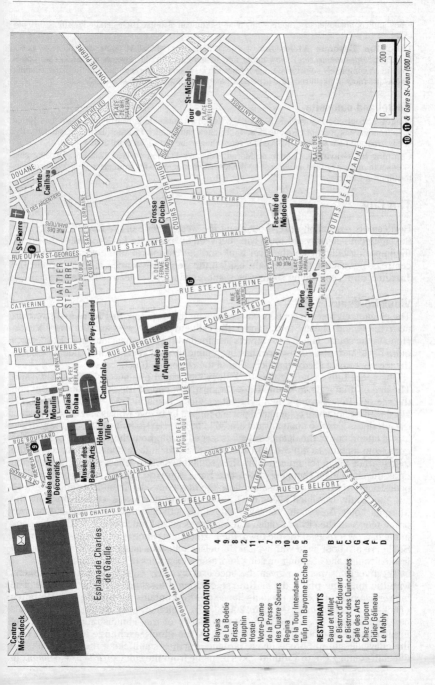

10 11 & Gare St-Jean (500 m) ▽

ACCOMMODATION

Blayais	4
de La Boétie	9
Bristol	8
Dauphin	2
Hostel	11
Notre-Dame	1
de la Presse	7
des Quatre Soeurs	3
Regina	10
de la Tour Intendance	6
Tulip Inn Bayonne Etche-Ona	5

RESTAURANTS

Baud et Millet	B
Le Bistrot d'Edouard	E
Le Bistrot des Quinconces	C
Café des Arts	G
Chez Dupont	A
Didier Gélineau	F
Le Mably	D

lobby and comfortable, airy rooms – all en suite. You can also use their garage for 40F/€6.10 per night. ③.

Tulip Inn Bayonne Etche-Ona, 4 rue Martignac (☎05.56.48.00.88, fax 05.56.48.41.60, *bayetche@bordeaux-hotel.com*). Now under new ownership, the old *Bayonne* and *Etche-Ona* hotels have been completely refurbished, the former in classy contemporary chic and the latter echoing its Basque roots in plush reds and greens. All mod cons and attentive service. ⑤–⑥.

Hostel and campsite

Hostel, 22 cours Barbey (☎05.56.91.59.51). Situated off cours de la Marne, the hostel is a 10min walk from gare St-Jean, or take bus #7 or #8. Kitchen and laundry facilities. Drawbacks include the seedy area and poor security. (Closed for renovations; due to reopen April 2001.)

Camping les Gravières, Chemin de Macau, Villenave-d'Ornon (☎05.56.87.00.36). Two-star site, 8km south of gare St-Jean, in a forest by the River Garonne. Bus #B from place de la Victoire to its terminus at Courejean.

The City

Bordeaux is reasonably spread out along the western side of the River Garonne, with the eighteenth-century **old town** lying between the **place de la Comédie** to the north, the imposing buildings of the river bank and the **cathedral** to the west. North of the centre is the vast open square of the **esplanade des Quinconces**, and further still, the **Jardin Public**, containing some very scant remains of Bordeaux's Roman past.

Vieux Bordeaux

The elegant, eighteenth-century city centres on the **quartier St-Pierre** and stretches up to the Grand Théâtre to the north, the cathedral to the west and the cours Victor-Hugo to the south. The narrow streets are lined with grand mansions from Bordeaux's glory days, and much of the area has been done up over recent years, though some of the streets remain seedy in anticipation of the restorer's touch.

The social hub of the eighteenth-century city was the impeccably classical **Grand Théâtre** on **place de la Comédie** at the northern end of rue Ste-Catherine. Built on the site of a Roman temple by the architect Victor Louis in 1780, this lofty building is faced with an immense colonnaded portico topped by twelve Muses and Graces. Inside, the interior is likewise opulently decorated in *trompe l'œil* paintings; the best way to see it is to attend one of the operas or ballets staged throughout the year, with seats in the gods from as little as 40F/€6.10 (☎05.56.00.85.95 for info & bookings), or ask at the tourist office about the guided tours they sometimes offer. Smart streets radiate from here: the city's main shopping street, **rue Ste-Catherine**, running south and partially pedestrianized to ease the consumer flow; the ritzy cours de l'Intendance running west; and the sandy, tree-lined allées de Tourny running northwest, commemorating the Marquis Louis Aubert de Tourny – the eighteenth-century administrator who was prime mover of the city's "Golden Age" and supervised much of the rebuilding. Back in the narrow streets of the old town, the harmonious **place du Parlement** and **place St-Pierre** are both lined with typical Bordelais mansions and peppered with wrought-iron balconies and arcading, making impressive examples of town planning.

The riverfront was also given the once-over by early eighteenth-century planners, with the imposing **place de la Bourse** creating a focal point on the quayside. The impressive bulk of the old customs house of 1733 contains the **Musée des Douanes** (Tues–Sun 10am–noon & 1–5/6pm; 20F/€3.05), which gives a rundown on Bordeaux's port and seafaring past and retraces the history of the administration and work of French Customs. The square is balanced by the **stock exchange** looking out over the quayside and the broad River Garonne. Further south along the river bank, the fifteenth-century **Porte Cailhau** takes its name from the stones (*cailloux – cailhaux* in dialect) unloaded on the neighbouring quay to be used as ballast for boats. Crossing the river just south of here, the only testimony to a nobler past is the impressive **Pont de Pierre** – "Stone Bridge", though in fact it's mostly brick – built at Napoléon's command during the Spanish campaigns, with seventeen arches in honour of his victories. The views of the river and quays from here are memorable, particularly when floodlit at night.

Place Gambetta, the cathedral and around

Cours de l'Intendance, a street lined with chic shops, links place de la Comédie with café-lined **place Gambetta**, a pivotal square for the city's museums, shops and the cathedral. Once a majestic space conceived as an architectural whole in the time of Louis XV, place Gambetta's house fronts are arcaded at street level and decorated with rows of carved masks. In the middle of the square a valiant attempt at an English garden adds some welcome relief, belying the fact that the guillotine lopped three hundred heads here at the time of the Revolution. In one corner stands the eighteenth-century arch of the **Porte Dijeaux**, an old city gate.

South of place Gambetta is the **Cathédrale St-André** (Mon–Sat 7.30–11.30am & 2–6/6.30pm), whose most eye-catching feature is the great upward sweep of the twin steeples over the north transept, an effect heightened by the adjacent but separate bell tower, the fifteenth-century **Tour Pey-Berland** (June–Sept daily 10am–6.30pm; rest of year Tues–Sun 10am–noon & 2–5pm; 25F/€3.81). The interior of the cathedral, begun in the twelfth century, is not particularly interesting, apart from the choir, which provides one of the few complete examples of the florid late Gothic style known as *Rayonnant*, and the north transept door and the Porte Royale to the right, which feature some fine carving.

The cream of Bordeaux's museums is to be found scattered in the streets around the cathedral. Directly behind the classical Hôtel de Ville, formerly Archbishop Rohan's palace, the **Musée des Beaux-Arts** (daily except Tues 11am–6pm; 20F/€3.05) has a small but worthy selection of European fine art, featuring works by Reynolds, Titian, Rubens, Matisse and Marquet (a native of the city), as well as Delacroix's superb painting of *La Grèce sur les ruines de Missolonghi*. More engaging, however, is the **Musée des Arts Décoratifs** (Mon & Wed–Fri 11am–6pm, Sat & Sun 2–6pm; 15F/€2.29), two blocks north in rue Bouffard and housed in a handsome eighteenth-century house. The extensive collection includes some beautiful, mainly French, porcelain and *faïence*, period furniture, glass, miniatures, Barye animal sculptures and prints of the city in its maritime heyday.

Continuing to circle clockwise round the cathedral, you'll pass the **Centre National Jean-Moulin** (Tues–Fri 11am–6pm, Sat & Sun 2–6pm; free), a moderately interesting museum dedicated to the local Resistance, before reaching the imaginatively laid-out **Musée d'Aquitaine**, on cours Pasteur (Tues–Sun 11am–6pm; 20F/€3.05), one of the city's best museums. A stimulating variety of objects and types of display emphasizes regional ethnography and covers the three main facets of the region's development: maritime, commercial and agricultural. Drawings and writings of the period enable you to see why eighteenth-century Bordeaux was so extolled by contemporary writers, who compared it to Paris. It's also worth taking a look at the section on the wine trade before venturing off on a vineyard tour in the region (see box on p.606). A couple of blocks east, rue St-James is straddled by a heavy Gothic tower, the fifteenth-century **Grosse Cloche**, originally part of the medieval town hall.

North of the centre

North of the Grand Théâtre, cours du 30-Juillet leads into the bare, gravelly – and frankly unattractive – expanse of the **esplanade des Quinconces**, said to be

Europe's largest municipal square. At the quayside end are two tall columns, erected in 1829 and topped by allegorical statues of Commerce and Navigation; at the opposite end of the esplanade is the **Monument aux Girondins**, a glorious *fin-de-siècle* ensemble of statues and fountains built in honour of the influential local deputies to the 1789 Revolutionary Assembly, later purged by Robespierre as moderates and counter-revolutionaries. During World War II, in a fit of anti-French spite, the occupying Germans made plans to melt the monument down, only to be foiled by the local Resistance, who got there first and, under cover of darkness, dismantled it piece by piece and hid it in a barn in the Médoc for the duration of the war.

To the northwest is the beautiful formal park, the **Jardin Public** (daily: April–Oct 7am–8/9pm; rest of year 7am–6pm; free), containing the city's botanical gardens. Behind it, to west and north, lies a quiet, provincial quarter of two-storey stone houses. Concealed among the narrow streets, on rue Dr-Albert-Barraud, is a large chunk of brick and stone masonry, the so-called **Palais Gallien**, in fact a third-century arena that's all that remains of *Burdigala*, Aquitaine's Roman capital. Nearby, on place Delerme, the unusual round **market hall** makes a focus for a stroll through the quarter. To the east of the gardens, closer to the river, the **Musée d'Art Contemporain** on rue Ferrère (Tues–Sun 11am–6pm; 30F/€4.57) occupies a converted nineteenth-century warehouse for colonial imports. The vast, arcaded hall provides a magnificent setting for the mostly post-1960 sculpture and installation-based work by artists such as Richard Long, Daniel Buren and Sol LeWitt. Few pieces from the permanent collection are on display at any one time, the main space being filled by temporary exhibitions, so it's hit or miss as to whether you'll like what's on offer. However, there's also a superb collection of glossy art books in the first-floor library and an elegant designer café-restaurant on the roof (lunch only).

Further out, the **Conservatoire International de la Plaisance**, in Dock no. 2 off bd Alfred-Daney (Wed–Sun 1–6pm; 30F/€4.57), an old German submarine base, with concrete walls and roof up to 9m thick, has been converted into an unusual museum combining pleasure boats and naval history.

Eating and drinking

Bordeaux is packed with numerous **restaurants**, many of them top-notch, and due to its position close to the Atlantic coast, fresh seafood features prominently on many a Bordelais menu. The best place to look for restaurants is around place du Parlement and place St-Pierre, where you'll find something to please all tastes and budgets. There are numerous sandwich bars and fast-food outlets at the south end of rue Ste-Catherine and spilling into studenty place de la Victoire. In recent summers, *guinguettes* – open-air **riverside stalls** selling shrimps, king prawns and other seafood snacks – have proved a huge success, and they set up along the quai des Chartrons. Surprisingly, Bordeaux lacks any truly grand, people-watching **cafés**. Though *Café Regent* on place Gambetta is the place to be seen, a nicer, cheaper alternative is to be found across the square at *Café Dijeaux* beside the city gate. For **picnic fodder**, there is a marvellous, round **market** in the place des Grand-Hommes, north of cours de l'Intendance. And on rue de Montesquieu, just off the square, Jean d'Alos runs the city's best *fromagerie*, with dozens of farm-produced cheeses.

Bordeaux's student population ensures a collection of young, lively **bars**, a host of which are found on and around place de la Victoire. Several offer live music and all are packed on Thursday nights. There's also a clutch of English, Irish and antipodean **pubs** now in Bordeaux and a low-key **gay scene** concentrated at the south end of rue des Remparts.

Cafés and restaurants

Baud et Millet, 19 rue Huguerie (☎05.56.79.05.77). The ultimate cheese-and-wine feast consumed around a few tables at the back of a wine shop where you choose your own bottle from the shelves. Most entrées and main courses are cheese-based – from a flaky-pastry starter filled with melted Jura and a creamy chive sauce to oven-baked Gouda with smoked salmon. Portions are generous and the food rich, so one dish goes a long way. Menus from 140F/€21.34. Closed Sun.

Le Bistrot d'Édouard, 16 place du Parlement. Undeniably touristy place, but in a great position on a lovely square, with outdoor seating in summer. There's a good-value, three-course menu (lunch 60F/€9.15; evening 70F/€10.67) offering a choice of regional dishes, as well as standard brasserie fare. If they're full, try the slightly more upmarket sister-restaurant, *L'Ombrière*, next door. Closed Sun evening Nov–Feb.

Le Bistrot des Quinconces, 4 place des Quinconces (☎05.56.52.84.56). Lively bistro which doubles as a daytime café and an early-evening tapas bar (7.30–8pm). In fine weather locals vie for the outdoor tables in a great spot facing the fountains. The modern, eclectic *carte* includes main dishes from around 70F/€10.67, with a three-course weekday lunch menu at 80F/€12.20.

Café des Arts, 138 cours Victor-Hugo. This café-brasserie on the corner of rue Ste-Catherine is one of the city's few old-style cafés, its unique ambience created from faded relics of the 1940s. The food is good, too, and the kitchens stay open till 1am, while twice-monthly free jazz concerts – mostly 1960s, acoustic – pack them in.

Chez Dupont, 45 rue de Notre-Dame (☎05.56.81.49.59). Bustling, old-fashioned restaurant in the Chartrons district, with wooden floors, old posters and waiters sporting colourful waistcoats. Their seasonal menus include *pot-au-feu*, *boudin*, foie gras and *crevettes* from Royan. Prices are very reasonable, with a two-course lunch for 62F/€9.45, and full menus from 140F/€21.34.

Didier Gélineau, 26 rue du Pas-St-Georges (☎05.56.52.84.25). One of the high spots of Bordeaux cuisine where you can eat exquisitely cooked, imaginative food at affordable prices. Seasonal dishes include foie gras, truffles, lobster and pigeon, all beautifully presented in an elegant dining room. Menus 130–300F/€19.82–45.73. Closed Sat lunch & Sun.

Le Mably, 12 rue Mably (☎05.56.44.30.10). Informal, friendly and popular restaurant with a warm, bistro atmosphere. Choose from a variety of *formules* starting with a *plat du jour* at 55F/€8.38 or three-course menus from 120F/€18.29. The food is plentiful and of excellent quality: lots of fish and local produce such as *magret* with acacia-flower honey or *rascass* topped with a knob of foie gras. Closed Sun & Mon.

Bars

Bar de l'Hôtel de Ville (BHV), 4 rue de l'Hôtel-de-Ville. Friendly little gay café-bar which stages a variety of free events every other Sunday (10.30pm).

Calle Ocho, 24 rue des Piliers-de-Tutelle (☎05.56.48.08.68). Bordeaux's best known and liveliest salsa bar is packed out on Friday and Saturday nights. They serve real Cuban rum and *mojitos*, a traditional drink of mint, lemon, sugar, sparkling water and lots of rum, and the music is loud.

Connemara, 18 cours d'Albret. For the homesick pining for a pint of Guinness, this is Bordeaux's liveliest Irish pub, with free concerts or some other event most nights. You can fill up on cheap bar-snacks, such as fish and chips, Guinness pie and apple crumble, or eat upstairs in the suitably green restaurant (Mon–Sat only; *plat du jour* 60F/€9.15 including beer and coffee).

Dick Turpin's, 72 rue du Loup. Opposite the wisteria-filled courtyard of the municipal archives, this is a pretty good rendition of an English town pub with a great atmosphere and an international clientele. There's the standard range of beers – Guinness, Bass and Newcastle Brown – in addition to well-priced bar meals, and tea and cakes in the quieter afternoons. Happy hour 5.30–8.30pm.

Le Plana, 22 place de la Victoire. One of the more relaxed student hangouts around the square, though, like everywhere else, it's jumping on Thursday nights. Free live music on Sun (jazz), Mon & Tues (various).

Nightlife and entertainment

Since Bordeaux's **dance clubs** are constantly changing – places often come and go within six months – it's best to ask around for the latest hotspots. There are one or two discos in the city centre, such as *Paris-Pékin*, at 10 rue de la Merci (☎05.56.44.19.88), but the majority of clubs are spread out along southerly quai du Paludate, where things don't really get going until two in the morning and continue till around four or five; Sunday is generally closing day. One of the district's longer-lived clubs is *La Plage* at no. 40 (☎05.56.49.02.46), a fun disco in a tropical-beach setting, while the wonderfully Baroque *Shadow Lounge*, 5 rue Cabannac (☎05.56.49.36.93), plays house and techno.

To find out the latest **events and happenings** in and around Bordeaux, get hold of a copy of the regional newspaper *Sud-Ouest*. Alternatively there are the fortnightly listings booklet *Spectaculair 33* (3F/€0.46), the free but less comprehensive *Bordeaux Plus* and *Clubs & Concerts*, also free, detailing the city's current favourite clubs. The tourist office issues *Bordeaux Magazine*, a free monthly with coverage of more highbrow cultural events around town. To buy **tickets** for city and regional events, contact the venue direct or head for the box office (☎05.56.48.26.26) in the nineteenth-century Galerie Bordelaise arcade, wedged between rue Ste-Catherine and rue des Piliers-de-Tutelle. Virgin Megastore (☎05.56.56.05.55) on place Gambetta also has a ticket outlet.

Jazz and blues fans should head south down the river to the *Comptoir du Jazz*, 59 quai de Paludate (05.56.49.15.55); entry is free but you are expected to buy at least a drink. Other options are the *Café des Arts* (see p.603) and the more frenetic *L'Alligator*, 3 place du Général-Sarrail (☎05.56.92.78.47), which blasts out the blues on Wednesday nights.

There's no shortage of more **contemporary music**, either. Rock is alive and kicking at *Le Barclay*, 57 cours de l'Argonne (☎05.56.31.44.66), a music-bar near place de la Victoire, and near the station at the *Rock School Barbey*, 18 cours Barbey (☎05.56.33.66.00). *Le Jimmy*, 68 rue de Madrid (☎05.56.98.20.83), meanwhile, is perhaps Bordeaux's most famous rock-bar, popular for its DJ nights and a programme ranging from heavy metal to techno.

Listings

Airlines Air France, 29 rue Esprit-des-Lois (☎05.56.44.05.69 or 08.02.80.28.02, *www.airfrance.com*); Air Liberté (☎08.03.80.58.05) has a desk at Mérignac airport (☎05.56.34.54.55); British Airways (☎08.02.80.29.02, *www.britishairways.com*) also has an airport desk.

Airport Bordeaux-Mérignac, 12km west of the city (☎05.56.34.50.50, *www.bordeaux.aeroport.fr*), is connected by half-hourly shuttle to and from the main tourist office (30–45min; 35F/€5.34).

Bike rental Bord'eaux Velo Loisirs (☎05.56.44.77.31), on quai Louis-XVIII beside the Quinconces boat dock, rents out everything from bikes to roller blades and baby-strollers (closed Mon & Thurs; open afternoons only Oct–May). Another option is Cycles Pasteur at 42 cours Pasteur (☎05.56.92.68.20).

Books and newspapers Maison de la Presse, at 61 rue Ste-Catherine and place Gambetta, sells the main English-language papers in addition to some regional guides and maps. Bordeaux's largest bookstore, Mollat, 15 rue Vital-Carles, has a good selection of local guides and maps. They also stock a few English-language titles, though there's a better choice at helpful Bradley's Bookshop, 8 cours d'Albret (*www.bradleys-bookshop.com*).

Car rental Numerous rental firms are located in and around the train station, including Avis (☎05.56.91.65.50); Budget (☎05.56.31.41.40); Europcar (☎05.56.31.20.30); Hertz (☎05.57.59.05.95); and National/Citer (☎05.56.92.19.62). They all have outlets at the airport as well: Avis (☎05.56.34.38.22); Budget (☎05.56.47.84.22); Europcar (☎05.56.34.05.79); Hertz (☎05.56.34.59.59); National/Citer (☎05.56.34.20.68).

Cinema You're most likely to find original-language (*version originale*, or *v.o.*) films at the wonderful art-house cinema Utopia, 5 place Camille-Jullian (☎05.56.52.00.03), in a converted church. Other good options include Trianon-Jean Vigo, 6 rue Franklin, near place des Grands-Hommes (☎05.56.44.35.17), and UGC Cinécité, 13–15 rue Georges-Bonnac (☎08.36.68.68.58). For more standard fare, there's the vast, new seventeen-screen Megarama (☎08.36.69.33.17) across the Pont de Pierre in the old Gare d'Orléans.

Consulates UK, 353 bd du Président-Wilson (☎05.57.22.21.10).

Emergencies To call an ambulance, phone SAMU on ☎15 or 05.56.96.70.70.

Hitching Allostop, 79 cours d'Argonne (☎05.57.95.60.74).

Hospital Centre Hospitalier Pellegrin-Tripode, place Amélie-Raba-Léon (☎05.56.79.56.79), to the west of central Bordeaux.

Internet *Cyberstation*, 23 cours Pasteur, is a friendly and helpful cyber café with rates from 5F/€0.76 for five minutes to 40F/€6.10 per hour.

Money exchange American Express, 14 cours de l'Intendance (Mon–Fri 8.45am–noon & 1.30–5.30pm), handles most travellers' cheques and foreign currencies. The main banks along cours de l'Intendance also offer exchange facilities and 24hr ATMs.

Police Commissariat Central, 87 rue Abbé-de-l'Épée (☎05.56.99.77.77), or call ☎17.

The Bordeaux wine region

Touring the **vineyards** and sampling a few local wines is one of the great pleasures of the Bordeaux region. The wine-producing districts lie in a great semi circle around the city, starting with the **Médoc** in the north, then skirting west through **St-Émilion**, before finishing south of the city among the vineyards of the **Sauternes**. In between, the less prestigious districts are also worth investigating, notably those of **Blaye**, to the north of Bordeaux, and **Entre-Deux-Mers**, to the west.

There's more to the region than its wine alone, however. Many of the Médoc's eighteenth-century châteaux are striking buildings in their own right, while the town of Blaye is dominated by a vast fortress, and there's a far older, more ruined castle at Villandraut on the edge of the Sauternes. St-Émilion is by far the prettiest of the wine towns, and has the unexpected bonus of a cavernous underground church. For scenic views, however, you can't beat the green, gentle hills of Entre-Deux-Mers and its ruined abbey, **La Sauve-Majeur**.

All these places are relatively well served by **public transport**. There are train lines from Bordeaux running north through the Médoc to Margaux and Pauillac, and south along the Garonne valley to St-Macaire and La Réole. St-Émilion, meanwhile, lies on the Bordeaux–Sarlat line, but the station is a couple of kilometres out of town. In addition, there's a very comprehensive regional bus network, with connections from Bordeaux to most of the towns mentioned below – you can pick up a route map at the tourist office in Bordeaux (see p.597). Though the buses are operated by several different companies, there's a central information service on ☎05.56.99.57.83.

The Médoc

The landscape of **the Médoc**, a slice of land northwest of Bordeaux wedged between the forests bordering the Atlantic coast and the Gironde estuary, is itself rather monotonous: its gravel plains, occupying the west bank of the brown, island-spotted estuary, rarely swell into anything resembling a hill. Paradoxically, however, this poor soil is ideal for viticulture – vines root more deeply if they don't find the sustenance they need in the topsoil and, firmly rooted, they are less subject to drought and flooding. The region's eight *appellations* – Médoc, Haut Médoc, St-Estèphe, Pauillac, St-Julien, Moulis en Médoc, Listrac-Médoc and Margaux – produce only red wines, from the grape varieties of Cabernet Sauvignon, Cabernet Franc, Merlot and, to a lesser degree, Petit Verdot. Cabernet Sauvignon gives body, bouquet, colour and maturing potential to the wine, while Merlot gives it its "animal" quality, making it rounder and softer. The D2 wine road, heading off the N15 from Bordeaux, passes through Margaux, St-Julien, Pauillac and St-Estèphe and, while the scenery might not be stunning, the many famous – albeit mostly inaccessible – châteaux are.

THE WINES OF BORDEAUX

With Burgundy and Champagne, the **wines of Bordeaux** form the "Holy Trinity" of French viticulture. Despite producing as many whites as reds, it is the latter – known as claret to the British – that have graced the tables of the discerning for centuries. The countryside that produces them encircles the city, enjoying near-perfect climatic conditions and soils ranging from limestone to sand and pebbles. It is the largest quality wine district in the world, turning out around 500 million bottles a year – over half the country's quality wine output.

The Gironde estuary, fed by the Garonne and the Dordogne, determines the lie of the land. The **Médoc** lies northwest of Bordeaux between the Atlantic coast and the River Gironde, with its vines deeply rooted in poor gravelly soil, producing good, full-bodied red wines; the region's eight *appellations* are Médoc, Haut Médoc, St-Estèphe, Pauillac, St-Julien, Moulis en Médoc, Listrac-Médoc and Margaux. Southwest of Bordeaux are the vast vineyards of **Graves**, producing the best of the region's dry white wines, along with some punchy reds, from some of the most prestigious communes in France – Pessac, Talence, Martillac and Villenave d'Ornon amongst them. They spread down to Langon and envelop the areas of **Sauternes** and **Barsac**, whose extremely sweet white dessert wines are considered among the world's best.

On the east side of the Gironde estuary and the Dordogne, the **Côtes de Blaye** feature some good-quality white table wines, mostly dry, and a smaller quantity of reds. The **Côtes de Bourg** specialize in solid whites and reds, spreading down to the renowned **St-Émilion** area. Here, there are a dozen producers who have earned the accolade of *Premiers Grands Crus Classés*, and their output is a full, rich red wine that doesn't have to be kept as long as the Médoc wines. Lesser-known neighbouring areas include the vineyards of **Pomerol**, **Lalande** and **Côtes de Francs**, all producing reds similar to St-Émilion but at more affordable prices.

Between Garonne and Dordogne is **Entre-Deux-Mers**, an area which yields large quantities of inexpensive, drinkable table whites, mainly from the Sauvignon grape. The less important sweet whites of **Ste-Croix du Mont** come out of the area south of

The problem of accommodation is much worse in the Médoc than in the rest of the wine region, but it's possible to visit the region on a day-trip from Bordeaux. Considering it's one of the most prestigious wine-growing areas in Bordeaux, it's surprisingly unwelcoming to visitors, with places to eat, and particularly affordable ones, also in short supply. There are regular bus services to Pauillac, but it's worth considering car rental (see Bordeaux "Listings", p.604).

Château Margaux and Fort Médoc

Easily the prettiest of the Bordeaux châteaux, **Château Margaux** is an eighteenth-century villa in extensive, sculpture-dotted gardens close to the west bank of the Gironde, some 20km north of Bordeaux. Its wine, a classified *Premier Grand Cru* and world-famous in the 1940s and 1950s, went through a rough patch in the two succeeding decades but improved in the 1980s after the estate was bought by a Greek family. The château (by appointment only Mon–Fri 10am–noon & 2–4pm; closed Aug and during harvest; ☎05.57.88.83.83, *www.chateau-margaux.com*; free) is not included in any tours, and it's best to book at least two weeks in advance.

In the small village of **MARGAUX** itself, there's an unusually friendly **Maison du Vin** (daily: July & Aug 9am–7pm; rest of year 9am–noon & 2–6pm; ☎05.57.88.70.82, fax 05.57.88.38.27, *syndicat.margaux@wanadoo.fr*) that can book accommodation and advise on visits to the *appellation*'s châteaux. At the other end of the village, the enterprising cellar La Cave d'Ulysse provides free tastings from a variety of Margaux

Cadillac. Stretching along the north bank of the Garonne, the vineyards of the **Côtes de Bordeaux** feature fruity reds and a smaller number of dry and sweet whites.

The **classification** of Bordeaux wines is an extremely complex affair. Apart from the usual *appellation d'origine contrôlée* (AOC) labelling – guaranteeing origin but not quality – the wines of the Médoc châteaux are graded into five *crus*, or growths. These were established as long ago as 1855, based on the prices the wines had fetched over the previous hundred years. Four were voted the best or *Premiers Grands Crus Classés*: Margaux, Lafitte, Latour and Haut-Brion. With the exception of Château Mouton-Rothschild, which moved up a class in 1973 to become the fifth *Premier Grand Cru Classé*, there have been no official changes, so divisions between the *crus* should not be taken too seriously. Since then, additional categories have been devised, for instance *Crus Bourgeois*, which has three categories of its own. The wines of Sauternes were also classified in 1855.

If you are interested in **buying wines**, it is possible to find bargains at some of the châteaux. Advantages of buying at source include the opportunity to sample before purchasing and to receive expert advice about different vintages. In Bordeaux, the best place to go is La Vinotèque (Mon–Sat 9.15am–7.30pm), next to the tourist office. In recent years tales of machine oil and chemical additives have shaken many people's confidence in wine drinking; as a result, there's a growing fashion for organic methods and "green" wines, already available on many good labels.

To **visit the châteaux**, Bordeaux's efficient Maison du Vin, just across the road from the tourist office (Mon–Fri 8.30am–5.30/6pm, late May to mid-Oct also Sat 9am–4.30pm), has various pamphlets detailing those châteaux which accept visitors. In addition, each wine-producing village has its own tourist office and Maison du Vin, which can provide the same service. Since getting to any of these places except St-Émilion without your own transport is hard work, the simplest thing is to take one of the Bordeaux tourist office's own half-day **guided tours**, covering a different area each day (May–Oct daily 1.30pm; rest of year Wed & Sat 1.30pm; 160F/€24.39). Generally interesting and informative, the guide translates into English the wine-maker's commentary and answers any questions. Tastings are generous, and expert tuition on how to go about it is part of the deal.

châteaux, giving you a chance to try and buy some very good wines. Margaux has a somewhat expensive but very comfortable **hotel**, *Le Pavillon de Margaux* (☎05.57.88.77.54, fax 05.57.88.77.73; ⑤), with a fine restaurant (menus from 89F/€13.57; closed Tues & Wed). Otherwise, try the *chambre d'hôte Domaine de Carrat* (☎ & fax 05.56.58.24.80; ④; closed Christmas & New Year) at **CASTELNAU-DE-MÉDOC**, 10km to the west. Besides the hotel, you can **eat** at Margaux's *Auberge de Savoie* (☎05.57.88.31.76; closed Sun, Mon evening out of season & last two weeks Feb), next to the Maison du Vin, with good traditional food and menus from 85F/€12.96.

The seventeenth-century **Fort Médoc**, off the D2 road between Margaux and St-Julien by the banks of the estuary, is a good place to tuck into a few purchases between châteaux. It was designed by the prolific military architect Vauban to defend the Gironde estuary against the British. The remains of the fort are scant but scrambleable, and in summer its Toytown aspect has a leafy charm, marred only by the view of a nuclear power station across the river to the north of Blaye. Since 1990, the annual Fort Médoc **jazz festival**, with big-name international acts, has been held here in mid-July (☎05.56.58.91.30 for details).

A couple of kilometres south, **LAMARQUE** is a very pretty village, full of flowers and with a sweet church. It's a pleasant place to stop for lunch, with a very agreeable restaurant, *L'Escale* (menus from 60F/€9.15; closed Wed & evenings off season), down by the port. From here at least four ferries (one way: passengers 18F/€2.74, cycles 9F/€1.37, cars 73F/€11.13) cross the Gironde daily to Blaye, another place fortified by Vauban, and an important, though less well-known, Bordeaux wine-growing centre (see opposite).

Pauillac and around

PAUILLAC is the largest town in the Médoc region and central to the most important vineyards of Bordeaux: no fewer than three of the top five *Grands Crus* come from around here. It has grown rapidly in recent years and, while its little harbour and riverfront are pretty enough, they can't counteract the presence of the nuclear power plant across the Gironde.

Pauillac has a huge **Maison du Tourisme et du Vin** along the waterfront (June & mid-Sept to Oct daily 9.30am–12.30pm & 2–6.30pm; July & Aug daily 9am–7pm; rest of year Mon–Sat 9.30am–12.30pm & 2–6pm, Sun 10am–12.30pm & 2.30–6pm; ☎05.56.59.03.08, fax 05.56.59.23.38, *www.pauillac-medoc.com*). It can provide you with a list of *gîtes*, rent out **bikes** and make appointments for you to visit the surrounding châteaux (25F/€3.81 per château). Pauillac itself is not a great **place to stay**, but should you wish to, try the *Hôtel de France et d'Angleterre*, opposite the little harbour (☎05.56.59.06.43, fax 05.56.59.02.31, *www.hotelfranceangleterre.com*; ④; closed Christmas & New Year), with a good restaurant serving menus from 75F/€11.43 (closed Sun & Mon off season), or the welcoming riverfront **campsite** further south on route de la Rivière (☎05.56.59.10.03; closed mid-Sept to March). Campsites are rare in the Médoc: the only other alternative is the two-star *Camping Le Bled* at **BERNOS** (☎05.56.59.41.33; closed mid-Sept to mid-June), 8km southwest near St-Laurent-de-Médoc, a peaceful, shady and clean option. Alternatively, there's an excellent *chambres d'hôte* about 8km northwest near the village of **CISSAC**: *Château Gugès* (☎05.56.59.58.04, fax 05.56.59.56.19; ④), in a large eighteenth-century house attached to a vineyard on the road to Gunes.

The most famous of the **Médoc châteaux** – Château Lafite-Rothschild (☎05.56.73.18.18), Château Latour (☎05.56.73.19.80) and Château Mouton-Rothschild (☎05.56.73.21.29) – can be visited by appointment only, either direct (all have English-speaking staff) or through the Maison du Vin. Their vineyards occupy larger single tracts of land than elsewhere in the Médoc, and consequently neighbouring wines can differ markedly: a good vintage Lafite is perfumed and refined, whereas a Mouton-Rothschild is strong and dark and should be kept for at least ten years. **Château Mouton-Rothschild** and its wine **museum** (April–Oct daily 9.30–11am & 2–4pm; rest of year closed Sat & Sun; 30F/€4.57, or 80F/€12.20 including one tasting) is the most absorbing of the big houses: as well as the viticultural stuff, you also get to see the Rothschilds' amazing collection of art treasures, all loosely connected with wine.

St-Estèphe

North of Pauillac, the wine commune of **ST-ESTÈPHE** is Médoc's largest *appellation*, consisting predominantly of *crus bourgeois* properties and growers belonging to the local *cave coopérative*, **Marquis de St-Estèphe**, on the D2 towards Pauillac (tastings July & Aug daily 9am–noon & 2–7pm; rest of year by appointment, ☎05.56.73.35.30). One of the *appellation*'s five *crus classés* is the distinctive **Château Cos d'Estournel**, with its over-the-top nineteenth-century French version of a pagoda; the *chais* can be visited by appointment (☎05.56.73.15.50; English spoken). The village of St-Estèphe itself is a sleepy affair dominated by its landmark, the eighteenth-century **church of St-Étienne**, with its highly decorative interior. The small, homespun **Maison du Vin** (April to mid-June & mid-Sept to Oct Mon–Fri 10am–noon & 2–6pm, Sat 2–6pm; mid-June to mid-Sept daily 9am–7pm; rest of year Mon–Fri 10am–noon & 2–5pm; ☎05.56.59.30.59) is hidden in the church square.

For an elegant place to **stay**, head for *Château Pomys* (☎05.56.59.73.44, fax 05.56.59.35.24; ④), just south of the village, a mansion set in its own park. There are also several good *chambres d'hôte* in the area, including *Clos de Puyzac* in Pez village (☎ & fax 05.56.59.35.28; ③) and, further along the same road near Vertheuil-en-Médoc, the hacienda-style *Cantemerle* (☎ & fax 05.56.41.96.24; ④), both with *tables d'hôte*.

Blaye

The green slopes north of the Garonne, the **Côtes de Bourg** and **Côtes de Blaye**, were home to wine production long before the Médoc was planted. The wine is a rather heavier, plummier red, and cheaper than anything found on the opposite side of the river, and the **Maison du Vin des Premières Côtes de Blaye** on cours Vauban (Mon–Sat 8.30am–12.15pm & 2–6pm), the main street of the pretty little town of **BLAYE**, serves up a representative selection of the local produce, with some ridiculously inexpensive wines – you can get a good bottle for 30–50F/€4.57–7.62.

The town was fortified again by Vauban, and the **citadelle** deserves a wander. People still live within it, and it's a strange combination of peaceful village and tourist attraction, typically with an old man sunning himself outside his tiny home, a revolving postcard rack only metres away. A beautiful spot, it has grass, trees, birds and a spectacular view over the Gironde estuary.

The riverfront **tourist office**, opposite the fort (July & Aug daily 9.30am–12.30pm & 2.30–7pm; rest of year Tues–Sat 9.30am–12.30pm & 2.30–6pm; ☎05.57.42.12.09, fax 05.57.42.91.94, *officedetourisme.blaye@wanadoo.fr*), is really helpful and can reserve rooms free of charge and give out details on wine-tasting. If you fancy **staying** here, try the *Auberge du Porche*, 5 rue Ernest-Régnier (☎05.57.42.22.69, fax 05.57.42.82.83; ③; closed one week in March & one week in Oct), a pleasant two-star further south along the riverfront with a good-value restaurant (closed Sun evening & Mon off season; from 58F/€8.84). Alternatively, there's the expensive *Hôtel La Citadelle* within the old fort with views over the Garonne (☎05.57.42.17.10, fax 05.57.42.10.34; ⑤; restaurant from 150F/€22.87). Finally, there's a small municipal **campsite** within the *citadelle* (☎05.57.42.00.20; closed Oct–April).

St-Émilion

ST-ÉMILION, 35km east of Bordeaux and a short trip by train from Bordeaux, is well worth a visit in its own right. The old grey houses of this fortified medieval town straggle down the south-hanging slope of a low hill, with the green froth of the summer's vines crawling over its walls. Many of the growers still keep up the old tradition of planting roses at the ends of the rows, which in pre-pesticide days served as an early-warning system against infection, the idea being that the commonest bug, *oidium*, went for the roses first, giving three days' notice of its intentions.

The Town

The town's **belfry** belongs to the rock-hewn subterranean **Église Monolithe** beneath it, which can be visited only on a **guided tour** from the tourist office (daily 10–11.30am & 2–5pm; 33F/€5.03). The tour starts in a dark hole in someone's backyard, supposedly the cave where St Émilion lived a hermit's life in the eighth century. A rough-hewn ledge served as his bed and a carved seat as his chair, where infertile women reputedly still come to sit in the hope of getting pregnant.

Above is the half-ruined thirteenth-century **Trinity Chapel**, which was built in honour of St Émilion and converted into a cooperage during the Revolution; fragments of frescoes are still visible, including a kneeling figure who is thought to be St Émilion,

On the other side of the yard, a passage tunnels beneath the belfry to the **catacombs**, where three chambers dug out of the soft limestone were used as ossuary and cemetery from the eighth to the eleventh centuries. In the innermost chamber – discovered by a neighbour enlarging his cellar some fifty years ago – an eleventh-century tombstone bears the inscription: "Aulius is buried between saints Valéry, Émilion and Avic", St Valéry being the patron saint of local wine-growers.

The ninth- and twelfth-century **church** itself is an incredible place. Simple and huge, the entire structure – barrel-vaulting, great square piers and all – has been hacked out of the rock. The impact has been somewhat diminished, however, by the installation of massive concrete supports after cracks were discovered in the bell tower above in 1990. The whole interior was painted once, but only faint traces survived the Revolution, when a gunpowder factory was installed here. These days, every June, the wine council – *La Jurade* – assembles in the church in distinctive red robes to evaluate the previous season's wine and decide whether each *viticulteur*'s produce deserves the *appellation contrôlée* rating.

Behind the tourist office, the town comes to an abrupt end with a grand view of the **moat** and old **walls**. To the right is the twelfth-century **collegiate church**, with a handsome but badly mutilated doorway and a lovely fourteenth-century **cloister**, accessed via the tourist office (same hours; free).

You should take advantage of the produce of this well-respected wine region, whose most famous wine originates at **Château Ausone**, immediately south of St-Émilion (not open to the public). If you are interested in visiting local vineyards, ask at the tourist office, which has detailed lists of those that are open, or at the **Maison du Vin** (Mon–Sat 9.30am–12.30pm & 2–6.30pm, Sun 10am–12.30pm & 2.30–6.30pm; ☎05.57.55.50.55), also at the top of the hill by the belfry.

Practicalities

The super-efficient **tourist office** on place des Créneaux by the belfry (daily: July & Aug 9.30am–8pm; rest of year 9.30am–12.30pm & 1.45–6/6.30pm; ☎05.57.55.28.28, fax 05.57.55.28.29, *st-emilion.tourisme@wanadoo.fr*) is a good source of information and organizes bilingual (French and English) vineyard tours in season (May–Sept; 51F/€7.77). They also have **bikes** for rent.

If you're short of funds or without your own transport, St-Émilion is best seen as a day-trip from Bordeaux, as there's a chronic shortage of budget **accommodation** within the town. However, the tourist office can furnish you with an extensive list of *chambres d'hôte* in the area, many of which are very reasonably priced. Within the town itself, the two-star *Auberge de la Commanderie* on rue des Cordeliers (☎05.57.24.70.19, fax 05.57.74.44.53; ④–⑤; closed mid-Jan to mid-Feb) offers the cheapest option. Three kilometres northwest in the village of Montagne, there's a fantastic three-star campsite, *La Barbanne* (☎05.57.24.75.80; closed mid-Oct to March), with its own swimming pool.

You should try the town's speciality while you're here: **macaroons** were devised here by the Ursuline sisters in 1620, and the one authentic place to buy them is at Blanchez, 9 rue Gaudet, where the tiny melt-in-the-mouth biscuits are baked to the original recipe. A good place for a **meal** is the relaxed contemporary-style bistro *L'Envers du Décor* (closed Sun Nov–April) on rue du Clocher, with *plats du jour* for 65F/€9.91 and local wine by the glass, which you can accompany with omelettes, cheese, salads and other light snacks.

Entre-Deux-Mers

The landscape of **Entre-Deux-Mers** (literally "between two seas") – so called because it is sandwiched between the tidal waters of the Dordogne and Garonne – is the prettiest of the Bordeaux wine regions, with its gentle hills and scattered medieval villages. Its wines, including the *Premières Côtes de Bordeaux*, are mainly dry whites produced by over forty *caves coopératives*, and are regarded as good but inferior to the Médocs or super-dry Graves to the south. It's also a region which can be explored, at least in part, by public transport, should you feel like avoiding the tourist office tour.

La Sauve-Majeure

The one place you should really try to see is the ruined **Abbey** (daily: June–Sept 10am–6.30pm; rest of year 10am–12.30pm & 2.30–5.30pm; 25F/€3.81) at **LA SAUVE-MAJEURE**, some 25km east of Bordeaux, an important stop for pilgrims en route to Santiago de Compostela in Spain. Once it was all forest here, the abbey's name being a corruption of the Latin *silva major* (big wood). It was founded in 1079, and the treasures of what remains are the twelfth-century Romanesque apse and apsidal chapels and the outstanding sculpted capitals in the chancel. The finest are the ones illustrating stories from the Old and New Testaments (Daniel in the lions' den, Delilah shearing Samson's hair and so on), while others show fabulous beasts and decorative motifs. There is a small **museum** at the entrance, with some excellent photos of the ruins, along with keystones from the fallen roofs. But what makes the visit so worthwhile is not just the capitals themselves, but the remote, undisturbed nature of the site.

St-Macaire and La Réole

If you're heading south through Entre-Deux-Mers, Langon is the first town of any size you come to. But **ST-MACAIRE**, across the Garonne from Langon, is far better for a rest or food stop. The village still has its original **gates** and **battlements** and a beautiful medieval church, the **Église-Prieuré**. The well-organized **tourist office**, 8 rue Canton (April–Sept Tues–Sat 10am–12.30pm & 2–6pm, Sun 2–7pm; rest of year Tues–Sat 10am–noon & 2–6pm; ☎05.56.63.32.14, fax 05.56.76.13.24), doubles as a Maison du Pays, promoting regional produce, which here means honey and wine. Staff can help arrange visits to the *chais*, and in season (April–June Sat & Sun; July & Aug daily) they organize tastings hosted by various local wine-makers. Opposite is a good **hotel**, *Les Feuilles d'Acanthe* (☎05.56.62.33.75, fax 05.56.76.12.02; closed Jan; ④), with a **restaurant** serving a choice of crêpes and more substantial regional dishes (weekday lunch menus from 50F/€7.62). Just below the walls is the small, two-star *Camping Les Remparts* (☎05.56.62.23.42; July & Aug only).

LA RÉOLE, on the north bank 18km further east, boasts a wealth of medieval architecture along a well-signposted walk through its narrow, hilly streets. France's oldest **town hall**, constructed for Richard the Lionheart in the twelfth century, and the well-preserved simple **Abbaye des Bénédictins** – with a fantastic view over the River Garonne and the surrounding countryside – reward a stroll through the town, although little remains of the fortified **castle**.

La Réole's **tourist office** is on place de la Libération (Easter–Oct Mon 3–6pm, Tues–Sat 9am–noon & 3–6pm, Sun 3–6pm; rest of year closed Sun; ☎05.56.61.13.55, fax 05.56.71.25.40), and it conducts tours of the sights in July and August. For **accommodation**, the two-star *Hôtel de l'Abbaye*, 42 rue Armand-Caduc (☎05.56.61.02.64, fax 05.56.71.24.40; ③), on the road up to the abbey, is a bit chaotic, but the rooms are clean and not too bad for the price. A good **restaurant** is *Les Fontaines* on rue du Verdun (closed Sun evening & Mon, also fifteen days in Feb & Nov), serving classic French cuisine, albeit with a modern touch, and a wide choice of menus from 85F/€12.96 to 240F/€36.59. A lively Saturday **market** on the esplanade des Quais along the Garonne provides good picnic provisions.

Sauternes and around

The **Sauternes** region, which extends southeast from Bordeaux for 40km along the left bank of the Garonne, is an ancient wine-making area, originally planted during the Roman occupation. The distinctive golden wine of the area is certainly sweet, but also round, full-bodied and spicy, with a long aftertaste. It's not necessarily a dessert wine, either: try it with some Roquefort cheese or with foie gras. Gravelly terraces with a limestone sub soil help create the delicious taste, but mostly it's due to a peculiar micro-climate of morning autumn mists and afternoons of sun and heat which causes *Botrytis cinerea* fungus, or "noble rot", to flourish on the grapes, letting the sugar concentrate and introducing some intense flavours. When they're picked, they're not a pretty sight: carefully selected by hand, only the most shrivelled, rotting bunches are taken. The wines of Sauternes make up some of the most highly sought-after in the world, with bottles of Château d'Yquem, in particular, fetching thousands of francs.

SAUTERNES itself is a fairly quiet little village surrounded by vines and dominated by the **Maison du Sauternes** (Mon–Fri 9am–7pm, Sat & Sun 10am–7pm; ☎05.56.76.69.83) at one end of the village, with a pretty church at the other. The *maison* is a room full of treasures, the golden bottles with white and gold labels being quite beautiful objects in themselves. Although they do offer tastings, staff are unfortunately rather snooty about it, unless you obviously intend to buy.

There are two good places to **eat** in Sauternes. By the church, the *Auberge Les Vignes* (☎05.56.76.60.06; closed Mon evening & Feb) is a typical country restaurant with regional specialities like *grillades aux Sauternes* (meats grilled over vine clippings), a great wine list and a menu at 65F/€9.91. The other option is the more refined *Le Saprien* (☎05.56.76.60.87; closed Christmas & Feb, also Mon and for dinner Sun & Wed), opposite the tourist office, combining regional-style elements with modern eclectic additions and featuring menus from 119F/€18.14.

Ten kilometres south of Sauternes, the ruinous curtain walls and corner towers of a colossal moated **Château** (daily: Jan–April & Oct–Dec 2–5pm; June & Sept 10am–12.30pm & 2–7pm; July & Aug 10am–7pm; 20F/€3.05) still dominate **VILLAN-DRAUT**. The castle was built by Pope Clement V, a native of the area who caused a schism by moving the papacy to Avignon in the fourteenth century. You can visit his tomb in the even smaller village of **UZESTE** on route to **BAZAS**, 15km east, with its laid-back, southern air. Bazas' most attractive feature is the wide, arcaded place de la Cathédrale, overlooked by the grey, lichen-covered **Cathédrale St-Jean-Baptiste**, which displays a harmonious blend of Romanesque, Gothic and classical styles in its west front.

For places to **stay** in Bazas try the cheap, friendly *Hostellerie St-Sauveur*, 14 cours du Général-de-Gaulle (☎05.56.25.12.18; ②; closed Sun Oct–June), or the plush *Domaine de Fompeyre*, on the southern edge of town (☎05.56.25.98.00, fax 05.56.25.16.25, *fompeyre@ot-sauternes.com*; ⑨; closed Sun evening Nov to mid-April), which has a restaurant (from 180F/€27.44). Other good places to **eat** are *Les Remparts*, off the central square (☎05.56.25.95.24; closed Sun evening & Mon, and evenings Nov–March), for delicious local specialities and menus from 70F/€10.67, and the cosy *Bistrot St-Jean* nearby (lunch only Oct–May; from 75F/€11.43).

The Côte d'Argent

The **Côte d'Argent** is the long stretch of coast from the mouth of the Gironde estuary to Biarritz, which – at over 200km – is the longest, straightest and sandiest in Europe. The endless beaches are backed by high sand dunes, while behind lies the largest forest in western Europe, **Les Landes**. Despite these attractions, the lack of conventional tourist sights means that outside July and August the coast gets comparatively few visitors, and away from the main resorts it is still possible to find deserted stretches of coastline.

Arcachon

On summer weekends, the Bordelais escape en masse to **ARCACHON**, the oldest resort on the Côte d'Argent and a forty-minute train ride across flat, sandy forest from Bordeaux. The beaches of white sand are magnificent but can be crowded, and its central jetties, Thiers and Eyrac, are busy with boats going off on an array of cruises to places like the Île aux Oiseaux and the Dune de Pyla.

The town itself is a sprawl of villas great and small, the most exclusive area being the **ville d'hiver** (winter town), whose wide shady streets are full of fanciful Second Empire mansions overlooking the seaside **ville d'été** (summer town). Well worth a wander, the area can be reached by following the lively pedestrianized and restaurant-filled rue de Maréchal-de-Lattre-de-Tassigny, running perpendicular to the seafront boulevard de la Plage; at the end of this mouthful of a street, a lift (daily 9am–12.45pm & 2.30–7pm) carries you up to the flower-filled, wooded **Parc Mauresque** (daily: April–Oct 7am–10pm; rest of year 8am–7.30pm; free), with the *ville d'hiver* beyond it. From the park, there are fine views over the seafront.

Practicalities

A well-stocked **tourist office**, esplanade Georges-Pompidou (July & Aug 9am–6pm, Sun 10am–1pm; rest of year Mon–Sat 9am–12.30pm & 2–6pm, Sun 10am–1pm; ☎05.57.52.97.97, fax 05.57.52.97.77, *tourisme@arcachon.com*), can be reached by following avenue Gambetta back from seafront place Thiers. In summer boats leave the jetties of Thiers and Eyrac on various **cruises**, including the Île aux Oiseaux (2hr; 75F/€11.43), an exploration of the Arcachon basin with a look at the Dune de Pyla (2hr 30min; 75F/€11.43), and a visit to an oyster farm with tasting (1hr 15min; 65F/€9.91). There's also a regular boat service from here to Cap Ferret on the opposite peninsula (30min; 60F/€9.15 return).

You'll be hard-pushed to find an inexpensive **hotel**, but a couple of reasonable ones are the small, friendly *Le Pergola*, 40 cours Lamarque-de-Plaisance (☎05.56.83.07.89, fax 05.56.83.14.21; ③), and the *St-Christaud*, 8 allée de la Chapelle (☎05.56.83.38.53; ①–②); half-board only July & Aug, ⑤), further out of town. Pricier options include the *Marinette*, 15 allée José-Maria-de-Hérédia (☎05.56.83.06.67, fax 05.56.83.09.59; ④; closed mid-Nov to mid-March), and the luxurious *Villa Térésa*, 4 allée Rebsomen (☎05.56.83.25.87, fax 05.57.52.22.41; ⑤), both in the *ville d'hiver*. Alternatively, there are many **holiday apartments** to rent; ask for the booklet *Clévacances* from the tourist office. **Camping** is another option, with plenty of sites around the Arcachon basin, though only the three-star *Le Camping Club*, allée de la Galaxie (☎05.56.83.24.15), is actually within the town; set in an expanse of bird-filled woodland beyond the *ville d'hiver*, it's worth the high summer prices. Hostellers can take the boat to Cap Ferret, where there's a small, basic **HI hostel** at 87 av de Bordeaux (☎05.56.60.64.62; July & Aug only).

A great **restaurant** to sample some of the local seafood is the colourful, jam-packed *La Marée*, 21 rue de Lattre-de-Tassigny (menus from 55F/€8.38 for weekday lunches, and 99F/€15.09 in the evening; closed Dec & Jan, also Mon & Tues evenings out of season); not only is it inexpensive, but if you're lucky you can sit out on one of two tiny wrought-iron balconies. Another good option, just round the corner at 17 rue Jehenne, is *La Plancha*, serving tapas (from 12F/€1.83 per dish), paella and other Spanish fare.

The Dune du Pyla and Le Teich

The Côte d'Argent's chief curiosity is the **Dune du Pyla**. At over 100m it is the highest sand dune in Europe – a veritable mountain of wind-carved sand, about 12km south

CHAPTER NINE

THE DORDOGNE, LIMOUSIN AND LOT

The land covered in this chapter forms a rough oval bordered to the east by the uplands of the Massif Central and to the west by the Atlantic plains. It is the area which was most in dispute between the English and the French during the Hundred Years War and which has been most in demand among English visitors and second-home buyers in recent times.

Although it does not coincide exactly with either the modern French administrative boundaries or the old provinces of Périgord and Quercy, which constitute the core of the region, the land has a physical and geographical homogeneity because of its great rivers: the **Dordogne**, the **Lot** and the **Aveyron**, all of which drain the waters of the western Massif Central into the mighty **Garonne**, which forms the southern limit covered by this chapter.

There are no great cities in the area: its charm lies in the landscapes and the dozens of harmonious small towns and villages. Some, like **Sarlat** and **Rocamadour**, are so well known that they are overrun with tourists. Others, like **Figeac**, **Villefranche-de-Rouergue**, **Gourdon**, **Montauban**, **Monflanquin** and the many *bastides* (fortified towns) that fill the area between the Lot and Dordogne, boast no single notable sight but are perfect organic ensembles.

The landscapes are surprisingly homogenous, too. From **Limoges** in the province of Limousin in the north to Montauban in the south towards Toulouse, the country is gently hilly, full of lush little valleys and miles of woodland, mainly oak. **Limousin**, at the north of this area, is slightly greener and wetter, the south more arid. But you can travel a long way without seeing a radical shift, except in the uplands of the **Plateau de Millevaches**, where the rivers plunge into gorges and the woods are beech, chestnut and conifer plantations. The other characteristic landscape is the *causses*, dry scrubby limestone plateaux like the **Causse de Gramat** between the Dordogne and the Lot and the **Causse de Limogne** between the Lot and Aveyron. Where the rivers have cut their way through the limestone, the valleys are walled with overhanging cliffs, riddled with fissures, underground stream-beds and caves. And in these caves – especially in the

---

ACCOMMODATION PRICE CODES

Each hotel and guesthouse in this book has been graded according to the following price codes, which indicate the price for the **cheapest double room available during the high season**.

① Under 160F/€24   ④ 300–400F/€46–61   ⑦ 600–700F/€91–107
② 160–220F/€24–34   ⑤ 400–500F/€61–76   ⑧ 700–800F/€107–122
③ 220–300F/€34–46   ⑥ 500–600F/€76–91   ⑨ Over 800F/€122

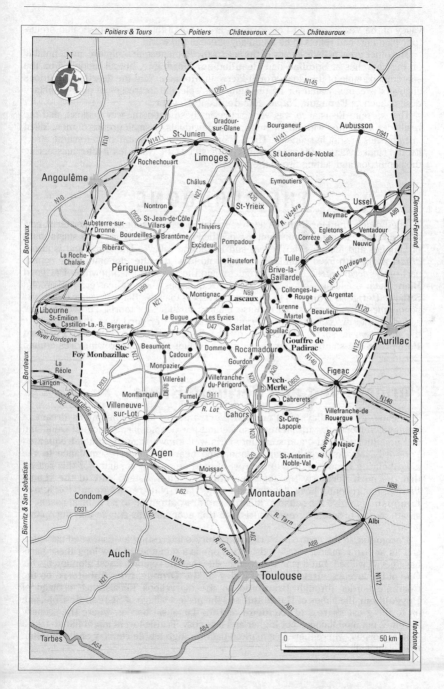

valley of the Vézère around **Les Eyzies** – are some of the most sophisticated prehistoric paintings and reliefs to be found anywhere in the world.

The other great artistic legacy of the area is the Romanesque sculpture, most notably on the churches at **Souillac** and **Beaulieu-sur-Dordogne**, but all modelled on the supreme example of the cloister of St-Pierre in **Moissac**. And the dearth of luxurious châteaux is compensated for by the numerous splendid fortresses of purely military design, such as **Bonaguil**, **Najac**, **Excideuil** and **Beynac**.

The wartime Resistance was very active in these out-of-the-way regions, and the roadsides are dotted with tiny memorials to individuals or small groups of men, killed in ambushes or shot in reprisals. There is one monstrous monument to wartime atrocity: the ruined village of **Oradour-sur-Glane**, still as the Nazis left it after massacring the population and setting fire to the houses.

THE DORDOGNE

To the French, the **Dordogne** is a river. To the British, it is a much looser term, covering a vast area roughly equivalent to what the French call Périgord. This starts south of Limoges and includes the Vézère and Dordogne valleys. The Dordogne is also a *département*, with fixed boundaries that pay no heed to either definition. The central part of the *département*, around Périgueux and the River Isle, is known as **Périgord Blanc**, after the light, white colour of its rock outcrops; the southeastern half around Sarlat as **Périgord Noir**, said to be darker in aspect than the Blanc because of the preponderance of oak woods. To confuse matters further, the tourist authorities have added another two colours to the Périgord patchwork: **Périgord Vert**, the far north of the *département*, so called because of its woods and pastureland; and **Périgord Pourpre** in the southwest, purple because it includes the wine-growing area around Bergerac.

Périgord Vert and Périgord Blanc

The close green valleys of **Périgord Vert** are like an Englishman's dream of England: very rural, with plenty of space and few people, large tracts of woodland and uncultivated land – and sunshine. Less well known than the much-frequented Périgord Noir, its largely granite landscape bears a closer resemblance to the neighbouring Limousin than to the rest of the Périgord. It is partly for this reason that the most northerly tip, together with the southwestern part of the Haute-Vienne, has recently been designated as the **Parc Naturel Régional Périgord-Limousin** – to give it a sense of identity and draw attention to its natural assets, in an attempt to promote "green" tourism in this economically fragile and depopulated area.

Périgueux, in the centre of **Périgord Blanc**, is interesting for its domed cathedral and its Roman remains, whose existence alone is a reminder of how long these parts have been civilized. But it is in the countryside that the region's finest monuments lie. One of the loveliest stretches is the **valley of the Dronne**, from **Aubeterre** on the Charente border through **Brantôme** to the marvellous Renaissance château of **Puyguilhem**, the abbey of **Boschaud** and the perfect village of **St-Jean-de-Côle**, and on to the great fortress of **Excideuil** and the Limousin border, where the scenery becomes not mountainous but higher and less cosy. Truffle-lovers might like to take a look at **Sorges**, where there is a marked path through truffle country and a museum to explain it all.

THE FOOD AND WINE OF PÉRIGORD

The two great stars of Périgord cuisine are **foie gras** and **truffles** (*truffes*). Foie gras is eaten on its own, in succulent slabs, often combined with truffles to accompany a huge variety of dishes from scrambled eggs to stuffed carp. In fact, you can be sure that this is what you are getting with any dish that has *sauce Périgueux* or *à la périgourdine* as part of its name. Truffles also come *à la cendre*, wrapped in bacon and cooked in hot ashes.

The other mainstay of Périgord cuisine is the grey Toulouse **goose**, whose fat is used in the cooking of everything, most commonly perhaps in the standard potato dish, *pommes sarladaises*. The goose fattens well: *gavé* or crammed with corn, it goes from six to ten kilos in weight in three weeks, with its liver alone weighing nearly a kilo. When the liver has been used for foie gras, the meat is cooked and preserved in its own thick yellow grease as *confits d'oie*, which you can either eat on its own or use in the preparation of other dishes, like *cassoulet*. **Duck** is used in the same way, both for foie gras and *confits*. *Magret de canard*, or duck breast fillet, is one of the favourite ways of eating duck and appears on practically every restaurant menu.

Another common goose delicacy is *cou d'oie farci* – goose neck stuffed with sausage meat, duck liver and truffles; a favourite salad throughout the region is made with warm *gésiers* or goose gizzards. Try not to be put off by fare such as this, or your palate will miss out on some delicious experiences – like *tripoux*, or sheep's stomach stuffed with tripe, trotters, pork and garlic, which is really an Auvergnat dish but is quite often served in neighbouring areas like the Rouergue. Other less challenging specialities include stuffed **cèpes**, or wild mushrooms; **ballottines**, or fillets of poultry stuffed, rolled and poached; the little flat discs of goat's cheese called *cabécou*; and the sweet light bread called *fouasse*, rather like the Greek *tsoureki*.

The **wines** should not be scorned either. There are the fine dark, almost peppery reds from Cahors, and both reds and whites from the vineyards of Bergerac, of which the sweet, white Monbazillac is the most famous. Pécharmant is the fanciest of the reds, but there are some very drinkable Côtes de Bergerac, much like the neighbouring Bordeaux and far cheaper. The same goes for the wines of Duras, Marmande and Buzet. If you are thinking of taking a stock of wine home, you could do much worse than make some enquiries in Bergerac itself, Ste-Foy, or any of the villages in the vineyard areas.

Périgueux

PÉRIGUEUX, capital of the *département* of the Dordogne and a central base for exploring the countryside of Périgord Blanc, is a small, busy and not particularly attractive market town for a province made rich by tourism and specialized farming. Its name derives from the Petrocorii, the local Gallic tribe, but it was the Romans who transformed it into an important settlement. A few Roman remains, as well as a medieval *vieille ville*, survive to this day.

Arrival, information and accommodation

The busiest and most interesting part of Périgueux is the square formed by the river, the allée de Tourny, boulevard Montaigne and cours Fénelon. At the junction of the two latter is the wide and unattractive place Francheville, with the **gare routière**, an underground car park and the **tourist office** (July & Aug Mon–Sat 9am–6pm, Sun 10am–6pm; rest of year closed Sun; ☎05.53.53.10.63, fax 05.53.09.02.50), next to the Tour Mataguerre, the last surviving bit of the town's medieval defences. Périgueux's **gare SNCF** lies to the west at the end of rue des Mobiles-du-Coulmiers, the continuation of rue Président-Wilson.

Opposite the train station, along rue Denis-Papin, you'll find a couple of reasonable **hotels**, the nicest of which are the *Régina* (☎05.53.08.40.44, fax 05.53.54.72.44; ③) and

a splurge, *Hercule Poireau*, 2 rue de la Nation (☎05.53.08.90.76), offers top-quality food at surprisingly affordable prices (menus from 99F/€15.09). And if you fancy a change from strictly French fare, *Le Chameau Gourmand*, 2 rue des Farges, serves excellent couscous (closed Mon; from 60F/€9.15), while *Le Canard Laqué*, 2 rue Lanmary, is a good and popular Chinese place with menus from 55F/€8.38 (closed Sun).

Brantôme and the valley of the Dronne

Although **Brantôme** itself is very much on the tourist trail, the country both to the west and east of the town along the **River Dronne** remains largely undisturbed. It is tranquil, very beautiful and restoring, best savoured at a gentle pace, perhaps by bike or even by canoeing along the river.

Brantôme

BRANTÔME, 27km north of Périgueux on the Angoulême road and beloved of British tourists, sits in a bend of the River Dronne, whose still, water-lilied surface mirrors the limes and weeping willows of the riverside gardens. On the north bank of the river are the church and convent buildings of the **ancienne abbaye** that for centuries has been Brantôme's focus. Its stone facades, now masking the secular offices of the **Hôtel de Ville**, have that pallor and blank stare so characteristic of the self-denying institutional life – not that self-denial was a virtue associated with this monastery's most notorious abbot, Pierre de Bourdeilles, the sixteenth-century author of scurrilous tales of life at the royal court. It's worth taking a look inside the **église abbatiale** for the palm-frond vaulting of the chapterhouse and the font made from a carved and grounded pillar capital. Also of architectural interest is a fine stone staircase at this end of the Hôtel de Ville, but Brantôme's best architectural feature is the Limousin-style Romanesque **belfry** standing behind the church against the wooded and cave-riddled scarp that forms the backdrop to the village.

Families with children may appreciate the **Musée de Rêve et Miniatures** in rue Puyjoli (April–June & Sept to mid-Nov daily except Fri 2–5/6pm; July & Aug daily 11am–6pm; 38F/€5.79), while a walk through the nearby **gardens** and along the pleasant balustraded **river banks** is a must. There are also **boat trips** on the river in summer (May–Sept; 35F/€5.34).

At least three **buses** a day (Mon–Sat) connect Brantôme with the TGV in Angoulême. The **tourist office** (Feb, March & Oct–Dec daily except Tues 10am–noon & 2–5pm; April–June & Sept daily except Tues 10am–12.30pm & 2–6pm; July & Aug daily 10am–7pm; closed Jan; ☎ & fax 05.53.05.80.52) is next to the abbey church. You can hire **canoes** and **bikes** from Brantôme Canoë (☎05.53.05.77.24).

The best cheap **accommodation** and **food** is to be had at the *Hôtel Versaveau*, 8 place de Gaulle, at the north end of town (☎05.53.05.71.42; ①; restaurant from 65F/€9.91, closed three weeks in Nov), though prettier and more comfortable rooms are available at *Hôtel Chabrol* across the river (☎05.53.05.70.15, fax 05.53.05.71.85; ③; closed Feb & mid-Nov to mid-Dec), whose restaurant, *Les Frères Charbonnel*, is in the gourmet class, with its cheapest menu at 165F/€25.15 (closed Sun evening & Mon Oct–June). If you're feeling rich, you could treat yourself to a meal for 240F/€36.59 plus at the beautiful *Moulin de l'Abbaye* hotel by the tourist office (☎05.53.05.80.22, fax 05.53.05.75.27, *moulin@relaischateaux.fr*; ⑨; closed Nov–April; restaurant closed Mon lunchtime). Under the same management, *Au Fil de l'Eau*, on quai Bertin, with tables down by the river, offers lighter meals at more affordable prices (closed Jan & Feb, also Mon evening & Tues; from 110F/€16.77). Campers should head for the well-run municipal **campsite** north of Brantôme on the D78 Thiviers road (☎05.53.05.75.24; closed Oct–April).

Bourdeilles

BOURDEILLES, 16km down the Dronne from Brantôme by a beautiful back road, is relatively hard to reach – perhaps the most appealing way is by canoe. It's a sleepy backwater, an ancient village clustering round its **Château** (early Feb to April & Oct–Dec daily except Tues 10am–12.30pm & 2–5.30pm; May, June & Sept daily except Tues 10am–12.30pm & 2–6.30pm; July & Aug daily 10am–7pm; closed Jan & early Feb; 30F/€4.57) on a rocky spur above the river. The château consists of two buildings: one a thirteenth-century fortress, the other an elegant Renaissance residence begun by the lady of the house as a piece of unsuccessful favour-currying with Catherine de Médicis – unsuccessful because Catherine never came to stay and the château remained unfinished. If you climb the octagonal keep, you can look down on the town's clustered roofs, the weir and the boat-shaped mill parting the current, and along the Dronne to the corn fields and the manors hidden among the trees.

The château is now home to an exceptional **collection of furniture** bequeathed to the state by its former owners. Among the more notable pieces are some splendid Spanish dowry chests; a sixteenth-century Rhenish Entombment with life-sized statues, embodying the very image of the serious, self-satisfied medieval burgher; and a fifteenth-century primitive Catalan triptych of an exorcism, with a bull-headed devil shooting skywards out of a kneeling princess.

For a **hotel**, *Les Tilleuls* (☎ & fax 05.53.03.76.40; ②; menus from 70F/€10.67), right opposite the château, makes a cheap and pleasant place to stay, or try the *Hostellerie Les Griffons* (☎05.53.45.45.35, fax 05.53.45.45.20, *www.griffons.fr*; ⑤; closed early Oct to Easter) in a sixteenth-century house beside the old bridge, with a restaurant serving top-notch regional cuisine (menus 134–195F/€20.43–29.73).

Ribérac

Surrounded by an intimate, hilly countryside of woods and hay meadows and drowsy hilltop villages, **RIBÉRAC**, 30km downstream from Bourdeilles, is a pleasant if unremarkable town, whose greatest claim to fame is its major Friday **market**, bringing in producers and wholesalers from all around. With a couple of decent **hotels**, it makes an agreeable base from which to explore the quiet, lush Dronne landscape. A good cheap option is the *Hôtel du Commerce* at 8 rue Gambetta on the corner of the wide central place de Gaulle (☎05.53.91.28.59; ①; closed Sun evening & Wed), with a nice restaurant from 55F/€8.38. More attractive and excellent value is the *Hôtel de France* on the opposite side of the square at 3 rue Marc-Dufraisse (☎05.53.90.00.61, fax 05.53.91.06.05; ②), with a terrace garden and a locally renowned restaurant, serving original cuisine (closed Mon & lunchtime Tues; menus 85F/€12.96). There's also a riverside municipal **campsite** on the Angoulême road outside Ribérac (☎05.53.90.50.08; closed Oct–May).

For further ideas about *chambres d'hôte* in the surrounding country, Ribérac's **tourist office** on place de Gaulle is the place to ask (July & Aug Mon–Sat 9am–noon & 2–7pm, Sun 10am–1pm; rest of year Mon–Sat 9am–noon & 2–6pm; ☎05.53.90.03.10, fax 05.53.91.35.13); they can also provide information about the numerous Romanesque churches in outlying villages that could provide a focus for leisurely wandering. **Bikes** can be rented from the campsite and Cycle Cum's, 35 rue du 26-Mars.

Aubeterre-sur-Dronne and around

Rather touristy, but very beautiful with its ancient galleried and turreted houses, **AUBETERRE-SUR-DRONNE** hangs on a steep hillside above the river, some 30km downstream of Ribérac. Its principal curiosity is the cavernous **Église Monolithe** (daily: mid-June to mid-Oct 9.30am–12.30pm & 2–7pm; rest of year 9.30am–12.30pm & 2–6pm; 20F/€3.05), carved out of the soft rock of the cliff face in the twelfth century, with its rock-hewn tombs going back to the sixth. A (blocked-off) tunnel connects with the **château** on the bluff overhead. There is also the extremely beautiful **church of St-Jacques**, with an eleventh-century façade sculpted and decorated in the richly carved Poitiers style on the street leading uphill from the square.

The **tourist office** is on the main square (July & Aug Mon 2.30–6.30pm, Tues–Sun 10am–noon & 2.30–6.30pm; rest of year daily 2–6pm; ☎05.45.98.57.18, fax 05.45.98.54.13), round the corner from attractive, old-fashioned *Hôtel de France*, now under Dutch ownership (☎05.45.98.50.43, *obakker@planete.net*; ②; menus from 85F/€12.96). There is a **campsite** (☎05.45.98.60.17; closed mid-Sept to mid-June) just below the village, and the delightful *Hôtellerie du Périgord*, beside the bridge (☎ & fax 05.45.98.50.46; ③), where you can eat well for around 110F/€16.77. On weekdays a daily **bus** runs to Angoulême, while Chalais, which is on the Angoulême train line, is only 12km away.

South of Aubeterre, towards **LA ROCHE-CHALAIS**, the country gradually changes. Farmland gives way to extensive forest of oak and sweet chestnut, bracken and broom, interspersed with sour, marshy pasture, very sparsely populated. It's ideal cycling and picnicking country. In La Roche-Chalais, the **tourist office** on the main square (May–Sept Mon 3–6pm, Tues–Sat 11am–noon & 3–6pm; rest of year Mon–Fri 3.30–5pm, Sat 9am–noon; ☎05.53.90.18.95) has information on local walking routes and farm visits. For an overnight **stay**, the *Hôtel Soleil d'Or*, across the square from the tourist office (☎05.53.90.86.71, fax 05.53.90.28.21; ④; restaurant from 130F/€19.82), has a magnificent view over the surrounding country and very comfortable rooms. Campers will find a **campsite** here (☎05.53.91.40.65; closed Nov–March) and another in **ST-AULAYE**, 12km northwest on the Aubeterre road (☎05.53.90.62.20; closed Oct–May), where the small **restaurant**, *Au Petit Gourmet*, on the central square (closed Sat evening & Sun, and mid-Sept to mid-Oct), serves good-value regional cuisine from 60F/€9.15.

Villars and around

A dozen kilometres northeast of Brantôme lies the hamlet of **VILLARS**, a village with no particular sights but which is surrounded by beautiful countryside and makes an excellent and not over-expensive base for visiting the **Château de Puyguilhem**. A short distance north of the hamlet are the **Grottes de Villars** (daily: April & Oct 2.30–6.30pm; May, June & Sept 10am–noon & 2–7pm; July & Aug 10am–7pm; 38F/€5.79), where local cavers discovered impressive stalactites and stalagmites, together with a few prehistoric paintings – notably of horses and bison – in 1958.

Villars' one **hotel**, *Le Relais de l'Archerie*, is housed in a nineteenth-century mini-château with terrace and gardens (☎05.53.54.88.64, fax 05.53.54.21.92; ②; closed Nov & Feb, also weekends Oct–March; restaurant from 80F/€12.20). There is alternative accommodation and food some 11km away in **ST-PARDOUX-LA-RIVIÈRE** at the simple *Hôtel de France* (☎05.53.56.70.15; ②; restaurant from 68F/€10.37).

The Château de Puyguilhem and Abbey of Boschaud

About a kilometre outside Villars, the appealing **Château de Puyguilhem** (early Feb to April & Oct–Dec Tues–Sun 10am–12.30pm & 2–5.30pm; May & June daily 10am–6.30pm; July & Aug daily 10am–7pm; Sept Tues–Sun 10am–12.30pm & 2–6.30pm; 30F/€4.57) sits on the edge of a valley backed by oak woods. The building you see today was erected at the beginning of the sixteenth century on the site of an earlier and more military fortress. With its octagonal tower, broad spiral staircase, steep roofs, magnificent fireplaces and false dormer windows it is a perfect example of French Renaissance architecture. From the gallery at the top of the stairs you get a close-up of the roof and window decoration, as well as a view down the valley, which once was filled by a lake.

In the next valley, and very much worth a visit, the ruined Cistercian **Abbey of Boschaud** lies on the edge of the woods, reached by a lane not much bigger than a farm track. Its charm lies as much in the fact that it is – for once – unfenced, unpampered and uncharged for, as in the pure, stark lines of its twelfth-century architecture.

St-Jean-de-Côle

Midway between Villars and Thiviers on the main Périgueux–Angoulême road, **ST-JEAN-DE-CÔLE** must rank as one of the loveliest villages in the Dordogne. Its ancient houses huddle together in typical medieval fashion around a wide sandy square dominated on one side by the huge **church of St-Jean-Baptiste**, built in the eleventh century, and the rugged-looking **Château de la Marthonie** (July & Aug daily 10.15am–noon & 2–7pm; 20F/€3.05) on the other. The château, first erected in the fourteenth century, has acquired various additions in a pleasingly organic kind of growth.

The **tourist office** (daily: April, May & Oct 9.30am–12.30pm & 2–5pm; June–Sept 10am–1pm & 2–7pm; ☎ & fax 05.53.62.14.15, *www.ville-saint-jean-de-cole.fr*) is also on the square, as well as two attractive **restaurants**: the *Coq Rouge* (☎05.53.62.32.71; closed Wed & Jan–March), whose excellent menus start at around 100F/€15.24, and *Le Templier*, serving a varied weekday lunch menu at 78F/€11.89, with dinner menus from 100F/€15.24 (closed Dec–Feb, also Mon & Tues). On the main road through the village you can also eat at the wisteria-covered *Hôtel St-Jean* (☎05.53.52.23.20; ②; restaurant from 70F/€10.67, closed Sun evening).

Thiviers and Sorges

If you're heading along the main N21 Périgueux–Limoges road, it's worth stopping off at the pretty village of **THIVIERS**, which styles itself as the foie gras capital of the region. Its helpful **tourist office**, on the central square (July & Aug Mon–Sat 9am–6.15pm, Sun 10am–1pm; rest of year Tues–Fri 9am–12.15pm & 2–6.15pm, Sat 9am–12.15pm & 3–6pm; ☎05.53.55.12.50), makes the most of this with a small **museum** dedicated to the history and production of foie gras (same hours; 10F/€1.52). If you're looking for somewhere to **stay**, try the attractive *Hôtel de France et de Russie*, 51 rue du Général-Lamy (☎05.53.55.17.80, fax 05.53.52.59.60; ③), between the tourist office and the **gare SNCF**, a couple of minutes' walk to the north.

SORGES, closer to Périgueux and strung out along the road, has less to offer aesthetically than Thiviers. However, the **tourist office** (July & Aug daily 9.30am–12.30pm & 2.30–6.30pm; rest of year Tues–Sun 10am–noon & 2–5pm; ☎05.53.05.90.11, fax 05.53.46.71.43) contains a fascinating **truffle museum** (same hours; 20F/€3.05), and can also direct you to a marked path that gives an idea of how and where truffles grow. There is a very reasonable **hotel**, *Auberge de la Truffe* on the main road (☎05.53.05.02.05, fax 05.53.05.39.27, *www.auberge-de-la-truffe.com*; ③), with an excellent restaurant (80–330F/€12.20–50.31), and with an annexe, *Hôtel de la Mairie*, by the church.

The Château de Hautefort

Forty kilometres northeast of Périgueux, the **Château de Hautefort** (daily: mid-Jan to March during school hols 2–6pm; April to mid-July & Sept 10am–noon & 2–6pm; mid-July to Aug 9.30am–7pm; Oct 2–6pm; Nov to mid-Dec Sun & hols 2–6pm; 35F/€5.34) enjoys a majestic position at the end of a wooded spur above its feudal village. A magnificent example of good living on a grand scale, the castle has an elegance

wine, best consumed with desserts or chilled as an apéritif, at the **Cave de Monbazillac** (closed Sun & Mon), 2km west on the D933 Marmande road.

Ste-Foy-la-Grande and Montcaret

Driving west from Bergerac along the River Dordogne, the first place you come to of any size is the *bastide* town of **STE-FOY-LA-GRANDE**, whose narrow central streets still retain a number of ancient houses. One of these, at 102 rue de la République, now houses the exceptionally helpful **tourist office** (mid-June to mid-Sept Mon–Sat 9.30am–12.30pm & 2.30–5.30pm, Sun 10.30am–12.30pm; rest of year closed Sun; ☎05.57.46.03.00, fax ☎05.57.46.53.77), which has lists of *chambres d'hôte* and local wine-tasting sessions. Another draw is the town's mouthwatering Saturday **market**, and there's a very pleasant place to **stay**, the *Grand Hôtel*, 117 rue de la République (☎05.57.46.00.08, fax 05.57.46.50.70, *www.grandhotel-mce.com*; ③; restaurant from 65F/E9.91), just east of the tourist office.

Thirteen kilometres from Ste-Foy lies **MONTCARET**, whose main attraction is a fourth-century **Gallo-Roman villa** (daily: April–June & Sept 9am–noon & 2–6pm; July & Aug 9am–1pm & 2–7pm; rest of year 10am–noon & 2–4pm; 25F/€3.81) with superb mosaics and baths plus an adjoining museum displaying the many objects exhumed on the site. It is another 3.5km to the **Château de Montaigne** (July & Aug daily 10am–6.30pm; rest of year Wed–Sun 10am–noon & 2–5.30pm; closed Jan; 20F/€3.05), where Michel de Montaigne wrote many of his chatty, digressive essays on the nature of life and humankind. All that remains of the original building is Montaigne's tower-study, its beams inscribed with his maxims; the rest of the château was rebuilt in pseudo-Renaissance style after a fire in 1885.

In the absence of a car, the best means of visiting Montcaret and the Château de Montaigne from Ste-Foy is by **bike**; rental outlets in Ste-Foy are Ets David, 29 rue Jean-Jacques-Rousseau, and Ets Vircoulon, 41 rue Victor-Hugo. The other option is to catch an early-morning **train** to Montcaret, but this leaves you with an eight-kilometre round-trip walk to the château, and then a long wait for the evening train back to Ste-Foy.

The bastide country

During the long struggles of the thirteenth and fourteenth centuries for control of southwest France, both the English and the French combatants constructed dozens of new towns – principally in the disputed "frontier" areas between the Dordogne and Garonne rivers – in an attempt to consolidate their hold on their respective territories. These towns, known as **bastides**, were essentially fortified settlements, walled and gated and built on a rational grid-plan round a central arcaded market square, in marked contrast to the haphazard organic growth of the usual medieval town. As an incentive to local people, anyone who was prepared to build, inhabit and defend them was granted various perks and concessions, including a measure of self-government remarkable in feudal times.

There is a heavy concentration of these settlements in the country to the south of Bergerac between the rivers Dordogne and Lot. Many retain no more than vestiges of their original aspect, but two of the finest, which are almost entirely intact, lie within a fifty-kilometre radius of Bergerac: **Monpazier** and **Monflanquin**.

Monpazier and around

MONPAZIER, founded in 1284 by King Edward I of England (who was also Duke of Aquitaine), is one of the most complete of the surviving *bastides*, and still relatively free of the commercialism that suffocates a place like Domme (see p.640). Picturesque and placid though it is today, the village has a hard and bitter history, being twice – in 1594 and 1637 – the centre of peasant rebellions provoked by the misery that followed the Wars of Religion. Both uprisings were brutally suppressed: the 1637 peasants' leader was broken on the wheel in the square. Sully, the Protestant general, describes a rare moment of light relief in the terrible wars, when the men of the Catholic *bastide* of Villefranche-de-Périgord planned to capture Monpazier on the same night as the men of Monpazier planned to capture Villefranche. By chance, both sides took different routes, met no resistance, looted to their hearts' content and returned home congratulating themselves on their luck and skill, only to find in the morning that things were rather different. The peace terms were that everyone should return everything to its proper place.

Monpazier is now severely depopulated. As the street ends the fields begin, and you look out over the surrounding country. There is an ancient *lavoir* where women used to wash clothes, a much-altered church and a gem of a central square – sunny, still and slightly menacing, like a Sicilian piazza at siesta time. Deep, shady arcades pass under all the houses, which are separated from each other by a small gap to reduce fire risk; at the corners the buttresses are cut away to allow the passage of laden pack animals.

The best place for an overnight **stay** in Monpazier is the *Hôtel de France*, 21 rue St-Jacques (☎05.53.22.60.06, fax 05.53.22.07.27; ③; closed mid-Nov to mid-Dec), with a fine regional restaurant from 90F/€13.72. There are two **campsites** in the vicinity: *Camping Véronne*, 3km north, signed off the D660 Bergerac road (☎05.53.22.62.22; closed mid-Sept to mid-June), and the more luxurious *Moulin de David*, roughly the same distance to the south (☎05.53.22.65.25; closed early Sept to mid-May).

Another possibility is to base yourself in one of the attractive villages within a twenty-kilometre radius. **BELVÈS** watches over the surrounding country from a ridge-top just 5km from Siorac on the Dordogne, and its *Hôtel Le Home*, on the through road at the top of the hill, provides good cheap **accommodation** and food (☎05.53.29.01.65, fax 05.53.59.46.99; ①–②; closed Sun; restaurant from 60F/€9.15). Make sure you take a look at the heart of the old village and place des Armes, with its old pillared **market** and the **tourist office** (June–Sept daily 10am–12.30pm & 3–5pm; rest of year closed Wed & Sun; ☎ & fax 05.53.29.10.20). The nearest **campsite** is at Les Nauves (☎05.53.29.07.87; closed mid-Sept to mid-May), 4.5km off the Monpazier road, and there's a small *camping à la ferme* called *Le Bon Accueil* (☎05.53.29.08.49; open all year) at the hamlet of Gratecap near St-Amand-de-Belvès.

VILLEFRANCHE-DU-PÉRIGORD lies 20km further south in the midst of wooded country above the River Lemance. Built in 1261 in lovely warm-coloured stone, it retains much of its *bastide* layout. At the end of the main street, whose medieval **halle** is splendid, is the good-value *Petite Auberge* (☎05.53.29.91.01, fax 05.53.28.88.10; ③; closed Fri evening & Sat lunch Dec–Feb; restaurant from 85F/€12.96), set among gardens 500m out of the village.

Biron, Villeréal and Monflanquin

Eight kilometres south of Monpazier, dominating the countryside for miles around, is the vast **Château de Biron** (early Feb to March & Oct–Dec Tues–Sun 10am–12.30pm & 2–5.30pm; April–June & Sept daily 10am–12.30pm & 2–5.30/6.30pm; July & Aug daily 10am–7pm; 30F/€4.57), begun in the eleventh century and added to piecemeal afterwards. You can take a guided tour (in French only) or borrow a written translation in English, which means you can wander at will around the rooms and the grassy courtyard, where there is a restored Renaissance chapel and guardhouse with tremendous views over the roofs of the feudal village below.

A single street runs through the village of **BIRON**, past a covered **market** on timber supports iron-hard with age, and out under an arched gateway. Well-manured vegetable plots interspersed with iris, lily and Iceland poppies lie under the tumbledown walls. At the bottom of the hill, another group of houses stands on a small square with a well in front of the village **church**, its Romanesque origins hidden by motley alterations. The *Auberge du Château*, back near the market hall, serves a good-value lunchtime menu at 60–70F/€9.15–10.67 (☎05.53.63.13.33; closed mid-Dec to mid-Feb & Sat Oct–April).

West of Biron, the *bastide* of **VILLERÉAL** was founded a decade or so earlier than Monpazier by Alphonse de Poitiers in an attempt to check English expansion in the Dordogne. It failed to do so and was taken by the English during the Hundred Years War. Its most outstanding feature is the oak-beamed *halles* in the central square, which dates from the fourteenth century. You can **stay** at the *Hôtel de l'Europe*, place Jean Moulin (☎05.53.36.00.35; ③; closed two weeks in Oct; restaurant from 70F/€10.67), or at one of the many nearby **campsites**, the closest of which is the *Camping du Pesquie Bas* (☎05.53.36.05.63; closed Oct–April), off the D207 to Issigeac and Bergerac.

Some 25km further south in the direction of Villeneuve-sur-Lot, pretty **MONFLAN-QUIN**, founded by Alphonse de Poitiers in 1256, is just as perfectly preserved as Monpazier, less touristy and even more impressively positioned on the top of a hill that rises sharply from the surrounding country and is visible for miles. It conforms to the regular pattern of right-angled streets leading from a central square to the four town gates. The square – **place des Arcades** – with its distinctly Gothic houses, derives a special charm from being on a slope and tree-shaded. The fortified **church** is also worth a look. The **tourist office** is on the place des Arcades (July & Aug daily 10am–12.30pm & 3–7pm; rest of year Mon–Sat 10am–noon & 2–5pm, Sun 2–5pm; ☎05.53.36.40.19, fax 05.53.36.42.91, *office.de.tourisme.monflanquin@wanadoo.fr*), and can furnish you with lists of *chambres d'hôte*. There's a **campsite** (☎05.53.36.47.35; closed Oct–May) just outside town at **COULON** on the Cancon road.

Beaumont and the Abbaye de Cadouin

BEAUMONT, 17km north of Villeréal on the D676, is another thirteenth-century English *bastide*, founded by Edward I. Like many *bastides*, its church, **Église St-Front**, was built for military as well as religious reasons – a kind of final outpost of defence in times of attack – hence the bulky tower at each of the four corners and the well inside. For **accommodation**, there's the creeper-covered *Hôtel Beaumontois* in rue Romier, with simple rooms and traditional Périgord cuisine (☎05.53.22.30.11, fax 05.53.22.38.99; ③; restaurant from 95F/€14.48), as well as a good **campsite**, *Les Remparts* (☎05.53.22.40.86; closed Oct–April), just southwest of town off the D676.

Around 15km northeast, and only 6km south of **LE BUISSON** on the Dordogne, is the twelfth-century Cistercian **Abbaye de Cadouin**. For 800 years until 1935 it drew flocks of pilgrims to wonder at a piece of cloth first mentioned by Simon de Montfort in 1214 and thought to be part of Christ's shroud. In 1935 the two bands of embroidery at either end of the cloth were shown to contain an Arabic text from around the eleventh century. Since then the main attraction has been the finely sculpted but badly damaged capitals of the flamboyant Gothic **cloister** (Feb–May & Oct–Dec daily except Tues 10am–12.30pm & 2–5.30pm; July & Aug daily 10am–7pm; 30F/€4.57). Beside it is a Romanesque **church** with a stark, bold front and wooden belfry roofed with chestnut shingles. (Chestnut trees abound around here – their timber was used in furniture-making and their nuts ground for flour in the formerly frequent famines.) Inside the church, the nave is slightly out of alignment; this is thought to be deliberate and per-haps a vestige of pagan attachments, for the three windows are aligned so that at the winter and summer solstices the sun shines through all three in a single shaft. There's a small municipal **campsite** on the Montferrand road (☎05.53.63.46.43; closed mid-Sept to mid-June).

Périgord Noir and the upper Dordogne

Périgord Noir encompasses the central part of the valley of the Dordogne, and the valley of the Vézère. This is the distinctive Dordogne country: deep-cut valleys enclosed within the water-smooth cliffs their rivers have eroded, with fields of maize in the alluvial bottoms and dense oak woods on the heights, interspersed with patches of not very fertile farmland. Plantations of walnut trees (cultivated for their oil), flocks of low-slung grey geese (their livers enlarged for foie gras) and prehistoric-looking stone huts called *bories* are other hallmarks of Périgord Noir, and beyond the region, along the **upper Dordogne valley** towards Argentat in the east.

In the **valley of the Vézère** the slightly overhanging cliffs have been worn away by frost action over the millennia and they are riddled with caves that have been used as dwellings and sanctuaries for thousands of years. It was here in the Vézère valley that the first skeletons of **Cro-Magnon people** – the first *Homo sapiens*, tall and muscular with a large skull – were unearthed in 1868 by labourers digging out the Périgueux–Agen train line, and here, too, that an incredible wealth of archeological and artistic evidence of the life of late Stone Age people has since been found.

The **prehistoric cave paintings** are the absolute highlight of Périgord Noir: they are remarkable not only for their great age, but also for their exquisite colouring and the skill with which they are drawn. However, the international renown of the caves and their paintings, combined with the well-preserved medieval architecture of **Sarlat**, has made this one of the most heavily touristed inland areas of France, with all the concomitant problems of crowds, high prices and tack. It is really worth coming out of season, but if you can't, seek accommodation away from the main centres, and always drive along the back roads – the smaller the better – even when there is a more direct route available.

Sarlat and around

SARLAT-LA-CANÉDA, capital of Périgord Noir, is held in a hollow between hills 10km or so back from the Dordogne valley. You hardly notice the modern town, as it is the mainly fifteenth- and sixteenth-century houses of the *vieille ville* in mellow, honey-coloured stone that draw the attention.

The **vieille ville** is an excellent example of medieval organic urban growth, violated only by the straight swath of the **rue de la République**, now thankfully pedestrianized, which cuts through its middle. The west side alone remains relatively un-chic; the east side is where most people wander. As you approach the old town from the station, turn right down rue Lakanal which leads to the large and unexciting **Cathédrale St-Sacerdos**, mostly dating from its seventeenth-century renovation. Opposite stands the town's finest house, the **Maison de La Boétie** once the home of Montaigne's friend Étienne de La Boétie, with its gabled tiers of windows and characteristic steep roof stacked with heavy limestone tiles (*lauzes*).

For a better sense of the medieval town, wander through the cool, shady lanes and courtyards – **cour des Fontaines** and **cour des Chanoines** – around the back of the cathedral. Directly behind the cathedral is the curious twelfth-century coned tower, the **Lanterne des Morts**, whose exact function has escaped historians, though the most popular theory is that it was built to commemorate St Bernard, who performed various miracles when he visited the town in 1147.

There are more wonderful old houses in the streets to the north, especially **rue des Consuls**, and up the slopes to the east. Eventually, though, Sarlat's labyrinthine lanes will lead you back to the central **place de la Liberté**, where the big Saturday **market** spreads its stands of geese, flowers, foie gras, truffles, walnuts and mushrooms in season, and where various people try to make a living from the hordes who hit Sarlat in the summer. The only other sight as such is the **Musée Automobile** (May, June & Sept daily except Tues 2.30–6.30pm; July & Aug daily 10am–noon & 2–6pm; 35F/€5.34), south of the centre on avenue Thiers, which features a wonderful collection of classic cars, dating from as far back as 1890.

Practicalities

The **gare SNCF** is just over 1km south of the old town. The **tourist office** lodges in the sixteenth-century Hôtel de Maleville on place de la Liberté (May–June & Sept–Nov daily 9am–7pm; July & Aug daily 9am–7.30pm; rest of year Mon–Sat 9am–noon & 2–6pm; ☎05.53.31.45.45, fax 05.53.59.19.44, *ot24.sarlat@perigord.tm.fr*). For a small fee, they'll help find a room in town or B&B accommodation in the surrounding area, though it's almost impossible to find cheap digs in season. You can rent **bicycles** from Cycles Sarladais, 36 av Thiers, and Christian Chapoulie, 4 av de Selves; the latter also has scooters.

The nicest and most reasonable place to **stay** in Sarlat is the *Hôtel des Récollets*, 4 rue J.-J.-Rousseau (☎05.53.31.36.00, fax 05.53.30.32.62, *otelrecol@aol.com*; ③), on the west-side of the old town. If they're full, try the more basic *Marcel* at 50 av de Selves, the

---

GÎTES D'ÉTAPE AROUND SARLAT

There are a number of **gîtes d'étape** in the vicinity of Sarlat, some on or near the GR6. For walkers, cyclists and campers they can provide much more enjoyable and hassle-free accommodation than anything in the towns.

Beynac: *La Grange*, five minutes east of the village towards Sarlat (☎05.53.49.40.93). Open all year; Nov–April minimum ten people.

Le Breuil: *Lo Cobano*, on the GR6 north of the D47 midway between Les Eyzies and Sarlat – turn north at Benives (☎05.53.29.66.23). Camping and meals.

Cénac: M. et Mme Sardan (☎05.53.28.32.77). Camping possible.

Castelnaud-la-Chapelle: *Camping Maisonneuve*, 1km below the castle on the GR64 towards Domme (☎05.53.29.51.29). Campsite offering well-equipped *gîte d'étape* accommodation.

---

northern extension of rue de la République (☎05.53.59.21.98; ③; closed mid-Nov to early Feb). At the other extreme, and closer to the old town, the *Hôtel de la Madeleine*, place de la Petite-Rigaudie (☎05.53.59.10.41, fax 05.53.31.03.62, *hotel.madeleine@wanadoo.fr*; ⑤), offers three-star comforts. There is a small **hostel** with dormitory accommodation at 77 av de Selves (☎05.53.59.47.59; closed Jan), a ten-minute walk from the *vieille ville*. The nearest **campsite**, *Les Périères*, on Sarlat's northern outskirts (☎05.53.59.05.84; closed Oct–Easter), is very well equipped but costs almost as much as a hotel; much better to try *Les Terrasses du Périgord*, about 2.5km north of Sarlat near Proissans village (☎05.53.59.02.25; closed Oct–April).

Restaurants are generally overpriced in Sarlat. However, *Chez Marc* in rue Tourny (☎05.53.59.02.71; closed Sun & Mon), south of the cathedral, with its menus at 55F/€8.38 and 85F/€12.96 and regional specialities, offers reasonable value for money, as does the slightly fancier *Le Bouffon*, behind the tourist office in rue Albéric-Cahuet, with a pretty courtyard (☎05.53.31.03.36; closed Dec & Wed off season; menus from 78F/€11.89). *Criquettamu's*, 5 rue des Armes (☎05.53.59.48.10; closed Mon & Nov–March; menus 80–180F/€12.20–27.44), is another safe bet, serving up foie gras, *magret* and *morilles* mushrooms, but for something a bit special try *Le Présidial*, rue Landry (☎05.53.28.92.47; closed Mon & Dec–Jan; menus from 115F/€17.53), east of place de la Liberté in a lovely seventeenth-century mansion and its walled garden.

A very pleasant alternative to both staying and eating in Sarlat would be to put up in the little hilltop hamlet of **MARQUAY** about halfway to Les Eyzies, at the *Hôtel des Bories* (☎05.53.29.67.02, fax 05.53.29.64.15; ②; closed Nov–March), with a marvellous view, swimming pool and an excellent attached restaurant, *L'Esterel* (closed Wed lunch; from 85F/€12.96); it is vital to book several months in advance for July and August.

Les Jardins d'Eyrignac

The *manoir* of **Eyrignac** is a very lovely seventeenth-century example of what, in English, would be called a country house. It lies in the hilly country to the northeast of Sarlat, about 13km by road. Its great glory is its **garden**, which is remarkable for its special effects and atmosphere (guided tours daily: June–Sept 9.30am–7pm; rest of year 10am–12.30pm & 2–7pm/dusk; 40F/€6.10; house closed to the public). The original formal garden was the work of an eighteenth-century Italian architect, but it was later converted to an English romantic garden as the owners – still the same family – followed subsequent fashions. What you see today is the work of the last forty years, the creation of the present owner's father in a combination of Italian and French styles. There are practically no flowers: the garden consists of evergreens – mainly box, hornbeam, cypress and yew – clipped and arranged in formal patterns of alleys and *parterres*. A work of art in its own right, it's now classified as a national monument.

Les Eyzies

The main base for visiting many of the prehistoric painted caves of the Vézère valley is **LES EYZIES-DE-TAYAC**, an unattractive one-street village completely dedicated to tourism. But while you're here, visit the **Musée National de Préhistoire** (daily except Tues: mid-March to June & Sept to mid-Nov 9.30am–noon & 2–6pm; July & Aug 9.30am–7pm; mid-Nov to mid-March 9.30am–noon & 2–5pm; 22F/€3.35), which exhibits numerous prehistoric artefacts and copies of one of the most beautiful pieces of Stone Age art, two clay bison from the Tuc d'Audoubert cave in the Pyrenees. Look out, too, for the small bas-relief of an exaggerated female figure holding what looks like a slice of watermelon, found near Laussel (see p.636), known as the Vénus à la Corne (Venus with the Horn of Plenty): the original is in the Musée d'Aquitaine in Bordeaux (see p.601).

In April 1990, local farmer M. Pataud opened his own extensive private collection of prehistoric finds, next door in the **Musée de l'Abri Pataud** (March–June & Sept–Nov Tues–Sun 10am–12.30pm & 1.30–5.30pm; July & Aug daily 10am–7pm; 30F/€4.57). Much of the stuff was discovered during archeological digs in the 1950s and 1960s on Pataud's own farmland, which, it transpired, lay over an *abri* (shelter) used by reindeer hunters for more than 20,000 years.

Practicalities

The **tourist office** is on Les Eyzies' one street (June–Sept Mon–Sat 9am–7/8pm, Sun 10am–noon & 2–6pm; rest of year Mon–Sat 9am–noon & 2–6pm; ☎05.53.06.97.05, fax 05.53.06.90.79). In addition to **bicycle rental**, they also give out information on local *chambres d'hôte* and *gîtes d'étape*. **Hotels** are pricey and may require *demi-pension* in high season. The cheapest is *Les Falaises*, in the main street (☎05.53.06.97.35; ②), but a nicer choice is the slightly more expensive *La Rivière*, about 1km away on the Périgueux road (☎05.53.06.97.14, fax 05.53.35.20.85; ②; closed Oct–Easter; simple meals from 68F/€10.37). Moving up a notch, the ivy-covered *Hôtel du Centre*, by the tourist office (☎05.53.06.97.13, fax 05.53.06.91.63; ③; closed Nov–Jan; restaurant 100–195F/€15.24–29.73), has small but very comfortable rooms, while just east of the centre, in a lovely spot by a mill race, *Le Moulin de la Beune* (☎05.53.06.93.39, fax 05.53.06.94.33; ④; closed Nov–Easter) has well-priced rooms and an excellent restaurant (closed Tues & Wed lunch; menus from 125F/€19.06). Alternatively, you could stay in **CAMPAGNE**, a pretty village 6km downstream, where you'll find big, bright rooms and regional menus at the *Hôtel du Château* (☎05.53.07.23.50, fax 05.53.03.93.69; ③; closed mid-Oct to Easter; restaurant from 100F/€15.24). The closest **campsite** to Les Eyzies is the well-tended *La Rivière* under the same management as the hotel (see above; closed Oct to March).

When it comes to **eating**, *La Grignotière*, near the tourist office, serves no-nonsense brasserie-style food. Otherwise, try *Le Chateaubriant* (☎05.53.35.06.11; closed Jan & for dinner Dec–March), a bit further north along the main street, with a nice terrace and lunch menus from 70F/€10.67, or one of the hotels mentioned above.

The caves around Les Eyzies

There are more **prehistoric caves** around Les Eyzies than you could possibly hope to visit in one day. Besides, the compulsory guided tours are tiring, so it's best to select just a couple of the ones listed below.

No one ever lived in these caves, and there are various theories as to why such inaccessible spots were chosen. Most agree that the caves were sanctuaries and, if not actually places of worship, they at least had religious significance. One theory is that making images of animals that were commonly hunted – like reindeer and bison – or feared – like bears and mammoths – was a kind of sympathetic magic intended to help men either catch or evade these animals. Another is that they were part of a fertility cult: sexual images of women with pendulous breasts and protuberant rumps are common, and it seems, too, that certain animals were associated with the feminine principle. Others argue that these cave paintings served educational purposes, making parallels with Australian aborigines who used similar images to teach their young vital survival information as well as the history and mythological origins of their people. But much remains unexplained – for instance, the abstract signs that appear in many caves and the arrows which clearly cannot be arrows, because Stone Age arrowheads looked different from these representations.

Grotte de Font-de-Gaume

Since its discovery in 1901, dozens of polychrome paintings have been found in the tunnel-like **Grotte de Font-de-Gaume** (daily except Wed: March & Oct 9.30am–noon & 2–5.30pm; April–Sept 9am–noon & 2–6pm; Nov–Feb 10am–noon & 2–5pm; 35F/€5.34; ☎05.53.06.86.00, fax 05.53.35.26.18; maximum twenty per tour), 1.5km along the D47 to Sarlat. Be aware that tickets sell out fast and only two hundred people are allowed to tour the cave each day; advance booking, several days ahead in peak season, is essential.

The cave was first settled by Stone Age people during the last Ice Age – about 25,000 BC – when the Dordogne was the domain of roaming bison, reindeer and mammoths. The cave mouth is no more than a fissure concealed by rocks and trees above a small lush valley. Inside, it's a narrow twisting passage of irregular height, and you quickly lose your bearings in the dark. The first painting you see is a frieze of bison, at about eye level: reddish-brown in colour, massive, full of movement, and very far from the primitive representations you might expect. Further on a horse stands with one hoof slightly raised, resting. But the most miraculous of all is a frieze of five bison discovered in 1966 during cleaning operations. The colour, remarkably sharp and vivid, is preserved by a protective layer of calcite. Shading under the belly and down the thighs is used to give three-dimensionality with a sophistication that seems utterly modern. Another panel consists of superimposed drawings, a fairly common phenomenon in cave painting, sometimes the result of work by successive generations, but here an obviously deliberate technique. A reindeer in the foreground shares legs with a large bison behind to indicate perspective.

Stocks of artists' materials have also been found: kilos of prepared pigments; palettes – stones stained with ground-up earth pigments; and wooden painting sticks. Painting was clearly a specialized, perhaps professional, business, reproduced in dozens and dozens of caves located in the central Pyrenees and areas of northern Spain.

Grotte des Combarelles

The **Grotte des Combarelles** (same hours as Font-de-Gaume; 35F/€5.34; maximum six people per tour), 2km along the D47 towards Sarlat, was discovered in 1910. The innermost part of the cave is covered with engravings from the Magdalenian period (about 12,000 years ago). Drawn over a period of 2000 years, many are superimposed one upon another. They include horses, reindeer, mammoths and stylized human figures – among the finest are the heads of a horse and a lioness.

As with Font-de-Gaume, prebooking is essential, especially in peak season (same phone and fax); collect tickets from Font-de-Gaume.

Abri du Cap Blanc and the Château de Commarque

Not a cave but a natural rock shelter, the **Abri du Cap Blanc** (daily: April–June, Sept & Oct 10am–noon & 2–6pm; July & Aug 9.30am–7pm; 31F/€4.73), lies on a steep wooded hillside about 7km east of Les Eyzies (turn left onto the D48 shortly after Les Combarelles). It contains a sculpted frieze of horses and bison dating from the Middle Magdalenian period, about 14,000 years ago. Of only ten surviving prehistoric sculptures in France, this is undoubtedly the best. The design is deliberate, with the sculptures polished and set off against a pock-marked background. But what makes this place extraordinary is not just the large scale, but the high relief of some of the sculptures. This was only possible in places where light reached in, which in turn brought the danger of destruction by exposure to the air. Cro-Magnon people actually lived in this shelter, and a female skeleton has been found that is some 2000 years younger than the frieze.

If you're looking for a non-cave detour, continue a little further up the heavily wooded Beune valley from Cap Blanc, to the elegant sixteenth-century **Château de Laussel** (closed to the public). On the opposite side of the valley stand the romantic ruins of the **Château de Commarque**, now undergoing extensive restoration. Built in the thirteenth century, it was occupied by the English during the Hundred Years War, and substantial sections of the fortifications still stand. You can reach it on foot via the GR6 footpath, which leaves the D47, past the Font-de-Gaume or – much quicker – by a path that starts in the left-hand corner of the field below Cap Blanc (flooded in wet weather).

Grotte du Grand Roc

As well as prehistoric cave paintings, you can see some truly spectacular stalactites and stalagmites in the area around Les Eyzies. Some of the best examples are off the D47 to Périgueux, 2km north of Les Eyzies, in the **Grotte du Grand Roc** (Feb, March, Nov & Dec daily except Tues 10am–5pm; April–June, Sept & Oct daily 9.30am–6pm; July & Aug daily 9.30am–7pm; 38F/€5.79), whose entrance is high up in the cliffs that line much of the Vézère valley. There's a great view from the mouth of the cave and, inside, along some 80m of tunnel, a fantastic array of rock formations.

Roque St-Christophe

The enormous prehistoric dwelling site, **La Roque St-Christophe** (daily: Jan, Feb, Nov & Dec 11am–5pm; March–June, Sept & Oct 10am–6/6.30pm; July & Aug 10am–7pm; 35F/€5.34), 9km northeast of Les Eyzies along the D706 to Montignac, is made up of about one hundred caves on five levels, hollowed out of the limestone cliffs. The whole complex is 700–800m long and about 80m above the ground, where the River Vézère once flowed. The earliest traces of occupation go back over 50,000 years. The view is pretty good, and the guided tour instructive, but most of the finds are on display at the Musée National de Préhistoire in Les Eyzies (see p.634).

Montignac and the Lascaux caves

Some 26km up the Vézère valley, **MONTIGNAC** is the main base for visiting the **Lascaux caves**. It's a more attractive place than Les Eyzies, with several wooden-balconied houses leaning appealingly over the river, and a lively annual **arts festival** in mid-July, featuring international folk groups. On place Bertran-de-Born in the old hospital, the **Musée Eugène-Le-Roy** (July to mid-Sept daily 9am–6.15pm; rest of year Mon–Sat 9–11.15am & 2–5.15pm; 10F/€1.52) displays local crafts and trades, and it includes a reconstruction of the household of Jacquou le Croquant, the peasant protagonist of the novel of the same name by Eugène le Roy, the Dordogne's native novelist, who lived and died here in Montignac. The novel describes the harshness of peasant life in the early nineteenth century and the depredations of the local squirearchy in spite of the reforms of the Revolution.

The **tourist office** shares the same building as the museum on place Bertran-de-Born (July to mid-Sept daily 9am–7pm; rest of year Mon–Sat 9am–noon & 2–6pm; ☎05.53.51.82.60, fax 05.53.50.49.72). Tickets for **Lascaux II** (see below) must be bought here, from the office on the ground floor.

Accommodation, as everywhere around here, can be a problem. The *Hôtel de la Grotte*, on rue du 4-Septembre (☎05.53.51.80.48, fax 05.53.51.05.96; ②; restaurant from 65F/€9.91), is the cheapest in town, with a pleasant stream-side garden. Then it's a big leap up to the three-star *Soleil d'Or*, also on the main rue du 4-Septembre (☎05.53.51.80.22, fax 05.53.50.27.54, *www.soleil-dor.com*; ④; closed mid-Jan to mid-Feb), whose restaurant menus start at 110F/€16.77. For not much more, however, you can stay in the pretty, period rooms of the ivy- and wisteria-clad *Hostellerie de la Roseraie*, across the river in quiet place d'Armes (☎05.53.50.53.92, fax 05.53.51.02.23; ⑤; closed Nov–March; restaurant from 175F/€26.68). And finally there is a cheap municipal **campsite** on the river bank 500m downstream (☎05.53.51.83.95; closed mid-Oct to March).

There are other worthwhile hotel options in the area. Two of the most attractive are *La Table du Terroir* at **LA CHAPELLE-AUBAREIL**, about 15km beyond the Lascaux caves (☎05.53.50.72.14, fax 05.53.51.16.23; ③; closed Nov–March), which has a swimming pool and an excellent restaurant (menus from 70F/€10.67), and *Hôtel Laborderie*, further south at **TAMNIÈS** on the Les Eyzies–St-Geniès road (☎05.53.29.68.59, fax 05.53.29.65.31; ②–⑤; closed Nov–March) offering equally good food (evening menus from 105F/€16.01). For other possibilities, ask the tourist office in Montignac for their extensive list of B&B and farm **campsites**. A particularly good spot for campers with a taste for luxury is the *Le Paradis* site (☎05.53.50.72.64; closed Nov–March) near the exquisite riverside village of **ST-LÉON-SUR-VÉZÈRE**, some 9km south of Montignac.

Grotte de Lascaux and Lascaux II

The **Grotte de Lascaux** was discovered in 1940 by four boys who were, according to popular myth, looking for their dog and fell into a deep cavern decorated with marvellously preserved animal paintings. Executed by Cro-Magnon people 17,000 years ago, the paintings are among the finest examples of prehistoric art in existence. There are five or six identifiable styles, and subjects include the bison, mammoth and horse, plus the biggest known prehistoric drawing, of a 5.5-metre bull with astonishingly expressive head and face. In 1948, the cave was opened to the public, and over the course of the next fifteen years more than a million tourists came to Lascaux. Sadly, because of deterioration from the body heat and breath of visitors, the cave had to be closed in 1963; now you have to be content with the replica known as **Lascaux II**, 2km south of Montignac on the D704 (early Feb to March & Nov–Dec Tues–Sun 10am–12.30pm & 2–5.30pm; April–June, Sept & Oct daily 9.30am–6.30pm; July & Aug daily 9am–8pm; 50F/€7.62, combined ticket with Le Thot – see below – 57F/€8.69). There are 2000 tickets on sale each day but these go fast in peak season; telephone bookings aren't accepted, but you can buy tickets in person a day or so in advance. Note also that in winter (Oct–March) tickets are normally on sale at the site, while in summer (April–Sept) they are available from an office underneath Montignac tourist office – the system varies from year to year, however, so check in Montignac before heading up to the cave.

Opened in 1983, Lascaux II was the result of eleven years' painstaking work by twenty artists and sculptors, under the supervision of Monique Peytral, using the same methods and materials as the original cave painters. While the visit can't offer the excitement of a real cave, the reconstruction – which cost over 500 million francs – rarely disappoints the thousands who trek here every year. The guided tour lasts forty minutes (commentary in French or English). If you have bought the joint ticket to

From the roof, there is a stupendous – and vertiginous – view upriver to the **Château de Marqueyssac**, whose beautiful seventeenth- and nineteenth-century gardens extend along the ridge-line (daily: mid-Feb to June & Sept to mid-Nov 10am–6/7pm; July & Aug 9am–8pm; mid-Nov to mid-Feb 2–5pm; 30F/€4.57).

In the main street below Beynac castle is the old-fashioned *Hôtel Bonnet* (☎05.53.29.50.01, fax 05.53.29.83.7; ④; closed Nov–March), with a good restaurant serving menus from 85F/€12.96, though you'll find quieter rooms in *Hôtel Pontet* on the road up to the castle (☎05.53.29.50.06, fax 05.53.28.28.52; ③; closed Jan). There's also a riverside **campsite**, *Le Capeyrou* (☎05.53.29.54.95, fax 05.53.28.36.27; closed mid-Sept to mid-May), immediately east of the town.

La Roque-Gageac

The village of **LA ROQUE-GAGEAC** is almost too perfect, its ochre-coloured houses sheltering under dramatically overhanging cliffs. Regular winner of France's prettiest village contest, it inevitably pulls in the tourist buses, and since the main road separates the village from the river, the noise and fumes of the traffic can become oppressive. The best way to escape is to slip away through the lanes and alleyways that wind up through the terraced houses. The other option is to hire a canoe and paddle over to the opposite bank, where you can picnic and enjoy a much better view of La Roque than from among the crowds milling around beneath the village, at its best in the burnt-orange glow of the evening sun.

Most people just come here for the afternoon, so there's usually space if you want to **stay** the night, most pleasantly at *La Belle Étoile* (☎05.53.29.51.44, fax 05.53.29.45.63; ④; closed Nov–March), whose restaurant serves good traditional cuisine (from 125F/€19.06). You can also **eat** well further along the riverfront at *La Plume d'Oie* (☎05.53.29.57.05; closed Dec to early Feb; menus from 195F/€29.73), though you'll need to book ahead. Of the many **campsites** in the vicinity, *Le Lauzier* (☎05.53.29.51.56; closed Oct to mid-June) is one of the closest, while *Le Beau Rivage* offers the greatest luxury; they're both east of La Roque on the D703 Sarlat road.

Domme

High on the scarp on the south bank of the river, **DOMME** is one of the best preserved of the *bastides*, although it's now wholly given over to tourism. Its attractions, in addition to its position, include three original thirteenth-century **gateways** and a section of the old **walls**. From the northern edge of the village, marked by a drop so precipitous that fortifications were deemed unnecessary, you look out over a wide sweep of river country. Beneath the village are hundreds of metres of **caves** (Feb to mid-Nov & Christmas hols daily 10.30am–noon & 2.15–5.15/6pm; 35F/€5.34) in which the townspeople took refuge in times of danger. You can enter the complex opposite the **tourist office** (Feb–June & Sept to mid-Nov daily 10am–noon & 2–6pm; July & Aug daily 10am–7pm; mid-Nov to Jan Mon–Fri 10am–noon & 2–6pm; ☎05.53.31.71.00, fax 05.53.31.71.09) on the main square, though there's not a lot to see.

At the top of the Grand'rue, *Le Nouvel Hôtel* (☎05.53.28.38.67, fax 05.53.28.27.13; ③; closed Sun evening & Mon; menus from 70F/€10.67) has several simple, reasonably priced **rooms** above a restaurant, while the smartest place to stay is *L'Esplanade*, right on the cliff edge (☎05.53.28.31.41, fax 05.53.28.49.92; ④; closed early Nov to mid-Feb; good restaurant from 180F/€27.44); note that rooms with a view cost double the price of those without. There's a municipal **campsite** (☎05.53.28.31.91; closed mid-Sept to mid-June) down by the river at **CÉNAC**. If you stay there, don't miss the round tile roof of the chapel or the beautifully proportioned twelfth-century **church** on rue St-Cybranet.

CANOEING ON THE DORDOGNE AND VÉZÈRE

Canoeing is hugely popular in the Dordogne, especially during the summer months when the Vézère and Dordogne rivers are shallow and slow-flowing – ideal for beginners. There are rental outlets at just about every twist in both rivers, and although it's possible to rent one-person kayaks or two-person canoes by the hour, it's best to take at least a half-day or longer, and simply cruise downstream. The company you book through will either take you to your departure point or send a minibus to pick you up from your final destination. Prices vary according to what's on offer; expect to pay 80–120F/€12.20–18.29 per day. Most places function daily in July and August, on demand in May, June and September, and are closed the rest of the year. All companies are obliged to equip you with lifejackets (*gilets*) and teach you basic safety procedures, most importantly how to capsize and get out without drowning. You must be able to swim. Below are just some of the choices on offer.

RIVER DORDOGNE

Canoë Dordogne, La Roque-Gageac (☎05.53.29.58.50). Choice of distances from 7 to 21km, including the stretch downstream past Castelnaud and Beynac.

Copeyre Canoë, Gluges (☎05.65.37.33.51, *canoe@mail.netsource.fr*). Thirteen bases from Argentat to Beynac; choose your own day-trip or longer outings of up to seven days.

Castelnaud Kayak-Club, Castelnaud-la-Chapelle (☎05.53.29.40.07). Groléjac–Castelnaud (full day); Vitrac–Castelnaud (half-day); Castelnaud–Les Milandes (half-day).

Randonnée Dordogne, Le Port de Domme (☎05.53.28.22.01). Carsac–Beynac (full day); Carsac–Cénac or Cénac–Beynac (half-day); longer accompanied trips possible.

Safaraid, Albas (☎05.65.30.74.47, *www.canoe-dordogne.com*). Eight bases from Argentat to Beynac; choose your own route, with rental available by the day, the week and the fortnight.

RIVER VÉZÈRE

Canoë Vallée Vézère, rte de Périgueux, Les Eyzies (☎05.53.05.10.11). You can choose your distance, starting anywhere between Montignac and Les Eyzies or, downstream, stopping anywhere from Les Eyzies to Trémolat.

Canoë-Kayak 7 Rives, Montignac (☎05.53.50.19.26). Choice of distances downstream to Thonac, St-Léon or La Roque St-Christophe.

Souillac

The first place of any size east of Sarlat is **SOUILLAC**, at the confluence of the Borrèze and Dordogne rivers and on a major road junction. Virginia Woolf stayed here in 1937, and was pleased to meet "no tourists . . . England seems like a chocolate box bursting with trippers afterward." There are still few tourists, since Souillac's only real point of interest is the twelfth-century **church of Ste-Marie**, just off the main road. Roofed with massive domes like the cathedrals of Périgueux and Cahors, its spacious interior creates just the atmosphere for cool reflection on a summer's day. On the back of the west door are some of the most wonderful Romanesque sculptures, including a seething mass of beasts devouring each other. The greatest piece of craftsmanship, though, is a bas-relief of Isaiah, fluid and supple, thought to be by one of the artists who worked at Moissac (see p.676). Behind the church, the **Musée de l'Automate** (Jan–March, Nov & Dec Wed–Sun 2–5pm; April, May & Oct Tues–Sun 10am–noon & 3–6pm; June & Sept daily 10am–noon & 3–6pm; July & Aug daily 10am–7pm; 30F/€4.57) contains a collection of mostly nineteenth-century mechanical dolls, which dance, sing and perform magical tricks, and which will appeal mainly to children.

The **tourist office** (July & Aug daily 9.30am–12.30pm & 2–7pm; rest of year Mon–Sat 10am–noon & 2–6pm; ☎05.65.37.81.56, fax 05.65.27.11.45, *souillac @wanadoo.fr*) is on the main boulevard Louis-Jean Malvy, next to the handsome, old

Grand Hôtel (☎05.62.32.78.30, fax 05.65.32.66.34; ②; closed Nov–March), with comfortable rooms and an excellent restaurant (closed Wed; from 75F/€11.43). There is cheaper **accommodation** at the *Auberge du Puits*, in the pretty place du Puits in the old quarter (☎05.65.37.80.32, fax 05.65.37.07.16, *aubpuits@souillac.net*; ①–②; closed Sun evening, Mon & Dec–Jan), with good food from 80F/€12.20. There's also a large riverside **campsite**, *Les Ondines* (☎05.65.37.86.44; closed Oct–April), and a *gîte d'étape* at Le Gachou on the Martel road (☎05.65.32.27.17). You can rent **bicycles** and **canoes** from Quercyland (☎05.65.32.72.61), next to the campsite, and bikes only from Carrefour du Cycle, 23 av de Gaulle (☎05.65.37.07.52).

Martel

About 15km east of Souillac and set back even further from the river, **MARTEL** is a minor medieval masterpiece, built in a pale, almost white, stone, offset by warm reddish-brown roofs, yet it suffers none of the crowds endured by the likes of Sarlat. Another Turenne-administered town (see p.655), its heyday came during the thirteenth and fourteenth centuries, when the viscounts established a court of appeal here.

The main square, **place des Consuls**, is mostly taken up by the large eighteenth-century covered *halles*, but on every side there are reminders of the town's illustrious past, most notably in the superb Gothic **Hôtel de la Raymondie**. Begun in 1280, it served as the Turenne law courts, though it doubled as the town's refuge, hence the distinctive corner turrets. Facing the *hôtel* is the **Tour des Pénitents**, one of the many medieval towers which gave the town its epithet, *la ville aux sept tours*. Henry Short-Coat (see box below) died in the striking building in the southeast corner of the square, the **Maison Fabri**. One block south, rue Droite leads east to the town's main church, the **church of St-Maur**, built in a fiercely defensive, mostly Gothic style, with a finely carved Romanesque tympanum depicting the Last Judgement above the west door.

If you'd rather **stay** here than in Souillac, head for the *Le Turenne* on avenue J.-Lavayssière (☎05.65.37.30.30; ②; closed Dec–Feb), with traditional cuisine from 75F/€11.43. There's a basic municipal **campsite**, *La Callopie* (05.65.37.30.03, fax 05.65.37.37.27; closed Oct–April), on the northern edge of town, and the little riverside *Camping les Falaises* (☎05.65.37.37.78; closed Oct–April), 5km away in the village of **GLUGES**. You'll find a nice hotel here as well, also called *Les Falaises* (☎05.65.27.18.44, fax 05.65.27.18.45; ③; closed Nov–March; restaurant from 120F/€18.29, evenings only), and you can rent **canoes** and **bikes** from Copeyre Canoë down by the water (☎05.65.37.33.51).

THE TALE OF HENRY SHORT-COAT

At the end of the twelfth century, Martel was the stage for one of the tragic events in the internecine conflicts of the Plantagenet family. When Henry Plantagenet (King Henry II of England) imprisoned his estranged wife Eleanor of Aquitaine, his sons took up arms against their father. The eldest son, **Henry Short-Coat** (Henri Court-Mantel), even went so far as to plunder the viscountcy of Turenne and Quercy. Furious, Henry II immediately stopped his allowance and handed over his lands to the third son, Richard the Lionheart. Financially insecure, and with a considerable army of soldiers to feed and clothe, Henry Short-Coat began looting the treasures of every abbey and shrine in the region. Finally, he decided to sack the shrine at Rocamadour, making off with various artefacts, including Roland's famous sword, Durandal. This last act was to be his downfall, for shortly afterwards he fled to Martel and fell ill with a fever. Guilt-ridden and afraid for his life, he confessed his crimes and asked his father for forgiveness. Henry II was busy besieging Limoges, but sent a messenger to pardon him. On the messenger's arrival in Martel, Henry Short-Coat died, and Richard the Lionheart became heir to the English throne.

Carennac and Castelnau-Bretenoux

CARENNAC is without doubt one of the most beautiful villages along this part of the Dordogne river. Elevated just above the south bank of the river, 13km or so east of Martel, it's best known for its typical Quercy architecture, its Romanesque priory, where the French writer Fénelon spent the best years of his life, and for its greengages.

Carennac's feature, as so often in these parts, is the Romanesque tympanum – in the Moissac style – above the west door of its church, the **église St-Pierre**. Christ sits in majesty with the Book of Judgment in his left hand, with the apostles and adoring angels below him. Next to the church, you can gain access to the old **cloisters and chapter house** (March–May & Sept–Oct daily 10am–noon & 1.30–6.30pm; June–Aug daily 10am–7pm; Nov–Feb Mon–Fri 10am–noon & 1.30–5.30pm, Sat & Sun 1.30–5.30pm; 10F/€1.52), which contain an exceptionally expressive life-size Entombment of Christ.

There are two comfortable and reasonably priced **hotels** in the village, both with good restaurants specializing in traditional regional cuisine: the *Auberge du Vieux Quercy*, to the south of the church (☎05.65.10.96.59, fax 05.65.10.94.05; ③; closed mid-Nov to mid-March), whose restaurant has a good-value menu at 98F/€14.94, and the more rustic *Hôtel Fénelon* on the main street (☎05.65.10.96.46, fax 05.65.10.94.86; ③; closed Jan to mid-March; restaurant from 100F/€15.24). There's also a **campsite**, *L'Eau Vive*, 1km east of Carennac (☎05.65.10.97.39; closed Oct–April).

Another 10km further upstream, the sturdy towers and machicolated red-brown walls of the eleventh-century **Château de Castelnau-Bretenoux** (daily: April–June & Sept 9.30am–12.15pm & 2–6.15pm; July & Aug 9.30am–6.45pm; Oct–March 10am–12.15pm & 2–5.15pm; 32F/€4.88) dominate a sharp knoll above the Dordogne, making a harmonious whole with the village piled at its feet. Most of it has now been restored and refurnished. Below, on the banks of the River Cère, you come to the graceful little *bastide* of **BRETENOUX**, with two sides of its cobbled and arcaded square still intact.

Beaulieu-sur-Dordogne

Beautifully situated on the banks of the Dordogne, 8km upriver from Castelnau-Bretenoux, **BEAULIEU-SUR-DORDOGNE** boasts another of the great masterpieces of Romanesque sculpture on the porch of the **church of St-Pierre** in the centre of town. This doorway is unusually deep-set, with a tympanum presided over by an oriental-looking Christ with one arm extended to welcome the chosen. All around him is a complicated pattern of angels and apostles, executed in characteristic "dancing" style, similar to that at Carennac. The dead raise the lids of their coffins hopefully, while underneath a frieze depicts monsters crunching heads. Take the opportunity also to wander north along rue de la Chapelle past some handsome sculpted facades and down to the river.

The most appealing **hotel** is the riverside *Les Charmilles*, on the northeast side of town (☎05.55.91.29.29, fax 05.55.91.29.30, *charme@dubinternet.fr*, ④; restaurant from 105F/€16.01), with *Le Turenne*, in a former abbey on central place Marbot (☎05.55.91.10.16, fax 05.55.91.22.42; ③; menus from 100F/€15.24), coming a close second. For cheaper rooms head further north to the *Hôtel Fournié*, on place de Champ-de-Mars (☎05.55.91.01.34; fax 05.55.91.23.57; ②; good restaurant from 100F/€15.24). The welcoming **HI hostel** is at the far end of rue de la Chapelle in a magnificent half-timbered and turreted building, with surprisingly modern rooms inside (☎05.55.91.13.82, fax 05.55.91.26.06; closed Oct–March). There are river-bathing and canoeing possibilities and a good riverside **campsite**, *Camping des Isles*, close by (☎05.55.91.02.65; closed Oct–April).

Around Limoges

There is a clutch of villages within a day's reach of Limoges. A route linking places of interest on the south bank of the Vienne, like the **châteaux** of **Rochebrune**, **Rochechouart** and **Châlus**, are detailed in the *Route Richard-Cœur-de-Lion* leaflet (available at local tourist offices), so called because of its associations with the English king. Visiting all of them really requires a car, but some at least are accessible by a combination of public transport and patient hitching.

Oradour-sur-Glane

Twenty-five kilometres northwest of Limoges and a few kilometres north of the N141 road to Angoulême, the village of **ORADOUR-SUR-GLANE** stands just as the soldiers of the SS left it on June 10, 1944, after killing all the inhabitants in reprisal for attacks by French *maquisards*. The village has been preserved both as a shrine and a chilling reminder of human brutality.

Before entering the village, the **Centre de la Mémoire**, immediately southeast of Oradour on the Limoges road (daily: Feb–April & mid-Oct to mid-Dec 9am–6pm; May to mid-Oct 9am–7pm; entry to village free, exhibition 30F/€4.57), sets the historical context and attempts to answer some of the questions. From here an underground passage leads into the **village** itself, where a sign admonishes, *Souviens-toi* ("Remember"), and the main street leads past roofless houses gutted by fire. Telephone poles, tram cables and gutters are fixed in tormented attitudes where the fire's heat left them; prewar cars rust in the garages; a yucca, grown into an enormous clump, still blooms in the notary's garden; last year's grapes hang wizened on a vine whose trellis has long rotted away.

Behind the square is a **memorial garden**, a plain rectangle of lawn hedged with beech. A dolmen-like slab on a shallow plinth covers a crypt containing relics of the dead, and the awful list of names. Beyond, by the stream, stands the **church** where the women and children – five hundred of them – were burnt to death.

The **modern village** of Oradour has been constructed beside the old, with a 1950s concrete church that tries to be impressive but struggles with the task of commemorating what happened here.

There are **buses** from Limoges to Oradour, although it might be more convenient to take the train to **ST-JUNIEN** and then bus back to Oradour. The *Hôtel au Rendez-vous des Chasseurs*, Pont-à-la-Planche (☎05.55.02.19.73, fax 05.55.02.06.98; ②; closed first week Aug & last two weeks Oct, also Sun evening & Fri), with a good restaurant specializing in game (from 65F–240F/€9.91–36.59), makes a decent place to put up in St-Junien. There's also a **hostel**, 13 rue de St-Amand (☎ & fax 05.55.02.22.79), in an old abbey 1.5km from the train station on the west side of town.

Rochechouart and Chassenon

ROCHECHOUART, a beautiful little walled town 11km southwest of St-Junien, has two claims to fame. Two hundred million years ago it was the site of impact of one of the largest meteorites ever to hit earth, a monster 1.5km in diameter and some 6000 million tonnes in weight. The traces of this cosmic pile-up still attract the curiosity of world's astronomers and moon-watchers. The only evidence that a layman might notice, however, is the unusual-looking breccia stone many of the region's older buildings are made of: the squashed, shattered, heat-transformed and reconstituted result of the collision.

One such building is Rochechouart's other source of pride: the handsome **château** that stands at the town's edge. It started life as a rough fortress before 1000 AD, was "modernized" in the thirteenth century (the sawn-off keep and entrance survive from this period) and civilized with Renaissance decoration and additions in the fifteenth. Until it was acquired as the Mairie in 1832, it had belonged to the de Rochechouart family for 800 years. Today it is not only the town hall, but also the very well-regarded and adventurous **Musée Départemental d'Art Contemporain** (closed for renovation at time of writing; check with tourist office for latest details), specializing in "land art" and the Arte Povera movement. For instance, in a room decorated with its original sixteenth-century frescoes of the Labours of Hercules, the British artist, Richard Long, has made a special installation of white stones, while in the garden strange bits of metal grapple with the trees.

The Rochechouart **tourist office** is at 6 rue Victor-Hugo (mid-June to mid-Sept daily 10am–12.30pm & 3–7pm; rest of year Mon–Sat 10am–noon & 2.30–5.30pm; ☎ & fax 05.55.03.72.73, *ot-rochechouart-pays-de-la-meteorite@wanadoo.fr*).Should you wish to **stay**, the *Hôtel de France*, just outside the old town centre on place Octave-Marquet, provides good board, comfortable lodgings and interesting food from 76F/€11.59 (☎05.55.03.77.40, fax 05.55.03.03.87; ③; restaurant closed Sun evening & Mon lunch). The same proprietors run another nice **restaurant**, *La Vallée de la Gorre* (☎05.55.00.01.27; closed for dinner Sun & Mon; from 76F/€11.59), in nearby **ST-AUVENT**.

One side trip worth making if you have come this far is to the **Roman baths** 5km along the Chabanais road at **CHASSENON** (daily guided tours: April, May & mid-Sept to mid-Nov 2–4.45pm; June to mid-Sept 10–11.15am & 2–6.15pm; 30F/€4.57). The site, known as Cassinomagus in Gallo-Roman times, stood at an important crossroads on the Via Agrippa, the Roman road that connected Lyon to Saintes via Clermont-Ferrand and Limoges. Only the baths survive: a grand temple and theatre were destroyed for their breccia stone. But the baths alone are ample testimony to the magnificence of the place. There are hot and cold pools with some of the original floor tiles in places, and waterproof plastering, boiler rooms and elaborate hypocaust piping systems; you can even see the marks of the shuttering used to make the vaults in some of the subterranean passages.

Châlus and Nexon

At **CHÂLUS**, 35km along the N21 from Limoges (1hr by bus), the principal point of interest is the ruined **Château Féodal** (daily: July & Aug 10am–7pm; rest of year 10am–noon & 2–6pm; 30F/€4.57), where in 1199 Richard the Lionheart was mortally wounded by an archer shooting from the still-extant keep. Richard, son of Eleanor of Aquitaine and as much French as English, was campaigning to suppress a local rebellion against English rule. The archer was flayed to death for his marksmanship. For real enthusiasts, there are two further castles, both private homes: **Brie**, with limited visiting days (April–Oct Sun & public hols 2–7pm; 25F/€3.81), 8km northwest of Châlus, and **Montbrun** (no visits), 8km southwest. For an overnight **stay** in Châlus, there's the basic but friendly *Hôtel du Centre*, 8 place de la Fontaine (☎05.55.78.41.61; ②), with good-value menus from 70F/€10.67 in its restaurant; or you can pitch a tent behind the Hôtel de Ville.

Eighteen kilometres east, past another early medieval fortress at Rilhac-Lastours, the village of **NEXON**, also directly accessible by bus and train from Limoges, is of more general interest, with a fine, heavily restored late medieval **Château** (now the Mairie), set in magnificent parklands once renowned for its stud farm breeding Anglo-Arabs. You can **camp** in Nexon at the *Étang de la Lande* (☎05.55.58.35.44; closed Oct–May). For a **meal**, try the *Dexet* at 17 av de Gaulle (closed for dinner Sat & Sun; lunch menus from 56F/€8.54, 118F/€17.99 on Sun), the main road heading north to the train station and Limoges, for good-value country cooking.

Chalusset and Solignac

A dozen kilometres south of Limoges in the lovely wooded valley of the Briance, the Château de Chalusset and the church of **SOLIGNAC** make the most attractive day's outing from the city. There are **trains** to Solignac-Le Vigen station, 1km away on the Limoges–Brive line, and infrequent **bus** services to Solignac itself; you'll have more choice if you take a bus to **LE VIGEN** and walk the final kilometre.

Approaching from Le Vigen you can see Solignac's Romanesque **abbey church** (daily 9am–6.30pm; free) ahead of you, with the tiled roofs of its octagonal apse and neat little brood of radiating chapels. The twelfth-century facade is plain with just a little sculpture, as the granite of which it is built does not permit the intricate carving of limestone. Inside it is beautiful, a flight of steps leading down into the nave with a dramatic view the length of the church. There are no aisles, just a single space roofed with three big domes, and no ambulatory either – an absolutely plain Latin cross in design. It is a simple, sturdy church, with the same feel of plain robust Christianity as the crypt of St-Eutrope in Saintes (see p.591).

There is a very pleasant, comfortable **hotel** opposite the church, *Le St Eloi* (☎05.55.44.52, fax 05.55.00.55.56; ③; closed three weeks in Jan & two weeks in Sept), with a good restaurant (closed Sun evening & Mon lunch; menus from 78F/€11.89). Alternatively, try the much simpler but welcoming *Les Sarrazins* (☎05.55.00.51.48; ①; closed three weeks in Aug), also in the village, which serves a generous meal for 60F/€9.15 (restaurant closed Fri evening, Sat & Sun).

The **Château de Chalusset** is a good five-kilometre walk up the valley of the Briance in the other direction – uphill quite a lot of the way along the D32 and D32a. After about 45 minutes, at the highest point of the climb, there is a dramatic view across the valley to the romantic, ruined keep of the castle, rising above the woods. It is a further kilometre down to the bridge on the Briance, where a path follows the river bank before climbing steeply up again into the woods. Built in the twelfth century, the château was in English hands during the Hundred Years War and, in the lawless aftermath, became the lair of a notorious local brigand, Perrot le Béarnais. Dismantled in 1593 for harbouring Protestants, it has recently been acquired by the local authorities who are in the midst of major restoration works, including an archeological dig, due for completion in 2005. It is still possible to visit, though you are restricted to safe areas along fenced-off paths.

St-Léonard-de-Noblat

ST-LÉONARD-DE-NOBLAT, twenty minutes by train from Limoges or 35 minutes by bus, is a beautiful little market town of narrow streets and medieval houses with jutting eaves and corbelled turrets. There's a very lovely eleventh- and twelfth-century **church**, whose six-storey tower looks out over the rising hills and woods where the River Vienne threads its course down from the heights of the Massif Central. The interior is strong and simple, with barrel vaults on big, square piles, a high dome on an octagonal drum and domed transepts – the whole in grey granite.

If you're in a car, St-Léonard can make a pleasant base for visiting Limoges. The **tourist office** on place du Champs-de-Mars (July & Aug Mon–Sat 9.30am–6.30pm, Sun 9.30am–12.30pm; rest of year Tues–Sat 9am–noon & 2–5pm; ☎05.55.56.25.06, fax 05.55.56.36.97) publishes route maps for local walks and will point you to *chambres d'hôte* possibilities round about. A good place to **stay** is the *Modern Hôtel* on the edge of the old town, 6 bd Pressemanne (☎05.55.56.00.25; ③; closed April), and you can **eat** well just round the corner at *Le Gay-Lussac*, rue de l'Égalité (☎05.55.56.98.45; closed Sun evening & Mon), which offers well-priced, imaginative menus from 65F/€9.91 at lunch and 95F/€14.48 in the evening. There's a municipal **campsite**

(☎05.55.56.02.79; closed mid-Sept to mid-June) beside the river a couple of kilometres out of town on the D39.

Aubusson

AUBUSSON is 90km east of Limoges and served by regular buses and trains. A neat grey-stone town in the bottom of a ravine formed by the River Creuse, it is of no great interest in itself. What makes it unique is its reputation as a centre for weaving tapestries, second only to the Gobelins in Paris. If you're interested, you should aim for the **Musée Départemental de la Tapisserie** in avenue des Lissiers (July & Aug Mon & Wed–Sun 10am–6pm, Tues 2–6pm; rest of year daily except Tues 9.30am–noon & 2–6pm; 20F/€3.05), which traces the history of Aubusson tapestries over six centuries, coming up to the modern day with works by Jean Lurçat, Pierre Baudouin and Sylvain Dubuisson. The **Maison du Tapissier** next to the tourist office (same hours as tourist office; 17F/€2.59) is also worth a quick look for its broad overview of weaving techniques and local history displayed in the sixteenth-century home of a master weaver.

For information about further exhibitions and workshop visits, ask at the **tourist office** in rue Vieille (July & Aug Mon–Sat 10am–7pm, Sun 10am–noon & 2.30–5.30pm; rest of year Mon–Sat 10am–noon & 2–6pm; ☎05.55.66.32.12, fax 05.55.83.84.51, *tourisme.aubusson@wanadoo.fr*). The smartest **hotel** in town is the *Hôtel de France* at 6 rue des Déportés (☎05.55.66.10.22, fax 05.55.66.88.64; ④), with elegant rooms and a very good restaurant (menus from 90F/€13.72). There are also two good, inexpensive **hotels** in the main Grande-Rue: the friendly *du Chapitre*, at no. 53 (☎05.55.66.18.54, fax 05.55.67.79.63; ②), and the older but well-kept *du Lissier*, at no. 84 (☎ 05.55.66.14.18, fax 05.55.66.33.87; ②; closed Sun evening & Mon; restaurant from 75F/€11.43). The town's **campsite** (☎05.55.66.18.00; closed Oct–March), is by the river on the Felletin road.

The Plateau de Millevaches

Millevaches, the plateau of a thousand springs, is undulating upland country 800–900m in altitude, a sort of step on the northern edge of the Massif Central. It is a wild and sparsely populated landscape, and the villages here are few and far between. The ones there are appear small, grey and sturdy, inured like their mainly elderly inhabitants to the buffeting of upland weather. It is a country of conifer plantations and natural woodland – of beech, birch and chestnut – interspersed with reed-fringed tarns, dam-created lakes and pasture grazed by sheep and cows, where you still find people haymaking with rake and pitchfork.

The small towns, like **Eymoutiers** and **Meymac**, have a primitive architectural beauty and an old-world charm largely untouched by modern development. It is an area to walk or cycle in, or at least savour at a gentle pace, and there are a surprisingly large number of attractive old-fashioned hotels.

Obviously, getting around by car is easiest, but there is access by public transport. **Ussel**, the largest town, is on the main road and rail link between Brive and Clermont-Ferrand, and is also connected by a cross-country line through Meymac and Eymoutiers to Limoges.

Ussel

On the southeastern edge of the plateau is USSEL, 90km west of Clermont-Ferrand and 60km northeast of Tulle, where the land begins its gradual descent to the uppermost reaches of the Dordogne valley, thickly wooded and cut by deep tributary valleys. The town is pleasant enough, with some attractive sixteenth- and seventeenth-century houses scattered about the central part. A giant battered granite eagle on the place Voltaire is all that remains of a Roman settlement hereabouts. It's not a place with much to see.

One building worth a look is the house of the local lords, the **Maison du Ducs de Ventadour**, who moved here from their draughty fortress in the hills to the south (see opposite). Just off place de la République behind the church, it has a very provincial and rather amateurish Renaissance grandeur, perhaps aping their rich metropolitan cousins. Also worth a quick look is the local **Musée du Pays d'Ussel** (July & Aug daily 10am–noon & 2–7pm; free), one half of which is dedicated to traditional crafts and trades of the region and located in the eighteenth-century Hôtel Bonnot de Bay on rue Michelet, parallel to avenue Thiers.

The N89, the main Clermont road, passes through the town centre. At the top of the hill, it becomes avenue Carnot and begins to descend towards the **gare SNCF**. The **tourist office** is on the wide place Voltaire (June & Sept daily 9am–noon & 2–5pm; July & Aug Mon–Sat 9am–12.30pm & 2–7pm, Sun 9am–12.30pm; rest of year Mon–Sat 9am–noon & 2–5pm; ☎05.55.72.11.50, fax 05.55.72.54.44, *ot-ussel@wanadoo.fr*).

The most comfortable place to **stay** is the striking 1970s *Les Gravades* (☎05.55.46.06.00, fax 05.55.46.06.10; ③; closed mid-Dec to Feb; restaurant from 95F/€14.48, closed Fri evening & Sat off season), a couple of kilometres east of Ussel on the N89 and set in its own grounds. Alternatively, try *Le Terminus*, next to the train station (☎ & fax 05.55.96.23.39; ②; restaurant from 60F/€9.15, closed Sun evening off season). There is a municipal **campsite** (☎05.55.72.30.05; closed Nov–Feb) just off the road to Tulle. Your best bet for **food** is one of the several brasseries on avenue Carnot, or the cluster of restaurants in front of the station.

Meymac and around

Pepperpot turrets and steep slate roofs adorn the ancient grey houses of **MEYMAC**, 17km west of Ussel. The village is packed tightly around its Romanesque **church**, whose porch is flanked by striking pink capitals. Adjoining it are the remains of the original Benedictine **abbey**, whose foundation a thousand years ago brought the town into being. Part of the abbey now houses the innovative **Centre National d'Art Contemporain** (daily except Tues: July & Aug 10am–noon & 2–7pm; rest of year 2–6pm; 25F/€3.81), featuring changing exhibitions of young, local artists as well as big-name retrospectives.

Grande-Rue, the main street, ends in steps that climb past the round **bell tower**, the town's landmark, to the lime-shaded square in front of the town hall. The **tourist office** is opposite, the other side of a prettily jetting fountain (July & Aug Mon–Sat 10am–12.30pm & 2–6.30pm, Sun 10am–12.30pm; rest of year Mon–Fri 10am–noon & 2–4pm; ☎05.55.95.18.43, fax 05.55.95.66.12), and has plenty of information on hiking amongst other things.

There's a pleasant **hotel** on the main road, the *Hôtel de Limousin*, 76 av Limousine (☎05.55.46.12.11, fax 05.55.46.12.12; ①–③; closed one week at Christmas; restaurant 69–150F/€10.52–22.87) and a municipal **campsite** (☎05.55.95.22.80; closed mid-Sept to mid-May) close at hand on the Sornac road.

One of the most touted sights in the area is the remains of a **Roman villa** and second-century **temple** at **CARS**. Although there is nothing very spectacular to see, the very presence of Roman influence here is interesting. And, if you want to stay, there is a simple, old-fashioned country **hotel** just a few kilometres away near **PÉROLS-SUR-VÉZÈRE**: the *Hôtel des Touristes* (☎05.55.95.51.71; ①–②; closed mid-Dec to mid-Jan), with genuine home-cooking from 60F/€9.15. A few kilometres further on, just outside **BUGEAT**, there is also a well-run riverside **campsite** (☎05.55.95.50.03; closed Nov–Easter).

Five kilometres northwest of Bugeat, the six houses of **VIAM** perch prettily on the shores of an artificial lake. Its innocence has been slightly marred by watersports, but

STEAM TRAINS ON MILLEVACHES

In July and August every year **steam-train trips** are run on the beautiful Limoges–Ussel mountain line. Prices are in the range of 50–220F/€7.62–33.54 (adults) and 30–120F/€4.57–18.29 (children), according to the length of the journey. There are various options, including Limoges–Meymac, Limoges–Eymoutiers, Eymoutiers–Bujaleuf and Meymac–Ussel. For dates and times, consult the brochure *Trains Touristiques à Vapeur en Limousin* or the tourist offices in Limoges, St-Léonard-de-Noblat, Bujaleuf, Pyrat-le-Château, Eymoutiers, Bugeat, Meymac or Treignac.

it has an exquisite and proportionately minute, lopsided **church**, whose door is blocked by a small iron gate, like Bugeat's church – presumably a local device to keep wandering farm animals out. There is no accommodation in Viam except a municipal **campsite** (☎05.55.95.52.05; closed mid-Sept to mid-June), but 6km on, towards Eymoutiers, there is a friendly **gîte d'étape** by the Étang de Goussolles (Mme Sarrazin; ☎05.55.95.54.99; closed Oct–May).

Eymoutiers

EYMOUTIERS, on the banks of the River Vienne, 45km from Limoges, is another attractive upland town of tall, narrow stone houses crowding round a much-altered Romanesque **church**. Not interesting enough for a prolonged stay, it nonetheless makes another agreeable stopover, especially for campers, as it has a simple but magnificently sited **campsite**, the *St-Pierre-Château* (☎05.55.69.27.81; closed Oct–May), on top of a hill overlooking the town (access off the Meymac–Tulle road). If you prefer a **hotel**, you'll find simple rooms and good food in the rustic setting of the *Hôtel des Touristes* (☎05.55.69.50.01; ①; closed one week in Nov & two weeks at Christmas; restaurant from 75F/€11.43) back on the St-Léonard road in the tiny village of **BUJALEUF**.

Château de Ventadour

The **Château de Ventadour,** like Chalusset (see p.650), is a magnificent ruin standing on the very tip of a high narrow spur way above the river valleys converging at its feet, with a lone tower rising above the trees. Built in the twelfth century, the château was abandoned in around 1600 by its owners, the dukes of Ventadour, in favour of a more comfortable house in Ussel. The celebrated troubadour Bernard de Ventadour was born here, child of a castle servant. The ruins are now undergoing lengthy restoration work to make them safe; you can get quite close but the site itself is fenced off.

The castle is about 6km from Egletons on the Tulle–Ussel road. You take the dead-end turning to the farming hamlet of Moustier. But far the most dramatic approach is from below, up the winding road from **NEUVIC** – itself an ancient village, rather spoilt by the presence of an artificial lake which has elevated it to resort status. It does, however, have an interesting **Musée de la Résistance**, based on the life of Henri Queuille, a former government minister and *résistant* (May–Oct daily 10am–noon & 3–6pm; 15F/€2.29).

There are **hotels** in Egletons, but it is much nicer to stay in Gimel-les-Cascades (see p.656).

Brive-la-Gaillarde and around

BRIVE-LA-GAILLARDE is a major rail junction and the nearest thing to an industrial centre for miles around, but it makes an agreeable base for exploring the Corrèze *département* and its beautiful villages, as well as the upper reaches of the Vézère and Dordogne rivers.

Though it has no commanding sights, Brive-la-Gaillarde does have a few distractions. Right in the middle of town is the much-restored **church of St-Martin**, originally Romanesque in style, though only the transept, apse and a few comically carved capitals survive from that era. St Martin himself, a Spanish aristocrat, arrived in pagan Brive in 407 AD on the feast of Saturnus, smashed various idols and was promptly stoned to death by the outraged onlookers.

Numerous streets fan out from the surrounding square, **place du Général-de-Gaulle**, with a number of turreted and towered houses, some dating back to the thirteenth century. The most impressive is the sixteenth-century **Hôtel de Labenche** on boulevard Jules-Ferry, now housing the town's archeological finds as well as a collection of seventeenth-century tapestries (daily except Tues: April–Oct 10am–6.30pm; rest of year 1.30–6pm; 27F/€4.12). There is also the **Centre National d'Etude Edmond Michelet** at 4 rue Champanatier (Mon–Sat 10am–noon & 2–6pm; free), based in the former house of this minister of de Gaulle, and one of the town's leading *résistants*, with exhibitions portraying the occupation and Resistance through photographs, posters and objects of the time.

From the **gare SNCF**, it's a ten-minute walk north along avenue Jean-Jaurès to the boulevard ringing the old town. A left turn here brings you to the pleasant square Auboiroux, with the **post office** nearby. The **tourist office** is north of the ring road on place 14-Juillet (July & Aug Mon–Sat 9am–12.30pm & 2–7pm, Sun 10am–1pm; rest of year Mon–Sat 9am–noon & 2–6pm; ☎05.55.24.08.80, fax 05.55.24.58.24), alongside a modern, timber-framed market.

There are numerous cheap **hotels** around the station, of which the grand, old *Hôtel Terminus* (☎05.55.74.21.14; ①) is the nicest, with its big rooms and high ceilings. Opposite, the *Hôtel de France* (☎05.55.74.08.13, fax 05.55.17.04.32; ①) offers more modern, functional accommodation above its brasserie restaurant (menus from 55F/€8.38). For something smarter, try *Le Chapon Fin*, near square Auboiroux (☎05.55.74.23.40, fax 05.55.23.42.52; ③; good restaurant from 75F/€11.43), or the very grand *La Truffe Noir*, 22 bd Anatole-France (☎05.55.92.45.00, fax 05.55.92.45.13, *www.la-truffe-noire.com*; ⑥), with a restaurant to match (menus from 140F/€21.34). In addition, there's a decent **HI hostel** on the other side of town from the train station at 56 av Maréchal-Bugeaud (☎05.55.24.34.00, fax 05.55.74.82.80), 25 minutes by foot from the *gare SNCF*, and a **campsite**, *Les Îles* (☎05.55.24.34.74), across the river.

For alternative places to **eat**, try *Le Boulevard* at 8 bd Jules-Ferry (closed Sun evening & Mon; menus from 65F/€9.91) or, tucked down an alley near St-Martin, *Les Viviers St-Martin*, 4 rue Traversière, with a wide range of menus starting at 59F/€8.99. Though you'll have to book ahead, *Chez Francis*, 61 av de Paris (☎05.55.74.41.72; closed Sun), towards the river, is a friendly, cluttered place – with graffiti by visiting artists on walls, ceilings and lampshades and imaginative takes on classic dishes – menus start at 85F/€12.96.

Uzerche and Arnac-Pompadour

A half-hour train ride north of Brive along the course of the bubbling River Vézère, the town of **UZERCHE** is impressively located above a loop in the river's course. It's worth a passing visit as the town has several fine old buildings. From the **gare SNCF**, the old town is a five-minute walk south along the main road. The **tourist office** (mid-June to Sept daily 10am–12.30pm & 1.30–6.30pm; rest of year Mon–Fri 10am–noon & 2–5pm; ☎05.55.73.15.71, fax 05.55.73.88.36, *ot.uzerche@wanadoo.fr*), behind the main church, provides a suggested walking route, but the place is so small you can easily find your own way around. If you need a place to **stay**, *Hôtel Teyssier*, by the river (☎05.55.73.10.05, fax 05.55.98.43.31; ③; closed Wed; restaurant from 95F/€14.48), is a good option, as is the slightly cheaper *Hôtel Ambroise* round the corner (☎05.55.73.28.60, fax 05.55.98.45.73; ①–②; restaurant from 80F/€12.20).

Roughly 20km west of Uzerche (40min by train, on a different line, from Brive), is **ARNAC-POMPADOUR**, a town dominated by its grey, turreted **château**, presented in 1745 by Louis XV to his mistress, Madame de Pompadour, though she never actually visited it. Set in the green countryside of southern Limousin – reminiscent of parts of Ireland – the château is home to one of France's best-known **stud farms** (*haras*), first created by Louis XV in 1761, where Anglo-Arabs were first bred. Only the château terraces are open to the public (daily: April–Sept 10–11.30am & 2–5.30pm; rest of year 2–4.30/5.30pm; 10F/€1.52), but it's more interesting to visit the *dépôt des étalons* where the stallions are kept (daily: July–Sept 10–11am & 2–5.30pm; rest of year 2.30–4.30pm; 25F/€3.81), across the square from the château. The mares live in the Jumenterie de la Rivière (mid-Feb to June 2–4.15/5pm; July–Sept 3–5pm; 20F/€3.05), 4km away near the village of Beyssac; in spring the fields around are full of mares and foals, the best being kept for breeding, the rest sold worldwide as two-year-olds. From May to October there are frequent race meetings on the magnificent track in front of the château, events and open days.

The **gare SNCF** is 500m southeast of the town, on the D7 Vigeois road. There's a reasonable place to **stay** and **eat**, the *Hôtel du Parc* (☎05.55.73.30.54, fax 05.55.73.39.79; ③; closed Christmas & New Year; restaurant from 85F/€12.96), behind the château.

Turenne

TURENNE, just 16km south of Brive, is the first of two very picturesque villages close to the town. Capital of the viscountcy of Turenne, whose most illustrious seigneur was Henri de la Tour d'Auvergne – the "Grand Turenne", whom Napoléon rated the finest tactician of modern times – the village today would still seem familiar to him. The same mellow stone houses still crowd in the lee of the sharp bluff on whose summit sprout the towers of their castle, one forming part of someone's house. The other, known as **La Tour de César**, can be visited (April–June, Sept & Oct daily 10am–noon & 2–6pm; July & Aug daily 10am–7pm; Nov–March Sun 2–5pm; 18F/€2.74), and it's worth climbing for vertiginous views away over the ridges and valleys to the mountains of Cantal.

Collonges-la-Rouge

COLLONGES-LA-ROUGE, 7km east of Turenne, is the epitome of rustic charm with its red-sandstone houses, pepperpot towers and pink-candled chestnut trees, although you need to time your visit carefully, as the village is now very much on the tourist bus circuit. Though small-scale, there is a grandeur about the place, as if the resident Turenne administrators were aping, within their means, the grandiloquence of their superiors. On the main square a twelfth-century **church** testifies to the imbecility of shedding blood over religious differences: here, side by side, Protestant and Catholic conducted their services simultaneously. Outside, the covered **market hall** still retains its old-fashioned baker's oven.

If you want to **stay** somewhere nearby, it's best to head downhill a few minutes to **MEYSSAC**, a town built in the same red sandstone, though less grandly, to the very pleasant *Relais du Quercy* (☎05.55.25.40.31, fax 05.55.25.36.22; ③; closed three weeks in Nov; restaurant from 80F/€12.20), or the **campsite**, *Moulin de Valane* (☎05.55.25.41.59; closed Oct–April).

On weekdays it's possible to get to Collonges by **bus** from Brive (2–4 buses daily); with an early start you can see the town and return by the late-afternoon service. The prettiest route on foot from Turenne is along the back lanes through meadow and walnut orchards via **SAILLAC** (3hr), whose Romanesque **church** sports an elaborately carved tympanum upheld by a column of spiralling animal motifs.

Tulle

Seen from the distance, **TULLE**, 29km east of Brive, is a strange, unattractive-looking place. Strung out along the bottom of the narrow and deep valley of the Corrèze, it looks grey, run-down and industrial. But once you get down to the riverside and the area around the cathedral, it reveals itself to be full of fascinating winding lanes and stairways bordered by very handsome houses – many as old as the fourteenth century – with an imposing **Hôtel de Ville** at the end of rue du Trech, the main commercial street. If not worth a prolonged stay, Tulle certainly makes an interesting stopover.

The **Cathédrale Notre-Dame**, whose construction was drawn out from Romanesque to Gothic periods, stands on the riverside quays in place Émile-Zola. The cloister beside it has a small **museum** (Mon–Tues, Thurs–Fri & Sun 9am–noon & 2–5/6pm, Wed & Sat 2–5/6pm; 15F/€2.29), containing a mishmash of exhibits ranging from archeology to accordions, along with a large contingent of firearms, which once formed one of the town's major industries, along with lace. Around the block, at 2 quai Edmond-Perrier, is a collection of documents to do with the Resistance at the **Musée Départemental de la Résistance et de la Déportation** (Mon–Fri 9am–noon & 2–6pm; free), particularly the terrible reprisals wreaked by the Germans when they recaptured the town from the Resistance on June 8, 1944, and hanged 99 people.

The **tourist office** is opposite the cathedral at 2 place Émile-Zola (July & Aug Mon–Sat 9.30am–7pm, Sun 10am–noon; rest of year Mon 2–6pm, Tues–Sat 9.30am–noon & 2–6pm; ☎05.55.26.59.61, fax 05.55.20.72.93), and you'll find the **bus and train stations** side by side on the southwest edge of the town on avenue Winston-Churchill. The **market** takes place every Wednesday and Saturday by the cathedral.

By far the most attractive place to **stay** is also the simplest: the *Hôtel au Bon Accueil*, 10 rue du Canton (☎05.55.26.70.57; ②; closed one week at Christmas; restaurant from 78F/€11.89), in an old beamed house with stone mullion windows, across the river from the cathedral. Other places to stay include *Hôtel de la Gare* (☎05.55.20.04.04, fax 05.55.20.15.87; ③; closed one week in Feb & two weeks in Sept; restaurant from 97F/€14.79), by the train station, and the *Toque Blanche* at 29 rue Jean-Jaurès (☎05.55.26.75.41, fax 05.55.20.93.95; ③; closed second half Jan & early July), overlooking the car park by the very unattractive municipal offices, but only five minutes from the cathedral. The rooms at the *Toque Blanche* are acceptable but nothing special, whereas the **restaurant** is renowned, with an affordable menu at 135F/€20.58 (closed Sun evening & Mon) – or you can try their brasserie, *L'Amadeus* (closed Sun, and Mon & Tues evenings; menus from 68F/€10.37), next door. There is a municipal **campsite** by the river on the Ussel side of town (☎05.55.26.75.97; closed Oct–April).

Gimel

If you're travelling by car, you might consider staying in one of the villages in the hilly wooded country northeast of Tulle. **GIMEL-LES-CASCADES**, in particular, is very beautiful and, out of season at least, very quiet. It is a minute hamlet, about 10km away and clinging to the edge of a steep valley beside a spectacular waterfall, the **Montane**, which has sadly been turned into a paying "sight" (March–Oct daily 10am–6pm, Wed from 11am; 20F/€3.05). There is also a superb twelfth-century reliquary, known as the *Chasse de St-Étienne*, in the treasury of the local **church**.

The attractive *Hostellerie de la Vallée* (☎05.55.21.40.60, fax 05.55.21.38.74; ③; closed Oct–March) in the village has a few simple rooms and a good restaurant from 85F/€12.96. A further possibility for **accommodation** is the friendly and unpretentious *Hôtel Maurianges*, near the defunct Monteil train station, one kilometre up the road from Gimel, serving copious home-cooked meals for 70F/€10.67 (☎05.55.21.28.88; ②; restaurant closed Sat & evenings out of season). There is also a campsite (☎05.55.26.42.12; July & Aug) by a beautiful lakelet, the Étang de Ruffaud, near Gimel, where you can swim and get a reasonable meal in the lakeside bar.

THE LOT

The core of this section is formed by the old provinces of Haut Quercy and Quercy: the land between the Dordogne and the Lot and between the Lot and the Garonne, Aveyron and Tarn. We have extended it slightly eastwards to include the gorges of the River **Aveyron** and Villefranche-de-Rouergue on the edge of the province of Rouergue.

The area is hotter, drier, less well known and, with few exceptions, less crowded than the Dordogne, which does not mean that it is less interesting. The cave paintings at **Pech-Merle** are on a par with those at Les Eyzies. **Najac**, **Penne** and **Peyrerusse** have ruined castles to rival those of the Dordogne. Towns like **Figeac** and **Villefranche-de-Rouergue** are without equal, as are villages like **Cardaillac** and **St-Antonin-Noble-Val**, and stretches of country like that below **Gourdon**, around **Les Arques** where Osip Zadkine had his studio, and the **Célé Valley**.

Again, without transport, many places are out of reach. Some consolation, however, is the existence of the Brive–Toulouse train line that makes Figeac, Villefranche-de-Rouergue and Najac accessible, while **Agen**, **Moissac** and **Montauban** are on the Bordeaux–Toulouse line.

Rocamadour and around

Half-way up a cliff in the deep and abrupt canyon of the Alzou stream, the spectacular setting of **ROCAMADOUR** is hard to beat; the town itself must have been beautiful once, too, but for centuries now it has been inundated by religious pilgrims (and latterly more secular-minded coach tours), whose constant stream has turned the place into something of a nightmare, with every house displaying mountains of unbelievable junk. The reason for its popularity since medieval times is the supposed miraculous ability of the cathedral's Black Madonna. Nowadays, pilgrims are outnumbered by tourists, who come here to wonder at the sheer audacity of its location, built almost vertically into its rocky backdrop.

Legend has it that the history of Rocamadour began with the arrival of Zacchaeus, husband of St Veronica, who fled to France to escape religious persecution and lived out his last years here as a hermit. When in 1166 a perfectly preserved body was found in a grave high up on the rock, it was declared to be Zacchaeus, who thereafter became known as St Amadour. Rocamadour soon became a major pilgrimage site and a staging post on the road to Santiago de Compostela in Spain. St Bernard, numerous kings of England and France and thousands of others crawled up the chapel steps on their knees to pay their respects and seek cures for their illnesses. Henry Short-Coat (see box on p.642) was the first to plunder the shrine, but he was easily outclassed by the Huguenots, who tried in vain to burn the saint's corpse and finally resigned themselves simply to hacking it to bits. What you see today, therefore, is not the real thing but a nineteenth-century reconstruction, carried out in the hope of reviving the flagging pilgrimage.

The Town

Rocamadour is easy enough to find your way around. There's just one street, rue de la Couronnerie, strung out between two medieval gateways. Above it, the steep hillside supports no fewer than seven churches. There's a lift dug into the rock-face (15F/€2.29 up and back), but it's far better to climb the 223 steps of the Via Sancta, up which the

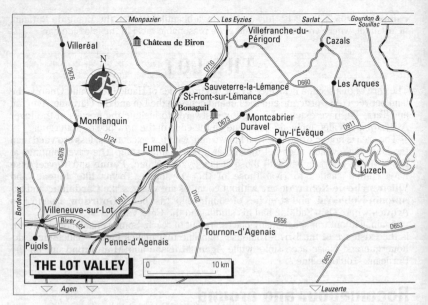

devout drag themselves on their knees to the smoke-blackened and votive-packed **Chapelle Notre-Dame** where the miracle-working twelfth-century Black Madonna resides. The tiny, macabre statue of walnut wood is appropriately lit in the mysterious half-light of her protective black cage, but the rest of the chapel is unremarkable. High up in the rock above the entrance to the chapel is a sword, supposedly Roland's legendary blade, Durandal.

There's no relief for the non-religious in the neighbouring **Musée d'Art Sacré** (Feb–June, Sept & Oct daily 10am–noon & 2–5pm; July & Aug daily 10am–7pm; Nov–Jan Mon–Fri 10am–noon & 2–5pm; 28F/€4.27), which contains sacred art treasures, reliquaries and various historical documents. It's dedicated to the French composer Francis Poulenc (1899–1963) because he was one of the modern pilgrims who received miraculous inspiration from the shrine, though in his case the results were musical rather than medical.

You can climb still further to the ancient **ramparts** above the chapel (daily 10am–noon & 2–5pm; 15F/€2.29) via the winding shady path, *La Calvarie*, past the Stations of the Cross, or take a more direct path: either way the views across the valley are stunning.

There are two different wildlife centres worth visiting above Rocamadour in L'Hospitalet: the **Rocher des Aigles** (daily: April–June & Sept daily 10am–noon & 2–5/6pm; July & Aug 10am–6pm; Oct 2–5/6pm; 40F/€6.10), a breeding centre for birds of prey – don't miss the falconry demonstrations – and the **Forêt des Singes**, off the D673 (daily: April–June & Sept 10am–noon & 1–6pm; July & Aug 10am–7pm; Oct 1–5pm; first two weeks Nov Sat & Sun 10am–noon & 1–5pm; 40F/€6.10), where more than a hundred Barbary apes roam the plateau in relative freedom.

Practicalities

Getting to Rocamadour without your own transport is awkward, unless you're prepared to walk or take a taxi the 4km from the Rocamadour-Padirac **gare SNCF** on the Brive–Capdenac line. If you arrive **by car**, you'll have to park in L'Hospitalet, 1.5km

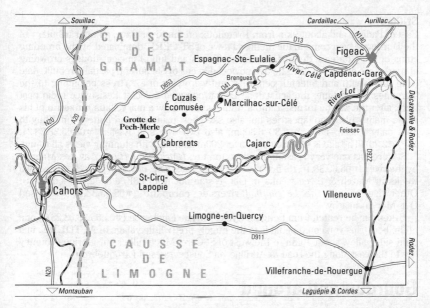

from Rocamadour (and with the best view of the town there is), or else in the car park, several hundred metres below the town. There are two **tourist offices**: the main one in l'Hospitalet (April–June & Sept daily 10am–noon & 2–5/6pm; July & Aug daily 10am–8pm; rest of year Mon–Fri 10am–noon & 2–5.30pm, Sat & Sun 2–5.30pm; ☎05.65.33.22.00, fax 05.65.33.22.01, *www.rocamadour.com*), and a second next to the Hôtel de Ville (daily: April to mid-July & Sept 10am–12.30pm & 1.30–6pm; mid-July to Aug 9.30am–7.30pm; Oct to mid-Nov 10am–noon & 2–5.30pm; mid-Nov to March 2.30–5.30pm; ☎05.65.33.63.26), on the main street.

Rocamadour's **hotels** are not too expensive but they're completely booked out in the summer and close for the winter months. If you ring ahead, you might get in at the *Lion d'Or*, Porte Figuier (☎05.65.33.62.04, fax 05.65.33.72.54; ②; restaurant from 68F/€10.37), or *Le Terminus des Pèlerins*, at the bottom of the *Via Sancta* (☎05.65.33.62.14, fax 05.65.33.72.10; ③; restaurant from 70F/€10.67), both closed from November to March. Up in L'Hospitalet, *Le Camp'hostel* (☎05.65.33.73.50, fax 05.65.33.69.60; ③; closed mid-Oct to March) has bright, modern rooms. They also run the neighbouring **campsite**, *Le Relais du Campeur* (☎05.65.33.63.28; closed Oct–March).

Gouffre de Padirac

The **Gouffre de Padirac** (daily guided tours: April to mid-July & Sept to mid-Oct 9am–noon & 2–5/6pm; last two weeks July 9am–6.30pm; Aug 8.30am–7pm; 48F/€7.32) is about 20km east of Rocamadour on the other side of the main Brive–Figeac road. It is an enormous limestone sinkhole, about 100m deep and over 100m wide. There are some spectacular formations of stalactites and waterfalls created by the accumulation of lime, and beautiful underground lakes, but it is very, very touristy – so much so that it's best avoided at weekends and other peak periods, or you'll wait an age for tickets. Visits are partly on foot, partly by boat, and the guided tours last an hour and a half. In wet weather you'll need a waterproof jacket. If you have no car, the nearest **gare SNCF** is Rocamadour-Padirac, more than 10km to the west; the only alternative is walking or hitching.

St-Céré

East of Padirac and about 9km from Bretenoux on the River Bave, a minor tributary of the Dordogne, you come to the medieval town of **ST-CÉRÉ**, dominated by the brooding ruins of the **Château de St-Laurent-les-Tours** and full of ancient houses crowding around place de Mercadial. The two powerful keeps of St-Laurent, partially rebuilt, date from the twelfth and fifteenth centuries and were part of a fortress belonging to the Turennes. In wartime, the artist Jean Lurçat operated a secret Resistance radio post here; after the war he turned it into a studio, and it's now a marvellous **museum** of his work, mainly his huge tapestries but also sketches, paintings and pottery (mid-July to Sept daily 9.30am–noon & 2.30–6.30pm; also two weeks at Easter; ☎05.65.38.28.21; 15F/€2.29). The site is spectacular at over 200m altitude, with stunning views all round.

St-Céré has one very reasonable place to **stay**: *Hôtel Victor Hugo*, 7 av des Maquis, by the river (☎05.65.38.16.15, fax 05.65.38.39.91, *www.hotel-victor-hugo.fr*, ③; closed two weeks in March & three weeks in Oct; restaurant from 88F/€13.42, closed Mon). Otherwise, there's the *Le Soulhol* riverside **campsite** (☎05.65.38.12.37; closed Oct–March) nearby.

Bikes can be rented from Peugeot Cycles, 45 rue Faidherbe (☎05.65.38.03.23) – one of the best trips you could pedal is to the hugely pretty little village of **AUTOURE**, in a tight side valley, about 10km to the west of St-Céré. Much hillier but glorious country lies to the east along the road to Aurillac via Sousceyrac and Laroquebrou.

Gourdon and around

GOURDON lies between Sarlat and Cahors, conveniently served by the Brive–Toulouse train line, and makes a quiet, pleasant base for visiting some of the major places in this part of the Dordogne and Lot. It's 17km south of the River Dordogne and pretty much at the eastern limit of the luxuriant woods and valleys of Périgord, which give way quite suddenly, at the line of the N20, to the arid limestone landscape of the **Causse de Gramat**.

In the Middle Ages, Gourdon was an important place, deriving wealth and influence from the presence of four monasteries. It was besieged and captured in 1189 by Richard the Lionheart, who promptly murdered its feudal lords. Legend has it that the archer who fired the fatal shot at him during the siege of Châlus was the last surviving member of this family. But more than anything it was the devastation of the Wars of Religion that dispatched Gourdon into centuries of oblivion.

Gourdon is a beautiful town, its medieval centre of yellow-stone houses attached like a swarm of bees to a prominent hilltop, neatly ringed by modern boulevards containing all the shops. From whichever direction you approach, all roads lead to place de la Libération in front of the fortified **gateway** over rue du Majou, the narrow main street of the old town. It is lined all the way up with splendid stone houses, some, like the **Maison d'Anglars** at no. 17, as old as thirteenth-century. At its upper end, rue du Majou debouches into a lovely square in front of the massive but not particularly interesting fourteenth-century **church of St-Pierre**, where there's a **market** on Tuesday mornings. The handsome **Hôtel de Ville** stands on one side of the square, and in place des Marronniers behind the church is the family home of the Cavaignacs, who supplied the nation with numerous prominent public figures in the eighteenth and nineteenth centuries, including the notoriously brutal general who put down the Paris workers' attempts to defend the Second Republic in June 1848. From the square, steps climb to the top of the hill, where the castle once stood and where there is a superb view over the Dordogne valley and surroundings.

A couple of kilometres along the Sarlat road in the direction of Cougnac from Gourdon, there is a very interesting **cave**, the **Grottes de Cougnac**, discovered in

1949 (daily: April–June, Sept & Oct 9.30–11am & 2–5pm; July & Aug 9.30am–6pm; 34F/€5.18). It has beautiful rock formations as well as some fine prehistoric paintings rather similar to those at Pech-Merle (see p.670).

Practicalities

The **tourist office** is on the left at the beginning of rue du Majou (July & Aug 10am–7pm, Sun 10am–noon; rest of year Mon–Sat 10am–noon & 2–5/6pm; ☎05.65.27.52.50, fax 05.65.27.52.52, *gramat@wanadoo.fr*), and has lists of B&B options in the area. **Bikes** can be rented from MJC (☎05.65.41.11.65), behind the tourist office.

For an overnight **stay**, the *Hôtel de la Promenade*, on the northwestern side of the ring road at 48 bd Galiot-de-Genouillac (☎05.65.41.41.44, fax 05.65.41.41.22; ③), is a cheerful place with immaculate rooms and a good restaurant (closed Sun lunch; menus from 71F/€10.82). On the opposite side of town, near the **post office**, is the agreeable *Hôtel Bissonnier*, 51 bd des Martyrs (☎05.65.41.02.48, fax 05.65.41.44.67; ③; closed Dec), with a restaurant serving such local specialities as *confits* and stuffed duck's neck (closed Sun evening & Mon lunch Oct–April; menu from 85F/€12.96). There is a good municipal **campsite**, *Ecoute s'il Pleut* (☎05.65.41.06.19; closed Oct–May), 1km north on the Sarlat road.

For a pleasant independent **restaurant**, with a tiny outside terrace, try the *Croque-Note* on the corner of rue Jean-Jaurès and boulevard Gabanès on the south side of the old town (menus from 65F/€9.91).

Les Arques

Twenty-five kilometres southwest of Gourdon on the Fumel road, you come to a pretty but not remarkable *bastide* called Cazals; a left turn here takes you along the bottom of the valley of the Masse and up its left flank to the exquisite hamlet of **LES ARQUES**. This is quiet, remote, small-scale farming country, emptied of people by the slaughter of rustic sons in World War I and by migration to the towns in search of jobs and money.

Les Arques' main claim to fame is the Russian Cubist/Expressionist sculptor Osip Zadkine, who bought the old house by the church here in 1934. Some of his sculptures adorn the space outside the church as well as its lovely interior, and there's also a **museum** with a number of his other works (daily: June–Sept 10am–1pm & 2–7pm; rest of year 2–5pm; 15F/€2.29).

The other reason to come here is the now superannuated village school, transformed into a most unusual **restaurant**, *La Récréation* (☎05.65.22.88.08; March–Sept daily except Wed, rest of year open Fri evening to Sun lunch), where you get a copious and delicious meal to eat beneath the wisterias and chestnut trees of the school yard for 90–140F/€13.72–21.34. On a summer night with the swifts screaming overhead, it is idyllic.

On the other side of the valley and well sign-posted, the tiny Romanesque **chapel of St-André-des-Arques** has some very lovely fifteenth-century frescoes discovered by Zadkine; get the key from the museum in Les Arques (see above).

Cahors and around

CAHORS, on the River Lot, was the capital of the old province of Quercy. In its time, it has been a Gallic settlement; a Roman town; a briefly held Moorish possession; a town under English rule; a bastion of Catholicism in the Wars of Religion, sacked in consequence by Henri IV; a university town for four hundred years; and birthplace of the politician Léon Gambetta (1838–82), after whom so many French streets and squares are named. Modern Cahors is a sunny southern backwater, with two interesting sights in its **cathedral** and the remarkable fourteenth-century **Pont Valentré**.

locomotives along this otherwise redundant line. Various round trips are available, including a boat trip at Cajarc, a walk along the towpath hewn into the rock at St-Cirq-Lapopie, or a visit to the château de Cénevières. Prices are 100–160F/€15.24–24.39 return, with departures from Cahors station or Capdenac. It's advisable to book in advance (☎05.65.23.94.72).

The cheapest **hotel** in Cahors is the basic *Hôtel de la Paix*, place de la Halle, near the cathedral (☎05.65.35.03.40, fax 05.65.35.40.88; ②; closed two weeks at Christmas; restaurant from 68F/€10.37, closed Sun), though if you can afford it *L'Escargot*, at the north end of boulevard Gambetta (☎05.65.35.07.66, fax 05.65.53.92.38; ③; restaurant from 62F/€9.45), offers better value for money. Near the station, the *Hôtel de France*, 252 av Jean-Jaurès (☎05.65.35.16.76, fax 05.65.22.01.08; ③; closed three weeks over Christmas), is another decent option, or you could splurge out on the lovely creeper-covered *Terminus*, 5 av Charles de Freycinet (☎05.65.53.32.00, fax 05.65.53.32.26; ⑥), boasting the famous *Le Balandre* restaurant (closed Sun evenings & Mon out of season; menus from 180F/€27.44). There's also a **HI hostel**, near the tourist office at 20 rue Frédéric-Suisse (☎05.65.35.64.71, fax 05.65.35.95.92), and an expensive **campsite** (☎05.65.30.06.30; closed Nov–March) across Pont Cabessut.

In addition to the hotel **restaurants** mentioned above, there's an unpretentious locals' place, *Le Troquet des Halles*, beside the *Hôtel de la Paix* (see above), serving good-value lunches for 60F/€9.15 (closed evenings & Sat), while *Lamparo*, on the south side of the square, is justifiably popular for its varied menus (from 65F/€9.91) and generous portions.

St-Cirq-Lapopie

If you have your own transport you could easily make a side trip from Cahors to the cliff-edge village of **ST-CIRQ-LAPOPIE**, 30km to the east, perched high above the south bank of the Lot. The village was saved from ruin when poet André Breton came to live here earlier this century, and it is now an irresistible draw for the tour buses with its cobbled lanes, half-timbered houses and gardens; but it's still worth the trouble, especially if you visit early or late in the day. **Public transport** in the form of an SNCF bus will get you from Cahors to Gare-St-Cirq in the valley bottom at Tour-de-Faure; thereafter, there's no alternative but to leg it up the steep hill. For **accommodation**, there is the very pretty *Auberge du Sombral* on the central square (☎05.65.31.26.08, fax 05.65.30.26.37; ④; closed mid-Nov to March), whose excellent restaurant (closed Tues & Wed out of season) has a menu at 100F/€15.24, and *La Pélissaria* (☎05.65.31.25.14, fax 05.65.30.25.52; ⑤; closed Nov–March), in a sixteenth-century house perched on the cliff at the eastern entrance to St-Cirq. There is also a very comfortable **gîte d'étape** in the village centre (☎05.65.31.21.51), and two well-run **campsites**: *Camping de la Plage* (☎05.65.30.29.51; all year), down by the river with swimming and canoeing possibilities, and *La Truffière* (☎05.65.30.20.22; closed Oct–April), 3km to the southeast over the rim of the valley.

Downstream from Cahors

West of Cahors the vine-cloaked banks of the Lot are dotted with small and ancient villages. The first of these, **Luzech** and the dramatic **Puy L'Évêque**, are served by an SNCF bus that threads along the valley from Cahors via Fumel to Monsempron-Libos, on the Agen–Périgueux train line. You'll need your own transport, however, to reach the splendid **Château de Bonaguil**, in the hills northwest of Puy-L'Évêque, worth the effort for its elaborate fortifications and spectacular position. From here on the Lot valley starts to get ugly and industrial, though **Villeneuve-sur-Lot** hides a surprisingly attractive old centre and provides a base for exploring the villages around. Prettiest are **Pujols**, to the south, which also boasts a number of excellent restaurants, and **Penne d'Agenais**, overlooking the Lot to the east.

Luzech, Puy L'Évêque and the Château de Bonaguil

Twenty kilometres downriver from Cahors you come to **LUZECH**, with scant Gaulish and Roman remains of the town of L'Impernal, and the **Chapelle de Notre-Dame-de-l'Île**, dedicated to the medieval boatmen who transported Cahors wines to Bordeaux. The town stands in a huge river loop, overlooked by a thirteenth-century **keep**, with some picturesque alleys and dwellings in the quarter opposite place du Canal.

Several bends in the river later – 15km by road – **PUY-L'ÉVÊQUE** is probably the prettiest village in the entire valley, with many grand houses built in honey-coloured stone and overlooked by both a **church** and the **castle** of the bishops of Cahors. For the best view, stand on the suspension bridge which crosses the Lot. For an overnight **stay**, the refurbished *Hôtel Bellevue*, perched on the cliff edge, has stylish rooms and a good restaurant (from 170F/€25.92, or 75F/€11.43 in the brasserie). For something cheaper, at the bottom of the town *Hôtel Henry* has cheap and decent rooms (☎05.65.21.32.24, fax 05.65.30.85.18; ②), or there's a Dutch-owned **campsite**, *Camping Les Vignes* (☎05.65.30.81.72; closed Oct–March), 3km south by the river.

With your own transport, follow the Lot as far as Duravel and then cut across country via the picturesque hamlet of St-Martin-le-Redon to reach the **Château de Bonaguil** (daily: Feb–May & Sept–Nov 10.30am–noon & 2.30–5pm; June 10am–noon & 2–5pm; July & Aug 10am–5.45pm; closed Dec & Jan; 30F/€4.57) some 15km later. It's spectacularly perched at the end of a wooden spur commanding two valleys, about 8km northeast of Fumel. Dating largely from the fifteenth and sixteenth centuries with a double ring of walls, five huge towers and a narrow boat-shaped keep designed to resist artillery, it was the last of the medieval castles to be constructed.

Villeneuve-sur-Lot and around

VILLENEUVE-SUR-LOT, 75km west and downstream from Cahors, is a pleasant, workaday sort of town but otherwise does not have a great deal to commend it: there are no very interesting sights, though the handful of attractive timbered houses in the old town go some way to compensate. If you're reliant on public transport note that there's no train station in Villeneuve itself, but SNCF runs regular bus services to Agen, which is on the Bordeaux–Toulouse line.

The town's most striking landmark is the red-brick tower of the **church of Ste-Catherine**, completed as late as 1937 in typically dramatic neo-Byzantine style, but rather unusually built on a north–south axis; inside, the church retains some attractive stained glass from the previous fourteenth-century building. In the streets around the main square, **place La Fayette**, a couple of towers alone survive from the fortifications of this originally *bastide* town, and to the south the main avenue, rue des Cieutats, crosses thirteenth-century **Pont des Cieutat**, resembling the Pont Valentré in Cahors but devoid of its towers.

The **tourist office** is opposite the theatre on boulevard de la République (June–Aug Mon–Sat 9am–7pm, Sun 10am–1pm; rest of year Mon–Sat 9am–noon & 2–6pm; ☎05.53.36.17.30, fax 05.53.49.42.98). The best place to look for **accommodation** is around the former train station, five minutes' walk south of centre, where the friendly *Hôtel la Résidence*, 17 av Lazare-Carnot (☎05.53.40.17.03, fax 05.53.01.57.34; ①–②; closed for Christmas & New Year), offers unbeatable value for money. If they're full, try the nearby *Hôtel le Terminus* (☎05.53.70.94.36, fax 05.53.70.45.13; ③; restaurant from

88F/€13.42), or, if you'd rather be closer to the centre, *Hôtel les Platanes*, 40 bd de la Marine (☎05.53.40.11.40, fax 05.53.70.71.95; ①–②; closed two weeks at Christmas; restaurant from 70F/€10.67), north along boulevard de la République from the tourist office. For **campers**, there's the *Camping du Rooy*, signed off the Agen road 1.5km south of centre (☎05.53.70.24.18; closed early Oct to mid-April).

When it comes to **eating**, *Chez Câline* in rue Notre-Dame, near the Pont des Cieutat, is a pretty little place offering menus from 75F/€11.43. For a bit more luxury and classic cuisine head north of the bridge to the *Aux Berges du Lot*, 3 rue de l'Hôtel-de-Ville (☎05.53.70.84.41; closed Sun evening & Mon), which does an 85F/€12.96 weekday lunch menu, starting at 130F/€19.82 for dinner. Alternatively, head south to Pujols (see below).

Pujols and Penne d'Agenais

Three kilometres south of Villeneuve the tiny hilltop village of **PUJOLS** makes a popular excursion, partly to see the faded Romanesque frescoes in the **church of Ste-Foy** and partly for the views over the surrounding country. But the main reason locals come here is for the quality of its **restaurants**. Top of the list is the excellent but expensive *La Toque Blanche* (☎05.53.49.00.30; closed Sun evening, Mon & Tues lunch; menus from 120–350F/€18.29–53.36), just south of Pujols with views back to the village. The views are even better, however, from their less formal outlet, *Lou Calel*, in Pujols itself, overlooking the Lot valley; for around 200F/€30.49 including wine you can sample some beautifully cooked traditional but light menus (☎05.53.70.46.14; closed Tues evening & Wed).

Another side trip could be to the beautiful but touristy old fortress town of **PENNE D'AGENAIS**, 8km upstream on a steep hill also on the south bank of the Lot, with remains of a thirteenth-century castle teetering on a cliff edge; without a car, you'll have to take the **bus** (Mon–Fri two daily; no service in Aug) from Villeneuve to St-Sylvestre on the north bank and walk across the bridge. There are great views from the top. The **tourist office**, in rue du 14-Juillet just inside the old town gate (June to mid-Sept Mon–Sat 9.30am–12.30pm & 2/3–7pm, Sun 3–7pm; rest of year Mon–Sat 9am–12.30pm & 2–6pm; ☎05.53.41.37.80, fax 05.53.49.38.37), can supply comprehensive lists of B&Bs and *gîtes* in the area. There's a **campsite** in St-Sylvestre by the river (☎05.53.41.22.23; closed Oct to mid-May) and a simple, modern **hotel**, *Le Compostelle* (☎05.53.41.12.41, fax 05.53.41.00.20; ③; closed Jan & Feb; restaurant from 65F/€9.91), near the **gare SNCF** on the Agen–Paris line.

Figeac and around

FIGEAC lies on the River Célé, 71km east of Cahors and some 8km north of the Lot. It's a beautiful town with an unspoilt medieval centre, not too encumbered by tourism. Like many other provincial towns hereabouts, it owes its beginnings to the foundation of an abbey in the early days of Christianity in France, one which quickly became wealthy because of its position on the pilgrim routes to both Rocamadour and Compostela. In the Middle Ages it became a centre of tanning, which partly accounts for the many houses whose top floors have *solelhos*, or open-sided wooden galleries used for drying skins and other produce. Again, as so often, it was the Wars of Religion that pushed it into eclipse, for Figeac threw in its lot with the nearby Protestant stronghold of Montauban and suffered the same punishing reprisals by the victorious royalists in 1662 (see p.673).

Roads and train line both funnel you automatically into the town centre, where the **Hôtel de la Monnaie** surveys place Vival. It is a splendid building whose origins go back to the thirteenth century, when the city's mint was located in this district. The building now houses the tourist office, as well as a none too exciting **museum** of old coins and archeological bits and pieces found in the surrounding area (May & June Mon–Sat 10am–noon & 2.30–6pm, Sun 10am–1pm; July to mid-Sept daily 10am–1pm & 2–7pm; rest of year Mon–Sat 10am–noon & 2.30–6pm; 10F/€1.52). In the streets radiating off to the north of the square – Caviale, République, Gambetta and their cross-streets – there is a delightful range of houses of the medieval and classical periods, both stone and half-timbered with brick noggings, adorned with carvings and colonnettes, ogees, and interesting bits of ironwork. At the end of these streets are the two small squares of **place Carnot** and **place Champollion**, both of great charm. The former is the site of the old *halles*, under whose awning cafés now spreads their tables.

Jean-François Champollion, who cracked Egyptian hieroglyphics by deciphering the triple text of the Rosetta Stone, was born in a house at 4 impasse Champollion, off the square, and the building now houses a very interesting **museum** dedicated to his life and work (March–June, Sept & Oct Tues–Sun 10am–noon & 2.30–6.30pm; July & Aug daily same hours; Nov–Feb Tues–Sun 2–6pm; 20F/€3.05). At the end of this alley, a larger-than-life reproduction of the Rosetta Stone forms the floor of the tiny **place des Écritures**, above which is a little garden planted with tufts of papyrus.

On the other side of place Champollion, rue Boutaric leads up to the cedar-shaded **church of Notre-Dame-du-Puy**, from where you get views over the roofs of the town. More interesting is the **church of St-Sauveur** off place des Herbes near the tourist office, with its lovely Gothic chapterhouse decorated with heavily gilded but dramatically realistic seventeenth-century carved wood panels illustrating the life of Christ.

Practicalities

The **gare SNCF** is a few minutes' walk to the south of place Vival across the river at the end of rue de la Gare and avenue des Poilus. SNCF **buses** leave from the train station, and others from the *gare routière* on avenue Maréchal-Joffre, a few minutes' walk west of place Vival. You'll find the **tourist office** in the Hôtel de la Monnaie on place Vival (May & June Mon–Sat 10am–noon & 2.30–6pm, Sun 10am–1pm; July to mid-Sept daily 10am–1pm & 2–7pm; rest of year Mon–Sat 10am–noon & 2.30–6pm; ☎05.65.34.06.25, fax 05.65.50.04.58, *figeac@wanadoo.fr*).

The nicest place to **stay** is the *Hôtel des Bains*, 1 rue du Griffoul (☎05.65.34.10.89, fax 05.65.14.00.45; ②; closed mid-Dec to mid-Jan), in a lovely riverside location just across from the old town. One block further back, the *Hôtellerie de l'Europe* at 51 allées Victor-Hugo (☎05.65.34.10.16, fax 05.65.50.04.57; ②; closed mid-Jan to mid-Feb), is better than it looks from the outside, with a 1930s lounge and excellent regional menus for 78–198F/€11.89–30.18 (restaurant closed Sat & Sun evening out of season). If you'd rather be more central, *Hôtel Champollion*, on place Champollion (☎05.65.34.04.37; ③), offers a few functional but clean rooms above a popular café. The tourist office can recommend *chambres d'hôte*, and there's a well-equipped **campsite**, *Les Rives du Célé* (☎05.65.34.59.00; closed Oct–March), by the river just east of town, with a restaurant, shop and swimming pool, by the sports ground, where you can also rent **canoes**.

For **eating** somewhere other than a hotel restaurant, the *Puce à l'Oreille*, 5 rue St-Thomas, behind place Carnot, offers some rich Quercy dishes in menus that range from 75F/€11.43 to 190F/€28.97 (☎05.65.34.33.08; closed one week in early Nov, and Sun evening & Mon out of season). For a lighter meal, try the crêperie *La Chandeleur* (about 50F/€7.62) in rue Boutaric, off place Champollion.

Cardaillac

Home of one of the great families of Quercy in the Middle Ages, the old part of the village of **CARDAILLAC**, about 10km to the north of Figeac off the N140, is gathered on

Grotte de Pech-Merle

Discovered in 1922, the **Grotte de Pech-Merle** (mid-Jan to March and Nov to mid-Dec by group reservation only; April–Oct daily 9.30am–noon & 1.30–5pm; ☎05.65.31.27.05; mid-June to mid-Sept 44F/€6.71, rest of year 38F/€5.79) is less accessible than the caves at Les Eyzies but still attracts sufficient visitors to warrant restricting numbers to 700 per day; it's advisable to book at least a day ahead in July and August. It is well hidden on the scrubby hillsides above Cabrerets, which lies 15km from Marcilhac and 4km from Conduché, where the Célé flows into the Lot.

The cave itself is far more beautiful than those at Padirac or Les Eyzies, with galleries full of the most spectacular stalactites and stalagmites – structures tiered like wedding cakes, hanging like curtains, or shaped like whale baffles, discs or cave pearls. On the downside, the cave is wired for electric light and the guides make sure you're processed through in the scheduled time.

The first **drawings** you come to are in the so-called Chapelle des Mammouths, executed on a white calcite panel that looks as if it's been specially prepared for the purpose. There are horses, bison charging head down with tiny rumps and arched tails, and tusked, whiskery mammoths. You then pass into a vast chamber where the glorious horse panel is visible on a lower level; it's a remarkable example of the way in which the artist used the contour and relief of the rock to do the work, producing an utterly convincing mammoth by just two strokes of black. The cave ceiling is covered with finger marks, preserved in the soft clay. You pass the skeleton of a cave hyena that has been lying there for 20,000 years – wild animals used these caves for shelter and sometimes, unable to find their way out, starved to death in them. And finally, the most spine-tingling experience at Pech-Merle: the footprints of a Stone Age adult and child preserved in a muddy pool.

The admission charge includes an excellent film and **museum**, where prehistory is illustrated by colourful and intelligible charts, a selection of objects (rather than the usual 10,000 flints), skulls and beautiful slides displayed in wall panels.

There's a **gîte d'étape** (☎05.65.31.27.04; closed Nov–Easter) and a **campsite** (☎05.65.31.26.61; closed Nov–March) close by at **CABRERETS**, a tiny place that also has a pair of two-star **hotels**: the *Auberge de la Sagne*, 1km outside the village on the road to the caves (☎05.65.31.26.62, fax 05.65.30.27.43; ④; closed mid-Sept to mid-May), which has an excellent restaurant (evenings only; menus at 90F/€13.72 & 130F/€19.82); and *Les Grottes* (☎05.65.31.27.02, fax 05.65.31.20.15; ③; closed Nov–March), down beside the river, also with a decent restaurant attached (menu from 89F/€13.57).

The valley of the Aveyron

Thirty-seven kilometres south of Figeac, **Villefranche-de-Rouerge** lies on a bend in the River Aveyron, clustered around its perfectly preserved, arcaded market square. From Villefranche the Aveyron flows south through increasingly deep, thickly wooded valleys, past the hilltop village of **Najac** and then turns abruptly west as it enters the Gorges de l'Aveyron. The most impressive stretch of this defile begins not far east of **St-Antonin-de-Noble-Val**, an ancient village caught between soaring limestone cliffs, and continues downstream to the villages of **Penne** and **Bruniquel**, perched beside their crumbling castles. Bruniquel marks the end of the gorges, as you suddenly break out into flat alluvial plains where the Aveyron joins the great rivers of the Tarn and Garonne.

Villefranche-de-Rouergue

No medieval junketing, not a craft shop in sight, **VILLEFRANCHE-DE-ROUERGUE** must be as close as you can get to what a French provincial town used to be like, and it's also where you are as likely to hear Occitan spoken as French. It's a small place, lying on a bend in the Aveyron, 35km due south of Figeac and 61km east of Cahors across the **Causse de Limogne**. Built as a *bastide* by Alphonse de Poitiers in 1252 as part of the royal policy of extending control over the recalcitrant lands of the south, the town became rich on copper from the surrounding mines and its privilege of minting coins. From the fifteenth to the eighteenth centuries, its wealthy men built the magnificent houses that grace the cobbled streets to this day.

Rue du Sergent-Bories and rue de la République, the main commercial street, are both very attractive, but they are no preparation for **place Notre-Dame**, the loveliest *bastide* central square in the region. It's built on a slope, so the uphill houses are much higher than the downhill, and you enter at the corners underneath the houses. All the houses are arcaded at ground-floor level, providing for a market (Thurs morning) where local merchants and farmers spread out their weekly produce. The houses are unusually tall and some are very elaborately decorated, notably the so-called **Maison du Président Raynal** on the lower side at the top of rue de la République.

The east side of the square is dominated by the **church of Notre-Dame** with its colossal porch and bell tower, nearly 60m high. The interior has some fine late fifteenth-century stained glass, carved choir stalls and misericords. Behind it is the marketplace. Thursday is **market** day, which, as the locals will tell you, is the quintessential Villefranche experience, where you'll hear little French spoken.

On the boulevard that forms the northern limit of the old town, the seventeenth-century **Chapelle des Pénitents-Noirs** (July–Sept daily 10am–noon & 2–6pm; 20F/€3.05) boasts a splendidly Baroque painted ceiling and an enormous gilded retable. Another ecclesiastical building worth the slight detour is the **Chartreuse St-Sauveur** (same hours; 20F/€3.05), about 1km out of town on the Gaillac road. It was completed in the space of ten years from 1450, giving it a singular architectural harmony, and has a very beautiful cloister and choir stalls by the same master as Notre-Dame in Villefranche, which, by contrast, took nearly 300 years to complete.

Aside from the pleasing details of many of the houses you notice as you explore the side streets, the town reserves one other most unexpected surprise. The **Médiathèque**, on rue Sénéchal (☎05.65.45.59.45), includes an amazing collection of jazz records, books, papers, recordings and documents belonging to the late Hugues Panassié, famous French jazz critic and one of the founders of the *Hot Club de France*. Much of the material is unrecorded or unobtainable elsewhere and is open to perusal by members. CD selections are on sale both here and at the tourist office.

Practicalities

Both the **gare SNCF** and **gare routière** are located a couple of minutes' walk south across the Aveyron from the old town. The **tourist office** sits just north of the river on promenade du Giraudet (May–Sept Mon–Fri 9am–noon & 2–6/7pm, Sat 9am–noon; rest of year closed Sat; ☎05.65.45.13.18, fax 05.65.45.55.58, *www.ville-franche.com*), beside the bridge. For those who want to stay overnight, there are two pleasant **hotels**: *L'Univers*, 2 place de la République at the end of the bridge opposite the tourist office (☎05.65.45.15.63, fax 05.65.45.02.21; ②), with a good traditional restaurant (from 89F/€13.57); and the more modest *Bellevue*, 3 av du Ségala (☎05.65.45.23.17, fax 05.65.45.11.19; ②; closed school hols in Feb & Nov, also Mon evening & Sun), also with a decent restaurant (menus 80–280F/€12.20–42.69), a little further out of town on the Rodez road. For an even more sumptuous meal and a comfortable sleep, despite its unpromising location, try *Le Relais de Farrou*, 3km out on the Figeac road (☎05.65.45.18.11, fax 05.65.45.32.59; ④; restaurant from 128F/€19.51). For cheaper accommodation, there's an excellent new *Foyer des Jeunes Travailleurs* **HI hostel** (☎05.65.45.09.68, fax 05.65.45.62.26), next to the *gare SNCF*. There is also a **gîte d'étape** by the river at La Gasse (☎05.65.45.10.80; closed

Oct–March), 3km out of town on the D269 back road to La Bastide-L'Évêque, at the start of **GR62b**, plus a **campsite**, 1.5km to the south on the D47 to Monteil (☎05.65.45.16.24; closed Oct–March). Finally, next to the covered market is a welcoming workers' diner, *Café des Halles*, where you can **eat** a substantial meal for 55F/€8.38 at shared tables.

Najac

NAJAC occupies an extraordinary site on a conical hill isolated in a wide bend in the deep valley of the Aveyron, 25km south of Villefranche-de-Rouergue and on the Aurillac–Toulouse train line, with one direct train to Paris every day. Its photogenic castle, which graces many a travel poster, sits right on the peak of the hill, while the half-timbered and stone-tiled village houses tail out in a single street along the narrow back of the spur that joins the hill to the valleyside. It's all very attractive and consequently touristy, with the inevitable resident knick-knack shops and craftspeople.

The **Château** (April, May & Sept daily 10am–12.30pm & 3–5.30pm; June daily 10am–12.30pm & 3–6.30pm; July & Aug daily 10am–1pm & 3–7pm; Oct Sun 3–5.30pm; last entry 30min before closing; 21F/€3.20) is a model of medieval defensive architecture and was endlessly fought over because of its commanding and impregnable position in a region once rich in silver and copper mines. You can see clearly all the devices for restricting an attacker once he was inside the castle: the covered passages and stairs within the thickness of the walls, the multistorey positions for archers and, of course, the most magnificent all-round view from the top of the keep. In one of the chambers of the keep you can see the stone portraits of St Louis, king of France, his brother Alphonse de Poitiers and Jeanne, the daughter of the count of Toulouse, whose marriage to Alphonse was arranged in 1229 to end the Cathar wars by bringing the domains of Count Raymond and his allies under royal control. It was Alphonse who "modernized" the castle and made the place we see today. Signatures of the masons who worked on it are clearly visible on many stones.

Below the rather dull central square stretches the **faubourg**, a sort of elongated square bordered by houses raised on pillars as in the central square of a *bastide*, which reduces to a narrow waist of a street overlooked by more ancient houses and leading past a fountain to the castle gate. At the foot of the castle, in the centre of what was the medieval village, stands the very solid-looking **church of St-Jean**, which the villagers of Najac were forced by the Inquisition to build at their own expense in 1258 as a punishment for their conversion to Catharism. In addition to a lovely silver reliquary and an extraordinary iron cage for holding candles – both dating from the thirteenth century – the church has one architectural oddity: its windows are solid panels of stone from which the lights have been cut out in trefoil form. Below the church, by a derelict farm, a stretch of **Roman road** survives and, at the bottom of the hill, a thirteenth-century **bridge** spans the Aveyron.

The **tourist office** is on the *faubourg* (April–June & Sept Mon–Sat 9am–noon & 2.30–5.30pm; July & Aug Mon–Sat 9am–noon & 2.30–5.30pm, Sun 10am–noon; Oct–March Mon–Sat 9am–noon; ☎05.65.29.72.05, fax 05.65.29.72.29). At the eastern entrance to the *faubourg* the modern village balances on the shoulder of the spur round an open square where you'll find the *Oustal del Barry* **hotel** (☎05.65.29.74.32, fax 05.65.29.75.32, *www.oustal-del-barry.com*; ④; closed Nov–March & Mon out of season), whose restaurant is renowned for its subtle and inventive cuisine (closed Mon & Tues lunch out of season; menus from 140F/€21.34). Below Najac there is a **campsite**, *Le Païsserou* (☎05.65.29.72.05; closed Oct–April), with a **gîte d'étape** (same phone no; open all year).

St-Antonin-Noble-Val

One of the finest and most substantial towns in the valley is **ST-ANTONIN-NOBLE-VAL**, 30km southwest of Najac. It sits on the bank of the Aveyron beneath the beetling cliffs of the **Roc d'Anglars**. It has endured all the vicissitudes of the old towns of the southwest: it went Cathar, then Protestant and each time was walloped by the alien power of the kings from the north. Yet, in spite of all, it recovered its prosperity, manufacturing cloth and leather goods, endowed by its wealthy merchants with a marvellous heritage of medieval houses in all the streets leading out from the lovely **place de la Halle** and its prolongation.

There's a café most conveniently and picturesquely placed at the end of the ancient *halle*, with a view of the town's finest building, the Maison des Consuls, whose origins go back to 1120. It now houses the town museum, **Musée du Vieux St-Antonin** (daily except Tues: May, June & Sept 2/3–6pm; July & Aug 10am–1pm & 3–6pm; 15F/€2.29), with collections of objects to do with the former life of the place, as well as a section on local prehistoric sites.

The **tourist office** is in the "new" town hall next to the church (June daily 10am–noon & 2–5.30pm; July to mid-Oct daily 9.30am–12.30pm & 2–6pm; rest of year Mon–Sat 2–5.30pm; ☎05.63.30.63.47, fax 05.63.30.66.33), and will supply information about B&Bs, canoeing on the Aveyron and walks in the region. By the bridge, as you cross from the Montauban road, there's a simple and attractive **hotel** immediately on the left, the *Hôtel Thermes* – so-called because there was once a spa next door – with a terrace overlooking the water (☎05.63.30.61.08, fax 05.63.68.26.23; ②; restaurant from 59F/€8.99). There are four local **campsites**, of which the riverside *Camping d'Anglars* is the closest, 1km upstream on the D115 (☎05.63.30.69.76; closed mid-Oct to mid-April).

Penne and Bruniquel

Twenty kilometres downstream of St-Antonin you come to the beautiful ridge-top village of **PENNE**, once a Cathar stronghold, with its ruined **castle** impossibly perched on an airy crag. Everything is old and leaning and bulging, but holding together nonetheless, with a harmony that would be impossible to create purposely.

Another hilltop **castle** commands its village at **BRUNIQUEL** (April, June & Sept Mon–Sat 2–6pm, Sun 10am–12.30pm & 2–6pm; May & Oct Sun only same hours; July & Aug daily 10am–12.30pm & 2–7pm; 15F/€2.29, or 20F/€3.05 including guided visit), a few kilometres further on. You can also visit a handsome house in the village, the aristocratic **Maison des Comtes de Payrol** (April–Sept daily 10am–6pm; rest of year Sat & Sun 10am–6pm; 15F/€2.29). If you want to **stay**, there's a *chambres d'hôte* (☎05.63.67.26.16; ③; closed Dec & Jan; meals from 95F/€14.48), whose proprietor is a mountain-biker and will take you out on trips, and *Le Payssel* **campsite** (☎05.63.67.25.95; closed Oct–April), about 700m south on the D964 to Albi.

Montauban and around

MONTAUBAN today is a prosperous middle-sized provincial city, capital of the largely agricultural *département* of Tarn-et-Garonne. It lies on the banks of the River Tarn, 53km from Toulouse, close to its junction with the Aveyron and their joint confluence with the Garonne, where the wide alluvial plain of the three rivers stretches boringly for miles around. But this is where the lines of communication run, and Montauban lies, conveniently, on the southwest Bordeaux–Toulouse *autoroute* and train line.

nearby, *Le Melvin* (☎05.63.94.75.60; closed Oct–May), and a **gîte d'étape** in the village for walkers on the GR65 (☎05.63.94.61.94).

Moissac

There is nothing very memorable about the modern town of **MOISSAC**, 30km north-west of Montauban, largely because of the terrible damage done by the flood of March 1930, when the Tarn, swollen by a sudden thaw in the Massif Central, burst its banks, destroying 617 houses and killing 120 people.

Luckily, the one thing that makes Moissac a household name in the history of art survived: the cloister and porch of the **abbey church of St-Pierre**, a masterpiece of Romanesque sculpture and the model for hundreds of churches and buildings else-where. Indeed, the fact that it has survived countless wars, including siege and sack by Simon de Montfort in 1212 during the crusade against the Cathars, is something of a miracle. During the Revolution it was used as a gunpowder factory and billet for sol-diers, who damaged many of the sculptures. In the 1830s it only escaped demolition to make way for the Bordeaux–Toulouse train line by a whisker.

Legend has it that Clovis the Frank first founded a monastery here, though it seems more probable that its origins belong to the seventh century, which saw the foundation of so many monasteries throughout Aquitaine. The first Romanesque church on the site was consecrated in 1063 and enlarged in the following century. The famous **south porch**, with its magnificent tympanum and curious wavy door jambs and pillars, dates from this second phase of building. It depicts Christ in Majesty, right hand raised in benediction, the book in his hand, surrounded by the evangelists and the elders of the Apocalypse as described by St John in the Book of Revelation. It is a display whose influence, assimilated with varying degrees of success, can be seen in the work of artists who decorated the porches of countless churches across the south of France. There is more fine carving in the capitals inside the porch, and the interior of the church, which was remodelled in the fifteenth century, is interesting too, especially for some of the wood and stone statuary it contains.

The adjoining **cloister** (same hours as tourist office – see below; 30F/€4.57) is entered through the tourist office, and if you want to experience the silent contempla-tion for which it was originally built, you must get there first thing in the morning. The cloister surrounds a garden shaded by a majestic cedar, and its pantile roof is support-ed by 76 alternating single and double marble columns. Each column supports a single inverted wedge-shaped block of stone, on which are carved with extraordinary delica-cy all manner of animals and plant motifs, as well as scenes from Bible stories and the lives of the saints: Daniel in the lions' den, the evangelists, St Peter being crucified upside down, John the Baptist being decapitated, and many, many others. An inscrip-tion on the middle pillar on the west side explains that the cloister was made in the time of Abbot Ansquitil in the year of Our Lord 1100.

Practicalities

The **tourist office** (daily: July & Aug 9am–7pm; rest of year 9am–noon & 2–5/6pm; ☎05.63.04.01.85, fax 05.63.04.27.10) is next to the cloister, with the **gare SNCF**, where buses also stop, further west along avenue Pierre-Chabrié. There's a weekend **market** in place des Récollets at the end of rue de la République, which leads away from the abbey, a marvel of colour and temptation.

Overlooking the south side of the square, *Le Chapon Fin* makes a pleasant place to **stay** (☎05.63.04.04.22, fax 05.63.04.58.44; ②; restaurant from 105F/€16.01, closed Sun Jan–March). Alternatively, try the slightly cheaper *Hôtel Le Luxembourg*, 2 av Pierre-Chabrié (☎05.63.04.00.27, fax 05.63.04.19.73; ②), with a well-rated traditional restaurant (menus 62–157F/€9.45–23.93). For **campers**, there's a shady site across the river on a little island, the *Île du Bidounet* (☎05.63.32.52.52; closed Oct–March), where there is also a **gîte d'étape** (walkers only). The nicest place to **eat** is the magnolia-shaded *Bistrot du Cloître* (closed Tues & lunch on Mon & Sat in winter, Mon & Tues evenings in summer; menus from 89F/€13.57), beside the tourist office.

Agen

AGEN, capital of the Lot-et-Garonne *département*, is a pleasanter town than it first appears. It was quartered by modern boulevards in the nineteenth century in its own version of a Haussmann clean-up, and it is down these roads that you're funnelled into the town, with the result that you see nothing of interest.

The town lies on the broad, powerful River Garonne halfway between Bordeaux and Toulouse, and lived through the Middle Ages racked by war with England and internecine strife between Catholics and Protestants. But it was able to extract some advantage from disputes in possession, as it see-sawed between the English and French, gaining more and more privileges of independence as the price of its loyalty – a tradition that it maintained during and after the Revolution by being staunchly republican (the churches still bear the legend: *Liberté, Fraternité, Égalité*).

Its pre-Revolutionary wealth derived from the manufacture of various kinds of cloth and its thriving port on the Garonne, which in those days was alive with river traffic. But the Industrial Revolution put paid to all of that. Agen's prosperity now is based on agriculture – in particular, its famous prunes and plums, said to have been brought back from Damascus during the Crusades.

The interesting part of Agen centres on **place Goya**, where boulevard de la République, leading to the river, crosses boulevard du Président-Carnot. On the south side of boulevard de la République, the main shopping area is around place Wilson, rue Garonne and the partly arcaded place des Laitiers. A left turn at the end of rue Garonne brings you to the wide place du Dr-Esquirol and an exuberant *fin-de-siècle* municipal **theatre**; opposite this is the **Musée Municipal des Beaux-Arts** (daily except Tues 10am–noon & 2–5/6pm; 20F/€3.05), magnificently housed in four adjacent sixteenth- and seventeeth-century mansions, with different roof angles, adorned with stair turrets and Renaissance window details. The collections include a rich variety of archeological finds, Roman and medieval, furniture and paintings – among the latter some Goyas and a Tintoretto rediscovered in the museum basement during an inventory in 1997. Not far from the museum, in place du Bourg at the end of rue des Droits-de-l'Homme, the cute little thirteenth-century **church of Notre-Dame** is also worth a look.

Behind the theatre, rue Beauville, with heavily restored but beautiful medieval houses, leads through to rue Voltaire, which is full of ethnic restaurants, and rue Richard-Cœur-de-Lion, leading to the **Église des Jacobins**, a big brick Dominican church of the thirteenth century, its barn-like interior divided by a single centre row of pillars, very like its counterpart in Toulouse; the deconsecrated church is now used for temporary art exhibitions. Beyond lie the river and the public gardens of **Le Gravier**, where a market is held every Saturday morning; there's a footbridge across the Garonne, from where you can see a **canal bridge** dating from 1839 further downstream.

Opposite place Wilson on the north side of boulevard de la République, the arcaded rue Cornières leads through to the **Cathédrale St-Caprais**, somewhat misshapen but with a finely proportioned Romanesque apse and radiating chapels still surviving. There is a piece of the original fortifications still showing in rue des Augustins close by – the **Tour du Chapelet** – dating from around 1100. Again nearby, in rue du Puits-du-

Saumon, is one of the finest houses in town, the fourteenth-century **Maison du Sénéchal**, with an elaborate open loggia on the first floor.

Practicalities

From the central place Goya, boulevard du Président-Carnot leads to the **gares SNCF** and **routière**. The **tourist office** is at 107 bd Carnot (July & Aug Mon–Sat 9am–7pm, Sun 10am–noon; rest of year Mon–Sat 9am–12.30pm & 2–6.30pm; ☎05.53.47.36.09, fax 05.53.47.29.98, *otsi.agen@wanadoo.fr*).

There are several reasonable **hotel** options in Agen. Near the tourist office, the *Ibis*, 16 rue Camille-Desmoulins (☎05.53.47.43.43, fax 05.53.47.68.54; ④), doesn't look much but is comfortable and welcoming. Also very central and in a more attractive street is the simple *Hôtel des Ambans*, 59 rue des Ambans (☎05.53.66.28.60, fax 05.53.87.94.01; ②), near place Goya. At the east end of bd de la République, close to the river, the attractive *Hôtel des Îles*, 25 rue Baudin (☎05.53.47.11.33, fax 05.53.66.19.25; ②), is less convenient but has light, airy rooms.

The best places to **eat** well at reasonable prices are *Les Mignardises*, 40 rue Camille-Desmoulins (closed Sun & Mon), popular for its good-value menus (from 56F/€8.54), and the more upmarket *Le Margotan*, 52 rue Richard-Cœur-de-Lion (☎05.53.48.11.55; closed Mon; from 90F/€13.72), which has a good range of seafood. Alternatively, try *Flo d'Argent*, 24 place J.-B.-Durand (menus 52.50–122F/€8–18.60), with an eclectic menu and Provencal decor, or, if you like crêpes, head for the *Crêperie des Jacobins*, right opposite the Église des Jacobins (closed Sun & Mon; 40–50F/€6.10–7.62).

travel details

Trains

Agen to: Belvès (3–4 daily; 1hr); Bordeaux (hourly; 1hr 10min–1hr 50min); Le Buisson (3–4 daily; 1hr 20min–1hr 45min); Les Eyzies (3–4 daily; 1hr 40min); Moissac (2–3 daily; 30min); Monsempron-Libos (6 daily; 30–45min); Montauban (every 1–2 hours; 40–50min); Périgueux (3–4 daily; 2hr 10min–2hr 20min); Toulouse (every 1–2 hours; 1hr–1hr 20min); Villefranche-du-Périgord (3–4 daily; 50min).

Bergerac to: Bordeaux (4–8 daily; 50min–1hr 30min); Montcaret (1–3 daily; 25–30min); St-Émilion (1–3 daily; 55min); Ste-Foy-la-Grande (5–10 daily; 20min); Sarlat (2–6 daily; 1hr–1hr 30min).

Brive to: Bordeaux (1–2 daily; 2hr 15min); Cahors (6–8 daily; 1hr–1hr 10min); Clermont-Ferrand (2–5 daily; 3hr 40min); Figeac (5–6 daily; 1hr 20min); Gourdon (7–11 daily; 40min); Limoges (10–15 daily; 1hr 10min); Montauban (6–8 daily; 1hr 50min); Paris-Austerlitz (10–15 daily; 4hr–4hr 45min); Périgueux (3–4 daily; 1hr); Rocamadour-Padirac (4–6 daily; 45min); Souillac (6–9 daily; 25min); Toulouse (6–8 daily; 2hr 30min); Uzerche (6–10 daily; 30min); Villefranche-de-Rouergue (2 daily; 2hr–2hr 20min).

Cahors to: Brive (6–8 daily; 1hr–1hr 10min); Montauban (7–14 daily; 40min); Toulouse (7–14 daily; 1hr 10min).

Figeac to: Aubin (3 daily; 30min–1hr); Brive (5–6 daily; 1hr 20min); Decazeville (4 daily; 20–50min); Najac (4–5 daily; 50min); Rodez (4–6 daily; 1hr–1hr 50min); Toulouse (5–6 daily; 2hr 30min); Villefranche-de-Rouergue (6–8 daily; 40min).

Limoges to: Angoulême (3–6 daily; 2hr); Bordeaux (6–7 daily; 2hr 30min); Brive (10–15 daily; 1hr 10min); Eymoutiers (4–5 daily; 50min); Meymac (3–4 daily; 1hr 40min); Nexon (6–11 daily; 15min); Paris-Austerlitz (10–14 daily; 3hr–3hr 40min); Périgueux (8–13 daily; 1hr–1hr 30min); Poitiers (3–5 daily; 2hr); Pompadour (1–2 daily; 1hr 10min); St-Junien (3–6 daily; 40min); St-Léonard (4–5 daily; 20min); Solignac-Le Vigen (1–3 daily; 10min); Thiviers (8–15 daily; 40min–1hr); Ussel (3–4 daily; 1hr 35min–2hr).

Montauban to: Agen (10–15 daily; 40–50min); Bordeaux (10–15 daily; 1hr 40min–2hr 30min); Moissac (4–7 daily; 20min); Toulouse (1–4 hourly; 25–35min).

Périgueux to: Agen (3–4 daily; 2hr 10min–2hr 20min); Belvès (2–4 daily; 1hr–1hr 15min); Bordeaux (10–16 daily; 1hr–1hr 25min); Brive (3–4 daily; 1hr); Le Buisson (2–7 daily; 45min–1hr); Les Eyzies (2–7 daily; 30–35min); Limoges (8–13 daily; 1hr–1hr 30min); Monsempron-Libos (2–4 daily; 1hr 30min); Villefranche-du-Périgord (2–4 daily; 1hr 15min).

Sarlat to: Bergerac (2–6 daily; 1hr–1hr 30min); Bordeaux (3–4 daily; 2hr 30min); Le Buisson (4–6 daily; 30–40min); Ste-Foy-la-Grande (4–6 daily; 1hr 30min–1hr 45min).

Buses

Agen to: Condom (Mon–Sat 3 daily; 50min); Mont-de-Marsan (daily except Sat; 2hr 20min); Villeneuve-sur-Lot (4–11 daily; 45min).

Argentat to: Beaulieu-sur-Dordogne (July & Aug Mon–Sat 2 daily; 40min); Tulle (1–5 daily; 40min–1hr).

Bergerac to: Marmande (1 daily; 2hr); Villeneuve-sur-Lot (Mon–Fri 1–2 daily; 1hr 15min).

Brive to: Argentat (Mon–Sat 2 daily; 1hr 20min); Arnac-Pompadour (Mon–Sat 1–2 daily; 1hr 45min); Collonges-le-Rouge (Mon–Sat 1–3 daily; 20–35min); Meyssac (Mon–Sat 1–3 daily; 30–40min); Turenne (Mon–Sat 2–3 daily; 45min); Uzerche (Mon–Sat 2 daily; 1hr–1hr 20min); Vayrac (Mon–Sat 3–4 daily; 1hr).

Cahors to: Cajarç (3–7 daily; 40min–1hr); Figeac (3–7 daily; 1hr 45min); Fumel (4–6 daily; 1hr 10min); Luzech (4–8 daily; 20min); Montauban (Mon–Fri 1 daily; 1hr 20min); Monsempron-Libos (4–6 daily; 1hr 20min); Puy-l'Évêque (4–8 daily; 45min); Rodez (Mon–Fri 1 daily; 2hr 40min); Villefranche-de-Rouergue (Mon–Sat 1–2 daily; 1hr 15min).

Limoges to: Aubusson (Mon–Sat 2–4 daily; 2hr); Châlus (Mon–Sat 2–3 daily; 1hr); Nexon (Mon–Sat 1–2 daily; 50min); Oradour-sur-Glane (4–9 daily; 30–50min); St-Junien (Mon–Fri 3 daily; 40min–1hr); St-Léonard (1–4 daily; 35min); Solignac (Mon–Sat school term only 1 daily; 30–45min); Le Vigen (Mon–Sat 2–4 daily; 25min).

Périgueux to: Angoulême (1–3 daily; 1hr 40min–2hr); Bergerac (Mon–Sat 2–4 daily; 1hr–1hr 20min); Brantôme (1–4 daily; 45min); Excideuil (Mon–Sat 3–5 daily; 1hr); Montignac (Mon–Sat 1–2 daily; 1hr); Sarlat (Mon–Sat 1–4 daily; 1hr); Sarlat (Mon–Sat 1–2 daily; 1hr 30min).

Ribérac to: Angoulême via Mareuil (Mon–Sat 1–3 daily; 1hr 30min–1hr 45min).

CHAPTER TEN

THE PYRENEES

Basque-speaking, wet and green in the west; craggy, snowy, Gascon-influenced in the middle; dry, Mediterranean and Catalan-speaking in the east – the **Pyrenees** are physically beautiful, culturally varied and considerably less developed than the Alps. The whole range is marvellous walkers' country, especially the central region around the **Parc National des Pyrénées**, with its 3000-metre peaks, streams, forests, flowers and wildlife. If you're a committed **hiker**, it's possible to traverse these mountains, from the Atlantic to the Mediterranean, along the **GR10** or the higher, more difficult **Haute Randonnée Pyrénéenne** (HRP). There are numerous local alpine resorts as well – **Cauterets**, **Luz-St-Sauveur**, **Barèges**, **Ax-les-Thermes** – with shorter hikes to suit all temperaments and abilities, as well as **skiing** opportunities in winter.

As for the more conventional of the tourist attractions, the **Côte Basque** is lovely but very popular, suffering from seaside sprawl and a surfeit of campsites. **St-Jean-de-Luz** is arguably the prettiest of the resorts, while once-elistist **Biarritz** is now enjoying a renaissance. **Bayonne**, which lies 6km inland, is an attractive, if heavily touristed town, with an excellent museum of Basque culture (set to reopen shortly). The foothill towns

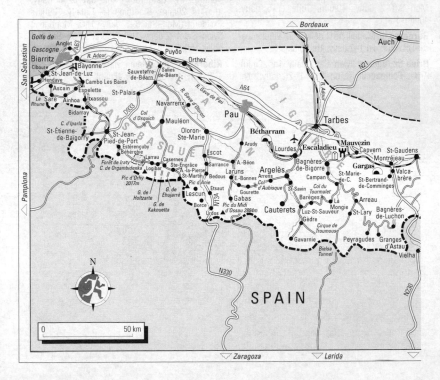

ACCOMMODATION PRICE CODES

Each hotel and guesthouse in this book has been graded according to the following price codes, which indicate the price for the **cheapest double room available during the high season**.

① Under 160F/€24   ④ 300–400F/€46–61   ⑦ 600–700F/€91–107
② 160–220F/€24–34   ⑤ 400–500F/€61–76   ⑧ 700–800F/€107–122
③ 220–300F/€34–46   ⑥ 500–600F/€76–91   ⑨ Over 800F/€122

are on the whole rather dull, although **Pau** merits at least a day or two, while **Lourdes** is such a monster of kitsch that it just has to be seen. The coast of Catalan-speaking **Roussillon** in the east has beaches every bit as popular as those of the Côte Basque, but on the whole is less inviting. Its interior, however, is another matter: craggy landscapes split by spectacular canyons, a crop of fine Romanesque abbeys – of which **St-Martin-de-Canigou** and **Serrabonne** are the most dramatic – and a climate bathed in Mediterranean heat and light.

Hiking in the Pyrenees

If you're planning on doing even very basic **walking** or other outdoor activities – canoeing, riding, cycling, paragliding – in the Pyrenees, a good contact point for **ideas**, **information** and **publications** (in French) is Randonnées Pyrénéennes, 4 rue Maye-Lane, 65420 Ibos, near Tarbes (☎05.62.90.09.90; information centre ☎05.62.90.09.92).

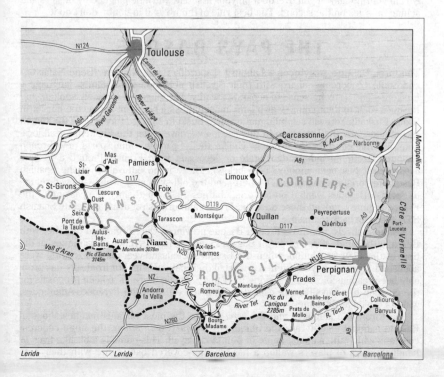

In addition, there are plenty of walkers' **guidebooks** to the area in both French and English (see p.1140). The most detailed **maps** are the French IGN 1:25,000 "TOP 25" series; #1547OT, #1647ET, #1647OT, #1748ET and #1748OT cover the Parc National des Pyrénées. Less demanding walkers can make do with Rando Éditions' *Cartes de Randonnées*, which covers the range at 1:50,000 in eleven sheets numbered from west to east.

The **walking season** usually lasts from mid-June through late September; earlier in the year, few staffed refuges function, and you will run into snow even on parts of the GR10. Whatever you intend, bear in mind that these are big mountains and should be treated with respect: to tackle any of the main walks **preparation** is crucial. Before taking to the hills, check weather forecasts, usually posted at the local tourist office, and be sure you are properly equipped with water, food, maps, bivvy bag, emergency signalling, whistle and knife, as well as warm, wetproof and windproof clothing and suitable boots – not to mention ice axe and crampons if you are going anywhere near permanent snow, which you shouldn't be doing unless you have experience in high-altitude mountaineering. Above all, don't take any chances: mountain conditions can change very quickly, and sunny, warm weather in the valley doesn't necessarily mean it will be the same higher up, three hours later. If you don't have any mountain-walking experience, it's probably best not to undertake anything more than a well-frequented path unless you're accompanied by someone who does.

One kilometre in twelve minutes (5kph) is a fairly average **walking pace** for level ground; if you're going uphill, allow an hour for every 500m in elevation gained. If you are out of condition it'll take longer. Work yourself in gently, otherwise you could easily ruin your holiday: if you overdo it on your first day, you'll be plagued by blisters and aching muscles on the second. The best rule of thumb is: if in doubt, don't do it.

THE PAYS BASQUE

The three **Basque provinces** – Labourd (Lapurdi), Basse Navarre (Behe Nafarroa) and Soule (Zuberoa) – share with their Spanish neighbours a common language – Euskera – and a strong sense of separate identity. The language is widely spoken, and Basques refer to their country as a land in itself, Euskal-herri, or, across the border in Spain, Euskadi. You will see bilingual French/Euskera signage throughout the region (sometimes only the latter), so in this section we have given the Euskera for all locations in brackets after the French. Unlike their Spanish counterparts, few French Basques favour an independent state or secession from France, though a Basque *département* has been mooted (see below). There is no equivalent of the Spanish Basque terrorist organization ETA here, and the old sympathy, which allowed refuge to Spanish Basques wanted on terrorist charges, has waned since the passing of the Franco regime – indeed these days the French authorities regularly extradite Spanish ETA suspects back to Spain.

Administratively, the three French Basque provinces were organized together with Béarn in the single *département* of Basses-Pyrénées, now Pyrénées-Atlantiques, at the time of the 1789 Revolution, when the Basques' thousand-year-old *fors* (rights) were abolished. It was a move designed to curtail their nationalism, but ironically has probably been responsible for preserving their unity. Of late there have been proposals for the creation of a Pays-Basque *département*, hived off from the Pyrénées-Atlantiques, with its capital at Bayonne.

Apart from the language and the *beret basque*, the most obvious manifestations of Basque national identity are the ubiquitous *trinquets* or *frontons*, the huge concrete courts in which the national game of **pelota** is played. This game is a bit like fives or handball: pairs of players wallop a hard leather-covered ball, either with their bare hands or a long basket-work extension of the hand called a *chistera*, against a high wall blocking one end of the court. It's extraordinarily dangerous – the ball travels at speeds of up to 200kph – and knockouts and worse are not uncommon. Trials of strength (*force Basque*), rather like Scottish Highland Games, are also popular: tugs-of-war, lifting heavy weights, turning massive carts, sawing through giant tree trunks and the like.

The Côte Basque

Barely 30km long, the **Basque coast** is easily accessible by air, bus and train, and reasonably priced hotel accommodation is not that difficult to find – though space should be reserved a month in advance during summer. **Bayonne**, slightly inland, is the cultural focus and only town with some life apart from tourism. **Biarritz** is the most prestigious and varied resort, flanked by magnificent beaches, but can be a rather noisy place to stay in high season. Families will probably prefer **St-Jean-de-Luz** to the south – an attractive and more manageable town in any case – or **Anglet** just to the north, with more fine beaches which attract surfers from near and far.

Bayonne (Baïona)

BAYONNE stands back some 6km from the Atlantic, a position that until recently protected it from any real exploitation by tourism. It bestrides the confluence of the River Adour, which rises to the east in the region of the Pic du Midi de Bigorre, and the much smaller Nive, whose source is the Basque Pyrénées above St-Jean-Pied-de-Port. Although purists dispute whether it is truly a Basque rather than a Gascon city, it is the effective economic and political capital of the Pays Basque. To the lay person, at least, there seems no doubt about its Basque flavour, with its tall half-timbered houses and woodwork painted in the peculiarly Basque tones of green and red. Here, too, Basques

---

THE FOOD OF THE BASQUE COUNTRY

Although **Basque cooking** shares many of the dishes of the southwest and the central Pyrenees – in particular **garbure**, a thick potato, cabbage and turnip soup enlivened with a piece of pork or duck or goose *confit* – it does have some distinctive recipes of its own. One of the best known is the Basque omelette, **pipérade**, made with tomatoes, chillis and sautéed Bayonne ham (salt-cured and resembling Parma ham), mixed into the eggs, so that it actually looks more like scrambled eggs. Another delicacy is sweet red peppers, or **piquillos**, stuffed whole with *morue* or cod. **Poulet basquaise** is also common, especially as takeaway food at the *traiteur*: it consists of pieces of chicken browned in pork fat and casseroled in a sauce of tomato, chilli, onions and a little white wine. And in season there is a chance of **palombe**, the wild doves netted or shot as they migrate north over the Pyrenees.

With the Atlantic close at hand, seafood is a speciality. The Basques inevitably have their version of fish soup, called *ttoro*. Another great delicacy is **elvers** or *piballes*, which are netted as they come up the Atlantic rivers from the Sargasso Sea. **Squid** are common, served here as *txiperons*, either in their own ink or stewed with onion, tomato, peppers and garlic. All the locally caught fish – tuna (*thon*), sea bass (*bor*), sardines (*sardine*) and anchovies (*anchois*) – are regular favourites, too.

Cheeses mainly comprise the delicious ewe's-milk *tommes* and *gasna* from the high pastures of the Pyrenees. Among sweets, one that is on show everywhere is the **gâteau basque**, a sweet flan pastry garnished with black cherries or filled with *crème pâtissière*.

As for alcohol, the only Basque **wine** is the very drinkable Irouléguy – as red, white or rosé – and the local *digestif* **liqueur** is the potent green or yellow Izzara.

in flight from Franco's Spain came without hesitation to seek refuge among their own. For many years the Petit Bayonne quarter on the right bank of the Nive was a hotbed of Basque nationalism, until the French government clamped down on such dangerous tendencies.

The city's origins go back to Roman times, since when its Latin name of Lapurdum, corrupted to Labourd (Lapurdi), has been extended to cover the whole of this westernmost of the three Basque provinces. For three centuries until 1451, which marked the end of the Hundred Years War, it enjoyed prosperity and security under English domination, and this wealth was consolidated when, around 1500, Sephardic Jews fleeing the Spanish Inquisition arrived, bringing their chocolate-manufacturing trade with them. The city reached the peak of its commercial success in the eighteenth century, when it was also a centre of the armaments industry (it gave its name to the bayonet). Later, its prestige suffered a blow in the 1789 Revolution when the anti-regionalist, centralizing Paris government subsumed the three Basque provinces under a single *département*, with its capital at Pau. More recently, economic activity has been based on the processing of by-products from the natural gas field at Lacq near Pau, although this has recently been through some hard times, leaving Bayonne with a higher-than-national-average level of unemployment.

These issues don't immediately impinge on the visitor, however, and first impressions are likely to be favourable. It's a small-scale, easily manageable city which can be explored on foot rather than bus, and, as the hub of all major road and rail routes from the north and east, it is worth considering as a base for a seaside sojourn.

Arrival, information and accommodation

The **gare SNCF** and **gare routière** for points in Béarn, Basse Navarre and Soule are next door to each other, just off place de la République on the north bank of the Adour, across the wide Pont St-Esprit from the city centre. In addition, a bus terminal in place des Basques on the Adour's south bank, serves destinations in the Nive valley. The **tourist office** is also in place des Basques (July & Aug Mon–Sat 9am–7pm, Sun 10am–1pm; rest of year Mon–Fri 9am–6.30pm, Sat 10am–6pm; ☎05.59.46.01.46), with a booth at the train station and the airport in summer only (July & Aug Mon–Sat 9.30am–12.30pm & 2–6.30pm); they organize several good bus trips up into the mountains – ask for their list.

The most agreeable budget **hotels** are the basic *Hôtel des Basques*, on place Paul-Bert (☎05.59.59.08.02; ①), the tiny *Hôtel du Port Neuf*, at 44 rue du Port-Neuf (☎05.59.25.65.83; ②), with just five rooms with bath or shower, and the *Hôtel Monbar*, at 24 rue Pannecau in Petit Bayonne (☎05.59.59.26.80; ②), with en-suite rooms. Pricier alternatives include *Hôtel des Basses-Pyrénées*, at 14 rue Tour-de-Sault (☎05.59.59.00.29, fax 05.59.59.42.02; ①–④), in a converted medieval building, and the top-end *Hôtel Frantour Loustau*, on place de la République (☎05.59.55.08.08, fax 05.59.55.69.36; ⑤), overlooking the river beside Pont St-Esprit; both have affordable attached restaurants (menus from under 100F/€15.25).

Hostellers can head for the **HI hostel** at 19 rte des Vignes in Anglet (see p.689), 6km west of town on the Biarritz road; the STAB bus #4 (direction "Biarritz Mairie") from the Hôtel de Ville stops right outside. The only **campsite** nearby is *La Chêneraie* (☎05.59.55.01.31; closed Oct–Easter), off the N117 Pau road close to the Bayonne-Nord exit from the *autoroute*, and also on the #4 bus route; take bus direction "Sainsontan" and get off at Navarre, from where the campsite is a 500-metre walk.

The City

Although there are no great sights in Bayonne, it's a pleasure to wander the deep narrow streets of the old town, bisected by the river Nive and still encircled by Vauban's

BAYONNE

ACCOMMODATION

des Basques	3
des Basses-Pyrénées	5
Frantour Loustau	1
Monbar	4
du Port Neuf	2

RESTAURANTS

Auberge du Cheval Blanc	C
Le Bistrot Ste-Cluque	A
Le Chistera	B
Au Clair de la Nive	D

defences. The cathedral is on the west bank in **Grand Bayonne**, and the museums east of the river in **Petit Bayonne**.

The **Cathédrale Ste-Marie** (Mon–Sat 10–11.45am & 3–5.45pm, Sun 3.30–5.45pm), on the magnolia-shaded place Pasteur, with its twin towers and steeple rising with airy grace above the houses, is best seen from a distance. Up close, the yellowish stone reveals bad weathering, with most of the decorative detail lost. Inside, its most impressive features are the height of the nave and some sixteenth-century glass, set off by the prevailing gloom. Like other southern Gothic cathedrals of the period (around 1260), it was based on more famous northern models, in this case Soissons and Reims. On the south side is a quiet, secretive **cloister** (daily 9am–5/6pm; 14F/€2.10), with a lawn, cypress trees and beds of begonias.

The smartest streets in town are those extending north from the cathedral: rue d'Espagne, the old commercial centre, and rue de la Monnaie, leading into rue Port-Neuf, with its aromatic pâtisseries and confiseries. Southwest of the cathedral, along rue des Faures and the streets above the old walls, there is a distinctly Spanish feel, with washing strung at the windows and strains of music drifting from dark interiors.

Below the cathedral, the riverside **quays** of the Nive are the city's most picturesque focus, with sixteenth-century arcaded houses on the Petit Bayonne side, one of which used to contain the excellent Basque ethnographic museum, the **Musée Basque** (closed for restoration; check with tourist office for latest details). Its exhibits illustrate Basque life through the centuries, and include reconstructed farm buildings, house interiors, implements, tools and *makhila*s – innocent-looking carved, wooden walking sticks with a concealed steel spear tip at one end, used by pilgrims and shepherds for self-protection if need be. There's also a section on Basque seagoing activities (Columbus's skipper was a Basque), and rooms on pelota – its history and stars – and famous Basques.

The city's second museum, the **Musée Bonnat**, close by at 5 rue Jacques-Lafitte (daily except Tues 10am–noon & 2.30–6.30pm, Fri till 8.30pm; 30F/€4.60), with an annexe at 9 rue Fredéric-Bastiat, provides an unexpected treasury of art. Thirteenth- and fourteenth-century Italian art is well represented, as are most periods before Impressionism. Highlights include Goya's *Self-Portrait* and *Portrait of Don Francisco de Borja*, Rubens' powerful *Apollo and Daphne* and *The Triumph of Venus*, plus works by Murrillo, El Greco and Ingrès. A whole gallery is devoted to high-society portraits by Léon Bonnat (1833–1922), whose personal collection formed the original core of the museum. There are also frequent temporary exhibits of the work of prominent artists, well worth catching.

Apart from savouring the wide river skies, there is little to draw you to the northern bank of the Adour. The **church of St-Esprit**, opposite the station, is all that remains of a hostel that once ministered to the sore feet and other ailments of the Santiago pilgrims – worth a peek inside for an interesting wood sculpture of *The Flight into Egypt*. Just behind the station is Vauban's massive **citadelle**; built in 1680 to defend the town against Spanish attack, it actually saw little action until the Napoleonic wars, when its garrison resisted a siege by Wellington for four months in 1813. Don't miss the beautiful **Jardin Botanique** inside the castle walls, with its huge collection of plants labelled in French, Basque and Latin (daily: mid-April to mid-Oct 9am–noon & 2–6pm; free).

If you have a car, it's worth making an evening trip northwest through the industrial suburb of **BOUCAU** and out to the breakwater, **La Barre**, that protects the mouth of the Adour. It's a pleasant place to sit and watch the leaden-hued Atlantic rollers come in; if you are tempted to swim off the beautiful white beach that stretches from here to Bordeaux, remember that there are lethal currents close inshore, so be extremely careful.

Eating, drinking and entertainment

The best area for eating and drinking is along the right bank (Petit Bayonne) of the Nive and in the back streets to either side of the river, especially along rue Pannecau, rue des Cordeliers and rue des Tonneliers in Petit Bayonne. Two of the best **restaurants** in this part of town are the *Auberge du Cheval Blanc*, 68 rue Bourgneuf (☎05.59.59.01.33; closed Sun evening, Mon in winter & one week in Aug; weekday lunch menus 125F/€19; booking essential), a durable gourmets' mecca specializing in decadent desserts; and *Au Clair de la Nive*, 28 quai Galuperie (closed Mon lunch & Sun; menu 98F/€14.95, à la carte 120–190F/€18.30–29), with a riverside terrace, serving tasty cuisine, such as roast anchovies, steamed cod in pepper sauce and delicate desserts. In Grand Bayonne, *Le Chistera*, 42 rue Port-Neuf (closed random weeks in Feb & May; menu 85F/€13, à la carte 100–120F/€15.25–18.30), is the best option, dishing up hearty Bayonnais specialities based on fish, pork and tripe, best ordered off the daily-specials board. The one culinary bright spot across the Adour is *Le Bistrot Ste-Cluque*, 9 rue Hughes (☎05.59.55.82.43; menu at 70F/€10.70, à la carte around

100F/€15.25; bookings essential), which is perennially packed for its excellent-value French cuisine and is also a popular gay hangout.

For **bar** snacks, head to *Bar du Marché*, 39 rue des Basques in Grand Bayonne (closed Sat evening & Sun), which begins serving food and drink at 5am to a mix of market sellers and bar-flies on their way home to bed, continuing with good-value *plats de jour* at lunchtime. Nearby is *Bodega Ibaia*, 49 quai Jauréguiberry, a lively, well-loved bar, with *plats de jour* for under 50F/€7.60 at lunchtime. If you fancy an afternoon drink, try *Chocolat Cazenave*, 19 rue du Port-Neuf, which serves hot cups of cocoa, and also sells every conceivable chocolate goodie to take home.

As far as **festivals** go, Bayonne's biggest bash of the year is the Fêtes Traditionelles, which starts on the first Wednesday in August and consists of five days and nights of continuous boozing and entertainment. This finishes up with a *corrida* on the following Sunday. Following the festival there are three or four more days of bullfighting beginning on August 15. A well-established jazz festival takes place in mid-July, and every October there is a Franco-Spanish theatre festival.

Biarritz (Miarritze)

A few minutes by rail or road from Bayonne, **BIARRITZ** was, until forty years ago, the Monte Carlo of the Atlantic coast, transformed by Napoléon III in the mid-nineteenth century into a playground for monarchs, aristos and glitterati. With the rise of the Côte d'Azur during the 1960s, however, the place went into seemingly terminal decline. It is only during the last decade that the city has been rediscovered by Parisian yuppies and the international surfing fraternity, who together fuel a respectable nightlife.

Arrival, information and accommodation

The **gare SNCF** is 3km southeast of the centre at the end of avenue Foch/avenue Kennedy in the *quartier* known as La Négresse (STAB bus #2 or #9 from square d'Ixelles). The **tourist office** is on square d'Ixelles (daily: July & Aug 8am–8pm; rest of year 9am–6.45pm; ☎05.59.22.37.10), in the vicinity of the casino.

Accommodation is heavily booked in July and August, but is less expensive than you might expect. The friendly and clean *Hôtel de la Marine*, with en-suite rooms, on the corner of rue des Goélands and rue du Port-Vieux (☎05.59.24.34.09; ②), is popular with backpackers and surfers. Nearby are the equally welcoming *Hôtel Palym* at 7 rue du Port-Vieux (☎05.59.24.16.56, fax 05.59.24.96.12; ②), with a variety of old-fashioned rooms, and, down the street at no. 10, the *Hôtel Atlantic* (☎05.59.24.34.08; ②); both have their own ground-floor bar-restaurant. Better value, and quieter than any of these is the Belle Époque *Hôtel Atalaye* at 6 rue des Goélands (☎05.59.24.06.76, fax 05.59.22.33.51; ③).

The nearest **HI hostel** (☎05.59.41.76.00) is 2km southwest of the centre on the shore of Lac Mouriscot, just walkable from the *gare SNCF*; otherwise take bus #2 from the centre and look out for the "Bois de Boulogne" stop. **Campers** should try *Biarritz-Camping*, at 28 route d'Harcet, the inland continuation of avenue de la Plage (☎05.59.23.00.12, fax 05.59.43.74.67; closed Oct–April), behind Plage de la Milady, to the south of town.

The Town

The focus of Biarritz is the **Casino Municipal**, just behind the Grande Plage, now restored to its 1930s grandeur. Inland, the town forms a surprisingly amorphous and workaday sprawl, with the sole point of interest the **Musée d'Art Oriental**, 1 rue Guy-Petit (Tues 10.30am–7pm, Wed–Fri 10.30am–1pm & 2.30–7/8pm, Sat 10.30am–1pm & 2.30–10/11pm, Sun 2.30–7/8pm; 45F/€6.85), exhibiting the collection of Indian and Tibetan art specialist Michel Postel.

Between here and the Plage du Port-Vieux are the only streets and squares conducive to relaxed strolling. At the far west end of **place Clemenceau**, one of several central squares, you can nibble a cake or sip a lemon tea at *Miremont's Salon de Thé* – a frightfully superior place epitomizing old-money Biarritz. To the west, the faded old-time hotels ringing the **place Attalaye**, high above the port, are worth a glance for their elegant facades, as is the characterful if touristy **rue du Port-Vieux** just below, leading down to its namesake beach (see below).

The **shore**, however, is undeniably beautiful. White breakers crash on sandy strands, where beautiful people bronze their limbs cheek by jowl with suburban families and surf bums, against a backdrop of casinos and ocean-liner hotels, ornate churches, Gothic follies and modern apartment blocks. The **beaches** – served by STAB buses #4 and #9 from Biarritz centre – extend northwards from Plage de la Milady through Plage Marbella, Côte des Basques, Plage du Port-Vieux, Grande Plage and Plage Miramar to the Pointe St-Martin. Most of the action takes place between the Plage du Port-Vieux and the Plage Miramar, overlooked by the huge **Hôtel du Palais** (formerly the Villa Eugénie), built by Napoléon III in the mid-nineteenth century for his wife, whom he met and courted in Biarritz.

Just beside the **Plage du Port-Vieux**, the most sheltered and intimate of the beaches, a rocky promontory sticks out into the sea, ending in the **Rocher de la Vierge**, an offshore rock topped by a white statue of the Virgin, and linked to the mainland by an Eiffel-built iron catwalk. Around it are scattered other rocky islets where the swell heaves and combs. On the bluff above the Virgin stands the **Musée de la Mer** (daily: July & Aug 9.30am–midnight; rest of year 9.30am–12.30pm & 2–6pm; 45F/€6.85), which contains interesting displays on the fishing industry and the region's birds, and an aquarium of North Atlantic fish.

Just below is the picturesque harbour of the **Port des Pêcheurs**, most easily approached by a switchback pedestrian lane. The fishermen have now gone, replaced by pleasure boats, but there's a scuba outfitter here and a clutch of pricey seafood restaurants. To the northeast lies the **Grande Plage**, an immaculate sweep of sand originally dubbed the "Plage des Fous" after the 1850s practice of taking mental patients to bathe here as a primitive form of thalassotherapy.

Eating, drinking and nightlife

There are some reasonable places to **eat** near the market *halles*, 200m southwest of place Clemenceau, and it's easy to eat well for a price, away from the touristy snack bars on rue du Port-Vieux. Two of the best options around the market are *Le St Amour*, at 26 rue Gambetta, a Lyonnais-style bistro with a sausage-strong menu at 75F/€11.45, and *Bistrot des Halles* (☎05.59.24.21.22), at 1 rue du Centre, which serves generously portioned, tasty fish dishes (count on 200F/€30.50 a head plus service). *Le Surfing*, behind Plage de Côte des Basques and festooned with antique boards, serves decent grills and *frites*, while clubbers repair to *Le Morgan*, at 4 rue du Helder off place Clemenceau, open 7pm until dawn, though the cheaper menus are only available until 10pm. Just south of the city limits on the Plage d'Ilbarritz, *Blue Cargo* (☎05.59.23.54.87; à la carte around 170F/€25.95) is currently the hottest place in town, serving mostly fish and salads on the terrace by an old villa, while the lower tent-bar gets going as a jampacked dance club after midnight.

More formal **nightlife** in the town centre includes *Cayo Coco*, a Cuban theme bar at 5 rue Jaulerry offering free salsa dance lessons, a slightly naff *Irish Pub* at 10 rue Victor-Hugo downhill from the *halles*, and *Ventilo Caffe* on rue du Port-Vieux, the favourite haunt of Parisian thirtysomethings. Whether you've slept the night before or not, the best start to the day is at *Salon de Thé L'Orangerie* at 1 rue Gambetta, serving all sorts of hot drinks and a great variety of breakfasts.

Anglet (Angelu)

Immediately north of Biarritz, **ANGLET** sprawls up the coast from the Pointe St-Martin to the mouth of the Adour. There is nothing to see except for two superb beaches – the **Chambre d'Amour**, so named for two lovers trapped in their trysting place by the tide, and the **Sables d'Or**, much favoured by the surfers and with boards for rent. Here, too, the swimming is very dangerous, so do heed the warning signs.

You can catch a #6 or #9 bus here from the central stops in Biarritz, or walk the distance in about thirty minutes, along avenue de l'Impératrice, avenue MacCroskey, then second left down to the seaside boulevard des Plages. Anglet has a **HI hostel** at 19 rte des Vignes (☎05.59.58.70.00; STAB bus #4, direction "Bayonne-Sainsontan" from Biarritz). There is also a **campsite**, the *Camping de la Chambre d'Amour*, on route de Bouney (☎05.59.03.71.66; closed Oct–April), 600m inland from the Plage de Chambre d'Amour. For **eating and drinking**, the most notable seaside establishments are the *Havana Café* at Chambre d'Amour, a permanently crowded bar that serves *plats du jour* at lunch for under 50F/€7.60, and the nearby *Café Bleu*, more of a proper eatery with a menu for 85F/€12.95. Inland, choose between long-running *Udala* at 165 av de l'Adour, for traditional Basque seafood (menu 100F/€15.25, à la carte 140F/€21.35), and the popular *La Fleur de Sel*, 5 av de la Forêt (closed Sun evening & Wed; weekday lunch menu 90F/€13.70, otherwise 148F/€22.60), in the Chiberta pine forest, serving more *nouvelle* dishes.

St-Jean-de-Luz (Donibane Lohitzun)

With its fine sandy bay and magnificent old quarter speckled with half-timbered mansions, **ST-JEAN-DE-LUZ** remains the most attractive resort on the Basque coast, despite being fairly overrun in peak season. As the only natural harbour between Arcachon and Spain, it has been a major port for centuries, with whaling and cod fishing the traditional preoccupations of its fleets. St-Jean remains one of the busiest fishing ports in France, and the principal one for landing anchovy and tuna.

Arrival, information and accommodation

St-Jean's **gare SNCF** is on the southern edge of the town centre, 500m from the beach. The somewhat harried **tourist office** is close by on place Maréchal-Foch, behind the Hôtel de Ville (July & Aug 9am–8pm, Sun 10.30am–1pm & 3–7pm; rest of year Mon–Sat 9am–12.30pm & 2–7pm; ☎05.59.26.03.16, *www.saint-jean-de-luz.com*). On Friday and Tuesday there is a **market** in the adjacent boulevard Victor-Hugo. **Bikes** can be rented at Luz Evasion on place Maurice-Ravel and ADO on avenue Labrouche, as well as at the *gare SNCF*. **Pelota** matches take place throughout the summer in both St-Jean and Ciboure; ask in the tourist office for details.

Opposite the train station, on and around avenue Verdun, are a few inexpensive (for St-Jean) if uninspiringly located **hotels**, among them the en-suite, recently renovated *Hôtel de Paris*, 1 bd du Comandant-Passicot, on the corner of av Labrouche (☎05.59.85.20.20, fax 05.59.85.20.25; ②; closed Jan–April). If you want a quieter old-town or sea-view location, you pay accordingly, and half-board is usually obligatory in peak season: about the cheapest of these is the *Trinquet Maïtena* at 42 rue du Midi, just east of pedestrianized Gambetta (☎05.59.26.05.13, fax 05.59.26.09.90; ②). Slightly more expensive are the English-run *Agur*, 96 rue Gambetta (☎05.59.51.91.11, fax 05.59.51.91.21; ④; closed Nov–March), and the *Ohartzia* (☎05.59.26.00.06, fax 05.59.26.74.75; ③), just inland from the beach, with a huge garden where breakfast is served. A more upmarket choice overlooking the Grande Plage, the *Hôtel de la Plage* (☎05.59.51.03.44, *www.hoteldelaplage.com*; ④; closed Jan–March), has its own (paying) car park and ground-floor brasserie. There are numerous **campsites**, all grouped in the so-called *zone des campings* to the left of the N10 between St-Jean and Guéthary.

The Town

The wealth and vigour of St-Jean's seafaring past is evident in the town, most notably in the surviving seventeenth- and eighteenth-century houses of the merchants and shipowners. One of the finest, adjacent to the Hôtel de Ville on the plane-tree-studded place Louis XIV, is the turreted **Maison Louis XIV** (guided tours: July & Aug Mon–Sat 10.30am–noon & 2.30–6.30pm; rest of year Mon–Sat 10.30am–noon & 2.30–5.30pm; 30F/€4.60), built for the shipowning Lohobiague family in 1643, but taking its name from the fact that the young King Louis stayed here for a month in 1660 during the preparations for his marriage to Maria Teresa, Infanta of Castile. She lodged in the equally impressive pink Italianate villa known as the **Maison de l'Infante** (June–Sept Mon & Sun 2.30–6.30pm, Tues–Sat 11am–12.30pm & 2.30–6.30pm; 15F/€2.30), overlooking the harbour on the quay of the same name. It also houses the **Musée Grévin** waxworks museum (daily: April–Oct 10am–noon & 2–6.30/8pm; rest of year 2–6pm; 37F/€5.65). The corner house on rue Mazarin, nearby, was the Duke of Wellington's HQ during the 1813–14 winter campaign against Marshal Soult.

In the school-book history of St-Jean-de-Luz, the wedding of King Louis and Maria Teresa was a major event. The couple were married in the **church of St-Jean-Baptiste** on pedestrianized **rue Gambetta**, the main shopping street today, though the door through which they left the church has been walled up ever since. The extravagance of the event defies belief. Cardinal Mazarin alone presented the queen with twelve thousand pounds of pearls and diamonds, a gold dinner service and a pair of sumptuous carriages drawn by teams of six horses – all paid for by money made in the service of France. Plain and fortress-like on the outside, this is the largest French Basque church inside, with a barn-like nave roofed in wood and lined on three sides with tiers of dark oak galleries. These are a distinctive feature of Basque churches, and were reserved for the men, while the women sat at ground level in the nave. Equally Basque is the elaborate gilded retable of tiered angels, saints and prophets behind the altar. The walled-up door through which Louis and his bride passed is on the right of the main entrance. Hanging from the ceiling is an *ex voto* model of the Empress Eugénie's paddle-steamer, the *Eagle*, which narrowly escaped being wrecked on the rocks outside St-Jean in 1867.

Ciboure (Ziburu), the docks and Urrugne (Urruña)

On the other side of the harbour, **CIBOURE** seems a continuation of St-Jean but is in fact a separate commune, terminating in the little fortress of Socoa, today home to a sailing club. Its streets are even prettier (and emptier), especially opposite the end of the bridge from St-Jean, the waterfront **quai Maurice-Ravel** (the composer was born at no. 12) and the parallel **rue Pocolette** behind. Wide-fronted, half-timbered, gaily painted and sometimes balconied, the houses epitomize the local Labourdian Basque style. The octagonal tower protruding above the houses belongs to the sixteenth-century **church of St-Vincent**, where you'll find more characteristic Basque galleries and a Baroque altarpiece; the entrance is in rue Pocolette through a paved courtyard with gravestones embedded in it.

From the Pont Charles de Gaulle linking St-Jean and Ciboure, the **fish dock** sticks out into the harbour, stacked with nets and blackened lobster traps, with grubby blue-painted tuna boats tied up alongside. Upstream, smaller boats lie keeled over on the tidal mudflats of the little River Nivelle against a backdrop of green fields and the emerald flanks of **La Rhune** (900m); to ascend the peak, catch a bus from the *gare SNCF* to Col de St-Ignace and Sare (2–3 buses daily; see p.692).

It is also interesting to visit the **Château d'Urtubie** (April–Oct daily except Tues 2–7pm; 30F/€4.60) at **URRUGNE**, just outside Ciboure, 3km southwest of St-Jean-de-Luz, which has belonged to the same family since its construction as a fortified château in 1341. It was enlarged and gentrified during the sixteenth and eighteenth centuries, and provided hospitality for the French King Louis XI, as well as for Soult and later Wellington during the Napoleonic Wars. If you fancy following in their footsteps, it is also a very upmarket **chambre d'hôtes** (☎05.59.54.31.15, fax 05.59.54.62.51; ⑤), with a restaurant offering dinner, including wine and a visit of the château, for 200F/€30.50.

Eating and drinking

There's ample scope in St-Jean for good-value **eating**, especially for seafood. The *Buvette de la Halle* (lunch only, closed Mon off season), on the corner of the market hall on boulevard Victor-Hugo, serves abundant meals of impeccably fresh crab, oysters and sardines, plus *pipérade*, drink and dessert for around 120F/€18.30, while nearby *La Bodega du Marché*, at 18 rue Harispe (closed Sun low season), is an all-purpose place, offering *plats du jour* at lunchtime, tapas, beer and sometimes music by night.

Leading off place Louis-XIV – with its cafés, sidewalk artists and free summertime **concerts** in the bandstand (Tues–Sun 10pm) – rue de la République also has numerous restaurants, among them the cheap and cheerful *La Ruelle* (closed Mon), at no. 19, with seafood menus at 85F/€12.95 and 145F/€22.10, and *L'Alcalde* at no. 22, serving mixed platters and seafood specials at 62–105F/€9.45–16. On the next street east, rue Tourasse, *La Vieille Auberge* at no. 22 (closed Tues lunch & Wed), offers six menus at 60–140F/€9.15–21.35, while *Le Tourasse*, at no. 25, is another classic for seafood and dessert (menus at 89F/€13.60 and 165F/€25.15).

Hendaye (Hendaïa) and the Spanish frontier

HENDAYE, 16km south of St-Jean-de-Luz, is the last town in France before the Spanish frontier. Neither the town itself, **Hendaye-Ville**, nor the seaside quarter, **Hendaye-Plage**, is of any intrinsic interest, though the latter has a fine, safe beach and modern tourist amenities.

The town, served by both the Paris–Bordeaux–Irún and Toulouse–Irún train lines, lies on the estuary of the River Bidassoa, which forms the border with Spain at this point. Just upstream, a tiny wooded island known as the **Île des Faisans** was once used as a meeting place for the monarchs of the two countries. François I, taken prisoner at the battle of Pavia in 1525, was ransomed here. In 1659 it was the scene of the signature of the Treaty of the Pyrénées and in the following year of the marriage contract between Louis XIV and Maria Teresa, when the painter Velázquez, responsible for the decor of the negotiations chamber, caught the cold which resulted in his death. Another interesting encounter was the meeting between Hitler and Franco at Hendaye station on October 23, 1940, when Hitler refused to commit himself to supporting Franco's colonial claims on Morocco, resulting in Franco's refusal to join the ranks of the Axis.

The main sight in the town itself is the **Château d'Abbadia**, home of the nineteenth-century Dublin-born explorer Antoine d'Abbadie, on the headland overlooking Hendaye Plage, just off the Route de la Corniche (guided visits: March–May & Oct Mon–Fri at 3pm & 4pm; June–Sept Mon–Sat at 11am, 3pm, 4pm & 5pm; 35F/€5.35). After expeditions in Ethiopia and Egypt, d'Abbadie had the château built between 1860 and 1870; the architect was Viollet-le-Duc, and the result is a bizarre Scottish Gothic folly, with Arabian boudoirs, Ethiopian frescoes and inscriptions over the doors and lintels inside in Irish, Basque, Arabic and Ethiopian. It is also filled with objects collected by d'Abbadie on his travels. He became president of the Académie des Sciences in 1891, to which he donated the château on his death in 1897.

Hendaye's **tourist office** is at 12 rue des Aubépines in Hendaye-Plage (July & Aug Mon–Sat 9am–8pm, Sun 10am–1pm; rest of year Mon–Fri 9am–12.30pm & 2–6.30pm, Sat 9am–12.30pm & 2–6pm; ☎05.59.20.00.34, *www.hendaye.com*). **Hotel** prices are cheaper in Hendaye-Ville, where accommodation clusters around the *gare SNCF*, but Hendaye-Plage is more pleasant. Worth a try here is the *Hôtel Les Buissonets*, 29 rue des Seringats (☎05.59.20.04.75, fax 05.59.20.79.72; ③), in a converted mansion behind the east end of boulevard de la Mer, with a pool and garden. The **campsites** are mainly grouped around Hendaye-Plage; *Le Moulin*, off the D658 (between the N10 and coastal D912), is one of the cheaper options.

Around Hendaye: up the coast and inland

The best thing about Hendaye is in fact getting there, for the stretch of **coast** from St-Jean south has remained miraculously unspoilt, especially in the region of the **Pointe Ste-Anne** promontory, accessible from the **Chemin Piéton Littoral** footpath, which runs parallel to the coastal D912 "Corniche Basque" road. It is equally accessible from the beach at Hendaye-Plage.

Inland, both trans-Pyrenean walking routes – the **GR10** and **HRP** – officially begin their course in Hendaye-Plage at the former casino on the front. The first, two-hour stage is dull and gives no sense of the glories that lie ahead: along boulevard Général-Leclerc, through the town on rue des Citronniers, under the rail line, then 50m east on the N10 before following the waymarks to the right towards the A63 *autoroute*. A cattle track passes underneath and continues to the tiny hilltop village of **BIRIATOU** (Biriatu), where the walking starts to get interesting. If you are not concerned about the romance of starting at the very beginning, splash out on a taxi and start at Biriatou. A short steep section leads to a Basque **church** with a collection of weather-worn Celtic-type tombstones, next door to the pretty *Auberge Hirribarren*, a temporary haven for many escaping Allied soldiers during World War II. From here the main footpaths and a number of local variations rise rapidly above the coast to semi-isolation, where only the buzzing power lines (soon left behind) and the occasional walker or jogger disturb the peace.

Inland: Labourd (Lapurdi) and Basse Navarre (Behe Nafarroa)

If you don't have your own transport, the simplest forays into the soft, seductive landscapes of the Basque hinterland are along the St-Jean-de-Luz–Sare bus route or the Bayonne–St-Jean-Pied-de-Port train line. Both give a representative sample of the area's main characteristics.

La Rhune (Larrun), Ascain (Azkaine), Sare (Sara) and Ainhoa

The 900-metre cone of **La Rhune**, straddling the frontier with Spain, is the last skyward thrust of the Pyrenees before they decline into the Atlantic. As *the* landmark of Labourd, in spite of its unsightly TV mast, and duly equipped with a rack-and-pinion rail service, it is predictably popular as a vantage point, offering fine vistas way up the Basque coast and east to the rising Pyrenees. Two or three **buses** a day (July & Aug Mon–Sat; rest of year Mon–Fri), run by Le Basque Bondissant, ply the thirty-minute route from the *gare SNCF* in St-Jean-de-Luz, stopping at Ascain, Col de St-Ignace and Sare.

ASCAIN, where Pierre Loti wrote his romantic novel *Ramuntcho*, is like so many Labourdan villages – pretty as a picture and in danger of caricaturing itself, with its galleried church, *fronton* and half-timbered houses. Loti's house is now one of several **hotel-restaurants** in town, the *de la Rhune* (☎05.59.54.00.04, fax 05.59.54.41.67; ③), with a garden at the back.

To shake off this sweetness you could walk up La Rhune from here in about two and a half hours, or take the little **tourist train** from **Col de St-Ignace** (daily: mid-March to June & Oct to mid-Nov 9am–3pm, according to demand and weather conditions; July–Sept about every 35mln from 8.30am; book on ☎05.59.54.20.26; one way 40F/€6.10, return 50F/€7.60). The ascent takes thirty minutes, but you need to allow up to two hours for the round trip. Be warned: it's massively popular in high season, with long waits and two snack bars near the base station taking advantage of a captive clientele.

With or without the bus, it's worth going on to **SARE**, another perfectly proportioned Basque hilltop village ringed by satellite hamlets. You can either walk on the **GR10** from the intermediate station below the summit of La Rhune in about an hour and a quarter or follow the 3km of road from St-Ignace in rather less time. If you plan to continue further east, you can make an overnight stop at one of the village's **hotels**: the *Pikassaria*, 1km southwest in Lehenbiscay hamlet (☎05.59.54.21.51, fax 05.59.54.27.40; ③), or the three-star *Arraya* on the village square (☎05.59.54.20.46, *www.arraya.com*; ⑤), a former hospice on the Santiago pilgrimage route. Alternatively, try the **campsites** just south of the village: *La Petite Rhune* (☎05.59.54.23.97; closed Oct–March) or *Telletchea* (☎05.59.54.26.01; July & Aug).

Instead of going back to St-Jean-de-Luz from Sare, an easy three-to-four-hour stint on the GR10 would take you on to **AINHOA** to link up with the valley of the Nive (see below). Another gem of a village, once patronized by the Duke of Windsor and now rather touristy in season, it consists of little more than a single street lined with substantial, mainly seventeenth-century houses, whose lintel plaques offer mini-genealogies as well as foundation dates. Take a look at the bulky towered **church** with its extravagant Baroque altarpiece of prophets and apostles in niches, framed by Corinthian columns. For **accommodation**, try the comfortable *Hôtel Oppoca* (☎05.59.29.90.72, fax 05.59.29.81.03; ③), with a good restaurant (four menus 90–175F/€13.70–26.70). **Campers** should head for *Camping Harazpy* near the village centre (☎05.59.29.89.38; closed mid-Sept to mid-June).

The valley of the Nive

The valley of the **River Nive** is the only public-transport artery southeast into the Basque interior, with four or five trains a day making the riverside journey from Bayonne to St-Jean-Pied-de-Port in about an hour. The luminous green landscape on the approach to the mountains is scattered with villages untouched by speculative development, and remains as peaceful and harmonious as in the lowlands.

Cambo-les-Bains (Kambo)

The first major stop is **CAMBO-LES-BAINS**, an old spa town whose favourable microclimate made it an ideal centre for the treatment of tuberculosis in the nineteenth century; the locals also claim that camellias flower a month earlier here than elsewhere in the region. It is an attractive town, green and open, but suffers from the usual genteel stuffiness of spas. The "new" town, with its ornate houses and hotels, radiates out from the baths over the heights above the River Nive, while the old quarter, typically Basque with its whitewashed houses and galleried church, lies beside the river.

The main thing to see here is the **Villa Arnaga**, 1.5km northwest of town on the Bayonne road (guided visits: Feb & March Sat & Sun 2.30–6.30pm; April–Sept daily 10am–12.30pm & 2.30–6.30pm; Oct to mid-Nov daily 2.30–6.30pm; 30F/€4.60), built for Edmond Rostand, author of *Cyrano de Bergerac*, who came here to cure his pleurisy in

1903. This larger-than-life Basque house overlooks an almost surreal formal garden with discs and rectangles of water and segments of grass punctuated by blobs, cubes and cones of box, lined by limes and blue cedars, with a distant view of green hills. Inside, it's very kitsch, with a minstrels' gallery, fake pilasters, allegorical frescoes, chandeliers, numerous portraits and various memorabilia.

The **tourist office** is in the Parc St-Joseph in the upper town centre (mid-July to Aug Mon–Sat 8.30am–noon & 2–6.30pm, Sun 10am–12.30pm; rest of year Mon–Sat 8.30am–noon & 2–5.30pm; ☎05.59.29.70.25). For an overnight **stay**, try the *Auberge de Tante Ursule* in the old quarter by the pelota court (☎05.59.29.78.23, fax 05.59.29.28.57; ①–③), with an excellent **restaurant** offering menus from 90F/€13.70. The nearest year-round **campsite** is *Ur-Hégia* on route des Sept-Chênes (☎05.59.29.72.03), also in Bas Cambo; *Camping Bixta Eder* is on the other side of town along avenue d'Espagne (☎05.59.29.94.23; closed mid-Oct to March).

Espelette (Ezpeleta) and Itxassou (Itsasu)

Buses cover the 5km southwest from Cambo to **ESPELETTE**, a somewhat traffic-plagued village of wide-eaved houses, with a **church** notable for its heavy square tower, carved doors, painted ceiling and disc-shaped gravestones. The village's principal source of renown is its large red **pimentos**, much used in Basque cuisine, and its **pottok** sales. *Pottoks* are a small stocky Basque breed of pony, once favoured for work in British coal mines but now reared mainly for meat and riding – herds of them are a common sight on the upland pastures. The annual sales take place on the last Tuesday and Wednesday in January; the pimento jamboree takes place on the last Sunday in October. There is a very good **hotel-restaurant** in the village, too, the *Euzkadi* on the through road at the northeast edge of the village (☎05.59.93.91.88, fax 05.59.93.90.19; ③; restaurant closed Mon), with quiet rear rooms, a pool, tennis courts and three menus (135–170F/€20.60–25.95) featuring Basque country cooking.

About the same distance from Cambo-les-Bains, next stop up the train line (though only one train a day stops here), is the delightful village of **ITXASSOU**, quieter than most of the others in the area, and surrounded by green wooded hills. Nearby, the River Nive cuts through a narrow looping defile by the so-called **Pas de Roland** – hardly more than a roadside boulder with a hole in it, supposedly struck by the hooves of the great knight's horse (see box on p.696). Somewhat more arresting is the little seventeenth-century **church of St-Fructueux**, about 1km out on the minor D349 road to the Pas de Roland, its white-plastered walls set in a lush green bowl; inside, its typical wooden galleries are worth a quick look. Itxassou is a great base for a gentle recharge of the batteries, with about a half-dozen **hotel-restaurants** scattered locally. These include the very central *Hôtel du Fronton* (☎05.59.29.75.10, fax 05.59.29.23.50; ②; closed Jan to mid-Feb), with its affiliated *Restaurant Bonnet*; and the remoter *Hôtel du Chêne* (☎05.59.29.75.01, fax 05.59.29.27.39; ③; closed Jan–Feb) and *Hôtel-Restaurant Ondoria* (☎05.59.29.75.39; 200F/€30.50), both a few hundred metres along the road to the Pas de Roland and Laxia hamlet.

Bidarray (Bidarrai) and St-Étienne-de-Baïgorry (Baigorri)

The GR10 from Ainhoa, as well as the train line (station Pont-Noblia), both call at **BIDARRAY**, which at first glance seems restricted to a few houses clustered around its medieval bridge. Further investigation, however, reveals the upper village, scattered appealingly on a ridge with superb views. On the way into the village on the GR10 is a **gîte d'étape**, *Auñamendi* (☎05.59.37.71.34; ①), while the central place de l'Église is flanked by the recently refurbished *Hôtel Restaurant Barberaenea* (☎05.59.37.74.86, fax 05.59.37.77.55; ②), where it's worth enduring leisurely service for the tasty five-course 135F/€20.60 *menu du terroir* served under the plane trees. Another good option down in the river-bank quarter, the welcoming *Hôtel-Restaurant du Pont d'Enfer* (☎05.59.37.70.88, fax 05.59.37.76.60; ③; closed Nov–Easter), also known as *Chez Anny* after the proprietress, has good-sized rooms and a restaurant serving on a river-view terrace in summer – among several menus, the 128F/€19.50 one is best value. A short walk east, equidistant from upper and riverside quarters, lies the *Camping Errekaldia* (☎05.59.37.72.36).

Bidarray is the preferred starting point for the classic **ridge walk** of the Basque country, the section of the GR10 running roughly south along the **Crête d'Iparla**, and then descending east to **ST-ÉTIENNE-DE-BAÏGORRY**. It's seven hours one way, and should only be attempted in settled conditions – when bad weather closes in, you won't get its famous views and close-range sightings of vultures, and you'll be at risk from lightning strikes or falling from the mist-shrouded brink, both of which kill hikers here regularly. Consult current SNCF schedules before setting out so that you coincide with one of the afternoon **rail-buses** that run the eight kilometres between St-Étienne and the train station of Ossès-St-Martin-d'Arrossa, one stop above Pont-Noblia.

Like most other Basque villages, St-Étienne is divided into quite distinct quarters, more like separate hamlets than a unified village. A prosperous, sleek place, its business is still predominantly agriculture rather than tourism, with the Pays Basque's only vineyards scattered all around, producing a good, strong wine named Irouléguy (Irulegi) after the eponymous village 5km east; a local shop, on the road north to St-Jean, offers **dégustation**. There's little specific to see here, other than a seventeenth-century **church** with a sumptuous Baroque retable and a picturesque medieval bridge posing against a backdrop of romantic castle and distant hills.

The **tourist office** is opposite the church (July & Aug Mon–Sat 9am–noon & 2–6pm, Sun 10am–noon & 3–6pm; rest of year closed Sun; ☎05.59.37.47.28). For budget **accommodation**, there's only the *Gîte d'étape Mendy* (☎05.59.37.42.39; ①), with camping space, in the northerly Lespars quarter. Other options include the tranquil *Hôtel-Restaurant Maechenea*, 4km north in the hamlet of Urdos (☎05.59.37.41.68, fax 05.59.37.46.03; ③), set on the bank of a stream, and the three-star *Hôtel-Restaurant Arcé*, on the west side of the river in St-Étienne (☎05.59.37.40.14, fax 05.59.37.40.27; ⑤), with English-speaking management and a **restaurant** serving menus at 110F/€16.80 and 170F/€25.95.

St-Jean-Pied-de-Port (Donibane Garazi)

The old capital of Basse Navarre, **ST-JEAN-PIED-DE-PORT** lies in a circle of hills at the foot of the Roncevaux pass into Spain. It owes its name to its position "at the foot of the *port*" – a Pyrenean word for "pass". Only part of France since the Treaty of the Pyrénées in 1659, it was an important centre for the pilgrimage to Santiago de Compostela in the Middle Ages. The routes from Paris, Vézelay and Le Puy converged just northeast of here at Ostabat, and it was the pilgrims' last port of call before struggling over the pass to the Spanish monastery of Roncesvalles (Roncevaux in French), where Roland, a general of Charlemagne celebrated in medieval romance, sounded his horn for aid in vain (see box on p.696).

The town lies on the River Nive, enclosed by walls of pinky-red sandstone. Above it rises a wooded hill crowned by the inevitable Richelieu-Vauban **fortress**, while to the east a further defensive system guards the road to Spain. The modern town spreads down across the main road onto lower ground; it's pleasant but unremarkable, and the seasonal throngs match anything on the coast.

The **old town** consists of a single cobbled street, **rue de la Citadelle**, running downhill from the fifteenth-century **Porte St-Jacques** – so named because it was the gate by which the pilgrims entered the town – to the **Porte d'Espagne**, commanding the bridge over the Nive, with a view of balconied houses overlooking the stream. Many of the painted houses bear inscriptions on their lintels from the sixteenth,

THE CHANSON DE ROLAND

Roland, with his sword Durandal, is the hero of the medieval **Chanson de Roland**. But he was also a historical character, warden of the Breton marches, who in 778 accompanied the Emperor Charlemagne on a campaign against the Moors in Spain, in the course of which the Navarrese capital of Pamplona was sacked. In revenge, the Basques ambushed and decimated Charlemagne's rearguard, commanded by Roland, as it withdrew through the gorges above Roncevaux. The chanson has it that infidel Muslim Saracens were the dastardly foe, but this was propaganda designed to make poor Roland's end more heroic.

seventeenth and eighteenth centuries. A fourteenth-century plain red church, **Notre-Dame-du-Bout-du-Pont**, stands beside the Porte d'Espagne and, opposite, a short street leads through the **Porte de Navarre** to place de-Gaulle and the modern road. Just to the north, beyond the dusky-pink Hôtel de Ville, is the *fronton* where a bare-handed **pelota match** – the most macho kind – is held every Monday at 5pm.

The **tourist office** is at 14 place de-Gaulle (July & Aug Mon–Sat 9am–noon & 2–7pm, Sun 10.30am–12.30pm & 3–6pm; rest of year closed Sun; ☎05.59.37.03.57), with the **gare SNCF** a ten-minute walk away at the end of avenue Renaud, on the northern edge of the centre. The least expensive **hotels** are *Les Remparts*, 16 place Floquet (☎05.59.37.13.79, fax 05.59.37.33.44; ③; closed mid-Oct to Jan), just before you cross the Nive coming into town on the Bayonne road, and not too noisy, and the recently renovated *Itzalpea*, 5 place du Trinquet (☎05.59.37.03.66, fax 05.59.37.33.18; ②), whose restaurant offers a wide choice of menus (average 120F/€18.30). More comfortable are the *Ramuntcho*, just inside the city walls at 1 rue de France (☎05.59.37.03.91, fax 05.59.37.35.17; ③), with a good and reasonably priced restaurant, and the posh *Central* on place de-Gaulle (☎05.59.37.00.22, fax 05.59.37.27.79; ④; closed mid-Dec to mid-Feb; restaurant 100–220F/€15.25–33.55), with some river-view rooms and free parking. There are also several budget options for hikers, among them the tiny, helpful *Gîte d'Étape Etchegoin* at 9 rte d'Uhart, on the Bayonne road (☎05.59.37.12.08), while the municipal **campsite**, the *Plaza Berri* (☎05.59.37.11.19, fax 05.59.37.99.78; closed Oct–May), is on the south bank of the Nive, beside the *fronton*.

Independent **restaurants** are apt to be slapdash and aimed at the day-tripper trade, but *Arbillaga* at 8 rue de l'Église just inside the walls (menus at 85–160F/€12.95–24.40; closed Tues evening, also Wed low season) is a high-standard exception.

Estérençuby, Béhérobie and the source of the Nive

From St-Jean, the D301 follows the deepening valley of the Nive to the southeast, past small red- and green-shuttered farms and attractive villages, while the GR10 stays well northeast of the river, first on paved lanes and then on track or trail along Handiamendi ridge. Both routes converge at **ESTÉRENÇUBY** (Esterenzubi), 8km from St-Jean and an attractive spot well supplied with **accommodation**. A good option here is the *Auberge Etchegoyen*, also known as the *Carricaburu* after the managing family (☎05.59.37.09.77; ②), with a streamside restaurant and the lively village bar.

Beyond Estérençuby the valley-floor road continues alongside the Nive, now no more than a mountain stream, tumbling down between steep green slopes, covered in hay and bracken. In late June and early July, you'll see entire families scything the meadows and turning the sweet-smelling hay with rakes. After 2km you'll pass another worthy establishment, the *Hôtel Artzain Etchea* (☎05.59.37.11.55, fax 05.59.37.20.16; ②; closed Feb), a modern but well-run place with a popular restaurant (menus 65–130F/€9.90–19.80).

THE GR65 FROM ST-JEAN

The mountains south of St-Jean towards the Spanish border are sheep country, and if you are interested in getting an idea of what the old pastoral life was like, this is a good place to do it. For walkers, the last French leg of the **GR65** pilgrim route starts from St-Jean and follows the line of the old Roman road across to Roncesvalles in Spanish Navarra, an easy day's walk.

Follow the Route de St-Michel out of St-Jean, soon adopting the D428; the typical yellow waymarks of the *Chemin St-Jacques* show the way. Though the climb is initially dull, on a tarmac lane, there are attractive farmhouses to look at, with immensely broad roofs, one side short, the other long enough to cover space for stalls and tools; it's all very quiet and rural, with long views out across the valleys. After a couple of hours you reach the tiny hamlet of **HONTO**, which for late starters in particular offers excellent **chambres d'hôte** and hearty evening meals at *Ferme Ithurburia* (☎05.59.37.11.17; ③). Beyond Honto, the grade sharpens, but there's only one brief path shortcut from the D428 before you finally leave the latter for a proper trail at Pic Urdanarré (1240m), some four hours along and just before the frontier.

Some 4km from Estérençuby the road reaches tiny **BÉHÉROBIE** before climbing up to the border and fizzling out. Here, the *Hôtel de la Source de la Nive* (☎05.59.37.10.57; ③; closed Jan, usually booked out in Oct for the wood-pigeon shooting season), beside the stream, is a marvellous place for a quiet stay, with a restaurant serving game-dominated menus (80–180F/€12.20–27.45).

Just before the bridge at Béhérobie, a lane leads to the left, signposted to the **Source de la Nive**. With a car, you can drive the 400m to the end of the asphalt, then continue on foot along the dirt track going left, not the one going over the bridge. After fifteen minutes, you'll reach the springs, where water percolates a thousand metres down through the karstic hillside to well up as surging rapids. Hidden in dense beech woods, it's a magic spot in any weather, with a faint mist often rising from the surface of the water.

Haute Soule

East of the Nive valley, you enter largely uninhabited country, known as the **Haute Soule**, threaded only by the GR10 and a couple of minor roads. The border between Basse Navarre and Soule skims the western edge of the **Forêt d'Iraty**, one of Europe's largest surviving beech woods, a popular summer retreat and winter cross-country skiing area. There are no shops or proper hotels until you reach **Larrau**, the only real village in these mountains, though the scattered hamlet of **Ste-Engrâce** in the east of the district has some facilities. There's even a downhill ski resort, westernmost in the Pyrenees, at **Arette-la-Pierre-St-Martin**, technically just over the border in Béarn but included here for convenience.

The Haute Soule is a land of open skies, where griffon vultures turn on the thermals high above countless flocks of sheep (their occasional corpses providing sustenance for the vultures), with three vast gorges to explore. Although the overall distance from the Nive valley to the Béarn is not very great, the slowness of the roads (there's no public transport) and the GR10 – it's a day-and-a-half minimum from Estérençuby to Larrau – and the grandeur of the scenery seem to magnify it. Carrying a tent would give you the greatest flexibility: no one objects if you pitch it discreetly, though to be on the safe side you can always ask the nearest shepherd. For the latest on **weather information** in the western Pyrenees, call ☎08.36.68.02.64.

The Forêt d'Iraty (Irati)

To drive to the **Forêt d'Iraty**, follow the D301 east out of the Nive valley from the junction near the *Hôtel Artzaïn Etchea* (see p.696), where the forest is signposted. The road is very steep, narrow and full of tight hairpins and ambling livestock – it's best avoided at night or in misty conditions – but as you climb higher up the steep spurs and round the heads of labyrinthine gullies, ever more spectacular views open beneath you. You can see way back over the valley of the Nive, St-Jean and the hills beyond. Stands of beech fill the gullies, shadowing the lighter grass whose green is so intense it seems almost theatrical – an effect produced, apparently, by the juxtaposition of outcrops of rock whose purplish hue brings out the cadmium yellow in the grass.

Along the cols and ridges stand ranks of shooting butts, from which the well-heeled urban bourgeoisie open fire every October on the millions of migrating *palombes*, as wood pigeons are called here, heading north over the western Pyrenees from Spain. Many other bird species can be seen too; among them honey buzzards, black kites, red kites, cranes and storks. Herds of healthy-looking horses and ponies, masses of sheep and big sleek caramel cows with bells at their throats on wooden collars marked with their owners' names, wander across the road. There are superb places to camp, with views west to the orange and crimson striations of the sunset and the revolving beacon of the Biarritz lighthouse visible in the dark.

Once past the north flank of **Occabé** (1456m), you're in Soule, and from here the road loops down to meet the D18 on the **plateau d'Iraty**, with its small lake, clutch of snack bars and flat ground to camp on. A minor road leads south to Ochagavia in Spain via the *Chalet Pedro* (1km), the best restaurant in the area, where the GR10 emerges from its descent of flat-topped Occabé (75min up from here), with its Iron Age **stone circle** and views across the forest and south to the Sierra de Abodi. Continuing east from the plateau, the D18 road enters the densest part of the forest, climbing past another small lake and a **campsite** half hidden in the magnificent beeches, to a collection of nine wooden chalets and a *gîte d'étape* at the **Col de Bargagiak**. An **information office** at the col (open all year; ☎05.59.28.51.29) takes bookings for the chalets and the *gîte d'étape*; across the parking lot is a small shop and inexpensive restaurant. From here you descend slightly to the nearby **Col d'Orgambidexka**, which is one of the prime viewing fields for the autumn bird migrations. As you emerge into the open beyond Bargagiak, the ground drops sharply away on the left into the **Valleé de**

TRANSHUMANCE IN THE PYRENEES

Like other shepherds in south European or Mediterranean climes, the Basques are forced to take their flocks to the high **mountain pastures** in summer in search of better grazing. They live out on the bare slopes in stone-hut sheepfolds called *cayolars*, with a couple of dogs, milking the ewes twice a day and making cheese, the *fromage de brebis*, whose soft and hard versions are a speciality throughout the pastoral Pyrenees. Most of the pastures today are accessible by car, at least at the gentler Basque end of the Pyrenees, so the shepherd's life is not as harsh and isolated as it used to be – though there are still areas in the higher mountains accessible only by mule or pony. A measure of the pre-eminence of sheep in the Basque economy is the Basque word for "rich", *aberats*, the literal meaning of which is "he who owns large flocks".

Much of the grazing is owned in common by various *communes*, who have over the centuries made elaborate agreements to ensure a fair share of the best pasture and avoid disputes. One of the oldest of these **faceries**, as they are called, concluded by the inhabitants of Spanish Roncal and French Barétous in 1326, is still in force and renewed each July 13 at the frontier **Col de la Pierre-St-Martin** on symbolic payment of three white heifers.

Larrau, 600m lower. To the right, the brilliant grassy swards of the **Pic d'Orhy** (2017m; allow 5hr return hike) culminate in swirling strata of rock below the summit, barring the way to Spain. And ahead, for the first breath-stopping time, you can see the serrated horizon of peaks that dominate the **Cirque de Lescun**, a harbinger of the central Pyrenees.

Larrau (Larrañe) to Arette-la-Pierre-St-Martin

The first thing you notice coming into **LARRAU** from the west is how different the architecture is. In contrast to the gaily painted facades and tiled roofs of Labourd and Basse Navarre, the houses here are grey and stuccoed, with steep-pitched slate roofs to shed heavy snow. And, although it's the biggest place since St-Jean, it is nonetheless very small and quiet – almost dead out of season.

There are two friendly **hotels**: the simple, old-fashioned *Hôtel Despouey* (☎05.59. 28.60.82; ②; closed mid-Nov to mid-Feb), with the local **shop** on the ground floor, and the fancier *Hôtel-Restaurant Etchémaïté* (☎05.59.28.61.45, fax 05.59.28.72.71; ③; closed late Jan), with a superb restaurant serving such treats as guinea-fowl roulade with braised bacon and cabbage, and artichokes stuffed with lamb sausage (closed Sun evening & Mon low season; menus 95F/€14.50 and 140F/€21.35; reservations advisable).

There is one **campsite** in Larrau, the *Ixtila* (☎05.59.28.63.09; closed mid-Nov to March), and a **gîte d'étape** – with restaurant – 3km away at **LOGIBAR** (☎05.59.28.61.14; closed Dec–Feb), close to the mouth of the **Gorges d'Holzarte**. This gorge is one of several in the region, cutting deep into northern slopes of the ridge that forms the frontier with Spain. A short track leads from Logibar across the turbulent and freezing stream to a car park, from where a steep, usually very busy path, a variant of the GR10, climbs through the beech woods to the junction of the Holzarte gorge with the Olhadybia (Olhadubi) in about 45 minutes. Slung across the mouth of the latter is a spectacular Himalayan-style **suspension bridge**, the *passerelle*, which bounces and swings dizzily as you walk out over the 180-metre drop. You can continue along the **GR10** to Ste-Engrâce in seven hours, or down to the beginning of the Gorges de Kakouetta in about six: it is definitely worth the walk – in June and July, the open spaces are full of flowers (columbines, cranesbills, orchids and vetches), and, if you're lucky, you might see the beautiful, long-stemmed *bimbette des Pyrénées*.

The Gorges de Kakouetta and Gorges d'Ehujarré

Ten kilometres by road east of Larrau, you reach the **Gorges de Kakouetta** (mid-March to mid-Nov daily 9am–nightfall; 25F/€3.80) by turning right off the D26 and up onto the D113. About 3km along the latter, the minuscule hamlet of **CASERNES** offers a food shop opposite the Mairie, and an attractive riverside **campsite**, the *Ibarra* (05.59.28.73.59; closed Nov–March).

Kakouetta is well established on the tourist trail, but do not be put off: the gorge is truly dramatic and, outside peak season, not crowded at all. It pays to be well shod, for the path is precarious and very slippery in places: you will be glad of the han drail. The walls of the gorge are very high – up to 300m and scarcely more than 5m apart in spots – and jungle-thick with luxuriant vegetation that thrives on the hothouse atmosphere, including a range of ferns that you wouldn't expect to see outside a houseplant nursery. Myriad seepages and waterfalls fill the air with a fine spray, refracting and filtering what sunlight gets in; the path continues for about an hour (2km) with a small cave at the end and just before it a full-blown waterfall spewing out of a hole in the rock.

There is a third, scarcely visited gorge, the **Gorges d'Ehujarré**, a short distance east at Senta, the easternmost of the three hamlets that comprise Ste-Engrâce (see p.700). It's a straightforward walk up – the route has been used for centuries for moving sheep up to the pastures of Pic Lakhoura – but is about a five-hour round trip.

Ste-Engrâce and Arette-la-Pierre-St-Martin

Le bout du monde – "the end of the earth" – is what they used to call the tiny settlement of **STE-ENGRÂCE**, locked in its cul-de-sac valley beneath the Spanish frontier at the easternmost extremity of the Basque country. And, although a road runs through it to Arette-la-Pierre-St-Martin, the place remains beautifully remote and peaceful. Life is not so idyllic for the locals – there is no work and the young won't stay – but for an outsider not caught in the rural poverty trap, it has great charm.

Ste-Engrâce's hallmark is the eleventh-century Romanesque **church** in the hamlet of **SENTA**, which features in all the coffee-table books on the Pyrenees. It stands just as it should, with its heavily buttressed walls, belfry and penthouse roof, a sharply defined and angular assertion of humanity against the often mist-shrouded bulwarks of the mountains behind. Very simple inside, it has some good carved column capitals, and the graveyard is full of traditional disc-shaped headstones. There's a **gîte d'étape** opposite the church, the *Auberge Elichalt* (☎05.59.28.61.63), with a few **chambres d'hôte** (③), a back garden to pitch a tent and a **café-bar** that serves light meals.

The road up to the ski resort of **ARETTE-LA-PIERRE-ST-MARTIN** gives fabulous views of the valley of Ste-Engrâce, through magnificent forests of pine and beech, though if the cloud is down, which it often is, you'll be lucky to see much at all. At a little col with a three-way junction, you're already in the ancient county of Béarn, and can glimpse the descent east into the Vallée d'Aspe (see p.707). The upper, right-hand turning leads into Arette, an ugly ski resort with eighteen pistes, and the excellent *Refuge-Gîte d'Étape Jeandel* (☎05.59.66.14.46; open all year by arrangement), mostly serving trekkers on the GR10, with enthusiastic management and meals (May to mid-Oct). The skiing here is better than you'd imagine at the modest altitude (2153m top point), owing to moist Atlantic exposure and some quite long runs for beginners and intermediates. There are also two nordic skiing areas nearby.

THE CENTRAL PYRENEES

The area immediately east of the Pays Basque – the **Central Pyrenees** – is home to the range's highest mountain peaks and is the most spectacular part of the region, with the southernmost part, by the border, protected within the **Parc National des Pyrénées Occidentales** (see box opposite). Getting to the area is simple enough, at least as far as the foothill towns, by train on the Bayonne–Toulouse line. But travelling uphill and around once there can be very slow. The few buses – and most other traffic – keep mainly to the north-south valleys, which is frustrating when you want to switch from one valley system to the next without having to come all the way out of the mountains each time.

The **GR10** provides a good lateral link if you are ready to walk all the way, and it's possible to hitch up the valleys and across the main passes at **Col d'Aubisque** and **Col du Tourmalet**, though you will find you often get left on the top by drivers, who come up for the view and go back the same way.

Highlights – apart from the lakes, torrents, forests and 3000-metre peaks around **Cauterets** – are the cirques of **Lescun**, **Gavarnie** and **Troumouse**, each with its distinctive character. And for less hearty interests, there is many a flower-starred mountain meadow accessible by car, especially near **Barèges** and **Bagnères-de-Luchon**, in which to picnic. The only real urban centres are **Pau**, a probable entry point to the area, and dull **Tarbes** and the tacky pilgrimage target of **Lourdes**. Great monuments of the bricks-and-mortar kind – with the exception of the fortified churches at **Luz-St-Sauveur**, **St-Savin** and **St-Bertrand-de-Comminges** – are equally scarce.

THE PARC NATIONAL DES PYRÉNÉES OCCIDENTALES

The **Parc National des Pyrénées Occidentales** was created in 1967 to protect at least part of the high Pyrenees from the development engendered by modern tourism – ski resorts, roads, mountain-top restaurants, car parks and other amenities. It runs for more than 100km along the Spanish border: from Pic de Laraille (2147m), south of Lescun, in the west, to beyond Pic de la Munia (3133m), east of Gavarnie. Varying in altitude between 1070m and 3298m at the Pic de Vignemale, south of Cauterets, the park takes in the spectacular cirques of Gavarnie and Troumouse, as well as over two hundred lakes, more than a dozen valleys and about 400km of marked walking routes.

Through the banning of hunting – apart from the traditional mountain peasants' pursuit of poaching or *braconnage* – and all dogs, the park has also provided sanctuary for many rare and endangered species of birds and mammals. Among them are chamois, marmots, genets, griffon vultures, golden eagles, eagle owls and capercaillies, to say nothing of the rich and varied flora. The most celebrated animal – and the most depleted by hunting – is the Pyrenean **brown bear**, whose prewar numbers ran to as many two hundred, but now amount to barely a half dozen individuals. Although largely herbivorous, bears will take sheep or cows when given the opportunity, and the mountain shepherds are their remorseless enemies. To appease them, the park pays prompt and generous compensation for any losses, but this is not always enough to overcome the atavistic fear of the bear (one was illegally shot in 1997). Park authorities have been criticized for not doing enough to protect the bears – an accusation which angers the hard-pressed rangers, who complain that distant armchair ecologists have no conception what it is really like trying to reconcile legitimate local economic needs with the protection of wild species and unsullied landscapes, to say nothing of coping with the litter, wear and tear on footpaths, illicit camping and other problems caused by modern tourism.

The **GR10** runs through the entire park on its 700-kilometre journey from coast to coast, starting at Argelès-sur-Mer on the Mediterranean and ending up at Hendaye-Plage on the Atlantic shore; the tougher trail of the **Haute Randonnée Pyrénéenne** (HRP) also finishes its course in Hendaye-Plage and runs roughly parallel to the GR10, but takes in much more rugged, alpine terrain. Hikers following either route are strongly advised to wear appropriate clothing, carry detailed maps and equipment and heed the words of warning on p.682. Though the Pyrenees have a modest maximum altitude by world-mountain standards, their climate can be as extreme as ranges twice their height – in short, not the place for a casual stroll.

There are **Maisons du Parc** in Etsaut, Cauterets, Luz-St-Sauveur, Gavarnie, Gabas and Arrens-Marsous, giving information about the park's wildlife and vegetation, lists of accommodation options and the best walks to do. There are over a dozen wardened refuges and plenty of hotels, campsites and *gîtes* throughout the park, listed in the text of this chapter or highlighted on the map on p.702. For an update on weather conditions in the *département* of Hautes-Pyrénées, telephone ☎08.36.68.02.65.

Pau and around

From humble beginnings as a crossing on the Gave de Pau for flocks en route to and from the mountains, **PAU** became the capital of the ancient viscountcy of Béarn in 1464, and of the French part of the kingdom of Navarre in 1512. In 1567 its sovereign, Henri d'Albret, married the sister of the king of France, Marguerite d'Angoulême, friend and protector of artists and intellectuals and herself the author of a celebrated Boccaccio-like tale (the *Heptameron*), who transformed the town into a centre of the arts and nonconformist thinking.

Their daughter was Jeanne d'Albret, an ardent Protestant, whose zeal offended her own subjects as well as attracting the wrath of the Catholic king of France, Charles X,

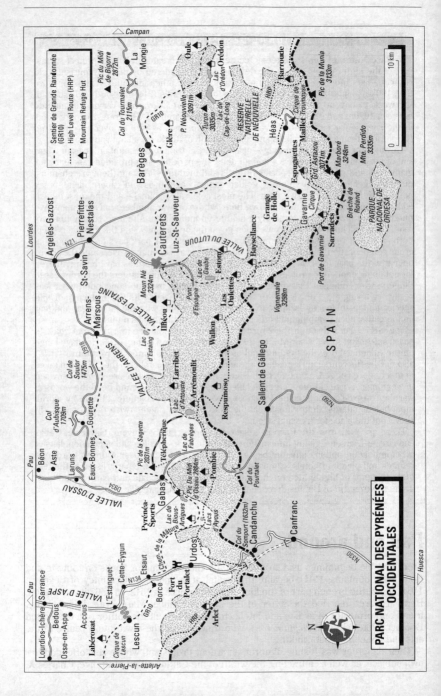

PARC NATIONAL DES PYRÉNÉES OCCIDENTALES

Legend:
- Sentier de Grande Randonnée (GR10)
- High Level Route (HRP)
- Mountain Refuge Hut

0   10 km

Campan
Lourdes
Pau
Arette-la-Pierre
Huesca

La Mongie
Pic du Midi de Bigorre 2872m
Col du Tourmalet 2115m
Barèges
Glère
Oule
Lac d'Orédon Orédon
Lac de Cap-de-Long
P. Néouvielle 3091m
Turon 3035m
RESERVE NATURELLE DE NÉOUVIELLE
Barroude
Pic de la Munia 3133m
Héas
Espuguettes
Cirque de
Maillet Troumouse
Grd. Astazou 3071m
Marboré 3248m
Mte. Perdido 3335m
Grange de Holle
Gavarnie
Cirque de Gavarnie
Bayssellance
Sarradets
Brèche de Roland
Port de Gavarnie
PARQUE NACIONAL DE ORDESA

Argelès-Gazost
Pierrefitte-Nestalas
Cauterets
Luz-St-Sauveur
St-Savin
N21
D920
VALLÉE DU LUTOUR
Lac de Gaube
Estom
Pont d'Espagne
Les Oulettes
Wallon
Moun Né 2324m
Ilhéou
VALLÉE DE L'ESTAING
Lac d'Estaing
Arrens-Marsous
Larribet
Lac d'Artouste
Arrémoulit
Respiumoso
Sallent de Gállego
N260

SPAIN

Col de Soulor 1475m
Col d'Aubisque 1709m
Gourette
VALLÉE D'ARRENS
D918
Pic de la Sagette 2031m
Lac de la Fabrèges
Téléphérique

Béon
Aste
Laruns
Eaux-Bonnes
VALLÉE D'OSSAU
D934
Pyrénéa-Sports
Gabas
Pombie
Pic Du Midi d'Ossau 2884m
Lac de Bious-Artigues
Lacs d'Ayous
Col du Pourtalet
Candanchu
Col du Somport (1632m)
Canfranc
N330

Lourdios-Ichère
Sarrance
Bedous
Osse-en-Aspe
Accous
Labérouat
Cirque de Lescun
Lescun
VALLÉE D'ASPE
L'Estanguet
Cette-Eygun
Etsaut
Borce
Fort du Portalet
Urdos
Chem. de la Mâture
N134
GR10
Arlet
HRP

N

thus embroiling Béarn in the Wars of Religion – whose resolution, albeit only temporary, had to await the accession to the French throne of her own son, Henri IV, in 1589. An adroit politician, he renounced his faith to facilitate this transition, quipping that "Paris is worth a Mass" and then appeasing the regional sensibilities of his Béarnais subjects by announcing that he was giving France to Béarn rather than Béarn to France. He did not incorporate Béarn into the French state; that was left to his son and successor, Louis XIII, in 1620. As Pau's most famous son, Henri acquired a suitably colourful reputation. He was baptized in traditional Béarnais style with the local Juraçon wine, and his infant lips were rubbed with garlic. In his adult life he was known as the *vert-galant* for his prowess as a lover. He also gave France one of its more famous recipes, *poule au pot* – chicken stuffed and boiled with vegetables: he is reputed to have said that he did not want anyone in his realm to be so poor as not to be able to afford a *poule* in the *pot* once a week.

The least-expected thing about Pau is its English connection, which dates from the arrival of Wellington and his troops after the defeat of Marshal Soult at Orthez in 1814. Seduced by its climate and persuaded of its curative powers by the Scottish doctor Alexander Taylor, the English flocked to Pau throughout the nineteenth century, bringing along their peculiar cultural obsessions – fox-hunting, horse-racing, polo, croquet, cricket, golf (the first eighteen-hole course in continental Europe in 1860 and the first in the world to admit women), tearooms and parks. When the rail line arrived here in 1866, the French came, too: writers and artists like Victor Hugo, Stendhal and Lamartine, as well as the socialites. The first French rugby club opened here in 1902, after which the sport spread throughout the southwest. During the 1950s, natural gas was discovered at nearby Lacq, bringing new jobs and subsidiary industries, as well as massive production of sulphur-dioxide-based pollution, now reduced by filtration but still substantial. In addition, there is a well-respected university, founded in 1972, whose eight thousand or so students give the town a youthful buzz.

Pau lies within easy reach of numerous small, picturesque villages in **northwest Béarn**, as well as the GR65 footpath that runs some 60km down to the Spanish border.

Arrival, information and accommodation

Pau's **airport**, to the north of town (☎05.59.33.33.00), is overshadowed by those nearby at Tarbes-Lourdes and Biarritz, so don't expect any international flights – just a few to Paris. The town lies on the A64 *autoroute Pyrénéenne* and on the main east–west rail route, with connections to Bayonne and Biarritz to the west, and Lourdes, Tarbes and Toulouse to the east, as well as to Bordeaux and Paris. The **gare SNCF** is on the southern edge of the city centre by the riverside: SNCF **buses** leave from here, and private buses from various kerbside terminals in rue Gachet, off place Clemenceau. Buses run south down the Vallée d'Ossau and to Oloron-Ste-Marie, with onward connections to the Vallée d'Aspe. A **free funicular** carries you up from the train station to the boulevard des Pyrénées, opposite place Royale, at the far end of which is the **tourist office** (July & Aug Mon–Sat 9am–6.30pm, Sun 9am–1pm & 2–6.30pm; rest of year Mon–Sat 9am–1pm & 2–6pm; ☎05.59.27.27.08). For information on walking and climbing try the local CAF, 5 rue René Fournets (Mon–Fri evenings only; ☎05.59.27.71.81), or Librairie des Pyrénées, 14 rue St-Louis, which stocks a wide range of books on the mountains. There is a central **Internet café**, *CyberSeventys*, at 7 rue Gambetta (*www.CyberSeventys.com*).

For a friendly, clean and quiet budget **hotel**, try the *Hôtel d'Albret*, 11 rue Jeanne-d'Albret, close to the castle (☎05.59.27.81.58; ①), which has large rooms mostly with basins. Two equally central alternatives are the *Hôtel le Matisse*, 17 rue Mathieu-Lalanne, opposite the Musée des Beaux-Arts (☎05.59.27.73.80; ①), and *Pomme d'Or* at 11 rue Maréchal-Foch (☎05.59.27.78.48; ①). Two-star, en-suite comfort is available at the *Commerce* at 9 rue Maréchal-Joffre (☎05.59.27.24.40, fax 05.59.83.81.74; ③) and the

terrace a ruined **castle** dominates the steep slope, its empty joist sockets making perfect pigeon holes. For **accommodation**, there is the excellent-value *Hostellerie du Château* in rue Léon-Bérard (☎05.59.38.52.10, fax 05.59.38.96.49; ③; closed mid-Jan to mid-Feb), and a municipal **campsite** by the medieval bridge (☎05.59.38.53.30; closed Oct–April). The *hostellerie* serves hearty menus based on sausage, trout and the like for 95–160F/€14.50–24.40.

Just across the river, the D936 bears southeast along the flat valley bottom to **NAVARRENX**, 20km away on the Pau–Mauléon bus route, a sleepy, old-fashioned market town built as a *bastide* in 1316 and still surrounded by its medieval **walls**; you enter by the fortified **Porte St-Antoine**. The *Hôtel du Commerce* by the Porte St-Antoine (☎05.59.66.50.16, fax 05.59.66.52.67; ③; closed mid-Oct to mid-Jan; excellent restaurant from 90F/€13.70), makes an agreeable place to **stay**, and there's also a municipal **campsite** in allée des Marronniers (☎05.59.66.10.00, fax 05.59.66.11.01; closed mid-Sept to March).

Lourdes

LOURDES, about 30km southeast of Pau, has just one function. Over seven million Catholic pilgrims arrive here each year, and the town is totally given over to looking after and exploiting them. Lourdes was hardly more than a village before 1858, when Bernadette Soubirous, the 14-year-old daughter of an ex-miller, had the first of eighteen visions of the Virgin Mary in the so-called Grotte de Massabielle by the Gave de Pau. Since then, Lourdes has grown a great deal, and it is now one of the biggest attractions in this part of France, many of its visitors hoping for a miraculous cure for conventionally intractable ailments.

The first large-scale **pilgrimage** took place in 1873, organized by a reactionary Catholic movement called the *Assomptionistes*, whose avowed purpose was to stem the advancing tide of republicanism and rationalism. They took over the management of Lourdes, shoving aside the local priest who had wanted to organize the pilgrimages himself. Adroit propagandists and agitators, they sought to promote their cause by publishing a cheap mass-circulation paper called *La Croix*, aimed at the poor and uneducated, and by organizing these massive pilgrimages.

Practically every shop is given over to the sale of indescribable religious kitsch: Bernadette in every shape and size, adorning barometers, thermometers, plastic tree trunks, key rings, empty bottles that you can fill with holy Lourdes water, bellows, candles, sweets and illuminated plastic grottoes. There's even a waxworks museum, the **Musée Grévin**, at 87 rue de la Grotte (daily: April–Oct 9–11.30am & 1.30–6.30pm; July & Aug also 8.30–10pm; 33F/€5), with over a hundred lifesize figures illustrating the lives of Bernadette and Christ. Clustered around the miraculous grotto are the churches of the **Cité Réligieuse**, an annexe to the town proper that sprang up last century. The first to be built was the flamboyant **Basilique du Rosaire et de l'Immaculée Conception** (1871–1883), swiftly followed by the massive subterranean **Basilique St-Pie-X**, which claims to be able to house 20,000 people at a time. The **Grotte de Massabielle** itself, where Bernadette had her visions, is the focus of the pilgrimages – a moisture-blackened overhang by the riverside with a statue of the Virgin in waxwork white and baby blue.

Lourdes' only secular attraction is its **castle**, poised on a rocky bluff guarding the approaches to the valleys and passes of the central Pyrenees. Briefly an English stronghold in the late fourteenth century, it later became a state prison. Inside, it houses the surprisingly excellent **Musée Pyrénéen** (guided visits: April–Sept daily 9–11.45am & 1.30–6.45pm; rest of year daily except Tues 9am–noon & 2–6pm; last tour 1hr before closing; 30F/€4.60). Its collections include Pyrenean fauna, all sorts of fascinating pastoral and farming gear, and an interesting section on the history of Pyrenean mountaineering.

In the rock garden outside are some beautiful models of various Pyrenean styles of house, as well as of the churches of St-Bertrand-de-Comminges and Luz-St-Sauveur.

Practicalities

Lourdes' **gare SNCF** is on the northeast edge of the town centre, at the end of avenue de la Gare; the **gare routière** is in the central place Capdevieille, and the not terribly helpful **tourist office** is in place Peyramale (Easter to mid-Oct Mon–Sat 9am–7pm, Sun 11am–6pm; rest of year Mon–Sat 9am–noon & 2–6pm; ☎05.62.42.77.40). Lourdes has more **hotels** than any city in France outside Paris. A good, comfortable hotel choice, opposite the food *halles*, some 300m south of place Peyramale, is the two-star *Hôtel d'Albret* (☎05.62.94.75.00, fax 05.62.94.78.45; ②), with the co-managed *Taverne de Bigorre* on the ground floor offering a range of menus (100F/€15.25 gets you three hearty courses), while *Hôtel Majestic*, 9 av Maransin (☎05.62.94.27.23, fax 05.62.94.64.91; ②; closed mid-Oct to mid-April), offers tastefully modernized rooms and decent home cooking downstairs, though it's in a somewhat noisy location. There's masses of cheap accommodation in the small central streets around the castle, while **hostel** accommodation can be had at the *Centre Pax Christi*, 4 rte de la Forêt (☎05.62.94.00.66, fax 05.62.42.94.44; closed mid-Oct to March), on the western edge of town. The nearest **campsite** is the *Poste*, 26 rue de Langelle, just south of the *gare SNCF* (☎05.62.94.40.35; closed mid-Oct to March).

Tarbes

Twenty minutes away by train to the north, **TARBES** is a relatively dull town dominated by its history as a military base, but useful as a base for visiting Lourdes or launching into the mountains to the south. There is an **airport** midway between Tarbes and Lourdes, which gets busy in winter with charter ski flights. The town's only real highlight is the Napoleonic stud farm, **Les Haras**, entered from chemin de Mauhourat (guided visits by appointment only: July & Aug Mon–Fri 10am–noon & 2–5pm, plus occasional days otherwise; last tour 1hr before closing; ☎05.62.56.30.80; 30F/€4.60), best known for the *cheval Tarbais*, bred from English and Moorish stock as a cavalry horse. You can watch them drilling during July and August at 3.15pm. World War I buffs may also want to visit the house, at 2 rue de la Victoire, where **Maréchal Foch**, supreme Allied commander in World War I, was born (guided tours Mon & Thurs–Sun: May–Sept 9am–noon & 2–6.30pm; rest of year 9am–noon & 2–5pm; 15F/€2.30), containing a dull repository of family and personal mementos.

The **gare SNCF** is on avenue Maréchal Joffre, north of the centre, and the **gare routière** on the other side of town on place au Bois, off rue Larrey. The **tourist office** is near the central place de Verdun, at 3 cours Gambetta (Mon–Sat 9am–12.30pm & 2–7pm; ☎05.62.51.30.31). Tarbes has some reasonable **hotels** in the vicinity of the station, such as the friendly, helpful *Hôtel de l'Avenue*, 80 av Bertrand-Barère (☎05.62.93.06.36; ②), and the more comfortable *Hôtel Isard*, 70 av Maréchal Joffre (☎05.62.93.06.69, fax 05.62.93.99.55; ②). There's also a **HI hostel** at 88 av Alsace-Lorraine (☎05.62.38.91.20). The *Isard*'s **restaurant** is decent, with a 65F/€9.90 *formule* and a more interesting 100F/€15.25 menu of the month.

The valleys of the Aspe and Ossau

The parallel north–south valleys of the **Aspe** and **Ossau** are the central Pyrenees at their most *sauvage*, and the region in which the Pyrenean brown bear most tenaciously resists extinction. About six survive on the slopes of the valleys, in the **Cirque de Lescun** and in the adjoining parts of Spain.

THE ZARAGOZA–BORDEAUX AUTOROUTE

A bitter controversy is raging between environmentalists and the constructors of the Zaragoza–Bordeaux **autoroute** along the Vallée d'Aspe. This has pitted many residents of this valley (and nearby regions of Spain), who claim to be hard pressed from lack of livelihood, against ecologists from elsewhere, in a protracted battle running since 1990. The hi-tech tunnel under the Col du Somport is now an accomplished fact and the focus of struggle has now shifted to lobbying for the rehabilitation of the long-abandoned transfrontier railway to carry high-speed trains and freight, and the simultaneous limiting in width of the monstrous proposed six-lane highway which would virtually flatten the Vallée d'Aspe.

Tourism is less developed here, especially in the Aspe valley, because unreliable snow conditions have precluded ski-resort construction – but what tourism has failed to do, a major road-building scheme threatens to achieve (see box above). To see the best of the region you should get out your map and walk perpendicular to the line of the valleys, using the handful of refuges or camping in permitted areas along the way.

Oloron-Ste-Marie

The valley of the Aspe begins at the grey town of **OLORON-STE-MARIE**, around 45km west of Lourdes, where the mountain streams of the Aspe and Ossau meet. It is served by train from Pau as well as by CITRAM buses, with five to seven daily SNCF buses continuing down the valley to Urdos, most of these continuing as far as Canfranc in Spain. The town's claim to fame is as the centre of the manufacture of the famous woollen pancake-shaped *beret basque*, once the standard headgear for all French men but now seldom seen on any but greybeards. However, the only real points of interest for the visitor are the town's two churches: **Ste-Croix**, one of the oldest Romanesque buildings in Béarn, with unusual interior vaulting copied from the Great Mosque at Cordoba, and the **Cathédrale Ste-Marie**, which boasts an unusually beautiful Romanesque portal in Pyrenean marble. In the upper arch, the elders of the Apocalypse play violins and rebecs, while in the second arch scenes from medieval life – a cooper, the slaying of a wild boar, fishing for salmon – are represented. The gallant knight on horseback over the outer column on the right is Gaston IV, Count of Béarn, who commissioned the portal on his return from the first Crusade at the beginning of the twelfth century, hence the reference to Saracens in chains among the sculptures. The magnificent studded doors were a present from Henri IV. Inside, well away from the main area of worship, is a stoup reserved for use by the Cagots, a stark reminder of centuries-long persecution and segregation of this mysterious group of people, thought by some to have been lepers and by others to have been perhaps of Visigothic origin.

Oloron's **tourist office** is in place de la Résistance (mid-July to Aug Mon–Sat 9am–7pm, Sun 9am–1pm; rest of year Tues–Sat 9am–noon & 2–7pm; ☎05.59.39.98.00). There are a couple of reasonable hotels in town – the *Hôtel de la Paix*, 24 av Sadi-Carnot, near the train station (☎05.59.39.02.63, fax 05.59.39.98.20; ②), and the nicer *Hôtel Bristol* at 9 rue Carréot (☎05.59.39.43.78, fax 05.59.39.08.19; ③) – and a **campsite**, the *Camping du Stade*, on the D919 Arrette road (☎05.59.39.11.26; closed Oct–March).

Villages of the upper Aspe valley

The narrow enclosed world of the valley proper begins south of Oloron at the village of **ESCOT**, where a beautiful side route, the D294, climbs east through beech woods to the **Col de Marie-Blanque** and down to Bielle in the Vallée d'Ossau. South of Escot, the road follows the river through narrow defiles, past the attractive riverside village of **SARRANCE**, where the **Eco-Musée du Vallée d'Aspe** (July to mid-Sept daily 10am–noon & 2–7pm; rest of year Sat & Sun 2–6pm; 25F/€3.80), devoted to valley history, is installed partly in the cloister of the ancient monastic church.

Some 7km south of Sarrance, **BEDOUS** is the largest settlement in the upper valley, with a miniature château, an arcaded Mairie and the *Gîte d'étape Le Mandragot*, on place de l'Église (☎05.59.34.59.33). Further *gîtes* can be found 1.5km southwest in Osse-en-Aspe – *Les Amis de Chaneü* (☎05.59.34.73.23) – and at the excellent *Auberge Cavalière-des Ecuyers Montagnards* (☎05.59.34.72.30, *www.pyrenees-online.fr/Auberge_Cavaliere*), 1km up the east flank of the valley from L'Estanguet, geared up for horse-riding and hiking holidays.

Beyond here, **CETTE-EYGUN** offers a bar-*gîte*, *La Goutte d'Eau* (☎05.59.34.78.83), occupying the disused train station between the road and the river, and run by the CSAVA (Coordination pour la Sauvegarde de la Vallée d'Aspe), the most vocal opponents of the road-building project in the valley. If you're desperate they can provide accommodation of dubious quality in an old train carriage parked on the tracks, camping space on the banks of the river and food if you're lucky at negotiable prices.

Beyond Cette-Eygun, the road curls southeast to **ETSAUT**, where there's a **Maison du Parc** (☎05.59.34.88.30) in the old *gare SNCF*, which has information on walks and accommodation in the Parc National des Pyrénées Occidentales (see box on p.701), a **gîte d'étape**, *La Maison de l'Ours* (☎05.59.34.86.38), a **hotel**, *des Pyrénées* (☎05.59.34.88.62, fax 05.59.34.86.96; ③), and a food shop. **BORCE**, a more attractive medieval village 1km away on the west flank of the valley, is home to another, communally run *gîte d'étape* (☎05.59.34.86.40) in the centre, and a campsite at the outskirts. Further upstream at one of the narrowest points of the Aspe squats the menacing **Fort du Portalet** (now privately owned), in which 1930s socialist premier Léon Blum was imprisoned by Pétain's Vichy government, and then Pétain himself after the liberation of France. Just before the fort, at the Pont de Cebers, the GR10 threads east along the **Chemin de la Mâture**, an eighteenth-century mule path hacked out of the precipitous rock slabs that form the sides of a dizzy ravine, facilitating the transport of tree trunks felled for use as ships' masts. The path is broad enough, but if you don't like heights keep away from the edge. The GR10 reaches the **Lacs d'Ayous refuge** opposite the Pic du Midi d'Ossau (see p.711) in about five hours.

Less than 2km south of the fort, **URDOS** is the last village on the French side of the frontier, and has arguably the best **hotel-restaurant** in the valley: the *Hôtel des Voyageurs* (☎05.59.34.88.05, fax 05.59.34.86.74; ③) – with an annexe across the road known as the *Hôtel Somport* – which serves a wonderful, four-course set meal (95F/€14.50). From here, you can continue through the new tunnel under the **Col de Somport** and on to Canfranc in Spain, the terminus for trains from Jaca.

Lescun

Six steep kilometres southwest of the N134 from L'Estanguet, the ancient grey-stone houses of **LESCUN** huddle tightly together on the north slopes of a huge and magnificent green cirque. The floor of the cirque and the lower slopes, dimpled with vales and hollows, have been gently and harmoniously shaped by generations of farming, while to the west it is overlooked by the great grey molars of **Le Billare** and **Le Petit Billare**, beyond whose shoulders bristle further leaning teeth of rock and the storm-lashed bulk of the **Pic d'Anie** (2504m). Below the village in the hollow of the cirque, the grassy *Camping Le Lauzart* (☎05.59.34.51.77; closed Oct–April) must be one of the best sites anywhere, with an uninterrupted view of the peaks and no sound to disturb beyond the chiming of cow bells. If you're on foot, be sure to take provisions with you – it is some way from the village and the only food shop. Lescun itself has a lovely old

hotel, the *Pic d'Anie* (☎05.59.34.71.54, fax 05.59.34.53.22; ③; closed Oct–March), with a decent restaurant and a **gîte d'étape** opposite (same number).

The obvious **walk** in the area is along the GR10 in the direction of La-Pierre-St-Martin. From Lescun, the path keeps close to the road as far as the *Refuge de Labérouat* (☎05.59.34.50.43) – around a two-hour walk – then crosses meadows before entering beech forest beneath the organ-pipe crags of **Les Orgues de Camplong**, with fantastic views of the pine-stippled ridges of the Billares. It emerges above the tree line in a long, flower-strewn, hanging valley by the primitive **Cabane d'Ardinet**, reaching the shepherds' hut at **Cap de la Baigt** (1700m) in a further ninety minutes. From there you can either continue on the GR towards La-Pierre-St-Martin, or swing south for the Col des Anies and the Pic d'Anie itself – a good two-and-a-half to three hours to the summit.

Along the Ossau

The **Ossau valley** is notable mainly for its distinctive **Pic du Midi** and some beautiful lakes set in rugged country. The valley is served by three **bus** companies: Sarl Canonge, CITRAM and SNCF. SNCF coaches ply once daily at weekends as far as Artouste-Fabrèges; CITRAM veers east to Gourette and the Col d'Aubisque every day from July to mid-September and again (to Gourette only) in the skiing season; while Sarl Canonge provides a summer-only link from Laruns to the Col du Pourtalet via Gabas and Fabrèges.

Pau to Laruns

Between Pau and Laruns, the only places worth stopping are **ARUDY**, for its **Maison d'Ossau** (July & Aug 10am–noon & 3–6pm; rest of year Mon 10am–noon, Tues, Thurs & Sat 2.30–5pm, Sun 3–6pm; 15F/€2.30), which offers a comprehensive account of the prehistoric Pyrenees and an exhibition of the flora and fauna of the Parc National, and **ASTE-BÉON** 2km upvalley, home to **La Falaise aux Vautours** (April daily 10am–1pm & 2–7pm; May & Sept daily 2.30–6.30pm; June–Aug daily 10am–1pm & 2–7pm; rest of year Sat 3–6pm; 39F/€5.95), a vulture-watching installation where the creatures are observed nesting naturally.

LARUNS, enclosed in the valley bottom by steep wooded heights, is of little interest in itself, though there are some fine old farms towards the river in the quarter known as Le Pon. The **tourist office** is in the main place de la Mairie (Mon–Sat 9am–12.30pm & 2–6.30pm, Sun 9.30am–12.30pm; ☎05.59.05.31.41). If you **stay** the night, try the central *Hôtel D'Ossau* (☎05.59.05.30.14; ②) or the characterful *Hôtel de France*, at the eastern end of town opposite the disused *gare* (☎05.59.05.33.71; ②; closed first two weeks of June & Dec). There's also the 28-bunk *Chalet-Refuge L'Embaradère* (☎05.59.05.41.88; cheap meals offered), more or less opposite the *Hôtel de France*, while the nearest **campsites** are *Ayguebere* (☎05.59.05.38.55) and *Pont Lauguère* (☎05.59.05.35.99), both in Le Pon quarter and open all year. For **food**, *L'Arrégalet* at 37 rue du Bourguet (closed Mon lunch) is strong on local recipes.

Gabas

The road to **GABAS**, 13km away, winds steeply into the upper reaches of the Gave d'Ossau valley, south of Laruns. On days when there is no bus, you should get a lift without much difficulty from other walkers or employees of the Parc National des Pyrénées Occidentales (see box on p.701), especially early in the morning. Primarily a base for climbers and walkers, there is nothing to it beyond a minuscule chapel, a **Maison du Parc** (mid-June to mid-Sept daily 10am–1pm & 2–7pm; ☎05.59.05.32.13), which has useful walking information, and a fair amount of **accommodation**. Of this, the best value is the CAF **refuge** (☎05.59.05.33.14) at the top of the hamlet, and *Hôtel*

Chez Vignau at the north entrance to town (☎05.59.05.34.06; ①). The latter also has the best **restaurant** locally, with delicacies such as frogs' legs and prune pie.

Pic du Midi d'Ossau

The **Pic du Midi**, with its rocky twin-peaked summit (2884m), is a classic Pyrenean landmark, visible for kilometres around. From Gabas, it is a steep 4.5-kilometre climb on a road up a wooded ravine (or take the daily Sarl Canonge bus) to the artificial **Lac de Bious-Artigues**, so named because it flooded the *artigue* – a Pyrenean word for "mountain pasture" – that formerly existed beside the infant *gave*. Just below the dam, where the bus stops, are the stony terraces of *Camping Bious-Oumettes* (☎05.59.05.38.76; closed mid-Sept to mid-June), which also has a small shop (roughly the same season). Beside the lake are the *Refuge Pyrénéa Sports* (☎05.59.05.32.12; daily mid-June to mid-Sept, weekends spring/autumn), and a good snack bar, the *Cantine de Bious*. The area within immediate reach of the road gets very crowded in summer and the refuges are likely to be full at weekends, so it's worth phoning ahead.

A round trip of the peak, excluding the summit, takes about seven hours. It can be broken by a **stay** at the CAF *Refuge de Pombie* (☎05.59.05.31.78; closed Oct to mid-June), below the vast southern walls of the mountain. From the lake, follow the GR10 up the left bank of the *gave* and past the turning to the Lacs d'Ayous (see below). Cross the Pont de Bious and continue upstream across an expanse of flat meadow until you come to a signpost indicating "Pombie Par Peyreget" to the left. There follows a steepish zigzagging climb to the timber line and a long traverse right to the junction with the HRP path (1hr from *Pyrénéa Sports*). Keep left, with the ground falling away on your right. At the **Lac de Peyreget**, you can either follow the HRP steeply left towards the **Col de Peyreget**, or alternatively keep right – due south – to the gentler **Col d'Iou**. From the latter, traverse leftwards, following the contour to the **Col de Soum**, where you turn due northwards towards the *Refuge de Pombie* (about 4hr). The path continues north, then west back to *Pyrénéa Sports* (about 3hr) via the **Col de Suzon** – where the standard ascent of the *pic* begins – the Col de Moundelhs and the Col Long de Magnabaigt.

There is a path south off the mountain from the Col du Soum, and another – part of the HRP – from the *Refuge de Pombie*. The latter leads due east down the valley of the Pombie stream, through meadows full of daffodils, orchids, violets and fritillaries in June, when you might also catch a glimpse of lizards. At the **Cabane de Puchéoux**, a shepherds' hut, cross to the left bank of the stream and carry on down to the next bridge. A non-HRP path continues on the left bank past the Cabane d'Arrégatiou and comes out at the southern end of the **Lac de Fabrèges**. The right-hand HRP crosses the bridge and descends through woods to the **Gave de Brousset** at Caillou de Soques (about 2hr from Pombie), where you meet the Col du Pourtalet road (which leads to the Spanish frontier) and can hitch back to Gabas.

The Lacs d'Ayous

Starting again from the *Refuge Pyrénéa Sports*, the walk up to the **Lacs d'Ayous** is another classic, in some ways more impressive than circling the Pic du Midi d'Ossau itself, especially if you spend the night by the lakes to get the quintessential dawn view of the peak silhouetted against the rising sun and reflected in the slaty waters of Lac Gentau.

It's a steady but manageable climb south, then west from *Pyrénéa Sports*, which will take around two hours in all. Instead of crossing the Pont de Bious, which you'll reach after 30 minutes, turn up the GR10 to the right – a sign says "Lacs d'Ayous 1hr 30min" – through woods of pine and beech, with ever-widening views of the valley scattered with herds of horses and cows and flocks of sheep. In early summer the meadows are full of orchids and the stream banks thick with azalea-like alpenrose. Near the top, you reach three small lakes, the third and largest of which is **Lac Gentau**, whose reddish shallows are full of minnows that turn into the trout so sought after by numerous fishermen. On its banks there's an expanse of flat, soft meadow for camping, while above it stands the *Refuge d'Ayous* at 1960m (☎05.59.05.37.00; closed mid-Sept to mid-June). Over the Col d'Ayous behind it, the GR10 continues west to the Chemin de la Mâture and the Aspe valley (see p.709).

Lac d'Artouste

Some 7km out of Gabas, the Pourtalet road passes the dammed **Lac de Fabrèges**, whence a *télécabine* swings up to the **Pic de la Sagette** (2031m) to connect with a **miniature rail line** that runs 10km southeast through the mountains to the **Lac d'Artouste**. Built in the 1920s to service a hydro-electric project which raised the lake level 25m, it was later converted for tourist purposes. Weather permitting, the train starts operating in early June and keeps going until late September. It is a beautiful trip, lasting about four hours, including time to walk down to the lake and back. Round-trip fares are 69–99F/€10.50–15.10 depending on the season; walkers may be able to negotiate one-ways. The first train leaves between 9 and 10am, but allow a half-hour for the *télécabine* (first departure 8.30–9.30am). Don't forget to take warm clothes, too, as you'll be at an altitude of over 2000m. In **winter** the same *télécabine* gives access to the small beginner-to-intermediate downhill **ski centre** on the northeast side of the Col de la Sagette.

The Col d'Aubisque and the road to the Gave de Pau

The only way of reaching the Gave de Pau by road without going back towards Pau is via the minor D918 over the **Col d'Aubisque**, a grassy, rounded ridge 17km from (and nearly 1000m above) Laruns. There's a café on the top, served by a single CITRAM bus from Laruns (July to mid-Sept). If you attempt to hitch on east, it's best to get a through ride the 18km to attractive Arrens-Marsous, where you'll find uninspiring accommodation and restaurants, among which *La Maison Camélat*, a *gîte d'étape* in a fine, rambling old house just off the central place (☎05.62.97.40.94, fax 05.62.97.43.01), is the best option. Between Laruns and the col, there are two resorts: the old Second Empire spa of Eaux-Bonnes, and the ugly ski centre of Gourette, which offers some thirty intermediate to advanced runs off Pic de Ger (2613m).

The col is a favourite place for slaughtering migrating wood pigeons in autumn, as the numerous shooting butts along the ridge bear witness. The Tour de France also usually passes this way, making the pass an irresistible challenge to any French cyclist worth his salt. You see swarms of them toiling up from the west, making it a matter of pride to find the breath for a cheery "Bonjour".

The Gave de Pau and around

From its namesake city, the **Gave de Pau** forges southeast towards the mountains, veering sharply south at Lourdes and shortly fraying into several tributaries: the **Gave d'Azun** (flowing down from Arrens), the **Gave de Cauterets**, the **Gave de Gavarnie** (draining its cirque) and the **Gave de Bastan**, dropping from the Col du Tourmalet. All four of these valleys, and the holiday bases in them, are served by SNCF buses from Lourdes. **Cauterets**, 30km due south of Lourdes, and **Gavarnie**, a further 20km southeast, are busy, established resorts on the edge of the Parc National des Pyrénées Occidentales, but the country they give access to is so spectacular that you should tolerate their congestion en route to the hills. If you want a smaller, more manageable base that's enjoyable in its own right, then **Barèges**, up a side valley from the spa resort of **Luz-St-Sauveur**, is a much better bet. All four towns are served by SNCF buses from Lourdes, via the valley of the **Gave de Pau** and its tributaries. As ever, if you pick your season right or even the time of day, you can still enjoy the most popular sites in relative solitude. At Gavarnie, for instance, few people stay the night, so it's quiet in the early morning and evening, and the **Cirque de Troumouse**, which is just as impressive in its way (though much harder to get to without a car), has very few visitors. By contrast, the spa of **Bagnères-de-Bigorre**, just east of the gave within striking distance of the Lourdes, is fairly dull, merely a gateway to the Vallée de Campan.

St-Savin

Between Lourdes and Cauterets, some 3km southeast of the dull, congested town of Argelès-Gazost, pleasant, sleepy **ST-SAVIN** merits a stop for its twelfth-century **abbey-church**, with later fortifications and a fine Romanesque doorway. The interior offers an interesting stoup, and an amusing organ cabinet carved with grotesque faces – supposedly those of damned souls – that were designed to grimace as the music played. For a fee of 12F/€1.85 you can view the **treasury**, installed in the vaulted former chapterhouse. Also worth a visit is the little hilltop chapel of **Nôtre-Dame-de-Piétat** (erratic hours; free), 1km south of the village, which has an elaborately painted ceiling, where birds perch on floral motifs covering every available space.

Cauterets and around

Thirty kilometres south of Lourdes, **CAUTERETS** is a pleasant if unexciting little town that owes its fame and its rather elegant Neoclassical architecture to its waters, still much in demand for the treatment of rheumatism and ear, nose and throat complaints. In modern times, it has also become one of the main Pyrenean ski and mountaineering centres.

Its origins as a spa began with Count Raymond de Bigorre's grant of land to the monks of St-Savin in 945 AD. In the seventeenth century, Marguerite d'Angoulême came to take the waters and wrote her *Heptameron* here. The eighteenth and nineteenth centuries were its heyday, especially the latter with its Romantic worship of mountains. Hugo visited, as did Chateaubriand, Baudelaire, Debussy, Edward VII and many other celebrities.

The modern town is so small that there is no difficulty in finding your way around. Most of it is still squeezed between the steep wooded heights that close the mouth of the Gave de Cauterets valley. Next door to the **gare routière** on the north edge of the centre, where SNCF coaches stop, the **Maison du Parc** (daily 9.30am–noon & 3.30–7pm; ☎05.62.92.52.56) has a small museum of flora and fauna (10F/€1.52), and film shows on Wednesday and Saturday in season (5.30pm; 20F/€3.04). In the centre, three minutes' walk from here, you'll find the **tourist office** in place Maréchal Foch (daily: July & Aug 9am–12.30pm & 1.30–7pm; rest of year 9am–12.30pm & 2–6.30pm; ☎05.62.92.50.27, *www.cauterets.com*); adjacent stands the Bureaux des Guides (daily: mid-June to mid-Sept 10.30am–12.30pm & 4.30–7.30pm; ☎05.62.92.62.02), which organizes walks and other activities.

Inexpensive **hotels** include *Le Bigorre*, 15 rue de Belfort (☎05.62.92.52.81; ②; closed Nov to mid-Dec & May), and *Le Centre et Poste*, 11 rue de Belfort (☎05.62.92.52.69, fax 05.62.92.05.73; ②). For something a little more upmarket, try the *César*, 3 rue César (☎05.62.92.52.57, fax 05.62.92.08.19; ③; closed May & Oct), or the atmospheric *Lion d'Or* nearby (☎05.62.92.52.87, fax 05.62.92.03.67; ③; closed Oct to mid-Dec). There are also a couple of **gîtes** – *Le Beau Soleil*, at 25 rue Maréchal-Joffre (☎05.62.92.53.52) and *Le Pas de l'Ours*, 21 rue de la Raillère (☎05.62.92.58.07, fax 05.62.92.06.49). There are several well-equipped **campsites** along the road north out of town, one of the quietest being *Les Bergeronnettes* (☎05.62.92.50.69; closed Oct–May), across the river on the right.

As most hotels require half-board, independent **restaurants** are thin on the ground: the *Giovanni Pizzeria* at 5 rue de la Raillère and *Casa Bodega Manolo* nearby at no. 11 are pretty much it. However, *La Brulerie du Gave*, at no. 7 on pedestrianized avenue de l'Esplanade, by the river, is an excellent spot for English breakfasts, crêpes, coffee, tea and juice.

Hikes around Cauterets

Most classic excursions around Cauterets begin up the Val de Jéret at the **Pont d'Espagne**, where the Gave de Gaube and Gave du Marcadau hurtle together in a boiling spume of spray, before rushing down to Cauterets over a series of spectacular waterfalls. In season there are six daily *navettes* from the town centre to the giant visitor centre and car park here; purists can walk there along an attractive, streamside section of the GR10, which doubles as a *parc national* path. This starts from the disused satellite spa of **LA RAILLÈRE**, 3km south of Cauterets, and takes two hours uphill through the forest (90min down).

From Pont d'Espagne, you can proceed southwest up the **Marcadau valley** along a bit of the GR10 to the *Refuge Wallon* (☎05.62.92.64.28; about 5hr round trip), or due south up into the alpine valley of the Gave de Gaube, with the lovely little **Lac de Gaube** backed by the snowy wall and glaciers of **Vignemale** (3298m). There is even a *télésiège* (28F/€4.25 return) to save you the first part of the ascent from Pont d'Espagne. Beyond the lake, the path continues to the *Refuge des Oulettes* below the north face of Vignemale (☎06.13.70.40.00; about 3hr from Pont d'Espagne), from where you can return to La Raillère via one of two routes. The HRP from *Refuge des Oulettes* goes over a high pass to the *Refuge de Bayssellance* (currently closed for renovation) and then loops broadly around to the *Refuge d'Estom* (☎05.62.92.75.07) in the beautiful and quieter **Lutour valley**; alternatively you can omit *Bayssellance* and head straight to *Estom* over the lower Col d'Arrailé. Even with a bus ride at the start and using this lower route, you should allow 8hr for the walking day; if you take in the high country around *Bayssellance*, it's best to schedule an overnight at *Oulettes* or *Estom*.

A less-frequented walk from Cauterets is to the **Lac d'Ilhéou** along the **GR10** (about 3hr). To avoid the initial steep climb you can take the Téléphérique du Lys (33F/€5 one way) to the **gare intermédiaire de Cambasque**, crossing the stream there and continuing up the right bank to the **Cabane de Courbet**, where you follow a track, first on the left bank, then on the right. After a short distance, the GR10 leaves the track and climbs up the slope to the left, steadily gaining height to cross a chute of boulders beside the long white thread of the **Cascade d'Ilhéou** waterfall. Over the rim of the chute, you come to a small lake, with the *Refuge d'Ilhéou* (☎05.62.92.75.07; closed Oct–May) in sight ahead on the shore – it's very pretty in June, with snow still on the surrounding peaks and ice floes drifting on its still surface.

Luz-St-Sauveur and the road south

The only road approach to Gavarnie and Troumouse, best known of the Pyrenean cirques, is through **LUZ-ST-SAUVEUR**, on the GR10 and a daily SNCF bus route from Lourdes. Like Cauterets, it was a nineteenth-century spa, patronized by Napoléon III and Eugénie, and the left-bank St-Saveur quarter owes its elegant Neoclassical facades to this period.

The principal sight, at the top of Luz's medieval, right-bank quarter, is the **church of St-André**. Built in the late twelfth century and fortified in the fourteenth by the Knights of St John, it's a classic of its kind, with a crenellated outer wall and two stout towers. The north entrance, beneath one of the towers, sports a handsome portal surmounted by a Christ in Majesty carved in fine-grained local stone. The lanes radiating down from the church are crammed with **market stalls** every Monday.

The **tourist office** (July & Aug Mon–Sat 9am–7.30pm, Sun 9am–12.30 & 4.30–7.30pm; rest of year daily 8.30/9am–noon & 2.30–6/7pm; ☎05.62.92.30.30), edges the central place du Huit-Mai, by the crossroads for Gavarnie or Barèges. Two central **hotels** to try are the quiet and atmospheric *Les Templiers* (☎05.62.92.81.52; ②; closed May & Oct), opposite the church, and *Les Cimes* (☎05.62.92.83.03; ②), 70m downhill on the same lane. There's also a **campsite** and **gîte d'étape**, *Les Cascades* (☎05.62.92.94.14), uphill from the church, and *Camping Le Toy*, near the tourist office (☎05.62.92.86.85; closed May & Oct–Dec). **Restaurants** are generally indifferent, catering to French day-trippers, though *Chez Christine* (closed May, Oct & Nov), near the post office, serves decent pizzas and salads.

Twelve kilometres south in tiny **GÈDRE**, where another side road veers off for the Cirque de Troumouse, there are two comfortable **hotels** – *Les Pyrénées* (☎05.62.92.48.51; ③; open all year) and *La Brèche de Roland* (☎05.62.92.48.54, fax 05.62.92.46.05; ③; closed late April & Oct–Dec), with a reasonable restaurant – plus a pair of highly rated **gîtes d'étape** nearby: *Le Saugué* (☎05.62.92.48.73; closed Nov–April), with camping space, and *L'Escapade* (☎05.69.92.49.37; closed April, May, Oct & Nov).

The Cirque de Gavarnie

South of Luz-St-Sauveur, and a further 8km up the ravine from Gèdre, **GAVARNIE** is connected with Luz by two daily **bus** services (Mon, Thurs & Sat only outside July & Aug), though you can walk it on the higher variant of the GR10 from Cauterets in two days. Either way you'll avoid the 20F/€3.05 levied on all drivers entering the huge car park at the entrance to the village. Once poor and depopulated, Gavarnie has found the attractions of mass tourism, much of it the excursion trade from Lourdes, too seductive to resist, and is now an unpleasant mess of pricey accommodation, souvenir shops and mediocre snack bars. The main street stinks, too, from the droppings of the dozens of mules, donkeys and horses used to ferry visitors up into the cirque. However, the **cirque** itself – Victor Hugo called it "Nature's Colosseum" – is magnificent, a natural amphitheatre scoured out by a glacier, of which barely the roots of the tongue remain. Nearly 1700m high, it consists of three sheer bands of rock discoloured by the striations of seepage and waterfalls, and separated by sloping ledges covered with snow. To the east, it is dominated by the jagged peaks of **Astazou** and **Marboré**, both over 3000m. In the middle, a corniced ridge sweeps round to Le Taillon, hidden behind the Pic des Sarradets, which stands slightly forward of the rim of the cirque, obscuring the **Brèche de Roland**, a curious vertical slash, 100m deep and about 60m wide, said to have been hewn from the ridge by Roland's sword, Durandal (see box on p.696). In winter, there is good **skiing** for beginners and intermediates at the nearby, nineteen-run resort of **Gavarnie-Gèdre**, with great views of the cirque from the top point of 2400m.

Practicalities

For those with a **tent**, there's the stunningly located *Camping La Bergerie* (☎05.62.92.48.41; closed Nov to mid-May) on the true right bank of the *gave*, on the cirque side of the village. The facilities leave a great deal to be desired, but the site is away from the crowds and has a view right into the cirque. The other campsite, *Le Pain de Sucre* (☎ & fax 05.62.92.47.55; closed Oct–Christmas & Easter–May), is on the Luz side of the village.

As for **hotels**, inexpensive options include the historic, though poorly maintained, *Les Voyageurs*, at the entrance of the village (☎05.62.92.48.01, fax 05.62.92.40.89; ②), which has been run by the same family since 1740; its "Golden Book" contains the signatures of Count Henry Russell, the eccentric pioneer of Pyrenean mountaineering, George Sand, Flaubert and Hugo among others. The beds here, so the whisper goes, witnessed the conception of Napoléon III in an illicit encounter between Hortense de Beauharnais and a local *berger*. Failing that, try the small *Hôtel Compostelle* by the church (☎05.62.92.41.13, *compostelle@gavarnie.com*; ②), whose management offers guided walks. Otherwise, the best bets are the CAF **refuge**, *Les Granges de Holle*, on the Port de Gavarnie road (☎05.62.92.48.77; closed Nov), which also does meals, and the high-standard **gîte d'étape** *Le Gypaète* (☎05.62.92.40.61), just below *Les Voyageurs*. The only surviving independent **restaurant** of note is *Le P'tit Toy*, beyond the *Compostelle*, with two appetizing menus below 120F/€18.30.

For **weather information and snow conditions**, ask the CRS mountain rescue unit opposite *La Bergerie* (or ring ☎08.36.68.02.65); for **general tourist information**, ask at the Maison du Parc (Mon–Sat 9.30am–noon & 1.30–6.30pm; ☎05.62.92.49.10) as you come into the village.

The cirque and around

It's an easy one-hour walk from Gavarnie to the cirque, using either the main or the west-bank trails beside the *gave* draining from it. Luckily, the scale of it is sufficient to dwarf the tourists, but for a bit of serenity it is still best to use the west-bank path, or go up before 10am or after 5pm, when the grandeur and silence are almost alarming. The track ends at the *Hôtel du Cirque et de la Cascade*, once a famous meeting place for mountaineers and now a popular snack bar in summer. To get to the foot of the cirque walls, you have to clamber over slopes of frozen snow. Take care not to stand too close, especially in the afternoon, because of falling stones. To the left, the **Grande Cascade**, at 423m the highest waterfall in Europe, wavers and plumes down the rock faces – a fine sight in the morning, when it appears to pour right out of the eye of the sun. Scaling the cliffs is obviously a matter for climbers, but the relatively intrepid can get a powerful impression of the majesty of the place – and a superb vantage point for photography – by climbing the first stage of the **HRP path** towards the **Refuge la Brèche de Roland**; the path begins in the right-hand corner of the cirque as you face it, at the edge of the first band of rock. The first, very exposed 100m or so could be a little nerve-racking if you are not used to heights, but in dry weather it is perfectly safe.

If you don't want to retrace your steps, an enjoyable and not too demanding walk back to Gavarnie is via the path from the *Hôtel du Cirque* up the east flank of the Gavarnie valley to the **Refuge des Espuguettes** (☎05.62.92.40.63; daily June–Sept, weekends Easter, May, Oct; 2hr). It is a beautiful path, cut into rocky, pine-shaded slopes; at the top, you emerge into open meadows tilting up to the refuge. The climb is well worth the effort for the views of the cirque and the Brèche de Roland. The committed may want to go from here on to **Piméné**, the bare peak above you. It's a couple of easy, if tedious, hours' climbing, but the view is fantastic: the Cirque d'Estaubé, Monte Perdido and away into Spain. To return to Gavarnie, turn right at the signposted trail fork below the refuge (allow 90min total).

La Brèche de Roland

La Brèche de Roland is *the* walk to do in Gavarnie. It is high, and involves crossing a glacier, which means being properly equipped with ice axe and crampons. It is, however, extremely popular in summer, so there is a good chance of being able to team up with someone more experienced.

There are three approaches to the *brèche*, all converging on the **Refuge de la Brèche de Roland**, aka *Refuge des Sarradets* (☎05.62.92.40.41; closed Oct–April); or contact the CRS in Gavarnie (☎05.62.92.48.24) for reservations at the refuge, which are always necessary in high season. The easiest route is up the road to the Port de

Gavarnie/Col de Boucharo, where a clear path climbs under the north face of Le Taillon to join the footpath coming directly from Gavarnie (1hr). The latter path starts beside the church, climbs steadily up the valley of Pouey Aspé, then zigzags steeply up to join the Port de Gavarnie path (2hr 45min). From the junction of these two paths, it's less than an hour to the refuge. The third and trickiest route (4hr 30min–5hr from Gavarnie to the hut) is via the **Échelle des Sarradets** section of the HRP path (see above). The *brèche* is about forty minutes above the refuge, with the glacier crossing occupying the final moments.

The Cirque de Troumouse

A vast, wild place, much bigger than Gavarnie and, in bad weather, rather intimidating, the **Cirque de Troumouse** lies up a desolate valley, whose only habitations are the handful of farmsteads and pilgrimage chapel that make up the hamlet of **HÉAS** – until the construction of the road in, one of the loneliest outposts in France. In Héas, two establishments offer **camping** space, **rooms** (②) and simple **meals**: *La Chaumière* (☎05.62.92.48.66, closed Nov–April) and *Auberge de la Munia* (☎05.62.92.48.39). As you reach the head of the valley there is a **tollgate** (9am–5pm; 23F/€3.50 per car), after which the road climbs in tight hairpins up treeless slopes 4km to the *Auberge du Maillet* (☎05.62.92.48.97; ①; closed mid-Oct to May), by the side of a small tarn. After this it climbs again, even more steeply over 3km, beneath bare shining crags, to a car park. Nearby, a prominent statue of the Virgin Mary crowns a grassy knoll, enclosed by the wide sweeping walls of the cirque and enough pasture to feed thousands of cows and sheep. The moorland turf is channelled with streams and cut into dingles and hummocks, where gentians and saxifrage, sedums and houseleeks grow among the rock crevices. Beneath the eastern walls of the cirque are scattered a half-dozen blue glacial lakelets, the **Lacs des Aires**. A Parc National path does the circuit from Héas (no toll for walkers, 4hr).

The Vallée de Bastan

Luz-St-Sauveur marks the start of the eighteen-kilometre climb east along the D918 through the **Vallée de Bastan**, culminating in the **Col du Tourmalet**, one of the major torments of the Tour de France and the fulcrum of a giant **skiing** *domaine*. North of the pass rises the landmark **Pic du Midi de Bigorre** (2872m), with its observatory and funicular. The only major village in between is **Barèges**, 7km along, linked with Lourdes by the SNCF bus to Luz. The **GR10** passes through Barèges, on its way southwest into the lake-filled **Néouvielle Massif**, part of France's oldest (1935) natural reserve, and highly recommended as a walking area.

Barèges

The attractive, one-street town of **BARÈGES** has been a popular spa since 1677, when it was visited by Madame de Maintenon with her infant charge, the seven-year-old Duc de Maine, son of Louis XIV. A military hospital opened here in 1744, as its waters became renowned for the treatment of gunshot wounds, and a low-key army connection endures – a mountain warfare training centre and an R&R facility face each other near the centre. But today it is primarily a skiing, mountaineering and paragliding centre, and by far the most congenial resort around the Gave de Pau.

The central **tourist office** (July & Aug Mon–Sat 9am–12.30pm & 2–7pm, Sun 10am–noon & 4–6pm; rest of year shorter afternoon hours; ☎05.62.92.16.00) can supply accommodation lists and ski-lift plans. The through road is lined with a half-dozen gracefully ageing **hotels**, all fairly similar in standards, opening season (May–Oct) and

---

SKIING AND HIKING AROUND BARÈGES

With its links to the adjacent resort of **LA MONGIE** just over the Col du Tourmalet, Barèges claims to offer access to the largest **skiing** area in the Pyrenees. The beginners' runs finishing in Barèges itself are much too low (1250m) to retain natural snow, so beginners and intermediates usually have to start from the areas of Tournaboup or Tourmalet a few kilometres east. New chair lifts were installed in autumn 2000, and runs regraded to make the resort more competitive, but La Mongie over the hill, despite its hideous purpose-built development, offers higher, longer pistes.

From Barèges, the **Réserve Naturelle du Néouvielle** is easily accessible via the GR10; you can cross it using this trail in one manic, eight-hour walking day, finishing at either the *Chalet-Refuge d'Orédon* (☎05.62.33.20.83; closed mid-Sept to mid-June), which serves superb meals, or the *Chalet-Hôtel de l'Oule* (☎05.62.98.48.62; closed mid-Sept to mid-Dec & mid-April to May).

---

price (typically ③). More interesting, perhaps, are two high-quality **gîtes d'étape**, open year-round except April and October: *L'Hospitalet* (☎05.62.92.68.08, fax 05.62.92.66.15), at the southern edge of town, somewhat institutional owing to its past as a military hospital, and the welcoming, Anglo-French-run *L'Oasis*, right behind the spa (☎05.62.92.69.47, fax 05.62.92.65.17, *andrea@gite-oasic.com*); both offer evening meals and reasonable half-board rates. Another possibility is the small, English-run inn *Les Sorbiers* on the main street (☎05.62.92.68.95, *sorbiers@sudfr.com*; ②; closed mid-Sept to mid-Dec & April to mid-May), which mainly handles one-week, pre-booked holidays, but accepts walk-ins and offers vegetarian meals on request.

The Col du Tourmalet and the Pic du Midi de Bigorre

Once past the Tournaboup area, the D918 climbs in earnest over denuded slopes to the **Col du Tourmalet**, at 2115m the highest road pass in the French Pyrenees. Even in summer it's apt to be a desolate, windy spot, flanked by a sporadically functioning café, and a rough-hewn, nude statue of the Unknown Cyclist, commemorating the first passage of the Tour through here in 1910. By the statue, a dirt road meanders off in the direction of the **Pic du Midi**, though the public can no longer use this to drive up to the observatory at the top, but must visit either on foot or by **téléphérique** (June–Sept daily 9.30am–4.30pm; *www.picdumidi.com*; 130F/€19.80, including admission to astronomical museum) from La Mongie. The venerable observatory, continuously staffed since opening in 1880 and still a serious research facility, long resisted commercialization but has now bowed to the inevitable with an on-site **astronomical museum**.

From the col the road descends past La Mongie, continuing through lovely woods of spruce, pine and beech, down into the gentle green Vallée de Campan (see p.719).

Bagnères de Bigorre and the Vallée de Campan

BAGNÈRES DE BIGORRE, nearly equidistant from Tarbes and Lourdes, is yet another Pyrenean spa town trying with mixed success to refurbish its somewhat faded image, but not a place to make a special stop.

It's served by frequent SNCF buses from Tarbes, which call at the disused **gare SNCF** on avenue de Belgique, 400m north of the town centre. The **tourist office** is at 3 allée Tournefort (daily: July & Aug Mon–Sat 9am–12.30pm & 2–7pm, Sun 9am–noon & 2–6pm; rest of year Mon–Sat 9am–12.15pm & 2–5.30pm; ☎05.62.95.50.71, *www.hautebigorre.com*), close to the leafy allées des Coustous, the main drag, lined with sidewalk **cafés**.

Hotels facing the spa tend to be overpriced, though the best of the budget options is *Les Petites Vosges* at 17 bd Carnot near the casino (☎05.62.95.28.31; ①), unchanged since World War II, but with showers in the pricier rooms. Otherwise, the quietest area is just north of the *halles*, itself 200m northwest of the tourist office, on rue de l'Horloge, where you'll find the old-fashioned *Hôtel l'Horloge* at no. 3bis (☎05.62.91.00.20; ①; closed Dec–Feb), and the similar *Hôtel de Nice* at no. 17 (☎05.62.95.04.65; ①; closed Nov–April). **Restaurants** aren't Bagnères' strong point: try *Le Bigourdan* (closed Mon) at 14 rue Victor-Hugo, corner rue de l'Horloge, with a great variety of menus (from 55F/€40, available lunch only), or next door at no. 12, the *Crêperie d'l'Horloge* for a range of *plats du jour* for under 50F/€7.60, plus of course crêpes to eat in or take away.

The Vallée de Campan

From Bagnères, regular daily summer buses serve the meadowy **Vallée de Campan**, upstream from town, whose architecture is quite distinct from the valleys to the west. Farm roofs are still slate, but house and barn are built in line as one building, with the balconied living quarters always to the right as you face the sun. The valley's "capital" is **CAMPAN**, with its interesting sixteenth-century covered market, old houses and another curious-looking fortified church with a presumed Cagot door in the west wall. **STE-MARIE-DE-CAMPAN**, 6km further along, has less character as a village but better **accommodation** and **eating** choices in its *Hôtel les Deux Cols* (☎05.62.91.85.60, fax 05.62.91.85.31; ①) and the *Gîte L'Ardoiserie* (☎05.62.91.88.88), both offering half-board.

The Comminges

Stretching from **Bagnères-de-Luchon** almost as far as Toulouse, the **Comminges** is an ancient feudal county that encompasses the upper valley of the River Garonne. It also boasts one of the finest buildings in the Pyrenees, the magnificent cathedral of **St-Bertrand-de-Comminges**, the product of three distinct periods of architecture. The mountainous southern part is what you will want to see, and access is via the unprepossessing little town of **MONTRÉJEAU**, from where there are daily bus and train services to Luchon.

Valcabrère

The village of **VALCABRÈRE** lies a short way south of Montréjeau on the main Bayonne–Toulouse rail line. It can be reached by SNCF bus (direction "Luchon") to the hamlet of Labroquère, by the Garonne, and then a short stroll across the river. It's a little place of rough stone barns and open lofts for hay-drying, with an exquisite Romanesque church of **St-Just** (March–June & Oct–Dec Sat & Sun 10am–noon & 2–6pm; July–Sept daily 9am–7pm; 12F/€1.80), whose square tower rises above a cemetery full of cypress trees. The north portal is elegantly sculpted and the apse, decorated with ten recessed arches, is quite remarkable. Both interior and exterior are full of recycled masonry from the old Roman settlement of **Lugdunum Convenarum**, whose remains are visible at the crossroads just beyond the village. Founded by Pompey in 72 BC, this was a town of some 60,000 inhabitants in its prime, making it one of the most important in Roman Aquitaine. Josephus, the Jewish historian, says it was the place of exile of Herod Antipas and his wife Herodias, who had John the Baptist decapitated. It was destroyed by Vandals in the fifth century and again by the Burgundians in the sixth century, after which it remained deserted until Bishop Bertrand, the future saint, appeared toward the end of the eleventh century.

St-Bertrand-de-Comminges and around

Further on is **ST-BERTRAND-DE-COMMINGES**, whose grey fortress-like **Cathedral** (March, April & Oct Mon–Sat 10am–noon & 2–6pm, Sun 2–6pm; May–Sept Mon–Sat 9am–7pm, Sun 2–6.30pm; Nov–Feb Mon–Sat 10am–noon & 2–5pm, Sun 2–5pm; admission to cloister and choir 20F/€3.05) commands the plain from the knoll ahead, the austere white-veined facade and heavily buttressed nave totally subduing the clutch of fifteenth- and sixteenth-century houses huddled at its feet. To the right of the west door a Romanesque cloister with engaging carved capitals looks out across a green valley to hills, where a local *maquis* unit had its lair during the war. In the aisleless interior, the small area at the west end reserved for the laity has a superbly carved sixteenth-century oak organ, pulpit and spiral stair, although the church's great attraction is the central choir, built by *toulousain* craftsmen and installed in 1535. The elaborately carved stalls – 66 in all – are a feast of virtuosity, mingling piety, irony and malicious satire, each one the work of a different craftsman. In the misericords and partitions separating them, the ingenuity and humour of their creators is best seen; each of the gangways dividing the misericords has a representation of a cardinal sin on top of the end partition. By the middle gangway on the south side, for example, Envy is represented by two monks, faces contorted with hate, fighting over the abbot's baton of office, pushing against each other foot to foot in a furious tug-of-war. The armrest on the left of the rood-screen entrance depicts the abbot birching a monk, while the bishop's throne has a particularly lovely back panel in marquetry, depicting St Bertrand himself and St John. In the ambulatory a fifteenth-century shrine depicts scenes from St Bertrand's life, with the church and village visible in the background of the top right panel.

During peak season cars are not allowed in the village itself, but a minibus operates a shuttle service from the car park at the base of the hill. In July and August the cathedral and St-Just in Valcabrère (see above), both with marvellous acoustics, host the musical **Festival du Comminges**; more details from the **tourist office** on the cathedral square (daily 10.30am–12.30pm & 3–7pm; ☎05.61.95.44.44; or for specific enquiries about the festival ☎05.61.88.32.00 in summer, ☎05.61.95.81.25 the rest of the year). **Staying** overnight is an attractive proposition, at least outside peak season. Opposite the cathedral, the *Hôtel du Comminges* (☎05.61.88.31.43, fax 05.61.94.98.22; ③; closed Nov–March) makes for a fine, old-fashioned overnight and has a reasonable restaurant (closed Oct–March). Otherwise the more modern *Hôtel L'Oppidum* (☎05.61.88.33.50, fax 05.61.95.94.04; ③; closed early Jan to late Feb & Wed out of season), north of the cathedral on rue de la Poste, has variable but engaging en-suite rooms, with an excellent ground-floor restaurant (allow 130F/€19.80 including drink), which doubles as a *salon de thé*. The nearest **campsite** – shady and well laid out – is *Es Pibous* (☎05.61.94.98.20; closed Oct–April), north of the road to St-Just. The only notable unaffiliated **restaurant** is *Chez Simone*, downhill from the *Hôtel du Comminges*, serving simpler fare (around 90F/€13.70) on its panoramic terrace.

The Grottes de Gargas

About 6km from St-Bertrand in the direction of Mazères-de-Neste, the **Grottes de Gargas** (45-minute guided tours daily: Jan–Easter & Oct–Nov 10am–noon & 2–5pm; Easter–June & Sept 10am–noon & 2–6pm; July & Aug 9.30am–12.30pm & 2–7pm; Dec 10am–noon & 2–4pm; last tour 45min before stated closing time; ☎05.62.39.72.39; 30F/€4.60; group maximum 25 persons) are renowned for their 231 prehistoric painted hand prints. Outlined in black, red, yellow or white, they mostly seem deformed – perhaps the result of leprosy, frostbite or ritual mutilation, though no one really knows why. There are representations of large animals as well.

Bagnères-de-Luchon

There's none of the usual spa-town fustiness about **BAGNÈRES-DE-LUCHON**, long one of the focuses of Pyrenean exploration. The main street, **allée d'Étigny**, lined with cafés and snack bars, has a distinctly metropolitan elegance and bustle. There is not, however, anything specific to see, apart from the slightly moth-eaten **Musée du Pays de Luchon** (daily 9am–noon & 2–6pm; group tour only) by the tourist office, which has an extraordinarily eclectic collection of archeological finds, old skis, art and natural history displays on the Pyrenees, and the nineteenth-century **baths** (guided tours Tues & Thurs 2pm; 30F/€4.60; bathing daily 4–8pm; 60F/€9.15) at the end of allée d'Étigny in the **Parc des Quinconces**. Luchon is best seen as a comfortable base for exploring the surrounding mountains in summer, and for **skiing** at the nearby centres of Superbagnères and Peyragudes in winter (see p.722). Because of the peculiar local topography, the valley here is also one of the major French centres for **paragliding** and **light aviation**.

Practicalities

The **gare SNCF**, which is also the **gare routière**, is in avenue de Toulouse across the River One in the northern part of the town. The **tourist office** is at 18 allée d'Étigny (April–June & Nov to mid-Dec Mon–Fri 9am–12.30pm & 2–6pm; July & Aug daily 9am–7pm; Sept & Oct daily 9am–1pm & 2–7pm; mid-Dec to March daily 8.30am–7pm; ☎05.61.79.21.21, *www.luchon.com*), and can give details about local skiing. Adjacent to the tourist office are the premises of the Bureau des Guides who organize walks and climbs. **Bikes** can be hired at Luchon Mountain Bike (☎05.61.79.88.56) and Cycles Demiguel (☎05.61.79.12.87), both on avenue Maréchal Foch, and Sun Park (☎05.61.79.81.41) on rue de Superbagnères.

You're best off forsaking the obvious **accommodation** on allée d'Étigny for better value in the quieter side streets. Possibilities include *Hôtel des Deux Nations* to the west at 5 rue Victor-Hugo (☎05.61.79.01.71, fax 05.61.79.27.89; ②), a well-kept, popular, en-suite one-star with a busy downstairs restaurant; *Hôtel Céleste*, to the east at 32 rue Lamartine (☎05.61.74.64.84, fax 05.61.79.34.44; ②), a bit well-worn but friendly; or, also east of the main street, the *Hôtel la Petite Auberge*, 15 rue Lamartine (☎05.61.79.02.88, fax 05.61.79.30.03; ②), installed in a Belle Époque mansion, with ample parking and a decent restaurant. However, perhaps the most appealing option is the romantically sited *Hôtel Le Jardin des Cascades*, above the church in Montauban-de-Luchon, 2km east (☎05.61.79.83.09, fax 05.61.79.79.16; ②; closed mid-Oct to early April), with just a half-dozen peaceful, wood-decor rooms in a lovely spot backed by a wild, hilly garden nurtured by the falls of the name.

There's no *gîte* or hostel in town, but there are ten **campsites** in the vicinity; least cramped, and with the best amenities, is *Camping La Lanette* (☎05.61.79.00.38; open most of year), 1.5km east over the Pique (down rue Lamartine) near Montauban-de-Luchon.

As with lodging, the best **eating-out** prospects are some distance away from the allée d'Etigny. Most central is *Le Clos du Silène*, 19 cours des Quinconces (closed Tues low season & mid-Nov to mid-Dec), a welcoming spot with sumptuous interior salons and a garden, offering three menus at 90–150F/€13.70–22.90. Alternatively, the shaded terrace restaurant at *Le Jardin des Cascades* (directions and phone as above) serves creative gourmet food, and offers sweeping views west and good service; there are cheaper lunch menus, but reckon normally on 210F/€32 per person, and mandatory reservations. Just out of town, try *L'Auberge de Castel-Vielh*, 2.5km south on the D125 (April–Oct daily; rest of year weekends only; menus at 100F/€15.25, 160F/€24.40 and 190F/€29), in a converted country house, serving excellent game and regional dishes, including snails and trout.

La-Bastide-de-Sérou and take the D15. It's a pretty road, but without a lift it'll take a good two hours on foot. Failing that, four Semvat buses a day run from Toulouse.

Secondary caves leading off the river cavern are the focus of historical interest; they were inhabited in prehistoric times for more than 20,000 years and used as a refuge by Cathars and Protestants in more recent times. As usual, the most important galleries are sealed off, though this hasn't stopped damage from road pollution, and those caves you can visit are interesting mainly for their sheer size (March, Oct & Nov Sun 2–6pm; April Mon–Fri 2–6pm, Sat & Sun 10am–noon & 2–6pm; May & June Mon–Sat 2–6pm, Sun 10am–noon & 2–6pm; July–Sept daily 10am–noon & 2–6pm; 40F/€6.10 including museum entry).

A few tools, animal bones and other objects found during excavation remain on view in glass cases in the caves, but the best pieces are now on display in the attractive, sleepy village of LE MAS-D'AZIL, 1km to the north, in the Musée de la Préhistoire (same hours as the cave; 30F/€4.58). Among other engraved tools and weapons, the museum's most outstanding exhibit is the beautiful carved antler known as *le faon aux oiseaux*, perhaps used as a spear-thrower. The only hotel in the hamlet is the *Hôtel Gardet* (☎05.61.69.90.05; ②; closed mid-Nov to mid-March), with a decent restaurant (menus 60–150F/€9.15–22.90), and there is a municipal campsite (☎05.61.69.71.37; closed mid-Sept to mid-June) a twenty-minute walk away. The best place to eat is *Le Jardin de Cadettou* (☎05.61.69.95.23; closed Sat noon, Sun evening & Mon), a homely restaurant with excellent menus of regional cuisine from 80F/€12.20.

Tarascon and around

TARASCON-SUR-ARIÈGE lies 16km south of Foix, where the N20 crosses the Ariège (a bypass diverts the worst of the traffic). Once a centre for the local iron-mining industry – there is still an aluminium plant in operation – it is a hot and unexciting little town enclosed by high wooded ridges. However, it is useful as a base for the Vicdessos valley and the prehistoric cave of Niaux (see below).

The cafés on the east bank of the river, dominated by the clock tower, are pleasant, sunny places to sit. Apart from that, it is worth taking a stroll up the narrow rue de Barri to the wide square by the church, a pleasant expanse with just one arcaded side and a single wooden house still standing, to the Porte d'Espagne, the only surviving piece of the town walls.

The gare SNCF is a few minutes' walk from the N20 bridge. The tourist office is west of the bridge on avenue des Pyrénées in the smart new Centre Multimédia François Mitterrand (July & Aug daily 9am–7pm; rest of year Mon–Sat 9am–6pm; ☎05.61.05.94.94, *pays.de.tarascon@wanadoo.fr*). Quietest and most attractive of the hotels is the *Confort* on the riverside quai Armand-Sylvestre (☎ & fax 05.61.05.61.90; ③), but for more comfort try the *Hostellerie de la Poste*, 200m north on the main through road (☎05.61.05.60.41, *pays.de.tarascon@wanadoo.fr*, ③). There's a campsite, *Pré Lombard* (☎05.61.05.61.94), on the left bank of the river, ten minutes' walk upstream from the bridge.

Niaux and the prehistoric caves

Just south of Tarascon, by the aluminium plant, the D8 cuts up right into the green valley of the Vicdessos past the riverside remains of a Catalan ironworks. The hamlet of NIAUX lies in the valley bottom, 5km further on. The tiny settlement has an interesting Musée Pyrénéen (daily: July & Aug 9am–8pm; rest of year 10am–noon & 2–6pm; 35F/€5.34), with an unrivalled collection of tools, furnishings, old photos and odds and ends illustrating the vanished traditions of peasant Ariège.

But the real reason people descend on the little hamlet is for the Grotte de Niaux, a huge cave complex under an enormous rock overhang high on the south flank of the valley (daily: July & Aug 8.30–11.30am & 1.30–5.15pm; Sept 10–11.30am & 1.30–5.15pm; rest of year visits at 11am, 3pm & 4.30pm; reservations essential, several days ahead in peak season, ☎05.61.05.88.37; 60F/€9.15). There are about 4km of galleries in all, with paintings of the Magdalenian period (circa 11,000 BC) widely scattered throughout, although the twenty people allowed in the cave at any one time are led through just a fraction of the complex. The paintings you can see are in a vast chamber, a slippery 800-metre walk from the entrance of the cave along a subterranean river bed. The subjects are horses, ibex, stags and bison. No colour is used, just a dark outline and shading to give body to the drawings, which have been executed with a "crayon" made of bison fat and manganese oxide. They are an extraordinary mix of bold impressionistic strokes and delicate attention to detail: the nostrils, pupils and the tendons on the inner thighs of the bison are all drawn in.

The village of **ALLIAT**, right across the valley from Niaux, is home to **La Grotte de la Vache** (Easter–June & Sept daily except Tues 3–4.30pm; July & Aug daily 10am–5.30pm; rest of year by appointment, ☎05.61.05.95.06; 45F/€6.86), a relatively rare example of an inhabited cave where you can observe hearths, bones, tools and other remnants *in situ*. If you want to stay locally, there's a well- equipped but somewhat expensive **campsite**, *Les Grottes* (☎05.61.05.88.21; closed mid-Sept to May), in the village.

Although it can't compete with visiting the caves themselves, the **Parc Pyrénéen de l'Art Préhistorique** (daily: April–June, Sept & Oct 10am–6pm; July & Aug 10am–6.30pm; 65F/€9.91), a few kilometres west of Tarascon on the road to Banat, provides a remarkable overview of cave art. Highlight is the "Grand Atelier", a compelling multi media exploration including recreations of Niaux's inaccessible Clastres system, with its enigmatic footprints, and the famous "Salon Noir" as it would have looked to its creators 10,000 years ago. The surrounding landscaped park, complete with Magdalenian flower meadow, footprints stream and hunting panorama, continues the prehistoric theme.

Into the Couserans

From Niaux, the road continues along the valley bottom, beneath the romantically pinnacled ruins of the Château of Miglos (unrestricted access), to Vicdessau and Auzat, the latter with an unsightly aluminium works. From Vicdessos, a really stunning route – the D18 – climbs the **valley of the Suc**, tunnelling through trees, past abandoned barns and occasional cottages in lush meadows, by waterfalls and streams, to the pass at the **Port de Lers** (1517m). On the far side, herds of grey cows graze the alpine meadows down to the Étang de Lers. Then the road climbs again to another col overlooking the head of the valley of the little **River Garbet**. Below, the steep slopes are luxuriant with beech, while directly south you look into a high-walled crenellated cirque formed by the **Pic Rouge de Bassiès** and the **Pic des Trois Comtes** above the **Étang de Garbet**, where the heights are underlined by wedges of snow lying beneath the sheerest faces. This is the beginning of the **Pays de Couserans**, one of the poorest, least developed and most depopulated regions of the Pyrenees. Its villages, **Aulus-les-Bains** in particular, were once renowned for their bear-trainers, who, driven by poverty, toured the lowland towns with their performing beasts.

Aulus-les-Bains

Once in the Garbet valley, the road drops quickly west to **AULUS-LES-BAINS**, a remote village lying among moist and fragrant meadows ringed by dramatic peaks. Like other spa towns, Aulus enjoyed its moment of glory and fell again into rustic somnolence, from which it is trying to resurrect itself once more. This is country for walking and enjoying the landscapes: there's nothing else, and, remote though it feels, it is not inaccessible – there are one to three daily buses (Mon–Sat) to St-Girons. The classic walk here involves heading south to the **Étang de Guzet** and then east to the **Cascade d'Ars** on a bit of the GR10, then returning to Aulus via the stream draining from it (round trip about 5hr).

For summer bike rental and information on other activities, consult the **tourist office** in the allée des Thermes (daily: July & Aug 10am–1pm & 2–7pm; rest of year 10am–noon & 2–6pm; ☎05.61.96.00.01). Among places to **stay**, try the *Hôtel de France* (☎05.61.96.00.90, fax 05.61.96.03. 29; ①; closed mid-Oct to mid-Dec), with a restaurant serving a hearty, four-course *menu de jour* for well under 100F/€15.25, or the more comfortable, antique-furnished *Hôtel La Terrasse* (☎05.61.96.00.98, fax 05 61 96.01.42; ③; closed Oct–May), both near the spa. There's also a **gîte d'étape** 150m downhill from the church, *La Presbytère* (☎05.61.96.02.21; open all year), and **camping** at *Le Couledous* (☎05.61.96.02.26; open all year), 500m west along the river.

St-Girons

With numerous SNCF buses a day from Boussens, on the main Tarbes–Toulouse rail line, and ordinary bus connections on to Aulus, Ustou, Massat and Sentein, **ST-GIRONS** may be your first taste of this out-of-the-way region. Apart from its long association with cigarette-paper manufacture, the most striking thing about St-Girons is its central pavements, made of a local reddish-pink marble with finely chiselled gutters to take the rainwater from down-pipes. And although there are no other memorable sights, it's a far from unpleasant town, with a **folklore festival** in mid-July and a **theatre festival** in early August.

The simplest centre for orientation is the **Pont-Vieux**, just below picturesque rapids on the River Salat. The bridge points you into the old commercial centre of the town on the right bank, with some marvellously old-fashioned shops, their fronts and fittings unchanged for generations. To the right, past the tiny cathedral, is the typically provincial **place des Poilus**, its cachet largely due to the faded elegance of the *Grand Hôtel de France* and the equally old-fashioned *Hôtel de l'Union*, opposite, where you can still stay (see below). The latter's ground-floor café is a splendid balconied period piece facing the riverside **Champ de Mars**, a wide gravelled *allée* of plane trees, which provides the site for a big general market on the second and fourth Mondays of every month, and for a regular produce market every Saturday morning.

Buses arrive at place des Capots on the left bank of the river. The well-stocked **tourist office** is inside the Maison de Couserans (Mon–Sat: July & Aug 9.30am–6.30pm; rest of year 9am–noon & 2–6pm; ☎05.61.96.26.60, *otCouserans @wanadoo.fr*), on the right bank, in place Alphonse-Sentein. If you want to **stay**, try the *Hôtel Mirouze* on the left bank, 300m southwest of the Pont-Vieux (☎05.61.66.12.77, fax 05.61.04.81.59; ②), with a decent restaurant serving a full range of menus, or the modern and comfortable two-star *La Clairière*, at the edge of town on the road to Seix (☎05.61.66.66.66, fax 05.34.14.30.32; ③), with a pool and the best restaurant in town (90–150F/€13.70–22.90 for gourmet fare). There's also a **campsite** at the Centre de Loisirs du Parc de Paletès (☎05.61.66.06.79), 2km out along avenue des Évadés, with an excellent affiliated terrace restaurant, *La Table de l'Ours*.

St-Lizier

ST-LIZIER, a five-minute ride by bus from the old *gare SNCF* on the St-Gaudens road, totally outclasses St-Girons in the tourism stakes. It sits on a hilltop, and is full of history; it's walled, arcaded, cobbled, cathedraled, half-timbered, pretty, and lifeless outside of summer.

Architecturally the most interesting building in town is the **Cathédrale de St-Lizier** (May–Oct daily 10am–noon & 2–7pm; rest of year Mon–Sat 10am–noon & 2–6pm; free), with its distinctive octagonal tower posing photogenically against the mountains to the south. Inside are some twelfth-century frescoes faded almost to invisibility, and a fine Romanesque cloister, also twelfth-century, with an array of unique, sculpted column capitals. A second cathedral, **Nôtre-Dame-de-Sède**, within the grounds of the bishop's palace, is closed indefinitely for renovation, though the palace is also home to the **Musée Départmentale de l'Ariège** on the first floor (April–June, Sept & Oct daily 2–5.30pm; July & Aug daily 10am–12.30pm & 2–6.30pm; rest of year weekends & hols 2–5.30pm; 25F/€3.80), which contains a permanent ethnographic collection devoted to the Vallée du Bethmale, not really worth the admission fee. It is, however, worth walking up to the palace anyway, for views over St-Lizier, and continuing on round the old **ramparts** (same hours; free).

The helpful **tourist office** is located by the lower cathedral (May–Oct Mon–Sat 10am–noon & 2–6pm, Sun 2–6pm; rest of year Sat & Sun 2–6pm; ☎05.61.96.77.77). There are some excellent **accommodation** options, including the recently renovated *Hôtel de la Tour* (☎05.61.66.38.02, fax 05.61.66.38.01, *hotel.de.la.tour@wanadoo.fr*, ②), down by the River Salat on rue du Pont, which features a gourmet yet affordable **restaurant** overlooking in the rapids; you can eat superbly for just 105F/€16, or resort to the 55F/€8.40 weekday lunch menu. For all hotels, you'll need to book ahead during the town's international music **festival** (information on ☎05.61.66.67.89) in the first half of August as rooms are much in demand.

Ax-les-Thermes

Twenty kilometres south of Tarascon, and still on the river, the spa town of **AX-LES-THERMES** is completely walled in by mountains. Its principal value is as a base for exploring the surrounding mountains and as a staging post on the way to Andorra or on down the N20 to Font-Romeu and, ultimately, Perpignan and the Mediterranean.

The town itself is small and pleasant enough, but there's little to see once you've wandered a couple of streets in the quarter to the right of the N20, which forms the main street, avenue Delcassé. Rue de l'École and rue de la Boucarie retain a few medieval buildings, and above place du Breilh, the **church of St-Vincent** is of architectural interest for its Romanesque tower. Just across the road you can dangle your feet for free in the **Bassin des Ladres**, a pool of hot sulphurous water which is all that remains of the hospital founded in 1260 by St Louis for soldiers wounded in the Crusades.

The **gare SNCF** is off avenue Delcassé on the northwest side of town. The **tourist office** on place du Breilh (May–June, Sept & Oct Mon–Sat 9am–noon & 2–7pm, Sun 9am–noon & 2–6pm; July & Aug daily 9am–1pm & 2–7pm; Nov Mon–Sat 9am–noon & 2–6pm; Dec–April daily 9am–noon & 2–6pm; ☎05.61.64.60.60, *www.vallees-ax.com*) has hiking information and lists of walks. A nice **place to stay** is the *Hôtel La Terrasse* at 7 rue Marcaillou (☎05.61.64.20.33; ④), with a decent restaurant (from 95F/€14.49). Another possibility is *Les Pyrénées*, on the main avenue Delcassé opposite the casino (☎05.61.64.21.01, fax 05.61.64.38.91; ④), with a restaurant from 85F/€12.96. There is also a **campsite**, *Le Malazéou* (☎05.61.64.09.14), on the river bank just before the *gare SNCF* as you come into town from Tarascon. The most atmospheric places to **eat** are the old *Grand Café*, next to *Hôtel Les Pyrénées*, and *Brasserie Le Club*, on place Roussel, which has live jazz.

Lavelanet and around

LAVELANET is a nondescript but not unattractive little town on the banks of the Touyre river, 20km from Foix to the west and 35km from Quillan to the east. However, it has little to offer beyond its bus connections – which include a route north to **Mirepoix** – and the easiest access to the famous Cathar castle of **Montségur**, 12km to the south. If you get stuck there, head for the very clean and modern municipal **camp-**

site (closed Oct–March), from which you can just see Montségur nudging over the brow of the intervening ridges. There is a **tourist office** (July & Aug Mon–Sat 9am–noon & 2–7pm, Sun 9am–noon; rest of year Mon–Sat 9am–noon & 2–7pm; ☎05.61.01.22.20, *lavelanet.tourisme@wanadoo.fr*), and a couple of restaurants off the main square.

Montségur

The **village** of MONTSÉGUR is strung out in terraced lines at the foot of its castle rock. Silent and depopulated now, the place comes to life only with the influx of tourists, most of them day-trippers. It's worth having a glance at the one-room **museum** (Feb daily 2–5.30pm; March, April, Oct & Nov daily 1–5.30pm; May–Aug daily 10am–noon & 2–5.30pm; Sept daily 10am–noon & 2–5.30pm; Dec Tues–Sun 2–5pm; free), with its collection of bits and pieces from the castle, before going up to the ruin itself.

A footpath from the top of the village shortens the way up to the saddle of the hill and the Prats des Cramats, the field where the Cathar martyrs were burnt (see box below). From here it's a steep half-hour climb to the **Château** (Feb & Nov daily 10am–4pm; March & Oct daily 10am–5pm; May–Aug daily 9am–7.30pm; Sept daily 9am–5.30pm; Dec Tues–Sun 10am–4pm; 22F/€3.36), of which all that remain are the stout and now truncated curtain walls and keep. The space within is terribly cramped, and one can easily imagine the sufferings of the besieged. A somewhat precarious stairway leads to the top of the walls, whence you look out over kilometres of forested hills and snowy peaks, giving a sense of solitude and airy isolation that is in itself highly evocative.

In summer there's a **tourist office** in the village (July–Sept daily 10am–1pm & 2–6pm; ☎05.61.03.03.03, *www.citaenet.com/montsegur*); at other times you'll have to go to the one in Lavelanet (see above). There are a couple of **hotels**, the nicest of them the old-fashioned *Hôtel Couquet* (☎05.61.01.10.28; ①), fronted by pollarded lime trees and with a café and restaurant on the first floor (menus from 65F/€9.91). The alternative is the more expensive *Hôtel Costes* (☎05.61.01.10.24, fax 05.61.03.06.28; ②; restaurant about 100F/€15.25), which also has a **gîte d'étape**. There's another *gîte d'étape* in the village (☎05.61.01.20.97).

THE FALL OF MONTSÉGUR

In the early years of the thirteenth century, Montségur's castle was reconstructed by a local feudal lord as a strongpoint for the **Cathars** (see p.779) under attack by the Crusade. In 1232 it became the capital of the banned Cathar Church, with a population of some five hundred people, bishops and clergy as well as ordinary believers on the run from the persecution of the Inquisition, under the protection of a garrison commanded by Pierre-Roger de Mirepoix.

Provoked by a raid on Avignonet in May 1242, in which several Inquisitors were killed, the forces of the Catholic Church and the king of France laid siege to the castle in the spring of 1243. By March 1244, Pierre-Roger, despairing of relief, agreed terms with them. At the end of a fortnight's truce, the 225 Cathars who still refused to recant were burnt on a communal pyre on March 16.

Four men who had made good their escape recovered the Cathar "treasure", which had been hidden in a cave for safekeeping since the preceding Christmas, and vanished. Two of them later reappeared in Lombardy, where it seems probable these funds were used to support the refugee Cathar community established there. But numerous legends have grown up, especially in German writings, identifying this "treasure" with the Holy Grail, and the Cathars themselves with the Knights of the Round Table.

FROM MONTSÉGUR TO THE TÊT

From Montségur, you can take a dramatic four-hour **walk** over the Montagne de la Frau (1950m) to Comus, just off the road between Ax-les-Thermes and Quillan in the Têt valley (see p.730). At the hairpin turn on the highway to the south of the village, take a small road south along the Lasset River. After about 1km, the GR7B branches off to the east, crossing the stream and heading across a ridge to the north of the Montagne de la Frau. The trail eventually descends to the farm of Pelail (signposted as Liam), just above the Hers river. Turning south, the trail continues up the Hers valley, following the D5 from Bélesta into the deep sunless ravine known as the **Gorges de la Frau**. When the highway ends, the path continues up the deep gully thickly wooded with beech, ash, wild cherry and fir, climbing until it reaches an old tarmac road which crosses the river by a farm. Here, turn east again, and you'll come to Comus after about 3km.

Mirepoix

If you are heading north from Lavelanet in the direction of Carcassonne, it is definitely worth taking a look at **MIREPOIX**, a late thirteenth-century *bastide* built around one of the loveliest surviving arcaded market squares in the country. The square is bordered by houses dating from between the thirteenth and the fifteenth centuries, and a relatively harmonious modern *halle* on one side, but its highlight is the medieval Maison des Consuls (council house), whose arcaded rafters are carved with hundreds of unique portrayals of animals, monsters, and caricatures of medieval social groups and professions, as well as ethnic groups from across the world.

There's a **tourist office** in the main square (Mon–Sat 9am–noon & 2–6pm; ☎05.61.68.83.76). If you're feeling extravagant, you could **stay** on the main square in the *Maison des Consuls* (☎05.61.68.81.81, fax 05.61.68.81.15; ⑤); otherwise head for the *Hôtel Le Commerce*, on the boulevard encircling the old town near the church (☎05.61.68.10.29, fax 05.61.68.20.29; ④; closed Jan & part Oct). There's a municipal **campsite** on the Limoux road (☎05.61.01.55.44; closed mid-Sept to mid-June). The best restaurant is the *Porte d'Aval* (☎05.61.68.19.19; closed Mon) on cours Maréchal de Mirepoix, which specializes in regional dishes from 80F/€12.20. Unfortunately, the only bus link from Mirepoix is to Pamiers – to get to Carcassonne without transport, you'll have to hitch.

Along the Aude

South of Carcassonne, the road and the rail line both climb steadily up the twisting valley of the **River Aude**, between scrubby hills and vineyards and ever deeper and more forested ravines to **Quillan**. From there, the road squeezes through the **Gorges de l'Aude** in a sunless bottom before emerging once again towards the river's headwaters above Les Angles on the east side of the Carlit Massif in the high Pyrenees. It is a magnificent drive, and quite hitchable, as it is one of the main routes to Andorra, though buses do make the run through to **Quérigut** three times a week.

Limoux

The first stop on the D118 road, 24km south of Carcassonne, **LIMOUX** is served several times daily by both the SNCF and the private Cars Teissier buses. It stands astride the Aude, which for much of the year is a powerful grey flood of snow melt. Life revolves around the pretty **place de la République** in the heart of the old town, with its Friday market, and the nineteenth-century **promenade du Tivoli**, in effect a bypass road. Known in the past for its woollens and the tanning of hides brought down from the mountains, the town's claim to fame today is the production of its excellent sparkling wine, Blanquette de Limoux, much cheaper than champagne.

The **tourist office**, on promenade du Tivoli (July & Aug Mon–Fri 9.30am–noon & 2–6pm, Sat & Sun 10am–noon & 2–5pm; rest of year Mon–Sat 9.30am–noon & 4–6pm; ☎04.68.31.11.82, *limoux@fnotsi.net*), shares a building with the **Musée Petiet** (same hours; 15F/€2.29), displaying a collection of local nineteenth-century paintings. The top two **hotel** choices are the splendid and stately *Modern & Pigeon* in place Général Leclerc (☎04.68.31.00.25, *modpig@chezcom*; ④; closed Wed), and the humbler *Des Arcades*, south of the church at 96 rue St-Martin (☎04.68.31.02.57, fax 04.68.31.66.42; ③); both are comfortable and have television in the rooms and garage parking. The municipal **campsite** (☎04.68.31.13.63; closed Oct to mid-May) is on the east bank of the river, south of the old bridge.

For an unusual and colourful place to **eat**, try the *Maison de la Blanquette*, on promenade du Tivoli, which sells local wines and serves excellent food (closed Wed; from 78F/€11.90); otherwise there are plenty of cafés and brasseries on the main square, or try one of the hotels above. If you are interested in sampling or buying any **wine**, the best place to go is the co-operative, Aimery-Sieur d'Arques, in avenue du Mauzac (daily 9am–noon & 2.30–7pm).

Alet-les-Bains and Rennes-le-Château

South of Limoux, road and rail track the Aude valley, skirting the minuscule thermal resort of **ALET-LES-BAINS**, with its half-timbered houses and excellent **hotel**, the *Hostellerie de l'Évêché* (☎04.68.69.90.25, fax 04.68.69.91.94; ③; closed Oct–April), standing beside the ruined cathedral.

If you've got your own transport it's worth taking a detour south of Alet, following the D52 as it climbs out of Couiza and spirals towards the mountain-top village of **RENNES-LE-CHÂTEAU**. The views alone repay the effort, but the primary reason for the jaunt is the mysterious **parish church** run by Abbé Saunière from 1885 until 1910, when he was suspended because of his inability to explain how he financed his comfortable lifestyle and the lavish restoration work on the church. The church is full of veiled symbols and secret codes, which, some say, indicate that he had discovered the lost treasure of Solomon, brought here by the Visigoths in the fifth century. This and a host of other theories are explored in a video shown in **Villa Bethania** (daily: May–Sept 10am–7pm; rest of year 10am–6pm; 25F/€3.81), built by Saunière as a retirement home for priests, and in the small museum next to the church (same hours and ticket). Strange events continue to surround the village, the latest being the discovery of aerial photos, dating back to 1967, which reveal the image of a Virgin and Child in a nearby field.

Quillan and Pont d'Aliès

Back on the main road, **QUILLAN**, 27km upstream from Limoux, is a pleasant little town, useful as a staging post on the way south into the mountains or east to the Cathar castles – it has daily bus connections with Perpignan via St-Paul-de-Fenouillet. The only monument of interest is the ruined **castle** that was burnt by the Huguenots in 1575 and partly dismantled in the eighteenth century. The **gare SNCF**, **gare routière** and **tourist office** (summer Mon–Sat 8am–noon & 2–7pm, Sun 9am–noon; ☎04.68.20.07.78) are all together on the main ring road, boulevard de-Gaulle. Good options on the same street are the *Canal*, 36 bd de-Gaulle (☎04.68.20.08.62, fax 04.68.20.08.27.96; ②), and the *Cartier*, at no. 31 (☎04.68.20.05.14, fax 04.68.20.22.57; ③), both with restaurants. The *Sapinette* **campsite** is at 21 rue René-Delpech (☎04.68.20.13.52; closed Nov–Feb).

There's another campsite by the river at **PONT D'ALIÈS** (☎04.68.20.53.27), a further 11km along the D117 by the junction for Axat and the Gorges de l'Aude (see below). At this junction you'll also find the Maison des Pyrénées Cathares for local **information** (July & Aug daily 8am–7pm; rest of year Mon–Fri 8am–noon & 2–6pm; ☎04.68.20.59.61).

The valley of the Rebenty and Gorges de l'Aude

From Pont d'Aliès there is a beautiful route west up the **valley of the Rebenty** on the tiny D107 through woods of beech, fir and oak, with a magnificent early summer display of orchids and other Pyrenean flowers. It's a marvellous cycling route, too, except for the agony of the climb out of the valley. The road continues to Ax-les-Thermes over the Col du Pradel, or you can escape onto the Plateau de Sault at **ESPEZEL**, some 20km west of Axat.

The narrowest and deepest stretch of the scenic **Gorges de l'Aude** is the eighteen or so kilometres between Axat and Usson. If you want to admire the scenery, don't drive: the road is much too dangerous to allow your eyes to wander. Towards the end there is a magnificent cave to investigate, the **Grotte de l'Aguzou**. It's expensive to visit, but as near the real thing as you can get without being a pukka caver – you spend the entire day underground, accoutred like a professional. Visits must be arranged a week in advance and there must be a minimum of four people (contact M. Moreno in Mijanès, ☎04.68.20.45.38; or the Quillan tourist office – see opposite; 200F/€30.50). Camping s*auvage* is allowed by the river.

On to Quérigut

Upstream, the road divides just after Usson-les-Bains. On a shaggy bluff between the arms of the fork, dwarfed in turn by the heights either side, stand the forlorn ruins of the Château d'Usson, allegedly the hiding place for the "Cathar treasure" during the 1243 siege of Montségur (see box on p.728). Passing its foot, a road winds up through the attractive grey tiers of houses at **MIJANÈS** – where there's a good **hotel**, the *Relais de Pailhères* (☎04.68.20.46.97; ①; restaurant from 70F/€10.68) – to the pass at the **Col de Pailhères**, which is at its loveliest in June when a cornice of snow still lines the crests above the small round lake.

From Mijanès another road branches up the valley to **QUÉRIGUT** passing through the village of Le Pla. There's also a thrice-weekly bus (Mon, Wed & Fri afternoons) from Quillan to Quérigut, run by Petit Charles of Carcanières, that passes through the village. Quérigut stands at the head of a slope of neglected terraces, guarded by the ruin of its **castle**, last refuge of the Cathars who held out for eleven years after the fall of Montségur. You'll find accommodation either at the village **campsite** or the *Hôtel du Donezan* (☎04.68.20.42.40, fax 04.68.20.47.06; ②). Above, the forest begins: kilometres of beech and pine, interspersed with lush meadows, stretching to the windy plateau above Font-Romeu. This is the **Donezan** region, beautiful but the poorest, most neglected and depopulated corner of Ariège.

Roussillon

The area that makes up the eastern fringe of the Pyrenees and the flatter stretch of land down to the Mediterranean coast is known as **Roussillon**, or **French Catalonia**. Catalan power first came into its own in the tenth century under the independent counts of Barcelona, who then became kings of Aragon as well in 1137. They attempted to create a joint power base with Occitan France under the counts of Toulouse, but that came to an unhappy end with the death of Pedro II at the battle of Muret in 1213, when he came to the aid of Raymond VI of Toulouse against Simon de Montfort during the anti-Cathar crusade. The height of Catalan power was reached in the thirteenth and fourteenth centuries, when the Franco-Catalan frontier was fixed along the base of the

Corbières hills north of Perpignan. But Jaime I made the mistake of dividing his kingdom between his two sons at his death. What is now the French part became the kingdom of Majorca with its capital at Perpignan, but, coveted by the rival brother, the king of Aragon, it sought alliance with the kings of France, who saw this as a splendid opportunity to straighten out their southern border, thus ensuring continuous squabbling that was only finally ended by the Treaty of the Pyrénées, negotiated by Louis XIV in 1659.

After the treaty, the French began a ruthless process of Frenchification, which was successful in Perpignan where the bourgeoisie tended to identify their commercial

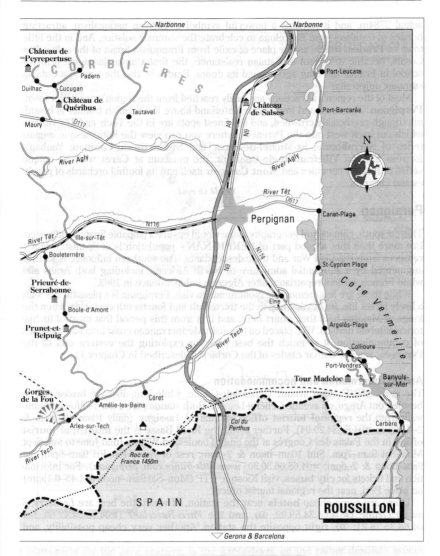

Château de Peyrepertuse

Duilhac   Cucugan   Padern

C O R B I E R E S

Château de Quéribus

Maury   D117   Tautavel

River Agly

River Têt   Ille-sur-Têt

Bouleternère

Prieuré-de-Serrabonne

Boule-d'Amont

Prunet-et-Belpuig

Gorges de la Fou

Arles-sur-Tech   Amélie-les-Bains   Céret

River Tech

Roc de France 1450m

S P A I N

△ Narbonne   △ Narbonne

Port-Leucate

Château de Salses   Port-Barcarès

River Agly

N9

River Têt   D617

Perpignan   Canet-Plage

N116

St-Cyprien Plage

N114

Elne

N9

Argelès-Plage

Collioure

Port-Vendres

Tour Madeloc

Banyuls-sur-Mer

Cerbère

Col du Perthus

N

Côte Vermeille

A9

ROUSSILLON

▽ Gerona & Barcelona

interest with a central power; the mountain hinterland, however, was left largely untouched until modern times, when the collapse of traditional agriculture, the introduction of compulsory education and the devastation of the vineyards by phylloxera combined to drive the peasantry off the land – a process which still continues today, albeit at a slower rate.

Although there is no real separatist impetus among French Catalans today, their sense of identity is still strong: the language is very much alive, and the national colours of yellow and red are much in evidence wherever you go. The **Pic du Canigou**, which completely dominates Roussillon, is much larger in presence than its

The City

The best place to begin your exploration of Perpignan is at **Le Castillet**, built as a gateway in the fourteenth century and now home to the **Casa Pairal** (daily except Tues: mid-June to mid-Sept 9.30am–7pm; rest of year 9am–6pm; 25F/€3.81), an interesting museum of Roussillon's Catalan folk culture, featuring religious art, agricultural and pastoral exposés, and all sorts of local crafts. From the roof there is a great view of the dominant pile of Canigou, while to the northwest you may be able to pick out the Château de Quéribus (see p.780), standing clear of its ridge. A short distance down rue Louis-Blanc you come to the **place de la Loge**, focus of the renovated and pedestrianized heart of the old town. Dominating the cafés and brasseries of the narrow square is Perpignan's most interesting building, the Gothic **Loge de Mer**. Designed to hold the city's stock exchange and maritime court, and decorated with gargoyles and lacy balustrades, its ground floor has been taken over by an incongruous fast-food joint. Side by side next door are the **Hôtel de Ville**, with its magnificent wrought-iron gates and Maillol's statue of *La Méditerranée* in the courtyard, and the fifteenth-century **Palais de la Députation**, once the parliament of Roussillon.

From place de la Loge, rue St-Jean runs down to the fourteenth-century **Cathédrale St-Jean** on place Gambetta (Mon & Wed–Sat 10am–noon & 2–5pm, Tues & Sun 2–5pm), its external walls built of bands of river stones sandwiched by brick. The interior is most interesting for its elaborate Catalan altarpieces, shadowy in the gloom of the dimly lit nave, and for the tortured wooden crucifix, known as the *Dévôt Christ*, in a side chapel to the south. Dating from around 1400, it's of Rhenish origin and was probably brought back from the Low Countries by a travelling merchant. Past the chapel, on the left is the entrance to the **Campo Santo**, one of France's oldest cemeteries, dating back some 600 years (same hours as cathedral).

From the cathedral, rue de la Révolution-Française and rue de l'Anguille lead into the close, dilapidated maze of the **Arab and Romany quarter**, where women congregate on the secluded inner lanes but are seldom seen on the more public thoroughfares. Here there are North African shops and cafés, especially on rue Lucia, and a daily **market** on **place Cassanyes**. At the heart of the quarter, the wide and grimy **place du Puig** is overlooked by a Vauban **barracks** converted into public housing. Just past it, at the top of a shady uphill street, is the elegant Catalan **church of St-Jacques**, dating from around 1200, on the edge of **La Miranda** gardens (July & Aug 8am–noon & 2.30–6.30pm; rest of year 8am–noon & 2.30–5.30pm), laid out on a section of the old city walls. It is from this church that the Procession de la Sanch (see opposite) sets out on Maundy (Holy) Thursday.

A twenty-minute walk away through place des Esplanades, crowning the hill that dominates the southern part of the old town, is the **Palais des Rois de Majorque** (daily: June–Sept 10am–6pm; rest of year 9am–5pm; 20F/€3.05). Although Vauban's walls surround it now, the two-storey palace and its great arcaded courtyard date originally from the late thirteenth century. Thanks to the Spanish–Moorish influence, there's a sophistication and finesse about the architecture and detailing – for instance in the beautiful marble porch to the lower of the two chapels – that you don't often find in the heavier styles of the north.

Finally, at 16 rue de l'Ange near place Arago, you'll find Perpignan's museum of art, the **Musée Rigaud** (Wed–Sun noon–7pm; 25F/€3.81), dedicated to the work of the locally born portraitist Hyacinthe Rigaud, who became official painter to the court of Versailles in the early eighteenth century. The collection also includes works by Dufy, Maillol, Picasso, Tapiès, Appel and others.

Eating, drinking and entertainment

For **eating**, there is nothing to beat the popular *Perroquet*, near the station at 1 av de Gaulle, which has a good selection of very reasonably priced Catalan dishes (closed

Wed Sept–April; menus from 55F/€8.39), with the *Expéditeurs* hotel-restaurant (see p.735; closed Sat evening & Sun; menus from 65F/€9.91) running a close second. For something smarter, head for the elegant *Côte de Théâtre*, at 7 rue du Théâtre (☎04.68.34.60.00; closed Sun and Mon lunch; menu from 148F/€22.57), which serves a splendid selection of local cuisine, or try *Les Trois Soeurs*, 2 rue Fontfroide (☎04.68.51.22.33; menus from 80F/€12.20), for elaborate seafood creations.

There are plenty of places for a leisurely **drink** in Perpignan. The *Bodega du Castillet*, in the rue Fabriques-Couvertes, is a favourite bar with the locals (and also serves good-value tapas), and there are several decent cafés on place Arago. On place de Verdun, under the plane trees in front of Le Castille, the *Grand Café de la Poste* is a great place to watch the world go by, and it is here, too, that on summer evenings you will see the Catalan dance, the *sardana*, being performed by kids, grandparents – anyone whom the spirit moves. There Is also **live street theatre and music** in the city centre every Thursday night during July and August (ask at the tourist office for details).

In midsummer, you can witness more music and general Catalan merrymaking at the festival of **Les Feux de St-Jean**, though Perpignan is better known for **La Procession de la Sanch**, the Maundy Thursday procession of penitents that goes from the church of St-Jacques to the cathedral between 3pm and 5pm.

Around Perpignan

CANET-PLAGE is the best place near Perpignan to test the waters of the Mediterranean, although there is nothing to recommend the place, except that its beach is wide and sandy and the sea is wet; take a 25-minute bus ride east from place Catalogne in Perpignan (CTP bus #1; hourly). The same goes for the other resorts around here: Port Leucate, Port Bacarès (complete with weathered Greek ferry beached to make a casino and nightclub) and St-Cyprien.

Perhaps more interesting, 15km north and served by several trains a day, is the **Château de Salses** (April, May & Oct daily 9.30am–12.30pm & 2–6pm; June & Sept 9.30am–6.30pm; July & Aug 9.30am–7pm; Nov–March 10am–noon & 2–5pm; 32F/€4.88). Built by the Catalans in the early fifteenth century, it was one of the first forts to be designed with a ground-hugging profile to protect it from artillery fire, and its superior design apparently put Vauban's nose so out of joint that he wanted it demolished, a task that proved impossible.

Another place, with not so much to see, but very moving because of its associations, is the vine-girt village of **TAUTAVEL**, 25km northwest off the St-Paul-de-Fenouillet road. In 1971 the remains of the oldest known European human being – dated to around 450,000 BC – were discovered near the village, and a reconstruction of the skull is on display in the village's **Musée de la Préhistoire** (daily: Jan–March & Oct–Dec 10am–12.30pm & 2–6pm; April–June & Sept 10am–7pm; July & Aug 9am–9pm; 45F/€6.86), along with various finds from the cave where he was unearthed, the **Caune d'Arago**, a few kilometres north, which can itself be visited in July and August (daily 10am–noon & 12.30–5.30pm) or by arrangement with the museum. The local **wines** are good, too, along with those of Estagel and Rivesaltes, and can be sampled at the numerous *domaines* in the area.

Thirteen kilometres to the south of Perpignan, on the way to the resorts of the Côte Vermeille (see p.738) and served by the same buses and trains, lies the town of **ELNE**. This small place once had the honour of seeing Hannibal camp at its walls en route for Rome, and used to be the capital of Roussillon. It was only overtaken by Perpignan when the latter became the seat of the kings of Majorca. Today, it's worth a stop for its fortified, partially Romanesque **cathedral** and extremely beautiful **cloister** (April & May daily 9.30am–5.45pm; June–Sept daily 9.30am–6.45pm; Oct daily 9.30am–noon &

2–5.45pm; Nov–March daily except Tues 10am–noon & 2–4.45pm; 27F/€4.12). Though only one side of the cloister is strictly Romanesque, immaculately carved with motifs such as foliage, lions, goats and biblical figures, the three fourteenth-century Gothic ones have been made to harmonize perfectly. It is the best introduction to Roussillon Romanesque you could want, especially if you're planning to visit places like Serrabonne and St-Michel-de-Cuxa further west. Below the cathedral there are still a few streets of the old town left, twisting back down to the drab and unremarkable modern development.

The Côte Vermeille

Known as the **Côte Vermeille**, the last few kilometres of shore before Spain, where the Pyrenees sweep down to the sea, once held a handful of attractive seaside villages. Tourism has put paid to that, though this does mean that all are well served by buses and trains from Perpignan. Travelling south, **Argelès** is the first resort you come to, but you're best off passing straight through and on to the fishing towns of **Collioure**, **Port-Vendres** and **Banyuls**.

Argelès and Collioure
ARGELÈS, the first of the resorts, with the last of the wide sandy beaches, on this stretch of coast, is lively and friendly but packed out with foreign tourists. The **Musée Casa des Albères** in rue de l'Égalité (June–Sept Mon–Fri 9am–noon & 3–6pm, Sat 9am–noon; 10F/€1.53) has some interesting exhibits of local arts and traditions.

A few kilometres south, **COLLIOURE**, set in its bay and once by far the prettiest of these places, inspired Matisse and Derain in 1905 to embark on their explosive Fauvist colour experiments; it is now overly quaint, to the point where you can follow the *Chemin de Fauvisme*, with reproductions of their works fixed to walls around the town. Palm trees line the curving beach, while behind the town, slopes of vines and olives rise to ridges crowned with ruined forts and watchtowers. The town is dominated by the **Château-Royal** (daily: July & Aug 10am–6pm; rest of year 9am–5pm; 20F/€3.05), which was founded by the Templars in the twelfth century and which has undergone numerous alterations, especially at the hands of the kings of Majorca and Aragon in the fourteenth century and again after the Treaty of the Pyrenees gave Collioure to France. Today, it is largely given over to summertime exhibitions. Collioure's other landmark is the distinctive round belfry of the seventeenth-century **church of Notre-Dame-des-Anges** (daily 9am–noon & 2–6pm), formerly the harbour lighthouse; inside the nave are some exuberant Baroque altarpieces. Behind it two small **beaches** are divided by a causeway leading to the **chapel of St-Vincent**, built on what used to be a rocky islet, while to the left a concrete path follows the rocky shore to the bay of **Le Racou** back towards Argelès.

Behind the château lies the **old harbour**, where half a dozen brightly painted lateen-rigged fishing boats are often beached, all that remains of Collioure's traditional fleet. The attractive surrounding streets of pink- and beige-washed houses are the centre of tourist activity. The **tourist office** is here on place de 18-Juin (July & Aug daily 9am–8pm; rest of year Mon–Sat 9am–noon & 2–6.30pm; ☎04.68.82.15.47, *www.little-france.com/collioure*). Two pleasant and comfortable places to **stay** are *Le Boramar* (☎04.68.82.07.06; ③; closed Nov–April) and the nearby *Triton*, 1 rue Jean-Bart (☎04.68.98.39.39, fax 04.68.82.11.32; ③). The best **campsite** is the seaside *La Girelle* (☎04.68.81.25.56, fax 04.68.81.87.02; closed Oct–March), but there are numerous others in the area, should it be full. Rue Camille-Pelletan, leading out to the harbour, has some cafés and **restaurants**. Off the main strip, try *El Capillo*, 22 rue St-Vincent (menus from 98F/€14.95), or the smarter *La Marinade*, on place 18-Juin (from 120F/€18.30), both serving Catalan dishes.

Port-Vendres and Banyuls

PORT-VENDRES, 3km further down the coast, is a functional sort of place. Although the harbour has never been as busy as it was in the nineteenth century, with colonial trade and ferries from North Africa, it still lands more fish than any other place on this stretch of coast. The boats come in between about 4.30pm and 6pm every day except Sunday; you can watch them unload and auction the catch on the dock at the far end of the harbour. Otherwise, there is little to see here.

South towards **BANYULS**, 7km further on, where the **GR10** finally comes down to the sea, the road winds through attractive scenery, with the Albères hills rising steeply on the right. The town itself, built round a broad sweep of pebble beach, is pleasant but lacks the charm of Collioure and the energy of more popular resorts. There are, however, several things to see and do there. One is the seafront **aquarium** of the Laboratoire Arago (daily: July & Aug 9am–noon & 2–10pm; rest of year 9am–noon & 2–6.30pm; 24F/€3.66), run by the Sorbonne's marine biology department, whose tanks contain a comprehensive collection of the region's fish and submarine life. Also worth a look are the works of the sculptor **Aristide Maillol**, who was born in Banyuls; they can be seen in front of the Mairie and on the port, as well as at the **museum** at Mas Maillol, 4km outside the town, where he is buried (daily: May–Sept 10am–noon & 4–7pm; rest of year 10am–noon & 2–5pm; 20F/€3.05). You could also sample the dark, full-bodied Banyuls **wine**, an *appellation* which, apart from Banyuls itself, applies only to the vineyards of Collioure, Port-Vendres and Cerbère. The best place to do this is the Cellier des Templiers, on route du Mas-Reig, just under the rail line at the foot of the steep brown-stone terraces of Banyuls' own vineyards (April–Oct daily 9am–7pm; rest of year Mon–Sat 9am–noon & 2–6pm).

For further information consult the **tourist office** opposite the Hôtel de Ville on the seafront (July & Aug daily 9.30am–12.30pm & 2.30–7pm; rest of year Tues–Sat 9.30am–12.30pm & 2–6.30pm; ☎04.68.88.31.58). Of the cheaper **hotels**, the best is *Le Manoir*, 20 rue de Maréchal-Joffre (☎04.68.88.32.98; ④; closed Nov & Dec), and there is a municipal **campsite** on avenue Guy Malé (☎04.68.88.32.13; closed mid-Oct to March). For somewhere to **eat**, try *Chez Rosa*, at 22 rue St-Pierre, which serves hearty fare at reasonable prices (from 85F/€12.96); alternatively, head for the more upmarket *La Pergola* (78F/€11.90) and *Al Fanal* (95F/€14.49), both on seafront avenue du Fontaulé.

A magnificent winding drive snakes up from Banyuls through the vineyards to the **Tour Madeloc**, a watchtower built by Jaime I of Majorca at the end of the thirteenth century on the crest of a ridge at about 650m. On a clear day, you can see down into Spain, along the coast, across to Montpellier and over the Corbières, with the castles of Quéribus and Peyrepertuse (see pp.780–1) easily visible.

Céret and the valley of the Tech

The first stop on the D115, the main road which follows the **Tech valley** inland all the way up to the Spanish border at Prats-de-Mollo, is **CÉRET**, capital of the Vallespir region, and served like the rest of the valley by regular buses from Perpignan's *gare routière*. It is a delightful place, friendly and bustling, with a wonderfully shady old town overhung by huge plane trees. The streets are typically narrow and winding, opening onto small squares like the **place des Neuf-Jets**, so called because of its trickling fountain. There's a large and varied Saturday **market**, which spills out of place Pablo-Picasso into the main street, avenue d'Espagne, where two remnants of the medieval walls, the **Porte de France** and **Porte d'Espagne**, are visible. In summer, Céret is also a big centre for *corridas*; the arena is on the other side of town from the market, out towards the Amélie-les-Bains road. Other high points include the Easter Sunday procession of the Resurrected Christ, at the time of year when Céret's famous cherry harvest is also getting under way. And there is an international *sardana* jamboree on the penultimate Sunday in August.

Céret's main sight, however, is the remarkable **Musée d'Art Moderne** (May to mid-June & mid-Sept to Oct daily 10am–6pm; mid-June to mid-Sept daily 10am–7pm; Nov–March daily except Tues 10am–6pm; 35F/€5.34), just off boulevard Maréchal-Joffre. In the early years of this century, Céret's charms, coupled with the presence here of the Catalan artist and sculptor Manolo, drew a number of avant-garde artists to the town, including Matisse and Picasso, who personally dedicated a number of pictures to the museum; it also contains work by Chagall, Dalí and Dufy, among others. Among the Picassos is a marvellous series of ceramic bowls illustrating bullfighting scenes and a sketch of a *sardana*.

You can get more information on the *corridas* and other aspects of the town from the **tourist office** on avenue Clemenceau (July & Aug Mon–Sat 9am–12.30pm & 2–7pm, Sun 10am–12.30pm; rest of year Mon–Fri 10am–noon & 2–5pm, Sat 10am–noon; ☎04.68.87.00.53, *www.ot-Ceret.fr*). If you wish to **stay**, try the very attractive and reasonably priced *Hôtel Vidal* in the place du 4-Septembre (☎04.68.87.00.85, fax 04.68.87.62.33; ③; restaurant from 80F/€12.20). For campers, there's a municipal **campsite** just out of town on the Maureillas road.

Eating options include a good, cheap restaurant-crêperie, *Le Pied dans le Plat*, on place des Neuf-Jets, while gourmets with money to spare can try the best food for miles around at *Les Feuillants* (☎04.68.87.37.88; closed Sun evening & Mon; from 275F/€41.94), serving utterly delicious Catalan cuisine.

Amélie-les-Bains and Arles-sur-Tech

West of Céret, past the leaping single span of its fourteenth-century **Pont du Diable**, the view opens north towards the towering imminence of the Canigou Massif. **AMÉLIE-LES-BAINS**, the next place you come to, is a rather stodgy health spa for the elderly and rheumatic, and is hardly worth a stop. If an **overnight stay** is necessary, however, you're best off heading for the attractive *Hôtel La Chaumière* at 2 av du Vallespir (☎04.68.39.05.35; ②), right on the river in the middle of town.

ARLES-SUR-TECH, 4km up the valley, is a more interesting proposition. It has a beautiful Romanesque **Abbey** (daily: March–June, Sept–Nov 10am–noon & 2–6pm; July & Aug Mon–Fri 8am–noon & 2–7pm, Sat 2–7pm; Dec–Feb by appointment through the tourist office – see below; 20F/€3.05), whose Carolingian origins in the ninth century are thought to account for its back-to-front alignment of altar at the west end and the entrance at the east. The massive interior is impressive, but the abbey's most renowned feature is the **cloister**, whose pointed white marble arches and twin columns prefigure the Gothic, showing its relative lateness compared to other examples of Romanesque in the region, like Serrabonne (see opposite). Twin towers flank the church, while against the wall outside the east front – whose plainness is beautifully relieved, as the sun turns, by the shadow of blind arcading – stands a very ancient (fourth- or fifth-century) sarcophagus, known as the **Ste Tombe**, which has the mysterious and scientifically inexplicable habit of slowly filling with very pure water. Every year, on 30 July, when Arles celebrates its fête dedicated to SS Abdon and Sennen, the water is siphoned out and distributed after Mass to the pilgrims who have come to worship. The town's other points of interest include the probably prehistoric **Fête de l'Ours**, a festival designed to exorcize human fear of the bear, traditionally held at the end of February when the bears woke from their winter hibernation. There is also a torchlight **Procession de la Sanch** at Easter. The **GR10** passes through Arles, climbing north towards the Cortalets refuge on Canigou and south towards the Roc de France.

The **tourist office** (Mon–Sat 9am–noon & 2–6pm; ☎04.68.39.11.99) is in rue Barjau. Your best **accommodation** option is the attractive *Hôtel les Glycines* on rue du Jeu-de-

Paume (☎04.68.39.10.09; ④), with a good restaurant (from 90F/€13.73) and wisteria-shaded terrace. There's a **campsite** on the west side of town.

A couple of kilometres out of Arles, on the road to Prats-de-Mollo, is the entrance to the **Gorges de la Fou**, some 2km in length, very narrow and up to 250m deep (Easter–Oct 10am–6pm; closed during bad weather; ☎04.68.39.16.21; 30F/€4.58). It's spectacular, but unfortunately something of a tourist trap, with a car park, admission charge, snacks and a metal catwalk all along the bottom of the gorge.

Prats-de-Mollo and the Spanish frontier

After the gorge, the road climbs on towards the border, between valley sides thick with walnut, oak and sweet chestnut, to **PRATS-DE-MOLLO**. Prats is the last French town before the border with Spain, and has a very Spanish atmosphere. Most of the population seems to sit around or play *pétanque* in **El Firal**, the main square. It's surprisingly unspoiled for a border town, and its **ville haute** makes for a wonderful wander, with steep cobbled streets and a weather-worn grey church with marvellous ironwork on the door under the porch. The encircling walls were rebuilt in the seventeenth century after the suppression of a local revolt against the taxation newly imposed by Louis XIV after the Treaty of the Pyrenees brought these lands under his sway. The **Fort Lagarde** (April–June 2–6pm; July & Aug 10am–7pm; Sept–March 2–5pm; 20F/€3.05), on the heights above the town, also dates from this period, built to keep the local population in check as much as keeping the Spanish out. For **accommodation**, try the *Bellevue* (☎04.68.39.72.48; ③; closed Nov–March), overlooking El Firal. If you're **camping**, head for the municipal site 1km along the road towards La Preste.

From Prats-de-Mollo it is only 13km to the border on the **Col d'Ares**. The next place of any size on the other side of the border is Camprodon, a village about 18km away. Alternatively, if you're feeling energetic, you can bus or hitch the 8km north to the spa town of La Preste, and then walk over the **Col Prégon**. It's about an hour's steep climb to the top, followed by another hour's more gentle descent down to the small village of Espinavell – leave the road at the first turning on the right before you get into La Preste, and then take the path from La Forge.

From the Tech to the Têt

The only practical route between the **valleys of the Tech and the Têt**, especially if you're hitching, is the D618 across the eastern spurs of Canigou from Amélie-les-Bains to Bouleternère. It's 43 slow kilometres of mountain road, twisting and climbing through magnificent woods of holm oak, cork oak, regular oak, chestnut, ash and cherry, with explosions of yellow broom and tangles of wild honeysuckle, past isolated half-derelict farms or *mas*, some still tenanted by survivors of the post-1968 migration from the towns. About halfway along, the three-house hamlet of **BELPUIG** stands on the road. One of its buildings is the **Chapelle de la Trinité**, a tiny, dark Romanesque church in grey and yellow stone with elaborate doors and a particularly fine crucifix from the twelfth century. Past the cemetery and up the hill beside a pine plantation, a path climbs to the ruined **Château de Belpuig**, some fifteen minutes' walk from the road with long-range views over the surrounding country.

From here the road descends into the valley bottom, through the pretty hamlet of Boule d'Amont, before climbing again to the remarkable **Prieuré de Serrabonne** (daily 10am–6pm; 10F/€1.53), some 4km up an asphalt lane above the road, one of the finest examples – perhaps the finest – of Roussillon Romanesque, and offering spectacular views over the rocky Boulès valley and into the valley of the Têt. The interior of the church (consecrated in 1151) is breathtakingly simple, making the beautiful carvings on the capitals of the pillars in the tribune even more striking: the carvings vividly depict lions, centaurs, griffins and human figures with oriental faces and haircuts –

motifs brought back from the Crusades – all in the local pink marble. The altar is made of the same stone, as are the pillars and equally elaborate capitals of the cloister, which is set to one side of the church on a high terrace. Despite the rigours of monastic life here – all abandoned now – the settlement was well developed, and the remains of terraced cultivation and irrigation systems are still visible.

The valley of the Têt and the Pic du Canigou

The upper part of the **Têt valley**, known as the **Pays de Conflent**, is utterly dominated by the **Pic du Canigou**. The valley bottoms are lush with peach and apple orchards – with the possibility of work as a picker from June onwards – but the mountain presides over all, vast and uncompromising.

Prades

The valley capital is **PRADES**, easily accessible by train and bus on the Perpignan–Villefranche–La Tour-de-Carol route, and the obvious starting point for all excursions in the Canigou region. It's an attractive place, although there are no great sights beyond the **church of St-Pierre** in the town centre, and it enjoys a standing way out of proportion to its size or economic power. This is largely thanks to the Catalan cellist Pau (Pablo) Casals, who set up home here as an exile and fierce opponent of the Franco regime in Spain. In 1950 he instituted the internationally renowned **music festival** now held every year in the abbey of St-Michel-de-Cuxa (see below) from late July to the middle of August. Today he is commemorated in a small **museum** (summer Mon–Sat 9am–noon & 2–6pm; winter Mon–Fri 9am–noon & 2–5pm; free). Prades is also a centre of ardent Catalan feeling, hosting a Catalan university in August and boasting the first Catalan-language primary school in France.

The **tourist office** at 4 rue Victor-Hugo (July & Aug Mon–Sat 9am–12.30pm & 2–7pm, Sun 9am–noon; rest of year Mon–Fri 9am–noon & 2–5pm; ☎04.68.05.41.02, *www.prades.com*) is a mine of information about the area and can sort out advance bookings for the music festival. For **accommodation**, try the *Hostalrich* (☎04.68.96.05.38, fax 04.68.96.00.73; ①), or the friendly and spotlessly clean *Les Glycines* (☎04.68.96.51.65, fax 04.68.96.45.57; ④), both on avenue de-Gaulle, at the south end of rue Victor-Hugo. If you have a car, you could try the delightful *Hôtel St Joseph*, across the river in Molitg-les-Bains (☎04.68.05.02.11, fax 04.68.05.05.23; ②), which has an excellent restaurant (from 80F/€12.20). The municipal **campsite** (☎04.68.96.29.83; closed Nov–April) is by the river on the road to Molitg.

Three kilometres south of Prades is one of the loveliest abbeys in the country, **St-Michel-de-Cuxa** (May–Sept Mon–Sat 9.30–11.50am & 2–6pm, Sun 2–6pm; rest of year Mon–Sat 9.30–11.50am & 2–5pm, Sun 2–5pm; 20F/€3.05), dating from around 1000. Although it was mutilated after the Revolution it is still beautiful, with its crenellated tower silhouetted against the wooded slopes of Canigou. The bare stone crypt and church – the altar slab was rediscovered doing duty as a balcony on a house in the village of Vinça – are impressive enough, but the glory of the place is the **cloister**. Although some of the capitals were shipped off to the Cloisters Museum in New York early in the twentieth century, those that remain are a feast for the eyes. Carved in the twelfth century in rose-pink marble from Villefranche, they are decorated with exact and highly stylized human, animal and vegetable motifs. The monastery is still inhabited by a small community of Benedictines from Monserrat in Spain.

Vernet-les-Bains and around

A quiet and not unpleasant little spa, **VERNET-LES-BAINS**, 15km along the D27 from Cuxa, can make a useful base for picking up provisions and information to climb the Pic

Canigou. It has a **tourist office** in place de la Mairie (Mon–Fri 9am–noon & 2–6pm; ☎04.68.05.55.35) and plenty of **eating and drinking** possibilities in the main square, place de la République. The town's two-star **hotels** offer a range of amenities and all are good value: two of the best are *Eden*, 2 promenade du Cady (☎04.68.05.54.09, fax 04.58.05.60.50; ④), and the *Princess*, rue de Lavandiers (☎04.68.05.56.22, fax 04.58.05.62.45; ④). There are several **campsites** around Vernet and a **gîte d'étape** (☎04.68.05.51.30) just up the road in Casteil. For a **meal**, try the popular *Le Pommier* in placette du Cady, just off the main square (from 60F/€9.15).

Just 2km from Vernet-les-Bains, or a half-hour walk above the hamlet of Casteil, is the stunning abbey of **St-Martin-du-Canigou**. Resurrected from its ruins at the turn of the century, the monastery occupies a narrow promontory of rock at over 1000m altitude. Quiet and serene, it is surrounded by the deep shade of chestnut and oak woods, and above it rise the precipitous slopes and eroded pinnacles of Canigou. Below, the ground drops sheer into the ravine of the Cady stream that rushes down from the Col de Jou. The buildings are visitable, in silent tours (hourly: June to mid-Sept 10am–noon & 2–5pm; rest of year 10am–noon & 2.30–4.30pm; 20F/€3.05). What you see is a beautiful little garden and cloister overlooking the ravine, a low dark atmospheric chapel beneath the church and the church itself. Founded in the tenth century, St-Martin was the inspiration for the Romanesque architecture of the region. The graves of the founder, Count Guifred of Cerdagne, and his wife lie in the rock by the church door.

From the reception building, a **path** leads up to a rocky viewpoint from which you can look down on the monastery and away across the valley to the surrounding mountains. As you go up, you pass a signpost to Moura on a path which leads first to the Col de Segalès on the GR10, then, on the HRP, to the *Cabane Arago* and finally to the summit of Canigou (see below). For a different route back to Casteil, a path drops down into the Cady ravine just at the start of the monastery buildings.

The Pic du Canigou

You can get at least part of the way up the **Pic du Canigou** by car or you can follow the trail heading up the river valley from Vernet on foot. **Cars** – and you would be well advised not to try it in a much-loved saloon – can get as far as the *Chalet des Cortalets* refuge either by the track from Villerach or the even steeper and rougher mining road that begins by the *Al Pouncy* **campsite** near Fillols and passes the *Refuge de Balatg* and the now vandalized *Cabane des Cortalets*, where herds of cows and horses graze untended. (They are the best barometer of mountain weather, descending to lower altitudes when bad weather is imminent.) Both routes take about an hour. Alternatively, you could **rent a jeep** and driver from Amalric (☎04.68.96.26.47) or Calas (☎60.46.05.27.08) in Prades, or Taurigna in Vernet-les-Bains (☎04.68.05.54.39) and Fillols (☎04.68.05.63.06). For **walkers**, the standard ascent is from Vernet on a path that begins about 1km along the road to Fillols, joining up with the **GR10** at the *Refuge de Bonaigua* (about 3hr) which you leave (about 90min) below the **Pic Joffre** to follow the HRP up the ridge to the summit (about 1hr). It is not for faint hearts, because the final ascent up a chimney is rather exposed. There is a five-hour alternative, starting from Casteil, passing the *Refuge Mariailles* (☎04.68.67.67.07; open all year; food served) on the GR10, then following the HRP for the last stretch via the *Cabane Arago*.

From the *Chalet des Cortalets* (☎04.68.96.36.19; closed Nov–April), which has a restaurant, it's an easy ninety-minute walk to the top. Strike west through the last trees, past a little lake, with a magnificent view into the cirque below the summit, round the back of the Pic Joffre, and up the long stony ridge to the cross and Catalan flag that crown the summit.

Although the **ascent** by this route is straightforward in good weather, you should be properly shod and clothed and have good large-scale maps. If you are not experienced and encounter frozen snow, turn back: a German couple slid to their deaths on the slopes between Pic Joffre and the summit in 1991. Midsummer is a great time to do the climb. On the night of June 23, which often coincides with the full moon, Catalans for kilometres around, including half the population of Barcelona, gather on the top to light the bonfire from which a flame is carried to kindle all the *feux de St-Jean* of the Catalan villages, though the scene around the refuge can be pretty horrendous, with tents, ghetto blasters and litter galore.

Villefranche-de-Conflent and the Petit Train Jaune

A medieval garrison town suffering from arrested development, **VILLEFRANCHE-DE-CONFLENT**, 6km up the Têt from Prades, is a tourist classic and lives off it, but it is nevertheless an interesting place. Founded around 1100 by the counts of Cerdagne to bar the road to Moorish invaders, remodelled by Vauban in the seventeenth century after rebelling against annexation by France, its streets and fortifications have remained untouched by subsequent development. Worth a look is the **church of St-Jacques**, with a primitively carved thirteenth-century baptismal font just inside the door, and you can walk the **walls** for a fee (daily: Feb, March, Nov & Dec 2–5pm; April, May, Sept & Oct 10am–noon & 2–6pm; June 10am–7pm; July & Aug 10am–8pm; 20F/€3.05). If you do so, you will see why Vauban constructed the **Libéria fortress** on the heights overlooking the town to protect it from "aerial" bombardment. Getting up to the Libéria (daily: June–Sept 9am–8pm; rest of year 10am–6pm; 30F/€4.58) involves climbing a stairway of a thousand steps beginning just across the old bridge and rail line at the end of rue St-Pierre. If you don't fancy the climb, look for the free minibus leaving from near the town's main gate.

The **tourist office** (Feb–Dec daily 10am–12.30 & 2–5.30pm; ☎04.68.96.22.96) is in place d'Église. For **accommodation**, try *Le Vauban* (☎04.68.96.18.03; ②; closed Oct–March) next door, or the magnificent old *Auberge du Cédre* (☎04.68.96.05.05; ③; closed Nov–April), situated just east of the old walls.

Villefranche is the terminus for trains from Perpignan. From here up to **La Tour-de-Carol** on the Spanish frontier, transport is by SNCF bus, or, far nicer, the narrow-gauge **Petit Train Jaune**, which climbs to the valley head at a pace that allows you a walker's or cyclist's proximity to the scenery, especially in summer when some of the carriages are open-air (late May to Sept 4–6 daily; ☎04.68.96.56.62, *www.ter.sncf.fr/trjaune*; 98F/€14.95).

On up the Têt

Just beyond Thuès-Entre-Valls, southwest of Villefranche on the left of the main N116, the wild wooded canyon of the **Gorges de la Carança** cuts south into the mountains towards Spain. A path follows the gorge to a junction with the GR10 at the refuge of the *Ras de la Carança* (3–4hr), while a further path continues on to meet the HRP on the frontier in another four hours.

At Fontpédrouse, 5km beyond Thuès, a road branches south across the river and up a grassy spur above the River Aigues towards the village of Prat-Balaguer. From the top of the rise directly opposite Fontpédrouse, a path leads down to the Aigues where water from **hot springs** forms three separate pools at different temperatures, where you can skinny-dip for free.

Another 10km up the main road brings you onto the wide **plateau of the Cerdagne**, whose once powerful counts controlled lands from Barcelona to Roussillon and endowed the monasteries of St-Michel-de-Cuxa, St-Martin-du-Canigou and Ripoll, now well inside Spain. It's an area that has never been sure whether it is Spanish or French. After the French annexation of Roussillon, it was partitioned, with Spain retaining – as it does today – the enclave of Lliva.

The first place you come to is the little garrison town of **MONT-LOUIS**, built by Vauban in 1679 and still used as a base for paratroops and marines. There isn't much to see, but it is a far pleasanter place to stay than the monstrous ski resort of Font-Romeu, just down the road. There's a **tourist office** (July & Aug daily 9.30am–noon & 2–7pm; rest of year Tues–Sat 10am–noon & 2–6pm; ☎04.68.04.21.97) and a good but expensive **hotel**, *La Taverne*, in rue Victor Hugo (☎04.68.04.23.67, fax 04.68.04.13.35; ④). **Campers** should head for the site at Pla de Barres, 3km away on the road to the Lac des Bouillousses (☎04.68.04.21.18; closed mid-Sept to mid-June), or there's a **gîte d'étape** at La Cassagne farm (☎04.68.04.21.40; ①), half an hour back down the main road. For **food**, *Lou Roubaillou*, near the barracks in rue des Écoles Laïques, serves up excellent mountain produce (menus 125–195F/€19.06–29.74).

Of things to do round about, there is a good four-hour walk from the pretty mountain village of **EYNE** up a valley renowned for its flowers and medicinal plants to the Col d'Eyne, and numerous walks in the **Carlit Massif** around the **Lac des Bouillousses** – where there's a CAF refuge (☎04.68.04.20.76), though the lake itself and parts accessible by car get very crowded in season. The region's curiosity is the **four solaire**, or solar power station (1hr guided tours daily: summer 10am–6.30pm, winter 10am–12.30pm & 2–6pm; 30F/€4.58), at **ODEILLO** just below Font-Romeu, although the most impressive part of this, a screen composed of thousands of mirrors, can in fact be seen from the road.

travel details

Trains

Bayonne to: Biarritz (13 daily; 10–15min); Bordeaux (8–9 daily; 1hr 40min–2hr); Boussens (4 daily; 3hr); Cambo-les-Bains (3–5 daily; 20min); Hendaye (13 daily; 35min); Lannemazan (4 daily; 2hr 40min); Lourdes (5–7 daily; 1hr 45min); Montréjeau (4 daily; 2hr 50min); Orthez (5–6 daily; 50min); Pau (5–7 daily; 1hr 15min); St-Gaudens (4 daily; 3hr); St-Jean-de-Luz (13 daily; 30min); St-Jean-Pied-de-Port (4–5 daily; 1hr); Tarbes (5–7 daily; 2hr); Toulouse (4–5 daily; 3hr 50min–4hr 10min).

Foix to: Ax-les-Thermes (5 daily; 45min); Barcelona (4 daily; 5hr 15min–6hr); Latour-de-Carol (5 daily; 1hr 40min–2hr); Tarascon (several daily; 20min); Toulouse (several daily; 40min–1hr).

Luchon to: Montréjeau (2 daily; 40min); Toulouse (2 daily; 2hr).

Montréjeau to: Luchon (2 daily; 40 min); Toulouse (10–13 daily; 1hr 20min).

Pau to: Bordeaux (7–9 daily; 2hr 10min–2hr 30min); Oloron-Ste-Marie (4–6 daily; 35min).

Perpignan to: Argelès (hourly; 20min); Banyuls (hourly; 40min); Barcelona (2–3 daily; 2hr 15min–5hr); Cerbère (hourly; 50min); Collioure (hourly; 25min); Elne (hourly; 10min); Leucate (hourly; 25min); Narbonne (hourly; 40min); Port-Bou (7–8 daily; 50min); Port-la-Nouvelle (hourly; 35min); Port-Vendres (hourly; 30min); Prades (7 daily; 40min); Rivesaltes (hourly; 10min); Salses (hourly; 15min); Villefranche-de-Conflent (7 daily; 40min).

Quillan to: Carcassonne (1–2 daily; 1hr); Limoux (1–2 daily; 30min).

Tarbes to: Bordeaux (6–7 daily; 3hr); Dax (6–7 daily; 1hr 30min); Lourdes (8–9 daily; 20min).

Buses

Bayonne to: Biarritz (every 10–20min on STAB; 15–20min); Cambo-les-Bains (several daily; 40min); Capbreton (hourly; 30min); Hendaye (3–7 daily; 30min); San Sebastian (1 daily Mon–Sat on ATCRB; 1hr 45min); St-Jean-de-Luz (6–14 daily on ATCRB; 40min).

Biarritz to: Hendaye (5–7 daily; 30min); Orthez (3 daily; 1hr 45min); Pau (3–4 daily; 2hr 30min); St-Jean-de-Luz (11–16 daily; 25min); Salies-de-Béarn (4 daily; 1hr 20min).

Foix to: Ax-les-Thermes (7–8 daily Mon–Sat; 1hr); Carcassonne (1 daily Mon–Sat; 2hr 35min); Lavelanet (1 daily Mon–Sat; 35min); Mirepoix (1 daily Mon–Sat; 1hr 30min); Pamiers (4–6 daily; 25min); Quillan (1 daily; 3hr); Tarascon (7 daily Mon–Sat; 20min); Toulouse (4–6 daily; 1hr 50min).

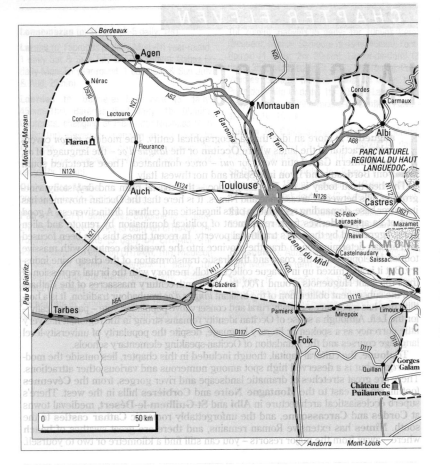

good introduction to the area, a hectic modern town impressive both for its Roman past and for some scattered attractions – the **Pont du Gard** for one – nearby. **Montpellier**, also, is worth a day or two, not so much for any historical attractions as for a heady vibrancy and ease of access to the ancient villages, churches and fine scenery of the upper **Hérault valley**. This was the part of Languedoc most affected by the spread of Protestantism in the sixteenth century, an experience that has marked the region's character more than any other. The Protestants, with their attachment to rationality and self-improvement, espoused the cause of French over Occitan, supported the Revolution and the Republic, fought Napoléon III's coup against the 1848 Revolution and adhered to the anticlerical and socialist movement under the Third Republic. They dominated the local textile industry in the nineteenth century and, interestingly, were extremely active in the Resistance to the Nazis.

They also suffered a great deal for their cause, as did the whole region. After the Revocation in 1685 of the Edict of Nantes – the treaty which had restored religious toleration at the end of the sixteenth century – persecution drove their most committed supporters, especially in the Cévennes to the north, to form clandestine *assemblées du*

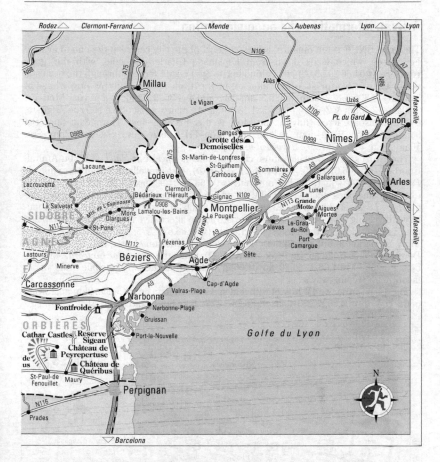

Désert, and finally, in 1702, to take up arms in the first guerrilla war of modern times, La Guerre des Camisards, conflicts which still resonate in the minds of both Huguenot and Catholic families.

Nîmes and around

On the border between Provence and Languedoc, the name of **NÎMES** is inescapably linked to two things – denim and Rome. The latter's influence is highly visible in some of the most extensive Roman remains in Europe, while the former (*de Nîmes*), equally visible on the backsides of the populace, was first manufactured in the city's textile mills, and exported to the southern USA in the nineteenth century to clothe slaves. It's worth a visit, in part for the ruins and, nowadays, for the city's new-found energy and direction, enlisting the services of a galaxy of architects and designers – including Norman Foster, Jean Nouvel and Philippe Starck – in a bid to wrest southern supremacy from neighbouring Montpellier.

Arrival, information and accommodation

The **gare SNCF** is ten minutes' walk southeast of the city centre at the end of avenue Feuchères, which leads down from Esplanade Charles-de-Gaulle, with the **gare routière** (☎04.66.29.52.00) just behind in rue Ste-Félicité (access through the train station). There's a **tourist office** annexe in the train station (July & Aug Mon–Sat 9.30am–12.30pm & 2–6pm, Sun 9.30am–12.30pm & 1.30–3.30pm; rest of year Mon–Fri 9.30am–12.30pm & 2–6pm; ☎04.66.84.18.13), and a main tourist office at 6 rue Auguste, by the Maison Carrée (July & Aug Mon–Wed & Fri 8am–8pm, Thurs 8am–9pm, Sat 9am–7pm, Sun 10am–6pm; rest of year Mon–Fri 8.30am–7pm, Sat 9am–7pm, Sun 10am–6pm; ☎04.66.67.29.11, *www.ot-nimes.fr*).

There are several decent **hotels**: clean and economical *Cat Hôtel*, at 22 bd Amiral-Courbet (☎04.66.67.22.85, fax 04.66.21.57.51; ②), is a travellers' favourite, while *de Provence*, at 5/7 square de la Couronne (☎04.66.76.04.92, fax 04.66.36.77.99; ②), has excellent amenities, such as cable TV, for its price. The old-fashioned but rather delightful *Hôtel Lisita*, at 2bis bd des Arènes (☎04.66.67.66.20, fax 04.66.76.22.30; ③), is popular with visiting bullfighters, and another attractive alternative is the *Central*, at 2 place du Château, close to the Protestant church (☎04.66.67.27.75, fax 04.66.21.77.79; ④). More upmarket is the atmospheric *Royal*, near the Maison Carrée at 3 bd Alphonse-Daudet (☎04.66.67.28.36, fax 04.66.21.68.97; ④), while the *Imperator Concorde*, on quai de la Fontaine (☎04.66.21.90.30, fax 04.66.67.70.25; ⑤), is the top of the pile – and an old favourite of Hemingway's.

There's an attractive **HI hostel** with tent space on chemin de la Cigale, 2km northwest of the centre (☎04.66.23.25.04, fax 04.66.23.84.27); take bus #2 direction "Alès/Villeverte"

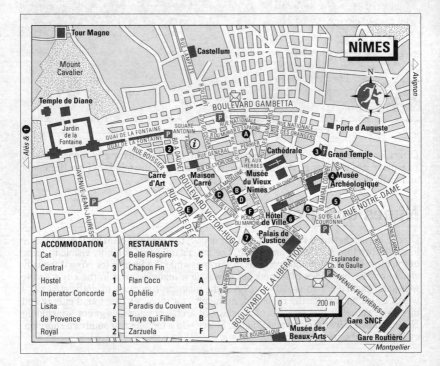

ACCOMMODATION		RESTAURANTS	
Cat	4	Belle Respire	C
Central	3	Chapon Fin	E
Hostel	1	Flan Coco	A
Imperator Concorde	6	Ophélie	D
Lisita	7	Paradis du Couvent	G
de Provence	5	Truye qui Filhe	B
Royal	2	Zarzuela	F

from the *gare SNCF* to stop "Stade" – the last bus goes at 8pm. The municipal **campsite** (☎04.66.38.09.21) is on rte de Générac, 5km south of the city centre, beyond the new Stade Costières and the *autoroute*.

The City

Most of what you'll want to see is contained within the boulevards de la Libération, Amiral-Courbet, Gambetta and Victor-Hugo, and there is much pleasure to be had from just wandering the narrow lanes that they enclose, discovering unexpected squares with their fountains and cafés. The focal point of the city, the first-century Roman arena, known as **Les Arènes** (daily: July & Aug 9am–6.30pm; rest of year 9am–noon & 2–5pm; closed during special events; 28F/€4.27), lies at the junction of boulevards de la Libération and Victor-Hugo. One of the best-preserved Roman arenas anywhere, its arcaded two-storey facade conceals massive interior vaulting, riddled with corridors and supporting raked tiers of seats with a capacity of more than 20,000 spectators, whose staple fare was the blood and guts of gladiatorial combat. When Rome's sway was broken by the barbarian invasions, the arena became a fortress and eventually a slum, home to an incredible 2000 people when it was cleared in the early 1800s. Today it has recovered something of its former role, with the passionate summer crowds still turning out for some real-life blood-letting – Nîmes is the premier European bullfighting scene outside Spain.

Behind the arena, through the beautiful little place du Marché, rue Fresque leads towards the city's other famous landmark, the **Maison Carrée** (daily: July & Aug 9am–noon & 2.30–7pm; rest of year 9am–12.30pm & 2–6pm; free), a neat, jewel-like temple, celebrated for its integrity and harmony of proportion. Built in 5 AD, it is dedicated to the adopted sons of Emperor Augustus – all part of the business of blowing up the imperial personality cult. No surprise, then, that Napoléon, with his love of flummery and ennobling his cronies to boost his own legitimacy, should have taken it as the model for the church of the Madeleine in Paris. The temple stands in its own small square opposite rue Auguste, where the Roman forum used to be. Around it are scattered pieces of Roman masonry. On the north side of place de la Maison Carrée, there's a new example of French architectural boldness, the **Carrée d'Art**, by English architect Norman Foster. In spite of its size, this box of glass, aluminium and concrete sits modestly among the ancient roofs of Nîmes, its slender portico echoing that of the Roman temple opposite. Light pours in through walls and roof, giving it a grace and weightlessness that makes it not in the least incongruous. Housed within the Carrée d'Art is the excellent **Musée d'Art Contemporain** (Tues–Sun 11am–6pm; 28F/€4.27), containing an impressive collection of French and Western European art of the last four decades. There is a roof-terrace café at the top, overlooking the Maison Carrée.

Though already a prosperous city on the Via Domitia, the main Roman road from Italy to Spain, constructed in 118 BC, Nîmes did especially well under Augustus. He gave the city its walls, remnants of which surface here and there, and its gates, as the inscription on the surviving **Porte d'Auguste** at the end of rue Nationale – the Roman main street – records. He also, indirectly, gave it the chained crocodile of its coat of arms. The device was copied from an Augustan coin struck to commemorate his defeat of Antony and Cleopatra after he settled veterans of that campaign on the surrounding land.

Running back east into the old quarter from the Maison Carrée, **rue de l'Horloge** leads to the delightful **place aux Herbes**, with two or three cafés and bars and a fine twelfth-century house on the corner of rue de la Madeleine. In the former bishop's palace, the **Musée du Vieux Nîmes** (daily 11am–6pm; 28F/€4.27) has displays of Renaissance furnishings and decor and documents to do with local history. Opposite,

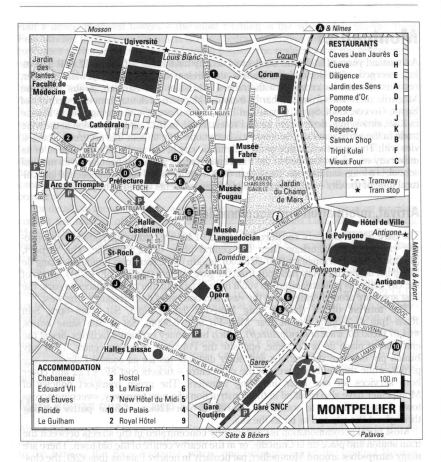

RESTAURANTS
Caves Jean Jaurès **G**
Cueva **H**
Diligence **E**
Jardin des Sens **A**
Pomme d'Or **D**
Popote **I**
Posada **J**
Regency **K**
Salmon Shop **B**
Tripti Kulai **F**
Vieux Four **C**

--- Tramway
★ Tram stop

ACCOMMODATION

Chabaneau	3	Hostel	1
Edouard VII	8	Le Mistral	6
des Étuves	7	New Hôtel du Midi	5
Floride	10	du Palais	4
Le Guilham	2	Royal Hôtel	9

MONTPELLIER

0   100 m

New Hôtel du Midi, 22 bd Victor-Hugo (☎04.67.92.69.61, fax 04.67.92.73.63, *www.new-hotel.com*). Very luxurious but good-value option right on the Comédie, in the old Grand Hôtel du Midi building. ⑥.

du Palais, 3 rue du Palais (☎04.67.60.47.38, fax 04.67.60.40.23). Tastefully renovated eighteenth-century mansion on the west side of the old town. ④.

Royal Hôtel, 8 rue Maguelone (☎04.67.92.13.36, fax 04.67.99.89.88, *www.hotel-centre-ville.fr*). Ageing but well-cared-for three-star hotel between the Comédie and the *gare SNCF*. ③.

Hostel

Hostel, rue des Écoles-Laïques (☎04.67.60.32.22, fax 04.67.60.32.30). Pricey but well-located in a renovated old building in impasse Petite Corraterie, off rue des Écoles Laïques (bus #6, stop "Ursalines"). There is a 2am curfew. Closed mid-Dec to mid-Jan.

The City

Montpellier's city centre – the **old town** – is small, compact, architecturally homogeneous, full of charm and teeming with life, except in July and August when the students are on holiday and everyone else is at the beach. And the place is almost entirely pedestrianized, so you can walk the narrow streets without looking anxiously over your shoulder.

At the hub of the city's life, joining the old part to its newer accretions, is **place de la Comédie**, or "L'Oeuf" to the initiated. This colossal, oblong square, paved with cream-coloured marble, has a fountain at its centre and cafés either side. One end is closed by the Opéra, an ornate nineteenth-century **theatre**; the other opens onto the **Esplanade**, a beautiful tree-lined promenade which ends in the Corum **concert hall**, dug into the hillside and topped off in pink granite, with splendid views from the roof. The city's most trumpeted museum, the **Musée Fabre** (Tues–Fri 9am–5.30pm, Sat & Sun 9.30am–5pm; 25F/€3.81), is close by on boulevard Sarrail and contains a large and historically important collection of seventeenth- to nineteenth-century French, Spanish, Italian, Dutch, Flemish and English painting, including works by Delacroix, Raphael, Jan van Steen and Veronese.

From the north side of L'Oeuf, **rue de la Loge** and **rue Foch**, opened in the 1880s in Montpellier's own Haussmann-izing spree, slice through the heart of the old city. Either side of them, a maze of narrow lanes slopes away to the encircling modern boulevards. Few buildings survive from before the 1622 siege, but the city's busy bourgeoisie quickly made up for the loss, proclaiming their financial power in lots of austere seventeenth- and eighteenth-century mansions. Known as "Lou Clapas" (rubble), the area is rapidly being restored and gentrified. It's a pleasure to wander through and come upon the secretive little squares like place St-Roch, place St-Ravy and place de la Canourgue.

First left off rue de la Loge is **Grande-Rue Jean-Moulin**, where Moulin, hero of the Resistance, lived at no. 21. To the left, at no. 32, the present-day Chamber of Commerce is located in one of the finest eighteenth-century *hôtels*, the Hôtel St-Côme, originally built as a demonstration operating theatre for medical students. On the opposite corner, rue de l'Argenterie forks up to **place Jean-Jaurès**. This square is a nodal point in the city's student life: on fine evenings between 6pm and 7pm you get the impression that the half of the population not in place de la Comédie is sitting here and in the adjacent place du Marché-aux-Fleurs. Through the Gothic doorway of no. 10 of place Jean-Jaurès, is the so-called palace of the kings of Aragon, who ruled Montpellier for a stretch in the thirteenth century. Close by is the **Halles Castellane**, a graceful, iron-framed market hall.

A short walk from place Jean-Jaurès, the Hôtel de Varenne, on place Pétrarque, houses two local history museums of somewhat specialized interest, the **Musée de Vieux Montpellier** (Tues–Sat 9am–noon & 1.30–5pm; free), concentrating on the city's history, and the more interesting, private **Musée Fougau** on the top floor (Wed & Thurs 3–6.30pm; free), dealing with the folk history of Languedoc and things Occitan. Off to the right, the lively little rue des Trésoriers-de-France has one of the best seventeenth-century houses, the **Hôtel Lunaret**, at no. 5, while round the block on rue Jacques Coeur you'll find the **Musée Languedocien** (Mon–Sat 2–5pm; 30F/€4.58), which houses a very mixed collection of Greek, Egyptian and other antiquities.

On the hill at the end of rue Foch, from which the royal artillery bombarded the Protestants in 1622, the formal gardens of the **Promenade du Peyrou** look out across the city and away to the Pic St-Loup, which dominates the hinterland behind Montpellier, with the distant smudge of the Cévennes beyond. At the farther end a swagged and pillared water tower marks the end of an eighteenth-century aqueduct modelled on the Pont du Gard. Beneath the grand sweep of its double tier of arches there is a pretty fruit and veg market (daily) and a huge Saturday **flea market**. At the city end of the promenade, a vainglorious **triumphal arch** shows Louis XIV-Hercules stomping on the Austrian eagle and the English lion, tactlessly reminding the locals of his victory over their Protestant "heresy".

Lower down the hill, on boulevard Henri-IV, the lovely but slightly run-down **Jardin des Plantes** (July & Aug Mon–Sat 8.30am–noon & 2–6pm; rest of year Mon–Sat 10am–5pm; free), with alleys of exotic trees, is France's oldest botanical garden. In the unexploited territory to make this coast a good getaway from the crowds, and many of the old towns which still depend on fishing have managed to sustain their character and traditions despite the summer onslaught.

La Grande-Motte, Grau-du-Roi and Aigues-Mortes

First-built of the new resorts, on the fringes of the Camargue, **LA GRANDE-MOTTE** is a 1960s vintage beach-side Antigone – a "futuristic" planned community which has aged as gracefully as the bean bag and eight-track tape. In summer, its seaside and streets are crowded with semi-naked bodies; in winter, it's a depressing, wind-battered place with few permanent residents. Both *Camping Louis Pibols* (☎04.67.56.50.08; closed Nov–March) and *Camping le Garden* (☎04.67.56.50.09; closed Nov–Feb) offer excellent facilities and are just a couple of minutes' walk from the beach.

A little way east are Port-Camargue, with a sparkling new marina, and **GRAU-DU-ROI**, which manages to retain something of its character as a working fishing port. Tourist traffic still has to give way every afternoon at 4.30pm when the swing bridge opens to let in the trawlers to unload the day's catch onto the quayside, whence it is whisked off to auction – *la criée* – conducted today largely by electronic means rather than the harsh-voiced shouting of former times. For a reasonable place to **stay**, try the *Hôtel Quai d'Azur*, on rue du Vidourle, near the harbour entrance (☎04.66.51.41.94, fax 04.66.53.41.94; ②; closed mid-Nov to Feb), or the huge *Camping L'Eden* (☎04.66.51.49.81; closed Nov–Feb), just east of town.

Eight kilometres inland lies the appealingly named town of **AIGUES-MORTES**, built as a fortress port by Louis IX in the thirteenth century for his departure on the Seventh Crusade. Its massive walls and towers remain virtually intact. Outside the walls, amid drab modern development, flat salt pans lend a certain otherworldly appeal, but inside all is geared to the tourist. If you visit, consider a climb up the **Tour de Constance** on the northwest corner of the town walls (daily: Pentecost to mid-Sept 9.30am–8pm; rest of year 10am–5pm; 32F/€4.88), where Camisard women were imprisoned (Marie Durand was incarcerated for 38 years), and a walk along the wall, where you can gaze out over the weird mist-shrouded flats of the Camargue.

Palavas and Maguelone

A dozen kilometres south of the city by road, **PALAVAS** is the bathing station for the citizens of Montpellier – a concrete sprawl with little to recommend it apart from the presence of the sea, though there is plenty of summertime activity in the discos and the rip-off quayside bars and restaurants. The best place to swim and sunbathe is a little way to the west off the long flat strand that borders the marsh, where some of Europe's few flamingos feed, and herons, egrets and other sea birds squabble and dive. Here stands the **Cathédrale de Maguelone** (daily 9am–7pm), dating mainly from the twelfth century, pale and grey and fortress-like on an island of vines and pines in the middle of the marsh. In the Middle Ages there was a thriving town here, and its cathedral was declared by Urban II to be "second only to that of Rome". However, the cathedral is all that remains of the settlement, which was largely destroyed by Louis XIII because of its Protestant leanings. Cavernous and cool, the strong, simple church interior is the venue for a music festival in the second half of June.

Sète

Some 28km southeast of Montpellier, twenty minutes away by train, **SÈTE** has been an important port for three hundred years. The upper part of the town straddles the slopes of the Mont St-Clair, which overlooks the vast Bassin de Thau, breeding ground of mussels and oysters, while the lower part is intersected by waterways lined with tall terraces and seafood restaurants. It has a lively workaday bustle in addition to its tourist activity, at its height during the summer *joutes nautiques*.

The pedestrian streets, crowded and vibrant, are scattered with café tables. A short climb up from the harbour is the **cimetière marin**, the sailors' cemetery, where poet Paul Valéry is buried. A native of the town, he called Sète his "singular island", and the **Musée Paul Valéry**, in rue Denoyer (Wed–Sun 10am–noon & 2–6pm; 10F/€1.53), opposite the cemetery, has a room devoted to him, as well as a small but strong collection of modern French paintings. If you're feeling energetic, you should keep going up the hill, through the pines to the top, for a view that's fabulous when it's not engulfed in sea mist. Below the sailors' cemetery, and neatly poised above the water, is Vauban's **Fort St-Pierre**, now home to an open-air theatre. Over on the west side of the hill, George Brassens, associate of Sartre and the radical voice of a whole French generation, is buried in the Cimetière le Py, in spite of his song *Plea to be Buried on the Beach at Sète*. In **Éspace Brassens** (Tues–Sun: June & Sept 10am–noon & 2–6pm; July & Aug 10am–noon & 2–7pm; 30F/€4.58), overlooking the cemetery, the locally born singer-songwriter lives again through his words and music, narrating his life-story on the museum's headsets.

Practicalities

The **gare routière** is awkwardly placed on quai de la République, and the **gare SNCF** further out still on quai Maréchal-Joffre – though it is on the main bus route, which circles Mont St-Clair (last bus about 7pm). **Ferries** for Morocco (1–2 weekly) and Mallorca (1–3 weekly) depart from the *gare maritime* at 4 quai d'Alger (☎04.67.46.68.00). Be warned that **hitching** out of Sète is horribly difficult; you're better off taking a train or bus to the nearest town and trying from there. The **tourist office**, at 60 Grand'Rue Mario-Roustan (July & Aug Mon–Sat 10am–1pm & 3–8pm, Sun 10am–1pm; Sept Mon–Fri 9.30am–noon & 2.30–6pm, Sat 9.30am–noon; rest of year Mon, Wed & Fri 9.30am–noon & 2.30–6pm, Sat 9.30am–noon; ☎06.12.57.46.32, *www.sete.org*), has a good array of English-language information.

For **accommodation**, try *Hôtel Family*, right on the quayside at 28 quai de Lattre-de-Tassigny (☎04.67.74.05.03, *andre.Schuller@wanadoo.fr*, ②), or the *Grand Hôtel de Paris* (☎04.67.74.98.10; ②; closed Oct–April) at 2 rue Frédéric-Mistral. For somewhere more comfortable, there's the Belle Époque splendour of the *Grand Hôtel*, 17 quai de Lattre-de-Tassigny (☎04.67.74.71.77, fax 04.67.74.29.27; ④), and *L'Orque Bleu* at 10 quai Aspirant-Herber (☎04.67.74.72.13; ④). The **HI hostel** (☎04.67.53.46.68, fax 04.67.51.34.01) is high up in the town on rue Général-Revest. Campers should ask the tourist office for details of the numerous campsites in the area.

There is a barrage of **restaurants** along quai Général-Duran, from the Pont de la Savonnerie right down to the fish market at the mouth of the pleasure port, all offering seafood in the 50–150F/€7.63–22.88 bracket. The *Marée Bleu* at no. 17 stands out, if only because they usually offer a free *apéritif* to pull in the punters. For a more upscale seafood meal, try *La Galinette*, 26 place des Mouettes (☎04.67.51.16.77; closed Sun evening, Fri lunch & Sat lunch out of season; menus from 220F/€33.55), on the north side of town.

Agde and around

Midway between Sète and Béziers, at the western end of the Bassin de Thau, **AGDE** is historically the most interesting of the coastal towns. Originally Phoenician, and maintained by the Romans, it thrived for centuries on trade with the Levant. Outrun as a seaport by Sète, it later degenerated into a sleepy fishing harbour.

Today, it is a major tourist centre with a good deal of charm, notably in the narrow back lanes between rue de l'Amour and the riverside, where fishing boats tie up. The town's most distinctive and surprising feature is its colour – black – from the volcanic stone of the Mont St-Loup quarries. But it has few sights apart from its impressively fortified **cathedral**, though the **waterfront** is attractive, and by the bridge you can watch the Canal du Midi slip quietly and modestly into the River Hérault on the very last leg of its journey from Toulouse to the Bassin de Thau and Sète.

The **tourist office** is in place Molière near the bridge (July & Aug 9am–7pm; rest of year Mon–Sat 9am–noon & 2–6pm; ☎04.67.94.29.68). Of the town's **hotels** *La Galoite* (☎04.67.21.30.28, *www.laGaliote.fr*, ③–⑤), located in the old bishop's palace on place J.-Jaurès, is the best, while *Le Donjon* (☎04.67.94.12.32, fax 04.67.94.34.54; ④), in another atmospheric old building comes a close second. For cheaper but still comfortable rooms, try *Hôtel des Arcades* (☎04.67.94.21.64; ③), in an old convent at 16 rue Louis-Bages. There are numerous places to **eat** around La Promenade, including *La Belle Agathoise* and *Les Remparts*, both with menus from around 60F/€9.15. *Casa Pépé*, in the centre of the old town at 29 rue Jean-Roger (☎04.67.21.17.67; menus from 80F/€12.20), serves ultra-fresh fish dishes in an intimate, stone-walled room.

An hourly **bus service** operates between the town and the sea at **Cap d'Agde** (see below); you can pick it up at the *gare SNCF* at the end of avenue Victor-Hugo, at the bridge and on La Promenade. To explore the **Canal du Midi**, take one of the boat trips organized by Bateaux du Soleil, 6 rue Chassefières (☎04.67.94.08.79).

Cap d'Agde

CAP D'AGDE, lies to the south of Mont St-Loup, 7km from Agde. The largest (and by far the most successful) of the new resorts, it sprawls laterally from the volcanic mound of St-Loup in an excess of pseudo-traditional modern buildings that offer every type of facility and entertainment – all expensive. It is perhaps best known for its colossal **quartier naturiste**, one of the largest in France, with the best of the beaches, space for 20,000 visitors, and its own restaurants, banks, post offices and shops. Access is possible, though expensive, if you're not actually staying there (50F/€7.63 per car, plus 13F/€1.98 for each passenger).

If you have time to fill, head for the **Musée de l'Éphèbe** (July & Aug daily 9am–12.30pm & 2.30–6.30pm; rest of year Wed–Sat 9am–noon & 2–6pm, Sun 2–6pm; 15F/€2.29), which displays antiquities discovered locally, many of them from beneath the sea. Alternatively, the **Fort de Brescou** (15F/€2.29), which dates back to 1680, lies on a rocky, seagull-infested island just off shore; it can be reached by ferries departing from the centre port at Cap d'Agde or from Grau d'Agde (daily except Wed 10.30am, 2.30 & 6.30pm; 35F/€5.34).

Inland from Montpellier

For getting out into the country of the Bas Languedoc, there are two good routes from Montpellier, both served by regular buses: the D986 **to Ganges** and the N109 **to Lodève**.

The Ganges route

The **Ganges road** weaves north across the Plateau des Garrigues, a landscape of scrubby trees, thorns and fragrant herbs cut by torrent beds. The plateau is dominated by the high limestone ridge of the **Pic St-Loup** until you reach the first worthwhile stopping place, **ST-MARTIN-DE-LONDRES**, 25km on, whose name derives from the old Celtic word for "swamp".

It's a lovely little place of arcaded houses and cobbled passageways set around the roadside place de la Fontaine. Its pride is an exceptionally handsome early Romanesque **church**, reached through a vaulted passage just uphill from the square. The honey-coloured stone is simply decorated with Lombard arcading, the plain rounded porch with a worn relief of St Martin on horseback, while the interior has an unusual clover-shaped ground plan. There's no hotel, only a **gîte**, *La Bergerie du Bayle* (☎ & fax 04.67.55.72.16, *bayle@tourismed.com*), which also serves good-value meals. The **campsite**, *Pic de Loup* (☎04.67.55.00.53; closed Oct–March), is just east of town on the main road.

About 6km south, off the Gignac road near Viols-le-Fort (on the bus route) and the Château de Cambous, there is a marvellous **prehistoric village** (May & June Sat & Sun 2–6pm; July to mid-Sept Tues, Wed & Fri–Sun 3.30–7pm; mid-Sept to April Sun 2–6pm; 15F/€2.29), dating from 2500 BC and only discovered in 1967. The site consists of a group of cabins, each about 20m long, their outlines clearly delineated, with the holes for the roof supports and the door slabs still in place. A reconstruction shows them to have been much like the sheep stalls in the old *bergeries* that dot the plateau.

Further north, almost as far as Ganges (see below), through dramatic river gorges, you reach the **Grotte des Demoiselles** (April–June & Sept 9am–noon & 2–6pm; July & Aug 9am–7pm; Oct–March 9.30am–noon & 2–5pm; *www.Desmoiselles.com*; 42F/€6.41), the most spectacular of the region's many caves: a set of vast cathedral-like caverns hung with stalactites descending with millennial slowness to meet the limpid waters of eerily still pools. Deep inside the mountain, it is reached by funicular (hourly departures).

GANGES itself, 46km from Montpellier and also connected by regular buses (which continue to Le Vigan on the southern edge of the Cévennes), is a rather non descript but busy market town (Friday's the day), whose old quarter is notable for its vaulted alleys designed for defence in the Wars of Religion. This, too, was a Protestant town, peopled by refugees from the plains, who made it famous for its silk stockings. It was here that the last-ditch revolt of the Camisards earned its name; the rebels sacked and pillaged a shirt factory and went off wearing the shirts (*chemises/camises*).

The **tourist office** (Mon–Fri 10am–noon & 2–6pm, Sat 10am–noon; ☎04.67.73.00.56) is on plan de l'Ormeau. On the same square you'll find a **hotel**, the basic *de la Poste* (☎04.67.73.85.88, fax 04.67.73.83.79; ②; closed Jan), although you'll be just as comfortable staying at the slightly cheaper *Auberge du Pont Vieux* (☎04.67.73.62.79; ②) on the route de Vigan on the edge of town. For somewhere to **eat**, try *Le Josyln' Melodie* (☎04.67.73.66.02; closed Wed; menus 82F/€12.51), a homely little Lyonnais place at 4 place Fabre d'Olivet.

The Lodève route

The second inland route runs due west from Montpellier, passing **Gignac** – the turn-off for the spectacular **Gorges de l'Hérault** and **St-Guilhem-le-Désert** – before reaching **Clermont-l'Hérault**, a transport hub from where you can access the Haut Languedoc to the west or the old cathedral town of **Lodève** further north.

Gignac and Aniane

The small town of **GIGNAC** lies 30km from Montpellier amid vineyards, and boasts a fine eighteenth-century bridge spanning the Hérault. There's just one **hotel**, the modern *Motel Vieux Moulin* (☎04.67.57.57.95, fax 04.67.57.69.19; ③) beside the river next door to *Camping du Pont* (☎04.67.57.52.40). For more upmarket accommodation, head 5km north to the town of **ANIANE**, home of the imposing classical **church of St-Sauveur** and the *Hostellerie St-Benoît* (☎04.67.57.71.63, fax 04.67.57.47.10; ③; closed late Dec to mid-Feb), which has a pool and a good restaurant (from 100F/€15.25).

Three kilometres further on is the eleventh-century **Pont du Diable**, supposedly the earliest medieval bridge in the country; children used to dive into the pool beneath until it was banned. The narrowest part of the Hérault gorge begins here.

St-Guilhem-le-Désert and around

The glorious abbey and village of **ST-GUILHEM-LE-DÉSERT** lies in a side ravine, 6km further on. A ruined **castle** spikes the ridge above, and the ancient tiled houses of the village ramble down the banks of the rushing Verdus, which is everywhere channelled into carefully tended gardens. The grand focus is the tenth- to twelfth-century **abbey church**, founded at the beginning of the ninth century by St Guilhem, comrade-in-arms of Charlemagne. The church is a beautiful and atmospheric building, though architecturally impoverished by the dismantling and sale of its cloister – now in New York – in the nineteenth century. It stands on place de la Liberté, surrounded by honey-coloured houses and arcades with traces of Romanesque and Renaissance domestic styles in some of the windows. The interior of the church is plain and somewhat severe compared to the warm colours of the exterior, best seen from rue Cor-de-Nostra-Dama/Font-du-Portal, where you get the classic view of the perfect apse.

There are a couple of easy and worthwhile **walks** you can make from here – up the valley of the Verdus into the red-stained walls of the **Cirque du Bout-du-Monde** (from place de la Liberté, take rue du Bout-du-Monde out of the village and continue for about 30min), or up the zigzagging path of the **GR74**, through the sweet-scented shrubs and flowers towards the castle ridge (also about 30min). From the crest of the ridge the view down onto the village is magnificent. The path divides here: one branch leads back right to the ruins of the castle, while the other continues along the GR74 to the Ermitage Notre-Dame-de-Belle-Grâce (90min), and on to join the GR7 at St-Maurice-Navacelles on the Causse de Larzac.

In season the village is on every tour operator's route, making early mornings and late afternoons the best times for visiting. A number of **gîtes** in and around St-Guilhem can put you up for the night, including the English-speaking *Gîte de la Tour* (☎& fax 04.67.57.34.00), located in a medieval tower in the village, and the CAP *gîte* (☎04.67.52.72.11), also in town. The nearest campsite is *Le Moulin de Siau* (☎04.67.57.51.08; closed mid-Sept to mid-June), near Aniane on the road back down to Gignac. Nearby, cave enthusiasts will enjoy the **Grotte de Clamouse** (daily: Feb–May & Oct 10am–5pm; June & Sept 10am–6pm; July & Aug 10am–7pm; Nov–Jan noon–5pm; 42F/€6.41).

Clermont-l'Hérault

Eight kilometres west of Gignac, the market town of **CLERMONT-L'HÉRAULT** – accessible by bus from Montpellier – is a rather dull little cantonal capital, whose only recommendation is that it is a good jumping-off point for visiting the area around **Lac Salagou** to the west. The only thing of interest you'll find here is a thirteenth-century **church**, fortified in the fourteenth century to defend it against the English.

The **tourist office** (Mon–Sat 9am–noon & 2–6pm, Sun 10am–noon; ☎04.67.96.23.86, fax 04.67.96.98.58) is at 9 rue René-Gosse, close to the cathedral. By far the best place to **stay** is *Le Terminus*, on allées Roger-Salengro, near the old station (☎04.67.88.45.00, fax 04.67.88.45.19; ③), with a good restaurant (from 87F/€13.27). If you're **camping**, head for the year-round site *Le Salagou* (☎04.67.96.13.13), northwest of Clermont near the lake. Reasonable **meals** can be had at the *Restaurant des Remparts*, on place de la République (closed Tues; menus from 65F/€9.91), or try *l'Arlequin*, tucked under the south wall of the cathedral on place St-Paul (closed Sun & Mon; menus from 80F/€12.20), for a more refined dining experience.

Around Clermont-l'Hérault

Three kilometres from Clermont-l'Hérault, along the main road to Bédarieux, lies **VILLENEUVETTE**, a model factory and workers' settlement created in the seventeenth century for the production of high-quality wool for sale in the Mediterranean. Initially successful, the factory eventually closed down in 1954, but the settlement still boasts 85 inhabitants. There is a very nice, if somewhat pricey, **hotel** tacked on to the village walls – *La Source* (☎04.67.96.05.07, fax 04.67.96.90.09; ③–⑦; closed mid-Nov to mid-Dec & mid-Jan to mid-March), with a good restaurant (from 100F/€15.25), pool and garden. Eight kilometres further west just off of the Bédarieux road, in the picturesque little village of **MOURÈZE**, you'll find an alternative hotel, *Les Hauts de Mourez* (☎04.67.94.04.84, fax 04.67.96.25.85; ④; closed Nov–March). Further accommodation options are available in **SALASC**, at the *Auberge Campagnard* (☎ & fax 04.67.96.15.62; ③ with breakfast), and at **OCTON** in the comfortable old hotel *La Calade* (☎ & fax 04.67.96.19.21; ③; closed mid-Dec to Feb) in the village centre (closed Tues & Wed out of season; lunch menu 73F/€11.13).

Three other interesting and little-visited places east of Clermont are only feasible if you have a car. The first is a very fine **dolmen** on the end of a low ridge overlooking the D32 – best reached from the village of **LE POUGET**, where it is signposted. Continuing along the D139, you come within sight of the pale grey ruins of the keep and chapel of the **Château d'Aumelas**, romantically silhouetted on the edge of the plateau of the *causse*. To reach it by road – considerably further – you need to bear right onto the D114 and then take a dirt track opposite a farm. It's a beautiful and silent place, and the chapel is in near-perfect condition.

Two kilometres further along the D114, down an unsigned and bumpy track leading right onto the *causse*, there is a marvellous and remote silvery chapel, **St-Martin-de-Cardonnet**, built in the twelfth century – all that remains of an ancient priory.

On to Lodève

Heading north from Clermont to **LODÈVE**, 19km away, the new A75 *autoroute* brings heavy traffic down from Clermont-Ferrand. It passes through countryside further scarred by uranium mining – the area around the village of St-Martin-du-Bosc has some of the highest soil concentration of radioactivity in the world.

Lodève, entirely enclosed by vine-terraced hills at the confluence of the Lergues and Soulondres rivers, is almost in the shadow of the **Causse de Larzac**. There are really no sights here, but Lodève is a pleasant old-fashioned place to pause on your way up to Le Caylar or La Couvertoirade on the *causse*. The **cathedral** – a stop on the route to Santiago de Compostela – is worth a look, as is the unusual World War I **Monument aux Morts**, in the adjacent park, by local sculptor Paul Dardé; more of his work is on display at the **town museum** in the Hôtel Fleury (Tues–Sun 9.30am–12.30pm & 2–6pm; 37F/€5.64) and the **Halle Dardé** (daily 9am–6pm; free) in the place du Marché. With a bit of organizing it's also possible to visit the **Annexe de la Savonnerie** (by appointment only Tues–Thurs 2–5pm; ☎04.67.96.40.40; 21F/€3.20), on the outskirts of Lodève, where priceless Gobelins tapestries are woven.

The **tourist office** is at 7 place de la République (July & Aug Mon–Fri 9am–noon & 2–6pm, Sat 9am–5pm, Sun 9.30am–1.30pm; rest of year closed Sun; ☎04.67.88.86.44, *www.lodeve.com*), next door to the **gare routière**, where you can catch buses to Montpellier, Béziers, Millau, Rodez and St-Afrique. The best place to **stay** in town is the newly renovated *Hôtel du Nord* (☎ & fax 04.67.44.10.08; ③) at 18 bd de la Liberté, or the family-run *Hôtel de la Paix* (☎04.67.44.07.46, fax 04.67.44.30.47; ③; closed Feb to mid-March) on 11 bd Montalangue. There is a big **market** on Saturdays, and three times weekly in summer local farmers bring in their produce.

SOUTHERN LANGUEDOC

Southern Languedoc presents an exciting and varied landscape, its watery coastal flats stretching south from the mouth of the Aude towards Perpignan, interrupted by occasional low, rocky hills. Just inland sits **Béziers**, its imposing cathedral set high above the languid Orb river, and girded on the north by the amazingly preserved Renaissance town of **Pézenas**, and on the south by the ancient pre-Roman settlement of the **Enseurune**. It is also a gateway to the spectacular uplands of the **Monts de l'Espinouse** and the **Parc Naturel Régional du Haut Languedoc**, a ramblers' paradise. Just south of Béziers, the ancient Roman capital of **Narbonne** guards the mouth of the Aude. Following the course of this river, which is shadowed by the historic **Canal du Midi**, you'll arrive at the quintessential medieval citadel, the famous fortress-town of **Carcassonne**. Once a shelter for renegade Cathar heretics, this town is a perfect departure point for the **Cathar castles** – a string of romantically ruined castles dotting the rugged hills to the south.

Béziers and around

Though no longer the rich city of its nineteenth-century heyday, **BÉZIERS** is still the capital of the Languedoc wine country and a focus for the Occitan movement, as well as being the birthplace of Resistance hero Jean Moulin. The fortunes of the movement and the vine have long been closely linked; Occitan activists have helped to organize the militant local vine-growers, and there were ugly events during the mid-1970s, when blood was shed in violent confrontations with the authorities over the importation of cheap foreign wines and the low prices paid for the essentially poor-grade local product. Things are calmer now, as the conservatism of Languedoc farmers has given way to more modern attitudes in the face of public demand for something better than the traditional table wine. As a result, some of the steam has also gone out of the movement; interest today is more in the culture than in anti-Paris separatist feelings. The town is also home to two great Languedocian adopted traditions: English **rugby** and the Spanish **corrida**, both of which it follows with a passion. The best time to visit is during the mid-August **feria**, a raucous four-day party which you will enjoy even if you don't find bullfighting to your tastes.

The City

The finest view of the old town is from the west, as you come in from Carcassonne: crossing the willow-lined River Orb by the Pont-Neuf, you can look upstream at the sturdy arches of the **Pont-Vieux**, above which rises a steep-banked hill crowned by the **Cathédrale St-Nazaire**, resembling a castle more than a church on account of its crenellated towers. The best approach to the cathedral is up the medieval lanes at the end of Pont-Vieux, rue Canterelles and passage Canterellettes. Its architecture is mainly Gothic, the original building having been burnt in 1209 during the sacking of Béziers, when Armand Amaury's crusaders massacred some seven thousand people at the church of the Madeleine for refusing to hand over about twenty Cathars. "Kill them all," the pious abbot is said to have ordered, "God will recognize his own!"

From the top of the cathedral **tower**, there's a superb view out across the vine-dominated surrounding landscape. Next door, you can wander through the ancient **cloister** (daily: May–Sept 10am–7pm; rest of year 10am–noon & 2–5pm; free) and out into the shady **bishop's garden** overlooking the river. In the adjacent **place de la Révolution**, a monument commemorates the people who died resisting Napoléon III's *coup d'état* in 1851 and their leader, Mayor Casimir Péret, who was shipped off to Cayenne where he drowned in a Papillon-style escape attempt. Also on the square, the Hôtel Fabrégat houses a **Musée des Beaux-Arts** (Tues–Fri 9am–noon & 2–6pm; 15F/€2.29), which, apart from an interesting collection of Greek Cycladic vases, won't keep you long. Nearby, **Hôtel Fayet**, at 9 rue Capus (same hours and ticket), has been pressed into service as an annexe to the museum, though it's as much of interest for its period interiors as its collection of nineteenth- and early twentieth-century art and works by local sculptor, Jean-Antoine Injalbert.

The city's other museum, the **Musée du Biterrois**, in the old St-Jacques barracks on avenue de la Marne near the train station (Tues–Sun: July & Aug 9am–7pm; rest of year 9am–noon & 2–6pm; 15F/€2.29), displays a variety of entertaining exhibits, ranging from Greek amphorae and nineteenth-century door knockers to distilling manuals, clogs and winepresses. Away from the medieval streets round the cathedral, the centre of life in Béziers is the **allées Paul-Riquet**, a broad, leafy esplanade lined with cafés, crêpes stalls, restaurants, banks and shops; it is named after the seventeenth-century tax collector who lost health and fortune in his obsession with building the Canal du Midi to join the Atlantic and the Mediterranean. Laid out in the last century, the *allées* runs from an elaborate nineteenth-century theatre on place de la Victoire to the gorgeous little park of the **Plateau des Poètes**, whose ponds, palms and lime trees were laid out in the so-called English manner by the man who created the Bois de Boulogne in Paris.

Practicalities

From the **gare SNCF** on boulevard Verdun, the best way into town is through the landscaped gardens of the Plateau des Poètes opposite the station entrance and up the allées Paul-Riquet. The **gare routière** is in place de Gaulle, at the northern end of the *allées*, while the **tourist office** is off the *allées* at 5 place Jean-Jaurès (July & Aug Mon–Sat 9am–7pm, Sun 10am–noon; rest of year Mon–Sat 9am–noon & 2–6.30pm; ☎04.67.28.05.97, *www.ville-beziers.fr*).

For a central place to **stay**, try the welcoming *Angleterre*, at 22 place Jean-Jaurès (☎04.67.28.48.42; ②), or the *Hôtel des Poètes*, 80 allées Paul-Riquet (☎04.67.76.38.66, fax 04.67.76.25.88; ③), at the south end overlooking the gardens. The *Hôtel du Théâtre*, at 13 rue Coquille (☎04.67.49.13.43, fax 04.67.49.31.58; ③), right beside the theatre, is smarter, while the town's deluxe option is *Hôtel Imperator* (☎04.67.49.02.25, fax 04.67.28.92.30; ④) at 28 allées Paul-Riquet. There's no **campsite** in town, but you'll find one at nearby Villeneuve-lez-Béziers (☎04.67.39.36.09; closed Nov–Feb).

For **food**, check out *Pizzeria da Patti* (from around 50F/€7.63), on the north side of place Jean-Jaurès, or head up into the old quarter where rue Viennet has a good choice of restaurants. Two specific places to try here are the elegant *Le Cep d'Or*, at no. 7, serving mostly seafood (closed Sun evening & Mon; menus from 78F/€11.90), and the *La Table Bretonne*, at no. 21 (closed Mon), a homely crêperie in the shadow of the cathedral, where you can eat well for around 60F/€9.15. *L'Ambassade*, at 22 bd de Verdun (☎04.67.76.06.24; closed Sun & Mon; menus from 145F/€22.11), is one of the town's best places, while *Le Bistrot des Halles*, further north on place de la Madeleine behind the market square, is popular for its varied, well-priced menus (closed Sun & Mon; from 90F/€13.73).

Béziers has one of the star **rugby** clubs in France, A.S.B.H., based at the Stade de la Méditerranée in the eastern suburbs (☎04.67.11.03.76). If you fancy pottering along the Canal du Midi, you can hire **bikes** at La Maison du Canal (☎04.67.62.18.18) beside the Port Neuf, south of the *gare SNCF*.

Pézenas and the Oppidum d'Ensérane

PÉZENAS lies 18km east of Béziers on the old N9. Market centre of the coastal plain, it looks across to rice fields and shallow lagoons, hazy with heat and dotted with pink flamingos. The town was catapulted to glory when it became the seat of the parliament of Languedoc and the residence of its governors in 1465, and it reached its zenith in the late seventeenth century when the prince Armand de Bourbon made it a "second Versailles". The legacy of this illustrious past can be seen in the town's exquisite array of fourteenth- to seventeenth-century mansions.

The town also plays up its association with Molière, who visited several times with his troupe in the mid-seventeenth century, when he enjoyed the patronage of Prince Armand. He put on his own plays at the **Hôtel d'Alfonce** on rue Conti, including the first performance of *Le Médecin Volant*, according to local tradition. The building is now privately owned, but in summer you can visit the courtyard which served as Molière's theatre (June–Sept Mon–Sat 10am–noon & 3–7pm; 10F/€1.53). When in town, he lodged at the Maison du Barbier-Gély, in the unspoiled **place Gambetta**, today occupied by the **tourist office** (July & Aug daily 9am–7pm; rest of year Mon–Sat 9.30am–noon & 2–6pm, Sun 2–5pm; ☎04.67.98.36.40, *www.ville-Pézenas.fr*). Although Molière features in the eclectic **Musée Vulliod St-Germain** (Mon–Sat 10am–noon & 3–7pm, Sun 3–7pm; 15F/€2.29), housed in a sixteenth-century palace just off the square, it's the grand salon, with its Aubusson tapestries and collection of seventeenth- and eighteenth-century furniture, that steals the show.

Seven kilometres southwest of Béziers on the N9 Narbonne road, a sign points the way up a hill to **L'Oppidum d'Ensérune**, the site of a 2600-year-old Gallo-Roman settlement, relics of which are displayed in a small **museum** (April, May & Sept daily 9.30am–6.30pm; June–Aug daily 9.30am–7.30pm; Oct–March daily except Tues 9.30am–5pm; 30F/€4.58). From the hill you can see the extraordinary, radial pattern of fields emanating from the now dry **Étang de Montady**, drained for cultivation in the thirteenth century.

Practicalities

The tourist office distributes a guide to all the town's eminent houses, taking in the former **Jewish ghetto** on rue des Litanies and rue Juiverie, but you can just as easily follow the explanatory plaques posted all over the centre, starting at the east end of rue François-Outrin where it leaves the town's main square, place du 14-Juillet. The **gare routière** is on the opposite side of the square on the river bank, with buses to Montpellier, Béziers and Agde, while an enormous **market** takes place each Saturday on cours Jean-Jaurès, a five-minute walk away.

There are two **hotels** in Pézenas: *Genieys*, at 9 rue Aristide-Briand (☎04.67.98.13.99, fax 04.67.98.04.80; ②), and the splendid *Molière*, on place du 14-Juillet (☎04.67.98.14.00, fax 04.67.98.98.28; ③). There are plenty of **restaurants** to choose from and all have menus for under 100F/€15.25. *Le Pomme d'Amour* (closed Jan & Feb), on rue Albert-Paul-Alliés, and *Brasserie Molière* (in the hotel of the same name) are good *terroir* restaurants, while *Le Conti*, 27 rue Conti (closed Sun), is a popular pizzeria. For those with a sweet tooth, there are two local delicacies to sample: flavoured sugar-drops called *berlingots*, and *petits pâtés* – bobbin-shaped pastries related to mince pies, reputedly introduced by the Indian cook in the household of Clive of India who stayed in Pézenas in 1770.

Narbonne and around

On the Toulouse–Nice main train line, 25km west of Béziers, is **NARBONNE**, once the capital of Rome's first colony in Gaul, Gallia Narbonensis, and a thriving port and communications centre in classical times and again in the Middle Ages. Plague, war with the English and the silting-up of its harbour finished it off in the fourteenth century, though a tentative prosperity returned in the late nineteenth century with the birth of the modern wine industry. Today, despite the ominous presence of the Malvesi nuclear power plant just 5km out of town, it's a pleasant provincial city with a small but well-kept old town, dominated by the great truncated choir of its cathedral and bisected by a grassy esplanade on the banks of the Canal de la Robine.

In the summer of 1991 Narbonne acquired notoriety as a new flash point in France's continuing problems with its ethnic minorities, as the Harkis – Algerians who had enlisted in the French forces and fought with them against their own people in the Algerian war of independence in the late 1950s – began angrily to protest official neglect of their community. The discontent has rumbled on, the most recent manifestation being a sit-in outside the Mairie during the winter of 1997.

The Town

One of the few Roman remnants in Narbonne is the **Horreum**, at the north end of rue Rouget-de-l'Isle (April–Sept daily 9.30am–12.15pm & 2–6pm; rest of year Tues–Sun 10am–noon & 2–5pm; 30F/€4.58, valid for three days and including entry to the museums in the Palais des Archévêques – see below), an unusual underground grain store divided into a series of small chambers leading off a rectangular passageway. At the opposite end of the same street, close to the attractive tree-lined banks of the **Canal de la Robine**, is Narbonne's other principal attraction, the enormous Gothic **Cathédrale St-Just-et-St-Pasteur**. With the Palais des Archévêques and its forty-metre keep, it forms a massive pile of masonry that completely dominates the restored lanes of the old town, and – like the cathedral of Béziers – can be seen for kilometres around. In spite of its size, it is actually only the choir of a much more ambitious church, whose construction was halted to avoid wrecking the city walls. The immensely tall interior has some beautiful fourteenth-century stained glass in the chapels on the northeast side of the apse and imposing Aubusson tapestries – one of the most valuable tapestries is kept in the **Salle du Trésor** (May–Dec Mon–Sat 10–11.45am & 2.30–5.30pm; 15F/€2.29), along with a small collection of ecclesiastical treasures. In summer the high north **tower** is open for a panoramic view of the surrounding vineyards (June–Sept daily 10am–5pm; rest of year by appointment only, ☎04.68.33.70.18; 15F/€1.53).

The adjacent **place de l'Hôtel-de-Ville** is dominated by the great towers of St-Martial, the Madeleine and Bishop Aycelin's keep. From there the passage de l'Ancre leads through to the **Palais des Archévêques** (Archbishops' Palace), housing a fairly ordinary **museum of art** and a good **archeology museum** (both museums have the same hours and tarifs as the Horreum), whose interesting Roman remains include a massive 3.5-metre wood and lead ship's rudder, and a huge mosaic. Across into the southern part of the town, beyond the bisecting Canal de la Robine and the built-over Pont des Marchands, the small early Christian crypt of the church of **St-Paul**, off rue de l'Hôtel-Dieu (Mon–Sat 9am–noon & 2–6pm; free), is worth a quick look, as is the eerily empty deconsecrated church of **Notre-Dame-de-Lamourguié**.

Practicalities

The **gare routière** and the **gare SNCF** are next door to each other on avenue Carnot on the northwest side of town. The **tourist office** is on place Salengro, next to the cathedral (April–Aug daily 9.30am–12.15pm & 2–6pm; rest of year Tues–Sun 10am–noon & 2–5pm; ☎04.68.65.15.60, fax 04.68.65.59.12, *www.Mairie-Narbonne.fr*).

The best budget **accommodation** is the modern and friendly *MJC Centre International de Séjour*, in place Salengro (☎04.68.32.01.00, fax 04.68.65.80.20; ①). A couple of reasonable hotels are *Will's Hotel*, 23 av Pierre-Sémard (☎04.68.90.44.50, fax

04.68.32.26.28; ③), a homely backpackers' favourite near the station, and the spruce *Hôtel de France*, 6 rue Rossini (☎04.68.32.09.75, *hotelfrance@bigfoot.com*; ③), beside the attractive market hall. A fancier option is the plush *La Résidence*, 6 rue du 1er-Mai (☎04.68.32.19.41, fax 04.68.65.18.48; ④), in a nineteenth-century renovated house, but the best is the magnificent *La Dorade*, 44 rue Jean-Jaurès, (☎04.68.32.65.95, fax 04.68.65.81.62; ③), facing the canal and set in a spectacular building built in 1648. The nearest **campsite** is *Les Roches Grises*, on the route de Perpignan to the southwest of town; take bus #2 from the Hôtel-de-Ville.

As for **food**, the best choice in Narbonne is *L'Alsace*, at 2 av Pierre-Sémard (☎04.68.65.10.24; closed Tues; menus from 110F/€16.78), with a great decor and mammoth servings of good, simple *terroir* and northeastern French dishes. Alternatively you'll find a string of alfresco snackeries and brasseries along the terraces bordering the Canal de la Robine in the town centre, while *L'Estagnol* (☎04.68.65.09.27; closed Sun; menus around 100F/€15.25), across the canal on Cours Mirabeau, attracts the crowds with its good-value, simple fare. For something a little fancier, try *Aux Trois Caves*, at 4 rue Benjamin-Crémieux (menus 120–240F/€18.30–36.30), with *terroir* dining in a medieval cellar, or the elegant *La Petite Cour*, north of the canal at 22 bd Gambetta (☎04.68.90.48.03), in a high-ceilinged room decked with seascape murals; seafood is the order of the day, with a good choice of menus around 75F/€11.44 at lunchtime, and 125F/€19.06 in the evening.

Fontfroide and the Étang de Bages

For a side trip from Narbonne – only 15km, but nigh impossible without transport of your own – the lovely **abbey** of **FONTFROIDE** enjoys a beautiful location, tucked into a fold in the dry cypress-clad hillsides. The extant buildings go back to the twelfth century, with some elegant seventeenth-century additions in the entrance and courtyards, and were in use from their foundation until 1900, first by Benedictines, then Cistercians. It was one of the Cistercian monks, Pierre de Castelnau, whose murder as papal legate set off the Albigensian Crusade against the Cathars in 1208.

Visits to the recently restored abbey are only possible with a guide (daily 10, 10.45 & 11.30am & 12.15, 1.45, 2.30, 4, 4.45 & 5.30pm; 37F/€5.64), and star features include the cloister, with its marble pillars and giant wisteria, the church itself, some fine ironwork and the rose garden. The stained glass in the windows of the lay brothers' dormitory consists of fragments from churches in north and eastern France damaged in World War I.

Just south of Narbonne, the **Étang de Bages et de Sigean** forms a large lagoon frequently visited by flamingos. A scenic drive leads out over the *étang* to **BAGES** village. It is a notably arty community with some houses featuring unusually decorous ceramic drainpipes. From Bages the road continues south along the edge of the *étang* to **PEYRIAC-DE-MER**, and the **Réserve Africaine Sigean** (daily 9am–9pm; 98F/€14.95), a better-than-average wildlife park with over 150 species from Africa and the rest of the world.

The coast: Valras to Gruissan

The coast close to Béziers and Narbonne enjoys the same attributes – and problems – as the rest of the Languedoc shoreline: fantastic sand but not a stitch of shade, and endless tacky development buffeted by a wind that would flay the shell off a tortoise.

For a quick escape from Béziers, you can take a thirty-minute bus ride across the flat vine-covered coastal plain to **VALRAS**, at the mouth of the River Orb, whose old-fashioned family resort status is still just discernible. Further south, St-Pierre and

Narbonne-Plage (reachable by bus from Narbonne) are uninspiring, modern resorts, and the only redeeming feature of this stretch of coast is the mini-landscape of the **Montagne de la Clape**, a former island, pine-covered and craggy, and not more than 200m above sea level, despite its name. At its far end the fishing village of **GRUISSAN**, 13km from Narbonne (there are buses), built in concentric rings around the hub of the Tour Barberousse, is the only real place of character left, and it, too, is under assault by the developers. Out along the beach, *plages des chalets*, is a section of houses originally built on stilts to keep them clear of the sea, but since the danger of flooding has receded many have now added ground floors.

The one really worthwhile thing to visit near Gruissan is the **Chapelle Notre-Dame-des-Auzils**. It's about 4km up a winding lane into the Montagne and stands in a quiet and highly atmospheric spot in the pine woods. All along the road leading to it are moving **memorials** to the people of Gruissan lost at sea in merchant ships, trawlers and warships, from Haiti to the Greek island of Skiros. If the chapel's open, take a peek inside at the *ex votos* offered by grateful seamen and their families, many of them now painted onto the walls, the originals having been stolen in the 1960s.

Parc Naturel Régional du Haut Languedoc

Embracing Mont Caroux in the east and the Montagne Noire in the west, the **Parc Naturel Régional du Haut Languedoc** is the southernmost extension of the Massif Central. The west, above Castres and Mazamet, is Atlantic in feel and climate, with deciduous forests and lush valleys, while the east is dry, craggy and calcareous. Except in high summer you can have it almost to yourself. Buses serve the **Orb valley** and cross the centre of the park to **La Salvetat** and **Lacaune**, but you really need transport of your own to make the most of it.

Bédarieux to St-Pons: the valleys of the Orb and Jaur

Some 34km north of Béziers, the pleasant if unremarkable town of **BÉDARIEUX** lies right on the edge of the park. Served by buses from both Béziers and Montpellier, and by train from Béziers, it makes a good base for entering the park, especially as the service continues along the Orb and Jaur valleys to St-Pons beneath the southern slopes of the Monts de l'Espinouse.

The best part of town is to the east of the river, where the tall and crumbly old houses are redolent of a rural France long since vanished in more prosperous areas. You'll find the **tourist office** on place aux Herbes (Mon, Tues, Thurs & Fri 9am–12.30pm & 2–7.30pm, Sat 9am–12.30pm; ☎04.67.95.08.79, *francis.ot@libertysurf.fr*). *Hôtel Le Central*, on place aux Herbes (☎04.67.95.06.76; ①), makes a cheap and atmospheric place to stay, and has a good, inexpensive restaurant. There's also a municipal **campsite** on boulevard Jean-Moulin (☎04.67.23.30.19; closed Oct to mid-June).

The Orb valley and Mons

Continuing **west**, the D908 is an easy hitch (if you don't want to wait for the bus) through spectacular scenery, with the peaks of the Monts de l'Espinouse rising up to 1000m on your right. The spa town of **LAMALOU-LES-BAINS**, 8km on, is notably livelier than neighbouring settlements, boasting the attraction of recuperative springs where the likes of André Gide, Dumas *fils* and crowned heads of Spain and Morocco soothed their aches and pains. At the west end of the town by the main road, the **cemetery** is an untypically grand necropolis crowned with ornate mausoleums, while the ancient **church** on the north side of town contains carvings left by Mozarab refugees from Spain.

At the village of Colombières, 5km to the west, a path leaves the road to take you up into the **Gorges de Madale**. Here it joins the GR7, which crosses the southern part of the park to Labastide-Rouairoux beyond St-Pons.

Seven or eight kilometres further along the D908 is **MONS**, which features a **gîte d'étape** (☎04.67.97.80.43) next to the church, and the small *Auberge des Gorges d'Héric* (☎04.67.97.72.98; ①; menus from 65F/€9.91) by the suspension bridge at Tarassac, 2km away on the D14, near the municipal **campsite** (☎04.67.97.72.64). From Mons a road climbs 5km up the dramatic **Gorges d'Héric** to the hamlet of Héric, with the **Gorges de l'Orb** winding their way southwards back to Béziers along the D14.

Olargues and St-Pons-de-Thomières

Five kilometres after Mons, you reach the medieval village of **OLARGUES**, scrambling up the south bank of the Jaur above its thirteenth-century single-span bridge. The steep twisting streets, presumably almost unchanged since the bridge was built, lead up to a thousand-year-old belfry crowning the top of the hill. With the river and gardens below, the ancient and earth-brown farms on the infant slopes of Mont Caroux beyond, and swifts screaming round the tower in summer, you get a powerful sense of age and history. There's a tiny **tourist office** on rue de la Place near the church (July & Aug daily 10am–noon & 4–7pm; rest of year Wed & Sat 10am–noon & 2–6pm; ☎04.67.97.71.26), as well as an old train station now served only SNCF **buses**. The *Laissac*, just outside of town in the Domaine de Rieumégé (☎04.67.97.71.26; ②; closed Nov–March), is a decent-enough **hotel**, but a better deal is Pauline Giles' homely *Les Quatr' Farceurs* in rue de la Comporte (☎ & fax 04.67.97.81.33, lqf@libertysurf.fr, ②), which also serves huge meals with free-flowing wine for 90F/€13.73. **Campers** should head for *Camping Le Baous*, down by the river (☎04.67.97.71.50; closed mid-Sept to mid-April).

ST-PONS-DE-THOMIÈRES, 18km further west, is a little larger and noisier: it's on the Béziers–Castres and Béziers–La Salvetat bus routes, as well as the Bédarieux–Mazamet route. This is the "capital" of the park, with the **Maison du Parc** at 13 rue du Cloître (Mon–Sat: July & Aug 10am–noon & 2–6pm; rest of year 10am–noon & 2–5pm; ☎05.63.37.45.76) by the **cathedral** – a strange mix of Romanesque and classical. It also boasts a small and reasonably interesting **museum of prehistory** (mid-June to Oct daily 10am–noon & 2.30–6pm; rest of year Wed, Sat & Sun 10am–noon & 2–5pm; 20F/€3.05), across the river from the **tourist office** on place du Forail (July & Aug daily 9am–7.30pm; rest of year Mon–Fri 10am–noon & 2.30–6pm, Sat 9am–noon; ☎04.67.97.06.65).

If you need to **stay**, try the basic *Le Somail*, near the tourist office (☎04.67.97.00.12; ②), or the much smarter *Les Bergeries de Ponderach*, 1km out of town on the Narbonne road (☎04.67.97.02.57, fax 04.67.97.29.75; ⑤), with a good restaurant. The municipal **campsite** (☎04.67.97.34.85) is on the main road east to Bédarieux. There's also a good *camping à la ferme*, *La Borio de Roque* (☎04.67.97.10.97; closed Oct to mid-June), 4km north of St-Pons on the D907, and *chambres d'hôte* 2km further on at *La Ferme de Tailhos* (☎04.67.97.27.62; ③). Continue along this road and you reach the Col du Cabaretou, with the stunningly situated *Auberge du Cabaretou* (☎04.67.97.02.31, fax 04.67.97.32.74; ③; closed mid-Jan to mid-Feb), with a *terroir* restaurant serving menus from 95F/€14.49. North of here the D907 leads to La Salvetat in the heart of the park.

The uplands of the park

The uplands of the park are a wild and little travelled area, dominated by the towering peak of **Mont Caroux** and stretching west along the ridge of the **Monts de l'Espinouse**. This is prime hiking territory, where thick forest of stunted oak alternates with broad mountain meadows, opening up on impressive vistas. Civilization appears again to the west in the upper Agout valley, where **Fraisse** and **La Salvetat** have become thriving bases for outdoor recreation, and to the north, at the medieval spa town of **Lacaune**. There's no transport which crosses the uplands, but the prettiest route through the park to Mont Caroux and L'Espinouse is the D180 from **Le Poujol-sur-Orb**, 2km west of Lamalou-les-Bains.

Combes, Douch and Héric

From Le Poujol, the D180 winds up through cherry orchards to the village of **COMBES**, where the *Auberge de Combes* (☎04.67.95.66.55, fax 04.67.95.63.49; ②; Oct–May weekends only; restaurant from 85F/€12.96) offers both *gîte d'étape* and *chambres d'hôte* accommodation, and on through the **Forêt des Écrivains-Combattants**, named after the French writers who died in World War I. Just above the hamlet of Rosis, the road levels out in a small mountain valley, whose slopes are brilliant yellow with broom in June.

A left fork leads to the hamlet of **DOUCH**, beneath the summit of Le Caroux – a perfect place where time seems really to have stood still. Half-a-dozen rough stone houses, inhabited by a handful of elderly residents, cluster tightly together for protection against the elements. There's a **gîte d'étape** (☎04.67.95.65.76) and a *ferme auberge* that provides meals in summer (by reservation only ☎04.67.95.21.41). In the meadows below nestles a picturesque **church** with an ancient cemetery full of graves like iron cots.

The University of Toulouse maintains a research unit here to survey the largest *mouflon* population in France. If you go out early in the morning or just before dark in the evening, you'll have a good chance of seeing these short-fleeced sheep, and wild boar, too, as they come out to feed. The road provides some good vantage points a little further north round the **Col de l'Ourtigas** and the Pas de la Lauze.

The best short **walk** to do from Douch is down the GR7 to the hamlet of **HÉRIC** in the gorge of the same name. The path starts on the left at the end of the road in Douch and follows the telephone line. Once over the col and into the head of the gorge it becomes a beautiful paved mule track looping down through beech and chestnut woods. In the past people lived off the chestnuts, selling them, eating them and making flour from them. It takes about forty minutes to reach the two or three brown-stone houses of Héric, inhabited for several generations by the Clavel family, and 90 minutes to climb back up. They run a *gîte d'étape* and can provide **meals**, too, on reservation (☎04.67.97.77.29). A good longer walk from Douch is the popular three-kilometre ascent of **Le Caroux** (1040m), south of the village with fine views from the summit along L'Espinouse (see below), south to Béziers, the sea and even the Pyrenees, on a clear day.

Into the Agout valley

Continuing north from Douch, the D180 climbs another 12km above deep ravines, offering spectacular views to the summit of **L'Espinouse**. The Col de l'Ourtigas is a good place to stretch your legs and take in the grandeur surrounding you. Here the landscape changes from Mediterranean cragginess to marshy moor-like meadow and big conifer plantations, and the road begins to descend west into the valley of the River Agout. It runs through tiny Salvergues, with plain workers' cottages and a striking fortress-church; Cambon, where the natural woods begin; postcard-pretty **FRAISSE-SUR-AGOUT** – home to the *Campotel* (☎04.67.69.64.29; ②) on the riverbank, and the small *Auberge de l'Espinouse* (☎04.67.97.56.14; ③; closed Nov–Feb); and thence to **LA SALVETAT-SUR-AGOUT**. Situated between the artificial lakes of La Raviège and Laouzas, this is another attractive mountain town built on a hill above the river, with car-wide streets and houses clad in huge slate tiles. It's usually half asleep except at holiday time, when it becomes a busy outdoor activities centre. With several **campsites** and the friendly, English-owned *La Pergola* hotel (☎04.67.97.60.57, fax 04.67.97.56.76; ①), it's a convenient stopover for the centre of the park. The municipal **campsite** (☎04.67.97.62.45; closed Sept–April) is by the sports ground off the D907, and there's a **tourist office** in place des Archers at the top of the hill (July & Aug Mon–Fri 9am–noon & 2–6pm, Sat & Sun 10am–noon & 2–5pm; rest of year closed Sun; ☎ & fax 04.67.97.64.44).

Lacaune

Twenty kilometres further north, **LACAUNE** makes another agreeable stop if you're heading for Castres. Surrounded by rounded wooded heights around the 1000m mark, it is very much a mountain town, one of the centres of Protestant Camisard resistance at the end of the seventeenth century, when its inaccessibility made the region ideal for clandestine worship. There are **bus** connections most days – not at very convenient times, usually afternoon or very early morning – to Castres, Albi and Bédarieux.

The air is fresh. The town, though somewhat grey in appearance because of the slates and greyish stucco common throughout the region, is cheerful enough. For a place to **stay**, try *Fusiés*, an erstwhile coaching inn opposite the church on rue de la République (☎05.63.37.02.03, *hotelfusies@grand-sud.com*; ④; closed Jan, Fri evening & Sun Nov–March), offering an old-fashioned classiness, or the simpler *Hôtel Calas*, a little way up the hill (☎05.63.37.03.28, fax 05.63.37.09.19; ③), which has a highly-rated restaurant (menus 45–240F/€6.86–36.60).

From here to Castres the most agreeable route is along the wooded **Gijou valley**, following the now defunct train track, past minuscule Gijounet and **LACAZE**, where a nearly derelict **château** strikes a picturesque pose in a bend of the river.

Carcassonne and around

Right on the main Toulouse–Montpellier train link, **CARCASSONNE** couldn't be easier to reach; and for anyone travelling through this region it is a must – one of the most dramatic, if also most-visited, towns in the whole of Languedoc. Carcassonne owes its division into two separate "towns" – the **Cité** and the **Ville Basse** – to the wars against the Cathars. Following Simon de Montfort's capture of the town in 1209, its people tried in 1240 to restore their traditional ruling family, the Trencavels. In reprisal King Louis IX expelled them, only permitting their return on condition they built on the low ground by the River Aude.

Arrival, information and accommodation

Arriving by **train**, you'll find yourself in the *ville basse* on the north bank of the Canal du Midi at the northern limits of the town. To reach the **town centre** from the train station, cross the canal bridge by an oval lock, pass the Jardin Chénier and follow rue Clémenceau, which will take you through the central **place Carnot** and out to the exterior boulevard on the southern side of town (a fifteen-minute walk). The **gare routière** is on boulevard de Varsovie on the northwest side of town, south of the canal, while the **airport** (☎04.68.25.04.53) lies just west of the city, on the #7 bus route (15min; 7.50F/€1.14).

The **tourist office** is at 15 bd Camille-Pelletan (July & Aug daily 9am–6pm; rest of year Mon–Sat 9am–12.15pm & 2–6.30pm; ☎04.68.10.24.30, fax 04.68.10.24.38, *www.tourisme.fr/carcassonne*), at the end of square Gambetta, where the main road from Montpellier enters the town across the Pont-Neuf and the River Aude. There's also an annexe (daily 9am–6pm) just inside the main gate to the medieval Cité, Porte Narbonnaise. For information on the **Cathars**, consult the Centre National d'Études Cathares, 53 rue de Verdun (☎04.68.47.24.66), while local bookshops offer plenty of Cathar literature and souvenir picture books, some in English.

Accommodation

With the exception of the modern, clean, but frequently booked-up **HI hostel** on rue Trencavel (☎04.68.25.23.16, *carcassonne@fuaj.org*), the price of staying in the Cité can be high; if you don't mind paying, try the **hotel** *Le Donjon*, 2 rue Comte-Roger (☎04.68.11.23.00, *hotel.donjon.best.western@wanadoo.fr*; ⑤). Just outside the walls, *du Pont Vieux*, at 32 rue Trivalle (☎04.68.25.24.99, fax 04.68.47.62.71; ③) is one of the best places in Carcassonne, set on a little street which winds up from the medieval bridge to the Cité.

There are, however, some very reasonably priced hotels in the *ville basse*. Pride of place goes to the *Grand Hôtel Terminus*, at 2 av de Maréchal Joffre (☎04.68.25.25.00, fax 04.68.75.53.09; ④; closed Dec–Feb), a station-side hotel of decaying steam-age luxury, with a splendid *fin-de-siècle* facade. The *Montségur*, 27 allée d'Iéna ☎04.68.25.31.41, fax 04.68.47.13.22; ③), is a comfortable nineteenth-century town house, with ample-sized rooms, but is not very close to the Cité. Good economy options include the centrally located *de la Poste*, at 21 rue de Verdun (☎04.68.25.12.18; ①), and the surprisingly well-equipped *St-Joseph*, at 81 rue de la Liberté (☎04.68.71.96.89, fax 04.68.71.36.28; ①).

The **campsite**, *Camping de la Cité*, on route St-Hilaire (☎04.68.25.11.17, fax 04.68.47.33.13), has good shady sites, a shop and some bungalows. Tucked off among parkland to the south of town it can be reached by local bus (line 8) or by foot (about 20min) from the Cité.

The Cité

The attractions of the well-preserved and lively *ville basse* notwithstanding, what everybody comes for is the **Cité**, the double-walled and turreted fortress that crowns the hill above the River Aude. From a distance it's the epitome of the fairytale medieval town. Viollet-le-Duc rescued it from ruin in 1844, and his "too-perfect" restoration has been furiously debated ever since. It is, as you would expect, a real tourist trap. Yet, in spite of the chintzy cafés, arty-crafty shops and the crowds, you'd have to be a very stiff-necked purist not to be moved at all.

To reach the Cité from the *ville basse*, take bus #2 from outside the station, or a *navette* from square Gambetta. Alternatively, you can walk it in under thirty minutes, crossing the Pont-Vieux and climbing rue Barbacane, past the church of St-Gimer to the sturdy bastion of the **Porte d'Aude**. This is effectively the back entrance – the main gate is **Porte Narbonnaise**, round on the east side.

There is no charge for admission to the streets or the grassy *lices* – "lists" – between the walls, though cars are banned from 10am to 6pm. However, to see the inner fortress of the **Château Comtal** and to walk the walls, you'll have to join a guided tour (daily: April, May & Oct 9.30am–6pm; June–Sept 9.30am–7.30pm; Nov–March 9.30am–5pm; 35F/€5.34). The seventy- to ninety-minute tours – several per day in English from June to September – assume some knowledge of French history, pointing out the various phases in the construction of the fortifications, from Roman to Visigothic to Romanesque and to the post-Cathar adaptations of the French kings.

In addition to wandering the narrow streets, don't miss the beautiful church of **St-Nazaire** (daily 9–11.45am & 1.45–6pm), towards the southern corner of the Cité at the end of rue St-Louis. It's a serene combination of Romanesque nave with carved capitals and Gothic transepts and choir adorned with some of the loveliest stained glass in Languedoc. In the south transept is a tombstone believed to belong to Simon de Montfort senior. You can also climb the **tower** (same hours; 10F/€1.53), for spectacular views over the Cité.

CANAL DU MIDI

The **Canal du Midi** runs for 240km from the River Garonne at Toulouse via Carcassonne to the Mediterranean at Agde. It was the brainchild of Pierre-Paul Riquet, a minor noble and tax collector, who succeeded in convincing Louis XIV (and more importantly, his first minister, Colbert) of the merits of linking the Atlantic and the Mediterranean via the Garonne.

The work, begun in 1667, took fourteen years to complete, using tens of thousands of workers. The crux of the problem from the engineering point of view was how to feed the canal with water, when its high point at Naurouze, west of Carcassonne, was 190m above sea level and 58m above the Garonne at Toulouse. Riquet responded by building a system of reservoirs in the Montagne Noire, channelling run-off from the heights down to Naurouze. He spent the whole of his fortune on the canal and, sadly, died just six months before its inauguration in 1681.

The canal was a success and sparked a wave of prosperity along its course, with traffic increasing steadily until 1857, when the Sète-Bordeaux railway was inaugurated, reducing trade on the canal to all but nothing. Today, the canal remains a marvel of engineering and beauty, incorporating no fewer than 99 locks (*écluses*) and 130 bridges, almost all of which date back to the first era of construction. A double file of trees lines most of its length, giving it a distinctive "Midi" look and impeding loss of water through evaporation, while the greenery is enhanced in spring by the bloom of yellow iris and wild gladioli. With all of this and the occasional glimpses afforded of a world beyond – a distant smudge of hills and the towers of Carcassonne – the canal is a pleasure to travel. You can follow it by road, and many sections have foot or bicycle paths, but the best way to travel it, of course, is by boat.

Outfits in all the major ports rent house-boats and barges, and there are many cruise options to choose from as well. For **boat rental and cruises**, contact Crown Blue Line, Le Grand Bassin, BP1201, 11492 Castelnaudary (☎04.68.94.52.72, *boathols@crown-blueline.com*), or Locaboat, Le Grand Bassin (☎03.86.91.72.72, *www.locaboat.com*), both of which have a number of branches in Languedoc and the Midi; or Nautic in Carcassonne (☎04.68.71.88.95, fax 04.67.94.05.91). Canal **information** can be found at the port offices of Voies Navigables de France, at 2 Port St-Étienne in Toulouse (☎05.61.36.24.24, *www.vnf.fr*), who also have English-speaking offices at the major canal ports.

Eating, drinking and entertainment

With over fifty **restaurants** within its walls, the Cité is a good place to look for somewhere to eat, though it tends to be on the expensive side. First choice is the *Auberge de Dame Carcas*, 3 place du Château (☎04.68.71.23.23; closed Sun evening, Mon lunch & Feb; menu at 85F/€12.96), a traditional bistro, offering cassoulet and other regional dishes. Otherwise try the *Jardin de la Tour*, 11 rue Porte d'Aude (closed Sun evening, Mon & Nov), with outside tables, or the smart *Brasserie du Donjon*, in the hotel of the same name (see above); both serve *terroir* menus from 80F/€12.20. There's a much greater variety of affordable places in the *ville basse*: among these *Le Petit Couvert*, at 18 rue de l'Aigle d'Or, has good cheap menus (closed Sun, Mon & March; from 65F/€9.91) and a small street-side terrace, while *La Bérbère*, 2 rue Denisse, is a friendly Moroccan restaurant and *salon du thé* (closed Sun & Mon; 55F/€8.39 menu). Nearby, at 29 bd Jean-Jaurès, the *Divine Comédie* serves a varied menu of pasta, pizzas and regional dishes in generous portions (closed Sun; from 80F/€12.20). For something more sophisticated, try *Chez Fred*, beside Jardin Chénier at 31 bd Omer Sarraut (menus from 98F/€14.95). For picnic provisions, head for the **market** on place Carnot (Tues, Thurs & Sat mornings).

Carcassonne hosts two major festivals: the month-long **Festival de la Cité** in July, with dance, theatre and music, whose highpoint is the mammoth fireworks display on

Bastille Day (July 14); and the elaborate medieval pageant, **Les Médiévales**, held in the first fortnight of August.

Castelnaudary

Thirty-six kilometres west of Carcassonne, on the main road from Toulouse, **CASTEL-NAUDARY** is one of those innumerable French country towns that boast no particular sights but are nonetheless a real pleasure to spend a couple of hours in, having coffee or shopping for a picnic in the market. Today it serves as an important a commercial centre for the rolling Lauragais farming country hereabouts, as it once was for the traffic on the Canal du Midi. In fact, the most flattering view of the town is still that from the canal's **Grand Bassin**, which makes it look remarkably like a Greek island town, with its ancient houses climbing the hillside from the water's edge.

In town you'll find some fine old **mansions**, a restored **windmill** and an eighteenth-century **semaphore** tower. However, Castelnaudary's chief claim to fame is as the world capital of **cassoulet**, which, according to tradition, must be made in an earthenware pot from Issel (a *cassolo*) with beans grown in Pamiers or Lavelanet, and cooked in a baker's oven fired with rushes from the Montagne Noire. To try it, go to the *Grand-Hôtel Fourcade*, 14 rue des Carmes (☎04.68.23.02.08, fax 04.68.94.10.67; closed part Jan & Sept–April Mon & Sun), where you can gorge yourself for 100F/€15.25, then sleep off the after-effects by taking a **room** upstairs (①). More attractive alternatives for spending the night are the modern *Hôtel du Canal*, 2 av Arnaut-Vidal (☎04.68.94.05.05, fax 04.68.94.05.06; ②), in a shady position beside the canal just west of the Grand Bassin, and the *Hôtel du Centre et du Lauragais* (☎04.68.23.25.95, fax 04.68.94.01.66; ③; closed Jan to mid-Feb), a converted nineteenth-century house, centrally located at 31 cours de la République, close to the post office. The **tourist office** is in Castelnaudary's central Halle aux Grains (mid-July to mid-Sept Mon–Sat 9.30am–12.30pm & 2.30–7pm, Sun 9.30am–12.30pm & 3–7pm; rest of year Mon–Sat 9.30am–12.30pm & 2–6.30pm; ☎04.68.23.05.73, *castelnaudary@fnotsi.net*).

Minerve

The village of **MINERVE** lies a dozen kilometres north of the canal du Midi, and halfway between Carcassonne and Béziers in the middle of the Minervois wine country. Its location is extraordinary, isolated on an island of rock between the gorges of the Briant and Cesse rivers, the latter of which has cut its course through two enormous tunnels in the rock known as the *Ponts Naturels*.

The village turned Cathar at the beginning of the thirteenth century, which made it a target for Simon de Montfort's crusade. On July 22, 1210, after a seven-week siege, he took the castle and promptly burnt 180 *parfaits* (or "purified souls"). There is a memorial to them by the **church** and, inside, one of the most ancient altars in Gaul, dated 456 – but you won't be allowed in for love nor money. Nothing remains of the castle but the ruins of a wall.

If you want to stay, you'll find free **camping** in the valley bottom by the cemetery and the *Relais Chantovent* (☎04.68.91.14.18, fax 04.68.91.81.99; ③; closed mid-Dec to mid-March), which is also one of the better places in town to get a meal (menus from 100F/€15.25). The **tourist office** (July & Aug daily 10am–noon & 2–6pm; ☎04.68.91.81.43) has information about other accommodation possibilities in the area.

The Montagne Noire

There are two good routes from Carcassonne into the **Montagne Noire**, which forms the western extremity of the Parc Naturel Régional du Haut Languedoc (see p.771):

Carcassonne–Revel and Carcassonne–Mazamet by the valley of the Orbiel. Neither is served by public transport, but both offer superlative scenery.

The Revel route

The **Revel route** follows the N113 out of Carcassonne, then the D629 through Montolieu (17km) and Saissac. **MONTOLIEU**, semi-fortified and built on the edge of a ravine, has set itself the target of becoming France's second-hand book capital, with shops overflowing with dog-eared and antiquarian tomes. Drop in at the Librairie Booth, by the bridge over the ravine.

SAISSAC, 8km further on, is much more an upland village. Conifers and beech wood, interspersed with patches of rough pasture, surround it, and gardens are terraced down its steep slopes. Remains of towers and fortifications poke out among the ancient houses, and on a spur below the village stand the romantic ruins of its castle and the church of St-Michel.

If you wish to **stay** in the area, try the rather aged *Hôtel de la Montagne Noire* (☎04.68.24.46.36, fax 04.68.24.46.20; ②) on the road through Saissac, with a good local restaurant open all year (menu from 75F/€11.44). More idyllic accommodation is available north of town at *Domaine du Lampy-Neuf* (☎04.68.24.46.07; ③), a *chambres d'hôte* by the banks of the Bassin du Lampy, which also functions as a *gîte*. There are also two **campsites**. If you have your own transport, the best place for miles around and an experience in itself is the *Camping du Bout du Monde* (☎04.68.94.20.92; all year round), at a beautiful tumbledown farm near Verdun-en-Lauragais, 5km west of Saissac. You camp among the broom at the edge of the woods.

Some 14km west of Saissac on the D103 (or just a few kilometres southwest of the *Bout du Monde* campsite), the ancient village of **ST-PAPOUL**, with its walls and Benedictine **abbey**, makes a gentle side trip. Though it's undergoing long-term restoration, you can visit the church and its pretty fourteenth-century cloister on a **guided tour** in French (daily: April–June, Sept & Oct 10am–noon & 2–6pm; July & Aug 10am–7pm; 20F/€3.05). Back on the "main" D629, the road winds down through the forest, past the Bassin de St-Férréol, constructed by Riquet to supply water to the Canal du Midi, and on to **REVEL**. Revel is a *bastide* dating from 1342, featuring an attractive arcaded central square with a superb wooden-pillared *halle* in the middle. Now a prosperous market town (market day is Saturday), it makes an agreeably provincial stopover. The *Auberge du Midi* at 34 bd Gambetta (☎05.61.83.50.50, fax 05.61.83.34.74; ③) is set in a refined old nineteenth-century mansion, and also has the town's best restaurant (menus from 90–180F/€13.73–27.45). Close by at 7 rue de Taur, you'll find the *Commanderie Hôtel* (☎05.63.46.61.24; ③), a good second choice, with an old timber-frame facade and a remodelled interior.

Lastours and the valley of the Orbiel

The alternative route from Carcassonne into the Montagne Noire takes you through the region known as the **Cabardès**. Cut by the deep ravines of the Orbiel and its tributary streams, it's covered with Mediterranean scrub lower down and forests of chestnut and pine higher up. The area is extremely poor and depopulated, with rough stone villages and hamlets crouching in the valleys. Until relatively recently, its people lived off beans and chestnut flour and the meat from their pigs, and worked from very ancient times in the region's copper, iron, lead, silver and gold mines. Nothing now remains of that tradition save for the gold mine at Salsigne, a huge and unsightly open pit atop a bleak windswept plateau.

The most memorable site in the **Orbiel valley** is the **Châteaux de Lastours**, the most northerly of the Cathar castles (see opposite), 16km north of Carcassonne. As the name suggests, there is more than one castle – four in fact, their ruined keeps jutting superbly from a sharp ridge of scrub and cypress that plunges to rivers on both sides.

The two oldest castles, Cabaret (mid-eleventh century) and Surdespine (1153), fell into de Montfort's hands in 1211, after their lords had given shelter to the Cathars. The other two, Tour Régine and Quertinheux, were added after 1240, when the site became royal property, and a garrison was maintained here as late as the Revolution. Today, despite their ruined state, they look as impregnable and beautiful as ever. A path winds up from the roadside, bright in early summer with iris, cistus, broom and numerous other flowers.

About 7km upriver from Lastours, the road and river divide. The left fork leads to the village of **MAS-CABARDÈS**, hunkered down defensively in the river bottom. The right goes to **ROQUEFÈRE**, whose ancient château hosts summertime theatre. From here a steep, serpentine road winds up through magnificent scenery to the tiny hamlet of **CUPSERVIES**, balanced on the edge of a sudden and deep ravine where the Rieutort stream drops some 90m into the bottom. A couple of kilometres further, by the cross-roads at **CANINAC**, there's a tenth-century chapel, **St-Sernin**, in the middle of the woods. To get here without transport, there's a marked footpath from Roquefère, which then returns via Labastide-Esparbairenque (a 4.5-hour round trip).

The Cathar castles

Romantic and ruined, the medieval fortresses which range in a broad arc around Carcassonne have come to be known as the **Cathar castles**, though in fact many of the castles in question were built after the Cathars' demise. The **Cathars** were a sect strong in this part of France, who were proscribed as heretics by Pope Innocent III. With papal blessing and the connivance of the French kings, hungry northern nobles descended on the area in a series of Albigensian crusades, beginning in 1208 and led for many years by the notoriously cruel Simon de Montfort. The name of the sect derives from the Greek word for "clean, pure", *katharos*, and they abhorred the materialism and worldly power of the established Church, proclaiming the simple and humble Christianity of the Sermon on the Mount. Although their adherents probably never accounted for more than ten percent of the population, there were many members of the nobility and the influential classes among them, which alarmed the powers that be.

Cathars who were caught were burnt in communal conflagrations, 100 or 200 at a time. Their lands were laid waste or seized by the northern nobles, de Montfort himself grabbing the properties of the count of Toulouse. The effect of this brutality was to unite both the Cathars and their Catholic neighbours in southern solidarity against the barbarian north. Though military defeat became irreversible with the capitulation of Toulouse in 1229 and the fall of the castle of Montségur (see box on p.728) in 1244, it took the informers and torturers of the Holy Inquisition another seventy years to root out Cathars completely.

The best of the castles are in the arid, herb-scented hills of the **Corbières** to the south of Carcassonne. **Walking** is undoubtedly the most direct way to experience them, and there are numerous paths, of which the **GR36**, crossing from Carcassonne to St-Paul-de-Fenouillet, and the Sentier Cathare, crossing east to west from Port La-Nouvelle to Foix, are the most exciting. The Sentier Cathare is divided into twelve stages with *gîtes d'étape*, described in *Sentier Cathare Topoguide* (Rando Editions), available in local bookstores.

Without transport or walking boots, the best way to tackle them is from the south, as the most spectacular ones are close to the **Perpignan–Quillan** road, which has a bus service. With transport it becomes possible to explore the wilder back roads and utterly ruinous castles like Durfort and Termes, and to cross the cols where orchids and cowslips shudder in the spring winds and the views southward all end in the snowy Pyrenean bulk of Canigou.

Puilaurens

From Quillan (see p.730), the road runs south through the incredibly narrow **défilé de Pierre-Lys** to the Pont d'Aliès before swinging 17km east to the village of Lapradelle and the first of the castles, the **Château de Puilaurens** (daily: April–June & Sept 10am–7pm; July & Aug 9am–8pm; Nov–March 10am–6pm; 20F/€3.05).

You can either drive up or there's a shorter and fairly gentle path from the hamlet of **PUILAURENS**. The castle is perched on top of a high, wooded hill at 700m, its fine crenellated walls built around the very top of the rock outcrops. Although the existence of a castle here dates from the tenth century, it seems more likely that it was fortified to something like its present extent in the early thirteenth century, when it passed from the king of France to the count of Roussillon, and then to the king of Aragon. It sheltered many Cathars up to 1256, when Chabert de Barbera, effective controller of power in the region, was captured and forced to hand over his strongholds here and at Quéribus further east, to secure his release. The castle remained strategically important, being close to the Spanish border, until 1659, when France annexed Roussillon and the frontier was pushed away to the south. The view from the battlements, which you can climb up to at one point, is quite breathtaking.

Five kilometres south of the village is the *Hostellerie du Grand Duc* in **GINCLA** (☎04.68.20.55.02, fax 04.68.20.61.22; ④; closed in winter), and a **gîte** (☎04.68.20.59.39) nearby at Col de Tuilla.

Quéribus, Cucugnan and Duilhac

The **Château de Quéribus** (Feb, March, Nov & Dec Sat, Sun & hols 10am–5pm; April & Oct daily 10am–6pm; May, June & Sept daily 10am–7pm; July & Aug daily 10am–7pm; 25F/€3.81), 30km further east towards Perpignan, stands on the ridge above the vine-ringed village of Cucugnan (see below), a few kilometres north of the main Quillan–Perpignan road – with a good chance of a lift up to the castle. Again, it is spectacularly situated, balanced on a pillar of rock above a sheer cliff, whose crevices nourish a variety of beautiful wild flowers. Until 1659 this was the border with Spain.

Because of the extreme, cramped topography of the rock, the space within the walls is stepped in terraces, dominated by the polygonal keep and accessible by a single stairway. Inside, at the heart of the keep, is the remarkable **chapel** of St-Louis-de-Quéribus, surprisingly high and wide when you consider the keep's tortured position, and supported by a single pillar. The stairs to the roof are broken, but from the window halfway up there are fantastic views to Canigou and Perpignan, with other castles and watchtowers of the Spanish Marches dotting the peaks and ridges. To the northwest you're within easy eyeshot of Peyrepertuse.

The history of Quéribus is similar to that of Puilaurens, though the fortifications visible today are thirteenth century. It was the last stronghold of Cathar resistance, holding out until 1255, eleven years beyond the fall of Montségur. Never reduced by siege, its role as a sanctuary for the Cathars ended with the capture of the luckless Chabert.

Entry to Quéribus also includes the **Théâtre Achille Mir** (same hours) in the small village of **CUCUGNAN**, in the valley to the north of the château. Through an imaginative slide-show the theatre retells the story of the Curé de Cucugnan, hero of Alphonse Daudet's book *Lettres de Mon Moulin*; locals claim he's based on their own nineteenth-century abbot Ruffié. The village also has a rare statue of a pregnant Virgin Mary in its pretty little church. There's **accommodation** at the *Auberge du Vigneron*, opposite the theatre (☎04.68.45.40.84, fax 04.68.45.01.52; ③; closed mid-Feb to mid-March), while the *Auberge de Cucugnan* (☎04.68.45.03.00, fax 04.68.45.01.52; ③; closed Feb), near the church, has a restaurant known for its hearty servings of game (from 100F/€15.25 including wine). The nearest other rooms are in **DUILHAC**, about 4km away below Peyrepertuse (see below), at the *Auberge du Vieux Moulin* (☎04.68.45.02.17, fax 04.68.45.02.18; ③; closed late Dec to early Feb; restaurant from 55–140F/€8.39–21.35). There is also an *alimentation* in the village, selling bread, open even on Sunday morning.

Peyrepertuse

If you only have time to visit one of the Cathar castles, then your best bet is **Château de Peyrepertuse** (daily: April–June & Sept 10am–7pm; July & Aug 9am–8pm; Nov–March 10am–6pm; 20F/€3.05), not only for its unbeatable site and stunning views, but also because the complex is unusually well preserved. The access road starts in Duilhac (see above) or, alternatively, you can walk up from Rouffiac village, on the north side, by the GR36; in summer it's a tough, hot climb that takes the best part of an hour. But either way the effort is rewarded, for Peyrepertuse is one of the most awe-inspiring castles anywhere in Europe, clinging to the crest of a long, wickedly jagged spine of rock on the top of a mountain ridge, surrounded by sheer drops of hundreds of metres.

You enter on the north side through thickets of boxwood. The heaviest fortifications enclose the lower eastern end of the ridge, with a keep and barbican controlling the main gate. The castle is much larger than the others despite its precarious hold on the earth, with extensive buildings inside the outer wall, culminating in a keep and tower shutting off the highest point of the ridge, where such a pit of air opens at your feet that no artificial defence is necessary.

Surprisingly, the castle was taken by the French without much difficulty in 1240, and most of the existing fortifications were built after that. Whatever you do, don't go up in a thunderstorm; there can be some fierce ones in summer, and the ridge brings down the lightning as surely as a high-tension cable.

If you need to **stay** the night, head for **ROUFFIAC**. The **hotel** here, the *Auberge de Peyrepertuse* (☎04.68.45.40.40; ②; closed late Dec to mid-Jan), also has dormitory accommodation (①), plus a restaurant (about 100F/€15.25). There are **bus** services on Wednesday and Saturday to St-Paul-de-Fenouillet on the main Perpignan D117 road, returning at 11am. Walkers can also call on the services of Balade Cathare (☎04.68.45.05.10), based in Rouffiac, which runs a minibus shuttling people and bags around the area; it helps if you can give them as much notice as possible.

Moving on from Peyrepertuse, by car or by the GR36, you can return to St-Paul-de-Fenouillet through the narrow **Gorges de Galamus**, and in many places you can get down to the river for a swim. On the way you pass the eagle's-nest **Hermitage St-Antoine**, built into the side of the ravine.

Alternatively, the drive eastwards offers more castles, including Padern and the especially fine **Aguilar**, near Tuchan, which overlooks the hills and vales of the Côtes de Roussillon-Villages wine area, with magnificent views from the twisty climbing roads. From here you have the possibility of heading either north towards Narbonne or south through Tautavel to Perpignan.

TOULOUSE AND WESTERN LANGUEDOC

With its own sunny, cosmopolitan charms, **Toulouse** is a very accessible kick-off point for any destination in the southwest of France. Of the immediately surrounding places, **Albi** is the number-one priority, with its highly original cathedral and comprehensive collection of Toulouse-Lautrec paintings. Once you've made it that far, it's worth the extra hop to the well-preserved medieval town of **Cordes**.

Toulouse

TOULOUSE, with its beautiful historic centre, is one of the most vibrant and metropolitan provincial cities in France. This is a transformation that has come about since the war, under the guidance of the French state, which has poured in money to make Toulouse the think-tank of high-tech industry and a sort of premier trans-national Euroville. Always an **aviation** centre – St-Exupéry and Mermoz flew out from here on their pioneering airmail flights over Africa and the Atlantic in the 1920s – Toulouse is now home to Aérospatiale, the driving force behind Concorde, Airbus and the Ariane space rocket. The national Space Centre, the European shuttle programme, the leading aeronautical schools, the frontier-pushing electronics industry... it's all happening in Toulouse, whose 110,000 students make it second only to Paris as a **university** centre. But it's not to the burgeoning suburbs of factories, labs, shopping and housing complexes that all these people go for their entertainment, but to the old **Ville Rose** – pink not only in its brickwork, but also in its politics.

This is not the first flush of pre-eminence for Toulouse. From the tenth to the thirteenth centuries the counts of Toulouse controlled much of southern France. They maintained the most resplendent court in the land, renowned especially for its troubadours, the poets of courtly love, whose work influenced Petrarch, Dante and Chaucer and thus the whole course of European poetry. Until, that is, the arrival of the hungry northern French nobles of the Albigensian Crusade; in 1271 Toulouse became crown property.

Arrival, information and accommodation

The train station, **gare Matabiau**, and **gare routière** (☎05.61.61.67.67), stand side by side in boulevard Pierre-Sémard on the bank of the tree-lined and imaginatively planted Canal du Midi. This is where you'll find yourself if you arrive by train, bus or air, for the **airport shuttle** (every 20min; 20min journey; 23F/€3.36) puts you down at the bus station (with stops also in allées Jean-Jaurès and at place Jeanne-d'Arc). It is also the best spot to aim for if you are in a car: leave the **boulevard périphérique** at exit 15.

To reach the city centre from the train station takes just five minutes by **métro** to stop Capitole (8F/€1.22, covering one hour's transport by métro and Semvat city buses within the city centre), or twenty minutes on foot. Turn left out of the station, cross the canal and head straight down allées Jean-Jaurès, through place Wilson and on into place du Capitole, the city's main square. Just before it lie the shady and much-frequented gardens of the square Charles-de-Gaulle, where the main **tourist office** (May–Sept Mon–Sat 9am–7pm, Sun 10am–1pm & 2–6.30pm; rest of year Mon–Fri 9am–6pm, Sat 9am–12.30pm & 2–6pm, Sun 10am–12.30pm & 2–5pm; ☎05.61.11.02.22, *www.Mairie-Toulouse.fr*) is housed in a sixteenth-century tower that has been restored to look like a castle keep; the Capitole métro stop is right outside.

The best guide to **what's on** in and around the city – and usually there is a lot, from opera to cinema – is the weekly listings magazines *Toulouse Hebdo* (3F/€0.46) and *Flash* (6F/€0.92). More highbrow interests are covered in the free monthly *Toulouse Culture*, available from the tourist office, among other places.

The best place to **stay** is in the city centre, where there are a number of excellent-value hotels, as well as many more upmarket establishments. The area around the train station, though charmless and still retaining some of its red-light seediness, has a few acceptable options if you're stuck. There is no hostel, but there are a number of accommodation centres for visitors who plan on staying for more than a few days: the CRIJ (see p.790, Listings, "Youth Information") and the Club UNESCO Midi-Pyrénées, forum des

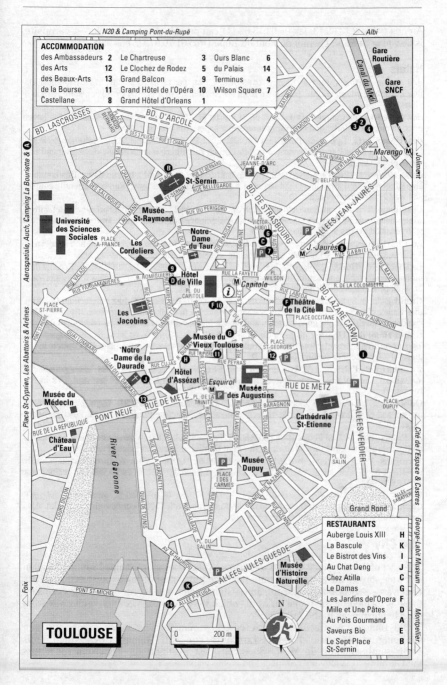

△ N20 & Camping Pont-du-Rupé △ Albi

ACCOMMODATION

des Ambassadeurs	2	Le Chartreuse	3	Ours Blanc	6
des Arts	12	Le Clochez de Rodez	5	du Palais	14
des Beaux-Arts	13	Grand Balcon	13	Terminus	4
de la Bourse	11	Grand Hôtel de l'Opéra	10	Wilson Square	7
Castellane	8	Grand Hôtel d'Orleans	1		

RESTAURANTS

Auberge Louis XIII	H
La Bascule	K
Le Bistrot des Vins	I
Au Chat Deng	J
Chez Atilla	C
Le Damas	G
Les Jardins del'Opera	F
Mille et Une Pâtes	D
Au Pois Gourmand	A
Saveurs Bio	E
Le Sept Place St-Sernin	B

TOULOUSE

0   200 m

Arènes (☎05.62.13.62.13, fax 05.62.13.62.14) can provide details. The closest **campsite** is *Camping de Rupé*, chemin du Pont du Rupé (☎05.61.70.07.35; bus #59, stop "Rupé").

Hotels

des Ambassadeurs, 68 rue Bayard (☎05.61.62.65.84, fax 05.61.62.97.38). Very friendly little hotel, run by a young couple. Just down from the station, its rooms all have TV, en-suite bath and phone. ②.

des Arts, 1bis rue Cantegril (☎05.61.23.36.21, fax 05.61.12.22.37). This is a top choice in the lower price range, with quirky and charming rooms in a superb old building. ①.

des Beaux-Arts, 1 place du Pont-Neuf (☎05.34.45.42.42, fax 05.34.45.42.43, *hba@internetclub.fr*). Elegant hotel housed in a 150-year-old building; each room here is individually decorated and has views of the Garonne. ⑤.

de la Bourse, 11 rue Clemence-Isaure (☎05.61.21.55.86). Basic and a bit run-down, this comfortable hotel is tucked away in a small street in a quiet part of the old town. Run by a friendly couple, and well located for the sights. ①.

Castellane, 17 rue Castellane (☎05.61.62.18.82, fax 05.61.62.58.04). A cheerful new hotel with a wide selection of room-types and -sizes, most of which are bright and quiet. One of the few hotels with disabled access in this price range. ⑤.

Le Chartreuse, 4bis bd Bonrepos (☎05.61.62.93.39, fax 05.61.62.58.17). Efficient and modern, if soulless, choice right by the station. Great value, considering the amenities and price. ②.

Le Clochez de Rodez, 14 place de Jeanne-d'Arc (☎05.61.62.42.92, fax 05.61.62.68.99). Freshly decorated, comfortable and central, with secure parking. Despite its size, it exudes a very personal hospitality, and has disabled access. ②.

Grand Balcon, 8 rue Romiguières (☎05.61.21.48.08, fax 05.61.21.59.98). Just off place du Capitole, this ageing classic was frequented by St-Exupéry and co in their pioneering days. It's now rather run-down, but definitely a good bargain, and smack in the centre of things. Closed most of Aug. ③.

Grand Hôtel de l'Opéra, 1 place du Capitole (☎05.61.21.82.66, fax 05.61.23.41.04, *www.grand-hotel -opera.com*). The elegant *grand dame* of Toulouse's hotels presides over the place du Capitole in the guise of a seventeenth-century convent. ⑦.

Grand Hôtel d'Orleans, 72 rue Bayard (☎05.61.62.98.47, fax 05.61.62.78.24, *www.grand-hotel -orleans.fr*). One of the better choices in the station zone, with a lift, and bar and TVs in the rooms. ④.

Ours Blanc, 25 place de Victor-Hugo (☎05.61.21.62.40, fax 05.61.23.62.34). Right by the covered market and steps from the Capitole, this cheerful and well-outfitted hotel is one of the city's better bargains. ④.

du Palais, 4 allées Paul-Feuga (☎05.62.26.56.57, fax 05.62.26.47.87). A great one-star hotel located on the southern edge of the old town by the Pont St-Michel. Reception closed Sun. ②.

Terminus, 13 bd Bonrepos (☎05.61.62.44.78, fax 05.61.63.18.06). This old three-star station-side hotel has good-value large, renovated rooms. Parking for 32F/€4.88 and a buffet breakfast for 42F/€6.41. ④.

Wilson Square, 12 rue d'Austerlitz (☎05.61.21.67.57, fax 05.61.21.16.23, *hotlwilson@aol.com*). Clean and well-kept place at the top end of rue Austerlitz, with TV, air-conditioning and a lift. Also features a great patisserie on the street level. ②.

The City

The part of the city you'll want to see forms a rough hexagon clamped round a bend in the wide, brown River Garonne and contained in a ring of inner nineteenth-century boulevards – Strasbourg, Carnot, Jules-Guesde and others. An outer ring enclosing these is formed by the Canal du Midi, which here joins the Garonne on its way from the Mediterranean to the Atlantic.

Old Toulouse is effectively quartered by two nineteenth-century streets: the long shopping street, **rue d'Alsace-Lorraine/rue du Languedoc**, which runs north–south; and **rue de Metz**, which runs east–west onto the Pont-Neuf and across the Garonne. It is all very compact and easily walkable.

In addition to the general pleasure of wandering the streets, there are three very good museums and some real architectural treasures in the churches of St-Sernin and Les Jacobins and in the magnificent Renaissance town houses – *hôtels particuliers* – of the merchants who grew rich on the woad-dye trade. This formed the basis of the city's economy from the mid-fifteenth to the mid-sixteenth century, when the arrival of indigo from the Indian colonies wiped it out.

Place du Capitole is the centre of gravity for the city's social life. Its smart cafés throng with people at lunchtime and in the early evening when the dying sun flushes the pink facade of the big town hall opposite. This is the scene of a mammoth Wednesday **market** for food, clothes and junk, and of a smaller organic foods market on Tuesday and Saturday mornings. From place du Capitole, a labyrinth of narrow medieval streets radiates out to the town's several other squares, such as place Wilson, the more intimate place St-Georges, the delightful triangular place de la Trinité and place St-Étienne in front of the cathedral.

For green space, you have to head for the sunny banks of the Garonne or the lovely formal gardens of the **Grand-Rond** and **Jardin des Plantes** in the southeast corner of the centre. A less obvious but attractive alternative is the towpath of the Canal du Midi; the best place to join it is a short walk southeast of the Jardin des Plantes, by the neo-Moorish pavilion of the **Georges-Labit museum**, which houses a good collection of Egyptian and Oriental art.

The Capitole and the hôtels particuliers

Occupying the whole of the eastern side of the eponymous square, the **Capitole** has been the seat of Toulouse's city government since the twelfth century. In medieval times it housed the *capitouls*, who made up the relatively democratic and independent city council, from which its name derives. This institution, under the name of *consulat*, was common to other Languedoc towns and may have been the inspiration for England's first parliamentary essays, often attributed to Simon de Montfort, son of the general who became familiar with these parts in the course of his merciless campaigns against the Cathar heretics in the early 1200s. Today, these medieval origins are disguised by an elaborate pink and white classical facade (1750) of columns and pilasters, from which the flags of Languedoc, the Republic and the European Union are proudly flown. If there are no official functions taking place, you can have a peek inside (Mon–Fri 9am–5pm, Sat 9am–1pm; free) at the Salle des Illustres and a couple of other rooms covered in flowery, late nineteenth-century murals and some more subdued Impressionist works by Henri Martin.

Many of the old *capitouls* built their **hôtels** in the dense web of now mainly pedestrianized streets round about. The material they used was almost exclusively the flat Toulousain brick, whose rosy colour gives the city its nickname of *Ville Rose*. It is an attractive material, lending a small-scale, detailed finish to otherwise plain facades, and setting off admirably any wood- or stonework. Although many of the *hôtels* survive, they are rarely open to the public, so you have to do a lot of nonchalant sauntering into courtyards to get a look at them. The best known, open to visitors thanks to its very handsome Bremberg collection of paintings, is the **Hôtel Assézat**, at the river end of rue de Metz (Tues, Wed & Fri–Sun 10am–6pm, Thurs 10am–9pm; 30F/€4.57, plus 20F/€3.05 for temporary exhibits). Started in 1555 under the direction of Nicolas Bachelier, Toulouse's most renowned Renaissance architect, and never finished, it is a sumptuous palace of brick and stone, sporting columns of the three classical orders of Doric, Ionic and Corinthian, plus a lofty staircase tower surmounted by an octagonal lantern. The paintings within include works by Cranach the Elder, Tintoretto and Canaletto as well as moderns like Pissarro, Monet, Gauguin, Vlaminck, Dufy and a roomful of Bonnards. From April to October there's also a *salon de thé* in the covered entrance gallery.

Other fine houses exist just to the south: on rue Pharaon, in place des Carmes, on rue du Languedoc and on rue Dalbade, where the Hôtel Clary (also known as de Pierre), at no. 25, is unusual for being built of stone. To the north, it's worth wandering along rue St-Rome, rue des Changes, rue de la Bourse and rue du May, where the Hôtel du May at no. 7 houses the **Musée du Vieux-Toulouse** (June–Sept Mon–Sat 2–6pm; 12F/€1.83), a rather uninspiring museum of the city's history.

The Musée des Augustins, the cathedral and the riverside

Right at the junction of rue de Metz and rue d'Alsace-Lorraine stands the **Musée des Augustins** (Mon & Thurs–Sun 10am–6pm, Wed 10am–9pm; *www.augustins.org*; 12F/€1.83). Outwardly unattractive, the nineteenth-century building incorporates two surviving cloisters of an Augustinian priory (one now restored as a monastery garden) and contains outstanding collections of Romanesque and medieval sculpture, much of it saved from the now-vanished churches of Toulouse's golden age. Many of the pieces form a fascinating, highly naturalistic display of contemporary manners and fashions: merchants with forked beards touching one another's arms in a gesture of familiarity, and the Virgin represented as a pretty, bored young mother looking away from the Child who strains to escape her hold.

To the south of the museum, just past the Chambre de Commerce, the pretty **rue Croix-Baragon**, full of smart shops and galleries, opens at its eastern end onto the equally attractive **place St-Étienne**, which boasts the city's oldest fountain, the Griffoul (1546). Behind it stands the lopsided **cathedral of St-Étienne**, whose construction was spread over so many centuries that it makes no architectural sense at all. But there is ample compensation in the quiet and elegant streets of the quarter immediately to the south, and in the **Musée Paul-Dupuy**, a few minutes' walk away along rue Tolosane and rue Mage at 13 rue de la Pléau (June–Sept Wed–Sun 10am–6pm; rest of year Wed–Sun 10am–5pm; 12F/€1.83), which has a beautifully displayed and surprisingly interesting collection of clocks, watches, clothes, pottery and furniture from the Middle Ages to the present day, as well as a good display of religious art.

If you follow the rue de Metz westward from the cathedral, you come to the **Pont-Neuf** – begun in 1544, despite its name – where you can cross over to the **St-Cyprien quarter** on the left bank of the Garonne. At the end of the bridge on the left, an old water tower, erected in 1822 to supply clean water to the city's drinking fountains, now houses the **Galerie Municipale du Château d'Eau** (Mon & Wed–Sun 2–7pm; 15F/€2.29), an influential photography exhibition space and information centre, with frequent changes of exhibition. Next door in the old hospital buildings, there's a small **medical museum** (Mon–Fri 5–7pm, Sat & Sun 1–7pm; free), housing a selection of surgical instruments and pharmaceutical equipment. But the star of the right bank is undoubtedly Toulouse's new contemporary art gallery, **Les Abattoirs**, at 76 allées Charles-de-Fitte (Tues–Sun noon–8pm; *www.lesabattoirs.org*; 20F/€3). This splendid venue, opened in July 2000, is not only one of France's best contemporary art museums, but a inspiring example of urban regeneration, constructed in a vast brick abattoir complex dating from 1828. The space itself is massive, with huge chambers perfectly suited to display even the largest canvases. The collection comprises over 2000 works (painting, sculpture, mixed- and multi media) by artists from 44 countries, but the most striking piece is undoubtedly Picasso's massive 14m by 20m theatre backdrop, *La dépouille du Minotaure en costume d'Arlequin*, painted in 1936 for Romain Rolland's *Le 14 Juillet*, which towers over the lower gallery.

The churches of Les Jacobins and St-Sernin

A short distance west of place du Capitole, on rue Lakanal, you can't miss the **church of the Jacobins**. Constructed in 1230 by the Order of Preachers (Dominicans) which St Dominic had founded here in 1216 to preach against Cathar heretics, the church is a huge fortress-like rectangle of unadorned brick, buttressed – like Albi cathedral – by plain brick piles, quite unlike what you'd normally associate with Gothic architecture. The interior is a single space divided by a central row of ultra-slim pillars from whose minimal capitals spring an elegant splay of vaulting ribs – 22 from the last in line – like palm fronds. Beneath the altar lie the bones of the philosopher St Thomas Aquinas. On the north side, you step out into the calming hush of a **cloister** with a formal array of box trees and cypress in the middle, and its adjacent art **exhibition hall** (daily 7am–7pm; 20F/€3.05, cloister only 14F/€2.14). Nearby, at the corner of rue Gambetta and rue Lakanal, poke your nose into the stone-galleried courtyard of the **Hôtel de Bernuy**, one of the city's most elaborate Renaissance houses.

From the north side of place du Capitole, **rue du Taur** leads past the belfry wall of **Notre-Dame-du-Taur**, whose diamond-pointed arches and decorative motifs represent the acme of Toulousain bricklaying skills, to place St-Sernin. Here you're confronted with the largest Romanesque church in France, the **basilica of St-Sernin**, begun in 1080 to accommodate the passing hordes of Santiago pilgrims, and one of the loveliest examples of its genre. Its most striking external features are the octagonal brick belfry with rounded and pointed arches, diamond lozenges, colonnettes and mouldings picked out in stone, and the apse with nine radiating chapels. Entering from the south, you pass under the Porte Miégeville, whose twelfth-century carvings launched the influential Toulouse school of sculpture. Inside, the great high nave rests on brick piers, flanked by double aisles of diminishing height, surmounted by a gallery running right around the building. The small fee for the **ambulatory** (daily 10am–6pm; 10F/€1.53) is well worth it for the exceptional eleventh-century marble reliefs on the end wall of the choir.

Right outside St-Sernin is the city's archeological museum, **Musée St-Raymond** (daily: June–Sept 10am–7pm; rest of year 10am–6pm; 12F/€1.83), housed in what remains of the block built for poor students' of the medieval university and containing a large collection of objects ranging from prehistoric to Roman, as well as an excavated necropolis in the basement. On Sunday mornings the whole of place St-Sernin turns into a marvellous, teeming **flea market**.

The suburbs

To see something of the modern face of Toulouse, it's necessary to venture out into the suburbs, where you can visit a high-tech amusement park and a very specialized but surprisingly interesting aircraft assembly plant. The first of these is the **Cité de l'Espace** (daily: July & Aug 9.30am–7pm; rest of year 9.30am–6pm; *www.cite -espace.com*; 69F/€10.52), beside exit 17 of the A612 *périphérique* on the road to Castres, or take bus #19 from place Marengo. The theme is space and space exploration, including satellite communications, space probes and, best of all, the opportunity to walk inside a mock-up of the Mir space station – fascinating, but absolutely chilling. Many of the exhibits are interactive and, though it's a bit on the pricey side, you could easily spend a half-day here, especially if you've got children in tow.

In 1970 Toulouse became home to **Aérospatiale**, which, along with the aerospace industries of Germany, Britain and Spain, now manufactures Airbus passenger jets. The planes are assembled, painted and tested in a vast hanger, L'Usine Clément Ader, before taking their maiden flights from next-door Blagnac airport. Members of the public are allowed inside the plant on a highly informative guided tour (occasionally in English; 55F/€8.39), but you need to apply at least two weeks before with your passport details, or a few days before for citizens of EU-member countries (July & Aug contact the tourist office; rest of year call the company direct on ☎05.61.18.06.01). After a brief bus tour round the site and a short PR film, you climb high above the eerily quiet assembly bays where just one hundred people churn out five planes a week, ably assisted by scores of computerized robots.

Eating, drinking and entertainment

Regular daytime **café-lounging** can be pursued around the popular student-arty hang-out of place Arnaud-Bernard, while place du Capitole is the early evening meeting place. Place St-Georges remains popular, though its clientele is no longer convincingly bohemian, and place Wilson also has its enthusiasts.

There are several good areas to look for a place to **eat**. One of the most attractive and fashionable, with a wide choice, is the rue de la Colombette, in the St-Aubin district just across boulevard Carnot, near the junction with allées Jean-Jaurès. Another is place Arnaud-Bernard and the tiny adjacent place des Tiercerettes, just north of St-Sernin. Rue du Taur has a number of Vietnamese places and sandwich bars, and the narrow rue du May has a crêperie, pasta place and restaurant. For lunch, however, there is no surpassing the row of five or six small restaurants jammed in line on the mezzanine floor above the gorgeous **food market** in place Victor-Hugo. They only function at lunchtime, are all closed on Monday, and cost as little as 58F/€8.85. Both food and atmosphere are perfect.

Cafés

Bibent, 5 place du Capitole. On the south side of the square, this is Toulouse's most distinguished café, with exuberant plasterwork, marble tables and cascading chandeliers.

Le Café des Artistes, place de la Daurade. Lively young café overlooking the Garonne. A perfect spot to watch the sun set on warm summer evenings, as floodlights pick out the brick buildings along the *quais*.

Le Florida, 12 place du Capitole. Relaxed café with a nicely retro air. One of the most pleasant places to hang out on the central square.

Jour de Fête, 43 rue de Taur. Trendy tea room and brasserie with a small street-side patio. Friendly service and a young university-set crowd.

au Trait d'Union, 12 rue des Gestes (*autraitdunion@wanadoo.fr*). Funky tea-house and art gallery down a small street just off the place du Capitole. Closed Sun & Mon.

Restaurants

Auberge Louis XIII, 1 rue Tripière (☎05.61.21.23.97). Good, uncomplicated home-cooking with local dishes in generous portions, and a nice courtyard for warm weather. Menus at 52F/€7.93, 70F/€10.68 and 86F/€13.12. Closed Sat & Sun.

La Bascule, 14 av Maurice-Hauriou (☎05.61.52.09.51). A Toulouse classic, serving well-cooked and well-presented regional dishes like cassoulet and *foie de canard*, along with oysters from the Bay of Arcachon. Menus from around 120F/€18.30. Closed Sun & Mon evenings.

Le Bistrot des Vins, place St-Étienne. An attractive, informal place with modern decor inside, plus tables on the pavement on the north side of the cathedral. Sells a huge selection of wines (8–40F/€1.22–6.10 per glass) and a *plat du jour* at around 50F/€7.63. Closed Sun & Mon.

au Chat Deng, 37 rue Peyrolières. Small, hip bistro, with cool blue decor, across from the *Petit Voisin* bar. Menus from 85F/€12.96, but considerably more à la carte. Closed Sun.

Chez Atilla, place Victor-Hugo. The best of the market restaurants, this no-nonsense lunch-time establishment is also one of Toulouse's best options for seafood. Menus from 58F/€8.85. Closed Mon & part Aug.

Le Damas, 32 rue Pollainaires (☎05.61.55.01.40). Great Syrian-Moroccan restaurant done up in gold and red, serving a wide selection of Middle Eastern and North African dishes and good vegetarian *plat* at 70F/€10.68.

Les Jardins de l'Opéra, 1 place du Capitole (☎05.61.23.07.76). The *Grand Hôtel*'s restaurant is one of Toulouse's best and most luxurious. It's expensive – starting with a basic menu of 220F/€33.55 – but worth it if your wallet allows. Closed Sun & part Aug.

Mille et Une Pâtes, 1 rue Mirepoix (☎05.61.21.97.83). Modern, unpretentious restaurant specializing in pasta (*pâtes*), with umpteen varieties on offer, even in the desserts. Count on around 100F/€15.25 for a full meal. Closed Sun.

Au Pois Gourmand, 3 rue Émile Heybrard (☎05.61.31.95.95). Pricey but high-quality French cuisine served in a great location in a riverside nineteenth-century house. Lunch around 130F/€19.83, dinner from 185F/€28.21. Closed Sat lunch & Sun.

Saveurs Bio, 22 rue Maurice-Fonvielle (☎05.61.12.15.15). Toulouse's best vegetarian place, with various set meals for under 100F/€15.25. Closed Sat evening & Sun.

Le Sept Place St-Sernin, 7 place St-Sernin (☎05.62.30.05.30). Lively and cheerful restaurant, concealed in a small house behind the basilica, serving inventive and original cuisine, followed by dazzling desserts. Menus 95–195F/€14.49–29.74. Closed Sun.

Bars and clubs

L'Ambassade, 22 bd de la Gare. Downbeat club where funk and soul rule. Live jazz on Sunday nights. Mon–Fri 7pm–2am, Sat & Sun 7pm–5am.

Arc en Ciel, 34 rue Teinturiers (☎05.61.42.77.34). One of Toulouse's best small venues for live rock music. Tues–Sat 9pm–2am.

Bagdam Café, 4 rue de la Croix (☎05.61.99.03.62). Bohemian place, catering for women only, with readings, music and drama as well as coffee, drinks and food. Tues–Sat from 7pm. Closed mid-Aug to mid-Sept.

Bar du Matin, 16 place des Carmes. Great old street-corner bar in the finest beer, peanuts and *pastis* tradition. A friendly and deservedly popular place. Mon–Sat 8am–11pm.

Bodega-Bodega, 1 rue Gabriel-Péri. The old *Telegraph* newspaper building makes a superb venue for this bar-restaurant, with its hugely popular disco after 10pm. Daily 7pm–2am, till 4am on Sat.

Le Chat d'Oc, 7 rue de Metz. Hip bar near the Garonne, attracting a mixed crowd which gets younger as the night progresses. Nightly *animations* include DJs and occasional live acts, with themes from grunge to Goth. Mon–Fri 7am–2am, Sat 9am–5am.

Erich Coffie, 9 rue Joseph-Vié (☎05.61.42.04.27). Just west of the river in the quartier St-Cyprien, this is one of the city's liveliest and most enjoyable music bars (food available), with an eclectic music policy. Live bands most evenings. Open Tues–Sat from 10pm.

Le Fair Play, 4 allées Paul-Feuga. A great bar for sports fans, which fills up whenever there is a football or rugby match or *jai alai* to watch. Happy hour Thurs 6–8pm.

The Frog & Rosbif, 14 rue de l'Industrie. Stop by this friendly British pub, just off bd Lazare-Carnot, for a pint of *Darktagnan* stout, or one of their other excellent home-brews. Quiz nights, football and fish and chips draw a surprisingly international crowd. Mon–Fri & Sun 5.30pm–2am, Sat 2pm–4am. Closed part Aug.

Hey Joe, place Héraclès. Popular disco with theme nights on Thursdays. Men pay 50F/€7.63, women get in free; happy hour midnight–1am. Open daily 11pm–5am.

José – fait jeter les Watts, 11 place des Puits Clos. Popular with the grunge set, this bar has a good patio by day and DJs by night. Mon–Sat 10am–2am.

Le Petit Voisin, 37 rue Peyrolières. A neighbourhood place, just like the name says, laid-back during the day, and with DJs at night. Open Mon–Fri 7.30am–2am, Sat 8am–4am. Closed mid-Aug.

Thélème, l'Abbaye, 41 rue Paradoux. Friendly bohemian refuge where customers and staff play guitar or piano. Fine wines and select light snacks are on offer. Occasional literary nights. Open Mon & Wed–Sun from 7pm.

L'Ubu, 16 rue St-Rome (☎05.61.23.26.75). Long-standing pillar of the city's dance scene, which remains as popular as ever. Mon–Sat 11pm till dawn.

Film, theatre and live music

Drinking and dancing aside, there is still plenty to do at night in Toulouse. Several **cinemas** regularly show *v.o.* films, including: ABC, 13 rue St-Bernard (☎05.61.29.81.00); Cinémathèque, 68 rue de Taur (☎05.62.30.30.10); Cratere, 95 Grande rue St-Michel (☎05.61.52.50.53); and Utopia, 24 rue Montardy (☎05.61.23.66.20). There is also an extremely vibrant **theatre** culture here. The tourist office can give you a full list of venues, which range from the official Théâtre de la Cité, 1 rue Pierre-Baudis (☎05,34.45.05.05, *www.tnt-cite.com*) to the workshop Nouveau Théâtre Jules-Julien, 6 av des Écoles-Jules-Juliens (Mon–Fri 9am–noon & 2–5pm; ☎05.61.25.79.92). The larger venues, such as Odyssud, 4 av du Parc Blagnac (☎05.61.71.75.15; bus #66), feature both theatre and **opera**, while the Orchestre National du Capitole has its base in the Halle aux Grains on place Dupuy (☎05.61.99.78.00, *www.onct.mairie-toulouse.fr*). The city's biggest **concert venue** (9000 seats), specializing in rock, is Zénith at 11 av Raymond Badiou (☎05.62.74.49.49; metro Arènes, Patte d'Oie; bus # 14, 46, 63–67), while Cave-Poesie at 71 rue de Taur (☎05.61.23.62.00) is home to literary workshops and gatherings of a decidedly bohemian spirit.

Listings

Airport Aéroport Toulouse-Blagnac (☎05.61.42.44.00, *www.toulouse.airport.fr*). For shuttle bus reservation call ☎05.34.60.64.00.

Bicycle rental Bikes and scooters available at Rev'moto, 14 bd de la Gare (☎05.62.47.07.08). Serious cyclists may want to contact the Association Vélo, 2 rue de la Daurade, 31000 Toulouse (☎05.61.11.87.09, *www.multimania.com/velotlse*).

Books For English-language books, Books and Mermaides, 3 rue Mirepoix, specializes in second-hand tomes and will exchange, while The Bookshop, 17 rue Lakanal, stocks new titles.

Car rental A2L, 81 bd Déodat-de-Séverac (☎05.61.59.33.99); Avis, *gare SNCF* (☎05.61.63.71.71); Budget, 49 rue Bayard (☎05.61.63.18.18); Europcar, 15 bd Bonrepos (☎05.61.62.52.89); Hertz, *gare SNCF* (☎05.61.62.94.12).

Consulates Canada, 30 bd de Strasbourg (☎05.61.99.30.16); Great Britain, c/o Lucas Aerospace, 20 chemin de la Porte (☎05.61.15.02.02); US, 25 allées Jean-Jaurès (☎05.34.31.36.50).

Internet *@fterbug*, 12 place St-Sernin (Mon–Fri noon–2am, Sat noon–5am, Sun 2–10pm; *afterbug @free.fr*).

Pharmacy Pharmacie de Nuit, 17 rue de Remusat (daily 8pm–8am; ☎05.61.21.81.20).

Police 23 bd de l'Embouchure (☎05.61.12.77.77).

Taxi ☎05.62.16.26.16 ("taxi touristique" tariff: 150F/€22.88 for a one-hour circuit and 300F/€45.96 for a two-hour circuit of the town).

Youth information CRIJ, 17 rue de Metz (Mon–Sat 10am–1pm & 2–7pm; ☎05.61.21.20.20).

Albi and around

ALBI, 77km and an hour's train ride northeast of Toulouse, is a small industrial town with two unique sights: a museum containing the most comprehensive collection of Toulouse-Lautrec's work (Albi was his birthplace); and one of the most remarkable Gothic cathedrals you'll ever see. Its other claim to fame comes from its association with Catharism; though not itself an important centre, it gave its name – Albigensian – to both the heresy and the crusade to suppress it.

The town hosts three good **festivals** over the course of the year: jazz in May, theatre at the end of June/beginning of July, and classical music at the end of July/beginning of August. During July and August there are also free organ recitals in the cathedral (Wed 5pm & Sun 4pm).

The Town

The **Cathédrale Ste-Cécile** (daily: June–Sept 8.30am–7pm; rest of year 8.30–11.45am & 2–5.45pm; entry to choir 5F/€0.80, to treasury 20F/€3.05), begun about 1280, is visible from miles around, dwarfing the town like some vast bulk carrier run aground, the belfry its massive superstructure. If the comparison sounds unflattering, perhaps it is not amiss, for this is not a conventionally beautiful building; it's all about size and boldness of conception. The sheer plainness of the exterior is impressive on this scale, and it is not without interest: arcading, buttressing, the contrast of stone against brick – every differentiation of detail becomes significant. Entrance is through the south portal, by contrast the most extravagant piece of Flamboyant sixteenth-century frippery. The interior, a hall-like nave of colossal proportions, is dominated by a huge mural of the *Last Judgement*, believed to be the work of Flemish artists in the late fifteenth century. Above, the vault is covered in richly colourful paintings of sixteenth-century Italian workmanship, while a rood screen, delicate as lace, shuts off the choir: Adam makes a show of covering himself, Eve strikes a flaunting model's pose beside the central doorway, and the rest of the screen is adorned with countless statuary.

Next to the cathedral, a powerful red-brick castle, the thirteenth-century **Palais de la Berbie**, houses the **Musée Toulouse-Lautrec** (June–Sept daily 10am–noon & 2–6pm; rest of year Wed–Sun 10am–noon & 2–5pm; 24F/€3.66), containing paintings, drawings, lithographs and posters from the earliest work to the very last – an absolute must for anyone interested in Belle Époque seediness and, given the predominant Impressionism of the time, the rather offbeat painting style of its subject. However, perhaps the most impressive thing about this museum is the building itself, its parapets, gardens and walkways giving stunning views over the river and its bridges.

Opposite the east end of the cathedral, rue Mariés leads into the shopping streets of the old town, most of it impeccably renovated and restored. The little square and covered passages by the **church of St-Salvy** are worth a look as you go by. Eventually you come to the broad **Lices Pompidou**, the main thoroughfare of modern Albi, which leads down to the river and the road to Cordes. Less touristy, this is the best place to look for somewhere to eat and drink.

Practicalities

From the **gare SNCF** on place Stalingrad it's a ten-minute walk into town along avenues Maréchal-Joffre and de-Gaulle; you'll see the **gare routière** on your right in place Jean-Jaurès as you reach the limits of the old town. The **tourist office** is in one corner of the Palais de la Berbie (July & Aug Mon–Sat 9am–7.30pm, Sun 10.30am–1pm & 3.30–6.30pm; rest of year Mon–Sat 9am–noon & 2–6pm, Sun 10.30am–12.30pm & 3.30–5.30pm; ☎05.63.49.48.80, *otsi.albi@wanadoo.fr*); ask for a copy of their English-language leaflet describing three walking tours round Albi.

There are two attractive **hotels** near the station on avenue Maréchal-Joffre: *La Régence*, at no. 27 (☎05.63.54.01.42, fax 05.63.54.80.48; ③), and the slightly more expensive *Georges V*, at no. 29 (☎05.63.54.24.16, *hotel.georgev@ilink.fr*; ③). On the opposite side of the town, on the north bank of the river, you'll find the luxurious *Mercure les Bastides* (☎05.63.47.66.66, *mercure.albi@wanadoo.fr*; ⑤) at 41 rue Porta. In the heart of old Albi near the cathedral, both the *Hotel St-Clair*, 8 rue St-Clair (☎05.63.54.25.66, fax 05.63.47.27.58; ③), and *Le Vieil Alby*, 25 rue Toulouse-Lautrec (☎05.63.54.15.69, fax 05.63.54.96.75; ③), are agreeable places to stay. Otherwise, there's a **hostel** at 13 rue de la République (☎05.63.54.53.65; HI membership obligatory) and a municipal **campsite** (☎05.63.60.37.06; closed mid-Oct to March) in the Parc de Caussels, about 2km east on the D999 Millau road.

Albi's cuisine is predominantly *terroir* – local cooking notable only for *lou tastou*, the local version of tapas. The best *terroir* restaurant is *Moulin de Mothe*, on rue de Lamothe (☎05.63.60.38.15; closed Sun noon; menus 140–380F/€21.35–57.95), on the north bank west from the *pont vieux*. Also serving *terroir*, *La Tête de l'Art*, 7 rue de la Piale (☎05.63.38.44.75; from 100F/€15.25), is set apart by unrestrained atmosphere and wacky decor, while *L'Esprit du Vin*, 11 quai Choiseul (☎05.63.54.60.44; closed mid-Feb to May; from 100F/€15.25), has imaginative *gastronomique* cuisine. For something different *La Casa Loca*, rue Puech Bérenguier (☎05.63.47.26.00; closed Sat lunch & Sun), features genuine Spanish food and tapas. *Tournesol*, off place du Vigan (☎05.63.38.44.60; closed Sat evening, Sun & Mon), is Albi's vegetarian option.

Cagnac-les-Mines and Cordes

The country between Albi and Carmaux, 16km to the north, has long been a coal-mining and industrial area, associated in particular with the political activity of Jean Jaurès, father figure of French socialism. Elected deputy for Albi in 1893, after defending the striking miners of Carmaux, he then championed the glassworkers in 1896 in a strike that led to the setting up of a pioneering workers' co-operative, La Verrerie Ouvrière, which still functions today. The tourist office in Albi can provide a list of interesting industrial sites in the area, including the pit at **CAGNAC-LES-MINES**, where visits include a fascinating trip into a reconstructed mine (Mon–Sat 10.30am, 11.30am & 2.30–4.30pm, Sun afternoon on the hour 3–5pm; 32F/€4.88).

Of more conventional tourist interest is the town of **CORDES**, perched on a conical hill 24km northwest of Albi, from which it's a brief trip by train (as far as Cordes-Vindrac, 5km away, with bike rental from the station) or bus (daily except Sun), or an easy hitch. Founded in 1222 by Raymond VII, Count of Toulouse, Cordes was a Cathar stronghold, and the ground beneath the town is riddled with tunnels for storage and refuge in time of trouble. As one of the southwest's oldest and best-preserved *bastides*, complete with thirteenth- and fourteenth-century houses climbing steep cobbled lanes, Cordes is inevitably a major tourist attraction: medieval banners flutter in the streets and artisans practise their crafts – unfortunately, the kiss of death. The **Musée Charles-Portal** (July & Aug daily 11am–noon & 3–6pm; rest of year Sun & hols 3–6pm; 15F/€2.29) depicts the history of the town. Lovers of the bizarre should take a look at the **Musée de l'Art du Sucre** (Feb–Dec daily 10am–noon & 2.30–6.30pm; 15F/€2.29), containing outrageous sugar-sculptures created by famous local *pâtissier*, Yves Thuriès, and his underlings. The nicest **hotel** in town is the *Grand Écuyer* (☎05.63.53.79.50, *grand.ecuyer@thuries.fr*; ⑨; closed Oct–Easter) in the former palace of Cordes' founder Raymond of Toulouse. Across from the Charles-Porte museum, *Hôtel de la Cité*, is a lower-priced alternative (☎05.63.56.03.53, fax 05.63.56.02.47; ③; closed Nov to mid-April), housed in a medieval building. There's also a **campsite** (☎ & fax 05.63.56.11.10; closed Oct–March) 1km southeast down the Gaillac road.

Castres and around

In spite of its industrial activities, **CASTRES**, 40km south of Albi, has kept a lot of its charm, in the streets on the right bank of the Agout and, in particular, the riverside quarter where the old tanners' and weavers' houses overhang the water. The centre is a bustling, businesslike sort of place, with a big morning **market** on Saturdays on place Jean-Jaurès. By the rather unremarkable old cathedral, the former bishop's palace holds the Hôtel de Ville and Castres' **Musée Goya** (July & Aug daily 9am–noon & 2–6pm; rest of year closed Mon; 20F/€3.50), which is home to the biggest collection of Spanish paintings in France outside the Louvre. Goya is represented by some lighter political paintings and a large collection of engravings, and there are also works by other famous Iberian artists, like Murillo and Velázquez.

Castres' other specialist museum is the **Musée Jean-Jaurès** (same hours as the Musée Goya; 10F/€1.52), dedicated to its famous native son. It's located in place Pélisson, and getting to it takes you through the streets of the old town, past the splendid seventeenth-century **Hôtel Nayrac**, on rue Frédéric-Thomas. The museum was opened in 1988 by President Mitterrand – appropriately enough, because Mitterrand's Socialist Party is the direct descendant of Jaurès' SFIO, founded in 1905, which split at the Congress of Tours in 1920, when the "Bolshevik" element left to form the French Communist Party. The museum, though slightly hagiographic as you might expect, nonetheless pays well-deserved tribute to one of France's boldest and best political writers, thinkers and activists of modern times. Jaurès supported Dreyfus (see p.1105), founded the newspaper *L'Humanité*, campaigned against the death penalty and colonialism, and was murdered for his courageous pacifist stance at the outbreak of World War I – oddly enough, by a man called Villain. There could be no better epitaph than his own last article in *L'Humanité*, in which he wrote: "The most important thing is that we should continue to act and to keep our minds perpetually fresh and alive . . . That is the real safeguard, the guarantee of our future."

Practicalities

Arriving from Toulouse by train, you'll find the **gare SNCF** a kilometre southwest of the town centre on avenue Albert-1er. The **gare routière** is on place Soult, with bus services to Mazamet and Lacaune. The **tourist office** is beside the Pont Vieux at 3 rue Milhau-Ducommun (April–Oct Mon–Sat 8.30am–7pm, Sun 10am–noon & 2–6pm; rest of year Mon–Sat 8.30am–12.30pm & 1.30–6.30pm, Sun 2–6pm; ☎05.63.62.63.62, fax 05.63.62.63.62).

There are several reasonable **hotels** in Castres. Among the cheapest are the basic, old-style *Le Périgord*, 22 rue Émile-Zola (☎05.63.59.04.74; ①; restaurant from 75F/€11.44), and the more comfortable *Hôtel Rivière*, 10 quai Tourcaudière (☎05.63.59.04.53, fax 05.63.59.61.97; ③). At the other end of the scale, try the stylish *Renaissance* at 17 rue Victor Hugo (☎05.63.59.30.42, fax 05.63.72.11.57; ④), just off place Jean-Jaurès. The municipal **campsite** (☎05.63.59.72.30; closed Oct–March) is in a riverside park 2km northeast of town on the road to Roquecourbe, which you can also reach by river-taxi (round trip 25F/€3.81).

For simple, inexpensive meals, you can't beat the upstairs dining room in the *Brasserie des Jacobins*, on place Jean-Jaurès. Alternatively, *Le Médiéval* (☎05.63.51.13.78; closed Sun & Mon), at 44 rue Milhau-Ducommun, has an eleventh-century dining room poised above the Agout, and offers reasonable *terroir* and *gastronomique* menus from 110F/€16.78.

Le Sidobre

Just east of Castres rises the westernmost extremity of the Parc Naturel Régional du Haut Languedoc (see p.771), cut by deep river valleys and covered with marvellous woods. This is **Le Sidobre**, an area renowned for its granite: huge boulders litter the woods, often carved by the millennia into zoomorphic or other shapes – Les Trois Fromages and l'Oie, for example – that give them commercial value in the eyes of the tourist industry. Exploration is best done on foot: the **GR36** footpath passes this way.

LACROUZETTE, 15km from Castres, is the main town and the capital of the granite industry. The demand for tombstones being impervious to recession, the town continues to prosper, though it's not the most beautiful place. However, if you're on your way up the Agout and Gijou valleys (see p.774) to Lacaze and Lacaune, the *Hôtel Relais du Sidobre*, 8 rte de Vabre (☎ & fax 05.63.50.60.06; ③; restaurant from 80F/€12.20), makes a convenient and pleasant stopover. For something more unique, head for the *chambres d'hôtes* of the luxurious fourteenth- to sixteenth-century castle in **BURLATS**, 10km northeast of Castres (☎05.63.35.29.20, fax 05.63.51.14.69; ④).

The Gers

West of Toulouse, the *département* of **Gers** lies at the heart of the historic region of Gascony. In the long struggle for supremacy between the English and the French in the Middle Ages it had the misfortune to form the frontier zone between the English base

ARMAGNAC

Armagnac is a dry, golden brandy distilled in the district extending into the Landes and Lot and Garonne *départements*, divided into three distinct areas: Haut-Armagnac (around Auch), Ténarèze (Condom) and Bas-Armagnac (Éauze), in ascending order of output and quality. Growers of the grape like to compare brandy with whisky, equating malts with the individualistic, earthy Armagnac distilled by small producers, and blended whiskies with the more consistent, standardized output of the large-scale houses. Armagnac grapes are grown on sandy soils and, importantly, the wine is distilled only once, giving the spirit a lower alcohol content but more flavour. Aged in local black oak, Armagnac matures quickly, so young Armagnacs are relatively smoother than corresponding Cognacs.

Armagnac was distilled originally for medicinal reasons, and many claims are made for its efficacy. Perhaps the most optimistic are those of the priest of Éauze de St-Mont, who held that the eau-de-vie cured gout and hepatitis. More reasonably, he also wrote that it "stimulates the spirit if taken in moderation, recalls the past, gives many joy above all else, conserves youth. If one retains it in the mouth, it unties the tongue and gives courage to the timid."

Many of the producers welcome visitors and offer tastings, whether you go to one of the bigger *chais* of Condom or Éauze, or follow a faded sign at the bottom of a farm track. For more **information**, contact the Bureau National Interprofessionnel de l'Armagnac, place de la Liberté, 32800 Éauze (☎05.62.08.11.00, fax 05.62.08.11.01, *www.cognacnet.com /armagnac/bnia*).

at Bordeaux and the French at Toulouse – hence the large number of fortified villages, or *bastides*, dominating the hilltops. It is attractive if unspectacular rolling agricultural land dotted with ancient, honey-stoned farms. Settlement is sparse and – with the exception of **Auch**, the capital – major monuments are largely lacking, which keeps it well off the beaten tourist trails.

The region's traditional sources of renown are its stout-hearted mercenary warriors – of whom Alexandre Dumas' d'Artagnan and Edmond Rostand's Cyrano de Bergerac are the supreme literary exemplars – its rich cuisine and its Armagnac. The food and brandy still flourish: Gers is the biggest producer of foie gras in the country. Other traditional dishes are *magret de canard*, Henri IV's *poule au pot* (the chicken that he promised to provide for every peasant's Sunday dinner), *confit* of duck and goose, thick *garbure* soup and *daube de por*. Then there's *croustade*, a tart of apple and Armagnac, the speciality of Gascon *pâtissiers*. And to wash it all down the red wines of Madiran, Buzet and St-Mont, and the whites of Pacherenc du Vic-Bilh.

Auch

The sleepy provincial capital of Gers, **AUCH**, is most easily accessible by rail from Toulouse, 78km to the east. The old town, which is the only part worth exploring, stands on a bluff overlooking the tree-lined River Gers, with the cathedral prominent at its edge.

It is this building – the **Cathédrale Ste-Marie** – which makes a trip to Auch worthwhile. Although not finished until the latter part of the seventeenth century, it is built in basically late Gothic style, with a classical facade. Of particular interest are the choir stalls (daily: April–June & Sept 10am–noon & 2–6pm, July & Aug 9am–6pm; Oct–March 9.30am–12.30pm & 2–5pm; 6F/€0.92) and the stained glass; both were begun in the early 1500s, though the windows are of clearly Renaissance inspiration, while the choir remains Gothic. The stalls are thought to have been carved by the same craftsmen who executed those at St-Bertrand-de-Comminges (see p.720), and show the same extraordinary virtuosity and detail. The eighteen windows, unusual in being a complete set, parallel the scenes and personages depicted in the stalls. They are the work of a Gascon painter, Arnaud de Moles, and are equally rich in detail.

Immediately south of the cathedral, in the tree-filled place Salinis, is the forty-metre-high **Tour d'Armagnac**, which served as an ecclesiastical court and prison in the fourteenth century. Descending from here to the river is a **monumental stairway** of 234 steps, with a statue of d'Artagnan gracing one of the terraces. From place de la République, in front of the cathedral's main west door, rue d'Espagne connects with rue de la Convention and what is left of the narrow medieval stairways known as the **pousterles**, which give access to the lower town. On the north side of place de la République, the tourist office inhabits a splendid half-timbered fifteenth-century house on the corner with rue Dessoles, a pedestrianized street boasting an array of fine buildings. Just down the steps to the east of rue Dessoles, on place Louis-Blanc, the former Couvent des Jacobins houses one of the best collections of pre-Columbian and later South American art in France, left to the town by an adventurous son, M. Pujos, who had lived in Chile in the last years of the nineteenth century. Now known as the **Musée d'Auch** (Tues–Sun: May–Sept 10am–noon & 2–6pm; rest of year 10am–noon & 2–5pm; 10F/€1.53), it also boasts a small collection of traditional Gascon furniture, religious artefacts and Gallo-Roman remains.

Practicalities

The **tourist office** (July & Aug daily 9am–noon & 2–6pm; rest of year Mon–Sat 9am–noon & 2–6pm; ☎05.62.05.22.89, fax 05.62.05.92.04) stands at the corner of place de la République and rue Dessoles. West of the tourist office, place de la Libération leads to the allées d'Étigny, with the **gare routière** off to the right.

For a very central place to stay, try the modest *Hôtel Sheherezade*, at 5 rue d'Espagne near the cathedral (☎05.62.05.13.25; ②; Moroccan restaurant downstairs). Slightly superior alternatives are the *Hôtel de Paris*, 38 av de la Marne (☎05.62.63.26.22, fax 05.62.60.04.27; ③; closed Nov), and *Le Relais de Gascogne*, 5 av de la Marne (☎05.62.05.26.81, fax 05.62.63.30.22; ③). To reach avenue de la Marne from the *gare SNCF*, turn right on avenue de la Gare, follow it to the end, then turn left.

There's also a rather drab **HI hostel**, *Foyer des Jeunes Travailleurs* (☎05.62.05.34.80), in the Le Garros housing development, about 25 minutes' walk from the station: turn left out of the station along avenue Pierre-Mendés-France, and then left again at the T-junction; after crossing the rail tracks, take the first right and keep straight ahead to find the hostel at the far end of rue du Bourget. The municipal **campsite** (☎05.62.05.00.22; closed mid-Nov to mid-April) is beside the river on the south side of town, and there's a GR653 **gîte d'étape** 4km east at the Château St-Cricq (☎05.62.63.10.17).

Avenue d'Alsace, in the lower town, is the best place to look for inexpensive **places to eat**. Alternatively, up by the cathedral, place de la République and place de la Libération boast a fair selection of cafés and brasseries; try *Café Daroles* by the fountain (menus from 70F/€10.68). For something a bit more traditional, *La Table d'Hôtes*, off rue Dessoles at 7 rue Lamartine, offers good Gascon fare from 68F/€10.37 (closed Sun evening & Wed).

Around Auch

Outside Auch is a handful of quiet country towns – **Fleurance**, **Lectoure** and **Condom** – with no great sights, but which, along with the surrounding countryside, make for a lazy taste of French provincial life. They are all connected by bus from Auch, but away from the main roads – the N21 for Fleurance and Lectoure, and the D930 for Condom – you'll be stymied without your own transport.

Fleurance and Lectoure

FLEURANCE, 24km north of Auch, has a typical *bastide* central square, **place de la République**, bordered by arcaded shops and houses, with the difference that its medieval *halle*, now the town hall, was successfully converted into mellow classical stone in the nineteenth century. The **church** is worth a look, too, for its octagonal Toulouse-style belfry and, more particularly, the three stained-glass windows executed by Arnaud de Moles, the artist of Auch cathedral. The **tourist office** is on the place de la République (July & Aug Mon–Sat 9am–6.30pm, Sun 9am–12.30pm; rest of year Mon–Sat 9am–1pm & 3.30–6pm; ☎05.62.64.00.00, fax 05.62.06.27.80). If you wish to stay, the only **hotels** are the central two-star *Le Relais* (☎05.62.06.05.08, fax 05.62.06.03.84; ③) and, just out of town on the route d'Agen, the large, modern *Le Fleurance* (☎05.62.06.14.85, *le.fleurance.hotel@libertysurf.fr*, ③).

Eleven kilometres further north sits **LECTOURE**, the smallest and prettiest of the three towns, built astride a high ridge looking out over the surrounding farmland. Capital of the colony of Novempopulania in Roman times and of the counts of Armagnac until their demise at the hands of Louis XI in 1473, it is now renowned for its melons. In the middle of the main street, the **Cathédrale de St-Gervais-et-de-St-Protais** raises its enormous tower above the town, while down the rue Fontelié, among scarcely altered medieval houses, you come to the **Fontaine de Diane**. Apart from the handsome Mairie, with its **Musée Lapidaire** (April–Sept daily 10am–noon & 2–5/6pm; rest of year closed Tues; 15F/€2.29), containing some interesting Roman bits and pieces, this pretty much exhausts the sights.

The **tourist office**, on place de la Cathédrale (Mon–Sat 8.30am–noon & 2–5/6pm, Sun 3–5pm; ☎05.62.68.76.98, fax 05.62.68.79.30), runs the GR65 **gîte d'étape** on nearby rue St-Gervais (same phone number). Just around the corner from the *gîte* is the superb but unfortunately named *Hôtel de Bastard* in rue Lagrange (☎05.62.68.82.44, fax 05.62.68.76.81; ④; closed Jan; menus from 88F/€13.42), while the *Auberge des Bouviers* (☎05.62.68.95.13; ②; closed Sun evening & Mon; restaurant from around 80F/€12.20), at 8 rue Montebello near the central market hall, makes for an atmospheric place to stay and eat.

Condom and around

Some 43km north of Auch and 21km west of Lectoure lies the town of **CONDOM**, whose road signs have predictably been interfered with by passing Brits: there's sadly no connection between the place and the device, though the mayor's considering opening a museum. Unremarkable in every other sphere, Condom is nonetheless good for a quick visit or an overnight stop, with an impressive cathedral and attractive old streets in the centre. Armagnac drinkers will be interested in the **Musée de l'Armagnac**, 2 rue Jules-Ferry (daily except Tues: Feb, March, Nov & Dec 2–5pm; April–Oct 10am–noon & 3–6pm; 13F/€1.98), and the **Chais Ryst-Duperon**, where the liquor is aged (July & Aug daily 9am–noon & 2–6.30pm; rest of year Mon–Sat 9am–noon & 2–6pm; free). For other places to taste and buy Armagnac, ask the **tourist office** in place Bossuet (July & Aug Mon–Sat 9am–12.30pm & 2–7pm, Sun 9am–12.30pm; rest of year Mon–Sat 9am–noon & 2–6pm; ☎05.62.28.00.80, fax 05.62.28.45.46).

The cheapest place to stay is the *Relais de la Ténaréze*, at 20 av d'Aquitaine (☎05.62.28.02.54, fax 05.62.28.46.96; ②). Two more appealing options, both with pools, are the *Hôtel Le Logis des Cordeliers*, in rue de la Paix (☎05.62.28.03.68, fax 05.62.68.29.03; ③; closed Jan), and, for a splurge, the *Hôtel des Trois Lys* (☎05.62.28.33.33, fax 05.62.28.41.85; ③; closed Feb; restaurant from 96F/€14.64). There's another GR65 **gîte d'étape** at the *Centre Salvandy* (☎05.62.28.23.80), and a municipal **campsite** (☎05.62.28.17.32; closed Nov–March) near the river on the road to Éauze. For a straightforward place to **eat**, try *Pizzéria l'Origan*, at 4 rue Cadéot in the town centre (closed Sun & Mon), or *Café des Sports*, on rue Charron by the cathedral, which does substantial salads and a *plat du jour* at 48F/€7.32. A more upmarket alternative is *Le Moulin du Petit Gascon* (☎05.62.28.28.42; closed Dec–Feb, also Sun evening & Mon; menus from 95F/€14.49), out of town by the campsite, and attractively sited beside a canal lock.

Just 5km west of Condom, the tiny twelfth-century village of **LARRESSINGLE** is certainly very pretty, but is totally given over to the heritage industry as the "Carcassonne du Gers", with twee tearooms inside – and it only takes one coachload of visitors to swamp it.

More interesting is the very fine abbey of **FLARAN**, 8km along the road to Auch (daily: Feb–June & Sept–Dec 10am–12.30pm & 2–6pm; July & Aug 9.30am–7pm; 25F/€3.81). Built by the Cistercians in 1151 in pale white stone, it has the same scrubbed, ascetic appeal as Fontenay in Burgundy (see p.528), with scarcely a hint of ornament – an effect totally destroyed by the decadent, incongruous plasterwork introduced into the monks' dormitory in the seventeenth century. Used as an Armagnac store until 1970, after undergoing many other vicissitudes in its long history, the monastery has only recovered its true identity in the last twenty years.

travel details

Trains

Béziers to: Agde (1–2 hourly; 15min); Arles (8–12 daily; 2hr); Avignon (4–10 daily; 2hr); Bédarieux (6–9 daily; 40min); Carcassonne (10–14 daily; 1hr); Marseille (8–12 daily; 2hr 30min); Millau (3–6 daily; 2hr); Montpellier (4–6 hourly; 1hr); Nîmes (1–3 hourly; 1hr 20min); Paris (10 daily; 5–10hr); Narbonne (4–6 hourly; 20min); Perpignan (2–3 hourly; 1hr); Sète (4–6 hourly; 30min).

Carcassonne to: Arles (6–8 daily; 2hr 40min); Béziers (10–14 daily; 1hr); Bordeaux (5 daily; 3hr 20min); Marseille (3–4 daily; 3hr 20min); Montpellier (1–2 hourly; 1hr 30min); Narbonne (1–2 hourly; 30min); Nîmes (1–2 hourly; 2hr 10min); Quillan (1–2 daily; 1hr); Sète (1–2 hourly; 1hr 30min); Toulouse (2–3 hourly; 45min).

Montpellier to: Arles (1–2 hourly; 1hr); Avignon (2 hourly; 1hr); Béziers (4–6 hourly; 1hr); Carcassonne (1–2 hourly; 1hr 30min); Lyon (8 daily; 2hr 30min); Marseille (2–3 hourly; 1hr 40min); Mende (2–3 daily; 3hr 40min); Narbonne (1–2 hourly; 1hr); Paris (5–6 TGVs daily; 4hr 20min); Perpignan (3–4 hourly; 2hr); Sète (3–4 hourly; 20min); Toulouse (8–12 daily; 2hr 20min).

Narbonne to: Arles (6–8 daily; 2hr); Avignon (4–11 daily; 2hr 20min); Béziers (4–6 hourly; 20min); Bordeaux (3–4 daily; 2hr 25min); Carcassonne (10–14 daily; 30min); Cerbère (1–2 hourly; 1hr–1hr 30min); Marseille (7–8 daily; 2hr 40min); Montpellier (1–2 hourly; 1hr 20min);

Nîmes (2–3 hourly; 1hr 50min); Perpignan (2–3 hourly; 30–40min); Port-Bou (1–2 hourly; 1hr 20min–1hr 40min); Sète (4–5 hourly; 40min); Toulouse (1–2 hourly; 1hr 20min–2hr).

Nîmes to: Arles (1–2 hourly; 30–40min); Avignon (1–2 hourly; 30min); La Bastide-St-Laurent (4–6 daily; 2hr 10min); Béziers (1–3 hourly; 1hr 20min); Carcassonne (1–2 hourly; 2hr 10min); Clermont-Ferrand (3 daily; 4–5hr); Génolhac (4–6 daily; 1hr 25min); Marseille (1–2 hourly; 1hr 20min); Montpellier (3–4 hourly; 30min); Narbonne (2–3 hourly; 1hr 50min); Paris via Alès (1–2 daily; 9hr); Paris (5–6 TGVs daily; 4hr 30min); Perpignan (6 daily; 2hr 30min); Sète (1–2 hourly; 40min); Vichy (1–2 daily; 6hr); Villefort (5–6 daily; 1hr 30min).

Sète to: Arles (6–8 daily; 1hr 15min); Avignon (8 daily; 1hr 30min); Béziers (4–6 hourly; 30min); Carcassonne (1–2 hourly; 1hr 30min); Marseille (7–10 daily; 2hr 10min); Montpellier (3–4 hourly; 20min); Narbonne (4–5 hourly; 40min); Nîmes (1–2 hourly; 40min); Perpignan (5–8 daily; 1hr 20min).

Toulouse to: Albi (9–19 daily; 1hr); Auch (4–7 daily; 1hr 30min); Ax-les-Thermes (5–7 daily; 1hr 45min); Barcelona (4 daily; 5hr–6hr 30min); Bayonne (5–6 daily; 3hr); Bordeaux (1–2 hourly; 2hr 45min); Brive (7–13 daily; 2hr 20min); Castres (5–10 daily; 1hr 20min); Foix (6–13 daily; 1hr 10min); Lourdes (6–10 daily; 2hr 20min); Lyon (3 daily; 5hr); Marseille (8–9 daily; 3hr 30min–4hr 20min); Mazamet (5–10 daily; 1hr 40min); Pamiers (6–13 daily; 50min); Paris (1 hourly; 5hr); Pau (5–8 daily; 2hr–2hr 30min); Tarascon (5–7 daily; 1hr 20min); Tarbes (6–13 daily; 2hr); La-Tour-de-Carol (4 daily; 2hr 35min).

Buses

Auch to: Agen (6–11 daily; 1hr 30min); Bordeaux (1 daily; 3hr 40min); Condom (1–2 daily; 40min); Fleurance (6–11 daily; 20min); Lannemezan (1 daily; 1hr 45min); Lectoure (6–11 daily; 40min); Montauban (Mon–Sat 1–3 daily; 2hr); Tarbes (3–4 daily; 2hr); Toulouse (1–3 daily; 1hr 30min).

Bédarieux to: Olargues (4–5 daily; 40min); Pont-de-Tarassac (4–5 daily; 30min); St-Pons-de-Thomières (4–5 daily; 1hr).

Béziers to: Castres (2 daily; 2hr 30min); Mazamet (2 daily; 2hr); Montpellier (4–12 daily; 1hr 40min); Narbonne (2 daily; 1hr); Pézenas (4–12 daily; 40min); St-Pons-de-Thomières (1–2 daily; 1hr 20min); La Salvetat (1–2 daily; 2hr 10min).

Carcassonne to: Castelnaudary (1–3 daily; 1hr); Quillan (2–3 daily; 1hr 20min); Toulouse (1 daily; 2hr).

Montpellier to: Aigues-Mortes (2–4 daily; 1hr); Bédarieux (3–4 daily; 1hr 35min); La Cavalerie (daily; 1hr 50min); Clermont-l'Hérault (3–4 daily; 1hr); Ganges (3–6 daily; 1hr 15min); Gignac (6–12 daily; 45min); La Grande-Motte (5–12 daily; 45min); Grau-du-Roi (4–11 daily; 1hr); Lodève (3–8 daily; 1hr 15min); Millau (1–5 daily; 2hr); Nîmes (Mon–Sat 2 daily; 1hr 30min); Palavas (10–15 daily; 35min); Rodez (1–3 daily; 3hr 55min); St-Martin-de-Londres (3–9 daily; 1hr); Sète (3–11 daily; 1hr); Le Vigan (3–5 daily; 1hr 40min); Viols-le-Fort (3–9 daily; 40min).

Narbonne to: Béziers (2 daily; 1hr); Carcassonne (1–4 daily; 1hr 30min); Gruissan (3–6 daily; 45min); Narbonne-Plage (2–3 daily; 45min); Perpignan (1 daily; 2hr).

Nîmes to: Aigues-Mortes (6 daily; 1hr); Avignon (2–4 daily; 1hr 30min); Ganges (1–5 daily; 1hr 40min); La Grande-Motte (5 daily; 1hr 20min); Grau-du-Roi (6 daily; 1hr 10min); Montpellier (Mon–Sat 2 daily; 1hr 30min); Pont-du-Gard (2–6 daily; 40min); Sommières (1–3 daily; 50min); Uzès (2–13 daily; 45min–1hr 20min); Le Vigan (1–5 daily; 2hr).

Sète to: Montpellier (3–11 daily; 1hr).

Toulouse to: Albi (6 daily; 1hr 30min); Auch (1–3 daily; 1hr 30min); Ax-les-Thermes (3–5 daily; 2hr 30min–3hr); Castres (1 daily; 1hr 30min); Foix (3–5 daily; 2hr); Pamiers (3–5 daily; 1hr 30min); Tarascon (3–5 daily; 2hr 20min).

CHAPTER TWELVE

THE MASSIF CENTRAL

One of the loveliest spots on earth . . . a country without roads, without guides, without any facilities for locomotion, where every discovery must be conquered at the price of danger or fatigue . . . a soil cut up with deep ravines, crossed in every way by lofty walls of lava, and furrowed by numerous torrents.

Thus one of George Sand's characters described the Haute-Loire, the central *département* of **the Massif Central**, and it's a description that could still be applied to some of the region. Thickly forested and sliced by numerous rivers and lakes, these once volcanic uplands are geologically the oldest part of France and culturally one of the most firmly rooted in the past. Industry and tourism have made few inroads here, and the people remain rural and taciturn, with an enduring sense of regional identity. They also have a largely unfounded reputation for unfriendliness.

The Massif Central takes up a huge portion of the centre of France, but only a handful of towns have gained a foothold in its rugged terrain: **Le Puy**, spiked with theatrical pinnacles of lava, is the most compelling, with its steep streets and majestic cathedral; the spa town of **Vichy** has an antiquated elegance and charm; even heavily industrial **Clermont-Ferrand**, the capital, has a certain cachet in the black volcanic stone of its historic centre and its stunning physical setting beneath the **Puy de Dôme**, a 1464-metre-high volcanic plug. There is pleasure, too, in the unpretentious provinciality of **Aurillac** and in the untouched medieval architecture of smaller places like **Murat, Besse, Salers, Orcival, Sauveterre-de-Rouergue, La Couvertoirade** and in the hugely influential abbey of **Conques**. But, above all, this is a country where the sights are landscapes rather than towns, churches and museums.

The heart of the region is the **Auvergne**, a wild and unexpected landscape of extinct volcanoes, stretching from the grassy domes and craters of the **Monts-Dômes** to the eroded skylines of the **Monts-Dore**, and deeply ravined **Cantal mountains** to the rash of darkly wooded pimples surrounding Le Puy. It is one of the poorest regions in France and has long remained outside the main national lines of communication: much of it is above 1000m in height and snowbound in winter, and it was only recently that construction began on an *autoroute* through the middle. There is little arable land, just thousands of acres of upland pasture, traditionally grazed by sheep brought up from the southern lowlands for the summer. Nowadays, cows far outnumber the sheep, some

ACCOMMODATION PRICE CODES

Each hotel and guesthouse in this book has been graded according to the following price codes, which indicate the price for the **cheapest double room available during the high season**.

① Under 160F/€24	④ 300–400F/€46–61	⑦ 600–700F/€91–107
② 160–220F/€24–34	⑤ 400–500F/€61–76	⑧ 700–800F/€107–122
③ 220–300F/€34–46	⑥ 500–600F/€76–91	⑨ Over 800F/€122

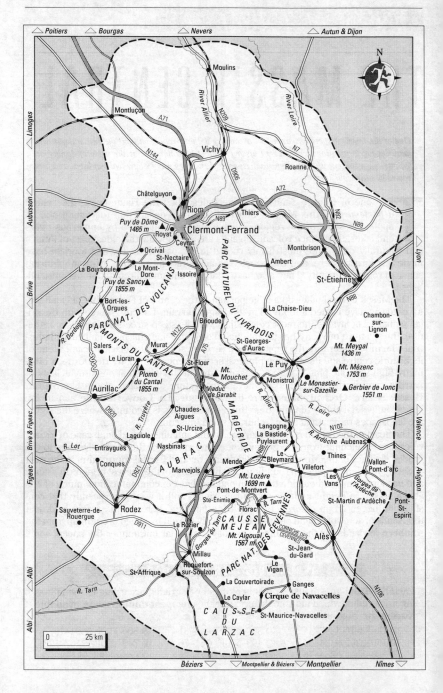

△ Poitiers △ Bourgas △ Nevers △ Autun & Dijon

◁ Limoges
◁ Aubusson
◁ Brive
◁ Brive
◁ Figeac
◁ Brive & Figeac
◁ Albi
◁ Albi

Lyon ▷
Valence ▷
Avignon ▷

▽ Béziers ▽ Montpellier & Béziers ▽ Montpellier ▽ Nîmes

N

Moulins

Montluçon A71

River Allier

N209

River Loire

N144

Vichy

N7

Roanne

D906

Châtelguyon

A72

Riom N89 Thiers

Puy de Dôme
1465 m
Royat
Clermont-Ferrand
Orcival Ceyrat
St-Nectaire
Le Mont- Issoire
La Bourboule Dore
Puy de Sancy
1855 m
Bort-les-
Orgues

Montbrison

Ambert

St-Étienne
N88

PARC NATUREL DU LIVRADOIS

R. Dordogne

PARC NAT. DES VOLCANS

MONTS DU CANTAL

N122

Brioude

La Chaise-Dieu

Chambon-
sur-
Lignon

Salers
Le Lioran
Murat

A75

St-Georges-
d'Aurac

Mt. Meygal
1436 m

St-Flour

Mt.
Mouchet

Le Puy

▲ Mt. Mézenc
1753 m

Plomb
du Cantal
1855 m

Monistrol

Le Monastier-
sur-Gazeille

▲ Gerbier de Jonc
1551 m

Aurillac

Viaduc
de Garabit

R. Allier

R. Loire

R. Truyère

Chaudes-
Aigues

MARGERIDE

St-Urcize

Langogne
La Bastide-
Puylaurent

N102

R. Ardèche Aubenas

Laguiole

Nasbinals

Thines

R. Lot

Entraygues

AUBRAC

Le
Bleymard

Villefort

Vallon-
Pont-d'arc

Conques

Marvejols

Mende

Mt. Lozère
1699 m ▲

Les
Vans

Gorges de
l'Ardèche

Sauveterre-de-
Rouergue

Rodez

Pont-de-Montvert

St-Martin d'Ardèche

Pont-
St-
Espirit

D911

Le Rozier

Ste-Énimie

Florac

R. Tarn

CAUSSE
MEJEAN

CORNICHE DES
CEVENNES

Alès

Gorges du Tarn

Mt. Aigoual
1567 m

PARC NAT. DES CEVENNES

St-Jean-
du-Gard

Millau
Roquefort-
sur-Soulzon

St-Affrique

R. Tarn

La Couvertoirade

Le
Vigan

Ganges

Cirque de Navacelles

Le Caylar

St-Maurice-Navacelles

C A U S S E
D U
L A R Z A C

N106

0 ___ 25 km

THE FOOD OF THE MASSIF CENTRAL

Don't expect anything very refined from the **cuisine of the Auvergne and Massif Central**: it is solid peasant fare as befits a poor and rugged region. The best-known dish is **potée auvergnate**, basically a kind of cabbage soup. It's easy to make and very nourishing. The ingredients – potatoes, pork or bacon, cabbage, beans, turnips – though added at different intervals, are all boiled up together. Another popular cabbage dish is **chou farci**, cabbage stuffed with pork and beef and cooked with bacon.

Two potato dishes are very common – **la truffade** and **l'aligot**. For *truffade*, the potatoes are sliced and fried in lard, then fresh Cantal cheese is added; for an *aligot*, the potatoes are puréed and mixed with cheese. Less palatable for the squeamish, there's **tripoux**, usually a stuffing of either sheep's feet or calf's innards, cooked in a casing of stomach lining. **Fricandeau**, a kind of pork pâté, is also wrapped in sheep's stomach.

By way of dessert, **clafoutis** is a popular fruit tart in which the fruit is baked with a batter of flour and egg simply poured over it. The classical fruit ingredient is black cherries, though pears, blackcurrants or apples can also be used.

The Auvergne and the Ardèche in the east produce some wines, though these are not of any great renown. **Cheese** is a different story. In addition to the four great cow's milk cheeses – St-Nectaire (see p.814), Cantal, Fourme d'Ambert and Bleu d'Auvergne – this region also produces the prince of all cheeses, **Roquefort**, made from sheep's milk at the edge of the Causse du Larzac (see p.835).

raised for beef and some still for the production of Auvergne's four great cheeses (see box above). The population has emigrated for generations, especially to Paris, where the café and restaurant trade has long been in the hands of Auvergnats. The same flight of population has affected the equally infertile but beautiful and more Mediterranean southern part of the region: the hills and valleys of the **Cévennes**, where Robert Louis Stevenson and his donkey made one of the more famous literary hikes in 1878.

Many of France's greatest rivers rise in the Massif Central: the **Dordogne** in the Monts-Dore, the **Loire** on the slopes of the Gerbier de Jonc in the east, and in the Cévennes the **Lot** and the **Tarn**. It is these last two rivers which create the distinctive character of the southern parts of the Massif Central, dividing and defining the special landscapes of the *causses*, or limestone plateaux, with their stupendous gorges.

This is territory, above all, for walkers and lovers of the **outdoors**, and everywhere you go tourist offices will supply ideas and routes for walks and bike rides, both long and short.

THE PARC DES VOLCANS D'AUVERGNE

The **Parc Naturel Régional des Volcans d'Auvergne** encompasses the whole of the western edge of the Massif Central, from **Vichy** in the north to **Aurillac** in the south. It consists of three groups of extinct volcanoes – the **Monts-Dômes**, the **Monts-Dore** and the **Monts du Cantal** – linked by the high plateaux of Artense and the Cézallier. It is big, wide-open country, sparsely populated and with largely treeless pasture grazed by the cows whose milk produces Cantal and St-Nectaire cheese.

The park organization, whose headquarters are at the **Maison du Parc**, Château de Montlosier, 20km southwest of Clermont-Ferrand just off the Mont-Dore road (May–Oct Mon–Fri 8.30am–12.30pm & 1–5pm; ☎04.73.65.64.00), oversees various subsidiary *maisons du parc*, each a kind of museum devoted to different themes or activities: fauna and flora, shepherd life, peat bogs and so on.

The best way to understand the park, its landscapes and activities is to walk or bike around it. Four **GR footpaths** cross or make circuits within the park. The **GR40** runs from north to south. The **GR441** makes a circuit round the Monts-Dômes, called the **Tour de la Chaîne des Puys**. The **GR400** encircles the Cantal mountains, and the **GR30** the lakes of the Artense plateau and Cézallier, under the title of the **Tour des Lacs d'Auvergne**. There are also lots of shorter walks; ask at local tourist offices for more information, and for details of where to rent mountain bikes.

The towns in the area are few and of secondary interest, although **Orcival**, **Murat** and **Salers** are unexpectedly attractive; **St-Nectaire** contains an exceptionally beautiful small church in the distinct Auvergne version of Romanesque; and **St-Flour** and Aurillac have an agreeable provincial insularity.

Clermont-Ferrand and around

CLERMONT-FERRAND lies at the northern tip of the Massif Central. Although its situation is magnificent, almost encircled by the wooded and grassy volcanoes of the **Monts-Dômes**, it has for a century been a typical smokestack industrial centre, the home base of Michelin tyres, which makes it a rather incongruous capital for the rustic, even backward province of the Auvergne.

Its roots, both as a spa and a communications and trading centre, go back to Roman times. It was just outside the town, on the plateau of Gergovia to the south, that the Gauls under the leadership of Vercingétorix won their only, albeit indecisive, victory against Julius Cæsar's invading Romans. In the Middle Ages, the two towns of Clermont and Montferrand were divided by commercial and political rivalry and ruled respectively by a bishop and the count of Auvergne. Louis XIII united them administratively in 1630, but it was not until the rapid industrial expansion of the late nineteenth century that the two really became indistinguishable. Indeed, it was Clermont that took the ascendancy, relegating Montferrand to a suburban backwater.

Michelin came into being thanks to the inventions of Charles Mackintosh, the Scotsman of raincoat fame. His niece married Édouard Daubrée, a Clermont sugar manufacturer, and brought with her some ideas about making rubber goods that she had learnt from her uncle. In 1889, the company became Michelin and Co, just in time to catch the development of the automobile and the World War I aircraft industry. The family ruled the town and employed 30,000 of its citizens until the early 1980s, when the industry went into decline. In the years since, the workforce has been halved, causing rippling unemployment throughout Clermont's economy. Many of those who have lost their jobs are Portuguese immigrants, imported over the last thirty years to fill the labour vacuum and well integrated with the local population.

As in many other traditional industrial towns hit by recession and changing global patterns of trade, Clermont has had to struggle to reorientate itself, turning to service industries and the creation of a university of 34,000 students. Nonetheless, many people have moved elsewhere in search of work, reducing the population by nearly a tenth. The town has changed physically, too, as many of the old factories have been demolished.

Arrival, information and accommodation

The **gare SNCF** is on avenue de l'Union Soviétique, from where it is a ten-minute bus journey to place de Jaude, at the western edge of the cathedral hill. The **gare routière** (☎04.73.35.05.62) is on boulevard François-Mitterrand, with a city transport information kiosk called Boutique T2C on place de Jaude (☎04.73.28.56.56). The city **airport**

(☎04.73.62.71.00, *www.clermont-fd.cci.fr*) is at Aulnat, 7km east, with daily flights to and from Paris and other internal destinations, as well as to London during the summer.

The main **tourist office** is opposite the cathedral in the place de la Victoire (June–Sept Mon–Sat 8.30am–7pm, Sun 9am–noon & 2–6pm; rest of year Mon–Fri 8.45am–6.30pm, Sat 9am–noon & 2–6pm, Sun 9am–1pm; ☎04.73.98.65.00, *www.ot -clermont-ferrand.fr*), and there is another conveniently placed annexe immediately to the left outside the train station exit (June–Sept Mon–Sat 9.15–11.30am & 12.15–5pm; rest of year closed Sat; ☎04.73.91.87.89). The **departmental office** is on the place de la Bourse (☎04.73.42.22.50), and the **regional office** at 44 av des Etats Unis (☎04.73.29.49.49, *www.crt-auvergne.fr*). Specific hiking or mountain-bike information is available from Chamina, 5 rue Pierre-le-Vénérable (☎04.73.92.81.44). You can access the **Internet** at *Internet@Café* at 34 rue Ballainvilliers (Mon & Sat 11am–11pm, Tues–Fri 8am–11pm; ☎04.73.92.42.80).

Most of Clermont's **hotels** are concentrated just off the lively place de Jaude, close to the town's main shops, and around the rather characterless station area. There's not a tremendous choice, but they are generally good value, ranging from small, family-run affairs to larger, modern concerns catering mostly to visiting Michelin workers. For budget travellers, there's a basic **HI hostel** just across the street from the train station at 55 av de l'Union Soviétique (☎04.73.92.26.39, fax 04.73.92.99.96; closed Nov–Feb), and a **foyer**, the *Home Dome*, at 12 place de Regensburg (☎04.73.31.57.00, fax 04.73.31.59.99, *perso.wanadoo.fr/home.dome*), in the southwest of town. For campers, there are municipal **campsites** at Royat (*L'Oclède*), 4km to the southwest (☎04.73.35.97.05, *www.camping.royat.com*; closed Nov–March; bus #41), Ceyrat (*Le Chanset*), 5km to the south (☎04.73.61.30.73; bus #4C & #41, stop "Preguille"), and Cournon (*Le Pré des Laveuses*), 10km to the east, on the River Allier (☎04.73.84.81.30; bus #3, stop "Plaine de jeux").

Hotels

Albert Elisabeth, 37 av Albert-Elisabeth (☎04.73.92.47.41, fax 04.73.90.78.32). Well-run family hotel, with pastel-decorated rooms; handy for the train station. ③.

Foch, 22 rue Maréchal-Foch (☎04.73.93.48.40, fax 04.73.35.47.41). Tucked away down a side street off place de Jaude, this is a good-value budget hotel, with bright, summery rooms. ②.

Lyon, 16 place de Jaude (☎04.73.93.32.55, fax 04.73.93.54.33). Tastefully furnished thoughout, though the lively bar and brasserie below can get a little noisy at night (*plats* around 55F/€8.38). ④.

des Puys d'Arverne, 16 place Delille (☎04.73.91.92.06, fax 04.73.91.60.25, *hotel-arverne@lhdcv.com*). A good, modern, top-of-the-range hotel, offering spacious rooms, some with balconies. Its first-rate gourmet restaurant has splendid views of the town and Le Puy de Dôme (from 98F/€14.94). ⑤.

Ravel, 8 rue de Maringues (☎04.73.91.51.33, fax 04.73.92.28.48). Opposite the old Marché St-Joseph, this friendly and recently refurbished hotel, offers attractive rooms, with sunny, Mediterranean decor. Closed Jan. ③.

Regina, 14 rue Bonnabaud (☎04.73.93.44.76, fax 04.73.35.04.63). Looks a little grubby from the outside, but inside, an elegant spiral staircase leads up to fresh, clean rooms. ③.

The City

The most dramatic and flattering approach to Clermont is from the Aubusson road or along the scenic rail line from Le Mont-Dore (see p.810), both of which cross the chain of the Monts-Dômes just north of the Puy de Dôme. This way you descend through the leafy western suburbs with marvellous views over the town, dominated by the black towers of the cathedral sitting atop the volcanic stump that forms the hub of the old town.

Clermont's reputation as a *ville noire* becomes immediately understandable when you enter the city's appealing medieval quarter, clustered in characteristic medieval muddle around the cathedral – it is due not to industrial pollution but to the black volcanic rock used in the construction of many of its buildings. The **Cathédrale Notre-Dame** stands at the centre and highest point of the old town; Freda White evocatively described its sombre grey-black-stone lava from the quarries at nearby Volvic (see p.808) as "like the darkest shade of a pigeon's wing". Begun in the mid-thirteenth century, it was not finished until the nineteenth, under the direction of Viollet-le-Duc, who was the architect of the west front and those typically Gothic crocketed spires, whose too methodically cut stonework at close range betrays the work of the machine rather than the mason's hand. The interior is swaddled in gloom, illuminated all the more startlingly by the brilliant colours of the rose windows in the transept and the stained-glass windows in the choir, most dating back to the fourteenth century. Remnants of medieval frescoes survive, too: a particularly beautiful Virgin and Child adorns the right wall of the Chapelle Ste-Madeleine and an animated battle scene between the crusaders and Saracens unfolds on the central wall of the Chapelle St-Georges.

If the day is fine, it's worth climbing the **Tour de la Bayette** (Mon–Fri 10am–6pm, Sun 3–6pm; 10F/€1.52) by the north transept door: you look back over the rue des Gras to the Puy de Dôme (see p.806) looming dramatically over the city, white morning mist retreating down its sides like seaweed from a rock.

A short step northeast of the cathedral, down the elegant old rue du Port, stands Clermont's other great church, the Romanesque **Basilique Notre-Dame-du-Port** – a century older than the cathedral and in almost total contrast both in style and substance, built from softer stone in pre-lava-working days and consequently corroding badly from exposure to Clermont's polluted air. For all that, it's a beautiful building in pure Auvergnat Romanesque style, featuring a Madonna and Child over the south door in the strangely stylized local form, both figures stiff and upright, the Child more like a dwarf than an infant. Inside, it exudes the broody mysteriousness so often generated by the Romanesque style. Put a coin in the slot and you can light up the intricately carved ensemble of leaves, knights and biblical figures on the church's pillars and capitals. It was here in all probability that Pope Urban II preached the First Crusade in 1095 to a vast crowd who received his speech with the Occitan cry of *Dios lo Volt* (God wills it) – a phrase adopted by the crusaders in justification of all subsequent massacres.

For general animation, shopping, drinking and eating, the streets between the cathedral and place de Jaude are best, with the main morning market taking place in the conspicuously modern **place St-Pierre** just off rue des Gras. **Place de Jaude** remains another monument to planners' aberrations in spite of the shops, the cafés well placed to take in the morning sun and an attempt to make it more attractive with trees and a fountain. Smack in the middle of the traffic, a romantic equestrian statue of Vercingétorix lines up with the Puy de Dôme.

Away from these central streets, there is nothing to tempt the pedestrian, save perhaps **rue Ballainvilliers**, whose eighteenth-century facades recall the sober, sombre elegance of Edinburgh and lead to the city's most interesting museum, the **Musée Bargoin** (Tues–Sun 10am–6pm; 30F/€4.57), with displays of archeological finds from round about. These include lots of fascinating domestic bits: Roman shoes, baskets, bits of dried fruit, glass and pottery, as well as a remarkable burial find from nearby Martres-de-Veyre dating back to the second century AD: a young girl's plaited blonde hair, her thigh-length boots, dress, belt and goatskin shoes. There is also an extraordinary collection of wooden limbs found during building operations, buried in a covered-over spring in the suburb of Chamalières: the gifts of people whose ailments had been cured thanks to these waters. Upstairs is a very handsome exhibition of oriental carpets and kilims.

The city's two other museums are not of great interest. **Musée Lecoq**, directly behind the Musée Bargoin (May–Sept Tues–Sat noon & 2–6pm, Sun 2–6pm; Oct–April 10am–noon & 2–5pm; 24F/€3.65), is devoted mainly to natural history – and named after the gentleman who also founded the public garden full of beautiful trees and formal beds just across the street. **Musée du Ranquet**, to the west of the cathedral at 34 rue des Gras (Tues–Sun 10am–6pm; free), is housed in a noble sixteenth-century house, containing, at its most interesting, a collection of traditional tools and domestic objects and two versions of seventeenth-century philosopher and scientist Blaise Pascal's calculating machine.

Montferrand is today little more than a suburb of larger Clermont, standing out on a limb to the north, but it's good for a stroll if you're feeling active. Built on the *bastide* plan, its principal streets, rue de la Rodade and rue Jules-Guesde (the latter named after the founder of the French Communist Party, as Montferrand was home to many of the Michelin factory workers), are still lined with the fine town houses of its medieval merchants and magistrates.

Eating and drinking

If you are staying **in the station area**, there are a couple of reasonable places to **eat**. The best is the oak-beamed, rustic-looking *Auvergnat*, 27 av de l'Union Soviétique (from 75F/€11.43), whose repertoire includes standard Auvergne dishes like *truffade*. Less expensive and very friendly, with a terrace at the back, is the *Hôtel des Commerçants*, opposite the station (from 65F/€9.91).

In **the centre of town**, the best of the cheaper places is the ever-popular *Crêperie 1513*, 3 rue des Chaussetiers, opposite the cathedral, which occupies a superb Renaissance mansion built in 1513 (lunchtime menu at 55F/€8.38), while in the same street, at no. 29, *Le Bougnat* offers local regional cuisine at affordable prices (closed Sun & Mon lunch; from 78F/€11.89). Close by at 36 rue des Gras, there's good pizza and pasta at *Le Bistrot Vénitien* from 79F/€12.04 (closed Sun). On the other side of the cathedral, you can get first-class Vietnamese cooking for around 50F/€7.62 at the *Mai Lan*, 41 bd Trudaine (closed Sun & Mon lunch), and crêpes for 35–60F/€5.34–9.15 at the *Pescajoux* in the old rue du Port at no. 13.

For a more specialized gastronomic experience, there's nothing to beat the refined and inventive cooking of *Gérard Anglard* at 17 rue Lamartine, off place de Jaude, especially the lunchtime menu at 110F/€16.77 (☎04.73.93.52.25; closed Sun & first two weeks Aug). Also good value, especially at lunchtime, is the *Clos St-Pierre*, next to the St-Pierre market below the cathedral (closed Sun and Mon; 60F/€9.15 at lunchtime, otherwise 205F/€31.25 plus). And, if you don't mind the drive – barely 5km southeast off the old N9 Issoire road – the *Petit Bonneval* at **Pérignat-lès-Sarliève** makes a delicious stop for dinner on a summer evening (☎04.73.79.11.11; closed Sun evening; menus from 125F/€19.06).

For a daytime **drink**, *Le Suffren*, on the corner of place de Jaude, is one of the most popular places to hang out. More unusual is *Les Goûters de Justine*, a *salon de thé*, tucked away in old rue Pascal and furnished with antique chairs, old sofas and oriental carpets. At night one of the most fashionable places is studenty *Le Dérailleur*, 9 av Georges-Clemenceau, while young rockers head for the suburban village of Orcines, beneath the Puy de Dôme, to long-standing *Phidias*, aka *Boudu's*, on route de la Baraque (☎04.73.62.18.34; until 5am; closed Sun & Mon).

The Puy de Dôme

Visiting Clermont without going to the top of the **Puy de Dôme** (1465m) would be like visiting Athens without seeing the Acropolis. And if you choose your moment – early in the morning or late in the evening – you can easily avoid the worst of the crowds.

Clearly signposted from place de Jaude, it is about 15km from the city centre by the D941. The last 6.5km is a private road and costs 30F/€4.57; when this is closed (July & Aug 10am–6pm) there is a shuttle service (21F/€3.20). If you are driving, make sure to pump your brakes on the descent; otherwise you may find yourself waiting for a long time before driving off, while your brakes cool down. Alternatively, you can leave the car at the **Col de Ceyssat** and climb the Puy on foot in about an hour.

The result of a volcanic explosion about 10,000 years ago, the Puy is an abrupt 400m from base to summit. Although the weather station buildings and enormous television mast are pretty ugly close up, the staggering views and sense of airy elevation more than compensate. Even if Mont Blanc itself is not always visible way to the east – it can be if conditions are favourable – you can see huge distances, all down the Massif Central to the Cantal mountains. Above all, you get a bird's-eye view of the other volcanic summits to the north and south, both the rounded domes, largely forested since the nineteenth century, and the perfect 100-metre-deep grassy crater of the **Puy de Pariou**, just to the north.

Immediately below the summit are the scant remains of a substantial **Roman temple** dedicated to Mercury (free entry), some of the finds from which are displayed in the Musée Bargoin in Clermont-Ferrand (see p.805). Beside it is a memorial commemorating the exploits of Eugène Renaux, who landed a plane here in 1911 in response to the offer of a 100,000 franc prize by the Michelin brothers. Today the aviators are hang-gliders and paragliding enthusiasts, drifting like gaudy birds around the stern of a ship.

Riom and around

Just 15km north of Clermont-Ferrand, **RIOM** is sedate and provincial. One-time capital of the entire Auvergne, its Renaissance architecture, fashioned out of the local black volcanic stone, now secures the town's status as a highlight of the northern Massif. In 1942, just before the first trains of Jewish deportees were shipped to Nazi Germany, Léon Blum, Jewish prime minister and architect of the Socialist Popular Front government, was put on trial in Riom by Marshal Pétain, France's collaborationist ruler, in an attempt to blame the country's defeat in 1940 on the Left. Defending himself, Blum turned the trial into an indictment of collaboration and Nazism. Under pressure from Hitler, Pétain called it off, but nonetheless deported Blum to Germany, an experience which he survived, to give evidence against Pétain himself after the war.

You may only want to spend a morning here, but Riom does provide a worthwhile stopover for lunch if you're on the way up to Vichy. It's an aloof, old-world kind of place, still Auvergne's judicial capital, with a nineteenth-century **Palais de Justice** that stands on the site of a grand palace built when the dukes of Berry controlled this region in the fourteenth century. Only the Gothic **Ste-Chapelle** survives of the original palace, with fine stained-glass windows taking up almost the entirety of three of the walls (guided visits only, every 30min: May Wed 3–5pm; June & Sept Wed–Fri 3–5pm; July & Aug daily 10am–noon & 2.30–5pm; 15F/€2.29).

The best way to admire the town's impressive ensemble of basalt-stone houses, with their red-tiled roofs, is to climb up to the viewing platform of the sixteenth-century **clock tower**, at 5 rue de l'Horloge, off the main street, rue du Commerce (May, June & Sept Mon & Sun 2–6pm, Tues–Sat 10am–noon & 2–6pm; July & Aug daily 10am–noon & 2–6pm; 5F/€0.76). There is an interesting museum on the region's folk traditions at 10bis rue Delille, the **Musée Régional d'Auvergne** (daily except Tues 10am–noon & 2.30–6pm; 26F/€3.97, or 36F/€5.49 joint ticket with the Musée Mandet, free on Wed), with the **Musée Mandet's** displays of Roman finds and unexciting paintings not far away at 4 rue de l'Hôtel-de-Ville (same hours; 26F/€3.97, free on Wed). At 44 rue du Commerce, the **church of Notre-Dame-du-Marthuret** holds Riom's most valued treasures, two statues of the Virgin and Child – one a Black Madonna, the other, the so-called *Vierge à l'Oiseau*, a touchingly realistic piece of carving that portrays the young Christ with a bird fluttering in his hands. A copy stands in the entrance hall of the church (its original site), where you can see it with the advantage of daylight.

Riom's **tourist office** is at 16 rue du Commerce (July & Aug Mon–Sat 9.30am–12.30pm & 2–6.30pm, Sun 10am–noon & 2.30–4pm; rest of year Mon–Sat 9.30am–12.30pm & 2–6pm; ☎04.73.38.59.45, fax 04.73.38.25.15). If you decide to **stay**, try the basic, but good-value *Hôtel du Square*, 26 bd Desaix (☎04.73.86.02.71, fax 04.73.86.18.80; ①), which runs a decent restaurant (crêpes and omelettes for around 50F/€7.62). For **dinner** or lunch, follow the locals to *au Bon Croûton*, on the corner of rue Gomot and rue Fleurs, where the speciality is fondue (menus from 95F/€14.48), or the nearby *Ane Gris* (closed Mon lunch and Sun), which serves *truffade* (78F/€11.89) and *aligot* (66F/€10.06).

Around Riom

From Riom SNCF buses run to **MOZAC**, on the edge of town, with a twelfth-century **abbey church** whose Romanesque sculpture is as beautiful as you'd expect, and continue to the bourgeois spa resort of **CHÂTEL-GUYON** in around twenty minutes. With thirty different **hot springs**, great views over the surrounding countryside and *puys*, and a couple of well-equipped **campsites**, this is as good a place as any if you want to rest up for a night. For an easy stroll from here, you can wander out along the leafy **valleys of the Sardon and Prades**.

The little town of **VOLVIC** is also close by, renowned for its spring water and the quarries that furnished the black rock for Clermont's cathedral, as well as so many other Auvergnat buildings. Its **Maison de la Pierre**, on rue Viallard (guided tours daily except Tues: mid-March to April & Oct to mid-Nov 10am–5.15pm; May–Sept 9.15am–6pm; 20F/€3.05), features a surprisingly engaging display about the use of lava rock, including a historical and geological explanation, as well as a tour of the disused quarries – a warm jacket is advised.

Vichy

VICHY is famous for two things: its World War II puppet government under Marshal Pétain, and its curative sulphurous springs, which attract thousands of ageing and ailing visitors, or *curistes*, every year. There's no mention of Pétain's government in town, but the fact that Vichy is one of France's foremost spa resorts colours everything you see here. The town is almost entirely devoted to catering for its largely elderly, genteel and rich population, which swells several-fold in summer; they come here to drink the water, wallow in it, inhale its steam or be sprayed with it. An attempt is now being made to rejuvenate the image of Vichy by appealing to a younger, more fitness-conscious generation.

The Town

All of this makes Vichy seem unappealing, and yet it has a certain element of charm. There's a real *fin-de-siècle* atmosphere about the place and a curious fascination in its continuing function. The town revolves around the **Parc des Sources**, a stately tree-shaded park that takes up most of the centre. At its north end stands the **Hall des Sources**, an enormous iron-framed greenhouse in which people sit and chat or read newspapers, while from a large tiled stand in the middle the various waters emerge from their spouts,

---

VOLVIC TO LASCHAMP WALK

For a good day's walk and a thorough exploration of the *puys*, take the train from Clermont to Volvic-Gare. Follow the D90 road beside the train line for about 1km until you join up with the **GR441** path, where the road turns right under the train line. Keep along your side of the train track for a few minutes longer and follow the GR441 round to the left, almost doubling back southwest along the line of the wooded Puys Nugères, Jumes and Coquille to the northern foot of the Puy de Chopine (2–3hr). Here you join up with the **GR4** and follow the combined GR4–441 across the Orcines–Pontgibaud road to the summit of the Puy de Dôme (about 2hr 30min from the road). From the Puy, descend to the Col de Ceyssat in half an hour (good chance of a lift back to Clermont), or continue to **LASCHAMP** (50min), where there is a **gîte d'étape** (7–8hr, though a fit and experienced walker could do it in 6hr).

You should not set off without either the relevant section of the GR4 *Topoguide* or, preferably, the IGN 1:25,000 map, the *Chaîne des Puys*, which also marks the GR441 from Volvic-Gare. If you don't feel up to a walk, there is a really beautiful train ride from Clermont to the town of Le Mont-Dore (see p.810), all round the chain of the *puys*.

beside the just-visible remains of the Roman establishment. The *curistes* line up to get their prescribed cupful, and for a small fee you can join them. The Célestins is the only one of the springs that is bottled and widely drunk: if you're into a taste experience, try the remaining five. They are progressively more sulphurous and foul, with the Source de l'Hôpital, which has its own circular building at the far end of the park, an almost unbelievably nasty creation. Each of the springs is prescribed for a different ailment and the tradition is that, apart from the Célestins, they must all be drunk on the spot to be efficacious – a dubious but effective way of drawing in the crowds.

Although all the springs technically belong to the nation and treatment is partially funded by the state, they are in fact run privately for profit by the Compagnie Fermière, first created in the nineteenth century to prepare for a visit by the Emperor Napoléon III. The Compagnie not only has a monopoly on selling the waters but also runs the casino and numerous hotels – even the chairs conveniently dotted around the Parc des Sources are owned by it.

Directly behind the Hall des Sources, on the leafy **Esplanade Napoléon III** (the emperor's interest in the waters brought Vichy to public notice in the mid-nineteenth century), is the enormous, Byzantine-style **Grand Établissement Thermal**, the former thermal baths, decorated with Moorish arches, gold-and-blue domes and blue ceramic panels of voluptuous mermaids. All that remains inside of the original baths is the grand entrance hall, with its fountain and two beautiful murals, *La Bain* and *La Source*, painted by Osberd in 1903. The arcades leading off either side of the hall, once the site of gyms and treatment rooms, now house expensive boutiques.

To provide distraction for the *curistes*, a grand **casino** and **opera house** were built at the southern end of the Parc des Sources. From May to September the opera house is the venue for regular concerts and opera productions, while lighter music oom-pahs out from the open-air bandstand in the park behind it.

After the waters, Vichy's curiosities are limited. There is pleasant, wooded riverside in the **Parc de l'Allier**, also created for Napoléon III. And, not far from here, the old town boasts the strange **church of St-Blaise**, actually two churches in one, with a 1930s Baroque structure built onto the original Romanesque one – an effect that sounds hideous but is rather imaginative. Inside, another Auvergne Black Virgin, Notre-Dame-des-Malades, stands surrounded by plaques offered by the grateful healed who stacked their odds with both her and the sulphur.

Practicalities

Vichy's **gare SNCF** is about a ten-minute walk from the centre, on the eastern edge of the city centre at the end of rue de Paris. The **gare routière** sits on the corner of rue Doumier and rue Jardet, by the central place Charles-de-Gaulle, and there is a public transport information line (☎04.70.30.17.30). The building that used to house the wartime Vichy government at 19 rue du Parc is now home to the **tourist office** (April–Sept Mon–Sat 9am–7pm, Sun 9.30am–12.30pm & 3–7pm; rest of year Mon–Sat 9am–noon & 1.30–6pm; ☎04.70.98.71.94, *www.ville-vichy.fr*).

There are so many **hotels** that finding a place to stay is not difficult. There are several around the station, but more pleasant are the friendly, grand neo-Baroque *Midland*, 4 rue de l'Intendance, in a quiet street off rue de Paris (☎04.70.97.48.48, fax 04.70.31.31.89; ③; closed mid-Oct to mid-April; good restaurant with menus from 85F/€12.96), and the *Hôtel Londres*, 7 bd de Russie, behind the casino (☎04.70.98.28.27, fax 04.70.98.29.37; ①; closed mid-Oct to March), which was the secret meeting place for Jean Moulin and fellow Resistance fighters in 1941. There's a municipal **campsite**, *La Graviere*, at the Centre Omnisports (☎04.70.59.21.00; closed Oct–Feb).

For **eating**, apart from the hotel-restaurants listed above, the simplest solution is to head for the area around the junction of rue Clemenceau and rue de Paris, where there are several brasseries and cafés. For something rather more elegant, the beautiful 1920s-style *Brasserie du Casino*, 4 rue du Casino (☎04.70.98.23.06; closed Wed & Sun evening & mid-Oct to mid-Nov; 85–145F/€12.95–22.10), is an interesting experience: dressing smartly is advisable, and you should book ahead if you're there during the opera season.

The Monts-Dore

The **Monts-Dore** lie about 50km southwest of Clermont. Also volcanic in origin – the main period of activity was around five million years ago – they are much more rugged and more obviously mountainous than their gentler, younger neighbours, the Monts-Dômes. Their centre is the precipitous, plunging valley of the River Dordogne, which rises on the slopes of the **Puy de Sancy**, at 1885m the highest point in the Massif Central, just above the little town of **Le Mont-Dore**.

In spite of their relative ruggedness, there are few crags and rock faces. Their upper slopes, albeit steep, are grassy and treeless for miles and miles. They are known as *montagnes à vaches* – mountains for cows – as they traditionally provided summer pasture land for herds of cows, raised above all for their milk and the production of **St-Nectaire** cheese. The herdsmen who milked them morning and evening and made the cheese set up their primitive summer homes in the dozens of (now mainly ruined) stone huts, or *burons*, that scatter the landscape.

Although these traditional activities still continue, many of the upland herds are now beef cattle being fattened for the autumn sales, often for export to Italy, Germany and Spain. And tourism has become an important part of the local economy, although mostly unobtrusive and low-key, with mainly walkers in summer and cross-country skiers in winter.

Le Mont-Dore and the Puy de Sancy

Squeezed out along the narrow wooded valley of the infant Dordogne, grey-slated **LE MONT-DORE**, 50km southwest of Clermont, is a long-established spa resort, with Roman remnants testifying to just how old it is. Its popularity goes back to the eighteenth century, when metalled roads replaced the old mule paths and made access possible, but reached its apogee with the opening of the rail line around 1900. It is an altogether wholesome and civilized sort of place.

The **Établissement Thermal** – the baths, which give the place its *raison d'être* – are right in the middle of town and are certainly worth visiting (guided tours Mon–Sat: mid-May to mid-Oct 2.30, 3.30, 4.30 & 5.30pm; 15F/€2.29). Early every morning, the *curistes* stream into its neo-Byzantine halls – an extravaganza of tiles, striped columns and ornate ironwork – hoping for a remedy in this self-proclaimed "world centre for treatment of asthma". For many Parisians, of all ages and walks of life, this is their annual mecca: whiling away their days sniffing sulphur from bunsen burner tubes, and sitting in thick steam.

Walkers also frequent the town, the principal attraction being the **Puy de Sancy** (1885m), whose jagged skyline blocks the head of the Dordogne valley, 3km away (mid-May to Sept; 4 buses daily from the tourist office; 18F/€2.74). Accessible by *téléférique* (38F/€5.80 return) since the 1930s, it's one of the busiest tourist sites in the country. As a result, the path from the *téléférique* station to the summit has had to be railed and paved with baulks of timber to prevent total erosion. Combined with the scars of access tracks for the ski installations, this has done little for its beauty.

However, with a little sweat and effort you can escape to wilder areas of the mountain. The **GR30** passes this way and on down to La Bourboule (see opposite), giving a good sense of the typical landscape: long views over meadows full of gentians and violets, grazed by sheep and cows. Start out along the summit path and at the first intermediate peak, take a right and go downhill. The GR30 is signposted. It follows the western ridge of the Dordogne valley for about an hour and a half, before turning ninety degrees left, away from the valley. Keep straight ahead at this point, go down a gravelly track, with the rocky dome of **Le Capucin**, above Le Mont-Dore, directly in front of you. The track enters the woods to the left of this bump by a ruined house. Five minutes later, on the right, just past a concrete water-pipe junction, a path drops steeply down through beech trees to Le Capucin *funiculaire* station and down again to Le Mont-Dore (3hr).

Practicalities

Without a car, Le Mont-Dore is most easily accessible by train from Clermont. The **train** and **bus stations** are at the entrance to the town. A ten-minute walk down avenue Michelet takes you to the centre, where the **tourist office** sits in the park on avenue de la Libération (July & Aug Mon–Sat 9am–7pm, Sun 10am–noon & 2–6pm; rest of year Mon–Sat 9am–12.30pm & 2–6.30pm, Sun 10am–noon & 4–6pm; ☎04.73.65.20.21, *www.mont-dore.com*); the helpful staff will advise about other walking and cycling possibilities (VTT rental), as well as day bus excursions to some otherwise rather inaccessible places round about.

Accommodation is not hard to come by, as the town is brimming with hotels. Close to the baths, at 8 rue Favart, *Hôtel aux Champs d'Auvergne* (☎04.73.65.00.37; ①; restaurant from 58F/€8,84) is very welcoming and serves copious breakfasts, while the elegant *Hôtel de la Paix*, nearby on rue Rigny (☎04.73.65.00.17, fax 04.73.65.00.31; ②), has comfortable, clean rooms and an excellent restaurant (menus from 85F/€12.96). Also good value, though slightly dowdier, is the *Nouvel Hôtel* on parallel rue Jean Moulin (☎04.73.65.11.34, fax 04.73.65.09.77; ①; closed Oct 10–Dec 20; restaurant from 60F/€9.15). There's an efficient modern **hostel** on the Puy de Sancy road, with a stunning view of the mountains (☎04.73.65.03.53, fax 04.73.65.26.39; meals), and a *gîte d'étape* (☎04.73.65.25.65, fax 04.73.65.03.94), on Chemin des Vergnes, not far from the municipal **campsite**, *Les Crouzets* (☎04.73.65.21.60), opposite the station. The other municipal campsite is *L'Esquiladou* (☎04.73.65.23.74; closed Nov–April), off to the right on the road to La Bourboule.

As far as **eating** is concerned, there are large numbers of brasseries and cafés in the centre offering *plats* for 40–50F/€6.10–7.62. A particularly pleasant place is rustic *Le Bougnat*, 23 av Clemenceau, which serves various Auvergnat traditional dishes, as well as raclette and fondue (☎04.73.65.28.19; closed Mon; menus from 79F/€12.05). A great place for a **drink** is atmospheric, 1940s-style *Café de Paris*, rue Jean Moulin.

La Bourboule

LA BOURBOULE is just 7km down the road from Le Mont-Dore. Known as the sister to Le Mont-Dore, it is another traditional spa – the "capital of allergies" – but with a more open feel and, because of its lower altitude, temperatures a degree or two warmer. The big **casino**, the domed **Grands Thermes baths** and several other Belle Époque buildings which once housed privately run baths are ornate, gilded and wonderfully vulgar, with a faded, permanently off-season look to them – much like the whole town. All in all, it's a cool, tranquil place to unwind: as the tourist office's leaflet says, "You will be able to put your vital node to rest in La Bourboule."

Behind the Hôtel de Ville, the large wooded **Parc Fenestre** has a *téléférique* taking you right up to **Plateau de Charlannes** (1300m), where it's possible to stroll in the woods or ski in winter; the **tourist office** in the Hôtel de Ville on place de la République (April–June & Sept daily 9am–noon & 1.30–6pm; July & Aug daily 9am–7pm;

WALKING AND SKIING AROUND LA BOURBOULE

Fit and serious walkers may want to conquer the **Puy de Sancy**, a six-hour hike south of La Bourboule on the GR30–41, passing after about two hours the two fine waterfalls of the **Cascade de la Vernière** and **Plat à Barbe** – themselves a satisfying destination. For the summit of Puy de Sancy, see the account of Le Mont-Dore (p.810). An easier walk out of La Bourboule is to the summit of the **Banne d'Ordanche** (1500m): pick up the GR path to the east of the town where it crosses the D130 road and the train line, then take the signposted GR41 where it diverges from the GR30.

During winter months, both Le Mont-Dore and La Bourboule double as ski resorts – centres of a **ski-de-fond** (cross-country) network of circular pistes, some over 20km long. Skiable paths also connect La Bourboule to other ski centres in the locality – Sancy, Besse, Chastreix and Picherande. Downhill skiing is possible, too, on the Puy de Sancy.

Oct–March Mon–Sat 9am–noon & 1.30–5.30pm, Sun 9.30am–12.30pm; ☎04.73.65.57.71, *www.bourboule.com*) sells a booklet of local walks.

Hotels here are plentiful, three good bargains being the *Aviation Hôtel*, in rue de Metz (☎04.73.81.32.32, fax 04.73.81.02.85, *www.sancy-info.fr/aviation*; ③; closed Oct–Dec 20; restaurant from 79F/€12.05), with indoor pool; the welcoming, Art Deco-style *Le Pavillon*, avenue d'Angleterre (☎04.73.65.50.18, fax 04.73.81.00.93; ③; closed mid-Oct to March; restaurant from 80F/€12.20); and *Des Fleurs* on avenue de Mussy (☎04.73.81.09.44, fax 04.73.65.52.03; ②; closed Oct 10–Dec 20; restaurant from 90F/€13.72). There is also a good selection of **campsites**, with the *Camping municipal* on avenue Maréchal Lattre-de-Tassigny (☎04.73.81.10.20), and another at Murat-le-Quaire, 4km away, along the Mont-Dore road (☎04.73.65.54.81).

Orcival

Twenty-seven kilometres southwest of Clermont and about 20km north of Le Mont-Dore, lush pastures and green hills punctuated by the abrupt eruptions of the *puys* enclose the village of **ORCIVAL**, the home town of ex-President Valéry Giscard d'Estaing. A pretty, well-visited, little place, founded by the monks of La Chaise-Dieu in the twelfth century, it makes a suitable base for hiking in the region.

Orcival is dominated by the stunning Romanesque **church of Notre-Dame**, built of the same dark-grey volcanic stone as the cathedral in Clermont and topped with a spire and fanned with tiny chapels. Inside, attention focuses on the choir, neatly and harmoniously contained by the semi-circle of pillars defining the ambulatory. Mounted on a stone column in the centre is the celebrated **Virgin of Orcival**, a gilded and enamelled statue of Mary enthroned, holding an adult-looking Child in her lap. The statue has been the object of a popular cult since the Middle Ages and is still carried through the streets on Ascension Day.

There is no public transport to Orcival itself; the nearest **bus station** is at Rochefort-Montagne, 6km away, served by buses from Clermont-Ferrand. There's modest **accommodation** at the *Hôtel des Touristes* (☎04.73.65.82.55, fax 04.73.65.91.11; ②; closed mid-Nov to mid-Feb; restaurant from 60F/€9.15) and the *Hôtel Vieux Logis* (☎04.73.65.82.03, fax 04.73.65.88.07; ①; closed Nov to mid-Dec), both near the church. One kilometre away on GR30–GR441, the **gîte d'étape** *La Fontchartoux* (☎04.73.65.83.04; ①) has an adjoining restaurant run by the *gîte* proprietor. There's a lakeside **campsite**, *Camping de l'Étang de Fléchat* (☎04.73.65.82.96; closed mid-Sept to April), 2km outside Orcival, but a better bet is the municipal site at St-Bonnet, 5km to the north of the village (☎04.73.65.83.32; closed Oct–April), set on a hillside with wonderful views of the surrounding mountains.

WALKS AROUND ORCIVAL

Walking possibilities from Orcival include trips to **Lac de Servières** and **Lac de Guéry**. The first takes two and a half hours, the second some five hours. For Lac de Servières, follow the **GR141–30** south through the woods above the valley of the Sioule. The lake is a beauty; it's 1200m up, with gently sloping shores surrounded by pasture and conifers. You can either head southeast to the **gîte d'étape** at Pessade (☎04.73.79.31.07), or continue to the larger Lac de Guéry, lent a slightly eerie air by the black basaltic boulders strewn across the surrounding meadows, where there is a romantically situated lakeside **hotel**, the *Lac de Guéry* (☎04.73.65.02.76, fax 04.73.65.08.78; ③; closed mid-Oct to mid-Jan; restaurant from 95F/€14.48).

If you are driving to Le Mont-Dore, only 9km further on from here, just before the Lac de Guéry, the road takes you round the head of the **Fontsalade valley**, where two prominent rocks composed of banks of basalt organ-pipes rise spectacularly from the woods: the **Roche Tuilière** and the **Roche Sanadoire**. A *Chamina* footpath takes you on a two-hour walk round the valley, starting from the roadside belvedere overlooking Sanadoire. A little higher up, on the bare slopes of the **Puy de l'Aiguiller**, a roadside memorial commemorates some English airmen killed in an accident while making a parachute drop to the *maquis* in March 1944.

St-Nectaire and around

ST-NECTAIRE lies some way to the south of Orcival, midway between Le Mont-Dore and Issoire. It comprises the tiny spa of **St-Nectaire-le-Bas**, whose main street is lined with grand but fading Belle Époque hotels, and the old village of **St-Nectaire-le-Haut**, overlooked by a magnificent Romanesque **church**. Like the church in Orcival and Notre-Dame-du-Port in Clermont, this is one of the jewels of the Auvergne's Romanesque architecture, with the same delightful features: patterned stonework, intricate arrangement of apse and radiating chapels and richly carved capitals within.

On the narrow valley floor, where the main street runs, two of the old **hotels** have been refurbished and provide a quiet and comfortable place to stay. One, in particular, the friendly *Hôtel Régina* (☎04.73.88.54.55, fax 04.73.88.50.56; ③; closed Nov–March) has an excellent restaurant with menus from 88F/€13.42. The *Thermalia* (☎04.73.88.30.28, fax 04.73.88.52.59; ③; closed mid-Oct to March), next door, has more character and also provides a good meal from 88F/€13.42. The best-value **campsite** is the *Clé des Champs* (☎04.73.88.52.33), and there is also a **gîte d'étape**, *Le Clos du Vallon* (☎04.73.88.50.92; closed Nov–March), for walkers on the GR30. This heads north from here to Lac Aydat in five hours, or west to the forest-girt **Lac Chambon** in three hours via Murol. There's another *gîte* on the way at Phialeix (☎04.73.79.32.43; closed Nov–March).

For shorter walks out of St-Nectaire, take the D150 past the church through the old village towards the **Puy de Mazeyres** (919m), and turn up a path to the right for the final climb to the summit (1hr), where you get a superb aerial view of the country round about. Alternatively, follow the D966 along the Couze de Chambon valley to **SAILLANT**, where the stream cascades down a high lava rock face in the middle of the village.

Murol

MUROL, 6km west of St-Nectaire by road (July & Aug twice-daily bus to Clermont), is an attractive, sleepy little place best known for its powerful medieval **château**, dramatically situated on top of a basalt cone commanding the approaches for kilometres around (May–Sept Mon–Sat 10am–noon & 1.30–6pm, Sun 2–5pm; rest of year daily 2–5pm; 20F/€3.05). In summer, a local organization re-enacts the medieval life of the castle in costume (45F/€6,86).

ST-NECTAIRE CHEESE

St-Nectaire is an *appellation contrôlée*, to which only cheeses made from herds grazing in a limited area to the south of the Monts-Dore are entitled. It is made in two stages. First, a white creamy cheese or *tomme* is produced. This is matured for two to three months in a cellar at a constant temperature, resulting in the growth of a mould on the skin of the cheese which produces the characteristic smell, taste and whitish or yellowy-grey colour.

There are two kinds: St-Nectaire **fermier** and St-Nectaire **laitier**. The *fermier* is the strongest and tastiest and some of it is still made entirely on the farm. Increasingly, however, individual farmers make the *tomme* stage, but then sell it on to wholesalers for the refining. The *laitier* is much more an "industrial" product, made from the milk of lots of different herds, sold onto a co-operative or cheese manufacturer for all its stages.

There are several small family-run **hotels** here. Try the *Hôtel des Pins*, on rue de Levat (☎04.73.88.60.50, fax 04.73.88.60.29; ①; closed mid-Oct to April; restaurant from 58F/€8.84), or the *Hôtel de Paris*, on place de l'Hôtel-de-Ville (☎04.73.88.60.09, fax 04.73.88.69.62; ③; closed mid-Sept to April). Of the **campsites**, the best value is the *Ribeyre*, a short distance away at **JASSAT** (☎04.73.88.64.29, *laribeyre.free.fr*, closed mid-Sept to April).

Besse

Eleven kilometres due south of Murol, **BESSE** is one of the prettiest and oldest villages in the region. Its fascinating winding streets of noble lava-built houses – some as old as the fifteenth century – sit atop the valley of the Couze de Pavin, with one of the original fortified town **gates** still in place at the upper end of the village.

Its wealth was due to its role as the principal market for the farms on the eastern slopes of the Monts-Dore. Its co-operative is still one of the main producers of St-Nectaire cheese (see box above), and the annual **festivals** of the Montée and Dévalade, marking the ascent of the herds to the high pastures in July and their descent in autumn, are still celebrated by the procession of the Black Virgin of Vassivière from the **church of St-André** in Besse to the chapel of **LA VASSIVIÈRE**, west of **Lac Pavin**, and back again in autumn (July 2 & the first Sun after Sept 21).

Lac Pavin lies 5km west of the village, on the way to the purpose-built ski resort of **SUPER-BESSE**. It's a perfect volcanic lake, filling the now wooded crater. The **GR30** goes through, passing by the **Puy de Montchal**, whose summit (1407m) gives you a fine view over several other lakes and the rolling plateau south towards **ÉGLISENEUVE-D'ENTRAIGUES**, 13km by road, where the Parc des Volcans' **Maison du Fromage** gives a blow-by-blow account of the making of the different cheeses of Auvergne (daily: mid-May to June & Sept 2–6pm; July & Aug 10am–12.30pm & 2.30–7pm; 18F/€2.75).

Besse's **tourist office** is next to the church on place du Dr Pipet (Mon–Sat 9am–noon & 2–6/6.30pm, Sun 10am–noon & 3–6pm; ☎04.73.79.52.84, *www.superbesse.com*), and will provide information and advice about walking, mountain biking and skiing. For a place to **stay**, there is none better than the attractive old *Hostellerie du Beffroi*, 24 rue Abbé-Blot (☎04.73.79.50.08, fax 04.73.79.57.87; ③), whose good restaurant serves up a range of local specialities from 100F/€15.25.

The Monts du Cantal

The **Cantal Massif** forms the most southerly extension of the Parc des Volcans. Still nearly 80km in diameter and once 3000m in height, it is one of the world's largest (albeit extinct) volcanoes, shaped like a wheel without a rim. The hub is formed by the three great conical peaks that survived the erosion of the original single cone: **Plomb du Cantal** (1885m), **Puy Mary** (1787m) and **Puy de Peyre-Arse** (1686m).

From this centre a series of deep-cut wooded valleys radiates out like spokes. The most notable are the **valley of Mandailles** and the **valleys of the Cère and Alagnon** in the southwest, where the road and rail line run, and in the north the **valleys of Falgoux and the Rhue**. Between the valleys, especially on the north side, are huge expanses of gently sloping grassland, most notably the **Plateau du Limon**, and it is these which for centuries have been the mainstay of life in the Cantal: summer pasture for the cows whose milk makes the firm yellow Cantal cheese, pressed in the form of great crusty drums. But this traditional activity has long been in serious decline; as elsewhere, many of the herds are now beef cattle. And tourism is on the increase, in particular walking, horse-riding and skiing.

The main walking routes are the fairly arduous **GR400**, which does a circuit of the whole massif, and the **GR4**, which crosses it from the north to the southeast. There are also more than fifty shorter routes, details of which are obtainable through Chamina publications (see p.803). The two main summits, Plomb du Cantal and Puy Mary, are – for better or worse – accessible to all: the former by *téléférique* from Super-Lioran, the latter by a veritable highway of a footpath from the road at Pas de Peyrol. The best section of the GR4–400 for an experienced hiker with limited time is the three-hour stretch between Super-Lioran and the Puy Mary, with the possibility of taking in a couple of extra summits on the way. For motorists, there's the long, sinuous **Route des Crêtes**, which does a rather wider circuit than the GR400. But, be warned, if you hit a period of bad weather, you'll drive a long way in low gear, seeing no more than white banks of mist illumined by your headlights.

The main centres within the massif lie on the N122 between Murat and Aurillac: **LE LIORAN**, where the road and rail tunnels begin, and **SUPER-LIORAN**, the downhill and cross-country ski centre, with the *Auberge du Tunnel* (☎04.71.49.50.02; ②; restaurant from 65F/€9.91) and two *gîtes d'étape*, as well as a **tourist office** (Mon–Sat: July & Aug 9.30am–12.30pm & 2–6.30pm; rest of year 8.30am–12.30pm & 1.30–6pm; ☎04.71.49.50.08, fax 04.71.49.51.01). **THIEZAC**, 10km south, also has a **tourist office** (June–Sept Mon–Sat 9.30am–12.30pm & 3.30–7.30pm; ☎04.71.47.03.50, fax 04.71.47.02.23), as well as the *Hôtel La Belle Vallée* (☎04.71.47.00.22, fax 04.71.47.02.08; ②; closed Nov–Dec 20; restaurant from 90F/€13.72), three *gîtes d'étape* and a municipal **campsite**, *La Bedisse* (☎04.71.47.00.41; closed mid-Sept to May). Further south at **VIC-SUR-CÈRE** there's a **tourist office** (Mon–Sat 9.30am–noon & 2.30–6pm; ☎04.71.47.50.68, fax 04.71.49.60.63), and **accommodation** at the *Hôtel des Bains*, 9 av de la Promenade (☎04.71.47.50.16, fax 04.71.49.63.82; ②; closed Oct–April; restaurant from 85F/€12.96), and the riverside municipal **campsite** (☎04.71.47.51.04; closed Oct–March).

Aurillac

AURILLAC, the provincial capital of the Cantal, lies on the west side of the mountains, 98km east of Brive and 160km from Clermont-Ferrand. In spite of its good mainline train connections and the fact that its population has almost doubled in the last forty years to around 30,000, it remains one of the most out-of-the-way French provincial capitals. It was until recently a major manufacturer of umbrellas, though that seems doomed to eventual extinction, like its older traditional lace-making and tanning industries. It is now mainly an administrative and commercial centre, with important cattle markets in the suburb of Sistrières on Mondays. Although there are no important sights, it makes a pleasant and unpretentious place to stop over on your way into the Massif Central from the west.

The most interesting part of town is the kernel of old streets, now largely pedestrianized and full of good shops, just to the north of the central **place du Square**. **Rue**

Duclaux leads through to the attractive **place de l'Hôtel-de-Ville**, where the big Wednesday and Saturday markets are held in the shadow of the handsome grey-stone **Hôtel de Ville**, built in restrained Republican-classical style in 1803. Beyond it, the continuation of **rue des Forgerons** leads to the beautiful little **place St-Géraud**, with a round twelfth-century fountain overlooked by a Romanesque house that was probably part of the original abbey guesthouse, and the externally rather unprepossessing **church of St-Géraud**, which nonetheless has a beautifully ribbed late Gothic ceiling.

At the back of the church, past a delightful small garden, **rue de la Fontaine** comes out on the river bank by the Pont du Buis, with a shady walk back along cours d'Angoulême on the other side to the Pont-Rouge and **place Gerbert**, where there is an ancient *lavoir*, or washing place. On a steep bluff overlooking this end of town towers the eleventh-century keep of the Château St-Étienne, containing the town's only worthwhile museum, the **Muséum des Volcans** (Jan to mid-June & mid-Sept to Dec Tues–Sat 2–6pm; mid-June to mid-Sept Mon–Sat 10am–6.30pm, Sun 2–6.30pm; 25F/€3.81), with a good section on volcanoes and a splendid view over the mountains to the east.

Southeast of the town towards Aubrac, the road leads through **Carlat**, once an important feudal fiefdom, as well as the particularly attractive villages of **Mur-de-Barrez**, **Brommat** and **Albinhac**, with some lovely old houses and curious churches in the latter two villages.

Practicalities

The **gare SNCF** and **gare routière** are together on place Sémard, a ten-minute walk from the central place du Square along avenue de la République and rue de la Gare. The **tourist office** occupies a small kiosk on the downhill side of place du Square (April–June & Sept Mon–Sat 9am–noon & 2–6.30pm, Sun 10am–noon & 2–5pm; July & Aug daily 9am–7pm; Oct–March Mon–Sat 9am–noon & 2–6.30pm; ☎04.71.48.46.58, *aurillac.tourisme@wanadoo.fr*), with a number of guidebooks and maps on sale, as well as a money-changing facility when the banks are closed. There's **Internet** access at the *Faisan Doré* cyber café, 8 place d'Aurigues.

For a **place to stay** in the centre of town, try the smart and comfortable *Le Square*, 15 place du Square (☎04.71.48.24.72, fax 04.71.48.47.57; ③; with a reasonable restaurant from 68F/€10.37), or the *Renaissance*, just next door (☎04.71.48.09.80, fax 04.71.48.54.81; ②). Another good option is the family-run *Hôtel Delcher*, just off the square at 20 rue des Carmes (☎04.71.48.01.69, fax 04.71.48.86.66; ③; closed Dec & last two weeks of July; good food from 72F/€10.98).

CATTLE RANCHING IN THE CANTAL: ALLANCHE

For an insider's view of the farming life of the Massif there's no better place to go than the age-old **cattle sales at Allanche**, little more than a straggling main street of ancient houses surrounded by windswept upland pastures, about 25km north of Murat (see opposite).

The September 7 sale, when the season's calves are sold off before winter, is typical. Activity starts at 1am or 2am with the clanging of cowbells, the cries of drivers and the thrumming of truck engines. By 4am two or three thousand cattle are tethered to the iron stanchions in the floodlit grassy marketplace, inspected and appraised by men in wellies and overalls and pancake-shaped berets. There is a great deal of bucking and bellowing and sudden uncontrollable charging as beasts are unloaded or loaded, some of them so big they'd have little trouble shifting a bulldozer. For information on other sales call the tourist office in Allanche (☎ & fax 04.71.20.48.43).

If you are tempted to **stay** to see the spectacle, there's a campsite at the south edge of the village (☎04.71.20.45.87; closed mid-Sept to mid-June) and, just beyond, the *Hôtel Le Foirail* (☎04.71.20.41.15; ①; restaurant from 70F/€10.67).

There are a number of **restaurants** where you can sample *auvergnat* specialities. Two of the most popular are the atmospheric *Le Terroir du Cantal*, 5 rue du Buis (closed Sun & Mon), with its rough-stone walls and wooden benches, and *Poivre et Sel*, 4 rue du 14-Juillet (closed Sun & Mon; menus from 63F/€9.60), featuring classic dishes such as *magret de canard*. The pretty, riverside *Birdland*, by the Pont-Rouge, done out in the French version of pub style, serves pizzas for around 40F/€6.10 and menus for 110F/€16.77 (closed Sun); if you're looking for **nightlife**, the *Bateau-Lavoir* disco is part of the same establishment (Thurs–Sun 11pm–4/5am; 50F/€7.62). Finally, Aurillac's most unexpected event is an annual international **street theatre festival** (*www.aurillac.net*) during the last full week in August, which attracts performers from all over Europe and fills the town with rather more exotic characters than are normally to be seen about its provincial streets.

Salers

SALERS lies 42km north of Aurillac, at the foot of the northwest slopes of the Cantal and within sight of the Puy Violent. Scarcely altered in size or aspect since its sixteenth-century heyday, it remains an extraordinarily homogeneous example of the architecture of that time. If it appears rather grand for a place so small, it's because the town became the administrative centre for the highlands of the Auvergne in 1564 and home of its magistrates. Exploiting this past is really all that is left to it, but Salers still makes a very worthwhile visit, despite the large numbers of tourists.

If you arrive by the Puy Mary road, you'll enter town by the **church**, which is worth a look for the super-naturalistic statuary of the *Entombment of Christ* (1496), hidden in a side chapel near the entrance. In front of you, the cobbled **rue du Beffroi** leads uphill, under the massive clock tower, and into the central **place Tyssandier-d'Escous**. It is a glorious little square, surrounded by the fifteenth-century mansions of the provincial aristocracy with pepper-pot turrets, mullioned windows and carved lintels, among them the sturdy **Maison du Bailliage**, and, nearby, the **Maison des Templiers**, housing the small Musée de Salers (April to mid-Nov daily 10.30am–12.30pm & 2.30–6.30pm; rest of year closed Tues; 20F/€3.05). Though the museum itself is rather dull, with exhibitions on the Salers cattle breed, traditional costumes and the local cheese-making industry, it's worth having a look at the vaulted ceiling of the entrance passageway, with its carved lions and heads of saints, such as St John the Baptist, framed by wild flowing hair. Before you are done, be sure to make your way to the **Promenade de Barrouze** for the view out across the surrounding green hills and the Puy Violent.

The **tourist office** is in place Tyssandier-d'Escous (Feb–May, Oct–Nov 11 & Dec 21–Jan 4 Mon–Sat 10am–noon & 2.30–7pm, Sun 2.30–5.30pm; June–Sept Mon–Sat 10am–noon & 2.30–7pm, Sun 10am–noon & 3–7pm (☎04.71.40.70.68, fax 04.71.40.70.94). If you are planning to **stay**, try the *Hôtel des Remparts*, near the Promenade de Barrouze (☎04.71.40.70.33, fax 04.71.40.75.32; ③; closed mid-Oct to mid-Dec), whose good restaurant specializes in Auvergnat cuisine (from 69F/€10.52); or the small *Hôtel du Beffroi*, in rue du Beffroi (☎04.71.40.70.11, fax 04.71.40.70.16; ③; closed mid-Nov to April), likewise with good solid regional food (from 65F/€9.91). There's a municipal **campsite** on the Puy Mary road (☎04.71.40.73.09; closed mid-Oct to mid-May).

Murat

MURAT, on the eastern edge of the Cantal, is the closest town to the high peaks. It is also the easiest to access, lying on the N122 road and main train line, about 12km northeast of Le Lioran. There is no one particular sight to see here. It's the ensemble of greystone houses that attracts, many dating from the fifteenth and sixteenth centuries. Crowded together on their medieval lanes, they make a magnificent sight, especially as you approach from the St-Flour road, with the backdrop of the steep basalt cliffs of the **Rocher Bonnevie**, once the site of the local castle and now surmounted by a huge white statue of the Virgin Mary. Facing the town, perched on the distinctive mound of the **Rocher Bredons**, on your left as you approach, there's the lovely Romanesque **Église de Bredons** (July & Aug daily 10am–noon & 2.30–6.30pm; 10F/€1.52), containing some fine eighteenth-century altarpieces. One of the finest of the old houses is now open to the public as the **Maison de la Faune** (July & Aug Mon–Sat 10am–noon & 3–7pm, Sun 3–7pm; rest of year Mon–Sat 10am–noon & 2–5pm; 22F/€3.35), full of stuffed animals and birds illustrating the wildlife of the Parc des Volcans area.

The **monument** to deportees on place de l'Hôtel-de-Ville and the name of the **avenue des 12-et-24-Juin-1944**, opposite the tourist office, both commemorate one of the blackest days in Murat's recent history. On June 12, 1944, a local Resistance group interrupted a German raid on the town and killed a senior SS officer. In reprisal, the Germans burnt several houses down on June 24 and arrested 120 people, 80 of whom died in deportation. Near the river, below the Rocher Bredons, a stone with an inscription marks the spot where the villagers were assembled before being deported.

The **tourist office** is on the place de l'Hôtel-de-Ville (May & June Mon–Sat 10am–noon & 2–6pm, Sun 10am–noon; July & Aug daily 9.30am–noon & 2–7pm; rest of year Mon–Sat 10am–noon & 2–6pm; ☎04.71.20.09.47, fax 04.71.20.21.94), and you can rent **mountain bikes** from La Godille, opposite, or from Bernard Escure, in place Gandilhon-Gens-d'Armes. The **gare SNCF** is on the main road, avenue du Dr-Mallet, where there are also some good places to **stay**. The most comfortable is the *Hôtel des Breuils*, a handsome, ivy-covered bourgeois house at no. 34 (☎04.71.20.01.25, fax 04.71.20.02.43; ③; closed Nov–Christmas & April), with a heated outdoor pool, while at no. 22, there is the equally friendly and simple *Les Globe-Trotters* (☎04.71.20.07.22, fax 04.71.20.16.88; ②; closed Oct 25–Nov 8). A few doors down at no. 18, *Les Messageries* (☎04.71.20.04.04, fax 04.71.20.02.81; ③) has somewhat clinical rooms, but the **restaurant** (from 78F/€11.89) serves up good hearty cooking, including home-made terrines and fruit tarts. The town's **campsite**, *Les Stalapos*, is southwest of the centre in rue du Stade (☎04.71.20.01.83; closed Oct–April).

St-Flour and the Margeride

Seat of a fourteenth-century bishopric, **ST-FLOUR** stands dramatically on a cliff-girt basalt promontory above the River Ander, 92km west of Le Puy and 92km south of Clermont-Ferrand. Prosperous in the Middle Ages because of its strategic position on the main road from northern France to Languedoc and the proximity of the grasslands of the Cantal whose herds provided the raw materials for its tanning and leather industries, it fell into somnolent decline in modern times, only partially reversed in the last thirty-odd years.

While the lower town that has grown up around the station is of little interest, the wedge of old streets that occupies the point of the promontory surrounding the cathedral has considerable charm. The best time to come is on a Saturday morning when the old town is filled with market stalls selling *saucissons*, cheese and other local produce. If you are in a car, the best thing is to leave it in the car park in the chestnut-shaded square, **Les Promenades**. One end of the square is dominated by the **memorial** to Dr Mallet, his two sons and other hostages and assorted citizens executed in reprisals by the Germans during World War II.

The narrow streets of the old town lead off from here and converge on the **place d'Armes**, where the fourteenth-century **Cathédrale St-Pierre** stands, backing onto the edge of the cliff, with a terrace giving good views out over the countryside. From the outside, the plain grey volcanic rock of the cathedral makes for a rather severe and uninspiring appearance; it's an impression that is partly mitigated inside by the fine vaulting of the ceiling and the presence of a number of works of art, most notably a carved, black-painted walnut figure of Christ with a strikingly serene expression, dating from the thirteenth century.

Facing the cathedral on the place d'Armes are some attractive old buildings, housing a couple of cafés under their arcades, while at the north and south extremities of the square stand the town's two museums. At the north end, the fine fourteenth-century building that was once the headquarters of the town's consuls contains the **Musée Alfred Douët's** somewhat ragbag collections of furniture, tapestries and paintings (mid-April to mid-Oct daily 9am–noon & 2–6/7pm; rest of year closed Sun; 20F/€3.05, joint ticket with Haute-Auvergne museum 35F/€5.35); the view from the cliffs behind the museum gives a sense of the impregnable position of the town. At the south end of the square, the current Hôtel de Ville, formerly the bishop's palace built in 1610, houses the more interesting **Musée de la Haute-Auvergne** (mid-April to mid-Oct daily 10am–noon & 2–6pm; rest of year closed Sun; same prices as above), whose collections include some beautifully carved Auvergnat furniture and exquisitely made traditional musical instruments, such as the *cabrette*, a kind of accordion peculiar to the Auvergne.

Practicalities

The **gare SNCF** is on avenue Charles de Gaulle in the lower town. A few trains from Clermont-Ferrand and Aurillac stop here, but most journeys involve changing at Neussargues onto a SNCF bus, which can drop you off on the Promenades in the old town, saving you the walk up. The **tourist office** is on the Promenades, opposite the memorial (July & Aug Mon–Sat 9am–8pm, Sun 10am–noon & 3–7pm; May to June & first two weeks Sept daily 9am–noon & 2–6pm; rest of year Mon–Sat 9am–noon & 2–6pm; ☎04.71.60.22.50, *www.st-flour.com*).

For a place to **stay**, try the *Hôtel du Nord*, at 18 rue des Lacs (☎04.71.60.28.00, fax 04.71.60.07.33; ②), with spacious, traditional rooms and a good, popular restaurant serving local specialities (from 65F/€9.91). The *Grand Hôtel de l'Europe*, on cours Spy des Ternes, on the edge of Les Promenades (☎04.71.60.03.64, fax 0471.60.03.45; ③; closed Dec–Feb), has rather chintzy rooms, though some have balconies overlooking the mountains, and there's also a decent restaurant, serving *pounti* – a terrine of minced pork and prunes – *chou farci* and other local dishes (menus from 81F/€12.35). Another congenial place to eat is *Chez Geneviève*, 25 rue des Lacs, where menus start at 85F/€12.96 and you can eat a *potée auvergnate* for 49F/€7.47. The town's municipal **campsite**, *Les Orgues*, is off avenue des Orgues in the old town (☎04.71.60.44.01; closed mid-Sept to mid-May).

The Margeride

South and west of St-Flour stretch the wild, rolling, sparsely populated wooded hills of the **Margeride**, one of the strongholds of the wartime Resistance groups. If you have your own transport, the D4 makes a slow but spectacular route east (92km) to Le Puy, crossing the forested heights of **Mont Mouchet**, at 1465m the highest point of the Margeride. A side turning, the D48 (signposted), takes you to the national Resistance **monument** by the woodman's hut that served as HQ to the local Resistance commander during the June 1944 battle to delay German reinforcements moving north to strengthen resistance to the D-day landings in Normandy. There is a **museum** here (May to mid-Sept daily 9.30am–noon & 2–7pm; mid-Sept to mid-Oct Mon–Fri 9.30am–noon & 2–7pm, Sat & Sun 10am–noon & 2–6pm; 25F/€3.81), sketching the progression of the Resistance movement in the area. The views back west from these heights to the Cantal are superb.

Further south, the new *autoroute* crosses the gorge of the River Truyère beside the delicate steel tracery of the **Viaduc de Garabit**, built by Gustave Eiffel (of Tower fame) in 1884 to carry the newly constructed rail line; experience he put to important use in the Tower. Not far away, about 20km south of St-Flour and perched above the waters of the lake created by the damming of the Truyère for hydroelectric power, are the romantic ruins of the keep of the **Château d'Alleuze**, stronghold in the 1380s of one Bernard de Garlan, a notorious leader of lawless mercenaries employed by the English in the Hundred Years War to sow panic and destruction in French-held parts of the country.

THE SOUTHWEST: AUBRAC AND ROUERGUE

In the southwest corner of the Massif Central, the landscapes start to change and the mean altitude begins to drop. The wild, desolate moorland of the **Aubrac** is cut and contained by the savage gorges of the **Lot and Truyère rivers**. To the south of them, the arid but more southern-feeling plateaux of the *causses* form a sort of intermediate step to the lower hills and coastal plains of Languedoc. And they in turn are cut by the dramatic trenches formed by the **gorges of the Tarn**, **Jonte** and **Dourbie**, along with the spectacular caves of the **Aven Armand** and **Dargilan**. These are places best avoided at the height of the holiday season, when they turn into overcrowded outdoor playgrounds for amateur canoeists, parties of schoolchildren, motorists and campers.

The bigger towns, like **Rodez** and **Millau** in the old province of the **Rouergue**, also have much more of a southern feel. Both are worth a visit, although their attractions need not keep you for more than half a day. Rodez has a fine cathedral and Millau is worth considering as a base for exploring the *causses* and river gorges of the Tarn and Jonte.

The two great architectural draws of the area are **Conques**, with its medieval village and magnificent abbey, which owes its existence to the Santiago pilgrim route (now the GR65), and the perfect little *bastide* town of **Sauveterre-de-Rouergue**.

The mountains of Aubrac

The **Aubrac** lies to the south of St-Flour, east of the valley of the River Truyère and north of the valley of the Lot. It is a region of bleak, windswept uplands with long views and huge skies, dotted with glacial lakes and granite villages hunkered down out of the weather. The highest points are between 1200m and 1400m, and there are more cows up here than people; you see them grazing the boggy, peaty pastures, divided by dry-stone walls and turf-brown streams. There are few trees: a scatter of willow and ash along the streams and the occasional stand of hardy beeches on the tops, and only abandoned shepherds' huts testify to more populous times. It is an area which in bad weather is invisible, but which, in good conditions, has a bleak beauty, little disturbed by tourism or modernization.

Once this was sheep country, where shepherds from the dry summer lowlands of Quercy and Languedoc brought their flocks for the season. They were displaced in the nineteenth century by cows, raised for their more commercially exploitable production of milk and cheese, destined for the growing towns. And these in turn, as available labour shrank with the depopulation of the villages, ceded the pastures to beef cattle, as in the Cantal further north.

Aumont-Aubrac and Aubrac

The waymarked **Tour d'Aubrac footpath** does a complete circuit of the area in around ten days, starting from the town of **AUMONT-AUBRAC**, where you'll find the **hotel** *Prunières* (☎04.66.42.80.14, fax 04.66.42.92.20; ②; restaurant from 65F/€9.91), the *Relais de Peyre*, at 9 rue Languedoc (☎04.66.42.85.88, fax 04.66.42.90.08; ②; closed Jan; restaurant from 70F/€10.67), and a municipal **campsite** (☎04.66.42.80.02). There is also a daily train connection on the Millau–St-Flour line.

The marathon **GR65** from Le Puy to Santiago de Compostela in Spain also crosses the area from northeast to southwest en route to Conques. In fact, the tiny village of **AUBRAC**, which gave its name to the region, owes its existence to this Santiago pilgrim route; around 1120, a way station was opened here for the express purpose of providing shelter for the pilgrims on these inhospitable heights. Little remains of it today, beyond the windy **Tour des Anglais**, into which is incorporated the friendly *Hôtel de la Dômerie* (☎05.65.44.28.42, fax 05.65.44.21.47; ③; closed Nov–April; restaurant from 100F/€15.25).

St-Urcize and Nasbinals

This is the wildest and most starkly beautiful part of the Aubrac. The close-huddled village of **ST-URCIZE**, 13km north of the town of Aubrac, hangs off the side of the valley of the River Lhère, with a lovely Romanesque church at its centre and a World War I **memorial**, with so many names on it you wouldn't have thought it possible such a small place could furnish so much cannon fodder. The village is ghostly out of season, for most of the unspoiled granite houses are owned by people who live elsewhere. Should you wish to **stay**, there is a campsite, a *gîte d'étape* (☎04.71.23.20.57) and the welcoming *Hôtel Remise* (☎04.71.23.20.02, fax 04.71.23.20.02; ②; excellent food from 80F/€12.20). Another hotel, the *Relais de l'Aubrac* (☎04.66.32.52.06, fax 04.66.32.56.58; ③; closed mid-Nov to mid-Feb; restaurant from 95F/€14.48), lies at the point where the road to Nasbinals crosses the River Bès at the Pont-du-Gournier, around 5km from St-Urcize.

NASBINALS, 8km to the southeast, is rather bigger and livelier, and something of a cross-country ski resort in winter. It, too, has a beautiful small-scale **church** of the twelfth century, joined onto the adjacent house with a round fortified tower incorporated in the transept wall by the entrance. Just above the building, the *Hôtel de La Route d'Argent* (☎04.66.32.50.03, fax 04.66.32.56.77; ②) provides comfortable accommodation and good food (from 69F/€10.52). The village **tourist office** is on the other side of the road (July & Aug Mon–Sat 9am–noon & 2–6.30pm, Sun 9am–noon; rest of year Tues–Sat 9am–noon & 1.30–4.30pm; ☎04.66.32.55.73) and can rent out mountain bikes. A **campsite** (☎04.66.32.50.17) and **gîte d'étape** (☎04.66.32.50.65; meals available) are located on the St-Urcize road.

Laguiole

Seventeen kilometres west of St-Urcize and 24km north of Espalion, **LAGUIOLE** passes for a substantial town in these parts. It is a name which means but one thing in France: knives, and specifically ones with a long, pointed, stiletto-like blade and bone handle that fits the palm; the genuine article should bear the effigy of a bull stamped on the clasp that holds the blade open. It is an industry that started in the nineteenth century, then moved to industrial Thiers, outside Clermont-Ferrand, before returning to Laguiole in 1987, when the Société Laguiole opened a factory designed by Philippe Starck on the St-Urcize road, with a giant knife projecting from the roof of the windowless all-aluminium building. Of all the numerous outlets selling knives in the village, only the Société's are made entirely in Laguiole. They have a shop on the main through-road, on the corner of the central marketplace opposite the **tourist office kiosk** (Mon–Sat 9am–12.30pm & 3–7pm, Sun 10.30am–noon & 2–7pm; ☎05.65.44.35.94, fax 05.65.44.35.76); their wares include pricey knives designed by Starck himself.

There is nothing of great significance to see in the village, though the **Musée du Haut-Rouergue** (July & Aug daily 3.30–6.30pm; 15F/€2.29), with its collection of objects illustrative of the pastoral life, might be of interest. Nonetheless, it is a relatively metropolitan base for exploring round about, with several **hotels** on the main street. Try the *Aubrac* opposite the marketplace (☎05.65.44.32.13, fax 05.65.48.48.74; ②; restaurant from 62F/€9.50), the nearby *Régis* (☎05.65.44.30.05, fax 05.65.48.46.44; ③; restaurant from 96F/€14.63) or the *Grand Hôtel Auguy* (☎05.65.44.31.11, fax 05.65.51.50.81; ③), 2 allée de l'Amicale, with a good restaurant from 130F/€19.82.

Alternatively, there's a sort of *chambre d'hôte* at Le Combaïre, in a quiet rural setting 3km west on the D42 (☎05.65.44.33.26, fax 05.65.44.37.38; ② half-board); *gîtes d'étape* at Le Vayssaire (☎05.65.48.44.69) and Soulages-Bonneval (☎05.65.44.42.18, fax 05.65.44.42.80; meals available), 5km away on the D54; and a municipal **campsite** (☎05.65.44.39.72; closed mid-Sept to mid-June) on the St-Urcize road. Communications, however, are not good, and if you don't have a car your only chance of getting in or out is the daily bus to Rodez.

Marvejols

MARVEJOLS lies at the southeast extremity of the Aubrac, on the main N9 road (the *autoroute* has not yet arrived) and the Paris–Béziers train line. The country changes drastically as you approach. The bare, granite-strewn plateau opens into a wide deep basin, wooded with pines and punctuated by the erosion-formed table-topped pinnacles known hereabouts as *trucs*. It is a small, undeveloped and unpretentious country town, whose ancient streets are contained within surviving medieval gates. There is little to do beyond savouring the atmosphere.

The **tourist office** is in the main gateway on the main road (June–Sept Mon–Sat 9am–noon & 2–7pm, Sun 10am–noon; rest of year Mon–Sat 9am–noon & 2–6pm; ☎04.66.32.02.14, fax 04.66.32.33.50). **Accommodation** comes in the form of the pleasant *Hôtel de la Gare et des Rochers* (☎04.66.32.10.58, fax 04.66.32.30.63; ②; good restau-

---

WOLVES AND THE BÉTE DU GÉVAUDAN

In Marvejols, at the junction of the bridge across the Colagne and the N9, there stands a hideous, flattened-out bronze statue of a semi-wolf, which represents the terrible legendary **Bête du Gévaudan**, supposedly the culprit of a series of horrific attacks in the eighteenth century. Between 1764 and 1767, the whole area between here and Le Puy was terrorized, and 25 women, 68 children and 6 men were slain. The king sent his dragoons, then his best huntsman, who eventually found and killed an enormous wolf, but the mysterious deaths continued until one Jean Chastel shot another wolf near Saugues.

It has never been established if a wolf was really guilty of these deaths – a wolf that attacked women and children almost exclusively, that moved about so rapidly, that never touched a sheep. Was it perhaps a human psychopath?

If you would like reassurance about the temperament of real wolves, visit the **Parc Zoologique du Gévaudan** in the hamlet of Ste-Lucie just off the N9, 9km north of Marvejols, where more than a hundred wolves live in semi-liberty (guided visits every one and a half hours: Feb–Dec daily 10am–5.30pm; 34F/€5.18), the first to do so in France since the beginning of the last century.

rant from 75F/€11.43), opposite the **gare SNCF**, which is 800m uphill to the right off the N9 in the direction of Chirac. There's also a municipal **campsite** beside a tributary stream on the other side of the River Colagne from the town.

Rodez and the upper valley of the Lot

A particularly beautiful and out-of-the-way stretch of country lies on the southwestern periphery of the Massif Central, bordered roughly by the valley of the **River Lot** in the north and the **Viaur** in the south. The upland areas are open and wide, with views east to the mountains of the Cévennes and south to the Monts de Lacaune and the Monts de l'Espinouse. **Rodez**, capital of the Rouergue, with a fine cathedral, is the only place of any size, accessible on the main train and bus routes. But the most dramatic places are in the river valleys, in particular the great abbey of **Conques** and the small towns of **Entraygues** and **Estaing**.

Rodez

Until the 1960s, **RODEZ** and the Rouergue were synonymous with back-country poverty and underdevelopment. Today it is an active and prosperous provincial town with a charming, renovated centre, even though the approach, through spreading commercial districts, is uninspiring.

Built on high ground above the River Aveyron, the **old town**, dominated by the massive red-sandstone **Cathédrale Notre-Dame**, is visible for kilometres around. No matter from what direction you approach, you will find yourself in the **place d'Armes**, where the cathedral's plain, fortress-like west front and the seventeenth-century bishop's palace sit side by side – both buildings were incorporated into the town's defences. The Gothic cathedral, its plain facade relieved only by an elaborately flowery rose window, was begun in 1277 and took three hundred years to complete. Towering over the square is the cathedral's 87-metre **belfry**, decorated with pinnacles, balustrades and statuary almost as fantastical as that of Strasbourg cathedral. The impressively spacious interior, architecturally as plain as the facade, is adorned with a magnificently extravagant seventeenth-century walnut organ loft and choir stalls that were crafted by André Sulpice in 1468.

Leaving by the splendid south porch, you find yourself in the tiny place Rozier in front of the fifteenth-century **Maison Cannoniale**, whose courtyard is guarded by jutting turrets. From the back of the cathedral to the north and the south, a network of well-restored medieval streets connects place de-Gaulle, place de la Préfecture and the attractive place du Bourg, with its fine sixteenth-century houses. In place Foch, just south of the cathedral, the Baroque chapel of the old **lycée** is worth a look for its amazing painted ceiling, while in place Raynaldy, the new **Hôtel de Ville** and the **médiathèque** are interesting examples of attempts to graft modern styles onto old buildings.

Practicalities

The **tourist office** is situated on place Foch, just off boulevard Gambetta and the place d'Armes, near the cathedral (July & Aug Mon–Sat 9am–1pm & 2–7pm, Sun 10am–noon; rest of year Mon–Fri 9am–noon & 2–6pm, Sat 10am–12.30pm & 3–5pm; ☎05.65.68.02.27, *officetourismerodez@wanadoo.fr*). The **gare routière** is on avenue V.-Hugo (☎05.65.68. 11.13), and the **gare SNCF** on boulevard Joffre, on the northern edge of town.

For reasonable, if somewhat charmless, hotel **accommodation**, try the *Hôtel Victor-Hugo* at 19 av V.-Hugo (☎05.65.68.14.59; ①), or the better *Hôtel du Clocher* to the left, off the east end of the cathedral at 4 rue Séguy (☎05.65.68.10.16, fax 05.65.68.64.27; ②),

More upmarket is *La Tour Maje*, in boulevard Gally, behind the tourist office (☎05.65.68.34.68, fax 05.65.68.27.56, *www.hotel.tour.maje.fr*, ④), a modern building tacked onto a medieval tower. Budget accommodation is available at the *Foyer Ste-Thérèse*, 21 rue Bonald, parallel to rue Séguy (☎05.65.77.14.00, fax 05.65.77.14.10), and at the **HI hostel** in **ONET-LE-CHÂTEAU**, 3km to the north, at 26 bd des Capucines, Quatre-Saisons (☎05.65.77.51.05, fax 05.65.67.37.97), with a good canteen serving local specialities for around 50F/€26.22, which you can reach by taking bus #1 or #3, direction "Quatre Saisons", stop "Marché d'Oc/Les Rosiers/Capucine". Rodez' municipal **campsite** (☎05.65.67.09.52; closed Oct–May) is on the river bank in the quartier Layoule, about 1km from the centre.

As for **eating**, one of the best places to sample local cuisine is *La Taverne*, 23 rue de l'Embergue (closed Sun; menus from 70F/€10.67), with an attractive terrace at the back, while the place to go for more gourmet food is the classy *Goûts et Couleurs*, 38 rue Bonald (closed Sun & Mon), where menus range from 99F/€15.10 to 360F/€54.88. *Le Bistroquet*, 17 rue du Bal, off place d'Olmet (closed Sun & Mon), does good salads and grills for around 80F/€12.20. For a **drink**, head for the *Café de la Paix*, on place Jean-Jaurès, or *au Bureau*, in the Tour Maje.

Sauveterre-de-Rouergue and the gorges of the Viaur

Forty kilometres southwest of Rodez and 6.5km northwest of Naucelle, **SAUVET-ERRE-DE-ROUERGUE** makes the most rewarding side trip in this part of the Rouergue. It is a perfect, otherworldly *bastide*, founded in 1281, with a large, wide central square, part cobbled, part gravelled, and surrounded by stone and half-timbered houses built over arcaded ground floors. Narrow streets lead off to the outer road, lined with stone-built houses the colour of rusty iron. On summer evenings, pétanque players come out to roll their bowls beneath chestnut and plane trees, while swallows and swifts swoop and dive overhead.

In summer, a **bus** runs once a weekday here in the late afternoon from Rodez. The **tourist office** is in the main square (June–Sept Mon 2.30–6pm, Tues–Fri 10am–12.30pm & 2.30–6pm, Sat 10am–12.30pm; ☎05.65.72.02.52). There are several agreeable **hotels**, including the cheap and charming *Hôtel La Grappe d'Or*, on the outer road (☎05.65.72.00.62; ②), whose restaurant (closed Oct–April) offers an excellent menu at 85F/€12.90, with dishes like *gésiers chauds*, *tripoux*, cheese, ice cream and *fouace* (a kind of sweet cake). More upmarket is the *Sénéchal*, at the entrance to the village (☎05.65.71.29.00, fax 05.65.71.29.09, *www.senechal.net*; ⑦; closed Jan & Feb), with an indoor pool and an excellent restaurant (closed Mon plus Tues lunch; from 150F/€22.87). There's also a **campsite**, just off the D997 (☎05.65.47.05.32).

The country round about, known as the **Ségala**, is high (around 500m) and wide, cut by sudden and deep river valleys full of lush greenery. The most spectacular of these is the valley of the **River Viaur** to the south and west of Sauveterre. A car is essential. If you are heading west towards Najac (see p.672), there is a marvellous back-country route through La Salvetat, crossing the Viaur at Bellecombe and again at Moulin-de-Bar, where there is a riverside **campsite**, *Le Gomvassou*. The wartime Resistance was very active hereabouts and there are numerous memorials to the Resistance fighters who lost their lives in the aftermath of the D-day landings. There is a particularly interesting one beside the tiny church in **JOUQUEVIEL**, further downstream, dedicated to a unit of Polish volunteers and 161 escaped Soviet POWs.

Conques

CONQUES, 37km north of Rodez, is one of the great villages of southwest France. It occupies a spectacular position on the flanks of the steep, densely wooded gorge of the little **River Dourdou**, a tributary of the Lot. The only public transport to the village is a daily service to Rodez, leaving there in the afternoon and returning the following morning; in July and August, there are also bus connections two or three times a week with Villefranche-de-Rouergue and Entraygues/Espalion, as well as Rodez, allowing you to visit Conques and return the same day.

It is the abbey which brought the village into existence. Its origins go back to a hermit called Dadon who settled here around 800 AD and founded a community of Benedictine monks, one of whom pilfered the relics of the martyred girl, Ste Foy, from the monastery at Agen. Known for her ability to cure blindness and liberate captives, Ste Foy's presence brought the pilgrims flocking to Conques in ever-increasing numbers, which earned the abbey a prime place on the pilgrimage route to Compostela.

The abbey church

At the village's centre, dominating the landscape, stands the renowned Romanesque **church of Ste-Foy**, whose giant pointed towers are echoed in those of the medieval houses that cluster tightly about it. Begun in the eleventh century, its plain fortress-like facade rises on a small cobbled square beside the tourist office (see below) and pilgrims' fountain, the slightly shiny silvery-grey schist prettily offset by the greenery and flowers of the terraced gardens.

In startling contrast to this plainness, the elaborately sculpted *Last Judgement* in the tympanum above the door admonishes all who see it to espouse virtue and eschew vice. Christ sits in judgement in the centre. On his right hand are the chosen, among them Dadon the hermit and the emperor Charlemagne, while his left hand directs the damned to Hell, as usual so much more graphically and interestingly portrayed with all its gory tortures than the boring bliss of Paradise, depicted in the bottom left panel.

The inside of the church was designed to accommodate the large numbers of pilgrims and channel them down the aisles and round the ambulatory. From here they could contemplate Ste Foy's relics displayed in the choir, encircled by a lovely wrought-iron screen, still in place. There is some fine carving on the capitals, especially in the triforium arches, too high up to see from the nave: you need to climb to the organ loft, which gives you a superb perspective on the whole interior. This is also a good place to admire the windows, designed by the Abstract artist Pierre Soulages, which consist of plain plates of glass that subtly change colour with the light outside.

The unrivalled asset of this church is the survival of its medieval treasure of extraordinarily rich, bejewelled **reliquaries**, including a statue of Ste Foy, bits of which are as old as the fifth century, and one known as the *A of Charlemagne*, because it is thought to have been the first in a series given as presents by the emperor to monasteries he founded. Writing in 1010, a cleric named Bernard d'Angers gave an idea of the effect of these wonders on the medieval pilgrim: "The crowd of people prostrating themselves on the ground was so dense it was impossible to kneel down . . . . When they saw it for the first time [Ste Foy], all in gold and sparkling with precious stones and looking like a human face, the majority of the peasants thought that the statue was really looking at them and answering their prayers with her eyes." The statue is kept in a room adjoining the now ruined cloister (daily 9am–1pm & 2–6pm; 31F/€4.73); the second part of the Conques museum, displayed on three floors of the house containing the tourist office, consists of a miscellany of tapestries, furnishings and architectural relics.

The village

The **village** of Conques is very small, largely depopulated and mainly contained within the medieval **walls**, parts of which still survive, along with three of its **gates**. The houses date mainly from the late Middle Ages. The whole ensemble of cobbled lanes and stairways is a pleasure to stroll through. There are two main streets, the old **rue**

Haute, or "upper street", which was the route for the pilgrims coming from Estaing and Le Puy and passing onto Figeac and Cahors through the **Porte de la Vinzelle**; and the lane, now **rue Charlemagne**, which leads steeply downhill through the **Porte de Barry** to the river and the ancient **Pont Romain**, with the little **chapel of St-Roch** off to the left, whence you get a fine view of the village and church. Better still: climb the road on the far side of the valley. The rather grandiose-sounding **European centre for medieval art and civilization**, hidden in a bunker right at the top of the hill (9am–noon & 2–6pm), sometimes has exhibitions and displays. Throughout August, the village hosts a prestigious **classical music festival**, most of the concerts taking place at the abbey church; contact the tourist office for more information.

Walkers can use sections of the **GR65** and **GR62**, both of which pass through the village; the tourist office will provide information about shorter local walks.

Practicalities

The **tourist office** is on the square beside the church (July & Aug daily 9am–7pm; rest of year Mon–Sat 9am–noon & 2–6pm; ☎05.65.72.85.00, fax 05.65.72.87.03). For somewhere central to **stay**, the *Auberge St-Jacques* (☎05.65.72.86.36, fax 05.65.72.82.47; ②), near the church, provides good-value, old-fashioned accommodation and also has a popular restaurant, with menus from 75F/€11.43 and *plats du jour* at 50–70F/€7.62–10.67. A good alternative is the *Auberge du Pont Romain*, on the main road below the hill on which Conques stands (☎05.65.69.84.07, fax 05.65.69.85.12; ②; closed first two weeks Nov; menus from 80F/€12.20) – it's a twenty-minute walk from here to the church. A little way upstream, the attractive *Moulin de Cambelong* (☎05.65.72.84.77, fax 05.65.72.83.91, *www.chateauxhotels.com/cambelong*; ④) offers more comfort – some rooms have spacious wooden balconies with great views of the river – and a first-rate restaurant, specializing in duck dishes (menus from 195F/€29.73).

There is **hostel**-type accommodation at the *Résidence Dadon* (☎05.65.72.82.98; ①) directly above the abbey, and a *gîte d'étape* next door (Mme Guibert; ☎05.65.72.82.98). There are several **campsites** in Conques: try *Beau Rivage*, on the banks of the Dourdou, just below the village (☎05.65.69.82.23; closed Oct–March), *St-Cyprien-sur-Dourdou* (☎05.65.72.80.52) or *Le Moulin*, at Grand-Vabre (☎05.65.72.87.28; closed Nov–March), 5km downstream.

The upper valley: Grand-Vabre to Entraygues and Espalion

The most beautiful stretch of the **Lot valley** is the 21.5km between the bridge of Coursavy, below **Grand-Vabre**, and **Entraygues**: deep, narrow and wild, with the river running full and strong, as yet unaffected by the dams higher up, with scattered farms and houses high on the hillsides among long-abandoned terracing.

There are two hotels 6.5km east in **VIEILLEVIE**, where canoe rental is also available: the *Hôtel de la Terrasse* (☎04.71.49.94.00, fax 04.71.49.99.81; ②; restaurant from 55F/€8.38) and the simpler *Le Canton au Relais des Pêcheurs* (☎04.71.49.98.82; ③; restaurant from 65F/€9.91). A further possibility is the delightful *Auberge du Fel*, some 10km further on, high on the north slopes of the valley in the hamlet of **LE FEL** (☎05.65.44.52.30, fax 05.65.48.64.96; ②; closed mid-Nov to March; excellent restaurant with menus from 70F/€10.67), which by an unexpected quirk of climate produces a little local wine. There is also a beautifully sited municipal **campsite** high on the hillside (☎05.65.44.51.86; closed Oct–May).

Entraygues and around

ENTRAYGUES, with its narrow riverside streets and attractive grey houses, has the feel of a sleepy mountain town. It lies right in the angle of the junction of the Lot with the equally beautiful River Truyère. The brown towers of a thirteenth-century **château** overlook the meeting of the waters. A magnificent four-arched **bridge** of the same date crosses the Truyère a little way upstream.

The **tourist office** is on the main street (June–Sept Mon 9am–12.30pm, Tues–Sat 9am–12.30pm & 2–6pm; rest of year Mon 1.30–5.30pm, Tues–Fri 9.30am–12.30pm & 1.30–5.30pm, Sat 9.30am–12.30pm; ☎05.65.44.56.10) and will provide information about walking, mountain biking and canoeing in the area. Reasonable **places to stay** include the *Hôtel du Centre*, on the main street (☎05.65.44.51.19, fax 05.65.48.63.09; ②; restaurant from 70F/€10.67), and the *Lion d'Or*, on the corner of the main street and the bank of the Lot (☎05.65.44.50.01, fax 05.65.44.55.43; ③), with an outdoor swimming pool and garden and attached restaurant (95F/€14.25). There is also a **campsite**, *Le Val-de-Saures* (☎05.65.44,56.92; closed Oct–April), and two **gîtes d'étape** – Mme Galan (☎05.65.44.50.73) and *Le Battedou* (☎05.65.48.61.62) – on the GR65 at **GOLINHAC**, about 7km south of Entraygues on the other side of the Lot. There is one **bus** per weekday to Aurillac in the north and Rodez to the south.

There are further accommodation options at **ESTAING**, another beautiful village huddled round a rocky bluff and castle in a bend of the Lot about 10km beyond Golinhac. The *Hôtel aux Armes d'Estaing*, named for the family who occupied the castle for five hundred years, offers attractive rooms and very good food in the centre of the village (☎05.65.44.70.02, fax 05.65.44.74.65, *perso.wanadoo.fr/remi.catusse/home*; ②; closed mid-Nov to Feb; restaurant from 68F/€10.40). There is also a municipal **campsite** (☎05.65.44.72.77; closed Oct–April) and **gîte d'étape** on the GR65 (☎05.65.44.71.74). A date to watch out for, however, is the first Sunday in July when the place fills up with people, many in medieval dress, who come to honour the relics of **St Fleuret**, bishop of Clermont, who died here in 621 AD and is buried in the fifteenth-century church by the castle.

Espalion

The substantial little town of **ESPALION** lies in a mild, fertile opening in the valley of the Lot, 10km from Estaing and 32km northeast of Rodez. It was the "first smile of the south" to the muleteers, pilgrims and other travellers coming down from the rude heights of the Massif Central and places north. Home town of the composer Francis Poulenc, as well as Benoît Rouquayrol and Auguste Denayrouze, inventors of diving suits, Espalion is best known in France for its exiles, in particular its countless sons and daughters who set up in the café business in Paris from the 1850s onwards.

The only interesting part of town is the **riverside quarter**, with its galleried and balconied old houses, once used as tanneries, hanging over the water. The finest view of the area is from the Pont Neuf, where the main road to Rodez crosses the Lot, for just upstream there is a lovely red sandstone packhorse **bridge** with a domed and turreted **château** dating from 1572 right behind it.

Surprisingly, there is an interesting museum dedicated principally to the life of the region: **Musée Joseph Vaylet**, in an old medieval church, on the main road, boulevard Poulenc (daily July–Sept 10am–noon & 2–7pm; rest of the year Tues, Sat & Sun 2–6pm; 15F/€2.29), which contains mainly furniture and domestic objects, plus an exhibition of diving gear (thanks to the two Espalionnais mentioned above).

Don't miss the glorious little Romanesque **church of St-Hilarion de Perse**, built on the spot, so the story goes, where, in the reign of Charlemagne, the Saracens lopped off the head of St Hilarion. It sits on the edge of the cemetery, about fifteen minutes' walk to the left of the bridge on the château side of the river, past the campsite. Built in red sandstone, with a wall belfry and wide porch with sculpted tympanum and dozens of figures adorning the corbel ends of the apse, it's a delight.

Also well worth a visit is the **Château de Calmont d'Olt** (May, June & Sept Wed–Fri, Sat & Sun 10am–noon & 2–6pm; July & Aug daily 9am–7pm; 30F/€4.57), for its unbeatable views of the town and the country beyond. It's a rough and atmospheric old fortress dating from the eleventh century, on the very peak of an abrupt bluff, 535m high and directly above the town on the south bank. There are reconstructions of medieval siege works and a catapult in the grounds.

The **tourist office** is just across the Pont Vieux in rue St-Antoine (Mon–Sat 9am–noon & 2–6pm; ☎05.65.44.10.63). For **accommodation**, there's no better place to stay than the *Hôtel Moderne* on the crossroads in the middle of town at 27 bd de Guizard (☎05.65.44.05.11, fax 05.65.48.06.94; ③; closed mid-Nov to mid-Dec). The rooms are comfortable, but, more importantly, its restaurant is first-rate, especially for its river fish (menus from 105F/€16.01).

Espalion has a second superb **restaurant** in the *Méjane*, by the old bridge (☎05.65.48.22.37; closed Sun evening & Mon, plus Feb, March & July; from 98F/€24.04), specializing in regional cuisine with a post-*nouvelle* influence, while for uncomplicated **eating**, there are several brasseries on the main through-street. There is a riverside **campsite**, Roc de l'Arche, behind the château (☎05.65.44.06.79; closed Sept to mid-April), but it's unnecessarily fancy and expensive and gets very crowded in season; better, if you have the time and the means, to go to the prettier, simpler and cheaper riverside *Belle Rive* (☎05.65.44.05.85; closed Oct–May) in the attractive village of **ST-CÔME D'OLT**, another 4km upstream, where there is also a **gîte d'étape** in a beautiful old house (☎05.65.44.07.24; closed Nov–Feb) lying on the GR65, GR6 and GR620.

Millau, Roquefort and the Gorges du Tarn

MILLAU, subprefecture of the Aveyron *département* and second town after Rodez in the old province of Rouergue, occupies a beautiful site in a bend of the River Tarn at its junction with the Dourbie. It is enclosed on all sides by impressive white cliffs, formed where the rivers have worn away the edges of the *causses*, especially on the north side, where the spectacular table-top hill of the **Puech d'Andan** stands sentinel over the town. From medieval until modern times, thanks to its proximity to the sheep pastures of the *causses*, the town was a major manufacturer of leather goods, especially gloves. Although outclassed by cheaper producers in the mass market and suffering serious unemployment as a result, Millau still leads in top-of-the-range goods. The town recently hit the headlines when one of its residents, 47-year-old **José Bové**, leader of the farm-workers' union, was put on trial and given a three-month sentence for his involvement in trashing a McDonald's restaurant that was being built in Millau in 1999. He was protesting against globalization and against *la mal bouffe* – junk food. Around 40,000 supporters turned out at his trial and he is regarded as a hero by many French farmers.

Arrival, information and accommodation

From the **bus and train stations** it's about a ten-minute walk down rue Alfred Merle to the main square, place du Mandarous. The **tourist office** is on place du Beffroi in the centre of the old town (July & Aug Mon–Sat 9am–7pm, Sun 10am–12.30pm & 1–6.30pm; rest of year Mon–Sat 9am–12.30pm & 2–6.30pm; ☎05.65.60.02.42, fax 05.65.60.95.08, *touristoffice@millau-clic.com*). **Bikes and outdoor equipment** can be rented from Roc et Canyon, 55 av Jean-Jaurès.

For an overnight **stay**, try the good-value *Hôtel Le Commerce*, 8 place du Mandarous (☎05.65.60.00.56, fax 05.65.60.96.50; ①), with clean, well-furnished rooms; it's best to take a room at the back, though, to avoid any noise from the square. A bit more expensive, but with more character, is *Les Causses*, in an attractive building on the N9 at 56 av Jean-Jaurès (☎05.65.60.03.19, fax 05.65.60,86.90; ③), which has a reasonable restaurant (from 65F/€9.91). Slightly further out of town, by the river at 115 rue du Rajol, the clean, traditional *Cévenol Hôtel* (☎05.65.60.74.44, fax 05.65.60.85.99, *www.cevenol.hotel.fr*; ④; restaurant from 75F/€11.25) offers a range of rooms, some with views of the *causses*. There's a good **hostel** about 1km down av Jean-Jaurès at 26 rue Lucien-Costes (☎05.65.61.27.74), and scattered round about are several **campsites**: one of the best is *Cureplat* (☎05.65.60.15.75; closed Oct–March) at 121 av de Millau Plage, on the left bank of the Tarn, north of the confluence with the Dourbie – take the bridge at the end of av Gambetta.

The Town

There are no remarkable sights in Millau; it is simply a very pleasant, lively provincial town whose clean and well-preserved old streets have a summery, southern charm. It owes its original prosperity to its position on the ford where the Roman road from Languedoc to the north crossed the Tarn, marked today by the truncated remains of a medieval **bridge** surmounted by a watermill jutting out into the river beside the modern bridge.

Whether you arrive from north or south, you will find yourself sooner or later in **place du Mandarous**, the main square, where avenue de la République, the road to Rodez, begins. South of here, the **old town** is built a little way back from the river to avoid the floods and contained within an almost circular ring of shady boulevards. The rue Droite cuts through the centre, linking the three squares: place Emma-Calvé, place des Halles and place Foch. The prettiest by far is **place Foch**, with its cafés, shaded by two big plane trees and bordered by houses supported on stone pillars; some are as old as the twelfth century. In one corner, the **church of Notre-Dame** is worth a look for its octagonal Toulouse-style belfry, originally Romanesque. In the other, there's the very interesting **Musée de Millau** (April–Sept daily 10am–noon & 2–6pm; rest of year closed Sun; 26.50F/€3.97), housed in a stately eighteenth-century mansion. Its collections revolve around the bizarre combination of archeology and gloves, and include the magnificent red pottery of the Graufesenque works (see below), as well as a complete 180-million-year-old plesiosaurus. Millau's other two squares have been the subject of some rather questionable attempts at reconciling old stones and Richard Rogers-inspired contemporary urban design. Off one of these squares, place Emma-Calvé, the **clock tower** (June & Sept Mon–Sat 10–11.30am & 3–5.30pm; July & Aug daily 10am–noon & 3.30–6pm; 15F/€2.29) is worth a climb for the great all-round view. Take a look also in the streets off the square – rue du Voultre, rue de la Peyrollerie and their tributaries – for a sense of the old working-class and bourgeois districts.

Clear evidence of the town's importance in Roman times is to be seen in the **Graufesenque pottery works**, just upstream on the south bank (daily 9am–noon & 2–6.30pm; 25F/€3.81), whose renowned red terracotta ware (*terra sigillata*) was distributed throughout the Roman world. It was a huge production line in its day, involving four hundred potters and a hundred kilns; today, there is an archeology museum with a permanent exhibition of the bowls, vases and cups that were produced.

Eating and drinking

If you are just looking for a quick **meal**, you'll find numerous brasseries and cafés on place du Mandarous. For something more traditional, try the *Auberge Occitane*, at 15 rue Peyrollerie (menus from 70F/€10.67), which serves excellent *aligot* and other local specialities, or the more upmarket *La Braconne*, on place Foch (☎05.65.60.30.93; closed Sun evening & Mon; from 98F/€14.94), offering high-calory fare such as stuffed goose and pork with juniper berries. Alternatively, head for boulevard de la Capelle on the northeast side of the old town, where two good establishments spread their tables under the trees: *La Mangeoire*, at no. 8 (from 78F/€11.70), which serves grilled fish, meat and game dishes; and next door, *La Marmite du Pêcheur*, featuring menus from 69F/€10.35, including the local potato and cheese dish, *aligot*. A popular place for a **drink** is *La Locomotive*, at 33 av Gambetta (till 2am), which has live music evenings in summer.

Roquefort-sur-Soulzon

Twenty-one kilometres south of Millau, the little village of **ROQUEFORT-SUR-SOULZON** has nothing to say for itself except cheese, and almost every building is devoted to the cheese-making process.

What gives the cheese its special flavour is the fungus, *penicillium roqueforti*, that grows exclusively in the fissures in the rocks created by the collapse of the sides of the valley on which Roquefort now stands. Legend has it that once upon a time a local shepherd one day forgot his lunch of bread and cheese, and found it some months later, covered with mould. He bit tentatively and discovered to his surprise that instead of ruining the cheese, the mould had much improved its taste.

While the sheep's milk used in the making of the cheese comes from different flocks and dairies as far afield as the Pyrenees, the crucial fungus is grown here, on bread. Just 2g of powdered fungus are enough for 4000 litres of milk, which in turn makes 330 Roquefort cheeses; they are matured in Roquefort's many-layered cellars, first unwrapped for three weeks and then wrapped up again. It takes three to six months for the full flavour to develop.

Two of the cheese manufacturers have organized **visits**: Société (daily: July & Aug 9.30am–6.30pm; rest of year 9.30–11.30am & 1.30–5pm; 15F/€2.29) and Papillon (April–June & Sept daily 9.30–11.30am & 1.30–5.30pm; July & Aug daily 9.30am–6.30pm, rest of year Mon–Fri 9–11.30am & 1.30–5pm; free). Each visit consists of a short film, followed by a tour of the cellars and tasting – not, in fact, very interesting.

The Gorges du Tarn

Jam-packed with tourists in July and August, but absolutely spectacular nonetheless, the **Gorges du Tarn** cut through the limestone plateaux of the Causse de Sauveterre and the Causse Méjean in a precipitous trench 400–500m deep and 1000–1500m wide. Its sides, cloaked with woods of feathery pine and spiked with pinnacles of eroded rock, are often sheer and always very steep, creating within them a microclimate in sharp distinction to the inhospitable plateaux above. The permanent population is tiny, though there is plenty of evidence of more populous times in abandoned houses and once-cultivated terraces. Because of the press of people and the subsequent overpricing of **accommodation**, the best bet, if you want to stay along the gorge, is to head up onto the Causse Méjean, where there are several small family-run hotels and *chambres d'hôte*, among which is the attractively sited *Auberge de la Cascade* in St-Chély-du-Tarn (☎04.66.48.52.82, fax 04.66.48.52.45; ②; closed mid-Oct to mid-March; restaurant from 75F/€11.43).

The most attractive section of the gorge runs for 53km from the pretty village of **LE ROZIER**, 21km northeast of Millau, to **ISPAGNAC**. If you want to **stay** in Le Rozier, try the *Hôtel Arnal* (☎05.65.62.66.00; ②; closed Oct–Easter) or *Hôtel Doussière* (☎05.65.62.60.25; ②; closed mid-Nov to Easter), or there's a municipal **campsite** (☎05.65.62.63.98, fax 05.65.62.60.83; closed Oct–April).

A narrow and very twisty road follows the right bank of the river from Le Rozier, but it's not the best way to see the scenery. For the car-borne, the best views are from the road to St-Rome-de-Dolan above Les Vignes, and from the roads out of La Malène and the attractive **STE-ÉNIMIE**, where you'll find a well-informed **tourist office** (July & Aug daily 10am–12.30pm & 2.30–7pm; rest of year Mon–Sat 9.30am–noon & 1.30–4.30pm; ☎04.66.48.53.44). La Malène has a municipal **campsite** (☎04.66.48.58.55; closed mid-Oct to March) and the nearby *La Blanquière* site

(☎04.66.48.54.93; closed mid-Sept to April), which is beautifully sited on the main road towards Les Vignes.

But it's best to walk if possible, or follow the river's course by boat or canoe – there are dozens of places to rent canoes. For walkers, the **GR6a**, a variant of the GR6 which crosses the *causses*, climbs steeply out of Le Rozier between the junction of the Tarn with the equally spectacular gorges of the River Jonte onto the Causse Méjean, then follows the rim of the Tarn gorge for a while before descending to rejoin the GR6 at Les Vignes (4–5hr).

Also eminently worth seeing are two beautiful **caves** about 25km up the Jonte from Le Rozier: the **Aven Armand** (daily: mid-March to June & Sept–Nov 9.30am–noon & 1.30–5/6pm; July & Aug 9.30am–7pm; 45F/€6.87), on the edge of the Causse Méjean, and the **Grotte de Dargilan** (daily March–June & Sept 9am–noon & 1.30–6pm; July & Aug 9am–7pm; Oct 10am–noon & 1.30–5pm; 39F/€5.95), on the south side of the river on the edge of the Causse Noir. **HYELZAS**, near the Aven Armand cave, has a *gîte d'é-tape* (M. Pratlong; ☎04.66.45.66.56).

THE CÉVENNES AND ARDÈCHE

The **Cévennes** mountains and River **Ardèche** form the southeastern defences of the Massif Central, overlooking the Rhône valley to the east and the Mediterranean littoral to the south. The bare upland landscapes of the inner or western edges are those of the central Massif. The outer edges, Mont Aigoual and its radiating valleys and the tributary valleys of the Ardèche, are distinctly Mediterranean: deep, dry, close and clothed in forests of sweet chestnut, oak and pine.

Remote and inaccessible country until well into the twentieth century, the region has bred rugged and independent inhabitants. For centuries it was the most resolute stronghold of Protestantism in France, and it was in these valleys that the persecuted Protestants put up their fiercest resistance to the tyranny of Louis XIV and Louis XV. In World War II, it was heavily committed to the Resistance, while in the aftermath of 1968, it became the promised land of the hippies – *zippies*, as the locals called them; they moved into the countless abandoned farms and hamlets, whose native inhabitants had been driven away by hardship and poverty. The odd hippy has stuck it out, true to the last to the alternative life. In more recent times, it has been colonized by Dutch and Germans.

The author Robert Louis Stevenson crossed it in 1878 with Modestine, a donkey he bought in miserable Le Monastier-sur-Gazeille near the astounding town of **Le Puy** and sold at journey's end in the former Protestant stronghold of **St-Jean-du-Gard**, a now-famous route described in *Travels with a Donkey* (see p.1135).

The Parc National des Cévennes

The **Parc National des Cévennes** was created in 1970 to protect and preserve the life, landscape, flora, fauna and architectural heritage of the Cévennes. North to south, it stretches from **Mende** on the Lot to **Le Vigan** and includes both **Mont Lozère** and **Mont Aigoual**. Access, to the periphery at least, is surprisingly easy, thanks to the Paris–Clermont–Alès–Nîmes train line and the Montpellier–Mende link.

Numerous walking routes crisscross the area: **GRs 7**, **6** and **60** cross all or part of the range, and other paths complete various circuits. The **GR66** does the tour of Mont Aigoual in 78.5km, the **GR68** of Mont Lozère in 110km. Another good route is the 130-kilometre **Tour des Cévennes** on the GR67. If you do go off hiking, remember that these are proper mountains for all their southerly latitude. You need good hiking boots, warm and weatherproof clothing, emergency shelter, adequate food, maps and guide-books. The current weather situation is obtainable on: ☎07.08.36.68.02 (Ardèche); ☎08.36.68.02.30 (Gard); ☎08.36.68.02.48 (Lozère).

The **main information office** for the park is at Florac (see opposite). It publishes numerous leaflets on the flora, fauna and traditions of the park, plus activities and routes for walkers, cyclists, caneoists and horse riders. It also provides a list of **gîtes d'étape** in the park and can provide information for those following Stevenson's route, including where to hire a donkey. In July and August, it is wise to book ahead for accommodation; otherwise you could find yourself sleeping out.

Mende and Mont Lozère

Capital of the Lozère *département*, **MENDE** lies well down in the deep valley of the Lot at the northern tip of the Parc des Cévennes, 28km east of Marvejols and 40km north of Florac, with train and bus links to the Paris–Nîmes and Clermont–Millau lines. It's a very attractive, unspoilt southern town, well worth a visit and a nice place to make an overnight stay.

Standing against the haze of the mountain background, the town's main landmark, the **Cathedral**, owes its construction to Pope Urban V, who was born locally and wished to give something back to his native soil. Although work began in 1369, progress was ham-pered by war and natural disasters and the building wasn't completed until the end of the nineteenth century. The most obvious signs of its patchy construction are the two unequal towers that frame the front entrance, from where there's a fine view back along the pine-clad Lot valley. Inside is a handsome choir, and, suspended from the clerestory, eight great Aubusson tapestries, depicting the life of the Virgin. She's also present in one of the side chapels of the choir in the form of a statue made from olive wood, thought to have been brought back from the Middle East during the crusades.

Aside from the cathedral, most pleasure resides in a quiet wander in the town's minuscule squares and narrow medieval streets, with their houses bulging outwards, as though buckling under the weight of the upper stories. In **rue Notre-Dame**, which separated the Christian from Jewish quarters in medieval times, the thirteenth-century house at no. 17 was once a synagogue. If you carry on down to the river, you'll see the medieval packhorse bridge, the **Pont Notre-Dame**, with its worn cobbles.

The **tourist office** is at 14 bd Henri-Bourrillon, to the right as you reach the centre of town from the N88 (July & Aug Mon–Sat 8.30am–12.30pm & 2–8pm, Sun 2.30–6.30pm; rest of year Mon–Fri 8.30am–12.30pm & 2–6pm, Sat 8.30am–12.30pm; ☎04.66.65.02.69, fax 04.66.65.02.69). The departmental tourist office is in the same building, with all the information you could want on the Lozère. The **gare SNCF** (☎04.66.49.00.39) lies across the river, north of the centre. **Buses** depart from either the station or place du Foirail, at the southern end of boulevard Henri-Bourrillon.

For a place to **stay**, try the recently refurbished *Hôtel Drakkar*, right in front of the cathedral on place Urbain-V (☎04.66.49.04.04, fax 04.66.65.24.43; ③; restaurant 60F/€9), or for more comfort the pretty *Hôtel de France* on boulevard Lucien-Arnault, the northern part of the inner ring road (☎04.66.65.00.04, fax 04.66.49.30.47; ③; closed Dec & Jan; restaurant from 105F/€16.01). Slightly further out of town, on the river at 2 av du 11 Novembre, the classy *Hôtel Pont-Roupt* (☎04.66.65.01.43, fax 04.66.65.22.96, *hotel-pont-roupt@wanadoo.fr*, ③) offers such luxuries as an indoor pool, terrace and good restaurant: dishes include *truite au lard* and *salade au Roquefort* (from 120F/€18.29). Apart from the hotel **restaurants**, the best food is served up at *Le Mazel* (closed Mon evening & Tues; from 79F/€11.85), though the setting – in the only mod-ern square in the old town – is a little disappointing. More atmospheric are *La Gogaille*, 5 rue Notre-Dame, where you can eat wholesome, traditional fare outside in a medieval arched courtyard (from 80F/€12), and *Les Voutes*, 13 rue d'Aigues-Passes, in a similar setting and specializing in pizzas (menus from 55F/€8.38).

Mont Lozère

Mont Lozère is a windswept and desolate barrier of granite and yellow grassland, rising to 1699m at the summit of **Finiels**, still grazed by herds of cows, but in nothing like the numbers of bygone years when half the cattle in Languedoc came up here for their summer feed. Snowbound in winter and wild and dangerous in bad weather, it has claimed many a victim among lost travellers. In some of the squat granite hamlets on the northern slopes, like Servies, Auriac and Les Sagnes, you can still hear the bells, known as *clochers de tourmente*, that tolled in the wind to give travellers some sense of direction when the cloud was low.

If you're travelling by car from Mende, the way to the summit is via the village of **LE BLEYMARD**, about 30km to the east on the bank of the infant River Lot, with accommodation in the form of *Hôtel La Remise* (☎04.66.48.65.80, fax 04.66.48.63.70; ③; restaurant from 75F/€11.25). From here, the D20 winds 7km up through the conifers to **LE CHALET**, with its *gîte d'étape* (☎04.68.48.62.84; food available), where it is joined by the GR7, which has taken a more direct route from Le Bleymard. This is the route that Stevenson took, waymarked as the "Tracé Historique de Stevenson". Road and footpath run together as far as the **Col de Finiels**, where the GR7 strikes off on its own to the southeast. The source of the River Tarn is about 3km east of the col, the summit of Lozère 2km to the west. From the col, the road and Stevenson's route drop down in tandem, through the lonely hamlet of **FINIELS** to the pretty but touristy village of **LE PONT-DE-MONTVERT**.

At Le Pont, a seventeenth-century **bridge** crosses the Tarn by a stone **tower** that once served as a tollhouse. In this building in 1702, the Abbé du Chayla, a priest appointed by the Crown to reconvert the rebellious Protestants enraged by the revocation of the Edict of Nantes, set up a torture chamber to coerce the recalcitrant. Incensed by his brutality, a group of them under the leadership of one Esprit Séguier attacked and killed him on July 23. Reprisals were extreme; nearly 12,000 were executed, thus precipitating the Camisards' guerrilla war against the state.

At the edge of the village, there is also an *écomusée* on the life and character of the region, the **Maison du Mont Lozère** (mid-April to Sept daily 10.30am–12.30pm & 2.30–6.30pm; 20F/€3.05). If you are tempted to **stay**, there's the small *Auberge des Cévennes* (☎04.66.45.80.01; ③; closed Nov–March; restaurant from 90F/€13.72), overlooking the bridge. There's also a *gîte d'étape* in the Maison du Mont Lozère (☎04.66.45.80.10; closed Jan & Feb; reservations obligatory).

Florac and Mont Aigoual

Situated 39km south of Mende, **FLORAC** lies in the bottom of the trench-like valley of the Tarnon just short of its junction with the Tarn. Behind it rises the steep wall that marks the edge of the Causse Méjean. When you get here, you will have already passed the frontier between the northern and Mediterranean landscapes; the dividing line seems to be the **Col de Montmirat** at the western end of Mont Lozère. Once you begin the descent, the scrub and steep gullies and the tiny abandoned hamlets, with their eyeless houses oriented towards the sun, speak clearly of the south.

The village, with some 2000 inhabitants, is strung out along the left bank of the Tarnon and the main street, **avenue Jean-Monestier**. There is little specific to see, though the close lanes of the village up towards the valley side have their charms, especially the plane-shaded **place du Souvenir**. A red-schist castle stands above the village, housing the **Centre d'Information du Parc National des Cévennes** (June to mid-Sept daily 9am–7pm; rest of year Mon–Fri 9am–noon & 2–7pm; ☎04.66.49.53.01, *www.bsi.fr/pnc*). The helpful **tourist office** is on avenue Jean-Monestier (June & Sept Mon–Sat 9am–noon & 2–5pm; July & Aug daily 9am–7.30pm; rest of year Mon–Fri 9am–noon & 2–5.30pm; ☎04.66.45.01.14, *www.florac-tourisme.com*). **Mountain bike rental** is available from Cévennes Evasion, in place Boyer (☎04.66.45.18.31).

The **accommodation** on offer is not fantastic. The best and cheapest place is *Chez Bruno*, on the tree-lined Esplanade (☎04.66.45.11.19, fax 04.66.45.06.65; ①; restaurant from 55F/€8.38). Alternatively try the *Hôtel du Parc* on avenue Jean-Monestier (☎04.66.45.03.05, fax 04.66.45.11.81; ②; closed Dec to March; restaurant from 92F/€14.03), with pleasant gardens and a pool, or the *Hôtel Central de la Poste*, on avenue Maurice Tour, which has a lovely terrace over the stream, though the rooms are a bit dowdy (☎04.66.45.00.01, fax 04.66.45.14.04; ③; closed Jan to Feb; restaurant from 75F/€11.43). A better bet is the *Lozérette*, in **COCURÈS**, 5km back towards Mont Lozère, on the Pont-de-Montvert road (☎04.66.45.06.04, fax 04.66.45.12.93; ④; closed Nov–April; restaurant from 88F/€13.42).

Three **gîtes d'etape** in and around Florac are *Le Presbytère*, 18 rue du Pêcher (☎04.66.45.24.54); the *gîte détape communal*, 1 rue du Four (☎04.66.45.14.93; closed Dec); and M. Serrano in Le Pont-du-Tarn, 1km north (☎04.66.45.20.89). The best-value **campsites** are the municipal one at Le Pont-du-Tarn out on the road towards Ispagnac (☎04.66.45.18.26, *lozere.net/pontdutarn.htm*; closed mid-Oct to March), and two more on the other side of town on the Corniche de Cévennes road, beside the River Tarnon.

Florac's Esplanade is a good place to look for somewhere to **eat**, or try *Le Chapeau Rouge*, on the corner of rue Théophile Roussel and avenue Jean-Monestier, offering *cévenoles* specialities (☎04.66.45.23.40; menus from 60F/€9.15). For something a bit more upmarket, there's *La Source du Pêcher* at 1 rue de Rémuret, in the old town beside the stream (☎04.66.45.03.01; menus from 89F/€13.57).

Mont Aigoual

By road it's 24km up the beautiful valley of the Tarnon to the **Col de Perjuret**, where a right turn will take you on to the **Causse Méjean** and to the strange rock formations of **Nîmes-le-Vieux**, and a left turn along a rising ridge a further 15km to the 1565-metre summit of **Mont Aigoual** (GR6, GR7, GR66), from where, they say, you can see a third of France, from the Alps to the Pyrenees, with the Mediterranean coast from Marseille to Sète at your feet. It is not a craggy summit, although the ground drops away pretty steeply into the valley of the River Hérault on the south side, but the view and the sense of exposure to the elements is dramatic enough. At the summit there is an **observatory**, which has been in use for over a century. A small but interesting **exhibition** (May–Sept daily 10am–6pm; free) shows modern weather-forecasting techniques alongside displays of old barometers and weather vanes. The observatory also harbours a **CAF refuge** and **gîte d'étape** (☎04.67.82.62.78; closed Oct–April).

The descent to Le Vigan (see p.836) by the valley of the Hérault is superb; a magnificent twisty road follows the deepening ravine through dense beech and chestnut woods, to come out at the bottom in rather Italianate scenery, with tall, close-built villages and vineyards beside the stream. The closest accommodation to the summit is the *Hôtel du Touring et de l'Observatoire* (☎04.67.82.60.04, fax 04.67.82.65.09; ③; restaurant from 70F/€10.67) at **L'ESPÉROU**, a rather soulless mountain resort just below the summit. Better to go down to the charming village of **VALLERAUGUE**, with its brown-grey schist houses and leafy riverside setting. There are a number of hotels here, including the welcoming *Petit Luxembourg* (☎04.67.82.20.44, fax 04.67.82.24.66; ③; menus 85–238F/€12.75–35.70).

The Causse du Larzac

In the 1970s, the **Causse du Larzac** was continually in the headlines over sustained political resistance to the high-profile presence of the French military. Originally there was a small military camp outside the village of **LA CAVALERIE** on the N9, long tolerated for the cash its soldiers brought in. But in the early 1970s the army decided to expand the place and use it as a permanent strategic base, expropriating a hundred or so farms. The result was explosive. A federation was formed – Paysans du Larzac – which attracted the support of numerous ecological, left-wing and regionalist groups in a protracted campaign of resistance under the slogan "Gardarem lo Larzac". Successful acts of sabotage were committed, and three huge peace festivals were held here, in 1973, 1974 and again in 1977. The army's plans were scotched by Mitterrand when he came to power in 1981, but you still find Larzac graffiti from here to Lyon, shorthand for opposition to the army, the state and the Parisian central government, and in favour of self-determination and independence for the south.

The best way to immerse yourself in the empty, sometimes eerie atmosphere of Larzac is to walk: **GRs 7, 71** and **74** cross the plateau, though you shouldn't attempt them without a *Topoguide*. If you have no time for anything else, the area between La Couvertoirade, Le Caylar and Ganges in the foothills of the Cévennes will give you a real sense of life on the *causse*.

LA COUVERTOIRADE lies 5km off the main road, a perfect Templar village, still completely enclosed by its towers and walls and almost untouched by renovation. Its forty remaining inhabitants live by tourism, and you have to pay to walk around the **ramparts** (daily: mid-March to June & Sept to mid-Nov 10am–noon & 2–5pm; July & Aug 10am–7pm; 15F/€2.29 including video presentation). Just outside the walls on the south side is a *lavogne*, a paved water hole of a kind seen all over the *causse* for watering the flocks, whose milk is used for Roquefort cheese (see p.830). If you want to stay, there's the GR71 **gîte d'étape** (☎05.65.62.28.06) in the far corner from the entrance. Half-a-dozen kilometres south, the village of **LE CAYLAR** clusters in similar fashion at the foot of a rocky outcrop, the top of which has been fashioned into a fortress – worth clambering up for the aerial view of the surrounding *causse*, where mean little patches of cultivated ground have been stolen from among the merciless upthrusts of rock.

If you've got your own transport and a good map, the back road from here, via St-Michel to St-Maurice-Navacelles, is strongly recommended. Wild box grows along the lanes, often meticulously clipped into hedges. Here and there among the scrubby oak and thorn or driving home along the road at milking time, you pass flocks of sheep. Occasional farmhouses materialize, like *Les Besses* – one of the few still in use – huge, self-contained and fortress-like, with the living quarters upstairs and the sheep stalls down below. **ST-MAURICE** itself, on the GR7 and GR74, is small and sleepy, with a shop in summer only and the *Hôtel des Tilleuls* (☎04.67.44.61.60; ②; closed Nov–Easter; meals from 55F/€8.38) opposite a fine World War I memorial by Paul Dardé. There is no official **campsite**, but if you ask you are directed to a grassy place by the cemetery, where a traditional *glacière* – a stone-lined pit for storing snow for use as ice before the days of refrigerators – has been restored. Its chief advantage is as a base for visiting the **Cirque de Navacelles**, 10km north on the D130 past the beautiful ruined seventeenth-century sheep farm of La Prunarède. The cirque is a widening in the 150-metre deep trench of the Vis gorges, formed by a now dry loop in the river that has left a neat pyramid of rock sticking up in the middle like a wheel hub. An ancient and scarcely inhabited hamlet survives in the bottom – a bizarre phenomenon in an extraordinary location, and you get literally a bird's-eye view of it from the edge of the cliff above. Both road and GR7 go through. Continuing to Le Vigan or Ganges via Montdardier, you pass a prehistoric **stone circle** on the left of the road, a silent and evocative place, especially in a close *causse* mist. There are other stones and dolmens in the vicinity.

Le Vigan and the Huguenot strongholds

Only 64km from Montpellier and 18km from Ganges, **LE VIGAN** makes a good starting point for exploring the southern part of the Cévennes. It's a leafy, cool and thoroughly agreeable place, at its liveliest during the **Fête d'Isis** at the beginning of August and the colossal fair that takes over the Parc des Châtaigniers on September 9 and 22.

The prettiest part of the town is around the central **place du Quai**, shaded by lime trees and bordered by cafés and brasseries. From here it's only a two-minute walk south, down rue Pierre-Gorlier, to reach the gracefully arched **Pont Vieux**, with beside it the **Musée Cévenol** (April–Oct daily except Tues 10am–noon & 2–6pm; rest of year Wed only 10am–noon & 2–6pm; 20F/€3.05), a well-presented look at traditional rural occupations in the area, including the woodcutter, butcher, shepherd and wolf-hunter. There's also a room devoted to the area's best-known twentieth-century writer, André Chamson, noted for his novels steeped in the traditions and countryside of the Cévennes. Interestingly, Coco Chanel also features in the museum: she had local family connections and it seems found inspiration for her designs in the *cévenol* silks (see below).

The **tourist office** occupies a modern block in the centre of the place du Marché, at the opposite end of the place du Quai from the church (July & Aug Mon–Sat 8.30am–12.30pm & 1.30–7pm, Sun 10am–12.30pm; rest of year Mon–Fri 8.30am–12.30pm & 1.30–6.30pm, Sat 9am–12.30pm & 2–5pm; ☎04.67.81.01.72, fax 04.67.81.86.79). For somewhere to **stay**, try the simple but attractive *Hôtel du Commerce*, with its wisteria-covered balcony and little garden, at 26 rue des Barris (☎04.67.81.03.28; ②). The best alternative is a couple of kilometres out of town, south towards Montdardier on the D48: the handsome old *Auberge Cocagne* in the village of **AVÈZE** (☎04.67.81.02.70, fax 04.67.81.07.67; ②; closed Dec 21–Feb; restaurant from 70F/€10.50). There are **campsites** in Avèze (☎04.67.81.95.01; closed mid-Sept to mid-June), or 2km upriver from Le Vigan, on the opposite bank, is the well-shaded riverside *Val de l'Arre* (☎04.67.81.02.77, *www.campingfrance.com/valdelarre*; closed Oct–March). There's a **gîte d'étape** at 1 rue de la Carrierrasse (☎04.67.81.01.71). One of the best places to **eat** is *Jardin des Cévennes*, in place du Terral, just off the main square; menus start at 95F/€14.25 and feature French classics with a local twist, such as *filet mignon* with a chestnut sauce. A good alternative is *Le Chandelier*, housed in a converted cellar on rue du Pouzadou; the 78F/€11.89 menu includes *confit de canard* and a choice of delicious desserts.

From Le Vigan, or more particularly from the Pont de l'Hérault bridge, a beautiful lane (D153) winds northeast through typical south Cévennes landscape – deep valleys thick with sweet chestnut and thinly peopled with isolated farms half-buried in greenery – from Sumène to St-Jean-du-Gard, a distance of around 45km, but very slow. **SUMÈNE** is a run-down but lovely old place, the entrance to its close, narrow streets still blocked by its medieval **gates**. It was once a centre for silk spinning, which for a couple of centuries until the 1900s was the mainstay of economic life in the Cévennes – that and the cultivation of the sweet chestnut, which provided the staple diet for the entire population.

There is a **gîte d'étape** at **COLOGNAC** (☎04.66.85.28.84) and another in the valley bottom outside the rather nondescript village of **LASALLE** (☎04.66.85.27.29), also home to the old-fashioned, well-established *Hôtel des Camisards* in the main street (☎04.66.85.20.50; ②; closed Nov–April; restaurant from 70F/€10.67).

St-Jean-du-Gard and around

Thirty-two kilometres west of Alès, **ST-JEAN-DU-GARD** was the centre of Protestant resistance during the Camisard war in 1702–04 (see below). It straggles along the bank of the River Gardon, crossed by a graceful, arched eighteenth-century bridge, with a number of picturesque old houses still surviving in the main street, **Grande-Rue**. One of them contains a splendid **Musée des Vallées Cévenoles** (April–Oct daily 10am–7pm; 22F/€3.30), a museum of local life, with displays of tools, trades, furniture, clothes, domestic articles and a fascinating collection of pieces related to the silk industry. The work of spinning the silk was done by women in factories and lists of regulations and rules on display give some idea of the tough conditions in which they had to work.

The **tourist office** is just off the main street by the post office (mid-June to mid-Sept Mon–Sat 9am–1pm & 2.30–7pm, Sun 9am–1pm; rest of year Mon–Sat 9am–5pm; ☎04.66.85.32.11, fax 04.66.85.16.28). They can advise you about the times of the **steam train** that operates between St-Jean and Anduze (March–Oct; 57F/€8.69 return). There is a big **market** all along Grande-Rue on Tuesday mornings.

The finest place to **stay** is on the Grande-Rue at the *Hôtel l'Oronge*, named after a rare edible mushroom found only in the Cévennes (☎04.66.85.30.34, fax 04.66.85.39.73; ③; closed Jan & Feb; good restaurant from 80F/€12.20). There is a *gîte d'étape* 3km north on the D907 at **LE MOULINET**; contact Mme Laurtay on ☎04.66.85.10.98.

The Musée du Désert

Signposts at St-Jean direct you to the museum at **MAS SOUBEYRAN**, a minuscule hamlet of beautiful rough-stone houses in a gully above the village of Mialet, about 12km east. The **Musée du Désert** (daily: March–June & Sept–Nov 9.30am–noon & 2–6pm; July & Aug 9.30am–7pm; 22F/€3.35), is in the house that once belonged to Rolland, one of the Camisards' self-taught but most successful military leaders, and it is pretty much the same as it would have been in 1704, the year of his death. It catalogues the appalling sufferings and sheer dogged heroism of the Protestant Huguenots in defence of their freedom of conscience; and the "desert" they had to traverse between the Revocation of the Edict of Nantes in 1685 and the promulgation of the Edict of Tolerance in 1787, which restored their original rights. Full emancipation came with the Declaration of the Rights of Man in the first heady months of the Revolution in 1789. During this period, they had no civil rights, unless they abjured their faith. They could not bury their dead, baptize their children or marry. Their priests were forced into exile on pain of death. The recalcitrant were subjected to the infamous *dragonnades*, which involved the forcible billeting of troops on private homes at the expense of the occupants. As if this were not enough, the soldiers would beat their drums continuously for days and nights in people's bedrooms in order to deprive them of sleep. Protestants were put to death or sent to the galleys for life; their houses were destroyed.

Not surprisingly, such brutality led to armed rebellion, inspired by the prophesying of the lay preachers who had replaced the banished priests, calling for a holy war. The rebels were hopelessly outnumbered and the revolt was ruthlessly put down in 1705. On display are documents, private letters and lists of those who died for their beliefs, including the names of five thousand who died as galley slaves (*galériens pour la foi*) and the women who were immured in the Tour de Constance prison in Aigues-Mortes. There are also the chains and rough uniform of a *galérien*.

Prafrance and the Mine Témoin

Twelve kilometres from St-Jean in the direction of Anduze, **PRAFRANCE** has an extraordinary and very appealing garden consisting exclusively of bamboos of all shapes and sizes: **La Bambouseraie** (March to mid-Nov daily 9.30am–6pm;

35F/€4.88), the result of its creator's pet passion. An easy way to get here is to take the steam train (see above) from St Jean du Gard; it just takes ten minutes.

If you want to leave the area by mainline train, the place to head for is **ALÈS** on the Nîmes–Paris line. This was a major coal-mining centre, though 25,000 jobs have been lost and all but two opencast pits closed in the last thirty-odd years. Today, it has a superb museum on the history and techniques of coal-mining, known as the **Mine Témoin**, in the underground workings of a disused mine on chemin de la Cité Ste-Marie in the Rochebelle district (tours daily: April, May & Sept to mid-Nov 9am–12.30pm & 2–5.30pm; June–Aug 10am–7pm; 38F/€5.79; last visit one and a half hours before closing). Tours conducted in English run on Wednesdays between 2 and 5pm during July and August.

Aubenas and the northern Cévennes

A small but prosperous and surprisingly industrial town of around 12,000 people, **AUBENAS** sits in the middle of the southern part of the Ardèche *département* high up on a hill overlooking the middle valley of the River Ardèche. It is 91km southeast of Le Puy and 42km west of Montélimar. With a character and non-tourist-dependent economy of its own, it makes a much better base than places further downstream around Vallon-Pont-d'Arc, with their nightmarish crowds.

The central knot of streets with their cobbles and bridges, occupying the highest point of town around **place de l'Hôtel-de-Ville**, have great charm, particularly towards place de la Grenette and place 14-Juillet. Place de l'Hôtel-de-Ville is dominated by the old feudal **château**, from which the local seigneurs ruled the area right up until the Revolution (guided tours: April–June & Sept Tues & Thurs–Sat tour at 2pm; July & Aug daily 11am–5pm; Oct & Dec–March Tues, Thurs & Sat tour at 2pm; 20F/€3.05). There's a magnificent view of the Ardèche snaking up the valley below from under an arch beside the castle, as there is from the end of **bd Gambetta** 200m downhill, where the **tourist office** is located on the corner (July & Aug daily 9am–12.30pm & 1.30–7pm; rest of year Mon–Sat 9am–noon & 2–6pm, Sun 10am–noon; ☎04.75.89.02.03, *ot.aubenas.ardeche@en-france.com*).

For somewhere to **stay**, it's hard to beat the old-fashioned *Hôtel des Négociants*, right next to the château on place de l'Hôtel-de-Ville (☎04.75.35.18.74; ③; closed Oct) which does nourishing meals from 42F/€6.40. A good alternative is *Hôtel l'Orangerie*, at 7 allées de la Guingette (☎04.75.35.30.42, fax 04.75.93.01.03; ③), in a fairly quiet location just outside the old town. There's a municipal **campsite** on Route de Lazuel (☎04.75.35.18.15). Cafés and brasseries line boulevard de Vernon on the south side of town; for fancier and more expensive places to **eat**, try *Le Fournil*, 34 rue du 4-Septembre, at the end of Béranger-de-la-Tour, in the heart of the old town (closed Sun evening & Mon; from 98F/€14.94), or *Le Chat Qui Pêche*, nearby on place de la Grenette (closed Tues & Wed except in July & Aug; from 98F/€14.94).

The Gorges de l'Ardèche

The **Gorges de l'Ardèche** begin at the **Pont d'Arc**, an extraordinary and very beautiful arch that the river has cut for itself through the limestone, just downstream from Vallon, itself 39km south of Aubenas. They continue for about 35km to **ST-MARTIN-D'ARDÈCHE** in the valley of the Rhône.

The gorges are fantastic. They wind back and forth with reptilian sinuosity, much of the time dropping 300m straight down like a knife cut in the almost dead-flat scrubby Plateau des Gras. But they are also an appalling tourist trap; the road which follows the rim, with spectacular viewpoints marked out at regular intervals, is jammed with traffic in summer. The river, down in the bottom, which is where you really want to be to appreciate the grandeur of the canyon, is likewise packed with canoes in high season. It is walkable, depending on the water level, but you would need to bivouac midway at either Gaud or Gournier. Generally speaking, if you can't go out of season, you're better off giving it a miss.

The plateau itself is riddled with caves. **Aven Marzal**, a stalactite cavern north of the gorge (daily 11am–5.30pm; 43F/€6.55, joint ticket with zoo 72F/€10.98), has a prehistoric **zoo**, which consists of reconstructions of dinosaurs and friends (April–Oct daily 10am–7.30pm; 43F/€6.55, joint ticket 72F/€10.98), but the frequency of visits to the cave depends on the number of visitors waiting – they are approximately every twenty minutes in July and August, falling to four per day in other months.

Best of the area's caves is the **Aven Orgnac**, to the south of the gorge (daily: March–June & Sept to mid-Nov 9.30am–noon & 2–6pm; July & Aug 9.30am–6pm; 47F/€7.20), one of France's most spectacular and colourful stalactite formations. There's also a very good prehistory **museum** (daily: March–June & Sept to mid-Nov 10am–noon & 2–6pm; July & Aug 10am–6pm; 31.50F/€4.80, joint ticket 57F/€8.69). Further upstream near **VALLON-PONT-D'ARC**, a complex series of cave paintings was discovered in December 1994, after being left untouched for 30,000 years, making the **Chauvet-Pont d'Arc cave** the oldest-known decorated cave in the world. The cave system is currently being investigated by archeologists and causing a major rethink about the history of art. The paintings depict woolly rhinos, bison, lions and bears, and display a remarkable mastery of perspective. It's unlikely that Chauvet-Pont d'Arc will ever be open to the public. However, there is a small but rewarding **exhibition** on the cave complex at Vallon, behind the Mairie. The highlight is a video taken inside the caves, showing many of the paintings close up (Tues–Sun 2–5.30pm; 25F/€3.81).

Accommodation in the area can be a problem during the high season. The cheapest place in Vallon itself is the *Hôtel du Parc*, on boulevard Alizon (☎04.75.88.02.17; ②), but by far the best is *Le Manoir du Raveyron*, rue Henri-Barbusse (☎04.75.88.03.59, fax 04.75.37.11.12; ③; closed mid-Nov to mid-March), with a good restaurant from 100F/€15.24. The river is lined with **campsites**, the cheapest being the municipal one (☎04.75.88.04.73; closed Oct–March). There's a **gîte d'étape** on place de la Mairie (☎04.75.88.07.87), and a **tourist office** on the south side of town (June to mid-Sept daily 9am–1pm & 3–7pm, Sun 10am–noon; rest of year Mon–Fri 9am–noon & 2–6pm, Sat 9am–noon; ☎04.75.88.04.01, *www.vallon-pont-darc.com*). Eight kilometres upstream, there is a well-priced municipal **campsite** at **RUOMS** (☎04.75.93.99.16; closed Oct to mid-May).

The valley of the Chassezac and the Corniche du Vivarais

Between Aubenas and Les Vans, 27km to the southwest, several wild mountain streams flow out of the northern part of the Cévennes to join the Ardèche. One of the most beautiful is the **Chassezac**, which rises north of Villefort and carves a dry, twisting ravine covered with pine, bracken and sweet chestnut down to **LES VANS**.

The centre of the town is occupied by the wide and cheerful **place Léopold-Ollier**, on one side of which is the eccentrically decorated *Hôtel des Cévennes* (☎04.75.37.23.09; ③), whose decor, friendly welcome and good cooking (from 80F/€12.20) make a stop here worthwhile. Other attractions are the remains of the old town and, just outside, the bizarre rock formations of the **Bois de Paiolive**. There is a **gîte d'étape** across the river at Chambonas (☎04.75.37.24.99).

Thines to the Col de Meyrand

THINES is a dozen twisting kilometres up the Chassezac from Les Vans, past isolated farms, abandoned terracing and numerous tumbling streams, then a further 5km or so up a side valley. The lane that leads to it is no wider than a car, and nature encroaches on either side. Traces remain of the old mule road, and in the torrent bed stand the stumps of packhorse bridges long since carried away. Among the scrubby oaks are bee-hives made from old tree trunks.

The village itself is at the end of the road high on a spur, looking back down the val-ley: just a handful of squat, grey-stone houses tightly grouped around a very lovely twelfth-century **church**, decorated with bands of red and white stone, the faces of its sculptures smashed during the Wars of Religion. At the top of the village, where the **GR4** and the local **GRP** enter from the scrubby heights behind, there is a strange **rock-cut relief** commemorating Resistance people killed here in August 1943. There's also a **gîte d'étape** (Mme Bacconnier; ☎04.75.36.94.33) and *ferme auberge* (Mme Archambault; ☎04.75.36.94.47; closed mid-Nov to Easter).

If your car is reasonably robust, you can get up onto the D4 on the 1000m ridge above Thines by a track that starts just above the bridge over the stream below the vil-lage. This is the so-called **Corniche du Vivarais Cévenol**, which you would otherwise have to make a long detour to reach. **SABLIÈRES**, another desolate Cévennes village, lies in the valley of the Drobie down to your right.

The landscape changes completely up here. The Mediterranean influence is left behind; it's windswept moorland, with natural beechwoods and mountain ash around the few bleak farms and plantations of conifers on the tops. The land rises steadily to over 1400m above the **Col de Meyrand**, itself at 1370m, whence it is possible to escape back down to the main road and train line at **LUC**, which is 18km to the west.

Le Puy-en-Velay and the northeast

Right in the middle of the Massif Central, 78km from St-Étienne and 132km from Clermont, **LE PUY-EN-VELAY**, often shortened to Le Puy, is one of the most remark-able towns in the whole of France. Both landscape and architecture are totally theatri-cal. Slung between the higher mountains to east and west, the landscape erupts in a chaos of volcanic acne: everywhere is a confusion of abrupt conical hills, scarred with dark outcrops of rock and topknotted with woods. Even in the centre of the town, these volcanic thrusts burst through.

In the past, Le Puy enjoyed influence and prosperity because of its ecclesiastical institutions. It was – and in a limited way, still is – a centre for pilgrims embarking on the 1600-kilometre trek to Santiago de Compostela. The actual starting point is place du Plot (also the scene of a lively Saturday market) and rue St-Jacques. History has it that Le Puy's Bishop Godescalk, in the tenth century, was the first pilgrim to make the journey. During the the Wars of Religion the town managed to resist the Protestant fervour of much of the Massif Central. Today, however, it has fallen somewhat on hard times, and its traditional industries – tanning and lace – have essentially gone bust.

Even today Le Puy is somewhat inaccessible for the capital of a *département*: the three main roads out all cross passes more than 1000m high, which causes problems in winter. But it is far from run-down. And it still produces its famous green lentils.

Arrival, information and accommodation

If you arrive at the **gare SNCF** or **gare routière** (☎04.71.09.25.60), facing each other in place Maréchal-Leclerc, you'll find yourself barely a ten-minute walk from the central place du Breuil and the **tourist office** (July & Aug Mon–Sat 8.30am–7.30pm, Sun 9am–noon & 2–6pm; rest of year Mon–Sat 8.30am–noon & 1.30–6.15pm, Sun

10am–noon; ☎04.71.09.38.41, fax 04.71.05.22.62, *www.ot-lepuyenvelay.fr*), with the **Comité Départemental du Tourisme** at 12 bd Philippe-Jourde (June–Aug Mon–Sat 8.30am–7.30pm, Sun 9am–noon & 2–6pm; rest of year Mon–Sat 8.30am–noon & 2–6pm; ☎04.71.09.38.41).

Le Puy doesn't have a superabundance of **hotels**, so it's wise to book ahead in peak season. Three to try on boulevard Maréchal-Fayolle, the main boulevard connecting the station and place Breuil, are the clean and pleasant *Dyke Hôtel*, at no. 37 (☎04.71.09.05.03, fax 04.71.02.58.66; ③), the basic *Régional*, at no. 36 (☎04.71.09.37.34; ①), and the rather handsome old *Régina*, at no. 34 (☎04.71.09.14.71, fax 04.71.09.18.57, *www.hotelrestregina.com*; ④–⑦; restaurant from 85F/€12.96). Alternatively, there's the *Bristol*, at 7 av Foch (☎04.71.09.13.38, fax 04.71.09.51.70; ③), with a restaurant offering an excellent regional set menu from 90F/€13.72. For those watching the pennies, there's a good **HI hostel** at the attractive *Centre Pierre-Cardinal*, 9 rue Jules-Vallès (☎04.71.05.52.40, fax 04.71.05.61.80), just off rue Lafayette, in the heart of the old town. **Campers** should head for the municipal *Camping d'Audinet*, near the River Loire in the northeast corner of town.

The Town

It would be hard to lose your bearings in Le Puy, for wherever you go there's no losing sight of the colossal, brick-red statue of the Virgin and Child that towers above the town on the **Rocher Corneille**, 755m above sea level and 130 abrupt metres above the lower town. The Virgin is cast from 213 guns captured at Sebastopol and painted red to match the tiled roofs below. You can climb up to the statue's base and, irreverent though it may seem, even up inside it (20F/€3.05). From here you get stunning views of the city, the church of St-Michel atop its needle-pointed pinnacle a few hundred metres north-west, and the surrounding volcanic countryside.

In the maze of steep cobbled streets and steps that terrace the Rocher, lace-makers – a traditional, though now commercialized, industry – do a fine trade, with doilies and lace shawls hanging enticingly outside souvenir shops. The main focus here, in the **old town**, is the Byzantine-looking **Cathédrale Notre-Dame-de-France**, begun in the eleventh century and decorated with parti-coloured layers of stone and mosaic patterns and roofed with a line of six domes. It is best approached up the rue des Tables, where you get the full theatrical force of its five-storeyed west front towering above you. In the rather exotic eastern gloom of the interior, a black-faced Virgin in spreading lace and golden robes stands upon the main altar, the copy of a revered original destroyed during the Revolution; the copy is still paraded through the town every August 15. Other lesser treasures are displayed at the back of the church in the sacristy, beyond which is the entrance to the exceptionally beautiful twelfth-century **cloister** (daily: April–June 9.30am–12.30pm & 2–6pm; July–Sept 9.30am–6.30pm; rest of year 9.30am–noon & 2–6.30pm; 25F/€3.81), with its carved capitals, cornices and magnificent views of the cathedral and the towering Virgin and Child overhead. The passageway to the cloisters takes you past the so-called **Fever Stone**, whose origins may have been as a prehistoric dolmen and which was reputed to have the power of curing fevers. The surrounding ecclesiastical buildings and the **place du For**, on the south side of the cathedral, all date from the same period and form a remarkable ensemble.

It's a ten-minute walk from the cathedral to the **church of St-Michel** (signposts lead the way), perched atop the 82-metre needle-pointed lava pinnacle of the **Rocher d'Aiguilhe**. The little Romanesque church, built on Bishop Godescalk's return from his pilgrimage (see opposite) and consecrated in 962, is a beauty in its own right, and its improbable situation atop this ridiculous needle of rock is quite extraordinary – it's a long haul up 265 steps to the entrance (daily: mid-March to mid-June 10am–noon & 2–5/7pm; mid-June to mid-Sept 9am–7pm; mid-Sept to mid-Nov 9.30am–5/6pm; mid-Nov to mid-March 2–4pm; 15F/€2.29).

In the new part of town, beyond the squat **Tour Pannessac**, which is all that remains of the city walls, **place de Breuil** joins **place Michelet** and forms a social hub backed by the spacious Henri Vinay public gardens, where the **Musée Crozatier** (May–Sept Mon & Wed–Sun Wed–Sat 10am–noon & 2–6pm, Sun 2–6pm; Oct–April Mon & Wed–Sat 10am–noon & 2–4pm, Sun 2–4pm; 20F/€3.04) is best known for its collections relating to the region's traditional lace-making activities. Busy boulevard Maréchal-Fayolle converges with place Cadelade, where there's another of Le Puy's crazier aspects: the extraordinary bulbous tower of what used to be the **Pagès Verveine distillery**. The *verveine* (verbena) plant is normally used to make *tisane* (herb tea), but in this region provides a vivid green, powerful digestive liqueur instead. Production has now moved to a distillery 5km outside Le Puy, which is open for guided tours and tasting (Mon–Fri 10am–noon & 1.30–6.30pm; 28F/€4.27). To get there take the N88 and exit at the *zone industrielle* Blavozy.

Eating and drinking

Apart from the hotel restaurants and the brasseries on the main street opposite the tourist office, there are several good and not too expensive places to **eat**. The best is the *Tournayre*, at 12 rue Chènebouterie (☎04.71.09.58.94; closed Sun evening, Mon & Jan), specializing in the region's cuisine (menus from 115F/€17.53). *La Parenthèse*, at 8 av de la Cathédrale (closed Sat & Sun; from 80F/€12.20), also does regional specialities and serves local wines. Two cheaper establishments, both in rue Raphaël, which begins at the bottom of rue des Tables, are the *Nom de la Rose*, at no. 48 (closed Tues & Nov–Feb), offering Mexican food, with menus from 69F/€10.52, and *La Felouque*, at no. 49 (closed Tues & Nov–Feb; from 50F/€7.62), which serves Middle Eastern dishes and excellent grilled salmon. At 29 rue Pannessac there's a vegetarian restaurant, *La Farandole*, serving mostly organic food and good fondues.

For a **drink** or light snack, the terrace of *Le Petit Gourmande*, at the bottom of rue des Tables, makes a pleasant stop in summer (closed Jan; galettes for 32F/€4.88). A good place for an evening drink is *Harry's Bar*, on rue Raphaël, near the corner with rue des Tables.

North of Le Puy

North of Le Puy, the D906 crosses a vast and terminally depopulated area of pine-clad uplands – now the Parc Naturel Régional Livradois-Forez – and continues all the way to Vichy, via the historic town of **La Chaise-Dieu** and the old industrial centres of **Ambert** and **Thiers**.

La Chaise-Dieu
After 42km you come to the little town of **LA CHAISE-DIEU**, renowned for the **abbey church of St-Robert** (daily: June–Sept 9am–noon & 2–7pm; rest of year 10am–noon & 2–5pm; 15F/€2.29), whose square towers dominate the town. Founded in 1044 and restored in the fourteenth century at the expense of Pope Clement VI, who had served as a monk here, the church was destroyed by the Huguenots in 1562, burnt down in 1692, and remained unfinished when the Revolution brought a wave of anticlericalism. It was only really finished in this century. Its interior contains the tomb of Clement VI, some magnificent Flemish tapes-

tries of Old and New Testament scenes hanging in the choir, which also boasts some fine Gothic stalls, and a celebrated fresco of the **Danse Macabre,** depicting Death plucking at the coarse plump bodies of 23 living figures, representing the different classes of society. "It is yourself", says the fifteenth-century text below, as indeed it might easily have been in an age when plague and war were rife.

Nearby on the place de l'Echo, the **Salle de l'Echo** (same times except closed Sun am; free) is another product of the risk of contagion – if not from plague, then from leprosy. For in this room, once used for hearing confession from the sick and dying, two people can turn their backs on each other and stand in opposite corners and have a perfectly audible conversation just by whispering.

A **classical music festival** takes place here in late August and early September, details of which are available from the **tourist office**, on place de la Mairie (April to mid-Sept Tues–Sun 10am–noon & 2–6pm; rest of year Tues–Sat 10am–noon & 2–6pm; ☎04.71.00.01.16, fax 04.71.00.03.45). The *Hôtel Monastère et Terminus*, on avenue de la Gare (☎04.71.00.00.73, fax 04.71.00.09.18; ②; closed Nov–March; restaurant from 67F/€10.21), and *Hôtel au Tremblant*, on the D906 (☎04.71.00.01.85, fax 04.71.00.08.59; ②; restaurant from 75F/€11.43), offer reasonable comfort for a night's stay. There's also a municipal **campsite** on the Vichy side of the D906 (☎04.71.00.07.88; closed Oct–May).

Ambert

Twenty-five kilometres north of La Chaise-Dieu, the little town of **AMBERT** was an important centre of cottage industry in the Middle Ages. From the fourteenth to eighteenth centuries it was the centre of papermaking in France, supplying in particular the printers of Lyon, a connection which brought the region into contact with new ideas, in particular the revolutionary teachings of the Reformed Church. Although those small-scale operations have long since been sidelined, there is still a **paper mill** in operation at Richard-de-Bas just east of the town, with its **Musée Historique du Papier** (daily: July & Aug 9am–6pm; rest of year 9am–noon & 2–6pm; 23F/€3.50), featuring exhibits and explanations from papyrus to handmade samples from medieval days. In the town itself, there's a small **museum** (July & Aug daily 10am–noon & 2–5pm; rest of year closed Mon; 25F/€3.81) devoted to the manufacture of the soft blue Fourme d'Ambert cheese, the region's speciality.

Thiers

THIERS, another 49km to the north, has an illustrious industrial history: it is the country's great manufacturer of knives. In spite of serious decline, especially since decolonization and the loss of such huge captive markets, it still accounts for some seventy percent of French production. It is an interesting little town, built over the steep slopes of the valley of the Durolle, whose water power drove the forges and blade-makers' wheels for centuries. There's the **Maison des Couteliers**, devoted to the knife, at 58 rue de la Coutellerie in the centre (daily 10am–noon & 2–6/6.30pm; Jan closed Mon; 21F/€3.20), while all along the deep valley bottom you can see where the old workshops were. You probably wouldn't want to stay overnight – there are frequent trains from Clermont Ferrand (30min).

East of Le Puy

East of Le Puy lies the barrier of the mountains of the Vivarais, rounded and wooded with beech, pine and fir, interspersed with open cow pastures. The highest points are the **Gerbier de Jonc** (1551m) and **Mont Mézenc** (1753m), with long views west across the whole of the Massif Central.

The Gerbier is a curious mound rising out of the otherwise flattish surrounding uplands, about 50km southeast of Le Puy, with the River Loire rising on its upper slopes. To get out there you take the D535 through **MONASTIER-SUR-GAZEILLE**, where R. L. Stevenson bought his donkey and started his famous journey. Although the village is pretty, with a particularly lovely church, there is something forlorn and unfriendly about it. The rather bleak *Hôtel de Provence* above the village would do for a night's stay (☎04.71.03.82.37; ②; restaurant from 65F/€9.91). The riverside municipal **campsite** (☎04.71.03.82.24; closed Oct–May) and **gîte d'étape** (☎04.71.03.82.24) are more welcoming.

Fifty kilometres further north, and about 40km east of Le Puy, behind the gentle bulk of **Mont Meygal** (1436m), lies the area known as the *Montagne Protestante*, because its people converted very early and have remained staunch Protestants ever since, albeit with some fairly far-out tendencies among them. Black-stone farmhouses stand in isolation among the pastures strewn with autumn crocus and the dark woods of fir. At the centre of the region lies **CHAMBON-SUR-LIGNON**, a rambling, rather unattractive village with a somewhat faded air, made famous, however, for its extraordinary wartime record as a haven for several thousand Jewish children. Everyone knew of their presence and was involved in protecting them, and no one ever betrayed them, bound together in their obdurate resolve by their strong Protestant beliefs. Their story is told in *Les Armes de l'Esprit*, a documentary film made by one of the surviving children who emigrated to the US, available from the Mairie. Albert Camus also stayed nearby in 1942 and wrote part of *La Peste* here. The **tourist office** is on the central square (Mon–Sat 9am–noon & 2/3–6/6.30pm, Sun 11am–noon; ☎04.71.59.71.56, fax 04.71.65.88.78). More local information can be had from the tourist office in **TENCE**, a rather more aesthetic village, 8km down the road (Tues–Sat 9am–noon & 2–6pm, Sun 10.30am–12.30pm; ☎04.71.59.81.99, fax 04.71.65.47.13).

St-Étienne

ST-ÉTIENNE, 78km northeast of Le Puy, is not a particularly appealing town. Almost unrelievedly industrial, it was a major armaments manufacturer, enclosed for kilometres around by mineworkings, warehouses and factory chimneys. However, like so many other industrial centres, it has fallen on hard times, and the demolition gangs have moved in to raze its archaic industrial past, which does not add to its charms.

The centre is bland, and the mood is that of decline since the closure of the coal fields, but its **Musée d'Art Moderne** at La Terrasse, in the north of the city (daily except Tues 10am–6pm; 28F/€4.27) justifies a detour for anyone with an interest in twentieth-century art – a quite unexpected treasure house of contemporary work, both pre- and post-World War II, with a good modern American section, in which Andy Warhol and Frank Stella figure prominently, along with work by Rodin, Matisse, Léger and Ernst, and rooms filled entirely with French art, imaginatively laid out to exciting effect. La Terrasse station is served by frequent trains from St-Étienne's central station, Châteaucreux. The **Musée d'Art et d'Industrie**, 2 place Louis-Comte, is also good on St-Étienne's industrial background, including the development of the revolutionary Jacquard loom, but was closed for renovation at the time of writing (contact the tourist office for latest details).

The **tourist office** on 16 av de la Liberation (Mon–Sat 9am–7pm, Sun 10am–1pm; ☎04.77.49.39.00, *www.tourisme-st-etienne.com*) is around ten minutes' walk from Châteaucreux train station along avenue D.-Rochereau. If you are forced to **stay**, try *Hôtel de la Tour*, 1 rue Mercière (☎04.77.32.28.48, fax 04.77.21.27.90; ②), *Le Cheval Noir*, 11 rue François-Gillet (☎04.77.33.41.72, fax 04.77.37.79.19; ③), or *Hôtel Terminus du Forez*, 29 av D.-Rochereau (☎04.77.32.48.47, fax 04.77.34.03.30, *hotel-terminus-du-forez@lhdcv.com*; ④).

travel details

Trains

Alès to: Genolhac (3–4 daily; 40min); Langogne (3–4 daily; 1hr 30min); Nîmes (6–7 daily; 35min); Villefort (3–4 daily; 1hr).

Aurillac to: Brive (4 daily; 1hr 40min).

Clermont-Ferrand to: Aurillac (6 daily; 2hr 30min); Béziers (1 daily; 6hr); Brive (3 daily; 3hr 40min); Limoges (2 daily; 3hr 30min); Le Lioran (6 daily; 2hr); Lyon (6 daily; 2hr 45min–3hr); Millau (3 daily; 4hr 20min); Le Mont Dore (6 daily; 1hr 30min); Murat (6 daily; 1hr 20min); Neussargues (6 daily; 1hr 30min); Paris (5 daily; 5hr); Le Puy (3 daily; 2hr 10min); Riom (10 daily; 10min); St-Flour-Chaudes-Aigues (5 daily; 2hr); Thiers (6 daily; 35min); Vic-sur-Cère (6 daily; 2hr 15min); Vichy (10 daily; 35min); Volvic (5 daily; 24min).

Mende to: La Bastide-Puylaurent (2–3 daily; 1hr); Langogne (2 daily; 1hr 30min); Marvejols (3 daily; 40min); Montpellier (several daily; 3hr); Nîmes (several daily; 2hr 30min–4hr).

Millau to: Aumont-Aubrac (5 daily; 1hr 30min); Béziers (4–5 daily; 2hr); Marvejols (5 daily; 1hr 10min); Paris (2 daily direct; 8hr–9hr 30min).

Le Puy to: St-Étienne (8 daily; 1hr 20min).

Rodez to: Millau (bus & train, 2 daily; 1hr 20min).

St-Étienne to: Clermont-Ferrand (3–6 daily; 2hr 40min); Lyon (3 daily TGVs; 45min); Paris (3 daily TGVs; 2hr 50min); St-Germain-des-Fosses (2 daily; 3hr).

St-Flour to: Neussargues (2–3 daily; 25min).

Vichy to: Clermont-Ferrand (frequent; 40min); Nîmes (1–2 daily; 7hr); Paris (4 daily; 3hr 30min).

Buses

Ambert to: St-Étienne (1 daily; 2hr).

Aubenas to: Alès (2–3 daily; 2hr 10min); Joyeuse (several daily; 25–40min); Privas (7 daily; 1hr); Valence (7 daily; 2hr); Vallon-Pont-d'Arc (1–2 daily; 45min); Les Vans (4 daily; 1hr 10min).

Aurillac to: Brommat, changing at Mut-de-Barrez (3 weekly; 2hr); Carlat (3–4 daily; 30min); Decazeville (1 daily; 2hr); Entraygues (1 daily; 1hr 30min); Mandailles (1 daily; 1hr 20min); Murat (1 daily; 1hr 40min); St-Flour (1 daily; 2hr 10min); Ste-Géneviève-sur-Argence, changing at Mur-de-

Barrez (3 weekly; 2hr 30min); Super-Lioran (1 daily; 1hr 20min); Thiézac (2 daily; 55min); Vic-sur-Cère (2–3 daily; 40min).

Chambon-sur-Lignon to: St-Agrève (4 daily; 20min); Valence (2 daily; 2hr 30min).

Clermont-Ferrand to: Ambert (1–2 daily: 1hr 45min); Aydat (1–2 daily; 40min); Besse (July & Aug 2 daily; 1hr 35min); Bort-les-Orgues (1–2 daily; 2hr 15min); La Chaise-Dieu (1 Mon; 2hr); Chaubon (July & Aug 2 daily; 1hr 35min); Mauriac (1–2 daily; 2hr 45min); Moulins (4 daily; 2hr 30min); Murol (July & Aug 2 daily; 1hr 10min); Le Puy (1 daily; 2hr 15min); St-Flour (2 weekly; 2hr); St-Nectaire (July & Aug 2 daily; 1hr); Superbesse (July & Aug 2 daily; 1hr 45min); Thiers (several daily; 1hr); Vichy (5 daily; 2hr).

Conques to: Entraygues (July & Aug Tues, Thurs & Sat 1 daily; 35min); Espalion (July & Aug Tues, Thurs & Sat 1 daily; 1hr 20min); Najac (July & Aug Tues & Fri 1 daily; 2hr 30min); Rodez (July & Aug Tues, Thurs & Sat 1 daily; 1hr); St-Geniez-d'Olt (July & Aug Tues, Thurs & Sat 1 daily; 2hr 15min); Villefranche-de-Rouergue (July & Aug Tues & Fri 1 daily; 2hr).

Florac to: Alès (1–2 daily; 1hr 30min).

Mende to: Langogne (2 daily; 1hr); Marvejols (3 daily; 50min); Le Puy (2 daily; 2hr); St-Chély-d'Apcher (1 daily; 1hr 10min); St-Étienne (1 daily; 3hr).

Millau to: Aven Armand (July & Aug 2 daily; 1hr 45min); Meyrueis (1–4 daily; 1hr 15min); Rodez (4 daily; 1hr 30min); Rozier (1–4 daily; 45min); Ste-Énimie (July & Aug 2 daily; 2hr 25min); Toulouse (2 daily; 4hr).

Neussargues to: Allanche (2–3 daily; 20min); Bort-les-Orgues (2–3 daily; 1hr 45min); Condat (2–3 daily; 30min); Riom-ès-Montagnes (2–3 daily; 1hr 15min); St-Flour (2–3 daily; 30min).

Le Puy to: Aubenas (2 weekly; 3hr 15min); La Chaise-Dieu (2 daily; 1hr); Clermont-Ferrand (1 daily; 3hr); Monistrol d'Allier (3 weekly; 45min); St-Étienne (4 daily; 2hr 10min); Saugues (3 weekly; 1hr 10min).

Rodez to: Albi (3 daily; 2hr); Conques (July & Aug Tues, Thurs & Sat 1 daily; 1hr); Entraygues (1 daily; 2hr); Espalion (3–4 daily; 45min); Laguiole (1 daily; 1hr 45min); Mende (1 daily; 3hr 30min);

Millau (4–5 daily; 1hr 30min); Montauban (1 daily; 3hr 15min); Montpellier (3 daily; 3hr 20min); Mur-de-Barrez (1 daily; 2hr 45min); Sauveterre-de-Rouergue (5 weekly; 55min); Séverac-le-Château (several daily; 45min); Toulouse (2–4 daily; 3hr 30min); Villefranche-de-Rouergue (1–2 daily; 1hr 30min).

St-Affrique to: Le Caylar (1 daily; 1hr 40min); Lodève (1 daily; 2hr 10min); Millau (2 daily; 50min); Montpellier (1 daily; 3hr 25min); Rodez (1 daily; 2hr 15min).

St-Agrève to: Chambon-sur-Lignon (4 daily; 20min); St-Étienne (4 daily; 2hr); Tence (4 daily; 35min).

St-Chély-d'Aubrac to: Espalion (1 daily; 30min).

St-Flour to: Chaudes-Aigues (2 daily; 1hr); Laguiole (Tues, Thurs & Sat 1 daily; 3hr); Massiac (3 daily; 35min).

St-Martin-d'Ardèche to: Avignon (1 daily; 1hr 40min); Pont St-Esprit (2 daily; 15min); Vallon-Pont-d'Arc (2 daily; 1hr 10min).

Vichy to: Ambert (5 daily; 2hr 10min); Thiers (several daily; 40min).

Le Vigan to: Ganges (4 daily; 25min); Montpellier (3 daily; 2hr); Nîmes (4 daily; 2hr); Valleraugue (July & Aug 1 daily; 30min).

Villefranche-de-Rouergue to: Conques (July & Aug Tues & Fri 1 daily; 2hr); Décazeville (July & Aug Tues & Fri 1 daily; 30min); Najac (July & Aug Tues & Fri 1 daily; 30min).

CHAPTER THIRTEEN

THE ALPS

Rousseau wrote in his *Confessions*, "I need torrents, rocks, pine trees, dark forests, mountains, rugged paths to go up and down, precipices at my elbow to give me a good fright", and he certainly found what he was looking for in **the Alps**. Formed by the collision of two continental plates two hundred million years ago, the range contains some of France's most dramatic landscapes, with roads, rail lines and population confined to the deep valley floors. To get the best out of this region you have to walk – or in winter, ski (the box on pp.870–1 has a short round-up of the resorts). There are four **national** or **regional parks** in the area covered by this chapter – Vanoise, Écrins, Queyras and Vercors – all with round-the-park trails, requiring one to two weeks' walking. The **Tour of Mont Blanc** path is of similar length. Then there are two transalpine routes: the **Route des Grandes Alpes**, which crosses all the major massifs from St-Gingolph on Lake Geneva to Nice, and **Le Balcon des Alpes**, a gentler, village-to-village itinerary through the western foothills.

All these routes are clearly marked, equipped with refuge huts and *gîtes d'étape*, and described in *Topoguides*. The CIMES office in Grenoble (see p.849) will provide information on all GR paths. In addition, local tourist offices often produce detailed maps of walks in their own areas. You should not undertake any high-level **long-distance hikes**, however, unless you are an experienced hill-walker; if you aren't, but nonetheless like the sound of some of these trails, read a specialized hiking book before making any plans, or simply limit your sights to more local targets. You can find plenty of day walks from bases in or close to the parks; and there are some spectacular road routes, too. The **Vercors**, **Chartreuse**, **Aravis**, **Faucigny** and **Chablais** areas are the gentlest and quietest introductions.

As for accommodation, you can **camp** freely on the fringes of the parks, but once inside you are supposed to pitch only in an emergency and move on after one night. **Hotels** are often seasonal (closed in late spring and late autumn), overbooked and overpriced – if you're on a budget but don't want to carry camping equipment, using **gîtes** and **refuges** is a better solution. The Alps are as crowded in midsummer as they are in winter (the **Chamonix-Mont Blanc** area is the worst black spot), but you are more or less obliged to go in high season if you want to walk: unreliable weather aside, anywhere above 2000m will be snowbound until the beginning of July. Drivers should remember that some high passes such as the **Col du Galibier** and the **Col de l'Iseran** in the east of the region can remain closed well into June, requiring long detours or excursions into Italy via Alpine tunnels.

ACCOMMODATION PRICE CODES

Each hotel and guesthouse in this book has been graded according to the following price codes, which indicate the price for the **cheapest double room available during the high season**.

① Under 160F/€24	④ 300–400F/€46–61	⑦ 600–700F/€91–107
② 160–220F/€24–34	⑤ 400–500F/€61–76	⑧ 700–800F/€107–122
③ 220–300F/€34–46	⑥ 500–600F/€76–91	⑨ Over 800F/€122

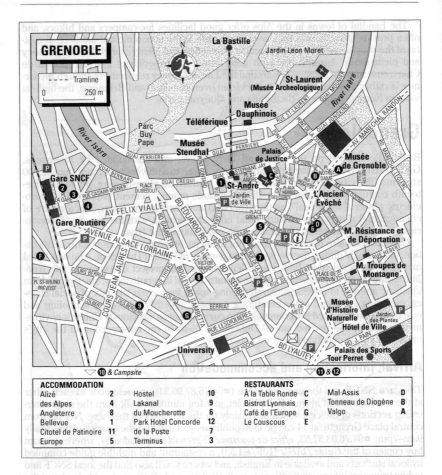

ACCOMMODATION				RESTAURANTS		
Alizé	2	Hostel	10	À la Table Ronde	C	Mal Assis	D
des Alpes	4	Lakanal	9	Bistrot Lyonnais	F	Tonneau de Diogène	B
Angleterre	8	du Moucherotte	6	Café de l'Europe	G	Valgo	A
Bellevue	1	Park Hotel Concorde	12	Le Couscous	E		
Citotel de Patinoire	11	de la Poste	7				
Europe	5	Terminus	3				

Hotels

Alizé, 1 place de la Gare (☎04.76.43.12.91, fax 04.76.47.62.79). Basic but clean hotel right by the *gare SNCF*. ②.

des Alpes, 45 av Félix-Viallet (☎04.76.87.00.71, fax 04.76.56.95.45, *www.hotel.desalpes@wanadoo.fr*). Good-value, family-run hotel near the *gare SNCF*, which is holding up well, despite its ageing decor. ③.

d'Angleterre, 5 place Victor-Hugo (☎04.76.87.37.21, fax 04.76.50.94.10, *www.hotel-angleterre .fr*). Newly renovated and very well-equipped hotel, convenient for both the sights and the stations. ⑦.

Bellevue, 1 rue de Belgrade (☎04.76.46.69.34, fax 04.76.85.20.12, *www.hotel-bellevue.fr*). Comfortable, small hotel on the banks of the Isère near the *téléférique*. ③.

Citôtel de Patinoire, 12 rue Marie-Chamoux (☎04.76.44.43.65, fax 04.76.44.44.77, *www.hotel -patinoire.com*). Excellent mid-range option with a generous breakfast at 35F/€5.34. ④.

de l'Europe, 22 place Grenette (☎ & fax 04.76.46.16.94, *hotel.europe.gre@wanadoo.fr*). Well-maintained and hospitable place smack in Grenoble's liveliest square. ②.

Lakanal, 26 rue de Bergers (☎04.76.46.03.42, fax 04.76.17.21.24). Comfortable and unassuming, this budget option often has space when others are full. A little bit off the beaten path, ten minutes' walk southwest of place Victor-Hugo, near the tram stop "Gambetta". ②.

du Moucherotte, 1 rue Auguste-Gaché, near place Ste-Claire (☎04.76.54.61.40, fax 04.76.44.62.52). An old-style small hotel, just steps from the city's tourist office. ②.

Park Hôtel Concorde, 10 place Paul-Mistral (☎04.67.85.81.23, fax 04.76.46.49.88, *www.park.hotel.fr*). Luxury hotel, with a magnificent facade looking out onto one of the old town's liveliest squares. ⑨.

de la Poste, 25 rue de la Poste (☎04.76.46.67.25). Tiny, friendly and rather old-fashioned establishment run by an English-speaking *patronne*, located on a pedestrian street, off place Vaucanson. ①.

Terminus, 10 place de la Gare (☎04.76.87.24.33, fax 04.76.50.38.28, *www.terminus-hotel-grenoble.fr*). Friendly and well-appointed old hotel, with spacious rooms; quiet, despite its station-side location. ⑤.

The City

The best way to start your stay is to take the **téléférique** (Jan to mid-March & Nov–Dec daily 11am–6.30pm; mid-March to May & Oct Mon 11am–7.30pm, Tues–Sat 9.45am–midnight, Sun 9.15am–7.30pm; June & Sept Mon 11am–midnight, Tues–Sat 9.15am–midnight, Sun 9.15am–7.30pm; July & Aug Mon 11am–12.30am, Tues–Sun 9.15am–12.30am; 35F/€5.34 single) from the riverside quai Stéphane-Jay to **Fort de la Bastille** on the steep slopes above the north bank of the Isère. The ride is hair-raising, as you are whisked steeply and swiftly into the air in a sort of transparent egg, which allows you to see very clearly how far you would fall in the event of an accident. If you don't like the sound of the cable car, you can climb the pleasant but steep footpath from the St-Laurent church (see below).

Although the fort is of little interest, the **view** is fantastic. At your feet the Isère, milky-grey and swollen with snow-melt, tears at the piles of the old bridges which join the St-Laurent quarter, colonized by Italian immigrants in the nineteenth century, to the nucleus of the medieval town, whose red roofs cluster tightly around the church of St-André. To the east, snowfields gleam in the gullies of the Belledonne massif (2978m). Southeast is Taillefer and south-southeast the dip where the *Route Napoléon* passes over the mountains to Sisteron and the Mediterranean – this is the road Napoléon took after his escape from Elba in March 1815 on his way to rally his forces for the campaign that led to his final defeat at Waterloo. To the west are the steep white cliffs of the Vercors massif; the highest peak, dominating the city, is Moucherotte (1901m). The jagged peaks at your back are the outworks of the Chartreuse massif. Northeast on a clear day you can see the white peaks of Mont Blanc up the deep glacial valley of the Isère, known as La Grésivaudan. It was in this valley that the first French hydroelectric project went into action in 1869. Heading back into town, there's a pleasant path down through the public gardens.

Upstream from the *téléférique* station is the sixteenth-century **Palais de Justice** (open to the public), with **place St-André** and the church of St-André behind. Built in

---

MUSEUM PASSES

The tourist office at Grenoble offers several discount packages on sights and transport. The basic one, the **Multipass Grenoble**, gives you free entrance to all of the city's museums, except for the Musées de Résistance and des Troupes de Montagne, a ride on the *petit train*, a return trip on the *téléférique*, a guided tour, unlimited city transport use and a 10F/€1.53 parking voucher (one-day pass 89F/€13.57, two-day 150F/€22.88). Another good deal is the **Pass Musées**, which for 50F/€7.63 gets you into sixteen museums in Grenoble and the surrounding area, and is valid for one year.

the thirteenth century and heavily restored, the church is of little architectural interest, but the narrow streets leading back towards places Grenette, Vaucanson and Verdun take you through the liveliest and most colourful quarter of the city. Life focuses on a chain of little squares – aux Herbes, Claveyson, de Gordes, Grenette and Notre-Dame – where people congregate at the numerous cafés and restaurants. The small produce **market** (Tues–Sun 6am–1pm) on place aux Herbes is a great place to stock up on inexpensive local produce.

Close to place St-André, in the former town hall at 1 rue Hector-Berlioz, in the corner of the Jardin de Ville gardens, is the **Musée Stendhal** (mid-July to mid-Sept Tues–Sat 9am–noon & 2–6pm; rest of year Tues–Sat 10am–noon, closed all hols; free), with one dusty room of objects associated with the author, who was born in Grenoble as Marie-Henri Beyle. You can also visit his grandfather's house, where he spent his childhood, at 20 Grand-Rue, just to the south (same hours; free)

On the east side of the bustling place Notre-Dame, Grenoble's newest museum, **L'Ancien Évêché** (Mon & Thurs–Sun 9am–7pm, Wed 9am–9pm; 20F/€3.05), housed in the old bishop's palace, offers a fleeting retrospective of Grenoble's history from the Stone Age to the seventeenth century. Among its prized exhibits are a good sixteenth-century triptych retable, known as the *Tours de Pins*, and a disappointing early Christian baptistery.

Other museums of note are the **Musée de Grenoble**, by the river at 5 place de Lavalette (Mon & Thurs–Sun 11am–7pm, Wed 11am–10pm; 25F/€3.81), and the **Musée Dauphinois**, 30 rue Maurice-Gignoux (daily except Tues: May–Oct 10am–7pm; rest of year 10am–6pm; 20F/€3.05), on the far bank of the Isère. The former is an enormous modern complex housing a gallery of mainly contemporary art. The building itself is impressive, but the collection is uneven, with many major schools of painting represented, though mostly by second-rate works. The best rooms are those of nineteenth- and twentieth-century artists (for example, Chagal and Matisse), but the contemporary section is marked by the mediocre work of local artists. The Musée Dauphinois lies up a cobbled path opposite the St-Laurent footbridge. Housed in the former convent of Ste-Marie-d'en-Haut, it is largely devoted to the history, arts and crafts of the province of Dauphiné; unlike neighbouring Savoie which was annexed only in 1860, Dauphiné has been French since the fourteenth century. There are exhibits on the life of the mountain people, *les gens de là-haut* ("the people from up there"), who (like most poor mountaineers) were obliged to travel the world as pedlars and knife-grinders. Many, too, were involved in smuggling, and there is a fascinating collection of body-hugging flasks used for contraband liquor. A well-produced audio-visual show, the *Roman des Grenoblois*, recounts the social and industrial history of the city, including the foundation of France's first trade union in 1803 by local glove-makers.

Also on the river's right bank, a few minutes' walk east of the Musée Dauphinoise, the **Musée Archéologique Église St-Laurent**, on place St-Laurent (Wed–Sun 9am–noon & 2–6pm; 20F/€3.05), is, for design and originality, Grenoble's best museum, and enjoyable both for adults and children. The history of the city is explained as you descend through various stages of excavations in this former church, passing through an early Christian necropolis, a high medieval cloister and an eighth-century crypt.

To the south of the old town lies the **Parc Paul-Mistral**, to one side of which is the Hôtel de Ville (1967), one of the earliest of France's now numerous and bold architectural experiments with its public buildings. In the park behind is an earlier and more frivolous structure, an 87-metre concrete **tower** designed in 1925 by Perret, one of the pioneers of avant-garde French architecture. The concrete looks shabby now and you could hardly call it attractive, but it is bold and unapologetically modern.

Across the road from the town hall, standing among the fine trees of the Jardin des Plantes is the **Muséum d'Histoire Naturelle** (Mon & Wed–Sat 9.30am–noon & 1.30–5.30pm, Sun 2–6pm; 15F/€2.29). It has a marvellous collection, though it's very badly displayed; and it includes all the Alpine birds of prey. Wedged between the park and the old town, you'll find the **Musée des Troupes de Montagne** at 19 rue Hébert (Mon–Fri 10am–noon & 2–5.30pm; free), a small museum devoted to the French mountain regiment, the Chasseurs Alpins. Just down the street at no. 14 is the **Musée de la Résistance et de la Déportation** (July & Aug 10am–6pm; rest of year Mon & Wed–Fri 9am–6pm, Sat & Sun 10am–6pm; 20F/€2.29), with a touching exhibition of photographs and memorabilia from the brutal Nazi occupation of the Dauphiné.

Eating, drinking and nightlife

Eating in Grenoble is a pleasure, with a wide variety of restaurants catering to all budgets and tastes – a call ahead is recommended for most of the places noted below. For something quick and cheap, head for the strip of near identical pizzerias on the north bank of the river.

Interesting, atmospheric places to **drink** are also easy to find, with places Grenette, St-André and Notre-Dame full of **café-bars**. On place St-André, *Le Bagatel* and *Le Perroquet* are particularly popular with the student set, as is the slightly tacky *Saxo Pub*, and the more reserved *Le Bibliothèque*, just behind the square. Another good spot is the *Café du Nord* in nearby place Claveyson, a typical old-style French café and a great place to people-watch. If you're feeling nostalgic for a pub and English voices, seek refuge at *Bukana*, on the riverside at 1 quai Créqui, while to find local bohemians, try the *Café des Arts* over the bridge at 36 rue St-Laurent. The popular gay establishment, *Le Queen's*, is west of the old town at 62 cours Jean-Jaurès. Grenoble's student population keeps the **nightlife** hopping during the academic year, with clubs like *L'Arkange*, 50 rue St-Laurent (Thurs–Sat), and *Le Vertigo*, 18 Grand-Rue (Wed–Sat 10.30pm–5.30am), among the liveliest venues.

Restaurants

Le Bistrot Lyonnais, 168 cours Berriat (☎04.76.21.95.33). Perhaps the best choice in town for a good-value traditional restaurant. Offers a good value *mini-carte* for only 75F/€11.44 and menus from 125F/€19.06. Closed Sat & Sun.

Café de l'Europe, 24 rue des Lesdiguères (☎04.76.43.03,35). Good fast service and subtle *gastronomique* cuisine are hallmarks of this respected establishment. Expect to spend 160F/€24.40 per person. Closed Sun, hols & Aug.

Le Couscous, 19 rue de la Poste. Popular and lively North African restaurant serving excellent couscous (*plat du jour* 45F/€6.86).

Le Jardin de Margaux, 10 rue de Pont Carpin (☎04.76.54.83.34). It's located on the far side of Parc Mistral, you'll need to take a cab, but once you arrive this understated *gastronomique* restaurant welcomes you with inexpensive and imaginative fare. Menus 90F/€13.73–130F/€19.83. Closed Mon, Wed & Sun evenings & Sat noon.

Le Mal Assis, 9 rue Bayard (☎04.76.54.75.93). A small and elegant traditional restaurant, serving dishes with a decidedly Provençal flavour and an excellent wine *carte*. The evening menu is 135F/€20.59. Closed Sun & Mon and mid-July to Aug.

La Mandragore, 11 rue Marx-Dormoy (☎04.76.96.18.95). The best of Grenoble's green cuisine, popular with local vegetarians and organic food fans, though it's à la carte only. Worth the long tram ride (line A to stop "St-Bruno"). Closed Sat evening, Sun & Mon.

à la Table Ronde, 7 place St-André (☎04.76.44.22.62). While not famous for its food – local fare which never quite rises above average quality – this is an atmospheric place, notable for being the second oldest restaurant in France (1739), numbering among its clients Rousseau and Léon Blum. Menus from 75F/€11.44 lunch and 105F/€16.01 evening.

Le Tonneau de Diogène, place Notre-Dame (☎04.16.42.38.40). A cheap standby, with uninspiring *steak frites*-type cuisine, but incredibly popular with tourists and a good place to meet fellow travellers. Closed Sun evening & Mon lunch.

Le Valgo, 2 rue St-Hughes (☎04.76.51.38.85). A cosy, rustic-styled haven in the heart of Grenoble, serving up traditional specialities of the Hautes-Alpes. Excellent value, with menus at 67–125F/€10.22–19.06. Closed Sun & Mon, Tues & Wed evenings, and Aug.

Listings

Bike rental Vélos de l'Isère, 14 rue des Arts (☎04.76.46.12.24).

Bookshop Decitre, 10 Grand-Rue, sells some English-language books.

Car rental ADA, 94 cours Jean-Jaurès (☎04.76.48.94.68); Auto Roule, 145 cours Jean-Jaurès (☎04.76.40.41.42); Avis, place de la Gare (☎04.76.47.11.33); Budget, 30 rue Emile Gueymard (☎04.76.46.66.90); Europcar, *gare SNCF* (☎04.76.86.27.81); Isère Location, 43 rue Nicolas Chorrier (☎04.76.21.78.38); Self Car, 24 rue Émile Gueymard (☎04.76.50.96.96).

Internet *New Age*, 16 place Notre-Dame (daily 7am–midnight).

Medical emergencies Centre Hospitalier Universitaire (☎04.76.76.75.75).

Police, 36 bd Maréchal Leclerc (☎04.76.60.40.40).

Pharmacy Pharmacie Bethalet, 8 place Victor-Hugo; Pharmacie de Château d'Eau, 6 place Grenette; late-night and holidays call the police for the "pharmacie de garde".

Taxi ☎04.76.54.42.54.

The Vercors and Chartreuse massifs

The **Vercors Massif** and **Chartreuse Massif** are very close to Grenoble, particularly the Vercors, which stretches out to the southwest, parallel to the River Drac on the west side of the N75. Chartreuse is northwest of the city, running up the west bank of the River Isère towards Chambéry.

Both ranges are relatively gentle and not too high, so if you're starting your Alpine ventures here, you can use them to break your feet in. The Grenoble CIMES office (see p.849) publishes route descriptions. Neither massif is heavily populated, and the lack of industry makes them authentic and unspoilt Alpine destinations, popular with all types of energetic outdoor enthusiasts from cavers to mountain bikers.

The Vercors Massif

The **Vercors Massif**, a limestone plateau featuring ridges, valleys and a variety of wildlife, is very pretty and undeveloped, but, unless you're walking, the only way to get around is to drive or hitch. CIMES leaflets detail a number of walks of varying difficulty around the area from the simplest and most accessible to St-Nizier, detailed below, to other good but more strenuous walks, such as Villard-de-Lans to Claix, near Grenoble (1700m descent; 7hr), and the circuit of Mont Aiguille, starting from Clelles (1hr by train south of Grenoble; 6hr 30min–9hr).

St-Nizier-du-Moucherotte

The easiest of the CIMES walks is a four-hour circular walk to **ST-NIZIER**, just over the rim of the Vercors Massif, with a fantastic view of the whole area. Start by taking bus #5 from place Victor-Hugo in Grenoble and get off in Seyssinet village by the school. The path starts about 200m uphill from the school on the right. For most of the way you follow **GR9** with its red and white waymarks. It is not difficult, but the path crosses the D106 a few times, and the continuation is not always obvious, so it is worth getting the leaflet. It is about two and a half hours to St-Nizier

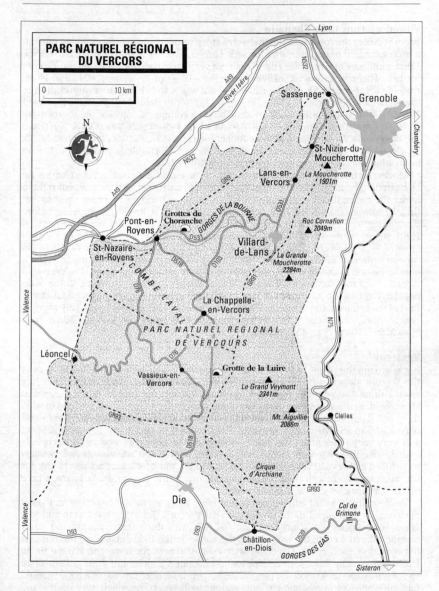

PARC NATUREL RÉGIONAL DU VERCORS

0   10 km

N

Lyon

River Isère

Sassenage

Grenoble

Chambéry

St-Nizier-du-Moucherotte

Lans-en-Vercors

La Moucherotte 1901m

Grottes de Choranche

GORGES DE LA BOURNE

Pont-en-Royens

Roc Cornafion 2049m

St-Nazaire-en-Royens

Villard-de-Lans

La Grande Moucherotte 2284m

COMBE LAVAL

La Chappelle-en-Vercors

PARC NATUREL RÉGIONAL DE VERCOURS

Léoncel

Vassieux-en-Vercors

Grotte de la Luire

Le Grand Veymont 2341m

Clelles

Mt. Aiguillie 2086m

Cirque d'Archiane

GR93

Die

Col de Grimone

Valence

Châtillon-en-Diois

GORGES DES GAS

Sisteron

(return the same way) through beautiful thick woods with long views back over Grenoble to the mountains beyond. The lovely purplish martagon lily blooms in the woods in early July. For a place to **stay** in St-Nizier, there's the unprepossessing *Hôtel Concorde* (☎04.76.53.42.61, fax 04.76.53.43.28; ③) and a small **campsite**. It is a further three and a half hours (there and back) to the top of **Moucherotte** on GR91.

Villard-de-Lans to La Chapelle

From St-Nizier the road winds up through a steep wooded gorge before coming out into a wide valley full of hay meadows towards Lans-en-Vercors and **VILLARD-DE-LANS**, 18km southwest of Grenoble. Villard makes a very good base for exploring the Vercors further. There is a **tourist office** (daily 9am–12.30pm & 2–7pm; ☎04.76.95.10.38, *www.ot-villard-de-lans.fr*) with information about walks and skiing. **Accommodation** in town includes the welcoming *Villa Primerose*, 147 av des Bains (☎04.76.95.13.17, closed Nov; ②), with self-catering facilities available in a communal kitchen; the inexpensive *Hôtel du Centre*, rue Gambetta (☎04.76.95.14.12; ③; closed part June, Oct & Nov); and the smart *Hôtel Le Pré Fleuri*, 509 rue Albert Piétri (☎04.76.95.10.96, fax 04.76.95.56.23; ④; closed May & Oct–Nov). For **food**, *Jack Burger*, 45 rue de la République, has an interesting selection of gourmet burgers from 40F/€6.10.

Moving on from Villard, turn right onto the Pont-en-Royans road into the **Gorges de la Bourne**. The gorge becomes rapidly deeper and narrower with the road cut right in under the rocks, the river running far below, and tree-hung cliffs almost shutting out the sky above. Take a left fork here and climb up to a lovely green valley before descending to St-Martin and **LA CHAPELLE**, where there's the reasonably priced *Hôtel de la Poste* (☎04.75.90.73.12; ③), and the more comfortable *Le Mistral* (☎04.75.01.22.42, fax 04.75.51.01.04; ③). From La Chapelle the road climbs again to the wide dry **plateau of Vassieux**, bordered to the east by a rocky ridge rising from thick pine forest and to the west by low hills covered with scrubby vegetation. Underground is interesting too: stay on the road to Pont-en-Royans and you will come to the over-popular **Grottes de Choranche**, renowned for the beauty of its gigantic stalactites. Part of the complex, the Grotte de Coufin, can be visited by **guided tour** (daily roughly hourly: April, May, Sept & Oct 9.30am–noon & 1.30–6pm; July & Aug 9.30am–6pm; Nov–March 10am–5pm; 43F/€6.56).

Vassieux

It was around the village of **VASSIEUX**, 10km south of La Chapelle, that the fighters of the Vercors *maquis* suffered a bloody and bitter defeat at the hands of the SS in July 1944. During 1942–43 they had been gradually turning the Vercors into a Resistance stronghold, to the annoyance of the Germans who finally, in June 1944, decided to wipe them out. They encircled and attacked the *maquisards* with vastly superior forces and parachuted an SS division into Vassieux. The French appealed in vain for Allied support and were very bitter about the lack of response. The Germans took vicious reprisals and, despite their attempts to disperse into the woods, 700 *maquisards* and civilians were killed and several villages razed. The Germans' most ferocious act was to murder the wounded, along with their nurses and doctors, in the **Grotte de la Liure**, a cave off the La Chapelle–Col de Rousset road.

Vassieux itself, a dull little village now rebuilt, has a memorial cemetery and small museum, the **Memorial de la Résistance du Vercors** (Jan–March & Oct to mid-Nov 10am–5pm; April–Sept 10am–6pm; 25F/€3.81), with documents, photos and other memorabilia to do with the *maquis* and the battle. In the field outside are the remains of two gliders used by the German paratroops. Also near the town, the **Musée de la Préhistoire** (daily: May, June & Sept 10am–12.30pm & 2–6pm; July & Aug 10am–6pm; Oct–April 10am–12.30pm & 2–5pm; 25F/€3.81) is built over the site of a 5000-year-old flint mine and axe works, and contains various tools and relics which have been found there. If you want to **stay**, try the comfortable *Hôtel Allard* in rue Abbé Gagnol (☎04.75.48.28.04, fax 04.75.48.27.49; ④).

Die to Grimone

From Vassieux, the **Col de Rousset** road winds south through 8km of woods of pine and fir before taking the final steep twisting descent of 10km to **DIE**, with terrific views of the white crags and pinnacles of the southeast end of the massif. Although it's an attractive little place, Die is worth no more than a brief stop – to sample the local *cré-mant*, Clairette de Die, which can be tasted and bought in the *caves* surrounding the town. There's a **tourist office** in place St-Pierre (May–Sept daily 9am–12.30pm & 2.30–7pm; rest of year Mon–Sat 9am–noon & 2–6pm, Sun 9.30am–12.30pm; ☎04.75.22.03.03). If you plan to **stay** the night here, there are five **campsites**, the cheapest being the *Camping municipal*, on the edge of town, as well as the modest but comfortable *Hôtel St-Domingue*, rue Camille Buffardel (☎04.75.22.03.08, fax 04.75.22.24.48; ③), with a restaurant serving menus from 90F/€13.73.

Six kilometres south along the River Drôme at the **Pont de Quart** the road forks left for **CHÂTILLON**, 6km away – not a bad place to take a break on a hot day, for you can swim in the river below the bridge. Châtillon village is lovely, lying in a narrow valley bottom surrounded by apple and peach orchards, vineyards, walnut trees and fields of lavender; it also has a couple of good **hotels** and a three **campsites**.

From here, the road enters the sunless trench of the **Gorges des Gats**, winding up between sheer rock walls to **GRIMONE**, a mountain hamlet on the flanks of a grassy valley with fir trees darkening the higher slopes. The **Col de Grimone** is visible above the village. A path cuts across the valley directly to the col from where it's about 7km down to the main Grenoble road, a tarmac trudge alleviated by the view eastwards to the mountains.

The Chartreuse Massif and Grande Chartreuse monastery

The **Chartreuse Massif**, designated in 1995 as the Parc Naturel Régional de Chartreuse, stretches north from Grenoble towards Chambéry and, like Vercors, it is not easy to visit without your own vehicle. The landscape, however, is spectacular, and very different to that of the Vercors: precipitous limestone peaks, mountain pastures and thick forest.

The main local landmark is the **Grande Chartreuse monastery**, situated up the narrow Gorges des Guiers Mort, southeast of St-Laurent-du-Port, and some 35km from Grenoble, one of seventeen Carthusian monasteries still functioning. The Carthusian Order, dating from the twelfth century, was the last great monastic reform movement, and was founded in answer to the degeneration of the Cistercian Order. Practising a strictly hermit-like existence, its members live in cells and meet only for Mass and a weekly communal meal, eaten in silence. Since 1605, however, the Carthusians have been better known as the producers of *Chartreuses* – powerfully alcoholic herbal elixirs, ranging from the better known green and yellow variants to a variety of gentler fruit liqueurs. The monastery is not open to the public, but near the village of **ST-PIERRE-EN-CHARTREUSE**, 5km back on the Grenoble road, you can visit the **Musée de la Grande Chartreuse**, formerly La Correrie monastery, which illustrates the life of the Carthusian Order (April–Oct daily 9.30am–noon & 2–6pm; 15F/€2.29). St-Pierre is also known for its annual festival devoted to Belgian-born singer Jacques Brel, which takes place in July. More information about the festival can be found at the **tourist office** at 58 cours Becquart-Castelban in **VOIRON**, the main town in the area, which is 30km west of St-Pierre (mid-June to Sept Mon–Fri & Sun 8.30am–noon & 2–6.30pm, Sat 8.30am–noon & 2–5.30pm; rest of year closed Sun; ☎04.76.05.00.38). While in Voisin, head for the **Caves de Chartreuse**, on boulevard Edgar-Kofler (daily: Easter–June, Sept & Oct 8.30–11.30am & 2–6pm; July & Aug 8.30am–6.30pm; Nov–Easter Mon–Fri 8.30–11.30am & 2–5.30pm), for a free visit and tasting of the sticky yellow or green liqueur. If you are looking for a **hotel**, St-Pierre has several options, the best of which is *Beau Site* (☎04.76.88.61.34, *christophesestier@csi.com*; ④; closed mid-Oct to Dec), while in Voiron you can stay at the small but comfortable *La Chaumière* (☎04.76.05.16.24, fax 04.76.05.13.27; ④).

Just south of St-Pierre, at the gorge's eastern end, a narrow road leads a couple of kilometres south to the village of **ST-HUGUES**. Its otherwise ordinary-looking **church** (Feb–Dec Wed–Sun 9am–noon & 2–7pm; free) has been transformed inside by local artist Jean-Marie Pirot (aka Arcabas), who was originally commissioned to redecorate the interior in 1953 and ended up making it his life's work. His paintings, tapestries, statues and, most notably, the stained glass make an unusual and striking impression and have earned Arcabas and the church a worldwide reputation.

Chambéry

CHAMBÉRY, 55km north of Grenoble, lies just south of the Lac du Bourget in a valley separating the Chartreuse Massif from the Bauges mountains, historically an important strategic position commanding the entrance to the big Alpine valleys leading to the passes into Italy. The present town grew up around the château built by Count Thomas of Savoie in 1232, when Chambéry became capital of the ancient province, and flourished particularly in the fourteenth century. Although superseded as capital by Turin in 1563, it remained an important commercial and cultural centre and the emotional focus of all French Savoyards: "the winter residence of almost all the nobility of Savoy", Arthur Young reported in 1789, before its mid-nineteenth-century incorporation into France. Today, however, Chambéry is a provincial town offering a couple of fairly good sights but otherwise little excitement.

The Town

Halfway down the broad, leafy boulevard de la Colonne is the splendidly extravagant **Fontaine des Éléphants**, an elaborate homage to himself by the Comte de Boigne, a native son who made a fortune in the French East India Company in the eighteenth century. Just south of this on square de Lannoy-de-Bissy is the **Musée Savoisien** (daily except Tues 10am–noon & 2–6pm; 20F/€3.05), which records the lost rural life of the Savoyard mountain communities. On the first floor are some very lovely paintings by Savoyard primitives and painted wood statues from various churches in the region; up above are tools, carts, hay-sledges, old photos, and some very fine furniture from a house in Bessans, including a fascinating kitchen range made of wood and lined with *lauzes* (slabs of schist).

Next to the museum, in the enclosed little place Métropole, the **cathedral** has a handsome, though much restored, Flamboyant facade. The inside is painted in elaborate nineteenth-century *trompe l'œil*, imitating the twisting shapes and whorls of the high Gothic style. The cathedral's **treasury** (May–Aug daily 3–6pm; free) is worth a look for a very early ivory diptych and a thirteenth-century pyx (a case for holding the Eucharist).

A passage leads from the square to **rue de la Croix-d'Or**, with numerous restaurants and the Italianate **Théâtre Charles Dullin**, named after the avant-garde director who was born in the region. To the right, there's the long, rectangular **place St-Léger**, with a fountain and more cafés, where street musicians and players perform on summer evenings. Rousseau and Mme de Warens lived here in 1735, and also had a country cottage, Les Charmettes, just 2km south of the town on the rustic chemin des Charmettes. It's now the **Musée Jean-Jacques Rousseau** (Wed–Sun: July & Aug 10am–noon & 2–6pm; rest of year 10am–noon & 2–4.30pm; 20F/€3.05), containing personal possessions of the famous philosopher.

Towards the northern end of the square, the town's smartest street, **rue de Boigne**, to the right, leads back to the Fontaine des Éléphants. But if you continue past this intersection, on the left, a narrow medieval lane, rue Basse-du-Château, brings you out beneath the elegant apse of the **Ste-Chapelle**, the castle chapel, whose lancet windows and star vaulting are in the same late Gothic style as the cathedral. It was built to house the Holy Shroud, that much-venerated and today highly controversial piece of linen brought back from the Crusades and reputed to bear the image of the dead Christ. The dukes took the original with them to Turin but a replica remains on display here. The chapel contains the biggest carillon in Europe, a 70-bell monster which you can hear in action on Saturdays at 10.30am and 6pm. To get into the chapel head left to the entrance of the **Château des Ducs de Savoie** (daily guided tours: May–Sept 2.30, 3.30 & 4.30pm; 25F/€3.81), which provides the only access. A massive and imposing structure, it was home to the dukes of Savoie until they transferred to Turin, and is now occupied by the *préfecture*. A short walk north from the door of the castle along promenade Veyrat is the **Musée des Beaux Arts** (Mon & Wed–Sat 10am–noon & 2–6pm; 20F/€3.05), a provincial museum with a collection of sixteenth- to eighteenth-century Italian works, including some good Renaissance paintings, as well as a number of less interesting nineteenth-century works. For those interested in medieval art, the church of **St-Pierre-de-Lemenc**, off boulevard de Lemenc (a twenty-minute walk north of the centre), is a must, featuring early Christian baptistery, Carolingian crypt and fourteenth-century sculpture (Sat 5–6pm, Sun 9.30–10.30am).

Practicalities

The **gare SNCF** is on rue Sommeiller, 500m north of the old town, with the **gare routière** (☎04.79.69.11.88) just outside in place de la Gare. Five minutes' walk away at no. 24 on the tree-lined boulevard de la Colonne, where all the **city buses** stop, is the **tourist office** (Mon–Sat 9am–12.30pm & 1.30–6.30pm, Sun 10am–12.30pm; ☎04.79.33.42.47, *www.mairie-chambery.fr*). If you are planning on exploring the Vanoise, the **Maison du Parc** at 135 rue Docteur-Juilland (☎04.79.62.30.54) can also help you out with maps and information.

There is plenty of inexpensive **accommodation** scattered about the centre of Chambéry: if you're on a budget, try the very basic *Le Mauriennais*, 2 rue Ste-Barbe (☎04.69.72.42.78, fax 04.69.72.46.85; ①), or *des Voyageurs*, 3 rue Doppet (☎04.79.33.57.00; ①), towards the *gares*. More expensive are the impersonal *Revard*, facing the train station at 41 av de la Boisse (☎03.79.62.04.64, fax 04.79.96.37.26; ④; restaurant from 62F/€9.46), and *Le Savoyard*, 35 place Monge (☎04.79.33.36.55, fax 04.79.85.25.70, *savoyard@cybercable.tm.fr*; ③), which is the best and most comfortable hotel, located south east of the cathedral. But for rural peace and a lovely view, head for *Hôtel aux Pervenches* (☎04.79.33.34.26, fax 04.79.60.02.52; ②), with a good restaurant serving menus from 95F/€14.49, in the village of **LES CHARMETTES**, where Rousseau used to live, 2km south of the centre. The nearest **campsite** is *Le Nivolet* (☎04.79.85.47.79) at **BASSENS**, reached on bus #C, direction "Albertville", from the tourist office.

Good **food** at decent prices is not hard to come by here. Mid-range Savoyard restaurants abound – many specializing in lake and river fish – the best of these being *La Chaumière*, 14–16 rue Denfert-Rochereau (☎04.79.33.16.26; closed Sun unless you reserve), and *Le Savoyard* in the hotel of the same name. If you fancy a splurge, however, truly exceptional *gastronomique* cuisine can be found at *Le St-Real*, in a converted seventeenth-century church at 86 rue St-Real (☎04.70.33.49.65; closed Sun), one of the best restaurants in the *département*, but pricey at 190–480F/€28.98–73.20. *Le Tonneau* on 4 rue St-Antoine (☎04.79.69.02.78), is a good alternative, with a similar cuisine, but at half the price.

Annecy and around

At the edge of the turquoise Lac d'Annecy, bounded to the east by the turreted peaks of La Tournette and to the west by the long wooded ridge of Le Semnoz, **ANNECY** is one of the most beautiful and popular resort towns of the French Alps, though the tourist traffic can get a bit wearing in high season. Historically, it enjoyed a brief flurry of importance in the early sixteenth century, when Geneva opted for the Reformation and the fugitive Catholic bishop decamped here with a train of ecclesiastics and a prosperous, cultivated elite.

Arrival, information and accommodation

The **gare SNCF** and **gare routière** complex is northwest of the centre, five minutes' walk north of the rue Royale. The road's continuation is the arcaded **rue Paquier**, which contains the modern shopping precinct of **Centre Bonlieu**, housing the **tourist office** (April to mid-June & last two weeks Sept Mon–Sat 9am–12.30pm & 1.45–6pm, Sun 10am–3pm; mid-June to mid-Sept Mon–Sat 9am–6.30pm, Sun 9am–noon & 1.45–6.30pm; Oct–March Mon–Sat 9am–12.30pm & 1.45–6pm; ☎04.50.45.00.33, *ancytour@cybercable.tm.fr*), who sell an excellent 1:25,000 map (57F/€8.69) of the Annecy area, showing walking trails. There are a number of **Internet cafés** in Annecy – in the old town try *l'emailerie*, faubourg des Annonciades (*www.emailerie.com*). There's **bike rental** from Sports Passion, 3 av de Parmelan (there are many other places to rent bikes around the lake – the tourist office has a complete list), and round-the-lake **boat trips** stopping off at various points along the lake – expect to pay around 35F/€5.34 per hour – from Compagnie des Bateaux or Bateaux Dupraz by the mouth of the Thiou canal.

There are a number of good, inexpensive **hotels** in Annecy. The cheapest in town is the small and serviceable *Rive du Lac*, behind the *gare* at 6 rue des Marquisats (☎04.50.51.32.85, fax 04.50.45.77.40; ②), but it's worth paying a bit more for better-located choices like the *Hôtel du Nord* (☎04.50.45.08.78, fax 04.50.51.22.04,

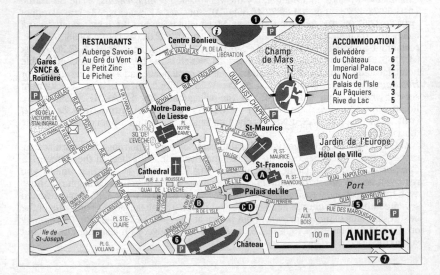

annecy.hotel.du.nord@wanadoo.fr; ③), and the *Hôtel Au Pâquiers*, 3 rue de Pâquier (☎04.50.51.09.67, fax 04.50.45.97.35; ③). Farther from the madding crowds, *Le Belvédère*, at 7 chemin de Belvédère (☎04.50.45.04.90, fax 04.50.45.67.25; ②; closed mid-Oct to April), has great views over the lake, while the homely *Hôtel du Château*, 16 rampe du Château (☎04.50.45.27.66, fax 04.50.52.75.26; ③; closed mid-Nov to mid-Dec), has a terrace overlooking the town. Upmarket options include the charming but cramped three-room *Hôtel du Palais du l'Isle*, 13 rue Perrière, in the heart of the medieval town (☎04.50.45.86.87, fax 04.50.51.22.04; ⑥), and the luxurious *L'Impérial Palace*, 32 av d'Albigny (☎04.50.09.30.00, fax 04.50.09.33.33; ⑨), in a beautiful mansion by the lakeside casino.

There is a modern **hostel** a short distance from the centre, just uphill past the Centre Hospitalier at 4 rte du Semnoz, overlooking the lake (☎04.50.45.33.19, fax 04.50.52.77.52; closed Christmas); follow the signs to Semnoz. The municipal **camp-site**, *Le Belvedere* (☎04.50.45.48.30), is situated off boulevard de la Corniche – turn right up the lane opposite chemin du Tillier; it's on the left past the *Hôtel du Belvédère*. There are other sites all around the shore of the lake.

The Town

The most picturesque part of Annecy lies at the foot of the castle hill, a warren of lanes, passages and arcaded houses, below and between which flow branches of the **Canal du Thiou**, draining the lake into the River Fier. The houses, ringed by canal-side rail-ings overflowing with geraniums and petunias, are incredibly beautiful, but the effect is marred by the fact that almost every shopfront in this area is a restaurant – at meal times it transforms into a vast outdoor mall.

From rue de l'Isle on the canal's south bank, the narrow Rampe du Château leads up to the **château**, former home of the counts of Genevois and the dukes of Nemours, a junior branch of the house of Savoy. There has been a castle on this site from the eleventh century. The Nemours, finding the old fortress too rough and unpolished for their taste, added living quarters in the sixteenth century, which now house the mis-cellaneous collections of the **Musée du Château** (April–Sept daily 10am–6pm; rest of year Wed–Sun 10am–noon & 2–6pm; 30F/€4.57), with archeological finds from the Iron and Bronze Ages and Roman period, to Savoyard popular art and woodwork. There is also an interesting and elaborate exhibition on the geography of the Alps.

At the base of the château is **rue Ste-Claire**, the main street of the old town, with arcaded shops and houses. At no. 18 is the **Hôtel Favre**, where in 1606 Antoine Favre, an eminent lawyer, and Bishop de Sales founded the literary-intellectual *Académie Florimontane* "because the Muses thrive in the mountains of Savoie". At the west end of the street is its original medieval gateway. Parallel to rue Ste-Claire, on the far side of the canal, rue J.-J. Rousseau passes the seventeenth-century former **bishop's palace** and the uninspiring **cathedral**, where Rousseau once sang as a chorister.

From the cathedral, you can either continue towards the train station on the far side of rue Royale, where the wider streets come as a welcome relief from the press of the alleys below the castle, or you could make your way back towards the canal. Here you'll find the picture-perfect Palais de l'Isle, a tiny twelfth-century fort which served in turn as palace, mint, court and prison (the latter as late as WWII), and now holds the **Musée de l'Histoire d'Annecy** (June–Sept daily 10am–6pm; rest of year daily except Tues 10am–noon & 2–6pm; 20F/€3.05), with a few unexciting exhibits relating to the town's past glories and, of more interest, the old prison cells. A few steps to the north, the fifteenth-century **church of St-Maurice** conceals some excellent fifteenth- and sixteenth-century religious art. Across the square to the east of the church from this, the **Hôtel de Ville** backs onto shady public gardens, from where a bridge crosses a canal to the lake side lawns of the extensive **Champ de Mars**.

Eating and drinking

Annecy's **restaurants** churn out rather unimaginative fare to feed all the tourists. You'll find a string of inexpensive **restaurants** overlooking the canal along quai Perrière, and rue Ste-Claire, among which *Le Pichet*, 13 rue Perrière (menus 78F–199F/€11.90–30.35), is dependable. One of the best venues is the *Auberge de Savoie* (☎04.50.45.03.05; closed Wed; menus around 200F/€30.50) on the far side of the canal at place St-François, serving Savoyard specialities and fish. *Le Petit Zinc* (☎04.50.51.12.93), nearby at 11 rue Pont-Morens, manages best to rise above the surrounding mediocrity, serving hearty Savoyard fare in a warm interior (lunch from 65F/€9.91, dinner from 150F/€22.88). For more adventurous cooking head to *Au Gré du Vent* (☎04.50.52.85.26; menus 85F–175F/€12.96–26.68), 2 place Ste Claire, with an exciting and varied *carte* that goes beyond the local *terroir* standards.

Rue Ste-Claire also has some of the town's liveliest **nightlife** in the music-bars *Pub Medievale* and *Red Zed*. And for a quiet coffee, the bohemian-flavoured *Café Cort*, by the old town gate at the end of the street, will fit the bill.

Around Annecy

While Annecy's high-season crowds may be bearable for only a day or two, the town's hinterland offers a number of agreeable ways to stretch your eyes and legs. As well as the **boat tours** mentioned above (see p.860), **cycling** is an enjoyable means of appreciating Lac Annecy. The forty-kilometre road circuit of the lake is a very popular Sunday morning activity among sporty Annéciens and a traffic-free cycle route follows the west bank of the lake. The surrounding hills offer walking and mountain-biking excursions (as well as more specialized pursuits) to suit all. The ascent of **La Tournette** (2351m) is one of the less demanding walks to be found in the forested **Semnoz mountains** on the lake's west side.

Ten kilometres west of Annecy, the **Gorges du Fier** and nearby Château Montrottier combine both natural and historical spectacle within a short distance of each other; and, if you're leaving Annecy to the north, the **Ponts de la Caille** are also worthy of a passing inspection.

Around the lake

Although a road rings Lake Annecy, a far more tranquil way of appreciating the lakeside is aboard one of the frequent boats that depart from Annecy's canal-side port, with the possibility of stopovers or returning later in the day.

On the east shore of the lake, signposted out of the village of **MENTHON-ST-BERNARD**, is the striking edifice of **Château de Menthon** (May, June & Sept Sat, Sun & hols 2–6pm; July & Aug daily noon–6pm; 30F/€4.57, 35F/€5.34 for weekend medieval costume shows). Inhabited since the twelfth century and birthplace of St Bernard (the patron saint of mountaineers for having established hospices on the Franco-Swiss mountain pass that now bears his name), the fortress was extensively renovated in the last century in the romantic Gothic-revival style and possesses a fine collection of period furniture and views across the lake back to Annecy. You can **eat** here at the lakeside *Buvette du Port*, which offers *plats du jour* for around 50F/€7.63. For a place to **stay**, continue a couple of kilometres down the road to the lovely lakeside village of **TALLOIRES**, whose ninth-century Benedictine abbey has been converted into the luxurious *Hôtel de l'Abbaye* (☎04.50.60.77.33, fax 04.50.60.78.81, *abbaye@alp-link.com*; ⑨; closed Nov to mid-April).

On the west side of the lake, the village of **DUINGT** occupies a peninsula where there are two more 1000-year-old **châteaux**, one in ruins and the other partly rebuilt. Like Menthon-St-Bernard and Talloires, it boasts a lakeside beach and gives the opportunity to rent pleasure craft. The town has a few good-value **hotels**, among them the *Hôtel Le Chalet* (☎04.50.68.66.51; ③; restaurant from 90F/€13.73). For a pricier but more tranquil overnight stay, head 7km south to the village of **DOUSSARD**, where the *Hôtel Grand Parc* (☎04.50.44.30.22, fax 04.50.44.85.03; ⑤) offers lakeside accommodation.

La Tournette and the Semnoz mountains

Experienced hill-walkers wanting a stiff but straightforward mountain ascent could tackle **La Tournette** (2351m), which dominates the east side of the lake with its patchy snowfields and crenellated summits. A road just north of Talloires crosses the **Col de la Forclaz**, doubles back to the left before the hamlet of **MONTMIN**, and ends in a steep but drivable track up to the **Col de l'Aulp**, less than 1000m from the summit. From the col, the climb is immediate, steep and clear, leading to a **refuge**, where late snow and increasing exposure demand extra care. Some scrambling (with fixed chains and handrails) is required to take you up to a broad, exposed shoulder. You cross some scree slopes and after a little more scrambling, arrive at the summit. To the east, the **Chaîne des Aravis** stretches before the snowbound massif of Mont Blanc on the horizon, just 50km away, while in the other direction the turquoise lake and Annecy itself lie at your feet.

Facing La Tournette on the lake's opposite shore, the wooded ridges of the **Semnoz mountains** offer less radical hiking. From the village of Duingt (see opposite), a four-hour walk leads southwards up the Taillefer ridge, involving just over 300m of ascent to the 765-metre summit of **Taillefer** itself. From the town church follow the signs for **Grotte de Notre Dame du Lac**, a steep walk up the ridge, and follow the red and yellow markers thereafter. Towards the summit of Taillefer, there is some scrambling, but nothing too difficult, and 1500m after the peak the path turns round and returns north via the hamlet of **LES MAISONS**.

The highest peak in the Semnoz is the **Crêt de Châtillon**, 16km directly south of Annecy along the D41. At 1699m it offers panoramic views, most impressively east past La Tournette towards Mont Blanc. A twenty-minute walk across meadows from the road's highest point leads to the cross on the summit and an orientation table pointing out the surrounding features.

The Gorges du Fier and Pont de la Caille

The River Fier, which trickles out of the lake through Annecy's picturesque canals, has cut a narrow crevice through the limestone rock at the **Gorges du Fier** (daily: mid-March to mid-June & mid-Sept to mid-Oct 9am–noon & 2–6pm; mid-June to mid-Sept 9am–7pm; 24F/€2.44). Signposted off the D14 at Lovagny, a footpath leads down into the 300-metre-long gorge which is traversed along a high-level walkway pinned to the gorge side. As you pass by the gorge, you'll catch glimpses of the **Château de Montrottier** (mid-March to June, Sept & Oct Wed–Sun 10am–1pm & 2–6pm; July & Aug daily 10am–1pm & 2–6pm; 30F/€4.57), which can be reached by continuing along the path for another 3km or by road from the car park. The castle, which dates from the thirteenth century, possesses an eclectic collection of furniture, earthenware and lace as well as exotic objects from former French colonies in West Africa and the Far East, amassed during the nineteenth century by one Léon Mares.

Sixteen kilometres north of Annecy, just after the N201 Geneva road parts from the *autoroute*, the highway spectacularly bridges the gorge of the River Usses, 140m below. Known as the **Pont de la Caille**, the present bridge was built in 1925, at which time it possessed one of the longest single spans in Europe. Next to it is the stunning spectacle of the original bridge, built under the orders of the King of Sardinia, Charles Albert, in 1839, and now disused. Its crenellated towers, supported by two dozen cables, are an impressive example of bold, mid-nineteenth-century engineering.

Northern pre-Alps: Samoëns and around

The **Northern pre-Alps**, climbing back from the shore of Lake Geneva, are softer, greener and a lot less crowded than the mighty ranges further south. A fine place to absorb the region's atmosphere is the gentle and attractive village of **SAMOËNS**, 21km from Cluses on the main Geneva–Chamonix road, lying at the foot of the Aiguille de Criou, with the tall peak of Le Buet in the distance. Its principal architectural claim to fame is its sixteenth-century Gothic **church** on a Romanesque base, with a doorway with crouching lions like those in the Queyras (see p.881).

The village is chiefly known, however, for its stonemasons and for Marie-Louise Cognacq-Jay, who left to seek her fortune in Paris at the age of 15 in 1853, and found it – as the founder of the famous French department store, La Samaritaine. There is a beautiful **botanical garden** (daily: summer 8am–noon & 1.30–7pm; winter 8am–noon & 1.30–5.30pm; free) on the slope above the old village centre, created by Madame Jay and planted with specimens of mountain flora from all over the world. Hers was an exceptional success, but migration was part of the pattern of local life. Up to World War I the men of the village would set out every spring with their tools on their backs to seek work in the cities of France and Switzerland. Their guild, *les frahans*, evolved its own peculiar dialect, *le mourne*, so they could communicate secretly among themselves.

For a **hotel**, try *Les Drugères* (☎04.50.34.43.84, fax 04.50.34.19.06; ④; closed May & Nov; restaurant from 75F/€11.44) or the *Gai Soleil* (☎04.50.34.40.74, fax 04.50.34.10.78; ④) at the north end of town, both of which have good-sized, comfortable rooms. There is a municipal **campsite** by the River Giffre, which meanders around the town, and a **gîte d'étape**, *Les Moulins*, 1km away on the road up to Les Allamands (☎04.50.34.95.69).

Sixt and the Cirque du Fer-à-Cheval

East of Samoëns, the valley narrows into the **Gorge des Tines** before opening out again at **SIXT**, 7km away, another pretty village on the confluence of two branches of the Giffre: the Giffre-Haut, which comes down from Salvagny; and the Giffre-Bas, which rises in the **Cirque du Fer-à-Cheval**.

The cirque begins about 6km from Sixt – there is a footpath along the left bank of the Giffre-Bas. It is a vast semi-circle of rock walls, up to 700m in height and 4–5km long, blue with haze on a summer's day and striated with the long chains of white water from the waterfalls. The left-hand end of the cirque is dominated by a huge spike of rock known as *La Corne du Chamois* (The Goat's Horn). At its foot the valley of the Giffre bends sharply north to its source in the glaciers above the Fond de la Combe. The bowl of the cirque is thickly wooded except for a circular meadow in the middle where the road ends.

There is a **tourist office** and a **park office** in **SIXT** (both Mon–Sat 9am–noon & 2–7pm; ☎04.50.34.40.28, fax 04.50.34.95.82). The park office produces a useful and well-illustrated folder of walks in the region. Sixt also has three *gîtes d'étape* and a **hotel**, the *Beau Site* (☎04.50.34.44.05, hotel.beau.site@wanadoo.fr; ④; closed mid-April to mid-June & mid-Sept to Dec), a modern chalet with an outdoor pool.

Abondance

The drive across country by the back roads from Samoëns to Évian takes you through some lovely scenery. If you are tempted to stay longer, **ABONDANCE**, in the middle of the Chablais region, is the place to make for. Remote and beautiful, it is renowned for its **abbey** and cloisters. There is a **gîte d'étape** here (☎04.50.73.12.93) and several **hotels**, the best of which are *La Rocaille* (☎04.50.73.01.74, fax 04.50.73.07.10; ②) and the *Hôtel L'Abbaye* (☎04.50.73.02.03, fax 04.50.81.60.46; ③).

Évian and Lake Geneva

Some 40km north of Annecy lies the dolphin-shaped expanse of **Lake Geneva** ("Lac Léman" to the French), forming a natural border with Switzerland. Around 70km long, 13km wide and an amazing 310m deep, the lake is fed and drained by the Rhône. It is a real inland sea, subject to violent storms, as Byron and Shelley discovered to their discomfort in 1816. On a calm day, though, sailing slowly across its silky-smooth surface is a serene experience.

There probably isn't any point in visiting **ÉVIAN** unless you are a well-heeled invalid or gambler, but it's actually a very unspoilt, peaceful town, and makes a pleasant base from which to take a leisurely trip on the lake. The mineral water for which the town is famous is now bottled at Amphion, 3km along the lakeside, but the **Source Cachat** still bubbles away behind the Évian company's beautiful nineteenth-century offices in rue Nationale, all wood, coloured glass, cupolas and patterned tiles. Anyone can go along and help themselves to spring water.

The **waterfront** is elegantly laid out with squares of billiard-table grass, brilliant flower beds and trees, mini-golf, water slides and other peaceful ways of amusing oneself. In summer, the **Centre Nautique** swimming pool complex also has outdoor film screenings by the lake. There are **ferries** to explore other towns around the lake, including Lausanne (9 daily; 104F/€15.86 return) and Geneva (2 daily; 160F/€24.40 return) in Switzerland and the medieval town of Yvoire (2 daily; 137.60F/€20.89 return) and Thonon-les-Bains on the French side (9 daily; 84F/€12.81 return). CGN Ferries also runs a number of sightseeing **cruises** (174–208F/€26.54–31.72), which do circuits of the lake, stopping at the most picturesque spots; enquire at the tourist office for routes and times.

The **tourist office** is in place d'Allinges (May–Sept Mon–Fri 8.30am–12.30pm & 2–7pm, Sat 9am–noon & 3–7pm, Sun 10am–noon & 3–6pm; rest of year Mon–Fri 8.30am–12.30pm & 2–7pm; ☎04.50.75.04.26, *www.eviantourism.com*). Évian has several **hotels** that can severely dent your wallet, but you can avoid these by heading straight for a wonderful place in the centre of town, the *Hôtel Continental*, 65 rue Nationale (☎04.50.75.37.54, fax 04.50.75.31.11, *hcontinental-evian@wanadoo.fr*; ③ summer, ④ winter), run by a friendly French-American couple, with rooms on the top floor that have a view of the lake. Alternatively, the *Terminus*, at 32 av le Gare (☎04.50.75.15.07, fax 04.50.74.63.23; ④), is a good, basic option and handy for the train station, while the water-side *Littoral*, quai Barron de Blonay (☎04.50.75.64.00, fax 04.50.75.30.04; ⑤), provides three-star amenities without breaking the bank. There is also a **hostel** on avenue de Neuvecelle (☎04.50.75.35.87, *jpteil@cur-archamps.fr*) – the D21 towards Abondance – and a **campsite**, the *Grande Rive*, off avenue Grande-Rive (closed Oct–March), less than 1km from the town centre.

Mont Blanc

Due east from Annecy, and 60km south of Évian, looms **Mont Blanc**, western Europe's highest peak, right on the Italian border. First climbed in 1786, this mountain is the biggest tourist draw in the Alps, but its grandeur is undiminished by the hordes of visitors, and if you're walking in the area, you can soon get away from the crowds. Annecy is the easiest place to approach the mountain from, and, of the two road routes, the one due east via the old ski resort of Megève is the more interesting. The two main approach roads to Mont Blanc come together at Le Fayet, a village just outside St-Gervais, where the **tramway du Mont Blanc** begins its 75-minute haul to the **Nid d'Aigle**, a vantage point on the northwest slope (132F/€20.13 return). **Chamonix-Mont Blanc**, the base camp for all Mont Blanc activities, is just 30km further on.

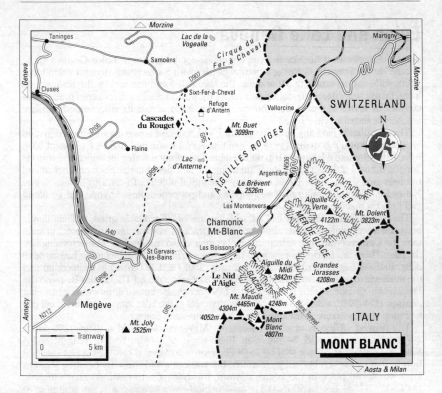

Chamonix-Mont Blanc

Expensive, tourist-choked **CHAMONIX** may have long since had its village identity submerged in a sprawl of tourist development, but the glaring snowfields, eerie green glaciers and ridges of shark-toothed *aiguilles* surrounding Mont Blanc are more than ample compensation. The town itself is of little interest, while being extremely expensive, and it crawls with tourists in the high summer season. The **Musée Alpin**, off avenue Michel-Croz in the town centre (daily: June to mid-Oct 2–7pm; Christmas–May 3–7pm; 10F/€1.52), will interest mountaineers, but its collection of equipment and documents is a bit disappointing. The star exhibit is Jacques Balmat's account of his first ascent of Mont Blanc in 1786, written in almost phonetically spelt French.

Practicalities

The **tourist office**, at 45 place du Triangle-de-l'Amitié (daily: July & Aug 8.30am–7.30pm; rest of year 8.30am–12.30pm & 2–7pm; ☎04.50.53.00.24, fax 04.50.53.58.90, *www.chamonix.com*), offers up-to-the minute **walking and climbing information**, as does the nearby Maison de la Montagne, which houses the Compagnie des Guides (☎04.50.53.00.88, fax 04.50.53.48.44, *info@cieguides-chamonix.com*), the Office de Haute Montagne (☎04.50.53.22.08, *ohm-info@chamonix.com*) and a meteorological service. The tourist office also publishes a **map** of summer walks in the area (25F/€3,81), while the guides run rock- and ice-climbing schools and will, if you wish, accompany you on any expedition they reckon is within your capabilities.

ACCOMMODATION

One of the biggest headaches in Chamonix can be **finding a bed**, especially if, as a walker or climber, you're having to sit out bad weather while waiting to get into the hills – the weather in Chamonix is notoriously fickle. All hotels need booking in advance and tend to be expensive; however, there is a fair supply of hostel or *gîte* accommodation. The best of the budget **hotels** are *La Boule de Neige*, 362 rue J. Vallot (☎04.50.53.04.48, fax 04.50.55.91.09, *laboule@claranet.fr*, ③), and *Hôtel Crèmerie Balmat*, 749 chemin des Crèmeries (☎04.50.53.24.44; ③). At 58 place de l'Église, *Hôtel le Chamonix* (☎04.50.53.11.07, fax 04.50.53.64.78; ④) offers simple comfort and a central location, while if you don't mind a bit of a walk *Le Relais de Gaillands*, 964 rte des Gaillands (☎04.50.53.13.58, fax 04.50.55.85.06; ④), is better value. Higher up on the price scale, try the luxurious and fully equipped chalets *Les Aiglons* at 270 av de Courmayeur (☎04.50.55.90.93, fax 04.50.53.51.08, *www.aiglons.com*; ⑦), or Chamonix's best hotel, the ultra-swish *Auberge du Bois Pins* (☎04.50.53.33.51, fax 04.50.53.48.75, *www .relaischateaux.fr/boisprin*; ⑨), at 79 chemin de l'Hernigne, both with great access to the *pistes*. There are further hotel options 3km north of central Chamonix in the suburb of Les Praz, including *La Bagna*, 337 rte des Gaudenays (☎04.50.53.62.90, fax 04.50.53.04.88; ②), while in Argentière, a further 5km towards Switzerland you'll find *Le Belvédère*, 501 rte du Plagnolet (☎ & fax 04.50.54.02.59, *PSCH296049@aol.com*; ②), and *La Boerne*, 288 Trelechamp (☎04.50.54.05.14, fax 04.50.54.15.53, *www.la-boerne.fr*; ②).

Gîte accommodation can be found not far from the centre, in rte de la Frasse: at *Le Chamoniard Volant*, 45 rte de la Frasse (☎04.50.53.14.09, fax 04.50.53.23.25; ④ with half-board compulsory), and *La Tapia*, 152 rte de la Frasse (☎04.50.53.18.19, fax 04.50.53.67.01; ④ half-board), which has wonderful views. For cheaper and more basic rooms, there's a *gîte d'étape*, the *Ski Station*, close to the Brévent cable-car station at 6 rte des Moussoux (☎04.50.53.20.25). The modern, comfortable and friendly **hostel** is at 127 Montée Jacques-Balmat, in the western part of town called Les-Pèlerins-en-Haut (☎04.50.53.14.52, fax 04.50.55.92.34, *chamonix@fuaj.org*; closed one week in mid-May & Nov to mid-Dec); take the bus to Les Houches and get off at "Pèlerins École" – the hostel is signposted from there.

Campsites are numerous, though in high season there may only be room for a small mountain tent. Two convenient sites are *Les Molliases*, on the left of the main road going west from Chamonix towards the Mont Blanc tunnel entrance (closed mid-Sept to May), and *Les Rosières* off the route des Praz (year round).

EATING AND DRINKING

For high-quality **dining**, head for *Atmosphère*, 123 place Balmat (☎04.50.55.97.97), offering elaborate dishes in a cosy setting for less than 150F/€22.88, or *Le Panier des Quatre Saisons* (☎04.50.53.98.77), which lacks atmosphere but serves up tasty affordable meals starting at 75F/€11.44. For a cheap meal, take advantage of hostel canteens where you can, or try *La Poêle*, 79 av de l'Aiguille-du-Midi, which specializes in omelettes (60–70F/€9.15–10.68), though it tends to become very crowded. Other possibilities are *La Belouga*, 56 rue Paccard, serving hearty sandwiches and *paninis*, and *Bistrot des Sports*, in rue Joseph-Vallot, a nice café with simple *plats*. Rue Joseph-Vallot has plenty of gourmet food shops with local cheeses and other Alpine delicacies. If you are after a **drink**, it's worth taking a look at *Le Choucas*, rue Paccard, right in the centre of town, or the *Wild Wallabies* bar in rue de la Tour, with pool tables, swimming pool, and Australian beers (summer 11.30am–2am; winter 4pm–2am).

Around Chamonix – the rack railway and cable car

There are a number of touristy but exhilarating excursions around Chamonix which you might want to experience – take your student card or hostelling card for reduced rates on some of the *téléfériques*. One is to take the **rack railway** from the Gare du

Montenvers through the pine woods up to the vast glacier known as the **Mer de Glace** (trains every 20min: May, June & Sept 8.30am–5.30pm; July & Aug 8am–6pm; Oct to mid-Nov & mid-Dec to April 10am–4pm; 116F/€17.68 return), a favourite with Victorian travellers. Once you get there you have the option of taking a short cable-car ride down into the **ice cave** carved out of the Mer de Glace every year.

A second excursion is to ride the very expensive *téléférique* (summer daily from 7am; return 200F/€30.50) to the **Aiguille du Midi** (3842m), one of the longest cable-car ascents in the world, rising no less than 3000m above the valley floor in two impossibly steep stages. Penny-pinching by buying a ticket only as far as the Plan du Midi, which is used principally by climbers heading up to the routes on the Aiguilles du Chamonix, is a waste of money: go all the way or not at all. If you do go up, make the effort to go before 9am, as the summits tend to cloud over towards midday, and huge crowds may force you to wait for hours if you go up later. Take warm clothes, for even on a summer day it will be well below zero on the top. You need a steady head, too: the drop beneath the little bubble of steel and glass is appalling.

The Aiguille is a terrifyingly exposed granite pinnacle on which the *téléférique* dock and a restaurant are precariously balanced. The view is incredible. At your feet is the snowy plateau of the **Col du Midi**, with the glaciers of the Vallée Blanche and Géant crawling off left at their millennial pace. To the right a steep snowfield leads to the easy ridge route to the summit with its cap of ice (4807m). Away to the front, rank upon rank of snow-and-ice-capped monsters recede into the distance. Most impressive of all, closing the horizon to your left, from the east to south, is a mind-blowing cirque of needle-sharp **peaks and precipitous cliffs**: the Aiguille Verte, Triollet, the Jorasses, with the Matterhorn and Monte Rosa visible in the far distance across a glorious landscape of rock, snow and cloud-filled valleys – the lethal testing ground of all truly crazed climbers.

A third – cheaper – alternative is to take the lift up to the **Glacier des Bossons** (daily: June 8.30am–6pm; July & Aug 8am–6pm; 50F/€7.62), where you can see the biggest precipice in Europe (a drop of 3500m), as well as the Alp's lowest ice face. A nature trail at the top, along with the spectacular views, makes for a good half-day outing.

Chamonix valley: some hikes

Opposite Mont Blanc, the north side of Chamonix valley is enclosed by the lower but nonetheless impressive **Aiguilles Rouges**, with another *téléférique* to **Le Brévent** (15min; 82F/€12.51 return), the 2525-metre peak directly above the town. Classic walks this side of the valley include the **Lac Blanc**, starting from Les Praz and the Flégère *téléférique* (20min; 57F/€8.85 return), and the **Grand** and **Petit Balcon Sud** trails, giving spectacular views of Mont Blanc. A highly recommended **two-day hike** is the **GR5** stage north from Le Brévent to the village of **SIXT** (see p.864) via **Lac d'Anterne**, with a night at the **Refuge d'Anterne**. The classic long-distance route is the two-week **Tour du Mont Blanc** (TMB), described in a *Topoguide*, Andrew Harvey's *Tour of Mont Blanc* and *Chamonix-Mont Blanc: A Walker's Guide*.

The Vanoise

The **Vanoise**, the rugged massif rising up to the southeast of **Albertville**, and over to the Italian border is a superb area for skiing and hiking. The dramatic range, whose highest peaks rise to altitudes in excess of 3500 metres is roughly diamond-shaped, hemmed in by the valley of the **Isère** to the northeast, where **Bourg-St-Maurice** is the best base for exploration, and the **Arc Valley** in the southwest. The glacier-capped southeast quadrant of the Vanoise, where both of these great rivers have their source has been incorporated in the **Parc National de la Vanoise**, across which lonely and spectacular GR trails offer unparalleled opportunities for seasoned hikers. Easiest road access to the region is from Chambéry or Grenoble, although driving the winding and precipitous old highways from Annecy or Chamonix is an adventure in itself.

The Isère valley

From **ALBERTVILLE**, 8km south of where the N508 from Annecy joins the N212 from Chaomnix, the N90 climbs southeast along the bends of the Isère River for 50km to **MOÛTIERS**, the turn-off for the massive Les Trois Vallées ski region (see box on p.871). Here the river course swings northeast, passing **AIME**, whose main Grande-Rue presents a pretty and little-spoilt succession of buildings. Six kilometres later, you reach **BOURG-ST-MAURICE**, the midpoint of the upper Isère valley, which is known as the Tarentaise. The town is of little interest itself, but it can be a useful place to stop. The big purpose-built ski resorts of **LES ARCS** and **LA PLAGNE** (see box on p.871) are nearby and the classic pass into the Italian Val d'Aosta, the **Col du Petit St-Bernard**, is right behind. It's a rather spooky crossing, reaching a height of 2188m, with a couple of barrack-like buildings and a row of statues of St Bernard. It's at its most dramatic when you're coming over from the Italian side in the early evening, right into the eye of the setting sun. (There is one daily bus crossing in July and August, from Bourg-St-Maurice to Courmayeur.) With its Swiss twin, the Grand St-Bernard, it was the only route around the Mont Blanc massif until the Mont Blanc tunnel was opened in 1965.

There are no very appealing **places to stay** in the town, with basic and functional *La Petite Auberge* just off the N90 on the Moûtiers side of town the best of a bad bunch (☎04.79.07.05.86; ②; restaurant from 80F/€12.20). There is also a **hostel**, *La Verdache*, just beyond Seez (☎04.79.41.01.93, fax 04.79.41.03.36, *seez-les-arcs@fuaj.org*; closed Oct to mid-Dec), 4km away on the dreary main road, avenue Leclerc, where you'll also find the **train and bus stations**, with the **tourist office** almost opposite (Mon–Sat 9.30am–noon & 2.30–6pm; ☎04.79.41.00.15, *www.ot-seez.fr*). The town's **campsite**, *Camping le Versoyen*, is on route des Arcs (☎04.79.07.03.45), on the right past the sports ground on the Val d'Isère road.

Twenty kilometres beyond Bourg-St-Maurice, a lane turns left into the valley bottom to **LA SAVINAZ** and **LA GURRAZ**, whose creamy church tower is a landmark for miles around. High above, though looking dangerously close, the green ice cliffs that terminate the Glacier de la Gurraz hang off the edge of **Mont Pourri** (3779m). From the turn, the lane veers steeply down through trees and hay meadows full of flowers, past ruined houses, to the river. The climb up the opposite bank is hard going, past impossibly steep fields. You take a right fork for La Gurraz across a rickety plank bridge in the jaws of a defile. It's about an hour's walk, once you're on the lane.

The village is tiny and untouched by tourism. Its dozen old houses have wide eaves and weathered balconies spread with sweet drying hay, and firewood stacked outside. The houses are all sited in the lee of a knoll for protection against the avalanches that come thundering off the glacier above, thousands of tonnes of snow and rock, almost sheer down into a cirque behind. If you are unlucky enough to be out of doors when an avalanche occurs, the blast knocks you off your feet and can even suffocate you. There are no provisions available, so bring your own. Other hamlets on the opposite flank of the valley are just as interesting, the prettiest being **LE MONAL**, in the mouth of a small hanging valley, also accessible by car from **LA THUILE**, further along the Bourg-St-Maurice road.

From La Gurraz, a signposted path climbs to **Refuge de la Martin** in an hour and a half. It zigzags up the slope behind the village of La Savinaz, onto a spur by a ruined chalet, where a right-hand path goes up the rocks overhead to the edge of the glacier. The refuge path continues left along the side of a deep gully, whose flanks are thick

SKIING IN THE ALPS

A home to downhill skiing since the beginnings of the sport, it was the Winter Olympics of 1992, based around Albertville, a grim, modern resort, which really brought the French Alps into the international skiing spotlight. High altitudes (ensuring good and lasting snow cover), long and varied runs, extensive lift-networks, excellent facilities, superb vistas and relatively mild weather make for some of the most enjoyable skiing in Europe. At any of the resorts you can simply turn up, buy a pass (150–250F/€22.88–38.13 a day, 800–1100F/€120–170 a week) and rent equipment by the day, though if you are planning on coming just to ski, your best bet is to arrange an accommodation/lift-ticket package from home; the price will be better and you will not have to look for accommodation, which can be hard to come by. High season covers the Christmas and New Year period and February through to mid-April, and should be avoided both for high prices and crowds; resorts usually remain open until at least the end of April. Finally, make sure your personal and travel insurance covers you for possible ski-related mishaps. Detailed ski information can be obtained from local ski clubs and organizations, or you could look online at *www.skifrance.fr*.

THE RESORTS
Most of the French resorts are ugly purpose-built affairs, but their layout is such that you can often ski straight out of your front door in the morning, and the lift systems are quick and efficient. There is also an emphasis on family skiing in France, with most resorts offering day-care facilities.

The best resorts lie along the Franco-Italian and Franco-Swiss borders. Of these **Val d'Isère** (*www.val-disere.com*) is deservedly known as one of the best ski stations, and, combined with Tignes, covers a massive area serviced by over 100 lifts, with a variety of runs, some as high as 3200m. Boasting many hotels, along with lively *après-ski*, the town is a good option for an impromptu stop. Its partner resort, **Tignes** (*www.tignes.net*), also features excellent skiing for all levels, but is more family-oriented, with fewer hotels and

with the white St Bruno's lily. It crosses a ferocious torrent by a plank bridge and follows a mule track up to the mountain pastures by the refuge, where cows and sheep graze. The **Mont Pourri glaciers** are directly above. Opposite is the big **Glacier de la Sassière** and up to your right Val d'Isère, with the Col de l'Iseran behind.

Tignes and Val d'Isère

Continuing south, climbing 10km further up the Isère valley from La Gurraz, you'll come to **TIGNES**, an unattractive, purpose-built resort on the artificial Lac de Chevril, which has little to offer aside from foot access to the Parc National da la Vanoise (see box on p.872) via the GR55, which passes through town, and a **hostel**, *Les Clarines* (☎04.79.41.09.93, fax 04.79.41.03.36, *tignes@fuaj.org*; closed three weeks in June). Linked to Tignes by ski-lifts, the resort of **VAL D'ISÈRE** sits in the shadow of the Col de l'Iseran on its north side; it is twelve kilometres further up river and is best reached by bus from Bourg-St-Maurice. Once a tiny mountain village, Val d'Isère is now a hideous agglomeration of cafés, supermarkets, apartments and chalets – with some of the finest skiing in Europe. It also makes a convenient centre for **walking** – details from the tourist office (☎04.79.06.06.50, *www.valdisere.com*) – but is no place to stay unless you're feeling extremely rich. In case you're not there's a **campsite** nearby on the edge of the resort at Le Laisinant.

The Col de l'Iseran

From Val d'Isère, both the D902 and the GR5 veer south from the river, climbing towards the **Col de l'Iseran**. Despite the dangers of weather and the arduous climb, bars. Despite its fame, **Chamonix** (*www.chamonix.com*), further north is not the most-user friendly of resorts, and access to the slopes is dependent on shuttle buses or having a car. That said, for advanced skiers, it is probably the best choice for its impressive range of challenging pistes, and with Mont Blanc looming above the scenery is unbeatable.

Further west from the Italian border, with good access to Chambéry and Albertville by road, Courchevel, Méribel and Val Thorens/Les Menuires make up **Les Trois Vallées**, the world's largest ski area. Its ingenious lift-network makes skiing from village to village easy, and near endless off-piste possibilities await the intrepid. Of the component resorts, **Courchevel** (*www.courchevel.com*) exudes expensive luxury, while **Méribel** (*www.meribel.net*) is traditionally British-dominated, with a good range of cheaper hotels and a lot of *après-ski* action. Ugly **Les Menuires** (*www.lesmenuires.com*) is family-oriented, with a fair number of cheap hotels, while younger crowds head for **Val Thorens** (*www.valthorens.com*), a hip resort particularly popular with the snowboard set, with a lively nightlife. North of the Trois Vallées, **Les Arcs** (*www.bourgstmaurice.com*), with its near identical concrete and glass hotels, is high on the list for North American travellers and snowboarders, and has a decidedly mellow *après-ski*.

On top of the famous centres, there are several less well-known but decent resorts. **Flaine**, north of St-Gervais (*www.flaine.com*), is a particularly good choice for novice skiers, with a generous selection of easier runs, though the town is shockingly ugly. **La Plagne** (*ot-laplagne@wanadoo.fr*), southwest of Bourg-St-Maurice in the Isère, is a huge ski-station, with a wide range of pistes for intermediates, though accommodation is dominated by apartments, and nightlife is minimal. For traditional Alpine atmosphere, La Clusaz and Megève, both of which are on the mountain route between St-Gervais and Annecy, are good choices. Although the pistes and snow conditions are not the best due to its relatively low altitude, **La Clusaz** (*www.laclusaz.com*) has managed to retain the feel of a village, and has a good range of moderately priced hotel accommodation. **Megève** (*www.megeve.com*) is the most beautiful French resort, with "olde worlde charm", a jet-set feel and a buzzing nightlife. Mediocre conditions are bolstered by extensive snow-making, but advanced skiers will be disappointed.

the pass has been used for centuries, being by far the quickest route between the remote upper valleys of the Isère and Arc. The volume of traffic was too small to disturb the nature of the tiny communities that eked out an existence on the approaches, but twentieth-century roads and the development of winter sports have changed all that. Small mountain communities have metamorphosed into monster modern developments, catering to an upmarket ski crowd.

From October to June, the pass is usually blocked by snow. But in summer, being the highest pass in the Alps (2770m), it is one of the sights that tourists with cars feel they must see; consequently it's relatively easy to hitch. A word of warning, though: if you do try, don't do it in light summer clothing, especially on a cool cloudy day, as temperatures can still hover around freezing point and blizzards are not unknown.

The GR5 reaches its zenith at the **Pointe des Lessières**, where on a clear day you have views of the Italian side of Mont Blanc and the whole of the frontier chain of peaks. Whether you head back or continue on to Bonneval (see p.872), the walk is a solid two and a half hours. If you continue south, a clear day will afford splendid views of the glaciers at the head of the Arc. As you descend along the Lenta stream through masses of anemones bloom in the stony ground, the riverbed winds through a desolate cirque, before dropping through a narrow defile towards the town.

The Arc valley

The **Arc valley** is wide and light below the col, though the treeless landscape can be more foreboding than joyous, especially under a stormy sky. Bare crags hang above the

THE PARC NATIONAL DE LA VANOISE

The **Parc National de la Vanoise** occupies the eastern end of the Vanoise Massif. It is extremely popular, with over 500km of marked paths, including the **GR5**, **GR55** and **GTA** (*Grande Traversée des Alpes*), with numerous refuges along the trails. For information on the spot, the tourist offices in Modane, Val d'Isère and Bourg-St-Maurice are helpful. The Maison du Parc in Chambéry (see p.859) also gives advice and sells maps.

To cross the park take the **GR5** from the northern edge of the transpontine section of Modane and follow it up to the **Refuge de l'Orgère**. Here a path joins up with the **GR55** leading north to Pralognan, over the **Col de la Vanoise** and right across the park to Val Claret on the Lac de Tignes – a tremendous walk. The GR5 itself keeps east of La Dent Parrachée mountain, describing a great loop past the **Refuge d'Entre-Deux-Eaux** before continuing up the north flank of the Arc valley and over the Col de l'Iseran to Val d'Isère.

steep meadows on the north flanks; glaciers threaten to the south and east. Descending through meadows and patches of cultivation in the valley bottom with the lighter foliage of larches gracing the mountainsides you pass through humble hamlets of squat rough grey-stone houses – the homes of people who have had to struggle to wring a living from harsh weather and unyielding soil. It is surprising at first to find such a wealth of exuberant **Baroque art** in the outwardly simple **churches** in small villages like Avrieux, Bramans, Termignon, Lanslevillard and Bessans. But probably it is precisely because of the harshness and poverty of their lives that the mountain people sought to express their piety with such colourful vitality. Schools of local artists flourished, particularly in the seventeenth and eighteenth centuries, inspired and influenced by itinerant Italian artists who came and went across the adjacent frontier.

The first settlement of any size as you descend into the valley is **BONNEVAL-SUR-ARC**, 1835m above sea level, at the foot of the Col de l'Iseran, which looks out on the huge glaciers of the **Sources de l'Arc** to the east. Better preserved and more obviously picturesque than other towns of the valley, Bonneval stops a lot of tourists on their way to and from the col. It is in danger of becoming twee, with its houses clustered tightly around the church, and only the narrowest of lanes between them. You sense how very isolated these places were until only a few years ago, cut off for months by heavy snow, forced in upon their own resources. Several graves in the churchyard record deaths by avalanche.

From here the valley descends to **BESSANS**, which retains its village character better than most. Its squat dwellings are built of rough stone with tiny windows, and roofed with heavy slabs to withstand the long hard winters. Most have south-facing balconies to make the most of the sun and galleries under deep eaves for drying *grebons*, the bricks of cow dung and straw used locally for fuel. The **church** has a collection of seventeenth-century painted wooden statues and a retable, signed by Jean Clappier. The Clappiers were a local family who produced several generations of artists. On the other side of the small cemetery, the **chapel of St-Antoine** has exterior murals of the Virtues and Deadly Sins and inside, some fine sixteenth-century frescoes; ask the priest to unlock the chapel – his house is on the right of the road leading east from the village square. Two kilometres beyond Bessans you pass the **chapel of Notre-Dame-des-Grâces** on the left, with another *ex voto* by Clappier. There is a small **tourist office** in the centre of Bessans (☎04.79.05.96.52, fax 04.79.05.53.11, *www.bessans.com*), and some **accommodation**, including the *Hôtel Le Mont Iseran* (☎04.79.05.95.97, fax 04.79.05.84.07; ④; closed mid-April to mid-June & Oct to mid-Dec). Alternatively, try the *gîte d'étape* in a handsome old farm on the opposite side of

the river from the village (☎04.79.05.95.84; meals available) in the nearby hamlet of Le Villaron.

In **LANSLEBOURG**, some 25km downstream from Bonneval, **Haute Maurienne Information**, in the town's old church (daily except Sat 3–7pm; ☎04.79.05.91.57, *www.hautemaurienne.com/culture*), organizes tours of the churches in Avrieux, Bramans, Termignon, Lanslevillard and Bessans, all within a twenty-kilometre radius of each other along the Arc valley. Lanslebourg is also the start of the climb to the **Mont Cenis pass** over to Susa in Italy, another ancient transalpine route. Last stop before the perils of the trek, it was once a prosperous and thriving town. Relief at finishing the climb from the French side was tempered by an alarming descent *en ramasse*, a sort of crude sledge, which shot downhill at breakneck speed, much to the alarm of travellers. "So fast you lose all sense and understanding", a terrified merchant from Douai recounted in 1518. Lanslebourg has a municipal **campsite** and a **hostel** with a fantastic view (☎04.79.05.90.96, *val-cenis@fuaj.org*; closed Oct to mid-Dec) and good rooms; alternatively, try the comfortable, rustic *Hôtel de la Vieille Poste* (☎04.79.05.93.47, fax 04.79.05.86.85; ③; closed Nov and weekends out of season; restaurant from 75F/€11.44).

MODANE, 20km downstream from Lanslebourg, is where the Arc valley starts to cut down dramatically through the high plateau, leading off towards Chambéry. It is a dreary little place, destroyed by Allied bombing in 1943 and now little more than a rail junction. Nonetheless, it's a good kicking-off point for walkers on the south side of the **Vanoise Massif**, the area contained between the upper valleys of the Isère and Arc rivers. It's easily accessible by **train** from Chambéry and has a **tourist office**, in place Sommeiller (Mon–Sat 9am–noon & 2–6pm; ☎04.79.05.28.58), which will give advice on walks in the surrounding area. If you want to **stay**, try the simple but clean *Hôtel Le Commerce*, 20 place Sommeiller (☎04.79.05.23.81, fax 04.79.05.00.78; ②), or the well-sited grassy municipal **campsite** just up the road to the Fréjus tunnel (which leads to Bardonecchia in Italy).

Briançon and the Écrins region

Only 26km south of Modane and nearly 100km east of Grenoble on the N91, you'll come to **BRIANÇON**, the capital of the Écrins. An imposing citadel set on a rocky height above the valleys of the Durance and Guisane only 10km from the Italian border, the town guards the road to the desolate and windswept **Col de Montgenèvre**, one of the oldest and most important passes into Italy. Originally a Gallic settlement, the town was fortified by the Romans to guard their *Mons Matrona* road from Milan to Vienne. During the Middle Ages, it was the capital of the République des Escartons, a federation of mountain communities grouped together for mutual defence and the preservation of their liberties and privileges. But, in marked contrast to the relatively untouristy Queyras (see p.880), Briançon and the other towns and villages on the northern side of the **Parc National des Écrins** are crawling with people in summer.

The **old town**, mainly eighteenth-century, is enclosed within a set of Vauban's stout walls. If you come in a car the best thing is to stop at the **Champ de Mars** at the top of the hill and look around from there. You enter the walls by the **Porte Pignerol**. In front of you the narrow main street, bordered by ancient houses, tips steeply downhill. It is known as the *grande gargouille* because of the stream running down the middle. To your right, you'll see the sturdy, plain **collegiate church**, designed under the supervision of Vauban, again with an eye to defence. Beyond it there is a fantastic **view** from the walls, especially on a clear starry night, when the snows on the surrounding barrier of mountains give off a silvery glow. Vauban's **citadel** above the Porte Pignerol, the highest point of the fortifications, can be visited for free at any time, and there are also daily guided tours in July and August at 3pm.

Practicalities

Briançon's **tourist office** is in the place du Temple close to the Porte Pignerol gateway (Mon–Sat 8.30am–noon & 1.30–6.30pm, Sun 10am–12.30pm & 2.30–6pm; ☎04.92.21.08.50, *www.briancon.com*). The mountain guides office is in Parc Chancel (☎04.92.20.15.73), and the Maison du Parc National des Écrins is in place Médecin-Général-Blanchard (☎04.92.21.42.15, *ecrins.brianconnais@espaces-naturels.fr*). There are a number of inexpensive **hotels** in Briançon, among which *Pension des Remparts*, in the citadel itself, 14 av Vauban (☎04.92.21.08.73; ②; closed Nov) is the best. The nearby *Hôtel aux Trois Chamois*, on the Champ de Mars, is another good choice (☎04.92.21.02.29, fax 04.92.23.45.89; ③), while down in the new town, closer to the station and services, *Auberge le Mont Prorel* (☎04.92.20.22.88, fax 04.92.21.27.76; ②) is a more basic place which attracts a youthful clientele. There's also a very nice **hostel** at Le Bez (Serre-Chevalier) (☎04.92.24.74.54, fax 04.92.24.83.39, *serre-chevalier@fuaj.org*), 8km north on the main Grenoble road – hitchable and also served by local buses. The nearest **campsite** is *Camping des 5 Vallées* at St-Blaise (☎04.92.21.06.27), 2km from town. There are a number of *gîtes d'étape*, including the cosy *Le Petit Phoque*, 2km along the Montgenèvre road at Le Fontenil (☎03.92.20.07.27).

As for **eating**, the old town has a number of good, affordable options. It's full of wonderful Italian cafés, with delicious cakes and pizzas, and there are plenty of reasonably priced restaurants such as *Les Templiers* and *Le Petit Bouchon*, both of which have patios on the place du Temple (beside the tourist office) and solid, cheap menus (from 65F/€9.91 and 75F/€11.44 respectively). Another good choice is *Le Pied de la Gargouille*, 64 Grande-Rue (closed Wed), where meats are roasted over the open fire in the centre of the dining room (menus from 75F/€11.44).

The Clarée valley

For a really beautiful day excursion from Briançon, head for the valley of the **River Clarée**. Without your own transport, you'll have to hitch or walk, but that should be no hardship because the scenery is truly magnificent.

Leave Briançon by the Montgenèvre road and take the left fork after 2km. A lane follows the wooded river bank along the bottom of a narrow ravine parallel to the Italian frontier. On foot you can follow the **GR5**, which passes through the main villages. If you want to spend a night up here, the depopulated and half-ruined hamlet of **PLAMPINET**, 11km from the beginning of the valley road, has both hotel and hostel-type **accommodation** in a vast renovated farm, *La Cleida* (☎04.92.21.32.48; ③; open mid-June to mid-Sept, and Christmas & Feb school hols), with comfortable beds, as well as better-equipped rooms at the *Auberge de la Clarée* by the bridge (☎04.92.21.37.71; ③). Alternatively, head for **NÉVACHE**, 6km past Plampinet, where the valley widens; it has already seen a good deal of holiday development, though the village's old nucleus of wide-roofed houses still huddles protectively around the **church**. This is worth a look for its carving, Baroque altarpiece and a few items in the treasury, including some eleventh-century doors. There are plenty of **gîtes** here, including *Le Creux des Souches* (☎04.92.21.16.34).

Beyond Névache, towards the head of the valley, the scenery becomes even finer – in May the meadows are carpeted with crocuses and run with snow melt, and fat marmots whistle from the rocks. Six kilometres past the village, there are more **refuges**, including two by the first bridge – *Fontcouverte* and *La Fruitière* – and another at the end of the road, as well as the CAF *Refuge des Drayères* on the slopes of Mont Thabor (☎04.92.21.36.01), none of which are open for much more than the summer season. A full list of refuges and *gîtes* with a map of their locations is available from the tourist office at Briançon.

The Parc National des Écrins

The **Parc National des Écrins** covers 93,000 hectares (230,000 acres) of Alpine terrain, some 50km southeast of Grenoble and 20km west of Briançon, its highest peaks rising to around 4100m in the **Massif de Pelvoux** in the north of the park. The easiest route into the park is from Argentières-la-Bessée, a scruffy, depressed little place, 16km south of Briançon. From here a small road cuts west into the valley towards Vallouise, with the ice-capped monster of **Mont Pelvoux** itself (3946m) rearing in front of you all the way. It's terrain for serious climbers and walkers.

La Bâtie and Les Vigneaux

The first place you come to on the road into the park from Argentières is **LA BÂTIE**, where there are remains of the so-called **Mur des Vaudois**. The origins of the wall are uncertain: it was probably built either to keep out companies of marauding soldiers–

turned-bandits, or to control the spread of plague in the fourteenth century. The wall has nothing, however, to do with the Valdois, a sect prominent in this part of the country (see box below).

A couple of kilometres beyond La Bâtie on the right is the lovely village of **LES VIGNEAUX**, surrounded by apple orchards and backed by the fierce crags of Montbrison. The village **church** has a fine old door and lock under a vaulted porch. Beside it on the exterior wall of the church are two bands of paintings depicting the Seven Deadly Sins. In the upper band, the sins are representations of men and women riding various beasts (a lion, hound and a monkey) and chained by the neck. A man carrying a leg of mutton and drinking wine from a flask represents Gluttony; a woman with rouged cheeks, green stockings and displaying an enticing expanse of thigh represents Lust. In the lower band they are all getting their comeuppance, writhing in the agonies of hellfire.

Vallouise

VALLOUISE lies under a steep wooded spur at the junction of two valleys, the Gyrond (or Gyr, as it is called upstream of Vallouise) and the Gérendoine, about 10km from Argentière. The great glaciered peaks visible up the latter valley are Les Bans; up in front is Mont Pelvoux. The nucleus of the old village – narrow lanes between sombre stone chalets – is again its **church**, fifteenth-century with a characteristic tower and steeple and a sixteenth-century porch on pink marble pillars. A fresco of the Adoration of the Magi adorns the tympanum above the door, itself a magnificent object, with carved Gothic panels along the top and an ancient lock-and-bolt with a chimera's head. Remains of an enormously long-legged figure, partially painted over, cover the end wall of the apse. Inside are some more frescoes, and at the back of the church six naive statues of painted wood.

The **GR54**, which does the circuit of the Écrins park, passes through Vallouise: the stage on from here to Le Monetier via **Lac de l'Eychauda** is one of the best. Another good walk is to the hamlet of **PUY AILLAUD**, high on the west flank of the Gyr valley. The path starts just to the right of the church and zigzags up the steep slope behind it with almost aerial views of the valley beneath.

Vallouise has a **campsite** and some **gîtes**, and several **hotels**: the *Edelweiss* is the least expensive (☎04.92.23.38.58, fax 04.92.23.33.46; ④ half-board; closed mid-Sept to mid-Dec), but all rooms in the village are likely to be full in July and August. The Vallouise Maison du Parc des Écrins provides **hiking information** and there is a **tourist office** in place de l'Eglise that opens sporadically (☎04.92.23.36.12). There is a minibus

---

THE VALDOIS

The **Valdois** ("Waldensians" in English) were a heretical sect founded in the late twelfth century by Pierre Valdo, a merchant from Lyon, who preached against worldly wealth and the corruption of the clergy, and, practising as he preached, gave his wealth to the poor. Excommunicated in 1186, the Valdois came more and more to deny the authority of the Church, and they sought refuge from persecution in the remote mountain valleys of Pelvoux, especially in the area around Vallouise and Argentières.

There was a crop of executions for sorcery in the early fifteenth century, and many of the victims were probably Valdois, burnt to death in wooden cabins built for this purpose. In 1488, Charles VIII launched a full-scale crusade against them. There is a spot west of Ailefroide (see opposite), known as **Baume Chapelue**, where they were smoked out by the military and butchered. After the Revocation of the Edict of Nantes, they were finally exterminated in the eighteenth century, when 8000 troops went on the rampage, creating total desolation and "leaving neither people nor animals".

service as far as Ailefroide in summer, starting from the bar next to the *Edelweiss* hotel; to walk takes two hours or so.

Ailefroide

The lane that continues another 6km up to **AILEFROIDE** is absolutely spectacular, as is the site of Ailefroide itself, overwhelmed by the daunting ridges, peaks and glaciers of Pelvoux and the **Barre des Écrins**, at 4102m the highest summit in the massif. The village is really no more than a huge campsite with a couple of shops and a climbing centre, overrun with climbers and walkers in July and August, and for that reason, it's not a particularly pleasant place to stay. Beyond Ailefroide, however, towards the end of the road at the Pré du Madame Carle and the old Refuge Cézanne, you'll be rewarded with some magnificent scenery.

The classic walk to do is the steep climb to the CAF **Refuge du Glacier Blanc** (☎04.92.23.50.24), right beside the beetling glacier, but it can be a real circus on a summer's day. Quieter, and a good deal longer, is the approach to the CAF **Refuge du Sélé** (04.92.23.39.49) and the Pointe du Sélé, due west of Ailefroide. But it cannot be over-emphasized that this is not afternoon-strollers' territory. The best guide is: if you haven't done it before, don't do it.

La Bérarde

To reach the tiny hamlet and mountaineering centre of **LA BÉRARDE**, right in the midst of the park's mightiest peaks at the end of the Vénéon valley, you leave the road from Grenoble some 6km after Le Bourg-d'Oisans (see below), and follow a very narrow lane for 38km up to the village. There you'll find a CAF refuge (☎04.76.79.53.83, *djacq@club-internetfr*; closed Oct–March), a mountain rescue base and the small *Hôtel Tairraz* (☎04.76.79.53.46; ④; closed Oct–March; restaurant from 90F/€13.73), which has adequate double rooms as well as dormitories. There are plenty of accessible valley walks without the need to risk your neck, including the approach to the back of the magnificent, near-4000-metre bulk of **La Meije**, with its dazzling glacier, the **Glacier Carré**.

North of the Écrins

Connecting Grenoble to Briançon, the **N91** twists through the precipitous valley of the Romanche and over the **Col du Lautaret** (2058m), which is kept open all year round and served regularly by the Grenoble–Briançon bus. As well as being an exciting foretaste of the high mountain scenery to come, this route offers the opportunity for some worthwhile detours, including the climb across the Col du Galibier to Valloire and hikes along the Valley of Guisane. Although it is not the biggest village along the route, **Le Bourg-d'Oisans** is an attractive town which is the traditional capital of the region. Sprawling **Les Deux-Alpes** is bigger, but has been wholly subsumed in the ski industry.

Le Bourg-d'Oisans

The first major settlement on the route, **LE BOURG-D'OISANS**, 20km southeast of Grenoble, is of no great interest in itself, but it's a good place to catch your breath. You can pick up information from the **tourist office**, on quai Girard, by the river in the middle of town (July & Aug 9am–7pm; rest of year Mon–Sat 9am–noon & 2–7pm; ☎04.76.80.03.25, *www.oisans.com*) and the **park information centre** on avenue Gambetta (July & Aug 9am–noon & 2–7pm; rest of year Mon–Fri 9am–noon & 2–7pm; ☎04.76.80.00.51). There are some good-value **hotels** here, among them *L'Oberland*, on avenue du Gare (☎04.76.80.24.24, fax 04.76.80.14.48, *www.oisans.com/hotel.oberland*;

③), the *Hôtel des Alpes* on the main road (☎04.76.80.00.16, fax 04.76.79.15.13; ③; restaurant from 68F/€10.37) and the *Hôtel Le Florentin* on rue Thiers (☎04.76.80.01.61, fax 04.76.80.05.49, *www.le-florentin.com*; ③; restaurant from 98F/€14.95). Campers are well catered for, with a municipal **campsite** on rue Humbert near the town centre and a concentration of sites across the river on the Alpe d'Huez road. The **restaurant** *Le Glandon*, specializing in grilled meats, also has rooms (☎ & fax 04.76.80.18.36; ③). If you like the idea of cycling in sharp mountain air, **bikes** can be rented from Cycles d'Oisans on rue Viennois – not such a crazy undertaking as you might think, for if you keep to the valley bottoms the gradients aren't too fearsome.

L'Alpe d'Huez

One place you're unlikely to be cycling to is the ski resort of **L'ALPE D'HUEZ**, signposted just outside Le Bourg. It is situated more than a vertical kilometre above the valley floor, and the eleven-kilometre road which crawls up the valley side is often used as a stage in the Tour de France. As you ascend through the 21 hairpins, you get a fine view of the acutely crumpled strata of rock exposed by passing glaciers on the south side of the Romanche valley. Undoubtedly a skier's paradise in winter, the purpose-built resort itself has little character in July and August, when it's only partially open. The extensive network of *télécabines*, extending as far as the 3327-metre **Pic du Lac Blanc**, at the bottom of the Chaîne des Rousses ridge north of the resort, does support some summertime skiing, but they can also be used to undertake some superb **high mountain walks**. Two recommended ones, detailed in the map *L'Oisans au bout des pieds* (15F/€2.29 from the tourist office – see below), are the eight-kilometre Lac Blanc and Refuge de la Fare walk, which winds through the bleak wilderness past the lakes encircling the Dôme des Petites Rousses to the east of the glacier-clad *chaîne*, or the less exposed ten-kilometre hike to the gorges of the Sarennes valley, to the east of the resort along the GR54. In addition to the locally published map, walkers should also pick up the IGN 3335E 1:50,000 map. A narrow and impressively scenic road through the Sarennes valley also offers an alternative descent back to the Romanche valley floor when the Col de Sarennes is free of snow. The **tourist office** in the Maison de l'Alpe, in place Papignon (July & Aug daily 9am–9pm; ☎04.76.11.44.44, *www.alpedhuez.com*), will give information about accommodation and walks.

La Grave and the Col du Lautaret

A few kilometres out of Le Bourg, southeast on the N91, the ascent into the **Gorges de l'Infernet** commences as the slate-black valley walls close around you, broadening out again as you cross the Barrage du Lac du Chambon, where roads diverge to the resort of **LES DEUX-ALPES** and the Col de Sarennes to the north. Continuing towards La Grave you'll pass two waterfalls issuing from the north side of the valley: early summer run-off will enhance the slender, 300-metre plume of the **Cascade de la Pisse**, while, 6km further on, the near-vertical fall of churning white water ironically called the **Saut de la Pucelle** ("the flea's leap") is a breathtaking sight.

    LA GRAVE, 26km from Le Bourg at the foot of the Col du Lautaret, faces the majestic glaciers of the north side of **La Meije**. It's a good base for walking: the **GR54** climbs up to Le Chazelet on the slopes northwest of the village and continues to the **Plateau de Paris** and the **Lac Noir**, which affords breathtaking views of La Meije. A similar and less energetic appreciation of these stunning vistas can be made by taking the **cable car** close to the 3200-metre summit of Le Rateau, just west of La Meije (late June to early Sept 108F/€16.47 return; late Dec to early May 187F/€28.52 return), a 35-minute ride that's very good value for money when you consider that the view of the barely accessible interior of the Écrins is normally seen by only the most intrepid mountain-walkers.

ASK IMAGES, TRIP

CHRIS PARKER, AXIOM

An alpine Ibex

Château de Peyrepertuse, Languedoc

M. HUGHES, TRAVEL INK

View from Salers, Auvergne

M. HUGHES, TRAVEL INK

NEIL SETCHFIELD

Mont Ste-Victoire, nr Aix-en-Provence

The cloisters of St-Trophime, Arles

CHRIS PARKER, AXIOM

Villefranche-sur-Mer, on the Côte d'Azur

Lavender fields in Provence

Olive market, Aix-en-Provence

The old town, Nice

M. HUGHES, TRAVEL INK

The old port of Marseille

A. SWAINE, TRIP

Calvi, Corsica

From La Grave it's only 11km to the top of the **Col du Lautaret**, a pass that's been in use for centuries. The Roman road from Milan to Vienne crossed it, and its name comes from the small temple (*altaretum*) the Romans built to placate the deity of the mountains. They called it *collis de altareto*. Around the col is a huge expanse of meadow long known to botanists for its glorious variety of Alpine flowers, seen at their best in mid-July. You'll also find a **Jardin Alpin** here, maintained by the University of Grenoble (daily 8am–noon & 2–6pm; July & Aug: 25F/€3.81, rest of year free), which includes plants from mountain ranges throughout the world. This is a great spot for picnicking or lounging while waiting for a ride, for the view into the glaciers hanging off La Meije is intoxicating.

The Galibier and Valloire

Turn north at Lauteret and you're on your way to the even higher **Col du Galibier** (no public transport), which is closed by snow from mid-October to mid-June – sometimes the snow lingers longer, making life for riders in the Tour de France yet more hellish. The road to the pass is a tremendous haul up to 2556m, utterly bare and wild, with the huge red-veined peak of the Grand Galibier rearing up on the right and a fearsome spiny ridge blocking the horizon beyond. The pass used to mark the frontier between France and Savoie, and you can see fine views of Mont Blanc to the north. A monument on the south side of the col commemorates Henri Desgranges, founder of the Tour de France. Crossing the col is one of the most gruelling stages in the race, with a long, brutal ascent and terrifying descent at breakneck speed. The road loops down in hairpin after hairpin, through **VALLOIRE**, a sizeable ski resort, whose church is one of the most richly decorated in Savoie, then over the **Col du Télégraphe** at 1570m and down into the deep wooded valley of the Arc, known as **La Maurienne**, with the Massif de la Vanoise rising abruptly behind. Valloire has pleasant, reasonably priced **hotels** in *Les Gentianes* (☎04.79.59.03.66, fax 04.79.83.36.55; ③; closed Oct, Nov & April to mid-June), and the *Christiania Hôtel* (☎04.79.59.00.57, fax 04.79.59.00.06; ④; restaurant from 85F/€12.96). There are *gîtes* nearby.

Le Casset

LE CASSET, back on the Briançon road about 12km beyond the Col du Lautaret, is a hamlet of dilapidated old houses clustered around a church with a bulbous dome. The site is superb: streams and meadows everywhere, reaching to the foot of the larch-covered mountainsides, the Glacier du Casset dazzling above the green of the larches. A good day's walk is to follow the **GR54** out of the village as far as the **Col d'Arsine** (about 3hr), from which point you can either turn back or go on down to La Grave on the north side of the park, making an overnight stop at the CAF *Refuge de Alpe/Villar d'Arène* (☎04.76.79.94.66), below the col.

The path from Le Casset crosses the Guisane and follows a track through dark woods, first on the left and later on the right bank of the Petit Tabuc stream. From the end of the track you cross some grassy clearings before entering the trees again and climbing up to a milky-looking lakelet, the **Lac de la Douche**, at the foot of the Glacier du Casset. From here a clear path zigzags up a very steep slope, coming out in a long valley and eventually leading to the Col d'Arsine. About halfway up are some tumble-down huts, the **Chalets d'Arsine**, by a series of blue-grey tarns. Up on the left from the chalets are a whole series of glaciers. The biggest is the **Glacier d'Arsine**, hanging from the walls of the long jagged ridge suspended between the Montagne des Agneaux and the Pic de Neige Cordier to the west.

For somewhere to stay in Le Casset, there's a **campsite** and **gîte d'étape**, *Le Casset* (☎04.92.24.45.74), near the church, with another (☎04.92.24.76.42) at neighbouring Les Boussardes. But provided you choose a spot where the hay has already been mown it seems you can camp anywhere. There are a café and grocery store in the village of Le

Casset, which is overcrowded in season. Other budget accommodation nearby includes a **gîte d'étape**, *Fourou* (☎04.92.24.41.13; closed Sept–Dec & May) in Monetier-les-Bains, and a **HI hostel** at Le Bez in the ski resort of Serre-Chevalier (see p.874).

Briançon to Queyras

The direct route from Briançon to Queyras, crossing the 2360m **Col d'Izoard**, is a beautiful trip, but you need a car do it – there are no buses. Leaving Briançon, the D902 begins to climb the steep Cerveyrette valley, the seemingly endless series of switch-backs entering an ever denser forest until it arrives at **LE LAUS**, a cluster of old stone houses with long, sloping, wooden roofs set in meadows beside the stream. Soon you reach the treeline and cross the 2360m **Col d'Izouard** to the **Casse Déserte**, a wild, desolate region with huge screes running down off the peaks and weirdly eroded orangey rocks. From the top the view extends over many kilometres of mountain landscape. Here you commence a vertiginous descent, entering another river valley, which is lined by a succession of tiny hamlets, **BRUNISSARD**, **LA CHALP** and, finally, larger **AVRIEUX**, lying in a high valley surrounded by fields and meadows, just 6km from Château-Queyras. A **church** with the characteristic tower and steeple stands guard at the entrance to the village. The **GR5** passes through, running a parallel route from Briançon; and if you do not have the energy to continue, the **hotel** *La Borne Ensoleilee* (☎04.92.46.72.89, fax 04.92.46.79.96; ③; closed Oct to mid-Dec), can put you up in no-frills style. If you started out late and can't reach Avrieux by nightfall, there are *gîtes* higher up in the valley: *La Teppio* (☎04.92.46.73.90) in La Chalp and *Les Bons Enfants* (☎04.92.46.73.85) in Brunissard. The **tourist office** in Arvieux (☎04.92.46.75.76, fax 04.92.46.83.03) can make further suggestions.

Parc Régional du Queyras

The **Parc Régional du Queyras** (*www.queyras.com*), spreading southeast of Briançon to the Italian border, is much more Mediterranean in appearance than the mountains to the north, with low scrub covering the mountainsides, poor shallow soil, white friable rock and a huge variety of flora. The park has some good walking opportunities, with the **GR58** path making a circuit of the park, running through **St-Véran** and L'Échalp, and the **GR5** crossing through Ceillac and **Arvieux** on its way from Briançon towards **Embrun**.

Mont-Dauphin and Embrun

From Briançon, the river Durance meanders leisurely through a wide valley, until some 27km later it passes **MONT-DAUPHIN**, a formidably **bastioned village**, and one of the many Alpine fortifications designed by Vauban in the seventeenth century, commanding the entrance to the valley of the Guil. From here **buses** leave for Ville-Vieille and St-Véran within the Queyras park. They meet the Paris–Briançon trains; the 7.40am bus going all the way to St-Véran (arriving 9.10am every day except Sun throughout the year), others only as far as Ville-Vieille (the 4.55pm operates only in the summer season). It is, however, easy to get a lift in these parts; there are always climbers and hikers with transport. There is a **tourist office** (☎04.92.45.17.80), a *gîte*, *Le Glacier Bleu* (☎04.92.45.01.58, fax 04.92.45.18.47), and several restaurants inside the walled perimeter.

Twenty kilometres further along its course the river reaches **EMBRUN**, 49km south of Briançon, a beautiful little town of narrow streets on a rocky bluff above the River Durance on the edge of both the Parc du Queyras and the Parc des Écrins. It has been

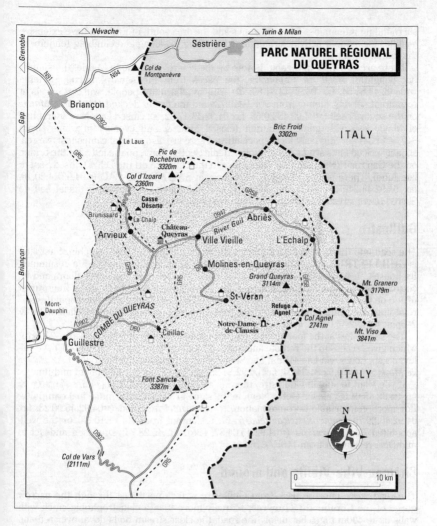

a fortress town for centuries. Hadrian made it the capital of the Maritime Alps, and from the third century to the Revolution it was the seat of an important archbishopric. Today it faces invading hordes of holiday-makers: the huge reservoir south of town, the Lac de Serre-Ponçon, has become the summer home of thousands of predominantly French caravan-dwellers. Its chief sight is its twelfth-century **cathedral** (concerts in summertime), with a porch in alternating courses of black and white marble in the Italian Lombard style, its roof supported on columns of pink marble resting on lions' backs – an arrangement that inspired numerous imitators throughout the region. The **tourist office**, in a former chapel of the Cordeliers on place Général-Dosse (July & Aug Mon–Sat 9am–7.30pm, Sun 9.30am–12.30pm & 4–7pm; rest of year Mon–Sat 9am–12.30pm & 2–6.30pm; ☎04.92.43.72.72, *www.ot-embrun.fr*), is next door to the bureau for **mountain guides**, which organizes a daily programme of walks in the surrounding mountains. The park zones and the area south of Embrun have extensive facilities for outdoor activities ranging from rafting to sailing and climbing (enquire at the tourist office).

There are two very agreeable **hotels** by the central place de la Mairie: the simple, but delightful *Hôtel du Commerce*, ten paces from the square in rue St-Pierre (☎04.92.43.54.54, fax 04.92.43.81.89; ②), run by charming people, with an excellent restaurant serving menus from 90F/€13.73; and the flower-decked *Hôtel de la Mairie* on the square itself (☎04.92.43.20.65, fax 04.92.43.47.02; ④; closed Oct–Nov & first half of May), also with good restaurant (closed Mon & Sun evening in winter; from 94F/€14.34) serving tasty local specialities. There are also several campsites: two reasonably priced ones are *Le Moulin* (closed mid-Sept to May), on the left after the bridge on the Gap road (N94), and *La Tour*, close to the Durance off the D994 (closed Sept to late June). There is also a **hostel** 10km away at **SAVINES-LE-LAC** (☎04.92.44.20.16, fax 04.92.44.24.54; closed Dec–March), overlooking the enormous artificial Lac de Serre-Ponçon created by damming and taming the wild Durance.

Guillestre

The road into the Queyras park follows the River Guil from Mont-Dauphin. First stop is **GUILLESTRE**, a pretty mountain village which only really comes to life in summer. Its houses, in typical Queyras style, have open granaries on the upper floors and its church has a lion-porch in emulation of the cathedral at Embrun. Head for the **tourist office** on the modern square at the top of the main street for information about the surrounding area (mid-June to Aug daily 9am–7pm; rest of year Mon–Sat 9am–noon & 2–6pm; ☎04.92.45.04.37, *www.pays-du-guil.net*).

The village lies at the foot of the long climb southwards to the **Col de Vars** (2108m), which gives access to the remote and beautiful walking country of the upper Ubaye valley; it's six hours, via Lac Miroir, Lac Ste-Anne and the Col Girardin, to the CAF *Refuge de Maljasset* (☎04.92.84.34.04, fax 04.92.84.35.28; closed Jan & mid-May to mid-June).

If you want to stay in Guillestre, there is a primitive **hostel**, *Les Quatre Vents* (☎ & fax 04.92.45.04.32; closed Oct & Nov), in the same grounds as the municipal **campsite**. For more comfortable accommodation, try the *Hôtel Martinet* (☎04.92.45.00.28, fax 04.92.45.29.79, *lemartinet@wanadoo/fr*; ③; restaurant from 70F/€10.68) or the well-appointed *Hôtel Barnières* (☎04.92.45.04.87, fax 04.92.45.28.74; ④; closed mid-Oct to mid-Dec; restaurant from 110F/€16.78).

Château-Ville-Vieille and around

The road route into the park from Guillestre strikes northeast through the narrow gorge of the **Combe du Queyras**, scarcely more than a claustrophobic crack with walls up to 400m high. Far below the road, the clear stream boils down over red and green rocks. It was only in the twentieth century that road-building techniques became sufficiently sophisticated to cope with these narrows – previously they had to be circumvented by a detour over the adjacent heights.

At the upper end of the Combe, the valley broadens briefly, and ahead you see the ruinous fort of **Château-Queyras** barring the way so completely that there is scarcely room for the road to squeeze around its base – Vauban at work again, though the original fortress was medieval. Just beyond is **CHÂTEAU-VILLE-VIEILLE**, where the road for St-Véran branches right over the Guil and up the ravine of the Aigue Blanche torrent. A smaller place than Guillestre, it has only a few old houses still intact and a **church** with its square tower and octagonal steeple flanked by four short triangular pinnacles – a style characteristic of this corner of the Alps. A Latin inscription in the porch says the church was destroyed in 1574 by the "impiety of the Calvinists" and restored by the "piety" of the Catholics. There is a painted sundial on the tower, which is also characteristic of the region.

Straight on, the road follows the Guil through the villages of Aiguilles, Abriès and La Monta (all with *gîtes d'étape*), to the **Belvédère du Viso**, close to the Italian border and **Monte Viso**, at 3841m the highest peak in the area. Above the Belvédère is the **Col de la Traversette**, where in 1480 the Marquis of Saluces drove a seventy-metre tunnel through the mountain. It has been reopened at various times through history, but is finally closed now.

East of L'Échalp, a variant of the **GR58**, which does the circuit of the park, climbs up to the **Col de la Croix**, used in former times by Italian peasants bringing their produce to market in Abriès. South of the village, the path climbs to the pastures of **Alpe de Médille**, where you can see across to Monte Viso, then on past the lakes of **Egourgéou**, **Bariche** and **Foréant** to **Col Vieux** and west to the **Refuge Agnel**; from here you can continue on to St-Véran.

St-Véran

At 2040m, **ST-VÉRAN** claims to be the highest permanently inhabited village in Europe. It lies on the east side of the valley of the Aigue Blanche, backed by hectares of steep lush mountain pasture, 7km south of Ville-Vieille. Opposite, rock walls and slopes of scree rise to snowy ridges. In the valley bottom and on any treeless patch of ground, no matter how steep, you can see the remains of abandoned terraces. They were in use up until World War II, though, as with most high Alpine villages, tradition-al farming activity has now practically died out. Today the principal economic activity is entertaining tourists. The route up from Ville-Vieille takes you through Molines, which – like its neighbours La Rua and Fontgillarde – seems to have preserved its traditional rural character better than St-Véran, with well-kept houses and hay meadows still neat-ly scythed by hand.

St-Veran's houses are part stone and part timber, and there are several refurbished old drinking fountains, made entirely of wood. The stone **church** stands prettily on the higher of the two "streets", its white tower silhouetted against the bare crags across the valley. The columns of its porch rest on crudely carved lions, one holding a man in its paws. The interior is surprisingly rich, with Baroque altars and retables.

Just south of the village, past a triple cross adorned with the instruments of Christ's Passion and an inscription urging the passer-by to choose between the devout or rebel-lious life ("l'homme révolté qui n'est jamais content"), the **GR58**, waymarked and easy to follow, turns right down to the river, beside which there are some good spots for **camping sauvage**. The path continues up the left bank through woods of pine and larch as far as the chapel of Notre-Dame-de-Clausis. There, above the timber-line, it crosses to the right bank of the stream and winds up damp grassy slopes to the **Col de Chamoussière**, about three-and-a-half hours from St-Véran. The ridge to the right of the col marks the frontier with Italy. In the valley below, you can see the *Refuge Agnel*, about an hour away, with the **Pain de Sucre** (3208m) behind it. From there you can continue to L'Échalp (see above). In early July, there are glorious flowers in the mead-ows leading up to the col: violets, Black Vanilla orchids, pinks and gentians.

It is hard to get good-value **accommodation** around St-Véran. The best deal for price is the *Auberge Monchu* (☎04.92.45.83.96, fax 04.92.45.80.09; ③ half-board per per-son; closed late April to early June & Oct to mid-Dec), which also provides *gîte d'étape* facilities. Otherwise, there's a couple of unremarkable **hotels** – *Le Grand Tétras* (☎04.92.45.82.42, fax 04.92.45.85.98; ⑤; closed Oct–May) and the *Coste Belle* (☎04.92.45.82.17, fax 04.92.45.86.62; ④; closed Oct & Nov) – and the *Les Gabelous gîte d'étape* (☎04.92.45.81.39). There are two small shops, and they have a tendency to run out of bread, fruit and vegetables.

travel details

Trains

Annecy to: Chambéry (several daily; 45min); Grenoble (several daily; 2hr); Lyon (several daily; 2hr); Paris (frequent; 4hr 30min); St-Gervais (10–12 daily; 1hr 15min–2hr).

Annemasse to: Annecy, changing at La-Roche-sur-Foron (4–5 daily; 1hr 30min); Évian (frequent; 35min); Paris (1 daily; 8hr).

Briançon to: Marseille (3 daily; 4hr 30min).

Chambéry to: Aix-les-Bains (frequent; 10min); Annecy (frequent; 45min); Bourg-St-Maurice (5 daily; 2hr); Geneva (several daily; 1hr 30min); Grenoble (several daily; 1hr); Lyon (frequent; 1hr 30min–2hr 30min); Modane (frequent; 40min–1hr 20min); Paris (frequent; 5hr 30min).

Evian to: Geneva (7 daily; 1hr).

Grenoble to: Annecy (several daily; 2hr); Briançon, changing at Veynes-Dévoluy (1–2 daily; 4hr); Chambéry (several daily; 1hr); Gap (1–2 daily; 2hr 30min); Lyon (frequent; 1hr 30min–1hr 45min); Paris-Lyon (several daily; 3hr 10min–7hr 15min).

St-Gervais to: Chamonix (5–7 daily; 35min).

Buses

Annecy to: Albertville (4 daily; 50min); Évian (4 daily; 1hr 30min); Lyon (2 daily; 2hr 30min); Telloires (6 daily; 50min).

Bourg-St-Maurice to: Aosta (1 daily July & Aug; 2hr 30min); Val d'Isère (1–2 daily; 50min–1hr 20min).

Chambéry to: Aix-les-Bains (several daily; 20min); Annecy (several daily; 1hr); Grenoble (several daily; 1hr).

Chamonix to: Annecy, via La-Roche-sur-Foron (3 daily; 3hr); Annecy, via Megève (1 daily; 3hr); Geneva (1 daily; 2hr 30min); Grenoble (1 daily; 3hr 30min).

Cluses to: Samoëns (3 daily; 35min); Sixt (3 daily; 45min).

Grenoble to: L'Alpe d'Huez (2 daily; 45min); Bourg-d'Oisans (4–6 daily; 1hr 20min); Briançon (several daily; 2hr); Chambéry (several daily; 1hr); Col du Lautaret (1 daily; 2hr); Gap (1 daily; 2hr 45min); La Grave (1 daily; 1hr 40min); Monetier-les-Bains (1 daily; 2hr 25min); Villard-de-Lans (at least 1 daily; 45min).

Mont-Dauphin to (summer only): Ceillac (2 daily; 35min); Guillestre (2–3 daily; 5min); St-Véran (2–3 daily; 1hr 30min); Vars (2 daily; 50min); Ville-Vieille (2–3 daily; 1hr 05min).

Valloire to (summer only): St-Michel-de-Maurienne (2 daily; 45min).

CHAPTER FOURTEEN

THE RHÔNE VALLEY AND PROVENCE

O f all the areas of France, **Provence** is the most irresistible. Geographically it ranges from the snow-capped mountains of the **southern Alps** to the delta plains of the **Camargue** and has the greatest European canyon, the **Gorges du Verdon**. Fortified towns guard its old borders; countless villages perch defensively on hilltops; and its great cities – **Aix-en-Provence** and **Avignon** – are full of cultural glories. The sensual inducements of Provence include warmth, food and wine, and the perfumes of Mediterranean vegetation. Along with its coast – which is covered in the following chapter – it has attracted the rich and famous, the artistic and reclusive, and countless arrivals who have found themselves unable to conceive of life elsewhere.

In appearance, despite the throngs of foreigners and French from other regions, **inland Provence** remains remarkably unscathed. The history of its earliest known natives, of the Greeks, then Romans, raiding Saracens, schismatic popes, and shifting allegiances to different counts and princes, is still in evidence. Provence's complete integration into France dates only from the nineteenth century and, though the Provençal language is only spoken by a small minority, the accent is distinctive even to a foreign ear. In the east the rhythms of speech become clearly Italian.

Unless you're intending to stay for months, the main problem with Provence is choosing where to go. In the west, along the **Rhône valley**, are the Roman cities of **Orange**, **Vaison-la-Romaine**, **Carpentras** and **Arles**, and the papal city of Avignon, with its brilliant summer festival. Aix-en-Provence is the mini-Paris of the region and was home to Cézanne, for whom the **Mont Ste-Victoire** was an enduring subject; Van Gogh's links are with **St-Rémy** and Arles. The Gorges du Verdon, the **Parc National du Mercantour** along the Italian border, **Mont Ventoux** northeast of Carpentras, and the flamingo-filled lagoons of the **Camargue** are just a selection of the diverse and stunning landscapes of this region.

Before you reach Provence from the north there are the **vineyards of the Rhône valley** and, before them, the French centre of gastronomy and second largest city of

---

ACCOMMODATION PRICE CODES

Each hotel and guesthouse in this book has been graded according to the following price codes, which indicate the price for the **cheapest double room available during the high season**.

① Under 160F/€24	④ 300–400F/€46–61	⑦ 600–700F/€91–107
② 160–220F/€24–34	⑤ 400–500F/€61–76	⑧ 700–800F/€107–122
③ 220–300F/€34–46	⑥ 500–600F/€76–91	⑨ Over 800F/€122

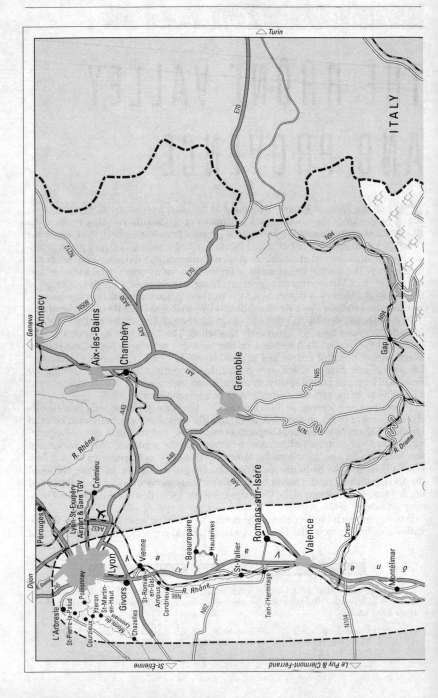

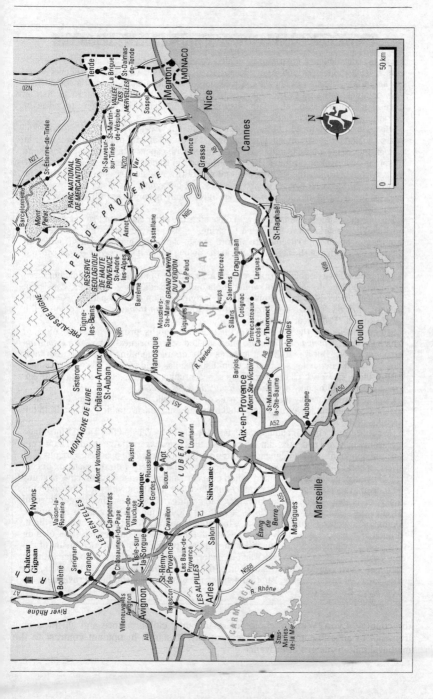

FOOD OF PROVENCE AND THE RHÔNE VALLEY

Lyon is renowned as a gastronomic centre, combining southern and northern ingredients. Its rich and hearty food is very meat- and offal-oriented, with sausages of every variety and a fine selection of cheeses. A Lyonnais salad includes bacon and a soft-cooked egg; potatoes also tend to be cooked with egg, cheeses and cream; and meat, fish or cheese are turned into fat, filling *quenelles*, or dumplings. Pâtisseries specialize in extremely rich chocolate gâteaux.

Olives were introduced to Provence by the ancient Greeks two and a half thousand years ago and today accompany the traditional Provençal apéritif of *pastis*; they appear in sauces and salads, on tarts and pizzas, and mixed with capers in a paste called *tapenade* to spread on bread or biscuits. They are also used in traditional meat stews, like *daube Provençale*. Olive oil is the starting point for most Provençal dishes; spiced with chillis or Provençal herbs (wild thyme, basil, rosemary and tarragon), it is also poured over pizzas, sandwiches and, of course, used in vinaigrette and mayonnaise with all the varieties of salad.

The ingredient most often mixed with olive oil is the other classic of Provençal cuisine: **garlic**. Whole markets are dedicated to strings of pale purple garlic. Two of the most famous concoctions of Provence are **pistou**, a paste of olive oil, garlic and basil, and **aïoli**, the name for both a garlic mayonnaise and the dish in which it's served with salt cod and vegetables.

Vegetables have double or triple seasons in Provence, often beginning while northern France is still in the depths of winter. Ratatouille ingredients – tomatoes, capsicum, aubergines, courgettes and onions – are the favourites, along with asparagus. Courgette flowers, or *fleurs de courgettes farcies*, stuffed with *pistou* or tomato sauce, are one of the most exquisite Provençal delicacies.

Sheep, taken up to the mountains in the summer months, provide the staple meat, of which the best is *agneau de Sisteron*, often roasted with Provençal herbs as a *gigot d'agneau aux herbes*. But it is **fish** that features most on traditional menus, with freshwater trout, salt cod, anchovies, sea bream, monkfish, sea bass and whiting all common, along with brilliant **seafood**: clams, periwinkles, sea urchins, oysters, spider crabs and langoustines piled into spiky sculptural *plateaux de fruits de mer*.

Cheeses are invariably made from goat's or ewe's milk. Two famous ones are Banon, wrapped in chestnut leaves and marinated in brandy, and the aromatic Picadon, from the foothills of the Alps.

Sweets of the region include chocolates, notably from Valrhona in Tain L'Hermitage and from Puyricard near Aix, almond sweets called *calissons* from Aix, candied fruit from Apt and nougat from Montélimar. As for **fruits**, the melons, white peaches, apricots, figs, cherries and Muscat grapes are unbeatable. Almond trees grow on the plateaux of central Provence, along with lavender, which gives Provençal **honey** its distinctive flavour.

Some of France's best **wine** is produced in the Côtes du Rhône vineyards, of which the most celebrated is the Crozes-Hermitage *appellation*. Once past the nougat town of Montélimar and into Provence, the best wines are to be found in the villages around the Dentelles, notably Gigondas, and at Châteauneuf-du-Pape. To the west are the light, drinkable, but not particularly special wines of the Côtes du Ventoux and the Côtes du Lubéron *appellations*. Huge quantities of wine are produced in Provence, many of the vineyards planted during World War I in order to supply every French soldier with his ration of a litre a day. With the exception of the Côteaux des Baux around Les Baux, and the Côtes de Provence in the Var *département*, the best wines of southern Provence come from along the coast.

the country, **Lyon**. With its choice of restaurants, clubs, culture and all the accoutrements of an affluent and vital Western city, it stands in opulent contrast to the medieval hilltop villages of Provence.

THE RHÔNE VALLEY

The **Rhône valley**, the north–south route of ancient armies, medieval traders and modern rail and road, is now as industrialized as the least attractive parts of the north. Though the river is still a means of transport, its waters now also cool the reactors of the Marcoule and Tricastin nuclear power station between **Montélimar** and Avignon and act as a dumping ground for the heavy industries along its banks. Following the River Rhône holds few attractions, with the exceptions of the stretch of **vineyards** and fruit orchards between the Roman city of **Vienne** and the distinctly southern city of **Valence**. But the big magnet is, of course, the gastronomic paradise of **Lyon**, with hundreds of sophisticated bars and restaurants.

Lyon

LYON is physically the second biggest city in France, a result of its uncontrolled urban sprawl. Viewed at high speed from the Autoroute du Soleil, the impression it gives is of a major confluence of rivers and roads, around which only petrochemical industries thrive. In fact, from the sixteenth century right up until the postwar dominance of metalworks and chemicals, silk was the city's main industry, generating the wealth which left behind a multitude of Renaissance buildings. But what has stamped its character most on Lyon is the commerce and banking that grew up with its industrial expansion. It is this that gives the town its staid, stolid and somewhat austere air.

The city is now busy forging a role for itself within a new Europe, with international schools and colleges, the new HQ for Interpol, a recently inaugurated eco-friendly tram system, a second TGV station with links to the north that bypass Paris, and high-tech industrial parks for international companies making it a modern city *par excellence*. More so than any other French city, it has embraced the monetarist vision of the European Union and is acting, with some success, as a postmodern city-state within it.

Most French people would find themselves in Lyon for business rather than for recreation: it's a get-up-and-go place, not a lie-back-and-rest one. You probably wouldn't plan a two-week stay – as you might in Provence's cities – but Lyon certainly has its charms. Foremost among these is **gastronomy**; there are more restaurants per Gothic and Renaissance square metre of the old town than anywhere else on earth, and the city could form a football team with its superstars of the international chef circuit. While the **textile museum** is the second famous reason for stopping here, Lyon's nightlife, cinema and theatre (including the famous Lyonnais puppets), its antique markets, music and other cultural festivities might tempt you to stay at least a few days. In addition it has been long established as the home of major **biennial festivals** of art and fashion.

Lyon is organized into *arrondissements*, of which there are nine. A visit to Lyon will necessarily take you into the Presqu'île (1e and 2e *arrondissements*), the area between the Rivers Saône and Rhône, and you are more than likely to spend some time in Vieux-Lyon (5e) on the west bank of the Saône, as well as the east bank of the Rhône (3e), including the modern development known as La Part-Dieu.

Arrival, information and city transport

The **Lyon-St Exupéry international airport** (☎04.72.22.72.21) and the new **TGV station** are off the Grenoble *autoroute*, 20km to the southeast of the city, with a 45-minute Satobus bus link to the town centre (50F/€7.53). The Paris to Lyon trip is actually

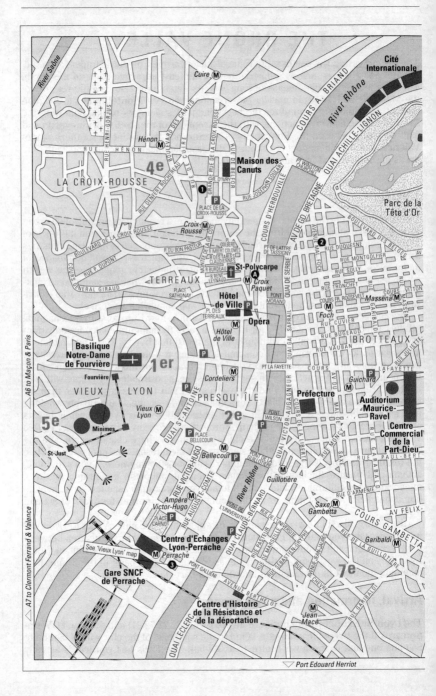

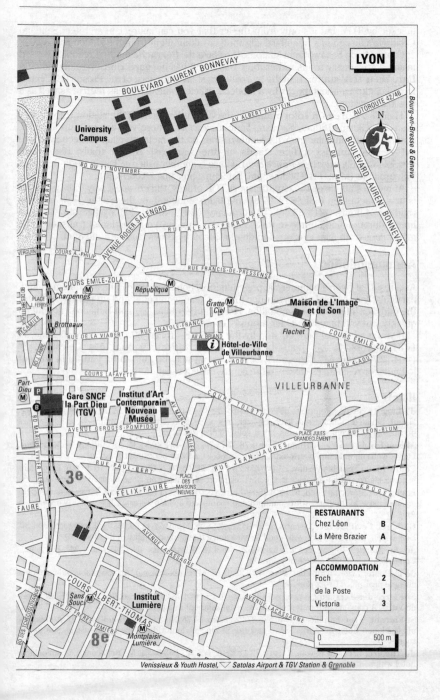

LYON

N

Bourg-en-Bresse & Geneva

BOULEVARD LAURENT BONNEVAY

AV ALBERT EINSTEIN

University
Campus

AUTOROUTE 42/46

RUE DU 8 MAI 1945

BOULEVARD LAURENT BONNEVAY

BD DU 11 NOVEMBRE

AVENUE ROGER SALENGRO

RUE ALEXIS-PERRONCEL

VERGUIN

COURS A.-PHILIP

RUE FRANCIS-DE-PRESSENSE

COURS EMILE-ZOLA

BD DES BROTTEAUX

PLACE
J. FERRY

Charpennes

République

*Gratte
Ciel*

Maison de L'Image
et du Son

RECAMIER

Brotteaux

RUE DE LA VIABERT

RUE ANATOLE-FRANCE

Flachet

COURS EMILE ZOLA

BD J. FAVRE

AV A. BRIAND

ⓘ Hôtel-de-Ville
de Villeurbanne

RUE DU 4-AOÛT

RUE DU 4-AOÛT

COURS LAFAYETTE

VILLEURBANNE

Part-
Dieu Ⓜ

P
Ⓑ

Gare SNCF
la Part Dieu
(TGV)

Institut d'Art
Contemporain
Nouveau
Musée

AV MARC-SAGLIER

COURS TOLSTOI

PLACE JULES
GRANDCLÉMENT

RUE LÉON-BLUM

BD MARIUS VIVIER MERLE

AVENUE GEROGES-POMPIDOU

RUE PAUL-BERT

RUE JEAN-JAURÈS

3e

AV FÉLIX-FAURE

PLACE
DES
MAISONS
NEUVES

AVENUE PAUL-KRÜGER

FAURE

AVENUE LACASSAGNE

RESTAURANTS	
Chez Léon	**B**
La Mère Brazier	**A**

AVENUE LACASSAGNE

BD DES TCHÉCOSLOVAQUES

COURS ALBERT-THOMAS

Sans
Souci Ⓜ

AV DES FRÈRES LUMIÈRE

Institut
Lumière

ACCOMMODATION	
Foch	**2**
de la Poste	**1**
Victoria	**3**

8e

Ⓜ
Montplaisir
Lumière

0   500 m

Venissieux & Youth Hostel   Satolas Airport & TGV Station & Grenoble quicker by TGV, but it's only from the air that you can appreciate architect Santiago Calatrava's design of a huge bird alighting or taking flight from the station roof.

Central Lyon has two train stations: the **Gare de Perrache** on the Presqu'île is used mainly for ordinary trains rather than TGVs, and has the **gare routière** alongside; **La Part-Dieu TGV station** is in the 3ᵉ *arrondissement* to the east of the Presqu'île. Central Lyon is linked to the suburbs by a modern, efficient and driverless **métro**, as well as a new **tram** system.

There's a **Bureau d'Information** in the Centre Perrache at the station (July & Aug Mon–Fri 7.30am–6.30pm, Sat 9am–5pm; *www.tcl.fr*), where you can pick up a métro, tram, bus and funicular map; it's just two stops on the métro to place Bellecour, where the **central tourist office** stands on the southeast corner (daily 10am–6pm; ☎04.72.77.69.69, *www.lyon-france.com*). There is another office at 3 av Aristide-Briand in Villeurbanne (Mon–Fri 9.30am–5pm, Sat 9am–5pm; ☎04.78.68.13.20).

At métro stations or the city transport TCL offices, the cheapest way to buy **tickets** is in a carnet of ten (68F/€10.37, discounts for students), or there's the *Ticket Liberté*, valid for 24 hours (24F/€3.66). The ordinary tickets (8F/€1.22) are flat-rate within an hour's duration and limited to three changes using any combination of transport. The métro runs from 5am to around midnight. Many bus lines close around 8pm.

Accommodation

As a result of Lyon's commercial pre-eminence, hotel **rooms** can be a problem to find, particularly on weekdays. If you don't book ahead, you could end up paying well over the odds for inferior accommodation. Hotels in Perrache (2ᵉ) and Bellecour (2ᵉ) fill up quickly, but you may be luckier around Terreaux (1ᵉʳ).

If you're on a real budget, stop by the **CROUS** offices, 59 rue de la Madeleine, 7ᵉ (☎04.72.80.13.13; Mᵒ Jean-Macé), or **CRIJ** offices, 9 quai des Celestins, 2ᵉ (☎04.72.77.00.66; Mᵒ Bellecour), both of whom may be able to fix you up in student lodgings or residences closer to the centre during vacation time.

Hotels

d'Ainay, 14 rue des Remparts d'Ainay, 2ᵉ (☎04.78.42.43.42, fax 04.72.77.51.90; Mᵒ Ampère Victor-Hugo). Situated in a pleasant, lively quarter, this place is preferable to its many cheap neighbours because of its decent-sized rooms, but it does fill fast. ③.

Alexandra, 49 rue Victor-Hugo, 2ᵉ (☎04.78.37.75.79, fax 04.72.40.94.34; Mᵒ Ampère Victor-Hugo). Large, well-run old hotel overlooking place Ampère – a lively pedestrian zone. ②.

Celtic, 10 rue François-Vernay, 1ᵉʳ (☎04.78.28.01.12, fax 04.78.28.01.34; Mᵒ Vieux-Lyon). Large, fairly comfortable and cheap place in the northern part of Vieux-Lyon close to place St-Paul. ①.

Foch, 59 av Maréchal-Foch, 6ᵉ (☎04.78.89.14.01, fax 04.78.93.71.69; Mᵒ Foch). Pleasant and superior hotel close to the park, with soundproofed rooms and a video library. Closed first two weeks in Aug. ④.

Globe et Cécil, 21 rue Gasparin, 2ᵉ (☎04.78.42.58.95, fax 04.72.41.99.06, *www.interhotel.com*; Mᵒ Bellecour). Attractive place with good service and a touch of originality in the decor. ⑤.

de la Marne, 78 rue de la Charité, 2ᵉ (☎04.78.37.07.46, fax 04.72.41.70.64; Mᵒ Perrache). Convenient, clean and excellent value. ②.

de la Poste, 1 rue Victor-Fort, 4ᵉ (☎04.78.28.62.67; Mᵒ Croix-Rousse). An acceptable old-fashioned cheapie near place Croix-Rousse. ②.

St-Pierre-des-Terreaux, 8 rue Paul-Chenavard, 1ᵉʳ (☎04.78.28.24.61, fax 04.72.00.21.07; Mᵒ Hôtel-de-Ville). A convenient if rather charmless establishment in a good location. ①.

St-Vincent, 9 rue Pareille, 1ᵉʳ (☎04.78.27.22.56, fax 04.78.30.92.87; Mᵒ Hôtel-de-Ville). A pleasant, old-fashioned hotel near the Saône and the St-Vincent footbridge. Marble fireplaces still in the rooms. ②.

du Théâtre, 10 rue de Savoie, 2ᵉ (☎04.78.42.33.32, fax 04.72.40.00.61; Mᵒ Bellecour). A comfortable hotel with some character, well run by a pleasant young couple. ③.

Vaubecour, 28 rue Vaubecour, 2ᵉ (☎04.78.37.44.91, fax 04.78.42.90.17; Mᵒ Ampère Victor-Hugo). One block back from the Saône quays, this place is comfortable, friendly and well-furnished for the price. ①.

Victoria, 3 rue Delandine, 2ᵉ (☎04.78.37.57.61, fax 04.78.42.91.07; Mᵒ Perrache). A decent two-star near the Perrache station. ②.

Hostels and campsites

HI hostel (Vieux Lyon), 41–45 Montée du Chemin Neuf, 5ᵉ (☎04.78.15.05.50, fax 04.78.15.05.51, *lyon@fuaj.org*; Mᵒ Vieux-Lyon-St-Jean/Minimes). A new modern hostel, with brilliant views over Lyon and access to an Internet terminal. Set in a steep part of the old town, the nearest métro station is Vieux-Lyon-St-Jean, but if you want to avoid the climb, get the funicular to Minimes and walk down the Montée du Chemin Neuf.

HI hostel, 51 rue Roger-Salengro, Vénissieux (☎04.78.76.39.23, fax 04.78.76.77.51, *lyon-venissieux@fuaj.org*; Mᵒ Gare de Vénissieux). Excellent hostel, with an unbeatable location, 4km southeast of the centre, and a full range of facilities.

Centre International de Séjour de Lyon, 103 bd Etats-Unis, 8ᵉ (☎04.37.90.42.42). Not far from the Vénissieux hostel, but a lot more expensive; the advantage is that it's out of earshot of the main ring road. Take bus #53 from Perrache or #36 from Part-Dieu, stop États-Unis-Beauvisage. Open 24hr.

Camping Porte de Lyon, Dardilly (☎04.78.35.64.55). East along the N6 from Lyon or by bus #89 (direction "Ecully-Dardilly") from the Hôtel de Ville. Pleasant though expensive, and has a tourist information bureau (daily June to mid-Sept 8am–11pm; rest of year 8am–8.30pm; ☎04.78.35.64.55).

The City

The centre of Lyon is the **Presqu'île**, or "peninsula", the tongue of land between the rivers Saône and Rhône, just north of their confluence. Most of it lies within the 2ᵉ *arrondissement*, but it's known by its *quartiers*, which include **Bellecour**, around the central square, and **Perrache** around the station. At the top end of the Presqu'île, as the Saône veers west, is the 1ᵉʳ *arrondissement*, known as **Terreaux**, centred on place des Terreaux and the Hôtel de Ville. On the west bank of the Saône is the old town, or **Vieux Lyon**, at the foot of Fourvière, on which the Romans built their capital of Gaul, Lugdunum. Vieux Lyon is made up of three villages: St-Paul, St-Jean and St-Georges, and forms the eastern end of the 5ᵉ *arrondissement*. The 9ᵉ lies to its north.

To the north of the Presqu'île is the old silk-weavers' district of **La Croix-Rousse**, the 4ᵉ *arrondissement*. **Modern Lyon** lies east of the Rhône, with the 7ᵉ and 8ᵉ *arrondissements* to the south, the 3ᵉ *arrondissement* in the middle, with **La Part-Dieu TGV station** amidst an assertive cultural and commercial centre, and the 6ᵉ *arrondissement*, known as **Brotteaux**, to the north. North of Brotteaux is Lyon's main open space, the **Parc de la Tête d'Or**. The district of **Villeurbanne**, home to the university and the Théâtre National Populaire, lies east of the 6ᵉ and the park.

The Presqu'île

The pink gravelly acres of **place Bellecour** were first laid out in 1617, and today form a focus on the peninsula, with views up to the looming bulk of Notre-Dame-de-Fourvière. The square is vast, dwarfing even the central statue of Louis XIV in the guise of a Roman emperor. Running south, **rue Auguste-Comte** is full of antique shops selling heavily framed eighteenth-century art works, and **rue Victor-Hugo** is a pedestrian precinct that continues north of place Bellecour on rue de la République all the way up to the back of the Hôtel de Ville below the area of La Croix-Rousse (see p.895).

South of place Bellecour on rue de la Charité, running parallel to rue Auguste-Comte on the Rhône side, is Lyon's best museum, the **Musée des Tissus** (Tues–Sun 10am–5.30pm; 20F/€4.57). It doesn't quite live up to its claim to cover the history of decorative cloth through the ages, but it does have brilliant collections from certain periods, most notably third-century Greek-influenced and sixth-century Coptic tapestries, woven silk and painted linen from Egypt. The fragment of woven wool *aux poissons* ("with fish"; second to third century AD) has an artistry unmatched in European work until at least the eighteenth century. There are silks from Baghdad contemporary with the *Thousand and One Nights*, and carpets from Iran, Turkey, India and China. The most boring stuff is that produced in Lyon itself: seventeenth- to eighteenth-century hangings and chair covers. Sadly, there's almost nothing from the period of the Revolution, but there are some lovely twentieth-century pieces – Sonia Delaunay's *Tissus Simultanés*, Michel Dubost's *L'Oiseau Bleu* and Raoul Dufy's *Les Coquillages*. The dull **Musée des Arts Décoratifs** next door (Tues–Sun 10am–noon & 2–5.30pm; same ticket as Musée des Tissus) displays seventeenth- and eighteenth-century tapestries, furniture and ceramics.

To the south, the station area around Perrache is of little interest, but across the adjacent pont Gallieni, at 14 av Berthelot, is the **Centre d'Histoire de la Résistance et de la Déportation** (Wed–Sun 9am–5.30pm; 25F/€3.81; M° Perrache/Jean-Macé). In addition to a library of books, videos, memoirs and other documents recording experiences of resistance, occupation and deportation to the camps, there's an exhibition space housed in the very cellars and cells in which Klaus Barbie, the Gestapo boss of Lyon, tortured and murdered his victims. Barbie was brought back from Uruguay a few years ago and tried in Lyon for crimes against humanity; the principal "exhibit" is a 45-minute video of the trial in which some of his victims recount their terrible ordeal at his hands – very moving and unsettling.

To the north of place Bellecour at the top of quai St-Antoine is the **quartier Mercière**, the old commercial centre of the town, with sixteenth- and seventeenth-century houses lining rue Mercière, and the **church of St-Nizier**, whose bells used to announce the nightly closing of the city's gates. In the silk-weavers' uprising of 1831 (see box opposite), workers fleeing the soldiers took refuge in the church, only to be massacred. The bourgeoisie had certainly been running scared, with only the area between the rivers, place des Terreaux and just north of St-Nizier still under their control. Unfortunately for the *canuts* (the silk workers), their employers were able to call on outside aid, and 30,000 extra troops arrived to quash the rebellion. Today, traces of this working-class life are rapidly disappearing as the district fills with fashionable bars and restaurants, as well as a row of smart shops all down the long pedestrian rue de la République. Close to St-Nizier, at 13 rue de la Poulaillerie, is the **Musée de l'Imprimerie et de la Banque** (Wed–Sun 9.30am–noon & 2–6pm; 25F/€3.81); unfortunately, its collection is unattractively displayed, which is a pity, for Lyon was both a leading publishing and banking centre in Renaissance times.

Further north, the monumental nineteenth-century **fountain** in front of the even more monumental **Hôtel de Ville** on place des Terreaux symbolizes rivers straining to reach the ocean. It was designed by Bartholdi, of Statue of Liberty fame, although the rows of watery leaks that sprout up unexpectedly across the rest of the square, are a modern addition. Opposite is the large bulk of the **Musée des Beaux-Arts** (Wed–Sun 10.30am–6pm; 25F/€3.81), housed in a former Benedictine abbey and whose collections are second in France only to those in the Louvre. The museum is organized roughly by genre, with nineteenth- and twentieth-century sculpture, represented by Canova, Barye and Rodin's *Temptation of St Anthony* in the ex-chapel on the ground floor. Medieval sculpture is on the first floor along with antiquities and *objets d'art*, including a particularly fine collection of sixth- to nineteenth-century Japanese, Korean and Chinese ceramics used in traditional tea ceremonies. In the painting collection, the twentieth century is particularly well represented: Gino Severini's *La Famille du Peintre* of 1939; spring and summer light in Bonnard's canvases beside wintry port scenes by Marquet; Van Dongens and de la Fresnayes throwing amused looks at their women friends; one of Monet's Thames series; *La Petite Niçoise* by Berthe Morisot; and

Degas' almost luminous pastel of the *Café-Concert aux Ambassadeurs*. This section was augmented considerably by the donation, in 1998, of Lyon-born actress Jaqueline Delubac's collection of thirty Impressionist pieces, including works by Picasso and Matisse. Of the early nineteenth-century collection, *La Maraichère*, attributed to David, is outstanding, and you can work your way back through Rubens, Zurbarán, El Greco, Tintoretto and a hundred others.

Behind the Hôtel de Ville, on the edge of several linked squares, stands Lyon's Neoclassical **opera house**, slightly uncertain of itself, having recently been redesigned by the architect Jean Nouvel. The Neoclassical exterior now supports a huge glass Swiss roll by way of a roof, and the interior – at least the only part accessible without a ticket – is now entirely black with silver stairways climbing into the darkness.

La Croix-Rousse

La Croix-Rousse is the old silk-weavers' district and spreads up the steep slopes of the hill above the northern end of the Presqu'île. It's still a working-class area, but barely a couple of dozen people operate the modern high-speed computerized looms that are kept in business by the restoration and maintenance of France's palaces and châteaux. You can watch traditional looms in mesmerizing action at **La Maison des Canuts** at 10–12 rue d'Ivry, north of place de la Croix-Rousse (Mon–Fri 8.30am–noon & 2–6.30pm, Sat 8.30am–noon & 2–6pm; 20F/€3.05; Mᵒ Croix-Rousse), and see some rare and beautiful cloths, including silk, damask and brocade, produced by this ancient home-weavers' co-operative.

The streets running down from **boulevard de la Croix-Rousse** – as well as many across the river in Vieux Lyon – are intersected by alleyways and tunnelled passages known as **traboules**. The original purpose of these was to provide shelter from the weather for the silk-weavers as they moved their delicate pieces of work from one part of the manufacturing process to another. Normally hidden by plain doors, they are impossible to distinguish from normal entryways; hence they proved an indispensable escape network for prewar gangsters, wartime Resistance fighters and, more recently, for political activists, who used them to thwart police efforts to prevent protests during the official visit of the Chinese ambassador in 2000. Try going up past the right of St-Polycarpe on **rue Réné-Leynaud** above place Terreaux, then take the *traboule* opposite 36 rue Burdeau, go right around **place Chardonnet**, through 55 rue des Tables-

---

THE SILK STRIKE OF 1831

The modern silk-weaving machines are no different in principle from the Jacquard loom of 1804, although they made it possible for one person to produce 25cm in a day instead of taking four people four days. But **silk workers**, or *canuts* – whether masters and apprentices, or especially women and child workers – were badly paid whatever their output. Over the three decades following the introduction of the Jacquard, the price paid for a length of silk was reduced by over fifty percent. Attempts to regulate the price were ignored by the dealers, even though hundreds of skilled workers were languishing in debtors' jails. On November 21, 1831, the *canuts* called an all-out strike. As they processed down the Montée de la Grande Côte with their black flags and the slogan "Live working or die fighting", they were shot at and three people died. After a rapid retreat uphill they built barricades, assisted by half the National Guard, who refused to fire canon at their "comrades of Croix-Rousse". For three days, until the reinforcements were brought in, the battle raged on all four banks, the silk workers using sticks, stones and knives to defend themselves. Some 600 people were killed or wounded, and in the end the silk industrialists were free to pay whatever pitiful fee they chose. But the uprising was one of the first instances of organized labour taking to the streets during the most revolutionary fifty years of French history.

Claudiennes, opposite 29 rue Imbert-Colomès and up the stairs into 14bis, across three more courtyards, and you should come out at **place Colbert**.

Officially the *traboules* of La Croix-Rousse and Vieux-Lyon are public thoroughfares during daylight hours – the tourist office distributes a free map of the *traboules* of the old town – though you may find some closed today for security reasons, especially as the area is gradually being gentrified. The long climb up the **Montée de la Grande Côte**, however, still gives an idea of what the *quartier* was like in the sixteenth century, when the *traboules* were first built. Take a look at the pretty **place Sathonay** at the bottom, where a public garden and a lively local café are overlooked by Croix-Rousse Mairie, and, if you have enough energy left, come down by the **rue Joséphin-Soulary**, which looks more like a lane in a country village and will bring you down a long flight of steps to the pont Winston-Churchill.

Vieux-Lyon

Reached by one of the three *passerelles* (footbridges) crossing the Saône from Terreaux and the Presqu'île, **Vieux Lyon** is made up of the three villages of St-Jean, St-Georges and St-Paul at the base of the hill overlooking the Presqu'île.

South of place St-Paul, the streets of Vieux Lyon, pressed close together beneath the hill of **Fourvière**, form a backdrop of Renaissance facades, bright night-time illumination and a swelling chorus of well-dressed Lyonnais in search of supper or a midday splurge. One of the most impressive buildings at the northern end is the sixteenth-century **Hôtel Paterin** at 4–6 rue Juiverie, a galleried mansion best viewed from the bottom of montée St-Barthélémy, just up from place St-Paul.

A short way south of the Hôtel Paterin, the **Musée Historique de Lyon**, on the ground floor of a fifteenth-century mansion on place du Petit-Collège (daily except Tues 10.45am–6pm; 25F/€3.81), has a good collection of Nevers ceramics, though the **Musée de la Marionnette**, on the first floor (same hours and ticket), is a lot more entertaining. As well as the eighteenth-century Lyonnais creations, *Guignol* and *Madelon* (the French equivalents of Punch and Judy), there are glove puppets, shadow puppets and rod-and-string toy actors from all over Europe and the Far East. If you want to see them in action, check out the times of performances at the **Théâtre de Guignol**, in the conservatory on rue Louis-Carrand by quai de Bondy (Oct–May Wed, Sat & Sun 3pm; for tickets and other puppet shows, ring ☎04.72.77.69.69 for information).

If you are *traboule*-hunting in Vieux-Lyon, two of the best can be found on two streets leading south from place du Petit-Collège: the winding passage behind the door at 27 rue de Bouef, and that at 24 rue St-Jean, which leads to the courtyard of a fifteenth-century palace. The central pedestrianized **rue St-Jean** ends at the twelfth- to fifteenth-century **Cathédrale St-Jean**. Though the west facade lacks most of its statuary as a result of various wars and revolutions, it's still impressive, and the thirteenth-century stained glass above the altar and in the rose windows of the transepts is in perfect condition. In the northern transept is a fourteenth-century astronomical clock, whose original mechanism has been covered by a lavish Baroque casing: it is capable of computing moveable feast days (such as Easter) till the year 2019, and most days on the strike of noon, 2pm and 3pm, the figures of the Annunciation go through an automated set piece. The cathedral treasury is also worth a look for its religious art and artefacts, ranging from Byzantine to the nineteenth-century (Tues–Fri 10am–noon & 2–6pm, Sat 10am–noon & 2–6/7pm; free).

Just beyond the cathedral, opposite avenue Adolphe-Max and pont Bonaparte, is the **funicular station** and the Vieux Lyon métro, from where you can ascend to the town's Roman remains (direction "St-Just", stop "Minimes"). The antiquities consist of two ruined **theatres** dug into the hillside (entrance at 6 rue de l'Antiquaille; mid-April to mid-Sept 7am–9pm; rest of year 7am–7pm; free) – the larger of which was built by Augustus and extended in the second century by Hadrian to seat 10,000 spectators –

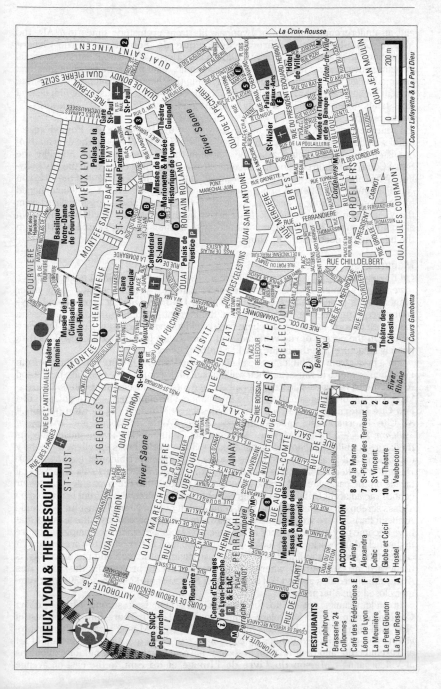

and an underground museum of Lyonnais life from prehistoric times to 7 AD, the **Musée Gallo-Romain et Parc Archéologique de Fourvière**, 17 rue Cléberg (Wed–Sun 9.30am–noon & 2–6pm; 20F/€3.05). Here, a mosaic illustrates various Roman games; bronze inscriptions detail economic, legal and administrative matters; and models aid the imagination in reconstructing the theatres outside. Nowadays, the ancient theatres are the focal point for the **Nuits de Fourvière** music and film festival that takes place annually in July and August (☎04.72.57.15.40, *www.nuits-de-fourviere.org*).

From the museum, it's just a moment's walk to the **Basilique de Fourvière**, an awful wedding-cake of a church built like the Sacré-Cœur in Paris in the aftermath of the 1871 Commune to emphasize the defeat of the godless socialists. And like the Sacré-Cœur, its hilltop position has become an almost defining element in the city's skyline. What makes a visit worthwhile, however, is the magnificent **view** of the city; you can distinguish the different quarters and see how they have grown and been shaped by the Saône and Rhône over the centuries. The Basilique is also accessible direct from the Vieux-Lyon funicular station: if you arrive by this route, it's worth walking down along the **montée St-Barthélemy** footpath, which winds back to Vieux Lyon through the hanging gardens below the church.

Modern Lyon

On the skyline from Fourvière, you'll see a gleaming cylinder with a pointed top – a tower that belongs to Lyon's home-grown Crédit Lyonnais bank – and other Manhattanish protuberances around it. This is **La Part-Dieu**, a business–culture—commerce conglomerate including one of the biggest public libraries outside Paris, a mammoth concert hall and a shopping centre said to be the largest in Europe (Mº Part-Dieu). On the corner of rue Garibaldi and cours Lafayette in front of these less than homely structures are the **main market halls** of Lyon.

For a break from city buildings head north to the **Parc de la Tête d'Or** (bus #4 from Part-Dieu or métro to Masséna, then walk up rue Masséna), where there are ponds and rose gardens, botanical gardens, a small zoo and lots of amusements for kids. It's overlooked by the bristling antennae of the international headquarters of Interpol, part of a new **Cité Internationale**, which also includes a new **Musée d'Art Contemporain**, at 81 Cité Internationale, quai Charles-de-Gaulle (Wed–Sun noon–7pm; *www.moca-lyon.org*; 25F/€3.81; bus #4, stop "Musée d'Art Contemporain"). The museum owns the largest public collection of installation art in the world, hosts excellent temporary exhibitions and is also the one of the homes of the *Lyon* art biennial (see opposite). Designed by Renzo Piano, it is a curious-looking structure with a 1930s Neoclassical facade on the park side and a pink concrete box tacked onto the river side. The colour echoes the adjacent **Palais des Congrès** conference centre, whose front is masked by a glass screen curving up over the roof, reminiscent of Jean Nouvel's Institut du Monde Arabe in Paris. There are some screens, catwalks and companionways: the features that have become part of the currency of architectural language since the Pompidou Centre first shocked the world. But it looks good, and will look better when the area around it ceases to resemble a building site. To the east, dividing the park and the university, is boulevard de Stalingrad, where antique-fanciers can browse in the **Cité des Antiquaires** arcades at no. 117 (Thurs, Sat & Sun 9.30am–12.30pm & 2.30–7pm; summer closed Sun afternoon).

In Villeurbanne, not far to the east of Part-Dieu, is a second **Musée d'Art Contemporain**, 11 rue Dr-Dolard (June–Sept Wed 1–8pm, Thurs–Sun 1–7pm; rest of year Wed–Sun 1–6pm; 25F/€3.80; bus #1, stop "Nouveau Musée"), where thought-provoking and engaging exhibitions by contemporary artists question the function of art and architecture and their relation to society. It's also worth looking out for exhibitions at Villeurbanne's **Maison du Livre de l'Image et du Son**, to the east on avenue

Émile-Zola (M° Flachet), which might feature anything from medieval illuminations to CD-ROMs.

Further south, on the edge of the 8ᵉ *arrondissement*, is the **Institut Lumière**, 25 rue du Premier-Film (Mon–Fri 9.30am–12.30pm, Sat & Sun 2–6pm; 25F/€3.81; M° Monplaisir/Lumière). The building was the home of Antoine Lumière, father of Auguste and Louis, who made the first films, and the exhibits feature early magic lanterns and the cameras used by the brothers, along with various art photographs. The Institut also hosts various film festivals.

Right down in the south of the city, in the **Gerland quartier** (7ᵉ), is a newly developed area with a marina and a park on the Rhône's east bank, which provides an illusion of nature around the mirrored Institut Pasteur and the thrusting wings and arches of the École Normale Supérieure. Across the bridge from the southern tip of the Presqu'île, just off place Antonin Perrin squats the massive **Tony Garnier Hall** (M° Debourg), whose 17,000 cubic metres is completely free of roof-supporting columns. Its walls graced with contemporary murals, it is now the main host to Lyon's art biennial – a major European show of new art convened here every other year (July–Sept in odd-numbered years).

Eating, drinking and entertainment

You'll find **restaurants** offering dishes from every region of France and overseas in Lyon. Vieux-Lyon is the area with the greatest concentration of eateries, though you'll find cheaper and less busy ones between place des Jacobins and place Sathonay at the top of the Presqu'île. The possibilities are endless, but on weekends booking ahead is always a good idea. The most affordable type of Lyonnais eating establishment, the **bouchon** (cork), derived its name from the vast quantities of Lyonnais wine consumed there. Tradition has it that wine bottles were lined up as the evening progressed, and at the end of the night the bill was determined by measuring from the first cork to the last. There are several *bouchons* located in the streets between Cordeliers and Terreaux, particularly in rue Mercière.

Lyon is almost as good a place for **nightlife** and **entertainment** as it is for eating, with a good range of clubs, cinema, opera, jazz, classical music concerts and theatre. The best places to wander if you are looking for a **bar** are rue Mercière and rue de la Monnaie and, most particularly, the streets of Vieux-Lyon, especially the southern part around the place Bertras. And make a point of crossing the river by the *passerelles*; the whole district looks magnificent at night.

The tourist office brings out a bimonthly brochure, *Le Progrèscope*, with broad mainstream listings. Alternatively buy a copy of the weekly *Lyon Poche*, available from newsagents (every Wed; 7F/€1.07).

Restaurants

L'Amphitryon, 33 rue St-Jean, 5ᵉ (☎04.78.37.23.68; M° Vieux-Lyon). Usually packed restaurant serving Lyonnais specialities; menu for under 100F/€15.25. Service till midnight.

Brasserie 24 Collonnes a la Une, 79 rue des Trois Maries, 5ᵉ (M° Vieux-Lyon). Near the cathedral, this friendly brasserie, with an early twentieth-century mirrored and stained-glass interior, becomes a jazzy piano-bar at night. Menus from 98F/€14.95. Open daily 10am–midnight.

Café des Fédérations, 8 rue du Major-Martin, 1ᵉʳ (☎04.78.28.26.00; M° Hôtel-de-Ville). Typical *bouchon* serving the earthiest of Lyonnais specialities (marinated tripe, black pudding and fish *quenelles*) in an atmosphere to match: there's even sawdust on the floor. Menu at 118F/€18 lunchtimes, 148F/€22.57 dinner. Closed Sat, Sun & Aug.

Chez Léon, Halles de la Part-Dieu, 102 cours Lafayette, 3ᵉ (☎04.78.62.30.28; M° Part-Dieu). Bar and restaurant in the market halls, whose specialities include seafood and snails. Around 150F/€22.88 for a good-sized meal. Closed May–Aug.

Léon de Lyon, 1 rue Pléney, 1er (☎04.78.28.11.33; M° Hôtel-de-Ville). Sophisticated and delicious eating, with original culinary creations as well as traditional Lyonnais recipes in this upmarket brasserie, whose huge interior is divided into intimate and warmly panelled smaller dining areas. Menus cost from 650F/€99.13, but there's a lunch menu for 290F/€44.23.

La Mère Brazier, 12 rue Royale, 1er (☎04.78.28.15.49; M° Croix-Paquet). A beautiful setting complements the excellent food, like Bresse chicken, artichoke hearts on foie gras, truffle crêpes – but it's very expensive. From 330F/€50.33, but you can easily spend twice as much. Closed Sun, Sat lunch & Aug.

La Meunière, 11 rue Neuve, 1er (☎04.78.28.62.91; M° Hôtel-de-Ville). Booking is essential in this excellent *bouchon*, but it's worth it for the 170F/€25.93 menu of course after course of Lyonnais specialities. Other menus start at 98F/€14.95. Closed Sun, Mon & July & Aug.

Paul Bocuse, 40 rue de la Plage, Collonges-au-Mont-d'Or (☎04.72.42.90.90). Lyon's most famous restaurant, named after its celebrity chef-owner, is 9km north of the city, on the west bank of the Saône. Traditional French gastronomy is the bill of fare, with stunning *crème brûlée* and *baba au rhum*. 520F/€79.30 upwards.

Le Petit Glouton, 56 rue St-Jean, 2e (☎04.78.74.30.12; M° Vieux-Lyon). A small but airy and unpretentious bistro in the heart of Vieux-Lyon. You can dine inside or on the small street-side terrace for under 100F/€15.25.

La Tour Rose, 22 rue Bœuf, 5e (☎04.78.37.25.90; M° Vieux-Lyon). Gastronomic palace with concoctions like asparagus with an oyster mousse or salad of lobster and spinach with a creamed truffle sauce. From 295F/€44.99. Closed Sun.

Bars and clubs

66 Road Café, 9 place des Terreaux, 1er (M° Hôtel-de-Ville). Not unconvincing Lyonnais version of a North American roadhouse bar. A lively and popular place with rock, R&B, blues, etc, plus billiards. Daily 2pm–3am.

Albion Public House, 12 rue Ste-Catherine, 1er (M° Hôtel-de-Ville). English pub with draught beer and a good selection of whiskies, where you can play darts and billiards, and listen to live jazz, R&B or soul on Wed nights. Nightly 5pm–3am; happy hour Mon–Thurs 5–8pm.

Coco Loco, 8 rue Joseph Serlin, 1er (M° Hôtel-de-Ville). Lively, multi-level Spanish-style disco featuring funk, rock and salsa. Special events include Brazilian nights and transvestite shows. Wed–Sat 10pm–dawn.

Les Écossais, 7 rue Charles-Dullin, 2e (just off place des Célestins; M° Bellecour). Scots-style piano bar serving a hundred different whiskies, and featuring jazz, Latin and live rock music. Mon–Sat 8pm–dawn; closed most of Aug.

Eden Rock Café, 68 rue Mercière, 2e (M° Cordeliers). Massive bar, decorated with memorabilia and modern art from the States, with cheap beer and food served until 1am. Live music Thurs–Sat with a heavy accent on rock, but also country and funk. Mon 5pm–1am, Tues & Wed noon–1am, Thurs noon–2am, Fri & Sat noon–3am; closed part Aug.

L'Épicerie, 2 rue Octavio-Mey, 5e (M° Vieux-Lyon). Lively cocktail bar hosting jazz and blues nights. Daily 5pm–1am.

L'Éspace Gerson, 1 place Gerson, 5e (☎04.78.27.96.99; M° Vieux-Lyon). Has café-théâtre some nights, otherwise jazz or performance art, plus darts and billiards. Cool modern design set within an antique building. 60F/€9.15 entry normally. Mon–Sat 8.30pm–3am.

FBI Café, 2 rue de la Monnaie, 2e (M° Cordeliers). Quintessential American-style bar – its deliberately clichéd decor makes it like stepping onto a sit-com set. Concerts, theme nights and DJs. Daily 1pm–3am.

Fish, opposite 21 quai Augagneur, 3e (*www.oxxo-kf.com*; M° Guillotière). One of Lyon's hippest night clubs, specializing in house. Admission 60F/€9.15, drinks 20–30F/€3.05-4.58. Open daily 10pm–5am; Thurs student night, Fri theme night and Sat garage.

Forum Bar, 15 rue des Quatre Chapeaux, 2e (M° Cordeliers). Popular bar with predominantly gay and lesbian clientele, tucked in an alley just north of the places des Jacobins and de la République. Mon–Thurs 5pm–2am, Fri & Sat 5pm–3am.

Hot Club, 26 rue du Lanterne, 1er (*www.hotclub.fr.st*; M° Hôtel-de-Ville). Jazz jam sessions and concerts of all varieties in a vaulted cellar, which is well ventilated to reduce smokiness. Tues–Sat 9pm–1am; closed July & Aug.

Paradiso Club, 24 rue Pizay, 1ᵉʳ (Mᵒ Hôtel-de-Ville). Funky music and transvestite or burlesque cabaret. Daily 10pm–dawn.

Theatre, music and film

Look out for **stage productions** by the Théâtre National Populaire (TNP), 8 place Lazare-Goujon (☎04.78.03.30.40; Mᵒ République), based across the street from Villeurbanne's town hall. Less radical stuff will be shown at the city's gilded Théâtre des Célestins, in place des Célestins, 2ᵉ (☎04.72.77.40.00; Mᵒ Bellecour). The **opera house**, one of the best in France, is on place de la Comédie, 1ᵉʳ (☎04.72.00.45.45; Mᵒ Hôtel-de-Ville), with cheap tickets sold just before performances begin. For avant-garde, classic and obscure **films**, usually in their original language, check the listings for the cinemas CNP Terreaux, Ambiance, Opéra and Le Cinéma. Also, look out for the Lyon dance biennial, which brings in hundreds of artists and troupes from around the world (last three weeks of Sept in even-numbered years; *www.biennale-de-lyon.org*).

Listings

Boat trips Bateaux-Mouches Lui, Société Naviginter, 13bis quai Rambaud, 2ᵉ (☎04.78.42.96.81). Leaving from quai des Célestins, boats run up the Saône or down to the confluence with the Rhône at the Île Barbe (daily April–Nov; 42F/€6.41). Another boat, *Elle*, run by the same company, heads down the Rhône to Vienne.

Books English bookshop, Eton, 1 rue du Plat, near Bellecour.

Car rental Europcar, 40 rue de la Villette, 3ᵉ (☎04.72.68.84.60); Hertz, 40 rue Vilette, 3ᵉ (☎04.72.33.89.89); Avis, Gare Part-Dieu, 3ᵉ (☎04.72.33.37.19); all the above also have offices at the airport and at the Perrache centre.

Changing money AOC, 20 rue Gasparin (Mon–Sat 9.30am–6.30pm, Sun 10am–5pm); AOC Opéra, 3 rue de la République (Mon–Fri 9am–6pm); Thomas Cook, gare de la Part-Dieu (Mon–Sat 8am–7pm, Sun 10.30am–7pm); the tourist office on Bellecour has a money-changing machine (open hours of tourist office, see p.892).

Consulates Ireland, 58 rue Victor-Lagrange, 7ᵉ (☎06.85.23.13.03); UK, 24 rue Childebert, 2ᵉ (☎04.72.77.81.70).

Disabled travellers For information on facilities for the disabled contact Délégation Régionale AGEFIPH, 29 rue Condorcet, 38090 Villefontaine (☎04.74.94.20.21, fax 04.74.94.08.93), or pick up the booklet *Lyon pratique* from the tourist office.

Emergencies SOS Médecins (☎04.78.83.51.51). Hospitals: Hôtel-Dieu, 1 place de l'Hôtel-Dieu, 2ᵉ; Hôpital Édouard-Herriot on place d'Arsonval, 3ᵉ (for both hospitals call ☎08.20.86.78.47).

Internet *Espace Connectik*, 19 quai St-Antoine, 2ᵉ (Mon–Sat 11am–7pm), has plenty of terminals but is rather expensive; *Raconte Moi de la Terre*, 38 rue Thomassin, 2ᵉ (Mon–Sat 10am–7.30pm), is cheaper and also serves snacks.

Lesbian and gay info Lésgayt'on (☎04.78.21.05.95, *www.multimania.com/lesgaysbb*).

Pharmacy Blanchet, 5 place des Cordeliers, 2ᵉ (daily till midnight).

Police The main commissariat is on rue de la Charité, 2ᵉ (☎04.78.42.26.56).

Post office PTT, place Antonin-Poncet, Lyon 69002.

Taxis ☎04.78.28.23.23 or 04.78.26.81.81.

Around Lyon

Within easy reach of the city, the **Monts du Lyonnais** to the south and west of Lyon may not reach spectacular heights, but they offer quiet and solitude among steep, forested hills and unassuming villages surrounded by cherry orchards, the region's main source of income. Tourism is low-key, but food and accommodation in the hostels of the mountain villages are rarely a problem for visitors to the area's parks and museums. **Bus** services from Lyon to the larger villages are reasonably frequent, and to the east of Lyon, the small medieval cities of **Pérouges** and **Crémieu** can easily be reached by train. The mountains can be visited every Sunday from June until the middle of September by steam train, leaving from **L'Arbresle**, just west of Lyon (frequent trains from Lyon-Perrache); it's a scenic service but not very useful for getting anywhere.

St-Pierre-la-Palud, Yzeron and St-Martin-en-Haut

Worth a visit if you're not returning straight to Lyon, the **Musée de la Mine** at **ST-PIERRE-LA-PALUD**, 15km west of the city (March–Nov Sat, Sun & hols 2–6pm; 25F/€3.81), is guaranteed to instil admiration for the endurance of the miners who put up with working conditions like those simulated in the reconstructed mine shaft which forms the main exhibit. Going down into the copper sulphate mine shaft while an ex-miner explains its workings in meticulous detail (2hr; in French) is not recommended if you're claustrophobic. Back on the surface, you move on to an exhibition about the former mining village and pit.

Most of the villages in the Lyonnais mountains have some form of *auberge* serving food and providing a bed for the night. A typical, attractive example is the tiny village of **YZERON**, 12km south of the wildlife park at Courzieu, on whose main square is the excellent *Auberge de Tonton* (☎04.78.81.01.42; ③), which serves duck and salmon as part of a 135F/€20.59 menu. There are another couple of hotels and restaurants in the village of **ST-MARTIN-EN-HAUT**, eight winding kilometres south of Yzeron, as well as a **tourist office** (Mon 2–4pm, Tues–Sat 9am–noon & 2–6pm, Sun 10am–noon; ☎04.78.48.64.32), and a municipal **campsite** just outside the village on the D122 (☎04.78.48.62.16; all year).

Pérouges and Crémieu

Twenty-nine kilometres northeast of Lyon on the N84, **PÉROUGES** is a pretty little town of cobbled alleyways, whose charm has not gone unnoticed by the French film industry – historical dramas like *The Three Musketeers* and *Monsieur Vincent* were filmed within the town walls – nor by some of the residents, who have fought long and hard for preservation orders on its most interesting buildings.

Local traditional life is also thriving in the hands of a hundred or so workers who still weave locally grown hemp. No particular monument stands out, but the central square, the **place du Halle**, and its main street, the **rue du Prince**, have some of the best-preserved French medieval remains. The **lime tree** on place du Halle is a symbol of liberty, planted in 1792. *The* place both to **stay** and eat in Pérouges, if you can afford it, is the *Ostellerie du Vieux Pérouges* (☎04.74.61.00.88, fax 04.74.34.77.90; ⑧), in a medieval town house on place Tilleul; its **restaurant** serves traditional mountain dishes of rabbit and carp, with menus from 190F/€28.98.

CRÉMIEU, to the south on the D517, is less compelling, despite its local sausages (*sabodet*), monumental architecture and early origins – the city can be traced back to 835 AD. It was once an important commercial centre, as signified by the fourteenth-century **market buildings** on rue du Lt-Col-Bel, and a border-post of the kingdom of Dauphiné; a number of imposing doorways are all that remain of the medieval fortifications.

Vienne and around

Heading south from Lyon on the A7, a twenty-kilometre stretch of oil refineries, steel, chemical and paper works, cement, fertilizer and textile factories, all spewing plumes of grey and orange pollution into the air, may well tempt you to make a bee-line for the lavender fields of Provence. However, a short detour off the *autoroute* brings you to

VIENNE MUSEUM PASS

The Théâtre Antique, Église and Cloître de St-André-le-Bas, Musée des Beaux-Arts et d'Archéologie and Église-Musée St-Pierre can be visited on a single ticket (25F/€3.81, or 29F/€4.42 if there is a temporary exhibition in any of the sites), which can be picked up at any of the sites.

VIENNE, which, along with **St-Romain-en-Gal**, across the river, makes for the most interesting stop on the Rhône before Orange.

With their riverside positions, Vienne and St-Romain prospered as Rome's major wine port and *entrepôt* on the Rhône, and many Roman monuments survive to attest to this past glory. Several important churches recall Vienne's medieval heyday as well: it was a bishop's seat from the fifth century and the hometown of twelfth-century Pope Calixtus II. Today, the compact old quarter is crisscrossed with pedestrian precincts which make for enjoyable menu-browsing around **rue des Clercs** and **place Charles-de-Gaulle**. And there's a feeling that despite the distant rumble of the *autoroute* calling you to sunnier climes, the town has maintained its character and sense of purpose.

The Town

Roman monuments are scattered liberally around the streets of Vienne, and it requires little effort to take in the magnificently restored **Temple d'Auguste** on place du Palais, a perfect, scaled-down version of Nîmes' Maison Carrée, or the scanty remains of the **Théâtre de Cybèle**, off place de Miremont. The **Théâtre Antique**, off rue du Cirque at the base of Mont Pipet to the north (April–Aug daily 9.30am–1pm & 2–6pm; Sept to mid-Oct Tues–Sun 9.30am–1pm & 2–6pm; mid-Oct to March Tues–Sat 9.30am–noon & 2–5pm, Sun 1.30–5.30pm; 12F/€1.83, or 25F/€3.81 combined ticket), is more of a haul but it's worth making the trip for the view of the town and river from the very top seats. The theatre is the venue of an **international jazz festival** for the first two weeks of July, when it plays host to some of the biggest names on the jazz circuit.

The **Église-Musée St-Pierre** (April–Aug daily 9.30am–1pm & 2–6pm; Sept to mid-Oct Tues–Sun 9.30am–1pm & 2–6pm; mid-Oct to March Tues–Sat 9.30am–noon & 2–5pm, Sun 1.30–5.30pm; 25F/€3.81 combined ticket) stands on the site of one of France's first cathedrals. Since its origins in the fifth century, the building has suffered much reconstruction and abuse, including a stint as a factory in the nineteenth century, though the monumental portico of the former church is still striking. Today it houses a forgettable collection of mostly broken and unremarkable Roman sculpture and epigraphy. Close by, is the most prominent – and vaunted – of Vienne's monuments, the **Cathédrale St-Maurice**, whose unwieldy facade, a combination of Romanesque and Gothic, appears as if its upper half has been dumped on top of a completely alien building. The interior, with its ninety-metre-long vaulted nave, is impressive though, and there are some superb stained-glass windows and fifteenth-century frescoes.

The **Église** (daily 9am–noon & 2–6pm; free) and **Cloître de St-André-le-Bas** (same hours and ticket as St-Pierre) on rue des Clercs, a few streets north of the cathedral, date from the ninth and twelfth centuries. The back tower of the church, on rue de la Table Ronde, is a remarkable monument, studded with tiny carved stone faces, while the cloister, entered through a space where temporary exhibits are held, is a beautiful little Romanesque affair, whose walls are decorated with local tombstones, some dating from the fifth-century.

The major museum in Vienne is the **Musée des Beaux-Arts et d'Archéologie** on place de Miremont (same hours and ticket as St-Pierre), with a preponderance of eighteenth-century French pottery, but also some attractive pieces of third-century

Roman silverware. More enlightening is the small textile museum, the **Musée de la Draperie** (April–Sept Tues–Sun 2.30–6.30pm; 12F/€1.83) in the Espace St-Germain to the south of the centre off rue Vimaine, which, with the aid of videos, working looms and weavers, illustrates the complete process of cloth-making as it was practised in the city for over two hundred years.

Practicalities

The cours Brillier runs at right angles to the river, with the **tourist office** at no. 3, near quai Jean-Jaurès (mid-June to mid-Sept daily 9am–12.30pm & 1.30–7pm; rest of year Mon–Sat 8.30am–noon & 2–6pm; ☎04.74.53.80.30, fax 04.74.53.80.31), and the **gare SNCF** at the other end. Halfway up the *cours*, rue Boson leads up to the west front of the cathedral.

If you plan to **stay**, the *Poste*, 47 cours Romestang (☎04.74.85.02.04, fax 04.74.85.16.17; ③), between the station and place de Miremont, has an excellent restaurant and good rooms overlooking the *cours*. One of the few other budget options is the *Ibis*, by the *gare routière* in place Camille-Jouffray (☎04.74.78.41.11, fax 04.78.85.42.28; ④), just down from the tourist office, while *Le Grand Hôtel du Nord* is a more upmarket central option at 9 place de Miremont (☎04.74.85.77.11, fax 04.74.53.23.62; ④). If you have your own transport, however, you should stay at the *Château des Sept Fontaines*, 5km northwest on the N7 at **SEYSSUEL** (☎04.74.85.25.70, fax 04.74.31.74.47; ④; closed Nov–March), with a large garden, sauna, gym and comfortable rooms. There's also an **HI hostel** on the other side of the park from the tourist office at 11 quai Riondet (☎04.74.53.21.97, fax 04.74.31.98.93; reserve ahead Fri–Sun mid-Sept to mid-May).

The old town has a number of promising places to **eat**, including a good selection of cheapies in rue de la Table Ronde (near St-André-le-Bas), among them *L'Estancot* at no. 4 (☎04.74.85.12.09; closed Mon & Sun) and *au Petit Chez Soi* at no. 6 (☎04.74.85.19.77; closed Sun), serving *moules frites* and menus under 100F/€15.25. Alternatively, *Le Bec Fin*, 7 place St-Maurice (☎04.74.85.76.72; closed Sun evening & Mon), offers filling menus of Lyonnais dishes from 98F/€14.95. However, if you fancy a splurge, head for the superlative restaurant in the hotel *La Pyramide*, 14 bd Fernand-Point (☎04.74.53.01.96; closed Tues & Wed), with weekday menus from 295F/€44.99 to 690F/€105.23; going à la carte will cost you at least 550F/€83.88. For **drinking**, there are a number of bars in town, including *Les 12 Mesures* in rue des Clercs and *The Celtic House* in rue Allmer.

St-Romain-en-Gal

Facing Vienne across the Rhône, several hectares of Roman ruins constitute the site of **ST-ROMAIN-EN-GAL**, also the name of the modern town surrounding it. The excavations (still ongoing), just across the road bridge from Vienne, attest to a significant community dating from the first century BC to the third AD, and give a vivid picture of the daily life and domestic architecture of Roman France. You enter through the **Musée Archéologique de St-Romain-en-Gal** (site & museum Tues–Sun 9.30am–6.30pm; 30F/€4.57; free English audioguide), which displays frescoes, mosaics and other objects recovered from the site, along with explanatory models. The ruins themselves are clearly laid out, with illuminating reconstructions and informative but not overly technical explanatory plaques in English – ideal for adults and children alike. Be sure to check out the Romans' lavishly decorated marble public toilets, by the entry ramp to the dig.

Between Vienne and Valence

Between Vienne and Valence are some of the oldest, most celebrated **vineyards** in France: the renowned Côte Rotie, Hermitage and Crozes-Hermitage *appellations*. If you've got any spare luggage space, it's well worth stopping to pick up a bottle from the local co-op; even their *vin ordinaire* is superlative and unbelievably cheap, considering its quality. Just south of Ampuis on the west bank, 8km south of Vienne, is the tiny area producing one of the most exquisite French white wines – Condrieu – and close by one of the most exclusive – Château-Grillet – an *appellation* covering just this single château (shop open Mon–Fri 8am–5pm; ☎04.74.59.51.56).

Between **St-Vallier** and **Tain l'Hermitage**, the Rhône becomes quite scenic, and after Tain you can see the Alps. In spring you're more likely to be conscious of orchards everywhere rather than vines. Cherries, pears, apples, peaches and apricots, as well as bilberries and strawberries, are cultivated in abundance.

Tain-l'Hermitage and around

TAIN-L'HERMITAGE, accessible from both the N7 and the A7, is unpretentious and uneventful. The only reason to stay here is to drink wine and eat chocolate. You can sample a good selection of the renowned Hermitage and Crozes-Hermitage **wines** at the Cave de Tain-l'Hermitage, 22 rte de Larnage (Mon–Sat 8am–noon & 2–6pm, Sun 9am–noon & 2–6pm; ☎04.75.08.20.87), and if your visit happens to fall on the last weekend in February you can try out wines from 78 vineyards in the Foire aux Vins des Côtes du Rhône Septentrionales. The celebrated **chocolates** in question are made by Valrhona and available at their shop (Mon–Fri 9am–7pm, Sat 9am–6pm) on avenue du Président-Roosevelt (the RN7), past the junction with the RN95 as you're heading south.

The **tourist office**, at 70 av Jean-Jaurès (Mon–Sat 9am–noon & 2–6pm; ☎04.75.08.06.81, fax 04.75.08.34.59), on the RN7 further north, can provide you with lists of vineyard addresses. If you need to **stay**, try the inexpensive hotel at 19 av du Dr Paul Durand, *Hôtel de la Gare* (☎04.75.08.50.93, fax 04.75.07.11.71; ②), or the slightly more upmarket *Les 2 Côteaux*, 18 rue Joseph-Péala, running off Jean-Jaurès south of place Taurobole (☎04.75.08.33.01, fax 04.75.08.44.20; ②). For a cheap **meal** in Tain try the crêperie *La Récré*, 8 place Taurobole, as an alternative to the stuffier establishments on avenue Jean-Jaurès. Tain's best restaurant, *Reynaud*, 82 av du Président-Roosevelt (☎04.75.07.22.10; closed Sun evening & Mon, and Jan), has an excellent-value 190F/€28.98 menu, with à la carte upwards of 300F/€45.75.

On the third weekend of September, the different wine-producing villages celebrate their cellars in the **Fête des Vendanges**. But at any time of the year you can go bottle-hunting along the N86 for some 30km north of Tain along the right bank, following the *dégustation* signs and then crossing back over between Serrières and Chanas.

Hauterives

HAUTERIVES, 25km northeast of Tain, is a small village with a remarkable creation – a manic, surreal **Palais Idéal** built by a local postman by the name of Ferdinand Cheval (1836–1912). The house is a truly bizarre structure, a bubbling frenzy reminscent of the *modernista* architecture of Spain, with features that recall Pharaonic temples. The eccentric building took him thirty years to carve, and he designed an equally bizarre tombstone which can also be seen. Various Surrealists have paid homage to the building; psychoanalysts have given it their all, but it defies all classification (daily: Jan & Dec 10am–4.30pm; Feb to mid-April & mid-Sept to Nov

9.30am–5.30pm; mid-April to mid-Sept 9am–7pm; *www.facteurcheval.com*; 30F/€4.57). If you want to **stay** here, you have the choice of the *Camping du Château* on the edge of town on the N538 (☎04.75.68.80.19, fax 04.75.68.90.94; closed mid-Oct to March) and a **hotel**, *Le Relais* (☎04.75.68.81.12, fax 04.75.68.92.42; ②; closed mid-Jan to Feb), in the village itself.

Romans-sur-Isère

South of Hauterives and 15km east of the Rhône at Tain is **ROMANS-SUR-ISÈRE**. It's not the most exciting of towns but it does have a fascinating museum of shoemaking – the industry that has kept Romans going for the last five centuries. The extensive **Musée Internationale de la Chaussure** is in the former Convent of the Visitation at 2 rue Ste-Marthe (July & Aug Mon–Sat 10am–6.30pm; rest of year Tues–Sat 9–11.45am & 2–5.45pm; 26F/€3.96) and also includes a permanent exhibition on the Resistance. Your toes will curl in horror at the extent to which women have been immobilized by their footwear from ancient times to the present on every continent, while at the same time you can't help but admire the craziness of some of the creations. Romans is also a good place to buy shoes, with several factory shops in the town.

Romans has plenty of beautiful old streets and buildings to admire, and its region has two gastronomic specialities: a ringed spongy bread flavoured with orange water, known as a *pogne*, and *ravioles*, cornflour-based ravioli with an eggy, cheesy, buttery filling. You can sample these at the **restaurant** *La Cassolette*, 16 rue Rebatte (☎04.75.02.55.71; closed Sun & Mon throughout the year & three weeks from last week in July; menus under 100F/€15.25).

There's a **tourist office** on place Jean-Jaurès (April–Oct Mon–Fri 9am–7pm, Sat 9am–6pm, Sun 9.30am–12.30pm; Nov–March Mon–Sat 9am–6pm, Sun 9.30am–12.30pm; ☎04.75.02.28.72), and several **hotels**, including *des Balmes*, northwest of the town centre in the *quartier* of the same name (☎04.75.02.29.52, fax 04.75.02.75.47; ③), with an excellent and inexpensive restaurant (closed Sun evening out of season). Cheaper options include the *Magdeleine*, 31 av Pierre-Sémard (☎04.75.02.33.53; ②; closed Sun evening out of season), and the *Karene* in St-Paul (☎04.75.05.12.50, fax 04.75.05.25.17; ②). The municipal **campsite**, *Les Chasses* (☎04.75.72.35.27; closed Oct–April), is 1km off the N92 northeast of the city, near the aerodrome.

Valence

At an indefinable point along the Rhône, there's an invisible sensual border, and by the time you reach **VALENCE**, you know you've crossed it. The quality of light is different and the temperature higher, bringing with it the scent of eucalyptus and pine, and the colours and contours suddenly seem worlds apart from the cold lands of Lyon and the north. Valence is the obvious place to celebrate your arrival in the Midi (as the French call the south), with plenty of good bars and restaurants in the old town, though it offers little else.

Arrival, information and accommodation

If you come in on the *autoroute*, running along the Rhône's left bank, you exit onto avenue Gambetta, with the old town, its ramparts replaced by boulevards, to your left. To the southeast of the old town you'll find the **gare routière**, the **gare SNCF** and the **tourist office** on parvis de la Gare (June–Aug Mon–Sat 9am–7pm, Sun 9am–noon; rest of year Mon 2–6.30pm, Tues–Sat 9am–12.30pm & 2–6.30pm; ☎04.75.44.90.40, *valence.tourisme@wanadoo.fr*).

For mid-range hotel **rooms**, try the *Europe*, 15 av Félix-Faure (☎04.75.43.02.16, fax 04.75.43.61.75; ③), with satellite TV and en-suite showers. If you want to splash out,

Yan's Hotel has spacious rooms in a stylish modern building with park and pool south of the city on the rte de Montéléger (☎04.75.55.52.52, fax 04.75.42.27.37; ⑥). Among the many budget options are the *Angleterre*, 11 av Félix-Faure (☎04.75.43.00.35, fax 04.75.43.75.17; ②), and the **HI hostel**, *L'Epervière*, on chemin de l'Epervière (☎04.75.42.32.00, fax 04.75.56.20.67), by the Rhône, 2km south of the city (bus line #1); the hostel is quite expensive but has good sports facilities – swimming pool, sailing – and bike rental. The municipal **campsite** is in the hostel grounds (same number; all year).

The Town

The focus of Vieux Valence, the **Cathédrale St-Apollinaire**, was consecrated in 1095 by Pope Urban II (who proclaimed the First Crusade), and largely reconstructed in the seventeenth century after a local baron went on the rampage, avenging the execution of three Protestants during the Wars of Religion. More work was carried out later, including the horribly mismatched nineteenth-century tower, but the interior still preserves its original Romanesque grace – especially the columns around the ambulatory.

Between the cathedral and **Église de St-Jean** at the northern end of Grande Rue, which has preserved its Romanesque tower and porch capitals, are some of the oldest and narrowest streets of Vieux Valence. They are known as **côtes**: côte St-Estève just northwest of the cathedral; côte St-Martin off rue du Petit-Paradis; and côte Sylvante off rue du Petit-Paradis' continuation, rue A.-Paré. Diverse characters who would have walked these steep and crooked streets include Rabelais, a student at the university founded here in 1452 and suppressed during the Revolution, and the teenage Napoléon Bonaparte, who began his military training as a cadet at the artillery school.

Though Valence lacks the cohesion of the medieval towns and villages further south, it does have several vestiges of the sixteenth-century city, most notably the Renaissance **Maison des Têtes** at 57 Grande Rue. Be sure to look at the ceiling in the passageway here, where sculpted roses transform into the cherub-like heads after which the palace is named. Also worth a look is the **Maison Dupré-Latour**, on rue Pérollerie, which has a superbly sculptured porch and spiral staircase. By contrast Valence's **Musée des Beaux-Arts**, near the cathedral on place des Ormeaux (Tues–Sun: May–Sept 10am–noon & 2–7pm; rest of year 10am–noon & 2–6pm; 15F/€2.29), contains a mishmash of unremarkable local art and archeological finds, and frankly is not worth the price of admission.

A good place if you need to fill in time is the **Parc Jouvet** overlooking the river (and the motorway) south of avenue Gambetta. At sunset, or even better at dawn, this is definitely the best place to be in the city – a tranquil oasis away from the town's bustle – with a bottle of Cornas or sparkling St-Peray from the vineyards across the water.

Eating and drinking

For **restaurants**, *L'Épicerie*, 18 place Belat (☎04.75.42.74.46; closed Sat lunch, Sun & Aug), is one of the most congenial places to eat, with art exhibitions on the fifteenth-century walls, jazz some nights and imaginative food on menus from 105F/€16.01 to 310F/€47.28. Another good option is *Père Joseph*, 9 place des Clercs (☎04.75.42.57.80), which serves excellent-value traditional food, with menus starting from 69F/€10.52, but if you want to eat very well and are prepared to pay over 700F/€106.75 for the pleasure (or 360F/€54.90 for a lunch weekday menu), *Restaurant Pic*, 285 av Victor-Hugo (☎04.75.44.15.32; closed Sun evening & three weeks in Aug), is the city's top-notch eating house: roast lobster with truffles, asparagus with hollandaise sauce and caviar, and frozen nougat are some of the delights. Valence also has several good old-fashioned brasseries with a wide range of dishes and prices, including *Café Victor-Hugo*, 30 av Victor-Hugo, and *Le Bistrot des Clercs*, 48 Grande Rue; plus an excellent *salon de thé*, *One Two Tea*, at 37 Grande Rue.

Montélimar

In **MONTÉLIMAR**, 40km south of Valence, every street proclaims the glory of the nougat that has been made here for centuries and is the town's chief *raison d'être*. It's a lively enough place with a pleasant *vieille ville* and a fascinating museum dedicated to miniaturization.

The main street of the old town, **rue Pierre-Julien**, runs from the one remaining medieval **gateway** on the nineteenth-century ring of boulevards at place St-Martin, south past the **church of Ste-Croix** with its well-populated square, and onto place Marx-Dormoy. At no. 19, opposite the post office, is the **Musée de la Miniature** (June to mid-Sept daily 10am–6pm; rest of year Wed–Sun 2–6pm; 30F/€4.57), whose tiny exhibits, some so small you have to use a microsope, have been created by leading contemporary artists. There's a grain of rice bearing a portrait of Pushkin and one of his poems and a table laid with a chess game is no bigger than a ten franc coin.

Leading off rue Pierre-Julien are many medieval lanes with sixteenth- and seventeenth-century town houses, and around the pastel facades and old arcades of **place du Marché** you'll find *Le Métro* bar, done up as an old Paris métro station with a young clientele playing chess and backgammon. Above the old town to the east is the impressive **Château des Adhémars** on rue du Château (mid-June to Sept 10am–1pm & 3–7pm; rest of year Wed–Sun 9.30–11.30am & 2–5.30pm; 12F/€1.83). Originally belonging to the family after whom the town ("Mount of the Adhémars") was named, the castle is mostly fourteenth-century, but also boasts a fine eleventh-century chapel and twelfth-century living-quarters. If you wish to find out more about the town's famous **nougat** (the word is a contraction of a phrase meaning "you spoil us"), you can visit the Nougats Gerbe d'Or facotry at 140 av Jean-Jaurès (daily 8am–noon & 2–6pm), where you will be shown around the plant and have a chance to sample (and buy) the end product.

Practicalities

The **gare SNCF** is a short way west of the old town, with the **tourist office** in the adjacent park on the allée Champs-de-Mars (mid-June to Aug daily 8.30am–7.30pm; rest of year Mon–Sat 8.30am–6.30pm; ☎04.75.01.00.20, *montelimar.tourisme@wanadoo.fr*). There are plenty of **hotels** around the boulevards, including the very pleasant *Sphinx*, in a seventeenth-century town house at 19 bd Marre-Desmarais (☎04.75.01.86.64, fax 04.75.52.34.21; ④; closed Jan & Feb), and *Le Printemps*, 8 chemin de la Manche (☎04.75.01.32.63, fax 04.75.46.03.14; ④). Within the old town you could try *Pierre*, 7 place des Clercs (☎04.75.01.33.16; ②) – peaceful, apart from the nearby bell of Ste-Croix tolling the hours. The **campsite**, *International Deux Saisons* (☎04.75.01.88.99; closed Dec–Feb) is 500m east on the D540, then right towards Alexis. For good traditional **food**, head for the *Relais de l'Empereur*, 1 place Max-Dormoy (☎04.75.01.29.00; closed mid-Nov to mid-Dec; menus from 139F/€21.20).

WESTERN PROVENCE

The richest area of Provence, the Côte d'Azur apart, is the **west**. Most of the large-scale production of fruit, vegetables and wine is based here in the low-lying plains beside the Rhône and the Durance rivers. The only heights are the rocky outbreaks of the **Dentelles** and the **Alpilles**, and the narrow east–west ridges of **Mont Ventoux**, the **Luberon** and the **Mont Ste-Victoire**. The two dominant cities of inland Provence, **Avignon** and **Aix**, both have rich histories and contemporary fame in their festivals of art; **Arles**, **Orange** and **Vaison-la-Romaine** have impressive Roman remains. Around the Rhône delta, the **Camargue** is a unique self-contained region, as different from the rest of Provence as it is from anywhere else in France.

Orange and around

ORANGE was the former seat of the counts of Orange, a title created by Charlemagne in the eighth century and passed to the Dutch crown in the sixteenth century. The family's most famous member was Prince William, who ascended the English throne with his consort Mary in 1689's "Glorious Revolution". Today the town is best known for its spectacular **Roman theatre**, which hosts the important summer Chorégies **music festival**. While the rest of the Orange is attractive enough, there's not a lot to detain you once you've visited the theatre and adjacent museum and taken a quick look at the Roman triumphal arch at the northern approach to the town centre. Unfortunately, the victory of Le Pen's Front National in the municipal elections of 1995 forced the May strip-cartoon festival, which brought in all kinds of weird and wonderful entertainment, to be abandoned, and led many artists to boycott Orange's festivals, creating strong and unpleasant divisions.

Arrival, information and accommodation

The **gare SNCF** is about 1500m east of the centre, at the end of avenue Frédéric-Mistral. The nearest bus stop is at the bottom of rue Jean-Reboul, the first left as you walk away from the station. Bus #2, direction "Nogent", takes you to the Théâtre Antique, opposite which there's a seasonal tourist office (April–Sept daily 10am–1pm & 2–7pm) and the next stop, "Gasparin", to the main **tourist office** on cours Aristide-Briand (April–Sept Mon–Sat 9am–7pm, Sun 10am–6pm; rest of year Mon–Sat 9am–5pm; ☎04.90.34.70.88, *www.provence-orange.com*). The **gare routière** is close to the centre on place Pourtoules.

Of the **hotels**, good options include small, appealing and good-value *Arcotel*, 8 place aux Herbes (☎04.90.34.09.23, fax 04.90.51.61.12; ③); *L'Arène*, on place de Langes (☎04.90.11.40.40, fax 04.90.11.40.45; ⑦), with spacious rooms and all mod cons; and the very comfortable *Le Glacier*, 46 cours Aristide-Briand (☎04.90.34.02.01, fax 04.90.51.13.80, *hotelgla@aol.com*; ⑤). Orange's **campsite**, *Le Jonquier*, rue Alexis-Carrel (☎04.90.34.49.08, fax 04.90.51.16.97; closed Oct–March), to the northwest, is equipped with tennis courts and a pool.

The Town

Days off in Orange circa 5 BC were most entertainingly spent from dawn to dusk watching farce, clownish improvisations, song and dance, and occasionally, for the sake of a visiting dignitary, a bit of Greek tragedy in Latin at the huge Roman **theatre** (daily: April–Sept 9am–6.30pm; rest of year 9am–noon & 1.30–5pm; 30F/€4.58 combined ticket with museum), built into the hill which squats on the south side of the old town. The acoustics allowed a full audience of 9000 to hear every word. The hill of St-Eutrope, into which the seats were built, plus a vast awning strung from the top of the stage wall, protected the spectators from the weather. It is one of the best-preserved examples in existence, with its stage wall still standing 103m across and 36m high, and completely plain like some monstrous prison wall when you see it from outside. The interior, although missing much of its original decoration, has its central, larger-than-life-size statue of Augustus, and niches for lesser statues.

The best view of the theatre in its entirety is from St-Eutrope hill. You can follow a path up the hill either from the top of cours Aristide-Briand (montée P. de Chalons) or from cours Pourtoules (montée Albert Lambert) until you are looking directly down

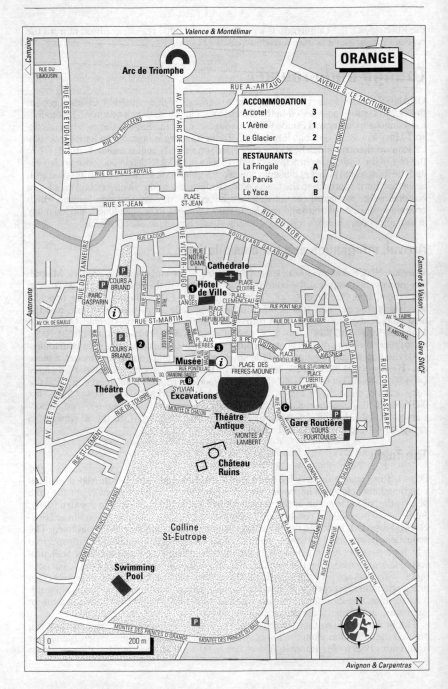

△ _Valence & Montélimar_

Camping ◁

RUE DU LIMOUSIN

Arc de Triomphe

RUE DES ÉTUDIANTS

RUE DES PHOCÉENS

AV. DE L'ARC DE TRIOMPHE

RUE A.-ARTAUD

AVENUE G. LE TACITURNE

RUE DE LA CONCORDE

ORANGE

ACCOMMODATION
Arcotel   3
L'Arène   1
Le Glacier   2

RESTAURANTS
La Fringale   A
Le Parvis   C
Le Yaca   B

RUE DE PALAIS-ROYALE

PLACE ST-JEAN

RUE ST-JEAN

RUE DU NOBLE

RUE LACOUR

BOULEVARD DALADIER

RUE VICTOR-HUGO

RUE NOTRE-DAME

Cathédrale

PLACE CLOITRE

RUE DES TANNEURS

RUE DE PLAISANCE

RUE GAMLET

Hôtel de Ville

PL. DE LANGES

PLACE CLEMENCEAU

RUE CARISTIE

RUE PONT NEUF

AV. H. FABRE

P COURS A BRIAND

P

PARC GASPARIN

(i)

RUE ST-MARTIN

PLACE DE LA RÉPUBLIQUE

RUE SECOND-WEBER

RUE DE LA RÉPUBLIQUE

AV. F. MISTRAL

Gare SNCF ▷

Camaret & Vaison ▷

AV. CH. DE GAULLE

RUE DE L'ANCIEN COLLÈGE

RUE DES VIEILLES...

P COURS A BRIAND

2

PL. AUX HERBES

RUE GOURMANDE

RT. PETIT FUSTERIE

PLACE CORDELIERS

RUE DES AVESNES

BOULEVARD DALADIER

(A)

3

Musée

(i)

R. TOURGAYRANNE

SQ. CHANOINE SAUTEL

RUE PONTILLAC

(B)

PLACE DES FRÈRES-MOUNET

RUE ST-FLORENT

PLACE LIBERTÉ

RUE DE L'HOPITAL

RUE CONTRASCARPE

AV DES THERMES

Théâtre

SYLVIAN Excavations

RUE DE TOURRE

MONTÉE DE CHALON

Théâtre Antique

(C)

Gare Routière

COURS POURTOULES

RUE POURTOULES

RUE ST-CLÉMENT

MONTÉE A LAMBERT

Château Ruins

AV. GÉNÉRAL LECLERC

BD DALADIER

MONTÉE DES PRINCES D'ORANGE

Colline St-Eutrope

RUE A. BLANC

RUE GAMBETTA

RUE DE CHÂTEAUNEUF

AV. MARÉCHAL FOCH

Swimming Pool

P

N

0   200 m

MONTÉE DES PRINCES D'ORANGE

MONTÉE DES PRINCES DU BAUX

Autoroute ◁

△ _Avignon & Carpentras_

onto the stage. The ruins around your feet are those of the short-lived seventeenth-century castle of the princes of Orange. Louis XIV had it destroyed in 1673 and the principality of Orange was officially annexed to France forty years later.

The **municipal museum**, across the road from the theatre entrance (daily: April–Sept 9.30am–7pm; rest of year 9.30am–noon & 1.30–5pm; 30F/€4.58 combined ticket with theatre), has documents concerning the Orange dynasty, including a suitably austere portrait of the founder of the Netherlands, William "the Silent". It also has Roman bits and pieces and a collection rotated on a yearly basis containing diverse items such as the contents of a seventeenth-century pharmacy and an unlikely selection of works by Frank Brangwyn, a Welsh painter who had no connections with Orange. The pictures here are stark portrayals of British workers early last century.

If you've arrived by road from the north you will have passed the town's second major Roman monument, the **Arc de Triomphe**, whose intricate frieze and relief celebrates imperial victories against the Gauls. It was built around 20 BC outside the town walls to recall the victories of the Roman Second Legion.

Orange's old town is very small, hemmed in between the theatre and the River Meyne, featuring some pretty fountain-adorned squares and houses with ancient porticoes and courtyards.

Eating, drinking and entertainment

For **food**, cheap *frites* with *plats du jour* to eat in or take away can be had at *La Fringale*, 10 rue de Tourre (closed Sun lunch, plus Wed lunch out of season), while *Le Yaca*, 24 place Silvain (☎04.90.34.70.03; closed Wed, plus Tues off-season & Nov), gives a generous choice of dishes for 125F/€19.06 or less in an old vaulted chamber. However, the best food you're likely to get in Orange is at *Le Parvis*, 3 cours des Pourtoules (☎04.90.34.82.00; closed Sun evening & Mon), with a weekday lunch menu from 98F/€14.95. For **drinking**, head for place de la République in the centre, where there's *Les Négociants* and the less expensive *Café de l'Univers*, painted in Provençal yellow. On the other side of cours Aristide-Briand, the *Café des Thermes*, 29 rue des Vieux-Fossés, has pool, a good selection of beers and a youngish clientele.

Orange's main festival is the **Chorégies**, a programme of opera, oratorios and orchestral concerts in July – details and tickets from the Bureau des Chorégies, 18 place Silvain (☎04.90.34.24.24).The theatre is also used throughout the year for jazz, film, folk and rock concerts. Prices range from 90F/€13.73 to 150F/€22.88, and some performances are free; details from the Service Culturel de la Ville, 14 place Silvain (☎04.90.51.57.57). Tickets for all events can be bought from FNAC shops in all big French cities, and at the theatre box office in Orange.

Sérignan-du-Comtat

The village of **SÉRIGNAN-DU-COMTAT**, 8km northeast of Orange (three buses daily from Orange and Avignon), was the final home of **Jean-Henri Fabre**, a remarkable self-taught scientist, famous for his insect studies, who also composed poetry, wrote songs and painted his specimens with artistic brilliance as well as scientific accuracy. In the 1860s he had to resign from his teaching post at Avignon because parents and priests thought his lectures on the fertilization of flowering plants were licentious, if not downright pornographic. In his **house**, which he named the *Harmas* (Mon & Wed–Sat 9–11.30am & 2–5pm; 15F/€2.29), you can see his jungly garden, his study, with his complete classification of the herbs of France, and, on the ground floor, a selection from his extraordinary watercolour series of the fungi of the Vaucluse. At the crossroads in the centre of the town (the *Harmas* is on the N976 towards Orange) there's a **statue** of Fabre in front of the red-shuttered buildings of the church and Mairie.

Châteauneuf-du-Pape

If you're heading down to Avignon, the slower route through **CHÂTEAUNEUF-DU-PAPE** (four buses daily) exerts a strong pull. The village takes its name from the summer palace of the Avignon popes, but neither the scant ruins of the fourteenth-century **château** (freely accessible) nor the medieval streets around **place du Portail** – the hub of the village – give Châteauneuf its special appeal. Rather it's the wines produced by the local vineyards, warmed at night by the large pebbles that cover the ground and soak up the sun's heat during the day, that are its real attraction. The rich ruby red is one of France's most renowned, but the white, too, is exquisite.

The *appellation* Châteauneuf-du-Pape does not, alas, come cheap, nor is there a centre where you can taste a good selection from the scores of *domaines*. For a casual introduction, the Cave Père-Anselme on avenue Bienheureux-Pierre-de-Luxembourg has a **Musée des Outils de Vigneron** (daily 9am–noon & 2–6pm; free), plus free tastings of its wines. Otherwise, the **tourist office** on place du Portail (July & Aug Mon–Sat 9am–7pm, Sun 10am–5pm; rest of year Mon–Sat 9am–12.30pm & 2–6pm; ☎04.90.83.71.08, fax 04.90.83.50.34), or the Fédération des Syndicats de Producteurs, 12 av Louis-Pasteur (☎04.90.83.72.21), can provide a complete list of producers, or you can visit an Association de Vignerons, such as Prestige et Tradition at 3 rue de la République (Aug & Sept daily 8am–noon & 2–6pm; rest of year closed Sun), who bottle the wine of ten producers.

If you can make your visit coincide with the first weekend of August you'll find free *dégustation* stalls throughout the village as well as parades, dances, equestrian contests, medieval entertainments and floats and so forth, all to celebrate the reddening of the grapes in the **Fête de la Véraison**. As well as wine, a good deal of grape liqueur – *marc* – gets consumed.

Accommodation is confined to four very pleasant but small **hotels**: *La Garbure*, 3 rue Joseph-Ducos (☎04.90.83.75.08, fax 04.90.83.52.34; ④); the four-star *Hostellerie du Château des Fines Roches* on route d'Avignon (☎04.90.83.70.23, fax 04.90.83.78.42, *fines-roches@en-provence.com*; ⑧); *La Mère Germaine* on avenue Cdt-Lemaitre (☎04.90.83.54.37, fax 04.90.83.50.27; ④); and *La Sommellerie* on route de Roquemaure (☎04.90.83.50.00, fax 04.90.83.51.85, *www.la-sommellerie.fr*; ⑧).

You can **eat** well for under 100F/€15.25 at the brasserie *La Mule du Pape*, 2 rue de la République (restaurant closed Sun evening & Mon), or pay a bit more at *La Mère Germaine* (see above; closed Wed), with its well-crafted Provençal dishes, and much more at *La Sommellerie* (see above; closed Sun evening & Mon out of season; menus from 170F/€25.93, à la carte around 320F/€48.80), where the cook is one of France's master chefs. Everything here is made on the premises, from the bread to the fine desserts, and meat is cooked on an outdoor wood fire.

Vaison-la-Romaine and around

VAISON-LA-ROMAINE lies 27km northeast of Orange and hit the headlines in 1992 when the River Ouvèze, which divides the medieval and eighteenth-century towns burst its banks, destroying riverside houses, the modern road bridge and an entire industrial quarter. Though the town has recovered remarkably, its character has changed. It seems much more commercialized and less friendly – perhaps because of the mass of ghoulish tourists who flocked to the town to see the damage.

It still, however, has the strong attractions of its medieval **haute ville**, with a ruined clifftop castle, a **Roman bridge** that held out against the floods, a cloistered former cathedral and the exceptional excavated remains of two **Roman districts**. Just south of Vaison there are sculptures in natural settings to be discovered at the **Crestet Centre d'Art**.

Arrival, information and accommodation

Buses to and from Carpentras, Orange and Avignon stop at the **gare routière** on avenue des Choralies near the junction with avenue Victor-Hugo, east of the town centre on the north side of the river. The **tourist office** is on place du Chanoine-Sautel (July & Aug daily 9am–12.30pm & 2–6.45pm; rest of year Mon–Sat 9am–noon & 2–5.45pm; ☎04.90.36.02.11, *vaison@wanadoo.fr*), between the two archeological sites in the north of the modern town.

There's not a great choice of **hotels** in Vaison, and few bargains. The town's best hotel and restaurant is *Le Beffroi*, a sixteenth-century residence on rue de l'Évêché in the *haute ville* (☎04.90.36.04.71, fax 04.90.36.24.78, *lebeffroi@wanadoo.fr*; ⑦; closed Jan to mid-March), while *Fête en Provence*, a restaurant in the *haute ville* also rents out rooms (☎04.90.36.36.43, fax 04.90.36.21.49, *lafetepce1@aol.com*; ⑦). You'll find cheaper accommodation at the *Centre Culturel à Cœur Joie* on route de St-Marcellin, 1km east of town down avenue Geoffroy from the Pont Romain (☎04.90.36.00.78, *centracj.France @wanadoo.fr*), which offers simple rooms. For **campers**, there's the central *Camping du Théâtre Romain* on chemin du Brusquet, off av des Choralies, Quartier des Arts (☎04.90.28.78.66; closed Nov to mid-March).

The Town

The *haute ville* lies on the south side of the river, with **rue du Pont** climbing up towards place des Poids and the fourteenth-century **gateway** to the town. More steep zigzags take you past the Gothic gate and overhanging portcullis of the **belfry** and into the heart of this sedately quiet, uncommercialized and rich *quartier*.

On the north bank from the **Pont Romain**, a Roman bridge that has been patched up over the years, Grande-Rue leads up to the central streets of rue de la République and cours Henri-Fabre, after which it becomes avenue Général-de-Gaulle. The two excavated **Roman residential districts** lie to either side of this avenue: Puymin to the east and La Villasse to the west (Jan, Feb, Nov & Dec Wed–Sun 10am–noon & 2–6.30pm; March–May & Oct daily 10am–12.30pm & 2–6pm; June–Sept daily 9.30am–6.30pm; ticket for both plus Puymin museum and cathedral cloisters 40F/€6.10).

The Puymin excavations contain the theatre, several mansions and houses, a colonnade known as the *portique de Pompée* and the museum for all the items discovered. The excavations of La Villasse reveal a street with pavements and gutters with the layout of a row of arcaded shops running parallel, more patrician houses (some with mosaics still intact), a basilica and the baths. The houses require a certain amount of imagination, but the street plan of La Villasse, the colonnade with its statues in every niche, and the theatre, which still seats 7000 people during the July festival, make it easy to visualize a comfortable, well-serviced town of the Roman ruling class.

Most of the detail and decoration of the buildings are displayed in the **museum** (same hours as ruins) in the Puymin district. Tiny fragments of painted plaster have been jigsawed together with convincing reconstructions of how whole painted walls would have looked. There are mirrors of silvered bronze, lead water pipes, taps shaped as griffins' feet, dolphin door knobs, weights and measures, plus impressive busts and statues.

Tickets can be bought at the Puymin entrance just by the tourist office or in the cloisters of the former **Cathédrale Notre-Dame**, west down chemin Couradou, which runs along the south side of La Villasse. The apse of the cathedral is a confusing overlay of sixth-, tenth- and thirteenth-century construction, using pieces quarried from the Roman ruins. The **cloisters** are fairly typical of early medieval workmanship – pretty enough but not wildly exciting. The only surprising feature is the large inscription visible on the north wall of the cathedral, a convoluted precept for the monks.

Eating and drinking

The **restaurant** to head for is *Le Bateleur*, 1 place Théodore-Aubanel, downstream from the Pont Romain on the north bank (☎04.90.36.28.04; closed Sun evening, Mon & mid-Nov to mid-Dec; weekday lunch menu 100F/€15.25, à la carte around 225F/€34.31); the lamb stuffed with almonds and the *rascasse soufflé* are highly recommended. Alternatively, *L'Auberge de la Bartavelle*, 12 place Sus-Auze (☎04.90.36.02.16; closed Mon & mid-Nov to mid-Dec), has specialities from southwest France for between 100F/€15.25 and 280F/€42.70, while salads and pizzas can by picked up at *Charlie's Pub*, 12 av Général-de-Gaulle (open 8am–3am), as well as traditional *plats* for around 65F/€9.91. You can get crêpes and pizzas in the old town and brasserie fare on place de Montfort, the obvious **drinking** place to gravitate towards. For a more local atmosphere, try *Vasio Bar* on cours Taulignan.

Le Crestet and the Centre d'Art

South of Vaison, 3.5km down the Malaucène road, a turning to the right leads up to the tiny hilltop village of **LE CRESTET** from where signs direct you the short distance to the **Crestet Centre d'Art** (permanent and free access), where modern sculptures have been placed, almost hidden, in an expanse of oak and pine woods. There is a map on the wall at the Centre but the idea is to wander freely: to start off, go behind the building and then turn sharp left within 20m. Some of the sculptures are formed from the trees themselves, others are startling metal structures such as a mobile and a Meccano cage.

Mont Ventoux

Mont Ventoux, whose outline repeatedly appears upon the horizon from the Rhône and Durance valleys, rises some 20km east of Vaison. White with snow, black with storm-cloud shadow or reflecting myriad shades of blue, the barren pebbles of the uppermost 300m are like a weathervane for all of western Provence. Winds can accelerate to 250km per hour around the meteorological, TV and military masts and dishes on the summit, but if you can stand still for a moment the view in all directions is unbelievable. A road, the D974, climbs all the way to the top, though no buses take it.

If you want to make the ascent on foot, the best path is from Les Colombets or Les Fébriers, two hamlets off the D974, east of **BEDOIN**, whose **tourist office** on the espace M.-L.-Gravier (July & Aug Mon–Fri 9am–1pm & 2–6pm, Sat 9am–noon & 2–6pm, Sun 9am–noon; rest of year Mon–Fri 9am–12.30pm & 2–6pm, Sat 9am–noon; ☎04.90.65.63.95) can give details of routes (including a once a week night-time ascent in July & Aug), plus addresses of campsites and *gîtes ruraux*.

Mont Ventoux is one of the challenges of the Tour de France, hence its appeal in summer for committed cyclists. Around the treeline is a **memorial** to the British cyclist Tommy Simpson, who died here from heart failure on one of the hottest days ever recorded in the race; according to race folklore his last words were "Put me back on the bloody bike."

The Dentelles and around

The **Dentelles**, a row of jagged limestone pinnacles, run across an arid, windswept and near-deserted upland area, the **Massif Montmirail-St-Amand**, just south of Vaison-la-Romaine. Their name refers to lace – the limestone protrusions were thought to resemble the contorted pins on a lace-making board – though the word's alternative connection with teeth (*dents* means "teeth") is equally appropriate.

The area is best known for its wines. On the western and southern slopes lie the wine-producing villages of **Gigondas**, **Beaumes-de-Venise**, **Sablet**, **Séguret**,

Vacqueyras and, across the River Ouvèze, **Rasteau**. Each one carries the distinction of having its own individual *appellation contrôlée* within the Côtes du Rhône or Côtes du Rhône Villages areas: in other words, their wines are exceptional. In addition, some of the villages are alluringly picturesque, with Séguret super-conscious of its Provençal beauty.

The most reputed red **wine** in the Dentelles is made at Gigondas – it's strong with an aftertaste of spice and nuts. You can taste the produce from forty different *domaines* at the **Caveau des Vignerons** on place de la Mairie in the village (daily 10am–noon & 2–6pm). The most distinctive wine, and elixir for those who like it sweet, is the pale amber-coloured Beaumes-de-Venise muscat which you can buy from the Cave des Vignerons (Mon–Sat 8.30am–noon & 2–6pm, Sun 9am–12.30pm & 2–6pm) on the D7 just outside Beaumes.

Besides *dégustation* and bottle-buying, you can go for long walks in the Dentelles, stumbling upon mysterious ruins or photogenic panoramas of Mont Ventoux and the Rhône valley. The pinnacles are favourite scaling faces for apprentice rock-climbers – though their wind-eroded patterns can be appreciated just as well without risking your neck on an ascent. Information on walking and climbing is available from *Le Gîte* (see below), as well as Gigondas' **tourist office** on place du Portail (July & Aug 10am–noon & 2–7pm; rest of year 10am–noon & 2–6pm; ☎04.90.65.85.46, *www.begond.fr/village /gigondas*), which also sells a local footpath map for 20F/€3.05.

Although it's possible to get to the villages by public transport from Vaison or Carpentras, your own vehicle is definitely an advantage. You can **rent bikes** at *Café du Court*, in the centre of Vacqueyras. **Hotel** possibilities include, in Beaumes, the old-fashioned and quiet *Auberge St-Roch*, on avenue Jules-Ferry (☎04.90.2.94.29; ①; closed Tues evening & Wed), and *Le Relais des Dentelles*, past the old village and over the river (☎04.90.62.95.27; ②; closed Mon). Gigondas has *Les Florets*, 2km from the village along the route des Dentelles (☎04.90.65.85.01, fax 04.90.65.83.80; ⑨, half-board obligatory in season), and the more upmarket *Hôtel Montmirail*, which you reach via Vacqueyras (☎04.90.65.84.01, fax 04.90.65.81.50; ⑤; closed Nov to late March). There are also **campsites** in Sablet (☎04.90.46.82.55), Beaumes (☎04.90.62.95.07) and Vacqueyras (☎04.90.65.84.24, fax 04.90.65.83.28), and a **gîte d'étape** at the entrance to Gigondas (☎04.90.65.80.85, fax 04.90.65.83.44, *www.provence-treking.com*; closed Jan & Feb), with double rooms and dormitory accommodation.

Besides the restaurants of the hotels mentioned above, places to stop to **eat** or drink are few and far between once you leave the villages. In Séguret *Le Bastide Bleue*, route de Sablet (☎04.90.46.83.43; closed Wed in winter; menus 70–120F/€10.68–18.30), is renowned for its use of fresh local ingredients. In Gigondas *L'Oustalet*, place du Portail (☎04.90.65.85.30; closed Mon & Sun evening; menus 85F/€12.96 lunch, 210F/€32.03 evening), has a pleasant shaded terrace and serves hearty home-style food; cheaper eats can be had at the *Café de la Poste* on rue Principale.

Carpentras

With a population of around 30,000, **CARPENTRAS** is a substantial city for this part of the world. It is also a very old city, its known history commencing in 5 BC as the capital of a Celtic tribe. The Greeks who founded Marseille came to Carpentras to buy honey, wheat, goats and skins, and the Romans had a base here. For a brief period in the fourteenth century, it became the papal headquarters and gave protection to Jews expelled from France.

For all its ancient remains, Carpentras seems incapable of working up an atmosphere to imbue the present with its past. The local history museum – the **Musée Comtadin** on boulevard Albin-Durand (daily except Tues: July & Aug 10am–noon & 2–6pm; rest of year 10am–noon & 2–4/6pm; 2F/€0.31) – is dark and dour. The erotic fantasies of a seventeenth-century cardinal frescoed by Nicolas Mignard in the **Palais de Justice**, formerly the episcopal palace, were effaced by a later incumbent. The *palais* is attached to the dull **Cathédrale St-Siffrein**, behind which, almost hidden in the corner, stands a **Roman arch** inscribed with scenes of prisoners in chains. Fifteen hundred years after its erection, Jews – coerced, bribed or otherwise persuaded – entered the cathedral in chains to be unshackled as converted Christians. The door they passed through, the **Porte Juif**, is on the southern side and bears strange symbolism of rats encircling and devouring a globe. The **synagogue** (Mon–Thurs 10am–noon & 3–5pm, Fri 10am–noon & 3–4pm; closed Jewish feast days; free), near the Hôtel de Ville, is a seventeenth-century construction on fourteenth-century foundations, making it the oldest surviving place of Jewish worship in France.

Carpentras cheers up, however, every Friday for the **market**, which from mid-November to March specializes in truffles, and during **festival** time in the second half of July. It also makes a useful base for excursions into the Dentelles, Mont Ventoux and the towns and villages south towards Apt.

Buses (trains are freight only) arrive either on avenue Victor-Hugo or place Terradou, a short walk away from place Aristide-Briand. The **tourist office** is at 170 allée Jean-Jaurès (July & Aug Mon–Sat 9am–7pm, Sun 9.30am–1pm; rest of year Mon–Fri 9am–1.30pm & 2–6.30pm, Sat 9am–noon & 2–6pm; ☎04.90.63.00.78, *tourist .carpentras@axit.fr*), which runs northeast from place Aristide-Briand. If you want to **stay**, rock-bottom options include *Le Théâtre*, 7 bd Albin-Durand (☎04.90.63.02.90; ③; closed Jan–March), and *Univers*, 10 place A.-Briand (☎04.90.63.00.05, fax 04.90.63.19.71; ②). For something much more pleasant, try *Le Fiacre*, 153 rue Vigne (☎04.90.63.03.15, fax 04.90.60.49.73; ⑤), an old town house with a garden, or *Safari Hotel*, 1 av J.-H.-Fabre (☎04.90.63.35.35, fax 04.90.60.49.99; ⑤), which is a bit characterless but has a pool and tennis courts. The local **campsite**, *Lou Comtadou*, is open year-round (☎04.90.67.03.16).

As far as **eating** goes, *Le Marijo* at 73 rue Raspail (☎04.90.60.42.65; closed Sun) is excellent, with menus from 80F/€12.20, while *Le Vert Galant*, 12 rue Clapies (☎04.90.67.15.50; closed Sat lunch, Sun evening, Mon lunch & weekends from May–Sept), serves more sophisticated fare, with a lunch menu for around 130F/€19.83, otherwise from 190F/€28.98. Takeaway Thai, Chinese and Vietnamese food is available from *La Perle d'Asie* on place du Théâtre. Café-crawling is best done on place Aristide-Briand or around the cathedral.

Avignon

AVIGNON, great city of the popes, and for centuries one of the major artistic centres of France, can be dauntingly crowded in summer and stiflingly hot. But it's worth braving for its spectacular monuments and museums, countless impressively decorated buildings, ancient churches, chapels and convents, and more places to eat and drink than you could cover in a month. During the **Festival d'Avignon** in July and the beginning of August, it is *the* place to be.

Immaculately preserved, central Avignon is enclosed by medieval walls, built in 1403 by the Anti-Pope Benedict XIII, the last of nine popes who based themselves here throughout most of the fourteenth century. The first pope to come to Avignon was Clement V in 1309, who was invited over by the astute King Philippe le Bel ("the Good"), ostensibly to protect Clement from impending anarchy in Rome. In reality, Philip saw a chance to extend his power over the Church by keeping the pope in the safety of Provence, during what came to be known as the Church's "Babylonian captivity". Clement's successors were a varied group, from the villainous John XXII (of Umberto Eco's *Name of the Rose* fame), to the dedicated Urban V, and later Gregory XI, who managed to re-establish the papacy in Rome in 1378. However, this was not the end

THE FESTIVAL OF AVIGNON

Unlike most provincial festivals of international renown, the **Festival d'Avignon** is dominated by theatre rather than classical music, though there is also plenty of that, as well as lectures, exhibitions and dance. It uses the city's great buildings as backdrops to performances, and takes place every year for three weeks from the second week in July. During festival time everything stays open late and everything gets booked up; there can be up to 200,000 visitors, and getting around or doing anything normal becomes virtually impossible.

The 2000 festival, which coincided with Avignon's turn as European Cultural Capital, saw theatrical interpretations as diverse as Euripides and Gogol, performed by companies from across Europe. As ever, heavywieght productions under the direction of figures such as Jacques Lasalle were balanced by the kinetic buffoonery of groups like the Footsbarn Travelling Theatre. The programme also included dance performances and lectures. The spotlighted culture of that year's festival was Eastern Europe; the programme *From the Baltic to the Balkans* was the debut of THEOREM (Theatres from the East and from the West), a European cultural venture designed to bring together the two halves of Europe on the stage, and it included theatre and dance groups from Lithuania to Romania, with strong Hungarian and Russian showings. As well as the mainstream festival, there's a fringe contingent known as the **Festival Off**, using a hundred different venues and the streets for a programme of innovative, obscure or bizarre performances.

The **main festival programme**, with details of how to book, is available from the second week in May from the Bureau du Festival d'Avignon, 8bis rue de Mons, 84000 Avignon (☎04.90.27.66.50, *www.festival-avignon.com*), or from the tourist office. Ticket prices are reasonable (between 130F/€19.83 and 200F/€30.50) and go on sale from the second week in June. As well as phone sales (11am–7pm; ☎04.90.14.14.14), they can be bought from FNAC shops in all major French cities. During the festival, tickets are available until 4pm for the same day's performances. The **Festival Off programme** is available from the end of June from Avignon Public Off BP5, 75521 Paris Cedex 11 (☎01.48.05.01.19, *www.avignon-off.org*). During the festival, the office is in the Conservatoire de Musique on place du Palais. Tickets prices range from 50F/€7.53 to 90F/€13.73 and a *Carte Public Adhérent* for 75F/€11.44 (50F/€7.53 during the festival) gives you thirty percent off all shows.

of the papacy here – after Gregory's death in Rome, dissident local cardinals elected their own pope in Avignon, provoking the Western Schism: a ruthless struggle for the control of the Church's wealth, which lasted until the pious Benedict fled Avignon for self-exile near Valencia in 1409.

As home to one of the richest courts in Europe, fourteenth-century Avignon attracted hordes of princes, dignitaries, poets and raiders, who arrived to beg from, rob, extort money from and entertain the popes. According to Petrarch, the overcrowded, plague-ridden papal entourage was "a sewer where all the filth of the universe has gathered". Burgeoning from within its low battlements, the town must have been a colourful, frenetic sight.

Arrival, information and accommodation

Both the **gare SNCF** on boulevard St-Roch and the adjacent **gare routière** (☎04.90.82.07.35) are close to Porte de la République, on the south side of the old city. In addition to the main *gare*, a new **TGV** station, which will cut travel to Paris down to two and half hours, is slated to open near the hospital 2km south of the city centre (consult *www.avignon-tourisme.com* for connection details). The city's two main local **bus stations** are by Porte de la République (stops "Poste", "Cité Administrative", "Gare Routière" and "Gare" are all within a five-minute walk) and place Pie, in the centre of

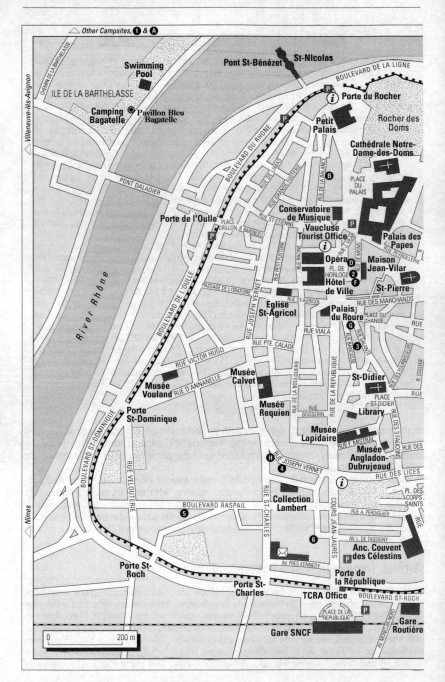

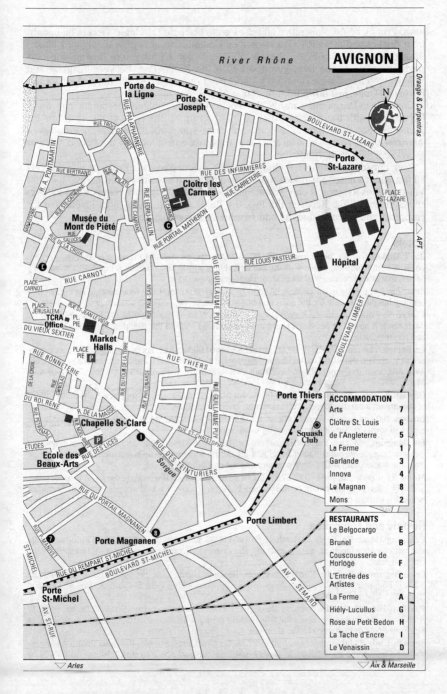

AVIGNON

River Rhône

N

△ Orange & Carpentras

Porte de la Ligne
Porte St-Joseph

BOULEVARD ST-LAZARE

RUE TROIS COLOMBES
RUE PALAPHARNERIE

Porte St-Lazare

PLACE ST-LAZARE

△ APT

R. A. PONTMARTIN
RUE BERTRAND
RUE 3 PILATS
RUE STE-CATHERINE
RUE DES CARMES
RUE DES INFIRMIERES

Cloître les Carmes

RUE CARRETERIE

BANASTERIE
RUE SALUCES
RUE LEDRU-ROLLIN
RUE CAMPANE

Musée du Mont de Piété

RUE PORTAIL MATHERON

C

RUE DE LA CROIX

RUE LOUIS PASTEUR

Hôpital

E

PLACE CARNOT

RUE CARNOT

RUE GUILLAUME PUY

RUE PALE-SAIN

BOULEVARD LIMBERT

PLACE JERUSALEM
RUE ST-JEAN LE VIEUX

TCRA Office

PL. PIE

DU VIEUX SEXTIER

Market Halls

PLACE PIE

P

RUE THIERS

RUE BONNETERIE

RUE DE LA CROIX

RUE GRIVOLAS

RUE DU ROUM DE LA TERRE

DU ROI RENE

R. DE LA MASSE

RUE PHILONARDE

RUE GUILLAUME PUY

Porte Thiers

RUE PETRAMALE

RUE NOEL BIRET

Chapelle St-Clare

P

RUE ST-CHRISTOPHE

Squash Club

ETUDES

RUE DES LICES

I

RUE DES TEINTURIERS

Ecole des Beaux-Arts

Sorgue

RUE DU PORTAIL MAGNANEN

ST-MICHEL

RUE MANUEL

7

Porte Magnanen

8

Porte Limbert

RUE DU REMPART ST-MICHEL

BOULEVARD ST-MICHEL

AV. P. SEMARD

Porte St-Michel

AV. ST-RUF

△ Arles

△ Aix & Marseille

ACCOMMODATION

Arts	7
Cloître St. Louis	6
de l'Angleterre	5
La Ferme	1
Garlande	3
Innova	4
Le Magnan	8
Mons	2

RESTAURANTS

Le Belgocargo	E
Brunel	B
Couscousserie de Horloge	F
L'Entrée des Artistes	C
La Ferme	A
Hiély-Lucullus	G
Rose au Petit Bedon	H
La Tache d'Encre	I
Le Venaissin	D

town. From Cité Administrative all buses go to place de l'Horloge. Tickets be bought from drivers and at TCRA (Transports en Commun de la Région d'Avignon) kiosks throughout town (6.50F/€0.99 each; 50F/€7.53 for 10). If you're driving, the best **parking** option is the free, guarded lot on the Île de Piot, between Avignon and Villeneuve; a free shuttle runs every 10min from 7am–2am between the parking lot and Porte de l'Oulle, just down from the Pont.

Cours Jean-Jaurès runs inside the Porte de la République becoming rue de la République, with the **tourist office** a little way up on the right at no. 41 (Mon–Fri 9am–6pm, Sat 9am–1pm & 2–5pm, Sun 9am–7pm; ☎04.32.74.32.74, *www.avignon -tourisme.com*). There's also an annexe at the other end of town by the Pont d'Avignon (May–Sept daily 9am–7pm).

Even outside festival time, finding a **room** in Avignon can be a problem: cheap hotels fill fast and it's never a bad idea to book in advance. It's worth remembering, too, that Villeneuve-lès-Avignon is only just across the river and may have rooms when its larger neighbour is full. Between the two, the Île de la Barthelasse is an idyllic spot for **camping**, and you may find the odd farmhouse advertising rooms.

Hotels

de l'Angleterre, 29 bd Raspail (☎04.90.86.34.31, fax 04.90.86.86.74, *www.hoteldangleterre.fr*). Located in the southeast corner of the old city, this is an old and traditional hotel with some very reasonably priced rooms, well away from night-time noise. ④.

Arts, 7 & 9 rue d'Aigarden (☎04.90.86.63.87, fax 04.90.82.90.15). Cosy little hotel in an eighteenth-century building. Handy for the train and bus stations. ③.

Cloître St Louis, 20 rue de Portail-Boquier (☎04.90.27.55.55, fax 04.90.82.24.01, *www.cloitre-saint -louis.com*). A large but personable and good-value hotel with all the facilities, including TV, phone and en-suite baths. ⑧.

La Ferme, chemin du Bois, Île de la Barthelasse (☎04.90.82.57.53, fax 04.90.27.15.47). A sixteenth-century farm on the island in the Rhône (signposted right off Pont Daladier as you cross over from Avignon), with well-equipped and pleasant rooms and greenery all around. Closed Nov to mid-March. ⑤.

Garlande, 20 rue Galante (☎04.90.85.08.85, fax 04.90.27.16.58). Delightful place right in the centre of the city on a narrow street. Well-known, so book in advance. ⑤.

Innova, 100 rue Joseph-Vernet (☎04.90.82.54.10, fax 04.90.82.52.39). A small, friendly hotel in the centre of town that's well worth booking in advance. ③.

Le Magnan, 63 rue Portail-Magnanen (☎04.90.86.36.51, fax 04.90.85.48.90, *www.avignon-et -provence.com/le-magnan*). Quiet hotel just inside the walls by Porte Magnanen a short way east from the station, and with a very pleasant shaded garden. ③.

Mons, 5 rue de Mons (☎04.90.82.57.16, fax 04.90.85.19.15, *hotelMons@wanadoo.fr*). A central, imaginatively converted thirteenth-century chapel. All the rooms are odd shapes, and you breakfast beneath a vaulted ceiling. ③.

Hostels and campsites

Camping Bagatelle, Île de la Barthelasse (☎04.90.86.30.39, fax 04.90.27.16.23). Three-star campsite, with laundry facilities, a shop and café; the closest to the city centre. Bus #20 "Bagatelle" stop. Open all year.

Camping municipal du Pont d'Avignon, Île de la Barthelasse (☎04.90.82.63.50, fax 04.90.85 .22.12). Four-star site, about 3km from the centre overlooking Pont St-Bénézet. Bus #20 to stop "Bénézet". Closed Nov–March.

Pavillon Bleu Bagatelle, camping Bagatelle, Île de la Barthelasse (☎04.90.86.30.39, fax 04.90.27 .16.23). Simple dormitory rooms for four to eight people with access to the campsite facilities. Bus #10 from Poste to Porte de l'Oulle, then bus #20 to "Bagatelle" stop.

Squash Club, 32 bd Limbert (☎04.90.85.27.78, fax 04.90.82.90.84). Not the most luxurious or central of options, but a good fall-back. Bus #2 east from the *gare SNCF* to stop "Thiers". 140F/€21.35 a night for a single.

The City

Avignon's low walls still form a complete loop around the city. Despite their menacing crenellations, they were never a formidable defence, even when sections were girded by a now-vanished moat. Nevertheless with the gates and towers all restored, the old ramparts still give a sense of cohesion and unity to the old town, dramatically marking it off from the modern spread of the city.

Rue de la République, the extension of cours Jean-Jaurès and the main axis of the old town, ends at **place de l'Horloge**, the city's main square. Beyond that is **place du Palais**, with the city's most imposing monument, the **Palais des Papes**, the **Rocher des Doms** park and the Porte du Rocher, overlooking the Rhône by the **pont d'Avignon**, or pont St-Bénézet as it's officially known.

The Palais des Papes and around

Rising high above the east side of place du Palais is the **Palais des Papes** (daily: last two weeks March 9.30am–6.30pm; April–Nov 9am–7pm; Nov to mid-March 9.30am–5.45pm; last ticket 1hr before closing; 46F/€7.02, including either an audio-guide or a guided tour at 11.30am or 4.45pm in English; 56F/€8.54 for palace and the Pont). With its massive stone vaults, battlements and sluices for pouring hot oil on attackers, the palace was built primarily as a fortress, though the two-pointed towers which hover above its gate are incongruously graceful. Close up it is simply too monstrous to take in all at once; to see it all, follow rue Peyrolerie around to the south end and look up. Inside the palace, so little remains of the original decoration and furnishings that you can be deceived into thinking that all the popes and their retinues were as pious and austere as the last official occupant, Benedict XIII. The denuded interior leaves hardly a whiff of the corruption and decadence of fat, feuding cardinals and their mistresses, the thronging purveyors of jewels, velvet and furs, musicians, chefs and painters competing for patronage, the riotous banquets and corridor schemings.

The visit begins in the **Pope's Tower**, otherwise known as the Tower of Angels. You enter the **Treasury** where the serious business of the church's deeds and finances went on. Four large holes found in the floor (covered over) of the smaller downstairs room served as safes. The same cunning storage device was used for the Chamberlain who lived upstairs in the **Chambre du Camérier** (just off the Jesus Hall), where the safes have been revealed. As he was the Pope's right-hand man, the quarters would have been lavishly decorated, but successive occupants have left their mark, most recently military whitewash, and what is now visible is a confusion of layers. The other door in this room leads into the **Papal Vestiary**, where the Pope would dress before sessions in the consistory. He also had a small library here and could look out onto the gardens below.

A door on the north side of the Jesus Hall leads to the **Consistoire** of the **Vieux Palais**, where sovereigns and ambassadors were received and the cardinals' council held. The only decoration that remains are fragments of frescoes moved from the cathedral, and a nineteenth-century line-up of the popes, in which all nine look remarkably similar thanks to the artist using the same model for each portrait. Some medieval

---

DISCOVERY PASSPORTS

The tourist offices in Avignon and Villeneuve-lès-Avignon distribute free **Discovery Passports**. After paying the full admission price for the first museum you visit, you and your family receive discounts of 20–50 percent on the entrance fees of all subsequent museums in Avignon. The pass also gives you discounts on tourist transport (such as *petits trains*, riverboats and bus tours), and is valid for two weeks after its first use.

artistry is in evidence, however, in the **Chapelle St-Jean**, off the Consistoire, and in the **Chapelle St-Martial** on the floor above. Both were decorated by a Sienese artist, Matteo Giovanetti, and commissioned by Clement VI, who demanded the maximum amount of blue – the most expensive pigment, derived from lapis lazuli. The **kitchen** on this floor also gives a hint of the scale of papal gluttony with its square walls becoming an octagonal chimneypiece for a vast central cooking fire. In the **Palais Neuf**, Clement VI's bedroom and study are further evidence of this pope's secular concerns, with wonderful food-oriented murals and painted ceilings. But austerity resumes in the cathedral-like proportions of the **Grande Chapelle**, or Chapelle Clementine, and in the **Grande Audience**, its twin in terms of volume on the floor below.

When you've completed the circuit, which includes a heady walk along the roof terraces, you can watch a glossy but informative film on the history of the palace (English headphones available). There are also concerts: programmes are available from the ticket office.

Next to the Palais des Papes, the **Cathédrale Notre-Dame-des-Doms** might once have been a luminous Romanesque structure, but the interior has had a bad attack of Baroque. In addition, nineteenth-century maniacs mounted an enormous gilded Virgin on the belfry, which would look silly enough anywhere, but when dwarfed by the fifty-metre towers of the popes' palace is absurd. There's greater reward behind, in the **Rocher des Doms** park. As well as ducks and swans and views over the river to Villeneuve and beyond, it has a sundial in which your own shadow tells the time.

The **Petit Palais** (daily except Tues: July & Aug 10am–1pm & 2–6pm; rest of year 9.30am–1pm & 2–5.30pm; 30F/€4.58), just below the Dom rock, contains a daunting collection of first-rate thirteenth- to fifteenth-century painting and sculpture, most of it by masters from northern Italian cities, like Florence, Bologna, Siena, Venice and Pisa. As you progress through the collection, you can watch as the masters wrestle with and finally conquer the representation of perspective – a revolution from medieval art, where the size of figures depended on their importance rather than position. Highlight of the collection, in room XVI, Botticelli's sublime *Virgin and Child* depicts a tender Mary, playfully coddling a smiling infant.

Behind the Petit Palais, and well signposted, is the half-span of Pont St-Bénézet, or the **Pont d'Avignon** of the famous song (daily: April, May & Oct 9am–7pm; June & July 9am–9pm; Aug & Sept 9am–8pm; Nov–March 9.30am–5.45pm; 20F/€3.05, 56F/€8.54 combined ticket with Palais des Papes). One theory has it that the lyrics say "*Sous le pont*" (under the bridge) rather than "*Sur le pont*" (on the bridge), and refer to the thief and trickster clientele of a tavern on the Île de la Barthelasse (which the bridge once crossed) dancing with glee at the arrival of more potential victims. Keeping the bridge in repair from the ravages of the Rhône was finally abandoned in 1660, three and a half centuries after it was built, and only four of the original 22 arches remain. Despite its limited transportational use, the bridge remained a focus of river boatmen, who constructed a chapel to their patroness on the first of the bridge's bulwarks.

Around place de l'Horloge

The café-lined **place de l'Horloge**, frenetically busy most of the time, is the site of the city's imposing **Hôtel de Ville** and **clock tower**, and the **Opéra**. Around the square, on rues de Mons, Molière and Corneille, famous faces appear in windows painted on the buildings. Many of these figures from the past were visitors to Avignon, and of those who recorded their impressions of the city it was the sound of over a hundred bells ringing that stirred them most. On a Sunday morning, traffic lulls permitting, you can still hear myriad different peals from churches, convents and chapels in close proximity. The fourteenth-century **church of St-Agricole**, just behind the Hôtel de Ville (Wed 10–11am, Sat 3.30–5pm), is one of Avignon's best Gothic edifices, though its lovely fifteenth-century façade is sadly scarred.

To the south, just behind rue St-Agricole on rue Collège du Roure, is the beautiful fifteenth-century **Palais du Roure**, a centre of Provençal culture. The gateway and the courtyard are definitely worth a look; there may well be temporary art exhibitions, and if you want a rambling tour through the attics to see Provençal costumes, publications and presses, photographs of the Carmargue in the 1900s and an old stagecoach, you need to turn up at 3pm on Tuesday (20F/€3.05).

To the west of place de l'Horloge are the most desirable Avignon addresses – both now and three hundred years ago. High, heavy facades dripping with cupids, eagles, dragons, fruit and foliage range along **rue Joseph-Vernet** and **rue Petite-Fusterie**, with expensive shops and restaurants to match.

The Banasterie and Carmes quartiers

The **quartier de la Banasterie**, lying behind the Palais des Papes, is almost solid seventeenth- and eighteenth-century, and the heavy wooden doors, with their highly sculptured lintels, today bear the nameplates of lawyers, psychiatrists and doctors.

Between Banasterie and **place des Carmes** are a tangle of tiny streets guaranteed to get you lost. Pedestrians have priority over cars on many of them, and there are plenty of tempting café or restaurant stops. At 24 rue Saluces, you'll find the peculiar **Musée du Mont de Piété**, an ex-pawnbroker's shop and now home to the town's archives (Mon–Fri 8.30–11.30am & 1.30–5.30pm; free). It has a small display of papal bulls and painted silk desiccators for determining the dry weight of what was the city's chief commodity.

Rue de la République to place Pie

Between rue de la République and the hideous **market hall** on **place Pie** (mornings Tues–Sun) is the main pedestrian precinct, centring around **place du Change**. **Rue des Marchands** and **rue du Vieux-Sextier** have their complement of chapels and late medieval mansions, in particular the **Hôtel des Rascas** on the corner of rue des Marchands and rue Fourbisseurs, and the **Hôtel de Belli** on the corner of rue Fourbisseurs and rue du Vieux-Sextier. The Renaissance **church of St-Pierre** on place St-Pierre has superb doors sculpted in 1551, and a retable dating from the same period. More Renaissance art is on show in the fourteenth-century **church of St-Didier** (Mon–Sat 9am–noon & 2–7pm, Sun 10–11am), chiefly *The Carrying of the Cross* by Francesco Laurana, commissioned by King René of Provence in 1478. There are also fourteenth-century frescoes in the left-hand chapel.

Musée Calvet and around

The excellent **Musée Calvet**, 65 rue Joseph-Vernet (daily except Tues 10am–1pm & 2–6pm; 30F/€4.58), and the impressive eighteenth-century palace housing it, are undergoing gradual restoration and transformation. Some of the collection will therefore be reshuffled. However, the **Galerie des Sculptures**, the first room, is completed and set to stay where it is. A better introduction to a museum couldn't be wished for, with a handful of languorous nineteenth-century marble sculptures, including Bosio's *Young Indian*, perfectly suited to this elegant space, lit from either side. The end of the gallery houses the Puech collection with a large selection of silverware, Italian and Dutch paintings and, more unusually, a Flemish curiosities cabinet, painted with scenes from the story of Daniel. Upstairs, the Provençal dynasties of the Mignards and the Vernets are well represented. Nicolas Mignard sets off with a fine set of seasons in the Joseph Vernet room, whilst Joseph Vernet himself sticks to representing the different times of the day. Further down, Horace Vernet donated the subtle *Death of Young Barra* by Jacques-Louis David as well as Géricault's *Battle of Nazareth*. On the way out don't miss the Victor Martin collection, including Vlaminck's *At the Bar*, Bonnard's *Winter Day* and the haunting *Downfall* by Chaïm Soutine. The rest of the eclectic collection – from an Egyptian mummy of a five-year-old boy to intricate wrought-iron work, taking in along the way Gallo-Roman pots and Gothic clocks – is due to be on show again by 2002.

Avignon's remaining museums are considerably less compelling. Next door to the Musée Calvet is the **Musée Requien** (Tues–Sat 9am–noon & 2–6pm; free); its subject is natural history and its sole advantage is in being free and having clean loos. With little more to recommend it is the **Musée Lapidaire**, a museum of Roman and Gallo-Roman stones housed in the Baroque chapel at 27 rue de la République (daily except Tues 10am–1pm & 2–6pm; April–Oct 10F/€1.53, rest of year free). Finally, at the **Musée Vouland**, at the end of rue Victor-Hugo near Porte St-Dominique (Tues–Sat: May–Oct 9am–noon & 2–6pm; rest of year 2–6pm; 20F/€3.05), you can feast your eyes on the fittings, fixtures and furnishings that French aristocrats enjoyed both before and after the Revolution. There's also some brilliant Moustiers faïence, exquisite marquetry and Louis XV ink-pots with silver rats holding the lids.

Southeast: to rue des Teinturiers

Between the noisy rue de la République and place St-Didier, on rue Labourer, is the **Musée Angladon-Dubrujeaud** (Wed–Sun 1–6pm, till 7pm in Aug; 30F/€4.58), displaying the remains of the private collection of Jacques Doucet. Although the collection, which once contained works like Picasso's *Demoiselles d'Avignon* and Douanier Rousseau's *The Snakecharmer* (now in the Musée d'Orsay), has seen better days, it is still very much worth a look. The visit begins with a series of rooms furnished and decorated as coherent units, the first Renaissance and the remainder eighteenth-century (including an orientalist room). The paintings which remain are alone worth the admission price, and include Foujita's *Portrait of Mme Foujita* and a *Self-Portrait*, Modigliani's *The Pink Blouse*, various Picassos and Van Gogh's *The Railroad Cars*, the only painting from Van Gogh's stay in Provence to be on permanent display in the region.

Through the park by the tourist office (where there's an old British red phone box) you come to **place des Corps-Saints**, a lively area of cafés and restaurants whose tables fill the square. Just to the north, rue des Lices runs eastwards, past the École des Beaux-Arts, to **rue des Teinturiers**, the city's most atmospheric street. Its name refers to the eighteenth- and nineteenth-century business of calico printing. The cloth was washed in the Sorgue which still runs alongside the street, turning the wheels of long-gone mills, and, although the water is fairly murky and sometimes smelly, this is still a great street for evening strolls, with a large number of cheap restaurants. Just west of the tourist office, down rue Violette, you'll find the **Collection Lambert** (Tues–Sun 11am–7pm; 15F/€2.29), Avignon's first (and rather unfortunate) attempt at a contemporary art gallery. The collection is disappointing and the admission price is hardly justified by displays such as an entire room of Robert Ryman's black canvases.

Eating and drinking

Good-value midday **meals** are easy to come by in Avignon and eating well in the evening needn't break the bank. The large terraced café-brasseries on place de l'Horloge, rue de la République, place du Change and place des Corps-Saints all serve quick basic meals. Rue des Teinturiers is good for menu-browsing if you're on a budget, and the streets between place de Crillon and place du Palais are full of temptation if you're not.

Restaurants

Le Belgocargo, 10 place des Châtaignes (☎04.90.85.72.99). Belgian restaurant, specializing in *moules frites* and beer; lunch menu with drink for under 50F/€7.53. Closed Sun out of season.

Brunel, 46 rue Balance (☎04.90.85.24.83). Superb regional dishes, with menus from 100F/€15.25. Closed Sun & Mon, and mid-July to mid-Aug.

Couscousserie de l'Horloge, 2 rue de Mons (☎04.90.85.84.86). Popular Algerian-run restaurant with a jovial atmosphere and excellent North African food. Try the delicious *tajine aux prunes* at 75F/€11.44.

L'Entrée des Artistes, 1 place des Carmes (☎04.90.82.46.90). Small, friendly bistro serving traditional French dishes; 92F/€14.03 weekday menu. Closed lunch Sat, Sun & first two weeks of Sept.

La Ferme, chemin du Bois, Île de la Barthelasse (☎04.90.82.57.53). A traditional farmhouse, serving well-prepared simple dishes. From 110F/€16.78. Closed Sat lunch.

Hiély-Lucullus, 5 rue de la République (☎04.90.86.17.07). This is one of Avignon's top gastronomic palaces, preparing beautiful Provençal cuisine. The Rhône wines are the very best, and will add a good whack to an already groaning bill if you order à la carte. 155F/€23.64 menu or else 320F/€48.80 *menu gourmand*. Closed Mon & Tues, and last two weeks of Jan & June.

Rose au Petit Bedon, 70 rue Joseph-Vernet (☎04.90.82.33.98). The *"Potbelly"* does the best meal for under 170F/€25.93 to be had anywhere in the city.

La Tache d'Encre, 22 rue des Teinturiers (☎04.90.85.97.13). The food isn't brilliant but the music – jazz, rock, chansons, African or salsa – usually is and the atmosphere is congenial. There's live music on Fri and Sat nights, occasionally weekdays, too; booking advisable. Menus from 92F/€14.03. Closed Mon.

Le Venaissin, 16 place de l'Horloge (☎04.90.86.20.99). In the height of summer, you'll be lucky to get a table here – it's the only cheap brasserie on place de l'Horloge that serves more than *steak frites*; two menus under 100F/€15.25. Closed mid-Nov to Jan.

Cafés, bars and salons de thé

Bloomsbury's, 11 rue de la Balance. As English a teahouse as you could find on this side of the Channel. Excellent cakes, and a good, quiet place to read the paper. Mon–Sat 1–6pm.

Les Célestins, place des Corps-Saints. Café-bar with a young, fairly trendy clientele. Mon–Sat 7am–1am.

Grand Café du Commerce, 21 rue St-Jean-de-Vieux. Pleasant café for all tastes.

Pub Z, cnr rue Bonneterie & rue Artaud (bus #58). Rock bar with black and white decor. Open till 1.30am; closed Sun & first three weeks of Aug.

Le Red Zone, 25 rue Carnot (☎04.90.27.02.44). Bar with DJs and weekly concerts. Thurs–Sat 7pm–1.30am.

Shakespeare, 155 rue Carreterie. English bookshop and *salon de thé*. Closed Sun, Mon & evenings.

Tapalocas, 10 rue Galante (☎04.90.82.56.84). Tapas at 12F/€1.83 a dish, and Spanish music, sometimes live. Daily 11.45am–1.30am.

Nightlife and entertainment

There's a fair amount of **nightlife** and cultural events in Avignon: the **Opéra**, on place de l'Horloge (☎04.90.82.23.44), mounts a good range of productions; Le Chêne Noir, 8bis rue Ste-Catherine (☎04.90.86.58.11), is a theatre company worth seeing, with mime, musicals or Molière on offer; and plenty of **classical concerts** are performed in churches, usually for free.

For **live music,** *AJMI Jazz Club,* La Manutention, rue Escalier-Ste-Anne (☎04.90.86.08.61), hosts live jazz every Thursday night and features major acts and some adventurous new groups. *Le Bistroquet,* quartier du Mouton on Île de la Berthelasse, is a rock bar with live gigs except in June, and the restaurant *La Tache d'Encre* (see above) has some good live sounds on Friday and Saturday nights. **Gay venues** include *L'Esclave Bar,* 12 rue du Limas (daily 10.30pm–5am; shows Wed & Sun), a bar and disco popular with gay men, and *The Cage,* a club in the *gare routière* building, with a gay and lesbian clientele. To find out what's on, get hold of the tourist office's free bi-monthly calendar *Rendez-Vous*. They may also have the weekly arts, events and music magazine *César* (also free), which is otherwise found in arts centres.

Listings

Bike rental Aymard, 80 rue Guillaume-Puy; Transhumance Voyages, 52 boul St-Roch (also scooters and motorbikes).

Boat trips Grands Bateaux de Provence, allée de l'Oulle (☎04.90.85.62.25, *bateaugpb@aol.com*), offering year-round trips upstream towards Châteauneuf-du-Pape and downstream to Arles; two-week advance booking recommended.

Car rental ADA, 23 bd St-Ruf (☎04.90.86.18.89); Hertz, 2a av Montclar (☎04.90.14.26.90); Rent a Car, 130 av Pierre Sémard (☎04.90.88.08.02); Sixt, 3 av St-Ruf (☎04.90.86.06.61).

Changing money Chaix Conseil, 43 cours Jean-Jaurès and place Carnot; automatic exchange at CIC, 13 rue République, and Caixa Bank, 64 rue Joseph-Vernet.

Emergencies Doctor/ambulance ☎15 or Médecins de Garde (☎04.90.87.75.00); hospital, Centre Hospitalier H.-Duffaut, 305 rue Raoul-Follereau (☎04.90.80.33.33); night chemist, call police at bd St-Roch (☎04.90.16.81.00) for addresses.

Internet *Cyber Highway*, 30 rue des Infirmières (*cyberhighway@wanadoo.fr*); *Le Pomme Bleue*, 5 place des Carmes (☎04.90.14.00.15).

Laundry 9 rue du Chapeau Rouge; 27 rue Portail-Magnanen; 113 av St-Ruf.

Police 10 place Pie (☎08.00.00.84.00).

Post office Poste, cours Président-Kennedy, Avignon 84000.

Swimming pool Piscine de la Barthelasse on the Île de la Barthelasse (May–Aug 10am–7pm).

Taxis place Pie (☎04.90.82.20.20).

Villeneuve-lès-Avignon

VILLENEUVE-LÈS-AVIGNON rises up a rocky escarpment above the west bank of the Rhône, looking down upon its older neighbour from behind far more convincing fortifications. Historically, Villeneuve operated largely as a suburb to Avignon, with palatial residences constructed by the cardinals and a great monastery founded by Pope Innocent VI.

To this day, Villeneuve is technically a part of Languedoc and not Provence, and would score better in the hierarchy of towns to visit were it further from Avignon, whose monuments it can almost match for colossal scale and impressiveness. In summer, at least, it benefits, providing venues for the Avignon Festival as well as alternatives for accommodation overspill; and it's certainly worth a day, whatever time of year you visit.

Arrival, information and accommodation

From Avignon's **gare SNCF** (see p.917) the half-hourly Villeneuve–Les Angles #10 bus (take care not to go in the direction Les Angles–Villeneuve) runs direct to place Charles-David ("Bellevue" stop), taking less than ten minutes, or five if you catch it from Porte d'Oulle. After 7pm you'll have to take a taxi or walk; it's only 3km. On place Charles-David you'll find the **tourist office** (July daily 10am–7pm; Aug daily 8.45am–12.30pm & 2–6pm; Sept–June Mon–Sat 8.45am–12.30pm & 2–6pm; ☎04.90.25 .61.55, *www.villeneuve.lez.avignon.tourisme@wanadoo.fr*), and a food **market** on Thursday morning and bric-a-brac on Saturday morning. Avenue Gabriel-Péri leads west off the square past the Mairie to place St-Marc. From here, the main street, rue de la République, runs due north.

If money is no object, the first choice for **accommodation** has to be *Le Prieuré*, 7 place du Chapitre (☎04.90.15.90.15, fax 04.90.25.45.39, *leprieure@relaischateaux.fr*, ⑧), both for the rooms and for its restaurant. For half the price, you could stay in equally ancient surroundings at *L'Atelier*, 5 rue de la Foire (☎04.90.25.01.84, fax 04.90.25.80.06;

MUSEUM PASS

A **Passeport pour l'Art** (45F/€6.86) gives you entry to the Fort St-André, Tour Philippe-le-Bel, La Chartreuse du Val de Bénédiction, the Collègiale Notre-Dame and its cloister and the Musée Pierre-de-Luxembourg. The ticket is available from each of the monuments and from the tourist office.

⑤), a sixteenth-century house with huge open fireplaces and a walled garden, or at a Louis XIV mansion, *Les Cèdres*, 39 bd Pasteur (☎04.90.25.43.92, fax 04.90.25.14.66, *lecedres.hotel@lemel.fr*; ⑤), with pool and restaurant. For a cheaper option, try the *Beauséjour*, 61 av Gabriel-Péri (☎04.90.25.20.56; ③), overlooking the river near the Pont du Royaume. The **YMCA hostel**, 7bis chemin de la Justice (☎04.90.25.46.20, fax 04.90.25.30.64), is an attractive alternative, beautifully situated overlooking the river by Pont du Royaume, with balconied rooms for two to six people and an open-air swimming pool (stop "Pont d'Avignon" on Les Angles–Villeneuve bus or "Général-Leclerc" on the Villeneuve-Les Angles bus). For **campers**, the three-star *Camping municipal de la Laune* is in chemin St-Honoré (☎ & fax 04.90.25.76.06; closed mid-Oct to March), off the D980, near the sports stadium and swimming pools.

The Town

For a good overview of Villeneuve – and Avignon – make your way to the **Tour Philippe-le-Bel** at the bottom of montée de la Tour (bus stop "Philippe-le-Bel"). This tower was built to guard the French end of Avignon's Pont St-Bénézet (or Pont d'Avignon; see p.922), and a climb to the top (Tues–Sun: April–Sept 10am–12.30pm & 3–7pm; rest of year 10am–noon & 2–7pm; 10F/€1.53) will be rewarded with stunning views.

Even more indicative of French distrust of its neighbours is the enormous **Fort St-André** (daily: April–Sept 10am–1pm & 2–6pm; rest of year 10am–noon & 2–5pm; 25F/€3.81), whose bulbous double-towered gateway and vast white walls loom over the town. Inside, refreshingly, there's not a hint of a postcard stall or souvenir shop – just tumbledown houses and the former **abbey**, with its gardens of olive trees, ruined chapels, lily ponds and dovecotes (Tues–Sun: July & Aug 10am–12.30pm & 2–6pm; rest of year 10am–noon & 2–5pm; 20F/€3.05). Its cliff-face terrace is the classic spot for artists to aim their brushes, or photographers their cameras, over Avignon. You can reach the approach to the fortress, montée du Fort, from place Jean-Jaurès on rue de la République, or by the "rapid slope" of **rue Pente-Rapide**, a cobbled street of tiny houses leading off rue des Recollets on the north side of place Charles-David.

Almost at the top of rue de la République, on the right, allée des Muriers leads from place des Chartreux to the entrance of **La Chartreuse du Val de Bénédiction** (daily: April–Sept 9am–6.30pm; rest of year 9.30am–5.30pm; 32F/€4.88). This Carthusian monastery, one of the largest in France, was founded by the sixth of the Avignon popes, Innocent VI (pope 1352–62), whose sharp profile is outlined on his tomb in the church. The buildings, which were sold off after the Revolution and gradually restored this century, are totally unembellished. With the exception of the Giovanetti frescoes in the chapel beside the refectory, all the paintings and treasures of the monastery have been dispersed, leaving you with a strong impression of the austerity of the Carthusian order. You're free to wander around unguided, through the three cloisters, the church, chapels, cells and communal spaces, which have little to see but plenty of atmosphere to absorb. It is one of the best venues in the Festival of Avignon.

Another festival venue is the fourteenth-century **Église Collégiale Notre-Dame** and its cloister (7F/€1.07) on place St-Marc close to the Mairie (Jan, March & Oct–Dec

Tues–Sun 10am–noon & 2–5.30pm; April to mid-June & last two weeks Sept Tues–Sun 10am–12.30pm & 3–7pm; mid-June to mid-Sept daily 10am–12.30pm & 3–7pm). Notre-Dame's most important treasure is a rare fourteenth-century smiling Madonna and Child made from a single tusk of ivory, now housed, along with many of the paintings from the Chartreuse, in the **Musée Pierre-de-Luxembourg**, just to the north along rue de la République (same hours as Église Collègiale Notre-Dame; 20F/€3.05). The spacious layout includes a single room, with comfortable settees and ample documentation, given over to the most stunning painting in the collection – *The Coronation of the Virgin*, painted in 1453 by Enguerrand Quarton as the altarpiece for the church in the Chartreuse.

Eating and drinking

There's a good choice of **eating** places in the town centre. Try *La Calèche*, 35 rue de la République (☎04.90.25.02.54; closed Nov & Sun out of season; menus around 100F/€15.25), or the *Le Fleur de Sel* on place V.-Basch (☎04.90.25.00.71; closed Sun out of season; around 80F/€12.20), both of which serve plentiful *terroir* meals. For a blowout meal, head for posh *La Magnanerie*, 37 rue Camp de Bataille (☎04.90.25.11.11), off rue de la Magnanerie, with a Provençal menu for 170F/€25.93 (à la carte over 400F/€61), or the luxurious restaurant of *Le Prieuré*, where subtly blended Mediterrean flavours dominate (menus from 200F/€30.50, à la carte over 400F/€61). Alternatively, *Aubertin*, 1 rue de l'Hôpital (☎04.90.25.94.84; closed Mon out of season), serves a 120F/€18.30 lunch menu in the shade of the old arcades by the Collègiale Notre-Dame (à la carte from 350F/€53.38).

St-Rémy-de-Provence and the Alpilles

The watery and intensely cultivated scenery of the Petite Crau plain south of Avignon changes abruptly with the eruption of the **Chaîne des Alpilles**, whose peaks look like the surf of a wave about to engulf the plain. At their northen foot nestles **ST-RÉMY**, a dreamy place whose old town is contained within a circle of boulevards no more than half a kilometre in diameter. Outside this ring, the modern town is sparingly laid out, so for once you don't have to plough your way through dense developments to reach the centre. It is a beautiful place, as unspoilt as the villages around it.

Arrival, information and accommodation

There's no train station in St-Rémy; **buses** from Avignon, Aix and Arles drop you in place de la République, the main square abutting the old town on the east. The **tourist office**, on place Jean-Jaurès (June–Sept Mon–Sat 9am–noon & 2–7pm, Sun 9am–noon; rest of year Mon–Sat 9am–noon & 2–6pm; ☎04.90.92.05.22, fax 04.90.92.38.52), is just south of the centre, reached by following boulevard Marceau/avenue Durand-Maillane; they have excellent free guides to **cycling and walking routes** in and around the Alpilles and can provide addresses for renting **horses**. If you want to rent a **bike**, try Telecycles (☎04.90.92.83.15). It's difficult to get to Glanum or Les Baux (see pp.930–1) except by foot or taxi (taxis ☎06.07.02.25.64 or 06.09.92.13.38).

St-Rémy has a fairly wide choice of **accommodation**, though real bargains are hard to come by. In the old town, pleasant hotels with some cheap rooms are *Les Arts-La Palette*, above the *Café des Arts* at 30 bd Victor-Hugo (☎04.90.92.08.50, fax 04.90.92.55.09; ④; closed Jan & Feb), and *Ville Verte*, on the corner of place de la République and avenue Fauconnet (☎04.90.92.06.14, fax 04.90.92.56.54; ③), which has facilities for the disabled, a garden and a pool, and also organizes walking, climbing and cycling trips. Outside the old town, try *Nostradamus*, 3 av Taillandier (☎04.90.92.13.23, fax 04.90.92.49.54; ③), to the north, with studios for two, or *Le Castellet des Alpilles*, 6 place Mireille (☎04.90.92.07.21, fax 04.90.92.52.03; ⑤; closed mid-Jan to mid-Feb), to the south past the tourist office, which is small and friendly, and has some rooms with great views. Finally, close by the tourist office, the *Antiques*, 15 av Pasteur (☎04.90.92.03.02, fax 04.90.92.50.40; ⑧; closed Nov–March), is a nineteenth-century mansion with huge grounds, pools and wonderfully aristocratic furnishings in the dining room and salons.

There are three functional and busy **campsites** near St-Rémy: the municipal *Le Mas de Nicolas*, 2km along route de Mollèges (☎04.90.92.27.05; closed Nov to mid-March); *Monplaisir*, 1km along route de Maillane (☎04.90.92.22.70, fax 04.90.92.18.57; closed Nov–Feb); and *Pegomas*, 1km along route de Noves (☎04.90.92.01.21, fax 04.90.92.56.17; closed Nov–Feb).

The Town

To reach the old town from place de la République, take avenue de la Résistance, which runs alongside the town's main church, the **Collégiale St-Martin** (organ recitals July–Sept Sat 5pm), and start wandering up the alleyways into immaculate, leafy squares. For an introduction to the region, a good first visit is to the **Musée des Alpilles** on place Favier, housed in the Hôtel Mistral de Mondragon (daily: April–June & Sept–Oct 10am–noon & 2–6pm; July & Aug 10am–noon & 2–7pm; Nov–Dec 10am–noon & 2–5pm; 18F/€2.75). The museum features interesting displays on folklore, festivities and traditional crafts, plus some intriguing local landscapes, some creepy portraits by Marshal Pétain's first wife and souvenirs of local boy Nostradamus.

You can buy a combined 40F/€6.10 ticket for the Musée des Alpilles and the neighbouring **Musée Archéologique** in the Hôtel de Sade (daily: Feb, March & Oct–Dec 9am–noon & 2–5pm; April–Sept 9am–noon & 2–6pm), displaying finds from the archeological digs at the Greco-Roman town of Glanum (see p.930). The hour or so which it takes to wander through the museum may be a bit much for the non-committed, but there are some stunning pieces, in particular the temple decorations. Entry to the archeological museum alone costs 15F/€2.29, while a 36F/€5.49 ticket includes entry to Glanum, and a 41F/€6.25 *forfait* includes entry to Glanum and the Musée des Alpilles.

In addition to the two fifteenth- to sixteenth-century *hôtels* that house the museums, you'll find more ancient stately residences as you wander through the old town, particularly along **rue Parage**. On rue Hoche is the birthplace of **Nostradamus**, though only the facade is contemporary with the savant, and the house is not open for visits. The Hôtel d'Estrine, 8 rue Estrine, houses the **Centre d'Art Présence Van Gogh** (April–Dec Tues–Sun 10.30am–12.30pm & 2.30–6.30pm; 20F/€3.05), which hosts contemporary art exhibitions and has a permanent exhibition of Van Gogh reproductions and extracts from letters, as well as audiovisual presentations on the painter.

Eating, drinking and festivals

You'll find plenty of **brasseries** and **restaurants** in and around old St-Rémy. There are a few good options on rue Carnot (leading from boulevard Victor-Hugo east through the old town to boulevard Marceau), including the Provençal *La Gousée d'Ail* at no. 25 (☎04.90.92.16.87; closed Wed), with live jazz on Thursday nights, and *La Maison Jaune* at no. 15 (☎04.90.92.56.14; closed Mon & Sun evening in winter, Mon & Tues in summer), with a 120F/€18.30 weekday lunch menu and a fabulous *menu dégustation provençal* for 275F/€41.94. Alternatively, *Le Jardin de Frédéric*, 8 bd Gambetta (☎04.90.92.27.76; closed Wed), which has a 130F/€19.83 lunch menu, usually has some interesting dishes on offer, and *Xa*, 24 bd Mirabeau (☎04.90.92.41.23; closed Wed & Nov–March; 140F/€21.35 menu), is a new modish restaurant with excellent food. For a scenic spot to dine on crêpes, try *Lou Planet*, 7 place Favier, by the Musée des Alpilles, and for brasserie fare head for *Le Bistrot des Alpilles*, 15 bd Mirabeau (open till midnight; closed Sun). For **café**-lounging, head for the *Café des Arts*, 30 bd Victor-Hugo (open till 12.30am; closed Tues & Feb), where the works of local painters are exhibited.

The best time to visit St-Rémy is during the **Fête de Transhumance** on Whit Monday, when a 2000-strong flock of sheep, accompanied by goats and donkeys, does a tour of the town before being packed off to the Alps for the summer. Another good time to come is for the **Carreto Ramado**, on August 15, a harvest thanksgiving procession in which the religious or secular symbolism of the floats reveals the political colour of the various village councils, while a pagan rather than workers' **May Day** is celebrated with donkey-drawn floral floats on which people play fifes and tambourines.

South of St-Rémy: Les Antiques, St-Paul-de-Mausole and Glanum

About 1.5km south of the old town, following avenue Vincent-Van-Gogh past the tourist office, you'll come to **Les Antiques** (free access), a triumphal arch supposedly celebrating the Roman conquest of Marseille, and a mausoleum thought to commemorate two grandsons of Augustus. Save for a certain amount of weather erosion, the mausoleum is perfectly intact, while on the arch you can still make out the sculptures of fruits and leaves representing the fertility of "the Roman Province" (hence "Provence"), and the figures of chained captives, symbolizing Roman might.

The arch would have been a familiar sight to **Vincent Van Gogh**, who in 1889 requested that he be put under medical care for several months. He was living in Arles at the time, and the hospital chosen by his friends was in the old monastery **St-Paul-de-Mausole**, a hundred metres or so east of the Antiques; it remains a psychiatric clinic today. Although the regime was more prison than hospital, Van Gogh was allowed to wander out around the Alpilles and painted prolifically during his twelve-month stay. The *Oliviers' Fields*, *The Reaper*, *The Enclosed Field* and *The Evening Stroll* are among the 150 canvases of this period. The church and cloisters can be visited (9am–6pm; free): take avenue Edgar-Leroy or allée St-Paul from avenue Vincent-Van-Gogh, go past the main entrance of the clinic and into the gateway on the left at the end of the wall.

Not very far beyond the hospital is a signposted farm called **Mas de la Pyramide** (daily: July & Aug 9am–noon & 2–7pm; rest of year 9am–noon & 2–5pm; 20F/€3.05). It's an old troglodyte farm in the Roman quarries for Glanum with a lavender and cherry orchard surrounded by cavernous openings into the rock filled with ancient farm equipment and rusting bicycles. The farmhouse is part medieval and part Gallo-Roman, with pictures of the owner's family who have lived there for generations.

One of the most impressive ancient settlements in France, **Glanum** (daily: April–Sept 9am–7pm; rest of year 9am–noon & 2–5pm; 32F/€4.88), was dug out from alluvial deposits at the very foot of the Alpilles. The site was originally a Neolithic homestead; then, between the second and first centuries BC, the Gallo-Greeks, probably from Massalia (Marseille), built a city here, on which the Gallo-Romans, from the end of the first century BC to the third century AD, constructed yet another town.

Though Glanum is one of the most important archeological sites in France, it can be very difficult to get to grips with. Not only were the later buildings moulded onto the earlier, but the fashion at the time of Christ was for a Hellenistic style. You can distinguish the Greek levels from the Roman most easily by the stones: the earlier civilization used massive hewn rocks while the Romans preferred smaller and more accurately shaped stones. The leaflet at the admission desk is helpful, as are the attendants if your French is good enough.

The site is bisected by a road running from north to south, with several **Hellenic houses** to the northwest. East of here are the **Thermes**, a complex of furnaces, bathing chambers and pools, and beyond this the **Maison du Capricorne** with some fine mosaics. A **forum** dating from Roman times is south of here, near a restored **theatre** and the superb sculptures on the Roman **Temples Geminées** (Twin Temples). The temples also have fragments of mosaics, fountains of both Greek and Roman periods and first-storey walls and columns. As the site narrows in the ravine at the southern end, you'll find a Grecian edifice around a **sacred spring** – the feature that made this location so desirable. Steps lead down to a pool, with a slab above for the libations of those too disabled to descend. An inscription records that Agrippa was responsible for restoring it in 27 BC and dedicating it to Valetudo, the Roman goddess of health.

Les Baux and the Val d'Enfer

At the top of the Alpilles ridge, 7km southwest of St-Rémy, lies the distinctly unreal fortified village of **LES BAUX**, where the ruined eleventh-century citadel is hard to distinguish from the edge of the plateau, whose rock is both foundation and part of the structure.

Once Les Baux lived off the power and widespread possessions in Provence of its medieval lords, who owed allegiance to no one. When the dynasty died out at the end of the fourteenth century, however, the town, which had once numbered 6000 inhabitants, passed to the counts of Provence and then to the kings of France. In 1632, Richelieu razed the feudal citadel to the ground and fined the population into penury for their disobedience. From that date until the nineteenth century, both citadel and village were inhabited almost exclusively by bats and crows. The discovery in the neighbouring hills of the mineral bauxite (whose name derives from "Les Baux") brought back some life to the village, and tourism has more recently transformed the place. Today the population stays steady at around 400, while the number of visitors exceeds 1.5 million each year.

The lived-in village has many very beautiful buildings. There are half a dozen museums, one of the best being the **Musée Yves Brayer** in the Hôtel des Porcelets (mid-Feb to March & Oct–Dec daily except Tues 10am–12.30pm & 2–5.30pm; April–Sept daily 10am–12.30pm & 2–6.30pm; 25F/€3.81), showing the paintings of the twentieth-century figurative artist whose work also adorns the seventeenth-century **Chapelle des Pénitents Blancs**. Changing exhibitions of contemporary Provençal artists' works are displayed in the Hôtel de Manville (hours vary, check with the tourist office; free). The museum of the **Fondation Louis Jou** in the fifteenth-century Hôtel Jean de Brion contains the presses, wood lettering blocks and hand-printed books of a master typographer (July & Aug daily 10am–noon & 2–5pm; rest of year visits by reservation only, ☎04.90.54.34.17; 20F/€3.05), while the **Musée des Santons** in the old Hôtel de Ville (daily 8am–7pm; free) displays traditional Provençal Nativity figures.

Following the signs to the Château will bring you to the entrance to the **Citadelle de la Ville Morte**, the main reason for coming to Les Baux (daily: Jan & Feb 9am–5pm; March–June, Sept & Oct 9am–7.30pm; July & Aug 9am–9.30pm; Nov & Dec 9am–6pm; 35F/€5.34) and where you can find ruins and several more museums. Pick of the bunch is the **Musée de l'Olivier** in the Romanesque Chapelle St-Blaise, featuring slide shows of paintings of olive trees and their artistic treatment by Van Gogh, Gauguin and Cézanne. The **Musée d'Histoire des Baux** in the vaulted space of Tour de Brau has a collection of archeological remains and models to illustrate the history from medieval splendour to bauxite works. The most impressive ruins are those of the feudal castle demolished on Richelieu's orders; there's also the partially restored **Chapelle Castrale** and the **Tour Sarrasine**, the cemetery, ruined houses half carved out of the rocky escarpment and some spectacular views, the best of which is out across the

Grande Crau from beside the statue of Provençal poet Charloun Riev at the southern edge of the plateau.

The **tourist office** is at the beginning of Grand-Rue (daily: July & Aug 9am–7pm; rest of year 9am–6pm; ☎04.90.54.34.39, *www.château-baux-provence.com*). You have to park – and pay – before entering the village. Nothing in Les Baux comes cheap, least of all **accommodation**. There is just one moderate option, the *Hostellerie de la Reine Jeanne*, by the entrance to the village (☎04.90.54.32.06, fax 04.90.54.32.33; ③; closed mid-Nov to mid-Feb), with a good restaurant (menus from 100F/€15.25). If you're feeling rich and want to treat yourself, head for the luxurious hotel-restaurant *Oustau de Baumanière*, just below Les Baux to the west on the road leading down to the Val d'Enfer (☎04.90.54.33.07, fax 04.90.54.40.46, *www.ostaudebaumaniere.com*; ⑨).

The Val d'Enfer

Within walking distance of Les Baux, along the D27 leading northwards, is the valley of quarried and eroded rocks named the **Val d'Enfer** – the Valley of Hell. One quarry has been turned into an audiovisual experience under the title of the **Cathédrale des Images** (mid-Feb to Dec daily 10am–7pm; 43F/€6.56), signposted to the right downhill from Les Baux's car park. The projection is continuous, so you don't have to wait to go in. You're surrounded by images projected all over the floor, ceilings and walls of these vast rectangular caverns, and by music that resonates strangely in the captured space. The content of the show, which changes yearly, does not really matter. It just is an extraordinary sensation, wandering on and through these changing shapes and colours. As an erstwhile work site put to good use, it couldn't be bettered.

Arles

ARLES is a major town on the tourist circuit, its fame sealed by the extraordinarily well-preserved Roman arena, **Les Arènes**, at the city's heart, and backed by an impressive variety of other stones and monuments, both Roman and medieval. It was the key city of the region in Roman times, then, with Aix, main base of the counts of Provence before unification with France. For centuries it was Marseille's only rival, profiting from the inland trade route up the Rhône whenever the enemies of France were blocking Marseille's port. Arles declined when the railway put an end to this advantage, and it was an inward-looking depressed town that **Van Gogh** came to in the late nineteenth century. Today it is a staid and conservative place, but comes to life for the **Saturday market**, which brings in throngs of farmers from the surrounding countryside, and during the various **festivals** of *tauromachie* between Easter and All Saints, when the town's frenzy for bulls rivals that of neighbouring Nîmes.

Arrival, information and accommodation

Arriving by train eases you gently into the city, with the **gare SNCF** conveniently located a few blocks to the north of the Arènes. Most buses also arrive here at the adjacent **gare routière** (☎04.90.49.38.01), though some, including all local buses, stop on the north side of boulevard Georges-Clemenceau just east of rue Gambetta. Rue Jean-Jaurès, with its continuation rue Hôtel-de-Ville, is the main axis of old Arles. At the southern end it meets boulevard Georges-Clemenceau and boulevard des Lices, with the **tourist office** directly opposite (Mon–Sat 9am–7pm, Sun 2–6pm; ☎04.90.18.41.20, *www.arles.org*); there's also an annexe in the *gare SNCF* (Mon–Sat 9am–1pm & 2–6pm). You can rent **bikes** from Peugeot, 15 rue du Pont, or Europbike, at the newspaper kiosk on esplanade Charles-de-Gaulle, and **cars** from Europcar (☎04.90.93.23.24), Eurorent (☎04.90.93.50.14) or Hertz (☎04.90.96.75.23), all on boulevard Victor-Hugo.

There's little shortage of **hotel** rooms at either end of the scale. The best place to look for cheap rooms is in the area around Porte de la Cavalerie near the station. If you get stuck, the tourist office will find you accommodation for a 5F/€0.76 fee.

Hotels

de l'Amphithéatre, 5 rue Diderot (☎04.90.96.10.30, fax 04.90.93.98.69, *www.hotelamphitheatre.fr*). Situated close to les Arènes, this place has recently been redecorated with plenty of warm colours, tiles and wrought ironwork. Closed Dec–March. ④.

d'Arlatan, 20 rue du Sauvage (☎04.90.93.56.55, fax 04.90.49.68.45, *www.hotel-arlatan.fr*). This may not be Arles' most expensive hotel, but it is probably the most luxurious, set in a beautiful old fifteenth-century mansion and decorated with antiques. ⑧.

Calendal, 22 place Pomme (☎04.90.96.11.89, fax 04.90.96.05.84, *contact@lecalendal,com*). Welcoming hotel with generous, air-conditioned rooms overlooking a garden. ⑤.

Le Cloître, 16 rue du Cloître (☎04.90.96.29.50, fax 04.90.96.02.88). A cosy hotel with some rooms giving views of St-Trophime. Closed Dec–March. ⑤.

Constantin, 59 bd de Craponne, off bd Clemenceau (☎04.90.96.04.05, fax 04.90.96.84.07). Pleasant, well-kept and comfortable hotel, with prices kept down by the proximity of the Nîmes highway (some traffic noise) and its location some distance from the centre. Closed mid-Nov to mid-March. ③.

du Forum, 10 place du Forum (☎04.90.93.48.95, fax 04.90.93.90.00, *forumarles@compuserve.com*). Spacious rooms in an old house at the ancient heart of the city, with a swimming pool in the garden. A bit noisy but very welcoming. Closed Nov–March. ⑥.

Gauguin, 5 place Voltaire (☎04.90.96.14.35, fax 04.90.18.98.87). Comfortable, cheap and well run. Advisable to book. ③.

Grand Hôtel Nord Pinus, 14 place du Forum (☎04.90.93.44.44, fax 04.90.93.34.00, *www.nord -pinus.com*). One of the most luxurious and elegant options, favoured by the *vedettes* of the bullring and decorated with their trophies. ⑨.

Musée, 11 rue du Grand-Prieuré (☎04.90.93.88.88, fax 04.90.49.98.15). Small, family-run place in a quiet location opposite Musée Réattu, offering slightly cramped but clean rooms. Closed Jan. ④.

Terminus & Van Gogh, 5 place Lamartine (☎04.90.96.12.32). A cheap option just outside one of the city gates, close to the train and bus stations. The Van Gogh theme is rather overplayed but at least it's colourful. Closed Dec & Jan. ②.

Hostel and campsites

HI hostel, 20 av Maréchal-Foch (☎04.90.96.18.25, fax 04.90.96.31.26). A rather dismal option, with rock-hard beds in large dorms and spartan facilities. Open all year; reception 7.30–10am and 5–11pm; 11pm curfew; take bus #3 from place Lamartine, direction "Fourchon", stop "Fournier". Closed late-Dec & Jan.

La Bienheureuse, 7km out on the N453 at Raphèles-les-Arles (☎04.90.98.35.64). Best of Arles' half-dozen campsites; the restaurant here is furnished with pieces similar to those displayed in the Museon Arlaten and full of pictures of popular Arlesian traditions. Open all year; regular buses from Arles.

Camping City, 67 rte de Crau (☎04.90.93.08.86, fax 04.90.93.91.07). The closest campsite to town on the Crau bus route. Closed Oct–March.

The City

The centre of Arles fits into a neat triangle between boulevard E.-Combes to the east, boulevards Clemenceau and des Lices to the south, and the Rhône to the west. The **Musée de l'Arles Antiques** is south of the expressway by the river, not far from the end of boulevard Clemenceau; **Les Alyscamps** is down across the train lines to the southeast. But these apart, all the **Roman and medieval monuments** are within easy walking distance in this very compact city centre.

Roman Arles

Roman Arles provided grain for most of the western empire and was one of the major ports for trade and shipbuilding. Under Constantine it became the capital of Gaul and

THE BULLFIGHT

Bullfighting, or more properly *tauromachie* (roughly, "the art of the bull"), comes in two styles in Arles and the Camargue. In the local *courses camarguaises*, which are held at *fêtes* from late spring to early autumn (the most prestigious of which is Arles' Cocarde d'Or in early July), *razeteurs* run at the bulls in an effort to pluck ribbons and cockades tied to the bulls' horns, cutting them free with special barbed gloves. The drama and grace of the spectacle is in the stylish way the men leap over the barrier away from the bull, and in the competition for prize money between the *razeteurs*. In this gentler bullfight, people are rarely injured and the bulls are not killed.

More popular, however, is the brutal Spanish-style *corrida* (late April, early July & September, at Arles), consisting of a strict ritual leading up to the all-but-inevitable death of the bull. After its entry into the ring, the bull is subjected to the *bandilleros* who stick decorated barbs in its back, the *picadors*, who lance it from horseback, and finally, the *torero*, who endeavours to lead the bull through as graceful a series of movements as possible before killing it with a single sword stroke to the heart. In one *corrida* six bulls are killed by three *toreros*, for whom injuries (sometimes fatal) are not uncommon. Whether you approve or not, *tauromachie*, which has a history of some centuries here, is your best way of taking part in local life and of experiencing the Roman arena in Arles (at 40–100F/€6.10–15.25 per seat). The tourist office, local papers and publicity around the arena will give you the details.

reached its height as a world trading centre in the fifth century. Once the empire crumbled, however, Arles found itself isolated between the Rhône, the Alpilles and the marshlands of the Camargue – an isolation that allowed its Roman heritage to be preserved.

A good place to start any tour of Roman Arles is the **Musée de l'Arles Antique** (daily: March–Oct 9am–7pm; rest of year 9am–5pm; 35F/€5.34), west of the town centre on the spit of land between the Rhône and the Canal de Rhône. It is housed in a resolutely contemporary building positioned on the axis of the second-century **Cirque Romaine**, an enormous chariot racetrack (currently being excavated) that stretches 450m from the museum to the town side of the expressway. The museum is a treat, open-plan, flooded with natural light and immensely spacious. It covers the prehistory of the area, then takes you through the five centuries of Roman rule, from Julius Cæsar's legionary base through Christianization to the period when spices and gems from Africa and Arabia were being traded here. Fabulous mosaics are laid out with walkways above; and there are numerous sarcophagi with intricate sculpting depicting everything from music and lovers to gladiators and Christian miracles.

Back in the centre of Arles, the most impressive Roman monument is the amphitheatre, known as the **Arènes** (see box for hours and price), dating from the end of the first century. To give an idea of its size, it used to shelter over two hundred dwellings and three churches built into the two tiers of arches that form its oval surround. This medieval quarter was cleared in 1830 and the Arènes was once more used for entertainment. Today, though missing its third storey and most of the internal stairways and galleries, it is a very dramatic structure and a stunning venue for performances. It can still seat 20,000 spectators.

The **Théâtre Antique** (see box for hours and price), just south of the Arènes, comes to life during July, with the Fête du Costume in which local folk groups parade in traditional dress, and the Mosaïque Gitane Romany festival. The theatre is nowhere near as well preserved as the arena, with only one pair of columns standing, all the statuary removed and the sides of the stage littered with broken bits of stone.

At the river end of rue Hôtel-de-Ville, the **Thermes de Constantin** (see box for hours and price), which may well have been the biggest Roman baths in Provence, are all that remain of the emperor's palace that extended along the waterfront. The Roman forum was up the hill on the site of **place du Forum**, still the centre of life in Arles. You can see the pillars of an ancient temple embedded in the corner of the *Nord-Pinus* hotel.

The Romans had their burial ground southwest of the centre, and it was used by well-to-do Arlesians well into the Middle Ages. Now only one alleyway, foreshortened by a train line, is preserved. To reach **Les Alyscamps** (see box for hours and price), follow avenue des Alyscamps from boulevard des Lices. Sarcophagi still line the shaded walk, whose tree trunks are azure blue in Van Gogh's rendering. There are numerous tragedy masks, too, though any with special decoration have long since been moved to serve as municipal gifts, as happened often in the seventeenth century, or to reside in the museums. But there is still magic to this walk, which ends at the ruins of a Romanesque church.

The cathedral, museums and medieval Arles

The doorway of the **Cathédrale St-Trophime** on Arles' central **place de la République** is one of the most famous examples of twelfth-century Provençal stonecarving in existence. It depicts the Last Judgement, trumpeted by angels playing with the enthusiasm of jazz musicians while the damned are led naked in chains down to hell and the blessed, all draped in long robes, process upwards. The cathedral itself was started in the ninth century on the spot where, in 597 AD, St Augustine was consecrated as the first bishop of the English, and it was largely completed by the twelfth century. A font in the north aisle and an altar illustrating the crossing of the Red Sea in the north transept were both originally Gallo-Roman sarcophagi. The nave is decorated with d'Aubusson tapestries, in which the one depicting Mary Magdalene bathing Christ's feet has a cat jumping from one oil container to another chased by a dog being ridden by a child. There is more superlative Romanesque and Gothic stonecarving in the extraordinarily beautiful **cloisters**, accessible from place de la République to the right of the cathedral (see box for hours and price).

Across place de la République from the cathedral stands the palatial seventeenth-century **Hôtel de Ville**, inspired by Versailles. You can walk through its vast entrance hall, with its flattened vaulted roof designed to avoid putting extra stress on the **Cryptoporticus du Forum** below. This is a huge, dark, dank and wonderfully spooky three-sided underground gallery, built by the Romans, possible as a food store, possibly as a barracks for public slaves, but certainly to provide sturdy foundations for the forum above. Access is from rue Balze (see box for hours and price), though it may be switched to the Musée Arlaten.

In case you feel that life stopped in Arles – if not after the Romans, then at least after the Middle Ages – head for the **Musée Arlaten** on rue de la République (daily: April–May & Sept 9.30am–12.30pm & 2–6pm; June–Aug 9.30am–1pm & 2–6.30pm;

MUSEUM PASSES AND OPENING HOURS

Two **global tickets** grant between ten and forty percent reductions to Arles' museums: the *Pass Monument* (65F/€9.91) includes the Arènes, Théâtre Antique, Musée de l'Arles Antique, Cryptoporticuss, Thermes de Constantin, Les Alyscamps, Musée Arlaten, Cloître St-Trophime and the Musée Réattu, while the *Circuit Arles Antique* (55F/€8.39) covers all but the last four. Museum opening hours, except for the Musée Arlaten and the Musée d'Arles Antique, are the same (daily: Jan & Dec 10am–noon & 2–4.30pm; Feb & Nov 10am–noon & 2–5pm; March & Oct 10am–12.30pm & 2–5.30pm; April to mid-June & last two weeks Sept 9am–12.30pm & 2–7pm; mid-June to mid-Sept 9am–7pm; the ticket offices close 30min before), as is the admission (20F/€3.05).

Oct–March 9.30am–12.30pm & 2–5pm; 25F/€3.81). The museum was set up in 1896 by Frédéric Mistral, the Nobel Prize-winning novelist who was responsible for the turn-of-the-twentieth-century revival of interest in all things Provençal, and whose statue stands in place du Forum. The collections of costumes, documents, tools, pictures and paraphernalia of Provençal life are alternately tedious and intriguing. The evolution of Arlesian dress is charted in great detail for all social classes from the eighteenth century to World War I and there's a mouthwatering life-size scene of a bourgeois Christmas dinner.

Another must-see in Arles is the main collection of the **Musée Réattu** (see box for hours and price), housed in a beautiful fifteenth-century priory opposite the Roman baths. Much of it comprises tedious and rigid eighteenth-century works by the museum's founder and his contemporaries, but dotted round this are some good modern works: Zadkine's study in bronze for the two Van Gogh brothers, Mario Prassinos' monochrome studies of the Alpilles, César's *Compression 1973* and, best of all, Picasso's *Woman with Violin* sculpture and 57 ink-and-crayon sketches made in Arles between December 1970 and February 1971. Amongst the split faces and clowns is a beautifully simple portrait of his mother.

Van Gogh in Arles

At the back of the Réattu museum, lanterns line the river wall where **Van Gogh** used to wander, wearing candles on his hat, watching the night-time light: *The Starry Night* is the Rhône at Arles. Much of the riverfront and its bars and bistros were destroyed during World War II. Another casualty of the bombing was the "Yellow House" on place Lamartine, where the artist lived before entering the hospital at St-Rémy. However, the café painted in *Café de Nuit* still stands in place du Forum. Van Gogh had arrived by train in February 1888 to be greeted by snow and a bitter mistral wind. But he started painting straight away, and in this period produced such celebrated canvases as *The Sunflowers, Van Gogh's Chair, The Red Vines* and *The Sower*. Van Gogh found few kindred souls in Arles and finally managed to persuade Gauguin to join him. No one knows what provoked the frenzied attack on his friend and the self-mutilation. He was packed off to the Hôtel-Dieu hospital on rue du Président-Wilson down from the Musée Arlaten, now the **Espace Van Gogh**, an academic and cultural centre with arty shops in its arcades and courtyard flower beds recreated according to Van Gogh's painting and descriptions of the hospital garden.

Arles has none of the artist's works but the **Fondation Vincent Van Gogh** (June–Sept daily 9am–7pm; rest of year Tues–Sun 9am–noon & 2–6.30pm; 30F/€4.58), facing the Arènes at 26 Rond-Point des Arènes, exhibits works by contemporary artists inspired by Van Gogh, including Francis Bacon, Jasper Johns, Hockney and Lichtenstein.

Eating and drinking

Arles has a good number of excellent-quality and cheap **restaurants**, and if you're looking for quick meals, or just want to watch the world go by, there's a wide choice of brasseries on the main boulevards. Place du Forum is the centre of café life; here you'll find *Le Café La Nuit*, immaculately recreated à la Van Gogh and open late, and the young and noisy *Bistrot Arlésien*.

L'Affenage, 4 rue Molière (☎04.90.96.07.67). Serves Provençal specialities in generous portions. Menus from 90F/€13.73. Closed Sun.

Boitel, 4 rue de la Liberté. A *salon de thé* with a whole pâtisserie full of goodies to go with the Earl Grey. Closed Sun.

Le Galoubet, 18 rue du Dr-Fanton (☎04.90.93.18.11). Pleasant, vine-covered terrace on which to taste the modern Provençal cuisine on a good-value 105F/€16.01 menu. Closed Sun.

La Gueule du Loup, 39 rue des Arènes (☎04.90.96.96.69). Cosy restaurant serving traditional dishes, with one menu under 130F/€19.83. Closed Sun & Mon lunch.

Le Jardin du Manon, 14 av des Alyscamps (☎04.90.93.38.68). Hospitable Provençal restaurant serving elaborate regional dishes and delicious desserts, which you can enjoy in a small patio garden. Menus from 98F/€14.95. Closed Wed.

Lou Marquès, *Hôtel Jules-César*, bd des Lices (☎04.90.93.43.20). The top gourmet palace in the top grand hotel. The specialities, which include *baudroie* (monkfish), langoustine salad and Camargue rice cake, are all served with the utmost pomposity. Menus from 150F/€22.88. The other restaurant in the hotel, *Le Cloître*, has a lunch menu at around 100F/€15.25. Both closed Nov & Dec.

La Paillote, 28 rue Dr-Fanton (☎04.90.96.33.15). Very friendly place with a good 96F/€14.64 menu. Closed Thurs.

The Camargue

The boundaries of **the CAMARGUE** are not apparent until you come upon them. Its horizons are infinite because land, lagoon and sea share the same horizontal plain. Both wild and human life have traits peculiar to this drained, ditched and now protected delta land. Today, the whole of the Camargue is a Parc Naturel Régional, with great efforts made to keep an equilibrium between tourism, agriculture, industry and hunting on the one hand, and the indigenous ecosystems on the other.

The Camargue is home to the **bulls** and to the **white horses** that the region's *gardiens*, or herdsmen, ride. Neither beast is truly wild, though both run in semi-liberty. The Camargue horse, whose origin is unknown, remains a distinct breed, born dark brown or black and turning white around its fourth year. It is never stabled, surviving the humid heat of summer and the wind-racked winter cold outdoors. The *gardiens* likewise are a hardy community. Their traditional homes, or *cabanes*, are thatched and windowless one-storey structures, with bulls' horns over the door to ward off evil spirits. They still conform, to some extent, to the popular cowboy myth, and play a major role in guarding Camarguais traditions. Throughout the summer they're kept busy in every village arena with spectacles involving bulls and horses, and the work carries local glamour. Winter is a good deal harder, and fewer and fewer Camarguais property owners can afford the extravagant use of land that bull-rearing requires.

The Camargue bulls and horses are just one element in the area's exceptionally rich **wildlife**, which includes flamingos, marsh and sea birds, waterfowl and birds of prey; wild boars, beavers and badgers; tree frogs, water snakes and pond turtles; and a rich flora of reeds, wild irises, tamarisk, wild rosemary and juniper trees. These last, which grow to a height of 6m, form the **Bois des Rièges** on the islands between the **Étang du Vaccarès** and the sea, part of the central national reserve to which access is restricted to those with professional credentials.

After World War II, the northern marshes were drained and re-irrigated with fresh water. The main crop planted was rice, and so successful was it that by the 1960s the Camargue was providing three-quarters of all French consumption of the grain. Vines were also reintroduced – in the nineteenth century they had survived the disease that devastated every other wine-producing region because their stems were under water. There are other crops – wheat, rapeseed and fruit orchards – as well as trees in isolated clumps. To the east, along the last stretch of the Grand Rhône, the chief business is the production of salt, which was first organized in the Camargue by the Romans in the first century AD. It's one of the biggest saltworks in the world, with salt pans and pyramids adding a somehow extraterrestrial aspect to the Camargue landscape.

Though the Étang du Vaccarès and the central islands are out of bounds, there are paths and sea dykes from which their inhabitants can be watched, and special nature trails (see p.940). The ideal months for bird-watching are the mating period of April to June, with the greatest number of flamingos present between April and September.

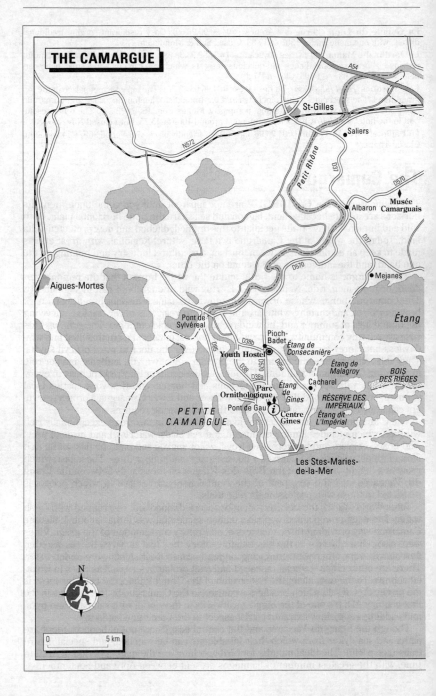

THE CAMARGUE

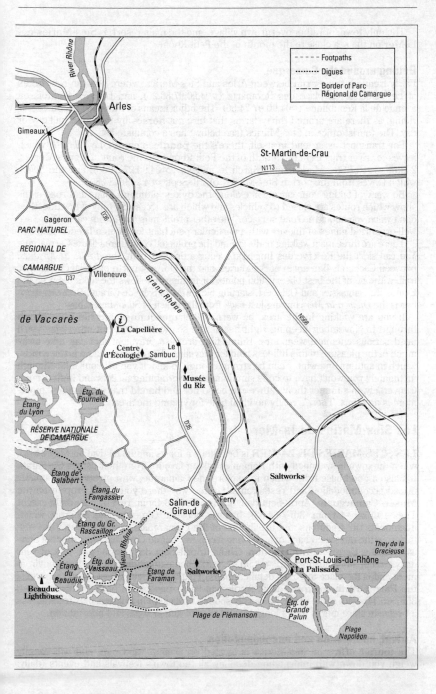

The only town, or rather overgrown village, and the main resort, is **Stes-Maries-de-la-Mer** on the sea close to the mouth of the Petit Rhône.

Getting around the Camargue

Fairly frequent **buses** run between Arles and Stes-Maries, where you can rent **bikes** at Le Vélociste on place des Remparts (☎04.90.97.83.26), and Le Vélo Sanitois on avenue de la République (☎04.90.97.74.56). The other means of transport to consider is riding, as there are around thirty farms that hire out **horses** by the hour, half-day or day. The tourist office in Stes-Maries (see below) has a complete list.

For transport as an end in itself, there's the **paddle steamer** *Le Tiki III*, which leaves for river trips from the mouth of the Petit Rhône, off the route d'Aigues-Mortes, 2.5km west of Stes-Maries (mid-March to mid-Nov; ☎04.90.97.81.68), and the *Soleil*, which leaves from the port in Stes-Maries (April–Sept; ☎04.90.97.85.89).

Be wary of taking your car or bike along the **dykes**: although maps and road signs show which routes are closed to vehicles and which are accessible only at low tide, they don't warn you about the road surface. The other problem is **theft** from cars. There are well-organized gangs of thieves with a particular penchant for foreign licence plates.

There are three main walking **trails** around the protected central area of the Carmargue. You can skirt the Réserve des Impériaux along a drovers' path, the *draille de Méjanes*, between Cacharel, 4km north of Ste-Maries, and the D37 just north of Méjanes. Another trail, with one of the best observation points for flamingos, follows the dyke between the Étangs du Fangassier and Galabert, starting 5km west of Salin-de-Giraud. Between these two is the *Digue à la Mer* running just back from the beach of Stes-Maries' bay.

If you are walking in the area, be warned that **mosquitoes** are rife from March through to November; keeping right beside the sea will be OK, but otherwise you'll need serious chemical weaponry. Biting flies are also prevalent and can take away much of the pleasure of this hill-less land for bicycling. The other problem is the **winds**, which in autumn and winter can be strong enough to knock you off your bike (though fortunately you won't have to cope simultaneously with biting insects and high winds). Conversely, in summer the weather can be so hot and humid that the slightest movement is an effort. There's really no ideal time for visiting the area.

Les Stes-Maries-de-la-Mer

LES STES-MARIES-DE-LA-MER is best known for its annual festival on May 24–25, when the town is swamped with Romanies asking favours from their patron Ste-Sarah. It's also a good base from which to explore the Camargue, with plenty of reasonably priced accommodation and restaurants. On the way there you could drop in on the **Musée Camarguais** (April–Sept daily 9.15am–5.45/6.45pm; rest of year daily except Tues 10.15am–4.45pm; 30F/€4.58), halfway between Gimeaux and Albaron, which documents the traditions and livelihoods of the Camarguais people through the centuries, in the old sheep barn of a working farm. At Pont de Gau, just 4km short of Stes-Maries, the **Centre d'Information Ginès** (April–Sept daily 9am–6pm; rest of year daily except Fri 9.30am–5pm; ☎04.90.97.86.32) has exhibitions on the local environment and is the place to go for detailed maps of paths and dykes. Just down the road is the **Parc Ornithologique** (daily: April–Sept 9am–sunset; rest of year 10am–sunset; 35F/€5.34), with some of the less easily spotted birds kept in aviaries, plus trails across a twelve-hectare marsh and a longer walk, all with ample signs and information.

Arrival, information and accommodation

The **tourist office** in Stes-Maries is located on avenue Van-Gogh, and will happily weigh you down with information detailing all the town's festivals and events (daily:

Jan, Feb, Nov & Dec 9am–5pm; March & Oct 9am–6pm; April–June & Sept 9am–7pm; July & Aug 9am–8pm; ☎04.90.97.82.55, *www.saintes-maries-camargue.enprovence.com*).

From April to October **rooms** in Stes-Maries should be booked in advance, and for the Romany festival, several months before. Prices go up considerably during the summer and at any time of the year are more expensive than at Arles. Outlying *mas* (farmhouses) renting out rooms tend to be quite expensive. **Camping** on the beach is not officially tolerated, but even at Stes-Maries people sleeping beneath the stars rarely get told to move on. The fifteen-kilometre seaside plage de Piemanson, also known as the plage d'Arles, south of Salin-de-Giraud, 10km east of Stes-Maries, is a favoured venue for *camping sauvage* in summer.

HOTELS

Camille, 13 av de la Plage (☎04.90.97.80.26, fax 04.90.97.98.01). Characterless cheapie but with a sea view. ④.

L'Estable Chez Kiki, 13 rte de Cacharel (☎04.90.97.83.27, fax 04.90.97.87.78). Nothing very special but serviceable and not expensive. Closed Nov–March. ④.

Hostellerie du Pont du Gau, rte d'Arles, Pont de Gau, 4km north of Stes-Maries (☎04.90.97.81.53, fax 04.90.97.98.54). Old-fashioned Camarguais decor, pleasant rooms and a good restaurant. Closed Jan & Feb. ③.

Mangio Fango, rte d'Arles (☎04.90.97.80.56, fax 04.90.97.83.60). Situated 600m from Stes-Maries, overlooking the Etang des Launes, with pool and patios. Closed mid-Nov to mid Dec & Jan. ⑥.

Mas des Rièges, rte de Cacharel (☎04.90.97.85.07, fax 04.90.97.72.26). An upmarket hotel in an old farmhouse, with swimming pool and garden. Down a track signed off the D85a close to Stes-Maries. Closed Dec–Feb. ⑤.

Les Vagues, 12 av T.-Aubunal (☎ & fax 04.90.97.84.40). A low-priced option overlooking the sea on the rte d'Aigues-Mortes. ③.

HOSTEL AND CAMPSITES

Hostel, on the Arles–Stes-Maries bus route, 10km north of Stes-Maries in the hamlet of Pioch-Badet (☎04.90.97.51.72, fax 04.90.97.54.88). Bike rental, horse rides and other excursions. Open all year.

Camping La Brise, rue Marcel-Carrière (☎04.90.97.84.67, fax 04.90.97.72.01). A three-star site, with a pool and laundry facilities, and tents and caravans for rent. On the Arles–Stes-Maries bus route, on the east side of the village (stop La Brise). Open all year.

Camping Le Clos du Rhône, at the mouth of the Petit Rhône, 2km west of the village on the rte d'Aigues-Mortes (☎04.90.97.85.99, fax 04.90.97.78.85). A busy four-star site with a pool, laundry and shop. Only two of the Arles–Stes-Maries buses continue to here (stop "Clos du Rhône"). Closed Oct–March.

The Town

Stes-Maries is an extremely pretty, if excessively commercialized town. Its streets of white houses and the grey-gold Romanesque church, with its strange outline of battlements and watchtower, have been turned into one long picture-postcard pose. It exploits its monopoly as the only Camargue resort and every leisure activity is catered for, to excess. There are kilometres of **beach**; a pleasure port with boat trips to the lagoons; horses – or bikes – to ride; watersports; the *arènes* for bullfights, cavalcades and other entertainment (events are posted on a board outside); and flamenco guitarists playing on the restaurant and café terraces – it can all be very good fun.

As for sights, the fortified **church of Stes-Maries** allows a look at Sarah's tinselled and sequined statue, which is carried into the sea each year (see box on p.942). It's at the back of the crypt on the right, and always surrounded by candles and abandoned crutches and callipers from the miraculously cured. The church itself has beautifully pure lines and fabulous acoustics. During the time of the Saracen raids it provided shel-

---

THE LEGEND OF SARAH

Sarah was the servant of Mary Jacobé, Jesus' aunt, and Mary Salomé, mother of two of the apostles, who, along with Mary Magdalene and various other New Testament characters, are said to have been driven out of Palestine by the Jews and put on a boat without sails or oars.

The boat apparently drifted to an island in the mouth of the Rhône, where the Egyptian god Ra was worshipped. Here Mary Jacobé, Mary Salomé and Sarah, who was herself Egyptian, settled to carry out conversion work, while the others headed off for other parts of Provence. In 1448 their relics were "discovered" in the fortress church of Stes-Maries on the erstwhile island, around the time that the Romanies were migrating to western Europe from the Balkans and from Spain.

Romanies have been making their **pilgrimage** to Stes-Maries since at least the sixteenth century. It's a time for weddings and baptisms, as well as music, dancing and fervent religious observance. After Mass on May 24, the shrines of the saints are lowered from the high chapel to an altar where the faithful stretch out their arms to touch them. Then the statue of Black Sarah is carried by the Romanies to the sea. On the following day the statues of Mary Jacobé and Mary Salomé, sitting in a wooden boat, follow the same route, accompanied by the mounted *gardiens* in full Camargue cowboy dress, Arlesians in traditional costume, and spectators. The sea, the Camargue, the pilgrims and the Romanies are blessed by the bishop from a fishing boat, before the procession returns to the church with much bell-ringing, guitar-playing, tambourines and singing. Another ceremony in the afternoon sees the shrines lifted back up to their chapel.

---

ter for all the villagers and even has its own freshwater well. Between March and Oct the church **tower** is open (10am–12.30pm & 2pm–sunset; 20F/€3.05), affording the best possible view over the Camargue.

A few steps south of the church on rue Victor-Hugo, the **Musée Baroncelli** (April to mid-Nov daily 10am–noon & 2–6pm; mid-Nov to March daily except Wed same hours; 10F/€1.53) is named after the man who, in 1935, was responsible for initiating the Romanies' procession down to the sea with Sarah. This was motivated by a desire to give a special place in the pilgrimage to the Romanies. The museum covers this event, other Camarguais traditions and the region's fauna and flora.

Eating and drinking

Few of the **restaurants** in Stes-Maries are bargains, though there are any number to choose from, and out of season the quality improves and prices come down. Right in the centre of town on place des Impériaux, *L'Impérial* (☎04.90.97.81.84; closed Nov–March & Tues except July & Aug) serves pleasant fish dishes on a 130F/€19.83 menu. Or try the tapas and bargain wine at *Kahlua Bodéga*, 1 rue Jean Roche (☎04.90.97.98.41; closed Jan & Feb, Wed out of season; around 100F/€15.25). The best places to try local fish specialities, however, are at the beach hut restaurants *Chez Juju* and *Chez Marc et Mireille* in **BEAUDUC**, over the dykes on the spit of sand on the opposite side of the bay from Stes-Maries.

From Avignon to Gordes

If you're heading east from Avignon towards Apt and the Luberon, two worthwhile stops are the exquisitely romantic **Fontaine-de-Vaucluse** and the picturesque **Gordes**, close to the **Abbaye de Sénanque**. Between Gordes and Apt are the old ochre-quarrying villages of **Roussillon** and **Rustrel**. Visiting all these places without your own transport is not that easy; Fontaine is accessible by bus from Avignon or from

L'Isle-sur-la-Sorgue's *gare SNCF* 6km away, Gordes from Cavaillon, 24km southwest of Avignon, and Roussillon only infrequently from Apt.

Fontaine-de-Vaucluse

The source of the Sorgue, the stream that runs alongside rue des Teinturiers in Avignon, is at **FONTAINE-DE-VAUCLUSE**, 29km southwest of Avignon, and one of the most powerful natural springs in the world. At the top of the gorge above the village is a mysterious tapering fissure deeper than the sheer 230-metre cliffs that barricade its opening. This is where the waters of the Sorgue appear, sometimes in spectacular fashion, bursting down the gorge (in March and April normally), other times seeping stealthily through subterranean channels to meet the river bed further down. The best time to admire it is in the early morning before the crowds arrive.

Fontaine-de-Vaucluse was once a rustic backwater where the fourteenth-century poet Petrarch pined for his Laura. It remains a supremely romantic place despite its hordes of visitors. If you're intrigued by the source of the river, visit the **Le Monde Souterrain** (hourly 45-minute tours in French; Feb–March & Sept–Nov Wed–Sun at 11am & 2–5pm; April–Aug daily 10am–noon & 2–6pm; closed Dec–Jan; 31F/€4.73) in the underground commercial centre alongside the chemin de la Fontaine, the path to the source. At the upper end of the centre, you'll find a re-creation of the medieval method of pulping rags to paper – using river power – with a vast array of printed matter on the product for sale.

On chemin de la Fontaine, there's also the impressive **Musée d'Histoire 1939–1945** (March to mid-April & mid-Oct to Dec Sat & Sun 10am–noon & 2–6pm; mid-April to June Wed–Sun 10am–noon & 2–6pm; July & Aug Wed–Sun 10am–7pm; Sept to mid-Oct Mon & Wed–Fri 10am–6pm, Sat & Sun 10am–noon & 2–6pm; 20F/€3.05), portraying life under the Vichy regime and commemorating the Resistance. Nearby you'll find the rather dull **Musée du Santon** (mid-April to mid-Oct Wed–Sun 9.30am–noon & 2–6.30pm; rest of year Sat & Sun 9.30am–noon & 2–6.30pm; 20F/€3.05), displaying an unremarkable collection of Provençal Nativity figures. Across the river, through an alleyway just past the bridge, is the much more interesting **Musée de Pétrarque** (mid-April to mid-Oct Wed–Sun 9.30am–noon & 2–6.30pm; rest of year weekends only; 20F/€3.05), with beautiful books dating back to the fifteenth century and pictures of Petrarch, his beloved Laura and of Fontaine, where he passed sixteen years of his unrequited passion.

The **tourist office** is on chemin de la Fontaine (Mon–Sat: July & Aug 9am–6pm; rest of year 10am–6pm; ☎04.90.20.32.22, *officetourisme.vaucluse@wanadoo.fr*). The cheapest and most characterful **hotel** in the village itself is the *Grand Hôtel des Sources* (☎04.90.20.31.84; ④), with a whole variety of *vieille France* rooms. On the road out towards Avignon, 3km from the village, are two hotels worth trying: *L'Ermitage* (☎04.90.20.32.20, fax 04.90.20.28.95; ③) and *Font de Lauro* (☎ & fax 04.90.20.31.49; ②). There's also a **hostel** on chemin de la Vignasse, 1km south on the road to Lagnes (☎04.90.20.31.65, fax 04.90.20.26.20; closed mid-Nov to mid-Feb), and a **campsite**, *Les Pres* (☎04.90.20.32.38; all year), 500m downstream from the village, with tennis courts and swimming pool. For **food**, you have a choice of several reasonably priced restaurants in town, including *Château* (☎04.90.20.13.54; closed Sun & Mon evenings out of season) and *Lou Fanau* (☎04.90.20.31.90; closed Wed), both of which have menus of solid regional food for under 100F/€15.25.

Gordes and around

GORDES, just 5km east of Fontaine as the crow flies, but 18km by road, is a picturesque Provençal village much favoured by Parisian media personalities, film directors, artists

animal life and buy recordings of Luberon birdsong. The centre also houses a small **Musée de la Paléontologie** (10F/€1.53), which is specifically designed to amuse children and is fun. A submarine-type "time capsule" door leads down to push-button displays that include magnified views of insect fossils and their modern descendants.

Given the region's general dearth of public transport, the only practical and pleasurable way to explore the park is by hiking or cycling. In Apt, **bikes** can be hired from Cycles Ricaud, 44 quai de la Liberté, Guy Agnel, 86 quai Général-Leclerc, or Cycles Peugeot, a few doors down.

The Abbaye de Silvacane

If you're heading for Aix-en-Provence from Apt, you'll pass close to another ancient Cistercian abbey contemporary with Sénanque (see p.944), 29km south of Apt, just across the Durance. After a long history of abandonment and evictions, the **Abbaye de Silvacane** (daily: April–Sept 9am–9pm; rest of year 10am–1pm & 2–5pm; 32F/€4.88) is once again a monastic institution. It is isolated from the surrounding villages on the bank of the Durance and its architecture has hardly changed over the last 700 years; you can visit the stark, pale-stoned splendour of the church, its cloisters and surrounding buildings.

Aix-en-Provence

AIX-EN-PROVENCE would be the dominant city of central Provence were it not for the great metropolis of Marseille, just 25km away. Historically, culturally and socially, the two cities are moons apart and the tendency is to love one and hate the other. Aix is complacently conservative and a stunningly beautiful place, its riches based on landowning and the liberal professions. The youth of Aix are immaculately dressed; hundreds of foreign students, particularly Americans, come to study here; and there's a certain snobbishness, almost of Parisian proportions.

From the twelfth century until the Revolution, Aix was the capital of Provence. In its days as an independent county, its most mythically beloved ruler, "Good" King René of Anjou (1409–80), held a brilliant court renowned for its popular festivities and patronage of the arts. René was an archetypal Renaissance man, a speaker of many languages (including Greek and Hebrew), a scientist, poet and economist; he also introduced the muscat grape to the region – today he stands in stone in picture-book medieval fashion, a bunch of grapes in his left hand, looking down the majestic seventeenth-century cours Mirabeau.

Arrival, information and accommodation

Cours Mirabeau, which replaced the town's old southern fortifications, is the main thoroughfare of Aix, with the multi-fountained place Général-de-Gaulle, or La Rotonde, at its west end, the main point of arrival. The **gare SNCF** is on rue Gustavo-Desplace at the end of avenue Victor-Hugo, the avenue leading south from the square; the **gare routière** is between the two western avenues – des Belges and Bonaparte – on rue Lapierre (☎04.42.27.17.91). **Driving** into Aix can be confusing: your best bet is to follow signs for the *gare*; taking avenue des Belges past the station will lead you to the tourist office in the centre of town – there is street parking on the ring road which hems in the old town. The **tourist office** is at 2 place Général-de-Gaulle (Mon–Sat 8.30am–7pm, Sun 8.30am–1pm & 2–6pm; ☎04.42.16.11.61, *www.aix-en-provence.com*), between avenue des Belges and avenue Victor-Hugo.

From mid-June to the end of July (festival time) your chances of getting a hotel **room** are pretty slim unless you've reserved a couple of months in advance at least. Outside this time, there is a decent range of accommodation to choose from.

Hotels

des Arts, 69 bd Carnot (☎04.42.38.11.77). Very welcoming, though slightly noisy hotel, with the cheapest rooms to be found in the centre of Aix. You can't book, so turn up early. ②.

La Caravelle, 29 bd Roi-René (☎04.42.21.53.05, fax 04.42.96.55.46). By the boulevards to the southeast of the city. The more expensive rooms overlook courtyard gardens. ④.

Cardinal, 24 rue Cardinale (☎04.42.38.32.30, fax 04.42.26.39.05, *hotel-cardinal@wanadoo.fr*). Clean, peaceful and welcoming establishment; great value. ⑤.

de France, 63 rue Espariat (☎04.42.27.90.15, fax 04.42.26.11.47). Right in the centre and with very comfortable rooms. ④.

Le Manoir, 8 rue d'Entrecasteaux (☎04.42.26.27.20, fax 04.42.27.17.97). Very smart and very comfortable ancient building which includes a fourteenth-century cloister. ⑤.

Number One, 10 cours des Minimes (☎04.42.64.45.01). Small family-run affair, one of the better bargains around. ②.

Paul, 10 av Pasteur (☎04.42.23.23.89, fax 04.42.63.17.80). Good value for Aix, with a garden. Rooms have private shower and phone and there are also some for three and four people. ②.

des Quatre-Dauphins, 54 rue Roux-Alphéran (☎04.42.38.16.39, fax 04.42.38.60.19). Old-world charm in the quartier Mazarin. ④.

St-Christophe, 2 av Victor-Hugo (☎04.42.26.01.24, fax 04.42.38.53.17, *SaintCristophe@francemarket.com*). Classy hotel, close to both the station and cours Mirabeau. ⑤.

Hostels and campsites

HI hostel, 3 av Marcel-Pagnol (☎04.42.20.15.99, fax 04.42.59.36.12). Located 2km from the centre, this hostel has small dorm rooms and no cooking facilities but it does have a TV room, bar, laundry facilities and a baggage deposit. Take bus #4, direction "Ojas de Bouffan", stop "Vasarely". Restaurant April–Oct. Closed Christmas–Feb.

CROUS, Cité Universitaire des Gazelles, 38 av Jules-Ferry (☎04,42.93.47.70). This student organization can sometimes find cheap rooms on campus during July & Aug. Take bus #5, direction "Bel Ormeau", stop "Pierre-Puget".

Camping Arc-en-Ciel, rte de Nice, Pont des Trois Sautets (☎04,42.26.14.28). Located 3km southeast of town on bus #3, this is not a particularly cheap site but has very good facilities. Closed Nov to mid-March.

Airotel Camping Chanteclerc, rte de Nice, Val St-André (☎04.42.26.12.98). Also 3km from the centre on bus #3 or #10, this site is equally expensive, with excellent facilities. Open all year.

The City

The whole of the **old city of Aix**, clearly defined by its ring of boulevards and the majestic cours Mirabeau, is the great monument here, far more compelling than any one single building or museum within it. With so many streets alive with people, so many tempting restaurants, cafés and shops, plus the best markets in Provence, it's easy to pass several days wandering around without the need for any itinerary or

---

MUSEUM PASS

Two different *Passeports Musées* give you ten to thirty-five percent reductions on the price of entry to Aix's museums: *Passeport 1* (50F/€7.53) covers Musée Granet, Pavillon Vendôme, Musée des Tapisseries and Ecole d'Art; *Passeport 2* (70F/€10.68) covers all of these, plus the L'Atelier Cézanne.

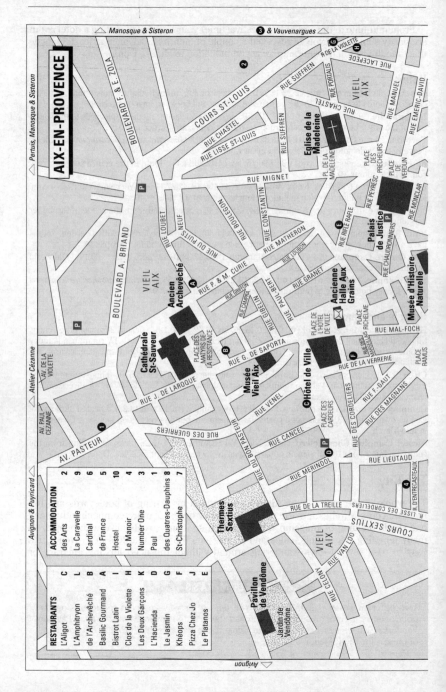

AIX-EN-PROVENCE

△ Manosque & Sisteron

❸ & Vauvenargues △

△ Pertuis, Manosque & Sisteron

△ Atelier Cézanne

△ Avignon & Puyricard

▽ Avignon

VIEIL AIX

VIEIL AIX

VIEIL AIX

VIEIL AIX

Ancien Archevêché

Cathédrale St-Sauveur

Musée Vieil Aix

Hôtel de Ville

Ancienne Halle Aux Grains

Musée d'Histoire Naturelle

Palais de Justice

Église de la Madeleine

Thermes Sextius

Pavillon de Vendôme

Jardin de Vendôme

PLACE DES MARTYRS DE LA RESISTANCE

PLACE DE L'HÔTEL DE VILLE

PLACE DES CARDEURS

PLACE RICHELME

PLACE DES PRECHEURS

PLACE DE VERDUN

PLACE RAMUS

PL. DE LA MADELEINE

RESTAURANTS

L'Aligot	C
L'Amphitryon	L
de l'Archevêché	B
Basilic Gourmand	A
Bistrot Latin	I
Clos de la Violette	H
Les Deux Garçons	K
L'Hacienda	D
Le Jasmin	G
Khéops	F
Pizza Chez Jo	J
Le Platanos	E

ACCOMMODATION

des Arts	2
La Caravelle	9
Cardinal	6
de France	5
Hostel	10
Le Manoir	4
Number One	3
Paul	1
des Quatres-Dauphins	8
St-Christophe	7

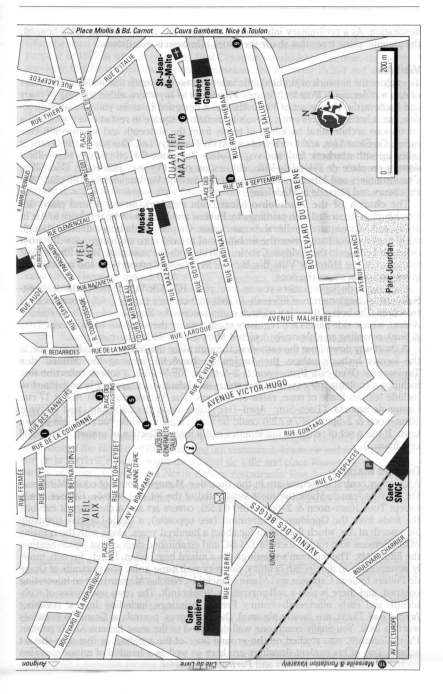

Le Clos de la Violette, 10 rue de la Violette (☎04.42.23.30.71). Aix's most renowned restaurant serves dishes that might not sound very seductive, like stuffed lamb's feet and *pieds et pâquets* (tripe and salt pork), but are in fact gastronomic delights. More obviously alluring are the puddings: a *clafoutis* of greengages and pistachios with peach sauce and a tart of melting dark chocolate. Lunch menu 250F/€38.13, otherwise menus start at 350F/€53.38 and à la carte from 450F/€68.63. Closed Mon lunch & Sun.

Les Deux Garçons, 53 cours Mirabeau. The erstwhile haunt of Camus is done up in faded 1900s style and still attracts a motley assortment of literati. Good brasserie food, but not cheap. Service daily till midnight.

L'Hacienda, cnr rue Mérindol & place des Cardeurs (☎04.42.27.00.35). Outdoor tables and a cheap lunch menu including wine, with delicious hacienda beef à la carte. Closed Sun.

Le Jasmin, 6 rue de la Fonderie (☎04.42.38.05.89). Tasty and distinctive Persian food for around 150F/€22.88. For dessert try the traditional Iranian *choleh zard*, a rice dish with saffron, spices and nuts. Closed Sat & Sun evening.

Khéops, 28 rue de la Verrerie (☎04.42.96.59.05). Egyptian cuisine featuring *falafel*, stuffed pigeon and gorgeous milk-based desserts. From 120F/€18.30. Closed Mon.

Pizza Chez Jo/Bar des Augustins, place des Augustins (☎04.42.26.12.47). This place is usually packed for its cheap pizzas and traditional *plats du jour*. Closed Sun.

Le Platanos, 13 rue Rifle-Rafle (☎04.42.21.33.19). Very cheap and popular Greek place with menus under 100F/€15.25. Closed Sun & Mon.

Nightlife and festivals

For **jazz**, the best club is *Hot Brass*, chemin de la Plaine-des-Verguetiers, rte d'Éguilles-Célony (☎04.42.21.05.57; 10.30pm onwards), or there's *Le Scat*, 11 rue de la Verrerie (☎04.42.23.00.23), with jazz, rock and funk. If you'd rather a more mainstream **disco**, head for *Le Richelme*, 24 rue de la Verrerie (☎04.42.23.49.29; from 9pm). For **pubs** with live music, try *Key Largo* and *Bugsy* at 34 and 25 rue de la Verrerie, respectively; *Pub Solferino*, place d'Armenie; or *Le Festival*, 67bis rue Espariat.

During the annual **music festivals**, Aix en Musique (rock, jazz, experimental and classical; mid-June to first week in July; ☎04.42.21.69.69) and the Festival International d'Art Lyrique (opera and classical concerts; last two weeks of July), the alternative scene – of street theatre, rock concerts and impromptu gatherings – turns the whole of Vieil Aix into one long party. Tickets for events range from 80F/€12.20 to 800F/€122 and can be obtained, along with programmes, from the Comité Officiel des Fêtes at Espace Forbin, 3 place John-Rewald, off cours Gambetta (☎04.42.63.06.75). Details of the Festival International Danse (two weeks in mid-July) are available from the same address.

Listings

Bike rental Cycles Zammit, 27 rue Mignet (☎04.42.23.19.53); Loca-velo, 16 rue Alain Savary (☎04.42.52.66.59, *locavelo.online.fr*).

Books Paradox Bookstore, 15 rue du 4-Septembre, for English books; Vents du Sud, place du Petit-Marché, is the best French bookshop.

Car rental ADA Discount, av Henri Mouret (☎04.42.52.36.36); Avis, 11 rue Gambetta (☎04.42.21.64.16); Europcar, 55 bd de la République (☎04.42.27.83.00); Rent a Car, 35 rue de la Molle (☎04.42.38.58.29).

Changing money American Express, 15 cours Mirabeau; Change d'Or, 22 rue Thiers; ATM outside Crédit Lyonnais, place Jeanne-d'Arc.

Emergencies Centre Hospitalier, av de Tamaris (☎04.42.33.90.28); SOS Médecins (☎04.42.26.24.00); for a late-night chemist, ring the gendarmerie on (☎04.42.26.31.96).

Internet *Le Hublot*, 15/17 rue Paul Bert (☎04.42.21.37.31); *Sam's Club*, 4 av des Belges (☎04.42.93.26.12).

Laundry 3 av St-Jérôme; 5 rue de la Fontaine; 60 rue Boulegon; 36 cours Sextius.

Police av de l'Europe (☎04.42.93.97.00).
Post office 2 rue Lapierre, 13100 Aix.
Taxis ☎04.42.21.61.61; ☎04.42.27.71.11 (24hr).

Mont Ste-Victoire

Mont Ste-Victoire, a rough pyramid whose apex has been pulled off-centre, lies 10km east of Aix. Ringed at its base by the dark green and orange-brown of pine woods and cultivated soil, the limestone rock reflects light, turning blue, grey, pink or orange. In the last years of his life **Cézanne** painted and drew Ste-Victoire more than fifty times, and, as part of his childhood landscape, it came to embody the incarnation of life within nature.

You may, however, be more interested in climbing Mont Ste-Victoire and in the view from it, though hiking on the Mont, and many other summits in the area, is forbidden from July to mid-September. The southern face has a sheer 500-metre drop, but from the north the two-hour walk requires nothing more than determination. The **GR9**, also called the Chemin des Venturiers, leaves from a small car park on the D10 just before **VAUVENARGUES**, 14km east of Aix. Having reached the 945-metre ridge, marked by a monumental nineteenth-century cross that doesn't figure in any of Cézanne's pictures, you can follow the path east along the ridge to the summit of the massif and then descend south to **PUYLOUBIER** (about 15km from the cross). Bring plenty of water and protection against the fierce sun if walking during summer.

At Vauvenargues, a perfect weather-beaten, red-shuttered fourteenth-century **château** (definitely not open to the public) stands just outside the village, with nothing between it and the slopes of Ste-Victoire. **Picasso** bought the château in 1958, lived there until his death and now lies buried in the gardens, his grave adorned with his sculpture *Woman with a Vase*. There is a friendly, good-value hotel in the village, *au Moulin de Provence*, 33 rue de Maquisards (☎04.42.66.02.22, fax 04.42.66.01.21; ②), whose owners speak English.

EASTERN PROVENCE

In **eastern Provence**, it is the landscapes not the towns that dominate. The gentle hills and villages of the **Haut-Var**, the northern half of the Var *département*, make for happy exploration by car or bike, before the foothills of the Alps gradually close in, eventually reaching heights of over 3000m in the far northeastern corner, around **Barcelonnette**. Winter visitors are almost exclusively skiers, while the summer brings a variety of dedicated hikers, bird-watchers, botanists and climbers. The **Parc National du Mercantour** is a conservation area in this mountainous terrain, but the most exceptional geographical feature is the **Gorges du Verdon** – Europe's answer to the Grand Canyon – in the heart of Provence.

Between Valence and Montélimar, the River Drôme joins the Rhône at **Livron-sur-Drôme**. Following the Drôme upstream by train towards **Sisteron**, or by road towards Sisteron or Barcelonnette, is one of the most dramatic ways of entering eastern Provence.

Haut-Var villages and Aups

Between **ST-MAXIMIN-DE-LA-STE-BAUME**, 35km east of Aix and famous for its supposed possession of the relics of Mary Magdalene, and **DRAGUIGNAN**, an eminently avoidable military town, a network of small roads links a dozen villages, all of which are ideal for Provençal-style loafing. The roads wind through farmland, vineyards and woods, alongside streams and lakes.

East of the **Lac de Carcès**, between Cabasse and Carcès, off the D19, lies the last of the three great Cistercian monasteries of Provence. Even more so than Silvacane and Sénanque, the **Abbaye du Thoronet** (daily 10am–noon & 2–7pm; 35F/€5.34) has been unscathed by the vicissitudes of time, and during the Revolution was kept intact as a remarkable monument of history and art; today it is occasionally used for concerts. It was first restored in the 1850s; a more recent campaign has brought it to clear-cut perfection. As with the other two abbeys, its interior spaces, delineated by walls of pale rose-coloured stone, are inspiring.

LORGUES, further east, has a serious gourmet stop in the **restaurant** *Chez Bruno* on route de Vidauban (☎04.94.85.93.93; closed Mon & Sun evening out of season; menu at 300F/€45.75, à la carte around 400F/€61), where the truffle reigns supreme, appearing in myriad forms, even in desserts. Heading 13km northwest, **ENTRE-CASTEAUX** has an ancient stone **laundry** by the river that's still used, and a very beautiful **château** (closed to the public).

COTIGNAC, 9km west of Entrecasteaux, is the Haut-Var village *par excellence*, with a shaded main square for pétanque and passages and stairways bursting with begonias, jasmine and geraniums leading through a cluster of medieval houses. More gardens sprawl at the foot of the bubbly rock cliff that forms the back wall of the village. You can **stay** in the village at the recently renovated *Lou Calen* at the bottom of cours Gambetta (☎04.94.79.60.40, fax 04.94.04.76.64: ③).

North of Cotignac, **SILLANS-LA-CASCADE** has a beautiful walk, signposted off the main road, to an immense waterfall and aquamarine pool (about 20min). **SALERNES**, 6km east of Sillans, makes tiles and pottery and has the good, old-fashioned *Grand Hôtel Allègre*, on route de Sillans (☎04.94.70.60.30, fax 04.94.70.78.84; ③; closed mid-Nov to mid-April). **VILLECROZE** and **TOURTOUR** to the northeast are both suitably picturesque. The *Auberge des Lavandes*, on place du Général-de-Gaulle in Villecroze (☎04.94.70.76.00, fax 04.94.70.57.66; ④; closed Jan & Feb), is one of the best-value hotels in the region, while in Tourtour, on route de Flayosc, you can shelter in total luxury at *La Bastide de Tourtour* (☎04.94.70.57.30, fax 04.94.70.54.90; ⑨). A second option in Tourtour, which won't break the bank, is *La Petite Auberge* (☎04.94.70.57.16, fax 04.94.70.54.52; ⑤). Between the two villages is a highly reputed **restaurant**, *Les Chênes Verts* (☎04.94.70.55.06; closed Tues evening & Wed), with menus from 250F/€38.13.

Aups

As a base for visiting the villages of Haut-Var or the Gorges du Verdon, the small town of **AUPS** is ideal, as long as you have your own transport. It has a lot of charm and still depends to a large extent on agriculture rather than tourism. Its speciality is truffles and, if you're here on a Thursday between November and mid-March, you can witness the **truffle market**.

On **place Martin-Bidauré**, which, along with **place Frédéric-Mistral** (Wed & Sat market), makes up the leafy open space before the start of the old town, a rare monument commemorates the town's citizens who died in 1851 defending the republic and its laws. The year was that of Louis Napoléon's *coup d'état*. Peasant and artisan resistance was strongest in Provence, and the defeat of the insurgents was followed by a bloody massacre of men and women. This might explain the enormous *République Française, Liberté, Egalité, Fraternité* sign on the **church of St-Pancrace**, proclaiming it as state property. The church was designed by an English architect 400 years ago, and has recently had its doors restored by two local British carpenters.

Surprisingly for such a small place, Aups has a museum of modern art, the **Musée Simon Segal** in the former chapel of a convent on avenue Albert-1er (mid-June to mid-Sept daily 10.30am–noon & 4–7pm; 15F/€2.29). The best works are those by the Russian-born painter Simon Segal, but there are interesting local scenes in the other paintings, such as the Roman bridge at Aiguines, now drowned beneath the artificial lake of Ste-Croix. Just outside Aups, 3.5km along the Tourtour road, is a **sculpture park** by local artist Maria de Faykod (daily except Tues: June–Sept 10am–noon & 3–7pm; rest of year 2–6pm; 35F/€5.34), with dramatic human forms in marble.

The **tourist office** is on place Frédéric-Mistral (April–June & Sept Mon 3–6pm, Tues–Sat 10am–noon & 3–6pm; July & Aug Mon–Sat 9am–noon & 3–7pm, Sun 9am–noon; Oct–March Mon 2–6pm, Tues–Sat 10am–noon & 2–6pm; ☎04.94.70.00.80, *otsiaups@easynet.fr*). All the **hotels** are good value: *Le Provençal* on place Martin-Bidauré (☎ & fax 04.94.70.00.24; ③) and the *Grand Hôtel* on place Duchâtel (☎04.94.70.10.82; ②) are both good inexpensive options. More comfort is to be had at *L'Escale du Verdon*, 1km out on the route de Sillans-la-Cascade (☎04.94.84.00.04, fax 04.94.84.00.05; ④; closed mid-Sept to mid-June). There are two **campsites** close to town: the two-star *Camping Les Prés*, to the right off allée Charles-Boyer towards Tourtour (☎04.94.70.00.93, fax 04.94.70.14.14; all year), which has **bikes** to rent, and the three-star *Saint Lazare* 2km along the Moissac road (☎04.94.70.12.86; closed Oct–March), which has a pool.

For **meals**, your first choice should be the hotel-restaurant *St-Marc* (☎04.94.70.06.08; ③; closed second & third week of June), a nineteenth-century mill on rue Aloisi. Serving local dishes, truffles and boar in season, it offers a very cheap lunch menu and evening menus from 130F/€19.83 (Sept–June closed Tues evening & Wed). For snacks, head for the boulangerie-pâtisserie at 20 av Albert 1er (closed Dec–April).

The Gorges du Verdon and around

From Aups, the road north leads to the western end of the **Gorges du Verdon**. A more dramatic approach crosses the vast military terrain of the Camp de Canjuers from Comps-sur-Artuby. The road runs west through 16km of deserted heath and hills, with each successive horizon higher than the last. When you reach the canyon, it is as if a silent earthquake had taken place during your journey.

From this vantage point, known as the **Balcons de la Mescla**, you look down 250m to the base of the V-shaped, 21-kilometre-long gorge incised by the River Verdon through piled strata of limestone. Ever changing in its volume and energy, the river falls from Rougon at the top of the gorge, disappearing into tunnels, decelerating for shallow, languid moments and finally exiting in full, steady flow at the **Pont de Galetas**. The huge artificial **Lac de Ste-Croix**, filled by the Verdon as it leaves the gorge, is great for swimming when the water levels are high; otherwise the beach becomes a bit sludgy. West from the Balcons runs the **Corniche sublime**, the D71, built expressly to give the most breathtaking and hair-raising views. On the north side, the **Route des Crêtes**, the D952, does the same, at some points looking down a sheer 800-metre drop to the sliver of water below.

The entire circuit around the gorge is 130km long and it's cycling country solely for the preternaturally fit. Even for drivers it's hard work, as the hidden bends and hairpins in the road are perilous and, in July and August, so is the traffic.

Public transport around the canyon is less than comprehensive. There's just one bus between Aix, Moustiers, La Palud, Rougon and Castellane on Monday, Wednesday and Saturday from July to mid-September; and one other bus daily except Sunday between La Palud, Rougon and Castellane in July and August.

The north side of the gorge: La Palud-sur-Verdon and Rougon

The loop of the Route des Crêtes joins at **LA PALUD-SUR-VERDON**, a tiny village on the northern face of the gorge and the best base from which to explore it. Life in the village revolves around the *Lou Cafetier* bar-restaurant. There are one or two other places to eat and a market on Wednesday morning around the church.

The **tourist office** is on the main road in La Palud (Easter–May & Sept to mid-Dec Thurs & Fri 10am–noon & 4–6pm, Sat 10am–noon; June–Aug daily 10am–noon & 4–6pm; ☎ & fax 04.92.77.32.02), with a nearby **Bureau des Guides** (Mon–Sat 10am–12.30pm & 2–5.30pm; ☎04.92.77.30.50), where you can find out about guided walks. UCPA (Union National de Centres Sportifs de Plein Air) in La Placette (☎04.92.77.31.66, *www.ucpa.com*) has information on all Verdon activities, and is another contact point for guides, as is the climbing shop, Le Perroquet Vert (☎04.92.77.33.39). If you want to **stay**, there's *Le Provence* on the route de la Maline (☎04.92.77.38.88, fax 04.92.77.31.05; ③) and the slightly cheaper *Auberge des Crêtes*, 1km east towards Castellane (☎04.92.77.38.47, fax 04.92.77.30.40; ③). The *Auberge du Point Sublime*, 8km to the east in **ROUGON** (☎04.92.77.60.35, fax 04.92.83.74.31; ③), is stunningly situated and not wildly expensive. The nearest **hostel**, *Le Trait d'Union*, with camping in its grounds, is 500m below La Palud (☎04.92.77.38.72; closed Nov–March), and there's a municipal **campsite**, *Le Grand Canyon*, 800m to the west of the village (☎04.92.77.38.13). If these are full, there are no fewer than six other campsites around the town. Two **gîtes** to try are *L'Étable*, on route des Crêtes in Palud (☎04.92.77.30.63), and *Le Wapiti*, just outside the village on the Moustiers road (☎04.92.77.30.02; closed mid-Nov to March). The *Chalet de la Maline*, on route des Crêtes just to the south of La Palud (☎04.92.77.38.05; closed mid-Nov to March), is a mountain **refuge** run by the Club Alpin Français.

The south side of the gorge: Aiguines and the Falaise des Cavaliers

AIGUINES, perched high above the **Lac de Ste-Croix** on its eastern side, has a turreted château (not open to the public) and a history of wood-turning – the boules for pétanque made from ancient boxwood roots used to be its speciality. You can find out more at the tiny **Musée des Tourneurs sur Bois** (mid-June to mid-Sept daily except Tues 10am–noon & 2–6pm; 10F/€1.53), a museum devoted to the intricate art, and there's some very expensive and beautiful woodwork, as well as pottery and faïence, to be viewed at the **Galerie d'Art** opposite the **tourist office** (July & Aug daily 10am–1pm & 4–7pm; rest of year Mon–Fri 10am–noon & 3–5pm; ☎04.94.70.21.64, *verdon.accueil@wanadoo.fr*).

For **rooms**, there's the hotel-restaurant *du Vieux Château* (☎04.94.70.22.95, fax 04.94.84.22.36; ⑤; closed Nov–March), or the rather characterless *Altitude 823* (☎ & fax 04.94.70.21.09; ⑦), half-board compulsory; closed Nov–March). Of the seven **campsites** in the vicinity, *Le Galetas* (☎04.94.70.20.48; closed mid-Nov to mid-March) is almost within diving distance of the lake, a long way down from the village.

However, the best place to stay on the south side – as long as you don't suffer from vertigo – is the *Hôtel du Grand Canyon du Verdon* by the dramatic **Falaise des Cavaliers** (☎04.94.76.91.31, fax 04.94.76.92.29; ④; closed mid-Nov to mid-March), on the Corniche Sublime, a good 20km from Aiguines, with stunning views. The restaurant serves reasonable food.

West of the gorge: Moustiers-Ste-Marie and Riez

MOUSTIERS-STE-MARIE is one place to avoid, particularly during high season, when the road west out of the gorge through the town is one long traffic jam and the village a tourist trap. There's a glut of hotels, restaurants, souvenir stands and a veritable surfeit of *ateliers* making glazed pottery – Moustiers' traditional speciality. The pottery, like the village itself, is pastel-coloured and pretty – and on sale in Liberty or Bloomingdales – but if you want to lug plates home with you, here's your chance.

A more pleasant option is low-key **RIEZ**, 15km west of Moustiers, where the main business is derived from the lavender fields that cover this corner of Provence. Just over the river on the road south is a lavender distillery making essence for the perfume industry. At the other end of the town, 1km along the road to Digne, is the **Maison de l'Abeille** (House of the Bee), a research and visitors' centre (daily 10am–12.30pm & 2.30–7pm; free). Visitors can buy various honeys (including the local speciality, lavender honey) and hydromel – the honey alcohol of antiquity made from nectar – and, if you show interest, you'll get an enthusiastic tour.

In size, Riez is more village than town, but it soon becomes clear that it was once more influential than it is now. Some of the houses on **Grande-Rue** and **rue du Marché** – the two streets above the main allées Louis-Gardiol – have rich Renaissance facades, and the **Hôtel de Ville** on place Quinquonces is a former episcopal palace. The sixth-century **cathedral** (Easter to mid-Sept; check with the tourist office for times), which was abandoned 400 years ago, has been excavated just across the river from allées Louis-Gardiol. Beside it is a **baptistery** (June–Sept Tues & Thurs 10am–noon; 15F/€2.29), restored in the nineteenth century but originally constructed, like the cathedral, around 600 AD. If you recross the river and follow it downstream, you'll find the even older and much more startling relics of four **Roman columns** standing in a field.

A rather more strenuous walk, heading first for the clock tower above Grande-Rue and then taking the path past the cemetery and on uphill (leaving the cemetery to your left), brings you to a cedar-shaded platform on the hilltop where the pre-Roman Riezians lived. The only building now occupying the site is the eighteenth-century **Chapelle Ste-Maxime**, with a gaudily patterned interior.

The **tourist office** is at 4 cours allées Louis-Gardiol (June–Sept Mon–Sat 9am–1pm & 2.30–6.30pm, Sun 9am–1pm; rest of year Tues–Sat 8am–noon & 1.30–5.30pm; ☎04.92.74.67.84, fax 04.92.74.60.65). For **accommodation**, there's an executive-style hotel on the other side of the river, the *Hôtel Carina* (☎04.92.77.85.43, fax 04.92.77.85.44; ④; closed Dec–March), with views and comfort to make up for its lack of character. Alternatively head out of town on the route de Valensole to the excellent-value *Château de Pontfrac* (☎04.92.77.78.77, fax 04.92.77.82.72; ④), offering a swimming pool and access to facilities such as riding stables. If you want to **eat** in the village, try *Les Abeilles* on allées Louis-Gardiol (☎04.92.77.89.29; open daily for lunch; summer open evenings also), a real treat with imaginative cooking, specialities like *aïoli* and menus including wine for under 100F/€15.25.

Castellane

Lying east of the gorge, 12km upstream from La Palud on the Route Napoléon (see p.958), **CASTELLANE**'s only distinguishing feature is the abrupt, massive rock to the east of the town. Since there's little else to do you might as well climb up to it – thirty minutes' worth from behind the modern church. The gorge itself is out of sight, but the view is still worth the trouble.

The **tourist office**, at the top of rue Nationale (April–June, Sept & Oct Mon–Fri 9am–noon & 2–6pm, Sat 10am–noon & 3–6pm; July & Aug Mon–Sat 9am–12.30pm & 2–7pm, Sun 10–12.30am; Nov–March Mon–Fri 9am–noon & 2–6pm; ☎04.92.83.61.14, *www.castellane.org*), can provide a full list of the many **hotels** and campsites in the village and its environs. The *Auberge Bon Accueil* on place Marcel-Sauvaire (☎ & fax 04.92.83.62.01; ②; closed Oct–March) is one of the cheapest, while the *Hôtel du Commerce* on place de l'Église (☎04.92.83.61.00, fax 04.92.83.72.82; ④; closed Dec–March) is the swanky option, and has an amazing restaurant serving a

120F/€18.30 menu with dishes such as artichoke hearts and ravioli stuffed with wild mushrooms and goat's cheese. The closest **campsite** to town, off the D952 or route de Moustiers, is *La Baume* (☎04.93.82.62.27). For **canoeing** and **rafting** on the Lac de Castellane and the Gorges de Verdon, Aqua-Verdon at 9 rue Nationale (☎04.92.83.72.75) is the place for information; it also rents out **bikes**.

The Route Napoléon to Sisteron

North of Castellane, the **Route Napoléon** passes through the barren scrubby rocklands of some of the most obscure and empty parts of Provence. The road was built in the 1930s to commemorate the great leader's journey north through Haute Provence on return from exile on Elba in 1815, in the most audacious and vain recapture of power in French history. Using mule paths still deep with winter snow, Napoléon and his 700 soldiers forged ahead towards **Digne-les-Bains** and **Sisteron** on their way to Grenoble – a total of 350km – in just six days. One hundred days later, he lost the battle of Waterloo and was permanently incarcerated on the island of St Helena.

At Barrème, the road is joined by the narrow-gauge **Chemin de Fer de Provence** (see box on p.1017), also known as the Train des Pignes, which runs between Nice and Digne-les-Bains. Other stations on the line are Annot and St-André-les-Alpes, both with bus connections to Castellane. Local tourist offices will have timetables.

Digne-les-Bains

DIGNE-LES-BAINS is the chief town of the Alpes-de-Haute-Provence *département*, and lies in a superb position between the Durance valley and the start of the real mountains. Though a somewhat dispiriting place, it has particular attractions for geologists and admirers of Tibet. Covering over 150,000 hectares to the north and east of Dignes, the **Réserve Naturelle Géologique de Haute Provence** is the largest geological reserve in Europe, with fossils dating back 300 million years. Guided day-trips are organized by the tourist office during July and August (not every day, so phone first), and just north of the city, down to the left after the bridge across the Bléone on the Barles road, is the **Centre de Géologie** (April–Oct daily 9am–noon & 2–5.30pm, closes Fri 4.30pm; rest of year Mon–Fri only; 25F/€3.81), with extremely good videos, workshops and exhibitions on the reserve. A couple of kilometres further along the Barles road you can see, on a bank to your left, a wall of ammonites.

The town's connection with Tibet is through the explorer Alexandra David-Neel, who managed to spend two months in the forbidden city of Lhasa disguised as a beggar in 1924. She spent the last years of her long life in Digne, dying there at the age of 101, and her house, Samten Dzong, at 27 av du Maréchal-Juin, is now home to the **Fondation Alexandra David-Neel** (guided visits daily except Sat 10am–noon & 2–4pm; free), devoted to her memory. The Dalai Lama himself has visited the place twice. Also a cut above the normal is the town's **municipal museum** at 64 bd Gassendi (closed for extended works), with some great sixteenth- to nineteenth-century paintings and homages to local seventeenth-century mathematician and savant Pierre Gassendi.

The **tourist office** is on the Rond-Point du 11-Novembre-1918 (Mon–Sat 8.45am–noon & 2–6pm, Sun 9am–noon; ☎04.92.36.62.62, *info@ot.dignelesbains.fr*), with the **gare routière** just to the north. The **gare SNCF** and the **Chemin de Fer de Provence** are both to the west over the river on avenue Pierre-Sémard. A very cheap

hotel option is the *Origan*, 6 rue Pied-de-Ville (☎ & fax 04.92.31.62.13; ①), with an excellent and inexpensive **restaurant** (closed Mon & Sun). *Le Grand Paris*, 19 bd Thiers (☎04.92.31.11.15, fax 04.92.32.32.82; ⑤ half-board; closed Dec–Feb), is considerably more luxurious and also has a good, though expensive, restaurant (closed Sun evening & Mon out of season; 120F/€18.30 lunchtime menu Mon–Sat, otherwise from around 220F/€33.55).

Sisteron

The Route Napoléon leads eventually to **SISTERON**, 25km northwest of Digne as the crow flies, and the most important mountain gateway to Provence. The site has been fortified since time immemorial and even now, half destroyed by the Anglo-American bombardment of 1944, its citadel stands as a fearsome sentinel over the city and the solitary bridge across the River Durance.

A visit to the **citadel** (daily: April–June & Sept to mid-Nov 9am–6pm; July & Aug 9am–7pm; 20F/€3.05) can easily take up half a day. There are no guides, just recordings in French attempting to recreate historic moments, such as Napoléon's march, of course, and the imprisonment in 1639 of Jan Kazimierz, the future king of Poland. Most of the extant defences were constructed after the Wars of Religion, and added to a century later by Vauban when Sisteron was a front-line fort against neighbouring Savoy. The eleventh-century castle was destroyed in the mid-thirteenth century during a pogrom against the local Jewish population.

The best views are from the Guérite du Diable lookout post. The outcrop on which the citadel sits abruptly stops here, 500m above the narrow passage of the Durance. In July and August, the festival known as Nuits de la Citadelle has open-air performances of music, drama and dance in the citadel grounds. There is also a **historical museum** with a room dedicated to Napoléon, and temporary art exhibitions in the vertiginous late medieval chapel, **Notre-Dame-du-Château**, restored to its Gothic glory and given very beautiful subdued stained-glass windows in the 1970s.

Back in Sisteron's old town, you'll see three huge **towers**, which belonged to the ramparts built in 1370. Beside them is the **Cathédrale Notre-Dame-des-Pommiers**, a well-proportioned twelfth-century church whose entryway is flanked by marble columns, but whose interior contains nothing of interest. From the cathedral, rue Deleuze leads to **place de l'Horloge**, where the Wednesday and Saturday **market** is held and which, on the second Saturday of every month, hosts a fair.

Arriving by train at Sisteron, turn right out of the **gare SNCF** along avenue de la Libération until you reach place de la République, where you'll find the **tourist office** (July & Aug Mon–Sat 9am–7pm, Sun 9am–noon & 2–5pm; rest of year Mon–Sat 9am–noon & 2–5pm; ☎04.92.61.12.03, *www.sisteron.com*) and the **gare routière**. Rooms come very cheap in the *Select'Hôtel* on place de la République (☎04.92.61.12.50, fax 04.92.61.53.62; ②), while the genteel and old-fashioned *Grand Hôtel du Cours* on allée de Verdon (☎04.92.61.04.51, fax 04.92.61.41.73; ④; closed Dec–Feb) is the best hotel in town. Sisteron's four-star **campsite** is across the river and 3km along the D951 (☎04.92.61.19.69; closed Nov–Feb).

The food in Sisteron's **restaurants** is nothing special, though the view down the valley from the terrace of the *Hôtel-Restaurant de la Citadelle*, 126 rue Saunerie, certainly is. *Le Cours*, on the allée de Verdon (☎04.92.61.00.50), serves copious meals, with the renowned *gigot d'agneau de Sisteron* included on a 120F/€18.30 menu, and you'll find plenty of eating places along rue Saunerie and on the squares around the clock tower. *Le Mondial* bar at the top of rue Droite stays open late, as does *L'Horloge* on place de l'Horloge. Finally, if you fancy a **swim**, there's a large artificial lake between the allée de Verdon and the river.

Northeast Provence

Depending on the season, the **northeastern corner of Provence** is two different worlds. In winter, the sheep and shepherds find warmer pastures, leaving the snowy heights to horned mouflons, chamois and the perfectly camouflaged ermine. The villages where shepherds came to summer markets are battened down for the long, cold haul, while modern conglomerations of Swiss-style chalet houses, sports shops and discotheques come to life around the ski lifts. From November to April many of the mountain road passes are closed, cutting off the dreamy northern town of **Barcelonnette** from its lower neighbours.

In spring, the fruit trees in the narrow valley orchards blossom, and melting waters swell the Vésubie, the Tinée and the Roya, sometimes flooding villages and carrying whole streets away. In summer and early autumn you move from the valleys to the snow-capped peaks through groves of chestnut and olive trees, then pine forests edged with wild raspberries and bilberries, up to moors and grassy slopes covered with Alpine flowers.

An uninhabited area of 68,500 hectares along the Italian border has been designated the **Parc National du Mercantour** (see box below). It can be explored from the small towns of **St-Étienne-de-Tinée**, **St-Martin-Vésubie**, **St-Sauveur-sur-Tinée** and from the **upper Roya valley**, but all the countryside in this mountainous region is breathtaking. To the south, the Italianate town of **Sospel** is a real delight.

Transport other than by foot or vehicle is a problem. Apart from the Turin–Nice train line down the Roya valley, there are regular bus connections going out from Barcelonnette or from Sospel but they don't meet, and there are only infrequent buses between villages on market days.

Barcelonnette

BARCELONNETTE is a place of immaculate charm, with snow-capped mountains visible at every turn. It is not very big, and a more ideal spot for doing nothing would be hard to find. The central square, **place Manuel**, has café tables from which to gaze at the blue sky or at the white clock tower commemorating the centenary of the 1848 Revolution. It's close to several ski resorts and to the northern edge of the Parc de Mercantour.

The **Maison du Parc** for the Mercantour (summer only daily 9am–noon & 2–5pm; ☎04.92.81.21.31) shares premises at 10 av de la Libération with the **Musée de la Vallée**

THE PARC NATIONAL DU MERCANTOUR

The **Parc National du Mercantour** is a long, narrow band of mountainland running for 75km close to the Italian border, from south of the town of Barcelonnette almost as far as Sospel, 16km north of the Mediterranean. The area is a haven for wildlife, with colonies of chamois, mouflon, ibex and marmots, breeding pairs of golden eagles and other rare birds of prey, great spotted woodpeckers and hoopoes, blackcocks and ptarmigan. The flora too is very special, with many unique species of lilies, orchids and Alpine plants, including the rare multi-flowering saxifrage.

It's crossed by numerous paths, including the GR5 and GR52, with refuge huts providing basic food and bedding for hikers. For more detailed information, contact the **Maisons du Parc** in Barcelonnette (see above), St-Étienne-de-Tinée (see p.962) or St-Martin-Vésubie (see p.963), which provide maps and accommodation details as well as advice on footpaths and weather conditions. Camping, lighting fires, picking flowers, playing radios or doing anything that might disturb the delicate environment is strictly outlawed.

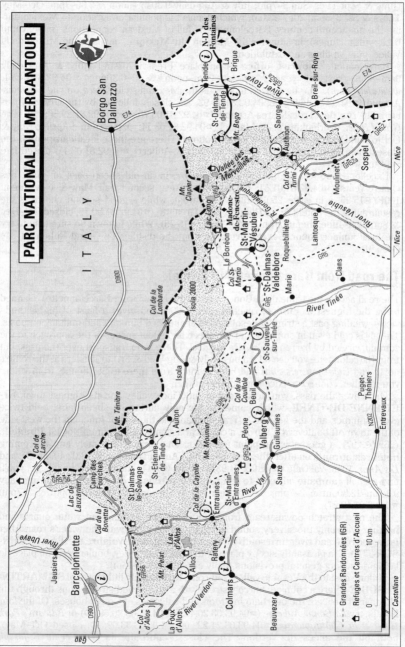

PARC NATIONAL DU MERCANTOUR

(June & Sept Tues–Sun 3–7pm; July & Aug daily 9.30am–noon & 2.30–7pm; Oct–May Thurs & Sat 3–6pm; 20F/€3.05), which details the popular emigration to Mexico during the nineteenth century. Barcelonnette is full of Mexican connections (many came back with fortunes); in summer the **Maison du Mexique**, opposite the Musée de la Vallée, puts on films and exhibitions.

Barcelonnette's **tourist office** is on place Frédéric-Mistral (July & Aug daily 9am–8pm; rest of year Mon–Sat 9am–noon & 2–6.30pm; ☎04.92.81.04.71, *www.ubaye.com*). The best place to **stay** is the Mexican-style *Azteca* on rue François-Arnaud (☎04.92.81.46.36, fax 04.92.81.43.92; ④), closely followed by the *Grande Épervière*, 18 rue des Trois-Fréres-Arnaud (☎04.92.81.00.70, fax 04.92.81.29.50; ③). The *Grand Hôtel*, overlooking place Manuel (☎04.92.81.03.14; ③; closed mid-April to May & Oct to mid-Dec), is one of the cheaper options. There are three local **campsites**, the closest being the three-star *Du Plan* at 52 av E.-Aubert (☎04.92.81.08.11; closed late Sept to late May).

Excellent **food** can be had at *La Mangeoire*, in an old sheep barn on place des Quatre-Vents (☎04.92.81.01.61; closed Mon, Tues, second half May & Nov; menu 100F/€15.25, à la carte 250F/€38.13 upwards), while a good second choice is the restaurant of the hotel *Cheval Blanc*, on rue Grenette (☎04.92.81.00.19; closed Oct–Dec & Sun Sept–June; menus from under 100F/€15.25). While in town be sure also to try the local juniper liquor, *Genepy*, available from the distiller Le Grand Ruben on rue Grenette.

The road from Barcelonnette to Sospel

The road across the Cime de la Bonette pass (the D2205 from Barcelonnette), claimed to be the highest in Europe, reaches over 2800m and gives a feast of high-altitude views, winding past a string of desolate and abandoned bunkers and military outposts. The air is cold even in summer and the green and silent spaces of the approach to the summit, circled by barren peaks, are magical. There is no transport over the pass, but from Barcelonnette you can take a bus (July & Aug Wed & Fri) to Jausiers at the route's north end (*info@jausiers.com*) and hike or hitch from there to St-Étienne, from where you can then connect to Nice and points between.

Once over the pass, you descend into the Tinée valley and its highest town, **ST-ÉTIENNE-DE-TINÉE**, which comes to life only during its sheep fairs, held twice every summer, and the Fête de la Transhumance at the end of June. On the west side of the town off boulevard d'Auron, a cable car ascends to the summit of **La Pinatelle** (26F/€3.97), a good starting point for walks. There are two homely and welcoming **hotel-restaurants** on offer: the *Regalivou*, bd d'Auron (☎ & fax 04.93.02.49.00; ③), and *Les Amis*, 1 rue Val-Gélé (☎ & fax 04.93.02.40.30; ③). On the edge of the village, you'll find a small **campsite** adjacent to and run by the **Maison du Parc** (July & Aug daily 9.30am–12.30pm & 2–7pm; rest of year Sat & Sun only 9.30am–12.30pm & 2–7pm; ☎04.93.01.42.27).

The next stretch downstream from St-Étienne has nothing but white quartz and heather, with only the silvery sound of crickets competing with the water's roar. After Isola, the road and river turn south through the **Gorges de Valabre** to **ST-SAUVEUR-SUR-TINÉE**, a pleasantly sleepy place, with a useful, if pricey, boulangerie on place de la Mairie selling general provisions (daily except Tues 1–4pm).

Shifting east to the Vésubie valley, you come to the lovely little town of **ST-MARTIN-VÉSUBIE** where a cobbled, narrow street with a channelled stream runs through the old quarter beneath the overhanging roofs and balconies of Gothic houses. Of the four **hotels**, try *La Bonne Auberge* (☎04.93.03.20.49, fax 04.93.03.20.69; ③) or *Edward's Park Hotel et la Châtaigneraie* (☎04.93.03.21.22, fax 04.93.03.33.99; ⑤; closed Oct–May), both on the allées de Verdon. The closest **campsite** is the *Ferme St-Joseph*

(☎04.93.03.20.14; all year), on the route de Nice by the lower bridge over La Madone. The most pleasant **restaurant** in St-Martin is *La Trappa* on place du Marché (closed Mon in term-time; around 100F/€15.25), which serves local dishes. The **tourist office** on place Félix-Faure (last two weeks June & first two weeks Sept daily 9am–noon & 2.30–5.30pm; July & Aug daily 9am–12.30pm & 5–7pm; mid-Sept to mid-June Mon–Sat 10am–noon & 2–5.30pm, Sun 10am–noon; ☎04.93.03.21.28, fax 04.93.03.20.01) provides details on walks and *gîtes*/refuges in the vicinity, and the **Maison du Parc** at 8 rue Kellerman provides practical information for exploring the Mercantour park (July–Sept daily 9.30am–12.30pm & 2–7pm; ☎04.93.03.23.15, *mercantour.vesubie@aol.com*).

Sospel and the Roya valley

The D2566 from the Vésubie valley joins the **Roya valley** at SOSPEL, a dreamy Italianate town spanning the gentle River Bévéra. You may find it over-tranquil after the excitements of the high mountains or the flashy speed of the Côte d'Azur, but it can make a pleasant break.

The main street, **avenue Jean-Médecin**, follows the river on its southern bank. The central bridge, the **Vieux Pont**, was built in the eleventh century to link the town centre on the south bank with its suburb across the river. The best approach to the old town is from the eastern place St-Pierre, along the gloomy, deeply shadowed rue St-Pierre. Suddenly it opens up into **place St-Michel**, one of the most beautiful series of peaches-and-cream Baroque facades in all Provence, made up of the **Église St-Michel**, two chapels and several arcaded houses. The road behind the church, rue de l'Abbaye, reached by steps between the chapels, leads up to an ivy-covered **castle** ruin, from which you get a good view of the town. An even better view can be had from the **Fort St-Roch**, part of the ignominious interwar Maginot Line, along chemin de St-Roch, which houses the **Musée de la Résistance**, illustrating the courageous local Resistance movement during the last war (April–May & Oct Sat & Sun 2–6pm; June–Sept Tues–Sun 2–6pm; 25F/€3.81).

The **gare SNCF** is southeast of the town on avenue A.-Borriglione, which becomes avenue des Martyrs-de-la-Résistance, before leading down to the park on place des Platanes opposite place St-Pierre. The **tourist office** is housed in the Vieux Pont (daily: Easter–Sept 10am–noon & 2–6pm; rest of year 10am–noon & 2–5pm; ☎04.93.04.15.80, fax 04.93.04.19.96). If you want to **stay**, the *Hôtel de France*, 9 bd de Verdun (☎04.93.04.00.01, fax 04.93.04.20.46; ③), and the *Auberge Provençale*, on route du Col de Castillon, 1500m uphill from the town (☎04.93.04.00.31, fax 04.93.04.24.54, *aubpro@aol.com*; ⑦ half-board compulsory), offer comparable quality, the latter with a pleasant garden and terrace from which to admire the town. There are five **campsites** around Sospel, the closest of which is *Le Mas Fleuri* in quartier La Vasta (☎ & fax 04.93.04.03.48; all year), with its own pool, 2km along the D2566 to Moulinet, following the river upstream.

There are various **eating** places along avenue Jean-Médecin. Alternatively, try *L'Escargot d'Or*, 3 rue de Verdun (☎04.93.04.00.43; closed Mon & Nov), just across the eastern bridge, where you can eat for between 70F/€10.68 and 165F/€25.16 on a terrace above the river.

The upper Roya valley

One of the strangest sights in the Provençal Alps is best approached from **ST-DALMAS-DE-TENDE** in the upper Roya valley, three stops on the train from Sospel. The first person to stumble upon the lakes and tumbled rocks of the **Vallée des Merveilles**, on the western flank of Mount Bego, was a fifteenth-century traveller who had lost his way. He described it as "an infernal place with figures of the devil and thousands of demons scratched on the rocks": a pretty accurate description, except that some of the carvings are of animals, tools, people working and mysterious symbols, dated to some time in the second millennium BC.

The easiest route into the valley is the ten-kilometre hike (5–7hr there and back) that starts at *Les Mesces Refuge*, about 8km west of St-Dalmas-de-Tende, on the D91. The engravings are beyond the *Refuge des Merveilles* (where you can get sustenance and shelter). You should note that certain areas are out of bounds unless accompanied by an official guide – and remember that blue skies and sun can always turn into violent hailstorms and lightning. **Guided walks** (one guide speaks English) are organized by the Bureau des Guides du Val des Merveilles in Tende (☎04.93.04.77.73; 35F/€5.34).

St-Dalmas is the nearest town to the Vallée des Merveilles and has a reasonably priced **hotel** on rue Martyres-de-la-Résistance, the *Terminus* (☎04.93.04.95.95, fax 04.93.04.95.96; ④).

LA BRIGUE, one stop up the line from St-Dalmas-de-Tende, is a good base for the Vallée des Merveilles, with some good-value hotels. While you're here, make the trip 4km east of town to the sanctuary of **Notre-Dame-des-Fontaines**, whose frescoes were executed by one Jean Canavéso at around the same time as the anonymous fifteenth-century traveller was freaking out about the demons of the Vallée des Merveilles. The frescoes, which cover the entire building, are akin to an arcade of video nasties. The goriest detail is a devil extracting Judas's soul from his disembowelled innards. The chapel is open in the summer (daily 2.30am–5.30pm; free), and in the winter you can visit it with a guide from the **tourist office** on place St-Martin (July & Aug Mon–Sat 9am–noon & 2–6pm; ☎04.93.04.36.07, fax 04.93.04.36.09). The three **hotels** in La Brigue are: *Le Mirval*, rue Vincent-Ferrier (☎04.93.04.63.71, fax 04.93.04.79.81; ④); and, on place St-Martin, the *Auberge St-Martin* (☎ & fax 04.93.04.62.17; ②) and the *Fleurs des Alpes* (☎04.93.04.61.05, ☎04.93.04.59.68; ②).

One more stop north on the train line brings you to **TENDE**, where the French spoken has a distinctly Italian accent. If you've missed the Vallée des Merveilles engravings you can see them reproduced outside the beautifully designed **Musée des Merveilles** on avenue du 16-Septembre-1947 (May to mid-Oct daily 10.30am–6.30pm; rest of year daily except Tues 10.30am–5pm; 30F/€4.58), a very contemporary museum covering the wildlife, prehistory and geology of the region. That apart, the old town is fun to wander through, looking at the symbols of old trades on the door lintels, the overhanging roofs and multiple balconies. The **tourist office** is on avenue du 16-Septembre-1947 (May–Sept Mon–Sat 9am–noon & 2–6pm; rest of year Mon–Sat 8.30am–noon & 1.30–5pm; ☎04.93.04.73.71, fax 04.93.04.35.09). To **stay**, there's the basic *du Centre* on place de la République (☎04.93.04.62.19; ②). Tende has plenty of shops and restaurants, though nothing very special on the gourmet front.

travel details

Trains

Aix-en-Provence to: Briançon (1–2 daily; 3hr 30min); Marseille (every 30min; 30–35min); Sisteron (3–4 daily; 1hr 15min–1hr 40min).

Arles to: Aix (6 daily; 1hr 15min); Avignon (9–13 daily; 20–45min); Marseille (10–12 daily; 45min).

Avignon to: Arles (hourly; 20–45min); Cavaillon (5–9 daily; 25min); L'Isle-sur-la-Sorgue (6–9 daily;

15–25min); Lyon (15–20 daily; 2hr 40min); Marseille (hourly; 50min–1hr); Orange (9–13 daily; 20–25min); Paris (8 daily; 4hr–7hr 30min); Valence (9–13 daily; 1hr 40min); Vienne (9–13 daily; 1hr 20min).

Digne to: Nice (4–5 daily; 3hr 20min).

Lyon (La Part-Dieu or Perrache) to: Annecy (7 daily; 1hr 25min); Arles (frequent; 2hr 45min);

Avignon (15–20 daily; 2hr 10min); Bordeaux (3 daily; 7–9hr); Bourg-en-Bresse (8–10 daily; 1hr 50min); Clermont-Ferrand (8–12 daily; 2hr 30min); Dijon (8–10 daily; 2hr); Grenoble (8–10 daily; 1hr 15min); Marseille (frequent; 3hr 40min); Montélimar (10–15 daily; 1hr 35min); Orange (7–9 daily; 2hr 30min); Paris (frequent; 2hr 10min–5hr); Roane (hourly; 1hr 30min); St-Étienne (8–10 daily; 45min); Strasbourg (5 daily; 5hr); Tain l'Hermitage (5 daily; 1hr 05min); Valence (8–10 daily; 55min); Vienne (7 daily; 20min).

Lyon (St Exupéry or La Part-Dieu) to: Lille-Europe (7 daily; 2hr 55min); Valence (5 daily; 40min).

Sospel to: La Brigue (4–5 daily; 45min–1hr); Nice (4–5 daily; 50min); St-Dalmas-de-Tende (4–5 daily; 40–55min); Tende (4–5 daily; 1hr 20min).

Valence to: Briançon (3 daily; 4hr 30min); Die (hourly; 1hr 10min); Gap (3 daily; 3hr); Grenoble (8–10 daily; 1hr 15min); Montélimar (6–8 daily; 20min).

Buses

Aix-en-Provence to: Apt (2 daily; 1hr 45min); Arles (3 daily; 2hr); Avignon (6 daily; 1hr–1hr 15min); Barcelonnette (2 daily; 4hr); Les Baux (1 daily; 1hr 10min); Draguignan (2 daily; 2hr 25min); Marseille (4 daily; 25min); Sisteron (3 daily; 2hr).

Arles to: Aix (3 daily; 1hr 55min–2hr); Avignon (6–10 daily; 20min–1hr 05min); Les Baux (4 daily; 30–40min); Marseille (5 daily; 2hr 05min–2hr 30min); Stes-Maries-de-la-Mer (7 daily; 55min); St-Rémy (1 daily; 35min).

Aups to: Aiguines (1 daily; 1hr 10min); Cotignac (2 daily; 20min); Draguignan (1–2 daily; 1hr–1hr 20min); Tourtour (1–2 daily; 20min); Sillans (1–2 daily; 10min).

Avignon to: Aix (4 daily; 1hr–1hr 15min); Apt (4 daily; 1hr–1hr 55min); Arles (frequent; 20min–1hr 05min); Les Baux (2 daily; 55min); Carpentras (frequent; 45min); Cavaillon (frequent; 45min); Châteauneuf-du-Pape (4 daily; 15min); Digne (2 daily; 3hr 30min); L'Isle-sur-la-Sorgue (hourly; 40min); Orange (4–6 daily; 45min); St-Rémy (8 daily; 40min); Vaison (1 daily; 1hr 15min).

Barcelonnette to: Digne (1 daily; 1hr 45min); Gap (3 daily; 1hr 20min); Marseille (2 daily; 3hr 55min).

Carpentras to: Aix (3 daily; 1hr 50min); Apt (3 weekly during school time; 1hr 05min); Beaumes (2 daily; 15min); Cavaillon (4 daily; 45min); Gigondas (2 daily; 40min); L'Isle-sur-la-Sorgue (3 daily; 20min); Orange (4 daily; 40min); Sablet (2 daily; 45min); Vacqueyras (2 daily; 25min); Vaison (2 daily; 45min).

Digne to: Avignon (2 daily; 3hr 30min); Barcelonnette (1 daily; 1hr 55min); Castellane (1 daily; 1hr 15min); Grenoble (1 daily; 4hr 30min); Marseille (4 daily; 2hr–2hr 40min); Nice (2 daily; 2hr 55min–3hr 15min).

Draguignan to: Aups (1–2 daily; 1hr 10min); Moustiers-Ste-Marie (1–2 daily; 2hr); Nice airport (2 daily; 1hr).

Gordes to: Cavaillon (2 daily; 45min).

Lyon to: Vienne (9–12 daily; 1hr 05min).

Orange to: Avignon (hourly; 45min); Carpentras (4 daily; 40min); Châteauneuf-du-Pape (4 daily; 25min); Sablet (3 daily; 50min); Seguret (3 daily; 55min); Sérignan (5 daily; 20min); Vaison (4 daily; 1hr 10min).

St Rémy to: Les Baux (1 daily July & Aug only; 20min).

Sospel to: Menton (3 daily; 50min).

Valence to: Tain l'Hermitage (3–6 daily; 25min).

CHAPTER FIFTEEN

THE CÔTE D'AZUR

The **Côte d'Azur** polarizes opinions like few other places in France. For some, it is the quintessential Mediterranean playground – the glamour queen of the coast – for others, it has become almost a parody of its image, an overdeveloped expensive victim of its own hype.

But in the gaps between the uncontrolled and often eclectic developments, and on the offshore islands, the remarkable beauty of the hills and land's edge, the scent of the plant life, the mimosa blossom in February and the impossibly blue water after which the coast is named, the Côte d'Azur remains undeniably captivating. The chance to see the works of innumerable artists seduced by the land and light also justifies the trip: Cocteau in **Menton** and **Villefranche**, Matisse and Chagall in **Nice** and **Vence**, Léger in **Biot**, Picasso in **Antibes** and **Vallauris**, and collections of Fauvists and Impressionists at **St-Tropez** and Hauts-de-Cagnes. And it must be said that **Monaco** and **Cannes**, places you either love or hate, certainly have an entertainment value, while the two great cities of **Marseille** and Nice have their own special magnetism.

The months to try to avoid are July and August, when hotels are booked up, overflowing campsites become health hazards, the locals get short-tempered, and the vegetation is at its most barren.

FROM MARSEILLE TO TOULON

From the vast and wonderful scruffiness of **Marseille** to the squalid naval base of **Toulon**, this stretch of the Mediterranean is definitely not what most people think of as the Côte d'Azur. There is no continuous corniche, few villas in the grand style, and work is geared to an annual rather than summer cycle. **Cassis** is the exception, but the overriding attraction here is Marseille – a city that couldn't be confused with any other, no matter where you are dropped in it.

Marseille

The most renowned and populated city in France after Paris, **MARSEILLE** has – like the capital – prospered and been ransacked over the centuries. It has lost its privileges

---

ACCOMMODATION PRICE CODES

Each hotel and guesthouse in this book has been graded according to the following price codes, which indicate the price for the **cheapest double room available during the high season**.

① Under 160F/€24   ④ 300–400F/€46–61   ⑦ 600–700F/€91–107
② 160–220F/€24–34   ⑤ 400–500F/€61–76   ⑧ 700–800F/€107–122
③ 220–300F/€34–46   ⑥ 500–600F/€76–91   ⑨ Over 800F/€122

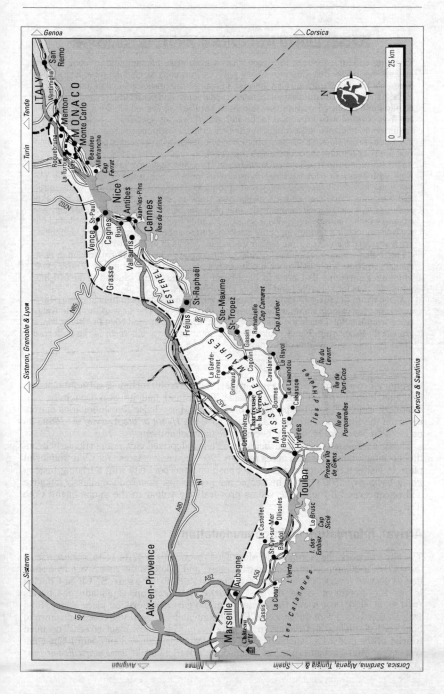

FOOD AND WINE OF THE COTE D'AZUR

The **Côte d'Azur**, as part of Provence, shares its culinary fundamentals of olive oil, garlic and the herbs that flourish in dry soil, its gorgeous vegetables and fruits, plus Menton's lemons, the goat's cheeses and, of course, the predominance of fish.

The fish soups of **bouillabaisse**, famous in Marseille, and **bourride**, served with a garlic and chilli-flavoured mayonnaise known as **rouille**, are served all along the coast, as are **fish** covered with Provençal herbs and grilled over an open flame. **Seafood** – from spider crabs to clams, sea urchins to crayfish, crabs, lobster, mussels and oysters – are piled onto huge *plateaux de mer*, which don't necessarily represent Mediterranean harvest, more the luxury associated with this coast.

The **Italian influence** is even stronger on the coast than it is inland, particularly in Nice, with delicate ravioli stuffed with asparagus, prawns, wild mushrooms or *pestou*, pizzas with wafer-thin bases and every sort of pasta as a vehicle for anchovies, olives, garlic and tomatoes. **Nice** has its own specialities, such as *socca*, a chickpea flour pancake, *pissaladière*, a tart of fried onions with anchovies and black olives, *salade niçoise* and *pan bagnat*, which combines egg, olives, salad, tuna and olive oil, and *mesclum*, a salad of bitter leaves including dandelion. *Petits farcies* – stuffed aubergines, peppers or tomatoes – are a standard feature on Côte d'Azur menus, as well as in inland Provence.

The Italian **dessert** tiramisu, made of mascapone cheese, chocolate and cream, appears in Nice, while St-Tropez has its own sweet speciality in the *tarte Tropezienne*. The sweet chestnuts that grow in the Massif des Maures are candied or turned into purée. Outlets for ice cream and sorbets are ubiquitous.

As for **wine**, the rosés of Provence might not have great status in the viniculture hierarchy, but for baking summer days they are hard to beat. The best of the Côte wines come from Bandol: Cassis too has its own *appellation*, and around Nice the Bellet wines are worth discovering. Fancy cocktails are a Côte speciality, and *pastis* is the preferred thirst quencher at any time of the day.

to sundry French kings and foreign armies, recovered its fortunes, suffered plagues, religious bigotry, republican and royalist Terror and had its own Commune and Bastille-storming. It was the presence of so many Marseillaise Revolutionaries marching from the Rhine to Paris in 1792 which gave the *Hymn of the Army of the Rhine* its name of *La Marseillaise*, later to become the national anthem.

Today, it's an undeniable fact that Marseille is a deprived city, not particularly beautiful architecturally, and with acres of grim 1960s housing estates. Yet it's a wonderful place to visit – a real, down-to-earth yet cosmopolitan port city with a trading history going back over 2500 years. The people are gregarious, generous, endlessly talkative and unconcerned if their style seems provocatively vulgar to the snobs of the Côte d'Azur.

Arrival, information and accommodation

The city's **airport**, the Aéroport de Marseille-Provence (☎04.42.14.14.14, *www.marseille .airport.fr*), is 20km northwest of the city centre, and linked to the *gare SNCF* by a shuttle bus service (every 20min 6.10am–9.50pm; 45F/€6.86). The **gare SNCF St-Charles** is on the northern edge of the 1er *arrondissement* on esplanade St-Charles (☎04.91.08.50.50), just round the corner from the **gare routière**, on place Victor-Hugo (☎04.91.08.16.40). From the *gare SNCF*, a monumental Art Deco staircase leads down to boulevard d'Athènes and thence to La Canebière, Marseille's main street. The main **tourist office** is at 4 La Canebière (July & Aug Mon–Sat 7am–7.30pm; Sun 10am–6pm; rest of year Mon–Sat 9am–7pm, Sun 10am–5pm; ☎04.91.13.89.00, *www.marseille-tourisme .fr*), down by the Vieux Port.

Marseille has an extensive **bus** network and two **métro** lines. The métro runs from 5am to 9pm, night buses from 9.25pm to around 12.30am (detailed in the *Fluobus* leaflet available from L'Espace Infos, 6 rue des Fabres, 1er; or métro sales points). Single **tickets**, known as *cartes solo* (9F/€1.37), are valid for any journeys made within an hour; a day pass (*carte journée*) costs 25F/€3.81; *cartes liberté*, for either 50F/€7.63 or 100F/€15.25, give you seven or fourteen hours' worth of journeys and can be shared among up to four people. Better value is the *Maestro* option on a *carte mistral* (52F/€7.93), which offers seven days' travel up to a maximum of 52 hours' worth of journeys, for which you'll need a passport photo. Métro stations, L'Espace Infos and many tabacs and bookshops sell tickets; *cartes solo* can also be bought on buses. All tickets must be punched in the machines at the start of your journey.

Since Marseille is not a great tourist city, **finding a room** in July or August is no more difficult than during the rest of the year. Hotels are plentiful, though if you get stuck the tourist office on La Canebière (see opposite) offers a free **accommodation service**. The most inexpensive options are the city's **hostels**, both quite a way from the centre. **Camping** is only possible at the Bois-Luzy hostel, for twenty tents only. Finally, if you are coming to town on a Friday, look out for the "Bonne Weekend en Ville" scheme, a two-nights-for-the-price-of-one package offered by many hotels in Marseille (check with the tourist office).

Hotels

Alizé, 35 quai des Belges, 1er (☎04.91.33.66.97, fax 04.91.54.80.06). Comfortable, soundproofed rooms, the more expensive looking out onto the Vieux Port. ④.

Le Béarn, 63 rue Sylvabelle, 6e (☎04.91.37.75.83, fax 04.91.81.54.98). Very good bargain for a pleasant, quiet hotel close to the centre. ③.

Le Corbusier, Cité Radieuse, 280 bd Michelet, 8e (☎04.91.16.78.00, fax 04.91.16.78.28). Simple rooms with great views on the third floor of the architect's prototype tower block (see p.978); book in advance. ③.

Edmond-Rostand, 31 rue Dragon, 6e (☎04.91.37.74.95, fax 04.91.57.19.04). Helpful management and good atmosphere; rooms come with TV and there is parking available. ③.

POWER AND POLITICS

Marseille has all the social, economic and political ills of France writ large. In addition, it has to contend with its notoriety for protection rackets and shoot-outs, corruption, drug-money laundering and prostitution. But the city's dangerous reputation is unfair – not because it's unfounded but because underworld activities flourish just as much, if not more, elsewhere on the Côte d'Azur.

The career of Marseille's most famous politician has been more spectacular than any gangster activities. Millionaire businessman **Bernard Tapie** entered politics in the 1980s with the express intention of seeing off the neo-fascist Le Pen. He became a *député* and MEP, and even held a cabinet post. He bought the city's football team, delighting the Marseillais with its success, but a match-rigging scandal in 1993 led to Olympique de Marseille's relegation from the First Division and investigations into not just the team's finances but the whole of Tapie's financial empire. The subsequent lifting of his parliamentary immunity and charges of fraud and tax evasion did nothing to dent his appeal, however, and in 1994 seventy percent of the Bouches-du-Rhône electorate voted for him. He then survived bankruptcy proceedings, and was convicted of bribery, embezzlement and misuse of funds, but got off with suspended sentences and a brief spell in jail. While defending his last case he entered a new career, starring in a film by Claude Lelouch, and finally resigned from parliament in 1996, faced with lengthy appeals against ongoing litigation. OM is now back again at the top of the French football league, having returned to compete in Europe in the 1998–99 season.

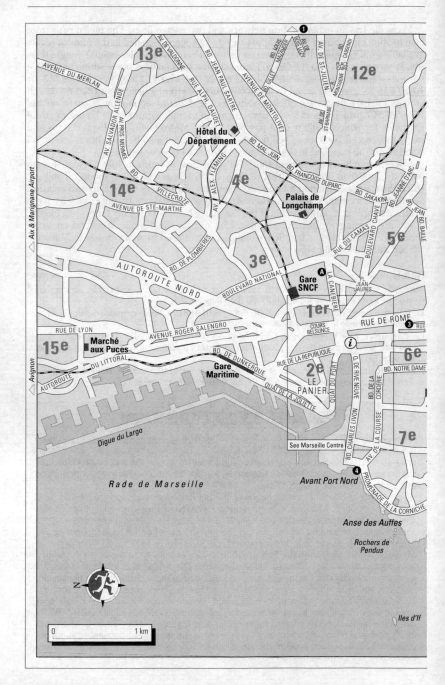

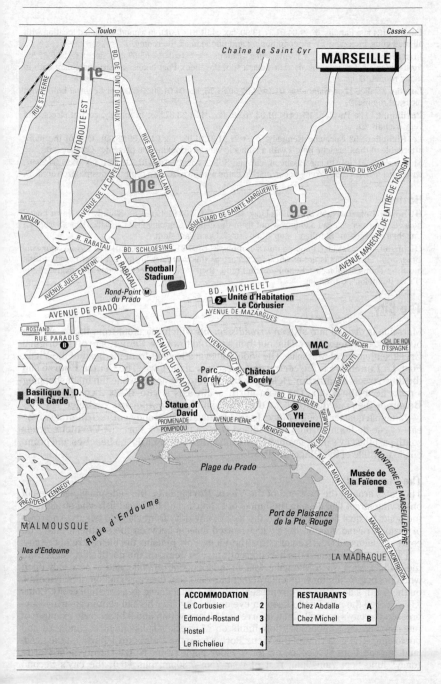

Esterel, 124 rue Paradis, 6e (☎ 04.91.37.13.90, fax 04.91.81.47.01). In a good, animated location with all mod cons, including TV, air-conditioning and phone in all the rooms. ③.

Frantour-Tonic Hotel, 42 quai des Belges, 1er (☎04.91.55.67.46, fax 04.91.55.67.56, *frantour.tonic.hotel@wanadoo.fr*). The smartest of the Vieux Port hotels; jacuzzi and steam bath in many rooms. ⑥.

Lutétia, 38 allée Léon-Gambetta, 1er (☎04.91.50.81.78, fax 04.91.50.23.52). Very central hotel, with pleasant rooms. ③.

Pavillon, 27 rue Pavillon, 1er (☎04.91.33.76.90, fax 04.91.33.87.56). In a lively, central street, and very friendly. ①.

Le Richelieu, 52 Corniche Kennedy, 7e (☎04.91.31.01.92, fax 04.91.59.38.09). One of the more affordable of the Corniche hotels with a fantastic view overlooking the plage des Catalans. ④.

St Ferréol's Hôtel, 19 rue Pisançon, cnr rue St-Ferréol, 1er (☎04.91.33.12.21, fax 04.91.54.29.97, *www.hotel-stferreol.com*). Pretty decor, marble baths with jacuzzis, in a central pedestrianized area. ⑤.

Hostels

HI hostel Bois Luzy, 76 av de Bois-Luzy, 12e (☎ & fax 04.91.49.06.18). Slightly run-down hostel housed in former château a long way out from the centre. Camping also available. Bus #8 from La Canebière, direction "St-Julien", stop "Bois Luzy". Open 7am–1am.

HI hostel, 47 av J.-Vidal, impasse du Dr-Bonfils, 8e (☎04.91.73.21.81, fax 04.91.73.97.23, *marseille @fuaj.org*). This hostel is not as cheap or secure as the *Bois Luzy* hostel, but its proximity to the beach is compensation. Mo Rond-Point-du-Prado, then bus #44 direction "Roy d'Espagne", stop "Place Bonnefon". Closed Jan.

The City

Marseille is divided into sixteen *arrondissements* which spiral out from the focal point of the city, the **Vieux Port**. Due north lies the old town, **Le Panier**, site of the original Greek settlement of Massalia. The wide boulevard leading from the head of the Vieux Port, **La Canebière** is the central east–west axis of the town. The **Centre Bourse** and the little streets of **quartier Belsunce** border it to the north, while the main shopping streets lie to the south. The main north–south axis is **rue d'Aix**, becoming **cours Belsunce** then **rue de Rome**, **av du Prado** and finally **boulevard Michelet**. The lively, youngish quarter around **place Jean-Jaurès** and the trendy **cours Julien** lie to the east of rue de Rome. From the headland west of the Vieux Port, the **Corniche** heads south past the city's most favoured residential districts towards the **beaches** and promenade nightlife of the **Plage du Prado**.

The Vieux Port

The cafés around the east end of the **Vieux Port** indulge the sedentary pleasures of observing street life, despite the fumes of exhausts and half-dead fish sold straight off the boats on quai des Belges, and the lack of any quay-front claim to beauty. The rows of seafood restaurants on the pedestrianized streets between the southern quay and cours d'Estienne-d'Orves ensure that the Vieux Port remains the life centre of the city.

Two **fortresses** guard the harbour entrance. **St-Jean**, on the north side, dates from the Middle Ages when Marseille was an independent republic, and is now only open when hosting exhibitions. Its enlargement in 1660, and the construction of **St-Nicolas**, on the south side of the port, represent the city's final defeat as a separate entity. Louis XIV ordered the new fort to keep an eye on the city after he had sent in an army, suppressed the city's council, fined it, arrested all opposition and – in an early example of rate-capping – set ludicrously low limits on Marseille's subsequent expenditure and borrowing. The best view of the Vieux Port is from the **Palais du Pharo**, on the headland beyond Fort St-Nicolas, or, for a wider angle, from **Notre-Dame-de-la-Garde** (daily: June–Sept 7am–9pm; rest of year 7am–7.30pm; bus #60), the city's Second

Empire landmark atop the hill south of the harbour. Crowned by a monumental gold Virgin that gleams to ships far out at sea, it is curious combination of draw-bridged fortification and church. Most curious are the paintings and drawings which line the chapels: dating from the eighteenth century to the present, they depict the often gory deaths or miraculous survivals of loved ones.

A short way inland from the Fort St-Nicolas, above the Bassin de Carénage, is Marseille's oldest church, the **Basilique St-Victor** (daily 8am–7.15pm; 10F/€1.53 entry for crypt). Originally part of a monastery founded in the fifth century on the burial site of various martyrs, the church was built, enlarged and fortified – a vital requirement given its position outside the city walls – over a period of 200 years from the middle of the tenth century. It looks and feels like a fortress, with some of the walls almost 3m thick, and it's no ecclesiastical beauty. You can descend to the **crypt** and **catacombs**, a warren of chapels and passages where the weight of stone and age – not to mention the photographs of skeletons exhumed – create an appropriate atmosphere in which to recall the sufferings of early Christians; St Victor himself, a Roman soldier, was slowly ground to death between two millstones.

Le Panier

To the north of the Vieux Port is the oldest part of Marseille, **Le Panier**, where, up until the last war, tiny streets, steep steps and houses of every era formed a *vieille ville* typical of the Côte. In 1943, however, with Marseille under German occupation, the quarter became an unofficial ghetto for *Untermenschen* of every sort, including Resistance fighters, Communists and Jews. The Nazis gave the 20,000 inhabitants one day's notice to quit; many were deported to the camps. Dynamite was carefully laid, and everything from the waterside to rue Caisserie was blown sky-high, except for three old buildings that appealed to the fascist aesthetic: the seventeenth-century **Hôtel de Ville**, on the quay; the **Hôtel de Cabre**, on the corner of rue Bonneterie and Grande-Rue; and the **Maison Diamantée**, on rue de la Prison. After the war, archeologists reaped some benefits from this destruction when they discovered the remains of a Roman dockside warehouse, equipped with vast food-storage jars, which can be seen *in situ* at the **Musée des Docks Romains**, on place de Vivaux (Tues–Sun: June–Sept 11am–6pm; rest of year 10am–5pm; 12F/€1.83).

At the junction of rue de la Prison and rue Caisserie, the steps of montée des Accoules lead up and across to **place de Lenche**, site of the Greek *agora* and a good café stop. At 29 montée des Accoules, the **Préau des Accoules**, a former Jesuit college, puts on wonderful exhibitions specially designed for children (Wed & Sat 1/1.30–5/5.30pm; free). What's left of old Le Panier is above here, though many of the tenements have recently been demolished. At the top of rue du Réfuge stands the restored **Hospice de la Vieille Charité**, a seventeenth-century workhouse with a gorgeous Baroque chapel surrounded by columned arcades in pink stone; only the tiny grilled exterior windows recall its original use. Local people say it was "beaucoup plus jolie" when it was lived in by a hundred families, all with ten children each. It's now a cultural centre, and alarmingly empty except during its major temporary exhibitions – usually brilliant – and evening concerts. It houses two museums (Tues–Sun: June–Sept 11am–6pm; rest of year 10am–5pm; 12F/€1.83, 18F/€2.75 during exhibitions, or 25–30F/€3.81–4.58 for both and the chapel): the **Musée d'Archéologie Méditerranéenne**, with some very beautiful pottery and glass and an Egyptian collection with a mummified crocodile, and the dark and spooky **Musée des Arts Africains, Océaniens et Amérindiens**.

The expansion of Marseille's **Joliette docks** started in the first half of the nineteenth century. Like the new cathedral, wide boulevards and Marseille's own Arc de Triomphe – the **Porte d'Aix** at the top of **Cours Belsunce**/rue d'Aix – the docks were paid for with the profits of military enterprise, most significantly the conquest of Algeria in

1830. Anyone fascinated by industrial architecture should join a tour of the docks run by the tourist office, or at least stop by the old warehouse building, **Les Docks** (follow rue République to the end), restored as a shopping and office complex. On the hill above looms the town's massive eighteenth-century **cathedral**, decorated by a distinctive pattern of alternating bands of stone (red and white outside, black and white inside).

La Canebière

La Canebière, the broad boulevard that runs for about a kilometre down to the port, is the undisputed hub of the town, its name taken from the hemp (*canabé*) that once grew here and provided the raw materials for the town's thriving rope-making trade. Fashioned originally with the Champs-Élysées in mind, La Canebière is a more patchwork affair of hotels, cafés and shops, neatly providing a division between the moneyed southern *quartiers* and the ramshackle **quartier Belsunce** to the north – an extraordinary, dynamic, mainly Arab area and a great trading ground. Hi-fis, suits and jeans from France and Germany are traded alongside spices, cloth and metalware from across the Mediterranean on flattened cardboard boxes in the streets – and not a French middleman in sight.

One block west, the **Centre Bourse** provides a stark contrast in a fiendish giant hypermall of noise, air-conditioning and over-lighting – useful, nevertheless, for mainstream shopping. Behind it is the **Jardin des Vestiges**, where the ancient port extended, curving northwards from the present quai des Belges. Excavations have revealed a stretch of the Greek port and bits of the **city wall** with the base of three square towers and a gateway, dated to the second or third century BC. In the Centre Bourse complex, the **Musée d'Histoire de Marseille** (Mon–Sat noon–7pm; free) presents the rest of the finds, including a third-century wreck of a Roman trading vessel. Further along La Canebière, where it crosses place de la Bourse, is the **Musée de la Marine** (Wed–Sun 10am–6pm; 12F/€1.83), housed on the ground floor of the Neoclassical stock exchange and filled with intricate models and paintings of ships on the high seas.

The Palais Longchamp and the Hôtel du Département

The **Palais Longchamp**, 2km east of the port at the end of boulevard Longchamp (bus #80 and #41, or M° Longchamp-Cinq-Avenues), forms the grandiose conclusion of an aqueduct that brought water from the Durance to the city. Although the aqueduct is no longer in use, water is still pumped into the centre of the colonnade connecting the two palatial wings. Below, an enormous statue looks as if it honours some great feminist victory – three muscular women above four bulls wallowing passively in a pool from which a cascade drops four or five storeys to ground level.

The palace's north wing is the city's **Musée des Beaux-Arts** (Thurs–Sun 10am–noon & 2–6.30pm; 10F/€1.53, free Sun morning), a hot and slightly stuffy place, but with a fair share of delights. Most unusual, and a very pleasant visual treat, are three paintings by Françoise Duparc (1726–76), whose first name has consistently found itself masculinized to François in catalogues both French and English. The nineteenth-century satirist from Marseille, Honoré Daumier, has a whole room for his cartoons. Plans for the city, sculptures and the famous profile of Louis XIV by Marseille-born Pierre Puget are on display along with graphic contemporary canvases of the plague that decimated the city in 1720.

Northwest of the Palais Longchamp, at the end of boulevard Mal-Juin, stands the new **Hôtel du Département** (M° St-Just). Deliberately set away from the centre of town in the run-down St-Just–Chartreux *quartier*, the seat of local government for the Bouches-du-Rhône *département* was the biggest public building to be erected in the French provinces in the twentieth century. It was designed by the English architect

William Alsop, who used his hallmark ovoid glass tube shapes above and alongside vast rectangular blocks of blue steel and glass. The Hôtel's great glass foyer is accessible during working hours, and the tourist office can arrange architectural tours.

South of La Canebière

The prime shopping district of Marseille is encompassed by three streets running **south from La Canebière**: rue Paradis, rue St-Ferréol and **rue de Rome**. Some of the smaller, intervening streets close to La Canebière are pretty seedy, with prostitutes on every corner day and night, but the atmosphere is usually friendly. Between rues St-Ferréol and Rome, on rue Grignan, is the city's most important art museum, the **Musée Cantini** (Thurs–Sun 10am–noon & 2–6.30pm; 15F/€2.29), with Fauvists and Surrealists well represented, plus works by Matisse, Léger, Picasso, Ernst, Le Corbusier, Miró and Giacometti.

A few blocks west of rue de Rome is one of the most pleasant places to idle in the city, **cours Julien** (Mᵒ N-D-du-Mont Cours Julien), with pools, fountains, pavement restaurant tables and enticing boutiques, populated by Marseille's arty and bohemian crowd and its diverse immigrant community. Streets full of bars and music shops lead west to **place Jean-Jaurès**, locally known as "la Pleine", where the daily market is a treat, particularly on Saturdays.

The corniche, beaches and Parc Borély

The most popular stretch of sand close to the city centre is the **plage des Catalans**, a few blocks south of the Palais du Pharo. This marks the beginning of Marseille's **corniche**, avenue J.-F.-Kennedy, which follows the cliffs past the dramatic statue and arch that frames the setting sun of the **Monument aux Morts des Orients**. South of the monument, steps lead down to an inlet, **Anse des Auffes**, which is the nearest Marseille gets to being picturesque. Small fishing boats are beached on the rocks, the dominant sound is the sea, and narrow stairways and lanes lead nowhere. The corniche then turns inland, bypassing the **Malmousque peninsula**, whose coastal path gives access to tiny bays and beaches – perfect for swimming when the mistral wind is not inciting the waves. You can see along the coast as far as Cap Croisette and, out to sea, the abandoned monastery on the Îles d'Endoume and the Château d'If (see below).

The corniche ends at the **Plage du Prado**, the city's main sand beach, where the water is remarkably clean. A short way up **avenue du Prado**, avenue du Park-Borély leads into the city's best green space, the **Parc Borély**, with a boating lake, rose gardens, palm trees and a botanical garden (daily 8am–9pm; free). The quickest way to the park and the beaches is by bus #19, #72 or #83 from Mᵒ Rd-Pt-du-Prado; for the corniche, take bus #83 from the Vieux Port.

The Château d'If

The **Château d'If** (daily: April–Sept 9.30am–6.30pm; rest of year 9.30am–5.30pm; 21F/€3.20), on the tiny island of If, is best known as the penal setting for Alexandre Dumas' *The Count of Monte Cristo*. Having made his watery escape after five years of incarceration as the innocent victim of treachery, the hero of the piece, Edmond Dantès, describes the island thus: "Blacker than the sea, blacker than the sky, rose like a phantom the giant of granite, whose projecting crags seemed like arms extended to seize their prey". The reality, for most prisoners, was worse: they went insane or died (and sometimes both) before reaching the end of their sentences. Only the nobles living in the less fetid upper-storey cells had much chance of survival, like de Niozelles, who was given six years for failing to take his hat off in the presence of Louis XIV, and Mirabeau, who was doing time for debt. The sixteenth-century castle and its cells are horribly well preserved, and the views back towards Marseille are brilliant. **Boats** for

If leave regularly from the quai des Belges on the Vieux Port (hourly 9am–6pm, last return at 6.40pm; journey time 15–20min; 50F/€7.63).

The Musée de la Faïence, the MAC and the Cité Radieuse

From the plage du Prado the promenade continues, with a glittering array of restaurants, clubs and cafés, all the way to the suburb of **Montredon** where the nineteenth-century Château Pastré, set in a huge park, contains the **Musée de la Faïence** (Tues–Sun: June–Sept 11am–6pm; rest of year 10am–5pm; 12F/€1.83). The eighteenth- and nineteenth-century ceramics, most produced in Marseille, are of an extremely high quality, and a small collection of novel modern and contemporary pieces is housed on the top floor. The entrance to the park (free) is at 157 av de Montredon (bus #19 from M° Rd-Pt-du-Prado, stop "Montredon-Chancel"). Along the coast from here are easily accessible *calanques* (rocky inlets), ideal for evening swims and supper picnics as the sun sets.

Between Montredon and **boulevard Michelet**, the main road out of the city, is the contemporary art museum, **MAC** (Tues–Sun: June–Sept 11am–6pm; rest of year 10am–5pm; 12F/€1.83) at 69 av d'Haïfa (bus #23 or #45 from M° Rd-Pt-du-Prado, stop "Haïfa" or "Marie-Louise"). The permanent collection, in perfect pure-white surrounds, includes works from the 1960s to the present day by Buren, Christo, Klein, Niki de Saint-Phalle, Tinguely and Warhol, as well as Marseillais artists César and Ben. There's also a cinema, the **Cinémac** (☎04.91.25.01.07), showing feature films, shorts and videos on different themes each month.

Set back just west of boulevard Michelet stands a building that broke the mould, Le Corbusier's seventeen-storey block of flats, the **Cité Radieuse**, designed in 1946 and completed in 1952. The Cité only fails to amaze now because so many architects the world over have tried to imitate Le Corbusier's revolutionary model. Each apartment has two levels and balconies on both sides of the building, with unhindered views of mountains and sea. On different floors there are shops, offices and a gymnasium; the third floor is now a hotel (see p.969); and the top floor features sculptural and ceramic roof decoration as well as a pool and a running track. To reach the Cité, take bus #21 from M° Rd-Pt-du-Prado to Le Corbusier.

Eating and drinking

The Marseillais **eat** just as well, if not better, than the ageing aristos and skin-stretched celebrities of the Riviera. Fish and seafood are the main ingredients, and the superstar of dishes is the city's own expensive invention, *bouillabaisse*, a saffron- and garlic-flavoured fish soup with bits of fish, croutons and *rouille* to throw in; theories conflict as to which fish should be included and where and how they must be caught, but one essential fish is the *rascasse* or scorpion fish. The other city speciality is the less exotic *pieds et paquets*, mutton or lamb belly and trotters.

Good **restaurant** hunting grounds to head for include cours Julien or place Jean-Jaurès (international options), the pedestrian precinct behind the Vieux Port's southern quay (a bit more upmarket and fishy), rue Pavillon (cheap lunches), the plage du Prado (glitzy and pricey) or Le Panier (snacks and old-time bistrots). Gourmet palaces lurk close to the corniche, while stalls on cours Belsunce sell chips and sandwiches with meaty fillings for under 20F/€3.05. Note that many Marseille restaurants take long summer breaks.

Cafés and bars

Bar de la Marine, 15 quai Rive Neuve, 1er. A favourite bar for Vieux Port lounging and the inspiration for Pagnol's celebrated Marseille trilogy of *Marius* (1929), *Fanny* (1931) and *César* (1936). Closed Sun.

Boulangerie, bd Baille. Open 24hrs, so ideal for late-night snacks.

Le Cadratin, 17 rue St-Saëns, 1er. Friendly and cheap bar with 1960s music playing on the jukebox and a great mix of people, both foreign and local.

Café Parisien, 1 place Sadi-Carnot, 2e. Very beautiful old-fashioned café, where people play cards and chess. Occasional painting exhibitions.

Le Petit Nice, 26 place Jean-Jaurès, 1er. Cosy, local bar overlooking the market.

La Samaritaine, 2 quai du Port, 2e. Sunny café, with the best panorama of the Vieux Port.

Restaurants

Les Arcenaulx, 25 cours d'Étienne-d'Orves, 1er (☎04.91.54.77.06). Superb food with menus from 135F/€20.59 in an intellectual haunt which is also a bookshop. Mixed gay and straight crowd. Closed Sun.

L'Atelier du Chocolat, 18 place aux Huiles, 1er (☎04.91.33.55.00). Gorgeous chocolate puddings to finish off an excellent meal; 100F/€15.25 menu including wine. Closed Sun, Mon & Tues evening.

La Athena, 2 rue de la République, 1er. Newly opened Armenian restaurant with meals from 60F/€9.15. Closed Sun & Mon lunch.

Auberge "In", 25 rue du Chevalier-Roze, 2e (☎04.91.90.51.59). In a health-food shop on the edge of Le Panier. Vegetarian *menu fixe* served lunchtimes and early evenings (around 60F/€9.15). Closed Sun.

Chez Abdalla, 17 rue Gui-Mocquet, 1er. Friendly Somali restaurant, tucked down a little alley. The food is inexpensive (huge *plats* for 35F/€5.34) and delicious.

Chez Angèle, 50 rue Calsserie, 2e (☎04.91.90.63.35). Packed Le Panier local, with a bargain *menu fixe* for basic French food. Closed Sat evening, Sun & Aug.

Chez Étienne, 43 rue Lorette, 2e. Old-fashioned Le Panier bistrot; hectic, cramped and crowded. Full meal from 100F/€15.25 as well as cheaper pizzas. No bookings. Closed Sun & Mon.

Chez Michel, 6 rue des Catalans, 7e (☎04.91.52.30.63). There's no debate about the *bouillabaisse* ingredients here. A basket of five fishes, including the elusive and most expensive one, the *rascasse*, is presented to the customer before the soup is made. Quite simply *the* place to eat this dish. Expect to pay 250F/€38.13 for the *bouillabaisse* alone.

Dar Djerba, 15 cours Julien, 6^e (☎04.91.48.55.36). Excellent Tunisian restaurant with beautiful tiling. Around 150F/€22.88.

Maurice Brun, 18 quai Rive-Neuve, 7^e (☎04.91.33.35.38). A Marseille institution serving authentic Provençal food; lunch menu 200F/€30.50, evening 250F/€38.13. Closed Sun, & Mon lunch.

Le Miramar, 12 quai du Port, 2e (☎04.91.91.10.40). This local favourite is not cheap, but with its portside location, and gregarious owner it is well worth the price (à la carte from 350F/€53). Best bet is the *bouillabaisse*.

Le Souk, 98 quai du Port, 2e (☎04.91.91.29.29). Top-notch North African restaurant with excellent quality food and smart service. Count on spending 200F/€30.50.

Nightlife

Marseille's **nightlife** has something for everyone, with plenty of live rock and jazz, as well as the more choice pastimes of theatre-, opera- and concert-going. Virgin Megastore, at 75 rue St-Ferréol (Mon–Thurs 9am–9pm, Fri & Sat 9am–midnight, Sun 9am–7pm), and the ticket bureau in the tourist office are the best places to go for **tickets and information** on gigs, concerts, theatre, free films and whatever cultural events are going on. Virgin also stocks a wide selection of English books and runs a café on the top floor. Other places with info are the book and record shop FNAC, on the top floor of the Centre Bourse (Mon–Sat 10am–7pm), the café, travel agency and comic shop La Passerelle, 26 rue des Trois-Mages (noon–midnight), and the New Age music shop *Tripsichord*, next door. At any of these places, you can pick up a copy of *Taktik*, Marseille's independent free weekly listings paper, which comes out on a Wednesday.

Practicalities

Buses from Marseille arrive at rond-point du Pressoir between the port and the beach. The **gare SNCF** is 3km out of town, with only two bus connections daily. The **tourist office** is on place Baragnon, 150m east of the port (June & Sept daily 9am–6pm; July & Aug daily 9am–8pm; Oct–May Mon–Fri 9am–12.30pm & 1.30–5pm, Sat 10am–12.30pm & 1.30–5pm; ☎04.42.01.71.17, *www.cassis.enprovence.com*).

Cheap **rooms** in high season don't exist in Cassis. The least expensive are at *Le Commerce*, 1 rue St-Clair (☎04.42.01.09.10, fax 04.42.01.14.17; ③), and *Le Provençal*, 7 av Victor-Hugo (☎01.42.01.72.13; ④), close to the port. For a little more money, and a view over the port, try *Le Golfe*, on quai Calendal (☎04.42.01.00.21, fax 04.42.01.92.08; ④; closed Nov–March). Further out, there's also the *Le Joli Bois*, route de la Gineste (☎04.42.01.02.68; ③; half-board obligatory in season), just off the main road to Marseille, 3km from Cassis and with few amenities. Far more isolated is the gorgeously scenic but rather inaccessible **hostel** *La Fontasse*, in the hills above the *calanques* west of Cassis (☎04.42.01.02.72; all year); from the D559 (stop "Les Calanques"), a road leads down towards the Col de la Gardiole, and when it becomes a track, take the left fork, and after another 2km you'll find the hostel. Rainwater, beds and electricity are the only mod cons, but if you want to explore this wild uninhabited stretch of limestone heights, the people running it are happy to give advice. To get to Cassis you can descend to the *calanques* and walk along the coast (about 1hr). If you're **camping**, don't bother going into town – the campsite, *Les Cigales* (☎04.42.01.07.34; closed mid-Nov to mid-March), is just off the D559 from Marseille before avenue de la Marne turns down into Cassis, a gruelling one-kilometre walk from the port.

Restaurant tables are in abundance along the portside quai des Baux; prices vary greatly, but if you can afford it your best bet has to be to follow your nose, and seek out the most enticing fish smells. The authentic Provençal *ratatouille* and freshly caught fish at *Chez Gilbert*, 19 quai Baux (☎04.42.01.71.36; closed Tues evening & Wed; menu 120F/€18.30), are hard to beat. *El Sol*, at no. 23 (☎04.42.01.76.10; closed Wed), with less elaborate *terroir* fare, costs a bit less, as do restaurants on the back streets, such as the family-run *La Boulangerie*, 19 rue Michel Arnaud (☎04.42.01.38.31), a pâtisserie which also does light regional dishes.

La Ciotat

You might not associate the building of 300,000-tonne oil and gas tankers with the pleasures of a Mediterranean resort. But it is one of the surprising charms of **LA CIOTAT** that the **Vieux Port**, below a golden stone old town, shelters the dramatic massive cranes and derricks of the former shipyards as well as the fishing fleet and the odd yacht or two. La Ciotat is not a town for keyed-up museum or monument motivation. It's a relaxing place with excellent **beaches** to loaf on and little glamour glitter.

In 1895, **August and Louis Lumière** filmed the first ever moving pictures here, including the arrival of a train at the *gare SNCF*, which had people jumping out of their seats in fright. The town celebrates its relatively unknown status as the cradle of cinema with an annual **film festival** (in mid-June) using the world's oldest movie house, the **Eden Cinema**, on the corner of boulevard A.-France and boulevard Jean-Jaurès. The brothers are commemorated by a solid 1950s monument on plage Lumière and in a mural on the covered market halls that house the modern cinema, visible as you walk up rue Regnier from boulevard Guérin north of the port.

The streets of the old town, apart from rue Poilus, are uneventful and a bit run-down. If you feel the need to do something constructive you can take a boat trip out to the tiny offshore **Île Verte** from the quai de Gaulle (departures every 20min; journey time 15min; ☎04.42.40.83.50), and to a number of nearby *calanques* from quai Ganteaume (☎04.42.83.54.50). Alternatively, take a walk through the **Parc du Mugel** (daily:

June–Sept 8am–8pm; rest of year 9am–6pm; free; bus #3 to La Garde, stop "Mugel"), with its strange cluster of rock formations on the promontory beyond the shipyards. A path leads up through overgrown vegetation to a narrow terrace overlooking the sea. Here, the cliff face looks like the habitat of some gravity-defying, burrowing beast rather than the erosions of wind and sea. If you continue on bus #3 to Figuerolles you can reach the **Anse de Figuerolles** *calanque* down the avenue of the same name, and its neighbour, the **Gameau**.

Practicalities

The **gare SNCF** is 5km from the Vieux Port, but a bus meets every train. The old town and port look out across the Baie de la Ciotat, whose inner curve provides the beaches and resort lifestyle of La Ciotat's modern extension, **La Ciotat Plage**. The **gare routière** is at the end of boulevard Anatole-France by the Vieux Port right beside the **tourist office** (Easter–May Mon–Sat 9am–6pm, Sun 10am–1pm; June–Sept Mon–Sat 9am–8pm, Sun 10am–1pm; Oct–Easter Mon–Sat 9am–noon & 2.30–6pm; ☎04.42.08.61.32, *www.altern.org/maisasso*).

For **hotels**, the cheapies are *La Marine*, 1 av Fernand Gassion (☎ & fax 04.42.08.35.11; ①), and *La Rotonde*, 44 bd de la République (☎04.42.08.67.50, fax 04.42.08.45.21, *info@asther.com*; ③), both in the old town. In La Ciotat Plage, *Miramar*, 3 bd Beaurivage (☎ & fax 04.42.83.33.79; ⑤; half-board compulsory in summer), is set amidst pines by the sea, while across the bay, on Corniche du Liouquet, you can stay in little villas in a park at *Ciotel Le Cap* (☎04.42.83.90.30, fax 04.42.83.04.17; ⑨). La Ciotat has nine **campsites**, three of them by the sea, of which *St-Jean*, 30 av St-Jean (☎04.42.83.13.01 fax 04.42.71.46.41; closed Oct to end March), is the closest to the centre (bus #4, stop "St-Jean Village").

La Ciotat's best **restaurant** is *La Fresque*, 18 rue des Combattants (☎04.42.08.00.60; closed Sun), with exquisite seafood dishes and menus from 120F/€18.30. Otherwise, *Coquillages Franquin*, 13 bd Anatole-France (☎04.42.83.59.50; closed Sun–Tues), serves perfectly respectable fish dishes, and there are plenty of cafés and brasseries around the Vieux Port and along boulevard Beaurivage in La Ciotat Plage.

Bandol

Across La Ciotat bay are the fine sand beaches and unremarkable family resort of **LES LECQUES**, an offshoot of the old town of **ST-CYR-SUR-MER**, behind. The **train station** is in St-Cyr, but the **tourist office** (July & Aug daily 9am–7pm; rest of year Mon–Sat 9am–6pm; ☎04.94.26.73.73, *www.saintcyrsurmer.com*) is on the place de l'Appel du 18 Juin, on the seafront in Les Lecques. St-Cyr has the cheapest **accommodation**, such as the rather basic but serviceable *Auberge Le Clos Fleurie* (☎ 04.94.26.27.46; ②), near the station on avenue Général-de-Gaulle, but there's a greater choice in Les Lecques. A ten-kilometre **coastal path** (signposted in yellow) runs from the east end of Les Lecques' beach through a rare villa-free stretch of secluded beaches and *calanques* to the unpretentious resort of **BANDOL**, while inland are **vineyards** producing some of the best wines on the Côte, the *appellation* Bandol. The *appellation* covers a large area stretching from St-Cyr to Le Castellet up in the hills to the edge of Ollioules, just east of Toulon; you'll see *dégustation* signs along the route. The reds are the most reputed, maturing for over ten years on a good harvest, with bouquets sliding between pepper, cinnamon, vanilla and black cherries.

In Bandol there are a number of cheap **hotel** options near the centre, including *Hôtel Florida* (☎04.94.29.41.72; ②) and *La Cigale Bleue* (☎04.94.29.41.40; ②), not to mention plenty of other middle-range hotels such as the *Hôtel Brise*, 12 bd Victor Hugo, close to the beach (☎04.94.29.41.70; ④), with en-suite bathrooms. The **tourist office**, on allée Vivien by the quayside (July & Aug daily 9am–1pm & 2–7pm; rest of year Mon–Sat

9am–noon & 2–6pm; ☎04.94.29.41.35, fax 04.94.32.50.39) will help if you are stuck during the busy high season.

The other stretch of **coastal path** this side of Toulon is along the southern edge of the **Sicié peninsula** from Le Brusc. The path climbs up to the sturdy clifftop chapel of Notre-Dame-du-Mai, once a primitive lighthouse, which affords fantastic views of the coast and hinterland. The chapel itself is only open in May and on certain special dates (Easter Monday, August 15, and for the pilgrimage on September 14).

Toulon

TOULON was half destroyed in the last war, and its rebuilt whole is dominated by the military and associated industries. The arsenal that Louis XIV created is today one of the major employers of southeast France, and the port is home to the French Navy's Mediterranean fleet. The shipbuilding yards of La Seyne have, however, been axed, closing the book on a centuries-old and at times notorious industry. Up until the eighteenth century, slaves and convicts were still powering the king's galleys, and following the Revolution, convicts were sent to Toulon with iron collars round their necks for sentences of hard labour. After 1854 convicts were deported to the colonies in whose conquest ships from Toulon played a major part.

Today, French nationals of non-European origin receive second-class treatment from the Town Hall, controlled since May 1995 by the Front National. Its victory – the most significant electoral gain for the extreme-right party to date – shocked the whole of France.

Toulon has never been a particularly pleasant city, and it isn't improving under its new masters. The museums are dull, motorway traffic crawls through the centre, it has all the paranoia of a big city with few of the charms, and is claustrophobic and ugly – in short, a place to avoid.

The **gare SNCF**, on place de l'Europe, and **gare routière**, on place Albert-1er, lie northeast of the town centre. There's a **tourist office** (June–Sept Mon–Sat 9am–6pm, Sun 10am–noon; rest of year Mon–Sat 9.30am–5.30pm, Sun 10am–noon; ☎04.94.18.53.00, *www.toulon.com*) on place Raimu, in the **old town**: head down rue Vauban, turn left at place d'Armes, follow the busy avenue that runs parallel to the coast, and turn left into rue Letuaire. Around place Victor-Hugo you'll find any number of cheap shops and places to eat, and a market (Tues–Sun).

If you do get stuck here, there's plenty of cheap **accommodation**: the *Foyer de la Jeunesse* hostel, 12 place d'Armes (☎04.94.22.62.00), just west of the old town; the *Hôtel des Allées*, 18 allées Amiral-Courbet (☎04.94.91.10.02; ②); or *Little Palace*, 6–8 rue Berthelot (☎04.94.92.26.62, fax 04.94.89.13.77; ③) – all very central.

THE CENTRAL RESORTS AND ISLANDS

Out of season, the stretch of coastline between **Hyères** and the **St-Raphael–Fréjus** conurbation and its backdrop of wooded hills hold their own against the cynicism engendered by tourist brochure overkill. The magic lies in the scented Mediterranean vegetation, silver beaches glimpsed between purple cliffs, secluded islands and medieval hilltop villages.

Hyères, which preserves a certain air of gentility, flashy St-Raphael and historic Fréjus are the only significant towns, though the urban sprawl around the erstwhile fishing villages of **Le Lavandou**, **Cavalaire-sur-Mer** and **Ste-Maxime** keeps any sense of wilderness at bay. But there are moments when it's almost possible to imagine the coastline of old: near the **Cap de Bregançon** south of **Bormes**, between **Le Rayol** and Cavalaire, in the **Domaine de Rayol gardens**, and around the southern tip of the **St-Tropez peninsula**. And out to sea, on the **Îles d'Hyères** (often called the Îles d'Or) you can experience untrammelled landscapes with some of the best fauna and flora in Provence. **La Croix-Valmer** is probably the most pleasant of the resorts, and **St-Tropez** is a must – for a day's visit at least. Inland, amidst the dense wooded hills of the **Massif des Maures**, are the gorgeous ancient villages of **Collobrières** and **La Garde Freinet**.

Sheer expense aside, **transport** is the one big problem. There are no trains, traffic is extremely slow in high season, and cycling doesn't get you very far unless you're Tour de France material.

Hyères

HYÈRES is the oldest resort on the Côte, listing Queen Victoria and Tolstoy among its early admirers, but the lack of a central seafront meant the town lost out when the foreign rich switched from winter convalescents to quayside strollers. It is, nevertheless, a very popular resort, but has the rare distinction, for this part of the world, of not being totally dependent on the summer influx. The town exports cut flowers and exotic plants, the most important being the date palm, which graces every street in the city – and numerous desert palaces in Arabia. The orchards, nursery gardens and vineyards, taking up land which elsewhere would have become a rash of holiday shelving units, are crucial to its economy. Hyères is consequently rather appealing.

Arrival, information and accommodation

The **gare SNCF** is on place de l'Europe, 1500m south of the town centre, with frequent buses to **place Clemenceau**, at the entrance to the old town, and to the **gare routière** on place Mal-Joffret, two blocks south (☎04.94.12.55.12). The modern Hyères–Toulon **airport** is between Hyères and Hyères-Plage, 3km from the centre (☎04.94.00.83.83), to which it's connected by a regular shuttle. The **tourist office** is next door to place Mal-Joffre in the Rotunde Jean-Salusse, on avenue de Belgique (July & Aug daily 9am–8pm; rest of year Mon–Fri 9am–noon & 2–6pm, Sat 10am–4pm; ☎04.94.65.18.55, fax 04.94.35.85.05). **Bikes** and **mopeds** can be rented from Holiday Bikes, on chemin du Palyestre, between the airport and the *gare SNCF* (☎04.94.38.79.45, *www.holidaybikes.com*).

Hotels in the old town include the *Hôtel le Soleil*, on rue du Rempart (☎04.94.65.16.26, fax 04.94.35.46.00; ③), in a renovated house at the foot of the parc St-Bernard, and the smaller *Hôtel du Portalet*, 4 rue de Limans (☎04.94.65.39.40, fax 35.86.33; ②). One kilometre from L'Almanarre beach, *La Québécoise*, on avenue Amiral (☎04.94.57.69.24, fax 04.94.38.78.27; ④; half-board obligatory in July & Aug), is a quiet and very pleasant hotel on the wooded slopes of Costabelle, with a pool and sea views. There are any number of **campsites** on the coast. Two smaller ones are *Camping-Bernard*, a two-star in Le Ceinturon (☎04.94.66.30.54; closed Oct–Easter), and *Clair de Lune*, avenue du Clair de Lune (☎04.94.58.20.19; closed mid-Nov to Jan), a three-star one on the Presqu'Île de Giens.

The Town

Walled and medieval **old Hyères** perches on the slopes of Casteou hill, 5km from the sea; below it lies the **modern town**, with avenue Gambetta the main north–south axis.

short-cut flights of steps. The mimosas here, and all along the Côte d'Azur, are no more indigenous than the people passing in their Porsches: the tree was introduced from Mexico in the 1860s, but the town still has some of the most luscious climbing flowers of any Côte town.

To the southwest of Bormes is one of those rare unbuilt-up stretches of coast around **BREGANÇON** and **CABASSON**, good wine-growing terrain, harbouring a presidential residence in the castle at **Cap de Bregançon**. Unfortunately, access to the sea is heavily controlled, with three **beaches** charging hefty parking fees (and a small charge for pedestrians and cyclists). The beach by the castle past Cabasson is the best.

Practicalities

Two reasonable **hotels** in old Bormes are *La Terrasse*, 19 place Gambetta (☎04.94.71.15.22; ②; closed Nov & Dec), with simple rooms; and the rather plain and old-fashioned *Bellevue*, on place Gambetta (☎04.94.71.15.15; ②; closed Oct–Jan). In Cabasson, there's also the very attractive and peaceful *Les Palmiers*, 240 chemin du Petit-Fort (☎04.94.64.81.94, fax 04.94.64.04.93.61; ⑤; closed mid-Nov to Dec; half-board compulsory in summer), with its own path to the beach. All **campsites** are just below the main road or in La Favière by the mindlessly ugly pleasure port, closer to Le Lavandou than to Bormes. One of the best options is the four-star *Clos-Mar-Jo* at 895 chemin de Bénat (☎04.94.71.53.39; closed Oct–March). For more information, the **tourist office** in Bormes is on place Gambetta (June & Sept daily 9am–12.30pm & 2.30–7pm; July & Aug daily 9am–12.30pm & 3–8pm; Oct–May Mon–Sat 9am–12.30pm & 2–6pm; ☎04.94.01.38.38, *www.provenceweb.fr/83/bormes*).

Good **restaurants** include *La Tonnelle des Délices*, on place Gambetta (☎04.94.71.34.84; closed Wed; menus from around 120F/€18.30), specializing in local honey-based recipes such as *lapin de blanc de Provence*; *L'Escoundudo*, 2 ruelle du Moulin (☎04.94.71.15.53; closed Mon & Tues midday out of season; 110F/€16.78 midday menu, otherwise 180F/€27.45), whose *carte* varies between traditional Provençal and *gastronomique*; and *Pâtes . . . et Pâtes*, on place du Bazar (☎04.94.64.85.75; closed Tues), which serves the best pasta in town for 100–150F/€15.25–22.88. More ordinary dinners can be had at the less expensive hotels listed above.

Le Lavandou to La Croix-Valmer

One of many Mediterranean fishing villages turned pleasure port, **LE LAVANDOU**, a few kilometres east of Bormes, has nothing wildly special to recommend it, apart from the seduction of its name (which comes from *lavoir* or "wash-house" rather than "lavender"), some tempting shops and a general Azur atmosphere. From the central promenade of quai Gabriel-Péri the sea is hardly visible for pleasure boats moored at the three harbours and it's only upmarket restaurant demand that keeps the dozen or so fishing vessels from a fleet, that once numbered fifty, still in business. If you want to indulge in watersports or nightlife, the **tourist office** on quai Gabriel-Péri (May–Sept Mon–Sat 9am–12.30pm & 2.30–7.30pm, Sun 10am–noon & 3.30–6.30pm; rest of year Mon–Sat 9am–noon & 2.30–6pm; ☎04.94.00.40.50, fax 04.94.00.40.59) will happily advise.

But if you're after the fabled silver beaches you need to head out of town and east along the classic Côte d'Azur corniche lined with pink oleander bushes and purple bougainvillaea, to **CAVALIÈRE**, **PRAMOUSQUIER**, **LE CANADEL** and **LE RAYOL**. It's hardly countryside, but you can explore the **Pointe du Layet** headland just east of Cavalière, follow the sinuous D27 up to the **Col du Canadel** for breathtaking views and beautiful cork-oak woodland, and, in Le Rayol, visit a superb garden, the **Domaine de Rayol** (daily: Jan–June & Sept to mid-Nov 9.30am–12.30pm & 2.30–6.30pm; July & Aug 9.30am–12.30pm & 4.30–8pm; 40F/€6.10), with plants from different parts of the world that share the Mediterranean climate.

Beyond Le Rayol the corniche climbs away from the coast through 3km of open countryside, scarred almost every year by fires. As abruptly as this wilderness commences, it ends with the choking, hideous sprawl of **Cavalaire-sur-Mer**. From here another exceptional sight of coastline, dressed only in its natural covering of rock and woodlands, is visible across the Baie de Cavalaire. This is the **Domaine de Cap Lardier**, a wonderful coastal conservation area around the southern tip of the St-Tropez peninsula, easily accessible from **La Croix-Valmer**. The resort's centre is some 2.5km from the sea, but this only adds to its charm, since some of the land in between is taken up by vineyards which produce a very decent *Côte de Provence*.

La Croix-Valmer's **tourist office** is in Les Jardins de la Gare (June–Sept Mon–Sat 9am–8pm, Sun 9am–1pm; rest of year Mon–Fri 9.15am–noon & 2–6pm, Sat & Sun 9.15am–noon; ☎04.94.55.22.00, *www.franceplus.com/golfe.de.st-tropez*) just up from the junction of the D559 and D93. A good-value **hotel** for this part of the world is *La Bienvenue* on rue L.-Martin (☎04.94.79.60.23, fax 04.94.79.70.08; ③; closed Nov–March) in the village centre. One of the least expensive options near the beach is the family-run *Hostellerie La Ricarde*, quartier de la Plage (☎04.94.79.64.07, fax 04.94.54.30.14; ③; closed Nov–March), whilst at the other end of the scale is *Le Château de Valmer*, on route de Gigaro (☎04.94.79.60.10, fax 04.94.54.22.68, *www.nova.fr/cjateua-valmer*; ⑨; closed Oct–April), a seriously luxurious old Provençal manor house in walking distance of the sea. You can **camp** at the four-star *Sélection*, on boulevard de la Mer (☎04.94.55.10.30, fax 04.94.55.10.39; closed mid-Oct to mid-April; booking advisable), 400m from the sea and with excellent facilities. Good, inexpensive pizzas are guaranteed at *L'Italien* (☎04.94.79.67.16) on plage de Gigaro, at almost the last commercial outlet before the conservation area. Two other good but expensive **restaurants** on this beach are *La Brigantine* and *Souleïas*.

The Massif des Maures

The secret of the Côte d'Azur is that however grossly vulgar the conglomeration of the coast, Provence is still just behind – old, sparsely populated, village-oriented and dependent on the land for produce, not real estate. Between Marseille and Menton, the most bewitching hinterland is the **Massif des Maures**, stretching from Hyères to Fréjus. The highest point of these hills stops short of 800m, but the quick succession of ridges, the sudden drops and views and then closure again, and the curling, looping roads, are pervasively mountainous. Where the lie of the land gives a wide bowl of sunlit slopes, vines are grown. Elsewhere the hills are thickly forested, with Aleppo and umbrella pines, holly, cork oaks and sweet chestnut trees. Amidst the brush lope the last of the Hermann's tortoises which once could be found along the whole of the northern Mediterranean coast – the few which escape predators and collectors can live to almost 100 years.

Much of the Massif is inaccessible even to walkers. However, the **GR9 footpath** follows the highest and most northerly ridge from Pignans on the N97 past Notre-Dame-des-Anges, La Sauvette, **La Garde-Freinet** and down to the head of the Golfe de St-Tropez. If you're **cycling**, the **D14** that runs for 42km through the middle, parallel to the coast, from Pierrefeu-du-Var, north of Hyères, to **Cogolin** near St-Tropez, is manageable and stunning, climbing from 150m to 411m above sea level.

Collobrières and La Chartreuse de la Verne

At the heart of the Massif is the ancient village of **COLLOBRIÈRES**, reputed to have been the first place in France to learn from the Spanish that a certain tree plugged into bottles allows a wine industry to grow. From the Middle Ages until very recent times,

St-Tropez and its peninsula

The origins of **ST-TROPEZ** are unremarkable: a little fishing village that grew up around a port founded by the Greeks of Marseille, which was destroyed by the Saracens in 739 and finally fortified in the late Middle Ages. Its sole distinction from the myriad other fishing villages along this coast was its inaccessibility. Stuck out on the southern shores of the Golfe de St-Tropez, away from the main coastal routes on a wide peninsula that never warranted real roads, St-Tropez could only easily be reached by boat. This held true as late as the 1880s, when the novelist Guy de Maupassant sailed his yacht into the port during his final high-living binge before the onset of syphilitic insanity.

Soon after de Maupassant's fleeting visit, the painter and leader of the neo-Impressionists, Paul Signac, was sailing down the coast when bad weather forced him to moor in St-Tropez. He instantly decided to build a house there, to which he invited his friends. Matisse was one of the first to accept, with Bonnard, Marquet, Dufy, Dérain, Vlaminck, Seurat and Van Dongen following suit, and by the eve of World War I St-Tropez was pretty well established as a hangout for bohemians. The 1930s saw a new influx of artists, this time of writers as much as painters: Cocteau, Colette and Anaïs Nin, whose journal records "girls riding bare-breasted in the back of open cars". In 1956 Roger Vadim arrived to film Brigitte Bardot in *Et Dieu Créa la Femme*. The international cult of Tropezian sun, sex and celebrities took off – even the 1960s hippies who flocked to the revamped Mediterranean Mecca of liberation managed to look glamorous – and the resort has been big-money mainstream ever since.

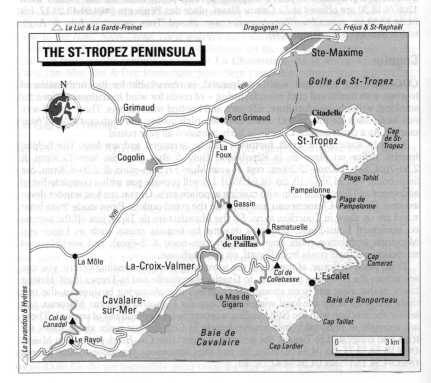

Arrival, information and accommodation

Buses run between the main coast road at **La Foux** and St-Tropez, 5.5km away, every two hours or so (in summer), dropping you at the **gare routière** on avenue Général-de-Gaulle. From here it's a short walk, along avenue du 8-Mai-1945, to the **Vieux Port**, where you'll find the **tourist office** opposite, on quai Jean-Jaurès (Jan–April & Nov–Dec 9am–12.30pm & 2–6pm; May, June, Sept & Oct 9am–1pm & 2.30–7pm; July & Aug 9.30am–1pm & 3–8.30pm; ☎04.94.97.45.21, *www.mova.fr/saint-tropez*). **Bikes** and **motorbikes** can be rented at Holiday Bikes at 14 av G. Leclerc (☎04.94.97.09.39, *www.holidaybikes.com*).

With more and more people wanting to pay homage to St-Tropez, **accommodation** is a problem; indeed, between April and September you won't find a room unless you've booked months in advance or are prepared to pay exorbitant prices. The tourist office can help with reservations, but, transport permitting, you might be better off staying in La Croix-Valmer or La Garde-Freinet (see pp.991 & 992). Out of season you may be luckier, though in winter few **hotels** stay open. One of the best-value places in town is *Lou Troupelen* (☎04.94.97.04.37, fax 04.94.97.41.76; ⑤; closed mid-Nov to April), a short walk from the centre, which has clean, comfortable rooms. If they're booked up, try the *Lou Cagnard*, 18 av Paul Roussel (☎04.94.97.04.24, fax 04.94.97.09.44; ⑤; closed Nov & Dec), which looks dreary from the outside but has a decent garden, or the rather scruffy *La Méditerranée*, 21 bd Louis-Blanc (☎04.94.97.00.44, fax 04.94.97.47.83; ④). If you're prepared to pay a bit more, *Le Baron*, 23 rue de l'Alïoli (☎04.94.97.06.57, fax 04.94.97.58.72; ⑥), overlooking the citadel, is a bit quieter than those in the centre, or there's the luxurious *La Ponche*, on place du Révelin (☎04.94.97.02.53, fax 04.94.97.78.61, *www.nova.fr/ponche*; ⑨; closed Nov–March), an old block of fishermen's houses with a host of famous arty names in its guest book.

Camping near St-Tropez is also a problem. The nearest are the two sites on the plage du Pampelonne, which charge extortionate rates and are massively crowded in high summer. Otherwise, 6km away on the N559 near Gassin is the three-star *Camping Parc Montana* (☎04.94.55.20.20, fax 04.94.56.34.77; closed Oct–March). Within a three-kilometre radius of Ramatuelle (see p.997) are *Les Tournels* on route de Camarat (☎04.94.55.90.90, fax ☎04.94.55.90.99) and *La Croix du Sud* on route des Plages (☎04.94.79.80.84, fax 04.94.79.89.21; closed Oct–April).

The Town

Beware of coming to St-Tropez in high summer, unless by yacht and with limitless credit. The road from Le Foux has traffic jams as bad as Nice or Marseille; the pedestrian jams to the port are not much better; the hotels and restaurants are full and very expensive; overnighting in vehicles is prohibited; the beaches are not the cleanest . . . So save your visit, if you can, for a spring or autumn day, and you'll understand why this place has had such history and such hype.

The **Vieux Port**, with the old town rising above the eastern quay, is where you'll get the classic St-Tropez experience: the quayside café clientele *face-à-face* with the yacht-deck martini sippers and the latest fashions parading in between, defining the French word *frimer*, which means to stroll ostentatiously in places like St-Tropez. It's surprising just how entertaining this spectacle can be.

Up from the port, at the end of quai Jean-Jaurès, you enter place de l'Hôtel-de-Ville, with the **Château Suffren**, originally built in 980 by Count Guillaume 1er of Provence (occasionally hosting art exhibitions), and the very pretty Mairie. A street to the left leads down to the rocky **baie de la Glaye**; while, straight ahead, rue de la Ponche passes through an ancient gateway to place du Revelin above the **fishing port** and its tiny beach. Turning inland and upwards, struggling past continuous shop-fronts, stalls and café tables, you finally reach the open space around the sixteenth-century **citadel**. Its maritime **museum** (daily: mid-June to mid-Sept 10am–6pm; rest of year 10am–5pm) is not much fun, but the walk round the ramparts on an overgrown path has the best views of the gulf and the back of the town – views that have not changed since their translations in oil onto canvas before the war.

Some of these paintings you can see at the marvellous **Musée de l'Annonciade**, in the deconsecrated sixteenth-century chapel on place Georges-Grammont, just west of the port (Wed–Sun: Jan–May, Oct & Dec 10am–noon & 3–6pm; June–Sept 10am–noon & 3–7pm; 25F/€3.81). It was originally Signac's idea to have a permanent exhibition space for the neo-Impressionists and Fauvists who painted here, though it was not until 1955 that the collections of various individuals were put together. The Annonciade features works by Signac, Matisse and most of the other artists who worked here: grey, grim, northern views of Paris, Boulogne and Westminster, and then local, brilliantly sunlit scenes by the same brush – a real delight and unrivalled outside Paris for the 1890–1940 period of French art.

The other pole of St-Tropez's life, south of the Vieux Port, is **place des Lices**. The café-brasseries have become a bit too Champs-Elysées in style, and a new commercial block has been added near the northern corner, but you can still sit on benches in the shade of sad but surviving plane trees and watch the boules games.

The beaches

The beach within easiest walking distance is **Les Graniers**, below the citadel just beyond the port des Pêcheurs along rue Cavaillon. From there, a path follows the coast around the **baie des Canoubiers**, with its small beach, to Cap St-Pierre, Cap St-Tropez, the very crowded **Les Salins** beach and right round to **Tahiti-Plage**, about 11km away.

Tahiti-Plage is the start of the almost straight, five-kilometre north–south **Pampelonne** beach, famous bronzing belt of St-Tropez and world initiator of the topless bathing cult. The water is shallow for 50m or so, and the beach is exposed to the wind, and sometimes scourged by dried sea vegetation, not to mention more distasteful garbage. But spotless glitter comes from the unending line of beach bars and restaurants, all with patios and sofas, serving cocktails and gluttonous ice creams (as well as full-blown meals).Though you'll stumble across people in the nude on all stretches of the beach, only some of the bars welcome people carrying wallets and nothing else.

Transport from St-Tropez to the beaches is provided by a frequent **minibus** service from place des Lices to Salins and Pampelonne, or a bus from the *gare routière* to Tahiti, Pampelonne and L'Escalet. If you're driving, you'll be forced to pay high parking charges at all the beaches, or to leave your car or motorbike some distance from the sea and easy prey to thieves.

Eating and drinking

There are **restaurants** to cover every budget in St-Tropez, as well as plenty of snack bars and takeaway outfits, particularly on rue Georges-Clemenceau and place des Lices.

Bistrot des Lices, 3 place des Lices (☎04.94.97.29.00). *Fin-de-siècle* decor for traditional preening and excellent but expensive eats; midday menu 99F/€15.10, otherwise from 300F/€45.75. Closed Thurs Jan–March & mid-Oct to Dec.

Café des Arts, place des Lices (☎04.94.97.02.25). The number-one brasserie on the square. Old-timers still gather in the bar at the back. Menus from 220F/€33.55.

Café Sénéquier, on the port. The top quayside café; horribly expensive, but sells sensational nougat (also on sale from the shop at the back).

Ghandi, 3 quai de l'Epi (☎04.94.97.71.71). Curries and tandoori, with a good selection of fish and shellfish on the menu. Lunch menu from 95F/€14.49 and dinner from 150F/€22.88. Closed Wed in summer, otherwise Tues & Wed.

Glaces Alfred, rue Sibille. Ice creams made on the premises.

L'Île aux Nattes, 3 rue du Petit-St-Jean (☎04.94.97.44.01). Spicy creole cooking from the French Carribean. Only open for dinner, with great seafood menus from 185F/€28.21 and 200F/€30.50 à la carte. Closed Jan & mid-Nov to mid-Dec.

Joseph, 1 place de l'Hôtel de Ville (☎04.94.97.01.66) & 5 rue du Cépoun Sanmartin (☎04.94.97.03.90). Good *bouillabaisse* and *bourride*, and great desserts; 180F/€27.45 menu, à la carte 250F/€38.13 upwards.

La Patate, rue Clemenceau. Snack bar with omelettes, pasta, *pain beignets* and so forth.

Le Petit Charron, 6 rue des Charrons (☎04.94.97.73.78). Tiny terrace and dining room serving beautifully cooked Provençal specialities. Midday menu under 195F/€29.74, otherwise from 220F/€33.55. Closed Wed out of season.

Regis et Lolo, montée de la Citadelle (☎04.94.97.15.53). Small, friendly bistro, usually full of exuberant youth; around 150F/€22.88.

La Tarte Tropezienne, 1 rue G.-Clemenceau. Pâtisserie claiming to have invented this sponge and cream custard cake.

Nightlife

In season St-Tropez stays up late, as you'd expect. You can spend the evening trying on fancy clothes in the amazing array of couturier shops; the boules games on place des Lices continue till well after dusk; and the portside spectacle doesn't falter till the early hours. If you're mad enough to want to pay to see – and be seen with – the **nightlife** creatures of St-Tropez, clubs include *Les Caves du Roy*, in the flashy *Hôtel Byblos* on rue Paul-Signac (the most expensive and exclusive); *L'Esquinade*, on rue du Four, which has been going strong since Bardot was young; and the **gay** disco *Le Pigeonnier*, 13 rue de la Ponche. All are open every night in summer, and usually Saturday only in winter.

Gassin and Ramatuelle

Though the coast of the **St-Tropez peninsula** sprouts second residences like a cabbage patch gone to seed, the interior is almost uninhabited, thanks to government intervention, complex ownerships and the value of some local wines. The best view of this richly green and flowering countryside is from the hilltop village of Gassin, its lower neighbour Ramatuelle, or the tiny road between them, the dramatic route des Moulins de Paillas, where three ruined windmills could once catch every wind.

GASSIN is the shape and size of a small ship perched on a summit; once an eighth-century Muslim stronghold, it is now, of course, highly chic. It's an excellent place for a blowout dinner, sitting outside by the village wall with a spectacular panorama east over the peninsula. Of the handful of **restaurants**, *Bello Visto*, 9 place des Barrys (☎04.94.56.17.30, fax 04.94.43.45.36; closed Tues), has very acceptable Provençal specialities on a 120F/€18.30 menu, plus nine **rooms** at excellent prices for this brilliant setting (④).

RAMATUELLE is bigger than its neighbour, though just as old, and is surrounded by some of the best Côte de Provence vineyards. The twisting, arcaded streets are full of arts and crafts of dubious talent, but it's all very pleasant nonetheless. The most beautiful French actor ever to have appeared on screen, Gérard Philippe (1922–59), is buried in Ramatuelle's **cemetery**. His ivy-covered tomb, shaded by a rose bush, is set against the wall on the right as you look down. **Hotels** worth trying are *Le Saint-Gilles*, 31 rue Clemenceau (☎04.94.79.20.46; ②), and *Lou Castellas*, route des Moulins (☎ & fax 04.94.79.20.67; ③). For **food**, great pasta dishes are to be had at *au Fil à la Pâte*, 27 rue Victor-Léon (☎04.94.79.27.81; closed Wed), with good *plats du jour* at 85F/€12.96.

Port Grimaud

At the head of the Golfe de St-Tropez, just north of La Foux on the main coast road, the ultimate Côte d'Azur property development half stands and half floats. **PORT GRI-MAUD** was created in the 1960s as a private lagoon pleasure city, with waterways for roads and yachts parked at the bottom of every garden. All the houses are in exquisitely tasteful old Provençal style and their owners, Joan Collins for example, more than just a little well-heeled. In a way it's surprising that the whole enclave isn't wired off and patrolled by Alsatian dogs.

The main visitors' entrance is 800m up the well-signed road off the N98. You don't have to pay to get in, but you can't explore all the islands without hiring a boat or joining a crowded boat tour (around 18F/€2.75). Even access to the church tower for views is controlled by an automatic paying barrier (5F/€0.76). However, if you want to **eat and drink**, there are rows upon rows of brasseries, restaurants and cafés, clearly designed for the visiting public rather than the residents, and not particularly good value (though affordable enough).

Ste-Maxime and around

Facing St-Tropez across its gulf, **STE-MAXIME** is the perfect Côte stereotype: palmed corniche and enormous pleasure-boat harbour, beaches crowded with confident bronzed windsurfers and waterskiers, and an outnumbering of estate agents to any other businesses by something like ten to one. It sprawls a little too much – like many of its neighbours – but the magnetic appeal of the water's edge is hard to deny.

To enjoy the resort, however, requires money. If your budget denies you the pleasures of promenade cocktail sipping and seafood-platter picking (not to mention water-skiing, wet-biking and windsurfing), you might as well choose somewhere rather prettier to swim, lie on the beach and walk along the shore.

For the spenders, **Cherry Beach** (or its five neighbours on the east-facing plage de la Nartelle, 2km west from the centre towards Les Issambres), is the strip of sand to head for. As well as paying for shaded cushioned comfort, you can enter the water on a variety of different vehicles, eat grilled fish, have drinks brought to your mattress and listen to a piano player as dusk falls. A further 4km on, **plage des Eléphants** has much the same facilities but is slightly cheaper.

Ste-Maxime's *vieille ville* has several good **markets**: a covered flower and food market on rue Fernand-Bessy (winter Tues–Sun 6am–1pm & 4.30–8pm); a fish market every morning on quai des Plaisanciers; a Thursday morning food market on and around place du Marché; bric-a-brac every second and third Saturday of the month on place Jean-Mermoz; and arts and crafts in the pedestrian streets (summer daily 10am–11pm).

High up in the Massif des Maures on the road to Le Muy, some 10km north of Ste-Maxime, the marvellous **Musée du Phonographe et de la Musique Mécanique**, in the parc St-Donat (Easter to mid-Oct Wed–Sun 10am–noon & 3–6pm; 15F/€2.29), is the result of one amazing woman's forty-year obsession with collecting audio equipment. She has amassed a wide selection of automata, musical boxes and pianolas, as well as various outstanding pieces: one of Thomas Edison's "talking machines" of 1878, the first recording machines of the 1890s and an amplified lyre (1903). Almost half the exhibits still work. If you get a tour from Madame herself, you'll find it hard to resist her enthusiasm for the history of this branch of twentieth-century technology. You can get the Le Muy bus to here from Ste-Maxime's place J.-Mermoz.

Practicalities

Buses into town stop outside the **tourist office** on the promenade Simon-Lorière (June & Sept daily 9am–12.30pm & 2–7pm; July & Aug Mon–Sat 9am–8pm, Sun 10am–noon & 4–7pm; Oct–May Mon–Sat 9am–12.30pm & 2–6pm; ☎ & fax 04.94.55.75.55, *www.sainte-maxime.com*), which can give you all the relevant information on trips and pleasures and will advise on hotel vacancies – once again, rare in summer. If you're heading for St-Tropez from Ste-Maxime, an alternative to the bus, at not much greater cost, is to go by **boat**; the twenty-minute service from Ste-Maxime's *gare maritime* on the port runs daily from April to October, with more frequent crossings in July and August. **Bikes** can be rented at Holiday Bikes, 8 av St-Euxpéry (☎04.94.43.90.19, *www.holidaybikes.com*).

As you would expect in such a popular Riviera destination, finding accommodation in Ste-Maxime can be a nightmare in high season: if you are coming in July or August, call as far ahead as possible to make a reservation. The best of the cheaper **hotels** is the good-value and welcoming *Auberge Provençale*, 49 rue Aristide Briand (☎04.94.55.76.90, fax 04.94.55.76.91; ④), with its own restaurant; or there's the small *Castellamar*, 21 av G.-Pompidou (☎04.94.96.19.97; ③; closed Nov–March), on the west side of the river but still close to the centre and the sea. For more comfortable surroundings, try the central *Hôtel de la Poste*, 11 bd Frédéric-Mistral (☎04.94.96.18.33, fax 04.94.96.41.68; ⑤), an ugly modern construction but with very nice rooms; or the small and unobstrusive *Marie-Louise*, 2km west in the Hameau de Guerre-Vieille (☎04.94.96.06.05, fax 04.94.49.40.85; ⑤), tucked away in greenery but in sight of the sea. For **camping**, *Les Cigalons*, in quartier de la Nartelle, is the three-star seaside option (☎04.94.96.05.51; closed mid-Sept to May).

For non-beach **eating**, the *Hostellerie de la Belle Aurore*, 4 bd Jean-Moulin (☎04.94.96.02.45; closed Wed lunctime & Oct–March; weekday menu 180F/€27.45), offers gourmet food on a sea-view terrace; or, less expensively, there are good fish dishes at *Le Sarrazin*, 7 place Colbert (☎04.94.96.10.84; closed Tues out of season & Jan; menus from 110F/€16.78).

Fréjus and St-Raphaël

The major conurbation of **St-Raphaël** on the coast and **Fréjus**, 3km inland, has a history dating back to the Romans. Fréjus was established as a naval base under Julius Cæsar and Augustus, St-Raphaël as a resort for its veterans. The ancient port at Fréjus, or Forum Julii, had 2km of quays and was connected by a walled canal to the sea, which was considerably closer then. After the battle of Actium in 31 AD, the ships of Antony and Cleopatra's defeated fleet were brought here.

The area between Fréjus and the sea is now the suburb of **Fréjus-Plage** with a hideous 1980s development of a marina, **Port-Fréjus**. Both Fréjus and Fréjus-Plage merge with St-Raphaël, which in turn merges with **Boulouris** to the east.

Despite the obsession with facilities for the seaborne rich – there were already two pleasure ports at St-Raphaël before Port-Fréjus was built – this is no bad place for a stopover. There's a wide price range of hotels and restaurants in St-Raphaël, good transport links and some interesting sightseeing to be done in Fréjus.

Fréjus

The population of **FRÉJUS**, remarkably, was greater in the first century BC than it is today if you just count the residents of the town centre, which lies well within the

Roman perimeter. But very little remains of the original Roman walls that once circled the city; and the harbour that made Fréjus an important Mediterranean port silted up early on and was finally filled in after the Revolution. It is the **medieval centre**, much more than the classical remnants, that evokes a feel for this ancient town.

Arrival, information and accommodation

About four trains a day stop at Fréjus' **gare SNCF**, just three to four minutes away from St-Raphaël. Buses between the two towns are much more frequent and take ten minutes on the St-Raphaël–Draguignan route. The **gare routière** is on the east side of the town centre on place Paul-Vernet (☎04.94.53.78.46), opposite which is the **tourist office**, at 325 rue Jean-Jaurès (June–Sept Mon–Sat 9am–noon & 2–7pm, Sun 10am–noon & 3.30–6pm; rest of year Mon–Sat 9am–noon & 2–6pm, Sun 10am–noon & 3–5.30pm; ☎04.94.51.83.83, *www.ville-frejus.fr*). Holiday Bikes, 943 av de Provence (☎04.94.52.30.65, *www.holidaybikes.com*), has **bikes** for rent. To connect to the **Internet**, head for *Cyber Bureau* at 213 rue Waldeck Rousseau (Mon–Fri 8am–7pm, Sat 8am–4pm; *infos@bureausworks.com*).

If you're looking to stay the night in Fréjus, three central **hotels** worth trying are the plush *Aréna*, 139 rue de Général-de-Gaulle (☎04.94.17.09.40, fax 04.94.52.01.52; ⑦), with pretty, if rather small rooms and a pool; *La Bellevue*, place Paul-Vernet (☎04.94.17.25.05, fax 04.94.17.23.75; ③), in a convenient though not particularly quiet location; and *La Riviera*, 90 rue Grisolle (☎04.94.51.31.46, fax 04.94.17.18.34; ②), very small and not very modern, but clean and perfectly acceptable. There's an **HI hostel** 2km northeast from the centre of Fréjus at chemin du Counillier (☎04.94.53.18.75, fax 04.94.53.25.86); bus #7 leaves quai 7 of the St-Raphaël *gare routière* at 6pm, or take a regular bus #4, #8 or #9 from St-Raphaël or Fréjus, direction "L'Hôpital" to stop "Les Chênes" and walk up avenue du Gal-d'Armée Jean-Calies – the chemin du Counillier is the first left. There is also a large **campsite** in the grounds. An alternative campsite is *Les Acacias*, 370 rue Henri-Giraud (☎04.94.53.21.22), 2.5km from the centre and open all year.

The Roman town

A tour of the Roman remains will give you a good idea of the extent of Forum Julii, but they are scattered throughout and beyond the town centre and take a full day to get around. Turning right out of the *gare SNCF* and then right down boulevard Severin-Decuers brings you to the **Butte St-Antoine**, against whose east wall the waters of the port would have lapped, and which once was capped by a fort. It was one of the port's defences, and one of the ruined **towers** may have been a lighthouse. A path around the southern wall follows the quayside (odd stretches are visible) to the medieval **Lanterne d'Auguste**, built on the Roman foundations of a structure marking the entrance of the canal into the ancient harbour.

In the other direction from the station, past the Roman **Porte des Gaules** and along rue Henri-Vadon, you come to the **amphitheatre** (Jan–March Mon–Fri 10am–noon & 1.30–5.30pm, Sat 9.30am–12.30pm & 1.30–5.30pm, Sun daylight hours; April–Oct Mon–Sat 10am–1pm & 2.30–6.30pm, Sun daylight hours; free), smaller than those at Arles and Nîmes, but still able to seat around 10,000. Today it's used for bullfights and concerts. Its upper tiers have been reconstructed in the same greenish local stone used by the Romans, but the vaulted galleries on the ground floor are largely original. The Roman **theatre** (same hours as amphitheatre; free) is north of the town, along avenue du Théâtre-Romain, its original seats long gone, though again it is still used for shows in summer. Northeast of it, at the end of avenue du XVème-Corps-d'Armée, a few arches are visible of the forty-kilometre **aqueduct**, once as high as the ramparts. Closer to the centre, on rue des Moulins, are the arcades of the **Porte d'Orée**, positioned on the former harbour's edge alongside what was probably a **bath complex**.

The medieval town

The **Cité Episcopale**, or cathedral close, takes up two sides of **place Formigé**, the marketplace and heart of both contemporary and medieval Fréjus. It comprises the cathedral flanked by the fourteenth-century bishop's palace, now the Hôtel de Ville, the baptistry, chapterhouse, cloisters and archeological museum. Visits to the cloisters and baptistry are guided (April–Sept daily 9am–7pm; rest of year Tues–Sun 9am–noon & 2–5pm; 25F/€3.81 including entrance to museum); access to the main body of the cathedral is free (9am–noon & 4–6pm).

The oldest part of the complex is the **baptistry**, built in the fourth or fifth century and so contemporary with the decline of the city's Roman founders. Its two doorways are of different heights, signifying the enlarged spiritual stature of the baptized. Bits of the early Gothic **cathedral** may belong to a tenth-century church, but its best features, apart from the bright diamond-shaped tiles on the spire, are Renaissance: the choir stalls, a wooden crucifix on the left of the entrance and the intricately carved doors with scenes of a Saracen massacre, protected by a wooden cover and only opened for the guided tours. Far the most beautiful and engaging component of the whole ensemble, however, are the **cloisters**. In a small garden of scented bushes around a well, slender marble columns, carved in the twelfth century, support a fourteenth-century ceiling of wooden panels painted with apocalyptic creatures. Out of the original 1200 pictures, 400 remain, each about the size of this page. The subjects include multi-headed monsters, mermaids, satyrs and scenes of bacchanalian debauchery. The **Musée Archéologique** on the upper storey of the cloisters is an archeological museum, whose star pieces are a complete Roman mosaic of a leopard and a copy of a double-headed bust of Hermes.

Eating, drinking and entertainment

One of the best **restaurants** in the old town is the tiny *Les Potiers*, 135 rue des Potiers (☎04.94.51.33.74), with menus of fresh seasonal ingredients from 165F/€25.16. The similarly priced restaurant at *L'Aréna* hotel (see opposite) is excellent for fish and seafood (closed Sat & Mon lunch in season, plus Sun evening out of season). Cheaper eats can be found on place Agricola, place de la Liberté and the main shopping streets. *L'Arcosolium*, rue V.-Paulin, offers a vegetarian menu at 90F/€13.73, as well as *moules* and seafood. At Fréjus-Plage there's a string of eating houses to choose from, with more upmarket *plateau des fruits de mer* outlets at Port-Fréjus. The *Bar du Marché*, on the place de la Liberté, is a good establishment for a bit of café lounging. The main **market days** are Wednesday and Saturday, plus Monday in summer. If you happen to be in town on July 14 and 15, you can take in a Spanish-style **bullfight** during the town's frenetic and jovial *fêtes*.

Around Fréjus

Unlikely remnants of the more recent past come in the shape of a **Vietnamese pagoda** and an abandoned **mosque**, both built by French colonial troops. The pagoda (daily: May–Sept 9am–noon & 2–6pm; rest of year 9am–noon & 2–5pm), still maintained as a Buddhist temple, is on the crossroads of the RN7 to Cannes and the D100, about 2km out of Fréjus. The Mosquée Missiri de Djenné is on the left off the D4 to Bagnols, in the middle of an army camp 2km from the RN7 junction. A strange, guava-coloured, fort-like building, it is a replica of a Sudanese mosque in Mali, decorated inside with fading murals of desert journeys gracefully sketched in white on the dark-pink walls.

Fréjus has a **modern art gallery** (summer Tues–Sun 2–6/7pm; winter Tues–Sat 2–6/7pm; free), bizarrely located in the *Zone Industrielle du Capitou* just by exit 38 from the motorway; from place Paul-Vernet, take bus #2 to Z.I. Capitou. It has no permanent collection but some quite interesting temporary exhibitions.

For children, there's a **zoo** just across the motorway from Capitou (daily: May–Sept 9.30am–6pm; rest of year 10am–5pm; 62F/€9.46, children under ten 38F/€5.80; bus #2), and a **water amusement park**, Aquatica (daily: June & Sept 10am–6pm; July & Aug 10am–7pm; 125F/€19.06, children 100F/€15.25; bus #19 or #29), off the RN98 to St-Aygulf. Toboggans and pedal boats, chutes into an enchanted river, lakes, a huge swimming pool with artificial waves, a beach for the less energetic and a Black Hole are some of its main attractions. In the same entertainment zone there's a **funfair** and a **go-cart track**, Azur Karting (mid-June to mid-Sept daily 11am–midnight; rest of year daily except Tues 11am–9pm; 150F/€22.88 per hour).

St-Raphaël

A large resort and now one of the richest towns on the Côte, **ST-RAPHAËL** became fashionable at the turn of the twentieth century. Its seafront Belle Époque mansions and hotels, flattened by bombardments in World War II, have mostly been rebuilt, while the **old town** beyond place Carnot on the other side of the railway line has suffered years of neglect. On rue des Templiers a crumbling fortified Romanesque church, the **Église St-Pierre**, has fragments of the Roman aqueduct that brought water from Fréjus in its courtyard along with a local history and underwater archeology **museum** (daily: June–Sept 10am–noon & 3–6.30pm; rest of year 10am–noon & 2–5.30pm; 20.20F/€3.08 for church and museum).

The **beaches** stretch between the old port in the centre and the newer **Port Santa Lucia**, with opportunities for every kind of watersport. You can also take boat trips to St-Tropez, the Îles d'Hyères and the much closer *calanques* of the Esterel coast from the *gare maritime* on the south side of the Vieux Port. When you're tired of sea and sand you can lose whatever money you have left on slot machines or blackjack at the **Grand Casino** on Square de Gand overlooking the Vieux Port (daily 11am–4am), or there's **bowling** at the Bowling Raphaëlois on promenade René-Coty, and plenty of snooty discotheques.

Practicalities

St-Raphaël's **gare SNCF**, in the centre of town, is the main station for the Marseille–Ventigmilia line; the **gare routière** is on square du Dr Régis, across the rail line behind the *gare SNCF*. Information on the surrounding region is available from the **tourist office**, just to the left out of the *gare SNCF* on rue W.-Rousseau (daily: July & Aug 9am–8pm; rest of year 9am–12.30pm & 2–6.30pm; ☎04.94.19.52.52, *www.saint-raphael.com*). **Bikes** can be hired from Patrick Moto, 280 av Général-Leclerc (☎04.94.53.65.99).

Seafront **accommodation** in St-Raphaël is available on promenade René-Coty at the *Beau Séjour* (☎04.94.95.03.75, fax 04.94.83.89.99; ③; closed Nov–March), one of the cheaper hotels along here, with a pleasant terrace; or at the *Excelsior* (☎04.94.95.02.42, fax 04.94.95.33.82, *www.excelsior-hotel.com*; ⑧), whose rooms are luxurious and well equipped. *Bellevue*, 22 bd Félix-Martin (☎04.94.19.90.10, fax 04.94.19.90.11; ②), is good value for its central location; and *La Bonne Auberge*, 54 rue de la Garonne (☎04.94.95.69.72; ③; closed Dec–Feb), is a cheapie close to the old port. East of the centre, the *Hôtel du Soleil*, 47 bd du Domaine de Soleil, off boulevard Christian-Lafon (☎04.94.83.10.00, fax 04.94.83.84.70; ④; closed Oct–March), is a small, pretty villa with its own garden. There's **hostel** accommodation and double rooms in Boulouris, 5km east of St-Raphaël, at the *Centre International Le Manoir*, impasse Raoul Blanchard, chemin de l'Escale (☎04.94.95.20.58, fax 04.94.83.85.06). The *Centre* has friendly, helpful staff and is close to the beach right by the Boulouris *gare SNCF* (trains or buses every 30min from St-Raphaël). A four-star **campsite** close to the beach, *Le Val Fleury*, on the N98 in Boulouris (☎04.94.95.21.52, fax 04.94.19.09.47), is open all year.

Food markets are held every day on place Victor-Hugo and place de la République. You'll find reasonably priced cafés and brasseries around these, and plenty of pizzerias, crêperies and restaurants of varying quality around Port Santa Lucia and along the promenades. Of the more expensive establishments, two of the best are *Le Sirocco*, 35 quai Albert-1ᵉʳ (☎04.94.95.39.99), a smart restaurant specializing in fish, with menus around 90–200F/€13.73–30.50 plus a view of the sea; and *Pastorel*, 54 rue de la Liberté (☎04.94.95.02.36; closed Sun & Mon), with menus from around 160F/€24.40, which has decently priced Provençal wines, *aïoli* on Fridays and wonderful hors d'œuvres.

For **drinking**, try the selection of beers at the *Blue Bar* on boulevard de la Libération plage du Veillat (open till 4am in summer); for expensive cocktails with piano accompaniment, there's the *Madison Club* at the Casino (7pm–4am) or the *Coco-Club* at Port Santa Lucia (till dawn); or there are a series of beachfront discos open in the summer along the promenade to the west of town. If you're staying outside the centre though, note that late-night **taxis** are almost impossible to come by in this part of the world.

THE RIVIERA

The **Riviera**, the seventy-odd kilometres of coast between **Cannes** and **Menton** by the Italian border, was once an inhospitable shore with few natural harbours, its tiny local communities preferring to cluster round feudal castles high above the sea. It wasn't until the nineteenth century that the first foreign aristocrats began to choose to winter in the region's mild climate. But the real transformation came with the onslaught of 1950s mass tourism. Nowadays, it's an almost uninterrupted promenade, lined by palms and megabuck hotels, with speeding sports cars on the corniche roads and yachts like ocean liners moored at each resort.

Attractions, however, still remain, most notably in the legacies of the artists who stayed here: Picasso, Léger, Matisse, Renoir and Chagall. **Nice**, too, has real substance as a major city.

Cannes and around

The film industry and all other manner of business junketing represent **CANNES**'s main source of income in an ever-multiplying calendar of festivals, conferences, tournaments and trade shows. The spin-offs from servicing the day and night needs of the jetloads of agents, reps, dealers, buyers and celebrities are even more profitable than providing the strictly business facilities. Cannes may be more than its film festival, but it's still a grotesquely overhyped urban blight on this once exquisite coast – a contrast reinforced by the sublime **Îles de Lérins**, a short boat ride offshore and the best reason for coming here.

The old town, known as **Le Suquet** after the hill on which it stands, provides a great panorama of the twelve-kilometre beach, and has, on its summit, the remains of the fortified priory lived in by Cannes' eleventh-century monks and the beautiful twelfth-century chapelle Ste-Anne. These house the **Musée de la Castre** (daily except Tues: April–June 10am–noon & 2–6pm; July–Sept 10am–noon & 3–7pm; Oct–March 10am–noon & 2–5pm; 10F/€1.53), which has an extraordinary collection of musical instruments from all over the world, along with pictures and prints of old Cannes and an ethnology and archeology section.

You'll find non-paying **beaches** to the west of Le Suquet, along the plages du Midi and just east of the Palais des Festivals. But the sight to see is **La Croisette**, the long boulevard along the seafront, with its palace hotels on one side and private beaches on the other. It is possible to find your way down to the beach without paying, but not easy (you

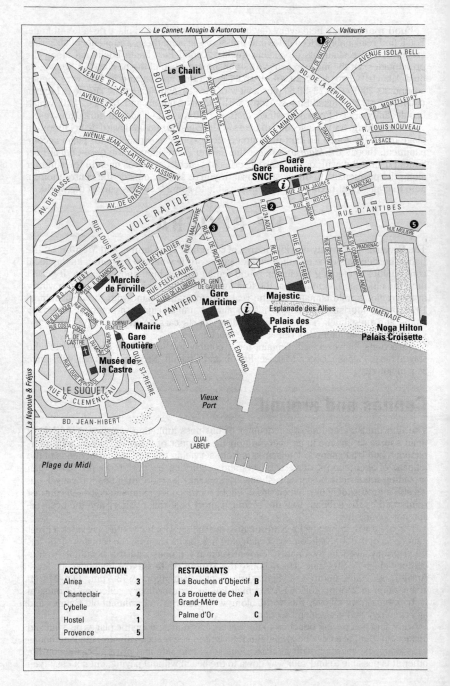

ACCOMMODATION	
Alnea	3
Chanteclair	4
Cybelle	2
Hostel	1
Provence	5

RESTAURANTS	
La Bouchon d'Objectif	B
La Brouette de Chez Grand-Mère	A
Palme d'Or	C

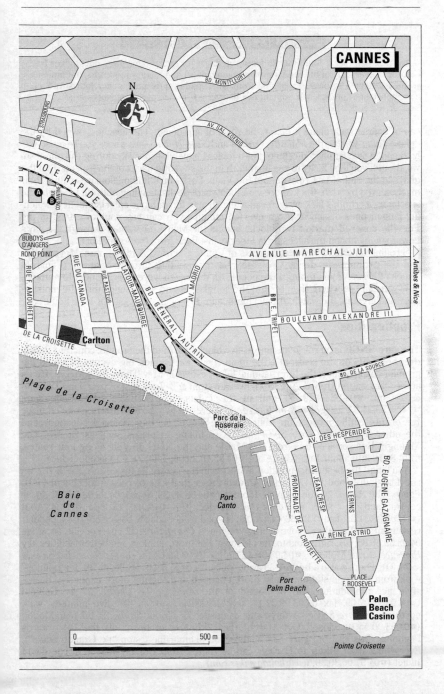

CANNES

N

BD. MONTFLEURY

AV. GAL KOENIG

VOIE RAPIDE

BD. C. STRASBOURG

RUE CONSTANTINE

A
B

DUBOYS
D'ANGERS
ROND POINT

AVENUE MARECHAL-JUIN

Antibes & Nice

RUE F. AMOURETTI

RUE DU CANADA

RUE PASTEUR

RUE DE LATOUR-MAUBOURGE

AV. MADRID

BD. GÉNÉRAL VAUTRIN

BD. E. TRIPET

BOULEVARD ALEXANDRE III

DE LA CROISETTE

Carlton

C

Plage de la Croisette

BD. DE LA SOURCE

Parc de la
Roseraie

AV. DES HESPERIDES

Baie
de
Cannes

Port
Canto

PROMENADE DE LA CROISETTE

AV. JEAN CRESP

AV. DE LERINS

BD. EUGENE GAZAGNAIRE

AV. REINE ASTRID

Port
Palm Beach

PLACE
F. ROOSEVELT

Palm
Beach
Casino

Pointe Croisette

0   500 m

MUSEUMS PASSPORT

An **Art'Pass** (price 140F/€21.35 for seven days; 70F/€10.68 for three days) gives free entry to over sixty of the region's most important art and history museums, monuments and gardens. The pass is available from participating museums, major tourist offices, branches of Thomas Cook exchange and several FNAC department stores.

can of course walk along it below the rows of sun beds). The beaches, owned by the deluxe *palais-hôtels* – the *Majestic, Carlton* and *Noga Hilton* – are where you're most likely to spot a face familiar in celluloid or a topless hopeful, especially during the film festival, though you'll be lucky to see further than the sweating backs of the paparazzi. At the quays at the end of La Croisette and the Vieux Port, you'll find millionaires eating their meals served by white-frocked crew on their yacht decks, feigning oblivion of landborne spectators a crumb's flick away. As an alternative to the dubious entertainment of watching langoustines disappear down overfed mouths, you can buy your own food in the **Forville covered market** two blocks behind the Mairie, or wander through the day's flower shipments on the allées de la Liberté, just back from the Vieux Port.

Strolling on and off the main streets of Cannes – **rue d'Antibes**, **rue Meynardier** and the **promenade de la Croisette** – is like wading through a hundred current issues of *Vogue*. If you thought the people on the beach were wearing next to nothing, now you can see where they bought the sunglasses and swimming suits, the moisturizers and creams, the watch, the perfume, and the collar and leash for little Fou-Fou.

Practicalities

The **gare SNCF** is on rue Jean-Jaurès, five blocks north of the orange, concrete **Palais des Festivals** on the seafront – the main venue for Cannes' big events, of which the premier celeb-puller is the International Film Festival in May. There are **tourist offices** at the train station (July & Aug Mon–Fri 9am–1pm & 3–7pm; rest of year 9am–12.30pm & 2–6pm; ☎04.93.99.19.77) and in the Palais des Festivals (daily 9am–8pm; ☎04.93.39.24.53, *www.cannes-on-line.com*). There are two **gare routières**: one on place B.-Cornut-Gentille between the Mairie and Le Suquet, serving coastal destinations; and the other next to the *gare SNCF* for buses inland to places such as Grasse. The Midnight Bus service runs from the Mairie and the Hôtel de Ville along four routes, from 8pm until about 1am (Bus Azur, ☎04.93.45.20.08; 7.50F/€1.14 single ticket).

You'll find the best concentration of **hotels** in the centre, between the *gare SNCF* on rue Jean-Jaurès and La Croisette, around the central axis of rues Antibes and Félix-Faure. The *Alnea*, 20 rue Jean de Riouffe (☎04.93.39.39.90, fax 04.92.98.07.05; ④), is central and has high standards of service; the *Cybelle*, 14 rue du 24 Août (☎04.93.38.31.33, fax 04.93.38.43.47; ③), is good value, if fairly basic, and has a popular restaurant; and another above-average option is *Chanteclair*, 12 rue Forville (☎ & fax 04.93.39.68.88; ③), right next to the old town. For more comfort and better facilities, try *Provence*, 9 rue Molière (☎04.93.38.44.35, fax 04.93.38.63.14, *contac@hotel-de-provence .com*; ⑥). There's also a **hostel**, 35 av de Vallauris (☎ & fax 04.93.99.26.79), ten minutes' walk from the train station; whilst more cramped and slightly more expensive hostel-style accommodation can be found at the *Auberge Le Chalit*, 27 av Galliéni (☎04.93.99.07.09, fax 04.93.99.22.11, *le_chalit@libertysurf.fr*; ①), five minutes' walk north of the *gare SNCF*. A three-star campsite, *Le Grand Saule*, 24 bd Jean-Moulin (☎04.93.90.55.10; closed Oct–March), lies 2km out of town, off the D9 towards Pégomas (bus #9 from *gare SNCF*, direction "Lamartine", stop "Le Grande Saule"). Everything from **bikes** to Harleys can be rented from Holiday Bikes, 16 rue du 14 Juillet (☎04.97.06.30.30, *www.holidaybikes.com*).

Cannes has hundreds of **eateries** catering for every budget. Rue Meynadier, Le Suquet and quai St-Pierre are good places to look. For menus under 100F/€15.25, try *au Bec Fin*, in the *Hôtel Cybele*, 12 rue du 24-Août (☎04.93.38.35.86; closed Sat evening & Sun), or *Le Bouchon d'Objectif*, 10 rue de Constantine (☎04.93.99.21.76; closed Sun evening & Mon). *La Brouette de Chez Grand-Mère*, 9 rue d'Oran (☎04.93.39.12.10; closed Sun) has a single very filling 195F/€29.74 menu including wine. If you'd just won a film festival prize the place to celebrate would be *La Palme d'Or* in the Hôtel Martinez, 73 La Croisette (☎04.92.98.74.14; closed Mon & Tues; 295F/€44.99 lunch menu except Sun; à la carte from 600F/€91.50).

Cannes has one of the oldest **gay** bars in France, *Le Zanzibar*, 85 rue Félix-Faure (6.30pm–5am), and a lesbian bar, *Exterieur Nuit*, 16 rue du Duquet (4pm–2am). A lively Gay Pride march is held annually on June 30,

Îles de Lérins

The **Îles de Lérins** would be lovely anywhere, but at fifteen minutes' ferry ride from Cannes, they're not far short of paradise facing purgatory. Planaria (*www.abbayedelerins.com*) runs the **boat service** to St-Honorat with departures from the old port (hourly: May–Sept 8am–5.30pm, last return 6pm; rest of year 8am–4.30pm, last return 5pm; 45F/€6.86). The Ste-Marguerite route, which also leaves from the old port, is operated by S.A.R.L. (hourly: May–Sept 9am–6.15pm, last return 7pm; rest of year 9am–4.15pm, last return 5pm; ☎04.92.98.71.36; 55F/€8.39), which also offers an hour-long circuit of the two islands with no stops (80F/€12.20). Taking a picnic is a good idea, as the handful of restaurants on the islands is overpriced.

Ste-Marguerite is far more commercial and touristy than its peaceful neighbour, St-Honorat. It is still beautiful, though, and large enough for visitors to find seclusion by following the trails that lead away from the congested port, through the Aleppo pines and woods of evergreen oak that are so thick they cast a sepulchral gloom. The western end is the most accessible, but the lagoon here is brackish, so the best points to swim are the rocky inlets across the island from the port.

The dominating structure of the island is the **Fort Ste-Marguerite** (daily except Tues 10.30am–noon & 2–4.30/6.30pm; 10F/€1.53), a Richelieu commission that failed to prevent the Spanish occupying both of the Lérin islands between 1635 and 1637. Later, Vauban rounded it off, presumably for Louis XIV's *gloire* – since the strategic value of greatly enlarging a fort facing your own mainland without upgrading the one facing the sea is pretty minimal. There are cells to see, including the one in which Dumas' *Man in the Iron Mask* is supposed to have been held, a small aquarium hosting specimens of local marine life and a **Musée de la Mer** (daily except Tues: April–June 10.30am–12.15pm & 2.15–5.30pm; July–Sept 10.30am–12.15pm & 2.15–6.30pm; Oct–March 10.30am–12.15pm & 2.15–4.30pm; 10F/€1.53), containing mostly Roman local finds but also remnants of a tenth-century Arab ship. Access is free to the grassy ramparts of this vast construction.

Owned by monks almost continuously since its namesake and patron founded a monastery here in 410 AD, **St-Honorat**, the smaller southern island, was home to a famous bishops' seminary, where St Patrick trained before setting out for Ireland. The present **abbey** buildings (daily: July to mid-Sept 10am–12.30pm & 2.30–5pm; rest of year 9.30am–4.30pm; free) date mostly from the nineteenth century, though some vestiges of the medieval and earlier constructions remain in the austere church (free to visit) and the cloisters. A shop sells the benevolent white wine, spirits and honey produced by the 28 Cistercian brothers of the monastic community. Behind the cloisters on the sea's edge stands an eleventh-century **fortress**, used by the monks in times of danger. Of all the protective forts against invaders built along this coast, this is the only one that looks as if it still might serve its original function. At the same time it shows its age without heavy-handed cosmetic reconstruction or being a picture-postcard ruin (daily: July & Aug 10.15am–noon & 2–5.30pm; rest of year 9.30am–5.30pm; 15F/€2.29 entrance June–Sept).

These days, the forces of this island are peace and silence, with pine leaves gently stirring and the sea mapping out its minuscule tide. Apart from one small restaurant near the landing stage, there are no bars, hotels or cars: just vines, lavender, herbs and olive trees mingled with wild poppies and daisies, and pine and eucalyptus trees shading the paths beside the white rock shore mixing with the scents of rosemary, thyme and wild honeysuckle.

Vallauris

Picasso spent ten years just northeast of Cannes in **VALLAURIS**, set in the hills above the Golfe Juan. It was here that he first began to use clay, thereby reviving one of the traditional crafts of this little town. Today the main street, **avenue Georges-Clemenceau**, sells nothing but pottery, much of it the garishly glazed bowls and figurines that could feature in souvenir shops anywhere. Picasso used to work in the **Madoura workshop**, on avenue des Ancien-Combattants-d'AFN, to the right as you come down avenue Georges-Clemenceau; it still has sole rights on reproducing Picasso's designs, which it sells, at a price, in the shop (Mon–Fri only).

The bronze statue of **Man with a Sheep**, Picasso's gift to the town, stands in the main square and marketplace, place de la Libération, beside the church and castle. The local authorities also suggested he should decorate the early medieval deconsecrated **chapel** in the castle courtyard (daily except Tues: June–Sept 10am–6.30pm; rest of year 10am–noon & 2–5pm; 17F/€2.59), which he finally did in 1952: his subject was war and peace. The space is tiny and has the architectural simplicity of an air-raid shelter, and at first glance it's easy to be unimpressed by the painted panels covering the vault – as many critics still are – since the work looks mucky and slapdash, with paint-runs on the plywood panel surface. But stay a while and the passion of this violently drawn pacifism slowly emerges. On the "War" panel, a music score is trampled by hooves and about to be engulfed in flames; a fighter's lance tenuously holds the scales of justice and a shield that bears the outline of a dove. "Peace" is represented by Pegasus, the winged horse of Greek myth; people dancing and suckling babies; trees bearing fruit; owls; books; and the freedom of the spirit to mix up images and concepts with well-intentioned mischief. The ticket for the chapel also gives admission to the **Musée de Céramique** in the castle (same hours; 17F/€2.59), which exhibits Picasso's and other ceramics.

There are regular buses from Cannes and from Golfe-Juan SNCF to place de la Libération. The **tourist office** is at the bottom of avenue Georges-Clemenceau on square du 8-Mai-1945 (July & Aug daily 7am–7pm; rest of year Mon–Sat 9am–noon & 2–6pm; ☎04.93.63.82.58, *www.crt-riviera.fr*).

Grasse

GRASSE, 16km inland from Cannes and with some stunning views over the Côte, is the world capital of *parfumiers* and has been for almost 300 years. These days it likes to flaunt itself, promoting its perfumed image as a chic eighteenth-century village with a medieval heart surrounded by hectares of scented flowers. Making perfumes is presented as a mysterious process, an alchemy, turning the soul of the flower into a liquid of luxury and desire, and the industry is at pains to keep quiet about modern innovations and techniques.

Grasse is the official starting point of the Route Napoléon (see p.958) but is equally easy to visit as a day-trip from the coast.

The Town

Vieux Grasse, despite its touristy shops and full range of restaurants, is surprisingly humble, a working-class enclave where lines of washing festoon the high, narrow streets – rates of pay for the pickers of raw ingredients for perfume essences are notoriously low. Inhabitants say it's like a village where everyone knows each other, and out of season that's certainly the atmosphere that prevails.

Place aux Aires, at the top of the old town, is the main meeting point for all and sundry and the venue for the daily flower and vegetable **market**. It is ringed by arcades of different heights and the elegant wrought-iron balcony of the *Hôtel Isnard* at no. 33, and at one time was the exclusive preserve of the tanning industry. At the opposite end of Vieux Grasse lie the **cathedral** – containing various paintings, including three by Rubens and a wondrous triptych by the sixteenth-century Niçois painter Louis Bréa – and the **bishop's palace**, now the Hôtel de Ville, both built in the twelfth century.

A museum you might like to take a quick flit through is the **Musée d'Art et d'Histoire de Provence**, 2 rue Mirabeau (Jan–Oct & Dec daily except Tues 10am–12.30pm & 2–5.30pm; 20F/€3.05), housed in a luxurious town house commissioned by Mirabeau's sister for her social entertainment duties. As well as all the gorgeous fittings and the original eighteenth-century kitchen, the historical collection adds a nice eclectic touch. It includes wonderful eighteenth- to nineteenth-century faïence from Apt and Le Castellet, Mirabeau's death mask, a tin bidet and six prehistoric bronze leg bracelets. The fascinating **Musée International de la Parfumerie**, 8 place du Cours (Jan–Oct & Dec daily except Tues 10am–12.30pm & 2–5.30pm; 20F/€3.05), displays perfume bottles from the ancient Greeks to the present via Marie-Antoinette and has a reconstruction of a perfume factory with a little test you can do on identifying fragrances. The guided tours are highly recommended.

The perfume factories

There are thirty major **parfumeries** in and around Grasse, most of them making not perfume but essences-plus-formulas which are then sold to Dior, Lancôme, Estée Lauder and the like, who make up their own brand-name perfumes. One litre of pure rose essence can cost as much as 125,000F/€19,000; perfume contains twenty percent essence (eau de toilette and eau de Cologne considerably less). The major cost in this multi-billion-dollar business is marketing. The grand Parisian couturiers, whose clothes, on strictly cost-accounting grounds, serve simply to promote the perfume, go to inordinate lengths to sell their latest fragrance, spending hundreds of millions of francs a year on advertising alone.

The ingredients that the "nose" – as the creator of the perfume's formula is known – has to play with include resins, roots, moss, beans, bark, civet (extract of cat genitals), ambergris (intestinal goo from whales), bits of beaver and musk from Tibetan goats. If that hasn't put you off, you can visit the various **showrooms**, with overpoweringly fragrant shops and free guided tours, in English, of the traditional perfume factory set-up (the actual working industrial complexes are strictly out of bounds). These visits are free and usually open daily without interruption in summer; a few to choose from are **Fragonard**, 20 bd Fragonard; **Galimard**, 73 rte de Cannes; and **Molinard** at 60 bd Victor-Hugo (*www.molinard-parfums.com*).

Practicalities

Grasse's **gare routière** is to the north of the old town at the Parking Notre-Dame-des-Fleurs. Head downhill on avenue Thiers becoming boulevard du Jeu de Ballon (where there's an annexe of the tourist office) and you'll find the museums and the main **tourist office** on cours Honoré-Cresp (July & Aug Mon–Sat 9am–7pm, Sun

9am–12.30pm & 1.30–6.30pm; rest of year Mon–Sat 9am–12.30pm & 1.30–6.30pm; ☎04.93.36.66.66, *Tourisme.Grasse@wanadoo.fr*).

Two possible **hotels** at the cheaper end of the market are: *Napoléon*, 6 av Thiers (☎04.93.36.05.87, fax 04.93.36.41.09; ②), right next to the *gare routière*, and *Les Palmiers*, 17 av Y.-Baudoin (☎ & fax 04.93.36.07.24; ②), with a pleasant garden and good views, if not particularly friendly. More expensively, the *Panorama*, on place du Cours (☎04.93.36.80.80, fax 04.93.36.92.04, *hotelpanorama@wanadoo.fr*; ⑤), offers rooms with views and all mod cons. There is also dorm accommodation available at *Altitude 500*, in the Centre Culturel G. Gibelin (☎04.93.36.35.64, fax 04.93.40.09.23).

Restaurants in the old town are good value, with several menus to choose from on rue de la Fontette. The best place in town, however, is *La Bastide de Saint Antoine*, 48 rue Henri Dunant (☎04.93.70.94.94), which serves regional dishes (menus from 260F/€39.65 and up) in a bright sophisticated decor. For tasty pizzas and *socca* (chick-pea pancakes) at reasonable prices, head for the relaxed *La Socca*, 17 rue Paul-Goby. For **drinks**, the bars on place aux Aires are friendly. At Maison Venturini, 1 rue Marcel Journet (closed Sun & Mon), you can buy fabulous sweet *fougassettes*, flavoured with the Grasse speciality of orange blossom, to take away.

Antibes and around

ANTIBES, or rather its promontory the **Cap d'Antibes**, is one of the select places on the Côte d'Azur where the *really* rich and the very, *very* successful still live, or at least have residences. Yet it's not immediately obvious why this area should be so desirable: it's just as built-up as the rest of the Riviera, with no open countryside separating Golfe Juan, **Juan-les-Pins** and Antibes. Long-time resident Graham Greene said it was the only town on the Côte that hadn't lost its soul; perhaps he was right, though he also gave his reason for living there as simply to be with the woman he loved. Be that as it may, Antibes is extremely animated, has one of the finest **markets** on the coast and the best **Picasso collection** in its ancient seafront castle; and the southern end of the Cap still has its woods of pine, in which the most exclusive mansions hide.

The sixteenth-century **Château Grimaldi** is a beautifully cool, light space, with hexagonal terracotta floor tiles, windows over the sea and a terrace garden with sculptures by Germaine Richier, Miró, César and others. In 1946, Picasso was offered the dusty building – by then already a museum – as a studio. Several extremely prolific months followed before he moved to Vallauris, leaving all his Antibes output to what is now the **Musée Picasso** (Tues–Sun: June–Sept 10am–6pm; rest of year 10am–noon & 2–6pm; 30F/€4.58). Although Picasso donated other works later on, the bulk of the collection belongs to this one period. There's an uncomplicated exuberance in the numerous still lifes of sea urchins, the goats and fauns in Cubist non-disguise and the wonderful *Ulysses and his Sirens* – a great round head against a mast around which the ship, sea and sirens swirl. Picasso himself is the subject of works here by other painters and photographers, including Man Ray and Bill Brandt; there are several anguished canvases by Nicholas de Staël, who stayed in Antibes for a few months from 1954 to 1955; and works by other contemporaries and more recent artists. Alongside the castle is the **cathedral**, built on the site of an ancient temple. The choir and apse survive from the Romanesque building that served the city in the Middle Ages while the nave and stunning ochre facade are Baroque. Inside, in the south transept, is a sumptuous medieval altarpiece surrounded by immaculate panels of tiny detailed scenes.

One block inland, the morning **covered market** on cours Masséna overflows with Provençal goodies and a profusion of cut **flowers**, the traditional and still-flourishing Antibes business (June–Aug daily; rest of year closed Mon). On Friday and Sunday (plus Easter–Sept Tues & Thurs) a craft market takes over in the afternoon. When the stalls are all packed up, café tables take their place.

Cap d'Antibes

Plage de la Salis, the longest Antibes beach, runs along the eastern neck of Cap d'Antibes, with no big hotels owning mattress exploitation rights – an amazing rarity on the Riviera. To the south, at the top of chemin du Calvaire, you can get superb views from the **Église de la Garoupe** (July & Aug 10am–noon & 2.30–6pm; rest of year 9.30am–noon & 2.30–5pm), which contains Russian spoils from the Crimean War and hundreds of *ex votos*. To the west, on boulevard du Cap between chemins du Tamisier and G.-Raymond, you can wander around the **Jardin Thuret** (Mon–Fri 8.30am–noon & 2.30–5.30pm; free), botanical gardens belonging to a national research institute. Back on the east shore, further south, a second beach, **plage de la Garoupe**, now heavily colonized by sun beds, is linked by a **footpath** to the peninsula's southern tip. There are more sandy coves and little harbours along the western shore, where you'll also find the **Musée Naval et Napoléonien** (Mon–Fri 9.30am–noon & 2.15–6pm, Sat 9.30am–noon; closed Oct; 30F/€4.58), at the end of avenue J.-F.-Kennedy. This documents the great return from Elba along with the usual Bonaparte paraphernalia of hats, cockades and signed commands.

Juan-les-Pins

JUAN-LES-PINS, less than 2km from the centre of Antibes, is another of those overloaded Côte d'Azur names: the summer St-Moritz, the night-time playground for the extravagantly outfitted front-page myths who retreat at dawn, like supernatural creatures, to their well-screened cages on Cap d'Antibes. Until this century it was nothing more than a pine grove on the western neck of Cap d'Antibes. A casino was built in 1908 and by the late 1920s Juan-les-Pins had taken off as the original summer resort of the Côte d'Azur. Revealing swimsuits, as opposed to swimming "dresses", were reputedly first worn here in the 1930s. Now, like so much of the Côte, it's so overcrowded and overbuilt that it's impossible to see what all the fuss is about – or to imagine it as a pine forest.

But its **international jazz festival** in the last two weeks of July is the best in the region and takes place in what's left of the pine forest, the **Jardin de La Pinède** (known simply as La Pinède), and **Square Gould** above the beach by the casino. This urban park and the 2km of sheltered sand beach are all that Juan-les-Pins has to offer for free, apart from the dizzying array of architectural styles along its streets.

Practicalities

Antibes's **gare SNCF** lies to the north of the old town at the top of avenue Robert-Soleau. Turn right out of the station and three minutes' walk along avenue R.-Soleau will bring you to place de Gaulle. The **tourist office** is on this square, at no. 11 (July & Aug daily 9am–7pm; rest of year Mon–Fri 9am–12.30pm & 2–6.30pm, Sat 9am–noon & 2–6pm; ☎04.92.90.53.00, *www.antibes-juanlespins.com*). The **gare routière** is off the adjoining place Guynemer (☎04.93.34.37.60), with frequent buses to and from the *gare SNCF* (Mon–Sat); otherwise it's a five-minute walk from the train station. Bus #2A goes to Cap d'Antibes; bus #1A and #3A to Juan-les-Pins, #10A to Biot. **Bikes** can be rented from three outlets on boulevard Wilson, at nos. 43, 93 and 122. Rue de la République leads into the heart of Vieux Antibes around place Nationale, from where rue Sade leads to cours Masséna, beyond which lie the cathedral, the castle and the sea. For **Internet** access, head to *Xtreme Café*, 6 rue Aubernon (Tues–Sat 3–11pm, Sun 10am–9pm),

The most economical **hotels** are both close to the *gare routière*: the *Hôtel de la Gare*, 6 rue du Printemps (☎04.93.61.29.96, fax 04.93.61.27.88; ②), and *Le Nouvel Hôtel*, 1 av du 24-Août (☎04.93.34.44.07, fax 04.93.34.44.08; ③). For greater comfort, try the *Mas Djoliba*, 29 av de Provence (☎04.93.34.02.48, fax 04.93.34.05.81, *info@hotel-pcastel -djoliba.com*; ⑥), between the old town and the beach, or *Le Ponteil*, 11 impasse Jean-Mensier (☎04.93.34.67.92. fax 04.93.34.49.47; ⑤), in a quiet location at the end of a cul-de-sac close to the sea.

There's a **hostel** on Cap d'Antibes, the *Relais International de la Jeunesse* on boule-vard de la Garoupe (☎04.93.61.34.40, fax 04.93.42.72.57; closed Oct–May; buses #1 & 2 stop right outside), which needs booking well in advance. All of Antibes' **campsites** are 3–5km north of the city in the *quartier* of La Brague (bus #10A or one train stop to Gare de Biot). The three-star *Logis de La Brague* (☎04.93.33.54.72; closed Oct–April) is clos-est to the station, while the two-star *Idéal-Camping* (☎04.93.74.27.07; closed Nov–Feb) is south of the station; both are on the route de Nice and close to the sea.

Place Nationale and cours Masséna are lined with **cafés**; rue James Close is nothing but **restaurants** and rue Thuret and its side streets also offer numerous menus to browse through. For pizzas, there's *Il Giardino*, 21 rue Thuret, though you may have a long wait to be served, and *La Famiglia*, a cheap family-run outfit at 34 av Thiers (closed Wed). *Le Romantic*, 5 rue Rostan (☎04.93.34.59.39; closed Wed lunch & Tues), lives up to its name and offers lunch menus from 95F/€14.49, although in the evening the *terroir*-dominated *carte* will bring the bill above 200F/€30.50. Another romantic option is *Le Relais du Postillon*, 8 rue Championnet (☎04.93.34.20.77; closed Sun evening & Mon lunch; menus from 155F/€23.64), which serves Provençal cuisine in a cosily restored eighteenth-century coachhouse. For something really special, *Les Vieux Murs*, near the castle on avenue Amiral-de-Grasse (☎04.93.34.06.73), does a superb meal for 220F/€33.55.

Juan-les-Pins has one of the **star restaurants** of the Côte, *La Terrasse*, on avenue Gallice (☎04.93.61.20.37; closed Mon–Wed; lunch menu 285F/€43.46, otherwise 450F/€68.63 minimum), with original 1930s decor, exquisite fish and seafood dishes and mouth-melting desserts. At the other end of the scale you can get brasserie food, crêpes, pizzas and similar snacks from **street stalls** till the early hours, and many shops and bars also keep going in summer till 3am or 4am. Juan-les-Pins is also one of the liveliest places along the coast for nightlife, with a whole host of **nightclubs** and bars for you to spend any dollars that are surplus to your budget. Entrance is typically 100F/€15.25 with a "complimentary" drink. You might like to try *Le Village/Voom Voom* at 1 bd de la Pinède, which attracts a young crowd and goes on till dawn; or *Le Pam-Pam*, 137 bd Président Wilson, with frequent live Brazilian bands.

Finally, if you've run out of reading material, Heidi's English Bookshop at 24 rue Aubernon in Antibes (daily 10am–7pm) is the cheapest English **bookshop** on the coast.

Biot

Frequent buses connect Antibes with the village of **BIOT**, 8km to the north, where Fernand Léger lived for a few years at the end of his life. A stunning collection of his intensely life-affirming works, created between 1905 and 1955, can be seen at the **Musée Fernand Léger**, built especially to display them (daily except Tues: July–Sept 10am–12.30pm & 2–6pm; rest of year 10am–12.30pm & 2–5.30pm; 30F/€4.58, 20F/€3.05 on Sun). The museum is just southeast of the village on the chemin du Val de Pome, stop "Fernand Léger" on the Antibes bus, or a thirty-minute walk from Biot's *gare SNCF*.

Few artists have had such consistency and power in their use of space and colour and the ability to change the relations between objects or figures without ever descending to surrealism. Léger's art has the capacity to inflict instant pleasure – the pattern of the shapes and the colours, particularly in his ceramic works – or harsh horror as in the charcoal black to brown on off-white paper in *Stalingrad*. It's interesting to compare his life and work with Picasso, fellow pioneer of Cubism and long-time comrade in the Communist Party. While Léger's commitment to collective working-class life never wavered, Picasso only nodded at it when he needed it. Picasso wanted to embrace the whole world and be embraced in return. He chose a complex, dominating, sometimes perverted persona in which to do it, while Léger stuck within the reality of himself and the world, an outlook captured by Alexander Calder's wire sculpture portrait of Léger in the museum. He was vocal on the politics of culture, arguing for museums to be open after working hours; for public spaces to be adorned with art; and for making all the arts more accessible to ordinary people.

The village of Biot is extremely beautiful and oozes with art in every form – architectural, sculpted, ceramic, jewelled, painted and culinary. The **tourist office**, on place de la Chapelle, at the far end of the main street, rue St-Sébastien (July & Aug Mon–Fri 10am–7pm, Sat & Sun 2.30–7pm; rest of year Mon–Fri 9am–noon & 2–6pm, Sat & Sun 2–6pm; ☎04.93.65.78.00, *www.biot-coteazur.com*), can provide copious lists of art galleries and glassworks (the traditional industry that brought Léger here, and which produces the famous hand-blown **bubble glass**). If you book well in advance you could **stay** at the very reasonable *Hôtel des Arcades*, 16 place des Arcades (☎04.93.65.01.04, fax 04.93.65.01.05; ④), full of old-fashioned charm and with huge rooms in the medieval centre of the village. Its **café-restaurant**, which also doubles as an art gallery, serves delicious traditional Provençal food (closed Sun evening & Mon; 170F/€25.93 menu).

Above the Baie des Anges

Between Antibes and Nice, the **Baie des Anges** laps at twentieth-century resorts with two fine examples of concrete corpulence: the giant petrified sails with viciously pointed corners of the Villeneuve-Loubet-Plage marina, and an apartment complex, 1km long and sixteen storeys high, barricading the stony beach.

The old towns and softer visual stimulation lie inland. **Cagnes** is another artists' town – associated in particular with Renoir – as is **St-Paul-de-Vence**, which houses the wonderful modern art collection of the Fondation Maeght. **Vence** has a small chapel decorated by Matisse, and is a relaxing place to stay, if quiet in the evenings.

Cagnes

CAGNES is made up of a nondescript coastal district known as Cros-de-Cagnes, Haut-de-Cagnes, the original medieval village overlooking the town from the northwest heights, and Cagnes-sur-Mer, the town centre situated inland between the two.

At the top of place de Gaulle, the main square in **Cagnes-sur-Mer**, avenue Auguste-Renoir runs right and crosses the road to La Gaude. A short way further on, chemin des Collettes leads off to the left up to **Les Collettes**, the house that Renoir had built in 1908 and where he spent the last twelve years of his life (bus #4 from square Bourdet, or stop "Béat-Les Collettes" on the Antibes or Nice bus). It's now a memorial **museum** (daily except Tues: Jan–June, Sept, Oct & Dec 10am–noon & 2–5pm; July & Aug 10am–noon & 2–6pm; 20F/€3.05; free entry to garden), and you're free to wander around the house and through the olive and rare orange groves that surround it. One of the two studios in the house – north-facing to catch the late afternoon light – is arranged as if Renoir had just popped out. Albert André's painting, *A Renoir Painting*, shows the ageing artist hunched over his canvas; plus there's a bust of him by Aristide Maillol, and a crayon sketch by Richard Guido. Bonnard and Dufy were also visitors to

Les Collettes; Dufy's *Hommage à Renoir*, transposing a detail of *Moulin de la Galette*, hangs here. Renoir's own work is represented by several sculptures, including *La Maternité* and a medallion of his son Coco, some beautiful, tiny watercolours in the studio and ten paintings from his Cagnes period.

Haut-de-Cagnes is a favourite haunt of successes in the contemporary art world, as well as those of decades past, and it lives up to everything dreamed of in a Riviera *village perché*. The ancient village backs up to a crenellated feudal **château** (Jan–June, Sept, Oct & Dec Tues–Sun 9am–noon & 2–5pm; July & Aug Tues–Sun 10am–noon & 2–6pm; 20F/€3.05; bus #9 from square Bourdet to "Le Château" or, by foot, the steep ascent along rue Général-Bérenger and montée de la Bourgade), with a stunning Renaissance interior, housing museums of local history, fishing and olive cultivation. In addition, if you're here between the end of November and January, you can see the entries from forty-odd countries for Haut-de-Cagnes' big event of the year, the **Festival International de la Peinture** (when the château is open daily).

Practicalities

The **gare SNCF** Cagnes-sur-Mer (one stop from the *gare SNCF* Cros-de-Cagnes) is southwest of the centre alongside the *autoroute*; turn right on the northern side of the *autoroute* along avenue de la Gare to head into town. If you want to rent a **bike**, take the second right, rue Pasqualini, where you'll find Cycles Marcel at no. 5 (☎04.93.20.64.07). The sixth turning on your right, rue des Palmiers, leads to the **tourist office** at 6 bd Maréchal-Juin (July & Aug Mon–Sat 9am–1pm & 3–7.30pm, Sun 9am–1pm & 3–7pm; rest of year Mon–Fri 8.30am–12.15pm & 2–6pm, Sat 8.30am–12.45pm & 2–5.30pm; ☎04.93.20.61.64, *www.cagnes.com*). Bus #2 runs from the *gare SNCF* to the **gare routière** on square Bourdet.

Budget **hotels** include *La Corrida*, 110 av de Nice (☎04.93.14.92.30; ②), and *Le Saratoga*, 111 av de Nice (☎04.93.31.05.70; ②), both on the busy N7, both in Cros-de-Cagnes (bus #2 from square Bourdet or Cagnes-sur-Mer *gare SNCF*). *Beaurivage*, also in Cros at 39 bd de la Plage (☎04.93.20.16.09, fax ☎04.93.22.98.20, *beaurivage@wanadoo.fr*; ④), has very pleasant rooms with views of the sea. If you're feeling extremely flush, you could try *Le Cagnard*, rue Pontis-Long (☎04.93.20.73.21, fax 04.93.22.06.39, *www.le-cagnard.com*; ⑨; closed Nov–Easter; menus from 310F/€47.30), a top-notch hotel with a restaurant in the ancient guard room of the château. **Campsites** are not marvellous, though there are plenty of them. The four-star *Panoramer*, chemin des Gros-Buaux (☎04.93.31.16.15; closed Nov–March), about 1km northeast of Cagnes-sur-Mer, is the closest, though not the cheapest.

The best places to **eat** are in Haut-de-Cagnes, and for café lounging, place du Château or place Grimaldi, to either side of the castle, are the obvious spots. The *Restaurant des Peintres*, 71 montée de la Bourgade (☎04.93.20.83.08; closed Sun evening & Mon), serves light Provençal delicacies and has menus from 148F/€22.57. *Le Clap*, despite the unfortunate name, at 4 rue Hippolyte-Guis, off montée de la Bourgade (☎04.92.02.06.28), has reasonable menus starting from 95F/€14.49.

In mid-July there are free **jazz concerts** on place du Château and, at the end of August, a bizarre **square boules** competition takes place down montée de la Bourgade.

St-Paul-de-Vence: the Fondation Maeght

Further into the hills, the fortified village of **ST-PAUL-DE-VENCE** is home to yet another artistic treat, and one of the best in the whole region: the remarkable **Fondation Maeght** created in the 1950s by Aimé and Marguerite Maeght, art collectors and dealers who knew all the great artists who worked in Provence (daily: July–Sept 10am–7pm; rest of year 10am–12.30pm & 2.30–6pm; 40F/€6.10, or 50F/€7.63 during exhibitions). The Nice–Vence **bus** has two stops in St-Paul: the Fondation is signposted from the second, and is approximately 1km from the old town. By **car or bike**, follow the signs just before you reach the village, off the D7 from La-Colle-sur-Loup or the D2 from Villeneuve. Admission includes the permanent collections, temporary exhibitions, bookshop, library and cinema, and it's worth every last centime.

Once through the gates, any idea of dutifully seeing the catalogue of priceless museum pieces crumbles. Alberto Giacometti's *Cat* is sometimes stalking along the edge of the grass; Miró's *Egg* smiles above a pond and his totemed *Fork* is outlined against the sky. It's hard not to be bewitched by the Calder mobile swinging over watery tiles, by Léger's *Flowers, Birds and a Bench* on a sunlit rough stone wall, by Zadkine's and Arp's metallic forms hovering between the pine trunks, or by the clanking tubular fountain by Pol Bury. The building itself is a superb piece of architecture: multi-levelled and flooded with daylight, making inside and outside hard to distinguish, and the collection it houses of works by Braque, Miró, Chagall, Léger and Matisse, along with more recent artists and the young up-and-comings, is fabulous. Not all the works are exhibited at any one time, and during the summer, when the main annual exhibition is mounted, none are on show, apart from those that make up the decoration of the building.

The other famous sight in this extremely busy tourist village is the hotel-restaurant **La Colombe d'Or** on place du Général-de-Gaulle (☎04.93.32.80.02, fax 04.93.32.77.78; ⑨; closed Nov–Christmas), where if you are prepared to splash out 400F/€61 for a mediocre meal or more than 1300F/€198 for a room, you can enjoy the Braques, Picassos, Matisses and Bonnards that hang from the walls, most of which were acquired by the establishment in the lean post-World War I years in lieu of the artists' unpaid bills.

Vence

A few kilometres north, with abundant water and the sheltering pre-Alps behind, **VENCE** has always been a significant city. The old town is blessed with numerous ancient houses, gateways, fountains, chapels and a **cathedral** (daily 9am–6pm) containing Roman funeral inscriptions and a Chagall mosaic. In the 1920s it became yet another haven for painters and writers: André Gide, Raoul Dufy, D.H. Lawrence (who died here in 1930 whilst being treated for tuberculosis contracted in England) and Marc Chagall were all long-term visitors, along with **Matisse** whose work is the reason most people come to Vence.

Towards the end of World War II, Matisse moved to Vence to escape the Allied bombing of the coast, and his legacy is the town's most famous and exciting building, the **Chapelle du Rosaire**, at 466 av Henri-Matisse, on the road to St-Jeannet from carrefour Jean-Moulin at the top of avenue des Poilus (Mon, Wed, Fri & Sat 2–5.30pm; Tues & Thurs 10–11.30am & 2.30–5.30pm, Sun briefly from 10.45am; free). The chapel was his last work – consciously so – and not, as some have tried to explain, a religious conversion. "My only religion is the love of the work to be created, the love of creation, and great sincerity," he said in 1952 when the five-year project was completed.

The drawings on the chapel walls – black outline figures on white tiles – were executed by Matisse with a paintbrush fixed to a two-metre long bamboo stick specifically to remove his own stylistic signature from the lines. He succeeded in this to the extent that many people are bitterly disappointed, not finding the "Matisse" they expect. The only source of colour in the chapel comes from the light diffused through green, blue and yellow stained-glass windows, which changes according to the time of day. Yet it is a total work – every part of the chapel is Matisse's design – and one that the artist was content with. It was his "ultimate goal, the culmination of an intense, sincere and difficult endeavour".

Vieux Vence has all the chic boutiques and arty restaurants worthy of an *haut-lieu* of the Côte aristocracy, but it also has an everyday feel about it, with ordinary people and run-of-the-mill cafés. On place du Frêne, by the western gateway, the fifteenth-century **Château de Villeneuve** (Tues–Sun: July–Oct 10am–6pm; rest of year 10am–12.30pm & 2–6pm; 25F/€3.81) provides a beautiful temporary exhibition space for the works of artists such as Matisse, Dufy, Dubuffet and Chagall.

Current artistic creation has a home at the **Centre d'Art VAAS**, 14 traverse des Moulins, just north of the old city (Tues–Sat 9.30am–noon & 2.30–6pm; free). A garden of sculptures leads to what was, from 1955 to 1970, Jean Dubuffet's studio. As well as a gallery of figurative art, this is a space for artists to meet and work, and the high-quality courses of art and sculpture it runs are open to anyone who wishes to pay the fees. It also gives the best view of the blue-tiled rooftop of the Chapelle du Rosaire.

Yet more art, this time by the likes of César, Klein, Arman, Ben, Tinguely and Warhol, are shown in changing temporary exhibitions at the **Galerie Beaubourg** in the Château Notre-Dame des Fleurs, halfway along the road from Vence to Tourettes-sur-Loup (April–Sept Mon–Sat 11am–7pm; rest of year Tues–Sat 11am–5.30pm; 30F/€4.58).

Practicalities

Arriving by bus, you'll be dropped near place du Frêne at the **gare routière** on place du Grand-Jardin, where you'll find the **tourist office** (Mon–Sat 9am–12.30pm & 2–6pm; ☎04.93.58.06.38, *www.nicetourism.com*) and **bike rental** at Vence Motocycles.

Vence is a real town, with affordable **places to stay**. If you're on a tight budget, your best bet is the rather down-at-heel *La Victoire*, on place du Grand Jardin (☎04.93.58.61.30, fax 04.93.58.74.68; ①); otherwise try the welcoming and peaceful *La Closerie des Genêts*, 4 impasse Maurel, off avenue M.-Maurel to the south of the old town (☎04.93.58.33.25, fax 04.93.58.97.01; ④), and *Le Provence*, 9 av M.-Maurel (☎04.93.58.04.21, fax 04.93.58.35.62; ④), with a pleasant garden. A little more luxury, including a pool, is available at *La Villa Roseraie*, 14 av Henri-Giraud (☎04.93.58.02.20, fax 04.93.58.99.31, *rvilla5536@aol.com*; ⑤). There's a **campsite**, *La Bergerie*, 3km west off the road to Tourettes-sur-Loup (☎04.93.58.09.36; closed mid-Oct to mid-March).

For a special, excellent-value **meal**, try *La Farigoule*, 15 av Henri-Isnard (☎04.93.58.01.27; closed Fri & Sat lunch out of season; menus from 120F/€18.30). Also good, and with menus from 130F/€19.83 (only 95F/€14.49 for residents), is the restaurant at *La Closerie des Genêts* hotel (see above; closed Sun evening). The fabled chef Jacques Maximin has opened a gourmet palace in Vence: imaginatively titled the *Maximin Restaurant*, 689 chemin de la Gaude (☎04.93.58.90.75), it prepares exquisite fare, with the cheapest menu starting at 250F/€38.13 and rising rapidly in price and indulgence. For more run-of-the-mill fare, try the astounding choice of pizzas at *Le Pêcheur du Soleil*, 1 place Godeau. You'll find plenty of **cafés** in the squares of Vieux Vence. *La Clemenceau*, on place Clemenceau, is the big café-brasserie-glacier, but you might find *Henry's Bar*, on place de Peyra, more congenial. *La Régence*, on place du Grand-Jardin, serves excellent coffee to sip beneath its stylish parasols.

Nice

The capital of the Riviera and fifth largest city in France, **NICE** scarcely deserves its glittering reputation. Living off inflated property values and fat business accounts, its ruling class has hardly evolved from the eighteenth-century Russian and English aristocrats who first built their mansions here; today it's the *rentiers* and retired people of various nationalities whose dividends and pensions give the city its startlingly high ratio of per capita income to economic activity.

Their votes ensured the monopoly of municipal power held for decades by the right-wing dynasty, whose corruption was finally exposed in 1990 when mayor Jacques

---

CHEMINS DE FER DE LA PROVENCE

The **Chemins de Fer de la Provence** runs one of France's most scenic and fun rail routes from the station on Nice's rue Alfred Binet, ten minutes' walk north of the *gare SNCF* (or buses #4 or #5). The line runs up the valley of the Var between **Nice** and **Digne-les-Bains** (see p.958), climbing through some spectacular scenery as it goes. Four trains run daily, year-round, and the whole journey takes 3hr 15min, and costs 218F/€33.25 (for more information call ☎04.93.82.10.17, or look online at *perso.club -internet.fr/dandesme*).

Médecin fled to Uruguay. He was finally extradited and jailed. Despite the disappearance of 400 million francs of taxpayers' money, public opinion remained in his favour. From his Grenoble prison cell, Médecin, who had twinned Nice with Cape Town during the height of South Africa's apartheid regime, backed the former Front National member and close friend of Jean-Marie Le Pen, Jacques Peyrat, in the 1995 local elections. Peyrat won with ease.

Politics apart, Nice has other reasons to qualify it as one of the more dubious destinations on the Riviera: it's a pickpocket's paradise; the traffic is a nightmare; miniature poodles appear to be mandatory; phones are always vandalized; and the beach isn't even sand. And yet Nice still manages to be delightful. The sun and the sea and the laidback, affable Niçois cover a multitude of sins. The medieval rabbit warren of the old town, the Italianate facades of modern Nice and the rich, exuberant, *fin-de-siècle* residences that made the city one of Europe's most fashionable winter retreats have all survived intact. It has also retained mementos from its ancient past, when the Romans ruled the region from here, and earlier still, when the Greeks founded the city. In addition, its bus and train connections make Nice by far the best base for visiting the rest of the Riviera.

Arrival, information and accommodation

Arriving by **air**, you can get different buses into town: bus #23 to the *gare SNCF* (8.50F/€1.30); a speedy *navette* (taking 15min; 26F/€3.97); or a bus (every 20min, 23F/€3.51) from outside the end door of Terminal 1 to the junction of avenue Gustav V and the promenade des Anglais, or on to the **gare routière**, which for once is very central, close to the old town beneath the promenade du Paillon on boulevard Jean-Jaurès (☎04.93.85.61.81). The **gare SNCF** is a little further out, a couple of blocks west of the top end of avenue Jean-Médecin (bus #12 to place Masséna). Both the bus and train stations have left-luggage counters.

You'll find the main **tourist office** beside the *gare SNCF* on avenue Thiers (daily: June–Sept 8am–8pm; rest of year 8am–7pm; ☎04.93.92.82.82, *www.nice-coteazur.org*). It's one of the most useful, helpful and generous of Côte tourist offices and has **annexes** at 5 promenade des Anglais (June–Sept Mon–Sat 8am–8pm, Sun 9am–6pm; rest of year Mon–Sat 9am–6pm; ☎04.92.14.48.00), another at Nice-Ferber (June–Sept Mon–Sat 8am–8pm, Sun 9am–6pm; rest of year Mon–Sat 10am–5pm; ☎04.93.83.32.64), further along the promenade des Anglais near the airport, and a third at Terminal 1 of the airport (daily: June–Sept 8am–8pm; rest of year 8am–10pm; ☎04.93.21.44.11). Any of these offices can supply you with a free listings magazine, *Le Mois à Nice*.

Buses operate frequent services around the city, running until 12.15am, with four lines running until 1.10am. Fares are flat-rate and you can buy a single ticket on the bus (8.50F/€1.30) or a carnet of ten tickets (55F/€8.38). There are also one-day (25F/€3.81; available on bus), five-day (85F/€12.96) or weekly passes (110F/€16.77), all of which can be bought at *tabacs*, kiosks, newsagents or from Sunbus, the transport

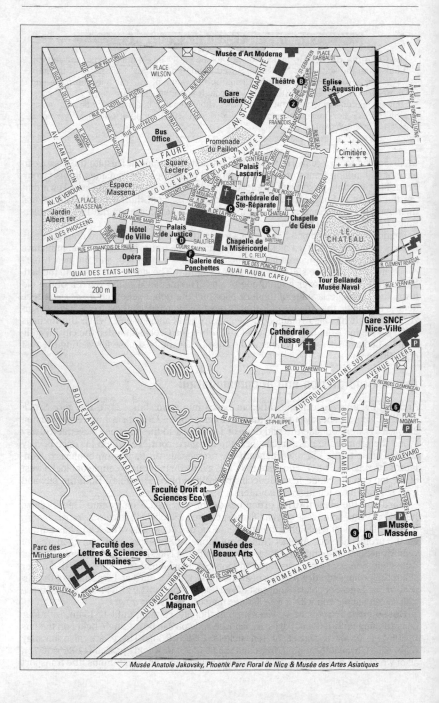

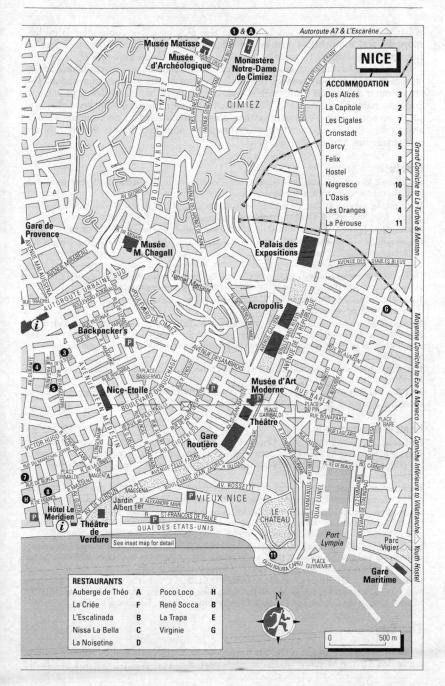

NICE

ACCOMMODATION

Des Alizés	3
La Capitole	2
Les Cigales	7
Cronstadt	9
Darcy	5
Felix	8
Hostel	1
Negresco	10
L'Oasis	6
Les Oranges	4
La Pérouse	11

RESTAURANTS

Auberge de Théo	A	Poco Loco	H
La Criée	F	René Socca	B
L'Escalinada	B	La Trapa	E
Nissa La Bella	C	Virginie	G
La Noisetine	D		

office at 10 av Félix-Faure, where you can also pick up a free route map. **Bicycles**, **mopeds** and **motorbikes** can be rented from Nicea Location Rent at 12 rue de Belgique (☎04.93.82.42.17, *nicealocation@aol.com*), just by the *gare SNCF*.

Before you start hunting around for **accommodation**, it's well worth taking advantage of the **reservation service** offered by the tourist office at the train station. The area around the station teems with cheap, seedy hotels, but it's perfectly possible to find reasonably priced rooms in Vieux Nice. In summer, there's a fairly good choice of youth accommodation. Sleeping on the beach, which used to be common though always illegal, is now difficult since it's brightly illuminated the whole length of the promenade des Anglais.

Hotels

des Alizés, 10 rue de Suisse (☎04.93.88.85.08). Excellent-value, hospitable, family-run hotel. Ask for a front room with a view of the square. ②.

Le Capitole, 4 rue de la Tour (☎04.93.80.08.15, fax 04.93.85.10.58). A good if potentially noisy location in Vieux Nice, with a warm atmosphere though not over-generous rooms. ③.

Les Cigales, 16 rue Dalpozzo (☎04.93.88.33.75). Clean, quiet and close to the beach. ③.

Cronstadt, 3 rue Cronstadt (☎04.93.82.00.30, fax 04.93.82.00.40). Extremely good-value place with old-fashioned clean and comfortable rooms hidden away one block away from the seafront. Has a charming *patronne* and offers free parking on street. ④.

Darcy, 28 rue Angleterre (☎04.93.88.67.06, fax 04.93.72.06.81, *hoteldarcy@hotmail.com*). Excellent-value hotel, close to the beach, but in a quieter neighbourhood away from the bustle. ②.

Félix, 41 rue Masséna (☎04.93.88.67.73, fax 04.93.16.15.78). A bit closer in than the *Darcy*. A small, quiet place with air-conditioning. ④.

Negresco, 37 promenade des Anglais (☎04.93.22.41.65, fax 04.93.88.35.68). This landmark of the Nice waterfront offers *fin-de-siècle* luxury for those who are prepared to pay. The service is excellent, the rooms are large (and mercifully not as garishly decorated as the lobby), and the ambience is pure Belle Époque. ⑨.

Les Orangers, 10bis av Durante (☎04.93.87.51.41, fax 04.93.82.57.82). A cheapie popular with American students. ②.

La Pérouse, 11 quai Rauba-Capeu (☎04.93.62.34.63, fax 04.93.62.59.41, *lp@hroy.com*). A wonderful location at the foot of Le Château, with views across the bay. Very luxurious. ⑨.

Hostels and campsite

HI hostel, rte Forestière du Mont-Alban (☎04.93.89.23.64, fax 04.93.04.03.10). Nice's HI hostel is 4km out of town and, for two people, not a lot cheaper than sharing a hotel room. The last bus from the centre leaves at 7.30pm; bus #14 from place Masséna, direction "Place du Mont-Boron", stop "L'Auberge".

Backpacker's Hotel, 32 rue Pertinax (☎04.93.80.30.72). Close to *gare SNCF*, this venerable backpacker's favourite has some double rooms, but mostly dorms. Kitchen facilities and no curfew.

Clairvallon Relais International de la Jeunesse, 26 av Scudéri (☎04.93.81.27.63, fax 04.93.53.35.88, *clajpaca@cote-dazur.com*). Located 10km north of the centre, but it's slightly cheaper than the HI hostel, pleasantly informal and has a pool; take bus #15 or #25, stop "Scudéri".

MJC Magnan, 31 rue Louis-de-Coppet (☎04.93.86.28.75, fax 04.93.44.93.22, *corrie@espacemagnan.com*). The least expensive of the hostel options: not too far from the centre and close to the beach. Take buses #12 or #23, stop "Magnan". Closed mid-Sept to mid-June.

Camping Terry, 768 rte de Grenoble, St-Isidore (☎04.93.08.11.58). The only campsite anywhere near Nice, 6.5km north of the airport on the N202; take the #700 bus from the *gare routière* to "La Manda" stop, or the Chemins de Fer de la Provence train to Bellet-Tennis des Combes.

The City

It doesn't take long to get a feel for the layout of Nice. Shadowed by mountains that curve down to the Mediterranean east of its port, it still breaks up more or less into old

MUSEUM PASSES

Entrance is free to all Nice's municipal **museums** on the first Sunday of each month; otherwise a single adult pays 25F/€3.81 (except where stated otherwise). A seven-day pass allowing a single entrance to all museums except the Chagall Museum costs 40F/€6.10. A museum pass, valid for fifteen visits of your choice within one year, is available from all the museums, price 120F/€18.30 (reduced rate 60F/€9.15). There is also a Carte Musée Côte d'Azur which gives you access to most museums and monuments (62 in total) in the region, for either three (80F/€12.20) or seven days (150F/€22.88).

and new. **Vieux Nice**, the old town, groups about the hill of **Le Château**, its limits signalled by **boulevard Jean-Jaurès**, built along the course of the River Paillon. Along the seafront, the celebrated **promenade des Anglais** runs a cool 5km until forced to curve inland by the sea-projecting runways of the airport. The central square, **place Masséna**, is at the bottom of the modern city's main street, **avenue Jean-Médecin**, while off to the north is the exclusive hillside suburb of **Cimiez**.

The château and Vieux Nice

For initial orientation, with brilliant sea and city views, fresh air and the scent of Mediterranean vegetation, the best place to make for is the **Château park** (daily: April, May & Sept 9am–7pm; June–Aug 9am–8pm; Oct–March 10am–5.30pm). It's where Nice began as the ancient Greek city of Nikea, hence the mosaics and stone vases in mock Grecian style. There's no château as such, but the real pleasure lies in looking down on the scrambled rooftops and gleaming mosaic tiles of Vieux Nice and along the sweep of the promenade des Anglais. To reach the park, you can either take the lift by the Tour Bellanda, at the eastern end of quai des Etats-Unis, or climb the steps from rue de la Providence or rue du Château in the old town.

Vieux Nice has been greatly gentrified over the last decade, but the expensive shops, smart restaurants and art galleries still coexist with little hardware stores selling brooms and bottled gas; tiny cafés are full of men in blue overalls; and washing is strung between the tenements. The streets are too narrow for buses and are best explored on foot.

The central square is **place Rossetti**, where the soft-coloured Baroque **Cathédrale de St-Réparate** (daily 8am–7pm) just manages to be visible in the concatenation of eight narrow streets. There are two cafés to relax in, with the choice of sun or shade, and a magical ice-cream parlour, *Fenocchio*, with an extraordinary choice of flavours. The real magnet of the old town, though, is **cours Saleya** and the adjacent place Pierre-Gautier and place Charles-Félix. These are wide-open, sunlit spaces alongside grandiloquent municipal buildings and Italianate chapels and the site of the city's main **market**. Every day except Monday from 6am to 1pm there are gorgeous displays of fruit, vegetables, cheeses and sausages, plus cut flowers and potted roses, mimosa and other scented plants displayed till 5.30pm; on Monday the stalls sell bric-a-brac and secondhand clothes. Café and restaurant tables fill the *cours* on summer nights, when literally thousands of people are enjoying the warmth and extraordinary animation.

To feast your eyes on Baroque splendour, pop into the **chapels** and **churches** of Vieux Nice: La Chapelle de la Miséricorde, on cours Saleya (open for Sunday Mass 10.30am or through the Palais Lascaris, see p.1022); L'Église du Gesu, on rue Droite (9am–6pm); or L'Eglise St-Augustine, on place St-Augustine (open for Mass Sat 4pm & Sun 9am), which also contains a fine *Pietà* by Louis Bréa. For contemporary graphic and photographic art, some of the best **art galleries** in Vieux Nice include Galerie Espace Ste-Réparate, 4 rue Ste-Réparate; Galerie Municipale Renoir, 8 rue de la Loge; and Galerie du Château, 14 rue Droite.

Also on rue Droite is the **Palais Lascaris** (Tues–Sun 10am–noon & 2–6pm; free; closed mid-Nov to mid-Dec), a seventeenth-century palace built by the Duke of Savoy's Field-Marshal, Jean-Paul Lascaris, whose family arms, engraved on the ceiling of the entrance hall, bear the motto "Not even lightning strikes us". It's all very sumptuous, with frescoes, tapestries and chandeliers, along with a collection of porcelain vases from an eighteenth-century pharmacy.

Place Masséna and around

The stately **place Masséna** is the hub of the new town, built in 1835 across the path of the River Paillon, with good views north past fountains and palm trees to the mountains. A balustraded terrace and steps on the south of the square lead to Vieux Nice; the new town lies to the north. It's a pretty and spacious expanse, without being very significant – in fact the only things of interest here are the sundry ice-cream vendors who shelter their goods under the arcades during summer. A short walk to the west lie the **Jardins Albert 1er**, on the promenade des Anglais, where the Théâtre de Verdune occasionally hosts concerts.

The covered course of the Paillon to the north of place Masséna has provided the sites for the city's more recent municipal prestige projects. At their worst, up beyond traverse Barla, they take the form of giant packing crates for high-tech goods, in the multi-media, mega-buck conference centre grotesquely called the **Acropolis**. Though theoretically a public building, with exhibition space, a cinema and bowling alley (11am–2am), international business often limits casual entry. There are, however, various modern sculptures outside the building on which to vent your critical frustration.

Downstream from the Acropolis is the vast marble **Musée d'Art Moderne et d'Art Contemporain**, or MAMAC (Wed–Sun 10am–6pm), with rotating exhibitions of avant-garde French and American movements from the 1960s to the present. New Realism (smashing, burning, squashing, wrapping, etc, the detritus or mundane objects of everyday life) and Pop Art feature strongly with works by, among others, Warhol, Klein, Lichtenstein, César, Arman and Christo. It's good fun, and the huge, light galleries are a delight to walk around.

Running north from place Masséna, **avenue Jean-Médecin** is the city's main shopping street, with nothing much to distinguish it from any other big French city high street. You'll find all the mainstream clothes and household accessory chains, plus FNAC for books and records, at the Nice-Étoile **shopping complex** between rue Biscarra and boulevard Dubouchage. **Couturier** shops are to be found west of place Masséna on rue du Paradis and avenue de Suède. Both these streets lead to the pedestrianized **rue Masséna** and the end of **rue de France** – all hotels, bars, restaurants, ice-cream and fast-food outlets, with no regard for quality or style.

Skirting this, the chief interest in western Nice is in the older architecture: eighteenth- and nineteenth-century Italian Baroque and Neoclassical, florid Belle Époque and unclassifiable exotic aristo-fantasy. The trophy for the most gilded, exotic and elaborate edifice goes to the **Russian Orthodox Cathedral**, off boulevard Tsaréwitch at the end of avenue Nicolas-II (daily: April, May, Sept & Oct 9.15am–noon & 2–5.30pm; July & Aug 9am–noon & 2.30–6pm; Nov–March 9.30am–noon & 2.30–5pm; Sun afternoon only; 12F/€1.83; bus #14 or #17, stop "Tsaréwitch").

The promenade des Anglais and the beaches

The point where the Paillon flows into the sea marks the beginning of the world-famous palm-fringed **promenade des Anglais**, created by nineteenth-century English residents for their afternoon's sea-breeze stroll along the Mediterranean sea coast. Today it's the city's unofficial high-speed racetrack, bordered by some of the most fanciful turn-of-the-twentieth-century architecture on the Côte d'Azur.

Most celebrated of all is the opulent **Negresco Hotel** at no. 37, built in 1906, and filling up the block between rues de Rivoli and Cronstadt. Though they will try to stop you if you are not deemed to be wearing *tenue correcte* (especially in the evenings), you can try wandering in to take a look at the Salon Louis XIV and the Salon Royale. The first, on the left of the foyer, has a seventeenth-century painted oak ceiling and mammoth fireplace, plus royal portraits, all from various French châteaux. The Salon Royale, in the centre of the hotel, is a vast domed oval room, decorated with 24-carat gold leaf and the biggest carpet ever to have come out of the Savonnerie workshops. The chandelier is one of a pair commissioned from Baccarat by Tsar Nicholas II – the other hangs in the Kremlin.

Just before the *Negresco*, with its entrance at 65 rue de France, stands the **Musée Masséna**, the city's art and history museum. Closed for major renovations until 2004, only its unexceptional, but shady gardens are open to the public (daily 9am–6pm).

A kilometre or so down the promenade and a couple of blocks inland at 33 av des Baumettes is the **Musée des Beaux-Arts** (Tues–Sun 10am–noon & 2–6pm; bus #38, stop "Chéret"). It has too many whimsical canvases by Jules Chéret, who died in Nice in 1932, a great many Belle Époque paintings to go with the building, a room dedicated to the Van Loos, plus modern works that come as unexpected delights: a Rodin bust of Victor Hugo and some very amusing Van Dongens, such as the *Archangel's Tango*. Monet, Sisley – one of his famous poplar alleys – and Degas also grace the walls. Continuing southwest along the promenade des Anglais towards the airport, you'll find the **Musée International d'Art Naïf Anatole Jakovsky** (daily except Tues 10am–noon & 2–6pm), home to a refreshingly different, and surprisingly good, collection of over six hundred pieces of amateur art from around the world.

The **beach** below the promenade des Anglais is all pebbles and mostly public, with showers provided. It's not particularly clean and you need to watch out for broken glass. There are, of course, the mattress, food and drinks concessionaries, but nothing like to the extent of Cannes. There's a small, more secluded beach on the west side of Le Château, below the sea wall of the port. But the best, and cleanest, place to swim, if you don't mind rocks, is the string of coves beyond the port that starts with the **plage de la Reserve** opposite parc Vigier (bus #32 or #3). From the water you can look up at the nineteenth-century fantasy palaces built onto the steep slopes of the **Cap du Nice**. Further up, past **Coco Beach** (bus #3 only, stop "Villa La Côte"), rather smelly steps lead down to a coastal path which continues around the headland. Towards dusk this becomes a gay pick-up place.

On the far side of the castle sits the **old port**, flanked by gorgeous red to ochre eighteenth-century buildings and headed by the Neoclassical Notre-Dame du Port; it's full of bulbous yachts but has little quayside life despite the restaurants along quai Lunel. On the hill to the east, prehistoric life in the region has been reconstructed on the site of an excavated fossil beach in the well-designed **Musée de Terra Amata**, 25 bd Carnot (Tues–Sun 9am–noon & 2–6pm).

Cimiez

The northern suburb of **Cimiez** has always been a posh place. Its principal streets, avenue des Arènes-de-Cimiez and boulevard Cimiez, rise between plush, high-walled villas to what was the social centre of the local elite some 1700 years ago, when the town was capital of the Roman province of Alpes-Maritimae. Part of a small amphitheatre still stands, and excavations of the **Roman baths** have revealed enough detail to distinguish the sumptuous and elaborate facilities for the top tax official and his cronies, the plainer public baths and a separate complex for women. All the finds, plus an illustration of the town's history up to the Middle Ages, are displayed in the impressive, modern **Musée d'Archéologie**, rue Monte-Croce (Tues–Sun: April–Sept 10am–noon & 2–6pm; rest of year 10am–1pm & 2–5pm; bus #15, #17, #20 or #22, stop "Arènes").

The seventeenth-century villa between the excavations and the arena is the **Musée Matisse** (Wed–Sun: March–Sept 10am–6pm; rest of year 10am–5pm). Matisse spent his winters in Nice from 1916 onwards, staying in hotels on the promenade – from where *A Storm at Nice* was painted – and then from 1921 to 1938 renting an apartment overlooking place Charles-Félix. It was here that he painted his most sensual, colour-flooded canvases of odalisques posed against exotic draperies. As well as the Mediterranean light, Matisse loved the cosmopolitan aspect of Nice, the rococo salons of the hotels and the presence of fellow artists Renoir, Bonnard and Picasso in neighbouring towns. He died in Cimiez in November 1954, aged 85. Almost all his last works in Nice were cut-out compositions, with an artistry of line showing how he could wield a pair of scissors with just as much strength and delicacy as a paintbrush.

The museum's collection, with work from every period, includes a great number of drawings and an almost complete set of his bronze sculptures. There are sketches for one of the *Dance* murals; models for the Vence chapel plus the priests' robes he designed; book illustrations; and excellent examples of his cut-out technique, of which the most delightful are *The Bees* and *The Créole Dancer*. Among the paintings are the 1905 portrait of Madame Matisse; the *Storm at Nice* (1919–20), which seems to get wetter and darker the further you step back from it; *Odalisk*; the 1947 *Still Life with Pomegranates*; and one of his two earliest attempts at oil painting, *Still Life with Books*, painted in 1890.

The Roman remains and the Musée Matisse back onto an old olive grove, one of the best open spaces in Nice and venue for the July **jazz festival**. At its eastern end are the sixteenth-century buildings and exquisite gardens of the **Monastère Notre-Dame de Cimiez** (Mon–Sat 10am–12.30pm & 3–7pm; free); the oratory has brilliant murals illustrating alchemy, while the church houses three masterpieces of medieval painting by Louis Bréa and Antoine Bréa.

At the foot of Cimiez hill, just off boulevard Cimiez on avenue du Docteur-Menard, **Chagall's Biblical Message** is housed in a museum built specially for the work and opened by the artist in 1972 (daily except Tues: July–Sept 10am–6pm; rest of year 10am–5pm; 30F/€4.58, or 38F/€5.80 for summer exhibitions; bus #15 stop "Musée Chagall"). The rooms are light, white and cool, with windows allowing you to see the greenery of the garden beyond the indescribable shades between pink and red of the *Song of Songs* canvases. The seventeen paintings are all based on the Old Testament and complemented with etchings and engravings. To the building itself, Chagall contributed a mosaic and stained-glass window.

The Phoenix Parc Floral de Nice

Right out by the airport is a vast tourist attraction, the **Phoenix Parc Floral de Nice**, 405 promenade des Anglais (daily: mid-March to mid-Oct 9am–7pm; rest of year 9am–5pm; 40F/€6.10; exit St-Augustin from the motorway or bus #9, #10, or #23 from Nice). It's a cross between botanical gardens, a bird and insect zoo and a tacky theme park: automated dinosaurs and mock Mayan temples along with alpine streams, ginkgo trees, butterflies and cockatoos. The greenhouse full of butterflies fluttering around is wonderful, but the assumption that the world's fauna and flora is yours to admire may make you feel a bit uneasy.

The best reason to make the trip out to the park is Nice's newest museum, the **Musée Départemental des Artes Asiatiques** (daily except Tues: May–Sept 10am–6pm; rest of year 10am–5pm; 35F/€5.34), designed by Japanese architect Kenzo Tange. It houses a collection of ethnographic artefacts, including silk goods and pottery, as well as traditional and contemporary art. The highlight is a pavilion designed to convey the peaceful philosophy of Zen.

Eating, nightlife and festivals

Nice is a great place for **food** indulgence, whether you're picnicking on market fare, snacking on Niçois specialities or dining in the palace hotels. The Italian influence is strong in all restaurants, with pasta on every menu; seafood is also a staple. For **snacks**, many of the cafés sell sandwiches with typically Provençal fillings such as fresh basil, olive oil, goat's cheese and *mesclum*, the unique green salad mix of the region. If you want to buy the best bread or croissants in town, seek out *Espuno*, 22 rue Vernier, in the old town.

Excellent restaurants can be found throughout most of Nice. Vieux Nice has a dozen on every street catering for a wide variety of budgets; the port quaysides have very good, but pricey, fish restaurants. In summer it's wise to book tables or turn up before 8pm, especially in Vieux Nice.

Given the city's staid, affluent population, the late-night scene tends to be dominated by luxury hotel **bars**. But **pubs** are popular with the young, and Vieux Nice has a wide choice of venues for drinking and dancing, though the music tends not to be very novel. A good place to set out is along rue Central in the old town, where many pubs have early evening happy hours. As for Niçois **nightclubs**, bouncers judging your wallet or exclusive membership lists are the rule.

Cafés and bars

Bar des Oiseaux, 9 rue St-Vincent. Named for the birds that fly down from their nests in the loft and the pet parrot and screeching myna bird that perch by the door. Serves delicious and copious baguette sandwiches. Erratic opening hours, sometimes closed all afternoon.

Caves Ricord, 2 rue Neuve. An old-fashioned wine bar with faded peeling posters and drinkers to match. A wide selection of wine by the glass, plus pizzas and other snacks. Closed Wed & mid-June to mid-July.

La Douche à l'Étage, 34 cours Saleya. A cyber café with four terminals linked up to the Internet while upstairs there really is a shower, plus comfy settees, billiards and music. Open till 12.30am.

Nocy-be, 2 rue Jules-Gilley. This New-Agey tea house has a cushioned interior which evokes a bedouin tent. Countless varieties of teas and infusions. Open Wed–Sun 4pm–12.30am.

Scarlet O'Hara, 22 rue Droite. Tiny Irish folk bar on the corner of rue Rosetti serving the creamiest, priciest Guinness this side of the Irish Sea. Daily 6pm–12.30am; closed Mon & first half of July.

Restaurants

L'Auberge de Théo, 52 av Cap-de-Croix (☎04.93.81.26.19). Pleasant Italian food up in Cimiez. 130F/€19.83 menu (except Sat & Sun evening). Closed Mon & third week Aug to second week Sept.

Chantecler and **La Rotonde**, *Hôtel Negresco*, 37 promenade des Anglais (☎04.93.16.64.00, *negresco@nicematin.fr*). *Chantecler* is the best restaurant in Nice and over 500F/€76 à la carte, but chef Dominique Le Stanc provides a lunchtime menu, wine and coffee included, for 250F/€38.13, which will give you a good idea of how sublime Niçoise food at its best can be. At *La Rotonde* you can taste less fancy but still mouthwatering dishes on 110F/€16.78 and 150F/€22.88 menus. Closed mid-Nov to mid-Dec.

La Criée, 22 cours Saleya (☎04.93.85.49.99). A cut above the hordes of near-identical seafood places whose patios cram the cours de Saleya. Great service and good prices, with menus from 100F/€15.25.

L'Escalinada, 22 rue Pairolière (☎04.93.62.11.71). Tucked away among the bustle of Old Nice's market street, this is the place for down-home Niçoise cooking in a relaxed and unpretentious atmosphere. Menus 120–160F/€18.30–24.40.

Nissa La Bella, 6 rue Ste-Réparate (☎04.93.62.10.20). *Socca*, pizzas and other real Niçoise specialities. From 80F/€12.20. Closed Sun lunch.

La Noisetine, cours Saleya, near rue Gassin. One of the cheapest places to eat on the cours Saleya with generous and tasty crêpes, huge salads, nice desserts and fresh fruit juices. Open till midnight.

Poco Loco, 2 rue Dalpozze (☎04.93.88.85.83, *www.poco-loco.com*). Lively place with authentic Mexican food at near-Mexican prices (60–95F/€9.15–14.49 for a menu). Just off the promenade des Anglais.

René Socca, 2 rue Miralhéti, off rue Pairolière. The cheapest meal in town: you can buy helpings of *socca*, *pissaladière*, stuffed peppers, pasta or *calamares* at the counter and eat with your fingers on stools ranged haphazardly across the street; the bar opposite serves the drinks. Closed Mon & Nov.

La Trapa, 12 rue Jules-Gilly (☎04.93.80.33.69). Cuban tapas bar and restaurant featuring live music on summer evenings and a delicious *plat du jour* at 70F/€10.68.

Virginie, 2 place A.-Blanqui (☎04.93.55.10.07). Excellent *plateau des fruits de mer*. From 60F/€9.15.

Clubs

B52, 8 Descente Crotti. Small dance floor, young clientele and good value. Daily 11pm–4am, free entry until 1am.

Le Baby Doll, 227 bd de la Madeleine. Lesbian disco, not exclusively female. Daily from 10pm.

Le Blue Boy, 9 rue Jean-Baptiste-Spinétta. Lesbians and heteros are welcome at this, Nice's best gay venue off boulevard François-Grosso. Two bars, two dance floors, DJs who know what's what, and a floorshow every Wed night. Daily 11pm–dawn; entrance charge around 40F/€6.10 Wed & weekends.

Blue Whales, 1 rue Mascoïnat (☎04.93.85.00.57). Intimate venue with friendly atmosphere, and live music after 10pm ranging from Latin to rock. Open till 2.30am.

L'Iguane, 5 quai des Deux-Emmanuel. Very stylish night bar with dance floor for the poseurs. Daily till 6am.

Subway, 19 rue Droite. Reggae, soul and rock; reasonably priced. Tues–Sat from 11.30pm.

Wayne's, 15 rue de la Préfecture (*www.waynes.fr*). Popular bar on the edge of the old town run by an expat who shares the French penchant for good old rock'n'roll. Live bands – of greatly varying quality – Fri and Sat nights. Daily 2.30pm–1am.

Festivals

Details of Nice's lively **festival** calendar are available from the pamphlet *Nice: vos rendez-vous* or the main tourist office. The **Mardi Gras Carnival** opens the year's events in February, with the last week of July taken up by the **Nice Jazz Festival** in the Parc de Cimiez (☎04.93.87.19.18 or *www.worldonline.fr* for info; or fax the main tourist office in May/June).

Listings

Airlines Air France (☎08.02.80.28.02); British Airways (☎08.25.82.54.00); British Midland (☎08.00.05.01.42); Delta (☎08.00.35.40.80); EasyJet (☎04.93.21.48.33); Virgin Express (☎08.00.52.85.28).

Airport information ☎04.93.21.30.12, *www.nice.aeroport.fr*.

Books The Cat's Whiskers, 30 rue Lamartine, and Top, 27 av Jean-Médecin, both sell English-language books.

Car rental Major firms are represented at the airport. Otherwise try: Avis, 2 av Phocéens (☎04.93.80.63.52); Budget, 23 rue Belgique (☎04.93.16.24.16); Europcar, 3 av Gustave V (☎04.92.14.44.50); Hertz, 12 av de Suède (☎04.93.87.11.87).

Cinema Rialo, 4 rue de Rivoli (☎04.93.88.08.41), the Cinémathèque de Nice, 3 esplanade Kennedy (☎04.93.24.06.66), and Le Nouveau Mercury, 16 place Garibaldi (☎08.36.68.81.06), all show *v.o.* films.

Consulates Canada, 64 av Jean Médecin (☎04.93.92.93.22); UK, 8 rue Alphonse Karr (☎04.93.82.32.04); US, 31 av Maréchal Joffre (☎04.93.88.89.55).

Disabled access Transport for people with reduced mobility ☎04.93.86.39.87 or 04.93.96.09.99

Emergencies Doctor: SOS Médecins ☎04.93.85.01.01; Casualty: Hôpital St-Roch, 5 rue Pierre-Dévoluy (☎04.92.03.33.75); Ambulance: ☎15 or ☎04.93.92.55.55.

Ferries to Corsica SNCM (☎04.93.13.66.66), or Corsica Ferries (☎04.92.00.43.76), both in the *gare maritime*, quai du Commerce.

Internet *Planete Cyber*, 16 rue Paganini (daily 9am–10pm; ☎04.93.16.89.81, *planetecyber@wanadoo .fr*), by the *gare*, also serves light meals.

Laundry Lavarie Automatique Assalit, 29 rue Assalit; Laverie du Mono, 8 rue Belgique.

Lost property 10 cours Saleya (☎04.93.80.65.50). SOS Voyageurs for help with lost or stolen luggage at *gare SNCF* (Mon–Fri 9am–noon & 3–6pm; ☎04.93.16.02.61).

Money exchange Change Halévy, 1 rue Halévy (daily 8am–7pm); Change Or, 17 av Thiers (daily 7am–midnight).

Pharmacy 7 rue Masséna (daily 7.30pm–8am; ☎04.93.87.78.94); 66 av J.-Médecin (☎04.93.62.54.44).

Police Commissariat Central de Police, 1 av Maréchal Foch (☎04.92.17.22.22).

Post office 21 av Thiers, 06000 Nice (Mon–Fri 8am–7pm, Sat 8am–noon).

Taxis ☎04.93.80.70.70 or ☎04.93.13.78.78.

Trains Information and reservations ☎08.36.35.35.35. For the scenic line to Digne: Chemins de Fer de la Provence, 4 bis rue Alfred Binet (☎04.93.88.34.72).

Youth information Centre Information Jeunesse, 19 rue Gioffredo (☎04.93.80.93.93).

The Corniches

Three **corniche roads** run east from Nice to the independent principality of Monaco and to Menton, the last town of the French Riviera. Napoléon built the **Grande Corniche** on the route of the Romans' Via Julia Augusta, and the **Moyenne Corniche** dates from the first quarter of the twentieth century, when aristocratic tourism on the Riviera was already causing congestion on the lower, coastal road, the **Corniche Inférieure**. The upper two are the classic location for executive car commercials, and for fatal car crashes in films. Real deaths occur too – most notoriously Princess Grace of Monaco, who died on the Moyenne Corniche.

Buses take all three routes; the **train** follows the lower corniche, and all three are superb means of seeing the most mountainous stretch of the Côte d'Azur. Staying in a **hotel** anywhere between Nice and Menton is expensive; it makes more sense to base yourself in Nice and treat these routes as pleasure rides.

The Corniche Inférieure

The characteristic Côte d'Azur mansions that represent the stylistically incompatible fantasies of their original owners parade along the **Corniche Inférieure**. Or they lurk screened from view on the promontories of **Cap Ferrat**, their gardens infested with killer cacti and piranha ponds if the plethora of "Défense d'entrer – Danger de Mort" signs is anything to go by.

VILLEFRANCHE-SUR-MER is just over the other side of Mont Alban from Nice, and has been spared architectural eyesores only to be marred by lurking US and French warships, attracted by the deep waters of the bay. But as long as your visit doesn't coincide with shore leave, the old town on the waterfront, with its active fleet of fishing boats, sixteenth-century citadel and its rue Obscure running beneath the houses, feels almost like the genuine article – an illusion which the quayside restaurants' prices quickly dispel.

The tiny fishing harbour is overlooked by the medieval **Chapelle de St-Pierre**, (April–Oct Mon & Wed–Fri 2.30–6.30pm, Sat 10am–1pm & 2.30–6.30pm; rest of year Mon & Wed–Fri 1.30–5.30pm, Sat 10am–1pm & 1.30–5.30pm; 12F/€1.83), decorated by Jean Cocteau in 1957 in shades he described as "ghosts of colours". The colours fill drawings in strong and simple lines portraying scenes from the life of St Peter and homages to the women of Villefranche and to the gypsies. Above the altar, Peter walks on water supported by an angel, to the outrage of the fish and to the amusement of Christ. The fishermen's eyes are drawn as fish; the ceramic eyes on either side of the

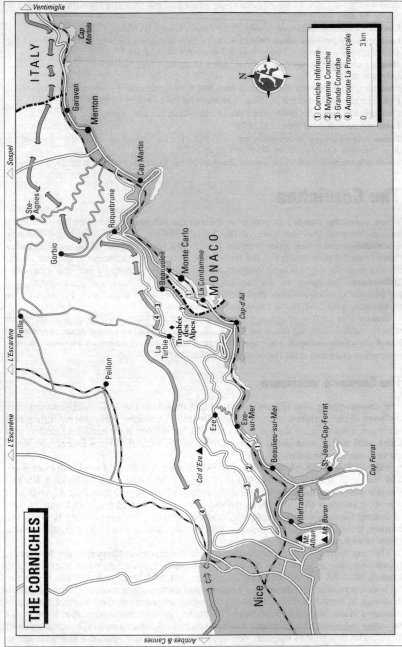

THE CORNICHES

① Corniche Inférieure
② Moyenne Corniche
③ Grande Corniche
④ Autoroute La Provençale

0   3 km

ITALY

Ventimiglia

Cap Mortola

Garavan

Menton

Cap Martin

Sospel

Ste-Agnes

Roquebrune

Gorbio

Beausoleil

Monte Carlo

La Condamine

MONACO

Peille

L'Escarène

Trophée des Alpes

La Turbie

Cap-d'Ail

Peillon

L'Escarène

Eze

Col d'Eze

Eze-sur-Mer

Beaulieu-sur-Mer

St-Jean-Cap-Ferrat

Cap Ferrat

Villefranche

Mt. Alban

Mt. Boron

Nice

Antibes & Cannes

N

door are the flames of the apocalypse; and the altar candelabras of night-time fishing forks rise above single eyes. The chapel is used just once a year, on June 29, when local fishermen celebrate the feast day of St Peter and St Paul with a Mass.

On the main road along the neck of the **Cap Ferrat peninsula**, between Villefranche and Beaulieu, stands the **Villa Éphrusi** (mid-Feb to mid-Nov 10am–6pm; rest of year Mon–Fri limited visit 2–6pm, Sat & Sun 10am–6pm; 50F/€7.63). Built in 1912 for a Rothschild heiress, it overflows with decorative art, paintings, sculpture and artefacts ranging from the fourteenth to the nineteenth centuries, and from European to Far Eastern origins. In addition, the villa is surrounded by huge, elaborate gardens.

BEAULIEU, overlooking the pretty Baie des Fourmis, is sheltered by a ring of hills that ensure some of the highest temperatures on the Côte. Its main point of interest is the **Villa Kérylos** (mid-Feb to June & Sept to mid-Nov daily 10.30am–6pm; July & Aug daily 10.30am–7pm; mid-Dec to mid-Feb Mon–Fri 2–6pm, Sat & Sun 10.30am–6pm; 45F/€6.86), a near-perfect reproduction of an ancient Greek villa, just east of the casino on avenue Gustav-Eiffel. Théodore Reinach, the archeologist who had it built, lived here for twenty years, eating, dressing and acting like an Athenian citizen, taking baths with his male friends and assigning separate suites to women. However perverse the concept, it's a visual knockout, with faithfully reproduced mosaics and vases and lavish use of marble and alabaster. The villa is only five minutes' walk from the **gare SNCF**. For those tempted to **stay** overnight, two economical options are the family-run *Hôtel Riviera*, at 6 rue Paul Doumer, right in the centre near the sea (☎04.93.01.04.92, fax 04.93.01.19.31, *m.hannoteux@wanadoo.fr*; ③), and the *Select*, 1 place Général-de-Gaulle (☎04.93.01.05.42, fax 04.93.01.34.30; ④), which is basic but clean, comfortable and excellent value for this part of the world.

The Moyenne Corniche

Of the three roads, the **Moyenne Corniche** is the most photogenic, a real cliff-hanging, car-chase highway. Eleven kilometres from Nice, the medieval village of **EZE** winds round its conical rock just below the corniche. No other *village perché* is more infested with antique dealers, pseudo-artisans and other caterers to the touristic rich, and it requires a major mental feat to recall that the labyrinth of tiny vaulted passages and stairways was designed not for charm but from fear of attack. At the summit, a cactus garden, the **Jardin Exotique** (daily: July & Aug 9am–8pm; rest of year 9am–noon & 2–5pm; 15F/€2.29) covers the site of the former castle.

From place du Centenaire, just outside the old village, you can reach the shore through open countryside via the **sentier Frédéric-Nietzsche**. The philosopher is said to have conceived part of *Thus Spoke Zarathustra*, his shaggy dog story against believing answers to ultimate questions, on this path – which isn't quite as hard going as the book. You arrive at the Corniche Inférieure at the eastern limit of Eze-sur-Mer (coming upwards, it's signposted to *La Village*).

The Grande Corniche

At every other turn on the **Grande Corniche**, you're invited to park your car and enjoy a *belvédère*. At certain points, such as **Col d'Eze**, you can turn off upwards for even higher views. Eighteen stunning kilometres from Nice, you reach the village of **LA TURBIE** and its **Trophée des Alpes**, a huge monument raised in 6 BC to celebrate the subjugation of the tribes of Gaul. Originally a statue of Augustus Cæsar stood on the 45-metre plinth, which was pillaged, ransacked for building materials and blown up over the centuries. Painstakingly restored in the 1930s, it now stands statueless, 35m high, and, viewed from a distance, still looks imperious. If you want a closer inspection, you'll have to buy a ticket (April–June daily 9.30am–6pm; July to mid-Sept daily

9.30am–7pm; mid-Sept to March Tues–Sun 10am–5pm; 25F/€3.81). Several buses a day run from here to Monaco and Nice, from Monday to Saturday.

As the corniche descends towards Cap Martin, it passes the eleventh-century castle of **ROQUEBRUNE**, its village nestling round the base of the rock. The **castle** (daily: Feb–May 10am–12.30pm & 2–6pm; June–Sept 10am–12.30pm & 3–7.30pm; Oct–Jan 10am–12.30pm & 2–5pm; 20F/€3.05) has been kitted out enthusiastically in medieval fashion, while the tiny vaulted passages and stairways of the village are almost too good to be true. One thing that hasn't been restored is the vast millennial **olive tree** that lies just to the east of the village on the chemin de Menton. To get to the *vieux village* from the **gare SNCF**, turn east and then right up avenue de la Côte d'Azur, then first left up escalier Corinthille, across the Grande Corniche and up escalier Chanoine-J.-B.-Grana. The only **hotel** worth trying in the old village is *Les Deux Frères*, place des Deux-Frères (☎04.93.28.99.00, fax 04.93.28.99.10; ⑤), which is worth booking in advance to try to get one of the rooms with the awesome view (rooms #1 or #2).

Southeast of the old town and the station is the peninsula of **Cap Martin**, with a **coastal path**, giving you access to a wonderful shoreline of white rocks and wind-bent pines. The path is named after **Le Corbusier**, who spent several summers in Roquebrune and died by drowning off Cap Martin in 1965. His grave – designed by himself – is in the **cemetery** (square J near the flagpole), high above the old village on promenade 1er-DFL.

A gourmet treat here is the panoramic **restaurant** *Le Vistaero*, on the Grande Corniche (☎04.92.10.40.20; closed Sun & mid-Jan to Feb), with a brilliant lunchtime menu for 200F/€30.50.

Monaco

Monstrosities are common on the Côte d'Azur, but nowhere – not even Cannes – can outdo **MONACO**. This tiny independent principality, no bigger than London's Hyde Park, has lived off gambling and catering for the desires of the idle international rich for the last hundred years. Meanwhile, it has become one of the greatest property speculation sites in the world – a sort of low-rise Manhattan-on-Sea with an incredibly dense concentration of *fin-de-siècle* Edwardian hotels standing in for the skyscrapers.

The principality has been in the hands of the ruling Grimaldi family since the thirteenth century, and legally Monaco would once again become part of France were the royal line to die out. The current ruler, Prince Rainier, is the one constitutionally autocratic ruler left in Europe, under whose nose every French law is passed for approval prior to being applied to Monaco. There is a parliament, but with limited functions and elected only by Monegasque nationals – about sixteen percent of the population. But there is no opposition to the ruling family. The citizens and non-French residents pay no income tax and their riches are protected by rigorous security forces; Monaco has more police per square metre than any other country in the world.

One time to avoid Monaco – unless you're a motor-racing enthusiast – is the last week in May, when racing cars burn around the port and casino for the Formula 1 **Monaco Grand Prix**. Every space in sight of the circuit is inaccessible without a ticket, making casual sightseeing out of the question.

PHONING MONACO

Monaco phone numbers have only eight digits and no -04 French area code. If you are phoning from France you must dial Monaco's international code 00377-, then the number (leaving out the first 0).

The Principality

The oldest part of the two-kilometre-long state is **Monaco-Ville**, around the palace on the high rocky promontory, with the new suburb and marina of **Fontvieille** in its western shadow. **La Condamine** is the old port quarter on the other side of the promontory; **Larvotto**, the bathing resort with artificial beaches of imported sand, reaches to the eastern border; and **Monte-Carlo** is in the middle.

Monte-Carlo

Monte-Carlo is the area of Monaco where the real money is flung about, and its famous **casino** (*www.casino-monte-carlo.com*; bus #1 or #2) demands to be seen. Entrance is restricted to over-21s and you may have to show your passport; dress code is rigid, with shorts and T-shirts frowned upon, and skirts, jackets and ties more or less obligatory for the more interesting sections. Bags and large coats are checked at the door.

Day-trippers and gambling *dilettantes* usually don't enter the casino proper, but head for the small room of one-armed bandits and poker machines (free) by the main entrance. Without further commitment you can also wander around the impressive entry hall, use the luxurious toilets and check out the small theatre (containing temporary exhibitions). The first gambling hall of the inner sanctum is the **Salons Européens** (open from noon; 50F/€7.63), where further slot machines surround the American roulette, craps and blackjack tables, the managers are Vegas-trained, the lights low and the air oppressively smoky. Above this slice of Nevada, however, the decor is *fin-de-siècle* Rococo extravagance, while the ceilings in the adjoining Pink Salon Bar are adorned with female nudes smoking cigarettes. The heart of the place is the **Salons Privés** (from 3pm), through the Salles Touzet. To get in, you have to look like a gambler, not a tourist (no cameras), and dispense with 100F/€15.25 at the door. Much larger and more richly decorated than the European Rooms, its early-afternoon or out-of-season atmosphere is that of a cathedral. No clinking coins, just sliding chips and softly spoken croupiers. Elderly gamblers pace silently, fingering hefty banknotes (the maximum unnegotiated stake here is 500,000F/€76,000), closed-circuit TV cameras above the chandeliers watch the gamblers watching the tables, and no one drinks. On midsummer evenings the place is packed out and the vice loses its sacred and exclusive touch.

Adjoining the casino is the gaudy **opera house**, and around the palm-tree-lined place du Casino are more casinos plus the city's palace-hotels and *grands cafés*. The *American Bar* of the **Hôtel de Paris** is, according to its publicity, the place where "the world's most elite society" meets. As long as you dress up and are prepared to be challenged if you haven't ordered a 200F/€30.50 drink, you can entertain yourself free of charge against the background of Belle Époque decadence by watching humans whose bank accounts are possibly the most interesting thing about them.

Monaco-Ville and Fontvieille

After the casino, the amusements of the glacé-iced **Monaco-Ville** (bus #1 or #2) where every other shop sells Prince Rainier mugs and assorted junk, are less rewarding. You can trail gasping round the state apartments of the **Palace** (daily: June–Sept 9.30am–6.20pm; Oct 10am–5pm; 30F/€4.58); look at waxwork princes in **L'Historial des Princes de Monaco**, 27 rue Basse (daily: Feb–Oct 9.30am–7pm; rest of year 10.30am–5pm; 24F/€3.66); watch a dreadful slide show on different aspects of the place in the **Monte Carlo Story** (daily: March–June, Sept & Oct 11am–5pm; July & Aug 11am–6pm; Nov–Feb 2–5pm; 38F/€5.80); or traipse around the tombs of the former princes and Princess Grace in the neo-Romanesque-Byzantine **cathedral**, whose right-hand transept features a reredos by Louis Bréa.

One point of real interest in the old town, however, is to be found on the place de la Visitation; the **Musée de la Chapelle de la Visitation** (Tues–Sun 10am–4pm;

20F/€3.05), displaying a part of the collection of religious art of Barbara Piasecka Johnson. This small but exquisite collection includes works by Zurbarán, Rivera, Rubens, and even an extremely rare, early religious work by Vermeer.

Perhaps the best site to visit in the whole of Monaco is the **aquarium** in the basement of the imposing **Musée Océanographique** (daily: July & Aug 9am–8pm; rest of year 9.30am–7pm; 60F/€9.15), where the fishy beings outdo the weirdest Kandinsky or Hieronymus Bosch creations. Less exceptional, but still peculiar, cactus equivalents can be viewed in the **Jardin Exotique**, on boulevard du Jardin Exotique high above Fontvieille (daily: mid-May to mid-Sept 9am–7pm; rest of year 9am–nightfall; 40F/€6.10; bus #2).

There are yet more museums in **Fontvieille**, the part of town just south of the palace, including collections of His Serene Highness's cars (daily 10am–6pm; 30F/€4.58), his coins and stamps (daily: July & Aug 10am–6pm; rest of year 10am–5pm; 20F/€3.05), his puppets (daily 10am–12.45pm & 2.30–6.30pm; 30F/€4.58) and his model ships (daily 10am–6pm; 25F/€3.81), plus a zoo of his rare wild animals (daily: Feb–May 10am–noon & 2–6pm; June–Sept 9am–noon & 2–7pm; Oct–Feb 10am–noon & 2–5pm; 20F/€3.05), at the **Terrasses de Fontvieille** (bus #6) by the port.

Near the Larvotto beach, the **Musée National**, 17 av Princesse Grace (daily: Easter–Sept 10am–6.30pm; rest of year 10am–12.15pm & 2.30–6.30pm; 30F/€4.58), is

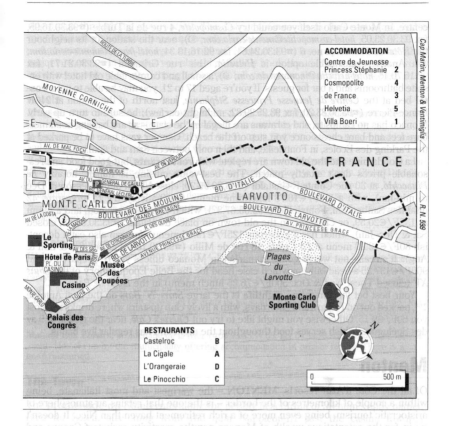

dedicated to the history of **dolls and automata**, and is better than sceptics would think: some of the dolls' house scenes and the creepy automata are quite surreal and fun.

Practicalities

The **gare SNCF** is on avenue Prince-Pierre in La Condamine, a short walk from the main **gare routière** on place d'Armes. Municipal buses ply the length of the principality from 7am to 8pm (8.50F/€1.30 single; four-trip card 21F/€3.20). Buses following the lower corniche stop at the *gare routière*; other routes have a variety of stations; all stop in Monte Carlo. Local bus #4 runs from the *gare SNCF* to the "Casino-Tourisme" stop, close to the **tourist office** at 2a bd des Moulins (Mon–Sat 9am–7pm, Sun 10am–noon; ☎92.16.61.66, fax 92.16.60.00, *www.monaco-congress.com*). One very useful public service is the incredibly clean and efficient **free lift** linking the lower and higher streets (marked on the tourist office map). **Bicycles** can be rented from Auto-Moto-Garage, 7 rue de Millo, off place d'Armes (☎93.50.10.80).

The best areas for **hotels** are La Condamine and Beausoleil, just across the northern boundary in France, where you'll find the pleasant *Villa Boeri*, at 29 bd du Général-Leclerc (☎04.93.78.38.10, fax 04.93.41.90.95; ①), only a couple minutes' walk from Monte Carlo

It can be visited without matrimonial intentions by asking the receptionist at the main door. On the wall above the official's desk, a couple face each other with strange topological connections between the sun, her headdress and his fisherman's cap. A *Saracen Wedding Party* on the right-hand wall reveals a disapproving mother of the bride, the spurned girlfriend of the groom and her armed, revengeful brother among the cheerful guests. On the left-hand wall is the story of *Orpheus and Eurydice* at the moment when Orpheus has just looked back. Meanwhile, on the ceiling are *Poetry Rides Pegasus* and tattered *Science Juggles with the Planets*, and *Love*, open-eyed, waiting with bow and arrow at the ready. Adding a little extra confusion, the carpet is mock panther-skin.

On avenue de la Madone, at the other end of the modern town, an impressive collection of paintings from the Middle Ages to the twentieth century can be seen in the **Palais Carnolès** (daily except Tues 10am–noon & 2–6pm; free; bus #3), the old summer residence of the princes of Monaco. Of the early works, the *Madonna and Child with St Francis* by Louis Bréa is exceptional. The most recent include canvases by Graham Sutherland, who spent some of his last years in Menton.

If it's cool enough to be walking outside, the public parks up in the hills and the gardens of **Garavan**'s once elegant villas make a change from shingle beaches. The best of all the Garavan gardens is **Les Colombières**, just north of boulevard de Garavan (Mon–Fri 10am–noon & 3–5pm; but check first with the Service du Patrimoine, ☎04.93.35.32.83, as it is sometimes closed for works; 20F/€3.05; bus #8, direction "Bd de Garavan", stop "Colombières"). Designed by the artist Ferdinand Bac, they lead you through every Mediterranean style of garden. There are staircases screened by cypresses; balustrades to lean against for the soaring views through pines and olive trees out to sea; fountains, statues and a frescoed swimming pool. The rest of the year, you'll have to make do with the public **Parc du Pian**, shaded by olive trees, nearer to the *vieille ville* on the same bus route as Les Colombières, and the **Jardin Exotique** (daily except Tues: June–Sept 10am–12.30pm & 3–6pm; rest of year 10am–12.30pm & 2–5pm; 20F/€3.05), both below boulevard de Garavan.

Eating and drinking

Surprisingly, Menton is not blessed with streets of gorgeous Provençal **restaurants**. If you're not bothered about what you eat as long as it's cheap, the pedestrianized rue St-Michel is promising ground. For a proper **restaurant** meal in very elegant surroundings, there's *Le Café Fiori* in *Hôtel Les Ambassadeurs*, 2 rue du Louvre (☎04.93.28.75.75; open summer evenings and winter daily lunch & dinner), with an evening bistro menu for 185F/€28.21. Menton also has two excellent Moroccan restaurants, both around the 200F/€30.50 mark: *Le Darkoum*, 23 rue St-Michel (☎04.93.35.44.88), and *La Mamounia*, 51 porte de France, Garavan (☎04.93.57.95.39).

travel details

Trains

Cannes to: Antibes (every 10–20min; 13min); Biot (every 10–20 min; 17min); Cagnes-sur-Mer (every 10–20min; 24min); Juan-les-Pins (every 10–20min; 10min); Marseille (every 10–20min; 1hr 05min); Monaco (every 10–20min; 1hr 10min); Menton (every 10–20min; 1hr 25min); Nice (every

10–20min; 25–40min); St-Raphaël (every 10–20min; 25–35min).

Marseille to: Aix (every 10–20min; 30–35min); Arles (every 10–20min; 45min); Avignon (every 10–20min; 55min–1hr 15min); Briançon (4–6 daily; 4hr 05min); Cannes (every 10–20min; 1hr 05min); Cassis (every 30min; 20–25min); Hyères

(2 daily; 1hr 25min); La Ciotat (every 30min; 25–30min); Les Arcs-Draguignan (hourly; 1hr 20min–2hr 15min); Lyon (8 daily; 2hr 35min); Menton (8 daily; 3hr 25min–4hr); Nice (every 10–20min; 2hr 20min–3hr 30min); Paris (10 daily; 4hr 20min–8 hr 35min; estimated 3hr 30min when TGV link completed – details from *www.sncf.fr*); St-Raphaël (every 10–20min; 1hr 45min); Toulon (every 10–20min; 40min–1hr 05min).

Nice to: Beaulieu-sur-Mer (every 10–20min; 13min); Cagnes-sur-Mer (every 10–20min; 15min); Cap d'Ail (every 10–20min; 18min); Cap Martin-Roquebrune (every 10–20min; 37min); Digne (4 daily; 3hr 10min); Eze-sur-Mer (every 10–20min; 18min); Draguignan (every 10–20min; 1hr 30min); Marseille (every 10–20min; 2hr 45min–3hr 15min); Menton (every 10–20min; 35min); Paris (7 daily; 10hr 40min–12hr); St-Raphaël (every 10–20min; 1hr–1hr 20min); Sospel (4 daily; 50min); Tende (4 daily, 2 changing at Breil-sur-Roya; 2hr 10min); Villefranche-sur-Mer (every 10–20min; 9min).

St-Raphaël to: Boulouris (9 daily; 4min); Cannes (every 10–20min; 35min); Marseille (every 10–20min; 1hr 45min); Nice (every 10–20min; 1hr–1hr 20min).

Toulon to: Hyères (4 daily; 20min); Marseille (every 10–20min; 1hr 05min).

Buses

Cannes to: Antibes (every 10–20min; 30min); Biot (every 10–20min; 40min); Cagnes-sur-Mer (every 20min; 50min); Grasse (every 10–20min; 45min); Golfe de Juan (every 10–20min; 15min); Nice (every 10–20min; 1hr 20min); Nice Airport (hourly; 45min–1hr 30min); St-Raphaël (3–7 daily; 1hr 10min); Vallauris (every 10–20min; 15min).

Hyères to: Bormes (every 10–20min; 25min); La Croix-Valmer (8 daily; 1hr 15min); Le Lavandou (every 10–20min; 35min); Le Rayol (8 daily; 55min); St-Tropez (8 daily; 1hr 35min–1hr 45min); Toulon (every 30min; 35–50min).

Le Lavandou to: Bormes (6 daily; 30min); Cogolin (2 daily; 40min); Grimaud (2 daily; 45min); Hyères (every 10–20min; 35min); La Croix-Valmer (8–9 daily; 40min); La Garde Freinet (2 daily; 1hr); Le Rayol (8–9 daily; 20min); St-Tropez (8 daily; 55min–1hr 05min); Toulon (every 10–20min; 1hr 10min).

Marseille to: Aix (every 10–20min; 25–30min); Arles (4 daily; 2hr 10min–2hr 30min); Aubagne (every 10–20min; 20–30min); Barcelonnette (2 daily; 3hr 55min); Cassis (7 daily; 50min); Digne (4 daily; 2hr–2hr 30min); Grenoble (1 daily; 3hr 55min); La Ciotat (8 daily; 1hr 05min); Sisteron (5–6 daily; 2hr 25min).

Menton to: Monaco (every 10–20min; 25min); Nice (every 10–20min; 1hr); Sospel (3 daily; 35–55min).

Monaco to: Eze-Village (7 daily; 35min); Menton (every 10–20min; 25min); Nice (every 10–20min; 30–40min); La Turbie (5–6 daily; 30min).

Nice to: Aix (3–5 daily; 2hr 20min–4hr 25min); Beaulieu (every 10–20min; 15–20min); Cagnes-sur-Mer (every 10–20min; 25–50min); Digne (1–2 daily; 2hr 55min–3hr 25min); Draguignan (3 weekly; 1hr 15min); Eze-sur-Mer (every 10–20min; 20min); Eze-Village (3–7 daily; 20min); Grasse (every 10–20min; 1hr 05min–1hr 15min); La Turbie (4 daily; 40min); Menton (every 10–20min; 1hr 05min); Monaco (every 10–20min; 30–40min); Roquebrune (every 10–20min; 40–55min); St-Jean (every 10–20min; 25min); St-Paul (every 10–20min; 40–45min); Sisteron (1–2 daily; 3hr 45min–4hr 10min); Toulon (2 daily from place Masséna; 2hr 30min); Vence (every 10–20min; 50min); Villefranche (14 daily; 10–15min).

St-Raphaël to: Cannes (10–13 daily; 1hr 10min); Cogolin (7 daily; 1hr–1hr 25min); Draguignan (10–12 daily; 1hr 15min–1hr 25min); La Foux (8 daily; 1hr 15min); Fréjus (every 10–20min; 10min); Grimaud (8 daily; 1hr); Nice Airport (3 daily; 1hr 05min); Ste-Maxime (10 daily; 30–40min); St-Tropez (8–10 daily; 1hr–1hr 25min).

St-Tropez to: Bormes (8 daily; 1hr 05min–1hr 15min); Cogolin (8 daily; 15min); Gassin (1 daily; 25min); Grimaud (8 daily; 20–35min); Hyères (8 daily; 1hr 30min–1hr 40min); La Croix-Valmer (8 daily; 20min); La Garde Freinet (1 daily; 45min); Le Lavandou (8 daily; 55min–1hr 05min); Le Rayol (8 daily; 40–55min); Ramatuelle (1 daily; 25min); Ste-Maxime (8 daily; 45min); St-Raphaël (8–10 daily; 1hr–1hr 25min); Toulon (8 daily; 2hr–2hr 15min).

Toulon to: Aix (4 daily; 1hr 15min); Draguignan (5 daily; 2hr 10min); Hyères (every 30min; 35–50min); La Croix-Valmer (7 daily; 1hr 50min); Le Lavandou (7 daily; 1hr 10min); Nice (2 daily; 2hr

30min); St-Raphaël (4 daily; 2hr); St-Tropez (8 daily; 2hr 15min).

Flights

Hyères to: Corsica (2 daily; 50min); Lille (April–Sept 1 weekly; 1hr 25min); Paris (10 daily; 1hr 25min).

Marseille to: London (4 daily; 1hr 30min); Lyon (3–5 daily; 40min); New York (4–6 daily; 8hr 30min); Paris (21 daily; 1hr 05min).

Nice to: Lille (1 daily; 1hr 30min); London (9 daily; 2hr 05min); Lyon (4 daily; 50min); New York (4 daily; 9hr); Ottawa (2 weekly; 8hr 30min); Paris (every 10–20min; 1hr 20min).

Ferries

For Îles d'Hyères and Îles de Lérins services, see box on p.987 & p.1007.

Marseille to: Corsica (4–10 weekly; 8–12 hr).

Nice to: Corsica (April–Sept daily; Oct–May 1 daily–3 weekly; 2hr 30min–11hr 30min).

Toulon to: Corsica (2–5 weekly; 7–11hr).

CHAPTER SIXTEEN

CORSICA

A round one-and-three-quarter million people visit Corsica each year, drawn by a climate that's mild even in winter and by some of the most astonishingly diverse landscapes in Europe. Nowhere in the Mediterranean are there beaches finer than Corsica's perfect half-moon bays of white sand and transparent water, or seascapes more inspiring than the granite cliffs of the west coast. Even though the annual influx of tourists now exceeds the island's population sevenfold, tourism has not spoilt the place: there are a few resorts, but overdevelopment is rare and high-rise blocks are confined to the main towns.

Set on the western Mediterranean trade routes, the island has always been of strategic and commercial appeal. Greeks, Carthaginians and Romans came in successive waves, driving native Corsicans into the interior. The Romans were ousted by Vandals, and for the following thirteen centuries the island was attacked, abandoned, settled and sold as a nation-state, with generations of islanders fighting against foreign government. Two hundred years of French rule have had a limited effect on Corsica, and the island's Baroque churches, Genoese fortresses, fervent Catholic rituals and a Tuscan-influenced indigenous language and cuisine show a more profound affinity with neighbouring Italy.

Corsica's uneasy relationship with its motherland has worsened in recent decades. Economic neglect and the French government's reluctance to encourage Corsican language and culture spawned a nationalist movement in the early 1970s, whose clandestine armed wings are still engaged in a bloody conflict with the central government. The violence seldom affects tourists but signs of the "troubles" are everywhere, from the black "Corsica Nazione" graffiti sprayed over roadsigns, to the bullet holes plastering public buildings.

The late 1990s also saw a marked upsurge in political assassinations, most of them episodes in long-standing vendetta-style feuds between rival separatist factions and their Mafia partners. Attempts by Alain Juppé's Gaullist government to diffuse the crisis became embroiled in controversy when the prime minister himself was accused of conducting secret negotiations with the nationalist paramilitaries, while outwardly insisting he "never talked to terrorists". Lionel Jospin's socialist government has fared little better. It kept alive an eight-month ceasefire, but this ended violently in February 1998 when the island's popular prefect (the de facto governor of Corsica) was shot dead on the streets of Ajaccio. Although none of the mutually loathing terrorist groups

---

ACCOMMODATION PRICE CODES

Each hotel and guesthouse in this book has been graded according to the following price codes, which indicate the price for the **cheapest double room available during the high season.**

① Under 160F/€24	④ 300–400F/€46–61	⑦ 600–700F/€91–107
② 160–220F/€24–34	⑤ 400–500F/€61–76	⑧ 700–800F/€107–122
③ 220–300F/€34–46	⑥ 500–600F/€76–91	⑨ Over 800F/€122

Bastia and around

The dominant tone of Corsica's most successful commercial town, **BASTIA**, is one of charismatic dereliction, as the city's industrial zone is spread onto the lowlands to the south, leaving the centre of town with plenty of aged charm. The old quarter, known as the Terra Vecchia, comprises a tightly packed network of haphazard streets, flamboyant Baroque churches and lofty tenements, their crumbling golden-grey walls set against a backdrop of *maquis*-covered hills. Terra Nova, the historic district on the opposite side of the old port, is a tidier area that's now Bastia's yuppie quarter.

The city dates from Roman times, when a base was set up at Biguglia to the south, although Bastia began to thrive under the Genoese, when wine was exported to the Italian mainland from Porto Cardo, forerunner of Bastia's Vieux Port, or Terra Vecchia. Despite the fact that in 1811 Napoléon appointed Ajaccio capital of the island, initiating a rivalry between the two towns which exists to this day, Bastia soon established a stronger trading position with mainland France. The Nouveau Port, created in 1862 to cope with the increasing traffic with France and Italy, became the mainstay of the local economy, exporting chiefly agricultural products from Cap Corse, Balagne and the eastern plain.

Arrival, information and accommodation

Bastia's **Poretta airport** is 16km south of town off the Route Nationale (☎04.95.54.54.54). Shuttle buses into the centre coincide with flights, dropping passengers opposite the train station for a fare of 50F/€7.60 (the journey takes thirty minutes); taxis charge around 200F/€30.40. **Ferries** arrive at the Nouveau Port, just a five-minute walk from the centre of town; the SNCM office is at 15 bd de Gaulle (☎04.95.54.66.88). Bastia doesn't have a proper **bus station**, which can cause confusion, with services arriving and departing from different locations around the north side of the main square. Buses from Ajaccio, Bonifacio, Porto-Vecchio and the east coast stop outside the travel agents opposite the post office (PTT) on avenue Maréchal-Sébastiani, whereas those coming from Calvi pull in outside the train station. Local suburban services, and those from St-Florent and Cap Corse, work out of a small square on the north side of avenue Maréchal-Sébastiani – which, confusingly, is referred to as the *gare routière*, even though it's little more than a lay-by. A summary of bus times and departure points is available at the **tourist office**, at the north end of place St-Nicolas (June to mid-Sept daily 8am–8pm; mid-Sept to May Mon–Sat 8am–6pm, Sun & holidays 9am–1pm; ☎04.95.31.81.34). You can access the **Internet** at *Gigatec*, 8 rue Fontaine-Neuve, just above the Vieux Port, one of Corsica's few Internet cafés (Mon–Sat 10am–8pm; minimum 40F/€6.08 for the first hour, and 20F/€3 per hour thereafter).

You can rent **cars** from Avis/Ollandini, 40 bd Paoli (☎04.95.32.57.30), or at the airport (☎04.95.54.55.46); and Europcar, 1 rue du Nouveau Port (☎04.95.31.50.91), or at the airport (☎04.95.30.09.50). **Bikes** can be rented from Locacycles, behind the Palais de Justice (☎04.95.32.30.64), and **scooters** and **motorcycles** from Plaisance Service Location, in the marina (☎04.95.31.49.01). **Luggage** may be left at the Nouveau Port's *gare maritime* (daily 8–11.30am & 2–7.30pm; 15F/€2.28 per item per day); there's another *consigne* at the train station, but it's a lot more expensive.

Although you are usually guaranteed to find somewhere to **stay** in Bastia, the choice of hotels is not great. Apart from the *Posta-Vecchia*, the classier places line the road to Cap Corse north of the port; the more basic ones are found in the centre of town, and there are a few even cheaper small *pensions* around the Nouveau Port.

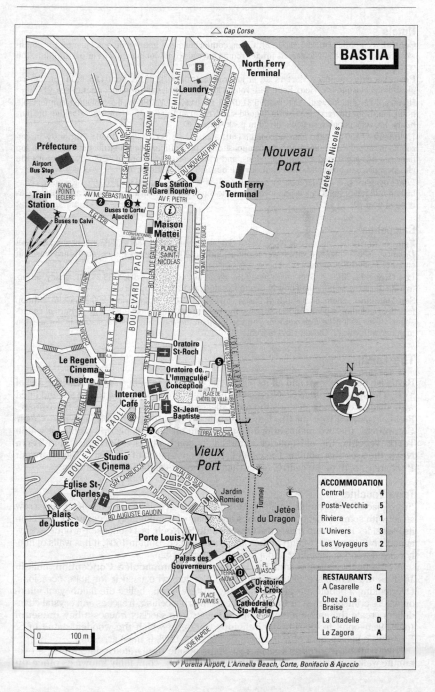

△ Cap Corse

BASTIA

North Ferry Terminal

Laundry

Nouveau Port

Préfecture

Airport Bus Stop

❶ Bus Station (Gare Routière)

South Ferry Terminal

Train Station

Buses to Corte/Ajaccio ❸

Buses to Calvi

❷

ⓘ

Maison Mattei

PLACE SAINT-NICOLAS

Jetée St. Nicolas

❹

RUE MIOT

Oratoire St-Roch

Le Regent Cinema Theatre

Oratoire de L'Immaculée Conception ❺

PLACE DE L'HÔTEL DE VILLE

Internet Café @

Ⓐ

St-Jean Baptiste

TERRA VECCHIA

Studio Cinema

Vieux Port

N

Église St-Charles

Jardin Romieu

Tunnel

Jetée du Dragon

Palais de Justice

Porte Louis-XVI

Palais des Gouverneurs

Ⓒ

TERRA NOVA

Ⓓ

PL GUASCO

Oratoire St-Croix

PLACE D'ARMES

Cathédrale Ste-Marie

VOIE RAPIDE

0   100 m

Poretta Airport, L'Arinella Beach, Corte, Bonifacio & Ajaccio

ACCOMMODATION	
Central	4
Posta-Vecchia	5
Riviera	1
L'Univers	3
Les Voyageurs	2

RESTAURANTS	
A Casarelle	C
Chez Jo La Braise	B
La Citadelle	D
Le Zagora	A

Hotels

Central, 3 rue Miot (☎04.95.31.71.12). Clean, comfortable and good-value hotel just off the south-west corner of place St-Nicolas. Its pricier rooms have air-conditioning and en-suite bathrooms; the rest share toilets. ③.

Posta-Vecchia, quai des Martyrs de la Libération (☎04.95.32.32.38, fax 04.95.32.14.05). Smart, plush hotel close to the Vieux Port, with rooms looking onto a narrow alley or out to sea. ④.

Riviera, 1 rue du Nouveau Port (☎04.95.31.07.16, fax 04.95.34.17.39). Well-established, comfortable hotel, handy for the ferry port, with 20 good-sized, clean and airy rooms (some overlooking the harbour). It's very popular, so book ahead in peak season. ④.

L'Univers, 3 av du Maréchal-Sébastiani (☎04.95.31.03.38, fax 04.95.31.19.91). Variously priced rooms in an old, institutional tenement opposite the post office. Their no-frills options on the top floor (no lift) are frayed around the edges, and traffic noise is a problem at the front, but it's the cheapest place in town and convenient for the bus and train stations. ③.

Les Voyageurs, 9 av Maréchal-Sebastiani (☎04.95.34.90.80, fax 04.95.30.00.65). Recently refurbished mid-range hotel in a prime location at the top of town. Their budget rooms are a particularly good deal. ④.

Campsites

Esperenza, rte de Pineto (☎04.95.36.15.09). Located about 20km south of Bastia, beyond the *San Damiano* (see below) and with fewer facilities, but close to the beach and cheap. Hourly buses in summer from the *gare routière*.

Les Orangers, Miomo, 5km north along the route to Cap Corse (☎04.95.33.24.09). Shady, attractive site near the sea; the half-hourly bus to Erbalunga will drop you here.

San Damiano, Pineto, 6km south of Bastia (☎04.95.33.68.02). Huge, pricey 200-place site with top facilities, including a pool and jacuzzi; take the road to the left across the bridge at Furiani roundabout. Buses as for the *Esperenza*, or you can jump on the train (the nearest station is Rocade, ten minutes' walk away). Closed Nov–March.

The Town

Bastia isn't a large town and all its sights can easily be seen in a day without the use of a car. The spacious **place St-Nicolas** is the focus of town life: open to the sea and lined with shady trees and cafés, it's the most pleasant spot for soaking up the atmosphere. Running parallel to it on the landward side are **boulevard Paoli** and **rue César Campinchi**, the two main shopping streets, but all Bastia's historic sights lie within **Terra Vecchia**, the old quarter immediately south of place St-Nicolas, and **Terra Nova**, the area surrounding the citadel. There's not much of interest in the **Nouveau Port** area, north of the centre, other than restaurants and downmarket bars.

Terra Vecchia

From place St-Nicolas the main route into Terra Vecchia is rue Napoléon, a narrow street with some ancient offbeat shops and a pair of sumptuously decorated chapels on its east side. The first of these, the **Oratoire de St-Roch**, is a Genoese Baroque extravagance, reflecting the wealth of the rising bourgeoisie. Built in 1604, it has walls of finely carved wooden panelling and a magnificent gilt organ.

A little further along stands the **Oratoire de L'Immaculée Conception**, built in 1611 as the showplace of the Genoese in Corsica, who used it for state occasions. Overlooking a pebble mosaic of a sun, the austere facade belies the flamboyant interior, where crimson velvet draperies, a gilt and marble ceiling, frescoes and crystal chandeliers create the ambience of an opera house. The sacristy houses a tiny **museum** (daily 9am–6pm; free) of minor religious works, of which the wooden statue of St Erasmus, a patron saint of fishermen, dating from 1788, is most arresting.

If you cut back through the narrow steps beside the Oratoire de St-Roch, a two-minute walk will bring you to place de l'Hôtel-de-Ville, commonly known as **place du**

Marché after the half-hearted farmers' **market** that takes place here each morning. Shouldering the south end of the square is the **church of St-Jean-Baptiste**, an immense ochre edifice that dominates the Vieux Port. Its twin campaniles are Bastia's distinguishing feature, but the interior is less than impressive – built in 1636, the church was restored in the eighteenth century in a hideous Rococo overkill of multicoloured marble. Decorating the walls are a few unremarkable Italian paintings from Napoléon's uncle, Cardinal Fesch, an avid collector of Renaissance art (see p.1072).

Around the church extends the oldest part of Bastia, a secretive zone of dark alleys, vaulted passageways and seven-storey houses. By turning right outside the church and following rue St-Jean you'll come to rue General-Carbuccia, the heart of Terra Vecchia. Corsican independence leader Pascal Paoli once lived here, at no. 7, and Balzac stayed briefly at no. 23 when his ship got stuck in Corsica on the way to Sardinia. Set in a small square at the end of the road is the **church of St-Charles**, a Jesuit chapel whose wide steps provide an evening meeting place for the locals; opposite stands the **Maison de Caraffa**, an elegant house with a strikingly graceful balcony.

The **Vieux Port** is easily the most photogenic part of town: soaring houses seem to bend inwards towards the water and peeling plaster and boat hulls glint in the sun, while the south side remains in the shadow of the great rock that supports the citadel. Site of the original Roman settlement of *Porto Cardo*, the Vieux Port later bustled with Genoese traders, but since the building of the ferry terminal and commercial docks it has become a backwater. The most atmospheric time to come here is early evening, when huge flocks of swifts swirl in noisy clouds above the harbour. Things liven up after sunset, with the glow and noise from the waterside bars and restaurants, which continue round the north end of the port along the wide **quai des Martyrs de la Libération**, where live bands clank out pop covers for the tourists in summer.

A small "Cuncolta" sign above a door on the north side of the Vieux Port marks the spot where a car bomb exploded in July 1996, killing a prominent nationalist, and seriously injuring Charles Pieri, national secretary of A Cuncolta, the political front of the island's main paramilitary movement, the FLNC. Fourteen other people were hurt in the blast, which was the first time a bomb had been planted in a public place, in broad daylight, since the begining of the troubles in Corsica.

Terra Nova

The military and administrative core of old Bastia, Terra Nova (or the citadel) has a distinct air of affluence, its lofty apartments now colonized by Bastia's yuppies. The area is focused on **place du Donjon**, which gets its name from the squat round tower that formed the nucleus of Bastia's fortifications and was used by the Genoese to incarcerate Corsican patriots – Sampiero Corso was held in the dungeon for four years in the early sixteenth century. Next to the tower, the strategically placed *Bar de la Citadelle* commands a magnificent view that extends to Elba on a clear day.

Facing the bar is the impressive fourteenth-century **Palais des Gouverneurs**. With its great round tower, arcaded courtyard and pristine peach-coloured paintwork, this building has a distinctly Moorish feel and was built for the governor and local bishop during the town's Genoese heyday. When the French transferred the capital to Ajaccio it became a prison, then was destroyed during the British attack of 1794 (in which an ambitious young captain named Horatio Nelson played a decisive part). The subsequent rebuilding was not the last, as parts of it were blown up by the Americans in 1943, and today the restorers are trying to regain something of the building's former grandeur. Part of the palace is given over to the **Musée d'Éthnographie** (daily: June–Aug 9am–6.30pm; Sept–May 9am–noon & 2–6pm; 18F/€2.74), which presents the history of Corsica from prehistoric times to the present day. Its vaulted chambers contain some fascinating historical tidbits, including a diminutive Roman sarcophagus decorated with hunting scenes, busts of famous Corsicans and an original 1755 Flag of Independence, with its distinctive Moorish emblem.

Back in place du Donjon, if you cross the square and follow rue Notre-Dame you'll come out at the **church of Ste-Marie**. Built in 1458 and overhauled in the seventeenth century, it was the cathedral of Bastia until 1801, when the bishopric was transferred to Ajaccio. The over-restored facade is an ugly shade of peach, and there's nothing of interest inside except a small silver statue of the Virgin. Virtually next door, in rue de l'Evêché, stands the **Oratoire Ste-Croix**, a sixteenth-century church decorated in Louis XV style, all rich blue paint and gilt scrollwork. It houses another holy item, the *Christ des Miracles*, a blackened oak crucifix which in 1428 was discovered floating in the sea surrounded by a luminous haze. Beyond the church, the narrow streets open out onto the tiny **place Guasco**, a delightful square at the heart of the citadel that typifies the exclusivity of Terra Nova. A few benches offer the chance of a rest before descending into the fray.

The beaches

Crowded with schoolchildren in the summer, the pebbly town **beach** in Bastia is only worth visiting if you're desperate for a swim. To reach it, go left at the flower shop on the main road south out of town, just beyond the citadel. A better alternative is the long beach of **L'Arinella** at Montesoro, a further 1km along the same road, the beginning of a sandy shore that extends along the whole east coast. A bus to L'Arinella leaves from outside *Café Riche* on boulevard Paoli every twenty minutes; just get off at the last stop and cross the train line to the sea. There are a couple of sailing and windsurfing clubs here, and a bar.

Eating and drinking

Numerous pizza vans are scattered about town, evidence of a strong Italian influence that's also apparent in the predominance of **pizzerias** and pasta places in the Nouveau Port area. The town also boasts some excellent inexpensive **restaurants** serving Corsican specialities: the posh places on the quai des Martyrs do the best *aziminu*, a Corsican version of *bouillabaisse*. Most of the good restaurants are to be found around the Vieux Port and on the quai des Martyrs, with a sprinkling in the citadel.

Drinking is serious business in Bastia, with the Casanis *pastis* factory on the outskirts of town in Lupino making the town's favourite drink. There are many bars and cafés all over town, varying from the stark and brightly lit bars of Terra Vecchia, which are the haunt of old men, to the elegant, dimly lit cafés on place St-Nicolas, which entertain a younger, more lively clientele. For a more sedate atmosphere, boulevard Paoli and rue Campinchi are lined with chi-chi *salons de thé* offering elaborate creamy confections, local chestnut cake and doughnuts.

Bars and cafés

Bar de la Citadelle, in front of the Palais des Gouverneurs. Basically a sandwich and ice-cream bar that would have little to recommend it were it not for its superb location overlooking the Vieux Port.

Café des Palmiers, place St-Nicolas. One of the few cafés along this stretch, with comfy wicker chairs that catch the sun at breakfast time and attentive service. Makes delicious fresh pastries.

Le Pub Assunta, 5 place Fontaine-Neuve. Large, lively bar with a good selection of draught beers, a snooker table on its mezzanine floor and a terrace opening onto the old quarter. Serves fast food indoors or on the shady terrace outside, and puts on live music nights with local bands on Thursdays.

Restaurants

A Casarella, 6 rue Ste-Croix (☎04.95.32.02.32). Innovative Corsican-French cuisine served on a terrace on the edge of the citadel. House specialities include *casgiate* (nuggets of fresh cheese baked in fragrant chestnut leaves) and the rarely prepared *storzzappretti* – balls of *brocciu*, spinach and herbs in tomato sauce. À la carte only; count on around 150F/€22.80 per head. Closed Sat & Sun lunchtimes.

Chez Jo La Braise, 7 bd Hyacinte-de-Montrea (☎04.95.31.36.97). Authentic Corsican pizzeria, whose succulent meat dishes and pizzas, cooked over wood grills with *maquis* herbs, have made its owner (a Choowawa-Indian Russian retired boxer) something of a local celebrity. The *tarte aux herbes* is a must for vegetarians, and Jo is deservedly proud of his banana *flambé*. Bank on around 100F/€15.20 for the full works. Closed Sun & Aug.

Le Citadelle, 6 rue du Dragon, Citadelle (☎04.95.31.44.70). Gorgeous gourmet restaurant at the heart of Terra Nova, serving classy French cuisine inside a vaulted cellar with mellow lighting. Prices are high (180F/€27.36 *menu fixe*, or around 220F/€33.44 à la carte without wine), but this is simply one of the finest places to eat on the island. Try one of their to-die-for desserts (the *mille-feuille aux fruits rouges* is sublime).

Le Zagora, Vieux Port. An attractively decorated Moroccan restaurant with great views over the harbour. Try their delicious veal with plums and almonds, washed down with mint tea. Around 150F/€22.80 per head.

La Marana, Mariana and the Étang de Biguglia

Traditionally the summer haunt of prosperous Bastia families, the sixteen-kilometre littoral known as **LA MARANA** lies a few kilometres south of Bastia. The beach here offers shady pine woods, restaurants and bars, though the sea is quite polluted. The whole of this part of the coast is divided into holiday residences or sections of beach attached to bars, the latter freely open to the public.

Fed by the rivers Bevinco and Golo, the **Étang de Biguglia** is the largest lagoon in Corsica, and one of its best sites for rare migrant birds. In summer, reed and cetti warblers nest in the reeds, while in winter, Biguglia supports a resident community of grey herons, kingfishers, great crested grebes, little grebes, water rails and various species of duck, such as the spectacular red-crested pochard, immediately identifiable by its red bill, red feet and a bright-red head.

The Roman town of **MARIANA**, just south of Étang de Biguglia, can be approached by taking the turning for Bastia's Poretta airport, 16km along the N193, or the more scenic coastal route through La Marana. It was founded in 93 BC as a military colony, but today's houses, baths and basilica are too ruined to be of great interest. It's only the square baptistry, with its remarkable mosaic floor decorated with dancing dolphins and fish looped around a bearded Neptune, that is worth seeking out.

Adjacent to Mariana stands the **church of Santa Maria Assunta**, known as La Canonica. Built in 1119 close to the old capital of Biguglia, it is the finest of around three hundred churches built by the Pisans in their effort to evangelize the island. Modelled on a Roman basilica, the perfectly proportioned edifice is decorated outside with Corinthian capitals plundered from the main Mariana site and with plates of Cap Corse marble, their delicate pink and yellow ochre hues fusing to stunning effect.

Marooned amid muddy fields about 300m to the south of La Canonica stands **San Parteo**, built in the eleventh and twelfth centuries over the site of a pagan burial ground. A smaller edifice than La Canonica, the church also displays some elegant arcading and fine sculpture – on the south side, the door lintel is supported by two writhing beasts reaching to a central tree, a motif of oriental origins.

Cap Corse

Until Napoléon III had a coach road built around **Cap Corse** in the nineteenth century, the promontory was effectively cut off from the rest of the island, relying on Italian maritime traffic for its income – hence its distinctive Tuscan dialect. Many *Capicursini* later left to seek their fortunes in the colonies of the Caribbean, which explains the distinctly ostentatious mansions, or *palazzus*, built by the successful emigrés (nicknamed "les Américains") on their return. For all the changes brought by the modern world, Cap Corse still feels like a separate country, with wild flowers in profusion, vineyards and quiet, traditional fishing villages.

Forty kilometres long and only fifteen across, the peninsula is divided by a spine of mountains called the Serra, which peaks at Monte Stello, 1037m above sea level. The coast on the east side of this divide is characterized by tiny ports, or *marines*, tucked into gently sloping river-mouths, alongside coves which become sandier as you go further north. The villages of the western coast are sited on rugged cliffs, high above the rough sea and tiny rocky inlets that can be glimpsed from the corniche road.

For those without transport, a circular-tour bus operates daily from Bastia during the summer. There are also buses throughout the year to **Erbalunga**, a placid fishing village on the east of Cap Corse where the buildings, ending in one of the ruined lookout towers for which the cape is famous, rise directly from the sea. In addition, sporadic services run from Bastia's *gare routière* to **Macinaggio** (Mon, Wed & Fri), on the far north tip of the cape, and to **Canari** (Mon & Wed), on the northwest side.

Erbalunga

Built along a rocky promontory 10km north of Bastia, the small port of **ERBALUNGA** is the highlight of the east coast, with aged, pale buildings stacked like crooked boxes behind a small harbour and ruined Genoese watchtower. A little colony of French artists lived here in the 1920s, and the village has drawn a steady stream of admirers ever since. It attracts a fair number of tourists throughout the year, and come summer it's transformed into something of a cultural enclave, with concerts and art events adding a spark to local nightlife. The town is most famous, however, for its Good Friday procession, known as the *Cerca* (Search), which evolved from an ancient fertility rite. Hooded penitents, recruited from the ranks of a local religious brotherhood, form a spiral known as a *Granitola*, or snail, which unwinds as the candlelit procession moves into the village square.

A port since the time of the Phoenicians, Erbalunga was once a more important trading centre than Bastia or Ajaccio. With the increasing exportation of wine and olive oil, in the eleventh century it became the capital of an independent village-state, ruled by the da Gentile family, who lived in the **palazzo** that dominates place de-Gaulle.

In the harbour, a few **bars** shaded by an enormous chestnut tree look out across the water to the tower. The one **hotel**, the stylish *Castel'Brando*, is sited at the entrance to the square (☎04.95.30.10.30, fax 04.95.33.98.18; ③; closed Nov–March): a beautifully restored Latin-American-style *palazzu*, it has plenty of period charm, but doesn't have a restaurant. For a **meal**, your best bet is *Le Pirate*, on the harbourside 30m from place de-Gaulle (☎04.95.33.24.20), which has been there for years and serves delicious seafood specialities. A less pricey option is *A Piazzetta*, in the tiny square behind (☎04.95.33.28.69), offering mainly pizzas and a generous selection of fresh pasta dishes from 60F/€9.12.

Macinaggio and around

A port since Roman times, well-sheltered **MACINAGGIO**, 20km north of Erbalunga, was developed by the Genoese in 1620 for the export of olive oil and wine to the Italian peninsula. The Corsican independence leader, Pascal Paoli, landed here in 1790 after his exile in England, whereupon he kissed the ground and uttered the words "*O ma patrie, je t'ai quitté esclave, je te retrouve libre*" ("Oh my country, I left you as a slave, I rediscover you a free man") – a plaque commemorating the event adorns the wall above the ship chandlers. There's not much of a historic patina to the place nowadays, but with its boat-jammed **marina** and its line of colourful seafront awnings, Macinaggio has a certain appeal, made all the stronger by its proximity to some of the best beaches on Corsica.

The best **hotel** is *Les Îles*, opposite the marina (☎04.95.35.43.02, fax 04.95.35.47.05; ③; closed Nov–Feb), which has cosy rooms overlooking the port and a good restaurant, specializing in imaginative seafood dishes. Another good choice is *U Libecciu*, behind the marina on the road that leads north off the D80 road to Rogliano (☎04.95.35.43.22, fax 04.95.35.46.08; ④; closed mid-Oct to March), with spacious rooms and an excellent restaurant. *U Ricordu*, on the south side of the road to Rogliano (☎04.95.35.40.20, fax 04.95.31.41.88; ⑤ including breakfast; closed Dec–March), is along the same lines, and has a swimming pool. There's also a **campsite**, *U Stazzu* (☎04.95.35.43.76), 1km north and with good access to the nearby town beach. As for **restaurants**, the *Pizzeria San Columbu*, at the end of the port facing out to sea, does a passable seafood pizza, or you can have a Corsican feast at *Les Îles* (see above).

North of the town lie some stunning stretches of white sand and clear sea. A marked footpath, known as **Le Sentier des Douaniers** because it used to be patrolled by customs officials, threads its way across the hills and caves along the coast, giving access to an area that cannot be reached by road. The **Baie de Tamarone**, 2km along this path, has deep clear waters, making it a good place for diving and snorkelling. Just behind the beach the road forks, and if you follow the left-hand track for twenty minutes you'll come to a stunning arc of turquoise sea known as the **rade de Santa Maria**, site of the isolated Romanesque **Chapelle Santa-Maria**. Raised on the foundations of a sixth-century church, the building comprises a tenth-century chapel and a twelfth-century chapel merged into one, hence the two discrepant apses. The bay's other principal landmark is the huge **Tour Chiapelle**. Dramatically cleft in half and entirely surrounded by water, the ruined three-storeyed tower was one of three built on the northern tip of the cape by the Genoese in the sixteenth century (the others are at Tollare and Barcaggio) as lookout posts against the increasingly troublesome Moorish pirates. As Macinaggio grew in importance, the *torri* began to be used also by health and customs officers, who controlled the maritime traffic with Genoa. Pascal Paoli established his garrison here in 1761, having been unsuccessful in his attempt to take Macinaggio, and contemplated building a rival port.

Centuri

From Macinaggio the main D80 winds west across the promontory via 8km of tortuous hairpin bends over the **Col St-Nicolas** (303m) and the **Col de Serra** (365m). Once over the second col you soon come to **CAMERA**, the first hamlet of the commune of Centuri, where the bizarre cylindrical turrets of the **Château de Général Cipriani** (not open to the public) peer from the woods beneath the road. The smaller hamlet of **CANELLE**, overlooking Centuri-Port and accessible from Camera along the road heading north or on foot from the port, is known for its enormous fig trees, whose drooping branches overhang the houses and shadow the road.

When Dr Johnson's biographer, James Boswell, arrived here from England in 1765, the former Roman settlement of **CENTURI-PORT** was a tiny fishing village, recommended to him for its peaceful detachment from the dangerous turmoil of the rest of Corsica. Not much has changed since Boswell's time: Centuri-Port exudes tranquillity despite a serious influx of summer residents, many of them artists who come to paint the fishing boats in the slightly prettified harbour, where the grey-stone wall is highlighted by the green serpentine roofs of the encircling cottages, restaurants and bars. The only drawback is that you'll find the small beach disappointingly muddy and not ideal for sunbathing (although it is an excellent spot for snorkelling).

Centuri-Port has more **hotels** than anywhere else on Cap Corse. *Hôtel-Restaurant du Pêcheur* (☎04.95.35.60.14; ④; closed Nov–March), the pink building in the harbour, is among the most pleasant and fills up quickly in the high season; its rooms are agreeably cool, with thick stone walls, and it has a popular restaurant. A slightly posher and pricier option is the *Vieux Moulin* (☎04.95.35.60.15, fax 04.95.35.60.24; ④; closed Oct–March), a restored *palazzu* that occupies a prime location behind the harbour (on the right as you enter the village), but the rooms can be stuffy in summer and the obligatory 150F/€22.80 menu is a poor deal. Otherwise you have *Hôtel La Jetée*, at the far end of the jetty (☎04.95.35.64.46; ③; closed Oct–Easter), whose rooms are pretty ordinary and don't have sea views, but are the cheapest in the village during high season. For **campers** there's *Camping l'Isolettu*, 400m south (☎04.95.35.62.81; open all year), an uninviting option but the only choice in the vicinity.

Nonza

Set high on a black rocky pinnacle that plunges vertically into the sea, the village of **NONZA**, 18km south of Centuri, is one of the highlights of the Cap Corse shoreline. It was formerly the main stronghold of the da Gentile family, and the remains of their **fortress** are still standing on the furthest rocks on the overhanging cliff.

Nonza is also famous for **St Julia**, patron saint of Corsica, who was martyred here in the fifth century. The story goes that she had been sold into slavery at Carthage and was being taken by ship to Gaul when the slavers docked here. A pagan festival was in progress, and when Julia refused to participate she was crucified; the gruesome legend relates that her breasts were then cut off and thrown onto a stone, from which sprang two springs, now enshrined in a chapel by the beach. To get there, follow the sign on the right-hand side of the road before you enter the square, which points to **La Fontaine de Ste-Julia**, down by the rocks. Reached by a flight of six hundred steps, Nonza's long grey **beach** is discoloured as a result of pollution from the now disused asbestos mine up the coast. This may not inspire confidence, but the locals insist it's safe (they take their own kids there in summer), and from the bottom you do get the best view of the tower, which looks as if it's about to topple into the sea.

You can **stay** in Nonza at *Auberge Patrizi* (☎04.95.37.82.16; ④ including breakfast; closed mid-Oct to March), run from the restaurant below the church: made up of two village houses, it's an old-fashioned place where half-board is obligatory, but the food is good and plentiful. The nearest campsite is *A Stella*, 9km south on the St-Florent Road (☎04.95.37.14.37; closed Nov–March), which is cheap and right next to a pebble beach.

The Nebbio

Taking its name from the thick mists that sweep over the region in winter, the **Nebbio** has for centuries been one of the most fertile parts of the island, producing honey, chestnuts and some of the island's finest wine. Tourism, however, has so far made little impact on this depopulated area, which comprises the amphitheatre of rippled hills, vineyards and cultivated valleys that converge on St-Florent, a handful of kilometres due west of Bastia. Aside from EU subsidies, the major money earner here is **viticulture**: some of the wines produced around the commune of **Patrimonio** rival those of Sartène, and *caves* offering wine tastings are a feature of the whole region.

A bishopric until 1790, **St-Florent** is a chic coastal resort at the base of Cap Corse. It remains the Nebbio's chief town, and is the obvious base for day-trips to the beautifully preserved Pisan church of **Santa Maria Assunta**, just outside the town, and the **Désert des Agriates**, a wilderness of parched *maquis*-covered hills whose rugged coastline harbours one of Corsica's least accessible, but most beautiful, beaches.

The only **public transport** serving Nebbio is the twice-daily bus from Bastia to St-Florent, which leaves the *gare routière* at 11am (or noon on Wed) and 5.30pm from Monday to Saturday.

St-Florent and around

Viewed from across the bay, **ST-FLORENT** (San Fiurenzu) appears as a bright line against the black tidal wave of the Tenda hills, the pale houses seeming to rise straight out of the sea, overlooked by a squat circular citadel. It's a relaxing place, blessed with a decent beach and a good number of restaurants, but the key to its success is the **marina**, which has made the town something of a low-key St-Tropez.

In Roman times, a town called Cersunam – referred to as Nebbium by chroniclers from the ninth century onwards – existed a kilometre east of the present village. Few traces remain of the settlement that grew up there, which in the fifteenth century was eclipsed by the port that developed around the new Genoese citadel. St-Florent, as it became known, prospered as one of Genoa's strongholds, and it was from here that Paoli set off for London in 1796, never to return.

Place des Portes, the centre of town life, has café tables facing the sea in the shade of plane trees, and in the evening fills with strollers and nonchalant pétanque players. In rue du Centre, which runs west off the square, parallel to the seafront and marina, you'll find some restaurants, a few shops and a couple of wine-tasting places – be sure to sample the sweet, *maquis*-scented Muscat made around here. The fifteenth-century circular **citadel** can be reached on foot from place Doria at the seafront in the old quarter. Destroyed by Nelson's bombardment in 1794, it was recently renovated and affords superb views from its terrace over the hills of the Nebbio and desert coast on the gulf's far shore.

Just a kilometre to the east of the town off a small road running off place des Portes, on the original site of Cersunum, the **church of Santa Maria Assunta** – the so-called cathedral of the Nebbio – is a fine example of Pisan Romanesque architecture. Built of warm yellow limestone, the cathedral has a distinctly barn-like appearance – albeit a superlatively elegant one. Gracefully symmetrical blind arcades decorate the western facade, and at the entrance twisting serpents and wild animals adorn the pilasters on each side of the door. The interior, too, appears deceptively simple. Carved shells, foliage and animals adorn the capitals of the pillars dividing the nave where, immediately to the right, you'll see a glass case containing the mummified figure of St Flor, a Roman soldier martyred in the third century.

Practicalities

Buses run from Bastia's *gare routière* to St-Florent twice daily (except Sun), and arrive in the village car park. The journey takes around forty-five minutes and costs 30F/€4.56 one way. The **tourist office** (May–Oct daily 8.30am–12.30pm & 2–7pm; Nov–April Mon–Fri 9am–noon & 2–5pm, Sat 9am–noon; ☎04.95.37.06.04) is in the same building as the **post office**, 100m north of place des Portes.

St-Florent is a popular resort, and **hotels** fill up quickly, especially at the height of summer when prior booking is essential. The *Hôtel Europe* in place des Portes (☎04.95.37.00.03; ④) is the most attractive option in town – and the only one open in winter. Otherwise, try *Hôtel du Centre*, just up the road from the *Europe* (☎04.95.37.00.68; ③; closed Nov–April), which has tiny rooms but is the cheapest place in town, or the more modern and swisher *Maxime*, just off place des Portes (☎04.95.37.05.30, fax 04.95.37.13.07; ④; closed Nov–April). A fair number of **campsites** are dotted about the coast, but are packed in August and closed out of season. *Camping Kallisté*, route de la Plage (☎04.95.37.03.08; closed Oct–May), is the closest to town and most congenial, but it's also a notch pricier than the others; the quickest way to get there on foot is via the bridge in the marina, from where you follow the beach as far as an (unmarked) white gate. To reach the scruffier *Camping U Pezzu* (☎04.95.37.01.65; closed Oct–May), follow the plage de la Roya road behind the *Kallisté* for 1km; the similarly priced *Aqua Dolce* (☎04.95.37.08.63; closed Oct–May), lies a further 500m in the same direction.

St-Florent is renowned for its crayfish and red mullet: a reasonably priced **restaurant** for excellent fish and Corsican specialities is *Le Cabestan* on the rue de Fornellu (☎04.95.37.05.70). More expensive is *La Marinuccia* (☎04.95.37.04.36) at the far end of the same street, which serves the best fish in St-Florent and has a terrace jutting out into the sea. Its entrance is on to the tiny place Doria, below the citadel, where another popular Corsican speciality restaurant, *Ind'e Lucia* (☎04.95.37.04.15), serves wonderful mountain charcuterie and, in season, melt-in-the-mouth sardines stuffed with *brocciu*, washed down with bargain-priced local AOC wine. Otherwise, try the cheap and cheerful (at least by St-Florent standards) *Pizzeria Citadel*, the fortress-shaped place just over the bridge south of the square, which dishes up pizzas from a wood-fired oven on a marina-side terrace.

Patrimonio

Leaving St-Florent by the Bastia road, the first village you come to, after 6km, is **PATRIMONIO**, centre of the first Corsican wine region to gain *appellation controlée* status. Apart from the renowned local Muscat, which can be sampled in the village or at one of the *caves* along the route from St-Florent, Patrimonio's chief asset is the sixteenth-century **church of St-Martin**, occupying its own little hillock and visible for kilometres around. The colour of burnt sienna, it stands out vividly against the rich green vineyards. In a garden 200m south of the church stands a limestone statue-menhir known as **U Nativu**, a late megalithic piece dating from 800–900 BC. A carved T-shape on its front represents a breastbone, and two eyebrows and a chin can also be made out.

The Désert des Agriates

Extending westwards from the Golfe de St-Florent to the mouth of the Ostriconi River, the **Désert des Agriates** is a vast area of uninhabited land, dotted with clumps of cacti and scrub-covered hills. It may appear inhospitable now, but during the time of the Genoese this rocky moonscape was, as its name implies, a veritable bread basket (*agriates* means "cultivated fields"). In fact, so much wheat was grown here that the Italian overlords levied a special tax on grain to prevent any build-up of funds that might have financed an insurrection. Fires and soil erosion eventually took their toll, however, and by the 1970s the area had become a total wilderness.

Numerous crackpot schemes to redevelop the Désert have been mooted over the years – from atomic weapon test zones to concrete Club-Med-style resorts – but during the past two decades the government has gradually bought up the land from its various owners (among them the Rothschild family) and designated it as a protected nature reserve. Nevertheless, species such as the Agriates' rare wild boar remain under threat, mainly from trigger-happy hunters and bush fires.

A couple of rough pistes wind into the desert, but without some kind of 4WD vehicle the only feasible way to explore the area and its rugged coastline, which includes two of the island's most beautiful **beaches**, is by foot. From St-Florent, a recently inaugurated pathway winds northwest to plage de Perajola, just off the main Calvi highway (N1197), in three easy stages. The first takes around 5hr 30min, and leads past the famous **Martello tower** and much-photographed **plage de Loto** to **plage de Saleccia**, a huge sweep of soft white sand and turquoise sea that was used a location for the invasion sequences in the film *The Longest Day*. There's a seasonal **campsite** here, *U*

TORRI

Crowning rocky promontories and clifftops from Cap Corse to Bonifacio, the 91 crumbling Genoese watchtowers that punctuate the Corsican coast have become emblematic of the island's picture-postcard tranquillity. Yet they date from an era when these shores were among the most troubled in Europe. During the fifteenth century, Saracen **pirates** from North Africa began to menace the coastal villages and became so common that many Corsicans fled the coast altogether, retreating to villages in the hills. To protect those that remained, as well as their threatened maritime trade, the Genoese erected a chain of watchtowers, or **torri**, at strategic points on the island. They were paid for by local villagers and staffed by watchmen whose job it was to signal the approach of any unexpected ships by lighting a fire on the crenellated rampart at the top of the tower. In this way, it was possible to alert the entire island in single hour.

Piracy more or less died out by the end of Genoese rule, but the *torri* remained in use long after, proving particularly effective during the Anglo-Corsican invasions of the late eighteenth century. The British were so impressed with the system that they erected similar structures along the south coast of England and Ireland to warn of attacks by the French. Named after the first Genoese watchtower ever built in Corsica – on the Pointe de Martella, protecting the port of St-Florent and the Nebbio – these **Martello towers** were later used as lookout towers in World War II.

Paradisu (☎04.95.37.82.51; closed Nov–April). From plage de Saleccia, it takes around three hours to reach the second night halt, **plage de Ghignu**, where a simple *gîte d'étape* (☎04.95.37.09.86) provides basic facilities for 50F/€7.60 per night. The last stretch to Perajola can be covered in under six hours.

Note that the only water sources along the route are at Saleccia and Ghignu, so take plenty with you. It's also worth knowing that between May and October, excursion **boats**, leaving throughout the day from the jetty in St-Florent marina (50F/€7.60), ferry passengers across the gulf to plage de Loto. If you time your walk well, you can pick one up for the return leg back to town.

The Balagne

The Balagne, the region stretching west from the Ostriconi valley as far as the red-cliffed wilderness of Scandola, has been renowned since Roman times as "Le Pays de l'Huile et Froment" (Land of Oil and Wheat). Backed by a wall of imposing, pale-grey mountains, the characteristic outcrops of orange granite punctuating its spectacular coastline shelter a string of idyllic beaches, many of them sporting ritzy marinas and holiday complexes. These, along with the region's two honeypot towns, **L'Île Rousse** and **Calvi**, get swamped in summer, but the scenery more than compensates. In any case, Calvi, with its cream-coloured citadel, stunning white-sand bay and mountainous backdrop, should not be missed.

Year-round **transport** in the Balagne is limited to the *Micheline* train, which descends the Ostriconi valley and runs west along the coast as far as Calvi, and a bus connection with Bastia, via Ponte Leccia. In July and August, you can also travel to Calvi from Porto by bus.

L'Île Rousse

Developed by Pascal Paoli in the 1760s as a "gallows to hang Calvi", the port of **L'ÎLE ROUSSE** (Isula Rossa) simply doesn't convince as a Corsican town, its palm trees, smart shops, neat flower gardens and colossal pink seafront hotel creating an atmosphere that has more in common with the French Riviera. Pascal Paoli had great plans for his new town on the Haute-Balagne coast, which was laid out from scratch in 1758 as a port to export the olive oil produced in the Balagne region. A large part of the new port was built on a grid system, featuring lines of straight parallel streets quite at odds with the higgledy-piggledy nature of most Corsican villages and towns. Thanks to the busy trading of wine and oil, it soon began to prosper and, two and a half centuries later, still thrives as a successful port. These days, however, the main traffic consists of holiday-makers, lured here by brochure shots of the nearby beaches. This is officially the hottest corner of the island, and the town is thus deluged by German and Italian sun-worshippers in July and August. Given the proximity of Calvi, and so much unspoilt countryside, it's hard to see why you should want to stop here for more than a couple of hours.

L'Île Rousse is easily accessible by **bus** from Bastia and Calvi, and the **train** pauses here on the Calvi–Ponte-Leccia line.

Arrival, information and accommodation

The **train station** (☎04.95.60.00.50) is on route du Port, 500m south of where the ferries arrive. The Bastia–Calvi **bus** stops just south of place Paoli in the town's main thoroughfare, avenue Piccioni. The SNCM office is on avenue J.-Calizi (☎04.95.60.09.56), and the **tourist office** on the south side of place Paoli (May, June, Sept & Oct Mon–Fri 9.30am–noon & 3–6pm; July & Aug daily 9am–1pm & 2.30–7.30pm; ☎04.95.60.04.35).

L'Île Rousse fills up early in the year and it can be difficult to find a **hotel** at any time from May to October. Most places are modern buildings, more functional than personable. The town has two main **campsites**: *Les Oliviers*, 1km east (☎04.95.60.19.92), and *Le Bodri* (☎04.95.16.19.70), 3km west off the main Calvi road (you can get to the latter site direct by rail – ask for "l'arrêt Bodri").

HOTELS

Le Grillon, 10 av Paul-Doumer (☎04.95.60.00.49, fax 04.95.60.43.69). The best budget hotel in town, just 1km from the centre on the St-Florent/Bastia road. Nothing special, but quiet and immaculately clean. Half-board in August, but at other times rates fall to 250F/€38 per double. Closed Nov–March. ④.

Napoléon Bonaparte, 3 place Paoli (☎04.95.60.06.09). Garish, converted *palazzu* which for years was the only luxury hotel on the island; although downgraded, it still has a certain old-fashioned appeal. Closed Nov–March. ⑥.

Santa Maria, in the port (☎04.95.60.13.49, fax 04.95.60.32.48). One of the larger and best-value three-star places, situated next to the ferry port. Rooms have air-conditioning and overlook a small garden and pool. Open all year. ⑤.

Splendid, 4 rue Comte-Valéry (☎04.95.60.00.24, fax 04.95.60.04.57). Well-maintained, 1930s-style building with small swimming pool and some sea views from upper floors; very reasonable tariffs given the location. Closed Nov–March. ⑤.

The town and beaches

All roads in L'Île Rousse lead to **place Paoli**, a shady square that's open to the sea and has as its focal point a fountain surmounted by a bust of "U Babbu di u Patria" (Father of the Nation), one of many local tributes to Pascal Paoli. There's a Frenchified covered **market** at the entrance to the square, which hosts a popular artisan-cum-antiques sale on Saturday mornings, while on the west side rises the grim facade of the **church of the Immaculate Conception**.

To reach the **Île de la Pietra**, the islet that gives the town its name, continue north, passing the station on your left. Once over the causeway connecting the islet to the mainland, you can walk through the crumbling mass of red granite as far as the lighthouse at the far end, from where the view of the town is spectacular, especially at sundown, when you get the full effect of the red glow of the rocks. Heading back along **A Marinella**, which follows the seafront behind the town beach, a ten-minute walk will bring you to the aquarium, the main sight in the town. The overpriced **Musée Océanographique** (May–Sept Mon–Fri 10.30am–1pm & 2–7pm; 45F/€6.90), situated at the north end of the beach, publicizes itself as the "Grotte aux Requins", but the only members of the shark family on display here are some timid dogfish. If the stiff entry charges don't put you off, then the decidedly cramped tanks housing the larger creatures probably will.

Although L'Île Rousse has a decent beach, the most popular one hereabouts is **plage de Rindara**, a fantastic duned strand with pale-green translucent water, 4km southwest of the town. Equally spectacular, **plage de Lozari**, a long semicircular sweep of white sand, lies 7km northeast. A decent road signposted "Lozari" leads down to the shore and a discreet holiday village.

Eating and drinking

Tourism has taken its toll here, hence the abundance of mediocre **eating** places crammed into the narrow alleys of the old town. A few restaurants do stand out, however, some offering classic gourmet menus and others serving superb fresh seafood. The best cafés are found in place Paoli along the southern side.

Le Grillon, av Paul-Doumer (☎04.95.60.00.09). High-ceilinged, blissfully cool air-conditioned hotel dining hall south of the centre with a limited, but consistently good menu of mainly French dishes. Their *steak au roquefort* and cod in spicy creole sauce are perennially popular, while for vegetarians there's a delicious courgette and basil pâté. Count on 110–150F/€16.72–22.80 per head.

La Jonque, rue Paoli. One of only a handful of Chinese/Vietnamese restaurants on the island. Drab, formulaic decor, but the food is fresh and spicy, and they do a good-value set menu (95F/€14.44).

L'Ostéria, place Santelli. Tucked away on a quiet square in the old quarter, this is the town's best Corsican speciality restaurant, serving a good-value set menu (117F/€17.78) that includes delicious *beignets de courgettes*, in a vaulted room adorned with farm implements. Closed Wed.

La Taverne Espgnole (Chez Paco), rue Paoli. Copious portions of tasty Spanish food (including paella; 170F/€25.84 for two) and spicy fish dishes (including *bouillabaisse*; 90F/€13.68) served under awnings in a quiet old town back street. Aperitifs and digestifs often on the house.

Calvi

Seen from the water, **CALVI** is a beautiful spectacle, with its three immense bastions topped by a crest of ochre buildings, sharply defined against a hazy backdrop of snow-capped mountains. Twenty kilometres west along the coast from L'Île Rousse, the town began as a fishing port on the site of the present-day *ville basse* below the citadel, and remained just a cluster of houses and fishing shacks until the Pisans conquered the island in the tenth century. Not until the arrival of the Genoese, however, did the town become a stronghold when, in 1268, Giovaninello de Loreto, a Corsican nobleman, built a huge citadel on the windswept rock overlooking the port and named it Calvi. A fleet commanded by Nelson launched a brutal two-month attack on the town in 1793, when Nelson lost his eye; he left saying he hoped never to see the place again.

The French concentrated on developing Ajaccio and Bastia during the nineteenth century, and Calvi became primarily a military base, used as a point for smuggling arms to the mainland in World War II. A hang out for European glitterati in the 1950s, the town these days has the ambience of a slightly kitsch Côte d'Azur resort, whose glamorous marina, souvenir shops and fussy boutiques jar with the down-to-earth villages of its rural hinterland. It's also an important base for the French Foreign Legion, and immaculately uniformed legionnaires are a common sight around the bars lining avenue de la République.

Arrival, information and accommodation

Ste-Catherine airport lies 7km south of Calvi (☎04.95.65.88.68); the only public transport into town is by taxi, which shouldn't cost more than 80F/€12.16 (or 120F/€18.24 at night). The **train station** (☎04.95.65.00.61) is on avenue de la République, close to the marina, where you'll find the **tourist office** on quai Landry (mid-June to Sept daily 9am–7pm; rest of year Mon–Fri 9am–noon & 2–5.30pm, Sat 9am–noon; ☎04.95.65.16.67). **Buses** from Bastia and towns along the north coast stop outside the train station on place de la Porteuse d'Eau, whereas those from Porto pull in at the marina.

Ferries, including NGV hydrofoils, dock at the Port de Commerce at the foot of the citadel, and the SNCM office is at quai Landry (☎04.95.65.01.38). You can rent **bikes** from Ambrosini on place Bel-Ombra, on the way out of town towards Porto (☎04.95.65.02.13), and **cars** from Hertz, 2 rue Maréchal-Joffre (☎04.95.65.06.64), or Budget at the airport (☎04.95.65.88.34).

Accommodation is easy to find in Calvi except during the jazz festival (third week of June). Hotels range from inexpensive pensions to luxury piles with pools and sweeping views of the bay. Prices are generally reasonable, apart from during high season when they go through the roof. If you're on a tight budget, take your pick from the

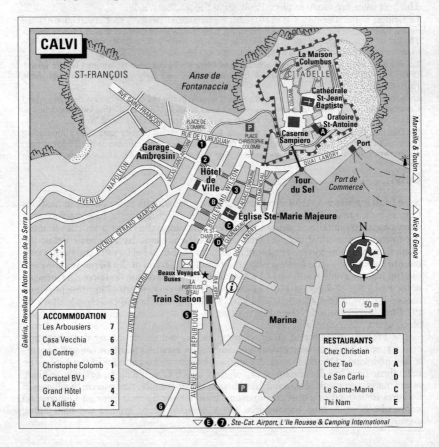

ACCOMMODATION	
Les Arbousiers	7
Casa Vecchia	6
du Centre	3
Christophe Colomb	1
Corsotel BVJ	5
Grand Hôtel	4
Le Kallisté	2

RESTAURANTS	
Chez Christian	B
Chez Tao	A
Le San Carlu	D
Le Santa-Maria	C
Thi Nam	E

town's two excellent **hostels**, or the dozen **campsites** within walking distance of the centre.

HOTELS

Les Arbousiers, rte de la Pietra-Maggiore (☎04.95.65.04.47, fax 04.95.65.26.14). Large, fading pink place set back from the main road, 1km south of town, with rooms ranged around a quiet courtyard. Good value outside July & Aug. ③.

Casa Vecchia, rte de Santore (☎04.95.65.09.33, fax 04.95.65.37.95). Small chalets set in leafy garden, 500m east of town, and a stone's throw from the beach. May, June & Sept doubles at 200F/€30.40. ④.

du Centre, 14 rue Alsace-Lorraine (☎04.95.65.02.01). Converted nineteenth-century *gendarmerie* bang in the middle of the old quarter, with lower tariffs and more character than most. Doubles at 190F/€28.88 outside July & Aug. ③.

Christophe Colomb, place Christophe-Colomb (☎04.95.65.06.04, fax 04.95.65.29.65). The best upmarket option close to the centre, offering spacious rooms and expansive views across the bay. Closed Nov–March. ④.

Grand Hotel, 3 bd Wilson (☎04.95.65.09.74, fax 04.95.65.25.18). Characterful *fin-de-siècle* hotel in the centre of town, with mostly period furniture and fittings. The rooms, though a bit dowdy, are huge and many have good views. Smaller than average price increases in peak season. Closed mid-Oct to mid-March. ④.

Le Kallisté, 1 av du Commandant-Marche (☎04.95.65.09.81, fax 04.95.65.35.65). Small dark rooms close to the citadel, but with its own restaurant and shady garden. Closed Nov–April. ④.

HOSTELS AND CAMPSITES

Corsotel BVJ, 43 av de la République (☎04.95.65.14.15, fax 04.95.65.33.72). Huge hostel in a prime position opposite the station and facing the sea. Very clean rooms for up to six people, some with balconies. Enormous breakfast included in 120F/€18.30 tariff. Book ahead (the staff speak English).

Relais International de la Jeunesse, 4km from the centre of town on rte de Pietra-Maggiore (☎04.95.65.14.16, fax 04.95.80.65.30). Follow the N197 for 2km, turn right at the sign for Pietra-Maggiore, and the hostel – two little houses with dormitories looking out over the gulf – is another 2km further on. Breakfast included in excellent-value 80F/€12.16 tariff, but obligatory half-board (150F/€22.80) in July & Aug. Closed Oct–May.

International Camping, opposite the *Balagne* hotel on rte de L'Île Rousse (☎04.95.65.01.75). Small and fairly central site (500m from centre), popular with bikers and backpackers. The bar is lively and stays open late, with live rock bands on weekends.

La Pinède, 2km east of Calvi between the beach and N197 (☎04.95.65.17.00, fax 05.96.65.19.60). Popular site in a pine forest, with bar, restaurant, supermarket, tennis courts and telephones. Catch the train out here, or request the last-but-two stop before Calvi coming from L'Île Rousse direction. Closed Nov–March.

The town and citadel

Social life in Calvi focuses on the restaurants and cafés of the **quai Landry**, a spacious seafront walkway linking the marina and the port. This is the best place to get the feel of the town, but as far as sights go there's not a lot to the *ville basse*. At the far end of the quay, under the shadow of the citadel, stands the sturdy **Tour du Sel**, a medieval lookout post once used to store imported salt. If you strike up through the narrow passageways off quai Landry, you'll come to **rue Clemenceau**, where restaurants and souvenir shops are packed into every available space. In a small square giving onto the street stands the pink-painted **Ste-Marie-Majeure**, built in 1774, whose spindly bell tower rises elegantly above the cafés on the quay but whose interior contains nothing of interest. From the church's flank, a flight of steps connects with **boulevard Wilson**, a wide modern high street which rises to **place Christophe-Colomb**, point of entry for the **ville haute**, or citadel.

Beyond the ancient **gateway** to the citadel, with its inscription of the town's motto, you come immediately to the enormous **Caserne Sampiero**, formerly the governor's palace. Built in the thirteenth century, when the great round tower was used as a dungeon, the **castle** was recently restored and is currently used for military purposes, and therefore closed to the public. The best way of seeing the rest of the citadel is to follow the ramparts, which connect the three immense bastions. From each bastion the views across the sea, the Balagne and the Cinto Massif are magnificent.

Within the walls the houses are tightly packed along tortuous stairways and narrow passages that converge on the diminutive place d'Armes. Dominating the square is the **Cathédrale St-Jean-Baptiste**, set at the highest point of the promontory and sitting uncomfortably amid the ramshackle buildings. This chunky ochre edifice was founded in the thirteenth century, but was partly destroyed during the Turkish siege of 1553 and then suffered extensive damage twelve years later, when the powder magazine in the governor's palace exploded. It was rebuilt in the form of a Greek cross, as you see today. The church's great treasure is the **Christ des Miracles**, housed in the chapel on the right of the choir; this crucifix was brandished at marauding Turks during the siege of 1553, an act which reputedly saved the day.

To the north of place d'Armes in rue de Fil stands the shell of the building that Calvi believes was **Christopher Columbus's birthplace**, as the plaque on the wall states, but the claim rides on pretty tenuous, circumstantial evidence. The house itself was destroyed by Nelson's troops during the siege of 1794, but as recompense a statue was erected on May 20, 1992, the 500th anniversary of Columbus's "discovery" of America; his alleged birthday, October 12, is now a public holiday in Calvi.

Calvi's outstanding **beach** sweeps right round the bay from the end of quai Landry, but most of the first kilometre or so is owned by bars which rent out sun loungers for a hefty price. To avoid these, follow the track behind the sand which will bring you to the start of a more secluded stretch. The sea might not be as sparklingly clear as at many other Corsican beaches, but it's warm, shallow and free of rocks. You can also sunbathe, and swim off the rocks, at the foot of the citadel, which have the added attraction of fine views across the bay.

Eating and drinking

Eating is a major pastime in Calvi, and you'll find a wide selection of restaurants and snack bars catering for all tastes. Fish restaurants predominate in the marina, where – at a price – you can eat excellent seafood fresh from the bay. It's cheaper to eat in the inland streets of the *ville basse* whose stairways and cramped forecourts hide a host of buzzing pizzerias and Corsican restaurants. **Cafés**, complete with raffia parasols, line the marina, becoming more expensive the nearer they are to the Tour du Sel.

CAFÉS AND BARS

Café Rex, at the top of bd Wilson, on the corner of place Christophe-Colomb. The most down-to-earth and animated bar in central Calvi, with a small but sunny terrace and a mixed clientele. A good breakfast venue for crowd-watching.

International Bar, *Camping International*, rte de l'Île Rousse. A campsite bar, but the most consistently fun spot on weekends, when local bands play thumping rock covers through the small hours. Drinks at regular prices, and an internationally mixed crowd.

RESTAURANTS

Chez Christian, place Marchal. A good option if you're on a tight budget, with a filling 75F/€11.40 menu, served in a small roadside square beneath the Mairie. As an accompaniment, try their light French cider.

Chez Tao, rue St-Antoine, in the citadel (☎04.95.65.00.73). Legendary nightclub, opened in the wake of the Crimean war by a Muslim White Russian, and long the haunt of the Riviera's glitterati. Now turned into pricey piano bar serving fussy nouvelle cuisine and local fish dishes, costing 100–150F/€15.20–22.80 à la carte. Outstanding view of the bay. June–Sept 7pm–midnight.

Le San Carlu, place St-Charles, off rue Clemenceau (☎04.95.65.92.20). Fine seafood and moderately priced French-Corsican cuisine served in the colonial-style garden of a sixteenth-century former Genoese hospital. Five *menus fixes* (85–130F/€12.92–19.76) and sixty à la carte dishes. Closed Nov–March.

Le Santa-Maria, on the square in front of Ste Marie-Majeure church, rue Clemenceau (☎04.95.64.04.19). Good-value four-course tourist menus (90F/€13.68), and filling paella (100F/€15.20), served in an atmospheric setting. Recommended on Saturday evenings, when jazz guitarists busk on the church steps.

Thi Nam, opposite Total petrol station, 1km east of town on the main road (☎04.95.65.38.62). Authentic, spicy Vietnamese main dishes for around 50–65F/€7.62–9.88. The interior's uninspiring; you'd do better to take away.

The Réserve Naturel de Scandola and Girolata

The **Réserve Naturel de Scandola** takes up the promontory west of Girolata, its name derived from the wooden tiles (*scandules*) that cover many of the island's mountain houses. But the area's roof-like rock formations are only part of its amazing geological repertoire: its stacked slabs, towering pinnacles and gnarled claw-like outcrops were formed by Monte Cinto's volcanic eruptions 250 million years ago, and subsequent erosion has fashioned shadowy caves, grottoes and gashes in the rock. Scandola's colours are as remarkable as the shapes, the hues varying from the charcoal grey of granite to the incandescent rusty purple of porphyry.

The headland and its surrounding water were declared a nature reserve in 1975 and now support significant colonies of seabirds, dolphins and seals, as well as 450 types of seaweed and some remarkable fish such as the grouper, a species more commonly found in the Caribbean. In addition, nests belonging to a rare kind of giant gull are visible on the cliffs, and you might see the odd osprey – there used to be only seven pairs here, but careful conservation has increased this number to 24.

Scandola is off-limits to hikers and can be viewed only by **boat**, which means taking one of the daily excursions from Calvi and Porto. These leave from Calvi at 9.15am and 2pm, and from Porto at 9.30am and 2.30pm (April–Oct), the first two stopping for two hours at Girolata (see below) and returning in the late afternoon. The later boat from Porto stops for only 45 minutes, but is a fascinating journey and well worth the 250F/€38, although it's a good idea to take a picnic, as the restaurants in Girolata are very pricey.

Girolata

Connected by a mere mule track to the rest of the island (90min on foot from the nearest road), the tiny fishing haven of **GIROLATA**, immediately west of Scandola, has a dreamlike quality that's highlighted by the vivid red of the surrounding rocks. A short stretch of stony beach and a few houses are dominated by a stately watchtower, built by the Genoese later in the seventeenth century in the form of a small castle on a bluff overlooking the cove. For most of the year, this is one of the most idyllic spots on the island, with only the odd yacht and party of hikers to threaten the settlement's tranquillity. From June through September, though, daily boat trips from Porto and Calvi ensure the village is packed during the middle of the day, so if you want to make the most of the scenery and peace and quiet, walk here and stay a night in one of the *gîtes*.

The head of the Girolata trail is at **Bocca â Crocce** (Col de la Croix), on the Calvi–Porto road, from where a clear path plunges downhill through dense *maquis* and forest to a flotsam-covered cove known as **Cala di Tuara** (30min). The more rewarding of the two tracks that wind onwards to Girolata is the more gentle one running left

THE GR20

Winding some 200km from Calenzana (12km from Calvi) to Conça (22km from Porto-Vecchio), the **GR20** is Corsica's most demanding long-distance footpath. Only one-third of the hikers who start it complete all sixteen stages (*étapes*), which can be covered in ten to twelve days if you're in good physical shape – if you're not, don't even think about attempting this route. Marked with red-and-white splashes of paint, it comprises a back-to-back series of harsh ascents and descents, sections of which exceed 2000m and become more of a climb than a walk, with stanchions, cables and ladders driven into the rock as essential aids. The going is made tougher by the necessity of carrying a sleeping bag, all-weather kit and two or three days' food with you. That said, the rewards more than compensate. The GR20 takes in the most spectacular mountain terrain in Corsica, from the shattered granite peaks of the central watershed to the fragrant pine forests and flower-spotted slopes of the island's highest valleys. Along the way you can expect to spot the elusive mouflon (mountain sheep), glimpse eagles wheeling around the crags, and swim in ice-cold torrents and waterfalls.

The first thing you need to do before setting off is get hold of the Parc Régional's indispensable **Topoguide**, published by the Fédération Française de la Randonnée Pédestre, which gives a detailed description of the route, along with relevant sections of IGN contour maps, lists of refuges and other essential information. Most good bookshops in Corsica stock them, or you can call in at the park office in Ajaccio (see p.1069).

The route can be undertaken in either **direction**, but most hikers start in the north at Calenzana, tackling the most demanding *étapes* early on. These first few days are relentlessly tough, but the hardship is alleviated by extraordinary mountainscapes as you round the Cinto massif, skirt the Asco, Niolo, Tavignano and Restonica valleys, and scale the sides of Monte d'Oro and Rotondo. At Vizzavona on the main Bastia–Corte–Ajaccio road, roughly the halfway mark, you can call it a day and catch a bus or train back to the coast, or press on south across two more ranges to the needle peaks of Bavella. With much of the forest east of here blackened by fire, hikers in recent years have been leaving the GR20 at Zonza, below the Col de Bavella (served by daily buses to Ajaccio and Porto-Vecchio), and walking to the coast along the less arduous Mare a Mare Sud trail.

Accommodation along the route is provided by **refuges**, where, for around 50F/€7.60, you can take a hot shower, use an equipped kitchen and bunk down on mattresses. Usually converted *bergeries* located hours away from the nearest road, these places are staffed by wardens during the peak period (July & Aug), when up to one thousand people per day may be using the GR20 at any one time. Advance reservation is not possible; beds are allocated on a first-come-first-served basis, so be prepared to bivouac if you arrive late. Better still, set off as early as possible to arrive before everyone else. Another reason to be on the trail soon after dawn is that it allows you to break the back of the *étape* before 2pm, when clouds tend to bubble over the mountains and obscure the views.

The **weather** in the high mountains is notoriously fickle, with extreme and sudden changes. A sunny morning doesn't necessarily mean a sunny day, and during July and August violent storms can rip across the route without warning, confining hikers to the refuges or sheltered rock crevices for hours or even days. It is therefore essential to take good wet-weather gear with you, as well as a hat, sunblock and shades for the baking heat that is the norm in summer. In addition, make sure you set off on each stage with adequate **food** and **water**. At the height of the season, many refuges sell basic supplies (*alimentation*), but you shouldn't rely on this service; ask hikers coming from the opposite direction where their last supply stop was and plan accordingly (basic provisions are always available at the main passes of Col de Vergio, Col de Vizzavona, Col de Bavella and Col de Verde). The refuge wardens (*gardiens*) will be able to advise you on how much water to carry at each stage.

Finally a word of **warning**: each year, injured hikers have to be air-lifted to safety off remote sections of the GR20, normally because they strayed from the marked route and got lost. Occasionally, fatal accidents also occur for the same reason, so always keep the paint splashes in sight, especially if the weather closes in – don't rely purely on the many cairns that punctuate the route, as these sometimes mark more hazardous paths to high peaks.

around the headland, but if you feel like stretching your legs, follow the second, more direct route uphill to a pass.

In Girolata, *La Cabane du Berger*, behind the beach, offers inexpensive **accommodation** in eucalyptus-shaded cabins (☎04.95.20.16.98; ① dorm bed or ② with half-board); meals are served in their quirky beachside restaurant, but the food isn't up to much, so make the most of the self-catering kitchen. If this place is full, try the equally pleasant *Le Cormorant gîte* at the north end of the cove (☎04.95.20.20.15; ①), whose beds are in four- to six-person dormitories.

Porto and around

The overwhelming proximity of the mountains, combined with the pervasive eucalyptus and spicy scent of the *maquis*, give **PORTO**, 30km south of Calvi, a uniquely intense, loaded atmosphere that makes it one of the most interesting places to stay on the west coast. Except for a watchtower built here by the Genoese in the second half of the sixteenth century, the site was only built upon with the onset of tourism since the 1950s; today the village is still so small that it can become claustrophobic in July and August, when overcrowding – thanks to predominantly German tourists – is no joke. Off-season, the place becomes eerily deserted, so you'd do well to choose your times carefully; the best months are May, June and September.

The crowds and traffic jams tend to be most oppressive passing the famous **Calanche**, a huge mass of weirdly eroded pink rock just southwest of Porto, but you can easily sidestep the tourist deluge in picturesque **Piana**, which overlooks the gulf from its southern shore, or by heading inland from Porto through the **Gorges de Spelunca**. Forming a ravine running from the sea to the watershed of the island, this spectacular gorge gives access to the equally grandiose **Forêt d'Aïtone**, site of Corsica's most ancient Laricio pine trees and a deservedly popular hiking area. Throughout the forest, the river and its tributories are punctuated by strings of *piscines naturelles* (natural swimming pools) – a refreshing, tranquil alternative to the beaches hereabouts, which tend to be cramped in peak season. If you're travelling between Porto and Ajaccio, a worthwhile place to break the journey is the clifftop village of **Cargèse** where the two main attractions are the Greek church and spectacular beach.

The Town

Eucalyptus-bordered **route de la Marine** links the two parts of the resort. The village proper, known as **Vaïta**, comprises a strip of supermarkets, shops and hotels 1km from the sea, but the main focus of activity is the small **marina**, located at the avenue's end. Overlooking the entrance to the harbour is the much-photographed **Genoese Tower** (Mon–Fri 10am–9pm, Sat & Sun noon–8pm; 10F/€1.52), a square chimney-shaped structure that was cracked by an explosion in the seventeenth century, when it was used as an arsenal. An awe-inspiring view of the crashing sea and *maquis*-shrouded mountains makes it worth the short climb. The **beach** consists of a pebbly cove south beyond the shoulder of the massive rock supporting the tower. To reach it from the marina, follow the little road that skirts the rock, cross the wooden bridge which spans the River Porto on your left, then walk through the car park under the trees. Although it's rather rocky and exposed, and the sea very deep, the great crags overshadowing the shore give the place a vivid edge.

Practicalities

Buses from Calvi, via Galéria, and from Ajaccio, via Cargèse, pull into the junction at the end of route de la Marine, opposite the Banco supermarket, en route to the marina.

Timetables are posted at the stops themselves, and at the **tourist office**, down in the marina (May, June & Sept daily 9am–noon & 3–7pm; July & Aug daily 9am–7pm; Oct–April Mon–Thurs 2–6pm; ☎04.95.26.10.55), where you can buy *Topoguides* and brochures for hikes in the area. Tickets for the **boat excursions** to Scandola, the Calanche and Girolata (depart 9.30am & 2.30pm) are available in advance from the operators at their office in the marina. Mountain **bikes** and **scooters**, ideal for day-trips up the Spelunca gorge, can be rented from the café opposite Timy supermarket, at the top of the village, though the cost is well over the odds (90F/€13.68 per day per bicycle or 300F/€45.60 for an 80cc step-through).

Porto has plenty of **hotels**, and stiff competition between them means that tariffs are surprisingly low outside peak season. The best all-round budget option is *Le Maquis*, above the village on the route d'Ota (☎04.95.26.12.19, fax 04.95.26.12.77; ③), which has plain but comfortable rooms with and without en-suite bathrooms. If it's full, then try *Le Colombo*, next door (☎04.95.26.10.14, fax 04.95.26.19.90; ④), an informal sixteen-room hotel overlooking the valley, imaginatively decorated with driftwood and flotsam sculpture. The *Panorama*, down in the marina (☎04.95.26.11.05; ③), is another good choice, with a wonderful little terrace restaurant on its ground floor, as is the *Brise de Mer* next door (☎04.95.26.10.28, fax 04.95.26.13.02; ③), which looks over the eucalyptus trees in the valley to the sea. Apart from the dismal *Camping municipal* behind the beach, Porto's **campsites** are all grouped in the village near the supermarkets. Pick of the bunch is the *Sol e Vista* (☎04.95.26.15.71), which has lots of shady terraces stacked up the hillside; *Le Porto* (☎04.95.26.13.67), on the opposite side of the road bridge, is almost as pleasant, and within easy reach of natural swimming pools in the river.

Pizzerias and standard hotel-restaurants make up the bulk of **eating places** in Porto, with prices generally increasing the nearer you get to the tower. Try the moderately priced *Le Maquis*, in the hotel of the same name at the top of the village, which serves honest, affordable home-cooking in a warm bar or on a tiny terrace overlooking the valley. Along the walkway leading from the square to the marina, *Le Sud* (☎04.95.26.15.11) is arguably the village's top restaurant, thanks to its policy of serving nothing except the freshest local food – hence the limited menu (if the local fishermen haven't landed anything, you won't find fish on the menu). Another place to eat that's well worth considering if you have transport, or are happy to walk 4km, is *Chez Félix* in Ota (☎04.95.26.12.92), which serves delicious local specialities such as *sanglier en daube*, a rich wild-boar stew, on a sunny terrace with stunning views across the valley to Capo d'Orto.

The Calanche

The UNESCO-protected site of the **Calanche**, 5km southeast of Porto, takes its name from *calanca*, the Corsican word for creek or inlet, but the outstanding characteristics here are the vivid orange and pink rock masses and pinnacles which crumble into the dark blue sea. Liable to unusual patterns of erosion, these tormented rock formations and porphyry needles, some of which soar 300m above the waves, have long been associated with different animals and figures, of which the most famous is the *Tête de Chien* (Dog's Head) at the north end of the stretch of cliffs. Other figures and creatures conjured up include a Moor's head, a monocled bishop, a bear and a tortoise.

One way to see the fantastic cliffs of the Calanche is by boat from Porto; excursions leave daily in summer, cost 100F/€15.20 and last about an hour. Alternatively, you could drive along the corniche road which weaves through the granite archways on its way to Piana. Eight kilometres along the road from Porto, the *Roches Bleues* café is a convenient landmark for walkers.

Piana

Picturesque **PIANA** occupies a prime location overlooking the Calanche, but for some reason does not suffer the deluge of tourists that Porto endures. Retaining a sleepy feel, the village comprises a cluster of pink houses ranged around an eighteenth-century church and square, from the edge of which the panoramic views over the Golfe de Porto are sublime.

If you want to **stay**, head straight for the *Hôtel les Roches Rouges*, at the entrance to the village on the Porto side (☎04.95.27.81.81, fax 04.95.27.81.76; ④; closed Nov–March). Built in the 1930s, this wonderfully dated place lay empty for nearly twenty years, but was recently reopened with most of its original fittings and furniture. The tariffs are exceptionally low, too, considering the hotel's situation and character. Even if your budget won't stretch to a room, drop in for coffee and a game of chess on the magnificent terrace. A cheaper alternative is the *Continental*, an old house with high wooden ceilings and a leafy garden, on the right as you leave Piana for Porto (☎04.95.27.89.00; ③). There's also an excellent **gîte d'étape** (☎04.95.27.82.05), where double rooms cost a mere 130F/€19.76 per night, and the friendly *patronne* offers good-value half-board for 175F/€26.60.

The Gorges de Spelunca

Spanning the 2km between the villages of Ota and Évisa, a few kilometres east of Porto, the **Gorges de Spelunca** are a formidable sight, with bare orange granite walls, 1km deep in places, plunging into the foaming green torrent created by the confluence of the rivers Porto, Tavulella, Onca, Campi and Aïtone. The sunlight, ricocheting across the rock walls, creates a sinister effect that's heightened by the dark jagged needles of the encircling peaks. The most dramatic part of the gorge can be seen from the road, which hugs the edge for much of its length.

ÉVISA's bright orange roofs emerge against a lush background of chestnut forests about 10km from Ota, on the eastern edge of the gorge, and the village makes the best base for hiking in the area. Situated 830m above sea level, it caters well for hikers and makes a pleasant stop for a taste of mountain life – the air is invariably crisp and clear, and the food particularly good.

The best place to **stay** is *La Chataigneraire*, a rambling schist and granite building with rooms set amid chestnut trees, on the west side of the village towards Porto (☎04.95.26.24.27, fax 04.95.26.33.11; ③; closed Nov–March). The smaller *Hôtel du Centre* (☎04.95.26.20.92; ③; closed Nov–Jan), opposite the statue in the centre of the village, is another good choice, with friendly proprietors and an excellent little restaurant serving wholesome Corsican specialities. A somewhat grander affair is the *Hôtel l'Aïtone*, at the north exit to the village (☎04.95.26.20.04, fax 04.95.20.24.18; ③; closed mid-Nov to Dec), which has luxurious rooms and a swimming pool boasting views over the valley. *Camping Paisolu d'Aïtone* 1km east of the village (☎04.95.26.20.39), is a well-situated year-round **campsite**.

Forêt d'Aïtone

Thousands of soaring Laricio pines, some of them as much as 50m tall, make up the **Forêt d'Aïtone**, just a few kilometres east of Évisa. The most beautiful forest in Corsica, it extends over ten square kilometres between Évisa and the Col de Verghio (1477m), the highest point in Corsica traversable by road. Well-worn tourist paths cross the forest at various points, but local wildlife still thrives here.

You can park 7km along the road from Évisa by the **Maison Forestière d'Aïtone**, the forest headquarters and information centre (June–Sept 9am–noon & 2–6pm) and a starting-off point for walks in the area. One of the most popular short hikes goes to the **Belvédère**, a great projecting rock 5km north of Évisa. To reach it, follow the sign-posted track leading into the forest, from beside a wide lay-by on the left-hand side of the road.

Just 4km beyond the *maison forestière*, the **Col de Verghio** borders the remote district of the Niolo and marks the limit of the **Fôret de Valdo-Niello**. The ugly concrete *Castellacciu* hotel (☎04.95.26.20.09; ②), situated at the point where the GR20 (see p.1062) makes one of its rare descents to road level, doubles as a refuge and basic ski station, but these days there's rarely enough snow to keep it in use.

Cargèse

Sitting high above a deep blue bay on a cliff scattered with olive trees, **CARGÈSE** (Carghjese), 20km southwest of Porto, exudes a lazy charm that attracts hundreds of well-heeled summer residents to its pretty white houses and hotels. The full-time locals, half of whom are descendants of Greek refugees who fled the Turkish occupation of the Peloponnese in the seventeenth century, seem to accept with nonchalance this inundation, and the proximity of a large Club Med complex, but the best times to visit are May and late September, when Cargèse all but empties.

Two churches stand on separate hummocks at the heart of the village, a reminder of the old antagonism between the two cultures (resentful Corsican patriots ransacked the Greeks' original settlement in 1715 because of the newcomers' refusal to take up arms against their Genoese benefactors). The **Roman Catholic church** was built for the minority Corsican families in 1828 and is one of the latest examples of Baroque with a *trompe l'œil* ceiling that can't really compete with the view from the terrace outside. The **Greek church**, however, is the more interesting of the two: a large granite neo-Gothic edifice built in 1852 to replace a building that had become too small for its congregation. Inside, the outstanding feature is an unusual iconostasis, a gift from a monastery in Rome, decorated with uncannily modern-looking portraits. Behind it hang icons brought over from Greece with the original settlers – the graceful Virgin and Child, to the right-hand side of the altar, is thought to date as far back as the twelfth century.

The best beach in the area, **plage de Pero**, is 2km north of the village – head up to the junction with the Piana road and take the left fork down to the sea. Overlooked by a Genoese tower, this white stretch of sand has a couple of bars and easily absorbs the crowds that descend on it in August. **Plage du Chiuni**, a further 2km along the same road, is much busier thanks to its windsurfing facilities and the presence of Club Med. A more secluded spot is **plage du Monachi**, 1km south of the village; this small, sandy cove is reached by climbing down the track at the side of the road past the little chapel on the cliffside.

Practicalities

There's a **tourist office** on rue Dr-Dragacci (daily: June–Sept 9am–noon & 4–7pm; Oct–May 2–5pm; ☎04.95.26.41.31), which can help find accommodation and sells tickets for summer boat trips to the Calanche (see p.1064), costing about 170F/€25.84. **Buses** for Ajaccio and Porto stop outside the **post office**, set back from the road in the main square.

All the best **hotels** are located within minutes of the centre, with the budget places at the top end of the village. The least expensive is the *Continental*, on the left as you descend into the main square from Porto (☎04.95.26.42.24; ③), which is a bit dingy but clean and comfortable enough. If you can afford to splash out a little more, head for the *Bel'Mare*, 400m out of the village towards Ajaccio (☎04.95.26.40.13; ④); all the rooms have superb sea views from balconies, and it offers good low-season discounts. An equally comfortable option is *Thalassa* on plage de Pero (☎04.95.26.40.08; ④ including meal; closed winter), an intimate little place with friendly owners. The nearest **campsite**, *Camping Torraccia* (☎04.95.26.42.39), is 4km north of Cargèse on the main road.

A fair number of **restaurants** are scattered about the village, as well as the standard crop of basic pizzerias. *A Volta*, behind the Catholic church on place Mattei, offers a good-value 100F/€15.20 menu, featuring seafood, game and pasta served on a spectacular terrace that juts out over the sea. Cargèse's most reputed, and expensive, restaurant is located down in the marina. Don't be fooled by *Chez Antoine*'s rustic fishing shack appearance; their *bouillabaisse* is legendary, and draws yachtles from the nearby moorings, and well-heeled Ajacciens in equal number. For a **drink**, go no further than the main square, where you can watch all the action from *Bar Chantilly*, whose breakfast customers munch takeaway croissants and *pains au chocolat* from the bakery opposite. Another equally atmospheric spot is the rear terrace of the *Bar au Bon Accueil*, on the main street, which affords optimum views over the old quarter and gulf.

Ajaccio

Edward Lear claimed that on a wet day it would be hard to find so dull a place as **AJAC-CIO** (Aiacciu), a harsh judgement with an element of justice. The town has none of Bastia's sense of purpose and can seem to lack a definitive identity of its own, but it is a relaxed and good-looking place, with an exceptionally mild climate, a wealth of cafés, restaurants and shops.

Although it's an attractive idea that Ajax once stopped here, the name of Ajaccio derives from the Roman *Adjaccium* (place of rest), a winter stop-off point for shepherds descending from the mountains to stock up on goods and sell their produce. This first settlement, to the north of the present town in the area called Castelvecchio, was destroyed by the Saracens in the tenth century, and modern Ajaccio grew up around the citadel that was founded in 1492. Napoléon gave Ajaccio international fame, but though the self-designated *Cité Impériale* is littered with statues and street names related to the Bonaparte family, you'll find the Napoleonic cult has a less dedicated following in his home town than you might imagine. The emperor is still considered by many Ajacciens as a self-serving Frenchman rather than as a Corsican, and his impact on the townscape of his birthplace isn't enormous.

From the early 1980s, the town has gained an unwelcome reputation for nationalist violence. The most infamous terrorist atrocity of recent years was the murder, in February 1998, of the French government's most senior official on the island, Claude Erignac, who was gunned down as he left the opera. However, separatist violence rarely (if ever) affects tourists, and for visitors Ajaccio remains memorable for the things that have long made it attractive – its battered old town, relaxing cafés and the encompassing view of its glorious bay.

Arrival, information and accommodation

Ajaccio's Campo dell'Oro **airport** (☎04.95.21.07.07) is 6km south of town; hourly buses provide a shuttle service into the centre, stopping on cours Napoléon, the main street – tickets cost 20F/€3.04, and the journey takes around fifteen minutes. Heading in the other direction, the best place to pick up buses to the airport is the parking lot adjacent to the main **bus station** (*terminal routière*), a five-minute walk north of the centre

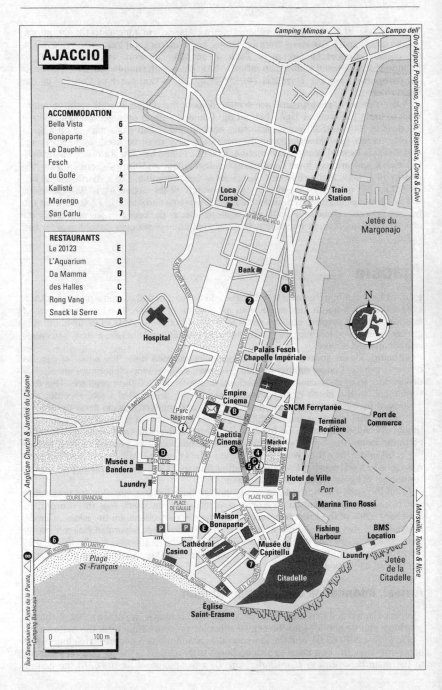

AJACCIO

ACCOMMODATION

Bella Vista	6
Bonaparte	5
Le Dauphin	1
Fesch	3
du Golfe	4
Kallisté	2
Marengo	8
San Carlu	7

RESTAURANTS

Le 20123	E
L'Aquarium	C
Da Mamma	B
des Halles	C
Rong Vang	D
Snack la Serre	A

Camping Mimosa

Campo dell'

Oro Airport, Propriano, Porticcio, Bastelica, Corte & Calvi

Loca Corse

Train Station

PLACE DE LA GARE

AV. BEVERINI VICO

Jetée du Margonajo

Bank

N

Hospital

Palais Fesch
Chapelle Impériale

AV. IMPÉRATRICE EUGÉNIE

R. IMPÉRATRICE EUGÉNIE

Empire Cinema

SNCM Ferrytanée

Port de Commerce

Parc Régional

Terminal Routière

Laetitia Cinema

Market Square

Musée a Bandera

Laundry

RUE GÉN. FIORELLA

COURS GRANDVAL

AV DE PARIS

Hotel de Ville

PLACE FOCH

Port

Marina Tino Rossi

PLACE DE GAULLE

Maison Bonaparte

Fishing Harbour

BMS Location

Cathédral

Casino

Musée du Capitellu

Laundry

Jetée de la Citadelle

BD ROSSINI

BD LANTIVY

Plage St-François

Citadelle

BOULEVARD PASCAL ROSSINI

Église Saint-Erasme

Anglican Church & Jardins du Casone

Iles Sanguinaires, Punta de la Parata, Camping Barbicaja

Marseille, Toulon & Nice

0   100 m

(☎04.95.21.28.01). **Ferries** also dock nearby, and the SNCM office is directly opposite at quai l'Herminier (☎04.95.29.66.88). The **gare SNCF** lies almost a kilometre north along boulevard Sampiero (☎04.95.23.11.03), a continuation of the quai l'Herminier. The **tourist office** on boulevard du Roi (May–Oct Mon–Sat 8am–8.30pm, Sun 9am–1pm; Nov–April Mon–Fri 8.30am–6pm, Sat 8.30am–1pm; ☎04.95 51.53.03) hands out large free glossy maps and posts transport timetables for checking departure times. Anyone planning a long-distance hike should head for the office of the national parks association, the **Parc Naturel Régional de Corse**, 2 rue Sergeant-Casalonga, around the corner from the Préfecture on cours Napoléon (Mon–Fri 8.15am–noon & 2–6pm; ☎04.95.51.79.00), where you can buy topo-guides, maps, guidebooks and leaflets detailing regional trail networks, and check the latest weather reports for the mountains. **Cars** can be rented from Rent-a-Car, at the *Hôtel Kallisté*, 51 cours Napoléon (☎04.95.51.34.45) and the airport (☎04.95.23.56.36); Aloha, at the airport only (☎04.95.23.57.19); Avis-Ollandini, 1 route d'Alata (☎04.95.23.92.50) and the airport (☎04.95.21.28.01); and Hertz-Locasud, 8 cours Grandval (☎04.95.21.70.94) and the airport (☎04.95.22.14.84).

Ajaccio suffers from a dearth of inexpensive **accommodation**, but there are a fair number of mid- and upscale places.

Hotels

Bella Vista, 20 bd Lantivy (☎04.95.21.07.97, fax 04.95.21.81.88). Large, imposing place slap on the seafront offering views of the gulf from its front rooms. Excellent value considering the location. ③.

Bonaparte, 1 rue Étienne-Conti (☎04.95.21.44.19). The rooms are a little overpriced, but immaculately clean and with views of the covered market; ask for one on the upper floor. Closed Nov–March. ③.

Le Dauphin, 11 bd Sampiero (☎04.95.21.12.94, fax 04.95.21.88.69). Easily Ajaccio's best budget hotel, directly opposite the ferry port and well placed for the airport bus. The bar downstairs serves inexpensive breakfasts. They also store luggage for no extra charge. Book in advance. ②.

Fesch, 7 rue Cardinal-Fesch (☎04.95.51.62.62, fax 04.95.21.83.36). Among the most appealing mid-range hotels in Ajaccio, with sheepskin furnishings and medieval-style decor designed by Corsicada, a group of local artisans. Closed mid-Dec to mid-Jan. ④.

du Golfe, 5 bd du Roi-Jérôme (☎04.95.21.47.64, fax 04.95.21.71.05). Popular with tour parties, this large, slick hotel has balconies overlooking the bay, televisions in every room and modern decor. Closed Feb. ⑤.

Kallisté, 51 cours Napoléon (☎04.95.51.34.45, fax 04.95.21.79.00). Recently revamped three-floor hotel, with an international atmosphere and parking space. Sound-proofed rooms for up to four people, plus studios with kitchenettes and TVs; Internet facilities in lobby. Proprietor speaks English. The best choice in this category. ④.

Marengo, 12 bd Mme-Mère (☎04.95.21.43.66, fax 04.95.21.51.26). Secluded, quiet and pleasant small hotel, a ten-minute walk west of centre, up a quiet side street off bd Mme-Mère. Slightly boxed in by tower blocks, but away from the city bustle. Closed mid-Nov to mid-March. ④.

San Carlu, 8 bd Danielle-Casanova (☎04.95.21.13.84, fax 04.95.21.09.99). Sited opposite the citadel and close to the beach, this three-star is the poshest option in the old town. Well-appointed rooms, own parking facilities and a special room for disabled guests in the easy-access basement. ⑦.

Campsites

Camping de Barbicaja, 4.5km west along the route des Sanguinaires (☎04.95.52.01.17). Crowded site, but close to the beach and easier to reach by bus (#5 from place de Gaulle) than *Les Mimosas*. Closed Oct–March.

Camping Les Mimosas, 3km northwest of town (☎04.95.20.99.85). A shady and well-organized site with clean toilet blocks, friendly management and fair rates, but rock-hard ground. It's a long trudge if you're loaded with luggage, but you can catch bus #4 from cours Napoléon to the "Brasilia" stop, and walk north from there to the roundabout at the bottom of the hill. After crossing the intersection, head up the lane on its far side and turn left at the signpost, passing a tennis club soon after on your right. The site lies another 1.5km uphill from there. Closed Nov–April.

The Town

The core of the **old town** holds the most interest in Ajaccio: a cluster of ancient streets spreading north and south of **place Foch**, which opens out to the seafront by the port and the marina. Nearby **place de Gaulle** forms the town centre and is the source of the main thoroughfare, **cours Napoléon**, which extends parallel to the sea almost 2km to the northeast. West of place de Gaulle stretches the modern part of town fronted by the **beach**, overlooked at its northern end by the citadel.

Around place de Gaulle and the new town.

Place de Gaulle (otherwise known as place du Diamant, after the Diamanti family who once owned much of the property in Ajaccio) is the most useful point of orientation, even if it's not much to look at – just a windy concrete platform surrounded by a shopping complex. The only noteworthy thing on the square is the huge, bronze equestrian statue, a pompous lump commissioned by Napoléon III in 1865 showing the first Napoléon in Roman attire, surrounded by his four brothers.

Devotees of Napoléon should take a stroll 1km up cours Grandval, the wide street rising west of place de Gaulle and ending in a square, the **Jardins du Casone**, where gaudily spectacular *son et lumière* shows take place in summer. An impressive **monument to Napoléon** dominates the square, standing atop an appropriately huge, proto-Fascist pedestal inscribed with the names of his battles. Behind the monument lies a graffiti-bedaubed cave where Napoléon is supposed to have frolicked as a child.

Place Foch

Once the site of the town's medieval gate, **place Foch** lies at the heart of old Ajaccio. A delightfully shady square sloping down to the sea and lined with cafés and restaurants, it gets its local name – place des Palmiers – from the row of palms bordering the central strip. Dominating the top end, a fountain of four marble lions provides a mount for the inevitable **statue of Napoléon**, this one by Ajaccien sculptor Maglioli. A humbler effigy occupies a niche high on the nearest wall – a figurine of Ajaccio's patron saint, **La Madonnuccia**, dating from 1656, a year in which Ajaccio's local council, fearful of infection from plague-struck Genoa, placed the town under the guardianship of the Madonna in a ceremony which took place on this spot.

At the northern end of place Foch is the **Hôtel de Ville** of 1826, with its prison-like wooden doors. The first-floor **Salon Napoléonien** (mid-June to mid-Sept Mon–Sat 9–11am & 2–5.45pm; rest of year Mon–Fri 9–11am & 2–4.45pm; 10F/€1.52) contains a replica of the ex-emperor's death mask in pride of place, along with a solemn array of Bonaparte family portraits and busts. A smaller medal room has a fragment from Napoléon's coffin and part of his dressing case, plus a model of the ship that brought his body back from St Helena, and a picture of the house where he died.

South of place Foch

The south side of place Foch, standing on the former dividing line between the poor district around the port and the bourgeoisie's territory, gives access to **rue Bonaparte**, the main route through the latter quarter. Built on the promontory rising to the citadel, the secluded streets in this part of town – with their dusty buildings and hole-in-the-wall restaurants lit by flashes of sea or sky at the end of the alleys – retain more of a sense of the old Ajaccio than anywhere else.

Napoléon was born in what's now the colossal **Maison Bonaparte**, on place Letizia (May–Sept Mon 2–6pm, Tues–Fri 9am–noon & 2–6pm, Sat 9–11.45am & 2–6pm, Sun 9am–noon; Oct–April Mon 2–6pm, Tues–Sat 10am–noon & 2–5pm, Sun 10am–noon;

NAPOLÉON AND CORSICA

Napoléon Bonaparte was born in Ajaccio in 1769, a crucial date in the history of Corsica as it was during this year that the French took over the island from the Genoese. They made a thorough job of it, crushing the Corsican leader Paoli's troops at Ponte Nuovo and driving him into exile. Napoléon's father Carlo, a close associate of Paoli, fled the scene of the battle with his pregnant wife in order to escape the victorious French army. But Carlo's subsequent behaviour was quite different from that of his former leader – he came to terms with the French, becoming a representative of the newly styled Corsican nobility in the National Assembly, and using his contacts with the French governor to get a free education for his children.

At the age of nine, Napoléon was awarded a scholarship to the Brienne military academy, an institution specially founded to teach the sons of the French nobility the responsibilities of their status, and the young son of a Corsican Italian-speaking household used his time well, leaving Brienne to enter the exclusive École Militaire in Paris. At the age of sixteen he was commissioned into the artillery. When he was twenty the Revolution broke out in Paris and the scene was set for a remarkable career.

Always an ambitious opportunist, he obtained leave from his regiment, returned to Ajaccio, joined the local Jacobin club and – with his eye on a colonelship in the Corsican militia – promoted enthusiastically the interests of the Revolution. However, things did not quite work out as he had planned, for Pascal Paoli had also returned to Corsica.

Carlo Bonaparte had died some years before, and Napoléon was head of a family that had formerly given Paoli strong support. Having spent the last twenty years in London, Paoli was pro-English and had developed a profound distaste for revolutionary excesses. Napoléon's French allegiance and his Jacobin views antagonized the older man, and his military conduct didn't enhance his standing at all. Elected second-in-command of the volunteer militia, Napoléon was involved in an unsuccessful attempt to wrest control of the citadel from royalist sympathizers. He thus took much of the blame when, in reprisal for the killing of one of the militiamen, several people were gunned down in Ajaccio, an incident which engendered eight days of civil war. In June 1793, Napoléon and his family were chased back to the mainland by the Paolists.

Napoléon promptly renounced any special allegiance he had ever felt for Corsica. He Gallicized the spelling of his name, preferring Napoléon to his baptismal Napoleone. And, although he was later to speak with nostalgia about the scents of the Corsican countryside, he put the city of his birth fourth on the list of places he would like to be buried.

22F/€3.34), off the west side of rue Napoléon. The house passed to Napoléon's father in the 1760s and here he lived, with his wife and family, until his death. But in May 1793, the Bonapartes were driven from the house by Paoli's partisans, who stripped the place down to the floorboards. Requisitioned by the English in 1794, Maison Bonaparte became an arsenal and a lodging house for English officers until Napoléon's mother Letizia herself funded its restoration. Owned by the state since 1923, the house now bears few traces of the Bonaparte family's existence.

One of the few original pieces of furniture left in the house is the wooden sedan chair in the hallway – the pregnant Letizia was carried back from church in it when her contractions started. Upstairs, there's an endless display of portraits, miniatures, weapons, letters and documents. Amongst the highlights of the first room are a few maps of Corsica dating from the eighteenth century, some deadly "vendetta" daggers and two handsome pairs of pistols belonging to Napoléon's father. The next-door Alcove Room was, according to tradition, occupied by Napoléon in 1799 when he stayed here for the last time, while in the third room you can see the sofa upon which the future emperor first saw the light of day on August 15, 1769. Adjoining the heavily restored long gallery is a tiny room known as the Trapdoor Room, whence Letizia and her children made their getaway from the marauding Paolists.

Napoléon was baptized in 1771 in the **Cathedral** (Mon–Sat 8am–6pm; no tourist visits on Sun), around the corner in rue Forcioli-Conti. Modelled on St Peter's in Rome, it was built in 1587–93 on a much smaller scale than intended, owing to lack of funds – an apology for its diminutive size is inscribed in a plaque inside, on the wall to the left as you enter. Inside, to the right of the door, stands the font where he was dipped at the age of 23 months; his sister, Elisa Baciochi, donated the great marble altar in 1811. Before you go, take a look in the chapel to the left of the altar, which houses a gloomy Delacroix painting of the Virgin.

A left turn at the eastern end of rue Forcioli-Conti brings you onto boulevard Danielle-Casanova. Here, opposite the citadel, an elaborately carved capital marks the entrance to **Musée Capitellu** (May–Oct Mon–Wed 10am–noon & 2–6pm; 25F/€3.80), a tiny museum mainly given over to offering a picture of domestic life in nineteenth-century Ajaccio. The house belonged to a wealthy Ajaccien family, the Baciochi, who were related to Napoléon through his sister's marriage. Amid the watercolour landscapes and marble busts, the glass display cases hold the most fascinating exhibits, including a rare edition of the first history of Corsica, written by Agostino Giustiniani, a bishop of the Nebbio who drowned in 1536, and the 1769 Code Corse, a list of laws set out by Louis XV for the newly occupied Corsica.

Opposite the museum, the restored **citadel**, a hexagonal fortress and tower stuck out on a wide promontory into the sea, is occupied by the military and usually closed to the public. Founded in the 1490s, the fort wasn't completed until the occupation of Ajaccio by Sampiero Corso and the powerful Marshal Thermes in 1553–58. The building overlooks the town **beach**, plage St-François, a short curve of yellow sand which faces the expansive mountain-ringed bay. Several flights of steps lead down to the beach from boulevard Danielle-Casanova.

North of place Foch

The dark narrow streets backing onto the port to the north of place Foch are Ajaccio's traditional trading ground. Each weekday and Saturday morning (and on Sundays during the summer), the square directly behind the Hôtel de Ville hosts a small farmers' **market** – a rarity in Corsica – where you can browse and buy top-quality fresh produce from around the island, including myrtle liqueur, wild-boar sauces, ewe's cheese from the Niolo valley and a spread of fresh vegetables, fruit and flowers.

Behind here, the principal road leading north is rue Cardinal-Fesch, a delightful meandering street lined with boutiques, cafés and restaurants. Halfway along the street, set back from the road behind iron gates, stands Ajaccio's best gallery, the **Musée Fesch** (April–June & Sept Mon 1–5.15pm, Tues–Sun 9.15am–12.15pm & 2.15–5.15pm; July–Sept Mon 1.30–6pm, Tues–Thurs 9am–6.30pm, Fri & Sat 10.30am–5.15pm, Sun 10.30am–6pm; Oct–March Tues–Sat 9.15am–12.15pm & 2.15–5.15pm; 35F/€5.32). Cardinal Joseph Fesch was Napoléon's step-uncle and bishop of Lyon, and he used his lucrative position to invest in large numbers of paintings, many of them looted by the French armies in Holland, Italy and Germany. His bequest to the town includes seventeenth-century French and Spanish masters, but it's the Italian paintings that are the chief attraction: Raphael, Titian, Bellini, Veronese and Botticelli all have a place here.

You'll need a separate ticket for the **Chapelle Impériale** (same hours; 10F/€1.52), which stands across the courtyard from the museum. With its gloomy monochrome interior the chapel itself is unremarkable, and its interest lies in the crypt, where various members of the Bonaparte family are buried. It was the cardinal's dying wish that all the Bonaparte family be brought together under one roof, so the chapel was built in 1857 and the bodies subsequently ferried in.

Eating, drinking and nightlife

Restaurants in Ajaccio vary from basic bistros to trendy pizzerias and pricey fish restaurants, the majority of which are found in the old town. **Bars** and **cafés** jostle for pavement space along cours Napoléon, generally lined with young people checking out the promenaders, and on place de Gaulle, where old-fashioned cafés and *salons de thé* offer a more sedate scene. If you fancy a view of the bay, check out one of the flashy cocktail bars that line the seafront on boulevard Lantivy, which, along with the casino, two cinemas and a handful of expensive euro-trashy clubs, comprise the sum total of Ajaccio's **nightlife**.

Bars and cafés

Le Dauphin, 11 bd Sampiero. An eccentric bar straight out of a 1950s French *policier*, complete with pinball machine, camp barman and sundry dodgy characters sipping *pastis* under a haze of Gauloise smoke.

L'Empereur, 12 place de Gaulle. Elegant Art Nouveau *salon du thé*, overlooking the main square.

Le Menestrel, 5 rue Fesch. Dubbed *"le rendez-vous des artistes"* because local musicians play here most evenings after 7pm – mostly café jazz, traditional mandolin and guitar tunes, with the odd popular singalong number "in the club style".

La Rade, 1 place Foch. The most congenial of the cafés fronting the Port de Plaisance and an ideal spot for crowd-watching over a chilled *pastis*.

Safari, 18 bd Lantivy. One of a row of lookalike cocktail bars next to the casino, overlooking the promenade. Good for a breezy coffee, and for watching Ajaccio's *beau monde* strut their stuff on Saturday nights.

Snack La Serre, 91 cours Napoléon. Popular budget-travellers' place, close to the train station, serving good-value bistro dishes and inexpensive snacks, including moussaka, roast lamb and adventurous salads.

Restaurants

Le 20123, 2 rue Roi de Rome (☎04.95.21.50.05). Decked out like a small hill village, complete with fountain and parked Vespa, the decor here is a lot more frivolous than the food: serious Corsican gastronomy (from charcuterie starter to chestnut-flour flan desserts) is featured on a single 175F/€26.60 menu.

L'Aquarium, rue des Halles (☎04.95.21.11.21). One of the best places in town for seafood – everything comes straight from the fish market across the square. Set menus 70–150F/€10.64–22.80. Closed Mon, except July & Aug.

des Halles, rue des Halles (☎04.95.21.42.68). Open since 1920, and the favourite lunch venue for market-stall holders and local office workers. They do a great value 77F/€11.70 menu with wild boar, fresh fish of the day and a choice of omelettes. Closed Sun in winter.

da Mamma, passage Guinghetta (☎04.95.21.39.44). Tucked away down a narrow passageway connecting cours Napoléon and rue Cardinal-Fesch, this sound budget choice serves authentic but affordable Corsican cuisine, such as *cannelloni al brocciu*, roast kid and seafood, on good-value set menus from 65F/€9.88 to 145F/€22.04 (the last one includes kid). The service is slick, the atmosphere lively, and the house wine's not bad either. Closed Sun in winter.

Rong Vang (Golden Dragon), opposite the Bandera Museum on rue Maréchal-d'Ornano. One of Corsica's few Chinese restaurants, serving French-influenced Cantonese cuisine (frogs legs *à la pékinoise* or with lemon curry). There are no set-menus, but à la carte dishes are reasonable at 60–95F/€9.12–14.44. Closed Sun.

Le Golfe de Valinco

From Ajaccio, the vista of white-washed villas and sandy beaches lining the opposite side of the gulf may tempt you out of town when you first arrive. On closer inspection, however, **Porticcio** turns out to be a faceless string of leisure settlement for Ajaccio's smart set, complete with tennis courts, malls and flotillas of jet-skis. Better to skip this stretch and press on south along the *route nationale* (RN194) which, after scaling the **Col de Celaccia**, winds down to the stunning **Golfe de Valinco**. A vast blue inlet bounded by rolling, scrub-covered hills, the gulf presents the first dramatic scenery along the coastal highway. It also marks the start of militant and Mafia-ridden south Corsica, more closely associated with vendetta, banditry and separatism than any other part of the island. Many of the mountain villages glimpsed from the roads hereabouts are riven with age-old divisions, exacerbated in recent years by the spread of organized crime and nationalist violence. But the island's seamier side is rarely discernible to the hundreds of thousands of visitors who pass through each summer, most of whom stay around the small port of **Propriano**, at the eastern end of the gulf. In addition to offering most of the area's tourist amenities, this busy resort town lies within easy reach of the menhirs at **Filitosa**, one of the western Mediterranean's most important prehistoric sites, and the secluded fishing village of **Campomorro**, on the opposite shore of the gulf, from where you can strike out south on foot to explore one of Corsica's wildest stretches of coast.

The Golfe de Valinco region is reasonably well served by **public transport**, with buses running four times per day between Ajaccio and Bonifacio, via Propriano and Sartène. Note, however, that outside July and August there are no services along this route on Sundays.

Propriano

Tucked into the narrowest part of the Golfe de Valinco, the small port of **PROPRIANO** (Prupria), 8km northwest of Sartène, centres on a fine natural harbour that was exploited by the ancient Greeks, Carthaginians and Romans, but became a prime target for Saracen pirate raids in the eighteenth century, when it was largely destroyed. Redeveloped in the 1900s, it now boasts a thriving marina, and handles ferries to Toulon, Marseille and Sardinia. The town around the port has also grown in importance, largely under the direction of a powerful coalition consisting of the mayor, a second-generation Italian immigrant named Émile Mocchi; his nephew, one of the leaders of a prominent nationalist group; and southern Corsica's most renowned godfather, Jean-Jérôme (aka "Jean-Jé") Colonna, veteran of the infamous "French Connection". Together, this alliance has somewhat held in check power struggles between the area's political and Mafia organizations, allowing Propriano to prosper as a tourist resort, although reports of mob and nationalist violence still crop up from time to time in the local press.

The occasional eruption of violence, however, doesn't deter the tourists, who come here in droves for the area's **beaches**. The nearest of these, **plage de Lido**, lies 1km west, just beyond the Port de Commerce; it's patrolled by lifeguards during the summer and is much safer and more appealing than the grubby **plage de Baracci**, 1km north of town, where the undertow is precariously strong. Just 3km beyond the Baracci beach, the D157 branches off to the left and continues along the coast, which is built up with hotels and package-tour holiday blocks until **Olmeto plage**, 10km west, where an abundance of campsites are on offer (see below). You can reach Olmeto on the three daily buses from Propriano to Porto.

Practicalities

Ferries from the mainland and Sardinia dock in the Port de Commerce, ten minutes' walk from where the **buses** stop at the top of rue du Général-de-Gaulle, the town's main street. The SNCM office is on quai Commandant-L'Herminier (☎04.95.76.04.36), while the **tourist office** is down in the harbour master's office in the marina (June & Sept

Mon–Sat 9am–noon & 3–7pm; July & Aug daily 8am–8pm; Oct–May Mon–Fri 9am–noon & 2–6pm; ☎04.95.76.01.49).

There's a reasonable choice of **hotels** in the centre of town, including the high-tech *Loft Hôtel*, 3 rue Camille-Pietri (☎04.95.76.17.48, fax 04.95.76.22.04; ④; closed Feb), directly behind the port; and the *Bellevue* on avenue Napoléon (☎04.95.76.01.86, fax 04.95.76.38.94; ③), overlooking the marina and with the cheapest central rooms. If you have a car, two other places worth trying are the *Arcu di Sole*, 3km northeast on the route de Baracci (☎04.95.76.05.10, fax 04.95.76.13.36; ⑤), which has a pool and gourmet restaurant, or the more modest *Centre Équestre Baracci* (☎04.95.76.09.48), an excellent *gîte d'étape* just down the road from the *Arc di Sole*, which offers beds in four-person dorms for 85F/€12.92, or double rooms for 210F/€31.92. **Campers** are well provided for, although the best sites are well out of town: for the best facilities go to *Camping Colomba* (☎04.95.76.06.42), 3km north along route de Baracci, which has a swimming pool. At Olmeta plage, the most appealing site is *U Libecciu* (☎04.95.74.01.28), the first place on the beach coming from Propriano, or you could try *Chez Antoine* (☎04.95.76.06.06) in Marina d'Olmeto, north of the beach.

Cafés and **restaurants** are concentrated along the marina's avenue Napoléon, where *Resto Nicoli* is just about the cheapest place to eat, with excellent omelettes and Italian specialities. For fresh seafood, though, you can't beat *L'Hippocampe* (☎04.95.76.11.01), tucked away behind the port on rue Pandolphi, which serves a superb-value 98F/€14.90 menu on a pretty rear terrace.

Filitosa

Set deep in the countryside of the fertile Vallée du Taravo, the extraordinary **Station Préhistorique de Filitosa** (March–Oct daily 8am–7.30pm; out-of-season visits are possible by arrangement; ☎04.95.74.00.91; 22F/€3.34), 17km north of Propriano, comprises a wonderful array of statue-menhirs and prehistoric structures encapsulating some eight thousand years of history. There's no public transport to this site. Vehicles can be left in the small car park in the hamlet of Filitosa, where you pay the entrance fee; from here it's a fifteen-minute walk to the entrance, where you'll find a café, a small museum and a workshop producing reproduction prehistoric ceramics.

The site was settled by Neolithic farming people who lived here in rock shelters until the arrival of navigators from the east in about 3500 BC. These invaders were the creators of the menhirs, the earliest of which were possibly phallic symbols worshipped by an ancient fertility cult. When the seafaring people known as the Torréens (after the towers they built on Corsica) conquered Filitosa around 1300 BC, they destroyed most of the menhirs, incorporating the broken stones into the area of dry-stone walling surrounding the site's two *torri* or towers, examples of which can be found all over the south of Corsica. The site remained undiscovered until a farmer stumbled across the ruins on his land in the late 1940s.

Filitosa V looms up on the right shortly after the main entrance to the site. The largest statue-menhir on the island, it's an imposing sight, with clearly defined facial features and a sword and dagger outlined on the body. Beyond a sharp left turn lies the oppidum or central monument, its entrance marked by the **eastern platform**, thought to have been a lookout post. The cave-like structure sculpted out of the rock is the only evidence of Neolithic occupation and is generally agreed to have been a burial mound. Straight ahead, the Torréen **central monument** comprises a scattered group of menhirs on a circular walled mound, surmounted by a dome and entered by a corridor of stone slabs and lintels. Nobody is sure of its exact function.

Nearby **Filitosa XIII** and **Filitosa IX**, implacable lumps of granite with long noses and round chins, are the most impressive of the menhirs. Filitosa XIII is typical of the figures carved just before the Torréen invasion, with its vertical dagger carved in relief

– **Filitosa VII** also has a clearly sculpted sword and shield. **Filitosa VI**, from the same period, is remarkable for its facial detail. On the eastern side of the central monument stand some vestigial Torréen houses, where fragments of ceramics dating from 5500 BC were discovered; they represent the most ancient finds on the site, and some of them are displayed in the museum.

The western monument, a two-roomed structure built underneath another walled mound, is thought to have been some form of Torréen religious building. A flight of steps leads to the foot of this mound, where a footbridge opens onto a meadow that's dominated by five statue-menhirs arranged in a semi-circle beneath a thousand-year-old olive tree. A bank separates them from the **quarry** from which the megalithic sculptors hewed the stone for the menhirs – a granite block is marked ready for cutting.

The **museum** is a shoddy affair, with poorly labelled exhibits and very little contextual information, but the artefacts themselves are fascinating. The major item here is the formidable Scalsa Murta, a huge menhir dating from around 1400 BC and discovered at Olmeto. Like other statue-menhirs of this period, this one has two indents in the back of its head, which are thought to indicate that these figures would have been adorned with headdresses. Other notable exhibits are **Filitosa XII**, which has a hand and a foot carved into the stone, and **Trappa II**, a strikingly archaic face.

Campomorro

Isolated at the mouth of the Golfe de Valinco, **CAMPOMORO**, 17km southwest of Propriano, ranks among the most congenial seaside villages on the island. The main attraction here is a two-kilometre-long **beach**, overlooked by an immense and well-preserved Genoese watchtower. In late July and August, it's swamped by Italian families from the adjacent campsites, but for the rest of the year Campomorro remains a tranquil enough place, with barely enough permanent residents to support a post office.

Another incentive to venture out here is the wild and windswept stretch of coast **south of Campomorro**, which is punctuated by outlandish rock formations and a string of empty pebble beaches. The absence of a road into the area, recently designated a regional nature reserve, means the only way to explore it is by boat or on foot, via the waymarked **coastal path** that begins below Campomorro's watchtower. From here, the path is easy to follow for the first eighty minutes or so as it threads through a series of dramatic granite outcrops, eroded into phantasmagorical shapes. But once you hit the **anse d'Eccia**, and its sandy bottle-necked cove, the going gets tougher. Determined, well-equipped hikers can walk all the way to Tizzano, 20km down the coast, via the much photographed **Senetosa Tower**, but to do so it's essential to take along a detailed map, plenty of fresh water and camping equipment in case you get lost. For additional route advice, contact the owner of Grand Bleu boat trips at his caravan near the tourist office in Propriano (☎04.95.76.04.26). He takes customers to anse d'Eccia by catamaran, and provides photographs to help you follow the trail back to Campomorro; the cost of this half-day trip is 140F/€21.28.

Practicalities

There are no bus services to Campomorro, but hitching is fairly reliable once you've turned off the main Propriano–Bonifacio road. The village possesses a couple of campsites and two **hotels**: *Le Ressac*, about 100m behind the chapel (☎04.95.74.22.25, fax 04.95.74.23.43; ③; closed Oct–May), a friendly family-run place with excellent views across the bay, is generally a better option than the more expensive, but less welcoming, *Le Campomorro*, overlooking the beach at the tower end of the village (☎04.95.74.20.89; ④). Of the two **campsites**, *Camping Peretto Les Roseaux*, 300m from the post office towards the tower (☎04.95.74.20.52; closed Nov–April) is the more peaceful. For **food**, try the popular *La Mouette* café opposite the church (☎04.95.74.22.26), which serves a selection of filling salads for under 50F/€7.60 on its beachside terrace. Alternatively, *Le Ressac*'s pricier restaurant is renowned for its *bouillabaisse*, which contains six or more kinds of fresh local fish, as well as lobster.

Sartène and around

Prosper Mérimée famously dubbed **SARTÈNE** (Sartè) *"la plus corses des villes corse"* (the most Corsican of Corsican towns), but the nineteenth-century German chronicler Gregorovius put a less complimentary spin on it when he described it as a "town peopled by demons". Sartène hasn't shaken off its hostile image, due in large part to a heavy presence of wealthy-looking godfather types. On the other hand it's a smart, clean place, noticeably better groomed than many small Corsican towns, its principal income coming from Sartène wine – the best on the island. The main square doesn't offer many diversions once you've explored the enclosed old town and prehistory museum, and the only time of year Sartène teems with tourists is at Easter for **U Catenacciu**, a Good Friday procession that packs the main square with onlookers.

Close to Sartène are some of the island's best-known prehistoric sites, most notably **Filitosa** (see above), the megaliths of **Cauria** and the **Alignement de Palaggiu** – Corsica's largest array of prehistoric standing stones.

The Town

Place Porta – its official name, place de la Libération, has never caught on – forms Sartène's nucleus. Once the arena for bloody vendettas, it's now a well-kept square opening onto a wide terrace that overlooks the rippling green valley of the Rizzanese. Flanking the south side of place Porta is the **church of Ste-Marie**, built in the 1760s but completely restored to a smooth granitic appearance. Inside the church, the most notable feature is the weighty wooden cross and chair carried through the town by hooded penitents during the Catenacciu procession.

A flight of steps to the left of the **Hôtel de Ville**, formerly the governor's palace, leads past the post office to a ruined **lookout tower**, which is all that remains of the town's twelfth-century ramparts. This apart, the best of the old town is to be found behind the Hôtel de Ville in the **Santa Anna district**, a labyrinth of constricted passageways and ancient fortress-like houses that rarely give any signs of life. Featuring few windows and often linked to their neighbours by balconies, these houses are entered by first-floor doors which would have been approached by ladders – dilapidated staircases have replaced these necessary measures against unwelcome intruders. To the left of rue des Frères-Bartoli are the strangest of all the vaulted passageways, where outcrops of rock block the paths between the ancient buildings. Just to the west of the Hôtel de Ville, signposted off the tiny place Maggiore, you'll find the **impasse Carababa**, a remarkable architectural puzzle of a passageway cut through the awkwardly stacked houses. A few steps away, at the western edge of the town, **place Angelo-Maria-Chiappe** offers a magnificent view of the Golfe du Valinco.

Sartène's only other cultural attraction is **Musée de la Préhistoire Corse** (closed at time of writing, pending a move to new premises across town; check with tourist office), Corsica's centre for archeological research. The museum contains a rather dry collection of mostly Neolithic and Torréen pottery fragments, with some bracelets from the Iron Age and painted ceramics from the thirteenth to sixteenth centuries.

Practicalities

If you're arriving in Sartène by **bus**, you'll be dropped either at the top of avenue Gabriel-Péri or at the end of cours Général-de-Gaulle. On the opposite side of place

Porta, a short way down rue Capitaine-Benedetti, is a tiny **tourist office** (May–Sept Mon–Fri 9am–noon & 3–7pm; ☎04.95.77.15.40).

The only **hotel** in Sartène itself is *Les Roches* on rue Jean-Jaurès, a large family-run place just below the old town (☎04.95.77.07.61, fax 04.95.77.19.93; ④); it commands panoramic views of the Vallée du Rizzanese and has a restaurant that serves hearty Corsican food. Otherwise try the *Villa Piana*, 1km out of town on the Propriano road (☎04.95.77.07.04, fax 04.95.73.45.65; ⑤; closed Nov to mid-April), an upmarket place, with a pool and tennis court, overlooking the Golfe de Valinco – or simply stay in Propriano (see p.1074), which has a wider choice of accommodation. The nearest **campsite**, *Camping Olva (Les Eucalyptus)*, lies 5km along the D69 to Castagna (☎04.95.77.11.58; closed Nov–April) – it offers a free bus service to and from Sartène.

As for **restaurants**, try the cheap and cheerful *aux Gourmets* (☎04.95.77.16.08), on the cours Sœur-Amélie, whose good-value 80F/€12.16 set menu includes wild-boar steak and chips. For a light lunch, you can't do better than the *Zia Paulina*, tucked away at the end of an atmospheric alleyway, rue des Frères-Bartoli, in the *vielle ville*: Corsican specialities dominate their set menus and there's a generous selection of local wines to choose from. *Pizza Porta*, on the square, is a good choice for quick snacks such as toasted sandwiches, fresh salads, crêpes and pizzas. **Cafés** cluster around place Porta, and are great places for crowd-watching.

The megalithic sites

Sparsely populated today, the rolling hills of the southwestern corner of Corsica are rich in prehistoric sites. The megaliths of **Cauria**, standing in ghostly isolation 10km southwest from Sartène, comprise the Dolmen de Fontanaccia, the best-preserved monument of its kind on Corsica, and the nearby alignments of **Stantari** and **Renaggiu** have an impressive congregation of statue-menhirs.

More than 250 menhirs can be seen northwest of Cauria at **Palaggiu**, another rewardingly remote site. Equally wild is the coast hereabouts, with deep clefts and coves providing some excellent spots for diving and secluded swimming.

The only public transport in this region is the twice-daily Ajaccio–Bonifacio **bus**.

Cauria

To reach the **Cauria megalithic site**, you need to turn off the N196 about 2km outside Sartène, at the Col de l'Albitrina (291m), taking the D48 towards Tizzano. Four kilometres along this road a left turning brings you onto a winding road through *maquis*, until eventually the **Dolmen de Fontanaccia** comes into view on the horizon, crowning the crest of a low hill amidst a sea of *maquis*. A blue sign at the parking space indicates the track to the dolmen, a fifteen-minute walk away.

Known to the locals as the **Stazzona del Diavolu** (Devil's Forge), a name that does justice to its enigmatic power, the Dolmen de Fontanaccia is in fact a burial chamber from around 2000 BC. This period was marked by a change in burial customs – whereas bodies had previously been buried in stone coffins in the ground, they were now placed above, in a mound of earth enclosed in a stone chamber. What you see today is the great stone table, comprising six huge granite blocks nearly 2m high, topped by a stone slab that remained after the earth eroded away.

The twenty "standing men" of the **Alignement de Stantari**, 200m to the east of the dolmen, date from the same period. All are featureless, except two which have roughly sculpted eyes and noses, with diagonal swords on their fronts and sockets in their heads where horns would probably have been attached.

Across a couple of fields to the south is the **Alignement de Renaggiu**, a gathering of forty menhirs standing in rows amid a small shadowy copse, set against the enormous granite outcrop of Punta di Cauria. Some of the menhirs have fallen, but all face north to south, a fact that seems to rule out any connection with a sun-related cult.

Palaggiu

To reach the **Alignement de Palaggiu**, the largest concentration of menhirs in Corsica, regain the D48 and head southwards past the Domaine la Mosconi vineyard (on your right, 3km after the Cauria turn-off), 1500m beyond which a green metal gate on the right side of the road marks the turning. From here a badly rutted dirt track leads another 1200m to the stones, lost in the *maquis*, with vineyards spread over the hills in the half-distance. Stretching in straight lines across the countryside like a battleground of soldiers, the 258 menhirs include three statue-menhirs with carved weapons and facial features – they are amidst the first line you come to. Dating from around 1800 BC, the statues give few clues as to their function, but it's a reasonable supposition that proximity to the sea was important – the famous Corsican archeologist Roger Grosjean's theory is that the statues were some sort of magical deterrent to invaders.

Bonifacio

BONIFACIO (Bonifaziu) enjoys a superbly isolated situation at Corsica's southernmost point, a narrow peninsula of dazzling white limestone creating a town site unlike any other. The much-photographed **haute ville**, a maze of narrow streets flanked by tall Genoese tenements, rises seamlessly out of sheer cliffs that have been hollowed and striated by the wind and waves, while on the landward side the deep cleft between the peninsula and the mainland forms a perfect natural harbour. A haven for boats for centuries, this inlet is nowadays a chic marina that attracts yachts from all around the Med. Separated from the rest of the island by a swathe of dense *maquis*, Bonifacio has maintained a certain temperamental detachment from the rest of Corsica, and is distinctly more Italian than French in atmosphere. The town retains Renaissance features found only here, and its inhabitants have their own dialect based on Ligurian, a legacy of the days when this was practically an independent Genoese colony.

Such a place has its inevitable drawbacks: exorbitant prices, overwhelming crowds in August and a commercial cynicism that's atypical of Corsica as a whole. However, the old town forms one of the most arresting spectacles in the Mediterranean, easily transcending all the tourist frippery that surrounds it, and warrants at least a day-trip. If you plan to come in peak season, try to get here early in the day before the bus parties arrive at around 10am.

Arrival, information and accommodation

Arriving by plane, you'll land at **Figari** airport, 17km north of Bonifacio. There's no bus service from here so you'll have to take a taxi into town – around 250F/€38. If you're coming by **bus** you'll be dropped at the car park by the **marina**, close to most of the hotels. The **tourist office** is up in the *haute ville*, in the Fort San Nicro at the bottom of rue F. Scamaroni (July–Sept daily 9am–8pm; Oct–June Mon–Fri 9am–12.30pm & 2–5.15pm); they will check for you which hotels have vacancies. **Cars** can be rented from Avis (☎04.95.73.01.28) or Hertz (☎04.95.73.06.41), both on quai Banda del Ferro, or Citer, quai Noel-Beretti (☎04.95.73.13.16). If you need to change money, note that Bonifacio's only ATM, at the Société Générale on the quai J. Comparetti, frequently runs out of money, so get here early in the day or you'll be at the mercy of the rip-off bureaux de change dotted around the town.

Finding a place to **stay** can be a chore, as Bonifacio's hotels are quickly booked up in high season; if you want to stay centrally, make sure you ring in advance. Better still,

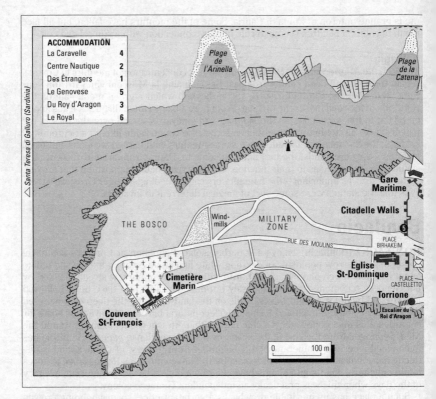

ACCOMMODATION

La Caravelle	4
Centre Nautique	2
Des Étrangers	1
Le Genovese	5
Du Roy d'Aragon	3
Le Royal	6

△ Santa Teresa di Galluro (Sardinia)

Plage de l'Arinella

Plage de la Catena

Gare Maritime

Citadelle Walls

THE BOSCO

Wind-mills

MILITARY ZONE

RUE DES MOULINS

PLACE BIRHAKEIM

Église St-Dominique

PLACE CASTELLETTO

Cimetière Marin

Torrione

Couvent St-François

Escalier du Roi d'Aragon

0   100 m

save yourself the trouble, and a considerable amount of money, by finding a room somewhere else and travelling here for the day; tariffs in this town are the highest on the island. The same applies to the large **campsites** dotted along the road to Porto-Vecchio, which can get very crowded.

Hotels

La Caravelle, 37 quai Comparetti (☎04.95.73.00.03, fax 04.95.73.00.41). Stylish olde-worlde place with an excellent restaurant in a prime location. Closed mid-Oct to Easter. ⑤.

Centre Nautique, on the marina (☎04.95.73.02.11, fax 04.95.73.17.47, *www.hotel.genovese.fr*). Chic but relaxed hotel on the waterfront, fitted out with wood and nautical charts. All rooms are tastefully furnished and consist of two storeys connected with a spiral staircase. ⑨.

des Étrangers, 4 av Sylvère-Bohn (☎04.95.73.01.09, fax 04 95 73 16 97). A swish place on the road to Ajaccio just past the port, whose (double-glazed) rooms are a bargain off season, but rather pricey and too close to the main road for comfort, especially during July and August, when the road is very busy. Closed Nov–March. ⑤.

Le Genovese, quartier de la Citadelle (☎04.95.73.12.34, fax 04.95.73.09.03, *www.oda.fr/aa/genovese*). The only luxury hotel in the *haute ville*, hence the sky-high rates. The views over the marina from some of the rooms are great. ⑧.

du Roy d'Aragon, 13 quai Comparetti (☎04.95.73.03.99, fax 04.95.73.07.94). A stylish, recently renovated three-star overlooking the marina, with better-than-average off-season discounts. ⑦.

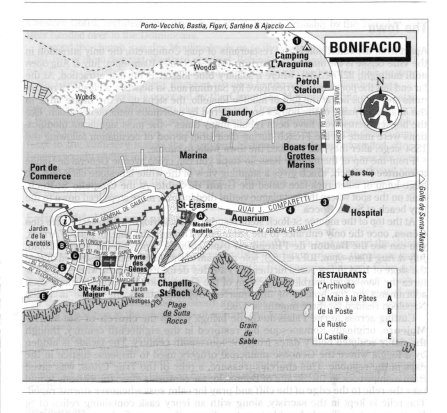

Le Royal, 8 rue Fred-Scamaroni, off the place Bonaparte (☎04.95.73.00.51, fax 04.95.73.04.68). Bright, clean place above a modern bar in the *ville haute*, with views of the citadel and the sea. All rooms air-conditioned. Good value by Bonifacio standards. ⑥.

Campsites

L'Araguina, av Sylvère-Bohn, opposite the Total service station near *Hôtel des Étrangers* (☎04.95.73.02.96). The closest site to town, but overcrowded, with stony ground and less than pleasant toilet blocks. Only worth considering if you can't get anywhere else.

Camping Asciaghju, route de Palombaggia (☎04.95.70.37.87). Basic but reasonably priced campsite, situated roughly midway between Bonifacio and Porto-Vecchio, on the road to Palombaggia beach. Offers access to a private beach – a godsend in summer. Closed Oct–May.

Camping Rondinara, Rondinara beach, signposted east off N198, 10km north of Bonifacio (☎04.95.70.43.15). One of the best-value, and best-situated, sites in the area, although quite a drive north. It has a pool, and is close to an exquisite shell-shaped beach (see p.1084). Closed Oct–May.

Campo di Liccia, opposite *U Farniente* (☎04.95.73.03.09). Well-shaded site, and large enough to guarantee you a place. They also run a free shuttle bus to the nearest beach in summer. Closed Oct–May.

U Farniente, Pertamina, 3km north along the road to Porto-Vecchio (☎04.95.73.05.47). Very flash four-star site with excellent facilities, including a pool – essential to book in summer. Closed Oct–May.

Heading **south of Porto-Vecchio** along the main N198, take the turning signposted for **Palombaggia**, a golden semicircle of sand edged by short twisted umbrella pines that are punctuated by fantastically shaped red rocks. This might be the most beautiful beach on the island were it not for the crowds, which pour on to it in such numbers that a wattle fence has had to be erected to protect the dunes. A few kilometres further along the same road takes you to **Santa Giulia**, a sweeping sandy bay backed by a lagoon. Despite the presence of several holiday villages and facilities for windsurfing and other noisier watersports, crowds are less of a problem here, and the shallow bay is an extraordinary turquoise colour.

North of Porto-Vecchio, the first beach worth a visit is **San Ciprianu**, a half-moon bay of white sand, reached by turning left off the main road at the Elf garage. Carry on for another 7km, and you'll come to the even more picturesque beach at **Pinarellu**, a uncrowded, long sweep of soft white sand with a Genoese watchtower and, like the less inspiring beaches immediately north of here, benefiting from the spectacular backdrop of the Massif de l'Ospédale.

The coast between Porto-Vecchio and Solenzara is also strewn with **prehistoric monuments**. The most impressive of these, **Casteddu d'Araggiu**, lies 12km north along the D759. From the site's car park (signposted off the main road), it's a twenty-minute stiff climb through *maquis* and scrubby woodland to the ruins. Built in 2000 BC and inhabited by a community that lived by farming and hunting, the *casteddu* consists of a complex of chambers built into a massive circular wall of pink granite, splashed with vivid green patches of lichen, from the top of which the views over the gulf are superb.

The route de Bavella

Starting from the picture-postcard-pretty mountain village of **ZONZA**, 40km northwest of Porto-Vecchio, and running northeast towards the coast, the D268 – known locally as the **route de Bavella** – is perhaps the most dramatic road in all Corsica. Well served by buses, it also affords one of the simplest approaches to the spectacular landscapes of the interior. The road penetrates a dense expanse of old pine and chestnut trees as it rises steadily to the **Col de Bavella** (1218m), where a towering statue of **Notre-Dame-des-Neiges** marks the windswept pass itself. An amazing panorama of peaks and forests spreads out from the col: to the northwest the serrated granite ridge of the Cirque de Gio Agostino is dwarfed by the pink pinnacles of the Aiguilles de Bavella; behind soars Monte Incudine.

Just below the pass, the seasonal hamlet of **BAVELLA** comprises a handful of congenial cafés, corrugated-iron-roofed chalets and hikers' hostels from where you can follow a series of waymarked **trails** to nearby viewpoints. Deservedly the most popular of these is the two-hour walk to the **Trou de la Bombe**, a circular opening that pierces the Paliri crest of peaks. From the car park behind the *Auberge du Col* (see opposite), follow the red-and-white waymarks of GR20 for 800m, then head right when you see orange splashes. Those with a head for heights should climb right into the hole for the dizzying view down the sheer 500m cliff on the other side. Even more amazing views may be had from the summit of the adjacent peak, **Calanca Murata**, which you can scale after a steep forty-minute haul from the head of the ravine just below Trou de la Bombe. Small stone cairns mark the route. At no stage do you need to climb, but the views, which take in the entire Bavella massif to the west and a huge sweep of the eastern plains, are on a par with those from any of the island's major peaks.

From Bavella, it's a steep descent through what's left of the **Forêt de Bavella**, which was devastated by fire in 1960 but still harbours some huge Laricio pines. The winding road offers numerous breathtaking glimpses of the Aiguilles de Bavella and plenty of places to pull over for a swim in the river.

The best place to **stay** locally is Zonza, which has a cluster of hotels, all with more than decent restaurants, such as *Le Tourisme*, set back on the west side of the Quenza road north of the village (☎04.95.78.67.72, fax 04.95.78.72.23; ④; closed Nov–March), or *L'Aiglon* in the village centre (☎04.95.78.67.79, fax 04.95.78.63.62; ③; closed Jan–March). For hikers, clean and comfortable dormitory accommodation is available at the *Auberge du Col* (☎04.95.57.43.87; closed Nov–March), the most pleasant of the small *gîtes d'étapes* at Bavella, below the pass. Regular **buses** run to Zonza from Ajaccio, Propriano, Sartène and Porto-Vecchio; for the current timetables ask at a tourist office.

Aléria

Built on the estuary at the mouth of the River Tavignano on the island's east coast, 40km southeast of Corte along the N200, **ALÉRIA** was first settled in 564 BC by a colony of Greek Phocaeans as a trading port for the copper and lead they mined from the land and the wheat, olives and grapes they farmed. After an interlude of Carthaginian rule, the Romans arrived in 259 BC, built a naval base and re-established its importance in the Mediterranean. Aléria remained the east coast's principal port right up until the eighteenth century. Little is left of the historic town except Roman ruins and a thirteenth-century Genoese fortress, which stands high against a background of chequered fields and green vineyards. To the south, a strip of modern buildings straddling the main road makes up the modern town, but it's the village set on the hilltop just west of here which holds most interest.

The best plan is to begin with the **Musée Jerôme Carcopino** (mid-May to Sept daily 8am–noon & 2–7pm; Oct to mid-May Mon–Sat 8am–noon & 2–5pm; 10F/€1.52, including Roman site), housed in the Fort Matra and crammed with remarkable finds from the Roman site, including Hellenic and Punic coins, rings, belt links, elaborate oil lamps decorated with Christian symbols, Attic plates and a second-century marble bust of Jupiter Ammon. Etruscan bronzes fill another room, with jewellery and armour from the fourth to the second century BC.

It's a stone's throw from here to the **Roman site** (closes 30min before museum; same ticket), where most of the excavation was done as recently as the 1950s, despite the fact that French novelist Prosper Merimée noticed signs of the Roman settlement during his survey of the island in 1830. Most of the site still lies beneath ground and is undergoing continuous excavation, but the *balneum* (bathhouse), the base of Augustus's triumphal arch, the foundations of the forum and traces of shops have already been unearthed.

First discovered was the arch, which formed the entrance to the governor's residence – the *praetorium* – on the western edge of the forum. In the adjacent *balneum*, a network of reservoirs and cisterns, the *caldarium* bears traces of the underground pipes that would have heated the room, and a patterned mosaic floor is visible inside the neighbouring chamber. To the north of the site lie the foundation walls of a large house, while at the eastern end of the forum the foundations of the temple can be seen, and at its northern edge, over a row of column stumps, are the foundations of the apse of an early Christian church.

Some traces of the **Greek settlement**, comprising the remains of an acropolis, have been discovered further to the east. It's believed that the main part of the town would have extended from the present site over to this acropolis and down to the Tavignano estuary. The port was located to the east of the main road, where the remnants of a second-century bathhouse have been found.

Of Aléria's few **hotels**, *Les Orangers* (☎04.95.57.00.31; ②), situated 50m north of the Cateraggio crossroads in the centre of the modern part, is the cheapest. *L'Atrachjata* (☎04.95.57.03.93, fax 04.95.57.08.03; ③), a little further north, does good meals;

bathe in the many pools fed by the cascading torrent of the River Restonica, easily reached by scrambling down the rocky banks.

From the *bergeries*, a well-worn path winds along the valley floor to a pair of beautiful glacial lakes. The first and larger, **Lac de Melo**, is reached after an easy hour's hike through the rocks. One particularly steep part of the path has been fitted with security chains, but the scramble around the side of the passage is perfectly straightforward, and much quicker. Once past Lac de Melo, press on for another forty minutes along the steeper marked trail over a moraine to the second lake, **Lac de Capitello**, the more spectacular of the pair. Hemmed in by vertical cliffs, the deep turquoise-blue pool affords fine views of the Rotondo massif on the far side of the valley, and in clear weather you can spend an hour or two exploring the surrounding crags, the haunt of rock pipits. Beyond here, the trail climbs higher to meet the GR20, and should only be attempted by well-equipped mountain-walkers.

Venaco and Vivario

Immediately south of Corte you ascend into a landscape of lush chestnut forests that lasts as far as the **Col de Bellagranjo** (723m), before the road sweeps through **VENACO**, an elegant village of rusty buildings emerging from deep green verdure on the slopes of Monte Padro. You might want to halt here to admire the vistas – from the terrace of the Baroque church there's a spectacular view of the lower Vallée du Tavignano in the east.

Five kilometres south of Venaco is the dizzying **Pont de Vecchiu** railway bridge at the foot of Monte Retondo, built by Gustave Eiffel (of Eiffel tower fame). Alongside it, the even more impressive new road bridge, opened in 1999, now spans the 222-metre-wide gorge at a height of 137.5m. A series of tortuous switchbacks beyond the bridges brings you to **VIVARIO**, located at the junction of the routes to the Forêt de Rospa Sorba and the Col de Verde. Straddling a nexus of the area's principal long-distance footpaths, this large but innocuous village makes a good base for walkers, who can stay at the basic *Macchje Monte* (☎04.95.47.22.00; ③; closed Jan & Feb). Vivario's attraction lies in its forest setting, a savage environment that once supported its own wild man. In 1800 a 10-year-old boy went missing here after arguing with his parents, and stayed on the run for twenty years until ensnared by a group of hunters down by the river. The only traversable spot across the **Gorge du Vecchiu**, a three-hour walk west of Vivario, is a three-metre jump still known as the **Saut du Sauvage**, or "wild man's leap".

A shorter walk from Vivario takes you to the **Fort de Pasciolo**, an evocative ruin 1km south of the village beside the N193. Set in a wild site facing a great circle of peaks and overlooking the deep Gorge du Vecchiu, the fort was built around 1770 by the French, and was transformed into a prison to incarcerate the rebels of Fiumorbo.

Vizzavona and its forest

Monte d'Oro dominates the route south of Vivario to **VIZZAVONA**, about 10km away. Shielded by trees, the village is invisible from the main road, so keep your eyes peeled for a turning on the right signposted for the train station – the place where the legendary bandit Bellacoscia surrendered to the police at the age of 75 (see opposite). With its handful of *gîtes d'étapes* and restaurants, Vizzavona is an ideal place to spend a few days walking in the forest, although it gets crowded in summer when it fills with hikers taking a break from the GR20, which passes nearby.

Among the **gîtes** here, top of the range is *I Laricci* (☎ & fax 04.95.47.21.12; ③; closed Nov–March) a recently converted alpine-style building with pitched roofs and charming Moroccan carpets decorating the walls of its dining room. A cheaper option is *Resto-Refuge-Bar "De la Gare"* (☎04.95.47.21.19, fax 04.95.47.22.20; ②; closed Nov–May), directly opposite the station, which offers a good half-board deal. For more atmosphere, head 3km further south along the main road to the hamlet of **LA FOCE**, where the venerable old *Monte d'Oro* (☎04.95.47.21.06, *www.sitec.fr/monte.oro*; ④) occupies a prime spot overlooking the valley – with its period furniture and fittings, *fin-de-siècle* feel and magnificent terrace looking out onto the mountain, it ranks among the most congenial hotels in Corsica. Adjacent to the *Monte d'Oro*, slap on the main road, is a little *gîte d'étape* (☎04.95.45.25.27; ②) that's nowhere near as gloomy as it looks and makes a handy fallback if the places down in the village are fully booked. The nearest bona fide **campsite** is the *Savaggio*, 4km north of Vizzavona (☎04.95.47.22.14); note that the train will make a special request stop at the site if you give the conductor plenty of warning.

The Forêt de Vizzavona

A glorious forest of beech and Laricio pine, the **Forêt de Vizzavona** is the most popular walking area in Corsica, thanks to the easy access by main road or train. A lot of people come here to tackle the ascent of 2389-metre-high **Monte d'Oro**, but there are many less demanding trails to follow, one of the most frequented of these being the walk to the **Cascade des Anglais**, connected to Vizzavona by a marked trail.

Less than a kilometre west of the hamlet of La Foce lies the highest pass on the Ajaccio–Bastia road, the **Col de Vizzavona** (1163m), usually jammed with picnickers. Fifteen minutes south of the col along the forest trail you come to a magnificent viewpoint over the forested peaks, with the ruins of the Genoese **Fort de Vizzavona** prominent on a rise in the valley below. You can reach the fort itself in just fifteen minutes along a wide path north of the picnic tables. A walk to **La Madonuccia** – a mound of scrambled rocks that's supposed to look like the Virgin – takes about thirty minutes from the col, following the trail signposted "Bergeries des Pozzi", which branches off southeast. Another marked path from the col takes you to the **Fontaine de Vitulo**, the source of the Foce stream, which joins the River Gravona further down the mountain.

Bocognano

From the Col de Vizzavona, the route winds southwards for 6km before reaching the ochre cottages of **BOCOGNANO** (Bucugnanu). Set on a plateau amidst a chestnut forest, the village gives a perfect panorama of Monte d'Oro's pale grey domes, and is well placed for walks to the **Cascade du Voile de la Mariée**, where the River Gravona crashes from a height of 150m in a series of cascades. The best approach to the falls is a thirty-minute walk south from the main road 3km south of Bocognano.

Bocognano is indissolubly associated with Antoine and Jacques Bellacoscia, born here in 1817 and 1832 respectively. Antoine, the elder son, took to the *maquis* in 1848, having killed the mayor of the village after an argument over some land. With his brother he went on to commit several more murders in full view of the hapless *gendarmes*, yet remained at liberty thanks to the support of the local population. In 1871, Jacques and Antoine managed to gain a safe pass into Ajaccio to organize an expedition to fight for the French in the war with Prussia. They returned from the war with their reputations restored, and took up residence in the family home, from where they continued to flout the law. In 1888, the police finally succeeded in ousting them from their house, which was converted into a prison. Antoine eventually surrendered at Vizzavona station on June 25, 1892, whereupon he was acquitted and exiled to Marseille in true Corsican tradition. The fate of Jacques is unknown.

travel details

Note that the details apply to June–Sept only; during the winter both train and bus services are considerably scaled down.

Trains

Ajaccio to: Bastia (4 daily; 3hr); Bocognano (4 daily; 50min); Calvi (2 daily; 4hr 35min); Corte (4 daily; 1hr 40min); L'Île Rousse (2 daily; 4hr); Venaco (4 daily; 1hr 20min); Vizzavona (4 daily; 1hr).

Bastia to: Ajaccio (2–4 daily; 3hr 40min); Bocognano (2–4 daily; 2hr 25min); Calvi (2 daily; 3hr); Corte (2–4 daily; 1hr 05min); L'Île Rousse (2 daily; 2hr 30min); Venaco (4 daily; 2hr 10min); Vivario (4 daily; 2hr 10min); Vizzavona (2–4 daily; 2hr 10min).

Calvi to: Ajaccio (2 daily; 4hr 40min); Bastia (2 daily; 3hr 15min); Corte (2 daily; 2hr 30min); L'Île Rousse (2 daily; 40min).

Corte to: Ajaccio (4 daily; 2hr); Bastia (4 daily; 1hr 30min); Bocognano (4 daily; 1hr); L'Île Rousse (2 daily; 1hr 55min); Venaco (4 daily; 15min); Vivario (4 daily; 20min); Vizzavona (4 daily; 40min).

L'Île Rousse to: Ajaccio (2 daily; 3hr 30min); Bastia (2 daily; 2hr 15min); Corte (2 daily; 2hr 15min).

Venaco to: Ajaccio (4 daily; 1hr 20min); Bastia (4 daily; 1hr 35min); Bocognano (4 daily; 1hr); Calvi (2 daily; 3hr 50min); Corte (4 daily; 15min); Vivario (4 daily; 15min); Vizzavona (4 daily; 25min).

Vizzavona to: Ajaccio (4 daily; 55min); Bastia (4 daily; 2hr); Bocognano (4 daily; 15min); Corte (4 daily; 1hr); Ponte Leccia (4 daily; 1hr 15min); Venaco (4 daily; 35min); Vivario (4 daily; 15min).

Buses

Ajaccio to: Bastia (2 daily; 3hr); Bonifacio (3 daily; 3–4hr); Cargèse (2–3 daily; 1hr 10min); Corte (2 daily; 1hr 45min); Évisa (1–3 daily; 2hr); Porto (1–2 daily; 2hr 10min); Porto-Vecchio (2–5 daily; 3hr 10min–3hr 45min); Propriano (2–6 daily; 1hr 50min); Sartène (2–6 daily; 2hr 15min); Vizzavona (2 daily; 1hr); Zonza (3 daily; 2hr 15min–3hr).

Aléria to: Bastia (2 daily; 1hr 30min); Corte (3 weekly; 1hr 25min); Porto-Vecchio (2 daily; 1hr 20min).

Bastia to: Ajaccio (2 daily; 3hr); Bonifacio (2–4 daily; 3hr 50min); Calvi (2 daily; 2hr 20min); Centuri (3 weekly; 2hr); Corte (2–3 daily; 1hr 50min); Erbalunga (hourly; 30min); L'Île Rousse (2 daily; 1hr 40min); Porto-Vecchio (2 daily; 3hr); St-Florent (2 daily; 1hr).

Bonifacio to: Ajaccio (2 daily; 3–4hr); Bastia (2–4 daily; 3hr 35min); Porto-Vecchio (1–4 daily; 30min); Propriano (2–4 daily; 1hr 40min–2hr 15min); Sartène (2 daily; 1hr 25min–2hr).

Calvi to: Bastia (1 daily; 2hr 15min); L'Île Rousse (2 daily; 40min); Porto (1 daily; 2hr 30min); St-Florent (1 daily; 1hr 20min).

Cargèse to: Ajaccio (1–2 daily; 1hr 10min); Porto (2–3 daily; 1hr).

Corte to: Ajaccio (2 daily; 2hr); Bastia (2 daily; 1hr 15min); Évisa (4 daily; 2hr); Porto (4 daily; 2hr 30min).

Évisa to: Ajaccio (1–3 daily; 1hr 45min).

Porto to: Ajaccio (1–2 daily; 2hr); Calvi (1 daily; 3hr); Cargèse (2–3 daily; 1hr 15min).

Porto-Vecchio to: Ajaccio (2–4 daily; 3hr 30min); Bastia (2 daily; 3hr); Bonifacio (1–4 daily; 30min); Propriano (2–4 daily; 2hr 10min); Sartène (2–4 daily; 40min).

Propriano to: Ajaccio (2–4 daily; 1hr 50min); Bonifacio (2–4 daily; 1hr 40min); Porto-Vecchio (2–4 daily; 2hr 10min); Sartène (2–4 daily; 20min).

Ferries

Marseille to: Ajaccio (3–7 weekly; 11hr overnight, 4hr 35min NGV); Bastia (1–3 weekly; 10hr); L'Île Rousse (1–3 weekly; 11hr 30min overnight); Porto-Vecchio (1–3 weekly; 14hr 30min overnight); Propriano (1 weekly; 12hr overnight).

Nice to: Ajaccio (1–6 weekly; 12hr overnight); Bastia (1–24 weekly; 6hr, or 2hr 30min NGV); Calvi (2–5 weekly; 2hr 45min NGV); L'Île Rousse (1–3 weekly; 7hr overnight, or 2hr 45min NGV).

Toulon to: Ajaccio (1–4 weekly; 10hr overnight); Bastia (1–3 weekly; 8hr 30min overnight).

PART THREE

THE
CONTEXTS

HISTORICAL FRAMEWORK

EARLY CIVILIZATIONS

Traces of human existence are rare in France until about 50,000 BC. Thereafter, beginning with the "Mousterian civilization", they become ever more numerous, with an especially heavy concentration of sites in the Périgord region of the Dordogne, where, near the village of Les Eyzies, remains were discovered of a late Stone Age people, subsequently dubbed "Cro-Magnon". Flourishing from around 25,000 BC, these cave-dwelling hunters seem to have developed quite a sophisticated culture, the evidence of which is preserved in the beautiful paintings and engravings on the walls of the region's caves.

By 10,000 BC human communities had spread out widely across the whole of France. The ice cap receded, the climate became warmer and wetter, and by about 7000 BC **farming and pastoral communities** had begun to develop. By 4500 BC, the first **dolmens** (megalithic stone tombs) showed up in Brittany; around 2000 BC copper made its appearance; and by 1800 BC the **Bronze Age** had arrived in the east and southeast of the country, and trade links had begun with Spain, central Europe and Wessex in Britain.

Significant population shifts occurred, too, at this time. Around 1200 BC the **Urnfield people**, who buried their dead in sunken urns, began to make incursions from the east. By 900 BC, they had been joined by the **Halstatt peo-**

ple who worked with iron and settled in Burgundy, Alsace and Franche-Comté near the principal ore **deposits**. At some point around 450 BC, the first Celts made an appearance in the region.

PRE-ROMAN GAUL

There were about fifteen million people living in **Gaul**, as the Romans called what we know as France (and parts of Belgium), when Julius Cæsar arrived in 58 BC to complete the Roman conquest.

The southern part of this territory – more or less equivalent to modern **Provence** – had been a colony since 118 BC and exposed to the civilizing influences of Italy and Greece for much longer. **Greek colonists** had founded Massalia (Marseille) as far back as 600 BC. But even the inhabitants of the rest of the country, what the Romans called "long-haired Gaul", were far from shaggy barbarians. Though the economy was basically rural, the **Gauls** had established large **hilltop towns** by 100 BC, notably at Bibracte near Autun, where archeologists have identified separate merchants' quarters.

The Gauls also invented the barrel and soap and were skilful manufacturers. By 500 BC they were capable of making metal-wheeled carts, as was proved by the "chariot tomb" of **Vix**, where a young woman was found buried lying on a cart with its wheels removed and propped against the wall. She was wearing rich gold jewellery and next to her were Greek vases and black figure pottery, dating the burial at around 500 BC and revealing the extent of commercial relations. Interestingly, too, the Gauls' money was based on the gold *staters* minted by Philip of Macedon, father of Alexander the Great.

ROMANIZATION

Gallic **tribal rivalries** made the Romans' job very much easier. And when at last they were able to unite under **Vercingétorix** in 52 BC, the occasion was their total and final defeat by **Julius Cæsar** at the battle of **Alésia**.

This event was one of the major turning points in the history of France. **Roman victory** fixed the frontier between Gaul and the Germanic peoples at the Rhine. It saved Gaul from disintegrating because of internal dissension and made it a Roman province. During the five centuries of peace that followed, the Gauls farmed, manufactured and traded, became urbanized and educated – and learnt Latin. Roman victory at Alésia laid the foundations of modern French culture and established them firmly enough to survive the centuries of chaos and destruction that followed the collapse of Roman power.

Augustus and **Claudius** were the emperors who set the process of **Romanization** going. Lugdunum (Lyon) was founded as the capital of Roman Gaul as early as 43 BC. Augustus founded numerous other cities – such as Autun, Limoges and Bayeux – built roads, settled Roman colonists on the land and reorganized the entire administration. Gauls were incorporated into the Roman army and given citizenship; Claudius made it possible for them to hold high office and become members of the Roman Senate, blurring the distinction and resentment between colonizer and colonized. Vespasian secured the frontiers beyond the Rhine, thus ensuring a couple of hundred years of peace and economic expansion.

Serious **disruptions** of the Pax Romana only began in the third century AD. Oppressive aristocratic rule and an economic crisis turned the destitute peasantry into gangs of marauding brigands – precursors of the medieval *jacquerie*. But most devastating of all, there began a series of incursions across the Rhine frontier by various restless **Germanic tribes**; first came the Alemanni, who pushed down as far as Spain, ravaging farmland and destroying towns.

In the fourth century the reforms of the emperor **Diocletian** secured some decades of respite from both internal and external pressures. Towns were rebuilt and fortified, an interesting development that foreshadowed feudalism and the independent power of the nobles since, due to the uncertainty of the times, big landed estates or *villae* tended to become more and more self-sufficient – economically, administratively and militarily.

By the fifth century, however, the Germanic invaders were back: **Alans**, **Vandals** and **Suevi**, with **Franks** and **Burgundians** in their wake. While the Roman administration assimilated them as far as possible, granting them land in return for military duties, they gradually achieved independence from the empire. Many Gauls, by now thoroughly Latinized, entered the service of the **Burgundian court of Lyon** or of the **Visigoth kings of Toulouse** as skilled administrators and advisers.

THE FRANKS AND CHARLEMAGNE

By 500 AD, the **Franks**, who gave their name to modern France, had become the dominant invading power. Their most celebrated king, **Clovis**, consolidated his hold on northern France and drove the Visigoths out of the southwest into Spain. In 507 he made the until-then insignificant little trading town of Paris his capital and became a Christian, which inevitably hastened the **Christianization** of Frankish society.

Under the succeeding **Merovingian** – as the dynasty was called – rulers, the kingdom began to disintegrate until in the eighth century the Pepin family, who were the Merovingians' chancellors, began to take effective control. In 732, one of their most dynamic scions, **Charles Martel**, reunited the kingdom and saved western Christendom from the northward expansion of Islam by defeating the Spanish Moors at the **battle of Poitiers**.

In 754 Charles's son, Pepin, had himself crowned king by the pope, thus inaugurating the **Carolingian dynasty** and establishing for the first time the principle of the divine right of kings. His son was **Charlemagne**, who extended Frankish control over the whole of what had been Roman Gaul, and far beyond. On Christmas Day in 800, he was crowned emperor of the **Holy Roman Empire**, though again, following his death, the kingdom fell apart in squabbles over who was to inherit various parts of his empire. At the Treaty of Verdun in 843, his grandsons agreed on a division of territory that corresponded roughly with the extent of modern France and Germany.

Charlemagne's administrative system had involved the royal appointment of counts and bishops to govern the various provinces of the empire. Under the destabilizing attacks of Normans/Norsemen/Vikings during the ninth century, Carolingian kings were obliged to delegate more power and autonomy to these **provincial governors**, whose lands, like **Aquitaine** and **Burgundy**, already had separate regional identities as a result of earlier invasions – the Visigoths in Aquitaine, the Burgundians in Burgundy, for example.

Gradually the power of these governors overshadowed that of the king, whose lands were confined to the Île-de-France. When the last Carolingian died in 987, it was only natural that they should elect one of their own number to take his place. This was Hugues Capet, founder of a dynasty that lasted until 1328.

THE RISE OF THE FRENCH KINGS

The years 1000 to 1500 saw the gradual extension and consolidation of the power of the **French kings**, accompanied by the growth of a centralized administrative system and bureaucracy. These factors also determined their foreign policy, which was chiefly concerned with restricting papal interference in French affairs and checking the English kings' continuing involvement in French territory. While progress towards these goals was remarkably steady and single-minded, there were setbacks, principally in the seesawing fortunes of the conflict with the English.

Surrounded by vassals much stronger than themselves, **Hugues Capet** and his successors remained weak throughout the eleventh century, though they made the most of their feudal rights. As dukes of the French, counts of Paris and anointed kings, they enjoyed a prestige their vassals dared not offend — not least because that would have set a precedent of disobedience for their own lesser vassals.

At the beginning of the twelfth century, having successfully tamed his own vassals in the Île-de-France, Louis VI had a stroke of luck. **Eleanor**, daughter of the powerful duke of Aquitaine, was left in his care on her father's death, so he promptly married her off to his son, the future Louis VII.

Unfortunately, the marriage ended in divorce and immediately, in 1152, Eleanor married Henry of Normandy, shortly to become **Henry II** of England. Thus the **English** crown gained control of a huge chunk of French territory, stretching from the Channel to the Pyrenees. Though their fortunes fluctuated over the ensuing three hundred years, the English rulers remained a perpetual thorn in the side of the French kings, with a dangerous potential for alliance with any rebellious French vassals.

Philippe Auguste (1179–1223) made considerable headway in undermining English rule by exploiting the bitter relations between Henry II and his three sons, one of whom was Richard the Lionheart. But he fell out with Richard when they took part in the **Third Crusade** together.

Luckily, Richard died before he was able to claw back Philippe's gains, and by the end of his reign Philippe had recovered all of Normandy and the English possessions north of the Loire.

For the first time, the royal lands were greater than those of any other French lord. The foundations of a systematic administration and civil service had been established in **Paris**, and Philippe had firmly and quietly marked his independence from the papacy by refusing to take any interest in the crusade against the heretic Cathars of Languedoc. When Languedoc and Poitou came under royal control in the reign of his son Louis VIII, France was by far the greatest power in western Europe.

THE HUNDRED YEARS WAR

In 1328 the Capetian monarchy had its first succession crisis, which led directly to the ruinous **Hundred Years War** with the English. Charles IV, last of the line, had only daughters as heirs, and when it was decided that France could not be ruled by a queen, the English king, **Edward III**, whose mother was Charles's sister, claimed the throne of France for himself.

The French chose **Philippe, Count of Valois**, instead, and Edward acquiesced for a time. But when Philippe began whittling away at his possessions in Aquitaine, Edward renewed his claim and embarked on war. Though, with its population of about twelve million, France was a far richer and more powerful country, its army was no match for the superior organization and tactics of the English. Edward won an outright victory at **Crécy** in 1346 and seized the port of Calais as a permanent bridgehead. Ten years later, his son, the Black Prince, actually took the French king, Jean le Bon, prisoner at the **battle of Poitiers**.

Although by 1375 French military fortunes had improved to the point where the English had been forced back to Calais and the Gascon coast, the strains of war and administrative abuses, as well as the madness of Charles VI, caused other kinds of damage. In 1358 there were **insurrections** among the Picardy peasantry (the *jacquerie*) and among the townspeople of Paris under the leadership of Étienne Marcel. Both were brutally repressed, as were subsequent risings in Paris in 1382 and 1412.

The king's madness led to the formation of two rival factions, following the murder of his brother, the duke of Orléans, by the duke of Burgundy. The **Armagnacs** gathered round the young Orléans, and the other faction round the **Burgundians**. Both factions called in the English to help them, and in 1415 Henry V of England inflicted another crushing defeat on the French army at **Agincourt**. The Burgundians seized Paris, took the royal family prisoner and recognized Henry as heir to the French throne. When Charles VI died in 1422, Henry's brother, the duke of Bedford, took over the government of France north of the Loire, while the young king Charles VII ineffectually governed the south from his refugee capital at Bourges.

At this point **Jeanne d'Arc** arrived on the scene. In 1429 she raised the English siege of the crucial town of Orléans and had Charles crowned at Reims. Joan fell into the hands of the Burgundians, who sold her to the English, resulting in her being tried and burnt as a heretic. But her dynamism and martyrdom raised French morale and tipped the scales against the English: except for a toehold at Calais, they were finally driven from France altogether in 1453.

By the end of the century, **Dauphiné**, **Burgundy**, **Franche-Comté** and **Provence** were under royal control, and an effective standing army had been created. The taxation system had been overhauled, and France had emerged from the Middle Ages a rich, powerful state, firmly under the centralized authority of an absolute monarch.

THE WARS OF RELIGION

After half a century of self-confident but inconclusive pursuit of military glory in Italy, brought to an end by the **Treaty of Cateau-Cambrésis** in 1559, France was plunged into another period of devastating internal conflict. The **Protestant** ideas of Luther and Calvin had gained widespread adherence among all classes of society, despite sporadic brutal attempts by François I and Henri II to stamp them out.

When **Catherine de Médicis**, acting as regent for Henri III, implemented a more tolerant policy, she provoked violent reaction from the ultra-Catholic faction led by the **Guise** family. Their massacre of a Protestant congregation coming out of church in March 1562 began a civil **war of religions** that, interspersed with ineffective truces and accords, lasted for the next thirty years.

Well organized and well led by the Prince de Condé and Admiral Coligny, the **Huguenots** – French Protestants – kept their end up very successfully, until Condé was killed at the battle of Jarnac in 1569. Three years later came one of the blackest events in the memory of French Protestants, even today: the **massacre of St Bartholomew's Day**. Coligny and three thousand Protestants who had gathered in Paris for the wedding of Marguerite, the king's sister, to the Protestant Henri of Navarre were slaughtered at the instigation of the Guises, and the bloodbath was repeated across France, especially in the south and west where the Protestants were strongest.

In 1584 the king's son died, leaving his brother-in-law, **Henri of Navarre**, heir to the throne, to the fury of the Guises and their Catholic league, who seized Paris and drove out the king. In retaliation, Henri III murdered the Duc de Guise, and found himself forced into alliance with Henri of Navarre, whom the pope had excommunicated. In 1589 Henri III was himself assassinated, leaving Henri of Navarre to become Henri IV of France. It took another four years of fighting and the abjuration of his faith for the new king to be recognized. "Paris is worth a Mass," he is reputed to have said.

Once on the throne Henri IV set about reconstructing and reconciling the nation. By the **Edict of Nantes** of 1598 the Huguenots were accorded freedom of conscience, freedom of worship in certain places, the right to attend the same schools and hold the same offices as Catholics, their own courts and the possession of a number of fortresses as a guarantee against renewed attack, the most important being La Rochelle and Montpellier.

KINGS, CARDINALS AND ABSOLUTE POWER

The main themes of the seventeenth century, when France was ruled by just two kings, **Louis XIII** (1610–43) and **Louis XIV** (1643–1715), were, on the domestic front, the strengthening of the centralized state embodied in the person of the king; and in external affairs, the securing of frontiers in the Pyrenees, on the Rhine and in the north, coupled with the attempt to prevent the unification of the territories of the Habsburg kings of Spain and Austria. Both kings had the good fortune to be served by capable, hardworking ministers dedicated to these objectives. Louis XIII had **Cardinal Richelieu** and Louis XIV had cardinals **Mazarin** and **Colbert**. Both reigns were disturbed in their early years by the inevitable aristocratic attempts at a coup d'état.

Having crushed revolts by Louis XIII's brother Gaston, Duke of Orléans, **Richelieu**'s commitment to extending royal absolutism brought him into renewed conflict with the Protestants. Believing that their retention of separate fortresses within the kingdom was a threat to security, he attacked and took La Rochelle in 1627. Although he was unable to extirpate their religion altogether, Protestants were never again to present a military threat.

The other important facet of Richelieu's domestic policy was the promotion of economic self-sufficiency – **mercantilism**. To this end, he encouraged the growth of the luxury craft industries, especially textiles, in which France was to excel right up to the Revolution. He built up the navy and granted privileges to companies involved in establishing **colonies** in North America, Africa and the West Indies.

In pursuing his foreign policy objectives, Richelieu adroitly kept France out of actual military involvement by paying substantial sums to the great Swedish king and general, Gustavus Adolphus, helping him to fund war against the Habsburgs in Germany. When in 1635, the French were finally obliged to commit their own troops, they made significant gains against the Spanish in the Netherlands, Alsace and Lorraine, and won Roussillon for France.

Richelieu died just a few months before Louis XIII in 1642. As Louis XIV was still an infant, his mother, Anne of Austria, acted as regent, served by Richelieu's protégé, **Cardinal Mazarin**, who was hated just as much as his predecessor by the traditional aristocracy and the *parlements*. These unelected bodies, which had the function of high courts and administrative councils, were protective of their privileges and angry that an upstart should receive such preferment. Spurred by these grievances, which were in any case exacerbated by the ruinous cost of the Spanish wars, various groups in French society combined in a series of revolts, known as the **Frondes**.

The first Fronde, in 1648, was led by the *parlement* of Paris, which took up the cause of the hereditary provincial tax-collecting officials – a group that resented the supervisory role of the

intendants, who had been appointed by the central royal bureaucracy to keep an eye on them. Paris rose in revolt but capitulated at the advance of royal troops. This was quickly followed by an aristocratic Fronde, supported by various peasant risings round the country. These revolts were suppressed easily enough. They were not really revolutionary movements but, rather, the attempts of various groups to preserve their privileges in the face of growing state power.

The economic pressures that contributed to their support were relieved when in 1659 Mazarin successfully brought the Spanish wars to an end with the **Treaty of the Pyrenees**, cemented by the marriage of Louis XIV and the daughter of Philip IV of Spain. On reaching the age of majority in 1661, **Louis XIV** declared that he was going to be his own man and do without a first minister. He proceeded to appoint a number of able ministers, with whose aid he embarked on a long struggle to modernize the administration.

The war ministers, Le Tellier and his son Louvois, provided Louis with a well-equipped and well-trained professional army that could muster some 400,000 men by 1670. But the principal reforms were carried out by **Colbert**, who set about streamlining the state's finances and tackling bureaucratic corruption. Although he was never able to overcome the opposition completely, he did manage to produce a surplus in state revenue. Attempting to compensate for deficiencies in the taxation system by stimulating trade, he set up a free-trade area in northern and central France, continued Richelieu's mercantilist economic policies, established the French East India Company, and built up the navy and merchant fleets with a view to challenging the world commercial supremacy of the Dutch.

These were all policies that the hard-working king was involved in and approved of. But in addition to his love of an extravagant court life at Versailles, which earned him the title of the **Sun King**, he had another obsession, ruinous to the state: the love of a prestigious military victory. There were sound political reasons for the **campaigns** he embarked on, but they did not help balance the budget.

Using his wife's Spanish connection, Louis demanded the cession of certain Spanish provinces in the Low Countries, and then embarked on a war against the Dutch in 1672. Forced to make peace at the **Treaty of Nijmegen** in 1678 by his arch-enemy, the Protestant William of Orange (later king of England), he nonetheless came out of the war with the annexation to French territory of **Franche-Comté**, plus a number of northern towns. In 1681 he simply grabbed Strasbourg, and got away with it.

In 1685, under the influence of his very Catholic mistress, Madame de Maintenon, the king removed all privileges from the **Huguenots** by revoking the Edict of Nantes. This incensed the Protestant powers, who combined under the auspices of the League of Augsburg. Another long and exhausting war followed, ending, most unfavourably to the French, in the **Peace of Rijswik** (1697).

No sooner was this concluded than Louis became embroiled in the question of who was to succeed the moribund Charles II of Spain. Both Louis and Leopold Habsburg, the Holy Roman Emperor, had married sisters of Charles. The prospect of Leopold acquiring the Spanish Habsburgs' possessions in addition to his own vast lands was not welcome to Louis or any other European power. However, when Charles died and it was discovered that he'd named Louis' grandson, Philippe, as his heir, that was a shift in the balance of power the English, Dutch and Austrians were not prepared to tolerate.

William of Orange, now king of England as well as ruler of the Dutch United Provinces, organized a Grand Alliance against Louis. The so-called **War of Spanish Succession** broke out and it went badly for the French, thanks largely to the brilliant generalship of the Duke of Marlborough. A severe winter in 1709 compounded the hardships with famine and bread riots at home, causing Louis to seek negotiations. The terms were too harsh for him and the war dragged on until 1713, leaving the country totally impoverished. The Sun King went out with scarcely a whimper.

LOUIS XV AND THE PARLEMENTS

While France remained in many ways a prosperous and powerful state, largely because of colonial trade, the tensions between central government and traditional vested interests proved too great to be reconciled.

The *parlement* of Paris became more and more the focus of opposition to the royal will,

eventually bringing the country to a state of virtual ungovernability in the reign of Louis XVI. Meanwhile, the diversity of mutually irreconcilable interests sheltering behind that parliamentary umbrella came more and more to the fore, bringing the country to a climax of tension which would only be resolved in the turmoil of **Revolution**.

The next king, **Louis XV**, was two when his great-grandfather died. During the **Regency**, the traditional aristocracy and the *parlements*, who for different reasons hated Louis XIV's advisers, scrabbled – successfully – to recover a lot of their lost power and prestige. An experiment with government by aristocratic councils failed, and attempts to absorb the immense national debt by selling shares in an overseas trading company ended in a huge collapse. When the prudent and reasonable **Cardinal Fleury** came to prominence upon the regent's death in 1726, the nation's lot began to improve. The Atlantic seaboard towns grew rich on trade with the American and Caribbean colonies, though industrial production did not improve much and the disparity in wealth between the countryside and the growing towns continued to increase.

In the mid-century there followed more disastrous military ventures, including the **War of Austrian Succession** and the **Seven Years War**, both of which were in effect contests with England for control of the colonial territories in America and India, contests that France lost. The need to finance the wars led to the introduction of a new tax, the Twentieth, which was to be levied on everyone. The *parlement*, which had successfully opposed earlier taxation and fought the Crown over its religious policies, dug its heels in again. This led to renewed conflict over Louis' pro-Jesuit religious policy. The Paris *parlement* staged a strike, was exiled from Paris, then inevitably reinstated. Disputes about its role continued until the *parlement* of Paris was actually abolished in 1771, to the outrage of the privileged groups in society, which considered it the defender of their special interests.

The division between the *parlements* and the king and his ministers continued to sharpen during the reign of **Louis XVI**, which began in 1774. Attempts by the enlightened finance minister Turgot to co-operate with the *parlements* and introduce reforms to alleviate the tax burden on the poor produced only short-term results. The national debt trebled between 1774 and 1787. Ironically, the one radical attempt to introduce an effective and equitable tax system led directly to the Revolution. Calonne, finance minister in 1786, tried to get his proposed tax approved by an **Assembly of Notables**, a device that had not been employed for more than a hundred years. His purpose was to bypass the *parlement*, which could be relied on to oppose any radical proposal. The attempt backfired. He lost his position, and the *parlement* ended up demanding a meeting of the **Estates-General**, representing the nobles, the clergy and the bourgeoisie, as being the only body competent to discuss such matters. The town responded by exiling and then recalling the *parlement* of Paris several times. As law and order began to break down, it gave in and agreed to summon the Estates-General on May 17, 1789.

REVOLUTION

Against a background of deepening economic crisis and general misery, exacerbated by the catastrophic harvest of 1788, controversy focused on how the **Estates-General** should be constituted. Should they meet separately as on the last occasion – in 1614? This was the solution favoured by the *parlement* of Paris, a measure of its reactionary nature: separate meetings would make it easy for the privileged, namely the clergy and nobility, to outvote the **Third Estate**, the bourgeoisie. The king ruled that they should hold a joint meeting, with the Third Estate represented by as many deputies as the other two Estates combined, but no decisions were made about the order of voting.

On June 17, 1789, the Third Estate seized the initiative and declared itself the National Assembly. Some of the lower clergy and liberal nobility joined them. Louis XVI appeared to accept the situation, and on July 9 the Assembly declared itself the National Constituent Assembly. However, the king then tried to intimidate it by calling in troops, which unleashed the anger of the people of Paris, the *sans-culottes* (literally, "without trousers").

On July 14 the *sans-culottes* stormed the fortress of the **Bastille**, symbol of the oppressive nature of the *ancien régime*. Similar insurrections occurred throughout the country, accompanied by widespread peasant attacks on landowners' châteaux and the destruction of records of debt and other symbols of their oppression. On the night of August 4, the Assembly abolished the feudal rights and privileges of the nobility – a momentous shift of gear in the Revolutionary process, although in reality it did little to alter the situation. Later that month they adopted the **Declaration of the Rights of Man**. In December church lands were nationalized, and the pope retaliated by declaring the Revolutionary principles impious.

Bourgeois elements in the Assembly tried to bring about a compromise with the nobility, with a view to establishing a constitutional monarchy, but these overtures were rebuffed. Émigré aristocrats were already working to bring about foreign invasion to overthrow the Revolution. In June 1791 the king was arrested trying to escape from Paris. The Assembly, following an initiative of the wealthier bourgeois **Girondin** faction, decided to go to war to protect the Revolution.

On August 10, 1792, the *sans-culottes* set up a **revolutionary Commune** in Paris and imprisoned the king. The Revolution was taking a radical turn. A new National Convention was elected and met on the day the ill-prepared Revolutionary armies finally halted the Prussian invasion at Valmy. A major rift swiftly developed between the **Girondins** and the **Jacobins** and *sans-culottes* over the abolition of the monarchy. The radicals carried the day. In January 1793, Louis XVI was executed. By June the Girondins had been ousted.

Counter-revolutionary forces were gathering in the provinces and abroad. A Committee of Public Safety was set up as chief organ of the government. Left-wing popular pressure brought laws on general conscription and price controls and a deliberate policy of de-Christianization. **Robespierre** was pressed onto the Committee as the best man to contain the pressure from the streets.

The **Terror** began. As well as ordering the death of the hated queen, Marie-Antoinette, Robespierre felt strong enough to guillotine his opponents on both Right and Left. But the effect of so many rolling heads was to cool people's faith in the Revolution; by mid-1794, Robespierre himself was arrested and executed, and his fall marked the end of radicalism. More conservative forces gained control of the government, decontrolled the economy, repressed popular risings, limited the suffrage, and established a five-man executive Directory (1795).

THE RISE OF NAPOLÉON

In 1799, one **General Napoléon Bonaparte**, who had made a name for himself as commander of the Revolutionary armies in Italy and Egypt, returned to France and took power in a coup d'état. He was appointed First Consul, with power to choose officials and initiate legislation. He redesigned the tax system and created the Bank of France, replaced the power of local institutions by a corps of *préfets* answerable to himself, made judges into state functionaries – in short, laid the foundations of the modern French administrative system.

Though Napoléon upheld the fundamental reforms of the Revolution, the retrograde nature of his regime became more and more apparent with the proscription of the Jacobins, granting of amnesty to the émigrés and restoration of their unsold property, reintroduction of slavery in the colonies, recognition of the Church and so on. Although alarmingly revolutionary in the eyes of the rest of Europe, his Civil Code worked essentially to the advantage of the bourgeoisie. In 1804 he crowned himself **emperor** in the presence of the pope.

Decline, however, came only with military failure. After 1808, Spain – under the rule of Napoléon's brother – rose in revolt, aided by the British. This signalled a turning of the tide in the long series of dazzling military successes. The nation began to grow weary of the burden of unceasing war.

In 1812, Napoléon threw himself into a **Russian campaign**, hoping to complete his European conquests. He reached Moscow, but the long retreat in terrible winter conditions annihilated his veteran Grande Armée. By 1814, he was forced to abdicate by a coalition of European powers, who installed **Louis XVIII**, brother of the decapitated Louis XVI, as monarch. In a last effort to recapture power, Napoléon escaped from exile in Elba and reorganized his armies, only to meet final defeat at **Waterloo** on June 18, 1815. Louis XVIII was restored to power.

THE RESTORATION AND 1830 REVOLUTION

The years following Napoléon's downfall were marked by a determined campaign, including the **White Terror**, on the part of those reactionary elements who wanted to wipe out all trace of the Revolution and restore the *ancien régime*. **Louis XVIII** resisted these moves and was able to appoint a moderate royalist minister, Decazes, under whose leadership the liberal faction that wished to preserve the Revolutionary reforms made steady gains. This process, however, was wrecked by the assassination of the Duc de Berry in an attempt to wipe out the Bourbon family. In response to reactionary outrage, the king dismissed Decazes. An attempted liberal insurrection was crushed and the four Sergeants of La Rochelle were shot by firing squad. Censorship became more rigid and education was once more subjected to the authority of the Church.

In 1824, Louis was succeeded by the thoroughly reactionary **Charles X**, who pushed through a law indemnifying émigré aristocrats for property lost during the Revolution. When the opposition won a majority in the elections of 1830, the king dissolved the Chamber and restricted the already narrow suffrage.

Barricades went up in the streets of Paris. Charles X abdicated and parliament was persuaded to accept **Louis-Philippe**, Duc d'Orléans, as king. On the face of it, divine right had been superseded by popular sovereignty as the basis of political legitimacy. The **1814 Charter**, which upheld Revolutionary and Napoleonic reforms, was retained, censorship abolished, the tricolour restored as the national flag, and suffrage widened.

However, the **Citizen King**, as he was called, had somewhat more absolutist notions about being a monarch. In the 1830s his regime survived repeated challenges from both attempted coups by reactionaries and some serious labour unrest in Lyon and Paris. The 1840s were calmer under the ministry of **Guizot**, the first Protestant to hold high office. It was at this time that **Algeria** was colonized.

Guizot, however, was not popular. He resisted attempts to extend the vote to enfranchise the middle ranks of the bourgeoisie. In 1846, economic crisis brought bankruptcies, unemployment and food shortages. Conditions were appalling for the growing urban working class, whose hopes of a more just future received a theoretical basis in the **socialist writings** and activities of Blanqui, Fourier, Louis Blanc and Proudhon, among others.

When the government banned an opposition *banquet*, the only permissible form of political meeting, in February 1848, workers and students took to the streets. When the army fired on a demonstration and killed forty people, civil war appeared imminent. The Citizen King fled to England.

THE SECOND REPUBLIC

A provisional government was set up and a **republic** proclaimed. The government issued a right-to-work declaration and set up national workshops to relieve unemployment. The vote was extended to all adult males – an unprecedented move for its time.

All was not plain sailing, though. By the time elections were held in April, a new tax designed to ameliorate the financial crisis had antagonized the countryside. A massive conservative majority was re-elected, to the dismay of the radicals. Three days of bloody street fighting at the barricades followed, when General Cavaignac, who had distinguished himself in the suppression of Algerian resistance, turned the artillery on the workers. More than 1500 were killed and 12,000 arrested and exiled.

A reasonably democratic constitution was drawn up and elections called to choose a president. To everyone's surprise, Louis-Napoléon, nephew of the emperor, romped home. In spite of his liberal reputation, he restricted the vote again, censored the press and pandered to the Catholic Church. In 1852, following a coup and further street fighting, he had himself proclaimed Emperor Napoléon III.

NAPOLÉON III AND THE COMMUNE

Through the 1850s, **Napoléon III** ran an authoritarian regime whose most notable achievement was a rapid growth in industrial and economic power. Foreign trade trebled, the rail system grew enormously, and the first investment banks were established. In 1858, in the aftermath of an attempt on his life by an Italian patriot, the emperor suddenly embarked on a policy of **liberalization**, initially of the economy, which alienated much of the business class. Reforms included the right to form trade unions and to strike, an extension of public education, lifting of censorship and the granting of

ministerial "responsibility" under a government headed by the liberal opposition.

Disaster, however, was approaching in the shape of the **Franco-Prussian** war. Involved in a conflict with Bismarck and the rising power of Germany, Napoléon III declared war. The French army was quickly defeated and the emperor himself taken prisoner in 1870. The result at home was a universal demand for the proclamation of a **third republic**. The German armistice agreement insisted on the election of a national assembly to negotiate a proper peace treaty. France lost Alsace and Lorraine and was obliged to pay hefty war reparations.

Outraged by the monarchist majority re-elected to the new Assembly and by the attempt of its chief minister, Thiers, to disarm the National Guard, the people of Paris created their own municipal government known as the **Commune**.

THE THIRD REPUBLIC

In 1889, the collapse of a company set up to build the Panama Canal involved several members of the government in a corruption scandal, which was one factor in the dramatic **socialist gains** in the elections of 1893. More importantly, the urban working class was becoming more class-conscious under the influence of the ideas of Karl Marx. The strength of the movement, however, was undermined by divisions, the chief one being Jules Guesde's Marxian Party. Among the independent socialists was **Jean Jaurès**, who joined with Guesde in 1905 to found the **Parti Socialiste**. The trade union movement, unified in 1895 as the **Confédération Générale du Travail** (CGT), remained aloof in its anarcho-syndicalist preference for direct action.

In 1894, **Captain Dreyfus**, a Jewish army officer, was convicted by court martial of spying for the Germans and shipped off to the penal colony of Devil's Island for life. It soon became clear that he had been framed – by the army itself – yet they refused to reconsider his case. The affair immediately became an issue between the Catholic Right and the Republican Left, with Jaurès, Émile Zola and Clemenceau coming out in favour of Dreyfus. Charles Maurras, founder of the fascist Action Française – precursor of Europe's Blackshirts – took the part of the army.

Dreyfus was officially rehabilitated in 1904, with his health ruined by penal servitude in the tropics. But in the wake of the affair the more radical element in the Republican movement had begun to dominate the administration, bringing the army under closer civilian control and dissolving most of the religious orders.

The country enjoyed a period of renewed prosperity in the years preceding World War I, yet there remained serious unresolved conflicts in the political fabric of French society. On the Right was Maurras' lunatic fringe with its strong-arm Camelots du Roi, and on the Left, the far bigger constituency of the working class – unrepresented in government. Although most workers now voted for it, the Socialist Party was not permitted to participate in bourgeois governments under the constitution of the Second International, to which it belonged. Several major strikes were brutally suppressed.

WORLD WAR I

With the outbreak of **World War I** in 1914, France found itself swiftly overrun by Germany and its allies, and defended by its old enemy, Britain. At home, the hitherto anti-militarist trade union and socialist leaders (Jaurès was assassinated in 1914) rallied to the flag and to the forces.

The cost of the war was even greater for France than for the other participants because it was fought largely on French soil. Over a quarter of the eight million men called up were either killed or crippled; industrial production fell to sixty percent of the prewar level. This – along with memories of the Franco-Prussian war of 1870 – was the reason that the French were more aggressive than either the British or the Americans in seeking war reparations from the Germans.

In the **postwar struggle for recovery** the interests of the urban working class were again passed over, save for Clemenceau's eight-hour-day legislation in 1919. An attempted general strike in 1920 came to nothing, and the workers' strength was again undermined by the formation of new Catholic and Communist unions, and most of all by the irreversible split in the Socialist Party at the 1920 Congress of Tours. The pro-Lenin majority formed the **French Communist Party**, while the minority faction, under the leadership of Léon Blum, retained the old SFIO (Section Française de l'Internationale Ouvrière) title. The bitterness caused by this split has bedevilled the French Left ever since. Both parties resolutely stayed away from government.

As the **Depression** deepened in the 1930s and Nazi power across the Rhine became more menacing, fascist thuggery and antiparliamentary activity increased in France, culminating in a pitched battle outside the Chamber of Deputies in February 1934. The effect of this fascist activism was to unite the Left, including the Communists led by the Stalinist Maurice Thorez, in the **Front Populaire**. When they won the 1936 elections with a handsome majority in the Chamber, there followed a wave of strikes and factory sit-ins – a spontaneous expression of working-class determination to get their just deserts after a century and a half of frustration.

Frightened by the apparently revolutionary situation, the major employers signed the **Matignon Agreement** with Blum, which provided for wage increases, nationalization of the armaments industry and partial nationalization of the Bank of France, a forty-hour week, paid annual leave and collective bargaining on wages. These **reforms** were pushed through parliament, but when Blum tried to introduce exchange controls to check the flight of capital, the Senate threw the proposal out and he resigned. The Left remained out of power, with the exception of coalition governments, until 1981. Most of the Front Populaire's reforms were promptly undone.

WORLD WAR II

The agonies of **World War II** were compounded for France by the additional traumas of **occupation, collaboration and Resistance** – in effect, a civil war.

After the 1940 defeat of the Anglo-French forces in France, **Maréchal Pétain**, a cautious and conservative veteran of World War I, emerged from retirement to sign an armistice with Hitler and head the collaborationist **Vichy government**, which ostensibly governed the southern part of the country, while the Germans occupied the strategic north and the Atlantic coast. Pétain's prime minister, Laval, believed it his duty to adapt France to the new authoritarian age heralded by the Nazi conquest of Europe.

There has been endless controversy over who collaborated, how much and how far it was necessary in order to save France from even worse sufferings. One thing at least is clear: Nazi occupation provided a good opportunity for the Maurras breed of out-and-out French fascist to go on the rampage, tracking down Communists, Jews, Resistance fighters, freemasons – indeed all those who, in their demonology, were considered "alien" bodies in French society.

While some Communists were involved in the **Resistance** right from the start, Hitler's attack on the Soviet Union in 1941 freed the remainder from ideological inhibitions and brought them into the movement on a large scale. Resistance numbers were further increased by young men taking to the hills to escape conscription as labour in Nazi industry. Général de Gaulle's radio appeal from London on June 18, 1940, rallied the French opposed to right-wing defeatism and resulted in the Conseil National de la Résistance, unifying the different Resistance groups in May 1943. The man to whom this task had been entrusted was Jean Moulin, shortly to be captured by the Gestapo and tortured to death by Klaus Barbie, who was convicted as recently as 1987 for his war crimes.

Although British and American governments found him irksome, **de Gaulle** was able to impose himself as the unchallenged spokesman of the Free French, leader of a government in exile, and to insist that the voice of France be heard as an equal in the Allied councils of war. Even the Communists accepted his leadership, though he was far from representing the kind of political interests with which they could sympathize.

Thanks, however, to his persistence, representatives of his provisional government moved into liberated areas of France behind the Allied advance after D-day, thereby saving the country from what would certainly have been at least localized outbreaks of civil war. It was also thanks to his insistence that Free French units, notably General Leclerc's Second Armoured Division, were allowed to perform the psychologically vital role of being the first Allied troops to enter Paris, Strasbourg and other emotionally significant towns in France.

THE AFTERMATH OF WAR

France emerged from the war demoralized, bankrupt and bomb-wrecked. The only possible provisional government in the circumstances was de Gaulle's **Free French** and the Conseil National de la Résistance, which meant a coalition of Left and Right. As an opening move to deal with the shambles, coal mines, air trans-

port and Renault cars were nationalized. But a new constitution was required and **elections**, in which French women voted for the first time, resulted in a large Left majority in the new Constituent Assembly – which, however, soon fell to squabbling over the form of the new constitution. De Gaulle resigned in disgust. If he was hoping for a wave of popular sympathy, he didn't get it.

The constitution finally agreed on, with little enthusiasm in the country, was not much different from the discredited Third Republic. And the new **Fourth Republic** appropriately began its life with a series of short-lived coalitions. In the early days the foundations for welfare were laid, banks nationalized and trade union rights extended. With the exclusion of the Communists from the government in 1947, however, thanks to the Cold War and the carrot of American aid under the Marshall Plan, France found itself once more dominated by the Right.

If the post-Liberation desire for political reform was quickly frustrated, the spirit that inspired it did bear fruit in other spheres. From being a rather backward and largely agricultural economy prewar, France in the 1950s achieved enormous industrial **modernization and expansion**, its growth rate even rivalling that of West Germany at times. In foreign policy France opted to remain in the US fold, but at the same time took the initiative in promoting closer **European integration**, first through the European Coal and Steel Community and then, in 1957, through the creation of the European Economic Community.

COLONIAL WARS

In its **colonial policy**, on the other hand, the Fourth Republic seemed firmly committed to nineteenth-century imperialism, despite the cosmetic reform of renaming the Empire the French Union.

On the surrender of Japan to the Allies in 1945, **Vietnam**, the northern half of the French Indochina colony, came under the control of Ho Chi Minh and his Communist organization Vietminh. Attempts to negotiate were bungled, and there began an eight-year armed struggle which ended with French defeat at Dien Bien Phu and partition of the country at the Geneva Conference in 1954 – at which point the Americans took over in the south, with well-known consequences.

In that year the government decided to create an **independent nuclear arsenal** and got embroiled in the **Algerian war of liberation**. If you want to take a charitable view, you can say that the situation was complicated from the French viewpoint by the legal fiction that Algeria was a *département*, an integral part of France, and by the fact that there were a million or so settlers, or *pieds noirs*, claiming to be French, plus there was oil in the south. But by 1958, half a million troops, most of them conscripts, had been committed to the war, with all the attendant horrors of torture, massacre of civilian populations and so forth.

When it began to seem in 1958 that the government would take a more liberal line towards Algeria, the hard-line Rightists among the settlers and in the army staged a putsch and threatened to declare war on France. Général de Gaulle, waiting in the wings to resume his mission to save France, let it be known that in its hour of need and with certain conditions – ie stronger powers for the president – the country might call upon his help. Thus, on June 1, 1958, the National Assembly voted him full powers for six months and the Fourth Republic came to an end.

DE GAULLE'S PRESIDENCY

As prime minister, then president of the **Fifth Republic** – with powers as much strengthened as he had wished – **de Gaulle** wheeled and dealed with the *pieds noirs* and Algerian rebels, while the war continued. In 1961, a General Salan staged a military revolt and set up the OAS (Secret Army Organization) to prevent a settlement. When his coup failed, his organization made several attempts on de Gaulle's life – thereby strengthening the feeling on the mainland that it was time to be done with Algeria.

An episode in the same year – covered up and censored until the 1990s – when between seventy and two hundred French Algerians were killed by the police in Paris, reinforced this feeling. This "secret massacre" began with a peaceful demonstration in protest against police powers to impose a curfew on any place in France frequented by North Africans. The police, it seems, went mad – shooting at crowds, batoning protesters and then throwing their bodies into the Seine. For weeks corpses were recovered, but the French media remained silent.

Eventually in 1962, a referendum gave an overwhelming yes to **Algerian independence**, and *pieds noirs* refugees flooded into France. Most of the rest of the French colonial empire had achieved independence by this time also, and the succeeding years were to see a resurgence of fascist and racist activity, both among the French "returnees" and the usual insular, anti-immigrant sectors. From the mid-1950s to the mid-1970s a French labour shortage led to massive recruitment campaigns for workers in North Africa, Portugal, Spain, Italy and Greece. People were promised housing, free medical care, trips home and well-paid jobs. When they arrived in France, however, these **immigrants** found themselves paid half as much as their French co-workers, accommodated in prison-style hostels and sometimes poorer than they had been at home. They had no vote, no automatic permit renewal, were subject to frequent racial abuse and assault and were forbidden to form their own organizations.

De Gaulle's leadership was haughty and autocratic in style, more concerned with *gloire* and grandeur than the everyday problems of ordinary lives. His quirky strutting on the world stage greatly irritated France's partners. He blocked British entry to the EC, cultivated the friendship of the Germans, rebuked the US for its imperialist policies in Vietnam, withdrew from NATO, refused to sign a nuclear test ban treaty and called for a "free Québec". If this projection of French influence pleased some, the very narrowly won presidential election of 1965 (in which Mitterrand was his opponent) showed that a good half of French voters would not be sorry to see the last of the general.

MAY 1968

Notwithstanding a certain domestic discontent, the sudden explosion of **May 1968** took everyone by surprise. Beginning with protests against the paternalistic nature of the education system by students at the University of Nanterre, the movement of revolt rapidly spread to the Sorbonne and out into factories and offices.

On the night of May 10, barricades went up in the streets of the Quartier Latin in Paris, and the CRS (riot police) responded by wading into everyone, including bystanders and Red Cross volunteers, with unbelievable ferocity. A **general strike** followed, and within a week more than a million people were out, with many factory occupations and professionals joining in with journalists striking for freedom of expression, doctors setting up new radically organized practices and so forth.

Autogestion – workers' participation – was the dominant slogan. More than specific demands for reform, there was a general feeling that all French institutions needed overhauling: they were too rigid, too hierarchical and too elitist.

De Gaulle seemed to lose his nerve and on May 27 he vanished from the scene. It turned out he had gone to assure himself of the support of the commander of the French army of the Rhine. On his return he appealed to the nation to elect him as the only effective barrier against left-wing dictatorship, and dissolved parliament. The frightened silent majority voted massively in his favour.

Although there were few short-term radical changes (except in education), the shock waves of May 1968 continued to be felt over the next two decades. Women's liberation, ecology groups, a relaxing of the formality of French society, a lessening of authoritarianism – all these can be traced to the heady days of May.

POMPIDOU AND GISCARD

Having petulantly staked his presidency on the outcome of yet another referendum (on a couple of constitutional amendments) and lost, de Gaulle once more took himself off to his country estate and retirement. He was succeeded as president by his business-oriented former prime minister, **Georges Pompidou**.

The new regime was devotedly capitalist. Pompidou hoped to eradicate the memory of 1968 in the creation of wealth, property and competition. His visions, however, had little time to attain reality. Having survived an election in 1972, Pompidou died, suddenly. His successor – and the 1974 presidential election winner by a narrow margin over the socialist François Mitterrand – was the former finance minister **Valéry Giscard d'Estaing**.

Having announced that his aim was to make France "an advanced liberal society", Giscard opened his term of office with some spectacular media coups, inviting Parisian trash collectors to breakfast, visiting prisons in Lyon and addressing the nation on television from his living room every evening. But, aside from reducing the voting age to 18 and liberalizing divorce laws, the advanced liberal society did not make a lot of progress. In the wake of the 1974 oil crisis the government introduced economic austerity measures. Giscard fell out with his ambitious prime minister, **Jacques Chirac**, who set out to challenge the leadership with his own RPR Gaullist party. And in addition to his superior, monarchical style, Giscard further compromised his popularity by accepting diamonds from the (literally) child-eating emperor of the Central African Republic, Bokassa, and by involvement in various other scandals.

The Left seemed well placed to win the coming 1978 elections, when the fragile union between the Socialists and Communists cracked, the latter fearing their roles as the coalition's junior partners. The result was another right-wing victory, with Giscard able to form a new government, with the grudging support of the RPR. Law and order and immigrant controls were the dominant features of Giscard's second term.

THE MITTERRAND ERA, 1981–95

When **François Mitterrand** won the presidential elections over Giscard in 1981, he embodied all the hopes of a generation of Socialists who had never seen their party in power. Headed by **Pierre Mauroy** as prime minister and including four Communist ministers, the **Socialists**' first government after 23 years in opposition started off bright, popular and optimistic. It was committed to an increase in state control over industry, high taxation for the rich, more power to local government, a public spending programme to raise the living standards of the least well-off and support for liberation struggles around the world. For Mitterrand, European integration was of great importance – France was after all, one of the founder members of the EEC – but was a primarily political rather than economic project, to ensure peace and security and to create a counterweight to American hegemony. By 1984, however, the flight of capital, inflation and budget deficits had forced a complete volte-face. The new prime minister, **Laurent Fabius**, presided over a cabinet of centrist to conservative "socialist" ministers, clinging desperately to power. Their 1986 election slogan was "Help – the Right is coming back", a bizarrely self-fulfilling message.

The Socialist government had lifted the ban on immigrants forming their own organizations, given a ten-year automatic renewal of permits and even promised voting rights. Able to organize for the first time, immigrant workers staged protests at the racist basis of lay-offs in the major industries. The Front National responded with the age-old bogey of foreigners taking jobs from the French; the Gaullists joined in with the spectre of falling birth rates (a French obsession since 1945); and both benefited in the 1986 elections. With a clear right-wing majority in parliament, Mitterrand appointed **Jacques Chirac** as prime minister, so beginning **cohabitation** – the head of state and head of government belonging to opposite sides of the political fence.

Although throughout 1987 the chances of Mitterrand's winning the presidential election in 1988 seemed very slim, Chirac's economic policies of **privatization** and monetary control failed to deliver the goods. He not only reversed the preceding socialist nationalizations, but also sold off banks and industries that de Gaulle had taken into the public sector after 1945. Unemployment rose steadily, and Chirac made the fatal mistake of flirting with the extreme Right.

As prime minister, Chirac instituted a series of **anti-immigration laws** that were jointly condemned by the Archbishop of Lyon and the head of the Muslim Institute in Paris. Several leading politicians in the government's coalition partners, including **Simone Weil**, a concentration-camp survivor, denounced Chirac's concessions to Le Pen and human rights groups. Churches and trade unions joined immigrants' groups in saying that France was on its way to becoming a police state. Mitterrand, the grand old man of politics, with decades of experience, played off all the groupings of the Right in an all-but-flawless campaign and won another mandate.

Mitterrand's party, however, failed to win an absolute majority in the parliamentary elections soon afterwards. The austerity measures of his new prime minister, **Michel Rocard**, upset traditional Socialist supporters in the public-service sector. He ruled out renationalization and allowed partial privatizations. Subsidies to large state-owned firms continued, but there was no coherent industrial strategy. Though Chirac's programmes were halted, they were not reversed. Strikes failed to halt lay-offs in the mines, shipyards, transport and the denationalized industries.

On returning to power, the Socialists also played electoral games with the immigration issue, reneged on the vote promise and failed to tackle the social and economic deprivation of France's immigrant ghettos. Polls showed over two-thirds of the adult French population to be in favour of deporting legal immigrants for any criminal offence or for being unemployed for over a year. Le Pen's proposals that immigrants should have second-class citizenship, segregated education and separate social security also received widespread support.

The 1980s ended with the most absurd blow-out of public funds ever – the **bicentennial celebrations of the French Revolution**. They symbolized a culture industry spinning mindlessly around the vacuum at the centre of the French vision for the future. And they highlighted the contrast between the unemployed and homeless begging on the streets and the limitless cash available for prestige projects.

In 1991, Mitterrand sacked Michel Rocard and appointed **Édith Cresson** as France's first woman prime minister. Her brand of left-wing nationalist rhetoric combined with centrist pragmatism made her highly unpopular at home and abroad. Furthermore, she jumped on the rampant racism bandwagon and said that special planes should be chartered to deport illegal immigrants. Kofi Yamgname, the minister for integration and only black member of the Socialist cabinet, suggested that immigrants who maintained traditional habits should go home. In 1992 the International Federation of Human Rights published a highly critical report on racism in the **French police** force and said France "was not the home of human rights".

Ironically, throughout the postwar years, France has maintained an independent and nationalist-oriented **foreign policy**, presenting its stance as a combination of French prestige and promotion of *liberté*, *égalité* and *fraternité*. In **major conflicts** France always tries to play a key role (and, as one of the five permanent members of the UN Security Council, it gets a say). However, high-profile diplomacy has given way to unprestigious military action, as in the **Gulf War** when the small French force was under American command. Mitterrand's visit, under gunfire, to Sarajevo in July 1992 was universally applauded, yet at the same time the French were reluctant to commit troops for UN actions in **former Yugoslavia**.

The important **Maastricht referendum,** held in 1992, split the Right and widened the gulf between the Socialists and Communists. Only the extreme end of the political spectrum, the Communists and the Front National remained determinedly anti-Europe. The voters divided along the lines of the poorer rural areas voting "No" and the rich urbanites voting "Yes". The very narrow margin in favour was a considerable disappointment to Mitterrand, but all the parties suffered.

Scandals over cover-ups and corruption that had erupted under Fabius continued to dog the Socialists, and in 1992 Cresson was replaced with **Pierre Bérégovoy**. He survived a wave of strikes by farmers, dockers, car workers and nurses, but then news broke of a private loan from a friend of Mitterrand accused of insider dealing. Mitterrand distanced himself from his prime minister, the Socialists were routed in the 1993 parliamentary elections, and Bérégovoy shot himself two months later, on May Day, leaving no note of explanation.

The new prime minister, **Edouard Balladur**, a fresh and fatherly face from the Right, soon lost the respect of his natural supporters after a series of U-turns following demonstrations by Air France workers, teachers, farmers, fishermen and school pupils, and the state's rescue of the Crédit Lyonnais bank after spectacular losses. Now popularly known as the Débit Lyonnais, the bank had to be bailed out to the tune of 100 billion FF (or £1000 per taxpayer), having run up colossal debts through dodgy speculative investments. Blame could also be laid at the Socialist administration's door – for failing to appoint competent management at Crédit Lyonnais.

The change in government in 1993 heralded a new privatization programme and ever greater reliance on **market forces**. The central French Bank was made independent in 1993; many now say it takes instructions straight from the Bundesbank. As in Britain, French banks, whether private or public, prefer short-term speculation in money and property markets rather than long-term investment in industry.

Mitterrand tottered on to the end of his presidential term, looking less and less like the nation's favourite uncle. Two months after Bérégovoy's suicide, Réné Bousquet, head of police in the Vichy government and responsible for the rounding up of Jews in 1942, was murdered. A personal friend of Mitterrand's, he was thought to have carried shady secrets about the president to his grave. On the twentieth anniversary of President Pompidou's death in April 1994, there was a wave of nostalgia for a time when "things were right and proper". Allegations of **corruption** against mayors, members of parliament, ministers and leading figures in industry were becoming an almost weekly occurrence. In 1994 a member of parliament leading a crusade against drugs and corruption on the Côte d'Azur was assassinated. Instead of increasing democracy, decentralization appeared to have licensed fraud and nepotism on an alarming scale. Several mayors ended up in jail, but it seemed as if the Paris establishment was above the law.

Meanwhile, France continued to stay outside NATO and sustain its own **nuclear arsenal**, for which there has long been cross-party consensus, and indeed national pride. In 1994 both sides in parliament approved huge increases in defence spending.

In 1994 a group of intellectuals, including the philosophers Bernard-Henri Lévy and André Glucksmann, ran a "Sarajevo" campaign to put **Bosnia** at the centre of the European debate, and received considerable support. By 1995 France was annoying its allies by taking unilateral action and accusing Britain and the US of Munich-style appeasement. In 1994, France sent troops into **Rwanda**, whose previous murderous government they had supported and armed. French troops were accused of giving protection to French-speaking Hutus responsible for the genocide, and of acting too late to save any of the English-speaking Tutsis. The policy backfired with the new regime in Rwanda taking an anti-French line and the unresolved conflicts spreading to the neighbouring former French colony, **Zaire**.

The fragmentation of the parties in the 1994 **European elections** saw the RPR/UDF lose votes to the anti-Europeans whilst the maverick left-wing crook **Bernard Tapie** took votes from the PS, which seemed to be in terminal decline.

In 1995, with Mitterrand dying from cancer but refusing to step down before the end of his term, revelations surfaced about his war record as an official in the Vichy regime before he joined the Resistance. A biography of Mitterrand, *Le Grand Secret*, detailing a whole host of scandals, was banned in France but avidly read on the Internet.

The Socialist Party was desperate for the popular **Jacques Delors**, who, as chair of the European Commission, saw Europe as having a strong social dimension, tackling unemployment, raising living standards, regulating the free play of global market forces and strengthening human rights, to stand as their presidential candidate and do the same on a national level. Instead they had to make do with **Lionel Jospin**, the rather uncharismatic former education minister, who performed remarkably well, topping the poll in the first round in which right-wing votes were split between Balladur, Chirac, the extremist Le Pen (who scored 15.5 percent) and the anti-European Philippe de Villiers. Chirac stole the Left's clothes by placing **unemployment and social exclusion** at the centre of his manifesto, and heaped promises of better times on every section of the electorate. He won, by a small margin, and was inaugurated as the new president of France in May 1995.

By the time Mitterrand finally stepped down, he had been the French head of state for fourteen years, presiding over two Socialist and two Gaullist governments. During the period of his presidency, official unemployment figures passed three million, crime and insecurity rose, and increasing numbers of people found themselves excluded from society by racism, poverty and homelessness. Corruption scandals touched the president, politicians of all parties and business chiefs; terrorist bombs went off in Paris; and, as faith in old left-wing certainties foundered, support for extreme Right policies propelled the Front National from a minority faction to a serious electoral force. Despite this, when he died in January 1996, Mitterrand was genuinely mourned as a man of culture and vision, a supreme political operator, and for his unwavering commitment to the vision of a united Europe – a certainty that has not been wholly shared by the succeeding generation of French politicians or by the French people.

CHIRAC'S PRESIDENCY

An immediate dramatic change wrought by Chirac was the **abolition of conscription**, to give France more efficient and effective armed forces. The move provoked impassioned responses by the PCF and other left-wingers for whom conscription represented social levelling, the useful acquisition of skills and the revolutionary spirit expressed in the words of the

national anthem – "Aux Armes, Citoyens . . ." Another early decision taken by President Chirac was to delay signing the Nuclear Non-Proliferation Treaty until France had carried out a new series of **nuclear tests** in the South Pacific. This provoked almost universal condemnation (Britain and China being the exceptions), boycotts of French goods, attacks on French embassy buildings in Australia and New Zealand, plus all-out riots in Tahiti. Chirac and most of the French press gloried in Gallic isolation, with no qualms at the French navy capturing Greenpeace's *Rainbow Warrior II*, almost ten years to the day after the bombing of *Rainbow Warrior I* in Auckland harbour by French secret service agents.

Chirac's new prime minister was **Alain Juppé**, a clever and clinical technocrat. It was down to him to square the circle of Chirac's election pledges of job creation, maintaining the value of pensions and welfare benefits, reducing the number of homeless, tax cuts, a continuing strong franc and a reduction in the budget deficit to stay on course for European monetary union. However, the Banque de France's control over interest rates and its commitment to the overvalued franc made Chirac's election promises to reduce unemployment difficult to fulfil. Not only was the French workforce terrified about job security and living standards, but French businesses were also up in arms at the cost of borrowing and the uncompetitiveness of their exports, leading to an epidemic of bankruptcies through the late 1990s. Even the indebted state-owned defence and electronics giant Thomson was put up for sale and its multimedia arm offered to the Korean company Daewoo for a symbolic 1F. People were scandalized and the deal was retracted, though Thomson was still sold, raising doubts about the government's commitment to retaining control over strategic industries.

In a television broadcast in October 1995, Chirac announced that rigorous economic measures to meet the criteria for European monetary union would have to take priority over social issues. Juppé then announced dramatic changes in social security provision and a "downsizing" of the state-owned railways, sparking off the **strikes** of November and December 1995. Students, teachers and nurses, workers in the transport, energy, post and telecommunications industries, bank clerks and civil servants took to the streets with the strong support of private-sector employees struggling to get to work. With five million people out over a period of 24 days, it was the strongest show of protest in France since May 1968. Though the slogan was *Tous ensembles* ("Everyone together"), and people were united in their opposition to arrogant, elitist politicians, their false election promises and the austerity measures emanating from the free-market philosophy, there were no united positive demands from the protesters, who ranged from working-class Front National supporters to middle-class Gaullists to Communist trade unionists.

The idea was propagated that Germany was responsible for imposing monetary union. As the government imposed increasingly severe austerity measures to meet the convergence criteria for a European single currency, views on Europe felt the wind of change. In the 1995 winter strikes, many protesters said that a repeat Maastricht referendum would show a clear majority against, and by 1996 even senior UDF politicians were beginning to question the commitment to monetary union at any price.

Juppé promised to clean up **corruption** and was almost immediately embroiled in a scandal involving his subsidized luxury flat in Paris. Accusations of cover-ups and perversion of the course of justice followed, punctuated by revelations of illegal funding of election campaigns, politicians taking bribes and dirty money changing hands during privatizations. In the past, politicians feathering their own nests never roused much public anger, but ordinary people, faced with job insecurity and falling living standards, were now becoming disgusted by the behaviour of the "elites". Even the normally obsequious right-wing press asked questions about the judiciary's independence, something Chirac had promised to uphold in his election manifesto. The consequences were twofold: a widening of the gulf between the governors and the governed, which was one of the key themes of the 1995 strikes; and a boost to the **Front National**'s popularity in the lead-up to the elections.

Municipal elections in June 1995 gave the Front National control of three towns, including the major port of Toulon. In 1996, a rare pact between Gaullists and Socialists prevented Jean-Pierre Stirbois from becoming the fourth FN mayor. The French constitution prevented FN town halls from fully carrying out their promised racial discrimination in housing, social services, etc, but local organizations, particularly those dealing with social integration, gay rights, AIDS support, feminism, contemporary art or the Jewish or Muslim communities – lost all their funding.

The **Algerian bomb attacks**, which rocked Paris in the mid-1990s, fuelled racism, added to the general feelings of insecurity, and diminished public confidence in the government as guardians of law and order. On the Right, Giscard used the potent word "invasion" and said that citizenship should be based on blood tles, not on place of birth. Chirac talked of the "noise and smell" of immigrants, and a UDF senator compared the four million immigrants in France to the German occupation. All of which boosted the confidence of Jean-Marie Le Pen and of the home affairs minister, **Charles Pasqua**, who reintroduced random identity checks, took away the automatic entitlement to French citizenship of those born in France and made it far harder for legal immigrants' families, asylum-seekers and students to enter France. Around 250,000 people living and working in France had their legal status removed. In March 1996 three hundred Malian immigrants, many of them failed asylum-seekers, sought refuge in a Paris church, and became known as the "*sans-papiers*". On the eve of the International Day Against Racism, they were forcibly evicted by truncheon-wielding riot police with the complicity of the local bishop and the curé of the church. In August ten immigrants from African countries, who had all legally worked and paid taxes in France, went on hunger strike in another Paris church (this time with the priest's support) against their **deportation**. Similar protests took place in other times and cities. In each case police action was swift and brutal. Trade unions, intellectuals and human rights groups denounced the government, which responded by announcing that three planes a month would be chartered to expel illegal immigrants. The Loi Debré was proposed so that all visiting foreign nationals' arrival and departure dates be notified, a law based on one passed during the Vichy regime. A wave of protest marches ensued. An amended version was still passed in March 1997, which the entire majority right-wing assembly voted for, and the left-wing minority voted against.

PARTIES AND POLITICIANS

ON THE LEFT

PS (Parti Socialiste). The Socialist Party to which **François Mitterrand** belonged but whose difficulties he chose to ignore during the *cohabitation* years. After an all-time electoral low in 1993 the party's fortunes were restored by **Lionel Jospin**'s creditable vote in the 1995 presidentials, several by-election successes and victory in the 1997 parliamentary elections. Following the 1997 elections Jospin attempted to create a "plural Left" of Socialists, Communists and Greens by including four Communist and two Green ministers in his cabinet. After an initial two years of phenomenal popularity, party divisions and scandals provoked a dramatic cabinet reshuffle in April 2000 in an attempt to forge a consensus among the divided Left. Jospin appointed long-time rival and former prime minister (1984–86) **Laurent Fabius** to finance, commerce and industry, while another rival, **Jean Chevènement**, the Left's *enfant terrible* was given the interior. Chevènement, who has a history of resigning from cabinet posts, as he did from defence in protest at 1991's Gulf War, is no easy bedfellow for Jospin, standing against the prime minister in the Corsica affair and resigning (for the fourth time) in autumn 2000. The flamboyant **Jack Lang**, who outraged some sectors by advocating the legalization of cannabis and ecstasy moved from education to culture, while the Green Party's **Guy Hascoët**

became minister of state for the social economy. **Elisabeth Guigou** – pegged by some as a future president – stayed in justice until she stepped into the employment portfolio vacated by **Martine Aubry**, daughter of **Jacques Delors**, and another possible future first woman president. The most widely-respected member of the cabinet is the Communist **Jean-Claude Gayssot**, who as transport minister gained accolades for diffusing the labour conflicts in the sector in summer and autumn 2000.

PCF (Parti Communiste Français). The veteran Stalinist leader **Georges Marchais** was succeeded by **Robert Hue** as party leader in 1994. Hue has proposed a new broad coalition with progressive Greens, Socialists, community groups, churches, etc, which constitutes a big break from the old line. The PCF remains influential within the trade union movement and in local government, and it now occupies key positions in Jospin's cabinet. The party counts on 10–12 percent support among the electorate.

Lutte Ouvrière. Trotskyist party whose presidential candidate **Arlette Laguillier** has stood in every contest since 1974 (with an identical workers' revolutionary programme). In 1995 she was credited with being the only honest candidate and won five percent of the vote in the first round, her highest-ever score.

ON THE RIGHT

UDF (Union pour la Démocratie Française). Confederation of Centre-Right parties in alliance with the RPR (see below) created by aloof, aristocratic **Valéry Giscard d'Estaing**, French president 1974–81. In 1995, members split their support between Balladur and Chirac and were then embroiled in a bitter leadership battle after Giscard stepped down in 1996. **François Léotard**, culture minister under Chirac and defence minister under Balladur (despite charges of corruption), is now the leader. **Raymond Barre**, mayor of Lyon and prime minister under Giscard, is an old stalwart who may yet return to high office. With the disappointing results of the 1997 elections, the party began to splinter, leading to the departure of some of its radical free market advocates and the triumph of the

moderate faction. This faction is led by **François Bayrou** and his Force Démocrate, which has combined the former CDS (Centre des Démocrates-sociaux) and PSD (Parti Social-démocrate) factions.

DL (Démocratie libérale). Economically right-wing group, which succeeded the now defunct **Parti Républicain** movement. It is led by **Alain Madelin**, the finance minister sacked by Juppé, who headed the pro-Chirac camp, and has now moved out of control of the UDF, with whom it retains a loose and uneasy coalition.

MPF (Mouvement pour la France). Another of the several small parties which have spintered off from the UDF, and a vehicle for the reactionary nationalist views of Catholic aristocrat and former Gaullist **Philippe de Villiers**.

Strongly anti-Europe, he campaigns for firmer borders, a tougher stance on crime, the absolute criminalization of drugs and the primacy of "Republican law". De Villiers and industrialist James Goldsmith won 12 percent of the vote in the 1994 Euro elections, but saw that rolled back significantly in 1998.

RPR (Rassemblement pour la République). Gaullist, conservative party headed by **Jacques Chirac**, mayor of Paris 1977–95, prime minister 1974–76 and 1986–88, and now president. **Edouard Balladur**, prime minister 1993–95, stood against Chirac in the presidentials. Chirac then appointed **Alain Juppé** as prime minister. Two key rivals to Juppé, both right-wing Eurosceptics, are **Phillipe Séguin**, speaker of the French parliament, and **Charles Pasqua**, home affairs minister under Chirac and Balladur. **Nicolas Sarkoszy**, former spokesman and current secretary-general of the party is the most influential of the up-and-coming younger generation. The flirtation of some of the party with the Le Pen and Mégret extremists has weakened party consensus and damaged its popular reputation.

FN (Front National). Extreme Right party led by nationalist and racist **Jean-Marie Le Pen**. Policies include: "Preference for the French" (meaning the ethnically French); expulsion of immigrants; greater police powers and resources; tougher sentences and the restoration of the death penalty; outlawing of abortion (for ethnically French women); higher defence spending; no European integration, lower taxation, a higher minimum wage and less state interference in family and business life; and proportional representation for parliamentary elections (the electoral system was changed after the 1986 elections to rid parliament of the 35 FN *députés*). With strong working-class support, it has eleven MEPs, and several hundred local councillors. However, the 13–15 percent popular support which it could once rely on has plummeted to around 7 per cent following the departure of former deputy Bruno Mégret.

MNR (Mouvement National Républicain). **Bruno Mégret**'s breakaway National Front party brings essentially the same platforms to voters as Le Pen's FN. The main difference is that the MNR, seeking to emulate Jörge Haider's Austrian Freedom Party, have been trying to adopt a more legitimate posture in an effort to draw legitimacy and support from the established, moderate right-wing parties. National support lingers at under 4 percent, however, reflecting the decline of the far-right in France as a result of Europeanization, bad management and scandal, and as a consequence of the split.

GREEN PARTIES

The environmental movement in France is patchy and divided, with the strongest support in Alsace, Brittany and Corsica. Though represented at, and good at campaigning on, a local level – against roads, protecting national parks, pollution control in cities, etc – they tend not to take on national issues such as **nuclear power**. With 70 percent of its energy produced by nuclear power (and 15 percent from hydropower), France scores very highly on global-warming pollutants, yet there is very little opposition to the nuclear industry, and a strong belief that French farming is clean and the French countryside unthreatened. The Greens did succeed in obtaining seven seats in the 1997 elections, and Green thinking has made some inroads into public consciousness, but ecology is not a national preoccupation. There are five splintered Green parties, of which the following are the main players:

GE (Génération Écologie). Aims to get environmental issues on the main political parties' agendas and is led by **Brice Lalonde**, who served in the Socialist government of 1988–91 as environment minister but switched allegiance in 1993 and supported Chirac for president in 1995, with whom he has maintained a tentative coalition ever since.

Les Verts. A more purist Green party with no leader as such. Put up shared candidates with GE in the 1993 parliamentary elections but with very disappointing results. Despite this, the separatist line of 1988 presidential candidate and MEP **André Waechter** was subsequently overturned. **Dominique Voynet** was the Greens' 1995 presidential candidate, scoring an unspectacular 3.3 percent. Since then the Greens have been taken into Jospin's Socialist coalition, where they occupy two cabinet positions.

The fate of immigrants and their French descendants was never so precarious. Fury and frustration at discrimination, assault, abuse and economic deprivation erupted into battles on the street. Several young blacks died at the hands of the police, while the right-wing media revelled in images of violent Arab youths. Two hundred French Muslims arrested on suspicion of involvement with the Algerian bomb attacks went on hunger strike to protest their innocence. Racist assaults became more common, and xenophobic opinions became accepted platitudes. In view of such attitudes it seems ironic that in 1996 France called for military intervention in Zaire – however, this was motivated less out of humanitarian concern than for fear that Americans were taking over a traditional French sphere of influence, with the concomitant threat of English gradually replacing French across Central Africa.

But the overriding **opposition to the government**, and to the political elite in general, came from the daily impact of economic policies on people's lives. Wages in former state-owned industries now in the hands of multinationals plummeted, deregulation led to deteriorating working conditions, and **unemployment** soared from 2.4 million in 1986 to 3.4 million (over 12 percent of the workforce) in 1996. Taking into account young people palmed off with training schemes and older people forced into early retirement, the true figure was close to five million. Six million people were living on or below the poverty line with at least another six million teetering on the edge of **poverty**. Furthermore, France experienced **negative growth** in 1996, taking it to the brink of a deflationary spiral. Some politicians, for the first time, called into question the strong franc policy, while the French public lost faith in any politician's ability to manage the economy and showed considerable sympathy for the strikes. Even the bully boys in Chirac and Juppé's own party, Séguin and Pasqua, started stirring trouble.

Amazingly, Juppé survived this "winter of discontent", abandoning some proposals and putting others on hold. A new tax to pay off the social security deficit was imposed, and cuts in the health service went ahead. More strikes and protests were held in 1996, but the three main trade unions (which in France are organized around political allegiance rather than occupation) returned to bickering amongst themselves, and Juppé was careful not to provoke public-sector workers.

In April 1997, Chirac unexpectedly dissolved the parliament and called early elections for May of that year, which had been due the following March. Even though Juppé announced his resignation whatever the outcome, Chirac spectacularly lost his gamble when the Socialists were elected. The Left was back in force with a strong majority, and the right-wing parties got their lowest score since 1958. There was a new *cohabitation*. **Lionel Jospin** took over as France's prime minister with election promises of job creation and economic growth. He immediately set about pursuing a strong pro-European policy despite members of the Communist party being in the coalition. Indeed, France, along with Germany and Spain, was one of the only countries to reach the **European Monetary Union** near-target deficit.

However, for all of the major parties the last few years have been characterized above all by **scandal** and popular dissaffection – encouraging popular apathy towards traditional institutions and increasing interest in alternative forms of political expresssion. The far-right Front National was the first to suffer, beginning in 1998, when Le Pen managed to alienate himself from the political scene by assaulting and punching a female Socialist candidate, who was running against his daughter in the April 1998 National Assembly elections, whilst the cameras were rolling. Consequently, he was temporarily stripped of his civic rights, including the ability to vote or run as a candidate in any election. In order to maintain his public influence and stature in the party, he had his wife stand in his place. This move sparked a revolt within the party. Bruno Mégret, Le Pen's lieutenant, who had seen his own chance to take the reins of the party when his master was banned from politics, was infuriated when Le Pen passed him over, and he set the wheels for a party revolt in motion. (Mégret, incidentally, was scarcely in a position to complain, given that he himself had nominated his own politically inexperienced wife to stand in the mayoral race of the town of Vitrolles in 1997 – a contest she won, thanks to the left-wing incumbent's own scandal-tainted record.) Mégret's machinations only served to divide the party, and with the municipal elections of April 1998, the extreme right suffered a number of reversals, including the loss of their former bastion of Toulon; in a pattern that was becoming all too familiar, the former mayor of that town, Le Chavallier, had been embroiled in his own legal difficulties and had nominated his wife to stand in his place, provoking the indignation of the electorate.

In July 1998, the seat was pulled out from under the Front National, when France's World Cup soccer victory, powered by a team made up to a great extent of immigrants, prompted a wave of popular patriotism which ran across the colour barrier. Even Le Pen couldn't think of anything to say as "Une France tricolore et multicolore" was celebrated with festivities all over the country, and the July 14 weekend was a lavish multi-ethnic event. The soccer final was not the end of Le Pen and company's streak of bad luck – the FN saw its logo temporarily hijacked in 1999 when the satirical weekly magazine *Charlie Hebdo* got wind that the copyright had expired and registered it for its own humorous ends, though the Front National managed to reclaim it after a court battle. In the meantime, Mégret's inability to wrest control of the party had prompted him to splinter off, trying to approach the moderate right parties by laying on a more centrist veneer. This shallow gambit failed, serving only to distance his own extreme-right followers. After the divorce between Le Pen and Mégret had become formal and *Charlie Hebdo* had been disposed of, the two fought for the right to use the Front National name and symbol. In the end Le Pen triumphed, and Mégret's party now runs under the banner of **Mouvement National Républicain**. Neither group did well in the 1999 European elections, however, where their aggregate popular vote dropped from 16 to 10 percent.

Nor has the moderate right fared much better. In 1998 the conservative Paris mayor **Jean Tiberi** was implicated in a scandal involving subsidized real-estate and salaries for fake jobs. This reflected badly on Chirac, recalling the string of scandals in the Mairie de Paris that took place whilst he was mayor. However, the revelation that Tiberi's wife earned money for a fake job led to a similar revelation about Jospin. In a cynical effort to whitewash the scandals, president and prime minister publicly united to impress upon the nation that France's real problems did not lie with these tabloid issues, which were better left forgotten.

But worse was yet to come for the president, when in September 2000 a journalist released a video-taped confession of the deceased RPR financier and former ally of Chirac, Jean-Claude Méry, disclosing an **influence-peddling** scandal leading directly to the president's office. The government reeled, lashing out with a judicial suit against the journalist and feverishly attempting to cut the trail before it could be traced back personally to Chirac. In the midst of this, a national referendum held to determine whether the presidential mandate should be limited to five years (it was decided in favour) was met by unprecedented voter apathy. Furthermore, progressive policies implemented by the government in the same year, including the legislation of a 35-hour working week and a 50:50 gender quota for representatives of political parties, encountered strenuous vocal resistance – this time from elements on the moderate right. The influences scandal provoked a serious fall in popularity for the president's party and a commensurate gain by Jospin and the Socialists, who redoubled their efforts to force Chirac to an early 2001 election.

As the new millennium dawned, Jospin may have been smiling – economic growth hit record levels in 2000, at three percent – but he had his own worries, too. Unemployment remained a worrying problem – official figures estimated it at ten percent of the population – despite numerous job creation schemes, and the government was suffering from a series of scandals. His cabinet had sustained a number of high-profile resignations, including employment minister Martine Aubray (author of the 35-hour working week), internationally respected finance minister Dominique Strauss-Kahn (caught up in a party funding scandal) and former prime minister Chevènement (in opposition to Jospin's plans for Corsica). Indeed, the **Corsican problem** had been the most thorny issue that Jospin had faced. At first he tried to counter the island's violent separatist movement with a low-level "dirty war", but later he shifted emphasis to negotiations for regional autonomy, an approach which provoked the ire of the Right – a no-confidence motion was tabled in 1999 against Jospin's attempts at compromise – and hopefulness among other regional nationalists (including Alsatians, Bretons and Basques). If Jospin's proposal succeeds (which it will not do if Chirac can help it), the island will have limited legislative power by 2004. Jospin's image was also hurt by comments he made on a state visit to Israel in 1999, when he characterized Hezbollah's campaign to free southern Lebanon as "terrorist" – Arab groups were outraged, and France's cultivated reputation as a paternalistic formal colonial power in the Middle East was seriously damaged. Nor was the Socialists' popularity aided by the trial in March 1999 of the Mitterrand-era cabinet ministers involved in the tragic **tainted blood scandal** of the mid-1980s. Through alleged stalling the government at the time failed to implement blood-screening, with the result that by the time of the trial four thousand transfusion recipients had contracted AIDS. The court doled out acquittals and suspended sentences for the three main defendants, including former prime minister Laurent Fabius; needless to say the verdict was greeted with outrage by the victims and their families and a wave of public cynicism. More skeletons tumbled out of the Socialists' Mitterrand closet, when Jean-Christophe Mitterrand, the former president's son was arrested on **criminal charges** in December 2000. Mitterrand *fils*, who was known during his father's presidency as "Papa m'a dit" ("Daddy told me") and "Monsieur Afrique", was a powerful behind-the-scenes mover for the Socialist regime's less salubrious African policies, which included buying illegal gems from repressive and murderous African regimes, selling arms and laundering money.

On the popular front, French reaction against American economic and cultural domination found an unlikely figurehead in **José Bové**, a political activist and farmer enraged at US sanctions against European products (like Roquefort cheese), who publicly vandalized a McDonald's restaurant in Millau in 1999. Quickly converted into a popular hero, his actions fanned the flames of anti-hamburger indignation and encouraged grass-roots environmentalists and agricultural protectionists to band together against America, environmental damage and *mal bouffe* (junk food). More violent acts followed, including the bombing of a McDonald's drive-through in Brittany in August

1999, in which a 22-year-old employee was killed. At his trial in September 2000, Bové received a very light sentence for the affair (serving only three months despite a prior record of civil disobedience). Ironically, the media-conscious Bové, who portrays himself as the champion of the Gallic *agriculteur*, was raised in the US by expat French academics and began his rural career only shortly before all the trouble began.

Elsewhere in 2000 there were strikes early in the year involving teachers and civil servants opposed to government plans to modernize and streamline their sectors. Then, when fuel prices escalated in October, taxi-drivers and truckers in France hit the streets in protest, disrupting highway flow and fuel distribution, and temporarily paralysing the country; their example led to similar actions across Europe. As the year closed, Bové's ruminations on the dangers of factory farming seemed all the more poignant as **mad cow** disease (BSE) began to appear in the nation's cattle stock.

All of this made for a tumultuous entry into the new millennium. Jospin and the Socialists seemed destined to gain on their conservative rivals in the next round of elections even if only by dint of the moderate Right's inability to keep a lid on public revelations of its own corruption. Whatever weaknesses Jospin's patchwork "plural Left" may have had, the centrifugal forces which were fragmenting the Right were far more serious, and Jospin had gained appeal among the middle class by establishing himself as someone who could undertake reform while reining in radical Left reaction. The far Right, always a minority and now divided, seemed to be fading out, as their xenophobic rantings rang increasingly hollow in the pluralistic European federation. Ironically, in view of the collapse of Communism in eastern Europe, the party which seemed destined to gain the most was the French Communist Party, which had enjoyed a resurgence in its traditional home of the south, and whose leader, Jean-Claude Gayssot, at the time minister of transport and housing, was hailed universally as the most competent member of the cabinet.

ART

From the Middle Ages to the twentieth century, France has held – with occasional gaps – a leading position in the history of European painting, with Paris, above all, attracting artists from the whole continent. The story of French painting is one of richness and complexity, partly due to this influx of foreign painters and partly due to the capital's stability as an artistic centre.

BEGINNINGS

In the late Middle Ages, the itinerant life of the nobles led them to prefer small and transportable works of art; splendidly **illuminated manuscripts** were much praised and the best painters, usually trained in Paris, continued to work on a small scale until the fifteenth century. In spite of the small size of the illuminated image, painters made startling steps towards a realistic interpretation of the world and in the exploration of new subject matters.

Many of these illuminators were also panel painters, foremost of whom was **Jean Fouquet** (c1420–1481), born in Tours in the Loire valley and the central artistic personality of fifteenth-century France. Court painter to Charles VIII, Fouquet drew from both Flemish and Italian sources, utilizing the new fluid oil technique that had been perfected in Flanders, and concerning himself with the problem of representing space convincingly, much like his Italian contemporaries. Through this he moulded a distinct personal style, combining richness of sur-

face with broad, generalized forms and, in his feeling for volume and ordered geometric shapes, laying down principles that became intrinsic to French art for centuries to come, from Poussin to Seurat and Cézanne.

Two other fifteenth-century French artists deserve brief mention here, principally for the broad range of artistic expression they embody. **Enguerrand Quarton** (c1410–c1466) was the most famous Provençal painter of the time; his art, profoundly religious in subject as well as feeling, already shows the impact of the Mediterranean sun in the strong light that pervades his paintings. His *Pietà* in the Louvre is both stark and intensely poignant, while the *Coronation of the Virgin* that hangs at Villeneuve-lès-Avignon is a vast panoramic vision not only of heaven but also of a very real earth, in what ranks as one of the first city/landscapes in the history of French painting: Avignon itself is faithfully depicted and the Mont Ste-Victoire, later to be made famous by Cézanne, is recognizable in the distance.

The **Master of Moulins**, active in the 1480s and 1490s, was noticeably more northern in temperament, painting both religious altarpieces and portraits commissioned by members of the royal family or the fast-increasing bourgeoisie.

MANNERISM AND ITALIAN INFLUENCE

At the end of the fifteenth and the beginning of the sixteenth centuries, the French invasion of Italy brought both artists and patrons into closer contact with the Italian Renaissance.

The most famous of the artists who were lured to France was **Leonardo da Vinci**, spending the last three years of his life (1516–19) at the court of François I. From the Loire valley, which until then had been his favourite residence, the French king moved nearer to Paris, where he had several palaces decorated. Italian artists were once again called upon, and two of them, **Rosso** and **Primaticcio**, who arrived in France in 1530 and 1532 respectively, were to shape the artistic scene in France for the rest of the sixteenth century.

Both artists introduced to France the latest Italian style, **Mannerism**, a sometimes anarchic derivation of the High Renaissance of Michelangelo and Raphael. Mannerism, with its emphasis on the fantastic, the luxurious and the large-scale decorative, was eminently compatible with the taste of the court, and it was first put to the test in the revamping of the old Château de Fontainebleau.

There, a horde of French painters headed by the two Italians came to form what was subsequently called the **School of Fontainebleau**. Most French artists worked at Fontainebleau at some point in their career, or were influenced by its homogeneous style, but none stands out as a personality of any stature, and for the most part the painting of the time was dull and fanciful in the extreme.

Antoine Caron (c1520–c1600), who often worked for Catherine de Médicis, the widow of Henri II, contrived complicated allegorical paintings in which elongated figures are arranged within wide, theatre-like scenery packed with ancient monuments and Roman statues. Even the Wars of Religion, raging in the 1550s and 1560s, failed to rouse French artists' sense of drama, and representations of the many massacres then going on were detached and fussy in tone.

Portraiture tended to be more inventive. The portraits of **Jean Clouet** (c1485–1541) and his son **François** (c1510–72), both official painters to François I, combined sensitivity in the rendering of the sitter's features with a keen sense of abstract design in the arrangement of the figure, conveying with great clarity social status and giving clues to the sitter's profession. Though influenced by sixteenth-century Italian and Flemish portraits, their work remains, nonetheless, very French in its general sobriety.

THE SEVENTEENTH CENTURY

In the **seventeenth century**, Italy continued to be a source of inspiration for French artists, most of whom were drawn to Rome – at that time the most exciting artistic centre in Europe. There, two Italian artists, especially, dominated the scene in the first decade of the century: Michelangelo Merisi da Caravaggio and Annibale Carracci.

Caravaggio (1571–1610) often chose lowlife subjects and treated them with remarkable realism, a realism that he extended to traditional religious subject matter and that he enhanced by using a strong, harsh lighting technique. Although he had to flee Rome in great haste under sentence for murder in 1606, Caravaggio had already had a profound effect

on the art of the age, both in terms of subjects and in his uncompromising use of realism.

Some French painters like **Moise Valentin** (c1594–1632) worked in Rome and were directly influenced by Caravaggio; others, such as the great painter from Lorraine, **Georges de la Tour** (1593–1652), benefited from his innovations at one remove, gaining inspiration from the Utrecht Caravaggisti who were active at the time in Holland. Starting with a descriptive realism in which naturalistic detail made for a varied painted surface, La Tour gradually simplified both forms and surfaces, producing deeply felt religious paintings in which figures appear to be carved out of the surrounding gloom by the magical light of a candle. Sadly, his output was very small – just some forty or so works in all.

Lowlife subjects and attention to naturalistic detail were also important aspects of the work of the **Le Nain brothers**, especially **Louis** (1593–1648), who depicted with great sympathy, but never with sentimentality, the condition of the peasantry. He chose moments of inactivity or repose within the lives of the peasants, and his paintings achieve timelessness and monumentality by their very stillness.

The other Italian artist of influence, the Bolognese **Annibale Carracci** (d. 1609), impressed French painters not only with his skill as a decorator but, more tellingly, with his ordered, balanced landscapes, which were to prove of prime importance for the development of the classical landscape in general, and in particular for those painted by **Claude Lorrain** (1604/5–82).

Claude, who started work as a pastry cook, was born in Lorraine, near Nancy. He left France for Italy to practise his trade, and worked in the household of a landscape painter in Rome, somehow persuading his master, who painted landscapes in the classical manner of Carracci, to let him abandon pastry for painting. Later he travelled to Naples, where the beauty of the harbour and bay made a lasting impression on him, the golden light of the southern port, and of Rome and its surrounding countryside, providing him with endless subjects of study which he drew, sketched and painted for the rest of his life. Claude's landscapes are airy compositions in which religious or mythological figures are lost within an idealized, Arcadian nature, bathed in a luminous, transparent light which, golden or silvery, lends a tranquil mood.

Landscapes, harsher and even more ordered, but also recalling the Arcadian mood of antiquity, were painted by the other French painter who elected to make Rome his home, **Nicolas Poussin** (1594–1665). Like Claude, Poussin selected his themes from the rich sources of Greek, Roman and Christian myths and stories; unlike Claude, however, his figures are not subdued by nature but rather dominate it, in the tradition of the masters of the High Renaissance, such as Raphael and Titian, whom he greatly admired. During the working out of a painting Poussin would make small models, arrange them on an improvised stage and then sketch the puppet scene – which may explain why his figures often have a still, frozen quality. Poussin only briefly returned to Paris, called by the king, Louis XIII, to undertake some large decorative works quite unsuited to his style or character. Back in Rome he refined a style that became increasingly classical and severe.

Many other artists visited Italy, but most returned to France, the luckiest to be employed at the court to boost the royal images of Louis XIII and XIV and the egos of their respective ministers, Richelieu and Colbert. **Simon Vouet** (1590–1649), **Charles Le Brun** (1619–90) and **Pierre Mignard** (1612–95) all performed that task with skill, often using ancient history and mythology to suggest flattering comparisons with the reigning monarch.

The official aspect of their works was paralleled by the creation of the new **Academy of Painting and Sculpture** in 1648, an institution that dominated the arts in France for the next few hundred years, if only by the way artists reacted against it. **Philippe de Champaigne** (1602–74), a painter of Flemish origin, alone stands out at the time as remotely different, removed from the intrigues and pleasures of the court and instead strongly influenced by the teaching and moral code of Jansenism, a purist and severe form of the Catholic faith. The apparent simplicity and starkness of his portraits hides an unusually perceptive understanding of his sitters' personalities. But it was the more courtly, fun-loving portraits and paintings by such artists as Mignard that were to influence most of the art of the following century.

THE EARLY EIGHTEENTH CENTURY

The semi-official art encouraged by the foundation of the Academy became more frivolous and light-hearted in the **eighteenth century**. The court at Versailles lost its attractions, and many patrons now were to be found among the hedonistic bourgeoisie and aristocracy living in Paris. History painting, as opposed to genre scenes or portraiture, retained its position of prestige, but at the same time the various categories began to merge and many artists tried their hands at landscape, genre, history or decorative works, bringing aspects of one type into another. **Salons**, at which painters exhibited their works, were held with increasing frequency and bred a new phenomenon in the art world – the art critic. The philosopher **Diderot** was one of the first of these arbiters of taste, doers and undoers of reputations.

Possibly the most complex personality of the eighteenth century was **Jean-Antoine Watteau** (1684–1721). Primarily a superb draughtsman, Watteau's use of soft and yet rich, light colours reveals how much he was struck by the great seventeenth-century Flemish painter Rubens. The open-air scenes of flirtatious love painted by Rubens and by the fifteenth/sixteenth-century Venetian Giorgione provided Watteau with precedents for his own subtle depictions of dreamy couples (sometimes depictions of characters from the Italian Comedy) strolling in delicate, mythical landscapes. In some of these *Fêtes Galantes* and in pictures of solitary musicians or actors (*Gilles*), Watteau conveyed a mood of melancholy, loneliness and poignancy that was largely lacking in the works of his many imitators and followers (Nicolas Lancret, J.-B. Pater).

The work of **François Boucher** (1703–70) was probably more representative of the eighteenth century: the pleasure-seeking court of Louis XV found the lightness of morals and colours in his paintings immensely congenial. Boucher's virtuosity is seen at its best in his paintings of women, always rosy, young and fantasy-erotic.

Jean-Honoré Fragonard (1732–1806) continued this exploration of licentious themes but with an exuberance, a richness of colour and a vitality (*The Swing*) that was a feast for the eyes and raised the subject to a glorification of love. Far more restrained were the paintings of **Jean-Baptiste-Siméon Chardin** (1699–1779), who specialized in homely genre scenes and still lifes, painted with a simplicity that belied his complex use of colours, shapes and space to promote a mood of stillness and tranquillity. **Jean-Baptiste Greuze** (1725–1805) chose stories that anticipated reaction against the laxity of the times; the moral, at times sentimental, character of his paintings was all-pervasive, reinforced by a stage-like composition well suited to cautionary tales.

NEOCLASSICISM

This new seriousness became more severe with the rise of **Neoclassicism**, a movement for which purity and simplicity were essential components of the systematic depiction of edifying stories from the classical authors. Roman history and legends were the most popular subjects, and though **Jacques-Louis David** (1748–1825), a pupil of an earlier exponent of Neoclassicism, J.-M. Vien, conformed to that to a certain extent, he was different in that he was also keenly sensitive to the changing mood and philosophies of his time and to the reaction against frivolity and self-indulgence. Many of his paintings are reflections of republican ideals and of contemporary history, from the *Death of Marat* to events from the life of Napoléon, who was his patron. For the emperor and his family, David painted some of his most successful portraits – *Madame Recamier* is not only an exquisite example of David's controlled use of shapes and space and his debt to antique Rome, but can also be seen as a paradigm of Neoclassicism.

Two painters, **Jean-Antoine Gros** (1771–1835) and **Baron Gérard** (1770–1837), followed David closely in style and in themes (portraits, Napoleonic history and legend), but often with a touch of softness and heroic poetry that pointed the way to Romanticism.

Jean-Auguste-Dominique Ingres (1780–1867) was a pupil of David; he also studied in Rome before coming back to Paris to develop the purity of line that was the essential and characteristic element of his art. His effective use of it to build up forms and bind compositions can be admired in conjunction with his recurrent theme of female nudes bathing, or in his magnificent and stately portraits that depict the nuances of social status.

ROMANTICISM

Completely opposed to the stress on drawing advocated by Ingres, two artists created,

through their emphasis on colour, form and composition, pictures that look forward to the later part of the nineteenth century and the Impressionists. **Théodore Géricault** (1791–1824), whose short life was still dominated by the heroic vision of the Napoleonic era, explored dramatic themes of human suffering in such paintings as *The Raft of the* Medusa, while his close contemporary, **Eugène Delacroix** (1798–1863), epitomized the **Romantic movement** – its search for emotions and its love of nature, power and change.

Delacroix was deeply aware of tradition, and his art was influenced, visually and conceptually, by the great masters of the Renaissance and the seventeenth and eighteenth centuries. In many ways he may be regarded as the last great religious and decorative French painter, but through his technical virtuosity, freedom of brushwork and richness of colours, he can also be seen as the essential forerunner of the Impressionists. For Delacroix there was no conflict between colour and design: David and Ingres saw these elements as separate aspects of creation, but Delacroix used colours as the basis and structure of his designs. His technical freedom was partly due to his admiration for two English painters, John Constable and his close friend, Richard Parkes Bonington, with whom he shared a studio for a few months. Bonington especially had a freshness of approach to colour and a free handling of paint, both of which had a strong impact on Delacroix. His numerous themes ranged from intimate female nudes, often with mysterious and erotic Middle Eastern overtones, to studies of animals and hunting scenes. Ancient and contemporary history supplied him with some of his most harrowing and dramatic paintings: *The Massacre at Chios* was based on an event that took place during the Greek War of Independence against the Turks, and *Liberty Guiding the People* was painted to commemorate the Revolution of 1830. Both paintings were his personal response to contemporary events and the human tragedies they entailed.

Other painters working in the Romantic tradition were still haunted by the Napoleonic legends, as well as by North Africa (Algeria) and the Middle East, which had become better known to artists and patrons alike during the Napoleonic wars. These were the subjects of paintings by **Horace Vernet** (1789–1863),

Jean-Louis-Ernest Meissonier (1815–91) and Théodore Chassériau (1819–56).

Among their contemporaries was **Honoré Daumier** (1808–79): very much an isolated figure, influenced by the boldness of approach of caricaturists, he was content to depict everyday subjects such as a laundress or a third-class rail car – caustic commentaries on professions and politics that work as brilliant observations of the times.

THE NINETEENTH CENTURY

Some painters of the first part of the **nineteenth century** were fascinated by other themes. Nature, in its true state, unadorned by conventions, became a subject for study, and running parallel to this was the realization that painting could be the visual externalization of the artist's own emotions and feelings. These two aspects, which until this time had only been very tentatively touched upon, were now more fully explored and led directly to the innovations of the Impressionists and later painters.

Jean-Baptiste-Camille Corot (1796–1875) started to paint landscapes that were fresh, direct and influenced as much by the unpretentious and realistic country scenes of seventeenth-century Holland as by the balanced compositions of Claude. His loving and attentive studies of nature were much admired by later artists, including Monet.

At the same time a whole group of painters developed similar attitudes to landscape and nature, helped greatly by the practical improvement of being able to buy oil paint in tubes rather than as unmixed pigments. Known as the **Barbizon School** after the village on the outskirts of Paris around which they painted, they soon discovered the joy and excitement of *plein-air* (open-air) painting.

Théodore Rousseau (1812–67) was their nominal leader, his paintings of forest undergrowth and forest clearings displaying an intimacy that came from the immediacy of the image. **Charles-François Daubigny** (1817–78), like Rousseau, often infused a sense of drama into his landscapes.

Jean-François Millet (1814–75) is perhaps the best-known associate of the Barbizon group, though he was more interested in the human figure than simple nature. Landscapes, however, were essential settings for his figures; indeed, his most famous pictures are those

exploring the place of people in nature and their struggle to survive. *The Sower*, for instance, was a typical Millet theme, suggesting the heroic working life of the peasant. As is so often the case for painters touching on new themes or on ideas that are uncomfortable to the rich and powerful, Millet enjoyed little success during his lifetime, and his art was only widely recognized after his death.

The moralistic and romantic undertone in Millet's work was something that **Gustave Courbet** (1819–77) strove to avoid. Courbet was a socialist and his frank, outspoken attitude led to his being accused of taking part in the destruction of the column in Paris's place Vendôme after the outbreak of the Commune and, eventually, to his exile. After an initial resounding success in the Salon exhibition of 1849, he endured constant criticism from the academic world and patrons alike: scenes of ordinary life, such as the *Funeral at Orléans*, which he often chose to depict, were regarded as unsavoury and deliberately ugly.

But Courbet had a deep admiration for the old masters, especially for Rembrandt and the Spanish painters of the seventeenth and eighteenth centuries. This link with tradition was probably one of the underlying themes of his large masterpiece, *The Studio*, which was emphatically rejected by the jury of the 1855 Exposition Universelle, and in which Courbet portrayed himself, surrounded by his model, his friends, colleagues and admirers, among them the poet Baudelaire. Courbet subsequently decided to hold a private exhibition of some forty of his works, writing at the same time a manifesto explaining his intentions of being true to his vision of the world and of creating "living art". Writing the word **Realism** in large letters on the door leading to the exhibition, he stated his intentions and gave a label to his art.

IMPRESSIONISM

Like Courbet, **Edouard Manet** (1832–83) was strongly influenced by Spanish painters, whose works had become more easily accessible to artists when a large collection belonging to the Orléans family was confiscated by the state in 1848. Unlike Courbet, though, he never saw himself as a socialist or indeed as a rebel or avant-garde painter, yet his technique and interpretation of themes was quite new and shocked as many people as it inspired. Manet used bold contrasts of light and very dark colours, giving his paintings a forcefulness that critics often took for a lack of sophistication. And his detractors saw much to decry in his reworking of an old subject originally treated by the sixteenth-century Venetian painter, Giorgione, *Le Déjeuner sur l'Herbe*. Manet's version was shocking because he placed naked and dressed figures together, and because the men were dressed in the costume of the day, implying a pleasure party too specifically contemporary to be "respectable".

Manet was not interested in painting moral lessons, however, and some of his most successful pictures are reflections of ordinary life in bars and public places, where respectability, as understood by the late nineteenth-century bourgeoisie, was certainly lacking. To Manet, painting was to be enjoyed for its own sake and not as a tool for moral instruction – in itself an outlook on the role of art that was quite new, not to say revolutionary, and marked a definite break with the paintings of the past. With Manet, the basis of our present expectations and understanding of modern art was established.

From the 1870s, Manet began to adopt the **Impressionist** techniques of painting out-of-doors, and his work became lighter and freer. Although it is doubtful whether Manet either wanted or expected to assume the role of leader, he found himself a much-admired member of that group of painters, one of whom was **Claude Monet** (1840–1926). Born in Le Havre, Monet came in contact with **Eugène Boudin** (1824–98), whose colourful beach scenes anticipated the way the Impressionists approached colour. He then went to Paris to study under Charles Gleyre, a respected teacher in whose studio he met many of the people with whom he formulated his ideas. Monet soon discovered that, for him, light and the way in which it builds up forms and creates an infinity of colours was the element that governed all representations. Under the impact of Manet's bright hues and his unconventional attitude, ("art for art's sake"), Monet soon began using pure colours side by side, blended together to create areas of brightness and shade.

In 1874, a group of some thirty artists exhibited together for the first time. Among them were some of the best-known names of this period of French art: Degas, Monet, Renoir,

Pissarro. One of Monet's paintings was entitled *Impression: Sun Rising*, a title that was singled out by the critics to ridicule the colourful, loose and unacademic style of these young artists. Overnight they became, derisively, the "Impressionists".

Camille Pissarro (1830–1903) was slightly older than most of them and seems to have played the part of an encouraging father-figure, always keenly aware of any new development or new talent. Not a great innovator himself, Pissarro was a very gifted artist whose use of Impressionist technique was supplemented by a lyrical feeling for nature and its seasonal changes. But it was really with **Monet** that Impressionist theory ran its full course: he studied endlessly the impact of light on objects and the way in which it reveals colours. To understand this phenomenon better, Monet painted the same motif again and again under different conditions of light, at different times of the day, and in different seasons, producing whole series of paintings such as *Grain Stacks*, *Poplars* and, much later, his *Waterlilies*. In the late 1870s and the early 1880s many other artists helped formulate the new style, though few remained true to its principles for very long.

Auguste Renoir (1841–1919), who started life as a painter of porcelain, was swept up by Monet's ideas for a while, but soon felt the need to look again at the old masters and to emphasize the importance of drawing to the detriment of colour. Renoir regarded the representation of the female nude as the most taxing and rewarding subject that an artist could tackle. Like Boucher in the eighteenth century, Renoir's nudes are luscious, but rarely, if ever, erotic. They have a healthy, uncomplicated quality that was, in his later paintings, to become cloyingly, almost overpoweringly, sickly and sweet. Better were his portraits of women fully clothed, both for their obvious and innate sympathy and for their keen sense of design.

Edgar Degas (1834–1917) was yet another artist who, although he exhibited with the Impressionists, did not follow their precepts very closely. The son of a rich banker, he was trained in the tradition of Ingres: design and drawing were an integral part of his art, and, whereas Monet was fascinated mainly by light, Degas wanted to express movement in all its forms. His pictures are vivid expressions of the body in action, usually straining under fairly exacting circumstances – dancers and circus artistes were among his favourite subjects, as well as more mundane depictions of laundresses and other working women.

Like so many artists of the day, Degas had his imagination fired by the discovery of **Japanese prints**, which could for the first time be seen in quantity. These provided him with new ideas of composition, not least in their asymmetry of design and the use of large areas of unbroken colour. **Photography**, too, had an impact, if only because it finally liberated artists from the task of producing accurate, exacting descriptions of the world.

Degas' extraordinary gift as a draughtsman was matched only by that of the Provençal aristocrat **Henri de Toulouse-Lautrec** (1864–1901). Toulouse-Lautrec, who had broken both his legs as a child, was unusually small, a physical deformity that made him particularly sensitive to free and vivacious movements. A great admirer of Degas, he chose similar themes: people in cafés and theatres, working women and variety dancers all figured large in his work. But, unlike Degas, Toulouse-Lautrec looked beyond the body, and his work is scattered with social comment, sometimes sardonic and bitter. In his portrayal of Paris prostitutes, there is sympathy and kindness; to study them better he lived in a brothel, revealing in his paintings the weariness and sometimes gentleness of these women.

POST-IMPRESSIONISM

Though a rather vague term, as it's difficult to date exactly when the backlash against Impressionism took place, **Post-Impressionism** represents in many ways a return to more formal concepts of painting – in composition, in attitudes to subject and in drawing.

Paul Cézanne (1839–1906), for one, associated only very briefly with the Impressionists and spent most of his working life in relative isolation, obsessed with rendering, as objectively as possible, the essence of form. He saw objects as basic shapes – cylinders, cones, etc – and tried to give the painting a unity of texture that would force the spectator to view it not so much as representation of the world but rather as an entity in its own right, as an object as real and dense as the objects surrounding it. It was this striving for pictorial unity that led him to

cover the entire surface of the picture with small, equal brush strokes which made no distinction between the textures of a tree, a house or the sky.

The detached, unemotional way in which Cézanne painted was not unlike that of the seventeenth-century artist Poussin, and he found a contemporary parallel in the work of **Georges Seurat** (1859–91). Seurat was fascinated by current theories of light and colour, and he attempted to apply them in a systematic way, creating different shades and tones by placing tiny spots of pure colour side by side, which the eye could in turn fuse together to see the colours mixed out of their various components. This **pointillist** technique also had the effect of giving monumentality to everyday scenes of contemporary life.

While Cézanne, Seurat and, for that matter, the Impressionists, sought to represent the outside world objectively, several other artists – the **Symbolists** – were seeking a different kind of truth, through the subjective experience of fantasy and dreams. **Gustave Moreau** (1840–98) represented, in complex paintings, the intricate worlds of the romantic fairy tale, his visions expressed in a wealth of naturalistic details. The style of **Puvis de Chavannes** (1824–98) was more restrained and more obviously concerned with design and the decorative. And a third artist, **Odilon Redon** (1840–1916), produced some weird and visionary graphic work that especially intrigued Symbolist writers; his less frequent works in colour belong to the later part of his life.

The subjectivity of the Symbolists was of great importance to the art of **Paul Gauguin** (1848–1903). He started life as a stockbroker who collected Impressionist paintings, a Sunday artist who gave up his job in 1883 to dedicate himself to painting.

During his stay in Pont-Aven in Brittany, Gauguin worked with a number of artists who called themselves the **Nabis**, among them **Paul Serusier** and **Émile Bernard**. He began exploring ways of expressing concepts and emotions by means of large areas of colour and powerful forms, and developed a unique style that was heavily indebted to his knowledge of Japanese prints and of the tapestries and stained glass of medieval art. His search for the primitive expression of primitive emotions took him eventually to the South Sea islands and

Tahiti, where he found some of his most inspiring subjects and painted some of his best-known canvases.

A similar derivation from Symbolist art and a wish to exteriorize emotions and ideas by means of strong colours, lines and shapes underlies the work of **Vincent Van Gogh** (1853–90), a Dutch painter who came to live in France. Like Gauguin, with whom he had an admiring but stormy friendship, Van Gogh started painting relatively late in life, lightening his palette in Paris under the influence of the Impressionists, and then heading south to Arles where, struck by the harshness of the Mediterranean light, he turned out such frantic expressionistic pieces as *The Reaper* and *Wheatfield with Crows*. In all his later pictures the paint is thickly laid on in increasingly abstract patterns that follow the shapes and tortuous paths of his deep inner melancholy.

Both Gauguin and Van Gogh saw objects and colours as means of representing ideas and subjective feelings. **Édouard Vuillard** (1868–1940) and **Pierre Bonnard** (1867–1947) combined this with Cézanne's insistence on unifying the surface and texture of the picture. The result was, in both cases, paintings of often intimate scenes in which figures and objects are blended together in a series of complicated patterns. In some of Vuillard's works, people dressed in checked material, for example, merge into the flowered wallpaper behind them, and in the paintings of Bonnard, the glowing design of the canvas itself is as important as what it's trying to represent.

THE TWENTIETH CENTURY

The **twentieth century** kicked off to a colourful start with the **Fauvist** exhibition of 1905, an appropriately anarchic beginning to a century which, in France above all, was to see radical changes in attitudes towards painting.

The painters who took part in the exhibition included, most influentially, **Henri Matisse** (1869–1954), **André Derain** (1880–1954), **Georges Rouault** (1871–1958) and **Albert Marquet** (1875–1947), and they were quickly nicknamed the Fauves (Wild Beasts) for their use of bright, wild colours that often bore no relation whatsoever to the reality of the object depicted. Skies were just as likely to be green as blue since, for the Fauves, colour was a way of composing, of structuring a picture, and not necessarily a reflection of real life.

Fauvism was just the beginning: the first decades of the twentieth century were times of intense excitement and artistic activity in Paris, and painters and sculptors from all over Europe flocked to the capital to take part in the liberation from conventional art that individuals and groups were gradually instigating. **Raoul Dufy** (1877–1953) used Fauvist colours in combination with theories of abstraction to paint an effervescent industrial age.

Pablo Picasso (1881–1973) was one of the first, arriving in Paris in 1900 from Spain and soon thereafter starting work on his first Blue Period paintings, which describe the sad and squalid life of intinerant actors in tones of blue. Later, while Matisse was experimenting with colours and their decorative potential, Picasso came under the sway of Cézanne and his organization of forms into geometrical shapes. He also learned from "primitive", and especially African, sculpture, and out of these studies came a painting that heralded a definite new direction, not only for Picasso's own style but for the whole of modern art – *Les Demoiselles d'Avignon*. Executed in 1907, this painting combined Cézanne's analysis of forms with the visual impact of African masks.

It was from this semi-abstract picture that Picasso went on to develop the theory of **Cubism**, inspiring artists such as **Georges Braque** (1882–1963) and **Juan Gris** (1887–1927), another Spaniard, and formulating a whole new movement. The Cubists' aim was to depict objects not so much as they saw them but rather as they knew them to be: a bottle and a guitar were shown from the front, from the side and from the back as if the eye could take in all at once every facet and plane of the object. Braque and Picasso first analysed forms into these facets (analytical Cubism), then gradually reduced them to series of colours and shapes (synthetic Cubism), among which a few recognizable symbols such as letters, fragments of newspaper and numbers appeared. The complexity of different planes overlapping one another made the deciphering of Cubist paintings sometimes difficult, and the very last phase of Cubism tended increasingly towards abstraction.

Spin-offs of Cubism were many: such movements as **Orphism**, headed by **Robert Delaunay** (1885–1941) and **Francis Picabia** (1879-1953), who experimented not with objects but with the colours of the spectrum, and **Futurism**, which evolved first in Italy, then in Paris, and explored movement and the bright new technology of the industrial age. **Fernand Léger** (1881–1955), one of the main exponents of the so-called School of Paris, had also become acquainted with modern machinery during **World War I**, and he exploited his fascination with its smoothness and power to create geometric and monumental compositions of technical imagery that were indebted to both Cézanne and Cubism.

The war, meanwhile, had affected many artists: in Switzerland, **Dada** was born out of the scorn artists felt for the petty bourgeois and nationalistic values that had led to the bloodshed, a nihilistic movement that sought to knock down all traditionally accepted ideas. It was best exemplified in the work of the Frenchman **Marcel Duchamp** (1887–1968), who selected ready-made, everyday objects and elevated them, without modification, to the rank of works of art by pulling them out of their ordinary context, or defaced such sacred cows as the *Mona Lisa* by decorating her with a moustache and an obscene caption.

Dada was also a literary movement, and through one of its main poets, André Breton, it led to the inception of **Surrealism**. It was the unconscious and its dark unchartered territories that interested the Surrealists: they derived much of their imagery from Freud and even experimented in words and images with free-association techniques.

Strangely enough, most of the "French" Surrealists were foreigners, primarily the German **Max Ernst** (1891–1976) and the Spaniard **Salvador Dalí** (1904–89), though Frenchman **Yves Tanguy** (1900–55) also achieved international recognition. Mournful landscapes of weird, often terrifying images evoked the landscape of nightmares in often very precise details and with an anguish that went on to influence artists for years to come. Picasso, for instance, shocked by the massacre at the Spanish town of Guernica in 1936, drew greatly from Surrealism to produce the disquieting figures of his painting of the same name.

World War II interrupted Paris's position as the artistic melting pot of Europe. Artists rushed there at the beginning of the twentieth century and after World War I, contributing by their individuality, originality and different nationalities to the richness and constant renewal of artistic endeavour. Although at the outbreak of World War II many artists emigrated to the US, where the economic climate was more favourable, Paris remained full of vibrant new work. Sculptors like the Romanian **Brancusi** (1876–1957) and the Swiss **Giacometti** (1886–1966) lived most of their lives in Paris, for example.

The last coherent French art movement of the century, largely of the 1950s and 1960s, was **Nouveau Réalisme**, which concentrated on the distortion of the objects and signs of contemporary culture, and loosely encompassed artists and sculptors such as Dubuffet, Arman, César, Jean Tinguely and Niki de Saint-Phalle.

Jean Dubuffet (1901–85) pioneered the depreciation of traditional artistic materials and methods, fashioning junk, tar, sand and glass into the shape of human beings. His work (which provoked much outrage) influenced both the French-born American, **Arman** (1928–) and **César** (1921–), both of whom made use of scrap metals – their output ranging from presentations of household debris to towers of crushed cars. Even more controversially, the Swiss **Daniel Spoerri** (1930–) used the remnants – including the crockery – of his dinners and glued them onto a canvas.

Nouveau Réaliste sculpture is best represented by the works of another Swiss, **Jean Tinguely** (1925–91) whose work was concerned mainly with movement and the machine, satirizing technological civilization. His most famous work, done in collaboration with **Niki de Saint-Phalle** (1926–) is the exuberant fountain outside the Pompidou Centre, featuring fantastical birds and beasts shooting water in all directions.

Later artists wanted to reassert their position as individuals and, though influenced by their cultural context, were not attached to any clear manifesto. Perhaps the most important post-World War II French artist is **Yves Klein** (1928–1962). He redefined the void and the immaterial as having a pure energy. He also patented his own colour, International Klein Blue, which he used on his monochromes, also signalling painting simply as pure colour. Klein and Duchamp laid the foundations for several currents in contemporary art.

Since Nouveau Réalisme, young French artists, like their counterparts abroad have shown a proclivity to mix styles as well as media. A number of smaller but less coherent movements have cropped up in France, notably **Support, Surface** and the graffiti-inspired **Figuration Libre**, while French artists have also been drawn towards the international currents of Italian-pioneered **Trans-Avant Gard**. The geometrically abstract Support, Surface emerged in Nice in 1969, founded by the likes of **Claude Villat** (1936–), and represented in sculpture by **Jean-Pierre Pincemin** (1944–). The Nantes artist **Jean-Charles Blais** (1956–) is one of the leaders of Figuration Libre (which began in 1981), and is known for high-relief abstracts which combine traditional painting techniques with the *montage* of found objects. **Louise Bourgeois** (1911–) is a major influence on young contemporary artists, a still-prolific sculptress producing oddly erotic and remarkable combinations of wrought iron, old clothes

and other material. A recent trend has been towards massive *mise-en-scène* works, such as **Christian Boltanski**'s (1944–) large, auto-referential installations, or the work of the Bulgarian **Christo** (1935–) and his wife and collaborator **Jeanne-Claude** (1935–), who cover buildings using different materials, and wrapped Paris's Pont-Neuf in woven polyamide fabric in 1985, in order to focus attention on the structure itself rather than its function. **Jean-Marc Bustamante** (1952–) constructs *in situ* installations, using building materials in his art, while **Jean-Luc Vilmout** (1952–) often co-opts the buildings themselves, resulting in a blurring of the aesthetic and the functional. Finally, in painting, the Lyonnais **Marc Desgrandchamps** (1960–) is a name to look out for, although he may be hard to spot given that his work runs a gamut of styles from abstract to photorealism.

ARCHITECTURE

France's architectural legacy is rich and important, reflecting the power and personality of successive kings, the Church and the state, vying to outdo their peers with bold, lavish statements in brick and stone. Many architectural trends filtered into France from Italy – Romanesque, Renaissance and Baroque – but they have been refined and developed by the French. Rococo grew from Baroque, Neoclassicism came from the Renaissance, and Art Nouveau was a brilliant, confused jumble of Baroque features combined with the newly developed cast-iron industry. Architecture this century has produced two great names – Auguste Perret and Le Corbusier – but France's contemporary scene is still thriving, with a host of new developments throughout the country.

THE ROMANS

The south of France was colonized by the **Romans** by around 120 BC in order to expand their trading operations, and they set up substantial settlements at Marseille, Narbonne, Orange, Arles, Fréjus, Glanum near St-Rémy, and Nice, with a network of roads linking them.

The Romans were fine town-planners, linking complexes of buildings with straight roads punctuated by decorative fountains, arches and colonnades. They built essentially in the Greek style, and their large, functional buildings were concerned more with strength and solidity than aesthetic. A number of substantial Roman build-

ing works survive: in **Nîmes** you can see the Maison Carrée, the best-preserved Roman temple still standing, and the Temple of Diana, one of just four vaulted Roman temples in Europe. Gateways remain at **Autun, Orange, Saintes** and **Reims**, and largely intact amphitheatres can be seen at Nîmes and **Arles**. The **Pont du Gard** aqueduct outside Nîmes is still a magnificent and ageless monument of civil engineering, built to carry the town's fresh water over the gorge, and Orange has its massive theatre, with Europe's only intact Roman façade. There are excavated archeological sites at **Glanum** near St-Rémy, **Vienne, Vaison-la-Romaine** and **Lyon**.

CAROLINGIAN AND ROMANESQUE

The **Carolingian dynasty** of Charlemagne attempted a revival of the symbols of civilized authority by recourse to Roman or "**Romanesque**" models. Of this era, practically nothing remains visible, though the motifs of arch and vault are carried on in their simplest forms, and the semi circular apse and the basilican plan of nave and aisles persist as the basis of the succeeding phases of Christian architecture. An interesting anomaly is the plan of the **church of St-Front** at Périgueux, a copy of St Mark's in Venice, brought by trading influence west along the Garonne in the early twelfth century.

Elsewhere development may be divided roughly north–south of the Loire. Southern Romanesque is naturally more Roman, with stone barrel vaults, aisleless naves and domes. **St-Trophime** at Arles (1150) has a porch directly derived from Roman models and, with the church at St-Gilles nearby, exhibits a delight in carved ornament peculiar to the south at this time. The cathedral at **Angoulême** typifies the use of all these elements.

The south, too, was the readiest route for the introduction of new cultural developments, and it is here that the pointed arch and vault first appear – from Spanish Muslim sources – in churches such as **Notre-Dame** at Avignon, the cathedral at **Autun** and **Ste-Madeleine** at Vézelay (1089–1206), which contains the earliest pointed cross vault in France.

In the north of the country, the nave with aisles is more usual, together with the development of twin western towers to mask the end of the aisles. The **Abbaye-aux-Hommes** at Caen good living, seductive painting and general "ooh-la-la", provides probably the most persistent image of France among the non-French.

In addition to the correct, official Classicism and the robust, exuberant and commercial Baroque, there is a third strand running through the nineteenth century that was ultimately more fruitful. The rational engineering approach, embodied in the official **School of Roads and Bridges** and invigorated by the teaching of Viollet-le-Duc, who reinterpreted Gothic style as pure structure, led to the development of new structural techniques out of which "modern" architectural style was born. Iron was the first significant new material, often used in imitation of Gothic forms and destined to be developed as an individual architectural style in America. In the **Eiffel Tower** (1889), France set up a potent symbol of things to come.

A more significantly French development was in the use of reinforced concrete towards the end of the century, most notably by **Auguste Perret**, whose 1903 apartment house at 25 rue Franklin, Paris 16ᵉ, turns the concrete structure into a visible virtue and breaks with conventional façades. Changes in the patterns of work and travel were making the need for new urban planning very acute in such cities as Paris. Perret and other **modernists** were all for the high-rise buildings that were going to better the haphazard layouts in America by a rational integration to new street systems. Some of their designs for gigantic skyscraper avenues and suburban rings now look like totalitarian horror-movie sets. But it was tradition, not charity, that blocked their projects at the time.

THE TWENTIETH CENTURY

The greatest proponent of the super New York scale, who also had genuine if mistaken concern for how people lived, was **Le Corbusier**, the most famous **twentieth-century** French architect. His stature may now appear diminished by the ascendancy of a blander style in concrete boxing, as well as by the significant technical and social failures of his buildings and his total disregard for historic streets and monuments.

But while his manifesto, *Vers une architecture moderne*, sounds like a call to arms for a new and revolutionary movement, Le Corbusier should perhaps be more fairly assessed as the original, inimitable and highly individual artist

he undoubtedly was. You should try to see some of his work – there's the **Cité Radieuse** in Marseille and plenty of examples in Paris – to make up your own mind about the man largely responsible for changing the face and form of buildings throughout the world.

One respect in which Paris at the turn of the century lagged behind London, Glasgow, Chicago and New York was in **underground transport**. First proposed in the 1870s, it took twenty years of furious debate before the Paris métro was finally realized in 1900. The design of the entrances was as controversial as every other aspect of the system, but the first commission went to **Hector Guimard**, renowned for his variations on the then-current fashion in style. The whirling metal railings, Art Nouveau lettering and bizarre antennae-like orange lamps were his creation. Conservatives were less amused when it came to sites such as the Opéra: **Charles Garnier**, architect of that edifice, demanded classical marble and bronze porticoes for every station, and his line was followed, on a less grandiose scale, wherever the métro steps surfaced by a major monument. Thus Guimard was out of a job. Some of the early ones remain (**Place des Abbesses**, 18ᵉ, is one), as do some of the white-tiled interiors, replaced after World War II in central stations by bright paint with matching seats and display cases.

Art Nouveau designs also found their way onto buildings – the early department stores in Paris are the best example – but the new materials and simple geometry of the modern or International Style favoured the **Art Deco** look; again, you're most likely to come across them in the capital.

Skipping the miserable 1950s and 1960s buildings everywhere, France again becomes one of the most exciting patrons of international **contemporary architecture**. The **Centre Beaubourg**, by **Renzo Piano** and **Richard Rogers**, derided, adored and visited by millions, maximizes space by putting the service elements usually concealed in walls and floors on the outside. The visible ducts, cables and pipes are painted in accordance with the colour code of architectural plans. You might think the whole thing is a professional in-joke, but the Beaubourg is one of the great contemporary buildings in western Europe – for its originality, popularity and practicality.

In **housing**, new styles and forms are to be seen in city suburbs and vacation resorts, many of them disastrous and visually unappealing, but interesting to look at when you don't have to live there. The latest state-funded projects confirm French seriousness about innovative design: just outside Poitiers is the postmodern **Futuroscope** cinema and virtual reality complex, and in Marseilles there's William Alsop's mammoth seat of regional government. Regional projects include Nîmes' **Carré d'Art** Modern Art museum by Sir Norman Foster, characterized by its simple transparent design. The **Cathédrale d'Evry**, masterminded by Swiss Mario Botta and finished in 1995, Is a huge cylindrical red-brick tower which houses an art centre, concert hall and cinema screen, besides the religious accoutrements that befit its function. Its roof is slanted at 45 degrees to receive more light, and is crowned by 24 trees emulating the laurel wreaths of Roman emperors Hadrian and Augustus. Its stained-glass window is at the foot of the building and symbolizes the roots of a tree.

President Mitterrand's "*grands travaux*" project foregrounded a new architectural era for Paris in the 1980s. He commissioned the **Cité de la Musique** from Christian de Fartzamparc as a finishing touch to the **Parc de la Villette** complex which was built under Giscard d'Estaing on the site of an old abbatoir, and which also houses the Cité de la Science and Bernard Tschemi's 21 "*folies*" of urban life. The **Institut du Monde Arabe**, by Jean Nouvel – who also did the Fondation Cartier building and the 426-metre high, 100-storey Tour Sans Fins in the Défense area – is made up of metal and glass facades positioned to emulate traditional Arabo-Islamic motifs, with light-sensitive shutters best admired in action on a sunny March day with racing clouds. The "**Grand Louvre**" project displaced the **Ministry of Finance** into a huge new building in Bercy, thus clearing the Richelieu wing of the Louvre for museum use, increasing exhibition space by 83 percent. leoh Ming Pei's glass **pyramid** in the Cour Napoléon is now loved by Parisians, and this new entrance to the museum takes visitors through the underground Carrousel du Louvre and its boutiques. The **Grande Arche de la Défense**, designed by Von Sprecklesen is a square arch aligned on the map and in mathematical proportions with the Arc de Triomphe – except that the former also has a fibreglass cloud hung in the space under the arch. Situated at the west of Paris, it is emblematic of the new business district – not quite the centre of communication that Mitterrand had wanted – housing 87,000 square metres of office space. The **Opéra Bastille** by Carlos Ott was designed to be a "modern and popular" alternative to the Opéra Garnier. Although the sound unfortunately resonates, the crowds still flock to see the performances.

The new **Bibliothèque Nationale** in the 13e *arrondissement* fits in extraordinarily well with the surrounding tower blocks. Designed by Dominique Perrault, it's a complex made up of four corners, which represent four open books. This apparently facile design is made up for by the complexity (and expense) of the detail. The aluminium shutters are covered in rare *oukoumé* reddish wood, which contrasts with the grey *ipé* and yellow *doussié* wood, to give the impression from a distance that the towers are bookshelves containing different bound volumes. By the year 2001, it will house more than 350,000 books stored under the four and is divided into separate sections for academics and the general public. The interior design is metallic and wood-based, and the library is a shrine to multimedia with excellent audiovisual research capacities.

The country's ever-advancing transport network has provided sites for some of the most high-tech office buildings with state-of-the-art engineering in Europe, as at **Eurolille**, the complex around Lille's TGV station, and in **Roissy**, around the Charles-de-Gaulle airport. The TGV **Lyon-Satolas** station is another typical 1990s creation, both elegant and thrustingly optimistic.

The new **European Parliament** building in Strasbourg, designed by the Architecture Studio group, was finished in 1997, and is a huge boomerang-shaped structure with a glass dome and metal tower. Most recently, the **Stade de France** in St-Denis, near Paris, was built to host many of the World Cup 98 matches, including, as it happened, the French victory in the final. Meanwhile, the futuristic **Antigone** housing and commercial development in Montpellier, laid out by Ricard Bofill and inaugurated in 1984, continues to grow, with the opening in autumn 2000 of Paul Chemetov's new library building.

But the French are also very good at preserving the past. Throughout the country you'll see far older period streets – medieval and Renaissance – that look as though they've never been touched. More often than not, the restoration has been carried out by the **Maisons de Compagnonage**, the old craft guilds, which have maintained traditional building skills, handing them down as of old from master to apprentice (and never to women), while also taking on new industrial skills.

Above all, though, bear in mind the extent and variety of architecture in France and don't feel intimidated by the established sights. If the empty grandeur of the Loire châteaux is oppres-sive, there are numerous smaller country houses open to the public, and such municipal buildings as the **Hôtels de Ville** tend to offer some charm or amusement, even in the smallest towns.

It is also possible in France to experience whole towns as consistent places of architecture, not only Carcassonne and Aigues-Mortes, Dinan and Nancy, but villages off the main roads in which time seems to have stopped long ago. And, besides, from any hotel bedroom you can simply delight in what Le Corbusier called "the magnificent play of forms seen in light", in the movement of morning sunlight over ordinary provincial tiles and chimneys.

BOOKS

Publishers are detailed below in the form of British publisher; American publisher, where both exist. Where books are published in one country only, UK or US follows the publisher's name.

Abbreviations: o/p (out of print); UP (University Press).

TRAVEL

James Boswell *An Account of Corsica*, current edition published as *The Journal of a Tour to Corsica* (In Print Publishing, UK). Typically robust and witty account of encounters with the Corsican people. Excerpts published in *Journals of James Boswell* (Mandarin/Yale UP).

Dorothy Carrington *Granite Island* (Penguin, UK, o/p). By far the best study of Corsica ever written in English. A fascinating and immensely comprehensive book, combining the writer's personal experiences with an evocative portrayal of historical figures and events.

Julien Green *Paris* (Marion Boyars). A collection of very personal sketches and impressions of the city, by an American who has lived all his life in Paris, writes in French, and is considered one of the great French writers of the century. Bilingual text.

Richard Holmes *Fatal Avenue* (Pimlico; Trafalgar Square). The phrase is de Gaulle's, used to describe France's northeast frontier whose notorious topographical vulnerability has made it the natural route for invaders since time began. From the Channel to Alsace, Holmes relates the wars and the personalities and the places as they are today, from the Hundred Years War to World War II. An exciting and informative read.

Richard Holmes *Footsteps* (Flamingo; Vintage). A marvellous mix of objective history and personal account, such as the tale of the author's own excitement at the events of May 1968 in Paris, which led him to investigate and reconstruct the experiences of the British in Paris during the 1789 Revolution.

Laurence Sterne *A Sentimental Journey Through France and Italy* (Penguin; Viking). Rambling tale by the eccentric eighteenth-century author of *Tristram Shandy* who, despite the title, never gets further than Versailles.

Robert Louis Stevenson *Travels with a Donkey* (OUP; Koneman). Mile-by-mile account of Stevenson's twelve-day trek in the Haute Loire and Cévennes uplands with the donkey Modestine. Devotees of Stevenson's footpaths – and there's a surprising number in France – might be interested in his first book, *Inland Voyage*, on the waterways of the north.

Freda White *Three Rivers of France* (Pavilion; Faber, o/p), *West of the Rhone* (Faber, US, o/p), *Ways of Aquitaine* (Faber, o/p). Freda White spent a great deal of time in France in the 1950s before tourism came along to the backwater communities that were her interest. These are all evocative books, slipping in the history and culture painlessly, if not always too accurately.

HISTORY

GENERAL

Alfred Cobban *A History of Modern France* (3 vols: 1715–99, 1799–1871 and 1871–1962; Penguin; Viking). Complete and very readable account of the main political, social and economic strands in French history from the death of Louis XIV to mid-de Gaulle.

Colin Jones *The Cambridge Illustrated History of France* (CUP, o/p). A political and social history of France from prehistoric times to the mid-1990s, concentrating on issues of regionalism, gender, race and class. Good illustrations and a friendly, non-academic writing style.

Theodore Zeldin *France 1845–1945* (OUP). Five thematic volumes on diverse French matters – all good reads.

Theodore Zeldin *The French* (Harvill; Kodansha). Urbane and witty survey of the French worldview – chapter titles include "How to be chic" and "How to appreciate a grandmother".

artistic detail to illustrate the painting, sculpture and architecture that emerged during the reigns of Louis XIII, XIV and XV.

Kenneth J. Comant *Carolingian and Romanesque Architecture, 800–1200* (Yale UP). Good European study with a focus on Cluny and the Santiago pilgrim route.

Norma Evenson *Paris: A Century of Change, 1878–1978* (Yale UP). A large, illustrated volume that makes the development of urban planning and the fabric of Paris an enthralling subject – mainly because the author's ultimate concern is always with people, not panoramas.

Edward Lucie-Smith *A Concise History of French Painting* (Thames & Hudson, US, o/p). If you're after an art reference book, this will do as well as any . . . though there are of course hundreds of books on particular French art movements.

John Richardson, *The Life of Picasso: Vol 1 1881–1906* (Pimlico; Random House) and *Vol 2 1907–17* (Cape; Random House). No twentieth-century artist has ever been subjected to scrutiny as close as Picasso receives in Richardson's exhaustive and brilliantly illustrated biography. The author has taken many years to complete the first two volumes, and there's a risk he'll never reach the end, but the mould-breaking years have now been covered, and it's impossible to imagine how anyone could surpass Richardson's treatment of them. Volumes 3 and 4 are in the pipeline.

Vivian Russell, *Monet's Garden* (Frances Lincoln; Stewart Tabori & Chang). Sumptuous colour photographs by the author, old photographs of the artist and reproductions of his paintings. Superb opening chapter on Monet as "poet of nature" and a detailed description of the garden's evolution, seasonal cycle and its current maintenance which will delight serious gardeners.

Gertrude Stein *The Autobiography of Alice B Toklas* (Penguin; Vintage). The goings-on at Stein's famous salon in Paris. The most accessible of her works, written from the point of view of Stein's long-time lover, gives an amusing account of the Paris art and literary scene of the 1910s and 1920s.

GUIDES

100 Walks in the French Alps (Hodder & Stoughton). A very good guide to hiking in the Alps, detailing which walks are appropriate for different abilities.

James Bromwich *The Roman Remains of Southern France* (Routledge). The only comprehensive guide to the subject – detailed, well illustrated and approachable. In addition to accounts of the famous sites, it will lead you off the map to little-known discoveries.

Glynn Christian *Edible France* (Grub Street; Interlink). A guide to food rather than restaurants: regional produce, local specialities, markets and best shops for buying goodies to bring back home.

Cicerone Walking Guides (Cicerone, UK). Neat, durable guides, with detailed route descriptions. Titles include *Tour of Mont Blanc*; *Chamonix-Mont Blanc*; *Tour of the Oisans* (GR54); *French Alps* (GR5); *The Way of Saint James* (GR65); *Tour of the Queyras*; *The Pyrenean Trail* (GR10); *Walks and Climbs in the Pyrenees*.

Robin G. Collomb *Corsica Mountains* (West Col, UK). Covers all the principal mountain peaks, with information on different approaches and ascents backed up with diagrams.

Elizabeth David *French Provincial Cooking* (Penguin, UK). A classic cookery book, written in 1960 by the English expert on French food. The recipes are in fine prose rather than manual speak, with excellent detail and warnings about tricky processes or the need for particular skills; and they work, even with non-French ingredients. She makes the subject of kitchen equipment fascinating and beautifully describes the different regional cuisines.

Mary Davis *The Green Guide to France* (Green Print, UK). Definitely not the Michelin, this is a resource guide to French national parks and wildlife reserves, veggie restaurants, communes and the like.

Emplois d'Été en France (published in France, distributed by Vacation Work, UK). Annual listings (in French) of thousands of summer jobs available in France.

Footpaths of Europe Series (16 titles; Robertson McCarta, UK). Route guides to most areas of France including Corsica, covering the system of GR footpaths, illustrated with 1:50,000 colour survey maps. These are English versions of the *Topoguides des Sentiers de Grande Randonnée* (CNSGR, Paris), which are widely available in France and not hard to follow with a working knowledge of French.

Mark Hampshell *Live and Work in France* (Vacation Work, UK, o/p). An invaluable guide for anyone considering residence or work in France; packed with ideas and advice on job hunting, bureaucracy, tax, health, etc.

Haute-Savoie & Mont Blanc (Two Wheels, UK, o/p). The only English-language guide to mountain-biking, detailing fifty off-road routes of varying difficulty in that region.

Louisa Jones *Gardens of the French Riviera* (Flammarion). The history and traditions of Riviera gardens accompanied by gorgeous photographs.

W. Lippert *Fleurs des Montagnes, Alpages et Forêts* (Miniguide Nathan Tout Terrain, Paris).

Best palm-sized colour guide if you want something to pack away with your gear in the mountains.

Carol Pineau & Maureen Kelly *Working in France* (AL Books, US, o/p). A practical guide, aimed at American readers, on how to get jobs in France, highlighting the cultural differences that affect job interviews and business practice generally.

Kev Reynolds *Walks and Climbs in the Pyrenees* (Cicerone Press, UK). The classic English guide for walking in the Pyrenees.

Georges Véron *Haute Randonnée Pyrénées* (Randonnées Pyrénéennes, Paris; Gastons-West Col, o/p). East-to-west description of the High Level route across the Pyrenees.

continued from previous page

TALKING TO PEOPLE

When addressing people you should always use *Monsieur* for a man, *Madame* for a woman, *Mademoiselle* for a young woman or girl. Plain *bonjour* by itself is not enough. This isn't as formal as it seems, and it has its uses when you've forgotten someone's name or want to attract someone's attention.

Excuse me	*Pardon*	OK/agreed	*d'accord*
Do you speak English?	*Parlez-vous anglais?*	please	*s'il vous plaît*
How do you say it in French?	*Comment ça se dit en français?*	thank you	*merci*
What's your name?	*Comment vous appelez-vous?*	hello	*bonjour*
		goodbye	*au revoir*
My name is...	*Je m'appelle...*	good morning/ afternoon	*bonjour*
I'm...	*Je suis...*	good evening	*bonsoir*
...English	*...anglais[e]*	good night	*bonne nuit*
...Irish	*...irlandais[e]*	How are you?	*Comment allez-vous?/Ça va?*
...Scottish	*...écossais[e]*		
...Welsh	*...gallois[e]*	Fine, thanks	*Très bien, merci*
...American	*...américain[e]*	I don't know	*Je ne sais pas*
...Australian	*...australien[ne]*	Let's go	*Allons-y*
...Canadian	*...canadien[ne]*	See you tomorrow	*A demain*
...a New Zealander	*...néo-zélandais[e]*	See you soon	*A bientôt*
yes	*oui*	Sorry	*Pardon, Madame/Je m'excuse*
no	*non*		
I understand	*Je comprends*	Leave me alone (aggressive)	*Fichez-moi la paix!*
I don't understand	*Je ne comprends pas*		
Can you speak slower?	*S'il vous plaît, parlez moins vite*	Please help me	*Aidez-moi, s'il vous plaît*

FINDING THE WAY

bus	*autobus/bus/car*	Where are you going?	*Vous allez où?*
bus station	*gare routière*	I'm going to...	*Je vais à ...*
bus stop	*arrêt*	I want to get off at...	*Je voudrais descendre à ...*
car	*voiture*		
train/taxi/ferry	*train/taxi/ferry*	the road to...	*la route pour...*
boat	*bâteau*	near	*près/pas loin*
plane	*avion*	far	*loin*
train station	*gare (SNCF)*	left	*à gauche*
platform	*quai*	right	*à droite*
What time does it leave?	*Il part à quelle heure?*	straight on	*tout droit*
What time does it arrive?	*Il arrive à quelle heure?*	on the other side of	*à l'autre côté de*
a ticket to...	*un billet pour...*	on the corner of	*à l'angle de*
single ticket	*aller simple*	next to	*à côté de*
return ticket	*aller retour*	behind	*derrière*
validate your ticket	*compostez votre billet*	in front of	*devant*
valid for	*valable pour*	before	*avant*
ticket office	*vente de billets*	after	*après*
how many kilometres?	*combien de kilomètres?*	under	*sous*
how many hours?	*combien d'heures?*	to cross	*traverser*
hitchhiking	*autostop*	bridge	*pont*
on foot	*à pied*		

QUESTIONS AND REQUESTS

The simplest way of asking a question is to start with *s'il vous plaît* (please), then name the thing you want in an interrogative tone of voice. For example:

Where is there a bakery?	*S'il vous plaît, la boulangerie?*	Question words	
Which way is it to the Eiffel Tower?	*S'il vous plaît, la route pour la tour Eiffel?*	where?	*où?*
		how?	*comment?*
		how many/how much?	*combien?*
Similarly with requests:		when?	*quand?*
Can we have a room for two?	*S'il vous plaît, une chambre pour deux?*	why?	*pourquoi?*
		at what time?	*à quelle heure?*
Can I have a kilo of oranges?	*S'il vous plaît, un kilo d'oranges?*	what is/which is?	*quel est?*

ACCOMMODATION

a room for one/two people	*une chambre pour une/deux personne(s)*	sheets	*draps*
a double bed	*un lit double*	blankets	*couvertures*
a room with a shower	*une chambre avec douche*	quiet	*calme*
		noisy	*bruyant*
a room with a bath	*une chambre avec salle de bain*	hot water	*eau chaude*
		cold water	*eau froide*
for one/two/three nights	*pour une/deux/trois nuits*	Is breakfast included?	*Est-ce que le petit déjeuner est compris?*
Can I see it?	*Je peux la voir?*	I would like breakfast	*Je voudrais prendre le petit déjeuner*
a room on the courtyard	*une chambre sur la cour*	I don't want breakfast	*Je ne veux pas de petit déjeuner*
a room over the street	*une chambre sur la rue*	Can we camp here?	*On peut camper ici?*
first floor	*premier étage*	campsite	*un camping/terrain de camping*
second floor	*deuxième étage*		
with a view	*avec vue*	tent	*une tente*
key	*clef*	tent space	*un emplacement*
to iron	*repasser*	youth hostel	*auberge de jeunesse*
do laundry	*faire la lessive*		

CARS

service station	*garage*	put air in the tyres	*gonfler les pneus*
service	*service*	battery	*batterie*
to park the car	*garer la voiture*	the battery is dead	*la batterie est morte*
car park	*un parking*	plugs	*bougies*
no parking	*défense de stationner/ stationnement interdit*	to break down	*tomber en panne*
		gas can	*bidon*
gas station	*poste d'essence*	insurance	*assurance*
fuel	*essence*	green card	*carte verte*
(to) fill it up	*faire le plein*	traffic lights	*feux*
oil	*huile*	red light	*feu rouge*
air line	*ligne à air*	green light	*feu vert*

HEALTH MATTERS

doctor	*médecin*	stomach ache	*mal à l'estomac*
I don't feel well	*Je ne me sens pas bien*	period	*règles*
medicines	*médicaments*	pain	*douleur*
prescription	*ordonnance*	it hurts	*ça fait mal*
I feel sick	*Je suis malade*	chemist	*pharmacie*
I have a headache	*J'ai mal à la tête*	hospital	*hôpital*

continued overleaf

continued from previous page

OTHER NEEDS

bakery	*boulangerie*	bank	*banque*
food shop	*alimentation*	money	*argent*
supermarket	*supermarché*	toilets	*toilettes*
to eat	*manger*	police	*police*
to drink	*boire*	telephone	*téléphone*
camping gas	*camping gaz*	cinema	*cinéma*
tobacconist	*tabac*	theatre	*théâtre*
stamps	*timbres*	to reserve/book	*réserver*

ARCHITECTURAL TERMS: A GLOSSARY

These are either terms you'll come across in the *Guide*, or come up against while travelling around.

ABBAYE abbey

AMBULATORY passage round the outer edge of the choir of a church

APSE semicircular termination at the east end of a church

BAROQUE High Renaissance period of art and architecture, distinguished by extreme ornateness

CAROLINGIAN dynasty (and art, sculpture, etc) named after Charlemagne; mid-eighth to early tenth centuries

CHÂTEAU mansion, country house, castle

CHÂTEAU FORT castle

CHEVET east end of a church

CLASSICAL architectural style incorporating Greek and Roman elements: pillars, domes, colonnades, etc, at its height in France in the seventeenth century and revived, as **Neoclassical**, in the nineteenth century

CLERESTORY upper storey of a church, incorporating the windows

DONJON castle keep

ÉGLISE church

FLAMBOYANT florid form of Gothic

MEROVINGIAN dynasty (and art, etc), ruling France and parts of Germany from sixth to mid-eighth centuries

NARTHEX entrance hall of church

NAVE main body of a church

PORTE gateway

RENAISSANCE art/architectural style developed in fifteenth-century Italy and imported to France in the sixteenth century by François I

RETABLE altarpiece

ROMAN Romanesque (easily confused with Romain – Roman)

ROMANESQUE early medieval architecture distinguished by squat, rounded forms and naïve sculpture, called Norman in Britain.

STUCCO plaster used to embellish ceilings, etc

TOUR tower

TRANSEPT transverse arms of a church

TYMPANUM sculpted panel above a church door

VOUSSOIR sculpted rings in arch over church door

INDEX

MUSIC ROUGH GUIDES ON CD

'Like the useful Rough Guide travel books and television shows, these discs delve right into the heart and soul of the region they explore'
– *Rhythm Music (USA)*

Available from book and record shops worldwide or order direct from World Music Network, Unit 6, 88 Clapham Park Road, London SW4 7BX
tel: 020 7498 5252 • fax: 020 7498 5353 • email: post@worldmusic.net

Hear samples from over 50 Rough Guide CDs at
WWW.WORLDMUSIC.NET

FOR STUDENTS AND YOUNG TRAVELLERS

250 BRANCHES WORLDWIDE

LOW COST FLIGHTS → ADVENTURE TOURS → TRAVEL PASSES
SKI → ISIC/YOUTH CARDS → ACCOMMODATION → INSURANCE
CAR HIRE → EXPERT ADVICE FROM WELL TRAVELLED STAFF

For Bookings and Enquiries:
0870 160 6070

Find fares, check availability, enter competitions, book online
or find your local branch @

www.statravel.co.uk

ABTA
9922/9

STA TRAVEL LTD